THE POPULATION OF THE UNITED STATES

Historical Trends and Future Projections

THE POPULATION OF THE UNITED STATES

Historical Trends and Future Projections

Donald J. Bogue

Director, Community and Family Study Center
The University of Chicago

Assisted by

George W. Rumsey
Odalia Ho
David Hartmann
Albert Woolbright

THE FREE PRESS
A Division of Macmillan, Inc.
NEW YORK

Collier Macmillan Publishers
LONDON

DEDICATION

This book is dedicated to the thousands of men and women (most of them in Washington, DC) who conscientiously produce a flow of high quality demographic information from censuses, surveys, vital registration systems, and other sources and make them available for analysis and public use.

The Free Press
A Division of Macmillan, Inc.
866 Third Avenue, New York, N. Y. 10022

Collier Macmillan Canada, Inc.

Printed in the United States of America

printing number

1 2 3 4 5 6 7 8 9 10

Library of Congress Cataloging in Publication Data

Bogue, Donald Joseph
The population of the United States: historical trends and future projections

1. United States–Population. 2. United States–Census, 20th, 1980. I. Title.
HB3505.B63 1985 304.6′2′0973 84-18688
ISBN 0-02-904700-5

Contents

Preface

Much of the history of a nation is recorded in its population censuses, surveys, and vital registration systems. These population data contain a high percentage of the factual information available about present social and economic conditions. As a consequence, members of almost all professions find it necessary to use data from these sources in order to make decisions, interpret change, and anticipate the future in their particular sphere of interest. Familiarity with population facts and figures is becoming an increasingly essential part of the training of students at the secondary, college, and post-graduate levels. Given the tremendous amount of information released each year, keeping up with population trends can be a difficult task. This volume is intended to be of service to all who find they need to know the fundamental facts of population growth, its composition and distribution in the United States, and to understand the implications of these facts for the present and the future. It is written in the belief that a vast number of people need and want a comprehensive statement of this type within the covers of a single book—and that such a book did not exist. This kind of book should not be over-simplified by the omission of basic information, yet it should spare the interested reader who may lack specific demographic training the many technical details having little effect on a correct understanding of the results. It should be complete enough in historical detail so that the reader need only consult other sources for the more specialized topics. It should select the most cogent information from all available sources, summarize it in easy-to-use statistical tables, and provide a comprehensive exposition of the fundamental details.

There are four principal ways in which this book can be used:

- **As a reference work** for anyone—from corporate executives and government workers to high school and college students writing research papers—who wishes to learn about a particular topic. The detailed index, bibliographies at the end of each chapter, and technical appendices where appropriate will all be valuable to such users. Where to obtain data released since the publication of this volume is indicated in each chapter.
- **As a refresher** for people who have followed U.S. population trends for some time, but who have not had a recent opportunity to "put it all together" to arrive at an up-to-date integrated understanding. Special care has been taken to present time series for statistics appearing in annual publications. Many users may disagree with particular interpretations, but will appreciate the convenience of having data spanning many years from scattered sources compiled in one text.
- **As a textbook** for students undergoing pre-professional and professional training at a more sophisticated level than the usual "population problems" approach. Basic concepts are defined in a separate Definition Box in each chapter, thereby making them available but not forcing informed readers to interrupt their reading of the text to review them.
- **As an introduction to the United States citizenry**, primarily for international readers and ethnographers seeking to become better acquainted with the nation. Such readers usually lack access to population materials found in U.S. libraries. Consulting the U.S. Bureau of the Census publications such as the *Statistical Abstract of the United States* or *Historical Statistics of the United States from Colonial Times to the Present* provides a highly incomplete set of statistical tables with no explanatory text. Readers of the present volume will learn about Americans, how they earn their living, their living conditions, and some of their social and economic problems as reflected in population statistics.

The United States has undergone such monumental population changes since World War I that it is now virtually a demographic pretzel! Major swings of war and peace, economic depression and prosperity, and "baby boom" and "baby bust" cycles have been coupled with the flow and ebb of migration to large cities, the arrival from overseas of new racial and ethnic groups, the death of certain occupations and industries and the birth of others, changes in living arrangements, the role of women, the education of the youth, and the survival of the elderly. Demographers, who are dauntless about predicting the future, forecast that there are more swings and swerves in store for the remainder of this century and the first quarter of the next. Tracing these changes through past censuses and surveys and peering into the future to predict what will happen has been most exciting and educational for the author, who hopes the reader will find this population story equally engrossing.

The discussion of most topics includes a comparison of data for whites, blacks, and Spanish-origin (Hispanic) people. Hence, the book provides a portrait of black and Hispanic demography as well as of the American population as a whole.

The materials are arranged in twenty chapters, grouped in five sections. Section I reviews the basic facts of growth, demographic composition, and spatial distribution. Section II analyzes each of the basic components and processes by which population change takes place: family formation, fertility, mortality, and migration. Section III studies the social aspects of population composition–ethnicity, educational attainment, school attendance, and household and family living arrangements. Section IV takes a similar approach to economic characteristics such as work force participation, occupation, industry, income, and unemployment. The last section explores selected important topics: poverty, politics, housing, and religion. It also contains a chapter on the population of Puerto Rico, which significantly influences what happens in the fifty official states because of its considerable population size and special relationship to the U.S.

Thanks to the rich annual harvest of statistical data from the U.S. Bureau of the Census *Current Population Reports* and the monthly or annual reports from the National Center for Health Statistics, the Bureau of Labor Statistics, and similar sources, this volume can provide information about changes since the census of 1980. Materials available as of July 1, 1984, have been incorporated into the volume. Readers are urged to consult the most recent issue of "Population Profile of the United States," published annually in the *Current Population Reports* (Series P-20), for a quick overview of demographic events since 1982-83.

A book, *The Population of the United States*, by the same author, was published in 1959. So different is the population situation in the 1980s that this volume is completely new and not a revision. The earlier volume will still be useful to anyone who needs more detailed data and interpretation for the years preceding and immediately following World War II. The present book places greatest analytical effort on the years since 1960, and hence can be regarded as a sequel to the first.

Because the author is indebted to so many people and organizations, a separate acknowledgments section follows.

Donald J. Bogue
October, 1984

Acknowledgments

Without generous and enthusiastic help from several organizations and persons this book could not have been completed in its present scope and detail. Acknowledging their aid is a pleasant obligation, which may be divided into four categories.

Data. Because of the inevitable delay between the collection of data and the appearance of published reports, much of the data needed for this volume was not available in published form when needed. In the early stages of writing this was true for 1980 census materials, and for post-1980 materials throughout. Generous help from the U.S. Bureau of the Census Population Division, the National Center for Health Statistics, and the Bureau of Labor Statistics made it possible to acquire copies of selected tabulations in advance of their publication. Because of the size of the book, the requests for materials encroached upon the normal limits of such service to users of these organizations' data. The National Opinion Research Center of the University of Chicago and the Center for Political Studies of the University of Michigan were generous in providing their data files in preparing Chapters 18 and 19, for which only limited official statistics are available.

Professional. An unknown editor, retained by the publisher, was a well-informed and astute demographer who made many corrections and suggestions that greatly improved the interpretation of data. Prof. José L. Vázquez, professor of demography at the University of Puerto Rico, gave such generous assistance in the writing of Chapter 20 that he has been listed as coauthor. Three advanced graduate students of demography at the University of Chicago not only performed and supervised large amounts of computation, but also read chapter drafts critically and made suggestions for improvement and correction. So great is the author's obligation to Odalia Ho, David Hartmann, and Albert Woolbright that they have been listed on the title page. They were assisted by the following junior demographers, who provided statistical computation:

Anita Brown-Isom
Chong Meng Chan
Yolanda Cordero
Rosario Garcia
Jaya Gujral
Allen Harden
Jeng-Koo Kang
Helene Kim
Ted Manley
Chang-Jin Moon
Wamucii Njogu
Cindy Rayman
Tony Tam.

Manuscript. Because of the highly statistical nature of this book, the only feasible way of publishing it was for the Community and Family Study Center to deliver camera-ready copy to the publisher. The laborious task of taking each chapter from rough draft through in-house editing and rewriting to final smooth copy, and of typing statistical tables, plotting graphs, justifying text, and then assembling everything as attractive and consistent completed page copy was performed by George Rumsey, whose contribution is so great that he heads the list of contributors on the title page. The final copy of the numerous graphs are also a product of Mr. Rumsey's creative abilities. He was assisted by the following persons, all of whom worked overtime to meet the publisher's deadlines:

Gretchen Balanoff–photographic copy and artwork
Yolanda Butts–composer typing and editing
Richard Dulaney–statistical and composer typing
Diane Kavanaugh–statistical typing and computation
Laura Pérez–statistical and composer typing
Elaine Tite–statistical typing and graphics.

Administrative. Isabel Garcia, administrator of the Community and Family Study Center, not only helped acquire materials and pay salaries and bills, but also gave constant and concerned encouragement to the entire staff to persevere for nearly three years of intense effort.

All of the above colleagues and friends must be excused from responsibility for any deficiencies that readers may find in this product of their sincere efforts.

DJB

Chapter 1

The Size and Growth of the United States Population

The Size of the U.S. Population

The population residing in the United States as of July 1, 1985, is estimated to be about 237 million persons.[1] Since the census of 1980 it has been growing at the rate of 2.2 million persons (1.0 percent) a year. These figures represent a comparatively small share of the earth's inhabitants and of the earth's population growth. Only about 4.9 percent (one-twentieth) of the world's people live in the United States (Table 1-1). In land area, the United States (3,539,289 square miles[2]) accounts for a slightly larger proportion of the world total than in population: The United States constitutes 7.0 percent of the land area of the world. Although it is the most populous nation in the Western Hemisphere, it contains only 35 percent of the population of North, Central, and South America combined and one-fifth of their combined land area.

Three nations—China, India, and the U.S.S.R.—have populations larger than that of the United States: China's population is 4.5 times, India's 3.2 times, and the Soviet Union's 1.2 times the size of the U.S. population.[3] (See Table 1-2 for statistics on and comparison of the largest nations of the world.) Together the four largest nations contain nearly one-half (48 percent) of the estimated number of people in the world. The estimated population of each nation, region, and continent of the world, for selected dates since 1950 and projected to 2025, is reported in Table 1-1.

Table 1-2 gives the estimated population in 1982 of the nations with 10 million or more inhabitants, ranked in order of size.[4] Figure 1-1 illustrates the size of the population of the United States in comparison with the nineteen other most populous nations of the world. Following the "big four," the next three largest nations—Indonesia, Brazil, and Japan—had populations above 100 million in 1983. Eleven others had populations between 50 million and 100 million. Together, the 59 largest nations listed in Table 1-2 contained 92 percent of the world's population. This means that only 8 percent of the world's people lived in the more than one hundred small nations, trust territories, possessions, and protectorates that have populations of less than 10 million.

The density of settlement (population per square mile) in the United States—65 per square mile in 1985—is slightly higher than the world average. However, the United States is less densely settled than the ten other largest nations except the U.S.S.R. and Brazil. Because of adverse climate, hostile topography, and lack of resources, much of the world's land is virtually uninhabited. Densities computed in terms of total land area are therefore only very crude measures of the relation of population to natural resources. Nevertheless, population densities are reported in Table 1-1 for each continent and nation. This table also notes, in terms of square miles, the estimated land area of each continent, region, and country.

Definitions

Each chapter of this book contains a "definition box," wherein demographic concepts and terms not defined in previous chapters are defined or explained. This avoids needless reading for those familiar with demographic terminology. The index specifies the page on which each item is defined.

Population Size. The total number of inhabitants of a specified area at a specified date.

Census Enumeration. An organized campaign to count the number of inhabitants residing within a specified area as of a specified date, enumerating their demographic, social, and economic characteristics in the process.

Population Density. The total population size divided by the total land area, in either square miles or square kilometers.

Population Change. Increase or decrease in population size between two dates.

Intercensal Population Change. Increase or decrease in population size between two censuses.

Intercensal Rate of Change. Percentage increase or decrease in population between two censuses.

Average Annual Rate of Change. The average percentage increase or decrease per annum required to account for the population change between two dates.

Components of Population Change. Births, deaths, immigration, and emigration.

Reproductive Change (Natural Increase). Births minus deaths.

Demographic Balancing Equation. Addition of the components of change between two censuses to the total of the earlier census in order to estimate the population count of the later census.

Error of Closure. Difference between the expected count, resulting from use of the demographic balancing equation, and the actual count at the later census.

Midyear Population. Estimate of population as of July 1 of a given year. Usually computed by averaging estimates of population at beginning and end of the calendar year.

Crude Birth Rate. Number of births during a year per 1,000 midyear population in that year.

Crude Death Rate. Number of deaths during a year per 1,000 midyear population in that year.

Net Migration Rate. Amount of net migration during a year per 1,000 midyear population in that year.

Population Projection. Estimate of what the population will be at a future date, based on assumptions about the future course of birth, death, and migration rates.

Recent Growth of the U.S. Population

Between the census taken April 1, 1970, and the census taken exactly ten years later in 1980, the U.S. population increased by 23.2 million persons (Table 1-3). This was a smaller numerical increase than took place over each of the two preceding decades, but greater than in any other decade from 1790 to 1950. It represented an intercensal growth of 11.4 percent over the 203.3 million inhabitants of 1970.[5] The rate of population growth between 1970 and 1980 is the lowest in the nation's history except for the decade 1930-40. The rather large numerical increase was produced by a rather low rate of increase being applied against a large population base.

Definitions of Population

The population may be defined in three ways: "total population," "resident population," and "civilian population." The way in which the population is defined affects the statistics of growth. For most purposes the "resident population" living within the national boundaries, including military personnel stationed there, is satisfactory. This is the definition used in the discussion so far and for the official census count. "Total population" includes population abroad (armed forces and federal civilian employees and their dependents stationed abroad, crews of merchant vessels, and U.S. ci-

Table 1-1. Population of the Countries of the World, Estimated 1950-80 and Projected 1985-2025

Region and country	Estimated population (000)							Land area (1,000 square miles) (1979)	Percent distribution (1979)		Density per square mile (1985)	Average annual growth rate (1980–1985)
	1950	1960	1970	1980	1985	2000	2025		Land area (1979)	Population		
World total	2,524,622	3,037,215	3,695,584	4,432,147	4,826,328	6,115,514	8,192,137	52,448.2	100.000	100.000	92	1.70
United States	152,271	180,671	204,879	223,233	234,548	263,829	305,841	3,675.5	7.008	4.860	64	0.99
More developed regions	831,855	944,909	1,047,217	1,131,339	1,170,153	1,268,824	1,373,856	22,004.6	41.955	24.245	53	0.68
Less developed regions	1,692,768	2,092,307	2,648,367	3,300,809	3,656,175	4,846,690	6,818,280	30,443.6	58.045	75,755	120	2.04
AFRICA	220,274	275,246	354,663	469,982	546,166	852,885	1,541,702	11,704.2	22.316	11.316	47	3.00
Eastern Africa	61,507	76,859	100,413	133,501	155,831	250,029	477,919	2,447.6	4.667	3.229	64	3.09
Burundi	2,426	2,913	3,485	4,241	4,824	7,207	13,310	10.7	0.020	0.100	451	2.57
Comoros	152	203	271	358	414	620	1,016	0.7	0.00	0.009	518	2.89
Ethiopia	16,253	20,093	25,450	31,468	35,631	54,666	93,633	471.8	0.900	0.738	76	2.49
Kenya	6,416	8,189	11,253	16,466	20,210	37,138	82,343	225.0	0.429	0.419	90	4.10
Madagascar	4,560	5,474	6,800	8,742	10,037	15,208	26,438	226.7	0.432	0.208	44	2.76
Malawi	2,701	3,419	4,511	6,162	7,290	12,014	22,997	45.7	0.087	0.151	160	3.36
Mauritius	487	664	830	959	1,041	1,248	1,568	0.8	0.002	0.022	1,301	1.63
Mozambique	5,709	6,546	8,140	10,473	12,013	18,701	36,260	302.3	0.590	0.249	40	2.75
Réunion	242	332	441	525	563	685	825	1.0	0.002	0.012	563	1.40
Rwanda	2,211	2,762	3,573	4,797	5,631	9,333	19,566	10.2	0.019	0.117	552	3.21
Somalia	1,907	2,274	2,789	4,637	5,588	7,156	13,418	246.2	0.469	0.116	23	3.73
Uganda	5,158	6,806	9,806	13,201	15,478	25,396	51,888	91.5	0.174	0.321	169	3.18
United Rep. of Tanzania	8,210	10,201	13,300	17,934	21,057	38,031	63,598	364.9	0.696	0.436	58	3.21
Zambia	2,519	3,207	4,242	5,766	6,819	11,276	21,777	290.6	0.554	0.141	23	3.35
Zimbabwe	2,415	3,605	5,308	7,396	8,805	14,726	28,435	150.8	0.288	0.182	58	3.49
Middle Africa	28,840	34,572	41,570	53,093	60,670	91,445	62,170	2,553.3	4.868	1.257	24	2.67
Angola	4,118	4,816	5,588	7,078	8,073	12,376	23,643	481.4	0.918	0.167	17	2.63
Central African Republic	1,388	1,538	1,857	2,294	2,593	3,914	7,399	240.5	0.459	0.054	11	2.45
Chad	2,639	3,032	3,643	4,455	4,954	7,063	12,195	495.8	0.945	0.103	10	2.12
Congo	824	969	1,198	1,537	1,760	2,717	5,204	132.0	0.252	0.036	13	2.71
Equatorial Guinea	211	244	291	363	411	613	1,129	10.8	0.021	0.009	38	2.47
Gabon	464	472	500	548	591	754	1,152	103.3	0.197	0.012	6	1.52
United Rep. of Cameroon	4,955	5,681	6,781	8,444	9,553	13,937	23,421	183.6	0.350	0.198	52	2.47
Zaïre	14,180	17,756	21,638	28,291	32,648	49,982	87,935	905.6	1.727	0.676	36	2.86

Table 1-1. Population of the Countries of the World, Estimated 1950-80 and Projected 1985-2025—continued

Region and country	Estimated population (000)							Land area (1,000 square miles) (1979)	Percent distribution (1979)		Density per square mile	Average annual growth rate (1980-1985)
	1950	1960	1970	1980	1985	2000	2025		Land area (1979)	Population	(1985)	
Northern Africa	52,061	65,227	82,968	109,017	125,825	186,160	295,916	3,291.5	6.276	2.607	38	2.87
Algeria	8,753	10,800	13,746	18,919	22,583	37,041	62,880	919.6	1.753	0.468	25	3.54
Egypt	20,461	25,929	32,820	41,963	47,240	64,421	94,933	386.7	0.737	0.979	122	2.37
Libya	1,029	1,349	1,982	2,978	3,611	6,077	10,934	679.4	1.295	0.075	5	3.85
Morocco	8,953	11,640	15,126	20,296	23,869	36,509	59,297	172.4	0.329	0.495	138	3.24
Sudan	9,322	11,256	14,090	18,371	21,211	32,328	54,435	967.5	1.845	0.439	22	2.88
Tunisia	3,530	4,221	5,127	6,354	7,156	9,556	13,072	63.2	0.120	0.148	113	2.38
Southern Africa	15,807	19,627	25,236	32,998	38,095	57,981	100,553	1,039.9	1.983	0.789	37	2.87
Botswana	430	507	622	807	946	1,597	3,432	231.8	0.442	0.020	4	3.18
Lesotho	746	869	1,061	1,341	1,519	2,222	3,732	11.7	0.022	0.031	130	2.50
Namibia	484	596	764	1,009	1,170	1,822	3,266	318.3	0.607	0.024	4	2.97
South Africa	13,863	17,310	22,358	29,285	33,800	51,320	88,260	471.4	0.899	0.701	72	2.88
Swaziland	283	345	430	557	647	1,020	1,863	6.7	0.013	0.013	97	3.00
Western Africa	62,059	78,960	104,476	141,372	165,746	267,271	505,144	2,371.9	4.522	3.434	70	3.18
Benin	1,648	2,050	2,646	3,530	4,127	6,756	13,927	43.5	0.083	0.086	95	3.13
Cape Verde	148	201	267	324	351	427	524	1.6	0.003	0.007	219	1.57
Gambia	269	327	449	603	686	1,046	1,970	4.4	0.008	0.014	156	2.58
Ghana	4,368	6,804	8,614	11,679	13,755	22,348	42,007	92.1	0.176	0.285	149	3.27
Guinea	2,815	3,213	3,921	5,014	5,734	8,823	16,841	95.0	0.181	0.119	60	2.69
Guinea-Bissau	511	520	487	573	628	859	1,432	13.9	0.027	0.013	45	1.82
Ivory Coast	2,666	3,300	5,341	8,034	9,418	14,775	26,727	124.5	0.237	0.195	76	3.18
Liberia	758	1,004	1,393	1,967	2,355	4,002	7,897	43.0	0.082	0.049	55	3.60
Mali	3,430	4,224	5,362	6,940	7,994	12,620	24,979	478.8	0.913	0.166	17	2.83
Mauritania	781	970	1,245	1,634	1,890	3,022	6,074	398.0	0.759	0.039	5	2.91
Niger	2,283	2,876	4,008	5,318	6,192	10,045	20,516	489.2	0.933	0.128	13	3.04
Nigeria	33,230	42,366	56,346	77,082	91,178	149,965	285,479	356.7	0.680	1.889	256	3.36
Senegal	2,536	3,076	4,267	5,661	6,474	9,747	16,771	75.8	0.145	0.134	85	2.68
Sierra Leone	1,809	2,165	2,692	3,474	3,997	6,090	10,675	27.7	0.053	0.082	144	2.80
Togo	1,213	1,506	2,020	2,625	3,061	4,844	8,854	21.6	0.04	0.063	142	3.07
Upper Volta	3,589	4,354	5,413	6,908	7,900	11,895	20,465	105.9	0.202	0.164	75	2.68

Table 1-1. Population of the Countries of the World, Estimated 1950-80 and Projected 1985-2025—continued

Region and country	Estimated population (000)							Land area (1,000 square miles) (1979)	Percent distribution (1979)		Density per square mile	Average annual growth rate (1980-1985)
	1950	1960	1970	1980	1985	2000	2025		Land area (1979)	Population	(1985)	
LATIN AMERICA	164,053	215,731	283,496	363,704	409,743	565,747	865,198	7,935.4	15.130	8.490	52	2.38
Caribbean	16,886	20,431	25,210	30,648	33,564	43,286	61,887	91.9	0.175	0.695	365	1.82
Barbados	211	231	239	263	277	320	381	0.2	*	0.006	1,385	1.06
Cuba	5,858	7,029	8,580	9,732	10,038	11,718	13,575	44.2	0.084	0.208	227	0.62
Dominican Republic	2,361	3,258	4,523	5,947	6,715	9,329	14,495	18.8	0.036	0.139	357	2.43
Guadeloupe	210	273	328	329	334	354	413	0.7	0.001	0.007	477	0.29
Haiti	3,097	3,723	4,605	5,809	6,585	9,860	18,312	10.7	0.020	0.136	615	2.51
Jamaica	1,043	1,629	1,869	2,188	2,358	2,872	3,764	4.2	0.008	0.049	561	1.50
Martinique	222	286	333	325	328	362	430	0.4	*	0.007	820	1.20
Puerto Rico	2,219	2,358	2,718	3,675	4,345	5,312	6,463	3.4	0.006	0.090	1,278	3.35
Trinidad and Tobago	636	843	1,027	1,168	1,272	1,483	1,789	2.0	0.004	0.026	636	1.39
Windward Islands	273	319	354	409	438	527	743	0.8	0.002	0.009	548	1.37
Other Caribbean	396	482	635	805	895	1,149	1,523	6.5	0.012	0.919	138	2.11
Middle America	36,101	49,299	68,093	92,538	106,848	155,709	242,909	963.5	1.837	2.214	111	2.88
Costa Rica	858	1,236	1,732	2,213	2,485	3,377	4,893	19.6	0.037	0.051	127	2.31
El Salvador	1,940	2,574	3,582	4,797	5,552	8,708	15,048	8.1	0.015	0.115	685	2.93
Guatemala	2,962	3,966	5,353	7,262	8,403	12,739	21,717	42.0	0.080	0.174	200	2.92
Honduras	1,401	1,942	2,640	3,691	4,372	6,978	13,293	43.3	0.083	0.091	101	3.39
Mexico	26,886	36,881	51,187	69,752	80,484	115,659	173,960	761.6	1.452	1.668	106	2.86
Nicaragua	1,109	1,472	1,970	2,733	3,218	5,154	9,752	50.2	0.096	0.067	64	3.27
Panama	825	1,095	1,464	1,896	2,117	2,823	3,937	29.8	0.057	0.044	71	2.20
Temperate South America	25,437	30,729	35,941	41,067	43,801	51,605	61,925	1,433.7	2.734	0.908	31	1.29
Argentina	17,150	20,611	23,748	27,036	28,689	33,222	39,058	1,068.3	2.037	0.594	27	1.19
Chile	6,091	7,585	9,368	11,104	12,074	14,934	18,758	292.3	0.557	0.250	41	1.68
Uruguay	2,194	2,531	2,824	2,924	3,036	3,448	4,108	68.5	0.13	0.063	44	0.75
Tropical South America	85,628	115,272	154,251	199,452	225,530	315,146	498,476	5,446.3	10.384	4.673	41	2.46
Bolivia	2,766	3,428	4,325	5,570	6,371	9,724	19,525	424.2	0.809	0.132	15	2.69
Brazil	52,842	71,513	95,322	122,320	137,233	187,494	291,252	3,286.5	6.266	2.843	42	2.30
Colombia	11,597	15,538	20,803	25,794	28,714	37,999	51,718	439.7	0.838	0.595	65	2.15
Ecuador	3,307	4,422	5,958	8,021	9,380	14,596	25,725	109.5	0.209	0.194	86	3.13
Guyana	375	538	709	883	979	1,238	1,620	83.0	0.158	0.020	12	2.06
Paraguay	1,371	1,778	2,290	3,168	3,681	5,405	8,552	157.0	0.299	0.076	23	3.00
Peru	7,988	10,181	13,461	17,625	20,273	30,703	56,036	496.2	0.946	0.420	41	2.80
Suriname	215	290	371	388	445	698	1,097	63.0	0.120	0.009	7	2.73
Venezuela	5,139	7,550	10,962	15,620	18,386	27,207	42,846	352.1	0.671	0.381	52	3.26

Table 1-1. Population of the Countries of the World, Estimated 1950-80 and Projected 1985-2025—continued

Region and country	Estimated population (000)							Land area (1,000 square miles) (1979)	Percent distribution (1979)		Density per square mile (1985)	Average annual growth rate (1980-1985)
	1950	1960	1970	1980	1985	2000	2025		Land area (1979)	Population		
EUROPE	391,955	425,129	459,425	483,704	491,915	512,017	522,199	1,881.9	3.588	10.192	261	0.34
Eastern Europe	88,500	96,713	103,312	110,024	113,440	121,362	130,672	382.3	0.729	2.350	297	0.61
Bulgaria	7,251	7,867	8,514	9,007	9,237	9,698	10,098	42.8	0.082	0.191	216	0.51
Czechoslovakia	12,389	13,654	14,362	15,336	15,738	16,839	18,489	49.4	0.094	0.326	319	0.52
German Democratic Republic	18,387	17,240	17,066	16,854	16,877	16,915	16,440	41.8	0.080	0.350	404	0.03
Hungary	9,338	9,984	10,353	10,754	10,877	10,964	10,938	35.9	0.068	0.225	303	0.23
Poland	24,824	29,561	32,657	35,805	37,558	41,217	45,685	120.7	0.230	0.778	311	0.96
Romania	16,311	18,407	20,360	22,268	23,153	25,728	29,021	91.7	0.175	0.480	252	0.78
Northern Europe	72,477	75,834	80,310	82,004	82,170	82,576	81,323	607.5	1.158	1.703	135	0.04
Denmark	4,271	4,581	4,929	5,122	5,164	5,249	5,142	16.6	0.032	0.107	311	0.16
Finland	4,009	4,430	4,606	4,863	4,964	5,058	4,849	130.1	0.248	0.103	38	0.41
Iceland	143	176	204	231	243	274	302	39.8	0.076	0.005	6	1.02
Ireland	2,969	2,834	2,954	3,308	3,498	4,118	4,993	27.1	0.052	0.072	129	1.11
Norway	3,265	3,581	3,877	4,079	4,143	4,312	4,405	125.2	0.239	0.086	33	0.31
Sweden	7,014	7,480	8,043	8,274	8,269	8,088	7,587	173.7	0.331	0.171	48	-0.01
U. K. of Great Britain and Northern Ireland	50,616	52,559	55,480	55,886	55,641	55,208	53,740	94.2	0.180	1.153	591	-0.09
Southern Europe	108,539	118,069	127,665	138,969	143,290	153,563	160,636	507.9	0.968	2.969	282	0.61
Albania	1,230	1,611	2,138	2,732	3,046	3,885	5,004	11.1	0.021	0.063	274	2.18
Greece	7,566	8,327	8,793	9,329	9,610	10,395	11,234	50.9	0.097	0.199	189	0.59
Italy	46,769	50,223	53,565	56,940	57,799	59,108	57,003	116.3	0.222	1.198	497	0.30
Malta	312	329	326	343	357	390	418	0.1	*	0.007		0.81
Portugal	8,405	8,826	8,628	9,836	10,198	11,154	12,261	35.6	0.068	0.211	286	0.72
Spain	27,868	30,303	33,779	37,378	38,999	43,362	48,310	194.9	0.372	0.808	200	0.85
Yugoslavia	16,346	18,402	20,371	22,328	23,192	25,168	26,289	98.8	0.188	0.481	235	0.76
Western Europe	122,439	134,513	148,138	152,707	153,015	154,516	149,569	384.2	0.733	3.170	398	0.004
Austria	6,935	7,048	7,447	7,481	7,451	7,425	7,112	32.4	0.062	0.154	230	-0.08
Belgium	8,639	9,153	9,638	9,833	9,866	9,964	9,732	11.8	0.002	0.204	836	0.07
France	41,736	45,684	50,670	53,508	54,282	56,252	57,106	211.2	0.403	1.125	257	0.29
Germany, Federal Republic	49,989	55,433	60,700	60,931	60,116	58,822	54,011	96.0	0.183	1.246	626	-0.27
Luxembourg	296	314	339	358	357	349	313	1.0	0.002	0.007	357	-0.06
Netherlands	10,114	11,480	13,032	14,079	14,400	15,180	15,207	15.8	0.030	0.298	911	0.45
Switzerland	4,694	5,362	6,267	6,466	6,488	6,461	6,008	15.9	0.030	0.134	408	0.07

Table 1-1. Population of the Countries of the World, Estimated 1950-80 and Projected 1985-2025—continued

Region and country	Estimated population (000)							Land area (1,000 square miles) (1979)	Percent distribution (1979)		Density per square mile	Average annual growth rate (1980–1985)
	1950	1960	1970	1980	1985	2000	2025		Land area (1979)	Population	(1985)	
NORTHERN AMERICA................	166,073	198,662	226,390	247,835	261,026	295,469	340,614	8,306.9	15.838	5.408	31	1.04
Canada......................	13,737	17,909	21,406	24,484	26,354	31,499	34,598	3,851.8	7.344	0.546	7	1.47
United States of America....	152,271	180,671	204,879	223,233	234,548	263,829	305,841	3,675.5	7.008	4.860	64	0.99
EAST ASIA......................	673,245	815,824	993,976	1,174,874	1,250,064	1,474,669	1,712,137	4,538.3	8.653	25.901	275	1.24
China........................	556,613	682,024	838,396	994,913	1,060,059	1,257,298	1,469,329	3,705.4	7.065	21.964	286	1.27
Japan........................	83,625	94,096	104,331	116,551	120,208	129,282	131,451	143.8	0.274	2.491	836	0.62
Other East Asia..............	33,006	39,704	51,249	63,410	69,797	88,089	111,356	689.1	1.314	1.446	101	1.92
Hong Kong..................	1,974	3,075	3,942	5,106	5,705	6,973	7,898	0.4	*	0.118	14,263	2.22
Dem. People's Rep. of Korea.	9,740	10,526	13,892	17,892	20,082	27,256	37,556	46.5	0.089	0.416	432	2.31
Republic of Korea..........	20,357	25,003	31,923	38,455	41,783	50,786	61,472	38.0	0.072	0.866	1,100	1.66
Mongolia...................	747	931	1,248	1,669	1,912	2,686	3,944	604.2	1.152	0.040	3	2.72
SOUTH ASIA.....................	716,300	876,506	1,116,605	1,403,736	1,564,692	2,074,789	2,819,265	6,188.2	11.799	32.420	253	2.17
Eastern South Asia...........	184,366	228,854	290,702	361,245	400,219	520,439	688,492	1,735.9	3.310	8.292	231	2.05
Burma......................	18,380	22,254	27,748	35,289	39,857	55,108	81,568	261.2	0.498	0.826	153	2.44
Democratic Kampuchea.......	4,346	5,433	6,938	6,747	7,635	10,609	14,125	69.9	0.133	0.158	109	2.47
East Timor.................	433	500	604	755	846	1,147	1,619	5.8	0.011	0.018	146	2.28
Indonesia..................	80,019	97,711	122,211	148,033	160,658	198,687	246,855	735.3	1.402	3.329	218	1.64
Lao People's Dem. Republic..	1,949	2,382	2,962	3,721	4,184	5,729	8,234	91.4	0.174	0.087	46	2.34
Malaysia...................	6,250	8,170	10,863	14,068	15,839	21,269	28,782	128.4	0.245	0.328	123	2.37
Philippines................	20,859	28,098	37,540	49,211	55,963	77,036	107,696	115.8	0.221	1.160	483	2.57
Singapore..................	1,022	1,634	2,075	2,390	2,552	2,967	3,259	0.2	*	0.053	12,760	1.31
Thailand...................	20,969	27,229	36,499	47,063	52,456	68,609	90,114	198.5	0.378	1.087	264	2.17
Viet Nam...................	30,094	35,351	43,128	53,740	59,950	78,894	105,743	127.2	0.243	1.242	471	2.19

Table 1-1. Population of the Countries of the World, Estimated 1950-80 and Projected 1985-2025—continued

Region and country	Estimated population (000)							Land area (1,000 square miles) (1979)	Percent distribution (1979)		Density per square mile	Average annual growth rate (1980-1985)
	1950	1960	1970	1980	1985	2000	2025		Land area (1979)	Population	(1985)	
Middle South Asia	489,502	591,797	752,243	944,141	1,050,850	1,386,257	1,867,011	2,620.7	4.997	21.773	401	2.14
Afghanistan	8,252	9,820	12,342	15,940	18,095	26,528	42,106	250.0	0.477	0.375	72	2.54
Bangladesh	40,574	51,446	68,278	88,164	101,366	148,361	221,750	55.6	0.106	2.100	1,823	2.79
Bhutan	750	857	1,045	1,296	1,450	2,030	3,166	19.3	0.037	0.030	75	2.25
India	368,458	439,441	552,469	684,460	752,938	960,611	1,233,790	1,269.3	2.420	15.601	593	1.91
Iran	16,913	21,554	28,359	38,126	44,383	64,916	99,420	636.3	1.213	0.920	70	3.04
Nepal	8,314	9,327	11,416	14,288	16,007	22,493	33,604	54.4	0.104	0.332	294	2.27
Pakistan	38,481	49,371	65,706	86,899	100,011	139,987	205,952	310.4	0.592	2.072	322	2.81
Sri Lanka	7,678	9,889	12,514	14,815	16,423	21,076	26,844	25.3	0.048	0.340	649	2.06
Western South Asia	42,432	55,856	73,660	98,350	113,623	168,093	263,762	1,831.6	3.492	2.354	62	2.89
Arab countries	19,871	25,659	34,760	48,539	57,494	91,801	155,114	1,518.6	2.895	1.191	38	3.39
Bahrain	116	156	220	313	360	515	774	0.2	*	0.007	1,800	2.77
Democratic Yemen	992	1,208	1,497	1,858	2,124	3,312	5,605	128.6	0.245	0.044	17	2.68
Iraq	5,158	6,847	9,356	13,072	15,475	24,198	40,396	167.9	0.320	0.321	92	3.38
Jordan	1,237	1,695	2,299	3,244	3,888	6,510	11,203	37.7	0.072	0.081	103	3.63
Kuwait	152	278	744	1,353	1,721	2,936	4,993	6.9	0.013	0.036	249	4.82
Lebanon	1,443	1,857	2,469	2,658	2,963	3,992	5,601	4.0	0.008	0.061	741	2.17
Oman	413	505	654	891	1,041	1,651	2,849	82.0	0.156	0.022	13	3.11
Qatar	25	45	111	237	285	425	664	4.2	0.008	0.006	68	3.70
Saudi Arabia	3,201	4,075	5,745	8,960	10,823	17,804	31,031	830.0	1.583	0.224	13	3.78
Syrian Arab Republic	3,495	4,561	6,258	8,977	10,903	18,677	32,685	71.5	0.136	0.226	152	3.89
United Arab Emirates	70	90	223	726	883	1,286	1,990	32.3	0.062	0.018	27	3.92
Yemen	3,324	4,039	4,835	5,812	6,536	9,828	16,342	75.3	0.144	0.135	87	2.35
Non-Arab countries	22,561	30,196	38,899	49,811	56,129	76,293	108,647	313.0	0.597	1.163	179	2.39
Cyprus	494	573	604	620	638	682	777	3.6	0.007	0.013	177	0.57
Israel	1,258	2,114	2,974	3,937	4,401	5,619	7,510	8.0	0.015	0.091	550	2.23
Turkey	20,809	27,509	35,321	45,254	51,091	69,991	100,361	301.4	0.575	1.059	170	2.43

Table 1-1. Population of the Countries of the World, Estimated 1950-80 and Projected 1985-2025—continued

Region and country	Estimated population (000)							Land area (1,000 square miles) (1979)	Percent distribution (1979)		Density per square mile (1985)	Average annual growth rate (1980-1985)
	1950	1960	1970	1980	1985	2000	2025		Land area (1979)	Population		
OCEANIA	12,649	15,784	19,330	22,820	24,521	29,701	36,064	3,284.8	6.263	0.508	7	1.44
Australia-New Zealand	10,127	12,687	15,371	17,756	18,802	21,819	24,633	3,071.6	5.856	0.390	6	1.15
Australia	8,219	10,315	12,552	14,488	15,345	17,795	19,943	2,967.9	5.659	0.318	5	1.15
New Zealand	1,908	2,372	2,820	3,268	3,457	4,024	4,690	103.7	0.198	0.072	33	1.12
Melanesia	1,830	2,189	2,779	3,645	4,177	6,007	9,236	201.5	0.384	0.087	21	2.72
Papua New Guinea	1,613	1,920	2,419	3,154	3,611	5,179	7,974	178.3	0.340	0.075	20	2.71
Other Melanesia	217	269	360	491	566	828	1,261	23.2	0.044	0.012	24	2.83
Micronesia-Polynesia	692	908	1,179	1,419	1,542	1,875	2,195	11.7	0.022	0.032	132	1.66
Micronesia	167	208	265	327	358	442	524	1.3	0.002	0.007	275	1.77
Polynesia	525	700	914	1,091	1,184	1,433	1,671	10.4	0.020	0.025	114	1.63
Fiji	289	394	520	630	684	817	928	7.1	0.014	0.014	96	1.65
Other Polynesia	236	306	394	462	500	616	743	3.3	0.006	0.010	152	1.60
UNION OF SOVIET SOCIALIST REPUBLICS	180,075	214,335	241,700	265,493	278,202	310,236	354,958	8,600.4	16.398	5.764	32	0.93

[a]Regional totals include data for some countries not listed. Eastern Africa includes British Indian Ocean Territory (except in land area data), Djibouti, and Seychelles. Middle Africa includes Sao Tome and Principe. Northern Africa includes Western Sahara. Western Africa includes St. Helena. Caribbean includes Antigua, Bahamas, British Virgin Islands, Cayman Islands, Dominica, Grenada, Montserrat, Netherland Antilles, St. Kitts-Nevis-Anguilla, Saint Lucia, St. Vincent-the Grenadines, Turks and Caicos Islands, and United States Virgin Islands. Middle America includes Belize. Temperate South America includes Falkland Islands (Malvinas). Tropical South America includes French Guiana. Northern America includes Bermuda, Greenland, and St. Pierre and Miquelon. Other East Asia includes Macau. Eastern South Asia includes Brunei. Middle South Asia includes Maldives. Northern Europe includes Channel Islands, Faeroe Islands, and Isle of Man. Southern Europe includes Andorra, Gibraltar, the Hole See, Malta, and San Marino. Western Europe includes Liechtenstein and Monaco. Melanesia includes New Caledonia, Norfolk Island, Papua New Guinea, Solomon Islands, and Vanuatu. Micronesia-Polynesia includes Guam, Kiribati, Nauru, Niue, Pacific Islands, and Tuvalu (Micronesia), as well as American Samoa, Cook Islands, Fiji, French Polynesia, Samoa, Tonga, and Wallis and Futuna Islands (Polynesia).

Note: * indicates less than 0.001 percent.

Source: United Nations. Demographic Indicators of Countries: Estimates and Projections as Assessed in 1980. New York: United Nations, 1982.

vilian citizens living abroad). For many purposes it is preferable to exclude the armed forces stationed within the nation from the resident population and deal with the resident "civilian population" only. Statistics of each of these three types of population are maintained by the Census Bureau and are presented in Table 1-4. In times of military mobilization the civilian population is diminished by inductions into the armed forces. At times of U.S. involvement in conflicts overseas the resident population is diminished by transfers abroad of military and civilian persons. A correct understanding of population changes requires information about the fluctuating size of the military population and whether it is stationed at home or abroad.

Commonwealth of Puerto Rico and Outlying Areas

Not included in the discussion so far is the population of the Commonwealth of Puerto Rico and the "outlying areas," which are under the political administration of the United States. Statistics of their population at recent censuses are presented in Table 1-5. Residents of those areas can migrate rather freely to the United States, so those areas affect U.S. growth rates and population composition. Because of its size and close ties with the nation, a special chapter in this volume is devoted to Puerto Rico.

Components of Population Change and Error of Closure

Changes in the size of an area's population involve two components, *reproductive change* (frequently called natural increase) and *net migration.*

- During any period a nation or community increases its population by means of live births. Over the same period it loses population by the death of some of its members. Reproductive change (natural increase) is equal to births minus deaths. It is the net result of two vital processes.
- During any period, a community increases its population by receiving immigrants from other nations or other areas.[6] During the same time, however, it loses population when emigrants go to other nations or other areas. Net migration is equal to immigration minus emigration. It is the net result of two redistributional processes. When a nation is the unit of study, its growth

Table 1-2. Population in 1983 and Estimated Rate of Growth of Nations with Ten Million Inhabitants or More: Estimated by United Nations and U.S. Bureau of the Census [ranked in order of size]

Country	Population in 1983 (000)		Average annual growth rate[a]		Estimated amount of yearly increase 1980-85 (000)
	United Nations	Census Bureau	United Nations	Census Bureau	
World total	4,665,375	4,721,887	1.70	1.8	83,117
China	1,033,699[b]	1,059,802	1.27	1.4	13,029
India	725,456	730,572	1.91	2.1	13,696
U.S.S.R.	273,125	272,308	0.84	0.8	2,542
UNITED STATES	229,949	234,193	1.0	0.9	2,263
Indonesia	155,564	160,932	1.6	2.1	2,525
Brazil	131,142	131,305	2.3	2.3	2,983
Japan	118,865	119,205	0.6	0.6	731
Bangladesh	95,898	96,539	2.8	3.1	2,640
Pakistan	94,656	94,780	2.8	2.8	2,622
Nigeria	85,215	85,219	3.4	3.4	2,819
Mexico	76,075	75,702	2.9	2.6	2,146
Germany, F.R.	60,395	61,543	-0.3	-0.2	-162
Italy	57,477	56,345	0.3	0.1	172
Vietnam	57,449	57,036	2.2	2.2	1,242
United Kingdom[c]	55,733	56,006	-0.1	0.0	-48
France	53,970	54,604	0.3	0.5	155
Philippines	53,226	53,162	2.3	2.5	1,350
Thailand	50,284	50,131	2.2	2.0	1,079
Turkey	48,692	49,155	2.4	2.2	1,167
Egypt	45,111	45,851	2.4	2.8	1,055
Iran	41,808	42,490	3.0	3.1	1,251
Korea, Rep.	40,445	41,366	1.7	1.5	666
Spain	38,366	38,234[d]	0.9	0.6	324
Burma	37,982	37,061	2.4	2.4	914
Poland	36,887	36,556	1.0	0.9	351
Ethiopia	33,765	31,305	2.5	2.4	833
South Africa	31,914	30,938	2.9	2.5	905
Zaire	30,821	31,250	2.9	2.9	871
Argentina	28,033	29,627	1.2	1.6	331
Colombia	27,515	27,663	2.2	2.1	584
Canada	25,605	24,882	1.5	1.0	374
Morocco	22,383	22,889	3.2	2.9	715
Yugoslavia	22,861	22,826	0.8	0.8	173
Romania	22,813	22,498	0.8	0.0	177
Algeria	21,027	20,695	3.5	3.1	733
Sudan	20,020	20,539	2.9	2.8	568
Tanzania	19,736	20,524	3.2	3.2	624
Korea, P.D.R.	19,185	19,185	2.4	2.3	438
Peru	19,161	19,161	2.8	2.8	529
Taiwan[b]	--	18,810	--	--	--
Kenya	18,612	18,580	4.1	4.1	749
Venezuela	17,257	17,993	3.3	3.2	580
Afghanistan	17,194	14,177	2.5	-0.2	431
Germany, D.R.	16,867	16,724	0.0	0.0	5
Sri Lanka	15,754	15,647	2.1	1.8	322
Czechoslovakia	15,591	15,420	0.5	0.3	80
Nepal	15,293	16,169	2.3	2.5	344
Malaysia	15,119	14,995	2.4	2.3	354
Australia	15,003	15,265	1.2	1.3	171
Uganda	14,511	13,819	3.2	3.0	455
Iraq	14,479	14,509	3.4	3.3	481
Netherlands	14,278	14,374	0.5	0.4	64
Ghana	12,878	13,367	3.3	3.2	415
Chile	11,682	11,486	1.7	1.5	194
Mozambique	11,359	13,047	2.8	2.7	308
Hungary	10,840	10,691	0.2	-0.1	25
Syria	10,084	9,739	3.9	3.4	385
Saudi Arabia	10,055	10,443	3.8	3.4	373
Portugal	10,055	10,008[e]	0.7	0.4	72

[a]Average annual growth rate is for 1980-85 for the United Nations, 1982-83 for the U.S. Bureau of the Census.

[b]U.N. figures for China include Taiwan.

[c]United Kingdom includes Great Britain and Northern Ireland.

[d]Census Bureau figures for Spain include Balearic and Canary Islands.

[e]Census Bureau figures for Portugal include Azores and Madeira Islands.

Source: United Nations. Demographic Indicators of Countries: Estimates and Projections as Assessed in 1980. New York: United Nations, 1982. U.S. Bureau of the Census. World Population 1983: Recent Demographic Estimates for the Countries and Regions of the World. Washington, DC: U.S. Government Printing Office, 1983.

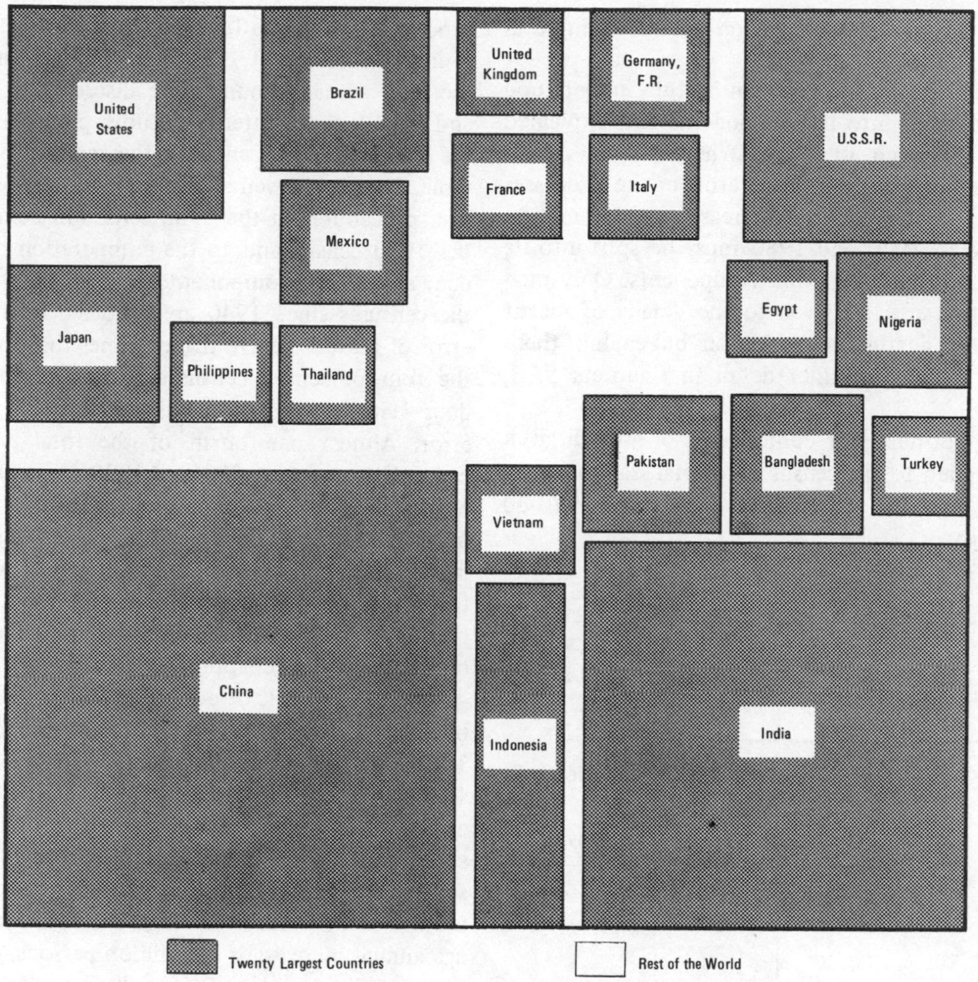

Figure 1-1. The United States in World Population: 1980

Table 1-3. Resident Population of the United States at Each Decennial Census

Census date	Number	Increase over preceding census: Number	Increase over preceding census: Percent	Average annual rate of increase
1980	226,545,805	23,243,774	11.4	1.08
1970	203,302,031	23,978,856	13.4	1.26
1960	179,323,175	27,997,377	18.5	1.70
1950	151,325,798	19,161,229	14.5	1.39
1940	131,669,275	8,894,229	7.2	0.70
1930	122,775,046	17,064,426	16.1	1.50
1920	105,710,620	13,738,354	14.9	1.39
1910	91,972,266	15,977,691	21.0	1.91
1900	75,994,575	13,046,861	20.7	1.88
1890	62,947,714	12,791,931	25.5	2.27
1880	50,155,783	10,337,334	26.0	2.31
1870	39,818,449	8,375,128	26.6	2.36
1860	31,443,321	8,251,445	35.6	3.04
1850	23,191,876	6,122,423	35.9	3.07
1840	17,069,453	4,203,433	32.7	2.83
1830	12,866,020	3,227,567	33.5	2.89
1820	9,638,453	2,398,572	33.1	2.86
1810	7,239,881	1,931,398	36.4	3.10
1800	5,308,483	1,379,269	35.1	3.01
1790	3,929,824	...	...	...

Source: U.S. Bureau of the Census. Statistical Abstract of the United States, 1982-83. Washington, DC: U.S. Government Printing Office, 1982, Table 1.

Table 1-4. Estimates of the Total Population, Resident Population, and Civilian Population [in thousands]

Date (July 1)	Total population (including abroad)	Resident population	Civilian population	Population abroad (including U.S. armed forces)	Armed forces residing in U.S.
1984 (April)	236,109	235,584	233,892	525	1,692
1983	234,249	233,722	232,039	527	1,683
1982	232,057	231,534	229,865	523	1,669
1981	229,849	229,348	227,700	501	1,648
1980	227,704	227,202	225,598	502	1,604
1979	225,055	224,567	222,969	488	1,598
1978	222,585	222,095	220,467	490	1,628
1977	220,239	219,760	218,106	479	1,654
1976	218,035	217,563	215,894	472	1,669
1975	215,973	215,465	213,788	508	1,677
1974	213,854	213,342	211,636	512	1,706
1973	211,909	211,357	209,600	552	1,757
1972	209,896	209,284	207,511	612	1,773
1971	207,661	206,827	204,866	834	1,961
1970	205,052	203,984	201,895	1,068	2,089

Source: U.S. Bureau of the Census. "Estimates of the Population of the United States to December 1, 1983" and "Estimates of the Population of the United States to April 1, 1984." Current Population Reports (Series P-25, nos. 943 and 953). Washington, DC: U.S. Government Printing Office, 1983 and 1984.

is affected by international migration but not by internal migration.

A change in population size can be fully understood only when divided into its components and explained with respect to each of them. Where possible, each component should be studied in terms of the processes it comprises. Thus, the total increase of 23.2 million persons between 1970 and 1980 must be split into its reproductive and net migration components. Only incidental attention can be given to the details of recent trends in births, deaths, and migration, but each of these processes is treated in fuller detail in Chapters 5, 6, and 7.

When the formulas for components of growth given above are applied to the census data, vital statistics, and immigration data, the following results for the 1970-80 decade emerge.

Components	Thousands of persons	
	Original	Revised
1970 census count.	203,235	203,302
Components of change:		
Births	+33,099	+33,499
Deaths	-19,322	-19,322
Net legal immigration. . . .	+3,018	+3,018
Net military movement to U.S..	+567	+567
Net increase	+17,762	+17,762
Expected 1980 census count . .	220,997	221,064
Actual 1980 census count . . .	226,505	226,505
Error of closure	5,508	5,441

Source: U.S. Bureau of the Census. "Coverage of the National Population in the 1980 Census, by Age, Sex, and Race: Preliminary Estimates by Demographic Analysis." Current Population Reports (Special Studies, Series P-23, no. 115). Washington, DC: U.S. Government Printing Office, 1982. Revised estimates provided in U.S. Bureau of the Census. "Estimates of the Population of the United States, by Age, Sex, and Race: 1980 to 1982." Current Population Reports (Series P-25, no. 929). Washington, DC: U.S. Government Printing Office, 1983.

The bottom line of the above "population accounting" is the "error of closure" between the two censuses. In most previous censuses, the figure has been *small* and usually *negative* (that is, net reproductive change and net immigration have predicted a total slightly higher than the actual census count). Between 1970 and 1980, however, the error of closure was *large* and *positive:* The 1980 census counted 5.4 million *more* persons than demographic accounting of births, deaths, and legal net immigration would have predicted. On the basis of vital processes and migration, the 1980 census should have found an increase of 17.8 million inhabitants instead of the 23.2 actually found. The discrepancy is a mystery and is still under intensive study; preliminary study by the Bureau of the Census in the report from which the table above is derived attributes it to improved enumeration procedures in the 1980 census in comparison with the 1970 census and to the enumeration of illegal resident aliens. The components of change between each of the censuses since 1940 are reported in Table 1-6. An error of closure nearly fifteen times that encountered in the four preceding censuses indicates either a tremendous leap forward in precision or a major processing error. Almost one-fourth of the total population increase between the 1970 and 1980 censuses is explained by comparative underenumeration in the 1970 census, inclusion of illegal aliens, and possible overenumeration in the 1980 census—or a combination of all. These factors must be continuously kept in mind when interpreting all measurements of the 1970-80 change throughout the remaining chapters of this report.

The components of population change as summarized by the Bureau of the Census for each calendar year from 1940 to 1982, including the population overseas, are shown in Table 1-7. Between 1970 and 1980, an annual average of 3.3 million births and 1.9 million deaths resulted in an average annual addition of 1.4 million persons to the population. To this must be added an annual average of 0.4 million net legal immigration, for an average annual increase of 1.8 million persons. An additional average adjustment of 0.55 million annually is required to account for the error of closure between the two censuses.

In order to interpret year-to-year changes in the components, it is customary to express them as *rates* per 1,000 population as of July 1 of the calendar year to which they refer. These are called "crude rates." Thus:

$$\text{Crude birth rate (CBR)} = \frac{\text{Births during year}}{\text{Midyear population}} \times 1{,}000$$

$$\text{Crude death rate (CDR)} = \frac{\text{Deaths during year}}{\text{Midyear population}} \times 1{,}000$$

$$\text{Net immigration rate} = \frac{\text{Immigrants minus emigrants}}{\text{Midyear population}} \times 1{,}000$$

The annual growth rate for a year is equal to CBR minus CDR, plus or minus net immigration. These rates (see Table 1-7) show that throughout the 1970-80 decade birth rates fluctuated between 14.5 and 18.2, ending

Table 1-5. Population and Area: United States and Outlying Areas, 1960-1980

Area	Resident population				Gross area (land and water), 1980 (sq. mi.)
	1960 (April 1)	1970 (April 1)	1980 (April 1)	Percent change, 1970-80	
Total	183,285,009	208,066,557	231,106,727	11.1	3,623,462
United States	179,323,175	203,302,031	226,545,805	11.4	3,618,770
Puerto Rico	2,349,544	2,712,033	3,196,520	17.9	3,515
Outlying areas	237,869	314,657	368,856	17.2	1,177
Territories	123,151	179,519	235,927	31.4	460
Guam	67,044	84,996	105,979	24.7	209
Virgin Islands of the U.S.	32,099	62,468	96,569	54.7	133
American Samoa	20,051	27,159	32,297	18.9	77
Trust Territory of the Pacific Islands	62,434	81,300	116,149	42.9	533
Northern Mariana Islands	8,290	9,640	16,780	74.1	184
U.S. population abroad	1,374,421	1,737,836	995,546	...	...
Federal employees	647,730	1,114,224	562,962	-49.5	...
Armed forces	609,720	1,057,776	515,408	-51.3	...
Civilians	38,010	56,448	47,554	-15.8	...
Dependents of Federal employees	506,393	371,366	432,584	16.5	...
Crews of merchant vessels	32,464	15,910	--	...	...
Other citizens	187,834	236,336	--	...	...

Note: -- indicates data not available. ... indicates data not applicable.

Source: U.S. Bureau of the Census. 1970 Census of Population (Vol. I) and 1980 Census of Population (Vol. I, Part A, PC80-1-a). Washington, DC: U.S. Government Printing Office, 1973 and 1983.

the decade at an intermediate between this range. This is considered *low* fertility—almost exactly the amount the population needs to maintain itself on a long-term basis (see Chapter 6). Death rates were only 60 percent as large as the birth rates and tended to decline slightly during the decade from 9.4 to 8.6 per 1,000 (see Chapter 5). The difference between birth and death rates is the chief component of the rate of increase. However, the contribution of net immigration was not insignificant. During the decade as a whole, 17 percent of the population increase (aside from error of closure) was contributed by legal net immigration from abroad (see Chapter 7). Had there been no immigration and no error of closure, the population of the United States would have grown by only 9.9 million between 1970 and 1980, or by only one-half the amount reported, and the annual rate of growth would have been by far the lowest in the nation's history.

Table 1-6. Components of Population Change and Error of Closure: Total Resident Population, 1940-50, 1950-60, 1960-70, and 1970-80 [in thousands]

Components of change	April 1, 1970 to 1980	April 1, 1960 to 1970	April 1, 1950 to 1960	April 1, 1940 to 1950
Population at beginning of period	203,235	179,323	151,326	132,166
Net change	17,762	23,912	27,997	19,160
Births	33,499	39,073	40,963	32,064
Deaths	19,322	18,209	15,608	14,294
Net civilian immigration	3,018	3,887	2,975	1,789
Net movement of Armed Forces	567	460	330	602
Error of closure	5,441	-379	-3	202
Population at end of period	226,505	203,235	179,323	151,326

Source: U.S. Bureau of the Census. "Estimates of the Population of the United States, by Age, Sex, and Race: 1980 to 1982." Current Population Reports (Series P-25, no. 929). Washington, DC: U.S. Government Printing Office, 1983. For 1960 to 1970, see U.S. Bureau of the Census. "Estimates of the Population of the United States and Components of Change: 1940 to 1978." Current Population Reports (Series P-25, no. 802). Washington, DC: U.S. Government Printing Office, 1979. For earlier years, see U.S. Bureau of the Census. "Estimates of the Population of the United States and Components of Change: 1940 to 1966." Current Population Reports (Series P-25, no. 331). Washington, DC: U.S. Government Printing Office, 1966.

Table 1-7. Estimated Components of Change for Selected Years: United States, 1940-1980

Calendar year	July 1 population	Rate per 1,000 midyear population					January 1 population	Population change during calendar year				
		Net change	Natural increase	Births	Deaths	Net civilian immigration		Net change	Natural increase	Births	Deaths	Net civilian immigration
1940. . .	132,594	9.2	8.6	19.4	10.8	0.6	132,054	1,221	1,138	2,570	1,432	77
1941. . .	133,894	10.3	9.7	20.3	10.6	0.4	133,275	1,382	1,301	2,716	1,415	60
1942. . .	135,361	12.7	11.8	22.2	10.4	0.6	134,657	1,714	1,595	3,002	1,407	83
1943. . .	137,250	13.1	11.8	22.7	10.9	1.1	136,371	1,799	1,615	3,118	1,503	148
1944. . .	138,916	11.5	9.9	21.3	11.4	1.5	138,170	1,597	1,372	2,954	1,582	202
1945. . .	140,468	10.4	9.4	20.5	11.0	1.2	139,767	1,462	1,324	2,873	1,549	162
1946. . .	141,936	15.3	14.2	24.1	9.9	1.1	141,229	2,165	2,018	3,426	1,409	151
1947. . .	144,698	18.3	16.4	26.5	10.1	1.6	143,394	2,653	2,379	3,834	1,455	238
1948. . .	147,208	17.2	15.0	24.8	9.9	1.9	146,047	2,533	2,201	3,655	1,453	280
1949. . .	149,767	17.1	14.8	24.5	9.7	2.2	148,580	2,556	2,215	3,667	1,452	323
1950. . .	152,271	16.3	14.3	23.9	9.6	2.0	151,135	2,486	2,177	3,645	1,468	299
1951. . .	154,878	17.4	15.1	24.8	9.7	2.2	153,622	2,688	2,344	3,845	1,501	335
1952. . .	157,553	16.9	15.4	25.0	9.6	1.5	156,309	2,663	2,421	3,933	1,512	242
1953. . .	160,184	17.0	15.3	24.9	9.6	1.6	158,973	2,717	2,457	3,989	1,531	261
1954. . .	163,026	17.8	16.0	25.2	9.1	1.8	161,690	2,898	2,613	4,102	1,489	287
1955. . .	165,931	17.6	15.6	24.9	9.3	2.0	164,588	2,925	2,591	4,128	1,537	337
1956. . .	168,903	18.1	15.8	25.1	9.3	2.3	167,513	3,058	2,672	4,244	1,572	387
1957. . .	171,984	17.2	15.6	25.2	9.5	1.6	170,571	2,961	2,691	4,332	1,641	272
1958. . .	174,882	16.7	15.0	24.5	9.5	1.7	173,533	2,915	2,623	4,279	1,655	292
1959. . .	177,830	16.5	14.9	24.3	9.4	1.6	176,447	2,939	2,650	4,313	1,663	292
1960. . .	180,671	16.1	14.4	23.8	9.5	1.8	179,386	2,901	2,599	4,307	1,700	328
1961. . .	183,691	16.1	14.2	23.5	9.3	2.0	182,287	2,955	2,615	4,317	1,703	373
1962. . .	186,538	14.9	13.2	22.6	9.4	1.9	185,242	2,771	2,455	4,213	1,758	351
1963. . .	189,242	14.0	12.3	21.9	9.6	1.9	188,013	2,655	2,327	4,142	1,815	361
1964. . .	191,889	13.3	11.8	21.2	9.4	1.7	190,668	2,555	2,271	4,070	1,799	317
1965. . .	194,303	11.9	10.1	19.6	9.4	1.9	193,223	2,315	1,972	3,801	1,830	373
1966. . .	196,560	11.2	9.0	18.5	9.5	2.3	195,539	2,197	1,773	3,642	1,869	455
1967. . .	198,712	10.4	8.5	17.9	9.4	2.1	197,736	2,072	1,694	3,555	1,861	414
1968. . .	200,706	9.7	7.9	17.6	9.7	2.0	199,808	1,952	1,587	3,535	1,948	398
1969. . .	202,677	10.3	8.3	17.9	9.5	2.2	201,760	2,089	1,692	3,626	1,934	453
1970. . .	205,052	12.8	8.9	18.3	9.4	2.1	203,849	2,617	1,830	3,757	1,927	438
1971. . .	207,661	11.8	8.0	17.2	9.3	1.9	206,466	2,451	1,651	3,581	1,930	387
1972. . .	209,896	9.9	6.3	15.6	9.4	1.5	208,917	2,068	1,317	3,282	1,965	325
1973. . .	211,909	9.2	5.6	14.9	9.3	1.6	210,985	1,947	1,185	3,159	1,974	331
1974. . .	213,854	9.3	5.8	14.9	9.0	1.5	212,932	1,999	1,248	3,183	1,935	316
1975. . .	215,973	10.0	5.9	14.7	8.8	2.1	214,931	2,164	1,273	3,167	1,894	449
1976. . .	218,035	9.6	5.9	14.6	8.8	1.6	217,095	2,084	1,281	3,191	1,910	353
1977. . .	220,239	10.4	6.6	15.2	8.6	1.8	219,179	2,298	1,451	3,352	1,901	394
1978. . .	222,585	10.8	6.4	15.1	8.7	2.3	221,477	2,403	1,430	3,358	1,928	508
1979. . .	225,055	11.4	7.1	15.6	8.5	2.2	223,880	2,564	1,606	3,520	1,914	499
1980. . .	227,704	10.7	7.3	16.0	8.7	2.9	226,444	2,434	1,653	3,639	1,986	654
1981. . .	229,849	9.5	7.3	16.0	8.6	2.3	228,878	2,181	1,686	3,673	1,987	520
1982. . .	232,057	9.5	7.5	16.1	8.6	2.1	231,059	2,199	1,745	3,731	1,986	480

Source: U.S. Bureau of the Census. "Projections of the Population of the United States, by Age, Sex, and Race: 1983 to 2080." Current Population Reports (Series P-25, no. 952). Washington, DC: U.S. Government Printing Office, 1984, Table 1.

U.S. Growth in Comparison with the World and with Other Nations

Population trends in the United States can be better appreciated if they are viewed from the perspective of population growth throughout the world. Tables 1-1 and 1-2 provide data for making international comparisons of recent population change. It is estimated that as of July 1, 1984, the world contained slightly more than 4.7 billion inhabitants. Both the rate at which world population is growing (1.70 percent a year) and the amounts by which it is growing (80 million a year) are striking. The world has acquired nearly one-half of its total present population in the last thirty years; 2.2 billion of the 4.7 billion has been added since 1950. At current rates of growth, world population would double within forty years. However, a trend toward slower growth is under way and is expected to continue. The population estimates of future years (2000 and 2025) projected by the United Nations are reported in Table 1-1. World populations of 6.1 billion in the year 2000 and 8.2 billion in 2025 are predicted. This increase is in sharp contrast to the slow population growth rate over the many thousands of years that elapsed between the origin of man and the middle of the seventeenth century, before the human species numbered even 500 million. Some demographers expect world population growth to become zero about the year 2100, with a total world population of 10 billion to 12 billion.

The great "population explosion," with each decade witnessing an ever growing increase in the number of people, resulted from the fact that death rates have declined faster, and by greater amounts, than birth rates. Nations all over the world are benefiting from modern knowledge of medicine and public health. The incidences of infectious diseases that once killed off infants, children, and young adults before they had a chance to marry and reproduce have been greatly reduced. As a result a much greater proportion of the infants who are born survive to age forty or older, to marry and have children. Meanwhile, birth rates have declined much more slowly than death rates and are still high enough to produce a substantial increase.

Table 1-1 includes summaries for the nations of the world divided into two categories, "more developed countries" (MDCs—Europe, North America, Japan, and Australia-New Zealand) and "less developed countries" (LDCs—the remaining nations of Asia, Latin America, and Africa). The components of growth for the two groups of nations are as follows:

Components of growth	Rates: 1980-85		
	World	More developed countries (MDC)	Less developed countries (LDC)
Crude birth rate. . .	27.5	15.8	31.4
Crude death rate. . .	10.6	9.6	11.0
Net migration rate. .	0.0	0.0	0.0
Annual rate of change (percent). .	1.69	0.62	2.04

It is evident that the rapid growth of world population is concentrated among the less developed nations. With a birth rate double that of the more developed nations and a death rate only slightly higher, the LDCs are growing at a pace more than three times as rapid as that of the MDCs.

The United States is a typical MDC. Its birth rates and death rates are slightly lower than the averages in the MDC column. However, its growth rates are higher than many nations of Europe, several of which have birth rates almost equal to their death rates, and are near or actually in a zero-growth situation. A nearly zero-growth situation now exists in Germany (both East and West), Sweden, Norway, Finland, Denmark, United Kingdom, Austria, Belgium, Hungary, and Switzerland. Given the present trends, it is unlikely (but not impossible) that the United States will have a zero-growth reproductive situation within this century or even in the early decades of the next; the positive rates—if they continue—may become very small.

As the more developed countries continue with their low growth rates into the future, and the less developed countries compound population with their high but declining growth rates, some dramatic shifts will occur in the world's population distribution. U.N. projections for the years 2000 and 2025 are as follows:

Region	Population (billions)		
	1984	2000	2025
Total.	4.746	6.116	8.192
Less developed countries . .	3.583	4.847	6.818
More developed countries . .	1.163	1.269	1.374
	Percent distribution		
Total.	100.0	100.0	100.0
Less developed countries . .	75.5	79.3	83.2
More developed countries . .	24.5	20.7	16.8

Thus as the LDCs grow in size, the more developed countries, including the United States, will shrink in comparison with world population because of slow growth. Only if large segments of LDC populations "graduate" into the ranks of MDCs will the growing imbalance be slowed or reversed.

The last column to the right in Table 1-2 shows the estimated amount of average annual increase in population. Despite its low growth rate in comparison with the LDCs, the United States still stands high among the world's nations in absolute annual growth. Because its growth starts from a large base, its low growth rates generate large numerical increments. When the sizable annual net migration is added in, the nation stands out as one of the world leaders in absolute population growth.

History of Population Growth in the United States

The recent population growth in the United States can be more readily appreciated when viewed in light of the nation's growth from 3.9 million in 1790 and, beyond that, the growth of the original settlements and colonies. Only four centuries ago, almost no people of European descent resided in the territory that is now the United States. Almost a century and a half passed before the first million people of European origin had accumulated (1610 to about 1745). Thereafter the population quickly doubled and redoubled. The history of the world had recorded no other population having grown to such a size, and at such a rate, over a comparable span of time. Unfortunately, the available statistics are not detailed enough to give a complete account of the nation's early demographic events.[7]

The population of the American colonies and settlements that eventually became the United States, with decennial increases and rates of increase, have been estimated as shown in Table 1-8. When the historical trend described in Table 1-3 is extended backward in time for an additional 140 years, decennial rates of increase above 30 percent characterize the colonial period (with interruptions in the 1690-1700 and 1770-1780 decades) as well as the early national period until 1860. Table 1-9 provides estimates for individual colonies.

The first census, taken in 1790, must be the starting point for formal analysis, but even the data provided by the first several censuses are much too sparse and incomplete to answer all significant questions. By considering the conditions that must have given rise to the events and trends that emerged, however, it is possible to build up a fairly complete and reliable history of population growth in terms of the components of this growth. Figure 1-2 compares the rates and sizes of the main components of growth from the colonial period to 1980.

Broadly speaking, the nation has passed through five distinct phases of growth and is now in a sixth. Each phase has grown out of the one that preceded it, and each represents a distinctive combination of the components of reproductive change and net migration. Table 1-10 reports the volume of growth during each decade since 1810, and its reproductive change and immigration components.

Table 1-8. Estimated Population and Rates of Increase of the American Colonies: 1630-1780

Year	Population (000)	Increase (000)	Decennial percent increase	Average annual rate of increase
1630	4.6	--	--	--
1640	26.6	22.0	478.3	17.55
1650	50.4	23.8	89.5	6.39
1660	75.1	24.7	49.0	3.99
1670	111.9	36.8	49.0	3.99
1680	151.5	39.6	35.4	3.03
1690	210.4	58.9	38.9	3.28
1700	250.9	40.5	19.2	1.76
1710	331.7	80.8	32.2	2.79
1720	466.2	134.5	40.5	3.40
1730	629.4	163.2	35.0	3.00
1740	905.6	276.2	43.9	3.64
1750	1,170.8	265.2	29.3	2.57
1760	1,593.6	422.8	36.1	3.08
1770	2,148.1	554.5	34.8	2.99
1780	2,780.4	632.3	29.4	2.58

Source: U.S. Bureau of the Census. Historical Statistics of the United States. Washington, DC: U.S. Government Printing Office, 1960, Table Z 1-19.

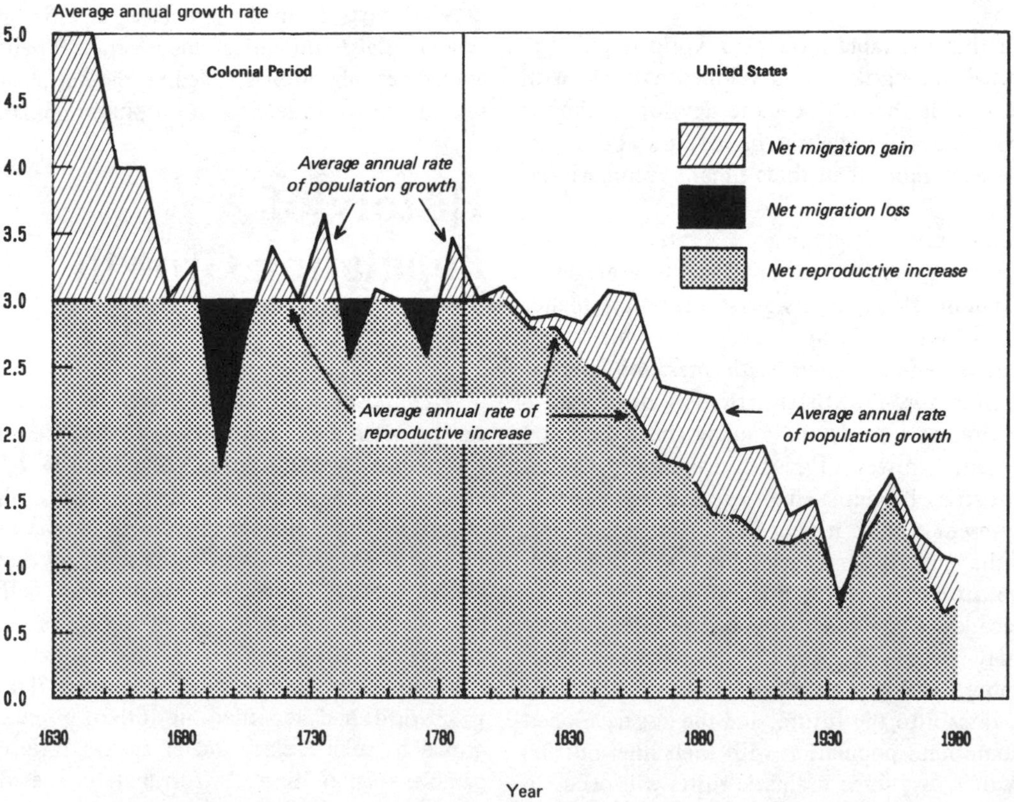

Figure 1-2. Estimated Components of Population Change in the Territory of the United States: 1630-1980

Table 1-9. Estimated Population of American Colonies: 1630-1780 [in thousands]

Colony	1780	1770	1760	1750	1740	1730	1720	1710	1700	1690	1680	1670	1660	1650	1640	1630
Total.	2,780.4	2,148.1	1,593.6	1,170.8	905.6	629.4	466.2	331.7	250.9	210.4	151.5	111.9	75.1	50.4	26.6	4.6
Percent change . .	29.4	34.8	36.1	30.0	43.9	35.0	40.5	32.2	19.3	38.9	35.4	49.1	49.0	89.1	473.3	...
Maine (counties) .	49.1	31.3	...	...	...	...	...	...	...	...	...	...	...	1.0	0.9	0.4
New Hampshire. . .	87.8	62.4	39.1	27.5	23.3	10.8	9.4	5.7	5.0	4.2	2.0	1.8	1.6	1.3	1.1	0.5
Vermont.	47.6	10.0	...	...	...	...	...	...	...	...	...	...	...	...	...	...
Plymouth and Massachusetts. .	268.6	235.3	222.6	188.0	151.6	114.1	91.0	62.4	55.9	56.9	46.2	35.3	22.0	15.6	10.0	0.9
Rhode Island . . .	52.9	58.2	45.5	33.2	25.3	17.0	11.7	7.6	5.9	4.2	3.0	2.2	1.5	0.8	0.3	...
Connecticut. . . .	206.7	183.9	142.5	111.3	89.6	75.5	58.8	39.4	26.0	21.6	17.2	12.6	8.0	4.1	1.5	...
New York	210.5	162.9	117.1	76.7	63.7	48.6	36.9	21.6	19.1	13.9	9.8	5.8	4.9	4.1	1.9	0.4
New Jersey	139.6	117.4	93.8	71.4	51.4	37.5	29.8	19.9	14.0	18.0	3.4	1.0	...	...	...	...
Pennsylvania . . .	327.3	240.1	183.7	119.7	85.6	51.7	31.0	24.4	18.0	11.4	0.7	...	...	...	...	...
Delaware	45.4	35.5	33.2	28.7	19.9	9.2	5.4	3.6	2.5	1.5	1.0	0.7	0.5	0.2	...	...
Maryland	245.5	202.6	162.3	141.1	116.1	91.1	66.1	42.7	29.6	24.0	17.9	13.2	8.4	4.5	0.6	...
Virginia	538.0	447.0	339.7	231.0	180.4	114.0	87.8	78.3	58.6	53.0	43.6	35.3	27.0	18.7	10.4	2.5
North Carolina . .	270.1	197.2	110.4	73.0	51.8	30.0	21.3	15.1	10.7	7.6	5.4	3.8	1.0	...	...	...
South Carolina . .	180.0	124.2	94.1	64.0	45.0	30.0	17.0	10.9	5.7	3.9	1.2	0.2	...	...	...	...
Georgia.	56.1	23.4	9.6	5.2	2.0	...	...	...	...	...	...	...	...	...	...	...
Kentucky	45.0	15.7	...	...	...	...	...	...	...	...	...	...	...	...	...	...
Tennessee.	10.0	1.0	...	...	...	...	...	...	...	...	...	...	...	...	...	...

Source: U.S. Bureau of the Census. Historical Statistics of the United States. Washington, DC: U.S. Government Printing Office, 1960, Table Z 1-19.

Table 1-10. Components of Population Change: 1810-1980

Time period	Total change in period	Components		Change per 1,000 population in base year			Percent of change due to natural increase
		Natural increase	Net immi-gration	Total in period	Natural increase	Net immi-gration	
1810 to 1820	2,399	2,328	71	33.1	32.1	1.0	97.0
1820 to 1830	3,228	3,105	123	33.5	32.2	1.3	96.2
1830 to 1840	4,203	3,710	493	32.7	28.8	3.8	88.3
1840 to 1850	6,122	4,702	1,420	35.9	27.5	8.3	76.8
1850 to 1860	8,251	5,614	2,593	35.6	24.2	11.2	68.4
1860 to 1870	8,375	6,291	2,102	26.6	20.0	6.7	75.0
1870 to 1880	10,337	7,675	2,622	26.0	19.3	6.6	74.5
1880 to 1890	12,792	7,527	4,966	25.5	15.0	9.9	60.2
1890 to 1900	13,047	9,345	3,711	20.7	14.8	5.9	71.7
1900 to 1910	15,978	9,656	6,294	21.0	12.7	8.3	60.5
1910 to 1920	13,738	11,489	2,484	14.9	12.5	2.7	82.2
1920 to 1930	17,064	14,500	3,187	16.1	13.7	3.0	88.2
1930 to 1940	8,894	9,962	-85	7.2	8.1	-0.6	100.8
1940 to 1950	19,429	17,426	1,801	14.7	13.2	1.4	89.7
1950 to 1960	28,289	25,310	2,983	18.6	16.7	2.0	89.5
1960 to 1970	23,912	20,864	3,887	13.3	11.6	2.2	87.3
1970 to 1980	16,795[a]	13,777	3,018	8.3	6.8	1.5	82.0

[a]Excludes error of closure and net military movement to the U.S.

Source: Estimates of natural increase and net immigration prior to 1910 from Warren S. Thompson and P.K. Whelpton. Population Trends in the United States. New York: McGraw-Hill Book Co., 1933, p. 303. For 1910 to 1960, Irene Taeuber and Contrad Taeuber. People of the United States in the 20th Century. Washington, DC: U.S. Bureau of the Census, U.S. Government Printing Office, 1971, p. 582. For 1960 to 1980, same sources as those in Table 1-6.

1. Colonial and Early National Phase, 1620-1830. High rates of reproductive change with initially high and then lower rates of net immigration characterized the colonial period.

Because the first official census of the United States was not taken until 1790, inferences about the earlier part of this period must rest upon fragmentary and incomplete data. In this earlier part of the period, birth rates were extremely high, approaching the average maximum of which the human race is biologically capable. Migrants to the New World appear to have considered children an economic asset in conquering the wilderness. Marriage probably occurred at an earlier age in America than in Europe, which meant that each married couple experienced a longer period of childbearing capability. In much of Europe deaths were almost as numerous as births, whereas death rates in America were only moderately high and permitted a rapid population growth. Plentiful food and a low density of settlement (conditions that help prevent epidemics) apparently caused death rates in the New World to be lower than they were in Europe and, at the same time, encouraged the rearing of large families. The high fertility of this population enabled the colonies to grow at an almost unprecedented rate for more than two centuries. Meanwhile, immigrants from Europe continued to enter the colonies. Rapid reproductive growth and immigration combined to produce a great population increase. While America was in this phase, its growth from national increase is assumed to have been about 3.0 percent per year from 1650 to 1820 (see Figure 1-2).

During the last portion of this phase, 1770 to 1830, the rate of immigration from abroad appears to have declined. The insecurity and uncertainty created by the Revolutionary War, the establishment of the Republic, and the War of 1812 tended to reduce temporarily the flow of migrants from abroad. Meanwhile the rate of reproductive growth continued to be very high.

Thompson and Whelpton estimate that at the beginning of the nineteenth century there were about 55 births and 25 deaths per 1,000 residents annually, which means that the United States had a net annual reproductive gain of 30 per 1,000, or 3 percent per annum.[8] Such a high rate of growth, phenomenal for any people at any stage of the world's history, had attracted worldwide attention even before the Revolutionary War. When Thomas Malthus looked around for proof that the human species, like other species, tended to increase geometrically, he found in the population of the newly established United States the evidence he sought. Thus, even though the net immigration from abroad had declined to a comparatively low point toward the end of the period, the decline had no seriously depressing effect upon population growth.

2. Frontier and Early Urbanization Phase, 1830-1900. Large but rapidly declining rates of reproductive increase and a very large volume of immigration from abroad characterize the second phase. The rapid growth of commerce and industry following the War of 1812 created almost unlimited opportunities for incoming migrants. Land was plentiful and easily obtained. During each decade except the first, 1830-40, the nation grew by about 5 percent as a result of immigration alone. In four of the decades the decennial rate due to net immigration was 8.3 percent or more. Meanwhile, the average annual rate of reproductive change was declining steadily and rapidly from the high point it had reached about 1800. It fell from about 2.9 percent in the 1830-40 decade to about 1.3 percent in the 1900-10 decade. This was a decline of 1.6 points, or more than half, in the span of eighty years. This precipitous drop represents a narrowing of the gap between birth rates and death rates. During this period, great medical discoveries began to be made. The germ theory of disease, epidemic control, antiseptic surgery, regulation of the water supply and waste disposal, better care of the sick, and greater interest in public health all began to exert a measurable influence on mortality during this era. Their combined effect was to lower the death rate considerably. For the rate of natural increase to fall while death rates were declining, birth rates had to fall much more rapidly than death rates. Such a drop in birth rates could have resulted only from lowered fertility. Thus, although the evidence is only crude and approximate, there is no mistaking the fact that *the really sharp reduction in American fertility took place in the nineteenth century rather than in the twentieth century* (see Figure 1-2). Because the population is known to have halved its rate of reproductive increase and to have enjoyed lower death rates during the sixty years between 1830 and 1890, the inference that birth rates were reduced drastically over that period is inescapable. If, during that period, the crude birth rate dropped from about 50 per 1,000 residents to about 28 per 1,000, and the death rate dropped from about 25 to 15 per 1,000, the annual rate of reproductive increase dropped from about 25 per 1,000 to about 13 per 1,000. Although the rates given for the beginning of the period are only guesses, they are probably accurate enough to illustrate the magnitude of change.

Demographers concerned with the problems involved in reducing fertility in underdeveloped and overpopulated countries might find it interesting that their own grandparents and great-grandparents reduced their fertility within a remarkably short time, and without the efficient devices available today. They seem to have lowered their birth rates by means of later marriages and the use of simple techniques which avoided, or at least postponed, pregnancy.

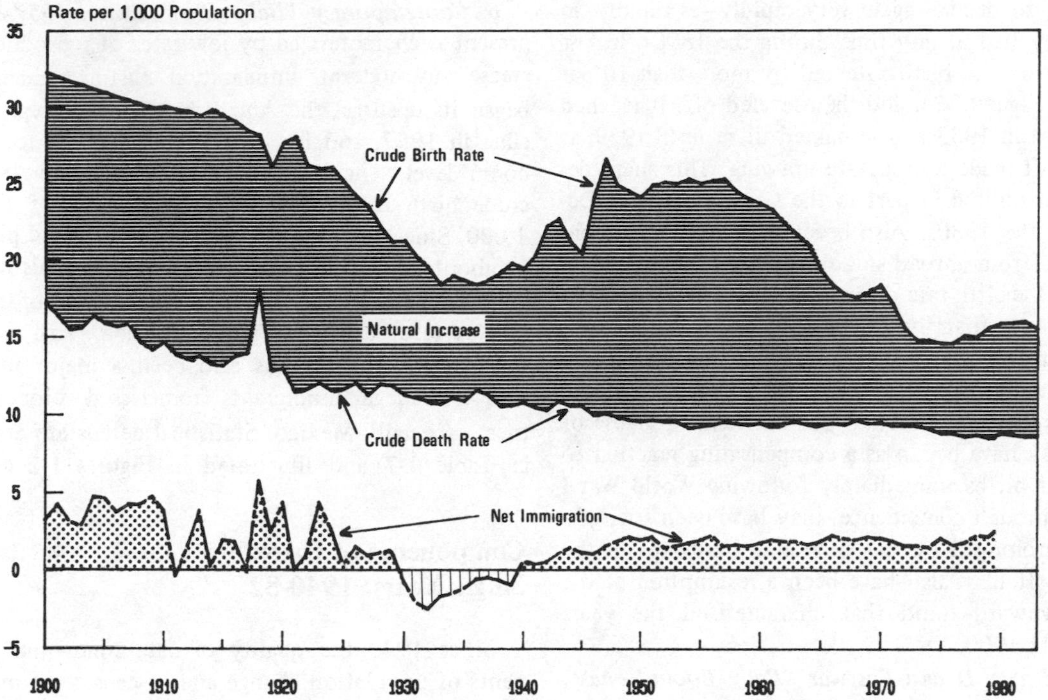

Figure 1-3. Components of Population Growth in the United States: 1900-1983

The period during which this drastic reduction in fertility took place was also the period during which the population became industrialized and urbanized. It has been generally assumed that birth control practices began in the cities and slowly diffused throughout the whole population, hence that urbanization and industrialization have been the factors underlying this fertility decline. However, there is evidence that birth rates fell as rapidly in early American rural communities as they did in the cities; even today many rural sections of the nation have lower birth rates than some large cities. The specific aspects of urban living to which declining fertility might be related are not clearly established—in fact, the association between city living and declining fertility has not been adequately researched. The exact motivation responsible for family limitation in the nineteenth century is not yet known.

3. Early Twentieth Century Phase, 1900-1925. Moderate and almost constant rates of reproductive increase were combined with declining immigration. This phase overlaps the one preceding it in that the rate of reproductive increase began to be steady at the turn of the century, but immigration did not begin to decline until after 1910.

During this period, both birth and death rates appear to have been declining moderately and at about the same rate. Consequently, between 1900 and 1925 the decennial rate of reproductive change remained steady at about 13 percent. (Far more factual data are available for evaluating the trends of this period than for previous periods. Figure 1-3 presents the estimates of the actual birth and death rates, from which more exact measurements of annual and decennial growth can be made.) With the exception of a temporary fluctuation during and after World War I, the birth rate appears to have leveled off from its previous steep decline and to have paralleled the more gradual decline of the death rate. Except for 1918, when the influenza epidemic caused a high death rate, death rates continued to decline. In this phase immigration from abroad slowed until it was about one-third of the average for the preceding period. In 1912 Congress passed a bill restricting immigration to a small quota for each foreign country. This combination of growth components resulted in national growth rates that were very moderate in comparison with those of the past; they were still very rapid in comparison with the rates in much of the world, however, and would be considered excessive if applied to a large population for any prolonged period.

4. Post-World War I Phase, 1925-40. Precipitous decline in birth rates and very low immigration marked the fourth phase. In 1919 birth rates had suffered a sharp but temporary decline because of the number of men who were overseas with the armed forces. In 1920 and 1921 birth rates increased abruptly as the armed forces were demobilized. Shortly thereafter, about 1925, birth rates began to decline again very rapidly—as rapidly, in fact, as they had at any time during the 1800s. In less than ten years the birth rate fell by more than 10 per 1,000 (see Figure 1-3), and then leveled off. It reached its low point in 1933 and remained there until 1939, at which time it made a moderate upswing. This sharp decline was attributed in part to the Great Economic Depression of the 1930s. Also because of the Depression, immigration from abroad shrank to very low levels. The behavior of the birth rate during this fifteen-year period—particularly the first five years of it—is an enigma that still has not been clarified by research. The fertility decline can hardly be attributed to the Depression alone, because the decline preceded the economic collapse of 1929. It may have begun as a compensating reaction to the wave of births immediately following World War I and then, through coincidence, may have been strengthened and prolonged by the economic hardships of the Depression. It may also have been a resumption of the steady downward trend that characterized the years from 1830 to 1900.

5. World War II and Postwar "Baby Boom" Phase, 1940-57. Moderately high rates of reproductive increase were combined with moderate immigration. An unexpected upsurge in population growth began about 1940 and lasted until 1957. Its cause was a rise in the birth rate (see Table 1-7 and Figure 1-3). Just how dramatic it was, as a reversal of the direction of trends in fertility and reproduction that had prevailed for at least a century and a quarter, may be more fully appreciated when it is viewed from the perspective of the nation's previous growth history. The following aspects of the upsurge, in comparison with previous trends, are especially significant:

- The reproductive change between 1940 and 1957 was sharply higher than the very small rate of growth from 1925 to 1940 (see Figure 1-3). But the nation did not return to the levels of rapid population growth of the nineteenth century in terms of either immigration or reproductive change.
- The rate of reproductive increase between 1940 and 1957 was quite similar to the rates that prevailed in the decades between 1890 and 1930. The difference was that the earlier rates were applied to a base of moderately high but declining birth and death rates, whereas the 1940 to 1957 rate of reproductive change was based upon very low death rates and moderately high birth rates. It is evident that the baby boom was a major deviation from more than a century of declining fertility.
- Immigration increased to a moderate level, largely explained by the entrance of refugees from World War II and the Korean War and of brides of servicement who married overseas.

6. Contemporary "Baby Bust" Phase, 1957-84. The present is characterized by low rates of reproductive increase and moderate immigration. Just as suddenly as it began its upsurge, the American birth rate began to decline in 1957, and by 1965 it had returned to the preboom level. The decline continued, and in 1976 the crude birth rate reached an all-time low of 14.5 per 1,000. Since then it has recovered slightly and plateaued at about 16.0. Meanwhile, immigration totals have sustained a moderate level, partially as a result of immigration of refugees from Viet Nam, Cuba, Haiti, and Central America. There has also been a major influx of legal and illegal immigrants from less developed countries, especially Mexico. Statistical details are contained in Table 1-7 and illustrated in Figures 1-2 and 1-3.

Components of Growth for Single Years: 1940-82

Since 1940 the quality of data concerning components of population change and of census enumerations is much superior to that for earlier years. As a consequence, it has been possible for the U.S. Bureau of the Census to prepare estimates of population size, change, and components of change for single years since 1940. These estimates are reported in Table 1-7. The left-hand panel of this table reports change and components in terms of rates based on midyear population. The right-hand panel reports change and components in terms of quantities of people, based on calendar years. With these data it is possible to study the last two phases of population change described above in terms of single years.

Projected Future Growth

By making what appear to be reasonable assumptions about the future trends in births, deaths, and net immigration, demographers prepare "population projections," which estimate or predict future population size. The U.S. Bureau of the Census makes such projections and revises them periodically as new perspectives are obtained on trends in the components of growth. Table 1-11 and Figure 1-4 show the growth projected for the future under "low," "intermediate," and "high" assumptions. All these assumptions presume that mortality rates will decline and that immigration will continue to be realistically within the range of recent experience. The chief variation is in assumptions about the future course of fertility. Some demographers expect another return to higher fertility (but not another baby boom). Others expect birth rates to decline even below the low level reached in 1976. The U.S. Bureau of the Census expects fertility to coast along at about 15 or 16 per 1,000, until the 1990s, and thereafter to decline gradually to a low rate of 12 and then to 11 by 2080.[9] Under this "moderate" or "most likely" projection of the U.S. Bureau of the Census the population will continue to grow to reach about 268 million in the year 2000 and about 301 million in 2025. If birth rates and net immigration are low and death rates improve very little, the population in 2025 can be as much as 40 million less; if fertility rises slightly above replacement, death rates fall a great deal, and net immigration is large, the population in 2025 can be as high as 50 million more than the intermediate projection. The author's opinion is that for the remainder of this century growth will be closer to the "low" than to the "medium" estimates of the Bureau of the Census. The reasons for this judgment ae presented in Chapter 7, where the basis for the projections of Tables 1-11 and 1-12 are examined in the light of Chapters 5, 6, and 7. Specifically, it is predicted that the population will grow slowly in the future to slightly above 255 million in the year 2000 and about 260 million in 2025, when growth will have declined to a zero-growth rate by about 2018 and become negative thereafter. It is debatable whether there will be population decline, however. The Bureau of the Census recommends its middle projections as the most likely. Table 1-12 provides detailed information about that projection in terms of its annual components.

Table 1-11. Projections of the Total Population of the United States: 1985-2025

Year	Projections (000)		
	Low	Medium	High
1985	234,605	238,631	239,959
1990	245,753	249,657	254,122
1995	251,876	259,559	268,151
2000	256,098	267,955	281,542
2025	260,904	301,394	355,503
2050	232,222	309,488	427,900
2080	191,118	310,762	531,178

Source: U.S. Bureau of the Census. "Projections of the Population of the United States, by Age, Sex, and Race: 1983 to 2080." Current Population Reports (Series P-20, no. 952). Washington, DC: U.S. Government Printing Office, 1984, Table 2.

Throughout the remaining chapters of this book, attention will be paid to the implications of these projections of growth both for population composition and for internal distribution. While growth rates are expected to be modest in comparison with the nineteenth century and the "baby boom" periods, the absolute population increase will be substantial under all three assumptions for the remainder of this century, because these low rates apply to what has become a very large population.

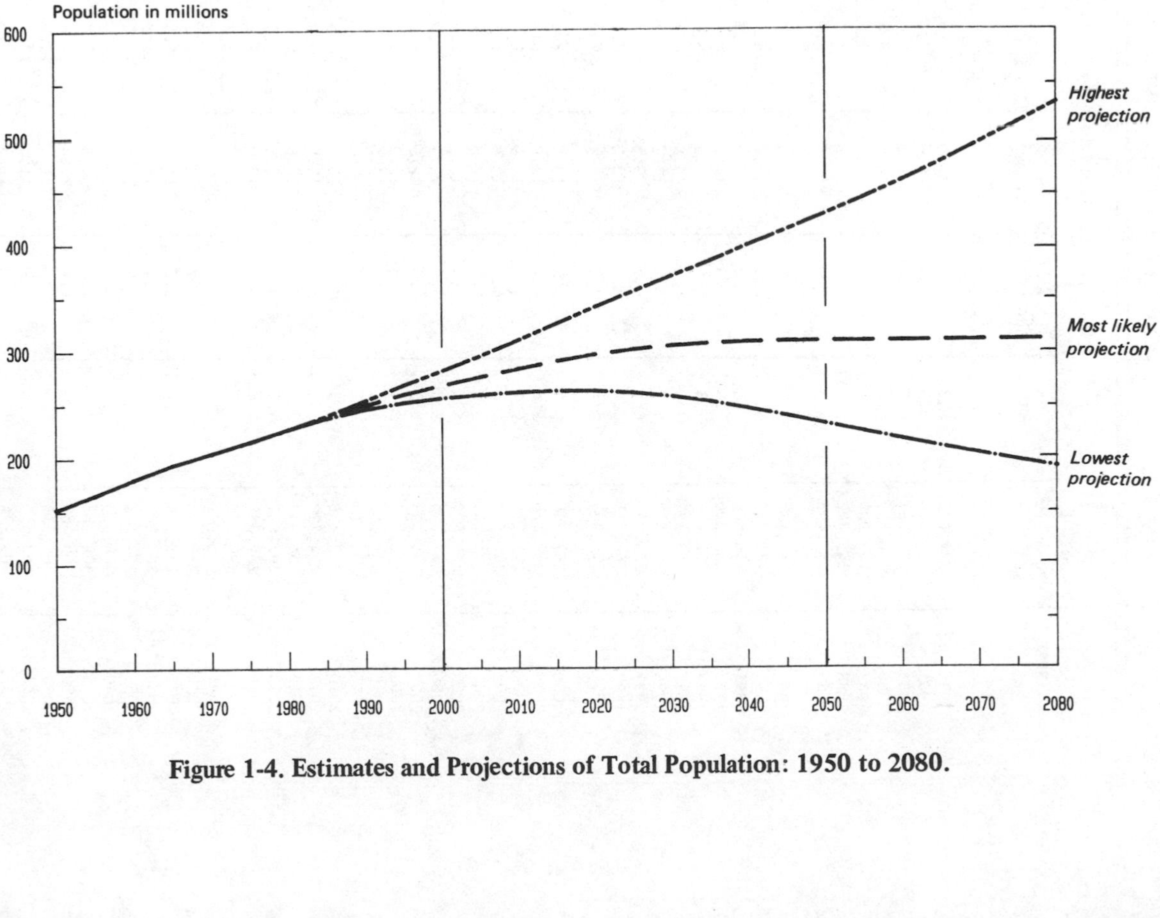

Figure 1-4. Estimates and Projections of Total Population: 1950 to 2080.

Table 1-12. Projections of the Total Population of the United States: 1983 to 2080.

Calendar year	July 1 population	Rate per 1,000 midyear population					January 1 population	Population change during calendar year				
		Net change	Natural increase	Births	Deaths	Net immi-gration		Net change	Natural increase	Births	Deaths	Net immi-gration
1983. . .	234,223	9.3	7.4	16.0	8.6	1.9	233,140	2,180	1,730	3,742	2,013	450
1984. . .	236,416	9.3	7.4	16.0	8.6	1.9	235,319	2,204	1,754	3,788	2,034	450
1985. . .	238,631	9.3	7.4	16.0	8.6	1.9	237,523	2,220	1,770	3,826	2,056	450
1986. . .	240,856	9.2	7.4	16.0	8.6	1.9	239,743	2,227	1,777	3,855	2,078	450
1987. . .	243,084	9.1	7.3	15.9	8.6	1.9	241,970	2,223	1,773	3,873	2,100	450
1988. . .	245,302	9.0	7.2	15.8	8.7	1.8	244,193	2,207	1,757	3,879	2,122	450
1989. . .	247,498	8.8	7.0	15.6	8.7	1.8	246,400	2,178	1,728	3,871	2,144	450
1990. . .	249,657	8.5	6.7	15.4	8.7	1.8	248,577	2,134	1,684	3,849	2,165	450
1991. . .	251,767	8.3	6.5	15.2	8.7	1.8	250,712	2,080	1,630	3,815	2,185	450
1992. . .	253,817	7.9	6.2	14.9	8.7	1.8	252,792	2,017	1,567	3,772	2,206	450
1993. . .	255,800	7.6	5.9	14.6	8.7	1.8	254,808	1,949	1,499	3,725	2,226	450
1994. . .	257,714	7.3	5.5	14.3	8.7	1.7	256,757	1,879	1,429	3,675	2,246	450
1995. . .	259,559	7.0	5.2	14.0	8.7	1.7	256,637	1,812	1,362	3,628	2,266	450
1996. . .	261,339	6.7	5.0	13.7	8.7	1.7	260,449	1,751	1,301	3,586	2,285	450
1997. . .	263,060	6.4	4.7	13.5	8.8	1.7	262,200	1,696	1,246	3,551	2,305	450
1998. . .	264,731	6.2	4.5	13.3	8.8	1.7	263,896	1,650	1,200	3,524	2,324	450
1999. . .	266,360	6.1	4.4	13.2	8.8	1.7	265,546	1,612	1,162	3,506	2,344	450
2000. . .	267,955	5.9	4.2	13.0	8.8	1.7	267,158	1,582	1,132	3,495	2,363	450
2001. . .	269,524	5.8	4.1	13.0	8.8	1.7	268,740	1,559	1,109	3,491	2,382	450
2002. . .	271,074	5.7	4.0	12.9	8.9	1.7	270,299	1,544	1,094	3,496	2,402	450
2003. . .	272,612	5.6	4.0	12.9	8.9	1.7	271,843	1,535	1,085	3,507	2,421	450
2004. . .	274,144	5.6	3.9	12.9	8.9	1.6	273,378	1,533	1,083	3,524	2,441	450
2005. . .	275,677	5.6	3.9	12.9	8.9	1.6	274,911	1,531	1,081	3,545	2,464	450
2006. . .	277,206	5.5	3.9	12.9	9.0	1.6	276,442	1,524	1,074	3,570	2,496	450
2007. . .	278,725	5.4	3.8	12.9	9.1	1.6	277,966	1,516	1,066	3,597	2,531	450
2008. . .	280,238	5.4	3.8	12.9	9.2	1.6	279,482	1,509	1,059	3,625	2,566	450
2009. . .	281,743	5.3	3.7	13.0	9.2	1.6	280,990	1,500	1,050	3,651	2,600	450
2010. . .	283,238	5.3	3.7	13.0	9.3	1.6	282,490	1,488	1,038	3,673	2,635	450
2011. . .	284,720	5.2	3.6	13.0	9.4	1.6	283,979	1,472	1,022	3,691	2,669	450
2012. . .	286,182	5.1	3.5	12.9	9.4	1.6	285,451	1,451	1,001	3,704	2,703	450
2013. . .	287,621	5.0	3.4	12.9	9.5	1.6	286,902	1,424	974	3,712	2,738	450
2014. . .	289,031	4.8	3.3	12.9	9.6	1.6	288,326	1,392	942	3,715	2,773	450
2015. . .	290,406	4.7	3.1	12.8	9.7	1.5	289,718	1,355	905	3,712	2,808	450
2020. . .	296,597	3.7	2.2	12.3	10.1	1.5	296,029	1,106	656	3,648	2,992	450
2025. . .	301,394	2.7	1.2	11.8	10.6	1.5	300,973	814	364	3,568	3,203	450
2030. . .	304,807	1.8	0.4	11.6	11.3	1.5	304,515	563	113	3,547	3,434	450
2035. . .	307,118	1.2	-0.3	11.6	11.9	1.5	306,924	370	-79	3,575	3,655	450
2040. . .	308,559	0.7	-0.8	11.6	12.4	1.5	308,446	212	-237	3,593	3,831	450
2045. . .	309,282	0.3	-1.2	11.5	12.7	1.5	309,235	85	-364	3,566	3,932	450
2050. . .	309,488	0.0	-1.4	11.4	12.8	1.5	309,482	10	-439	3,517	3,957	450
2055. . .	309,513	0.0	-1.4	11.3	12.7	1.5	309,509	11	-438	3,492	3,932	450
2060. . .	309,652	0.2	-1.3	11.3	12.6	1.5	309,630	48	-401	3,490	3,892	450
2065. . .	309,974	0.2	-1.2	11.3	12.5	1.5	309,936	76	-373	3,492	3,866	450
2070. . .	310,358	0.2	-1.2	11.2	12.4	1.4	310,322	71	-378	3,480	3,860	450
2075. . .	310,639	0.1	-1.3	11.1	12.4	1.4	310,618	40	-409	3,457	3,866	450
2080. . .	310,762	0.0	-1.4	11.1	12.5	1.4	310,756	7	-442	3,435	3,878	450

Source: U.S. Bureau of the Census. "Projections of the Population of the United States, by Age, Sex, and Race: 1983 to 2080." Current Population Reports (Series P-25, no. 952). Washington, DC: U.S. Government Printing Office, 1984, Table 2.

Notes

1. U.S. Bureau of the Census. "Projections of the Population of the United States: 1983 to 2080 (Advance Report)." *Current Population Reports* (Series P-25, no. 952). Washington, DC: U.S. Government Printing Office, 1984.

The Bureau of the Census annually issues a report entitled "Estimates of the Population of the United States to July 1, [Year]." These estimates are highly accurate (within a small fraction of 1 percent). They appear in a publication called *Current Population Reports: Population Estimates and Projections* (Series P-25). Annual estimates of the sex, age, and color composition of the current national population and estimates as to the size of the current population of states and regions also appear in this series. By obtaining the most recent reports in this series, either directly from the Bureau or from a library, the reader can supplement the materials in this chapter and gain an "up-to-the-minute" picture of present population size, recent growth, and projections of anticipated future trends.

2. This figure represents the land area in square miles. The gross area–including bodies of water–for the United States in 1980 is 3,618,770 square miles. See U.S. Bureau of the Census. *Statistical Abstract of the United States: 1982-83.* Washington, DC: U.S. Government Printing Office, 1982, Table 1.

3. These comparisons are approximate; data concerning the reported size of the Chinese and Soviet Union populations are still being evaluated.

4. The United Nations, through its annual publication *Demographic Yearbook* and its quarterly *Population and Vital Statistics Reports,* Series E (both prepared in the Statistical Office of the United Nations), is an invaluable source of information about world population trends. The U.S. Bureau of the Census, which maintains a research unit in international demography, publishes a series entitled *International Population Reports* (Series P-91), which reports estimates of past, present, and future populations of nations for which sufficient data are available. By consulting the most recent issues of these publications, the reader can quickly bring up to date the materials concerning the populations of other nations that are presented in this volume.

5. There was a major inconsistency between the 1970 and 1980 census counts. See "Components of Population Change and Error of Closure."

6. The terms "immigration" and "emigration" are usually employed to designate movement into or out of a nation. The terms "in-migration" and "out-migration" are employed to designate internal movement within a nation.

7. The bibliography lists works that have used the incomplete evidence available to arrive at estimates.

8. Warren S. Thompson and P.K. Whelpton. *Population Trends in the United States* (New York: McGraw-Hill, 1933), Chapter 1.

9. A more detailed exposition of expected future trends in the components of growth and the implications for populations is given in later chapters.

Bibliography

Callahan, Daniel (ed.). *The American Population Debate.* Garden City, NY: Doubleday and Company, 1971.

Campbell, Arthur A. "Baby Boom to Birth Dearth and Beyond." *Annals of the American Academy of Political and Social Science* 435 (1978):40-60.

Coale, Ansley J., and Zelnick, Melvin. *New Estimates of Fertility and Population in the U.S.* Princeton, NJ: Princeton University Press, 1963.

Commission on Population Growth and the American Future. *Population and the American Future.* (Chapter 2, "Population Growth.") Washington, DC: U.S. Government Printing Office, 1972.

Dulbin, Louis I. (ed.). *The American People: Studies in Population.* Philadelphia: The American Academy of Political and Social Science, 1936.

Easterlin, Richard A. "Long Swings in the United States Demographic and Economic Growth: Some Findings in Historical Pattern." *Demography* 2 (1965):490-507.

Frejka, Tomas. "Reflections on the Demographic Conditions Needed to Establish a U.S. Stationary Population Growth." *Population Studies* 22 (1968):379-97.

Hauser, Philip M. *Population Perspectives.* (Chapter 2, "The United States Population Explosion: The Facts.") New Brunswick, NJ: Rutgers University Press, 1960.

Lorimer, Frank; Winston, Ellen; and Kiser, Louise K. *Foundations of American Population Policy.* (Chapter 2, "Population Trends in the United States.") New York: Harper and Brothers, 1940.

National Resources Committee. *The Problems of a Changing Population.* (Chapter 1, "The Trend of Population.") Washington, DC: U.S. Government Printing Office, 1938.

Population Reference Bureau. "U.S. Population: Where We Are; Where We're Going" (symposium). *Population Bulletin* 37 (1982):3-50.

Ryder, Norman B. "A Demographic Optimum Population for the United States." In *Demographic and Social Aspects of Population Growth,* edited by Charles Westoff and Robert Parke, Jr. Research reports of the

U.S. Commission on Population Growth and the American Future, volume 6. Washington, DC: U.S. Government Printing Office, 1972.

Spengler, Joseph J. *Facing Zero Population Growth.* Durham, NC: Duke University Press, 1978.

———. *Population and America's Future.* San Francisco: W.H. Freeman and Company, 1975.

Sternlieb, George, and Hughes, James W. *Current Population Trends in the United States.* New Brunswick, NJ: Center for Urban Policy Research, 1978.

Taeuber, Conrad, and Taeuber, Irene B. *The Changing Population of the United States.* New York: John Wiley and Sons, 1958.

Taeuber, Irene B., and Taeuber, Conrad. *People of the United States in the 20th Century.* (Chapter I, "Increase, Expansion, and Concentration," and Chapter XI, "Population Change.") Washington, DC: U.S. Bureau of the Census, 1971.

Thompson, W.S., and Whelpton, P.T. *Population Trends in the United States.* New York: McGraw-Hill, 1933.

U.S. Bureau of the Census. *A Century of Population Growth from the First Census of the United States to the Twelfth, 1790-1900.* Washington, DC: U.S. Government Printing Office, 1909.

———. "Coverage of the National Population in the 1980 Census, by Age, Sex and Race: Preliminary Estimates by Demographic Analysis." *Current Population Reports, Special Studies* (Series P-23, no. 115). Washington, DC: U.S. Government Printing Office, 1982.

———. "Estimates of the Population of the United States and Components of Change: 1940 to 1966." *Current Population Reports, Population Estimates and Projections* (Series P-25, no. 331). Washington, DC: U.S. Government Printing Office, 1966.

———. "Estimates of the Population of the United States and Components of Change: 1940 to 1978." *Current Population Reports, Population Estimates and Projections* (Series P-25, no. 802). Washington, DC: U.S. Government Printing Office, 1978.

———. *Historical Statistics of the United States: Colonial Times to 1970.* Washington, DC: U.S. Government Printing Office, 1975.

———. *1980 Census of Population.* Volume 1, Chapter A, Number of Inhabitants, Part 1 (United States Summary). Washington, DC: U.S. Government Printing Office, 1983.

———. "Population Profile of the United States: 1982." *Current Population Reports, Population Characteristics* (Series P-23, no. 170). Washington, DC: U.S. Government Printing Office, 1984.

———. "Projections of the Population of the United States." *Current Population Reports* (Series P-25, no. 952). Washington, DC: U.S. Government Printing Office, 1984.

———. "Provisional Projections of the Population of States, by Age and Sex: 1980 to 2000." *Current Population Reports* (Series P-25, no. 937). Washington, DC: U.S. Government Printing Office, 1983.

———. *Statistical Abstract of the United States: 1984.* Washington, DC: U.S. Government Printing Office, 1984.

Westoff, Charles F. (ed.). *Towards the End of Growth.* Englewood Cliffs, NJ: Prentice Hall, 1973.

Technical Appendix 1-1

An Overview of the 1980 Census

A very large share of the materials analyzed in this book are derived from the censuses of the United States, and especially the 1980 census. Following is a synthesis of materials issued by the U.S. Bureau of the Census describing the procedures by which the census was taken and processed and the forms and instructions used in collecting the data in the field. Similar descriptions can be found in appendices to the volumes for the 1970 and earlier censuses.

DATA COLLECTION PROCEDURES

The 1980 census was conducted primarily through self-enumeration. A census questionnaire was delivered by postal carriers to every housing unit several days before Census Day, April 1, 1980. This questionnaire included explanatory information and was accompanied by an instruction guide. Spanish-language versions of the questionnaire and instruction guide were available on request. The questionnaire was also available in narrative translation in 32 languages.

In most areas of the United States, altogether containing about 95 percent of the population, the householder was requested to fill out and mail back the questionnaire on Census Day. Approximately 83 percent of these households returned their forms by mail. Households that did not mail back a form and vacant housing units were visited by an enumerator. Households that returned a form with incomplete or inconsistent information that exceeded a specified tolerance were contacted by telephone or, if necessary, by a personal visit, to obtain the missing information.

In the remaining (mostly sparsely settled) area of the country, which contained about 5 percent of the population, the householder was requested to fill out the questionnaire and hold it until visited by an enumerator. Incomplete and unfilled forms were completed by interview during the enumerator's visit. Vacant units were enumerated by a personal visit and observation.

Each housing unit in the country received one of two versions of the census questionnaire: a short-form questionnaire containing a limited number of basic population and housing questions or a long-form questionnaire containing these basic questions as well as a number of additional questions. A sampling procedure was used to determine those units which were to receive the long-form questionnaire. Two sampling rates were employed. For most of the country, one in every six housing units (about 17 percent) received the long form or sample questionnaire; in counties, incorporated places and minor civil divisions estimated to have fewer than 2,500 inhabitants, every other housing unit (50 percent) received the sample questionnaire to enhance the reliability of sample data in small areas.

Special questionnaires were used for the enumeration of persons in group quarters such as colleges and universities, hospitals, prisons, military installations, and ships. These forms contained the population questions but did not include any housing questions. In addition to the regular census questionnaires, the Supplementary Questionnaire for American Indians was used in conjunction with the short form on Federal and State reservations and in the historic areas of Oklahoma (excluding urbanized areas) for households that had at least one American Indian, Eskimo, or Aleut household member.

A more detailed description of the data collection and processing procedures can be obtained from the 1980 Census of Population and Housing, *Users' Guide,* PHC80-R1.

USUAL PLACE OF RESIDENCE

In accordance with census practice dating back to the first U.S. census in 1790, each person enumerated in the 1980 census was counted as an inhabitant of his or her "usual place of residence," which is generally construed to mean the place where the person lives and sleeps most of the time. This place is not necessarily the same as the person's legal residence or voting residence. In the vast majority of cases, however, the use of these different bases of classification would produce substantially the same statistics, although there might be appreciable differences for a few areas.

PROCESSING PROCEDURES

The 1980 census questionnaires were processed in a manner similar to that for the 1970 and 1960 censuses. They were designed to be processed electronically by the Film Optical Sensing Device for Input to Computer (FOSDIC). For most items on the questionnaire, the information supplied by the respondent or obtained by the enumerator was indicated by marking the answers in predesignated positions that would be "read" by FOSDIC from a microfilm copy of the questionnaire and transferred onto computer tape with no intervening manual processing. The computer tape did not include information on individual names and addresses.

The tape containing the information from the questionnaires was processed on the Census Bureau's computers through a number of editing and tabulation steps. Among the products of this operation were computer tapes from which the tables in this report (and most others in the 1980 census publications) were prepared on phototypesetting equipment at the Government Printing Office.

SOURCES OF ERROR

Since 1980 population data shown in this report were tabulated from the entries for persons on all questionnaires, these data are not subject to sampling error. In any large-scale statistical operation such as a decennial census, human and mechanical errors occur. These errors are commonly referred to as nonsampling errors. Such errors include failure to enumerate every housing unit or person in the population, not obtaining all required information from respondents, obtaining incorrect or inconsistent information, and recording information incorrectly. Errors can also occur during the field review of the enumerators' work, the clerical handling of the census questionnaires, or the electronic processing of the questionnaires.

In an attempt to reduce various types of nonsampling error in the 1980 census, a number of techniques were introduced on the basis of experience in previous censuses and in tests conducted prior to the census. These quality control and review measures were utilized throughout the data collection and processing phases of the census to minimize undercoverage of the population and housing units and to keep the errors at a minimum.

EDITING OF UNACCEPTABLE DATA

The objective of the processing operation is to produce a set of statistics that describes the population as accurately and clearly as possible. To meet this objective, certain unacceptable entries were edited.

In the field, questionnaires were reviewed for omissions and certain inconsistencies by a census clerk or an enumerator and, if necessary, a followup was made to obtain missing information. In addition, a similar review of questionnaires was done in the central processing offices. As a rule, however, editing was performed by hand only when it could not be done effectively by computer.

There are two means by which incomplete or inconsistent data on the questionnaires were corrected during the computer editing process: allocation and substitution. Allocations, or assignments of acceptable codes in place of unacceptable entries, were needed most often when an entry for a given item was lacking or when the information reported for a person on that item was inconsistent with other information for the person. As in previous censuses, the general procedure for changing unacceptable entries was to assign an entry for a person that was consistent with entries for other persons with similar characteristics. The assignment of acceptable codes in place of blanks or unacceptable entries, it is believed, enhances the usefulness of the data.

Please fill out this official Census Form and mail it back on Census Day, Tuesday, April 1, 1980

1980 Census of the United States

If the address shown below has the wrong apartment identification, please write the correct apartment number or location here:

DO	A1	A2	A4	A5	A6
				L	

Your answers are confidential

By law (title 13, U.S. Code), census employees are subject to fine and/or imprisonment for any disclosure of your answers. Only after 72 years does your information become available to other government agencies or the public. The same law requires that you answer the questions to the best of your knowledge.

Para personas de habla hispana

(For Spanish-speaking persons):
SI USTED DESEA UN CUESTIONARIO DEL CENSO EN ESPAÑOL llame a la oficina del censo. El número de teléfono se encuentra en el encasillado de la dirección.

O, si prefiere, marque esta casilla ☐ y devuelva el cuestionario por correo en el sobre que se le incluye.

A message from the Director, Bureau of the Census . . .

We must, from time to time, take stock of ourselves as a people if our Nation is to meet successfully the many national and local challenges we face. This is the purpose of the 1980 census.

The essential need for a population census was recognized almost 200 years ago when our Constitution was written. As provided by article I, the first census was conducted in 1790 and one has been taken every 10 years since then.

The law under which the census is taken protects the confidentiality of your answers. For the next 72 years — or until April 1, 2052 — only sworn census workers have access to the individual records, and no one else may see them.

Your answers, when combined with the answers from other people, will provide the statistical figures needed by public and private groups, schools, business and industry, and Federal, State, and local governments across the country. These figures will help all sectors of American society understand how our population and housing are changing. In this way, we can deal more effectively with today's problems and work toward a better future for all of us.

The census is a vitally important national activity. Please do your part by filling out this census form accurately and completely. If you mail it back promptly in the enclosed postage-paid envelope, it will save the expense and inconvenience of a census taker having to visit you.

Thank you for your cooperation.

U.S. Department of Commerce
Bureau of the Census
Form D-2

Form Approved
O.M.B. No. 41-S78006

Please continue →

Page 1

How to fill out your Census Form

See the filled-out example in the yellow instruction guide. This guide will help with any problems you may have.

If you need more help, call the Census Office. The telephone number of the local office is shown at the bottom of the address box on the front cover.

Use a black pencil to answer the questions. Black pencil is better to use than ballpoint or other pens.

Fill circles "O" completely, like this: ●

When you write in an answer, print or write clearly.

Make sure that answers are provided for everyone here.

See page 4 of the guide if a roomer or someone else in the household does not want to give you all the information for the form.

Answer the questions on pages 1 through 5, and then starting with pages 6 and 7, fill a pair of pages for each person in the household.

Check your answers. Then write your name, the date, and telephone number on page 20.

Mail back this form on Tuesday, April 1, or as soon afterward as you can. Use the enclosed envelope; no stamp is needed.

Please start by answering Question 1 below.

Question 1

List in Question 1

- Family members living here, including babies still in the hospital.
- Relatives living here.
- Lodgers or boarders living here.
- Other persons living here.
- College students who stay here while attending college, even if their parents live elsewhere.
- Persons who usually live here but are temporarily away (including children in boarding school below the college level).
- Persons with a home elsewhere but who stay here most of the week while working.

Do Not List in Question 1

- Any person away from here in the Armed Forces.
- Any college student who stays somewhere else while attending college.
- Any person who usually stays somewhere else most of the week while working there.
- Any person away from here in an institution such as a home for the aged or mental hospital.
- Any person staying or visiting here who has a usual home elsewhere.

1. What is the name of each person who was living here on Tuesday, April 1, 1980, or who was staying or visiting here and had no other home?

____

____

____

____

____

____

____

____

____

____

____

____

____

Note

If everyone here is staying only temporarily and has a usual home elsewhere, please mark this box ☐.

Then please:
- answer the questions on pages 2 through 5 only, and
- enter the address of your usual home on page 20.

Please continue ↗

ALSO ANSWER →

Here are the QUESTIONS ↓ These are the columns for ANSWERS → *Please fill one column for each person listed in Question 1.*	PERSON in column 1 Last name First name Middle initial	PERSON in column 2 Last name First name Middle initial
2. How is this person related to the person in column 1? *Fill one circle.* *If "Other relative" of person in column 1, give exact relationship, such as mother-in-law, niece, grandson, etc.*	*START in this column with the household member (or one of the members) in whose name the home is owned or rented. If there is no such person, start in this column with any adult household member.*	If relative of person in column 1: ○ Husband/wife ○ Father/mother ○ Son/daughter ○ Other relative ○ Brother/sister If not related to person in column 1: ○ Roomer, boarder ○ Other nonrelative ○ Partner, roommate ○ Paid employee
3. Sex *Fill one circle.*	○ Male ○ Female	○ Male ○ Female
4. Is this person — *Fill one circle.*	○ White ○ Asian Indian ○ Black or Negro ○ Hawaiian ○ Japanese ○ Guamanian ○ Chinese ○ Samoan ○ Filipino ○ Eskimo ○ Korean ○ Aleut ○ Vietnamese ○ Other — *Specify* ○ Indian (Amer.) *Print tribe* →	○ White ○ Asian Indian ○ Black or Negro ○ Hawaiian ○ Japanese ○ Guamanian ○ Chinese ○ Samoan ○ Filipino ○ Eskimo ○ Korean ○ Aleut ○ Vietnamese ○ Other — *Specify* ○ Indian (Amer.) *Print tribe* →
5. Age, and month and year of birth *a. Print age at last birthday.* *b. Print month and fill one circle.* *c. Print year in the spaces, and fill one circle below each number.*	a. Age at last birthday b. Month of birth ○ Jan.—Mar. ○ Apr.—June ○ July—Sept. ○ Oct.—Dec. c. Year of birth 1: 1 ● 8 ○ 9 ○ 0 ○ 1 ○ 2 ○ 3 ○ 4 ○ 5 ○ 6 ○ 7 ○ 8 ○ 9 ○ 0 ○ 1 ○ 2 ○ 3 ○ 4 ○ 5 ○ 6 ○ 7 ○ 8 ○ 9 ○	a. Age at last birthday b. Month of birth ○ Jan.—Mar. ○ Apr.—June ○ July—Sept. ○ Oct.—Dec. c. Year of birth 1: 1 ● 8 ○ 9 ○ 0 ○ 1 ○ 2 ○ 3 ○ 4 ○ 5 ○ 6 ○ 7 ○ 8 ○ 9 ○ 0 ○ 1 ○ 2 ○ 3 ○ 4 ○ 5 ○ 6 ○ 7 ○ 8 ○ 9 ○
6. Marital status *Fill one circle.*	○ Now married ○ Separated ○ Widowed ○ Never married ○ Divorced	○ Now married ○ Separated ○ Widowed ○ Never married ○ Divorced
7. Is this person of Spanish/Hispanic origin or descent? *Fill one circle.*	○ No (not Spanish/Hispanic) ○ Yes, Mexican, Mexican-Amer., Chicano ○ Yes, Puerto Rican ○ Yes, Cuban ○ Yes, other Spanish/Hispanic	○ No (not Spanish/Hispanic) ○ Yes, Mexican, Mexican-Amer., Chicano ○ Yes, Puerto Rican ○ Yes, Cuban ○ Yes, other Spanish/Hispanic
8. Since February 1, 1980, has this person attended regular school or college at any time? *Fill one circle. Count nursery school, kindergarten, elementary school, and schooling which leads to a high school diploma or college degree.*	○ No, has not attended since February 1 ○ Yes, public school, public college ○ Yes, private, church-related ○ Yes, private, not church-related	○ No, has not attended since February 1 ○ Yes, public school, public college ○ Yes, private, church-related ○ Yes, private, not church-related
9. What is the highest grade (or year) of regular school this person has ever attended? *Fill one circle.* *If now attending school, mark grade person is in. If high school was finished by equivalency test (GED), mark "12."*	**Highest grade attended:** ○ Nursery school ○ Kindergarten Elementary through high school *(grade or year)* 1 2 3 4 5 6 7 8 9 10 11 12 ○ ○ ○ ○ ○ ○ ○ ○ ○ ○ ○ ○ College *(academic year)* 1 2 3 4 5 6 7 8 or more ○ ○ ○ ○ ○ ○ ○ ○ ○ Never attended school — *Skip question 10*	**Highest grade attended:** ○ Nursery school ○ Kindergarten Elementary through high school *(grade or year)* 1 2 3 4 5 6 7 8 9 10 11 12 ○ ○ ○ ○ ○ ○ ○ ○ ○ ○ ○ ○ College *(academic year)* 1 2 3 4 5 6 7 8 or more ○ ○ ○ ○ ○ ○ ○ ○ ○ Never attended school — *Skip question 10*
10. Did this person finish the highest grade (or year) attended? *Fill one circle.*	○ Now attending this grade *(or year)* ○ Finished this grade *(or year)* ○ Did not finish this grade *(or year)*	○ Now attending this grade *(or year)* ○ Finished this grade *(or year)* ○ Did not finish this grade *(or year)*
	CENSUS USE ONLY A. ○ I ○ N ○ ○	*CENSUS USE ONLY* A. ○ I ○ N ○ ○

Name of Person 1 on page 2: ______________________
Last name First name Middle initial

11. In what State or foreign country was this person born?
Print the State where this person's mother was living when this person was born. Do not give the location of the hospital unless the mother's home and the hospital were in the same State.

____
Name of State or foreign country; or Puerto Rico, Guam, etc.

12. *If this person was born in a foreign country –*
a. Is this person a naturalized citizen of the United States?
○ Yes, a naturalized citizen
○ No, not a citizen
○ Born abroad of American parents

b. When did this person come to the United States to stay?
○ 1975 to 1980 ○ 1965 to 1969 ○ 1950 to 1959
○ 1970 to 1974 ○ 1960 to 1964 ○ Before 1950

13a. Does this person speak a language other than English at home?
○ Yes ○ No, only speaks English – *Skip to 14*

b. What is this language?
____
(For example – Chinese, Italian, Spanish, etc.)

c. How well does this person speak English?
○ Very well ○ Not well
○ Well ○ Not at all

14. What is this person's ancestry? *If uncertain about how to report ancestry, see instruction guide.*

____
(For example: Afro-Amer., English, French, German, Honduran, Hungarian, Irish, Italian, Jamaican, Korean, Lebanese, Mexican, Nigerian, Polish, Ukrainian, Venezuelan, etc.)

15a. Did this person live in this house five years ago (April 1, 1975)?
If in college or Armed Forces in April 1975, report place of residence there.
○ Born April 1975 or later – *Turn to next page for next person*
○ Yes, this house – *Skip to 16*
○ No, different house

b. Where did this person live five years ago (April 1, 1975)?
(1) State, foreign country, Puerto Rico, Guam, etc.: ______________
(2) County: ______________
(3) City, town, village, etc.: ______________
(4) Inside the incorporated (legal) limits of that city, town, village, etc.?
○ Yes ○ No, in unincorporated area

16. When was this person born?
○ Born before April 1965 – *Please go on with questions 17-33*
○ Born April 1965 or later – *Turn to next page for next person*

17. In April 1975 *(five years ago)* **was this person –**
a. On active duty in the Armed Forces?
○ Yes ○ No
b. Attending college?
○ Yes ○ No
c. Working at a job or business?
○ Yes, full time ○ No
○ Yes, part time

18a. Is this person a veteran of active-duty military service in the Armed Forces of the United States?
If service was in National Guard or Reserves only, see instruction guide.
○ Yes ○ No – *Skip to 19*

b. Was active-duty military service during –
Fill a circle for each period in which this person served.
○ May 1975 or later
○ Vietnam era *(August 1964–April 1975)*
○ February 1955—July 1964
○ Korean conflict *(June 1950–January 1955)*
○ World War II *(September 1940–July 1947)*
○ World War I *(April 1917–November 1918)*
○ Any other time

19. Does this person have a physical, mental, or other health condition which has lasted for 6 or more months and which . . .

	Yes	No
a. Limits the kind or amount of work this person can do at a job?	○	○
b. Prevents this person from working at a job?	○	○
c. Limits or prevents this person from using public transportation?	○	○

20. *If this person is a female –*
How many babies has she ever had, not counting stillbirths?
Do not count her stepchildren or children she has adopted.
None 1 2 3 4 5 6
○ ○ ○ ○ ○ ○ ○
7 8 9 10 11 12 or more
○ ○ ○ ○ ○ ○

21. *If this person has ever been married –*
a. Has this person been married more than once?
○ Once ○ More than once
b. Month and year of marriage? ______ *(Month)* ______ *(Year)*
Month and year of first marriage? ______ *(Month)* ______ *(Year)*
c. *If married more than once –* **Did the first marriage end because of the death of the husband (or wife)?**
○ Yes ○ No

22a. Did this person work at any time last week?
○ Yes – *Fill this circle if this person worked full time or part time. (Count part-time work such as delivering papers, or helping without pay in a family business or farm. Also count active duty in the Armed Forces.)*
○ No – *Fill this circle if this person did not work, or did only own housework, school work, or volunteer work.* – *Skip to 25*

b. How many hours did this person work last week (at all jobs)?
Subtract any time off; add overtime or extra hours worked.
______ Hours

23. At what location did this person work last week?
If this person worked at more than one location, print where he or she worked most last week.
If one location cannot be specified, see instruction guide.
a. Address *(Number and street)* ______________
If street address is not known, enter the building name, shopping center, or other physical location description.
b. Name of city, town, village, borough, etc.
____
c. Is the place of work inside the incorporated (legal) limits of that city, town, village, borough, etc.?
○ Yes ○ No, in unincorporated area
d. County ______________
e. State ______ **f. ZIP Code** ______

24a. Last week, how long did it usually take this person to get from home to work (one way)?
______ Minutes

b. How did this person usually get to work last week?
If this person used more than one method, give the one usually used for most of the distance.
○ Car ○ Taxicab
○ Truck ○ Motorcycle
○ Van ○ Bicycle
○ Bus or streetcar ○ Walked only
○ Railroad ○ Worked at home
○ Subway or elevated ○ Other – *Specify* ______
If car, truck, or van in 24b, go to 24c. Otherwise, skip to 28.

FOR CENSUS USE ONLY

Per. No.	11.	13b.	14.	15b.	23. ○ VL	24a.
	0 0 0	0 0 0	0 0 0 0 0 0	0 0 0 0 0 0	0 0 0 0 0 0 0 0 0	0 0
1	1 1 1	1 1 1	1 1 1 1 1 1	1 1 1 1 1 1	1 1 1 1 1 1 1 1 1	1 1
2	2 2 2	2 2 2	2 2 2 2 2 2	2 2 2 2 2 2	2 2 2 2 2 2 2 2 2	2 2
3	3 3 3	3 3 3	3 3 3 3 3 3	3 3 3 3 3 3	3 3 3 3 3 3 3 3 3	3 3
4	4 4 4	4 4 4	4 4 4 4 4 4	4 4 4 4 4 4	4 4 4 4 4 4 4 4 4	4 4
5	5 5 5	5 5 5	5 5 5 5 5 5	5 5 5 5 5 5	5 5 5 5 5 5 5 5 5	5 5
6	6 6 6	6 6 6	6 6 6 6 6 6	6 6 6 6 6 6	6 6 6 6 6 6 6 6 6	6 6
7	7 7 7	7 7 7	7 7 7 7 7 7	7 7 7 7 7 7	7 7 7 7 7 7 7 7 7	7 7
0	8 8 8	8 8 8	8 8 8 8 8 8	8 8 8 8 8 8	8 8 8 8 8 8 8 8 8	8 8
	9 9 9	9 9 9	9 9 9 9 9 9	9 9 9 9 9 9	9 9 9 9 9 9 9 9 9	9 9

c. When going to work last week, did this person usually —

○ Drive alone — *Skip to 28* ○ Drive others only
○ Share driving ○ Ride as passenger only

d. How many people, including this person, usually rode to work in the car, truck, or van last week?

○ 2 ■ ○ 4 ○ 6 ■
○ 3 ○ 5 ○ 7 or more

After answering 24d, skip to 28.

25. Was this person temporarily absent or on layoff from a job or business last week?

○ Yes, on layoff
○ Yes, on vacation, temporary illness, labor dispute, etc.
○ No

26a. Has this person been looking for work during the last 4 weeks?

○ Yes ○ No — *Skip to 27*

b. Could this person have taken a job last week?

○ No, already has a job ■
○ No, temporarily ill
○ No, other reasons *(in school, etc.)* ■
○ Yes, could have taken a job

27. When did this person last work, even for a few days?

○ 1980 ○ 1978 ○ 1970 to 1974 }
○ 1979 ○ 1975 to 1977 ○ 1969 or earlier } *Skip to 31d*
○ Never worked }

28–30. Current or most recent job activity

Describe clearly this person's chief job activity or business last week. If this person had more than one job, describe the one at which this person worked the most hours. If this person had no job or business last week, give information for last job or business since 1975.

28. Industry

a. For whom did this person work? *If now on active duty in the Armed Forces, print "AF" and skip to question 31.*

____
(Name of company, business, organization, or other employer)

b. What kind of business or industry was this?
Describe the activity at location where employed.

____
(For example: Hospital, newspaper publishing, mail order house, auto engine manufacturing, breakfast cereal manufacturing) ■

c. Is this mainly — *(Fill one circle)*

○ Manufacturing ■ ○ Retail trade
○ Wholesale trade ○ Other — *(agriculture, construction, service, government, etc.)*

29. Occupation

a. What kind of work was this person doing?

____
(For example: Registered nurse, personnel manager, supervisor of order department, gasoline engine assembler, grinder operator)

b. What were this person's most important activities or duties?

____
(For example: Patient care, directing hiring policies, supervising order clerks, assembling engines, operating grinding mill)

30. Was this person — *(Fill one circle)*

Employee of private company, business, or individual, for wages, salary, or commissions ..... ○ ■
Federal government employee ..... ○
State government employee ..... ○
Local government employee *(city, county, etc.)* ..... ○
Self-employed in own business, professional practice, or farm —
Own business not incorporated ..... ○
Own business incorporated ..... ○
Working without pay in family business or farm ..... ○

CENSUS USE

21b.
I 0 0
○ 1 1
2 2
II 3 3
○ 4 4
III 5 5
○ 6 6
7 7
IV 8 8
○ 9 9

22b.
0 0
1 1
2 2
3 3
4 4
5 5
6 6
7 7
8 8
9 9

28.
A B C
○ ○ ○
D E F
○ ○ ○
G H J
○ ○ ○
K L M
○ ○ ○

0 0 0
1 1 1
2 2 2
3 3
4 4
5 5
6 6
7 7
8 8
9 9

AF ○
NW ○

29.
N P Q
○ ○ ○
R S T
○ ○ ○
U V W
○ ○ ○
X Y Z
○ ○ ○

0 0
1 1
2 2
3 3 3
4 4 4
5 5 5
6 6 6
7 7 7
8 8 8
9 9 9

31a. Last year (1979), did this person work, even for a few days, at a paid job or in a business or farm?

○ Yes ■ ○ No — *Skip to 31d*

b. How many weeks did this person work in 1979?
Count paid vacation, paid sick leave, and military service.

__________ Weeks

c. During the weeks worked in 1979, how many hours did this person usually work each week?

__________ Hours

d. Of the weeks not worked in 1979 (if any), how many weeks was this person looking for work or on layoff from a job?

__________ Weeks

32. Income in 1979 —
Fill circles and print dollar amounts.
If net income was a loss, write "Loss" above the dollar amount.
If exact amount is not known, give best estimate. For income received jointly by household members, see instruction guide.

During 1979 did this person receive any income from the following sources?

If "Yes" to any of the sources below — **How much did this person receive for the entire year?**

a. Wages, salary, commissions, bonuses, or tips from all jobs . . . *Report amount before deductions for taxes, bonds, dues, or other items.*

○ Yes ➔ $ ______.00
○ No *(Annual amount – Dollars)*

b. Own nonfarm business, partnership, or professional practice . . . *Report net income after business expenses.*

■ ○ Yes ➔ $ ______.00
○ No *(Annual amount – Dollars)*

c. Own farm. . .
Report net income after operating expenses. Include earnings as a tenant farmer or sharecropper.

○ Yes ➔ $ ______.00
○ No *(Annual amount – Dollars)*

d. Interest, dividends, royalties, or net rental income . . .
Report even small amounts credited to an account.

○ Yes ➔ $ ______.00
○ No *(Annual amount – Dollars)*

e. Social Security or Railroad Retirement . . .

■ ○ Yes ➔ $ ______.00
○ No *(Annual amount – Dollars)*

f. Supplemental Security (SSI), Aid to Families with Dependent Children (AFDC), or other public assistance or public welfare payments . . .

○ Yes ➔ $ ______.00
○ No *(Annual amount – Dollars)*

g. Unemployment compensation, veterans' payments, pensions, alimony or child support, or any other sources of income received regularly . . .
Exclude lump-sum payments such as money from an inheritance or the sale of a home.

■ ○ Yes ➔ $ ______.00
○ No *(Annual amount – Dollars)*

33. What was this person's total income in 1979?
Add entries in questions 32a through g; subtract any losses.
$ ______.00 *(Annual amount – Dollars)*
If total amount was a loss, write "Loss" above amount. OR ○ None

CENSUS USE ONLY

31b.	31c.	31d.
0 0	0 0	0 0
1 1	1 1	1 1
2 2	2 2	2 2
3 3	3 3	3 3
4 4	4 4	4 4
5 5	5 5	5 5
6	6 6	6
7	7 7	7
8	8 8	8
9	9 9	9

32a. ■	32b.
0 0 0 0	0 0 0 0
1 1 1 1	1 1 1 1
2 2 2 2	2 2 2 2
3 3 3 3	3 3 3 3
4 4 4 4	4 4 4 4
5 5 5 5	5 5 5 5
6 6 6 6	6 6 6 6
7 7 7 7	7 7 7 7
8 8 8 8	8 8 8 8
9 9 9 9	9 9 9 9
A ○	○ A ○

32c.	32d.
0 0 0 0	0 0 0 0
1 1 1 1	1 1 1 1
2 2 2 2	2 2 2 2
3 3 3 3	3 3 3 3
4 4 4 4	4 4 4 4
5 5 5 5	5 5 5 5
6 6 6 6	6 6 6 6
7 7 7 7	7 7 7 7
8 8 8 8	8 8 8 8
9 9 9 9	9 9 9 9
○ A ○	○ A ○

32e.	32f.
0 0 0 0	0 0 0 0
1 1 1	1 1 1
2 2 2	2 2 2
3 3 3	3 3 3
4 4 4	4 4 4
5 5 5	5 5 5
6 6 6	6 6 6
7 7 7	7 7 7
8 8 8	8 8 8
9 9 9	9 9 9

32g.	33.
0 0 0 0	0 0 0 0
1 1 1 1	1 1 1 1
2 2 2 2	2 2 2 2
3 3 3 3	3 3 3 3
4 4 4 4	4 4 4 4
5 5 5 5	5 5 5 5
6 6 6 6	6 6 6 6
7 7 7 7	7 7 7 7
8 8 8 8	8 8 8 8
9 9 9 9	9 9 9 9
■	○ A ○

1 1	1 1	1 1 1
2 2	2 2	2 2 2
3 3	3 3	3 3 3
4 4	4 4	4 4 4
5 5	5 5	5 5 5
6 6	6 6	6 6 6
7 7	7 7	7 7 7
8 8	8 8	8 8 8
9 9	9 9	9 9 9

INSTRUCTIONS FOR QUESTIONS 1 THROUGH 10

1. List in question 1 (on page 1), the names of all the people who usually live here. Then turn to pages 2 and 3 where there are columns to list up to seven persons. In the first column print the name of one of the household members in whose name this home is owned or rented. If no household member owns or rents the living quarters, list in the first column any adult household member who is not a roomer, boarder, or paid employee. Print the names of the other household members, if any, in the columns which follow, using question 1 as a checklist.

2. Fill a circle to show how each person is related to the person in column 1.

   A stepchild or legally adopted child of the person in column 1 should be marked **Son/daughter**. Foster children or wards living in the household should be marked **Roomer, boarder**.

3. Be sure to fill a circle for the sex of each person.

4. Fill the circle for the category with which the person most closely identifies. If you fill the **Indian (American)** or **Other** circle, be sure to print the name of the specific Indian tribe or specific group.

5. Enter age at last birthday in the space provided (enter "0" for babies less than one year old). Also enter month and year of birth, *and* fill the appropriate circles. For an illustration of how to complete question 5, see the example on pages 4 and 5. If age or month or year of birth is not known, give your best estimate.

6. If the person's only marriage was annulled, mark **Never married**.

7. A person is of Spanish/Hispanic origin or descent if the person *identifies* his or her ancestry with one of the listed groups, that is, Mexican, Puerto Rican, etc. Origin or descent (ancestry) may be viewed as the nationality group, the lineage, or country in which the person or the person's parents or ancestors were born.

8. Do not count enrollment in a trade or business school, company training, or tutoring unless the course would be accepted for credit at a regular elementary school, high school, or college. A *public* school is any school or college which is controlled and supported primarily by a local, county, State, or Federal Government.

9. Fill only one circle. Mark the highest grade *ever* attended even if the person did not finish it. If the person is still in school, mark the grade in which now enrolled. Schooling received in foreign or ungraded schools should be reported as the equivalent grade or year in the regular American school system. If uncertain whether a Head Start program is for nursery school or kindergarten, mark the circle for **Nursery school**.

   If the person skipped or repeated grades, mark the highest grade ever attended regardless of how long it took to get there. Persons who did not attend any college but who completed high school by finishing the 12th grade or by passing an equivalency test, such as the General Educational Development (GED) examination, should fill the circle for the 12th grade.

10. Mark **Finished this grade (or year)** only if the person finished the *entire* grade or year marked in question 9 or if the highest grade was completed by passing a high school equivalency test.

INSTRUCTIONS FOR QUESTIONS 11 THROUGH 14

11. *For persons born in the United States:*
    Print the name of the State in which this person's mother was living when this person was born. For persons born in a hospital, do not give the State in which the hospital was located unless the hospital and the mother's home were in the same State or the location of the mother's home is not known. For example, if a person was born in a hospital in Washington, D.C., but the mother's home was in Virginia at the time of the person's birth, enter "Virginia."

    For persons born outside the United States:
    Print the full name of the foreign country or Puerto Rico, Guam, etc., where the person was born. Use international boundaries as now recognized by the United States. Specify whether Northern Ireland or Ireland (Eire); East or West Germany; England, Scotland or Wales (*not* Great Britain or United Kingdom). Specify the particular island in the Caribbean, *not*, for example, West Indies.

12. This question is only for persons born in a foreign country. Fill the **Yes, a naturalized citizen** circle only if the person has *completed* the naturalization process and is now a citizen.

    If the person has entered the U.S. more than once, fill the circle for the year he or she came to stay permanently.

13a. Mark **No, only speaks English** if the person always speaks English *at home*; then skip to question 14.

   Mark **Yes** if the person speaks a language other than English *at home*. Do *not* mark **Yes** for a language spoken only at school or if speaking ability is limited to a few expressions or slang.

b. Print the non-English language spoken *at home*. If this person speaks two or more non-English languages *at home* and cannot determine which is spoken most often, report the first language the person learned to speak.

c. Fill the circle that best describes the person's *ability* to speak English.

   (1) The circle **Very well** should be filled for persons who have no difficulty speaking English.

   (2) The circle **Well** should be filled for persons who have only minor problems which do not seriously limit their ability to speak English.

   (3) The circle **Not well** should be filled for persons who are seriously limited in their ability to speak English.

   (4) The circle **Not at all** should be filled for persons who do not speak English at all.

14. Print the ancestry group with which the person *identifies*. Ancestry (or origin or descent) may be viewed as the nationality group, the lineage, or the country in which the person or the person's parents or ancestors were born before their arrival in the United States. Persons who are of more than one origin and who cannot identify with a single group should print their multiple ancestry (for example, German-Irish).

    Be specific; for example, if ancestry is "Indian," specify whether American Indian, Asian Indian, or West Indian. Distinguish Cape Verdean from Portuguese, and French Canadian from Canadian.

    A religious group should not be reported as a person's ancestry.

INSTRUCTIONS FOR QUESTIONS 15 THROUGH 20

15a. Mark **Yes, this house** if this person lived in this same house or apartment on April 1, 1975, but moved away and came back between then and now. Mark **No, different house** if this person lived in the same building but in a different apartment (or in the same mobile home or trailer but on a different trailer site).

b. If this person lived in a different house or apartment on April 1, 1975, give the location of this person's usual home at that time.

Part (1) If the person was living in the United States on April 1, 1975, print the name of the State. If the person did *not* live in the United States on April 1, 1975, print the full name of the foreign country or Puerto Rico, Guam, etc.

Part (2) If in Louisiana, print the parish name. If in Alaska, print the borough name. If in New York City – print the borough name if the county name is not known. If an independent city, leave blank.

Part (3) If in Connecticut, Maine, Massachusetts, New Hampshire, Rhode Island or Vermont, print the name of the town rather than the name of the village or city, unless the name of the town is unknown.

Part (4) Mark **Yes** if you know that the location is *now* inside the limits of a city, town, village or other incorporated place, even if it was not inside the limits on April 1, 1975.

17a. Mark **Yes** only if this person was on *active* duty in the U.S. Army, Navy, Air Force, Marine Corps, or Coast Guard. Mark **No** if the person was in the National Guard or the reserves.

b. Mark **Yes** if the person was attending a college or university either full or part time and was enrolled for credit toward a degree. Mark **No** if the person was taking only non-credit courses or was attending a vocational or trade school, such as secretarial school.

c. Mark **Yes, full time** if the person worked full time (35 hours or more per week). Mark **Yes, part time** if the person worked part time (less than 35 hours per week). Mark **No** if the person only did unpaid volunteer work, housework or yard work at own home, or if the only work done was as a resident of an institution.

18a. Mark **Yes** if this person was ever on active duty in the U.S. Army, Navy, Air Force, Marine Corps, or Coast Guard, even if the time served was short. For persons in the National Guard or military reserve units, mark **Yes** *only* if the person was ever called to active duty; mark **No** if the only service was active duty for training.

b. If this person served during more than one period, fill all circles which apply, even if service was for a short time.

19. The term "health condition" refers to any physical or mental problem which has lasted for 6 *or more* months. A serious problem with seeing, hearing, or speech should be considered a health condition. Pregnancy or a temporary health problem such as a broken bone that is expected to heal normally should *not* be considered a health condition.

20. Count all children born alive, including any who have died (even shortly after birth) or who no longer live with her.

INSTRUCTIONS FOR QUESTIONS 21 THROUGH 26

21. If the exact date of marriage is not known, give your best estimate.

22a. Mark **Yes** if the person worked, either full or part time, on any day of last week (Sunday through Saturday).

Count as work:

Work for someone else for wages, salary, piece rate, commission, tips, or payments "in kind" (for example, food, lodging received as payment for work performed).

Work in own business, professional practice, or farm.

Any work in a family business or farm, paid or not.

Any part-time work including babysitting, paper routes, etc.

Active duty in Armed Forces.

Do not count as work:

Housework or yard work at home.

Unpaid volunteer work.

Work done as a resident of an institution.

b. Give the *actual* number of hours worked at *all jobs last week*, even if that was more or fewer hours than usually worked.

23. If the person worked at several locations, but reported to the same location each day to begin work, print where he or she reported. If the person did not report to the same location each day to begin work, print the words "various locations" for 23a, and give as much information as possible in the remainder of 23 to identify the area in which he or she worked *most* last week.

If the person's employer operates in more than one location (such as a grocery store chain or public school system), give the exact address of the location or branch where the person worked.

If the person worked in a foreign country or Puerto Rico, Guam, etc., print the name of the country in 23e and leave the other parts of 23 blank.

24a. Travel time is from door to door. Include time taken waiting for public transportation, picking up passengers in carpools, etc.

b. Mark **Worked at home** for a person who works on a farm where he or she lives, or in an office or shop in the person's home.

c. If the person was driven to work by someone who then drove back home or to a non-work destination, mark **Drive alone**.

d. Do not include riders who rode to school or some other non-work destination.

25. If the person works only during certain seasons or on a day-to-day basis when work is available, mark **No**.

26a. Mark **Yes** if the person tried to get a job or to start a business or professional practice at any time in the last *four* weeks; for example, registered at an employment office, went to a job interview, placed or answered ads, or did anything toward starting a business or professional practice.

b. Mark **No, already has a job** if the person was on layoff or was expecting to report to a job within 30 days.

Mark **No, temporarily ill** if the person expects to be able to work within 30 days.

Mark **No, other reasons** if the person could not have taken a job because he or she was going to school, taking care of children, etc.

INSTRUCTIONS FOR QUESTIONS 27 THROUGH 29

27. Look at the instructions for 22a to see what to count as work. Mark **Never worked** if the person: (1) never worked at any kind of job or business, either full or part time, (2) never did any work, with or without pay, in a family business or farm *and* (3) never served in the Armed Forces.

28a. If the person worked for a company, business, or government agency, print the name of the company, not the name of the person's supervisor. If the person worked for an individual or a business that has no company name, print the name of the individual worked for. If the person worked in his or her own business, print "self-employed."

b. Print two or more words to tell what the business, industry, or individual employer named in 28a does. If there is more than one activity, describe only the major activity *at the place where the person works.* Enter what is made, what is sold, or what service is given.

Some examples of what is needed to make an answer acceptable are shown on the census form and here.

Unacceptable	Acceptable
Furniture company	Metal furniture manufacturing
Grocery store	Wholesale grocery store
Oil company	Retail gas station
Ranch	Cattle ranch

c. Mark **Manufacturing** if the factory, plant, mill, etc., mostly makes things, even if it also sells them.

Mark **Wholesale trade** if the business mostly sells things to stores or other companies.

Mark **Retail trade** if the business mostly sells things (not services) to individuals.

Mark **Other** if the main activity of the employer is not making or selling things. Some examples of **Other** are farming, construction, and services such as those provided by hotels, dry cleaners, repair shops, schools, and banks.

29a. Print two or more words to describe the kind of work the person does. If the person is a trainee, apprentice, or helper, include that in the description.

Some examples of what is needed to make an answer acceptable are shown on the census form and here.

Unacceptable	Acceptable
Clerk	Production clerk
Helper	Carpenter's helper
Mechanic	Auto engine mechanic
Nurse	Registered nurse

b. Print the most important things that the person does on the job. Some examples are shown on the census form.

INSTRUCTIONS FOR QUESTIONS 30 THROUGH 33

30. If the person was an employee of a *private* nonprofit organization, such as a church, fill the first circle.

Mark **Local government employee** for a teacher working in an elementary or secondary public school.

31a. Look at the instructions for question 22a to see what to count as work.

b. Count every week in which the person did any work at all, even for an hour.

c. If the hours worked each week varied considerably, give the best estimate of the hours usually worked most weeks.

d. Count every week in which the person did not work at all, but spent any time looking for work or on layoff from a job. *Looking for work* means trying to get a job or start a business or professional practice; *layoff* includes either temporary or indefinite layoff.

32. Fill the **Yes** or **No** circle for each part and enter the appropriate amount. If income from any source was received jointly by household members, report if possible, the appropriate share for each person; otherwise, report the whole amount for only one person and mark **No** for the other person, unless the other person has additional income of the same type.

a. Include sick leave pay. Do not include reimbursement for business expenses and pay "in kind," (for example, food, lodging received as payment for work performed).

b. Include net earnings (gross earnings minus business expenses) from a nonfarm business. If business lost money, write "Loss" above the amount.

c. Include net earnings (gross receipts minus operating expenses) from a farm. If farm lost money, write "Loss" above the amount.

d. Include interest and dividends credited to the person's account (for example, from savings accounts and stock shares), net royalties, and net income from rental property.

e. Include Social Security or Railroad Retirement payments to retired persons, to dependents of deceased insured workers and to disabled workers.

f. Include public assistance or welfare payments received from Federal, State, or local agencies. Do not include private welfare payments.

g. Include all other regular payments, such as government employee retirement, union or private pensions and annuities; unemployment benefits; worker's compensation; Armed Forces allotments; private welfare payments; regular contributions from persons not living in the household; etc.

Do not include lump-sum payments received from the sale of property (capital gains), insurance policies, inheritances, etc.

33. If no income was received in 1979, fill the **None** circle. If total income was a loss, write "Loss" above the amount.

Chapter 2

Demographic Composition: Race/Ethnicity, Sex, and Age

Introduction to Population Composition

Treating population simply as numbers of people, which was the approach in Chapter 1, is a necessary first step, but for the purposes of population study it is not sufficient. Population characteristics are no less important than numbers of inhabitants. The next step is to divide the total population into categories, or subpopulations, by classifying the individuals according to selected characteristics. Such categorization, of course, can go no farther than the information supplied by census or sample survey questionnaires. Demographers customarily divide the study of population composition into three branches, each dealing with a set of population traits.[1] In the present account, the following organization of traits will be followed:

1. *Demographic characteristics*
   a. Race
   b. Ethnicity
   c. Sex
   d. Age
2. *Social characteristics*
   e. Marital status
   f. Household and family status
   g. School enrollment
   h. Educational attainment
3. *Economic characteristics*
   i. Employment status
   j. Industry of employment
   k. Occupation
   l. Income.

This chapter will provide an overview of the demographic characteristics of the U.S. population. These traits, unlike the other two sets of traits, are physiologically determined at birth, and the individual is powerless to change them. Because they are such fundamental subdivisions, they are used to cross-classify each of the other traits in the analysis of both social characteristics and economic characteristics. In other words, when social characteristics such as educational attainment or economic characteristics such as income are studied, special interest is given to comparisons between the race, ethnic, sex, and age subpopulations. Therefore, it is necessary to know the population's demographic composition before proceeding to the study of the other two branches of composition.

Definitions

Race. All persons were asked to identify themselves according to the following race categories on the 1980 questionnaire: White, Black or Negro, American Indian, Eskimo, Aleut, Japanese, Chinese, Filipino, Korean, Asian Indian, Vietnamese, Hawaiian, Guamanian, Samoan, and Other. The "Other" category includes Malayan, Polynesian, Thai, and groups not included in the specific categories listed on the questionnaire. The concept of race reflects self-identification by respondents; it does not denote any clear-cut scientific definition of biological stock. For persons with parents of different races who could not provide a single response to the race question, the race of the person's mother was used. In 1970, when persons with parents of different races were in doubt as to their classification, the race of the father was used. Also in 1970 there were no categories for Vietnamese, Asian Indian, Guamanian, or Samoan; Eskimo and Aleut appeared only on questionnaires used in Alaska. In 1970 persons who did not report a specific race but wrote in Hispanic categories were assigned to White; for 1980 these persons remained in the "other" category.

Spanish-origin. All persons were asked to identify themselves as being either of Spanish or non-Spanish origin or descent. If the person reported a multiple origin and could not provide a single origin, the origin of the person's mother was used. Four categories of Spanish-origin were specified: Mexican, Puerto Rican, Cuban, or Other Spanish. The Spanish-origin question was asked on a 100-percent basis for the first time in 1980. A similar question was asked on the 1970 5-percent sample questionnaire.

Sex Ratio. The number of males per 100 or per 1,000 females. This ratio may be computed for age groups, race groups, or any other trait or combinations of traits subclassified by sex.

Age. Completed years of age as of last birthday, based on replies to a question on month and year of birth. Respondents who failed to provide this information were requested to specify "age at last birthday." This response was used only when date of birth was not provided, because of the tendency of some people in reporting their ages to round off to "0" or "5" (and to report even rather than odd numbers).

Dependency Ratio. Number of persons under age fifteen or over sixty-five per 100 population aged 15-64. Some demographers employ age under twenty instead of under fifteen in computing this ratio.

Age Pyramid. A diagram illustrating the age and sex composition of a population. Single-year or five-year age groups are stacked successively atop each other, beginning with the youngest age. Number (or percent) of the total population is used as a scale. Male population is plotted on the left and female population on the right side of the diagram. For examples, see Figure 2-7.

Birth Cohort. A subpopulation born in a particular year or set of years which therefore are the same age group and pass through the life cycle together. Their progress may be charted by following them at successively older ages in consecutive censuses or enumerations.

Racial Composition

At the 1980 census all persons were asked to classify themselves as belonging to one of the fifteen "race" categories shown in Table 2-1. The resulting data therefore show how the respondents identified themselves by race, as they interpreted the census question.* The categories obviously are not a scientific classification of distinctive, genetically determined biological stocks. It is, rather, a set of categories deemed to be important for social, economic, and administrative purposes in one or more of the fifty states. Because the 1980 census was primarily one of self-enumeration, because public ideas of what constitute categories of race probably are subject to great variation, and because the word "race" was not contained in the census question about race, the data may have substantial response errors. For example, many respondents who should have classified themselves as white (especially nonblack Spanish-speaking) apparently regarded it as a nationality question, and when they did not find their nation of origin mentioned, simply marked "other."

*See question 4 of the 1980 census form, reproduced in the Technical Appendix to Chapter 1.

Table 2-1, which is a tabulation of responses to this question of race, makes clear that the basic racial contrast is between "white" (83 percent) and "black" (Negro, 12 percent). All of the other specific racial categories combined amounted only to 2 percent, with 3 percent in the unspecified "other" category. As a consequence, many of the tables in this and later chapters will make use of a trichotomy: "white," "black," and "other," or simply the dichotomy "white" and "black" and other races," or "black" and "white and other races."

Because of the different way of collecting race information in the 1980 census in comparison with 1970, the U.S. Census Bureau has modified 1980 census counts for race to distribute the artificially large "other" category in a way that more nearly conforms to the 1970 definitions. Primarily, the adjustment consisted of allocating the Spanish-origin population that erroneously classified itself as "other race" almost entirely into the white population, with a very small allocation to the black population. Table 2-2 reports the modified counts and the implied measures of change between 1970 and 1980. This adjustment increases the white component to 86 percent. During the 1970-80 decade the black population grew at a rate nearly twice as fast as the white population (see Figure 2-1). Nevertheless, the black population still remains very much a minority group, comprising only one-ninth of the total. The Asian and American Indian populations nearly doubled in size between 1970 and 1980, but because of small initial size they still accounted for only 2.1 percent of the total at the end of the decade.

The change in U.S. racial composition from 1790 to 1983 is presented in Table 2-3.

Table 2-1. Racial Composition of the U.S. Population: 1980 [resident population]

Race	Number of persons (000)	Percent distri-bution	Percent female
Total.	226,546	100.00	51.4
White.	188,372	83.15	51.3
Black (Negro). . .	26,495	11.70	52.7
American Indian, Aleut, Eskimo. .	1,420	0.63	50.6
American Indian	1,364	0.60	50.6
Eskimo	42	0.02	48.9
Aleut.	14	0.01	49.4
Asian and Pacific Islander	3,500	1.55	51.6
Japanese	701	0.31	54.2
Chinese.	806	0.36	49.4
Filipino	775	0.34	51.7
Korean	355	0.16	58.3
Asian Indian . .	362	0.16	48.3
Vietnamese . . .	262	0.12	48.2
Hawaiian	167	0.07	50.7
Guamian.	32	0.01	48.4
Samoan	42	0.02	49.3
Other races. . . .	6,758	2.98	48.9

Source: U.S. Bureau of the Census. "General Population Characteristics: United States Summary." 1980 Census of Population. Washington, DC: U.S. Government Printing Office, 1983, Table 38.

Black Population

When the nation was founded, and for its first half-century, almost one resident in five was black (preponderantly slaves). When the importation of slaves was forbidden and as the floodgates of immigration from Europe were opened, this proportion declined by almost half (see Figure 2-2). Its lowest point was reached in 1930. During the most recent half-century, higher black than white fertility, with reduced immigration from abroad, has caused the proportion of blacks to climb back to about the proportion it was in 1890, nearly 12 percent. Were it not for the continuing inflow of white immigrants from Latin America and other nations the proportion would climb more quickly toward the 1790 figure because of the substantially higher fertility among black than among white residents (see Chapter 6).

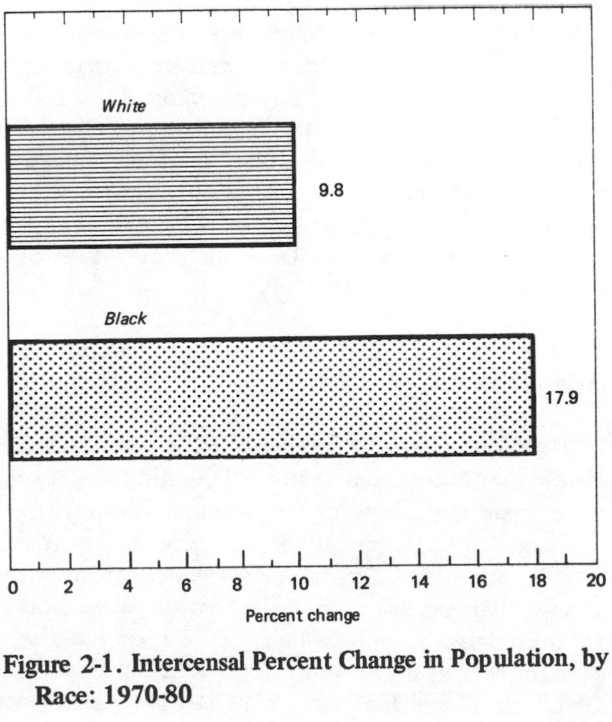

Figure 2-1. Intercensal Percent Change in Population, by Race: 1970-80

Table 2-2. Racial Composition of the United States: 1980 and 1970 *

Race	Number (000)			Percent distribution		Percent change 1970-80
	1980	1970	1970-80	1980	1970	
Total, all races.	226,505	203,212	23,293	100.0	100.0	11.5
White	195,141	177,749	17,392	86.2	87.5	9.8
Black	26,624	22,580	4,403	11.8	11.1	17.9
American Indian, Eskimo, Aleut. .	1,418	2,883	1,858	0.6	1.4	64.5
Asian and Pacific Islanders . . .	3,322			1.5		

*1980 count has been modified to be consistent with 1970 census. See U.S. Bureau of the Census. "Preliminary Estimates of the United States by Age, Sex and Race: 1970 to 1981." Current Population Report (Series P-25, no. 917). Washington, DC: U.S. Government Printing Office, 1982.

Source: U.S. Bureau of the Census. "Preliminary Estimates of the United States by Age, Sex and Race: 1970 to 1981." Current Population Report (Series P-25, no. 917). Washington, DC: U.S. Government Printing Office, 1982. Also U.S. Bureau of the Census. "General Population Characteristics: United States Summary." 1980 Census of Population. Washington, DC: U.S. Government Printing Office, 1983, Table 40.

American Indians

American Indians appeared to be almost an endangered group at the close of the Civil War (1870), with only 26,000 reported in the census. The enumeration of this group at the various censuses has been erratic and, until 1960, incomplete. In recent censuses the group has increased to a more substantial size, showing phenomenal growth. Some people have said that light-skinned black residents (many of whom have Indian blood) who report themselves as American Indian may account for part of the growth. The self-identification method of enumerating race in 1980, when almost a doubling of the American Indian population within a decade was recorded, may have contributed to such a practice.

Asian-Origin Population

The Chinese population entered the United States in a wave that lasted from 1870 to 1900. Almost as it subsided, there was a wave of Japanese immigration, which continued, with temporary interruption during World War II, into the 1950s, as many servicemen returned from military service in the Orient with Japanese brides. Once established, each of these populations has grown by natural increase as well as by additional migration. Both Chinese and Japanese groups have increased in size at a rapid rate since World War II. The Filipino population, which began entering the nation in large numbers in the 1920s, has grown especially rapidly since 1950. It appears to have increased by 125 percent in the 1970-80 decade. In 1980 Koreans numbered 0.36 million and Vietnamese 0.26 million, while Asian Indians were 0.36 million. Most of this immigration is known to have occurred primarily since 1960.

Spanish-Origin Population

Because of a steady and comparatively large inflow of immigrants from Latin America, the Spanish-origin population has come to constitute a comparatively important ethnic minority in the United States. It has four principal components: Mexicans, Puerto Ricans, Cubans, and persons with origins in other Latin American nations or Spain. Residents of Brazilian or Portuguese origin are not included. The 1980 census undertook to enumerate this population separately by asking a special question on Hispanic origin (see "definitions"*). A similar question was asked at the 1970 census for a 15 percent sample of respondents. The responses obtained at both enumerations are summarized in Table 2-4.

***Also see question 7 of the 1980 census form, reproduced in the Technical Appendix to Chapter 1.**

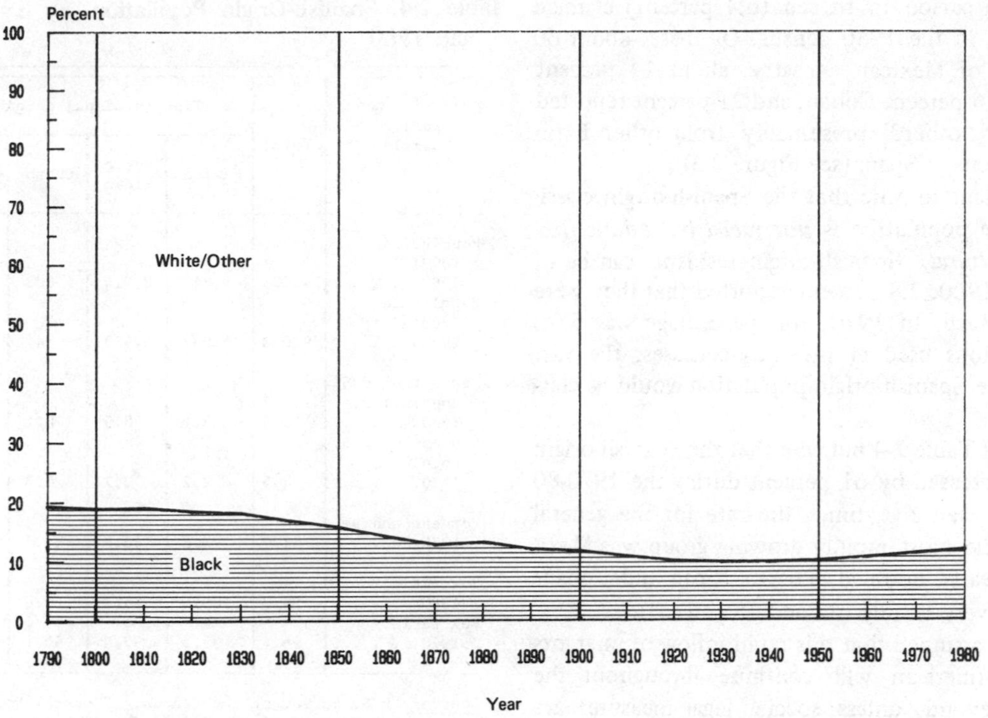

Figure 2-2. Racial Composition of the U.S. Population: 1790 to 1980

Table 2-3. Racial Composition of the Population of the United States: 1790 to 1983

Year	Number (000)							Percent distribution			Percent change since preceding date		
	White	Black	American Indian	Japanese	Chinese	Filipino	Other	White	Black	Other[a]	White	Black	Other[a]
1980. .	195,141	26,624	1,364	701	806	775	1,134	86.1	11.8	2.1	9.8	17.9	85.8
1970. .	177,749	22,580	793	591	435	343	410	87.5	11.1	1.4	11.9	19.7	58.9
1960. .	158,832	18,871	524	464	237	176	218	88.6	10.5	0.9	17.5	25.4	43.1
1950. .	135,150	15,045	357	326	150	123	175	89.3	9.9	0.8	14.2	16.9	20.2
1940. .	118,358	12,866	345	285	106	99	106	89.6	9.7	0.7	7.2	8.2	2.8
1930. .	110,396	11,892	343	279	102	108	83	89.6	9.7	0.7	16.3	13.6	39.9
1920. .	94,904	10,464	244	221	85	26	78	89.5	9.9	0.6	16.0	6.5	11.2
1910. .	81,812	9,829	277	153	94	3	61	88.7	10.7	0.6	22.3	11.3	15.3
1900. .	66,869	8,834	237	86	119	--	68	87.7	11.6	0.7	21.4	18.0	42.5
1890. .	55,101	7,489	249	2	107	--	0	87.5	11.9	0.6	27.0	13.8	108.1
1880. .	43,403	6,581	66	0	106	--	0	86.5	13.1	0.4	29.2	34.9	91.1
1870. .	33,589	4,880	26	0	64	--	0	87.1	12.7	0.2	24.8	9.9	13.9
1860. .	26,923	4,442	44	0	35	--	0	85.6	14.1	0.3	37.7	22.1	--
1850. .	19,553	3,639	--	--	--	--	--	84.3	15.7	--	37.7	26.6	--
1840. .	14,196	2,874	--	--	--	--	--	83.2	16.8	--	34.7	23.4	--
1830. .	10,537	2,329	--	--	--	--	--	81.9	18.1	--	33.9	31.4	--
1820. .	7,867	1,772	--	--	--	--	--	81.6	18.4	--	34.2	28.6	--
1810. .	5,862	1,378	--	--	--	--	--	81.0	19.0	--	36.1	37.5	--
1800. .	4,306	1,002	--	--	--	--	--	81.1	18.9	--	35.8	32.4	--
1790. .	3,172	757	--	--	--	--	--	80.7	19.3	--	...	...	...

[a]Includes American Indians, Japanese, and Chinese.

Note: -- indicates data not available. ... indicates data not applicable.

Source: Data for 1790 to 1890 from U.S. Bureau of the Census. Historical Statistics of the United States, Part I (Series A 91-104). Washington, DC: U.S. Government Printing Office, 1975. Total, white, and black populations from Table 2-2 in this chapter. Other data for 1900 to 1980 from U.S. Bureau of the Census. "General Population Characteristics: United States Summary." 1980 Census of Population. Washington, DC: U.S. Government Printing Office, 1983, Table 40.

About one person in fifteen (6.4 percent) claimed Spanish origin in the 1980 census. Of these, about 60 percent were of Mexican ancestry, about 14 percent Puerto Rican, 6 percent Cuban, and 21 percent reported themselves as "other," presumably from other Latin American nations or Spain (see Figure 2-3).

It is important to note that the Spanish-origin classification of the population is *not racial but ethnic (linguistic and cultural).* Spanish-origin residents can be of any race. (In 1980, 2.8 percent reported that they were of the black race. In 1970, this percentage was 5.0.) Under definitions used in previous censuses, the vast majority of the Spanish-origin population would be classified as white.

The data of Table 2-4 indicate that the Spanish-origin population increased by 61 percent during the 1970-80 decade—more than five times the rate for the general population. The most rapidly growing group was Mexican, which nearly doubled. Puerto Rican and Cubans also increased very rapidly (41 and 48 percent).

It is widely assumed that this rapid inflow of migrants from Latin American will continue throughout the 1980s and beyond, unless special legal measures are taken to curtail it. Because it is now the second largest minority group in the population and still growing rapidly, throughout this book special attention will be given to the Spanish-origin, as well as the black, in comparison with the majority white population.

Table 2-4. Spanish-Origin Population, by Type: 1970 and 1980

Spanish-origin population	Total	Type (national origin)			
		Mexican	Puerto Rican	Cuban	Other
Population (000), 1980. . . .	14,609	8,740	2,014	803	3,051
Population (000), 1970. . . .	9,073	4,532	1,429	545	2,566
Percent of U.S. population, 1980. . . .	6.4	3.9	0.9	0.4	1.3
Percent of U.S. population, 1970. . . .	4.5	2.2	0.7	0.3	1.3
Percent change, 1970-80 . . .	61.0	92.8	40.9	47.5	18.9
Sex ratio, 1980. . . .	99.3	103.4	95.2	90.8	93.3
Sex ratio, 1970. . . .	96.4	98.2	97.3	90.1	94.2

Source: U.S. Bureau of the Census. "General Population Characteristics: United States Summary." 1980 Census of the Population. Washington, DC: U.S. Government Printing Office, 1983, Table 39; U.S. Bureau of the Census. "Special Reports, Spanish-origin Population." 1970 Census of the Population. Washington, DC: U.S. Government Printing Office, 1973, Table 1.

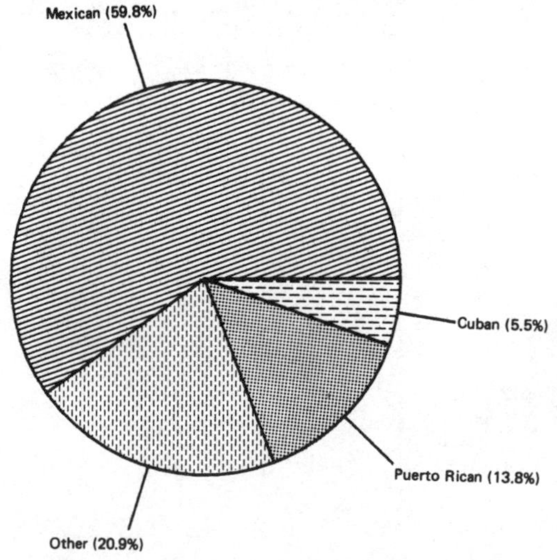

Figure 2-3. Percent Distribution of the Spanish-Origin Population by Type of Origin: 1980

Sex Composition

Females outnumber males in the United States, as in almost all other industrialized nations. In 1980, 48.6 percent of the population was male and 51.4 percent female. It is conventional to express a population's sex composition in terms of the *sex ratio,* or the number of males per 100 females. The sex ratio for the United States in 1980 was 94.5 males per 100 females.

At least four factors influence the sex ratio:

1. *Sex ratio at birth.* Among live-born infants, males outnumber females in the ratio of about 106 to 100. Because of this initial preponderance of males at birth, the sex ratio of the population would always be higher than 100 if it were not for other factors. (Details on sex ratio at birth are provided in Chapter 6.)

2. *Differential mortality between the sexes.* From conception on, death takes a greater toll of males than females. The initially high sex ratio is gradually reduced by death rates, which are higher for boys than for girls, and for men than for women. (Details on sex differences in mortality are provided in Chapter 5.) At about age thirty, the preponderance of males due to sex ratio at birth is counterbalanced by differential mortality, and

at ages older than this women progressively come to outnumber men (see section on "Age" below).

3. *Immigration.* Throughout the nineteenth century and until 1910, immigration to the United States was predominantly male. During the past half-century, however, the situation has been reversed, and more females than males have entered the United States legally. (Details are provided in Chapter 7.) Thus, immigration is contributing to the low sex ratio in the nation.

4. *Armed forces overseas and war losses.* Because armed forces are preponderantly male, expansion in the size of these forces overseas reduces the sex ratio of the population residing in the United States. Loss of armed forces in combat makes a part of this a permanent rather than a temporary reduction. In times of comparative peace, the number of the population in the armed forces is a small part of the total, and consequently in 1980 the sex ratio of the total population, with armed forces overseas included, was 94.85, versus 94.47 for the resident population and 93.32 for the civilian population.

5. *Sex differences in underenumeration.* Before 1980 there was a tendency for the census to undercount (to some extent) young men between the ages of twenty and thirty-five, in comparison with the enumeration of women for the same ages. The effect is to produce a lower overall sex ratio than would otherwise exist.

Four of the five factors (all but the first) that affect the sex ratio have operated throughout most of the twentieth century to lower the sex ratio, and their combined effect accounts for the present level of the sex ratio.

Sex ratios for the entire population and by major racial groups from 1790 to 1980 are presented in Table 2-5. Throughout the nation's history until the year 1950, males had outnumbered females in the white population by a considerable margin (see Figure 2-4). Although sex ratios for the Japanese, Chinese, and Filipino populations in the United States were not abnormal in 1980, during the first waves of immigration of these groups in the later decades of the nineteenth century, males outnumbered females by a wide margin, and hence the sex ratios were extremely high.

The sex ratio of the black population has been consistently below 100 and lower than that of the white population since 1840 (see Figure 2-4). The reasons for this long-time preponderance of women among the black population are not fully understood. The sex ratio at birth of the black population is somewhat lower than that of whites. On the other hand, the sex differential in mortality is less severe among blacks than among whites; this would tend to counterbalance the lower sex ratios at birth. It had generally been presumed that serious underenumeration of black males at young adult ages was a factor. However, despite the improved enumeration of the 1980 census the sex ratio for the black population was extremely low—89.6 males for each 100 females.

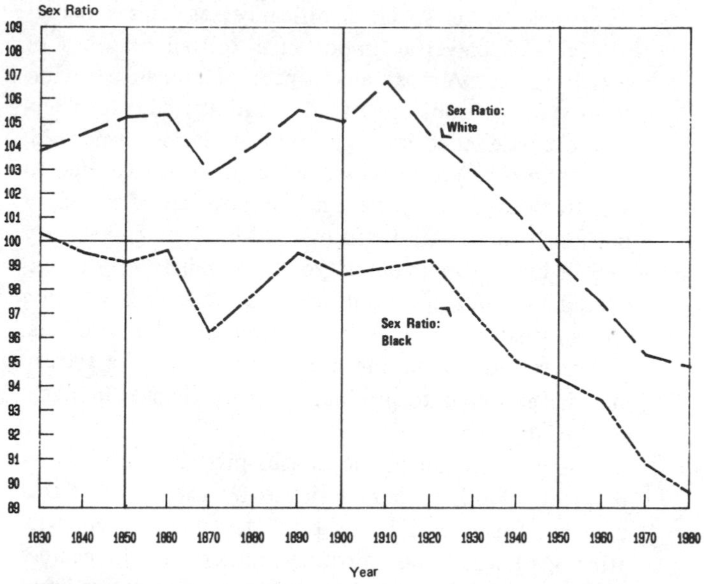

Figure 2-4. 150 Years of Sex Composition in the U.S.

The sex ratio for the Spanish-origin population is considerably above the average for the general population (see Table 2-4). However, there is much variation among its subgroups. In the Mexican group, males outnumber females; for the other sources (particularly Puerto Rican) the sex ratios are well below the average for the nation. It is believed that these differences in sex composition are caused by sex selectivity in migration to the United States from Spanish-origin places. Sex selectivity in return migration to Mexico and Puerto Rico also is very probably involved.

Age Composition

Aging as a Process

Like other species, human beings have a distinct life cycle. In its purely physiological aspect, it is a process of bodily growth, maturation to adulthood, slow decline in vigor, and death. But the life cycle also has a socioeconomic aspect pertaining to the roles the members of the society are expected to fill at each stage of life. Every society places its own interpretations and prescriptions on the biological process of aging. The age at which it is appropriate to enter the labor force or to perform gainful work, to end formal schooling, to marry, or to retire from the labor force is determined only in part by the biological aspects of age.

Because of its social significance, age has a fundamental and universal importance for all branches of social science. Almost any aspect of human behavior, from states of subjective feeling and attitudes to objective characteristics such as income, home ownership, occupation, or group membership, may be expected to vary with age. Thus, the age composition of a society has much to do with its form and functioning. A society with a high proportion of young members may be expected to differ in its outlook and mode of life from a society that has a high proportion of older members. Extensive changes in the age composition of a society may be expected to produce adaptive changes in many areas of its behavior.

The U.S. Bureau of the Census provides cross-tabulations of all other characteristics by age, to meet this demand. (See "definitions box" for mode of enumerating age.) Age at last birthday, rather than the nearest birthday, is taken as the reference point in determining age because this procedure makes easier the computing and interpreting of the averages, rates, and ratios that are associated with demographic work.

A basic goal in analyzing age structure is to learn what proportion of the total population is in each stage of the life cycle, how these proportions have been changing, how they differ from place to place, and what factors are responsible for a given age composition or for a change in age composition. A full comprehension of how a population has arrived at its present age structure, or exactly why its age composition is changing as it is requires a study of the components of growth–births, deaths, and migration for the past century. Each component is studied in considerable detail in later chapters. The present chapter provides an overview.

All three components of population growth tend to be heavily concentrated at particular stages of the life cycle. Every person must enter a population at age zero. He may die at any phase of the life cycle–from a moment after birth to more than a century after birth–but the probability of his death is much greater when he is a very young infant or after he has reached fifty years of age. The span of life over which he does live affects the age composition. If he lives to reproduce, both the age at which he does so and the number of his offspring have an important effect upon maintaining or changing the age composition. If he migrates, he removes one person from his age group in one place and adds one to his age group in another; this too can alter age structure. Thus, both short-term and long-term fluctuations in birth, death, and migration rates are reflected in the age composition.

A sudden rise or fall in the birth rate produces an extraordinarily large or small crop of children in particular years. This group ages with the passing of time

Table 2-5. Sex Composition of the Population of the United States, by Race: 1790 to 1980

Year	Race							
	Total	White	Black	Indian	Japanese	Chinese	Filipino	Other races
1980.	94.5	94.8	89.6	97.5	84.5	102.3	93.4	102.8
1970.	94.8	95.3	90.8	96.2	84.8	110.7	123.4	102.6
1960.	97.1	97.4	93.4	101.2	93.9	133.2	175.4	111.4
1950.	98.7	99.1	94.3	108.5	108.6	168.1	271.3	109.3
1940.	100.8	101.2	95.0	105.5	119.1	224.5	456.7	108.6
1930.	102.6	102.9	97.0	105.1	128.9	296.4	706.1	114.7
1920.	104.1	104.4	99.2	104.8	159.6	465.7	485.2	116.6
1910.	106.2	106.7	98.9	103.5	349.2	925.8	944.2	129.2
1900.	104.6	105.0	98.6	101.5	487.1	1,385.1	--	106.9
1890.	103.6	105.5	99.5	102.6	656.4	2,678.9	--	--
1880.	103.4	104.0	97.8	104.8	957.1	2,106.8	--	--
1870.	102.2	102.8	96.2	94.8	587.5	1,283.3	--	--
1860.	104.7	105.3	99.6	119.0	--	1,858.1	--	--
1850.	104.3	105.2	99.1	--	--	--	--	--
1840.	103.7	104.5	99.5	--	--	--	--	--
1830.	103.1	103.8	100.3	--	--	--	--	--
1820.	103.3	103.2	103.4	--	--	--	--	--
1810.	--	104.0	--	--	--	--	--	--
1800.	--	104.0	--	--	--	--	--	--
1790.	--	103.8	--	--	--	--	--	--

Note: -- indicates data not available.

Source: Data for 1900 to 1980 from U.S. Bureau of the Census. "General Population Characteristics: United States Summary." 1980 Census of Population. Washington, DC: U.S. Government Printing Office, 1983, Table 40. Data for 1790 to 1890 from U.S. Bureau of the Census. Historical Statistics of the United States, Part I (Series A 91-104). Washington, DC: U.S. Government Printing Office, 1975, p. 14.

and constitutes a wave or a trough in the age structure. At the first census after its occurrence, this rise or fall will appear as an unusually large or small complement of children. At the next it will constitute a disproportionately large or small youth group. At a third census it will have passed into the adult category, and at succeeding censuses it will reappear at successively later phases of the life cycle until it has died out at the oldest ages. Consequently, unusually large or small "birth cohorts" (see "definitions") of several decades ago may be represented in the present age structure as a disproportionately large or small age group. As an unusually large or unusually small generation passes through adulthood, it tends to produce a correspondingly large or small crop of children, thereby creating a secondary wave or trough in the age structure, with a lag of 20 to 35 years behind the original one.

Any catastrophe that kills off large numbers of particular age groups, such as military losses among young men in a war, leaves a trough in the age structure that persists until that generation has died. A sudden improvement in methods of prolonging life, such as the use of antibiotics, has the opposite effect: Instead of dying, an increased proportion of persons lives on into the next age group.

The arrival of a large group of migrants has the same effect as an unusually large birth cohort from two to three decades earlier (because migrants tend to be concentrated at young adult ages), and the children of these migrants can constitute a secondary wave. The departure of migrants has the reverse effect. Thus, the age structure of a population at any given time is a composite resulting from all the factors that have influenced fertility, mortality, and migration over the century or more preceding the date of the census to which the data refer.

The following principles will prove helpful in interpreting age statistics:

1. If birth rates fall, children will account for a smaller proportion of the total population, and this necessarily increases the proportion of people in the adult and older ages. A rise in birth rates has the opposite effect: The proportion of people in the younger ages tends to increase, and the proportion of adults tends to decrease.

2. A decline in death rates at any age has the effect of passing on to the next age class a larger proportion of the individuals of the given age than in preceding years. Since death rates have an age pattern (the rates being different at different ages), the nature of the pattern has much to do with the age composition, and changes in this pattern lead to changes in age composition. In comparison with the past, therefore, a differential decline in death rates has the *direct* effect of increasing the proportion of people in the particular ages where the decline in death rates was greatest, *and also of increasing it in all later ages.* A rise in death rates for any particular age group has the opposite result.

3. Changes in the death rates for persons younger than forty to fifty also have an *indirect* effect upon age composition, for they alter the number of potential parents.

4. Most migration streams tend to decrease the size of the young adult age groups in the areas from which these streams depart, and tend to augment the young adult age groups of the population to which they migrate. Where migrants have an older age composition, they exert their additive and subtractive effect upon the age groups in which they fall; young adult migrants also affect the childhood and youth ages, because they often take children with them when they move.

5. Because all age groups, especially those above forty, are steadily depleted by mortality, the waves and troughs created at birth tend to become progressively less important, in relation to the total population, as they pass into the upper ages. If the population is growing rapidly, the phenomenon of declining importance is even more pronounced, for the differences are expressed as percentages of a progressively larger base population.

Median Age of the U.S. Population

In order to give a quick and approximate answer to the question, "Is the population old or young in its age composition?" demographers sometimes report the median age of a population. This is the age above which 50 percent of the population fall, and below which 50 percent fall. The median age of the U.S. population in 1983 and at each census since 1790 is reported in Table 2-6 and graphed by race in Figure 2-5 for 1830 to 1980.

The median age of the nation's population has been at an all-time high beginning in 1981. The figures in Table 2-6 show that the median age of the white population was only 16.0 years in 1790. From the perspective of a nation with low birth and low death rates, it may be somewhat surprising to discover that at the time of the Revolutionary War and immediately afterward one-half of the population of the United States was sixteen or younger. This median age was produced primarily by the extraordinarily high fertility rates. By 1950 the median age had risen to 30.2 years, also primarily because of the long-term decline in fertility described in Chapter 1. Between 1950 and 1960 this trend of 150 years' duration was interrupted; the median age in 1960 was almost one year lower than in 1950. By

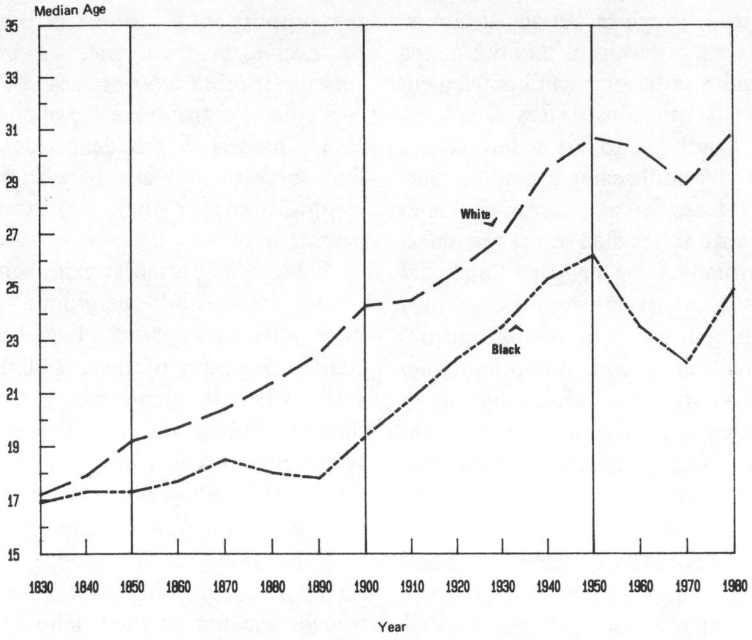

Figure 2-5. 150 Years of Median Age in the U.S.

Table 2-6. Median Age of the U.S. Population, by Race: 1790-1983

Year	All races	White	Black	Change since preceding date: total	Race differential
1983. . .	30.8	31.8	25.7	0.2	6.1
1982. . .	30.6	31.5	25.5	0.3	6.0
1981. . .	30.3	31.2	25.2	0.3	6.0
1980. . .	30.0	30.9	24.9	0.5	6.0
1970. . .	28.0	28.9	22.1	-1.5	6.5
1960. . .	29.5	30.3	23.5	-1.0	6.8
1950. . .	30.2	30.7	26.2	1.2	4.5
1940. . .	29.0	29.5	25.3	2.5	4.2
1930. . .	26.4	26.9	23.5	1.2	3.4
1920. . .	25.3	25.6	22.3	1.2	3.3
1910. . .	24.1	24.5	20.8	1.2	3.7
1900. . .	22.9	23.4	19.4	0.9	4.9
1890. . .	22.0	22.5	17.8	1.1	4.7
1880. . .	20.9	21.4	18.0	0.7	3.4
1870. . .	20.2	20.4	18.5	0.8	1.9
1860. . .	19.4	19.7	17.7	0.5	2.0
1850. . .	18.9	19.2	17.3	1.1	1.9
1840. . .	17.8	17.9	17.3	0.6	0.6
1830. . .	17.2	17.2	16.9	0.5	0.3
1820. . .	16.7	16.5	17.2	...	...
1810. . .	--	16.0	--	...	...
1800. . .	--	16.0	--	...	...
1790. . .	--	--	--	...	...

Note: -- indicates data not available. ... indicates data not applicable.

Source: U.S. Bureau of the Census. Statistical Abstract of the United States, 1982-83. Washington, DC: U.S. Government Printing Office, 1983, Table 28. For data since 1980 see U.S. Bureau of the Census. "Population Estimates." Current Population Reports (Series P-25, no. 917). Washington, DC: U.S. Government Printing Office, 1982.

1970 the median age had declined still further to 28.0. This sudden reversal (see Figure 2-5) must be attributed to the rise in fertility ("baby boom") that took place starting in the late 1940s. It was preceded by an unusually large rise in the median age between 1930 and 1940, which resulted from the cumulative effects of lower birth rates and death rates in earlier years.

The upward trend in median age was resumed in the 1970s as birth rates fell. By 1981 the level of 1950 had been regained, and since then the median age has risen to new heights. In 1983, the white population set an all-time record, surpassing the previous record of 1950, while the black population was below its 1950 record.

In the rise and fall of the median age, the white and black populations have followed similar trends, with the white population having a higher median age, caused by its lower fertility. The white-black differential in median age reached a peak in 1960, and has declined since. When the nation was founded, fertility was high among both white and black residents, and their age composition was similar. As fertility has declined more rapidly in the white than in the black population, the gap between their median ages has gradually widened. If their birth rates converge, this age differential will shrink further.

Age Composition of the U.S. Population in Terms of the Life Cycle

The median age is a useful device for giving a general indication of the age level of the population, but it cannot give detailed information about age structure or the distribution of the population among the various stages of the life cycle. A more informative procedure is to study the proportions of the population in each of a set of age groupings. These age groupings may be single years of age, five-year age groups (0-4, 5-9, 10-14), or age intervals that refer to major transitions and status changes in the life cycle. Although the process of aging is continuous, some qualitative differences may be associated with various points in it. Those qualitative differences may be designated as phases or stages of the life cycle, representing cultural definitions of the physiological processes. In Table 2-7 the entire life span of the U.S. population has been subdivided into eleven *stages* of the life cycle. The age span of each stage is intended to represent present cultural definitions in the United States. Although the definitions are imposed on the population data of each census since 1880, their applicability to earlier years is only approximate. For example, in 1880 a high proportion of the "late adolescent" and the "early old age" groups was active participants in the labor force, whereas today a small fraction of these age groups is gainfully employed. In comparing, over a period of time, the changing proportions of the population in each stage of the life cycle, the changing connotation of the life cycle classification itself must be kept in mind. For purposes of broad and general comparison, the eleven stages have been grouped into four major categories: childhood, youth, adulthood, and old age.

A comparison of the age composition of the United States population in 1980, 1960, and 1940 with the age composition in 1880 may be made as follows:

Major stages of the life cycle	1980	1960	1940	1880
Total percent . . .	100.0	100.0	100.0	100.0
Childhood	12.9	19.8	14.4	24.4
Youth	15.2	16.1	16.2	19.4
Adulthood	60.6	55.1	62.5	52.8
Old age	11.3	9.0	6.8	3.4

Figure 2-6 illustrates the change in each stage of the life cycle over this interval of time. In 1880 the adult population was proportionately smaller than now, whereas children and youth were a much larger part of the total population than today. The aged were a very small part (about one-thirtieth) of the population. Since 1880 the proportion of children and youth has declined by about 60 percent, while the old age component is now more than three times what it was then. This difference in age composition at the younger ages is due largely to the historical decline in the birth rate. At the older ages the differences are a result of lowered death rates combined with lowered birth rates. Note the effect of the

Table 2-7. Age Composition of the United States Population in Terms of Life Cycle: 1980 [statistics for 1950 based on a 20 percent sample]

Stages in the life cycle	Age span (years)	Percent distribution										
		1980	1970	1960	1950	1940	1930	1920	1910	1900	1890	1880
All ages.	...	100.0	100.0	100.0	100.0	100.0	100.0	100.0	100.0	100.0	100.0	100.0
Childhood	0-8	12.9	16.2	19.8	18.0	14.4	17.5	19.7	20.2	21.6	22.1	24.4
Infancy	Under 1	1.6	1.7	2.3	2.1	1.5	1.8	2.1	2.4	2.5	2.5	2.9
Early childhood	1-5	7.1	8.6	11.2	10.5	8.1	9.6	11.0	11.4	11.9	12.2	13.6
Late childhood.	6-8	4.3	5.9	6.3	5.4	4.8	6.2	6.5	6.4	7.1	7.4	7.9
Youth	9-17	15.2	18.0	16.1	13.2	16.2	17.5	17.5	17.7	18.8	19.7	19.4
Preadolescence.	9-11	4.9	6.2	5.8	4.6	5.1	6.0	6.1	5.9	6.6	6.6	7.0
Early adolescence	12-14	4.8	6.1	5.5	4.4	5.5	5.8	6.0	6.0	6.2	6.8	6.7
Late adolescence.	15-17	5.5	5.8	4.7	4.2	5.6	5.7	5.4	5.8	6.0	6.3	5.7
Adulthood	18-64	60.6	55.9	55.1	60.6	62.5	59.5	58.0	57.6	55.3	54.1	52.8
Early maturity.	18-24	13.3	11.7	8.7	10.5	12.6	12.6	12.3	13.9	13.6	14.1	14.4
Maturity.	25-44	27.7	23.6	26.2	29.9	30.1	29.4	29.6	29.2	28.0	26.9	25.8
Middle age.	45-64	19.6	20.6	20.3	20.2	19.8	17.4	16.1	14.6	13.7	13.1	12.6
Old age	65-over	11.3	9.9	9.0	8.2	6.8	5.4	4.7	4.3	4.1	3.8	3.4
Early old age	65-74	6.9	6.1	6.0	5.6	4.8	3.9	3.3	3.0	2.9	2.7	2.4
Advanced old age.	75-over	4.4	3.8	3.0	2.6	2.0	1.5	1.4	1.2	1.2	1.1	1.0
Not reported.	...	...	...	...	...	...	0.1	0.1	0.2	0.3	0.3	...

Note: ... indicates data not applicable.

Source: U.S. Bureau of the Census. "General Population Characteristics: United States Summary." 1980 Census of Population. Washington, DC: U.S. Government Printing Office, 1983, Table 42.

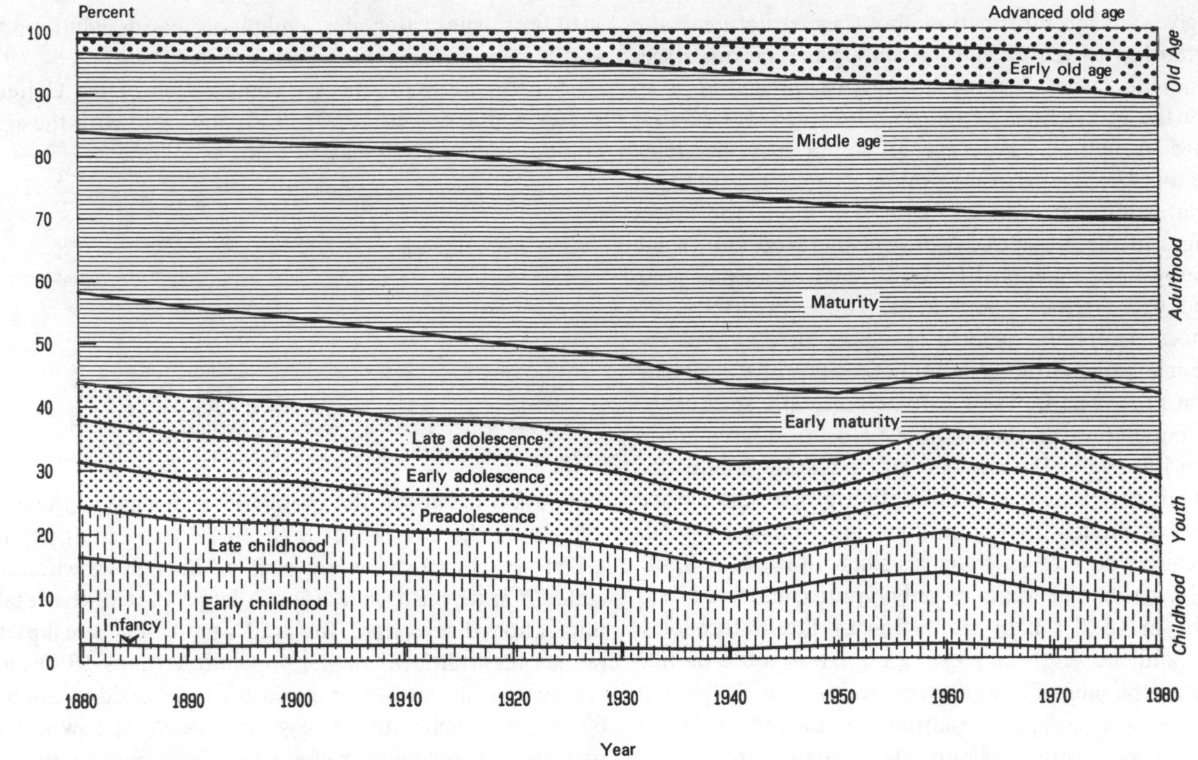

Figure 2-6. Age Composition of the U.S. Population in Terms of Life Cycle: 1880-1980

baby boom and the baby bust in causing a fluctuation in age composition between 1940 and 1980.

By providing life cycle age data by race and Spanish-origin for 1960, 1970, and 1980, Table 2-8 permits a more intensive examination of recent changes in age composition. Table 2-9 provides measures of intercensal percent change in each life cycle stage for the two decades. The effect on age composition of the roller coaster decline-rise-plunge-plateau in birth rates over the past half-century is clearly manifest. By 1980 the children born during the baby boom of 1940-60 had moved into adulthood, causing rapid expansion during the 1970s in the "early maturity" and during the 1980s in the "maturity" group. Meanwhile, the decline in fertility after 1960 caused sharp drops during the 1970s in both the proportion and the absolute numbers of children. During the 1980s this decline extended to both children and adolescents. The recent plateau in fertility causes the proportion of infants to be about the same in 1980 as 1970.

The small birth cohorts of the 1930s are often under-appreciated in considerations of U.S. age composition. By 1980 people born during the 1930s had aged into the "middle age" category and created a pronounced reduction between 1970 and 1980 in the share of population in this category. Between 1980 and 2000 this smallish cohort will move progressively into the upper ages, causing the old-age population to grow more slowly than previously. Unless there are as yet unforeseen medical breakthroughs in prolonging life to spectacularly older ages, the oft-expressed fear that the nation will be inundated with oldsters will not occur in this century, although it may early in the next century when the baby boom babies become sixty-five and older.

Tables 2-8 and 2-9 show that the overall fluctuations in age composition have been similar for black and white populations, except that because of higher fertility the proportions of persons in the younger ages have been lower for the black population than for the white. The large absolute and relative declines in child population since 1960 are much more heavily concentrated in the white than in the black population.

As Chapter 6 on fertility will show, the Spanish-origin population has comparatively high fertility. Combined with rapid immigration of working-age adults from Mexico, other Latin American countries, and Puerto Rico, the result is an extremely young median age with proportions of youth and adolescents that resemble the U.S. population in the mid-nineteenth century. However, the Spanish-origin population is aging at a rapid rate because of the passage into later maturity and old age of generations of migrants who arrived during World War II and in a continuous stream since. The future age composition of this group will of course be strongly influenced by un-

Table 2-8. Life Cycle Composition of the U.S. Population, by Race and Spanish-Origin: 1980, 1970, and 1960

Stages in the life cycle	Age span (years)	1980				1970				1960			
		Total	White	Black	Spanish-origin	Total	White	Black	Spanish-origin	Total	White	Black	Spanish-origin
All ages.	...	100.0	100.0	100.0	100.0	100.0	100.0	100.0	100.0	100.0	100.0	100.0	100.0
Childhood	0-8	12.9	12.0	16.5	19.7	16.2	15.6	20.5	22.8	19.8	19.2	24.8	27.2
Infancy	Under 1	1.6	1.4	2.0	2.5	1.7	1.7	2.2	2.5	2.3	2.2	3.0	3.3
Early childhood . . .	1-5	7.1	6.6	9.0	11.0	8.6	8.3	11.0	12.3	11.2	10.9	14.2	15.7
Late childhood. . . .	6-8	4.3	4.0	5.6	6.2	5.9	5.7	7.3	8.0	6.3	6.1	7.6	8.2
Youth	9-17	15.2	14.6	18.9	18.8	18.0	17.6	21.6	21.3	16.1	15.8	17.8	19.6
Preadolescence.	9-11	4.9	4.7	6.0	6.3	6.2	6.0	7.5	7.7	5.8	5.7	6.9	7.6
Early adolescence . .	12-14	4.8	4.6	6.1	6.0	6.1	5.9	7.4	7.1	5.5	5.4	5.9	6.4
Late adolescence. . .	15-17	5.5	5.3	6.8	6.5	5.8	5.7	6.7	6.5	4.7	4.7	5.1	5.6
Adulthood	18-64	60.6	61.2	56.7	56.6	55.9	56.5	51.0	51.4	55.1	55.4	51.2	49.6
Early maturity. . . .	18-24	13.3	12.9	14.8	15.3	11.7	11.6	12.0	12.3	8.7	8.6	9.3	10.9
Maturity.	25-44	27.7	27.7	26.1	27.9	23.6	23.7	22.5	26.0	26.2	26.3	25.0	26.6
Middle age.	45-64	19.6	20.6	15.8	13.4	20.6	21.2	16.5	13.0	20.3	20.6	16.8	12.1
Old age	65-over	11.3	12.2	7.9	4.9	9.9	10.3	6.9	4.5	9.0	9.6	6.2	3.6
Early old age	65-74	6.9	7.4	5.1	3.1	6.1	6.3	4.6	3.0	6.0	6.4	4.3	2.5
Advanced old age. . .	75-over	4.4	4.8	2.8	1.7	3.8	4.0	2.3	1.5	3.0	3.3	1.9	1.1

[a] An approximate age composition for the 1960 Spanish-origin population was estimated by adding age data for Puerto Rican and Spanish-surname populations from the Bureau of the Census "Subject Reports: Puerto Ricans in the United States" and "Spanish Surname Population in the United States" (1960). Although the total of these groups is not correct, a percent distribution based on the total is believed to be reasonably accurate.

Source: 1980 data from U.S. Bureau of the Census. 1980 Census of Population. Washington, DC: U.S. Government Printing Office, 1983. Other data from U.S. Bureau of the Census. 1970 Census of Population. Washington, DC: U.S. Government Printing Office, 1973. Spanish-origin data for 1970 from U.S. Bureau of the Census. "Subject Reports: Persons of Spanish Origin." 1970 Census of Population. Washington, DC: U.S. Government Printing Office, 1973.

certain future migration as well as fertility trends. Should fertility decline rapidly and migration be sharply curtailed, the Spanish-origin population will take on an old age composition at a very rapid pace. If fertility and migration remain high, it will retain an age composition that is considerably younger than both the black and white populations.

Age Composition in Terms of Five-Year Age Groups, with Single Years for Younger Ages

It has become customary to summarize age-data in five-year age groups, as illustrated in Table 2-10, which presents data for a more detailed classification of race. Although the five-year groupings do not match the life cycle definitions as nicely as the categories of Tables 2-8 and 2-9, they have an important advantage in studying change: A particular five-year age group enumerated at one census retains its identity at exactly ten years older at the next census. (For example, persons 15-19 years old in 1970 were 25-29 years old in 1980, and so on.) By manipulating the data in five-year groupings, the entire life cycle is summarized succinctly in categories with uniform intervals. However, the numerous administrative and research concerns with children, youth, and young adults make it important to have data also available for single years at the younger ages, to permit individual researchers to make their own definitions of the early stages of the life cycle. It has therefore become Census Bureau practice to provide single-year-of-age data for the first twenty years or so, with five-year summaries, and then five-year summaries only for ages twenty-five and over. It is often important to have such data by sex and race. Such data are reproduced for the censuses of 1940 to 1980 in Appendix Table 1 in the statistical appendix to this volume.

Table 2-10 shows the American Indian-Eskimo-Aleut population to have a very young age composition, similar to that of the Spanish-origin population. The Asian-Pacific Islander population, in contrast, has an age composition intermediate between that of the black population and the white, conforming somewhat more closely to the latter. It also shows the Asian population to be more highly concentrated in the adult working ages 25-49 than any other racial group.

Table 2-11 provides intercensal rates of change by five-year age groups for race groups, 1930-80. It reveals the five-year cohort consistency between censuses, as well as the erratic birth cohort pattern of age growth rates for all recent censuses.

Table 2-9. Percent Change in Life Cycle Composition, by Race and Spanish-Origin: 1970-80 and 1960-70

Stages in the life cycle	Age span (years)	1970-80				1960-70			
		Total	White	Black	Spanish-origin	Total	White	Black	Spanish-origin
All ages.	...	11.5	6.0	17.3	61.0	13.3	11.9	19.8	--
Childhood	0-8	-11.2	-18.2	-5.4	39.1	-7.1	-8.7	-1.2	--
Infancy	Under 1	1.4	-7.3	9.0	59.4	-15.6	-16.1	-13.6	--
Early childhood	1-5	-8.6	-15.8	-4.5	43.7	-13.3	-14.8	-7.4	--
Late childhood.	6-8	-18.6	-25.2	-10.9	25.5	7.0	4.9	15.2	--
Youth	9-17	-6.0	-12.4	2.8	42.0	27.3	24.9	45.6	--
Preadolescence.	9-11	-11.8	-17.7	-6.0	32.3	20.0	18.2	31.3	--
Early adolescence	12-14	-11.6	-17.8	-2.3	35.6	25.7	22.3	50.2	--
Late adolescence.	15-17	6.1	-1.0	18.3	60.2	38.0	36.1	59.8	--
Adulthood	18-64	20.9	14.9	30.4	77.4	14.9	14.0	19.4	--
Early maturity.	18-24	26.7	18.0	44.0	100.0	52.1	50.5	54.6	--
Maturity.	25-44	30.7	24.0	36.3	72.6	2.3	1.0	7.7	--
Middle age.	45-64	6.4	3.1	12.4	65.8	15.1	15.3	17.2	--
Old age	65-over	27.3	25.2	33.9	75.3	23.8	19.8	33.5	--
Early old age	65-74	25.3	23.3	28.6	69.8	14.6	11.4	28.5	--
Advanced old age.	75-over	30.6	28.2	44.6	86.4	42.4	36.3	44.9	--

Note: -- indicates data not available.

Source: Appendix Table 1.

Table 2-10. Age Composition of the Population, by Race and Spanish-Origin: 1980

Age	Population (000)						Percent distribution					
	Total	White	Black	American Indian[a]	Asian[b]	Spanish-origin	Total	White	Black	American Indian[a]	Asian[b]	Spanish-origin
Total, all ages. .	226,546	188,372	26,495	1,420	3,500	14,609	100.0	100.0	100.0	100.0	100.0	100.0
0-4 years.	16,348	12,634	2,436	149	293	1,663	7.2	6.7	9.2	10.5	8.4	11.4
5-9 years.	16,700	13,033	2,491	147	302	1,537	7.4	6.9	9.4	10.3	8.6	10.5
10-14 years.	18,242	14,461	2,673	156	280	1,475	8.1	7.7	10.1	11.0	8.0	10.1
15-19 years.	21,168	16,962	2,985	170	289	1,606	9.3	9.0	11.3	12.0	8.2	11.0
20-24 years.	21,319	17,289	2,725	149	320	1,586	9.4	9.2	10.3	10.5	9.1	10.9
25-29 years.	19,521	15,985	2,321	125	369	1,376	8.6	8.5	8.8	8.8	10.5	9.4
30-34 years.	17,561	14,645	1,889	107	371	1,129	7.8	7.8	7.1	7.5	10.6	7.7
35-39 years.	13,965	11,761	1,458	84	277	854	6.2	6.2	5.5	5.9	7.9	5.8
40-44 years.	11,669	9,826	1,251	69	221	712	5.2	5.2	4.7	4.9	6.3	4.9
45-49 years.	11,090	9,457	1,143	58	181	622	4.9	5.0	4.3	4.1	5.2	4.3
50-54 years.	11,710	10,158	1,129	52	158	564	5.2	5.4	4.3	3.6	4.5	3.9
55-59 years.	11,615	10,238	1,037	45	130	454	5.1	5.4	3.9	3.2	3.7	3.1
60-64 years.	10,088	8,976	871	34	98	321	4.5	4.8	3.3	2.4	2.8	2.2
65-69 years.	8,782	7,812	777	28	80	264	3.9	4.1	2.9	2.0	2.3	1.8
70-74 years.	6,798	6,095	564	20	58	193	3.0	3.2	2.1	1.4	1.7	1.3
75-79 years.	4,794	4,310	387	14	39	136	2.1	2.3	1.5	1.0	1.1	0.9
80-84 years.	2,935	2,685	200	7	21	67	1.3	1.4	0.8	0.5	0.6	0.5
85 years and over. .	2,240	2,045	159	6	14	49	1.0	1.1	0.6	0.4	0.4	0.3

[a] Includes American Indian, Eskimo, and Aleut.

[b] Includes Asian and Pacific Islands.

Source: U.S. Bureau of the Census. "General Population Characteristics: United States Summary." 1980 Census of Population. Washington, DC: U.S. Government Printing Office, 1983, Table 43.

Table 2-11. Intercensal Percent Change in Age Groups, by Race: 1930-1950

Age	Black population					White population				
	1970-80	1960-70	1950-60	1940-50	1930-40	1970-80	1960-70	1950-60	1940-50	1930-40
0-4 years. . . .	0.15	-10.6	44.0	51.4	1.5	-12.4	-16.9	22.2	53.8	-9.0
5-9 years. . . .	-9.3	14.9	56.3	18.2	-5.4	-22.9	5.0	38.5	24.3	-16.4
10-14 years. . .	-4.9	42.4	45.9	1.6	6.3	-18.2	20.7	50.9	-6.3	-3.2
15-19 years. . .	23.2	61.9	22.1	-6.0	4.3	3.6	41.0	24.2	-14.9	7.0
20-24 years. . .	50.2	49.7	-1.6	3.0	0.7	21.1	50.7	-7.2	-1.5	7.6
25-29 years. . .	62.5	21.2	-5.6	9.1	6.9	35.3	23.6	-12.7	10.4	13.8
30-34 years. . .	50.7	2.1	11.2	11.1	14.8	46.9	-5.8	2.0	12.6	12.2
35-39 years. . .	21.9	-2.1	7.2	15.5	10.7	21.0	-12.7	10.6	18.2	2.9
40-44 years. . .	4.4	10.2	11.7	19.3	18.6	-1.4	1.8	13.2	15.9	9.2
45-49 years. . .	1.8	10.8	17.4	24.6	10.0	-12.8	10.8	19.6	8.5	18.0
50-54 years. . .	14.1	16.2	21.3	27.6	9.1	1.6	15.0	15.2	12.8	22.7
55-59 years. . .	18.7	15.1	47.2	29.7	28.4	13.7	18.0	13.9	23.4	25.7
60-64 years. . .	18.7	33.6	42.7	30.1	22.2	15.0	19.1	15.8	28.0	26.3
65-69 years. . .	23.9	28.6	19.8	37.1	91.2	24.0	9.7	25.0	31.0	34.2
70-74 years. . .	35.5	28.2	47.0	35.4	64.4	22.3	13.5	37.9	32.5	30.1
75-79 years. . .	52.2	25.3	55.5	-16.4	166.1	21.3	25.3	-7.8	24.0	38.7
80-84 years. . .	38.8	59.4	38.4	--	--	26.7	43.2	--	--	--
85 years + . . .	35.4	87.4	45.3	--	--	48.5	60.5	61.0	--	--

Note: -- indicates data included in the preceding age category.

Source: Appendix Table 1-A, B, and C.

The Dependency Ratio

Age statistics are used frequently to compute a measure of the dependency load that the population of working age must carry. The dependency load, comprising children, youth, and people of retirement age, is measured approximately by the "dependency ratio," defined as the ratio of the number of persons under fifteen or over sixty-five years of age to the number in the 15-64 age group, multiplied by 100. This is not a measure of the number of persons each worker must support in addition to himself. However, it is a rough indication of the average number of dependents that each 100 adult persons would be required to support and care for if the load were equally divided among the adult population, and if all persons under fifteen and over sixty-five were dependent, and no one between fifteen and sixty-four was dependent. None of these conditions is met completely, and the degree to which they are approximated varies from one population to another, and over time, within the same population. Nevertheless, in the absence of more detailed information with which to estimate actual dependence, this ratio is useful for making general comparisons.

The dependency ratios for the United States, for selected dates since 1800, are shown in Table 2-12. Note that there was a relatively steady decline in the total dependency ratio from 1800 until 1940 (with the exception of the data for 1870). Because of the baby boom, it rose between 1940 and 1960, and then declined. As an example, the dependency load in 1980 for the white population (50.4) was only one-half as large as in 1800. Because a higher proportion of persons under fifteen and over sixty-five were economically active in the nineteenth and early twentieth centuries, the decline of the actual dependency load was not as great as indicated by the index. Nevertheless, these statistics may be used to illustrate the general magnitude of the decline in dependency, and the time pattern of that decline. The decline over the 180-year period from 1800 to 1980 consisted of a net balance between two opposing trends: a fall in the dependency load for the youth, and a rise in the dependency load for the aged. The youth dependency ratio has always been 80 percent or more of the total. Taking the data for the total population from 1870 to 1940, the youth dependency ratio fell by 14.2 points, while the old-age dependency ratio increased by only 3.8 points; the net result was a large decline in the total dependency ratio.

One direct result of fertility control is an almost immediate lessening of the overall burden of dependency, since such control lowers the large burden of youth dependency. In fact, the result is a temporary situation in which the dependency load is unusually light. There are fewer children and many adults, and there is a delay in the increase in the ratio of older persons to adults in the 15-64 age groups. Later, when the aging process passes the spate of adult workers into the older ages, the dependency ratio will tend to rise somewhat, provided the fertility level remains low. The statistical series for the United States shown in Table 2-12 illustrates the important principle that the dependency ratio in a low fertility/low mortality population is far lower than the dependency ratio in a high fertility/high mortality population because of the reduction in the large dependency load for children. Although the transition from high fertility and mortality rates to low fertility and mortality rates raises the dependency load for the aged by a few points, this increase is more than offset by the much greater reduction in the youth dependency load. The recent discussion of the aging of the American population as if it were a severe social problem is somewhat out of perspective. A really onerous dependency load is borne by nations where high death rates remove children of all ages before they have a chance to make a productive contribution. From the dependency point of view, the deaths of a ten-year-old boy and a seventy-five-year-old man are not identical events. One has consumed for ten years as a dependent without contributing any return; the other has consumed for thirty years as a dependent, but has also produced for forty-five years. As a result of demographic processes the American people for more than a century have borne a smaller dependency load than most populations of the world have been carrying. Between 1940 and 1960 three-fourths of the increase of 20.9 points in the total dependency ratio was created by the resurgency of fertility and the increased youth dependency load, and only one-fourth of the increase was due to the growing number of persons past sixty-five. Considering the present and proposed schemes of social security and retirement, plus the near-universal tendency of workers to invest at least a portion of their income against their retirement, it is impossible that the aged population of the United States will become an oppressive net economic burden to the working-age adult population during this century, and very probably not in the next, in view of the simultaneous reduction in child and youth dependency. As of 1983, the dependency ratios for both black and white populations were nearly at the all-time low set in 1940.

Table 2-12. Percent of Youth and Old Age and Dependency Ratio, by Race: 1800 to 1983

Year	Total			White			Black		
	Percent 0-14	Percent 65-over	Dependency ratio	Percent 0-14	Percent 65-over	Dependency ratio	Percent 0-14	Percent 65-over	Dependency ratio
1983.	22.0	11.7	50.9	21.0	12.4	50.3	27.9	7.9	55.7
1980.	22.6	11.3	51.3	21.3	12.2	50.3	28.7	7.9	57.7
1970.	28.5	9.9	62.3	27.6	10.3	61.0	35.4	6.9	73.3
1960.	31.1	9.2	67.5	30.3	9.6	66.4	37.6	6.2	77.9
1950.	26.9	8.1	53.8	26.3	8.4	53.3	31.8	5.8	60.3
1940.	25.0	6.8	46.6	24.5	7.1	46.1	30.1	4.8	53.6
1930.	29.4	5.4	53.4	29.0	5.7	53.1	32.4	3.1	55.0
1920.	31.8	4.7	57.5	31.5	4.8	57.1	34.9	3.2	61.6
1910.	32.1	4.3	57.3	31.5	4.5	56.2	37.4	3.0	67.8
1900.	34.5	4.1	62.7	33.8	4.2	61.3	40.0	3.0	75.2
1890.	35.6	3.9	65.2	34.7	4.0	63.2	42.7	2.8	83.7
1880.	38.1	3.4	70.9	37.1	3.6	68.6	--	--	--
1870.	39.2	3.0	73.0	38.7	3.1	71.8	43.0	2.5	83.7
1860.	40.6	--	68.3[a]	40.0	--	66.7[a]	44.4	--	79.7[a]
1850.	41.5	--	71.1[a]	40.9	--	69.3[a]	44.8	--	81.0[a]
1840.	--	--	--	43.7	--	77.6[a]	--	--	--
1830.	--	--	--	45.0	--	81.8[a]	--	--	--
1820.	--	--	--	48.9[b]	--	95.7[a]	--	--	--
1810.	--	--	--	50.0[b]	--	100.1[a]	43.0	--	75.4[a]
1800.	--	--	--	50.1[b]	--	100.4[a]	--	--	--

[a] Plus α, which is greater than 0.

[b] 0-15 years old.

Source: U.S. Bureau of the Census. *Historical Statistics of the United States, Part I* (Series A 119-134). Washington, DC: U.S. Government Printing Office, 1975. 1980 data from U.S. Bureau of the Census. "General Population Characteristics: United States Summary." *1980 Census of Population.* Washington, DC: U.S. Government Printing Office, 1983, Table 44.

Sex Composition by Age

The overall age composition of the population, discussed above, varies consistently by sex. At the very youngest ages males outnumber females, but because of differential mortality favoring females, the sex ratio of males per 100 females declines steadily to the point where females outnumber males two-to-one or more at ages beyond eighty-five. Sex ratios by age are reported for each major racial group for 1980 in Table 2-13. All races show the same age pattern of sex ratios, but with variations. The black population manifests its below-average sex ratio for all ages up to age seventy-five, beyond which the survival of black males in comparison with black females appears to be superior to the same ratio for white males. American Indians tend to have a slightly lower than average sex ratio at ages below fifty but considerably above average ratios for older ages. The Asian-origin population has a very irregular pattern of sex ratios by age. Below age twenty the ratios are very similar to those for the white population. Because of a preponderance of female over male immigrants, the ratio is unusually low between ages twenty and sixty. At the oldest ages the ratio is very high, as the remnants of the old male-dominated immigration at the end of the last century and the beginning of the present one brought fewer female immigrants.

The Spanish-origin population has near-average sex ratios except for above average proportions of males at the migratory ages of 15-29 and at ages seventy and older.

Age Composition in Comparison with Other Nations

Each nation has its demographic history impressed upon its age structure. An overall comparison of the age structure of the U.S. population with the age structures of other countries may be made, using the information provided in Table 2-14 and Figure 2-7. Age and sex composition data for nations with a population of 10 million or more in 1980 are reported in Table 2-14. The data are estimates as of 1985. Figure 2-7 comprises three population pyramids (see "definitions"). Figure 2-7A illustrates the two panels of age composition by sex of (1) the "more developed countries" and (2) the "less developed countries" as defined by the United Nations. Figure 2-7B portrays (3) the U.S. population in 1980. Most of the principles concerning the forces that affect age composition are illustrated in these graphs. Several noteworthy findings may be derived from Figure 2-7 and Table 2-14.

Table 2-13. Sex Ratios for Age Groups, by Race and Spanish-Origin: 1980

Age	Total	Race/Ethnicity				
		White	Black	American Indian	Asian	Spanish-origin
All ages	94.5	94.8	89.6	97.8	93.7	99.3
0-4 years	104.7	105.4	101.6	103.2	102.0	104.0
5-9 years	104.6	105.3	101.6	102.4	103.5	103.8
10-14 years	104.4	105.0	101.2	102.6	105.6	102.6
15-19 years	103.3	103.7	99.5	102.6	106.9	106.0
20-24 years	100.1	100.9	91.3	100.7	96.5	106.8
25-29 years	98.9	100.3	87.7	97.1	85.5	102.8
30-34 years	97.7	99.4	85.6	95.6	83.7	97.9
35-39 years	96.6	98.3	83.3	95.5	90.6	94.8
40-44 years	95.8	97.5	82.8	94.8	95.5	93.8
45-49 years	94.5	96.3	82.1	92.6	84.1	93.4
50-54 years	92.3	93.9	80.8	93.9	79.2	91.8
55-59 years	89.4	90.1	81.8	91.7	88.7	91.6
60-64 years	86.2	86.9	79.3	89.4	85.7	84.7
65-69 years	80.0	80.4	74.5	83.1	96.6	78.0
70-74 years	72.3	72.0	71.2	80.1	114.4	78.0
75-79 years	62.7	62.0	65.1	79.6	100.5	76.2
80-84 years	53.2	52.4	59.9	68.2	74.7	70.0
85 years and over	43.7	42.9	50.0	64.9	60.0	61.3

Source: U.S. Bureau of the Census. "General Population Characteristics: United States Summary." 1980 Census of Population. Washington, DC: U.S. Government Printing Office, 1983, Table 43.

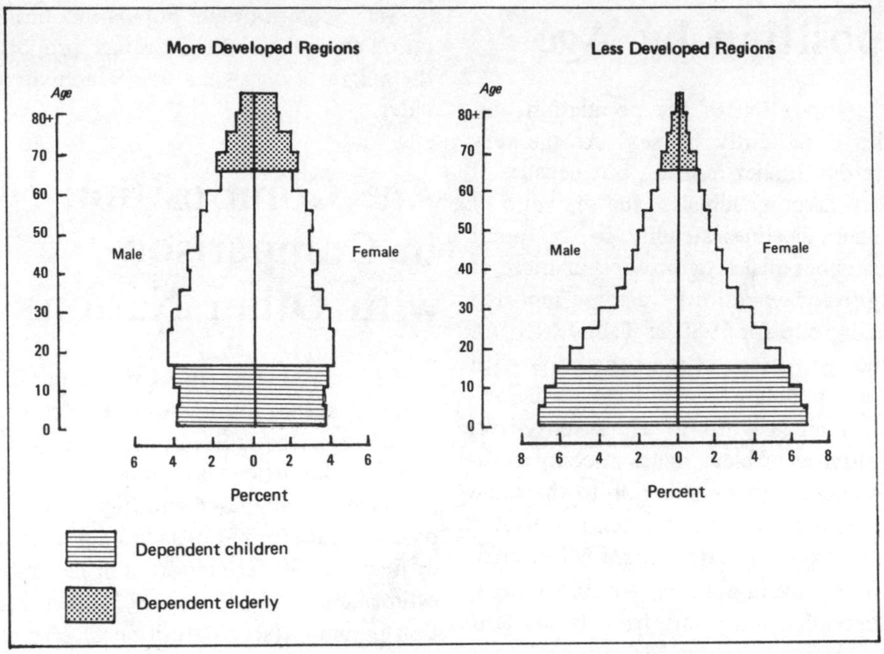

Figure 2-7A. Percentage Distribution of Population by Age and Sex: More Developed and Less Developed Regions: 1980 [From Population Division, Department of International Economic and Social Affairs, United Nations Secretariat, 1982]

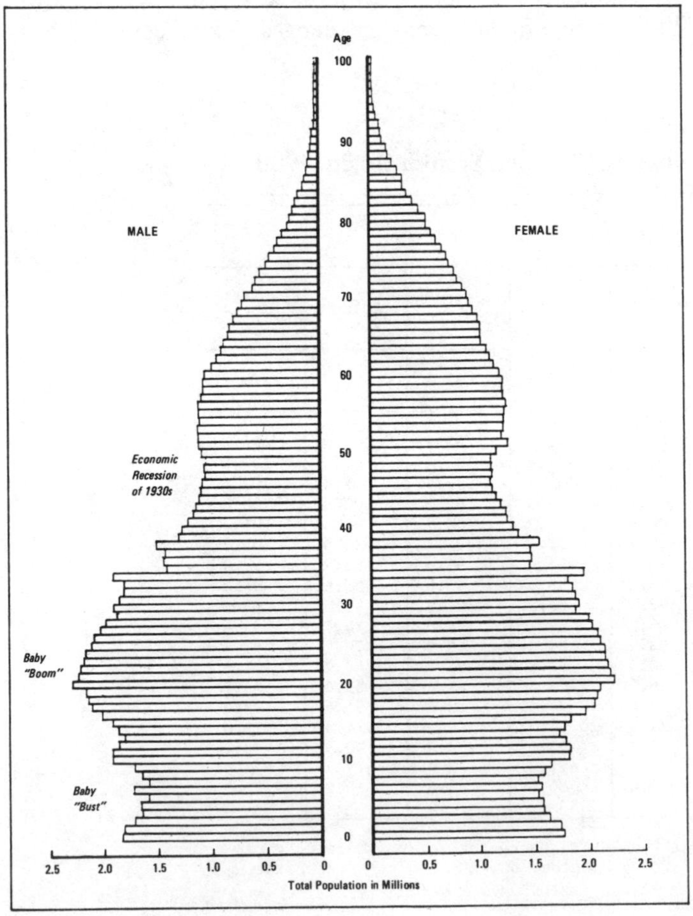

Figure 2-7B. Distribution of the Total U.S. Population by Age and Sex: July 1, 1981

Table 2-14. Age and Sex Composition of Nations with 10 Million or More Inhabitants: Estimates as of 1985

Country	Median age	Percent distribution			Dependency ratio			Sex ratio
		0-14	15-64	65-over	Youth 0-14	Aged 65-over	Total	
World total	23.5	33.6	60.5	5.8	55.6	9.6	65.2	100.9
More developed countries	32.4	22.4	66.6	11.1	33.6	16.7	50.3	94.4
Less developed countries	21.0	37.2	58.6	4.2	63.5	7.1	70.6	103.1
China	24.8	29.7	64.3	6.0	46.1	9.3	55.4	104.2
India	20.5	38.0	58.8	3.2	64.6	5.4	70.0	107.3
U.S.S.R.	30.3	24.8	65.6	9.6	37.8	14.6	52.4	89.1
UNITED STATES	31.0	22.9	66.1	11.0	34.7	16.7	51.3	95.4
Indonesia	21.1	36.6	59.9	3.5	61.0	5.9	66.9	99.0
Brazil	20.9	37.5	58.2	4.3	64.5	7.3	71.8	101.3
Japan	35.0	21.6	68.7	9.7	31.5	14.2	45.6	97.4
Bangladesh	17.2	45.0	52.4	2.6	86.0	5.0	91.0	106.5
Pakistan	17.7	44.0	53.2	2.8	82.8	5.4	88.1	107.9
Nigeria	16.1	47.8	49.7	2.5	96.1	5.0	101.1	98.0
Mexico	18.2	42.9	53.6	3.4	80.0	6.4	86.4	100.9
Germany, Federal Rep. of	37.6	15.8	70.6	13.6	22.3	19.3	41.7	92.9
Italy	35.7	19.6	66.8	13.5	29.4	20.2	49.6	96.4
Vietnam	19.5	40.7	55.5	3.8	73.4	6.8	80.2	95.2
United Kingdom	35.5	18.6	66.4	15.0	28.0	22.5	50.5	96.7
France	33.7	21.0	66.6	12.5	31.5	18.7	50.2	96.6
Philippines	19.4	40.4	56.6	2.9	71.4	5.2	76.6	102.0
Thailand	20.2	38.0	58.8	3.3	64.6	5.6	70.1	100.4
Turkey	21.0	38.2	57.6	4.2	66.3	7.3	73.6	102.2
Egypt	20.5	38.8	57.4	3.7	67.6	6.5	74.1	102.2
Iran	17.3	45.1	52.0	3.0	86.8	5.7	92.5	103.3
Korea, Republic of	23.8	31.7	64.0	4.3	49.5	6.8	56.3	101.7
Spain	31.1	24.3	64.3	11.4	37.8	17.7	55.4	96.2
Burma	19.4	41.0	55.1	3.9	74.4	7.1	81.5	99.0
Poland	31.0	25.0	65.7	9.3	38.1	14.2	52.3	95.9
Ethiopia	17.3	45.3	52.2	2.5	86.9	4.8	91.7	99.0
South Africa	19.0	42.0	53.8	4.2	77.9	7.8	85.7	98.9
Zaire	17.5	44.8	52.2	2.9	85.8	5.5	91.3	97.2
Argentina	29.0	27.6	63.1	9.3	43.7	14.7	58.4	99.3
Colombia	20.7	37.2	59.1	3.8	62.9	6.4	69.3	100.7
Canada	30.1	22.5	68.3	9.2	32.9	13.5	46.4	99.0
Morocco	17.1	45.5	51.5	3.0	88.4	5.8	94.2	100.2
Yugoslavia	31.7	23.3	68.3	8.4	34.1	12.4	46.5	97.5
Romania	31.7	25.0	65.4	9.5	38.3	14.6	52.9	97.8
Algeria	16.3	47.1	49.6	3.3	95.0	6.6	101.7	99.7
Sudan	17.7	44.6	52.4	2.9	85.0	5.6	90.7	102.9
Tanzania	16.8	46.4	50.5	3.1	91.9	6.2	98.1	98.2
Korea, Dem. People's Rep.	20.6	38.1	58.1	3.8	65.5	6.6	72.1	98.3
Peru	18.9	41.4	55.3	3.3	74.9	5.9	80.9	100.7
Taiwan[a]	--	--	--	--	--	--	--	--
Kenya	14.3	51.8	45.5	2.6	113.8	5.7	119.6	98.0
Venenzuela	19.2	41.0	56.0	2.9	73.2	5.2	78.5	100.0
Afghanistan	17.4	44.9	52.6	2.4	85.3	4.6	90.0	104.8
German Democratic Rep.	35.2	18.7	67.1	14.2	27.8	21.1	49.0	90.0
Sri Lanka	22.4	34.0	61.7	4.3	55.2	6.9	62.1	104.4
Czechoslovakia	32.8	24.5	64.2	11.3	38.1	17.7	55.8	96.0
Nepal	18.7	42.2	54.8	3.1	77.0	5.6	82.6	105.4
Malaysia	20.4	38.3	58.0	3.7	66.0	6.4	72.4	101.6
Australia	30.3	24.1	66.2	9.7	36.5	14.7	51.2	100.8
Uganda	17.1	45.6	51.2	3.1	89.1	6.1	95.3	98.3
Iraq	16.8	46.1	51.2	2.6	90.1	5.1	95.1	103.0
Netherlands	33.4	19.4	68.7	11.9	28.2	17.3	45.5	98.7
Ghana	16.4	47.1	50.1	2.8	94.0	5.5	99.5	98.0
Chile	24.5	31.2	63.1	5.7	49.5	9.0	58.5	98.1
Mozambique	17.9	44.2	52.4	3.4	84.2	6.5	90.7	97.2
Hungary	35.3	21.6	65.9	12.5	32.8	19.0	51.8	95.0
Syrian Arab Republic	16.0	48.0	49.1	2.9	97.6	5.9	103.5	104.1
Saudi Arabia	18.2	43.7	53.5	2.8	81.8	5.2	86.9	116.4
Portugal	30.0	24.8	64.6	10.6	38.3	16.4	54.8	90.6

[a]Data for Taiwan not available from the United Nation's estimates.

Source: United Nations. Demographic Indicators of Countries: Estimates and Projections as Assessed in 1980. New York: United Nations, 1982.

1. Great variation in age composition among the nations, at all phases of the age cycle, is illustrated in Figure 2-7. Where birth and death rates are high, as in the less developed countries, the age pyramid is broad at the base and rises rapidly to a peak. Where birth and death rates are low, as in the more developed nations, the age pyramid is narrow at the bottom and rises almost vertically before narrowing at the older ages. Where there has been an earlier upsurge in fertility following a decline, as in the United States, a previously constricted base is again broadened as an "echo" when the babies born during the boom reach reproductive age. This gives the age pyramid a narrow section in the center.

2. Most nations of Western Europe have an age composition roughly similar to that of the more developed nations: lower proportions of children and youth and higher proportions of old age than are found in most other parts of the world. Germany, Austria, France, England and Wales, and Sweden all have lower proportions of population under fifteen and a larger proportion over sixty-five than does the United States. These differences between the age composition of the United States and most nations of Western Europe result from lower birth rates and a longer period of declining births in Western Europe than in the United States. Dependency load for the countries of Europe and for populations of European descent tends to be low in comparison with other nations; the median age of these European peoples tends to be high. In several nations of Europe, loss of life in World War II has contributed to a high median age.

3. The less industrialized and more rural nations for which data are available tend to have a much higher proportion of children and youth and a smaller proportion of "old-age" population than does the United States. Their median age is lower, and their dependency ratios higher than those of the United States or of European nations. These differences reflect higher rates of fertility and higher death rates. Several of the LDCs have an age composition in 1985 very similar to that of the United States in 1800. All of the developing nations carry a heavy dependency load, consisting almost entirely of children and youth.

4. The proportion of population in the most vigorous working ages, 15-64 years, is roughly the same for all nations—between 55 and 65 percent of the total population. The nations with low fertility tend to have a larger share of their population in the working age group than do the high fertility countries. Moreover, a higher proportion of these workers are middle aged and hence are more seasoned and experienced workers.

5. The right-hand column of Table 2-14 reports sex ratios for the larger nations. The sex ratio of the U.S. coincides almost exactly with that of the average for developed nations.

Components of Population Growth, by Race

Chapter 1 discussed the growth of the population in terms of its components of births, deaths, and net immigration, with data for single calendar years from 1940 to 1982. Growth of the white and black populations can be studied separately in terms of the same components for single calendar years for 1950 to 1982 with the use of new estimates prepared by the U.S. Bureau of the Census. These data for the white population are contained in Table 2-15 and for the black population in Table 2-16; for the period 1950-60, data are available only for the nonwhite population (black plus other nonwhite races). The left panel of these tables reports the growth components in terms of rates and the right panel in terms of amounts. Figure 2-8 charts the trends of each of the components in a way that permits comparison of the trends for the two race groups, with a panel for each component. The series begin just as the baby boom was cresting (1950-57) and traces the decline of fertility into the baby bust of the 1960s. The white population entered the baby bust phase suddenly and swiftly sank below replacement. The black population had the fantastically high birth rate of 35 per 1,000 at the peak of the baby boom. It coasted more gradually into a decline and has stayed well above the rate for whites. The rate of 22 per 1,000 for 1982 is 40 percent above replacement and is still very high for a population in a developed nation.

Meanwhile, because of rapid aging of the white population (caused by the rapidly declining fertility), the crude death rate of the black population fell below that of the white population about 1971. In the 1950s and 1960s the white population was receiving a considerably larger growth boost than the black population from net immigration. However, even this evaporated during the 1970s, as immigration from the Caribbean began to bring in larger numbers of black arrivals, resulting in immigration rates for blacks substantially higher than the rates for whites. Thus, as of 1983, all of the components of growth—fertility, mortality, and immigration—were more favorable to the growth of the black than of the white population. As a consequence the black population was experiencing a net annual increase of 1.6 percent while the white population was growing at only 0.75 percent, or less than half as fast.

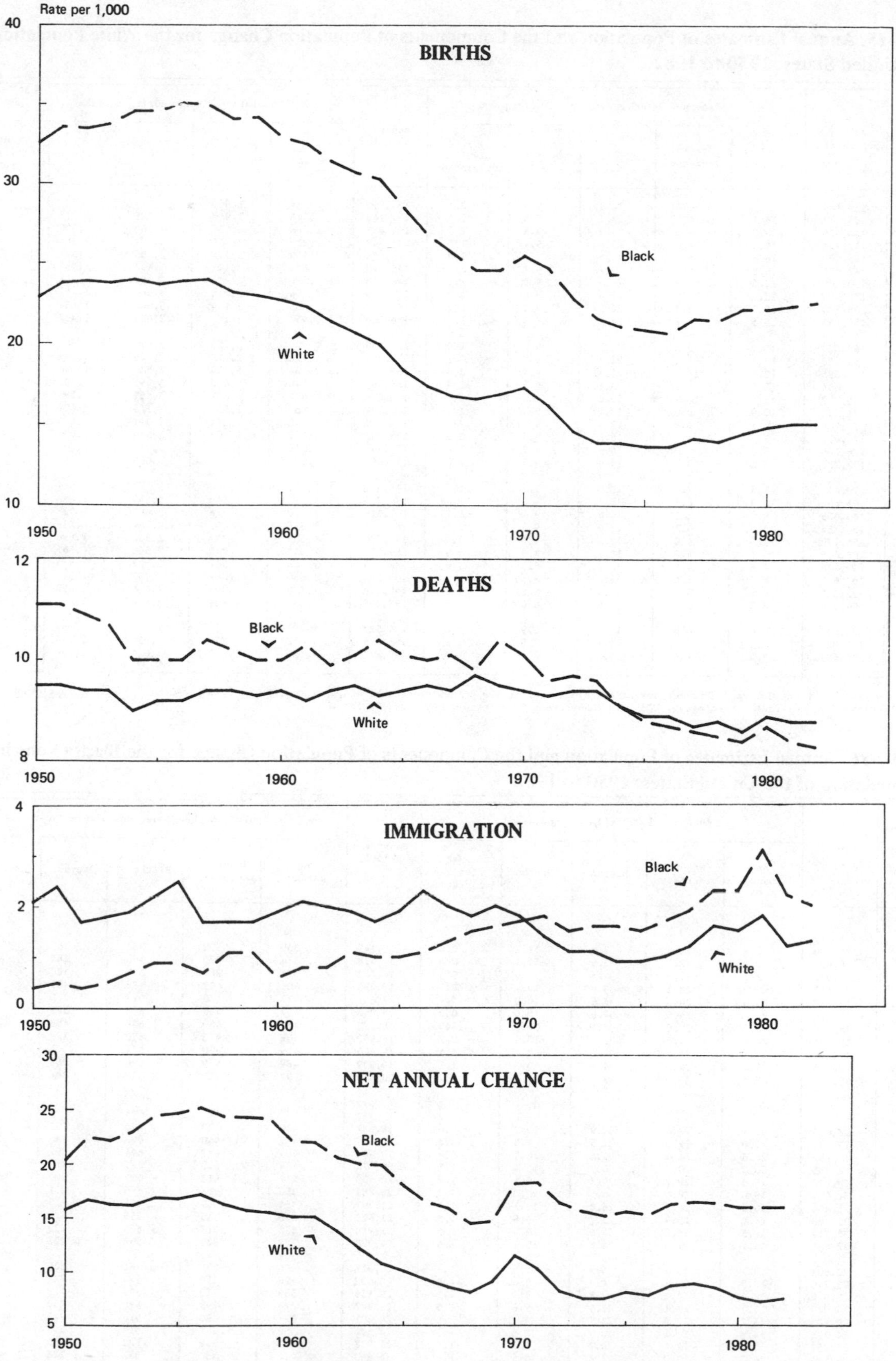

Figure 2-8. Trends in the Components of Population Growth: 1950-1983

Table 2-15. Annual Estimates of Population and the Components of Population Change for the White Population of the United States: 1950 to 1982

Calendar year	July 1 population	Rate per 1,000 midyear population					January 1 population	Population change during calendar year				
		Net change	Natural increase	Births	Deaths	Net civilian immigration		Net change	Natural increase	Births	Deaths	Net civilian immigration
1950. . .	135,984	15.8	13.4	22.9	9.5	2.1	134,990	2,154	1,827	3,114	1,287	292
1951. . .	138,221	16.7	14.2	23.8	9.5	2.4	137,144	2,313	1,969	3,285	1,316	326
1952. . .	140,526	16.3	14.5	23.9	9.4	1.7	139,457	2,286	2,037	3,363	1,326	236
1953. . .	142,773	16.2	14.4	23.8	9.4	1.8	141,743	2,316	2,056	3,401	1,345	252
1954. . .	145,193	16.9	15.0	24.0	9.0	1.9	144,059	2,460	2,174	3,485	1,311	274
1955. . .	147,653	16.8	14.5	23.7	9.2	2.2	146,519	2,474	2,141	3,495	1,354	321
1956. . .	150,163	17.2	14.7	23.9	9.2	2.5	148,993	2,586	2,203	3,587	1,384	371
1957. . .	152,769	16.3	14.5	24.0	9.4	1.7	151,579	2,494	2,218	3,660	1,442	259
1958. . .	155,200	15.7	13.9	23.2	9.4	1.7	154,073	2,435	2,154	3,608	1,454	271
1959. . .	157,655	15.5	13.7	23.0	9.3	1.7	156,508	2,451	2,161	3,623	1,462	270
1960. . .	160,023	15.1	13.3	22.7	9.4	1.9	158,959	2,409	2,123	3,625	1,502	304
1961. . .	162,533	15.1	13.1	22.3	9.2	2.1	161,367	2,448	2,127	3,626	1,499	345
1962. . .	164,885	13.8	12.0	21.4	9.4	2.0	163,815	2,281	1,984	3,530	1,546	322
1963. . .	167,104	13.0	11.2	20.7	9.5	1.9	166,096	2,170	1,870	3,462	1,592	324
1964. . .	169,257	12.2	10.7	20.0	9.3	1.7	168,266	2,070	1,811	3,391	1,580	284
1965. . .	171,205	10.8	9.0	18.4	9.4	1.9	170,336	1,850	1,538	3,145	1,607	333
1966. . .	172,998	10.1	7.9	17.4	9.5	2.3	172,187	1,740	1,371	3,011	1,640	390
1967. . .	174,695	9.3	7.5	16.8	9.4	2.0	173,927	1,621	1,305	2,940	1,636	343
1968. . .	176,246	8.6	7.0	16.6	9.7	1.8	175,548	1,519	1,225	2,930	1,705	317
1969. . .	177,782	9.1	7.4	16.9	9.5	2.0	177,067	1,626	1,315	3,009	1,694	354
1970. . .	179,644	11.5	7.9	17.3	9.4	1.8	178,692	2,057	1,420	3,107	1,687	327
1971. . .	181,663	10.3	6.8	16.2	9.3	1.4	180,749	1,867	1,243	2,935	1,692	255
1972. . .	183,326	8.2	5.2	14.6	9.4	1.1	182,616	1,510	946	2,669	1,723	199
1973. . .	184,782	7.5	4.5	13.9	9.4	1.1	184,126	1,394	835	2,564	1,729	195
1974. . .	186,170	7.5	4.8	13.9	9.1	0.9	185,520	1,395	892	2,590	1,698	175
1975. . .	187,629	8.1	4.8	13.7	8.9	0.9	186,915	1,515	905	2,566	1,661	173
1976. . .	189,074	7.8	4.8	13.7	8.9	1.0	188,430	1,468	907	2,582	1,675	184
1977. . .	190,649	8.7	5.5	14.2	8.7	1.2	189,898	1,650	1,042	2,707	1,665	223
1978. . .	192,335	8.9	5.2	14.0	8.8	1.6	191,548	1,720	1,006	2,696	1,690	300
1979. . .	194,098	8.5	5.9	14.5	8.6	1.5	193,268	1,655	1,148	2,824	1,676	294
1980. . .	195,637	7.6	6.0	14.9	8.9	1.8	194,923	1,492	1,183	2,915	1,732	347
1981. . .	197,022	7.2	6.2	15.1	8.8	1.2	196,415	1,412	1,226	2,966	1,740	238
1982. . .	198,483	7.5	6.4	15.1	8.8	1.3	197,827	1,479	1,268	3,006	1,738	258

Source: U.S. Bureau of the Census. "Projections of the Population of the United States, by Age, Sex, and Race: 1983 to 2080." Current Population Reports (Series P-25, no. 952). Washington, DC: U.S. Government Printing Office, 1984, Table 1.

Table 2-16. Annual Estimates of Population and the Components of Population Change for the Black (Nonwhite) Population of the United States: 1950 to 1982

Calendar year	July 1 population	Rate per 1,000 midyear population					January 1 population	Population change during calendar year				
		Net change	Natural increase	Births	Deaths	Net civilian immigration		Net change	Natural increase	Births	Deaths	Net civilian immigration
Nonwhite												
1950. . .	16,288	20.4	21.5	32.6	11.1	0.4	16,145	333	350	531	181	7
1951. . .	16,657	22.5	22.5	33.6	11.1	0.5	16,478	374	375	560	185	9
1952. . .	17,026	22.2	22.6	33.5	10.9	0.4	16,852	378	384	570	186	6
1953. . .	17,411	23.0	23.1	33.8	10.7	0.5	17,230	401	402	588	186	9
1954. . .	17,833	24.5	24.6	34.6	10.0	0.7	17,631	437	439	617	178	13
1955. . .	18,279	24.7	24.6	34.6	10.0	0.9	18,068	452	450	633	183	16
1956. . .	18,740	25.2	25.0	35.1	10.0	0.9	18,520	472	469	657	188	16
1957. . .	19,215	24.4	24.6	35.0	10.4	0.7	18,992	468	473	672	199	13
1958. . .	19,682	24.3	23.9	34.1	10.2	1.1	19,460	479	470	671	201	21
1959. . .	20,175	24.2	24.2	34.2	10.0	1.1	19,939	489	489	690	201	22
1960. . .	20,648	23.8	23.0	33.0	10.0	1.1	20,428	492	475	682	206	24
Black												
1960. . .	19,006	22.1	22.6	32.9	10.3	0.6	18,817	420	429	625	195	12
1961. . .	19,437	22.0	22.6	32.5	9.9	0.8	19,237	427	440	633	193	16
1962. . .	19,852	20.6	21.3	31.4	10.1	0.8	19,664	409	422	624	201	15
1963. . .	20,255	20.0	20.3	30.7	10.4	1.1	20,074	404	410	621	211	22
1964. . .	20,672	19.9	20.2	30.3	10.1	1.0	20,478	411	418	627	209	21
1965. . .	21,064	18.0	18.4	28.5	10.0	1.0	20,889	380	388	599	211	20
1966. . .	21,434	16.5	16.7	26.8	10.1	1.1	21,269	354	357	575	217	24
1967. . .	21,780	15.9	15.9	25.7	9.8	1.3	21,623	346	345	559	214	28
1968. . .	22,117	14.5	14.2	24.6	10.4	1.5	21,968	320	315	545	230	33
1969. . .	22,431	14.7	14.5	24.6	10.1	1.6	22,288	329	325	552	227	36
1970. . .	22,801	18.2	15.6	25.5	9.9	1.7	22,617	416	355	581	226	39
1971. . .	23,240	18.3	15.1	24.7	9.6	1.8	23,033	426	350	574	224	42
1972. . .	23,646	16.4	13.1	22.8	9.7	1.5	23,459	388	310	539	229	35
1973. . .	24,029	15.6	12.1	21.6	9.6	1.6	23,847	374	290	520	230	38
1974. . .	24,402	15.2	12.0	21.1	9.1	1.6	24,221	371	292	515	223	39
1975. . .	24,778	15.6	12.1	20.9	8.8	1.5	24,592	386	301	519	218	38
1976. . .	25,157	15.3	12.0	20.7	8.7	1.7	24,978	385	302	522	220	42
1977. . .	25,559	16.3	13.0	21.6	8.6	1.9	25,363	416	332	552	220	48
1978. . .	25,984	16.5	13.0	21.5	8.5	2.3	25,779	429	339	560	221	60
1979. . .	26,417	16.4	13.8	22.2	8.4	2.3	26,208	432	365	586	221	61
1980. . .	26,847	16.0	13.6	22.2	8.7	3.1	26,640	431	365	598	233	82
1981. . .	27,275	16.0	14.0	22.4	8.4	2.2	27,071	437	382	612	230	60
1982. . .	27,712	16.0	14.4	22.6	8.3	2.0	27,508	444	398	627	229	55

Source: U.S. Bureau of the Census. "Projections of the Population of the United States, by Age, Sex, and Race: 1983 to 2080." Current Population Reports (Series P-25, no. 952). Washington, DC: U.S. Government Printing Office, 1984, Table 1.

Future Race-Sex-Age Composition

In making its population projections (published in 1984), the U.S. Bureau of the Census looked an entire century into the future in terms of race, age, and sex. Its projections are assumptions made about the plausible future course of fertility, mortality, and migration rates. The "middle" projections appear to be within the realm of high probability and should be taken seriously as a guide to long-term planning and policy-making. The projections for the first fifty years, from 1980 to to 2030, are much more likely to come true than those for 2030 to 2080. Even the latter are instructive for showing where the population's race-sex-age composition is headed if current trends continue without adaptive changes. Some of the results are routine and to be expected, but others (particularly those for future age composition) are shocking by today's demographic standards. The materials of this section extend and elaborate on the projections reported in Chapter 1.

Future Race Composition of the Population

By taking into account the higher fertility and younger age composition in 1982 of the black population, assuming a gradual convergence of the fertility and mortality rates of the two races, and making assumptions about racial composition of future immigrants, projections can be made for the total, white, and black populations as shown in Tables 2-17, 2-18, and 2-19. Data for single years of age are given for the first twenty years of life; for the remaining ages, five-year age groupings are used. Projections for 1985 and for each decennial year from 1990 to 2030 are provided. These tables are an informed estimate of the number of persons of each race that the census will enumerate in the 1990 and subsequent censuses, by age (medium assumptions).

Because of its below-replacement fertility, the white population is projected to grow at progressively slower rates until it attains zero absolute growth about the year 2030, after which absolute decline will set in. However, because of its above-replacement and moderately high fertility, the black/other population continues to grow continuously for the next one hundred years, with the rate of growth tending toward zero at the end of that period. As a consequence of this differential growth, the proportion of the population that is white declines steadily from 86 percent in 1980 to 75 percent in 2080. The percentage of the population that is nonwhite rises from 14 percent in 1980 to 25 percent in 2080. This nonwhite population is predominantly black in 1980, but because of immigration from Asia, the Middle East, and other areas (and the rapid growth of the American Indian population), the proportion of the nonwhite population comprised by other races is expected to rise.

Subtracting the projections for white and black populations from the projections for the total population makes it possible to infer the following percent distributions for a racial trichotomy:

Race	1980	2000	2030	2080
Total. . . .	100.0	100.0	100.0	100.0
White.	85.9	83.1	79.3	74.5
Black.	11.8	13.3	15.6	17.9
Other nonwhite	2.3	3.6	5.1	7.5

Should the fertility of the black population converge with that of the white at a more rapid pace, the proportion black would rise more slowly and could even stabilize. However, if fertility for the total population should rise, it would create an increase in the proportion black, since black fertility would probably rise more than that of the white population. Thus, under the most plausible assumption the black population will be a minority racial group in the United States for the foreseeable future, although increasingly influential in proportion. Meanwhile, the category of Asian/other nonwhite races, which until now has been almost insignificant, will assume much more importance, becoming one-third as large as the black population by the year 2030.

Future Spanish-Origin Population

These computations fail to take into account that a significant and rapidly growing portion of the white population comprises persons of Spanish origin. The Bureau of the Census did not undertake to project the growth of this population, and perhaps to do so would be an exercise in futility. Later chapters will provide evidence that persons of Spanish-origin are intermarrying and otherwise rapidly being assimilated into the general population, including loss of the use of the Spanish language. For the remainder of this century, however, the flow of immigrants from Latin America is expected to be steady and large; combined with high fertility, this could produce a situation wherein the proportion of persons who self-consciously identify themselves as of Spanish-origin with ethnic self-interests comparable to those of the black population could possibly rise to a point where they would almost equal in size the black population by the turn of the century or certainly by

Table 2-17. Population Projection for All Races: 1985-2030 [numbers in thousands]

Age	Projected population						Percent change				
	1985	1990	2000	2010	2020	2030	1980-90	1990-00	2000-10	2010-20	2020-30
All ages	238,631	249,657	267,955	283,238	296,597	304,807	10.2	7.3	5.7	4.7	2.8
Under 5 years	18,453	19,198	17,626	17,974	18,357	17,695	17.4	-8.2	2.0	2.1	-3.6
Under 1 year	3,776	3,832	3,474	3,639	3,635	3,526	8.4	-9.3	4.7	-0.1	-3.0
1 year	3,734	3,847	3,490	3,617	3,654	3,528	17.6	-9.3	3.6	1.0	-3.4
2 years	3,688	3,851	3,516	3,594	3,673	3,535	19.4	-8.7	2.2	2.2	-3.8
3 years	3,651	3,843	3,552	3,572	3,691	3,546	20.9	-7.6	0.6	3.3	-3.9
4 years	3,604	3,825	3,595	3,551	3,705	3,560	21.7	-6.0	-1.2	4.3	-3.9
5 to 9 years	16,611	18,591	18,758	17,597	18,590	18,105	11.3	0.9	-6.2	5.6	-2.6
5 years	3,576	3,797	3,645	3,534	3,716	3,577	20.0	-4.0	-3.0	5.1	-3.7
6 years	3,374	3,761	3,700	3,521	3,722	3,597	21.0	-1.6	-4.8	5.7	-3.4
7 years	3,244	3,717	3,755	3,513	3,723	3,619	13.6	1.0	-6.4	6.0	-2.8
8 years	3,261	3,681	3,806	3,512	3,719	3,643	8.4	3.4	-7.7	5.9	-2.0
9 years	3,157	3,635	3,852	3,518	3,711	3,688	-3.3	6.0	-8.7	5.5	-1.2
10 to 14 years	16,797	16,793	19,519	17,957	18,306	18,689	-7.9	16.2	-8.0	1.9	2.1
10 years	3,219	3,610	3,887	3,532	3,698	3,693	-2.9	7.7	-9.1	4.7	-0.1
11 years	3,150	3,409	3,909	3,554	3,681	3,718	-4.8	14.7	-9.1	3.6	1.0
12 years	3,277	3,281	3,917	3,584	3,662	3,741	-6.8	19.4	-8.5	2.2	2.2
13 years	3,399	3,299	3,911	3,622	3,642	3,761	-9.4	18.6	-7.4	0.6	3.3
14 years	3,753	3,195	3,895	3,667	3,623	3,777	-15.5	21.9	-5.9	-1.2	4.3
15 to 19 years	18,416	16,968	18,943	19,114	17,958	18,948	-19.8	11.6	0.9	-6.0	5.5
15 years	3,755	3,257	3,868	3,718	3,607	3,788	-19.8	18.8	-3.9	-3.0	5.0
16 years	3,655	3,187	3,832	3,772	3,594	3,794	-23.8	20.2	-1.6	-4.7	5.6
17 years	3,568	3,311	3,787	3,826	3,585	3,795	-21.6	14.4	1.0	-6.3	5.9
18 years	3,658	3,431	3,751	3,877	3,584	3,790	-19.3	9.3	3.4	-7.6	5.7
19 years	3,780	3,783	3,705	3,921	3,589	3,781	-15.0	-2.1	5.8	-8.5	5.3
20-24 years	21,301	18,580	17,145	19,857	18,308	18,654	-12.8	-7.7	15.8	-7.8	1.9
25-29 years	21,838	21,522	17,396	19,362	19,533	18,389	10.3	-19.2	11.3	0.9	-5.9
30-34 years	19,950	22,007	19,019	17,616	20,301	18,769	25.3	-13.6	-7.4	15.2	-7.5
35-39 years	17,894	20,001	21,753	17,696	19,644	19,816	43.2	8.8	-18.7	11.0	0.9
40-44 years	14,110	17,846	21,990	19,076	17,699	20,352	52.9	23.2	-13.3	-7.2	15.0
45-49 years	11,647	13,980	19,763	21,522	17,559	19,478	26.1	41.4	8.9	-18.4	10.9
50-54 years	10,817	11,422	17,356	21,424	18,621	17,307	-2.5	52.0	23.4	-13.1	-7.1
55-59 years	11,245	10,433	13,280	18,825	20,507	16,778	-10.2	27.3	41.8	8.9	-18.2
60-64 years	10,943	10,618	10,487	16,023	19,791	17,247	5.3	-1.2	52.8	23.5	-12.9
65-69 years	9,214	9,996	9,096	11,703	16,620	18,133	13.8	-9.0	28.7	42.0	9.1
70-74 years	7,641	8,039	8,581	8,615	13,235	16,402	18.3	6.7	0.4	53.6	23.9
75-79 years	5,556	6,260	7,295	6,782	8,824	12,619	30.6	16.5	-7.0	30.1	43.0
80-84 years	3,501	4,089	5,023	5,544	5,662	8,815	39.3	22.8	10.4	2.1	55.7
85 years and over	2,697	3,313	4,926	6,551	7,081	8,612	47.9	48.7	33.0	8.1	21.6

Source: U.S. Bureau of the Census. "Projections of the Population of the United States, by Age, Sex, and Race: 1983 to 2080." Current Population Reports (Series P-25, no. 952). Washington, DC: U.S. Government Printing Office, 1984, Table 6.

Table 2-18. Projection for the White Population: 1985-2030 [numbers in thousands]

Age	Projected population						Percent change				
	1985	1990	2000	2010	2020	2030	1980-90	1990-00	2000-10	2010-20	2020-30
All ages.	203,113	210,790	222,654	231,540	238,739	241,647	11.9	5.6	4.0	3.1	1.2
Under 5 years	14,813	15,390	13,843	13,865	14,055	13,351	21.8	-10.1	0.2	1.4	-5.0
Under 1 year.	3,040	3,065	2,715	2,806	2,777	2,656	12.7	-11.4	3.4	-1.0	-4.4
1 year.	3,008	3,082	2,735	2,789	2,795	2,660	21.9	-11.3	2.0	0.2	-4.8
2 years	2,972	3,088	2,761	2,772	2,813	2,667	23.7	-10.6	0.4	1.5	-5.2
3 years	2,916	3,084	2,796	2,756	2,829	2,677	24.5	-9.3	-1.4	2.6	-5.4
4 years	2,877	3,071	2,836	2,742	2,841	2,691	26.5	-7.7	-3.3	3.6	-5.3
5 to 9 years.	13,573	14,895	14,883	13,628	14,275	13,737	14.3	-0.1	-8.4	4.7	-3.8
5 years	2,908	3,051	2,882	2,730	2,851	2,707	24.2	-5.5	-5.3	4.4	-5.1
6 years	2,761	3,023	2,931	2,722	2,857	2,726	25.4	-3.0	-7.1	5.0	-4.6
7 years	2,657	2,989	2,979	2,720	2,859	2,746	17.7	-0.3	-8.7	5.1	-4.0
8 years	2,668	2,935	3,025	2,723	2,857	2,768	10.4	3.1	-10.0	4.9	-3.1
9 years	2,580	2,897	3,066	2,733	2,851	2,790	-2.4	5.8	-10.9	4.3	-2.1
10 to 14 years.	13,737	13,688	15,588	14,049	14,072	14,262	-5.3	13.9	-9.9	0.2	1.4
10 years.	2,633	2,928	3,098	2,750	2,841	2,813	-0.6	5.8	-11.2	3.3	-1.0
11 years.	2,572	2,783	3,119	2,774	2,829	2,835	-2.2	12.1	-11.1	2.0	0.2
12 years.	2,667	2,680	3,129	2,804	2,815	2,855	-3.8	16.8	-10.4	0.4	1.4
13 years.	2,778	2,692	3,127	2,840	2,800	2,873	-6.8	16.2	-9.2	-1.4	2.6
14 years.	3,085	2,603	2,115	2,881	2,787	2,887	-13.0	19.6	-7.5	-3.3	3.6
15 to 19 years.	15,186	13,840	15,113	15,104	13,855	14,500	-18.4	9.2	-0.1	-8.3	4.7
15 years.	3,111	2,657	3,095	2,927	2,776	2,897	-17.8	16.5	-5.4	-5.2	4.4
16 years.	3,015	2,595	3,068	2,976	2,768	2,903	-22.4	18.2	-3.0	-7.0	4.9
17 years.	2,940	2,689	3,033	3,024	2,765	2,904	-20.5	12.8	-0.3	-8.6	5.0
18 years.	3,015	2,797	2,978	3,069	2,768	2,901	-18.1	6.5	3.1	-9.8	4.8
19 years.	3,105	3,102	2,939	3,108	2,777	2,894	-13.5	-5.3	5.8	-10.6	4.2
20-24 years	17,697	15,270	13,889	15,781	14,254	14,277	-11.7	-9.0	13.6	-9.7	0.2
25-29 years	18,388	17,815	14,076	15,345	15,336	14,098	11.4	-21.0	9.0	-0.1	-8.1
30-34 years	16,935	18,474	15,514	14,156	16,030	14,515	26.1	-16.0	-8.8	13.2	-9.5
35-39 years	15,396	16,951	17,929	14,242	15,499	15,490	44.1	5.8	-20.6	8.8	-0.1
40-44 years	12,224	15,341	18,426	15,524	14,183	16,034	56.1	20.1	-15.7	-8.6	13.1
45-49 years	10,080	12,106	16,739	17,733	14,116	15,355	28.0	38.3	5.9	-20.4	8.8
50-54 years	9,449	9,888	14,923	17,964	15,158	13,865	-2.7	50.9	20.4	-15.6	-8.5
55-59 years	9,958	9,122	11,512	15,969	16,928	13,500	-10.9	26.2	38.7	6.0	-20.3
60-64 years	9,801	9,414	9,093	13,800	16,633	14,065	4.9	-3.4	51.8	20.5	-15.4
65-69 years	8,307	8,968	7,966	10,158	14,130	15,002	14.8	-11.2	27.5	39.1	6.2
70-74 years	6,881	7,258	7,623	7,477	11,414	13,812	19.1	5.0	-1.9	52.7	21.0
75-79 years	5,031	5,644	6,554	5,940	7,661	10,734	31.0	16.1	-9.4	29.0	40.1
80-84 years	3,178	3,708	4,539	4,923	4,911	7,595	38.1	22.4	8.5	-0.2	54.7
85 years and over	2,477	3,019	4,444	5,880	6,229	7,256	47.6	47.2	32.3	5.9	16.5

Source: U.S. Bureau of the Census. "Projections of the Population of the United States, by Age, Sex, and Race: 1983 to 2080." Current Population Reports (Series P-25, no. 952). Washington, DC: U.S. Government Printing Office, 1984, Table 6.

Table 2-19. Projection for the Black Population: 1985-2030 [numbers in thousands]

Age	Projected population						Percent change				
	1985	1990	2000	2010	2020	2030	1980-90	1990-00	2000-10	2010-20	2020-30
All ages	29,074	31,412	35,753	40,033	44,175	47,598	18.6	13.8	12.0	10.3	7.7
Under 5 years	3,057	3,215	3,079	3,302	3,413	3,360	32.0	-4.2	7.2	3.4	-1.6
Under 1 year	631	646	617	672	680	673	21.7	-4.5	8.9	1.2	-1.0
1 year	623	646	614	666	681	672	32.6	-5.0	8.5	2.3	-1.3
2 years	614	645	614	660	683	672	34.9	-4.8	7.5	3.5	-1.6
3 years	600	642	615	654	684	672	36.3	-4.2	6.3	4.6	-1.8
4 years	589	637	619	648	685	672	35.5	-2.8	4.7	5.7	-1.9
5 to 9 years	2,486	3,064	3,174	3,162	3,419	3,385	23.0	3.6	-0.4	8.1	-1.0
5 years	548	631	623	643	686	673	34.8	-1.3	3.2	6.7	-1.9
6 years	503	624	629	637	686	675	33.3	0.8	1.3	7.7	-1.6
7 years	480	616	635	632	685	677	23.7	3.1	-0.5	8.4	-1.2
8 years	485	602	641	627	683	679	18.7	6.5	-2.2	8.9	-0.6
9 years	470	592	646	624	680	681	7.6	9.1	-3.4	9.0	0.1
10 to 14 years	2,518	2,509	3,247	3,113	3,336	3,447	-6.1	29.4	-4.1	7.2	3.3
10 years	479	551	650	621	677	684	2.8	18.0	-4.5	9.0	1.0
11 years	471	507	651	620	672	687	-1.4	28.4	-4.8	8.4	2.2
12 years	500	485	651	621	667	690	-6.4	34.2	-4.6	7.4	3.4
13 years	512	491	649	623	662	692	-8.7	32.2	-4.0	6.3	4.5
14 years	556	476	645	627	657	694	-16.2	35.5	-2.8	4.8	5.6
15 to 19 years	2,703	2,546	3,114	3,225	3,213	3,469	-14.7	22.3	3.6	-0.4	8.0
15 years	534	485	640	633	652	695	-18.5	32.0	-1.1	3.0	6.6
16 years	534	477	634	639	647	695	-20.5	32.9	0.8	1.3	7.4
17 years	526	506	626	645	642	695	-15.7	23.7	3.0	0.5	8.3
18 years	540	517	613	651	638	693	-12.2	18.6	6.2	-2.0	8.6
19 years	570	561	602	656	634	690	-6.5	7.3	9.0	-3.4	8.8
20-24 years	3,029	2,720	2,558	3,291	3,158	3,380	-0.2	-6.0	28.7	-4.0	7.0
25-29 years	2,824	3,036	2,579	3,144	3,255	3,244	30.8	-15.1	21.9	3.5	-0.3
30-34 years	2,388	2,824	2,737	2,584	3,309	3,182	49.5	-3.1	-5.6	28.1	-3.8
35-39 years	1,935	2,380	3,025	2,588	3,148	3,261	63.2	27.1	-14.4	21.6	3.6
40-44 years	1,469	1,915	2,786	2,714	2,571	3,286	53.1	45.5	-2.6	-5.3	27.8
45-49 years	1,237	1,437	2,310	2,949	2,535	3,087	25.7	60.8	27.7	-14.0	21.8
50-54 years	1,099	1,189	1,814	2,656	2,600	2,476	5.3	52.6	46.4	-2.1	-4.8
55-59 years	1,055	1,032	1,314	2,134	2,738	2,371	-0.5	27.3	62.4	28.3	-13.4
60-64 years	948	966	1,041	1,613	2,377	2,345	10.9	7.8	54.9	47.4	-1.3
65-69 years	761	833	851	1,108	1,817	2,348	7.2	2.2	30.2	64.0	29.2
70-74 years	649	642	738	820	1,287	1,914	13.8	15.0	11.1	57.0	48.7
75-79 years	452	520	583	618	819	1,356	34.4	12.1	6.0	32.5	65.6
80-84 years	279	327	392	472	536	856	63.5	19.9	20.4	13.6	59.7
85 years and over	189	257	412	541	645	831	61.6	60.3	31.3	19.2	28.8

Source: U.S. Bureau of the Census. "Projections of the Population of the United States, by Age, Sex, and Race: 1983 to 2080." Current Population Reports (Series P-25, no. 952). Washington, DC: U.S. Government Printing Office, 1984, Table 6.

the year 2020. By 2030 it is almost certain that persons of Spanish-origin will outnumber the black population, unless massive immigration from Latin America slackens dramatically, fertility rates of the Spanish-origin population decline swiftly, or assimilation causes them not to identify themselves as of Spanish origin on census questionnaires.

In summary, the white non-Spanish population will progressively cease to be the overwhelming majority of the population it is now. A century from now the race-ethnic composition of the United States could well be two blacks, two Hispanics, and one Asian/other non-white persons for every five white non-Hispanic residents.

Future Sex Composition of the Population

The least informative aspect of population projections is future sex composition, because the results depend heavily on assumptions made about differences in mortality rates between men and women at older ages. The Bureau of the Census projections assume these differences diminish rather than widen. The result is a projection wherein the ratio of males to females remains almost unchanged over the entire century for which the projections are made. The following summary of sex ratios by race demonstrates this:

Year	Total	White	Black/ other
1983	94.8	95.4	90.3
1990	94.8	95.5	90.5
2000	94.9	95.7	91.1
2010	95.1	95.9	91.7
2020	95.0	95.8	92.1
2030	94.3	95.0	92.1
2080	93.2	94.0	91.8

Although the Bureau of the Census projections provide separate projections for males and females, the changes in sex composition are so minor that no sex-specific data by age and race for future years are included in this report.

Future Changes in Age Composition

Far more radical than the changes in race-ethnicity composition predicted by the projections are the changes in age composition that are almost certain to take place. Every phase of the life cycle will be strongly affected by changing age composition over the course of the next half-century. Tables 2-17, 2-18 and 2-19 provide age data for the total, white, and black populations for this period, and Figure 2-9 graphs the projected change in age composition for the century 1980-2080 under the middle assumptions of the Bureau of the Census.

The following age synopsis from Table 2-17 shows that the recent decline in the proportion of the population comprised of youth is scheduled to stabilize and remain at about 25-26 percent for the remainder of this century, and then to begin a new trend downward.

Year	Percent of population by age			
	Total	Under 18 years	18-64 years	65+ years
1980	100.0	28.0	60.7	11.3
1985	100.0	26.3	61.7	12.0
1990	100.0	25.8	61.5	12.7
1995	100.0	25.9	61.1	13.1
2000	100.0	25.1	61.8	13.0
2010	100.0	22.9	63.3	13.8
2020	100.0	22.3	60.4	17.3
2030	100.0	21.6	57.2	21.2
2050	100.0	21.0	57.3	21.8
2080	100.0	20.3	56.2	23.5

Similarly, there is comparatively little change predicted in the relative size of the working-age population or of the retirement age population until the year 2010. Between 2010 and 2020 a revolutionary change in age composition is scheduled to set in, with the proportion elderly rising swiftly from 13-14 percent to 21-22 percent. This is linked to the passing of the baby boom generation into retirement ages (for details see below).

The effects of these age changes upon dependency ratios are minimal between 1980 and 2020. Until that date, small declines in proportions under age eighteen offset small rises in proportions above sixty-five. But after 2020 that is no longer true. From 2030 to 2050 the baby boom babies create a dependency load that causes a large absolute rise in the dependency ratio. The following tabulation summarizes the trend:

Year	Number of dependents per 100 persons 18-64		
	Total	Under 18 years	65+ years
1980	64.6	46.0	18.6
1985	62.1	42.7	19.4
1990	62.5	41.9	20.6
1995	63.7	42.3	21.4
2000	61.8	40.7	21.1
2010	58.1	36.2	21.9
2020	65.6	36.9	28.7
2030	74.8	37.8	37.0
2050	74.6	36.6	38.0
2080	78.1	36.2	41.9

A more detailed study of the projected population by age reveals a number of noteworthy findings. In order to study the documentation for these changes, the reader should examine the trends in size and intercensal percent change provided in Table 2-17. The following changes can be observed separately for the white and black populations in Tables 2-18 and 2-19.

1. The persons born during the baby boom (1945-57) are twenty-eight to forty years of age in 1985. These are ages of declining fertility but vigorous labor force participation. During the 1980-90 decade they are causing high rates of increase in ages 30-54, which will shift to successively older ages. For the remainder of this century the baby boom generation will comprise the core of the work force, but will contribute little to fertility.

2. The "baby bust" generation, born since 1957 (and especially since 1960) are ten to twenty-five years of age in 1985. They are the generations now and for the next twenty years attending school, marrying, and entering the labor force. Between 1980 and 1990 there will be negative rates of growth for ages 10-24, particularly at ages 14-24. Because of these reduced numbers, the quantities of everything involving this group will continue to be reduced in amount, especially classrooms and educational facilities.

3. The "baby bust" generation will place much more modest demands for expansion on the labor force than did the baby boom generation. As a consequence teenage unemployment may decline after 1985, since it may be easier then for succeeding generations to find jobs. If conditions of full employment exist, the pressure for women to join the labor force may be stronger than ever, which could have an additional depressing effect on fertility. As the "baby bust" generation passes into the peak childbearing years, the number of births can be expected to sink, even though birth rates may remain the same.

4. The smallish bulge of "baby boom echo" babies born since 1975 are eight years of age or younger in 1985. They are in preschool and the lower grades of elementary school, causing moderate increases. They will gradually pass through the school system in later decades providing a slight and temporary relief or recovery from the retrenchment of the preceding decade.

5. The smaller cohorts of persons born during the Great Depression and the strong fertility decline of the 1920s will be entering retirement age between 1990 and 2010. As a result, the expansion of the elderly population will be moderate. Growth in the old age population will come more from increased longevity, not larger cohorts entering old age. But this is only the calm before the hurricane.

6. Beginning about 2010-15 the large cohorts born during the baby boom will begin to reach retirement.

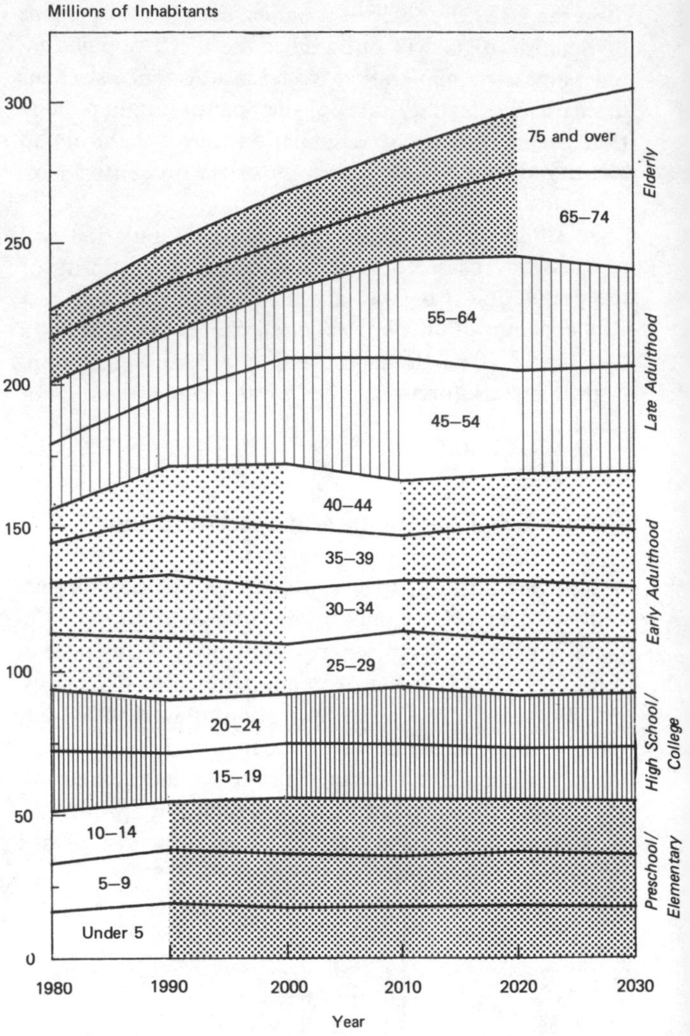

Figure 2-9. Projected Change in Age Composition: 1980-2030

The number and proportion of persons over sixty-five years of age will skyrocket, especially if assumptions of increased longevity materialize. This huge segment of elderly persons will be "supported" by a small labor force made up of persons born during the "baby bust." If bankruptcy capsizes Social Security, Medicare, and public and private retirement schemes for demographic reasons, that is much more likely to occur in the decades of the 2020s and 2030s than in this century. Figure 2-10 illustrates the phenomenal increase in the number of persons aged sixty-five and over that will occur between 2020 and 2030. After 2030 most of the "baby boom" will be deceased, and thereafter the age distribution will have a more "normal" shape, without huge major waves unless a new baby boom occurs.

As the elderly population increases, the proportion of those who are extremely elderly—eighty-five or older—

will also climb very quickly, as the following tabulation shows:

Year	Percent 65+ who are age 85+	Year	Percent 65+ who are age 85+
Estimates		Projections	
1950. . . .	4.8	1985. . . .	9.4
1955. . . .	5.3	1990. . . .	10.5
1960. . . .	5.6	1995. . . .	12.0
1965. . . .	5.9	2000. . . .	14.1
1970. . . .	7.1	2010. . . .	16.7
1975. . . .	8.0	2030. . . .	13.3
1980. . . .	8.8	2050. . . .	23.8
1982. . . .	9.1	2080. . . .	24.9

The increase is substantial but more or less regular until the year 2050, which will show a tremendous increase in the number of extremely elderly.

The baby boom generation illustrates the economic and social problems that severe fluctuations in fertility create by causing "waves" in the age distribution. Members of this generation have suffered hardships and will continue to do so. They had difficulties obtaining adequate schooling. They had trouble finding jobs in the 1980s, suffering from unemployment. It appears they will not even be able to retire in peace, and when they begin to suffer terminal illnesses (about 2030), hospital and medical facilities may be insufficient to accomodate them.

These problems have been caused by the large number of people in comparison with preceding generations. For the first time in the nation's history, the elderly will outnumber youths aged 0-18 and by a considerable margin. Unless more of them stay in the labor force to help support themselves, the elderly population may be despised as a heavy economic burden.

Components of Growth in the Future

Table 2-20 reports the annual components of growth implied by the Bureau of the Census middle population projection. The crude birth rate is projected to decline steadily and to fall progressively further below the replacement level, reaching a low of 11-12 per 1,000 in 2020 and remaining on that plateau. Meanwhile, because of aging of the baby boom generation, the death rate is projected to shoot up and surpass the birth rate, with the result that negative natural increase occurs in 2040. Absolute population loss is avoided only by assumed continued net immigration. Because immigration is assumed to be at the level of 450,000 per year, it becomes a progressively smaller rate as the population base slowly expands.

Summary

The age composition of the U.S. population during the 1980s is highly distorted by "waves" introduced into it by the extraordinary fluctuations of birth rates over the past half-century. Because of these fluctuations, a number of imbalances and rapid changes have occurred and will retain their imprint on age composition as the

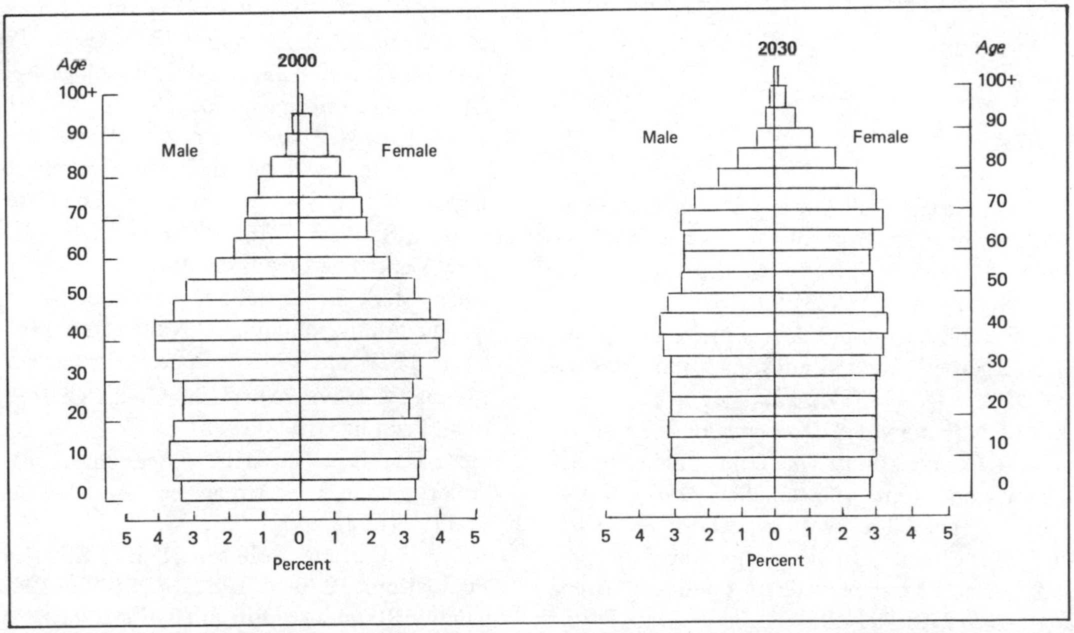

Figure 2-10. Percentage Distribution of Population by Age and Sex: 2000 and 2030

Table 2-20. Components of Population Change for Middle Projections of the Total Population: 1983-2080 [numbers in thousands]

Calendar year	Rate per 1,000 midyear population						Population change during calendar year					
	July population	Net change	Natural increase	Births	Deaths	Net immigration	January 1 population	Net change	Natural increase	Births	Deaths	Net immigration
1983.	234,223	9.3	7.4	16.0	8.6	1.9	233,140	2,180	1,730	3,742	2,013	450
1984.	236,416	9.3	7.4	16.0	8.6	1.9	235,319	2,204	1,754	3,788	2,034	450
1985.	238,631	9.3	7.4	16.0	8.6	1.9	237,523	2,220	1,770	3,826	2,056	450
1986.	240,856	9.2	7.4	16.0	8.6	1.9	239,743	2,227	1,777	3,855	2,078	450
1987.	243,084	9.1	7.3	15.9	8.6	1.9	241,970	2,223	1,773	3,873	2,100	450
1988.	245,302	9.0	7.2	15.8	8.7	1.8	244,193	2,207	1,757	3,879	2,122	450
1989.	247,498	8.8	7.0	15.6	8.7	1.8	246,400	2,178	1,728	3,871	2,144	450
1990.	249,657	8.5	6.7	15.4	8.7	1.8	248,577	2,134	1,684	3,849	2,165	450
1991.	251,767	8.3	6.5	15.2	8.7	1.8	250,712	2,080	1,630	3,815	2,185	450
1992.	253,817	7.9	6.2	14.9	8.7	1.8	252,792	2,017	1,567	3,772	2,206	450
1993.	255,800	7.6	5.9	14.6	8.7	1.8	254,808	1,949	1,499	3,725	2,226	450
1994.	257,714	7.3	5.5	14.3	8.7	1.7	256,757	1,879	1,429	3,675	2,246	450
1995.	259,559	7.0	5.2	14.0	8.7	1.7	258,637	1,812	1,362	3,628	2,266	450
1996.	261,339	6.7	5.0	13.7	8.7	1.7	260,449	1,751	1,301	3,586	2,285	450
1997.	263,060	6.4	4.7	13.5	8.8	1.7	262,200	1,696	1,246	3,551	2,305	450
1998.	264,731	6.2	4.5	13.3	8.8	1.7	263,896	1,650	1,200	3,524	2,324	450
1999.	266,360	6.1	4.4	13.2	8.8	1.7	265,546	1,612	1,162	3,506	2,344	450
2000.	267,955	5.9	4.2	13.0	8.8	1.7	267,158	1,582	1,132	3,495	2,363	450
2010.	283,238	5.3	3.7	13.0	9.3	1.6	282,490	1,488	1,038	3,673	2,635	450
2020.	296,597	3.7	2.2	12.3	10.1	1.5	296,029	1,106	656	3,648	2,992	450
2030.	304,807	1.8	0.4	11.6	11.3	1.5	304,515	563	113	3,547	3,434	450
2040.	308,559	0.7	-0.8	11.6	12.4	1.5	308,446	212	-237	3,593	3,831	450
2050.	309,488	0.0	-1.4	11.4	12.8	1.5	309,482	10	-439	3,517	3,957	450
2060.	309,652	0.2	-1.3	11.3	12.6	1.5	309,630	48	-401	3,490	3,892	450
2070.	310,358	0.2	-1.2	11.2	12.4	1.4	310,322	71	-378	3,480	3,860	450
2080.	310,762	0.0	-1.4	11.1	12.5	1.4	310,756	7	-442	3,435	3,878	450

Source: U.S. Bureau of the Census. "Projections of the Population of the United States, by Age, Sex, and Race: 1983 to 2080." Current Population Reports (Series P-25, no. 952). Washington, DC: U.S. Government Printing Office, 1984, Table 12.

population ages in future decades. The chapters which follow will trace some of these changes and point out their implications for both the present and future.

Note

1. Fertility, mortality, and migration do not fall into this classification because they are processes, not traits or statuses.

Bibliography

Bean, Frank D.; King, Allan G.; and Passel, Jeffrey S. "The Number of Illegal Migrants of Mexican Origin in the United States: Sex Ratio-Based Estimates for 1980." *Demography* 20 (1983):99-109.

Blumstein, J.F., and Salamon, L.M. (eds.). "Growth Policy in the Eighties" (symposium). *Law and Contemporary Problems* 43 (1979):2-252.

Bogue, Donald J. *Principles of Demography*. (Chapter 7, "Population Composition: The Demographic Variables.") New York: John Wiley and Sons, 1969.

Brown, D.L. "Metropolitan Reclassification: Some Effects on the Characteristics of the Population in Metropolitan and Nonmetropolitan Counties." *Rural Sociology* 44 (1979):791-801.

Frazier, E. Franklin. *The Negro in the United States.* New York: Macmillan Co., 1957.

Gelfang, Donald E. *Aging: The Ethnic Factor.* Boston: Little, Brown and Co., 1982.

Guttentag, Marcia, and Secord, Paul F. *Too Many Women? The Sex Ratio Question.* Beverly Hills: Sage Publications, 1983.

Jaffee, Abram J. et al. *Spanish-Americans in the United States: Changing Demographic Characteristics.* New York: Research Institute for the Study of Man, 1976.

Jennings, Jerry T. "Social and Economic Characteristics of the Older Population: 1978." *Current Population Reports* (Series P-23, no. 85). Washington, DC: U.S. Government Printing Office, 1979.

Kreps, Juanita M. *Economics of a Stationary Population.* A report to the National Science Foundation. Washington, DC: U.S. Government Printing Office, 1977.

Lieberson, Stanley. *Ethnic Patterns in American Cities.* New York: The Free Press, 1963.

Littman, Mark S. "Social and Economic Characteristics of the Metropolitan and Nonmetropolitan Population: 1977 and 1970." *Current Population Reports* (Series P-23, no. 75). Washington, DC: U.S. Government Printing Office, 1978.

Massey, Douglas. "Residential Segregation of Spanish-Americans in U.S. Urbanized Areas." *Demography* 16 (1979):553-563.

Matney, W.C., and Johnson, D.L. "America's Black Population: 1970 to 1982." *Crisis* 90 (1983):10-18.

Population Reference Bureau (Barberis, M.). "America's Elderly: Policy Implications." *Population Bulletin* 35 (1981):2-13.

______ (Bouvier, Leon F.). "America's Baby Boom Generation: the Fateful Bulge." *Population Bulletin* 35 (1980).

______ (Davis, Cary; Haub, Carl; and Willette, JoAnne). "U.S. Hispanics: Changing the Face of America." *Population Bulletin* 38 (1983).

______. "Population Age Composition." *Population Bulletin* 37 (1982):29-32.

______ (Reid, John). "Black America in the 1980's." *Population Bulletin* 37 (1982).

______ (Soldo, B. J.). "America's Elderly in the 1980s." *Population Bulletin* 35 (1980):2-47.

Sheldon, Harry D., and Tibbits, Clark. *The Older Population in the United States.* New York: John Wiley and Sons, 1958.

Siegel, J.S. "Estimates of Coverage of the Population by Sex, Race, and Age in the 1970 Census." *Demography* 11 (1979):1-23.

Siegel, J.S., and Passel, J. "Coverage of the Hispanic Population of the United States in the 1970 Census." *Current Population Reports* (Series P-23, no. 82). Washington, DC: U.S. Government Printing Office, 1970.

Siegel, J.S.; Passel, Jeffrey S.; and Robinson, J. Gregory. "Preliminary Review of Existing Studies of the Number of Illegal Residents in the United States." Appendix E (Papers on Illegal Immigration to the U.S.). In *U.S. Immigration Policy and the National Interest.* The Staff Report to the Select Commission on Immigration and Refugee Policy. Washington, DC, 1979.

Sly, D.F. et al. (ed.). "Metropolitan and Regional Change in the United States." *Social Science Quarterly* 61 (1980):369-675.

Taeuber, Cynthia M. "Older Workers: Force of the Future?" Paper presented at the meeting of the Population Association of America, May, 1984.

Taeuber, Irene B., and Taeuber, Conrad. *People of the United States in the 20th Century.* (Chapter 4, "Age: Formation, Structure, Differentiation.") Washington, DC: U.S. Bureau of the Census, 1971.

Taeuber, Karl E., and Taeuber, A.F. *Negroes in Cities.* Chicago: Aldine Publishing Co., 1965.

United States Congress, Senate, Special Committee on Aging. *The Graying of Nations: Implications.* Washington, DC: U.S. Government Printing Office, 1978.

United States Women's Bureau. *Women of Spanish-Origin in the United States.* Washington, DC: U.S. Department of Labor, 1976.

Urban Associates for Department of Health, Education and Welfare. *A Study of Socioeconomic Characteristics of Ethnic Minorities Based on the 1970 Census.* (3 vols.: "Spanish-Americans in the United States," "Asian Americans," "Indians of North America.") Washington, DC: U.S. Government Printing Office, 1974.

U.S. Bureau of the Census. "America in Transition: An Aging Society." *Current Population Reports* (Series P-23, no. 128). Washington, DC: U.S. Government Printing Office, 1983.

______. "Coverage of the Hispanic Population of the United States in the 1970 Census: A Methodological Analysis." *Current Population Reports* (Series P-23, no. 82). Washington, DC: U.S. Government Printing Office, 1970.

______ (Miller, Louisa). "Estimates of the Population of the United States by Age, Sex and Race: 1980 to 1982." *Current Population Reports* (Series P-25, no. 929). Washington, DC: U.S. Government Printing Office, 1983.

______. "Persons of Spanish-Origin in the United States: March 1979." *Current Population Reports* (Series P-20, no. 354). Washington, DC: U.S. Government Printing Office, 1979.

______. "Population Profile of the United States: 1982." *Current Population Reports* (Series P-23, no. 130). Washington, DC: U.S. Government Printing Office, 1984.

______. "Projections of the Population of the United States, by Age, Sex and Race: 1983 to 2080." *Current Population Reports* (Series P-25, no. 952). Washington, DC: U.S. Government Printing Office, 1984.

______ (Siegel, Jacob S., and Davidson, Maria). "Demographic and Socioeconomic Aspects of Aging in the United States." *Current Population Reports* (Series P-23). Washington, DC: U.S. Government Printing Office, 1985.

______. "Social and Economic Characteristics of the Metropolitan and Nonmetropolitan Population: 1974 and 1970." *Current Population Reports* (Series P-23, no. 55). Washington, DC: U.S. Government Printing Office, 1975.

U.S. Department of Health, Education and Welfare, and Office of Human Development, Administration on Aging. *Indicators of the Status of the Elderly in the U.S.* Washington, DC: U.S. Government Printing Office: 1974.

Wilson, William J. *The Declining Significance of Race.* Chicago: University of Chicago Press, 1980.

Technical Appendix 2-1

The Bureau of Census Current Population Survey

One of the unique resources for population data for the United States is the Current Population Survey (CPS) maintained by the Bureau of the Census. Once each month a probability sample of the national population is interviewed to collect population data. This monthly CPS deals mainly with labor force data for the civilian noninstitutional population. Its principal purpose is to keep a finger on the pulse of the labor market, especially to measure the rate of unemployment and obtain data concerning the characteristics and problems of the labor force. Inasmuch as the sample is large and highly sophisticated, it yields data that have a comparatively small sampling error, and provides such data for areal subdivisions of the nation as well as for the national total.

In 1982-83 the number of housing units interviewed was 59,000. The sample was drawn from 629 sample areas, chosen to provide coverage in each state and the District of Columbia. By a system of gradually rotating households in the sample, it is possible to conduct short longitudinal studies of particular households and individuals.

However, the CPS is not confined to collecting labor force data. While the interviewers are in the households, they ask an additional set of questions. By using a different set of special questions each month, the CPS covers almost all of the major subfields of demographic in the course of a year. By always using a particular month to obtain data about a particular topic, it generates series of data exactly one year apart. For example, the CPS schedule includes the following:

March–mobility and migration, households, marital status, and income
June–fertility
October–school enrollment and education
November–voting.

The monthly data concerning employment and unemployment are published by the Bureau of Labor Statistics in a publication titled *Employment and Earnings.* Additional data are published in four sets of the *Current Population Reports:*

Series P-20–"Population Characteristics"
Series P-23–"Special Reports"
Series P-27–"Farm Population"
Series P-60–"Consumer Income."

Following are the titles of some reports that have been produced from the Current Population Survey:

Series P-20 and Series P-23

Marital Status and Living Arrangements
Fertility of American Women
Household and Family Characteristics
School Enrollment: Social and Economic Characteristics of Students
Educational Attainment in the United States
Voting and Registration
Geographic Mobility
Major Field of Study of College Students
Persons of Spanish Origin in the United States
Travel to School
Relative Progress of Children in School
Marriage, Divorce, Widowhood, and Remarriage
Trends in Childspacing
Nursery School and Kindergarten Enrollment of Children and Labor Force Status of Their Mothers
Divorces in the United States
Daytime Care of Children
College Plans of High School Seniors
Characteristics of the Population by Ethnic Origin
Undergraduate Enrollment in Two-Year and Four-Year Colleges

Fertility Histories and Birth Expectancies of American Women
Labor Union Membership
Population Profile of the United States

Series P-27
Farm Population of the United States

Series P-60
Money Income of Households, Families, and Persons in the United States
Poverty States of the United States Population
Projections of Income Size Distribution
Lifetime Earnings Estimates for Men and Women
Receipt of Noncash Benefits
Characteristics of Households and Persons Receiving Noncash Benefits

These titles illustrate the variety of topics covered. An examination of the reports will show that a great deal of creativity has gone into the design of the tables and the categorization of the variables. As a result, over the course of a year most of the topics covered in the decennial census are updated with an impressive degree of rich detail.

The Population of the United States relies heavily upon the data of the Current Population Survey, particularly for the years since the 1980 census. For this volume, publications received as of July 1, 1984, were included. Readers may update the materials of most chapters by obtaining more recent editions of the Current Population Survey reports cited in the tables. The highlights of these reports are summarized each year in the *Statistical Abstract of the United States*, which can be consulted if the reader does not have access to the CPS reports.

Chapter 3

Population Distribution: An Overview

Population distribution is the pattern by which the population is arranged within the physical space of the national boundaries. It takes three forms:

1. Differential density of settlement
2. Differential population composition
3. Differential rates of growth and change.

This chapter presents an overview of the distribution of the U.S. population in each of the three forms in terms of the demographic variables discussed in Chapter 2. It also introduces each of five principal systems of classification used to portray distribution and lays the groundwork for a distributional analysis of each of the topics to be discussed in subsequent chapters.

The unique aspect of distributional analysis is that the population is divided into subareas, according to some criterion, and the population that inhabits each subarea is studied as a separate entity. Instead of a single population total for the nation, there is a subtotal for each areal subdivision. The U.S. Bureau of the Census and the National Center for Health Statistics are generous in providing population data and vital statistics for subareas of the population, so that almost as much information is available about the principal areal parts of the nation as for the national total.

Five ways of dividing the area of the United States are used for studying the pattern of population distribution:

1. States, geographic divisions, and regions
2. Urban and rural residence; urbanized areas
3. Metropolitan and nonmetropolitan areas
4. Counties or county equivalents
5. Census tracts, blocks, and enumeration districts.

This chapter provides definitions of all five systems and makes a distributional analysis for each of the first three. Because of the enormous numbers of measurements involved, only general descriptions are presented for the fourth and fifth systems.

In this chapter, as in all following chapters, the statistical tables contain far too much detail to be fully discussed in the text. They have been selected and prepared to provide a comprehensive record, enabling each reader to study aspects of particular interest, guided by the general interpretive comments focusing on highlights and major differences and changes.

States, Geographic Divisions, and Regions

Because the United States is a union of states, there are both legal and administrative reasons why as much information should be provided for each state as for the nation, insofar as resources and data permit. Thus the fifty states are primary areal subdivisions for the study of population distribution. For a combination of reasons involving differences in geography, economy, history, and the characteristics of the inhabitants, the states tend to be clustered into regions of coterminous states. Two such regional systems of delimitation are in common use: the nine geographic divisions, which in turn can be combined to form four geographic regions. Figure 3-1 illustrates how the states are grouped into these clusters. Table 3-1A reports the total population of these units as enumerated at each census of the last 190 years.

Definitions

Urban and Rural Residence. As defined for the 1980 census, the urban population comprises all persons living in urbanized areas and in places of 2,500 or more inhabitants outside urbanized areas. The population not classified as urban constitutes the rural population.

In censuses prior to 1950, the urban population comprised all persons living in incorporated places of 2,500 or more inhabitants and areas (usually minor civil divisions) classified as urban under special rules relating to population size and density. A definition of urban population restricted to incorporated places having 2,500 or more inhabitants excludes a number of large and densely settled areas merely because they are not incorporated. Prior to 1950, an effort was made to avoid some of the more obvious omissions by inclusion of selected areas which were classified as urban under special rules. Even with these rules, however, the inhabitants of many large and closely built-up areas were excluded from the urban population.

To improve its measure of the urban population, the Bureau of the Census in1950 adopted the concept of the urbanized area and delineated boundaries for unincorporated places.

Urbanized Areas. An urbanized area consists of a central city or cities and surrouding closely settled territory or "urban fringe."

There are 366 urbanized areas delineated in the United States for the 1980 census.

The following criteria are used in determining the eligibility and definition of the 1980 urbanized areas.

An urbanized area comprises an incorporated place and adjacent densely settled surrounding area that together have a minimum population of 50,000. The densely settled surrounding area consists of:

1. Contiguous incorporated places or census designated places having:
   a. A population of 2,500 or more; or,
   b. A population of fewer than 2,500 but having either a population density of 1,000 persons per square mile, a closely settled area containing a minimum of 50 percent of the population, or a cluster of at least 100 housing units.
2. Contiguous incorporated area which is connected by road and has a population density of at least 1,000 persons per square mile.
3. Other contiguous unincorporated area with a density of less than 1,000 persons per square mile, provided that it:
   a. Eliminates an enclave of less than 5 square miles which is surrounded by built-up area.
   b. Closes an indentation in the boundary of the densely settled area that is no more than 1 mile across the open end and encompasses no more than 5 square miles.
   c. Links an outlying area of qualifying density, provided that the outlying area is:
      (1) Connected by road to, and is not more than 1½ miles from, the main body of the urbanized area.
      (2) Separated from the main body of the urbanized area by water or other undevelopable area, is connected by road to the main body of the urbanized area, and is not more than 5 miles from the main body of the urbanized area.
4. Large concentrations of nonresidential urban area (such as industrial parks, office areas, and major airports), which have at least one-quarter of their boundary contiguous to an urbanized area.

Standard Metropolitan Statistical Areas. The general concept of a metropolitan area is one of a large population nucleus, together with adjacent communities which have a high degree of economic and social integration with that nucleus. The standard metropolitan statistical area (SMSA) classification is a statistical standard, developed for use by Federal agencies in the production, analysis, and publication of data on metropolitan areas. The SMSAs are designated and defined by the Office of Management and Budget, following a set of official published standards developed by the interagency Federal Committee on Standard Metropolitan Statistical Areas.

Continued on next page

Definitions

Each SMSA has one or more central counties containing the area's main population concentration: an urbanized area with at least 50,000 inhabitants. An SMSA may also include outlying counties which have close economic and social relationships with the central counties. The outlying counties must have a specified level of commuting to the central counties and must also meet certain standards regarding metropolitan character, such as population density, urban population, and population growth. In New England, SMSAs are composed of cities and towns rather than whole counties.

There are 318 SMSAs designated in the United States for the 1980 census.

The population living in SMSAs may also be referred to as the metropolitan population. This population is subdivided into "inside central city (or cities)" and "outside central city (or cities)." The population living outside SMSAs constitutes the nonmetropolitan population.

SMSA Titles. Most SMSAs have at least one central city. The titles of SMSAs include up to three city names, as well as the names of each state into which the SMSA extends. For the 1980 census, central cities of SMSAs are those named in the titles of the SMSAs, with the exception of Nassau-Suffolk, N.Y., which has no central city, and Northeast Pennsylvania, the central cities of which are Scranton, Wilkes-Barre, and Hazleton. Data on central cities of SMSAs include the entire population within the legal city boundaries. In Hawaii, where there are no incorporated places recognized by the Bureau of the Census, census designated places are recognized as central cities.

Standard Consolidated Statistical Areas. In some parts of the country, metropolitan development has progressed to the point that adjoining SMSAs are themselves socially and economically interrelated. These areas are designated standard consolidated statistical areas (SCSAs) by the Office of Management and Budget, and are defined using standards included as part of the new SMSA standards described above.

Table 3-1B shows a percentage distribution of the population among the various areas. Table 3-1C reports the intercensal growth rates for this same period of time. Table 3-1D reports land area and density for selected dates. The history of the settlement of the nation is contained in these four tables. Tables 3-2A and 3-2B report the race composition of each state, division, and region in 1980 in numbers and as a percent distribution. Table 3-3 provides the same information for the Spanish-origin population by nation of origin. Table 3-4 presents summary age and sex statistics for each of these areal units. In analyzing all of these tables, the central point of reference, for comparison purposes, is the totals for the nation; regional differences consist in deviations from the average statistics for the nation. Secondary comparisons can then be made among and between the areal units.

Population Growth

Between 1970 and 1980 the Northeast region had very nearly zero growth, and the North Central region grew very little. Almost all of the population increase of the country took place in the South and West. The fastest-growing states were Nevada, Arizona, Florida, Wyoming, Utah, Alaska, Idaho, and Colorado, which all grew by 30 percent or more during the decade. All of the older industrial states of the Atlantic Seaboard, from Massachusetts to Maryland, had practically zero growth, and New York suffered a major absolute decline. Figure 3-2 divides the states into two main classes: those that grew faster in 1970-80 than they did in 1960-70 (above the diagonal) and those that grew slower (below the diagonal). The westward drift of population is of many decades' duration, as old as the nation itself, but the drift from the Northeast and North into the "Sunbelt" of the South and West is primarily a phenomenon that began in the 1950s and has remained strong since. As later chapters will make clear, for most states these growth differences are primarily the product of migration, both internal and international.

Table 3-1C shows that the West region, especially the Pacific division, has grown at rates roughly double those for the nation during every decade since 1850. The Northeast, by contrast, has managed to grow only at rates well below the national level in most decades, arriving at zero growth between 1970 and 1980. This has been caused primarily by prolonged outmigration to regions in the West. The North Central region grew rapidly during the phase of its settlement (1800-1900) but has

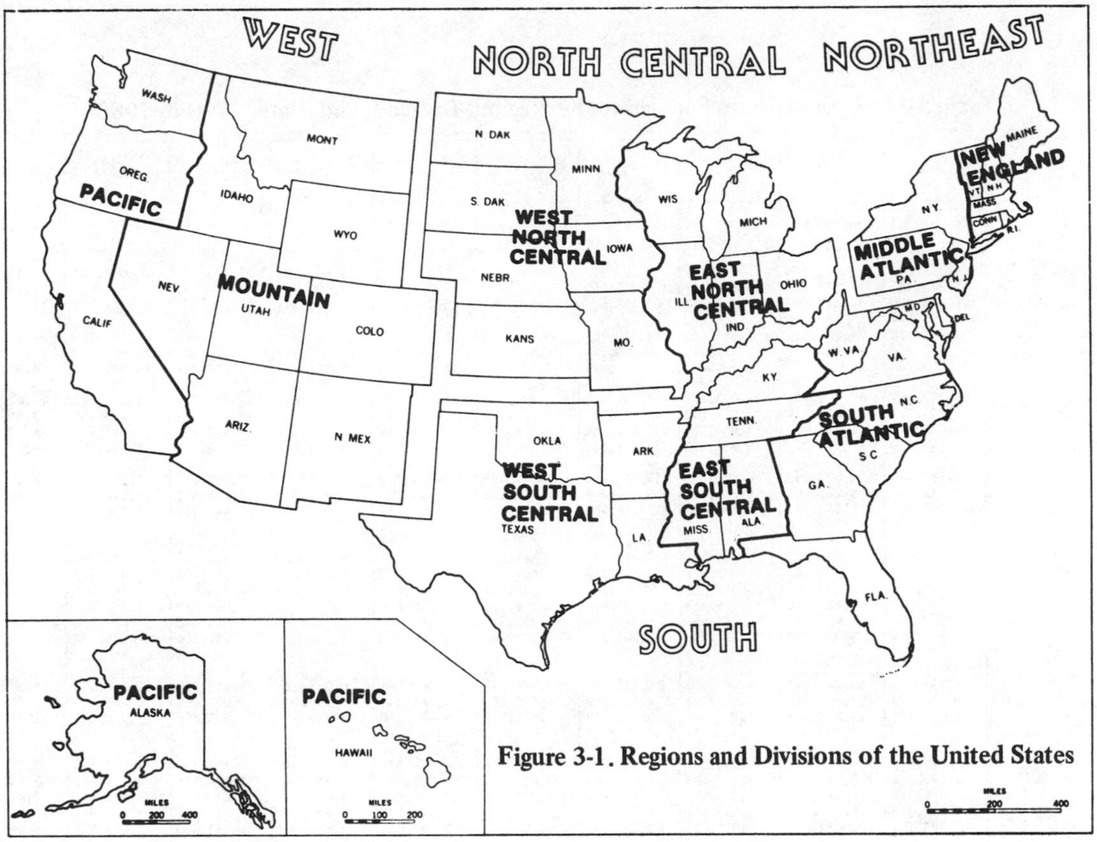

Figure 3-1. Regions and Divisions of the United States

Source: U.S. Bureau of the Census. "General Population Characteristics: United States Summary." 1980 Census of the Population. Washington, DC: U.S. Government Printing Office, 1983, Figure 1.

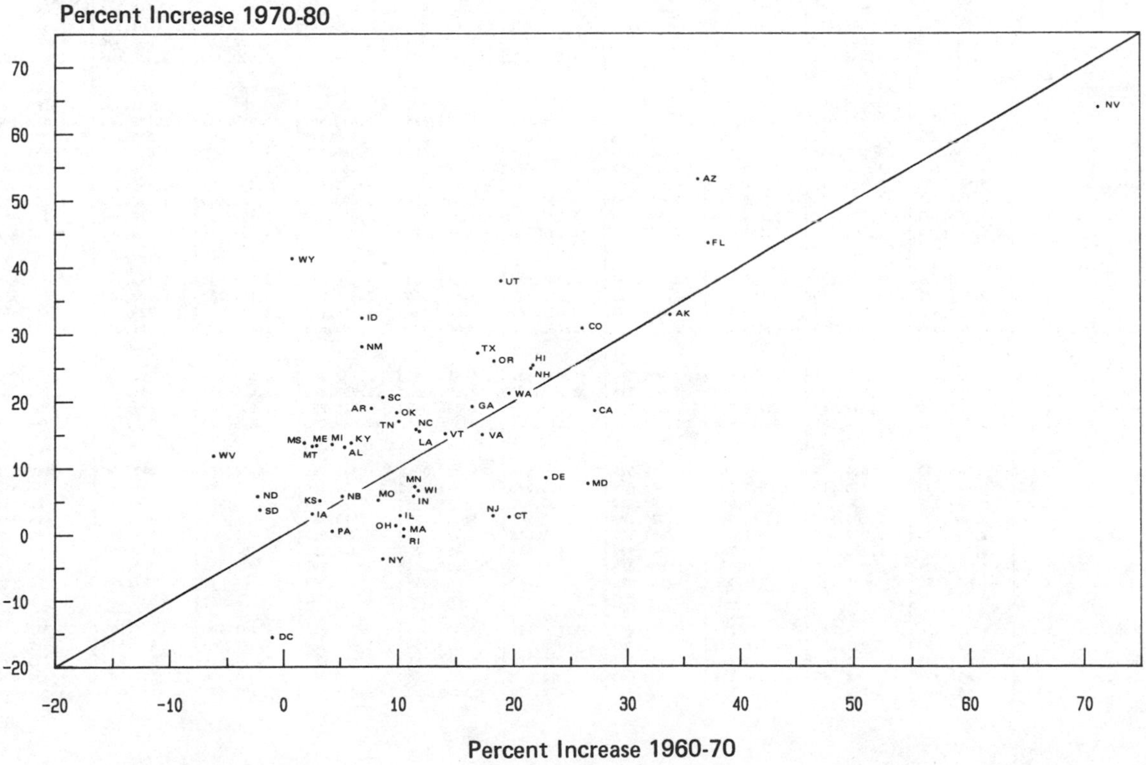

Figure 3-2. Percent Increase in the Population of the States: 1970-80 Against 1960-70

Table 3-1A. United States Population, by Region, Division, and State: 1790 to 1980

Region, division, and state	1980	1970	1960	1950	1940	1930	1920	1910	1900	1890
United States, total.	226,545,805	203,302,031	179,323,175	151,325,798	132,164,569	123,202,624	106,021,537	92,228,496	76,212,168	62,979,766
Northeast region.	49,135,283	49,060,514	44,677,819	39,477,986	35,976,777	34,427,091	29,662,053	25,868,573	21,046,695	17,406,969
New England	12,348,493	11,847,245	10,509,367	9,314,453	8,437,290	8,166,341	7,400,909	6,552,681	5,592,017	4,700,749
Middle Atlantic	36,786,790	37,213,269	34,168,452	30,163,533	27,539,487	26,260,750	22,261,144	19,315,892	15,454,678	12,706,220
North Central region.	58,865,670	56,590,294	51,619,139	44,460,762	40,143,332	38,594,100	34,019,792	29,888,542	26,333,004	22,410,417
East North Central.	41,682,217	40,262,747	36,225,024	30,399,368	26,626,342	25,297,185	21,475,543	18,250,621	15,985,581	13,478,305
West North Central.	17,183,453	16,327,547	15,394,115	14,061,394	13,516,990	13,296,915	12,544,249	11,637,921	10,347,423	8,932,112
South region.	75,372,362	62,812,980	54,973,113	47,197,088	41,665,901	37,857,633	33,125,803	29,389,330	24,523,527	20,028,059
South Atlantic.	35,959,123	30,628,826	25,971,732	21,182,335	17,823,151	15,793,589	13,990,272	12,194,895	10,443,480	8,857,922
East South Central.	14,666,423	12,808,077	12,050,126	11,477,181	10,778,225	9,887,214	8,893,307	8,409,901	7,547,757	6,429,154
West South Central.	23,746,816	19,326,077	16,951,255	14,537,572	13,064,525	12,176,830	10,242,224	8,784,534	6,532,290	4,740,983
West region	43,172,490	34,838,243	28,053,104	20,189,962	14,378,559	12,323,800	9,213,889	7,082,051	4,308,942	3,134,321
Mountain.	11,372,785	8,289,901	6,855,060	5,074,998	4,150,003	3,701,789	3,336,101	2,633,517	1,674,657	1,213,935
Pacific	31,799,705	26,548,342	21,198,044	15,114,964	10,228,556	8,622,011	5,877,788	4,448,534	2,634,285	1,920,386
New England										
Maine	1,124,660	993,722	969,265	913,774	847,226	797,423	768,014	742,371	694,466	661,086
New Hampshire	920,610	737,681	606,921	533,242	491,524	465,293	443,083	430,572	411,588	376,530
Vermont	511,456	444,732	389,881	377,747	359,231	359,611	352,428	355,956	343,641	332,422
Massachusetts	5,737,037	5,689,170	5,148,578	4,690,514	4,316,721	4,249,614	3,852,356	3,366,416	2,805,346	2,238,947
Rhode Island.	947,154	949,723	859,488	791,896	713,346	687,497	604,397	542,610	428,556	345,506
Connecticut	3,107,576	3,032,217	2,535,234	2,007,280	1,709,242	1,606,903	1,380,631	1,114,756	908,420	746,258
Middle Atlantic										
New York.	17,558,072	18,241,391	16,782,304	14,830,192	13,479,142	12,588,066	10,385,227	9,113,614	7,268,894	6,003,174
New Jersey.	7,364,823	7,171,112	6,066,782	4,835,329	4,160,165	4,041,334	3,155,900	2,537,167	1,883,669	1,444,933
Pennsylvania.	11,863,895	11,800,766	11,319,366	10,498,012	9,900,180	9,631,350	8,720,017	7,665,111	6,302,115	5,258,113
East North Central										
Ohio.	10,797,630	10,657,423	9,706,397	7,946,627	6,907,612	6,646,697	5,759,394	4,767,121	4,157,545	3,672,329
Indiana	5,490,224	5,195,392	4,662,498	3,934,224	3,427,796	3,238,503	2,930,390	2,700,876	2,516,462	2,192,404
Illinois.	11,426,518	11,110,285	10,081,158	8,712,176	7,897,241	7,630,654	6,485,280	5,638,591	4,821,550	3,826,352
Michigan.	9,262,078	8,881,826	7,823,194	6,371,766	5,256,106	4,842,325	3,668,412	2,810,173	2,420,982	2,093,890
Wisconsin	4,705,767	4,417,821	3,951,777	3,434,575	3,137,587	2,939,006	2,632,067	2,333,860	2,069,042	1,693,330
West North Central										
Minnesota	4,075,970	3,806,103	3,413,864	2,982,483	2,792,300	2,563,953	2,387,125	2,075,708	1,751,394	1,310,283
Iowa.	2,913,808	2,825,368	2,757,537	2,621,073	2,538,268	2,470,939	2,404,021	2,224,771	2,231,853	1,912,297
Missouri.	4,916,686	4,677,623	4,319,813	3,954,653	3,784,664	3,629,367	3,404,055	3,293,335	3,106,665	2,679,185
North Dakota.	652,717	617,792	632,446	619,636	641,935	680,845	646,872	577,056	319,146	190,983
South Dakota.	690,768	666,257	680,514	652,740	642,961	692,849	636,547	583,888	401,570	348,600
Nebraska.	1,569,825	1,485,333	1,411,330	1,325,510	1,315,834	1,377,963	1,296,372	1,192,214	1,066,300	1,062,656
Kansas.	2,363,679	2,249,071	2,178,611	1,905,299	1,801,028	1,880,999	1,769,257	1,690,949	1,470,495	1,428,108
South Atlantic										
Delaware.	594,338	548,104	446,292	318,085	266,505	238,380	223,003	202,322	184,735	168,493
Maryland.	4,216,975	3,923,897	3,100,698	2,343,001	1,821,244	1,631,526	1,449,661	1,295,346	1,188,044	1,042,390
District of Columbia.	638,333	756,668	763,956	802,178	663,091	486,869	437,571	331,069	278,718	230,392
Virginia.	5,346,818	4,651,448	3,966,949	3,318,680	2,677,773	2,421,851	2,309,187	2,061,612	1,854,184	1,655,980
West Virginia	1,949,644	1,744,237	1,860,421	2,005,552	1,901,974	1,729,205	1,463,701	1,221,119	958,800	762,794
North Carolina.	5,881,766	5,084,411	4,556,155	4,061,929	3,571,623	3,170,276	2,559,123	2,206,287	1,893,810	1,617,949
South Carolina.	3,121,820	2,590,713	2,382,594	2,117,027	1,899,804	1,738,765	1,683,724	1,515,400	1,340,316	1,151,149
Georgia	5,463,105	4,587,930	3,943,116	3,444,578	3,123,723	2,908,506	2,895,832	2,609,121	2,216,331	1,837,353
Florida	9,746,324	6,791,418	4,951,560	2,771,305	1,897,414	1,468,211	968,470	752,619	528,542	391,422
East South Central										
Kentucky.	3,660,777	3,220,711	3,038,156	2,944,806	2,845,627	2,614,589	2,416,630	2,289,905	2,147,174	1,858,635
Tennessee	4,591,120	3,926,018	3,567,089	3,291,718	2,915,841	2,616,556	2,337,885	2,184,789	2,020,616	1,767,518
Alabama	3,893,888	3,444,354	3,266,740	3,061,743	2,832,961	2,646,248	2,348,174	2,138,093	1,828,697	1,513,401
Mississippi	2,520,638	2,216,994	2,178,141	2,178,914	2,183,796	2,009,821	1,790,618	1,797,114	1,551,270	1,289,600
West South Central										
Arkansas.	2,286,435	1,923,322	1,786,272	1,909,511	1,949,387	1,854,482	1,752,204	1,574,449	1,311,564	1,128,211
Louisiana	4,205,900	3,644,637	3,257,022	2,683,516	2,363,880	2,101,593	1,798,509	1,656,388	1,381,625	1,118,588
Oklahoma.	3,025,290	2,599,463	2,328,284	2,233,351	2,336,434	2,396,040	2,028,283	1,657,155	790,391	258,657
Texas	14,229,191	11,198,655	9,579,677	7,711,194	6,414,824	5,824,715	4,663,228	3,896,542	3,048,710	2,235,527
Mountain										
Montana	786,690	694,409	674,767	591,024	559,456	537,606	548,889	376,053	243,329	142,924
Idaho	943,935	713,015	667,191	588,637	524,873	445,032	431,866	325,594	161,772	88,548
Wyoming	469,557	332,416	330,066	290,529	250,742	225,565	194,402	145,965	95,531	62,555
Colorado.	2,889,964	2,209,596	1,753,947	1,325,089	1,123,296	1,035,791	939,629	799,024	539,700	413,249
New Mexico.	1,302,894	1,017,055	951,023	681,187	531,818	423,317	360,350	327,301	195,310	160,282
Arizona	2,718,215	1,775,399	1,302,161	749,587	499,261	435,573	334,162	204,354	122,931	88,243
Utah.	1,461,037	1,059,273	890,627	688,862	550,310	507,847	449,396	373,351	276,749	210,779
Nevada.	800,493	488,738	285,278	160,083	110,247	91,058	77,407	81,875	42,335	47,355
Pacific										
Washington.	4,132,156	3,413,244	2,853,214	2,378,963	1,736,191	1,563,396	1,356,621	1,141,990	518,103	357,232
Oregon.	2,633,105	2,091,533	1,768,687	1,521,341	1,089,684	953,786	783,389	672,765	413,536	317,704
California.	23,667,902	19,971,069	15,717,204	10,586,223	6,907,387	5,677,251	3,426,861	2,377,549	1,485,053	1,213,398
Alaska.	401,851	302,583	226,167	128,643	72,524	59,278	55,036	64,356	63,592	32,052
Hawaii.	964,691	769,913	632,772	499,794	422,770	368,300	255,881	191,874	154,001	...

Table 3-1A. United States Population, by Region, Division, and State: 1790 to 1980—continued

Region, division, and state	1880	1870	1860	1850	1840	1830	1820	1810	1800	1790
United States, total. .	50,189,209	38,558,371	31,443,321	23,191,876	17,063,353	12,860,702	9,638,453	7,239,881	5,308,483	3.929,214
Northeast region.	14,507,407	12,298,730	10,594,268	8,626,851	6,761,082	5,542,381	4,359,916	3,486,675	2,635,576	1,968,040
New England	4,010,529	3,487,924	3,135,283	2,728,116	2,234,822	1,954,717	1,660,071	1,471,973	1,233,011	1,009,408
Middle Atlantic	10,496,878	8,810,806	7,458,985	5,898,735	4,526,260	3,587,664	2,699,845	2,014,702	1,407,565	958,632
North Central region. . .	17,364,111	12,981,111	9,096,716	5,403,595	3,351,542	1,610,473	859,305	292,107	51,006	...
East North Central. . .	11,206,668	9,124,517	6,926,884	4,523,260	2,924,728	1,470,018	792,719	272,324	51,006	...
West North Central. . .	6,157,443	3,856,594	2,169,832	880,335	426,814	140,455	66,586	19,783	...	...
South region.	16,516,568	12,288,020	11,133,361	8,982,612	6,950,729	5,707,848	4,419,232	3,461,099	2,621,901	1,961,174
South Atlantic.	7,597,197	5,853,610	5,364,703	4,679,090	3,925,299	3,645,752	3,061,063	2,674,891	2,286,494	1,851,806
East South Atlantic . .	5,585,151	4,404,445	4,020,991	3,363,271	2,575,445	1,815,969	1,190,489	708,590	335,407	109,368
West South Central. . .	3,334,220	2,029,965	1,747,667	940,251	449,985	246,127	167,680	77,618	...	...
West region	1,801,123	990,510	618,976	178,818	...	...	...	...	...	...
Mountain.	653,119	315,385	174,923	72,927	...	...	...	...	...	...
Pacific	1,148,004	675,125	444,053	105,891	...	...	...	...	...	...
New England										
Maine	648,936	626,915	628,279	583,169	501,793	399,455	298,335	228,705	151,719	96,540
New Hampshire	346,991	318,300	326,073	317,976	284,574	269,328	244,161	214,460	183,858	141,885
Vermont	332,286	330,551	315,098	314,120	291,948	280,652	235,981	217,895	154,465	85,425
Massachusetts	1,783,085	1,457,351	1,231,066	994,514	737,699	610,408	523,287	472,040	422,845	378,787
Rhode Island.	276,531	217,353	174,620	147,545	108,830	97,199	83,059	76,931	69,122	68,825
Connecticut	622,700	537,454	460,147	370,792	309,978	297,675	275,248	261,942	251,002	237,946
Middle Atlantic										
New York.	5,082,871	4,382,759	3,880,735	3,097,394	2,428,921	1,918,608	1,372,812	959,049	589,051	340,120
New Jersey.	1,131,116	906,096	672,035	489,555	373,306	320,823	277,575	245,562	211,149	184,139
Pennsylvania.	4,282,891	3,521,951	2,906,215	2,311,786	1,724,033	1,348,233	1,049,458	810,091	602,365	434,373
East North Central										
Ohio.	3,198,062	2,665,260	2,339,511	1,980,329	1,519,467	937,903	581,434	230,760	45,365	...
Indiana	1,978,301	1,680,637	1,350,428	988,416	685,866	343,031	147,178	24,520	5,641	...
Illinois.	3,077,871	2,539,891	1,711,951	851,470	476,183	157,445	55,211	12,282	...	...
Michigan.	1,636,937	1,184,059	749,113	397,654	212,267	31,639	8,896	4,762	...	...
Wisconsin	1,315,497	1,054,670	775,881	305,391	30,945	...	...	...	...	...
West North Central										
Minnesota	780,773	439,706	172,023	6,077	...	...	...	...	...	...
Iowa.	1,624,615	1,194,020	674,913	192,214	43,112	...	...	...	...	...
Missouri.	2,168,380	1,721,295	1,182,012	682,044	383,702	140,455	66,586	19,783	...	...
North Dakota.	36,909	2,405	...	...	...	...	...	...	...	...
South Dakota.	98,268	11,776	4,837	...	...	...	...	...	...	...
Nebraska.	452,402	122,993	28,841	...	...	...	...	...	...	...
Kansas.	996,096	364,399	107,206	...	...	...	...	...	...	...
South Atlantic										
Delaware.	146,608	125,015	112,216	91,532	78,085	76,748	72,749	72,674	64,273	59,096
Maryland.	934,943	780,894	687,049	583,034	470,019	447,040	407,350	380,546	341,548	319,728
District of Columbia. .	177,624	131,700	75,080	51,687	33,745	30,261	23,336	15,471	8,144	...
Virginia.	1,512,565	1,225,163	1,219,630	1,119,348	1,025,227	1,044,054	938,261	877,683	807,557	691,737
West Virginia	618,457	442,014	376,688	302,313	224,537	176,924	136,808	105,469	78,592	55,873
North Carolina.	1,399,750	1,071,361	992,622	869,039	753,419	737,987	638,829	555,500	478,103	393,751
South Carolina.	995,577	705,606	703,708	668,507	594,398	581,185	502,741	415,115	345,591	289,073
Georgia	1,542,180	1,184,109	1,057,286	906,185	691,392	516,823	340,989	252,433	162,686	82,948
Florida	269,493	187,748	140,424	87,445	54,477	34,730	...	...	...	...
East South Central										
Kentucky.	1,648,690	1,321,011	1,155,684	982,405	779,828	687,917	564,317	406,511	220,955	73,677
Tennessee	1,542,359	1,258,520	1,109,801	1,002,717	829,210	681,904	422,823	261,727	105,602	35,691
Alabama	1,262,505	996,992	964,201	771,623	590,756	309,527	127,901	9,046	1,250	...
Mississippi	1,131,597	827,922	791,305	606,526	375,651	136,621	75,448	31,306	7,600	...
West South Central										
Arkansas.	802,525	484,471	435,450	209,897	97,574	30,388	14,273	1,062	...	...
Louisiana	939,946	726,915	708,002	517,762	352,411	215,739	153,407	76,556	...	...
Oklahoma.	...	...	...	...	...	...	...	...	...	...
Texas	1,591,749	818,579	604,215	212,592	...	...	...	...	...	...
Mountain										
Montana	39,159	20,595	...	...	...	...	...	...	...	...
Idaho	32,610	14,999	...	...	...	...	...	...	...	...
Wyoming	20,789	9,118	...	...	...	...	...	...	...	...
Colorado.	194,327	39,864	34,277	...	...	...	...	...	...	...
New Mexico.	119,565	91,874	93,516	61,547	...	...	...	...	...	...
Arizona	40,440	9,658	...	...	...	...	...	...	...	...
Utah.	143,963	86,786	40,273	11,380	...	...	...	...	...	...
Nevada.	62,266	42,491	6,857	...	...	...	...	...	...	...
Pacific										
Washington.	75,116	23,955	11,594	1,201	...	...	...	...	...	...
Oregon.	174,768	90,923	52,465	12,093	...	...	...	...	...	...
California.	864,694	560,247	379,994	92,597	...	...	...	...	...	...
Alaska.	33,426	...	...	...	...	...	...	...	...	...
Hawaii.	...	...	...	...	...	...	...	...	...	...

Source: U.S. Bureau of the Census. "Number of Inhabitants: United States Summary." 1980 Census of Population. Washington, DC: U.S. Government Printing Office, 1983, Table 8.

Table 3-1B. Percent Distribution of the Population, by Region, Division, and State: 1790 to 1980

Region, division, and state	1980	1970	1960	1950	1940	1930	1920	1910	1900	1890
United States, total	100.00	100.00	100.00	100.00	100.00	100.00	100.00	100.00	100.00	100.00
Northeast region	21.69	24.13	24.91	26.09	27.22	27.94	27.98	28.05	27.62	27.64
New England	5.45	5.83	5.86	6.16	6.38	6.63	6.98	7.10	7.34	7.46
Middle Atlantic	16.24	18.30	19.05	19.93	20.84	21.32	21.00	20.94	20.28	20.18
North Central	25.98	27.84	28.79	29.38	30.37	31.33	32.09	32.41	34.55	35.58
East North Central	18.40	19.80	20.20	20.09	20.15	20.53	20.26	19.79	20.98	21.40
West North Central	7.58	8.03	8.58	9.29	10.23	10.79	11.83	12.62	13.58	14.18
South	33.27	30.90	30.66	31.19	31.53	30.73	31.24	31.07	32.18	31.80
South Atlantic	16.31	15.09	14.48	14.00	13.49	12.82	13.20	13.22	13.70	14.06
East South Central	6.47	6.30	6.72	7.58	8.16	8.03	8.39	9.12	9.90	10.21
West South Central	10.48	9.51	9.45	9.61	9.89	9.88	9.66	9.52	8.57	7.53
West	19.06	17.14	15.64	13.34	10.88	10.00	8.69	7.68	5.65	4.98
Mountain	5.02	4.08	3.82	3.35	3.14	3.00	3.15	2.86	2.20	1.93
Pacific	14.04	13.06	11.82	9.99	7.74	7.00	5.54	4.82	3.46	3.05
New England										
Maine	0.50	0.49	0.54	0.60	0.64	0.65	0.72	0.80	0.91	1.05
New Hampshire	0.41	0.36	0.34	0.35	0.37	0.38	0.42	0.47	0.54	0.60
Vermont	0.23	0.22	0.22	0.25	0.27	0.29	0.33	0.39	0.45	0.53
Massachusetts	2.53	2.80	2.87	3.10	3.27	3.45	3.63	3.65	3.68	3.56
Rhode Island	0.42	0.47	0.48	0.52	0.54	0.56	0.57	0.59	0.56	0.55
Connecticut	1.37	1.49	1.41	1.33	1.29	1.30	1.30	1.21	1.19	1.18
Middle Atlantic										
New York	7.75	8.97	9.36	9.80	10.20	10.22	9.80	9.88	9.54	9.53
New Jersey	3.25	3.53	3.38	3.20	3.15	3.28	2.98	2.75	2.47	2.29
Pennsylvania	5.24	5.80	6.31	6.94	7.49	7.82	8.22	8.31	8.27	8.35
East North Central										
Ohio	4.77	5.24	5.41	5.25	5.23	5.39	5.43	5.17	5.46	5.83
Indiana	2.42	2.56	2.60	2.60	2.59	2.63	2.76	2.93	3.30	3.48
Illinois	5.04	5.46	5.62	5.76	5.98	6.19	6.12	6.11	6.33	6.08
Michigan	4.09	4.37	4.36	4.21	3.98	3.93	3.46	3.05	3.18	3.32
Wisconsin	2.08	2.17	2.20	2.27	2.37	2.39	2.48	2.53	2.71	2.69
West North Central										
Minnesota	1.80	1.87	1.90	1.97	2.11	2.08	2.25	2.25	2.30	2.08
Iowa	1.29	1.39	1.54	1.73	1.92	2.01	2.27	2.41	2.93	3.04
Missouri	2.17	2.30	2.41	2.61	2.86	2.95	3.21	3.57	4.08	4.25
North Dakota	0.29	0.30	0.35	0.41	0.49	0.55	0.61	0.63	0.42	0.30
South Dakota	0.30	0.33	0.38	0.43	0.49	0.56	0.60	0.63	0.53	0.55
Nebraska	0.69	0.73	0.79	0.88	1.00	1.12	1.22	1.29	1.40	1.69
Kansas	1.04	1.11	1.21	1.26	1.36	1.53	1.67	1.83	1.93	2.27
South Atlantic										
Delaware	0.26	0.27	0.25	0.21	0.20	0.19	0.21	0.22	0.24	0.27
Maryland	1.86	1.93	1.73	1.55	1.38	1.32	1.37	1.40	1.56	1.66
District of Columbia	0.28	0.37	0.43	0.53	0.50	0.40	0.41	0.36	0.37	0.37
Virginia	2.36	2.29	2.21	2.19	2.03	1.97	2.18	2.24	2.43	2.63
West Virginia	0.86	0.86	1.04	1.33	1.44	1.40	1.38	1.32	1.26	1.21
North Carolina	2.60	2.50	2.54	2.68	2.70	2.57	2.41	2.39	2.48	2.57
South Carolina	1.38	1.27	1.33	1.40	1.44	1.41	1.59	1.64	1.76	1.83
Georgia	2.41	2.26	2.20	2.28	2.36	2.36	2.73	2.83	2.91	2.92
Florida	4.30	3.34	2.76	1.83	1.44	1.19	0.91	0.82	0.69	0.62
East South Central										
Kentucky	1.62	1.58	1.69	1.95	2.15	2.12	2.28	2.48	2.82	2.95
Tennessee	2.03	1.93	1.99	2.18	2.21	2.12	2.21	2.37	2.65	2.81
Alabama	1.72	1.69	1.82	2.02	2.14	2.15	2.21	2.32	2.40	2.40
Mississippi	1.11	1.09	1.21	1.44	1.65	1.63	1.69	1.95	2.04	2.05
West South Central										
Arkansas	1.01	0.95	1.00	1.26	1.47	1.51	1.65	1.71	1.72	1.79
Louisiana	1.86	1.79	1.82	1.77	1.79	1.71	1.70	1.80	1.81	1.78
Oklahoma	1.34	1.26	1.30	1.48	1.77	1.94	1.91	1.80	1.04	0.41
Texas	6.28	5.51	5.34	5.10	4.85	4.73	4.40	4.22	4.00	3.55
Mountain										
Montana	0.35	0.34	0.38	0.39	0.42	0.44	0.52	0.41	0.32	0.23
Idaho	0.42	0.35	0.37	0.39	0.40	0.36	0.41	0.35	0.21	0.14
Wyoming	0.21	0.16	0.18	0.19	0.19	0.18	0.18	0.16	0.12	0.10
Colorado	1.28	1.09	0.98	0.88	0.85	0.84	0.89	0.87	0.71	0.66
New Mexico	0.58	0.50	0.53	0.45	0.40	0.34	0.34	0.35	0.26	0.25
Arizona	1.20	0.87	0.73	0.50	0.38	0.35	0.32	0.22	0.16	0.14
Utah	0.64	0.52	0.50	0.46	0.42	0.41	0.42	0.40	0.36	0.33
Nevada	0.35	0.24	0.16	0.11	0.08	0.07	0.07	0.09	0.06	0.08
Pacific										
Washington	1.82	1.68	1.59	1.57	1.31	1.27	1.28	1.24	0.68	0.57
Oregon	1.16	1.03	0.99	1.01	0.82	0.77	0.74	0.73	0.54	0.50
California	10.45	9.82	8.76	7.00	5.23	4.61	3.23	2.58	1.95	1.93
Alaska	0.18	0.15	0.13	0.09	0.05	0.05	0.05	0.07	0.08	0.05
Hawaii	0.43	0.38	0.35	0.33	0.32	0.30	0.24	0.21	0.20	...

Table 3-1B. Percent Distribution of the Population, by Region, Division, and State: 1790 to 1980—continued

Region, division, and state	1880	1870	1860	1850	1840	1830	1820	1810	1800	1790
United States, total. .	100.00	100.00	100.00	100.00	100.00	100.00	100.00	100.00	100.00	100.00
Northeast region.	28.91	31.90	33.70	37.20	39.62	43.10	45.23	48.16	49.65	50.09
New England	7.99	9.05	9.97	11.76	13.09	15.20	17.22	20.33	23.23	25.69
Middle Atlantic	20.91	22.85	23.73	25.43	26.53	27.90	28.01	27.83	26.42	24.40
North Central region. . .	34.60	33.67	28.93	23.30	19.64	12.52	8.92	4.03	0.96	...
East North Central. . .	22.33	23.66	22.03	19.50	17.14	11.43	8.22	3.76	0.96	...
West North Central. . .	12.27	10.00	6.90	3.80	2.50	1.09	0.69	0.27	...	...
South region.	32.91	31.87	35.41	33.73	40.73	44.38	45.85	47.81	49.39	49.91
South Atlantic.	15.14	15.18	17.06	20.18	23.00	28.35	31.76	36.95	43.07	47.13
East South Central. . .	11.13	11.42	12.79	14.50	15.09	14.12	12.35	9.79	6.32	2.78
West South Central. . .	6.64	5.26	5.56	4.05	2.64	1.91	1.74	1.07	...	...
West region	3.59	2.57	1.97	0.77	...	...	...	...	...	...
Mountain.	1.30	0.82	0.56	0.31	...	...	...	...	...	...
Pacific	2.29	1.75	1.41	0.46	...	...	...	...	...	...
New England										
Maine	1.29	1.63	2.00	2.51	2.94	3.11	3.10	3.16	2.86	2.46
New Hampshire	0.69	0.83	1.04	1.37	1.67	2.09	2.53	2.96	3.46	3.61
Vermont	0.66	0.86	1.00	1.35	1.71	2.18	2.45	3.01	2.91	2.17
Massachusetts	3.55	3.78	3.92	4.29	4.32	4.75	5.43	6.52	7.97	9.64
Rhode Island.	0.55	0.56	0.56	0.64	0.64	0.76	0.86	1.06	1.30	1.75
Connecticut	1.24	1.39	1.46	1.60	1.82	2.31	2.86	3.62	4.73	6.06
Middle Atlantic										
New York.	10.13	11.37	12.34	13.36	14.23	14.92	14.24	13.25	11.10	8.66
New Jersey.	2.25	2.35	2.14	2.11	2.19	2.49	2.88	3.39	3.98	4.69
Pennsylvania.	8.53	9.13	9.24	9.97	10.10	10.48	10.89	11.19	11.35	11.05
East North Central										
Ohio.	6.37	6.91	7.44	8.54	8.90	7.29	6.03	3.19	0.85	...
Indiana	3.94	4.36	4.30	4.26	4.02	2.67	1.53	0.34	0.11	...
Illinois.	6.13	6.59	5.45	3.67	2.79	1.22	0.57	0.17	...	...
Michigan.	3.26	3.07	2.38	1.71	1.24	0.25	0.09	0.07	...	...
Wisconsin	2.62	2.74	2.47	1.32	0.18	...	...	...	...	...
West North Central										
Minnesota	1.56	1.14	0.55	0.03	...	...	...	...	...	...
Iowa.	3.24	3.10	2.15	0.83	0.25	...	...	...	...	...
Missouri.	4.32	4.46	3.76	2.94	2.25	1.09	0.69	0.27	...	...
North Dakota.	0.07	0.01	...	...	...	...	...	...	...	...
South Dakota.	0.20	0.03	0.02	...	...	...	...	...	...	...
Nebraska.	0.90	0.32	0.09	...	...	...	...	...	...	...
Kansas.	1.98	0.95	0.34	...	...	...	...	...	...	...
South Atlantic										
Delaware.	0.29	0.32	0.36	0.39	0.46	0.60	0.75	1.00	1.21	1.50
Maryland.	1.86	2.03	2.19	2.51	2.75	3.48	4.23	5.26	6.43	8.14
District of Columbia. .	0.33	0.34	0.24	0.22	0.20	0.24	0.24	0.21	0.15	...
Virginia.	3.01	3.18	3.88	4.83	6.01	8.12	9.73	12.12	15.21	17.60
West Virginia	1.23	1.15	1.20	1.30	1.32	1.38	1.42	1.46	1.48	1.42
North Carolina.	2.79	2.78	3.16	3.75	4.42	5.74	6.63	7.67	9.01	10.02
South Carolina.	1.98	1.83	2.24	2.88	3.48	4.52	5.22	5.73	6.51	6.34
Georgia	3.07	3.07	3.36	3.91	4.05	4.02	3.54	3.49	3.06	2.10
Florida	0.54	0.49	0.45	0.38	0.32	0.27	...	...	...	...
East South Central										
Kentucky.	3.28	3.43	3.68	4.24	4.57	5.35	5.85	5.61	4.16	1.88
Tennessee	3.07	3.26	3.53	4.32	4.86	5.30	4.39	3.62	1.99	0.91
Alabama	2.52	2.59	3.07	3.33	3.46	2.41	1.33	0.12	0.02	...
Mississippi	2.25	2.15	2.52	2.62	2.20	1.06	0.78	0.43	0.14	...
West South Central										
Arkansas.	1.60	1.26	1.39	0.91	0.57	0.24	0.15	0.01	...	...
Louisiana	1.87	1.89	2.25	2.23	2.07	1.68	1.59	1.06	...	...
Oklahoma.	...	...	...	...	...	...	...	...	...	...
Texas	3.17	2.12	1.92	0.92	...	...	...	...	...	...
Mountain										
Montana	0.08	0.05	...	...	...	...	...	...	...	...
Idaho	0.06	0.04	...	...	...	...	...	...	...	...
Wyoming	0.04	0.02	...	...	...	...	...	...	...	...
Colorado.	0.39	0.10	0.11	...	...	...	...	...	...	...
New Mexico.	0.24	0.24	0.30	0.27	...	...	...	...	...	...
Arizona	0.08	0.03	...	...	...	...	...	...	...	...
Utah.	0.29	0.23	0.13	0.05	...	...	...	...	...	...
Nevada.	0.12	0.11	0.02	...	...	...	...	...	...	...
Pacific										
Washington.	0.15	0.06	0.04	0.01	...	...	...	...	...	...
Oregon.	0.35	0.24	0.17	0.05	...	...	...	...	...	...
California.	1.72	1.45	1.21	0.40	...	...	...	...	...	...
Alaska.	0.07	...	...	...	...	...	...	...	...	...
Hawaii.	...	...	...	...	...	...	...	...	...	...

Note: ... indicates data not applicable.

Source: U.S. Bureau of the Census. "Number of Inhabitants: United States Summary." 1980 Census of Population. Washington, DC: U.S. Government Printing Office, 1983, Table 10.

Table 3-1C. Decennial Rates of Change in Population, by Region, Division, and State: 1790 to 1980

Regions, division, and state	Change 1970 to 1980		Percent change							
	Population	Percent	1960 to 1970	1950 to 1960	1940 to 1950	1930 to 1940	1920 to 1930	1910 to 1920	1900 to 1910	1890 to 1900
United States, total	23,243,774	11.4	13.4	18.5	14.5	7.3	16.2	15.0	21.0	21.0
Northeast	74,769	0.2	9.8	13.2	9.7	4.5	16.1	14.7	22.9	20.9
New England	501,248	4.2	12.7	12.8	10.4	3.3	10.3	12.9	17.2	19.0
Middle Atlantic	426,479	-1.1	8.9	13.3	9.5	4.9	18.0	15.2	25.0	21.6
North Central	2,275,376	4.0	9.6	16.1	10.8	4.0	13.4	13.8	13.5	17.5
East North Central	1,419,470	3.5	11.1	19.2	14.2	5.3	17.8	17.7	14.2	18.6
West North Central	855,906	5.2	6.1	9.5	4.0	1.7	6.0	7.8	12.5	15.8
South	12,559,382	20.0	14.3	16.5	13.3	10.1	14.3	12.7	19.8	22.4
South Atlantic	6,280,297	20.5	18.1	22.6	18.8	12.9	12.9	14.7	16.8	17.9
East South Central	1,858,346	14.5	6.3	5.0	6.5	9.0	11.2	5.7	11.4	17.4
West South Central	4,420,739	22.9	14.0	16.6	11.3	7.3	18.9	16.6	34.5	37.8
West	8,334,247	23.9	24.2	38.9	40.4	16.7	33.8	30.1	64.4	37.5
Mountain	3,082,884	37.2	20.9	35.1	22.3	12.1	11.0	26.7	57.3	38.0
Pacific	5,251,363	19.8	25.2	40.2	47.8	18.6	46.7	32.1	68.9	37.2
New England										
Maine	130,938	13.2	2.5	6.1	7.9	6.2	3.8	3.5	6.9	5.0
New Hampshire	182,929	24.8	21.5	13.8	8.5	5.6	5.0	2.9	4.6	9.3
Vermont	66,724	15.0	14.1	3.2	5.2	-0.1	2.0	-1.0	3.6	3.4
Massachusetts	47,867	0.8	10.5	9.8	8.7	1.6	10.3	14.4	20.0	25.3
Rhode Island	-2,569	-0.3	10.5	8.5	11.0	3.8	13.7	11.4	26.6	24.0
Connecticut	75,359	2.5	19.6	26.3	17.4	6.4	16.4	23.9	22.7	21.7
Middle Atlantic										
New York	-683,319	-3.7	8.7	13.2	10.0	7.1	21.2	14.0	25.4	21.1
New Jersey	193,711	2.7	18.2	25.5	16.2	2.9	28.1	24.4	34.7	30.4
Pennsylvania	63,129	0.5	4.3	7.8	6.0	2.8	10.5	13.8	21.6	19.9
East North Central										
Ohio	140,207	1.3	9.8	22.1	15.0	3.9	15.4	20.8	14.7	13.2
Indiana	294,832	5.7	11.4	18.5	14.8	5.8	10.5	8.5	7.3	14.8
Illinois	316,233	2.8	10.2	15.7	10.3	3.5	17.7	15.0	16.9	26.0
Michigan	380,252	4.3	13.5	22.8	21.2	8.5	32.0	30.5	16.1	15.6
Wisconsin	287,946	6.5	11.8	15.1	9.5	6.8	11.7	12.8	12.8	22.2
West North Central										
Minnesota	269,867	7.1	11.5	14.5	6.8	8.9	7.4	15.0	18.5	33.7
Iowa	88,440	3.1	2.5	5.2	3.3	2.7	2.8	8.1	-0.3	16.7
Missouri	239,063	5.1	8.3	9.2	4.5	4.3	6.6	3.4	6.0	16.0
North Dakota	34,925	5.7	-2.3	2.1	-3.5	-5.7	5.3	12.1	80.8	67.1
South Dakota	24,511	3.7	-2.1	4.3	1.5	-7.2	8.8	9.0	45.4	15.2
Nebraska	84,492	5.7	5.2	6.5	0.7	-4.5	6.3	8.7	11.8	0.3
Kansas	114,608	5.1	3.2	14.3	5.8	-4.3	6.3	4.6	15.0	3.0
South Atlantic										
Delaware	46,234	8.4	22.8	40.3	19.4	11.8	6.9	10.2	9.5	9.6
Maryland	293,078	7.5	26.5	32.3	28.6	11.6	12.5	11.9	9.0	14.0
District of Columbia	-118,335	-15.6	-1.0	-4.8	21.0	36.2	11.3	32.2	18.8	21.0
Virginia	695,370	14.9	17.3	19.5	23.9	10.6	4.9	12.0	11.2	12.0
West Virginia	205,407	11.8	-6.2	-7.2	5.4	10.0	18.1	19.9	27.4	25.7
North Carolina	797,355	15.7	11.6	12.2	13.7	12.7	23.9	16.0	16.5	17.1
South Carolina	531,107	20.5	8.7	12.5	11.4	9.3	3.3	11.1	13.1	16.4
Georgia	875,175	19.1	16.4	14.5	10.3	7.4	0.4	11.0	17.7	20.6
Florida	2,954,906	43.5	37.2	78.7	46.1	29.2	51.6	28.7	42.4	35.0
East South Central										
Kentucky	440,066	13.7	6.0	3.2	3.5	8.8	8.2	5.5	6.6	15.5
Tennessee	665,102	16.9	10.1	8.4	12.9	11.4	11.9	7.0	8.1	14.3
Alabama	449,534	13.1	5.4	6.7	8.1	7.1	12.7	9.8	16.9	20.8
Mississippi	303,644	13.7	1.8	--	-0.2	8.7	12.2	-0.4	15.8	20.3
West South Central										
Arkansas	363,113	18.9	7.7	-6.5	-2.0	5.1	5.8	11.3	20.0	16.3
Louisiana	561,263	15.4	11.9	21.4	13.5	12.5	16.9	8.6	19.9	23.5
Oklahoma	465,827	18.2	9.9	4.3	-4.4	-2.5	18.1	22.4	109.7	205.6
Texas	3,030,536	27.1	16.9	24.2	20.2	10.1	24.9	19.7	27.8	36.4
Mountain										
Montana	92,281	13.3	2.9	14.2	5.6	4.1	-2.1	46.0	54.5	70.3
Idaho	230,920	32.4	6.9	13.3	12.1	17.9	3.0	32.6	101.3	82.7
Wyoming	137,141	41.3	0.7	13.6	15.9	11.2	16.0	33.2	57.7	47.9
Colorado	680,368	30.8	26.0	32.4	18.0	8.4	10.2	17.6	48.0	30.6
New Mexico	285,839	28.1	6.9	39.6	28.1	25.6	17.5	10.1	67.6	21.9
Arizona	942,816	53.1	36.3	73.7	50.1	14.6	30.3	63.5	66.2	39.3
Utah	401,764	37.9	18.9	29.3	25.2	8.4	13.0	20.4	34.9	31.3
Nevada	311,755	63.8	71.3	78.2	45.2	21.1	17.6	-5.5	93.4	-10.6
Pacific										
Washington	718,912	21.1	19.6	19.9	37.0	11.1	15.2	18.8	120.4	45.0
Oregon	541,572	25.9	18.3	16.3	39.6	14.2	21.8	16.4	62.7	30.2
California	3,696,833	18.5	27.1	48.5	53.3	21.7	65.7	44.1	60.1	22.4
Alaska	99,268	32.8	33.8	75.8	77.4	22.3	7.7	-14.5	1.2	98.4
Hawaii	194,778	25.3	21.7	26.6	18.2	14.8	43.9	33.4	24.6	...

Table 3-1C. Decennial Rates of Change in Population, by Region, Division, and State: 1790 to 1980–continued

Regions, division, and state	Percent change									
	1880 to 1890	1870 to 1880	1860 to 1870	1850 to 1860	1840 to 1850	1830 to 1840	1820 to 1830	1810 to 1820	1800 to 1810	1790 to 1800
United States, total	25.5	30.2	22.6	35.6	35.9	32.7	33.4	33.1	36.4	35.1
Northeast	20.0	18.0	16.1	22.8	27.6	22.0	27.1	25.0	32.3	33.9
New England	17.2	15.0	11.2	14.9	22.1	14.3	17.7	12.8	19.4	22.2
Middle Atlantic	21.0	19.1	18.1	26.5	30.3	26.2	32.9	34.0	43.6	46.3
North Central	29.1	33.8	42.7	68.3	61.2	108.1	87.4	194.2	472.7	...
East North Central	20.3	22.8	31.7	53.1	54.7	99.0	85.4	191.1	433.9	...
West North Central	45.1	59.7	77.7	146.5	106.3	203.9	110.9	236.6	...	...
South	21.3	34.4	10.4	23.9	29.2	21.8	29.2	27.7	32.0	33.7
South Atlantic	16.6	29.8	9.1	14.7	19.2	7.7	19.1	14.4	17.0	23.5
East South Central	15.1	26.8	9.5	19.6	30.6	41.8	52.5	68.0	111.3	206.7
West South Central	42.2	64.3	16.2	85.9	109.0	82.8	46.8	116.0	...	...
West	74.0	81.8	60.0	246.1	...	...	...	...	...	...
Mountain	85.9	107.1	80.3	139.9	...	...	...	...	...	...
Pacific	67.3	70.0	52.0	319.3	...	...	...	...	...	...
New England										
Maine	1.9	3.5	-0.2	7.7	16.2	25.6	33.9	30.4	50.7	57.2
New Hampshire	8.5	9.0	-2.4	2.5	11.7	5.7	10.3	13.8	16.6	29.6
Vermont	--	0.5	4.9	0.3	7.6	4.0	18.9	8.3	41.1	80.8
Massachusetts	25.6	22.4	18.4	23.8	34.8	20.9	16.6	10.9	11.6	11.6
Rhode Island	24.9	27.2	24.5	18.4	35.6	12.0	17.0	8.0	11.3	0.4
Connecticut	19.8	15.9	16.8	24.1	19.6	4.1	8.1	5.1	4.4	5.5
Middle Atlantic										
New York	18.1	16.0	12.9	25.3	27.5	26.6	39.8	43.1	62.8	73.2
New Jersey	27.7	24.8	34.8	37.3	31.1	16.4	15.6	13.0	16.3	14.7
Pennsylvania	22.8	21.6	21.2	25.7	34.1	27.9	28.5	29.5	34.5	38.7
East North Central										
Ohio	14.8	20.0	13.9	18.1	30.3	62.0	61.3	152.0	408.7	...
Indiana	10.8	17.7	24.5	36.6	44.1	99.9	133.1	500.2	334.7	...
Illinois	24.3	21.2	48.4	101.1	78.8	202.4	185.2	349.5	...	...
Michigan	27.9	38.2	58.1	88.4	87.3	570.9	255.7	86.8	...	...
Wisconsin	28.7	24.7	35.9	154.1	886.9	...	...	...	...	...
West North Central										
Minnesota	67.8	77.6	155.6	2,730.7	...	...	...	...	...	...
Iowa	17.7	36.1	76.9	251.1	345.8	...	...	...	...	...
Missouri	23.6	26.0	45.6	73.3	77.8	173.2	110.9	236.6	...	...
North Dakota	417.4	1,434.7	...	...	...	...	...	...	...	...
South Dakota	254.7	734.5	143.5	...	...	...	...	...	...	...
Nebraska	134.9	267.8	326.5	...	...	...	...	...	...	...
Kansas	43.4	173.4	239.9	...	...	...	...	...	...	...
South Atlantic										
Delaware	14.9	17.3	11.4	22.6	17.2	1.7	5.5	0.1	13.1	8.8
Maryland	11.5	19.7	13.7	17.8	24.0	5.1	9.7	7.0	11.4	6.8
District of Columbia	29.7	34.9	75.4	45.3	53.2	11.5	29.7	50.8	90.0	...
Virginia	9.5	23.5	0.5	9.0	9.2	-1.8	11.3	6.9	8.7	16.7
West Virginia	23.3	39.9	17.3	24.6	34.6	26.9	29.3	29.7	34.2	40.7
North Carolina	15.6	30.7	7.9	14.2	15.3	2.1	15.5	15.0	16.2	21.4
South Carolina	15.6	41.1	0.3	5.3	12.5	2.3	15.6	21.1	20.1	38.8
Georgia	19.1	30.2	12.0	16.7	31.1	33.8	51.6	35.1	55.2	97.1
Florida	45.2	43.5	33.7	60.6	60.5	56.9	...	...	...	...
East South Central										
Kentucky	12.7	24.8	14.3	17.6	26.0	13.4	21.9	38.8	84.0	199.9
Tennessee	14.6	22.6	13.4	10.7	20.9	21.6	61.3	61.6	147.8	195.9
Alabama	19.9	26.6	3.4	25.0	30.6	90.9	142.0	1,313.9	623.7	...
Mississippi	14.0	36.7	4.6	30.5	61.5	175.0	81.1	141.0	311.9	...
West South Central										
Arkansas	40.6	65.6	11.3	107.5	115.1	221.1	112.9	1,244.0	...	...
Louisiana	19.0	29.3	2.7	36.7	46.9	63.4	40.6	100.4	...	...
Oklahoma	...	...	...	...	...	...	...	...	...	...
Texas	40.4	94.5	35.5	184.2	...	...	...	...	...	...
Mountain										
Montana	265.0	90.1	...	...	...	...	...	...	...	...
Idaho	171.5	117.4	...	...	...	...	...	...	...	...
Wyoming	200.9	128.0	...	...	...	...	...	...	...	...
Colorado	112.7	387.5	16.3	...	...	...	...	...	...	...
New Mexico	34.1	30.1	-1.8	51.9	...	...	...	...	...	...
Arizona	118.2	318.7	...	...	...	...	...	...	...	...
Utah	46.4	65.9	115.5	253.9	...	...	...	...	...	...
Nevada	-23.9	46.5	519.7	...	...	...	...	...	...	...
Pacific										
Washington	375.6	213.6	106.6	865.4	...	...	...	...	...	...
Oregon	81.8	92.2	73.3	333.8	...	...	...	...	...	...
California	40.3	54.3	47.4	310.4	...	...	...	...	...	...
Alaska	-4.1	...	...	...	...	...	...	...	...	...
Hawaii	...	...	...	...	...	...	...	...	...	...

Note: -- indicates data not available. ... indicates data not applicable.

Source: U.S. Bureau of the Census. "Number of Inhabitants: United States Summary." 1980 Census of Population. Washington, DC: U.S. Government Printing Office, 1983, Table 9.

Table 3-1D. Area, 1980, and Population Density, by Region, Division, and State: Selected Years, 1800 to 1980

Region, division, and state	1980 Area (square miles)			Population per square miles of land area							
	Total	Land	Inland water	1980	1970	1960	1950	1940	1900	1850	1800
United States, total. . .	3,618,770	3,539,289	79,481	64.0	57.5	50.6	50.7	44.2	25.6	7.9	6.1
Northeast region.	168,876	162,745	6,131	301.9	300.5	273.4	242.6	221.1	129.3	53.0	16.2
New England	66,672	63,012	3,660	196.0	188.2	166.8	147.8	133.9	88.7	43.3	19.6
Middle Atlantic	102,203	99,733	2,470	368.9	371.0	340.2	302.4	276.1	155.0	59.1	14.1
North Central region. . . .	766,365	752,093	14,272	76.3	75.3	68.6	59.1	53.4	35.0	7.2	...
East North Central. . . .	248,540	243,961	4,579	170.9	164.9	148.2	124.6	109.1	69.6	18.5	0.2
West North Central. . . .	517,825	508,132	9,693	33.8	32.2	30.3	27.7	26.6	20.4	1.7	...
South region.	898,575	873,005	25,570	86.3	71.9	62.8	54.1	47.7	28.1	10.3	3.0
South Atlantic.	278,926	266,910	12,017	138.5	114.9	97.1	79.4	66.8	39.1	17.5	8.6
East South Central. . . .	181,947	178,824	3,123	82.0	71.6	67.2	64.2	60.3	42.2	18.8	1.9
West South Central. . . .	437,701	427,271	10,430	55.6	45.2	39.5	34.0	30.6	15.3	2.2	...
West region	1,784,955	1,751,446	33,509	24.6	19.9	16.0	11.5	8.2	2.5	0.1	...
Mountain.	863,563	855,193	8,369	13.3	9.7	8.0	5.9	4.9	2.0	0.1	...
Pacific	921,392	896,253	25,140	35.5	29.8	23.8	16.9	11.4	2.9	0.1	...
New England											
Maine	33,265	30,995	2,270	36.3	32.1	31.3	29.4	27.3	23.2	19.5	5.1
New Hampshire	9,279	8,993	286	102.4	81.7	67.2	59.1	54.5	45.6	35.2	20.4
Vermont	9,614	9,273	341	55.2	48.0	42.0	40.7	38.7	37.7	34.4	16.9
Massachusetts	8,284	7,824	460	733.3	727.0	657.3	596.2	545.9	349.0	123.7	52.6
Rhode Island.	1,212	1,055	158	897.8	905.4	819.3	748.5	674.2	401.6	138.3	64.8
Connecticut	5,018	4,872	147	637.8	623.7	520.6	409.7	348.9	188.5	76.9	52.1
Middle Atlantic											
New York.	49,108	47,377	1,731	370.6	381.4	350.6	309.3	281.2	152.5	65.0	12.4
New Jersey.	7,787	7,468	319	986.2	953.5	805.5	642.8	553.1	250.7	65.2	28.1
Pennsylvania.	45,308	44,888	420	264.3	262.4	251.4	233.1	219.8	140.6	51.6	13.4
East North Central											
Ohio.	41,330	41,004	325	263.3	260.1	236.6	193.8	168.0	102.1	48.6	1.1
Indiana	36,185	35,932	253	152.8	143.9	128.8	108.7	94.7	70.1	27.5	0.0
Illinois.	56,345	55,645	700	205.3	199.3	180.4	155.8	141.2	86.1	15.2	...
Michigan.	58,527	56,954	1,573	162.6	156.3	137.7	111.7	92.2	42.1	6.9	...
Wisconsin	56,153	54,426	1,727	86.5	81.1	72.6	62.8	57.3	37.4	5.5	...
West North Central											
Minnesota	84,402	79,548	4,854	51.2	48.0	43.1	37.3	34.9	21.7	0.0	...
Iowa.	56,275	55,965	310	52.1	50.5	49.2	46.8	45.3	40.2	3.5	...
Missouri.	69,697	68,945	752	71.3	67.8	62.6	57.1	54.6	45.2	9.9	...
North Dakota.	70,702	69,300	1,403	9.4	8.9	9.1	8.8	9.2	4.5	...	...
South Dakota.	77,116	75,952	1,164	9.1	8.7	9.0	8 5	8.4	5.2	...	...
Nebraska.	77,355	76,644	711	20.5	19.4	18.4	17.3	17.2	13.9	...	...
Kansas.	82,277	81,778	499	28.9	27.5	26.6	23.2	21.9	18.0	...	...

Table 3-1D. Area, 1980, and Population Density, by Region, Division, and State: Selected Years, 1800 to 1980–continued

Region, division, and state	1980 Area (square miles)			Population per square miles of land area							
	Total	Land	Inland water	1980	1970	1960	1950	1940	1900	1850	1800
South Atlantic											
Delaware.	2,045	1,932	112	307.6	276.5	225.2	160.8	134.7	94.0	46.6	32.7
Maryland.	10,460	9,837	623	428.7	396.7	313.5	237.1	184.2	119.5	58.6	34.4
District of Columbia. . .	69	63	6	10,132.3	12,404.4	12,523.9	13,159.5	10,870.3	3,972.3	891.2	156.6
Virginia.	40,767	39,704	1,063	134.7	116.9	99.6	83.2	67.1	46.1	22.1	13.7
West Virginia	24,232	24,119	112	80.8	72.5	77.2	83.3	79.0	39.9	...	...
North Carolina.	52,669	48,843	3,826	120.4	104.2	93.2	82.7	72.7	38.9	17.8	9.8
South Carolina.	31,113	30,203	909	103.4	85.7	78.7	69.9	62.1	44.0	21.9	11.3
Georgia	58,910	58,056	854	94.1	79.0	67.8	58.9	53.4	37.7	15.4	1.5
Florida	58,664	54,153	4,511	180.0	125.6	91.5	51.1	35.0	9.6	1.6	...
East South Central											
Kentucky.	40,410	39,669	740	92.3	81.2	76.2	73.9	70.9	53.4	24.4	5.5
Tennessee	42,144	41,155	989	111.6	95.0	86.2	78.8	69.5	48.5	24.1	2.5
Alabama	51,705	50,767	938	76.7	67.9	64.2	59.9	55.5	35.7	15.0	...
Mississippli.	47,689	47,233	457	53.4	46.9	46.0	46.1	46.1	33.5	13.1	0.3
West South Central											
Arkansas.	53,187	52,078	1,109	43.9	37.0	34.2	36.3	37.0	25.0	4.0	...
Louisiana	47,752	44,521	3,230	94.5	81.1	72.2	59.4	52.3	30.4	11.4	...
Oklahoma.	69,956	68,655	1,301	44.1	37.2	33.8	32.4	33.7	11.4	...	...
Texas	266,807	262,017	4,790	54.3	42.7	36.4	29.3	24.3	11.6	0.8	...
Mountain											
Montana	147,046	145,388	1,658	5.4	4.8	4.6	4.1	3.8	1.7	...	...
Idaho	83,564	82,412	1,153	11.5	8.6	8.1	7.1	6.3	1.9	...	...
Wyoming	97,809	96,989	820	4.8	3.4	3.4	3.0	2.6	0.9	...	...
Colorado.	104,091	103,595	496	27.9	21.3	16.9	12.8	10.8	5.2	...	...
New Mexico.	121,593	121,335	258	10.7	8.4	7.8	5.6	4.4	1.6	0.3	...
Arizona	114,000	113,508	492	23.9	15.7	11.5	6.6	4.4	1.1	...	...
Utah.	84,899	82,073	2,826	17.8	12.9	10.8	8.4	6.7	3.4	0.0	...
Nevada.	110,561	109,894	667	7.3	4.4	2.6	1.5	1.0	0.4	...	...
Pacific											
Washington.	68,139	66,511	1,627	62.1	51.3	42.8	35.6	25.9	7.8	...	...
Oregon.	97,073	96,184	889	27.4	21.7	18.4	15.8	11.3	4.3	0.0	...
California.	158,706	156,299	2,407	151.4	127.7	100.4	67.5	44.1	9.5	0.6	...
Alaska.	591,004	570,833	20,171	0.7	0.5	0.4	0.2	0.1	0.1	...	...
Hawaii.	6,471	6,425	46	150.1	119.8	98.5	78.0	66.0	24.0	...	...

Note: ... indicates data not applicable. To calculate population density for regions and divisions from 1800 to 1950, the region and division population totals (obtained from "Number of Inhabitants: U.S. Summary," 1980 Census of Population, Table 8), were divided by appropriate land areas per square mile (Table 11 of the same volume).

Source: U.S. Bureau of the Census. "Number of Inhabitants: U.S. Summary." 1980 Census of Population. Washington, DC: U.S. Government Printing Office, 1975, Table A1-5, pp. 195-209.

Table 3-2A. Race of Population, by Region, Division, and State: 1980

Region, division, and state	Total persons	White	Black	American Indian	Eskimo	Aleut	Japanese	Chinese
United States, total . .	226,545,505	188,371,622	26,495,025	1,364,033	42,162	14,205	700,974	806,040
Northeast region	49,135,283	42,326,288	4,848,431	77,430	890	718	46,926	217,737
New England.	12,348,493	11,585,633	474,549	21,108	277	212	7,832	32,969
Middle Atlantic.	36,786,790	30,740,655	4,373,882	56,322	613	506	39,094	184,768
North Central region . . .	58,865,670	52,194,799	5,337,095	246,345	1,286	762	44,462	72,938
East North Central . . .	41,682,217	36,150,455	4,548,546	104,547	834	526	34,520	57,606
West North Central . . .	17,183,453	16,044,344	788,549	141,798	452	236	9,942	15,332
South region	75,372,362	58,960,346	14,047,787	369,603	1,158	1,046	44,652	90,588
South Atlantic	36,959,123	28,659,351	7,651,969	117,457	772	497	25,137	50,526
East South Central . . .	14,666,423	11,702,269	2,868,960	22,164	201	112	4,801	7,567
West South Central . . .	23,746,816	18,598,726	3,526,858	229,982	608	437	14,714	32,495
West region.	43,172,490	34,890,189	2,261,712	670,655	38,405	11,679	564,934	424,777
Mountain	11,372,785	9,961,018	268,790	363,199	799	383	26,958	19,511
Pacific.	31,799,705	24,929,171	1,992,922	307,456	37,606	11,296	537,976	405,266
New England								
Maine.	1,124,660	1,109,850	3,128	4,057	17	13	336	484
New Hampshire.	920,610	910,099	3,990	1,297	41	14	448	790
Vermont.	511,456	506,736	1,135	968	8	8	227	271
Massachusetts.	5,737,037	5,362,836	221,279	7,483	129	131	4,483	25,015
Rhode Island	947,154	896,692	27,584	2,872	14	12	474	1,718
Connecticut.	3,107,576	2,799,420	217,433	4,431	68	34	1,864	4,691
Middle Atlantic								
New York	17,558,072	13,960,868	2,402,006	38,967	330	285	24,524	148,105
New Jersey	7,364,823	6,127,467	925,066	8,176	130	88	9,905	23,369
Pennsylvania	11,863,895	10,652,320	1,046,810	9,179	153	133	4,665	13,294
East North Central								
Ohio	10,797,630	9,597,458	1,076,748	11,985	167	87	5,479	9,917
Indiana.	5,490,224	5,004,394	414,785	7,682	107	47	2,361	3,986
Illinois	11,426,518	9,233,327	1,675,398	15,846	242	195	18,571	28,597
Michigan	9.262,078	7,872,241	1,199,023	39,714	208	128	5,872	11,009
Wisconsin.	4,705,767	4,443,035	182,592	29,320	110	69	2,237	4,097
West North Central								
Minnesota.	4,075,970	3,935,770	53,344	34,831	118	67	2,789	4,835
Iowa	2,913,808	2,839,225	41,700	5,369	59	27	1,049	2,110
Missouri	4,916,686	4,345,521	514,276	12,129	119	73	2,649	4,280
North Dakota	652,717	625,557	2,568	20,120	32	6	230	305
South Dakota	690,768	639,669	2,144	44,948	17	3	262	271
Nebraska	1,569,825	1,490,381	48,390	9,145	26	24	1,378	1,106
Kansas	2,363,679	2,168,221	126,127	15,256	81	36	1,585	2,425
South Atlantic								
Delaware	594,338	487,817	95,845	1,307	13	8	421	998
Maryland	4,216,975	3,158,838	958,150	7,823	113	85	4,305	14,485
District of Columbia . .	638,333	171,768	448,906	996	19	16	752	2,476
Virginia	5,346,818	4,229,798	1,008,668	9,211	156	87	5,207	9,360
West Virginia.	1,949,644	1,874,751	65,051	1,555	37	18	404	881
North Carolina	5,881,766	4,457,507	1,318,857	64,536	57	59	3,186	3,176
South Carolina	3,121,820	2,147,224	948,623	5,665	70	22	1,415	1,404
Georgia.	5,463,105	3,947,135	1,465,181	7,442	108	66	3,368	4,324
Florida.	9,746,324	8,184,513	1,342,688	18,922	199	136	5,579	13,422
East South Central								
Kentucky	3,660,777	3,379,006	259,477	3,518	59	33	1,056	1,318
Tennessee.	4,591,120	3,835,452	725,942	5,013	62	29	1,657	2,909
Alabama.	3,893,888	2,872,621	996,335	7,502	52	29	1,401	1,505
Mississippi.	2,520,638	1,615,190	887,206	6,131	28	21	687	1,835
West South Central								
Arkansas	2,286,435	1,890,322	373,768	9,364	47	17	755	1,275
Louisiana.	4,205,900	2,912,172	1,238,241	11,951	59	55	1,482	3,298
Oklahoma	3,025,290	2,597,791	204,674	169,292	107	60	1,975	2,461
Texas.	14,229,191	11,198,441	1,710,175	39,375	395	305	10,502	25,461
Mountain								
Montana.	786,690	740,148	1,786	37,153	79	38	754	346
Idaho.	943,935	901,641	2,716	10,418	76	27	2,585	905
Wyoming.	469,557	446,488	3,364	7,057	27	10	600	392
Colorado	2,889,964	2,571,498	101,703	17,734	236	98	9,870	3,897
New Mexico	1,302,894	977,587	24,020	105,976	88	55	1,286	1,442
Arizona.	2,718,215	2,240,761	74,977	152,498	138	109	4,074	6,820
Utah	1,461,037	1,382,550	9,225	19,158	81	17	5,474	2,730
Nevada	800,493	700,345	50,999	13,205	74	29	2,315	2,979
Pacific								
Washington	4,132,156	3,779,170	105,574	58,186	1,253	1,365	26,378	18,114
Oregon	2,633,105	2,490,610	37,060	26,591	407	316	8,433	8,036
California	23,667,902	18,030,893	1,819,281	198,155	1,734	1,480	261,822	322,309
Alaska	401,851	309,728	13,643	21,869	34,144	8,090	1,595	522
Hawaii	964,691	318,770	17,364	2.655	68	45	239,748	56,285

Table 3-2A. Race of Population, by Region, Division, and State: 1980—continued

Region, division, and state	Filipino	Korean	Asian Indian	Vietnamese	Hawaiian	Guamian	Samoan	Other
United States, total	774,652	354,593	361,531	261,729	166,814	32,158	41,948	6,758,319
Northeast region	75,104	66,151	120,758	24,855	3,786	1,637	804	1,321,768
New England	8,504	8,647	15,531	6,070	762	425	265	185,709
Middle Atlantic	66,600	59,504	105,227	18,785	3,024	1,212	539	1,136,059
North Central region	79,970	62,214	85,175	36,657	5,175	2,157	1,242	695,393
East North Central	68,782	45,897	71,498	19,339	3,488	1,343	511	574,325
West North Central	11,188	16,317	13,677	17,318	1,687	814	731	121,068
South region	82,602	70,381	83,606	80,264	10,507	5,066	2,156	1,522,177
South Atlantic	56,537	44,664	46,213	28,451	5,329	2.645	1,134	268,441
East South Central	5,750	6,710	8,577	5,095	1,624	651	304	31,638
West South Central	20,315	19,007	28,816	46,718	3,554	1,770	718	1,222,098
West region	636,976	153,847	71,992	119,953	147,346	23,298	37,746	3,218,981
Mountain	13,821	12,993	7,306	11,104	3,894	1,470	1,376	680,163
Pacific	523,155	140,854	64,686	108,849	143,452	21,828	36,370	2,538,818
New England								
Maine	666	481	392	465	58	49	16	4,648
New Hampshire	314	515	563	209	64	13	13	2,240
Vermont	101	288	343	85	18	14	8	1,246
Massachusetts	3,073	4,544	8,387	3,172	374	197	145	95,678
Rhode Island	1,218	592	851	314	71	51	14	14,672
Connecticut	3,132	2,116	4,995	1,825	177	101	69	67,220
Middle Atlantic								
New York	33,956	34,157	60,505	6,644	1,566	773	296	845,090
New Jersey	24,377	12,845	29,510	2,844	632	234	92	200,048
Pennsylvania	8,267	12,502	15,212	9.257	826	205	151	90,921
East North Central								
Ohio	7,435	7,257	13,106	3,509	768	232	117	63,365
Indiana	3,626	3,295	4,296	2,338	475	126	54	42,652
Illinois	43,857	23,989	35,749	7,034	1,063	606	187	341,857
Michigan	11,166	8,174	14,690	4,209	799	226	105	93,974
Wisconsin	2,698	2,642	3,657	2,249	383	153	48	32,477
West North Central								
Minnesota	2,677	6,319	3,670	5,866	243	97	40	25,304
Iowa	1,225	2,259	2,147	2,476	182	70	59	15,851
Missouri	4,029	3,519	4,099	3,179	633	230	478	21,472
North Dakota	446	342	294	283	46	20	13	2,455
South Dakota	282	258	182	386	45	28	24	2,249
Nebraska	867	993	928	1,438	160	105	27	14,857
Kansas	1,662	2,627	2,357	3,690	378	264	90	38,880
South Atlantic								
Delaware	813	490	1,071	205	65	43	6	5,236
Maryland	10,965	15,089	13,705	4,131	616	400	82	27,688
District of Columbia	1,297	338	950	505	237	66	15	9,992
Virginia	18,901	12,550	8,483	10,000	903	535	270	32,689
West Virginia	1,313	587	1,641	253	74	27	14	3,038
North Carolina	2,542	3,581	4,720	2,391	839	500	241	19,574
South Carolina	3,696	1,390	2,152	1,072	439	189	77	8,382
Georgia	2,792	5,968	4,347	2,294	778	409	177	18,716
Florida	14,218	4,671	9,144	7,600	1,378	476	252	143,126
East South Central								
Kentucky	1,443	2,102	2,225	1,090	342	265	129	8,714
Tennessee	1,901	2,237	3,195	1,391	432	158	83	10,659
Alabama	964	1,795	1,994	1,333	520	152	70	7,615
Mississippi	1,442	576	1,163	1,281	330	76	22	4,650
West South Central								
Arkansas	918	583	832	2,051	258	62	6	6,177
Louisiana	2,614	1,729	2,873	10,884	563	214	122	19,643
Oklahoma	1,687	2,698	2,880	4,671	515	301	87	36,091
Texas	15,096	13,997	22,231	29,112	2,218	1,193	503	1,160,187
Mountain								
Montana	458	301	162	275	135	48	24	4,983
Idaho	680	610	310	429	318	52	59	23,109
Wyoming	253	235	176	167	102	29	15	10,642
Colorado	2,908	5,316	2,298	4,026	861	567	173	168,779
New Mexico	1,182	706	806	1,043	217	82	61	188,343
Arizona	3,342	2,449	2,102	1,932	808	353	146	227,700
Utah	928	1,319	830	2,108	844	80	763	34,930
Nevada	4,064	2,057	622	1,124	609	259	135	21,677
Pacific								
Washington	24,374	13,083	4,002	9,838	2,976	1,942	1,830	84,071
Oregon	4,257	4,428	1,938	5,564	1,488	387	244	43,346
California	357,492	103,845	57,901	89,601	23,086	17,673	20,089	2,362,541
Alaska	3,092	1,536	241	383	402	149	134	6,323
Hawaii	133,940	17,962	604	3,463	115,500	1,677	14,073	42,537

Source: U.S. Bureau of the Census. "General Population Characteristics: United States Summary." 1980 Census of Population. Washington, DC: U.S. Government Printing Office, 1983.

Table 3-2B. Percent Distribution of Each Racial Group Among, Regions, Divisions, and States: 1980

Region, division, and state	Total population	White	Black	Indian	Eskimo	Aleut	Japanese	Chinese	Filipino	Korean	Asian, Indian	Vietnamese	Hawaiian, Guamian, Samoan	Other
United States, total. . .	100.00	100.00	100.00	100.00	100.00	100.00	100.00	100.00	100.00	100.00	100.00	100.00	100.00	100.00
Northeast region.	21.69	22.47	18.30	5.68	2.11	5.05	6.69	27.00	9.70	19.22	33.41	9.50	2.58	19.56
New England	5.45	6.15	1.79	1.55	0.66	1.49	1.12	4.09	1.10	2.44	4.30	2.32	0.60	2.75
Middle Atlantic	16.24	16.32	16.51	4.13	1.45	3.56	5.57	22.91	8.60	16.78	29.11	7.18	1.98	16.81
North Central region. . . .	25.98	27.71	20.15	18.06	3.05	5.36	6.34	9.05	10.32	17.54	23.56	14.01	3.56	10.29
East North Central. . . .	18.40	19.19	17.17	7.66	1.98	3.70	4.92	7.15	8.88	12.94	19.78	7.39	2.22	8.50
West North Central. . . .	7.58	8.52	2.98	10.40	1.07	1.66	1.42	1.90	1.44	4.60	3.78	6.62	1.34	1.79
South region.	33.27	31.30	53.02	27.09	3.75	7.37	6.37	11.24	10.66	19.85	23.12	30.67	7.36	22.52
South Atlantic.	16.32	15.22	28.88	8.61	1.83	3.50	3.59	6.27	7.30	12.60	12.78	10.87	3.78	3.97
East South Central. . . .	6.47	6.21	10.83	1.62	0.48	0.79	0.68	0.94	0.74	1.89	2.37	1.95	1.07	0.47
West South Central. . . .	10.48	9.87	13.31	16.86	1.44	3.08	2.10	4.03	2.62	5.36	7.97	17.85	2.51	18.08
West region	19.06	18.52	8.53	49.17	91.09	82.22	80.60	52.71	69.32	43.39	19.91	45.83	86.50	47.63
Mountain.	5.02	5.29	1.01	26.63	1.90	2.70	3.85	2.42	1.78	3.66	2.02	4.24	2.80	10.06
Pacific	14.04	13.23	7.52	22.54	89.19	79.52	76.75	50.29	67.52	39.73	17.89	41.59	83.70	37.57
New England														
Maine	0.50	0.59	0.01	0.30	0.04	0.09	0.05	0.06	0.09	0.14	0.11	0.18	0.05	0.07
New Hampshire	0.41	0.48	0.02	0.10	0.10	0.10	0.06	0.10	0.04	0.15	0.16	0.08	0.04	0.03
Vermont	0.23	0.27	0.00	0.07	0.02	0.06	0.03	0.03	0.01	0.08	0.09	0.03	0.02	0.02
Massachusetts	2.53	2.85	0.84	0.55	0.31	0.92	0.64	3.10	0.40	1.31	2.32	1.21	0.30	1.42
Rhode Island.	0.42	0.48	0.10	0.21	0.03	0.08	0.07	0.21	0.16	0.17	0.24	0.12	0.06	0.22
Conneticut.	1.37	1.49	0.82	0.32	0.16	0.24	0.27	0.58	0.40	0.60	1.38	0.70	0.14	0.99
Middle Atlantic														
New York.	7.75	7.41	9.07	2.86	0.78	2.01	3.50	18.37	4.38	9.63	16.74	2.54	1.09	12.50
New Jersey.	3.25	3.25	3.49	0.60	0.31	0.62	1.41	2.90	3.15	3.62	8.16	1.10	0.40	2.96
Pennsylvania.	5.24	5.65	3.95	0.67	0.36	0.94	0.67	1.65	1.07	3.53	4.21	3.54	0.49	1.35
East North Central														
Ohio.	4.77	5.09	4.06	0.88	0.40	0.61	0.78	1.23	0.96	2.05	3.63	1.34	0.46	0.94
Indiana	2.42	2.66	1.57	0.56	0.25	0.33	0.34	0.49	0.47	0.93	1.19	0.89	0.27	0.63
Illinois.	5.04	4.90	6.32	1.16	0.57	1.37	2.65	3.55	5.66	6.77	9.89	2.69	0.77	5.06
Michigan.	4.09	4.18	4.53	2.91	0.49	0.90	0.84	1.37	1.44	2.46	4.06	1.61	0.47	1.39
Wisconsin	2.08	2.36	0.69	2.15	0.26	0.49	0.32	0.51	0.35	0.75	1.01	0.86	0.24	0.48
West North Central														
Minnesota	1.80	2.09	0.20	2.55	0.28	0.47	0.40	0.60	0.35	1.78	1.02	2.24	0.16	0.37
Iowa.	1.29	1.51	0.16	0.39	0.14	0.19	0.15	0.26	0.16	0.64	0.59	0.95	0.13	0.23
Missouri.	2.17	2.31	1.94	0.89	0.28	0.51	0.38	0.53	0.52	0.99	1.13	1.21	0.56	0.32
North Dakota.	0.29	0.33	0.00	1.48	0.08	0.04	0.03	0.04	0.06	0.10	0.08	0.11	0.03	0.04
South Dakota.	0.30	0.34	0.00	3.30	0.04	0.02	0.04	0.03	0.04	0.07	0.05	0.15	0.04	0.03
Nebraska.	0.69	0.79	0.18	0.67	0.06	0.17	0.20	0.14	0.11	0.28	0.26	0.55	0.12	0.22
Kansas.	1.04	1.15	0.48	1.12	0.19	0.25	0.23	0.30	0.21	0.74	0.65	1.41	0.30	0.58
South Atlantic														
Delaware.	0.26	0.26	0.36	0.10	0.03	0.06	0.06	0.12	0.10	0.14	0.30	0.08	0.04	0.08
Maryland.	1.86	1.68	3.62	0.57	0.27	0.60	0.69	1.80	1.42	4.26	3.79	1.58	0.46	0.41
District of Columbia. . .	0.28	0.09	1.69	0.07	0.05	0.11	0.11	0.31	0.17	0.10	0.26	0.19	0.13	0.15
Virginia.	2.36	2.25	3.81	0.68	0.37	0.61	0.74	1.16	2.44	3.54	2.35	3.82	0.71	0.48
West Virginia	0.86	1.00	0.25	0.11	0.09	0.13	0.06	0.11	0.17	0.17	0.45	0.10	0.05	0.04
North Carolina.	2.60	2.37	4.98	4.73	0.14	0.42	0.45	0.39	0.33	1.01	1.31	0.91	0.66	0.29
South Carolina.	1.38	1.14	3.58	0.42	0.17	0.15	0.20	0.17	0.48	0.39	0.60	0.41	0.29	0.12
Georgia	2.41	2.10	5.53	0.55	0.26	0.46	0.48	0.54	0.36	1.68	1.20	0.88	0.57	0.28
Florida	4.30	4.34	5.07	1.39	0.47	0.96	0.80	1.67	1.84	1.32	2.53	2.90	0.87	2.12
East South Central														
Kentucky.	1.62	1.79	0.98	0.26	0.14	0.23	0.15	0.16	0.19	0.59	0.62	0.42	0.31	0.13
Tennessee	2.02	2.04	2.74	0.37	0.15	0.20	0.24	0.36	0.25	0.63	0.88	0.53	0.28	0.16
Alabama	1.72	1.52	3.76	0.55	0.12	0.20	0.20	0.19	0.12	0.51	0.55	0.51	0.31	0.11
Mississippi	1.11	0.86	3.35	0.45	0.07	0.15	0.10	0.23	0.19	0.16	0.32	0.49	0.18	0.07
West South Central														
Arkansas.	1.01	1.00	1.41	0.69	0.11	0.12	0.11	0.16	0.12	0.16	0.23	0.78	0.14	0.09
Louisiana	1.86	1.55	4.67	0.88	0.14	0.39	0.21	0.41	0.34	0.49	0.79	4.16	0.37	0.29
Okalahoma	1.34	1.38	0.77	12.41	0.25	0.42	0.28	0.31	0.22	0.76	0.80	1.78	0.37	0.53
Texas	6.28	5.94	6.45	2.89	0.94	2.15	1.50	3.16	1.95	3.95	6.15	11.12	1.62	17.17
Mountain														
Montana	0.35	0.39	0.01	2.72	0.19	0.27	0.11	0.04	0.06	0.08	0.04	0.11	0.09	0.07
Idaho	0.42	0.48	0.01	0.76	0.18	0.19	0.37	0.11	0.09	0.17	0.09	0.16	0.18	0.34
Wyoming	0.21	0.24	0.01	0.52	0.06	0.07	0.09	0.05	0.03	0.07	0.05	0.06	0.06	0.16
Colorado.	1.27	1.37	0.38	1.30	0.56	0.69	1.41	0.48	0.38	1.50	0.64	1.54	0.66	2.50
New Mexico.	0.58	0.52	0.09	7.77	0.21	0.39	0.18	0.18	0.15	0.20	0.22	0.40	0.15	2.79
Arizona	1.20	1.19	0.28	11.18	0.33	0.77	0.58	0.85	0.43	0.69	0.58	0.74	0.54	3.37
Utah.	0.64	0.73	0.03	1.40	0.19	0.12	0.78	0.34	0.12	0.37	0.23	0.81	0.70	0.52
Nevada.	0.35	0.37	0.19	0.97	0.18	0.20	0.33	0.37	0.52	0.58	0.17	0.43	0.42	0.32
Pacific														
Washington.	1.82	2.01	0.40	4.27	2.97	9.61	3.76	2.25	3.15	3.69	1.11	3.76	2.80	1.24
Oregon.	1.16	1.32	0.14	1.95	0.97	2.22	1.20	1.00	0.55	1.25	0.54	2.13	0.88	0.64
California.	10.45	9.57	6.87	14.53	4.11	10.42	37.35	39.99	46.15	29.29	16.02	34.23	25.26	34.96
Alaska.	0.18	0.16	0.05	1.60	80.98	56.95	0.23	0.06	0.40	0.43	0.07	0.15	0.28	0.10
Hawaii.	0.43	0.17	0.07	0.19	0.16	0.32	34.20	6.98	17.29	5.07	0.17	1.32	54.48	0.63

Note: The sum of the totals may not add to 100.00 due to rounding error.

Source: U.S. Bureau of the Census. "General Population Characteristics: U.S. Summary." 1980 Census of Population. Washington, DC: U.S. Government Printing Office, 1983, Table 62.

consistently grown less rapidly than the nation during every decade in this century. Within this region, the East North Central states have grown more nearly like the nation than those of the West North Central division, some of which (especially North Dakota and South Dakota) have suffered absolute population losses during some decades since 1930. During the 1970-80 decade the West North Central division of this region showed relatively more growth strength than during the preceding decade, but the East North Central division showed far less.

The South, which as a region grew only at average rates or below until 1960 but has grown more rapidly than the nation since, has had a mixed internal pattern of growth. Paced by Florida, the South Atlantic division has grown comparatively rapidly since 1930 and explosively since 1970. Other states of this division (West Virginia, South Carolina, Georgia) stagnated until the 1960s and 1970s but have accelerated since. The states of the East South Central division grew only sluggishly until 1970; through the 1970-80 decade, they grew moderately above national rates. The West South Central division (except Texas) has been slow growing between 1930 and 1960 (this region suffered severe outmigration during the great drought of the 1930s), but all states grew at well above the average rates between 1970 and 1980, with Texas being among the ten fastest-growing states.

The most striking growth during the 1970-80 decade has been in the Mountain division of the West region. Nevada, Arizona, Wyoming, Utah, Idaho, Colorado, and New Mexico have been seven of the ten fastest-growing states in the nation. In all previous decades of this century, California and the Pacific division grew faster than the Mountain division; in the 1970-80 decade the Mountain states grew at almost double the rates of the Pacific division. Within the Pacific division, Alaska and Hawaii continued their long-term trend of high growth rates. California, although the volume of its growth was large, grew at a slower rate than during any other decade of its entire history. Washington and Oregon continued above-average growth, as in their entire history as states.

In interpreting the growth rates for the decade 1970-80 of Table 3-1C, the reader should keep in mind the "error of closure" between the 1970 and 1980 censuses described in Chapter 1. Some instances of apparent recovery of growth or acceleration of previously slow growth (West Virginia, Kentucky, Tennessee, Alabama, Mississippi, and Arkansas) could be due to an important degree to the differences in coverage between the two censuses. In the 1980-90 decade some of these states appear to have reverted to their former pattern of slow or negative growth (see below).

Throughout the remainder of this book particular attention will be paid to the differences between the stagnating, the slow growing, and the rapidly growing regions, in order to uncover some of the concomitants and implications of this dramatic abandonment of the Eastern portion of the nation for the West, and of the Northern portion for the South.

Proportional Distribution and Density

The long-term growth pattern has had the effect of distributing the population more evenly among the regions. States with high densities have tended to grow less rapidly than states with low densities (except in the northern Great Plains). Table 3-1B summarizes the entire regional history of population distribution by showing the percentage of population in each state, division, and region at each census from 1790 (or the first census in the state or territory) until 1980. The pattern of regional distribution is graphed in Figures 3-3A and 3-3B. The long-term shift of the demographic weight from the Northeast to the West and the major gains of the South between 1960 and 1980 are evident. The fifteen most populous and least populous states, and their share of the nation's population, are as follows:

Most populous	Percent	Least populous	Percent
Total.	65.66	Total.	5.21
California . . .	10.45	Alaska	0.18
New York	7.75	Wyoming.	0.21
Texas.	6.28	Vermont.	0.23
Pennsylvania . .	5.24	Delaware	0.26
Illinois	5.04	D. of Columbia .	0.28
Ohio	4.77	North Dakota . .	0.29
Florida.	4.30	South Dakota . .	0.30
Michigan	4.09	Nevada	0.35
New Jersey . . .	3.25	Montana.	0.35
North Carolina .	2.60	New Hampshire. .	0.41
Massachusetts. .	2.53	Rhode Island . .	0.42
Indiana.	2.42	Idaho.	0.42
Georgia.	2.41	Hawaii	0.43
Virginia	2.36	Maine.	0.50
Missouri	2.17	New Mexico . . .	0.58

The average population density of each region, division, and state is reported in Table 3-1D. Despite its many decades of slower growth, the Northeast is still about five times as densely settled as the rest of the nation and the national average. Despite its phenomenal growth throughout this century, the West region is still less than one-half as densely settled as the national average.

Race Composition

The number of persons of each race living in each region, division, and state is reported in Table 3-2A. Table 3-2B shows the percentage distribution of each race among the states, that is, how many persons of each race were residing in each state and in which states the people of each particular racial group are concentrated. Figure 3-4 graphs the regional distribution of the major race groups and the Spanish-origin population. All the Asian race groups except Asian Indians are concentrated in the Pacific division. Almost one-half of all American Indians are found in the West region. Despite many decades of outmigration to the North and West, more than one-half of the black population still resides in the South, and nearly 30 percent is in the South Atlantic states.

The percentage of population classed as black (Negro) for states at each census since 1850 is reported in Table 3-5A, and the intercensal rate of increase in the black population is reported in Table 3-5B. The change between 1970 and 1980 in the regional pattern of growth rates in comparison with the northward-exodus days of the 1940s, 1950s, and (to a lesser degree) 1960s is remarkable. This change, together with the acceleration in the rates of growth in the Mountain and Pacific states, is perhaps indicative of a major turning point in the population redistribution pattern of the black population.

Aside from the District of Columbia (70 percent black), the states with the highest and lowest proportions black population are:

Table 3-3. Spatial Distribution of Spanish-Origin Population: 1980

Region, division, and state	Number (000)	Percent Spanish-origin	Percent of Spanish-origin				Percent black	Percent distribution
			Mexican	Puerto-Rican	Cuban	Other		
United States, total. . .	14,609	6.4	59.8	13.8	5.5	20.9	2.7	100.00
Northeast region.	2,604	5.3	3.4	57.4	6.8	32.4	5.5	17.82
New England	299	2.4	5.5	57.5	4.5	32.5	4.4	2.05
Middle Atlantic	2,305	6.3	3.1	57.4	7.1	32.5	5.6	15.78
North Central region. . . .	1,277	2.2	64.3	16.1	2.6	17.0	3.2	8.74
East North Central. . . .	1,068	2.6	63.0	18.5	2.8	15.8	3.2	7.31
West North Central. . . .	209	1.2	70.8	4.2	2.0	23.0	3.1	1.43
South region.	4,474	5.9	69.2	4.0	11.7	15.1	3.7	30.62
South Atlantic.	1,194	3.2	16.7	11.8	41.3	30.2	7.8	8.17
East South Central. . . .	120	0.8	55.3	7.1	4.1	33.5	27.4	0.82
West South Central. . . .	3,160	13.3	89.6	1.0	0.7	8.7	1.2	21.63
West region	6,254	14.5	75.7	2.1	1.1	21.1	0.7	42.81
Mountain.	1,443	12.7	66.4	1.0	0.5	32.1	0.4	9.88
Pacific	4,811	15.1	78.5	2.5	1.3	17.7	0.8	32.93
New England								
Maine	5	0.4	30.7	14.3	4.1	50.9	1.4	0.03
New Hampshire	6	0.7	20.6	23.6	5.9	49.9	2.3	0.04
Vermont	3	0.6	19.0	9.8	4.4	66.8	1.1	0.02
Massachusetts	141	2.5	5.2	54.2	4.7	36.1	5.4	0.97
Rhode Island.	20	2.1	6.8	23.4	2.8	66.9	4.4	0.13
Connecticut	124	4.0	3.6	71.0	4.5	20.9	3.6	0.85
Middle Atlantic								
New York.	1,659	9.4	2.3	59.4	4.6	33.6	6.2	11.36
New Jersey.	492	6.7	2.7	49.6	16.4	31.3	3.6	3.37
Pennsylvania.	154	1.3	12.6	59.7	3.6	24.2	6.1	1.05
East North Central								
Ohio.	120	1.1	44.5	27.1	2.7	25.8	6.5	0.82
Indiana	87	1.6	66.2	14.6	2.2	17.0	3.4	0.60
Illinois.	636	5.6	64.2	20.3	3.0	12.4	2.1	4.35
Michigan.	162	1.8	69.1	7.6	2.6	20.7	5.1	1.11
Wisconsin	63	1.3	65.2	16.6	1.6	16.6	2.3	0.43
West North Central								
Minnesota	32	0.8	63.6	4.8	2.5	29.1	2.4	0.22
Iowa.	26	0.9	71.1	2.8	1.9	24.2	1.6	0.17
Missouri.	52	1.1	62.0	4.9	2.9	30.2	6.6	0.35
North Dakota.	4	0.6	59.4	6.3	1.5	32.8	0.8	0.03
South Dakota.	4	0.6	59.7	5.7	1.1	33.5	1.0	0.03
Nebraska.	28	1.8	80.0	2.2	1.3	16.4	1.6	0.19
Kansas.	63	2.7	78.8	4.6	1.5	15.1	2.1	0.43

Highest	Percent	Lowest	Percent
Mississippi. . .	35.2	Vermont.	0.2
South Carolina .	30.4	Montana.	0.2
Louisiana. . . .	29.4	Maine.	0.3
Georgia.	26.8	South Dakota . .	0.3
Alabama.	25.6	Idaho.	0.3
Maryland	22.7	North Dakota . .	0.4
North Carolina .	22.4	New Hampshire. .	0.4
Virginia	18.9	Utah	0.6
Arkansas	16.3	Wyoming.	0.7
Delaware	16.1	Minnesota. . . .	1.3
Tennessee. . . .	15.8	Oregon	1.4
Illinois	14.7	Iowa	1.4
Florida.	13.8	Hawaii	1.8
New York	13.8	New Mexico . . .	1.8
Michigan	12.9	Washington . . .	2.6

The Spanish-Origin Population

Chapter 2 introduced the Spanish-origin population as the second great minority group in the nation. It increased in size very rapidly between 1970 and 1980.[1] Table 3-3 shows the distribution of this ethnic group among the regions, divisions, and states, and its nationality composition among these units. The states with the highest proportion of residents of Spanish-origin population and the states where the Spanish-origin population is most concentrated are as follows:

Table 3-3. Spatial Distribution of Spanish-Origin Population: 1980—continued

Region, division, and state	Number (000)	Percent Spanish-origin	Percent of Spanish-origin: Mexican	Puerto-Rican	Cuban	Other	Percent black	Percent distri-bution
South Atlantic								
Delaware.	10	1.6	15.9	49.7	6.2	28.2	10.4	0.07
Maryland.	65	1.5	19.1	13.9	8.2	58.8	11.9	0.44
District of Columbia. . .	18	2.8	17.7	8.1	5.5	68.7	21.2	0.12
Virginia.	80	1.5	30.2	12.8	6.2	50.8	13.1	0.55
West Virginia	13	0.7	49.2	5.2	2.3	43.3	3.5	0.09
North Carolina.	57	1.0	49.1	13.1	5.5	32.3	25.2	0.39
South Carolina.	33	1.1	52.4	12.3	5.0	30.3	38.9	0.23
Georgia	61	1.1	45.1	12.9	9.6	32.4	27.8	0.42
Florida	858	8.8	9.3	11.0	54.8	24.9	2.9	5.87
East South Central								
Kentucky.	27	0.7	51.6	10.0	3.5	34.9	7.9	0.19
Tennessee	34	0.7	54.5	7.0	4.5	34.0	20.8	0.23
Alabama	33	0.9	56.7	6.9	4.6	31.8	38.0	0.23
Mississippi	25	1.0	58.8	4.3	3.5	33.4	43.8	0.17
West South Central								
Arkansas.	18	0.8	60.8	4.6	3.4	31.1	21.1	0.12
Louisiana	99	2.4	28.8	4.6	8.0	58.6	14.8	0.68
Oklahoma.	57	1.9	67.9	5.0	1.4	25.7	2.8	0.39
Texas	2,986	21.0	92.2	0.8	0.5	6.6	0.6	20.44
Mountain								
Montana	10	1.3	64.8	2.9	0.8	31.5	0.7	0.07
Idaho	37	3.9	76.9	1.1	0.3	21.7	0.1	0.25
Wyoming	25	5.3	65.1	1.2	0.3	33.4	0.3	0.17
Colorado.	340	11.8	61.0	1.2	0.4	37.3	0.5	2.32
New Mexico.	477	36.6	49.0	0.3	0.1	50.5	0.2	3.27
Arizona	441	16.2	89.9	0.9	0.2	8.9	0.4	3.02
Utah.	60	4.1	63.1	2.5	0.5	34.0	0.4	0.41
Nevada.	54	6.7	60.7	3.4	6.9	29.0	1.0	0.37
Pacific								
Washington.	120	2.9	67.6	4.2	1.0	27.1	1.3	0.82
Oregon.	66	2.5	68.6	2.7	1.6	27.1	0.8	0.45
California.	4,544	19.2	80.1	2.0	1.3	16.6	0.8	31.11
Alaska.	10	2.5	48.5	10.2	1.7	39.6	2.3	0.07
Hawaii.	71	7.4	12.1	27.2	0.6	60.1	1.0	0.49

Source: U.S. Bureau of the Census. "General Population Characteristics: United States Summary." 1980 Census of Population. Washington, DC: U.S. Government Printing Office, 1983, Table 63.

States with highest percent Spanish-origin population	Percent	States with largest shares of U.S. Spanish-origin population	Percent
New Mexico . . .	36.6	California . . .	31.10
Texas.	21.0	Texas.	20.44
California . . .	19.2	New York	11.36
Arizona.	16.2	Florida.	5.87
Colorado	11.8	Illinois	4.85
New York	9.5	New Jersey . . .	3.37
Florida.	8.8	New Mexico . . .	3.27
Hawaii	7.4	Arizona.	3.06
Nevada	6.7	Colorado	2.32
New Jersey . . .	6.7	Michigan	1.11
Illinois	5.6	Pennsylvania . .	1.05
Wyoming.	5.2	Massachusetts. .	0.97
Utah	4.1	Connecticut. . .	0.85
Connecticut. . .	4.0	Ohio	0.82
Idaho.	3.9	Washington . . .	0.82

In five states the proportion of population that is Spanish-origin exceeds 10 percent. All are in the West or Southwest. In ten additional states, 4.0 percent or more of the population is Spanish-origin. Except Florida, they are all either in the old industrial belt or in the West and Southwest.

The geographic concentration of the Spanish-origin population was pronounced in 1980. More than one-half of all Spanish-origin residents were found in California and Texas, and three-fourths were found in the six states with the largest concentrations. It cannot yet be predicted whether this population will retain this tendency to congregate in old industrial cities and along the southern border of the United States or will diffuse more evenly throughout the population as it becomes more bilingual and assimilated.

Table 3-3 also shows the nationality of origin of the Spanish-origin population. Figure 3-5 graphs the nationality composition of the U.S. population by region. In the Northeast, Puerto Ricans and immigrants from Latin American countries other than Mexico and Cuba predominate. Florida (and to a lesser degree New Jersey, Louisiana, Maryland, and Nevada) has a strong concentration of Cubans. Mexicans are overwhelmingly predominant in California and most of the states of the Western region. In Illinois and the East North Central division, Mexicans predominate, but there is a strong infusion of Puerto Ricans and other nationalities. Along the Atlantic Seaboard south of New Jersey, the mixture is about equal between "other" Latin Americans and Mexicans, with strong elements of Puerto Ricans and Cuban residents.

It was noted in Chapter 2 that a small fraction of the Spanish-origin population (2.7 percent) reported themselves as of the black race. This tendency is very strong in all states of the Southern region except Texas, West Virginia, and Oklahoma. This may be related to incorrect self-reporting to the Census, or it may be that the small fraction of Spanish-origin population that is black does reside predominantly in the South.

Sex Composition

Because of young age composition, race composition (black population), and possibly selective migration, a few states have unusually high sex ratios, and a few have unusually low sex ratios, in comparison with the national average in 1980 of 94.5 males per 100 females.

High sex ratios		Low sex ratios	
Wyoming.	118.2	D. of Columbia .	86.1
Alaska	112.8	New York	90.5
Hawaii	105.2	Massachusetts. .	90.8
Nevada	102.4	Rhode Island . .	91.0
North Dakota . .	101.3	Pennsylvania . .	91.9
Idaho.	99.7	New Jersey . . .	92.2
Montana.	99.6	Florida.	92.2
Washington . . .	98.7	Alabama.	92.5
Colorado	98.5	Missouri	92.7
Utah	98.4	Missippi	92.9
South Dakota . .	97.3	Delaware	93.1
California . . .	97.2	Connecticut. . .	93.1
New Mexico . . .	97.2	Tennessee. . . .	93.3
Oregon	97.0	Arkansas	93.5
Arizona.	96.9	Ohio	93.5

The sex composition history of the nation is portrayed in Table 3-6, which shows that during the early years of settlement each state or region has tended to have high sex ratios but, with the passage of time, has tended to regress toward the national mean.

Age Composition

Although all of the states have roughly similar age compositions based on low fertility and low mortality, there are substantial differences among them. Some have a higher than average proportion of young population, while others have an unusually large proportion of old population. These variations are a result of past differences in fertility, migration, and mortality. The states having higher fertility and substantial inmigration of young workers have a younger age composition. States that suffer outmigration and have low fertility (usually with high life expectancy) have older age compositions. These rules are modified by the tendency for people of retirement ages to move to warmer climates: Florida's high proportion of aged population is the focal point of such migration. Table 3-4 documents these present interstate differences in age composition, separately for males and females.

Tables 3-7A and 3-7B report statistics with which to trace the changing age composition of each state since

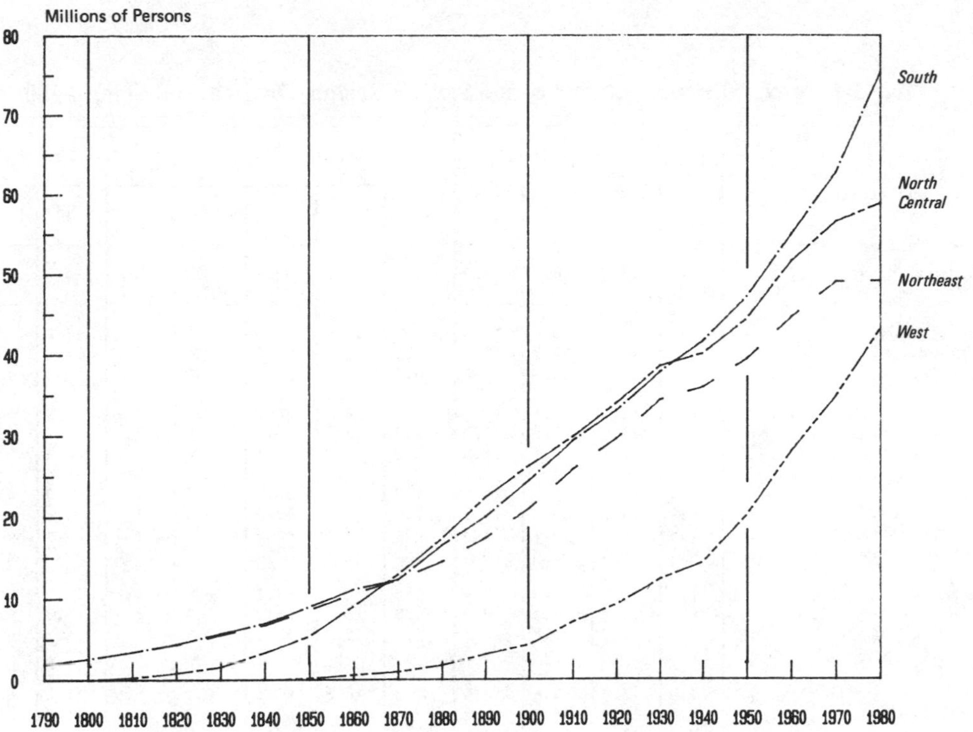

Figure 3-3A. Population of Geographical Regions: 1790-1980

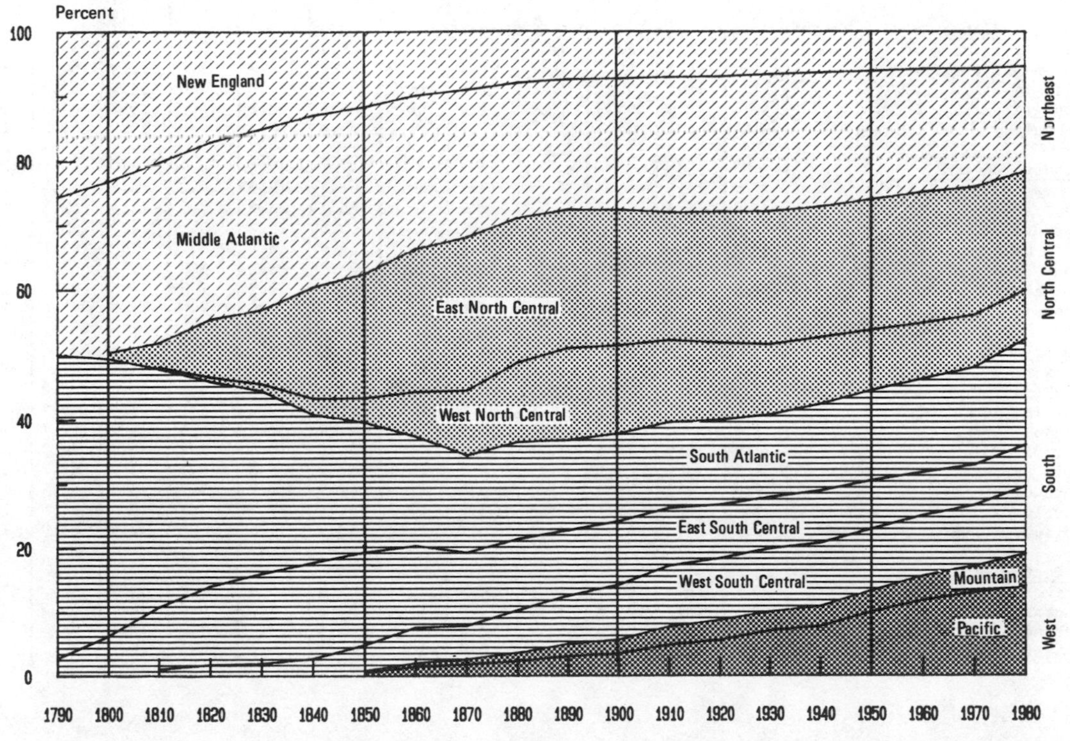

Figure 3-3B. Percent Distribution of Population Among Geographical Regions: 1790-1980

Table 3-4. Percent Distribution of Age and Sex, by Region, Division, and State: 1980

Region, division, and state	Total				Males				Females			
	0-4	5-14	15-64	65+	0-4	5-14	15-64	65+	0-4	5-14	15-64	65+
United States, total	7.2	15.5	66.2	11.3	7.6	16.3	66.8	9.3	6.9	14.7	65.3	13.0
Northeast region	6.3	14.8	66.6	12.3	6.8	15.9	67.3	10.1	5.9	13.8	65.6	14.4
New England	6.1	14.9	66.7	12.3	6.5	15.9	67.8	9.8	5.7	14.0	65.7	14.6
Middle Atlantic	6.4	14.8	66.4	12.4	6.8	15.8	67.2	10.2	6.0	13.8	65.8	14.4
North Central region	7.4	15.7	65.4	11.5	7.8	16.5	66.2	9.4	7.1	14.9	64.9	13.3
East North Central	7.4	15.9	65.9	10.8	7.8	16.8	66.5	8.9	7.0	15.1	65.3	12.6
West North Central	7.6	15.1	64.5	12.8	8.0	15.9	65.5	10.6	7.2	14.4	63.5	14.9
South region	7.4	15.8	65.5	11.3	7.7	16.7	66.1	9.5	7.0	15.0	65.1	13.0
South Atlantic	6.7	15.2	66.3	11.8	7.1	16.0	67.0	9.9	6.4	14.4	65.7	13.5
East South Central	7.6	16.4	64.7	11.3	8.1	17.3	65.2	9.4	7.2	15.5	64.3	13.0
West South Central	8.2	16.4	65.0	10.4	8.5	17.1	65.7	8.7	7.8	15.7	64.5	12.0
West region	7.7	15.1	67.3	9.9	8.0	15.6	68.2	8.4	7.4	14.6	66.6	11.5
Mountain	8.7	16.2	65.8	9.3	9.0	16.7	66.2	8.1	8.5	15.8	65.2	10.5
Pacific	7.3	14.7	67.8	10.2	7.6	15.2	68.7	8.5	7.1	14.2	66.9	11.8
New England												
Maine	7.0	15.9	64.6	12.5	7.4	16.8	65.6	10.3	6.6	15.0	63.7	14.6
New Hampshire	6.8	15.7	66.3	11.2	7.1	16.6	67.3	9.0	6.5	14.9	65.4	13.2
Vermont	7.0	15.7	65.8	11.4	7.4	16.5	66.6	9.3	6.7	14.9	65.1	13.3
Massachusetts	5.9	14.6	66.9	12.7	6.3	15.6	68.1	9.9	5.5	13.6	65.8	15.2
Rhode Island	6.0	14.3	66.3	13.4	6.4	15.4	67.5	10.7	5.6	13.4	65.2	15.9
Connecticut	6.0	14.9	67.4	11.7	6.3	15.8	68.4	9.6	5.6	14.0	66.6	13.8
Middle Atlantic												
New York	6.5	14.8	66.5	12.3	7.0	15.9	67.1	10.1	6.0	13.8	65.9	14.3
New Jersey	6.3	15.1	66.9	11.7	6.7	16.1	67.6	9.6	5.9	14.2	66.3	13.6
Pennsylvania	6.3	14.6	66.2	12.9	6.7	15.6	67.0	10.7	5.9	13.7	65.4	15.0
East North Central												
Ohio	7.3	15.8	66.1	10.8	7.7	16.8	66.7	8.9	6.9	14.9	65.5	12.7
Indiana	7.6	16.2	65.5	10.7	8.1	17.0	66.2	8.7	7.2	15.4	64.9	12.5
Illinois	7.4	15.5	66.1	11.0	7.8	16.3	66.9	9.0	7.0	14.7	65.3	13.0
Michigan	7.4	16.5	66.3	9.8	7.8	17.3	66.6	8.3	7.1	15.7	65.8	11.4
Wisconsin	7.4	15.7	64.9	12.0	7.7	16.4	65.8	10.1	7.0	15.0	64.2	13.8
West North Central												
Minnesota	7.5	15.4	65.3	11.8	7.9	16.1	66.1	9.9	7.2	14.8	64.4	13.6
Iowa	7.6	15.2	63.9	13.3	8.0	16.0	65.1	10.9	7.2	14.4	62.8	15.6
Missouri	7.2	15.0	64.6	13.2	7.7	15.9	65.5	10.9	6.8	14.1	63.8	15.3
North Dakota	8.4	15.3	64.0	12.3	8.6	15.7	64.9	10.8	8.2	15.0	62.9	13.9
South Dakota	8.5	15.5	62.8	13.2	8.7	16.0	64.0	11.3	8.2	15.1	61.7	15.0
Nebraska	7.8	15.2	63.8	13.1	8.2	15.6	65.1	10.9	7.5	14.5	62.8	15.2
Kansas	7.7	14.6	64.8	13.0	8.0	15.3	66.1	10.6	7.3	13.9	63.6	15.2
South Atlantic												
Delaware	6.9	15.3	67.8	10.0	7.3	16.2	68.4	8.1	6.6	14.5	67.3	11.7
Maryland	6.5	15.4	68.8	9.4	6.8	16.2	69.3	7.6	6.1	14.6	68.2	11.0
District of Columbia	5.4	12.3	70.6	11.6	5.9	13.5	71.5	9.2	5.0	11.4	69.9	13.7
Virginia	6.7	15.3	68.5	9.5	7.1	16.0	69.4	7.6	6.4	14.7	67.7	11.2
West Virginia	7.5	15.9	64.5	12.2	7.9	16.9	64.9	10.4	7.1	15.0	64.0	13.9
North Carolina	6.9	15.8	67.1	10.3	7.2	16.6	67.9	8.3	6.5	15.0	66.3	12.1
South Carolina	7.6	16.7	66.5	9.2	8.0	17.5	67.2	7.3	7.3	15.9	65.9	11.0
Georgia	7.6	16.8	66.1	9.5	8.0	17.7	66.8	7.5	7.2	15.9	65.6	11.3
Florida	5.9	13.4	63.4	17.3	6.2	14.3	63.9	15.6	5.5	12.6	63.0	18.9
East South Central												
Kentucky	7.7	16.1	64.9	11.2	8.0	16.9	65.6	9.4	7.6	15.9	63.2	13.3
Tennessee	7.1	15.7	65.9	11.3	7.6	16.6	66.5	9.4	6.7	14.8	65.5	13.1
Alabama	7.6	16.5	64.6	11.3	8.0	17.6	65.0	9.4	7.2	15.5	64.2	13.1
Mississippi	8.5	17.7	62.3	11.5	9.0	18.7	62.5	9.7	8.1	16.7	62.1	13.1

Table 3-4. Percent Distribution of Age and Sex, by Region, Division, and State: 1980–continued

Region, division, and state	Total				Males				Females			
	0-4	5-14	15-64	65+	0-4	5-14	15-64	65+	0-4	5-14	15-64	65+
West South Central												
Arkansas	7.7	16.0	62.7	13.7	8.2	16.9	62.9	12.0	7.2	15.1	62.4	15.2
Louisiana	8.6	17.1	64.7	9.6	9.0	17.9	65.1	8.0	8.2	16.3	64.3	11.2
Oklahoma	7.7	15.2	64.6	12.4	8.1	16.0	65.6	10.3	7.3	14.5	63.7	14.5
Texas	8.2	16.5	65.6	9.6	8.5	17.1	66.3	8.0	7.9	15.9	65.0	11.2
Mountain												
Montana	8.2	15.6	65.5	10.7	8.4	16.0	66.2	9.4	8.0	15.2	64.8	12.1
Idaho	9.9	17.2	63.0	9.9	10.2	17.6	63.3	8.9	9.6	16.7	62.7	10.9
Wyoming	9.6	16.3	66.3	7.9	9.5	16.4	67.4	6.7	9.6	16.2	65.1	9.2
Colorado	7.5	15.2	68.8	8.6	7.7	15.6	69.6	7.0	7.3	14.8	67.9	10.1
New Mexico	8.8	17.2	65.1	8.9	9.1	17.7	65.3	7.9	8.5	16.6	65.0	9.9
Arizona	7.9	15.8	65.0	11.3	8.2	16.4	65.3	10.2	7.6	15.3	64.7	12.4
Utah	13.0	18.6	60.9	7.5	13.5	19.1	61.0	6.4	12.6	18.1	60.8	8.5
Nevada	7.0	14.7	70.1	8.2	7.1	14.8	70.6	7.5	6.9	14.5	69.6	9.0
Pacific												
Washington	7.4	15.0	67.2	10.4	7.6	15.4	68.1	8.8	7.2	14.5	66.3	12.1
Oregon	7.5	14.9	66.1	11.5	7.9	15.5	66.7	10.0	7.2	14.3	65.5	13.0
California	7.2	14.6	68.0	10.2	7.5	15.1	69.0	8.4	7.0	14.1	67.1	11.9
Alaska	9.7	17.3	70.2	2.9	9.4	16.7	71.2	2.7	10.0	17.8	69.1	3.1
Hawaii	8.1	15.3	68.7	7.9	8.1	15.4	68.8	7.8	8.1	15.3	68.6	8.0

Source: U.S. Bureau of the Census. "General Population Characteristics: United States Summary." *1980 Census of Population*. Washington, DC: U.S. Government Printing Office, 1983, tables 67, 55, and 45.

1850. Table 3-7A provides data on the proportion of persons under fifteen years of age, and Table 3-7B provides similar data on persons sixty-five and over. Following are lists of states having unusually high proportions of young and old populations in 1980:

High proportion of population under 15		High proportion of population 65 or older	
Utah	31.6	Florida	17.3
Idaho	27.1	Arkansas	13.7
Alaska	26.9	Rhode Island	13.4
Mississippi	26.2	Iowa	13.3
New Mexico	25.9	Missouri	13.2
Wyoming	25.8	South Dakota	13.2
Louisiana	25.7	Nebraska	13.1
Texas	24.7	Kansas	13.0
Georgia	24.4	Pennsylvania	12.9
South Carolina	24.3	Massachusetts	12.7
Alabama	24.1	Maine	12.5
South Dakota	24.0	Oklahoma	12.4
Kentucky	23.9	North Dakota	12.3
Michigan	23.9	New York	12.3
Montana	23.8	West Virginia	12.2
Indiana	23.8	Wisconsin	12.0

Most of the states with young age composition are in the West and South, while most of those with concentrations of older population are in the Northeast and North Central regions.

Urban-Rural Residence

A highly useful classification for studying population distribution is one that separates city dwellers from country dwellers. The separation is achieved by setting up a definition of the residential places that are to be considered urban and classifying the rest as rural. In the United States, with mass use of automobiles and a highway system that permits a wide choice of locations for residence with relation to any given place of work, urban and rural localities shade into each other as more of a continuum than two clearly demarcated categories. Whatever dividing line is placed between the two is therefore arbitrary. Before 1950 the U.S. Bureau of the Census defined urban population as the residents of incorporated places numbering 2,500 or more inhabitants in that particular census. Suburban overflow across city boundaries into contiguous unincorporated territory prompted the Census Bureau for the 1950 census to use the term "urbanized areas," defined as the city plus its "urban fringe." This urban fringe is the contiguous, closely settled surrounding suburban territory. A population density of at least 1,000 persons per square mile is the principal criterion for establishing the urbanized area boundaries. However, the boundaries are also drawn

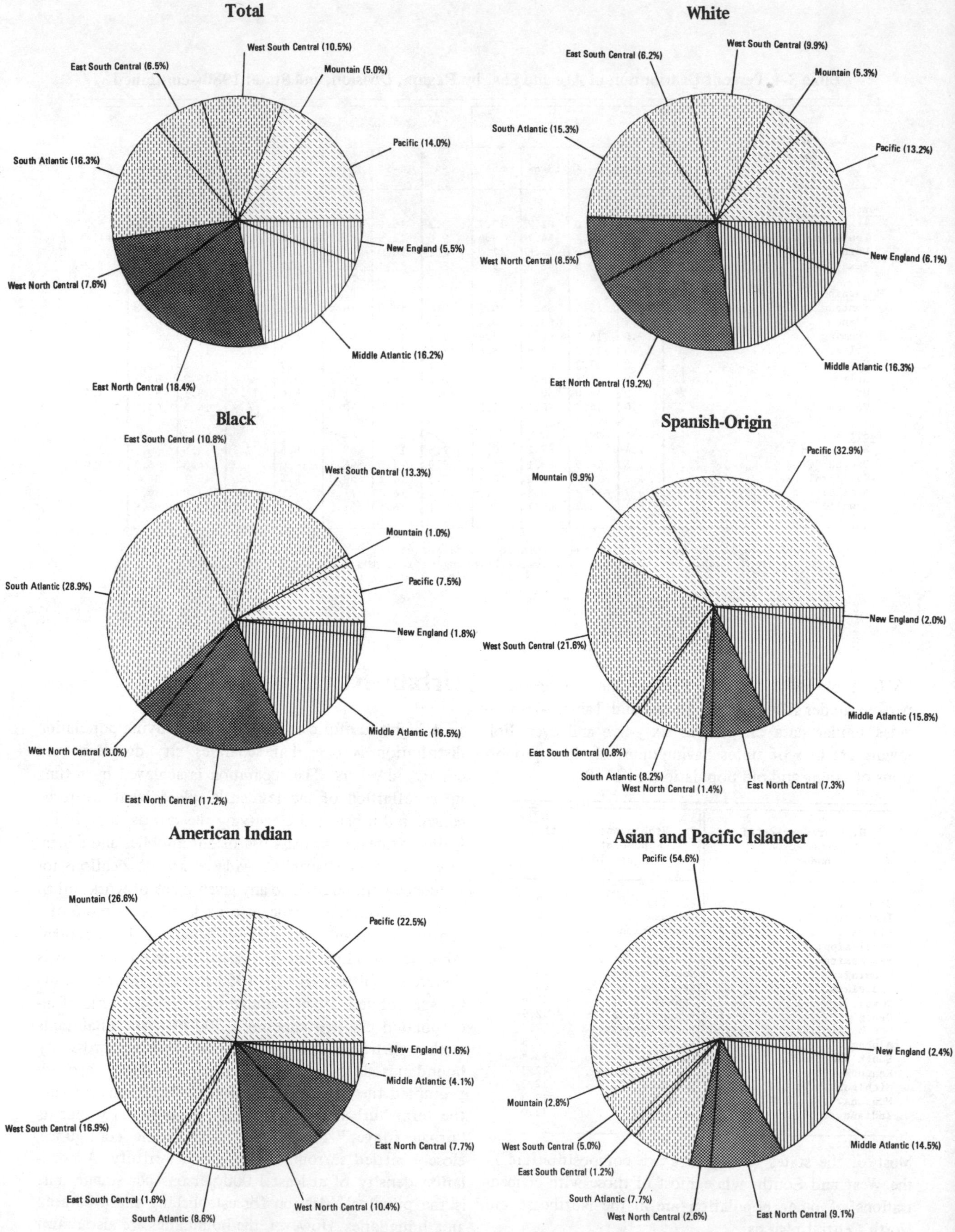

Figure 3-4. Distribution of Race-Ethnicity Groups Among Geographical Regions: 1980

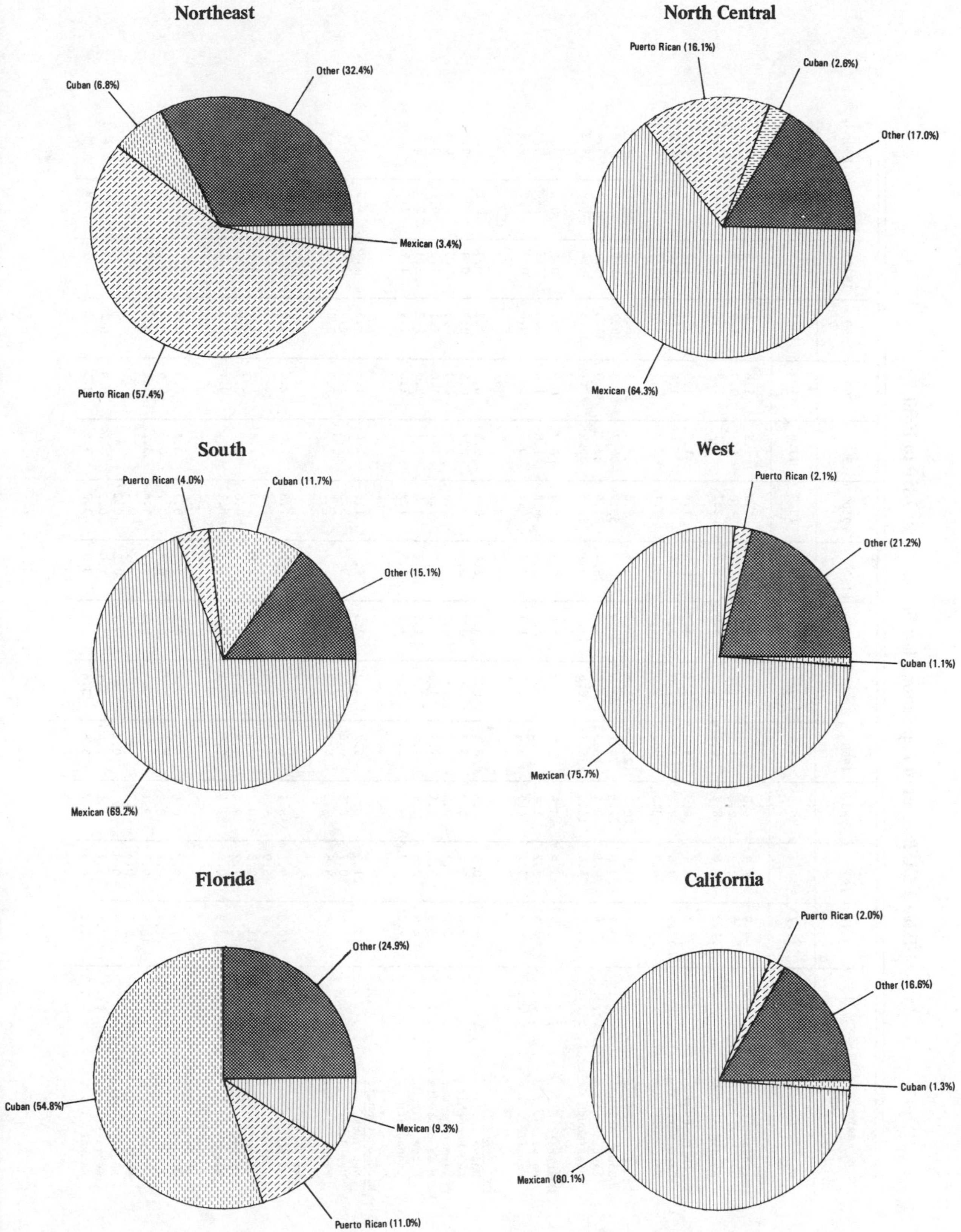

Figure 3-5. Ethnic Composition of the Spanish-Origin Population: Regions, 1980

Table 3-5A. Percent of Population Classified as Black: 1850 to 1980

Regions, division, and state	1980	1970	1960	1950	1940	1930	1920	1910	1900	1890	1880	1870	1860	1850
United States, total. . .	11.7	11.1	10.5	9.9	9.7	9.7	9.9	10.7	11.6	11.9	13.1	12.7	14.1	15.7
Northeast region.	9.9	8.9	6.8	5.1	3.8	3.3	2.3	1.9	1.8	1.6	1.6	1.5	1.5	1.7
New England	3.8	3.3	2.3	1.5	1.2	1.2	1.1	1.0	1.1	0.9	1.0	0.9	0.8	0.9
Middle Atlantic	11.9	10.6	8.2	6.2	4.6	4.0	2.7	2.2	2.1	1.8	1.8	1.7	1.8	2.2
North Central region. . . .	9.1	8.1	6.7	5.0	3.5	3.3	2.3	1.8	1.9	1.9	2.2	2.1	2.0	2.5
East North Central. . . .	10.9	9.6	8.0	5.9	4.0	3.7	2.4	1.6	1.6	1.5	1.6	1.4	0.9	1.0
West North Central. . . .	4.6	4.3	3.6	3.0	2.6	2.5	2.2	2.1	2.3	2.5	3.3	3.7	5.6	10.2
South region.	18.6	19.1	20.6	21.7	23.8	24.7	26.9	29.8	32.3	33.8	36.0	36.0	36.8	37.3
South Atlantic.	20.7	20.8	22.5	24.1	26.4	28.0	30.9	33.7	35.7	36.8	38.7	37.9	38.4	39.8
East South Central. . . .	19.6	20.1	22.4	23.5	25.8	26.9	28.4	31.5	33.1	33.0	34.4	33.2	34.7	33.4
West South Central. . . .	14.9	15.6	16.3	16.7	18.6	18.7	20.1	22.6	25.9	29.1	32.6	36.4	36.9	39.2
West region	5.2	4.9	3.9	2.8	1.2	1.0	0.9	0.7	0.7	0.9	0.7	0.6	0.6	0.6
Mountain.	2.4	2.2	1.8	1.3	0.9	0.8	0.9	0.8	1.0	1.0	0.5	*	*	*
Pacific	6.3	5.7	4.5	3.4	1.3	1.1	0.8	0.7	0.6	0.7	0.5	0.6	0.9	0.9
New England														
Maine	0.3	0.3	0.3	0.1	0.1	0.1	0.1	0.1	0.1	0.2	0.2	0.3	0.2	0.2
New Hampshire	0.4	0.4	0.3	0.2	*	0.2	0.2	0.2	0.2	0.3	0.3	0.3	*	0.3
Vermont	0.2	0.2	0.3	*	*	0.3	0.3	0.6	0.3	0.3	0.3	0.3	0.3	0.3
Massachusetts	3.9	3.1	2.2	1.6	1.3	1.2	1.2	1.1	1.1	1.0	1.1	1.0	0.8	0.9
Rhode Island.	2.9	2.6	2.1	1.8	1.5	1.5	1.7	1.8	2.1	2.0	2.2	2.3	2.3	2.7
Connecticut	7.0	6.0	4.2	2.6	1.9	1.8	1.5	1.3	1.7	1.6	1.9	1.9	2.0	2.2
Middle Atlantic														
New York.	13.7	11.9	8.4	6.2	4.2	3.3	1.9	1.5	1.4	1.2	1.3	1.2	1.3	1.6
New Jersey.	12.6	10.7	8.5	6.6	5.5	5.2	3.7	3.5	3.7	3.3	3.4	3.4	3.7	4.9
Pennsylvania.	8.8	8.6	7.5	6.1	4.7	4.5	3.3	2.5	2.5	2.1	2.0	1.8	2.0	2.3
East North Central														
Ohio.	10.0	9.1	8.1	6.5	4.9	4.6	3.2	2.3	2.3	2.4	2.5	2.4	1.6	1.3
Indiana	7.6	6.9	5.8	4.4	3.6	3.5	2.8	2.2	2.3	2.1	2.0	1.5	0.8	1.1
Illinois.	14.7	12.8	10.3	7.4	4.9	4.3	2.8	1.9	1.8	1.5	1.5	1.1	0.5	0.6
Michigan.	12.9	11.2	9.2	6.9	4.0	3.5	1.6	0.6	0.7	0.7	0.9	1.0	0.9	0.8
Wisconsin	3.9	2.9	1.9	0.8	0.4	0.4	0.2	0.1	0.1	0.1	0.2	0.2	0.1	0.3
West North Central														
Minnesota	1.3	0.9	0.6	0.5	0.4	0.4	0.4	0.3	0.3	0.3	0.3	0.2	*	*
Iowa.	1.4	1.2	0.9	0.8	0.7	0.7	0.8	0.7	0.6	0.6	0.6	0.5	0.1	*
Missouri.	10.5	10.3	9.1	7.5	6.4	6.2	5.2	4.8	5.2	5.6	6.7	6.9	10.1	13.2
North Dakota.	0.4	0.3	0.2	*	*	*	*	0.2	*	*	*	*	*	*
South Dakota.	0.3	0.3	0.1	0.2	*	0.1	0.2	0.2	*	*	*	*	*	*
Nebraska.	3.1	2.7	2.1	1.4	1.1	1.0	1.0	0.7	0.6	0.8	0.4	0.8	*	*
Kansas.	5.3	4.8	4.2	3.8	3.6	3.5	3.3	3.2	3.5	3.5	4.3	4.7	0.9	*

Table 3-5A. Percent of Population Classified as Black: 1850 to 1980–continued

Regions, division, and state	1980	1970	1960	1950	1940	1930	1920	1910	1900	1890	1880	1870	1860	1850
South Atlantic														
Delaware	16.1	14.2	13.7	13.8	13.5	13.9	13.5	15.3	16.8	16.7	17.7	18.4	19.6	21.7
Maryland	22.7	17.8	16.7	16.5	16.6	16.9	16.8	17.9	19.8	20.7	22.5	22.4	24.9	28.3
District of Columbia	70.3	71.1	53.9	35.0	28.2	27.1	25.1	28.4	31.2	33.0	33.7	32.6	18.7	26.9
Virginia	18.9	18.5	20.6	22.1	24.7	26.8	29.9	32.5	35.7	38.3	41.8	41.9	45.0	47.1
West Virginia	3.3	3.8	4.8	5.7	6.2	6.7	5.9	5.2	4.5	4.3	4.2	4.1	*	*
North Carolina	22.4	22.2	24.5	25.8	27.5	29.0	29.8	31.6	32.9	34.7	37.9	36.6	36.5	36.4
South Carolina	30.4	30.5	34.8	38.8	42.8	45.7	51.4	55.2	58.4	59.9	60.6	58.9	58.5	58.9
Georgia	26.8	25.9	28.5	30.9	34.7	36.8	41.6	45.1	46.7	46.8	47.0	46.0	44.1	42.5
Florida	13.8	15.3	17.8	21.8	27.1	29.4	34.0	41.0	43.7	42.5	47.2	48.9	45.0	46.0
East South Central														
Kentucky	7.1	7.2	7.1	6.9	7.5	8.6	9.8	11.4	13.3	14.4	16.4	16.8	20.4	22.5
Tennessee	15.8	15.8	16.5	16.1	17.5	18.3	19.3	21.6	23.8	24.4	26.1	25.6	25.5	24.5
Alabama	25.6	26.2	30.0	32.0	34.7	35.7	38.4	42.5	45.2	44.8	47.5	47.7	45.4	44.7
Mississippi	35.2	36.8	42.1	45.3	49.2	50.2	52.2	56.1	58.5	57.6	57.4	53.6	55.2	51.2
West South Central														
Arkansas	16.3	18.3	21.8	22.4	24.8	25.8	26.9	28.1	28.0	27.4	26.3	25.2	25.5	22.9
Louisiana	29.4	29.9	31.9	32.9	35.9	36.9	38.9	43.1	47.1	50.0	51.5	50.1	49.4	50.6
Oklahoma	6.8	6.7	6.6	6.5	7.2	7.2	7.3	8.3	7.1	8.5	*	*	*	*
Texas	12.0	12.5	12.4	12.7	14.4	14.7	15.9	17.7	20.4	21.8	24.7	30.9	30.3	27.7
Mountain														
Montana	0.2	0.3	0.1	0.2	0.2	0.2	0.4	0.5	0.8	0.7	*	*	*	*
Idaho	0.3	0.3	0.3	0.2	0.2	0.2	0.2	0.3	*	*	*	*	*	*
Wyoming	0.7	0.9	0.6	1.0	0.4	0.4	0.5	1.4	1.1	1.6	*	*	*	*
Colorado	3.5	3.0	2.3	1.5	1.1	1.2	1.2	1.4	1.7	1.5	1.0	*	*	*
New Mexico	1.8	2.0	1.8	1.2	0.9	0.7	1.7	0.6	1.0	1.3	0.8	*	*	*
Arizona	2.8	3.0	3.3	3.5	3.0	2.5	2.4	1.0	1.6	1.1	*	*	*	*
Utah	0.6	0.7	0.4	0.4	0.2	0.2	0.2	0.3	0.4	0.5	*	*	*	*
Nevada	6.4	5.7	4.6	2.5	0.9	1.1	*	1.2	*	*	*	*	*	*
Pacific														
Washington	2.6	2.1	1.7	1.3	0.4	0.4	0.5	0.5	0.6	0.6	*	*	*	*
Oregon	1.4	1.2	1.0	0.8	0.3	0.2	0.3	0.1	0.2	0.3	*	*	*	*
California	7.7	7.0	5.6	4.4	1.8	1.4	1.1	0.9	0.7	0.9	0.7	0.7	1.1	1.1
Alaska	3.4	3.0	3.1	*	*	*	*	*	*	*	*	*	*	*
Hawaii	1.8	1.0	0.8	0.6	*	0.3	*	0.5	*	*	*	*	*	*

Note: * indicates less that 0.1.

Source: U.S. Bureau of the Census. Historical Statistics of the United States, Colonial Times to 1970, Part I. Washington, DC: U.S. Government Printing Office, 1975, table series A 195–209, 172–194, 91–118 for data prior to 1980. U.S. Bureau of the Census. "General Population Characteristics: United States Summary." 1980 Census of Population. Washington, DC: U.S. Government Printing Office, 1983, table 61.

Table 3-5B. Decennial Rates of Change in the Black Population, by Region, Division, and State: 1850 to 1980

Regions, division, and state	1980	1970	1960	1950	1940	1930	1920	1910	1900	1890	1880	1870	1860	1850
United States, total. . .	17.3	19.7	25.5	16.9	8.2	13.6	6.5	11.2	18.0	13.8	34.9	9.9	22.0	26.4
Northeast region.	11.6	43.5	50.0	47.3	19.4	68.9	40.3	25.7	42.6	17.9	27.2	15.4	4.0	5.6
New England	21.9	60.1	71.1	42.0	6.4	19.0	17.9	13.6	34.1	10.0	21.2	32.0	4.2	4.3
Middle Atlantic	10.6	42.0	48.6	47.9	20.4	75.5	43.5	28.2	44.2	18.9	28.4	13.0	3.1	5.8
North Central region. . . .	16.7	32.7	54.7	56.9	12.5	59.1	46.0	9.5	15.1	11.7	41.4	48.4	35.3	52.8
East North Central. . . .	17.5	34.2	60.0	68.8	14.8	80.9	71.3	15.8	25.7	12.6	39.7	104.7	42.2	55.2
West North Central. . . .	12.9	24.8	32.1	21.1	5.7	19.1	14.4	2.5	5.3	11.4	41.3	18.2	34.4	50.0
South region.	17.4	5.8	10.6	3.2	5.8	5.0	1.9	10.4	17.2	13.6	34.7	7.9	22.2	26.9
South Atlantic.	19.8	9.3	14.7	8.5	6.2	2.3	5.1	10.3	14.3	10.9	32.7	7.7	10.6	16.4
East South Central. . . .	11.6	-4.7	0.0	-2.9	4.6	5.3	-4.8	6.1	17.9	10.2	31.4	5.0	24.1	35.0
West South Central. . . .	17.2	6.6	13.8	0.3	6.3	10.6	3.9	17.1	23.0	26.7	47.2	14.8	74.5	72.4
West region	33.5	56.1	90.2	233.9	42.5	51.9	54.9	70.0	11.1	125.0	100.0	50.0	300.0	--
Mountain.	48.6	48.4	84.8	78.4	19.4	1.0	36.4	29.4	41.7	33.3	--	--	--	--
Pacific	31.6	57.2	89.6	279.1	47.3	89.6	60.0	100.0	7.1	133.3	50.0	0.0	300.0	--
New England														
Maine	*	*	*	*	*	*	*	*	*	*	*	*	*	*
New Hampshire	*	*	*	*	*	*	*	*	*	*	*	*	*	*
Vermont	*	*	*	*	*	*	*	*	*	*	*	*	*	*
Massachusetts	25.6	57.1	53.4	32.7	5.8	15.6	18.4	18.8	45.5	15.8	35.7	40.0	11.1	0.0
Rhode Island.	12.0	38.9	28.6	27.3	10.0	0.0	0.0	11.1	28.6	16.7	20.0	*	*	*
Connecticut	19.9	69.2	101.9	60.6	13.8	38.1	40.0	0.0	25.0	0.0	20.0	11.1	12.5	0.0
Middle Atlantic														
New York.	10.7	53.0	54.5	60.8	38.3	108.6	47.8	35.4	41.4	7.7	25.0	6.1	0.0	-2.0
New Jersey.	20.1	49.5	61.4	40.5	8.6	78.6	30.0	28.6	45.8	23.1	25.8	24.0	4.2	9.1
Pennsylvania.	2.9	19.2	33.7	35.7	9.0	51.2	46.9	23.6	45.4	25.6	32.3	14.0	5.6	12.5
East North Central														
Ohio.	10.0	23.4	53.2	51.3	9.7	66.1	67.6	14.4	11.5	8.8	27.0	70.3	48.0	47.1
Indiana	16.2	32.7	54.6	42.6	8.9	38.3	35.0	3.4	28.9	15.4	56.0	127.3	0.0	57.1
Illinois.	17.5	37.5	60.5	66.9	17.6	80.8	67.0	28.2	49.1	23.9	58.6	262.5	60.0	*
Michigan.	21.0	38.0	62.4	112.5	23.1	181.7	252.9	6.3	6.7	0.0	25.0	71.4	*	*
Wisconsin	43.0	70.7	167.9	133.3	9.1	120.0	*	*	*	*	*	*	*	*
West North Central														
Minnesota	51.4	59.1	57.1	40.0	11.1	0.0	28.6	40.0	*	*	*	--	--	--
Iowa.	27.3	32.0	25.0	17.6	0.0	-10.5	26.7	15.4	18.2	10.0	66.7	*	--	--
Missouri.	7.1	22.8	31.6	21.7	8.9	25.8	13.4	-2.5	7.3	3.4	22.9	-0.8	32.2	50.0
North Dakota.	*	*	*	*	*	*	*	*	*	*	--	--	--	--
South Dakota.	*	*	*	*	*	*	*	*	*	*	--	--	--	--
Nebraska.	20.0	37.9	52.6	35.7	0.0	7.7	62.5	33.3	-33.3	*	*	--	--	--
Kansas.	17.8	17.6	24.7	12.3	-1.5	13.8	7.4	3.8	4.0	16.3	152.9	*	--	--

Table 3-5B. Decennial Rates of Change in the Black Population, by Region, Division, and State: 1850 to 1980—continued

Regions, division, and state	1980	1970	1960	1950	1940	1930	1920	1910	1900	1890	1880	1870	1860	1850
South Atlantic														
Delaware	23.1	27.9	38.6	22.2	9.1	10.0	-3.2	0.0	10.7	7.7	13.0	4.5	10.0	0.0
Maryland	37.1	34.9	34.2	27.8	9.4	13.1	5.2	-1.3	8.8	2.9	20.0	2.3	3.6	8.6
District of Columbia	83.5	30.6	46.6	50.3	41.7	20.0	17.0	8.0	14.5	26.7	39.5	207.1	0.0	40.0
Virginia	17.2	5.5	11.2	11.0	1.7	-5.8	2.8	1.5	4.1	0.5	23.2	-6.6	4.2	5.0
West Virginia	-3.0	-24.7	-22.6	-2.5	2.6	33.7	34.4	48.8	30.3	26.9	44.4	--	--	--
North Carolina	17.1	0.9	6.6	6.7	6.7	20.4	9.3	11.9	11.2	5.6	35.5	8.3	14.6	17.5
South Carolina	20.3	-4.8	0.9	1.0	2.5	-8.2	3.5	6.9	13.5	14.1	45.2	1.0	4.6	17.6
Georgia	23.4	5.7	5.6	-2.0	1.3	-11.2	2.5	13.7	20.5	18.5	33.0	17.0	21.0	35.6
Florida	28.9	18.4	45.9	17.3	19.0	31.3	6.5	33.8	39.2	30.7	38.0	46.0	57.5	48.1
East South Central														
Kentucky	12.1	6.9	6.9	-5.6	-5.3	-4.2	-9.9	-8.1	6.3	-1.1	22.1	-5.9	6.8	16.3
Tennessee	16.9	5.8	10.5	4.3	6.5	5.8	-4.4	-1.5	11.4	6.9	25.2	13.8	15.0	30.2
Alabama	10.3	-7.9	0.0	-0.3	4.0	4.9	-0.8	9.8	22.0	13.0	26.1	8.7	27.0	34.8
Mississippi	8.7	-10.9	-7.1	-8.3	6.4	8.0	-7.3	11.1	22.2	14.3	46.4	1.6	40.5	57.9
West South Central														
Arkansas	6.3	-9.5	-8.9	-11.6	1.0	1.3	6.5	20.7	18.8	46.4	73.0	9.9	131.3	140.0
Louisiana	13.9	4.6	17.8	3.9	9.4	10.9	-2.0	9.7	16.5	15.5	33.0	4.0	33.6	35.1
Oklahoma	19.2	12.4	4.8	-13.6	-1.7	15.4	8.0	146.4	154.5	--	--	--	--	--
Texas	27.7	17.9	21.5	5.7	8.1	15.2	7.5	11.1	27.3	24.2	55.3	38.3	210.2	--
Mountain														
Montana	*	*	*	*	*	*	*	*	*	--	--	--	--	--
Idaho	*	*	*	*	*	*	*	*	*	--	--	--	--	--
Wyoming	*	*	*	*	*	*	*	*	*	*	*	*	--	--
Colorado	54.5	65.0	100.0	66.7	0.0	9.1	0.0	22.2	50.0	*	*	*	--	--
New Mexico	20.0	17.6	112.5	60.0	*	*	*	*	*	*	--	--	--	--
Arizona	41.5	23.3	65.4	73.3	36.4	37.5	*	*	*	--	--	--	--	--
Utah	*	*	*	*	*	*	*	*	*	*	*	*	*	*
Nevada	82.1	115.4	*	*	*	--	--	--	--	--	--	--	--	--
Pacific														
Washington	47.9	44.9	58.1	342.9	0.0	0.0	16.7	*	*	*	*	*	*	--
Oregon	42.3	44.4	*	*	*	*	*	*	*	*	*	*	*	*
California	29.9	58.4	91.3	272.6	53.1	107.7	77.3	100.0	0.0	83.3	*	*	*	--
Alaska	55.6	28.6	--	--	--	--	--	--	--	--	--	--	--	--
Hawaii	112.5	60.0	*	--	--	--	--	--	--	--	--	--	--	--

Note: -- indicates data not available. * indicates fewer than 5,000 blacks.

Source: U.S. Bureau of the Census. Historical Statistics of the United States, Colonial Times to 1970, Part I. Washington, DC: U.S. Government Printing Office, 1975. For 1980 data, U.S. Bureau of the Census. "General Population Characteristics: United States Summary." 1980 Census of Population. Washington, DC: U.S. Government Printing Office, 1983, Table 61.

Table 3-6. Sex Ratio of the Population, by Region, Division, and State: 1860 to 1980

Regions, division, and state	1980	1970	1960	1950	1940	1930	1920	1910	1900	1890	1880	1870	1860
United States, total. . .	94.5	95.8	97.8	99.2	100.9	102.5	104.1	106.0	104.4	105.0	103.6	102.2	104.7
Northeast region.	91.5	92.4	94.7	96.1	98.6	100.0	100.6	102.2	100.0	99.5	97.5	97.8	98.8
New England	92.2	93.2	95.0	95.6	97.0	97.2	98.5	99.3	97.7	97.0	95.5	96.1	96.9
Middle Atlantic	91.3	92.2	94.5	96.2	99.1	100.9	101.4	103.3	100.9	100.4	98.2	98.5	99.7
North Central region. . . .	94.6	95.0	97.4	99.5	102.0	104.2	105.9	107.5	106.6	107.7	108.0	104.5	106.0
East North Central. . . .	94.4	94.9	97.3	99.3	101.9	104.1	105.7	106.1	104.7	105.4	105.5	105.1	107.8
West North Central. . . .	95.0	95.1	97.7	100.1	102.1	104.2	106.1	109.9	109.7	111.2	112.7	103.1	100.2
South region.	94.3	94.9	97.0	98.5	99.6	100.9	102.6	103.2	102.3	102.1	100.3	98.3	103.2
South Atlantic.	93.7	95.0	97.1	98.2	99.1	99.6	101.2	101.2	100.0	101.8	97.8	96.0	100.3
East South Central. . . .	93.6	94.2	96.2	97.9	99.2	100.2	101.1	101.9	101.9	101.8	100.0	99.0	104.0
West South Central. . . .	95.8	95.3	97.4	99.5	100.8	103.3	105.8	107.2	106.7	107.7	107.0	103.8	110.6
West region	98.0	97.7	100.7	102.4	105.6	109.1	113.1	123.9	125.5	133.0	135.7	149.4	196.2
Mountain.	98.7	97.9	101.3	104.4	107.5	111.2	115.6	125.0	127.9	141.4	160.2	154.0	161.2
Pacific	97.8	98.0	100.5	101.7	104.9	108.3	111.7	121.5	124.0	128.0	123.8	147.3	212.7
New England													
Maine	94.4	94.9	97.8	98.7	101.2	101.3	102.6	103.3	102.3	101.5	99.7	99.7	101.9
New Hampshire	95.0	95.8	96.4	96.7	99.2	99.1	100.5	100.9	99.5	98.4	97.2	95.7	96.4
Vermont	94.9	95.6	97.0	98.9	102.8	104.0	102.9	105.8	103.6	103.7	101.2	100.6	101.9
Massachusetts	90.8	91.5	93.4	93.8	94.9	95.1	96.3	96.7	95.1	94.5	92.8	93.4	94.2
Rhode Island.	91.0	96.3	96.4	97.5	95.9	95.2	97.1	99.3	96.8	94.9	92.4	92.9	93.3
Connecticut	93.1	94.2	96.4	97.0	99.0	99.4	101.5	102.4	100.0	98.1	96.5	97.4	96.6
Middle Atlantic													
New York.	90.5	91.5	93.8	95.4	98.5	100.6	99.8	101.2	98.9	98.6	97.2	97.4	99.3
New Jersey.	92.2	93.7	96.0	97.1	99.0	101.0	101.5	102.8	100.0	99.6	98.1	98.7	99.4
Pennsylvania.	91.9	92.4	94.8	97.0	100.0	101.3	103.2	105.9	103.5	102.9	99.6	99.7	100.1
East North Central													
Ohio.	93.5	94.1	96.4	97.8	100.4	102.3	105.5	104.4	102.3	102.1	101.9	100.8	103.6
Indiana	94.4	95.1	97.3	99.1	101.3	102.6	103.3	104.9	104.4	104.1	104.3	104.3	107.4
Illinois.	94.0	94.2	96.6	98.3	100.4	103.1	103.9	106.8	105.3	106.4	106.4	107.7	116.6
Michigan.	95.1	96.1	98.6	101.6	105.2	108.4	110.8	107.3	106.6	109.0	111.2	109.2	111.6
Wisconsin	96.0	96.3	98.9	101.1	104.1	105.8	106.4	107.5	106.7	107.7	107.1	106.9	110.6
West North Central													
Minnesota	96.1	96.0	98.4	101.4	104.6	105.6	109.1	114.7	113.8	114.4	115.7	115.2	117.7
Iowa.	94.6	94.6	97.2	99.9	101.7	103.2	104.6	106.6	107.6	108.4	109.3	110.2	110.6
Missouri.	92.7	93.2	95.3	96.4	98.8	100.9	102.5	105.1	105.6	107.0	108.3	108.6	111.1
North Dakota.	101.3	102.0	104.5	108.8	109.1	112.1	112.1	122.3	124.6	124.7	--	--	--
South Dakota.	97.3	98.5	102.4	107.0	107.4	110.6	112.7	118.7	116.8	119.5	--	--	--
Nebraska.	95.2	95.4	98.5	101.4	102.5	105.1	107.9	111.3	112.5	117.8	122.7	132.1	141.7
Kansas.	95.9	96.2	98.5	100.2	101.2	104.5	105.7	110.1	109.5	111.6	117.0	124.7	122.9

Table 3-6. Sex Ratio of the Population, by Region, Division, and State: 1860 to 1980–continued

Regions, division, and state	1980	1970	1960	1950	1940	1930	1920	1910	1900	1890	1880	1870	1860
South Atlantic													
Delaware.	93.1	95.0	98.2	97.5	101.5	103.4	104.6	104.0	103.3	103.6	101.4	101.6	101.8
Maryland.	94.0	95.5	97.8	99.2	101.0	101.2	101.3	98.9	98.3	97.9	97.7	97.2	98.6
District of Columbia. . .	86.1	86.7	88.2	89.2	91.9	91.0	87.2	91.3	89.8	90.9	89.4	88.6	87.5
Virginia.	96.0	97.7	99.5	101.9	101.5	100.8	102.4	100.9	99.8	99.0	97.3	95.1	102.0
West Virginia	94.1	93.9	96.8	100.7	103.9	106.1	108.8	111.6	108.5	104.6	103.3	101.8	--
North Carolina.	94.4	95.9	97.3	98.6	98.6	98.7	99.9	99.1	98.3	97.6	96.6	93.9	99.8
South Carolina.	94.7	96.5	97.4	96.7	96.9	96.3	99.2	98.4	98.5	98.8	97.0	95.0	97.5
Georgia	93.5	94.6	95.5	96.2	96.6	97.4	99.6	100.1	99.1	100.3	97.9	95.7	101.3
Florida	92.2	93.2	96.9	97.4	98.8	101.0	104.7	110.1	108.7	106.9	102.3	102.2	109.0
East South Central													
Kentucky.	95.6	96.3	98.6	100.3	101.8	102.4	103.2	103.0	103.1	102.9	102.1	101.7	105.2
Tennessee	93.3	93.7	95.3	97.2	98.4	99.5	100.9	102.0	102.2	101.8	99.5	98.1	102.9
Alabama	92.5	93.3	95.0	96.4	97.7	98.8	99.8	100.9	100.5	100.3	97.3	96.3	102.9
Mississippi	92.9	94.0	96.2	97.7	98.6	100.0	100.5	101.7	101.4	101.6	100.5	99.5	105.5
West South Central													
Arkansas.	93.5	94.0	96.9	99.4	101.8	102.7	104.4	106.0	106.1	108.1	107.8	105.1	109.6
Louisiana	94.2	94.7	95.6	96.7	98.4	99.4	100.9	101.7	101.2	100.0	99.6	99.2	109.5
Oklahoma.	95.4	94.9	97.3	99.8	102.3	106.0	109.1	113.7	115.3	117.6	--	--	--
Texas	96.8	95.9	98.1	100.4	100.8	103.7	106.9	107.4	107.4	110.3	111.1	107.3	112.7
Mountain													
Montana	99.6	100.0	103.9	109.6	115.0	120.1	120.5	152.3	161.3	186.0	254.6	425.0	--
Idaho	99.7	99.7	102.7	106.3	111.7	113.9	118.2	132.9	136.8	151.4	200.0	400.0	--
Wyoming	105.1	100.6	105.0	114.0	116.4	123.8	131.0	170.4	170.6	181.8	200.0	350.0	--
Colorado.	98.5	97.4	98.5	100.8	102.5	105.1	110.3	117.1	120.9	147.3	198.5	166.7	1650.0
New Mexico.	97.2	97.3	101.9	104.2	104.6	107.4	111.8	115.1	114.3	116.2	116.4	104.4	111.4
Arizona	96.9	96.8	101.2	102.2	107.1	113.2	121.9	138.4	141.2	134.2	233.3	233.3	--
Utah.	98.4	97.6	99.8	102.1	102.6	104.8	106.9	111.9	105.2	113.1	108.7	102.3	100.0
Nevada.	102.4	102.9	107.2	113.3	124.5	139.4	148.4	182.8	152.9	176.5	210.0	320.0	600.0
Pacific													
Washington.	98.7	98.8	101.2	106.0	109.2	112.1	118.2	136.4	142.1	163.2	158.6	166.7	266.7
Oregon.	97.0	96.0	99.0	103.2	106.8	110.1	113.4	132.9	128.7	137.3	145.1	139.5	152.4
California.	97.2	96.9	99.5	100.1	103.7	107.6	112.5	125.4	123.5	137.6	149.3	165.4	255.1
Alaska.	112.8	119.0	133.0	161.2	143.3	150.0	175.0	255.6	255.6	146.2	--	--	--
Hawaii.	105.2	108.1	114.6	121.2	137.6	152.7	143.8	178.3	220.8	--	--	--	--

Note: -- indicates data not available.

Source: U.S. Bureau of the Census. Historical Statistics of the United States, Colonial Times to 1970, Part I. Washington, DC: U.S. Government Printing Office, 1975, table series A 195-209 for data prior to 1980. U.S. Bureau of the Census. "General Population Characteristics: United States Summary." 1980 Census of Population. Washington, DC: U.S. Government Printing Office, 1983, Table 67.

Table 3-7A. Percent of Population under Fifteen Years of Age, by Region, Division, and State: 1850 to 1980

Region, division, and state	1980	1970	1960	1950	1940	1930	1920	1910	1900	1890	1880	1870	1860	1850
United States, total	22.6	28.5	31.1	26.9	25.0	29.4	31.8	32.0	34.4	35.5	38.1	39.2	40.5	41.5
Northeast region	21.1	27.2	28.5	23.7	22.1	27.2	29.5	28.5	29.8	29.8	32.6	34.5	36.2	36.8
New England	21.0	27.9	29.8	24.3	22.4	27.2	28.5	27.2	27.4	26.8	29.1	30.9	32.7	33.6
Middle Atlantic	21.2	27.0	28.3	23.5	22.0	27.2	29.8	29.0	30.6	30.9	33.9	35.9	37.7	38.2
North Central region	23.1	29.2	31.4	26.3	23.8	27.9	30.0	30.4	33.6	35.3	38.3	41.1	42.5	43.2
East North Central	23.3	29.4	31.5	25.9	23.3	27.5	29.4	29.5	32.5	34.1	37.2	40.5	42.0	44.2
West North Central	22.7	28.6	31.2	27.2	24.7	28.7	31.1	31.9	35.4	37.1	41.0	42.5	44.0	--
South region	23.2	28.9	32.6	30.3	29.6	33.9	36.7	38.1	39.8	41.2	43.4	42.3	43.6	44.6
South Atlantic	21.9	28.3	32.2	29.9	29.1	34.1	43.8	37.6	39.0	40.8	42.6	41.5	43.2	44.0
East South Central	24.0	29.2	33.2	31.7	30.9	34.6	37.1	38.1	39.7	41.6	43.9	43.2	44.6	46.2
West South Central	24.6	29.6	33.0	29.9	29.0	33.2	36.5	38.8	41.3	41.3	44.6	42.7	42.8	42.0
West region	22.8	28.5	31.6	25.7	21.9	25.1	27.2	25.9	28.7	28.8	31.4	33.9	28.1	22.9
Mountain	25.0	29.6	34.6	30.6	28.5	31.7	33.2	31.1	33.6	30.3	32.0	33.9	35.1	41.1
Pacific	22.0	27.8	30.7	25.3	20.7	24.0	25.5	24.4	27.3	27.9	30.8	33.8	25.9	10.4
New England														
Maine	22.8	28.8	31.1	27.8	26.1	28.7	28.3	27.4	27.4	27.5	29.9	32.4	35.4	38.1
New Hampshire	22.5	29.0	30.0	25.5	23.4	26.9	27.1	26.2	25.7	24.7	26.5	28.3	30.7	32.1
Vermont	22.8	29.7	31.5	28.0	25.9	28.1	28.7	27.5	27.6	28.0	30.7	32.0	33.7	35.7
Massachusetts	20.5	27.6	28.7	23.6	21.8	26.5	28.0	27.0	27.3	26.4	28.7	30.5	32.0	31.7
Rhode Island	20.3	26.4	28.4	23.5	22.2	28.0	28.8	27.4	28.0	27.8	30.0	30.4	32.0	33.1
Connecticut	20.8	28.1	29.5	23.8	21.2	27.8	30.1	27.7	28.1	27.1	29.7	31.1	31.7	31.8
Middle Atlantic														
New York	21.2	26.7	27.6	22.6	20.6	25.0	27.8	27.3	29.0	28.8	31.7	34.0	35.8	36.3
New Jersey	21.4	27.8	28.8	23.2	21.0	27.1	30.2	29.1	30.6	30.7	34.1	36.4	37.5	38.8
Pennsylvania	20.9	26.9	29.1	25.0	24.2	30.0	32.1	30.9	32.4	33.2	36.4	38.2	40.1	40.7
East North Central														
Ohio	23.1	29.2	31.7	25.9	22.9	27.5	28.5	28.2	30.9	33.0	36.5	39.3	41.2	43.2
Indiana	23.8	29.5	31.8	26.8	24.0	27.7	28.9	29.5	32.3	34.7	38.1	42.0	43.9	46.6
Illinois	22.9	28.5	29.8	24.0	21.6	26.0	29.2	29.5	33.0	34.5	38.0	41.5	42.4	45.4
Michigan	23.9	30.5	33.1	27.4	25.0	29.0	30.0	29.6	31.9	33.2	35.4	38.1	39.3	42.5
Wisconsin	23.0	29.8	32.1	27.0	24.9	28.9	31.2	32.1	35.8	36.4	38.3	42.0	43.3	41.6
West North Central														
Minnesota	23.0	30.2	32.8	27.6	24.7	28.9	31.2	31.9	36.4	36.5	39.4	43.0	42.4	33.3
Iowa	22.8	28.6	31.1	26.9	24.6	28.3	29.9	30.9	34.0	36.0	39.3	42.8	44.7	46.9
Missouri	22.2	27.6	29.3	24.9	23.4	26.7	29.4	31.1	34.8	37.3	40.6	43.2	44.2	46.0
North Dakota	23.7	30.1	34.5	31.0	29.8	34.4	39.0	36.6	39.5	37.2	--	--	--	--
South Dakota	24.0	29.6	33.5	29.3	27.8	32.3	34.7	34.2	38.3	36.4	--	--	--	--
Nebraska	23.1	28.3	30.9	26.3	25.2	29.6	32.1	32.7	36.5	38.0	40.7	39.0	37.9	--
Kansas	22.2	27.4	30.8	26.2	24.4	28.8	31.2	31.8	34.9	38.0	41.5	40.7	42.1	--

Table 3-7A. Percent of Population under Fifteen Years of Age, by Region, Division, and State: 1850 to 1980—continued

Region, division and state	1980	1970	1960	1950	1940	1930	1920	1910	1900	1890	1880	1870	1860	1850
South Atlantic														
Delaware	22.2	30.1	32.1	25.8	22.5	26.9	28.7	29.2	31.4	32.7	35.4	39.2	41.1	41.3
Maryland	21.9	29.5	32.0	26.7	23.8	28.2	29.7	31.0	33.2	34.6	37.0	38.5	39.7	40.7
District of Columbia	17.7	25.0	25.4	20.1	17.8	20.5	20.6	23.3	24.7	27.8	33.1	34.9	36.0	38.5
Virginia	22.1	28.5	32.0	29.1	28.6	33.8	35.8	37.0	38.3	40.2	42.4	40.6	56.4	55.3
West Virginia	23.4	27.2	32.2	31.7	31.3	35.9	37.2	36.7	38.3	40.8	43.5	43.9	--	--
North Carolina	22.7	28.6	33.4	32.3	32.5	37.9	40.4	40.5	41.3	42.8	43.4	41.8	44.1	45.0
South Carolina	24.3	30.4	35.7	34.8	33.7	38.5	40.9	41.5	42.8	44.7	45.3	41.9	43.5	43.7
Georgia	24.4	29.9	33.6	31.6	30.6	34.7	38.4	39.9	41.3	43.0	44.7	43.4	45.4	46.8
Florida	19.3	25.8	29.6	26.2	25.0	29.8	33.4	35.6	38.6	40.4	43.9	43.6	44.3	44.8
East South Central														
Kentucky	23.9	28.6	32.2	30.8	30.4	34.0	35.2	35.9	37.7	39.3	42.0	43.2	44.6	45.7
Tennessee	22.8	28.0	31.6	30.1	29.4	33.2	36.1	36.9	38.8	41.0	43.8	43.1	45.1	46.9
Alabama	24.1	29.6	33.9	32.7	32.3	35.9	39.1	39.8	41.1	43.1	44.7	43.0	45.1	46.0
Mississippi	26.2	31.6	35.8	34.0	32.6	35.4	38.4	40.3	41.9	44.2	45.9	43.4	43.2	46.3
West South Central														
Arkansas	23.7	28.1	31.9	31.9	31.0	34.8	38.3	39.5	41.5	43.9	45.8	43.6	46.9	48.1
Louisiana	25.7	31.7	35.2	31.4	29.7	33.6	36.2	38.5	40.5	41.9	42.9	40.2	38.1	37.8
Oklahoma	22.9	26.9	30.0	28.6	29.2	33.8	37.6	39.0	41.4	9.3	--	--	--	--
Texas	24.7	29.7	33.1	29.1	28.0	32.2	35.4	38.6	41.6	43.4	45.1	44.4	45.4	46.0
Mountain														
Montana	23.8	30.2	34.6	28.8	25.4	29.6	32.4	27.1	29.2	22.4	25.6	14.3	--	--
Idaho	27.1	30.3	34.6	31.7	28.6	32.8	35.4	33.1	36.4	33.7	30.3	13.3	--	--
Wyoming	25.8	29.5	33.9	28.9	26.7	30.1	31.4	26.7	31.2	28.6	23.8	22.2	--	--
Colorado	22.7	29.2	32.4	27.5	25.6	29.0	29.9	28.5	30.2	28.3	25.3	30.0	--	--
New Mexico	25.9	33.4	38.0	34.8	34.6	36.6	36.9	36.7	39.0	35.0	37.5	40.2	40.4	40.3
Arizona	23.7	30.4	34.8	31.9	30.1	32.8	33.5	31.9	33.3	21.6	25.0	20.0	--	--
Utah	31.6	33.3	37.5	33.5	31.5	35.6	37.6	37.3	40.8	40.3	45.1	48.3	50.0	45.5
Nevada	21.7	29.4	30.5	25.6	22.7	24.2	24.7	20.7	26.2	25.5	24.2	16.7	0.0	*
Pacific														
Washington	22.4	28.1	31.3	26.3	21.1	24.9	27.4	26.4	30.5	28.9	36.0	37.5	33.3	--
Oregon	22.4	27.3	30.8	26.6	21.2	24.4	27.2	25.7	30.4	32.1	36.0	41.8	44.2	41.7
California	21.8	27.7	30.3	24.6	19.8	22.8	23.8	22.9	26.3	27.2	30.5	32.3	23.2	6.5
Alaska	26.9	34.3	35.4	27.1	28.8	28.8	29.1	18.8	17.2	--	--	--	--	--
Hawaii	23.4	30.0	34.4	31.2	31.0	36.1	35.5	29.7	22.7	--	--	--	--	--

Note: -- indicates data not available. * indicates under 15 years less than 500.

Source: U.S. Bureau of the Census. "Supplementary Report," PC 80-51-1." 1980 Census of Population. Washington, D.C.: U.S. Government Printing Office, 1981, Table 3-4 for 1980. U.S. Bureau of the Census. Historical Statistics of the United States, Colonial Times to 1970. Washington, D.C.: U.S. Government Printing Office, 1975, table series 195-209.

Table 3-7B. Percent of Population Sixty-Five Years of Age or Older, by Region, Division, and State: 1850 to 1980

Region, division and state	1980	1970	1960	1950	1940	1930	1920	1910	1900	1890	1880	1870	1860	1850
United States, total. . .	11.3	10.4	9.2	8.1	6.8	5.4	4.7	4.4	4.0	3.8	3.8	3.0	0.4	0.4
Northeast region.	12.4	10.6	10.1	8.7	7.2	5.6	4.9	4.8	4.8	5.1	4.8	4.1	0.5	0.5
New England	12.3	10.7	10.7	9.7	8.5	6.7	5.8	5.9	5.9	6.3	6.3	5.6	0.7	0.7
Middle Atlantic	12.4	10.6	9.9	8.4	6.8	5.2	4.6	4.4	4.5	4.6	4.3	3.6	0.4	0.4
North Central region. . . .	11.4	12.5	9.8	8.9	7.7	6.2	5.3	4.9	4.3	3.8	3.0	2.4	0.2	0.2
East North Central. . . .	10.8	12.9	9.3	8.5	7.4	6.0	5.3	5.1	4.6	4.3	3.4	2.7	0.2	0.2[a]
West North Central. . . .	12.8	11.7	11.2	9.8	8.2	6.6	5.2	4.6	3.9	3.1	2.3[a]	1.7[a]	0.2[a]	0.1[a]
South region.	11.3	9.6	8.3	6.9	5.5	4.2	3.8	3.6	3.1	3.0	2.8	2.6	0.4	0.4
South Atlantic.	11.8	9.6	8.1	6.6	5.4	4.3	4.0	3.6	3.5	3.4	3.3	3.0	0.5[a]	0.5[a]
East South Central. . . .	11.3	9.9	8.7	7.1	5.7	4.4	4.1	4.7	3.2	3.0	2.7[a]	2.4[a]	0.3[a]	0.3[a]
West South Central. . . .	10.4	9.5	8.4	7.1	5.5	4.0	3.4	2.8	2.4	2.2	2.0[a]	1.8[a]	0.2[a]	0.2[a]
West region	10.0	8.9	8.6	8.0	7.4	5.9	4.7	3.9	3.7	2.5	2.0	1.3	1.1	*
Mountain.	9.3	8.4	7.7	7.1	6.0	4.9	3.6	3.0	2.7	2.0	1.9[a]	2.2[a]	1.1[a]	...
Pacific	10.2	9.1	8.8	8.4	7.9	6.3	5.3	4.4	4.3	2.9[a]	2.0[a]	1.1[a]	...	...
New England														
Maine	12.5	11.6	11.0	10.3	9.4	8.7	8.1	8.2	7.9	7.9	7.6	6.2	0.6	0.7
New Hampshire	11.2	10.1	11.2	10.9	10.0	9.0	8.0	7.9	7.8	8.5	8.4	7.9	0.9	0.9
Vermont	11.4	10.6	11.3	10.6	9.5	8.6	8.5	8.1	8.1	8.4	7.8	6.6	1.0	1.0
Massachusetts	12.7	11.2	11.1	10.0	8.5	6.4	5.3	5.2	5.1	5.4	5.4	4.7	0.6	0.6
Rhode Island.	13.4	11.0	10.4	8.8	7.6	5.8	5.0	4.6	4.7	5.0	5.0	4.6	0.6	0.7
Connecticut	11.7	9.5	9.6	8.8	7.5	5.8	5.0	5.4	5.6	6.0	5.9	5.4	0.7	0.8
Middle Atlantic														
New York.	12.3	10.8	10.0	8.5	6.8	5.3	4.7	4.6	4.8	5.0	4.6	3.8	0.4	0.4
New Jersey.	11.7	9.7	9.2	8.1	6.7	5.0	4.2	4.2	4.2	4.3	4.0	3.3	0.4	0.6
Pennsylvania.	12.9	10.8	10.0	8.4	6.8	5.3	4.5	4.3	4.2	4.3	4.0	3.4	0.4	0.4
East North Central														
Ohio.	10.8	9.4	9.2	9.0	7.8	6.2	5.5	5.5	5.0	4.8	4.0	3.4	0.3	0.3
Indiana	10.7	9.5	9.6	9.2	8.4	7.2	6.3	5.5	4.7	4.2	3.1	2.5	0.2	0.2
Illinois.	11.0	9.8	9.7	8.7	7.2	5.5	4.6	4.3	4.0	3.6	2.8	2.0	0.2	0.1
Michigan.	9.8	8.5	8.2	7.3	6.3	5.3	5.2	5.6	5.0	4.4	3.5	2.8	0.3	0.3
Wisconsin	12.0	10.7	10.1	9.0	7.7	6.5	5.3	5.1	5.0	4.8	3.8	2.7	0.1	*
West North Central														
Minnesota	11.8	10.7	10.4	9.0	7.6	6.4	4.7	4.1	3.8	3.2	2.4	1.8	*	*
Iowa.	13.3	12.4	12.0	10.4	9.0	7.4	6.0	5.6	4.7	4.1	2.9	2.0	0.1	*
Missouri.	13.2	12.0	11.6	10.3	8.6	6.8	5.5	4.6	3.6	3.0	2.3	1.6	0.1	0.1
North Dakota.	12.3	10.7	9.3	7.7	6.0	4.4	3.0	2.3	2.2	2.1	...	...	...	...
South Dakota.	13.2	12.0	10.2	8.4	6.8	5.3	4.1	3.3	3.2	2.3	...	...	...	...
Nebraska.	13.1	12.4	11.6	9.8	8.1	6.2	4.9	4.3	3.3	2.2	1.5	0.8	...	...
Kansas.	13.0	11.8	11.0	10.2	8.7	6.9	6.0	5.2	4.1	2.8	1.7	1.1	...	...

Table 3-7B. Percent of Population Sixty-Five Years of Age or Older, by Region, Division, and State: 1850 to 1980—continued

Region, division, and state	1980	1970	1960	1950	1940	1930	1920	1910	1900	1890	1880	1870	1860	1850
South Atlantic														
Delaware.	10.0	8.0	8.1	8.2	7.8	7.1	5.4	5.0	4.3	4.8	4.1	3.2	...	...
Maryland.	9.4	7.6	7.3	7.0	6.8	5.6	5.0	4.7	4.2	4.2	3.6	3.1	0.4	0.5
District of Columbia. . .	11.6	9.4	9.0	7.1	6.0	5.5	4.8	5.1	4.3	4.0	3.4	3.0	...	...
Virginia.	9.5	7.8	7.3	6.5	5.8	4.9	4.3	4.1	3.9	3.9	3.7	3.5	0.6	0.7
West Virginia	12.2	11.2	9.3	6.9	5.3	4.3	3.8	3.4	3.3	3.4	3.0	2.9	...	...
North Carolina.	10.3	8.1	6.8	5.5	4.4	3.7	3.9	3.5	3.5	3.5	3.4	3.2	0.5	0.6
South Carolina.	9.2	7.4	6.3	5.4	4.3	3.3	3.1	2.9	3.0	3.0	3.2	3.0	0.4	0.2
Georgia	9.5	8.0	7.4	6.4	5.1	3.9	3.5	3.1	3.0	2.8	2.9	2.5	0.4	0.3
Florida	17.3	14.6	11.1	8.6	6.9	4.8	4.2	2.9	2.6	2.6	2.2	2.1	...	...
East South Central														
Kentucky.	11.2	10.4	9.6	8.0	6.6	5.4	4.8	4.1	3.6	3.4	2.9	2.6	0.3	0.4
Tennessee	11.3	9.8	8.7	7.1	5.9	4.5	4.3	3.8	3.3	3.1	2.8	2.5	0.4	0.4
Alabama	11.3	9.5	8.0	6.5	4.8	3.7	3.5	3.0	3.0	2.8	2.7	2.3	0.3	0.3
Mississippi	11.5	10.0	8.7	7.0	5.2	4.3	3.7	3.0	2.9	2.7	2.5	2.1	0.3	0.2
West South Central														
Arkansas.	13.7	12.4	11.0	7.9	5.5	4.1	3.5	2.9	2.4	2.0	1.6	1.4	0.2	...
Louisiana	9.6	8.4	7.4	6.6	5.0	3.6	3.3	3.0	2.9	2.9	2.7	2.3	0.3	0.2
Oklahoma.	12.4	11.7	10.7	8.7	6.2	4.0	3.2	2.5	1.9	0.4	...	...	...	...
Texas	9.6	8.9	7.8	6.7	5.4	4.0	3.5	2.8	2.4	2.1	1.8	1.5	0.2	...
Mountain														
Montana	10.7	9.9	9.6	8.6	6.4	5.0	3.1	2.4	2.1	1.4	...	...	...	...
Idaho	9.9	9.5	8.7	7.5	6.1	4.9	3.5	2.8	2.5	2.2	...	...	...	...
Wyoming	7.9	9.0	7.9	6.2	5.2	4.0	3.1	2.1	2.2	2.0	...	...	...	...
Colorado.	8.6	8.5	9.0	8.6	7.7	6.0	4.4	3.4	2.6	2.2	1.0	...	...	...
New Mexico.	8.9	7.0	5.4	5.5	4.3	4.0	3.3	3.0	3.0	2.5	2.5	2.2	1.1	...
Arizona	11.3	9.1	6.9	5.9	4.8	3.7	3.0	2.9	2.4	1.1	...	...	...	...
Utah.	7.5	7.4	6.7	6.1	5.5	4.5	3.6	3.2	3.6	3.3	2.8	2.3	...	...
Nevada.	8.2	6.3	6.3	6.9	6.4	5.5	3.9	3.7	4.8	2.1	1.6	...	...	...
Pacific														
Washington.	10.4	9.4	9.8	8.7	8.3	6.5	4.4	3.2	2.9	1.7	1.3	...	...	...
Oregon.	11.5	10.9	10.4	8.7	8.5	7.0	5.5	4.2	3.9	2.8	2.3	1.1	...	...
California.	10.2	9.0	8.8	8.5	8.0	6.4	5.8	5.3	5.2	3.3	2.0	1.1	...	...
Alaska.	2.9	2.3	2.2	3.9	5.5	5.1	3.6	1.6	1.6	...	...	...	...	...
Hawaii.	7.9	5.7	4.6	4.0	3.1	2.2	2.0	1.6	1.9	...	...	...	...	...

[a]Based on existing figures because figures for some states are not available before 1890.

Note: ... indicates data not available. * indicates fewer than 500 people.

Source: U.S. Bureau of the Census. Historical Statistics of the United States, Colonial Times to 1970, Part I. Washington, DC: U.S. Government Printing Office, 1975, table series 172-209. Also U.S. Bureau of the Census. "Supplementary Report, PC80-S1-1." 1980 Census of Population. Washington, DC: U.S. Government Printing Office, 1989, table 3-4.

Table 3-8A. Percent of Population Classified as Urban, by Region, Division, and State: 1850 to 1980[a]

Region, division, and state	1980	1970	1960	1950	1940	1930	1920	1910	1900	1890	1880	1870	1860	1850
United States, total. . .	73.7	73.6	69.9	64.0	56.5	56.1	51.2	45.6	39.6	35.1	28.2	25.7	19.8	15.3
Northeast region.	79.2	80.6	80.2	79.5	76.6	77.6	75.5	71.8	66.1	59.0	50.8	44.3	35.7	26.5
New England	75.1	76.6	76.4	76.2	76.1	77.3	75.9	73.3	68.6	61.6	52.4	44.4	36.6	28.8
Middle Atlantic	80.6	81.8	81.4	80.5	76.8	77.7	75.4	71.2	65.2	58.0	50.2	44.2	35.4	25.5
North Central region. . . .	70.5	71.6	68.7	64.1	58.4	57.9	52.3	45.1	38.6	33.1	24.2	20.8	13.9	9.2
East North Central. . . .	73.3	74.8	73.0	69.7	65.5	66.4	60.8	52.7	45.2	37.9	27.5	21.6	14.1	9.0
West North Central. . . .	63.9	63.7	58.8	52.0	44.3	41.8	37.7	33.2	28.5	25.8	18.2	18.9	13.4	10.3
South region.	66.9	64.8	58.5	48.6	36.7	34.1	28.1	22.5	18.0	16.3	12.2	12.2	9.6	8.3
South Atlantic.	67.1	64.1	57.2	49.1	38.8	36.1	31.0	25.4	21.4	19.5	14.9	14.4	11.5	9.8
East South Central. . . .	55.7	54.7	48.4	39.1	29.4	28.1	22.4	18.7	15.0	12.7	8.4	8.8	5.9	4.2
West South Central. . . .	73.4	72.7	67.7	55.6	39.8	36.4	29.0	22.3	16.2	15.1	12.5	13.3	12.3	15.1
West region	83.9	83.1	77.7	69.5	58.5	58.4	51.8	47.9	39.9	37.0	30.2	25.8	16.0	6.4
Mountain.	76.4	73.1	67.1	54.9	42.7	39.4	36.5	35.9	32.3	29.3	21.6	12.3	10.1	6.2
Pacific	86.6	86.2	81.1	74.4	64.9	66.6	60.5	55.0	44.7	41.9	35.2	32.1	18.4	6.4
New England														
Maine	47.5	50.8	51.3	51.7	40.5	40.3	39.0	35.3	33.5	28.1	22.6	21.0	16.6	13.5
New Hampshire	52.2	56.4	58.3	57.5	57.6	58.7	56.5	51.8	46.7	39.3	30.0	26.2	22.1	17.1
Vermont	33.8	32.2	38.5	36.4	34.3	33.0	31.2	27.8	22.1	15.2	10.0	6.9	2.0	1.9
Massachusetts	83.8	84.6	83.6	84.4	89.4	90.2	90.0	89.0	86.0	82.0	74.7	66.7	59.6	50.7
Rhode Island.	87.0	87.1	86.4	84.3	91.6	92.4	91.9	91.0	88.3	85.3	82.0	74.6	63.3	55.6
Connecticut	78.8	78.4	78.3	77.6	67.8	70.4	67.8	65.6	59.9	50.9	41.9	33.0	26.5	16.0
Middle Atlantic														
New York.	84.6	85.7	85.4	85.5	82.8	83.6	82.7	78.9	72.9	65.1	56.4	50.0	39.3	28.2
New Jersey.	89.0	88.9	88.6	86.6	81.6	82.6	79.9	76.4	70.6	62.6	54.4	43.7	32.7	17.6
Pennsylvania.	69.3	71.5	71.6	70.5	66.5	67.8	65.1	60.4	54.7	48.6	41.6	37.3	30.8	23.6
East North Central														
Ohio.	73.3	75.3	73.4	70.2	66.8	67.8	63.8	55.9	48.1	41.1	32.2	25.6	17.1	12.2
Indiana	64.2	64.9	62.4	59.9	55.1	55.5	50.6	42.4	34.3	26.9	19.5	14.7	8.6	4.5
Illinois.	83.3	83.2	80.7	77.6	73.6	73.9	67.9	61.7	54.3	44.9	30.6	23.5	14.3	7.6
Michigan.	70.7	74.0	73.4	70.7	65.7	68.2	61.1	47.2	39.3	34.9	24.8	20.1	13.3	7.3
Wisconsin	64.2	65.9	63.8	57.9	53.5	52.9	47.3	43.0	38.2	33.2	24.1	19.6	14.4	9.4
West North Central														
Minnesota	66.9	66.5	62.2	54.2	49.8	49.0	44.1	41.0	34.1	33.8	19.1	16.1	9.4	0.0
Iowa.	58.6	57.2	53.0	47.7	42.7	39.6	36.4	30.6	25.6	21.2	15.2	13.1	8.9	5.1
Missouri.	68.1	70.1	66.6	61.5	51.8	51.2	46.6	42.3	36.3	32.0	25.2	25.0	17.2	11.8
North Dakota.	48.8	44.3	35.2	26.6	20.6	16.6	13.6	11.0	7.3	5.6	...	...	...	...
South Dakota.	46.4	44.6	39.3	33.2	24.6	18.9	16.0	13.1	10.2	8.2	...	...	...	...
Nebraska.	62.9	61.5	54.3	46.9	39.1	35.3	31.3	26.1	23.7	27.4	13.6	18.0	0.0	...
Kansas.	66.7	66.1	61.0	52.1	41.9	38.8	34.8	29.1	22.4	18.9	10.5	14.2	9.4	...

Table 3-8A. Percent of Population Classified as Urban, by Region, Division, and State: 1850 to 1980[a]—continued

Region, division, and state	1980	1970	1960	1950	1940	1930	1920	1910	1900	1890	1880	1870	1860	1850
South Atlantic														
Delaware	70.6	72.2	65.6	62.6	52.3	51.7	54.2	48.0	46.4	42.2	33.4	24.7	18.9	15.3
Maryland	80.3	76.6	72.7	69.6	59.3	59.8	60.0	50.8	49.8	47.6	40.2	37.8	34.0	32.3
District of Columbia	100.0	100.0	100.0	100.0	100.0	100.0	100.0	100.0	100.0	100.0	90.0	91.6	93.0	93.6
Virginia	66.0	63.2	55.6	47.0	35.3	32.4	29.2	23.1	18.3	17.1	12.5	11.9	9.5	8.0
West Virginia	36.2	39.1	38.2	34.6	28.1	28.4	25.2	18.7	13.1	10.7	8.7	8.1	5.3	3.8
North Carolina	48.0	45.5	39.5	33.7	27.3	25.5	19.2	14.4	9.9	7.2	3.9	3.4	2.5	2.4
South Carolina	54.1	48.3	41.2	36.7	24.5	21.3	17.5	14.8	12.8	10.1	7.5	8.6	6.9	7.3
Georgia	62.4	60.3	55.3	45.3	34.4	30.8	25.1	20.6	15.6	14.0	9.4	8.4	7.1	4.3
Florida	84.3	81.7	73.9	65.5	55.1	51.7	36.5	29.1	20.3	19.8	10.0	8.1	4.1	0.0
East South Central														
Kentucky	50.9	52.3	44.5	36.8	29.8	30.6	26.2	24.3	21.8	19.2	15.2	14.8	10.4	7.5
Tennessee	60.4	59.1	52.3	44.1	35.2	34.3	26.1	20.2	16.2	13.5	7.5	7.5	4.2	2.2
Alabama	60.0	58.6	54.8	43.8	30.2	28.1	21.7	17.3	11.9	10.1	5.4	6.3	5.1	4.6
Mississippi	47.3	44.5	37.7	27.9	19.8	16.9	13.4	11.5	7.7	5.4	3.1	4.0	2.6	1.8
West South Central														
Arkansas	51.6	50.0	42.8	33.0	22.0	20.6	16.6	12.9	8.5	6.5	4.0	2.6	0.9	0.0
Louisiana	68.6	66.5	63.3	54.8	41.5	39.7	34.9	30.0	26.5	25.4	25.5	27.9	26.1	26.0
Oklahoma	67.3	68.0	62.9	51.0	37.6	34.3	26.5	19.2	7.4	3.7	...	...	...	...
Texas	79.6	79.7	75.0	62.7	45.4	41.0	32.4	24.1	17.1	15.6	9.2	6.7	4.4	3.6
Mountain														
Montana	52.9	53.4	50.2	43.7	37.8	33.7	31.3	35.5	34.7	27.1	17.8	15.1	...	...
Idaho	54.0	54.1	47.5	42.9	33.7	29.1	27.6	21.5	6.2	0.0	0.0	0.0	...	...
Wyoming	62.7	60.5	56.8	49.8	37.3	31.1	29.4	29.6	28.8	34.3	29.6	0.0	...	...
Colorado	80.6	78.5	73.7	62.7	52.6	50.2	48.2	50.3	48.3	45.0	31.4	11.9	13.9	...
New Mexico	72.1	69.8	65.9	50.2	33.2	25.2	18.0	14.2	14.0	6.2	5.5	5.2	5.0	7.4
Arizona	83.8	79.6	74.5	55.5	34.8	34.4	36.1	31.0	15.9	9.4	17.3	33.4	--	--
Utah	84.4	80.4	74.9	65.3	55.5	52.4	48.0	46.3	38.1	35.7	23.4	18.4	20.5	0.0
Nevada	85.3	80.9	70.4	57.2	39.3	37.8	19.7	16.3	17.0	33.8	31.1	16.6	0.0	...
Pacific														
Washington	73.5	73.4	68.1	63.2	53.1	56.6	54.8	53.0	40.8	35.6	9.5	0.0	0.0	0.0
Oregon	67.9	67.1	62.2	53.9	48.8	51.3	49.8	45.6	32.2	27.9	14.8	9.1	5.5	0.0
California	91.3	90.9	86.4	80.7	71.0	73.3	67.9	61.8	52.3	48.6	42.9	37.2	20.7	7.4
Alaska	64.3	56.9	37.9	26.6	24.0	13.2	5.6	9.5	24.5	0.0	...	...	--	--
Hawaii	86.5	83.1	76.5	69.0	62.5	53.7	36.1	30.7	25.5	...	...	...	...	...

[a]1950-1980 from current definition, before 1950 from previous urban definition.

Note: -- indicates data not available. ... indicates data not applicable.

Source: U.S. Bureau of the Census. "Number of Inhabitants: U.S. Summary." 1980 Census of Population. Washington, DC: U.S. Government Printing Office, 1983, Table 13.

Table 3-8B. Percent Change in Urban Population from Preceding Decade, by Region, Division, and State: 1850 to 1980[a]

Region, division, and state	1980	1970	1960	1950	1940	1930	1920	1910	1900	1890	1880	1870	1860	1850
United States, total. . .	11.6	19.5	29.3	20.6	8.0	27.5	29.0	39.2	36.7	56.5	42.7	59.3	75.4	92.1
Northeast region.	-1.5	10.2	14.2	8.0	3.2	19.2	20.7	33.4	35.5	39.3	35.3	43.8	65.5	82.7
New England	2.1	13.0	13.1	8.6	1.7	12.3	17.0	25.3	32.5	37.6	35.7	34.9	46.4	80.8
Middle Atlantic	-2.6	9.5	14.6	7.9	3.7	21.5	22.0	36.5	36.7	40.0	35.1	47.7	75.5	83.7
North Central region. . . .	2.5	14.2	24.5	16.0	4.9	25.7	31.8	32.7	37.0	76.7	55.4	113.9	152.9	286.0
East North Central. . . .	1.4	14.0	24.8	15.6	3.9	28.7	35.7	33.2	41.2	66.0	56.2	102.5	137.9	262.3
West North Central. . . .	5.7	14.9	23.8	17.1	7.9	17.6	22.2	31.3	27.7	106.2	53.1	152.1	221.0	448.2
South region.	23.9	26.6	40.1	37.8	18.5	38.8	40.4	49.8	35.6	61.7	34.8	40.3	43.4	60.7
South Atlantic.	26.3	32.3	42.9	34.0	21.5	31.4	40.2	38.5	29.2	53.0	34.3	36.8	33.6	51.7
East South Central. . . .	16.6	20.2	30.0	28.9	13.9	39.3	26.7	39.2	38.4	74.3	21.5	63.1	67.1	161.6
West South Central. . . .	24.1	22.4	42.1	48.3	17.5	49.1	51.8	85.0	47.7	71.2	55.2	25.1	51.5	34.9
West region	25.2	32.7	55.3	43.8	16.8	50.8	40.8	97.4	48.0	113.2	113.0	157.8	772.8	...
Mountain.	43.4	31.6	65.1	40.9	21.5	19.7	28.9	74.5	52.2	152.6	262.0	120.7	288.2	...
Pacific	20.4	33.0	52.9	44.5	15.6	61.5	45.4	107.9	46.1	99.5	86.2	165.8	1,095.4	...
New England														
Maine	5.9	1.4	5.3	9.2	6.7	7.3	14.2	12.6	25.4	26.7	11.3	26.2	32.2	100.6
New Hampshire	15.5	17.6	15.3	10.3	3.7	9.0	12.2	16.1	30.0	42.1	24.7	15.8	32.6	90.4
Vermont	20.9	-4.7	8.9	11.7	3.8	8.0	11.2	30.4	49.8	51.8	45.3	269.5	1.7	...
Massachusetts	*	11.8	8.7	5.3	0.7	10.5	15.8	24.2	31.4	37.8	37.0	32.6	45.5	80.3
Rhode Island.	-0.1	11.0	11.3	5.4	2.8	14.5	12.4	30.5	28.4	30.1	39.8	46.7	34.7	72.2
Connecticut	3.1	19.7	27.4	20.1	2.3	20.9	28.0	34.6	43.1	45.7	47.2	45.1	105.9	52.3
Middle Atlantic														
New York.	-4.9	9.0	13.0	6.6	6.1	22.5	19.5	35.7	35.5	36.3	31.0	43.6	74.5	85.3
New Jersey.	2.9	18.6	28.4	15.4	1.7	32.4	30.1	45.9	46.9	47.0	55.4	80.2	155.0	118.0
Pennsylvania.	-2.6	4.1	9.4	6.1	0.8	15.2	22.5	34.3	34.8	43.4	35.8	46.7	64.3	76.8
East North Central														
Ohio.	-1.3	12.7	27.7	15.9	2.3	22.6	38.0	33.4	32.3	46.5	50.9	70.5	65.2	190.4
Indiana	4.5	15.9	23.5	17.5	5.1	21.1	29.6	32.6	46.2	52.8	55.9	113.7	159.7	316.5
Illinois.	2.9	13.7	20.4	11.7	3.1	28.0	26.5	33.0	52.2	82.8	57.8	142.7	281.1	570.6
Michigan.	-0.2	14.4	27.4	20.6	4.6	47.3	68.9	39.3	30.4	80.1	70.4	138.7	243.5	218.9
Wisconsin	3.8	15.4	26.9	16.1	8.1	24.8	24.0	27.1	40.5	77.3	53.2	85.1	290.9	...
West North Central														
Minnesota	7.6	19.3	30.6	15.6	10.5	19.6	23.7	42.2	35.0	197.8	110.2	336.1	...	...
Iowa.	5.7	10.5	16.9	13.4	10.7	11.9	28.7	18.8	41.1	64.0	58.3	160.4	516.9	...
Missouri.	2.2	13.9	18.2	16.8	5.5	17.2	13.9	23.5	31.6	57.0	27.1	111.1	152.6	389.1
North Dakota.	16.4	22.8	35.1	24.9	16.4	28.4	39.5	170.1	120.0	295.2	...	...	...	...
South Dakota.	8.1	11.0	23.3	36.7	20.8	28.5	33.2	86.8	43.4	296.2	...	...	...	...
Nebraska.	8.2	19.1	23.2	18.0	5.8	19.9	30.4	23.0	-13.4	374.7	177.0	...	...	...
Kansas.	6.1	11.8	33.8	19.8	3.3	18.4	25.2	49.3	22.3	156.8	102.3	416.4	...	...

Table 3-8B. Percent Change in Urban Population from Preceding Decade, by Region, Division, and State: 1850 to 1980[a]—continued

Region, division, and state	1980	1970	1960	1950	1940	1930	1920	1910	1900	1890	1880	1870	1860	1850
South Atlantic														
Delaware	6.1	35.1	47.0	6.1	13.2	2.0	24.4	13.3	20.6	45.1	58.8	45.1	52.1	67.1
Maryland	12.7	33.3	39.5	32.0	10.8	12.1	32.1	11.3	19.3	31.9	27.2	26.6	24.1	65.1
District of Columbia	-15.6	-1.0	-4.8	21.0	36.2	11.3	32.2	18.8	21.0	44.1	32.6	72.6	44.4	57.7
Virginia	20.1	33.3	41.3	45.6	20.3	16.6	41.4	40.1	20.3	49.5	29.8	25.7	29.8	25.8
West Virginia	3.5	-4.2	2.4	19.9	8.7	33.2	61.7	81.9	54.2	50.5	50.1	79.4	75.6	45.0
North Carolina	22.2	28.2	31.7	27.1	20.3	65.2	54.0	70.5	61.4	110.0	52.2	47.5	16.3	58.6
South Carolina	35.1	27.4	26.2	40.1	25.6	26.2	30.8	31.3	47.4	55.9	22.2	25.6	-1.0	46.0
Georgia	23.2	27.0	39.8	32.8	19.9	23.0	35.1	55.5	34.5	77.5	45.0	32.6	93.5	58.1
Florida	48.1	51.4	101.9	49.8	37.6	114.9	61.4	104.7	38.4	187.1	76.4	167.6	...	...
East South Central														
Kentucky	10.6	24.4	24.8	16.1	6.3	26.1	14.1	18.8	31.1	42.7	27.6	62.4	63.4	138.5
Tennessee	19.6	24.3	28.4	23.1	14.6	46.7	38.6	35.0	37.0	105.5	23.1	102.5	111.7	217.3
Alabama	15.9	12.6	33.6	43.5	15.0	46.1	37.5	70.9	42.4	122.2	9.3	28.2	39.0	177.6
Mississippi	20.9	20.2	35.2	39.0	27.8	41.1	15.8	72.7	71.6	102.3	4.0	60.7	92.9	196.9
West South Central														
Arkansas	22.8	25.6	21.4	42.9	12.8	31.8	43.3	81.4	52.7	128.5	158.6	232.2	...	...
Louisiana	19.2	17.5	40.0	40.8	17.6	32.7	26.5	35.6	29.0	18.6	18.2	9.5	37.6	27.6
Oklahoma	16.9	18.8	28.5	25.9	7.1	52.7	68.7	446.0	516.0	...	...	...	...	...
Texas	27.0	24.1	48.6	58.4	21.8	58.0	61.2	80.1	49.0	138.1	169.2	104.9	247.2	...
Mountain														
Montana	12.3	9.5	31.2	19.6	16.8	5.2	28.9	57.8	118.0	455.1	125.0	...	...	...
Idaho	32.2	21.6	25.6	32.5	36.4	8.8	70.3	598.8	...	...	...	...	...	...
Wyoming	46.5	7.2	29.7	54.5	33.5	22.8	32.1	62.1	24.1	249.2	...	...	...	...
Colorado	34.4	34.1	55.5	28.6	13.6	14.7	12.7	54.3	40.2	205.0	1,181.0	0.2	...	...
New Mexico	32.6	13.1	83.2	78.4	65.1	64.4	39.5	70.1	174.6	50.3	39.2	2.8	2.1	...
Arizona	61.7	45.2	133.3	57.4	16.1	24.1	90.9	224.5	134.8	18.5	117.3	...	...	...
Utah	44.8	27.6	48.3	41.7	14.7	23.5	24.7	64.0	40.3	123.2	110.7	94.0	...	...
Nevada	72.8	97.0	119.0	94.2	25.6	125.9	14.1	85.8	-55.1	-17.2	174.6	...	...	...
Pacific														
Washington	21.4	28.7	29.3	38.2	4.2	19.1	22.7	186.3	66.3	1,686.0	...	...	...	...
Oregon	27.5	27.5	34.3	37.7	8.6	25.5	27.1	130.6	50.5	242.3	211.7	188.6	...	...
California	19.1	33.7	58.9	47.1	17.8	78.8	58.5	89.0	31.8	59.1	77.8	165.0	1,053.2	...
Alaska	51.2	99.4	150.3	97.2	121.6	156.3	-50.2	-60.6	...	...	...	...	...	...
Hawaii	30.7	32.0	40.3	30.5	33.5	114.6	56.5	49.9	...	...	...	...	...	...

[a]1960–1980 current urban definition, 1950 and before from previous urban definition.

Note: ... indicates data not applicable. * indicates less than 0.1.

Source: U.S. Bureau of the Census. "Number of Inhabitants: U.S. Summary." 1980 Census of Population. Washington, DC: U.S. Government Printing Office, 1983, Table 13.

Table 3-8C. Percent Change in Rural Population from Preceding Decade, by Region, Division, and State: 1850 to 1980

Region, division, and state	1980	1970	1960	1950	1940	1930	1920	1910	1900	1890	1880	1870	1860	1850
United States, total. . .	11.1	-0.9	-0.8	6.5	6.3	4.4	3.2	9.1	12.5	13.4	25.8	13.6	28.4	29.1
Northeast region.	7.3	7.8	9.0	15.3	8.9	6.4	-0.6	2.4	-0.1	0.1	4.2	0.6	7.4	15.1
New England	11.3	11.7	12.0	16.3	8.8	4.1	1.9	-0.6	-2.8	-5.3	-1.6	-2.4	2.2	7.9
Middle Atlantic	5.7	6.3	7.9	15.0	9.0	7.1	-1.5	3.3	0.8	2.0	6.5	1.9	9.7	18.5
North Central region. . . .	8.1	-0.5	1.1	3.4	2.8	*	-1.0	1.4	7.8	13.9	28.1	31.2	59.7	52.2
East North Central. . . .	10.1	3.4	6.3	11.5	8.0	0.9	-2.4	-1.5	4.8	3.0	13.6	20.1	44.7	46.3
West North Central. . . .	4.6	-6.6	-6.0	-6.4	-2.8	-1.0	0.6	5.0	11.7	31.5	61.2	66.3	138.0	92.5
South region.	13.0	-3.2	-5.9	-1.0	5.7	4.7	4.7	13.3	19.9	15.6	34.4	7.2	22.2	27.0
South Atlantic.	10.2	-0.9	3.0	9.2	8.0	4.6	6.1	10.9	15.2	10.2	29.0	5.5	12.6	16.5
East South Central. . . .	12.1	-6.8	-11.1	-2.8	7.1	3.0	0.9	6.5	14.3	9.7	27.3	6.2	17.5	27.8
West South Central. . . .	19.7	-3.6	-15.2	-13.2	1.4	6.6	6.5	24.7	36.0	38.0	65.6	14.9	92.0	131.6
West region	18.2	-6.0	1.7	35.7	16.5	15.4	20.3	42.4	31.3	57.0	71.0	41.4	210.4	...
Mountain.	20.7	-1.2	-1.5	8.4	6.0	5.9	25.4	49.0	32.0	67.5	85.3	75.8	130.0	...
Pacific	16.6	-8.7	3.6	53.7	24.6	24.1	16.0	37.4	30.7	49.8	62.4	26.4	265.9	...
New England														
Maine	21.0	3.3	6.9	7.0	5.9	1.6	-2.4	4.0	-2.9	-5.4	1.4	-5.5	3.9	9.0
New Hampshire	36.9	27.1	11.8	6.1	8.4	-0.2	-7.1	-5.4	-4.1	-5.9	3.4	-7.6	-3.6	3.0
Vermont	12.4	25.6	-0.1	1.8	-2.0	-0.7	-5.7	-4.0	-5.0	-5.7	-2.8	-0.4	0.3	5.5
Massachusetts	5.7	3.9	15.7	36.6	9.3	9.1	3.4	-5.8	-2.6	-10.5	-7.0	-2.5	1.5	7.1
Rhode Island.	1.1	4.5	-6.5	71.7	15.2	5.7	1.2	-2.8	-1.1	1.5	-9.7	-13.8	-2.1	7.0
Connecticut	0.3	19.3	22.5	11.9	16.0	6.9	16.0	5.0	-0.5	1.2	0.5	6.6	8.5	14.9
Middle Atlantic														
New York.	3.4	6.5	14.1	26.4	12.0	15.0	-6.7	-2.3	-5.8	-5.5	1.0	-6.9	6.0	13.6
New Jersey.	1.6	14.8	6.7	19.8	9.0	10.8	5.8	7.9	2.6	4.8	1.1	12.8	12.1	20.9
Pennsylvania.	8.5	4.4	4.0	6.0	7.0	1.6	0.4	6.3	5.7	8.0	13.1	9.8	13.8	24.8
East North Central														
Ohio.	9.6	1.7	9.1	13.3	7.3	2.7	-0.9	-2.6	-0.1	-0.2	9.3	2.2	11.6	21.0
Indiana	7.9	4.0	11.1	11.5	6.8	-0.3	-7.0	-5.8	3.2	0.6	11.1	16.1	30.8	39.8
Illinois.	2.5	-4.1	-0.6	6.6	4.6	-4.2	-3.6	-2.1	4.7	-1.4	10.0	32.6	86.3	68.7
Michigan.	17.4	10.8	11.5	22.4	16.9	7.9	-3.8	1.0	7.7	10.7	30.2	45.7	76.2	81.4
Wisconsin	11.8	5.4	-1.2	1.8	5.3	-0.1	4.3	4.0	13.1	13.3	17.8	27.6	139.9	794.4
West North Central														
Minnesota	6.1	-1.4	-4.9	-1.9	7.3	-2.2	9.0	6.3	33.0	37.2	71.3	136.8	2,463.8	...
Iowa.	-0.2	-6.7	-5.5	-4.3	-2.5	-2.4	-1.0	-6.9	10.2	9.4	32.7	68.8	237.0	323.3
Missouri.	12.0	-3.1	-5.2	-8.7	3.0	-2.6	-4.3	-4.0	8.6	12.3	25.6	32.0	62.7	63.8
North Dakota.	-2.9	-16.0	-9.9	-10.8	-10.1	1.6	8.7	73.7	64.0	427.1	1,322.7	...	...	...
South Dakota.	0.3	-10.8	-5.2	-10.0	-13.7	5.1	5.4	40.7	12.7	251.5	673.3	...	...	...
Nebraska.	1.9	-11.5	-8.3	-10.3	-10.1	0.1	1.1	8.3	5.5	97.1	287.8	249.7	...	...
Kansas.	3.4	-10.4	-6.8	-4.3	-9.0	-0.1	-3.8	5.1	-1.5	30.0	185.1	221.7	...	...

Table 3-8C. Percent Change in Rural Population from Preceding Decade, by Region, Division, and State: 1850 to 1980–continued

Region, division, and state	1980	1970	1960	1950	1940	1930	1920	1910	1900	1890	1880	1870	1860	1850
South Atlantic														
Delaware	14.4	-0.6	29.0	33.9	10.3	12.7	-2.9	6.3	1.6	-0.2	3.7	3.5	17.3	11.2
Maryland	-9.6	8.5	16.5	23.8	12.8	13.2	-8.9	6.8	9.2	-2.2	15.2	7.0	14.9	10.9
District of Columbia	...	...	...	...	...	...	...	...	...	-100.0	59.7	112.8	57.4	8.2
Virginia	6.3	-3.0	0.2	12.1	5.9	0.1	3.2	4.7	10.3	3.8	22.6	-2.2	7.2	7.9
West Virginia	17.1	-7.5	-12.3	-0.2	10.5	13.1	10.3	19.1	22.3	20.7	39.0	13.9	22.6	34.3
North Carolina	10.4	0.6	2.2	8.7	10.0	14.1	9.6	10.6	13.6	11.7	29.9	6.9	14.2	14.6
South Carolina	6.9	-4.4	4.6	2.1	4.8	-1.6	7.7	10.4	13.0	12.4	42.9	-1.6	5.8	10.5
Georgia	12.8	3.3	-6.5	-1.5	1.8	-7.1	4.7	10.7	18.4	13.1	28.9	10.4	13.2	30.1
Florida	23.2	-3.5	34.8	41.4	20.2	15.2	15.3	26.6	34.2	29.5	40.6	28.0	54.1	60.5
East South Central														
Kentucky	17.2	-8.9	-9.4	-1.9	10.0	1.8	2.8	3.3	11.8	7.4	24.3	8.7	13.9	21.3
Tennessee	13.2	-5.7	-7.4	7.4	9.8	-0.4	-1.0	2.9	10.8	7.2	22.5	9.5	8.4	19.3
Alabama	9.1	-3.3	-14.3	-7.3	3.9	3.4	4.0	9.7	18.4	14.0	27.8	2.1	24.3	27.4
Mississippi	7.9	-9.4	-13.6	-9.9	4.8	7.8	-2.5	11.1	17.3	11.2	38.0	3.1	29.3	60.1
West South Central														
Arkansas	15.0	-5.7	-20.2	-14.8	3.1	0.7	6.6	14.3	13.7	36.9	63.2	9.4	105.7	115.1
Louisiana	8.2	1.9	-1.3	-5.8	9.1	8.3	0.9	14.2	21.6	19.2	33.6	0.3	36.4	55.2
Oklahoma	20.9	-5.1	-21.1	-22.7	-7.5	5.6	11.4	82.8	193.8	...	...	...	...	...
Texas	27.3	-4.9	-16.7	-11.6	2.0	9.0	6.5	17.0	34.0	30.5	89.1	32.3	181.9	...
Mountain														
Montana	14.4	-3.7	1.0	-2.8	-2.4	-5.4	55.3	52.8	52.5	223.7	84.0	...	...	...
Idaho	32.7	-6.6	4.2	1.8	10.3	0.9	22.3	68.5	71.4	171.5	117.4	...	...	...
Wyoming	33.2	-7.9	-2.3	-7.2	1.1	13.2	33.6	56.0	60.4	180.6	60.5	...	...	...
Colorado	18.2	2.8	-6.6	6.1	3.2	6.1	22.6	42.2	22.7	70.5	279.9	18.9	...	...
New Mexico	18.1	-5.3	-4.3	3.1	12.3	7.1	5.2	67.2	11.7	33.1	29.6	-2.0	55.9	...
Arizona	21.4	9.2	-0.6	46.3	13.8	33.9	51.2	36.4	29.4	139.1	419.6	...	...	...
Utah	9.7	-7.0	-6.5	4.5	1.3	3.3	16.7	17.0	26.3	23.0	55.8	121.0	181.5	...
Nevada	25.8	10.4	23.5	13.5	18.3	-8.9	-9.3	95.0	12.2	-27.0	21.1	416.9	...	...
Pacific														
Washington	20.6	-0.2	3.9	35.7	19.9	10.6	14.4	75.0	33.3	238.3	183.8	106.6	865.4	...
Oregon	22.7	3.0	-4.8	41.4	20.3	18.1	7.5	30.4	22.3	53.9	80.2	66.6	310.1	...
California	13.9	-15.6	4.8	68.4	32.2	37.9	21.0	28.4	13.5	26.3	40.4	16.7	251.3	...
Alaska	10.8	-7.9	48.4	71.1	7.2	-1.0	-10.7	21.3	49.7	-4.1	...	...	...	...
Hawaii	0.2	-12.7	-3.9	-2.3	-7.0	4.1	23.1	15.9	...	...	...	...	...	...

Note: ... indicates data not applicable. * indicates less than 0.1.

Source: U.S. Bureau of the Census. "Number of Inhabitants: U.S. Summary." 1980 Census of Population. Washington, DC: U.S. Government Printing Office, 1983, Table 13.

to include contiguous or enclosed urban land use areas not intended primarily for residence (industrial parks, railroad yards, storage areas, and so forth), even though the density may be below 1,000 per square mile. In order to qualify as an urbanized area at the 1980 census, the agglomeration of city and suburbs must have at least 50,000 inhabitants. The city around whose periphery the urban fringe is delimited is termed the "central city" of the urbanized area. At the 1970, 1960, and 1950 censuses only cities with 50,000 or more inhabitants (or "twin cities" totaling 50,000) were eligible to have an urbanized area delimitation. For the 1980 census no minimum population size is required for the central city of the urbanized area. Also, in 1970 and 1980 for certain "extended cities" that have incorporated large expanses of land with low residential density, the Census Bureau removed this low-density portion and reclassified it as rural. The official definitions of urban and rural populations are presented in the Definition Box.

Urban-Rural Population Growth

In 1980, 73.7 percent of the population was classed as urban and 26.3 percent as rural (see Table 3-8A). These proportions were almost identical with those reported for the 1970 census. Tables 3-8B and 3-8C show the change in percent urban and rural from 1850 to 1980. During the 1970-80 decade the rural population grew almost as rapidly as the urban population, despite the fact that numerous places passed from the rural to the urban category simply by adding a few more persons during the decade to attain the minimum 2,500 persons needed to be reclassified as urban, and the growth of places to a size that qualified them to have an urban fringe delimited for them. *This represented the halt of a steady trend toward increasing urbanization that had been under way since the nation's founding,* with only a minor setback between 1810 and 1820 (Table 3-9 and Figure 3-6).

Table 3-8A reports the proportion of the population classed as urban at each census since 1850 for each state, division, and region. Table 3-8B reports rates of growth (intercensal percent of increase) in urban population for each intercensal period since 1850. Together, these tables summarize the historical urbanization movement in the nation. In 1790, when the nation was 95 percent rural, most of the urban settlements were on the Atlantic Coast. The urban population grew at rates above the average national growth rate in almost every state at almost every census. However, the more agricultural and less industrialized states remain substantially less urbanized today. Following is a list of the most urban and least urban states:

Most urban	Percent urban	Least urban	Percent urban
D. of Columbia .	100.0	Vermont.	33.8
California . . .	91.3	West Virginia. .	36.2
New Jersey . . .	89.0	South Dakota . .	46.4
Rhode Island . .	87.0	Mississippi. . .	47.3
Hawaii	86.5	Maine.	47.5
Nevada	85.3	North Carolina .	48.0
New York	84.6	North Dakota . .	48.8
Utah	84.4	Kentucky	50.9
Florida.	84.3	Arkansas	51.6
Massachusetts. .	83.8	New Hampshire. .	52.2
Arizona.	83.8	Montana.	52.9
Illinois	83.3	Idaho.	54.0
Colorado	80.6	South Carolina .	54.1
Maryland	80.3	Iowa	58.6
Texas.	79.6	Alabama.	60.0

Although the South is still somewhat less urban than the Northeast, North Central, and West regions, there are very urban and quite rural states in each of the regions.

In studying the urbanization trend in the United States, the effect of the change in definition between 1940 and 1950 (recognition of urbanized areas) must be taken into account. This change affected some states comparatively little but made substantial changes in others. Table 3-9 provides data under both old and new definitions for 1950 and 1960.

Size of Place

Urban places range in size from small cities of 2,500 to New York City's 7 million persons. Within the rural areas there are many thousands of hamlets and villages of various sizes, all with less than 2,500 inhabitants. Table 3-10 provides a detailed report of this distribution of urban and rural sizes of place, both for 1970 and 1980. This table presents the following facts:

1. There was an absolute decline in the population of cities of 500,000 or more, and cities of 100,000 to 500,000 grew very slowly.
2. The great majority of the urban growth that took place occurred in the urban fringes. The central city population grew slowly.
3. Within the urban fringe, the fastest growth occurred in the smaller (rather than the larger) suburban places.
4. Surprisingly, the smaller urban places outside urbanized areas suffered almost a 10 percent decline in population during the decade. This could have been caused in part by the absorption of numerous urban centers into the expanding urban fringes.
5. In the rural areas population centers of all sizes grew, but the most rapid growth occurred in the relatively open country, outside the villages and hamlets recognized as separate entities.

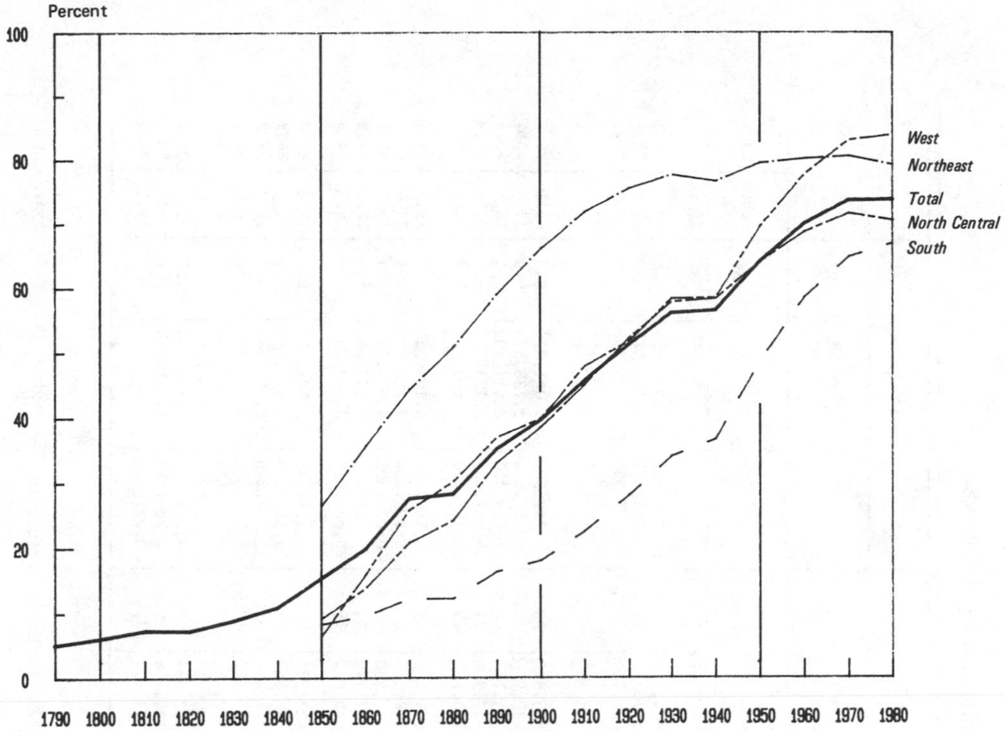

Figure 3-6. Population Percent Urban, by Region: 1790-1980

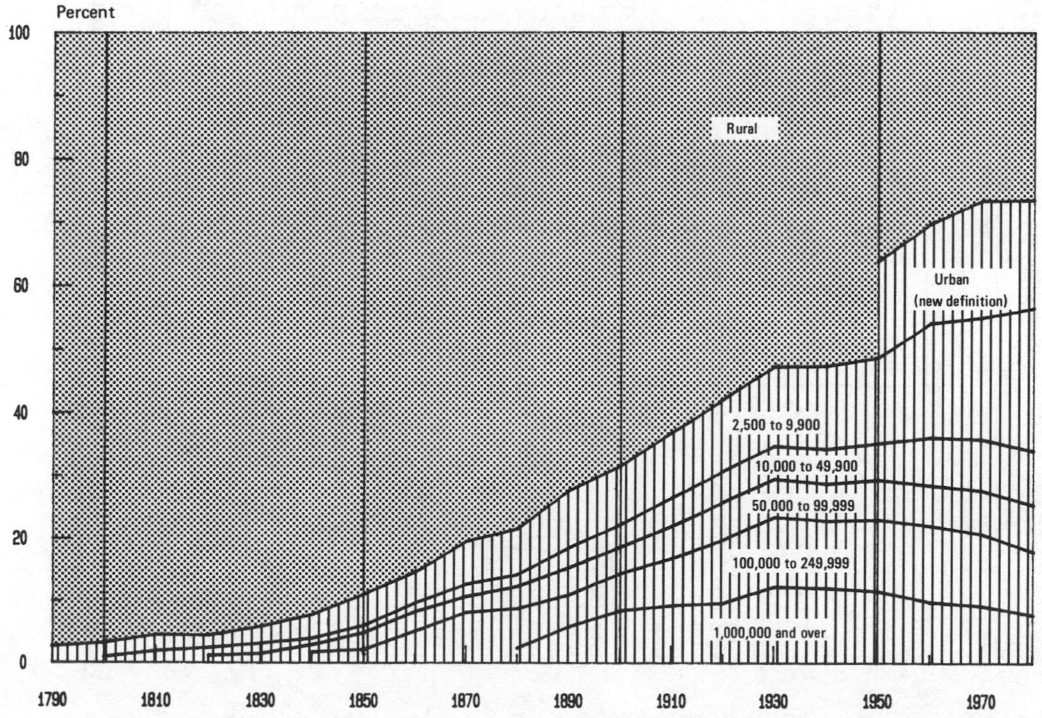

Figure 3-7. Population of the United States by Size of Place of Habitation: 1790-1980

Table 3-9. Urban and Rural Population of the United States: 1790-1980

Year	United States			Urban				Rural			Percent of total population	
	Total population	Change from preceding census		Places of 2,500 or more	Population	Change from preceding census		Population	Change from preceding census			
		Number	Per-cent			Number	Per-cent		Number	Per-cent	Urban	Rural
Current urban definition:												
1980 (Apr. 1).	226,545,805	23,243,774	11.4	7.749	167,050,992	17,404,363	11.6	59,494,813	5,929,516	11.1	73.7	26.3
1970 (Apr. 1).	203,302,031	23,978,856	13.4	6.434	149,646,629	23,377,879	19.5	53,565,297	-489,128	-0.9	73.6	26.4
1960 (Apr. 1).	179,323,175	27,997,377	18.5	5.445	125,268,750	28,421,933	29.3	54,045,054	-424,556	-0.8	69.9	30.1
1950 (Apr. 1).	151,325,798	19,161,229	14.5	4,307	96,846,817	...	...	54,478,981	...	...	64.0	36.0
Previous urban definition:												
1960 (Apr. 1).	179,323,175	27,997,377	18.5	5,023	113,063,593	22,935,399	25.4	66,259,582	5,061,978	8.3	63.1	36.9
1950 (Apr. 1).	151,325,798	19,161,229	14.5	4,077	90,128,194	15,422,856	20.6	61,197,604	3,738,373	6.5	59.6	40.4
1940 (Apr. 1).	132,164,569	8,961,945	7.3	3,485	74,705,338	5,544,739	8.0	57,459,231	3,417,206	6.3	56.5	43.5
1930 (Apr. 1).	123,202,624	17,181,087	16.2	3,183	69,160,599	14,907,317	27.5	54,042,025	2,273,770	4.4	56.1	43.9
1920 (Jan. 1).	106,021,537	13,793,041	15.0	2,728	54,253,282	12,189,281	29.0	51,768,255	1,603,760	3.2	51.2	48.8
1910 (Apr. 15)	92,228,496	16,016,328	21.0	2,269	42,064,001	11,849,169	39.2	50,164,495	4,167,159	9.1	45.6	54.4
1900 (June 1).	76,212,168	13,232,402	21.0	1,743	30,214,832	8,108,567	36.7	45,997,336	5,123,835	12.5	39.6	60.4
1890 (June 1).	62,979,766	12,790,557	25.5	1,351	22,106,265	7,976,530	56.5	40,873,501	4,814,027	13 4	35.1	64.9
1880 (June 1).	50,189,209	11,630,838	30.2	940	14,129,735	4,227,374	42.7	36,059,474	7,403,464	25.8	28.2	71.8
1870 (June 1).	38,558,371	7,115,050	22.6	663	9,902,361	3,685,843	59.3	28,656,010	3,429,207	13.6	25.7	74.3
1860 (June 1).	31,443,321	8,251,445	35.6	392	6,216,518	2,672,802	75.4	25,226,803	5,578,643	28.4	19.8	80.2
1850 (June 1).	23,191,876	6,128,523	35.9	236	3,543,716	1,698,661	92.1	19,648,160	4,429,862	29.1	15.3	84.7
1840 (June 1).	17,063,353	4,202,651	32.7	131	1,845,055	717,808	63.7	15,218,298	3,484,843	29.7	10.8	89.2
1830 (June 1).	12,860,702	3,222,249	33.4	90	1,127,247	433,992	62.6	11,733,455	2,788,257	31.2	8.8	91.2
1820 (Aug. 7).	9,638,453	2,398,572	33.1	61	693,255	167,796	31.9	8,945,198	2,230,776	33.2	7.2	92.8
1810 (Aug. 6).	7,239,881	1,931,398	36.4	46	525,459	203,088	63.0	6,714,422	1,728,310	34.7	7.3	92.7
1800 (Aug. 4).	5,308,483	1,379,269	35.1	33	322,371	120,716	59.9	4,986,112	1,258,553	33.8	6.1	93.9
1790 (Aug. 2).	3,929,214	...	...	24	201,655	...	...	3,727,559	...	...	5.1	94.9

Note: ... indicates data not applicable.

Source: U.S. Bureau of the Census. "Number of Inhabitants: United States Summary." 1980 Census of Population. Washington, DC: U.S. Government Printing Office, 1983, Table 3.

Table 3-10. Population of the United States, by Size of Place: 1980 and 1970

Urban and rural areas, by size of place	1980				1970			
	Places	Population	Percent of total population	Percent distribution	Places	Population	Percent of total population	Percent distribution
United States								
Total.	22,529	226,545,805	100.0	...	20,768	203,302,031	100.0	...
Urban.	8,765	167,050,992	73.7	100.0	7,129	149,646,629	73.6	100.0
Inside urbanized areas	4,938	139,170,683	61.4	83.3	3,456	120,724,546	59.4	80.7
Central cities	431	67,035,302	29.6	40.1	340	65,061,444	32.0	43.5
Cities of--								
1,000,000 or more. . . .	6	17,530,248	7.7	10.5	6	18,769,365	9.2	12.5
500,000 to 1,000,000 . .	16	10,834,121	4.8	6.5	20	12,966,746	6.4	8.7
250,000 to 500,000 . . .	33	11,900,309	5.3	7.1	30	10,441,689	5.1	7.0
100,000 to 250,000 . . .	82	12,295,543	5.4	7.4	78	11,484,410	5.7	7.7
50,000 to 100,000. . . .	125	8,649,031	3.8	5.2	125	8,630,741	4.2	5.8
Less than 50,000	169	5,826,050	2.6	3.5	81	2,768,493	1.4	1.9
Urban fringe	4,507	72,135,381	31.8	43.2	3,116	55,663,102	27.4	37.2
Places of 2,500 or more. . .	3,491	58,212,417	25.7	34.8	2,421	39,432,356	19.4	26.4
100,000 or more.	36	4,976,800	2.2	3.0	22	2,801,623	1.4	1.9
50,000 to 100,000.	165	11,137,456	4.9	6.7	115	8,093,137	4.0	5.4
25,000 to 50,000	424	14,539,729	6.4	8.7	280	9,572,936	4.7	6.4
10,000 to 25,000	1,087	17,232,991	7.6	10.3	743	11,700,845	5.8	7.8
5,000 to 10,000.	1,108	7,900,939	3.5	4.7	769	5,499,732	2.7	3.7
2,500 to 5,000	671	2,424,502	1.1	1.5	492	1,764,083	0.9	1.2
Places of less than 2,500. .	1,016	1,260,246	0.6	0.8	695	835,318	0.4	0.6
2,000 to 2,500	183	406,475	0.2	0.2	124	174,742	0.1	0.2
1,500 to 2,000	210	367,921	0.2	0.2	122	210,663	0.1	0.1
1,000 to 1,500	238	297,473	0.1	0.2	157	195,235	0.1	0.1
Less than 1,000.	385	188,377	0.1	0.1	292	154,678	0.1	0.1
Other urban.	...	12,662,718	5.6	7.6	...	15,395,428	7.6	10.3
Outside urbanized areas. . . .	3,827	27,880,309	12.3	16.7	3,673	28,922,083	14.2	19.3
Places of--								
25,000 or more	118	3,773,752	1.7	2.3	175	5,816,108	2.9	3.9
10,000 to 25,000	642	9,708,035	4.3	5.8	626	9,417,075	4.6	6.3
5,000 to 10,000.	1,073	7,455,198	3.3	4.5	1,069	7,414,564	3.6	5.0
2,500 to 5,000	1,994	6,943,324	3.1	4.2	1,803	6,274,336	3.1	4.2
Rural.	13,764	59,494,813	26.3	100.0	13,639	53,565,297	26.4	100.0
Places of 1,000 to 2,500 . . .	4,434	7,037,840	3.1	11.8	4,128	6,551,504	3.2	12.2
2,000 to 2,500	918	2,048,678	0.9	3.4	863	1,924,254	0.9	3.6
1,500 to 2,000	1,318	2,280,677	1.0	3.8	1,239	2,142,712	1.1	4.0
1,000 to 1,500	2,198	2,708,485	1.2	4.6	2,026	2,484,538	1.2	4.6
Places of less than 1,000. . .	9,330	3,863,470	1.7	6.5	9,511	3,849,112	1.9	7.2
Other rural.	...	48,593,503	21.4	81.7	...	43,164,681	21.2	80.6
Urbanized areas								
Total.	366	139,170,683	61.4	100.0	275	120,724,546	59.4	100.0
Areas of--								
1,000,000 or more.	29	80,088,652	35.4	57.5	25	70,828,671	34.9	58.7
500,000 to 1,000,000	24	16,049,079	7.1	11.5	21	14,419,672	7.1	11.9
250,000 to 500,000	45	15,751,665	7.0	11.3	35	12,478,948	6.1	10.3
100,000 to 250,000	107	16,341,905	7.2	11.7	97	15,776,393	7.8	13.1
Less than 100,000.	161	10,939,382	4.8	7.9	97	7,220,862	3.6	6.0

Note: ... indicates data not applicable.

Source: U.S. Bureau of the Census. "Number of Inhabitants: United States Summary." 1980 Census of Population. Washington, DC: U.S. Government Printing Office, 1983, Table 4.

The growth of urban and rural population by size of place from 1790 to 1980 is reported in Table 3-11 and graphed in Figure 3-7. For each decennial date, this table reports the number of places, the population in each size group, and the percent of population in each size class. The nation did not have a city of 1 million inhabitants until 1880 (New York); now there are six such cities and 173 cities with more than 100,000 inhabitants. In 1940 there were only 93 cities that large.

Until 1930 there was a tendency for rapid growth to take place in the larger places and their environs. This diminished during the 1940-50 decade, as a "decentralization" movement set in (including growth of places in the South and Southwest that had previously been slow to urbanize). By 1970 population began to drift away from many of the largest concentrations. Between 1970 and 1980 there were no new additions to the ranks of cities with 250,000 or more inhabitants, but the number of smaller and medium ones growing into the urban category increased substantially during the decade. Despite the addition of more than 1,300 urban entities during the decade, the rural population grew as rapidly as the urban.

In rural areas 80 percent of the population has traditionally been widely dispersed in individual homes located on the land, and not clustered into village settlements. That pattern persists today and is being perpetuated by the open-country nature of rural growth.

Table 3-11. Urban and Rural Population of the United States, by Size of Place: 1790-1980

Urban and rural areas, by size of place	1980	1970	1960	1950 Current urban definition	1950 Previous urban definition	1940	1930	1920	1910	1900
Number of places										
Urban, total	8,765	7,129	6,041	4,764	4,077	3,485	3,183	2,725	2,266	1,740
Places of 2,500 or more	7,749	6,434	5,445	4,307	4,077	3,485	3,183	2,725	2,266	1,740
1,000,000 or more	6	6	5	5	5	5	5	3	3	3
500,000 to 1,000,000	16	20	16	13	13	9	8	9	5	3
250,000 to 500,000	34	30	30	23	23	23	24	13	11	9
100,000 to 250,000	117	100	81	66	68	56	57	43	31	23
50,000 to 100,000	290	240	201	126	129	107	98	77	60	40
25,000 to 50,000	675	520	432	253	284	213	186	143	119	83
10,000 to 25,000	1,765	1,385	1,134	779	832	666	609	466	369	281
5,000 to 10,000	2,181	1,838	1,394	1,184	1,137	970	853	715	606	465
2,500 to 5,000	2,665	2,295	2,152	1,858	1,586	1,436	1,343	1,256	1,062	833
Places of less than 2,500	1,016	695	596	457	...	...	...	...	...	...
Rural, total	13,764	13,639	13,749	13,851	13,279	13,328	13,468	12,872	11,843	8,933
Places of 1,000 to 2,500	4,434	4,128	4,151	4,186	3,436	3,233	3,111	3,034	2,723	2,130
Places of less than 1,000	9,330	9,511	9,598	9,665	9,843	10,095	10,357	9,838	9,120	6,803
Cumulative summary										
Places of										
1,000,000 or more	6	6	5	5	5	5	5	3	3	3
500,000 or more	22	26	21	18	18	14	13	12	8	6
250,000 or more	56	56	51	41	41	37	37	25	19	15
100,000 or more	173	156	132	107	109	93	94	68	50	38
50,000 or more	463	396	333	233	238	200	192	145	110	78
25,000 or more	1,138	916	765	486	522	413	378	288	229	161
10,000 or more	2,903	2,301	1,899	1,265	1,354	1,079	987	754	598	442
5,000 or more	5,084	4,139	3,293	2,449	2,491	2,049	1,840	1,469	1,204	907
2,500 or more	7,749	6,434	5,445	4,307	4,077	3,485	3,183	2,725	2,266	1,740
Population										
Urban, total	167,050,992	149,646,629	125,268,750	96,846,817	90,128,194	74,705,338	69,160,599	54,253,282	42,064,001	30,214,832
Places of 2,500 or more	153,128,028	133,415,883	114,272,899	88,924,799	90,128,194	74,705,338	69,160,559	54,253,282	42,064,001	30,214,832
1,000,000 or more	17,530,248	18,769,365	17,484,059	17,404,450	17,404,450	15,910,866	15,064,555	10,145,532	8,501,174	6,429,474
500,000 to 1,000,000	10,834,121	12,966,746	11,110,991	9,186,945	9,186,945	6,456,959	5,763,987	6,223,769	3,010,667	1,645,087
250,000 to 500,000	12,157,578	10,441,689	10,765,881	8,241,560	8,241,560	7,827,514	7,956,228	4,540,838	3,949,839	2,861,296
100,000 to 250,000	17,015,074	14,286,033	11,652,426	9,726,696	9,971,804	7,971,976	7,678,548	6,519,187	4,840,458	3,272,490
50,000 to 100,000	19,786,487	16,723,878	13,835,902	8,930,823	9,137,541	7,343,917	6,491,448	5,347,228	4,231,098	2,709,338
25,000 to 50,000	23,435,654	17,860,912	14,950,612	8,834,919	9,903,043	7,417,093	6,425,693	5,075,041	4,023,397	2,839,933
10,000 to 25,000	27,644,903	21,414,545	17,568,286	11,877,759	12,779,084	9,990,251	9,116,668	7,045,099	5,548,868	4,350,738
5,000 to 10,000	15,356,137	12,914,296	9,779,714	8,192,636	7,885,742	6,712,485	5,910,028	4,970,683	4,224,165	3,204,195
2,500 to 5,000	9,367,826	8,038,419	7,580,028	6,529,011	5,618,025	5,074,277	4,753,444	4,385,905	3,734,335	2,902,281
Places of less than 2,500	1,260,246	835,318	689,746	577,992	...	...	...	...	...	...
Other urban	12,662,718	15,395,428	9,851,105	7,344,026	...	...	...	...	...	...
Rural, total	59,494,813	53,565,297	54,054,425	54,478,981	61,197,604	57,459,025	54,042,025	51,768,255	50,164,495	45,997,336
Places of 1,000 to 2,500	7,037,840	6,551,504	6,496,788	6,515,474	5,424,796	5,067,057	4,851,746	4,718,651	4,242,798	3,301,314
Places of less than 1,000	3,863,470	3,849,112	3,893,090	4,036,760	4,134,661	4,321,471	4,368,170	4,262,255	3,933,993	3,003,479
Other rural	48,593,503	43,164,681	43,664,547	43,926,747	51,638,147	48,070,703	44,822,109	42,787,349	41,987,704	39,692,543
Percent of total population										
Urban	73.7	73.6	69.9	64.0	59.6	56.5	56.1	51.2	45.6	39.6
Places of 2,500 or more	67.6	65.7	64.0	58.8	59.6	56.5	56.1	51.2	45.6	39.6
1,000,000 or more	7.7	9.2	9.8	11.5	11.5	12.0	12.2	9.6	9.2	8.4
500,000 to 1,000,000	4.8	6.4	6.2	6.1	6.1	4.9	4.7	5.9	3.3	2.2
250,000 to 500,000	5.4	5.1	6.0	5.4	5.4	5.9	6.5	4.3	4.3	3.8
100,000 to 250,000	7.5	7.0	6.5	6.4	6.6	6.0	6.2	6.1	5.2	4.3
50,000 to 100,000	8.7	8.2	7.7	5.9	6.0	5.6	5.3	5.0	4.6	3.6
25,000 to 50,000	10.3	8.8	8.3	5.8	6.5	5.6	5.2	4.8	4.4	3.7
10,000 to 25,000	12.2	10.5	9.8	7.8	8.4	7.6	7.4	6.6	6.0	5.7
5,000 to 10,000	6.8	6.4	5.5	5.4	5.2	5.1	4.8	4.7	4.6	4.2
2,500 to 5,000	4.1	4.0	4.2	4.3	3.7	3.8	3.9	4.1	4.0	3.8
Places of less than 2,500	0.6	0.4	0.4	0.4	...	...	...	...	...	...
Other urban	5.6	7.6	5.5	4.9	...	...	...	...	...	...
Rural	26.3	26.4	30.1	36.0	40.4	43.5	43.9	48.8	54.4	60.4
Places of 1,000 to 2,500	3.1	3.2	3.6	4.3	3.6	3.8	3.9	4.5	4.6	4.3
Places of less than 1,000	1.7	1.9	2.2	2.7	2.7	3.3	3.5	4.0	4.3	3.9
Other rural	21.4	21.2	24.3	29.0	34.1	36.4	36.4	40.4	45.5	52.1

Table 3-11. Urban and Rural Population of the United States, by Size of Place: 1790-1980–continued

Urban and rural areas, by size of place	1890	1880	1870	1860	1850	1840	1830	1820	1810	1800	1790
Number of places											
Urban, total	1,348	939	663	392	236	131	90	61	46	33	24
Places of 2,500 or more	1,348	939	663	392	236	131	90	61	46	33	24
1,000,000 or more	3		...	...	...	...	...	...	...	...	...
500,000 to 1,000,000	1	3	2	2	1	...	...	...	...	...	...
250,000 to 500,000	7	4	5	1	...	1	...	...	...	...	...
100,000 to 250,000	17	12	7	6	5	2	1	1	...	...	...
50,000 to 100,000	30	15	11	7	4	2	3	2	2	1	...
25,000 to 50,000	66	42	27	19	16	7	3	2	2	2	2
10,000 to 25,000	230	146	116	58	36	25	16	8	7	3	3
5,000 to 10,000	340	249	186	136	85	48	33	22	17	15	7
2,500 to 5,000	654	467	309	163	89	46	34	26	18	12	12
Places of less than 2,500	...	...	...	...	...	...	...	...	...	...	...
Rural, total	6,495	--	--	--	--	--	--	--	--	--	--
Places of 1,000 to 2,500	1,605	--	--	--	--	--	--	--	--	--	--
Places of less than 1,000	4,890	--	--	--	--	--	--	--	--	--	--
Cumulative summary											
Places of											
1,000,000 or more	3	1	...	...	...	...	...	...	...	...	...
500,000 or more	4	4	2	2	1	...	...	...	...	...	...
250,000 or more	11	8	7	3	1	1	...	...	...	...	...
100,000 or more	28	20	14	9	6	3	1	1	...	...	...
50,000 or more	58	35	25	16	10	5	4	3	2	1	...
25,000 or more	124	77	52	35	26	12	7	5	4	3	2
10,000 or more	354	233	168	93	62	37	23	13	11	6	5
5,000 or more	694	472	354	229	147	85	56	35	28	21	12
2,500 or more	1,348	939	663	392	236	131	90	61	46	33	24
Population											
Urban, total	22,106,265	14,129,735	9,902,361	6,216,518	3,543,716	1,845,055	1,127,247	693,255	525,459	322,371	201,655
Places of 2,500 or more	22,106,265	14,129,735	9,902,361	6,216,518	3,543,716	1,845,055	1,127,247	693,255	525,459	322,371	201,655
1,000,000 or more	3,662,115	1,206,299	...	...	...	...	...	...	...	...	...
500,000 to 1,000,000	806,343	1,917,018	1,616,314	1,379,198	515,547	...	...	...	...	...	...
250,000 to 500,000	2,447,608	1,300,809	1,523,820	266,661	...	312,710	...	...	...	...	...
100,000 to 250,000	2,781,894	1,786,783	989,855	992,922	659,121	204,506	202,589	123,706	...	...	...
50,000 to 100,000	2,027,569	947,918	768,238	452,060	284,355	187,048	222,474	126,540	150,095	60,515	...
25,000 to 50,000	2,268,786	1,446,366	930,119	670,293	611,328	235,424	105,243	70,474	80,342	67,734	61,653
10,000 to 25,000	3,451,258	2,189,447	1,709,541	884,433	560,783	404,822	240,371	121,613	108,980	54,479	48,182
5,000 to 10,000	2,383,685	1,717,146	1,278,145	976,436	596,086	328,744	230,859	155,035	116,271	94,394	47,569
2,500 to 5,000	2,277,007	1,617,949	1,086,329	594,515	316,496	171,801	125,711	95,887	69,771	45,249	44,251
Places of less than 2,500	...	...	...	...	...	...	...	...	...	...	...
Other urban	...	...	...	...	...	...	...	...	...	...	...
Rural, total	40,873,501	36,059,474	28,656,010	25,226,803	19,648,160	15,218,298	11,733,455	8,945,198	6,714,422	4,986,112	3,727,559
Places of 1,000 to 2,500	2,511,085	--	--	--	--	--	--	--	--	--	--
Places of less than 1,000	2,250,090	--	--	--	--	--	--	--	--	--	--
Other rural	36,112,326	--	--	--	--	--	--	--	--	--	--
Percent of total population											
Urban	35.1	28.2	25.7	19.8	15.3	10.8	8.8	7.2	7.3	6.1	5.1
Places of 2,500 or more	35.1	28.2	25.7	19.8	15.3	10.8	8.8	7.2	7.3	6.1	5.1
1,000,000 or more	5.8	2.4	...	...	...	...	...	...	...	...	...
500,000 to 1,000,000	1.3	3.8	4.2	4.4	2.2	...	...	...	...	...	...
250,000 to 500,000	3.9	2.6	4.0	0.8	...	1.8	...	...	...	...	...
100,000 to 250,000	4.4	3.6	2.6	3.2	2.8	1.2	1.6	1.3	...	...	...
50,000 to 100,000	3.2	1.9	2.0	1.4	1.2	1.1	1.7	1.3	2.1	1.1	...
25,000 to 50,000	3.6	2.9	2.4	2.1	2.6	1.4	0.8	0.7	1.1	1.3	1.6
10,000 to 25,000	5.5	4.4	4.4	2.8	2.4	2.4	1.9	1.3	1.5	1.0	1.2
5,000 to 10,000	3.8	3.4	3.3	3.1	2.6	1.9	1.8	1.6	1.6	1.8	1.2
2,500 to 5,000	3.6	3.2	2.8	1.9	1.4	1.0	1.0	1.0	1.0	0.9	1.1
Places of less than 2,500	...	...	...	...	...	...	...	...	...	...	...
Other urban	...	...	...	...	...	...	...	...	...	...	...
Rural	64.9	71.8	74.3	80.2	84.7	89.2	91.2	92.8	92.7	93.9	94.9
Places of 1,000 to 2,500	4.0	--	--	--	--	--	--	--	--	--	--
Places of less than 1,000	3.6	--	--	--	--	--	--	--	--	--	--
Other rural	57.3	--	--	--	--	--	--	--	--	--	--

Note: -- indicates data not available. ... indicates data not applicable.

Source: U.S. Bureau of the Census. "Number of Inhabitants: United States Summary." 1980 Census of Population. Washington, DC: U.S. Government Printing Office, 1983, Table 5.

Regional and State Differences in Type of Urban and Rural Population

There are major differences among regions, divisions, and states in the composition of the urban and rural population. In the Northeast and North Central regions, a high percentage of urban population is found in urbanized areas, and urban fringes tend to be almost as populous as the central cities they surround. In the South, a higher percentage of the urban population is found outside the urbanized areas. The details, state by state, are provided in Table 3-12.

Race Differences in Urban-Rural Residence

The apparent stagnation between 1970 and 1980 in urbanization was in reality a balancing of opposing trends for the races. The white population actually became substantially more rural in its residence, while the black population, already highly urbanized, became even more so (85.3 percent from 81.3 percent. See Table 3-13 and Figure 3-8). White populations were abandoning central cities and moving to urban fringes and rural communities, while simultaneously a significant share of the comparatively small black populations still residing in rural communities were moving into cities and urban fringes. Thus, the urban fringes grew rapidly, by inmovement of both white and black populations. For many central cities, the exodus of white population surpassed the influx of black population by a considerable margin. Although the black population made up only one-ninth of the total at the national level, in central cities black population had come to comprise almost one-fourth. More than one-half of the black population now lives in central cities of urbanized areas.

However, the net movement of the black population into central cities between 1970 and 1980 was only moderate, not the big influx that took place in the 1940s and 1950s, as the old agricultural system of the South underwent change. Most of the urban expansion of the black population occurred in urban fringes. For the decade, the rate of growth of the black population in urban fringes was almost 100 percent. (It should be kept in mind that the base is small.) Thus, by losing white population by their exodus to both urban fringe and rural areas, and failing to gain black population to the extent of previous censuses, central cities suffered extremely low rates of growth, and many had absolute declines. The fact that birth rates were low throughout the decade made it difficult to replace the migration losses by natural reproductive increases.

Individual Urban Localities: Cities of 100,000 or More

Table 3-14 lists each of 170 cities with 100,000 or more inhabitants in 1980 and reports its population at each census since 1790 or the decade of its incorporation. The cities are ranked in order of size. Principal characteristics of these cities are provided in Table 3-15 (arranged alphabetically). This table provides information on:

Change and rate of change, 1970-80
Population in 1970 and 1980
Percent black, 1970 and 1980
Spanish-origin population, percent 1980
Proportions of youth and old age, 1980
Density, 1980
Number of households, 1980.

Among the important findings to be derived from this table are the following:

1. A total of 81 of the 170 cities (48 percent) suffered an absolute decline in population during the 1970-80 decade. Most of these places were central cities of urbanized areas, where growth occurred primarily in the fringe areas.

2. A total of 103 of the 170 cities (60 percent) had a higher percentage of population classed as black than the national proportion of 11.7 percent. In nine places, the black population was an absolute majority:

City	Percent
Gary, IN.	70.8
Washington, DC.	70.3
Atlanta, GA	66.6
Detroit, MI	63.1
Newark, NJ.	58.2
Birmingham, AL.	55.6
New Orleans, LA	55.3
Baltimore, MD	54.8
Richmond, VA.	51.3

The black population accounted for 40 percent to 50 percent of the total in the following additional cities:

City	Percent
Savannah, GA.	49.0
Memphis, TN	47.6
Durham, NC.	47.1
Jackson, MS	47.0
Oakland, CA	46.9
St. Louis, MO	45.6
Portsmouth, VA.	45.1
Macon, GA	44.5
Cleveland, OH	43.8
Flint, MI	41.4
Shreveport, LA.	41.1
Winston-Salem, NC	40.2
Columbia, SC.	40.2

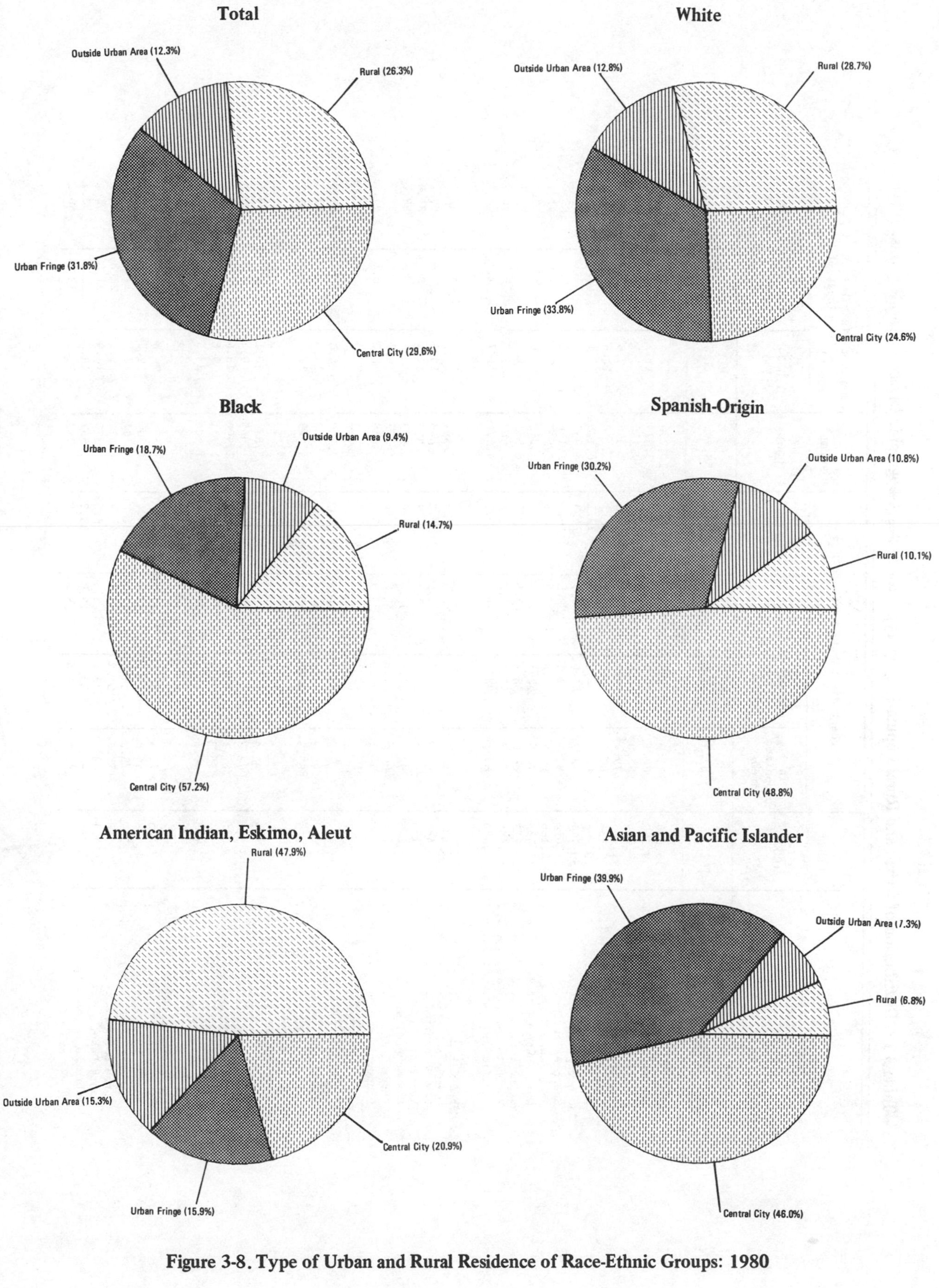

Figure 3-8. Type of Urban and Rural Residence of Race-Ethnic Groups: 1980

Table 3-12. Distribution of Urban and Rural Population, by Type, for States, Geographic Divisions, and Regions: 1980

Region, division, and state	Urban population (000)	Percent distribution of urban: In urbanized areas	Central cities of UA	Fringe of UA	Outside UA	Rural population (000)	Percent distribution of rural in places of: 1,000–2,500	Under 1,000	Other rural
United States total	167,051	83.3	40.1	43.2	16.7	59,495	11.8	6.5	81.7
Northeast region	38,906	91.0	39.9	51.1	9.0	10,230	12.5	2.8	84.7
New England	9,269	88.1	36.8	51.3	11.9	3,079	11.1	0.5	88.4
Middle Atlantic	29,636	92.0	40.8	51.2	8.0	7,150	13.1	3.8	83.1
North Central region	41,520	79.4	39.2	40.2	20.6	17,346	13.6	11.0	75.4
East North Central	30,534	83.7	40.3	43.4	16.3	11,148	11.6	7.5	80.9
West North Central	10,986	67.5	36.2	31.3	32.5	6,198	17.1	17.1	65.8
South region	50,414	78.7	42.0	36.7	21.3	24,958	10.0	5.1	84.9
South Atlantic	24,813	83.9	33.1	50.8	16.1	12,146	9.1	3.9	87.0
East South Central	8,166	69.5	45.6	23.9	30.5	6,500	8.1	4.5	87.4
West South Central	17,435	75.5	52.8	22.7	24.5	6,312	13.6	8.2	78.2
West region	36,211	86.0	38.9	47.1	14.0	6,961	13.0	5.8	81.2
Mountain	8,685	76.2	42.0	34.2	23.8	2,687	15.2	8.2	76.6
Pacific	27,526	89.1	38.0	51.1	10.9	4,274	11.7	4.2	84.1
New England									
Maine	534	46.7	29.1	17.6	53.3	591	13.8	*	86.2
New Hampshire	480	61.0	47.7	13.3	39.0	440	10.9	*	89.1
Vermont	173	44.3	21.8	22.5	55.7	339	14.1	4.1	81.8
Massachusetts	4,808	92.4	34.0	58.4	7.6	929	11.4	*	88.6
Rhode Island	824	96.0	41.8	54.2	4.0	123	4.7	*	95.3
Connecticut	2,450	94.5	41.0	53.5	5.5	658	8.2	0.1	91.7
Middle Atlantic									
New York	14,858	92.8	56.2	36.6	7.2	2,700	15.3	3.7	81.0
New Jersey	6,557	95.9	11.6	84.3	4.1	807	10.6	1.4	88.0
Pennsylvania	8,221	87.2	36.4	50.8	12.8	3,643	12.1	4.4	83.5
East North Central									
Ohio	7,918	82.6	38.7	43.9	17.4	2,879	10.1	6.3	83.6
Indiana	3,525	73.8	43.7	30.1	26.2	1,965	9.4	7.0	83.6
Illinois	9,518	87.1	42.7	44.4	12.9	1,908	18.0	14.7	67.3
Michigan	6,552	88.3	33.0	55.3	11.7	2,711	9.0	3.7	87.3
Wisconsin	3,021	77.4	48.4	29.0	22.6	1,685	13.5	8.2	78.3
West North Central									
Minnesota	2,725	75.4	31.7	43.7	24.6	1,351	15.3	14.6	70.1
Iowa	1,708	54.6	39.5	15.1	45.4	1,206	19.5	20.9	59.6
Missouri	3,350	78.2	36.1	42.1	21.8	1,567	13.2	11.8	75.0
North Dakota	318	55.6	51.9	3.7	44.4	334	21.1	22.8	56.1
South Dakota	321	43.2	39.9	3.3	56.8	370	16.9	21.0	62.1
Nebraska	988	64.2	49.2	15.0	35.8	582	19.0	22.5	58.5
Kansas	1,576	54.2	28.4	25.8	45.8	788	21.7	18.1	60.2

Table 3-12. Distribution of Urban and Rural Population, by Type, for States, Geographic Divisions, and Regions: 1980—continued

Region, division, and state	Urban population (000)	Percent distribution of urban				Rural population (000)	Percent distribution of rural in places of:		
		In urbanized areas	Central cities of UA	Fringe of UA	Outside UA		1,000–2,500	Under 1,000	Other rural
South Atlantic									
Delaware	420	87.6	16.7	70.9	12.4	175	15.5	6.2	78.3
Maryland	3,387	92.8	25.9	66.9	7.2	830	11.2	2.9	85.9
District of Columbia	638	100.0	100.0	...	...	...	...	...	...
Virginia	3,529	86.3	33.6	52.7	13.7	1,817	7.0	2.5	90.5
West Virginia	705	57.2	33.4	23.8	42.8	1,244	11.4	4.6	84.0
North Carolina	2,823	70.9	44.1	26.8	29.1	3,059	7.4	3.8	88.8
South Carolina	1,689	70.4	21.6	48.8	29.6	1,433	9.5	3.4	87.1
Georgia	3,409	76.4	31.8	44.6	25.6	2,054	8.3	6.0	85.7
Florida	8,212	90.5	30.7	59.8	9.5	1,534	12.0	2.8	85.2
East South Central									
Kentucky	1,862	66.2	30.8	35.4	33.8	1,799	7.3	3.8	88.9
Tennessee	2,774	75.2	59.0	16.2	24.8	1,818	8.4	3.7	87.9
Alabama	2,338	75.5	48.5	27.0	24.5	1,556	8.8	5.8	85.4
Mississippi	1,193	49.4	31.9	17.5	50.6	1,328	8.2	4.9	86.9
West South Central									
Arkansas	1,180	47.8	36.7	11.1	52.2	1,107	11.1	10.7	78.2
Louisiana	2,887	76.3	44.4	31.9	23.7	1,319	10.2	5.0	84.8
Oklahoma	2,035	62.3	43.2	19.1	37.7	990	16.2	13.2	70.6
Texas	11,333	80.5	58.3	22.2	19.5	2,896	15.3	7.0	77.7
Mountain									
Montana	416	50.1	37.7	12.4	49.9	370	15.2	8.2	76.6
Idaho	510	36.9	29.2	7.7	63.1	434	13.0	10.7	76.3
Wyoming	295	40.0	33.4	6.6	60.0	175	16.7	10.3	73.0
Colorado	2,330	86.6	44.3	42.3	13.4	560	13.4	11.5	75.1
New Mexico	940	55.9	45.3	10.6	44.1	363	11.9	4.9	83.2
Arizona	2,279	84.0	51.0	33.0	16.0	439	13.4	0.7	85.9
Utah	1,233	85.1	28.7	56.4	14.9	228	34.0	17.6	48.4
Nevada	683	87.1	38.9	48.2	12.9	118	11.2	1.5	87.3
Pacific									
Washington	3,037	86.3	37.4	48.9	13.7	1,095	9.4	4.2	86.4
Oregon	1,788	70.9	33.6	37.3	29.1	845	10.3	5.6	84.1
California	21,608	91.5	37.5	54.0	8.5	2,060	11.9	0.4	87.7
Alaska	259	65.8	65.8	*	34.2	143	21.3	40.4	38.3
Hawaii	835	82.5	51.6	30.9	17.5	130	24.6	16.3	59.1

Note: ... indicates data not applicable. * indicates less than 0.1.

Source: U.S. Bureau of the Census. "Number of Inhabitants: United States Summary." 1980 Census of Population. Washington, DC: U.S. Government Printing Office, 1983, Tables 14 and 15.

3. The Spanish-origin population is a high proportion (20 percent or more) of the total in a few selected cities:

City	Percent
Hialeah City, FL.	74.3
El Paso, TX	62.5
Miami, FL	55.9
San Antonio, TX	53.7
Corpus Christi, TX.	46.6
Santa Ana, CA	44.5
Oxnard, CA.	44.4
Pueblo, CO.	35.5
Albuquerque, NM	33.8
Patterson, NJ	28.7
Los Angeles, CA	27.5
Elizabeth, NJ	26.7
San Bernardino, CA.	25.4
Tucson, AZ.	24.9
Fresno, CA.	23.6
San Jose, CA.	22.3
Stockton, CA.	22.1
Hartford, CT.	20.5
New York, NY.	19.9

4. In the age composition, there is far more variation among cities than among states:

Cities with young age composition	Percent 0-14 years
El Paso, TX	35.0
Gary, IN.	34.9
Sterling Heights, MI.	34.5
Newark, NJ.	34.1
Garland, TX	33.7
Oxnard, CA.	33.2
Patterson, NJ	32.9
Corpus Christi, TX.	32.4
San Antonio, TX	32.2
Flint, MI	31.9
Chesapeake, VA.	31.9
Anchorage, AK	31.5
Pasadena, TX.	31.4
San Jose, CA.	31.0
Virginia Beach, VA.	30.7
Santa Ana, CA	30.6
Detroit, MI	30.3
Shreveport, LA.	30.3

Cities with old age composition	Percent 65+ years
St. Petersburg, FL.	25.8
Hollywood, FL	25.1
Fort Lauderdale, FL	19.1
St. Louis, MO	17.6
Miami, FL	17.0
Albany, NY.	16.5
Worcester, MA	16.3
Glendale, CA.	16.3
Allentown, PA	16.1
Pittsburgh, PA.	16.0
Roanoke, VA	15.6
Waterbury, CT	15.5
San Francisco, CA	15.4
Minneapolis, MN	15.4
Seattle, WA	15.4
Providence, RI.	15.3
Louisville, KY.	15.3
Spokane, WA	15.3
Portland, OR.	15.3
Evansville, IN.	15.2
Buffalo, NY	15.0
St. Paul, MN.	15.0

The young age composition arises from large Spanish-origin population, large student populations, and higher-than-average fertility. The concentration of old age populations is due to migration after retirement, to aging of resident populations, and to extensive outmigration of youth.

Metropolitan and Nonmetropolitan Areas

Urbanologists have long discussed the "metropolitanization" of the American economic and social life. As the number of large cities has increased and as they have grown in size, it is observed that they "dominate" a broad region surrounding themselves.

A fundamental and familiar aspect of metropolitan dominance is the tendency for areas located very near the metropolis to be closely integrated with the metropolis both economically and socially. The effect of the metropolis upon the adjacent area is so direct and so strong that, for many purposes, it is highly important to look separately at this area.

There are many practical, as well as theoretical, reasons for separating the metropolises and their immediate environs from the rest of the nation and for treating them as units in studying the distribution of population and economic activities. Labor force experts, transportation and traffic specialists, metropolitan newspapers, television and FM radio broadcasters, experts in industrial location, city planners, and business people interested in outlying shopping centers are only a few of those interested in metropolitan areas. The area to be included in this delimitation is considerably larger than the closely built-up urban fringe described in the preceding section. It more nearly corresponds to what one would regard as the labor market area or commuting radius of the metropolis. Automobile transportation and rapid transit make it possible for people to live many miles distant from where they work. Many office and factory workers in the central business district now choose to live beyond the densely settled suburbs. Since the early 1940s open-country areas surrounding large metropolises have been the sites of a tremendous building boom—industrial as well as residential and commercial. Many old industrialized cities have lost manufacturing plants to their own suburbs. Factories need a metropolitan location but not necessarily a downtown or inner-city location. As industry has decentralized into suburban areas, many residents of nearby open-country rural areas commute to work there. In many newer metropolitan areas industries locate by choice in the suburbs. Many firms prefer to locate in the periphery, where land is plentiful and cheaper, and often where a

Table 3-13. Urban and Rural Population, by Race: 1980 and 1970

Year and race	Total population	Urban population: Total urban	Inside urbanized areas (UA): Total UA	Central cities	Urban fringe	Other urban outside UA	Rural population
Total population							
1980	226,546	167,051	139,171	67,035	72,135	27,880	59,495
1970	203,212	149,325	118,447	63,922	54,525	30,878	53,887
Change, 1970-1980	23,334	17,726	20,724	3,113	17,610	-2,998	5,608
Percent change, 1970-1980	11.5	11.9	17.5	4.9	32.3	-9.7	10.4
Percent distribution							
1980	100.0	73.7	61.4	29.6	31.8	12.3	26.3
1970	100.0	73.5	58.3	31.5	26.8	15.2	26.5
Change, 1970-1980	...	0.2	3.1	-1.9	5.0	-2.9	-0.2
White population							
1980	188,372	134,322	110,149	46,409	63,740	24,173	54,050
1970	177,749	128,773	100,952	49,547	51,405	27,822	48,976
Change, 1970-1980	10,623	5,549	9,197	-3,138	12,335	-3,649	5,074
Percent change, 1970-1980	6.0	4.3	8.1	-6.3	24.0	13.1	10.4
Percent distribution							
1980	100.0	71.3	58.5	24.6	33.9	12.8	28.7
1970	100.0	72.4	56.8	27.9	28.9	15.7	27.6
Change, 1970-1980	...	-1.1	1.7	-3.3	5.0	-2.9	1.1
Black population							
1980	26,495	22,594	20,106	15,144	4,962	2,488	3,901
1970	22,580	18,367	15,693	13,145	2,548	2,675	4,213
Change, 1970-1980	3,915	4,227	4,413	1,999	2,414	-187	-312
Percent change, 1970-1980	17.3	23.0	28.1	15.2	94.7	-7.0	-7.4
Percent distribution							
1980	100.0	85.3	75.9	57.2	18.7	9.4	14.7
1970	100.0	81.3	69.5	58.2	11.3	11.8	18.7
Change, 1970-1980	...	4.0	6.4	-1.0	7.4	-2.4	-4.0
Percent black							
1980	11.7	13.5	14.4	22.6	6.9	8.9	6.6
1970	11.1	12.3	13.2	20.6	4.7	8.7	7.8
Change, 1970-1980	0.6	1.2	1.2	2.0	2.2	0.2	-1.2

Source: U.S. Bureau of the Census. "General Population Characteristics: United States Summary." 1980 Census of Population. Washington, DC: U.S. Government Printing Office, 1983, Table 43. Also U.S. Bureau of the Census. "General Population Characteristics: United States Summary." 1970 Census of Population. Washington, DC: U.S. Government Printing Office, 1973, Table 52.

superior quality of labor force resides and is available at salaries lower than in the central city. Quite often the suburban governments provide tax and other incentives to attract companies to locate in their environs.

In the areas just beyond the urban fringe but adjacent to it is a ring of rapid population growth that can be several miles in breadth. A high proportion of the population in that outer ring is rural. Scattered dwellings are built in long strings and on large lots along main highways leading into the metropolis. Even the rural farm population in this outer zone of direct metropolitan influence tends to have different characteristics from those of the rural farm populations in areas outside the orbit of direct metropolitan dominance. Farms in this zone tend to produce for sale in the nearby metropolitan market. Many farms are operated as part-time ventures, with one or more breadwinners in the family employed in the metropolis or a suburban center.

The Standard Metropolitan Statistical Area

In order to acknowledge the metropolitanized aspect of the economy and to provide separate statistics for areas under direct metropolitan dominance, the Bureau of the Census recognized, beginning in 1950, a new entity then termed "standard metropolitan areas" and subsequently renamed "standard metropolitan statistical areas" (SMSAs). These usually are one or more whole counties containing the central city (metropolis) and extending into the hinterland sufficiently far to encompass the immediate "trade area," "commuting area,"

Table 3-14. Rank and Population of Cities of 100,000 or More in 1980: 1790 to 1980

1980 rank	City	1980	1970	1960	1950	1940	1930	1920	1910	1900	1890
1	New York city, NY.	7,071,639	7,895,563	7,781,984	7,891,957	7,454,995	6,930,446	5,620,048	4,766,883	3,437,202	2,507,414
2	Chicago city, IL	3,005,072	3,369,357	3,550,404	3,620,962	3,396,808	3,376,438	2,701,705	2,185,283	1,698,575	1,099,850
3	Los Angeles city, LA	2,966,850	2,811,801	2,479,015	1,970,358	1,504,277	1,238,048	576,673	319,198	102,479	50,395
4	Philadelphia city, PA. . . .	1,688,210	1,949,996	2,002,512	2,071,605	1,931,334	1,950,961	1,823,779	1,549,008	1,293,697	1,046,964
5	Houston city, TX	1,595,138	1,233,535	938,219	596,163	384,514	292,352	138,276	78,800	44,633	27,557
6	Detroit city, MI	1,203,339	1,514,063	1,670,144	1,849,568	1,623,452	1,568,662	993,678	465,766	285,704	205,876
7	Dallas city, TX.	904,078	844,401	679,684	434,462	294,734	260,475	158,976	92,104	42,638	38,067
8	San Diego city, CA	875,538	697,471	573,224	334,387	203,341	147,995	74,361	39,578	17,700	16,159
9	Phoenix city, AZ	789,704	584,303	439,170	106,818	65,414	48,118	29,053	11,134	5,544	3,152
10	Baltimore city, MD	786,775	905,787	939,024	949,708	859,100	804,874	733,826	558,485	508,957	434,439
11	San Antonio city, TX	785,880	654,153	587,718	408,442	253,854	231,542	161,379	96,614	53,321	37,673
12	Indianapolis city, IN. . . .	700,807	736,856	476,258	427,173	386,972	364,161	314,194	233,650	169,164	105,436
13	San Francisco city, CA . . .	678,974	715,674	740,316	775,357	634,536	634,394	506,676	416,912	342,782	298,997
14	Memphis city, TN	646,356	623,988	497,524	396,000	292,942	253,143	162,351	131,105	102,320	64,495
15	Washington city, DC.	638,333	756,668	763,956	802,178	663,091	486,869	437,571	331,069	278,718	188,932
16	Milwaukee city, WI	636,212	717,372	741,324	637,392	587,472	578,249	457,147	373,857	285,315	204,468
17	San Jose city, CA.	629,442	459,913	204,196	95,280	68,457	57,651	39,642	28,946	21,500	18,060
18	Cleveland city, OH	573,822	750,879	876,050	914,808	878,336	900,429	796,841	560,663	381,768	261,353
19	Columbus city, OH.	564,871	540,025	471,316	375,901	306,087	290,564	237,031	181,511	125,560	88,150
20	Boston city, MA.	562,994	641,071	697,197	801,444	770,816	781,188	748,060	670,585	560,892	448,477
21	New Orleans city, LA	557,515	593,471	627,525	570,445	494,537	458,762	387,219	339,075	287,104	242,039
22	Jacksonville city, FL. . . .	540,920	504,265	201,030	204,517	173,065	129,549	91,558	57,699	28,429	17,201
23	Seattle city, WA	493,846	530,831	557,087	467,591	368,302	365,583	315,312	237,194	80,671	42,837
24	Denver city, CO.	492,365	514,678	493,887	415,786	322,412	287,861	256,491	213,381	133,859	106,713
25	Nashville-Davidson, TN . . .	455,651	426,029	154,563	174,307	167,402	153,866	118,342	110,364	80,865	76,168
26	St. Louis city, MO	453,085	622,236	750,026	856,796	816,048	821,960	772,897	687,029	575,238	451,770
27	Kansas City city, MO	448,159	507,330	475,539	456,622	399,178	399,746	324,410	248,381	163,752	132,716
28	El Paso city, TX	425,259	322,261	276,687	130,485	96,810	102,421	77,560	39,279	15,906	10,338
29	Atlanta city, GA	425,022	495,039	487,455	331,314	302,288	270,366	200,616	154,839	89,872	65,533
30	Pittsburgh city, PA.	423,938	520,089	604,332	676,806	671,659	669,817	588,343	533,905	321,616	238,617
31	Oklahoma City city, OK . . .	403,213	368,164	324,253	243,504	204,424	185,389	91,295	64,205	10,037	4,151
32	Cincinnati city, OH.	385,457	453,514	502,550	503,998	455,610	451,160	401,247	363,591	325,902	296,908
33	Fort Worth city, TX.	385,164	393,455	356,268	278,778	177,662	163,447	106,482	73,312	26,688	23,076
34	Minneapolis city, MN	370,951	434,400	482,872	521,718	492,370	464,356	380,582	301,408	202,718	164,738
35	Portland city, OR.	366,383	379.967	372,676	373,628	305,394	301,815	258,288	207,214	90,426	46,385
36	Honolulu (CDP), HI	365,048	324,871	294,194	248,034	179,326	137,582	83,327	52,183	39,306	22,907
37	Long Beach city, CA.	361,334	358,879	344,168	250,767	164,271	142,032	55,593	17,809	2,252	564
38	Tulsa city, OK	360,919	330,350	261,685	182,740	142,157	141,258	72,075	18,182	1,390	...
39	Buffalo city, NY	357,870	462,768	532,759	580,132	575,901	573,076	506,775	423,715	352,387	255,664
40	Toledo city, OH.	354,635	383,062	318,003	303,616	282,349	290,718	243,164	168,497	131,822	81,434
41	Miami city, FL	346,865	334,859	291,688	249,276	172,172	110,637	29,571	5,471	1,681	...
42	Austin city, TX.	345,496	253,539	186,545	132,459	87,930	53,120	34,876	29,860	22,258	14,575
43	Oakland city, CA	339,337	361,561	367,548	384,575	302,163	284,063	216,261	150,174	66,900	48,682
44	Albuquerque city, NM	331,767	244,501	201,189	96,815	35,449	26,570	15,157	11,020	6,238	3,785
45	Tucson city, AZ.	330,537	262,933	212,892	45,454	35,752	32,506	20,292	13,193	7,531	5,150
46	Newark city, NJ.	329,248	381,930	405,220	438,776	429,760	442,337	414,524	347,469	246,070	181,830
47	Charlotte city, NC	314,447	241,420	201,564	134,042	100,899	82,675	46,338	34,014	18,091	11,557
48	Omaha city, NB	314,255	346,929	301,598	251,117	223,844	214,006	191,601	124,096	102,555	140,452
49	Louisville city, KY.	298,451	361,706	390,639	369,129	319,077	307,745	234,891	223,928	204,731	161,129
50	Birmingham city, AL.	284,413	300,910	340,887	326,037	267,583	259,678	178,806	132,685	38,415	26,178
51	Wichita city, KS	279,272	276,554	254,698	168,279	114,966	111,110	72,217	52,450	24,671	23,853
52	Sacramento city, CA.	275,741	257,105	191,667	137,572	105,958	93,750	65,908	44,696	29,282	26,386
53	Tampa city, FL	271,523	277,714	274,970	124,681	108,391	101,161	51,608	37,782	15,839	5,532
54	St. Paul city, MN.	270,230	309,866	313,411	311,349	287,736	271,606	234,698	214,744	163,065	133,156
55	Norfolk city, VA	266,979	307,951	304,869	213,513	144,332	129,710	115,777	67,452	46,624	34,871
56	Virginia Beach city, VA. . .	262,199	172,106	8,091	5,390	2,600	1,719	846	320	...	...
57	Rochester city, NY	241,741	295,011	318,611	332,488	324,975	328,132	295,750	218,149	162,608	133,896
58	St. Petersburg city, FL. . .	238,647	216,159	181,298	96,738	60,812	40,425	14,237	4,127	1,575	273
59	Akron city, OH	237,177	275,425	290,351	274,605	244,605	255,040	208,435	69,067	42,728	27,601
60	Corpus Christi city, TX. . .	231,999	204,525	167,690	108,287	57,301	27,741	10,522	8,222	4,703	4,387
61	Jersey City city, NJ	223,532	260,350	276,101	299,017	301,173	316,715	298,103	267,779	206,433	163,003
62	Baton Rouge city, LA	219,419	165,921	152,419	125,629	34,719	30,729	21,782	14,897	11,269	10,478
63	Anaheim city, CA	219,311	166,408	104,184	14,556	11,031	10,995	5,526	2,628	1,456	1,273
64	Richmond city, VA.	219,214	249,332	219,958	230,310	193,042	182,929	171,667	127,628	85,050	81,388
65	Fresno city, CA.	218,202	165,655	133,929	91,669	60,685	52,513	45,086	24,892	12,470	10,818
66	Colorado Springs city, CO. .	215,150	135,517	70,194	45,472	36,789	33,237	30,105	29,078	21,085	11,140
67	Shreveport city, LA.	205,820	182,064	164,372	127,206	98,167	76,655	43,874	28,015	16,013	11,979
68	Lexington-Fayette, KY. . . .	204,165	108,137	62,810	55,534	49,304	45,736	41,534	35,099	26,369	21,567
69	Santa Ana city, CA	203,713	155,710	100,350	45,533	31,921	30,322	15,485	8,429	4,933	3,628
70	Dayton city, OH.	203,371	243,023	262,332	243,872	210,718	200,982	152,559	116,577	85,333	61,220
71	Jackson city, MS	202,895	153,968	144,422	98,271	62,107	48,282	22,817	21,262	7,816	5,920
72	Mobile city, AL.	200,452	190,026	194,856	129,009	78,720	68,202	60,777	51,521	38,469	31,076
73	Yonkers city, NY	195,351	204,297	190,634	152,798	142,598	134,646	100,176	79,803	47,931	32,033
74	Des Moines city, IA.	191,003	201,404	208,982	177,965	159,819	142,559	126,468	86,368	62,139	50,093
75	Grand Rapids city, MI. . . .	181,843	197,649	177,313	176,515	164,292	168,592	137,634	112,571	87,565	60,278
76	Montgomery city, AL.	177,857	133,386	134,393	106,525	78,084	66,079	43,464	38,136	30,346	21,883
77	Knoxville city, TN	175,030	174,587	111,827	124,769	111,580	105,802	77,818	36,346	32,637	22,535
78	Anchorage city, AK	174,431	48,081	44,237	11,254	3,495	2,277	1,856	...	...	...
79	Lubbock city, TX	173,979	149,101	128,691	71,747	31,853	20,520	4,051	1,938	...	...
80	Fort Wayne city, IN.	172,196	178,269	161,776	133,607	118,410	114,946	86,549	63,933	45,115	35,393
81	Lincoln city, NB	171,932	149,518	128,521	98,884	81,984	75,933	54,948	43,973	40,169	55,154
82	Spokane city, WA	171,300	170,516	181,608	161,721	122,001	115,514	104,437	104.402	36,848	19,922
83	Riverside city, CA	170,876	140,089	84,332	46,764	34,696	29,696	19,341	15,212	7,973	4,683
84	Madison city, WI	170,616	171,809	126,706	96,056	67,447	57,899	38,378	25,531	19,164	13,426
85	Huntington Beach city, CA. .	170,505	115,960	11,492	5,237	3,738	3,690	...	...	...	...
86	Syracuse city, NY.	170,105	197,297	216,038	220,583	205,967	209,326	171,717	137,249	108,374	88,143
87	Chattanooga city, TN	169,565	119,923	130,009	131,041	128,163	119,798	57,895	44,604	30,154	29,100
88	Columbus city, GA.	169,441	155,028	116,779	79,611	53,280	43,131	31,125	20,554	17,614	17,303

Table 3-14. Rank and Population of Cities of 100,000 or More in 1980: 1790 to 1980—continued

1980 rank	City	1880	1870	1860	1850	1840	1830	1820	1810	1800	1790
1	New York city, NY.	1,911,698	1,478,103	1,174,779	696,115	391,114	242,278	152,056	119,734	79,216	49,401
2	Chicago city, IL	503,185	298,977	112,172	29,963	4,470	...	...	...	...	...
3	Los Angeles city, CA	11,183	5,723	4,385	1,610	...	...	...	...	...	...
4	Philadelphia city, PA. . . .	847,170	647,022	565,529	121,376	93,665	80,462	63,802	53,722	41,220	28,522
5	Houston city, TX	16,513	9,382	4,845	2,396	...	...	...	...	...	...
6	Detroit city, MI	116,340	79,577	45,619	21,019	9,102	2,222	1,422	...	...	...
7	Dallas city, TX.	10,358	...	...	...	...	...	...	...	...	...
8	San Diego city, CA	2,637	2,300	731	...	...	...	...	...	...	...
9	Phoenix city, AZ	...	...	...	...	...	...	...	...	...	...
10	Baltimore city, MD	332,313	267,354	212,418	169,054	102,313	80,620	62,738	46,555	26,514	13,503
11	San Antonio city, TX	20,550	12,256	8,235	3,488	...	...	...	...	...	...
12	Indianapolis city, IN. . . .	75,056	48,244	18,611	8,091	2,692	...	...	...	...	...
13	San Francisco city, CA . . .	233,959	149,473	56,802	34,776	...	...	...	...	...	...
14	Memphis city, TN	33,592	40,226	22,623	8,841	...	...	...	...	...	...
15	Washington city, DC.	147,293	109,199	61,122	40,001	23,364	18,826	13,247	8,208	3,210	...
16	Milwaukee city, WI	115,587	71,440	45,246	20,061	1,712	...	...	...	...	...
17	San Jose city, CA.	12,567	9,089	...	...	...	...	...	...	...	...
18	Cleveland city, OH	160,146	92,829	43,417	17,034	6,071	1,076	606	...	...	...
19	Columbus city, OH.	51,647	31,274	18,554	17,882	6,048	2,435	...	...	...	...
20	Boston city, MA.	362,839	250,526	177,840	136,881	93,383	61,392	43,298	33,787	24,937	18,320
21	New Orleans city, LA	216,090	191,418	168,675	116,375	102,193	46,082	27,176	17,242	...	...
22	Jacksonville city, FL. . . .	7,650	6,912	2,118	1,045	...	...	...	...	...	...
23	Seattle city, WA	3,533	1,107	...	...	...	...	...	...	...	...
24	Denver city, CO.	35,629	4,759	4,749	...	...	...	...	...	...	...
25	Nashville-Davidson, TN . . .	43,350	25,865	16,988	10,165	6,929	5,566	...	...	345	...
26	St. Louis city, MO	350,518	310,864	160,773	77,860	16,469	4,977	...	...	...	...
27	Kansas City city, MO	55,785	32,260	4,418	...	...	...	...	...	...	...
28	El Paso city, TX	736	...	...	...	...	...	...	...	...	...
29	Atlanta city, GA	37,409	21,789	9,554	2,572	...	...	...	...	...	...
30	Pittsburgh city, PA.	156,389	86,076	49,221	46,601	21,115	12,568	7,248	4,768	1,565	...
31	Oklahoma city, OK.	...	...	...	...	...	...	...	...	...	...
32	Cincinnati city, OH.	255,139	216,239	161,044	115,435	46,338	24,831	9,642	2,540	...	...
33	Fort Worth city, TX.	6,663	...	...	...	...	...	...	...	...	...
34	Minneapolis city, MN	46,887	13,066	2,564	...	...	...	...	...	...	...
35	Portland city, OR.	17,577	8,293	2,874	...	...	...	...	...	...	...
36	Honolulu (CDP), HI	...	...	...	...	...	...	...	...	...	...
37	Long Beach city, CA.	...	...	...	...	...	...	...	...	...	...
38	Tulsa city, OK	...	...	...	...	...	...	...	...	...	...
39	Buffalo city, NY	155,134	117,714	81,129	42,261	18,213	8,668	2,095	1,508	...	...
40	Toledo city, OH.	50,137	31,584	13,768	3,829	1,222	...	...	...	...	...
41	Miami city, FL	...	...	...	...	...	...	...	...	...	...
42	Austin city, TX.	11,013	4,428	3,494	629	...	...	...	...	...	...
43	Oakland city, CA	34,555	10,500	1,543	...	...	...	...	...	...	...
44	Albuquerque city, NM	...	...	...	...	...	...	...	...	...	...
45	Tucson city, AZ.	7,007	3,224	...	...	...	...	...	...	...	...
46	Newark city, NJ.	136,508	105,059	71,941	38,894	17,290	10,953	...	...	...	...
47	Charlotte city, NC	7,094	4,473	2,265	1,065	...	...	...	...	...	...
48	Omaha city, NB	30,518	16,083	1,883	...	...	...	...	...	...	...
49	Louisville city, KY.	123,758	100,753	68,033	43,194	21,210	10,341	4,012	1,357	359	200
50	Birmingham city, AL.	3,086	...	...	...	...	...	...	...	...	...
51	Wichita city, KS	4,911	...	...	...	...	...	...	...	...	...
52	Sacramento city, CA.	21,420	16,283	13,785	6,820	...	...	...	...	...	...
53	Tampa city, FL	720	796	...	...	...	...	...	...	...	...
54	St. Paul city, MN.	41,473	20,030	10,401	1,112	...	...	...	...	...	...
55	Norfolk city, VA	21,966	19,229	14,620	14,326	10,920	9,814	8,478	9,193	6,926	2,959
56	Virginia Beach city, VA. . .	...	...	...	...	...	...	...	...	...	...
57	Rochester city, NY	89,366	62,386	48,204	36,403	20,191	9,207	...	...	...	...
58	St. Petersburg city, PA. . .	...	...	...	...	...	...	...	...	...	...
59	Akron city, OH	16,512	10,006	3,477	3,266	...	...	...	...	...	...
60	Corpus Christi city, TX. . .	3,257	2,140	175	...	...	...	...	...	...	...
61	Jersey City city, NJ	120,722	82,546	29,226	6,856	3,072	...	...	...	...	...
62	Baton Rouge city, LA	7,197	6,498	5,428	3,905	2,269	...	...	...	...	...
63	Anaheim city, CA	833	881	...	...	...	...	...	...	...	...
64	Richmond city, VA.	63,600	51,038	37,910	27,570	20,153	16,060	12,067	9,735	5,737	3,761
65	Fresno city, CA.	1,112	...	...	...	...	...	...	...	...	...
66	Colorado Springs city, CO. .	4,226	...	...	...	...	...	...	...	...	...
67	Shreveport city, LA.	8,009	4,607	2,190	1,728	...	...	...	...	...	...
68	Lexington-Fayette, KY. . . .	16,656	14,801	9,321	8,159	6,997	6,026	5,279	4,326	1,795	834
69	Santa Ana city, CA	...	...	...	...	...	...	...	...	...	...
70	Dayton city, OH.	38,678	30,473	20,081	10,977	6,067	2,950	1,000	383	...	...
71	Jackson City, MS	5,204	4,234	3,191	1,881	...	...	...	...	...	...
72	Mobile city, AL.	29,132	32,034	29,258	20,515	12,672	3,194	...	...	...	...
73	Yonkers city, NY	18,892	12,733	8,218	...	...	...	...	...	...	...
74	Des Moines city, IA.	22,408	12,035	3,965	...	...	...	...	...	...	...
75	Grand Rapids city, MI. . . .	32,016	16,507	8,085	2,686	...	...	...	...	...	...
76	Montgomery city, AL.	16,713	10,588	8,843	8,728	2,179	...	...	...	...	...
77	Knoxville city, TN	9,693	8,682	...	2,076	...	...	...	...	...	...
78	Anchorage city, AK	...	...	...	...	...	...	...	...	...	...
79	Lubbock city, TX	...	...	...	...	...	...	...	...	...	...
80	Fort Wayne city, IN.	26,880	17,718	9,121	4,282						
81	Lincoln city, NB	13,003	...	...	...	...	...	...	...	...	...
82	Spokane city, WA	...	...	...	...	...	...	...	...	...	...
83	Riverside city, CA	...	...	...	...	...	...	...	...	...	...
84	Madison city, WI	10,324	9,176	6,611	1,525	...	...	...	...	...	...
85	Huntington Beach city, CA. .	...	...	...	...	...	...	...	...	...	...
86	Syracuse city, NY.	51,792	43,051	28,119	22,271	...	...	...	...	...	...
87	Chattanooga city, TN	12,892	6,093	...	...	...	...	...	...	...	...
88	Columbus city, GA.	10,123	7,401	9,621	5,942	3,114	...	...	...	...	...

Table 3-14. Rank and Population of Cities of 100,000 or More in 1980: 1790 to 1980—continued

1980 rank	City	1980	1970	1960	1950	1940	1930	1920	1910	1900	1890
89	Las Vegas city, NV.	164,674	125,787	64,405	24,624	8,422	5,165	2,304	...	...	...
90	Salt Lake City city, UT . . .	163,033	175,885	189,454	182,121	149,934	140,267	118,110	92,777	53,531	44,843
91	Worcester city, MA.	161,799	176,572	186,587	203,486	193,694	195,311	179,754	149,986	118,421	84,655
92	Warren city, MI	161,134	179,260	89,246	727	582	515	326	297	350	...
93	Kansas city, KS	161,087	168,213	121,901	129,553	121,458	121,857	101,177	82,331	51,418	38,316
94	Arlington city, TX.	160,113	90,229	44,775	7,692	4,240	3,661	3,031	1,794	1,079	664
95	Flint city, MI.	159,611	193,317	196,940	163,143	151,543	156,492	91,599	38,550	13,103	9,803
96	Aurora city, CO	158,588	74,974	48,548	11,421	3,437	2,295	983	679	202	...
97	Tacoma city, WA	158,501	154,407	147,979	143,673	109,408	106,817	96,965	83,743	37,714	36,006
98	Little Rock city, AK.	158,461	132,483	107,813	102,213	88,039	81,679	65,142	45,941	38,307	25,874
99	Providence city, RI	156,804	179,116	207,498	248,674	253,504	252,981	237,595	224,326	175,597	132,146
100	Greensboro city, NC	155,642	144,076	119,574	74,389	59,319	53,569	19,861	15,895	10,035	3,317
101	Fort Lauderdale city, FL. . .	153,279	139,590	83,648	36,328	17,996	8,666	2,065	...	...	...
102	Mesa city, AZ	152,453	63,049	33,772	16,790	7,224	3,711	3,036	1,692	722	...
103	Springfield city, MA.	152,319	163,905	174,463	162,399	149,554	149,900	129,614	88,926	62,059	44,179
104	Gary city, IN	151,953	175,415	178,320	133,911	111,719	100,426	55,378	16,802	...	...
105	Raleigh city, NC.	150,255	122,830	93,931	65,679	46,897	37,379	24,418	19,218	13,643	12,678
106	Stockton city, CA	149,779	109,963	86,321	70,853	54,714	47,963	40,296	23,253	17,506	14,424
107	Amarillo city, TX	149,230	127,010	137,969	74,246	51,686	43,132	15,494	9,957	1,442	482
108	Hialeah city, FL.	145,254	102,452	66,972	19,676	3,958	2,600	...	...	...	...
109	Newport News city, VA	144,903	138,177	113,662	42,358	37,067	34,417	35,596	20,205	19,635	4,449
110	Bridgeport city, CT	142,546	156,542	156,748	158,709	147,121	146,716	143,555	102,054	70,996	48,866
111	Huntsville city, AL	142,513	139,282	72,365	16,437	13,050	11,554	8,018	7,611	8,068	7,995
112	Savannah city, GA	141,390	118,349	149,245	119,638	95,996	85,024	83,252	65,064	54,244	43,189
113	Rockford city, IL	139,712	147,370	126,706	92,927	84,637	85,864	65,651	45,401	31,051	23,584
114	Glendale city, CA	139,060	132,664	119,442	95,702	82,582	62,736	13,536	2,746	...	...
115	Garland city, TX.	138,857	81,437	38,501	10,571	2,233	1,584	1,421	804	819	478
116	Paterson city, NJ	137,970	144,824	143,663	139,336	139,656	138,513	135,875	125,600	105,171	78,347
117	Hartford city, CT	136,392	158,017	162,178	177,397	166,267	164,072	138,036	98,915	79,850	53,230
118	Springfield city, MO.	133,116	120,096	95,865	66,731	61,238	57,527	39,631	35,201	23,267	21,850
119	Fremont city, CA.	131,945	100,869	43,790	...	...	...	...	...	...	...
120	Winston-Salem city, NC. . . .	131,885	133,683	111,135	87,811	79,815	75,274	48,395	22,700	13,650	10,729
121	Evansville city, IN	130,496	138,764	141,543	128,636	97,062	102,249	85,264	69,647	59,007	50,756
122	Lansing city, MI.	130,414	131,403	107,807	92,129	78,753	78,397	57,327	31,229	16,485	13,102
123	Torrence city, CA	129,881	134,968	100,991	22,241	9,950	7,271	...	...	...	...
124	Orlando city, FL.	128,291	99,006	88,135	52,367	36,736	27,330	9,282	3,894	2,481	2,856
125	New Haven city, CT.	126,109	137,707	152,048	164,443	160,605	162,655	162,537	133,605	108,027	86,045
126	Peoria city, IL	124,160	126,963	103,162	111,856	105,087	104,969	76,121	66,950	56,100	41,024
127	Carden Grove city, CA	123,307	121,155	84,238	...	...	...	...	...	...	...
128	Hampton city, VA.	122,617	120,779	89,258	5,966	5,898	6,382	6,138	5,505	2,764	2,513
129	Hollywood city, CA.	121,323	106,873	35,237	14,351	6,239	2,869	...	...	...	...
130	Erie city, PA	119,123	129,265	138,440	130,803	116,955	115,967	93,372	66,525	52,733	40,634
131	Pasadena city, CA	118,550	112,951	116,407	104,577	81,864	76,086	45,354	30,291	9,117	4,882
132	Beaumont city, TX	118,102	117,548	119,175	94,014	59,061	57,732	40,422	20,640	9,427	3,296
133	San Bernardino city, CA . . .	117,490	106,869	91,922	63,058	43,646	37,481	18,721	12,779	6,150	4,012
134	Macon city, GA.	116,896	122,423	69,764	70,252	57,865	53,829	52,995	40,665	23,272	22,746
135	Youngstown city, OH	115,436	140,909	166,689	168,330	167,720	170,002	132,358	79,066	44,885	33,220
136	Topeka city, KS	115,266	125,011	119,484	78,791	67,833	64,120	50,022	43,684	33,608	31,007
137	Chesapeake city, VA	114,486	89,580	...	...	...	...	...	...	...	...
138	Lakewood city, CO	112,860	92,743	...	...	...	...	...	...	...	...
139	Pasadena city, TX	112,560	89,957	58,737	22,483	3,436	1,647	...	...	...	...
140	Independence city, MO	111,806	111,630	62,328	36,963	16,066	15,296	11,686	9,859	6,974	6,380
141	Cedar Rapids city, IA	110,243	110,642	92,035	72,296	62,120	56,097	45,566	32,811	25,656	18,020
142	Irving city, IA	109,943	97,260	45,985	2,621	1,089	731	357	...	...	...
143	South Bend city, IN	109,727	125,580	132,445	115,911	101,268	104,193	70,983	53,684	35,999	21,819
144	Sterling Heights city, MI . .	108,999	61,365	...	...	...	...	...	...	...	...
145	Oxnard city, CA	108,195	71,225	40,265	21,567	8,519	6,285	4,417	2,555	...	...
146	Ann Arbor city, MI.	107,966	100,035	67,340	48,251	29,815	26,944	19,516	14,817	14,509	9,431
147	Tempe city, AZ.	106,743	63,550	24,897	7,684	2,906	2,495	1,963	1,473	885	...
148	Sunnyvale city, CA.	106,618	95,976	52,898	9,829	4,373	3,094	...	...	...	...
149	Modesto city, CA.	106,602	61,712	36,585	17,389	16,379	13,842	9,241	4,034	2,024	2,402
150	Elizabeth city, NJ.	106,201	112,654	107,698	112,817	109,912	114,589	95,783	73,409	52,130	37,764
151	Eugene city, OR	105,624	79,028	50,977	35,879	20,838	18,901	10,593	9,009	3,236	...
152	Bakersfield city, CA.	105,611	69,515	56,848	34,784	29,252	26,015	18,638	12,727	4,836	2,626
153	Livonia city, MI.	104,814	110,109	66,702	17,534	...	...	...	...	...	...
154	Portsmouth city, VA	104,577	110,963	114,773	80,039	50,745	45,704	54,387	33,190	17,427	13,268
155	Allentown city, PA.	103,758	109,871	108,347	106,756	96,904	92,563	73,502	51,913	35,416	25,228
156	Berkeley city, CA	103,328	114,091	111,268	113,805	85,547	82,109	56,036	40,434	13,214	5,101
157	Waterbury city, CT.	103,266	108,033	107,130	104,477	99,314	99,902	91,715	73,141	45,859	28,646
158	Davenport city, IA.	103,264	98,469	88,981	74,549	66,039	60,751	56,727	43,028	35,254	26,872
159	Concord city, CA.	103,255	85,164	36,000	6,953	1,373	1,125	912	703	...	...
160	Alexandria city, VA	103,217	110,927	91,023	61,787	33,523	24,149	18,060	15,329	14,528	14,339
161	Stamford, CT.	102,453	108,798	92,713	74,293	47,938	46,346	35,096	25,138	15,997	10,396
162	Boise City city, ID	102,451	74,990	34,481	34,393	26,130	21,544	21,393	17,358	...	...
163	Fullerton city, CA.	102,034	85,937	56,180	13,958	10,442	10,860	4,415	1,725	...	...
164	Albany city, NY	101,727	115,781	129,726	134,995	130,577	127,412	113,344	100,253	94,151	94,923
165	Puehlo city, CO	101,686	97,774	91,181	63,685	52,162	50,096	43,050	41,747	28,157	24,558
166	Waco city, TX	101,261	95,326	97,808	84,706	55,982	52,848	38,500	26,425	20,686	14,445
167	Columbia city, SC	101,208	113,542	97,433	86,914	62,396	51,581	37,524	26,319	21,108	15,353
168	Durham city, NC	100,831	95,438	78,302	71,311	60,195	52,037	21,719	18,241	6,679	5,485
169	Reno city, NV	100,756	72,863	51,470	32,497	21,317	18,529	12,016	10,867	4,500	3,563
170	Roanoke city, VA.	100,220	92,115	97,110	91,921	69,287	69,206	50,842	34,874	21,495	16,159

Table 3-14. Rank and Population of Cities of 100,000 or More in 1980: 1790 to 1980—continued

1980 rank	City	1880	1870	1860	1850	1840	1830	1820	1810	1800	1790
89	Las Vegas city, NV.	...	...	...	...	...	...	...	...	...	...
90	Salt Lake city, UT.	20,768	12,854	8,236	...	...	...	...	...	...	...
91	Worcester city, MA.	58,291	41,105	24,960	17,049	7,497	4,173	2,962	2,577	2,411	2,095
92	Warren city, MI	...	...	...	...	...	...	...	...	...	...
93	Kansas City city, KS.	3,200	...	...	...	...	...	...	...	...	...
94	Arlington city, TX.	...	...	...	...	...	...	...	...	...	...
95	Flint city, MI.	8,409	5,386	2,950	...	...	...	...	...	...	...
96	Aurora city, CO	...	...	...	...	...	...	...	...	...	...
97	Tacoma city, WA	...	...	...	...	...	...	...	...	...	...
98	Little Rock city, AK.	13,138	12,380	3,727	2,157	...	...	...	...	...	...
99	Providence city, RI	104,857	68,904	50,666	41,513	23,171	15,833	11,767	10,071	7,614	6,380
100	Greensboro city, NC	2,105	497	...	...	...	...	...	...	...	...
101	Fort Lauderdale city, FL.	...	...	...	...	...	...	...	...	...	...
102	Mesa city, AZ	...	...	...	...	...	...	...	...	...	...
103	Springfield city, MA.	33,340	26,703	15,199	11,766	10,985	6,784	3,914	2,767	2,312	1,574
104	Gary city, IN	...	...	...	...	...	...	...	...	...	...
105	Raleigh city, NC.	9,265	7,790	4,780	4,518	2,244	1,700	2,674	...	669	...
106	Stockton city, CA	10,282	10,066	3,679	...	...	...	...	...	...	...
107	Amarillo city, TX	...	...	...	...	...	...	...	...	...	...
108	Hialeah city, FL.	...	...	...	...	...	...	...	...	...	...
109	Newport News city, VA	...	...	...	...	...	...	...	...	...	...
110	Bridgeport city, CT	27,643	18,969	12,106	6,080	3,294	...	...	...	...	...
111	Huntsville city, AL	4,977	4,907	3,634	2,863	...	...	...	...	...	...
112	Savannah city, GA	30,709	28,235	22,292	15,312	11,214	7,303	7,523	5,215	5,146	...
113	Rockford city, IL	13,129	11,049	6,979	...	...	...	...	...	...	...
114	Glendale city, CA	...	...	...	...	...	...	...	...	...	...
115	Garland city, TX.	...	...	...	...	...	...	...	...	...	...
116	Paterson city, NJ	51,031	33,579	19,586	11,334	7,596	...	...	...	...	...
117	Hartford city, CT	42,015	37,180	26,917	13,555	9,468	7,074	4,726	3,955	3,523	2,683
118	Springfield city, MO.	6,522	5,555	...	415	...	...	...	...	...	...
119	Fremont city, CA.	...	...	...	...	...	...	...	...	...	...
120	Winston-Salem city, NC.	4,194	433	...	...	...	...	...	...	...	...
121	Evansville city, IN	29,280	21,830	11,484	3,235	...	...	...	...	...	...
122	Lansing city, MI.	8,319	5,241	3,074	...	...	...	...	...	...	...
123	Torrance city, CA	...	...	...	...	...	...	...	...	...	...
124	Orlando city, FL.	...	...	...	...	...	...	...	...	...	...
125	New Haven city, CT.	62,882	50,840	39,267	20,345	12,960	10,180	7,147	5,772	4,049	4,487
126	Peoria city, IL	29,259	22,849	14,045	5,095	1,467	...	...	...	...	...
127	Garden Grove city, CA	...	...	...	...	...	...	...	...	...	...
128	Hampton city, VA.	...	...	...	...	...	...	...	...	...	...
129	Hollywood city, FL.	...	...	...	...	...	...	...	...	...	...
130	Erie city, PA	27,737	19,646	9,419	5,858	3,412	1,465	635	394	81	...
131	Pasadena city, CA	...	...	...	...	...	...	...	...	...	...
132	Beaumont city, TX	...	...	...	...	...	...	...	...	...	...
133	San Bernardino city, CA	1,673	...	...	...	...	...	...	...	...	...
134	Macon city, GA.	12,749	10,810	8,247	5,720	3,927	...	...	...	...	...
135	Youngstown city, OH	15,435	8,075	2,759	...	...	...	...	...	...	...
136	Topeka city, KS	15,452	5,790	759	...	...	...	...	...	...	...
137	Chesapeake city, VA	...	...	...	...	...	...	...	...	...	...
138	Lakewood city, CO	...	...	...	...	...	...	...	...	...	...
139	Pasadena city, TX	...	...	...	...	...	...	...	...	...	...
140	Independence city, MO	3,146	3,184	3,164	...	...	...	...	...	...	...
141	Cedar Rapids city, IA	10,104	5,940	1,830	...	...	...	...	...	...	...
142	Irving city, TX	...	...	...	...	...	...	...	...	...	...
143	South Bend city, IN	13,280	7,206	3,832	1,652	...	...	...	...	...	...
144	Sterling Heights city, MI	...	...	...	...	...	...	...	...	...	...
145	Oxnord city, CA	...	...	...	...	...	...	...	...	...	...
146	Ann Arbor city, MI.	8,061	7,363	5,097	...	...	...	...	...	...	...
147	Tempe city, AZ.	...	...	...	...	...	...	...	...	...	...
148	Sunnyvale city, CA.	...	...	...	...	...	...	...	...	...	...
149	Modesto city, CA.	...	...	...	...	...	...	...	...	...	...
150	Elizabeth city, NJ.	28,229	20,832	11,567	5,583	4,184	3,455	3,515	2,977	...	...
151	Eugene city, OR	1,117	861	...	...	...	...	...	...	...	...
152	Bakersfield city, CA.	...	...	...	...	...	...	...	...	...	...
153	Livonia city, MI.	...	...	...	...	...	...	...	...	...	...
154	Portsmouth city, VA	11,390	10,590	9,496	8,626	6,477	...	...	...	...	...
155	Allentown city, PA.	18,063	13,884	8,025	3,779	2,493	1,544	...	...	...	...
156	Berkeley city, CA	...	...	...	...	...	...	...	...	...	...
157	Waterbury city, CT.	17,806	10,826	10,004	...	...	...	...	...	...	...
158	Davenport city, IA.	21,831	20,038	11,267	1,848	...	...	...	...	...	...
159	Concord city, CA.	...	...	...	...	...	...	...	...	...	...
160	Alexandria city, VA	13,659	13,570	12,652	8,734	8,459	8,241	8,218	7,227	4,971	2,748
161	Stamford city, CT	2,540	...	...	...	...	...	...	...	...	...
162	Boise City city, IN	1,899	995	...	...	...	...	...	...	...	...
163	Fullerton city, CA.	...	...	...	...	...	...	...	...	...	...
164	Albany city, NY	90,758	69,422	62,367	50,763	33,721	24,209	12,630	10,762	5,289	3,498
165	Pueblo city, CO	3,217	...	...	...	...	...	...	...	...	...
166	Waco city, TX	7,295	3,008	...	...	...	...	...	...	...	...
167	Columbia city, SC	10,036	9,298	8,052	6,060	4,340	3,310	...	...	...	...
168	Durham city, NC	2,041	...	...	...	...	...	...	...	...	...
169	Reno city, NV	1,302	1,035	...	...	...	...	...	...	...	...
170	Roanoke city, VA.	669	...	...	...	...	...	...	...	...	...

Note: ... indicates data not applicable.

Source: U.S. Bureau of the Census. "Number of Inhabitants: United States Summary." 1980 Census of Population. Washington, DC: U.S. Government Printing Office, 1982, Table 27.

and "zone of daily influence" of the metropolitan center just described. (The complete definition of these areas is provided in the Definition Box.) Once recognized, these units have been described by the U.S. Census Bureau with detailed tabulations similar to those provided for states. At periodic intervals new metropolitan areas are recognized and delimited. For the 1980 census there was a total of 318 SMSAs.

The counties termed "nonmetropolitan" are all those that have not been declared parts of metropolitan areas. The nonmetropolitan counties contain smaller urban places and rural populations.

The SMSA may be thought of as having two principal components, the "central city" (metropolis) and the "metropolitan ring" (the balance of the SMSA remaining when the central city is deducted). Sometimes it is found convenient to divide the ring population into urban and rural. Because most central cities of SMSAs are also the central cities for urbanized areas, it is possible to subdivide the urban population of the ring into "urban fringe" and "other urban."

The main difference between the SMSA classification and the urban definitions is that each individual SMSA is recognized by the Bureau of the Census as a primary unit for data tabulation, similar to states. Almost all the data available for the state or nation are also available for each SMSA, or at least each of the larger ones, as they are not for individual urbanized areas. SMSA statistics therefore enable people to study metropolises one by one, rather than simply as a residential category that is pooled for tabulating data for states, divisions, regions, and the national total. SMSAs may be either pooled like the urban definition or treated individually in great demographic detail.

Population Growth in SMSAs

The number of SMSAs recognized at each census and the percent of population classed as metropolitan and nonmetropolitan, with rates of population growth, are as follows:

SMSA growth	Year				
	1980	1970	1960	1950	1940[a]
Number of SMSAs. . . .	318	243	212	168	168
Percent of population:					
Metropolitan	74.8	68.6	63.0	56.1	52.8
Nonmetropolitan. . .	25.2	31.4	37.0	43.9	47.2
Intercensal percent change:					
Metropolitan	21.5	23.6	33.0	22.0	...
Nonmetropolitan. . .	-10.5	-4.0	-0.1	7.0	...

[a]1950 delimitations extended backward to 1940.

When the SMSA was introduced, the metropolitan population outnumbered the nonmetropolitan by only a small margin. In 1980 the ratio had shifted to three-fourths metropolitan and one-fourth nonmetropolitan. This is due only in part to population growth within the metropolitan areas. Pressures to gain metropolitan status are strong, and medium-size cities have been able to make persuasive arguments that the definition should be extended to include their areas. As medium-size places have grown, more of them are able to qualify. As a result the number of places recognized as SMSAs in 1980 was 90 percent greater than in 1950. Each SMSA added subtracts an equivalent amount of population from the nonmetropolitan category. With such large transfers of population by reclassification, it is only to be expected that the nonmetropolitan population will fail to grow and the percent classed as metropolitan will increase.

The SMSA delimitation reveals how strongly aggregated around and oriented toward larger cities the U.S. population actually is. The following statistics tell the story:

Year and type of area	Percent distribution		
	Land area	Population	Density (Pop/sq. mi.)
1980 (318 SMSAs):			
Metropolitan	16.0	74.8	300
Nonmetropolitan.	84.0	25.2	19
Total.	100.0	100.0	64
1970 (243 SMSAs):			
Metropolitan	10.9	68.6	360
Nonmetropolitan.	89.1	31.4	20
Total.	100.0	100.0	57

Source: U.S. Bureau of the Census. Statistical Abstract of the United States, 1982-83. Washington, DC: U.S. Government Printing Office, 1982, table 18.

The three-fourths of the population classed as metropolitan lives on one-sixth of the land area at an average density of 300 persons per square mile, while the one-fourth classed as nonmetropolitan is diffused over five-sixths of the land area at a density of 19 per square mile. Between 1970 and 1980, 5.1 percent of the land area, with its dense settlement, was transferred from nonmetropolitan status to metropolitan status. Because the new SMSAs added were smaller and lower in population density, the expanded classification lowered average density within the SMSA category during the decade despite population growth in those areas. It also lowered slightly the average density of nonmetropolitan areas.

Table 3-15. Cities with 100,000 Inhabitants or More in 1980: Population, 1970 and 1980, and Households, 1980

City	Population										Households, 1980	
	1970		1980									
						Percent						
	Total (1,000)	Percent black	Total (1,000)	Rank	Percent change, 1970–1980	Black	Spanish-origin	Under 18 years	65 years and over	Per square mile	Total (1,000)	Persons per household
Akron, OH	275	17.5	237	59	-13.9	22.2	0.6	26.4	13.5	4,125	91	2.56
Albany, NY	116	12.2	102	164	-12.1	16.1	1.6	20.5	16.4	4,710	41	2.28
Albuquerque, NM	245	2.2	332	44	35.7	2.5	33.8	27.8	8.4	3,485	124	2.65
Alexandria, VA	111	14.1	103	160	-7.0	22.3	3.9	18.3	9.2	6,867	49	2.07
Allentown, PA	110	1.8	104	155	-5.6	3.1	5.1	22.4	16.1	5,929	41	2.42
Amarillo, TX	127	5.3	149	107	17.5	5.5	9.2	29.0	10.1	1,863	56	2.63
Anaheim, CA	166	*	219	63	31.8	1.2	17.2	26.5	7.7	5,259	80	2.71
Anchorage, AK	48	5.9	174	78	262.8	5.3	3.0	31.5	2.0	101	60	2.80
Ann Arbor, MI	100	6.7	108	146	7.9	9.3	2.1	19.1	5.9	4,389	39	2.42
Arlington, TX	90	0.6	160	94	77.5	2.9	4.1	28.5	4.5	2,024	59	2.69
Atlanta, GA	495	51.3	425	29	-14.1	66.6	1.4	26.8	11.5	3,244	163	2.51
Aurora, CO	75	1.2	159	96	111.5	6.9	5.0	29.5	4.3	2,657	59	2.67
Austin, TX	254	11.8	345	42	36.3	12.2	18.7	24.5	7.5	2,978	134	2.45
Bakersfield, CA	70	13.3	106	152	51.9	10.6	15.0	29.1	9.2	1,435	40	2.62
Baltimore, MD	905	46.4	787	10	-13.1	54.8	1.0	26.9	12.8	9,793	281	2.74
Baton Rouge, LA	166	27.8	219	62	32.2	36.5	1.8	27.3	8.7	3,562	79	2.67
Beaumont, TX	118	30.7	118	132	0.5	36.6	3.5	28.3	11.4	1,620	43	2.68
Berkeley, CA	114	23.5	103	156	-9.4	20.1	5.1	15.4	10.8	9.458	45	2.11
Birmingham, AL	301	42.0	284	50	-5.5	55.6	0.8	26.6	13.9	2,887	107	2.61
Boise City, ID	75	0.4	102	162	36.6	0.5	2.3	26.8	10.2	2,607	40	2.50
Boston, MA	641	16.3	563	20	-12.2	22.4	6.4	21.6	12.7	11,928	218	2.40
Bridgeport, CT	157	16.3	143	110	-8.9	21.0	18.7	27.9	13.4	9,697	52	2.65
Buffalo, NY	463	20.4	358	39	-22.7	26.6	2.7	25.2	15.0	8,561	141	2.46
Cedar Rapids, IA	111	1.6	110	141	-0.4	2.3	0.9	27.6	11.0	2,045	42	2.58
Charlotte, NC	241	30.3	314	47	30.2	31.0	1.1	27.8	8.6	2,251	118	2.64
Chattanooga, TN	120	35.8	170	87	41.4	31.7	0.8	26.7	12.7	1,370	62	2.63
Chesapeake, VA	90	23.1	114	137	27.8	27.6	0.9	31.9	7.1	337	36	3.11
Chicago, IL	3,369	32.7	3,005	2	-10.8	39.8	14.0	28.4	11.4	13,174	1,093	2.71
Cincinnati, OH	454	27.6	385	32	-15.0	33.8	0.8	25.2	14.5	4,935	158	2.35
Cleveland, OH	751	38.3	574	18	-23.6	43.8	3.1	27.8	13.0	7,264	218	2.58
Colorado Springs, CO	136	5.2	215	66	58.8	5.6	8.5	28.3	8.3	2,081	81	2.59
Columbia, SC	114	29.9	101	167	-10.9	40.2	2.2	20.3	10.4	945	30	2.47
Columbus, GA	155	26.2	169	88	9.3	34.2	2.1	29.5	8.9	779	59	2.76
Columbus, OH	540	18.5	565	19	4.6	22.1	0.8	25.8	8.9	3,123	217	2.49
Concord, CA	85	0.3	103	159	21.2	1.7	7.2	27.8	7.3	3,515	38	2.68
Corpus Christi, TX	205	5.1	232	60	13.4	5.1	46.6	32.4	8.2	2,237	77	2.98
Dallas, TX	844	24.9	904	7	7.1	29.4	12.3	27.0	9.5	2,715	355	2.51
Davenport, IA	98	4.2	103	158	4.9	6.1	2.8	29.1	10.5	1,736	38	2.65
Dayton, OH	243	30.5	203	70	-16.2	36.9	0.9	27.4	11.8	4,202	78	2.51
Denver, CO	515	9.1	492	24	-4.3	12.0	18.8	22.5	12.6	4,452	212	2.27
Des Moines, IA	201	5.7	191	74	-5.2	6.8	1.8	25.9	12.5	2,890	75	2.46
Detroit, MI	1,514	43.7	1,203	6	-20.5	63.1	2.4	30.3	11.7	8,874	433	2.73
Durham, NC	95	36.8	101	168	5.7	47.1	0.9	23.2	12.1	2,484	38	2.46
Elizabeth, NJ	113	15.5	106	150	-5.7	18.2	26.7	25.7	13.2	9,060	39	2.69
El Paso, TX	322	2.3	425	28	32.0	3.2	62.5	35.0	6.9	1,778	128	3.28
Erie, PA	129	6.6	119	130	-7.8	9.7	1.1	27.3	13.4	5,490	44	2.68
Eugene, OR	79	0.8	106	151	33.7	1.1	2.1	22.4	9.5	3,250	42	2.36
Evansville, IN	139	7.3	130	121	-6.0	8.8	0.5	24.6	15.2	3,499	51	2.46
Flint, MI	193	28.1	160	95	-17.4	41.4	2.5	31.9	10.0	4,911	58	2.74
Fort Lauderdale, FL	140	14.6	153	101	9.6	21.0	4.2	19.3	19.1	4,795	68	2.22
Fort Wayne, IN	178	10.6	172	80	-3.4	14.6	2.2	28.0	11.9	3,274	66	2.55
Fort Worth, TX	393	19.9	385	33	-2.1	22.8	12.6	27.1	11.8	1,604	144	2.60
Fremont, CA	101	*	132	119	30.8	2.5	14.0	30.1	5.2	1,683	44	2.96
Fresno, CA	166	9.6	218	65	31.7	9.5	23.6	27.9	10.9	3,326	82	2.59
Fullerton, CA	86	0.8	102	163	18.7	1.6	13.5	24.2	8.0	4,620	38	2.64
Garden Grove, CA	121	*	123	127	1.8	0.8	13.5	28.3	7.4	7,046	42	2.93
Garland, TX	81	3.7	139	115	70.5	5.3	6.3	33.7	4.1	2,495	46	3.01
Gary, IN	175	52.8	152	104	-13.4	70.8	7.1	34.9	8.2	3,857	49	3.06
Glendale, CA	133	*	139	114	4.8	0.3	17.8	20.8	16.3	4,540	59	2.30
Grand Rapids, MI	198	11.3	182	75	-8.0	15.7	3.2	27.4	13.4	4,190	66	2.63
Greensboro, NC	144	28.2	156	100	8.0	33.0	0.8	25.3	9.8	2,581	57	2.58
Hampton, VA	121	25.4	123	128	1.5	34.3	1.4	29.1	7.0	2,390	42	2.83
Hartford, CT	158	27.9	136	117	-13.7	33.9	20.5	29.0	11.4	7,662	51	2.53
Hialeah, FL	102	1.1	145	108	41.8	1.5	74.3	24.2	11.4	7,482	48	2.99
Hollywood, FL	107	3.7	121	129	13.5	4.1	5.3	19.8	25.1	5,249	51	2.37
Honolulu, HI	325	0.7	365	36	12.4	1.2	5.2	23.1	10.4	4,196	127	2.79
Houston, TX	1,234	25.7	1,595	5	29.3	27.6	17.6	28.4	6.9	2,867	603	2.62
Huntington Beach, CA	116	*	171	85	47.0	0.7	7.9	27.9	5.9	6,291	61	2.78
Huntsville, AL	139	12.1	143	111	2.3	20.7	1.0	28.9	7.0	1,256	50	2.78
Independence, MO	112	0.6	112	140	0.2	0.7	1.4	27.2	10.9	1,389	42	2.62
Indianapolis, IN	737	18.0	701	12	-4.9	21.8	0.9	28.6	10.3	1,990	260	2.65
Irving, TX	97	1.0	110	142	13.0	1.5	7.4	29.1	4.7	1,635	40	2.70
Jackson, MS	154	39.7	203	71	31.8	47.0	0.7	29.6	9.7	1,910	71	2.76
Jacksonville, FL	504	22.3	541	22	7.3	25.4	1.8	28.8	9.6	712	197	2.70
Jersey City, NJ	260	21.0	224	61	-14.1	27.7	18.6	29.4	11.8	16,934	81	2.74
Kansas City, KS	168	20.4	161	93	-4.2	25.3	4.9	29.6	11.7	1,499	60	2.68
Kansas City, MO	507	22.1	448	27	-11.7	27.4	3.3	26.5	12.3	1,417	175	2.51
Knoxville, TN	175	12.7	175	77	0.3	14.6	0.7	21.9	13.8	2,270	69	2.40
Lakewood, CO	93	0.1	113	138	21.7	0.5	5.9	27.6	7.2	3,174	41	2.70

Table 3-15. Cities with 100,000 Inhabitants or More in 1980: Population, 1970 and 1980, and Households, 1980—continued

City	Population										Households, 1980	
	1970		1980									
						Percent						
	Total (1,000)	Percent black	Total (1,000)	Rank	Percent change, 1970–1980	Black	Spanish-origin	Under 18 years	65 years and over	Per square mile	Total (1,000)	Persons per house-hold
Lansing, MI	131	9.3	130	122	-0.8	13.9	6.3	29.2	8.7	3,694	50	2.61
Las Vegas, NV	126	11.2	165	89	30.9	12.8	7.8	27.9	8.3	2,994	62	2.63
Lexington-Fayette, KY	108	17.0	204	68	88.8	13.3	0.7	25.3	8.6	717	75	2.56
Lincoln, NB	150	1.5	172	81	15.0	2.0	1.6	23.5	10.3	2,866	65	2.46
Little Rock, AK	132	25.0	158	98	19.6	32.2	0.8	28.0	11.0	1,996	61	2.55
Livonia, MI	110	*	105	153	-4.8	0.1	0.9	28.4	7.8	3,018	33	3.18
Long Beach, CA	359	5.3	361	37	0.7	11.3	14.0	22.9	14.0	7,256	152	2.31
Los Angeles, CA	2,812	17.9	2,967	3	5.5	17.0	27.5	25.1	10.6	6,384	1,135	2.55
Louisville, KY	362	23.8	298	49	-17.5	28.2	0.7	25.0	15.3	4,974	117	2.48
Lubbock, TX	149	7.3	174	79	16.7	8.2	18.8	27.7	7.8	1,920	61	2.70
Macon, GA	122	37.3	117	134	-4.5	44.5	0.7	28.7	11.9	2,357	42	2.71
Madison, WI	172	1.5	171	84	-0.7	2.7	1.3	20.5	8.7	3,165	66	2.38
Memphis, TN	624	38.9	646	14	3.6	47.6	0.8	29.1	10.4	2,-47	230	2.76
Mesa, AZ	63	1.2	152	102	141.8	1.2	9.1	30.1	11.2	2,250	54	2.80
Miami, FL	335	22.7	347	41	3.6	25.1	55.9	21.4	17.0	10,113	134	2.54
Milwaukee, WI	717	14.7	636	16	-11.3	23.1	4.1	27.0	12.5	6,641	242	2.56
Minneapolis, MN	434	4.4	371	34	-14.6	7.7	1.3	20.0	15.4	6,732	162	2.19
Mobile, AL	190	35.4	200	72	5.5	36.2	1.1	29.0	11.1	1,630	71	2.75
Modesto, CA	62	1.9	107	149	72.7	2.1	10.5	29.5	9.7	4,281	39	2.68
Montgomery, AL	133	33.4	178	76	33.3	39.2	0.9	30.2	10.1	1,386	63	2.76
Nashville-Davidson, TN	426	19.6	456	25	7.0	23.3	0.8	25.0	11.0	950	170	2.57
New Haven, CT	138	26.3	126	125	-8.4	31.9	8.0	25.3	13.1	6,672	47	2.48
New Orleans, LA	593	45.0	558	21	-6.1	55.3	3.4	28.8	11.7	2,796	206	2.63
New York, NY	7,896	21.1	7,072	1	-10.4	25.2	19.9	25.0	13.5	23,455	2,789	2.49
Bronx Borough	1,472	24.3	1,169	...	-20.6	31.8	33.9	29.2	12.9	28,006	429	2.66
Brooklyn Borough	2,602	25.2	2,231	...	-14.3	32.4	17.6	28.3	12.5	31,762	828	2.67
Manhattan Borough	1,539	24.7	1,428	...	-7.2	21.7	23.5	17.7	14.3	64,395	705	1.96
Queens Borough	1,987	13.0	1,891	...	-4.8	18.7	13.9	23.1	14.9	17,411	712	2.63
Staten Island Borough	295	5.3	352	...	19.2	7.3	5.4	29.1	10.0	5,995	115	3.00
Newark, NJ	382	54.2	329	46	-13.8	58.2	18.6	34.1	8.8	13,662	111	2.93
Newport News, VA	138	28.4	145	109	4.9	31.5	1.8	28.4	7.8	2,219	51	2.73
Norfolk, VA	308	28.3	267	55	-13.3	35.2	2.3	24.6	9.2	5,037	88	2.65
Oakland, CA	362	34.5	339	43	-6.1	46.9	9.6	24.3	13.2	6,296	142	2.34
Oklahoma City, OK	368	13.7	403	31	9.5	14.6	2.8	27.0	11.3	668	160	2.48
Omaha, NB	347	9.9	314	48	-9.4	12.0	2.3	27.5	12.2	3,457	118	2.59
Orlando, FL	99	29.5	128	124	29.6	30.0	3.9	24.0	12.7	3,248	48	2.45
Oxnard, CA	71	6.0	108	145	51.9	6.1	44.4	33.2	6.6	4,508	33	3.21
Pasadena, CA	113	16.1	119	131	5.0	20.7	18.4	23.1	14.9	5,154	47	2.42
Pasadena, TX	90	0.1	113	139	25.1	0.8	17.0	31.4	4.8	2,974	39	2.88
Paterson, NJ	145	26.9	138	116	-4.7	34.1	28.7	32.9	10.3	16,623	46	2.96
Peoria, IL	127	11.5	124	126	-2.2	16.7	1.4	27.6	12.3	3,028	46	2.57
Philadephia, PA	1,949	33.6	1,688	4	-13.4	37.8	3.8	25.9	14.1	12,413	620	2.66
Phoenix, AZ	584	4.8	790	9	35.2	4.8	14.8	29.0	9.3	2,437	285	2.74
Pittsburgh, PA	520	20.2	424	30	-18.5	24.0	0.8	21.4	16.0	7,652	166	2.44
Portland, OR	380	5.6	366	35	-3.6	7.6	2.1	21.8	15.3	3,547	159	2.25
Portsmouth, VA	111	39.9	105	154	-5.8	45.1	1.0	28.7	10.7	3,498	37	2.79
Providence, RI	179	8.9	157	99	-12.5	11.8	5.8	23.2	15.3	8,297	60	2.44
Pueblo, CO	98	2.1	102	165	4.0	2.1	35.5	28.5	12.3	3,063	37	2.66
Raleigh, NC	123	22.7	150	105	22.3	27.4	0.9	22.3	8.3	2,793	55	2.46
Reno, NV	73	2.2	101	169	38.3	2.7	5.1	20.1	10.5	3,250	44	2.24
Richmond, VA	249	42.0	219	65	-12.1	51.3	1.0	22.4	14.1	3,650	86	2.43
Riverside, CA	140	5.2	171	83	22.0	6.9	16.2	29.2	8.8	2,380	61	2.75
Roanoke, VA	92	19.3	100	170	8.8	22.0	0.7	24.4	15.6	2,326	40	2.46
Rochester, NY	295	16.8	242	57	-18.1	25.8	5.4	26.6	14.0	7,068	95	2.45
Rockford, IL	147	8.3	140	113	-5.2	13.2	2.9	27.8	12.6	3,601	52	2.61
Sacramento, CA	257	10.7	276	52	7.2	13.4	14.2	24.6	13.6	2,869	113	2.39
St. Louis, MO	622	40.9	453	26	-27.2	45.6	1.2	26.1	17.6	7,379	178	2.49
St. Paul, MN	310	3.5	270	54	-12.8	4.9	2.9	24.1	15.0	5,157	106	2.44
St. Petersburg, FL	216	14.8	239	58	10.4	17.2	1.8	20.4	25.8	4,300	104	2.24
Salt Lake City, UT	176	1.2	163	90	-7.3	1.5	7.6	24.2	14.7	2,168	68	2.35
San Antonio, TX	654	7.6	786	11	20.1	7.3	53.7	32.2	9.5	2,992	259	2.97
San Bernardino, CA	107	14.0	117	133	9.9	14.9	25.4	28.1	11.9	2,208	43	2.63
San Diego, CA	697	7.6	876	8	25.5	8.9	14.9	24.1	9.7	2,736	321	2.53
San Francisco, CA	716	13.4	679	13	-5.1	12.7	12.3	17.2	15.4	14,636	299	2.19
San Jose, CA	460	2.5	629	17	36.9	4.6	22.3	31.0	6.2	3,984	210	2.96
Santa Ana, CA	156	4.3	204	69	30.8	4.0	44.5	30.6	7.4	7,435	64	3.12
Savannah, GA	118	44.9	141	112	19.5	49.0	1.3	29.6	11.4	2,489	51	2.73
Seattle, WA	531	7.1	494	23	-7.0	9.5	2.6	17.6	15.4	3,415	219	2.15
Shreveport, LA	182	34.1	206	67	13.0	41.1	1.3	30.3	11.7	2,544	75	2.72
South Bend, IN	126	14.1	110	143	-12.6	18.3	2.4	26.8	14.8	3,014	42	2.56
Spokane, WA	171	1.3	171	82	0.5	1.6	1.5	24.5	15.3	3,313	71	2.35
Springfield, MA	164	12.6	152	103	-7.1	16.6	9.1	27.5	13.8	4,805	55	2.66
Springfield, MO	120	2.0	133	118	10.8	2.1	0.7	23.2	13.2	2,051	52	2.40
Stamford, CT	109	12.3	102	161	-5.8	15.0	5.6	24.5	12.0	2,689	38	2.65
Sterling Heights, MI	61	0.1	109	144	77.6	0.2	0.9	34.5	4.5	2,978	34	3.20

Table 3-15. Cities with 100,000 Inhabitants or More in 1980: Population, 1970 and 1980, and Households, 1980—continued

City	Population										Households, 1980	
	1970		1980									
						Percent						
	Total (1,000)	Percent black	Total (1,000)	Rank	Percent change, 1970-1980	Black	Spanish-origin	Under 18 years	65 years and over	Per square mile	Total (1,000)	Persons per house-holds
Stockton, CA	110	11.0	150	106	36.2	10.4	22.1	29.2	11.0	3,744	55	2.62
Sunnyvale, CA.	96	0.8	107	148	11.1	2.4	11.5	23.0	8.2	4,650	43	2.46
Syracuse, NY	197	10.8	170	86	-13.8	15.7	1.7	23.3	14.6	7,147	67	2.38
Tacoma, WA	154	6.8	159	97	2.7	9.2	2.4	26.8	13.5	3,323	63	2.44
Tampa, FL.	278	19.7	272	53	-2.2	23.5	13.3	25.1	14.8	3,217	106	2.51
Tempe, AZ.	64	0.7	107	147	68.0	1.8	8.2	24.7	4.7	2,822	37	2.73
Toledo, OH	383	13.8	355	40	-7.4	17.4	3.0	28.1	12.5	4,212	133	2.62
Topeka, KS	125	8.4	115	136	-7.8	9.5	4.6	25.2	13.9	2,333	46	2.39
Torrance, CA	135	*	130	123	-3.8	0.7	8.3	23.8	8.5	6,341	50	2.60
Tucson, AZ	263	3.5	331	45	25.7	3.7	24.9	25.5	11.7	3,356	125	2.57
Tulsa, OK.	330	10.6	361	38	9.3	11.8	1.7	25.8	10.8	1,945	145	2.43
Virginia Beach, VA	172	9.1	262	56	52.3	10.0	2.0	30.7	4.5	1,025	85	2.97
Waco, TX	95	19.9	101	166	6.2	21.8	11.1	24.3	14.3	1,367	38	2.51
Warren, MI	179	*	161	92	-10.1	0.2	0.9	27.8	8.0	4,680	54	2.99
Washington, DC	757	71.1	638	15	-15.6	70.3	2.8	22.5	11.6	10,181	253	2.40
Waterbury, CT.	108	10.1	103	157	-4.4	11.6	6.7	25.8	15.5	3,611	38	2.67
Wichita, KS.	277	9.7	279	51	1.0	10.8	3.5	26.3	10.6	2,754	110	2.49
Winston-Salem, NC.	134	34.3	132	120	-1.3	40.2	0.8	25.3	12.1	2,169	50	2.50
Worchester, MA	177	1.9	162	91	-8.4	2.9	4.3	23.6	16.3	4,326	59	2.56
Yonkers, NY.	204	6.4	195	73	-4.4	10.5	8.7	23.1	14.8	10,655	74	2.61
Youngstown, OH	141	25.2	115	135	-18.1	33.3	3.3	26.3	14.6	3,346	42	2.70

Note: ... indicates data not applicable. * indicates less than .05 percent.

Source: U.S. Bureau of the Census. Statistical Abstract of the United States, 1982-83. Washington, DC: U.S. Government Printing Office, 1982, Table 26.

A valid measure of growth trends inside and outside metropolitan areas is to take a sample of SMSAs as recognized and delimited for a particular census, tabulate data for those same areas at two censuses, and compare the results. This is accomplished in Table 3-16. The SMSAs as delimited in 1970 and 1980 are tabulated for both the preceding and current censuses. This permits the study of growth trends, holding the SMSAs' definitions constant. The SMSAs are classified according to their size as of the more recent of the pair of censuses. Keeping in mind that the annual decennial rate of change in 1970-80 was 11.4 percent, it is clear that the 318 SMSAs as a group grew slightly less rapidly than the nation; the nonmetropolitan population grew slightly more rapidly than the metropolitan. However, it may be seen that this is due entirely to an absolute population decline in the top size class, the seven supermetropolises of 3.0 million or more inhabitants. SMSAs smaller than that grew at rates slightly larger than the nation's, with the most rapid growth occurring in the medium-size SMSAs having between 100,000 and 250,000 population.

A similar comparison for the 1960-70 decade for the 243 metropolises recognized at the 1970 census shows a similar pattern. The national growth rate of 13.4 for the 1960-70 decade was not attained by the largest size group of SMSAs but was surpassed by all other size groups except the smallest, those below 100,000 population. However, in the 1960-70 decade, the most rapid growth occurred in the three groups between 250,000 and 3,000,000. Thus the very largest SMSAs have grown at less than average rates for two decades, while those smaller in size (especially the middle-size SMSAs) have grown at rates moderately more rapid than the nation.

In 1960-70 the nonmetropolitan area as a category grew substantially less rapidly than the metropolitan area. Hence, the upsurge of nonmetropolitan population growth (which is linked to the rural growth of population discussed in the preceding section) is a reversal of a long-term trend.

Metropolitanization, 1900 to 1950

Efforts have been made to trace the metropolitanization of the population for decades before the SMSA delimitations were established by extending the definition backward to 1900 in order to obtain data for the first half of this century.[2]

By combining county statistics from each census since 1900, the standard metropolitan area definitions were applied to the results of each census. This permitted a study of the growth of population in metropolitan and nonmetropolitan areas from 1900 to 1950. To make this

Table 3-16. Number and Population of SMSAs, 1970 and 1980, and Change, 1960 to 1980

Population-size class of SMSAs	243 SMSAs[a]				318 SMSAs[c]				
	Number, 1970[b]	Population, 1970			Number, 1980[b]	Population, 1970 (mil.)	Population, 1980		
		Total (mil.)	Percent in each class	Percent change, 1960-70			Total (mil.)	Percent in each class	Percent change, 1970-80
Total SMSAs	243	139.4	100.0	16.6	318	153.7	169.4	100.0	10.2
3,000,000 or more. . . .	6	37.7	27.0	11.9	7	39.3	39.1	23.1	0.5
1,000,000-3,000,000. . .	27	42.9	30.8	21.4	31	47.3	53.8	31.7	13.8
500,000-1,000,000. . . .	32	21.9	15.7	18.0	41	25.1	28.1	16.6	11.8
250,000-500,000.	60	19.8	14.2	16.3	71	21.4	24.6	14.5	14.7
100,000-250,000.	92	15.0	10.7	14.5	140	18.5	21.6	12.7	16.4
Less than 100,000. . . .	26	2.1	1.5	12.3	28	2.1	2.4	1.4	13.3

[a]As defined in 1970 census publications.

[b]Based on size class in 1970 and 1980, respectively.

[c]Includes all SMSAs as defined by U.S. Office of Management and Budget, June 30, 1981.

Source: U.S. Bureau of the Census. Statistical Abstract of the United States, 1982-83. Washington, DC: U.S. Government Printing Office, 1982, Table 16.

study of trends, it was necessary to redelimit the 16 standard metropolitan areas of New England along county boundaries rather than town lines, because data for the town units were not available in all cases. Since in some instances two or more New England standard metropolitan areas fall in the same county, in order to form a few of the county-equivalent areas it was necessary to combine two or more SMAs. This reduced the total number of SMAs from 168 to 162. The SMA definition was extended to earlier censuses only for "principal standard metropolitan areas," that is, SMAs with a total population of 100,000 or more at any census. (In 1950 this eliminated 15 small SMAs that had less than 100,000 population, and for the 1940 and earlier censuses required that areas have 100,000 population at the census date before they could be defined as metropolitan.) There were 147 principal SMAs at the 1950 census.

Between 1900 and 1950, there was a steady trend toward an increase in the number of standard metropolitan areas, and toward a rise in the proportion of the total population residing in such areas. The record of this trend is contained in Table 3-17A. Had the SMA delimitation been in effect in 1900, there would have been an estimated 52 areas, and these areas would have contained less than one-third of the total population. At each succeeding census, from 10 to 23 new SMAs would have been added as a result of additional areas attaining 100,000 population and qualifying as SMAs under the definition.

The extent to which metropolitan centers tended to agglomerate population about themselves during the first five decades of this century may be appreciated by comparing the growth rates of metropolitan and nonmetropolitan areas, and by noting what proportion of the nation's total population increase for each decade was claimed by the standard metropolitan areas. The right-hand column of Table 3-17A reports this information. During every decade except one, the SMAs grew 50 percent faster than the nonmetropolitan areas, and claimed a disproportionately large share of the total national growth.

Central City Versus Ring Growth

The study cited above also undertook to compare growth patterns for central cities and rings within SMSAs, as retrojected to 1900. The data are reproduced in Table 3-17B.

Between 1920 and 1930 there was a remarkable reversal in the pattern of growth within metropolitan areas. During the 1900-10 and the 1910-20 decades central cities were growing faster than their rings. In each decade since 1920 rings have grown faster than central cities. Table 3-17B documents this shift. Early in the century rings had only about one-ninth of the population of the nation. Between 1900-10 the rings claimed only about one-sixth of the national population growth; in 1940-50 they claimed almost one-half. The relative gap between the growth rate of central cities and rings has become very large; in 1940-50 rings grew almost two

Table 3-17A. Growth Data for Standard Metropolitan Areas, Retrojected to Earlier Censuses: 1900-50

Census year	Number of SMAs	Population (millions)	Percent of U.S. population	Rate of growth (percent change) during preceding decade			Percent U.S. growth claimed by SMAs in preceding decade
				U.S. total	Standard metro areas	Nonmetro areas	
All SMAs, 1950. .	162	85.6	56.8	14.5	21.8	6.0	80.6
Principal SMAs							
1950.	147	84.3	56.0	14.5	21.8	6.3	79.3
1940.	125	67.1	51.1	7.2	8.3	6.2	57.7
1930.	115	61.0	49.8	16.1	27.0	7.1	76.2
1920.	94	46.1	43.7	14.9	25.2	8.1	67.6
1910.	71	34.5	37.6	21.0	32.6	15.0	53.1
1900.	52	24.1	31.9	20.7	...	...	...

Source: Donald J. Bogue. The Growth of Standard Metropolitan Areas: 1900-1950, with an explanatory analysis of urbanized areas. Washington, DC: U.S. Government Printing Office, 1953.

Table 3-17B. Growth Data for Central Cities and Rings of Standard Metropolitan Areas, Retrojected to Earlier Censuses: 1900-50

Census year	Number of SMAs	Percent of U.S. population		Rate of growth (percent change) during preceding decade			Percent of U.S. population growth claimed by SMAs during preceding decade	
		Central cities	Rings	Metro areas, total	Central cities	Rings	Central cities	Rings
All SMAs, 1950. . .	162	32.8	24.0	21.8	13.9	34.7	31.6	49.0
Principal SMAs								
1950.	147	32.3	23.8	21.8	13.7	34.8	30.7	48.6
1940.	125	31.6	19.5	8.3	5.1	13.8	22.8	34.9
1930.	115	31.8	18.0	27.0	23.3	34.2	43.3	32.9
1920.	94	28.9	14.8	25.2	26.7	22.4	46.8	20.8
1910.	71	25.0	12.7	32.6	35.3	27.6	37.4	15.7
1900.	52	21.2	10.7	...	...	...	...	...

Note: ... indicates data not applicable.

Source: Donald J. Bogue. The Growth of Standard Metropolitan Areas: 1900-1950, with an explanatory analysis of urbanized areas. Washington, DC: U.S. Government Printing Office, 1953.

and one-half times as fast as central cities. In making these comparisons it should be noted also that in both the 1930-40 and 1940-50 decades the growth rates for central cities were below the national average, while the growth rates for rings were well above it.

Figures 3-9A and 3-9B integrate the results of this early retrojection study with the results of the censuses of 1960-80.

Regional Variations in Metropolitan-Nonmetropolitan Growth

Because the differences noted above have great regional and even state-to-state variations, it is worthwhile to examine the growth of metropolitan and nonmetropolitan populations both for 1970-80 and 1960-70 in terms of regions, divisions, and states. Table 3-18 provides the data for such an analysis. For this table the 318 SMSAs of 1980 were tabulated by states from data for 1960 and 1970 censuses, thereby permitting measures of change with constant (1980) boundaries and a constant SMSA list. From this table the following can be learned:

1. The population loss for large SMSAs, noted above, occurred largely in the Middle Atlantic division (New York City), with other losses in Pennsylvania, Ohio, and the District of Columbia.

2. SMSAs as a group grew at below national rates of growth in the Northeast region and the North Central region, but New Hampshire, Vermont, North Dakota, and South Dakota in these regions had substantial metropolitan growth.

3. There was little evidence of sluggishness in metropolitan growth between 1970 and 1980 in the regions of the South and West. All states in those regions enjoyed metropolitan growth at rates in excess of the nation, except for the following states of the South:

Delaware	West Virginia
Maryland	Kentucky.
District of Columbia	

4. In the 1960-70 decade metropolitan growth was quite strong in all regions, though below the national growth rate (in many cases only by a small amount) for the following states:

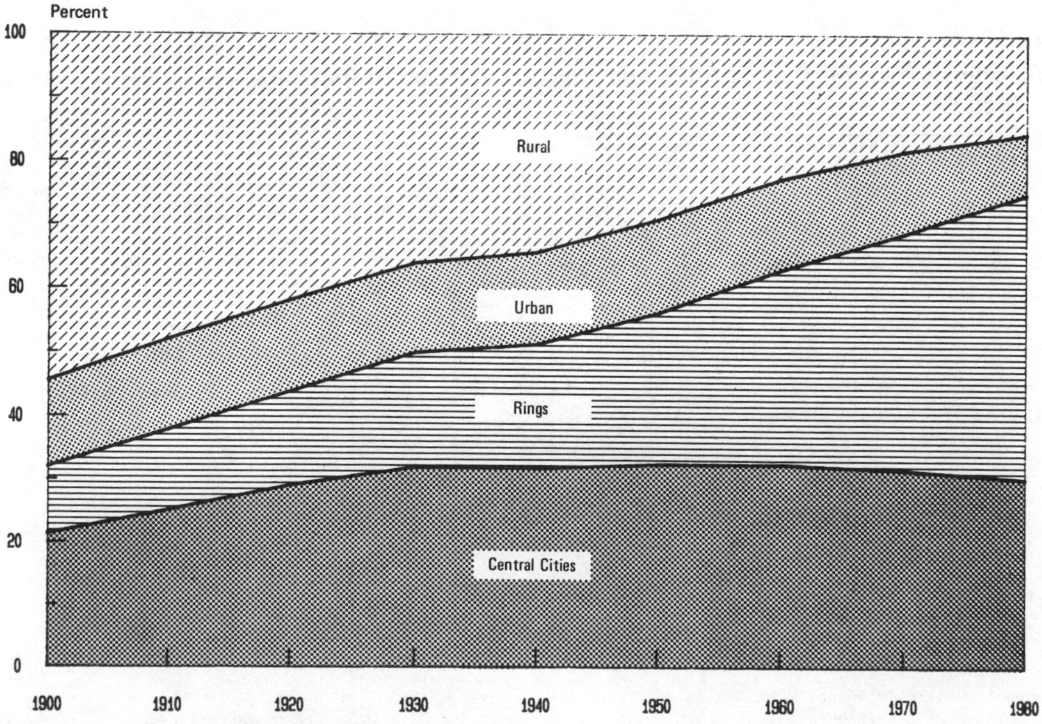

Figure 3-9A. Percent of Population in Central Cities and Rings of Metropolitan Areas, and Urban and Rural Portions of Nonmetropolitan Areas: 1900-1980

Maine
Massachusetts
Rhode Island
New York
New Jersey
Pennsylvania
Ohio
Indiana
Illinois
Michigan
Wisconsin
Iowa
Missouri
Kansas
North Dakota
South Dakota
West Virginia
South Carolina
Kentucky
Tennessee
Alabama
Louisiana
Montana
Wyoming
District of Columbia.

5. The tendency for nonmetropolitan areas to grow faster than metropolitan areas is found in about two-thirds of the states. The exceptions are primarily the states of the West North Central and Mountain divisions. In the following states, nonmetropolitan areas failed to grow as rapidly as or more rapidly than metropolitan areas:

State	Rate of growth: Metropolitan	Rate of growth: Nonmetropolitan
Idaho.	54.2	28.3
North Dakota . . .	19.1	-0.9
Mississippi. . . .	26.1	9.7
Nevada	66.5	52.3
New Mexico	36.7	22.5
Texas.	29.8	17.1
South Dakota . . .	14.3	1.8
Alaska	38.0	29.1
South Carolina . .	24.0	15.6
Louisiana.	17.9	11.4
Oklahoma	20.6	15.0
Georgia.	21.3	15.9
Nebraska	8.8	3.4
Arkansas	22.1	16.9
Arizona.	54.2	49.8
Iowa	5.8	1.4
Colorado	31.6	27.6
Kansas	7.0	3.5
North Carolina . .	16.3	15.0
Vermont.	16.0	14.7
Minnesota.	7.4	6.6
Alabama.	13.5	12.4

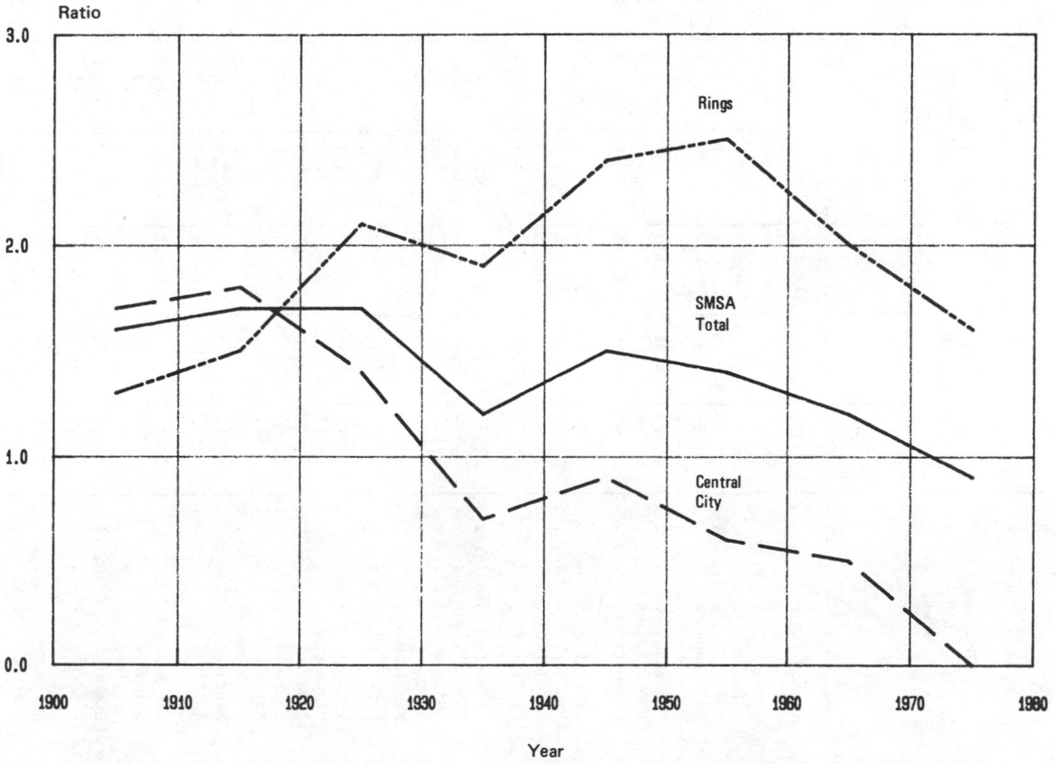

Figure 3-9B. Ratio of Central City and Ring Rates of Growth to the Nation: 1900 to 1980

Table 3-18. Metropolitan and Nonmetropolitan Area Population, by Divisions and States: 1960-80

Division and state	Metropolitan area population							Nonmetropolitan area population						
	Total (1,000)			Percent change		Percent of state or division		Total (1,000)			Percent change		Percent of state or division	
	1960	1970	1980	1960–1970	1970–1980	1970	1980	1960	1970	1980	1960–1970	1970–1980	1970	1980
United States	131,319	153,694	169,431	17.0	10.2	75.6	74.8	47,992	49,608	57,115	3.4	15.1	24.4	25.2
New England	8,323	9,369	9,461	12.6	1.0	79.1	76.6	2,187	2,479	2,887	13.3	16.5	20.9	23.4
Maine	339	349	371	3.0	6.2	35.2	33.0	630	644	754	2.3	17.0	64.8	67.0
New Hampshire	295	377	467	27.7	23.8	51.1	50.7	312	361	454	15.7	25.8	48.9	49.3
Vermont	74	98	114	33.0	16.0	22.1	22.3	316	346	397	9.6	14.7	77.9	77.7
Massachusetts	4,563	4,980	4,892	9.1	-1.8	87.5	85.3	586	709	845	21.1	19.1	12.5	14.7
Rhode Island	786	867	873	10.3	0.7	91.3	92.2	73	83	74	13.1	-10.5	8.7	7.8
Connecticut	2,265	2,697	2,744	19.1	1.8	88.9	88.3	270	335	363	24.1	8.4	11.1	11.7
Middle Atlantic	30,384	33,178	32,280	9.2	2.7	89.2	87.8	3,784	4,035	4,506	6.6	11.7	10.8	12.2
New York	15,245	16,614	15,828	9.0	-4.7	91.1	90.1	1,538	1,627	1,730	5.8	6.3	8.9	9.9
New Jersey	5,807	6,756	6,733	16.3	-0.3	94.2	91.4	260	415	632	59.6	52.1	5.8	8.6
Pennsylvania	9,333	9,808	9,719	5.1	-0.9	83.1	81.9	1,987	1,993	2,145	0.3	7.6	16.9	18.1
East North Central	28,365	31,954	32,558	12.7	1.9	79.4	78.1	7,861	8,308	9,124	5.7	9.8	20.6	21.9
Ohio	7,835	8,704	8,666	11.1	-0.4	81.7	80.3	1,871	1,953	2,131	4.4	9.1	18.3	19.7
Indiana	3,226	3,660	3,832	13.5	4.7	70.5	69.8	1,436	1,535	1,658	6.9	8.0	29.5	30.2
Illinois	8,074	9,053	9,251	12.1	2.2	81.5	81.0	2,007	2,057	2,176	2.5	5.8	18.5	19.0
Michigan	6,590	7,518	7,664	14.1	1.9	84.6	82.8	1,233	1,364	1,598	10.6	17.1	15.4	17.2
Wisconsin	2,640	3,019	3,145	14.4	4.2	68.3	66.8	1,312	1,399	1,561	6.6	11.6	31.7	33.2
West North Central	7,562	8,674	9,154	14.7	5.5	53.1	53.3	7,832	7,653	8,029	-2.3	4.9	46.9	46.7
Minnesota	2,052	2,451	2,632	19.5	7.4	64.4	64.6	1,362	1,355	1,444	-0.6	6.6	35.6	35.4
Iowa	990	1,105	1,169	11.6	5.8	39.1	40.1	1,767	1,720	1,745	-2.7	1.4	60.9	59.9
Missouri	2,801	3,155	3,210	12.6	1.8	67.4	65.3	1,519	1,523	1,706	0.3	12.1	32.6	34.7
North Dakota	171	196	234	14.7	19.7	31.7	35.9	462	422	418	-8.6	-0.9	68.3	64.1
South Dakota	87	95	109	10.0	14.9	14.3	15.8	594	571	581	-3.9	1.8	85.7	84.2
Nebraska	542	637	693	17.4	8.8	42.9	44.1	869	849	877	-2.4	3.4	57.1	55.9
Kansas	920	1,035	1,107	12.5	7.0	46.0	46.8	1,259	1,214	1,257	-3.5	3.5	54.0	53.2
South Atlantic	17,114	21,551	26,032	25.9	20.8	70.2	70.4	8,845	9,128	10,927	3.2	19.7	29.8	29.6
Delaware	307	386	398	25.5	3.2	70.4	67.0	139	162	196	16.9	20.9	29.6	33.0
Maryland	2,758	3,544	3,745	28.5	5.7	90.3	88.8	342	380	472	10.9	24.4	9.7	11.2
District of Columbia	764	757	638	-1.0	-15.6	100.0	100.0	*	*	*	...	...	*	*
Virginia	2,617	3,268	3,721	24.8	13.9	70.2	69.6	1,337	1,384	1,626	3.5	17.5	29.8	30.4
West Virginia	704	687	723	-2.4	5.2	39.4	37.1	1,157	1,057	1,227	-8.6	16.0	60.6	62.9
Ncrth Carolina	2,196	2,663	3,098	21.3	16.3	52.4	52.7	2,360	2,421	2,783	2.6	15.0	47.6	47.3
South Carolina	1,295	1,504	1,865	16.1	24.0	58.0	59.8	1,087	1,087	1,256	-0.1	15.6	42.0	40.2
Georgia	2,130	2,701	3,276	26.9	21.3	58.9	60.0	1,814	1,886	2,187	4.0	15.9	41.1	40.0
Florida	4,343	6,041	8,568	39.1	41.8	89.0	87.9	609	750	1,179	23.3	57.1	11.0	12.1

Table 3-18. Metropolitan and Nonmetropolitan Area Population, by Divisions and States: 1960-80—continued

Division and state	Metropolitan area population							Nonmetropolitan area population						
	Total (1,000)			Percent change		Percent of state or division		Total (1,000)			Percent change		Percent of state or division	
	1960	1970	1980	1960–1970	1970–1980	1970	1980	1960	1970	1980	1960–1970	1970–1980	1970	1980
East South Central . . .	5,968	6,679	7,612	11.9	14.0	52.1	51.9	6,082	6,129	7,055	0.8	15.1	47.9	48.1
Kentucky	1,324	1,511	1,628	14.1	7.8	46.9	44.5	1,714	1,710	2,032	-0.2	18.9	53.1	55.5
Tennessee.	2,216	2,497	2,884	12.7	15.5	63.6	62.8	1,351	1,429	1,707	5.7	19.4	36.4	37.2
Alabama.	1,987	2,129	2,415	7.1	13.5	61.8	62.0	1,280	1,316	1,479	2.8	12.4	38.2	38.0
Mississippi.	441	543	684	23.0	26.1	24.5	27.1	1,737	1,674	1,836	-3.6	9.7	75.5	72.9
West South Central . . .	10,942	13,239	16,723	21.0	26.3	68.5	70.4	6,009	6,087	7,024	1.3	15.4	31.5	29.6
Arkansas	622	734	896	18.0	22.1	38.2	39.2	1,164	1,189	1,390	2.1	16.9	61.8	60.8
Louisiana.	1,985	2,262	2,666	14.0	17.9	62.1	63.4	1,272	1,382	1,540	8.6	11.4	37.9	36.6
Oklahoma	1,232	1,468	1,770	19.1	20.6	57.4	58.5	1,096	1,091	1,255	-0.4	15.0	42.6	41.5
Texas.	7,103	8,775	11,390	23.5	29.8	78.4	80.0	2,477	2,424	2,840	-2.1	17.1	21.6	20.0
Mountain	3,782	5,072	7,173	34.1	41.4	61.2	63.1	3,073	3,217	4,200	4.7	30.5	38.8	36.9
Montana.	152	169	189	11.0	11.6	24.4	24.0	522	525	598	0.6	13.8	75.6	76.0
Idaho.	93	112	173	20.1	54.2	15.7	18.3	574	601	771	4.7	28.3	84.3	81.7
Wyoming.	50	51	72	3.3	40.2	15.4	15.3	280	281	398	0.3	41.5	84.6	84.7
Colorado	1,326	1,776	2,337	34.0	31.6	80.4	80.9	428	433	553	1.1	27.6	19.6	19.1
New Mexico	336	403	551	19.8	36.7	39.6	42.3	615	614	752	-0.1	22.5	60.4	57.7
Arizona.	929	1,323	2,040	42.4	54.2	74.5	75.1	373	453	678	21.3	49.8	25.5	24.9
Utah	683	843	1,154	23.4	36.9	79.6	79.0	207	216	307	4.3	42.0	20.4	21.0
Nevada	212	394	657	86.2	66.5	80.7	82.0	74	94	144	28.4	52.3	19.3	18.0
Pacific.	18,880	23,977	28,436	27.0	18.6	90.3	89.4	2,318	2,572	3,364	10.9	30.8	9.7	10.6
Washington	2,241	2,752	3,322	22.8	20.7	80.6	80.4	612	661	810	8.0	22.5	19.4	19.6
Oregon	1,112	1,375	1,708	23.6	24.2	65.8	64.9	656	716	925	9.1	29.2	34.2	35.1
California	14,943	19,092	22,469	27.8	17.7	95.6	94.9	774	879	1,199	13.5	36.5	4.4	5.1
Alaska	83	126	174	52.6	38.0	41.8	43.4	143	176	227	22.9	29.1	58.2	56.6
Hawaii	500	631	763	26.0	20.9	81.9	79.0	132	139	202	5.3	45.0	18.1	21.0

Note: ... indicates data not applicable. * indicates zero.

Source: U.S. Bureau of the Census. Statistical Abstract of the United States, 1982–83. Washington, DC: U.S. Government Printing Office, 1982, Table 19.

Note that the statistics are distorted, because unusually rapid growth of a medium-size city classed as nonmetropolitan prior to 1980 would have caused it to be reclassified as metropolitan in 1980. Thus the "nonmetropolitan" areas of 1980 exclude some of the rapid-growing nonmetropolitan areas throughout the decade.

In only seven of the states listed above did the nonmetropolitan areas grow more slowly than the national rate of 11.4 percent. For most of the exceptions the entire state was enjoying above-average growth—in both metropolitan and nonmetropolitan areas.

Investigators have noted that the trend toward rural and nonmetropolitan growth in competition with large urban clusters is weak in states that are themselves rural and have inferred that much (if not most) of the resurgence of rural growth is simply an extension of metropolitan dominance across the boundaries of the SMSA into adjoining nonmetropolitan counties. This may explain a part, but certainly not all, of the rural and nonmetropolitan resurgence.

Central Cities and Metropolitan Rings

The same type of growth differential found between the central cities and their urban fringe exists for central cities and their suburban rings. The comparison is similar, except that for SMSAs a broader hinterland is included in addition to the urban fringe. Table 3-19 provides summary data on the comparative growth, between 1970 and 1980, of the central cities and metropolitan rings. During the decade central cities as a whole had almost zero growth (0.2 percent), whereas the metropolitan rings grew by about 18 percent—60 percent faster than the national average rate. The metropolitan rings grew 20 percent faster than the nonmetropolitan areas. Thus, although the central cities have lost most of their power to attract new population growth, their peripheries still have not lost their attraction, although it is being challenged by the resurgence of growth in nonmetropolitan territory, either adjacent to the SMSA or elsewhere in the hinterland.

The slow growth or loss of population of central cities, especially those of the North East and North Central regions, is a movement toward decongestion and de-densification that has been under way for a long time, as evident in Table 3-17. Many demographers and urbanologists regard it as a favorable social change, leading to an overall improvement in the quality of urban life. It is also a symptom that a high proportion of the land available for residential land use in the inner city has been consumed, and that further expansion without increasing densities can occur only at the periphery.

Overall comparisons based on aggregate data such as those of Table 3-19 can be very deceiving, however. Some central cities did grow comparatively rapidly between 1970 and 1980, and some metropolitan rings were stagnant along with their central cities. SMSAs located in regions of population expansion tended to grow throughout. Younger and smaller SMSAs also tended to have both central city and ring growth. Only by looking at individual SMSAs and noting the variation among them and explaining this variation in terms of their characteristics and regional contexts can a full explanation of the forces working to determine growth rates of central cities and rings, and hence of the entire SMSA, be developed.

Race-Ethnicity Distribution

Table 3-19 also provides a summary of the distribution of the major race-ethnic groups between metropolitan and nonmetropolitan areas and within SMSAs. Figure 3-10 graphically depicts the metropolitanization of the population by race. All of the minority populations except American Indians are far more concentrated in metropolitan areas than is the white population. Most metropolitanized is the Asian population, followed by the Spanish-origin population and then the black population. Some readers may be surprised at the statistics for the Spanish-origin population, having assumed that a major reason for immigration to the United States from Mexico would be agricultural labor. Those who acquire legal residence settle in larger urban places, most of which are metropolitan areas. Only 12 percent of Spanish-origin and 9 percent of Asian populations live outside SMSAs, as against 27 percent of the white population.

Of those who live in metropolitan areas, the black population is more strongly concentrated within the central cities than the others. The proportion of the SMSA population living in central cities, for each group, was as follows in 1980:

Race-ethnicity	Central city	Ring
Total.	40	60
White.	35	65
Black.	71	29
American Indian. .	43	58
Asian.	51	49
Spanish-origin . .	58	42

The overall race-ethnicity composition of SMSAs, central cities, rings, and nonmetropolitan territory in 1980 was

Table 3-19. Population by Metropolitan-Nonmetropolitan Residence, 1970 and 1980, and by Race and Spanish-Origin: 1980

Residence	1970, total[a]	1980								
		Total		Race					Spanish-origin[b]
		Number	Percent change, 1970-80	White	Black	American Indian, Eskimo, Aleut	Asian and Pacific Islander	Other	
Total	203.3	226.5	11.4	188.4	26.5	1.4	3.5	6.8	14.6
Inside SMSAs	153.7	169.4	10.2	138.1	21.5	0.7	3.2	6.0	12.8
Central cities. . .	67.9	68.0	0.2	47.0	15.3	0.3	1.6	3.7	7.4
Outside central cities.	85.8	101.5	18.2	91.0	6.2	0.4	1.6	2.3	5.4
Outside SMSAs	49.6	57.1	15.1	50.3	5.0	0.7	0.3	0.8	1.8
Percent Distribution									
Total	100.0	100.0	...	100.0	100.0	100.0	100.0	100.0	100.0
Inside SMSAs	75.6	74.8	...	73.3	81.1	49.0	91.4	88.7	87.6
Central cities. . .	33.4	30.0	...	25.0	57.8	21.0	46.3	54.7	50.4
Outside central cities.	42.2	44.8	...	48.3	23.3	28.1	45.0	34.0	37.3
Outside SMSAs	24.4	25.2	...	26.7	18.9	51.0	8.6	11.3	12.4

[a]Includes revisions made since publication of 1970 census reports.

[b]Persons of Spanish-origin may be of any race.

Source: U.S. Bureau of the Census. Statistical Abstract of the United States, 1982-83. Washington, DC: U.S. Government Printing Office, 1982, Table 17.

Race-ethnicity	Percent distribution			
	SMSA total	Central city	Metro ring	Nonmetro total
Total. . . .	100.0	100.0	100.0	100.0
White.	81.5	69.2	89.6	88.1
Black.	12.7	22.5	6.1	8.8
American Indian . . .	0.4	0.4	0.4	1.2
Asian and Pacific. . .	1.9	2.4	1.6	0.5
Other.	3.5	5.5	2.3	1.4
Spanish-origin . . .	7.6	10.9	5.3	3.2

Thus the famed "white flight" of the majority population from the central cities to the metropolitan ring leaves the minority populations concentrated in the central cities, but comprising only a tiny fraction of the population of the ring and of the nonmetropolitan area.

Individual SMSAs

Appendix Table 2, "Population Growth in Individual Standard Metropolitan Statistical Areas: 1960-1980," lists each of the SMSAs recognized in 1980 and provides basic growth information for each. This table, intended to be a reference table for particular places, reports population data for the SMSA total and separately for central city and ring for both 1970 and 1980. Growth rates for 1960-70 and 1970-80 are provided for the SMSA, central city, and metropolitan ring. Finally, a percent rural is reported for the 1980 ring population. From this large volume of data, it is readily apparent that there is great diversity not only from region to region but even between SMSAs in the same state. Hence, knowledge of general tendencies is a poor indicator of what happened in a particular SMSA during the past two decades. This table provides specific indicators of growth for each SMSA.

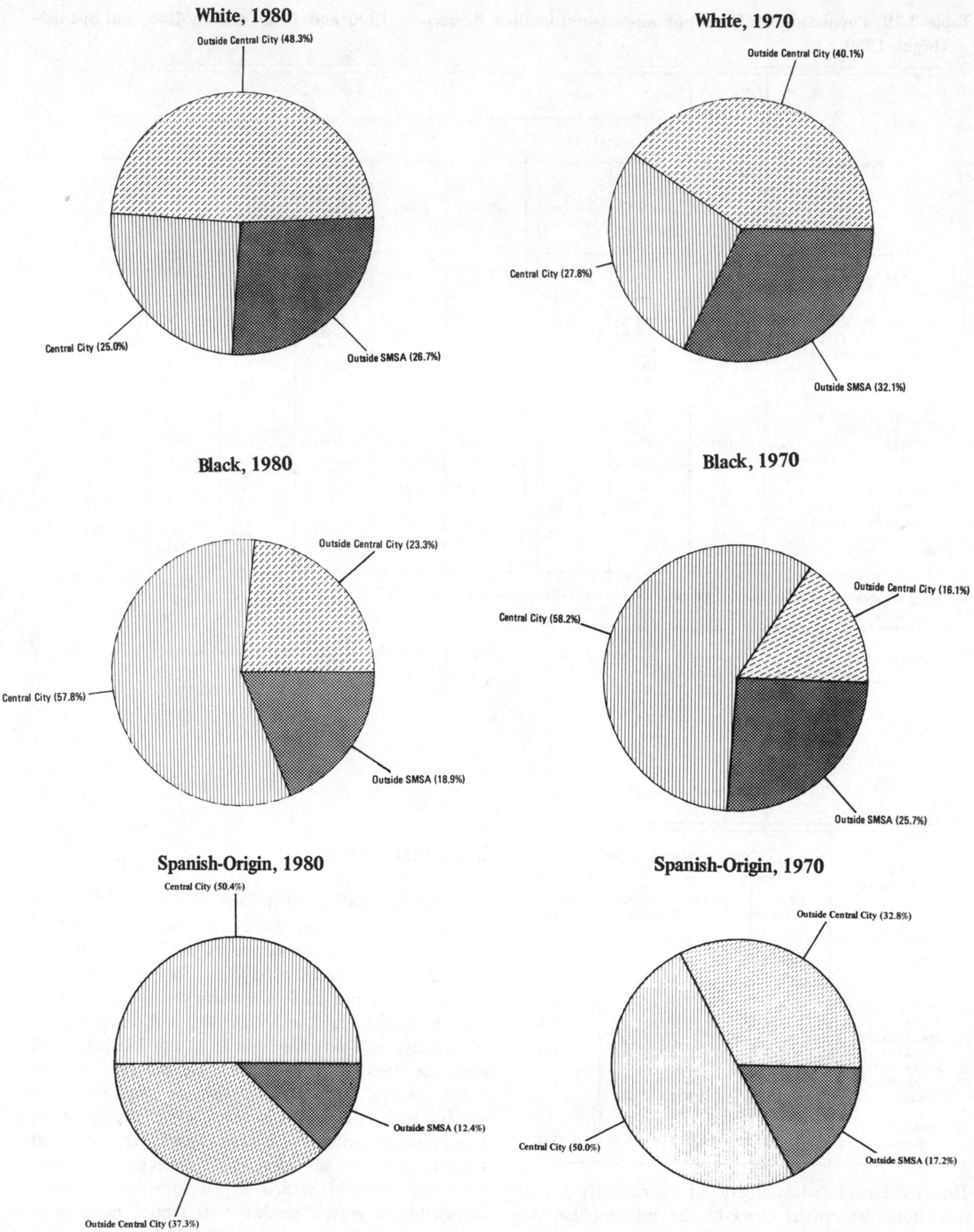

Figure 3-10. Distribution of the Population Among Central City, Metropolitan Ring, and Nonmetropolitan Areas for Race-Ethnic Groups: 1970 and 1980

Composition of Population in Individual SMSAs

Appendix Table 3, "Demographic Characteristics of SMSAs, Central Cities, and Metropolitan Ring: 1980," provides data on race-ethnicity, sex, and age composition of SMSAs, with statistics for central cities and suburban rings. This table contains information for each of the 318 SMSAs recognized at the 1980 census. Like Appendix Table 2, it is a reference table to provide information about each SMSA and its components.

Counties and County Equivalents

Counties are important administrative units, and the U.S. Census of Population provides a substantial amount of population data for each of them. They are highly useful for demographic analysis for subdividing the large nonmetropolitan population in order to study internal variation within a state or region. Because there are more than 3,100 counties, it is beyond the scope of this book to provide data for them or to discuss intercounty variation. Readers interested in population distribution by counties should consult the state volumes for each decennial census. In addition, the U.S. Bureau of the Census periodically issues a summary volume entitled *City and County Data Book,* which provides data on population size and composition for each of the larger cities and for counties.

In some states there are no county units. Working with local organizations, the U.S. Census Bureau has delimited county-equivalent areas.

Census Tracts, City Blocks, and County Subdivisions

For many purposes, all of the areal units discussed in the preceding sections are too large. Instead of talking about whole states, whole metropolitan areas, whole central cities or metropolitan rings, or whole counties, the researcher will want information about *neighborhoods,* or small segments of the population. This branch of population work is sometimes called "microdemography." It is known that within every SMSA (and within central cities and rings), there is great internal diversity. Because of segregation (self-imposed or imposed by socioeconomic processes), neighborhoods tend to contain persons with similar socioeconomic, racial, ethnic, family, and other characteristics. Each neighborhood has distinctive sources of employment, housing stock, and locational characteristics within the broader community.

Census Tracts

The U.S. Bureau of the Census provides data for subparts of urban areas, called "census tracts." A census tract has an average of about 4,000 residents. The tracts are delimited by local persons who desire to have the tract statistics produced, according to specifications laid down by the Census. Hence they reflect the structure of the metropolis as viewed by those most familiar with it. For 1970 and 1980 the entire territory of the SMSAs was tracted. Thus, a typical SMSA with 250,000 population would have between 600 and 750 tracts. With such data for small areas, place-to-place variations can be mapped, correlated, and analyzed for causes and implications. Census tract reports provide printed data for each tract; in addition, the data are available on computer tape.

Block Data

For some purposes, even census tracts are too large—especially for housing studies. In larger and built-up areas with a street pattern, the Census Bureau publishes data for individual blocks. These data are very simple, providing only a count of population and a very few facts about composition (sex, race-ethnicity, income, and broad age groups). The block data are available either as publications or on tape.

Data for subdivisions of counties are available for territories outside SMSAs and not tracted. Limited amounts of summary data for individual urban places, for townships, or analogous units are published in decennial census volumes. More detailed information can be obtained from computer tapes if not published.

Population Distribution Since the 1980 Census

Once each year the Bureau of the Census prepares estimates of the population of each state as of July 1 of that year, using special demographic procedures. It also uses data from its Current Population Surveys to obtain indications of changes in population distribution since the last census. By consulting the most recent releases in the *Current Population Reports* (Series P-25), a reader can update the materials provided above for 1980 and before. This information for the period 1980-83, derived from these sources, is summarized by state in Table 3-20 (right-hand column).

Table 3-20. Projections of the Resident Population of Regions, Divisions, and States: 1980-2000

Region, division, and state	Population projections		Percent change		Components 1980-90		Components 1990-2000		Percent change 1980-83
	1990	2000	1980-90	1990-2000	Natural increase	Net migration	Natural increase	Net migration	
United States	249,203,000	267,461,600	9.72	7.33	17,132,400	8,541,700	14,413,300	11,283,700	3.3
Northeast region	48,423,300	46,400,600	-1.66	-4.18	1,882,300	-1,970,400	1,072,800	-1,797,400	0.8
New England	12,733,100	12,775,200	2.90	0.33	507,100	55,400	313,900	93,900	1.1
Middle Atlantic	35,690,200	33,625,400	-3.19	-5.79	1,375,200	-2,025,800	758,900	-1,891,300	0.7
North Central region	60,265,400	59,714,000	2.11	-0.91	4,234,000	-2,112,300	3,250,800	-2,132,100	0.1
East North Central	42,371,800	41,646,600	1.39	-1.71	3,018,700	-1,828,100	2,268,500	-1,834,600	-0.4
West North Central	17,893,600	18,067,300	2.85	0.97	1,215,300	-284,200	982,300	-297,500	1.4
South region	87,594,200	98,827,800	15.92	12.82	6,239,100	6,969,500	5,329,300	8,584,900	5.5
South Atlantic	43,144,400	48,974,800	16.51	13.51	2,328,800	4,378,400	1,563,500	5,591,300	5.0
East South Central	16,121,300	17,174,000	9.62	6.53	1,165,200	457,700	992,100	521,500	1.9
West South Central	28,328,500	32,679,100	18.90	15.36	2,745,100	2,133,400	2,773,600	2,472,100	8.6
West region	52,920,200	62,519,200	22.20	18.14	4,777,000	5,654,900	4,760,400	6,628,300	6.5
Mountain	15,404,100	20,139,900	34.96	30.74	1,690,200	2,536,500	1,905,100	3,410,500	8.4
Pacific	37,516,100	42,379,300	17.63	12.96	3,086,800	3,118,400	2,855,300	3,217,800	5.8
New England									
Maine	1,229,400	1,308,000	9.05	6.39	65,000	56,600	53,600	62,700	1.9
New Hampshire	1,138,800	1,363,500	23.37	19.74	74,800	159,000	75,900	189,600	4.1
Vermont	574,600	625,000	12.03	8.78	39.100	31,700	34,100	34,500	2.7
Massachusetts	5,703,900	5,490,400	-0.77	-3.71	193,200	-144,800	97,200	-153,000	0.5
Rhode Island	950,800	925,800	0.19	-2.62	29,300	-12,000	11,800	-10,500	0.9
Connecticut	3,135,600	3,062,400	0.70	-2.34	105,700	-35,100	42,200	-29,400	1.0
Middle Atlantic									
New York	16,456,700	14,990,200	-6.47	-8.91	673,200	-1,578,800	432,000	-1,485,300	0.6
New Jersey	7,513,100	7,427,600	1.81	-1.14	302,800	-58,300	174,600	-55,000	1.4
Pennsylvania	11,720,400	11,207,600	-1.43	-4.37	399,200	-388,700	152,300	-351,000	0.3
East North Central									
Ohio	10,763,100	10,356,800	-0.60	-3.78	706,400	-614,000	477,900	-594,900	-0.5
Indiana	5,679,300	5,679,200	3.43	-0.00	412,500	-157,800	316,700	-157,100	-0.2
Illinois	11,502,500	11,187,500	0.45	-2.74	872,700	-661,400	681,700	-690,000	0.5
Michigan	9,394,300	9,207,600	1.16	-1.99	686,900	-445,800	516,100	-447,800	-2.1
Wisconsin	5,032,700	5,215,500	6.66	3.63	340,200	50,900	276,100	56,100	1.0
West North Central									
Minnesota	4,358,400	4,489,400	6.47	3.12	322,500	10,200	266,600	-700	1.7
Iowa	2,983,300	2,972,100	2.13	-0.38	187,100	-78,800	152,700	-78,400	-0.3
Missouri	5,076,800	5,080,000	2.99	0.06	298,000	-78,000	221,300	-77,400	1.1
North Dakota	678,400	682,000	3.60	0.53	57,500	-23,100	48,100	-25,000	4.3
South Dakota	698,500	687,000	0.90	-1.56	62,800	-46,300	52,200	-43,800	1.3
Nebraska	1,639,800	1,661,900	4.16	1.35	119,100	-29,300	101,800	-32,800	1.7
Kansas	2,463,400	2,494,400	3.96	1.26	168,300	-38,900	139,600	-39,400	2.6

Table 3-20. Projections of the Resident Population of Regions, Divisions, and States: 1980-2000—continued

Region, division, and state	Population Projections		Percent change		Components 1980-90		Components 1990-2000		Percent change 1980-83
	1990	2000	1980-90	1990-2000	Natural increase	Net migration	Natural increase	Net migration	
South Atlantic									
Delaware.	629,800	638,200	5.51	1.34	44,400	-2,500	28,200	-2,500	1.9
Maryland.	4,491,100	4,581,900	6.24	2.02	259,800	63.900	161,400	50,400	2.1
District of Columbia. .	501,500	376,500	-21.44	-24.94	19,500	-152,500	7,800	-125,000	-2.4
Virginia.	5,960,900	6,389,400	11.20	7.19	370,300	312,100	278,300	320,400	3.8
West Virginia	2,037,400	2,067,700	4.21	1.48	112,600	1,100	86,800	2,300	0.8
North Carolina.	6,473,400	6,867,800	9.90	6.09	364,200	305,500	231,400	346,300	3.4
South Carolina.	3,559,600	3,907,100	13.75	9.76	291,100	181,000	231,000	216,400	4.5
Georgia	6,174,600	6,708,200	12.64	8.64	520,100	243,400	443,900	262,000	4.9
Florida	13,316,000	17,438,000	36.55	30.76	346,800	3,426,400	94,700	4,521,000	9.6
East South Central									
Kentucky.	4,073,500	4,399,900	10.91	8.01	295,200	65,500	267,400	183,300	1.5
Tennessee	5,072,600	5,419,600	10.20	6.84	305,300	233,600	245,100	250,100	2.1
Alabama	4,213,800	4,415,300	8.01	4.78	298,800	64,700	240,000	77,100	1.7
Mississippi	2,761,400	2,939,200	9.55	6.44	265,900	-6,100	239,600	11,000	2.6
West South Central									
Arkansas.	2,579,800	2,835,400	12.59	9.91	157,600	164,800	136,700	195,800	1.8
Louisiana	4,747,000	5,159,800	12.49	8.69	509,600	70,000	466,800	78,300	5.5
Oklahoma.	3,503,400	3,944,500	15.48	12.59	254,800	264,600	249,400	301,700	9.0
Texas	17,498,200	20,379,400	22.54	18.52	1,823,100	1,634,000	1,920,800	1,896,300	10.5
Mountain									
Montana	888,400	963,000	12.55	8.39	77,900	35,400	68,500	33,700	3.8
Idaho	1,213,800	1,512,200	28.02	24.59	148,800	134,500	178,800	163,100	4.8
Wyoming	701,300	1,002,200	48.26	42.90	89,800	149,500	121,100	208,900	9.5
Colorado.	3,755,100	4,656,600	29.54	24.01	336,700	580,700	355,100	681,000	8.6
New Mexico.	1,536,000	1,727,300	17.68	12.45	177,500	76,600	157,500	83,100	7.4
Arizona	3,993,700	5,582,500	46.46	39.78	359,300	972,400	376,900	1,374,900	9.0
Utah.	2,040,300	2,777,400	38.73	36.13	392,800	202,000	529,900	286,100	10.8
Nevada.	1,275,400	1,918,800	59.08	50.44	107,400	385,400	117,300	579,700	11.3
Pacific									
Washington.	5,011,800	5,832,500	20.98	16.37	369,500	578,500	344,700	643,900	4.1
Oregon.	3,318,600	4,025,300	25.67	21.30	232,900	497,800	238,600	584,800	1.1
California.	27,525,600	30,613,100	15.95	11.22	2,272,200	1,938,900	2,053,800	1,905,200	6.4
Alaska.	522,100	630,700	29.66	20.80	89,100	37,500	98,000	27,600	19.2
Hawaii.	1,138,000	1,277,700	17.49	12.27	123,100	65,700	120,200	56,300	6.1

Note: Percent changes extend from July 1 to July 1 and are based on the population at the beginning of the interval.

Source: U.S. Bureau of the Census. "Estimates of the Population of States, by Age, July 1, 1981 to 1983" and "Provisional Projections of the Population of States, by Age and Sex: 1980-2000." Current Population Reports (Series P-25, nos. 951 and 937). Washington, DC: U.S. Government Printing Office, 1984 and 1983.

States

Between 1980 and 1983 the population increased from 226.4 to 233.9 million, or by 7.4 million persons (3.3 percent). More than one-half of this growth occurred in three states: Florida, California, and Texas. Following are some rankings of growth:

Faster growing		Slower growing	
Alaska.	19.2	D. of Columbia .	-2.4
Nevada.	11.3	Michigan	-2.1
Utah.	10.8	Ohio	-0.5
Texas	10.5	Iowa	-0.3
Florida	9.6	Indiana.	-0.2
Wyoming	9.5	Pennsylvania . .	0.3
Oklahoma.	9.0	Illinois	0.5
Arizona	9.0	Massachusetts. .	0.5
Colorado.	8.6	New York	0.6
New Mexico. . . .	7.4	West Virginia. .	0.8
California. . . .	6.4	Rhode Island . .	0.9
Hawaii.	6.1	Connecticut. . .	1.0
Louisiana	5.5	Missouri	1.1
Georgia	4.9	Oregon	1.1
Idaho	4.8	South Dakota . .	1.3
South Carolina. .	4.5	New Jersey . . .	1.4
North Dakota. . .	4.3	Kentucky	1.5
New Hampshire . .	4.1	Alabama.	1.7
Washington . . .	4.1	Minnesota. . . .	1.7
		Nebraska	1.7
		Arkansas	1.8
		Maine.	1.9
		Delaware	1.9
		Tennessee. . . .	2.1
		Maryland	2.1

All of the faster-growing states were also faster-growing in the 1970-80 decade, but some that previously were fast growing fell out of that position or sank much lower during that period. Examples are Oregon, Washington, Kentucky, Tennessee, Maryland, Alabama, Mississippi, and Arkansas; even California and Florida are lower in the list of faster growing states. Oklahoma, which previously was a slow-growing state, stands higher in the list than either of them. All of the fast-growing states except New Hampshire and North Dakota are in either the South or the West.

The slow growth of the Northeast and North Central regions is a continuation of trends from the previous decade, perhaps accentuated in Michigan, Ohio, and Indiana by the economic recession in heavy industry.

Projection of the Future Population of States

Taking into account recent trends, the Bureau of the Census has prepared projections to the year 2000 of the population of each state. These projections are reported in Table 3-20. The implied rates of growth for each decade and estimated components of change for the 1980-90 and 1990-2000 periods are also reported. In general the pattern of projection (reported in column 1 of this table) is similar to 1970-80 trends. Some of the estimated trends since 1980 are not consistent with the projections. (The current estimates and the projections are prepared independently, with the current estimates being more precise.) Examples are New York and Pennsylvania, which since 1980 are not losing population as predicted, and Michigan, Indiana, and Iowa, which are losing population despite predictions to the contrary. Washington and Oregon are growing more slowly than the projections forecast, and Louisiana and Oklahoma are growing faster than predicted. However, the 1980-83 trends may represent temporary distortions caused by economic recession. Decennial projections could still materialize. The substantial regional change that these projections call for is shown by the following summary of regional distribution:

Region	Year		
	1980	1990	2000
Total	100.0	100.0	100.0
Northeast	21.7	19.4	17.4
North Central	26.0	24.2	22.3
South	33.3	35.2	37.0
West	19.1	21.2	23.4

The share of the population residing in the South and West combined is expected to jump from 51 percent to 60 percent. It is predicted that the Northeast and North Central regions each will lose about 4 percent of the nation's population. As Table 3-20 shows, most of this change is caused by net migration. Many states are expected to lose population by net migration but are kept from doing so by positive natural increases. Those states that truly grow rapidly are the ones combining large natural increases with large net immigration.

The Farm Population

One of the miracles of industrialization is the ability of developed nations to feed their population and grow agricultural industrial products with only a small fraction of their population devoted to farming.[4] The number of persons living on farms in rural areas of the United States was estimated to be 5,620,000 for April

1982. Only 2.4 percent of the nation's total population is farm population. In 1920, 30.2 percent of the nation's population lived on farms. By 1950 this proportion had fallen to 15.3 percent, and at the 1980 census it was 2.7 percent. This downward trend, during a time of rapid population growth, has been made possible by modern technology of agroindustry. Figure 3-11 charts this decline. Between 1940 and 1960 the descent was very rapid. During the two decades since 1960, the descent has been more gradual.

At one time the rural farm population formed most of the rural population, and the Bureau of the Census carried it as a principal areal classification in its decennial census reports. It is now such a small part of the total population that it receives only secondary attention in census population tabulations. As farms have become larger, more highly mechanized, and more productive per person engaged, the demographic significance of the farm population has fallen far below the economic significance of the agricultural industry it maintains.

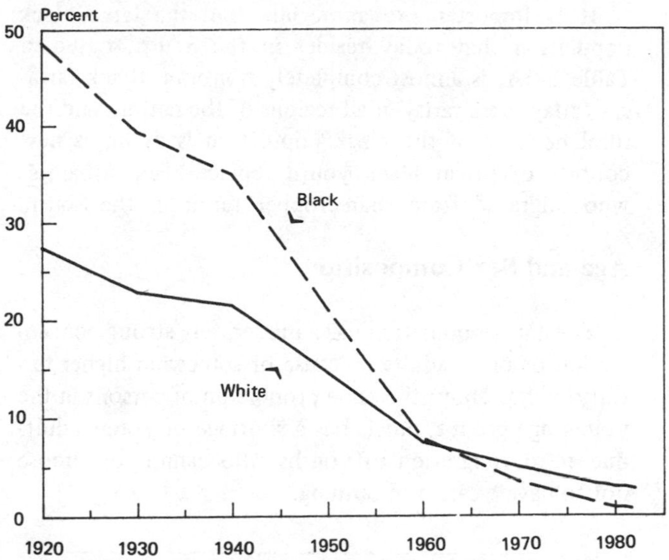

Figure 3-11. Decline in the Farm Population, by Race: 1920-82

Regional Distribution

In 1982 the percent distribution of the farm population was:

Region	Percent distribution, 1982: Farm population	Total population
Total.	100.0	100.0
Northeast.	7.5	21.4
North Central. . .	44.8	25.5
South.	34.8	33.7
West	13.0	19.4

Thus the farm population is concentrated in the North Central region. The South, which until about 1965 contained a higher proportion of the farm population than any other region, lost large quantities through outmigration to the North and West between 1920 and 1960; now it has only its proportionate share. Especially the Northeast but also the West have deficits of farm population in comparison to the total population.

Metropolitan-Nonmetropolitan Distribution

Farm population is overwhelmingly nonmetropolitan in its distribution; only 18 percent lived inside SMSAs in 1982, as against 68 percent of the total population. Yet despite their concencentration there, even in nonmetropolitan areas the farm population is a minority—only 6.2 percent of the total nonmetropolitan population.

Race Composition

The farm population has an excess of white and a deficit of black and Spanish-origin residents, in comparison with the total population:

Race	Farm population	Total population
White.	95.9	85.6
Black.	3.2	11.8
Spanish-origin . .	2.3	6.3

Until 1950 a higher proportion of the black than of the white population lived on farms. Migration from farms to cities, especially from the South to other regions, which has continued unrelentingly from World War I to the present, was especially severe during the 1940-60 decades (see Figure 3-11). The reduction of the traditional system of sharecropping was particularly important in the urbanization of the black population and its transfer to central cities of all regions. Even in 1982, after much outmigration, the black population that remains on farms is much less economically secure than the white farm population, and future years will possibly see its virtual elimination.

It is important to appreciate that the large black population that today resides in the South, noted in Table 3-2A, is almost completely nonfarm. Black farmers today are a rarity in all regions of the nation, and the rural heritage of the black population is dying as new cohorts of urban black youth replace black urbanites who migrated from sharecropper farms in the South.

Age and Sex Composition

The farm population has a moderately strong concentration of older adults. Because of somewhat higher fertility, it has about the same proportion of persons in the young age groups, but it has a shortage of young adults due to outmigration of youths who cannot or choose not to have a career in farming.

Age	Farm population	Nonfarm population
Total.	100.0	100.0
Under 20 years	31.2	31.1
20 to 34 years	18.6	26.3
35 to 44 years	11.9	12.1
45 to 54 years	12.1	9.8
55 to 64 years	13.1	9.5
65 years and over. . .	13.0	11.1

In 1940 and before the farm population was a young population, with high proportions of the population in ages under thirty-five. Heavy outmigration in the 1940-60 decades, and continued more moderate migration from 1960 to the present, created the current age structure. However, the proportion of the population aged sixty-five and over is relatively small, given the long history of outmigration. This results from the tendency of farm couples who retire to move to a nonfarm residence. Even if they remain in the same residence, the mere act of cessation of farming causes them to be reclassified from farm to nonfarm.

Because farming provides less employment to women (except as wives of farmers) than to men, there is a tendency for the sex ratio to be higher in the farm population than in the general population. In 1982 it was 108, as against 93 for the nonfarm population. Sex ratios are high even in the older age groups fifty-five and older, where women tend to outnumber men because of differential mortality. Women who lose a spouse through widowhood or divorce tend to migrate to nonfarm residences or to cease farming even if they remain in the same house.

Other Characteristics

Farm populations differ significantly from the nonfarm populations in most social and economic characteristics. These will be noted in subsequent chapters dealing with such characteristics.

Conclusion

Together, the five systems of areal subdivision described in this chapter—by states, divisions, and regions; by urban and rural residence; by metropolitan and nonmetropolitan areas; by counties and county equivalents; and by census tracts, blocks, and enumeration districts—are able to meet a wide variety of needs for population information for the study of spatial distribution and composition. The materials of this chapter have synthesized this field and sketched the broad outlines. Each of the subsequent chapters will return to the subject of geographical distribution in order to show the internal patterns that form within the grand totals for the nation. The recent and projected trends in distribution are a context in which all other changes have and will take place.

Notes

1. Because data for Spanish origin were collected only for a five-percent sample in 1970 and the enumeration procedure was not identical with 1980, the distributional and compositional changes indicated by the statistics must be interpreted cautiously.

2. Donald J. Bogue. *The Growth of Standard Metropolitan Areas: 1900-1950, With an Explanatory Analysis of Urbanized Areas.* Washington, DC: U.S. Government Printing Office, 1953. This monograph presents statistics for each standard metropolitan area, its central city, and the urban and rural parts of its ring for each decade from 1900 to 1950.

3. Calvin L. Beale is widely credited for having been the first demographer to note this shift as the shift to nonmetropolitan growth.

4. The materials summarized below have been taken from U.S. Bureau of the Census. "Farm Population of the United States: 1982." *Current Population Reports* (Series P-27, no. 56). Washington, DC: U.S. Government Printing Office, 1984. This report is based on tabulations and estimates prepared jointly by the U.S. Department of Agriculture Research Service and the Bureau of the Census.

Bibliography

Beale, Calvin L. *The Revival of Population Growth in Nonmetropolitan America.* Washington, DC: U.S. Department of Agriculture, 1975.

Beale, Calvin, L., and Fugitt, Glenn V. "The New Pattern of Nonmetropolitan Population Change." In *Social Demography*, edited by Karl E. Taeuber, Larry Bumpass, and James A. Sweet. New York: Academic Press, 1978.

Berry, B.J.L. "Urbanization and Counterurbanization in the United States." *American Academy of Political and Social Science Annual* 451 (1980):13-20.

Berry, Brian J.L., and Dahmann, Donald C. "Population Redistribution in the United States in the 1970s." *Population and Development Review* 3 (1977): 443-71.

Beyers, W.B. "Contemporary Trends in the Regional Economic Development of the United States." *Professional Geographer* 31 (1979):33-44.

Bogue, Donald J. *Principles of Demography.* (Chapter 15, "Population Distribution and Urban-Rural Residence.") New York: John Wiley and Sons, 1969.

Boone, M.S. "Introduction: Metropolitan Ethnography." *Anthropological Quarterly* 54 (1981):55-9.

Coughlin, R.E. "Farming on the Urban Fringe: Where Are the Farmlands Going?" *Environment* 22 (1980): 33-42.

Farley, Reynolds. "Residential Segregation in Urbanized Areas of the United States in 1970: An Analysis of Social Class and Racial Differences." *Demography* 14 (1977):497-518.

Fisher, J.S., and Mitchelson, R.L. "Forces of Change in the American Settlement Pattern." *Geographical Review* 71 (1981):298-310.

Frisbie, W.P., and Poston, D.L. "Components of Sustenance Organization and Nonmetropolitan Population Changes: A Human Ecological Investigation." *American Sociological Review* 40 (1975):773-84.

Fugitt, G.V., and Kasarda, J.D. "Community Structure in Response to Population Growth and Decline: A Study in Ecological Organization." *American Sociological Review* 46 (1981):600-15.

Gans, H.J. et al. "State of the Nation's Cities" (symposium). *Urban Affairs Quarterly* 18 (1982):163-280.

Haren, Claude C., and Holling, Ronald W. "Industrial Development in Nonmetropolitan America: A Locational Perspective." In *Nonmetropolitan Industrialization*, edited by Richard E. Lonsdale and H.L. Seyler. Washington, DC: V.H. Winston and Sons, 1979.

Hawley, Amos H. *Urban Society: An Ecological Approach.* New York: Ronald Press, 1971.

Hawley, Amos H., and Rock, V.P. (eds.). *Metropolitan America in Contemporary Perspective.* New York: John Wiley and Sons, 1975.

Kasarda, J.D. "Implications of Contemporary Redistribution Trends for National Urban Policy." *Social Science Quarterly* 61 (1980):373-400.

Kasarda, John. "The Theory of Ecological Expansion: An Empirical Test." *Social Forces* 51 (1972).

Laconte, P. (ed.). "Changing Cities: A Challenge to Planning" (symposium). *American Academy of Political and Social Science Annual* 451 (1980):1-151.

Lichter, D.T., and Fuguitt, G.V. "Transition to Nonmetropolitan Population Deconcentration." *Demography* 19 (1982):211-21.

Littman, Mark S. "Social and Economic Characteristics of the Metropolitan and Nonmetropolitan Population: 1977-1970." *Current Population Reports, Special Studies* (Series P-23, no. 71). Washington, DC: U.S. Government Printing Office, 1978.

Long, Larry, and Diane DeAre. "Repopulating the Countryside: a 1980 Census Trend." *Science* 217 (1982):1111-1116.

Massey, D.S. "Effects of Socioeconomic Factors on the Residential Segregation of Blacks and Spanish-Americans in U.S. Urbanized Areas." *American Sociological Review* 44 (1979):1015-22.

Massey, D.S. "Residential Segregation of Spanish-Americans in United States Urbanized Areas." *Demography* 16 (1979):553-63.

McCarthy, Kevin F., and Morrison, Peter A. *The Changing Demographic and Economic Structure of Nonmetropolitan Areas in the United States.* Santa Monica, CA: Rand Corporation, 1979.

McKenzie, R.B. "Myths of Sunbelt and Frostbelt." *Policy Review* 20 (1982):103-14.

McWorter, G. "Racism and the Numbers Game: Black People and the 1980 Census." *Black Scholar* 11 (1980):61-71.

Morrison, Peter A. *Emerging Public Concerns Over U.S. Population Movements in an Era of Slowing Growth.* Santa Monica, CA: Rand Corporation, 1977.

Population Reference Bureau (Long, Larry). "Population Redistribution in the U.S.: Issues for the 1980s." *Occasional Papers in Population Trends and Public Policy,* March, 1983.

Population Reference Bureau. "Population Distribution and Internal Migration." *Population Bulletin* 37 (1982):24-9.

Schnore, Leo F. "The Socioeconomic Status of Cities and Suburbs." *American Sociological Review* 28 (1963):79-85.

Scott, A.J. "Production System Dynamics and Metropolitan Development." *Association of American Geographers Annual* 72 (1982): 185-200.

Simmie, J.M. "Beyond the Industrial City?" *American Planning Association Journal* 49 (1983):59-76.

Sly, D.F. et al. (eds.). "Metropolitan and Regional Change in the United States" (symposium). *Social Science Quarterly* 61 (1980):369-675.

Sly, D.F., and Tayman, J. "Metropolitan Morphology and Population Mobility: The Theory of Ecological Expansion Reexamined." *American Journal of Sociology* 86 (1980):119-38.

South, S.J., and Poston, D.L. "U.S. Metropolitan System: Regional Change, 1950-1970." *Urban Affairs Quarterly* 18 (1982):187-206.

Sternlieb, G., and Hughes, J.W. "New Regional and Metropolitan Realities of America." *American Institute of Planning Journal* 43 (1977):227-41.

Taeuber, Irene B., and Taeuber, Conrad. *People of the United States in the 20th Century.* (Chapter 1, "Increase, Expansion, Concentration," and Chapter 2, "Urbanization.") Washington, DC: U.S. Bureau of the Census, 1971.

Theodorson, George A. *Urban Patterns: Studies in Human Ecology.* Pennsylvania: Pennsylvania State Press, 1982.

Tolley, G.S. et al. "Urban Growth Question." *Law and Contemporary Problems* 43 (1979):211-38.

U.S. Bureau of the Census. "Farm Population of the United States: 1982." *Current Population Reports* (Series P-27, no. 56). Washington, DC: U.S. Government Printing Office, 1984.

_____ (Long, John F.). *Population Deconcentration in the United States.* Washington, DC: U.S. Government Printing Office, 1981.

_____ (Long, Larry, and DeAre, Diane). *The Economic Base of Recent Population Growth in Nonmetropolitan Settings.* Washington, DC: Center for Demographic Studies, 1982.

_____. "Projections of the Population of States, by Age and Sex: 1980 to 2000." *Current Population Reports* (Series P-25, no. 937). Washington, DC: U.S. Government Printing Office, 1983.

_____. "Projections of the Population of the United States, by Age, Sex, and Race: 1983-2080." *Current Population Reports* (Series P-25, no. 952). Washington, DC: U.S. Government Printing Office, 1984.

U.S. Department of Agriculture, Economic Research Service, and the U.S. Bureau of the Census. "Farm Population of the United States: 1982." *Current Population Reports* (Series P-27, no. 56). Washington, DC: U.S. Government Printing Office, 1984.

Vining, D.R. Jr., and Kontuly, T. "Population Dispersal from Major Metropolitan Regions: An International Comparison." *International Regional Science Review* 3 (1978):49-73.

Williams, James D., and Sofranko, Andrew J. "Motivations for the Immigration Component of Population Turnaround in Nonmetropolitan Areas." *Demography* 16 (1979):239-55.

Windsor, D. "Critique of *The Costs of Sprawl.*" *American Planning Association Journal* 45 (1979):279-92.

Zimmer, Basil G. "The Metropolitan Community: Changing Spatial Orientation of Residents?" Paper presented at Population Association of America Conference, May, 1983.

Zuiches, James J. "Residential Preferences in the United States." In *Metropolitan America in Transition*, edited by Amos H. Hawley and Sara Mills Mazie. Chapel Hill, NC: University of North Carolina Press, 1981.

Chapter 4

Marriage, Divorce, and Marital Status

Four marital statuses are enumerated and reported by the U.S. Bureau of the Census: single, married, divorced, and widowed.[1] Arrival at each of these statuses represents a major life cycle transition. For the great majority of the population, marriage (transition from bachelorhood to the married state) signals the formation of a family and anticipation of having children. Divorce or death of a spouse signals the dissolution of that particular family or a drastic change in its structure. Few events in the life cycle require more extensive changes and adjustments in activities, responsibilities, and living habits (or cause greater alterations in attitudes, reranking of values, and alterations of outlook on life) than do marriage, divorce, and death of spouse. Marriage and divorce are considered so important that they are made the occasion for specified social-legal ceremonies. These events are registered, tabulated statistically, and reported as a part of the demographic "vital statistics." Socially and demographically, marriage is a validation of the privilege of childbearing with full social approval. To be sure, a significant and growing proportion of children are being born out of wedlock (see Chapter 6), and a much greater proportion are conceived out of wedlock. Nevertheless, the belief that children need and deserve to have both a father and a mother living together and cooperating in their upbringing seems to be almost universally endorsed, backed by the full force of custom, tradition, and law, despite the exceptions. Consequently divorce (which has also become more common) has come to be viewed with concern for child welfare as well as for the welfare of the adults involved.

Marriage and divorce may be studied from two points of view: statically as a classification into marital status categories at points in time, and *dynamically* as rates at which the processes of marriage, divorce, and widowhood are occurring per unit of time. The first section of this chapter begins with a static approach to show the marital status composition of the population now and as it has been in the past.[2] The second section will then take up the study of marriage as a dynamic process of family formation, and the third section will deal with divorce as a dynamic process of marriage dissolution. Sections two and three will reveal the forces at work that explain the prevalence of the particular marital statuses of "married" and "divorced." Later, Chapter 5 will discuss the processes that determine the prevalence of the "widowed" status. Because the divorced and widowed statuses can be revoked by remarriage, the study of the dynamic processes can be confusing unless preceded by a comprehension of long-term trends in the marital status composition.

Definitions

Marital Status. The data on marital status were derived from answers to question 6, which was asked of all persons (see Technical Appendix, Chapter 1). A similar question is asked in the Current Population Survey reports. The marital status classification refers to the status at the time of enumeration. Persons classified as "Now married" include those who have been married only once and have never been widowed or divorced as well as those currently married persons who remarried after having been widowed or divorced. Persons reported as separated are those living apart because of marital discord, with or without a legal separation. Persons in common-law marriage are classified as now married, persons whose only marriage had been annulled are classified as never married, and persons under fifteen years old are classified as never married. All persons classified as never married are shown as "single." When marital status was not reported it was allocated according to the relationship to householder and sex and age of that person.

MARRIAGE RATES

Crude Marriage Rate (CMR). Number of marriages in a year per 1,000 population as of the midpoint of that year.

General Marriage Rate (GMR). Number of marriages in a year per 1,000 females aged fifteen and over as of the midpoint of that year.

General Nuptiality Rate (GNR). Number of marriages per 1,000 unmarried females aged 15-44 as of the midpoint of that year.

Age-Specific Nuptiality Rate. Number of marriages to women of a given age per 1,000 unmarried females of the same age as of the midpoint of that year. (May be computed also for males.)

First Marriage Rate. Number of first marriages per 1,000 never-married women as of the midpoint of that year. (May be computed on age-specific basis, and also for males.)

Remarriage Rate (RMR). Number of marriages of previously married persons per 1,000 widowed or divorced population as of the midpoint of that year.

Age-Specific Remarriage Rate. Number of remarriages to previously married women of a given age per 1,000 widowed or divorced women of the same age as of the midpoint of that year. (May be computed also for males.)

DIVORCE RATES

Crude Divorce Rate. Number of divorces per 1,000 population as of the midpoint of that year.

General Divorce Rate (GDR). Number of divorces per 1,000 married women (aged fifteen and over) as of the midpoint of that year.

Marital Status

Information about the marital status of the population has been collected and reported for each decennial census since 1890. Annual estimates for years since 1947 are available from the Current Population Survey of the Census Bureau. The question "Is he now married, widowed, divorced, separated, or has he never been married?" evokes the response that the census tabulates. (For details, see "marital status" in the Definition Box.)

Since marital status is self-reported (or reported for members of the household), it is possible that some mature or elderly never married persons (especially those with children) may be classed as divorced or widowed and that some divorced or widowed persons may be classed as single. Demographers frequently refer to the "ever married" population. This is the population that has been married at some time in its life. It is equal to the sum of the married, widowed, separated, and divorced, or to the total population minus the single (never married) population.

Overview

Table 4-1 summarizes the census data since 1890 for marital status, and Figure 4-1 illustrates the change that has occurred. The third and fourth columns of the table shows that there was a steady decrease during the sixty-five years from 1890 to 1955 in the proportion of the population that was single, and a corresponding increase in the proportions married and ever married. In 1890, 44 percent of males and 34 percent of females fourteen years of age or older were single. This higher prevalence of bachelorhood was caused by delayed marriages and high proportions never marrying. During the half-century to 1940 there was a slow decline in the proportion single, as marriage became more nearly universal and occurred at earlier ages.

For all recent censuses, men tend to be single (never married) in greater proportions than women. The reason for this is that women tend to marry about 2.5 years younger than men. Women tend to be widowed or divorced in greater proportions than men. This is caused by their greater longevity and by the greater tendency for men with broken marriages to remarry.

Not as widely publicized as the "baby boom" of the 1940s to the 1960s was the "marriage boom" that accompanied it. Beginning suddenly in the early 1940s, marriage became tremendously popular at all ages, and the proportion of the population single shrank dramatically. This marriage boom was a sudden acceleration of the long-term downward trend in the proportion of single (never married) adults described above. It lasted until about 1957, at which time only about 24 percent of males and 18 percent of females were classed as single—far below the proportions of 1890. This was followed by a decade (1957-1967) of plateau, during which the proportion of the population classified as never married remained smaller than at any time in the nation's history. Figure 4-1 illustrates the effect of the marriage boom in shrinking the single population and expanding the "married" category.

By 1960 the proportion of single was clearly rising again, reversing the marriage boom. About 1970 the tendency toward bachelorhood accelerated until by 1980 the proportions single were approximately those that existed in the early 1940s, before the marriage boom began. Many persons today view these recent changes with alarm, as if marriage and the family were losing their social and moral attractiveness and force. Table 4-1 and Figure 4-1 show that in 1980 and since, the institution of marriage is still more prevalent than in 1890 by a considerable margin.

Table 4-1. Marital Status of the Population and Estimated Median Age at First Marriage: United States, 1890-1983

Year	Median age at first marriage		Percent distribution by marital status							
			Single		Married		Widowed		Divorced	
	Male	Female	Male	Female	Male	Female	Male	Female	Male	Female
1983	25.4	22.8	30.0	22.9	62.3	57.9	2.3	11.7	5.4	7.5
1982	25.2	22.5	29.7	22.5	62.6	58.3	2.2	11.7	5.5	7.5
1981	24.8	22.3	29.4	22.5	63.0	58.5	2.3	11.9	5.3	7.1
1980	24.7	22.0	29.3	22.4	63.4	59.0	2.5	11.9	4.8	6.6
1975	23.5	21.1	29.5	22.8	64.8	60.4	2.4	12.1	3.3	4.8
1970	23.2	20.8	28.1	22.1	66.9	61.7	2.9	12.5	2.2	3.5
1965	22.8	20.6	26.6	20.7	67.9	63.9	3.3	12.5	2.2	2.9
1960	22.8	20.3	25.3	19.0	69.1	65.6	3.7	12.8	1.9	2.6
1955	22.6	20.2	24.1	18.2	69.9	66.9	4.2	12.6	1.8	2.3
1950	22.8	20.3	26.2	19.6	68.2	66.1	4.0	12.1	1.6	2.2
1940	24.3	21.5	34.8	27.6	59.7	59.5	4.2	11.3	1.2	1.6
1930	24.3	21.3	35.8	28.4	58.4	59.5	4.5	10.8	1.1	1.3
1920	24.6	21.2	36.9	29.4	57.6	58.9	4.6	10.8	0.6	0.8
1910	25.1	21.6	40.4	31.8	54.2	57.1	4.4	10.3	0.5	0.6
1900	25.9	21.9	42.0	33.3	52.8	55.2	4.5	10.9	0.3	0.5
1890	26.1	22.0	43.6	34.1	52.1	54.8	3.8	10.6	0.2	0.4

[a] Figures before 1980 are for persons 14 years old and over. Figures since 1980 are for persons 15 years old and over.

Source: U.S. Bureau of the Census. "Marital Status and Living Arrangements: March (various years)." Current Population Reports (Series P-20, nos. 389 (1983), 380 (1982), 372 (1981), 365 (1980), 287 (1975 and 1970), 144 (1965 and 1960), 62 (1955), and 35 (1890-1950)). Washington, DC: U.S. Government Printing Office, 1984, 1983, 1982, 1981, 1975, 1965, 1955, and 1951 (respectively).

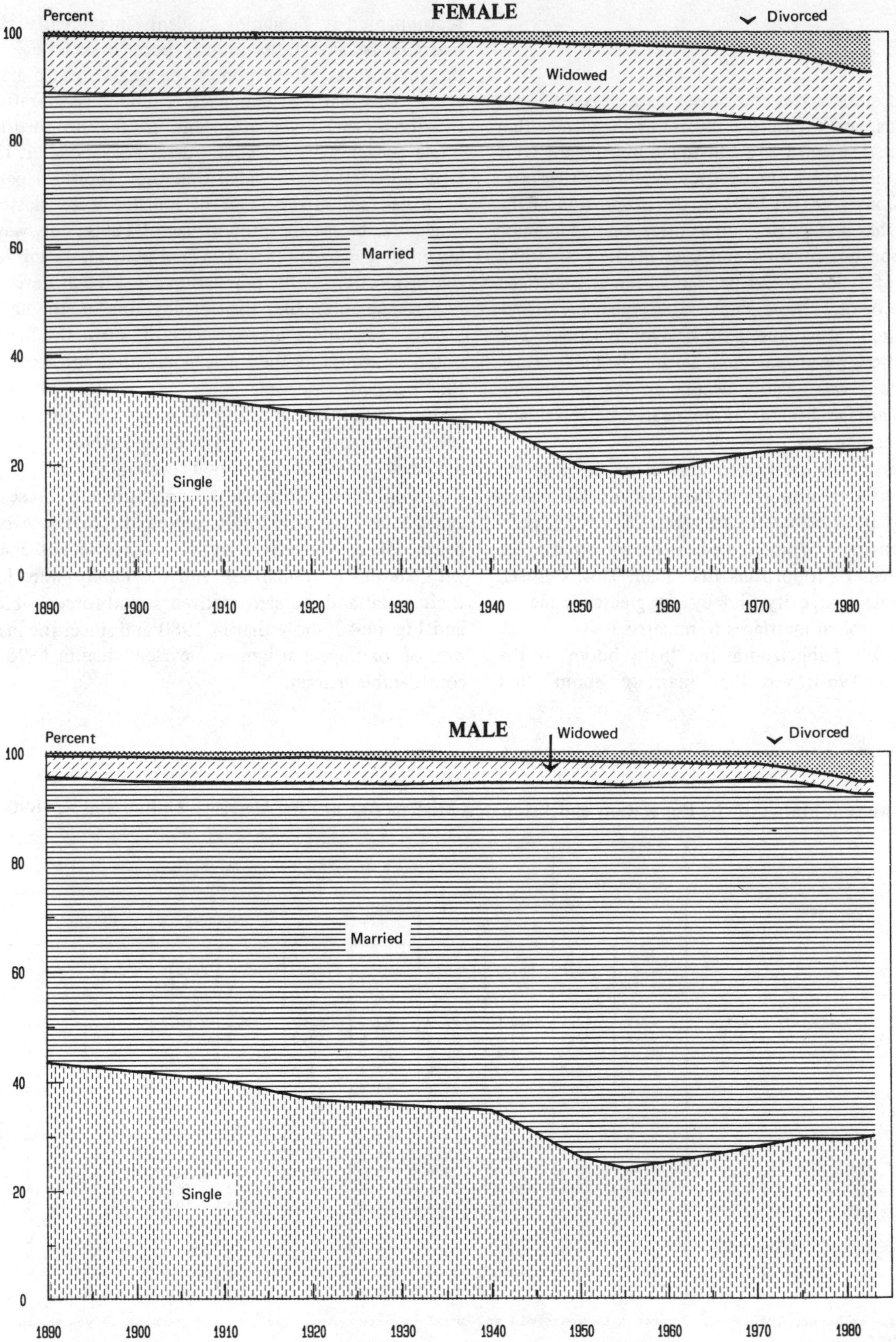

Figure 4-1. Marital Status of the United States Population Fourteen Years of Age and Over: 1890-1983

Meanwhile, the proportion of divorced persons has increased dramatically, especially since 1970. In 1890 divorced persons were practically nonexistent. By 1940 divorce had become the status for 1.2 percent of the male population and 1.6 percent of the female, having risen from less than 0.5 percent in 1900. By 1980 these proportions had more than quadrupled, to 4.8 percent for all males and 6.6 percent for all females fifteen years of age and over. The following statistics summarize the change that has taken place with respect to divorce:

Sex	Percent of population 15 years and over		
	1890	1940	1980
Male.	0.2	1.2	4.8
Female.	0.4	1.6	6.6

These data are for divorced persons who have not (yet) remarried. The percentage of ever-divorced persons is even greater.

Widowhood is a very common status for women. Because of their tendency to outlive their husbands, about one woman in nine is a widow who has not remarried. This proportion has changed comparatively little since 1890. Widowhood among men is much less and has diminished in recent decades. This decline is linked both to the dramatic increase in longevity of women (wives) and to the propensity for widowed men to remarry.

Another aspect of marital status worthy of particular notice is the category "separated." As defined in recent censuses and in recent sample surveys, this category measures roughly the number of marriages disrupted by marital discord that have not been terminated permanently by divorce. (Statistics for the separated population are reported in Table 4-4C.) As of 1982, about 1.9 percent of all adult males and 3.0 percent of all adult females were separated, and nearly 1 percent were living apart from their spouses because of work away from home, military service, and other reasons. The number of separated persons is about 40 percent as large as the number divorced and not remarried. Hence, as a measure of broken marriages, the divorce statistics are quite incomplete. Also, in discussing married persons it is well to remember that nearly 1 percent of all married persons are not living with their spouses because of military service, work away from home, and other reasons not necessarily linked to marital discord.

The Age Pattern of Marital Status

Each of the marital statuses has a characteristic age pattern. Figure 4-2 illustrates these patterns. Table 4-2 presents statistics of marital status by age from 1890 to 1980, by sex. This table has four parts; one part is devoted to each marital status. Until about age fifteen almost all of the population is single. (For the 1980 census, population under fifteen was assumed to be single—see Definition Box.) In the ten years between ages fifteen and twenty-five, the proportion married rises very swiftly and reaches a peak about age thirty to thirty-five. Although the age pattern is similar for males and females, the transition from single to married begins at an earlier age and rises more quickly for women than for men (compare Figures 4-2 and 4-3). The loss of marriage partners through death begins to be evident about age thirty, and at each year of age thereafter a larger proportion of the population is widowed. The proportion divorced also increases in size during the middle-age years. Finally, at ages seventy for women and eighty-five and over for men, the majority of the population is widowed, a comparatively small part is single, and the balance is married. Comparison among the four parts of Table 4-2 will show that for each age up to fifty-five a smaller proportion of the population was single in 1960 than in 1890. The change was especially large at the younger ages (fifteen to thirty).

From 1960 to 1980 the pattern at these young ages has been reversed, and the proportion single at ages under forty (those married since 1960) has risen while those at ages under thirty are higher than at any census since 1920. The effect of fluctuations in the proportion single over the decades upon the proportion married at each of these ages may be observed from Table 4-2B. In 1940, for example, only 51.3 percent of women twenty to twenty-four were married, but in 1950, 65.6 percent of this age group were married. However, by 1980 only 44.4 percent of this age group were married.

Cohort Analysis of Marital Status

The data of Table 4-2 make it clear that the various generations have behaved unlike each other with respect to marriage. Some appear to have rushed into marriage at unusually early ages, while others delayed marriage. In interpreting such tables, it is useful to study the tables from a generational or "cohort analysis" perspective. Instead of simply comparing age groups across censuses (horizontal comparisons), it is useful to make such comparisons in terms of the behavior of generations. An age group of persons (such as persons aged 15-19 at one census) will be ten years older at the next census and twenty years older after two censuses. Therefore, by reading Tables 4-2 and 4-4 diagonally and comparing how the groups differ from each other as they have proceeded through life, it is possible to gain a better perspective on differences in the life-cycle behavior between various generations. This can be done for each marital status. Studying the tables in this fashion will show that:

1. The "marriage boom" of the 1940s and 1950s affected all age groups. A higher percentage of people who had delayed marriage until after age thirty-five became married than in previous generations.

2. The "marriage boom" had its greatest impact in the early marriage of persons under twenty-five. Table 4-1, which reports the estimated median age at first marriage, verifies this.

3. The "marriage market" behavior of the most recent entering generation of women has been to remain single in proportions not manifested since 1890-1910 and may even surpass that level. For males the proportions are similar to the groups who became of marriageable age in the 1930s.

4. The age distribution of marital status in 1980 reflects the past behavior of at least four types of generations (ages are as of 1980):

- *Ages 15-25,* the oncoming generation, which is tending to postpone or forgo marriage more frequently than in previous generations
- *Ages 25-55,* the "marriage boom" cohorts, who married young and for whom marriage was apparently a very attractive status (more attractive than at any previous time in the last century)
- *Ages 55-70,* persons who married in the 1920s and 1930s, when marriage was becoming economically difficult and declining in popularity
- *Ages 70 and older,* persons who had delayed marriage in their youth, perhaps because of economic reasons and as a fertility control measure.

For most precise cohort analysis, it is preferable to deal with generations as persons in single-year rather than five-year age groups. Table 4-3 provides single-year age data for the percentage single for white and black women for the 1940-80 period. These data provide details of the marriage "boom" and "bust" of the late 1970s and the 1980s. The "marriage bust" was already underway for white women aged 17-25 and for black women of all ages in 1970. The marriage bust between 1970 and 1980 has been far more drastic among the black than among the white population.

Bachelorhood: Proportions Never Marrying

A certain proportion of the population goes through its entire life without ever marrying. This tendency also has fluctuated with the generations. In general, those generations that tend to marry very early in life also tend to have higher proportions ever marrying, while

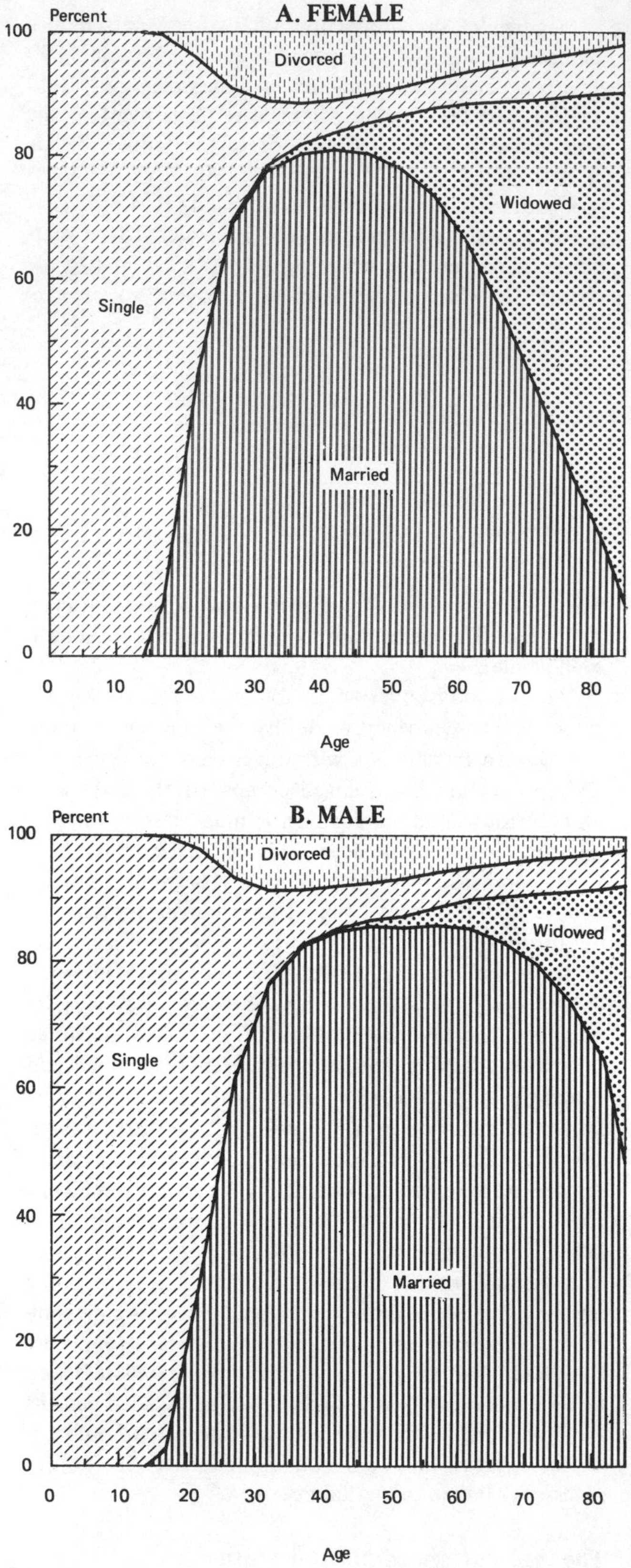

Figure 4-2. Marital Status of the U.S. Population: 1980

Table 4-2A. Percent of the Population Classified as Single, by Age: 1890-1980

Marital status and age	1980[a]	1970	1960	1950	1940	1930	1920	1910	1900	1890
Percent single male										
Total	29.7	28.6	24.9	26.4	34.8	35.8	36.9	40.4	42.0	43.6
14 years.	--	98.8	99.4	99.1	99.9	99.9	99.7	99.9	99.9	100.0
15 to 19 years.	97.2	95.9	96.1	96.7	98.3	98.0	97.7	98.3	98.8	99.4
20 to 24 years.	68.2	55.5	53.0	59.1	72.2	70.8	70.7	74.9	77.6	80.7
25 to 29 years.	32.1	19.6	20.8	23.8	36.0	36.7	39.4	42.8	45.8	46.0
30 to 34 years.	14.9	10.7	11.9	13.2	20.7	21.2	24.1	26.0	27.6	26.5
35 to 39 years.	8.7	8.2	8.8	10.1	15.3	15.4	16.1	16.7	17.0	15.3
40 to 44 years.	6.7	7.5	7.3	9.0	12.6	13.1				
45 to 49 years.	6.0	6.6	7.1	8.7	11.2	11.9	12.0	11.1	10.3	9.1
50 to 54 years.	6.0	6.2	7.6	8.3	11.0	10.9				
55 to 59 years.	5.6	6.4	8.2	8.3	10.8	10.3	9.8	8.3	7.6	6.8
60 to 64 years.	5.2	6.6	7.6	8.6	10.5	9.9				
65 to 69 years.	5.4	7.1	7.7	8.7	10.3	9.3				
70 to 74 years.	5.5	7.3	7.8	8.3	9.9	8.6				
75 to 79 years.	5.6	7.3	7.9	8.1	9.5		7.3	6.2	5.7	5.6
80 to 84 years.	5.7	7.6	7.4	7.4	8.7	7.0				
85 years and over . . .	5.6	10.8	7.1	7.7	7.9					
Percent single female										
Total	22.9	22.6	19.0	20.0	27.6	28.4	29.4	31.8	33.3	34.1
14 years.	--	98.6	98.9	99.3	99.7	99.6	99.4	99.6	99.4	99.8
15 to 19 years.	91.2	88.1	83.9	82.9	88.1	86.8	87.0	87.9	88.7	90.3
20 to 24 years.	51.2	36.3	28.4	32.3	47.2	46.0	45.6	48.3	51.6	51.8
25 to 29 years.	21.6	12.2	10.5	13.3	22.8	21.7	23.0	24.9	27.5	25.4
30 to 34 years.	10.6	7.4	6.9	9.3	14.7	13.2	14.9	16.1	16.6	15.2
35 to 39 years.	6.7	5.9	6.1	8.4	11.2	10.4	11.4	11.4	11.1	9.9
40 to 44 years.	5.3	5.4	6.1	8.3	9.5	9.5				
45 to 49 years.	4.7	5.3	6.5	7.9	8.6	9.0	9.6	8.5	7.8	7.1
50 to 54 years.	4.6	5.7	7.6	7.7	8.7	9.2				
55 to 59 years.	4.7	6.5	8.2	7.7	8.7	9.0	8.4	7.1	6.6	5.8
60 to 64 years.	5.2	7.2	7.7	8.2	9.3	8.9				
64 to 69 years.	5.9	7.4	7.9	8.4	9.4	8.4				
70 to 74 years.	6.6	7.8	8.4	9.0	9.5	8.4				
75 to 79 years.	7.0	8.4	8.8	9.4	9.2		7.1	6.3	6.0	5.6
80 to 84 years.	7.3	8.8	9.5	9.4	9.2	7.3				
85 years and over . . .	7.9	10.7	9.6	9.7	8.0					

[a]Prior to 1980, the total equals 14 years and over; in 1980 the total is for 15 years and over.

Source: Data for 1980 from U.S. Bureau of the Census. "Detailed Population Characteristics: United States Summary." 1980 Census of Population. Washington, DC: U.S. Government Printing Office, 1983. Data for 1970 from U.S. Bureau of the Census. "Detailed Population Characteristics: United States Summary." 1970 Census of Population. Washington, DC: U.S. Government Printing Office, 1973. Data for 1890-1960 from U.S. Bureau of the Census. "Detailed Population Characteristics: United States Summary." 1960 Census of Population. Washington, DC: U.S. Government Printing Office, 1965.

Table 4-2B. Percent of the Population Classified as Married, by Age: 1890-1980

Marital status and age	1980[a]	1970	1960	1950	1940	1930	1920	1910	1900	1890
Percent married male										
Total	62.5	65.7	69.6	67.5	59.7	58.4	57.6	54.2	52.8	52.1
14 years.	--	1.0	0.6	0.6	0.1	0.1	0.3	0.1	0.1	*
15 to 19 years.	2.7	3.9	3.8	3.1	1.7	1.7	2.1	1.1	1.0	0.5
20 to 24 years.	29.5	42.9	45.9	39.9	27.4	28.1	28.3	24.0	21.6	18.9
25 to 29 years.	61.1	77.1	77.2	74.2	62.7	61.3	58.7	55.5	52.6	52.7
30 to 34 years.	76.3	85.7	85.7	84.3	77.2	76.0	73.2	71.4	69.8	71.3
35 to 39 years.	82.4	87.9	88.3	86.8	81.6	81.0	79.8	79.2	78.8	80.9
40 to 44 years.	84.7	87.9	89.1	87.1	83.2	82.1				
45 to 49 years.	85.6	88.3	88.5	86.2	83.6	82.1	81.0	81.5	82.2	84.3
50 to 54 years.	85.4	87.9	87.0	85.0	81.9	81.0				
55 to 59 years.	85.8	86.6	84.8	83.1	79.9	79.5	77.9	79.0	79.7	82.3
60 to 64 years.	85.3	84.5	82.9	79.3	76.7	76.2				
65 to 69 years.	83.0	80.6	79.4	74.0	71.9	71.5				
70 to 74 years.	79.6	75.8	73.1	67.5	64.9	64.7				
75 to 79 years.	73.6	68.8	64.7	59.0	56.1		64.7	65.6	67.1	70.5
80 to 84 years.	64.4	58.0	53.7	48.2	45.8	50.4				
85 years and over . . .	48.4	43.4	38.7	33.6	33.0					
Percent married female										
Total	57.8	61.2	66.0	65.8	59.5	59.5	58.9	57.1	55.2	54.8
14 years.	--	1.1	1.1	0.7	0.3	0.4	0.5	0.4	0.5	0.2
15 to 19 years.	8.4	11.3	15.7	16.7	11.6	12.6	12.5	11.3	10.9	9.5
20 to 24 years.	44.4	60.5	69.5	65.6	51.3	51.6	52.3	49.7	46.5	46.7
25 to 29 years.	68.8	82.5	86.2	83.3	74.1	74.3	73.4	71.8	68.9	71.4
30 to 34 years.	77.3	86.1	88.7	86.2	80.4	81.5	80.1	79.0	78.0	79.8
35 to 39 years.	80.1	86.6	88.1	85.5	81.5	82.3	80.3	80.1	79.5	80.6
40 to 44 years.	80.8	85.3	85.9	83.1	80.6	80.6				
45 to 49 years.	80.2	83.2	82.5	79.8	78.3	77.6	74.0	74.8	73.9	73.9
50 to 54 years.	77.7	78.7	77.0	75.0	73.3	72.3				
55 to 59 years.	73.4	72.2	69.9	69.1	67.2	66.2	61.2	62.2	60.5	60.4
60 to 64 years.	65.7	63.1	61.4	60.1	58.0	56.9				
65 to 69 years.	54.8	52.0	51.6	48.9	46.5	46.6				
70 to 74 years.	42.7	40.0	39.1	36.6	34.3	35.0				
75 to 79 years.	29.5	27.9	27.4	24.7	23.0		33.9	35.0	34.2	35.4
80 to 84 years.	17.7	17.2	16.2	14.2	13.5	18.2				
85 years and over . . .	8.4	10.7	8.2	7.0	6.7					

[a]Prior to 1980, the total equals 14 years and over; in 1980 the total is for 15 years and over.

Note: * indicates less than 0.1 percent.

Source: Same as Table 4-2A.

Table 4-2C. Percent of the Population Classified as Widowed, by Age: 1890-1980

Marital status and age	1980	1970	1960	1950	1940	1930	1920	1910	1900	1890
<u>Percent widowed male</u>										
Total	2.5	3.0	3.4	4.1	4.2	4.5	4.6	4.4	4.5	3.8
14 years.	--	0.1	*	0.2	*	*	*	*	*	*
15 to 19 years.	*	0.1	*	0.1	*	*	*	*	*	*
20 to 24 years.	0.1	0.2	0.1	0.2	0.1	0.3	0.5	0.4	0.4	0.2
25 to 29 years.	0.1	0.3	0.2	0.3	0.4	0.8	1.1	1.1	1.2	1.0
30 to 34 years.	0.2	0.3	0.3	0.4	0.7	1.3	1.8	1.8	2.0	1.8
35 to 39 years.	0.3	0.5	0.5	0.7	1.3	2.0	3.0	3.2	3.6	3.3
40 to 44 years.	0.5	0.8	0.8	1.2	2.1	3.0				
45 to 49 years.	1.0	1.3	1.4	2.1	3.2	4.3	5.8	6.4	6.8	6.0
50 to 54 years.	1.8	2.1	2.3	3.7	5.1	6.3				
55 to 59 years.	2.8	3.2	3.8	5.9	7.4	8.4	11.2	11.7	11.9	10.2
60 to 64 years.	4.6	5.2	6.5	9.6	11.1	12.4				
65 to 69 years.	7.3	8.8	10.2	15.0	16.2	17.8				
70 to 74 years.	11.2	13.8	16.7	22.2	23.8	25.4				
75 to 79 years.	17.6	21.2	25.3	31.4	33.3		26.9	27.1	26.4	23.3
80 to 84 years.	27.3	32.0	37.2	43.3	44.7	41.5				
85 years and over . . .	43.8	43.4	52.8	57.9	58.5					
<u>Percent widowed female</u>										
Total	12.3	12.3	12.1	11.8	11.3	10.8	10.8	10.3	10.9	10.6
14 years.	--	0.3	*	0.1	*	*	*	*	*	*
15 to 19 years.	0.1	0.2	0.1	0.1	0.1	0.2	0.3	0.2	0.2	0.1
20 to 24 years.	0.2	0.7	0.3	0.4	0.6	1.0	1.4	1.2	1.4	1.2
25 to 29 years.	0.5	1.1	0.7	0.9	1.3	2.1	2.6	2.4	2.9	2.8
30 to 34 years.	0.9	1.5	1.2	1.6	2.5	3.3	3.9	3.9	4.6	4.5
35 to 39 years.	1.6	2.2	2.2	2.7	4.6	5.3	7.2	7.5	8.6	8.9
40 to 44 years.	2.8	3.7	4.0	5.0	7.3	8.0				
45 to 49 years.	5.0	5.9	6.7	8.6	10.7	11.6	15.3	15.7	17.6	18.4
50 to 54 years.	8.7	10.0	11.1	13.9	15.9	16.9				
55 to 59 years.	14.2	16.1	17.9	20.5	22.4	23.4	29.5	30.0	32.3	33.3
60 to 64 years.	22.6	24.9	27.6	29.7	31.3	33.1				
65 to 69 years.	33.8	36.5	37.9	41.1	43.1	44.1				
70 to 74 years.	46.2	49.0	50.4	53.3	55.5	55.9				
75 to 79 years.	60.0	61.1	62.2	65.1	67.3		58.4	58.1	59.3	58.6
80 to 84 years.	72.3	71.9	73.1	75.9	77.1	73.9				
85 to 89 years.	81.8	76.9	81.4	82.9	85.1					

[a]Prior to 1980, the total equals 14 years and over; in 1980 the total is for 15 years and over.

Note: * indicates less than 0.1 percent.

<u>Source:</u> Same as Table 4-2A.

Table 4-2D. Percent of the Population Classified as Divorced, by Age: 1890-1980

Marital status and age	1980	1970	1960	1950	1940	1930	1920	1910	1900	1890
Percent divorced male										
Total	5.3	2.7	2.1	2.0	1.2	1.1	0.6	0.5	0.3	0.2
14 years.	--	0.1	*	0.1	*	*	*	*	*	*
15 to 19 years.	0.1	0.1	0.1	0.1	*	*	*	*	*	*
20 to 24 years.	2.2	1.4	1.0	0.9	0.3	0.4	0.2	0.1	0.1	*
25 to 29 years.	6.7	3.0	1.8	1.7	0.9	1.0	0.5	0.4	0.2	0.2
30 to 34 years.	8.7	3.3	2.2	2.1	1.4	1.4	0.7	0.5	0.4	0.2
35 to 39 years.	8.6	3.4	2.5	2.4	1.8	1.5	0.9	0.7	0.5	0.3
40 to 44 years.	8.0	3.8	2.7	2.7	2.0	1.6				
45 to 49 years.	7.5	3.8	3.0	2.9	2.0	1.7	1.0	0.8	0.6	0.4
50 to 54 years.	6.8	3.9	3.1	3.0	2.0	1.6				
55 to 59 years.	5.8	3.9	3.1	2.7	1.9	1.6	1.0	0.8	0.6	0.5
60 to 64 years.	5.0	3.6	3.0	2.5	1.7	1.5				
65 to 69 years.	4.4	3.5	2.7	2.3	1.6	1.3	0.7	0.7	0.5	0.4
70 to 74 years.	3.7	3.1	2.4	1.9	1.3	1.1				
75 to 79 years.	3.2	2.7	2.1	1.5	1.1	0.8				
80 to 84 years.	2.6	2.4	1.7	1.1	0.8					
85 years and over . . .	2.1	2.4	1.4	0.8	0.6					
Percent divorced female										
Total	7.1	3.9	2.9	2.4	1.6	1.3	0.8	0.6	0.5	0.4
14 years.	--	0.1	*	*	*	*	*	*	*	*
15 to 19 years.	0.4	0.3	0.3	0.3	0.1	0.2	0.1	0.1	0.1	*
20 to 24 years.	4.2	2.5	1.8	1.7	0.9	1.1	0.6	0.5	0.4	0.2
25 to 29 years.	9.1	4.3	2.6	2.5	1.8	1.8	0.9	0.7	0.6	0.4
30 to 34 years.	11.2	5.0	3.1	3.0	2.4	1.9	1.0	0.8	0.7	0.5
35 to 39 years.	11.6	5.3	3.6	3.5	2.8	1.9	1.1	0.9	0.7	0.6
40 to 44 years.	11.1	5.6	4.0	3.7	2.7	1.8				
45 to 49 years.	10.1	5.5	4.3	3.6	2.4	1.7	1.0	0.8	0.6	0.5
50 to 54 years.	9.0	5.5	4.2	3.3	2.0	1.5				
55 to 59 years.	7.7	5.2	3.9	2.7	1.7	1.3	0.8	0.6	0.5	0.4
60 to 64 years.	6.5	4.8	3.3	2.1	1.4	1.0				
65 to 69 years.	5.5	4.1	2.7	1.5	1.0	0.8	0.4	0.4	0.3	0.3
70 to 74 years.	4.5	3.3	2.1	1.1	0.7	0.5				
75 to 79 years.	3.6	2.7	1.5	0.7	0.4	0.3				
80 to 84 years.	2.7	2.1	1.1	0.5	0.3					
85 years and over . . .	2.0	1.7	0.8	0.4	0.2					

[a]Prior to 1980, the total equals 14 years and over; in 1980 the total is for 15 years and over.

Note: * indicates less than 0.1 percent.

Source: Same as Table 4-2A.

those generations with later ages at marriage tend to have higher proportions never marrying. Demographers tend to take the proportion of persons aged 50-54 as an indicator of the tendency to remain single permanently. (For ages older than this, the data may be biased by misreporting of marital status and because of selective mortality.) This statistic is a crude indicator of the proportion of the men and women who do not significantly participate in childbearing. By examining the proportions of persons single at age 50-54 (from Table 4-2A), one can see that the proportions vary as follows:

Males–between 6 and 11 percent
Females–between 4 and 9 percent

Since permanent single status tends to be a generational phenomenon, one cannot take the percentage single at age 50-54 in 1980 as a tendency for permanent bachelorhood among persons younger than this in 1980. By coincidence, the group of persons aged 50-54 in 1980, who were born in 1925 to 1930, were the cohort that launched the marriage boom in 1940-50. Hence, it is likely that for those aged 25-55 in 1980 (the marriage boom cohort) the proportions will be toward the lower end of the range, while for those generations under 25 in 1980 the proportions ultimately never marrying may be expected to fall toward the upper end of this range–or even somewhat beyond it. As yet there is little evidence that the percentage of the younger generations that will remain unmarried throughout their lives will be higher than what was considered "normal" in 1940 because of the late marriage of persons (aged 50-54) in 1940 who were married between 1905 and 1920.

Race-Ethnic Differentials in Marital Status

There are substantial differences in marital status among the major race-ethnic categories, even when sex and age are taken into consideration. Tables 4-3 and 4-4A through 4-4F report the percentage of each group in each marital status. (One table is devoted to each marital status, showing data for that status by age, sex, and three race-ethnicity groups.) From these tables, it can be determined that:

Single (Never Married). Spanish-origin individuals tend to marry at younger ages than whites. This is indicated by lower percent-single figures in comparison with the white group. Bachelorhood is highest among the black population, especially at ages 45-54; it is about equal for the white and Spanish-origin groups. (Bachelorhood at age 45-54 is less for Spanish-origin males, but greater for Spanish-origin females, than for the respective sexes in the white population.)

Widowed. Widowhood is considerably more prevalent among the black population than among the white or Spanish-origin population at all ages older than thirty-five. This is true for both sexes but is especially pronounced for females. It is about equal for the white and Spanish-origin populations, when considered age group by age group. However, because of the much older age composition of the white population, the prevalence for all ages combined is nearly twice as high among whites as among those of Spanish-origin.

Divorced. Divorce is much more prevalent among the black population than among the white population at all ages beyond thirty for both males and females. For the Spanish-origin population younger than thirty-five, a smaller proportion is divorced than for the white population, but at ages fifty-five and over the difference is reversed. In all race-ethnic groups, the proportion divorced is higher for women than for men, except at the very oldest ages, where all converge toward a very small percentage.

Separated. For both the black and the Spanish-origin population, there is a very strong tendency for a substantial part of the population to be married but separated from their spouses. In fact, for the black population the prevalence of separation at most ages is higher than for divorce. (Separation is sometimes called "the poor person's divorce.") The white population, although it has a substantial percentage of separation, tends to have more divorce than separation. The status is at its maximum at ages 25-44 for women and 30-54 for men. Table 4-4C separated category does not include those separated from spouse because the spouse is in the armed forces or is just away from home because of work.

Married, spouse present. Table 4-4B shows that the black population falls far below the other race-ethnic groups in this status. Because of the propensity not to marry at all and to suffer all of the forces of marital dissolution (widowhood, divorce, and separation) more acutely, less than one-half of the black women at prime childbearing ages are married and living with their spouses. Only 55 to 65 percent of black men are in this status. This has profound implications for the bearing of children out of wedlock, as Chapter 6 will show.

The white population has the highest prevalence of adults married and living with spouse during the prime childbearing and childrearing ages (25-54). The Spanish-origin population, although it has much higher proportions than the black population, suffers greater attrition from separation, divorce, and widowhood at these ages and hence is lower than the white.

Because of the great differences in their age composition and because the proportions of each marital status differ so radically by age, one can arrive at very erroneous implications by looking only at the marital status totals for all ages by race-ethnicity. Only by comparing the race-ethnic groups in terms of their age-specific patterns can a proper interpretation be made. Even such detailed analysis should be done on a cohort basis if trends are to be assessed.

Urban-Rural Residence and Marital Status

The patterns of marital status described above take significantly different forms in urban and rural areas. Table 4-5 provides percentage distributions by marital status according to several categories of residence. The data are provided for five racial groups by sex. In all categories the following generalization apply with only minor exceptions.

In general urban areas tend to be more "anti-nuptial" and rural areas to be more "pro-nuptial." In fact there is a continuum of this pattern, with anti-nuptiality being highest in central cities and pro-nuptiality being highest in open-country rural areas, with urbanized fringes, small cities, and small urban areas falling sequentially along the continuum. This pattern is consistent for each category of the race-ethnic groups. Each group preserves the differences noted above, but the following differentials are quite uniformly patterned within each race-ethnic group:

1. In rural areas the proportion of persons who are single is considerably lower than in urban areas. Thus persons who live in rural places either marry or migrate to urban places.

2. In rural areas the proportion of persons who are divorced is considerably lower than in urban areas. Although divorce is not inconsequential in the rural areas, it is only one-half as prevalent as in urban areas (4 percent as compared to 9 percent overall).

3. In rural areas the proportion of persons separated is considerably lower than in urban areas. Again, although separation is not uncommon in rural areas, it is much less prevalent than in urban areas (1.3 versus 2.2 percent overall).

4. In rural areas the proportion of persons classed as "married and living with spouse" is higher than in urban areas.

5. Rural areas and central cities tend to have a higher prevalence of widowhood among females. This is primarily an indirect effect of age composition.

All of these differentials are more intense for the white than for the other race-ethnic groups.

Thus, Table 4-5 shows that the crest of the wave of marriage bust that has swept the nation has its locus in central cities and its trough in rural open-country areas. This is true for each sex and for all race-ethnic groups.

Table 4-3. Percent Single (Never Married) for Single Years of Age 15-29 Females, by Race: 1940-80

Age, by race	1980	1970	1960	1950	1940
White women					
15 years. . . .	98.7	98.3	97.7	98.1	99.0
16 years. . . .	97.4	96.2	94.3	94.2	96.6
17 years. . . .	93.9	91.6	88.0	87.5	92.0
18 years. . . .	87.0	82.3	75.5	76.4	83.8
19 years. . . .	77.7	70.2	59.4	63.2	74.5
20 years. . . .	67.2	56.1	45.2	32.4	64.6
21 years. . . .	57.6	43.5	33.7	39.2	55.7
22 years. . . .	47.4	30.9	24.5	30.4	47.5
23 years. . . .	38.7	23.2	18.3	24.0	39.8
24 years. . . .	31.6	18.5	14.6	19.4	33.7
25 years. . . .	26.1	14.7	12.2	16.5	29.2
26 years. . . .	21.6	11.8	10.5	14.6	25.6
27 years. . . .	18.2	10.2	9.4	12.8	22.4
28 years. . . .	15.5	9.0	8.7	11.6	20.4
29 years. . . .	13.6	8.2	8.2	10.3	18.0
Black women[a]					
15 years. . . .	98.5	98.0	97.1	96.8	97.4
16 years. . . .	98.5	95.6	93.2	90.7	92.4
17 years. . . .	96.9	91.1	86.4	81.3	83.6
18 years. . . .	93.5	83.1	76.4	68.8	71.1
19 years. . . .	88.3	72.1	61.7	56.1	60.7
20 years. . . .	81.6	59.8	51.4	44.4	49.6
21 years. . . .	74.8	49.7	41.3	36.7	42.4
22 years. . . .	66.6	41.3	33.7	30.3	35.8
23 years. . . .	60.0	33.9	27.0	24.6	30.4
24 years. . . .	53.0	28.0	23.3	20.8	26.6
25 years. . . .	45.6	26.3	19.8	18.1	24.1
26 years. . . .	40.6	23.2	17.2	16.0	21.0
27 years. . . .	36.4	19.8	15.2	13.1	18.7
28 years. . . .	32.1	19.8	13.5	12.1	17.2
29 years. . . .	29.0	16.8	12.7	10.8	15.3

[a]Nonwhite for 1960 and preceding years.

Source: U.S. Bureau of the Census. "United States Summary." 1980, 1970, 1960, 1950, and 1940 Censuses of Population. Washington, DC: U.S. Government Printing Office, 1983, 1973, 1964, 1952, and 1942.

Marital Status of American Indians and Asian-Pacific Islander Races

The above discussion of race-ethnic differences overlooked the American Indian and the Asian and Pacific Islander races. Table 4-5 provides information for both. American Indians are unique in having a higher proportion divorced, both in urban and rural areas, than any other race-ethnic groups; it also has high proportions separated. Marital instability appears to be almost equal-great among rural Indians as among rural black families, and nearly as great among urban American Indians as among urban blacks. In both rural and urban areas, American Indian marital disruption is higher than Spanish-origin disruption.

Table 4-4A. Marital Status of the Population, by Sex, Race, Spanish-Origin, and Age: Single, 1940-1982 [percent distribution]

Race-ethnicity and age	Males								Females							
	1982	1980	1978	1975	1970	1960	1950	1940	1982	1980	1978	1975	1970	1960	1950	1940
All races, single																
15 and over	29.7	29.3	30.6	29.5	28.2	24.9	26.4	34.8	22.5	22.4	23.9	22.8	22.1	19.0	20.0	27.6
15-17 years	99.3	99.4	99.6	99.3	99.3	96.7	97.1	98.5	97.2	97.0	97.4	97.1	97.3	86.4	85.6	90.0
18-19 years	94.9	94.2	94.4	93.1	92.5				84.9	82.8	81.3	77.7	75.5			
20-24 years	72.0	68.6	65.8	59.9	55.2	53.0	59.1	72.2	53.4	50.2	47.6	40.3	35.9	28.4	32.3	47.2
25-29 years	36.1	32.4	27.8	22.3	19.7	20.8	23.8	36.0	23.4	20.8	18.0	13.8	10.7	10.5	13.3	22.8
30-34 years	17.3	15.7	12.8	11.1	9.6	11.9	13.2	20.7	11.6	9.5	8.4	7.5	6.4	6.9	9.3	14.7
35-44 years	8.9	7.4	7.6	7.9	7.2	8.1	9.6	14.0	5.6	5.6	5.4	4.9	5.2	6.1	8.3	10.4
45-54 years	5.4	6.4	6.8	6.3	7.6	7.4	8.5	11.1	4.1	4.7	4.4	4.6	4.9	7.0	7.8	8.7
55-64 years	4.6	5.7	5.4	6.5	7.6	8.0	8.4	10.7	4.2	4.6	4.8	5.1	6.8	8.0	7.9	9.0
65 and over	4.4	5.1	5.4	4.7	7.8	7.7	8.4	9.8	5.6	5.9	6.2	5.8	7.7	8.5	8.9	9.3
White, single																
15 and over	28.1	28.0	29.2	28.4	27.1	24.3	26.1	34.7	20.8	20.9	22.4	21.6	21.3	18.6	19.9	27.7
15-17 years	99.3	99.4	99.5	99.2	99.3	96.7	97.2	98.7	96.8	96.7	97.1	97.1	97.2	86.5	86.1	90.8
18-19 years	94.2	93.6	93.8	92.5	92.0				83.1	81.5	80.2	77.0	75.5			
20-24 years	70.1	66.9	64.2	58.9	54.5	52.5	59.5	73.5	50.5	47.2	44.5	38.2	34.7	27.4	32.4	48.4
25-29 years	34.1	31.1	25.9	21.0	17.9	20.0	23.6	36.7	20.6	18.3	15.8	12.2	9.5	9.8	13.2	23.2
30-34 years	16.5	14.6	12.0	10.1	9.4	11.3	13.1	20.7	10.0	8.2	7.2	6.7	5.7	6.6	9.3	15.0
35-44 years	8.1	6.6	7.3	7.6	6.4	7.7	9.6	13.8	4.6	4.8	4.4	4.3	4.7	6.0	8.5	10.7
45-54 years	4.8	5.8	6.0	6.0	7.3	7.2	8.6	11.1	3.6	4.4	4.1	4.5	4.9	7.2	8.2	9.0
55-64 years	4.4	5.6	5.3	6.5	7.5	7.8	8.6	10.8	3.9	4.4	4.8	5.1	7.0	8.2	8.2	9.3
65 and over	4.2	5.0	5.2	4.5	7.8	7.8	8.6	10.1	5.7	6.1	6.5	5.8	8.0	8.8	9.3	9.7
Black, single																
15 and over	41.2	40.2	41.2	38.2	36.6	30.2	28.5	35.5	35.1	33.4	35.4	31.4	28.0	21.9	20.7	26.1
15-17 years	99.6	99.4	99.8	99.7	99.5	96.7	96.3	97.3	98.8	98.3	98.8	97.3	98.2	86.2	82.3	84.1
18-19 years	98.7	97.7	97.8	96.1	95.8				96.0	90.9	88.4	81.4	73.9			
20-24 years	82.3	79.0	74.8	65.4	59.4	56.8	54.7	60.4	71.5	68.7	67.2	54.7	43.3	35.2	31.2	37.2
25-29 years	48.3	42.7	40.4	31.7	32.0	27.4	25.2	30.5	40.6	37.2	34.4	25.8	19.0	15.7	14.1	19.4
30-34 years	23.2	26.7	19.3	18.1	9.5	17.1	14.4	21.3	23.3	19.0	18.7	13.2	10.8	9.6	8.9	12.6
35-44 years	16.1	14.7	11.7	11.3	13.6	11.2	9.8	15.5	13.9	10.6	12.7	8.5	9.5	7.1	6.4	7.9
45-54 years	11.4	12.3	13.8	8.9	10.3	8.7	7.7	10.8	7.7	7.6	7.1	6.1	4.5	6.0	4.6	5.2
55-64 years	6.3	7.0	6.4	6.6	7.5	9.3	6.2	8.7	6.8	5.7	5.7	5.1	4.7	6.0	4.1	4.5
65 and over	4.4	5.8	6.8	5.4	5.6	6.5	5.5	7.0	4.6	4.5	3.9	4.8	4.1	4.4	4.4	4.1
Spanish-origin, single																
15 and over	34.2	32.6	34.9	36.3	32.2	--	--	--	25.5	27.6	27.8	27.1	26.5	--	--	--
15-17 years	98.8	98.5	98.7	95.6	95.8	--	--	--	94.1	94.6	95.9	88.4	89.2	--	--	--
18-19 years	87.8	92.2	89.0		87.4	--	--	--	74.4	79.2	72.5		70.6	--	--	--
20-24 years	65.6	59.9	58.1	55.8	49.9	--	--	--	44.7	42.9	40.3	37.9	33.4	--	--	--
25-29 years	31.1	26.9	23.9	25.8	19.4	--	--	--	20.3	22.5	16.2	13.4	13.7	--	--	--
30-34 years	11.7	11.2	12.1	11.9	11.0	--	--	--	10.2	11.3	10.2	7.6	8.4	--	--	--
35-44 years	8.1	5.7	7.4	10.0	7.3	--	--	--	6.3	7.4	7.0	6.3	6.6	--	--	--
45-54 years	4.1	6.5	7.1	3.7	6.2	--	--	--	6.3	7.1	6.8	6.0	6.1	--	--	--
55-64 years	4.7	4.4	3.5	7.3	6.0	--	--	--	5.9	7.9	3.5	5.8	6.7	--	--	--
65 and over	3.2	9.7	4.5	3.5	8.9	--	--	--	6.7	5.0	7.3	5.3	7.7	--	--	--

Note: -- indicates data not available.

Source: U.S. Bureau of the Census. "Marital Status and Living Arrangements: March (1982, 1980, 1978, 1975, and 1970)," and "Persons of Spanish-origin in the United States: March, 1975." Current Population Reports (Series P-20, nos. 380, 365, 338, 312, and 212; and Series P-20, no. 290). Washington, DC: U.S. Government Printing Office, 1983, 1981, 1979, 1976, and 1971; and 1976. 1940-1960 data from U.S. Bureau of the Census. "U.S. Summary." 1960 Census of Population. Washington, DC: U.S. Government Printing Office, 1964.

Table 4-4B. Marital Status of the Population, by Sex, Race, Spanish-Origin, and Age: Married, 1940-1982 [percent distribution]

Race-ethnicity and age	Males								Females							
	1982	1980	1978	1975	1970	1960	1950	1940	1982	1980	1978	1975	1970	1960	1950	1940
All races, married (spouse present)																
15 and over.	59.9	60.8	60.0	62.3	64.1	69.6	67.5	59.7	54.5	55.4	54.8	56.9	58.4	66.0	65.8	59.5
15-17 years.	0.2	0.2	0.1	0.3	0.2	} 3.2	2.7	1.4	2.2	2.3	2.0	2.2	2.2	} 13.2	14.0	9.8
18-19 years.	3.7	5.1	5.0	6.4	6.8				12.5	14.7	16.4	19.6	20.8			
20-24 years.	24.9	27.9	30.0	36.7	41.5	45.9	39.9	27.4	39.0	42.0	43.9	51.0	56.0	69.5	65.6	51.3
25-29 years.	54.7	59.1	62.9	69.8	75.2	77.2	74.2	62.7	62.1	64.9	68.2	74.0	79.7	86.2	83.3	74.1
30-34 years.	69.7	72.6	76.6	80.4	84.4	85.7	84.3	77.2	70.3	72.7	75.2	78.8	83.5	88.7	86.2	80.4
35-44 years.	77.9	80.9	81.6	83.0	86.0	88.7	87.0	82.4	73.7	76.2	76.8	79.7	82.8	87.1	84.3	81.0
45-54 years.	81.5	81.9	82.1	84.3	84.6	87.8	85.7	82.8	74.1	75.0	76.2	76.2	77.9	79.9	77.6	76.0
55-64 years.	83.5	82.4	83.1	81.8	83.0	84.0	81.4	78.5	67.7	67.1	67.2	66.7	63.7	66.0	65.0	63.0
65 and over.	77.6	75.5	74.8	77.3	68.4	70.8	65.7	63.8	38.5	38.0	36.7	37.6	33.7	37.4	35.7	34.3
White, married (spouse present)																
15 and over.	62.2	63.0	62.3	64.2	66.0	70.3	67.9	59.9	57.2	58.1	57.5	59.3	60.2	66.7	66.2	59.8
15-17 years.	0.2	0.3	0.2	0.3	0.2	} 3.2	2.6	1.3	2.5	2.6	2.2	2.2	2.4	} 13.2	13.6	9.0
18-19 years.	4.2	5.7	5.5	6.9	7.4				14.1	15.9	17.6	20.3	20.9			
20-24 years.	26.6	29.5	31.7	37.8	42.6	46.3	39.4	26.1	41.7	45.0	47.6	54.1	58.0	70.5	65.6	50.3
25-29 years.	56.8	60.7	65.6	71.8	77.5	78.1	74.4	62.1	65.6	68.8	71.9	77.3	82.5	87.2	83.7	74.1
30-34 years.	71.2	74.4	78.1	82.7	85.6	86.4	84.6	77.3	73.7	76.2	78.5	82.0	86.5	89.6	86.5	80.7
35-44 years.	79.8	82.9	83.4	84.1	88.5	89.3	87.2	82.8	77.1	79.8	80.3	83.2	85.7	87.9	84.9	81.8
45-54 years.	83.5	84.3	84.6	86.6	86.2	88.3	85.9	83.1	77.4	78.2	79.4	79.1	80.1	80.7	78.4	76.9
55-64 years.	85.6	84.3	84.3	83.1	83.6	84.6	81.6	78.7	70.4	69.6	69.4	68.6	65.3	66.9	65.8	63.8
65 and over.	79.3	77.1	77.2	79.2	69.7	71.2	65.8	63.8	39.6	39.0	37.8	38.8	34.6	37.9	36.2	34.8
Black, married (spouse present)																
15 and over.	41.7	42.3	41.3	45.5	48.6	62.8	64.4	58.2	33.4	34.0	33.4	36.7	42.0	60.5	62.0	56.9
15-17 years.	0.0	0.0	0.0	0.1	0.4	} 3.2	3.5	2.6	0.6	0.8	0.8	2.2	1.1	} 13.4	17.3	15.4
18-19 years.	0.7	1.7	1.8	3.9	3.0				2.7	7.2	8.4	15.9	21.0			
20-24 years.	15.7	17.2	19.4	30.5	35.3	42.4	43.9	38.7	22.3	23.5	20.9	29.3	42.6	62.3	65.7	59.6
25-29 years.	40.7	46.7	42.5	54.4	57.7	70.4	72.4	67.6	39.7	38.5	41.2	48.2	59.7	78.8	80.2	74.3
30-34 years.	56.9	54.8	62.5	62.7	75.3	79.3	82.2	75.6	44.8	45.1	48.5	52.5	61.3	82.2	83.1	77.0
35-44 years.	59.0	60.7	63.2	70.4	64.4	83.3	85.1	79.1	47.4	49.2	49.9	53.4	58.3	80.3	80.0	74.3
45-54 years.	63.3	60.1	60.5	62.1	67.3	83.1	83.3	79.6	46.9	48.5	48.9	50.5	56.9	72.1	69.2	65.5
55-64 years.	61.5	61.2	68.2	66.1	76.6	77.5	78.4	76.0	43.5	42.9	45.2	46.8	46.3	56.9	54.3	52.5
65 and over.	60.7	60.9	53.8	59.3	54.6	66.7	64.4	63.7	26.4	27.7	27.1	25.6	21.5	32.1	29.0	27.4
Spanish-origin, married (spouse present)																
15 and over.	55.3	58.2	55.9	55.7	58.4	--	--	--	52.3	52.1	52.4	53.6	54.5	--	--	--
15-17 years.	0.6	0.9	0.7	} 3.6	3.2	--	--	--	5.2	4.7	3.6	} 9.2	8.3	--	--	--
18-19 years.	7.7	7.6	11.0		10.2	--	--	--	20.1	16.0	24.7		23.1	--	--	--
20-24 years.	29.7	35.2	37.3	40.4	43.0	--	--	--	44.7	46.6	47.7	52.5	55.3	--	--	--
25-29 years.	58.6	65.4	68.9	66.7	71.4	--	--	--	63.1	62.4	66.8	68.0	72.4	--	--	--
30-34 years.	75.7	76.4	78.0	76.3	79.7	--	--	--	67.4	69.1	70.7	75.0	75.9	--	--	--
35-44 years.	79.4	83.2	79.6	78.7	82.9	--	--	--	67.7	71.0	72.9	72.9	75.1	--	--	--
45-54 years.	81.6	81.3	79.0	84.0	82.1	--	--	--	67.7	64.6	65.3	70.7	70.1	--	--	--
55-64 years.	79.9	81.8	78.0	79.6	78.9	--	--	--	53.4	57.9	60.7	55.2	55.7	--	--	--
65 and over.	69.6	66.8	77.3	83.8	63.8	--	--	--	33.3	35.3	33.6	39.0	30.8	--	--	--

Note: -- indicates data not available.

Table 4-4C. Marital Status of the Population, by Sex, Race, Spanish-Origin, and Age: Separated, 1940-1982 [percent distribution]

Race-ethnicity and age	Males								Females							
	1982	1980	1978	1975	1970	1960	1950	1940	1982	1980	1978	1975	1970	1960	1950	1940
All races, separated																
15 and over.	1.9	1.8	1.8	1.6	1.3	--	--	--	3.0	2.8	2.8	2.8	2.2	--	--	--
15-17 years.	--	--	--	--	--	--	--	--	0.2	0.2	0.1	0.3	0.1	--	--	--
18-19 years.	0.4	0.1	--	--	0.2	--	--	--	0.9	0.9	0.8	0.9	1.0	--	--	--
20-24 years.	1.1	1.1	1.1	1.1	1.0	--	--	--	3.0	3.0	3.2	3.6	2.5	--	--	--
25-29 years.	2.2	2.1	2.3	2.7	1.5	--	--	--	4.4	4.3	4.2	4.5	3.5	--	--	--
30-34 years.	2.8	2.8	2.5	2.1	1.3	--	--	--	4.6	4.7	4.2	4.7	3.3	--	--	--
35-44 years.	2.6	2.6	2.9	2.4	2.0	--	--	--	4.9	4.3	4.4	4.4	2.9	--	--	--
45-54 years.	2.4	2.6	2.4	1.9	1.7	--	--	--	3.7	3.3	3.4	3.1	3.0	--	--	--
55-64 years.	2.1	2.1	1.9	2.1	1.6	--	--	--	2.4	2.0	2.3	2.0	2.5	--	--	--
65 and over.	1.4	1.2	1.7	1.2	1.5	--	--	--	0.9	0.9	1.1	1.0	0.9	--	--	--
White, separated																
15 and over.	1.5	1.4	1.3	1.1	0.9	--	--	--	2.2	1.9	1.9	1.8	1.3	--	--	--
15-17 years.	--	--	--	--	--	--	--	--	0.2	0.1	0.1	0.3	0.1	--	--	--
18-19 years.	0.4	0.1	--	--	0.2	--	--	--	1.0	0.9	0.6	1.0	0.8	--	--	--
20-24 years.	1.2	1.0	1.0	1.0	0.9	--	--	--	2.9	2.7	2.7	2.6	1.8	--	--	--
25-29 years.	2.1	1.8	1.6	2.1	1.1	--	--	--	3.6	2.9	3.1	3.2	2.2	--	--	--
30-34 years.	2.4	2.3	1.9	1.2	1.0	--	--	--	3.5	3.2	3.1	3.1	1.7	--	--	--
35-44 years.	2.0	2.1	2.1	1.7	1.1	--	--	--	3.4	2.6	2.8	2.6	1.4	--	--	--
45-54 years.	1.7	1.6	1.5	1.0	0.9	--	--	--	2.5	2.0	2.0	1.9	1.8	--	--	--
55-64 years.	1.3	1.4	1.3	1.4	1.3	--	--	--	1.4	1.4	1.5	1.2	1.6	--	--	--
65 and over.	1.0	0.7	1.0	0.7	1.3	--	--	--	0.5	0.6	0.8	0.7	0.6	--	--	--
Black, separated																
15 and over.	5.3	6.0	6.6	6.7	5.0	--	--	--	9.2	9.8	9.6	10.6	10.0	--	--	--
15-17 years.	--	--	--	--	--	--	--	--	--	0.3	0.1	0.4	0.1	--	--	--
18-19 years.	0.3	--	--	--	0.3	--	--	--	--	1.0	2.0	0.5	2.5	--	--	--
20-24 years.	0.8	2.4	2.1	2.7	1.7	--	--	--	3.5	5.0	6.8	10.1	8.3	--	--	--
25-29 years.	3.2	5.1	8.1	9.2	5.1	--	--	--	9.9	13.7	12.4	15.3	13.9	--	--	--
30-34 years.	7.5	7.2	8.0	12.1	3.5	--	--	--	13.1	16.6	13.1	17.7	16.1	--	--	--
35-44 years.	8.5	8.1	11.5	9.2	10.2	--	--	--	17.2	17.2	16.4	18.0	14.9	--	--	--
45-54 years.	8.6	11.4	10.4	11.4	10.5	--	--	--	13.6	13.7	15.9	14.3	14.3	--	--	--
55-64 years.	11.3	10.3	9.2	9.6	5.0	--	--	--	12.2	8.5	11.0	10.5	12.5	--	--	--
65 and over.	6.4	6.3	9.5	6.7	4.8	--	--	--	4.8	4.7	4.6	4.6	3.8	--	--	--
Spanish-origin, separated																
15 and over.	2.8	2.1	2.6	1.4	1.8	--	--	--	6.2	5.4	5.5	5.8	4.2	--	--	--
15-17 years.	--	--	0.2	--	0.2	--	--	--	--	0.3	--	1.3	0.6	--	--	--
18-19 years.	2.4	--	--	--	0.4	--	--	--	2.8	2.6	0.4	1.3	1.6	--	--	--
20-24 years.	2.0	2.2	1.8	1.5	1.5	--	--	--	4.7	5.1	4.1	5.1	3.8	--	--	--
25-29 years.	4.4	1.8	2.4	0.9	2.3	--	--	--	7.7	6.7	9.5	8.5	5.6	--	--	--
30-34 years.	2.8	2.4	2.5	1.4	2.3	--	--	--	8.6	6.9	6.7	10.2	6.1	--	--	--
35-44 years.	3.5	2.7	3.7	3.0	2.3	--	--	--	8.7	7.0	6.9	7.6	5.9	--	--	--
45-54 years.	2.9	3.0	4.3	1.6	2.4	--	--	--	6.8	7.1	8.2	5.7	5.4	--	--	--
55-64 years.	2.3	3.5	5.5	1.8	2.6	--	--	--	6.4	5.8	6.5	7.3	4.9	--	--	--
65 and over.	5.5	2.7	2.4	1.1	2.3	--	--	--	4.1	3.0	3.5	2.8	2.6	--	--	--

Note: -- indicates data not available.

Source: Same as Table 4-4A.

Table 4-4D. Marital Status of the Population, by Sex, Race, Spanish-Origin, and Age: Widowed, 1940-1982 [percent distribution]

Race-ethnicity and age	Males								Females							
	1982	1980	1978	1975	1970	1960	1950	1940	1982	1980	1978	1975	1970	1960	1950	1940
All races, widowed																
15 and over	2.2	2.5	2.3	2.4	3.0	3.4	4.1	4.2	11.7	11.9	11.6	12.1	12.5	12.2	11.8	11.3
15-17 years	--	--	--	--	--	--	0.1	--	--	--	--	--	*	} 0.1	0.1	0.1
18-19 years	--	--	--	*	--				--	0.1	--	0.1	*			
20-24 years	--	--	0.1	0.1	*	0.1	0.2	0.1	0.1	0.2	0.2	0.3	0.3	0.3	0.4	0.6
25-29 years	--	0.1	0.1	0.1	0.1	0.2	0.3	0.4	0.5	0.4	0.6	0.5	0.3	0.7	0.9	1.3
30-34 years	0.1	0.1	0.2	0.1	0.1	0.3	0.4	0.7	0.7	1.2	0.6	0.9	0.8	1.2	1.6	2.5
35-44 years	0.3	0.4	0.4	0.4	0.6	0.7	0.9	1.7	1.9	2.2	2.2	2.8	2.5	3.0	3.8	5.9
45-54 years	1.5	1.6	1.6	1.7	1.6	1.8	2.8	4.1	6.8	7.0	7.2	8.5	8.1	8.8	11.1	13.1
55-64 years	3.5	4.0	3.2	4.0	3.9	5.0	7.6	9.0	17.3	18.9	18.4	20.3	21.3	22.3	24.7	26.4
65 and over	12.4	13.6	14.2	13.6	18.1	19.1	24.1	25.1	50.4	51.0	52.0	52.5	54.6	52.1	54.3	55.6
White, widowed																
15 and over	2.1	2.3	2.2	2.2	2.9	3.3	4.0	4.1	11.7	11.8	11.6	12.0	12.4	11.9	11.5	10.8
15-17 years	--	--	--	--	--	} --	0.1	--	--	--	--	--	*	} 0.1	0.1	0.1
18-19 years	--	--	--	*	--				--	0.1	--	--	*			
20-24 years	--	--	--	0.1	--	0.1	0.1	0.1	0.1	0.2	0.2	0.3	0.3	0.3	0.3	0.4
25-29 years	--	0.1	0.1	0.1	0.1	0.1	0.2	0.3	0.5	0.3	0.5	0.4	0.3	0.5	0.7	0.9
30-34 years	0.1	0.1	0.2	0.2	0.1	0.2	0.3	0.6	0.5	1.1	0.4	0.7	0.6	0.9	1.3	1.9
35-44 years	0.3	0.3	0.4	0.3	0.4	0.5	0.7	1.5	2.0	1.8	2.0	2.2	1.9	2.6	3.1	4.8
45-54 years	1.3	1.2	1.3	1.2	1.4	1.5	2.5	3.8	5.9	6.1	6.5	7.7	7.4	8.0	9.9	11.8
55-64 years	3.1	3.6	3.1	3.5	3.7	4.5	7.1	8.7	16.4	17.7	17.6	19.4	20.6	21.3	23.6	25.4
65 and over	11.6	13.1	13.1	12.7	17.0	18.7	23.7	24.8	49.6	50.3	51.2	51.8	53.6	51.3	53.4	54.7
Black, widowed																
15 and over	3.5	3.9	3.5	4.2	4.3	4.6	5.2	5.3	12.4	13.0	12.0	13.3	13.5	13.9	14.6	15.4
15-17 years	0.2	--	--	--	--	} 0.1	0.1	--	0.2	--	--	--	--	} 0.1	0.2	0.3
18-19 years	--	--	--	--	--				--	--	--	0.7	--			
20-24 years	--	--	0.4	--	0.2	0.2	0.5	0.5	0.2	0.4	0.6	0.4	0.4	0.7	1.1	2.0
25-29 years	0.2	--	0.2	--	--	0.4	0.7	1.1	0.5	0.8	1.8	1.5	0.3	1.8	2.3	4.2
30-34 years	0.4	0.8	0.2	--	0.6	0.8	1.1	1.9	1.8	2.4	2.5	2.5	2.0	3.3	4.1	7.7
35-44 years	0.5	1.4	0.9	0.8	2.3	1.8	2.4	3.8	5.1	5.4	4.0	7.2	7.3	7.0	9.5	15.2
45-54 years	3.7	5.3	4.2	6.6	4.3	4.4	6.2	7.9	13.8	14.5	12.8	16.2	15.4	16.3	22.8	27.3
55-64 years	7.8	8.9	4.9	9.8	4.9	9.8	12.9	14.0	26.0	30.9	26.4	29.4	28.5	33.2	39.4	41.7
65 and over	21.8	19.6	22.6	23.2	31.9	24.3	28.6	28.3	58.8	57.5	58.7	60.2	67.3	61.5	65.6	67.9
Spanish-origin, widowed																
15 and over	1.1	1.4	1.3	1.2	2.0	--	--	--	6.2	6.4	6.2	6.8	7.6	--	--	--
15-17 years	--	--	--	} --	0.1	--	--	--	--	--	--	} --	0.2	--	--	--
18-19 years	--	--	--		0.1	--	--	--	--	--	--		0.2	--	--	--
20-24 years	--	--	--	0.2	0.1	--	--	--	0.4	0.9	0.4	--	0.7	--	--	--
25-29 years	--	0.3	0.3	--	0.2	--	--	--	0.9	0.3	0.6	0.9	1.0	--	--	--
30-34 years	0.1	0.3	0.5	--	0.3	--	--	--	1.8	1.4	1.3	1.1	1.5	--	--	--
35-44 years	0.5	0.7	0.3	0.1	0.7	--	--	--	3.0	2.0	1.6	3.2	3.1	--	--	--
45-54 years	1.4	1.3	0.8	2.0	1.7	--	--	--	5.2	8.7	8.1	9.1	8.4	--	--	--
55-64 years	3.0	3.4	4.4	4.1	4.7	--	--	--	20.0	15.8	17.3	22.5	22.8	--	--	--
65 and over	11.9	13.1	7.1	9.0	18.2	--	--	--	45.4	49.8	49.0	43.8	53.2	--	--	--

Note: -- indicates data not available. * indicates data less than 0.05 percent.

Source: Same as Table 4-4A.

Table 4-4E. Marital Status of the Population, by Sex, Race, Spanish-Origin, and Age: Divorced, 1940-1982 [percent distribution]

Race-ethnicity and age	Males								Females							
	1982	1980	1978	1975	1970	1960	1950	1940	1982	1980	1978	1975	1970	1960	1950	1940
All races, divorced																
15 and over	5.5	4.8	4.2	3.3	2.2	2.1	2.0	1.2	7.5	6.6	6.0	4.8	3.5	2.9	2.4	1.6
15-17 years	--	0.1	--	*	--	} 0.1	0.1	--	0.1	0.1	0.1	0.1	*	} 0.3	0.3	0.1
18-19 years	0.1	0.2	0.2	--	*				0.7	0.6	0.6	0.6	0.4			
20-24 years	1.3	1.6	1.9	1.4	1.1	1.0	0.9	0.3	3.5	3.6	3.6	3.6	2.3	1.8	1.7	0.9
25-29 years	6.0	5.3	5.9	4.2	2.3	1.8	1.7	0.9	8.8	8.5	8.1	6.5	4.3	2.6	2.5	1.8
30-34 years	9.2	7.9	6.9	5.0	2.9	2.2	2.1	1.4	12.1	11.1	10.5	7.1	4.6	3.6	3.0	2.4
35-44 years	9.4	8.0	6.2	5.0	2.9	2.6	2.5	1.9	12.6	10.8	10.2	7.6	5.4	3.8	3.6	2.7
45-54 years	8.2	6.7	5.8	4.9	3.6	3.1	3.0	2.0	10.6	9.2	7.9	6.9	4.9	4.3	3.5	2.2
55-64 years	5.4	5.0	5.5	4.5	3.0	3.1	2.6	1.8	7.7	6.7	6.4	5.3	4.5	3.6	2.4	1.6
65 and over	3.2	3.7	2.9	2.5	2.4	2.3	1.9	1.3	3.8	3.4	3.2	2.6	2.3	2.0	1.1	0.7
White, divorced																
15 and over	5.3	4.7	4.1	3.3	2.2	2.1	2.0	1.3	7.3	6.4	5.8	4.6	3.4	2.8	2.4	1.6
15-17 years	--	--	--	*	--	} 0.1	0.1	--	0.1	0.1	0.1	0.1	*	} 0.3	0.3	0.1
18-19 years	0.2	--	0.2	--	0.1				0.8	0.7	0.6	0.6	0.4			
20-24 years	1.4	1.7	2.0	1.5	1.0	1.0	0.9	0.3	3.8	3.9	3.7	3.8	2.4	1.8	1.6	0.9
25-29 years	6.1	5.5	5.9	4.3	2.4	1.8	1.8	0.9	9.0	8.7	8.1	6.4	4.1	2.5	2.4	1.7
30-34 years	9.1	7.8	6.8	5.1	2.7	2.1	2.1	1.4	11.7	10.7	10.0	6.5	4.6	2.9	2.9	2.4
35-44 years	9.0	7.5	5.7	4.9	2.5	2.5	2.5	1.9	12.3	10.3	9.7	7.0	5.1	3.6	3.5	2.7
45-54 years	7.8	6.3	5.4	4.4	3.4	3.0	3.0	2.0	9.9	8.6	7.2	6.4	4.7	4.1	3.5	2.2
55-64 years	4.8	4.6	5.1	4.4	2.9	3.0	2.7	1.8	7.5	6.2	6.1	5.2	4.5	3.6	2.4	1.6
65 and over	3.0	3.5	2.6	2.3	2.5	2.3	1.9	1.3	3.8	3.2	3.0	2.5	2.3	2.0	1.1	0.7
Black, divorced																
15 and over	7.3	6.4	5.9	4.4	2.9	2.4	1.9	1.0	8.9	8.7	8.2	6.5	4.3	3.6	2.7	1.7
15-17 years	--	0.4	--	--	--	} 0.1	0.1	--	--	0.2	--	--	--	} 0.2	0.2	0.2
18-19 years	--	0.1	0.4	--	--				--	--	0.5	0.3	0.2			
20-24 years	0.4	0.9	1.6	0.7	1.5	0.7	0.9	0.4	1.8	2.1	2.9	2.0	1.5	1.7	1.9	1.2
25-29 years	6.1	4.0	7.1	3.8	1.9	1.7	1.7	0.8	8.3	8.0	8.1	7.7	5.6	3.6	3.4	2.1
30-34 years	11.6	9.7	7.8	5.4	4.6	2.9	2.4	1.2	15.6	15.9	15.0	12.0	5.4	4.8	3.9	2.7
35-44 years	14.8	13.9	11.0	7.3	5.5	3.7	2.8	1.6	15.4	15.7	14.9	11.5	8.1	5.7	4.2	2.6
45-54 years	12.0	9.5	9.5	10.4	5.9	3.9	2.8	1.7	17.0	14.3	14.2	11.8	7.1	5.5	3.4	2.0
55-64 years	12.0	9.7	9.5	6.1	3.4	3.4	2.5	1.4	10.1	11.3	10.3	7.1	5.5	3.9	2.2	1.3
65 and over	4.9	5.4	5.9	3.9	1.8	2.4	1.5	1.0	4.5	4.9	5.0	4.0	2.5	2.0	1.0	0.6
Spanish-origin, divorced																
15 and over	4.4	3.5	3.4	2.8	2.3	--	--	--	8.1	6.9	6.6	5.3	4.4	--	--	--
15-17 years	--	0.1	--	} 0.3	0.1	--	--	--	0.3	0.1	0.1	} 0.6	0.2	--	--	--
18-19 years	--	--	--		0.2	--	--	--	0.8	0.3	1.0		0.7	--	--	--
20-24 years	0.9	0.7	1.6	0.7	1.4	--	--	--	3.4	2.5	4.3	2.1	2.6	--	--	--
25-29 years	4.1	3.3	3.2	3.0	2.6	--	--	--	7.0	5.8	6.5	7.8	4.5	--	--	--
30-34 years	7.5	5.2	3.1	7.6	2.8	--	--	--	10.0	10.3	9.4	3.9	5.4	--	--	--
35-44 years	6.3	5.6	5.4	3.4	3.1	--	--	--	12.3	11.4	10.6	8.9	6.5	--	--	--
45-54 years	7.7	4.3	7.2	4.7	3.6	--	--	--	12.6	11.2	9.7	7.6	7.4	--	--	--
55-64 years	5.9	5.1	6.3	4.8	4.1	--	--	--	12.0	10.3	8.9	7.8	7.0	--	--	--
65 and over	6.7	6.9	5.6	1.5	3.5	--	--	--	9.2	5.6	5.6	6.9	3.9	--	--	--

Note: -- indicates data not available. * indicates data less than 0.05 percent.

Source: Same as Table 4-4A.

Table 4-5. Marital Status, by Residence, Sex, Race, and Spanish-Origin: 1980 [percent distribution]

Place of residence: 1980	Females 15 years and over					Males 15 years and over				
	Single	Married[a]	Separated	Widowed	Divorced	Single	Married[a]	Separated	Widowed	Divorced
White										
United States	21.2	57.4	1.8	12.6	7.0	28.2	62.5	1.4	2.5	5.4
Urban total	22.8	54.0	2.0	13.3	7.9	29.8	60.4	1.6	2.5	5.8
Central cities	25.1	49.0	2.3	14.7	9.0	32.8	55.6	1.9	2.9	6.9
Urban fringe	22.0	57.6	1.9	11.3	7.3	28.3	62.9	1.4	2.2	5.1
Places 10,000 and over[b]	22.9	53.2	1.7	14.7	7.5	30.0	60.7	1.3	2.5	5.5
Places 2,500-10,000[b]	18.5	56.7	1.6	16.5	6.7	25.7	65.0	1.3	3.0	5.0
Rural total	16.9	66.5	1.2	10.8	4.5	24.2	68.0	1.2	2.3	4.3
Places 1,000-2,499	16.8	59.1	1.5	16.7	5.9	23.9	67.1	1.2	3.2	4.7
Other rural	16.9	67.6	1.2	10.0	4.3	24.2	68.1	1.2	2.2	4.3
Black										
United States	34.4	35.1	8.7	12.8	9.0	41.1	42.6	6.1	3.8	6.4
Urban total	34.7	33.9	9.2	12.4	9.8	41.2	42.0	6.3	3.6	6.9
Central cities	35.4	31.9	9.8	12.6	10.3	41.6	40.2	6.9	3.8	7.4
Urban fringe	33.6	39.9	7.7	9.2	9.6	39.4	46.7	5.1	2.5	6.3
Places 10,000 and over[b]	33.7	34.1	8.0	16.3	7.9	42.4	42.1	5.4	4.5	5.6
Places 2,500-10,000[b]	32.5	35.2	7.9	17.9	6.5	41.8	43.1	5.3	5.0	4.7
Rural total	32.1	42.5	6.0	15.1	4.4	40.4	46.3	4.9	4.5	3.9
Places 1,000-2,499	32.0	36.3	7.5	18.5	5.7	40.1	44.8	5.4	5.4	4.4
Other rural	32.1	43.3	5.8	14.6	4.2	40.4	46.5	4.9	4.4	3.8
American Indian[c]										
United States	28.9	48.0	4.1	8.9	10.1	37.3	49.6	2.9	2.5	7.6
Urban total	28.6	45.6	4.8	8.3	12.7	36.8	48.6	3.3	2.1	9.2
Central cities	30.8	41.0	5.8	8.2	14.2	39.0	44.1	4.1	2.3	10.6
Urban fringe	26.0	50.7	4.3	6.5	12.5	33.9	52.9	3.0	1.5	8.7
Places 10,000 and over[b]	29.3	45.3	4.1	9.5	11.8	37.7	48.7	2.6	2.3	8.6
Places 2,500-10,000[b]	27.6	47.8	3.8	10.8	10.1	36.5	51.3	2.2	2.7	7.4
Rural total	29.2	51.0	3.2	9.7	7.0	38.0	50.8	2.4	3.0	5.8
Places 1,000-2,499	29.5	47.3	3.2	11.0	9.1	38.3	49.6	2.3	3.2	6.6
Other rural	29.1	51.4	3.2	9.5	6.7	37.9	50.9	2.5	3.0	5.7

Table 4-5. Marital Status, by Residence, Sex, Race, and Spanish-Origin: 1980 [percent distribution]—continued

Place of residence: 1980	Females 15 years and over					Males 15 and over				
	Single	Married[a]	Separated	Widowed	Divorced	Single	Married[a]	Separated	Widowed	Divorced
Asian and Pacific Islander										
United States	25.0	61.7	1.7	7.6	4.0	35.5	58.8	1.3	1.6	2.8
Urban total	25.6	61.1	1.7	7.6	4.1	35.6	58.7	1.4	1.6	2.7
Central cities.	28.2	56.7	1.9	8.7	4.5	38.1	55.5	1.5	1.9	3.0
Urban fringe.	22.8	65.9	1.6	6.1	3.6	32.0	63.4	1.2	1.1	2.3
Places 10,000 and over[b] . .	24.9	61.8	1.4	7.9	4.1	40.5	53.5	1.1	1.9	2.9
Places 2,500-10,000[b]. . . .	21.4	65.7	1.4	7.6	3.9	35.4	58.2	1.1	2.1	3.2
Rural total	17.8	69.7	1.2	8.0	3.3	33.1	60.0	1.2	2.4	3.3
Places 1,000-2,499.	19.0	66.2	1.2	9.7	3.9	32.4	60.0	1.3	2.9	3.5
Other rural	17.5	70.5	1.2	7.6	3.1	33.3	60.0	1.1	2.3	3.3
Spanish-origin										
United States	27.5	52.8	5.0	7.2	7.5	35.6	55.2	2.7	1.7	4.8
Urban total	27.8	51.9	5.3	7.2	7.8	35.8	54.9	2.8	1.6	4.9
Central cities.	29.0	48.6	6.4	7.5	8.4	37.0	52.8	3.3	1.7	5.2
Urban fringe.	26.5	55.7	4.0	6.5	7.3	34.4	57.4	2.3	1.3	4.7
Places 10,000 and over[b] . .	26.4	55.6	3.6	8.0	6.4	34.7	57.0	2.1	1.9	4.3
Places 2,500-10,000[b]. . . .	25.1	57.3	3.3	8.6	5.7	33.7	58.5	1.9	2.1	3.7
Rural total	24.9	61.6	2.3	7.1	4.1	34.4	57.6	2.0	2.1	3.9
Places 1,000-2,499.	24.8	58.7	2.8	8.8	5.0	33.6	58.7	1.8	2.3	3.6
Other rural	24.9	62.2	2.2	6.7	4.0	34.6	57.5	2.0	2.0	4.0

[a]Married includes separated, hence married, spouse present.

[b]Urban places outside urbanized areas.

[c]Includes Eskimos and Aleuts.

Source: U.S. Bureau of the Census. "General Population Characteristics: United States Summary." 1980 Census of Population. Washington, DC: U.S. Government Printing Office, 1983, Table 46.

In contrast the Asian and Pacific Islander groups have the *lowest* prevalence of divorce and separation of any other group, including the white.

Marital Disruption and Remarriage Ratios

The proportion of persons reported as divorced or widowed at a census or survey greatly understates the magnitude of marital disruption since many persons who have suffered a broken marriage have remarried. In order to measure the total impact of disruption, the 1980 census asked a "marital history" question, wherein each ever-married person was asked whether he or she had been married more than once, and if so, how the previous marriage ended. (See question 21 of the 1980 census questionnaire at the end of Chapter 1.) Table 4-6 reports the percent of ever-married persons aged 15-54 who have ever had a marital termination. The proportions are much higher than the sum of widowed and divorced at these ages as reported in Tables 4-2 and 4-4, and for all ages in Table 4-5. Nearly one-fourth of all ever-married white persons have suffered marital disruption. For American Indians the proportion is nearly one-third. It is lowest for Asian and Pacific Island groups and intermediate for Spanish-origin persons. For all of the groups it is substantially higher in urban than in rural areas.

The extent of remarriage is indicated by remarriage ratios for females, shown in Table 4-7. A remarriage ratio for divorced persons was derived in two steps:

First, a divorce ratio was derived by taking the ratio of persons currently divorced at the time of the 1980 census to persons reported as having ever been divorced.

Then, this ratio was subtracted from 1.000 and the result multiplied by 100 to get a measure of the percentage of ever-divorced persons who had subsequently remarried. A similar procedure was used to compute the remarriage ratio for widowed persons (lower panel of Table 4-7). Such ratios were computed by age for each of five major race-ethnic groups. The following inferences may be made:

1. A high percentage of persons who divorce eventually remarry. The proportion tends to rise with age because of the longer exposure time for remarriage following divorce. It is above 50 percent for the white population for all ages above twenty-five years. Remarriage tends to be less for the Spanish-origin than for the other populations.

2. Widowed persons remarry in lower proportions than divorced persons. Persons who become widowed while still young tend to remarry much more frequently than persons who become widowed at an older age; hence the ratios decline with age. Widowed black persons are much less inclined to remarry than those of other race-ethnic groups.

3. Although divorce causes a great deal of marital disruption, it is only a turnover in marital partners in

Table 4-6. Marital Disruption Ratios, by Race-Ethnicity: Persons Aged 15-54 Years, 1980

Residence	White	Black	American Indian	Asian and Pacific Islander	Spanish-origin
Total	23.1	26.3	32.7	10.9	18.8
Urban, total.	24.5	27.8	37.4	10.9	19.0
Central cities. . . .	27.4	28.9	40.0	11.6	19.7
Urban fringe.	22.7	26.7	37.2	9.9	18.8
Other urban	24.0	23.4	33.7	12.2	16.5
Rural, total.	19.9	16.8	26.3	11.9	16.2
Rural, nonfarm. . . .	20.7	16.9	26.4	12.2	16.4
Farm.	11.6	13.6	24.3	7.9	12.9

Source: U.S. Bureau of the Census. "General Social and Economic Characteristics." 1980 Census of Population. Washington, DC: U.S. Government Printing Office, 1983.

Table 4-7. Remarriage Ratios for Females, by Type of Marital Disruption, Age, and Race-Ethnicity: 1980

Age	White	Black	American Indian	Asian and Pacific Islander	Spanish-origin
Remarriage of divorced					
20-24 years	40.3	24.1	37.5	38.0	33.9
25-29 years	50.4	28.9	48.5	46.6	42.8
30-34 years	56.0	34.0	53.5	51.4	47.4
35-39 years	57.1	37.5	55.5	53.5	48.2
40-44 years	57.6	41.3	56.0	53.6	48.5
45-49 years	57.7	46.3	54.3	52.4	48.5
50-54 years	58.7	51.4	55.7	52.4	47.3
55-59 years	60.1	56.2	58.7	55.8	48.0
60-64 years	61.8	60.4	58.7	56.2	48.8
65-69 years	63.5	64.3	62.1	57.9	47.7
70-74 years	65.2	69.1	68.5	61.5	51.3
75-79 years	66.2	71.5	69.4	65.5	52.0
80-84 years	67.2	76.5	67.3	60.0	56.4
85 years and over.	69.5	77.5	72.1	59.0	61.4
Remarriage of widowed					
20-24 years	31.9	8.7	20.8	25.2	23.1
25-29 years	44.3	16.0	40.7	38.9	31.8
30-34 years	52.6	22.2	51.1	43.8	36.6
35-39 years	49.3	21.6	46.5	39.3	36.8
40-44 years	43.4	19.7	42.6	32.2	34.6
45-49 years	36.7	18.2	35.4	27.4	28.6
50-54 years	30.5	17.0	30.6	21.5	25.3
55-59 years	25.8	15.2	25.0	15.7	19.4
60-64 years	19.2	12.9	19.7	11.2	15.1
65-69 years	13.8	10.3	15.5	6.6	11.6
70-74 years	9.4	8.4	10.0	4.8	7.3
75-79 years	5.9	6.1	5.4	3.4	5.8
80-84 years	3.2	3.9	5.1	1.8	3.1
85 years and over.	1.5	2.2	3.9	1.3	1.7

Source: U.S. Bureau of the Census. "Detailed Population Characteristics." 1980 Census of Population. Washington, DC: U.S. Government Printing Office, 1983. Table 264.

about two cases out of three. Thus the marital status of "divorced" is for most persons only a temporary status, occupied for a comparatively short time until a new partner is found. Those whose first marriage is a failure tend to try again. This is also true (to a lesser degree) for persons who are widowed before age sixty.

Marital Status as a Variable in Subsequent Chapters

Because of its importance in marking life cycle transitions, marital status is treated as a variable by which most of the topics to be discussed in later chapters of this book are cross-classified. Fertility, educational attainment, mortality, migration, labor force participation, occupation, and income are examples. The reader who is interested in learning about the relationships between marital status and other population characteristics and events should consult the index, where the portions of the chapters dealing with marital status are identified.

Marriage as a Demographic Event

The preceding discussion has treated marriage and divorce as *statuses* that persons occupy at the time of a census or other enumeration. In this section and the next they are studied as *events*. An official record is made of each marriage and divorce, hence they can be counted and tabulated. Each year in the early 1980s about 2,400,000 marriages and 1,200,000 divorces occurred in the United States. The National Center for Health Statistics of the U.S. Public Health Service, which bears responsibility for assembling information on marriage and divorce from each of the states, publishes an annual summary that includes data concerning certain characteristics of the brides and grooms and of persons involved in divorce.[3] A technical appendix at the end of this chapter explains the data collection and reporting procedures.

The appropriate statistics for measuring the incidence of the marriage and divorce events are rates—the number of events per 1,000 persons "exposed" to the occurrence of the event. Table 4-8 reports estimates of the number of marriages and divorces, with the rates, for each year since 1920. Unfortunately, there is no obviously best denominator that specifies the "exposed" population. The National Center for Health Statistics provides four versions of marriage rates and two versions of divorce rates:

Marriage

$$\text{Crude marriage rate (CMR)} = \frac{\text{Number of marriages}}{\text{Total population}} \times 1{,}000$$

$$\text{Crude nuptiality rate (CNR)} = \frac{\text{Number of marriages}}{\text{Women 15+}} \times 1{,}000$$

$$\text{General marriage rate (GMR)} = \frac{\text{Number of marriages}}{\text{Unmarried females 15+}} \times 1{,}000$$

$$\text{General nuptiality rate (GNR)} = \frac{\text{Number of marriages}}{\text{Unmarried females 15-44}} \times 1{,}000$$

Divorce

$$\text{Crude divorce rate (CDR)} = \frac{\text{Number of divorces}}{\text{Total population}} \times 1{,}000$$

$$\text{General divorce rate (GDR)} = \frac{\text{Number of divorces}}{\text{Married females 15+}} \times 1{,}000$$

The general nuptiality rate and the general divorce rate have the most precisely defined denominators and hence should be regarded as the best measures of the force of the marriage and divorce processes upon the population.[4]

The remainder of this section is devoted to an analysis of marriage as events; the next section deals with divorce in the same way.

Marriage as a Dynamic Process

The marriage boom of the 1940s and 1950s, followed by the marriage relapse of the 1970s and early 1980s, is clearly evident from Figure 4-3A, which graphically illustrates the trend of the crude marriage rate (CMR), and Figure 4-3B, which traces the history of the general marriage rate (GMR) and the general nuptiality rate (GNR). Before 1920, when a small marriage boom was caused by the military demobilization of World War I, the historical trend of marriage was at a plateau. This was followed by a gradual decline during the 1920s until 1930, when a sharp decline coincided with the economic depression. However, in the late 1930s the rates began to climb despite the economic depression, and they climbed further during the war years. The rates peaked in 1946, at the same time as demobilization following World War II. Large numbers of postponed marriages were celebrated in that one year. Marriage rates remained high during the immediate postwar years. Although they declined gradually, they remained above

Table 4-8. Number of Marriages and Divorces, and Rates: 1920-1983

Year	Marriages					Divorces		
		Rates					Rates	
	Number	Per 1,000 population (CMR)	Per 1,000 women 15+ years (CNR)	Per 1,000 unmarried women 15+ years (GMR)	Per 1,000 unmarried women 15-44 (GNR)	Number	Per 1,000 population (CDR)	Per 1,000 married women 15+ years (GDR)
1983	2,444,000	10.5	26.2	62.3	101.0	1,179,000	5.0	21.9
1982	2,495,000	10.8	27.1	64.9	105.6	1,180,000	5.1	21.9
1981	2,422,145	10.6	25.8	61.7	103.1	1,213,000	5.3	22.6
1980	2,390,252	10.6	26.1	61.4	102.6	1,189,000	5.2	22.6
1979	2,331,337	10.4	26.1	63.6	107.9	1,181,000	5.3	22.8
1978	2,282,272	10.5	26.2	64.1	109.1	1,130,000	5.1	21.9
1977	2,178,367	10.1	25.4	63.6	109.8	1,091,000	5.0	21.1
1976	2,154,807	10.0	25.5	65.2	113.4	1,083,000	5.0	21.1
1975	2,152,662	10.1	25.9	66.9	118.5	1,036,000	4.9	20.3
1974	2,229,667	10.5	27.3	72.0	128.4	977,000	4.6	19.3
1973	2,284,108	10.9	28.4	76.0	137.3	915,000	4.4	18.2
1972	2,282,154	11.0	28.9	77.9	141.3	845,000	4.1	17.0
1971	2,190,481	10.6	28.2	76.2	138.9	773,000	3.7	15.8
1970	2,158,802	10.6	28.4	76.5	140.2	708,000	3.5	14.9
1969	2,145,000	10.6	28.9	80.0	149.1	639,000	3.2	13.4
1968	2,069,000	10.4	28.3	79.1	147.2	584,000	2.9	12.5
1967	1,927,000	9.7	26.9	76.4	145.2	523,000	2.6	11.2
1966	1,857,000	9.5	26.4	75.6	145.1	499,000	2.5	10.9
1965	1,800,000	9.3	26.0	75.0	144.3	479,000	2.5	10.6
1964	1,725,000	9.0	25.3	74.6	146.2	450,000	2.4	10.0
1963	1,654,000	8.8	24.7	73.4	143.3	428,000	2.3	9.6
1962	1,577,000	8.5	23.9	71.2	138.4	413,000	2.2	9.4
1961	1,548,000	8.5	24.0	72.2	145.4	414,000	2.3	9.6
1960	1,523,000	8.5	24.0	73.5	148.0	393,000	2.2	9.2
1959	1,494,000	8.5	23.8	73.6	149.8	395,000	2.2	9.3
1958	1,451,000	8.4	23.5	72.0	146.3	368,000	2.1	8.9
1957	1,518,000	8.9	24.9	78.0	157.4	381,000	2.2	9.2
1956	1,585,000	9.5	26.4	82.4	165.6	382,000	2.3	9.4
1955	1,531,000	9.3	25.8	80.9	161.1	377,000	2.3	9.3
1954	1,490,000	9.2	25.4	79.8	154.3	379,000	2.4	9.5
1953	1,546,000	9.8	26.7	83.7	163.3	390,000	2.5	9.9
1952	1,539,318	9.9	26.8	83.2	159.9	392,000	2.5	10.1
1951	1,594,694	10.4	28.1	86.6	164.9	381,000	2.5	9.9
1950	1,667,231	11.1	29.8	90.2	166.4	385,144	2.6	10.3
1949	1,579,798	10.6	28.5	86.7	158.0	397,000	2.7	10.6
1948	1,811,155	12.4	33.0	98.5	174.7	408,000	2.8	11.2
1947	1,991,878	13.9	36.8	106.2	182.7	483,000	3.4	13.6
1946	2,291,045	16.4	42.8	118.1	199.0	610,000	4.3	17.9
1945	1,612,992	12.2	30.5	83.6	138.2	485,000	3.5	14.4
1944	1,452,394	10.9	27.8	76.5	124.5	400,000	2.9	12.0
1943	1,577,050	11.7	30.6	83.0	133.5	359,000	2.6	11.0
1942	1,772,132	13.2	34.8	93.0	147.6	321,000	2.4	10.1
1941	1,695,999	12.7	33.7	88.5	138.4	293,000	2.2	9.4
1940	1,595,879	12.1	32.3	82.8	122.4	264,000	2.0	8.8
1939	1,403,633	10.7	28.8	73.8	113.1	251,000	1.9	8.5
1938	1,330,780	10.3	27.7	71.0	108.2	244,000	1.9	8.4
1937	1,451,296	11.3	30.6	78.5	119.2	249,000	1.9	8.7
1936	1,369,000	10.7	29.3	75.2	113.5	236,000	1.8	8.3
1935	1,327,000	10.4	28.8	74.0	111.0	218,000	1.7	7.8
1934	1,302,000	10.3	28.6	73.7	110.0	204,000	1.6	7.5
1933	1,098,000	8.7	24.5	63.1	93.7	165,000	1.3	6.1
1932	981,903	7.9	22.2	57.3	84.6	164,241	1.3	6.1
1931	1,060,914	8.6	24.4	62.9	92.3	188,003	1.5	7.1
1930	1,126,856	9.2	26.3	67.8	99.0	195,961	1.6	7.5
1929	1,232,559	10.1	29.3	75.5	109.9	205,876	1.7	8.0
1928	1,182,497	9.8	28.6	73.7	107.0	200,176	1.7	7.8
1927	1,201,053	10.1	29.6	76.2	110.4	196,292	1.6	7.8
1926	1,202,574	10.2	30.2	77.6	112.2	184,678	1.6	7.5
1925	1,188,334	10.3	30.5	78.1	112.6	175,449	1.5	7.2
1924	1,184,574	10.4	31.0	79.3	114.0	170,952	1.5	7.2
1923	1,229,784	11.0	32.8	83.9	120.3	165,096	1.5	7.1
1922	1,134,151	10.3	30.9	78.9	112.7	148,815	1.4	6.6
1921	1,163,863	10.7	32.4	82.6	117.6	159,580	1.5	7.2
1920	1,274,476	12.0	36.2	92.3	131.0	170,505	1.6	8.0

Note: -- indicates data not available. GMR and GNR for years 1920-1939 were estimated by the author. CNR for 1982 and 1983 were also estimated by the author.

Source: National Center for Health Statistics. Vital Statistics of the United States: 1978; "Advance Report of Final Marriage Statistics," "Advance Report of Final Divorce Statistics" (1980 and 1981), and "Births, Marriages, Divorces, and Deaths for 1983." Monthly Vital Statistics Report. Washington, DC: U.S. Government Printing Office, 1982, 1983, and 1984.

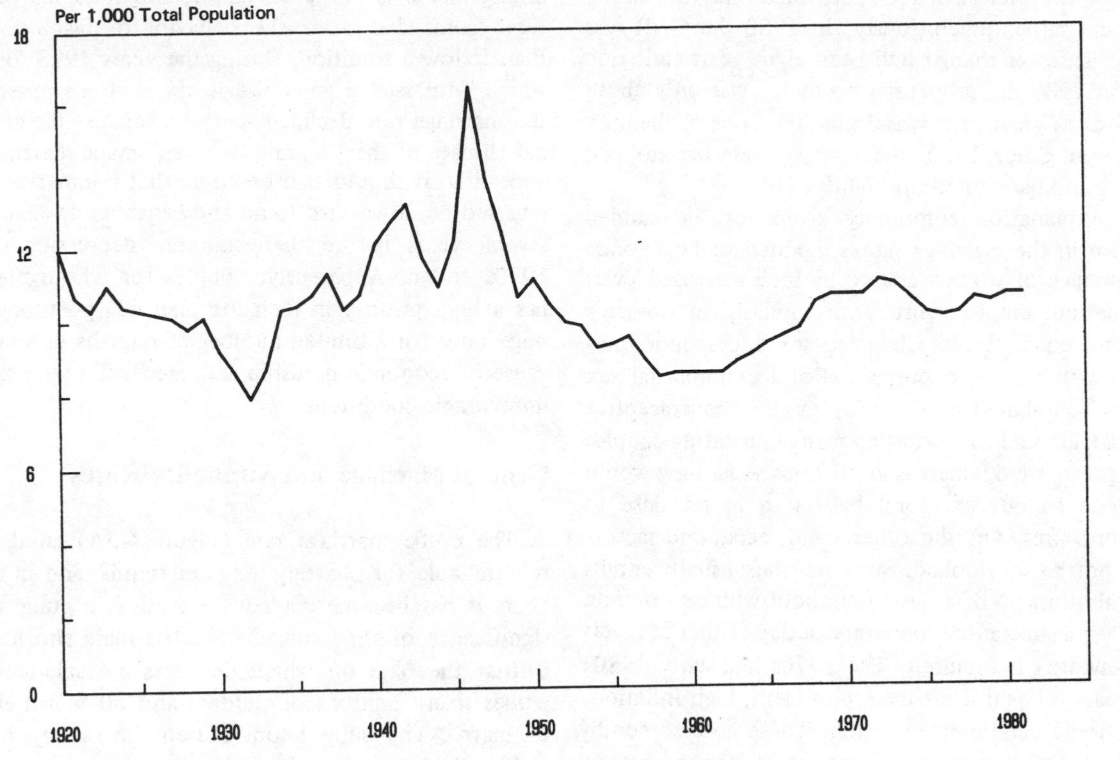

Figure 4-3A. Crude Marriage Rate: 1920-1983

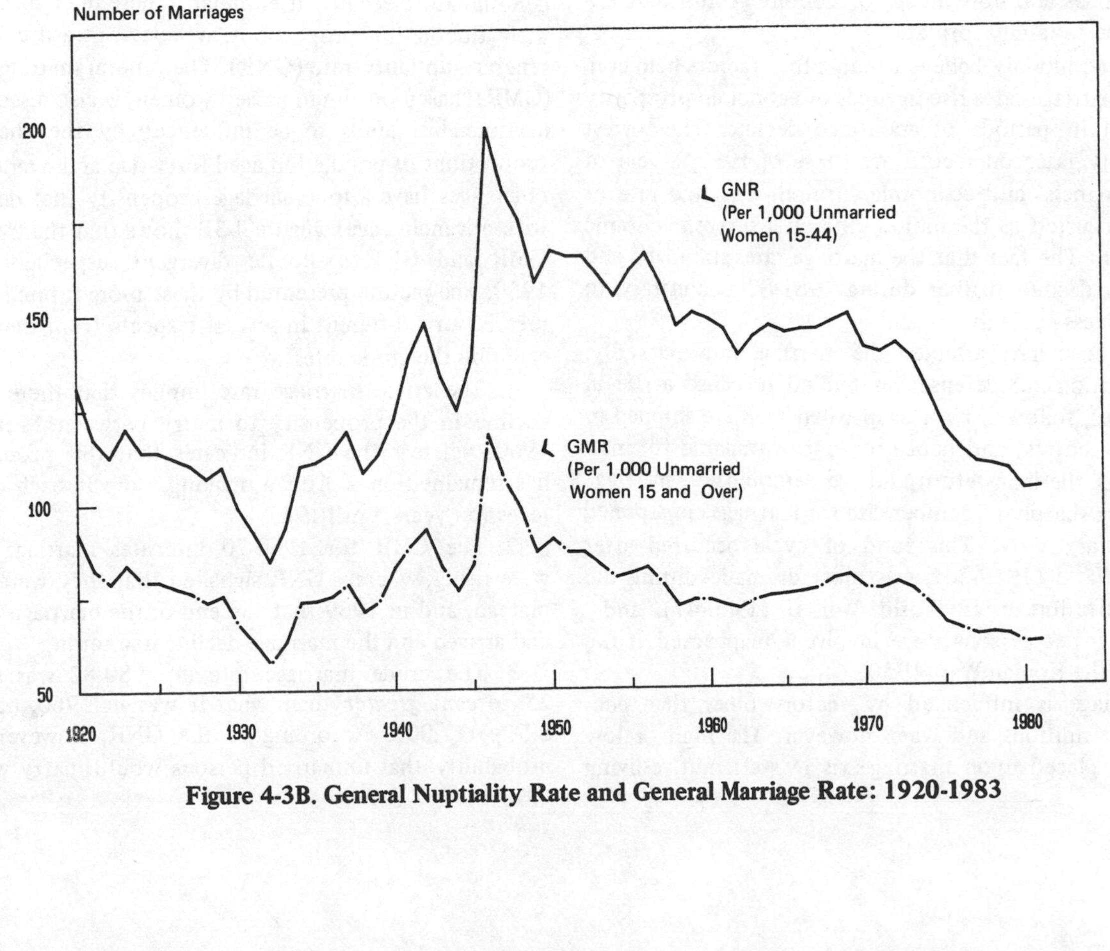

Figure 4-3B. General Nuptiality Rate and General Marriage Rate: 1920-1983

the long-term level until 1957, at which time they began to decline rather precipitously. In 1980 the GNR was 27 percent lower than it had been eight years earlier, in 1972. In 1980 the propensity to marry was only about two-thirds as great as it was during the years of the marriage boom. Since 1980, the marriage rate has stopped declining and has turned up slightly.

The explanation commonly given for the sudden downturn in the marriage rate is the increased economic independence of women caused by their increased levels of education, employment, and emphasis on women's rights and equal status. Changing sex codes, more permissive with regard to premarital and extramarital sex relations (combined with use of modern contraceptive methods), are said to be causing many cohabiting couples not to get married, whereas in previous years they would have done so out of moral beliefs or in response to social pressures. On the other hand, economic factors should not be overlooked. Since marriage usually entails the establishment of a new household with appropriate amenities, a substantial monetary outlay (either in credit or in savings) is required. The 1970s and early 1980s were years of significant unemployment, high inflation, and periodic economic recession. These adverse conditions had their greatest impact upon young persons leaving school and seeking to join the work force. Thus, an urgent research need is to determine how much the lower marriage rates in the 1980s are attributable to new social codes and how much to economic conditions unfavorable to family formation.

It is commonly believed that, other factors held constant, marriage rates rise in times of economic prosperity and fall in periods of economic decline. The lowest nuptiality rates on record are those of 1932, a year of great financial and economic turmoil. The low rate of 1980 occurred as the nation entered a severe economic recession. The fact that the marriage rates stabilized and did not decline further during 1981-82 is contrary to the business cycle theory.

Wars also have affected the marriage rate markedly. Mobilization for defense has tended to cause a rise in marriages, followed by a drop when men are shipped to combat centers, and hence no longer available for marriage. As the men return and are demobilized, marriage rates rise sharply to compensate for marriages postponed by military duty. This kind of cycle occurred after World War I (1919-20), was most dramatic during the demobilization after World War II (1946-47), and—though fewer persons were involved—reappeared at the time of the Korean War (1950).

Marriage is influenced by factors other than economic conditions and wars, however. The high or low priority placed upon marriage vis-a-vis alternative living arrangements is one such factor, and it seems to fluctuate somewhat after the behavior of fashion rather than follow a tradition. During the years 1923 to 1929, which witnessed a great rise in the nation's prosperity, the marriage rate declined—perhaps because the attitudinal climate of the "roaring twenties" made marriage less appealing. It should also be noted that the marriage rate reversed its downward trend and began an upward trend several years before the economic depression of the 1930s ended. Apparently, couples for whom marriage has a high priority in their life plan will postpone marriage only for a limited number of months or years because of economic hardship and then will marry despite unfavorable conditions.

General Marriage and Nuptiality Rates

The crude marriage rate (Figure 4-3A) cited above is unreliable for charting long-run trends, and in recent years it has become inadequate even as a guide to the significance of short-run changes. Its main shortcoming is that the base on which the rates are calculated includes many millions of children and other not eligible to marry. The baby boom caused the rate to decline artificially because of the larger child population in the denominator; subsequent fertility decline is now causing the CMR to understate the extent of marriage rate decline because of the shrinking child population in the denominator. Because it eliminates these ineligibles with their fluctuating proportions, a better measure is the general nuptiality rate (GNR). The general marriage rate (GMR), based on all unmarried women, is also a sensitive measure but tends to be influenced by the changing proportions of population aged forty-five and over (these older ages have a low marriage propensity that declines with advancing age). Figure 4-3B shows that the trend of GMR and GNR are quite divergent, especially since 1950. The picture presented by these more refined measures is very different in several respects from that indicated by the crude rates:

1. The crude marriage rate implies that there was a decline in the propensity to marry between 1950 and 1960, whereas the GNR indicates that this propensity has remained on a plateau, making a dip in each of the recession years, until 1957.

2. The CMR for 1960-70 indicates marriage rates were rising, whereas GNR signalled that they were on a plateau, and in 1969 that the end of the marriage boom had arrived and the marriage decline had set in.

3. The crude marriage rate in 1980-82 was about 25 percent *greater* than what it was in 1960, namely 8.5 per 1,000. According to the GNR, however, the probability that unmarried persons would marry within

Table 4-9. Median Age and Previous Marital Status of Bride and Groom: 1952-1981

Year	Median age		Previous marital status of bride			Previous marital status of groom		
	Bride	Groom	Single	Widowed	Divorced	Single	Widowed	Divorced
1981.	24.1	26.3	69.6	3.2	27.1	68.0	3.0	29.0
1980.	23.7	25.9	70.7	3.4	25.9	69.3	3.1	27.6
1979.	23.4	25.8	70.9	3.6	25.3	69.2	3.5	27.3
1978.	23.2	25.5	71.7	3.6	24.8	69.9	3.2	26.9
1977.	22.9	25.2	71.7	3.8	24.4	70.0	3.5	26.5
1976.	22.7	25.0	72.5	4.0	23.5	70.7	3.6	25.7
1975.	22.4	24.7	73.3	4.2	22.5	72.0	3.8	24.1
1974.	22.0	24.2	75.1	4.3	20.6	74.1	3.7	22.2
1973.	21.9	24.1	76.2	4.2	19.6	75.4	3.7	20.9
1972.	21.7	23.8	77.8	4.2	18.0	77.0	3.7	19.3
1971.	21.7	23.7	78.0	4.5	17.4	77.5	4.0	18.5
1970.	21.7	23.6	78.4	4.7	16.9	78.1	4.1	17.8
1969.	21.6	23.5	77.2	5.2	17.6	77.1	4.5	18.5
1968.	21.5	23.6	77.9	5.2	17.2	77.7	4.6	17.9
1967.	21.4	23.8	77.7	5.4	16.9	77.6	4.7	17.7
1966.	21.5	23.8	77.6	5.5	17.0	77.4	4.8	17.7
1965.	21.4	23.6	77.8	5.7	16.6	77.6	5.0	17.3
1964.	21.4	23.6	77.4	5.8	16.8	77.6	5.1	17.3
1963.	21.3	23.7	77.2	5.9	17.0	77.8	5.2	17.0
1962.	21.5	24.0	79.9	5.3	14.8	80.4	4.6	15.0
1961.	21.3	23.9	80.0	5.1	15.0	80.2	4.5	15.3
1960.	21.5	24.1	80.5	5.2	14.3	81.4	4.8	13.8
1959[a]	21.6	24.2	76.9	6.3	16.8	77.9	5.5	16.6
1958[a]	21.6	24.2	78.8	6.1	15.1	79.5	5.5	15.0
1957[a]	21.8	24.3	76.9	6.5	16.5	77.9	5.8	16.4.
1956[a]	21.9	24.4	77.6	6.4	16.0	78.6	5.6	15.8
1955[a]	22.0	24.5	76.1	6.7	17.2	77.3	5.9	16.8
1954[a]	22.1	24.6	74.7	7.2	18.0	76.0	6.4	17.6
1953[a]	22.2	24.7	72.8	7.4	19.8	74.2	6.3	19.5
1952[a]	22.5	24.8	76.1	7.0	16.9	77.1	6.4	16.5

[a]Indicates number of states reporting varies between 28 and 15.

Source: National Center for Health Statistics. Vital Statistics of the United States (1952-1981). Washington, DC: U.S. Government Printing Office, 1955-1984.

one year was 31 percent *less* in 1980 than in 1960. These examples illustrate that the general nuptiality rate is a more valid statistic for studying marriage trends and differences, because it more nearly reflects the exposed population.

The data for GNR show that the propensity to marry has plummeted since 1972. The probability that an unmarried person will get married within a year declined by at least 25 percent in the eight years between 1972 and 1980—notwithstanding the fact that the crude marriage rate for the two years is nearly identical. Whether this leveling out of 1981-82 is a long-term or even a reversal is not predictable at present.

First Marriage and Remarriage

Only about 70 percent of the marriages that occur are first marriages for either the bride or the groom. In all other cases one or both of the partners have been married previously. Table 4-9, based on a tabulation of marriage returns for states tabulating these data as far back as data are reported, shows that the proportion of remarriages among all marriages has increased moderately. There has been a decline in the proportion of widowed and an increase in the proportion of divorced persons among those marrying. A summary of the previous marital status of marriage partners as of 1981 (for whom previous status of both partners was reported) may be made as follows:

Previous marital status	1978	1981
Total.	100.0	100.0
First marriage for both bride and groom.	61.1	58.3
First marriage for bride, not for groom.	10.2	10.9
First marriage for groom, not for bride.	8.5	9.4
Remarriage for both bride and groom.	20.2	21.4

It is important to realize that widows and divorcees have been much more prone to remarry since World War II than they were previously. Among those members of the population who remarry, the ratio of divorced persons to widows is more than 5 to 1, for both men and women. Since this ratio is much higher than that found among the general population, it must be concluded that divorced persons are much more inclined to remarry than widowed persons. A major element in this differential is the fact that divorced persons are considerably younger on the average than widowed persons. There appears to be a tendency for previously married persons to marry persons who have been married before. In fact, there seems to be a tendency for widowed persons to marry widowed persons, and for divorced persons to marry divorced persons.

Age-Specific Marriage Rates

Table 4-10A reports the nuptiality rates that prevailed between 1971 and 1980, in each of several age groups, for grooms. Table 4-10B reports the same information for brides. The rates for first marriages and for remarriages are given separately. In computing these age-specific nuptiality rates, at each age the appropriate unmarried population has been used as the denominator. The rates of first marriage have been based on the single (never married) population, while the rates of remarriage have been based on the widowed and divorced population (see "definitions"), subdivided into age groups. The bottom two panels give rates for widowed and divorced persons as separate groups. Figure 4-4 illustrates these rates. The data of Tables 4-10A and 4-10B are not reported for all states. The rates reported are probably not

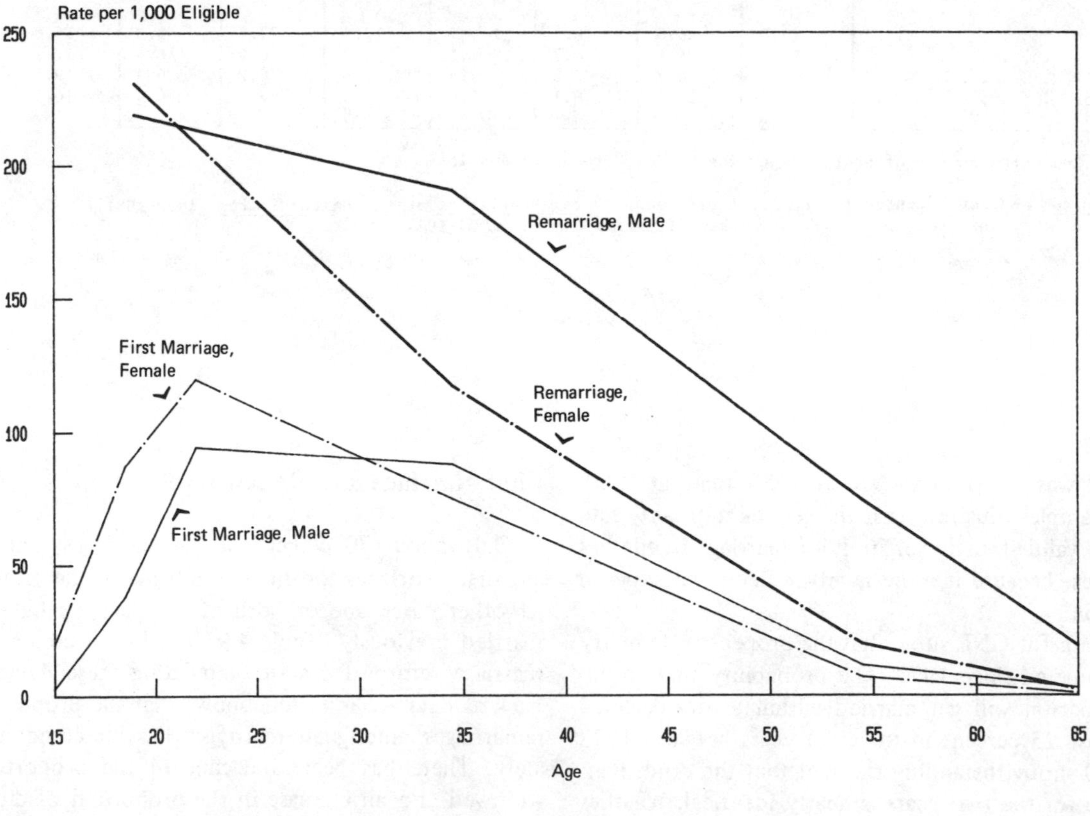

Figure 4-4. Age Profile of Marriage Rates: 1980

Table 4-10A. Marriage Rates, by Previous Marital Status and Age of Groom: Marriage-Registration Area, 1965-1980

Previous marital status and age	Groom											
	1980[a]	1979	1978	1977	1976	1975	1974	1973	1972	1971	1970	1965
All marriages												
14 and over. . . .	66.8	65.1	64.9	65.1	66.6	68.8	73.8	78.6	80.7	78.8	80.8	74.7
14-17 years. . .	3.0	2.5	2.7	2.9	3.2	3.5	4.2	4.5	4.5	4.2	4.0	3.0
18-19 years. . .	39.2	42.7	45.0	47.6	52.4	58.5	67.9	73.7	77.1	73.0	74.4	69.5
20-24 years. . .	100.4	109.0	112.2	115.4	121.5	129.6	150.9	165.0	176.1	177.5	205.7	199.0
25-44 years. . .	121.2	129.5	134.5	138.3	141.2	146.3	148.4	160.3	160.5	156.4	164.0	150.5
45-64 years. . .	49.1	51.4	50.6	50.8	53.7	52.7	54.3	60.8	62.8	58.4	54.9	49.0
65 and over. . .	15.2	16.2	13.2	14.2	15.6	16.8	17.2	16.6	16.4	16.7	15.6	14.2
Median age	25.9	25.8	25.5	25.2	25.0	24.7	24.2	24.1	23.8	23.7	23.6	23.6
Mean age	29.4	29.5	29.1	29.0	28.9	28.7	28.3	28.1	27.9	27.8	27.8	28.1
First marriages												
14 and over. . . .	54.7	52.0	51.9	52.0	53.1	56.0	61.8	66.8	69.7	67.9	72.1	68.2
14-17 years. . .	2.9	2.4	2.7	2.8	3.2	3.4	4.2	4.4	4.4	4.1	3.9	3.0
18-19 years. . .	38.4	41.9	44.3	46.7	51.0	57.4	66.6	72.2	75.6	71.2	73.0	68.4
20-24 years. . .	94.5	102.4	105.2	107.7	113.0	121.7	141.8	155.6	166.2	165.6	195.7	191.8
25-44 years. . .	87.9	89.5	91.1	91.9	91.7	96.7	100.4	109.9	111.6	106.9	119.6	110.5
45-64 years. . .	11.6	10.8	10.3	11.8	12.4	13.0	12.6	15.6	16.5	14.6	14.1	13.1
65 and over. . .	2.9	3.0	2.5	2.5	3.1	3.0	3.5	3.6	3.7	3.2	3.4	3.9
Median age	23.6	23.4	23.2	23.0	22.9	22.7	22.5	22.5	22.4	22.5	22.5	22.5
Mean age	24.8	24.6	24.4	24.3	24.1	24.0	23.8	23.8	23.7	23.7	23.8	24.0
All remarriages												
14 and over. . . .	108.3	120.2	121.8	122.4	127.6	129.8	129.1	133.3	133.9	130.6	116.5	103.8
14-19 years. . . 20-24 years. . .	219.2	334.5	336.3	361.0	384.3	371.4	367.1	398.5	467.3	536.9	350.9	466.1
25-44 years. . .	190.6	226.6	242.4	253.4	274.5	284.1	281.9	311.3	318.5	327.5	298.0	326.0
45-64 years. . .	74.4	84.6	85.2	82.0	86.8	88.0	93.3	104.4	109.7	105.8	95.6	95.7
65 and over. . .	19.0	20.6	16.8	18.5	19.6	21.5	21.4	20.6	20.7	21.6	19.9	17.3
Median age	35.2	35.3	35.1	34.9	35.1	35.5	35.7	36.3	36.5	36.9	37.5	39.6
Mean age	38.7	38.9	38.5	38.6	38.8	39.1	39.4	39.6	39.8	40.3	40.6	42.0
Widowed												
14 and over. . . .	32.2	35.3	32.7	35.3	37.6	40.4	38.9	39.3	40.6	42.5	40.6	37.2
14-24 years. . . 25-44 years. . .	106.7	157.8	146.1	159.3	204.6	173.3	136.1	148.9	175.3	201.3	107.8	198.4
45-64 years. . .	59.2	60.6	64.9	66.3	68.9	71.4	69.6	77.3	86.8	85.8	79.2	78.6
65 and over. . .	17.8	19.9	15.6	17.7	18.6	19.5	19.2	18.8	18.4	19.6	19.4	15.4
Median age	61.2	61.7	59.7	60.1	60.0	59.4	59.2	59.3	59.1	59.1	58.7	57.8
Mean age	59.6	60.0	58.4	58.9	58.6	58.2	58.2	58.1	58.0	57.7	57.7	56.7
Divorced												
14 and over. . . .	142.1	165.6	168.6	173.4	185.0	189.8	198.7	221.3	229.0	230.7	204.5	215.3
14-19 years. . . 20-24 years. . .	217.6	318.1	307.4	347.9	391.8	368.2	365.8	431.3	486.7	527.8	402.2	513.5
25-44 years. . .	188.8	224.1	236.6	252.9	270.2	278.2	286.9	321.4	324.6	338.4	325.4	354.6
45-64 years. . .	79.1	92.8	89.2	85.1	91.5	94.0	101.6	117.3	123.2	119.5	108.7	109.2
65 and over. . .	22.8	23.3	20.8	21.9	26.1	31.4	34.6	32.0	38.3	38.6	23.6	36.5
Median age	34.0	33.9	33.8	33.6	33.7	33.6	33.6	33.9	34.0	34.1	34.5	36.0
Mean age	36.5	36.4	36.2	36.1	36.2	36.3	36.3	36.4	36.5	36.6	36.7	37.8

[a] Categories for 1980 begin at 15 years of age instead of 14 as in preceding years.

Source: National Center for Health Statistics. Vital Statistics of the United States (1965, 1970-78). Also "Advance Report of Final Marriage Statistics (1979 and 1980)." Monthly Vital Statistics Reports (Vol. 30, no 4; and Vol. 32, no. 5). Washington, DC: U.S. Government Printing Office, 1968, 1974-82, 1979, and 1980.

Table 4-10B. Marriage Rates, by Previous Marital Status and Age of Bride: Marriage-Registration Area, 1965-1980

Previous marital status and age	Bride											
	1980[a]	1979	1978	1977	1976	1975	1974	1973	1972	1971	1970	1965
<u>All marriages</u>												
14 and over. . . .	54.2	53.6	53.3	53.7	55.1	56.9	61.0	64.9	66.6	65.2	64.8	63.6
14-17 years. . .	20.2	16.7	17.7	18.9	20.3	22.3	25.9	27.9	29.0	27.0	26.3	27.1
18-19 years. . .	90.9	94.8	99.2	103.6	110.1	119.6	138.9	150.4	157.1	156.6	156.7	171.8
20-24 years. . .	130.8	134.6	136.0	140.1	148.2	157.5	174.6	194.1	209.4	216.6	234.2	251.8
25-44 years. . .	96.5	102.0	102.3	104.8	109.2	113.5	116.7	125.2	124.6	120.6	111.3	118.3
45-64 years. . .	17.3	19.0	19.1	19.4	20.8	20.6	21.4	22.8	22.4	21.4	20.9	20.3
65 and over. . .	2.2	2.7	2.0	2.2	2.2	2.4	2.3	2.4	2.4	2.4	2.4	2.3
Median age	23.7	23.4	23.2	22.9	22.7	22.4	22.0	21.9	21.7	21.7	21.7	21.4
Mean age	26.7	26.7	26.3	26.2	26.1	25.9	25.6	25.5	25.2	25.1	25.1	25.2
<u>First marriages</u>												
14 and over. . . .	66.0	62.1	62.1	62.7	64.8	68.1	74.8	81.0	84.5	82.8	82.9	84.4
14-17 years. . .	19.8	16.3	17.3	18.4	19.8	21.7	25.2	27.2	28.3	26.2	25.6	26.6
18-19 years. . .	87.3	91.7	95.6	99.6	105.1	115.0	133.5	144.8	151.9	150.3	151.4	166.9
20-24 years. . .	119.8	121.9	123.0	125.6	133.4	143.8	159.5	177.1	192.9	197.7	220.1	237.3
25-44 years. . .	74.9	76.8	77.1	78.6	81.8	81.7	85.7	94.8	94.2	89.2	82.5	96.4
45-64 years. . .	7.0	7.8	7.9	8.6	9.3	9.2	9.6	11.3	10.8	9.5	8.8	9.0
65 and over. . .	0.9	0.9	1.0	1.0	1.1	1.2	0.8	1.0	1.1	1.4	1.1	1.3
Median age	21.8	21.6	21.4	21.1	21.0	20.8	20.6	20.6	20.5	20.5	20.6	20.4
Mean age	22.7	22.5	22.3	22.2	22.1	21.9	21.7	21.7	21.6	21.6	21.6	21.6
<u>All remarriages</u>												
14 and over. . . .	38.3	40.8	40.0	40.0	39.7	40.1	40.0	40.6	39.3	37.3	36.6	33.7
14-19 years. . . / 20-24 years. . .	} 231.0	312.6	321.5	323.5	324.4	319.9	332.1	391.2	398.0	405.9	317.6	471.0
25-44 years. . .	117.3	127.5	126.8	129.0	133.2	144.5	147.3	154.3	155.3	152.6	142.3	139.6
45-64 years. . .	19.7	21.7	21.9	22.1	23.5	23.5	24.4	25.7	25.4	24.6	24.8	24.5
65 and over. . .	2.3	3.0	2.1	2.4	2.3	2.5	2.5	2.5	2.6	2.5	2.5	2.4
Median age	32.0	31.9	31.5	31.4	31.7	32.0	32.1	32.3	32.8	32.9	33.3	35.5
Mean age	35.0	35.4	34.9	35.0	35.3	35.5	35.7	36.0	36.2	36.4	36.6	37.7
<u>Widowed</u>												
14 and over. . . .	6.7	7.7	7.1	7.6	7.9	8.3	9.1	9.3	9.4	9.6	10.2	10.2
14-24 years. . . / 25-44 years. . .	} 51.0	52.6	55.3	57.3	56.0	61.7	61.8	60.7	65.1	70.4	54.1	65.5
45-64 years. . .	12.2	13.6	13.6	14.0	15.2	14.9	16.3	16.5	16.3	16.5	17.7	16.6
65 and over. . .	2.1	2.6	1.8	2.1	2.1	2.1	2.2	2.2	2.2	2.2	2.3	2.0
Median age	53.6	55.2	52.6	53.1	53.0	52.4	51.9	52.1	51.4	51.8	51.2	50.1
Mean age	52.2	53.4	51.4	51.8	51.8	51.2	51.0	51.0	50.7	50.6	50.3	49.7
<u>Divorced</u>												
14 and over. . . .	91.3	104.0	105.0	107.3	111.3	117.2	121.7	131.0	130.6	132.8	123.3	129.7
14-19 years. . . / 20-24 years. . .	} 236.4	309.1	313.7	347.3	339.4	319.6	336.3	394.0	406.3	443.9	413.4	535.3
25-44 years. . .	122.8	135.2	134.4	137.3	144.0	158.6	166.0	177.7	177.1	176.1	179.6	175.5
45-64 years. . .	30.3	35.1	35.6	35.6	37.5	40.1	41.0	46.1	47.2	46.5	42.6	47.7
65 and over. . .	5.3	7.4	6.4	6.4	6.9	9.1	6.7	8.3	9.5	9.3	6.1	9.4
Median age	31.0	30.8	30.5	30.2	30.1	30.2	30.0	30.2	30.3	30.2	30.1	31.7
Mean age	32.8	32.8	32.6	32.5	32.5	32.7	32.5	32.8	32.9	32.8	32.8	33.6

[a]Categories for 1980 begin at 15 years of age instead of 14 as in preceding years.

Source: Same as Table 4-10A.

exactly the same as complete national rates, but the age patterns are probably almost identical to the unknown national age-at-marriage patterns.

According to the estimates of Tables 4-10A and 4-10B, the rates for first marriage begin low (at ages 14-17), climb quickly to reach a peak at ages 20-24 for brides and 25-29 for grooms, and then decline gradually with advancing age. The peak rate is reached earlier in the case of females than in the case of males. The trend at all ages, and for the greatest relative decline to take place at the earliest ages. Between the ages of fifteen and twenty-four, the probability that a single woman will marry within a year is greater than that for men. But after they pass their twenty-fifth birthday, single women have nuptiality rates much lower than those for men, and the female rates decline more swiftly. In the years after age sixty-five the probability of a single woman marrying during a one-year period is only one-third as great as that for men, but it is very low for both.

Rates of remarriage are not very trustworthy before age twenty-five, because the number of previously married persons is so small that the numbers are unstable. Tables 4-7A and 4-7B show that the rate of remarriage is higher for males than for females at all ages. Remarriage rates are higher than first marriage rates, moreso for males than females. As a group, previously married men remarry at a rate more than three times as high as previously married women. Despite the fact that a very high proportion of remarriages occur after age thirty (see below), the *rate* of remarriage is at its peak in the twenties and thirties and declines very sharply after age forty-five. At every age the rate of remarriage is higher for both men and women than the rate of first marriage. Remarriage of divorced persons has a higher rate than for widowed persons, at every age. These data imply that once they have entered the married state, both sexes try to remain there. If their marriage is broken, they tend to remarry rather promptly if they are younger than forty-five, and at a significant rate at older ages. However, remarriage rates have declined since 1971 for both males and females and at all ages. The reduction has been particularly large at the younger ages.

Nuptiality Rates by Single Years

First marriage is concentrated into such a short segment of the life cycle that groups of ages do not portray accurately the shape of the age-specific nuptiality curve. First marriage nuptiality rates for individual years (first marriages of persons of a given age per 1,000 unmarried persons of the same age) are estimated in Table 4-11. Marriages are tabulated by single years of age in the interval 18-29 years by the National Center for Health Statistics, but appropriate denominators can be obtained only by making estimates. This has been done for Table 4-11.

Although approximate, the data of Table 4-11 reveal the dynamics of the marriage boom and the subsequent decline in much finer detail than do Tables 4-10A and 4-10B. Figure 4-5, which graphs some of these data, il-

Table 4-11. Estimated Age-Specific Nuptiality Rates for First Marriages: 1970 to 1980

Age and marriage order	Brides				Grooms			
	1980	1978	1975	1970	1980	1978	1975	1970
Under 18 years	15.80	18.64	25.06	20.64	2.42	2.93	4.02	3.18
18 years	65.31	72.88	93.72	109.38	23.16	27.34	40.01	44.66
19 years	74.19	78.98	96.05	136.26	40.12	45.64	60.50	77.21
20 years	80.57	87.25	102.57	154.38	55.15	61.22	79.90	105.42
21 years	88.21	96.32	112.58	186.07	68.60	77.90	96.91	158.58
22 years	100.48	101.04	118.01	199.29	82.81	89.16	105.85	179.21
23 years	97.69	98.64	104.00	176.21	89.29	93.96	107.31	195.04
24 years	91.19	89.06	94.64	144.46	88.59	94.23	105.51	178.84
25 years	82.35	78.96	78.48	113.86	88.38	87.54	97.20	155.33
26 years	72.83	68.13	66.84	98.67	85.76	82.73	92.07	137.80
27 years	61.93	56.91	55.11	83.09	77.77	71.57	82.39	126.39
28 years	57.50	45.68	51.89	66.34	72.40	69.55	76.08	109.11
29 years	45.64	38.46	38.98	57.05	60.75	57.47	58.78	100.07
30-34 years	29.90	25.42	25.54	37.37	46.27	42.21	42.25	60.76
35-44 years	11.63	11.44	11.87	15.08	19.89	18.24	18.56	23.34
45-54 years	4.03	3.85	4.81	5.33	6.08	6.26	7.63	7.54
55-64 years	1.36	1.41	2.00	1.49	2.60	2.39	3.39	2.63
65 years and over	0.23	0.22	0.32	0.27	1.04	0.89	1.12	1.16

Source: National Center for Health Statistics. Vital Statistics of the United States. Washington, DC: U.S. Government Printing Office, annual volumes for years cited.

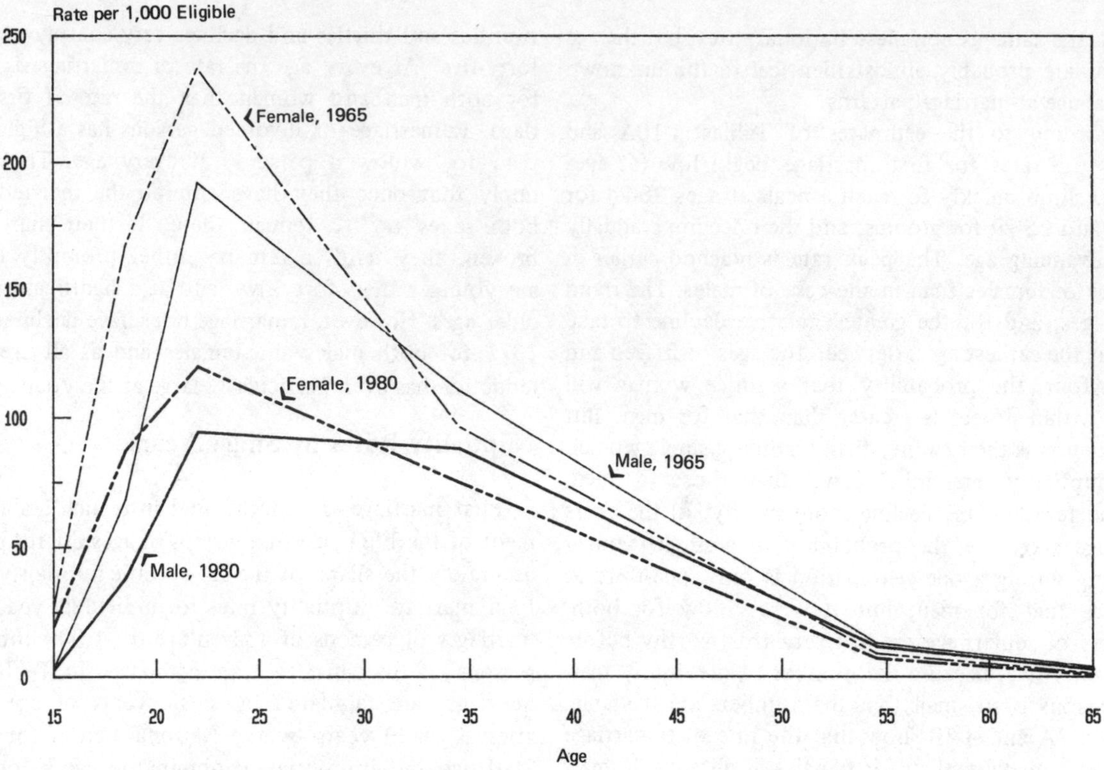

Figure 4-5A. Age-Specific First Marriage Rates, by Sex: 1965 and 1980

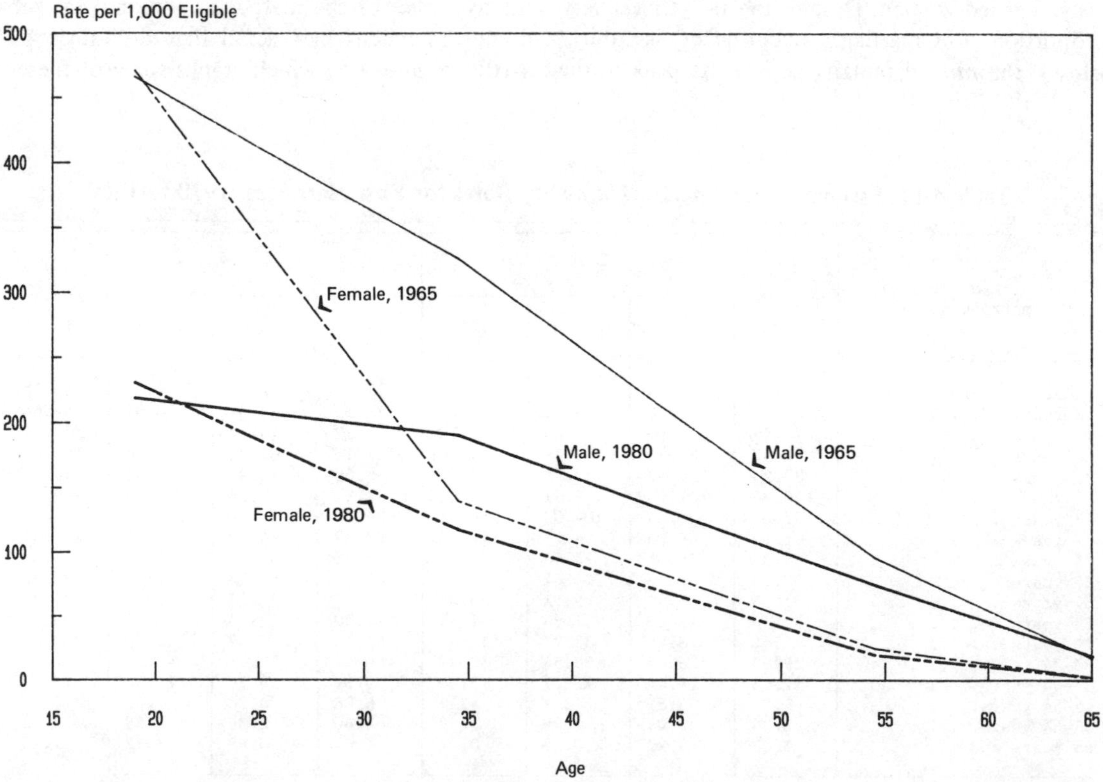

Figure 4-5B. Age-Specific Remarriage Rates, by Sex: 1965 and 1980

Table 4-12A. Marriages by Previous Marital Status of Bride by Previous Marital Status of Groom, by Race: 1960-1981

Marital status of bride and year	Previous marital status of white grooms of white brides				Previous marital status of black grooms of black brides			
	Total	Single	Widowed	Di-vorced	Total	Single	Widowed	Di-vorced
Single								
1981.	100.0	82.7	0.5	16.8	100.0	83.4	1.2	15.4
1979.	100.0	83.9	0.6	15.5	100.0	84.1	1.2	14.7
1978.	100.0	84.4	0.6	15.0	100.0	84.1	1.3	14.5
1975.	100.0	86.5	0.6	12.9	100.0	86.1	1.4	12.4
1970.	100.0	90.4	0.8	8.8	100.0	89.8	1.9	8.3
1965.	100.0	91.8	1.0	7.2	100.0	90.3	2.5	7.2
1960.	100.0	92.5	1.2	6.3	100.0	89.6	2.2	8.2
Widowed								
1981.	100.0	12.5	44.5	43.0	100.0	25.7	37.4	36.8
1979.	100.0	11.3	48.2	40.5	100.0	25.3	34.0	40.7
1978.	100.0	12.2	44.2	43.6	100.0	24.1	31.7	44.2
1975.	100.0	13.9	45.6	40.5	100.0	28.7	34.1	37.2
1970.	100.0	15.2	47.1	37.8	100.0	26.8	43.2	30.0
1965.	100.0	18.4	46.0	35.6	100.0	29.5	44.0	26.4
1960.	100.0	22.9	45.9	31.2	100.0	28.9	46.6	24.5
Divorced								
1981.	100.0	29.9	4.1	66.0	100.0	39.5	5.9	54.6
1979.	100.0	29.2	4.9	65.9	100.0	39.8	7.2	53.0
1978.	100.0	29.1	4.8	66.1	100.0	40.0	6.6	53.4
1975.	100.0	29.0	6.1	64.9	100.0	36.9	10.2	52.9
1970.	100.0	32.3	7.3	60.4	100.0	41.7	11.8	46.5
1965.	100.0	34.6	8.8	56.6	100.0	40.7	15.2	44.1
1960.	100.0	38.3	9.0	52.7	100.0	42.5	15.8	41.7

Source: National Center for Health Statistics. Vital Statistics of the United States: Marriage and Divorce. Washington, DC: U.S. Government Printing Office, annual volumes for years cited.

lustrates the phenomenal decline in teenage marriage and shows how the peak age of marriage has been pushed later into the 20-24 year age interval, while undergoing lowering of rates and a flattening of the peaks.

Tables 4-12A and 4-12B show the previous marital status of both partners. For each previous marital status of bride (single, widowed, or divorced), the previous marital status of the groom is reported as a percent distribution. This is shown for both white and black marriages, and for a twenty-year period. The evidence is strong that single persons tend to marry single persons, widowed to marry widowed, and divorced to marry divorced. Figure 4-6 illustrates this tendency. Age selectivity, perhaps more than marital status selectivity, is involved. The long-term trend has been toward an increased proportion of divorced grooms, irrespective of the marital status of the bride.

First Marriage and Remarriage, by Race

The changing nuptiality rates for marriage and remarriage, described above, cause a distinctive pattern in the composition of marriages. This impact differs for marriages of black and white couples. Because a few states do not report marriage statistics by race, the race statistics are not complete and should be generalized to the nation with some caution. Table 4-13 reports the race data for the proportion of all marriages that are remarriages. A higher proportion of the marriages of white couples involves remarriage than of marriages of blacks. For both races a higher proportion of the grooms than of the brides are remarrying. The trend has been toward an increasing proportion of remarriage for both races.

Age Composition of Marriages

The concentration of high marriage rates for first marriages within the few years of late adolescence and early adulthood, accompanied by remarriage of persons who have been divorced, causes marriages to have an age composition heavily concentrated at the younger ages for first marriages and spread throughout the entire age

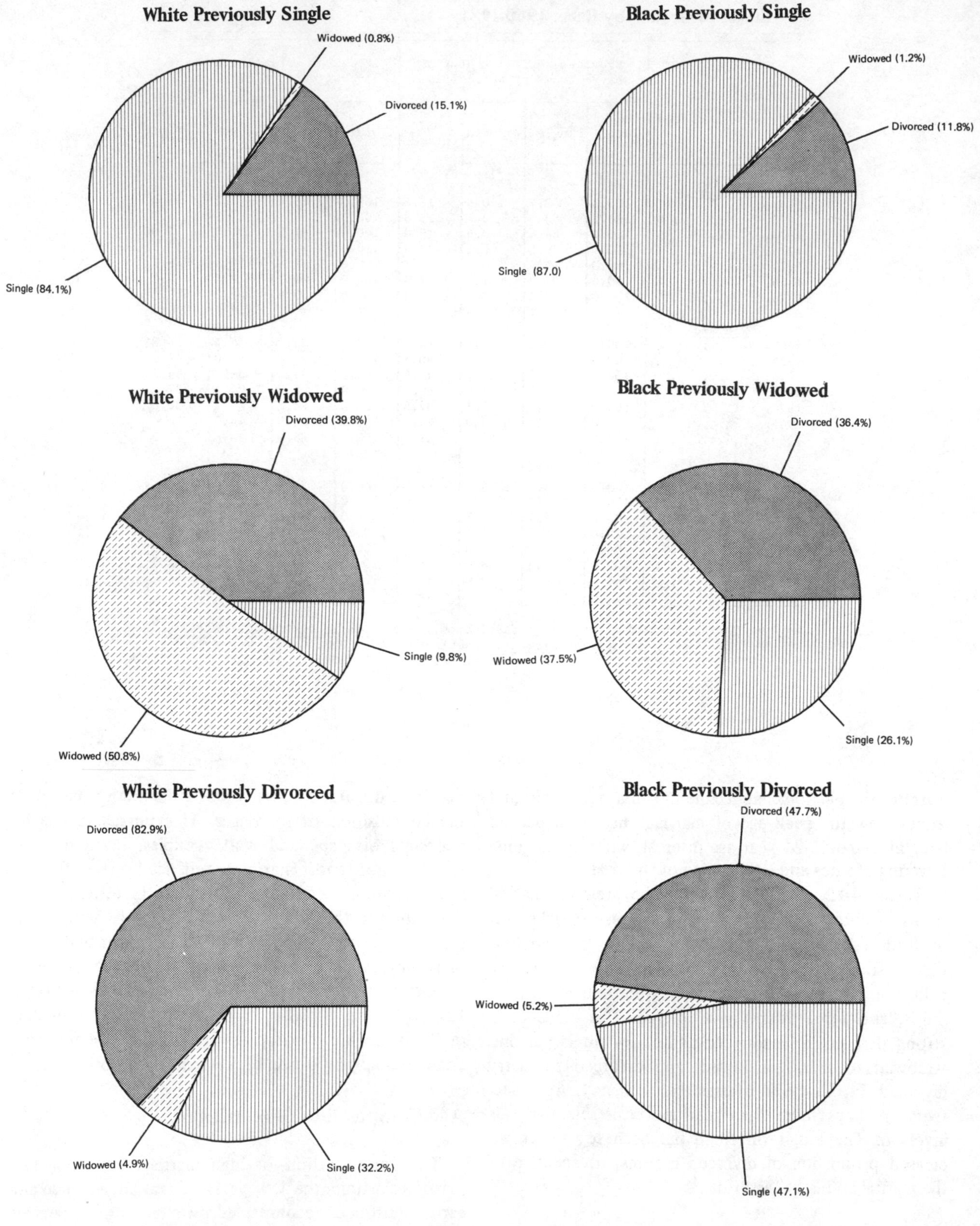

Figure 4-6. Previous Marital Status of Grooms According to Previous Marital Status of Brides, by Race: 1981

Table 4-12B. Marriages by Previous Marital Status of Groom by Previous Marital Status of Bride, by Race: 1960-1981

Marital status of groom and year	Previous marital status of white brides of white grooms				Previous marital status of black brides of black grooms			
	Total	Single	Widowed	Divorced	Total	Single	Widowed	Divorced
Single								
1981.	100.0	84.1	0.8	15.1	100.0	87.0	1.2	11.8
1979.	100.0	85.9	0.8	13.3	100.0	87.5	1.2	11.3
1978.	100.0	86.2	0.8	13.0	100.0	87.6	1.3	11.2
1975.	100.0	87.8	1.0	11.2	100.0	88.8	1.7	9.4
1970.	100.0	90.4	1.1	8.4	100.0	91.4	1.7	7.0
1965.	100.0	91.9	1.3	6.9	100.0	92.2	2.0	5.8
1960.	100.0	91.1	1.6	7.3	100.0	90.1	2.3	7.7
Widowed								
1981.	100.0	9.6	50.8	39.6	100.0	26.1	37.5	36.4
1979.	100.0	9.4	54.5	36.1	100.0	25.1	33.6	41.3
1978.	100.0	10.7	50.6	38.7	100.0	28.2	33.9	37.9
1975.	100.0	10.4	52.2	37.4	100.0	23.9	33.6	42.6
1970.	100.0	13.0	55.6	31.3	100.0	29.1	40.9	30.0
1965.	100.0	17.0	53.4	29.7	100.0	32.9	39.2	28.0
1960.	100.0	19.8	51.7	28.5	100.0	25.5	42.0	32.5
Divorced								
1981.	100.0	32.2	4.9	62.9	100.0	47.3	5.2	47.7
1979.	100.0	32.5	5.8	61.7	100.0	47.3	6.2	46.5
1978.	100.0	32.1	5.9	62.0	100.0	46.8	7.2	46.0
1975.	100.0	31.8	7.1	61.1	100.0	44.9	7.9	47.3
1970.	100.0	32.2	10.0	57.8	100.0	46.7	10.3	43.0
1965.	100.0	34.6	11.6	53.8	100.0	47.9	11.7	40.4
1960.	100.0	33.7	11.5	54.7	100.0	46.6	11.0	42.5

Source: National Center for Health Statistics. Vital Statistics of the United States: Marriage and Divorce. Washington, DC: U.S. Government Printing Office, annual volumes for years cited.

span for remarriages. The trend in the composition is reported for all marriages in Table 4-14 and for marriages of white and black couples in Table 4-15. The trend has been for the proportion of first marriages of brides at ages below twenty to decline and for the proportions in ages 20-24 and 25-29 to increase. For grooms, the proportion under age twenty-five has declined, and the proportion aged 25-29 and 30-34 has increased. For both sexes, the proportion of first marriages occurring at ages older than thirty-five is slight, because by these ages the proportion of population remaining single is small and marriage rates are low. Remarriages, in contrast, are tending to occur in larger proportions at younger ages, especially in the 25-29 groups. However, at least one-fourth of all remarriages takes place in later adulthood—ages 45-64.

Further insight into the relationships that exist between previous marital status and age at marriage may be obtained from the median age statistics of Tables 4-10A and 4-10B, in which the median ages of brides and grooms at time of marriage are reported by previous marital status. According to this table, the average bride who is marrying for the first time is twenty-one years of age, and her husband is two years older. But the bride who has been divorced and is remarrying is thirty-two years old, and the groom is thirty-five.

Age at Marriage and Previous Marital Status

The ratio of remarriages to all marriages varies greatly with age, as is shown by Table 4-16. At ages below twenty years, about 97 percent of all marriages for women are first marriages, and only 3 percent are remarriages. During the years 20-29, first marriages are predominant, but an increased proportion for each successively older age group consists of remarriage. By ages 30-34, among both women and men, the majority of marriages are remarriages, and the great bulk of these are remarriages of divorced persons. At ages older than forty-five, nearly 90 percent or more of all marriages are remarriages. Of the comparatively few marriages that occur after age sixty-five, 95 percent or more are remarriages.

Table 4-13. Percent of All Marriages That Are Remarriages, by Sex and Race: 1955-1981

Year	Brides			Grooms		
	Total	White	Black	Total	White	Black
1981	33.6	37.0	26.4	35.2	38.0	30.1
1980	32.6	35.6	26.2	34.1	36.6	29.1
1979	32.4	35.2	25.8	34.2	36.0	29.2
1978	31.8	34.7	25.8	33.7	36.0	29.1
1977	31.7	34.5	25.7	33.5	35.8	28.7
1976	30.8	33.6	25.3	32.7	34.9	28.6
1975	30.0	32.4	25.1	31.3	33.3	27.5
1974	28.0	30.4	22.3	29.1	31.1	24.9
1973	26.8	29.1	20.7	27.6	29.6	22.9
1972	25.1	27.2	19.5	25.9	27.6	21.9
1971	24.4	26.1	18.3	25.1	26.1	20.8
1970	23.9	25.5	19.5	24.2	25.5	20.8
1969	23.1	24.6	19.3	23.2	24.3	21.5
1968	22.5	24.1	18.4	22.6	23.7	20.2
1967	22.7	24.3	18.5	22.8	24.0	20.4
1966	22.8	23.9	18.6	22.9	23.8	20.4
1965	22.6	22.7	18.9	22.8	22.7	20.6
1964	23.1	23.2	19.3	22.9	22.8	21.3
1963	23.2	23.3	20.1	22.6	22.3	22.0
1962	23.1	22.8	22.3	22.4	22.3	23.4
1961	23.0	22.7	20.5	22.7	22.3	21.6
1960	22.9	22.5	22.7	21.9	21.3	23.4
1955	23.3	23.3	23.8	22.2	21.9	24.6

Note: Nonwhite instead of black used in 1955-1969 tabulations

Source: National Center for Health Statistics. Vital Statistics of the United States: Marriage and Divorce. Washington, DC: U.S. Government Printing Office, annual volumes for years cited.

Number of Times Married, by Age at Marriage

One might want to know what proportions, among the population that remarries, are marrying for the third or higher-order time. In 1981 the proportion was 20.5 percent for females and 20.2 for males. Table 4-17 shows the long-term trend toward a slow rise in the proportion of third or higher-order marriages among those who remarry. These proportions vary greatly with age.

Differences in Age of Brides and Grooms

To say that, on the average, the groom tends to be two years older than the bride is to make a very crude generalization. There is wide variation among couples in the differences in age of partners. The pattern of age difference between the marriage partners varies according to the age group concerned and also according to whether the marriage is a first marriage or a remarriage. In Table 4-18, the age of the groom is reported according to how many years older or younger he is than his bride. The table is divided into two panels. The upper panel compares the ages of brides and grooms in marriages that are first marriages for both partners. The lower panel compares the ages of brides and grooms whose marriages involve a remarriage for one or both partners. For lack of data at other ages, the table deals only with ages 18-29.

The highest degree of similarity between the ages of bride and groom at first marriage is found among brides who marry at ages twenty-two and twenty-three; among this group 20.2 percent of the couples are of the same age, and for 29 percent more the age of the groom is within one year (plus or minus) of the bride's age. At ages younger than twenty the groom tends to be considerably older than the bride, while at ages older than twenty the correlation between the ages of bride and groom becomes progressively lower and rather large disparities become more common (see Figure 4-7). In the case of brides who are twenty-nine years of age, for example, 5.2 percent of the grooms are ten to fourteen years younger and 10.3 percent are ten or more years older than the bride.

When one or both of the parties involved are marrying for a second or third time, the correlation between the ages of bride and groom is much lower than when the marriage is a first marriage for both. Among those who remarry, the ages deviate in either direction—the groom may be considerably younger than the bride, or he may be considerably older. Such small correlation as does exist tends to reach its highest point at about age twenty-six or twenty-seven and then becomes progressively lower as age of bride increases. Among remarriages there tends to be more cases where the groom is considerably older than the bride. The computations for the upper panel of Table 4-18B were performed for the year 1978, and a comparison made by subtracting the

Table 4-14. Percent Distribution of Marriages by Age at Marriage and Median Age of Bride and Groom, by Marriage Order: 1955-1981

Age and marriage order	1981	1980	1979[a]	1978	1975	1970	1965	1960	1955
All marriages[b]									
Bride	100.0	100.0	100.0	100.0	100.0	100.0	100.0	100.0	100.0
Under 20 years. . .	19.3	21.1	22.5	24.1	29.2	32.5	36.8	40.2	36.9
20-24 years	36.5	37.1	37.1	37.2	36.1	39.1	36.0	32.0	33.5
25-29 years	19.7	18.7	17.6	16.9	14.4	10.6	9.1	8.8	10.5
30-34 years	10.3	9.3	8.7	8.2	6.7	4.9	4.7	5.0	5.8
35-44 years	8.3	7.8	7.6	7.3	6.7	6.2	6.5	7.2	7.2
45-64 years	5.0	5.0	5.3	5.4	6.0	5.9	6.1	5.9	5.5
65 years and over .	1.0	1.0	1.2	0.9	1.0	0.8	0.9	0.9	0.7
Median age.	24.1	23.7	23.4	23.2	22.4	21.7	21.8	21.5	22.0
Groom	100.0	100.0	100.0	100.0	100.0	100.0	100.0	100.0	100.0
Under 20 years. . .	7.7	8.5	9.2	10.0	13.0	13.7	13.8	13.6	11.0
20-24 years	34.2	35.7	36.2	37.4	38.8	45.6	45.7	44.0	43.6
25-29 years	24.3	23.8	23.0	22.1	20.3	15.9	17.0	17.0	20.0
30-34 years	13.3	12.3	11.7	11.1	9.1	6.8	6.8	7.4	8.0
35-44 years	11.2	10.5	10.2	10.0	8.9	7.7	8.3	8.1	8.4
45-64 years	7.7	7.4	7.7	7.8	8.1	7.5	7.4	7.9	7.3
65 years and over .	1.7	1.8	2.0	1.6	1.9	1.7	2.1	2.0	1.7
Median age.	26.3	25.9	25.8	25.5	24.7	23.7	24.0	24.1	24.5
First marriages									
Bride	100.0	100.0	100.0	100.0	100.0	100.0	100.0	100.0	100.0
Under 20 years. . .	28.1	30.4	32.4	34.2	40.4	41.9	46.2	50.7	46.1
20-24 years	47.3	47.3	47.1	46.6	44.1	45.4	41.4	36.9	38.5
25-29 years	17.4	16.0	14.5	13.6	10.6	7.9	7.1	6.8	8.5
30-34 years	4.7	4.0	3.6	3.3	2.6	2.2	2.3	2.6	3.1
35-44 years	1.8	1.6	1.6	1.5	1.4	1.6	1.9	2.0	2.5
45-64 years	0.6	0.6	0.7	0.7	0.8	1.0	1.0	0.9	1.0
65 years and over .	0.1	0.1	0.1	0.1	0.1	0.1	0.1	*	0.1
Median age.	22.0	21.8	21.6	21.4	20.8	20.6	20.5	19.9	20.5
Groom	100.0	100.0	100.0	100.0	100.0	100.0	100.0	100.0	100.0
Under 20 years. . .	11.8	12.7	13.8	14.8	18.7	17.9	17.6	17.4	13.8
20-24 years	48.7	50.0	50.9	51.8	52.2	56.9	56.1	53.9	53.0
25-29 years	26.9	25.7	24.3	22.9	19.9	16.4	16.0	17.9	21.0
30-34 years	8.2	7.5	7.0	6.4	5.0	4.4	4.9	5.3	6.1
35-44 years	3.1	2.9	2.8	2.8	2.6	2.9	3.6	3.7	4.1
45-64 years	1.1	1.1	1.1	1.1	1.4	1.5	1.7	1.7	1.8
65 years and over .	0.1	0.1	0.1	0.1	0.1	0.2	0.2	0.2	0.1
Median age.	23.9	23.6	23.4	23.2	22.7	22.6	22.9	23.0	23.4
Remarriages									
Bride	100.0	100.0	100.0	100.0	100.0	100.0	100.0	100.0	100.0
Under 20 years. . .	1.4	1.7	1.6	1.9	2.6	2.9	3.2	3.2	3.3
20-24 years	14.5	15.3	15.6	16.6	17.2	19.2	16.9	15.0	15.9
25-29 years	24.4	24.4	24.1	24.3	23.4	19.0	16.2	16.0	17.4
30-34 years	21.5	20.6	19.6	19.0	16.3	13.5	13.2	13.3	15.3
35-44 years	21.5	20.8	20.2	19.9	19.3	20.5	22.9	25.3	23.9
45-64 years	13.8	14.3	15.3	15.7	18.1	21.7	23.9	23.3	21.4
65 years and over .	2.8	2.9	3.6	2.6	3.1	3.2	3.8	3.9	2.9
Median age.	32.1	32.0	31.9	31.5	32.0	33.2	35.2	35.9	34.4
Groom	100.0	100.0	100.0	100.0	100.0	100.0	100.0	100.0	100.0
Under 20 years. . .	0.2	0.2	0.3	0.2	0.3	0.3	0.3	0.3	0.2
20-24 years	6.8	7.2	7.5	8.4	9.1	10.3	9.2	8.8	8.0
25-29 years	19.2	20.1	20.3	20.6	21.1	19.0	15.6	14.2	16.0
30-34 years	22.7	21.9	21.1	20.6	18.0	14.5	13.7	14.8	15.1
35-44 years	26.4	25.6	24.7	24.6	22.7	22.8	24.7	23.8	24.8
45-64 years	20.0	20.0	20.5	21.0	22.9	26.4	28.1	30.0	28.4
65 years and over .	4.7	5.1	5.7	4.7	5.7	6.7	8.4	8.2	7.6
Median age.	35.3	35.2	35.3	35.1	35.5	37.2	39.5	40.1	39.0

[a]Figures by marriage order exclude data for Iowa.

[b]Figures include marriage order not stated.

Note: * indicates less than 0.1.

Source: National Center for Health Statistics. Vital Statistics of the United States: Marriages and Divorces (1978, 1975, 1970, 1965, 1960, and 1955); also Monthly Vital Statistics Report (1981). Washington, DC: U.S. Government Printing Office, 1982, 1979, 1974, 1968, 1964, and 1957; 1984.

Table 4-15. Percent Distribution of Marriages, by Age at Marriage and Race of Bride and Groom: 1970-1981

Age and marriage order	White						Black					
	1981	1980	1979	1978	1975	1970	1981	1980	1979	1978	1975	1970
Bride												
First marriages.	100.0	100.0	100.0	100.0	100.0	100.0	100.0	100.0	100.0	100.0	100.0	100.0
Under 18 years . .	9.8	10.5	11.8	12.8	15.8	14.9	4.6	5.6	6.4	7.5	11.0	15.7
18-19 years. . . .	23.7	25.0	26.0	26.8	29.7	30.7	16.0	17.6	19.5	19.9	24.9	26.2
20-24 years. . . .	46.8	46.6	45.7	45.1	42.5	45.3	46.1	45.7	44.9	44.9	40.4	40.0
25-29 years. . . .	14.6	13.4	12.2	11.3	8.6	6.1	20.3	19.8	17.7	17.1	13.8	9.6
30-34 years. . . .	3.4	2.9	2.6	2.4	1.8	1.3	7.8	6.3	5.9	5.5	4.4	3.4
35-44 years. . . .	1.2	1.1	1.1	1.0	0.9	1.0	3.5	3.4	4.0	3.4	3.5	3.2
45-54 years. . . .	0.3	0.3	0.3	0.3	0.4	0.5	1.1	1.1	1.2	1.3	1.4	1.3
55-64 years. . . .	0.1	0.1	0.2	0.2	0.2	0.2	0.4	0.4	0.4	0.4	0.4	0.5
65 years and over.	0.1	0.1	0.1	0.1	0.1	0.1	0.1	0.1	0.1	0.1	0.1	0.1
Remarriages. . .	100.0	100.0	100.0	100.0	100.0	100.0	100.0	100.0	100.0	100.0	100.0	100.0
Under 20 years . .	1.9	2.2	2.2	2.6	3.4	3.6	0.3	0.6	0.5	0.7	0.8	0.9
20-24 years. . . .	16.5	17.3	17.6	18.3	19.0	20.5	9.2	9.0	10.0	10.7	12.6	11.5
25-29 years. . . .	24.4	23.9	23.5	24.0	22.9	18.7	23.1	22.6	24.3	23.5	21.3	16.2
30-34 years. . . .	20.2	19.6	18.4	18.1	15.6	12.6	22.8	21.9	19.7	19.9	16.3	14.4
35-44 years. . . .	20.7	20.0	19.6	19.1	18.5	19.4	24.8	23.8	23.3	23.2	22.8	25.6
45-54 years. . . .	8.9	9.3	9.5	10.0	11.4	13.7	11.5	13.3	12.8	13.5	14.9	17.7
55-64 years. . . .	4.6	4.7	5.6	5.2	6.1	7.8	5.6	6.0	6.3	6.1	8.0	10.1
65 years and over.	2.8	3.0	3.6	2.7	3.1	3.6	2.7	2.9	3.1	2.4	3.4	3.6
Groom												
First marriages.	100.0	100.0	100.0	100.0	100.0	100.0	100.0	100.0	100.0	100.0	100.0	100.0
Under 18 years . .	1.8	1.9	2.1	2.4	3.0	2.6	0.3	0.5	0.6	0.6	1.0	2.1
18-19 years. . . .	12.8	13.7	14.7	15.6	18.7	17.8	7.1	7.8	9.2	9.1	13.6	16.9
20-24 years. . . .	50.9	52.0	52.6	53.3	53.3	58.6	47.0	47.3	47.7	49.7	48.9	51.2
25-29 years. . . .	24.4	23.2	21.8	20.4	17.7	14.7	27.8	27.1	25.4	24.5	21.1	17.0
30-34 years. . . .	6.7	6.2	5.7	5.3	4.1	3.2	10.0	9.4	8.7	8.2	7.0	5.7
35-44 years. . . .	2.5	2.1	2.1	2.1	2.0	2.1	5.1	5.1	5.5	5.3	5.1	4.4
45-54 years. . . .	0.6	0.6	0.6	0.6	0.8	0.7	1.7	1.9	1.9	1.7	2.0	1.8
55-64 years. . . .	0.2	0.2	0.3	0.2	0.3	0.3	0.8	0.8	0.8	0.7	0.9	0.6
65 years and over.	0.1	0.1	0.1	0.1	0.1	0.1	0.2	0.2	0.2	0.3	0.3	0.3
Remarriages. . .	100.0	100.0	100.0	100.0	100.0	100.0	100.0	100.0	100.0	100.0	100.0	100.0
Under 20 years . .	0.2	0.3	0.3	0.3	0.5	0.4	*	0.1	0.1	*	0.1	0.1
20-24 years. . . .	8.0	8.4	8.9	9.6	10.2	11.5	4.1	4.3	4.6	5.3	6.1	5.8
25-29 years. . . .	20.0	20.7	20.7	21.1	21.7	19.0	17.9	18.4	18.7	18.1	18.7	13.9
30-34 years. . . .	22.2	21.5	20.5	20.3	18.0	14.2	23.3	20.4	20.4	20.2	16.9	12.6
35-44 years. . . .	25.4	24.7	23.9	23.7	21.7	22.2	26.4	27.0	26.6	26.2	23.1	24.1
45-54 years. . . .	12.8	12.6	12.7	13.2	14.6	16.0	13.4	14.4	14.9	15.2	16.0	19.3
55-64 years. . . .	6.7	6.8	7.2	7.1	7.7	9.6	8.9	9.2	8.6	9.9	11.7	14.3
65 years and over.	4.7	5.0	5.8	4.8	5.5	7.3	5.9	6.3	6.2	5.2	7.3	9.9

Note: * indicates less than 0.1.

Source: National Center for Health Statistics. Vital Statistics of the United States (1981, 1980, 1979, 1978, 1975, and 1970). Washington, DC: U.S. Government Printing Office, 1984, 1982, 1979, and 1974.

Table 4-16. Percent of All Marriages That Are Remarriages, by Age and Sex: 1955-1980

Sex and age	1981	1980	1978	1975	1970	1965	1960	1955
Brides.	33.6	32.6	31.8	30.0	32.9	22.6	22.6	23.3
Under 20.	2.5	2.5	2.5	2.7	2.1	1.8	} 5.8	2.0
20-24 years	13.0	13.1	13.9	14.1	11.1	9.9		10.5
25-29 years	40.5	41.3	44.5	48.1	43.2	40.2	38.7	36.7
30-34 years	68.4	69.9	71.5	72.4	66.3	63.9	58.5	59.8
35-44 years	84.6	84.7	84.4	84.8	80.4	77.2	75.6	73.7
45-54 years	89.6	} 90.6	89.5	89.4	87.0	86.0	85.0	84.4
55-64 years	90.8		90.8	91.2	91.1	89.0	89.2	90.2
65 and over	93.4	93.6	92.8	94.0	92.9	92.8	93.8	93.1
Grooms.	35.2	34.1	33.7	31.3	24.3	22.8	21.6	22.1
Under 20.	0.8	0.9	0.7	0.8	0.6	0.5	} 3.2	0.4
20-24 years	6.8	6.6	7.4	7.3	5.3	4.2		3.9
25-29 years	27.1	27.9	30.6	32.3	26.3	21.2	16.4	16.8
30-34 years	58.8	58.8	60.9	61.7	52.3	46.1	41.1	39.7
35-44 years	80.9	80.8	80.4	79.4	71.8	67.2	62.7	62.0
45-54 years	88.9	} 89.0	87.9	86.7	84.2	81.8	81.5	77.9
55-64 years	90.4		91.1	90.2	90.2	88.8	87.8	86.8
65 and over	93.6	94.0	93.2	95.1	93.3	93.2	91.8	93.1

Source: National Center for Health Statistics. Vital Statistics of the United States: Marriages and Divorces (1978, 1975, 1970, 1965, 1960, and 1955); also "Advance Report of Final Marriage Statistics." Monthly Vital Statistics Report (1981 and 1980). Washington, DC: U.S. Government Printing Office, 1982, 1979, 1974, 1968, 1964, and 1957; 1984 and 1983.

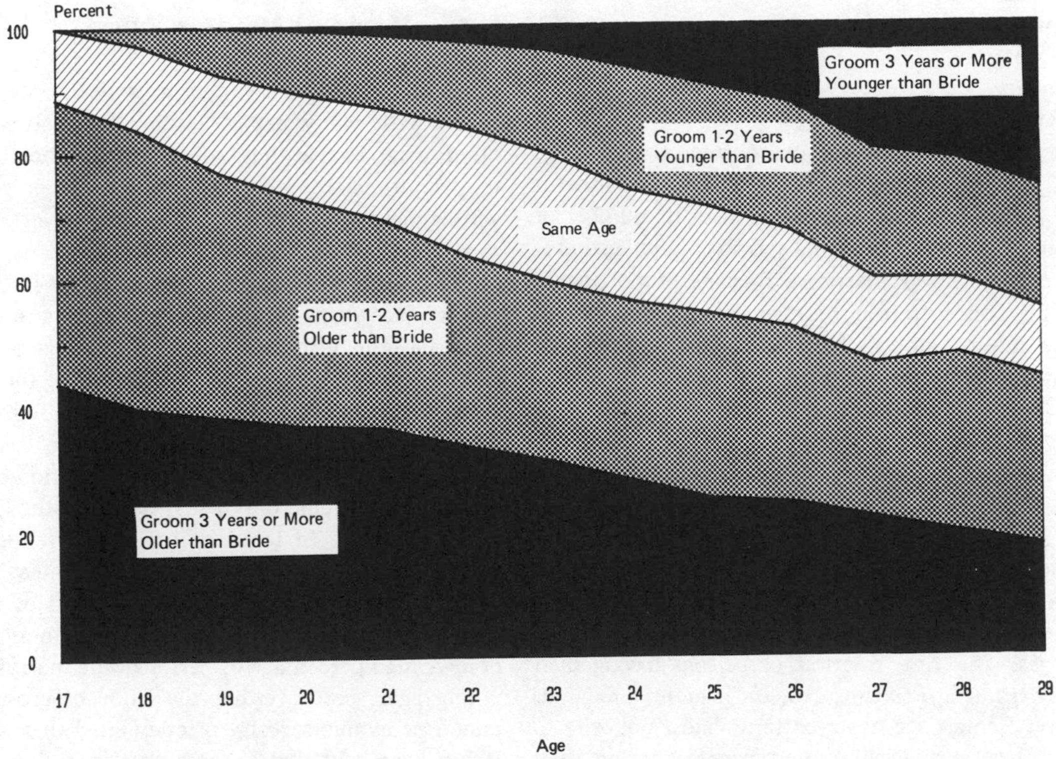

Figure 4-7. Comparison of Age of Bride and Groom, by Age of Bride: 1978

data for 1956 from the data for 1978 to get a measure of change. In 1978 a higher percentage of couples were the same age and a higher proportion of grooms were younger (smaller proportions older) than the bride than was the case in 1956.

Month and Season of Marriage

If couples were to consider no particular month of the year more appropriate than any other as a time to marry, roughly one-twelfth (8.3 percent) of all marriages would occur each month. Variations in the number of days in the month would affect these proportions slightly, and the monthly proportions would probably vary from year to year as a result of changes in the number of weekends in the respective months. Table 4-19 reports the percent of marriages occurring in each month, showing which months are preferred for marriages, and by how much. When they are ranked in descending order of preference, the months fall into the following order:

1. June
2. August
3. September
4. October
5. May
6. December
7. July
8. November
9. April
10. February
11. January
12. March.

The month of June is so popular (based on an average for 1970, 1975, and 1980 reported in Table 4-19) that it attracts 49 percent more marriages than its number of days would suggest, while January is so unpopular that it has 34 percent fewer marriages than its proportionate share. This concentration of marriages in the summer and early autumn months tends to have a slight seasonal effect on the distribution of births by months.

Type of Marriage Ceremony

Table 4-20 reports that about 80 percent of all first marriages are performed as religious ceremonies, but for remarriages this percentage declines to 60 percent. For first marriages, having a civil rather than a religious ceremony tends to increase with age, except at the very oldest ages. The tiny fraction of persons having their first marriage at age sixty-five or older prefer a religious ceremony. Remarriage has a pattern almost opposite to that for first marriages: Young persons having their second marriage tend to prefer a civil ceremony in a higher proportion of cases, but at progressively older ages the religious ceremony becomes more popular. At all ages a majority of ceremonies are religious.

Table 4-17. Percent of Remarriages That Are Second and Higher Order Marriages: 1955-1981

Year	Number of this marriage			
	Brides		Grooms	
	Second	Higher order	Second	Higher order
1981	79.5	20.5	79.8	20.2
1980	79.8	20.2	80.2	19.8
1979	80.2	19.8	80.5	19.5
1978	81.2	18.8	81.2	18.8
1975	81.6	18.4	82.7	17.3
1970	82.4	17.6	84.1	15.9
1965	82.1	17.9	83.8	16.2
1960	82.2	17.8	82.5	17.5
1955	86.3	13.7	86.6	13.4

Source: National Center for Health Statistics. Vital Statistics of the United States: Marriages and Divorces (Vol. III, Tables 1-27, 1-28, 1-44, 2-24 and Vol. I, Table 10). Washington, DC: U.S. Government Printing Office, annual reports for the years cited.

Future Trend of Marriage Rates

As of 1984, marriage rates appeared to be at a crossroads, with many experts asking themselves and each other what course they will follow in the future. Will they continue to decline, because younger generations will become even less supportive of marriage and family as a way of life? Will they stabilize at or near their present level, with marriages occurring at later ages but taking place eventually? Or will there be a resurgence of marriage popularity, with another marriage boom? Plausible arguments can be made for each of these alternatives. In assessing these possibilities, the following considerations should be kept in mind.

1. In many respects the present situation of delayed marriage is extreme only when viewed in the light of the marriage boom. In terms of long-term trends it is still within the realm of past history, hence "normal."

2. Many sociologists and psychologists of the family were extremely critical of the marriage boom phenomenon. A high percentage of persons were marrying at very young ages, before either the bride or groom had attained economic security or completed their education. It has been said that because they were immature and insecure, these couples have experienced much marital discord and dissolution. Those who support greater civil

Table 4-18. Age of Groom in Relation to Age of Bride: First Marriages and Remarriages for Brides under Thirty Years of Age, 1978 [percent distribution]

Age of bride	Groom younger than bride: 7 or more years	6 years	5 years	4 years	3 years	2 years	1 year	Same age	Groom older than bride: 1 years	2 years	3 years	4 years	5 years	6 years	7-9 years	10-14 years	15 or more years
First marriages																	
Under 18 years. . . .	--	--	--	--	--	--	--	11.3	21.3	22.6	16.4	11.2	6.6	4.3	4.5	1.2	0.6
18 years. . .	--	--	--	--	--	--	2.9	13.4	20.4	19.4	16.0	10.3	6.4	4.4	5.0	1.4	0.5
19 years. . .	--	--	--	--	--	1.0	6.5	15.5	20.3	18.0	13.6	9.1	5.8	3.8	4.5	1.3	0.5
20 years. . .	--	--	--	--	0.5	2.6	7.6	16.6	19.7	17.2	12.0	8.4	5.1	3.7	4.6	1.6	0.4
21 years. . .	--	--	--	0.1	1.2	3.3	8.4	17.6	20.7	15.8	11.3	7.3	4.8	2.9	4.0	1.9	0.6
22 years. . .	--	--	0.1	0.6	1.8	3.8	9.9	20.2	19.2	14.3	10.0	6.7	4.5	3.1	3.0	2.2	0.5
23 years. . .	--	0.1	0.3	1.1	2.5	5.3	11.1	20.2	18.1	13.1	8.7	5.9	4.3	2.9	3.3	2.5	0.6
24 years. . .	0.0	0.3	0.9	2.1	3.4	6.9	12.5	17.6	16.1	12.0	9.0	5.8	3.7	3.4	3.1	1.6	1.5
25 years. . .	0.3	0.7	1.4	2.8	4.6	7.5	11.8	16.8	14.2	10.9	8.4	6.2	2.4	2.4	7.2	1.2	1.3
26 years. . .	1.4	1.1	2.4	2.9	4.7	8.2	12.2	15.2	13.7	10.8	7.7	4.7	3.9	3.1	4.3	1.9	1.9
27 years. . .	2.1	2.9	3.5	5.2	6.4	8.2	12.4	13.2	13.1	8.9	4.7	4.7	3.8	3.8	2.4	2.5	2.5
28 years. . .	3.7	2.3	3.5	4.7	7.2	9.4	9.6	11.7	11.6	8.0	6.7	5.3	4.0	2.7	2.6	4.4	2.5
29 years. . .	5.2	2.8	4.1	5.6	8.2	8.7	10.7	10.7	9.5	7.9	6.3	4.7	3.2	2.2	3.9	3.3	3.1
Remarriages																	
Under 18 years. . . .	--	--	--	--	--	--	--	2.6	7.9	8.4	9.8	9.7	10.3	9.7	18.1	11.9	11.5
18 years. . .	--	--	--	--	--	--	0.5	4.4	6.7	8.7	11.8	10.2	8.5	9.0	17.7	13.3	9.2
19 years. . .	--	--	--	--	--	0.5	1.9	6.0	9.1	10.3	10.3	8.8	8.4	7.8	17.3	12.8	7.1
20 years. . .	--	--	--	--	0.2	1.2	3.6	6.4	8.5	9.1	8.6	9.6	7.6	7.5	17.3	13.3	7.2
21 years. . .	--	--	--	0.1	1.2	2.1	4.2	6.9	8.5	9.5	9.8	9.3	8.1	6.8	13.8	12.5	7.3
22 years. . .	--	--	0.1	0.7	1.7	3.1	5.3	7.9	8.7	10.1	8.8	8.7	7.2	6.0	13.0	11.7	7.3
23 years. . .	--	0.1	0.5	1.4	2.2	3.3	5.1	7.7	8.6	8.8	8.4	8.2	6.8	6.8	12.0	11.0	9.1
24 years. . .	0.2	0.2	0.9	1.5	2.6	4.2	5.8	8.6	9.0	9.2	8.5	7.3	6.6	2.0	15.4	9.8	8.2
25 years. . .	0.3	0.9	1.6	2.0	3.4	4.1	5.9	8.5	8.9	7.8	7.6	8.0	5.6	5.6	13.7	6.9	9.3
26 years. . .	0.8	1.3	2.4	2.7	3.7	5.4	6.5	8.4	8.8	8.6	7.8	4.0	4.5	5.1	13.4	8.0	8.9
27 years. . .	1.8	1.5	2.0	3.4	3.9	5.0	6.3	8.5	9.3	6.8	5.3	5.3	5.8	5.8	10.9	9.5	9.0
28 years. . .	3.4	2.0	2.8	3.1	4.8	5.7	5.7	7.2	7.9	5.2	5.7	6.2	6.8	7.3	6.5	10.9	9.0
29 years. . .	3.8	2.3	3.0	3.9	4.7	5.4	6.2	7.0	5.8	6.2	6.7	7.2	7.7	2.2	7.5	13.4	7.2

Source: National Center for Health Statistics. Vital Statistics of the United States: 1978. Washington, DC: U.S. Government Printing Office, 1982, Tables 19 and 20.

and social rights for women emphasize later marriage to permit women to get more education and work experience. In many respects the increasing ages at which marriage is taking place in the 1980s would tend to be defined as almost ideal by these experts. Marriage appears to be being postponed until education is completed, employment is secured, and savings accumulated. Supposedly those who do enter marriage under these circumstances do so out of a sincere desire for family living. This may serve to reduce divorce rates in later years. It may separate those who are serious about childbearing from those who are not, with beneficial effects for future generations of children.

3. Low and late marriage rates do not necessarily predestine low fertility rates. The United States had high fertility rates in the period between 1890 and 1920, when marriage postponement was popular.

4. Economic stagnation combined with inflation in the 1970s, followed by the acute economic recession of the early 1980s, may have caused substantial postponement of marriages, which will take place in the later 1980s even if economic conditions do not improve. This phenomenon occurred in the late years of the Great Depression.

5. There appears to be a strong element of generational "attitude climate" or "life-style" that can fluctuate cyclically rather than follow a uniform pattern. Many moralists who saw marriage rates declining in the 1920s and the liberal political movement among young persons during the 1930s forecast a great deemphasis of marriage and the family. As a consequence the marriage boom of the 1940s and 1950s was wholly unpredicted and ran counter to moralists' as well as theorists' expectations. It was a spontaneous shift in social thinking at

Table 4-18B. Change in Age of Groom in Relation to Age of Bride: First Marriages, 1956-1978 [percent distribution for 1956 subtracted from percent distribution for 1978]

Age of bride	Groom younger than bride						Same age	Groom older than bride							
	6 or more years	5 years	4 years	3 years	2 years	1 year		1 year	2 years	3 years	4 years	5 years	6-9 years	10-14 years	15 or more years
18 years. . .	--	--	--	--	--	-1.7	-3.2	-5.6	-4.1	5.7	2.0	2.4	3.6	0.8	0.0
19 years. . .	--	--	--	--	-0.5	-2.2	-4.0	-5.2	1.8	1.6	2.3	2.1	3.6	0.9	-0.1
20 years. . .	--	--	--	-0.3	-1.1	-2.4	-4.5	-0.8	-0.4	1.7	3.7	2.1	2.8	0.6	0.1
21 years. . .	--	--	0.0	-0.5	-1.3	-3.1	0.7	-2.3	-0.4	0.6	1.6	1.8	3.1	0.1	-0.1
22 years. . .	--	--	-0.2	-0.7	-0.8	-0.4	-3.4	-2.8	-0.2	1.1	1.7	1.5	3.9	0.3	0.2
23 years. . .	--	-0.1	-0.4	-0.8	0.2	-0.8	-4.6	-3.1	0.3	1.7	1.9	1.3	3.8	0.5	0.2
24 years. . .	-0.1	-0.4	-0.8	0.5	-0.4	-1.9	-2.2	-1.6	-0.1	0.4	1.4	1.2	3.2	1.4	-0.5
25 years. . .	-0.3	-0.6	0.0	0.2	-0.2	-0.4	-2.3	-1.4	-0.5	-0.4	0.3	2.4	0.6	2.7	0.0
26 years. . .	-1.2	0.1	0.2	-4.5	-0.1	-1.3	-1.8	-2.0	-1.2	0.2	1.5	0.1	2.4	2.1	-0.5
27 years. . .	-2.4	-0.8	-0.9	-0.1	0.6	-1.2	-0.5	-3.0	-0.4	1.9	0.7	0.9	4.1	1.9	-1.1
28 years. . .	-1.8	-0.2	-0.7	-1.0	-1.1	0.3	0.0	-1.9	-0.1	0.0	0.3	0.1	4.9	0.4	-0.3
29 years. . .	-6.4	-0.4	-0.2	-0.5	0.1	-1.9	-0.3	-1.1	-1.1	0.0	0.4	0.8	0.5	1.3	-0.7

Note: -- indicates data not available.

Source: 1978 data from National Center for Health Statistics. Vital Statistics of the United States: 1978. Washington, DC: U.S. Government Printing Office, 1982. 1956 data from Donald J. Bogue. Population of the United States. Glencoe, IL: The Free Press, 1959.

the grassroots level, which could reappear, equally unexpected and equally contrary to predictions based on trends and the philosophy of current generations.

6. The movement toward greater equality for women has forced many women to choose between marriage and self-realization. It is quite possible that continued social change will produce new living and work patterns to reduce this conflict, with the result that marriage in early adulthood can be a normal and consistent part of "women's liberation."

7. Living in a nonfamily situation (either as unmarried adults with a "relationship" or alone) carries a number of economic, personal, and even mental and emotional risks for many of its practitioners. These include long-term economic and social insecurity for women, possible anxiety about stability and duration of intense personal relationships, and more uncertainty in developing a life plan. The problems of remaining single appear to increase with age. There are plausible limits to the proportion of the population (particularly males) that will choose this lifestyle for an entire lifetime.

8. Much delayed marriage in the early part of this century was necessary because the couple lacked income to establish a family at their desired level of living. With modern reductions in poverty, the option to marry under economically adequate conditions is now open to the vast majority of young adults, should they choose to do so. As indicated above, they may begin to exercise this option in larger numbers.

Considering all of the above, it would appear that the marriage rates of the early 1980s may be below the long-term trend they will follow over the next quarter-century. On such an assumption, one could predict a moderate rise in the rates during the last half of the 1980s in comparison with those that prevailed during the first half.

Another facet of marriage is the phenomenon of remarriage. Given today's high divorce rates (see next section) and the propensity for divorced persons to remarry, it will be much more common in future years for couples to have three or more marriages.

Divorce as a Demographic Event

The population exposed to divorce is currently married couples. Hence, the appropriate rate is the general divorce rate (GDR), defined in the opening of the last section. Although a crude divorce rate, based on total population, is published, it can be misleading because of the marked change in age composition that the American population has undergone.

The phenomenal increase in divorce that has taken place since 1940, and especially since 1970, is reported by the statistics of Table 4-21 and illustrated in Figure 4-8. The number of divorces in 1980 was 68 percent greater than in 1970, and the general divorce rate in-

Table 4-19. Month of Marriage, by Marriage Order and Race: Brides [percent of marriage occurring in each month]

Marriage order and race	January	February	March	April	May	June	July	August	September	October	November	December
All marriages												
1980	4.9	6.0	6.7	7.2	10.2	12.1	8.8	12.1	8.7	8.4	7.8	7.1
1978	4.8	5.4	6.3	8.0	8.7	11.8	10.3	10.5	10.1	8.1	7.6	8.4
1975	5.4	6.0	6.8	7.2	9.6	12.2	8.8	12.1	8.1	7.9	8.0	7.9
1970	6.3	6.3	6.3	7.1	8.4	12.8	8.8	11.6	8.6	8.1	7.5	8.2
1965	6.3	6.6	5.7	6.8	8.5	12.0	10.1	10.9	9.0	8.5	7.7	7.9
1960	6.3	6.9	5.1	7.5	8.1	12.2	9.8	9.9	9.6	8.7	7.7	8.2
1955	6.5	6.5	5.6	8.0	8.0	11.9	9.3	9.1	9.5	8.9	7.9	8.7
1950	5.8	6.2	5.2	7.8	7.5	11.5	9.2	9.9	11.3	8.8	8.1	8.7
First marriages, white												
1980	4.4	5.4	6.5	7.2	10.8	13.1	8.6	12.5	8.9	8.5	7.6	6.4
1978	4.5	5.1	6.0	8.0	9.0	13.0	10.3	11.0	10.4	8.1	7.2	7.4
1975	5.1	5.6	6.4	7.0	10.0	13.5	8.8	12.8	8.3	7.8	7.6	7.1
1970	6.4	5.9	6.0	6.9	8.6	14.7	8.5	12.3	8.4	7.7	7.1	7.7
1965	6.1	6.5	5.2	6.5	9.0	13.9	10.5	11.8	9.1	7.8	6.9	6.7
1960	5.9	6.9	4.5	7.5	8.0	12.9	10.1	10.2	10.2	8.5	7.4	7.8
First marriages, black												
1980	6.0	6.7	7.2	7.3	7.9	11.7	10.1	11.6	7.8	6.9	7.9	8.9
1978	5.9	6.0	7.1	7.5	7.6	10.9	10.4	10.0	9.8	7.1	7.5	10.2
1975	6.8	6.5	7.7	7.3	7.7	12.3	9.8	11.1	7.6	6.6	7.4	9.3
1970	7.2	6.9	7.6	7.8	8.2	12.4	8.5	10.7	7.8	7.1	7.1	8.7
1965	7.3	7.3	7.5	7.3	7.8	10.3	9.9	10.5	8.0	7.6	7.3	9.2
1960	7.9	6.5	6.6	7.2	7.3	11.2	9.2	10.2	8.5	8.5	8.1	8.7
All remarriages												
1980	6.0	7.3	7.4	7.2	9.5	10.4	8.6	10.5	7.6	8.3	8.6	8.8
1978	5.5	6.2	7.3	8.1	8.4	10.3	9.8	9.1	9.0	7.9	8.4	10.1
1975	5.9	6.7	7.3	7.4	9.3	10.1	8.6	10.4	7.4	7.8	9.0	10.0
1970	6.5	6.9	7.0	7.4	8.7	9.9	9.1	9.5	8.2	8.7	8.4	9.8
1965	6.8	6.8	6.7	7.6	8.4	9.5	9.8	9.1	8.0	8.8	8.8	9.7
1960	6.8	6.9	6.4	7.7	8.2	10.1	9.1	8.9	8.5	9.3	8.7	9.3
Remarriages, white												
1980	6.1	7.3	7.4	7.3	9.5	10.2	8.5	10.1	7.6	8.3	8.8	8.8
1978	5.6	6.3	7.5	8.2	8.4	10.4	9.7	8.7	9.0	7.9	8.3	10.0
1975	6.1	6.8	7.4	7.4	9.4	9.8	8.7	10.2	7.3	8.1	9.0	10.0
1970	6.7	6.9	7.1	7.5	9.0	10.0	9.1	9.4	8.1	8.4	8.3	9.4
1965	6.9	6.8	6.8	8.0	8.5	9.6	10.2	9.1	7.9	8.8	8.1	9.3
1960	7.1	6.6	6.5	7.5	8.4	10.2	9.4	9.4	8.4	8.9	8.3	9.3
Remarriages, black												
1980	6.8	6.6	7.5	7.9	8.5	10.5	9.3	11.0	7.7	7.4	8.0	8.8
1978	6.1	5.2	8.4	8.7	8.0	9.9	9.6	9.8	8.8	7.6	7.8	10.1
1975	6.7	6.6	8.2	7.4	8.1	10.3	8.9	10.0	8.2	6.9	8.9	9.6
1970	7.1	7.5	7.7	7.7	8.9	11.2	8.4	8.4	7.8	8.6	6.9	9.6
1965	7.7	5.7	8.4	8.1	8.4	9.2	9.0	10.1	7.9	8.2	7.7	9.6
1960	5.6	9.1	4.5	8.9	5.5	9.3	7.5	7.5	7.7	11.0	11.3	12.1

Note: Nonwhite instead of black for years 1960 and 1965. Data for 1955 is for 36 reporting states.

Source: National Center for Health Statistics. Vital Statistics of the United States: Marriage and Divorce. Washington, DC: U.S. Government Printing Office, annual volumes for years cited.

Table 4-20. Percent of First Marriages and Remarriages Performed as Civil Ceremonies, by Age of Bride: 1960-1980

Age	First marriages							Remarriages						
	1980	1979	1978	1975	1972	1965	1960	1980	1979	1978	1975	1972	1965	1960
All ages.	22.1	21.6	20.8	21.0	20.0	19.4	16.4	40.0	39.5	39.7	40.9	40.6	42.5	38.4
Under 20 years. . .	25.7	25.0	24.0	23.3	22.3	22.0	17.9	44.2	44.4	49.5	46.7	45.8	46.5	44.6
20-24 years	17.7	16.9	16.0	15.9	15.0	14.3	12.4	42.4	42.4	41.0	41.9	42.1	45.0	36.7
25-29 years	22.7	22.5	22.8	24.5	23.7	22.8	17.1	39.8	39.3	40.0	40.9	41.6	45.9	42.3
30-34 years	32.6	34.1	33.1	35.1	35.2	29.1	23.8	40.5	39.9	40.6	42.8	43.4	45.5	42.2
35-44 years	42.8	43.5	43.0	44.9	44.4	33.6	35.5	41.5	41.6	41.2	43.8	43.9	44.8	40.2
45-54 years	46.6	48.4	45.3	43.1	40.6	39.2	17.3	39.8	39.8	38.9	40.0	39.2	38.7	36.2
55-64 years	43.2	44.8	44.3	45.5	37.1	37.2	37.1	33.1	31.9	32.4	31.8	28.0	32.6	28.3
65 years and over .	31.8	30.7	31.3	36.8	23.6	25.2	11.9	24.8	23.6	23.0	24.1	22.5	25.6	27.6

Source: National Center for Health Statistics. Vital Statistics of the United States: Marriage and Divorce. Washington, DC: U.S. Government Printing Office, annual volumes for years cited.

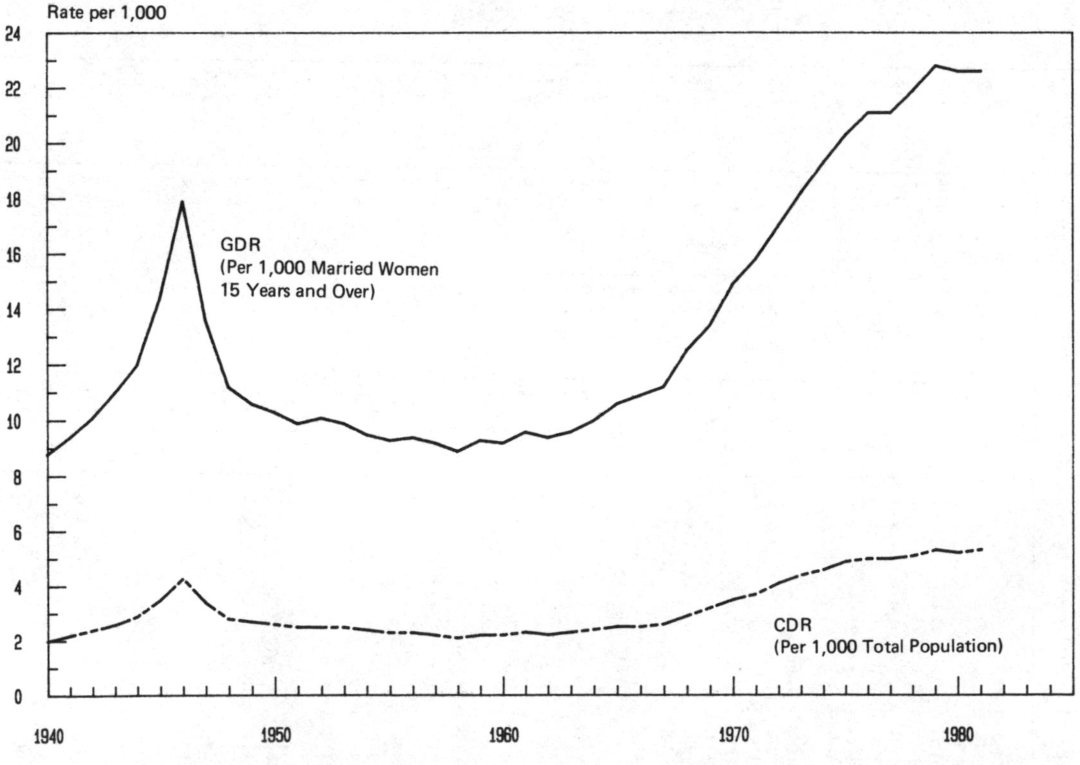

Figure 4-8. General Divorce Rate and Crude Divorce Rate: United States, 1940-1981

Table 4-21. Trends in Basic Divorce Measures: 1940-1983

Year	Number (000)	Rates		Median duration of marriage	Median age at time of decree		Median age at time of marriage		Duration of marriage			
		Crude rate	General rate		Husband	Wife	Husband	Wife	Under 5 years	5-9 years	10-14 years	15+ years
1983	1,179	5.0	21.9	--	--	--	--	--	--	--	--	--
1982	1,180	5.1	21.9	--	--	--	--	--	--	--	--	--
1981	1,213	5.3	22.6	7.0	33.1	30.6	23.4	21.1	37.7	27.3	15.3	19.6
1980	1,189	5.2	22.6	6.8	32.7	30.3	23.3	20.9	38.1	27.8	14.8	19.3
1979	1,181	5.3	22.8	6.8	32.5	30.1	23.2	20.9				
1978	1,130	5.1	21.9	6.6	32.0	29.7	23.0	20.7	39.1	28.0	13.9	19.0
1977	1,091	5.0	21.1	6.6	32.4	29.9	23.1	20.7	39.1	27.9	13.5	19.5
1976	1,083	5.0	21.1	6.5	32.3	29.7	23.1	20.7	39.8	27.4	13.3	19.5
1975	1,036	4.9	20.3	6.5	32.2	29.5	23.0	20.6	39.5	27.2	13.6	19.8
1974	977	4.6	19.3	6.5	32.2	29.5	23.0	20.6	39.6	26.7	13.1	20.6
1973	915	4.4	18.2	6.6	32.4	29.7	22.9	20.5	39.3	26.0	13.2	21.3
1972	845	4.1	17.0	6.7	32.6	29.8	23.0	20.5	39.7	25.1	13.3	21.9
1971	773	3.7	15.8	6.7	32.9	29.8	23.0	20.5	39.2	24.9	13.5	22.2
1970	708	3.5	14.9	6.7	32.9	29.8	23.0	20.4	38.9	25.2	13.8	21.9
1969	639	3.2	13.4	6.9	33.5	30.1	23.6	20.7	39.0	24.6	13.8	22.6
1968	584	2.9	12.5	7.0	33.9	30.5	23.7	20.7	38.8	24.3	14.2	22.9
1967	523	2.6	11.2	7.1	33.6	30.1	23.5	20.3	38.3	23.3	14.4	23.8
1966	499	2.5	10.9	7.1	33.8	30.4	23.5	22.8	38.1	23.8	14.1	24.0
1965	479	2.5	10.6	7.2	34.1	30.5	23.7	20.4	38.1	23.6	13.7	24.4
1964	450	2.4	10.0	7.4	34.0	30.6	23.7	20.4	36.6	24.8	14.6	24.0
1963	428	2.3	9.6	7.5	34.8	31.3	23.9	20.6	36.5	23.9	14.9	24.8
1962	413	2.2	9.4	7.3	34.5	31.0	24.0	20.7	36.2	25.3	15.1	23.5
1961	414	2.3	9.6	7.1	34.0	30.8	23.8	20.6	38.0	24.7	15.5	21.9
1960	393	2.2	9.2	--	34.1	30.9	24.2	20.9	37.5	24.5	17.0	20.9
1959	395	2.2	9.3	7.0	--	--	--	--	38.6	24.3	16.2	20.9
1958	368	2.1	8.9	6.4	--	--	--	--	41.8	23.5	15.2	19.4
1957	381	2.2	9.2	6.7	--	--	--	--	40.2	24.7	15.1	20.1
1956	382	2.3	9.4	6.5	--	--	--	--	40.9	26.1	14.1	18.9
1955	377	2.3	9.3	6.4	--	--	--	--	41.9	26.9	12.8	18.4
1954	379	2.4	9.5	--	--	--	--	--	41.9	27.2	12.6	18.2
1953	390	2.5	9.9	--	--	--	--	--	42.2	26.8	12.8	18.2
1952	392	2.5	10.1	--	--	--	--	--	42.3	26.2	13.0	18.5
1951	381	2.5	9.9	--	--	--	--	--	42.9	25.3	12.7	19.1
1950	385	2.6	10.3	--	--	--	--	--	46.4	22.6	12.2	18.6
1949	397	2.7	10.6	--	--	--	--	--	--	--	--	--
1948	408	2.8	11.2	--	--	--	--	--	--	--	--	--
1947	483	3.4	13.6	--	--	--	--	--	--	--	--	--
1946	610	4.3	17.9	--	--	--	--	--	--	--	--	--
1945	485	3.5	14.4	--	--	--	--	--	--	--	--	--
1944	400	2.9	12.0	--	--	--	--	--	--	--	--	--
1943	359	2.6	11.0	--	--	--	--	--	--	--	--	--
1942	321	2.4	10.1	--	--	--	--	--	--	--	--	--
1941	293	2.2	9.4	--	--	--	--	--	--	--	--	--
1940	264	2.0	8.8	--	--	--	--	--	--	--	--	--

Note: -- indicates data not available. General rate for 1982 and 1983 is estimated by the author.

Source: National Center for Health Statistics. Vital Statistics of the United States. Washington, DC: U.S. Government Printing Office, annual volumes for the years cited.

creased by 52 percent. Thus population growth played an insignificant part in the increase. The attrition rate on marriage is 2.6 times the level of 1940, and the 1940 rates are above those that prevailed earlier in the century. It is this development that has caused media commentators to speak of the "epidemic" of divorce, which has swept the nation since World War II.

Before discussing the causes of this development and trying to forecast its future course, certain basic facts about divorce need to be understood. These are summarized in Tables 4-21 through 4-25. Because the reporting of divorce statistics is more incomplete than marriage data, and fewer characteristics are tabulated, far less is known about divorce as a demographic event than is desirable to know. These tables synthesize what has been assembled by the National Center for Health Statistics as a result of decades of intensive efforts to develop better reporting.

Duration

Only a small proportion of divorces results from immediate negative reaction to marriage. The median duration of marriage is almost six years. Summary data are presented in Table 4-21, and much more detailed data are in Table 4-22. The percentages are highest at the durations of one to four years. One-fifth of all divorces are granted to couples who have been married less than three years. However, it must not be concluded that couples who have lived together for a long time are immune to divorce. In 1980, 5.7 percent of all divorces were granted to couples who had been married for twenty-five years or more, and about one-fifth of all divorces granted to couples who had been married for fifteen years or longer.

Actually, the duration pattern has not changed much during the recent "epidemic," although there is a slight

Table 4-22. Duration of Marriage: 1950-1980 [percent distribution]

Year	Under 1 year	1 year	2 years	3 years	4 years	5 years	6 years	7 years	8 years	9 years	10–14 years	15–19 years	20–24 years	25–29 years	30 years and over
1980	4.4	8.4	9.1	8.4	7.8	7.0	6.2	5.6	4.8	4.1	14.8	8.3	5.3	3.0	2.7
1979	4.5	8.1	8.8	8.6	7.8	7.1	6.5	5.5	4.8	4.4	14.4	8.1	5.4	3.1	2.8
1978	4.6	8.3	9.1	8.9	8.2	7.3	6.4	5.5	4.8	4.1	13.9	7.8	5.3	3.1	2.8
1977	4.4	8.1	9.0	9.2	8.4	7.2	6.2	5.7	4.7	4.1	13.5	8.0	5.4	3.3	2.8
1976	4.4	8.3	9.6	9.2	8.3	7.1	6.5	5.4	4.6	3.8	13.3	7.8	5.5	3.6	2.6
1975	4.5	8.6	9.4	8.9	8.1	7.4	6.2	5.2	4.4	4.0	13.6	8.0	5.6	3.7	2.5
1974	4.6	8.7	9.1	8.7	8.5	7.2	6.1	5.1	4.4	3.8	13.1	8.2	5.9	3.8	2.7
1973	4.7	8.3	9.0	9.2	8.1	6.9	5.8	5.1	4.4	3.8	13.2	8.6	6.1	3.9	2.7
1972	4.7	8.3	9.8	9.2	7.7	6.5	5.8	4.9	4.3	3.7	13.3	8.9	6.5	3.8	2.7
1971	4.6	8.8	9.5	8.8	7.5	6.4	5.9	4.8	4.1	3.7	13.5	9.0	7.0	3.6	2.6
1970	4.8	8.5	9.4	8.5	7.7	6.9	5.6	5.0	4.1	3.6	13.8	9.0	7.0	3.3	2.6
1969	5.2	8.6	9.2	8.5	7.5	6.4	5.4	4.7	4.2	3.8	13.8	9.5	7.1	3.5	2.5
1968	5.1	8.7	9.3	8.5	7.2	6.0	5.5	4.8	4.3	3.7	14.2	9.6	7.3	3.6	2.4
1967	5.8	9.1	8.4	8.1	6.9	6.0	5.3	4.7	3.9	3.4	14.4	10.0	7.1	3.9	2.8
1966	5.6	8.9	8.9	7.8	6.9	6.0	5.4	4.6	4.0	3.8	14.1	10.8	6.7	3.7	2.8
1965	5.3	9.3	8.6	8.0	6.9	5.9	5.1	4.5	4.2	3.9	13.7	11.2	6.5	3.6	3.1
1964	5.3	8.8	8.4	7.3	6.8	6.2	5.2	5.0	4.6	3.8	14.6	11.4	6.3	3.4	2.9
1963	5.2	8.6	8.4	7.5	6.8	5.7	5.5	5.0	4.0	3.7	14.9	11.5	6.8	3.5	3.0
1962	5.1	8.6	8.3	7.6	6.6	7.0	5.1	4.9	4.4	3.9	15.1	10.3		(13.2)	
1961	5.6	9.4	8.0	7.7	7.3	6.1	5.6	4.9	4.0	4.0	15.5	9.7		(12.2)	
1960	6.2	8.1	8.1	7.9	7.3	6.4	5.0	4.9	4.3	3.9	17.0	8.9		(12.0)	
1959	5.9	8.2	9.1	8.3	7.1	6.0	5.4	4.7	4.3	3.9	16.2	9.0	5.6	3.1	3.2
1958	7.6	9.4	10.1	8.2	6.6	6.0	5.1	4.7	4.1	3.6	15.2	8.5	5.4	2.7	2.8
1957	6.1	9.8	9.2	8.0	7.1	6.2	5.4	4.7	4.3	4.1	15.1	8.6	5.4	2.9	3.2
1956	6.4	9.7	9.4	8.2	7.1	6.4	5.4	4.8	4.7	4.8	14.1	8.1	4.8	2.8	3.2
1955	6.3	9.7	10.0	8.5	7.4	6.2	5.4	5.3	5.3	4.7	12.8	7.8	4.7	3.0	2.9
1954	6.4	10.1	9.7	8.5	7.2	6.1	6.1	5.9	5.5	3.6	12.6	7.8	4.6	2.9	2.9
1953	7.0	10.1	9.8	8.1	7.2	7.0	6.7	6.1	4.0	3.0	12.8	7.7	4.6	3.1	2.8
1952	7.1	9.9	9.0	8.3	8.0	7.7	7.0	4.5	3.6	3.4	13.0	7.6	4.8	3.1	3.0
1951	6.6	9.5	9.0	9.0	8.8	8.1	5.1	4.2	4.0	3.9	12.7	7.7	5.1	3.3	3.0
1950	6.4	10.3	10.3	10.0	9.4	5.9	4.5	4.3	4.3	3.6	12.2	7.3	5.2	3.1	3.0

Source: National Center for Health Statistics. *Vital Statistics of the United States.* Washington, DC: U.S. Government Printing Office, annual volumes for the years cited.

Table 4-23. Age-Specific Divorce Rates: 1970-1980 [rates per 1,000 married persons of age]

Year	20-24 years	25-29 years	30-34 years	35-39 years	40-44 years	45-49 years	50-54 years	55-59 years	60-64 years	65 and years
Male										
1980.	51.05	47.12	38.18	30.79	24.03	16.97	11.03	6.69	4.26	2.12
1979.	51.90	48.28	37.85	30.13	23.62	16.99	11.07	6.69	4.46	2.23
1978.	52.62	47.72	36.31	28.36	21.48	15.88	10.76	6.71	4.05	2.05
1977.	50.16	46.18	35.36	27.20	20.94	15.97	11.10	6.89	4.29	2.35
1976.	50.74	48.19	33.94	26.42	20.70	16.36	11.12	7.06	4.42	2.33
1975.	48.79	47.40	33.51	24.75	19.28	15.65	11.16	6.54	4.39	2.29
1974.	47.01	43.76	31.99	23.72	18.65	14.87	10.67	6.28	4.62	2.33
1973.	43.95	40.26	30.57	22.51	18.05	14.71	10.30	6.31	4.33	2.15
1972.	40.88	37.91	28.10	21.06	17.05	13.48	9.85	6.01	4.13	2.07
1971.	39.25	33.18	25.32	20.35	16.01	12.82	9.12	5.81	3.69	1.93
1970.	34.71	31.87	23.82	19.04	14.76	11.46	8.14	5.43	3.64	1.97
Female										
1980.	52.21	43.38	33.30	26.74	19.15	12.59	7.82	4.54	3.02	1.61
1979.	52.54	44.17	32.77	25.87	19.19	12.76	7.81	4.75	3.13	1.49
1978.	53.36	42.68	30.87	24.04	17.32	12.08	7.92	4.41	2.86	1.45
1977.	50.27	41.74	30.78	22.52	17.09	12.27	7.89	4.97	3.10	1.67
1976.	49.95	43.15	29.27	22.44	17.07	12.49	8.16	4.98	3.07	1.60
1975.	47.71	42.19	28.23	21.30	15.73	12.01	8.14	5.02	3.02	1.60
1974.	45.65	39.08	27.07	19.89	15.31	11.75	7.63	4.88	3.18	1.65
1973.	42.69	36.40	25.40	19.22	15.01	11.48	7.77	4.55	2.97	1.42
1972.	40.06	33.25	23.37	18.20	14.40	10.95	7.23	4.32	2.91	1.42
1971.	38.30	28.77	21.76	17.11	13.29	10.23	6.87	4.11	2.42	1.35
1970.	34.93	27.46	20.10	15.72	12.69	9.21	5.99	3.76	2.41	1.35

Note: Since the divorce registration area does not include all states in the United States, the estimated age-specific divorce rates had to be calculated as follows: (1) The total number of divorces for a specified year for the entire United States was divided by the number of divorces for a specified year for the divorce registration area. This provided an adjustment factor that was applied to all divorce registration area age groups to achieve the U.S. total. (2) The 1970 and 1980 censuses were then used as the points from which to interpolate data for intervening years. (3) Step 1 was divided by Step 2 for each age group for each sex to obtain the age-specific divorce rates.

Source: National Center for Health Statistics. Vital Statistics of the United States: Marriage and Divorce. Washington, DC: U.S. Government Printing Office, annual volumes for years cited.

trend toward shorter duration–seeking divorce after fewer years of marriage. The great majority of couples have apparently made an earnest effort at succeeding in marriage, and termination comes only after some years of marriage.

Age at Divorce

As a consequence of the years of duration that elapse before divorce is attained, Table 4-21 shows the typical wife to be near thirty and the husband thirty-two or thirty-three years of age at the time of divorce. Table 4-23 is an estimated set of age-specific divorce rates for each age. These rates are highly approximate because of the estimating required to develop them (see explanation in the footnote to the table). However, they are superior to simply percentage distribution of divorced persons by age, because they measure the strength of the attrition force on each age group. They show that married persons 20 to 29 years of age are subject to very high rates and that the curve declines sharply with age. They also suggest that the divorce rate peaked about 1978 and has remained on a plateau for the younger ages but risen slightly for older (30-49) years.

Age at Marriage of Divorced Persons

The median age at marriage of women involved in divorce was 20-21 years, and the median age of the man is twenty-three. This is about one-half year or more younger than the typical age at marriage that prevailed seven years earlier, when the average divorced couple was married. Estimated divorce rates specific for age at marriage are reported in Table 4-24. The data of this table suggest that marriages contracted before age twenty are subject to very high attrition from divorce. This differential is of long standing and does not appear to have changed much over the years. Marriages when the bride and groom were 20-24 years of age at marriage appear to be more stable than marriages entered into at older ages. Table 4-24 shows that the increase in divorce rates has occurred in all age-at-marriage categories except the few which occur at ages forty-five and over. An important implication of Table 4-24 is that as of about 1974-75, the probability that a given marriage will end in divorce rose above the 50-50 mark, and that since that date there is a slightly greater probability that newly contracted marriages will end in divorce than in lasting until death parts the partners.

Table 4-24. Age-at-Marriage Specific Divorce Rates, by Sex: 1970-1978 [divorces per 1,000 persons married at indicated ages seven years earlier]

Sex and year	Age at marriage						
	All ages	Under 20	20-24 years	25-29 years	30-34 years	35-44 years	45 and over
Female							
1978 . . .	515.9	669.1	453.4	514.7	524.5	410.2	210.5
1977 . . .	505.4	655.7	432.8	517.1	563.6	417.5	226.5
1976 . . .	504.9	658.6	425.4	512.3	583.4	433.0	234.2
1975 . . .	500.7	659.8	423.6	483.5	534.5	425.9	241.9
1974 . . .	507.0	661.0	434.8	515.2	534.3	386.7	244.9
1973 . . .	492.7	605.5	447.9	493.5	500.5	389.2	232.7
1972 . . .	469.4	581.5	418.5	480.8	484.6	383.7	219.7
1971 . . .	448.1	570.8	382.8	481.6	469.7	349.9	214.3
1970 . . .	428.1	553.4	356.2	466.2	412.8	348.7	210.1
Male							
1978 . . .	515.9	695.9	506.4	540.4	554.6	483.4	234.0
1977 . . .	505.4	670.8	490.4	525.5	581.5	476.6	258.7
1976 . . .	504.9	684.0	485.3	519.0	582.3	483.5	266.1
1975 . . .	500.7	684.9	487.7	508.2	551.0	450.9	271.3
1974 . . .	507.0	696.7	506.7	500.4	548.9	436.5	263.4
1973 . . .	492.7	612.1	513.2	483.3	529.4	422.2	257.0
1972 . . .	469.4	658.4	463.5	486.0	487.5	406.2	242.3
1971 . . .	448.1	686.2	429.4	458.8	494.0	393.1	232.6
1970 . . .	428.1	650.2	412.2	433.9	444.3	384.1	229.3

Note: Rates were calculated by the author.

Source: National Center for Health Statistics. *Vital Statistics of the United States.* Washington, DC: U.S. Government Printing Office, annual volumes for the years 1963-78.

Children Involved in Divorce

Each year since 1970, about one million children under eighteen years of age are involved in divorce. This is an average of about one child per divorce and includes about 1.7 percent of all children under eighteen. A child exposed for seventeen years to a 1.7 per 1,000 annual probability of having his parents divorce will have more than a 20 percent chance of being involved in a divorce before attaining adulthood. Table 4-25 shows the trend over three decades.

The average number of children per divorce has been declining since 1964. This is an indirect consequence of declining fertility. The proportion of children under eighteen involved in a divorce is rising rapidly because of the increased number of divorces, not because parents with children are getting more inclined to divorce. A more accurate picture of the trend can be obtained from the right-hand panel of Table 4-25, which shows the number of children the couple had born at the time of divorce. Nearly one-half of all divorcing couples are childless. This proportion declined from 1950 to 1964, but has risen somewhat since then. This is an indirect result of the fact that the couples exposed to divorce are the same couples that caused the baby boom. Now that couples which caused the baby bust are becoming increasingly exposed to divorce, childlessness in divorce is on the increase. Also, if the duration of marriage before divorce continues to shorten, the proportion of children involved in divorce will decline because more divorces take place before children are born. The old-fashioned solution of waiting until the children are grown before divorcing appears to be less popular in the 1980s.

The Future Trend of Divorce Rates

In interpreting today's high divorce rates, one should keep in mind the following facts:

1. The divorce epidemic is not being created by today's younger generation. It has been created by today's population aged thirty or more, who married in the 1960s and before. The generation that was 30-45 in 1980 has been a volatile generation that distinguished itself for nonconformist activity and is quite unlike today's more pragmatic generation. High divorce rates in the 1980s may represent a continuation of this nonconformist idealism. This would suggest that divorce rates will decline as this generation ages and is replaced by more conservative cohorts in the divorce-prone ages.

2. High divorce is linked to early marriage, low education, and poverty (to be validated in later chapters). The younger generations are marrying at later ages; they are better educated and at least as economically secure if not more so than young persons a decade ago. Hence, one would expect a decline in divorce rates.

3. The tendency of unmarried young persons to live together (see Chapter 11) may be a form of trial marriage in which incompatible unions can be dissolved without having to become a matter of public record. Marriage, when it does occur, may be more durable because it is based on mature, experienced decisions rather than impulse. Such marriages may have less divorce.

On the basis of these considerations, it is predicted that divorce rates will level off during the last half of the 1980s, and decline from their present high proportions. This could, of course, be overturned by oncoming generations.

Notes

1. An additional status, "separated," is also recognized in recent censuses and surveys to identify those married persons living apart primarily because of marital discord.

2. Marital status should also be thought of as an important social characteristic of the type to be considered in Part III of this book.

3. The fifty states do not report marriage and divorce statistics as completely or as accurately as they do births and deaths. In order to obtain national totals, the National Center for Health Statistics is forced to make estimates (which are very reasonable) for some items of information. For details, see the technical appendix to this chapter.

Table 4-25. Children and Divorce: 1950-1981

Year	Estimated number of children involved	Average number of children per decree	Rate per 1,000 children under 18 years	Percent distribution of number of children reported						
				None	One	Two	Three	Four	Five	Six or more
1981	1,180,000	0.97	18.7	44.8	25.7	20.3	6.7	1.8	(0.7)	
1980	1,174,000	0.98	17.3	44.4	25.9	20.1	6.9	2.0	0.5	0.2
1979	1,181,000	1.00	18.9	44.6	25.5	19.7	7.2	2.2	0.6	0.3
1978	1,147,000	1.01	18.1	44.3	25.4	19.5	7.4	2.3	0.7	0.3
1977	1,095,000	1.00	17.0	45.1	25.3	18.8	7.3	2.5	0.7	0.4
1976	1,117,000	1.03	17.1	44.4	25.3	18.9	7.4	2.7	0.9	0.4
1975	1,123,000	1.08	16.9	42.9	25.5	18.9	8.0	3.0	1.0	0.6
1974	1,099,000	1.12	16.3	42.0	25.5	18.8	8.3	3.5	1.2	0.7
1973	1,079,000	1.17	15.8	40.5	25.5	19.0	9.0	3.7	1.4	0.9
1972	1,021,000	1.20	14.8	39.9	25.6	18.9	9.0	4.0	1.6	1.0
1971	946,000	1.22	13.6	40.1	24.9	18.7	9.5	4.0	1.7	1.1
1970	870,000	1.22	12.5	40.1	24.6	18.7	9.5	4.3	1.7	1.1
1969	840,000	1.31	11.9	39.4	23.5	18.6	10.1	4.9	2.0	1.6
1968	784,000	1.34	11.1	39.0	23.2	18.6	10.4	5.1	2.2	1.6
1967	701,000	1.34	9.9	39.0	23.3	18.4	10.4	5.2	2.1	1.6
1966	669,000	1.34	9.5	39.7	22.8	18.2	10.4	5.3	2.1	1.5
1965	630,000	1.32	8.9	40.2	23.2	18.0	10.2	4.9	2.0	1.4
1964	613,000	1.36	8.7	37.4	24.1	18.6	11.1	5.2	2.2	1.5
1963	562,000	1.31	8.2	38.4	23.9	18.7	10.7	5.0	2.0	1.4
1962	532,000	1.29	7.9	39.8	23.3	18.9	10.2	4.5	(3.3)	
1961	516,000	1.25	7.8	39.7	25.1	18.6	9.3	4.6	(2.7)	
1960	463,000	1.18	7.2	43.3	23.0	17.4	9.7	4.0	(2.6)	
1959	468,000	1.18	7.5	40.9	25.5	18.4	8.8	3.8	1.5	1.0
1958	398,000	1.08	6.5	44.9	24.6	16.9	8.0	3.5	1.2	0.8
1957	379,000	0.99	6.4	49.1	23.1	15.5	7.2	3.0	1.1	0.9
1956	361,000	0.95	6.3	51.1	22.6	14.8	6.8	2.8	1.1	0.7
1955	347,000	0.92	6.3	51.9	22.8	14.5	6.8	2.3	0.9	0.8
1954	341,000	0.90	6.4	52.2	23.1	14.4	6.3	2.4	1.0	0.7
1953	330,000	0.85	6.4	54.5	22.3	13.6	5.7	2.2	(1.6)	
1952	318,000	0.81	6.2	55.4	22.5	13.3	5.3	2.4	(1.1)	
1951	304,000	0.80	6.1	56.1	22.6	12.9	5.0		(3.5)	
1950	299,000	0.78	6.3	56.0	23.8	12.2	5.0	1.7	(1.4)	

Source: National Center for Health Statistics. Vital Statistics of the United States (1950-80), and Monthly Vital Statistics Report (1981). Washington, DC: U.S. Government Printing Office, 1954-84.

4. Because only about 6 percent of all marriages occur to women forty-five or older, an upper age limit of forty-four is specified for the GNR.

Bibliography

Beale, Calvin L. "Increased Divorce Rates Among Separated Persons as a Factor in Divorce Since 1940." *Social Forces* 19 (1950):72-74.

Becker, G.; Landes, E.; and Michael, R. "An Economic Analysis of Marital Instability." *Journal of Political Economy* 85 (1977):1141-87.

Bernardo, D.H. "Divorce and Remarriage at Middle Age and Beyond." *American Academy of Political and Social Science Annals* 464 (1982):132-39.

Bernard, Jessie S. *Marriage and Family Among Negroes.* Englewood Cliffs, NJ: Prentice Hall, 1966.

Bogue, Donald J. *Principles of Demography.* (Chapter 17, "Marriage and Marital Dissolution.") New York: John Wiley & Sons, 1969.

Bumpass, Larry L., and Sweet, James A. "Differentials in Marital Instability: 1970." *American Sociological Review* 37:754-66.

Carter, Hugh, and Glick, Paul C. *Marriage and Divorce: A Social and Economic Study.* Cambridge, MA: Harvard University Press, 1976.

Cherlin, Andrew S. *Marriage, Divorce and Remarriage.* Cambridge, MA: Harvard University Press, 1981.

Davis, Kingsley. "Statistical Perspective on Marriage and Divorce." *Annals of the American Academy of Political and Social Science* 272 (1950):12-15.

Ferriss, A.L. "An Indicator of Marriage Dissolution by Marriage Cohort." *Social Forces* 48 (1970):356-64.

Frieden, A. "The United States Marriage Market." *Journal of Political Economy* 82 (1974):534-53.

Frisbie, W. "Recent Changes in Marital Stability Among Mexican Americans: Convergence with Black and Anglo Trends." *Social Forces* 58 (1980):1205-20.

———; Bean, Frank D.; and Eberstein, Isaac W. "Patterns of Marital Instability Among Mexican Americans, Blacks, and Anglos." In *The Demography of Racial and Ethnic Groups*, edited by Frank D. Bean and W. Parker Frisbie. New York: Academic Press, 1978.

Glick, Paul C. *American Families*. New York: John Wiley & Sons, 1957.

———, and Norton, A.J. "Marrying, Divorcing, and Living Together in the U.S. Today." *Population Bulletin* 32 (1977):3-39.

———. "Perspectives on the Recent Upturn in Divorce and Remarriage." *Demography* 10 (1973):301-14.

Hajnal, John. "The Marriage Boom." *Population Index* 19 (1953):80.

Hogan, D. "Order of Events in the Life Course." *American Sociological Review* 43 (1978):573-86.

Jacobson, Paul H. *American Marriage and Divorce*. New York: Rinehart, 1959.

Kitagawa, E.M. "New Life-Styles: Marriage Patterns, Living Arrangements, and Fertility Outside of Marriage." *American Academy of Political and Social Science Annual* 453 (1981):1-27.

Koo, H., and Suchindran, C. "Effects of Children and Women's Remarriage Prospects." *Journal of Family Issues* 1:497-515.

Marini, M.M. "Transition to Adulthood: Sex Differences in Educational Attainment and Age at Marriage." *American Sociological Review* 43 (1978):483-507.

McCarthy, J. "A Comparison of the Probability of the Dissolution of First and Second Marriages." *Demography* 15 (1978):345-60.

Menken, J.; Trussel, J.; Stempel, D.; and Babakol, O. "Proportional Hazards Life Table Models: An Illustrative Analysis of Socio-Demographic Influences on Marital Dissolution in the United States." *Demography* 18 (1981):181-200.

Monahan, Thomas P. "When Married Couples Part: Statistical Trends and Relationships in Divorce." *American Sociological Review* 27 (1962):625-33.

Mott, F., and Moore, S. "The Causes of Marital Disruption Among Young American Women: An Interdisciplinary Perspective." *Journal of Marriage and the Family* 41 (1979):355-65.

———. "Tempo of Remarriages Among Young American Women." *Journal of Marriage and the Family* 45: (1983):427-36.

Mueller, C., and Pope, H. "Marital Instability: A Study of Its Transmission Between Generations." *Journal of Marriage and the Family* 39 (1977):83-93.

Nock, Stephen L. "The Family Life Cycle: Empirical or Conceptual Tool?" *Journal of Marriage and the Family* 44 (1979):15-26.

Plateris, Alexander A. "Divorce by Marriage Cohort." *Vital and Health Statistics* (Series 21, no. 34). Washington, DC: U.S. Government Printing Office, 1979.

———. "Duration of Marriage Before Divorce: United States." *Vital and Health Statistics* (Series 21, no. 38.) Washington, DC: U.S. Government Printing Office, 1981.

———. "100 Years of Marriage and Divorce Statistics: 1867-1967." *Vital and Health Statistics* (Series 21, no. 24). Washington, DC: U.S. Government Printing Office, 1981.

Pope, H., and Mueller, C. "The Intergenerational Transmission of Marital Instability: Comparisons by Race and Sex." *Journal of Social Issues* 32 (1976):49-66.

Preston, S., and McDonald, J. "The Incidence of Divorce Within Cohorts of American Marriages Contracted Since the Civil War." *Demography* 16 (1979):1-25.

Rawlings, Steve W. "Perspectives on American Husbands and Wives." *Current Population Reports* (Series P-23, no. 77). Washington, DC: U.S. Government Printing Office, 1978.

Rele, J.R. "Some Correlates of the Age at Marriage in the United States." *Eugenics Quarterly* 12 (1965):1-6.

Schultz, Theodore W. (ed.). "Marriage, Family, Human Capital, and Fertility." Proceedings of a Conference, June 4-5, 1973. *Journal of Political Economy* 82 (1974):51-5233.

Spanier, G.B., and Glick, P.C. "The Life Cycle of American Families: An Expanded Analysis." *Journal of Family History* 5 (1980):97-111.

Stouffer, S.A., and Spencer, L.M. "Recent Increases in Marriage and Divorce." *American Journal of Sociology* (1939): 551-54.

Sweet, J. *Differentials in Remarriage Probabilities*. Madison, WI: University of Wisconsin, Center for Demography and Ecology, 1973.

Taeuber, Irene B., and Taeuber, Conrad. *People of the United States in the 20th Century*. (Chapter 7, "Marital Stutus.") Washington, DC: U.S. Bureau of the Census, 1971.

Thornton, A. "Decomposing the Remarriage Process." *Population Studies* 31 (1977):383-92.

U.S. Bureau of the Census. "Household and Family Characteristics: March 1977." *Current Population Reports* (Series P-20, no. 326). Washington, DC: U.S. Government Printing Office, 1978.

———. "Household, Families, Marital Status and Living Arrangements." *Current Population Reports* (Series P-20, no. 382). Washington, DC: U.S. Government Printing Office, 1983.

______. "Households and Families by Type: March 1980 (Advance Report)." *Current Population Reports* (Series P-20, no. 57). Washington, DC: U.S. Government Printing Office, 1980.

______. "Marital Status and Living Arrangements," (March 1977; 1979; and 1981). *Current Population Reports* (Series P-20, nos. 323; 349; and 372). Washington, DC: U.S. Government Printing Office, 1978; 1980; and 1982.

______. "Marriage, Divorce, Widowhood, and Remarriage by Family Characteristics." *Current Population Reports* (Series P-20, no. 312). Washington, DC: U.S. Government Printing Office, 1975.

______. "Number, Timing and Duration of Marriages and Divorces in the United States: June, 1975." *Current Population Reports* (Series P-20, no. 297). Washington, DC: U.S. Government Printing Office, 1976.

______. "Social and Economic Variations in Marriage, Divorce and Remarriage: 1967." *Current Population Reports* (Series P-20, no. 223). Washington, DC: U.S. Government Printing Office, 1971.

______. "Subject Reports: Age at First Marriage." *1970 Census of Population*. Washington, DC: U.S. Government Printing Office, 1973.

______. "Subject Reports: Age at First Marriage, Data on Duration of Marriage, Times Married, Difference in Age Between Husband and Wife." *1960 Census of Population*. Washington, DC: U.S. Government Printing Office, 1966.

______. "Subject Reports: Marital Status." *1970 Census of Population*. Washington, DC: U.S. Government Printing Office, 1972.

U.S. National Center for Health Statistics. "Advance Report of Final Marriage Statistics (Annual)." *Monthly Vital Statistics Report*. (Report for 1980, Vol. 32, no. 5, Supplement.) Washington, DC: U.S. Government Printing Office, 1983.

____ (Weed, James). "National Estimates of Marriage Dissolution and Survivorship: United States." *Vital and Health Statistics* (Series 3, no. 19). Washington, DC: U.S. Government Printing Office, 1980.

____. "Remarriage of Women 15-44 Years of Age Whose First Marriage Ended in Divorce: United States 1976." (Advance Data Number 58.) Washington, DC: U.S. Government Printing Office, 1980.

Waite, L., and Spitze, G. "Young Women's Transition to Marriage." *Demography* 18 (1980):681-94.

Weitzman, L.J. *The Marriage Contract*. New York: Free Press, 1981.

White, L.K. "Note on Racial Differences in the Effect of Female Economic Opportunity on Marriage Rates." *Demography* 18 (1981):349-54.

Wilson, Barbara F., and Hume, Elaine. "First Marriages: United States, 1968-1976." *Vital and Health Statistics* (Series 21, no. 35). Washington, DC: U.S. Government Printing Office, 1979.

Wolfe, W., and MacDonald, M. "The Earnings of Men and Remarriage." *Demography* 16 (1979):389-99.

Technical Appendix 4-1

Statistics from Vital Registration of Marriages and Divorces

The material reported below was extracted from Technical Appendix 4 of Volume III, Vital Statistics of the United States: 1978 (Marriages and Divorces). *The reader is referred to the full report for a complete account of the effort to develop a vital statistics reporting system comparable in scope and quality to the one used for births and deaths.*

Marriage and divorce statistics from vital registration are based on information from three sources: (1) complete counts of events obtained from all states, (2) samples of marriage and divorce certificates from states meeting specified reporting criteria, and (3) precoded machine-readable data for all marriages and all divorces occurring in states participating in the Cooperative Health Statistics System (CHSS).

State and local officials annually provide complete counts of marriages and divorcesby county of occurrence and marriages by month of occurrence. From these counts, marriage and divorce totals are derived and rates are computed for each state, geographic division, region, and the United States. For marriages a total is also derived for the marriage-registration area.

Sample records are obtained by the National Center for Health Statistics (NCHS) from microfilm copies of the original certificates received from the registration offices of states and areas comprising the marriage registration area (MRA) and the divorce registration area (DRA). The statistical information on these records, including data on the characteristics of marriages and divorces and of the persons involved in them, is edited, classified, transferred to tape for computer processing, and tabulated in NCHS. Exceptions to this procedure are statistics from those states in the MRA or DRA that submit precoded machine-readable data to NCHS through CHSS.

Marriage and divorce statistics for the United States, for the registration areas, and for individual states are limited to events occurring during the year and registered within the specified area. All tabulations are by place of occurrence and include events occurring to nonresidents. Marriages or divorces of members of the Armed Forces or other U.S. nationals that occur outside the United States are excluded. "United States" refers to the fifty states and the District of Columbia. Alaska has been included in the U.S. tabulations since 1959 and Hawaii since 1960.

Nationwide Counts

The total counts of marriages by state and county were obtained from central files of marriage records for the states maintaining them and from the District of Columbia. The registration officials of Manhattan supplied the counts for the five boroughs of New York City. In the states without central files, counts are obtained from the counties by state officials or by NCHS.

Although total counts of marriages performed are requested from each county registration official, a small number of counties report instead the number of marriage licenses issued. The number of marriage licenses issued is usually 1 or 2 percent greater than the number of marriages performed.

Beginning with final marriage statistics for 1978, nonlicensed (confidential) marriages registered in California are included in national and geographic totals and rates. Section 4213 of the California Civil Code allows unmarried couples who have been living together to be married confidentially without obtaining a marriage license or health certificate. In 1972 this section was amended to require county clerks to keep sealed records of these marriages and periodically to report the total number to the California State Department of Health Services. These records may not be opened to inspection without a court order on a showing of good cause.

Total counts of divorces by state and county include decrees of absolute divorce and of annulment as well as decrees of marriage dissolution newly introduced in many states. These counts are obtained from central files of the states maintaining them and from the District of Columbia. Either local or state officials provided the county totals for the states without central files of divorce records.

Registration Areas

Registration areas for the collection of marriage and divorce statistics were established in 1957 and 1958, respectively. These areas include states with adequate programs for collecting marriage and divorce statistics. Criteria for participation in the registration areas are

1. A central file of marriage or divorce records
2. A statistical report form conforming closely in content to the Standard License and Certificate of Marriage (Figure 4-A) or Standard Certificate of Divorce, Dissolution of Marriage, or Annulment (Figure 4-B)
3. Regular reporting to the state office by all local areas in which marriages or divorces are recorded
4. Tests for completeness and accuracy of marriage or divorce registration carried out in cooperation with NCHS.

In 1978 the MRA comprised forty-one states, the District of Columbia, Puerto Rico, and Virgin Islands. The DRA included twenty-eight states and Virgin Islands.

In the statistical tabulations in 1978, *marriage registration area* refers only to the forty-one states and Dis-

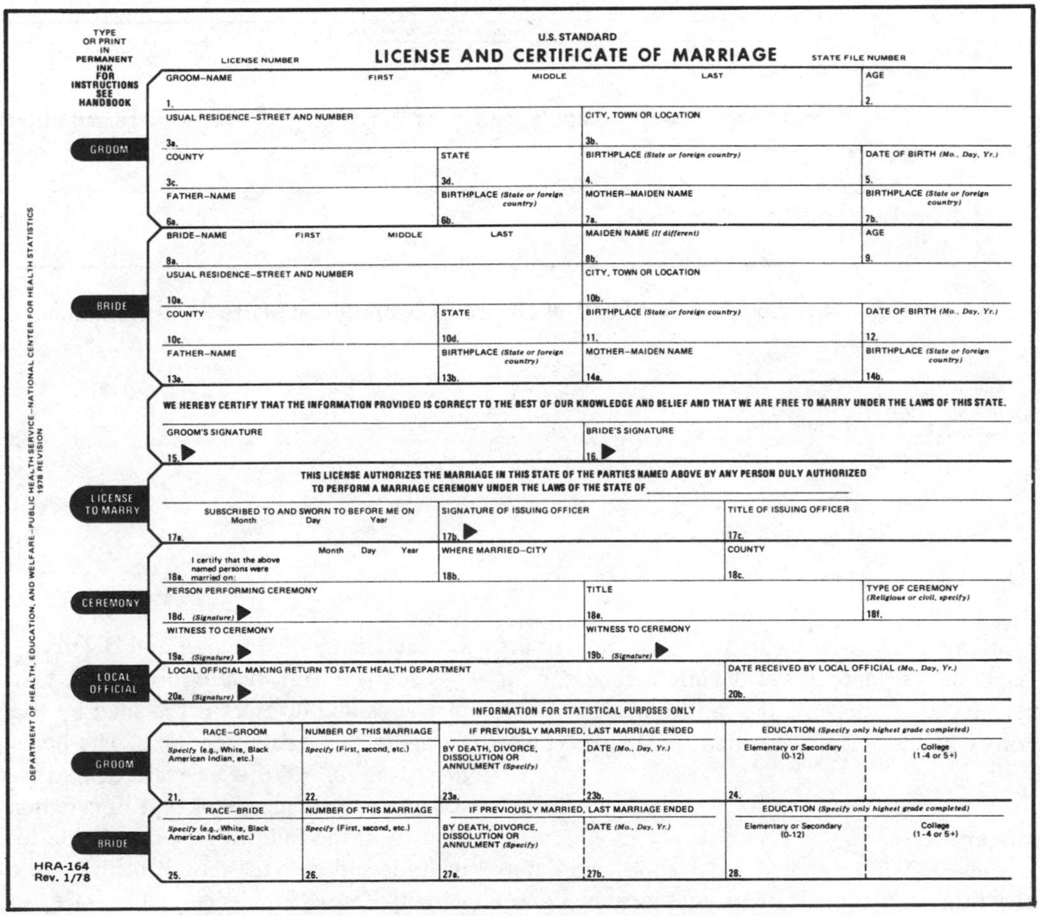

TYPE OR PRINT IN PERMANENT INK
FOR INSTRUCTIONS SEE HANDBOOK

U.S. STANDARD
LICENSE AND CERTIFICATE OF MARRIAGE
LICENSE NUMBER
STATE FILE NUMBER

GROOM
1. GROOM–NAME FIRST MIDDLE LAST
2. AGE
3a. USUAL RESIDENCE–STREET AND NUMBER
3b. CITY, TOWN OR LOCATION
3c. COUNTY
3d. STATE
4. BIRTHPLACE (*State or foreign country*)
5. DATE OF BIRTH (*Mo., Day, Yr.*)
6a. FATHER–NAME
6b. BIRTHPLACE (*State or foreign country*)
7a. MOTHER–MAIDEN NAME
7b. BIRTHPLACE (*State or foreign country*)

BRIDE
8a. BRIDE–NAME FIRST MIDDLE LAST
8b. MAIDEN NAME (*If different*)
9. AGE
10a. USUAL RESIDENCE–STREET AND NUMBER
10b. CITY, TOWN OR LOCATION
10c. COUNTY
10d. STATE
11. BIRTHPLACE (*State or foreign country*)
12. DATE OF BIRTH (*Mo., Day, Yr.*)
13a. FATHER–NAME
13b. BIRTHPLACE (*State or foreign country*)
14a. MOTHER–MAIDEN NAME
14b. BIRTHPLACE (*State or foreign country*)

WE HEREBY CERTIFY THAT THE INFORMATION PROVIDED IS CORRECT TO THE BEST OF OUR KNOWLEDGE AND BELIEF AND THAT WE ARE FREE TO MARRY UNDER THE LAWS OF THIS STATE.
15. GROOM'S SIGNATURE
16. BRIDE'S SIGNATURE

LICENSE TO MARRY
THIS LICENSE AUTHORIZES THE MARRIAGE IN THIS STATE OF THE PARTIES NAMED ABOVE BY ANY PERSON DULY AUTHORIZED TO PERFORM A MARRIAGE CEREMONY UNDER THE LAWS OF THE STATE OF ____________
17a. SUBSCRIBED TO AND SWORN TO BEFORE ME ON Month Day Year
17b. SIGNATURE OF ISSUING OFFICER
17c. TITLE OF ISSUING OFFICER

CEREMONY
18a. I certify that the above named persons were married on: Month Day Year
18b. WHERE MARRIED–CITY
18c. COUNTY
18d. PERSON PERFORMING CEREMONY (*Signature*)
18e. TITLE
18f. TYPE OF CEREMONY (*Religious or civil, specify*)
19a. WITNESS TO CEREMONY (*Signature*)
19b. WITNESS TO CEREMONY (*Signature*)

LOCAL OFFICIAL
20a. LOCAL OFFICIAL MAKING RETURN TO STATE HEALTH DEPARTMENT (*Signature*)
20b. DATE RECEIVED BY LOCAL OFFICIAL (*Mo., Day, Yr.*)

INFORMATION FOR STATISTICAL PURPOSES ONLY

GROOM
21. RACE–GROOM: *Specify* (e.g., White, Black American Indian, etc.)
22. NUMBER OF THIS MARRIAGE: *Specify* (First, second, etc.)
IF PREVIOUSLY MARRIED, LAST MARRIAGE ENDED
23a. BY DEATH, DIVORCE, DISSOLUTION OR ANNULMENT (*Specify*)
23b. DATE (*Mo., Day, Yr.*)
24. EDUCATION (*Specify only highest grade completed*): Elementary or Secondary (0-12) | College (1-4 or 5+)

BRIDE
25. RACE–BRIDE: *Specify* (e.g., White, Black American Indian, etc.)
26. NUMBER OF THIS MARRIAGE: *Specify* (First, second, etc.)
IF PREVIOUSLY MARRIED, LAST MARRIAGE ENDED
27a. BY DEATH, DIVORCE, DISSOLUTION OR ANNULMENT (*Specify*)
27b. DATE (*Mo., Day, Yr.*)
28. EDUCATION (*Specify only highest grade completed*): Elementary or Secondary (0-12) | College (1-4 or 5+)

DEPARTMENT OF HEALTH, EDUCATION, AND WELFARE–PUBLIC HEALTH SERVICE–NATIONAL CENTER FOR HEALTH STATISTICS
1978 REVISION
HRA-164
Rev. 1/78

Figure 4-A. Standard License and Certificate of Marriage

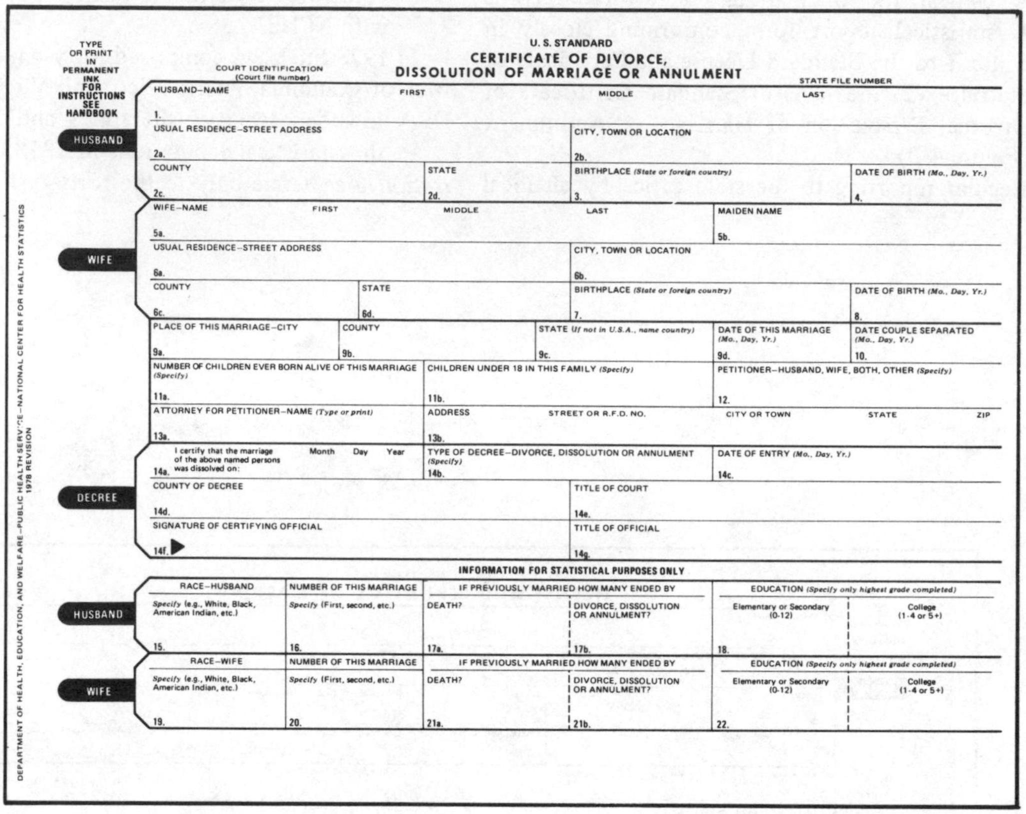

TYPE OR PRINT IN PERMANENT INK FOR INSTRUCTIONS SEE HANDBOOK

U. S. STANDARD
CERTIFICATE OF DIVORCE,
DISSOLUTION OF MARRIAGE OR ANNULMENT

COURT IDENTIFICATION (Court file number)

STATE FILE NUMBER

HUSBAND

HUSBAND–NAME FIRST MIDDLE LAST 1.

USUAL RESIDENCE–STREET ADDRESS 2a. | CITY, TOWN OR LOCATION 2b.

COUNTY 2c. | STATE 2d. | BIRTHPLACE (State or foreign country) 3. | DATE OF BIRTH (Mo., Day, Yr.) 4.

WIFE

WIFE–NAME FIRST MIDDLE LAST 5a. | MAIDEN NAME 5b.

USUAL RESIDENCE–STREET ADDRESS 6a. | CITY, TOWN OR LOCATION 6b.

COUNTY 6c. | STATE 6d. | BIRTHPLACE (State or foreign country) 7. | DATE OF BIRTH (Mo., Day, Yr.) 8.

PLACE OF THIS MARRIAGE–CITY 9a. | COUNTY 9b. | STATE (If not in U.S.A., name country) 9c. | DATE OF THIS MARRIAGE (Mo., Day, Yr.) 9d. | DATE COUPLE SEPARATED (Mo., Day, Yr.) 10.

NUMBER OF CHILDREN EVER BORN ALIVE OF THIS MARRIAGE (Specify) 11a. | CHILDREN UNDER 18 IN THIS FAMILY (Specify) 11b. | PETITIONER–HUSBAND, WIFE, BOTH, OTHER (Specify) 12.

ATTORNEY FOR PETITIONER–NAME (Type or print) 13a. | ADDRESS STREET OR R.F.D. NO. CITY OR TOWN STATE ZIP 13b.

DECREE

I certify that the marriage of the above named persons was dissolved on: Month Day Year 14a. | TYPE OF DECREE–DIVORCE, DISSOLUTION OR ANNULMENT (Specify) 14b. | DATE OF ENTRY (Mo., Day, Yr.) 14c.

COUNTY OF DECREE 14d. | TITLE OF COURT 14e.

SIGNATURE OF CERTIFYING OFFICIAL 14f. | TITLE OF OFFICIAL 14g.

INFORMATION FOR STATISTICAL PURPOSES ONLY

HUSBAND

RACE–HUSBAND Specify (e.g., White, Black, American Indian, etc.) 15. | NUMBER OF THIS MARRIAGE Specify (First, second, etc.) 16. | IF PREVIOUSLY MARRIED HOW MANY ENDED BY DEATH? 17a. DIVORCE, DISSOLUTION OR ANNULMENT? 17b. | EDUCATION (Specify only highest grade completed) Elementary or Secondary (0-12) College (1-4 or 5+) 18.

WIFE

RACE–WIFE Specify (e.g., White, Black, American Indian, etc.) 19. | NUMBER OF THIS MARRIAGE Specify (First, second, etc.) 20. | IF PREVIOUSLY MARRIED HOW MANY ENDED BY DEATH? 21a. DIVORCE, DISSOLUTION OR ANNULMENT? 21b. | EDUCATION (Specify only highest grade completed) Elementary or Secondary (0-12) College (1-4 or 5+) 22.

DEPARTMENT OF HEALTH, EDUCATION, AND WELFARE–PUBLIC HEALTH SERVICE–NATIONAL CENTER FOR HEALTH STATISTICS 1978 REVISION

Figure 4-B. Standard Certificate of Divorce, Dissolution of Marriage, or Annulment

trict of Columbia. *Divorce registration area* refers to the twenty-eight states. Marriages in the MRA accounted for 79 percent of all marriages in the United States in 1978, and divorces in the DRA accounted for 48 percent of all divorces.

Standard Certificates

Each state and independent registration area determines the form and content of its vital records. Consequently the records vary in certain details. Although modified in each state as required by particular needs or by special provisions of the state vital statistics law, the marriage and divorce certificates of most states in the MRA and DRA conform closely to the standard certificates.

Characteristics of Marriages and Divorces

Each year statistical information on characteristics of marriages and divorces is provided by the states participating in the registration areas. The items processed for marriages for 1978 were state of marriage; month and day of week of marriage; type of ceremony, civil or religious; and the following items relating to characteristics of bride and groom: state of birth, date of birth or age, nativity status, residence status, race, number of this marriage, previous marital status, and education.

For divorces (including absolute divorces, annulments, and decrees of marriage dissolution) the items processed for 1978 were state in which divorce was granted, number of children under eighteen years of age, month and year of marriage (from which duration of marriage and age at marriage are obtained), month and year of separation (from which duration of marriage to separation and duration of separation to divorce are obtained), place of marriage, and the following items relating to husband and wife: date of birth or age, race, number of this marriage, and education.

Information about previous marriages of the bride and groom is obtained from two items: number of this marriage and previous marital status. For the District of Columbia and the thirty-four states that requested both items on their marriage certificates, first marriages and remarriages could be identified if either item was stated.

Race is generally not well reported on either marriage or divorce certificates. The item appears on the marriage forms of all states in the MRA except California, Iowa, Maryland, Massachusetts, Michigan, New York, and Ohio. The District of Columbia no longer reports race on its marriage certificates. Race appears as an item on the divorce certificates of all states in the DRA except Michigan and Ohio.

Percents and Rates

Rates for 1940, 1950, and 1970 are based on the population enumerated as of April 1 in the censuses of those years. Rates for all other years are based on the estimated midyear (July 1) population for the respective years. Rates are based on population estimates including Armed Forces stationed in the United States but excluding Armed Forces abroad, except divorce rates for 1941-46, which are based on populations including Armed Forces abroad.

Children Involved in Divorces

To obtain national estimates for 1970 through 1978, the average number of children under eighteen years of age per decree for the DRA was multiplied by the national divorce total. From 1965 to 1969 the average number of children per decree was computed for the sixteen states that had reported children with a satisfactory degree of completeness in 1965 (Alaska, Hawaii, Idaho, Iowa, Kansas, Michigan, Missouri, Montana, Nebraska, Ohio, Oregon, South Dakota, Tennessee, Virginia, Wisconsin, and Wyoming) and the national divorce total was multiplied by this average.

The race of a child involved in a divorce is inferred from the race of the husband and wife. When spouses are both in the same racial category, the child is assigned to that category. When the husband is white and the wife is not, the child is assigned to the wife's race. When the husband is not white, the child is assigned to the husband's race. When the race of only one spouse is stated, the child is assigned to the stated race.

Chapter 5

Mortality

Overview

Mortality in the United States is very low and declining. Two summary measures of the force of mortality upon a population, the crude death rate (CDR) and the expectation of life at birth (identified by the symbol $\mathring{e}_0$), are reported in Tables 5-1 and 5-2 respectively, and illustrated graphically in Figure 5-1. (For explanations of CDR and expectation of life at birth, see "definitions.") In both tables, measures are provided for each sex and for white and black/other populations for selected years in this century.[1] Because death is concentrated in the older ages, the crude death rate is strongly affected by changing age composition. Although CDR is useful in understanding growth rate, expectation of life at birth is a more precise measure of mortality.[2]

Tables 5-1 and 5-2 and Figure 5-1 divulge the following:

1. The CDR in 1983 stood at 8.6 per 1,000 population, and the life expectation at birth was above seventy-four years. Because of changing age composition, the CDR has declined by only one point since 1950, yet life expectation has risen substantially.

2. Since 1970 the United States has been in a phase of modest improvement in life expectation. This was preceded by a decade of nearly zero or only slight improvement, which caused speculation that some biological maximum to length of life was being approached.

3. Mortality decline has not been steady and uniform. There were periods of more rapid improvement in mortality conditions spanning 1900-15, 1940-50, and 1970-83, with periods of slower improvement between.

4. Male mortality has been consistently higher than female mortality. As of 1982 male life expectation was 7.4 years less than (only 91 percent of) that of females.

5. Black mortality has been consistently higher than white mortality. As of 1982 life expectation of the white population was 4.2 years higher (6 percent) than that of the black/other population.

6. Year-to-year fluctuations in death rates were common occurrences before World War I (especially with the influenza epidemic of 1918). With the passage of time, these fluctuations have diminished.

7. The race differences in mortality were greater in the past than in more recent years, but the sex differences are greater now than ever before.

All of these points will be explored in considerable detail in this chapter.

Definitions

Crude Death Rate (CDR). The number of annual deaths per 1,000 midyear population in a given year. This rate may be computed separately for each sex, for specific races, or for each geographic area of a nation. Also called "general death rate" or simply "death rate."

Age-Specific Death Rate (ASDR). The number of annual deaths at a given age per 1,000 midyear population of that age. Deaths and population usually are grouped into 5-year or 10-year age groups.

Age-Sex Specific Death Rates. Age-specific death rates computed separately for each sex.

Death Probability. The proportion of persons alive at a given birth date who will die before reaching the end of that year of life. These probabilities are derived from age-specific death rates in order to compute life tables. Also called "age-specific mortality rate" or "proportion dying at age (x)."

Life Table. A statistical procedure for summarizing mortality rates for a particular date. A hypothetical cohort of 100,000 persons is assumed to be subject to the age-specific death probabilities observed for an actual population during the particular time period. The number who would die at each age and who would survive to be exposed to death at later ages is computed. From such statistics, it is possible to compute life expectation. Such life tables are termed "cross-section" or "period" life tables. Generational life tables may also be computed, using age-specific death probabilities of real cohorts. (For details see Appendix 5-1.)

Life Expectation ($\mathring{e}_x$). The average number of additional years a person will live if he or she is exposed for an entire remaining lifetime to the age-specific death probabilities of a given year, derived from a life table. Life expectation can be computed for each age (x).

Life Expectation at Birth ($\mathring{e}_0$). Life expectation of a person at age 0 (birth), derived from a life table for a specific year. This is the best single summary measure of the overall effect of mortality on a population.

Cause of Death. The disease or event that caused death. Causes are categorized and assigned according to internationally established coding procedures. World Health Organization regulations specify that cause of death be categorized according to the current revision of the *International Statistical Classification of Diseases, Injuries, and Causes of Death* (see Technical Appendix 5-2).

Cause-Specific Death Rates. The annual number of deaths from a given cause per 100,000 midyear population. Cause-specific rates may be reported for age groups, by sex, race, or other categories.

Infant Mortality Rate (IMR). The annual number of deaths to infants under one year of age per 1,000 or per 100,000 live births in the same year. This rate is similar to, but not identical with, the age-specific death rate for age 0-1.

Neonatal Mortality Rate. Annual number of deaths to infants under 28 days of life per 100,000 live births during the year. It is commonly (not wholly correctly) assumed that deaths during the first month of life are caused primarily by factors relating to physiology, prenatal care, and delivery.

Post-Neonatal MortalityRate. Annual number of deaths to infants 28 days to 365 days of life per 100,000 live births during the year. It is commonly (not wholly correctly) assumed that deaths during this period are caused by environmental, nutritional, and health care conditions. The neonatal rate plus the post-neonatal mortality rate equals the infant mortality rate.

Fetal Mortality Rate. The annual number of stillborn infants (born dead) after 28 weeks or more of gestation per 100,000 live births during the same year.

Perinatal Mortality Rate. The sum of the fetal mortality rate and the neonatal mortality rate.

Maternal Mortality Rate.(MMR). Annual number of deaths to women as a result of childbirth per 100,000 births in that year.

Table 5-1. Crude Death Rates, by Color and Sex: United States, 1900-1983[a]

Year	Total			White			Black/other			Ratio male to female	Ratio black/other to white
	Both sexes	Male	Female	Both sexes	Male	Female	Both sexes	Male	Female		
1983 . . .	8.6	9.5	7.8	8.8	9.6	8.1	7.3	8.6	6.1	1.22	0.83
1982 . . .	8.6	9.4	7.7	8.7	9.5	8.0	7.3	8.7	6.0	1.22	0.84
1981 . . .	8.7	9.6	7.8	8.9	9.7	8.0	7.5	8.9	6.3	1.24	0.85
1980 . . .	8.7	9.8	7.8	8.9	9.8	8.0	7.8	9.4	6.5	1.26	0.88
1979 . . .	8.5	9.6	7.5	8.7	9.6	7.7	7.7	9.2	6.4	1.27	0.89
1978 . . .	8.7	9.8	7.6	8.8	9.8	7.8	7.9	9.4	6.5	1.28	0.90
1975 . . .	8.8	10.0	7.6	8.9	10.0	7.8	8.2	9.9	6.7	1.32	0.93
1970 . . .	9.5	10.9	8.1	9.5	10.9	8.1	9.4	11.2	7.8	1.35	0.99
1965 . . .	9.4	10.9	8.0	9.4	10.9	8.0	9.7	11.2	8.2	1.36	1.03
1960 . . .	9.5	11.0	8.1	9.5	11.0	8.0	10.1	11.5	8.7	1.36	1.06
1955 . . .	9.3	10.8	7.9	9.2	10.7	7.8	10.0	11.3	8.8	1.37	1.09
1950 . . .	9.6	11.1	8.2	9.5	10.9	8.0	11.2	12.5	9.9	1.35	1.18
1945 . . .	10.6	12.6	8.8	10.4	12.5	8.6	11.9	13.5	10.5	1.43	1.14
1940 . . .	10.8	12.0	9.5	10.4	11.6	9.2	13.8	15.1	12.6	1.26	1.33
1935 . . .	10.9	12.0	9.9	10.6	11.6	9.5	14.3	15.6	13.0	1.21	1.35
1930 . . .	11.3	12.3	10.4	10.8	11.7	9.8	16.3	17.4	15.3	1.18	1.51
1925 . . .	11.7	12.4	10.9	11.1	11.8	10.4	17.4	18.2	16.6	1.14	1.57
1920 . . .	13.0	13.4	12.6	12.6	13.0	12.1	17.7	17.8	17.5	1.06	1.40
1915 . . .	13.2	14.0	12.3	12.9	13.7	12.0	20.2	20.8	19.5	1.14	1.57
1910 . . .	14.7	15.6	13.7	14.5	15.4	13.6	21.7	22.3	21.0	1.14	1.50
1905 . . .	15.9	16.7	15.0	15.7	16.5	14.8	25.5	26.8	24.3	1.11	1.62
1900 . . .	17.2	17.9	16.5	17.0	17.7	16.3	25.0	25.7	24.4	1.08	1.47

[a]Data for 1930 and earlier are for death registration states; increased in number from ten states and the District of Columbia in 1900 to the entire conterminous United States in 1933.

Note: 1980-83 figures are based on 10 percent sample of deaths.

Source: National Center for Health Statistics. Vital Statistics of the United States: Mortality (1976--Vol. II, Part A, Table 6); and Monthly Vital Statistics Report (Vol. 30, no. 13, Table 5; Vol. 32, no. 12, Table 5). Washington, DC: U.S. Government Printing Office, 1980; 1982 and 1984.

Table 5-2. Expectation of Life and Birth, by Race and Sex: 1900-1982

Year	Total			White			Black/other			Ratio male to female	Ratio black/other to white
	Both sexes	Male	Female	Both sexes	Male	Female	Both sexes	Male	Female		
1982 . . .	74.5	70.8	78.2	75.1	71.4	78.7	70.9	66.5	75.2	0.91	0.94
1981 . . .	74.1	70.3	77.9	74.7	71.0	78.5	70.3	66.1	74.5	0.90	0.94
1980 . . .	73.7	70.0	77.5	74.4	70.7	78.1	69.5	65.3	73.6	0.90	0.93
1979 . . .	73.9	70.0	77.8	74.6	70.8	78.4	69.8	65.4	74.1	0.90	0.94
1978 . . .	73.5	69.6	77.3	74.1	70.4	78.0	69.3	65.0	73.5	0.90	0.94
1977 . . .	73.3	69.5	77.2	74.0	70.2	77.9	68.9	64.7	73.2	0.90	0.93
1976 . . .	72.9	69.1	76.8	73.6	69.9	77.5	68.4	64.2	72.7	0.90	0.93
1975 . . .	72.6	68.8	76.6	73.4	69.5	77.3	68.0	63.7	72.4	0.90	0.93
1974 . . .	71.9	68.1	75.8	72.7	68.9	76.6	67.0	62.9	71.3	0.90	0.92
1973 . . .	71.3	67.5	75.2	72.1	68.4	76.1	65.9	61.8	70.1	0.90	0.91
1972 . . .	71.1	67.4	75.0	72.0	68.2	75.9	65.6	61.4	69.9	0.90	0.91
1971 . . .	71.1	67.4	75.0	71.9	68.2	75.8	65.6	61.6	69.7	0.90	0.91
1970 . . .	70.8	67.1	74.7	71.7	68.0	75.6	65.3	61.3	69.4	0.90	0.91
1965 . . .	70.2	66.8	73.8	71.1	67.6	74.8	64.3	61.2	67.6	0.91	0.90
1960 . . .	69.7	66.6	73.1	70.6	67.4	74.1	63.6	61.1	66.3	0.91	0.90
1955 . . .	69.6	66.7	72.8	70.5	67.4	73.7	63.7	61.4	66.1	0.92	0.90
1950 . . .	68.2	65.6	71.1	69.1	66.5	72.2	60.8	59.1	62.9	0.92	0.88
1945 . . .	65.9	63.6	67.9	66.8	64.4	69.5	57.7	56.1	59.6	0.94	0.86
1940 . . .	62.9	60.8	65.2	64.2	62.1	66.6	53.1	51.5	54.9	0.93	0.83
1935 . . .	61.7	59.9	63.9	62.9	61.0	65.0	53.1	51.3	55.2	0.94	0.84
1930 . . .	59.7	58.1	61.6	61.4	59.7	63.5	48.1	47.3	49.2	0.94	0.78
1925 . . .	59.0	57.6	60.6	60.7	59.3	62.4	45.7	44.9	46.7	0.95	0.75
1920 . . .	54.1	53.6	54.6	54.9	54.4	55.6	45.3	45.5	45.2	0.98	0.83
1915 . . .	54.5	52.5	56.8	55.1	53.1	57.5	38.9	37.5	40.5	0.92	0.71
1910 . . .	50.0	48.4	51.8	50.3	48.6	52.0	35.6	33.8	37.5	0.93	0.71
1905 . . .	48.7	47.3	50.2	49.1	47.6	50.6	31.3	29.6	33.1	0.94	0.64
1900 . . .	47.3	46.3	48.3	47.6	46.6	48.7	33.0	32.5	33.5	0.96	0.69

Note: Data for 1900-1925 are for death registration states. The 1970-1980 period excludes nonresidents. 1981-82 figures are based on a 10 percent sample of deaths. 1972 figures are based on a 5 percent sample of deaths.

Source: National Center for Health Statistics. Vital Statistics of the United States: Mortality (1978--Vol. II, Part A, Table 5-5); and Monthly Vital Statistics Report (Vol. 31, no. 13, Table 5). Washington, DC: U.S. Government Printing Office, 1982; 1983.

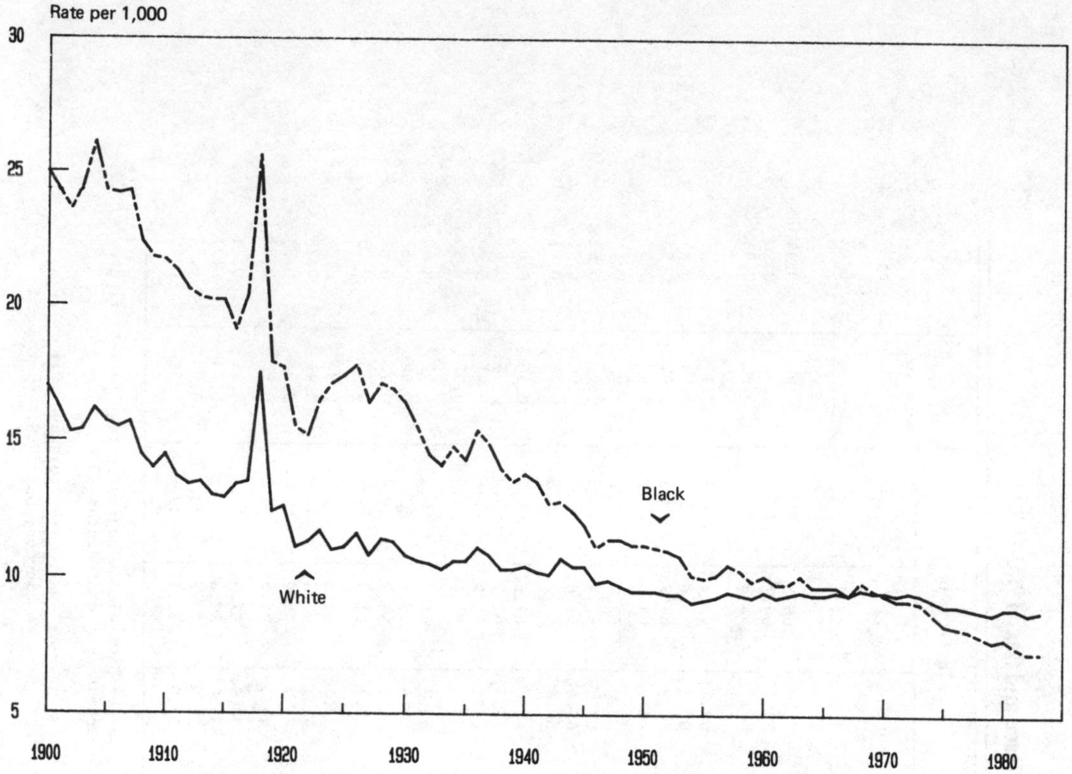

Figure 5-1A. Trends in Race Differentials in Crude Death Rates: 1900-1983

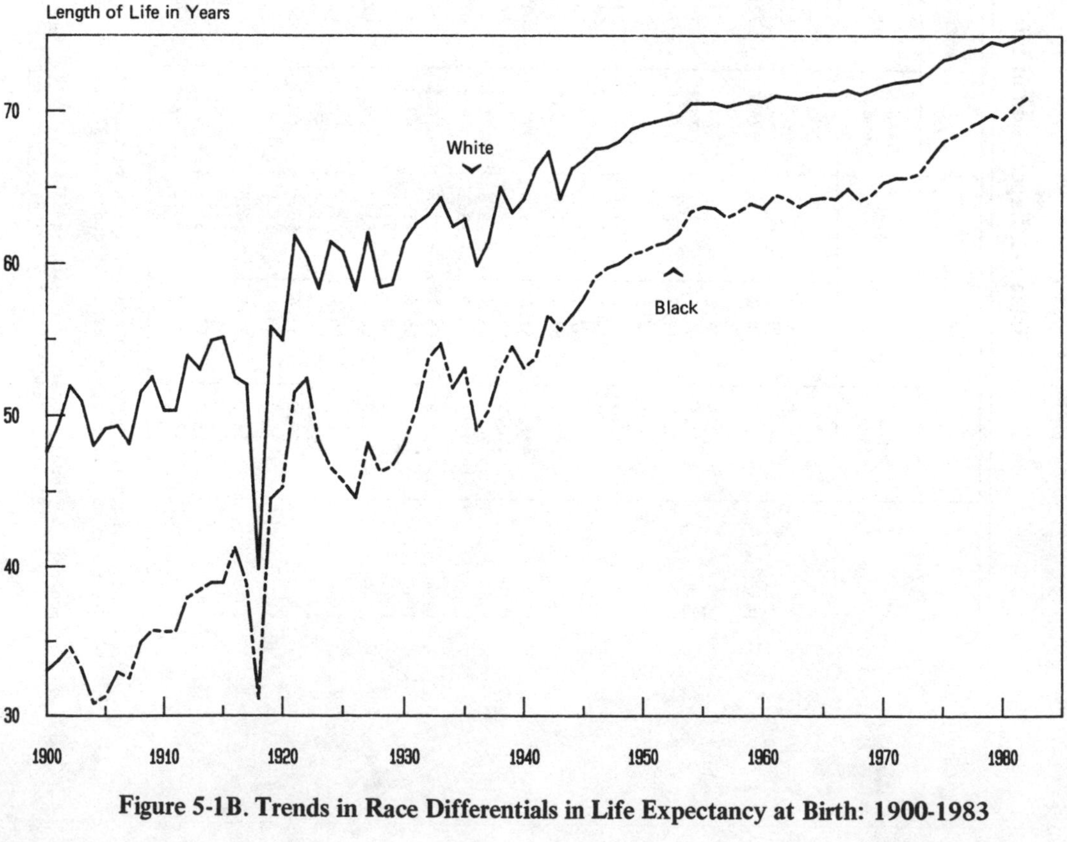

Figure 5-1B. Trends in Race Differentials in Life Expectancy at Birth: 1900-1983

Sources of Mortality Data

The principal source of statistical information about deaths is the annual report, *Vital Statistics of the United States: Mortality* (Volume II), published by the National Center for Health Statistics (NCHS). That report is made up of two parts, each bound separately: Part A contains detailed analytical tables for each of the major mortality topics pertaining primarily to the nation as a whole; Part B presents mortality statistics in geographical detail. Mortality statistics here are based on information obtained directly from copies of certificates of death or coded from those certificates, received from the registration office of each state. In addition, NCHS publishes summary mortality statistics in its *Monthly Vital Statistics Report.* An annual issue in this series presents advance yearly totals pending the release (after a delay of three or four years) of the final volume of vital statistics.* The reader may update the analysis of this chapter by consulting these sources. *Statistical Abstract of the United States* summarizes some of this information. A technical appendix to this chapter provides more information about these data.

International Comparisons

Estimates by the United Nations of crude death rate and life expectation at birth for the entire world (by region and for nations with life expectation above 72 years) are reported in Table 5-3. (The United Nations estimates higher levels of mortality for the United States than the official statistics reported in Tables 5-1 and 5-2.) Table 5-3 shows that mortality conditions in the United States—as well as in Europe, North America, and Oceania—as measured by life expectation at birth are much better than in Africa, South Asia, and Latin America. Because of extremely young age composition, the values of CDR for developing countries are artificially low, and they obscure the fact that death rates actually are moderately high, despite unprecedented declines since World War II.

However, far from being a leader in low mortality, the United States appears to be surpassed in life expectation by at least seventeen nations—most noticeably by Japan, the Scandinavian countries, Netherlands, and Switzerland. Although the data are not precise, it appears that several less wealthy countries such as Cuba, Puerto Rico, Greece, Spain, and Italy all have lower mortality than the United States. Although mortality is strongly affected by level of living and economic well-being, these international comparisons suggest that great wealth, high education, and elaborate medical technology may explain most, but not all, of the place-to-place variations in death rates. Table 5-3 shows that from 1950-55 to 1980-85, life expectancy in the world increased by twelve years, or four years per decade. However, important gains took place primarily in the least developed regions of Africa, Latin America, and Asia. The United States gained only 4.2 years of life expectancy in the three decades, or only a little more than one year of life expectancy per decade. In the more developed nations, medical technology and improved quality of life have made slower progress in extending life than have the simple improvements in health, medical care, and living conditions in the less developed countries.

Age Pattern of Mortality

Age-specific death rates (ASDR, see "definitions") show a characteristic curve of the type graphed in Figure 5-2. The ASDR is high for the first year of life, then falls to a very low level for ages one to about forty-four years. Thereafter, the rate rises with increasing age until it becomes very high at the oldest ages. This general shape is characteristic of the age-curves of the death rates of all human populations under normal conditions. However, there can be great variation from one population to another or at different times within the same population, of the height of the curve at each age. Table 5-4 reports the schedule of age-specific rates in the United States for selected years from 1900 to 1982. It shows ASDR data by sex and race. Figure 5-2 graphs the age curves for the U.S. population in 1980 and 1900, to show the pattern of change that has occurred. It is easy to see that the decline in mortality rates has not been evenly distributed among the age groups. There has been a most remarkable reduction in the death rate for infants under one year of age. The rate for this group in 1900 was 162.4; it has declined to 12.9 in 1980, or by 92 percent. There have been impressive declines at the older ages also. Although the size of decline is small for the intermediate ages (because the rates are normally lower at these ages), the percentage declines at these ages have also been impressive, as Table 5-5 shows.

Table 5-5 specifies the long-term trends in age patterns of mortality in the United States. The gains during the 40 years 1900-40 were primarily at ages below fifty-five. The gains during the 40 years 1940-80 have been primarily at ages older than fifty-five years, plus continued improvement in mortality during the first year of life. In addition, Table 5-4 shows that the mortality de-

*The author acknowledges with gratitude the staff of the National Center for Health Statistics for their assistance in obtaining copies of tabulations of mortality data for recent years.

Table 5-3. Summary Mortality Measures for the United States in Comparison With the World, Regions, and Selected Countries: 1950-55 and 1980-85

Regions and nations	Crude death rate (CDR)		Life expectation at birth ($\mathring{e}_0$)		Percent change	
	1980-85	1950-55	1980-85	1950-55	CDR	$\mathring{e}_0$
World, total . .	10.6	18.9	59.2	47.1	-44	26
Africa	15.6	27.4	50.8	37.3	-43	36
Latin America. . .	8.2	15.4	64.1	51.2	-47	25
Northern America .	9.1	9.4	73.3	69.0	-3	6
East Asia.	6.7	19.2	69.9	47.5	-65	47
South Asia	13.2	25.8	52.8	39.4	-49	34
Europe	10.7	10.9	72.7	65.4	-2	11
Oceania.	8.8	12.4	66.7	60.7	-29	10
USSR	9.4	9.2	70.0	61.7	+2	13
Japan.	6.7	9.4	76.3	64.0	-29	19
Iceland.	7.0	7.5	76.3	72.0	-7	6
Hong Kong.	5.0	8.9	76.0	60.9	-44	25
Sweden	11.8	9.8	75.5	71.8	+20	5
Norway	10.8	8.2	75.4	72.6	+32	4
Netherlands. . . .	8.9	7.5	75.1	72.1	+19	4
Switzerland. . . .	10.3	10.1	75.0	69.3	+2	8
Denmark.	11.0	9.0	74.5	70.9	+22	5
France	10.9	12.8	74.2	66.5	-15	12
Canada	7.6	8.7	74.0	69.1	-13	7
Australia.	8.0	9.4	73.6	69.6	-15	6
New Zealand. . . .	8.0	9.3	73.4	70.6	-14	4
Spain.	8.4	10.2	73.4	65.2	-18	13
Greece	9.9	7.2	73.4	65.7	+38	12
Italy.	9.8	9.9	73.4	66.0	-1	11
Cuba	6.4	11.0	73.4	58.8	-42	25
Puerto Rico. . . .	5.5	9.0	73.4	64.4	-39	14
Finland.	10.0	9.7	73.2	66.2	+3	11
United Kingdom . .	12.3	11.7	73.0	69.0	+5	6
UNITED STATES. . .	9.2	9.5	73.2	69.0	-3	6
Ireland.	9.8	12.6	72.9	66.9	-22	9
Cyprus	9.0	10.5	72.8	67.0	-14	9
Israel	7.3	6.9	72.7	65.4	+6	11
Germany, Fed. Rep.	12.9	10.8	72.6	67.5	+19	8
Bulgaria	10.3	10.2	72.6	64.1	+1	13
Belgium.	12.2	12.2	72.5	67.5	0	7
Austria.	12.8	12.3	72.4	65.9	+4	10
Germany, Dem. Rep.	13.2	11.9	72.4	66.4	+11	9
Luxembourg	12.0	11.7	72.3	66.0	+3	10

Source: United Nations. Demographic Indicators of Countries. New York: United Nations, 1982.

clines for ages above forty-five years are continuing past 1980 to the last year for which data are available—for both sexes and for whites and blacks/others. However, the gains since 1980 have been made at all ages, with greatest improvement in infant mortality and at ages under one year and age seventy-five and above.

Age Pattern of the Male-Female Mortality Differential

The sex differential in mortality, in which males have higher death rates than females, is shown in Table 5-6 and graphed in Figure 5-3. Its presence is strong for all ages and for both the white and the black/other populations, without exception. However, it reaches peak intensity at ages of early adulthood and early old age (55-64 and 65-74 years) and then diminishes at the older ages, especially at ages eighty-five and above. This differential has existed since 1900, but the discrepancy was more modest until 1940 (20 percent or less). From 1945 until 1970 the differential was above 30 percent. Since 1970 the sex differential appears to be declining again: as of 1980 it was at the same level as in 1930-35. The sex differential has declined further in the years since 1980. This does not mean that death rates for females are rising; the differential occurred because earlier progress in reducing mortality was more rapid for females than for males, but in recent years this imbalance has eased. However, there is substantial evidence of not only a physiological basis for the sex differential but sex-related differences in life-style and health-impairing activities. This phenomenon is considered in more detail later, when causes of death are examined.

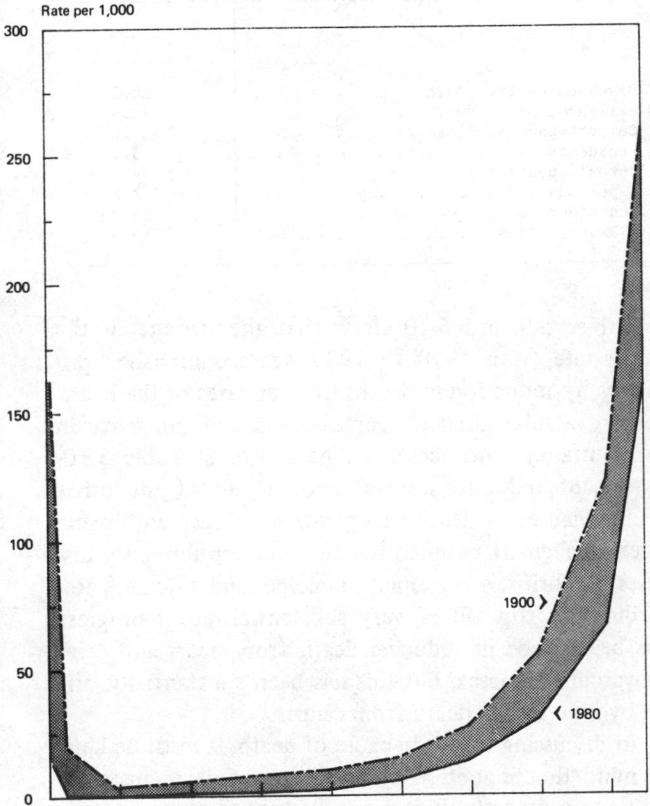

Figure 5-2. Change in Age-Specific Mortality Rates: United States, 1900 and 1980

Age Pattern of the Race Mortality Differential

The average tendency for the nonwhite (black/other) population[3] to have higher overall mortality rates than whites is not found at all ages. It is relatively great at the ages of infancy, youth, and adulthood to age sixty-five. At the most advanced ages the death rates are considerably *lower* among the black/other population than for the white. This pattern of apparently higher survival of blacks at advanced ages has been long-standing; it was manifest in 1900 and has continued. Formerly, demographers believed it was due in large part to defects in death registration and errors in age declarations on death certificates and at census enumerations. The fact that it has persisted during the past eighty years—despite improved educational attainment and better procedures for collection of vital statistics and census data—creates doubt that this is a complete explanation.

On the basis of crude death rates, the race differential appears to have disappeared; the crude death rate for the black population today is *lower* than that of the white population. This is true for both sexes. This reversal has existed since about 1972. However, it is in part artificial—a result of the younger age composition of the black than of the white population. Nevertheless, the race differentials persist, and at very high levels, for all ages under sixty-five.

The ratios of Table 5-7 imply that the relative deprivation of blacks in comparison with whites is only moderately less severe today than at the turn of the century. However, it is important not to overlook the very great decline in the *absolute difference* between the white and black/other groups (compare the rates of Table 5-4 and see Figure 5-4). As the age-specific death rates at ages below fifty have declined toward nearly zero, the black/other group has shared in this by the same amount as whites (and often more). Consequently, on an absolute basis the age-specific death rates for the white population are only a few points below those for the black/other. It is precisely because the absolute differentials between the races are now so low—combined with a younger age composition and an apparent advantage of blacks at the older ages—that the crude death rates of the black/other population has been lower than that of the white population in each year since 1972, rendering the crude death rate useless as an overall measure of the race differential.

The race differential in mortality is analyzed in more detail later as a part of the study of the causes of death.

Life Expectation

The life table technique for analyzing mortality(see Technical Appendix 5-2) can estimate the average number of years remaining to be lived by any person who has survived to a particular age. It is able to answer such questions as, "How many years does a man who has just retired on his sixty-fifth birthday have to live in the state of retirement?" Table 5-8 provides the data as of 1980 for an average male; irrespective of his color, he can look forward to about fourteen years. If this question were asked for a women, the answer would be 18.5 years for a white female, 17.3 years for a black/other female. Table 5-8 provides expectation of life data for five-year age intervals for four dates. It also gives measures of absolute and percentage change for two broad periods of time, 1900-40 and 1940-80. This table shows that:

1. Earlier in this century, survival of the first year of life added greatly to life expectancy, but infant mortality is now so low that it adds very little.

2. By far the biggest gains in life expectancy have been at the younger ages, especially during the first four decades of this century. Advances in reducing mortality at older ages manage only to postpone death for a year or two.

3. Recent gains in mortality control have benefited the black population considerably more than the white population.

4. Recent gains in mortality control have benefited males and females about equally, with females still enjoying some net gains in comparisons with males.

5. Life expectance for black/other males is lower than that for white males until about age seventy-five; thereafter life expectancy is greater for black/other populations. Life expectancy for black/other females is lower than that for white females until about age seventy-five; thereafter black/other females have a higher life expectancy than white females.

6. The sex differential persists at all ages. Although it declines in absolute size with advancing age, the relative differential (percentage difference) increases.

Between 1980 and 1982 further progress was made in extending life at a pace just as fast as in the preceding decade. The trend toward moderation of race and sex differentials continued.

Causes of Death

Since death results from many different diseases or events, an understanding of mortality levels and trends requires a subdivision of the death rate into causes. With such cause-specific death rates (see "definitions"), it is possible to disaggregate the crude death rate and the age-specific death rate into cause-of-death components. U.S. vital statistics of death are reported by cause-of-death categories according to the *International Statistical Classification of Diseases, Injuries and Causes of Death.* (This classification system is revised periodically, which affects comparability; the most recent revision was for 1979—see Technical Appendix 5-1.[4]) Table 5-9 is a report of the rate of death per 100,000 population in 1980 and 1970, from each of seventy-two cause-of-death categories. The data for 1980 are reported not only for the total population but also for sex and color groupings. Although the list of disease categories is lengthy, the rates for most of them are quite low. Table 5-10 reports the rates for the fifteen leading causes of death and the proportion of deaths resulting from each cause. Data for 1970 are also reported in this table, in order to permit measurement of change. Three-fourths of all deaths result from five causes:

Cause	Proportion of deaths
Total.	100.0
Diseases of the heart.	38.2
Malignant neoplasms.	20.9
Cerebrovascular diseases	8.6
Accidents.	5.3
Chronic obstructive pulmonary diseases	2.8
Ten other leading causes	13.2
All other causes	10.9

Tables 5-9 and 5-10 show that the decline in the death rate from 1970 to 1980 was accomplished primarily by reduction in deaths from diseases of the heart, cerebrovascular diseases, certain causes of mortality in early infancy, and accidents. As shown in Table 5-10, significant reductions were made in all of the other leading causes of death except for six causes with rising rates: malignant neoplasms, obstructive pulmonary diseases, nephritis, septicemia, homicide, and suicide.[5] Regarding the top killers, very substantial recent progress has been made in reducing death from heart and cerebrovascular diseases, but this has been substantially offset by increases in death from cancer.

In discussing trends in cause of death, it must be kept in mind that reduction in one cause of death may not result in a dramatic increase in life expectancy, because the survivors are meanwhile exposed to death from other diseases. Thus, cancer may claim the lives of persons saved from diseases of the heart, diabetes, or other causes on which progress has been made.

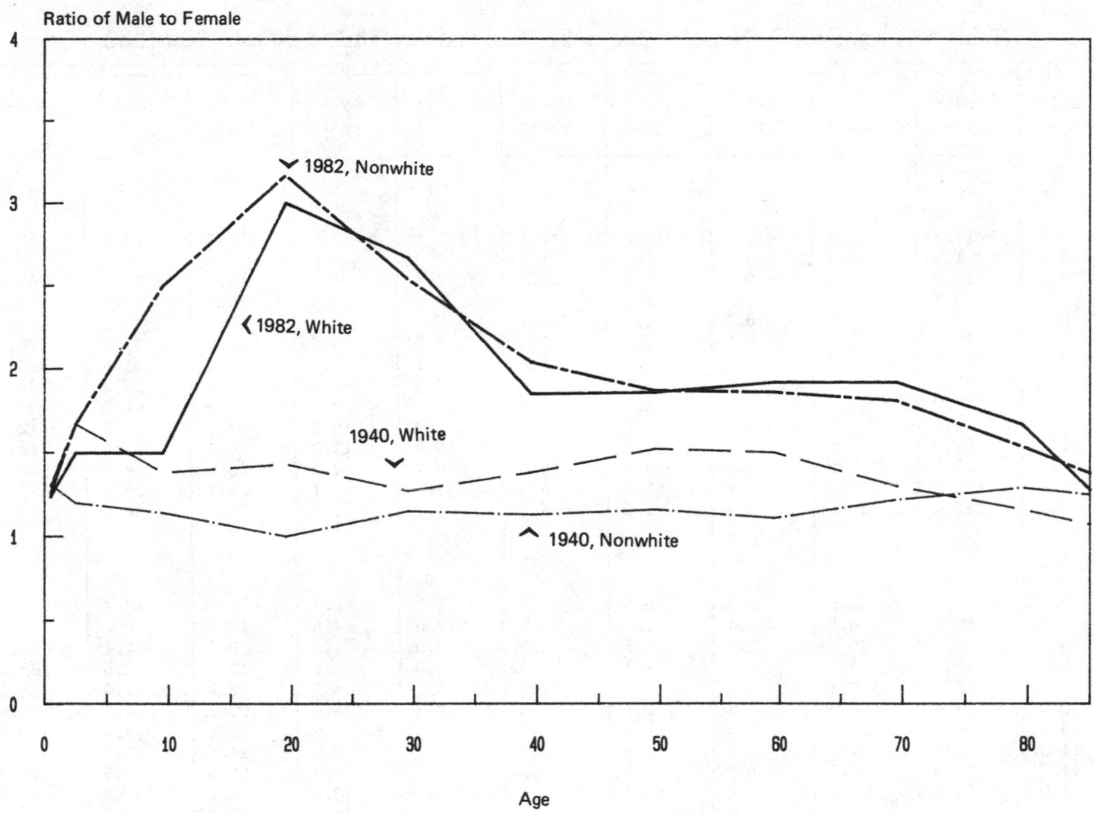

Figure 5-3. Sex Differentials in Mortality: 1940 and 1982 [ratio of male to female age-specific death rates]

Note: Between ages one and thirty-five years, age-specific rates for both white and black populations in 1982 are extremely low–less than 2.0 per 1,000.

In order to understand changes in the pattern of causes of death, it is necessary to consider age, sex, and race for each cause. Each broad category of cause is discussed in a subsection below. The rate of death from each cause is reported by age in Table 5-11 and shown in Figure 5-5. This is a most useful table. If compared by rows, it shows how the age pattern of death from one cause differs from the age pattern for other causes. Compared by columns, it shows how the cause of death at one age differs from cause of death at other ages. This analysis is refined by two supplementary tables. Table 5-12 reports the trend in the sex differential in mortality for 1970-78 by age groups, and Table 5-13 reports the trend in the race differential in mortality for 1970-78 by age groups. Table 5-12 and 5-13 are confined to a comparison of 1970 and 1978, both coded by the eighth revision of the classification system and hence comparable. Table 5-12 is the ratio of male to female age-sex-cause specific rates for each of the two periods. Because the rates were so low at the younger ages, the rates for ages 1 to 19 and 20 to 24 were summed before taking the ratios. Table 5-13 is the ratio of black to white rates, developed in the same way as the ratios of Table 5-12.

With Tables 5-11, 5-12, and 5-13, it is possible to isolate more precisely the age-race-sex patterns of causes of death. These materials are used in the following discussion of each major cause-of-death grouping.

Table 5-4. Age-Specific Mortality Rates, by Race and Sex: United States, 1900-1982

Year, sex, and race	All ages	Under 1 year	1-4 years	5-14 years	15-24 years	25-34 years	35-44 years	45-54 years	55-64 years	65-74 years	75-84 years	85 years and over
Total												
1982. . .	8.6	11.4	0.6	0.3	1.0	1.3	2.1	5.6	12.9	29.0	63.5	152.3
1981. . .	8.7	11.9	0.6	0.3	1.1	1.4	2.3	5.8	13.4	29.4	64.3	153.6
1980. . .	8.8	12.9	0.6	0.3	1.2	1.4	2.3	5.8	13.5	29.9	66.9	159.8
1979. . .	8.5	13.3	0.6	0.3	1.1	1.3	2.3	5.9	13.4	29.3	65.0	149.6
1978. . .	8.7	13.8	0.7	0.3	1.2	1.3	2.4	6.1	13.9	30.2	67.1	154.8
1975. . .	8.8	16.0	0.7	0.4	1.2	1.4	2.7	6.5	14.8	31.8	70.3	156.6
1970. . .	9.5	21.4	0.8	0.4	1.3	1.6	3.1	7.3	16.6	35.8	80.0	163.4
1960. . .	9.5	27.0	1.1	0.5	1.1	1.5	3.0	7.6	17.4	38.2	87.5	198.6
1950. . .	9.6	33.0	1.4	0.6	1.3	1.8	3.6	8.5	19.0	41.0	93.3	202.0
1940. . .	10.8	54.9	2.9	1.0	2.0	3.1	5.2	10.6	22.3	48.0	112.0	235.7
1930. . .	11.3	69.0	5.6	1.7	3.3	4.7	6.8	12.2	24.0	51.4	112.7	228.0
1920. . .	13.0	92.3	9.9	2.6	4.9	6.8	8.1	12.2	23.6	52.5	118.9	248.3
1910. . .	14.7	131.8	14.0	2.9	4.5	6.5	9.0	13.7	26.2	55.6	122.2	250.3
1900. . .	17.2	162.4	19.8	3.9	5.9	8.2	10.2	15.0	27.2	56.4	123.3	260.9
Male												
1982. . .	9.5	12.7	0.6	0.3	1.5	1.8	2.7	7.3	17.3	39.7	84.7	180.5
1981. . .	9.6	13.4	0.7	0.4	1.6	1.9	3.0	7.6	17.8	40.2	85.4	182.8
1980. . .	9.8	14.3	0.7	0.4	1.7	2.0	3.0	7.8	18.2	41.1	88.2	188.0
1979. . .	9.6	14.8	0.7	0.4	1.7	1.9	3.0	7.8	18.2	40.5	85.7	176.0
1978. . .	9.8	15.3	0.8	0.4	1.7	1.9	3.1	8.0	18.8	41.8	88.4	182.1
1975. . .	10.0	17.9	0.8	0.4	1.7	2.0	3.5	8.6	20.2	44.1	91.5	181.3
1970. . .	10.9	24.1	0.9	0.5	1.9	2.2	4.0	9.6	22.8	48.7	100.1	178.2
1960. . .	11.0	30.6	1.2	0.6	1.5	1.9	3.7	9.9	23.1	49.1	101.8	211.9
1950. . .	11.1	37.3	1.5	0.7	1.7	2.2	4.3	10.7	24.0	49.3	104.3	216.4
1940. . .	12.0	61.9	3.1	1.2	2.3	3.4	5.9	12.5	26.2	54.2	121.3	246.4
1930. . .	12.3	77.0	6.0	1.9	3.5	4.9	7.5	13.6	26.6	55.8	119.1	236.7
1920. . .	13.4	103.6	10.3	2.8	4.8	6.4	8.2	12.6	24.6	54.5	122.1	253.0
1910. . .	15.6	145.5	14.6	3.0	4.8	6.9	10.0	15.2	28.7	58.7	127.4	255.8
1900. . .	17.9	179.1	20.5	3.8	5.9	8.2	10.7	15.7	28.7	59.3	128.3	268.8
Female												
1982. . .	7.7	10.2	0.5	0.2	0.5	0.7	1.5	3.9	9.1	20.9	51.1	140.4
1981. . .	7.8	10.3	0.5	0.2	0.5	0.8	1.6	4.1	9.4	21.2	51.9	141.2
1980. . .	7.9	11.4	0.5	0.2	0.6	0.8	1.6	4.1	9.3	21.4	54.4	147.5
1979. . .	7.5	11.8	0.6	0.2	0.6	0.7	1.6	4.1	9.2	20.7	52.7	137.9
1978. . .	7.6	12.2	0.6	0.3	0.6	0.8	1.7	4.3	9.5	21.3	54.4	142.5
1975. . .	7.6	14.1	0.6	0.3	0.6	0.8	1.9	4.6	9.9	22.4	57.4	144.5
1970. . .	8.1	18.6	0.8	0.3	0.7	1.0	2.3	5.2	11.0	25.8	66.8	155.2
1960. . .	8.1	23.2	1.0	0.4	0.6	1.1	2.3	5.3	12.0	28.7	76.3	190.1
1950. . .	8.2	28.5	1.3	0.5	0.9	1.4	2.9	6.4	14.0	33.3	84.0	191.9
1940. . .	9.5	47.7	2.7	0.9	1.8	2.7	4.5	8.6	18.1	41.9	103.7	227.6
1930. . .	10.4	60.7	5.2	1.5	3.2	4.4	6.1	10.6	21.2	46.8	106.6	221.4
1920. . .	12.6	80.7	9.5	2.5	5.0	7.1	8.0	11.7	22.4	50.5	115.9	244.7
1910. . .	13.7	117.6	13.4	2.9	4.2	6.1	7.9	12.1	23.7	52.4	117.4	246.0
1900. . .	16.5	145.4	19.1	3.9	5.8	8.2	9.8	14.2	25.8	53.6	118.8	255.2
White male												
1982. . .	9.6	11.3	0.6	0.3	1.5	1.6	2.4	6.7	16.5	38.9	85.1	183.3
1981. . .	9.7	11.9	0.6	0.4	1.5	1.7	2.6	7.0	17.0	39.5	86.0	185.6
1980. . .	9.8	12.3	0.7	0.4	1.7	1.7	2.6	7.0	17.3	40.4	88.3	191.0
1979. . .	9.6	12.8	0.6	0.4	1.7	1.7	2.6	7.1	17.3	39.9	86.2	179.2
1978. . .	9.8	13.0	0.7	0.4	1.6	1.6	2.7	7.4	18.0	41.2	89.2	185.9
1975. . .	10.0	15.5	0.7	0.4	1.6	1.7	3.0	7.9	19.4	43.4	92.7	185.6
1970. . .	10.9	21.1	0.8	0.5	1.7	1.8	3.4	8.8	22.0	48.1	101.0	185.5
1960. . .	11.0	26.9	1.0	0.5	1.4	1.6	3.3	9.3	22.3	48.5	103.0	217.5
1950. . .	10.9	34.0	1.4	0.7	1.5	1.9	3.8	9.8	23.0	48.6	105.3	221.2
1940. . .	11.6	56.7	2.8	1.1	2.0	2.8	5.1	11.4	25.2	54.0	122.0	251.4
1930. . .	11.7	71.5	5.5	1.8	3.0	4.1	6.5	12.3	25.5	55.1	119.2	237.6
1920. . .	13.0	98.1	9.8	2.7	4.2	5.9	7.7	12.0	24.2	54.2	122.5	253.6
1910. . .	15.4	143.0	14.2	3.0	4.7	6.7	9.7	15.0	28.4	58.6	127.6	257.9
1900. . .	17.7	175.9	20.2	3.8	5.8	8.1	10.6	15.5	28.5	59.1	128.2	269.2

Table 5-4. Age-Specific Mortality Rates, by Race and Sex: United States, 1900-1982—continued

Year, sex, and race	All ages	Under 1 year	1-4 years	5-14 years	15-24 years	25-34 years	35-44 years	45-54 years	55-64 years	65-74 years	75-84 years	85 years and over
White female												
1982. . .	8.0	9.1	0.4	0.2	0.5	0.6	1.3	3.6	8.6	20.3	50.9	142.8
1981. . .	8.0	9.2	0.5	0.2	0.5	0.7	1.4	3.7	8.8	20.5	51.8	143.0
1980. . .	8.1	9.6	0.5	0.2	0.6	0.7	1.4	3.7	8.8	20.7	54.0	149.8
1979. . .	7.7	9.9	0.5	0.2	0.6	0.6	1.4	3.7	8.6	20.0	52.6	140.3
1978. . .	7.8	10.3	0.5	0.2	0.6	0.7	1.5	3.9	8.9	20.5	54.5	145.0
1975. . .	7.8	11.9	0.6	0.3	0.6	0.7	1.7	4.1	9.3	21.4	57.9	147.5
1970. . .	8.1	16.1	0.7	0.3	0.6	0.8	1.9	4.6	10.1	24.7	67.0	159.8
1960. . .	8.0	20.1	0.9	0.3	0.5	0.9	1.9	4.6	10.8	27.8	77.0	194.8
1950. . .	8.0	25.7	1.1	0.5	0.7	1.1	2.4	5.5	12.9	32.4	84.8	196.8
1940. . .	9.2	43.6	2.4	0.8	1.4	2.2	3.7	7.5	16.8	41.5	104.8	235.0
1930. . .	9.8	56.0	4.8	1.4	2.5	3.6	5.2	9.2	19.9	46.0	107.6	225.1
1920. . .	12.1	76.1	9.0	2.3	4.3	6.5	7.3	10.9	21.7	49.9	116.4	247.0
1910. . .	13.6	115.2	13.0	2.8	4.1	5.9	7.7	11.8	23.4	52.2	117.8	248.1
1900. . .	16.3	142.6	18.7	3.8	5.6	8.1	9.6	14.0	25.5	53.4	118.9	256.7
Black/ other male												
1982. . .	8.8	18.2	1.0	0.5	1.9	3.3	5.1	11.8	24.4	47.1	81.1	155.1
1981. . .	8.9	19.6	0.9	0.4	1.8	3.4	5.7	12.3	25.9	45.9	79.2	153.2
1980. . .	9.4	23.5	1.0	0.4	2.0	3.6	5.9	13.1	26.1	47.5	86.9	157.7
1979. . .	9.2	24.7	1.0	0.5	1.9	3.7	6.2	13.3	25.6	45.8	79.7	142.6
1978. . .	9.4	26.5	1.1	0.5	2.0	3.6	6.4	13.6	26.7	47.5	79.8	143.6
1975. . .	9.9	29.7	1.1	0.6	2.4	4.4	7.2	14.5	27.6	50.4	79.6	138.6
1970. . .	11.2	40.2	1.4	0.7	3.0	5.0	8.7	16.5	30.5	54.7	89.8	114.1
1960. . .	11.5	51.9	2.1	0.8	2.1	3.9	7.3	15.5	31.5	56.6	86.6	152.4
1950. . .	12.5	59.9	2.7	1.0	2.9	5.0	8.6	18.6	34.8	57.9	90.3	160.2
1940. . .	15.1	101.2	5.3	1.6	5.0	8.5	13.2	24.5	39.5	56.5	108.8	199.7
1930. . .	17.4	122.3	10.0	2.7	7.8	12.1	17.0	26.3	40.4	67.3	117.6	228.5
1920. . .	17.8	167.7	15.0	3.7	9.9	12.2	14.4	20.1	31.1	60.2	116.0	247.1
1910. . .	22.3	257.6	30.1	5.4	10.0	12.6	17.5	24.8	38.7	66.3	113.8	174.1
1900. . .	25.7	369.3	43.4	7.8	11.8	12.5	14.2	24.7	42.1	71.6	131.4	249.3
Black/ other female												
1982. . .	6.1	14.4	0.6	0.2	0.6	1.3	2.5	6.3	13.1	26.0	52.6	112.0
1981. . .	6.3	14.4	0.7	0.3	0.7	1.4	2.7	6.2	14.2	27.3	53.1	119.5
1980. . .	6.6	19.4	0.8	0.3	0.7	1.4	2.9	6.9	14.2	28.6	58.6	119.2
1979. . .	6.4	20.5	0.9	0.3	0.7	1.3	2.9	6.9	13.9	27.6	54.2	108.3
1978. . .	6.5	21.5	0.9	0.3	0.7	1.4	3.1	7.1	14.6	28.4	54.3	112.4
1975. . .	6.7	24.9	0.9	0.3	0.8	1.6	3.6	7.8	15.8	31.8	52.7	108.5
1970. . .	7.8	31.7	1.2	0.4	1.1	2.2	4.9	9.8	18.9	36.8	63.9	102.9
1960. . .	8.7	40.7	1.7	0.5	1.1	2.6	5.5	11.4	24.1	39.8	67.1	128.7
1950. . .	9.9	47.5	2.3	0.8	2.2	3.9	7.5	15.5	27.6	46.1	70.6	133.7
1940. . .	12.6	77.4	4.4	1.4	5.0	7.4	11.7	21.1	35.7	46.3	84.1	159.7
1930. . .	15.3	97.9	8.7	2.6	8.2	11.1	15.3	25.2	41.4	60.0	91.4	187.2
1920. . .	17.5	131.1	14.2	3.9	10.8	13.5	16.0	23.4	35.8	60.4	106.4	221.2
1910. . .	21.0	221.4	26.6	5.9	10.5	11.6	16.4	24.3	38.2	61.9	93.9	177.9
1900. . .	24.4	299.5	43.5	10.1	11.2	11.7	15.6	23.9	42.1	66.4	113.2	195.8

Note: 1981-82 figures are based on a 10 percent sample of deaths.

Source: National Center for Health Statistics. Vital Statistics of the United States: Mortality (1950--Vol. III, Table 8.40); and Monthly Vital Statistics Report (Vol. 31, no. 13, Table 6). Washington, DC: U.S. Government Printing Office, 1953; 1983.

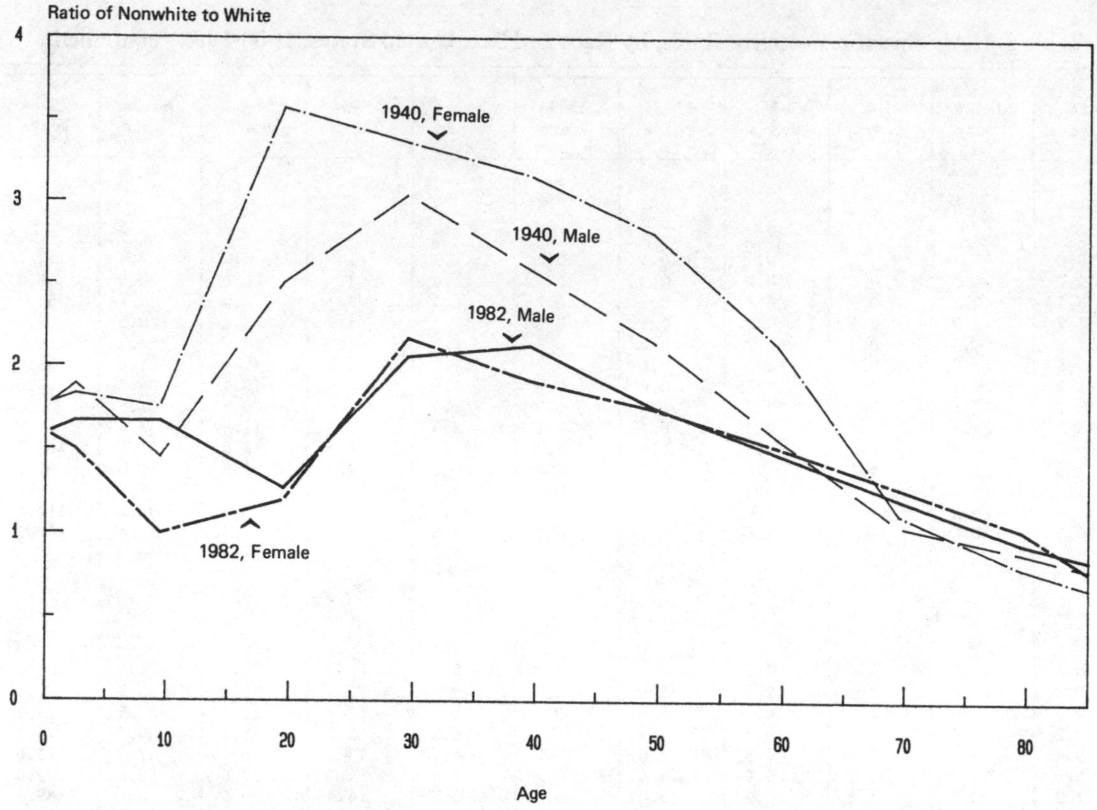

Figure 5-4. Race Differential in Mortality: 1940 and 1982 [ratio of nonwhite to white age-specific death rates]

Note: Between ages one and thirty-five years, age-specific rates for both white and black populations in 1982 are extremely low—less than 2.0 per 1,000.

Table 5-5. Absolute and Relative Decline in Age-Specific Death Rates of the United States: 1900-40, 1940-80, and 1980-82

Age	Decline in rate (points)			Percent decline		
	1900-40	1940-80	1980-82	1900-40	1940-80	1980-82
All ages.	-6.4	-2.0	-0.2	-37.2	-18.5	-2.3
Under 1 year.	-107.5	-42.0	-1.5	-66.2	-76.5	-11.6
1 to 4 years.	-16.9	-2.3	0.0[a]	-85.4	-79.3	0.0[a]
5 to 14 years	-2.9	-0.7	0.0[a]	-74.4	-70.0	0.0[a]
15 to 24 years.	-3.9	-0.8	-0.2	-66.1	-40.0	-16.7
25 to 34 years.	-5.1	-1.7	-0.1	-62.2	-54.8	-7.1
35 to 44 years.	-5.0	-2.9	-0.2	-49.0	-55.8	-8.7
45 to 54 years.	-4.4	-4.8	-0.2	-29.3	-45.3	-3.4
55 to 64 years.	-4.9	-8.8	-0.6	-18.0	-39.5	-4.4
65 to 74 years.	-8.4	-18.1	-0.9	-14.9	-38.3	-3.0
75 to 84 years.	-11.3	-45.1	-3.4	-9.2	-40.8	-5.1
85 years and over . . .	-25.2	-75.9	-7.5	-9.7	-33.6	-4.7

[a]Declines occured in rates per 100,000, but do not show up in rates per 1,000.

Source: National Center for Health Statistics. Vital Statistics of the United States: Mortality (1950, Table 8.40); and Monthly Vital Statistics Report (Vol. 31, no. 13, Table 6). Washington, DC: U.S. Government Printing Office, 1953 and 1983.

Table 5-6. Sex Differential in Mortality—Ratio of Male Age-Specific Death Rates to Corresponding Rates for Females, by Race: United States, 1900-1982

Year	All ages	Under 1 year	55-64 years	65-74 years	75-84 years	85 years and over
White						
1982.	1.20	1.24	1.92	1.92	1.67	1.28
1981.	1.21	1.29	1.93	1.93	1.66	1.30
1970.	1.22	1.28	1.97	1.95	1.64	1.27
1979.	1.25	1.29	2.01	2.00	1.64	1.28
1978.	1.26	1.27	2.02	2.01	1.64	1.28
1977.	1.27	1.30	2.04	2.02	1.64	1.28
1976.	1.27	1.27	2.06	2.03	1.62	1.26
1975.	1.30	1.30	2.09	2.03	1.60	1.26
1970.	1.34	1.31	2.18	1.95	1.51	1.16
1960.	1.37	1.34	2.06	1.74	1.34	1.12
1950.	1.36	1.32	1.78	1.50	1.24	1.12
1940.	1.26	1.30	1.50	1.28	1.16	1.07
1930.	1.19	1.28	1.28	1.12	1.11	1.06
1920.	1.07	1.29	1.12	1.21	1.05	1.03
1910.	1.13	1.24	1.21	1.12	1.08	1.04
1900.	1.09	1.23	1.12	1.11	1.08	1.05
Black/other						
1982.	1.44	1.26	1.86	1.81	1.54	1.38
1981.	1.41	1.36	1.82	1.68	1.49	1.28
1980.	1.42	1.21	1.83	1.66	1.48	1.32
1979.	1.45	1.20	1.85	1.66	1.47	1.32
1978.	1.45	1.23	1.83	1.68	1.47	1.28
1977.	1.44	1.22	1.81	1.62	1.47	1.32
1976.	1.45	1.20	1.81	1.63	1.47	1.26
1975.	1.47	1.19	1.75	1.58	1.51	1.28
1970.	1.44	1.27	1.61	1.49	1.40	1.11
1960.	1.32	1.28	1.31	1.42	1.29	1.18
1950.	1.26	1.26	1.26	1.26	1.28	1.20
1940.	1.20	1.31	1.11	1.22	1.29	1.25
1930.	1.14	1.25	0.98	1.12	1.29	1.22
1920.	1.02	1.28	0.87	1.00	1.09	1.12
1910.	1.06	1.16	1.01	1.07	1.21	0.98
1900.	1.05	1.23	1.00	1.08	1.16	1.27

Source: Table 5-4.

Table 5-7. Race Differential in Mortality—Ratio of Black/Other Age-Specific Death Rates to Corresponding Rates for Whites, by Sex: United States, 1900-1982

Year	All ages	Under 1 year	45-54 years	55-64 years	65-74 years	75-84 years	85 years and over
Male							
1982.	0.91	1.62	1.76	1.48	1.21	0.95	0.85
1981.	0.91	1.64	1.75	1.53	1.16	0.92	0.83
1980.	0.95	1.91	1.87	1.51	1.18	0.98	0.83
1979.	0.96	1.93	1.87	1.48	1.15	0.92	0.80
1978.	0.96	2.04	1.85	1.48	1.15	0.89	0.77
1977.	0.97	1.95	1.87	1.48	1.15	0.87	0.79
1976.	0.97	1.98	1.88	1.45	1.16	0.86	0.75
1975.	0.98	1.91	1.84	1.42	1.16	0.86	0.75
1970.	1.03	1.90	1.86	1.38	1.14	0.89	0.61
1960.	1.05	1.93	1.66	1.42	1.17	0.84	0.70
1950.	1.15	1.76	1.89	1.51	1.19	0.86	0.72
1940.	1.30	1.78	2.15	1.57	1.05	0.89	0.79
1930.	1.49	1.71	2.14	1.58	1.22	0.99	0.96
1920.	1.37	1.71	1.68	1.29	1.11	0.95	0.97
1910.	1.45	1.80	1.65	1.36	1.13	0.89	0.68
1900.	1.45	2.10	1.59	1.48	1.21	1.02	0.93
Female							
1982.	0.76	1.59	1.76	1.52	1.28	1.03	0.78
1981.	0.79	1.56	1.66	1.60	1.33	1.02	0.84
1980.	0.82	2.02	1.85	1.62	1.38	1.09	0.80
1979.	0.82	2.08	1.83	1.61	1.38	1.03	0.77
1978.	0.83	2.09	1.82	1.64	1.38	1.00	0.78
1977.	0.86	2.09	1.88	1.67	1.43	0.98	0.77
1976.	0.85	2.09	1.90	1.65	1.44	0.94	0.75
1975.	0.87	2.09	1.88	1.70	1.48	0.91	0.74
1970.	0.95	1.96	2.12	1.86	1.49	0.95	0.64
1960.	1.09	2.03	2.50	2.23	1.43	0.87	0.66
1950.	1.24	1.85	2.85	2.14	1.42	0.83	0.68
1940.	1.37	1.78	2.81	2.13	1.12	0.80	0.68
1930.	1.56	1.75	2.74	2.08	1.30	0.85	0.83
1920.	1.45	1.72	2.15	1.65	1.21	0.91	0.90
1910.	1.54	1.92	2.06	1.63	1.19	0.80	0.72
1900.	1.50	2.10	1.71	1.65	1.24	0.95	0.76

Source: Table 5-4.

Table 5-8. Average Number of Years of Life Remaining at Selected Ages, by Sex and Race: 1900-1982 [with measures of absolute and relative change]

Age, race, and sex	Average number of years					Absolute change			Relative change		
	1982	1980	1969-71	1939-41	1900-02	1980-82	1940-80	1900-40	1980-82	1940-80	1900-40
White male											
0 . . .	71.4	70.7	67.94	62.81	48.23	0.7	7.89	14.58	1.0	12.56	30.23
1 . . .	--	70.6	68.33	64.96	54.61	--	5.64	10.35	--	8.68	18.95
5 . . .	--	66.8	64.55	61.68	54.43	--	5.12	7.25	--	8.30	13.32
10. . .	--	61.9	59.69	57.03	50.59	--	4.87	6.44	--	8.54	12.73
15. . .	--	57.0	54.83	52.33	46.25	--	4.67	6.08	--	8.92	13.15
20. . .	--	52.4	50.22	47.76	42.19	--	4.64	5.57	--	9.72	13.20
25. . .	--	47.8	45.70	43.20	38.52	--	4.52	4.76	--	4.97	12.36
30. . .	--	43.2	41.07	38.80	34.88	--	4.40	3.92	--	11.34	11.24
35. . .	--	38.6	36.43	34.36	31.29	--	4.24	3.07	--	12.34	9.81
40. . .	--	34.0	31.87	30.03	27.74	--	3.97	2.29	--	13.22	8.26
45. . .	--	29.4	27.48	25.87	24.21	--	3.53	1.66	--	13.65	6.86
50. . .	--	25.2	23.34	21.96	20.76	--	3.24	1.20	--	14.75	5.78
55. . .	--	21.2	19.51	18.34	17.42	--	2.86	0.92	--	15.59	5.28
60. . .	--	17.5	16.07	15.05	14.35	--	2.45	0.70	--	16.28	4.88
65. . .	--	14.2	13.02	12.07	11.51	--	2.13	0.56	--	17.65	4.87
70. . .	--	11.3	10.38	9.42	9.03	--	1.88	0.39	--	19.96	4.32
75. . .	--	8.8	8.06	7.17	6.84	--	1.63	0.33	--	22.73	4.82
80. . .	--	6.7	6.18	5.38	5.10	--	1.32	0.28	--	24.54	5.49
85. . .	--	5.0	4.63	4.02	3.81	--	0.98	0.21	--	24.38	5.51
White female											
0 . . .	78.7	78.1	75.49	67.29	51.08	0.6	10.81	16.21	0.8	16.06	31.73
1 . . .	--	77.9	75.66	68.93	56.39	--	8.97	12.54	--	13.01	22.24
5 . . .	--	74.0	71.86	65.57	56.03	--	8.43	9.54	--	12.86	17.03
10. . .	--	69.1	66.97	60.85	52.15	--	8.25	8.70	--	13.56	16.68
15. . .	--	64.2	62.07	56.07	47.79	--	8.13	8.28	--	14.50	17.33
20. . .	--	59.4	57.24	51.38	43.77	--	8.02	7.61	--	15.61	17.39
25. . .	--	54.5	52.42	46.78	40.05	--	7.72	6.73	--	16.50	16.80
30. . .	--	49.7	47.60	42.21	36.42	--	7.49	5.79	--	17.74	15.90
35. . .	--	44.9	42.82	37.70	32.82	--	7.20	4.88	--	19.10	14.87
40. . .	--	40.1	38.12	33.25	29.17	--	6.85	4.08	--	20.60	13.99
45. . .	--	35.4	33.54	28.90	25.51	--	6.50	3.39	--	22.49	13.29
50. . .	--	30.9	29.11	24.72	21.89	--	6.18	2.83	--	25.00	12.93
55. . .	--	26.5	24.85	20.73	18.43	--	5.77	2.30	--	27.83	12.48
60. . .	--	22.4	20.79	17.00	15.23	--	5.40	1.77	--	31.76	11.62
65. . .	--	18.5	16.93	13.56	12.23	--	4.94	1.33	--	36.43	10.87
70. . .	--	14.8	13.37	10.50	9.59	--	4.30	0.91	--	40.95	9.49
75. . .	--	11.5	10.21	7.92	7.33	--	3.58	0.59	--	43.20	3.05
80. . .	--	8.6	7.59	5.88	5.50	--	2.72	0.38	--	46.26	6.91
85. . .	--	6.3	5.54	4.43	4.10	--	1.96	0.24	--	45.16	5.85
All other male											
0 . . .	66.5	65.3	60.98	52.33	32.54	1.2	12.97	19.79	1.8	24.79	60.82
1 . . .	--	65.7	62.13	56.05	42.46	--	9.65	13.59	--	17.22	32.01
5 . . .	--	61.9	58.48	53.13	45.06	--	8.77	8.07	--	16.51	17.91
10. . .	--	57.1	53.67	48.54	41.90	--	8.56	6.64	--	17.63	15.85
15. . .	--	52.2	48.84	43.95	38.26	--	8.25	5.69	--	18.77	14.87
20. . .	--	47.5	44.37	39.74	35.11	--	7.76	4.63	--	19.53	13.19
25. . .	--	43.1	40.29	35.94	32.21	--	7.16	3.73	--	19.92	11.58
30. . .	--	38.8	36.20	32.25	29.25	--	6.55	3.00	--	20.31	10.26
35. . .	--	34.5	32.16	28.67	26.16	--	5.83	2.51	--	20.33	9.59
40. . .	--	30.3	28.29	25.23	23.12	--	5.07	2.11	--	20.10	9.13
45. . .	--	26.3	24.64	22.02	20.09	--	4.28	1.93	--	19.44	9.61
50. . .	--	22.6	21.24	19.18	17.34	--	3.42	1.84	--	17.83	10.61
55. . .	--	19.3	18.14	16.67	14.69	--	2.63	1.98	--	15.78	13.48
60. . .	--	16.2	15.35	14.38	12.62	--	1.82	1.76	--	12.66	13.95
65. . .	--	13.5	12.87	12.18	10.38	--	1.32	1.80	--	10.84	17.34
70. . .	--	11.1	10.68	10.06	8.33	--	1.04	1.73	--	10.34	20.77
75. . .	--	8.9	8.99	8.09	6.60	--	0.81	1.49	--	10.01	22.58
80. . .	--	6.9	7.57	6.46	5.12	--	0.44	1.34	--	6.81	26.17
85. . .	--	5.3	6.04	5.08	4.04	--	0.22	1.04	--	4.33	25.74

Table 5-8. Average Number of Years of Life Remaining at Selected Ages, by Sex and Race: 1900-1982 [with measures of absolute and relative changes] –continued

Age, race, and sex	Average number of years					Absolute change			Relative change		
	1982	1980	1969-71	1939-41	1900-02	1980-82	1940-80	1900-40	1980-82	1940-80	1900-40
All other female											
0 . . .	75.2	73.6	69.05	55.51	35.04	1.6	18.09	20.47	2.2	32.59	58.42
1 . . .	--	73.9	70.01	58.47	43.54	--	15.43	14.93	--	26.39	34.29
5 . . .	--	70.2	66.34	55.47	46.04	--	14.73	9.43	--	26.55	20.48
10. . .	--	65.3	61.49	50.83	43.02	--	14.47	7.81	--	28.47	18.15
15. . .	--	60.4	56.60	46.22	39.79	--	14.18	6.43	--	30.68	16.16
20. . .	--	55.5	51.85	42.14	36.89	--	13.36	5.25	--	31.70	14.23
25. . .	--	50.7	47.19	38.31	33.90	--	12.39	4.41	--	32.34	13.01
30. . .	--	46.0	42.61	34.52	30.70	--	11.48	3.82	--	33.26	12.44
35. . .	--	41.4	38.14	30.83	27.52	--	10.57	3.31	--	34.28	12.03
40. . .	--	36.8	33.87	27.31	24.37	--	9.49	2.94	--	34.75	12.06
45. . .	--	32.4	29.80	24.00	21.36	--	8.40	2.64	--	35.00	12.36
50. . .	--	28.3	25.97	21.04	18.67	--	7.26	2.37	--	34.51	12.69
55. . .	--	24.4	22.37	18.44	15.88	--	5.96	2.56	--	32.32	16.12
60. . .	--	20.7	19.02	16.14	13.60	--	4.56	2.54	--	26.39	18.68
65. . .	--	17.3	15.99	13.95	11.38	--	3.35	2.57	--	24.01	22.58
70. . .	--	14.2	13.30	11.81	9.62	--	2.39	2.19	--	20.24	22.77
75. . .	--	11.4	11.06	9.80	7.90	--	1.60	1.9	--	16.33	24.05
80. . .	--	9.0	9.01	8.00	6.48	--	1.00	1.52	--	12.50	23.46
85. . .	--	7.0	7.07	6.38	5.10	--	0.62	1.28	--	9.72	25.10

Source: National Center for Health Statistics. Vital Statistics of the United States: Mortality (1978--Vol. II, Part A, Table 5-4); and Monthly Vital Statistics Report (Vol. 31, no. 13, Table 5; and Vol. 32, no. 4, Table 2). Washington, DC: U.S. Government Printing Office, 1982 and 1983.

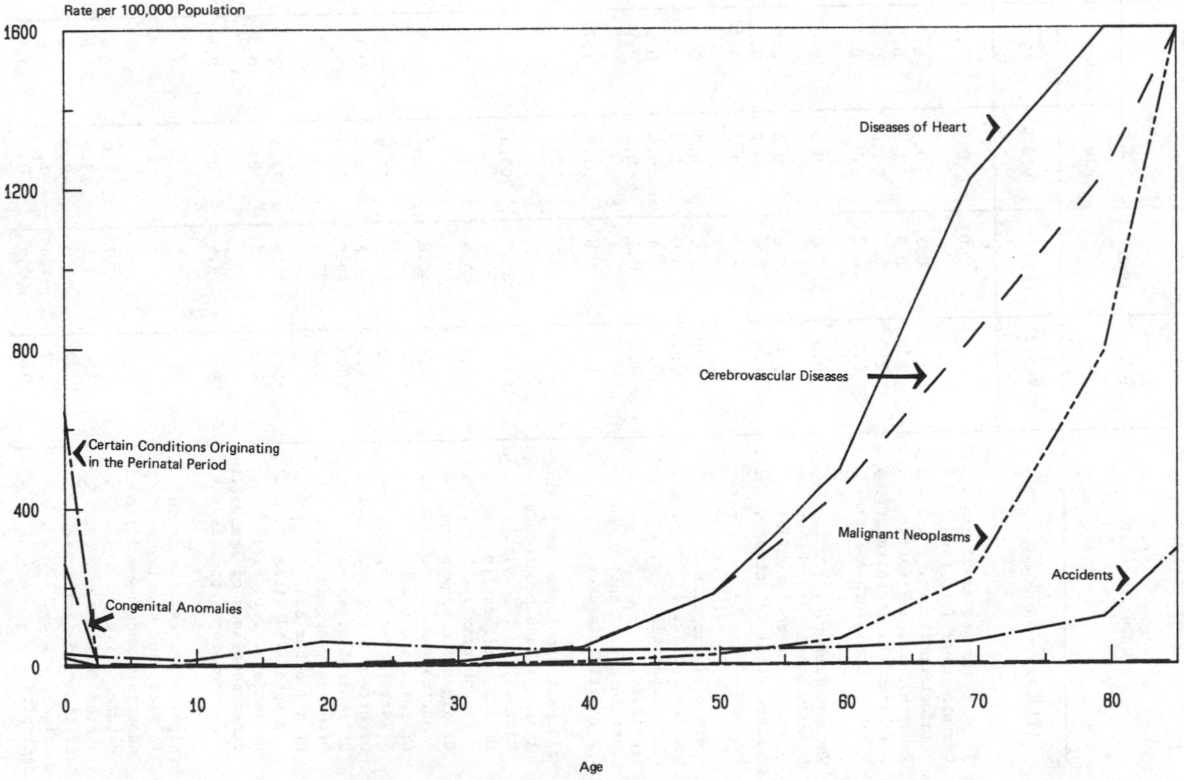

Figure 5-5. Profile of Selected Age-Specific Causes of Death

Table 5-9. Death Rates for 72 Selected Causes, by Sex and Race: 1970 and 1980 [rates per 100,000 population]

Cause of death	1970	1980	Sex		White			Other (nonwhite)			Ratio male to female	Ratio nonwhite to white
			Male	Female	Total	Male	Female	Total	Male	Female		
All causes	945.3	878.3	976.9	785.3	892.5	983.3	806.1	791.7	936.5	660.6	1.24	0.89
Shigellosis and amebiasis	0.0	0.0	0.0	0.0	0.0	0.0	0.0	0.0	0.0	0.0	0.00	0.00
Certain other intestinal infections	1.3	0.2	0.1	0.2	0.1	0.1	0.2	0.2	0.3	0.2	0.50	2.00
Tuberculosis, all forms	2.6	0.9	1.2	0.6	0.6	0.9	0.4	2.3	3.2	1.5	2.00	3.83
Tuberculosis/respiratory	2.0	0.7	1.0	0.4	0.5	0.8	0.3	1.8	2.6	1.1	2.50	3.60
Tuberculosis/other forms	0.5	0.2	0.2	0.1	0.1	0.1	0.1	0.5	0.5	0.5	2.00	5.00
Whooping cough	0.0	0.0	0.0	0.0	0.0	0.0	0.0	0.0	0.0	0.0	0.00	0.00
Streptococcal sore throat/scarlatina and erysipelas	0.0	0.0	0.0	0.0	0.0	0.0	0.0	0.0	0.0	0.0	0.00	0.00
Meningococcal infection	0.3	0.2	0.2	0.2	0.2	0.2	0.1	0.3	0.3	0.2	1.00	1.50
Septicemia	1.7	4.2	4.3	4.1	3.8	3.9	3.8	6.2	6.7	5.8	1.05	1.63
Acute poliomyelitis	0.0	0.0	0.0	0.0	0.0	0.0	0.0	0.0	0.0	0.0	0.00	0.00
Measles	0.0	0.0	0.0	0.0	0.0	0.0	0.0	0.0	0.0	0.0	0.00	0.00
Viral hepatitis	0.5	0.4	0.4	0.3	0.3	0.4	0.3	0.4	0.4	0.5	1.33	1.33
Syphilis	0.2	0.1	0.1	0.1	0.1	0.1	0.0	0.2	0.3	0.1	1.00	2.00
Other infective and parasitic diseases	1.5	1.8	1.9	1.7	1.7	1.8	1.6	2.5	2.6	2.4	1.12	1.47
Malignant neoplasms (including lymphatic and hematopoietic tissues)	162.8	183.9	205.3	163.6	189.0	208.7	170.3	152.3	184.1	123.6	1.25	0.81
Of lip, oral cavity and pharynx	3.7	3.8	5.4	2.3	3.7	5.1	2.4	4.3	7.1	1.8	2.35	1.16
Of digestive organs and peritoneum	46.6	48.8	52.7	45.2	49.7	52.9	46.7	43.4	51.2	36.3	1.17	0.87
Of respiratory and intrathoracic organs	34.2	47.9	71.9	25.2	49.4	73.4	26.5	38.9	62.5	17.5	2.85	0.79
Of breast	14.7	15.8	0.2	30.6	16.7	0.2	32.3	10.9	0.2	20.5	0.01	0.65
Of genital organs	20.3	20.5	21.5	19.6	20.3	20.8	19.7	21.9	25.6	18.5	1.10	1.08
Of urinary organs	7.6	7.9	10.6	5.3	8.4	11.4	5.5	4.6	5.6	3.6	2.00	0.55
Of all other and unspecified sites	19.2	22.4	24.5	20.3	23.2	25.4	21.1	17.1	18.9	15.5	1.21	0.74
Leukemia	7.1	7.3	8.4	6.3	7.7	8.8	6.7	4.6	5.3	3.9	1.33	0.60
Other neoplasms of lymphatic and hematopoietic tissues	9.2	9.5	10.1	8.8	9.9	10.5	9.3	6.7	7.7	5.9	1.15	0.68
Benign neoplasms, carcinoma in situ, and neoplasms of uncertain and unspecified nature	2.4	2.7	2.6	2.8	2.8	2.6	2.9	2.6	2.4	2.7	0.93	0.93
Diabetes mellitus	18.9	15.4	13.0	17.6	14.8	12.8	16.8	18.9	14.6	22.7	0.74	1.28
Nutritional deficiencies	1.2	1.0	0.9	1.2	1.0	0.8	1.2	1.1	1.2	1.0	0.75	1.10
Anemias	1.7	1.4	1.3	1.6	1.3	1.1	1.5	2.2	2.2	2.1	0.81	1.69
Meningitis	0.8	0.6	0.7	0.5	0.5	0.6	0.4	1.2	1.5	1.1	1.40	2.40

Table 5-9. Death Rates for 72 Selected Causes, by Sex and Race: 1970 and 1980 [rates per 100,000 population]—continued

Cause of death	1970	1980	Sex		White			Other (nonwhite)			Ratio male to female	Ratio nonwhite to white
			Male	Female	Total	Male	Female	Total	Male	Female		
Major cardiovascular diseases	496.0	436.4	457.7	416.2	453.5	473.9	434.1	330.9	355.7	308.4	1.10	0.73
Diseases of heart	362.0	336.0	368.6	305.1	350.8	384.0	319.2	245.0	271.8	220.7	1.21	0.70
Rheumatic fever and rheumatic heart disease	7.3	3.5	2.4	4.4	3.7	2.6	4.8	2.0	1.6	2.4	0.55	0.54
Hypertensive heart disease	4.1	9.3	8.1	10.5	8.0	6.7	9.3	17.1	16.5	17.6	0.77	2.14
Hypertensive heart and renal disease	3.2	1.6	1.4	1.9	1.5	1.2	1.7	2.5	2.1	2.9	0.74	1.67
Ischemic heart disease	328.1	249.7	282.4	218.9	266.4	300.9	233.7	147.1	165.8	130.2	1.29	0.55
Acute miocardial infarction	175.8	132.2	162.3	104.0	141.7	174.2	110.7	74.5	86.3	63.7	1.56	0.53
Other acute and subacute forms of ischemic heart disease	2.1	2.1	2.7	1.5	2.1	2.7	1.5	2.3	3.0	1.6	1.80	1.10
Angina pectoris	0.1	0.2	0.3	0.2	0.3	0.3	0.2	0.2	0.1	0.2	1.50	0.67
Old myocardial infarction and other forms of chronic ischemic heart disease	150.1	115.1	117.2	113.2	122.4	123.7	121.2	70.2	76.4	64.7	1.04	0.57
Other diseases of endocardium	3.3	3.2	3.4	3.0	3.3	3.5	3.2	2.1	2.4	1.8	1.13	0.64
All other heart disease	15.9	68.7	71.0	66.4	67.8	69.1	66.5	74.1	83.5	65.7	1.07	1.09
Hypertension with or without renal disease	4.1	3.5	3.3	3.6	3.1	3.0	3.3	5.3	5.1	5.6	0.92	1.71
Cerebrovascular diseases	101.9	75.1	63.6	86.1	76.3	63.3	88.8	67.7	65.5	69.7	0.74	0.89
Intracerebral and other intracranial hemorrhage	20.4	9.2	8.6	9.7	8.8	8.0	9.6	11.4	12.2	10.6	0.89	1.30
Cerebral thrombosis and unspecified occlusion of cerebral arteries	28.5	15.0	12.5	17.4	15.6	12.8	18.3	11.5	10.8	12.1	0.72	0.74
Cerebral embolism	0.4	0.4	0.3	0.4	0.4	0.3	0.4	0.3	0.3	0.3	0.75	0.75
All other cerebrovascular	52.7	50.6	42.2	58.5	51.6	42.2	60.5	44.6	42.2	46.8	0.72	0.86
Atherosclerosis	15.6	13.0	10.5	15.3	13.9	11.1	16.6	7.5	7.0	7.9	0.69	0.54
Other diseases of arteries, arterioles and capillaries	12.5	8.8	11.8	6.0	9.4	12.6	6.3	5.4	6.2	4.6	1.97	0.57
Acute bronchitis and bronchiolitis	0.6	0.3	0.3	0.3	0.3	0.3	0.3	0.2	0.3	0.2	1.00	0.67
Pneumonia and influenza	30.9	24.1	25.1	23.2	24.8	25.1	24.6	19.7	25.0	14.9	1.08	0.79
Pneumonia	29.0	22.9	24.2	21.7	23.5	24.1	23.0	19.4	24.7	14.5	1.12	0.83
Influenza	1.8	1.2	0.9	1.5	1.3	1.0	1.6	0.3	0.3	0.4	0.60	0.23
Chronic obstructive pulmonary diseases, allied conditions	15.2	24.7	35.1	15.0	26.9	37.9	16.4	11.6	17.6	6.2	2.34	0.43
Bronchitis, chronic and unspecified	2.9	1.6	2.2	1.2	1.8	2.3	1.3	0.7	1.0	0.4	1.83	0.39
Emphysema	11.2	6.1	9.2	3.2	6.8	10.1	3.6	2.2	3.6	0.8	2.88	0.32
Asthma	1.1	1.3	1.2	1.4	1.2	1.1	1.3	1.9	1.9	1.9	0.86	1.58
Other chronic obstructive pulmonary diseases and allied conditions	...	15.7	22.6	9.2	17.1	24.4	10.2	6.9	11.1	3.0	2.46	0.40

Table 5-9. Death Rates for 72 Selected Causes, by Sex and Race: 1970 and 1980 [rates per 100,000 population]—continued

Cause of death	1970	1980	Sex		White			Other (nonwhite)			Ratio male to female	Ratio nonwhite to white
			Male	Female	Total	Male	Female	Total	Male	Female		
Ulcer of stomach and duodenum	4.2	2.7	3.1	2.3	2.8	3.2	2.5	1.8	2.4	1.2	1.35	0.64
Appendicitis	0.7	0.3	0.3	0.3	0.3	0.3	0.3	0.4	0.5	0.4	1.00	1.33
Hernia of abdominal cavity and intestinal obstruction without mention of hernia	3.6	2.4	2.0	2.8	2.4	1.9	3.0	2.1	2.3	1.9	0.71	0.88
Chronic liver disease and cirrhosis	15.5	13.5	18.0	9.3	13.0	17.3	8.8	16.8	22.3	11.9	1.94	1.29
Cholelithiasis/other disorders of gallbladder	2.0	1.5	1.3	1.6	1.5	1.4	1.6	0.9	0.8	1.0	0.81	0.60
Nephritis/nephrotic syndrome/nephrosis	4.4	7.4	7.8	7.0	6.7	7.2	6.3	11.4	11.9	11.0	1.11	1.70
Acute glomerulonephritis/nephrotic syndrome	0.7	0.1	0.1	0.1	0.1	0.1	0.1	0.2	0.2	0.2	1.00	2.00
Chronic glomerulonephritis/nephritis/nephropathy, not specified as acute/chronic, and renal schlerosis, unspecified	...	1.0	1.0	1.0	0.9	0.9	0.8	1.7	1.7	1.6	1.00	1.89
Renal failure/disorders resulting from impaired renal function/small kidney of unknown cause	...	6.3	6.7	5.9	5.7	6.1	5.3	9.5	9.9	9.2	1.14	1.67
Infections of kidney	4.0	1.2	0.9	1.5	1.2	0.9	1.6	1.2	1.0	1.3	0.60	1.00
Hyperplasia of prostate	1.1	0.3	0.7	...	0.3	0.7	...	0.3	0.7	...	...	1.00
Complications of pregnancy, childbirth and puerperium	0.4	0.1	...	0.3	0.1	...	0.2	0.4	...	0.8	...	4.00
Pregnancy with abortive outcome	0.1	0.0	...	0.1	0.0	...	0.0	0.1	...	0.2	...	...
Other complications of pregnancy, childbirth, and the puerperium	0.3	0.1	...	0.2	0.1	...	0.2	0.3	...	0.6	...	3.00
Congenital anomalies	8.3	6.2	6.8	5.5	5.9	6.5	5.3	7.8	8.7	7.0	1.24	1.32
Certain conditions originating in the perinatal period	21.3	10.1	11.9	8.4	7.9	9.4	6.5	23.3	27.2	19.8	1.42	2.95
Birth trauma/intrauterine hypoxia/birth asphyxia/respiratory distress syndrome	11.2	3.3	4.1	2.6	2.8	3.5	2.2	6.5	7.7	5.5	1.58	2.32
Other conditions originating in the perinatal period	10.0	6.7	7.8	5.8	5.1	5.9	4.4	16.8	19.5	14.4	1.34	3.29
Symptoms/signs/ill-defined conditions	12.7	12.7	15.0	10.6	10.7	12.6	8.9	24.9	29.7	20.6	1.42	2.33
All other diseases (residual)	49.8	50.9	53.2	48.7	50.2	51.5	48.9	55.3	63.7	47.7	1.09	1.10
Accidents/adverse effects	56.4	46.7	67.4	27.1	46.3	66.3	27.2	49.1	74.4	26.3	2.49	1.06
Motor vehicle accidents	26.9	23.5	35.3	12.3	24.1	35.9	12.8	19.9	31.5	9.3	2.87	0.83
All other accidents/adverse effects	29.5	23.2	32.1	14.8	22.2	30.4	14.4	29.3	42.9	16.9	2.17	1.32
Suicide	11.6	11.9	18.6	5.5	12.7	19.9	5.9	6.4	10.6	2.6	3.38	0.50
Homicide/legal intervention	8.3	10.7	17.3	4.5	7.0	10.9	3.2	33.8	57.8	12.1	3.84	4.83
All other external causes	2.7	1.6	2.4	0.9	1.4	2.1	0.8	2.8	4.4	1.3	2.67	2.00

Note: ... indicates data not applicable or not specified in 1970.

Source: National Center for Health Statistics. Monthly Vital Statistics Report (Vol. 31, no. 6 Supplement, Table 8; Vol. 32, no. 4 Supplement, Table 8). Washington, DC: U.S. Government Printing Office, 1982 and 1983.

Table 5-10. Mortality from Fifteen Leading Causes of Death, United States, 1980, and Change in Rates from Those Causes, 1970-1980

Rank order 1980	Cause of death	Rate per 100,000 population				Percent of total deaths	
		1980	1970	Change 1970-80		1980	1970
				Absolute	Percent		
	All causes.	878.3	945.3	-67.0	-7.1	100.0	100.0
1	Diseases of heart	336.0	362.0	-26.0	-7.2	38.2	38.3
2	Malignant neoplasms, including neoplasms of lymphatic and hematopoietic tissues	183.9	162.8	21.1	13.0	20.9	17.2
3	Cerebrovascular diseases.	75.1	101.9	-26.8	-26.3	8.6	10.8
4	Accidents and adverse effects	46.7	56.4	-9.7	-17.2	5.3	6.0
	Motor vehicle accidents	23.5	26.9	-3.4	-12.6	2.7	2.8
	All other accidents and adverse effects	23.2	29.5	-6.3	-21.4	2.6	3.1
5	Chronic obstructive pulmonary diseases and allied conditions.	24.7	15.2	9.5	62.5	2.8	1.6
6	Pneumonia and influenza	24.1	30.9	-6.8	-22.0	2.7	3.3
7	Diabetes mellitus	15.4	18.9	-3.5	-18.5	1.8	2.0
8	Chronic liver disease and cirrhosis	13.5	15.5	-2.0	-12.9	1.5	1.6
9	Atherosclerosis	13.0	15.6	-2.6	-16.7	1.5	1.7
10	Suicide	11.9	11.6	0.3	2.6	1.4	1.2
11	Homicide and legal intervention . . .	10.7	8.3	2.4	28.9	1.2	0.9
12	Certain conditions originating in the perinatal period	10.1	21.3	-11.2	-52.6	1.1	2.3
13	Nephritis, nephrotic syndrome, and nephrosis	7.4	4.4	3.0	68.2	0.8	0.5
14	Congenital anomalies.	6.2	8.3	-2.1	-25.3	0.7	0.9
15	Septicemia.	4.2	1.7	2.5	147.1	0.5	0.2
	All other causes.	95.6	110.5	-14.9	-13.5	10.9	11.7

Source: 1980 data from National Center for Health Statistics. Monthly Vital Statistics Report (Vol. 32, no. 4, supplement, Table B). Washington, DC: U.S. Government Printing Office, 1983. 1970 data from National Center for Health Statistics. Monthly Vital Statistics Report (Vol. 31, no. 6, supplement, Table 8). Washington, DC: U.S. Government Printing Office, 1982.

Table 5-11. Death Rates for 72 Selected Causes, by Ten-Year Age Groups: United States, 1980 [rates per 100,000 population]

Cause of death	All ages[a]	Under 1 year	1–4 years	5–14 years	15–24 years	25–34 years	35–44 years	45–54 years	55–64 years	65–74 years	75–84 years	85 years and over
All causes	878.3	1,288.3	63.9	30.6	115.4	135.5	227.9	584.0	1,346.3	2,994.9	6,692.6	15,980.3
Shigellosis and amebiasis	0.0	0.1	0.0	0.0	0.0	0.0	0.0	0.0	0.0	0.0	0.1	0.0
Enteritis/other diarrheal	0.2	3.2	0.2	0.0	0.0	0.0	0.0	0.1	0.1	0.3	0.8	3.0
Tuberculosis, all forms	0.9	0.1	0.0	0.0	0.0	0.1	0.0	1.1	1.7	3.5	5.6	9.6
Tuberculosis/respiratory	0.7	*	*	*	0.0	0.1	0.3	0.9	1.4	2.9	4.8	8.3
Tuberculosis/other forms	0.2	0.1	0.0	0.0	0.0	0.0	0.1	0.2	0.2	0.6	0.9	1.3
Whooping cough	0.0	0.3	0.0	*	*	*	*	*	*	*	*	*
Streptococcal sore throat/ scarlatina/erysipelas	0.0	0.0	*	0.0	*	*	0.0	0.0	0.0	0.0	0.1	0.1
Meningococcal infections	0.2	2.2	0.9	0.1	0.1	0.1	0.0	0.1	0.1	0.1	0.2	0.3
Septicemia	4.2	6.8	0.6	0.1	0.2	0.4	0.9	2.3	5.8	13.7	35.5	87.8
Acute poliomyelitis	0.0	*	*	*	*	*	0.0	0.0	0.0	0.0	0.0	*
Measles	0.0	0.1	0.0	0.0	0.0	0.0	*	*	*	*	*	*
Viral hepatitis	0.4	0.3	0.1	0.0	0.2	0.2	0.3	0.5	0.7	1.0	1.5	1.6
Syphilis and its sequelae	0.1	0.1	*	*	0.0	0.0	0.0	0.0	0.1	0.3	0.7	1.0
Other infectious and parasitic diseases	1.8	6.6	0.8	0.3	0.4	0.6	0.9	1.7	3.1	5.5	8.8	18.7
Malignant neoplasms (including neoplasms of lymphatic and hematopoietic tissues)	183.9	3.2	4.5	4.3	6.3	13.7	48.6	180.0	436.1	817.9	1,232.3	1,594.6
Of bucal cavity and pharynx	3.8	*	0.0	0.0	0.0	0.1	1.2	5.3	11.6	16.0	18.5	23.3
Of digestive organs and peritoneum	48.8	0.3	0.2	0.1	0.4	1.7	8.0	35.8	102.6	221.5	389.5	565.6
Of respiratory system	47.9	0.2	0.1	0.0	0.1	0.8	9.6	56.5	144.3	243.1	251.4	184.5
Of breast	15.8	*	*	0.0	0.0	1.7	9.2	25.0	43.2	57.7	80.3	118.6
Of genital organs	20.5	*	0.0	0.0	0.5	1.6	4.6	14.1	35.9	88.3	177.2	267.0
Of urinary organs	7.9	0.3	0.2	0.1	0.1	0.2	1.0	5.3	15.4	35.8	65.2	98.2
Of all other and unspecified sites	22.4	1.5	2.3	1.7	2.3	4.0	8.9	24.3	50.9	89.2	133.6	187.0
Leukemia	7.3	0.9	1.5	1.9	1.7	1.9	2.9	5.3	11.8	25.9	50.7	78.2
Other neoplasms of lymphatic and hematopoietic tissues	9.5	0.1	0.2	0.4	1.0	1.8	3.3	8.4	20.4	40.3	66.0	72.2
Benign neoplasms, carcinoma in situ, and neoplasms of uncertain behaviour and of unspecified nature	2.7	1.9	0.3	0.3	0.3	0.5	1.0	2.4	4.9	10.1	19.8	31.2
Diabetes mellitus	15.4	0.1	0.1	0.1	0.3	1.5	3.5	9.6	26.7	64.9	131.1	221.9
Nutritional deficiencies	1.0	0.8	0.1	0.0	0.0	0.0	0.1	0.3	0.7	2.4	9.4	42.9
Anemias	1.4	0.7	0.5	0.2	0.3	0.4	0.4	0.6	1.3	3.8	11.9	33.7
Meningitis	0.6	12.5	1.7	0.1	0.1	0.1	0.2	0.3	0.7	1.1	1.5	2.0

Table 5-11. Death Rates for 72 Selected Causes, by Ten-Year Age Groups: United States, 1980 [rates per 100,000 population]—continued

Cause of death	All ages[a]	Under 1 year	1–4 years	5–14 years	15–24 years	25–34 years	35–44 years	45–54 years	55–64 years	65–74 years	75–84 years	85 years and over
Major cardiovascular diseases . .	436.4	27.8	3.2	1.3	4.1	11.5	54.9	212.0	581.0	1,513.4	4,020.1	10,951.9
Diseases of heart	336.0	22.8	2.6	0.9	2.9	8.3	44.6	180.2	494.1	1,218.6	2,993.1	7,777.1
Rheumatic fever/rheumatic heart disease	3.5	0.1	0.0	0.1	0.2	0.4	1.3	3.7	7.8	15.7	22.2	23.9
Hypertensive heart disease. .	9.3	0.0	*	0.0	0.0	0.3	1.9	6.3	15.8	34.8	80.7	176.3
Hypertensive heart and renal disease	1.6	*	0.0	*	0.0	0.0	0.1	0.5	1.5	4.9	16.5	53.1
Ischemic heart disease.	249.7	0.8	0.1	0.0	0.3	3.2	29.1	131.9	372.4	930.6	2,254.8	5,652.1
Acute myocardial infarction .	132.2	0.6	0.1	0.0	0.2	2.1	19.6	89.6	245.8	570.1	1,126.6	1,961.5
Other acute/subacute forms of ischemic heart disease .	2.1	*	*	*	0.0	0.1	0.5	2.1	4.5	8.2	15.1	31,0
Angina pectoris	0.2	*	*	*	*	0.0	0.1	0.1	0.4	1.0	2.4	4.2
Chronic disease of endocardium/other myocardial insufficiency	115.1	0.3	0.0	0.0	0.1	1.0	9.0	40.1	121.7	351.4	1,110.7	3,655.3
Other diseases of endocardium .	3.2	0.2	0.0	0.0	0.2	0.3	0.6	1.5	4.6	12.0	30.1	57.3
All other heart disease	68.7	21.6	2.4	0.8	2.1	4.0	11.5	36.3	92.0	220.7	588.8	1,814.4
Hypertension with or without renal disease	3.5	0.1	0.0	0.0	0.0	0.2	0.6	1.8	4.3	11.2	31.7	91.5
Cerebrovascular diseases. . . .	75.1	4.4	0.5	0.3	1.0	2.6	8.5	25.2	65.2	219.5	788.6	2,288.9
Cerebral/cranial hemorrhage . .	9.2	2.6	0.2	0.1	0.3	0.8	3.1	8.4	16.0	32.8	74.1	141.1
Cerebral thrombosis/unspecified occlusion of cerebral arteries	15.0	0.4	0.1	0.0	0.1	0.2	0.5	2.4	10.5	41.3	167.5	517.7
Cerebral embolism	0.4	0.0	*	0.0	0.0	0.0	0.1	0.2	0.4	1.2	3.7	6.9
All other/late effects of cerebrovascular disease . . .	50.6	1.3	0.2	0.1	0.6	1.6	4.9	14.3	38.4	144.1	543.3	1,623.3
Atherosclerosis	13.0	0.1	*	*	0.0	0.0	0.2	1.2	4.8	23.6	125.5	656.5
Other diseases of arteries, arterioles, and capillaries . .	8.8	0.5	0.1	0.1	0.2	0.4	1.0	3.6	13.3	40.6	81.3	137.9
Acute bronchitis / bronchiolitis .	0.3	2.5	0.3	0.0	0.0	0.0	0.0	0.1	0.3	0.6	1.9	7.3
Pneumonia and influenza	24.1	28.6	2.1	0.6	0.8	1.5	3.5	7.7	18.6	55.6	220.0	885.7
Pneumonia	22.9	28.3	2.0	0.5	0.8	1.5	3.4	7.6	18.1	53.6	208.9	828.2
Influenza	1.2	0.3	0.1	0.0	0.0	0.0	0.1	0.1	0.5	2.1	11.1	57.5
Chronic obstructive pulmonary diseases/allied conditions. . .	24.7	1.6	0.4	0.2	0.3	0.5	1.6	9.8	42.7	129.1	224.4	274.0
Bronchitis, chronic and unspecified	1.6	1.2	0.2	0.0	0.0	0.0	0.1	0.6	2.6	7.6	14.8	25.8
Emphysema	6.1	0.1	*	0.0	0.0	0.1	0.3	2.4	11.3	33.5	55.1	56.9
Asthma.	1.3	0.2	0.2	0.2	0.2	0.4	0.6	1.4	2.4	4.9	7.7	9.9
Other chronic obstructive pulmonary obstructive diseases/allied conditions . . .	15.7	0.1	0.0	0.0	0.0	0.1	0.6	5.4	26.4	83.1	146.7	181.4
Ulcer of stomach and duodenum . .	2.7	0.3	0.1	0.0	0.1	0.2	0.6	1.6	4.1	9.9	23.8	55.1
Appendicitis.	0.3	0.3	0.1	0.1	0.1	0.1	0.1	0.2	0.6	0.9	2.2	4.5
Hernia of abdominal cavity/intestinal obstruction without mention of hernia	2.4	3.7	0.2	0.1	0.1	0.1	0.4	0.9	2.3	6.6	22.1	71.0

Table 5-11. Death Rates for 72 Selected Causes, by Ten-Year Age Groups: United States, 1980 [rates per 100,000 population]—continued

Cause of death	All ages[a]	Under 1 year	1–4 years	5–14 years	15–24 years	25–34 years	35–44 years	45–54 years	55–64 years	65–74 years	75–84 years	85 years and over
Chronic liver disease/cirrhosis	13.5	0.9	0.1	0.0	0.3	3.5	13.6	30.9	41.6	43.1	30.6	19.9
Cholelithiasis/other disorders of gallbladder	1.5	0.0	*	*	0.0	0.1	0.2	0.5	1.5	4.6	14.6	40.1
Nephritis, nephrotic syndrome/nephrosis	7.4	6.4	0.2	0.1	0.3	0.7	1.4	3.6	9.0	24.6	67.8	174.1
Acute glomerulonephritis/nephrotic syndrome	0.1	0.2	0.0	0.0	0.0	0.0	0.0	0.1	0.2	0.4	1.3	2.9
Chronic glomerulonephritis/nephritis/nephropathy, not specified as acute/chronic, and renal schlerosis, unspecified	1.0	*	0.0	0.0	0.1	0.1	0.3	0.5	1.2	3.4	9.0	22.2
Renal failure/disorders resulting from impaired renal function/small kidney of unknown cause	6.3	6.2	0.1	0.1	0.2	0.5	1.1	3.0	7.7	20.8	57.5	149.1
Infections of kidney	1.2	0.2	*	0.0	0.0	0.1	0.2	0.4	0.9	3.4	12.4	38.5
Hyperplasia of prostate	0.3	*	*	*	*	*	*	0.0	0.1	0.8	4.0	12.5
Complications of pregnancy, childbirth and puerperium	0.1	*	*	*	0.3	0.4	0.2	0.0	*	*	*	*
Pregnancy with abortive outcome	0.0	*	*	*	0.0	0.1	0.0	*	*	*	*	*
Other complications of pregnancy, childbirth, and the puerperium	0.1	*	*	*	0.2	0.3	0.2	0.0	*	*	*	*
Congential anomalies	6.2	260.9	8.0	1.6	1.4	1.3	1.3	1.7	2.2	2.9	3.7	4.6
Certain conditions originating in the perinatal period	10.1	643.7	0.7	0.0	0.0	0.0	0.0	0.0	0.0	0.0	*	0.0
Birth trauma/intrauterine hypoxia/birth asphyxia/respiratory distress syndrome	3.3	213.5	0.2	0.0	0.0	*	*	0.0	0.0	*	*	*
Other conditions originating in the perinatal period	6.7	430.2	0.5	0.0	0.0	0.0	0.0	*	0.0	0.0	*	0.0
Symptoms/signs/ill-defined conditions	12.7	172.3	2.2	0.4	2.1	3.4	4.4	8.5	16.4	31.0	62.1	169.8
All other diseases (residual)	50.9	59.3	7.6	3.7	5.9	10.0	19.0	39.2	74.9	162.0	377.0	903.2
Accidents/adverse effects	46.7	33.0	25.9	15.0	61.7	46.3	37.3	39.0	42.6	57.7	120.3	292.5
Motor vehicle accidents	23.5	7.0	9.2	7.9	44.8	29.1	20.9	18.6	17.4	19.2	28.1	27.6
All other accidents/adverse effects	23.2	26.0	16.7	7.1	16.9	17.2	16.4	20.4	25.2	38.5	92.2	264.9
Suicide	11.9	*	*	0.4	12.3	16.0	15.4	15.9	15.9	16.9	19.1	19.2
Homicide/legal intervention	10.7	5.9	2.5	1.2	15.6	19.6	15.1	11.1	7.0	5.7	5.2	5.3
All other external causes	1.6	1.9	0.8	0.2	1.7	2.4	2.1	1.9	1.8	1.6	2.0	2.7

[a]Figures for ages not states are included in "All ages" but not distributed among age groups.

Note: * indicates zero cases reported.

Source: National Center for Health Statistics. Monthly Vital Statistics Report (Vol. 32, no. 4 Supplement, Table 6). Washington, DC: U.S. Government Printing Office, 1983.

Table 5-12. Sex Differentials in Mortality, by Age: 1970 and 1978 [ratio of male to female age-cause specific rates]

Cause of death	Age in 1978							Age in 1970						
	Total	1-19 years	20-44 years	45-64 years	65-74 years	75-84 years	85 years and over	Total	1-19 years	20-44 years	45-64 years	65-74 years	75-84 years	85 years and over
All causes	1.28	1.83	2.15	1.93	1.97	1.61	1.27	1.35	1.75	1.97	2.01	1.89	1.49	1.15
Bacillary dysentery/amebiasis	--	0.00	--	--	1.00	1.00	--	--	1.00	--	2.00	1.00	1.00	1.00
Enteritis/other diarrheal	1.00	1.20	1.75	0.88	1.25	1.15	0.99	1.00	1.00	1.00	1.27	1.10	1.03	0.79
Tuberculosis, all forms	2.00	1.00	2.10	2.87	2.89	2.84	2.40	2.71	1.00	1.76	3.30	3.41	3.77	3.80
Tuberculosis/respiratory	2.50	0.00	1.78	3.52	3.13	3.21	2.51	2.82	1.00	1.93	3.78	4.01	4.08	3.26
Tuberculosis/other forms	2.00	0.00	2.00	1.50	2.53	1.94	2.00	1.75	3.00	1.11	2.08	2.00	2.72	2.19
Whooping cough	--	--	--	--	--	--	--	--	--	--	--	--	--	--
Streptococcal sore throat/ scarlet fever	--	--	--	--	--	--	--	--	--	--	--	--	--	1.00
Meningococcal infections	1.00	1.36	2.00	0.75	0.67	0.50	0.33	1.50	1.25	3.00	1.00	1.00	2.00	--
Septicemia	1.15	1.11	1.15	1.44	1.56	1.66	1.49	1.33	1.25	0.95	1.61	1.70	1.81	1.44
Acute poliomyelitis	--	--	--	--	--	--	--	--	--	--	--	--	--	--
Measles	--	--	--	--	--	--	--	--	1.00	--	--	--	--	--
Syphilis and its sequelae	1.00	--	0.00	4.00	1.50	1.80	2.25	1.50	--	0.50	2.10	3.00	1.96	1.63
Other infective and parasitic diseases	1.10	0.92	1.09	1.23	1.52	1.63	1.29	1.16	1.00	0.97	1.28	1.70	1.53	1.39
Malignant neoplasms (including lymphatic and hematopoietic tissues)	1.26	1.36	0.89	1.32	1.85	1.94	1.88	1.26	1.34	0.88	1.34	1.82	1.78	1.57
Of buccal cavity and pharynx	2.50	0.00	2.13	3.05	3.12	3.07	2.42	2.80	1.00	2.16	3.14	4.00	3.25	2.45
Of digestive organs and peritoneum	1.16	0.83	1.39	1.59	1.63	1.48	1.38	1.21	1.75	1.37	1.57	1.59	1.43	1.26
Of respiratory system	3.15	2.00	1.84	2.99	4.70	5.54	4.56	4.52	3.00	2.62	4.53	7.53	6.11	3.81
Of breast	0.01	--	0.00	0.00	0.01	0.02	0.03	0.01	--	0.00	0.01	0.01	0.02	0.02
Of genital organs	1.05	1.25	0.22	0.35	1.50	3.46	5.30	0.84	1.50	0.23	0.29	1.26	3.02	4.50
Of urinary organs	2.06	0.71	1.95	2.69	2.92	2.95	2.54	2.08	0.90	1.95	2.67	3.04	2.53	2.35
Of all other and unspecified sites	1.17	1.22	1.39	1.47	1.53	1.37	1.41	1.15	1.28	1.30	1.41	1.43	1.27	1.12
Leukemia	1.37	1.43	1.40	1.57	1.98	1.87	1.98	1.34	1.27	1.28	1.59	1.84	1.72	1.64
Other neoplasms of lymphatic and hematopoietic tissues	1.19	2.08	1.76	1.46	1.47	1.45	1.50	1.31	1.89	1.73	1.54	1.47	1.51	1.39
Benign neoplasms and neoplasms of unspecified nature	0.96	1.08	0.97	1.06	1.42	1.25	1.19	0.96	1.06	0.75	1.05	1.39	1.28	1.07
Diabetes mellitus	0.74	0.80	1.33	1.07	1.00	0.92	0.92	0.73	0.62	1.39	0.97	0.88	0.86	0.93
Avitaminoses/other nutritional deficiencies	0.73	1.00	0.83	1.23	1.38	1.15	1.04	0.92	2.00	1.57	1.11	1.32	1.32	1.00
Anemias	0.88	1.07	1.12	0.96	1.39	1.24	1.33	0.94	1.06	0.84	1.07	1.30	1.34	1.33
Meningitis	1.33	1.67	1.38	1.21	1.26	1.37	0.96	1.43	1.17	2.67	1.54	1.40	1.26	1.00
Major cardiovascular diseases	1.14	1.19	2.42	2.63	2.00	1.45	1.14	1.24	1.26	2.19	2.59	1.86	1.37	1.06
Diseases of heart	1.27	1.12	3.14	2.98	2.14	1.53	1.20	1.39	1.24	2.92	2.95	2.00	1.44	1.11
Active rheumatic fever/ chronic rheumatic disease	0.81	1.00	1.12	1.05	1.01	1.02	1.02	0.91	1.22	1.07	1.05	1.05	1.00	0.89
Hypertensive heart disease	0.76	--	2.09	1.40	1.14	0.83	0.67	0.73	--	1.15	1.19	1.10	0.78	0.58
Hypertensive heart and renal disease	0.88	--	2.00	1.11	1.61	1.35	1.36	0.88	--	1.25	1.45	1.48	1.19	1.02
Ischemic heart disease	1.29	2.00	4.38	3.26	2.21	1.55	1.20	1.42	1.50	4.03	3.24	2.05	1.46	1.12
Acute myocardia infarction	1.64	3.00	4.86	3.54	2.39	1.75	1.41	1.82	3.00	4.69	3.65	2.29	1.69	1.33
Other acute/subacute	1.92	--	4.50	3.77	3.20	1.76	1.32	1.80	--	3.63	3.75	2.17	1.66	1.35
Chronic ischemic	1.05	--	3.76	2.88	2.01	1.41	1.11	1.08	2.00	2.82	2.53	1.75	1.29	1.02
Angina pectoris	1.00	--	--	2.25	2.00	1.37	1.25	1.00	--	--	2.67	1.75	1.30	0.94
Chronic disease of endocardium/other myocardial insufficiency	1.06	1.20	1.41	1.86	1.62	1.27	1.10	1.06	1.17	1.73	1.77	1.56	1.24	1.04
All other heart disease	1.27	1.06	1.79	2.21	2.03	1.62	1.30	1.38	1.29	1.64	2.19	2.05	1.50	1.17
Hypertension	0.92	--	1.50	1.38	1.45	1.42	1.36	1.13	0.00	1.13	1.48	1.61	1.53	1.36
Cerebrovascular diseases	0.76	1.33	1.05	1.27	1.41	1.15	0.98	0.87	1.41	1.00	1.37	1.36	1.15	0.94
Cerebral hemorrhage	0.86	1.13	1.34	1.23	1.32	1.05	0.99	0.94	1.67	1.26	1.42	1.34	1.10	0.91
Cerebral thrombosis	0.74	--	0.94	1.66	1.50	1.12	0.94	0.84	2.00	1.27	1.63	1.39	1.13	0.94
Cerebral embolism	0.75	--	0.00	1.40	1.74	1.10	0.82	0.80	--	0.00	1.36	1.05	1.44	0.93
All other cerebrovascular	0.75	1.53	0.94	1.21	1.40	1.17	0.99	0.85	1.33	0.86	1.27	1.36	1.18	0.95
Arteriosclerosis	0.70	--	5.00	1.99	1.62	1.25	1.03	0.81	--	1.20	2.10	1.49	1.27	0.98
Other diseases of arteries, arterioles, capillaries	1.53	1.00	1.45	2.49	2.78	2.23	1.36	1.70	0.83	1.30	2.83	3.01	1.93	1.19
Acute bronchitis/bronchiolitis	1.33	1.00	1.50	2.00	2.00	2.21	1.41	1.40	1.36	1.14	1.85	2.44	1.25	1.43
Influenza and pneumonia	1.18	1.13	1.61	2.03	2.29	1.94	1.52	1.34	1.22	1.52	2.04	2.22	1.84	1.31
Influenza	0.76	0.50	1.00	1.22	1.60	1.30	0.94	1.12	1.60	0.83	1.43	1.84	1.51	1.03
Pneumonia	1.23	1.14	1.66	2.09	2.34	2.01	1.58	1.36	1.23	1.56	2.10	2.25	1.86	1.33
Bronchitis, emphysema, asthma	2.44	1.33	0.97	1.96	3.67	4.83	3.79	3.81	1.22	1.03	3.37	6.40	6.92	4.33
Chronic and unqualified bronchitis	1.86	3.00	1.50	1.65	2.75	3.32	2.43	2.87	1.83	1.30	2.78	4.79	5.01	2.73
Emphysema	3.17	--	2.00	2.50	4.50	6.31	5.50	5.16	--	1.89	4.55	8.05	8.72	5.68
Asthma	0.10	1.50	0.61	0.60	0.98	1.09	0.98	0.77	1.10	0.53	0.80	1.14	1.27	1.61
Peptic ulcer	1.43	1.00	2.40	2.45	2.19	1.89	1.57	2.07	1.00	2.24	2.92	2.96	2.39	1.73
Appendicitis	1.33	1.00	1.33	1.91	2.00	2.14	1.42	1.80	1.17	1.75	2.50	2.56	1.72	1.76
Hernia/intestinal obstruction	0.76	1.66	1.00	1.15	1.25	0.99	0.94	0.92	1.50	1.12	1.14	1.22	1.06	1.06
Cirrhosis of liver	2.00	1.33	2.11	2.14	2.57	2.27	2.34	1.94	0.56	1.69	2.14	2.75	2.19	2.11
Cholelithiasis, cholecystitis, and cholangitis	0.80	--	1.50	1.36	1.63	1.14	1.09	0.77	--	0.40	1.08	1.16	1.13	0.94
Nephritis and nephrosis	1.22	0.83	1.45	1.26	1.69	2.06	1.97	1.26	1.21	1.44	1.43	1.60	1.70	1.64
Acute nephritis and nephrotic syndrome	1.38	1.00	1.17	1.40	1.85	2.04	1.80	1.33	1.20	1.67	1.56	1.86	1.65	2.40
Chronic and unqualified nephritis and renal sclerosis	1.21	0.80	1.46	1.22	1.64	2.06	2.04	1.24	1.22	1.43	1.41	1.57	1.71	1.56
Infections of kidney	0.75	0.00	0.57	0.67	1.10	1.18	1.34	0.84	0.25	0.56	0.83	1.13	1.29	1.39
Hyperplasis of prostate	--	--	--	--	--	--	--	--	--	--	---	--	--	--
Complication of pregnancy, childbirth, puerperium	--	--	--	--	--	--	--	--	--	--	--	--	--	--
Abortions	--	--	--	--	--	--	--	--	--	--	--	--	--	--
Other complications	--	--	--	--	--	--	--	--	--	--	--	--	--	--

Table 5-12. Sex Differentials in Mortality, by Age: 1970 and 1978—continued

Cause of death	Age in 1978							Age in 1970						
	Total	1-19 years	20-44 years	45-64 years	65-74 years	75-84 years	85 years and over	Total	1-19 years	20-44 years	45-64 years	65-74 years	75-84 years	85 years and over
Congenital anomalies	1.20	1.14	1.25	1.13	1.11	1.41	1.82	1.18	1.10	1.14	1.11	1.07	1.36	1.62
Certain causes of mortality in early infancy	1.45	3.00	--	--	--	--	--	1.48	--	--	--	--	--	--
Birth injury, difficult labor, other anoxic and hypoxic conditions	1.47	3.00	--	--	--	--	--	1.57	--	--	--	--	--	--
Other causes of mortality in early infancy	1.32	--	--	--	--	--	--	1.39	--	--	--	--	--	--
Symptoms and ill-defined conditions	1.43	1.51	1.81	2.27	2.15	1.74	1.25	1.53	1.07	1.48	2.28	2.29	1.75	1.20
All other diseases	1.36	1.30	1.38	1.67	2.07	2.04	1.63	1.32	1.21	1.31	1.64	1.83	1.60	1.34
Accidents	2.46	2.28	3.88	2.78	2.14	1.74	1.48	2.41	2.39	4.04	2.87	2.17	1.50	1.14
Motor vehicle accidents	2.83	2.18	3.56	2.55	2.15	2.52	4.22	2.70	2.19	3.58	2.54	2.19	2.55	3.51
All other accidents	2.17	2.45	4.48	2.96	2.13	1.56	1.33	2.19	2.70	4.92	3.21	2.16	1.28	1.02
Suicide	3.02	4.00	2.84	2.46	4.29	6.70	9.47	2.55	3.03	2.20	2.53	4.02	6.36	7.19
Homicide	3.63	2.00	4.21	4.34	2.85	1.67	1.86	3.94	2.55	4.26	4.69	3.93	2.27	2.96
Other external causes	2.25	2.87	2.55	1.89	2.37	3.04	3.25	2.60	2.44	2.73	2.22	3.17	2.95	1.66

Note: -- indicates ratios not computed.

Source: National Center for Health Statistics. Vital Statistics of the United States: Mortality (1978 and 1970--Vol. II, Part A, Table 1-8). Washington, DC: U.S. Government Printing Office, 1982 and 1974.

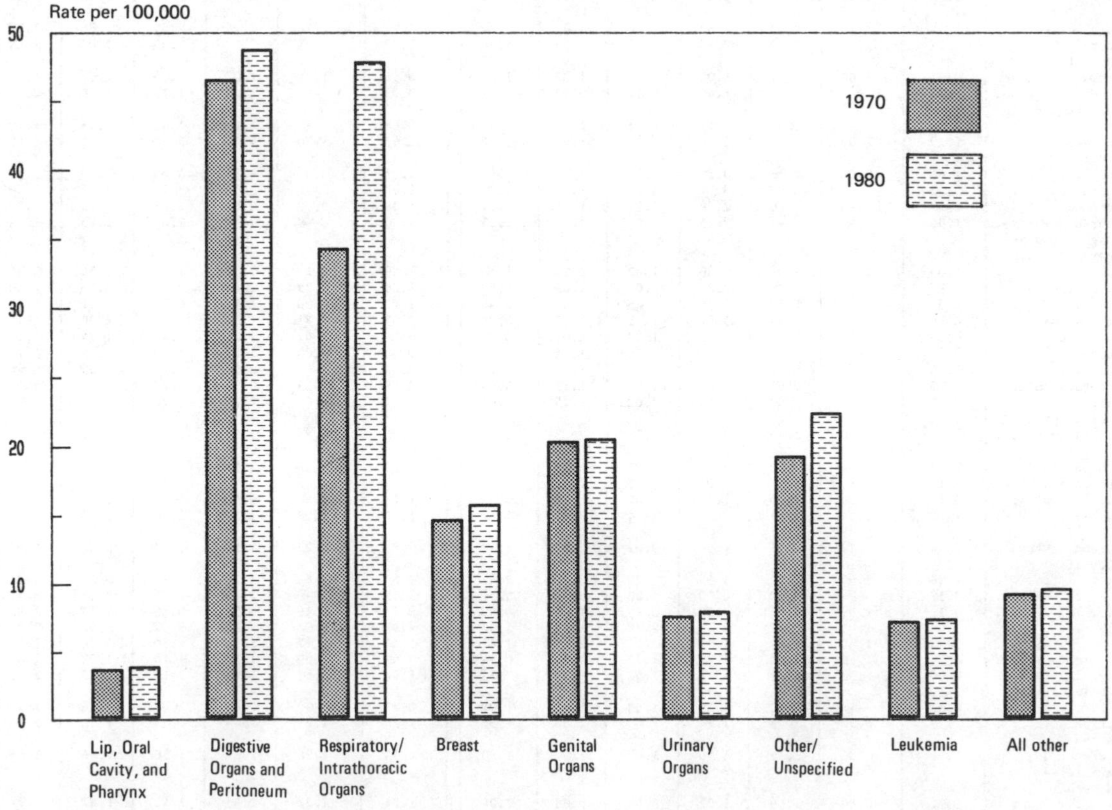

Figure 5-6. Change in Mortality Due to Malignant Neoplasms: 1970-1980

Infectious and Parasitic Diseases

Equal in significance to the chief causes of death are the causes that do *not* rank high. Infections and parasitic diseases (first thirteen causes listed in Table 5-9) have been reduced to almost zero. They were already very low in 1970 and have been reduced still more since. Diseases such as tuberculosis, dysentery and diarrhea, measles, whooping cough, scarlet fever, poliomyelitis, and meningitis, which were once major killers, especially of children, now account for only about 1 percent of all deaths. Immunization, antibiotics, improved sanitation and public health, and improved levels of nutrition and living standards have been responsible for the great decline in this category of disease.

One exception to this optimistic picture, however, is septicemia, which ranks fifteenth in the leading causes of death. The death rate from this disorder has risen remarkably in recent years. Although the rate is still low, it increased by 147.1 percent in the 1970-80 period. Septicemia afflicts infants in their first year of life and continues to be a leading cause of infant mortality (see later section). However, it strikes most frequently at ages sixty-five and over. At both the youngest and the oldest ages it attacks the black population with nearly double the force as the white (see Table 5-13) and occurs with greater frequency among men than among women. In recent years, the sex differential has tended to narrow at most ages, but the race differential has tended to decrease only at ages under forty-five and to increase at older ages.

Malignant Neoplasms

Death rates from malignant neoplasms (cancer) of all types and at all sites rose more than 10 percent between 1970 and 1980 (see Figure 5-6). Males have a death rate from cancer that is 28 percent higher than that of females (Tables 5-9 and 5-12). Only at ages 20-44 is the rate for females higher than that for males (because of breast cancer). This sex differential becomes very high (80-95 percent higher among males) at ages above sixty-five (Table 5-12). Cancer mortality is much lower among the black/other population than among the white—only 81 percent as high in 1978 (Table 5-13). This race differential has a particular age pattern; the black/other population has moderately higher rates at ages 20-74, but very much lower rates at ages eighty-five and over.

Although cancer is primarily a disease of old age, it is nevertheless a leading cause of death at all ages. Age-specific mortality rates for malignant neoplasms by type (site) are shown in Table 5-11. Neoplasm of the respiratory system, including lung cancer, is the most common form of cancer resulting in death at ages 40-69; thereafter, death from neoplasms of the digestive system are more common. Also, death rates for cancer of the genital organs, which is quite low in comparison with other types, becomes very important at advanced ages.

Between 1970 and 1980 the rate of cancer of each type either increased or remained unchanged. For no important type of cancer was there a substantial decrease in the death rate. Nearly 60 percent of the overall increase in death from malignant neoplasms was due to an increase in rates for neoplasms of the respiratory system. Because of this dramatic increase, rates for 1970 and 1980 are shown separately for age-sex-race groups in Table 5-14. The rates for males are five times as high as rates for females at ages above seventy. This table shows that the rates increased for both sexes and for both races for every age group forty-five and above. Females experienced a doubling in the rate of mortality from lung cancer in this decade. The increase was proportionately greater among black/other males than among white males but greater among white females than among black/other females. This dramatic increase has been attributed to changing smoking habits of women and to duration and intensity of exposure of both sexes to air pollution. Medical technology for detection and treatment of respiratory cancer has been conspicuously unable to halt the rising incidence of this type of disease.

Cancer of the breast occurs rarely in males but is a very important cause of death among females and has increased by 8 percent between 1970 and 1980. It has a comparatively low rate at ages under forty, but rises steadily and swiftly after age forty-five until it attains a very high level after age fifty-five with further increments with each advance in age. It is a cause of death for black/other females only about two-thirds as often as for white females. Table 5-15 shows the 1970 and 1980 rates separately for race group by age. This table reveals some progress in reducing death rates at ages under sixty, but the death rates at ages seventy and over were significantly higher in 1980 than in 1970. This was true both for white and for black/other women.

Tables 5-10, 5-11, 5-12, and 5-13 show that the other leading causes of death by cancer, not specifically discussed above, increased moderately or maintained nearly the same rate, while keeping the same age pattern and the same sex-race differentials in 1978-80 as in 1970. Clearly, the long-sought "breakthrough" in cancer control has not yet arrived, while pollution in the environment, the rising age composition, and the conquest of other diseases are causing cancer to become an increasingly significant cause of death.

Table 5-13. Race Differentials in Mortality, by Age: 1970 and 1978 [ratio of black to white age-cause specific rate]

Cause of death	Age in 1978							Age in 1970						
	Total	1-19 years	20-44 years	45-64 years	65-74 years	75-84 years	85 years and over	Total	1-19 years	20-44 years	45-64 years	65-74 years	65-74 years	85 years and over
All causes	0.90	1.22	2.09	1.64	1.27	1.01	0.60	0.99	1.54	2.50	1.66	1.30	0.91	0.64
Bacillary dysentery/amebiasis	--	--	--	--	--	--	9.00	--	1.00	2.00	4.00	1.00	2.33	7.00
Enteritis/other diarrheal	2.43	0.50	1.00	2.85	1.16	1.46	0.63	2.27	2.06	1.13	1.78	1.27	1.02	0.80
Tuberculosis, all forms	2.73	4.00	12.67	5.51	3.07	2.55	1.83	2.86	4.67	9.23	4.25	3.12	2.30	1.80
Tuberculosis/respiratory	2.88	--	20.67	5.80	3.35	2.28	1.61	3.06	6.00	10.83	4.37	3.41	2.39	1.83
Tuberculosis/other forms	3.00	--	7.00	4.54	2.27	3.48	3.15	2.75	7.00	8.80	3.77	2.18	1.88	1.61
Whooping cough	--	--	--	--	--	--	--	--	--	--	--	--	--	--
Streptococcal sore throat/ scarlet fever	--	--	--	--	--	--	--	--	--	--	--	--	--	--
Meningococcal infections	1.50	1.15	3.50	0.75	1.33	1.00	2.00	2.50	1.50	1.50	4.00	2.50	4.75	--
Septicemia	1.81	1.67	3.90	3.22	2.66	2.18	1.28	2.13	2.13	4.13	3.02	2.50	1.43	1.10
Acute poliomyelitis	--	--	--	--	--	--	--	--	--	--	--	--	--	--
Measles	--	--	0.00	--	--	--	--	--	2.67	--	--	--	--	--
Syphilis and its sequelae	2.00	--	--	17.00	7.50	4.90	5.50	3.50	--	--	8.56	5.58	7.16	6.43
Other infective and parasitic diseases	1.60	1.36	3.45	2.37	1.57	1.42	0.93	1.94	1.73	3.62	2.24	1.91	1.56	0.68
Malignant neoplasms (including lymphatic and hematopoietic tissues)	0.81	0.93	1.41	1.37	1.16	1.03	0.69	0.81	0.78	1.37	1.29	1.11	0.90	0.72
Of buccal cavity and pharynx	1.05	0.00	4.00	1.90	1.11	0.87	0.40	0.89	1.00	2.91	1.40	0.90	0.89	0.59
Of digestive organs and peritoneum	0.86	1.40	1.94	1.65	1.25	1.01	0.69	0.84	0.67	1.86	1.53	1.17	0.89	0.67
Of respiratory system	0.80	1.00	1.60	1.36	0.99	0.94	0.66	0.79	1.66	1.73	1.21	0.93	0.85	0.80
Of breast	0.67	--	1.46	0.99	0.84	0.84	0.63	0.63	--	1.27	0.86	0.75	0.70	0.58
Of genital organs	1.07	0.80	1.63	1.64	1.79	1.62	1.03	1.13	1.00	1.77	1.79	1.80	1.39	1.02
Of urinary organs	0.59	2.25	1.43	0.99	1.01	0.72	0.40	0.60	1.33	1.21	1.04	0.87	0.63	0.49
Of all other and unspecified sites	0.80	0.94	0.96	1.26	1.22	1.03	0.67	0.80	0.88	0.98	1.21	1.17	0.87	0.77
Leukemia	0.60	0.75	1.13	1.02	0.76	0.64	0.41	0.61	0.62	0.97	1.00	0.87	0.51	0.43
Other neoplasms of lymphatic and hematopoietic tissues	0.66	1.22	0.91	1.06	1.00	0.81	0.66	0.65	0.86	0.74	1.08	0.83	0.72	0.60
Benign neoplasms and neoplasms of unspecified nature	0.87	1.00	1.61	1.50	1.19	1.04	0.66	1.04	1.35	1.83	1.56	1.30	0.94	0.66
Diabetes mellitus	1.25	1.75	2.27	2.63	2.07	1.49	0.78	1.25	1.00	2.55	2.88	1.84	1.07	0.70
Avitaminoses/other nutritional deficiencies	1.15	5.00	2.50	2.60	2.55	1.39	1.09	1.33	2.33	3.67	2.30	2.25	1.57	0.80
Anemias	1.64	5.88	10.50	3.08	1.72	1.14	0.59	2.00	7.44	10.76	2.98	1.57	0.97	0.76
Meningitis	2.50	1.68	2.71	3.59	2.26	3.21	0.92	2.86	1.63	3.75	4.17	2.95	2.65	2.47
Major cardiovascular diseases	0.73	1.67	2.35	1.61	1.26	0.95	0.55	0.79	2.09	2.75	1.67	1.30	0.86	0.60
Diseases of heart	0.70	2.06	2.16	1.45	1.15	0.91	0.55	0.73	2.57	2.35	1.43	1.16	0.82	0.59
Active rheumatic fever/ chronic rheumatic disease	0.62	4.67	2.24	1.02	0.59	0.69	0.40	0.71	4.43	1.98	0.86	0.62	0.60	0.47
Hypertensive heart disease	1.83	--	5.83	4.40	3.32	1.99	0.96	2.19	--	14.00	5.75	3.34	1.82	1.09
Hypertensive heart and renal disease	1.13	--	4.50	5.60	2.59	1.59	0.65	1.32	--	12.00	5.22	2.78	1.31	0.70
Ischemic heart disease	0.64	2.00	1.79	1.34	1.08	0.85	0.52	0.67	2.25	1.97	1.32	1.09	0.78	0.57
Acute myocardia infarction	0.52	4.00	1.31	0.94	0.80	0.69	0.49	1.53	6.00	1.40	0.92	0.76	0.63	0.54
Other acute/subacute	1.00	--	2.10	1.73	1.52	1.45	0.78	1.10	--	2.87	2.02	1.49	1.19	0.63
Chronic ischemic	0.74	--	2.71	2.02	1.44	0.97	0.53	0.83	--	3.80	2.28	1.59	0.91	0.59
Angina pectoris	1.00	--	--	1.14	1.63	1.05	1.00	1.00	--	--	0.80	0.91	1.10	0.39
Chronic disease of endocardium/other myocardial insufficiency	0.95	1.80	3.13	1.97	1.30	0.87	0.75	1.06	2.33	3.30	2.00	1.78	1.10	0.77
All other heart disease	1.24	1.95	3.31	2.39	1.87	1.51	0.83	1.61	2.21	4.21	2.96	2.35	1.45	0.94
Hypertension	1.61	--	10.14	5.61	2.73	1.56	0.69	2.11	1.00	13.76	6.38	2.95	1.29	0.88
Cerebrovascular diseases	0.91	1.04	3.08	2.82	1.91	1.12	0.60	1.01	1.59	3.85	3.07	1.92	1.00	0.64
Cerebral hemorrhage	1.23	1.00	4.30	2.77	1.70	1.08	0.61	1.25	1.67	5.12	3.05	1.78	1.01	0.66
Cerebral thrombosis	0.73	1.00	2.57	2.-8	1.66	0.99	0.54	0.79	--	3.74	3.05	1.73	0.88	0.60
Cerebral embolism	0.50	--	3.00	2.20	0.65	0.36	0.42	0.40	--	--	1.31	0.80	0.66	0.46
All other cerebrovascular	0.91	1.16	2.55	2.84	2.05	1.18	0.62	1.04	1.58	3.25	3.12	2.12	1.07	0.65
Arteriosclerosis	0.51	--	1.00	1.80	1.44	0.88	0.47	0.54	--	2.60	2.15	1.68	0.82	0.42
Other diseases of arteries, arterioles, capillaries	0.63	0.60	2.00	1.31	0.87	0.85	0.59	0.66	1.60	2.11	1.42	0.89	0.68	0.63
Acute bronchitis/bronchiolitis	0.75	1.67	2.33	1.40	0.65	0.62	0.37	3.00	2.70	2.00	1.32	0.92	0.56	0.25
Influenza and pneumonia	0.85	1.92	3.59	2.44	1.47	0.93	0.49	1.32	2.36	3.65	2.55	1.70	0.95	0.57
Influenza	0.45	1.00	1.67	1.29	0.91	0.44	0.31	1.06	2.20	1.87	1.86	1.77	1.02	0.83
Pneumonia	0.89	1.90	3.65	2.51	1.51	0.97	0.51	1.33	2.36	3.80	2.61	1.69	0.95	0.55
Bronchitis, emphysema, asthma	0.46	2.38	3.04	0.97	0.51	0.46	0.41	0.52	2.93	3.19	0.88	0.47	0.52	0.48
Chronic and unqualified bronchitis	0.41	2.00	2.20	0.82	0.42	0.39	0.31	2.48	1.63	1.64	0.92	0.40	0.44	0.45
Emphysema	0.36	--	1.67	0.80	0.48	0.41	0.42	0.38	--	2.04	0.65	0.43	0.50	0.49
Asthma	1.63	2.40	4.81	2.63	1.27	1.56	0.74	2.30	4.00	5.22	3.03	1.72	1.15	0.42
Peptic ulcer	0.67	3.00	1.80	1.47	1.04	0.75	0.44	0.70	1.00	2.44	1.23	0.89	0.62	0.38
Appendicitis	1.67	1.50	2.00	3.15	1.46	1.65	0.76	1.29	2.40	2.88	2.15	1.57	1.42	1.24
Hernia/intestinal obstruction	0.92	1.75	3.00	2.24	1.67	1.14	0.49	0.97	1.29	2.86	2.05	1.42	0.97	0.53
Cirrhosis of liver	1.33	2.50	3.83	1.61	0.90	0.68	0.52	1.30	1.57	4.01	1.33	0.75	0.61	0.28
Cholelithiasis, cholecystitis, and cholangitis	0.57	--	1.75	1.56	1.19	0.57	0.45	0.43	--	1.70	1.04	0.60	0.59	0.35
Nephritis and nephrosis	2.23	1.40	5.46	5.16	3.35	2.62	1.44	2.46	2.31	5.57	4.36	3.14	2.08	1.59
Acute nephritis and nephrotic syndrome	1.44	3.00	3.75	2.97	1.90	1.79	1.11	1.83	1.60	4.63	2.80	2.23	1.49	1.73
Chronic and unqualified nephritis and renal sclerosis	2.54	1.00	6.39	5.81	3.88	2.94	1.57	2.58	2.44	5.69	4.63	3.34	2.18	1.57
Infections of kidney	1.07	--	2.00	2.41	2.28	1.39	0.80	1.50	0.50	4.48	3.92	2.79	1.33	0.83
Hyperplasis of prostate	1.00	--	--	5.00	2.85	1.70	0.88	1.00	--	--	3.80	2.46	1.62	0.55
Complication of pregnancy, childbirth, puerperium	5.00	8.00	5.30	--	--	--	--	4.67	5.50	5.58	--	--	--	--
Abortions	--	--	--	--	--	--	--	--	4.00	8.75	--	--	--	--
Other complications	5.00	7.00	5.00	--	--	--	--	5.00	7.00	5.00	--	--	--	--

Table 5-13. Race Differentials in Mortality, by Age: 1970 and 1978—continued

Cause of death	Age in 1978							Age in 1970						
	Total	1-19 years	20-44 years	45-64 years	65-74 years	75-84 years	85 years and over	Total	1-19 years	20-44 years	45-64 years	65-74 years	75-84 years	85 years and over
Congenital anomalies.	1.33	1.05	1.20	1.03	1.04	1.06	0.49	1.21	1.14	1.20	1.14	1.16	0.61	0.76
Certain causes of mortality in early infancy.	2.96	2.00	--	--	--	--	--	2.39	3.00	--	--	--	--	--
Birth injury, difficult labor, other anoxic and hypoxic conditions. . .	2.64	1.50	--	--	--	--	--	2.17	--	--	--	--	--	--
Other causes of mortality in early infancy.	3.36	--	--	--	--	--	--	2.64	--	--	--	--	--	--
Symptoms and ill-defined conditions.	2.36	2.00	3.33	3.27	3.30	3.17	2.09	3.27	3.32	4.66	4.47	4.36	4.08	3.31
All other diseases.	0.99	1.23	3.30	1.85	1.17	0.99	0.70	1.20	1.40	3.36	1.87	1.27	0.90	0.71
Accidents	1.07	0.96	1.22	1.70	1.46	1.03	0.55	1.26	1.24	1.56	1.66	1.35	0.88	0.52
Motor vehicle accidents . . .	0.89	0.66	0.99	1.44	1.16	1.08	0.69	1.07	0.89	1.24	1.45	1.08	0.73	0.77
All other accidents	1.26	1.44	1.60	1.90	1.64	1.01	0.54	1.44	1.73	2.08	1.84	1.52	0.93	0.50
Suicide	0.51	0.52	0.73	0.41	0.34	0.33	0.32	0.45	0.67	0.68	0.34	0.28	0.35	0.45
Homicide.	5.29	3.81	6.13	5.42	4.96	3.41	2.03	8.07	7.76	9.41	7.92	5.96	2.93	3.40
Other external causes	1.88	2.20	2.16	1.80	1.71	2.22	1.15	2.73	3.73	3.74	2.06	1.68	1.19	0.54

Note: -- indicates ratios not computed.

Source: National Center for Health Statistics. Vital Statistics of the United States: Mortality (1978 and 1970--Vol. II, Part A, Table 1). Washington, DC: U.S. Government Printing Office, 1982 and 1974.

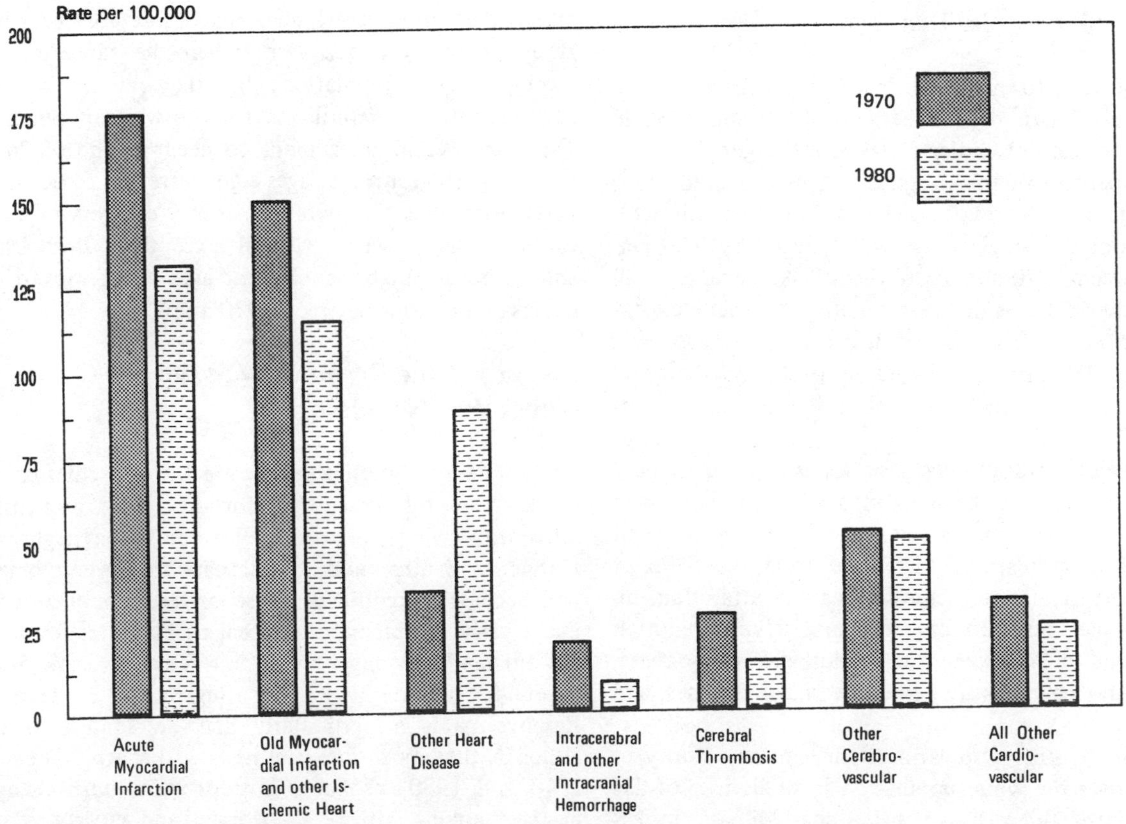

Figure 5-7. Change in Mortality Due to Heart Disease: 1970-1980

Table 5-14. Mortality Rates for Malignant Neoplasms of the Respiratory System, by Sex and Race: 1980 and 1970 [rates per 100,000 population]

Age	White male		White female		Black/other male		Black/other female	
	1980	1970	1980	1970	1980	1970	1980	1970
Total.	73.4	58.3	26.5	13.1	62.5	47.6	17.5	9.5
40-44 years. . .	18.1	22.6	10.8	7.9	35.2	44.5	10.8	13.1
45-49 years. . .	47.6	46.8	23.3	16.7	85.5	82.5	32.7	19.6
50-54 years. . .	99.6	90.2	43.7	27.9	164.0	148.2	49.3	27.6
55-59 years. . .	170.8	162.9	62.9	36.9	258.8	210.6	70.7	35.6
60-64 years. . .	266.7	242.3	87.0	42.1	359.9	256.5	83.1	34.9
65-69 years. . .	375.5	325.2	106.4	44.8	444.6	293.5	84.6	41.5
70-74 years. . .	477.0	371.0	110.1	46.0	470.8	312.8	92.9	57.0
75-79 years. . .	522.3	380.6	105.0	55.9	474.4	293.4	79.5	55.3
80-84 years. . .	505.0	325.4	90.5	58.2	449.4	252.8	91.6	49.8
85 years and over	391.5	221.8	96.8	57.4	334.1	158.8	90.2	45.8

Source: National Center for Health Statistics. Vital Statistics of the United States: Mortality (1980 and 1970--Vol. II, Part A). Washington, DC: U.S. Government Printing Office, 1984 and 1974.

Major Cardiovascular Diseases

In contrast to malignant neoplasms, there was an impressively sharp decline between 1970 and 1980 in deaths from cardiovascular diseases (see Figure 5-7). Almost 73 percent of this progress was due to a reduction in death from acute myocardial infarction (heart attack). Death from this single cause was reduced by 32.9 percent between 1970 and 1980. Significant declines in all of the other diseases in this category were made except for two: death from hypertensive heart disease was higher in 1980 than it had been in 1970, and there was an increase in deaths from "all other forms of heart diseases."

The major cardiovascular diseases as a group are only moderately more fatal among men than among women (Table 5-12). Yet the two sexes suffer from different forms of these diseases. Males die from the form of ischemic heart disease, acute myocardial infarction. Instead females tend to die comparatively more often from several of the lesser forms–rheumatic heart disease, hypertensive heart disease, cerebrovascular diseases, and arteriosclerosis.

The black/other population maintains superiority or equality over the white population in all diseases of this group except three: hypertensive heart disease, hypertension, and cerebral hemorrhage (Table 5-13). However, for most of the cardiovascular diseases, rates for the black/other group are higher than those for the white group at the younger ages (when the rates are low throughout the population), but they fail to rise with advancing age as rapidly as for the white population. This crossover in rates tends to occur at the 65-74 or the 75-84 age groups. At ages eighty-five and over, blacks have lower rates than whites of every category of major cardiovascular disease without exception. Both black and white populations of most ages have enjoyed significant reductions between 1970 and 1980.

Diseases of the Respiratory System (Other than Neoplasms)

Pneumonia and emphysema are the two chief causes of death in this category. Mortality from bronchitis, influenza, and asthma is so low as to be negligible. (Influenza deaths tend to fluctuate from year to year and become a significant cause of death only in infrequent years of epidemic outbreaks.) The rates for males are outstandingly higher than for females (Table 5-12) except for asthma, which has a higher rate for females. Emphysema is a particularly male-dominated disease, although the sex differential narrowed sharply between 1970 and 1980, probably in connection with changes in the smoking history of women and environmental changes. The black/other population tended to have higher rates than the white for most of these diseases

Table 5-15. Mortality Rates among Females for Malignant Neoplasms of the Breast, by Race: 1970 and 1980 [rates per 100,000 population]

Age	White females		Black/other females	
	1980	1970	1980	1970
Total.	32.3	29.9	20.5	18.3
40-44 years. . . .	22.8	26.0	29.8	29.3
45-49 years. . . .	37.8	45.2	38.2	40.7
50-54 years. . . .	57.6	61.5	58.2	59.0
55-59 years. . . .	75.9	77.9	71.9	59.8
60-64 years. . . .	87.4	80.8	75.5	64.3
65-59 years. . . .	99.8	92.2	73.3	71.1
70-74 years. . . .	108.5	100.3	82.9	75.9
75-59 years. . . .	119.9	124.2	99.2	95.5
80-84 years. . . .	141.2	138.4	114.8	99.5
85 years and over.	171.7	161.9	139.9	103.0

Source: National Center for Health Statistics. Vital Statistics of the United States: Mortality (1980 and 1970--Vol. II, Part A). Washington, DC: U.S. Government Printing Office, 1984 and 1974.

(especially pneumonia) in 1970, but by the end of the decade their rates had fallen below those for whites except for one minor case: asthma. At the younger ages, the rates for blacks tend to be higher than for whites, but at ages seventy-five and over the black/other group enjoys equality or advantages for every disease except asthma (and influenza when there is an epidemic). At these advanced ages the surviving black population may have a less negative history of smoking than the white population, perhaps because of selective survival.

Causes Related to Pregnancy and Birth

Childbirth now presents very little risk to mothers but still poses dangers to infants. Most of these risks have been reduced greatly since 1970. Complications of pregnancy, birth injury, and other causes of mortality during early infancy were all reduced by 50 percent or more during this time. Deaths from congenital anomalies were reduced by 29 percent. Male infants are much more subject to death from this group of causes than female infants, and black/other infants have significantly higher rates than white infants. A later section on infant mortality deals with this group of causes in more detail.

Other Diseases and Disorders

Among the leading causes of death from disease not discussed previously are diabetes mellitus, cirrhosis of the liver, and nephritis.[6] All experienced significant reductions between 1970 and 1980. Diabetes affects women considerably more than men (Table 5-12) and blacks/others considerably more than whites (Table 5-13).

External Causes of Death (Nondisease)

A very significant proportion of deaths (8 percent) result from one of four external causes: accidents, suicide, homicide, or other nondisease causes. Accident ranks fourth, suicide ranks tenth, and homicide ranks eleventh among the fifteen leading causes of death (see Table 5-10). Because of incomplete and possibly biased reporting, these external causes may be underreported or misreported more than causes based primarily on a physician's diagnosis.

Accidents

About one-half of accidental deaths are by motor vehicles, and one-half from all other forms of accident. Between 1970 and 1980 significant reductions in deaths from all categories of accidents were made. Reduction in motor vehicle deaths has been attributed to lowering the legal speed limits (imposed as an energy conservation measure) and to stricter enforcement in many parts of the country of driving-under-the-influence laws. Deaths involving motor vehicles tend to be about the same at all ages, but deaths from other accidental causes tend to be highest during infancy and at ages above seventy-five. Males are more than twice as "accident-prone" as females (Table 5-12). The black/other population has a slightly lower death rate from automobile accidents than whites, but a 26 percent higher death rate from other accidents.

Table 5-16A provides data on accidents for motor vehicles and all other causes combined by age, race, and sex for 1970 and 1980. Motor vehicle accidents take many more male than female lives, and they kill black males at a higher rate than white males, except at the very oldest ages. There was a uniform decline in motor accidents for all ages, both sexes, and both races between 1970 and 1980. Table 5-16B provides a detailed age classification, by sex and race, for each of several major categories of accidents for 1980. Accidents from falls cause death in swiftly rising frequency after age seventy. Death from fire and flames among the black population is nearly triple that for whites, and for both groups becomes an important cause of death after age seventy-five. Accidental drowning is a cause of death associated with youth and early adulthood—much more frequent in males than in females and more common among the black male than among the white male population. Suffocation from inhaling or ingesting food or other objects

Table 5-16A. Death Rates for Accidental Causes–Motor Vehicles and Other Causes Combined, by Age, Sex, and Race: 1970 and 1980 [rates per 100,000 population]

Age	Death rates for accidental causes 1980							
	Motor vehicles				All other accidents			
	White male	White female	Other male	Other female	White male	White female	Other male	Other female
Less than 1. . .	7.0	7.1	8.8	4.8	23.9	18.2	53.4	42.8
1-4.	9.5	7.7	13.6	9.9	18.6	11.4	27.8	19.7
5-9.	8.7	5.7	12.7	6.6	7.7	4.0	15.9	7.9
10-14.	10.9	5.7	8.2	4.9	10.0	3.1	14.4	5.6
15-19.	69.1	25.6	28.9	8.4	24.6	4.8	24.9	5.4
20-24.	78.5	20.5	49.7	10.7	31.3	5.2	36.3	7.0
25-29.	53.1	13.7	46.6	12.7	29.9	5.0	39.2	7.8
30-34.	39.5	10.6	41.1	10.9	24.3	5.0	44.0	8.4
35-39.	31.8	10.3	39.2	8.4	23.5	4.8	45.2	10.1
40-44.	29.3	10.8	38.3	11.2	25.3	6.3	47.8	12.5
45-49.	27.8	10.0	34.5	9.2	26.5	7.8	58.9	13.1
50-54.	24.9	10.4	40.6	10.2	30.2	9.1	69.3	16.0
55-59.	24.4	10.8	40.0	10.1	33.1	10.1	69.0	21.1
60-64.	23.3	10.2	37.2	10.7	36.7	14.3	80.5	27.6
65-69.	23.7	11.7	42.8	8.5	45.2	18.8	89.0	34.4
70-74.	28.7	15.6	38.9	9.5	60.0	29.1	93.3	63.1
75-79.	40.3	19.0	53.0	11.0	91.1	54.4	147.4	95.8
80-84.	49.6	19.0	45.9	16.2	154.2	102.5	207.4	136.7
85 and over. . .	57.3	15.3	42.8	14.3	321.9	243.0	311.0	208.2

Age	Death rates for accidental causes 1970							
	Motor vehicles				All other accidents			
	White male	White female	Other male	Other female	White male	White female	Other male	Other female
Less than 1. . .	9.1	10.2	10.8	11.3	48.1	40.6	131.6	103.5
1-4.	12.2	9.6	17.0	12.3	21.6	13.4	36.1	28.8
5-9.	12.6	7.1	19.2	11.9	11.2	5.2	17.8	10.9
10-14.	12.6	6.6	12.3	6.4	15.1	4.2	23.9	7.0
15-19.	67.1	24.4	45.4	12.4	31.7	5.0	52.4	10.0
20-24.	84.9	20.7	80.8	18.0	36.1	5.6	72.0	11.2
25-29.	53.4	13.1	70.4	14.8	30.8	5.5	63.6	14.0
30-34.	39.5	12.2	64.0	14.5	31.0	6.3	68.9	13.9
35-39.	36.1	12.5	54.5	16.1	32.5	6.8	74.7	17.3
40-44.	34.4	12.1	60.9	17.1	34.6	9.0	79.1	15.1
45-49.	34.9	13.4	60.8	15.6	37.0	10.7	78.3	20.2
50-54.	34.3	15.2	60.3	17.7	41.9	14.0	95.5	19.8
55-59.	38.3	15.5	60.5	16.2	48.3	14.9	87.9	19.7
60-64.	39.7	16.8	59.3	17.3	54.4	19.2	97.2	30.1
65-69.	42.5	19.8	56.3	18.0	65.6	25.9	93.6	44.1
70-74.	51.1	24.8	59.3	16.1	82.7	41.6	118.1	65.7
75-59.	66.2	28.1	55.3	14.4	124.6	83.3	138.2	97.3
80-84.	74.6	28.2	58.6	14.8	203.1	172.7	164.2	136.6
85 and over. . .	65.5	18.1	41.5	16.5	383.4	370.5	189.5	186.9

Source: National Center for Health Statistics. Vital Statistics of the United States: Mortality (1980 and 1970--Vol. II, Part A). Washington, DC: U.S. Government Printing Office, 1984 and 1974.

Table 5-16B. Death Rates for Selected Accidental Causes, by Type of Accident, Sex, Race, and Age: 1980 [rates per 100,000 population]

Age	Accidental poisoning				Accidental falls				Accidents caused by fire and flames			
	White male	White female	Other male	Other female	White male	White female	Other male	Other female	White male	White female	Other male	Other female
Under 1 year. . .	0.6	0.5	0.9	1.0	1.1	0.9	3.1	1.3	2.6	4.0	10.6	10.5
1-4	0.6	0.4	1.5	1.1	0.7	0.7	2.2	1.1	4.6	2.9	13.9	11.3
5-9	0.2	0.1	0.1	0.2	0.3	0.3	0.4	0.3	1.1	1.3	5.4	4.1
10-14	0.2	0.1	0.2	0.3	0.4	0.1	0.2	0.1	0.9	0.8	1.3	1.7
15-19	2.0	0.9	1.3	1.1	1.9	0.2	0.9	0.2	1.1	0.8	1.3	1.2
20-24	3.8	1.4	3.7	1.3	2.6	0.3	2.4	0.2	2.2	0.9	2.6	1.5
25-29	5.3	1.3	6.0	2.5	2.8	0.3	3.0	0.5	2.2	0.7	3.1	1.5
30-34	4.3	1.3	6.1	2.1	2.0	0.3	4.8	0.4	1.8	0.8	4.2	1.6
35-39	2.9	1.2	5.6	1.9	2.4	0.6	6.4	1.2	2.0	0.6	4.7	2.4
40-44	3.2	1.4	5.3	2.5	3.3	0.9	9.1	2.0	2.1	1.0	8.0	2.0
45-49	2.4	1.4	5.4	1.3	4.1	1.3	12.0	2.4	2.6	1.3	7.8	2.0
50-54	2.7	1.8	5.0	1.3	5.6	1.7	14.4	2.7	3.1	1.3	11.3	3.4
55-59	2.5	1.6	3.6	1.5	7.5	2.5	11.2	2.7	3.1	1.4	11.0	5.4
60-64	1.9	1.5	3.8	2.3	9.2	4.3	17.2	4.1	4.1	2.0	12.9	3.2
65-69	2.0	1.4	4.7	1.6	12.6	5.8	16.3	4.6	5.1	2.7	18.2	7.3
70-74	2.7	1.5	2.2	3.5	21.6	11.4	19.6	11.1	5.6	3.4	13.4	10.6
75-79	2.1	2.0	6.1	4.2	41.1	27.8	28.5	20.5	7.9	4.7	30.1	13.7
80-84	4.3	2.7	10.3	2.8	77.6	63.8	58.5	27.5	12.0	6.1	37.8	26.8
85 and above. . .	6.1	3.5	14.8	4.2	208.8	179.9	97.1	68.3	16.4	7.2	52.7	32.0

Age	Accidental drowning and submersion				Inhalation and ingestion of food or other object causing obstruction of respiratory tract or suffocation				Water transport accidents			
	White male	White female	Other male	Other female	White male	White female	Other male	Other female	White male	White female	Other male	Other female
Under 1 year. . .	3.2	1.8	5.0	1.0	7.4	5.0	15.0	13.6	0.1	*	*	0.3
1-4	7.5	4.1	4.5	2.0	1.1	0.8	1.6	1.6	0.2	0.1	0.2	*
5-9	3.0	0.8	7.5	1.6	0.1	0.2	0.3	0.3	0.2	0.1	0.3	0.1
10-14	2.5	0.6	8.0	2.2	0.2	0.1	0.3	0.3	0.3	0.1	0.7	0.1
15-19	7.8	0.9	12.2	1.2	0.3	0.1	0.5	0.2	1.4	0.2	1.3	0.1
20-24	7.0	0.6	13.5	1.1	0.5	0.2	0.6	0.5	2.1	0.3	1.7	0.4
25-29	4.9	0.6	10.1	0.7	0.5	0.2	0.5	0.1	1.8	0.2	1.2	0.3
30-34	2.9	0.6	9.6	1.1	0.6	0.2	1.2	0.6	1.5	0.1	2.9	0.2
35-39	2.5	0.4	6.5	1.2	0.9	0.3	1.9	0.9	1.3	0.1	1.1	0.1
40-44	2.3	0.5	5.3	0.6	0.9	0.6	1.1	1.1	1.4	0.1	2.4	0.1
45-49	2.2	0.5	5.2	0.9	1.4	0.8	3.2	1.2	1.4	0.1	2.7	0.1
50-54	2.0	0.5	5.3	0.4	1.7	0.8	2.5	1.5	1.1	0.2	2.2	*
55-59	2.6	0.4	4.7	0.8	2.2	1.0	5.6	2.4	1.0	0.1	2.4	*
60-64	1.8	0.6	5.6	0.2	2.9	1.4	4.7	3.0	1.0	0.0	2.5	*
65-69	2.4	0.8	4.2	1.0	4.7	2.4	8.0	2.0	1.0	*	1.0	*
70-74	2.7	0.7	4.4	1.4	5.2	2.8	7.6	6.2	0.6	0.1	2.2	0.3
75-79	2.5	0.7	6.7	0.8	8.2	4.7	12.8	4.9	0.7	0.0	0.6	*
80-84	4.5	1.1	4.6	3.5	14.2	7.6	16.0	4.2	0.3	0.1	1.1	*
85 and over . . .	4.5	1.4	6.6	2.5	24.8	15.6	26.3	15.2	0.2	0.1	*	*

Table 5-16B. Death Rates for Selected Accidental Causes, by Type of Accident, Sex, Race, and Age: 1980 [rates per 100,000 population]–continued

Age	Air and space transport accidents				Misadventures during medical care, abnormal reactions, and late complications				Accidents caused by firearms (non-handgun)			
	White male	White female	Other male	Other female	White male	White female	Other male	Other female	White male	White female	Other male	Other female
Under 1 year. . .	0.1	*	*	0.3	0.7	0.7	2.2	1.3	0.1	0.1	*	*
1-4	0.1	0.1	*	*	0.2	0.2	0.2	0.1	0.2	0.2	0.6	0.3
5-9	0.1	0.1	0.1	*	0.1	0.1	0.1	0.1	0.5	0.1	0.9	0.3
10-14	0.2	0.1	0.1	0.3	0.1	0.1	0.2	0.1	1.7	0.2	1.1	0.3
15-19	0.5	0.2	0.1	0.1	0.1	0.1	0.1	*	2.7	0.3	2.1	0.6
20-24	1.4	0.4	0.4	0.1	0.1	0.1	0.2	0.2	2.2	0.3	3.0	0.5
25-29	2.4	0.4	0.6	0.3	0.1	0.2	0.4	0.5	1.7	0.3	3.0	0.4
30-34	2.7	0.4	0.7	0.1	0.1	0.3	0.3	0.6	1.3	0.2	2.2	0.4
35-39	2.5	0.3	0.4	*	0.2	0.3	0.8	0.9	0.9	0.2	2.2	0.2
40-44	2.7	0.4	0.4	*	0.4	0.3	0.4	1.1	1.2	0.1	1.1	0.4
45-49	2.2	0.5	0.2	*	0.5	0.4	0.8	0.8	1.1	0.2	1.9	0.1
50-54	1.9	0.3	0.2	*	0.9	0.7	2.7	0.5	0.5	0.1	1.2	0.1
55-59	1.4	0.2	0.2	0.2	1.6	0.9	2.5	1.5	0.9	0.1	0.4	*
60-64	0.6	0.1	*	*	2.5	1.4	4.5	3.6	0.6	0.1	1.1	0.5
65-69	0.5	0.1	*	*	3.4	2.0	6.2	4.0	0.7	0.1	1.8	*
70-74	0.1	0.1	*	*	5.9	3.5	7.3	4.6	0.7	*	1.1	*
75-79	0.1	0.0	*	*	7.1	5.6	11.2	5.7	1.0	0.0	1.7	*
80-84	*	0.1	*	*	11.8	7.2	8.0	9.2	0.9	0.1	2.3	*
85 and above. . .	*	0.1	*	*	19.2	12.6	32.9	15.2	0.6	*	*	*

Note: * indicates zero cases reported.

Source: National Center for Health Statistics. Vital Statistics of the United States: Mortality (1980--Vol. II, Part A). Washington, DC: U.S. Government Printing Office, 1984.

is a hazard of infancy and old age. At the older ages, it is far more common among males than among females, and at all ages tends to be more common among the black than among the white population. Transport accidents, both water and space, are negligible at all ages. Deaths from firearm accidents are rare (excluding homicide and illegal use) and occur primarily to black males. Adverse reactions to medication and medical treatment tends to be an accidental cause of death primarily among the very elderly.

Suicide

Between 1970 and 1980 the rate of death from suicide increased by 7.8 percent. Suicide before age fifteen is rare. The rate is roughly similar for all ages above fifteen, rising slightly after age sixty-five. Men are three times as likely as women to commit suicide, and this differential increases with age. At age eighty-five and over the suicide rate among men is nearly ten times that of women (Table 5-12). Suicide rates among the white population are more than twice that among the black/other, and this race differential also increases with age. At ages eighty-five and over the black/other group commits suicide with only one-third the frequency of the white group.

Homicide

Homicide death rates also increased significantly between 1970 and 1980. Homicide victims are concentrated between the ages of fifteen and fifty-five, although the rate is substantial at all ages, even among infants. Men are nearly four times more likely to be victims than are women, but the racial differential is even greater: 5 to 1 between black/other and white.

Infant Mortality Rate

The infant mortality rate (see "definitions") has declined remarkably in recent years to a low level previously thought to be almost medically impossible to attain. By 1983, of each 1,000 live-born babies, only eleven die during their first year of life. This is about one-half the rate of only fifteen years earlier and less than one-eighth the rate of 1915-19. Table 5-17 and Figure 5-8 report the impressive conquest of infant deaths made in this century, which continues to the present.

Despite this progress, during the first year of life infants incur a risk of death greater than the combined risk of the next forty-five years of life. (Causes for these deaths are discussed below.) These risks are 25 percent greater for male than for female infants. Black/other infants suffer a grave disadvantage; their rate is 75 percent higher than that of white infants. These differentials have persisted at approximately the same magnitudes since 1900, when data first became available. Thus, there has been an impressive convergence of absolute differences in mortality between the sexes and the black/white races, but a maintenance of substantial and inflexible relative differentials.

Age and Infant Mortality

Infant mortality is far from uniform throughout the first year of life. It is greatest during the twenty-four hours following birth and declines daily for the first week, weekly for the first month, and monthly for the first year. Table 5-18 reports rates by day, week, and month of age for 1980. The pattern of sex differentials remains almost unchanged throughout the first year, but the race differential is highest at the first day and converges toward the rate for whites as time passes.

Because more than two-thirds of infant mortality occurs during the first month of life, and because medical and health experts have noted differentials in causes of death between the first month and the following eleven months, it has become customary to divide the infant mortality rate into two periods, the neonatal (first twenty-eight days) and the post-neonatal (remainder of the first year) periods (see "definitions"). Table 5-19 analyzes trends in these two classes of rates for the past several years, separately for white and nonwhite births. For whites and males, the ratio of neonatal to post-neonatal are higher than for black/other and females. This is interpreted to imply that physiological factors are relatively more important in the first pair, and that environmental factors are relatively more important in the second pair. For all groups the ratio of neonatal to post-neonatal rates have been declining. Improved prenatal care, delivery of babies under medical supervision, and new medical procedures for caring for problem deliveries have reduced the mortality during the first month more rapidly than the fall in infant mortality for the other eleven months.

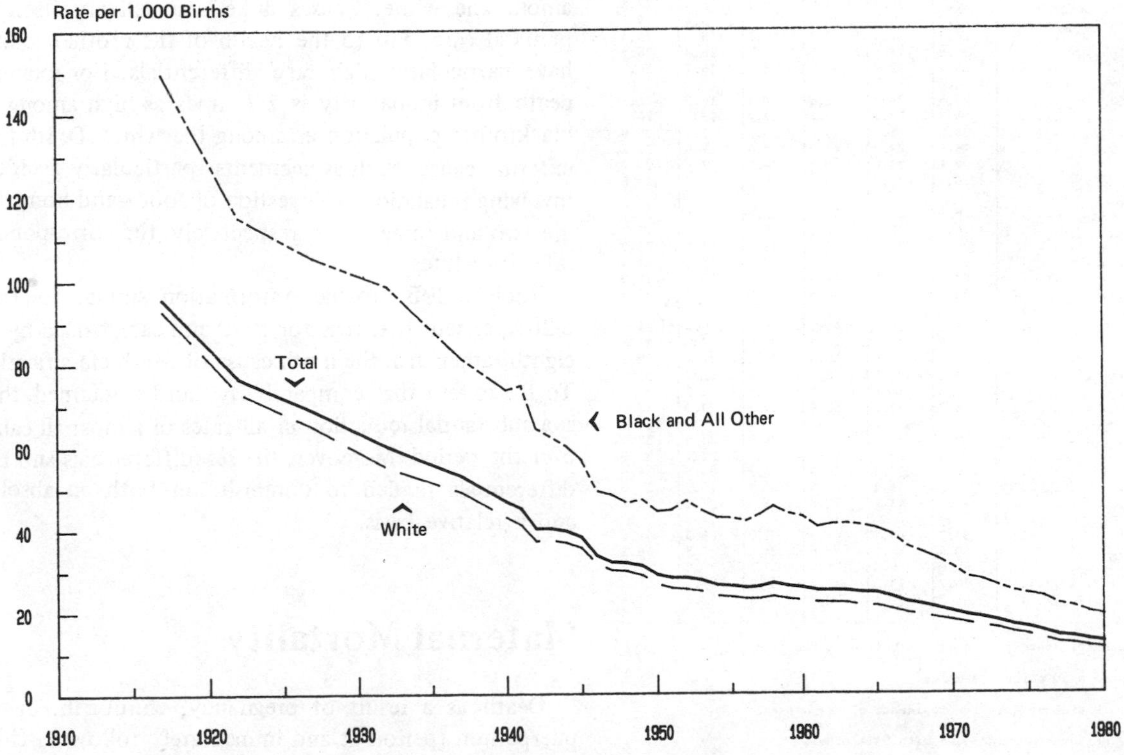

Figure 5-8. Decline in Infant Mortality: 1915-1980

Causes of Infant Deaths

Infants have a unique cause-of-death pattern. They die from several causes from which adults are not at risk. Table 5-20A reports infant mortality rates for selected causes of death in 1980, by sex and race. This table permits the infant mortality rate to be broken down into its constituent causes, allowing a cause-specific analysis by sex and race over time. The largest single cause of infant death is a category of ailments entitled "certain causes of mortality in early infancy." This category accounts for about one-half of all infant deaths. The chief ailments within it are immaturity, respiratory distress syndrome, asphyxia of newborn, hyaline membrane disease, condition of the placenta, and birth injuries. Causes pertaining to the health or condition of the mother or to difficulties of labor or delivery are minor causes of infant death. Congenital anomalies are the second largest category of causes of death. Among these are anomalies of heart, circulatory system, and respiratory system, and anacephalus. Causes of death that pertain to the environment into which the infant is born and the care it receives in the home tend to be of secondary importance in the list of causes. Among the leading environment-linked causes are pneumonia, accidents, septicemia, diarrheal diseases, and meningitis.

For only three causes in the list do female infants have significantly higher rates than males: whooping cough, anacephalus, and spina bifida. Males have higher death rates in all other categories.

The higher infant mortality rates of black/other infants is quite unequally distributed by cause. Black/other babies actually have *lower* death rates than white infants from congenital anomalies, although they do tend to have higher rates for particular types of anomalies (those of the circulatory and digestive systems). In contrast, death from the special group of early infancy causes of death is nearly double among the black/other than among the white. Causes linked to delivery itself, to prenatal care, and to the health of the mother tend to have particularly high race differentials. For example, death from immaturity is 2.7 times as high among the black/other population as among the white. Death from external causes such as accidents—particularly accidents involving inhalation or ingestion of food—and homicides are two and three times, respectively, the corresponding rates for whites.

Table 5-20B provides information similar to Table 5-20A, except that it is for 1970 and categorized by the eighth rather than the ninth cause-of-death classification. To the extent that comparability can be assumed, there is a substantial reduction in all rates of almost all causes over the period. Moreover, the sex differentials and race differentials tended to diminish, on both an absolute and a relative basis.

Table 5-17. Infant and Neonatal Mortality Rates, by Race: Birth Registration States or United States, 1915-1980 [rate per 1,000 births]

Year	Infant mortality rate			Neonatal mortality rate		
	Total	White	All other	Total	White	All other
1980[a]	12.6	11.0	19.1	8.5	7.5	12.5
1979[a]	13.1	11.4	19.8	8.9	7.9	12.9
1978[a]	13.8	12.0	21.1	9.5	8.4	14.0
1977[a]	14.1	12.3	21.7	9.9	8.7	14.7
1976[a]	15.2	13.3	23.5	10.9	9.7	16.3
1975[a]	16.1	14.2	24.2	11.6	10.4	16.8
1974[a]	16.7	14.8	24.9	12.3	11.1	17.2
1973[a]	17.7	15.8	26.2	13.0	11.8	17.9
1972[a, b]	18.5	16.4	27.7	13.6	12.4	19.2
1971[a]	19.1	17.1	28.5	14.2	13.0	19.6
1970[a]	20.0	17.8	30.9	15.1	13.8	21.4
1969	20.9	18.4	32.9	15.6	14.2	22.5
1968	21.8	19.2	34.5	16.1	14.7	23.0
1967	22.4	19.7	35.9	16.5	15.0	23.8
1966	23.7	20.6	38.8	17.2	15.6	24.8
1965	24.7	21.5	40.3	17.7	16.1	25.4
1964	24.8	21.6	41.1	17.9	16.2	26.5
1963[c]	25.2	22.2	41.5	18.2	16.7	26.1
1962[c]	25.3	22.3	41.4	18.3	16.9	26.1
1961	25.3	22.4	40.7	18.4	16.9	26.2
1960	26.0	22.9	43.2	18.7	17.2	26.9
1959	26.4	23.2	44.0	19.0	17.5	27.7
1958	27.1	23.8	45.7	19.5	17.8	29.0
1957	26.3	23.3	43.7	19.1	17.5	27.8
1956	26.0	23.2	42.1	18.9	17.5	27.0
1955	26.4	23.6	42.8	19.1	17.7	27.2
1954	26.6	23.9	42.9	19.1	17.8	27.0
1953	27.8	25.0	44.7	19.6	18.3	27.4
1952	28.4	25.5	47.0	19.8	18.5	28.0
1951	28.4	25.8	44.8	20.0	18.9	27.3
1950	29.2	26.8	44.5	20.5	19.4	27.5
1949	31.3	28.9	47.3	21.4	20.3	28.6
1948	32.0	29.9	46.5	22.2	21.2	29.1
1947	32.2	30.1	48.5	22.8	21.7	31.0
1946	33.8	31.8	49.5	24.0	23.1	31.5
1945	38.3	35.6	57.0	24.3	23.3	32.0
1944	39.8	36.9	60.3	24.7	23.6	32.5
1943	40.4	37.5	62.5	24.7	23.7	32.9
1942	40.4	37.3	64.6	25.7	24.5	34.6
1941	45.3	41.2	74.8	27.7	26.1	39.0
1940	47.0	43.2	73.8	28.8	27.2	39.7
1935-39	53.2	49.2	81.3	31.0	29.5	41.4
1930-34[d]	60.4	55.2	98.6	34.4	32.5	48.2
1925-29	69.0	65.0	105.4	37.2	36.0	47.9
1920-24	76.7	73.3	115.3	39.7	38.7	51.1
1915-19	95.7	92.8	149.7	43.4	42.3	58.1

[a]Excludes deaths of nonresidents of the United States.

[b]Deaths based on a 50 percent sample.

[c]Figures by race exclude data for residents of New Jersey.

[d]For 1932-34, Mexicans are included with "All other."

Source: National Center for Health Statistics. Vital Statistics of the United States: Mortality (1980--Vol. II, Part A). Washington, DC: U.S. Government Printing Office, 1984.

Maternal Mortality

Death as a result of pregnancy, childbirth, or the puerperium (period at and immediately following childbirth) are now so low in the United States (as in other developed nations) as to present only minor risks, espe-

Table 5-18. Infant Mortality Rates, by Age, Race, and Sex: United States, 1980 [rates per 100,000 live births in specified group]

Age	All races			White			All other					
							Total			Black		
	Both sexes	Male	Female	Both sexes	Male	Female	Both sexes	Male	Female	Both sexes	Male	Female
Under 1 year	1,260.3	1,392.8	1,120.8	1,099.8	1,227.4	964.8	1,912.5	2,073.0	1,746.8	2,137.5	2,326.8	1,942.6
Under 28 days.	847.0	931.2	759.6	748.1	829.1	662.4	1,251.8	1,351.0	1,149.4	1,408.2	1,532.3	1,280.5
Under 1 day.	463.2	505.8	418.3	400.1	437.9	360.2	719.2	784.9	651.5	814.9	896.2	731.3
Under 1 hour	129.3	134.1	124.2	116.9	121.3	112.3	179.5	187.0	171.8	198.1	205.7	190.3
1-23 hours	333.9	371.6	294.2	283.2	316.6	247.9	539.7	597.8	479.7	616.8	690.6	541.0
1 day.	79.9	89.3	70.0	70.9	80.3	60.9	116.6	126.6	106.3	129.6	142.8	116.0
2 days	65.0	75.4	55.3	60.0	70.0	49.3	88.4	97.4	79.2	101.8	112.7	90.5
3 days	36.4	42.7	29.8	33.4	39.7	26.8	48.6	54.9	42.2	53.9	61.2	46.5
4 days	24.2	25.8	22.5	22.5	24.3	20.7	31.0	32.0	29.9	32.9	34.4	31.3
5 days	20.7	22.0	19.3	18.9	20.9	16.8	27.6	26.2	29.1	30.7	29.8	31.7
6 days	15.6	16.9	14.6	14.5	15.3	13.7	20.9	23.4	18.2	23.1	25.7	20.3
7-13 days.	73.3	79.2	67.1	67.8	74.6	60.7	95.6	98.2	92.9	107.2	110.4	103.9
14-20 days	40.4	43.9	36.8	36.5	40.3	32.5	56.5	59.0	53.8	61.6	64.5	58.5
21-27 days	28.2	30.3	25.9	23.4	25.9	20.8	47.4	48.3	46.4	52.6	54.5	50.6
28 days-1 month.	100.7	113.0	87.9	83.9	97.2	69.8	100.3	177.9	160.4	189.6	197.0	182.0
2 months	81.4	90.5	71.9	68.5	77.8	58.8	133.8	142.6	124.8	148.4	158.2	138.3
3 months	62.4	72.8	51.4	53.9	63.8	43.4	96.8	109.8	83.5	105.0	120.1	91.5
4 months	43.9	49.4	38.1	37.4	42.9	31.4	70.4	75.9	64.7	77.2	82.6	71.6
5 months	29.5	33.4	25.3	24.5	27.0	21.9	49.5	59.6	39.0	54.3	65.9	42.3
6 months	24.6	26.6	22.6	21.8	23.4	20.1	36.3	40.0	32.5	39.7	43.1	36.1
7 months	19.2	20.6	17.7	16.3	16.9	15.7	30.8	35.6	25.9	34.9	41.5	28.3
8 months	16.1	17.6	14.5	14.1	15.3	12.9	24.0	27.0	20.8	25.9	28.4	23.4
9 months	13.0	13.9	12.0	12.1	12.5	11.7	16.5	19.6	13.4	17.3	20.1	14.5
10 months.	11.0	12.4	9.5	9.5	11.1	7.7	17.1	17.4	16.8	18.5	19.7	17.2
11 months.	11.0	11.8	10.3	9.7	10.4	8.9	16.1	16.6	15.7	17.5	18.1	16.9

Source: National Center for Health Statistics. Vital Statistics of the United States: Mortality (1980--Vol. II, Part A). Washington, DC: U.S. Government Printing Office, 1984.

cially before age thirty-five. Table 5-21 presents maternal mortality rates, by race, for the United States, 1915-1980. In 1915-1919, the risk to a white woman bearing a child was 105 times as great as in 1980. For a black/other woman, the risk was 63 times as great. Despite these wonderful accomplishments in lifesaving, attributable to both prenatal self-care and medical care (especially at delivery and after), there still remains a major differential between the races. Among black/other women, the maternal mortality rate in 1980 was 3.0 times that for white women. Although the absolute difference in rates has declined over the years, the relative differential has increased.

Following is the maternal mortality rate by age and race:

Age	Total	White	Black/other	Ratio black/other to white
Total.	9.2	6.7	19.8	3.0
Under 20 years	7.8	5.9	11.8	2.0
20-24 years.	5.8	4.3	11.9	2.8
25-29 years.	7.7	5.5	19.4	3.5
30-34 years.	13.6	9.4	35.1	3.7
35-39 years.	31.3	21.2	72.3	3.4
40-44 years.	60.6	51.0	91.9	1.8

Table 5-19A. Trends in Neonatal and Post-Neonatal Infant Mortality Rates by Year [rate per 1,000 Births]

Year	Infant mortality rate	Neonatal mortality rate	Post-neonatal mortality rate
1983.	10.9	7.3	3.6
1982.	11.3	7.6	3.7
1981.	11.8	7.9	3.9
1980.	12.6	8.5	4.1
1979.	13.1	8.9	4.2
1978.	13.8	9.5	4.3
1977.	14.1	9.9	4.2
1976.	15.2	10.9	4.3
1975.	16.1	11.6	4.5
1974.	16.7	12.3	4.4
1973.	17.7	13.0	4.7
1972.	18.5	13.6	4.9
1971.	19.1	14.2	4.9
1970.	20.0	15.1	4.9
1965.	24.7	17.7	7.0
1960.	26.0	18.7	7.3
1955.	26.4	19.1	7.3
1950.	29.2	20.5	8.7
1940.	47.0	28.8	18.2

Source: National Center for Health Statistics. Vital Statistics of the United States: Mortality (1978--Vol. II, Part A, Table 2-1); and Monthly Vital Statistics Report (Vol. 31, no. 12, Table 7; Vol. 32, no. 4, Table 12). Washington, DC: U.S. Government Printing Office, 1982; 1983 and 1984.

Table 5-19B. Trends in Neonatal and Post-Neonatal Infant Mortality, by Race and Sex: United States, 1960-1980 [rate per 1,000 births]

Year	White				Nonwhite			
	Neonatal		Post-neonatal		Neonatal		Post-neonatal	
	Male	Female	Male	Female	Male	Female	Male	Female
1980.	8.3	6.6	4.0	3.0	13.5	11.5	7.2	6.0
1979.	8.8	6.9	4.0	3.0	13.9	11.8	7.6	6.3
1978.	9.3	7.4	4.0	3.2	15.6	12.1	7.7	6.4
1977.	9.8	7.6	4.1	3.1	16.2	13.2	7.8	6.3
1976.	10.7	8.5	4.1	3.2	17.6	14.7	8.1	6.2
1975.	11.7	9.0	4.2	3.3	18.5	15.4	8.2	6.9
1970.	15.5	11.9	4.4	3.5	23.8	18.9	10.7	8.6
1960.	19.7	14.7	8.1	6.5	30.0	23.6	17.8	14.8

Note: Nonwhite rates computed for 1960-79 by first computing total live births, then subtracting white live births, then adding nonwhite deaths and computing rates.

Source: National Center for Health Statistics. Vital Statistics of the United States: Mortality (1978, 1977, 1976, 1975, 1970, and 1960--Vol. II, Part A); and Monthly Vital Statistics Report. Washington, DC: U.S. Government Printing Office, 1982, 1981, 1980, 1979, 1974, and 1963; 1984 and 1983.

Table 5-20A. Infant Mortality Rates for Selected Causes, by Race and Sex: 1980 [rate per 100,000 births]

Cause of death	Both sexes	Sex: Male	Sex: Female	Color: White	Color: Black/other	Ratio male to female	Ratio black/other to white
All causes	1,260.3	1,390.0	1,120.0	1,099.8	1,912.5	1.24	1.74
Certain intestinal infections	3.1	3.4	2.8	2.2	6.9	1.21	3.14
Whooping cough	0.3	0.2	0.4	0.2	0.4	0.50	2.00
Meningococcal infection	2.1	2.4	1.9	2.1	2.4	1.26	1.14
Septicemia	6.7	8.1	5.2	5.1	13.3	1.56	2.61
Viral diseases	3.8	3.9	3.6	3.5	4.8	1.08	1.37
Congenital syphillis	0.1	0.1	0.1	0.0	0.1	1.00	...
Remainder of infectious and parasitic diseases	3.2	3.2	3.2	2.7	5.5	1.00	2.04
Malignant neoplasms, including neoplasms of lymphatic and hematopoietic tissues	3.1	3.6	2.7	3.1	3.2	1.33	1.03
Benign neoplasms, carcinoma in situ, and neoplasms of uncertain behavior and of unspecified nature	1.9	1.9	1.8	1.8	2.0	1.06	1.11
Diseases of thymus gland	0.2	0.3	0.1	0.2	0.3	3.00	1.50
Cystic fibrosis	1.1	1.1	1.1	1.3	0.3	1.00	0.23
Diseases of blood and blood-forming organs	2.7	2.9	2.4	2.0	5.3	1.21	2.65
Meningitis	12.3	13.5	10.9	10.1	20.9	1.24	2.07
Other diseases of nervous system and sense organs	14.8	16.1	13.5	13.7	19.5	1.19	1.42
Acute upper respiratory infections	2.2	2.0	2.3	1.5	4.9	0.87	3.27
Bronchitis and bronchiolitis	3.6	4.1	3.0	3.1	5.3	1.37	1.71
Pneumonia and influenza	28.0	32.2	23.5	20.5	58.7	1.37	2.86
Pneumonia	27.7	31.8	23.2	20.2	58.0	1.37	2.87
Influenza	0.3	0.4	0.3	0.2	0.7	1.33	3.50
Remainder of diseases of respiratory system	14.0	16.1	11.8	11.7	23.4	1.36	2.00
Hernia of abdominal cavity and intestinal obstruction without mention of hernia	3.6	4.2	3.0	3.2	5.3	1.40	1.66
Gastritis/duodenitis/noninfections	5.1	6.2	3.9	3.3	12.5	1.59	3.79
Remainder of diseases of digestive system	6.9	7.5	6.3	5.9	11.4	1.19	1.93
Congenital anomalies	255.2	267.6	241.5	258.7	249.2	1.11	0.96
Anencephalus and similar anomalies	21.9	18.6	25.3	24.2	12.6	0.74	0.52
Spina bifida	7.1	6.6	7.7	7.9	3.9	0.86	0.49
Congential hydrocephalus	9.0	10.2	7.7	8.6	10.8	1.32	1.26
Other congenital anomalies of central nervous system and eye	8.7	7.8	9.8	7.9	12.1	0.80	1.53
Congenital anomalies of heart	79.6	87.3	71.2	80.3	76.4	1.23	0.95
Other congenital anomalies of circulatory system	25.9	27.7	24.0	24.5	32.0	1.15	1.31
Congenital anomalies of respiratory system	17.7	21.4	13.9	16.9	21.3	1.54	1.26
Congenital anomalies of digestive system	7.9	8.1	7.8	7.6	9.5	1.04	1.25
Congenital anomalies of genitourinary system	12.5	16.8	8.0	13.2	9.7	2.10	0.73
Congenital anomalies of musculoskeletal system	17.7	18.6	16.8	18.5	14.9	1.11	0.81
Down's syndrome	3.4	3.3	3.5	3.3	3.8	0.94	1.15
Other chromosomal anomalies	14.7	12.4	17.0	14.9	13.9	0.73	0.93
All other and unspecified congenital anomalies	28.9	28.9	28.9	29.0	28.5	1.00	0.98
Certain conditions originating in the perinatal period	629.7	699.4	554.3	530.1	1,034.0	1.26	1.95
Newborn affected by maternal conditions which may be unrelated to present pregnancy	3.9	4.4	3.4	3.4	6.0	1.29	1.76
Newborn affected by maternal complications of pregnancy	43.5	46.4	40.4	36.4	72.3	1.15	1.99

Table 5-20A. Infant Mortality Rates for Selected Causes, by Race and Sex: 1980 [rate per 100,000 births]—continued

Cause of death	Both sexes	Sex		Color		Ratio male to female	Ratio black/ other to white
		Male	Female	White	Black/ other		
Newborn affected by complications of placenta, cord and membranes.	27.3	29.3	25.0	25.2	35.7	1.17	1.42
Newborn affected by other complications of labor and delivery	3.9	4.2	3.6	3.8	4.3	1.17	1.13
Slow fetal growth/fetal malnutrition. .	1.4	1.1	1.6	1.1	2.2	0.69	2.00
Disorders relating to short gestation and unspecified low birth weight. . .	101.0	108.0	93.4	74.7	207.7	1.16	2.78
Disorders relating to long gestation and high birth weight	0.1	0.1	0.1	0.1	*	1.00	...
Birth trauma.	29.3	33.0	25.3	26.3	41.3	1.30	1.57
Intrauterine hypoxia/birth asphyxia . .	41.4	45.0	37.6	36.6	61.0	1.20	1.67
Fetal distress in liveborn infant . .	7.8	9.2	6.4	6.9	11.8	1.44	1.71
Birth asphyxia.	33.6	35.8	31.2	29.8	49.2	1.15	1.65
Respiratory distress syndrome	138.1	163.4	111.0	125.8	187.9	1.47	1.49
Other respiratory conditions of newborn.	102.3	115.2	88.5	84.8	173.5	1.30	2.05
Infections specific to the perinatal period.	26.9	30.0	23.6	23.4	40.9	1.27	1.75
Neonatal hemorrhage	26.8	30.3	22.9	22.7	43.4	1.32	1.91
Hemolytic disease of newborn, due to isoimmunization and other perinatal jaundice	2.5	2.7	2.3	2.2	3.8	1.17	1.73
Syndrome of "infant of a diabetic mother"/neonatal diabetes mellitus. .	0.5	0.8	0.2	0.6	0.3	4.00	0.50
Hemorrhagic disease of newborn.	0.3	0.4	0.2	0.3	0.3	2.00	1.00
All other/ill-defined conditions originating in the perinatal period. . .	80.4	85.1	75.3	62.5	153.2	1.13	2.45
Symptoms/signs/ill-defined conditions .	168.5	192.8	142.5	140.4	282.8	1.35	2.01
Sudden infant death syndrome.	152.5	175.6	127.8	128.3	251.0	1.37	1.96
Symptoms, signs, and all other ill-defined conditions.	16.0	17.2	14.7	12.1	31.8	1.17	2.63
Accidents and adverse effects	32.3	35.5	28.8	28.2	48.9	1.23	1.73
Inhalation and ingestions of food or other object causing obstruction of respiratory tract or suffocation.	7.5	8.5	6.4	6.2	12.8	1.33	2.06
Accidental mechanical suffocation . .	4.7	5.3	3.9	3.9	7.6	1.36	1.95
Other accidental causes and adverse effects	20.1	21.7	18.5	18.0	28.6	1.17	1.59
Homicide.	5.8	6.1	5.5	4.3	11.9	1.11	2.77
Child battering/other maltreatment. .	2.3	2.4	2.2	1.8	4.2	1.09	2.33
Other homicide.	3.5	3.8	3.2	2.5	7.7	1.19	3.08
All other causes (residual)	50.0	55.4	44.1	42.7	79.3	1.26	1.86

Note: * indicates zero cases reported.

Source: National Center for Health Statistics. Vital Statistics of the United States: Mortality (1980--Vol. II, Part A). Washington, DC: U.S. Government Printing Office, 1984.

Table 5-20B. Infant Mortality Rates for Selected Causes, by Race and Sex: 1970 [rate per 100,000 births]

Cause of death	Both Sexes	Sex: Male	Sex: Female	Race: White	Race: Black/other	Ratio male to female	Ratio black/other to white
All causes	2,001.1	2,237.0	1,752.2	1,775.2	3,091.8	1.28	1.74
Diarrheal diseases	20.4	23.4	17.3	12.5	58.6	1.35	4.69
Whooping cough	0.2	0.1	0.3	0.2	0.3	0.33	1.50
Meningococcal infections	3.3	3.8	2.8	3.3	3.6	1.36	1.09
Tetanus	0.2	0.3	*	0.1	0.5	*	5.00
Septicemia	23.2	24.4	21.9	19.3	41.9	1.11	2.17
Viral diseases	7.3	7.9	6.6	6.2	12.5	1.20	2.02
Congenital syphilis	0.3	0.4	0.2	0.1	1.2	2.00	12.00
Other infective and parasitic diseases	6.2	7.2	5.3	4.7	13.7	1.36	2.91
Malignant neoplasms (including lymphatic and hematopoietic tissues)	4.4	4.1	4.7	4.6	3.4	0.87	0.74
Benign neoplasms and neoplasms of unspecified nature	2.0	2.2	1.7	2.0	1.9	1.29	0.95
Diseases of thymus gland	1.3	1.5	1.0	1.3	1.2	1.50	0.92
Cystic fibrosis	3.1	3.5	2.8	3.5	1.4	1.25	0.40
Diseases of the blood and blood-forming organs	3.8	4.2	3.5	2.9	8.4	1.20	2.90
Meningitis	15.7	18.0	13.3	12.2	32.8	1.35	2.69
Other diseases of nervous system and sense organs	15.0	16.4	13.5	14.6	16.9	1.21	1.16
Acute upper respiratory infections	5.7	6.6	4.7	4.3	12.3	1.40	2.86
Bronchitis and bronchiolitis	15.7	17.3	14.0	9.7	44.8	1.24	4.62
Influenza and pneumonia	168.9	188.8	148.0	128.5	364.3	1.28	2.84
Influenza	2.2	2.5	2.0	1.6	5.5	1.25	3.44
Pneumonia	166.7	186.3	146.0	126.9	358.8	1.28	2.83
Other chronic interstitial pneumonia	0.6	0.6	0.6	0.5	0.9	1.00	1.80
All other diseases of respiratory system	18.0	21.0	14.8	15.6	29.4	1.42	1.88
Hernia and intestinal obstruction	16.8	18.5	15.0	16.6	17.7	1.23	1.07
Gastritis, duodenitis, and colitis of noninfectious origin	1.1	1.1	1.0	0.9	1.9	1.10	2.11
Other diseases of digestive system	11.3	13.1	9.4	9.4	20.5	1.39	2.18
Congenital anomalies	301.7	314.2	288.5	309.0	266.7	1.09	0.86
Anencephalus	26.9	21.6	32.5	30.2	10.9	0.66	0.36
Spina bifida	18.0	13.9	22.4	19.6	10.3	0.62	0.53
Congenital hydrocephalus	15.1	15.1	15.0	15.4	13.3	1.01	0.86
Other congenital anomalies of central nervous system and eye	11.6	10.9	12.2	11.9	9.7	0.89	0.82
Congenital anomalies of heart	119.0	133.2	104.1	120.2	113.4	1.28	0.94
Other congenital anomalies of circulatory system	19.8	22.3	17.2	19.8	19.8	1.30	1.00
Congenital anomalies of respiratory system	11.8	12.4	11.2	11.8	12.0	1.11	1.02
Congenital anomalies of digestive system	19.1	19.5	18.6	18.8	20.5	1.05	1.09
Congenital anomalies of genitourinary system	10.0	13.5	6.3	10.5	7.7	2.14	0.73
Congenital anomalies of musculoskeletal system	10.0	10.5	9.5	10.9	5.5	1.11	0.50
Down's disease	3.6	3.6	3.6	3.7	3.1	1.00	0.84
Other congenital syndromes affecting multiple systems	30.0	30.3	29.7	29.2	33.9	1.02	1.16
Other and unspecified congenital anomalies	6.8	7.3	6.3	6.9	6.6	1.16	0.96

Table 5-20B. Infant Mortality Rates for Selected Causes, by Race and Sex: 1970 [rate per 100,000 births]—continued

Cause of death	Both Sexes	Sex		Race		Ratio male to female	Ratio black/other to white
		Male	Female	White	Black/other		
Certain causes of mortality in early infancy	1,157.1	1,316.6	988.9	1,041.1	1,715.9	1.33	1.65
Chronic circulatory diseases in mother	0.3	0.4	0.2	0.2	0.6	2.00	3.00
Other maternal conditions unrelated to pregnancy	12.3	14.4	10.2	12.4	12.2	1.41	0.98
Syphilis	0.2	0.2	0.1	*	0.9	2.00	*
Diabetes mellitus	7.1	8.8	5.4	7.6	4.7	1.63	0.62
Rubella	0.4	0.5	0.4	0.5	0.3	1.25	0.60
All other maternal conditions unrelated to pregnancy	4.6	4.9	4.3	4.3	6.2	1.14	1.44
Toxemia of pregnancy	5.3	5.7	4.8	4.4	9.7	1.19	2.20
Maternal antepartum and intrapartum infection	7.5	6.9	8.0	6.2	13.3	0.86	2.15
Difficult labor	18.0	21.0	14.9	17.0	22.8	1.41	1.34
With mention of birth injury	6.6	7.6	5.5	6.2	8.3	1.38	1.34
Without mention of birth injury	11.5	13.4	9.4	10.8	14.5	1.43	1.34
All other complications of pregnancy and childbirth	131.7	148.5	113.9	118.8	193.9	1.30	1.63
Conditions of placenta	61.1	69.6	52.2	60.7	63.4	1.33	1.04
Conditions of umbilical cord	12.2	14.3	10.0	11.5	15.6	1.43	1.36
Birth injury without mention of cause	57.6	69.2	45.4	51.1	89.2	1.52	1.75
Hemolytic disease of newborn	22.2	23.8	20.6	24.2	12.8	1.16	0.53
Hyaline membrane disease	142.1	175.9	106.6	142.6	140.0	1.65	0.98
Respiratory distress syndrome	119.5	139.7	98.2	110.9	161.2	1.42	1.45
Asphyxia of newborn, unspecified	252.9	282.2	222.0	223.2	396.6	1.27	1.78
All other anoxic and hypoxic conditions not elsewhere classifiable	20.4	22.6	18.1	17.0	36.7	1.25	2.16
Immaturity, unqualified	234.6	257.4	210.4	192.9	435.5	1.22	2.26
Postmaturity	0.1	0.1	0.1	*	0.3	1.00	*
Hemorrhagic disease of newborn	13.2	14.6	11.7	11.5	21.4	1.25	1.86
All other conditions of newborn	46.0	50.2	41.6	36.8	90.6	1.21	2.46
Symptoms and ill-defined conditions	94.2	109.1	78.5	67.6	222.8	1.39	3.30
Accidents	61.5	65.4	57.4	51.3	110.6	1.14	2.16
Inhalation and ingestion of food or other object causing obstruction or suffocation	18.9	19.9	17.8	15.3	36.1	1.12	2.36
Accidental mechanical suffocation	15.2	16.9	13.4	12.6	27.5	1.26	2.18
Other accidental causes	27.4	28.6	26.1	23.3	47.0	1.10	2.02
Homicide	4.0	4.2	3.9	2.7	10.2	1.08	3.78
All other causes (residual)	37.9	43.0	32.5	30.1	75.5	1.32	2.51

Note: * indicates zero cases reported.

Source: National Center for Health Statistics. Vital Statistics of the United States: Mortality (1973 and 1970--Vol. I, Table 1-18; Vol. II, Part A, Table 2-4 and Table 2-5). Washington, DC: U.S. Government Printing Office, 1977 and 1974.

Table 5-21. Maternal Mortality Rates, by Race: Birth Registration States or United States, 1915-1980 [rate per 100,000 deliveries]

Year	All races	White	All other
1980[a]	9.2	6.7	19.8
1979[a]	9.6	6.4	22.7
1978[a]	9.6	6.4	23.0
1977[a]	11.2	7.7	26.0
1976[a]	12.3	9.0	26.5
1975[a]	12.6	9.1	29.0
1974[a]	14.6	10.0	35.1
1973[a]	15.2	10.7	34.6
1972[a,b]	18.8	14.3	38.5
1971[a]	18.8	13.0	45.3
1970[a]	21.5	14.4	55.9
1969	22.2	15.5	55.7
1968	24.5	16.6	63.6
1967	28.0	19.5	69.5
1966	29.1	20.2	72.4
1965	31.6	21.0	83.7
1964	33.3	22.3	89.9
1963[c]	35.8	24.0	96.9
1962[c]	35.2	23.8	95.9
1961	36.9	24.9	101.3
1960	37.1	26.0	97.9
1959	37.4	25.8	102.1
1958	37.6	26.3	101.8
1957	41.0	27.5	118.3
1956	40.9	28.7	110.7
1955	47.0	32.8	130.3
1954	52.4	37.2	143.8
1953	61.1	44.1	166.1
1952	67.8	48.9	188.1
1951	75.0	54.9	201.3
1950	83.3	61.1	221.6
1949	90.3	68.1	234.8
1948	116.6	89.4	301.0
1947	134.5	106.6	334.6
1946	156.7	130.7	358.9
1945	207.2	172.1	454.8
1944	227.9	189.4	506.0
1943	245.2	210.5	509.9
1942	258.7	221.8	544.0
1941	316.5	266.0	678.1
1940	376.0	319.8	773.5
1935-39	493.9	439.9	875.5
1930-34[d]	636.0	575.4	1,080.7
1925-29	668.6	615.0	1,163.7
1920-24	689.5	649.2	1,134.3
1915-19	727.9	700.3	1,253.5

[a]Excludes deaths of nonresidents of the U.S.

[b]Deaths based on a 50 percent sample.

[c]Figures by race exclude data for residents of New Jersey; see original source for explanation.

[d]For 1932-35, Mexicans are included with "All other."

Source: National Center for Health Statistics. Vital Statistics of the United States: Mortality (1980--Vol. II, Part A). Washington, DC: U.S. Government Printing Office, 1984.

Maternal mortality is lowest at ages 20-24 years. The risk of death from childbearing is quite low for ages under thirty-five (though teenagers are at greater risk than women in their early twenties), but rises sharply for ages 35-39 and older. Women 35-39 have five times the risk of death than women 20-24, and for women 40-44 the risk is nearly ten times as great. White mothers have a better than 3:1 ratio over black/other mothers at all ages, except at age forty and over, when it is 2:1. The advantage of white mothers is greatest at 30-34 years, when it is 4:1.

Table 5-22 reports cause-specific rates of maternal mortality for each racial group. From this table it can be learned:

1. About one-third of maternal deaths arise from a general category named "all other complications of pregnancy, childbirth, and the puerperium." Although toxemia, hemorrhage, and sepsis each are causes of some significance, they all have rates of only 1 or 2 per 100,000. However, at ages thirty-five and over, they become much more important.

2. Death from abortion, both induced and spontaneous, is the least important of the specified causes. In 1980 there was one death reported from illegally induced abortion and five from legally induced abortion for the entire nation. There may be underreporting.

3. Black/other mothers are at a great disadvantage in comparison with white mothers for all of the causes. Their disadvantage is somewhat worse for ectopic pregnancy. hemorrhage, and sepsis, and the few abortion-related deaths that do occur are predominantly among black/other mothers.

4. The number of maternal deaths each year is impressively small, in comparison with all deaths. In 1980 there were only 334 maternal deaths out of a total of 914,763 female deaths.

Future Mortality Trends

Because of the acceleration in longevity that has taken place since 1970, it is necessary to consider future trends in mortality more carefully than demographers have in the past. In making its population projections, the U.S. Bureau of the Census considered carefully the recent mortality trends and made what appeared to be plausible possible projections. The Office of the Actuary, Social Security Administration, has performed research on which the Bureau of the Census relied heavily.[7] These studies envisage that the expectation of life will continue to rise steadily and reasonably rapidly for the remainder of this century, but about the year 2005 would begin to decelerate toward an upper limit. However, the exact amount of the improvement in

Table 5-22. Maternal Mortality Rates for Selected Causes, by Five-Year Age Groups and Race: United States, 1980 [rates per 100,000 deliveries]

Cause of death and race	Rate per 100,000 live births							
	Total	Under 20 years	20-24 years	25-29 years	30-34 years	35-39 years	40-44 years	45 years and over[a]
Complications of pregnancy/ childbirth/puerperium.	9.2	7.6	5.8	7.7	13.6	31.3	60.6	166.7
White.	6.7	5.9	4.3	5.5	9.4	21.2	51.0	112.2
All other.	19.8	11.6	11.9	19.4	35.1	72.3	91.9	323.6
Black.	21.5	12.8	13.4	21.4	41.9	91.7	100.3	490.2
Pregnancy with abortive outcome. .	1.7	0.5	1.4	1.7	2.5	6.4	*	*
White.	0.9	0.3	0.9	1.1	0.9	2.7	*	*
All other.	4.9	1.2	3.3	5.1	11.0	21.7	*	*
Black.	5.3	1.3	3.3	5.9	14.0	25.5	*	*
Ectopic pregnancy.	1.3	0.4	1.1	1.4	1.8	4.3	*	*
White.	0.8	0.3	0.8	0.9	0.7	1.8	*	*
All other.	3.4	0.6	2.1	4.0	7.7	14.5	*	*
Black.	3.4	0.6	1.9	4.4	9.3	15.3	*	*
Spontaneous abortion	0.1	0.2	0.1	0.1	*	*	*	*
White.	0.0	*	*	0.1	*	*	*	*
All other.	0.3	0.6	0.4	*	*	*	*	*
Black.	0.3	0.6	0.5	*	*	*	*	*
Legally induced abortion	0.1	*	0.2	0.1	0.2	0.7	*	*
White.	0.0	*	*	0.1	*	*	*	*
All other.	0.6	*	0.8	*	1.1	3.6	*	*
Black.	0.7	*	1.0	*	1.6	5.1	*	*
Illegally induced abortion . . .	0.0	*	*	0.1	*	*	*	*
White.	*	*	*	*	*	*	*	*
All other.	0.1	*	*	0.6	*	*	*	*
Black.	0.2	*	*	0.7	*	*	*	*
Other pregnancy with abortive outcome.	0.2	*	0.1	0.1	0.5	1.4	*	*
White.	0.1	*	0.1	*	0.2	0.9	*	*
All other.	0.6	*	*	0.6	2.2	3.6	*	*
Black.	0.7	*	*	0.7	3.1	5.1	*	*
Direct obstetric causes.	7.2	6.9	4.1	5.9	10.7	23.4	56.3	166.7
White.	5.6	5.6	3.2	4.3	8.3	17.7	51.0	112.2
All other.	14.0	10.0	7.8	14.3	23.0	47.0	73.6	323.6
Black.	15.3	10.9	9.1	15.5	26.4	61.1	75.2	490.2
Hemorrhage of pregnancy and childbirth	1.2	0.4	0.6	0.8	2.4	4.3	17.3	*
White.	0.9	0.3	0.7	0.3	1.7	5.3	11.3	*
All other.	2.4	0.6	1.2	3.4	5.5	*	36.8	*
Black.	2.0	0.6	1.4	3.7	3.1	*	25.1	*
Toxemia of pregnancy	1.7	2.1	0.9	1.3	2.9	2.8	8.7	83.3
White.	1.2	1.8	0.4	1.0	2.2	2.7	11.3	112.2
All other.	3.4	2.9	2.9	2.9	6.6	3.6	*	*
Black.	3.9	3.2	3.3	3.7	7.8	5.1	*	*
Obstructed labor	*	*	*	*	*	*	*	*
White.	*	*	*	*	*	*	*	*
All other.	*	*	*	*	*	*	*	*
Black.	*	*	*	*	*	*	*	*
Complications of the puerperium.	2.6	2.8	1.1	2.4	3.6	8.5	17.3	83.3
White.	2.1	2.0	0.9	2.0	3.5	7.1	11.3	*
All other.	4.3	4.7	1.6	4.6	4.4	14.5	36.8	323.6
Black.	5.1	5.1	1.9	5.2	6.2	20.4	50.1	490.2
Other direct obstetric	1.8	1.6	1.3	1.4	1.8	7.8	13.0	*
White.	1.2	1.5	1.1	1.0	0.9	2.7	17.0	*
All other.	3.9	1.8	2.1	3.4	6.6	28.9	*	*
Black.	4.2	1.9	2.4	2.9	9.3	35.7	*	*
Indirect obstetric causes.	0.3	0.2	0.3	0.1	0.4	1.4	4.3	*
White.	0.2	*	0.2	0.1	0.2	0.9	*	*
All other.	0.8	0.6	0.8	*	1.1	3.6	18.4	*
Black.	1.0	0.6	1.0	*	1.6	5.1	25.1	*

[a]Rates computed by relating deaths of women 45 years and over to live births among women 45-49 years.

Note: * indicates zero cases reported.

Source: National Center for Health Statistics. Vital Statistics of the United States: Mortality (1980--Vol. II, Part A). Washington, DC: U.S. Government Printing Office, 1984.

Table 5-23. Projection of Life Expectancy at Birth and at Age 65, by Race and Sex: 1980 to 2080

Projections	Life expectancy at birth						Life expectancy at 65					
	Total		White		Black		Total		White		Black	
	Male	Female	Male	Female	Male	Female	Male	Female	Male	Female	Male	Female
1980.	70.0	77.5	70.7	78.1	63.7	72.3	14.1	18.3	14.2	18.5	12.9	16.5
Low mortality assumption												
1985.	71.2	78.7	72.0	79.3	65.5	74.6	14.8	19.2	14.9	19.4	13.7	18.2
1990.	72.2	79.8	72.9	80.3	67.0	76.2	15.3	20.0	15.4	20.1	14.3	19.0
1995.	73.2	80.9	73.9	81.4	68.5	77.7	15.8	20.8	15.9	20.9	14.9	20.0
2000.	74.3	82.0	74.9	82.5	70.1	79.3	16.4	21.7	16.4	21.7	15.6	20.9
2010.	75.7	83.7	76.2	84.0	72.2	81.5	17.2	22.9	17.3	23.0	16.5	22.4
2020.	76.4	84.7	76.8	85.0	73.4	82.8	17.8	23.8	17.8	23.9	17.2	23.3
2030.	77.1	85.7	77.5	85.9	74.6	84.1	18.3	24.7	18.4	24.8	17.8	24.3
2050.	78.6	87.8	78.8	87.9	77.0	86.8	19.6	26.6	19.6	26.7	19.2	26.3
2080.	80.8	91.0	80.8	91.0	80.8	91.0	21.6	29.8	21.6	29.8	21.6	29.8
Middle mortality assumption												
1985.	71.0	78.5	71.8	79.0	65.2	74.4	14.7	19.1	14.8	19.2	13.6	18.0
1990.	71.6	79.2	72.4	79.7	66.3	75.4	15.0	19.5	15.1	19.6	14.0	18.6
1995.	72.3	79.8	73.0	80.3	67.3	76.5	15.3	20.0	15.4	20.1	14.4	19.1
2000.	72.9	80.5	73.6	81.0	68.5	77.6	15.7	20.5	15.7	20.6	14.8	19.7
2010.	73.8	81.5	74.4	81.8	70.0	79.1	16.1	21.2	16.2	21.3	15.4	20.6
2020.	74.2	82.0	74.7	82.3	71.0	79.9	16.5	21.7	16.5	21.8	15.8	21.1
2030.	74.6	82.5	75.0	82.8	71.9	80.8	16.8	22.1	16.8	22.2	16.2	21.7
2050.	75.5	83.6	75.7	83.8	73.8	82.5	17.4	23.1	17.5	23.1	17.1	22.8
2080.	76.7	85.2	76.7	85.2	76.7	85.2	18.5	24.6	18.5	24.6	18.5	24.6
High mortality assumption												
1985.	70.8	78.3	71.6	78.8	65.0	74.1	14.6	18.9	14.7	19.0	13.5	17.8
1990.	71.1	78.6	71.9	79.1	65.7	74.8	14.7	19.1	14.8	19.2	13.7	18.2
1995.	71.4	78.9	72.1	79.4	66.3	75.5	14.9	19.4	15.0	19.5	14.0	18.5
2000.	71.7	79.2	72.4	79.7	67.0	76.1	15.0	19.6	15.1	19.7	14.2	18.8
2010.	72.1	79.6	72.7	80.1	68.1	77.1	15.3	19.9	15.3	20.0	14.5	19.2
2020.	72.3	79.9	72.8	80.2	68.8	77.6	15.4	20.1	15.5	20.1	14.8	19.5
2030.	72.5	80.1	73.0	80.4	69.6	78.2	15.5	20.3	15.6	20.3	15.0	19.8
2050.	72.9	80.5	73.2	80.7	71.1	79.4	15.8	20.6	15.9	20.7	15.5	20.3
2080.	73.5	81.2	73.5	81.2	73.5	81.2	16.2	21.2	16.2	21.2	16.2	21.2

Source: U.S. Bureau of the Census. "Projections of the Population of the United States, by Age, Sex, and Race: 1983 to 2080." Current Population Reports (Series P-25, no. 952). Washington, DC: U.S. Government Printing Office, 1984, Table B-5.

mortality until 2005 and the slower progress thereafter is difficult to specify. Accordingly, the Bureau of the Census made three assumptions: high, medium, and low mortality assumptions (a low mortality assumption presumes high survivorship). Table 5-23 reports the life expectancy at birth and at age sixty-five, by race and sex, derived from the life tables that the Bureau of the Census used for making projections. These assumptions represent good predictions about the future course of mortality. They put to rest some of the speculation that expectation of life will surpass 100 years, based on extrapolation of the most recent trends. The results for the medium mortality assumptions may be summarized as follows:

Year	Males	Females	Difference
1980	70.0	77.5	7.5
2000	72.9	80.5	7.6
2050	75.5	83.6	8.1
2080	76.7	85.2	8.5

Thus, from 1980 to 2080, the Bureau of the Census anticipates an increase of about seven years in life expectancy, with one year more of improvement for females than for males. Women would live 8.5 years longer than men in 2080, instead of 7.5 years as now. However, these assumptions have strong implications for the survival of the elderly. In 1980 a person aged sixty-five could expect to live 14.1 more years if a male and 18.5 more years if a female. By 2080 this would have increased to 18.5 years for men and 24.6 years for women. Table 5-23 shows the time trend of these gains. This table also illustrates that if the low mortality assumptions were to materialize, the survival of the aged would increase much more, by 53 percent for men and 63 percent for women.

Conclusion

It can be said with confidence that progress in reducing mortality at ages under thirty-five is rapidly drawing to a close, simply because the death rates for these ages are so close to zero that little more can be done. Mortality rates at ages sixty-five and over are still very high, because they represent the organic failures associated with inevitable death. Surprising progress in postponing death at these upper ages, except in the case of cancer, still is being made, and few care to predict what the ultimate upper limit will be, if one is encountered. Two by-products of this trend are of special interest to demographers. First, the combination of increasing length of life and low birth rates will lead to a much older age composition than at present or at any time in the past. Second, improved health and medical care is permitting the elderly to lead active and satisfying lives for many more years after the typical retirement age than previously thought possible. This has important implications for family life, housing, labor force participation, social security, and politics.

Notes

1. The National Center for Health Statistics did not report data separately for the black population until recently. For historical trends data are for "white" and "other" (black and other nonwhite races). Since 95 percent or more of this residual category is black, for all practical purposes the "black/other" category can be interpreted as "black."

2. When the median age is low (because of high recent fertility), the crude death rate is lower than when the median age is higher (because of recent low fertility), even when the death rate at each age is the same in both populations.

3. For historical trends it is necessary to combine data for the black population with those of races other than white.

4. The data for years before 1979 reported in this chapter are based on the eighth revision, while those for 1980 are based on the ninth revision. The comparability of the two systems of classification are explained and comparability ratios provided in *Monthly Vital Statistics Report* (Volume 31, no. 6), published by the National Center for Health Statistics (Washington, DC: U.S. Government Printing Office, 1983).

5. The indicated rise in death rates from nephritis and chronic pulmonary conditions is due to lack of comparability between the eighth and ninth revisions of the cause-of-death classifications. See Table 22 of *Monthly Vital Statistics Report* (Volume 31, no. 6, 1983).

6. Changes in coding procedures between the eighth and ninth revisions seriously affect the statistics for nephritis.

7. Joseph F. Faber and John C. Wilken. "Social Security Area Population Projections, 1981." *Social Security Administration Office of the Actuary, Actuarial Studies no. 85.* Also Joseph F. Faber. "Life Tables for the United States: 1900-2050." *Social Security Administration Office of the Actuary, Actuarial Studies no. 87.* Washington, DC: U.S. Government Printing Office, 1981 and 1982.

Bibliography

Arthur, W.B. "Economics of Risks to Life." *American Economic Review* 71 (1981):54-64.

Boone, M.S. "Socio-Medical Study of Infant Mortality Among Disadvantaged Blacks." *Human Organization* 41 (1982):227-36.

Brooks, C.H. "Social, Economic, and Biological Correlates of Infant Mortality in City Neighborhoods." *Journal of Health and Social Behavior* 21 (1980): 2-11.

Chang, H.C., and Pendleton, B.F. "Demographic, Environmental, and Sex-Specific Correlates of Noninfant Mortality in the North Central Region." *Sociology and Social Research* 66 (1981):52-68.

Cooper, R. et al. "Is the Period of Rapidly Declining Adult Mortality in the United States Coming to an End?" *American Journal of Public Health* 73 (1983): 1091-93.

Crimmins, E.M. "The Changing Pattern of American Mortality Decline, 1940-1977, and Its Implications for the Future." *Population and Development Review* 7 (1981):229-54.

Demeny, P., and Guingrich, P. "A Reconsideration of

Negro-White Mortality Differentials in the United States." *Demography* 4 (1967):820-37.

Dorn, Harold F. "Ecological Factors in Morbidity and Mortality from Cancer." In *Trends and Differentials in Mortality*. New York: Milbank Memorial Fund, 1956.

Erhardt, Carl L. *Mortality and Morbidity in the United States*. Cambridge, MA: Harvard University Press, 1974.

Feinleib, Manning; Fabsitz, Richard; and Sharrett, A. R. *Mortality from Cardiovascular and Noncardiovascular Diseases for U.S. Cities 1949-50, 1959-61 and 1969-71 with Selected Environmental Descriptors*. Washington, DC: U.S. Public Health Service, 1979.

Fingerhut, L.A. "Changes in Mortality Among the Elderly: United States, 1940-78." *Vital and Health Statistics* (Series 3, no. 22). Hyattsville, MD: National Center for Health Statistics, 1982.
Government Printing Office, 1982.

Garfinkel, Joseph; Chabot, Marion J.; and Pratt, Margaret W. *Infant, Maternal and Childhood Mortality in the United State, 1968-1973*. Washington, DC; U.S. Government Printing Office, 1975.

Gittelsohn, A.M. "On the Distribution of Underlying Causes of Death." *American Journal of Public Health* 72 (1982):133-40.

Hamilton, C. Horace. "Ecological and Social Factors in Mortality Variation." *Eugenics Quarterly* 2 (1955): 212-23.

Hedderson, J., and Daudistel, H.C. "Infant Mortality of the Spanish Surname Population." *Social Science Journal* 19 (1982):19-67.

Helsing, K.J. et al. "Factors Associated with Mortality after Widowhood." *American Journal of Public Health* 71 (1981):802-09.

Holinger, P.C., and Klemen, E.H. "Violent Deaths in the United States, 1900-1975: Relationships Between Suicide, Homicide and Accidental Deaths." *Social Science and Medicine* 16 (1982):1929-38.

Hunt, Eleanor P., and Huyck, Earl E. "Mortality of White and Nonwhite Infants in Major U.S. Cities." *Health, Education and Welfare Indicators* . Washington, DC: U.S. Government Printing Office, 1966.

Keyfitz, Nathan (International Union for the Scientific Study of Population). "Cause of Death in Future Mortality." International Population Conference. Mexico City, 1977.

Kitagawa, Evelyn M., and Hauser, Philip M. *Differential Mortality in the United States. A Study in Socioeconomic Epidmiology*. Cambridge, MA: Harvard University Press, 1973.

Klebba, A.J.; Maurer, J.D.; and Glass, E.J. "Mortality Trends: Age, Color, and Sex, United States, 1950-69." *Vital and Health Statistics* (Series 20, no. 15). Washington, DC: U.S. Government Printing Office, 1973.

———. "Mortality Trends for Leading Causes of Death, United States, 1950-69." *Vital and Health Statistics* (Series 20, no. 16). Washington, DC: U.S. Government Printing Office, 1973.

Knowles, J.H. (ed.). *Doing Better and Feeling Worse: Health in the United States*. New York: Norton, 1977.

Kohn, R.R. "Cause of Death in Very Old People." *Journal of the American Medical Association* 247 (1982): 2793-97.

Lave, Lester B., and Seskin, Eugene P. *Air Pollution and Human Health*. Baltimore, MD: Johns Hopkins University Press, 1977.

Logan, W.P.D. "Social Class Variations in Mortality." *Public Health Reports* 59 (1954): 1217-23.

Manton, K.G. "Changing Concepts of Morbidity and Mortality in the Elderly Population." *Health and Society (Milbank Memorial Fund Quarterly)*. 60 (1982):183-244.

———. "Temporal and Age Variation of United States Black/White Cause-Specific Mortality Differentials: A Study of the Recent Changes in the Relative Health State of the United States Black Population." *Gerontologist* 22 (1982):170-79.

Manton, K.G., and Stallard, E. "Temportal Trends in U.S. Multiple Cause of Death Mortality Data: 1968 to 1977." *Demography* 19 (1982):527-47.

Mare, R.D. "Socioeconomic Effects on Child Mortality in the United States." *American Journal of Public Health* 72 (1982):539-47.

McMillen, Marilyn M. (Mortality Statistics Branch, National Center for Health Statistics). "Twentieth Century Trends in United States Mortality." Paper presented at the Annual Meeting for the Population Association of America, 1984.

Milbank Memorial Fund. *Trends and Differentials in Mortality*. New York: Milbank Memorial Fund, 1956.

Moriyama, Iwao M. "Recent Changes in Infant Mortality Trends." *Public Health Reports* 75 (1960):391-405.

Nam, C.B.; Weatherby, N.L.; and Ockay, K.A. "Causes of Death Which Contribute to the Mortality Crossover Effect." *Social Biology* 25 (1978):306-14.

National Center for Health Statistics. *Health–United States–1981*. Washington, DC: U.S. Government Printing Office, 1981.

National Center of Vital Statistics. "Death Rates by Age, Race and Sex, United States, 1900-1953: Selected Causes." *Vital and Health Statistics Special Reports* (Volume 43, nos. 1-31). Washington, DC: U.S. Government Printing Office, 1956.

Population Bulletin. "Mortality." *Population Bulletin* 37 (1982):15-24.

Preston, Samuel H. *Mortality Patterns in National Populations: With Special Reference to Recorded Causes of Death.* New York: Academic Press, 1976.

———. "Mortality Trends." In *Annual Review of Sociology* (Volume 3). A. Inkeles, J. Coleman, and S. Smelser (eds.). Palo Alto, CA: Annual Reviews, Inc. 1977.

Rao, S.L.N. "On Long Term Mortality Trends in the United States, 1950-68." *Demography* 10 (1973): 405-19.

Retherford, Robert D. *The Changing Sex Differntial in Mortality.* Westport, CT: Greenwood Press, 1975.

Rosenwaike, I. "Note on New Estimates of the Mortality of the Extreme Aged." *Demography* 18 (1981): 257-66.

Ross, C.E., and Duff, R.S. "Medical Care, Living Conditions, and Children's Well-Being." *Social Forces* 61 (1982):456-74.

Safer, M.A. "Evaluation of the Health Hazard Appraisal Based on Survey Data from a Randomly Selected Population." *Public Health Reports* 97 (1982):31-37.

Shapiro, Sam et al. "Infant and Perinatal Mortality in the United States." *Analytical Studies.* Washington, DC: U.S. Government Printing Office, 1965.

Shepard, D.S., and Zeckhauser, R.J. "Long-Term Effects of Intervention to Improve Survival in Mixed Populations." *Journal of Chronic Diseases* 33 (1980): 413-33.

Sheps, Mindel C. "Marriage and Mortality." *American Journal of Public Health* 59 (1954):1217-23.

Siegel, J.S. *Demographic Aspects of the Health of the Elderly to the Year 2000 and Beyond.* Geneva, Switzerland: World Health Organization, 1982.

Singer, R.B., and Levinson, L. *Medical Risks: Patterns of Mortality Survival.* Lexington, MA: Lexington Books, 1976.

Sintonen, H. "Approach to Measuring and Valuing Health States." *Social Science and Medicine* 15C (1981):55-65.

Spiegelman, Mortimer. "Mortality Trends and Prospects and Their Implications." *Annals of the American Academy of Political and Social Science* 316 (1958): 25-33.

Stolnitz, George J. "A Century of International Mortality Trends: II." *Population Studies* 10 (1976): 17-42.

Taeuber, Conrad, and Taeuber, Irene B. *The Changing Population of the United States.* (Chapter 14, "Mortality.") New York: John Wiley and Sons, 1958.

U.S. Public Health Service. *Smoking and Health.* Washington, DC: U.S. Government Printing Office, 1963.

Verbrugge, L.M. "Recent Trends in Sex Mortality Differentials in the United States." *Women and Health* 5 (1981):17-37.

———. "The Social Roles of the Sexes and Their Relative Health and Mortality." Pp. 221-45 in *Sex Differentials in Mortality: Trends, Determinants, and Consequences.* A. Lopez, and L. Ruzicka (eds.). Canberra, Australia: Department of Demography, Australian National University, 1983.

———. "Women and Men: Mortality and Health of Older People." Pp. 139-64 in *Aging Society: Selected Reviews of Recent Research.* M.W. Riley, B.B. Hess, and K. Bond (eds.). Hillsdale, NJ: Lawrence Erlbaum Associates, 1983.

Wagner, E. et al. "Assessment of Health Hazard/Health Risk Appraisal." *American Journal of Public Health* 72 (1982):337-39, 347-52.

Wing, S., and Manton, K.G. "Contribution of Hypertension to Mortality in the U.S.: 1968, 1977." *American Journal of Public Health* 73 (1983):140-44.

Wolinsky, F.D., and Zusman, M.E. "Toward Comprehensive Health Status Measures." *Sociological Quarterly* 21 (1980):607-21.

World Health Organization, and United Nations. *Levels and Trends of Mortality Since 1950.* New York: United Nations, Department of International Economical Social Affairs, 1982.

Technical Appendix 5-1

Sources of Mortality Statistics: Vital Registration

The information provided below is an annotated extract of Section 7, "Technical Appendix" to the annual reports of Vital Statistics of the United States, Volume II–Mortality. *The report for 1979 was used in preparing this Appendix. Readers are urged to consult the 1980 report (not available when this Appendix was prepared) because it will describe changes made in relation to the 1980 census. Procedures are presented here as those in effect for the 1970s, which differ in minor respects from procedures for earlier decades. For a full history of changes in definitions and procedures, readers should consult the original sources.*

Death and Fetal-Death Statistics

Mortality statistics are based on information from all death records received by the National Center for Health Statistics (NCHS). The records are furnished by all the states, the District of Columbia, and the independent registration area of New York City.

The United States vital statistics system covers the fifty states, the District of Columbia, Puerto Rico, the Virgin Islands, and Guam.

Standard Certificates and Reports

The Standard Certificate of Death and the Standard Report of Fetal Death, issued by the Public Health Service, have served for many years as the principal means of attaining uniformity in the content of the documents used to collect information on these events. They have been modified in each state to the extent necessitated by the particular needs of the state or by special provisions of the state vital statistics law. However, the certificates or reports of most states conform closely in content and arrangement to the standards.

The Standard Certificate of Death has been revised periodically by the national vital statistics agency through consultation with state health officers and registrars; Federal agencies concerned with vital statistics; national, state, and county medical societies; and others working in such fields as public health, social welfare, demography, and insurance. This revision procedure has assured careful evaluation of each item in terms of its current and future usefulness for registration, identification, legal, medical, and research purposes. New items have been added where necessary, and old items have been modified to ensure better reporting, or in some cases have been dropped when their usefulness appeared to be limited.

The Standard Certificate of Death is shown in Figure 5-A. The certificate of death is for use by either a physician or a medical examiner or a coroner.

Classification of Data

The principal value of vital statistics data is realized through the presentation of rates, which are computed by relating the vital events of a class to the population of a similarly defined class. Vital statistics and population statistics must therefore be classified according to similarly defined systems and tabulated in comparable groups. Even when the variables common to both, such as geographic area, age, race, and sex, have been similarly classified and tabulated, differences between the enumeration method of obtaining population data and the registration method of obtaining vital statistics data may result in significant discrepancies.

Classification by Occurrence and Residence

Tabulations for the United States and specified geographic areas in this report are by place of residence unless stated as by place of occurrence. Deaths of nonresidents of the United States are not included in tables by place of residence.

Residence error–Results of a 1960 study show that the classification of residence information on the death certificates correspond closely to the residence classification of the census records for the decedents whose records were matched.

Cause of Death

Cause-of-death classification–Since 1949, cause-of-death statistics have been based on the underlying cause of death, which is defined as "(a) the disease or injury

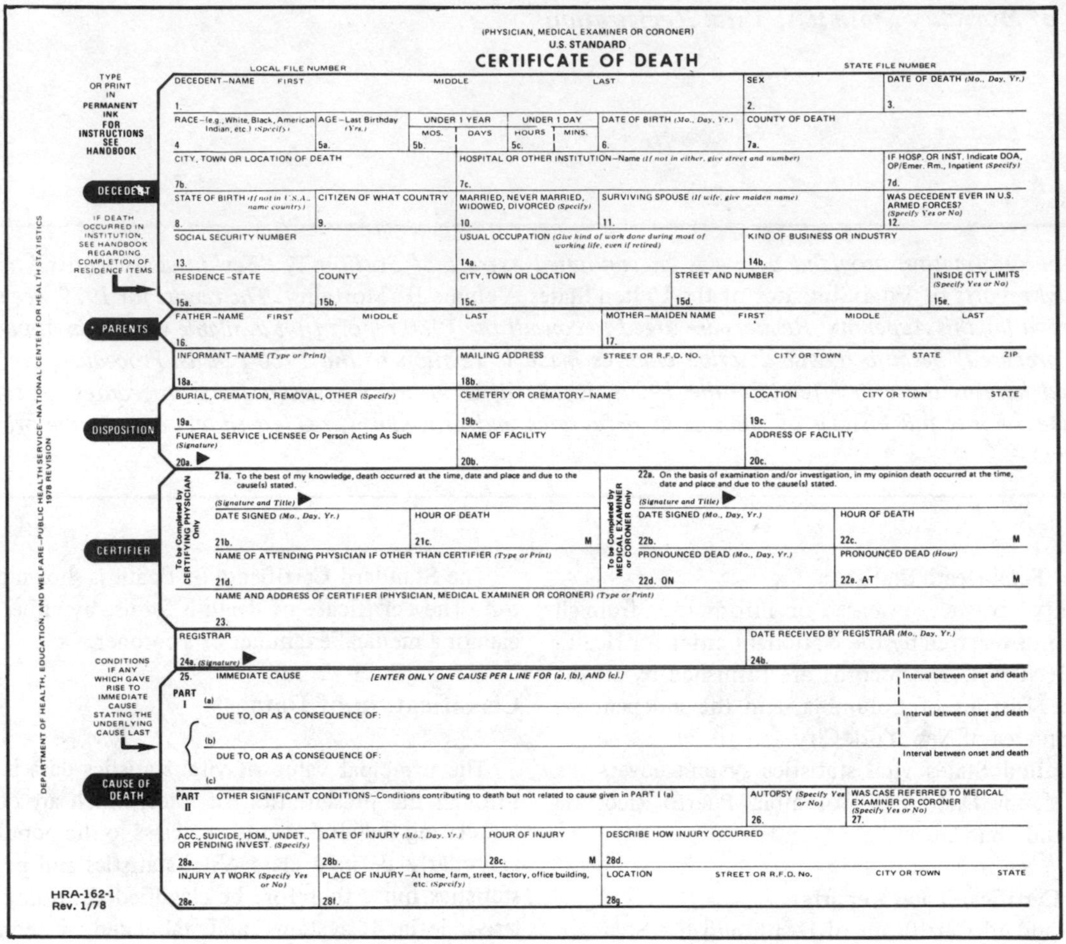

(PHYSICIAN, MEDICAL EXAMINER OR CORONER)
U.S. STANDARD
CERTIFICATE OF DEATH

LOCAL FILE NUMBER | STATE FILE NUMBER

TYPE OR PRINT IN PERMANENT INK
FOR INSTRUCTIONS SEE HANDBOOK

DECEDENT

DECEDENT–NAME FIRST MIDDLE LAST 1. | SEX 2. | DATE OF DEATH (Mo., Day, Yr.) 3.
RACE–(e.g., White, Black, American Indian, etc.) (Specify) 4 | AGE–Last Birthday (Yrs.) 5a. | UNDER 1 YEAR MOS. DAYS 5b. | UNDER 1 DAY HOURS MINS. 5c. | DATE OF BIRTH (Mo., Day, Yr.) 6. | COUNTY OF DEATH 7a.
CITY, TOWN OR LOCATION OF DEATH 7b. | HOSPITAL OR OTHER INSTITUTION–Name (If not in either, give street and number) 7c. | IF HOSP. OR INST. Indicate DOA, OP/Emer. Rm., Inpatient (Specify) 7d.
STATE OF BIRTH (If not in U.S.A., name country) 8. | CITIZEN OF WHAT COUNTRY 9. | MARRIED, NEVER MARRIED, WIDOWED, DIVORCED (Specify) 10. | SURVIVING SPOUSE (If wife, give maiden name) 11. | WAS DECEDENT EVER IN U.S. ARMED FORCES? (Specify Yes or No) 12.
SOCIAL SECURITY NUMBER 13. | USUAL OCCUPATION (Give kind of work done during most of working life, even if retired) 14a. | KIND OF BUSINESS OR INDUSTRY 14b.

IF DEATH OCCURRED IN INSTITUTION, SEE HANDBOOK REGARDING COMPLETION OF RESIDENCE ITEMS

RESIDENCE–STATE 15a. | COUNTY 15b. | CITY, TOWN OR LOCATION 15c. | STREET AND NUMBER 15d. | INSIDE CITY LIMITS (Specify Yes or No) 15e.

PARENTS

FATHER–NAME FIRST MIDDLE LAST 16. | MOTHER–MAIDEN NAME FIRST MIDDLE LAST 17.
INFORMANT–NAME (Type or Print) 18a. | MAILING ADDRESS STREET OR R.F.D. NO. CITY OR TOWN STATE ZIP 18b.

DISPOSITION

BURIAL, CREMATION, REMOVAL, OTHER (Specify) 19a. | CEMETERY OR CREMATORY–NAME 19b. | LOCATION CITY OR TOWN STATE 19c.
FUNERAL SERVICE LICENSEE Or Person Acting As Such (Signature) 20a. | NAME OF FACILITY 20b. | ADDRESS OF FACILITY 20c.

CERTIFIER

To be Completed by CERTIFYING PHYSICIAN Only
21a. To the best of my knowledge, death occurred at the time, date and place and due to the cause(s) stated.
(Signature and Title)
DATE SIGNED (Mo., Day, Yr.) 21b. | HOUR OF DEATH 21c. M
NAME OF ATTENDING PHYSICIAN IF OTHER THAN CERTIFIER (Type or Print) 21d.

To be Completed by MEDICAL EXAMINER or CORONER Only
22a. On the basis of examination and/or investigation, in my opinion death occurred at the time, date and place and due to the cause(s) stated.
(Signature and Title)
DATE SIGNED (Mo., Day, Yr.) 22b. | HOUR OF DEATH 22c. M
PRONOUNCED DEAD (Mo., Day, Yr.) 22d. ON | PRONOUNCED DEAD (Hour) 22e. AT M

NAME AND ADDRESS OF CERTIFIER (PHYSICIAN, MEDICAL EXAMINER OR CORONER) (Type or Print) 23.
REGISTRAR 24a. (Signature) | DATE RECEIVED BY REGISTRAR (Mo., Day, Yr.) 24b.

CAUSE OF DEATH

CONDITIONS IF ANY WHICH GAVE RISE TO IMMEDIATE CAUSE STATING THE UNDERLYING CAUSE LAST

25. IMMEDIATE CAUSE [ENTER ONLY ONE CAUSE PER LINE FOR (a), (b), AND (c).] | Interval between onset and death
PART I (a)
DUE TO, OR AS A CONSEQUENCE OF: | Interval between onset and death
(b)
DUE TO, OR AS A CONSEQUENCE OF: | Interval between onset and death
(c)
PART II OTHER SIGNIFICANT CONDITIONS–Conditions contributing to death but not related to cause given in PART I (a) | AUTOPSY (Specify Yes or No) 26. | WAS CASE REFERRED TO MEDICAL EXAMINER OR CORONER (Specify Yes or No) 27.
ACC., SUICIDE, HOM., UNDET., OR PENDING INVEST. (Specify) 28a. | DATE OF INJURY (Mo., Day, Yr.) 28b. | HOUR OF INJURY 28c. M | DESCRIBE HOW INJURY OCCURRED 28d.
INJURY AT WORK (Specify Yes or No) 28e. | PLACE OF INJURY–At home, farm, street, factory, office building, etc. (Specify) 28f. | LOCATION STREET OR R.F.D. No. CITY OR TOWN STATE 28g.

DEPARTMENT OF HEALTH, EDUCATION, AND WELFARE–PUBLIC HEALTH SERVICE–NATIONAL CENTER FOR HEALTH STATISTICS
1978 REVISION

HRA-162-1
Rev. 1/78

Figure 5-A. Standard Certificate of Death

which initiated the train of events leading directly to death, or (b) the circumstances of the accident or violence which produced the fatal injury." For a given death the underlying cause is selected from an array of conditions given in the cause-of-death section on the death certificate. These conditions are translated into medical codes through use of the classification structure and selection and modification rules contained in the applicable revision of the *International Classification of Diseases* (ICD) published by the World Health Organization (WHO). Selection rules guide the coder in systematically identifying the underlying cause of death in terms of the format of reported conditions and their causal relationship. Modification rules are intended to improve the usefulness of mortality statistics by giving preference to certain classification categories over others and/or to consolidate two or more conditions on the certificate into a single classification category.

As a statistical datum, the underlying cause of death is a simple, one dimensional statistic, which is conceptually easy to understand, and is a well accepted measure of mortality. It identifies the initiating cause of death and is therefore most useful to public health officials in developing measures to prevent the chain of events leading to death from starting. The rules for coding underlying causes of death are included with the ICD as a means of standardizing classification, which contributes toward uniformity in mortality medical statistics among countries.

Beginning with data year 1979 the cause-of-death statistics published by the National Center for Health Statistics have been classified in accordance with the 1975 *Revision of the International Classification of Diseases* (ICD-9). In addition to specifying that the Classification be used, WHO–in an effort to promote international comparability–recommended a basic list for tabulation of mortality data.

Five cause lists have been developed for tabulation and publication of mortality data by NCHS: The Each-Cause List, List of 282 Selected Causes, List of 61 Selected Causes of Infant Death, and the List of 34 Selected Causes. These lists were designed to be as comparable as possible to the NCHS lists more recently in use under the Eigth Revision.

Ninth Revision.–Cause of death statistics begin with the Ninth Revision. In the Ninth Revision, as in the Eighth Revision, the Classification is arranged in seventeen main sections or chapters. The first deals with diseases caused by well-defined infectious and parasitic agents. The next two deal with categories for neoplasms and for endocrine, nutritional and metabolic diseases, and immunity disorders. Most of the remaining chapters are arranged according to the principal anatomical sites of diseases with special chapters for mental disorders; complications of pregnancy, childbirth, and the puerperium; congenital anomalies; certain conditions originating in the perinatal period; and a chapter for symptoms, signs, and ill-defined conditions.

The last chapter (XVII), on injury and poisoning, consists of titles for nature of injury as part of the main classification.

In many ways, the Ninth and Eighth Revisions are similar. The essential basis of the Eighth Revision was retained as much as possible. Thus, overall blocks of classification numbers previously allocated to each chapter were retained. The Ninth Revision is more specific.

Maternal Deaths

Maternal deaths are those for which the certified physician has designated a maternal conditions as the underlying cause of death. In the Ninth Revision, WHO defined a maternal death as follows:

> A maternal death is defined as the death of a woman while pregnant or within 42 days of termination of pregnancy, irrespective of the duration and the site of the pregnancy, from any cause related to or aggravated by the pregnancy or its management but not from accidental or incidental causes.

Fetal Deaths

In May, 1950, the World Health Organization recommended the adoption for international use of the definition of fetal death as "death prior to the complete expulsion or extraction from its mother of a product of conception, irrespective of the duration of pregnancy; the death is indicated by the fact that after such separation, the fetus does not breathe or show any other evidence of life such as beating of the heart, pulsation of the umbilical cord, or definite movement of voluntary muscles." The term "fetal death" was defined on an all-inclusive basis to end confusion arising from usage of such terms as still-birth, abortion, and miscarriage.

Quality of Data

Completeness of Registration

All states have adopted laws that require the registration of births, deaths, and fetal deaths. It is believed that over 99 percent of the births and deaths occurring in this country are registered.

Reporting requirements for fetal deaths vary somewhat from state to state. Overall registration completeness is not as good for fetal deaths as for births and deaths; but it is believed to be relatively complete for fetal deaths of 20 weeks gestation or more. National statistical data on fetal deaths include only those fetal deaths of 20 weeks gestation or more.

Population Bases

The death rates are computed on the basis of population statistics published or made available by the U.S. Bureau of the Census. Rates for 1940, 1950, 1960, and 1970 are based on the populations enumerated as of April 1 in the censuses of those years. Rates for all other years are based on the estimated midyear (July 1) population for the respective years. Population estimates for 1971-79 are based on the results of the *1970 Census of Population*, estimates of census coverage, and data for components of change. The rates and life table values for 1971-79 will subsequently be revised due to the large difference between the 1980 census enumeration and the previously estimated population for 1980.

Generally, the revised life tables would show higher life expectancy, especially for the black population, and higher survival probabilities.

Technical Appendix 5-2

Life Tables

The mortality rates for a specific period may be summarized by the life table method to obtain measures of comparative longevity. There are two types of life tables–the generation or cohort life table and the current life table. The generation life table provides a "longitudinal" perspective in that it follows the mortality experience of a particular cohort, all persons born in the year 1900, for example, from the moment of birth through consecutive ages in successive calendar years. Based on age-specific death rates observed during consecutive calendar years, the generation life table reflects the mortality experience of a cohort from birth until no lives remain in the group.

The better known current life table may, by contrast, be characterized as "cross-sectional." Unlike the generation life table, the current life table does not represent the mortality experience of an actual cohort. Rather, the current life table considers a hypothetical cohort and assumes that it is subject to the age-specific mortality rates observed for an actual population during a particular period. Thus, for example, a current life table for 1980 assumes a hypothetical cohort subject throughout its lifetime to the age-specific mortality rates prevailing for the actual population in 1980. The current life table may thus be characterized as rendering a "snapshot" of current mortality experience. In this section the term "life table" refers to the current life table only and not to the generation life table.

The Life Table Program

There are three series of life tables prepared in the National Center for Health Statistics–complete, provisional abridged, and final abridged life tables. The complete life tables for the U.S. population contain life table values for single years of age and are based on decennial census data and deaths for a 3-year period about the census year and have been prepared since 1900. The provisional abridged life tables contain values by age groups and are based on a 10-percent sample of deaths. The final abridged life tables (referred to in this section as "abridged life tables") also contain values by age groups but are based on a complete count of all reported deaths.

Numerous requests have been received annually for current life table statistics that are more detailed than those available in the abridged life tables. Therefore tables showing l_x and $\mathring{e}_x$ values by single years of age interpolated from the abridged life tables have been published since 1960.

The demand for information regarding up-to-date life table values has been responsible for the introduction of a third series, provisional abridged life tables. Starting with 1958 provisional abridged life tables have been published, for the total population only, in the "Annual Summary for the United States," *Monthly Vital Statistics Report*. Values in these life tables are based on population estimates provided by the Bureau of the Census and on the estimated number of deaths derived from the "Current Mortality Sample" (CMS). The CMS consists of one-tenth of the death certificates filed in the vital statistics registration offices of each state, Washington, D.C., and New York City. The sample is taken by selecting one certificate out of every ten death certificates received between two dates a month apart.

Life Table Values

The data used to prepare the abridged U.S. life tables for a given year are the final mortality statistics and the midyear estimates of the population by age, race, and sex prepared by the U.S. Bureau of the Census.

Explanation of the Columns of the Life Table

Column 1–Age interval (x to $x + n$).–The age interval shown in column 1 is the interval between the two exact ages indicated. For instance, "20-25" means the 5-year interval between the 20th birthday and the 25th.

Column 2. Proportion dying ($_nq_x$).–This column shows the proportion of the cohort who are alive at the beginning of an indicated age interval and who will die before reaching the end of that age interval. For example, for males in the age interval 20-25, the proportion dying is 0.0101–out of every 1,000 males alive and exactly 20 years old at the beginning of the period about 10 will die before reaching their 25th birthday. In other words, the $_nq_x$ values represent *probabilities* that persons who are alive at the beginning of a specific age interval will die before reaching the beginning of the next age interval. The "proportion dying" column forms the basis of the life table; the life table is so constructed that all other columns are derived from it.

Column 3–Number surviving (l_x).–This column shows the number of persons, starting with a cohort of 100,000 live births, who survive to the exact age marking the beginning of each age interval. The l_x values are computed from the $_nq_x$ values, which are successively applied to the remainder of the original 100,000 persons still alive at the beginning of each age interval. Thus out of 100,000 male babies born alive, 98,600 will complete the first year of life and enter the second; 98,317 will begin the sixth year; 97,261 will reach age 20; and 17,783 will live to age 85.

Column 4–Number dying ($_nd_x$).–This column shows the number dying in each successive age interval out of 100,000 live births. Out of 100,000 males born alive, 1,400 die in the first year of life, 283 in the succeeding 4 years, 986 in the 5-year period between exact ages 20 and 25, and 17,783 die after reaching age 85. Each figure in column 4 is the difference between two successive figures in column 3.

Columns 5 and 6–Stationary population ($_nL_x$ and T_x).–Suppose that a group of 100,000 individuals like that assumed in columns 3 and 4 is born every year and that the proportions dying in each such group in each age interval throughout the lives of the members are exactly those shown in column 2. If there were no migration and if the births were evenly distributed over the calendar year, the survivors of these births would make up what is called a stationary population–stationary because in such a population the number of persons living in any given age group would never change. When an individual left the group, either by death or by growing older and entering the next higher age group, his place would immediately be taken by someone entering from the next lower age group. Thus a census taken at any time in such a stationary community would always show the same total population and the same numerical distribution of that population among the various age groups. In such a stationary population supported by 100,000 annual births, column 3 shows the number of persons who, each year, reach the birthday which marks the beginning of the age interval indicated in column 1, and column 4 shows the number of persons who die each year in the indicated age interval.

Column 5 shows the number of persons in the stationary population in the indicated age interval. For example, the figure given for males in the age interval 20-25 is 483,870. This means that in a stationary population of males supported by 100,000 annual births and with proportions dying in each age group always in accordance with column 2, a census taken on any date would show 483,870 persons between exact ages 20 and 25.

Column 6 shows the total number of persons in the stationary population (column 5) in the indicated age interval and all subsequent age intervals. For example, in the stationary population of males referred to in the last illustration, column 6 shows that there would be at any given moment a total of 5,033,709 persons who have passed their 20th birthday. The male population at all ages 0 and above (in other words, the total male population of the stationary community) would be 6,995,933.

Column 7–Average remaining lifetime ($\mathring{e}_x$).–The average remaining lifetime (also called expectation of life) at any given age is the average number of years remaining to be lived by those surviving to that age on the basis of a given set of age-specific rates of dying. In order to arrive at this value, it is first necessary to observe that the figures in column 5 of the life table can also be interpreted in terms of a single life table cohort without introducing the concept of the stationary population. From this point of view, each figure in column 5 represents the total time (in years) lived between two indicated birthdays by all those reaching the earlier birthday among the survivors of a cohort of 100,000 live births. Thus the figure 483,870 for males in the age interval 20-25 is the total number of years lived between the 20th and 25th birthdays by the 97,261 (column 3) who reached the 20th birthday out of 100,000 males born alive. The corresponding figure (5,033,709) in column 6 is the total number of years lived after attaining age 20 by the 97,261 reaching that age. This number of years divided by the number of persns (5,033,709 divided by 97,261) gives 51.8 years as the average remaining lifetime of males at age 20.

Table 5-A. Abridged Life Tables by Sex: United States, 1980

Age interval	Proportion dying	Of 100,000 born alive		Stationary population		Average remaining lifetime
Period of life between two exact ages stated by years, race, and sex	Proportion of persons alive at beginning of age interval dying during interval	Number living at beginning of age interval	Number dying during age interval	In the age interval	In this and all subsequent age intervals	Average number of years of life remaining at beginning of age interval
(1)	(2)	(3)	(4)	(5)	(6)	(7)
x to x + n	$_nq_x$	l_x	$_nd_x$	$_nL_x$	T_x	$\mathring{e}_x$
All races						
0 to 1	0.0127	100,000	1,266	98,901	7,371,986	73.7
1 to 5	0.0025	98,734	250	394,355	7,273,085	73.7
5 to 10.	0.0015	98,484	150	492,017	6,878,730	69.8
10 to 15	0.0015	98,334	152	491,349	6,386,713	64.9
15 to 20	0.0049	98,182	482	489,817	5,895,364	60.0
20 to 25	0.0066	97,700	648	486,901	5,405,547	55.3
25 to 30	0.0066	97,052	638	483,665	4,918,646	50.7
30 to 35	0.0070	96,414	672	480,463	4,434,981	46.0
35 to 40	0.0091	95,742	875	476,663	3,954,518	41.3
40 to 45	0.0139	94,867	1,321	471,250	3,477,855	36.7
45 to 50	0.0222	93,546	2,079	462,857	3,006,605	32.1
50 to 55	0.0351	91,467	3,209	449,811	2,543,748	27.8
55 to 60	0.0530	88,258	4,676	430,230	2,093,937	23.7
60 to 65	0.0794	83,582	6,638	402,081	1,663,707	19.9
65 to 70	0.1165	76,944	8,965	363,181	1,261,626	16.4
70 to 75	0.1694	67,979	11,517	312,015	898,445	13.2
75 to 80	0.2427	56,462	13,702	248,534	586,430	10.4
80 to 85	0.3554	42,760	15,197	175,192	337,896	7.9
85 and over.	1.0000	27,563	27,563	162,704	162,704	5.9
Male						
0 to 1	0.0140	100,000	1,400	98,787	6,995,933	70.0
1 to 5	0.0029	98,600	283	393,749	6,897,146	70.0
5 to 10.	0.0018	98,317	173	491,124	6,503,397	66.1
10 to 15	0.0019	98,144	188	490,340	6,012,273	61.3
15 to 20	0.0071	97,956	695	488,224	5,521,933	56.4
20 to 25	0.0101	97,261	986	483,870	5,033,709	51.8
25 to 30	0.0098	96,275	939	478,990	4,549,839	47.3
30 to 35	0.0098	95,336	932	474,430	4,070,849	42.7
35 to 40	0.0122	94,404	1,149	469,323	3,596,419	38.1
40 to 45	0.0180	93,255	1,681	462,351	3,127,096	33.5
45 to 50	0.0288	91,574	2,640	451,697	2,664,745	29.1
50 to 55	0.0462	88,934	4,110	435,061	2,213,048	24.9
55 to 60	0.0707	84,824	5,997	409,935	1,777,987	21.0
60 to 65	0.1061	78,827	8,365	374,082	1,368,052	17.4
65 to 70	0.1571	70,462	11,068	325,406	993,970	14.1
70 to 75	0.2259	59,394	13,420	263,862	668,564	11.3
75 to 80	0.3149	45,974	14,476	193,303	404,702	8.8
80 to 85	0.4354	31,498	13,715	121,742	211,399	6.7
85 and over.	1.0000	17,783	17,783	89,657	89,657	5.0
Female						
0 to 1	0.0113	100,000	1,126	99,021	7,748,490	77.5
1 to 5	0.0022	98,874	215	394,990	7,649,469	77.4
5 to 10.	0.0013	98,659	126	492,954	7,254,479	73.5
10 to 15	0.0011	98,533	113	492,411	6,761,525	68.6
15 to 20	0.0027	98,420	261	491,492	6,269,114	63.7
20 to 25	0.0031	98,159	305	490,045	5,777,622	58.9
25 to 30	0.0034	97,854	334	488,463	5,287,577	54.0
30 to 35	0.0042	97,520	412	486,634	4,799,114	49.2
35 to 40	0.0062	97,108	601	484,140	4,312,480	44.4
40 to 45	0.0100	96,507	963	480,283	3,828,340	39.7
45 to 50	0.0160	95,544	1,524	474,134	3,348,057	35.0
50 to 55	0.0247	94,020	2,322	464,624	2,873,923	30.6
55 to 60	0.0369	91,698	3,381	450,481	2,409,299	26.3
60 to 65	0.0558	88,317	4,931	429,330	1,958,818	22.2
65 to 70	0.0828	83,386	6,902	400,651	1,528,888	18.3
70 to 75	0.1261	76,484	9,643	359,605	1,128,237	14.8
75 to 80	0.1937	66,841	12,950	303,049	768,632	13.5
80 to 85	0.3088	53,891	16,639	228,072	465,583	8.6
85 and over.	1.0000	37,252	37,252	237,511	237,511	6.4

Source: National Center for Health Statistics. Vital Statistics of the United States: Mortality (1980--Vol. II, Part A). Washington, DC: U.S. Government Printing Office, 1984.

Chapter 6

Fertility and Reproduction

Overview

In order for the human race to perpetuate itself, each person who dies must be replaced by a birth. If births outnumber deaths, the population grows. When births and deaths are exactly equal, a condition of zero growth occurs. If zero growth continues for a sustained time, demographers characterize the population as "stationary." In such conditions fertility is said to be at the "replacement level"—able to neutralize the effects of death, but insufficient for growth. The population of the United States appears to be approaching a stationary state, and fertility is hovering around the replacement level. Although there are differentials in fertility levels among the various races, socioeconomic groups, and regional sectors of the population, with only a few exceptions these differentials are minor variations on the dominant theme of replacement-level fertility.

Bearing and rearing children has been a major personal ambition and social expectation throughout the nation's history, and currently is still stronger than in the northwestern European nations of its colonial origin. Having replacement-level fertility does not necessarily signify that a population is repudiating child-rearing and abandoning cultural expectations about population replacement, but it does imply significant changes in ideal family size, the age composition of the population, and almost every other topic on which this book focuses. This chapter not only describes the facts of fertility trends but also reviews the evidence concerning the more subjective aspects of the value of children and intentions to bear children in the changing American value system. The remaining chapters will discuss the implications of fertility change, topic by topic.

This chapter is divided into three sections. The first describes fertility in the United States as an aggregate demographic process. The second section describes fertility in terms of the attitudes, behaviors, and expectations of individuals and families. The third combines information about mortality from Chapter 5 with information about fertility from the present chapter to discuss reproduction and long-term prospects for population growth or decline in the nation.

Definitions

Crude Birth Rate (CBR). Number of births in a year per 1,000 total midyear population residing in an area.

General Fertility Rate (or Fertility Rate)(GFR). Number of births in a year per 1,000 women aged 15-44 residing in an area as of midyear.

Age-Specific Fertility Rate (ASFR). The number of live births in a year to women of a specified age (or grouping of ages) per 1,000 women in the same age or age grouping residing in an area at midyear. In the United States it is customary to declare age fifteen as the lower age limit for fertility statistics and to include the comparatively small number of births to females under fifteen in this group. Similarly age forty-four is defined as the oldest age in the reproductive span, and the few births occurring to women age forty-five and over are included in this group. The United Nations defines forty-nine as the upper limit for reproduction and sometimes has birth rates for an age group under fifteen years of age.

Total Fertility Rate (TFR). The sums of age-specific birth rates across the entire reproductive span. If ASFRs are reported in five-year age groups, their sum is multiplied by five. This rate specifies how many children 1,000 women would bear if they experienced the age-specific fertility rates for a given year throughout their reproductive lives. When divided by 1,000, TFR reports the average number of children each woman in the population would bear under these assumptions.

Cumulative Fertility Rate. Number of live births ever born per 1,000 women in a cohort (hypothetical or real) from the onset of their potential childbearing (age fifteen) to a specified age. This statistic is derived by summing age-specific fertility rates.

Completed Fertility Rate. The cumulative fertility rate of a cohort of women who have passed their forty-fifth birthday. For hypothetical cohorts it is equal to TFR.

Cohort Fertility Rate. Fertility to real cohorts of women, obtained by tracing them longitudinally from year to year. Cohort rates may be age-specific or cumulative. For completed cohorts (which have passed their forty-fifth birthday) it is possible to compute GFR, TFR, and other summary measures.

Birth Order. The ordinal order of a birth to a particular woman (first, second, and so on).

Order-Specific Fertility Rate. Number of live births of a given birth order in a year (1, 2, 3, and so on) per 1,000 women aged 15-44 years.

Nuptial Fertility Rate (NFR). The number of live births in a year to married women aged 15-44. This rate may be made specific for age, race, and birth order.

Parity. The number of children a woman has ever born. This is a fertility characteristics of women. (Zero parity represents childlessness, parity 1 represents having born one child, and so on.)

Out-of-Wedlock (Illegitimacy) Birth Rate (OWBR). Number of live births to unmarried women per 1,000 unmarried women aged 15-44. This rate may be made specific for age, race, and birth order.

Out-of-Wedlock Birth Ratio. The ratio of out-of-wedlock births in a year per 1,000 total live births during the same year. This ratio may be made specific for age, race, and birth order.

Child-Woman Ratio (CWR). Number of children aged 0-4 per 1,000 women aged 20-44 or 20-49 years. This is a reasonably precise indicator of fertility when birth data are not available. It assumes that the children were born by the women of those ages, and that mortality is equal among all groups being compared since living children rather than births are taken as indicators of fertility.

Children Ever Born. The cumulative number of children women have born at the time they are interviewed in a census or survey. This measure is a form of cumulative fertility that may be reported on an age-specific basis or on a cumulative basis.

Birth Probabilities. The probability that a woman will have a live birth within a specified year of age.

Parity-Specific Fertility Rate or Parity-Specific Birth Probability. Annual number of live births of a given order per 1,000 women of a parity one child lower than the birth order (for example, first births to zero parity women). Such measures may be computed either as rates or as probabilities.

Continued on next page

Definitions

Sex Ratio at Birth. Number of male live-born infants per 100 or per 1,000 female live-born infants in a given year. *Proportion female* for births is the proportion of all births that were female in a specified year.

Gross Reproduction Rate (GRR). The sums of age-specific birth rates by five-year age groups of mothers multiplied by five and by the proportion of births that were female. These rates represent the average number of daughters that a hypothetical cohort of women would bear if they all survived from birth to the end of the childbearing period and if throughout their lives they experienced the age-specific fertility rates for a given year.

Net Reproduction Rate (NRR). The sum of age-specific birth rates by five-year age groups of mothers multiplied by five and the probability (as determined from the life table for the year) of women surviving to a specified age group and by the proportion of births that were female. These rates represent the average number of daughters that a hypothetical cohort of women would bear if they experienced a given set of age-specific mortality and fertility rates until attaining age forty-five.

Intrinsic Birth, Death, and Natural Increase Rates. The rates of birth, death, and natural increase that would eventually prevail if a population were to experience the age-specific mortality and fertility rates for a given year over a long period of time, without migration.

Sources of Fertility Data

The principal source of statistical information about births is the annual volume *Vital Statistics of the United States: Volume I-Natality,* published by the National Center for Health Statistics of the U.S. Department of Health and Human Services. The book presents a tabulation of actual births as documented on birth certificates. In addition, the U.S. Bureau of the Census periodically publishes "Fertility of American Women," based on sample surveys with a cross section of the population. These reports are published in *Current Population Reports* (Series P-20). The National Institute of Health and Human Development sponsors periodic national fertility surveys. These are supplemented by other surveys taken by private survey organizations, sometimes with subsidies from the federal government. This chapter will present the highlights of the findings from these sources. Technical Appendix 6-1 at the end of this chapter describes in more detail how fertility data are collected and disseminated.

Fertility as a Demographic Process

In addition to the crude birth rate (CBR) (introduced in Chapter 1), three widely used measures of fertility are the general fertility rate (GFR), the age specific fertility fertility rates (ASFR), and the total fertility rate (TFR). These rates are defined in the Definition Box. Because the crude birth rate is strongly affected by age and sex composition, the GFR and TFR are preferred summary measures of fertility, because they are based on women of childbearing age. They are highly correlated and usually lead to almost identical conclusions. (For most years, the TFR is roughly thirty times the GFR, because GFR represents the rate of childbearing in one year and TFR estimates the results of such childbearing if it were to continue unchanged for the thirty years of the reproductive span of ages fifteen to forty-four.) Many demographers prefer to use TFR because of its clear implications for average family size.

Table 6-1 provides statistics on the number of births and the crude birth rate for each year since 1909. Data are provided separately for the white and black populations. (Before 1959 birth data for the black population were pooled with births to the "other nonwhite" populations–American Indian, Chinese, Japanese, and so on. Because the black population was 95 percent or more of the residual remaining after the white population was subtracted from the total population, the "all other" total and the black categories yield almost identical rates and trends, as the data since 1959 indicate.) Table 6-2 reports the general fertility rate and the total fertility rate for the same years, by race. Figure 6-1 graphs the trend of the total number of births and the crude birth rate, and Figure 6-2A graphs the trend of the general fertility rate for the white and the black (other races) population.

In this century fertility may be said to have passed through four phases:

Table 6-1. Live Births and Crude Birth Rates: United States, 1909-1983 [birth rates per 1,000 population residing in area for specified group]

Year[a]	Number				Crude birth rate[b]			
	All races	White	All other		All races	White	All other	
			Total	Black			Total	Black
1983	3,614,000	--	--	--	15.5	--	--	--
1982	3,704,000	--	--	--	16.0	--	--	--
1981	3,629,238	2,908,669	720,569	587,797	15.8	14.8	22.0	21.6
1980	3,612,258	2,898,732	713,526	589,616	15.9	14.9	22.5	22.1
1979	3,494,398	2,808,420	685,978	577,855	15.6	14.5	22.2	22.0
1978	3,333,279	2,681,116	652,163	551,540	15.0	14.0	21.6	21.3
1977	3,326,632	2,691,070	635,562	544,221	15.1	14.1	21.6	21.4
1976	3,167,788	2,567,614	600,174	514,479	14.6	13.6	20.8	20.5
1975	3,144,198	2,551,996	592,202	511,581	14.6	13.6	21.0	20.7
1974	3,159,958	2,575,792	584,166	507,162	14.8	13.9	21.2	20.8
1973	3,136,965	2,551,030	585,935	512,597	14.8	13.8	21.7	21.4
1972	3,258,411	2,655,558	602,853	531,329	15.6	14.5	22.8	22.5
1971	3,555,970	2,919,746	636,224	564,960	17.2	16.1	24.6	24.4
1970	3,731,386	3,091,264	640,122	572,362	18.4	17.4	25.1	25.3
1969	3,600,206	2,993,614	606,592	543,132	17.9	16.9	24.5	24.4
1968	3,501,564	2,912,224	589,340	531,152	17.6	16.6	24.2	24.2
1967	3,520,959	2,922,502	598,457	543,976	17.8	16.8	25.0	25.1
1966	3,606,274	2,993,230	613,044	558,244	18.4	17.4	26.1	26.2
1965	3,760,358	3,123,860	636,498	581,126	19.4	18.3	27.6	27.7
1964	4,027,490	3,369,160	658,330	607,556	21.1	20.0	29.2	29.5
1963	4,098,020	3,326,344	638,928	580,658	21.7	20.7	29.7	--
1962	4,167,362	3,394,068	641,580	584,610	22.4	21.4	30.5	--
1961	4,268,326	3,600,864	667,462	611,072	23.3	22.2	31.6	--
1960	4,257,850	3,600,744	657,106	602,264	23.7	22.7	32.1	31.9
1959	4,286,000	3,619,000	666,000	605,962	24.2	23.1	33.9	--
1958	4,246,000	3,595,000	651,000	--	24.5	23.3	34.0	--
1957	4,300,000	3,646,-00	654,000	--	25.3	24.0	35.0	--
1956	4,210,000	3,570,000	640,000	--	25.2	24.0	35.1	--
1955	4,097,000	3,485,000	613,000	--	25.0	23.8	34.5	--
1954	4,071,000	3,472,000	599,000	--	25.3	24.2	34.7	--
1953	3,959,000	3,387,000	572,000	--	25.1	24.0	33.9	--
1952	3,909,000	3,356,000	553,000	--	25.1	24.1	33.4	--
1951	3,820,000	3,275,000	545,000	--	24.9	23.9	33.7	--
1950	3,632,000	3,108,000	524,000	--	24.1	23.0	33.3	--
1949	3,649,000	3,136,000	513,000	--	24.5	23.6	33.0	--
1948	3,637,000	3,141,000	495,000	--	24.9	24.0	32.4	--
1947	3,817,000	3,347,000	469,000	--	26.6	26.1	31.2	--
1946	3,411,000	2,990,000	420,000	--	24.1	23.6	28.4	--
1945	2,858,000	2,471,000	388,000	--	20.4	19.7	26.5	--
1944	2,939,000	2,545,000	394,000	--	21.2	20.5	27.4	--
1943	3,104,000	2,704,000	400,000	--	22.7	22.1	28.3	--
1942	2,989,000	2,605,000	384,000	--	22.2	21.5	27.7	--
1941	2,703,000	2,330,000	374,000	--	20.3	19.5	27.3	--
1940	2,559,000	2,199,000	360,000	--	19.4	18.6	26.7	--
1939	2,466,000	2,117,000	349,000	--	18.8	18.0	26.1	--
1938	2,496,000	2,148,000	348,000	--	19.2	18.4	26.3	--
1937	2,413,000	2,071,000	342,000	--	18.7	17.9	26.0	--
1936	2,355,000	2,027,000	328,000	--	18.4	17.6	25.1	--
1935	2,377,000	2,042,000	334,000	--	18.7	17.9	25.8	--
1934	2,396,000	2,058,000	338,000	--	19.0	18.1	26.3	--
1933	2,307,000	1,982,000	325,000	--	18.4	17.6	25.5	--
1932	2,440,000	2,099,000	341,000	--	19.5	18.7	26.9	--
1931	2,506,000	2,170,000	335,000	--	20.2	19.5	26.6	--
1930	2,618,000	2,274,000	344,000	--	21.3	20.6	27.5	--
1929	2,582,000	2,244,000	339,000	--	21.2	20.5	27.3	--
1928	2,674,000	2,325,000	349,000	--	22.2	21.5	28.5	--
1927	2,802,000	2,425,000	377,000	--	23.5	22.7	31.1	--
1926	2,839,000	2,441,000	398,000	--	24.2	23.1	33.4	--
1925	2,909,000	2,506,000	403,000	--	25.1	24.1	34.2	--
1924	2,979,000	2,577,000	401,000	--	26.1	25.1	34.6	--
1923	2,910,000	2,531,000	380,000	--	26.0	25.2	33.2	--
1922	2,882,000	2,507,000	375,000	--	26.2	25.4	33.2	--
1921	3,055,000	2,657,000	398,000	--	28.1	27.3	35.8	--
1920	2,950,000	2,566,000	383,000	--	27.7	26.9	35.0	--
1919	2,740,000	2,387,000	353,000	--	26.1	25.3	32.4	--
1918	2,948,000	2,588,000	360,000	--	28.2	27.6	33.0	--
1917	2,944,000	2,587,000	357,000	--	28.5	27.9	32.9	--
1916	2,964,000	2,599,000	365,000	--	29.1	28.5	--	--
1915	2,965,000	2,594,000	371,000	--	29.5	28.9	--	--
1914	2,966,000	2,588,000	378,000	--	29.9	29.3	--	--
1913	2,869,000	2,497,000	372,000	--	29.5	28.8	--	--
1912	2,840,000	2,467,000	373,000	--	29.8	29.0	--	--
1911	2,809,000	2,435,000	374,000	--	29.9	29.1	--	--
1910	2,777,000	2,401,000	376,000	--	30.1	29.2	--	--
1909	2,718,000	2,344,000	374,000	--	30.0	29.2	--	--

[a] Births prior to 1959 have been adjusted for underregistration.

[b] For 1917-1919 and 1941-1946, rates based on population including armed forces abroad.

Sources: National Center for Health Statistics. "Births, Marriages, Divorces and Deaths: 1983." *Monthly Vital Statistics Report* (Vol. 32, no.12); "Advance Report of Final Natality Statistics: 1981." *Monthly Vital Statistics Report* (Vol. 32, no. 9 supplement, Table 1); and *Vital Statistics of the United States: 1979* (Table 1-1). Washington, DC: U.S. Government Printing Office, 1984 and 1983.

Table 6-2. General Fertility Rate and Total Fertility Rate, by Race: United States, 1909-1981

Year[a]	General fertility rate				Total fertility rate			
	All races	White	All other		All races	White	All other	
			Total	Black			Total	Black
1981.	67.4	63.9	86.4	85.4	1,815.0	1,726.0	2,274.5	2,206.0
1980.	68.4	64.7	88.6	88.1	1,839.5	1,748.5	2,323.0	2,266.0
1979.	67.2	63.4	88.5	88.3	1,808.0	1,715.5	2,309.5	2,263.2
1978.	65.5	61.7	87.0	86.7	1,760.0	1,667.5	2,264.5	2,218.0
1977.	66.8	63.2	87.7	88.1	1,789.5	1,703.0	2,278.5	2,251.0
1976.	65.0	61.5	85.8	85.8	1,738.0	1,652.0	2,222.5	2,187.0
1975.	66.0	62.5	87.7	87.9	1,774.0	1,686.0	2,276.0	2,243.0
1974.	67.8	64.2	89.8	89.7	1,835.0	1,748.5	2,338.5	2,298.5
1973.	68.8	64.9	93.4	93.6	1,879.0	1,783.0	2,443.0	2,411.0
1972.	73.1	68.9	99.5	99.9	2,010.0	1,906.5	2,627.5	2,601.0
1971.	81.6	77.3	109.1	109.7	2,266.5	2,160.5	2,919.5	2,902.0
1970.	87.9	84.1	113.0	115.4	2,480.0	2,385.0	3,066.7	3,098.7
1969.	86.1	82.2	111.6	112.1	2,455.5	2,360.3	3,061.2	3,042.8
1968.	85.2	81.3	111.9	112.7	2,464.2	2,365.6	3,108.4	3,099.8
1967.	87.2	82.8	117.1	118.5	2,557.7	2,446.9	3,299.2	3,311.8
1966.	90.8	86.2	123.5	124.7	2,721.4	2,602.9	3,531.5	3,545.3
1965.	96.3	91.3	131.9	133.2	2,912.6	2,783.4	3,807.9	3,828.5
1964.	104.7	99.8	140.0	142.6	3,190.5	3,065.0	4,070.2	4,138.6
1963.	108.3	103.6	143.7	--	3,318.8	3,193.5	4,203.0	--
1962.	112.0	107.5	147.8	--	3,461.3	3,341.3	4,340.1	--
1961.	117.1	112.3	153.0	--	3,620.3	3,496.9	4,496.8	--
1960.	118.0	113.2	153.6	153.5	3,653.6	3,532.9	4,522.1	4,541.8
1959.	119.9	114.5	160.7	--	3,670.0	3,544.0	4,595.0	--
1958.	120.0	114.8	159.1	--	3,701.0	3,560.0	4,727.0	--
1957.	122.7	117.6	161.7	--	3,767.0	3,625.0	4,798.0	--
1956.	121.0	115.9	159.7	--	3,689.0	3,546.0	4,730.0	--
1955.	118.3	113.7	154.3	--	3,580.0	3,446.0	4,550.0	--
1954.	117.9	113.5	152.2	--	3,543.0	3,415.0	4,474.0	--
1953.	115.0	110.9	146.4	--	3,424.0	3,306.0	4,283.0	--
1952.	113.8	110.0	142.7	--	3,358.0	3,250.0	4,147.0	--
1951.	111.4	107.7	141.7	--	3,269.0	3,157.0	4,091.0	--
1950.	106.2	102.3	137.3	--	3,091.0	2,977.0	3,928.0	--
1949.	107.1	103.6	135.1	--	3,110.0	3,009.0	3,855.0	--
1948.	107.3	104.3	131.6	--	3,109.0	3,022.0	3,742.0	--
1947.	113.3	111.8	125.9	--	3,274.0	3,230.0	3,575.0	--
1946.	101.9	100.4	113.9	--	2,943.0	2,901.0	3,238.0	--
1945.	85.9	83.4	106.0	--	2,491.0	2,421.0	3,017.0	--
1944.	88.8	86.3	108.5	--	2,568.0	2,501.0	3,075.0	--
1943.	94.3	92.3	111.0	--	2,718.0	2,664.0	3,128.0	--
1942.	91.5	89.5	107.6	--	2,628.0	2,577.0	3,022.0	--
1941.	83.4	80.7	105.4	--	2,399.0	2,328.0	2,956.0	--
1940.	79.9	77.1	102.4	--	2,301.0	2,229.0	2,870.0	--
1939.	77.6	74.8	100.1	--	--	--	--	--
1938.	79.1	76.5	100.5	--	--	--	--	--
1937.	77.1	74.4	99.4	--	--	--	--	--
1936.	75.8	73.3	95.9	--	--	--	--	--
1935.	77.2	74.5	98.4	--	--	--	--	--
1934.	78.5	75.8	100.4	--	--	--	--	--
1933.	76.3	73.7	97.3	--	--	--	--	--
1932.	81.7	79.0	103.0	--	--	--	--	--
1931.	84.6	82.4	102.1	--	--	--	--	--
1930.	89.2	87.1	105.9	--	--	--	--	--
1929.	89.3	87.3	106.1	--	--	--	--	--
1928.	93.8	91.7	111.0	--	--	--	--	--
1927.	99.8	97.1	121.7	--	--	--	--	--
1926.	102.6	99.2	130.3	--	--	--	--	--
1925.	106.6	103.3	134.0	--	--	--	--	--
1924.	110.9	107.8	135.6	--	--	--	--	--
1923.	110.5	108.0	130.5	--	--	--	--	--
1922.	111.2	108.8	130.8	--	--	--	--	--
1921.	119.8	117.2	140.8	--	--	--	--	--
1920.	117.9	115.4	137.5	--	--	--	--	--
1919.	111.2	--	--	--	--	--	--	--
1918.	119.8	--	--	--	--	--	--	--
1917.	121.0	--	--	--	--	--	--	--
1916.	123.4	121.8	--	--	--	--	--	--
1915.	125.0	123.2	--	--	--	--	--	--
1914.	126.6	124.6	--	--	--	--	--	--
1913.	124.7	122.4	--	--	--	--	--	--
1912.	125.8	123.3	--	--	--	--	--	--
1911.	126.3	123.6	--	--	--	--	--	--
1910.	126.8	123.8	--	--	--	--	--	--
1909.	126.8	123.6	--	--	--	--	--	--

[a]Births prior to 1959 have been adjusted for underregistration.

Note: -- indicates data not available.

Source: National Center for Health Statistics. Vital Statistics of the United States: 1979 (Vol. I, Tables 1-1 and 1-6); and "Advance Report of the Final Natality Statistics: 1981," Monthly Vital Statistics Report (Vol 32, no. 9 supplement, Tables 1 and 4). Washington, DC: U.S. Government Printing Office, 1984 and 1982. Also U.S. Bureau of the Census. Historical Statistics of the United States: Colonial Times to 1970. Washington, DC: U.S. Government Printing Office, 1975.

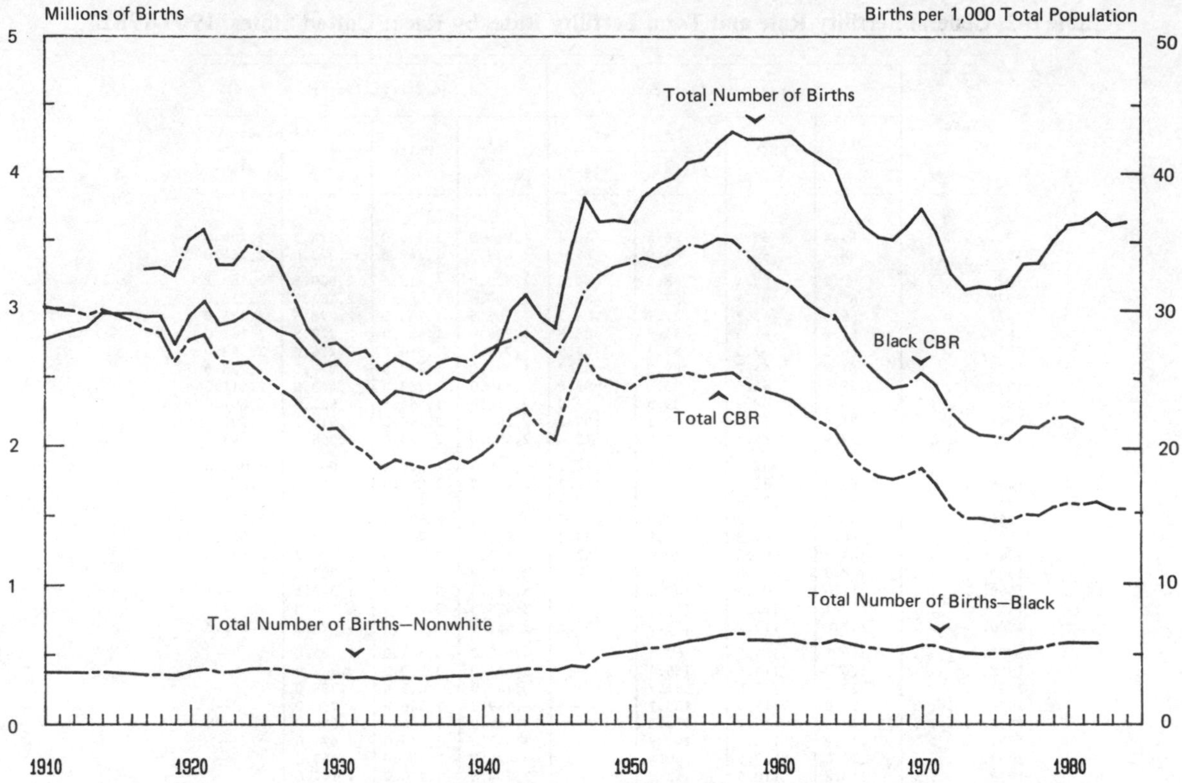

Figure 6-1. Race Differentials in Total Births and Crude Birth Rate

1. Gradual decline from high to replacement level fertility, from 1900 to 1933, with a small upsurge following World War I
2. The "baby boom," from 1940 to 1957, with rising rate and number of births
3. The "baby bust," from 1957 to 1976, with declining rate and number of births.
4. Low-level plateau ("baby boom echo"), from 1976 to 1983, with a level rate and rising number of births.

It has already been shown (in Chapter 2) how these fluctuations have created "waves" in the population age distribution. Starting about 1977, an "echo wave" began to be created in the number of births, even though fertility rates were low, because the women born during the "baby boom" were passing through the prime childbearing years. Because the number of women of childbearing age increased, the number of births each year rose.

A total fertility rate of 2,100 (2.1 births per woman) represents replacement. At this rate adults are able to replace themselves, with a small margin for infants and children who die before reaching reproductive age. A general fertility rate of 70 also approximately represents replacement, which corresponds roughly to a crude birth rate of 15.5 or 16.0 births per 1,000 total population per year. A basic demographic theorem is that any population with a crude death rate of 15.0 is either very close to or slightly below replacement level, and any population with a crude birth rate of 17.0 or more is above replacement. Thus, it can be seen from Table 6-2 that as of about 1972 the fertility in the United States sank below the replacement level and has remained there for more than a decade. The number of births has continued to be higher than the number of deaths only because of the young age composition of the population, left over from the baby boom. Between 1969 and 1971 there was a significant rise in fertility rates, leading to speculation that a new baby boom was developing, but in 1972-76 there was a relapse to lower levels. A low point in fertility (CBR of 14.6, GFR of 65.0, and TFR of 1,738) occurred in 1976; after 1976 there was a slight rise to a point closer to but still below replacement level. Following the recovery between 1976 and 1980, the birth rate wandered along on a plateau for two years with no apparent trend. In 1983 it took another dip, perhaps in reaction to the severe recession of 1982 and 1983, then it recovered sharply in early 1984 to the plateau levels of 1980-83. Figure 6-2B, which graphs the monthly fluctuations since 1980 in the seasonally adjusted fertility rate (see Definition Box), illustrates the fertility rate's path since 1980.

As of 1984 demographers were hesitant about pre-

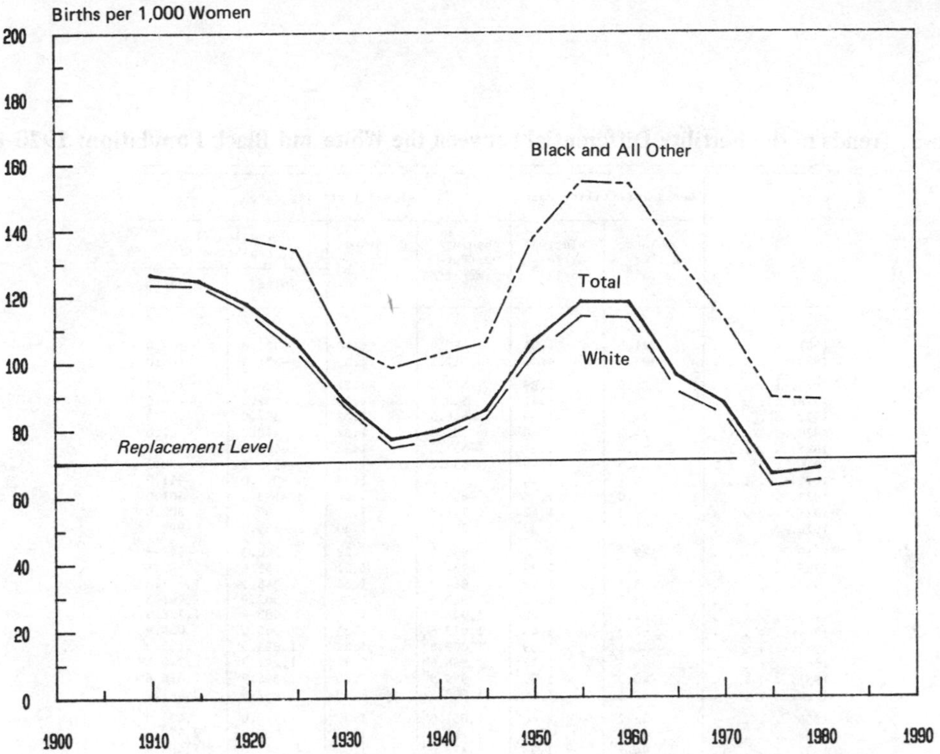

Figure 6-2A. Trends of the General Fertility Rate and the Total Fertility Rate, by Race: 1900-1983

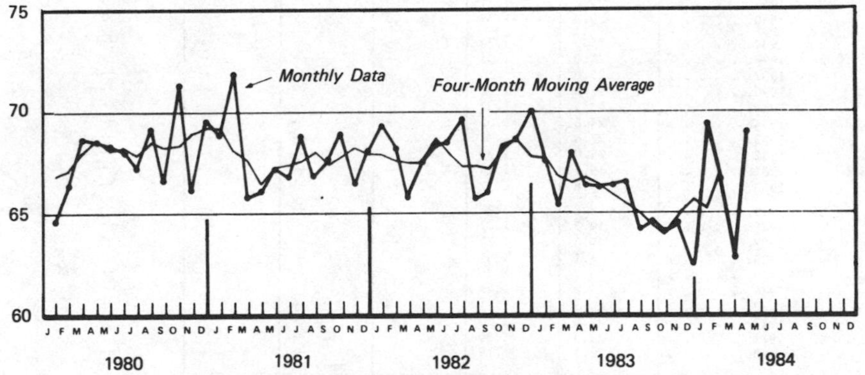

Figure 6-2B. Seasonally Adjusted Fertility Rate per 1,000 Women Aged 15-44

dicting what course the birth rate would take for the remainder of the decade. Because of apparently impending recovery from the severe economic recession during 1980-83 some were foreseeing a small rise, while others predicted further declines because of the trends toward later marriage (described in Chapter 4). Most agreed that no "baby boom" based on a resurgence of fertility rates was on the horizon, but there was still little evidence of "demographic suicide" through refusal to reproduce. Instead, the prospect seemed to be small ripples in a plateau hovering just at or moderately below the replacement level.

Table 6-3. Trends in the Fertility Differential between the White and Black Population: 1920-1981

Year	General fertility rate		Total fertility rate			
	Absolute differential[a]	Relative differential[b]	Absolute differential[a]	Relative differential[b]	Deviation from replacement[c]	
					White	Black
1981.	21.5	1.34	480.0	1.28	-374.0	106.0
1980.	23.4	1.36	517.5	1.30	-351.5	166.0
1979.	24.9	1.39	547.7	1.32	-384.5	163.2
1978.	25.0	1.41	550.5	1.33	-432.5	118.0
1977.	24.9	1.39	548.0	1.32	-397.0	151.0
1976.	24.3	1.40	535.0	1.32	-448.0	87.0
1975.	25.4	1.41	557.0	1.33	-414.0	143.0
1974.	25.5	1.40	550.0	1.31	-351.5	198.5
1973.	28.7	1.44	628.0	1.35	-317.0	311.0
1972.	31.0	1.45	694.5	1.36	-193.5	501.0
1971.	32.4	1.42	741.5	1.34	60.5	802.0
1970.	31.3	1.37	713.7	1.30	285.0	998.7
1969.	29.9	1.36	682.5	1.29	260.3	942.8
1968.	31.4	1.39	734.2	1.31	265.6	999.8
1967.	35.7	1.43	864.9	1.35	346.9	1,211.8
1966.	38.5	1.45	942.4	1.36	502.9	1,445.3
1965.	41.9	1.46	1,045.1	1.38	683.4	1,728.5
1964.	42.8	1.43	1,073.6	1.35	965.0	2,038.6
1963.	40.1[d]	1.39[d]	1,009.5[d]	1.32[d]	1,093.5[d]	2,103.0[d]
1962.	40.3[d]	1.37[d]	998.8[d]	1.30[d]	1,241.3[d]	2,240.1[d]
1961.	40.7[d]	1.36[d]	999.9[d]	1.29[d]	1,396.9[d]	2,396.8[d]
1960.	40.3	1.36	1,008.9	1.29	1,432.9	2,441.8
1959.	46.2[d]	1.40[d]	1,051.0[d]	1.30[d]	1,444.0[d]	2,495.0[d]
1958.	44.3[d]	1.39[d]	1,167.0[d]	1.33[d]	1,460.0[d]	2,627.0[d]
1957.	44.1[d]	1.38[d]	1,173.0[d]	1.32[d]	1,525.0[d]	2,698.0[d]
1956.	43.8	1.38	1,184.0	1.33	1,446.0	2,630.0
1955.	40.6	1.36	1,104.0	1.32	1,346.0	2,450.0
1954.	38.7	1.34	1,059.0	1.31	1,315.0	2,374.0
1953.	35.5	1.32	977.0	1.30	1,206.0	2,183.0
1952.	32.7	1.30	897.0	1.28	1,150.0	2,047.0
1951.	34.0	1.32	934.0	1.30	1,057.0	1,991.0
1950.	35.0	1.34	951.0	1.32	877.0	1,828.0
1949.	31.5	1.30	846.0	1.28	909.0	1,755.0
1948.	27.3	1.26	720.0	1.24	922.0	1,642.0
1947.	14.1	1.13	345.0	1.11	1,130.0	1,475.0
1946.	13.5	1.13	337.0	1.12	801.0	1,138.0
1945.	22.6	1.27	596.0	1.25	321.0	917.0
1944.	22.2	1.26	574.0	1.23	401.0	975.0
1943.	18.7	1.20	464.0	1.17	564.0	1,028.0
1942.	18.1	1.20	445.0	1.17	477.0	922.0
1941.	24.7	1.31	628.0	1.27	228.0	856.0
1940.	25.3	1.33	641.0	1.29	129.0	770.0
1939.	25.3	1.34	--	--	--	--
1938.	24.0	1.31	--	--	--	--
1937.	25.0	1.34	--	--	--	--
1936.	22.6	1.31	--	--	--	--
1935.	23.9	1.32	--	--	--	--
1934.	24.6	1.32	--	--	--	--
1933.	23.6	1.32	--	--	--	--
1932.	24.0	1.30	--	--	--	--
1931.	19.7	1.24	--	--	--	--
1930.	18.8	1.22	--	--	--	--
1929.	18.8	1.22	--	--	--	--
1928.	19.3	1.21	--	--	--	--
1927.	24.6	1.25	--	--	--	--
1926.	31.1	1.31	--	--	--	--
1925.	30.7	1.30	--	--	--	--
1924.	27.8	1.26	--	--	--	--
1923.	22.5	1.21	--	--	--	--
1922.	22.0	1.20	--	--	--	--
1921.	23.6	1.20	--	--	--	--
1920.	22.1	1.19	--	--	--	--

[a]Absolute differential is FR of black population minus FR of white population.

[b]Relative differential is FR of black population divided by FR of white population.

[c]Deviation from replacement is TFR minus 2,100.

[d]Nonwhite instead of black, and for all years prior to 1956.

Source: Table 6-2.

Differentials in Fertility Between the Black and White Population

In 1981 the TFR for black women was 2,206, which is 5 percent above the replacement level of 2,100. In contrast, the TFR of white women was 1,726, which is 18 percent below replacement level. If this differential were to persist, black females would bear an average of 0.48 child more than white females, an excess in the fertility rate of 28 percent above the white population (see Table 6-2). This differential is due less to the high (above replacement) level of the black population than to the below replacement fertility of the white population.

One of the impressive facts about fertility trends in the United States has been the tendency for black and white birth rates to follow parallel paths, fluctuating upward and downward almost simultaneously. Figure 6-2 illustrates this propensity. However, the trends are not wholly parallel, and the differentials by race have changed over time. Table 6-3 and Figure 6-3 examine these differentials in more detail. The differentials are expressed in three ways:

1. Absolute differential: black fertility minus white fertiltiy
2. Relative differential: black fertility divided by white fertility
3. Deviation from replacement: TFR minus 2,100.

Although these three series of data emphasize the similarity of the trends, with both racial groups tending toward replacement, certain significant points need to be mentioned.

At the onset of the "baby boom" the absolute differentials tended to widen. Although the fertility of both black and white populations rose, the fertility of the black population rose by a larger *amount* while the *ratio* of black-to-white fertility remained almost unchanged. Since the onset of the "baby bust" in 1958 there has been a steady narrowing of the absolute differentials while the relative differential has remained the same. This means that the birth rate of the black population has declined by a greater *amount* than the white population and that the rates are converging, but the *ratio* is constant. In 1955-58, at the height of the baby boom, the birth rate of black population was truly explosive (4.8 births per woman)–not far below the rates of the developing nations of Asia and Latin America (though well below those of Africa). In those days there was widespread fear that the white population would reduce its fertility and the black population would not, with the result that the growth differential between the two would become huge. Instead, the fertility of the black population was headed down toward replacement, and by greater annual absolute amounts than that of the white population. A close examination

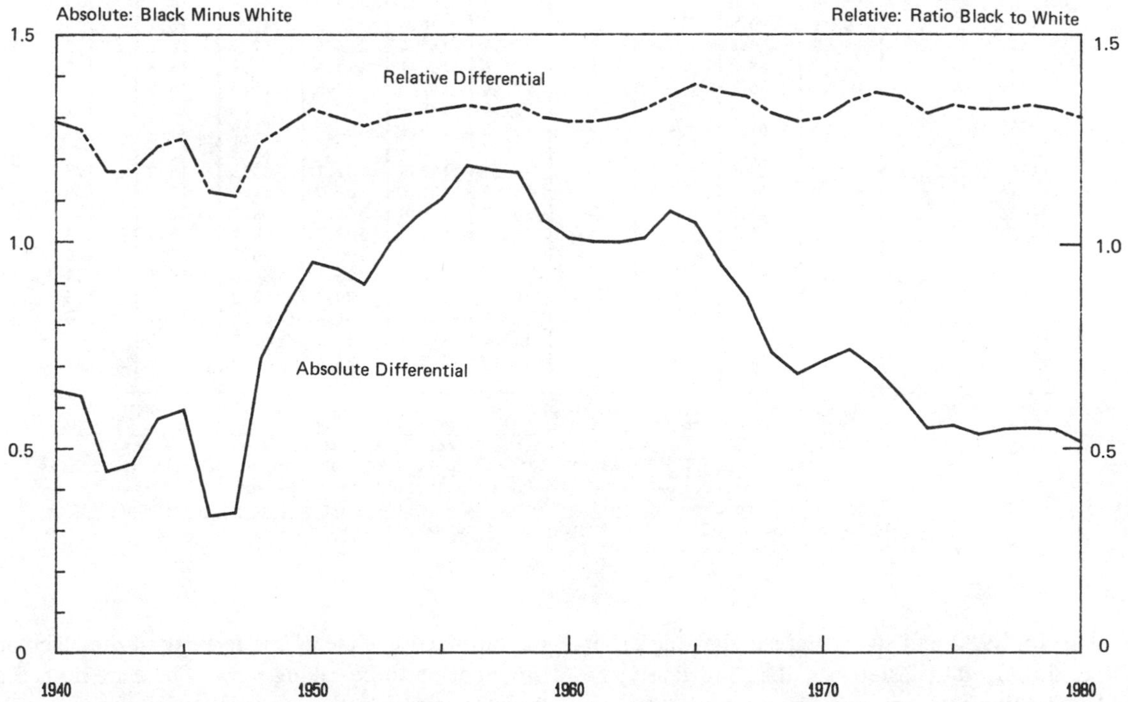

Figure 6-3. Absolute and Relative Differences between White and Black Total Fertility Rates: 1940-1982

Table 6-4A. Age-Specific Fertility Rates of the United States Population: All Races, 1940-1981

Year	10-14 years	15-19 years			20-24 years	25-29 years	30-34 years	35-39 years	40-44 years	45-49 years
		Total	15-17 years	18-19 years						
1981.	1.1	52.7	32.1	81.7	111.8	112.0	61.4	20.0	3.8	0.2
1980.	1.1	53.0	32.5	82.1	115.1	112.9	61.9	19.8	3.9	0.2
1979.	1.2	52.3	32.3	81.3	112.8	111.4	60.3	19.5	3.9	0.2
1978.	1.2	51.5	32.2	79.8	109.9	108.5	57.8	19.0	3.9	0.2
1977.	1.2	52.8	33.9	80.9	112.9	111.0	56.4	19.2	4.2	0.2
1976.	1.2	52.8	34.1	80.5	110.3	106.2	53.6	19.0	4.3	0.2
1975.	1.3	55.6	36.1	85.0	113.0	108.2	52.3	19.5	4.6	0.3
1974.	1.2	57.5	37.3	88.7	117.7	111.5	53.8	20.2	4.8	0.3
1973.	1.2	59.3	38.5	91.2	119.7	112.2	55.6	22.1	5.4	0.3
1972.	1.2	61.7	39.0	96.9	130.2	117.7	59.8	24.8	6.2	0.4
1971.	1.1	64.5	38.2	105.3	150.1	134.1	67.3	28.7	7.1	0.4
1970.	1.2	68.3	38.8	114.7	167.8	145.1	73.3	31.7	8.1	0.5
1969.	1.0	65.5	35.7	112.4	165.7	143.0	73.5	33.1	8.8	0.5
1968.	1.0	65.6	35.1	113.5	166.5	140.0	74.2	35.4	9.6	0.6
1967.	0.9	67.5	35.3	116.7	172.9	142.1	78.7	38.3	10.6	0.7
1966.	0.8	70.3	35.7	120.3	185.6	148.2	85.1	41.9	11.7	0.7
1965.	0.8	70.5	--	--	195.3	161.6	94.4	46.2	12.8	0.8
1964.	0.9	73.1	--	--	217.5	178.7	103.4	49.9	13.8	0.8
1963.	0.9	76.7	--	--	229.1	185.1	105.8	51.2	14.2	0.9
1962.	0.8	81.4	--	--	241.9	191.1	108.6	52.6	14.9	0.9
1961.	0.9	88.6	--	--	251.9	197.5	113.2	55.6	15.6	0.9
1960.	0.8	89.1	--	--	258.1	197.4	112.7	56.2	15.5	0.9
1959.	0.9	89.1	--	--	257.5	198.6	114.4	57.3	15.3	0.9
1958.	0.9	91.4	--	--	258.2	198.3	116.2	58.3	15.7	0.9
1957.	1.0	96.3	--	--	260.6	199.4	118.9	59.9	16.3	1.1
1956.	1.0	94.6	--	--	253.7	194.7	117.3	59.3	16.3	1.0
1955.	0.9	90.5	--	--	242.0	190.5	116.2	58.7	16.1	1.0
1954.	0.9	90.6	--	--	236.2	188.4	116.9	57.9	16.2	1.0
1953.	1.0	88.2	--	--	224.6	184.1	113.4	56.6	15.8	1.0
1952.	0.9	86.1	--	--	217.6	182.0	112.6	55.8	15.5	1.3
1951.	0.9	87.6	--	--	211.6	175.3	107.9	54.1	15.4	1.1
1950.	1.0	81.6	--	--	196.6	166.1	103.7	52.9	15.1	1.2
1949.	1.0	83.4	--	--	200.1	165.4	102.1	53.5	15.3	1.3
1948.	1.0	81.8	--	--	200.3	163.4	103.7	54.5	15.7	1.3
1947.	0.9	79.3	--	--	209.7	176.0	111.9	58.9	16.6	1.4
1946.	0.7	59.3	--	--	181.8	161.2	108.9	58.7	16.5	1.5
1945.	0.8	51.1	--	--	138.9	132.2	100.2	56.9	16.6	1.6
1944.	0.8	54.3	--	--	151.8	136.5	98.1	54.6	16.1	1.4
1943.	0.8	61.7	--	--	164.0	147.8	99.5	52.8	15.7	1.5
1942.	0.7	61.1	--	--	165.1	142.7	91.8	47.9	14.7	1.6
1941.	0.7	56.9	--	--	145.4	128.7	85.3	46.1	15.0	1.7
1940.	0.7	54.1	--	--	135.6	122.8	83.4	46.3	15.6	1.9

Source: National Center for Health Statistics. Vital Statistics of the United States: Natality (1979, Vol. I, Tables 1-1 and 1-6); and "Advance Report of the Final Natality Statistics: 1981." Monthly Vital Statistics Report (Vol. 32, no. 9, supplement, Tables 1 and 4). Washington, DC: U.S. Government Printing Office, 1984 and 1982. Also U.S. Bureau of the Census. Historical Statistics of the United States: Colonial Times to 1970. Washington, DC: U.S. Government Printing Office, 1975.

of the data for 1980 and since suggests that the differential has shrunk at a faster rate than previously, because the fertility rates of the black population have continued to decline while those of the white population have remained almost unchanged. Thus convergence due to continued decline of the fertility of the black population appears to be taking place. There are hints that this decline may be both absolutely and relatively greater in the balance of the 1980s than that of the white population.

Table 6-4B. Age-Specific Fertility Rates of the United States Population: White, 1940-1981

Year	10-14 years	15-19 years: Total	15-19 years: 15-17 years	15-19 years: 18-19 years	20-24 years	25-29 years	30-34 years	35-39 years	40-44 years	45-49 years
1981.	0.5	44.6	25.1	71.9	106.3	111.3	60.2	18.7	3.4	0.2
1980.	0.6	44.7	25.2	72.1	109.5	112.4	60.4	18.5	3.4	0.2
1979.	0.6	43.7	24.7	71.0	107.0	110.8	59.0	18.3	3.5	0.2
1978.	0.6	42.9	24.9	69.4	104.1	107.9	56.6	17.7	3.5	0.2
1977.	0.6	44.1	26.1	70.5	107.7	110.9	55.3	18.0	3.8	0.2
1976.	0.6	44.1	26.3	70.2	105.3	105.9	52.6	17.8	3.9	0.2
1975.	0.6	46.4	28.0	74.0	108.2	108.1	51.3	18.2	4.2	0.2
1974.	0.6	47.9	28.7	77.3	113.0	111.8	52.9	18.9	4.4	0.2
1973.	0.6	49.0	29.2	79.3	114.4	112.3	54.4	20.7	4.9	0.3
1972.	0.5	51.0	29.3	84.3	124.8	117.4	58.4	23.3	5.6	0.3
1971.	0.5	53.6	28.5	92.3	144.9	134.0	65.4	26.9	6.4	0.4
1970.	0.5	57.4	29.2	101.5	163.4	145.9	71.9	30.0	7.5	0.4
1969.	0.4	54.7	26.4	99.2	161.3	143.7	71.9	31.5	8.1	0.5
1968.	0.4	54.9	25.6	100.5	162.1	140.3	72.4	33.7	8.9	0.5
1967.	0.3	56.9	25.7	104.0	167.9	141.0	76.4	36.5	9.8	0.6
1966.	0.3	60.4	26.6	108.2	180.0	146.0	82.5	39.9	10.8	0.7
1965.	0.3	60.6	--	--	189.0	158.4	91.6	44.0	12.0	0.7
1964.	0.3	63.4	--	--	211.6	175.9	100.5	47.6	13.0	0.7
1963.	0.3	68.2	--	--	223.5	181.1	102.6	48.8	13.4	0.8
1962.	0.4	73.2	--	--	237.0	187.4	105.2	50.1	14.2	0.8
1961.	0.4	79.2	--	--	246.7	194.2	110.1	53.1	14.8	0.9
1960.	0.4	79.4	--	--	252.8	194.9	109.6	54.0	14.7	0.8
1959.	0.4	79.2	--	--	251.7	195.5	111.3	55.1	14.7	0.9
1958.	0.5	81.0	--	--	251.4	194.8	113.0	55.8	14.8	0.8
1957.	0.5	85.2	--	--	253.8	195.8	115.9	57.4	15.4	0.8
1956.	0.3	83.2	--	--	247.1	190.6	114.4	57.0	15.4	0.8
1955.	0.3	79.2	--	--	236.0	186.8	114.1	56.7	15.4	0.9
1954.	0.4	79.0	--	--	230.7	185.0	115.1	56.2	15.4	0.9
1953.	0.4	77.2	--	--	219.6	181.5	111.9	55.1	15.0	0.9
1952.	0.4	75.0	--	--	212.5	180.5	111.4	54.4	14.8	0.9
1951.	0.4	75.9	--	--	206.0	174.2	106.5	52.6	14.6	1.0
1950.	0.4	70.0	--	--	190.4	165.1	102.6	51.4	14.5	1.0
1949.	0.4	72.1	--	--	194.6	165.2	101.5	52.2	14.6	1.1
1948.	0.4	71.1	--	--	195.5	163.9	103.6	53.5	15.2	1.1
1947.	0.4	69.8	--	--	207.9	179.1	113.0	58.4	16.1	1.2
1946.	0.3	50.6	--	--	179.8	164.0	110.0	58.4	15.9	1.3
1945.	0.3	42.1	--	--	134.7	133.1	100.5	56.3	16.0	1.4
1944.	0.3	45.3	--	--	147.9	137.7	98.2	54.1	15.5	1.2
1943.	0.3	52.1	--	--	161.1	150.7	100.2	52.2	15.0	1.3
1942.	0.3	51.8	--	--	162.9	145.6	92.3	47.2	14.1	1.3
1941.	0.2	47.6	--	--	141.6	130.1	85.2	45.1	14.3	1.4
1940.	0.2	45.3	--	--	131.4	123.6	83.4	45.3	15.0	1.6

Source: Same as Table 6-4A.

Age-Specific Fertility Rates

Fertility has a very distinctive age pattern. It begins at nearly zero for ages under fifteen, is low for ages 15-17, considerably higher for ages 18-19, and peaks in the 20-24 and 25-29 ages. At ages thirty and above, the rate declines swiftly to be again nearly zero at ages 40-44 (see Figure 6-4). This age pattern is strongly influenced by the pattern of age at first marriage and by the gradual decline in ability to conceive as the age of menopause is approached. However, exposure to the risk of pregnancy and physiological factors pertaining to conception only establish broad limits: within these limits the level of fertility can and does vary greatly, depending upon the prevalence and effectiveness of fertility regulation practiced. Table 6-4 shows the age-specific fertility rates for the U.S. population, by race, for each year since 1940. This table has four parts. Table 6-4A is for all races;

Table 6-4C. Age-Specifie Fertility Rates of the United States Population: Nonwhite [All Other], 1940-1981

Year	10-14 years	15-19 years			20-24 years	25-29 years	30-34 years	35-39 years	40-44 years	45-49 years
		Total	15-17 years	18-19 years						
1981.	3.6	91.8	65.2	130.8	140.8	115.9	68.5	27.6	6.3	0.4
1980.	3.9	94.6	68.3	133.2	145.0	115.5	70.8	27.9	6.5	0.4
1979.	4.1	96.5	70.5	134.9	144.3	114.6	68.3	27.3	6.4	0.4
1978.	4.0	96.0	70.4	134.4	142.1	111.9	65.2	26.9	6.4	0.4
1977.	4.3	99.5	74.8	136.8	142.3	111.5	63.4	27.3	6.9	0.5
1976.	4.3	99.9	75.5	137.2	138.9	107.6	59.5	26.9	6.9	0.5
1975.	4.7	106.4	80.5	146.1	141.0	108.7	58.8	27.6	7.5	0.5
1974.	4.6	111.3	84.9	153.1	145.5	109.5	59.9	28.8	7.6	0.5
1973.	5.0	117.5	90.5	160.9	151.6	111.2	63.2	30.9	8.6	0.6
1972.	4.7	123.8	93.8	173.3	163.4	119.3	68.9	34.8	9.9	0.7
1971.	4.7	128.5	94.0	185.6	184.0	134.6	79.3	40.2	11.7	0.9
1970.	4.8	133.4	95.2	195.4	196.8	140.1	82.5	42.2	12.6	0.9
1969.	4.5	131.3	91.8	195.1	195.9	138.2	83.6	44.1	13.7	1.0
1968.	4.3	132.3	92.8	197.5	197.7	138.6	85.9	46.9	14.8	1.2
1967.	4.1	135.0	93.8	203.6	208.7	149.2	93.9	50.9	16.7	1.2
1966.	4.0	136.4	92.7	210.9	224.7	163.0	102.1	56.3	18.4	1.4
1965.	4.0	138.4	--	--	239.2	183.5	113.0	62.7	19.3	1.5
1964.	4.0	141.5	--	--	258.6	198.0	122.7	66.8	20.9	1.6
1963.	4.0	142.6	--	--	268.4	208.7	125.7	68.7	21.1	1.5
1962.	3.9	147.1	--	--	276.9	215.2	130.0	71.8	21.8	1.5
1961.	4.0	155.2	--	--	286.6	220.4	134.7	74.9	22.3	1.4
1960.	4.0	158.2	--	--	294.2	214.6	135.6	74.2	22.0	1.7
1959.	4.2	160.5	--	--	297.9	220.2	138.1	75.0	21.2	1.8
1958.	4.3	167.3	--	--	305.2	224.2	142.3	78.4	21.8	1.9
1957.	5.6	172.8	--	--	307.0	228.1	143.5	78.7	23.5	2.0
1956.	4.7	172.5	--	--	299.1	225.9	139.4	78.8	23.6	2.0
1955.	4.8	168.3	--	--	283.4	219.6	133.5	75.4	22.1	2.1
1954.	4.9	170.3	--	--	274.7	215.7	131.3	72.9	22.5	2.1
1953.	5.1	165.4	--	--	261.4	206.4	125.7	70.0	23.0	2.2
1952.	5.2	162.9	--	--	254.0	194.2	122.0	66.6	21.9	2.2
1951.	5.4	166.7	--	--	252.5	184.2	117.9	66.5	22.6	2.2
1950.	5.1	163.5	--	--	242.6	173.8	112.6	64.3	21.2	2.6
1949.	5.1	162.8	--	--	241.3	167.0	107.3	63.9	21.1	2.5
1948.	4.9	157.3	--	--	237.0	159.6	104.1	62.5	20.4	2.8
1947.	4.6	146.6	--	--	223.7	150.6	102.4	62.7	21.4	3.1
1946.	3.7	121.9	--	--	197.3	139.2	99.3	61.0	21.8	3.5
1945.	3.9	117.5	--	--	172.1	125.4	97.1	61.3	22.3	3.7
1944.	3.9	121.5	--	--	182.4	126.8	97.3	58.4	21.5	3.2
1943.	4.0	133.4	--	--	187.2	125.1	93.9	56.9	21.5	3.7
1942.	3.9	131.8	--	--	182.3	119.6	88.1	54.0	20.8	4.0
1941.	4.0	128.3	--	--	175.0	118.1	86.2	54.1	21.5	4.1
1940.	3.7	121.7	--	--	168.5	116.3	83.5	53.7	21.5	5.2

Source: Same as Table 6-4A.

Table 6-4B is for the white population; Table 6-4C is for the black and other population; and Table 6-4D is for the black population. The fluctuations in fertility have tended to occur at all ages, the curve for one date stacked neatly below or above the curve for another. However, a detailed examination of the age specific fertility rates for two recent points of time is instructive: (1) at the peak of the baby boom (1957), and (2) at a subsequent low point of fertility of 1981. These data are graphed in Figure 6-4. Birth rates only twenty-five years apart can be seen to fluctuate widely: The value of TFR at the peak is 2.1 times the TFR at the trough. This comparison shows that

1. The declines from the peak to the trough encompass all ages. Absolute declines are greatest at ages 20-24 and 25-29, while the greatest relative decline occurs at ages thirty-five and over.
2. Teenage pregnancy (ages 15-19) declines less, both

Table 6-4D. Age-Specific Fertility Rates of the United States Population: Black, 1960-1981[a]

Year	10-14 years	15-19 years: Total	15-19 years: 15-17 years	15-19 years: 18-19 years	20-24 years	25-29 years	30-34 years	35-39 years	40-44 years	45-49 years
1981	4.1	97.1	70.6	135.9	141.2	108.3	60.4	24.2	5.6	0.3
1980	4.3	100.0	73.6	138.8	146.3	109.1	62.9	24.5	5.8	0.3
1979	4.6	101.7	75.7	140.4	146.3	108.2	60.7	24.7	6.1	0.4
1978	4.4	100.9	75.0	139.7	143.8	105.4	58.3	24.3	6.1	0.4
1977	4.7	104.7	79.6	142.9	144.4	106.4	57.5	25.4	6.6	0.5
1976	4.7	104.9	80.3	142.5	140.5	101.6	53.6	24.8	6.8	0.5
1975	5.1	111.8	85.6	152.4	142.8	102.2	53.1	25.6	7.5	0.5
1974	5.0	116.5	90.0	158.7	146.7	102.2	54.1	27.0	7.6	0.6
1973	5.4	123.1	96.0	166.6	153.1	103.9	58.1	29.4	8.6	0.6
1972	5.1	129.8	99.5	179.5	165.0	112.4	64.0	33.4	9.8	0.7
1971	5.1	134.5	99.4	192.6	186.6	128.0	74.8	38.9	11.6	0.9
1970	5.2	147.7	101.4	204.9	202.7	136.3	79.6	41.9	12.5	1.0
1969	4.8	137.0	96.9	202.5	198.0	132.3	79.1	42.9	13.5	1.0
1968	4.7	138.7	98.2	206.1	199.8	133.1	82.2	45.8	14.5	1.2
1967	4.4	141.8	99.5	213.4	211.9	145.3	91.1	50.1	16.6	1.2
1966	4.2	142.7	97.9	219.2	227.9	159.0	100.3	55.4	18.2	1.4
1965	4.3	144.6	--	--	243.1	180.4	111.3	61.9	18.7	1.4
1964	4.3	147.6	--	--	264.7	198.5	123.5	66.8	20.8	1.5
1963	--	--	--	--	--	--	--	--	--	--
1962	--	--	--	--	--	--	--	--	--	--
1961	--	--	--	--	--	--	--	--	--	--
1960	4.3	156.1	--	--	295.4	218.6	137.1	73.9	21.9	1.1

[a]Data not available for black only between 1940-1959.

Source: Same as Table 6-4A

absolutely and relatively, than pregnancy in any of the other age groups lower than thirty-five years of age.

The trend of change in each of the six age-specific fertility rates is charted in Figure 6-5A. That all age groups between twenty and forty-five and over have shared a common trend over time is made evident by this figure. Also the recent upturn in fertility since 1975 is shown to be localized in the age groups 25-29 and 30-34, with only modest upturns in ages 40-44. Thus it is not caused by earlier onset of childbearing, but childbearing at intermediate ages at a higher rate than in the years immediately preceding.

The race differential in fertility can better be understood in terms of its age-specific components. Figure 5-5B graphs the trend of fertility rates for white and black population by age between 1940 and 1980. Table 6-5 shows the absolute and relative measures of differential fertility between the races for each age group. Data are presented for three points in time: (1) the peak of the baby boom, 1956; (2) the trough of the baby bust, 1976; and (3) 1981. Figure 6-6 graphs the ASFR for blacks and whites as of 1981.

Among teenage women, fertility for the black population is more than double that for the white (at ages 15-17, it is nearly triple). At ages 20-24 the fertility of black women is about one-third higher than that of the white population. At ages 25-29, the race differential almost disappears—the rates are practically the same for both groups. At ages thirty-five and over, although the rates are low for both races, the nonwhite fertility tends to be 30 percent or more greater than white fertility. Thus the race differential is sharp only at the youngest and oldest ages of the childbearing span. More than 80 percent of the difference between the races is generated by fertility among those under twenty-five years of age. (Fertility at ages under twenty has a component of childbearing out of wedlock, a topic discussed in a later section of this chapter.)

Did the various age groups of the black and white populations behave differently during the transition from the peak of the baby boom in 1956 to the trough of the baby bust in 1976? The answer to this question, supplied in Table 6-6, reveals that in absolute terms the decline was greater at all age groups among the black than among the white population. However, in relative

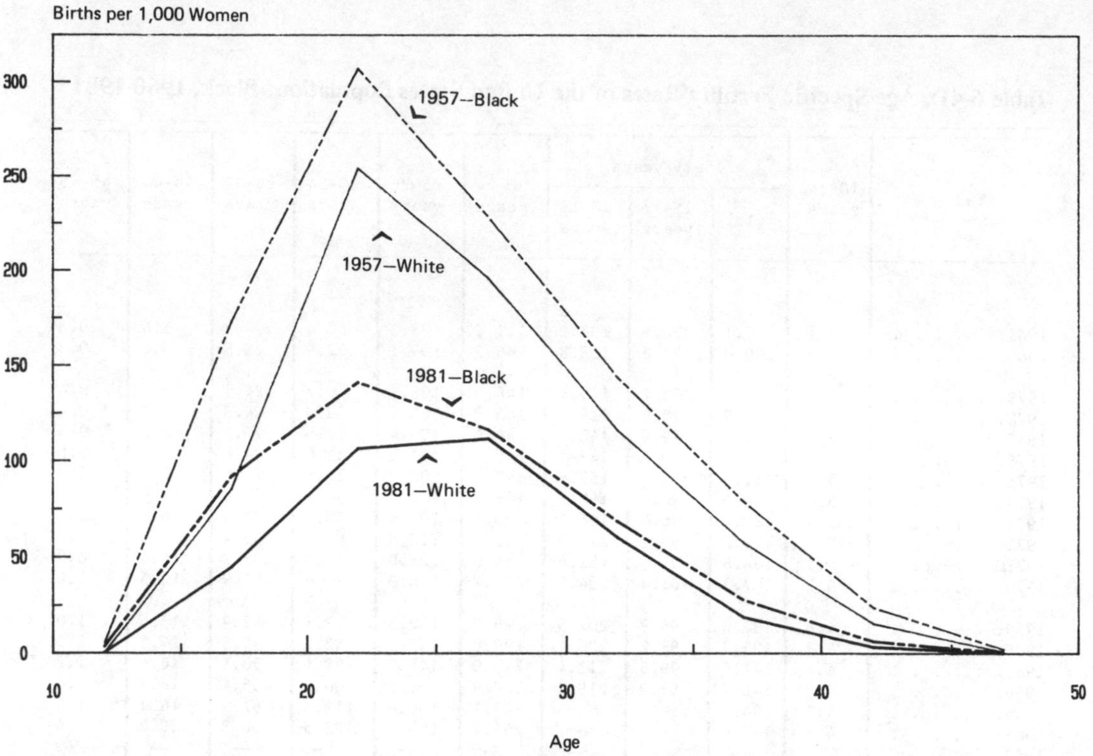

Figure 6-4. Age-Specific Fertility Rates of the Population, by Race: 1957 and 1981

Table 6-5. Absolute and Relative Measures of Differential Fertility between the Black and White Races, by Age Group for Specified Years

Age	Absolute differential[a]			Relative differential[b]		
	1956[c]	1976	1981	1956[c]	1976	1981
Total Fertility Rate. . . .	1184.0	535.0	480.0	1.33	1.32	1.28
15-19 years	89.3	60.8	52.5	2.07	2.38	2.18
15-17 years	--	54.0	45.5	--	3.05	2.81
18-19 years	--	72.3	64.0	--	2.03	1.89
20-24 years	52.0	35.2	34.9	1.21	1.33	1.33
25-29 years	35.3	-4.3	-3.0	1.19	0.96	0.97
30-34 years	25.0	1.0	0.2	1.22	1.02	1.00
35-39 years	21.8	7.0	5.5	1.38	1.39	1.29
40-44 years	8.2	2.9	2.2	1.53	1.74	1.65

[a]Absolute differential is the age-specific fertility rate of the black population minus the age-specific fertility rate of the white population.

[b]Relative differential is the age-specific fertility rate of the black population divided by the age-specific fertility rate of the white population.

[c]1956 data refers to nonwhite instead of black fertility rates.

Note: -- indicates data not available.

Source: National Center for Health Statistics. Vital Statistics of the United States: Natality (1979, Vol. I, Tables 1-1 and 1-6); and "Advance Report of the Final Natality Statistics: 1981." Monthly Vital Statistics Report (Vol. 32, no. 9, supplement, Tables 1 and 4). Washington, DC: U.S. Government Printing Office, 1984 and 1982. Also U.S. Bureau of the Census. Historical Statistics of the United States: Colonial Times to 1970. Washington, DC: U.S. Government Printing Office, 1975.

Table 6-6. Comparison of Age-Specific Fertility Rates, at Peak of Baby Boom and through Baby Bust.

Age	White population		Black population		Absolute change 1956-1976		Relative change 1956-1976	
	1956	1976	1956[a]	1976	White	Black	White	Black
Total fertility rate.	3,546.0	1,652.0	4,730.0	2,187.0	-1,894.0	-2,543.0	-53.4	-53.8
10-14 years	0.3	0.6	4.7	4.7	0.3	0.0	100.0	0.0
15-19 years	83.2	44.1	172.5	104.9	-39.1	-67.6	-47.0	-39.2
15-17 years	--	26.3	--	80.3	...	...	...	...
18-19 years	--	70.2	--	142.5	...	...	...	...
20-24 years	247.1	105.3	299.1	140.5	-141.8	-158.6	-57.4	-53.0
25-29 years	190.6	105.9	225.9	101.6	-84.7	-124.3	-44.4	-55.0
30-34 years	114.4	52.6	139.4	53.6	-61.8	-85.8	-54.0	-61.5
35-39 years	57.0	17.8	78.8	24.8	-39.2	-54.0	-68.8	-68.5
40-44 years	15.4	3.9	23.6	6.8	-11.5	-16.8	-74.7	-71.2

[a]Nonwhite instead of black in 1956.

Note: -- indicates data not available. ... indicates data not applicable.

Source: Table 6-4.

terms (percent decline) the performances of the two race groups was nearly identical—both declined roughly by the same percentage at each age. The main exception was in the 15-19 age group. Despite the fact that this group for the black population had a much larger absolute decline in teenage fertility than the same ages for the white population, the relative size of the decline was smaller, perhaps because of the initial very high rate. To a lesser degree, the same phenomenon characterized the 20-24 age group.

Birth Order

With fertility rates below replacement level, it is not surprising to find that more than 40 percent of all births are first births, more than 30 percent are second births, and only about 5 percent of all births are fifth and higher order children. Table 6-7 presents data on the fertility rates by birth order (see "Parity-specific fertility rates" in the Definition Box). These rates, in effect, subdivide the GFR into components, showing the part of the general fertility rate due to births of each order. Figure 6-7 illustrates the trend in the order-specific rates, by race. By tracing the trend in the order-specific components over time, one can gain insight into the impact of the baby boom and the baby bust.

In 1940, before the onset of the baby boom, the order-specific rates were quite similar to those of 1981 for the first three birth orders. The baby boom changed that dramatically. There was a substantial increase in first births, followed a few years later by an increase in second births. There was a progressive increase in all birth orders, but the absolute increase was substantial only for the first four birth orders. This means that there was no important tendency toward a return to the really large family with five children or more.

As the baby bust developed, the process was reversed. The rates for fourth and higher-order births declined sharply to levels below those of 1940. In 1975 the rate for third and higher-order births dropped to points below that of 1940. The slight "recovery" of fertility rates since 1975 is due to increase in the birth rates for first, second, and third births, with the rates for fourth and higher-order births remaining on a plateau or continuing to decline.

For the black population the order-specific pattern for 1981 is a radical change from 1940 and the intervening years. Between 1940 and 1965 the rates for higher order births rose substantially. Beginning in 1965 the rates for fourth and higher order births have declined sharply to very low levels. The recent trend has been toward a convergence of white and black order-specific rates.

Table 6-7 emphasizes that the American public (both white and black) has not abandoned childbearing. It has simply forgone bearing large numbers of children, especially of fourth and higher-order parities, and perhaps is postponing the bearing of those fewer children to the late twenties and early thirties instead of rushing into childbearing at ages 20-24.

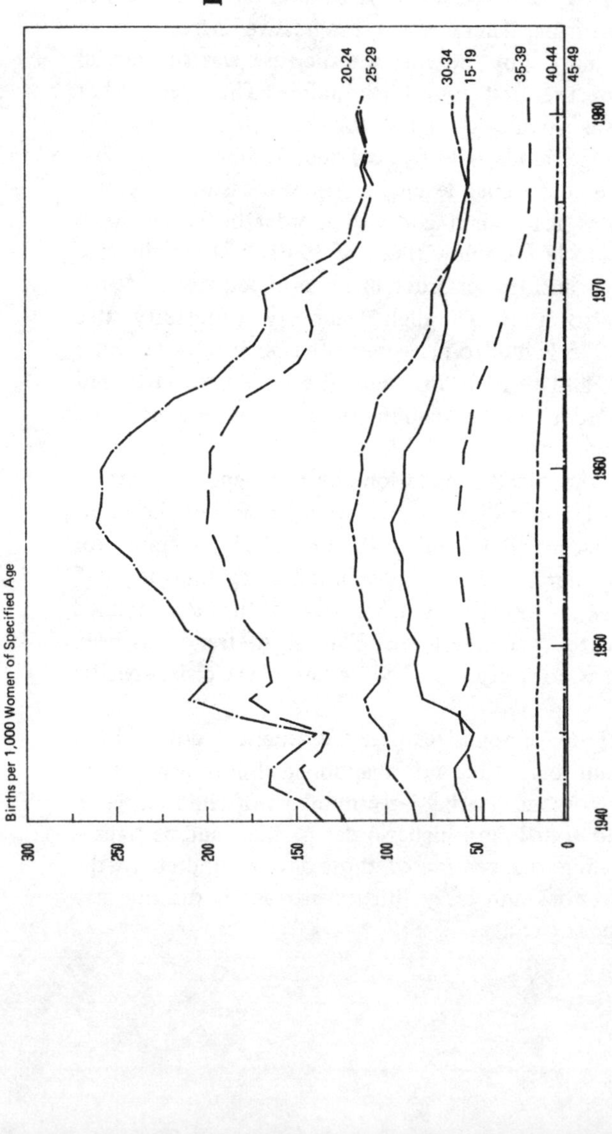

Figure 6-5A. Time Trends in the Age-Specific Fertility Rate: 1940-1981

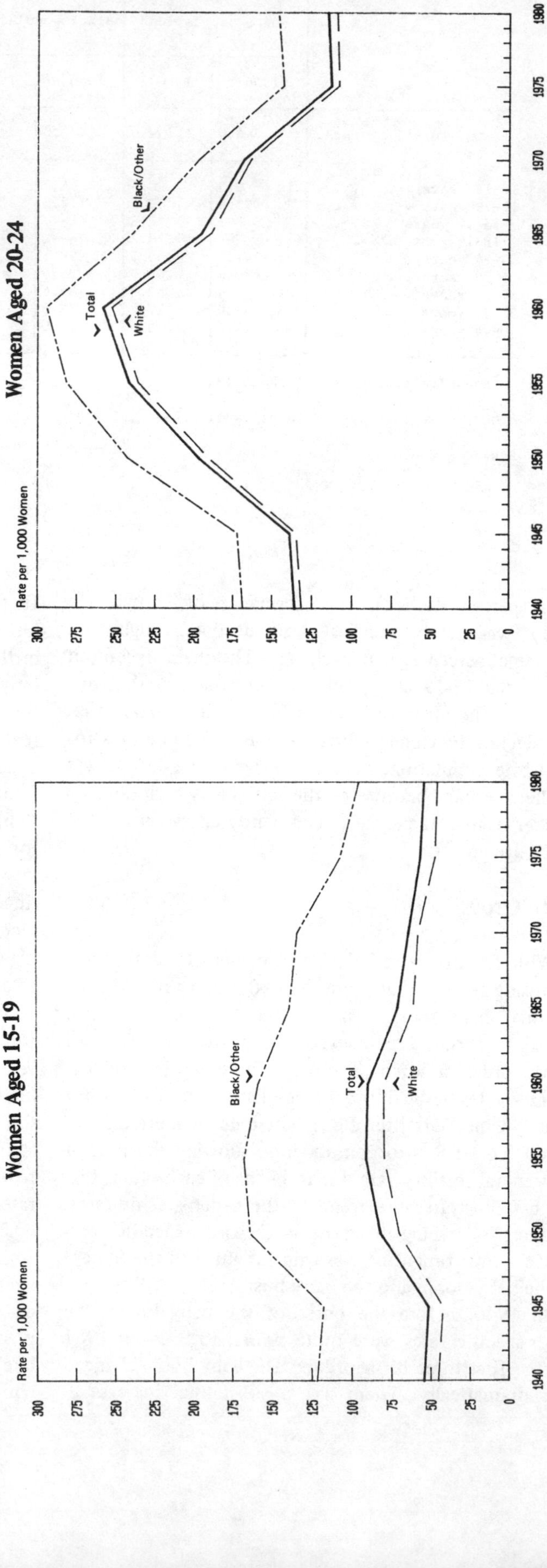

Figure 6-5B. Fertility Rates of Women for Specified Ages: 1940-1981

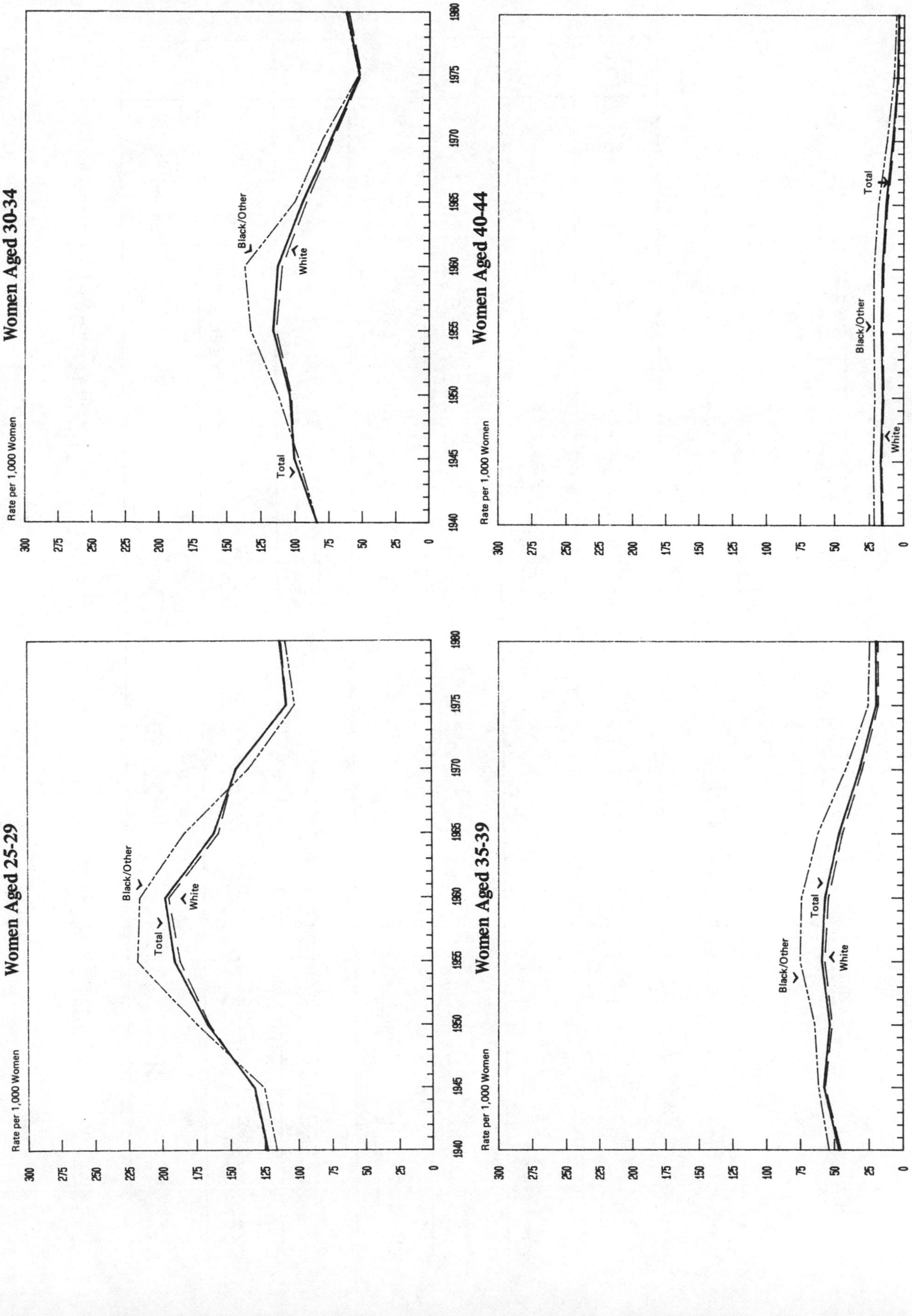

Figure 6-5B. Fertility Rates of Women for Specified Ages: 1940-1981—continued

Table 6-7. Birth Rates, by Live-Birth Order and Race of Child: United States, 1940-1981

Year	Birth order							
	Total (GFR)	1	2	3	4	5	6 and 7	8 and over
All races								
1981	67.4	29.0	21.6	10.2	3.8	1.5	0.9	0.4
1980	68.4	29.5	21.8	10.3	3.9	1.5	1.0	0.4
1979	67.2	28.6	21.6	10.1	3.8	1.5	1.0	0.4
1978	65.5	27.8	21.1	9.8	3.8	1.5	1.0	0.4
1977	66.8	28.2	21.6	10.0	3.8	1.6	1.1	0.5
1976	65.0	27.5	20.8	9.5	3.8	1.6	1.2	0.6
1975	66.0	28.1	20.9	9.4	3.9	1.7	1.3	0.7
1974	67.8	28.7	21.4	9.5	4.1	1.9	1.5	0.8
1973	68.8	28.6	21.0	9.8	4.5	2.2	1.8	0.9
1972	73.1	29.8	21.4	10.6	5.3	2.6	2.2	1.2
1971	81.6	32.0	23.1	12.5	6.4	3.3	2.8	1.5
1970	87.9	34.2	24.2	13.6	7.2	3.8	3.2	1.8
1969	86.1	32.6	23.3	13.4	7.3	4.0	3.5	2.0
1968	85.2	31.9	22.4	13.1	7.5	4.2	3.9	2.3
1967	87.2	30.7	22.5	13.9	8.3	4.8	4.5	2.7
1966	90.8	30.9	22.4	14.7	9.1	5.4	5.2	3.1
1965	96.3	29.7	23.3	16.6	10.7	6.4	6.0	3.7
1964	104.7	30.3	25.1	18.7	12.2	7.3	6.9	4.1
1963	108.3	29.9	26.1	19.9	13.1	7.8	7.3	4.3
1962	112.0	29.9	26.9	21.0	13.8	8.2	7.6	4.5
1961	117.1	30.9	28.3	22.4	14.6	8.5	7.9	4.5
1960	118.0	31.1	29.2	22.8	14.6	8.3	7.6	4.3
1959	118.8	31.5	29.9	23.0	14.5	8.2	7.4	4.2
1958	120.2	32.2	30.6	23.3	14.4	8.1	7.3	4.2
1957	122.9	33.7	31.7	23.9	14.4	7.9	7.1	4.2
1956	121.2	33.5	31.9	23.6	13.9	7.6	6.8	4.0
1955	118.5	32.9	31.9	23.1	13.3	7.2	6.4	3.8
1954	118.1	33.6	32.4	22.7	12.8	6.8	6.0	3.8
1953	115.2	33.4	32.5	21.9	12.0	6.3	5.5	3.6
1952	113.9	34.0	32.7	21.3	11.3	5.8	5.2	3.6
1951	111.5	34.9	32.6	20.0	10.2	5.3	5.0	3.6
1950	106.2	33.3	32.1	18.4	9.2	4.8	4.7	3.6
1949	107.1	36.2	32.1	17.1	8.6	4.7	4.7	3.7
1948	107.3	39.6	30.9	16.1	8.0	4.5	4.6	3.6
1947	113.3	46.7	30.3	15.6	7.9	4.5	4.6	3.7
1946	101.9	38.5	27.9	14.5	7.8	4.5	4.7	3.8
1945	85.9	28.9	22.9	13.4	7.5	4.5	4.8	4.0
1944	88.8	30.2	23.8	13.8	7.6	4.5	4.9	4.0
1943	94.3	34.7	25.5	13.5	7.4	4.4	4.8	4.0
1942	91.5	37.5	22.9	11.9	6.6	4.1	4.6	3.9
1941	83.4	32.2	20.7	11.2	6.4	4.1	4.7	4.1
1940	79.9	29.3	20.0	10.9	6.4	4.1	4.8	4.3
White								
1981	63.9	28.1	20.9	9.4	3.3	1.2	0.8	0.3
1980	64.7	28.4	21.0	9.5	3.4	1.3	0.8	0.3
1979	63.4	27.4	20.8	9.4	3.4	1.3	0.8	0.3
1978	61.7	26.6	20.2	9.2	3.3	1.3	0.8	0.3
1977	63.2	26.9	20.9	9.4	3.4	1.4	0.9	0.4
1976	61.5	26.3	20.2	8.9	3.4	1.4	1.0	0.4
1975	62.5	26.7	20.3	8.8	3.5	1.5	1.1	0.5
1974	64.2	27.2	20.8	9.0	3.8	1.7	1.2	0.6
1973	64.9	27.0	20.4	9.2	4.1	1.9	1.5	0.7
1972	68.9	28.1	20.9	10.1	4.9	2.3	1.8	0.8
1971	77.3	30.5	22.5	12.0	6.0	3.0	2.3	1.0
1970	84.1	32.9	23.7	13.3	6.8	3.4	2.7	1.2
1969	82.2	31.4	22.9	13.1	7.0	3.6	2.9	1.4
1968	81.3	30.8	22.0	12.8	7.1	3.8	3.2	1.6
1967	82.8	29.6	22.1	13.5	7.8	4.3	3.7	1.8
1966	86.2	30.0	21.9	14.3	8.6	4.9	4.3	2.1
1965	91.3	28.9	22.9	16.2	10.1	5.8	5.0	2.4
1964	99.8	29.8	24.8	18.4	11.7	6.7	5.7	2.7
1963	103.6	29.4	25.9	19.6	12.6	7.1	6.1	2.9
1962	107.5	29.6	26.8	20.8	13.3	7.5	6.3	3.0
1961	112.3	30.6	28.3	22.2	14.0	7.7	6.4	3.0
1960	113.2	30.8	29.2	22.7	14.1	7.5	6.1	2.8

Table 6-7. Birth Rates, by Live-Birth Order and Race of Child: United States, 1940-1981—continued

Year	Birth order							
	Total (GFR)	1	2	3	4	5	6 and 7	8 and over
White (continued)								
1959	113.9	31.2	29.9	22.9	13.9	7.3	5.9	2.8
1958	114.9	31.9	30.6	23.1	13.8	7.2	5.7	2.7
1957	117.7	33.4	31.7	23.7	13.7	7.0	5.6	2.7
1956	116.0	33.2	31.9	23.4	13.1	6.6	5.2	2.6
1955	113.8	32.6	32.0	22.9	12.6	6.2	4.9	2.5
1954	113.6	33.3	32.8	22.6	12.0	5.9	4.6	2.5
1953	111.0	33.3	32.9	21.6	11.1	5.4	4.3	2.5
1952	110.0	34.1	33.1	21.0	10.4	5.0	4.0	2.5
1951	107.7	35.0	32.9	19.5	9.4	4.5	3.9	2.5
1950	102.3	33.3	32.3	17.9	8.4	4.1	3.7	2.5
1949	103.6	36.3	32.2	16.6	7.9	4.0	3.8	2.7
1948	104.3	39.9	31.1	15.7	7.4	3.9	3.7	2.6
1947	111.8	47.8	30.8	15.3	7.4	4.0	3.8	2.7
1946	100.4	39.5	28.5	14.4	7.3	4.0	3.9	2.8
1945	83.4	29.0	23.3	13.2	7.0	3.9	4.0	3.0
1944	86.3	30.4	24.2	13.6	7.1	4.0	4.1	3.1
1943	92.3	35.2	25.9	13.2	6.9	3.9	4.0	3.1
1942	89.5	38.3	23.1	11.5	6.1	3.6	3.8	3.1
1941	80.7	32.5	20.7	10.7	5.9	3.6	3.9	3.2
1940	77.1	29.4	20.0	10.5	5.9	3.6	4.1	3.5
All other, nonwhite								
1981	86.4	34.3	25.9	14.2	6.4	2.8	2.0	0.8
1980	88.6	35.6	26.2	14.4	6.5	2.9	2.1	0.9
1979	88.5	35.7	26.2	14.2	6.4	2.9	2.1	1.0
1978	87.0	35.0	25.8	13.8	6.3	2.9	2.2	1.1
1977	87.7	35.6	25.7	13.5	6.2	3.0	2.4	1.3
1976	85.8	35.2	24.7	12.8	6.0	3.0	2.5	1.5
1975	87.7	36.7	24.6	12.6	6.1	3.1	2.8	1.8
1974	89.8	37.7	24.7	12.5	6.3	3.3	3.1	2.1
1973	93.4	38.8	24.4	13.0	6.9	3.9	3.7	2.6
1972	99.5	40.6	25.0	13.7	7.7	4.6	4.6	3.4
1971	109.1	41.6	26.8	15.5	9.0	5.6	5.9	4.6
1970	113.0	42.4	26.9	15.9	9.7	6.1	6.7	5.3
1969	111.6	41.0	25.6	15.4	9.8	6.5	7.2	6.1
1968	111.9	39.5	24.6	15.3	10.1	6.8	8.3	7.2
1967	117.1	37.6	25.3	16.5	11.2	7.9	9.9	8.8
1966	123.5	36.6	25.5	17.7	12.6	9.2	11.4	10.5
1965	131.9	35.3	26.2	19.3	14.4	10.7	13.6	12.4
1964	140.0	34.4	27.1	20.9	15.8	12.0	15.6	14.3
1963	143.7	33.5	27.4	21.6	16.8	13.0	16.4	15.0
1962	147.8	32.9	27.8	22.7	17.7	13.6	17.5	15.6
1961	153.0	33.5	28.7	23.6	18.7	14.0	18.4	16.0
1960	153.6	33.6	29.3	24.0	18.6	14.1	18.4	15.6
1959	156.0	33.9	29.8	24.4	19.1	14.5	18.7	15.6
1958	160.5	34.7	31.0	25.4	19.5	14.9	19.1	15.9
1957	163.0	36.1	31.6	25.7	19.8	15.3	19.0	15.6
1956	160.9	35.9	31.7	25.2	19.7	15.0	18.7	15.0
1955	155.3	35.0	30.7	24.4	19.1	14.6	17.4	14.1
1954	153.2	35.6	29.7	24.4	19.1	14.2	16.5	13.5
1953	147.2	34.1	29.5	23.8	18.4	13.3	15.4	12.8
1952	143.3	33.1	29.2	24.0	18.1	12.4	14.2	12.4
1951	142.1	34.1	29.9	23.9	16.9	11.2	13.5	12.2
1950	137.3	33.8	30.3	22.9	15.3	10.4	12.6	12.0
1949	135.1	35.4	30.8	21.2	14.0	9.8	12.2	11.8
1948	131.6	37.3	29.5	19.4	12.9	9.2	11.7	11.6
1947	125.9	38.4	26.2	17.3	12.1	8.8	11.4	11.6
1946	113.9	31.1	23.4	16.0	11.8	8.7	11.3	11.7
1945	106.0	27.9	20.1	14.7	11.3	8.7	11.3	11.9
1944	108.5	28.7	21.1	15.6	11.7	8.6	11.3	11.6
1943	111.0	31.0	22.2	15.5	11.4	8.4	11.0	11.6
1942	107.6	31.0	21.1	14.9	10.8	8.1	10.5	11.1
1941	105.4	29.8	20.6	14.5	10.6	8.0	10.6	11.3
1940	102.4	28.6	19.6	14.1	10.5	7.8	10.4	11.3

Table 6-7. Birth Rates, by Live-Birth Order and Race of Child: United States: 1940-1981—continued

Year	Birth order							
	Total (GFR)	1	2	3	4	5	6 and 7	8 and over
Black								
1981.	85.4	33.8	25.2	14.3	6.6	2.9	2.0	0.8
1980.	88.1	35.2	25.7	14.5	6.7	3.0	2.1	0.9
1979.	88.3	35.3	25.8	14.4	6.6	3.0	2.2	1.0
1978.	86.7	34.6	25.4	13.9	6.5	3.0	2.3	1.1
1977.	88.1	35.6	25.5	13.6	6.4	3.1	2.4	1.4
1976.	85.8	35.2	24.4	12.9	6.2	3.1	2.6	1.5
1975.	87.9	36.9	24.2	12.6	6.3	3.2	2.9	1.9
1974.	89.7	37.7	24.2	12.6	6.5	3.4	3.3	2.2
1973.	93.6	38.9	24.0	13.0	7.0	4.0	3.9	2.8
1972.	99.9	40.7	24.6	13.7	7.9	4.7	4.8	3.6
1971.	109.7	41.7	26.6	15.5	9.2	5.7	6.2	4.8
1970.	115.4	43.3	27.1	16.1	10.0	6.4	7.0	5.6
1969.	112.1	41.2	25.4	15.4	9.9	6.6	7.4	6.3
1968.	112.7	39.8	24.4	15.3	10.2	7.0	8.5	7.5
1967.	118.5	38.0	25.3	16.5	11.4	8.1	10.1	9.1
1966.	124.7	36.9	25.5	17.7	12.7	9.4	11.7	10.8
1965.	133.9	35.6	26.1	19.3	14.5	10.9	14.0	12.7
1964.	142.6	35.0	27.3	21.1	16.1	12.3	16.1	14.7
1963.	--	--	--	--	--	--	--	--
1962.	--	--	--	--	--	--	--	--
1961.	--	--	--	--	--	--	--	--
1960.	153.5	33.6	29.3	24.0	18.6	14.1	18.4	15.6

Source: National Center for Health Statistics. "Advance Report of Final Natality Statistics: 1981." Monthly Vital Statistics Report (Vol. 32, no. 9, supplement, Table 5). Washington, DC: U.S. Government Printing Office, 1983. Also, U.S. Bureau of the Census. Historical Statistics of the United States: Colonial Times to 1970 (Series B20-27). Washington, DC: U.S. Government Printing Office, 1975.

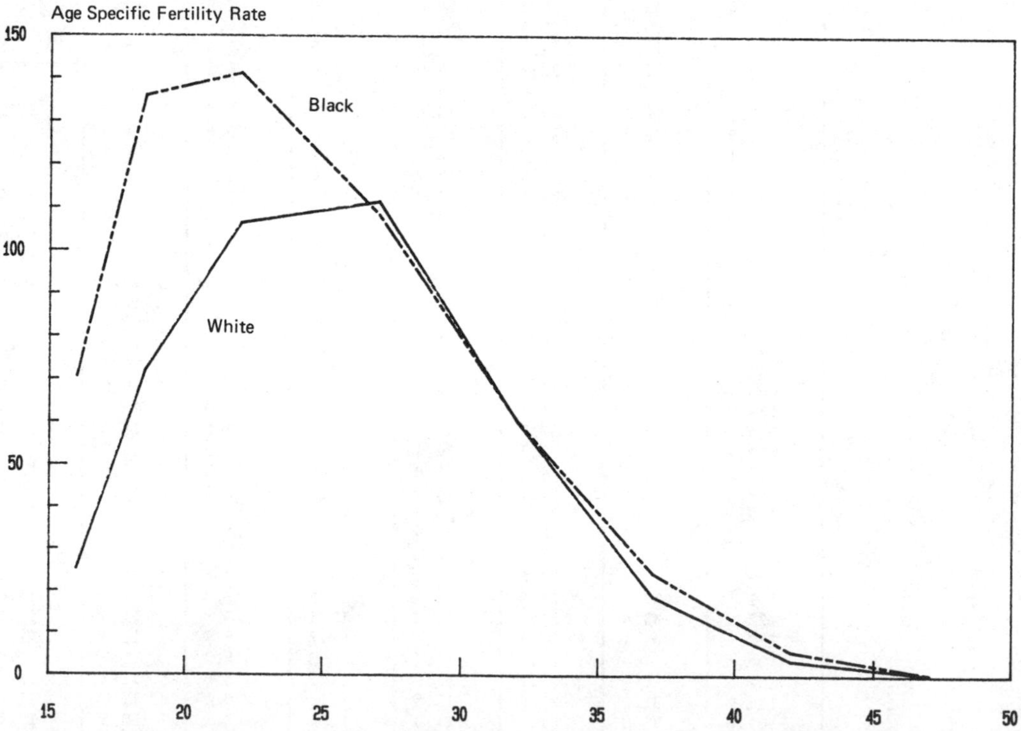

Figure 6-6. Age-Specific Fertility Rates of the Population, by Race: 1981

Median Age of Mother at Birth of Children

The typical mother in the United States is over twenty-five or twenty-six years old at the time of childbearing (see Table 6-8). Despite the fact that the median age at marriage has fluctuated over a range of more than three years since 1940 and the level of fertility has risen and fallen sharply, the overall median age at childbearing has been only moderatly affected. The median age at motherhood does not necessarily rise when the birth rate falls, because lower fertility means fewer higher-order births at older ages. At the height of the baby boom it declined by slightly more than one year, and it has continued to decline into the 1980s. As explained below, this decline is caused by cessation of childbearing at later ages rather than the earlier onset of childbearing.

The median age at childbearing becomes progressively older with increasing birth order. For example, the median age of mothers at the birth of their first child was 23.3 years (for white) and 21.4 years (for nonwhite) in 1980. For the second birth the median age was about three years later, and for the third and fourth children about two years later than the preceding birth. The median age at first birth is more sensitive to age at marriage than the higher orders.

In all cases the median age of bearing children of a given order is higher for the white than for the other populations. These differentials have been steadily shrinking, however. The median age at bearing second children and children of each higher order has risen steadily since 1960, while the median age for white women for the same order has also risen, but more slowly.

With the onset of the baby boom the median age at the birth of a first, second, third, and fourth child declined in comparison with 1940. With the beginning of the baby bust the process was reversed, and the median age at childbearing at each order became practically identical with what existed in 1940. Median age of mothers at each order has risen substantially since 1960 as fertility declined, especially for second and third births. This implies both later age at the start of childbearing (with consequent later age at bearing second child or additional children) and greater spacing between births.

Overall, as fertility declines and most women bear only one or two children, the ages at which those births occur are drifting slowly upward. However, the rarity of third and higher-order births means that a high percentage of all childbearing is being compressed into ages 25-29 years with some spillover into 30-34 years.

Table 6-8. Median Age[a] of Women at Childbirth, by Race and Birth Order

Race and year	All children	Order of birth: First	Second	Third	Fourth	Fifth	Sixth and seventh	Eighth and over
White								
1980	25.9	23.3	26.3	28.4	30.5	32.4	34.6	37.8
1975	25.6	22.7	25.8	28.1	30.4	32.4	34.5	37.3
1970	25.6	22.3	25.0	27.7	29.8	31.7	33.4	36.4
1965	25.9	22.2	24.4	27.3	29.2	31.0	32.7	35.9
1960	25.5	22.0	24.2	26.9	28.8	30.5	32.4	35.8
1950	26.1	22.8	25.7	28.1	29.9	31.6	33.3	37.2
1940	26.9	23.6	26.1	28.0	29.6	31.5	33.7	37.7
Other-than-white								
1980	24.6	21.4	24.7	26.9	28.5	30.3	32.8	37.1
1975	24.2	20.6	23.9	26.1	28.0	29.9	32.8	36.5
1970	24.3	20.4	23.2	25.2	27.4	28.9	31.2	35.4
1965	25.0	20.1	22.7	24.4	26.4	27.9	29.8	34.3
1960	24.9	19.9	22.5	24.1	25.9	27.6	29.6	34.2
1950	24.6	19.8	22.5	24.1	26.2	28.1	30.5	35.6
1940	24.8	19.4	22.2	23.9	26.2	28.4	31.0	36.4

[a]Median age computed from birth rates by 5-year age groups of women.

Source: National Center for Health Statistics. Vital Statistics of the United States: Natality (1979, Vol. I); and "Advance Report of Final Natality Statistics, 1980." Monthly Vital Statistics Report (Vol. 31, no. 8, supplement). Washington, DC: U.S. Government Printing Office, 1984 and 1982.

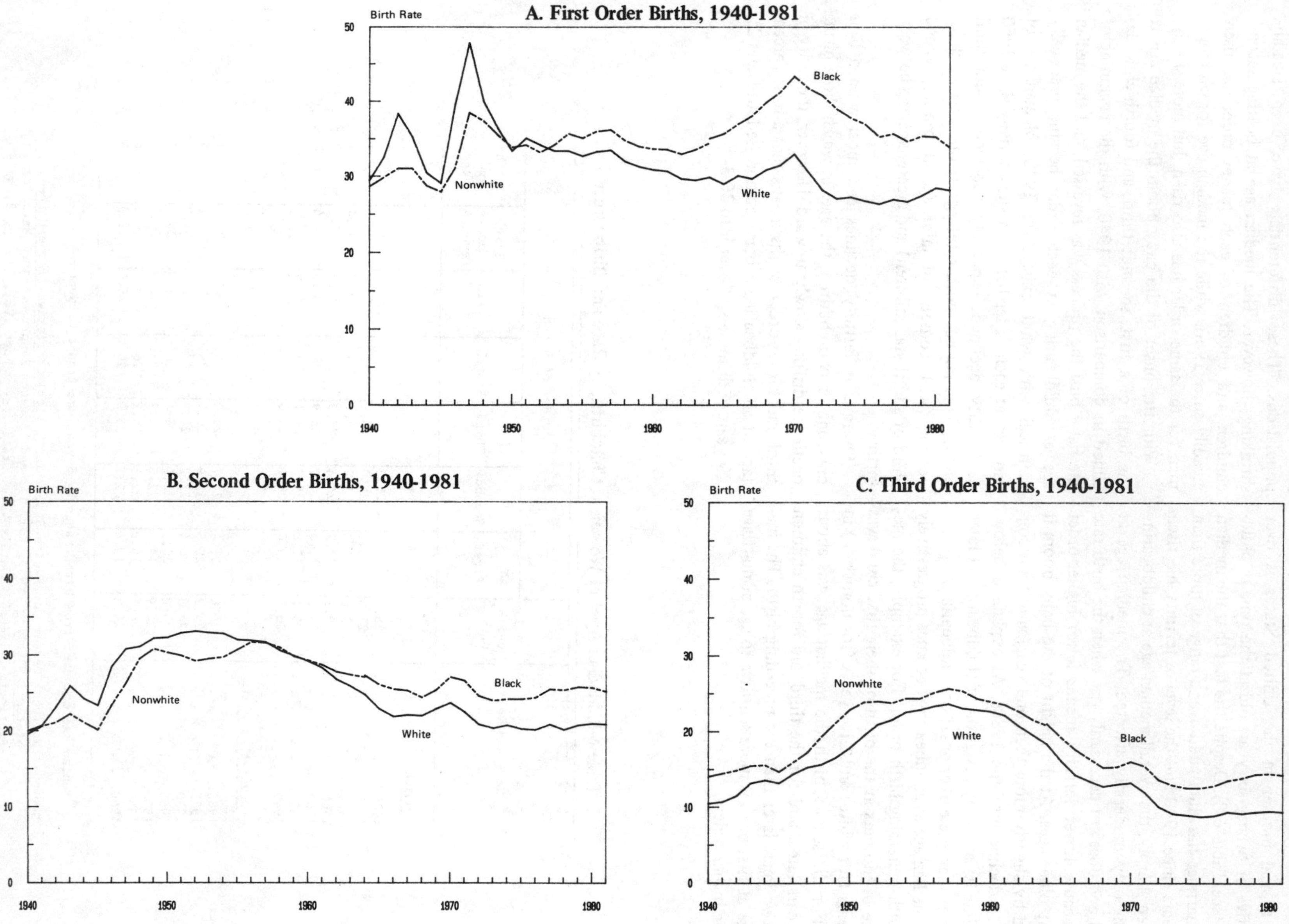

Figure 6-7. Order-Specific Birth Rates per 1,000 Women Aged 15-44, by Race

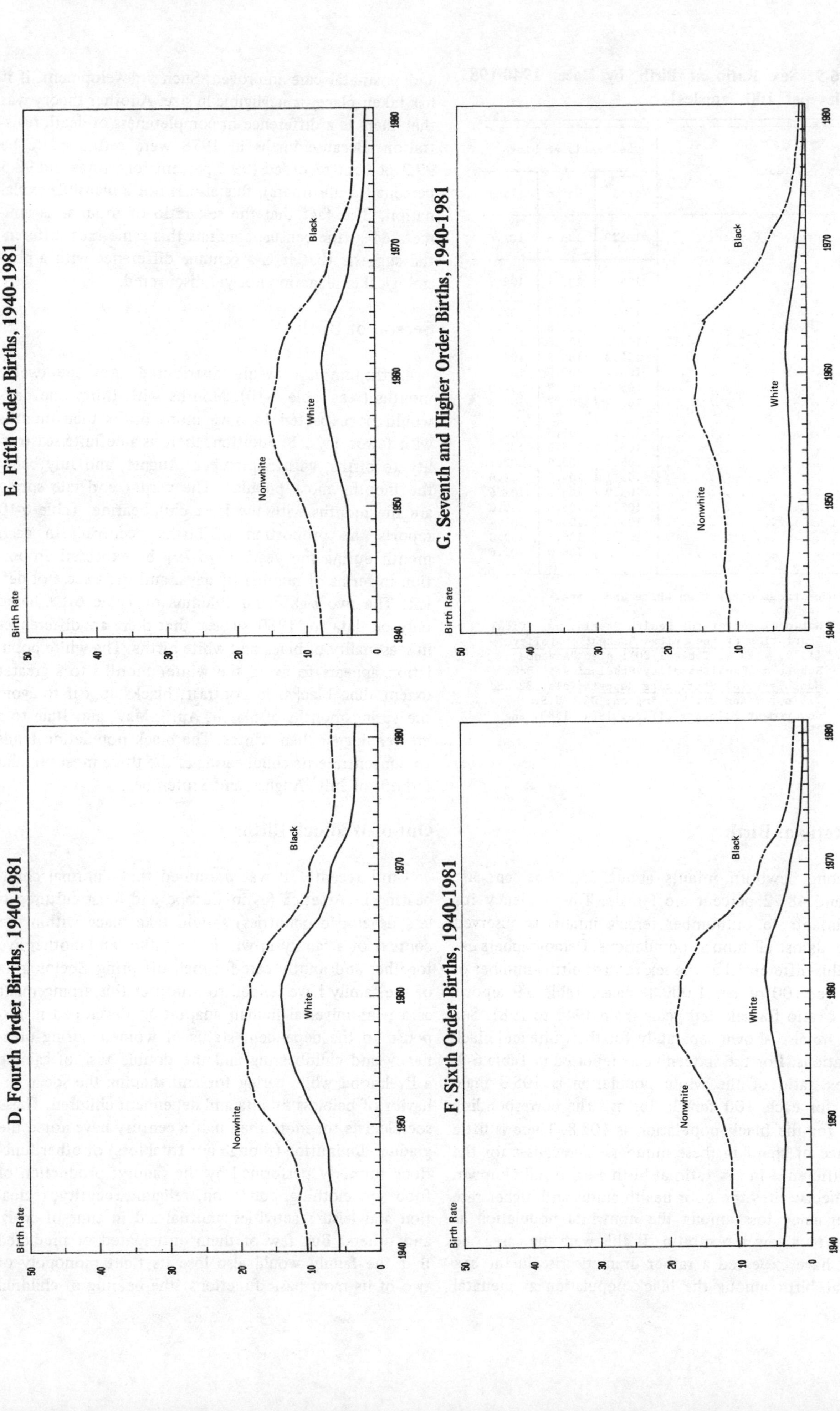

Figure 6-7. Order-Specific Birth Rates per 1,000 Women Aged 15-44, by Race–continued

Table 6-9. Sex Ratio at Birth, by Race: 1940-1981 [males per 100 females]

Year	Sex ratio at birth		
	Total[a]	White	Black
Average (18 years) . . .	105.3	105.8	102.8
1981	105.2	105.7	102.7
1980	105.3	105.8	102.9
1979	105.2	105.7	102.7
1978	105.3	105.8	102.9
1977	105.3	105.8	102.6
1976	105.3	105.8	102.7
1975	105.4	105.9	102.0
1974	105.5	105.9	102.0
1973	105.2	105.7	102.8
1972	105.1	105.7	102.4
1971	105.2	105.6	102.8
1970	105.5	105.9	102.1
1965	105.1	105.6	102.6
1960	105.9	105.5	101.6
1955	105.1	105.6	102.0
1950	105.4	105.8	102.4
1945	105.5	106.1	102.0
1940	105.5	106.0	102.6

[a]Includes races other than white and black.

Source: National Center for Health Statistics. Vital Statistics of the United States: Natality (1979, Vol. I, Table 1-20); also "Advance Report of Final Natality Statistics: 1980." Monthly Vital Statistics Report (Vols. 32 and 31, no. 9 and 8). Washington, DC: U.S. Government Printing Office, 1984, 1983, and 1982.

Sex Ratio at Birth

Among newborn infants about 51.28 percent are male and 48.72 percent are female. This tendency for male infants to outnumber female infants is observed among almost all human populations. Demographers express this differential as the sex ratio at birth—number of males per 100 or per 1,000 females. Table 6-9 reports the sex ratio for selected years from 1940 to 1981. Sex ratios are also shown separately for the white and black populations. For the sixteen years reported in Table 6-9, the sex ratio of the white population is 105.3 male births for each 100 female births. The corresponding figure for the black population is 102.8. There is little evidence of trend in these numbers. The causes for the race difference in sex ratio at birth are not fully known. One theory cites the poor health status and higher rate of pregnancy loss among the nonwhite population as leading to a lower sex ratio. If this were the case, one would have expected a rather dramatic rise in the sex ratio at birth among the black population as prenatal and postnatal care improved. Such a development, if it has taken place, is negligible in size. Another theory was that there is a difference in completeness of death registration. Because births in 1978 were estimated to be 99.3 percent recorded (99.5 percent for whites and 98.5 percent for all others), this also is not a plausible explanation. The fact that the sex ratio of infants, as enumerated at the census, contains this same race differential suggests that it is a genuine difference with a physiological explanation not yet discovered.

Season of Birth

Births are not evenly distributed over the twelve months (see Table 6-10). Months with thirty-one days would be expected to have more births than months with fewer days. In addition, there is a definite seasonality to births, with September, August, and July being the months most popular. The winter and late spring are the months with the least childbearing. Table 6-10 reports the proportion of births occurring in each month during the years 1975-79, the expected proportion in terms of number of days, and the excess or deficit. The two right-hand columns of Table 6-10, based only on data for 1980, suggest that there are differences in seasonality of black and white births. The white population appears to avoid the winter months to a greater extent than blacks. In contrast, blacks appear to avoid the spring months of March, April, May, and June to a greater degree than whites. The black population tends to concentrate its childbearing in the three most popular months of July, August, and September.

Out-of-Wedlock Births

Until recently it was presumed that "normal childbearing in America (as in Europe and most cultures in less developed countries) should take place within the context of a family in which the father and mother live together and jointly care for their offspring. Sociologists of the family have tended to interpret this arrangement as a near-universal human adaptation developed in response to the dependent status of women during pregnancy and childbearing and the double task of gaining a livelihood while caring for and shaping the social behavior of helpless infants and dependent children. These sociologists for more than half a century have noted the gradual diminution (though not total loss) of other functions formerly performed by the family: production of food and clothing, education, religion, security, recreation and leisure activities, mutual aid in time of crisis, and others. But few of them anticipated or predicted that the family would also lose its tight monopoly of two of its most basic functions: the bearing of children

Table 6-10. Season of Birth Indicators: 1975-1980

Month	Proportion of annual births 1975 to 1979				Amount of difference 1980	
	Actual	Expected	Amount	Percent	White	Black
January	8.160	8.493	-0.333	-3.9	-0.484	0.037
February	7.562	7.671	-0.109	-1.4	0.054	0.268
March	8.296	8.493	-0.197	-2.3	-0.229	-0.365
April	7.790	8.219	-0.429	-5.2	-0.193	-0.687
May	8.174	8.493	-0.319	-3.8	-0.279	-0.794
June	8.129	8.219	-0.090	-1.1	-0.083	-0.214
July	8.830	8.493	0.337	4.0	0.368	0.689
August	9.000	8.493	0.507	6.0	0.415	0.657
September	8.801	8.219	0.582	7.1	0.633	0.733
October	8.654	8.493	0.161	1.9	0.137	-0.023
November	8.171	8.219	-0.048	-0.6	-0.211	-0.237
December	8.437	8.493	-0.056	-0.7	-0.126	-0.061

Note: The difference is actual minus expected. Also, percent difference is percent amount' of difference of expected.

Source: National Center for Health Statistics. "Advance Report of Final Natality Statistics: 1980." Monthly Vital Statistics Report (Vol. 31, no. 8, Table 8). Washington, DC: U.S. Government Printing Office, 1982.

Table 6-11. Estimated Number and Ratio of Births to Unmarried Women, by Race: United States, 1940-1981

Year	Number				Ratio per 1,000 births			
	All races	White	All other		All races	White	All other	
			Total	Black			Total	Black
1981	686,605	337,050	349,555	328,879	189.2	115.9	485.1	559.5
1980	665,747	320,063	345,684	325,737	184.3	110.4	484.5	552.5
1979	597,800	263,000	334,800	315,800	171.1	93.6	488.1	546.5
1978	543,900	233,600	310,200	293,400	163.2	87.1	475.6	532.0
1977	515,700	220,100	295,500	281,600	155.0	81.8	464.9	517.4
1976	468,100	197,100	271,000	258,800	147.8	76.8	451.5	503.0
1975	447,900	186,400	261,600	249,600	142.5	73.0	441.7	487.9
1970	398,700	175,100	223,600	215,100	106.9	56.6	349.3	375.8
1965	291,200	123,700	167,500	--	77.4	39.6	263.2	--
1960	224,300	82,500	141,800	--	52.7	22.9	215.8	--
1955	183,300	64,200	119,200	--	45.3	18.6	202.4	--
1950	141,600	53,500	88,100	--	39.8	17.5	179.6	--
1945	117,400	56,400	60,900	--	42.9	23.6	179.3	--
1940	89,500	40,300	49,200	--	37.9	19.5	168.3	--

Note: -- indicates data not available.

Source: National Center for Health Statistics. Vital Statistics of the United States: Natality (1979, Vol. I); and "Advance Report of Final Natality Statistics" (1980 and 1981). Monthly Vital Statistics Report (Vol. 31, no. 8; and Vol 32, no. 9). Washington, DC: U.S. Government Printing Office, 1984; 1982 and 1983.

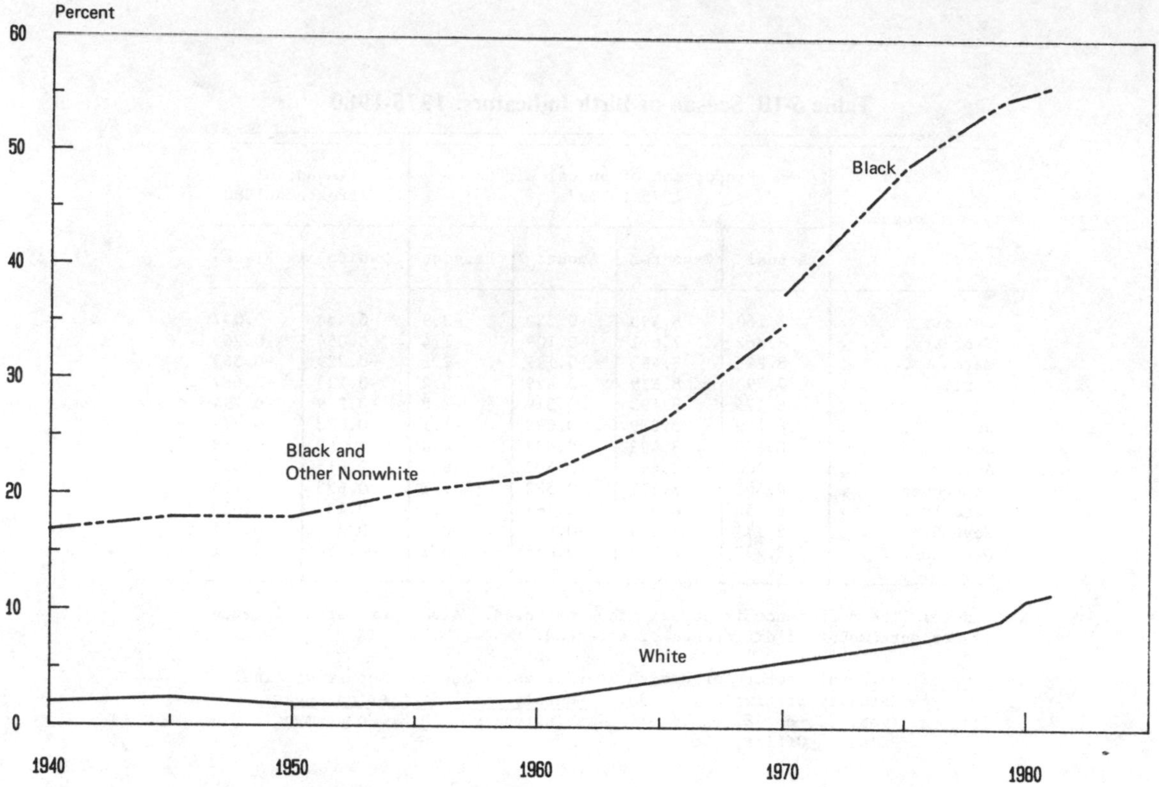

Figure 6-8. Percent of Births Born Out of Wedlock, by Race: 1940-1981

and sex relations. Chapter 11 documents the dramatic increase in premarital and extramarital conjugal living arrangements that have emerged in recent years. This has been paralleled by an unprecedented propensity to bear children out of wedlock. Demographers, sociologists, and social welfare experts now discuss changing arrangements for bearing and rearing children in terms of a "revolution" in family life. As of 1981 one child in six in the United States was born out of wedlock. For the white population the ratio was one in nine, and for the black population it was more than one in two.

Out-of-wedlock childbearing may be measured from two perspectives: from the perspective of the children thus born and from that of the unmarried women who bear them. When viewed from the perspective of children, the appropriate measure is the "out-of-wedlock birth ratio" (formerly called the "illegitimacy ratio"). When viewed from the perspective of women, the appropriate statistic is a "birth rate for unmarried women" or "out-of-wedlock birth rate," which relates the births to the number of unmarried women (see Definition Box). Table 6-11 presents data on number of children born out of wedlock and the out-of-wedlock birth ratio for selected years since 1940. Figure 6-8 graphs the rise, widely viewed as a tragic and socially undesirable situation, of this phenomenon. Since 1940 the out-of-wedlock birth ratio has risen fivefold. During the first two decades of that period the increase was gradual, but in the twenty years since 1960 it has been enormous.

It appears that out-of-wedlock births among the black population have always been higher than among the white population, but in 1940 and before the proportions were a comparative minority of all births to the black population. In other words, blacks followed the traditional two-parent prescription in five out of six families, and only one family in six was an exception to this pattern. Since 1976 the norm for childbearing in the black population has become one of out-of-wedlock fertility; the number of black children born into two-parent families is fewer than the number born out of wedlock.

Out-of-wedlock births, by age of mother and by race, are reported in Table 6-12 as percent distributions and out-of-wedlock ratios. Table 6-13 reports age-specific out-of-wedlock fertility rates by race for selected years. From these tables certain additional important facts emerge.

1. Out-of-wedlock childbearing has two principal forms: premarital childbearing by single (never married) women, mostly in their teens and early twenties, and childbearing by separated, divorced, and widowed women primarily twenty-five or older. Table 6-12 makes

Table 6-12. Distribution by Age of Births to Unmarried Women and Age-Specific Out-of-Wedlock Ratios, by Race: 1981

Age of mother	Out-of-wedlock births percent distribution				Ratio of out-of-wedlock births per 1,000 live births			
	All races	White	All other		All races	White	All other	
			Total	Black			Total	Black
All ages	100.0	100.0	100.0	100.0	189.2	115.9	485.1	559.5
Under 15 years	1.3	0.9	1.6	1.6	891.7	763.2	981.8	988.2
15–19 years	37.7	38.3	37.3	37.5	491.5	348.6	827.6	861.8
15 years	3.0	2.7	3.3	3.4	791.7	643.3	966.5	976.5
16 years	5.9	5.8	5.9	6.0	674.0	521.5	929.8	948.9
17 years	8.4	8.7	8.2	8.2	568.4	422.5	882.5	911.2
18 years	10.0	10.4	9.7	9.7	469.7	333.5	814.9	851.7
19 years	10.4	10.7	10.2	10.2	370.9	250.2	722.7	766.0
20–24 years	36.0	35.6	36.3	36.4	203.7	124.0	519.8	574.2
25–29 years	15.9	15.6	16.2	16.1	96.8	55.6	310.3	379.0
30–34 years	6.6	6.8	6.4	6.2	77.9	47.5	231.0	303.9
35–39 years	2.1	2.3	1.9	1.8	97.8	66.5	226.6	295.1
40 years and over	0.4	0.5	0.4	0.4	126.6	89.8	244.1	306.4

Source: National Center for Health Statistics. "Advance Report of Final Natality Statistics: 1981." Monthly Vital Statistics Report (Vol. 32, no. 9). Washington, DC: U.S. Government Printing Office, 1983.

it clear that teenagers account for a large part (nearly 40 percent) but by no means a majority of the out-of-wedlock childbearing. Table 6-13 reveals that the rates remain high for unmarried women aged 20-24, 25-29, and 30-34 who are primarily separated and divorced. The right-hand panel of Table 6-12 shows that the ratio of out-of-wedlock births to all births is nearly 100 percent of all births to black females under eighteen years of age and is more than 50 percent for white females under seventeen years of age. The out-of-wedlock ratio declines rapidly for white females after age eighteen and plateaus at about 5 percent after age twenty-five. For black women the rate exceeds 50 percent through ages 20-24 and only declines to about 30 percent after age thirty.

2. The *rate* of bearing children out of wedlock (Table 6-13) has apparently leveled off or is rising very slowly since about 1976. For the black population there has been a significant absolute decline in the out-of-wedlock birth rate for ages under twenty-five. For the white population the rates still appear to be rising rapidly for all ages. Thus, in terms of exposure to the bearing of an illegitimate child, the young black unmarried female population appears to be decreasing its exposure to the risk of bearing an out-of-wedlock child, probably by more prevalent and more effective practice of contraception (which can only still be low), while the young unmarried white population is increasing its exposure as a result of premarital sexual activity, possibly with only moderately prevalent use of contraception.

3. The numbers of out-of-wedlock births are nevertheless continuing to climb each year far more rapidly than the rates because of the increase in the size of the unmarried population and the steady rise in the proportion of the younger age group that is black. The delay in marriage and the increase in separation and divorce (described in Chapter 4) are causing these rates to apply to a quickly growing base.

4. As discussed in Chapter 4, there is a possibility that the rates of marital dissolution will decline in future years and that postponement of marriage will plateau. If this happens and if the rates of out-of-wedlock childbearing stabilize or decline, there can be a leveling off and sizable decline of the number of out-of-wedlock births in the late 1980s and thereafter.

Most demographers and sociologists who have reviewed the rising tide of out-of-wedlock childbearing have reached the conclusion that the "existence of the family is not threatened." That is not the relevant point; the increasing prevalence of out-of-wedlock childbearing is creating a situation whereby the state and the local community are forced to provide economic and

Table 6-13: Estimated Birth Rates for Unmarried Women, by Age of Mother and Race: 1940-1981

Race and year	15-44 years[a]	Age of mother							
		15-19 years			20-24 years	25-29 years	30-34 years	35-39 years	40-44 years[b]
		Total	15-17 years	18-19 years					
All races									
1981.	29.6	28.2	20.9	39.9	40.9	34.7	20.8	9.8	2.6
1980.	28.4	27.5	20.7	38.7	39.7	31.4	18.5	8.4	2.3
1979.	27.2	26.4	19.9	37.2	37.7	29.9	17.7	8.4	2.3
1978.	25.7	24.9	19.1	35.1	35.3	28.5	16.9	8.2	2.2
1977.	25.6	25.1	19.8	34.6	34.0	27.7	16.9	8.4	2.4
1976.	24.3	23.7	19.0	32.1	31.7	26.8	17.5	9.0	2.5
1975.	24.5	23.9	19.3	32.5	31.2	27.5	17.9	9.1	2.6
1970.	26.4	22.4	17.1	32.9	38.4	37.0	27.1	13.6	3.5
1965.	23.4	16.7	--	--	39.6	49.1	37.2	17.4	4.5
1960.	21.6	15.3	--	--	39.7	45.1	27.8	14.1	3.6
1955.	19.3	15.1	--	--	33.5	33.5	22.0	10.5	2.7
1950.	14.1	12.6	--	--	21.3	19.9	13.3	7.2	2.0
1940.	7.1	7.4	--	--	9.5	7.2	5.1	3.4	1.2
White									
1981.	18.2	17.1	12.4	24.5	24.9	21.6	13.6	6.9	1.8
1980.	16.2	15.9	11.7	22.8	22.4	17.3	10.5	5.3	1.4
1979.	14.9	14.6	10.8	21.0	20.3	15.9	10.0	5.1	1.4
1978.	13.7	13.6	10.3	19.3	18.1	14.8	9.4	4.8	1.3
1977.	13.5	13.4	10.5	18.7	17.4	14.4	9.3	4.9	1.4
1976.	12.6	12.3	9.7	16.9	15.8	14.0	10.1	5.5	1.4
1975.	12.4	12.0	9.6	16.5	15.5	14.8	9.8	5.4	1.5
1970.	13.8	10.9	7.5	17.6	22.5	21.1	14.2	7.6	2.0
1965.	11.6	7.9	--	--	22.0	24.3	16.6		4.9
1960.	9.2	6.6	--	--	18.2	18.2	10.8		3.9
1955.	7.9	6.0	--	--	15.0	13.3	8.6		2.8
1950.	6.1	5.1	--	--	10.0	8.7	5.9		2.0
1940.	3.6	3.3	--	--	5.7	4.0	2.5		1.2
All other									
1981.	75.4	79.2	60.3	109.0	104.5	80.1	45.6	19.7	5.7
1980.	78.0	83.0	64.0	113.4	108.2	79.1	46.2	18.5	5.3
1979.	78.2	83.9	64.8	115.3	107.1	77.7	44.8	19.1	5.7
1978.	76.5	81.2	63.2	111.6	104.9	76.4	43.6	18.2	5.6
1977.	77.4	84.0	67.2	112.7	103.1	74.4	43.7	18.5	6.6
1976.	76.4	82.5	67.5	108.9	101.1	74.0	43.4	18.7	6.9
1975.	79.0	86.3	70.7	114.3	102.1	73.2	47.9	20.0	6.9
1970.	89.9	90.8	73.3	126.5	121.0	93.8	69.8	32.0	10.7
1965.	97.4	77.1	--	--	147.8	161.0	131.9		38.7
1960.	98.3	76.5	--	--	166.5	171.8	104.0		35.6
1955.	87.2	77.6	--	--	133.0	125.2	100.9		25.3
1950.	71.2	68.5	--	--	105.4	94.2	63.5		20.0
1940.	35.6	42.5	--	--	46.1	32.5	23.4		9.3
Black									
1981.	81.4	86.8	66.9	117.6	112.5	86.4	47.2	20.4	5.8
1980.	83.2	90.3	70.6	121.8	116.0	82.9	47.0	18.5	5.5
1979.	83.0	91.0	71.0	123.3	114.1	80.0	44.8	19.3	5.9
1978.	81.1	87.9	68.8	119.6	111.4	79.6	43.9	18.5	6.2
1977.	82.6	90.9	73.0	121.7	110.1	78.6	45.7	19.0	6.6
1976.	81.6	89.7	73.5	117.9	107.2	78.0	45.0	19.2	7.0
1975.	84.2	93.5	76.8	123.8	108.0	75.7	50.0	20.5	7.2
1970.	95.5	96.9	77.9	136.4	131.5	100.9	71.8	32.9	10.4

[a]Rates computed by relating total births to unmarried mothers, regardless of the age of mother, to unmarried women aged 15-44 years.

[b]Rates computed by relating births to unmarried mothers aged forty years and over to unmarried owmen aged 40-44 years.

Note: -- indicates data not available.

Sources: Data for 1970-81 from National Center for Health Statistics. "Advance Report of Final Natality Statistics, 1981." Monthly Vital Statistics Report (Vol. 32, no. 9 supplement). Washington, DC: U.S. Government Printing Office, 1983. Data for 1940-65 from National Center for Health Statistics. Vital Statistics of the United States: Natality (1979, Vol. I). Washington, DC: U.S. Government Printing Office, 1984.

Table 6-14. Estimated Birth Rates for Married Women, by Age of Mother and Race: 1950-1980

Year	Age of mother								
	15-44 years	15-19 years			20-24 years	25-29 years	30-34 years	35-39 years	40-44 years[a]
		Total	15-17 years	18-19 years					
All races									
1980.	97.8	350.0	481.5	319.7	204.0	146.3	73.2	22.3	4.5
1979.	96.4	331.8	473.4	299.2	196.7	143.3	71.3	22.0	4.5
1978.	93.6	323.1	489.8	284.7	187.5	137.0	67.5	21.2	4.6
1977.	94.9	309.2	471.6	271.1	188.2	138.2	64.8	21.4	4.9
1976.	91.6	307.6	490.6	265.8	178.3	129.3	60.7	20.9	4.9
1975.	92.1	313.1	482.1	270.6	178.5	129.7	58.6	21.3	5.3
1970.	121.1	443.7	720.3	386.3	246.6	164.3	79.2	34.2	9.5
1965.	130.2	462.7	--	--	273.6	178.6	100.4	49.9	14.8
1960.	156.6	530.6	--	--	353.6	221.0	123.9	61.8	18.3
1955.	153.7	460.2	--	--	332.1	213.7	126.8	64.8	19.3
1950.	141.0	410.4	--	--	282.6	191.8	115.7	59.0	18.3
White									
1980.	97.4	352.0	*	*	201.5	146.9	72.0	21.0	4.1
1979.	95.8	331.8	*	*	193.3	143.5	70.2	20.8	4.2
1978.	92.9	318.4	*	*	184.3	137.3	66.5	20.0	4.2
1977.	94.3	305.2	*	*	185.6	138.8	64.0	20.1	4.5
1976.	91.1	303.9	*	*	176.5	129.8	60.0	19.7	4.6
1975.	91.5	309.4	*	*	177.0	130.1	58.2	20.1	4.9
1970.	119.6	431.8	*	*	244.0	164.9	78.2	32.7	8.8
1965.	127.5	443.2	--	--	270.9	177.3	98.9	30.8	
1960.	153.6	513.0	--	--	352.5	220.5	121.6	39.7	
1955.	150.6	440.9	--	--	328.5	211.2	126.2	42.2	
1950.	139.3	398.5	--	--	281.2	193.1	115.9	39.3	
Black									
1980.	94.0	332.3	*	*	216.9	130.1	71.4	27.5	6.3
1979.	95.6	315.3	*	*	222.8	131.9	69.9	27.6	6.8
1978.	94.0	353.4	*	*	212.3	124.4	65.9	27.5	6.5
1977.	94.7	337.3	*	*	207.7	125.1	63.1	28.8	7.3
1976.	90.4	313.0	*	*	191.5	115.5	56.9	27.5	7.2
1975.	91.8	318.8	*	*	188.7	117.3	54.3	27.6	8.3
1970.	130.3	533.3	*	*	263.2	148.3	81.0	44.6	14.2
1965.	--	--	--	--	--	--	--	--	--
1960.	--	--	--	--	--	--	--	--	--
1955.	--	--	--	--	--	--	--	--	--
1950.	--	--	--	--	--	--	--	--	--
All other									
1980.	100.5	331.7	*	*	224.0	141.5	81.7	31.9	7.3
1979.	101.2	332.2	*	*	226.0	141.7	79.6	31.2	7.1
1978.	99.4	369.0	*	*	214.3	135.1	75.0	30.8	7.2
1977.	99.2	347.5	*	*	208.8	133.9	71.4	31.3	7.6
1976.	95.4	339.3	*	*	192.3	125.6	65.4	30.4	7.5
1975.	96.2	342.5	*	*	189.1	126.8	62.1	30.4	8.3
1970.	132.8	522.4	*	*	267.6	159.3	86.7	46.1	14.5
1965.	150.9	602.4	--	--	293.3	188.6	110.3	42.9	
1960.	180.9	659.3	--	--	361.8	225.0	142.1	5 .5	
1955.	180.2	598.2	--	--	360.5	235.4	131.8	53.7	
1950.	155.8	475.2	--	--	292.4	180.2	113.9	46.9	

[a]Rates are computed by relating births to married women aged 40 and over to married women aged 40-44 years. Rates by race for years prior to 1969 are computed by relating birth to married women aged 25 years and over to women aged 25-44 years.

Note: -- indicates data not available. * indicates figure does not meet standards of reliability or precision.

Source: National Center for Health Statistics. Vital Statistics of the United States: Natality (1981, Vol. I). Washington, DC: U.S. Government Printing Office, 1985.

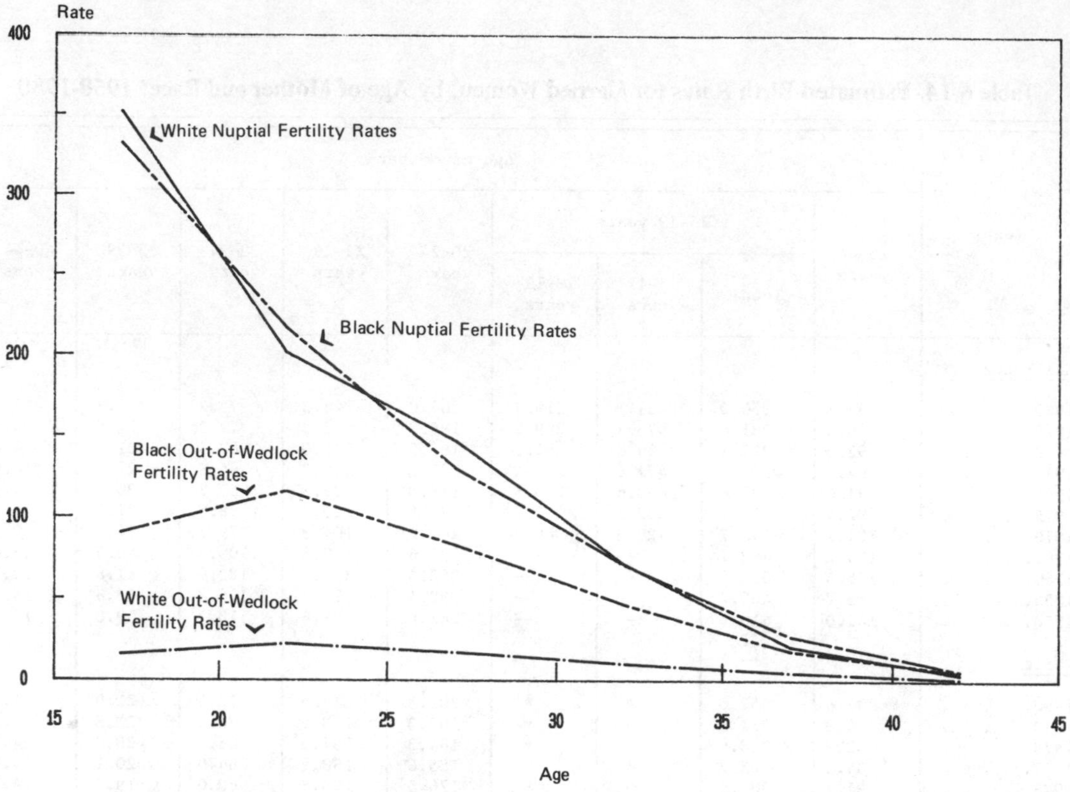

Figure 6-9. Age-Specific Nuptial and Out-of-Wedlock Fertility Rates, by Race: 1980

social necessities formerly provided by two-parent families–as a protection for the child-citizens born in this socially anomalous status. Out-of-wedlock parenthood can no longer be viewed as a minor and temporary aberration but has now become an established and widespread family type, with a new procedure for bearing, financing, and rearing children, which shows signs of gaining additional moral, economic, and political power with the passage of time and to which a cultural adjustment will be made.

The data presented in this chapter show that out-of-wedlock childbearing has shared very little in the recent overall trends of fertility described in previous sections. The "baby bust" of the years since 1958 occurred despite increases in out-of-wedlock childbearing. For example, were it not for the 320,000 illegitimate white births that occurred in 1980, the birth rate of the white population would have been 11 percent lower, yielding a birth rate so far below replacement that there could have been a serious public outcry against "white reproductive suicide." Were it not for the 326,000 black illegitimate births in 1980, the birth rate of the black population would have been only 10 per 1,000, or only one baby per woman per lifetime, leading to very rapid race extinction. Clearly the dominant fertility trends are not being created solely by the childbearing of married couples.

Nuptial Fertility

Nuptial fertility is the ratio of "legitimate" births to married women of childbearing age. Because it deals with a universe of women who are highly exposed to childbearing, the rates are much higher than rates based on total women. Table 6-14 reports age-specific nuptial fertility rates for the population, by race. For very young women the rates are extremely high because many are pregnant at the time of marriage or make immediate efforts to become pregnant without delay. As a consequence in a given year about 50 percent of all married girls aged 15-17 bear a child. The rate drops sharply for the successive age groups. This table provides evidence to support the following important observations:

1. Despite the high rates of out-of-wedlock births for the black population and the rising rates for the white, nuptial fertility rates are far higher at each age for married than for not-married women (Figure 6-9). Thus, a prominent indirect cause for fertility decline has been postponement of marriage, even though that postponement meant more out-of-wedlock childbearing.

2. The race differential in fertility is much lower among the married than among the unmarried population. In fact, at ages 25-29 and 30-34 (peak childbearing years), black nuptial fertility is *lower* than that of white.

For younger ages there is moderately higher black than white fertility within marriage.

3. This near-equality of black and white nuptial fertility rates at ages twenty-five and over is not of recent origin. It dates as far back as 1950 and has persisted since. The main source of the race differential in nuptial fertility has been in the greater childbearing of black wives under twenty-five years of age. For the age group 20-24 the race differential has been quite modest—even during the baby boom.

4. The decline in fertility since 1960—the baby bust—is a joint contribution of both black and white married couples of all ages. The absolute decline has been greater, on an absolute basis (change in fertility rate), for the black than for the white married couples. The relative decline (percentage change in fertility rate) has been roughly equal.

Cohort Fertility

The measures of fertility discussed thus far are all "cross-sectional" or "static," because they refer to the rate of childbearing in a particular year. In order to develop summary measures such as the total fertility rate, it has been necessary to imagine a hypothetical situation where a group of women go through life exposed to the conditions of fertility that happen to be in effect in a single year. An alternative approach is to study *real cohorts* of women, tracing them from year to year and observing their birth rates as they change in response to increasing age, number of children already born, and changing social and economic conditions. Real cohorts may differ from each other: One cohort may be exposed to a set of social and economic conditions greatly different from that faced by another, with the result that

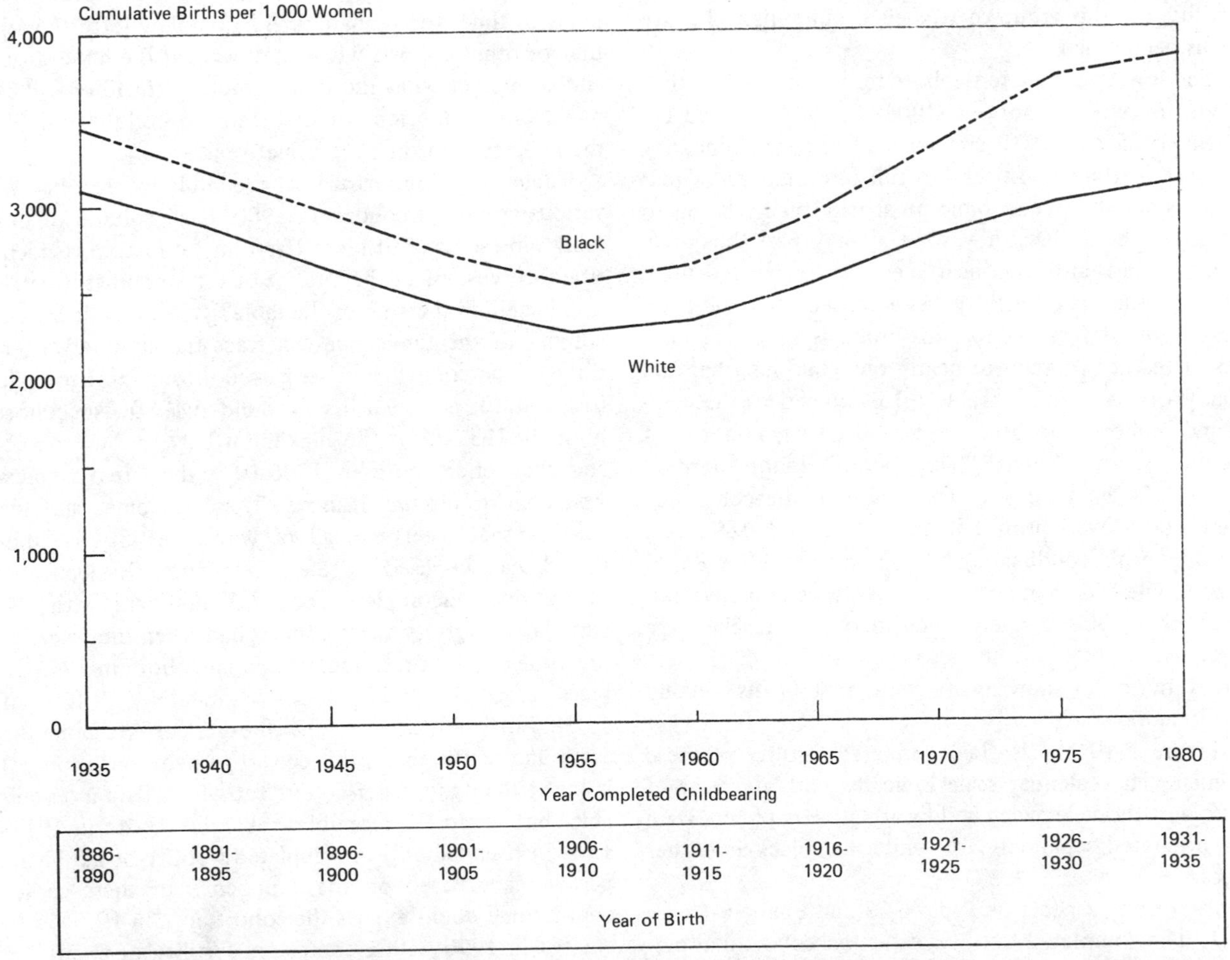

Figure 6-10. Completed Cohort Fertility of Birth Cohorts Reaching Age 40-44 between 1935 and 1980

its fertility may be stimulated or retarded. Changing attitudes and values with respect to marriage, family life, childbearing, and women's status may cause one cohort to behave very differently from another with respect to fertility.

Completed Real Cohort Fertility

If the births that occur to a cohort of women, such as those born between 1931 and 1935, are cumulated statistically, by 1980 those women all passed their forty-fifth birthday and the children they have born per 1,000 women can be termed their "completed cohort fertility." The particular cohort of women mentioned above happens to be the cohort that produced much of the peak fertility of the baby boom. They married early (see Chapter 4) and were at prime childbearing age (22 to 27) when the baby boom reached its pinnacle in 1957. They continued to bear children at a time when birth rates were declining moderately. When the "baby bust" period began in earnest (1970) these women had already reached ages 35-40 and hence were not greatly affected by it. As a consequence the completed cohort fertility for this group of women is quite high–3.2 live births per woman.

The lowest completed cohort fertility on record thus far is for women born in 1906-10. They married between 1925 and 1930 and reached prime childbearing age just in time to suffer the full impact of the Great Depression. When economic prosperity finally began to return in the 1940s, they were already past thirty-five years of age and too near menopause to participate much in the rising fertility. As a consequence the completed cohort fertility for this group is very low–only 2.3 births per woman, or nearly one child less than the "baby boom" cohort. Table 6-15 summarizes the completed cohort fertility of ten five-year cohorts of women, of which the "baby boom" cohort born in 1931-35 is the youngest. The oldest of the cohorts in Table 6-15 was born between 1886 and 1890 and reached peak childbearing during and just after World War I. These data report not only the cumulative fertility per 1,000 women when they had reached age forty-five or beyond, but also the distribution of these births by order–how many were first births, second births, and so on.

Figure 6-10 charts the completed fertility of these women. The calendar scale indicates both the year of birth and the year when childbearing is completed. Data are presented separately for white and black-and-other races.

Interesting aspects of Table 6-15 and Figure 6-10 are

1. The completed fertility of the real cohort that participated most in the baby boom was attained in 1980 at the height of a "baby bust."

2. The oldest cohort (1886-90) had fertility slightly lower than that of the baby boom cohort. Thus, the women who created the baby boom had a larger average number of children upon completing fertility than any generation of women born since 1885.

3. The cohort fertility of the black population follows the same historical trend as that of the white, but with an important difference: The baby boom boosted the completed fertility of black women born in 1931-35 to a peak far higher than that of any generation of black women on record–3.8 births per woman. The disparity between the two races narrowed during the years of declining fertility but widened dramatically during the years of the baby boom generations.

Cumulative Fertility

One difficulty in studying real cohorts is that it is impossible to know how many children the real cohort will bear until it has reached age forty-four–much too far in the future to be useful except for historical study. Analyses are therefore forced to compare the cumulative fertility of cohorts (see Definition Box) up to a given point in time, to compare such incomplete fertility with that of other cohorts when they were at the same stage, and to predict what the final completed fertility will be based on assumptions of their rates of childbearing for the remainder of their reproductive lives.

Table 6-16 summarizes the cumulative fertility of various groups of cohorts in 1980. Each column of this table represents a different five-year set of cohorts identified by year of birth. The age of these cohorts in 1980 is indicated in the stub of the table. By reading down the column of the table, one can trace the cumulative fertility of the cohort as it has passed through its life cycle to the status at which it was found in 1980. The cohort born in 1931-35 is the maximum baby boom cohort, and the cohort born in 1906-10 is the Great Depression cohort, discussed above. These extremes and the cohorts that intervene, all of whose fertility is completed, can be used as reference points. One can ask, "How does incomplete cohort *X* compare with the cumulative fertility these cohorts had when they were at the same age?" For example, the cohort born in 1951-55 (ages 25-29 in 1980) had a cumulative fertility of 1,058.5 in 1980. Compared with other cohorts along the same line of the table, this cohort (a baby bust cohort) is lower than any other cohort for which data are available, but it closely resembles the cohort born in 1911-15, which ended with a completed fertility of 2.3 births per woman. Based on the experience of these earlier cohorts one could expect the cohort born in 1951-55 to emerge in 1990 with a completed fertility of about 2.3 children per woman or less.

Table 6-16 makes it clear that the cohort of women

Table 6-15. Completed Cohort (Cumulative) Fertility Rate and Live Birth Order, by Race: 1935-1980 [cohorts born between 1886 and 1935 reaching age 45-49 between 1935 and 1980]

Exact age of woman, cohort, and race	As of Jan. 1	Total	Live-birth order 1	2	3	4	5	6	7	8 and over
White 45-49 years										
1931-35. . . .	1980	3,101.0	921.5	824.7	593.6	357.1	191.2	100.7	52.5	59.7
1926-30. . . .	1975	2,985.8	905.9	791.7	551.6	329.3	180.5	99.3	54.8	72.7
1921-25. . . .	1970	2,793.1	905.8	755.1	490.6	281.8	153.8	85.9	49.1	71.0
1916-20. . . .	1965	2,525.9	865.4	689.5	420.8	235.6	129.1	73.8	43.5	68.2
1911-15. . . .	1960	2,312.2	822.6	617.6	363.5	204.5	116.5	70.5	43.1	73.9
1906-10. . . .	1955	2,247.4	792.1	574.0	340.8	201.9	122.3	77.7	49.7	88.9
1901-05. . . .	1950	2,397.5	802.0	582.5	364.2	228.4	146.1	96.7	63.7	114.5
1896-1900. . .	1945	2,629.1	806.8	614.7	408.8	267.3	178.3	123.1	82.0	148.1
1891-95. . . .	1940	2,888.0	808.2	640.7	456.1	314.7	216.7	152.4	104.6	194.6
1886-90. . . .	1935	3,092.9	790.9	646.6	486.3	353.9	253.7	183.4	128.6	249.5
Black and other 45-49 years										
1931-35. . . .	1980	3,835.5	854.9	761.5	620.7	480.2	358.5	280.2	181.8	317.7
1926-30. . . .	1975	3,717.9	812.6	701.7	571.6	450.5	344.2	258.4	189.1	389.8
1921-25. . . .	1970	3,314.1	782.2	618.8	487.0	378.8	289.7	221.0	164.7	371.9
1916-20. . . .	1965	2,921.6	733.7	531.7	410.8	319.6	247.0	189.3	144.4	345.1
1911-15. . . .	1960	2,638.0	703.8	471.5	355.1	276.8	212.5	166.5	127.5	324.3
1906-10. . . .	1955	2,525.5	712.5	445.8	331.2	258.0	197.9	154.3	118.7	307.1
1901-05. . . .	1950	2,702.5	749.5	473.6	355.8	274.8	212.4	169.3	130.2	336.9
1896-1900. . .	1945	2,960.9	772.4	517.5	403.2	305.7	231.4	192.4	149.8	388.5
1891-95. . . .	1940	3,204.3	777.5	570.9	458.4	343.8	251.1	210.7	162.1	429.8
1886-90. . . .	1935	3,451.4	768.1	592.2	486.3	389.7	296.4	244.0	166.0	488.7

Source: National Center for Health Statistics. Vital Statistics of the United States: Natality (1981, Vol. I). DC: U.S. Government Printing Office, 1985, Table 1-15.

Table 6-16. Cumulative Rates for Women in Five-Year Cohorts Born between 1906 and 1965, by Age and Race of Mother: United States, 1940-1980

Age in 1980	Year of birth 1961-65	1956-60	1951-55	1946-50	1941-45	1936-40	1931-35	1926-30	1921-25	1916-20	1911-15	1906-10
White												
15-19 years . . .	58.8	65.7	63.8	76.0	92.1	85.7	75.4	51.1	50.0	--	--	--
20-24 years . . .	...	438.4	490.6	621.7	823.1	893.9	788.3	641.4	522.1	459.8	--	--
25-29 years . . .	...	...	1,058.5	1,297.6	1,660.6	1,999.8	1,933.9	1,637.1	1,394.7	1,197.2	1,084.8	--
30-34 years . . .	...	...	...	1,739.9	2,146.3	2,570.4	2,699.4	2,422.4	2,138.1	1,872.2	1,672.7	1,666.5
35-39 years . . .	...	...	...	...	2,328.8	2,790.9	3,007.1	2,837.1	2,586.1	2,296.7	2,090.3	2,021.4
40-44 years . . .	...	...	...	...	...	2,846.5	3,091.4	2,969.2	2,765.0	2,489.6	2,273.8	2,210.9
45-49 years . . .	...	...	...	...	...	...	3,101.0	2,985.8	2,793.1	2,525.9	2,312.2	2,247.4
Black and other												
15-19 years . . .	168.7	202.3	208.6	213.6	233.1	236.9	219.8	183.0	169.8	--	--	--
20-24 years . . .	...	857.5	958.7	1,095.6	1,254.6	1,349.6	1,230.3	1,055.8	912.0	830.3	--	--
25-29 years . . .	...	...	1,619.3	1,835.5	2,151.0	2,543.6	2,459.7	2,125.3	1,755.2	1,569.8	1,475.5	--
30-34 years . . .	...	...	...	2,291.1	2,641.9	3,169.9	3,304.9	2,982.8	2,495.6	2,155.0	1,968.9	1,952.3
35-39 years . . .	...	...	...	...	2,869.5	3,448.8	3,689.4	3,497.4	3,020.1	2,610.1	2,350.8	2,271.6
40-44 years . . .	...	...	...	...	...	3,538.9	3,817.0	3,688.2	3,268.4	2,866.5	2,582.5	2,475.9
45-49 years . . .	...	...	...	...	...	...	3,835.5	3,717.9	3,314.1	2,921.6	2,638.0	2,525.5

Note: -- indicates data not available. ... indicates data not applicable.

Source: National Center for Health Statistics. Vital Statistics of the United States: Natality (1980, Vol. 1). Washington, DC: U.S. Government Printing Office, 1984.

Table 6-17. Birth Probabilities, by Parity, Exact Age, and Race: Specific Years 1940-1965 and Each Year 1970-1980 [white population]

Exact age of woman as of January 1 and race	Parity							
	0	1	2	3	4	5	6	7+
White								
15-19 years								
1980. . . .	38	183	*	*	*	*	*	*
1979. . . .	37	178	*	*	*	*	*	*
1978. . . .	37	171	*	*	*	*	*	*
1977. . . .	38	173	*	*	*	*	*	*
1976. . . .	38	164	*	*	*	*	*	*
1975. . . .	40	165	*	*	*	*	*	*
1974. . . .	42	167	*	*	*	*	*	*
1973. . . .	43	164	*	*	*	*	*	*
1972. . . .	45	173	*	*	*	*	*	*
1971. . . .	47	195	*	*	*	*	*	*
1970. . . .	50	216	*	*	*	*	*	*
1965. . . .	51	270	255	*	*	*	*	*
1960. . . .	62	351	331	*	*	*	*	*
1955. . . .	62	326	308	*	*	*	*	*
1950. . . .	54	292	*	*	*	*	*	*
1945. . . .	35	205	*	*	*	*	*	*
1940. . . .	36	256	*	*	*	*	*	*
20-24 years								
1980. . . .	83	197	136	138	*	*	*	*
1979. . . .	80	196	133	134	*	*	*	*
1978. . . .	78	189	125	130	*	*	*	*
1977. . . .	80	195	126	132	*	*	*	*
1976. . . .	79	185	118	128	*	*	*	*
1975. . . .	82	185	115	131	*	*	*	*
1974. . . .	86	188	115	124	*	*	*	*
1973. . . .	88	182	115	128	*	*	*	*
1972. . . .	98	187	123	138	*	*	*	*
1971. . . .	115	210	149	162	*	*	*	*
1970. . . .	128	228	161	177	*	*	*	*
1965. . . .	141	272	194	190	209	*	*	*
1960. . . .	179	340	263	267	289	*	*	*
1955. . . .	175	317	243	257	288	*	*	*
1950. . . .	143	253	214	246	*	*	*	*
1945. . . .	102	169	177	226	*	*	*	*
1940. . . .	92	194	206	262	*	*	*	*
25-29 years								
1980. . . .	94	174	88	84	102	*	*	*
1979. . . .	92	173	87	83	98	*	*	*
1978. . . .	91	167	83	81	95	*	*	*
1977. . . .	94	171	83	81	92	*	*	*
1976. . . .	93	165	78	75	85	*	*	*
1975. . . .	96	165	77	74	83	*	*	*
1974. . . .	100	172	78	74	83	94	*	*
1973. . . .	100	171	81	76	83	101	*	*
1972. . . .	105	176	90	84	93	111	*	*
1971. . . .	117	192	108	102	111	130	*	*
1970. . . .	126	207	120	109	117	137	*	*
1965. . . .	129	223	145	132	139	165	194	*
1960. . . .	146	262	181	179	193	237	283	*
1955. . . .	144	241	167	174	201	251	*	*
1950. . . .	142	198	141	156	189	241	*	*
1945. . . .	99	156	126	159	199	250	*	*
1940. . . .	92	133	121	162	202	263	*	*

Exact age of woman as of January 1 and race	Parity							
	0	1	2	3	4	5	6	7+
White (con.)								
30-34 years								
1980. . . .	61	101	43	41	51	75	*	*
1979. . . .	59	100	43	41	48	71	*	*
1978. . . .	57	97	42	39	44	61	*	*
1977. . . .	55	97	43	39	43	60	*	*
1976. . . .	54	94	41	37	41	57	70	*
1975. . . .	53	94	41	36	40	52	71	*
1974. . . .	54	95	43	37	41	52	66	105
1973. . . .	54	94	45	40	43	56	71	102
1972. . . .	66	97	49	44	49	61	75	112
1971. . . .	69	99	58	53	58	71	87	126
1970. . . .	64	105	65	58	52	76	90	136
1965. . . .	69	115	80	80	88	113	137	189
1960. . . .	68	125	96	105	121	158	191	269
1955. . . .	83	126	99	110	128	168	204	272
1950. . . .	75	122	86	95	114	155	187	273
1945. . . .	61	112	88	101	129	176	209	289
1940. . . .	54	79	65	86	113	163	196	280
35-39 years								
1980. . . .	20	29	13	14	18	25	39	79
1979. . . .	20	28	13	13	17	24	34	65
1978. . . .	19	27	13	12	16	21	33	60
1977. . . .	19	28	13	13	16	22	29	55
1976. . . .	19	27	13	13	16	22	28	59
1975. . . .	20	27	14	13	16	23	28	55
1974. . . .	20	27	14	14	17	23	29	57
1973. . . .	20	29	15	15	19	25	34	60
1972. . . .	21	29	17	18	21	29	37	67
1971. . . .	23	32	20	21	26	35	43	77
1970. . . .	25	35	22	24	29	38	49	84
1965. . . .	27	38	30	37	48	66	83	145
1960. . . .	31	41	38	51	67	91	116	186
1955. . . .	31	49	45	58	72	96	118	193
1950. . . .	30	47	41	51	65	90	115	200
1945. . . .	28	48	44	55	71	99	125	213
1940. . . .	22	29	29	40	58	86	111	198
40-44 years								
1980. . . .	3	4	2	2	3	5	8	18
1979. . . .	4	4	2	2	3	5	8	19
1978. . . .	4	4	2	2	3	5	7	17
1977. . . .	4	4	2	3	3	5	7	18
1976. . . .	4	4	2	3	4	6	6	19
1975. . . .	4	4	2	3	4	6	8	19
1974. . . .	4	4	3	3	4	6	8	21
1973. . . .	4	5	3	3	4	7	11	24
1972. . . .	4	5	3	4	5	8	13	26
1971. . . .	4	6	3	4	7	10	13	30
1970. . . .	4	6	4	5	8	11	16	34
1965. . . .	7	7	6	10	15	22	31	60
1960. . . .	6	8	9	13	21	31	46	74
1955. . . .	6	9	10	15	23	31	38	77
1950. . . .	6	9	9	13	19	28	36	78
1945. . . .	7	8	9	13	18	29	39	87
1940. . . .	4	5	6	10	16	25	32	78

Table 6-17. Birth Probabilities, by Parity, Exact Age, and Race: Specific Years 1940-1965 and Each Year [black/all other] –continued

Exact age of woman as of January 1 and race	Parity							
	0	1	2	3	4	5	6	7+
All other								
15–19 years								
1980. . . .	81	194	246	*	*	*	*	*
1979. . . .	82	192	240	*	*	*	*	*
1978. . . .	82	187	232	*	*	*	*	*
1977. . . .	85	185	224	*	*	*	*	*
1976. . . .	86	178	212	*	*	*	*	*
1975. . . .	92	181	215	*	*	*	*	*
1974. . . .	97	185	213	*	*	*	*	*
1973. . . .	102	193	223	*	*	*	*	*
1972. . . .	106	211	231	*	*	*	*	*
1971. . . .	107	236	259	*	*	*	*	*
1970. . . .	108	258	284	*	*	*	*	*
1965. . . .	96	356	388	*	*	*	*	*
1960. . . .	98	383	423	457	*	*	*	*
1955. . . .	105	372	416	*	*	*	*	*
1950. . . .	99	392	382	*	*	*	*	*
1945. . . .	78	283	312	*	*	*	*	*
1940. . . .	82	254	395	*	*	*	*	*
20–24 years								
1980. . . .	125	163	165	172	184	*	*	*
1979. . . .	124	162	162	169	177	*	*	*
1978. . . .	121	158	157	166	174	*	*	*
1977. . . .	123	158	152	156	171	*	*	*
1976. . . .	123	151	143	149	160	*	*	*
1975. . . .	127	152	143	148	152	*	*	*
1974. . . .	132	156	144	151	143	*	*	*
1973. . . .	131	159	151	160	157	*	*	*
1972. . . .	148	168	160	174	174	*	*	*
1971. . . .	158	198	188	199	199	*	*	*
1970. . . .	163	206	201	217	213	*	*	*
1965. . . .	141	274	276	302	305	395	*	*
1960. . . .	148	311	336	365	371	488	*	*
1955. . . .	137	316	331	364	385	489	*	*
1950. . . .	113	261	318	348	370	482	*	*
1945. . . .	80	168	248	312	344	*	*	*
1940. . . .	80	172	283	363	407	*	*	*
25–29 years								
1980. . . .	141	126	96	96	104	137	*	*
1979. . . .	138	125	95	94	97	127	*	*
1978. . . .	135	121	91	92	94	115	*	*
1977. . . .	132	122	92	90	93	115	*	*
1976. . . .	128	117	89	88	87	101	120	*
1975. . . .	126	118	86	88	88	103	112	*
1974. . . .	120	121	89	89	89	103	110	140
1973. . . .	110	121	93	95	96	117	121	147
1972. . . .	106	129	101	108	111	134	137	160
1971. . . .	103	142	120	126	134	154	161	192
1970. . . .	102	150	125	134	141	168	172	00
1965. . . .	86	160	158	181	205	248	265	298
1960. . . .	77	187	190	226	267	316	342	373
1955. . . .	67	169	196	251	292	337	362	407
1950. . . .	61	130	184	238	280	335	348	393
1945. . . .	39	76	143	215	273	321	342	387
1940. . . .	32	60	139	225	265	338	357	441

Exact age of woman as of January 1 and race	Parity							
	0	1	2	3	4	5	6	7+
All other (con.)								
30–34 years								
1980. . . .	125	89	57	50	52	61	79	115
1979. . . .	106	88	56	49	51	59	68	104
1978. . . .	87	86	54	48	49	59	65	92
1977. . . .	74	85	54	50	49	59	65	91
1976. . . .	62	84	52	47	48	56	58	85
1975. . . .	57	83	52	48	48	56	60	86
1974. . . .	54	86	53	49	48	58	62	83
1973. . . .	48	84	56	53	55	64	69	94
1972. . . .	48	87	61	58	63	74	75	103
1971. . . .	47	90	71	69	73	87	94	126
1970. . . .	48	89	73	73	80	92	95	129
1965. . . .	34	91	84	97	115	140	164	221
1960. . . .	30	88	100	126	153	189	228	295
1955. . . .	32	71	106	146	180	226	250	319
1950. . . .	28	53	99	133	166	204	246	309
1945. . . .	19	33	73	118	156	218	253	328
1940. . . .	13	20	54	96	136	192	232	312
35–39 years								
1980. . . .	29	38	25	22	23	27	28	48
1979. . . .	24	38	24	21	22	26	28	44
1978. . . .	23	38	24	22	23	26	28	46
1977. . . .	21	36	24	22	23	25	28	45
1976. . . .	19	35	24	21	22	27	28	45
1975. . . .	19	34	24	22	23	27	29	45
1974. . . .	18	34	24	23	25	29	31	49
1973. . . .	17	31	26	25	27	31	35	55
1972. . . .	16	34	28	28	31	36	40	65
1971. . . .	15	34	30	31	36	43	51	77
1970. . . .	14	36	32	35	40	45	53	84
1965. . . .	11	33	39	48	60	74	89	151
1960. . . .	12	27	46	66	82	111	132	210
1955. . . .	13	26	53	77	100	127	155	231
1950. . . .	12	20	46	71	86	123	152	244
1945. . . .	9	12	33	59	80	117	148	269
1940. . . .	7	8	23	42	67	108	131	239
40–44 years								
1980. . . .	4	7	5	5	6	6	7	13
1979. . . .	4	7	5	5	6	6	8	14
1978. . . .	4	7	5	5	6	7	8	14
1977. . . .	3	7	5	5	6	7	9	15
1976. . . .	3	6	5	5	6	7	9	16
1975. . . .	3	6	5	5	7	8	9	17
1974. . . .	3	7	4	6	6	7	9	18
1973. . . .	2	6	5	6	8	10	11	21
1972. . . .	2	7	6	7	9	11	14	24
1971. . . .	2	7	6	9	9	13	15	31
1970. . . .	2	6	7	10	12	14	16	33
1965. . . .	3	5	9	15	19	26	30	61
1960. . . .	3	4	12	19	26	33	44	81
1955. . . .	3	5	12	20	25	37	41	88
1950. . . .	2	3	9	15	20	32	42	90
1945. . . .	2	2	7	12	19	30	38	98
1940. . . .	2	2	4	8	13	30	35	90

Source: National Center for Health Statistics. Vital Statistics of the United States: Natality (1981, Vol. I, Table 1-12). Washington, DC: U.S. Government Printing Office, 1985.

who created the baby boom will have passed out of the childbearing years within the 1980-90 decade and will be replaced in the 1990s by cohorts of women who will have lower cumulative fertility. This implies replacement-level fertility or below by the year 2000 for the white portion of the younger cohorts as of 1980, and a completed fertility of 2.5 children or less per woman for the black-and-other population. However, should age-specific birth rates for women aged 30-39 rise or decline, these forecasts could be altered substantially.

Age-Parity Birth Probabilities

The cohort approach described above emphasizes that the future fertility behavior of women is influenced not only by their age but also by the number of children they have already born when they reach a particular age. Therefore, one of the most sensitive ways of studying birth trends is to examine the changes that take place in birth probabilities (see Definition Box), made specific for both parity and age. Table 6-17 presents such probabilities, by race, for selected years between 1940 and 1980. Data for each calendar year 1970-80 are reported so recent trends can be viewed, with data for every fifth year for the preceding decades. In interpreting this table one should view the years as follows:

1940–Emergence from the Great Depression
1955–Peak of the baby boom
1976–Bottom of the baby bust
1980–Moderate rise following baby bust.

In this table each calendar year represents a particular cohort passing through the age interval specified. Page 284 gives the data for the white population, and page 285 provides data for the black/other population. From Table 6-17 the following specific points can be learned:

White Racial Group

1. In 1980 there was a higher probability that young women who had never born a child (0 parity) would have a child than was the case at the bottom of the baby bust in 1976. This greater propensity to bear children is exhibited at all ages between fifteen and twenty-five years. Thus the "fertility recovery" encompassed childless young women as well as women who had already born a child.

2. A similar increase in age-parity birth probabilities occurs for all ages under thirty-five years and for all parities from one to four. Thus, recovery from the baby bust appears to have taken place along a broad front–encompassing all of the years of peak reproduction and the bearing of higher-order children.

3. There is no evidence of renewed interest in childbearing following the baby bust among women aged thirty-five years or over. These are the women who created the baby boom and whose cumulative fertility is already high. Those few who had not yet born a child or had only one child maintained a small and almost unchanged probability of bearing a child. Those who had already born two to four children showed no higher birth probability. However, those who had already born five or more children did show a slightly increased probability to bear still another.

4. The size of the "recovery" from the baby bust is slight. As of 1980 the probabilities for most ages and parities had risen from their 1976 nadir only to the already low level of 1972, which is still below replacement level.

5. Some demographers have interpreted the rise in fertility between 1976 and 1980 as due to the bearing of children by educated and working women who had postponed childbearing but were being faced after passing their 25th to 35th birthday with the choice of bearing children then or forgoing them altogether. The probabilities of Table 6-17 give only moderate support for this hypothesis. Although there was a small rise in the probabilities for childless women aged 25-29 and 30-34 between 1976 and 1980, there was a larger probability for bearing a second child by one-parity women (women with one child) at all ages and particularly ages 20-24, 25-29, and 30-34 years. The broad spread of the increase among all age groups under thirty-five and for parities one to four betoken more of a renewed interest in maintaining the two-child family and replacement-level fertility.

6. As the older cohorts, the champion childbearers of the baby boom, are replaced by new cohorts with lower cumulative fertility, there may be more childbearing in the later ages (particularly the 35-39 age group) by women who will be having smaller families but spacing their children more widely after having begun childbearing at later ages.

Black-and-Other Race Group

The points made above for birth probabilities of the white population also characterize the black population. However, the "recovery" from the baby bust appears to have been much more robust among the black population. Black women who had already born one child were much more likely to bear another, irrespective of parity for all ages from fifteen to thirty-five years. Women thirty-five or older showed revived fertility only if they were childless. Also childless black women 25-29 and 30-34 showed higher birth probabilities.

Summary

An analysis of cohorts and of age-parity probability

Table 6-18. Percent Distribution of Live Births, by Interval since Last Live Birth, and Age and Race of Mother: 47 Reporting States and the District of Columbia, 1979

Interval since last live birth and race	Total, 2nd and higher order births[a]	Age of mother							
		Under 15 years	15-19 years	20-24 years	25-29 years	30-34 years	35-39 years	40-44 years	45-49 years
All races[b]	100.0	100.0	100.0	100.0	100.0	100.0	100.0	100.0	100.0
0 months (plural deliveries) .	1.5	20.3	2.6	1.5	1.4	1.4	1.3	0.9	0.6
1-11 months	1.7	14.1	6.4	2.3	1.1	0.8	0.7	0.5	0.5
12-17 months.	10.9	49.0	29.4	15.1	8.4	5.9	5.3	3.5	1.5
18-23 months.	13.6	16.7	23.7	17.1	12.7	9.4	7.8	5.3	2.8
24-35 months.	23.7	*	25.8	27.6	24.6	19.3	13.8	10.6	8.3
36-47 months.	15.7	*	9.1	16.8	17.0	15.3	10.4	8.8	7.0
48-59 months.	10.1	*	2.4	10.0	11.3	11.2	8.6	7.3	6.6
60-71 months.	6.6	*	0.5	5.3	7.7	8.2	7.1	5.9	6.0
72 months and over. . .	16.2	*	0.1	4.2	15.8	28.5	44.9	57.1	66.7
White	100.0	100.0	100.0	100.0	100.0	100.0	100.0	100.0	100.0
0 months (plural deliveries) .	1.4	24.0	2.7	1.5	1.4	1.3	1.3	0.9	0.6
1-11 months	1.4	16.0	6.2	2.1	1.0	0.7	0.7	0.4	0.6
12-17 months.	10.2	42.0	29.4	14.9	8.1	5.6	5.1	3.2	1.1
18-23 months.	13.9	18.0	24.6	17.9	13.2	9.6	8.0	5.3	2.2
24-35 months.	24.8	*	26.3	29.0	26.2	20.3	14.3	10.5	8.8
36-47 months.	16.2	*	8.5	17.0	17.7	16.0	10.6	8.8	7.2
48-59 months.	10.2	*	1.8	9.5	11.3	11.4	8.6	7.2	6.0
60-71 months.	6.5	*	0.3	4.8	7.4	8.2	7.1	5.8	5.2
72 months and over. . .	15.4	*	0.1	3.4	13.8	27.0	44.5	57.9	68.3
Black	100.0	100.0	100.0	100.0	100.0	100.0	100.0	100.0	100.0
0 months (plural deliveries) .	1.8	18.7	2.5	1.7	1.6	1.7	1.5	1.1	0.6
1-11 months	2.8	13.7	6.8	3.2	1.9	1.1	1.0	0.8	*
12-17 months.	13.4	51.8	29.2	15.4	9.2	7.0	6.4	4.6	2.2
18-23 months.	12.1	15.8	22.1	14.1	9.0	7.4	6.7	5.1	4.5
24-35 months.	18.5	*	25.1	22.5	15.7	12.3	10.6	10.0	6.2
36-47 months.	13.3	*	10.0	16.4	13.0	10.6	8.6	8.4	6.7
48-59 months.	10.1	*	3.3	11.9	11.4	9.6	7.8	7.6	9.0
60-71 months.	7.4	*	0.8	7.5	9.8	8.1	6.7	6.0	9.0
72 months and over. . .	20.5	*	0.2	7.3	28.4	42.1	50.7	56.3	61.8

[a]Excludes not stated birth order.

[b]Includes races other than white and black.

Note: * indicates insufficient cases to report.

Source: National Center for Health Statistics. Vital Statistics of the United States: Natality (1979, Vol. I, Table 1-26). Washington, DC: U.S. Government Printing Office, 1984.

shows that the propensity to bear children or not tends to rise and fall over a broad spectrum of the childbearing population. It is not narrowly confined to any one set or segment of the population such as educated white-collar women. This implies that the cohorts comprising the baby bust generation could, if conditions were propitious and if they desired it, still achieve replacement-level fertility or slightly higher. On the other hand, the fertility of the black population could either sink to the replacement level as a continuation of past age-parity trends or could rebound to higher levels in response to the same circumstances that would promote a return to replacement-level fertility among the white population.

Birth Intervals

Instead of measuring fertility in terms of fertility rates, demographers often study it in terms of the intervals between live births. Some couples appear to be more fecund (conceive more readily) than others. As a result the interval between one birth and the next is very short, unless the couple does something to postpone conception. Some deliberately have births at a rapid pace, while others space them farther apart or postpone them until particular objectives have been attained. Hence the study of the changing length between intervals reveals changes in the timing and spacing of births. Table 6-18 provides statistics that reveal the pattern of birth spacing and how it has changed over time.

Nearly one-quarter of all births have an interval of 24-35 months (2-3 years) from the preceding live birth, with wide dispersion between 12-24 months on one side and 36-60 months of the other (Table 6-18). A small but significant percentage of births occur after extremely long intervals of seven years or more. If an interval of at least two years is accepted as minimally desirable for the health of both the mother and child, then one-quarter of all births in the United States are too closely spaced. Close spacing is somewhat more prevalent among the black than among the white population, but the black population also has higher proportions with extremely long spacing. Spacing is likely to be short for women under twenty-five who bear children (and very short for teenage mothers). For ages thirty and above spacing tends to increase sharply with age. A high proportion of such births occur to women who bore their last child in their twenties and then have another in their late thirties. Long spacing is particularly prevalent among older black women.

Contrary to what may be common belief, the average interval between births of the various orders is about the same for all birth orders between the second and seventh births (see total column of Table 6-19 and Figure 6-11A). Also contrary to popular belief, the interval between black births is practically identical with that of white births, or even longer. This is true for each age group and for most birth orders (see Figure 6-11B).

However, there is a rapid decrease in the length of intervals between births of a given parity when age is controlled. This is necessary for couples to crowd a larger number of births within the fixed span of time between onset of childbearing and current age. However, intervals increase systematically with age, irrespective of parity. This reflects declining ability to conceive and increased use of contraception.

Birth intervals do not change a great deal when birth rates fluctuate widely. This may be verified from Tables 6-20A and 6-20B, which provide distributions of birth intervals obtained from two different sources. The data for Table 6-20A are from vital statistics; those for Table 6-20B are from the Bureau of the Census Current Population Survey of June, 1980, and are based on retrospective reporting of pregnancy histories. Both show essentially the same phenomenon of almost constant intervals between births of all orders after the first.

However, the same cannot be said for the baby bust

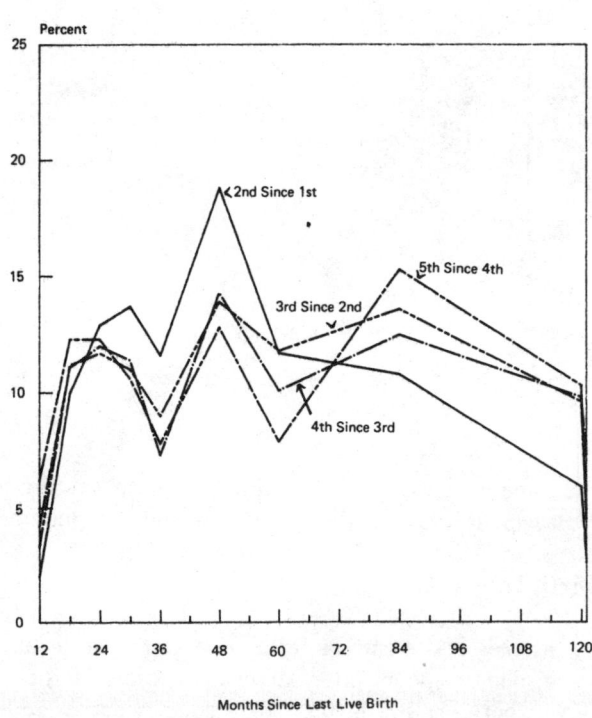

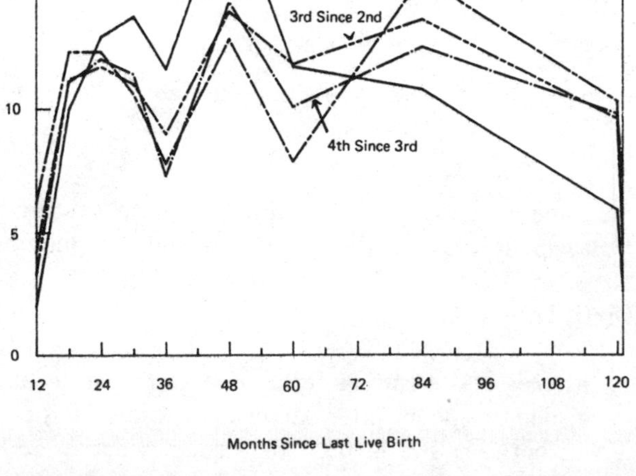

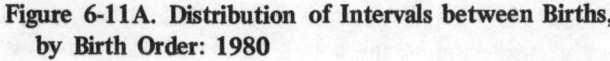

Figure 6-11A. Distribution of Intervals between Births, by Birth Order: 1980

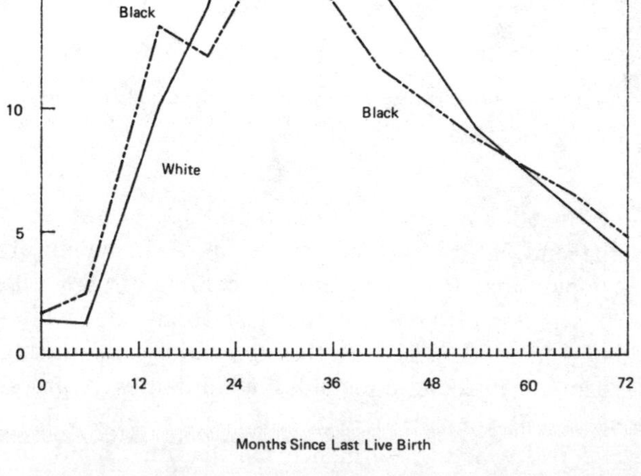

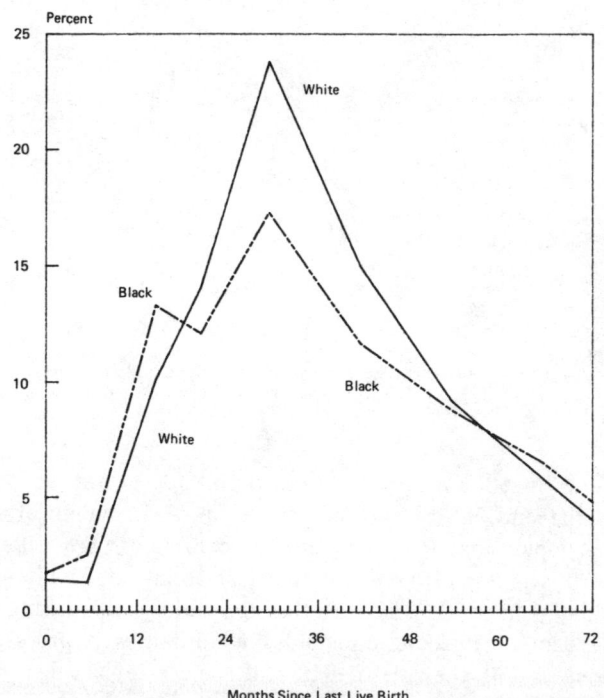

Figure 6-11B. Distribution of Intervals between Births, by Race: 1980

Table 6-19. Mean Interval Since Last Live Birth, by Age of Mother, Live-Birth Order, and Race: 47 Reporting States and the District of Columbia, 1979

Live-birth order and race	Total	Age of mother							
		Under 15 years	15-19 years	20-24 years	25-29 years	30-34 years	35-39 years	40-44 years	45-49 years
All races[a]									
Mean interval since birth of last child, all births of second and higher order[b]	45.2	14.5	23.0	33.6	44.6	57.2	76.6	98.7	112.6
Mean interval between first and second births . .	43.4	14.4	23.5	35.5	46.9	58.7	77.9	107.2	144.1
Mean interval between second and third births . .	47.7	17.4[c]	20.4	30.4	44.6	62.1	89.1	122.2	153.9
Mean interval between third and fourth births . .	47.2	13.0[c]	19.2	25.8	37.3	53.9	82.3	122.0	135.0
Mean interval between fourth and fifth births . .	48.7	*	18.3	23.3	32.6	47.7	74.8	111.4	132.8
Mean interval between fifth and sixth births. . .	47.5	*	21.2[c]	21.6	29.0	41.1	63.1	93.5	119.5
Mean interval between sixth and seventh births. .	46.7	*	18.0[c]	22.8	26.1	36.6	55.1	84.8	112.8
Mean interval since birth of last child, eighth and higher order births.	42.3	*	19.5[c]	26.1	24.9	30.9	42.0	59.2	80.4
White									
Mean interval since birth of last child, all births of second and higher order[b]. . . .	44.6	14.4	22.7	32.9	43.1	55.8	76.0	100.5	115.8
Mean interval between first and second births . .	42.4	13.9	23.0	34.3	45.0	56.8	75.7	106.5	146.2
Mean interval between second and third births . .	47.7	19.7[c]	20.2	29.7	43.2	60.8	89.2	125.9	157.4
Mean interval between third and fourth births . .	47.7	*	19.1	25.4	35.8	52.2	81.4	123.8	139.6
Mean interval between fourth and fifth births . .	49.6	*	19.3	23.5	31.4	45.8	73.2	110.6	132.6
Mean interval between fifth and sixth births. . .	48.0	*	24.6[c]	22.1	28.2	38.9	60.7	93.2	119.6
Mean interval between sixth and seventh births. .	46.1	*	*	24.9	25.6	34.3	51.4	83.0	112.8
Mean interval since birth of last child, eighth and higher order births.	41.7	*	17.3[c]	28.9	26.5	30.1	40.2	57.5	80.9
Black									
Mean interval since birth of last child, all births of second and higher order[b]. . . .	48.1	14.5	23.6	36.7	54.0	69.4	84.2	96.0	108.4
Mean interval between first and second births . .	49.1	14.5	24.5	41.6	64.4	82.5	101.4	131.2	163.2[c]
Mean interval between second and third births . .	47.8	14.0[c]	20.7	32.4	53.1	75.1	97.3	115.4	155.4[c]
Mean interval between third and fourth births . .	46.1	*	19.2	26.7	42.9	64.6	90.7	119.0	111.8[c]
Mean interval between fourth and fifth births . .	46.9	*	17.8	23.1	35.4	56.3	84.0	118.1	147.2[c]
Mean interval between fifth and sixth births. . .	46.8	*	19.8[c]	21.4	30.7	48.0	74.1	97.0	115.0
Mean interval between sixth and seventh births. .	49.0	*	18.0[c]	21.5	27.0	42.8	68.0	93.3	114.4[c]
Mean interval since birth of last child, eighth and higher order births.	43.9	*	21.3[c]	23.9	22.8	32.8	46.9	63.8	82.1

[a]Includes races other than white and black.

[b]Excludes births with birth order not stated and interval not stated.

[c]Figure does not meet standards of reliability.

Note: * indicates quantity zero.

Source: National Center for Health Statistics. Vital Statistics of the United States: Natality (1979, Vol. I, Table 1-24). Washington, DC: U.S. Government Printing Office, 1984.

era. Table 6-20B indicates there has been a very substantial lengthening of the intervals between births of all parities since the baby bust began in the years following 1965. As of 1975-79 the intervals for all events (including marriage to first birth) have lengthened to a degree not previously observed (see Figure 6-12). This trend is manifest for the white, black, and Spanish-origin populations alike. These are cross-sectional and not cohort data, but they suggest that the modern couple wishing to have a four- or five-child family will tend to space the births rather evenly over the childbearing years at intervals of about forty months instead of 30-33 months, as was the custom from 1930 to 1960.

The explanation for the apparent paradox that birth intervals did not become shorter during the baby boom than in the preceding years lies in the phenomenon of the "open intervals." The data of Tables 6-18, 6-19, 6-20A, and 6-20B refer only to intervals *between births.* Much low fertility is caused by *termination* of childbearing, bearing a first or second child and then never having another. This creates a very long "open interval" following the last birth in which no other birth has occurred at the time the woman is interviewed or a census taken. Also by *postponement* of marriage or of *exposure* to childbearing, a longer open interval is created between the menarche and the birth of the first child, which can also reduce fertility. For this reason, closed birth interval statistics provide little information about fertility trends, unless the open intervals (for which data cannot be obtained in vital

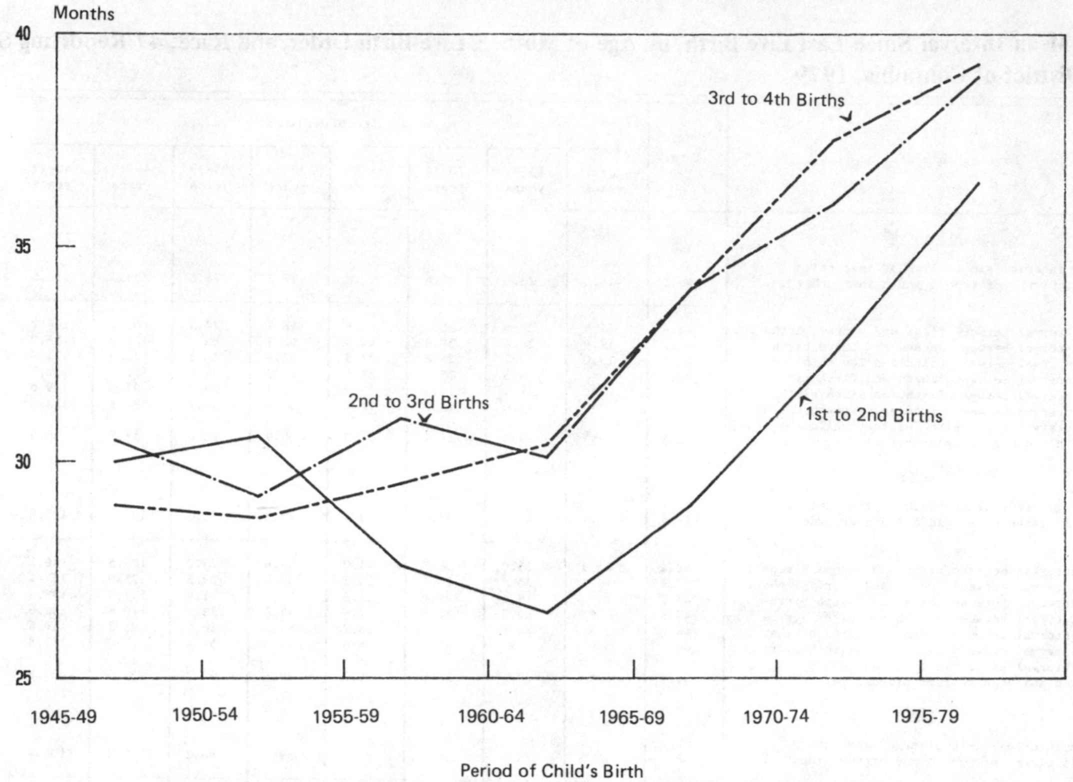

Figure 6-12. Median Interval in Months Since Birth of Previous Child, for Births Occurring from 1945-1949 to 1975-1979

registration) are also taken into account. They are useful primarily for estimating the number and characteristics of births spaced at extremely short or unusually long intervals but are unreliable and useless as indicators of fertility levels or trends.

Family Building Patterns

Figure 6-13 attempts to graph schematically the "family formation strategy" (or pattern) followed by couples who ultimately bear a certain number of children in their lifetime, based on birth intervals for 1975-79 from Table 6-20B. Those who bear only one child tend to do so at a late age, followed by an open interval that lasts for the remainder of their reproductive life. At the other extreme, those who set out to (or who ultimately) acquire a family of five children tend to bear their first child at a young age and to have a shorter open interval between their last child and the onset of menopause. However, within the childbearing span of their lives they tend to space their births by roughly the same number of months. Thus, having a small family is achieved by starting later and stopping sooner, rather than extraordinarily long spacing between births over the entire reproductive span.

One highly significant corollary of Figure 6-13 is that even with today's delayed marriage and wider spacing of births, there is plenty of time within the reproductive span for women to bear five children or more should they wish. Only rigorous control of the open interval will prevent it.

The reader may be puzzled at the long average interval between births (three to four years), even when birth rates are high. Several factors account for this. One is that there is always a period of "postpartum amenorrhea" after the birth of a child (temporary infertility when ovulation has not resumed following childbirth.) This averages at least three months in the United States. Another factor is that, when couples decide to have another child, they do not always succeed the first month they begin trying to get pregnant. (This is the "waiting time" in birth interval analysis: the time it takes couples to conceive once they decide to have another pregnancy by terminating birth control.) A significant proportion of couples are "subfecund" and must wait long periods of time (often undergoing medical treatment) before conception takes place; such lengthy intervals increase the average substantially. In addition, once conceived, it takes nine months before the child is delivered. If to this is added a year or eighteen months

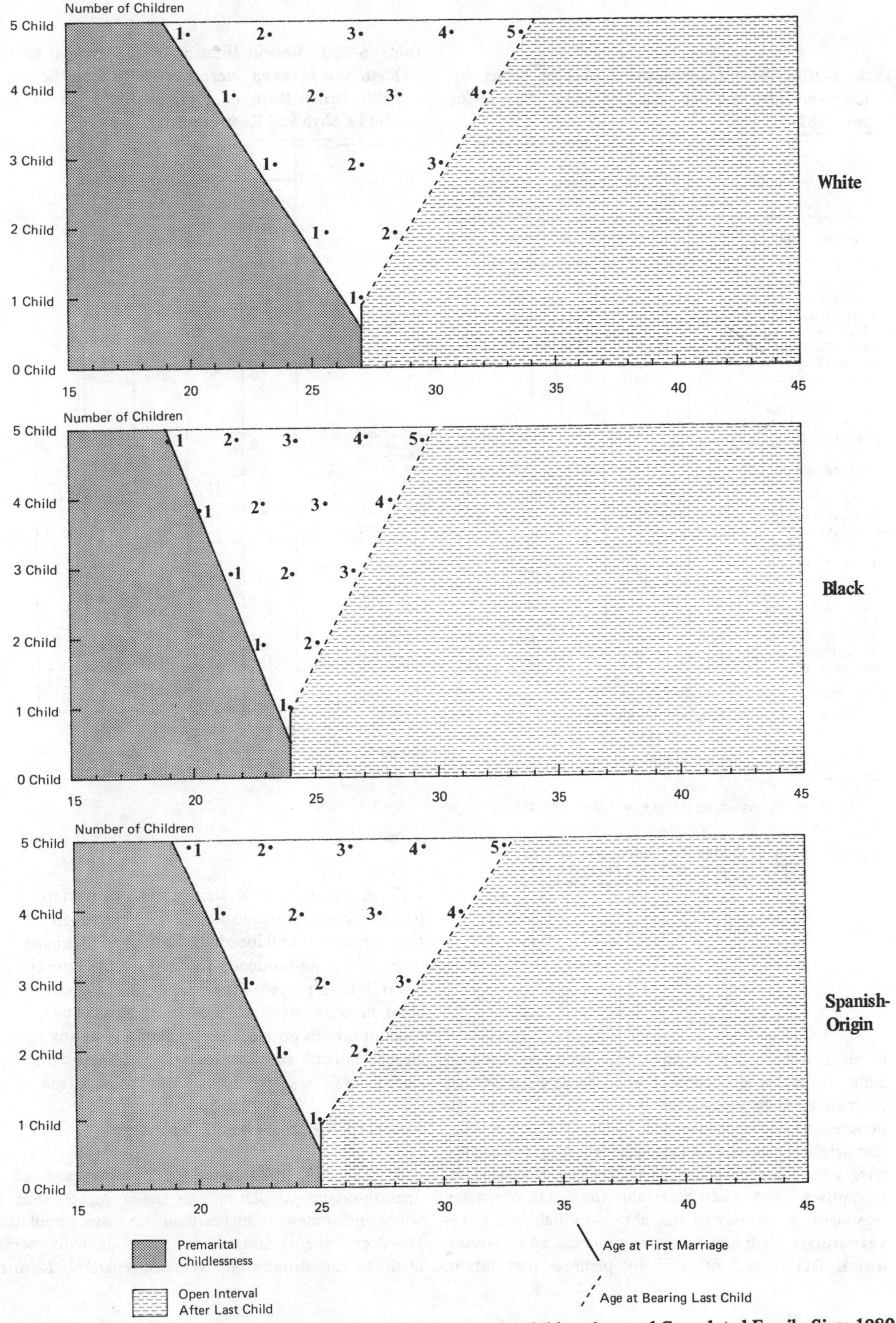

Figure 6-13. A Model of Family Building Patterns, by Average Age, Childspacing, and Completed Family Size: 1980

Table 6-20A. Percent Distribution of Live Births, by Race and Interval Since Last Live Birth: 1969, 1976, and 1981

Interval	Recovery 1981[a]	Baby bust 1976[b]	Baby boom 1969[c]
White, total	100.0	100.0	100.0
0 months (plural deliveries).	1.4	1.3	{ 2.9
1 to 11 months	1.3	1.4	
12 to 17 months.	10.1	9.3	12.6
18 to 23 months.	14.1	12.0	13.3
24 to 35 months.	23.8	22.5	23.1
36 to 47 months.	15.0	16.0	14.7
48 to 59 months.	9.2	10.8	9.6
60 to 71 months.	5.8	7.6	6.2
72 and over months . . .	14.1	14.1	11.9
Not stated	5.3	5.0	5.7
Black, total	100.0	100.0	100.0
0 months (plural deliveries).	1.7	1.4	{ 5.5
1 to 11 months	2.5	2.7	
12 to 17 months.	13.3	12.3	18.2
18 to 23 months.	12.1	11.6	14.1
24 to 35 months.	17.3	17.9	18.6
36 to 47 months.	11.7	13.3	11.2
48 to 59 months.	8.8	10.0	7.6
60 to 71 months.	6.5	7.6	4.8
72 and over months . . .	19.3	16.3	9.9
Not stated	6.7	6.9	10.2

[a]Total of 49 reporting states and the District of Columbia.

[b]Total of 43 reporting states and the District of Columbia.

[c]Total of 36 reporting states and the District of Columbia.

Source: National Center for Health Statistics. "Advance Report of Final Natality Statistics, 1981." Monthly Vital Statistics Report (Vol. 32, no. 9, Table 17); Vital Statistics of the United States: Natality (1976 and 1969, Vol. 1). Washington, DC: U.S. Government Printing Office, 1983, 1980, and 1972.

of planned contraception to permit the previously born child to mature and the mother to prepare for another pregnancy, three years have elapsed. Couples can postpone pregnancy by abstinence, by use of rhythm, or by comparatively unreliable methods, which on the average have some delaying effect. With modern, effective contraceptives, couples can determine the length of spacing reasonably accurately. Thus, about one-half of a three-year average birth interval seems to be caused by physiological factors and one-half by planned intervention.

Table 6-20B. Median Interval from Marriage to First Birth and between Successive Births from Second to Fifth Order Birth of Previous Child, by Year of Child's Birth and Race-Ethnicity

Year of child's birth	Interval since preceding birth					Percent first births before marriage
	Marriage to first birth	Second birth	Third birth	Fourth birth	Fifth birth	
White						
1975 to 1979	25.0	35.7	40.1	42.2	41.0	5.5
1970 to 1974	18.6	33.2	36.2	39.4	39.0	8.6
1965 to 1969	15.2	29.6	34.9	35.2	38.3	7.7
1960 to 1964	14.9	26.6	31.7	31.7	32.0	6.2
1955 to 1959	16.4	28.2	31.9	30.5	31.5	5.3
1950 to 1954	18.9	31.3	30.5	29.6	33.4	4.5
1945 to 1949	19.1	30.9	31.9	29.5	33.2	4.6
1940 to 1944	19.2	30.7	31.7	29.6	35.5	4.8
1935 to 1939	17.6	28.8	31.2	29.3	32.5	5.3
1930 to 1934	15.9	28.0	27.3	24.0	29.3	5.7
Black						
1975 to 1979	10.1	39.1	37.2	28.2	29.1	25.1
1970 to 1974	4.1	31.1	32.8	27.7	30.7	39.9
1965 to 1969	4.4	26.4	28.7	27.0	29.9	41.0
1960 to 1964	6.6	25.3	22.9	23.3	29.0	29.9
1955 to 1959	7.7	23.4	25.6	24.1	28.4	35.0
1950 to 1954	12.4	24.1	23.4	24.7	27.6	26.8
1945 to 1949	9.8	23.9	24.2	23.7	31.2	26.4
1940 to 1944	10.7	23.7	24.7	24.6	*	24.2
1935 to 1939	9.1	22.2	24.1	23.4	*	35.5
1930 to 1934	10.9	24.7	25.5	*	*	27.3
Spanish-origin						
1975 to 1979	14.0	34.0	37.2	42.1	*	11.0
1970 to 1974	11.4	28.6	33.4	36.6	35.2	18.4
1965 to 1969	10.8	26.4	27.8	28.9	28.6	14.2
1960 to 1964	13.2	25.5	25.9	23.9	29.5	8.3
1955 to 1959	11.8	25.4	26.8	24.7	*	19.6
1950 to 1954	13.4	23.3	26.5	25.1	*	13.5
1945 to 1949	15.1	25.5	22.6	23.1	*	11.6
1940 to 1944	13.7	24.3	*	*	*	15.0
1935 to 1939	12.8	*	*	*	*	12.5
1930 to 1934	*	*	*	*	*	*

Note: * indicates base too small to show derived measure.

Source: U.S. Bureau of the Census. "Childspacing Among Birth Cohorts of American Women: 1905 to 1959." Current Population Reports (Series P-20, no. 385, Tables 9 and 10). Washington, DC: U.S. Government Printing Office, 1984.

Contraception, surgical sterilization, and infertility together account for almost all of the long "open interval" that terminates childbearing. Returning to Figure 6-13, it would be old-fashioned to interpret the long childless interval that precedes the bearing of only one or two children as due solely to "marriage postponement." With modern contraception, people can marry at any age they choose and still end their reproductive years with almost exactly the size of family they want to have (see below).

Births of Spanish-Origin Parentage

It has long been known that birth rates of the Spanish-origin population are much higher than the white and somewhat higher than the black populations. However, direct measurement was difficult because births to this ethnic group were not separately identified until 1978, when births to Hispanic parents began to be identified in seventeen states with large Hispanic populations; by 1980 the number of states had expanded to twenty-two. It is estimated that these states account for 90 percent of all Spanish-origin births in the United States. Meanwhile, completeness of reporting improved with the result that the vital statistics for births of Hispanic parentage are useful and informative. Births are classified according to the origin of the mother. The data are not only for the Hispanic population as a whole but for the chief place-of-origin groups within that population.

Table 6-21 (first panel) provides age-specific fertility rates and total fertility rates for the Spanish-origin population by subgroups as of 1980; TFRs are shown in Figure 6-14. General fertility rates are provided in the second panel. Hispanics have a TFR 34 percent higher than the national average. However, there appears to be great diversity among the subgroups. Those of Mexican ancestry have a TFR of 2.9 children per woman, while Puerto Ricans have nearly one child per woman less; Cubans are reported to have extremely low fertility, far below replacement (1.3 children per woman). "Other Hispanics" from Central and South American and those whose origin was not specified have near replacement fertility of 2.0 births per woman. Thus, the so-called high fertility of Hispanics is due almost exclusively to the Mexican ancestry group. All other Hispanics have below replacement fertility, considerably lower than that of the black population. The high Mexican fertility occurs at every age.

An interesting facet of Table 6-21 is the fertility rates for the white non-Hispanic population. Earlier in this chapter the TFR for the white population in 1980 was reported to be 1,749 births per 1,000 women. Because Mexicans are predominantly classified as white, their fertility helps to inflate the TFR for the white population. When they are removed, the non-Hispanic white TFR sinks to 1,692 births per 1,000 women or a reduction of 3.4 percent. Without the contribution of the Mexican fertility, the white population is even farther below replacement than previously indicated.

Birth Order of Hispanic Births

Order-specific birth rates (second panel) and percentage distribution of births by order (third panel) are provided in Table 6-21. As would be expected from knowl-

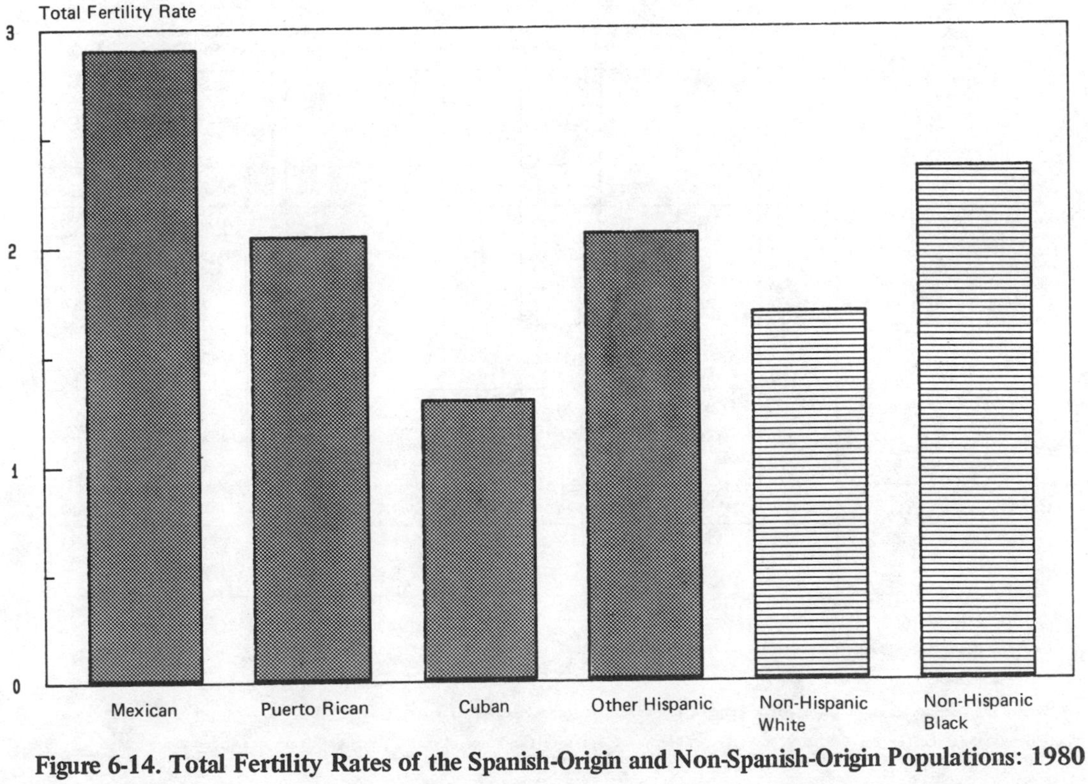

Figure 6-14. Total Fertility Rates of the Spanish-Origin and Non-Spanish-Origin Populations: 1980

Table 6-21. Birth Rates and Fertility Indicators for the Spanish-Origin Population: 22 Reporting States, 1980

TOTAL FERTILITY AND BIRTH RATES BY AGE OF MOTHER, BY HISPANIC-ORIGIN OF MOTHER, AND BY RACE OF CHILD FOR MOTHERS OF NON-HISPANIC ORIGIN

Fertility indicator: Age of mother	Origin of mother: All origins[a]	Hispanic: Total	Hispanic: Mexican	Hispanic: Puerto Rican	Hispanic: Cuban	Hispanic: Other Hispanic[b]	Non-Hispanic: Total[c]	Non-Hispanic: White	Non-Hispanic: Black
Total fertility rate. . . .	1,893.5	2,534.0	2,900.5	2,045.5	1,296.0	2,061.0	1,814.5	1,692.0	2,353.5
10-14 years	1.2	1.7	1.9	2.3	0.3	0.9	1.1	0.4	4.6
15-19 years	55.2	82.2	95.6	83.0	25.3	52.3	51.5	41.2	105.1
15-17 years[d]	33.9	52.1	--	--	--	--	31.3	22.4	77.2
18-19 years[d]	85.7	126.9	--	--	--	--	80.2	67.7	146.5
20-24 years	117.8	156.4	176.8	133.3	80.2	123.7	112.8	105.5	152.2
25-29 years	114.1	132.1	147.1	98.5	84.1	118.6	111.9	110.6	111.7
30-34 years	64.4	83.2	95.2	58.7	48.4	74.1	62.2	59.9	65.2
35-39 years	21.5	39.9	48.4	26.9	17.2	33.9	19.6	17.7	25.8
40-44 years	4.3	10.6	14.2	6.1	3.6	8.0	3.6	3.0	5.8
45-49 years	0.2	0.7	0.9	0.3	0.1	0.7	0.2	0.1	0.3

BIRTH RATES BY LIVE-BIRTH ORDER BY HISPANIC-ORIGIN OF MOTHER, AND BY RACE OF CHILD, FOR MOTHERS OF NON-HISPANIC-ORIGIN

Live-birth order	All origins[a]	Hispanic: Total	Mexican	Puerto Rican	Cuban	Other Hispanic[b]	Non-Hispanic: Total[c]	White	Black
All orders (GFR).	70.2	95.4	111.3	77.0	41.9	75.3	67.1	62.4	90.7
First child	30.0	36.1	40.4	30.3	21.1	31.3	29.3	28.0	35.7
Second child.	22.1	27.2	30.8	22.6	14.0	23.2	21.5	20.4	26.4
Third child	10.6	16.1	19.0	13.7	4.8	12.2	9.9	9.0	15.0
Fourth child.	4.2	7.8	9.8	6.0	1.3	4.9	3.7	3.1	7.1
Fifth child	1.7	3.7	5.0	2.4	0.4	1.9	1.4	1.1	3.2
Sixth child and over.	1.6	4.5	6.3	2.1	0.3	1.8	1.3	0.9	3.2

PERCENT DISTRIBUTION OF LIVE BIRTHS BY LIVE-BIRTH ORDER, BY HISPANIC-ORIGIN OF MOTHER, AND BY RACE OF CHILD FOR MOTHERS OF NON-HISPANIC-ORIGIN

Live-birth order	All origins[a]	Hispanic: Total	Mexican	Puerto Rican	Cuban	Central and South American	Other and unknown Hispanic	Non-Hispanic: Total[c]	White	Black
Total	100.0	100.0	100.0	100.0	100.0	100.0	100.0	100.0	100.0	100.0
First child	42.8	37.8	36.3	39.3	50.4	41.5	41.6	43.6	44.7	39.3
Second child.	31.5	28.5	27.7	29.4	33.4	31.8	30.0	32.0	32.7	29.2
Third child	15.1	16.9	17.1	17.7	11.5	16.3	16.1	14.8	14.4	16.6
Fourth child.	5.9	8.2	8.8	7.8	3.0	6.2	6.8	5.6	4.9	7.9
Fifth child	2.4	3.9	4.4	3.1	0.9	2.2	2.7	2.1	1.8	3.5
Sixth child and over.	2.3	4.7	5.7	2.7	0.8	2.0	2.8	1.9	1.4	3.5

PERCENT DISTRIBUTION BY RACE OF CHILD, BY HISPANIC-ORIGIN OF MOTHER

Race of child	All origins[a]	Hispanic: Total	Mexican	Puerto Rican	Cuban	Central and South American	Other and unknown Hispanic	Non-Hispanic	Not stated
All races	100.0	100.0	100.0	100.0	100.0	100.0	100.0	100.0	100.0
White	79.7	95.1	98.1	90.4	95.5	79.2	90.4	76.3	84.2
Black	16.2	2.9	1.2	7.4	3.1	12.2	3.4	19.1	12.3
Other	4.1	2.0	0.8	2.2	1.4	8.6	6.1	4.6	3.5

[a] Includes origin not stated.

[b] Includes Central and South American and other and unknown Hispanic.

[c] Includes races other than white and black.

[d] Population data to compute rates not available for specific Hispanic-origin groups.

Source: National Center for Health Statistics. "Births of Hispanic Parentage, 1980." Monthly Vital Statistics Report (Vol. 32, no. 6 supplement). Washington, DC: U.S. Government Printing Office, 1983, Tables 4, 5, 6, and 8.

edge of the total fertility and general fertility rates, the order-specific rates for Mexicans are far above the other Spanish-origin groups; rates for fifth children are double and those for sixth children are triple those for Puerto Ricans. Cubans have extremely low birth rates for first, second, and third children and practically zero rates for fourth and higher-order children. The third panel, which reports the percentage distribution of births by order, shows that one-half of all Cuban babies are first births, one-third are second order, and births of orders above four are practically nonexistent—much lower even than for the non-Hispanic white population.

Again the order-specific rates for the white population with Hispanics removed are very instructive in comparison with the black population (also with Hispanics removed). The general fertility rate of 90.7 for the non-Hispanic black population (second panel of Table 6-21) is 45 percent higher than the rate of 62.4 for the non-Hispanic white population. On an order-specific basis the ratio of black to white fertility is as follows:

All orders (GFR)	1.45
First child	1.28
Second child	1.29
Third child	1.67
Fourth child	2.29
Fifth child	2.91
Sixth child and over	3.56

In the bearing of first and second children, the rates for the black population are between 25 and 30 percent higher than for the white population, but at orders above this the rates soar to progressively higher ratios. That the ratios are extremely large should not be confused with the fact that at these higher orders the order-specific rates for both white and black populations are comparatively low. The ratios emphasize that there are remnants of extremely high-fertility mothers in the black population, but they are very rare among the non-Hispanic white population.

Race Composition of Hispanic Births

The lower panel of Table 6-21 reports the white-black composition of births to each Spanish-origin group as of 1980. Almost all Mexican births (98 percent) were classed as white. Likewise, 96 percent of Cuban births were classed as white. For Puerto Ricans the proportion was lower (90 percent), and for the Central American and South American group it was much lower (79 percent). Overall, 95 percent of Hispanic births were classed as white and hence contributed far more to the growth of the white population than of the black population. (Incidentally, non-Hispanic white births were only 76 percent of all births in 1980.)

Out-of-Wedlock Births to Hispanic Mothers

Both Mexican and Puerto Rican women are much more likely to bear children out of wedlock than are the white non-Hispanic women. However, Puerto Rican women are nearly 50 percent more likely to bear children out of wedlock than are Mexican women. Table 6-22 (second panel), which provides details, also shows Cuban women are much less inclined to bear children out of wedlock than the general population. The top panel of Table 6-22 reports out-of-wedlock birth ratios. For all groups the ratios are extremely high for the teenage population. Teenage ratios are lower for Cubans than for the non-Hispanic whites, and far higher for Puerto Ricans than for any other Spanish-origin group and only moderately lower than for the black population. At ages thirty and above the out-of-wedlock ratios for Puerto Ricans are higher than for the black population.

For all Spanish-origin groups the age distribution of out-of-wedlock births is similar (third panel of Table 6-22). About one-third are to teenagers, one-third to young women 20-24, and the remaining one-third to older women, extending significantly even to the late thirties. This pattern of even distribution among all ages is even more pronounced than for the black population.

Considering that 95 percent of all Spanish-origin births are classed as white, a minor contributing factor to the rising tide of out-of-wedlock births among the white population is the contribution of the Spanish-origin population, which has increased substantially in number over the years of the fertility rise. However, the age-specific ratios and percent for the non-Hispanic white population provided in Table 6-22 give unbiased estimates of the incidence and prevalence of out-of-wedlock childbearing among the white population with the Spanish-origin influence removed, and they show out-of-wedlock childbearing of substantial magnitude. Out-of-wedlock childbearing among the white population is more heavily concentrated in the teenage years than in other groups, but 59 percent occurs in the adult years, especially during ages 20-29.

Socioeconomic Differentials

Birth certificates contain comparatively little information about the social and economic characteristics of the mothers and fathers of children. Hence, to study socioeconomic differentials in fertility, it is necessary to turn either to sample surveys or to census sources. One of the most detailed sources of information is the 1980 census, which asked "How many children have you born?" of a large sample of women. This information has been cross-classified by age of mother and a lengthy list of characteristics, reported in Table 6-23, which provides a wealth of detail.

Table 6-22. Out-of-Wedlock Birth Ratios, Rates, and Distributions for the Spanish-Origin Population, by Age, Spanish-Origin of Mother, and Race for Mothers of Non-Spanish-Origin: 1980

Age of mother	All[a] origins	Hispanic						Non-Hispanic		
		Total	Mexican	Puerto Rican	Cuban	Central and South American	Other Hispanic	Total[b]	White	Black
OUT-OF-WEDLOCK BIRTH RATIOS (OUT-OF-WEDLOCK BIRTHS PER 1,000 TOTAL BIRTHS TO A GROUP)										
All ages	192.4	236.1	203.4	463.1	99.5	271.3	224.0	185.2	93.2	564.3
Under 15 years . . .	885.3	736.3	687.9	884.7	428.6	888.9	827.2	922.0	776.9	986.7
15-19 years.	480.2	418.7	370.4	662.0	238.1	494.9	458.0	496.7	309.1	854.6
15 years	775.6	608.9	536.2	882.6	580.6	840.0	699.0	819.6	630.1	971.0
16 years	655.7	537.4	483.5	762.0	378.0	614.5	614.5	684.3	482.7	938.8
17 years	550.5	459.7	412.8	671.2	268.0	543.9	518.7	574.8	379.7	900.9
18 years	455.6	393.3	346.5	637.8	221.0	479.4	420.3	472.3	292.5	843.5
19 years	363.1	342.1	296.9	588.8	181.6	438.3	363.9	369.6	217.7	757.2
20-24 years.	202.6	238.1	202.8	462.6	100.0	305.0	231.1	196.6	98.3	570.2
25-29 years.	98.6	158.9	129.3	355.1	60.5	244.7	140.0	88.9	40.1	378.9
30-34 years.	83.4	152.3	123.3	336.6	63.9	222.0	115.9	71.9	34.5	306.3
35-39 years.	103.0	161.6	132.6	344.2	88.4	213.8	142.5	88.8	46.0	291.0
40 years and over. .	131.8	158.5	125.5	376.3	69.0	257.3	157.9	122.1	70.6	306.5
RATE OF BIRTHS TO UNMARRIED WOMEN										
15-44 years[c]	30.3	52.0	54.5	74.5	9.3	40.9		27.7	--	--
15-19 years.	29.1	39.7	41.8	62.4	6.6	27.0		27.7	--	--
15-17 years. . . .	21.7	28.3	29.9	43.9	4.3	18.6		20.8	--	--
18-19 years. . . .	41.4	60.5	63.9	96.8	10.6	41.1		39.0	--	--
20-24 years.	42.5	76.5	79.5	114.1	14.0	58.6		38.7	--	--
25-29 years.	34.2	71.1	72.0	94.8	14.8	64.2		30.2	--	--
30-34 years.	22.0	53.9	56.2	64.8	11.4	49.3		18.5	--	--
35-44 years.	6.9	19.6	22.0	22.3	4.1	17.2		5.5	--	--
PERCENT DISTRIBUTION OF OUT-OF-WEDLOCK MOTHERS BY AGE										
All ages	100.0	100.0	100.0	100.0	100.0	100.0	100.0	100.0	100.0	100.0
Under 15 years . . .	1.3	1.1	1.3	1.2	0.4	0.3	1.0	1.4	0.9	1.8
15-19 years.	38.2	33.0	35.3	32.4	30.9	15.2	34.8	39.7	41.0	39.2
15 years	3.2	2.7	2.9	2.8	2.5	0.7	3.0	3.4	2.9	3.8
16 years	6.0	5.2	5.7	5.1	4.3	1.8	5.5	6.2	6.2	6.3
17 years	8.5	7.2	7.9	6.9	5.8	2.7	7.5	8.8	9.3	8.6
18 years	10.0	8.5	9.1	8.4	8.3	4.2	8.9	10.4	11.0	10.1
19 years	10.5	9.3	9.8	9.2	10.0	5.8	9.8	10.8	11.5	10.3
20-24 years.	35.5	35.1	35.2	35.2	34.2	34.1	35.4	35.6	35.4	35.8
25-29 years.	15.5	17.6	16.3	17.9	18.5	26.7	17.2	14.9	14.2	15.2
30-34 years.	6.7	8.9	8.0	9.2	9.5	16.1	7.6	6.1	6.1	5.9
35-39 years.	2.2	3.5	3.2	3.4	5.3	6.1	3.2	1.9	1.9	1.8
40 years and over. .	0.5	0.8	0.8	0.7	1.1	1.5	0.8	0.4	0.4	0.4

[a]Includes origin not stated.

[b]Includes races other than white and black.

[c]Rates computed by relating total births to unmarried mothers, regardless of age of mother, to unmarried women 15-44 years.

Note: -- indicates data not available.

Source: National Center for Health Statistics. "Births of Hispanic Parentage, 1980." Monthly Vital Statistics Report (Vol. 32, no. 6 supplement, Tables 7 and 11). Washington, DC: U.S. Government Printing Office, 1983.

Table 6-23A. Indices of Differential Fertility, by Socioeconomic Characteristics and Race-Ethnicity: 1980

Characteristics	Age 25 to 34 years			Age 35 to 44 years		
	White	Black	Spanish-origin	White	Black	Spanish-origin
Marital status						
Total	0.95	1.26	1.30	0.96	1.21	1.21
Single	0.09	0.82	0.48	0.07	0.76	0.46
Now married	1.12	1.45	1.48	1.02	1.28	1.29
Husband present	1.13	1.42	1.48	1.02	1.25	1.28
Wife married once	1.11	1.40	1.47	1.02	1.25	1.28
Wife married more than once	1.24	1.58	1.58	1.05	1.26	1.31
Husband absent	1.04	1.55	1.50	1.05	1.38	1.35
Separated	1.09	1.61	1.59	1.08	1.40	1.39
Other	0.91	1.27	1.29	0.97	1.24	1.21
Widowed	1.17	1.73	1.65	1.05	1.45	1.38
Divorced	0.87	1.39	1.25	0.92	1.17	1.13
Age at first marriage						
Total ever married	1.10	1.45	1.46	1.01	1.27	1.28
Under 15 years	1.73	2.13	2.32	1.34	1.71	1.83
15 to 17 years	1.60	1.97	2.05	1.27	1.65	1.70
18 and 19 years	1.30	1.58	1.62	1.11	1.39	1.43
20 and 21 years	1.07	1.35	1.37	1.00	1.21	1.27
22 to 24 years	0.79	1.13	1.13	0.88	1.06	1.12
25 and 26 years	0.55	1.02	0.93	0.76	0.97	1.00
27 to 29 years	0.51	1.06	0.94	0.68	0.95	0.91
30 years and over	0.49	1.12	0.92	0.53	0.93	0.80
Years of school completed						
Total	0.95	1.26	1.30	0.96	1.21	1.21
Elementary 0 to 7 years	1.41	1.69	1.81	1.19	1.54	1.53
Elementary 8 years	1.59	1.96	1.70	1.22	1.62	1.32
High school 1 to 3 years	1.48	1.78	1.57	1.19	1.49	1.29
High school 4 years	1.08	1.26	1.17	0.98	1.11	1.03
College 1 to 3 years	0.83	1.01	0.87	0.89	0.98	0.92
College 4 years	0.57	0.63	0.60	0.78	0.76	0.81
College 5 or more years	0.40	0.55	0.55	0.60	0.64	0.70
Labor force						
Women 16 to 44 years	0.95	1.26	1.30	0.96	1.21	1.21
In labor force	0.73	1.12	1.06	0.90	1.12	1.09
Not in labor force	1.34	1.62	1.63	1.07	1.43	1.39
Occupation of employed women						
Employed women 16 to 44 years	0.72	1.09	1.03	0.90	1.10	1.07
Managerial and professional specialty occupations	0.49	0.76	0.68	0.74	0.84	0.88
Executive, administrative, managerial	0.51	0.79	0.73	0.77	0.88	0.91
Professional specialty	0.48	0.76	0.65	0.73	0.83	0.85
Technical, sales, administrative support	0.71	0.99	0.90	0.88	0.97	0.94
Technicians and related support	0.58	1.03	0.80	0.84	1.01	0.91
Sales	0.85	1.08	1.03	0.97	1.09	1.04
Administratuve support occupations, including clerical	0.69	0.97	0.88	0.86	0.94	0.91
Service occupations	0.99	1.36	1.23	1.07	1.31	1.20
Private household occupations	1.08	1.40	1.03	1.01	1.27	1.03
Protective service occupations	0.78	1.11	0.99	1.03	1.17	1.10
Service occupations, except for protective and household	0.99	1.36	1.26	1.08	1.32	1.22
Farming, forestry, fishing occupations	1.08	1.54	1.60	1.12	1.50	1.63
Precision production, craft, and repair	0.86	1.24	1.21	0.97	1.16	1.09
Operators, fabricators, and laborers	1.07	1.37	1.32	1.05	1.27	1.19
Machine operators, assemblers, and inspectors	1.06	1.36	1.31	1.04	1.25	1.18
Transportation and material moving	1.13	1.44	1.24	1.15	1.37	1.20
Handlers, equipment cleaners, helpers, and laborers	1.04	1.39	1.35	1.06	1.30	1.25

Table 6-23A. Indices of Differential Fertility, by Socioeconomic Characteristics and Race-Ethnicity: 1980–continued

Characteristics	Age 25 to 34 years			Age 35 to 44 years		
	White	Black	Spanish-origin	White	Black	Spanish-origin
Occupation of employed husband						
Women 16 to 44 years with employed husband present	1.12	1.40	1.47	1.01	1.23	1.26
Managerial and professional specialty occupations	0.96	1.11	1.12	0.93	0.97	1.03
Executive, administrative, managerial	1.02	1.15	1.18	0.95	1.01	1.05
Professional specialty	0.89	1.06	1.05	0.91	0.92	0.99
Technical, sales, administratove support	1.01	1.23	1.21	0.96	1.06	1.08
Technicians and related support	0.95	1.19	1.11	0.94	0.97	1.05
Sales	1.02	1.18	1.21	0.96	1.05	1.08
Administrative support occupations, including clerical	1.04	1.26	1.26	0.97	1.08	1.09
Service occupations	1.14	1.41	1.47	1.04	1.25	1.26
Private household occupations	1.17	1.62	1.66	1.05	1.19	1.10
Protective service occupations	1.13	1.28	1.27	1.01	1.11	1.13
Service occupations, except for protective and household	1.15	1.47	1.53	1.06	1.30	1.29
Farming, forestry, fishing occupations	1.39	1.92	1.93	1.20	1.73	1.77
Precision production, craft, and repair	1.24	1.47	1.55	1.07	1.28	1.29
Operators, fabricators, and laborers	1.28	1.52	1.63	1.10	1.33	1.37
Machine operators, assemblers, and inspectors	1.28	1.50	1.62	1.08	1.29	1.34
Transportation and material moving	1.30	1.54	1.59	1.12	1.32	1.34
Handlers, equipment cleaners, helpers, and laborers	1.26	1.54	1.68	1.11	1.39	1.45
Family income in 1979 for married couple families[a]						
Only husband worked in 1979	1.46	1.76	1.74	1.09	1.44	1.38
Less than $10,000	1.55	1.85	1.83	1.18	1.51	1.46
$10,000 to $14,999	1.49	1.77	1.78	1.13	1.44	1.41
$15,000 to $19,999	1.45	1.71	1.69	1.08	1.41	1.37
$20,000 to $24,999	1.45	1.69	1.67	1.07	1.39	1.33
$25,000 to $34,999	1.45	1.63	1.63	1.08	1.41	1.35
$35,000 to $49,999	1.42	1.60	1.54	1.09	1.46	1.39
$50,000 or more	1.38	1.58	1.58	1.06	1.41	1.21
Husband and wife worked in 1979	0.95	1.31	1.30	0.98	1.16	1.19
Less than $10,000	1.17	1.58	1.58	1.07	1.35	1.36
$10,000 to $14,999	1.11	1.47	1.44	1.04	1.31	1.31
$15,000 to $19,999	1.05	1.37	1.37	1.01	1.26	1.23
$20,000 to $24,999	0.99	1.29	1.27	0.98	1.19	1.18
$25,000 to $34,999	0.87	1.20	1.16	0.97	1.11	1.14
$35,000 to $49,999	0.73	1.11	1.03	0.96	1.05	1.12
$50,000 or more	0.73	1.12	1.03	0.92	1.07	1.08

[a]Limited to married couples where both husband and wife are 16 years and over.

Source: U.S. Bureau of the Census. "Detailed Population Characteristics: United States Summary." 1980 Census of Population. Washington, DC: U.S. Government Printing Office, 1983, Table 271.

Census and survey data on children ever born (see Definition Box) are a source of cumulative fertility information. Because demographers are usually interested only in knowing current or recent differentials, they focus attention on the responses made by younger women. As a result, children-ever-born rates are incomplete measures of fertility and have very little usefulness or meaning other than to show differences between groups having dissimilar characteristics. So that the data in Table 6-23A will be easy to interpret, the children-ever-born data have been reduced to indices in which the average number of children ever born to women of a particular age group in the entire nation is taken as an index value of 1.00. A ratio in excess of 1.00 indicates the relative excess of cumulative fertility over all women of the same age, while a ratio less than 1.00 indicates relative

Table 6-23B. Fertility Status at Time of First Marriage for Women First Married at Ages 14-19, by Period of First Marriage and Race-Ethnicity

Race and period of first marriage	Fertility status at marriage		
	Already bore a child	Pregnant	Other
White			
1975-79.	7.2	13.0	79.8
1970-74.	6.8	13.8	79.4
1965-69.	5.9	14.6	79.5
1960-64.	5.3	12.9	81.8
1955-59.	4.4	10.0	85.7
1950-54.	3.9	8.2	87.9
1945-49.	3.8	5.8	90.5
1940-44.	2.7	5.0	92.3
1935-39.	4.0	6.0	90.0
1930-34.	3.0	7.0	90.0
Black			
1975-79.	43.6	11.8	44.6
1970-74.	38.7	17.1	44.2
1965-59.	32.7	21.9	45.4
1960-64.	29.5	25.9	44.5
1955-59.	33.0	16.5	50.5
1950-54.	24.1	14.5	61.4
1945-49.	17.9	15.3	66.8
1940-44.	16.5	13.9	69.6
1935-39.	22.3	12.0	65.7
1930-34.	16.3	9.8	74.0
Spanish-origin			
1975-79.	16.4	13.5	70.1
1970-74.	12.4	15.6	72.1
1965-69.	10.5	23.2	66.3
1960-64.	12.9	13.5	73.6
1955-59.	9.5	14.0	76.5
1950-54.	13.8	7.8	78.4
1945-49.	5.2	5.6	89.2
1940-44.	9.6	5.6	84.8
1935-39.	9.2	7.0	83.8
1930-34.	2.5	10.6	87.0

Source: U.S. Bureau of the Census. "Childspacing Among Birth Cohorts of American Women: 1905-1959." Current Population Reports (Series P-20, no. 385). Washington, DC: U.S. Government Printing Office, 1984, Table 8.

deficit. For example, according to the first line of Table 6-23A, fertility among white women aged 25-34 is reported to be 95 percent of the average (deficit of 5 percent), while fertility among black women is reported to be 26 percent above average and that of Spanish-origin women 30 percent above average. These differentials are somewhat reduced if ages 35-44 are used for comparison. Because the age groupings are broad, age composition is only partially controlled.

Marital Status

Among white women being single reduces fertility to only 9 percent of the average; among black women, being single reduces fertility very little to only 82 percent of the average. Highest fertility is found among women who have married more than once and are living with a husband. High fertility is also indicated for those who are widowed, probably because they have an older age composition within each of the two age groups. In comparison with being married once and living with husband, being divorced suppresses fertility by about 22 percent among white women but very little among black women and only moderately among Spanish-origin women. For white and Spanish-origin women, being separated is associated with fertility higher than being married once and living with husband. These differentials suggest that childbearing is involved in marital dissolution as well as marriage formation, in particularly complex ways, for the black and Spanish-origin populations.

Age at First Marriage

Women who married at a very early age have a longer time of exposure to childbearing and hence tend to bear more children. This inverse relationship between age at first marriage and number of children born is especially strong at the younger ages, because it truncates the age distribution, but it remains valid even for the age group 35-44. It affects white, black, and Spanish-origin groups equally.

Years of School Completed

There is a strong inverse relationship between the amount of education women have and their fertility. This is true for each race-ethnicity group. In fact the size of the race-ethnicity differential shrinks substantially with increasing education and practically disappears for the level of four years or more of college. The relationship is exaggerated for the 25-34 age group by delayed marriage to complete school but is also found with reduced impact in the older age groups (see Figure 6-15).

Labor Force Participation

The number of children ever born tends to be substantially higher among women who are not in the labor force than among women who are in the labor force. However, this is a difficult statistic to interpret:

1. A substantial number of women in the labor force are single, and hence are less exposed to childbearing.
2. Many women work until they have a child and then deliberately withdraw from the labor force to care for the child. The direction of causality is therefore unclear.
3. Many women who are widowed, separated, di-

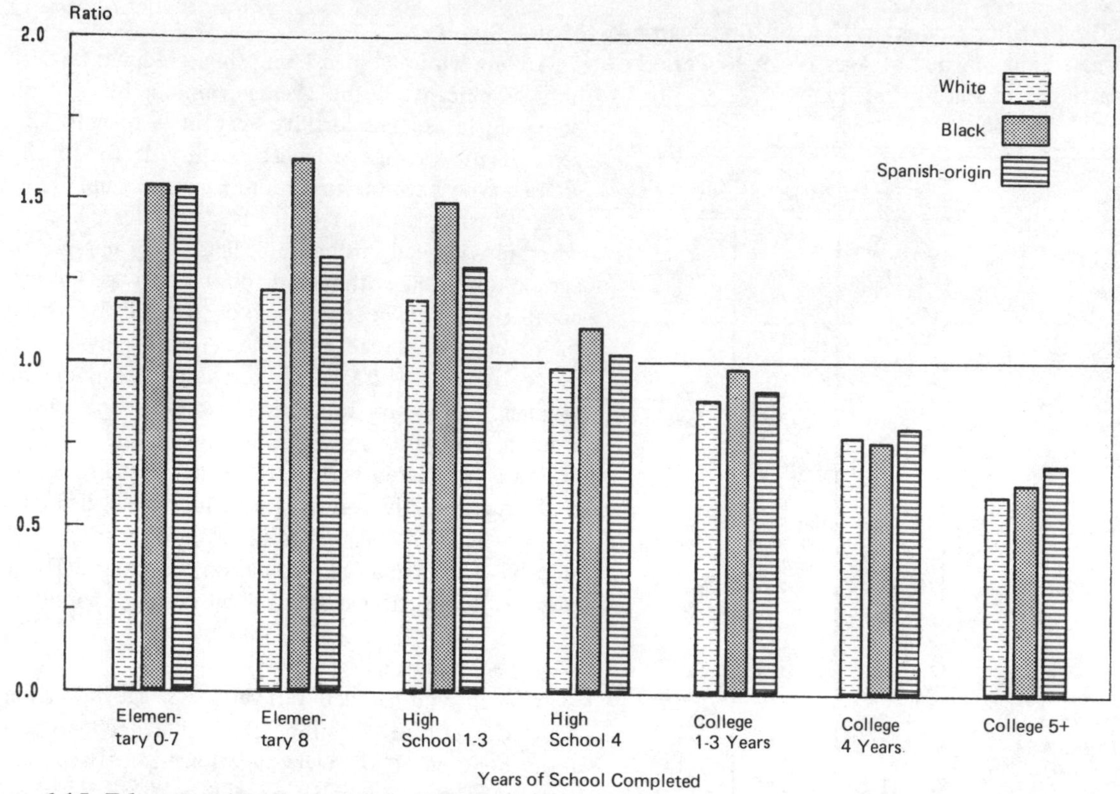

Figure 6-15. Educational Differentials in Fertility [ratio of children ever born to national average of children ever born for women aged 35-44, by educational attainment and race: 1980]

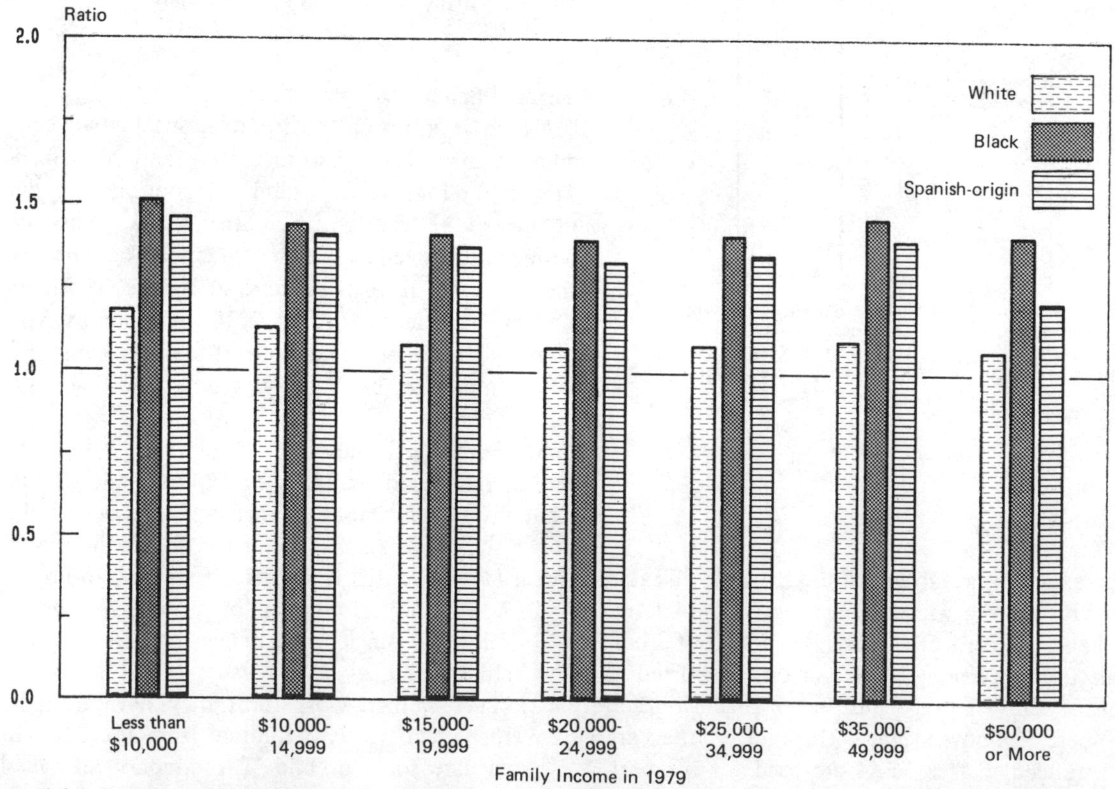

Figure 6-16. Income Differentials of Fertility [ratio of children ever born to national average of children ever born for women aged 30-44, by family income and race: 1980]

vorced, or otherwise less exposed are forced to work to support themselves.

4. Many women who are sterile or subfecund work as an involuntary substitute for having children.

It is therefore naive to assume that the act of being employed directly "causes" lower fertility, although it is undoubtedly an influencing factor.

Occupation of Women

Women who hold high-prestige white-collar positions (managers, professional workers, technicians, and administrative workers) tend to have lower fertility than women who have blue-collar and service occupations. A part of this could be an indirect reflection of the amount of education the woman has received.

Occupation of Husband

Married women with husbands present were tabulated according to the husbands' occupations. The results are similar to those reported for the occupation of women.

Income

Contrary to what might have been expected, there is comparatively little difference in fertility according to the size of family income where the husband works but the wife does not (see Figure 6-16). However, in such families the level of fertility is above average. At the lower end of the income scale (less than $20,000) fertility rates are above average, and at the very top ($35,000 or more) they are below average—but the differential is quite small when compared with those noted above for education and occupation. Also, when income is controlled the differences between races are greatly reduced.

The bottom panel of Table 6-23A shows a strong inverse relationship between family income with both husband and wife working and fertility. Where the income is high, fertility is low; where the income is low, fertility is high. This inverse relationship is stronger for younger women than for older. It may reflect education, occupation, and amount of full-time work by the wife, or it may represent an insistence upon childbearing by low-income families even though the wife is working.

A noteworthy finding in Table 6-23A is that fertility differentials between socioeconomic groups are comparatively small. This is especially true for the age group 35-44, where the truncating and autocorrelation effects of age at marriage, school enrollment, marital status, and

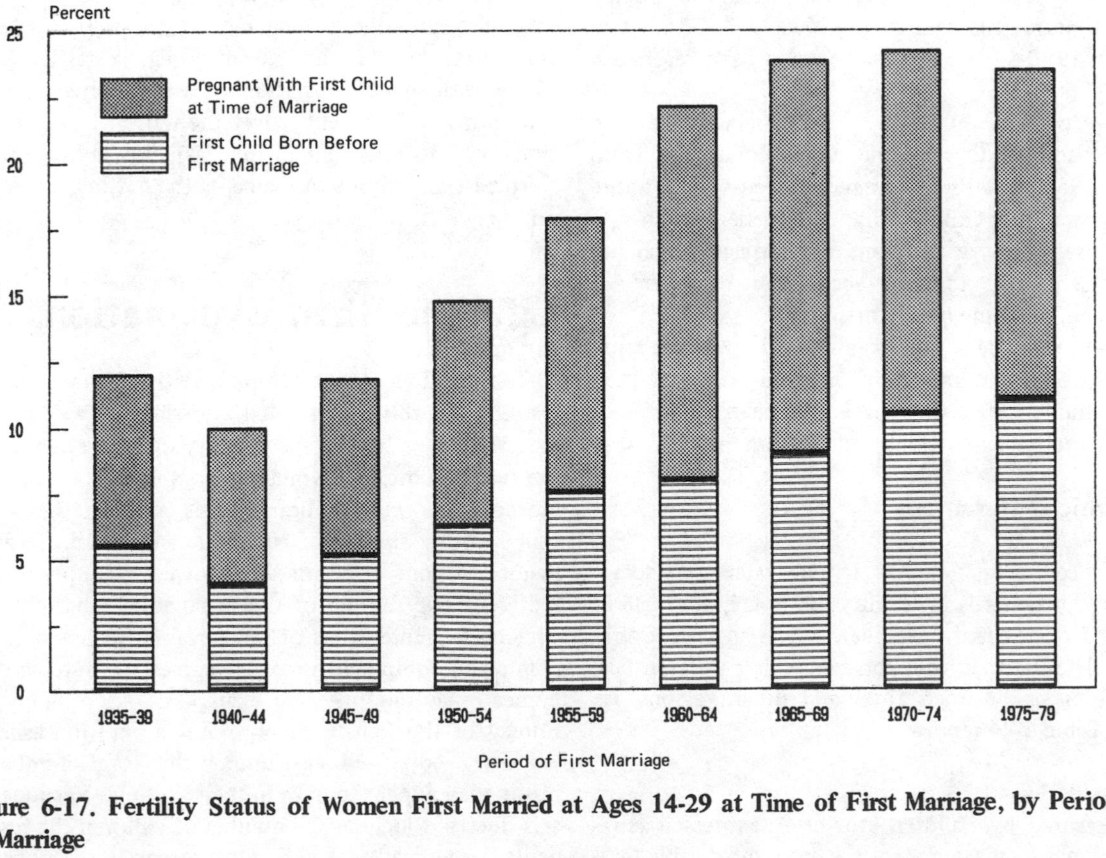

Figure 6-17. Fertility Status of Women First Married at Ages 14-29 at Time of First Marriage, by Period of First Marriage

self-selection into or out of the labor force are reduced. This is consistent with studies for earlier censuses, which have also found differentials to be of modest size and apparently converging toward average values over time.

Pregnancy Status at First Marriage

There has been a great deal of speculation about the proportion of women who are pregnant at the time they were first married, and the number of women who eventually marry after having born a child out of wedlock. The Bureau of the Census provides rough estimates of both items, reported in Table 6-23B and shown in Figure 6-17. As of 1975-79, about one white woman in five either had already born a child or was pregnant at the time of marriage. For all three groups there is a long-term trend toward having already born a child at the time of marriage; this is especially characteristic of black women. This set of data carries the following implications:

1. A substantial share of children born out of wedlock eventually get absorbed into a married couple situation, even if temporarily or belatedly. Having born a child out of wedlock appears to be less of a barrier to ultimate marriage than might be supposed.
2. Pregnancy at the time of marriage is less than might have been predicted, and is roughly the same for all race-ethnic groups—about 12-13 percent. Pregnancy at time of marriage is significantly lower in 1975-79 than it was in 1960-69, when it appears to have reached a peak.
3. The pattern of the Spanish-origin population closely resembles that of the white population from 1940 to 1950, but thereafter has tended to veer more toward premarital childbearing. It experienced an episode of pregnancy at the time of marriage which has been subsequently reduced—accompanied by greatly increased childbearing before marriage.
4. There may be a great reduction in pressure from pregnant women to marry the natural father of their unborn child. Instead, the mother may marry a different man after the out-of-wedlock child is born.

Geographic Differentials

The preceding section has demonstrated that socioeconomic differentials in fertility are now quite small in the United States and have been converging for several decades. The same is true for geographic differentials. The differences between rural and urban regions are small, as Table 6-24 reports.

White Population

As measured by children ever born, expressed as ratios to the national average for the age group, Table 6-24 shows that fertility in urban areas was consistently below that of rural areas and that the differences are larger for younger than for older women. However, teenage/youth fertility is lower in the urban fringe and in the rural farm areas than in central cities and in rural nonfarm areas. Teenage fertility is lowest in the Northeast and highest in the South. For ages 35-44, the urban-rural and regional differentials all tend to converge to comparatively low values. This could be a cohort effect of the baby boom generation, or it could be the fact that by this age women have had an opportunity to overcome initial differences due to age at marriage and child-spacing.

Black Population

Unlike the white population, teenage/youth fertility among the black population is above average in central cities, but like the white population it is low in urban fringes and rural farm areas. For intermediate and advanced ages, the differential shifts to strictly urban-rural; black fertility is 15-24 percent higher in rural than in urban areas, whereas it is 2-3 percent below the national average in urban areas.

Spanish-Origin Population

The Spanish-origin population shows lower fertility for teenagers who live in urban fringes; otherwise all areas have about the same rate of teenage/youth fertility. At intermediate and advanced ages rural fertility is 16 percent above the national average, while in urban fringes it is 6-8 percent below the national average. Regionally, Spanish-origin fertility is below average in the Northeast and about the same as the national average in other regions.

Lifetime Birth Expectations

There is urgent need to predict the future course of fertility, yet this is difficult to do simply by extrapolating past trends because of the very different behavior of the recent cohorts of women in comparison with preceding cohorts. One solution to this problem that works well in other spheres of economic and social life where major decisions or events are involved, is simply to ask a representative sample of the population what they expect to do. (Intentions of industrialists to invest in new plants and equipment or of consumers to purchase new homes or automobiles are examples.) Accordingly, the Bureau of the Census incorporates a question asked of women aged 18-34 concerning the total number of births they expect to have in their lifetime. Responses to this question include the number of children the respondents have already born. For this reason the responses of

Table 6-24. Differentials in Urban, Rural, and Regional Fertility: Ratios of Children Ever Born per 1,000 Women of Areal Grouping to Children Ever Born Rate for National Total, by Age Groupings

RURAL AND URBAN, 1970 AND 1980.

Age and race	1980 Urban	1980 Rural	1980 Ratio of rural to urban	1970 Urban	1970 Rural	1970 Ratio of rural to urban	Percent change 1970–80 Urban	Percent change 1970–80 Rural
White								
15-24 years. . . .	0.90	1.30	1.44	0.92	1.25	1.36	-23.7	-19.2
25-34 years. . . .	0.92	1.21	1.32	0.95	1.14	1.20	-35.1	-28.9
35-44 years. . . .	0.96	1.09	1.13	0.96	1.10	1.14	-12.0	-12.8
Black								
15-24 years. . . .	0.99	1.04	1.05	1.01	0.96	0.95	17.5	24.4
25-34 years. . . .	0.98	1.17	1.19	0.96	1.27	1.33	-23.2	-30.7
35-44 years. . . .	0.97	1.24	1.28	0.94	1.36	1.46	-5.8	-16.9

TYPE OF PLACE AND RACE-ETHNICITY: 1980.

Type of place	White 15-24 years	White 25-34 years	White 35-44 years	Black 15-24 years	Black 25-34 years	Black 35-44 years	Spanish-origin 15-24 years	Spanish-origin 25-34 years	Spanish-origin 35-44 years
U.S. total . . .	1.00	1.00	1.00	1.00	1.00	1.00	1.00	1.00	1.00
Urban-rural									
Urban total. . . .	0.90	0.92	0.96	0.99	0.98	0.97	1.00	0.99	0.98
Central cities .	0.92	0.83	0.92	1.01	0.98	0.96	1.04	0.98	0.98
Urban fringe . .	0.78	0.93	0.96	0.89	0.91	0.91	0.87	0.94	0.92
Rural total. . . .	1.30	1.21	1.09	1.04	1.17	1.24	1.03	1.16	1.19
Farm	0.84	1.35	1.18	0.98	1.15	1.23	1.06	1.24	1.17
Regions									
Northeast.	0.70	0.90	0.96	0.84	0.91	0.87	0.97	0.93	0.87
North Central. . .	1.0	1.06	1.06	1.07	1.03	1.00	1.04	1.04	1.04
South.	1.15	1.03	0.98	1.05	1.04	1.08	0.95	1.02	1.01
West	1.07	0.97	0.99	0.87	0.89	0.91	1.04	1.01	1.05

Sources: U.S. Bureau of the Census. "General Social and Economic Characteristics: U.S. Summary." 1980 Census of the Population (Table 121, 131, and 204), and "General Social and Economic Characteristics: U.S. Summary." 1970 Census of the Population (Vol. I, part 1, Tables 76 and 89). Washington, DC: U.S. Government Printing Office, 1983 and 1973.

younger persons (18-24) with low cumulative fertility are accepted as an "early warning" of significant changes upward or downward in the birth rate. Fairly rigorous tests of the stability and validity of these responses indicate that women have firm opinions on this topic, these opinions are quite stable over time for particular cohorts, and they may be accepted as good indicators of eventual completed family size. Table 6-25 reports the number of lifetime births expected per 1,000 women for selected years since 1967. The trend of birth expectations for all age groups and all race-ethnic groups has been steadily downward. For white women 18-24 and 25-29, the expectation is for below replacement-level fertility (2.1 live births per woman). For black and Spanish-origin women, 18-24 year olds expect replacement-level fertility or below.

The birth expectation data are published as rates for two groups: all women and currently married women. In general currently married women tend to have slightly higher birth expectations than all women. However, even the married women of each race-ethnic group have lowered their fertility expectations over time, and in 1982 black and Spanish-origin women expressed expectations far below the total fertility rates their groups now exhibit.

The trend in birth expectations during 1980, 1981, and 1982 are of special interest, because those years were the years of a slight upturn in birth rates. Have women raised their fertility expectations? Are they thinking of having larger families than was the case for the same age groups in earlier years? There is no evidence that this is the case. In fact, for each age group in each race-ethnic group the expectations are significantly lower in 1982 than in 1980. In 1979 and again in 1980 there was an across-the-board rise in birth expectations in comparison with the preceding year. This elevated expectation continued into 1981 but appears to have completely collapsed in 1982, with expectations falling to a lower level for each age group for every race-ethnic group than at any time since the Bureau of the Census started collecting data on this subject. (A minor exception is white women 25-29 years of age, who in 1982 expected 2,148 births per 1,000 instead of 2,146 as in 1980).

In sum, in 1982 American women expected to bear children at or slightly below replacement level for the remainder of their reproductive lifetime, with their expectations tending to decline with each passing year. Among the currently married, birth expectations for women 18-24 are lower than those for older age groups, but as of 1982 the birth expectations for all age groups were essentially the same. Black women aged 18-24 have even lower birth expectations than white women of the same age, and the birth expectations of Spanish-origin women for this young age group are only 0.04 child higher. However, at older ages both black and Spanish-origin women expect to bear more children primarily because of the larger number of births they already had accumulated when interviewed. The picture that emerges from Table 6-25 is that there is no evidence of a strong upward or downward trend in fertility during the foreseeable future—to the degree that women are able to predict and report their own reproductive future. Instead, the range of fluctuating about the replacement level, which has characterized the years 1979-83, is expected to continue well into the future. The emergence of new young cohorts with different ideas could of course change this outlook.

The fact that birth expectations have declined only slightly during recent years, despite a significant rise in

Table 6-25. Lifetime Births Expected per 1,000 Women: 1967 and 1971-1982 [age of women at survey date]

Years, race, and Spanish origin	Total, 18 to 34 years	18 to 24 years	25 to 29 years	30 to 34 years
All women				
All races				
1982	2,023	1,994	2,026	2,059
1981	2,048	2,033	2,012	2,106
1980	2,059	2,023	2,022	2,150
1979	2,072	2,033	2,033	2,170
1976	2,160	2,030	2,098	2,445
White				
1982	2,003	2,016	1,986	2,002
1981	2,024	2,049	1,971	2,044
1980	2,036	2,028	1,984	2,101
1979	2,049	2,034	1,998	2,126
1976	2,138	2,038	2,062	2,390
Black				
1982	2,149	1,845	2,271	2,478
1981	2,207	1,944	2,289	2,531
1980	2,227	1,997	2,298	2,557
1979	2,237	2,013	2,310	2,528
1976	2,348	1,974	2,422	2,994
Spanish-origin[a]				
1982	2,274	2,053	2,282	2,562
1981	2,343	2,114	2,407	2,638
1980	2,362	2,152	2,329	2,743
1979	2,352	2,138	2,304	2,833
1976	2,504	2,227	2,320	3,189
Currently married women				
All races				
1982	2,158	2,096	2,166	2,195
1981	2,189	2,162	2,164	2,233
1980	2,187	2,134	2,166	2,248
1979	2,217	2,164	2,193	2,282
1975	2,344	2,173	2,260	2,610
1972	2,521	2,255	2,452	2,915
1971	2,638	2,375	2,619	2,989
1967	3,052	2,852	3,037	3,288
White				
1982	2,143	2,090	2,148	2,178
1981	2,165	2,166	2,128	2,198
1980	2,169	2,130	2,146	2,223
1979	2,195	2,145	2,169	2,259
1975	2,311	2,147	2,233	2,564
1972	2,483	2,243	2,420	2,842
1971	2,601	2,353	2,577	2,936
1967	3,015	2,859	3,001	3,200
Black				
1982	2,289	2,054	2,294	2,447
1981	2,451	2,106	2,531	2,642
1980	2,378	2,155	2,426	2,522
1979	2,505	2,361	2,554	2,580
1975	2,751	2,489	2,587	3,212
1972	2,963	2,398	2,830	3,749
1971	3,071	2,623	3,112	3,714
1967	3,465	2,787	3,407	4,257
Spanish-origin[a]				
1982	2,553	2,324	2,522	2,746
1981	2,609	2,348	2,670	2,806
1980	2,600	2,428	2,495	2,909
1979	2,660	2,450	2,562	3,064
1975	2,668	2,223	2,607	3,238
1973	3.040	2,582	2,881	3,784

[a]Persons of Spanish origin may be of any race.

Source: U.S. Bureau of the Census. "Fertility of American Women: June 1982." Current Population Reports (Series P-20, no. 387). Washington, DC: U.S. Government Printing Office, 1984.

the age at marriage and a decline in fertility at ages under twenty-five, suggests that women expect to make up for these changes by bearing more children in their late twenties, early thirties, or even beyond. Tables 6-26, 6-27, and 6-28 report on birth expectations of women according to social and economic characteristics.

Marital Status

Table 6-27 shows that marital status affects birth ex-expectations than currently married women. Also single black women twenty-one years of age and under expect than single, divorced, separated, or widowed women of the same age. Among black women those who are divorced, separated, or widowed have significantly higher expectations than current married women. Also, single black women twenty-one years of age and under expect to have fewer children than white women of the same ages; the same is true for Spanish-origin women eighteen and nineteen years of age. Although these expectations may all be unrealistic in the sense that they could easily change, it appears that young unmarried women of all race-ethnic groups are entering the early years of family formation with the expectation of bearing children at below-replacement fertility, while currently married women in their early twenties expect to adhere almost exactly to replacement-level fertility.

Educational Attainment

A fairly strong inverse relationship exists between expectations of completed fertility and amount of education. High school graduates and those with less education expect to have replacement fertility or above; all groups with some college education expect to have below replacement-level fertility, and college graduates expect even fewer children.

Table 6-26. Births Expected per 1,000 Women, by Marital Status, Race, and Age: 1982

Marital status and age	White	Black	Spanish-origin
Women currently married			
Total, 18-34 years	2,143	2,289	2,553
18-24 years	2,090	2,054	2,324
18 and 19 years	1,943	*	*
20 and 21 years	2,148	1,874	2,318
22-24 years	2,091	2,148	2,396
25-29 years	2,148	2,294	2,522
30-34 years	2,178	2,447	2,746
Women widowed, divorced, or separated			
Total, 18-34 years	1,799	2,544	2,093
18-24 years	1,868	2,088	*
18 and 19 years	*	*	*
20 and 21 years	1,758	*	*
22-24 years	1,896	*	*
25-29 years	1,785	2,514	*
30-34 years	1,780	2,682	2,249
Women never married			
Total, 18-34 years	1,783	1,920	1,762
18-24 years	1,975	1,768	1,833
18 and 19 years	2,040	1,766	1,613
20 and 21 years	2,036	1,684	2,075
22-24 years	1,835	1,835	1,805
25-29 years	1,428	2,142	1,713
30-34 years	758	2,229	*

Note: * indicates base too small to show derived measure.

Source: U.S. Bureau of the Census. "Fertility of American Women: June 1982." Current Population Reports (Series P-20, no. 387). Washington, DC: U.S. Government Printing Office, 1984.

Table 6-27. Lifetime Births Expected per 1,000 Women, by Educational Attainment and Labor Force Status: 1982

Subject	Lifetime births expected	Percent expecting	
		No lifetime births	No future births
Educational attainment			
White			
Total, 18-34 years	2,003	11.8	49.2
Not a high school graduate	2,215	8.8	61.7
High school, 4 years	2,004	10.5	52.4
College: 1-3 years	1,982	13.3	41.2
College: 4 years or more	1,815	16.4	38.5
4 years	1,888	14.9	36.4
5 years or more	1,646	19.7	43.3
Black			
Total, 18-34 years	2,149	10.0	64.0
Not a high school graduate	2,570	7.9	74.4
High school, 4 years	2,118	8.8	66.9
College: 1-3 years	1,887	11.6	52.7
College: 4 years or more	1,742	19.1	47.0
4 years	1,631	22.7	52.6
5 years or more	*	*	*
Spanish-origin			
Total, 18-34 years	2,274	8.0	55.4
Not a high school graduate	2,523	5.9	64.0
High school, 4 years	2,170	9.1	54.3
College: 1-3 years	1,956	11.0	41.8
College: 4 years or more	1,787	9.3	32.2
4 years	*	*	*
5 years or more	*	*	*
Labor force status			
White			
Total, 18-34 years	2,003	11.8	49.2
In labor force	1,879	14.3	44.7
Employed	1,870	14.6	44.3
Unemployed	1,963	11.3	48.0
Not in labor force	2,276	6.2	59.1
Black			
Total, 18-34 years	2,149	10.0	64.0
In labor force	1,991	10.4	61.8
Employed	1,960	10.4	60.6
Unemployed	2,074	10.3	64.8
Not in labor force	2,471	9.3	68.4
Spanish-origin			
Total, 18-34 years	2,274	8.0	55.4
In labor force	2,076	11.0	51.1
Employed	2,072	11.3	49.2
Unemployed	2,099	9.6	60.3
Not in labor force	2,545	3.8	61.4

Note: * indicates base is too small to show derived measure.

Source: U.S. Bureau of the Census. "Fertility of American Women: June, 1982." Current Population Reports (Series P-20, no. 387, Table 4). Washington, DC: U.S. Government Printing Office, 1984.

Table 6-28. Lifetime Births Expected per 1,000 Wives 18-34 Years of Age, by Selected Characteristics: 1982 [data limited to "reporting" women]

Characteristic	Lifetime births expected		
	Wives 18 to 24 years old	Wives 25 to 29 years old	Wives 30 to 34 years old
Age at first marriage			
Total	2,096	2,166	2,195
Under 18 years	2,174	2,397	2,733
18 and 19 years	2,073	2,304	2,317
20 and 21 years	2,094	2,167	2,207
22 to 24 years	2,039	1,998	1,951
25 or more years	...	1,909	1,808
Years of school completed by civilian husband[a]			
Total years of school	2,092	2,173	2,200
Not a high school graduate	2,088	2,281	2,649
High school, 4 years	2,074	2,144	2,149
College: 1 to 3 years	2,088	2,154	2,157
4 or more years	2,135	2,145	2,056
4 years	2,143	2,152	2,057
5 or more years	2,111	2,134	2,054
Record not located	2,207	2,425	2,376
Major occupation group of employed civilian husband[a]			
Total employed[b]	2,084	2,165	2,185
White-collar workers	2,078	2,144	2,085
Prof., tech. and kindred wkrs	2,097	2,186	2,054
Man., admin., except farm	2,081	2,194	2,132
Sales worker	2,035	1,921	2,061
Clerical and kindred wkrs.	2,078	2,108	2,067
Blue-collar workers	2,092	2,162	2,268
Craftsmen	2,089	2,136	2,202
Operatives, inc. transport.	2,102	2,186	2,304
Laborers, except farm	2,073	2,197	2,473
Service, inc. pvt. hhld.	1,866	2,197	2,103
Farm workers	2,356	2,493	2,788
Family income for wives in married-couple families			
Wife in labor force			
Total income	2,004	2,005	2,015
Under $15,000	2,022	2,185	2,353
Under $5,000	2,030	*	*
$5,000 to $9,999	2,099	2,209	2,365
$10,000 to $14,999	1,980	2,189	2,266
$15,000 and over	1,998	1,956	1,948
$15,000 to $19,999	1,934	2,061	2,212
$20,000 to $24,999	1,994	2,000	2,146
$25,000 and over	2,047	1,898	1,821
Not reported	*	*	*
Wife not in labor force			
Total income	2,230	2,434	2,474
Under $15,000	2,204	2,471	2,687
Under $5,000	2,161	2,299	2,786
$5,000 to $9,999	2,155	2,484	2,892
$10,000 to $14,999	2,263	2,511	2,575
$15,000 and over	2,264	2,409	2,385
$15,000 to $19,999	2,285	2,446	2,621
$20,000 to $24,999	2,272	2,463	2,379
$25,000 and over	2,222	2,338	2,315
Not reported	*	*	*
Births to date			
Total	2,096	2,166	2,195
Childless	1,852	1,562	792
One child	2,102	1,839	1,397
Two children	2,430	2,261	2,104
Three children	3,220	3,237	3,087
Four or more children	*	4,538	4,562

[a]For wives in married-couple families.

[b]Excludes wives for whom husband's record was not located.

Note: ... indicates data not applicable. * indicates data too small to make accurate measurement.

Source: U.S. Bureau of the Census. "Fertility of American Women, June 1982." Current Population Reports (Series P-20, no. 387). Washington, DC: U.S. Government Printing Office, 1984.

Labor Force Status

Women currently employed have lower fertility expectations than those who are unemployed, who in turn have lower expectations than women not in the labor force. However, as a group, currently employed women expect to bear children almost at the replacement level.

Age at First Marriage

Those who married at an early age expect to have more children than those who marry later.

Occupation of Husband

Women have almost the same birth expectations irrespective of their husband's occupation, except wives of farm workers, who have the highest expectations, and wives of sales workers, who have the lowest.

Family Income

There is a mild inverse relationship between family income and fertility both when the wife is in the labor force and when she is not. However, the size of the differential is quite small except at the lowest and highest categories.

Children Already Born

The number of children a woman already has born affects her expectations. Childless young women expect to bear nearly two children, which is a vote of confidence for fertility in the future. However, older childless women, who may suspect themselves of being subfecund, have very low birth expectations. Women who have two children expect to maintain almost perfect contraception for the remainder of their lives, for they anticipate almost no additional children.

Summary

In short, the birth expectations of the current generation of young women call for a massive convergence toward replacement or slightly below replacement fertility levels, regardless of race, education, income, occupation, and other socioeconomic traits. This prospect results from the fact that groups with above-average fertility expect to reduce their childbearing. Women in groups that already have below replacement fertility anticipate some further reduction, but not a great deal.

Contraception and Fertility

Contraceptive Prevalence

One cannot fully comprehend or trust the birth expectation data just reviewed without also knowing the scope and nature of actions being taken by cohabiting

Table 6-29. Number of Currently Married Women[a] Aged 15-44 and Percent Distribution, by Current Contraceptive Status and Race: United States, 1973, 1976, and 1982 [statistics are based on samples of the household population of the coterminous United States]

Contraceptive status	All races[b]			White			Black		
	1982	1976	1973	1982	1976	1973	1982	1976	1973
Total	100.0	100.0	100.0	100.0	100.0	100.0	100.0	100.0	100.0
Contraceptors	67.9	67.7	69.6	68.8	68.8	70.5	61.0	58.6	60.0
Pregnant, post partum, seeking pregnancy . .	14.0	13.3	14.3	13.8	12.7	14.2	14.6	16.4	14.0
Contraceptively sterile	13.1	11.4	7.5	12.9	11.4	7.4	14.6	11.7	8.1
Other nonusers.	5.0	7.6	8.7	4.5	7.1	7.8	9.8	13.3	17.9
All women	28,231	27,488	26,646	25,195	24,795	24,249	2,130	2,169	2,081

[a]Includes a small nubmer of unmarried women living together with a partner in 1976 and 1973.

[b]Includes formally married women only in 1982.

Source: Christine A. Bachrach. "Contraceptive Practice: 1982." Paper presented at the annual meeting of the Population Association of America, May 3-5, 1984.

Table 6-30. Number of Currently Married Women[a] Aged 15-44 Using Contraception and Percent Distribution, by Method and Race: United States, 1973, 1976, and 1982

Contraceptive method	All races[b]			White			Black		
	1982	1976	1973	1982	1976	1973	1982	1976	1973
Total	100.0	100.0	100.0	100.0	100.0	100.0	100.0	100.0	100.0
Female sterilization. . . .	25.7	14.1	12.3	24.7	13.9	11.6	34.4	18.7	22.7
Male sterilization.	15.4	13.3	11.2	16.2	14.2	11.9	3.6[c]	3.0	1.0
Pill.	19.8	33.2	36.1	19.5	32.9	35.6	25.5	38.0	43.8
IUD	7.0	9.3	9.6	6.9	9.2	9.5	9.6	10.6	12.7
Diaphragm	6.7	4.2	3.4	6.8	4.4	3.6	5.4	3.0	2.0
Condom.	14.4	10.8	13.5	14.8	10.9	14.1	7.1	7.9	5.3
Foam.	2.9	4.4	5.0	3.0	4.2	5.0	3.4[c]	6.5	5.0
Periodic abstinence	4.7	5.0	4.0	4.8	5.1	4.1	3.9[c]	2.4	1.3[c]
Withdrawal.	1.8[c]	3.0	2.1	1.8[c]	3.0	2.2	2.0[c]	3.1	0.7[c]
Douche.	0.2[c]	1.0	0.8	0.1[c]	0.8	0.7	1.7[c]	4.6	3.0
Other	1.5[c]	1.5	1.9	1.3[c]	1.5	1.9	3.5[c]	2.3[c]	1.6
All contraceptors	19,143	18,609	18,548	17,311	17,051	17,107	1,294	1,269	1,249

[a]Includes a small number of unmarried women living together with a partner in 1976 and 1973; includes formally married women only in 1982.

[b]Includes white, black, and other races.

[c]Denotes percentages with relative standard errors of 0.30 or more.

Source: Christine A. Bachrach. "Contraceptive Practice: 1982." Paper presented at the annual meeting of the Population Association of America, May 3-5, 1984.

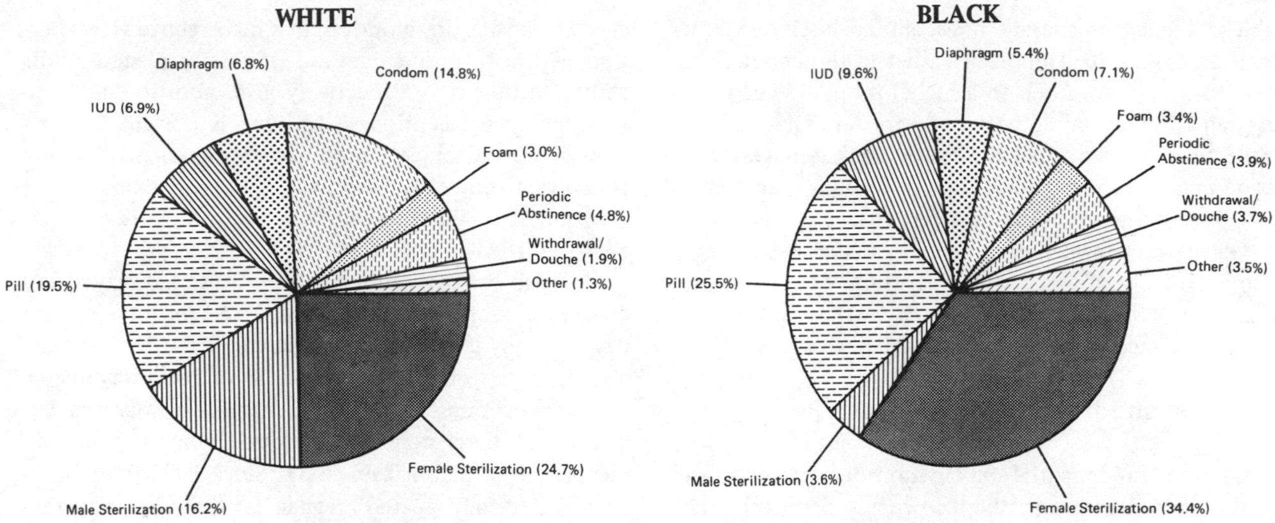

Figure 6-18. Percent Distribution of Contraceptive Methods in the United States: 1982

American couples to keep fertility under control. The National Center for Health Statistics periodically sponsors a "National Survey of Family Growth" in order to collect data on fertility, contraceptive practice, and aspects of maternal and child health. A cycle was conducted in 1973, another in 1976, and one in 1982.[1] Table 6-29 reveals that 81 percent of currently married women aged 15-44 are protected from pregnancy either by contraception or by sterilization for noncontraceptive reasons. Only 19 percent are actively seeking pregnancy, are already or recently pregnant, or else are neglecting to attempt fertility regulation. These proportions changed little in the nine years between 1973 and 1982. They are practically identical for the black and white populations.

Contraceptive Methods Used

The contraceptive methods that the American public uses to keep its fertility at near-replacement levels are reported in Table 6-30. Sterilization (male or female) accounts for nearly 40 percent, with oral pills and condoms accounting for an additional one-third. The IUD and the diaphragm protect an additional 14 percent of the population. Only about 10 percent of the population uses methods known to give only moderate or poor protection. Thus, with 80 percent of the population protected and nearly 90 percent of them using modern, reliable methods, it is quite accurate to say that fertility is highly controlled in the American culture. When women say they expect to have only one child, they are prepared to cause the prediction to come true.

A large-scale shift from use of the pill to the use of sterilization, which as Table 6-30 indicates occurred between 1973 and 1982, represents a transition from a reversible to a permanent method, a step taken by couples who have decided they have all the children they wish and who do not want to risk accidental pregnancy. Concern about the long-term effects of the oral pills on health has also stimulated a shift to sterilization and other methods. Figure 6-18 graphs the contraceptive profiles of the black and white populations. Birth rates cannot rise unless some of this intensive application of contraception diminishes.

Teenage Pregnancy and Contraception

The only significant group of reproductive age whose fertility is not being tightly regulated is the premaritally or extramaritally sexually active. The "National Survey of Family Growth" of 1982 obtained data on the prevalence of premarital sexual experience and the utilization of family planning services by women 15-19 years of age.[2] Of this group 46 percent reported having premarital sexual intercourse. This proportion, although high, appears not to have increased significantly since a 1979 survey. Among those young women who were sexually active, three-fourths had visited a family planning services center before having their first intercourse. Apparently they learned contraception subsequently, some only after becoming pregnant. At these rates of contraception, fertility among sexually active teenagers could be as high as among young married women, because the proportions using contraception are roughly the same.

The higher pregnancy rates among black teenagers than among white (reported earlier in this chapter) appear to be due as much to a higher proportion engaging in premarital sexual activity as to greater neglect of contraception. In fact, sexually active black teenagers were using family planning services in as high (or even higher) proportions as their white counterparts.

Given the prevalence of teenage sexual activity, the number of out-of-wedlock births would be even greater were it not for extensive, though by no means universal, use of contraception by sexually active teenagers.

Abortion and the Birth Rate

Another fundamental explanation of how birth rates in the United States are kept low is by abortion. Since 1973 abortion has been available as a normal medical procedure in all states of the nation. Before 1967 all states in the nation had laws prohibiting abortion except for extreme situations, usually to save the life of the mother. Between 1967 and 1973 some states passed more liberal abortion laws, but the Supreme Court decided in 1973 that state laws restricting the right of a woman to choose abortion rather than childbirth during the first three months of pregnancy were unconstitutional. The trough of the baby bust coincides with the widespread availability of this additional choice for dealing with unwanted pregnancies when contraceptives failed or were neglected. It is impossible to say how much downward impetus the birth rate received from the partial and then full liberalization of abortion, but it must be considered substantial. There is the presumption that available abortion would have an immediate effect by removing a certain percentage of unwanted pregnancies. Under this presumption, it is incorrect to view abortion as "just another method of family planning"; its ability to function retroactively gives abortion a dimension that contraception lacks. One important facet of the widespread objection to abortion-on-demand is the contention, not fully disproved, that some persons use abortion as a substitute for contraception rather than as a last resort when contraception fails.

A rough indicator of the role abortion has played and continues to play in influencing U.S. fertility may be developed by combining the data for live births and legal abortions to get a rough estimate of medically recognized conceptions, and by expressing abortions as a percentage of these conceptions. Such computations, by race, are presented in Table 6-31. Since 1972 the proportion of medically treated pregnancies that are terminated in abortion has risen from 15 to nearly 30 percent. Each year the proportion has been much higher among the black than among the white population. The proportion for black/other women has been 36 to 85 percent greater than for white women. This is consistent with the hypotheses that use of contraception is somewhat lower among the black population but that their birth expectations are almost identical.

The high proportions of abortions among pregnancies have two other important implications. First, the picture presented earlier of fertility under tight control through contraception is only partially accurate. There must be a great deal of neglect or carelessness in contraceptive use to have such a volume of abortion practiced. Secondly, with such high abortion proportions combined with such a high prevalence of contraception, comparatively few babies that are truly unwanted are allowed to be born. The incidence of unwanted babies can only have diminished remarkably during the 1970s.

Table 6-31. Proportion of Medically Recorded Pregnancies Terminated by Legal Abortion [abortions as a percent of live births plus abortions]

Year	All races	White	Black	Ratio black/white
1980	30.0	27.4	43.8	1.60
1979	30.0	27.4	42.9	1.57
1978	29.7	26.5	44.4	1.68
1977	28.4	24.8	44.0	1.77
1976	27.1	23.4	43.4	1.85
1975	24.8	21.5	39.4	1.83
1974	22.1	19.6	34.7	1.77
1973	19.2	17.7	27.6	1.56
1972	15.3	14.6	19.9	1.36

Source: U.S. Bureau of the Census. Statistical Abstract of the United States: 1984. Washington, DC: U.S. Government Printing Office, 1983, Table 98.

Synthesis

From the evidence presented it can be inferred that a substantial proportion of first births are unplanned or conceived out of carelessness, ignorance, or lack of appreciation of the implications of pregnancy—especially among births to teenagers. However, once attaining adulthood or having born a child, a very high percentage of women take full control of their conception risks and use effective modern methods of contraception (and abortion when necessary) in order to keep their childbearing at the level of one or two children, to which most aspire. Demographically teenage pregnancy probably has very little effect upon population growth, other than to lengthen the time during which contraception must be practiced, with some increased risk of additional pregnancies. The key factor is the long-run fertility intentions that the couples have. These seem to be focused on the ideal of the two-child family, with a substantial minority opting for one child or no child (see below).

Childlessness

In all societies a significant proportion of women remain childless throughout their lifetime. This may be caused by inability to conceive due to either male or female sterility or by a combination of lifetime abstinence or contraception. Because of rising age at marriage and postponement of childbearing, the proportion of young women who are still childless by the time they reach thirty is rising. This has caused some demographers to predict that lifetime childlessness may reach very high proportions, as much as 30 percent.[3]

Following is the estimated proportion childless among real cohorts of ever-married women who reached 40-44 at selected dates, and by race for 1981 and 1982:

Year	Proportion childless
All races	
1950	20.0
1954	17.8
1960	14.1
1965	11.0
1970	8.6
1975	7.0
1980	6.6
1981	5.9
1982	7.6
By race-ethnicity	
White, 1981	5.9
White, 1982	7.4
Black, 1981	6.5
Black, 1982	8.9
Spanish-origin, 1981	6.5
Spanish-origin, 1982	6.6

Source: U.S. Bureau of the Census. Statistical Abstract of the United States, 1984. Also, "Fertility of American Women: June, 1981." Current Population Reports (Series P-20, no. 378). Washington, DC: U.S. Government Printing Office, 1983.

Thus, until the onset of the baby boom, childlessness was a state for a high percentage of women who arrived at their fortieth birthday. The Great Depression, with its delayed marriage, low fertility rates, and high proportions of women never marrying, created the situation where about one-fifth of all women arrived at menopause without having had a child. This proportion declined steadily from 1950 to 1981; as a result of the "marriage boom" described in Chapter 4 and the baby boom described earlier in this chapter, a much higher proportion of women than ever before were exposed to the likelihood of pregnancy. Throughout this time childlessness was substantially higher among the black than among the white population. Physiologists estimate that roughly 5 percent of all women are unable to bear children because either they or their husbands are sterile. Thus in 1981 the proportion childless was not far from the estimated biological minimum. Clearly, there had been a great deal of childlessness, through choice or necessity, in the preceding years.

According to the above data beginning in 1982 the proportion of childlessness began to rise again for the white and the black populations. The Current Population Survey of 1983 found that 10.1 percent of all women aged 40-44 were childless, which implies that the reversal that started in 1982 has continued. Childlessness *is* on the rise. Whether or not it will return to its former very high levels, however, is questionable. Two sets of data should be examined in this connection: differentials in current childlessness and childless expectations of women.

Current Childlessness

Table 6-32 reports the proportion childless in 1982 among women aged 30-44 having selected characteristics. A fairly consistent pattern emerges. Childlessness is highest among women who have the following characteristics when they reach menopause: never married, living in a central city, having a college or postgraduate degree, and employed as a white-collar worker. In none of these groups except the never-married and women with five years or more of college does childlessness reach 30 percent. The maximum proportion of childlessness ranges between 15 and 18 percent among the categories more prone to childlessness, in which large sectors of the population now and in the future will be concentrated. It should be noted that on a cross-sectional rather than a cohort basis, childlessness among the black population is now equal to or even lower than among the white; whatever was causing high proportions of childlessness among black women in earlier cohorts seems to have vanished. It should also be noted that never having been married is a very powerful factor in determining childlessness among the white population (89.5 percent childless), but 72 percent of never-married black women has born a child by ages 35-44 (only 28.1 percent childless).

Future Expectations of Childlessness

Table 6-27 reports the proportion of women 18-34 years of age who reported in 1982 they expected to bear no children in their lifetime (second column of data). Of these women, only 11.8 percent expected to

Table 6-32. Percent Childless among Women Aged 35-44, by Race-Ethnicity: 1982

Characteristics	White	Black	Spanish-origin
Total.	13.1	10.9	10.1
Marital status			
Ever married	9.1	8.4	6.5
Never married.	89.5	28.1	*
Residence			
Metropolitan	14.6	11.5	10.3
Central city	18.5	12.0	11.9
Metro ring	12.8	10.1	7.9
Nonmetropolitan.	10.0	8.4	8.9
Farm-nonfarm			
Farm	5.9	--	--
Nonfarm.	13.2	--	--
Educational attainment			
Not a high school graduate	9.4	8.4	7.8
High school graduate . . .	9.7	10.2	8.8
College 1-3 years.	15.3	11.0	18.6
College 4 years.	17.7	} 20.5	*
College 5 years or more.	30.3		
Labor force status			
In labor force	15.3	11.9	11.2
Employed	15.3	12.9	12.0
Unemployed	15.2	3.6	*
Not in labor force	8.6	8.1	8.8
Occupation			
White collar workers . . .	17.2	15.7	16.5
Blue collar workers. . . .	12.8	13.4	12.5
Service workers.	9.3	7.3	5.1
Farm workers	7.9	*	*

Notes: -- indicates data not available. * indicates sample too small for reliable measure.

Source: U.S. Bureau of the Census. "Fertility of American Women: June 1982." Current Population Reports (Series P-20, no. 387). Washington, DC: U.S. Government Printing Office, 1984.

remain childless, which is slightly higher than the proportion actually childless among women aged 40-44. The proportions climbed to above 20 percent only for women with five years or more of college; for college graduates it was 16 percent. Those who were employed showed average proportions of childlessness, as did women with 1-3 years of college. To the extent that childlessness, like childbearing, is under the ability of women to control, the proportions expecting to remain childless are higher than in 1980, but not by a large amount.

In reporting the results of the 1982 survey, the Bureau of the Census compared expectations of childlessness with the 1976 survey. It found that although the proportions of women 25-29 and 30-34 who were still childless at those ages increased between the two surveys, the proportion of women in these ages who reported they expected to remain childless declined. This implies that a substantial proportion of the women who were childless at these ages still planned to marry and bear a child before the end of their reproductive life. Only if these women postpone marriage to such an advanced age that they will have difficulty in bearing children or if there is an "epidemic" of couples refusing to marry, both the birth expectations and the childlessness expectations suggest that childlessness may rise moderately but will not rise much above one-half of the 25-30 percent that characterized earlier generations (see Figure 6-19).

Reproduction Rates

Population growth can be measured in a more precise way than simply subtracting the crude death rate from the crude birth rate to get the rate of reproductive change (natural increase), as introduced in Chapter 1. Temporary effects of age composition need to be controlled, and fertility and mortality need to be measured in age-specific terms rather than as crude rates. Demographers have developed two refined measures, the net reproduction rate (NRR) and the intrinsic rates of birth, death, and increase (see Definition Box). Both of these rates reveal what the long-term growth trends in the population would be if the age-specific birth and death rates were applied to the population's future age distribution. Table 6-33 reports these measures each year since 1960. Both rates measure the extent to which the population is replacing itself on a long-term basis, given its present birth and death rates.

Net Reproduction Rate

Using an age distribution that would result if the population were exactly replacing itself (stationary population) at current fertility and mortality, the net reproduction rate states how many daughters 1,000 women bear each year (1,000 represents exact replacement). As of 1979 the numbers are estimated to be as follows:

Total.	884
Black.	1,140
White.	837

The white population is 837/1,000 or 16.3 below replacement. Correspondingly, the black population is 1,140/1,000 or about 14.0 percent above replacement. Thus the black population replaces itself at 1,173/864, or 1.362 times (36.2 percent greater), the rate of the white population.

Table 6-33A. Net Reproduction Rates, by Race: United States, 1940-1979

Year	Total	White	All other
Registered births			
1979	884	837	1,140
1978	856	810	1,109
1977	868	825	1,113
1976	839	797	1,078
1975	853	810	1,098
1974	879	837	1,120
1973	897	852	1,164
1972	956	908	1,247
1971	1,075	1,026	1,374
1970	1,168	1,125	1,433
1969	1,161	1,113	1,473
1968	1,166	1,116	1,495
1967	1,213	1,158	1,582
1966	1,288	1,231	1,678
1965	1,376	1,314	1,802
1964	1,507	1,447	1,923
1963	1,564	1,506	1,973
1962	1,633	1,577	2,033
1961	1,704	1,648	2,100
1960	1,715	1,662	2,093
1959	1,722	1,667	2,118
Births adjusted for underregistration			
1959	1,742	1,679	2,200
1958	1,736	1,675	2,178
1957	1,765	1,701	2,206
1956	1,729	1,665	2,184
1955	1,676	1,617	2,101
1954	1,657	1,601	2,062
1953	1,597	1,546	1,959
1952	1,563	1,516	1,897
1951	1,521	1,472	1,865
1950	1,435	1,387	1,780
1949	1,439	1,397	1,743
1948	1,430	1,400	1,679
1947	1,505	1,492	1,594
1946	1,344	1,331	1,435
1945	1,132	1,106	1,323
1944	1,163	1,139	1,334
1943	1,228	1,211	1,348
1942	1,185	1,171	1,293
1941	1,075	1,052	1,242
1940	1,027	1,002	1,209

Source: National Center for Health Statistics. Vital Statistics of the United States (1979, Vol. I, Table 1-4). Washington, DC: U.S. Government Printing Office, 1983.

Intrinsic Rate of Increase

Similar findings are obtained when the intrinsic birth, death, and natural increase rates are computed. Using an age distribution that would result if current fertility and mortality rates were to be in effect for a prolonged period of time (stable population), the birth rate would stabilze at (see Table 6-33B for details):

Rate of increase	-4.7
Intrinsic birth rate	11.2
Intrinsic death rate	15.9

Thus, although the crude birth and death rates of 1979 show a positive but small gain, both the net reproduction rate and the intrinsic rate of increase show that on a long-term basis the population is not reproducing itself. The extent of this shortfall is about 4.7 per 1,000, or 0.5 percent per year. This loss is due entirely to the below-replacement level of the white population. The black population continues to grow at the rate of about 2.0 percent a year, while the white population loses at the rate of 6.8 percent a year. It is this differential growth which, when projected into the future, results in the gradual increase in the proportion of the population that is black as noted in Chapter 2.

Conclusion: Future Trend of Fertility

Despite the great amount of information available about fertility and the insights into trends and causes that intensive research and rich data sources provide, it is impossible to predict with any high degree of confidence whether fertility rates will rise, fall, or stay the same in the next decade or until the year 2000. It is quite unlikely that they will change radically from their present levels. When making its hundred-year projections of population, the U.S. Bureau of the Census made three assumptions about the possible future course of the TFR: these merit attention as a possible set of boundaries to use in "bracketing" the range of future trends.

Year	Low	Middle	High
White			
1983	1,717	1,763	1,812
1985	1,707	1,801	1,875
1990	1,682	1,873	2,013
2000	1,633	1,897	2,167
2025	1,600	1,900	2,300
Black			
1983	2,223	2,286	2,349
1985	2,192	2,309	2,406
1990	2,117	2,345	2,526
2000	1,974	2,293	2,630
2025	1,767	2,098	2,540

Source: U.S. Bureau of the Census. "Projections of the Population of the United States, by Age, Sex, and Race: 1983 to 2080." Current Population Reports (Series P-25, no. 952). Washington, DC: U.S. Government Printing Office, 1984.

The Census Bureau based these assumptions after reviewing the data on fertility trends and future expecta-

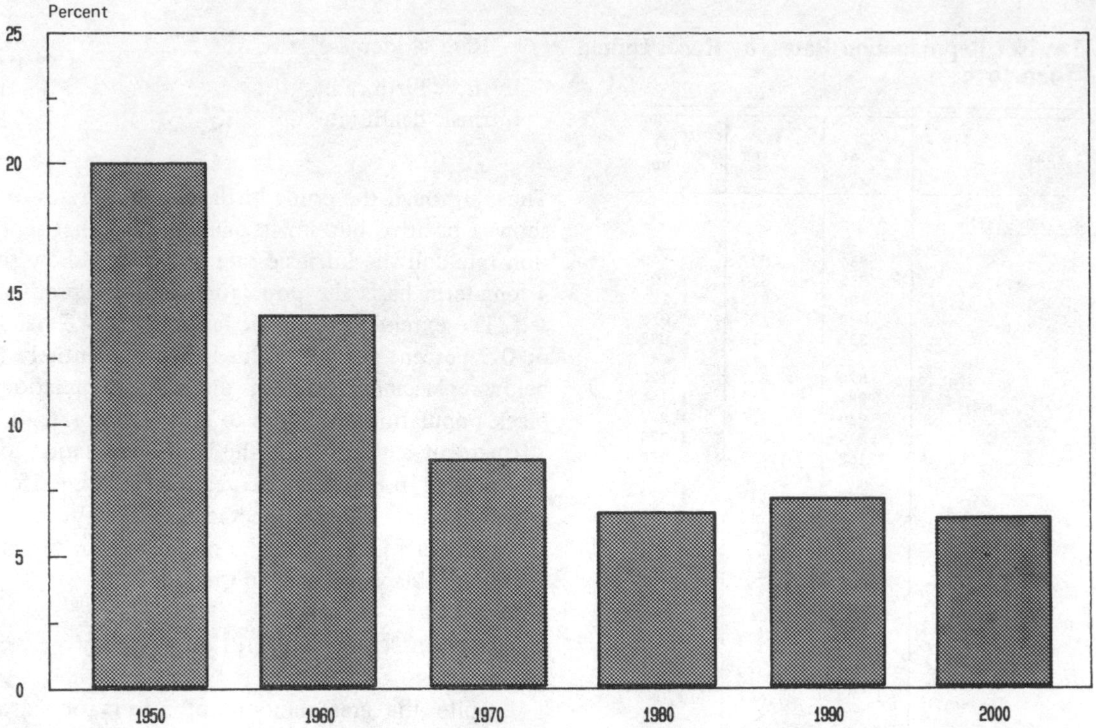

Figure 6-19. Prevalence of Childlessness in the United States: Past Levels and Future Expectations

Table 6-33B. Intrinsic Rates of Birth, Death, and Natural Increase, by Race: United States, 1940, 1950, and 1960-1979

Year	Intrinsic rate of natural increase			Intrinsic birth rate			Intrinsic death rate		
	Total	White	All other	Total	White	All other	Total	White	All other
1979	-4.7	-6.8	5.2	11.2	10.2	17.3	15.9	16.9	12.1
1978	-6.0	-8.0	4.1	10.7	9.7	16.8	16.7	17.7	12.7
1977	-5.4	-7.4	4.3	11.1	10.0	17.0	16.5	17.4	12.7
1976	-6.7	-8.6	3.0	10.5	9.5	16.3	17.2	18.2	13.3
1975	-6.1	-8.1	3.7	10.8	9.8	16.9	16.9	17.9	13.1
1974	-5.0	-6.8	4.6	11.4	10.4	17.6	16.4	17.3	13.0
1973	-4.2	-6.1	6.1	11.9	10.8	18.8	16.1	17.0	12.7
1972	-1.7	-3.7	8.9	13.2	12.0	20.7	14.9	15.7	11.8
1971	2.8	1.0	12.8	15.6	14.4	23.4	12.8	13.5	10.6
1970	6.0	4.5	14.4	17.6	16.5	24.6	11.6	12.0	10.2
1969	5.7	4.1	15.4	17.5	16.3	25.5	11.7	12.2	10.1
1968	5.9	4.2	16.0	17.6	16.4	26.0	11.7	12.2	10.0
1967	7.4	5.6	18.2	18.5	17.2	27.5	11.1	11.6	9.4
1966	9.7	7.9	20.4	20.0	18.7	29.4	10.4	10.8	9.0
1965	12.1	10.3	23.1	21.7	20.3	31.5	9.6	9.9	8.4
1964	15.6	14.0	25.7	24.2	22.8	33.7	8.5	8.8	8.0
1963	17.1	15.6	26.7	24.6	23.2	33.8	7.5	7.7	7.1
1962	18.8	17.4	27.9	25.8	24.6	34.8	7.0	7.1	6.9
1961	20.5	19.1	29.2	27.1	25.8	35.9	6.6	6.7	6.7
1960	20.8	19.5	29.2	27.4	26.2	36.1	6.6	6.7	6.9
Births adjusted for underregistration									
1950	13.7	12.3	23.0	22.6	21.3	31.8	8.9	9.0	8.9
1940	1.0	0.1	7.4	--	--	--	--	--	--

Source: National Center for Health Statistics. Vital Statistics of the United States: Natality (1979, Vol. I, Table 1-5). Washington, DC: U.S. Government Printing Office, 1983.

tions that have been reviewed in this chapter. These assumptions presumed a gradual narrowing of race differentials to a point where they disappear about the year 2030. It seems plausible to conclude that for the remainder of this century and far into the next the white population will continue to reproduce at below replacement level, that both the black and the Spanish-origin populations will decline toward replacement level, perhaps at a faster pace and arriving earlier than envisaged in the Census Bureau projections. It is this prospect that underlies the very slow rates of population growth predicted by these projections.

Notes

1. Christine A. Bachrach. "Contraceptive Practice: 1982." Paper presented at the annual meeting of the Population Association of America, May, 1984.
2. William F. Pratt and Gerry E. Hendershot. "The Use of Family Planning Services by Sexually Active Teenage Women." Paper presented at the annual meeting of the Population Association of America, May, 1984.
3. Charles F. Westoff. "Some Speculation on the Future of Marriage and Fertility." *Family Planning Perspectives* 10 (1978):79-83.

Bibliography

Ahlburg, Dennis A. "Forecasting Regional Births from National Birth Forecasts." Paper presented at the International Conference on Forecasting Regional Population Change and Its Economic Determinants and Consequences. 1982.

Anderson, John E. "Planning Status of Marital Births, 1975-1976." *Family Planning Perspectives* 13 (1981).

Anderson, K.H. "Sensitivity of Wage Elasticities to Selectivity Bias and Assumption of Normality: An Example of Fertility Demand Estimation." *Journal of Human Resources* 17 (1982):594-605.

Bachrach, Christine A. "Contraceptive Practice: 1982." Paper presented at meeting of Population Association of America, Minneapolis, May, 1984.

Baldwin, Wendy H. "Adolescent Pregnancy and Childbearing–Growing Concerns for Americans." *Population Bulletin* 2 (1976):3-48.

Baldwin, Wendy H., and Cain, Virginia S. "The Children of Teenage Parents." *Family Planning Perspectives* 1A (1980):34-43.

Bean, Frank D., and Marcum, John P. "Differential Fertility and the Minority Group Status Hypothesis: An Assessment and Review." Pp. 189-211 in *The Demography of Racial and Ethnic Groups*. Frank D. Bean and W. Parker Frisbie (eds.). New York: Academic Press, 1978.

Bean, Frank D., and Swicegood, Gray. "Generation, Female Education and Mexican American Fertility." *Social Science Quarterly* 63 (1982):131-44.

Becker, G.S. "An Economic Analysis of Fertility." In *Demographic and Economic Change in Developed Countries*. Universities National Bureau Conference Series II. Princeton, NJ: Princeton Universtiy Press, 1960.

Birdsall, S.S. "An Analysis of Population Age Balance." *Professional Geography* 32 (1980):467-70.

Blake, Judith. "Is Zero Preferred? American Attitudes Toward Childlessness in the 1970s." *Journal of Marriage and the Family* 41 (1979):245-57.

Blake J., and Del Pinal, J. "Educational Attainment and Reproductive Preferences: Theory and Evidence." In *Determinants of Fertility Trends: Theories Re-Examined*. C. Hohn and R. Mackensen (eds.). Liege, Belgium: IUSSP, 1982.

———. "Predictors of Family-Size Preferences, 1945-1977: A Multivariate Analysis." *Social Biology* 26 (1979):302-13.

Bloom, David E. "Age Patterns of Women at First Birth." *Genus*. (Forthcoming.)

———. "What's Happening to the Age at First Birth in the United States? A Study of Recent Cohorts." *Demography* 19 (1982):351-70.

Bloom, David E., and Pebley, Anne R. "Voluntary Childlessness: A Review of the Evidence and Implications." *Population Research and Policy Review* 1 (1982):203-24.

Bouvier, Leon F. "America's Baby Boom Generation: The Fateful Bulge." *Population Bulletin* 35 (1980): 1-35.

Bouvier, Leon F., and Rao, S.L.N. *Socioreligious Factors in Fertility Decline*. Cambridge, MA: Ballinger Publishing Company, 1975.

Brackbill, Yvonne, and Howell, Embry M. "Religious Differences in Family Size Preference Among American Teenagers." *Sociological Analysis* 35 (1974):35-44.

Braun, H.I. "Regression-Like Analysis of Birth Interval Sequences." *Demography* 17 (1980):207-23.

Busby, R.C., and Mode, C.J. "Theory and Applications of a Computationally Efficient Cohort Simulation Model of Human Reproduction." *Mathematical Biosciences*. (Forthcoming.)

Butz, W.P., and Ward, Michael. "The Emergence of Countercyclical U.S. Fertility." *American Economic Review* 69 (1979):318-28.

Cain, G., and Dooley, M. "Estimation of a Model of Labor Supply, Fertility, and Wages of Married Women." *Journal of Political Economy* 84 (1976): 5179-99.

Caldwell, J. *The Theory of Fertility Decline*. New York:

Academic Press, 1981.

Campbell, Arthur A. "Baby Boom to Baby Bust and Beyond." *Annals of the American Academy of Political and Social Science* 435 (1978):40-59.

Carlson, E. "Dispersion of Childbearing Outside Marriage." *Sociology and Social Research* 66 (1982): 335-47.

Casterline, John, and Trussell, James. "Age at First Birth." *Comparative Studies* 15 (1980).

Cho, Lee-Jay; Grabill, Wilson H.; and Bogue, Donald J. *Differential Current Fertility in the United States.* Chicago: Community and Family Study Center, University of Chicago, 1970.

Cochrane, Susan H. "Effects of Education and Urbanization on Fertility." In *Determinants of Fertility in Developing Countries.* Rodolfo Bulatao and Ronald D. Lee (eds.). New York: Academic Press, 1983.

Coombs, L.C., and Fernandez, D. "Husband-Wife Agreement about Reproductive Goals." *Demography* 15 (1978):57-73.

Cooney, R.S. et al. "Puerto Rican Fertility: An Examination of Social Characteristics, Assimilation, and Minority Status Variables." *Social Forces* 59 (1981): 57-73.

Cramer, J.C. "Fertility and Female Employment: Problems of Causal Direction." *American Sociological Review* 45 (1980):167-90.

Cummings, M., and Cummings, S. "Family Planning Among the Urban Poor: Sexual Politics and Social Policy." *Family Relations* 32 (1983):47-58.

Cymrot, D.J., and Seiver, D.A. "Fertility Conflict in American Households, 1976." Paper presented at the meetings of the Population Association of America, San Diego, April, 1982.

DeFronzo, J. "Female Labor Force Participation and Fertility in 48 States: Cross-Sectional and Change Analysis for the 1960-70 Decade." *Sociology and Social Research* 64 (1980):263-78.

———. "Testing the Economic Theory of Fertility with Cross-Sectional and Change Data." *Social Biology* 23 (1976):226-34.

DeJong, Gordon F., and Sell, Richard R. "Changes in Childlessness in the United States: A Demographic Path Analysis." *Population Studies* 31 (1977): 129-41.

Devaney, Barbara. "An Analysis of Variations in U.S. Fertility and Female Labor Participation Trends." Duke University, Durham, NC, 1980. (Mimeographed.)

Dixon, B.D. "Teenage Pregnancy and Adolescent Risk-Taking: The Influence of Alienation, Feminist Ideology, Contraceptive Orientation, Socioeconomic Status, and Traditional Fundamentalist Religion Upon the Adolescent Woman's Decision Whether to Contracept." Washington, DC: University Microfilms International, 1981.

Dooley, M.D. "Labor Supply and Fertility of Married Women: An Analysis with Grouped and Individual Data from the 1970 U.S. Census." *Journal of Human Resources* 17 (1982):499-532.

Dryfoos, John G. "Contraceptive Use, Pregnancy Intentions and Pregnancy Outcomes Among U.S. Women." *Family Planning Perspectives* 14 (1982):81-93.

Easterlin, Richard A. *Birth and Fortune: The Impact of Numbers on Personal Welfare.* New York: Basic Books, 1980.

———. *Population, Labor Force and Long Swings in Economic Growth.* New York: National Bureau of Economic Research, 1968.

———. "Relative Economic Status and the American Fertility Swing." In *Family Economic Behavior.* Eleanor Sheldon (ed.). Philadelphia: J.B. Lippincott Co., 1973.

———. "What Will 1984 Be Like? Socioeconomic Implications of Recent Twists in Age Structure." *Demography* 15 (1978):397-432.

Feeney, G. "Population Dynamics Based on Birth Intervals and Parity Progression." *Population Studies* 35 (1982):65-78.

Freedman, D.S., and Thornton, A. "Income and Fertility: The Elusive Relationship." *Demography* 19 (1982):65-78.

Freedman, D.S. et al. "Age at First Birth and Family Size: Evidence from a Longitudinal Study." *Social Biology* 28 (1981):217-27.

Fried, E.S., and Udry, J.R. "Wives' and Husbands' Expected Costs and Benefits of Childbearing as Predictors of Pregnancy." *Social Biology* 26 (1979): 265-74.

Furstenberg, F.F. Jr. "Parenting Apart: Patterns of Childbearing after Divorce." Paper presented at the Annual Meeting of the American Sociological Association, San Francisco, September, 1982.

Gurak, Douglas T. "Sources of Ethnic Fertility Differences: An Examination of Five Minority Groups." *Social Science Quarterly* 59 (1978):294-310.

Hendershot, G.E., and Placek, P.J. *Predicting Fertility.* Lexington, MA: Lexington Books, 1981.

Hofferth, Sandra L., and Moore, Kristin A. "Early Childbearing and Later Economic Well-Being." *American Sociological Review* 44 (1979):784-815.

Huber, J. "Will U.S. Fertility Decline Toward Zero?" *Sociological Quarterly* 21 (1980):481-92.

Isaac, L. et al. "Period Effects on Race- and Parity-Specific Birth Probabilities of American Women, 1917-1976: A New Measure of Fertility." *Social Science Research* 11 (1982):176-200.

Isserman, A. "Multiregional Demoeconomic Modeling

with Endogenously Determined Birth and Migration Rates: Theory and Prospects." Paper presented at the International Conference on Regional Population Change and Its Economic Determinants and Consequences. 1982.

Jain, A.K. "Effect of Female Education on Fertility: A Simple Explanation." *Demography* 18 (1981): 577-95.

James, W.H. "Causes of the Decline in Fecundability with Age." *Social Biology* 26 (1979):330-34.

———. "Distributions of Coital Rates and of Fecundability." *Social Biology* 28 (1981):334-41.

Janssen, S.G., and Hauser, R.M. "Religion, Socialization, and Fertility." *Demography* 18 (1981):511-28.

Joerding, W. "Lifetime Consumption, Labor Supply and Fertility: A Complete Demand System." *Economic Inquiry* 20 (1982):255-76.

Johnson, N.E. "Minority-Group Status and the Fertility of Black Americans, 1970: A New Look." *American Journal of Sociology* 84 (1979):1386-400.

———. "Religious Differentials in Reproduction: The Effects of Sectarian Education." *Demography* 19 (1982):495-509.

Joseph, H. "Estimation of Fertility Using a Stock-Adjustment Model." *Review of Economic Studies* 62 (1980):545-54.

Keyfitz, N. "On the Momentum of Population Growth." *Demography* 7 (1971):71-80.

Kitagawa, Evelyn M. "New Life-Styles: Marriage Patterns, Living Arrangements, and Fertility Outside of Marriage." *American Academy of Political and Social Science Annals* 453 (1981):1-27.

Kleinbaum, R. *The Emergence of Countercyclical Fertility Revisited* (Research Report no. 82-27). Ann Arbor, MI: Population Studies Center, University of Michigan, 1982.

Lee, Ronald D. "Demographic Forecasting and the Easterlin Hypothesis." *Population and Development Review* 2 (1976):459-68.

———. "Forecasting Births in Post-Transition Populations: Stochastic Renewal with Serially Correlated Fertility." *Journal of the American Statistical Association* 69 (1974):607-17.

Lehrer, E. "Behavioral and Biological Effects of Child Mortality on Spacing by Parity: A Cox-Regression Analysis." 1982. (Mimeographed.)

Loftin, C., and Ward, S.K. "Spatial Autocorrelation Model of the Effects of Population Density on Fertility." *American Sociological Review* 48 (1983): 121-28.

Lopez, D.E., and Sabagh, G. "Untangling Structural and Normative Aspects of the Minority Status-Fertility Hypothesis." *American Journal of Sociology* 83 (1978):1491-97.

Marcum, J.P. "Explaining Fertility Differences Among U.S. Protestants." *Social Forces* 60 (1981):532-43.

Marcum, J.P., and Radosh, M. "Religious Affiliation, Labor Force Participation, and Fertility." *Sociological Analysis* 42 (1981):353-62.

Marini, M.M. "Effects of the Number and Spacing of Children on Marital and Parental Satisfaction." *Demography* 17 (1980):225-42.

———. "Effects of the Timing of Marriage and First Birth on Fertility." *Journal of Marriage and the Family* 43 (1981):27-46.

Masnick, George. "Historical Trends in Cohort Parity Distribution: Implications for Fertility in the 1980s." 1980. (Mimeographed.)

———. "Social Determinants of the Timing of the First Birth." 1980. (Mimeographed.)

McCabe, J.L., and Rosezweig, M.R. "Female Employment Creation and Family Size." Pp. 322-55 in *Population and Development: The Search for Selective Intervention*. R. Ridker (ed.). Baltimore: Johns Hopkins Press, 1976.

McDonald, John. "The Emergence of Countercyclical Fertility: A Reassessment of the Evidence." *Journal of Macroeconomics* (1983).

McLaughlin, S.D. "Differential Patterns of Female Labor-Force Participation Surrounding the First Birth." *Journal of Marriage and the Family* 44 (1982):407-20.

Mineau, G.P., and Trussel, T.J. "A Specification of Marital Fertility by Parent's Age, Age at Marriage, and Marital Duration." *Demography* 19 (1982): 335-49.

Moore, Kristin A., and Hofferth, Sandra L. *The Consequences of Age at First Childbirth: Final Research Summary* (Report no. NICHD/CPR/CPR/BSB/79-7). Springfield, VA: U.S. NTIS, 1978.

Moore, Kristin A., and Waite, Linda J. "Early Childbearing and Educational Attainment." *Family Planning Perspectives* 9 (1977):220-25.

———. "Marital Dissolution, Early Motherhood, and Early Marriage." *Social Forces* 60 (1981):20-40.

Morgan, S. Philip. "Parity-Specific Fertility Intentions and Uncertainty: The United States, 1970 to1975." *Demography* 19 (1982):315-34.

Morgan, S. Philip, and Rindfuss, Ronald R. "Delayed Childbearing in the United States: 'Depression'-Style Childbearing in the 1970s and 1980s." 1982. (Mimeographed.)

Mosher, William D., and Bachrach, Christine A. "Childlessness in the United States: Estimates from the National Survey of Family Growth." *Journal of Family Issues* 3 (1982):517-43.

Nag, M. "How Modernization Can Also Increase Fertility." *Current Anthropology* 21 (1980):571-87.

Namboodiri, N.K. "On Factors Affecting Fertility at Different States in the Reproduction History: An Exercise in Cohort Analysis." *Social Forces* 59 (1981): 1114-29.

National Institutes of Child Health and Human Development. "Fertility Change after the Baby Boom: The Role of Economic Stress, Female Employment, and Education." *Population and Environment* 3 (1980).

O'Connell, Martin. "Comparative Estimates of Teenage Illegitimacy in the United States, 1940-44 to 1970-74." *Demography* 17 (1980):13-23.

———. "Regional Fertility Patterns in the United States: Convergence or Divergence?" *International Regional Science Review* 6 (1981).

O'Connell, Martin, and Rogers, Carolyn C. "Differential Fertility in the United States: 1976-1980." *Family Planning Perspectives* 14 (1982):281-86.

Pebley, A. "Changing Attitudes Toward the Timing of First Births." *Family Planning Perspectives* 13 (1981):171-75.

Pickens, G.T. "A Stochastic Model of Natural Marital Fertility: Theory and Analysis of Some Historical Population Data." *Mathematical Biosciences* 48 (1980):129-51.

Pittenger, D.B. "An Exponential Model of Female Sterility." *Demography* 10 (1973):113-21.

Population Reference Bureau. "Fertility." *Population Bulletin* 37 (1982):7-11.

Potter, R.G., and Kobrin, F.E. "Some Effects of Spouse Separation on Fertility." *Demography* 19 (1982): 79-85.

Preston, S.H. *The Effects of Infant and Child Mortality on Fertility*. New York: Academic Press, 1978.

Public Health Report. "1980 Rate of Childbearing for U.S. Unmarried Women Highest Ever Observed." *Public Health Reports* 98 (1983):196.

Pullum, T.W. "Adjusting Stated Fertility Preferences for the Effect of Actual Family Size with Applications to World Fertility Survey Data." Paper presented at the meetings of the Population Association of America, Philadelphia, 1979.

———. "Separated Age, Period, and Cohort Effects in White U.S. Fertility, 1920-1970." *Social Science Research* 9 (1980):225-44.

Reid, John. "Black America in the 1980s." *Population Bulletin* 37 (1982).

Repetto, R. "Interaction of Fertility and the Size Distribution of Income." *Journal of Development Studies* 14 (1978):22-39.

Rindfuss, Ronald R., and Bumpass, Larry. "How Old Is Too Old? Age and the Sociology of Fertility." *Family Planning Perspectives* 8 (1976):43-55.

Rindfuss, Ronald R.; Bumpass, Larry; and St. John, Craig. "Education and Fertility: Implications for the Roles Women Occupy." *American Sociological Review* 45 (1980):431-47.

Rindfuss, Ronald R., and St. John, Craig. "Social Determinants of the Timing of the First Birth." *Journal of Marriage and the Family* 45 (1983).

Rindfuss, Ronald R., and Sweet, James. *Postwar Fertility Trends and Differentials in the United States*. New York: Academic Press, 1977.

Ritchy, P. Neal. "The Effect of Minority Group Status on Fertility: Causal Inferences from Household Models." *Journal of Political Economy* 88 (1980): 328-48.

Rosenzweig, M.R., and Wolpin, K.I. "Testing the Quantity-Quality Fertility Model: The Use of Twins as a Natural Experiment." *Econometrica* 48 (1980): 227-40.

Samuelson, P.A. "An Economist's Non-Linear Model of Self-Generated Fertility Waves." *Population Studies* 30 (1976):243-48.

Scanzoni, J. "Work and Fertility Control Sequences Among Younger Married Women." *Journal of Marriage and the Family* 41 (1979):739-48.

Schultz, T. Paul. *Economics of Population*. Reading, MA: Addison-Wesley, 1981.

Schultz, T. W. "The High Value of Human Time: Population Equilibrium." *Journal of Political Economy* 82 (1974):5233-51.

Sheps, M.C., and Menken, J.A. *Mathematical Models of Conception and Birth*. Chicago: University of Chicago Press, 1973.

Smith-Lovin, L., and Tickamyer, A.R. "Fertility and Patterns of Labor Force Participation Among Married Women." *Social Biology* 28 (1981):81-95.

St. John, Craig. "Race Differences in Age at First Birth and the Pace of Subsequent Fertility: Implications for the Minority Group Status Hypothesis." *Demography* 19 (1982):301-14.

Teachman, Jay. "Early Marriage, Premarital Fertility, and Marital Dissolution: Results for Blacks and Whites." *Journal of Family Issues*. (Forthcoming.)

Thompson, Warren S., and Whelpton, P.K. *Population Trends in the United States*. New York: McGraw-Hill, 1933.

Thadani, V.N. "Property and Progeny: An Exploration of Intergenerational Relations." *Population Council Center for Policy Studies* (Working Paper 62). New York: The Population Council, 1980.

Thomson, E. "Individual and Couple Utility of Children." Paper presented at the meeting of the Population Association of America, San Diego, April, 1982.

Thornton, Arland D. "The Influence of First Generation Fertility and Economic Status on Second Generation Fertility." 1984. (Mimeographed.)

Thornton, Arland D. "Marital Dissolution, Remarriage,

and Childbearing." *Demography* 15 (1978):361-80.

Tilly, C. (ed.). *Historical Studies of Changing Fertility*. Princeton, NJ: Princeton University Press, 1978.

Tomes, N. "Model of Fertility and Children's Schooling." *Economic Inquiry* 19 (1981):209-34.

Treas, J. "Great American Fertility Debate: Generational Balance and Support of the Aged." *Gerontologist* 21 (1981):98-103.

———. "Postwar Trends in Family Size." *Demography* 18 (1981):321-34.

Trussell, James, and Bloom, David E. "Estimating the Covariates of Age at Marriage and First Birth." *Population Studies*. (Forthcoming.)

Trussell, T.J., and Menken, J. "Early Childbearing and Subsequent Fertility." *Family Planning Perspectives* 10 (1978):209-18.

Trussell, James; Menken, Jane; and Coale, Ansley J. "A General Model for Analyzing the Effect of Nuptiality on Fertility." In *Nuptiality and Fertility: Proceedings of a Conference*. L. Ruzicka (ed.). Liege, Belgium: Ordina Editions, 1982.

Turchi, B.A. *The Demand for Children: The Economics of Fertility in the United States*. Cambridge, MA: Ballinger Publishing Company, 1975.

Tyler, Carl W.W. "Planned Parenthood: Ideas for the 1980s." *Family Planning Perspectives* 14 (1982): 221-23.

U.S. Bureau of the Census (Moore, Maurice J., and O'Connell, Martin). *Perspectives on American Fertility* (Series P-23, no. 70). Washington, DC: U.S. Government Printing Office, 1978.

U.S. Department of Health and Human Services. *National Survey of Family Growth, Cycle II: Sample Design, Estimation Procedures, and Variance Estimation* (Series 2, no. 87). Washington, DC: U.S. Government Printing Office, 1981.

Veevers, Jean E. "Voluntary Childlessness: A Review of Issues and Evidence." *Marriage and Family Review* 2 (1979):2-26.

Waite, Linda J., and Stolzenberg, Ross M. "Intended Childbearing and Labor Force Participation of Young Women." 1984. (Mimeographed.)

Weller, Robert H., and Bouvier, Leon F. *Population Demography and Policy*. New York: St. Martin's Press, 1981.

Westoff, Charles F. "Some Speculation on the Future of Marriage and Fertility." *Family Planning Perspectives* 10 (1978):79-83.

———. "The Predictability of Fertility in Developed Countries." *Population Bulletin of the United Nations* 11 (1978):1-6.

Westoff, Charles F., and Jones, E. "The End of 'Catholic' Fertility." *Demography* 16 (1979):209-17.

Westoff, Charles F., and Ryder, Norman B. *The Contraceptive Revolution*. Princeton, NJ: Princeton University Press, 1977.

———. "The Predictive Validity of Reproductive Intentions." *Demography* 14 (1977):431-54.

Wilkie, Jane R. "The Trend Toward Delayed Parenthood." *Journal of Marriage and the Family* 43 (1981):583-92.

Willigan, J.D.; Mineau, G.P.; Anderton, D.L.; and Bean, L.L. "A Macrosimulation Approach to the Investigation of Natural Fertility." *Demography* 19 (1982): 161-76.

Yoder, Michael L. "Religion as a Determinant of Fertility Among White Americans, 1965." Madison, WI: University of Wisconsin and University Microfilms, 1980.

Zelnik, Melvin, and Kantner, John. "Sexuality, Contraception and Pregnancy Among Young Unwed Females in the U.S." In *Demographic and Social Aspects of Population Growth* (Vol. 1, Commission on Population Growth and the American Future, Research Reports). Charles Westoff and Robert Parks, Jr. (eds.). Washington, DC: U.S. Government Printing Office, 1972.

Zimmer, B.G., and Fulton, J. "Size of Family, Life Changes, and Reproductive Behavior." *Journal of Marriage and the Family* 42 (1980):657-70.

Zlotnik, H., and Hill, K. "Use of Hypothetical Cohorts in Estimating Demographic Parameters Under Conditions of Changing Fertility and Mortality." *Demography* 18 (1981):103-22.

Technical Appendix 6-1

Registration and Tabulation of Natality Statistics

A large part of the data presented in this chapter is derived from statistics of birth based on registration in each of the fifty states, as published by the National Center for Health Statistics. Following is an abstract of Section 4 of the Natality *volume for 1979, describing the procedures by which these data are collected and tabulated.*

Definition of Live Birth

Every product of conception that gives a sign of life after birth, regardless of the length of the pregnancy, is considered a live birth. This concept is embraced by the definition set forth by the World Health Organization as follows:

> Live birth is the complete expulsion or extraction from its mother of a product of conception, irrespective of the duration of the pregnancy, which, after such separation, breathes or shows any other evidence of life.

This definition distinguishes a live birth from a fetal death.

Birth-Registration Area

At present the birth-registration system of the United States covers the fifty states, the District of Columbia, Puerto Rico, the U.S. Virgin Islands, and Guam. However, in the statistical tabulations, United States refers only to the aggregate of the fifty states and the District of Columbia. Tabulations for Puerto Rico, the Virgin Islands, and Guam are shown separately.

The national birth-registration area was established in 1915, and completed in 1933. The organized territories of Hawaii and Alaska were admitted in 1929 and 1950. (Additional states were admitted as the required completeness of registration and other requirements were achieved.)

The original birth-registration area of 1915 consisted of ten states and the District of Columbia.

Because of the growth of the area for which data have been collected and tabulated, a national series of geographically comparable data prior to 1933 can be obtained only by estimation. These estimates include adjustments for underregistration as well as for states not in the birth-registration area before 1933.

Natality Statistics

Natality statistics are based on information provided by the individual states. As of 1979, for all but eight states and the District of Columbia, statistics are based on information derived from computer data tapes coded by the states and provided to the National Center for Health Statistics (NCHS) through the vital statistics cooperative program. Data from these states are based on the total file of records. Statistics for the remaining states—Arizona, Arkansas, California, Delaware, Georgia, New Mexico, North Dakota, and South Dakota—and the District of Columbia are based on information obtained from a 50-percent sample of microfilm copies of all certificates of live birth filed in these states. The Center receives these tapes and microfilm copies from the registration offices of each state, the District of Columbia, and New York City.

Standard Certificate of Live Birth

The Standard Certificate of Live Birth, issued by the Public Health Service, has served for many years as the principal means of attaining uniformity in the content of the documents used to collect information on births in the United States. It has been modified in each state to the extent required by the particular needs of the state, or by special provisions of the state vital statistics law. However, the certificates of most states conform closely to the content of the Standard Certificate.

CLASSIFICATION OF DATA

Classification by Occurrence and Residence

Natality tabulations for states and other areas within the United States are by place of residence unless otherwise specified in the tables. Births to U.S. residents occurring outside this country are not reallocated to the United States. In tabulations by place of residence, births occurring within the United States to U.S. citizens and to resident aliens are allocated to the usual place of residence of the mother in the United States as reported on the birth certificate. Beginning in 1970, births to nonresidents of the United States occurring in the United States are excluded from these tabulations.

Incomplete residence.–Beginning in 1973 where only the state of residence is reported with no city or country specified, and the state named is different from the state of occurrence, the birth is allocated to the largest city of the state of residence. For years prior to 1973, such births were allocated to the exact place of occurrence.

Race or National Origin and Color

Births in the United States in 1978 are classified for statistical purposes according to the race or national origin of the parents. The categories are "White," "Black," "American Indian," "Chinese," "Japanese," "Hawaiian," "Filipino," "Other Asian or Pacific Islander," and "Other."

The newborn child is ordinarily assigned to the race or national origin of the parents. If the parents are of different races or national origins, the following rules apply: (1) When only one parent is white, the child is assigned the other parent's race or national origin. (2)

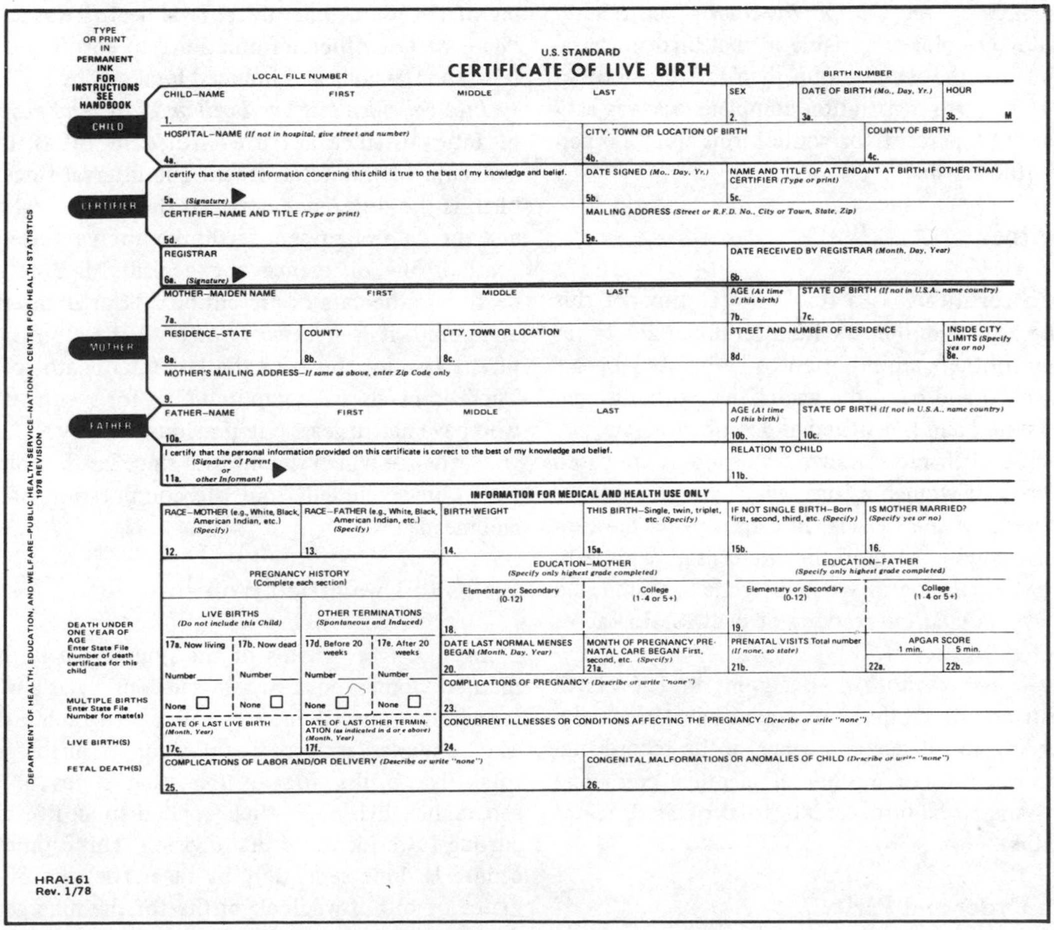
TYPE OR PRINT IN PERMANENT INK
FOR INSTRUCTIONS SEE HANDBOOK

U.S. STANDARD
CERTIFICATE OF LIVE BIRTH

LOCAL FILE NUMBER — BIRTH NUMBER

CHILD
1. CHILD–NAME FIRST MIDDLE LAST | 2. SEX | 3a. DATE OF BIRTH (Mo., Day, Yr.) | 3b. HOUR M
4a. HOSPITAL–NAME (If not in hospital, give street and number) | 4b. CITY, TOWN OR LOCATION OF BIRTH | 4c. COUNTY OF BIRTH

CERTIFIER
I certify that the stated information concerning this child is true to the best of my knowledge and belief.
5a. (Signature) | 5b. DATE SIGNED (Mo., Day, Yr.) | 5c. NAME AND TITLE OF ATTENDANT AT BIRTH IF OTHER THAN CERTIFIER (Type or print)
5d. CERTIFIER–NAME AND TITLE (Type or print) | 5e. MAILING ADDRESS (Street or R.F.D. No., City or Town, State, Zip)
6a. REGISTRAR (Signature) | 6b. DATE RECEIVED BY REGISTRAR (Month, Day, Year)

MOTHER
7a. MOTHER–MAIDEN NAME FIRST MIDDLE LAST | 7b. AGE (At time of this birth) | 7c. STATE OF BIRTH (If not in U.S.A., name country)
8a. RESIDENCE–STATE | 8b. COUNTY | 8c. CITY, TOWN OR LOCATION | 8d. STREET AND NUMBER OF RESIDENCE | 8e. INSIDE CITY LIMITS (Specify yes or no)
9. MOTHER'S MAILING ADDRESS–If same as above, enter Zip Code only

FATHER
10a. FATHER–NAME FIRST MIDDLE LAST | 10b. AGE (At time of this birth) | 10c. STATE OF BIRTH (If not in U.S.A., name country)
I certify that the personal information provided on this certificate is correct to the best of my knowledge and belief.
11a. (Signature of Parent or other Informant) | 11b. RELATION TO CHILD

INFORMATION FOR MEDICAL AND HEALTH USE ONLY
12. RACE–MOTHER (e.g., White, Black, American Indian, etc.) (Specify) | 13. RACE–FATHER (e.g., White, Black, American Indian, etc.) (Specify) | 14. BIRTH WEIGHT | 15a. THIS BIRTH–Single, twin, triplet, etc. (Specify) | 15b. IF NOT SINGLE BIRTH–Born first, second, third, etc. (Specify) | 16. IS MOTHER MARRIED? (Specify yes or no)

PREGNANCY HISTORY (Complete each section)
LIVE BIRTHS (Do not include this Child): 17a. Now living Number ___ None ☐ | 17b. Now dead Number ___ None ☐
OTHER TERMINATIONS (Spontaneous and Induced): 17d. Before 20 weeks Number ___ None ☐ | 17e. After 20 weeks Number ___ None ☐
17c. DATE OF LAST LIVE BIRTH (Month, Year) | 17f. DATE OF LAST OTHER TERMINATION (as indicated in d or e above) (Month, Year)

18. EDUCATION–MOTHER (Specify only highest grade completed) Elementary or Secondary (0-12) | College (1-4 or 5+)
19. EDUCATION–FATHER (Specify only highest grade completed) Elementary or Secondary (0-12) | College (1-4 or 5+)
20. DATE LAST NORMAL MENSES BEGAN (Month, Day, Year) | 21a. MONTH OF PREGNANCY PRENATAL CARE BEGAN First, second, etc. (Specify) | 21b. PRENATAL VISITS Total number (If none, so state) | APGAR SCORE 22a. 1 min. 22b. 5 min.
23. COMPLICATIONS OF PREGNANCY (Describe or write "none")
24. CONCURRENT ILLNESSES OR CONDITIONS AFFECTING THE PREGNANCY (Describe or write "none")
25. COMPLICATIONS OF LABOR AND/OR DELIVERY (Describe or write "none") | 26. CONGENITAL MALFORMATIONS OR ANOMALIES OF CHILD (Describe or write "none")

DEATH UNDER ONE YEAR OF AGE Enter State File Number of death certificate for this child
MULTIPLE BIRTHS Enter State File Number for mate(s)
LIVE BIRTH(S)
FETAL DEATH(S)

DEPARTMENT OF HEALTH, EDUCATION, AND WELFARE–PUBLIC HEALTH SERVICE–NATIONAL CENTER FOR HEALTH STATISTICS
1978 REVISION

HRA-161
Rev. 1/78

Figure 6-A. Certificate of Live Birth.

When neither parent is white, the child is assigned the father's race or national origin with one exception; if the mother is Hawaiian or part-Hawaiian, the child is assigned to Hawaiian. If race is missing for one parent, the child is assigned the race of the parent for whom race is given.

White.—The category "White" comprises births reported as white, Mexican, Puerto Rican, Cuban, and before 1964, all births for which race or national origin was not stated.

All other.—The category "All other" comprises black, American Indian, Chinese, Japanese, Hawaiian and part-Hawaiian, Filipino, other Asian or Pacific Islander, and "Other." Beginning in 1964, Aleuts and Eskimos are included in "American Indian," significantly increasing the births in this category when comparisons are made with previous years. Alaska is particularly affected in this regard. Before 1964, Aleuts and Eskimos were assigned to the "Other" category.

Nearly all statistics by color and race or national origin for the United States as a whole in 1962 and 1963 are affected by a lack of information for New Jersey. Birth rates by color for those years are computed on a population base which excludes New Jersey.

Completeness of registration by color.—The quality of birth data by color is variable in that birth registration is higher for the white group than for the all other group. In 1979 birth-registration completeness was estimated to be 99.5 percent for white births and 98.6 percent for all other births.

Age of Mother

The birth certificate asks for "Age (at time of this birth)." The age of mother is edited for upper and lower limits. When mothers are reported to be below 10 years of age or age 50 and over, the age of the mother is considered not stated and is assigned as described below.

Age-specific birth rates shown in this report are based on populations of women by age, which are prepared by the U.S. Bureau of the Census. In census years the census decennial counts are used. In intercensal years, estimates of the population of women by age are published in the *Current Population Reports* of the U.S. Bureau of the Census.

Not stated age of mother.—Beginning in 1964 birth records with age of mother not stated have been allocated according to the age appearing on the record previously processed for a mother of identical color and having the same total-birth order (total of fetal deaths and live births).

Live-Birth Order and Parity

Birth order and parity classifications refer to the total number of live births the mother has had. Fetal deaths are excluded.

Birth order indicates what number the present birth represents, e.g., a baby born to a mother who has had two previous live births (even if one or both are not now living) has a birth order of three.

Parity indicates how many live births a mother has had. Before delivery a mother having her first baby has a parity of zero and a mother having her third baby has a parity of two. After delivery the mother of a baby who is a first live birth has a parity of one and the mother of a baby who is a third live birth has a parity of three.

Birth order and parity are ascertained from two items on the birth certificate. "Live births now living" and "Live births—now dead."

Dates of Last Live Birth and Last Fetal Death

Date of last live birth and date of last fetal death were added to the Standard Certificate of Live Birth in 1968 for the purpose of providing information on child spacing and pregnancy intervals. Tabulations on these items were presented for the first time in 1969. In 1978 wording of the item "date of last fetal death" was changed to "date of last other termination" to ensure inclusion of both spontaneous and induced fetal deaths.

Interval since last live birth and last fetal death.—Data on intervals since last live birth, date of last live birth, and date of last fetal death. The interval since last live birth is the difference between the date of last live birth and the date of present birth; the interval since last fetal death is the difference between the date of last fetal death and the date of present birth. For an interval to be computed, it is necessary for both the month and year of the last live birth or the last fetal death to be valid. These intervals are computed only for events to mothers who have had at least one previous delivery.

Births for which the interval since last live birth is not stated are excluded from the computation of percents and means.

Births to Unmarried Women

In making estimates of the number of births to unmarried women occurring in the country as a whole, the states are grouped into the nine geographic divisions. The combined ratio of out-of-wedlock births per 1,000 total live births for all reporting states in a single geographic division is then applied to all live births occurring to residents of that division. This estimating procedure is done separately by race. The sum of the estimates of out-of-wedlock births for the nine geographic divisions comprises the estimates for the United States.

In processing the data no adjustments are made for

errors in the reporting of marital status on the birth record or for failure to register births to unmarried women because the extent of such reporting problems is unknown. A mother whose marital status is not stated is considered to be married. (However, this procedure is modified for years following 1980). Out-of-wedlock births for each reporting state are based on births occurring to its residents within the reporting area.

When out-of-wedlock births are reported as second or higher order births, it is not known whether previous deliveries to the mother occurred out of wedlock since the marital status of the mother at the time of these earlier births is not available from the birth record.

Attendant at Birth

The tabulations of births by attendant at birth combine information about place of delivery and the person in attendance at birth. Births occurring in hospitals, institutions, clinics, centers, or homes are included in the category "In hospital." In this context the word "homes" does not refer to the mother's residence but to an institution such as a home for unwed mothers.

Birth Weight

In practically all areas birth weight is reported in terms of pounds and ounces rather than in grams. However, the metric system has been used in tabulating and presenting the statistics to facilitate comparison with data published by other groups.

For purposes of classification, infants weighing 2,500 grams or less at birth are considered to be of low birth weight.

Period of Gestation

The period of gestation is defined as beginning with the first day of the last normal menstrual period (LMP) and ending with the day of the birth. The LMP is used as the initial date since it can be more accurately determined than the date of conception, which usually occurs 2 weeks after the LMP.

An examination of the period of gestation information reported in terms of weeks or months in previous years shows a substantial heaping at 40 weeks. This bias results from the fact that the gestation period is frequently not carefully observed and that the newborn infant of normal size is generally assumed to have had a gestation period of 40 weeks or 9 months, depending on conventional usage. Such errors in reporting are minimized in areas where this item on the birth certificate requests the "date last normal menses began" as suggested on the 1968 revision of the U.S. Standard Certificate of Live Birth.

Births occurring prior to 37 weeks of gestation are considered to be "preterm" or "premature" for purposes of classification.

QUALITY OF DATA

While vital statistics data are useful for a variety of administrative and scientific purposes, they cannot be correctly interpreted unless various qualifying factors and methods of classification are taken into account.

Most of the factors limiting the use of data arise from imperfections in the original records or from the impracticability of tabulating these data in very detailed categories. These defects should not be ignored, but their existence does not vitiate the value of the data for most general purposes.

Completeness of Registration

It is estimated that 99.3 percent of all births occurring in the United States in 1979 were registered. This estimate is based on the results of the 1964-68 test of birth-registration completeness according to place of delivery (in or out of hospital) and color and on the 1979 proportions of births in these categories.

Discontinuation of adjustment for underregistration, 1960.—Adjustment for underregistration of births was discontinued in 1960, when birth registration for the United States was estimated to be 99.1 percent complete. This removed a bias introduced into age-specific rates when adjusted births classified by age were used. Age-specific rates are calculated by dividing the number of births to an age group of mothers by the population of women in that age group. Tests have shown that population figures are likely to be understated through census undercounts; these errors compensate for underregistration of births. Adjustment for underregistration of births, therefore, removes the compensating effect of underenumeration, biasing the age-specific rates more than when uncorrected birth and population data are used.

Differential Reporting

Not all of the fifty states collect or report statistics for all of the items of information specified above (particularly dates of last live birth and marital status of mother). Tabulations are based on the states for which information is available. In some instances estimates for the nonreporting states are made in order to arrive at national totals.

Chapter 7

Internal and International Migration

Overview: The Nonvital Demographic Process

Chapter 1 has already introduced the basic concept of mobility and migration as one of the three components of population change. The first two, birth and death, are vital processes, but mobility and migration involve no more than a simple change of residence and can recur to the same individual. The mobile person simply removes himself from one population subgroup (household, family, neighborhood, or community) and places himself in another subgroup, thereby diminishing the size of the first and increasing the second. The demographic process is one of redistribution rather than increment or attrition to the system as a whole, yet there are analogies: A person's migration may be viewed as a "death" to the community he leaves and as a "birth" to the community at which he arrives. Like the vital processes, mobility can be expressed as rates having a distinctive age curve; there are significant differentials associated with the other demographic, social and economic traits.

Moreover, a change of residence is not an insignificant act. The forces that induce or "cause" population motion to occur are varied and complex, involving all of the fields of social science. This chapter cannot review or analyze these causes in detail but must remain primarily descriptive, as has been the case for fertility, mortality, and nuptiality. The bibliography at the end of the chapter cites numerous studies that have tried to discover why people move–ranging from the departure of a child from home to attend college, through the movement ot that same child to his first full-time employment, and ultimately in old age to his removal to a retirement community or nursing home. In between there may be mobility because of "white flight" to avoid racial integration, improvement or deterioration in employment conditions or income, discovery of new opportunities elsewhere, increase in family size, service in the military, dislike for the climate or other community traits, need for special facilities or technical services, widowhood, divorce, remarriage, employment or change of employment of spouse, inconvenience or cost of commuting, development of a physical handicap, imprisonment, and numerous other causes. This chapter glosses over such mobility stimuli to present a picture of the objective result such factors produce: streams of movement and population redistribution.

Definitions

Mobility Status (General Mobility). A classification of the population based on a comparison between the place of residence of each individual at the time of a census enumeration or survey (destination) and the place of residence as of some specified earlier date (origin). Mobility status falls into four main categories:

1. *Nonmovers (nonmobile persons)* are persons who are living in the same house at the time of the census as at the date of origin. *Movers (mobile persons)*, persons living in a different house are further classified as to where they were living at the earlier date.
2. *Local movers* are mobile persons who are living in the same county at census time as at the date of origin.
3. *Migrants* are mobile persons who were living in a different county at census time from the county of residence at the date of origin. Migrants may be subclassified further:
   a. *Intrastate migrants* are persons living in a different county but within the same state.
   b. *Interstate migrants* are persons living in a different state.
   c. *Interregional migrants* are persons living in a different geographic division or census geographic region.
4. *International migrants (movers from abroad)* are persons who were living in a foreign country at the census date.

Mobility Interval. The time elapsed between the date specified for previous residence and the date of enumeration, usually one year or five years. Recent census enumerations specify five years, and the Current Population Surveys have specified intervals of one, two, three, four, and five years.

Metropolitan Mobility. A system of subdividing mobile persons into categories according to their place of residence with respect to standard metropolitan statistical areas at the beginning and end of the mobility interval, as follows:

1. Within same SMSA
2. Between SMSAs
3. From outside SMSAs to SMSAs
4. From SMSAs to outside SMSAs
5. Outside SMSAs at both dates
6. Movers from abroad: (a) to SMSAs or (b) To areas outside SMSAs

Mobility Rates. The number of persons in a specified mobility status per 100 or per 1,000 population of the area in which they resided as of the end of the mobility interval. Such rates may refer to any of the categories of nonmobile or mobile persons specified above. Mobility rates may be specific for age, race, sex, or other trait. The denominator may also be the origin date or the midpoint of the migration interval.

Central City Mobility. As a refinement of metropolitan mobility, mobile persons who resided inside an SMSA both at the beginning and the end of the mobility interval may be classified as follows:

1. Nonmobile (same house)
   a. Central cities
   b. Metropolitan ring (balance of SMSA)
2. Movers within and between central cities
   a. Within same SMSA
   b. Between SMSAs
3. Movers within and between metropolitan rings (balance of SMSA)
   a. Within same SMSA
   b. Between SMSAs
4. Movers from central cities to balance of SMSAs
   a. Within same SMSA
   b. Between SMSAs

Continued on next page

Definitions

5. Movers from balance of SMSAs to central cities
    a. Within same SMSA
    b. Between SMSAs

Detailed Mobility. A set of categories developed by the Bureau of the Census for use in combining the categories of metropolitan mobility and central city mobility (see definitions above).

Mobility Streams. The number of migrants who move from one specified type of place of origin (residence at beginning of mobility period) to a different specified type of place of destination (residence at end of mobility period).

Inmigration. Internal migrants arriving at a particular place of destination, with no reference to the place of origin.

Outmigration. Internal migrants departing from a particular place of origin, with no reference to the place of their destination.

Immigration. Migrants who have arrived in a country from a residence abroad.

Emigration. Migrants who have departed from the country to reside abroad from a former residence inside the country.

Net Internal Migration. The balance of inmigration and outmigration, obtained by subtracting outmigration from inmigration. The resulting numbers may be either positive or negative. Negative numbers indicate net loss through migration; positive numbers represent net gain through migration.

Foreign Born. Immigrants born as citizens of a country other than the United States.

How Mobile Is the Population of the United States?

Only Canada and Australia have populations as mobile as that of the United States.[1] In a single year about 37,000,000 (17 percent) of the nation's inhabitants move from one house or apartment to another, and about 14,000,000 (6 percent) change their county of residence. At current mobility rates the average American lives at fourteen different addresses during his lifetime. Of these thirteen moves, three will be as a dependent moving because his parents change their residence, and ten will be on his own volition.[2] People who have spent their entire lives in the same houses or apartments account for no more than 2 or 3 percent of the adult population, and perhaps no more than 10 to 15 percent spend their entire lives in their county of birth. The materials in this chapter pertain to the argument that residential mobility in the United States follows a definite pattern, intimately related to population redistribution and to social change and adjustment, and is not simply restless or aimless wandering.

In addition to this internal movement, each year the United States receives about 1,300,000 persons from abroad. Perhaps one-third to one-half of these are immigrants from other countries seeking permanent residence, while the remainder are American citizens returning from residence abroad. No other nation accepts immigrant foreigners as permanent residents at the volume and rate as the United States. Because the flow from abroad has been voluminous throughout the nation's history, a substantial share of the population is foreign-born or of foreign origin.

This chapter deals with internal mobility and international migration in separate sections. The next chapter will deal with ethnic composition resulting from immigration.

Internal Mobility

A "mobile person" is one who has changed his place of residence between two specified dates (see "mobility status" in the Definition Box). It is customary to collect mobility statistics with reference to movement within a single year or within the five years preceding the enumeration. Mobility data come from two sources: decennial censuses and an annual measurement/report from the Current Population Survey. It is customary for the decennial census to study mobility over a five-year period. The Current Population Survey has measured mobility over a variety of periods–one-year, two-year, three-year, four-year, and five-year periods.

Demographers divide residential mobility within the nation into two parts: (1) *local mobility,* or the changing of residence from one part of a community to another, and (2) *internal migration,* or the changing of residence from one community to another within the nation. For the sake of greater ease in collecting statistics concerning mobility, it has become customary to define as a migrant any person who changes his residence from one county to another, and as a local mover any person who changes residence within the same county. Both of these types of residential mobility are significant and worthy of attention. Migration usually involves the complete severance of a person's economic and social ties with the community he leaves and requires that he adjust to a new job, a new set of community institutions, and a new group of people. Also, migration can change the size or the composition of a particular population rather quickly. Such changes can result from a mass exodus of people, a mass invasion of people, or a large-scale selective interchange of people with other areas. For these

Table 7-1. One Year Mobility Status of the Civilian Population: Selected Years, 1947-1982 [percent of population age one year and over]

Years	Non-mobile (same house)	Mobile--different house						Percent of migration interstate
		Total mobile	Local (same county)	Internal migration			Migration from abroad	
				Total	Within state	Interstate		
1981-82 (March). . . .	83.0	16.6	10.3	6.2	3.3	3.0	0.5	47.5
1980-81 (March). . . .	82.8	16.6	10.4	6.2	3.4	2.8	0.6	44.8
1975-76 (March). . . .	82.3	17.1	10.8	6.4	3.4	3.0	0.6	46.4
1970-71 (March). . . .	81.3	17.9	11.4	6.5	3.1	3.4	0.8	52.8
1969-70 (March). . . .	80.9	18.4	11.7	6.7	3.1	3.6	0.8	53.1
1968-69 (March). . . .	81.0	18.3	11.7	6.6	3.2	3.4	0.7	51.2
1967-68 (March). . . .	80.5	18.8	11.8	7.0	3.4	3.6	0.7	51.6
1966-67 (March). . . .	81.0	18.3	11.6	6.7	3.3	3.4	0.7	51.0
1965-66 (March). . . .	80.2	19.3	12.7	6.6	3.3	3.3	0.5	50.0
1964-65 (March). . . .	79.3	20.1	13.4	6.8	3.5	3.3	0.5	48.2
1963-63 (March). . . .	79.9	19.6	13.0	6.6	3.3	3.3	0.5	49.4
1962-63 (March). . . .	80.0	19.4	12.6	6.8	3.1	3.6	0.6	53.8
1961-62 (April). . . .	80.4	19.1	13.0	6.1	3.0	3.1	0.5	50.5
1960-61 (March). . . .	79.4	20.0	13.7	6.3	3.1	3.2	0.6	51.2
1959-60 (March). . . .	80.1	19.4	12.9	6.4	3.3	3.2	0.5	49.1
1958-59 (April). . . .	80.3	19.2	13.1	6.1	3.2	3.0	0.5	48.3
1957-58 (March). . . .	79.7	19.8	13.1	6.7	3.4	3.3	0.5	49.7
1956-57 (April). . . .	80.1	19.4	13.1	6.2	3.2	3.1	0.5	49.4
1955-56 (March). . . .	79.0	20.5	13.7	6.8	3.6	3.1	0.6	46.3
1954-55 (April). . . .	79.6	19.9	13.3	6.6	3.5	3.1	0.6	47.0
1953-54 (April). . . .	80.7	18.6	12.2	6.4	3.2	3.2	0.6	50.4
1952-53 (April). . . .	79.4	20.1	13.5	6.6	3.0	3.6	0.5	54.4
1951-52 (April). . . .	79.7	19.8	13.2	6.6	3.2	3.4	0.4	51.3
1950-51 (April). . . .	78.8	21.0	13.9	7.1	3.6	3.5	0.2	49.6
1949-50 (March). . . .	80.9	18.7	13.1	5.6	3.0	2.6	0.3	47.1
1948-49 (April). . . .	80.8	18.8	13.0	5.8	2.8	3.0	0.3	52.1
1947-48 (April). . . .	79.8	19.9	13.6	6.4	3.3	3.1	0.3	48.5

Source: U.S. Government Printing Office. "Geographical Mobility: March 1970 to March 1971;" "Geographical Mobility: March 1975 to March 1976;" "Geographical Mobility: March 1980 to March 1981;" and "Geographical Mobility: March 1981 to March 1982." Current Population Reports (Series P-20, nos. 235; 305; 377; and 384). Washington, DC: U.S. Government Printing Office, 1972, Table 1; 1977, Table 6; 1983, Table 6; and 1984, Table 6.

reasons migration tends to receive more popular, as well as more scientific, attention than local moving. Nevertheless, local moving can change the internal distribution of population within a community and can cause particular neighborhoods to undergo rather dramatic changes within a comparatively short time. For this reason, local moving is coming to the fore as a subject considered worthy of more intensive research.

One-Year Mobility

Table 7-1 reports the mobility status of the civilian population for selected years from 1947 to 1982, as measured by special surveys. By comparing the place of residence one year earlier, it is possible to determine what percentage of the population are migrants (living in a different county), what percentage are local movers (living in a different house in the same county), and what share are nonmobile (living in the same house). This table shows that the percentages of nonmobile, locally mobile, and migratory people have fluctuated remarkably little over a prolonged period. Over the years the rate of local mobility has declined from 13 percent in the 1950s and 1960s to 10 percent in the 1980s. However, the rate of internal migration has remained at about the same level throughout–6 to 6.5 percent per year (see Figure 7-1). About one-half of each year's 14,000,000 migrants change the state of their residence. Movers from abroad amount to about 0.6 percent of the population, double the rate of three decades ago.

Five-Year Mobility

Measuring mobility in terms of one-year intervals (place of residence a year ago) conforms to the procedures used in the study of birth, death, and marriage, and leads to annual rates comparable to those of the vital processes. One-year mobility data are superior for studying the characteristics of migrants and getting precise mobility rates. However, there are also good research reasons for measuring migration in five-year intervals (place of residence five years ago). Because the five-year intervals is a broader span of time, it can embrace long-term trends and changes better than single-year intervals. Since the census is taken only every ten years, it asks migration questions in terms of these five-year intervals. The Current Population Survey has also collected mobility information for 1970-75 and 1975-80, thereby spanning the decade in a manner permitting a comparison of the two halves.

When the five-year mobility interval is used, the mobility rates are not five times as large as those for a

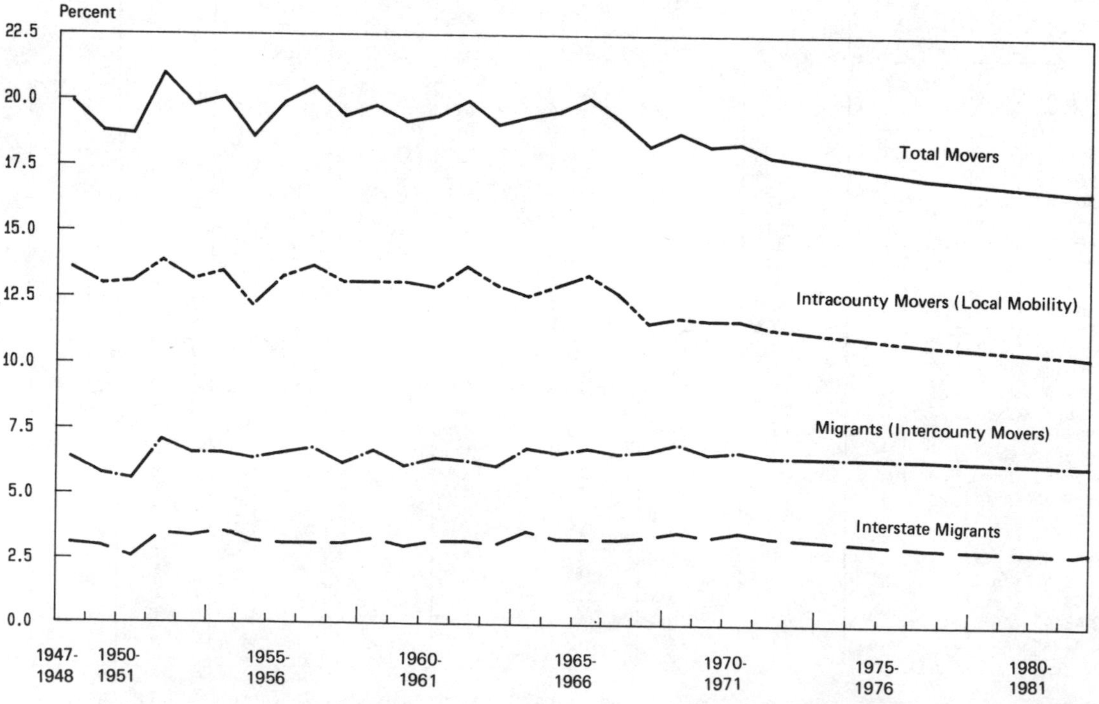

Figure 7-1. Mobility of the U.S. Population: 1947-1982 [data available for dates indicated in Table 7-1]

Table 7-2. Mobility Status of the Population, by Race: 1940, 1960, 1970, and 1980

Race and census	Mobility status: residence 5 years ago					Percent migration interstate[a]
	Total	Nonmobile (same house)	Local mobility (same county)	Migration (different county)	Immigration abroad	
All races						
1980.	100.0	53.5	25.1	19.5	1.9	49.7
1970.	100.0	55.9	24.6	18.0	1.5	50.7
1960.	100.0	50.6	30.3	17.8	1.3	50.9
1940.	100.0	[86.6[b]]		13.1	0.3	41.3
White						
1980.	100.0	53.8	24.3	20.6	1.3	49.3
1970.	100.0	56.0	23.6	18.9	1.5	50.3
1960.	100.0	50.9	29.2	18.6	1.3	50.5
1940.	100.0	[86.2]		13.5	0.3	41.3
Black						
1980.	100.0	56.7	29.4	12.7	1.2	55.4
1970.	100.0	56.1	32.5	10.4	1.0	55.8
1960.	100.0	49.3	38.6	11.1	1.0	56.3
1940.	100.0	[90.4]		9.5	0.1	41.0

[a] Ratio of different state to different county multiplied by 100.

[b] Persons living in the same house in 1935 and persons living in a different home in the same county or quasi-county (cities of 100,000 or more and the balance of their counties) in 1935 not tabulated separately.

Source: U.S. Bureau of the Census. "General Social and Economic Characteristics: United States Summary." 1980 Census of Population. Washington, DC: U.S. Government Printing Office, 1983, Table 80. For 1940, U.S. Bureau of the Census. "General Social and Economic Characteristics: United States Summary." 1960 Census of Population. Washington, DC: U.S. Government Printing Office, 1963, Table 71.

single year because persons who move several times within the interval are counted only once (a disproportionately large part of all mobility is created by a group of persons who move frequently). Still, over the five-year interval a large proportion of the population is defined as mobile, locally and as migrants. This conclusion is confirmed by the data of Table 7-2, obtained in decennial censuses that refer to change of residence over a five-year period. Nearly one-half of the population is mobile over a five-year period, and more than one-fifth are migrants, either internal or from abroad. These five-year data also reflect a decrease in local mobility between 1960 and 1980 (from 30 to 25 percent), with a rise in internal migration from 13 percent in 1940 to nearly 20 percent in 1980.

The two Current Population Surveys spanning the 1970-80 decade yield the following results:

Mobility status	1975-80	1970-75	Change
Total.	100.0	100.0	...
Nonmobile (same house) .	53.0	51.5	+1.5
Locally mobile (same county).	25.8	24.2	+1.6
Migratory (different county).	19.3	17.1	+2.2
Same state	10.2	8.4	+1.8
Different state. . . .	9.1	8.6	+0.5
Abroad	1.9	7.2[a]	-5.3

[a] Includes mobility status not reported.

Note: ... indicates data not applicable.

Source: U.S. Bureau of the Census. "Geographical Mobility: 1970-75" and "Geographical Mobility: 1975-1980." Current Population Reports (Series P-20, nos. 285 and 368). Washington, DC: U.S. Government Printing Office, 1975 and 1982.

Table 7-3A. Sex Differential in Mobility Status, 1970-1982

Mobility status	1981-82		1975-76		1970-71	
	Male	Female	Male	Female	Male	Female
Total.	100.0	100.0	100.0	100.0	100.0	100.0
Nonmobile.	82.5	83.4	81.9	82.7	80.6	81.9
Local mobility	10.5	10.1	10.9	10.6	11.5	11.3
Migration, total	6.5	6.0	6.6	6.2	6.7	6.3
Same state	3.3	3.2	3.5	3.3	3.2	3.0
Between states	3.1	2.8	3.0	2.9	3.5	3.4
Noncontiguous.	2.2	2.0	2.1	1.9	2.6	2.4
Abroad	0.6	0.4	0.6	0.5	1.1	0.5

Source: U.S. Bureau of the Census. "Geographical Mobility: March 1970 to March 1971;" "Geographical Mobility: March 1975 to March 1976;" and "Geographical Mobility: March 1981 to March 1982." Current Population Reports (Series P-20, nos. 235; 305; and 384). Washington, DC: U.S. Government Printing Office, 1972; 1977; and 1984.

Table 7-3B. Race Differential in Mobility Status: 1970-1982

Mobility status	1981-82		1975-76		1970-71	
	White	Black	White	Black	White	Black
Total.	100.0	100.0	100.0	100.0	100.0	100.0
Nonmobile.	83.3	81.7	82.6	81.7	81.7	78.8
Local mobility	9.8	13.9	10.3	14.2	10.7	16.6
Migration, total	6.5	4.0	6.7	3.9	6.9	3.9
Same state	3.4	2.2	3.6	2.1	3.3	1.7
Between states	3.1	1.8	3.1	1.8	3.6	2.2
Abroad	0.4	0.4	0.5	0.3	0.7	0.8

Source: U.S. Bureau of the Census. "Geographical Mobility: March 1970 to March 1971;" "Geographical Mobility: March 1975 to March 1976;" and "Geographical Mobility: March 1981 to March 1982." Current Population Reports (Series P-20, nos. 235; 305; and 384). Washington, DC: U.S. Government Printing Office, 1972; 1977; and 1984.

Although there is some indication of decreased mobility during the decade, it is confounded by a rather substantial element of "mobility status not reported." If one assumes that the unknowns are distributed proportionately, during the 1970s local mobility appears to have remained almost unchanged; however, there was some acceleration in migration, particularly within the same state. This finding is consistent with the trends of Table 7-2, but not of Table 7-1. Tentatively, one can conclude that since 1980 there has been no diminution in the tendency to migrate but there has been an apparent reduction in local mobility.

The frequently heard statement that the population of the United States is fluid appears to be warranted by the facts. However, local moving, as well as long-distance migration, is responsible for that characteristic. The present rates of residential mobility are so high that the annual volume of local movement and migration involves about 40 million persons. Over a period of only five years, mobility involves half of the population (125 million persons); over a period of a lifetime it involves almost everybody.

Which Segments of the Population Are Most Mobile?

Census surveys taken in recent years have provided data about the total residential mobility of the population, classified according to several characteristics.

Sex Differences

Men appear to be more mobile with respect to residence than women, but the difference in rates between the sexes is very small. This difference has consisted largely of a slight preponderance of males over females among mobile persons who are migrants. There is very little evidence that either sex has been a great deal more mobile than the other at the local level. The year-to-year fluctuations in mobility rates tended to affect each sex in the same way and by about the same amount.

Race Differences

Total residential mobility for the nonwhite population has been somewhat higher than for the white population. In 1970 they were about equally mobile, but the 1980 census reports the black population to be less mobile than the white. This difference is an average of two different patterns, however. The nonwhite population, on the average, has been considerably more mobile locally (within the same county) than the white population. On the other hand, the white population has been equally or even more mobile with respect to migration than the nonwhite population. Table 7-3B, reporting for three surveys, reveals this pattern clearly. Table 7-4, pertaining to the five years preceding the 1980 census shows a similar differential. In 1980 blacks were 5 percentage points more locally mobile than whites, but the whites were 8 percentage points more migratory than blacks, causing them to have an overall higher mobility index than blacks.

Table 7-4. Mobility Status of the Population, by Race-Ethnicity and Metropolitan-Nonmetropolitan Residence: 1975-1980

Race, ethnicity, and residence	Mobility status: residence in 1975					Percent migration interstate[a]
	Total	Nonmobile (same house)	Local mobility (same county)	Migration (different county)	Immigration abroad	
White, total.	100.0	53.8	24.3	20.6	1.3	49.3
Inside SMSAs.	100.0	53.2	25.0	20.3	1.5	51.3
Central cities.	100.0	51.6	27.1	19.2	2.1	56.1
Metropolitan rings.	100.0	54.1	23.9	20.8	1.2	49.0
Outside SMSAs	100.0	55.7	22.3	21.4	0.6	43.9
Black, total.	100.0	56.7	29.4	12.7	1.2	55.4
Inside SMSAs.	100.0	55.0	30.9	12.8	1.3	57.1
Central cities.	100.0	56.3	32.7	9.8	1.2	59.8
Metropolitan rings.	100.0	51.4	26.7	20.3	1.6	53.9
Outside SMSAs	100.0	64.7	22.7	12.1	0.5	47.7
Spanish-origin, total . . .	100.0	44.7	32.2	14.3	8.8	46.1
Inside SMSAs.	100.0	43.9	33.3	13.5	9.3	46.4
Central cities.	100.0	44.4	34.4	11.3	9.9	45.6
Metropolitan rings.	100.0	42.9	32.0	16.5	8.6	47.1
Outside SMSAs	100.0	51.5	23.9	19.7	4.7	44.9

[a]Ratio of different state to different county multiplied by 100.0

Source: U.S. Bureau of the Census. "General Social and Economic Characteristics: United States Summary." 1980 Census of Population. Washington, DC: U.S. Government Printing Office, 1983, tables 142 and 152. Spanish-origin comes from Table 152.

Spanish-Origin Population

Far more mobile than either the white or the black population are those members of both races classed as of Spanish origin (Table 7-4). Rates of local mobility are very high (32 percent). Because of steady immigration, a high percentage (9 percent) is classed as movers from abroad. Coupled with this are rates of internal migration, which are higher than for the black population, though considerably lower than for the white population.

Other Races

Table 7-5 reports mobility rates for the U.S. Bureau of the Census detailed race classification. American Indians are slightly more mobile (both locally and as migrants) than the white population. High proportions of all the groups from Asia and the Pacific Islands reported in the 1980 census arrived from abroad during the preceding five years. This is particularly true for Vietnamese and Korean groups. However, all these racial groups also show a substantial amount of local mobility and internal migration; only a minority (primarily Japanese and Hawaiians) can be said to have low mobility.

Spatial Differences in Mobility

Mobility rates differ considerably according to place of residence.

Metropolitan-Nonmetropolitan Residence

Table 7-4 reports rates of mobility for residence inside and outside SMSAs, by race. For all groups, mobility of residents inside SMSAs is higher than for those outside. Almost all of this difference is explained by the greater local mobility of those living in metropolitan areas. Within metropolitan areas, local mobility is considerably higher among those living in central cities than among those living in the metropolitan suburban rings outside the central city but within the metropolitan area. In contrast, the residents of the metropolitan rings are considerably more migratory than residents of the central city. The above real differences tend to be valid for white, black, and Spanish-origin populations alike. Thus, each race-ethnic group manifests its own mobility pattern while conforming to the mobility patterns of the community in which it resides.

Table 7-5. Mobility Status, by Detailed Race Classification: 1975-1980

Detailed race classification	Mobility status: residence in 1975					Percent migration interstate[a]
	Total	Nonmobile (same house)	Local mobility (same county)	Migration (different county)	Immigration abroad	
American Indian	100.0	47.0	28.7	23.2		49.5
Eskimo	100.0	53.8	28.9	16.9	0.4	47.0
Aleut	100.0	44.3	30.5	23.2	2.0	52.5
Asian and Pacific Islander						
Japanese	100.0	56.1	21.0	12.7	10.2	52.0
Chinese	100.0	39.1	20.6	18.1	22.2	50.7
Filipino	100.0	31.7	26.6	19.2	22.5	52.9
Korean	100.0	18.1	21.1	19.8	41.0	57.1
Asian	100.0	25.3	20.6	23.2	30.9	58.4
Vietnamese	100.0	7.0	10.8	12.1	70.1	63.4
Hawaiian	100.0	52.6	30.6	15.5	1.3	57.7
Guamian	100.0	28.0	24.4	18.0	29.6	60.0
Samoan	100.0	37.5	27.0	17.4	18.1	72.8
Other	100.0	12.3	14.8	14.5	58.4	60.7

[a]Ratio of different state to different county multiplied by 100.

Source: U.S. Bureau of the Census. "General Social and Economic Characteristics: United States Summary." 1980 Census of Population. Washington, DC: U.S. Government Printing Office, 1983, Table 161.

Urban-Rural Residence

Rural populations, especially rural farm populations, tend to be less mobile than urban (Table 7-6). Within the urban category, local mobility is highest in the central cities of urbanized areas and lowest in the suburban fringes of urbanized areas and in the small towns of 2,500 to 9,999 inhabitants outside urbanized areas. This low local mobility is counterbalanced, in part, by a tendency for these areas to have above-average migration rates. The rural farm population, however, has extremely low migration rates and local mobility rates, with the result that it is by far the least mobile sector (77 percent nonmobile).

Racial difference in urban-rural mobility patterns may be studied with the five-year data in Table 7-7. The pattern described above tends to characterize each race group and the Spanish-origin population as well.

Age and Mobility

Persons in their late teens, their twenties, and their early thirties are much more mobile than the general population. Persons who are fourteen to seventeen years old and those who are thirty-five and over tend to be less mobile than average, and the elderly are only about one-half as mobile as the general population. The validity of these statements has been documented frequently. It is not always recognized, however, that in addition to migration local mobility is also more common among persons at the young adult ages, and that it varies with age following much the same pattern as migration. Table 7-8 and Figure 7-2 show that the annual mobility enumeration of the census reveals this same pattern. *Thus, residential mobility is primarily a phenomenon of late adolescence and early maturity.* The high degree of mobility prevailing among the young adult population is a fundamental aspect of population dynamics. Each year 35 percent or more of the population aged twenty to twenty-four changes residence, and nearly one-half of this change is migratory. By way of contrast 5 percent or less of the population aged sixty-five years and over changes residence within a year, and most of that is local mobility. Only about 2 percent or less of the elderly become migrants.

The higher-than-average mobility of children under ten years of age is evidently due to the movement, both local and migratory, of their parents.

The age pattern of mobility is understandable in view

Table 7-6. Mobility Status of the Population, by Urban-Rural Residence: 1975-1980

Residence in 1980	Mobility status: residence in 1975					Percent migration interstate[a]
	Total	Nonmobile (same house)	Local mobility (same county)	Migration (different county)	Immigration abroad	
Urban, total.	100.0	52.0	26.2	19.5	2.3	52.9
Inside urbanized areas. . . .	100.0	52.3	26.5	18.7	2.5	54.4
Central cities.	100.0	51.8	28.7	16.6	2.9	56.4
Urban fringe.	100.0	52.7	24.5	20.6	2.2	52.9
Outside urbanized areas . . .	100.0	50.4	24.8	23.5	1.3	46.9
Places of 10,000 or more. .	100.0	48.1	25.6	24.8	1.5	46.7
Places of 2,500 to 9,999. .	100.0	52.6	24.0	22.3	1.1	47.0
Rural, total.	100.0	58.1	21.8	19.5	0.6	40.9
Places 1,000 to 2,499	100.0	57.0	22.7	19.6	0.7	42.2
Rural farm.	100.0	76.9	13.5	9.3	0.3	33.2
Inside SMSAs.	100.0	52.7	26.0	19.1	2.2	51.7
Outside SMSAs	100.0	56.2	22.4	20.6	0.8	44.2

[a]Ratio of different state to different county multiplied by 100.

Source: U.S. Bureau of the Census. "General Social and Economic Characteristics: United States Summary." 1980 Census of Population. Washington, DC: U.S. Government Printing Office, 1983, Table 101.

Table 7-7. Mobility Status of the Population, by Race and Urban-Rural Residence: 1975-1980

Residence in 1980 and race-ethnicity	Mobility status: residence in 1975					Percent migration interstate[a]
	Total	Nonmobile (same house)	Local mobility (same county)	Migration (different county)	Immigration abroad	
White, total	100.0	53.8	24.3	20.6	1.3	49.3
Urban, total	100.0	52.4	25.2	20.8	1.6	52.5
Urbanized areas	100.0	53.0	25.3	20.0	1.7	54.1
Central cities	100.0	51.6	27.1	19.2	2.1	56.2
Urban fringe	100.0	54.0	24.0	20.5	1.5	52.7
Other urban	100.0	50.1	24.6	24.4	0.9	46.4
Rural total	100.0	57.5	21.9	20.1	0.5	40.8
Farm	100.0	77.1	13.4	9.3	0.2	33.1
Black, total	100.0	56.7	29.4	12.7	1.2	55.4
Urban, total	100.0	54.8	31.0	12.9	1.3	57.5
Urbanized areas	100.0	54.4	31.7	12.6	1.3	58.2
Central cities	100.0	56.4	32.7	9.7	1.2	59.7
Urban fringe	100.0	48.4	28.6	21.3	1.7	56.2
Other urban	100.0	57.8	25.9	15.3	1.0	52.7
Rural, total	100.0	68.3	19.8	11.5	0.4	42.0
Farm	100.0	78.4	14.3	7.2	0.1	39.4
Spanish-origin, total	100.0	44.7	32.2	14.3	8.8	46.2
Urban, total	100.0	44.1	33.2	13.6	9.1	47.0
Urbanized areas	100.0	43.5	33.9	13.0	9.6	47.5
Central cities	100.0	44.4	34.4	11.3	9.9	45.6
Urban fringe	100.0	41.1	33.4	15.9	9.6	49.1
Other urban	100.0	48.7	27.6	18.3	5.4	44.0
Rural, total	100.0	51.2	23.3	20.1	5.4	41.0
Farm	100.0	57.2	21.4	14.6	6.8	30.2

[a]Ratio of different state to different county multiplied by 100.

Source: U.S. Bureau of the Census. "General Social and Economic Characteristics: United States Summary." 1980 Census of Population. Washington, DC: U.S. Government Printing Office, 1983, tables 122 and 132. Spanish-origin comes from Table 132.

of the fact that eighteen years is the median age for graduating from high school. A change of residence is often involved in either going to college or seeking work. Furthermore, the median age of marriage for women and men alike falls in the 20-25 age interval, and marriage usually involves a change of residence for either bride or groom, if not both. The gradual transitions from smaller to larger living quarters and from the status of renter to that of homeowner are made by a great many families while the adult members are between the ages of twenty-five and thirty-five. The arrival of a second or third child may require a family to change residence. It should be noted that migration is a much larger proportion of all mobility at the ages 18-29 than at other ages.

The two types of mobility do not have identical age patterns, however. The child population and the older adult population tend to exhibit rates of local mobility that are nearer the average for all ages than are the migration rates of these two age groups. This suggests the hypothesis that local mobility is more routine readjustment to minor problems or transitions, whereas migration involves major life cycle adjustments, primarily in the transition from youth to adulthood.

Sex differences in age patterns of mobility are reported in Table 7-9. Data for single years of age are shown in order to show the detail of the age pattern at the high-mobility ages. Females tend to become mobile at an earlier age than males. Beginning with age twelve

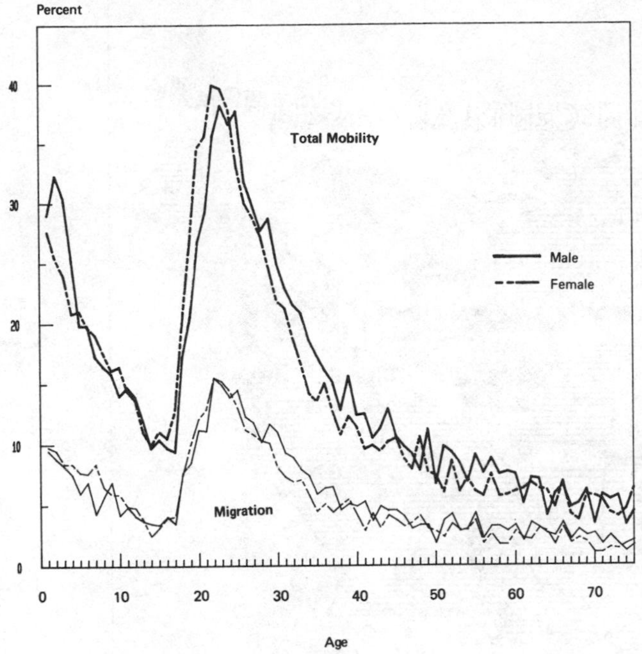

Figure 7-2. Age Curve of Mobility Rates, by Sex: 1981-1982

and continuing through age twenty-four, women tend to be both more locally mobile and more migratory than males. However, males catch and surpass females in mobility around the age of twenty-five and maintain higher rates until they reach forty-four. At ages forty-five and over the sex differences become comparatively small, as the rates for both decline to small numbers. At the most advanced ages females tend to be more mobile than males, perhaps because of widowhood.

Socioeconomic Characteristics and Migration

Migration tends to vary with particular social and economic characteristics. For example, mobility differences are associated with household and family relationships, educational attainment, employment status, occupation, income, and poverty status or receipt of public assistance. These mobility differentials are reported in the respective chapters dealing with the characteristics in question.

Migration and Regional Redistribution of Population

Internal migration includes inmigration, which brings people to a community from other places, and outmigration, which takes them away from a community to live

Table 7-8. Mobility Status of the Population, by Age: 1975-1976 and 1981-1982

Age	Mobility status (percent of total)							
	Nonmobile		Local mobility		Migration, total		Migration, different state	
	1981-82	1975-76	1981-82	1975-76	1981-82	1975-76	1981-82	1975-76
Total.	83.0	82.3	10.3	10.8	6.2	6.4	3.0	3.0
Under 5 years. . .	74.3	72.3	16.3	17.6	8.8	9.2	4.2	4.1
5-9 years.	81.3	80.9	11.6	12.0	6.6	6.7	3.1	3.3
10-14 years. . . .	86.7	86.9	8.7	7.9	4.2	4.8	2.0	2.3
15-19 years. . . .	84.5	83.3	9.3	10.4	5.7	5.7	2.6	2.6
20-24 years. . . .	63.6	60.6	21.8	23.2	13.7	14.8	6.5	6.7
25-29 years. . . .	69.0	66.5	18.4	20.8	11.6	11.7	5.5	5.1
30-34 years. . . .	79.2	79.1	12.2	12.8	8.0	7.5	3.6	3.5
35-44 years. . . .	86.8	86.1	7.9	8.1	4.8	5.3	2.4	2.7
45-54 years. . . .	91.2	91.3	5.2	5.2	3.3	3.2	1.6	1.5
55-64 years. . . .	93.1	92.8	4.0	4.1	2.7	2.9	1.2	1.3
65 and over. . . .	94.6	94.3	3.3	3.5	2.0	2.1	0.9	0.9

Source: U.S. Bureau of the Census. "Geographical Mobility, March 1981 to March 1982," and "Geographical Mobility, March 1975 to March 1976." Current Population Reports (Series P-20, no. 384; and Series P-20, no. 305). Washington, DC: U.S. Government Printing Office, 1984, Table 6; and 1977, Table 6.

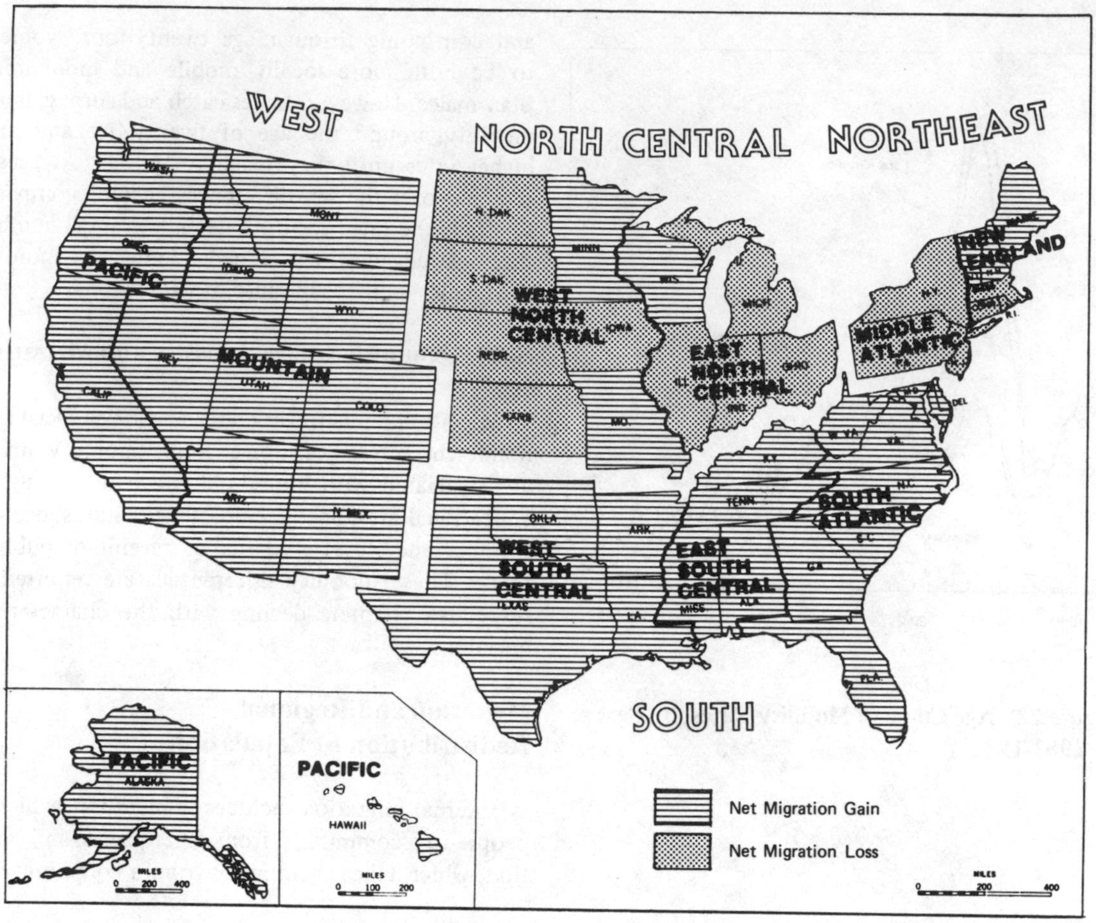

Figure 7-3. States Gaining and Losing Population Through Net Migration: 1970-1980

in other places (see "mobility stream" in the Definition Box). Its effect, therefore, is made clear by an examination of net migration, which is inmigration minus outmigration (see Definition Box). If migration were a completely random process, one would expect every place to receive as many inmigrants as it loses outmigrants, so that the net effect would be zero. This certainly has not happened in the United States as is shown by Table 7-10, which reports that the estimated net gain or loss of population through migration for each of the states for each decade since 1870. The table documents the historic westward movement of population and the exodus from the South and the North during the late nineteenth century and the first decades of the present century. Equally important, it reveals important changes that have taken place recently—in the 1970-80 decade, a period when several historic trends were reversed or greatly modified.

Three large interregional flows of internal migration have been occurring in the United States not only during the 1970-80 decade but for many decades; the behavior of these flows may be inferred from Figure 7-3 and Table 7-10.

Westward Movement

There long has been a high-volume flow of persons into the Pacific region and the southwestern states of the Mountain region. California has been the chief recipient. Until 1940 this flow consisted primarily of white persons, but after 1940 many blacks joined the stream. During the 1970-80 decade the volume of westward movement exceeded that of any previous decade, despite the fact that movement to California was less than at any time since the 1940-50 decade. Mountain states that previously had been suffering losses (Montana, Idaho, Wyoming, New Mexico, Utah) all made

Table 7-9. Mobility Status of the Population, by Age and Sex: 1981-82 (percent of age-sex total)

Year	Nonmobile		Local mobility		Migration total		Migration non-contiguous states	
	Male	Female	Male	Female	Male	Female	Male	Female
Total	82.5	83.4	10.5	10.1	6.5	6.1	2.2	2.0
1 year	70.1	71.9	19.5	17.8	9.5	9.8	2.6	3.2
2 years.	74.1	73.6	16.5	15.8	8.8	9.5	2.8	3.4
3 years.	76.4	76.0	14.9	15.5	8.2	8.4	2.4	3.6
4 years.	74.3	79.1	17.7	12.4	7.5	8.4	3.7	2.3
5 years.	79.7	78.4	13.8	13.3	6.0	7.7	1.8	2.4
6 years.	79.9	79.4	12.9	12.1	6.9	7.6	3.0	2.6
7 years.	82.6	80.2	12.9	10.6	4.3	8.4	1.5	3.0
8 years.	83.2	82.1	10.7	11.0	5.7	6.5	2.0	1.6
9 years.	84.1	83.4	8.9	10.2	6.9	5.9	2.6	1.7
10 years.	85.5	83.1	9.8	10.5	4.2	5.9	1.1	1.6
11 years.	85.0	85.5	9.8	9.5	4.9	4.9	2.1	1.9
12 years.	85.7	85.7	9.8	8.8	4.1	4.8	1.6	1.2
13 years.	87.9	88.7	8.2	7.2	3.7	3.8	1.4	1.4
14 years.	89.9	89.7	6.2	7.4	3.5	2.5	1.2	0.6
15 years.	89.4	88.8	7.0	7.9	3.4	3.2	1.2	0.8
16 years.	90.0	89.1	5.6	6.5	4.1	4.0	1.7	1.3
17 years.	90.0	86.7	5.9	8.6	3.5	4.1	1.1	0.7
18 years.	82.0	79.1	9.5	12.5	7.7	7.5	2.6	2.4
19 years.	78.7	72.5	12.0	16.7	8.5	10.0	2.8	3.6
20 years.	72.1	64.8	15.6	22.5	11.2	12.1	3.4	4.3
21 years.	69.1	64.0	18.1	22.7	11.1	12.9	4.2	3.7
22 years.	62.8	59.2	20.1	24.4	15.5	15.5	5.3	4.8
23 years.	60.9	59.7	23.3	24.4	14.9	15.2	5.1	5.3
24 years.	62.1	61.8	22.7	23.5	13.9	14.4	5.0	4.8
25 years.	60.6	66.3	23.2	20.1	14.5	13.0	4.1	5.0
26 years.	66.9	68.6	19.5	18.8	12.3	11.2	4.9	3.6
27 years.	69.4	70.5	18.0	18.0	11.8	10.8	3.9	3.1
28 years.	71.1	72.2	17.5	16.9	10.2	10.3	3.1	3.5
29 years.	70.6	74.8	17.0	14.4	11.7	10.1	4.4	3.2
30 years.	74.3	77.6	13.9	13.7	11.0	8.1	3.8	2.4
31 years.	75.8	78.2	13.6	13.9	9.3	7.3	3.7	2.3
32 years.	77.7	80.3	12.6	11.8	8.9	6.9	3.1	2.3
33 years.	78.2	83.2	12.9	9.5	7.9	7.1	2.5	2.3
34 years.	80.8	85.3	11.2	8.4	7.4	5.8	1.8	1.9
35 years.	81.5	86.0	11.4	9.0	5.9	4.5	2.0	1.7
36 years.	83.2	84.2	9.7	9.9	6.4	5.1	2.5	1.8
37 years.	84.6	87.0	8.6	8.3	6.5	4.4	2.3	1.4
38 years.	86.6	89.1	8.2	5.8	4.6	5.0	1.7	1.8
39 years.	84.4	87.4	10.5	6.8	5.1	5.5	1.9	1.6
40 years.	87.0	88.2	7.5	7.2	4.9	4.2	2.4	1.3
41 years.	86.7	90.0	7.2	6.7	5.3	2.9	2.3	0.7
42 years.	89.1	90.0	6.8	5.6	3.7	4.3	0.8	1.5
43 years.	88.7	90.6	6.4	6.3	4.9	3.1	2.8	1.5
44 years.	86.2	89.4	8.4	6.1	4.5	4.1	1.2	1.0
45 years.	88.6	89.1	6.1	6.8	4.5	3.7	1.5	1.5
46 years.	90.1	90.8	5.8	5.6	4.0	3.2	1.5	1.2
47 years.	90.4	91.8	6.2	4.4	3.0	3.5	0.8	1.2
48 years.	91.1	89.0	4.5	6.5	3.3	4.1	1.3	1.6
49 years.	88.8	91.6	7.9	4.7	3.3	3.0	0.9	1.0
50 years.	93.4	92.1	4.9	4.6	1.8	2.8	0.6	0.7
51 years.	89.9	93.8	6.1	3.7	3.7	2.3	0.5	0.9
52 years.	90.2	91.4	5.1	5.2	4.2	3.4	1.8	1.1
53 years.	91.4	93.9	5.6	3.2	2.8	2.9	0.6	1.2
54 years.	93.1	92.8	3.9	4.3	3.0	2.9	1.2	0.6
55 years.	90.8	93.7	4.8	2.4	4.3	3.7	1.2	1.1
56 years.	92.4	93.8	5.4	3.9	2.2	1.8	0.6	0.3
57 years.	91.2	92.5	5.6	4.9	3.2	2.6	0.9	1.0
58 years.	92.3	94.2	4.3	4.0	3.2	1.7	1.2	0.9
59 years.	92.2	93.7	4.9	4.1	2.8	1.7	0.7	0.6
60 years.	92.3	93.8	4.2	3.3	3.3	2.8	1.2	1.1

Table 7-9. Mobility Status of the Population, by Age and Sex: 1981-82–continued

Year	Nonmobile		Local mobility		Migration total		Migration non-contiguous states	
	Male	Female	Male	Female	Male	Female	Male	Female
61 years.	94.5	93.8	3.1	4.1	2.0	2.2	0.7	0.9
62 years.	92.9	92.8	3.6	4.7	3.5	2.1	1.2	0.6
63 years.	92.8	93.6	4.0	3.3	3.1	3.0	1.0	0.8
64 years.	95.4	93.8	1.5	3.4	2.6	2.8	1.0	1.2
65 years.	94.1	95.1	3.5	3.1	2.4	1.7	0.6	0.5
66 years.	93.4	93.0	3.1	3.8	3.5	3.1	1.7	0.8
67 years.	95.1	95.8	2.7	2.4	2.1	1.8	0.7	0.8
68 years.	94.3	96.0	2.2	1.5	2.9	2.2	0.9	1.0
69 years.	93.8	94.2	3.8	3.9	2.4	1.9	0.1	0.5
70 years.	96.5	93.9	1.8	3.1	1.6	2.6	1.0	1.0
71 years.	94.2	94.3	4.1	4.4	1.7	1.0	0.5	0.4
72 years.	93.7	95.7	3.0	2.9	2.4	1.4	1.2	0.5
73 years.	94.1	95.9	4.0	2.7	1.7	1.3	0.8	0.4
74 years.	96.4	95.5	2.2	2.9	1.1	1.7	0.4	0.7
75 years.	95.6	93.6	2.8	4.3	1.6	2.0	0.7	0.7

Source: U.S. Bureau of the Census. "Geographical Mobility: March 1975 to March 1980." Current Population Reports (Series P-20, no. 368, Table 5). Washington, DC: U.S. Government Printing Office, 1981.

big positive gains. In Colorado, Nevada, and Arizona the large gains of the previous decade continued.

Northward Movement from the South

Between the close of the Civil War and 1950, the South region lost population heavily, and a very large share of it was absorbed by industrial centers in the Northeast and East North Central regions. The great industrial and commercial expansion that took place on the Atlantic coast and in the cities on the Great Lakes attracted many millions of persons from the three regions of the South to the Northern industrial centers. Both white and black migrants have flowed along this channel in great numbers. (Texas, Florida, Maryland, and Delaware were exceptions to the general loss through migration. Between 1970 and 1980 the net flow of movement completely dried up and disappeared. On the one hand, the South appears to be retaining people and on the other, people from the South migrated West instead of North. Every industrial state in the Northeast and North Central regions suffered a net migration loss during the decade. This had been adumbrated by mixed low positive and small negative net migration for these states in the 1950-60 decade.

The Southward Movement to the Gulf Coast and the Southern Atlantic Seaboard

The entire Gulf Coast–from the mouth of the Rio Grande in Texas, past Corpus Christi and Houston, across the coastal portions of lower Louisiana, Mississippi, and Alabama, and on to include all of Florida–has undergone a much more rapid and intensive economic development than the Southern and Southeastern parts of the United States lying away from the coast. This movement was already under way in 1870 and has continued without interruption since. It accelerated greatly during the 1950-60 and 1960-70 decades and became explosive in 1970-80. Instead of being confined simply to coastal areas and Texas, it expanded to include all of the South. Every state in all three geographic divisions of the South region gained population in unprecedented amounts during that decade. The cessation of the northward movement coincided with accelerated economic growth throughout the South. For the first time the volume of net movement to Florida exceeded that of movement to California. Interior states like Kentucky, Tennessee, and Arkansas, which all had suffered net migration losses since 1870, gained by net migration in the 1970-80 decade.

In short, as of 1980 there are only two regional migration streams instead of three: movement toward the South and Southwest and movement toward the West. The Northeast and the North Central Regions are the source from which these migrants come.

Regional Changes Since 1980

Estimates of net migration in 1980-82 for each state (shown below) indicated that the pattern of movement

Table 7-10A. Estimated Net Intercensal Migration of Total Population, by State: 1870-1980 [in thousands]

Total population by state	Components of change method				Survival rate method								
	1970–1980	1960–1970	1950–1960	1940–1950	1950–1960	1940–1950	1930–1940	1920–1930	1910–1920	1900–1910	1890–1900	1880–1890	1870–1880
New England													
Maine	76	-69	-67	-27	-70.5	-35.8	-1.2	-39.3	-8.3	10.6	4.1	-15.9	-33.3
New Hampshire	136	69	12	*	-2.1	-9.1	9.1	-10.2	-3.6	3.2	20.4	20.7	10.1
Vermont	38	15	-38	-19	-38.4	-23.8	-18.7	-20.6	-17.6	-3.7	-2.4	-13.3	-26.2
Massachusetts	136	74	-96	23	-154.0	-29.5	-69.5	22.1	192.2	307.3	334.9	295.7	140.2
Rhode Island	33	13	-26	11	-36.5	2.7	-2.3	11.4	12.8	66.1	45.9	42.5	27.9
Connecticut	52	214	234	113	-172.7	89.5	39.2	64.1	122.1	112.7	90.8	72.9	22.4
Middle Atlantic													
New York	-1,542	-101	210	270	1.2	83.8	396.3	1,062.1	467.4	1,061.0	604.8	395.4	61.7
New Jersey	114	488	578	294	409.9	200.7	-28.2	442.3	278.2	376.1	218.3	151.3	48.4
Pennsylvania	292	-378	-475	-355	-594.0	-447.2	-301.0	-252.9	51.9	444.6	262.0	285.1	19.1
East North Central													
Ohio	543	-126	407	245	265.9	151.6	-56.6	214.7	499.4	207.7	77.7	41.9	-12.9
Indiana	87	-16	61	97	21.0	56.7	10.6	-0.9	16.0	-54.4	33.4	-86.7	-70.2
Illinois	402	-43	124	75	-10.1	-22.1	-60.8	414.0	255.6	223.0	340.0	170.3	-59.0
Michigan	294	27	155	336	88.0	251.4	17.1	549.6	465.2	117.2	62.0	172.3	161.4
Wisconsin	15	4	-53	-84	85.2	-95.1	-10.9	-17.9	37.6	9.2	84.3	100.8	9.0
West North Central													
Minnesota	9	-25	-98	-173	-109.2	-160.9	36.0	-106.2	59.1	72.6	148.4	264.1	156.2
Iowa	58	-183	-234	-196	-220.7	-178.8	-73.4	-167.2	-18.3	-207.5	21.7	-5.6	85.1
Missouri	15	2	-134	-190	-150.0	-168.6	-20.8	-98.7	-134.7	-163.8	-17.2	56.4	-30.4
North Dakota	17	-94	-105	-121	-91.0	-109.4	-105.8	-76.3	-46.0	137.3	63.8	{ 243.4	86.8
South Dakota	26	-94	-95	-79	-76.1	-71.2	-101.4	-45.0	-31.2	86.9	0.3		
Nebraska	12	-73	-117	-135	-102.4	-123.0	-139.5	-78.1	-34.5	-28.8	-153.9	362.5	204.4
Kansas	19	-130	-44	-91	-29.6	-86.8	-163.8	-83.1	-74.5	20.0	-149.8	159.7	366.8
South Atlantic													
Deleware	7	38	63	21	51.1	14.5	16.0	-3.5	5.1	2.7	-1.2	4.3	-2.3
Maryland	55	385	321	270	231.1	213.3	87.0	10.2	43.1	-8.3	8.2	-10.7	-11.2
District of Columbia	150	-100	-160	49	-115.1	78.5	157.8	27.3	97.0	41.0	34.3	36.1	18.1
Virginia	354	141	15	169	-2.0	152.0	0.2	-231.6	-27.7	-73.7	-91.5	-80.9	-51.1
West Virginia	113	-265	-446	-235	-401.6	-210.8	-73.6	-53.8	-1.7	46.1	17.2	-4.8	24.0
North Carolina	402	-94	-328	-258	-277.6	-202.8	-85.4	-7.9	-74.3	-80.4	-88.8	-57.7	-14.4
South Carolina	274	-149	-222	-230	-179.1	-172.4	-102.5	-256.9	-80.9	-80.6	-75.5	-35.9	25.7
Georgia	442	51	-212	-290	-169.7	-224.3	-134.1	-414.9	-98.1	-41.7	-56.1	-19.5	-40.0
Florida	722	1,326	1,616	578	2,385.6	510.9	280.3	297.6	101.6	103.5	36.9	51.1	12.1
East South Central													
Kentucky	208	-153	-390	-366	-350.2	-319.2	-93.5	-206.1	-167.1	-177.8	-65.1	-96.8	-47.2
Tennessee	394	-45	-274	-143	-252.6	-102.8	-14.9	-113.8	-131.2	-156.9	-95.4	-77.7	-91.8
Alabama	180	-233	-369	-342	-332.3	-271.0	-165.3	-149.2	-113.9	-47.8	-40.4	-11.5	-60.7
Mississippi	85	-267	-433	-433	-369.6	-349.9	-90.3	-101.6	-199.3	-46.4	-44.5	-60.6	-5.6
West South Central													
Arkansas	233	-71	-433	-415	-353.0	-320.4	-128.8	-191.3	-74.7	-27.2	-82.8	75.1	84.0
Louisiana	190	-130	-49	-147	-39.0	-112.1	5.7	-23.2	-64.7	10.6	1.4	-3.0	-12.0
Oklahoma	295	13	-219	-434	-196.0	-356.1	-269.4	-51.8	62.4	491.5	501.3	44.5	--
Texas	1,781	146	121	73	174.5	132.9	-72.8	243.5	114.3	131.1	147.7	151.2	308.5
Mountain[a]													
Montana	33	-58	-25	-40	-25.3	-42.2	-19.3	-72.9	90.1	86.5	63.5	70.6	12.1
Idaho	130	-42	-40	-27	-39.3	-29.6	-20.5	-50.6	37.3	104.1	39.8	34.2	11.7
Wyoming	95	-39	-20	-1	-18.7	-4.6	-0.1	-1.2	20.7	33.3	15.6	28.7	7.2
Colorado	447	215	164	41	132.4	32.4	1.0	-16.6	39.8	159.8	51.9	146.8	119.1
New Mexico	144	-1	52	16	51.7	9.8	18.6	-22.9	-20.2	63.1	1.2	6.4	-3.3
Arizona	112	228	329	137	289.3	117.4	-3.5	23.5	75.4	50.7	21.4	10.9	19.8
Utah	149	-11	9	9	4.9	6.4	-30.5	-30.8	-0.2	24.9	8.9	17.9	16.7
Nevada	259	144	86	34	74.9	28.8	12.5	6.9	-6.4	32.9	-5.1	-15.6	6.6
Pacific[a]													
Washington	476	249	87	392	49.5	351.3	109.2	81.6	97.5	464.7	80.4	205.4	28.7
Oregon	397	159	16	286	1.2	244.0	94.1	96.5	56.0	189.9	43.0	85.9	39.0
California	2,078	2,113	3,142	2,658	2,573.1	2,339.1	974.6	1,695.2	804.1	694.1	172.7	214.2	129.6
Alaska	37	16	41	...	48.0	...	...	...	...	...	...	...	...
Hawaii	176	11	3	...	47.9	...	...	...	...	...	...	...	...

[a]For 1870-1890, only white population in Mountain and Pacific states; no estimates made for blacks.

Note: * indicates less than 1,000. -- indicates data not available. ... indicates data not applicable.

Source: U.S. Bureau of the Census. Historical Statistics of the United States: Colonial Times to 1970. Washington, DC: U.S. Government Printing Office, 1975. Also, data for 1970-1980 from U.S. Bureau of the Census. Statistical Abstract of the United States: 1984 (Table 13). Washington, DC: U.S. Government Printing Office, 1983.

described above continued in the 1980s, with some modifications:

	NET TOTAL MIGRATION
United States	9,279
Regions:	
Northeast	-1,918
North Central	-1,417
South	7,583
West	5,031
New England	29
Maine	76
New Hampshire	136
Vermont	38

Table 7-10B. Estimated Net Intercensal Migration of Native White Population, by State: 1870-1970 [in thousands]

Native white population by state	Components of change method			Survival rate method								
	1960-1970	1950-1960	1940-1950	1950-1960	1940-1950	1930-1940	1920-1930	1910-1920	1900-1910	1890-1900	1880-1890	1870-1880
New England												
Maine	-69	-69	-27	-71.4	-41.6	-2.2	-46.6	-22.7	-18.4	-20.6	-40.8	-46.5
New Hampshire	68	11	-1	-2.7	-12.6	8.3	-14.4	-12.8	-15.7	-2.5	-7.1	-7.1
Vermont	14	-38	-20	-38.1	-25.8	-14.6	-25.2	-19.7	-17.2	-10.9	-21.9	-24.7
Massachusetts	23	-122	8	-185.0	-73.8	-45.6	-101.7	-6.0	-23.3	46.9	31.9	13.5
Rhode Island	4	-28	9	-34.2	-0.2	0.8	-8.7	-10.5	5.1	3.3	2.4	4.1
Connecticut	166	195	98	106.6	49.0	30.2	6.4	18.7	-10.9	5.4	2.8	-6.5
Middle Atlantic												
New York	-638	-72	-6	-392.6	-270.8	140.3	138.1	-76.5	-74.9	-18.6	-146.4	-167.4
New Jersey	336	466	231	214.5	88.6	-18.8	179.3	72.0	71.4	46.3	9.4	-8.9
Pennsylvania	-423	-552	-467	-657.9	-531.3	-260.9	-380.2	-199.4	-178.1	-60.2	-70.0	-105.2
East North Central												
Ohio	-191	274	110	116.8	28.5	-58.6	58.2	233.4	-40.4	-29.6	-96.7	-92.8
Indiana	-58	17	57	-24.6	15.0	7.1	-43.3	-33.1	-111.9	-7.6	-120.4	-101.2
Illinois	-215	-64	-142	-229.6	-202.9	-58.7	80.3	-36.2	-198.9	44.0	-170.7	-192.5
Michigan	-124	28	146	-57.7	51.7	18.1	239.9	181.5	-35.9	-26.8	-19.7	25.8
Wisconsin	-29	-82	-96	-120.8	-110.3	-10.0	-53.2	-37.3	-103.3	-25.7	-75.6	-78.8
West North Central												
Minnesota	-39	-102	-175	-111.1	-163.1	27.1	-113.6	-1.2	-61.4	25.9	37.2	38.2
Iowa	-189	-236	-198	-218.3	-180.9	-70.5	-164.0	-45.9	-249.1	-29.9	-108.2	2.7
Missouri	-25	-161	-222	-173.7	-197.4	-36.8	-141.4	-173.7	-228.1	-50.0	2.4	-43.2
North Dakota	-94	-103	-119	-87.5	-103.6	-99.1	-72.8	-46.3	81.8	20.4	{ 126.0	43.5
South Dakota	-92	-90	-74	-74.0	-71.3	-96.8	-46.1	-33.7	59.6	-26.5		
Nebraska	-76	-121	-139	-106.0	-125.9	-135.5	-81.1	-53.2	-62.4	-159.2	244.3	139.2
Kansas	-139	-49	-96	-33.6	-90.1	-156.2	-84.6	-86.9	-18.2	-156.6	106.3	290.1
South Atlantic												
Delaware	32	57	17	43.6	11.2	12.8	-3.8	0.3	-3.0	-3.7	-11.0	-2.6
Maryland	290	284	231	187.6	167.6	72.2	-4.5	16.8	-26.9	-5.8	-29.4	-16.1
District of Columbia	-137	-213	-14	-165.4	6.7	101.2	5.5	69.3	22.2	20.1	18.1	8.6
Virginia	206	85	194	58.4	169.1	33.7	-111.7	-9.5	-35.6	-25.8	-33.6	-16.5
West Virginia	-247	-406	-219	-361.3	-193.0	-66.7	-62.7	-29.3	-6.2	3.5	-12.3	18.1
North Carolina	81	-121	-95	-109.9	-81.6	-27.1	5.2	-47.7	-54.4	-41.7	-19.8	-7.6
South Carolina	44	-4	-24	-0.7	-15.7	-8.7	-52.4	-8.0	-10.5	-10.8	-17.5	9.1
Georgia	198	-8	-49	-10.8	-38.2	-44.2	-155.1	-27.4	-30.8	-31.4	-35.1	-20.8
Florida	1,340	1,516	564	1,152.8	438.7	208.4	221.1	84.5	46.6	10.1	24.8	7.
East South Central												
Kentucky	-158	-375	-349	-334.8	-299.1	-83.8	-188.4	-153.1	-159.9	-58.9	-85.6	-39.6
Tennessee	1	-217	-97	-201.6	-68.6	-24.4	-100.6	-103.2	-127.3	-76.7	-64.9	-67.0
Alabama	-5	-145	-140	-142.5	-108.6	-101.0	-69.7	-45.3	-32.8	-41.1	-12.1	-25.9
Mississippi	10	-110	-108	-104.8	-94.3	-32.0	-33.8	-70.3	-19.0	-35.8	-47.7	-22.7
West South Central												
Arkansas	38	-283	-259	-243.8	-207.1	-95.5	-144.4	-74.4	-55.2	-77.6	25.3	53.0
Louisiana	26	43	-2	23.0	-4.7	15.3	2.9	-17.8	15.8	9.2	-12.2	-11.8
Oklahoma	-4	-193	-361	-179.5	-319.5	-253.4	-51.2	54.5	414.2	404.3	39.6	--
Texas	92	147	173	155.3	134.4	-1.7	197.5	-28.4	60.5	95.5	90.9	233.9
Mountain												
Montana	-57	-23	-36	-23.5	-41.9	-14.8	-66.9	75.4	51.0	37.1	39.8	8.2
Idaho	-44	-41	-28	-39.5	-30.7	20.8	-49.5	31.5	81.9	31.0	24.6	8.5
Wyoming	-39	-19	-2	-17.0	-5.6	2.2	-1.8	19.9	19.8	11.7	19.1	5.5
Colorado	187	149	32	110.1	21.1	7.4	-17.6	29.2	108.8	33.1	101.1	86.7
New Mexico	-120	53	17	43.3	3.8	22.5	-17.2	32.0	52.7	-2.3	2.7	-5.9
Arizona	248	339	135	255.5	97.6	12.4	31.8	39.9	25.7	15.1	7.2	11.7
Utah	-16	8	6	-2.0	1.0	-27.5	-31.5	-7.6	2.8	-2.5	2.7	0.6
Nevada	136	80	31	66.0	24.2	13.8	5.1	-6.1	21.5	-3.9	-10.0	0.8
Pacific												
Washington	220	69	375	27.8	303.9	100.3	49.2	51.9	311.4	54.0	133.2	20.8
Oregon	145	10	278	-4.5	222.9	90.4	74.3	38.2	132.0	29.2	57.4	25.7
California	1,528	2,788	2,373	1,964.6	1,874.7	899.5	1,244.5	537.7	425.2	96.3	109.6	56.0
Alaska	22	42	...	41.1	...	...	...	...	...	...	...	...
Hawaii	58	55	...	44.5	...	...	...	...	...	...	...	...

Note: -- indicates data not available. ... indicates data not applicable.

Source: U.S. Bureau of the Census. Historical Statistics of the United States: Colonial Times to 1970. Washington, DC: U.S. Government Printing Office, 1975.

Massachusetts	-136
Rhode Island	-33
Connecticut	-52
Middle Atlantic	-1,947
New York	-1,542
New Jersey	-114
Pennsylvania	-292
East North Central	-1,312
Ohio	-543
Indiana	-87
Illinois	-402
Michigan	-294
Wisconsin	15
West North Central	-106
Minnesota	9
Iowa	-58
Missouri	15
North Dakota	-17

Table 7-10C. Estimated Net Intercensal Migration of Black Population, by State: 1870-1970 [in thousands]

Black population by state	Components of change method			Survival rate method									
	1960–1970	1950–1960	1940–1950	1950–1960	1940–1950	1930–1940	1920–1930	1910–1920	1900–1910	1890–1900	1880–1890	1870–1880
New England												
Maine	-2	2	*	1.4	-0.1	0.2	-0.2	0.1	0.2	0.3	-0.1	-0.2
New Hampshire	*	1	*	0.7	0.2	-0.3	0.2	**	**	0.1	**	0.1
Vermont	*	*	*	**	0.1	-0.2	**	-0.9	0.8	-0.1	**	**
Massachusetts	33	20	12	16.8	10.6	2.7	2.9	6.9	5.9	9.9	4.4	3.0
Rhode Island	2	1	1	0.3	1.2	0.6	-0.7	0.6	0.6	1.5	1.2	0.8
Connecticut	38	37	15	28.5	12.9	2.2	5.2	5.3	0.5	2.5	1.1	0.8
Middle Atlantic												
New York	396	255	266	243.8	243.6	135.9	172.8	63.1	35.8	33.8	9.9	7.6
New Jersey	120	107	61	92.2	53.6	9.5	67.0	24.5	18.5	17.7	8.4	2.9
Pennsylvania	25	75	107	60.4	89.6	20.3	101.7	82.5	32.9	39.2	20.8	8.7
East North Central												
Ohio	45	129	131	107.4	106.7	20.7	90.7	69.4	15.6	5.2	5.2	2.6
Indiana	32	42	39	35.3	32.1	8.6	23.2	20.3	4.1	8.1	3.9	6.6
Illinois	127	182	203	159.2	179.8	49.4	119.3	69.8	23.5	22.7	8.4	8.7
Michigan	124	122	186	109.9	163.3	28.0	86.1	38.7	1.9	0.4	-1.2	1.6
Wisconsin	27	29	14	23.5	11.9	1.0	4.4	2.2	0.5	3.0	0.1	1.3
West North Central												
Minnesota	7	5	4	3.6	2.7	1.0	0.6	2.1	2.3	5.9	1.5	1.5
Iowa	2	2	2	0.9	1.0	-0.4	-1.9	3.9	2.1	1.6	0.4	2.3
Missouri	14	24	31	19.2	25.7	19.2	35.9	27.2	1.0	**	-4.0	-4.3
North Dakota	1	1	*	0.3	0.1	-0.1	-0.1	-0.1	0.3	4.9	{ **	0.3
South Dakota	*	*	*	0.2	0.2	-0.1	-0.2	**	0.3	14.0		
Nebraska	2	4	4	3.6	3.0	0.6	**	5.2	1.6	-2.3	7.3	1.2
Kansas	-1	2	4	2.4	2.3	-0.1	6.0	5.4	2.6	-0.6	2.7	14.7
South Atantic												
Delaware	4	6	4	4.6	2.4	2.4	0.5	-0.6	-0.4	-0.7	0.3	-1.4
Maryland	79	31	37	24.9	29.9	10.7	5.0	7.0	-11.4	-6.5	-7.5	-7.5
District of Columbia	36	51	61	51.3	61.2	47.5	16.0	18.3	9.8	8.7	13.4	6.2
Virginia	-79	-74	-29	-71.1	-30.6	-36.9	-117.2	-27.2	-49.3	-70.8	-53.4	-37.6
West Virginia	-20	-41	-17	-36.8	-16.7	-4.1	12.8	15.5	15.3	5.8	3.6	2.1
North Carolina	-175	-204	-164	-171.3	-127.3	-60.0	-15.7	-28.9	-28.4	-48.7	-38.4	-7.9
South Carolina	-197	-218	-208	-180.8	-159.0	-94.4	-204.3	-74.5	-72.0	-65.5	-18.6	15.7
Georgia	-154	-205	-243	-165.1	-191.2	-90.3	-260.0	-74.7	-16.2	-27.3	12.3	-20.3
Florida	-32	96	12	79.8	7.2	49.9	54.2	3.2	40.7	23.4	15.8	1.4
East South Central												
Kentucky	1	-16	-18	-16.6	-22.8	-9.1	-16.6	-16.6	-22.3	-12.2	-22.4	-13.1
Tennessee	-51	-59	-48	-52.2	-38.2	8.6	-14.0	-29.3	-34.3	-19.0	-18.7	-24.6
Alabama	-231	-224	-204	-191.6	-165.4	-63.8	-80.7	-70.8	-22,1	-1.7	-5.8	-36.1
Mississippi	-279	-323	-326	-264.2	-258.2	-58.2	-68.8	-129.6	-30.9	-10.4	-13.2	17.6
West South Central												
Arkansas	-112	-150	-158	-108.6	-116.1	-33.3	-46.3	-1.0	22.5	-7.9	44.7	25.4
Louisiana	-163	-93	-147	-66.2	-113.8	-8.4	-25.5	-51.2	-16.1	-21.6	3.3	-1.3
Oklahoma	-3	-21	-47	-18.8	-38.9	-13.0	1.9	0.8	54.8	79.3	2.3	--
Texas	-4	-33	-107	-19.6	-67.2	4.9	9.7	5.2	-10.2	7.1	12.6	21.0
Mountain												
Montana	*	*	*	**	0.1	**	-0.2	-0.1	0.3	...	...	...
Idaho	*	*	*	0.1	0.3	**	-0.1	0.3	0.3	...	...	...
Wyoming	*	-1	2	-0.8	1.3	-0.2	-0.1	-0.6	1.2	...	...	...
Colorado	16	13	7	11.0	6.1	0.9	0.8	0.7	3.1	...	...	...
New Mexico	-4	4	2	4.1	2.3	1.5	-2.9	4.1	--	...	...	...
Arizona	-4	4	6	7.0	6.7	3.5	1.9	5.8	0.2	...	...	...
Utah	1	1	1	0.5	1.1	0.2	-0.3	0.4	0.5	...	...	...
Nevada	6	6	3	5.3	2.8	0.2	0.2	-0.1	0.4	...	...	...
Pacific												
Washington	10	8	21	6.7	17.8	1.2	0.2	1.1	3.4	...	...	...
Oregon	4	3	8	2.4	6.9	0.5	0.2	0.7	0.5	...	...	...
California	272	255	289	220.4	258.9	41.2	36.4	16.1	9.8	...	...	...
Alaska	*	*	...	5.2	...	...	...	...	...	...	...	...
Hawaii	1	*	...	1.2	...	...	...	...	...	...	...	...

Note: * indicates less than 500. ** indicates less than 50. -- indicates data not available. ... indicates data not applicable.

Source: U.S. Bureau of the Census. Historical Statistics of the United States: Colonial Times to 1970. Washington, DC: U.S. Government Printing Office, 1975.

South Dakota	-26
Nebraska	-12
Kansas	-19
South Atlantic	4,220
Delaware	7
Maryland	55
District of Columbia	-150
Virginia	354
West Virginia	113
North Carolina	402
South Carolina	274
Georgia	442
Florida	2,722
East South Central	867
Kentucky	208
Tennessee	394
Alabama	180
Mississippi	85
West South Central	2,497
Arkansas	233

Table 7-11. Mobility Status of the Population, by Race and Place of Residence in 1982

Residence in March, 1982	Mobility rates-total population				Mobility rates-black population			
	Non-mobile	Local mobility	Migra-tion	From abroad	Non-mobile	Local mobility	Migra-tion	From abroad
United States (all regions)								
Total	83.0	10.3	6.2	0.5	81.7	13.9	4.0	0.4
Inside SMSAs	82.7	10.7	5.9	0.6	80.7	14.8	4.0	0.5
Central cities	80.4	13.2	5.6	0.8	81.2	15.0	3.2	0.5
Balance of SMSAs	84.3	9.1	6.1	0.5	79.4	14.2	6.0	0.4
Outside SMSAs	83.5	9.4	6.9	0.2	85.1	11.0	3.9	0.1
Northeast region								
Total	88.4	7.5	3.6	0.5	84.4	12.4	2.5	0.7
Inside SMSAs	88.4	7.7	3.4	0.6	84.5	12.2	2.5	0.7
Central cities	86.3	9.7	3.3	0.7	84.1	13.1	2.1	0.7
Balance of SMSAs	89.7	6.4	3.5	0.4	86.2	9.2	4.0	0.7
Outside SMSAs	88.6	6.8	4.4	0.2	80.0	17.3	1.9	0.9
North central region								
Total	84.5	10.2	5.1	0.2	78.2	17.6	4.1	0.1
Inside SMSAs	84.6	10.6	4.5	0.3	78.4	17.5	4.1	0.1
Central cities	80.2	14.7	4.8	0.4	78.8	17.8	3.3	*
Balance of SMSAs	87.4	7.9	4.4	0.3	76.5	16.1	7.1	0.3
Outside SMSAs	84.2	9.4	6.2	0.1	76.0	19.1	4.9	*
South region								
Total	81.3	10.5	7.7	0.5	83.7	12.3	3.5	0.4
Inside SMSAs	79.7	11.3	8.2	0.8	82.2	13.7	3.4	0.7
Central cities	78.8	13.5	6.8	0.9	82.7	13.5	2.9	0.9
Balance of SMSAs	80.4	9.6	9.3	0.6	81.0	14.3	4.3	0.4
Outside SMSAs	83.3	9.5	7.0	0.2	86.0	10.2	3.7	0.1
West region								
Total	77.7	13.3	8.2	0.7	73.1	17.6	9.0	0.3
Inside SMSAs	78.1	13.6	7.5	0.8	73.0	17.9	8.8	0.3
Central cities	76.3	15.0	7.5	1.2	75.1	17.9	6.9	0.2
Balance of SMSAs	79.2	12.8	7.4	0.6	69.7	17.8	12.0	0.6
Outside SMSAs	76.7	12.2	10.6	0.4	73.6	11.2	15.2	*

Note: * indicates less than 0.1.

Source: U.S. Bureau of the Census. "Geographical Mobility: March 1981 to March 1982." Current Population Reports (Series P-20, no. 384). Washington, DC: U.S. Government Printing Office, 1984, Table 3.

Louisiana	190	*New Mexico*	144
Oklahoma	295	*Arizona*	712
Texas	1,780	*Utah*	149
Mountain	1,968	*Nevada*	259
Montana	33	**Pacific**	3,063
Idaho	130	*Washington*	476
Wyoming	95	*Oregon*	397
Colorado	447	*California*	2,078

Alaska	37
Hawaii	76

(In order to make a rough comparison, one can divide the amounts for 1970-80 shown in Table 7-10A by five to make the numbers comparable with those provided above.) The volume of loss in Massachusetts, New York, and New Jersey seems to have slackened somewhat. Meanwhile, the volume of loss in the North Central states appears to be even more severe than during the 1970-80 decade. Net migration gain in the South is less universal than in the 1970-80 decade. For example, the East South Central states resumed their long-term pattern of population loss. However, the great flow to Florida and Texas continues in great volume, as does migration to the Southwest. The Pacific states appear to be gaining more slowly than during the 1970s.

The following estimates of inmigration, outmigration, and net migration for five-year intervals between 1965 and 1980 summarize the direction and movement of regional population flows.

(numbers in thousands)

Interregional migration	North-east	North Central	South	West
1965-70				
Inmigrants	1,273	2,024	3,142	2,309
Outmigrants. . . .	1,988	2,661	2,486	1,613
Net migration. . .	-715	-637	+656	+696
1970-75				
Inmigrants	1,057	1,731	4,082	2,347
Outmigrants. . . .	2,399	2,926	2,253	1,639
Net migration. . .	-1,342	-1,195	+1,829	+708
1975-80				
Inmigrants	1,106	1,993	4,204	2,838
Outmigrants. . . .	2,592	3,166	2,440	1,945
Net migration. . .	-1,486	-1,173	+1,764	+893

Source: U.S. Bureau of the Census. "Geographical Mobility: March 1975 to March 1980." Current Population Reports (Series P-20, no. 368). Washington, DC: U.S. Government Printing Office, 1984.

During each half of the 1970-80 decade the ouflow of migrants from the Northeast and North Central states was almost equal, and also almost double the amount lost in 1965-70. Meanwhile, the rate of flow into the West region increased only moderately. Of the 5.2 million persons lost to the Northeast and North Central regions during the decade, 3.6 million (70 percent) went to the South and 1.6 million (30 percent) went to the West.

The above summary reveals a very important piece of information that should not be overlooked: There was a very large influx of inmigrants into the Northeast and North Central regions (1.1 and 2.0 million respectively between 1975 and 1980) from other regions. Hence, the Northeast and North Central regions still attract population from each other and from the South and West, but considerably less than the population that moves out.

A summary for the interregional movement of the black population, matching that for the total population provided above, reveals a very dramatic turnaround in the interregional flow of the black population during the 1970s.

(numbers in thousands)

Interregional migration of blacks	North-east	North Central	South	West
1965-70				
Inmigrants	146	203	162	150
Outmigrants. . . .	110	111	378	61
Net migration. . .	+36	+92	-216	+89
1970-75				
Inmigrants	118	150	302	153
Outmigrants. . . .	182	202	288	51
Net migration. . .	-64[a]	-52[a]	+14[a]	+102
1975-80				
Inmigrants	99	170	415	193
Outmigrants. . . .	274	221	220	163
Net migration. . .	-175	-51[a]	+195	+30[a]

[a]Difference from zero not statistically significant at the 0.05 level.

The 1965-70 period indicated a continuation (at a low volume) of the traditional northward flow of the black population, with a net loss to the South. Between 1970 and 1975 this appeared to be reveresed, becoming slightly positive. By 1975-80 the volume was such that the reversal was unmistakable: For the first time in history the South gained black population through net inmigration and both the Northeast and North Central appear to have lost black population through net outmigration. Meanwhile, what had been a substantial flow toward the West appeared to slacken substantially.

Metropolitan-Nonmetropolitan Migration

In Chapter 3 the upsurge of growth in nonmetropolitan areas, with resultant near-equality of metropolitan-nonmetropolitan population increase, was described, and the changing patterns of mobility were cited as the cause. The course of this new trend between 1965 and 1980, by five-year periods, is estimated to have been as follows:

Metropolitan and Nonmetropolitan Migration	1965-70	1970-75	1975-80
Metropolitan			
Inmigrants	5,457	5,127	5,993
Outmigrants.	5,809	6,721	7,337
Net migration.	-352	-1,594	-1,344
Nonmetropolitan			
Inmigrants	5,809	6,721	7,337
Outmigrants.	5,457	5,127	5,993
Net migration.	+352	+1,594	+1,344

The rather modest net loss from metropolitan areas due to internal migration between 1965 and 1970 was greatly increased during both five-year periods of the 1970s. This increase in the net migration out of metropolitan areas may be partially due to the fact that the data for all three five-year periods between 1965 and 1980 use the 1970 definition of standard metropolitan statistical areas; much of the movement from metropolitan to nonmetropolitan areas was to counties redefined as metropolitan since 1970 or adjacent to existing SMSAs. However, this accounts for only a fraction of the new stream of migratory movement.

During this interval the metropolitan-nonmetropolitan flow of the black population has been undergoing a major transformation also, as the following summary reveals.

(numbers in thousands)

Metropolitan and nonmetropolitan migration of blacks	1965-70	1970-75	1975-80
Metropolitan			
Inmigrants	452	463	469
Outmigrants.	234	325	353
Net migration.	+218	+138[a]	+116[a]
Nonmetropolitan			
Inmigrants	234	325	353
Outmigrants.	452	463	469
Net migration.	-218	-138[a]	-116[a]

[a]Difference from zero not statistically significant at the 0.05 level

Whereas the migratory flow of black population resulted in substantial gains in metropolitan areas during the 1960s, that flow has greatly decreased in the 1970s and may in fact have become zero. The number of black inmigrants to metropolitan areas remained about the same over the three five-year periods while the number of black persons leaving metropolitan areas increased significantly, creating a situation of approximately zero net migration.

Table 7-11 provides some information showing that this pattern was still strongly in effect in 1982. Areas outside SMSAs have higher rates of migration (inmigration) than areas within SMSAs. This is true for each region except the South, which appears still to have a net movement toward metropolitan areas and away from nonmetropolitan areas. This growth of nonmetropolitan areas by immigration is strongest in the West. It is stronger among the white than among the black population, but the black population also appears to be moving into nonmetropolitan areas more rapidly than into metropolitan areas in the North Central, the South, and the West regions.

What effect is this having upon the redistribution of population? The following summary for 1982 suggests that nonmetropolitan areas are continuing to gain at the expense of metropolitan areas, and that this gain is confined to white population, since the black population appears to be still showing a small positive (possibly zero) net migration with respect to SMSAs:

Migration	Total	White	Black
Inmigration to SMSAs from outside SMSAs	2,217	2,035	134
Outmigration from SMSAs to outside SMSAs	2,366	2,190	112
Net migration with respect to SMSAs. . .	-149	-155	+22

Source: U.S. Bureau of the Census. "Geographic Mobility: March 1981 to March 1982." *Current Population Reports* (Series P-20, no. 384, Table 8). Washington, DC: U.S. Government Printing Office, 1982.

Table 7-12 reports this information for each region. Because of sampling errors, these results are only roughly indicative. They indicate that net migration is contributing to nonmetropolitan growth more than to metropolitan growth in the Northeast, the North Central, and the South regions, but not in the West. (Apparently inmigration to the West is rapid to both metropolitan and nonmetropolitan areas.) This growth in nonmetropolitan areas through net migration is largely that of white population, except in the South, where there appears to be a net movement of black population from metropolitan to nonmetropolitan areas and a reverse net movement of white population from nonmetropolitan to metropolitan areas.

Central City Mobility

Chapter 3 also described the population declines of central cities and the growth of population in the metropolitan rings outside central cities during the 1970s. This was attributed to movement from the central city to the suburbs. Following is a summary of the inmigration, outmigration, and net migration for central cities and their suburban rings for the 1970-80 decade:

(numbers in thousands)

Central city and suburban migration	1970-75	1975-80
Central cities		
Inmigrants	5,987	6,891
Outmigrants	13,005	13,237
Net migration	-7,018	-6,346
Suburbs		
Inmigrants	12,732	13,628
Outmigrants	7,309	8,627
Net migration	+5,423	+5,001

Source: U.S. Bureau of the Census. "Geographical Mobility: 1970-75" and "Geographical Mobility: 1975-1980." Current Population Reports (Series P-20, nos. 285 and 368). Washington, DC: U.S. Government Printing Office, 1975 and 1982.

In both parts of the decade central cities lost and the suburban rings gained. The process seems to have slackened somewhat during the last half of the decade. This was caused *not* by a slowing of the flow of outmigrants from central cities, but by an apparent increase in inmigrants. The Spanish-origin population undoubtedly contributed to this easing of migration loss of central cities.

Central cities also showed a net loss of black in both 1970-75 and 1975-80, and suburbs had a corresponding net gain of blacks due to internal migration. However, the net gain of blacks to the suburbs was greater than the net loss from the central cities:

(numbers in thousands)

Central city and suburban migration of blacks	1970-75	1975-80
Central cities		
Inmigrants	737	724
Outmigrants	980	1,163
Net migration	-243	-439
Suburbs		
Inmigrants	827	1,123
Outmigrants	446	567
Net migration	+381	+556

It was this excess of suburbanization that caused the apparently small increase in the metropolitan black population through migration. These data suggest that a substantial part of black suburbanization is caused by the movement of blacks to suburbs directly from nonmetropolitan areas, rather than via the central city route.

If the sample results from the Current Population Survey are correct, the process described above has continued since the 1980 census, as the following summary shows:

(numbers in thousands)

Movers between central cities, suburbs, and nonmetropolitan areas	1981-82
Movers to central cities	2,693
From suburbs	1,831
From nonmetropolitan areas	862
Movers from central cities	5,202
To suburbs	4,001
To nonmetropolitan areas	1,201
Net for central cities	-2,509
Movers to suburbs	5,356
From central cities	4,001
From nonmetropolitan areas	1,355
Movers from suburbs	2,996
To central cities	1,831
To nonmetropolitan areas	1,165
Net for suburbs	+2,360
Movers to nonmetropolitan areas	2,366
From central cities	1,201
From suburbs	1,165
Movers from nonmetropolitan areas	2,217
To central cities	862
To suburbs	1,355
Net for nonmetropolitan areas	+149[a]

[a]Not significantly different from zero.

However, these results indicate that the net movement toward nonmetropolitan from metropolitan areas has slowed greatly and may be nearly zero. It also suggests that the annual net loss of central cities and the annual net gain of suburbs will be even greater in the 1980s than during the 1970s, if these figures turn out to be typical for the decade.

Table 7-13 and Figure 7-4 examine the above trends in terms of opposing *streams* of migrants. They show that:

1. Suburban rings gain two inmigrants from the central city for every person who moves from the ring to the central city, resulting in heavy net loss for the central cities and rapid gain for the suburbs.

2. Metropolitan rings gain about five inmigrants from nonmetropolitan areas for every four they lose to nonmetropolitan areas, thereby having a net gain in exchange with nonmetropolitanareas.

3. Nonmetropolitan areas gain about four migrants

Table 7-12. Streams of Migration to and from Standard Metropolitan Statistical Areas, by Race and Region: 1981-1982

Migration stream and race	United States total	North-east	North Central	South	West
Total					
In-migration to SMSAs . .	2,217	187	446	1,039	545
Out-migration from SMSAs.	2,366	276	541	1,058	491
Net migration	-149	-89	-95	-19	+54
White					
In-migration to SMSAs . .	2,035	167	418	968	482
Out-migration from SMSAs.	2,190	264	531	945	451
Net migration	-155	-97	-113	+23	+31
Black					
In-migration to SMSAs . .	134	21	27	63	24
Out-Migration from SMSAs.	112	3	8	93	7
Net migration	+22	+18	+19	-30	+17

Source: U.S. Bureau of the Census. "Geographical Mobility: March 1981 to March 1982." Current Population Reports (Series P-20, no. 384). Washington, DC: U.S. Government Printing Office, 1984, Table 8.

for every three they send to the central city, thereby enjoying a net gain in exchange with central cities.

4. The net gain of nonmetropolitan areas with respect to central cities is slightly larger than their net loss to the suburbs, thereby giving a small overall net gain to nonmetropolitan areas.

5. Because they suffer a net loss both with respect to nonmetropolitan areas and suburban rings, central cities continue to lose population rapidly through net outmigration.

6. Sampling difficulties make it difficult to assess the pattern for the black population exactly. Suburbanization of the black population appears to be continuing, but much less rapidly than for whites, with apparent "return" migration to the central cities. Nonmetropolitan areas appear to gain about as much black population as they lose to central cities and suburbs (small loss to central cities, small gain from suburbs).

Another significant facet of Table 7-13 (also illustrated in Figure 7-4) is the substantial amount of "circular" mobility or internal turnover within central cities, metropolitan rings, and nonmetropolitan areas alike.

Summary

The materials presented in this section indicate that internal mobility patterns during the 1980s are continuing along the same general lines as during the late 1970s, but with modifications. The movement to the South and West appears to be less strong and more selective in destination. Correspondingly, the net loss of the Northeast region seems to be less severe. Meanwhile, nonmetropolitanization of the population appears to have been slowed, while suburbanization is continuing but not with much acceleration, if any, above 1970-80. The recent declines in local mobility are not easy to explain with available information. They may reflect increased home ownership; increased difficulties in renting or purchasing a different residence because of inflation and high interest rates; recession; unemployment; postponement of marriage; lower fertility; or increased satisfaction with present living arrangements—or a combination of all.

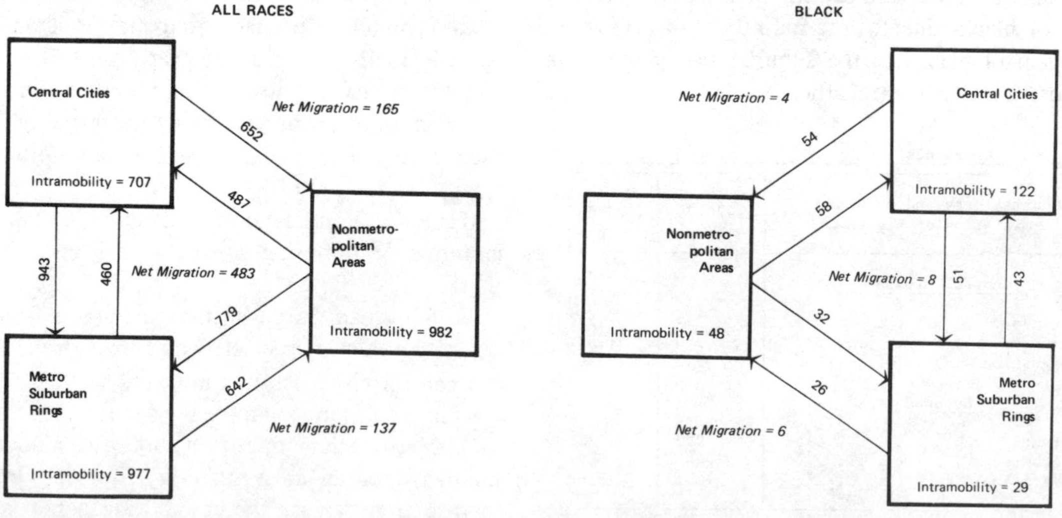

Figure 7-4. Migration Streams between Central Cities, Suburban Rings, and Nonmetropolitan Areas, by Race: 1981-1982

Table 7-13. Streams of Movement between Metropolitan and Nonmetropolitan Areas and between Central Cities and Rings: 1981-1982

Residence in 1981	Total				Black			
	Inside SMSAs			Outside SMSAs	Inside SMSAs			Outside SMSAs
	Total	Central cities	Metro-politan rings		Total	Central cities	Metro-politan rings	
All regions.	4,353	1,654	2,699	2,274	336	224	113	128
SMSAs total.	3,087	1,167	1,920	1,293	245	165	80	80
Central cities	1,648	707	943	652	173	122	51	54
Metropolitan rings . . .	1,439	460	977	641	72	43	29	26
Outside SMSAs.	1,267	487	779	982	90	58	32	48

Source: U.S. Bureau of the Census. "Geographical Mobility: March 1981 to March 1982." Current Population Reports (Series P-20, no. 384). Washington, DC: U.S. Government Printing Office, 1984, Table 3.

International Migration to the to the United States

Since the 1950s immigration to the United States has risen to levels unrecorded since the years before World War I. The nations from which these migrants are coming are quite different from those of previous migration flows: Latin America and Asia instead of Europe. This section describes the flow of migrations from abroad and their sources. The characteristics of these migrants and the significance of their ethnic and nationality origins in determining the composition of the U.S. population are described in the next chapter.

Although the flow of immigration is now controlled, it is still large in comparison with the number of immigrants admitted by most other nations. Two features of recent decades have been large migrations from Puerto Rico and Mexico and a relaxation of immigration quotas in order to admit some of the many thousands of displaced persons and refugees left by World War II, the Cuban revolution, and the Vietnamese conflict. Chapter 1 introduced net immigration as a component of national growth and provided a great deal of data.

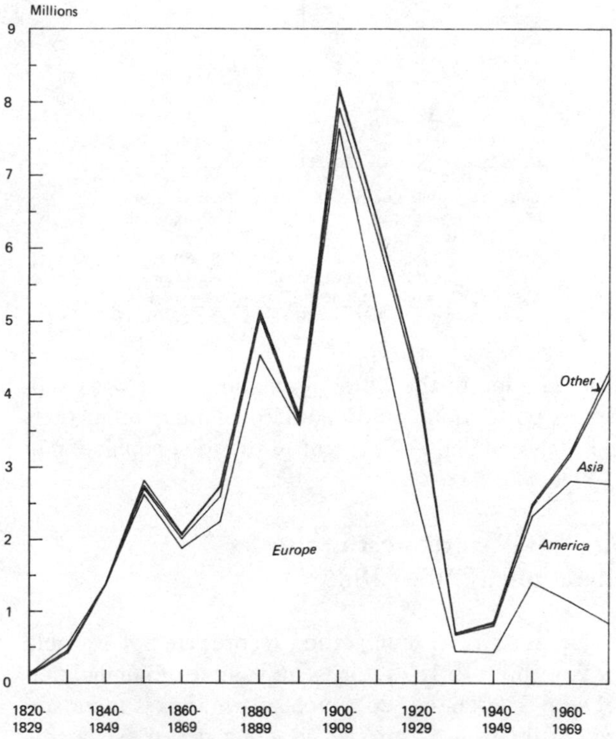

Figure 7-5. Number of Immigrants, by Continent: 1820-1979

A Brief History of United States Immigration

As a nation whose population is composed of immigrants and the descendents of immigrants, the United States has a complex migration history. An understanding of this history is indispensable to anyone attempting to appreciate the present ethnic and racial background of the population. Moreover, ethnic origin is still an important factor in the lives of a great many people. The fact that all but a small fraction of United States citizens are now native born (93.8 percent in 1980) and that foreign-born population has comprised less than 10 percent of the population since 1949 does not mean that complete cultural homogeneity has been achieved. The number of foreign-born persons is still quite large, and the number who are children and grandchildren of foreign-born persons is much larger still.

In 1790, when the Republic was formed, the white population was preponderantly British in descent. There were comparatively few Germans, Irish, and Dutch; very small groups of French, Canadians, Belgians, Swiss, Mexicans, and Swedes; and almost no others. The following table estimates the composition of the population in 1790:

Country of origin	Percent of white population
Total	100.0
Great Britain and Northern Ireland. . .	77.0
Germany	7.4
Irish Free State. . . .	4.4
Netherlands	3.3
France.	1.9
Canada.	1.6
Belgium	1.5
Switzerland	0.9
Mexico.	0.7
Sweden.	0.5
All others.	0.8

Source: 70th Cong., 2d Sess., Senate Document 259. "Immigration Quotas on the Basis of National Origin," p. 5, as reported by W.S. Thompson and P.K. Whelpton. Population Trends in the United States. New York: McGraw-Hill, 1933, p. 91.

In addition to the white population, there was a substantial population comprised of involuntary immigrants and their children: 19 percent of the total population in 1790 was black.

The "Old" Northwest European Migration: 1820 to 1885

Because official immigration records are not available for years prior to 1820, the exact volume of immigration between 1790 and 1820 is not known, nor is there any way of knowing from which countries the migrants came. It is believed, however, that there were very few migrants, and that they came primarily from England and Ireland. The statistical record of immigration, by country of origin, is summarized in Table 7-14. According to this table, not until the nineteenth century was well under way (about 1830) did the many and diverse national groups begin their massive exodus to the United States. About 1830 the Germans and the Irish began to arrive in greatly increasing numbers, far outstripping the migrants from England. The Irish immigration reached a peak near the middle of the century; a total number of 1,350,000 Irish are recorded as having arrived in the United States during the eight years from 1847 to 1854. The German immigration reached its peak between 1880 and 1892, although it had been quite high since 1830; in those twelve years more than 1,770,000 Germans came to this country. Large numbers of both Irish and German immigrants continued to arrive for some time even after these peak years but in somewhat less than "flood" proportions.

A moderate-sized Chinese migration began in about 1855, and continued at a rather impressive rate for thirty years. Landing on the West Coast, these migrants provided much of the unskilled labor needed for the swift development of the West. Scandinavians joined the stream of immigrants heading for America's Midwest, and immediately after the Civil War great numbers of Swedes, Norwegians, and Danes flowed into Wisconsin, Minnesota, the Dakotas, Iowa, Nebraska, and the territory even farther west.

Between 1830 and 1885 immigration came preponderantly from Northwestern Europe and Germany. Since there was comparatively little restriction on immigration, the number of new arrivals varied with changes in economic and political conditions, in both the United States and Europe. As Table 7-14 illustrates, the flow of immigrants was very erratic—in some years it was a veritable flood and in others, a comparative trickle. When there was financial panic, depression, or war in the United States, migration from Europe slackened; when there was famine or political upheaval across the Atlantic and prosperity in the United States, migration tended to be large. New land to settle was not the only opportunity the United States offered to immigrants; there were railroads to build, forests to convert into lumber, mines to work, and cities to build. The course of economic development paced the flow of immigration.

The "Intermediate" Migration from Southern and Eastern Europe: 1885-1940

Although many of the migrants from Northwestern Europe and Germany met with temporary hostility and, in scattered instances, mistreatment, it was recognized that they were needed to help man the expanding econ-

Table 7-14A. Immigrants, by Country: 1820-1970

[For years ending June 30, except: 1820–1831 and 1844–1849, years ending Sept. 30; 1833–1842 and 1851–1867, years ending Dec. 31; 1832 covers 15 months ending Dec. 31; 1843, 9 months ending Sept. 30; 1850, 15 months ending Dec. 31; 1868, 6 months ending June 30]

Year	All countries [1]	Europe											
		Total	Northwestern Europe				Central Europe			Eastern Europe		Southern Europe	
			Great Britain	Ireland [2]	Scandinavia [3]	Other Northwestern [4]	Germany [5]	Poland	Other Central [6]	U.S.S.R. and Baltic States [7]	Other Eastern [8]	Italy	Other Southern [9]
	89	90	91	92	93	94	95	96	97	98	99	100	101
1970	373,326	110,653	14,089	1,583	2,110	6,961	10,632	2,013	10,411	836	1,357	27,369	33,292
1969	358,579	114,052	15,072	1,981	2,149	5,944	10,380	2,115	8,889	574	1,158	27,033	38,757
1968	454,448	129,022	26,025	2,995	4,203	9,873	16,590	3,676	5,659	974	883	25,882	32,262
1967	361,972	128,775	23,004	2,765	4,230	9,881	16,595	4,356	5,116	876	899	28,487	32,566
1966	323,040	115,898	18,777	3,267	4,549	9,049	17,654	8,490	3,972	768	878	26,447	22,047
1965	296,697	101,468	24,135	5,187	5,853	11,526	22,432	7,093	3,693	632	859	10,874	9,184
1964	292,248	108,215	25,758	6,055	5,497	11,120	24,494	7,097	3,248	763	1,054	12,769	10,360
1963	306,260	109,066	22,708	5,746	5,208	11,938	24,727	6,785	3,244	591	996	16,175	10,948
1962	283,763	103,989	18,066	5,118	4,716	13,117	21,477	5,660	2,533	753	753	20,119	11,677
1961	271,344	108,532	18,719	5,738	4,943	14,635	25,815	6,254	2,911	996	620	18,956	8,945
1960	265,398	120,178	19,967	6,918	6,185	17,234	29,452	4,216	9,073	856	761	13,369	12,147
1959	260,686	138,191	18,325	6,595	6,100	14,217	32,039	2,800	30,738	775	726	16,804	9,072
1958	253,265	115,198	24,147	9,134	5,873	11,364	29,498	1,470	3,508	641	673	23,115	5,775
1957	326,867	169,625	24,020	8,227	6,189	25,109	60,353	571	15,498	663	558	19,624	8,813
1956	321,625	156,866	19,008	5,607	5,681	15,254	44,409	263	10,284	643	394	40,430	14,893
1955	237,790	110,591	15,761	5,222	5,159	10,707	29,596	129	4,133	523	134	30,272	8,955
1954	208,177	92,121	16,672	4,655	5,459	11,853	33,098	67	2,873	475	104	13,145	3,720
1953	170,434	82,352	16,639	4,304	5,537	11,145	27,329	136	2,885	609	86	8,432	5,250
1952	265,520	193,626	22,177	3,526	5,416	12,476	104,236	235	23,529	548	137	11,342	10,004
1951	205,717	149,545	14,898	3,144	5,502	10,973	87,755	98	10,365	555	223	8,958	7,074
1950	249,187	199,115	12,755	5,842	5,661	10,857	128,592	696	17,792	526	277	12,454	3,663
1949	188,317	129,592	21,149	8,678	6,665	12,288	55,284	1,673	7,411	694	246	11,695	3,809
1948	170,570	103,544	26,403	7,534	6,127	13,721	19,368	2,447	6,006	897	485	16,075	4,481
1947	147,292	83,535	23,788	2,574	4,918	14,562	13,900	745	4,622	761	249	13,866	3,550
1946	108,721	52,852	33,552	1,816	1,278	8,651	2,598	335	511	153	98	2,636	1,224
1945	38,119	5,943	3,029	427	224	365	172	195	206	98	97	213	917
1944	28,551	4,509	1,321	112	281	619	238	292	316	157	109	120	944
1943	23,725	4,920	974	165	239	1,531	248	394	206	159	54	49	901
1942	28,781	11,153	907	83	371	5,622	2,150	343	396	197	117	103	864
1941	51,776	26,541	7,714	272	1,137	9,009	4,028	451	786	665	299	450	1,730
1940	70,756	50,454	6,158	839	1,260	7,743	21,520	702	3,628	898	491	5,302	1,913
1939	82,998	63,138	3,058	1,189	1,178	5,214	33,515	3,072	5,334	1,021	620	6,570	2,367
1938	67,895	44,495	2,262	1,085	1,393	3,352	17,199	2,403	5,195	960	542	7,712	2,392
1937	50,244	31,863	1,726	531	971	2,512	10,895	1,212	3,763	629	533	7,192	1,899
1936	36,329	23,480	1,310	444	646	1,745	6,346	869	2,723	378	424	6,774	1,821
1935	34,956	22,778	1,413	454	688	1,808	5,201	1,504	2,357	418	453	6,566	1,916
1934	29,470	17,210	1,305	443	557	1,270	4,392	1,032	1,422	607	347	4,374	1,461
1933	23,068	12,383	979	338	511	1,045	1,919	1,332	981	458	352	3,477	991
1932	35,576	20,579	2,057	539	938	1,558	2,670	1,296	1,749	636	592	6,662	1,882
1931	97,139	61,909	9,110	7,305	3,144	4,420	10,401	3,604	4,500	1,396	1,192	13,399	3,438
1930	241,700	147,438	31,015	23,445	6,919	9,170	26,569	9,231	9,184	2,772	2,159	22,327	4,647
1929	279,678	158,598	21,327	19,921	17,379	9,091	46,751	9,002	8,081	2,450	2,153	18,008	4,435
1928	307,255	158,513	19,958	25,268	16,184	9,079	45,778	8,755	7,091	2,652	1,776	17,728	4,244
1927	335,175	168,368	23,669	28,545	16,860	9,134	48,513	9,211	6,559	2,933	1,708	17,297	3,939
1926	304,488	155,562	25,528	24,897	16,818	8,773	50,421	7,126	6,020	3,323	1,596	8,253	2,807
1925	294,314	148,366	27,172	26,650	16,810	8,548	46,068	5,341	4,701	3,121	1,566	6,203	2,186
1924	706,896	364,339	59,490	17,111	35,577	16,077	75,091	28,806	32,700	20,918	13,173	56,246	9,150
1923	522,919	307,920	45,759	15,740	34,184	12,469	48,277	26,538	34,038	21,151	16,082	46,674	7,008
1922	309,556	216,385	25,153	10,579	14,625	11,149	17,931	28,635	29,363	19,910	12,244	40,319	6,477
1921	805,228	652,364	51,142	28,435	22,854	29,317	6,803	95,089	77,069	10,193	32,793	222,260	76,409
1920	430,001	246,295	38,471	9,591	13,444	24,491	1,001	4,813	5,666	1,751	3,913	95,145	48,009
1919	141,132	24,627	6,797	474	5,590	5,126	52	(10)	53	1,403	51	1,884	3,197
1918	110,618	31,063	2,516	331	6,506	3,146	447	(10)	61	4,242	93	5,250	8,471
1917	295,403	133,083	10,735	5,406	13,771	6,731	1,857	(10)	1,258	12,716	369	34,596	45,644
1916	298,826	145,699	16,063	8,639	14,761	8,715	2,877	(10)	5,191	7,842	1,167	33,665	46,779
1915	326,700	197,919	27,237	14,185	17,883	12,096	7,799	(10)	18,511	26,187	2,892	49,688	21,441
1914	1,218,480	1,058,391	48,729	24,688	29,391	25,591	35,734	(10)	278,152	255,660	21,420	283,738	55,288
1913	1,197,892	1,055,855	60,328	27,876	32,267	28,086	34,329	(10)	254,825	291,040	18,036	265,542	43,526
1912	838,172	718,875	57,148	25,879	27,554	22,921	27,788	(10)	178,882	162,395	20,925	157,134	38,249
1911	878,587	764,757	73,384	29,112	42,285	25,549	32,061	(10)	159,057	158,721	21,655	182,882	40,051
1910	1,041,570	926,291	68,941	29,855	48,267	23,852	31,283	(10)	258,737	186,792	25,287	215,537	37,740
1909	751,786	654,875	46,793	25,033	32,496	17,756	25,540	(10)	170,191	120,460	11,659	183,218	21,729
1908	782,870	691,901	62,824	30,556	30,175	22,177	32,309	(10)	168,509	156,711	27,345	128,503	32,792
1907	1,285,349	1,199,566	79,037	34,530	49,965	26,512	37,807	(10)	338,452	258,943	36,510	285,731	52,079
1906	1,100,735	1,018,365	67,198	34,995	52,781	23,277	37,564	(10)	265,138	215,665	18,652	273,120	29,975
1905	1,026,499	974,273	84,189	52,945	60,625	24,693	40,574	(10)	275,693	184,897	11,022	221,479	18,156
1904	812,870	767,933	51,448	36,142	60,096	23,321	46,380	(10)	177,156	145,141	12,756	193,296	22,197
1903	857,046	814,507	33,637	35,310	77,647	17,009	40,086	(10)	206,011	136,093	12,600	230,622	25,492
1902	648,743	619,068	16,898	29,138	54,038	10,322	28,304	(10)	171,989	107,347	8,234	178,375	14,423
1901	487,918	469,237	14,985	30,561	39,234	9,279	21,651	(10)	113,390	85,257	8,199	135,996	10,685
1900	448,572	424,700	12,509	35,730	31,151	5,822	18,507	(10)	114,847	90,787	6,852	100,135	8,360
1899	311,715	297,349	13,456	31,673	22,192	5,150	17,476	(10)	62,491	60,982	1,738	77,419	4,772
1898	229,299	217,786	12,894	25,128	19,282	4,698	17,111	4,726	39,797	29,828	1,076	58,613	4,633
1897	230,832	216,397	12,752	28,421	21,089	5,323	22,533	4,165	33,031	25,816	943	59,431	2,893
1896	343,267	329,067	24,565	40,262	33,199	7,611	31,885	691	65,103	51,445	954	68,060	5,292
1895	258,536	250,342	28,833	46,304	26,852	7,313	32,173	790	33,401	35,907	768	35,427	2,574
1894	285,631	277,052	22,520	30,231	32,400	9,514	53,989	1,941	38,638	39,278	1,027	42,977	4,537
1893	439,730	429,324	35,189	43,578	58,945	17,888	78,756	16,374	57,420	42,310	625	72,145	6,094
1892	579,663	570,876	42,215	51,383	66,295	21,731	119,168	40,536	76,937	81,511	1,331	61,631	8,138
1891	560,319	546,085	66,605	55,706	60,107	21,824	113,554	27,497	71,042	47,426	1,222	76,055	5,047

Table 7-14A. Immigrants, by Country: 1820-1970—continued

Year	Asia: Total	Asia: Turkey in Asia [11]	Asia: China [12]	Asia: India	Asia: Japan [13]	Asia: Other Asia	America: Total	America: Canada and Newfoundland	America: Mexico	America: West Indies	America: Other America
	102	103	104	105	106	109	110	111	112	113	114
1890	4,448	1,126	1,716	43	691	872	3,833	183	(18)	3,070	580
1889	1,725	593	118	59	640	315	5,459	28	(18)	4,923	508
1888	843	273	26	20	404	120	5,402	15	(18)	4,880	507
1887	615	208	10	32	229	136	5,270	9	(18)	4,876	385
1886	317	15	40	17	194	51	3,026	17	(18)	2,734	275
1885	198	...	22	34	49	93	41,203	38,336	323	2,477	67
1884	510	...	279	12	20	199	63,339	60,626	430	2,208	75
1883	8,113	...	8,031	9	27	46	71,729	70,274	469	903	83
1882	39,629	...	39,579	10	5	35	100,129	98,366	366	1,291	106
1881	11,982	5	11,890	33	11	43	127,577	125,450	325	1,680	122
1880	5,839	4	5,802	21	4	8	101,692	99,744	492	1,351	105
1879	9,660	31	9,604	15	4	6	33,043	31,286	556	1,123	78
1878	9,014	7	8,992	8	2	5	27,204	25,592	465	1,019	128
1877	10,640	3	10,594	17	7	19	24,065	22,137	445	1,390	93
1876	22,943	8	22,781	25	4	125	24,686	22,505	631	1,382	168
1875	16,499	1	16,437	19	3	39	26,640	24,097	610	1,790	143
1874	13,838	6	13,776	17	21	18	35,339	33,020	386	1,777	156
1873	20,325	3	20,292	15	9	6	40,335	37,891	606	1,634	204
1872	7,825	–	7,788	12	17	5	42,205	40,204	569	1,322	110
1871	7,240	4	7,135	14	78	9	48,835	47,164	402	1,169	100
1870	15,825	–	15,740	24	48	13	42,658	40,414	463	1,679	102
1869	12,949	2	12,874	3	63	7	23,767	21,120	320	2,233	94
1868	5,171	...	5,157	–	–	14	3,415	2,785	129	419	82
1867	3,961	...	3,863	2	67	29	24,715	23,379	292	817	227
1866	2,411	...	2,385	17	7	2	33,582	32,150	239	895	298
1865	2,947	...	2,942	5	–	–	22,778	21,586	193	851	148
1864	2,982	...	2,975	6	–	1	4,607	3,636	99	718	154
1863	7,216	...	7,214	1	–	1	4,147	3,464	96	491	96
1862	3,640	...	3,633	5	–	2	4,175	3,275	142	585	173
1861	7,528	...	7,518	6	1	3	2,763	2,069	218	358	118
1860	5,476	...	5,467	5	...	4	6,343	4,514	229	1,384	216
1859	3,461	...	3,457	2	...	2	5,466	4,163	265	879	159
1858	5,133	...	5,128	5	...	–	5,821	4,603	429	647	142
1857	5,945	...	5,944	1	...	–	6,811	5,670	133	923	85
1856	4,747	...	4,733	13	...	1	9,058	6,493	741	1,337	487
1855	3,540	...	3,526	6	...	8	9,260	7,761	420	887	192
1854	13,100	...	13,100	–	...	–	8,533	6,891	446	1,036	160
1853	47	...	42	5	...	–	6,030	5,424	162	406	38
1852	4	...	–	4	...	–	7,695	6,352	72	1,232	39
1851	2	...	–	2	...	–	9,703	7,438	181	1,929	155
1850	7	...	3	4	...	–	15,768	9,376	597	3,171	2,624
1849	11	...	3	8	...	–	8,904	6,890	518	1,073	423
1848	8	...	–	6	...	2	7,989	6,473	24	1,338	154
1847	12	...	4	8	...	–	5,231	3,827	62	1,251	91
1846	11	...	7	4	...	–	5,525	3,855	222	1,351	97
1845	6	...	6	–	...	–	5,035	3,195	498	1,241	101
1844	6	...	3	1	...	2	3,740	2,711	197	771	61
1843	11	...	3	2	...	6	2,854	1,502	398	880	74
1842	7	...	4	2	...	1	3,994	2,078	403	1,410	103
1841	3	...	2	1	...	–	3,429	1,816	352	1,042	219
1840	1	...	–	1	...	–	3,815	1,938	395	1,446	36
1839	...	...	–	–	...	–	3,617	1,926	353	1,289	49
1838	1	...	–	1	...	–	2,990	1,476	211	1,231	72
1837	11	...	–	11	...	–	3,628	1,279	627	1,627	95
1836	4	...	–	4	...	–	4,936	2,814	798	1,178	146
1835	17	...	8	8	...	1	3,312	1,193	1,032	938	149
1834	6	...	–	6	...	–	2,779	1,020	885	791	83
1833	3	...	–	3	...	–	3,282	1,194	779	1,264	45
1832	4	...	–	4	...	–	2,871	608	827	1,256	180
1831	1	...	–	1	...	–	2,194	176	692	1,281	45
1830	...	...	–	–	...	–	2,296	189	983	937	187
1829	2	...	1	1	...	–	3,299	409	2,290	517	83
1828	3	...	–	3	...	–	2,090	267	1,089	652	82
1827	1	...	–	1	...	–	580	165	127	227	61
1826	1	...	–	1	...	–	831	223	106	427	75
1825	1	...	1	–	...	–	846	314	68	389	75
1824	1	...	–	1	...	–	559	155	110	259	35
1823	...	...	–	–	...	–	382	167	35	160	20
1922	1	...	–	1	...	–	378	204	5	159	10
1821	...	...	–	–	...	–	303	184	4	107	8
1820	5	...	1	1	...	3	387	209	1	164	13

Table 7-14A. Immigrants, by Country: 1820-1970—continued

Year	Asia								America				
	Total	Turkey in Asia [11]	China [12]	India	Japan [13]	Korea [14]	Philippines	Other Asia	Total	Canada and New-foundland [15]	Mexico	West Indies	Other America
	102	103	104	105	106	107	108	109	110	111	112	113	114
1970	90,215	495	6,427	8,795	4,731	8,888	30,507	30,372	161,727	26,850	44,821	56,614	33,442
1969	72,959	556	5,264	5,205	4,095	5,854	20,263	31,722	164,045	29,303	45,748	53,190	35,804
1968	56,298	325	4,851	4,165	3,810	3,592	16,086	23,469	262,736	41,716	44,716	140,827	35,477
1967	57,574	491	7,118	4,129	4,125	3,845	10,336	27,530	170,235	34,768	43,034	61,987	30,446
1966	40,113	365	2,948	2,293	3,468	2,414	5,894	22,731	162,551	37,273	47,217	37,999	40,062
1965	20,040	365	1,611	467	3,294	2,139	2,963	9,201	171,019	50,035	40,686	31,141	49,157
1964	21,279	331	2,684	488	3,774	2,329	2,862	8,811	158,644	51,114	34,448	24,067	49,015
1963	23,242	307	1,605	965	4,147	2,560	3,483	10,175	169,966	50,509	55,986	22,951	40,520
1962	20,249	304	1,356	390	4,054	1,463	3,354	9,328	155,871	44,272	55,805	20,917	34,877
1961	19,495	296	900	292	4,490	1,442	2,628	9,447	139,580	47,470	41,476	20,520	30,114
1960	21,604	200	1,380	244	5,699	1,410	2,791	9,880	119,525	46,668	32,708	13,636	26,513
1959	25,259	229	1,702	351	6,248	1,614	2,503	12,612	93,061	34,599	22,909	12,109	23,444
1958	20,870	197	1,143	323	6,847	1,470	2,034	8,856	113,132	45,143	26,791	16,983	24,215
1957	20,008	77	2,098	196	6,829	577	1,874	8,357	134,160	46,354	49,321	18,362	20,123
1956	17,327	48	1,386	185	5,967	579	1,792	7,370	144,713	42,363	61,320	19,512	21,518
1955	10,935	54	568	194	4,150	263	1,598	4,108	110,436	32,435	43,702	12,876	21,423
1954	9,970	33	254	144	3,846	175	1,234	4,284	95,587	34,873	30,645	8,411	21,658
1953	8,231	13	528	104	2,579	75	1,074	3,858	77,650	36,283	17,183	8,628	15,556
1952	9,328	12	263	123	3,814	47	1,179	3,890	61,049	33,354	9,079	6,672	11,944
1951	7,149	3	335	109	271	21	3,228	3,182	47,631	25,880	6,153	5,902	9,696
1950	4,508	13	1,280	121	100	24	729	2,241	44,191	21,885	6,744	6,206	9,356
1949	7,595	40	3,415	175	529	39	1,157	2,240	49,334	25,156	8,083	6,733	9,362
1948	11,907	16	7,203	263	423	44	1,168	2,790	52,746	25,485	8,384	6,932	11,945
1947	6,733	22	3,191	432	131	---	910	2,047	52,753	24,342	7,558	6,728	14,125
1946	2,108	16	252	425	14	---	475	926	46,066	21,344	7,146	5,878	11,698
1945	461	13	71	103	1	---	19	254	29,646	11,530	6,702	5,452	5,962
1944	231	15	50	41	4	---	4	117	23,084	10,143	6,598	3,198	3,145
1943	342	36	65	71	20	---	8	142	18,162	9,761	4,172	2,312	1,917
1942	615	31	179	36	44	---	51	274	16,377	10,599	2,378	1,599	1,801
1941	1,971	16	1,003	94	289	---	170	399	22,445	11,473	2,824	4,687	3,461
1940	2,050	7	643	52	102	---	137	1,109	17,822	11,078	2,313	2,675	1,756
1939	2,281	15	642	36	102	---	119	1,367	17,139	10,813	2,640	2,231	1,455
1938	2,492	11	613	34	93	---	116	1,625	20,486	14,404	2,502	2,110	1,470
1937	1,149	13	293	47	132	---	84	580	16,903	12,011	2,347	1,322	1,223
1936	793	20	273	13	91	---	72	324	11,786	8,121	1,716	985	964
1935	682	31	229	32	88	---	(16)	302	11,174	7,782	1,560	931	901
1934	597	22	187	28	86	---	---	274	11,409	7,945	1,801	861	802
1933	552	27	148	44	75	---	---	258	9,925	6,187	1,936	862	940
1932	1,931	43	750	87	526	---	---	525	12,577	8,003	2,171	1,029	1,374
1931	3,345	139	1,150	123	653	---	---	1,280	30,816	22,183	3,333	2,496	2,804
1930	4,535	118	1,589	110	837	---	---	1,881	88,104	65,254	12,703	5,225	4,922
1929	3,758	70	1,446	103	771	---	---	1,368	116,177	66,451	40,154	4,306	5,266
1928	3,380	80	1,320	102	550	---	---	1,328	144,281	75,281	59,016	4,058	5,926
1927	3,669	73	1,471	102	723	---	---	1,300	161,872	84,580	67,721	4,019	5,552
1926	3,413	37	1,751	93	654	---	---	878	144,393	93,368	43,316	3,222	4,487
1925	3,578	51	1,937	65	723	---	---	802	141,496	102,753	32,964	2,106	3,673
1924	22,065	2,820	6,992	183	8,801	---	---	3,269	318,855	200,690	89,336	17,559	11,270
1923	13,705	2,183	4,986	257	5,809	---	---	470	199,972	117,011	63,768	13,181	6,012
1922	14,263	1,998	4,406	360	6,716	---	---	783	77,448	46,810	19,551	7,449	3,638
1921	25,034	11,735	4,009	511	7,878	---	---	901	124,118	72,317	30,758	13,774	7,269
1920	17,505	5,033	2,330	300	9,432	---	---	410	162,666	90,025	52,361	13,808	6,472
1919	12,674	19	1,964	171	10,064	---	---	456	102,286	57,782	29,818	8,826	5,860
1918	12,701	43	1,795	130	10,213	---	---	520	65,418	32,452	18,524	8,879	5,563
1917	12,756	393	2,237	109	8,991	---	---	1,026	147,779	105,399	17,869	15,507	9,004
1916	13,204	1,670	2,460	112	8,680	---	---	282	137,424	101,551	18,425	12,027	5,421
1915	15,211	3,543	2,660	161	8,613	---	---	234	111,206	82,215	12,340	11,598	5,053
1914	34,273	21,716	2,502	221	8,929	---	---	905	122,695	86,139	14,614	14,451	7,491
1913	35,358	23,955	2,105	179	8,281	---	---	838	103,907	73,802	11,926	12,458	5,721
1912	21,449	12,788	1,765	175	6,114	---	---	607	95,926	55,990	23,238	12,467	4,231
1911	17,428	10,229	1,460	524	4,520	---	---	695	94,364	56,830	19,889	13,403	4,242
1910	23,533	15,212	1,968	1,696	2,720	---	---	1,937	89,534	56,555	18,691	11,244	3,044
1909	12,904	7,506	1,943	203	3,111	---	---	141	82,208	51,941	16,251	11,180	2,836
1908	28,365	9,753	1,397	1,040	15,803	---	---	372	59,997	38,510	6,067	11,888	3,532
1907	40,524	8,053	961	898	30,226	---	---	386	41,762	19,918	1,406	16,689	3,749
1906	22,300	6,354	1,544	216	13,835	---	---	351	24,613	5,063	1,997	13,656	3,897
1905	23,925	6,157	2,166	190	10,331	---	---	5,081	25,217	2,168	2,637	16,641	3,771
1904	26,186	5,235	4,309	261	14,264	---	---	2,117	16,420	2,837	1,009	10,193	2,381
1903	29,966	7,118	2,209	94	19,968	---	---	577	11,023	1,058	528	8,170	1,267
1902	22,271	6,223	1,649	93	14,270	---	---	36	6,698	636	709	4,711	642
1901	13,593	5,782	2,459	22	5,269	---	---	61	4,416	540	347	3,176	353
1900	17,946	3,962	1,247	9	12,635	---	---	93	5,455	396	237	4,656	166
1899	8,972	4,436	1,660	17	2,844	---	---	15	4,316	1,322	161	2,585	248
1898	8,637	4,275	2,071	–	2,230	---	---	61	2,627	352	107	2,124	44
1897	9,662	4,732	3,363	–	1,526	---	---	41	4,537	291	91	4,101	54
1896	6,764	4,139	1,441	–	1,110	---	---	74	7,303	278	150	6,828	47
1895	4,495	2,767	539	–	1,150	---	---	39	3,508	244	116	3,096	52
1894	4,690	–	1,170	–	1,931	---	---	1,589	3,551	194	109	3,177	71
1893	2,392	–	472	–	1,380	---	---	540	2,593	(17)	(18)	2,593	–
1892	(17)	---	---	---	---	---	---	---	(17)	(17)	(18)	(17)	(17)
1891	7,678	2,488	2,836	42	1,136	---	---	1,176	5,082	234	(18)	3,906	942

Table 7-14A. Immigrants, by Country: 1820-1970–continued

Year	All countries[1]	Europe											
		Total	Northwestern Europe				Central Europe			Eastern Europe		Southern Europe	
			Great Britain	Ireland[2]	Scandinavia[3]	Other Northwestern[4]	Germany[5]	Poland	Other Central[6]	U.S.S.R. and Baltic States[7]	Other Eastern[8]	Italy	Other Southern[9]
	89	90	91	92	93	94	95	96	97	98	99	100	101
1890	455,302	445,680	69,730	53,024	50,368	20,575	92,427	11,073	56,199	35,598	723	52,003	3,960
1889	444,427	434,790	87,992	65,557	57,504	22,010	99,538	4,922	34,174	33,916	1,145	25,307	2,725
1888	546,889	538,131	108,692	73,513	81,924	23,251	109,717	5,826	45,811	33,487	1,393	51,558	2,959
1887	490,109	482,829	93,378	68,370	67,629	17,307	106,865	6,128	40,265	30,766	2,251	47,622	2,248
1886	334,203	329,529	62,929	49,619	46,735	11,737	84,403	3,939	28,680	17,800	670	21,315	1,702
1885	395,346	353,083	57,713	51,795	40,704	13,732	124,443	3,085	27,309	17,158	941	13,642	2,561
1884	518,592	453,686	65,950	63,344	52,728	18,768	179,676	4,536	36,571	12,689	388	16,510	2,526
1883	603,322	522,587	76,606	81,486	71,994	24,271	194,786	2,011	27,625	9,909	163	31,792	1,944
1882	788,992	648,186	102,991	76,432	105,326	27,796	250,630	4,672	29,150	16,918	134	32,159	1,978
1881	669,431	528,545	81,376	72,342	81,582	26,883	210,485	5,614	27,935	5,041	102	15,401	1,784
1880	457,257	348,691	73,273	71,603	65,657	15,042	84,638	2,177	17,267	5,014	35	12,354	1,631
1879	177,826	134,259	29,955	20,013	21,820	9,081	34,602	489	5,963	4,453	29	5,791	2,063
1878	138,469	101,612	22,150	15,932	12,254	6,929	29,313	547	5,150	3,048	29	4,344	1,916
1877	141,857	106,195	23,581	14,569	11,274	8,621	29,298	533	5,396	6,599	32	3,195	3,097
1876	169,986	120,920	29,291	19,575	12,323	10,923	31,937	925	6,276	4,775	38	3,015	1,842
1875	227,498	182,961	47,905	37,957	14,322	11,987	47,769	984	7,658	7,997	27	3,631	2,724
1874	313,339	262,783	62,021	53,707	19,178	15,998	87,291	1,795	8,850	4,073	62	7,666	2,142
1873	459,803	397,541	89,500	77,344	35,481	22,892	149,671	3,338	7,112	1,634	53	8,757	1,759
1872	404,806	352,155	84,912	68,732	28,575	15,614	141,109	1,647	4,410	1,018	20	4,190	1,928
1871	321,350	265,145	85,455	57,439	22,132	7,174	82,554	535	4,887	673	23	2,816	1,457
1870	387,203	328,626	103,677	56,996	30,742	9,152	118,225	223	4,425	907	6	2,891	1,382
1869	352,768	315,963	84,438	40,786	43,941	10,585	131,042	184	1,499	343	18	1,489	1,638
1868	138,840	130,090	24,127	32,068	11,985	4,293	55,831	–	192	141	4	891	558
1867	315,722	283,751	52,641	72,879	8,491	12,417	133,426	310	692	205	26	1,624	1,040
1866	318,568	278,916	94,924	36,690	14,495	13,648	115,892	412	93	287	18	1,382	1,075
1865	248,120	214,048	82,465	29,772	7,258	7,992	83,424	528	422	183	14	924	1,066
1864	193,418	185,233	53,428	63,523	2,961	5,621	57,276	165	230	256	11	600	1,162
1863	176,282	163,733	66,882	55,916	3,119	3,245	33,162	94	85	77	16	547	590
1862	91,985	83,710	24,639	23,351	2,550	4,386	27,529	63	111	79	11	566	425
1861	91,918	81,200	19,675	23,797	850	3,769	31,661	48	51	34	5	811	499
1860	153,640	141,209	29,737	48,637	840	5,278	54,491	82	----------	65	4	1,019	1,056
1859	121,282	110,949	26,163	35,216	1,590	3,727	41,784	106	----------	91	10	932	1,330
1858	123,126	111,354	28,956	26,873	2,662	4,580	45,310	9	----------	246	17	1,240	1,461
1857	251,306	216,224	58,479	54,361	2,747	6,879	91,781	124	----------	25	11	1,007	810
1856	200,436	186,083	44,658	54,349	1,330	12,403	71,028	20	----------	9	5	1,365	916
1855	200,877	187,729	47,572	49,627	1,349	14,571	71,918	462	----------	13	9	1,052	1,156
1854	427,833	405,542	58,647	101,606	4,222	23,070	215,009	208	----------	2	7	1,263	1,508
1853	368,645	361,576	37,576	162,649	3,396	14,205	141,946	33	----------	3	15	555	1,198
1852	371,603	362,484	40,699	159,548	4,106	11,278	145,918	110	----------	2	3	351	469
1851	379,466	369,510	51,487	221,253	2,438	20,905	72,482	10	----------	1	2	447	485
1850	369,980	308,323	51,085	164,004	1,589	11,470	78,896	5	----------	31	15	431	797
1849	297,024	286,501	55,132	159,398	3,481	7,634	60,235	4	----------	44	9	209	355
1848	226,527	218,025	35,159	112,934	1,113	9,877	58,465	–	----------	1	3	241	232
1847	234,968	229,117	23,302	105,536	1,320	24,336	74,281	8	----------	5	2	164	163
1846	154,416	146,315	22,180	51,752	2,030	12,303	57,561	4	----------	248	4	151	82
1845	114,371	109,301	19,210	44,821	982	9,466	34,355	6	----------	1	3	137	320
1844	78,615	74,745	14,353	33,490	1,336	4,343	20,731	36	----------	13	10	141	292
1843	52,496	49,013	8,430	19,670	1,777	4,364	14,441	17	----------	6	5	117	186
1842	104,565	99,945	22,005	51,342	588	5,361	20,370	10	----------	28	2	100	139
1841	80,289	76,216	16,188	37,772	226	6,077	15,291	15	----------	174	6	179	288
1840	84,066	80,126	2,613	39,430	207	7,978	29,704	5	----------	–	1	37	151
1839	68,069	64,148	10,271	23,963	380	7,891	21,028	46	----------	7	1	84	477
1838	38,914	34,070	5,420	12,645	112	3,839	11,683	41	----------	13	–	86	231
1837	79,340	71,039	12,218	28,508	399	5,769	23,740	81	----------	19	–	36	269
1836	76,242	70,465	13,106	30,578	473	5,189	20,707	53	----------	2	3	115	239
1835	45,374	41,987	8,970	20,927	68	3,369	8,311	54	----------	9	–	60	219
1834	65,365	57,510	10,490	24,474	66	4,468	17,686	54	----------	15	1	105	151
1833	58,640	29,111	4,916	8,648	189	5,355	6,988	1	----------	159	1	1,699	1,155
1832	60,482	34,193	5,331	12,436	334	5,695	10,194	34	----------	52	–	3	114
1831	22,633	13,039	2,475	5,772	36	2,277	2,413	–	----------	1	–	28	37
1830	23,322	7,217	1,153	2,721	19	1,305	1,976	2	----------	3	2	9	27
1829	22,520	12,523	3,179	7,415	30	1,065	597	–	----------	1	1	23	212
1828	27,382	24,729	5,352	12,488	60	4,700	1,851	1	----------	7	6	34	230
1827	18,875	16,719	4,186	9,766	28	1,829	432	1	----------	19	1	35	422
1826	10,837	9,751	2,319	5,408	26	968	511	–	----------	4	2	57	456
1825	10,199	8,543	2,095	4,888	18	719	450	1	----------	10	–	75	287
1824	7,912	4,965	1,264	2,345	20	671	230	4	----------	7	2	45	377
1823	6,354	4,016	1,100	1,908	7	528	183	3	----------	7	2	33	245
1822	6,911	4,418	1,221	2,267	28	522	148	3	----------	10	4	35	180
1821	9,127	5,936	3,210	1,518	24	521	383	1	----------	7	–	63	209
1820	8,385	7,691	2,410	3,614	23	452	968	5	----------	14	1	30	174

– Represents zero.

[1] For 1820–1867 excludes returning citizens; therefore, for those years, does not agree with series C 120 and C 138.

[2] Comprises Eire and Northern Ireland.

[3] Comprises Norway, Sweden, Denmark, and Iceland.

[4] Comprises Netherlands, Belgium, Luxembourg, Switzerland, and France.

[5] Includes Austria, 1938 to 1945.

[6] Comprises Czechoslovakia (since 1920), Yugoslavia (since 1920), Hungary (since 1861), and Austria (since 1861, except for the years 1938–1945, when Austria was included with Germany).

[7] Comprises U.S.S.R. (excluding Asian U.S.S.R. between 1931 and 1963, Latvia, Estonia, Lithuania, and Finland).

[8] Comprises Romania, Bulgaria, and Turkey in Europe.

[9] Comprises Spain, Portugal, Greece, and other Europe, not elsewhere classified.

[10] Between 1899 and 1919, included with Austria-Hungary, Germany, and Russia.

Table 7-14A. Immigrants, by Country: 1820-1970–continued

Year	Africa, total	Australasia			All other countries
		Total	Australia and New Zealand	Other Pacific Islands	
	115	116	117	118	119
1970	7,099	3,632	2,693	939	
1969	4,460	3,061	2,278	783	2
1968	3,220	3,172	2,374	798	
1967	2,577	2,811	2,128	683	
1966	1,967	2,500	1,894	606	11
1965	1,949	2,199	1,803	396	22
1964	2,015	2,070	1,767	303	25
1963	1,982	1,977	1,642	335	27
1962	1,834	1,819	1,427	392	1
1961	1,851	1,881	1,556	325	5
1960	1,925	2,140	1,892	248	26
1959	1,992	2,162	1,878	284	21
1958	2,008	2,045	1,783	262	12
1957	1,600	1,458	1,228	230	16
1956	1,351	1,346	1,171	175	22
1955	1,203	1,028	932	96	3,597
1954	1,248	910	845	65	8,341
1953	989	782	742	40	430
1952	931	578	545	33	8
1951	845	527	490	37	20
1950	849	517	460	57	7
1949	995	776	661	115	25
1948	1,027	1,336	1,218	118	10
1947	1,284	2,960	2,821	139	27
1946	1,516	6,106	6,009	97	73
1945	406	1,663	1,625	38	
1944	112	615	577	38	
1943	141	160	120	40	
1942	473	163	120	43	
1941	564	255	194	61	
1940	202	228	207	21	
1939	218	222	213	9	
1938	174	248	228	20	
1937	155	174	145	29	
1936	105	165	147	18	
1935	118	141	132	9	63
1934	104	147	130	17	3
1933	71	137	122	15	
1932	186	303	291	12	
1931	417	652	616	36	
1930	572	1,051	1,026	25	
1929	509	636	619	17	
1928	475	606	578	28	
1927	520	746	712	34	
1926	529	591	556	35	
1925	412	462	416	46	
1924	900	679	635	44	58
1923	548	759	711	48	15
1922	520	915	855	60	25
1921	1,301	2,281	2,191	90	130
1920	648	2,185	2,066	119	702
1919	189	1,310	1,234	76	46
1918	299	1,090	925	165	47
1917	566	1,142	1,014	128	77
1916	894	1,574	1,484	90	31
1915	934	1,399	1,282	117	31
1914	1,539	1,446	1,336	110	136
1913	1,409	1,340	1,229	111	23
1912	1,009	898	794	104	15
1911	956	1,043	984	59	39
1910	1,072	1,097	998	99	43
1909	858	892	839	53	49
1908	1,411	1,179	1,098	81	17
1907	1,486	1,989	1,947	42	22
1906	712	1,733	1,682	51	[19] 33,012
1905	757	2,166	2,091	75	161
1904	686	1,555	1,461	94	90
1903	176	1,349	1,150	199	25
1902	37	566	384	182	103
1901	173	498	325	173	1
1900	30	428	214	214	13
1899	51	810	456	354	217
1898	48	201	153	48	
1897	37	199	139	60	
1896	21	112	87	25	
1895	36	155	155		
1894	24	244	244		70
1893	(17)	248	248	(17)	5,173
1892	(17)	267	267	(17)	8,520
1891	103	1,301	777	524	70
1890	112	1,167	699	468	62
1889	187	2,196	1,000	1,196	70
1888	65	2,387	697	1,690	61
1887	40	1,282	528	754	73
1886	122	1,136	522	614	73
1885	112	679	449	230	71
1884	59	900	502	398	98
1883	67	747	554	193	79
1882	60	889	878	11	99
1881	33	1,191	1,188	3	103
1880	18	954	953	1	63
1879	12	816	813	3	36
1878	18	606	606	–	15
1877	16	914	912	2	27
1876	89	1,312	1,205	107	36
1875	54	1,268	1,104	164	76
1874	58	1,193	960	233	128
1873	28	1,414	1,135	279	160
1872	41	2,416	2,180	236	164
1871	24	21	18	3	85
1870	31	36	36		27
1869	72				17
1868	3				161
1867	25				3,270
1866	33				3,626
1865	49				8,298
1864	37				559
1863	3				1,183
1862	12				448
1861	47				380
1860	126				486
1859	11				1,395
1858	17				801
1857	25				22,301
1856	6				542
1855	14				334
1854					658
1853	8				984
1852					1,420
1851	3				248
1850					45,882
1849	3				1,605
1848	10				495
1847					608
1846	1				2,564
1845	4				25
1844	14				110
1843	6				612
1842	3				616
1841	14				627
1840	6				118
1839	10				294
1838	10				1,843
1837	2				4,660
1836	6				831
1835	14				44
1834	1				5,069
1833	1				26,243
1832	2				23,412
1831	2				7,397
1830	2				13,807
1829	1				6,695
1828	6				554
1827	4				1,571
1826					254
1825	1				808
1824					2,387
1823					1,956
1822					2,114
1821	2				2,886
1820	1				301

– Represents zero.
[11] No record of immigration from Turkey in Asia until 1869.
[12] Beginning 1957, includes Taiwan.
[13] No record of immigration from Japan until 1861.
[14] No record of immigration from Korea prior to 1948.
[15] Prior to 1920, Canada and Newfoundland were recorded as British North America.
[16] Philippines included in "All other countries" prior to 1936.
[17] Included in "All other countries."
[18] No record of immigration from Mexico for 1886 to 1893.
[19] Includes 32,897 persons returning to their homes in the United States.

Source: U.S. Bureau of the Census. Historical Statistics of the United States: Colonial Times to 1970. Washington, DC: U.S. Government Printing Office, 1975, pp. 105-09.

Table 7-14B. Immigrants, by Country of Last Permanent Residence: 1820-1979 [numbers in thousands]

Country	1820-1979, total	1951-1960, total	1961-1970, total	1971-1979, total	1970	1971	1972	1973	1974	1975	1976	1977	1978	1979	Percent		
															1820-1979	1961-1970	1971-1979
Total.	49,125	2,515.5	3,321.7	3,962.5	373.3	370.5	384.7	400.0	394.9	386.2	398.6	462.3	601.4	460.3	100.0	100.0	100.0
Europe	36,267	1,325.6	1,123.4	728.2	109.8	91.5	86.3	91.2	80.4	72.8	73.0	74.0	76.2	64.2	73.8	33.8	18.4
Austria.	4,317	67.1	20.6	9.1	5.3	1.9	2.3	1.6	0.7	0.5	0.5	0.5	0.5	0.5	8.8	0.6	0.2
Hungary.		36.6	5.4	5.8	0.5	0.5	0.5	1.0	0.9	0.6	0.6	0.5	0.6	0.5		0.2	0.1
Belgium.	203	18.6	9.2	4.7	0.7	0.6	0.5	0.4	0.4	0.4	0.5	0.5	0.6	0.6	0.4	0.3	0.1
Czechoslovakia .	138	0.9	3.3	5.0	0.8	0.7	1.2	0.9	0.4	0.3	0.3	0.3	0.4	0.5	0.3	0.1	0.1
Denmark.	365	11.0	9.2	3.9	0.6	0.5	0.5	0.4	0.5	0.3	0.4	0.4	0.4	0.4	0.7	0.3	0.1
Finland.	34	4.9	4.2	2.3	0.4	0.3	0.3	0.3	0.2	0.2	0.2	0.2	0.3	0.3	0.1	0.1	0.1
France	753	51.1	45.2	22.7	3.7	2.8	2.9	2.6	2.2	1.8	2.0	2.7	2.7	2.9	1.5	1.4	0.6
Germany.	6,985	477.8	190.8	67.9	10.6	8.6	7.8	7.6	7.2	5.9	6.6	7.4	7.6	7.2	14.2	5.7	1.7
Great Britain. .	4,948	204.5	214.5	121.9	14.5	12.3	11.5	11.9	11.7	12.2	13.0	14.0	16.4	15.5	10.1	6.5	3.1
Greece	661	47.6	86.0	87.7	15.4	15.0	10.5	10.3	10.6	9.8	8.6	7.8	7.0	5.9	1.3	2.6	2.2
Ireland.	4,691	57.3	37.5	10.6	1.2	1.2	1.4	1.6	1.3	1.1	1.0	1.0	0.9	0.8	9.5	1.1	0.3
Italy.	5,300	185.5	214.1	123.9	27.4	22.8	22.4	22.3	15.0	11.0	8.0	7.4	7.0	6.0	10.8	6.4	3.1
Netherlands. . .	361	52.3	30.6	9.5	1.3	1.1	1.0	1.0	1.0	0.8	0.9	1.0	1.2	1.2	0.7	0.9	0.2
Norway	857	22.9	15.5	3.5	0.5	0.4	0.4	0.4	0.4	0.4	0.3	0.3	0.4	0.4	1.7	0.5	0.1
Poland	518	10.0	53.5	32.5	2.0	1.9	3.8	4.1	3.5	3.5	3.2	3.3	4.5	3.9	1.1	1.6	0.8
Portugal	452	19.6	76.1	93.3	12.3	10.5	9.5	10.0	10.7	11.3	11.0	10.0	10.5	7.1	0.9	2.3	2.4
Soviet Union . .	3,375	0.6	2.3	28.4	0.4	0.3	0.4	0.9	0.9	4.7	7.4	5.4	4.7	1.9	6.9	0.1	0.7
Spain.	263	7.9	44.7	37.4	5.3	3.7	4.3	5.5	4.7	2.6	2.8	5.6	4.3	3.3	0.5	1.3	0.9
Sweden	1,273	21.7	17.1	5.8	0.8	0.6	0.7	0.6	0.6	0.5	0.6	0.6	0.6	0.8	2.6	0.5	0.1
Switzerland. . .	350	17.7	18.5	7.7	1.2	1.1	1.0	0.7	0.7	0.7	0.8	0.8	0.9	0.8	0.7	0.6	0.2
Yugoslavia . . .	115	8.2	20.4	28.5	3.8	3.3	2.8	5.2	5.0	2.9	2.3	2.3	2.2	1.9	0.2	0.6	0.7
Other Europe . .	308	1.8	4.7	16.1	1.2	1.2	0.9	1.9	1.9	1.3	2.0	2.0	2.5	1.8	0.6	0.1	0.4
Asia	3,037	150.1	427.8	1,352.1	91.1	98.1	116.0	120.0	127.0	129.2	146.7	150.8	243.6	183.0	6.2	12.9	34.1
China.	540	9.7	34.8	96.7	6.4	7.6	8.5	9.2	10.0	9.2	9.9	12.5	14.5	12.3	1.1	1.0	2.4
Hong Kong. . . .	200	15.5	75.0	109.5	9.7	8.0	10.9	10.3	10.7	12.5	13.7	12.3	11.1	16.8	0.4	2.3	2.8
India.	182	2.0	27.2	141.4	8.8	13.1	15.6	12.0	11.7	14.3	16.1	16.8	19.1	18.6	0.4	0.8	3.6
Iran	48	3.4	10.3	34.9	1.7	2.3	2.9	2.9	2.5	2.2	2.6	4.2	5.9	8.3	0.1	0.3	0.9
Israel	90	25.5	29.6	34.2	3.2	2.3	3.0	2.9	2.9	3.5	5.2	4.4	4.5	4.3	0.2	0.9	0.9
Japan.	411	46.3	40.0	45.4	4.7	4.6	5.0	6.1	5.4	4.8	4.8	4.5	4.5	4.5	0.8	1.2	1.1
Jordan	41	5.8	11.7	24.0	2.4	2.3	2.4	2.1	2.5	2.3	2.4	2.9	3.2	3.2	0.1	0.4	0.6
Korea.	276	6.2	34.5	235.4	8.9	13.7	18.1	22.3	27.5	28.1	30.6	30.7	28.8	28.7	0.6	1.0	5.9
Lebanon.	58	4.5	15.2	37.3	3.3	2.8	3.0	2.6	3.0	4.0	5.0	5.5	4.8	4.8	0.1	0.5	0.9
Philippines. . .	431	19.3	98.4	312.7	30.5	27.7	28.7	30.2	32.5	31.3	36.8	38.5	36.6	40.8	0.9	3.0	7.9
Turkey	387	3.5	10.1	11.1	1.3	1.1	1.5	1.4	1.4	1.1	1.0	1.0	1.0	1.3	0.8	0.3	0.3
Vietnam.	134	2.7	4.2	129.3	--	--	--	--	--	2.7	2.4	3.4	87.6	19.1	0.3	0.1	3.3
Other Asia . . .	239	8.1	36.7	140.3	10.1	12.7	16.3	18.0	16.9	13.2	16.2	14.1	22.0	20.3	0.5	1.1	3.5
America.	9,248	996.9	1,716.4	1,778.3	161.7	171.7	173.2	179.7	178.8	174.7	169.2	223.2	266.5	197.1	18.8	51.7	44.9
Argentina. . . .	97	19.5	49.7	27.2	4.0	2.5	2.5	2.9	2.9	2.8	2.7	3.1	4.1	3.1	0.2	1.5	0.7
Brazil	59	13.8	29.3	16.4	2.7	2.2	1.8	1.8	1.6	1.4	1.4	1.9	2.2	1.8	0.1	0.9	0.4
Canada	4,125	378.0	413.3	156.2	26.9	22.7	18.6	14.8	12.3	11.2	11.4	18.0	23.5	20.2	8.4	12.4	3.9
Colombia	156	18.0	72.0	66.0	6.7	6.5	5.2	5.3	5.9	6.4	5.7	8.2	10.9	10.5	0.3	2.2	1.7
Cuba	539	78.9	208.5	249.7	14.6	21.7	19.9	22.5	17.4	25.6	28.4	66.1	27.5	14.0	1.1	6.3	6.3
Dominican Rep. .	235	9.9	93.3	130.8	10.4	12.6	10.8	14.0	15.7	14.1	12.4	11.6	19.5	17.5	0.5	2.8	3.3
Ecuador.	91	9.8	36.8	44.0	4.2	5.0	4.4	4.2	4.8	4.7	4.5	5.2	5.7	4.4	0.2	1.1	1.1
El Salvador. . .	50	5.9	15.0	28.4	1.7	1.8	2.0	2.0	2.3	2.4	2.4	4.4	5.9	4.5	0.1	0.5	0.7
Guatemala. . . .	44	4.7	15.9	22.2	2.2	2.2	1.7	1.8	1.7	1.9	2.0	3.7	4.1	2.6	0.1	0.5	0.6
Haiti.	89	4.4	34.5	49.8	6.3	7.0	5.5	4.6	3.8	5.0	5.3	5.2	6.1	6.1	0.2	1.0	1.3
Honduras	37	6.0	15.7	14.8	1.3	1.2	1.0	1.4	1.4	1.4	1.3	1.6	2.7	2.5	0.1	0.5	0.4
Mexico	2,176	299.8	453.9	583.7	44.8	50.3	64.2	70.4	71.9	62.6	58.4	44.6	92.7	52.5	4.4	13.7	14.7
Panama	51	11.7	19.4	19.8	1.7	1.5	1.6	1.7	1.7	1.7	1.8	2.5	3.3	3.5	0.1	0.6	0.5
Peru	52	7.4	19.1	25.1	1.0	1.2	1.5	1.8	2.0	2.3	2.6	3.9	5.1	4.0	0.1	0.6	0.6
West Indies. . .	895	29.8	133.9	237.4	25.3	25.1	24.2	21.6	24.4	22.3	19.6	27.1	34.6	33.5	1.8	4.0	6.0
Other America. .	552	99.2	106.2	106.9	8.9	8.1	8.3	8.7	9.3	8.9	9.3	16.1	18.6	16.4	1.1	3.2	2.7
Africa	143	14.1	29.0	66.7	7.1	5.8	5.5	5.5	5.2	5.9	5.7	9.6	10.3	11.2	0.3	0.9	1.7
Australia and New Zealand.	121	11.5	19.6	21.6	2.7	2.4	2.6	2.5	2.0	1.8	2.1	2.5	2.6	2.5	0.2	0.6	0.5
All other.	309	17.2	5.7	15.7	0.9	1.0	1.2	1.3	1.4	1.8	1.8	2.1	2.2	2.4	0.6	0.2	0.4

Note: In 1938-45, Austria included with Germany; 1899-1919, Poland included with Austria-Hungary, Germany, and U.S.S.R. Beginning in 1952, Great Britain includes data for United Kingdom not specified, formerly included with "Other Europe." Ireland comprises Eire and Northern Ireland. Soviet Union includes parts of Europe and Asia. Beginning in 1957, China includes Taiwan. Prior to 1951, Hong Kong, Iran, Israel, Jordan, Korea, and Lebanon included with "Other Asia." Prior to 1951, Philippines included with "All Other." Prior to 1953, data for Vietnam not available. Prior to 1951, Argentina, Brazil, Colombia, Ecuador, El Salvador, Guatemala, Honduras, Panama, and Peru included with "Other America." Prior to 1951, Haiti included with "Other West Indies."

Source: U.S. Bureau of the Census. Statistical Abstract of the United States: 1984 and Statistical Abstract of the United States: 1976. Washington, DC: U.S. Government Printing Office, 1983 and 1975.

omy, and they were generally accepted as potential good citizens. Around 1880, however, the ethnic and national composition of the migration streams began to change drastically; the flow of immigrants from Italy, Poland, Russia, and the Baltic states, and Southern Europe began to assume substantial proportions, and by 1900 these new arrivals dwarfed migration from all other sources. In 1907, for example, the estimated 1,200,000 migrants received from Europe were divided by origin as follows:

Origin	Number of persons
Old sources	
Northwestern Europe	190,000
Germany	38,000
New sources	
Poland and other Central Europe . .	338,000
Italy	286,000
U.S.S.R. and the Baltic states. . .	259,000
Other Eastern and Southern Europe .	89,000

Thus, only about one-fifth of the total flow of immigrants was coming from the sources that had provided the old immigration. Whereas a large proportion of the old migration were Protestants (except for Irish Catholics and some Catholic Germans), an overwhelming percentage of the new immigrants were Catholic, Jewish, or Greek Orthodox in religious affiliation. Meanwhile, from about 1900 the Japanese began to arrive in greatly increased numbers, and in 1908 Mexicans began to cross the border in unprecedentedly large mass immigrations. Once the first arrivals had established themselves, all of these "new" sources began to account for large quantities of each year's immigrants. Native-born Americans and immigrants from Northwestern Europe began to be apprehensive, feeling that this different and unprecedentedly large flood of newcomers was somehow a threat to the cultural and economic progress of the nation. They attempted to set up restrictions and regulations concerning which nationalities, and how many of each, could enter, which led to the imposition of the migration "quotas." (Figure 7-5 illustrates the change in the sources of immigrants between 1820 and 1980.)

Immigration by Quota

After the turn of the century public sentiment in favor of restricting the numbers and regulating the source of immigration became extremely intense and widespread. The empty lands of the Midwest had all been homesteaded, and the colonization of the West and the Southwest was well under way. The great railroads had been built, and the end of the forests was already in sight. The "new" migration flowed into the large cities, where ethnic islands were established. New York City, Chicago, and other large metropolises each came to have its "Little Italy," "Little Poland," and the likes, which were separate neighborhoods and communities. In these enclaves, native languages and the customary dress, food, and ritual were kept alive. Schools, newspapers, and churches were established to serve the needs of particular ethnic groups. The community at large developed antipathies toward the ethnic groups. and students of society predicted that their separatism would make assimilation very slow and difficult for the members of such colonies. Prejudice against the Chinese had already led to their exclusion by law and treaty, beginning in 1882. The inflow of Japanese workers was "voluntarily" curtailed by Japan in 1907 in response to pressure from the United States. Sentiment in favor of limiting immigration from Southern and Eastern Europe mounted, and such a limitation was imposed by the Immigration Act of 1921. Support for the legislation came from many different segments of the population—from labor unions and labor groups, from farmers and businessmen, and from "race haters"—and arguments in its favor invoked everything from economics to eugenics.

The annual "quota" of immigrants that the act established for each country was set at 3 percent of the number of people born in that country who were residents in the United States as reported by the 1910 Census of Population. (Before 1921 the restrictions on immigration were largely qualitative or "undesirable" persons, irrespective of national origins.) Since the quotas of 1921 still gave the "new" migration sources a large share of the total of 150,000 persons to be admitted each year, the law was revised in 1924; it followed the same principle as the Act of 1921 but based the quotas on the national origins of the foreign-born population as of 1890. (In 1890 the stream of "new" immigrants had not been flowing long enough to build up a large foreign-born population of Southern and Eastern European origin.) The Act of 1924 also called for a study that would determine more exactly the national origins of the population and specified that, beginning July 1, 1929, the quota for any country should have the same ratio to 150,000 as the number of persons in the United States of that national origin to the total population of the United States. The act also established minimum quotas of 100 persons for all quota areas and continued the exclusion of Orientals.

There was much criticism of the quota system and of the philosophy on which the quotas are based. Many argued that cultural homogeneity is not necessarily a good thing (and perhaps perilous to a democracy) and that the United States should continuously absorb persons from all of the world's cultures in order to avoid losing insight into the problems faced by other peoples.

Whatever opinions one may have concerning the course of events it set in motion, the quota system did have the intended effect of curtailing sharply the flow of immigration from Southern, Eastern, and Central Europe (except Germany). However, it did not revive migration from the "old" sources. The quotas set for the nations of Northern and Western Europe exceeded the numbers applying for admission, and those nations failed regularly to fill their allotted quotas; in almost every year between 1925 and the abolition of quotas in 1965 the total quota allotted to these nations was undersubscribed by a rather large margin. During the years of the economic depression, 1930 to 1939, the margin was wide. For example, the volume of migration from Great Britain was so small that only between 5 and 40 percent of the large quota of 65,000 was used in any year since 1925. Not all of the great decline in immigration during the years 1925 to 1945 was a direct result of the quota system. Part of it was caused by economic recession, war, and the disinclination of Northwestern Europeans to leave the country of their birth and seek citizenship in America. Their reluctance has been due, in no small part, to the greatly improved level of living achieved by many of these countries. Life in Sweden, England, or Denmark may have been less luxurious in certain ways than in the United States, but the economic opportunities for the citizen with education or skill appear to have been as great there as in the United States, if not greater.

In addition to the quota immigration, a substantial number of persons were permitted to enter each year as nonquota immigrants. This category consisted of immigrants born in Canada, Mexico, Cuba, Haiti, the Dominican Republic, the Canal Zone, and the countries of Central and South America, and their spouses and children under age twenty-five if accompanying, or following to join, such immigrants; spouses and children of citizens of the United States; ministers of religious denominations and their spouses and children if accompanying or following to join such ministers; and certain refugees admitted by special legislation.

Immigration After World War II: Displaced Persons or Refugees

World War II caused many millions of people to be "transferred" from one nation to another. For example, millions of Jews fled from Germany before the war, and Germans fled from Easter Europe and Poland after the war to what is now West Germany. Many thousands were left homeless or stateless. The nations of the world, as an act of humanity and under pressure from the United Nations, cooperated to provide asylum for these refugees. In the United States, the Displaced Persons Act of 1948 authorized the entry of displaced persons and other refugees without regard to the current availability of places for them on the quotas of their countries of origin, but made their entry chargeable against future annual quotas. Between 1948 and 1955, 406,000 persons entered the United States under this program. The program was renewed in 1953, and the original act was replaced by a new Displaced Persons Act authorizing the issuance of 214,000 special nonquota visas to refugees and expellees from the Soviet Union and other Communist-dominated countries. Between 1954 and 1957 a total of 187,700 persons were granted asylum under this program. Thus, the number of immigrants coming to this country from certain nations was considerably in excess of the quotas allotted to the nations they came from. Most of those nations are ones that have been historically considered sources of "new" migration rather than of the "old" migration. A very large percentage of these displaced persons and refugees were born in Poland, Germany, the U.S.S.R., Yugoslavia, Latvia, Lithuania, Hungary, Estonia, Czechoslovakia, Romania, Greece, and Austria. Table 7-14 reports that almost 2 million immigrants were admitted between 1950 and 1957. In only six of the forty years of mass immigration (between 1830 and 1870) did the number of immigrants exceed the 327,867 admitted by the United States in 1957.

Contemporary "Worldwide" Immigration (Latin America and Asia): 1955 to the Present

Unfavorable implications of the quota system for international relations, the greater involvement of the United States in economic and political events in all parts of the globe, the rising tide of unrestricted Latin American immigration permitted under the quota system, and other factors led to the abolition of the quota system. In its place a new act, passed in 1965 to become effective in 1968, imposed an annual numerical limitation of 170,000 immigrants from the Eastern Hemisphere, with no more than 20,000 immigrants to come from any one country. This act imposed a similar limitation of 120,000 annually on Western Hemisphere immigration. This was the first immigration limitation imposed on immigration from U.S. neighbors in its own hemisphere. The 1965 act gave persons from every country within each hemisphere an equal chance to immigrate to the United States. However, a series of special acts were passed permitting some additional immigration exempt from the numerical limitations. These acts pertained primarily to exemptions of immediate relatives of U.S. citizens, various categories of refugees, and special immigrants (ministers of religion, employees of the U.S.

Government abroad, and others). Refugees from Cuba, Vietnam, Laos, and Cambodia have been given special exemptions. For immigrants subject to numerical limitations, numbers are allocated on a basis of seven preference categories, four of which provide for reunion of families of U.S. citizens and resident aliens, two for specified workers needed in the United States, and one for refugees. Numbers not used by these seven preferences are then available to qualified nonpreference immigrants.

Effective October, 1978, the separate hemisphere limits were abolished in favor of a worldwide limit of 290,000. This limit was lowered to 280,000 for the fiscal year 1980. Thus the contemporary immigration policy is worldwide in scope, with equal opportunity for entrance, subject to the special preferences and exemptions described above.

A Refugees Act, effective April 1, 1980, provides for a uniform admission procedure for refugees of all countries, based on the United Nations' definition of refugees. Authorized admission ceilings are set annually by the President in consultation with Congress. After one year of residence in the United States, refugees are eligible for immigrant status.

The legislation and immigration administration procedures have now lost any semblance of being officially targeted in favor of or against particular nationalities or ethnic groups, although in actual practice there are still differences in chances of admission between residents of various countries. The demand for entrance, especially from Mexico and countries of Latin America and Asia, has become very great, with the result that a large volume of illegal immigration has occurred and continues to occur.

Table 7-14B shows the substantial change as well as the continuities with past immigration during the "contemporary" period. Although immigration from Europe has been reduced sharply, the flow from Great Britain, Greece, Italy, Portugal, and Spain has been copious. Meanwhile, immigration from Asia has nearly tripled, with large streams from China, Hong Kong, India, Korea, the Philippines, and Vietnam. Total immigration from the Western Hemisphere as a whole has remained about the same, but immigration from Canada has been halved, and that from Latin America has expanded greatly. Migration from Africa, although still comparatively small, is quadruple the volume under the quota system.

In summary, the immigration policy of the United States today is more receptive than before to newcomers from less developed nations throughout the world and offers a refuge to persons displaced by political upheavals.

Table 7-15. Immigrants, by Selected Characteristics: 1951-1979

Characteristic	Percent		
	1951-1960	1961-1970	1971 1979
Total	100.0	100.0	100.0
Male	45.9	44.8	46.9
Married	19.6	19.6	23.0
Single	24.9	24.6	23.3
Other	1.3	0.6	0.6
Female	54.1	55.2	53.1
Married	26.7	26.6	29.2
Single	24.1	25.8	21.3
Other	4.4	2.9	2.6
Males per 1,000 females	847	884	879
Age			
Under 16 years	22.9	25.5	26.1
16-44 years	63.5	60.7	59.3
45 years and over	21.6	13.8	14.6
Median age (year)	25.8[a]	25.0	25.4
Occupation[b]			
Professional, tech. and kindred	7.3	10.1	10.3
Managers and administrators[c]	2.1	2.0	2.9
Sales workers	--	--[d]	0.7
Clerical and kindred workers	7.8	7.4[d]	4.1
Craftsmen and kindred workers	7.8	6.2	4.0
Operatives, except transport	6.7	4.9[e]	5.6
Transport equipment operatives	--	--[e]	0.6
Laborers, except farm	5.3	3.9	3.6
Farmers and farm managers	1.9	0.7	0.2
Farm laborers and farm foremen	1.7	1.7	1.7
Service workers except private households	2.8	3.3	3.9
Private household workers	3.7	3.8	2.1
No occupation[f]	52.8	55.9	60.0

[a]1954-1960.

[b]Beginning 1974, based on Bureau of the Census 1970 index of occupations; prior years based on 1950 and 1960 indexes.

[c]Except farm.

[d]Sales workers included in "Clerical and kindred workers.

[e]Transport equipment operatives included in "Operatives, except transport."

[f]Includes dependent women and children, and other aliens without occupation not reported.

Note: -- indicates data not available.

Source: U.S. Bureau of the Census. Statistical Abstract of the United States: 1984 (Table 127). Washington, DC: U.S. Government Printing Office, 1983.

Characteristics of Immigrants

Table 7-15 summarizes selected characteristics of immigrants. The typical immigrant to the United States is a well educated, highly trained person with professional or technical skills, or the child or spouse of such a person. Contrary to the trend throughout most of the nineteenth and early twentieth century, females outnumber males among immigrants. Since refugee immigration came to be an important element, children under sixteen years of age have increased in relation to the total.

It is perhaps precisely because of this selectivity for legal immigrants that such a large proportion of illegal immigrants from Latin America tend to fall lower in the socioeconomic scale.

Emigration

It would certainly be incorrect to leave the impression that all immigrants to the United States have remained here and become citizens. Large numbers found the country not to their liking and returned home. Others may be successful older persons going back to their country of birth to retire. Many came with the sole intention of working a few years in order to save some money or send money home to support their families over a financial crisis; many of these immigrants returned when they had accomplished their objectives. As a result, each stream of immigration from a nation has had its backflow. The size of the backflow has depended on a variety of factors. The most important factor at any given time has been the total number of foreign-born persons of a particular nationality who have immigrated and are present in the country. Probably the largest emigration in the nation's history occurred right after the turn of the century. For example, during the eight years from 1908 to 1915, a total of 2.3 million aliens departed from the United States, most of them undoubtedly dissatisfied or homesick Italians, Poles, Germans, and so on.

Unfortunately, statistics concerning emigration have been kept only sporadically, and the last episode of attempting to assemble them ended in 1957. However, the number of long-term residents who annually leave the country for more than temporary tourist or other reasons cannot be less than half a million. Chapter 1 showed that between 1970 and 1980 the nation gained 3.0 million persons through net immigration from abroad (Table 1-6). This chapter has shown that during the same decade, annual Current Population Surveys reported that about 1.1 million persons moved from abroad. (The March, 1976, survey reported that one year earlier 1,148,000 persons had been living abroad.) Thus, during the course of the decade there must have been a total of about 10 million arrivals. In order to have a net gain of 3 million there must have been about 7 million departures, or about 700,000 per year. A typical year during the 1980s (excluding tourtists) might be

Immigrants	1,300,000
Emigrants	800,000
Net immigration	500,000

Some of these arrivals and departures may represent routine turnover involving embassy, military, business, or other personnel. Whatever the causes, the total volume of international movement is considerably larger than (about quadruple) the size of the net movement might suggest.

Conclusion

The population of the United States is now so large that the admission of 600,000 persons a year would appear to be of little demographic, economic, or social significance. However, this is far from true. Because birth rates are now so low, the annual increment from immigration accounts for a quarter to a third of the annual growth and helps prevent severe below-replacement depopulation. Because the contemporary immigration is highly concentrated in Latin America and Asian nationalities, it is changing the ethnic composition cumulatively. As all of the chapters in this book demonstrate, the Spanish-origin population is now an important second minority, to be taken into account in almost all demographic discussions. The sizable Asian population is also a significant cultural socioeconomic element in national life, which will increase over the coming years as the new worldwide immigration policy continues to enlarge the entrance of nationalities that formerly were restricted.

Opinions differ concerning the future of immigration into the United States. Some observers predict a virtual closing of the borders to all except temporary workers, as is the policy in most of Europe. Others predict that the pressure of the Third World nations for entrance will mount, with the result that the annual limits set will rise as a part of international relations policy. A compromise of these two views leads to the prediction that immigration will continue to be a significant source of growth and change in population composition and distribution for the remainder of this century, perhaps at about present levels of 350,000-550,000 persons per year.

Notes

1. Long, Larry, and Boertlein, Celia G. "The Geographical Mobility of Americans: An International Comparison." *Current Population Reports* (Special Studies, Series P-23, no. 64). Washington, DC: U.S. Government Printing Office, 1976.

2. *Ibid.*

3. The terms "inmigration" and "outmigration" are used in the analysis of internal migration to avoid confusion with international "immigration" and "emigration.

Bibliography

A. Internal Mobility and Migration

Barsby, Steve L., and Cox, Dennis R. *Interstate Migration of the Elderly: An Economic Analysis.* Lexington, MA: Lexington Books, 1975.

Beale, Calvin L., and Fugitt, Glenn V. "The New Pattern of Nonmetropolitan Change." In *Social Demography.* Karl E. Taeuber, Larry Bumpass, and James A. Sweet (eds.). New York: Academic Press, 1978.

Bellante, Don. "The North-South Differential and the Migration of Heterogeneous Labor." *American Economic Review* 69 (1979):166-75.

Bender, Lloyd D. "The Effect of Trends in Economic Structure on Population Change in Rural Areas." Pp. 137-62 in *New Directions in Urban-Rural Migration: The Population Turnaround in Rural America.* David L. Brown and John M. Wardwell (eds.). New York: Academic Press, 1980.

Berry, Brian J.L., and Dahman, Donald C. "Population Redistribution in the United States in the 1970s." In *Population Redistribution and Public Policy.* Brian J.L. Berry and Lester P. Silverman (eds.). Washington, DC: National Academy of Sciences, 1980.

Berry, Brian J.L., and Silverman, Lester P. *Migration Population Redistribution and Public Policy.* Washington, DC: National Academy of Sciences, 1980.

Blackwood, Larry G., and Carpenter, Edwin H. "The Importance of Anti-Urbanism in Determining Residential Preferences and Migration Patterns." *Rural Sociology* 43 (1978):31-47.

Bogue, Donald J. "Internal Migration." Pp. 486-509 in *The Study of Population: An Inventory and Appraisal.* Philip M. Hauser and Otis Dudley Duncan (eds.). Chicago: University of Chicago Press, 1959.

Bowles, Gladys K. *Farm Population, Net Migration for the Rural Farm Population, 1940-50.* Washington, DC: U.S. Government Printing Office, 1956.

Bowles, Gladys K.; Beale, Calvin L.; and Lee, Everett S. *Net Migration of the Population, 1960-70, by Age, Sex, and Color.* Washington, DC: U.S. Government Printing Office, 1975.

Cebula, R.J. "Geographic Mobility and the Cost of Living: An Exploratory Note." *Urban Studies* 17 (1980):353-55.

———. "Real Earnings and Human Migration in the United States." *International Migration Review* 16 (1982):189-96.

Chalmers, J.A., and Greenwood, M.J. "Economics of the Rural to Urban Migration Turnaround." *Social Science Quarterly* 61 (1980):524-44.

Chernoff, M.L., and Reitzes, D.C. "Revised View of Distance-Density Relationships." *Sociology and Social Research* 64 (1980):389-404.

Chevan, Albert, and Fischer, Lucy Rose. "Retirement and Interstate Migration." Paper presented at the annual meeting of the Population Association of America, Atlanta, GA, 1978.

Clark, W.A.V., and Moore, E.G."Residential Mobility and Public Programs: Current Gaps between Theory and Practice." *Journal of Social Issues* 38 (1982): 35-50.

Congdon, P. "Model for the Interaction of Migration and Commuting." *Urban Studies* 20 (1983):185-95.

Conner, R. "Migration and North America's Future." *Futurist* 14 (1980):23-24.

Creamer, Daniel C. *Migration and Planes of Living.* Philadelphia: University of Pennsylvania Press, 1935.

DaVanzo, Julie S. "Does Unemployment Affect Migration? Evidence from Micro Data." *Review of Economics and Statistics* 60 (1978):504-14.

———. "Repeat Migration in the United States: Who Moves Back and Who Moves on?" *The Review of Economics and Statistics* 65 (1983):552-59.

———. "Why Families Move: A Model of Geographic Mobility of Married Couples." *Report No. R-1972-DOL.* Santa Monica, CA: RAND Corporation, 1976.

DaVanzo, Julie S., and Morrison, P.A. "Return and Other Sequences of Migration in the United States, Other Sequences of Migration in the United States." *Demography* 18 (1981):85-101.

DeJong, Gordon F., and Gardner, Robert W. (eds.). *Migration Decision Making: Multidisciplinary Approaches to Microlevel Studies in Developed and Developing Countries.* New York: Pergamon Press, 1981.

Eldridge, Hope T. *Net Intercensal Migration for States and Geographic Divisions of the United States, 1940-60.* Philadelphia: Population Studies Center, University of Pennsylvania Press, 1965.

Falaris, E.M. "Migration and Regional Wages." *Southern Economic Journal* 48 (1982):670-86.

Farley, R. "School Desegregation and White Flight: An Investigation of Competing Models and Their Discrepant Findings." *Sociology of Education* 53 (1980):123-39.

Fisher, J.S., and Mitchelson, R.L. "Forces of Change in the American Settlement Pattern." *Geographical Review* 71 (1981):298-310.

Fliegel, F.C. et al. "Population Growth in Rural Areas and Sentiments of the New Migrants Toward Further Growth." *Rural Sociology* 46 (1981):411-29.

Frey, William H. "Mover Destination Selectivity and the Changing Suburbanization of Metropolitan Whites and Blacks." *Research Reports.* Ann Arbor: Population Studies Center, University of Michigan, 1983.

———. "Population Movement and City-Suburb Redistribution: An Analytic Framework." *Demography* 15 (1978):571-88.

Frisbie, William P., and Poston, Dudley L. Jr. *Migration in Nonmetropolitan America.* Iowa City: University of Iowa Press, 1978.

Gill, Flora. *Economics of the Black Exodus: An Analysis of Negro Emigration from the Southern United States, 1910-70.* New York: Garland Publishing Company, 1979.

Goodman, J.L., and Streitwieser, M.L. "Explaining Racial Differences: A Study of City-to-Suburb Residential Mobility." *Urban Affairs Quarterly* 18 (1983):184-99.

Goss, E., and Chang, H.S. "Changes in Elasticities of Interstate Migration: Implications of Alternative Functional Forms." *Journal of Regional Science* 23 (1983):223-32.

Greenwood, Michael J. *Migration and Economic Growth in the United States National, Regional and Metropolitan Perspectives.* New York: Academic Press, 1981.

———. "Research on Internal Migration in the United States: A Survey." *Journal of Economic Literature* 13 (1979):397-433.

Hawley, Amos N., and Mazie, Sara Mills (eds.). *Nonmetropolitan America in Transition.* Chapel Hill: University of North Carolina Press, 1981.

Heaton, T. et al. "Residential Preferences, Community Satisfaction, and the Intention to Move." *Demography* 16 (1979):565-73.

———. "Temporal Shifts in the Determinants of Young and Elderly Migration in Nonmetropolitan Areas." *Social Forces* 60 (1981):41-60.

Hinze, Kenneth E. *Causal Factors in the Net Migration Flow to Metropolitan Areas of the United States, 1960-70.* Chicago: Community and Family Study Center, University of Chicago, 1977.

Jones, Marcus E. *Black Migration in the United States With Emphasis on Selected Central Cities.* Sarasota, CA: Century Twenty-One, 1980.

Johnson, Daniel M., and Campbell, Rex R. *Black Migration in America: A Social Demographic History.* Durham, NC: Duke University Press, 1981.

Johnson, Gary T. *Mobility, Residential Location and Urban Change: A Partially Annotated Bibliography.* Chicago: CPL Bibliographies, 1981.

Karp, Herbert H., and Kelly, Dennis. *Toward an Ecological Analysis of Intermetropolitan Migration.* Chicago: Markham Publishing Co., 1971.

Keeley, M.C. "Effect of a Negative Income Tax on Migration." *Journal of Human Resources* 15 (1980): 695-706.

Kobrin, F.E., and Speare, A. "Out-Migration and Ethnic Communities." *International Migration Review* 17 (1983):425-44.

Krumm, R.J. "Regional Labor Markets and the Household Migration Decision." *Journal of Regional Science* 23 (1983):361-76.

Lee, Everett S. "A Theory of Migration." *Demography* 3 (1966):47-57.

Lichter, D.T. "Migration of Dual-Worker Families: Does the Wife's Job Matter?" *Social Science Quarterly* 63 (1982):48-57.

Lichter, D.T. et al. "Trends in the Selectivity of Migration Between Metropolitan and Nonmetropolitan Areas: 1955-1975." *Rural Sociology* 44 (1979): 646-66.

Liu, B.C. "Differential Net Migration Rates and the Quality of Life." *The Review of Economics and Statistics* 57 (1975):329-37.

Long, J. "The Effects of College and Military Populations on Models of Interstate Migration." *Socio-Economic Planning.* (Forthcoming.)

Long, Larry H. "The Influence of Number and Ages of Children on Residential Mobility." *Demography* 9 (1972):371-382.

Long, Larry H., and DeAre, Diana. *Migration and Nonmetropolitan Areas: Appraising the Trend and Reasons for Moving* (Special Demographic Analyses, CDS 80-2). Washington, DC: U.S. Government Printing Office, 1980.

Lord, J.D., and Catau, J.C. "School Desegregation Policy and Intra-School District Migration." *Social Science Quarterly* 57 (1977):784-96.

Markham, W.T. et al. "Note on Sex, Geographic Mobility and Career Advancement." *Social Forces* 61 (1983):1138-46.

McAuley, W.J., and Nutty, C.L. "Residential Preferences and Moving Behavior: A Family Life-Cycle Analysis." *Journal of Marriage and the Family* 44 (1982):301-09.

McMillen, D.B. "The Myths of Elderly Migration." Paper presented at the meetings of the American Statistical Association, 1983.

Miller, Ann R. "Net Intercensal Migration to Large Urban Areas of the United States, 1930-40, 1940-50. 1950-60." *Analytical and Technical Reports VIII.* Philadelphia: Population Studies Center, University of Pennsylvania Press, 1964.

Mincer, Jacob. "Family Migration Decisions." *Journal of Political Economy* 86 (1978):749-73.

Nakosteen, R.A., and Zimmer, M. "Migration and Income: The Question of Self-Selection." *Southern Economic Journal* 46 (1980):840-51.

Population Bulletin. "Population Distribution and Internal Migration." *Population Bulletin* 37 (1982):24-29.

Porell, F.W. "Intermetropolitan Migration and Quality of Life." *Journal of Regional Science* 22 (1982): 137-58.

Poston, D.L. Jr."Ecological Analysis of Migration in Metropolitan America, 1970-1975" *Social Science Quarterly* 61 (1980):418-33.

Pursell, D.E. "Age and Educational Dimensions in Southern Migration Patterns, 1965-1970." *Southern Economic Journal* 44 (1977):148-54.

Ravenstein, E.G. "The Laws of Migration." *Journal of the Royal Statistical Society* 52 (1889):241-301.

Ritchey, P. Neal. "Explanation of Migrations." *Annual Review of Sociology* 2 (1976):363-404.

Roof, W.C. "Southern Birth and Racial Residential Segregation: The Case of Northern Cities." *American Journal of Sociology* 86 (1980):350-58.

Roseman, Curtis C. *Changing Migration Patterns Within the United States.* Washington, DC: Association of American Geographers, 1977.

Rossi, P.H. *Why Families Move.* New York: Free Press, 1955.

Rossi, P.H., and Schlay, A.B. "Residential Mobility and Public Policy Issues: *Why Families Move* Revisited." *Journal of Social Issues* 38 (1982):21-34.

Sandefur, Gary D., and Scott, W.J. "A Dynamic Analysis of Migration: An Assessment of the Effects of Age, Family and Career Variables." *Demography* 18 (1981):355-68.

Schachter, J., and Althaus, P.G. "Neighborhood Quality and Climate as Factors in U.S. Net Migration Patterns, 1974-76." *American Journal of Economics and Sociology* 41 (1982):387-400.

Schlottmann, A.M., and Herzog, H.W. Jr. "Employment Status and the Decision to Migrate." *Review of Economics and Statistics* 63 (1981):590-98.

Schnore, Leo F. "Components of Population Change in Large Metropolitan Suburbs." *American Sociological Review* 23 (1958):57-73.

Shaw, P.R. *Migration Theory and Fact: A Review and Bibliography of the Current Literature* (Bibliography Series No. 5). Philadelphia: Regional Science Institute, 1975.

Shin, Ewi-Hang. "Effects of Migration on the Educational Levels of the Black Resident Population at the Origin and Destination, 1955-1960 and 1965-1970." *Demography* 15 (1978):41-56.

Shryock, Henry S. *Population Mobility Within the United States.* Chicago: Community and Family Study Center, University of Chicago, 1964.

Smither, R. "Human Migration and the Acculturation of Minorities." *Human Relations* 35 (1982):57-68.

Sofranko, A.J., and Williams, J.D. *Rebirth of Rural America: Rural Migration in the Midwest.* Ames, IA: North Central Regional Center for Rural Development, Iowa State University, 1980.

Sommers, P.M. "Analysis of Net Interstate Migration Revisited." *Social Science Quarterly* 62 (1981):294-302.

Speare, Alden Jr. "Home Ownership, Life Cycle Stage. and Residential Mobility." *Demography* 7 (1970): 449-458.

Speare, Alden Jr. et al. "Influence of Socioeconomic Bonds and Satisfaction on Interstate Migration." *Social Forces* 61 (1982):551-74.

Speare, Alden Jr.; Goldstein, Sidney; and Frey, William H. *Residential Mobility, Migration, and Metropolitan Change.* Cambridge, MA: Ballinger Publishing Company, 1974.

Sternlieb, G., and Hughes, J.W. "Some Economic Effects of Recent Migration Patterns in Central Cities." *Research in Population Economics* 3 (1981):184-207.

Taeuber, Karl E. *Migration in the United States: An Analysis of Residential Histories.* Washington, DC: U.S. Government Printing Office, 1968.

Thomas, Dorothy. "Age and Economic Differential in Interstate Migration." *Population Index* 24 (1958): 313-25.

Thompson, Warren S. *Research Memorandum on Internal Migration in the Depression* (Bulletin no. 30). New York: Social Science Research Council, 1957.

Thornthwaite, C. Warren. *Internal Migration in the United States.* Philadelphia: University of Pennsylvania Press, 1934.

Uhlenberg, Peter. "Noneconomic Determinants of Migration: Sociological Considerations for Migration Theory." *Rural Sociology* 45 (1980):296-311.

U.S. Bureau of the Census. "Geographical Mobility: March 1975 to March 1980." *Current Population Reports* (Series P-20, no. 368). Washington, DC: U.S. Government Printing Office, 1981.

———. "Geographical Mobility: March 1981 to March 1982." *Current Population Reports* (Series P-20, no. 384). Washington, DC: U.S. Government Printing Office, 1984.

———. "Mobility of the Population of the United States: March 1970 to March 1975." *Current Population Reports* (Series P-20, no. 285). Washington, DC: U.S. Government Printing Office, 1975.

———. "Reasons for Moving: March 1962 to March 1963." *Current Population Reports* (Series P-20, no. 235). Washington, DC: U.S. Government Printing Office, 1966.

Varady, D.P. "Determinants of Residential Mobility Decisions: The Role of Government Services in Relation to Other Factors." *American Planning Association Journal* 49 (1983):184-99.

Wang, C.S.Y., and Sewell, W.H. "Residence, Migration, and Earnings." *Rural Sociology* 45 (1980):185-206.

Wardwell, J.M., and Gilchrist, C.J. "Employment Deconcentration in the Nonmetropolitan Migration Turnaround." *Demography* 17 (1980):145-58.

Way, Peter O. "Inter-Regional Migration and the South, 1965-70." Ph.D. dissertation, University of Chicago, 1977.

Wermuth, D., and Wermuth, M. "Some Determinants and the Migration of Professional Manpower." *Demography* 12 (1975):615-28.

Wertheimer, Richard F. *The Monetary Rewards of Migration Within the U.S.* Washington, DC: Urban Institute, 1970.

White, R.B. "Family Size Composition Differentials Between Central City-Suburb and Metropolitan-Nonmetropolitan Migration Streams." *Demography* 19 (1982):29-36.

Wilber, George W. "Migration Expectancy in the United States." *Journal of the American Statistical Association* 58 (1963):444-53.

Williams, J.D. "Nonchanging Determinants of Nonmetropolitan Migration." *Rural Sociology* 46 (1981): 183-202.

Williams, James D., and Sofranko, Andrew J. "Motivations for the Inmigration Component of Population Turnaround in Nonmetropolitan Areas." *Demography* 16 (1979):239-55.

Wood, C.H. "Structural Changes and Household Strategies: A Conceptual Framework for the Study of Rural Migration." *Human Organization* 40 (1981): 338-44.

Zipf, Geogre K. "The P[1]P[2]/D Hypothesis: On the Intercity Movement of Persons." *American Sociological Review* 11 (1946):677-85.

B. International Migration

Axelrod, Bernard. "Historical Studies of Emigration from the United States." *International Migration Review* Spring (1972):32-49.

Bean, F.D. et al. "Number of Illegal Migrants of Mexican Origin in the United States: Sex Ratio Based Estimates for 1980." *Demography* 20 (1983):99-109.

Bustamante, J.A., and Martinez, G.G. "Undocumented Immigration from Mexico: Beyond Borders But Within Systems." *Journal of Internal Affairs* 33 (1979): 265-84.

Cebula, Richard J. *The Determinants of Human Migration.* Lexington, MA: Lexington Books, 1979.

Chiswick, Barry R. *Human Capital and the Labor Market Adjustment of Immigrants: Testing Alternative Hypothesis.* Cambridge, MA: Center for Population Studies, Harvard University.

Cornelius, W.A. "Mexican Migration to the United States." *Academy of Political Science Proceedings* 34 (1981):67-77.

Cuthbert, R.W., and Stevens, J.B. "Net Economic Incentive for Illegal Mexican Migration: A Case Study." *International Migration Review* 15 (1981):543-50.

Gerking, S.D., and Mutti, J.H. "Costs and Benefits of Illegal Immigration: Key Issues for Government Policy." *Social Science Quarterly* 61 (1980):71-85.

Graham, O.L. Jr., and Piore, M. "New Immigration: An Exchange." *Dissent* 27 (1980):341-51.

Gutierrez, G.G. "Undocumented Immigrant: The Limits of Cost-Benefit Analysis." *Public Management* 62 (1980):8-11.

Jones, R.C. "Undocumented Migration from Mexico: Some Geographical Questions." *Association of American Geographers Annual* 72 (1982):77-87.

Kuznets, Simon, and Rubin, Ernest. "Immigration and the Foreign Born." *National Bureau of Economic Research, Occasional Paper 46.* New York: National Bureau of Economic Research, 1954.

Kuznets, Simon, and Thomas, Dorothy Swain. *Population Redistribution and Economic Growth, 1870-1950.* Philadelphia: The American Philosophical Society, 1957-64.

Massey, D.S. "Dimensions of the New Immigration to the United States and the Prospects for Assimilation." *Annual Review of Sociology* 7 (1981):57-85.

Massey, D.S., and Schnabel, K.M. "Recent Trends in Hispanic Migration to the United States." *International Migration Review* 17 (1983):212-44.

Office of the U.S. Coordinator for Refugee Affairs. *Overview of the World Refugee Situation.* Washington, DC: U.S. Government Printing Office, 1980.

Reimers, D.M. "Post-World War II Immigration to the United States: America's Latest Newcomers." *American Academy of Political and Social Science Annals* 454 (1981):1-12.

Riche, M.F. "Immigration Waves." *Perspectives* 13 (1981):46-48.

Schultz, T.P. "The Schooling and Health of Children of U.S. Immigrants and Natives in 1976." *Immigration Policy and the National Interest*. Select Commission on Immigration and Refugee Policy. Washington, DC: U.S. Government Printing Office, 1981.

Teitelbaum, M.S. "Right Versus Right: Immigration and Refugee Policy in the United States." *Foreign Affairs* 59 (1980):21-59.

Thomas, Brinley. *Migration and Economic Growth.* Cambridge, England: Cambridge University Press, 1954.

Thomas, Dorothy. "International Migration." In *Population and World Politics.* Philip M. Hauser (ed.). Glencoe, IL: The Free Press, 1958.

United Nations. *International Migration Policies and Programmes: A World Survey*. New York: United Nations, 1982.

———. *Trends and Characteristics of International Migration Since 1950.* New York: United Nations, 1978.

Warren, Robert, and Passel, Jeffrey S. (Population Division, U.S. Bureau of the Census). "Estimates of Illegal Aliens from Mexico Counted in the 1980 United States Census." Paper presented at the Annual Meeting of the Population Association of America, April, 1983.

Warren, Robert, and Peck, Jennifer M. "Emigration from the United States: 1960 to 1970." *Demography* (1980):71-84.

Chapter 8

Nativity and Ethnicity: Ancestry

It is true that most citizens of the United States are descendents of immigrants from other continents, but much of the migration of their forebears occurred a century or more ago and has been followed by intermarriage and assimilation into a national entity. Therefore, the public at large has only incomplete knowledge of its ethnic roots. Even if a complicated genealogical question were to be included in the census, most persons would lack the information requested. The statistics collected on this subject must be comparatively simple and hence incomplete.

The 1980 census approached this task by identifying the following four population characteristics (see the definitions box for more details):

Nativity: whether native born or foreign born
Country of birth: asked of the foreign born
Ancestry: self-identification of ethnicity
Language spoken at home and *ability to speak English.*

Supplementary items of information, particularly about the foreign born, were asked (year of immigration and whether or not respondents have become naturalized citizens). This chapter summarizes the information collected and reported about these topics. Special reports, scheduled to be published later by the Bureau of the Census, will amplify the information contained in this chapter. A section is devoted to each of the four topics listed above.

Nativity

The 14.1 million foreign-born residents of the United States in 1980 exceeded the number of such residents counted by all previous censuses except one—the 1930 census, which showed the cumulative effects of rapid immigration from 1890 to 1920. Table 8-1 provides data on numbers and proportions of foreign born since 1850. The large number in 1980, an increase of nearly 4.5 million people over 1970, is the cumulative result of the increased flow of immigrants, both refugee and under quotas, since World War II and especially since the Vietnam War. However, because the population is now so much larger than before, foreign-born persons comprise only 6 percent of the total, whereas in 1910, at the height of the influx from Southern and Eastern Europe, foreign-born persons accounted for 15 percent of the total population. Figure 8-1 illustrates the sources of immigration, by continent, for the 1950-80 period.

The slackening of immigration during the Depression of the 1930s and the aging and dying off of the larger contingents of migrants from the late nineteenth century caused the proportion of foreign born to decline to only 5 percent by 1970. The opening of the migration gate a crack wider during the 1970s has caused a reversal or suspension of this trend. Unless the volume of inflow becomes even larger, however, the proportion will again decline in 1980-90 because of increasing population size.

Definitions

Nativity. Classification as native or foreign born, according to place of birth. The "native" category comprises persons born in the United States, Puerto Rico, or possessions of the United States, as well as the small number of persons born at sea or in a foreign country with at least one American parent. Persons not classifiable as "native" are classified as "foreign born."

Country of Birth. For the native population, the United States, broken down further as persons born in the state in which they were residing at the time of the census; persons born in a different state, by region; and persons born abroad or at sea with at least one American parent. For the foreign born, the country of birth is identified according to international boundaries as recognized by the United States government on April 1, 1980, rather than boundaries that existed at the time of birth or emigration or a country reported as a matter of national preference.

Ancestry. A person's nationality group, lineage, or the country in which the person's parents or ancestors were born before their arrival in the United States, regardless of the number of generations removed from country of origin. Responses to the ancestry question in the 1980 census reflected the ethnic group(s) with which persons identified and not necessarily the degree of attachment or association the person had with the particular group. Persons reporting a particular ancestry may be of any race or country of birth and may report any language spoken at home.

Language Spoken at Home; Ability to Speak English. Data derived from answers to the following questions from the 1980 census questionnaire: (13a) "Does this person speak a language other than English at home?" (13b) If yes, "What is this language?" (13c) "How well does this person speak English?"

Language Spoken at Home. Answers to question 13b, coded in accordance with a detailed language list that distinguished approximately 400 languages. In most reports only a few of the most widely used languages can be shown separately; the rest of the languages reported specifically have been grouped in an "other specified language" category. Languages not on the detailed language list, not identified by the respondent, or not otherwise identifiable based on other information supplied by the person were placed in an "unspecified language" category.

Ability to Speak English. Respondents' subjective evaluations of facility in English in homes where a language other than English was reported as spoken. These responses were a person's own perception about his or her ability or, because census forms are usually filled by only one household member, the perception of another household member.

Mother Tongue (Previous Censuses). For most census years, 1910-40 and in 1960 and 1970, the language spoken in childhood or the language spoken before a foreign-born person immigrated to the United States. In the 1910 and 1920 censuses statistics on mother tongue were published for the foreign stock (foreign born and native of foreign or mixed parentage) white population; in 1930 for the foreign-born white population; in 1940 for native white of native parentage and the white foreign stock; in 1960 for all foreign-born persons; and in 1970 for all persons. Ability to speak English, a simple "yes" or "no" question, was asked in the censuses of 1890 through 1930.

Citizenship and Year of Immigration. Data derived from answers to questions 12a and 12b of the 1980 census questionnaire: "(If this person was born in a foreign country) 12a. Is this person a naturalized citizen of the United States? 12b. When did this person come to the United States to stay?" Persons born abroad or at sea with at least one American parent were to report themselves as "born abroad of American parents."

Citizenship. Status as belonging to one of two categories: citizens and noncitizens; citizens are further classified as native or naturalized. (It was assumed that all native persons were citizens.) Questions on citizenship were asked in the decennial censuses of 1820, 1830, 1870, 1890-1950, and 1970.

Year of Immigration. The year the respondent came to stay permanently in the United States. A question on year of immigration was asked in each decennial census from 1890 to 1930 and in 1980.

Parentage (1970 and earlier censuses). According to birthplace of parents, the native population is divided into two categories: native of native parentage (both parents born in the United States) and native

Continued on next page

Definitions

of foreign or mixed parentage (one or both parents foreign born). The rules for determining the nativity of parents are generally the same as those for determining the nativity of the person.

Foreign Stock (1970 and earlier censuses). A category that includes the foreign-born population and the native population of foreign or mixed parentage, thus comprising all first- and second-generation Americans. When classified according to country of origin, second-generation Americans whose parents were born in different foreign countries are classified according to the country of birth of the father, and those with one native parent classified according to the country of birth of the foreign-born parent.

Race and Foreign Birth

A significant new development, resulting from the new immigration policies described in Chapter 7, is the renewal of black immigration. As Table 8-1 shows, before World War II almost all immigration was white; immigration of black population was negligible. Not since the end of the slave trade had large numbers of black persons immigrated to the United States. After World War II black immigrants from the Caribbean began to alter this pattern. Opening up the quotas to immigrants from Africa in the 1970s helped to cause a rise in the percentage of all foreign born who are black from 2.6 in 1970 to 5.8 percent in 1980. In 1960 and before it was customary and valid to think of the foreign-born population as a white population. By 1980 this presumption was outdated.

More than one-half of the Asian and Pacific Islander race group (59 percent) and more than one-quarter (29 percent) of the Spanish-origin residents were foreign born in 1980, as Table 8-2 shows. The two groups have been prominent in immigration since World War II and especially during the 1970s.

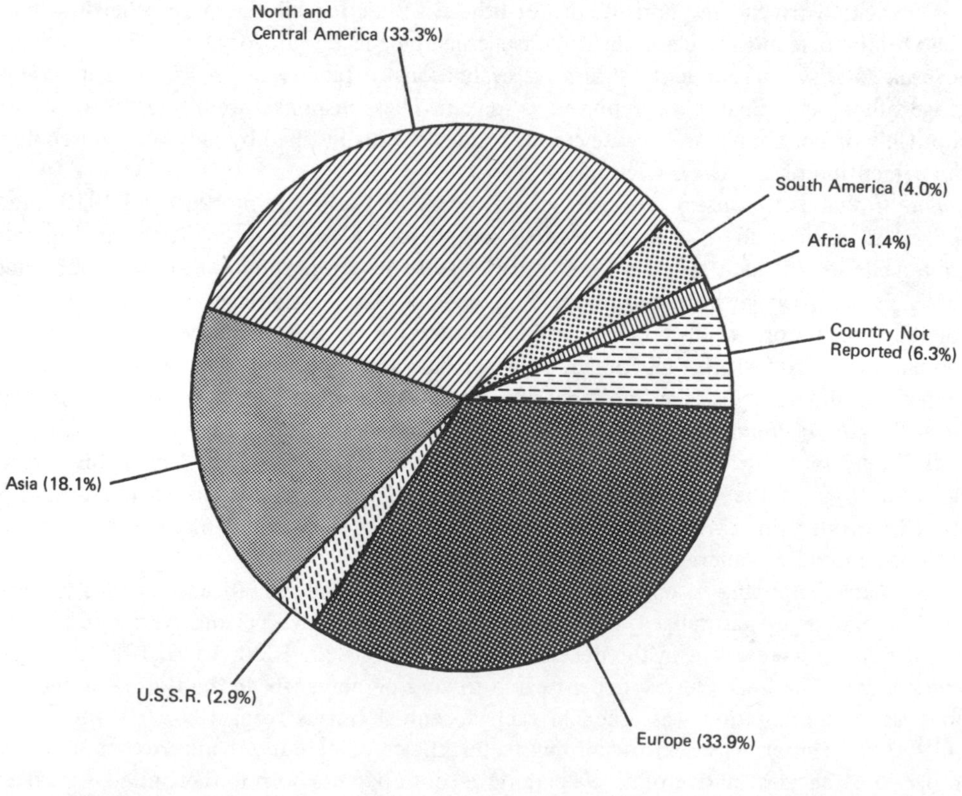

Figure 8-1. Percent Distribution of Immigrants, by Continent: 1950-1980

Table 8-1. Foreign-Born Population, by Race: 1850-1980 [numbers in thousands]

Year	Foreign-born population			Percent foreign born			Percent foreign born, black
	Total	White	Black	Total	White	Black	
1980. . .	14,080	9,324	816	6.2	4.9	3.1	5.8
1970. . .	9,619	8,734	253	4.7	4.9	1.1	2.6
1960. . .	9,738	9,294	125	5.4	5.9	0.7	1.3
1950. . .	10,431	10,095	114	6.9	7.5	0.8	1.1
1940. . .	11,657	11,419	84	8.8	9.6	0.7	0.7
1930. . .	14,283	13,983	99	11.6	12.7	0.8	0.7
1920. . .	14,020	13,713	74	13.2	14.5	0.7	0.5
1910. . .	13,630	13,346	40	14.8	16.3	0.4	0.3
1900. . .	10,445	10,214	20	13.7	15.3	0.2	0.2
1890. . .	9,250	9,122	--	14.7	16.6	--	--
1880. . .	6,680	6,560	14	13.3	15.1	0.2	0.2
1870. . .	5,567	5,494	10	14.4	16.4	0.2	0.2
1860. . .	--	4,097	--	--	15.2	--	--
1850. . .	--	2,241	--	--	11.5	--	--

Note: -- indicates data not available.

Source: U.S. Bureau of the Census. "General Social and Economic Characteristics: United States Summary." 1980 Census of Population. Washington, DC: U.S. Government Printing Office, 1983, Table 77. Data for 1980 and before from Historical Statistics of the United States: Colonial Times to 1970. Washington, DC: U.S. Government Printing Office, 1975.

Age and Foreign Birth

Table 8-2 shows that the proportion of foreign-birth residents rises with age for the white, Asian, and Spanish-origin populations. This reflects the past history of immigration and the fact that a disproportionate share of most immigrants are adult. The numbers of immigrating children usually are significant only in refugee movements. The high proportion of foreign born white population at ages seventy and over consists of the migrants from Italy, Poland, and other countries of Europe who arrived between 1890 and 1920.

Country of Birth of the Foreign Born

The countries of birth of the 14.1 million foreign-born persons are shown in Table 8-3. For each nationality group, a percentage distribution of the year of immigration is provided. A final column reports what percentage of the group has become naturalized U.S. citizens. The multiethnic nature of the United States population can be fully appreciated when the number of residents from the various nations of the world are noted. All continents and all major nations of all continents (except for the Middle East and Africa) are well represented. The nations with at least 100,000 immigrants residing in the United States in 1980 are as follows:

Nation	Foreign born (000)
Mexico	2,199
Germany	849
Canada	843
Italy	832
United Kingdom	669
Cuba	608
Philippines	501
Poland	418
U.S.S.R.	406
Korea	290
China	286
Vietnam	231
Japan	222
Greece	211
India	206
Ireland	198
Jamaica	197
Portugal	177
Dominican Republic	169
Yugoslavia	153
Austria	146
Hungary	144
Colombia	144
Iran	122
France	120
Czechoslovakia	113
Netherlands	103

Table 8-2. Percent Foreign-Born and Percentage of Foreign-Born Naturalized, by Race and Age: 1980

Age	Percent foreign born				Percent foreign born naturalized			
	White	Black	Asian & Pacific Islander	Spanish-origin	White	Black	Asian & Pacific Islander	Spanish-origin
All ages.	4.9	3.1	58.6	28.6	59.8	43.8	33.3	30.0
Under 5 years	0.8	0.8	18.4	5.1	30.3	60.1	13.8	20.5
5-9 years	1.4	1.3	40.7	11.2	25.9	48.5	17.1	17.9
10-14 years	1.9	2.0	50.1	16.0	27.7	39.4	22.4	18.9
15-19 years	2.6	2.8	52.0	24.0	31.1	37.2	25.1	20.2
20-24 years	3.7	3.6	58.3	33.7	35.7	34.1	23.8	22.9
25-29 years	4.3	4.3	69.7	38.0	37.7	32.1	22.4	25.6
30-34 years	5.0	4.8	76.3	38.7	44.4	34.6	31.2	28.4
35-39 years	5.6	5.1	77.3	42.1	47.0	40.9	42.2	32.4
40-44 years	6.5	4.8	77.1	43.2	52.9	45.2	48.5	36.1
45-49 years	6.1	4.1	69.5	40.5	58.1	50.4	52.6	37.3
50-54 years	6.0	3.6	59.1	37.8	65.6	54.9	51.5	39.8
55-59 years	6.2	3.3	50.9	38.5	72.5	59.2	44.2	42.2
60-64 years	5.2	3.1	51.7	40.7	74.4	63.7	37.4	43.5
65-69 years	7.5	2.7	60.8	46.3	79.8	66.1	40.4	44.5
70-74 years	10.4	2.5	67.4	52.3	84.3	67.8	47.9	44.2
75-79 years	14.5	3.0	67.2	57.4	87.1	73.7	51.0	46.0
80-84 years	16.7	3.6	67.9	56.2	88.9	79.0	51.2	51.3
85 years and over . . .	19.1	3.4	70.7	58.3	87.9	76.6	48.6	47.9

Source: U.S. Bureau of the Census. "Detailed Population Characteristics: United States Summary." 1980 Census of Population. Washington, DC: U.S. Government Printing Office, 1983, Table 253.

The oldest immigrant groups (50 percent or more immigrated before 1950) are:

Nation	Percentage arriving before 1950
Lithuania	71
Sweden.	71
Austria	70
Norway.	67
Czechoslovakia.	61
England	58
U.S.S.R..	58
Ireland	57
Wales	57
Finland	56
Poland.	56
Scotland.	55
Denmark	54
Italy	52

The newest immigrant groups (those with the highest percentage having arrived between 1975 and 1980), some of which have attracted comparatively little public attention, are:

Nation	Percentage arriving between 1975 and 1980
Vietnam	91
Iran.	72
Korea	52
El Salvador	51
Lebanon	49
Thailand.	46
Guyana.	46
India	44
Guatemala	40
Hong Kong	35
Haiti	34
Israel.	34
Philippines	34
Mexico.	33
Egypt	32
Brazil.	32
Japan	32
Peru.	32
Dominican Republic.	31
Jamaica	31
Barbados.	30
Colombia.	30

The groups with the highest percentages of naturalized citizens are, of course, the older migrants from Europe.

Table 8-3. Country of Birth, Year of Immigration, and Citizenship of the Foreign Born: 1980

Country of birth	Foreign-born persons	Percent immigrated							Percent natural-ized
		Total	1975 to 1980	1970 to 1974	1965 to 1969	1960 to 1964	1950 to 1959	Before 1950	
Total	14,079,906	100.0	23.7	15.8	12.8	9.4	13.6	24.7	50.5
Europe.	4,743,550	100.0	8.1	7.5	9.9	9.2	21.4	43.8	72.3
Austria	145,607	100.0	2.7	1.8	3.1	4.5	17.7	70.2	87.0
Azores.	32,531	100.0	18.1	17.7	26.2	7.7	9.7	20.7	43.1
Belgium	36,487	100.0	10.6	4.6	6.0	8.7	21.3	48.9	72.4
Czechoslovakia. . . .	112,707	100.0	3.3	4.3	10.4	4.6	16.3	61.2	87.4
Denmark	42,732	100.0	8.4	3.9	6.3	8.8	18.3	54.4	72.5
Finland	29,172	100.0	10.4	4.7	7.1	8.0	14.2	55.7	69.4
France.	120,215	100.0	13.9	7.2	10.1	13.8	22.6	32.4	64.1
Germany	849,384	100.0	6.2	4.4	8.0	12.6	32.4	36.3	78.6
Greece.	210,998	100.0	12.9	19.1	19.9	7.9	16.6	23.7	65.0
Hungary	144,368	100.0	3.8	4.5	5.4	5.4	34.4	46.6	86.0
Ireland	197,817	100.0	3.7	3.6	5.1	9.4	20.8	57.3	81.2
Italy	831,922	100.0	4.0	8.1	10.0	8.1	17.7	52.0	77.4
Latvia.	34,349	100.0	1.5	0.9	1.6	2.7	51.4	41.8	80.6
Lithuania	48,194	100.0	1.5	1.2	1.8	3.0	21.9	70.8	83.9
Netherlands	103,136	100.0	8.3	4.4	7.3	13.9	33.0	33.0	68.2
Norway.	63,316	100.0	6.0	2.3	3.9	5.7	15.0	67.3	77.8
Poland.	418,128	100.0	6.0	5.0	6.3	8.2	18.5	56.0	77.8
Portugal.	177,437	100.0	22.5	24.4	26.2	8.0	6.9	12.0	37.3
Rumania	66,994	100.0	17.0	10.2	9.1	7.7	17.8	38.3	73.4
Spain	73,735	100.0	17.1	17.9	19.5	15.0	9.3	21.4	49.1
Sweden.	77,157	100.0	7.9	2.8	4.3	4.5	9.5	71.0	76.8
Switzerland	42,804	100.0	14.3	5.8	7.8	9.5	19.0	43.5	67.8
United Kingdon. . . .	669,149	100.0	12.7	7.0	10.8	10.7	18.4	40.5	60.0
England	442,499	100.0	14.3	7.6	11.2	10.8	18.6	37.5	58.0
Northern Ireland. .	19,831	100.0	8.3	7.0	8.7	11.0	21.4	43.6	66.0
Scotland.	142,001	100.0	5.9	4.2	8.1	9.6	16.9	55.3	71.4
Wales	13,528	100.0	8.6	5.0	7.9	7.5	13.8	57.2	67.4
Yugoslavia.	152,967	100.0	7.4	16.2	16.4	7.5	26.6	25.8	67.6
Other European. . . .	62,244	100.0	10.5	8.3	10.5	7.0	24.1	39.7	70.0
U.S.S.R..	406,022	100.0	21.1	3.2	2.3	3.0	12.6	57.8	72.6
Asia.	2,539,777	100.0	47.0	22.4	12.0	6.0	6.4	6.1	34.8
China	286,120	100.0	27.2	20.3	17.1	10.1	10.6	14.6	50.3
Hong Kong	80,380	100.0	34.9	27.6	22.1	8.8	4.6	2.0	38.3
India	206,087	100.0	43.7	33.1	14.8	4.4	2.6	1.3	24.0
Iran.	121,505	100.0	71.9	12.7	5.9	3.8	3.6	2.1	14.6
Isreal.	66,961	100.0	34.1	18.9	15.1	9.9	14.5	7.5	51.8
Japan	221,794	100.0	31.6	13.6	10.8	11.9	21.8	10.3	43.3
Korea	289,885	100.0	52.3	31.6	8.7	4.3	2.6	0.4	34.6
Lebanon	52,674	100.0	48.9	18.1	8.4	4.5	5.9	14.1	41.0
Philippines	501,440	100.0	34.4	29.2	17.0	5.5	5.4	8.4	44.7
Thailand.	54,803	100.0	46.3	38.3	12.5	1.6	1.1	0.2	19.7
Turkey.	51,915	100.0	22.7	15.4	12.6	8.6	8.0	32.7	54.6
Vietnam	231,120	100.0	90.5	7.1	1.8	0.4	0.2	0.1	11.1
Other Asia.	375,093	100.0	59.0	18.5	9.2	5.8	4.6	3.0	26.8
North and Central America	4,664,903	100.0	25.3	20.9	16.4	11.8	10.7	14.9	34.9
Canada.	842,859	100.0	9.8	5.4	9.1	11.1	18.6	46.1	61.0
El Salvador	94,447	100.0	51.3	25.9	11.1	5.7	3.3	2.8	14.3
Guatemala	63,073	100.0	40.1	29.2	18.3	6.0	4.1	2.3	17.9
Mexico.	2,199,221	100.0	33.0	24.7	13.0	8.9	10.1	10.2	23.6
West Indies	1,258,363	100.0	18.6	24.1	27.7	17.8	7.1	4.7	38.9
Barbados.	26,847	100.0	29.5	26.3	18.1	6.3	6.2	13.6	42.4
Cuba.	607,814	100.0	6.3	20.5	32.2	28.2	9.4	3.4	45.1
Dominican Republic.	169,147	100.0	31.0	25.8	24.9	12.3	3.9	2.1	25.5
Haiti	92,395	100.0	33.6	31.0	23.4	7.4	3.3	1.3	26.1
Jamaica	196,811	100.0	30.6	28.0	24.1	5.6	5.2	6.4	36.3
Trinidad and Tobago.	65,907	100.0	27.6	34.2	25.8	5.0	3.4	4.0	29.3
Other West Indies . . .	99,442	100.0	25.2	22.0	19.8	9.0	8.9	15.1	46.8
Other North and Central America . .	206,940	100.0	29.8	19.2	16.5	13.5	12.7	8.3	38.6

Table 8-3. Country of Birth, Year of Immigration, and Citizenship of the Foreign Born: 1980—continued

Country of birth	Foreign-born persons	Percent immigration							Percent natural-ized
		Total	1975 to 1980	1970 to 1974	1965 to 1969	1960 to 1964	1950 to 1959	Before 1950	
South America	561,011	100.0	32.6	23.6	20.4	12.6	6.6	4.1	28.9
Argentina	68,887	100.0	25.3	17.9	20.9	19.4	10.1	6.4	38.8
Brazil.	40,919	100.0	32.1	16.0	18.4	12.9	9.3	11.3	35.3
Colombia.	143,508	100.0	29.5	25.4	24.2	13.0	5.7	2.2	24.9
Ecuador	86,128	100.0	25.5	27.7	26.0	13.1	5.7	1.9	24.7
Guyana.	48,608	100.0	46.1	26.4	17.5	3.1	2.9	4.0	31.2
Peru.	55,496	100.0	31.7	27.7	15.9	15.0	6.8	2.9	28.8
Other South America	117,465	100.0	40.9	21.4	15.2	10.7	6.9	4.9	27.9
Africa.	199,723	100.0	43.8	21.2	11.9	7.3	7.6	8.2	37.0
North Africa.	71,450	100.0	35.1	19.3	17.4	10.6	10.7	6.8	51.3
Egypt	43,424	100.0	32.4	24.1	20.6	9.8	8.0	5.1	55.2
Other Africa.	128,273	100.0	48.7	22.2	8.9	5.5	5.8	8.9	29.1
All other countries . .	78,896	100.0	35.7	16.6	12.3	7.2	9.1	19.1	40.7
Country not reported.	886,024	100.0	22.0	13.8	12.2	9.3	13.7	29.0	68.7

Source: U.S. Bureau fo the Census. "Detailed Population Characteristics: United States Summary." 1980 Census of Population. Washington, DC: U.S. Government Printing Office, 1983.

The lowest percentages of naturalized citizens belong to the groups from the following countries:

Nation	Percentage of natural-ized citizens
Vietnam	11
El Salvador	14
Iran.	15
Guatemala	18
Thailand.	20
India	24
Mexico.	24
Ecuador	25
Colombia.	25

Place of Residence of the Foreign Born

The foreign-born population is not evenly distributed throughout the United States. Particular nationality groups, in fact, tend to be concentrated in particular localities. Table 8-4A presents these patterns in broad outline. The distribution of each foreign-born group by country of birth is shown for regions, by residence in metropolitan and nonmetropolitan areas, and by urban-rural residence. The table shows:

1. Groups from Northwest Europe are more evenly distributed throughout the regions and are more inclined to live in suburbs and nonmetropolitan areas and in rural areas than other foreign-born groups.

2. Immigrants from Asia are highly concentrated in the West region and in central cities of other regions.

3. Immigrants from Italy, Poland, and other nations of Eastern and Southern Europe are most inclined to live in the Northeast and North Central regions, in central cities, or in metropolitan rings, but not in nonmetropolitan areas.

4. Immigrants from Mexico and Latin America are inclined to concentrate in the South and West and in central cities of all regions.

Many of these details have already been described in Chapter 2 as a part of race-ethnicity composition. Table 8-4A simply provides more nation-of-origin detail.

Table 8-4B provides a distribution of the country of birth of the foreign-born population for each of the fifteen largest cities of the nation in 1980. No two of these largest places have similar proportions and distributions of foreign-born persons.

Characteristics of the Foreign Born, by Country

Selected indicators of population composition or population dynamics for the principal countries or origin of the foreign-born population, in comparison with the native-born population, are provided in Table 8-5. The

Table 8-4A. Place of Residence of the Foreign-Born Population: 1980

Country of origin	Region				Metropolitan		Nonmetropolitan	Urban	Rural
	Northeast	North central	South	West	Central city	Metro ring			
Number of foreign born persons	4,505,923	2,114,190	2,894,757	4,565,036	6,424,775	5,593,356	1,159,721	12,914,965	1,164,941
Percent of population foreign born	9.2	3.6	3.8	10.6	9.6	7.8	2.0	7.7	2.0
Total foreign-born	100.0	100.0	100.0	100.0	100.0	100.0	100.0	100.0	100.0
Europe	47.7	46.8	24.0	20.0	29.4	37.2	37.5	32.9	42.0
Austria.	1.5	1.5	0.8	0.5	1.0	1.1	1.0	1.0	1.3
Czechoslovakia	1.1	1.6	0.5	0.4	0.7	0.9	0.9	0.8	1.1
France	0.9	0.8	1.1	0.7	0.7	0.9	1.1	0.8	1.2
Germany.	6.0	9.2	6.7	4.1	4.3	6.6	10.1	5.5	11.6
Greece	2.4	2.4	1.0	0.5	1.7	1.5	0.8	1.6	0.6
Hungary.	1.4	1.7	0.7	0.6	0.9	1.2	0.8	1.0	1.2
Ireland.	2.8	1.3	0.6	0.6	1.4	1.5	1.0	1.4	1.2
Italy.	12.6	5.7	2.1	1.8	5.7	7.0	4.0	6.1	3.7
Netherlands.	0.5	1.2	0.5	0.9	0.4	0.9	1.2	0.6	1.7
Poland	4.8	5.9	1.5	0.8	3.4	2.9	1.8	3.0	2.1
Portugal	3.1	0.1	0.2	0.7	1.3	1.3	1.1	1.3	0.9
Sweden	0.4	1.1	0.4	0.5	0.4	0.6	1.2	0.5	1.1
United Kingdom	4.9	5.4	4.9	4.2	3.1	5.8	6.7	4.5	7.9
England.	2.9	3.5	3.5	3.0	2.1	3.7	4.8	2.9	5.5
Northern Ireland . .	0.2	0.1	0.1	0.1	0.1	0.2	0.2	0.1	0.2
Scotland	1.3	1.3	0.9	0.7	0.6	1.4	1.3	1.0	1.4
Wales.	0.1	0.1	0.1	0.1	0.1	0.1	0.1	0.1	0.2
Yugoslavia	1.1	3.3	0.3	0.6	1.1	1.2	0.6	1.1	0.9
U.S.S.R.	4.3	3.5	2.2	1.7	3.5	2.6	2.2	2.9	2.2
Asia	11.7	18.7	15.5	25.6	18.8	18.8	14.2	18.6	11.3
China.	2.1	1.2	1.0	3.0	2.8	1.6	0.7	2.2	0.6
India.	1.6	2.4	1.6	0.8	1.2	1.9	1.1	1.5	1.0
Japan.	0.7	1.2	1.3	2.7	1.4	1.7	1.8	1.6	1.6
Korea.	1.2	2.5	2.1	2.6	1.8	2.4	1.9	2.1	1.8
Philippines.	1.3	2.8	2.0	7.1	3.6	3.7	3.2	3.6	2.8
Vietnam.	0.5	1.5	2.4	2.4	1.8	1.6	1.4	1.7	0.9
North and Central America.	22.6	20.8	42.9	43.0	34.9	30.4	33.4	33.2	32.0
Canada	6.1	7.4	4.6	6.1	3.7	6.8	12.3	5.4	12.3
Mexico	0.4	10.2	18.2	31.5	16.3	12.7	18.3	15.5	17.3
West Indies.	14.1	2.1	17.4	1.6	11.4	8.8	1.7	9.6	1.5
Cuba	3.1	1.0	13.7	1.1	3.9	6.1	0.8	4.6	0.6
Dominican Republic	3.4	0.1	0.4	0.1	2.2	0.5	0.1	1.3	0.1
Jamaica.	3.1	0.5	1.4	0.2	2.0	1.0	0.3	1.5	0.4
South America.	6.2	2.0	4.3	2.5	4.6	4.2	1.6	4.2	1.5
North Africa	0.6	0.5	0.5	0.5	0.5	0.5	0.3	0.5	0.3
Other Africa	0.9	1.1	1.3	0.6	1.1	0.8	1.0	0.9	0.7
All other countries. .	0.2	0.4	0.4	1.1	0.5	0.6	0.6	0.6	0.7
Country not reported	5.7	6.2	8.9	5.3	6.8	5.0	9.0	6.0	9.4

Sources: U.S. Bureau of the Census. "General Social and Economic Characteristics: United States Summary," and "Detailed Population Characteristics: United States Summary." 1980 Census of Population. Washington, DC: U.S. Government Printing Office, 1983.

foreign born are divided into recent (1970-80) and older (before 1970) arrivals. Furthermore, immigrants from principal "sending" nations and regions are shown separately.

Sex Ratio

In the very recent immigration, males outnumber females by a small margin. This is a reversal of a strong tendency for females to outnumber males (and to outsurvive males) for the older groups of immigrants. The predominance of males seems to be contributed primarily by Mexico, augmented by migrants from Greece, Italy, India, Vietnam, and Africa. Very low sex ratios are reported for Vietnamese migrants who came between 1970 and 1975 and for migrants from Korea, the Philippines, Cuba, Dominican Republic, Jamaica, and Canada.

Living Arrangements

Immigrants often provide living space in their homes for remote relatives or even nonrelatives who are later arrivals. That is particularly true of the immigrants during the 1970-80 decade, as is clear from Table 8-5. Of the immigrants who arrived during that decade, 11 percent were living as "other relatives" in the families of others, and 6 percent as "nonrelatives." Chinese, Filipinos, Vietnamese, Mexicans, Haitians, and Dominican

Table 8-4B. Foreign-Born Population in the Fifteen Largest Cities of the United States: 1980

Country of origin	New York City	Chicago	Los Angeles	Phila-delphia	Houston	Detroit	Dallas	San Diego	Phoenix	Bal-timore	San Antonio	Indian-apolis	San Fran-cisco	Memphis	Wash-ington DC
Number of foreign-born persons. . .	1,946,800	744,930	1,664,793	242,658	220,861	282,766	124,697	235,593	82,536	73,804	76,944	18,905	509,352	11,686	249,994
Percent of population foreign-born.	21.3	10.5	22.3	5.1	7.6	6.5	4.2	12.7	5.5	3.4	7.2	1.6	15.7	1.3	8.2
Total, foreign-born.	100.0	100.0	100.0	100.0	100.0	100.0	100.0	100.0	100.0	100.0	100.0	100.0	100.0	100.0	100.0
Europe.	37.7	40.9	13.0	54.8	11.7	47.9	16.4	18.5	30.6	45.4	13.8	43.3	23.8	29.0	26.9
Austria	1.6	1.2	0.4	1.6	0.3	1.2	0.4	0.4	0.9	1.1	0.3	1.1	0.6	0.6	0.8
Czechoslovakia. . .	1.0	1.4	0.3	0.8	0.3	0.9	0.4	0.3	0.7	1.2	0.3	0.5	0.4	0.4	0.6
France.	0.8	0.5	0.5	0.9	0.7	0.7	0.9	0.7	1.4	1.0	0.8	1.4	1.1	1.4	1.8
Germany	4.3	6.0	2.1	9.4	2.6	6.3	5.0	3.7	7.2	11.2	5.8	13.8	4.2	9.4	6.2
Greece.	2.4	3.2	0.4	2.5	0.7	2.1	0.5	0.5	0.8	4.4	0.2	1.3	0.8	1.0	1.9
Hungary	1.3	0.9	0.7	1.6	0.3	1.6	0.4	0.4	1.2	1.0	0.2	1.2	0.5	0.4	0.7
Ireland	2.7	2.0	0.3	3.8	0.2	1.0	0.4	0.5	0.9	1.4	0.5	1.4	1.2	0.6	0.7
Italy	10.5	6.0	1.3	14.9	0.7	8.0	0.7	2.0	3.4	6.4	0.6	1.6	3.3	3.6	2.4
Netherlands	0.2	0.5	0.5	0.5	0.5	0.6	0.5	0.7	0.9	0.7	0.2	1.5	0.8	1.0	0.6
Poland.	4.6	8.4	1.0	4.7	0.5	7.6	0.6	0.7	1.8	4.4	0.5	1.4	0.6	1.7	1.1
Portugal.	0.5	0.1	0.2	0.9	0.1	*	*	0.8	0.1	0.1	0.1	*	1.4	0.2	0.6
Sweden.	0.2	0.9	0.2	0.3	0.1	0.3	0.2	0.5	0.5	0.4	0.1	0.5	0.6	0.3	0.3
United Kingdon. . .	2.5	2.5	2.8	7.8	3.2	8.1	4.6	4.7	6.4	6.9	3.0	9.7	4.1	6.3	5.2
England	1.6	1.6	1.9	4.6	2.2	4.4	3.4	3.2	4.3	4.7	2.3	6.6	2.8	4.9	3.6
Northern Ireland	0.1	0.1	0.1	0.5	*	0.2	0.1	0.1	0.1	0.1	0.1	0.4	0.1	0.2	0.1
Scotland. . . .	0.6	0.6	0.5	2.1	0.4	3.0	0.6	1.0	1.4	1.3	0.3	1.5	0.7	0.6	0.7
Wales	*	*	*	0.2	0.1	0.2	0.1	0.1	0.1	0.2	*	0.3	0.1	0.1	0.1
Yugoslavia. . . .	1.3	3.0	0.6	1.0	0.2	3.7	0.2	0.5	1.1	0.4	0.1	0.9	0.5	0.2	0.3
U.S.S.R..	4.9	3.3	2.1	8.9	0.7	3.5	0.9	0.9	2.1	6.0	0.5	2.9	1.9	4.5	1.8
Asia.	13.1	17.2	20.4	16.7	21.7	18.3	21.2	27.4	12.7	25.7	9.7	26.2	42.3	31.5	32.0
China	3.3	1.2	2.0	1.4	2.1	0.9	1.5	1.0	1.6	1.8	0.5	2.1	11.0	3.0	2.8
India	1.4	2.9	0.6	2.7	3.5	2.2	2.4	0.4	0.8	3.2	0.6	3.3	1.3	2.4	3.6
Japan	0.9	0.8	2.0	0.9	1.1	0.6	1.5	2.8	1.5	1.7	1.7	1.8	2.7	4.4	1.6
Korea	1.2	2.3	3.0	3.4	1.4	1.1	2.0	0.9	1.6	7.6	1.1	4.9	1.8	2.8	5.9
Philippines	1.3	4.3	4.4	2.1	1.9	2.0	1.8	13.0	1.3	3.9	1.7	4.0	13.2	4.3	3.6
Vietnam	0.2	0.6	1.7	1.4	5.3	0.4	3.8	3.3	1.6	1.5	1.5	3.1	2.2	2.8	3.6
North and Central America	27.4	28.7	54.8	9.5	51.0	23.1	48.5	44.9	44.6	10.2	69.4	13.4	21.9	13.1	17.4
Canada.	1.2	2.2	3.4	3.2	2.3	19.9	3.8	5.9	10.8	3.2	1.6	6.8	4.1	7.2	3.3
Mexico.	0.4	21.6	41.9	0.6	42.4	1.7	40.0	36.9	31.9	0.2	64.9	2.3	11.0	1.3	0.9
West Indies	22.6	3.2	2.7	4.8	3.8	1.2	2.8	0.9	0.8	5.6	1.3	2.8	1.0	2.4	8.4
Cuba.	2.8	1.9	2.1	1.2	2.0	0.3	2.0	0.3	0.3	0.9	0.7	1.6	0.6	1.5	2.0
Dominican Republic. . . .	6.6	0.1	*	0.3	0.1	0.1	0.1	0.1	0.1	0.2	0.1	0.1	*	0.1	0.5
Jamaica	5.1	0.6	0.2	1.7	0.5	0.4	0.2	0.2	0.1	2.0	0.2	0.4	0.2	0.3	2.8
South America . . .	8.8	2.5	3.5	2.5	3.9	1.0	2.4	1.7	1.9	3.3	1.0	3.0	2.5	1.7	9.6
North Africa. . . .	0.6	0.3	0.6	0.5	0.5	0.4	0.6	0.3	0.3	0.7	0.3	0.5	0.5	0.3	1.3
Other Africa. . . .	0.7	0.8	0.5	1.1	1.7	0.5	1.5	0.5	0.6	1.6	0.3	1.6	0.6	1.1	3.8
All other countries	0.2	0.2	0.5	0.3	0.3	0.2	0.5	1.0	0.6	0.6	0.3	0.6	1.6	1.3	0.8
Country not reported	6.5	6.2	4.7	5.6	8.5	5.0	7.9	4.8	6.6	6.4	4.8	8.5	4.9	17.4	6.4

Note: * indicates amount less than 0.1 percent.

Source: U.S. Bureau of the Census. "General Social and Economic Characteristics: United States Summary." 1980 Census of Population. Washington, DC: U.S. Government Printing Office, 1983.

Republic immigrants are particularly likely to shelter other relatives, while Vietnamese, Haitians, Mexicans, South Americans, and Africans tend to reside as nonrelatives as well.

Size of Household and Family

The average size of the household or family for the foreign born is nearly 20 percent greater than for the native born. This can be a result of sheltering additional family members (see above), greater fertility, or both. Largest size of families (four persons or more) is found among immigrants from Mexico, Vietnam, and the Philippines.

Families Headed by a Female Householder

In general, immigrants are less prone than native Americans to have families headed by a female householder. Outstanding exceptions (perhaps dictated by the sex composition of the migration stream) are people from the Dominican Republic (36 percent), Jamaica (26 percent), and Vietnam (36 percent for those who immigrated between 1970 and 1974).

Table 8-5. Selected Characteristics of Native and Foreign-Born Populations: 1980

Characteristic	Native born	Immigrated 1970–80	Immigrated before 1970	North and Central America							South America	Africa
				Total	Canada	Cuba	Dominican Rep.	Haiti	Jamaica	Mexico		
Number of persons	212,465,899	5,560,363	8,519,543	2,153,322	127,905	163,224	96,014	59,729	115,456	1,270,246	315,602	129,874
Sex ratio	94.9	101.8	79.6	106.0	88.7	87.9	88.5	99.7	89.0	121.0	93.4	153.2
Living arrangements (percent)												
Other relatives	3.8	11.2	6.3	12.8	2.1	12.6	15.8	15.7	11.1	13.6	10.6	6.3
Nonrelatives	2.6	6.0	2.3	6.8	5.3	2.7	4.6	7.3	5.3	7.2	6.2	6.7
Inmate of institution	1.1	0.3	2.2	0.2	0.4	0.2	0.2	0.1	0.3	0.2	0.2	0.1
Other group quarters	1.4	2.2	1.1	1.5	4.2	0.4	0.6	1.4	2.3	1.2	1.9	4.4
Persons per household	2.73	3.36	2.68	3.74	2.65	3.04	3.45	3.49	3.22	4.21	3.15	2.61
Persons per family	3.25	3.81	3.30	4.04	3.17	3.43	3.70	3.81	3.73	4.39	3.58	3.36
Percent families with female head of household, no husband	13.9	11.6	14.2	14.7	7.0	14.3	35.8	23.1	25.6	9.7	14.3	6.4
Percent families with subfamilies	2.3	5.4	1.7	6.0	1.3	5.4	6.3	5.4	7.7	6.3	4.7	1.9
Children ever born, per 1,000												
15–24 years	313	429	330	566	186	207	451	342	319	726	259	338
25–34 years	1,470	1,519	1,626	1,974	1,113	1,175	1,628	1,593	1,525	2,378	1,271	1,375
35–44 years	2,652	2,571	2,478	3,338	2,036	1,965	3,014	2,744	2,691	4,341	2,182	2,223
Education, persons 25+ years												
Percent less than 5 years	2.9	11.1	12.8	21.7	0.9	11.4	21.3	10.9	4.0	32.9	4.5	2.7
Percent high school graduates	67.7	51.5	56.9	33.2	78.0	40.2	27.1	55.9	60.7	17.0	66.2	88.5
Percent 4+ years of college	16.3	13.2	22.2	6.9	30.0	10.3	3.4	9.5	9.7	2.7	18.3	43.3
Percent speaking non-English language at home	6.8	61.7	83.7	84.0	23.7	98.4	98.3	96.1	6.2	98.5	84.8	78.9
Percent non-English speakers who also speak English	90.6	77.8	59.6	43.2	94.0	44.4	39.1	69.5	90.4	38.5	64.8	89.2
Percent in labor force												
Males	75.1	65.2	77.6	83.8	73.1	73.2	75.7	78.2	76.7	88.2	75.0	64.6
Females	50.4	39.9	50.8	50.5	47.7	51.5	49.2	63.1	66.5	44.8	51.6	48.2
Percent unemployed												
Males	6.6	5.3	7.2	8.7	3.9	6.8	11.4	12.3	9.8	8.8	6.4	7.0
Females	6.4	6.3	9.4	11.6	5.1	10.4	13.5	14.6	7.9	13.9	10.2	10.2
Mean weeks of unemployment	14.0	15.0	14.0	14.6	11.6	14.3	15.1	18.0	15.9	14.4	13.6	14.5
Mean number of workers per family	1.6	1.5	1.6	1.7	1.5	1.7	1.5	1.7	1.8	1.7	1.6	1.5
Median income per family ($)	20,069	18,959	15,244	12,455	23,910	14,510	9,569	11,966	16,094	11,782	14,795	15,109
Mean income per family ($)	23,183	23,299	18,626	15,020	29,777	16,795	11,719	13,889	17,976	13,512	18,058	19,574
Percent families below poverty level	9.4	8.7	20.7	25.1	8.4	20.5	36.1	25.6	15.7	28.2	18.4	21.1
Percent unrelated individuals below poverty level	24.7	24.3	40.1	42.7	30.6	50.3	42.7	45.0	32.5	44.6	39.8	45.7
Persons below poverty level	25,250,116	888,579	1,253,885	574,101	13,960	34,078	30,920	15,105	18,394	388,332	60,384	32,459

Table 8-5. Selected Characteristics of Native and Foreign-Born Populations: 1980–continued

Characteristic	Europe					Asia						
	Total	Greece	Italy	Portugal	United Kingdom	Total	China	India	Korea	Philip-pines	Vietnam	
											1970–74	1975–80
Number of persons	741,570	67,428	100,453	83,235	131,796	1,763,129	136,029	158,333	243,299	319,039	16,428	209,214
Sex ratio	96.0	129.8	114.0	103.2	90.4	97.2	97.9	112.0	69.0	71.7	47.5	118.2
Living arrangements (percent)												
Other relatives	6.7	10.6	7.4	7.9	3.4	11.8	14.6	8.8	7.5	18.1	3.8	15.7
Nonrelatives	4.3	2.7	1.4	1.4	4.7	4.8	4.0	2.8	1.9	4.1	3.6	6.2
Inmate of institution	0.2	0.1	0.1	*	0.2	0.1	0.1	*	*	0.1	0.1	0.1
Other group quarters	1.3	1.2	0.6	0.4	1.5	2.5	2.1	1.4	1.6	2.2	0.7	1.6
Persons per household	2.98	3.23	3.52	3.71	2.67	3.33	3.47	3.12	3.48	3.63	3.08	4.44
Persons per family	3.46	3.60	3.79	3.84	3.20	3.84	3.86	3.48	3.85	4.04	3.58	4.78
Percent familes with female head of household, no husband	6.4	3.2	3.8	4.6	7.4	9.1	8.0	2.3	9.6	14.0	35.6	13.3
Percent families with subfamilies	3.7	5.7	4.6	4.7	1.9	6.1	7.9	4.0	4.4	13.6	1.8	5.4
Children ever born, per 1,000												
15–24 years	347	582	347	302	228	271	150	267	245	306	399	289
25–34 years	1,283	1,557	1,643	1,606	1,150	1,262	1,111	1,269	1,234	1,143	1,801	1,700
35–44 years	1,990	1,932	2,479	2,551	1,943	2,285	2,393	2,069	2,097	2,011	2,396	3,661
Education, persons 25+ years												
Percent less than 5 years	11.7	9.9	17.7	51.0	0.8	7.4	15.8	2.8	4.2	5.8	8.8	10.6
Percent high school graduates	60.4	41.5	33.4	19.3	88.6	74.5	59.7	87.2	77.4	77.1	66.6	60.8
Percent 4+ years of college	20.4	10.6	8.3	2.8	30.5	37.4	27.6	63.1	31.6	47.9	18.5	11.2
Percent speaking non-English language at home	73.7	96.6	95.5	98.2	8.2	92.3	98.5	90.0	88.4	89.9	72.0	96.8
Percent non-English speakers who also speak English	67.9	64.3	61.4	46.9	94.8	72.7	48.2	90.3	65.3	90.2	88.0	54.4
Percent in labor force												
Males	84.0	83.9	85.2	89.5	85.4	70.0	76.5	88.3	75.9	81.4	83.7	63.9
Females	50.8	41.8	49.0	71.5	48.5	51.0	54.5	55.1	53.4	66.9	59.4	45.5
Percent unemployed												
Males	5.7	7.0	8.2	6.7	3.2	5.6	3.9	3.9	4.4	4.6	2.8	8.3
Females	8.1	9.2	11.0	6.7	5.9	7.1	4.8	10.5	7.6	4.8	6.8	8.7
Mean weeks of unemployment	13.5	15.1	15.3	12.5	11.0	13.4	14.2	12.5	13.0	12.1	12.6	13.8
Mean number of workers per family	1.7	1.7	1.8	2.0	1.6	1.7	1.9	1.7	1.7	2.1	1.6	1.5
Median income per family ($)	20,226	16,204	18,418	18,939	25,431	17,861	15,237	23,935	18,342	24,480	15,077	12,026
Mean income per family ($)	23,568	18,575	21,149	19,907	29,892	21,364	18,792	28,061	21,316	26,704	18,931	14,474
Percent families below poverty level	10.1	14.0	9.9	9.0	6.9	19.2	17.8	6.7	15.4	6.2	19.1	38.1
Percent unrelated individuals below poverty level	30.1	35.8	30.5	27.9	22.0	42.8	38.8	25.2	39.2	22.8	28.7	52.9
Persons below poverty level	90,560	9,839	11,554	8,493	12,475	368,425	25,644	12,914	31,446	21,258	2,027	84,267

Note: * indicates insufficient cases.

Source: U.S. Bureau of the Census. "General Population Characteristics: United States Summary." 1980 Census of Population. Washington, DC: U.S. Government Printing Office, 1983.

Subfamilies

Providing shelter to a married child or other relative with a family is much more common among recent immigrants than among the native population. This is especially common among Philippine, Jamaican, Dominican Republic, and Chinese families.

Children Ever Born

Children ever born per 1,000 women of specified ages is a crude measure of fertility. Fertility levels among immigrants (both recent and long term) are not significantly higher than for the native-born population. Only Mexicans and Vietnamese show evidence of high fertility. Migrants from Europe and all of Asia, including China, India, Korea, and the Philippines, show indicators of below-average fertility. This is also true of migrants from South America, Canada, and Africa. On balance, the newer migrants to the United States are not contributing to a baby boom or even to a buoying of the sagging native birth rate.

Educational Attainment

There is wide variation in the educational attainment of immigrants. Persons coming from China, India, Korea, the Philippines, Canada, the United Kingdom, and Africa tend to be very well educated (20 percent or more with college education). In contrast, the immigration from Mexico, the Dominican Republic, Portugal, and Italy tends to have large concentrations of persons with less than a grammar school education and very few college graduates. The operation of the new immigration laws clearly are functioning to act as a "brain drain" from many developing countries of Africa, South America, and Asia.

Female Labor Force Participation

Women who migrated to the United States before 1970 exhibit participation rates in the labor force similar to the native women. The immigrant women who came between 1970 and 1980 are much less likely to be participating than native women. Highest rates are shown for those from the Philippines, Portugal, Jamaica, Haiti, and Vietnam. Much lower participation rates are reported for women from Greece and Mexico.

Unemployment

Overall the foreign born have about the same rate of unemployment as the native born or even lower rates. Above-average rates are experienced by Haitian, Dominican Republic, Mexican, Jamaican, and Italian immigrants. Lowest rates are shown by those from the United Kingdom, China, the Philippines, and Canada.

Income and Poverty

Immigrants who arrived before 1970 tend to have lower incomes, and the proportion below the poverty line is twice that of the native population. Immigrants from Haiti, the Dominican Republic, Cuba, Mexico, Korea, and Vietnam have the highest percentage of poor people. Those with less poverty than the native population are immigrants from the Philippines, the United Kingdom, and India.

Summary

From the above indicators, the immigrants who are entering the United States (except for those from Mexico and Central America) are well-educated middle-class persons who have good work qualifications, who quickly find employment and overcome whatever financial handicaps they may have had when they entered the country. Immigration, on balance, is not contributing a great deal to the poverty load of the nation.

Ancestry

Before 1980 the Bureau of the Census attempted to use objective definitions to determine the ancestry of the population. This was done through the concepts of "parentage" and "foreign stock" (see Definition Box). By 1980 the population had become so mixed by intermarriage that this approach was abandoned in favor of a subjective approach in which people were simply asked to report their ethnic origins in broad categories, as they perceived themselves. This was done by using an ancestry question.

When asked to specify ancestry in 1980, 83 percent of the population complied. The remaining 17 percent of the population included 7 percent who reported "American" or "United States" and 10 percent who did not provide any ancestry. Only 52 percent reported a single ancestry, and 31 percent indicated multiple ancestry–intermarriage of nationality groups.

The regular 1980 census tabulations provide only limited information about ancestry. However, the Current Population Survey for 1979 collected ancestry information as a special supplement. A report, "Ancestry and Language in the United States: November, 1979," published in *Current Population Reports, Special Studies* (Series P-23, no. 116), provides much of the information from which the materials of this section are derived.

Table 8-6 summarizes the ancestry composition of the population as reported in the Current Population Survey in 1979. Overall 179.1 million of the 216.6 million population (82.7 percent) reported an ancestry; 54 percent of that number reported a single ancestry

Table 8-6. Ancestry of the United States Population: 1979 [civilian noninstitutional population in thousands]

Ancestry	Number of persons reporting ancestry			Percent of persons reporting ancestry		
	Total[a]	Single ancestry	Multiple ancestry	Total[a]	Single ancestry	Multiple ancestry
Reported at least one specific ancestry	179,078	96,496	82,582	100.0	100.0	46.1
Afro-American, African.	16,193	15,057	1,136	9.0	15.6	7.0
American Indian. . .	9,900	2,053	7,847	5.3	2.1	79.3
Asian Indian	182	156	26	0.1	0.2	14.3
Austrian	1,070	385	685	0.6	0.4	64.0
Belgian.	448	113	335	0.3	0.1	74.8
Canadian	609	228	381	0.3	0.2	62.6
Chinese, Taiwanese.	705	540	165	0.4	0.6	23.4
Czechoslovakia . . .	1,695	794	901	0.9	0.8	53.2
Danish	1,672	438	1,234	0.9	0.5	73.8
Dutch.	8,121	1,362	6,759	4.5	1.4	83.2
English.	40,004	11,501	28,503	22.3	11.9	71.3
Filipino	764	525	239	0.4	0.5	31.3
Finnish	616	225	361	0.3	0.3	58.6
French	14,047	3,047	11,000	7.8	3.2	78.3
French Canadian. . .	1,053	582	471	0.6	0.6	44.7
German	51,649	17,160	34,489	28.8	17.8	66.8
Greek.	990	567	423	0.6	0.6	42.7
Hungarian	1,592	534	1,058	0.9	0.6	66.5
Iranian.	118	103	15	0.1	0.1	12.7
Irish.	43,752	9,760	33,992	24.4	10.1	77.7
Italian, Sicilian	11,751	6,110	5,641	6.6	6.3	48.0
Jamaican	184	158	26	0.1	0.2	14.1
Japanese	680	529	151	0.4	0.5	22.2
Korean	265	230	35	0.1	0.2	13.2
Lebanese	322	179	143	0.2	0.2	44.4
Lithuanian	832	317	515	0.5	0.3	61.9
Norwegian.	4,120	1,232	2,888	2.3	1.3	70.1
Polish	8,421	3,498	4,923	4.7	3.6	58.5
Portuguese	946	493	453	0.5	0.5	47.9
Rumanian	335	132	203	0.2	0.1	60.6
Russian.	3,466	1,496	1,970	1.9	1.6	56.8
Scandinavian . . .	340	110	230	0.2	0.1	67.6
Scottish	14,205	1,615	12,590	7.9	1.7	88.6
Slavic	722	300	422	0.4	0.3	58.4
Spanish.	12,493	9,762	2,731	7.0	10.0	21.9
Colombian. . . .	117	101	16	0.1	0.1	13.7
Cuban.	675	558	117	0.4	0.6	17.3
Dominican. . . .	119	107	12	0.1	0.1	10.1
Mexican.	6,682	5,889	793	3.7	6.1	11.9
Puerto Rican . . .	1,333	1,107	226	0.7	1.1	17.0
Other Spanish. . .	3,566	2,000	1,566	2.0	2.1	43.9
Swedish.	4,886	1,216	3,670	2.7	1.3	75.1
Swiss.	1,228	312	916	0.7	0.3	74.6
Ukranian	525	231	294	0.3	0.2	56.0
Vietnamese	198	177	21	0.1	0.2	10.6
Welsh.	2,568	455	2,113	1.4	0.5	82.3
West Indian. . . .	193	129	64	0.1	0.1	33.2
Yugoslavian. . . .	467	283	184	0.3	0.3	39.4
Other specified ancestry groups. .	4,942	2,372	2,571	2.8	2.5	52.0

[a]Number and percent by ancestry groups do not add to total, as persons may be counted in more than one ancestry group.

Source: U.S. Bureau of the Census. "Ancestry and Language in the United States: 1979." Current Population Reports (Series P-23, no. 116). Washington, DC: U.S. Government Printing Office, 1982.

and 46 percent a multiple ancestry. The fact that the 1980 census produced the same proportions suggests that the subjective response elicited by the ancestry question represents firmly held beliefs about one's own origins. The principal ancestry categories used by the Bureau of the Census in reporting how Americans identified themselves are listed in Table 8-6, together with the number of persons who identified themselves with each nationality. The numbers in the first column of this table add to much more than the total, because those who reported multiple ancestry are counted in both (or more) of the ancestry groups they indicated. (For example, "Scotch-Irish" were counted under both "Scottish" and "Irish.") Ranked in order of percentage reporting, either as single or multiple identification, the leading ancestry roots of the nation are as follows:

Nation	Percentage of those reporting ancestry	Percentage reporting multiple ancestry
German	28.8	66.8
Irish.	24.4	77.7
English.	22.3	71.3
Afro-American, African . .	9.0	7.0
Scottish	7.9	88.6
French	7.8	78.3
Italian, Sicilian.	6.6	48.0
American Indian.	5.3	79.3
Polish	4.7	58.5
Dutch.	4.5	83.2
Mexican.	3.7	11.9
Swedish.	2.7	75.1
Norwegian.	2.3	70.1
"Other Spanish".	2.1	43.9
Russian.	1.9	56.8
Welsh.	1.4	82.3
Czechoslovakia	0.9	53.2
Danish	0.9	73.8
Hungarian.	0.9	66.5
Puerto Rican	0.7	17.0
Swiss.	0.7	74.6
Austrian	0.6	64.0
French Canadian.	0.6	44.7
Greek.	0.6	42.7
Lithuanian	0.5	61.9
Portuguese	0.5	47.9

The listing shows that German, Irish, English, and Afro-American (black) ancestry are by far the largest structural components of the nation, with strong supplementary additions from Northwest Europe, Italy, Poland, and Mexico. One American in twenty claims some American Indian ancestry.

Single-nationality ancestry is rare in the principal ancestry categories, as is shown by the percentage reporting mixed ancestry in those categories. The German-Irish-English and other Northwest European groups have freely intermarried, with the result that less than 30 percent of them report "pure" (single) ancestry. American Indian ancestry also is highly mixed, that group being second only to Scottish in the tendency to intermarry with other nationality groups. East and South European ancestry groups report less but still substantial intermixture (40 to 60 percent). Mexican, Puerto Rican, and Afro-American groups show little multiple ancestry.

Table 8-7. Selected Social and Economic Characteristics of Ancestry Groups: 1979

Ancestry group	Nativity and parentage			Residence			Percent households nonfamily	Percent families female householder	Percent living "other relative"
	Native of native parents	Native of mixed parentage	Foreign born	Central cities	Metropolitan ring	Nonmetropolitan			
Single ancestry groups	80.4	10.9	5.4	14.3	23.7	32.5	25.7	14.7	19.0
English	89.9	6.2	3.8	7.8	19.2	42.8	25.3	10.0	12.4
French	79.4	15.3	5.1	7.4	17.4	41.6	21.6	11.6	10.9
German	85.3	10.7	4.0	8.7	23.5	38.7	22.5	8.3	11.9
Irish	86.8	10.4	2.7	12.4	23.7	37.4	27.6	12.0	13.6
Italian	42.7	44.1	13.1	20.4	37.8	13.7	23.8	10.0	16.0
Polish	48.7	40.3	10.8	23.6	36.3	16.8	26.8	9.9	15.0
Scottish	75.2	14.2	10.5	10.3	20.1	37.0	22.3	6.4	8.9
Spanish	44.4	25.1	30.3	30.9	23.7	15.6	15.2	20.7	19.9
Other	71.3	16.0	12.3	27.5	20.8	23.6	25.5	21.0	19.4
Multiple ancestry groups	91.1	7.6	1.2	9.2	26.9	32.6	28.2	14.3	22.0
Ancestry not specified	77.1	3.0	1.7	13.4	17.9	41.1	25.6	15.8	20.3
Selected multiple ancestry									
American Indian and other	97.2	2.4	0.4	7.7	17.2	43.9	23.0	19.4	20.3
Dutch and other	94.8	4.2	1.0	5.0	19.2	42.3	28.9	15.7	21.7
English and other	93.4	5.7	0.9	7.8	26.3	33.4	29.0	13.9	22.0
French and other	92.1	6.8	1.0	8.7	23.6	33.2	28.9	16.2	21.3
German and other	93.5	5.9	0.6	8.7	28.2	32.9	27.4	13.5	22.6
Irish and other	95.0	4.5	0.5	8.1	25.8	34.4	28.7	15.3	21.8
Italian and other	89.5	9.9	0.6	11.6	38.8	19.1	30.3	15.4	27.0
Polish and other	84.5	13.9	1.6	15.5	36.8	19.3	24.1	11.0	25.4
Scottish and other	92.8	6.1	1.0	7.1	25.0	34.6	30.2	12.7	20.8

Source: U.S. Bureau of the Census. "Ancestry and Language in the United States: 1979." *Current Population Reports* (Series P-23, no. 116). Washington, DC: U.S. Government Printing Office, 1982, Table 3.

Characteristics of Ancestry Groups

It is to be expected that those ancestry groups that have been most diluted by intermarriage and most assimilated through long-time residence in the United States would come closest to the national average composition for the various population characteristics, while those least diluted and assimilated would be more likely to show distinctively different traits. Tables 8-7, 8-8, and 8-9, presenting selected characteristics for the main single- and multiple-ancestry groups, confirm this expectation.

Nativity and Parentage

Ancestry at the 1970 census and before was determined by questions on nativity and parentage (see Definition Box). Table 8-7 (first three columns) presents this classification for the 1979 Current Population Survey, for purposes of comparison of the two modes of measuring ancestry. The diminished usefulness of the old system is evident from this table, since 80 percent of all people claiming ancestry were native born of native parents, and 91 percent of those claiming multiple ancestry are native born of native parents. Thus, the old nativity-parentage categories simply classify most of those who are not foreign born as native Americans of native parents. The only important exception to this general finding is the Spanish-origin population.

Residence

The ancestry groups with most intermarriage and longest residence in the United States (Northwest European) are much more inclined to be residing in the suburban ring of metropolitan areas or in nonmetropolitan areas. Immigrants from Southern and Eastern Europe and from Latin America are much more likely to be found in central cities. The Italian, Polish, and Spanish groups exemplify this latter pattern strongly. American Indians of multiple ancestry (and presumably even more those of single ancestry) are more decentralized—more are found outside metropolitan areas—even though they too, like all of the ancestry groups, are predominantly metropolitan in residence.

Living Arrangements

The living arrangements of Northwest European ancestry groups differ little from those of the general population. However, there is a tendency for persons of Italian, Polish, and Spanish ancestry to have other relatives living in the household. Also, the tendency toward living in nonfamily households is greater among the Northwest European ancestry groups. The family headed by a female householder is rare in all of the ancestry groups reported except American Indians and Spanish.

Educational Attainment

The Spanish-origin population has extraordinarily low educational attainment. For both sexes combined, 45 percent have eight years of elementary education or less, and only 40-44 percent have graduated from high school. This is the only ethnic group with low educational attainment. (This low accomplishment is due primarily to the Mexican ethnic group; Cubans and Puerto Ricans tend to be much better educated.)

There are no important differences among the other ancestry groups in level of educational attainment, except those associated with race and age. Those with older age composition tend to have smaller percentages of persons in the upper educational groups. In addition, persons of American Indian ancestry tend to have less education than those of other ancestry groups. Contrary to what may be the general impression, Italian and Polish ancestry groups tend to show above average educational level when linked as multiple ancestry groups.

Table 8-8. Educational Attainment of Ancestry Groups: Persons 25 Years and Over, 1979 [percent distribution by educational level]

Ancestry group	Males				Females			
	Elementary 0 to 8 years	High school 1 to 3 years	High school 4 years	College 1 or more years	Elementary 0 to 8 years	High school 1 to 3 years	High school 4 years	College 1 or more years
Single ancestry groups								
English	13.5	11.9	32.8	41.8	11.5	11.9	42.6	34.1
French.	18.6	14.4	36.3	30.7	20.5	13.8	43.0	22.7
German.	15.5	12.1	37.8	34.6	15.9	12.0	46.4	25.6
Irish	17.2	14.0	33.5	35.3	15.8	14.2	43.9	26.1
Italian	20.6	16.8	34.1	28.6	23.0	16.6	43.8	16.5
Polish.	19.7	15.9	34.5	29.8	26.1	14.8	37.7	21.4
Scottish.	9.1	9.7	31.2	50.0	9.5	12.4	38.4	39.7
Spanish	44.7	12.8	22.1	20.3	44.6	14.8	27.3	13.3
Other	21.1	15.2	30.8	32.9	20.9	16.3	36.4	26.4
Multiple ancestry groups.	10.5	11.1	33.4	44.9	9.2	12.6	43.8	34.4
Ancestry not specified	25.1	15.7	32.1	27.1	23.0	18.4	38.0	20.6
Selected multiple ancestry								
American Indian and other	21.0	16.7	37.8	24.5	19.1	19.6	43.4	17.9
Dutch and other . . .	16.2	15.3	37.0	31.5	16.0	16.0	42.2	25.8
English and other . .	9.0	10.1	32.3	48.6	6.8	11.4	41.9	40.0
French and other. . .	10.8	12.0	34.3	42.9	9.0	14.4	41.9	34.7
German and other. . .	9.4	10.8	35.0	44.8	7.7	11.8	46.6	33.9
Irish and other . . .	12.8	12.6	34.1	40.6	10.7	13.8	44.9	30.6
Italian and other . .	5.1	9.5	35.2	50.2	5.4	10.8	49.4	34.3
Polish and other. . .	8.9	6.7	32.3	52.2	6.2	9.8	44.2	39.9
Scottish and other. .	8.4	10.1	30.6	50.9	7.6	11.3	41.8	39.2

Source: U.S. Bureau of the Census. "Ancestry and Language in the United States: 1979." Current Population Reports (Series P-23, no. 116). Washington, DC: U.S. Government Printing Office, 1982.

Table 8-9. Selected Economic Characteristics of Ancestry Groups: 1979

Ancestry group	Percent in labor force	Percent unem- ployed	Family income						
			Median	Under $5,000	$5,000 to $9,999	$10,000 to $14,999	$15,000 to $19,999	$20,000 to $24,999	$25,000 and over
Single ancestry group									
English	49.3	4.3	16,891	6.9	16.8	19.4	15.2	15.5	26.2
French.	51.9	6.2	15,571	8.6	17.7	21.0	17.5	17.7	17.5
German.	51.9	3.9	17,531	5.2	14.6	19.7	18.0	18.6	23.9
Irish	49.3	5.8	16,092	7.7	17.3	20.2	17.0	16.3	21.5
Italian	48.6	6.4	16,993	4.9	17.0	18.6	19.5	16.9	23.0
Polish.	49.2	5.6	16,977	6.4	12.9	22.0	18.4	15.9	24.5
Scottish.	46.0	2.2	20,018	5.2	14.2	16.4	14.0	16.0	34.1
Spanish	47.9	11.3	10,607	18.8	27.5	22.8	12.8	9.0	8.9
Other	51.5	8.7	13,755	14.3	20.3	19.6	14.7	12.5	18.7
Multiple ancestry groups.	55.5	6.4	17,810	6.4	14.7	18.5	16.3	16.7	27.3
Ancestry not specified	50.0	6.6	13,454	14.1	19.8	21.8	15.2	13.0	16.1
Selected multiple ancestry									
American Indian and other	57.8	10.0	13,641	13.1	20.8	21.5	16.9	15.0	12.8
Dutch and other . . .	51.9	7.3	15,868	8.8	19.1	18.6	15.5	16.4	21.6
English and other . .	53.2	5.6	18,680	5.3	14.5	17.9	15.6	16.0	30.7
French and other. . .	54.3	7.4	17,048	7.2	15.5	19.6	15.9	16.0	25.8
German and other. . .	57.3	6.2	18,375	5.3	13.8	18.5	16.9	17.0	28.6
Irish and other . . .	54.0	6.7	16,860	7.2	16.2	19.4	16.3	16.2	24.7
Italian and other . .	65.0	7.5	17,833	7.8	12.9	16.0	20.6	16.6	26.0
Polish and other. . .	63.8	5.9	19,968	4.6	10.0	17.4	18.0	20.1	29.9
Scottish and other. .	50.3	5.0	19,148	5.6	14.2	17.3	14.9	17.1	30.9

Source: U.S. Bureau of the Census. "Ancestry and Language in the United States: 1979." Current Population Reports (Series P-23, no. 116). Washington, DC: U.S. Government Printing Office, 1982, Table 3.

Table 8-10. Persons Five Years and Over Speaking Various Languages at Home, by Age: 1979 [civilian noninstitutional population in thousands]

Language spoken at home	Persons 5 years old and over	Total, percent	5 to 13 years	14 to 17 years	18 to 24 years	25 to 44 years	45 to 64 years	65 to 74 years	75 years and over
Total	200,812	...	30,414	15,955	27,988	59,385	43,498	15,053	8,519
Percent	...	100.0	15.1	7.9	13.9	29.6	21.7	7.5	4.2
Speaking English only .	176,319	100.0	15.4	8.0	14.1	29.5	21.5	7.4	4.0
Speaking other language	17,985	100.0	14.4	6.9	12.6	30.8	21.8	7.5	6.0
Chinese	514	100.0	12.5	5.8	15.8	34.8	21.2	6.8	3.1
French.	987	100.0	8.1	5.5	10.2	29.9	30.4	9.9	6.0
German.	1,261	100.0	5.4	7.1	10.8	24.3	27.4	12.8	12.2
Greek	365	100.0	16.7	4.9	10.4	38.1	21.9	4.4	3.6
Italian	1,354	100.0	7.5	4.9	8.1	19.3	31.5	15.1	13.7
Japanese.	265	100.0	7.9	6.8	7.9	27.2	36.6	9.4	3.8
Korean.	191	100.0	16.2	5.8	17.8	35.6	19.9	3.7	1.0
Philippine languages.	419	100.0	10.7	5.3	8.6	40.8	20.3	7.2	6.9
Polish.	731	100.0	2.7	1.4	3.7	13.8	45.7	21.6	10.9
Portuguese.	245	100.0	15.9	8.6	12.2	33.9	22.0	3.7	3.3
Spanish	8,768	100.0	20.2	8.8	15.4	34.6	15.8	3.1	2.2
Yiddish	234	100.0	8.5	0.4	3.0	15.8	20.9	29.1	21.8
Other	2,651	100.0	10.0	4.9	10.8	30.3	23.3	10.1	10.6
Not reported.	6,508	100.0	11.1	8.4	13.5	26.9	25.1	9.5	5.6

Note: ... indicates data not applicable.

Source: U.S. Bureau of the Census. "Ancestry and Language in the United States: 1979." Current Population Reports (Series P-23, no. 116). Washington, DC: U.S. Government Printing Office, 1982.

Labor Force Participation of Women

Women who claim multiple ancestry (more assimilated and younger) are more likely to be in the labor force than women who claim single ancestry or who claim no ancestry. Italian and Polish women with multiple ancestry particularly are in the labor force in outstandingly high proportions. Chapter 12 should be consulted in interpreting these data.

Family Income

The Scottish, English, and German heritage groups tend to have high family incomes, both on single and multiple ancestry classifications. However, contrary to Protestant work ethic theory, the income for Polish multiple ancestry is equally high, although income for Irish, Italian, and French is moderately lower, in conformity with that hypothesis. Chapter 15 contains a full exposition of income distribution, and Table 8-9 should be reviewed in connection with that information.

Language Spoken in the Home

As a measure of assimilation, the census has inquired about language spoken at home. Prior to 1980 the question was posed in terms of language spoken in *childhood* home, and was termed "mother tongue." At the 1980 census the question was changed to measure *current* language spoken at home. The special survey of the *Current Population Report* (1979) collected information according to both systems, for purposes of comparison.

Language spoken in home	Number (millions)	Percentage of population
Mother tongue other than English	32	19.0
Current language other than English	18	9.0

Note: Mother tongue data refer to persons fourteen years of age and over, and current language data refer to persons five years of age and over.

Clearly, more than half of the persons who spoke a language other than English in their childhood home speak only English currently. This is evidence of strong assimilation.

The ten most common mother tongue languages, with corresponding percentage of current use, are as follows:

Language	Mother tongue	Current use
Spanish	4.5	4.4
German.	3.0	0.6
Italian	2.4	0.7
Polish.	1.4	0.4
French.	1.4	0.5
Yiddish	0.7	0.1
Norwegian	0.3	*
Swedish	0.3	*
Chinese	0.3	0.3
Czechoslovakian	0.3	*

Note: * indicates number to small to be reported.

All of the mother tongue languages except Spanish and Chinese show a dramatic decline between childhood home and current use.

Table 8-10 reports the numbers of persons currently speaking major languages at home and their composition by age. The languages shown above spoken by immigrants from Europe all tend to be concentrated in the older ages—suggesting that only families with older immigrant/ethnic members tend to cling to another language, and that younger families use English. However, Spanish, Chinese, Greek, Korean, and Portuguese appear to be active current languages used by young as well as older family members. Of these, Spanish is by far the most used; it is used almost as much as all other non-English languages combined. Because of the size of the Hispanic population and the currency of use, Spanish is an important and pervasive language in contemporary American life.

Ability to Speak English

An important question is the bilingual ability of persons who currently speak a language other than English at home. Table 8-11 provides data on this point. A majority (more than 50 percent) of persons in all language groups report they speak English "very well" except Korean and Philippine language speakers, and of these a large proportion report they speak the language "well." Overall nearly 80 percent of those who currently speak another language in their homes report that they speak English "very well" or "well." Only 6 percent speak no English at all. As Table 8-11 shows, those with English language handicaps tend to be the older persons. Among youths of high school age, difficulty with English is reported for only a small portion of the population.

Among the Asian populations, the Chinese and Japanese youths (14-17 years of age) tend to speak English well in a very high percentage of cases. Among Korean youths, however, more than one-half cannot speak

English well. English is spoken with difficulty among all Asian groups at older ages.

Of particular interest, because of the size of the group, are those who speak Spanish. Among youths of high school age, only 8 percent report deficiency in English, whereas for those in the working ages the proportion is three or four times greater. Thus there is ample evidence of very rapid language assimilation of the Spanish-speaking population. It is likely that within a decade the English-speaking abilities of this group will be similar to those for Italian and Polish and by the year 2000 will resemble those for German, French, and Yiddish—nearly complete fluency in English, with another language still used in the home.

Conclusion

The worldwide immigration policy of the United States over recent decades has resulted in the emergence of a large number of new foreign-born, ancestry, and language groups. However, they appear to assimilate rapidly into most aspects of American life. Like the generations of immigrants before them, all but a small fraction of them are bilingual. Very quickly, all but the older adults gain some proficiency in English if they are not already bilingual when they arrive. The younger generation rapidly is losing whatever language handicaps it may have. In many respects the great concern being shown for the bilingual education of the Spanish-speaking population may be misplaced. According to Census Bureau estimates in 1979 only 354,000 children under fourteen who spoke Spanish at home spoke English "not well" or "not at all." Given the rapid pace at which assimilation appears to be progressing, by 1985 the number will be no larger or even greatly reduced, despite rapid growth in the Spanish population as a result of both high fertility and the arrival of new immigrants. Perhaps more urgent are special programs to improve abilities to speak English for the many thousands of working-age adults whose English-speaking skills clearly place them under a handicap in earning a living and participating in national life.

Bibliography

Alba, R.D., and Chamlin, M.B. "Preliminary Examination of Ethnic Identification Among Whites." *American Sociological Review* 48 (1983):240-47.

Alba, R.D., and Moore, G. "Ethnicity in the American Elite." *American Sociological Review* 47 (1982): 373-83.

Bahr, Howard M., and Chadwick, Bruce A. (eds.). *American Ethnicity*. Lexington, MA: Heath, 1979.

Brye, David L. *European Immigration and Ethnicity in the United States and Canada: A Historical Bibliography*. Santa Barbara, CA: ABC-Clio Information Services, 1982.

Burma, John. *Spanish-Speaking Groups in the United States*. Durham, NC: Duke University Press, 1954.

Dashefsky, Arnold (ed.). *Ethnic Identity in Society*. Chicago: Rand McNally, 1976.

Duncan, Otis D., and Lieberson, Stanley. "Ethnic Segregation and Assimilation." *American Journal of Sociology* 64 (1959):364-74.

Garcia, P. "Trends in the Relative Income Position of

Table 8-11. English Speaking Ability of Persons Who Speak a Language Other Than English at Home, by Language Spoken at Home: 1979 [percent distribution by educational level]

Language	Ability to speak English				Percent who speak not well or not at all				
	Very well	Well	Not well	Not at all	5 to 13 years	14 to 17 years	18 to 24 years	25 to 64 years	65 and over
Chinese	51.0	20.8	20.2	7.8	12.5	6.7	17.3	29.9	70.6
French	76.4	18.0	4.6	1.0	0.0	0.0	4.0	4.5	15.3
German	80.4	15.7	3.5	0.4	1.5	0.0	1.5	3.1	8.2
Greek	60.8	16.2	19.7	3.3	0.0	0.0	13.2	27.9	58.6
Italian	65.5	18.3	12.8	3.3	0.0	1.5	4.6	16.9	24.6
Japanese	52.5	24.2	20.8	2.6	0.0	5.6	33.3	20.6	52.8
Korean	30.4	25.1	34.6	10.5	32.3	54.5	32.4	46.7	100.0
Philippine	45.6	40.3	12.9	1.2	6.7	0.0	13.9	12.1	35.6
Polish	70.2	13.3	11.8	4.8	20.0	20.0	37.0	12.2	22.2
Portuguese	56.3	15.1	22.9	6.1	5.1	0.0	36.7	35.8	44.4
Spanish	50.7	21.0	18.7	9.5	16.7	7.6	24.0	34.4	60.2
Yiddish	76.9	12.8	9.0	0.9	25.0	0.0	0.0	9.3	7.6
Other	62.9	21.0	12.2	4.0	20.5	10.0	17.1	13.8	21.2

Source: U.S. Bureau of the Census. "Ancestry and Language in the United States: 1979." Current Population Reports (Series P-23, no. 116). Washington, DC: U.S. Government Printing Office, 1982, Table 7.

Mexican-Origin Workers in the U.S.: The Early Seventies." *Sociology and Social Research* 66 (1982): 467-83.

Glazer, Nathan, and Moynihan, Daniel P. (eds.). *Ethnicity: Theory and Experience.* Cambridge, MA: Harvard University Press, 1975.

Greeley, Andrew M., and Baum, Gregory (eds.). *Ethnicity.* New York: Seabury Press, 1977.

Handlin, Oscar. *The American People in the Twentieth Century.* Cambridge, MA: Harvard Unirsity Press, 1954.

Hardley, J. Nixon. "Demography of the American Indians." Pp. 1-165 of *American Indians and American Life. Annals of the American Academy of Politicial and Social Science* (Vol. 311). George E. Simpson and J. Milton Yinger (eds.). May, 1957.

Hayes, Marion. "A Century of Change: Netroes in the U.S. Economy, 1860-1960." *Monthly Labor Review* 85 (1962):1359-65.

Jafee, A.J.; Cullen, Ruth M.; and Boswell, Thomas D. *The Changing Demography of Spanish Americans.* New York: Academic Press, 1980.

Kobrin, Frances E., and Goldscheider, Calvin. *The Ethnic Factor in Family Structure and Mobility.* Cambridge, MA: Ballinger Publishing Company, 1978.

Lieberson, Stanley. *Ethnic Patterns in American Cities.* New York: Free Press, 1963.

Massey, D.S. "Research Note on Residential Succession: The Hispanic Case." *Social Forces* 61 (1983):825-33.

Miller, A.T. "Social and Economic Status of the Black Population in the U.S.: An Historical View, 1790-1978." *Review of Black Political Economy* 10 (1980):314-17.

Montero, D. "Japanese Americans: Changing Patterns of Assimilation over Three Generations." *American Sociological Review* 46 (1981):829-39.

Nampeeo, D.R., McKenney et al. "The Social and Economic Status of the Black Population in the United States, 1974." *Current Population Reports* (Series P-23, no. 54). Washington, DC: U.S. Government Printing Office, 1975.

Nelson, K.P. "Recent Suburbanization of Blacks: How Much, Who, and Where." *American Planning Association Journal* 46 (1980):287-300.

Peach, Ceri; Robinson, Vaughan; and Smitt, Susan. *Ethnic Segregation in Cities.* Athens, GA: University of Georgia Press, 1981.

Roof, W.C., and Spain, D. "Research Note on City-Suburban Socioeconomic Differences Among American Blacks." *Social Forces* 56 (1977):15-20.

Rosen, Philip. *The Neglected Dimension: Ethnicity in American Life.* South Bend, IN: Notre Dame Press, 1980.

Ross, J.A. "Urban Development and the Politics of Ethnicity: A Conceptual Approach." *Ethnic & Racial Studies* 5 (1982):440-56.

Salgado de Snyder, N., and Padilla, A.M. "Cultural and Ethnic Maintenance of Interethnically Married Mexican Americans." *Human Organization* 41 (1982): 359-62.

Sampson, W.A., and Rossi, P.H. "Race and Family Social Standing." *American Sociological Review* 40 (1975):201-14.

Tienda, M., and Angel, R. "Headship and Household Composition Among Blacks, Hispanics, and Other Whites." *Social Forces* 61 (1982):508-31.

U.S. Bureau of the Census. "The Social and Economic Status of the Black Population in the United States: An Historical View, 1790-1978." *Current Population Reports* (Special Report, Series P-23, no. 80). Washington, DC: U.S. Government Printing Office, 1979.

U.S. Department of Health, Education, and Welfare. Office of the Assistant Secretary for Planning and Evaluation. Office of Special Concerns. *A Study of Selected Socio-Economic Characteristics of Ethnic Minorities Based on the 1970 Census.* (In 4 vols.) Washington, DC: Urban Associates, Inc., 1974.

Chapter 9

School Enrollment

Every technologically advanced nation requires a citizenry that is well educated. Even unskilled workers are expected to be literate. Routine tasks in factories and offices demand knowledge and skills that those with a complete secondary education command more fully than those with less education. "High technology," professionalization of work, and complicated systems of record-keeping and data management presuppose additional technical training beyond high school, either in colleges and universities or in special courses.

In each decennial census since 1940 and in its Current Population Survey the Bureau of the Census has obtained information about the school attendance activities of persons of all ages (see Definition Box). These data measure only the quantity, not the quality, of school attendance, so they answer some but not all of the questions being asked about educational trends.

At the turn of the century only half or slightly more of the children of school age, 5-19 years, were attending school. During the ensuing seven decades, school enrollment rates (the percentage of school-age children enrolled in school) rose steadily. Between 1970 and 1980, however, they remained stable. The record of changes in school enrollment is summarized in the following table:

Year	Percent of population aged 5-19 enrolled in school	Inter-censal change
1980	88.6	0.7
1970	87.9	3.9
1960	84.0	5.3
1950	78.7	3.9
1940	74.8	4.9
1930	69.9	5.6
1920	64.3	5.1
1910	59.2	9.7
1900	50.5	-3.8
1890	54.3	-3.5
1880	57.8	...

Source: U.S. Bureau of the Census. Historical Statistics of the United States. Washington, DC: U.S. Government Printing Office, 1975, Table H-433-441.

The small gain of the 1970-80 decade contrasts sharply with the preceding decades of the century. A key question is, Is some upper level of saturation being approached, or has there been some social change to slow the increase and prevent the proportion from nearing 100 percent? This issue is explored in the sections below.

Definitions

The following definitions were used by the 1980 census; modifications or amplifications by the Current Population Survey (CPS) are noted.

School Enrollment. Pursuant to answers to questions 8, 9, and 10 (see appendix to Chapter 1), persons are classified as enrolled in school if they reported attending a "regular" school or college at any time between February 1, 1980, and the time of enumeration. Regular schooling includes nursery school, kindergarten, elementary school, and schooling that leads to a high school diploma or college degree. The CPS counts as enrolled anyone who was enrolled at any time during the current term or school year in any type of graded public, parochial, or other private school in the regular school system. Attendance may be either full time or part time and during the day or night.

Level and Year of School in Which Enrolled. The levels separately identified are nursery school, kindergarten, elementary school, high school, and college. Children in "Head Start" or similar programs were counted under "nursery school" or kindergarten," as appropriate. Elementary school includes grades 1-8, and high school includes grades 9-12. Junior high school pupils are reported in elementary school or high school according to their grade. The term "college" includes junior or community colleges, four-year colleges, universities, and graduate or professional schools.

Years of School Completed. Data derived from answers to questions 9 and 10, which applied only to progress in "regular" schools as defined under the definition for school enrollment. Question 9 called for the highest grade attended, regardless of "skipped" or "repeated" grades. Question 10 asked whether or not the highest grade attended had been finished. A "no" answer meant the respondent had completed only part of the year, had dropped out, or had failed to pass the last grade attended. If the person was still attending school in that grade, he or she answered "Now attending." The number in each category of highest grade of school completed represents the combination of (a) persons who reported the indicated grade as the highest grade attended and that they had finished it, (b) those who had attended the next higher grade but had not finished it, and (c) those still attending the next higher grade. Persons who have not completed the first year of elementary school are classified as having no years of school completed.

College Enrollment (CPS). Persons reporting themselves as attending or enrolled in college, including anyone who had been enrolled at any time during the current term or school year, except those who had left for the remainder of the term. Regular college enrollment includes those persons attending a four-year or two-year college, university, or professional school (such as medical or law school), or in courses that may advance the student towards a recognized college or university degree (e.g. B.A. or M.A.). Attendance may be either full time or part time, during the day or night.

Full-Time and Part-Time Attendance (CPS). Attending college full time means taking twelve or more hours of classes during the average school week, and part time means taking less than twelve hours of classes during the average school week.

Two-Year and Four-Year Colleges (CPS). Students in the first three years of college were asked to report whether the college in which they were enrolled was a two-year college (junior or community college) or a four-year college or university; those in the fourth or later academic year of college were assumed to be in a four-year college or university.

Modal Grade. The year of school in which the largest proportion of students of a given age is enrolled, hence a standard against which to measure relative progress in school.

School Enrollment Rates. The percentage of persons in a particular category of population who are enrolled in school, as defined above. Rates may be specific for sex, age, race-ethnicity, residential categories, or other traits. Rates may be computed for families that contain members of school-going ages (ages three to thirty-four).

Public, Church-Related, or Other Private School. In general, a "public" school is defined as any school controlled and supported primarily by a local, state, or Federal government agency; a "church-related" school is a private school controlled or supported primarily by a religious organization; and an "other private" school is a school controlled or supported primarily by private groups other than religious organizations.

Age and School Enrollment

Nearly all children between the ages of seven and fourteen (second to eighth grade) are attending school (see Figure 9-1 and Table 9-1). The law of almost every state compels school attendance at those ages, and in several states attendance is mandatory until age sixteen. Attendance at those ages has not always been so nearly universal. In 1910 parents appear to have been much less insistent than they are today that their children between six and nine years of age attend school, and at age twelve (now the age at which attendance is at its peak rate) only 91 percent were enrolled in school. From age fourteen to age fifteen, among both boys and girls, there was a sharp drop in school attendance. At those ages children were economically useful for farm work and could help to lighten the housework attendant upon raising large families.

From 1920 to 1970 there was a persistent upward trend in the proportion of children remaining in school after passing the age of compulsory attendance. For example, in 1910 only 34 percent of boys seventeen years of age were still in school, but by 1970 the proportion had reached almost 90 percent. Similarly, the proportion of persons aged eighteen or nineteen enrolled in school rose from 19 percent in 1910 to 57 percent in 1970. *However, between 1970 and 1980 the rates of attendance at ages sixteen to nineteen changed very little or actually declined.* Thus there was no improvement in attendance rates of persons aged eighteen and nineteen, the ages of finishing high school and entering college. As Chapter 12 will show, there is a tendency to enter the labor force during these years instead of continuing in school.

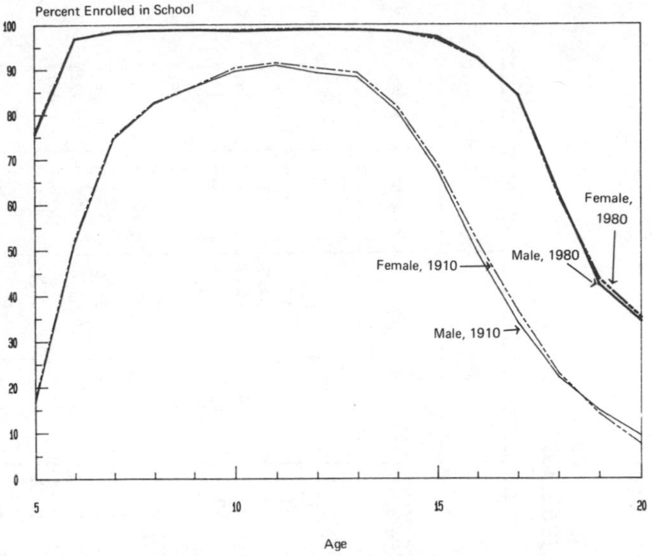

Figure 9-1. Percent Attending School, by Sex and Age: 1910 and 1980

Table 9-1. Percent Enrolled in School by Single Years of Age and Sex for the United States: 1910-1980

Age	Both sexes					Males								Females							
	1980	1970	1960	1950	1940	1980	1970	1960	1950	1940	1930	1920	1910	1980	1970	1960	1950	1940	1930	1920	1910
5 to 20 years, total	84.7	85.2	81.8	75.2	70.8	84.8	86.2	82.6	75.9	71.2	70.2	64.1	59.1	84.5	84.2	80.9	74.4	70.4	69.7	64.5	59.4
5 years	75.8	54.5	44.8	34.3	18.0	75.5	54.5	44.7	33.9	17.5	19.5	18.3	16.7	76.2	55.0	45.0	34.7	18.4	20.5	19.3	17.4
6 years	96.9	89.9	83.2	76.8	69.1	96.9	89.1	83.0	76.4	68.2	65.5	62.8	51.7	97.0	89.3	83.4	77.2	70.1	67.1	63.9	52.4
7 years	98.5	97.1	97.0	94.4	92.4	98.5	96.6	96.9	94.2	92.2	89.0	83.1	74.7	98.6	96.5	97.1	94.5	92.7	89.7	83.5	75.2
8 years	98.8	97.9	97.8	95.6	94.8	98.8	97.1	97.8	95.6	94.7	94.0	88.3	82.5	98.8	97.2	97.9	95.7	95.0	94.3	88.6	82.8
9 years	98.9	97.9	98.0	96.1	95.6	98.9	97.3	97.9	96.0	95.5	95.4	90.3	86.1	98.9	97.4	98.0	96.2	95.7	95.7	90.5	86.3
10 years.	98.7	95.7	97.9	96.0	95.7	98.6	97.0	97.8	95.9	95.6	96.9	92.9	89.6	98.8	97.1	97.9	96.2	95.8	97.2	93.2	90.4
11 years.	98.9	97.6	97.8	96.3	95.9	98.8	97.5	97.7	96.1	95.8	97.4	93.8	90.9	99.0	97.7	97.8	96.4	96.0	97.6	94.1	91.5
12 years.	99.0	97.6	97.5	95.9	95.5	98.9	97.5	97.4	95.6	95.3	96.9	93.0	89.2	99.0	97.6	97.6	96.3	95.7	97.3	93.4	90.3
13 years.	98.8	97.7	96.9	95.9	94.8	98.8	97.4	96.9	95.7	94.6	96.4	92.4	88.3	98.9	97.4	97.0	96.0	95.1	96.7	92.7	89.3
14 years.	98.5	98.7	95.3	94.8	92.5	98.5	96.3	95.4	94.7	92.2	92.9	86.2	80.7	98.6	96.0	95.3	94.9	92.8	92.9	86.5	81.8
15 years.	97.1	97.6	92.9	91.4	87.6	97.3	95.7	93.1	91.5	87.3	84.8	71.9	67.5	96.8	95.3	92.6	91.2	88.0	84.5	73.9	69.0
16 years.	92.6	93.5	86.3	80.9	76.2	92.6	92.3	86.5	80.6	75.5	65.8	48.2	49.3	92.5	91.8	86.0	81.1	76.8	66.8	53.3	51.9
17 years.	84.2	87.1	75.6	68.2	60.9	84.2	86.8	76.3	67.9	60.5	47.1	32.1	34.0	84.3	85.8	74.8	68.4	61.3	48.8	37.2	36.6
18 years.	62.1	65.2	30.6	39.8	36.4	62.3	70.1	54.8	42.4	38.1	31.1	20.5	22.1	61.8	61.0	46.5	37.2	34.7	30.3	22.8	23.0
19 years.	43.0	46.7	32.8	24.7	20.9	42.3	51.4	37.5	27.8	23.2	20.8	14.0	14.8	43.6	43.1	28.4	21.8	18.7	18.8	13.6	14.1
20 years.	34.7	32.8	23.5	17.9	12.5	34.3	38.3	28.1	21.2	14.4	14.6	9.3	9.3	35.2	29.3	19.3	14.9	10.6	11.7	7.5	7.5

Source: U.S. Bureau of the Census. "Detailed Population Characteristics: United States Summary." 1980 Census of Population. Washington, DC: U.S. Government Printing Office, 1983, Table 260. Data for 1970 from U.S. Bureau of the Census. "Detailed Population Characteristics: United States Summary." 1970 Census of Population. Washington, DC: U.S. Government Printing Office, 1973, Tables 197 and 50. Data for 1960, 1950, 1940, 1930, and 1920 from U.S. Bureau of the Census. "Detailed Population Characteristics: United States Summary." 1960 Census of Population. Washington, DC: U.S. Government Printing Office, 1963, Table 166. Data for 1910 from Donald J. Bogue. The Population of the United States. Glencoe, IL: The Free Press, 1959.

Table 9-2. Percent Enrolled in School, by Age, Race, and Spanish-Origin: 1950, 1960, 1970, and 1980

Age	1980						1970				1960		1950	
	Total	Black	White	American Indian	Asian/ Pac. Is.	Spanish-origin	Total	Black	White	Spanish-origin	Black[a]	White	Black[a]	White
3 years. . . .	23.2	27.9	22.7	19.9	28.8	16.6	7.5	8.4	7.3	6.4	--	--	--	--
4 years. . . .	42.5	49.6	41.3	41.7	52.0	35.6	17.4	19.8	16.8	16.1	--	--	--	--
5 years. . . .	75.8	79.0	75.2	74.6	82.5	73.9	54.5	49.3	55.4	53.3	42.5	45.2	25.5	35.5
6 years. . . .	96.9	95.5	97.3	94.6	96.7	95.7	89.9	85.4	90.8	86.4	78.4	84.0	71.1	77.6
7 years. . . .	98.5	97.4	98.8	97.4	97.7	97.8	97.1	95.4	97.6	95.2	94.7	97.3	91.3	94.7
8 years. . . .	98.8	98.0	99.1	97.5	98.0	98.1	97.9	96.8	98.3	96.3	96.4	98.0	93.8	95.9
9 years. . . .	98.9	98.1	99.1	97.9	98.3	98.4	97.8	97.1	98.2	96.6	96.7	98.2	94.7	96.3
10 years . . .	98.7	97.9	98.9	97.6	97.8	98.1	95.7	93.3	96.3	96.3	96.5	98.1	94.5	96.3
11 years . . .	98.9	97.9	99.1	98.0	98.6	98.2	97.6	96.4	98.0	97.0	96.3	98.0	95.0	96.4
12 years . . .	99.0	98.1	99.2	97.6	98.4	98.4	97.6	96.4	98.0	96.7	95.8	97.8	94.3	96.2
13 years . . .	98.8	97.9	99.1	96.7	98.4	98.0	97.7	96.4	98.1	96.5	94.8	97.2	94.2	96.1
14 years . . .	98.5	97.5	98.9	95.7	98.4	97.0	98.7	97.2	99.1	94.7	92.2	95.8	91.9	95.2
15 years . . .	97.1	96.3	97.5	92.0	97.5	93.5	97.5	95.4	98.1	93.0	88.0	93.6	85.9	92.1
16 years . . .	92.6	92.6	93.0	83.1	95.5	86.6	93.5	90.0	94.3	87.9	79.8	87.1	72.6	82.1
17 years . . .	84.2	83.3	85.0	70.6	91.3	73.9	87.1	81.1	88.2	78.2	66.6	76.8	55.8	69.9
18 years . . .	62.1	61.8	62.5	48.0	77.0	53.1	65.2	55.1	66.7	58.6	46.3	51.2	32.3	40.8
19 years . . .	43.0	41.6	43.4	29.3	64.8	34.6	46.7	37.6	48.0	39.6	29.3	33.3	19.7	25.3
20 years . . .	34.7	31.0	35.5	20.6	57.0	25.7	32.8	19.7	34.5	21.8	18.1	24.3	12.5	18.6
21 years . . .	30.1	25.8	31.0	17.8	51.2	21.3	27.0	14.8	28.6	16.2	13.5	19.4	8.3 (21–24 years)	12.2 (21–24 years)
22 years . . .	22.0	19.6	22.3	15.3	42.8	17.3	18.2	10.3	19.1	12.2	9.5	12.9		
23 years . . .	16.1	15.0	16.1	11.7	35.8	14.1	13.4	8.2	13.9	10.3	7.9	9.9		
24 years . . .	13.7	12.8	13.6	10.8	29.5	12.5	11.1	6.8	11.5	8.3	6.7	8.6		
25–29 years. .	10.3	10.6	10.1	9.6	19.9	9.7	7.5	5.4	7.6	6.8	5.6	6.2	--	--
30–34 years. .	7.1	8.5	6.8	7.8	11.6	7.1	4.5	4.2	4.4	4.6	3.6	3.1	--	--
35–39 years. .	4.8	6.1	4.6	5.8	8.1	5.0	--	--	--	--	--	--	--	--
40–44 years. .	3.7	4.8	3.4	4.5	6.7	3.8	--	--	--	--	--	--	--	--
45–54 years. .	2.2	3.2	2.0	3.0	4.2	2.7	--	--	--	--	--	--	--	--
55–64 years. .	1.0	1.7	1.0	1.5	2.0	1.6	--	--	--	--	--	--	--	--
65 years and over	0.7	1.0	0.7	0.9	1.3	1.1	--	--	--	--	--	--	--	--

[a] Includes nonwhite.

Note: -- indicates data not available.

Source: U.S. Bureau of the Census. "Detailed Population Characteristics: United States Summary." 1980 Census of Population. Washington, DC: U.S. Government Printing Office, 1983, Table 260. Data for 1970 from U.S. Bureau of the Census. "Detailed Population Characteristics: United States Summary." 1970 Census of Population. Washington, DC: U.S. Government Printing Office, 1973, Table 197 and 50. Data for 1960 from U.S. Bureau of the Census. "Detailed Population Characteristics: United States Summary." 1960 Census of Population. Washington, DC: U.S. Government Printing Office, 1963, Tables 166 and 165.

Preschool Attendance

At the youngest ages there has been a steady increase in school enrollment. At ages five and six attendance in 1980 was at unprecedented high levels, having risen from much lower levels that, until 1950, were comparatively unchanging (Table 9-1). This phenomenon, which is primarily preschool attendance, extends to children of even younger ages and is analyzed in more detail below.

School Enrollment at Ages Twenty and Above

In contrast to the relative standstill in school enrollment at ages sixteen to nineteen, there has been an uninterrupted rise in enrollment for the 20-34 age group. Table 9-2 reports data for enrollment at those ages as well as for younger age groups. These are ages of college attendance and postgraduate training. Data presented below show that this trend has extended to all adult ages. At a time when older teenagers were not improving their enrollment rates, there was a surge in adult education, embracing even the postretirement years to a small extent.

Sex Differences in School Enrollment

Between the ages of seven and fourteen, girls have a slightly higher rate of school enrollment than boys, but the difference is small (Table 9-1 and Figure 9-1). At ages eighteen and above, boys traditionally have had a substantially higher enrollment rate than girls. This difference resulted largely from the fact that many girls beyond the age of seventeen withdrew from school to marry, especially after they had graduated from high school. During the late 1970s and early 1980s this situation changed: The enrollment rates for females became higher than for males at age eighteen and nineteen and only moderately lower in the twenties. The proportion of female high school graduates who enter college is now equal to or higher than the corresponding proportion of males.

In 1910 girls had higher enrollment rates than males up to age nineteen, and the difference between the sexes with respect to school enrollment at elementary and higher school ages was not very large; however, between 1940 and 1950 male enrollment increased more rapidly than female. Table 9-1 demonstrates that the standstill in enrollment rates at ages eighteen and nineteen between 1970 and 1980 (described above) was equally strong among females and males. However, the analysis below will show that there has been a great acceleration in college enrollment of women since 1975, with the result that the pattern of higher female than male school enrollment has been reestablished for ages twenty and above.

Race and Ethnic Differences in School Enrollment

Unlike the situation in past decades, the rate of school attendance for minority populations is now nearly identical to that for the white population (Table 9-2 and Figure 9-2). Among the black population preschool attendance is considerably higher at ages three to five than among the white population. From age six to sixteen attendance rates for the black population is only one percentage point below that of whites, and both are close to the 100 percent level. Attendance at ages seventeen and above is lower among the black than among the white youths, but only 10 to 15 percent lower. Similarly, the Spanish-origin population has near saturation rates of school attendance between ages six and fifteen. However, for all ages older than fifteen the Spanish-origin group has substantially lower attendance rates than either the black or the white population. This signifies lower attendance at high school and greater dropout from high school. Also, there is less preschool attendance for Spanish-origin persons than for blacks or whites.

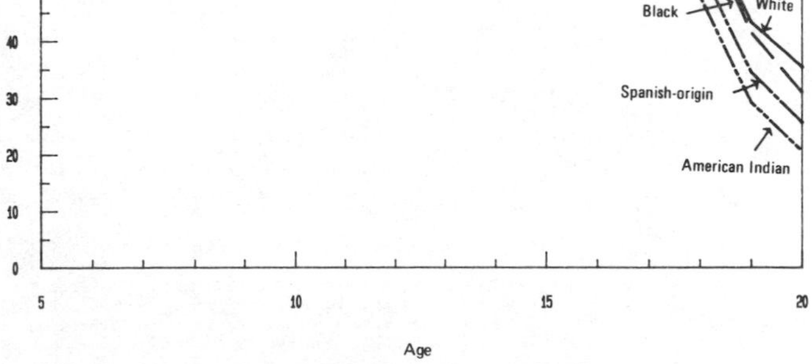

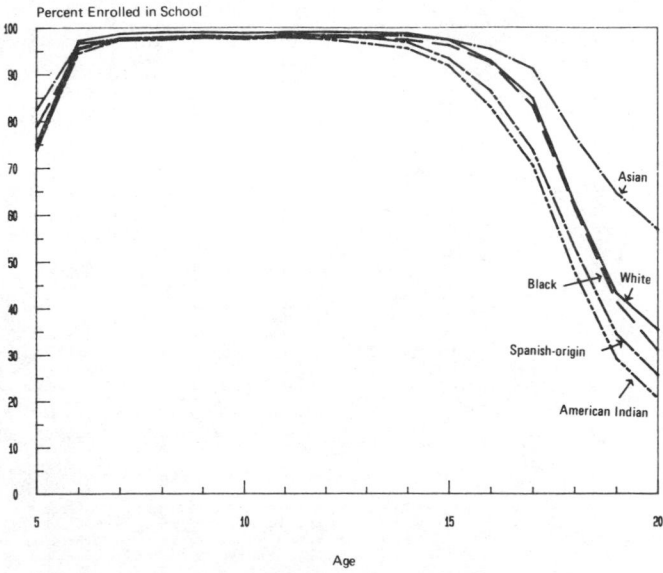

Figure 9-2. Percent Attending School, by Race-Ethnicity: 1980

Table 9-3. Percent of Persons 3-34 Years of Age Enrolled in School, by Age, Sex, Race, Spanish-Origin, and Mexican-Origin: 1970, 1980, and 1982

Percent enrolled in school	Both sexes			Male			Female		
	1970	1980	1982	1970	1980	1982	1970	1980	1982
All races, total . .	56.4	49.7	48.6	59.7	50.9	49.7	53.2	48.5	47.5
3 to 4 years	20.5	36.7	36.4	21.2	37.8	36.4	19.8	35.5	36.4
5 to 6 years	89.5	95.7	95.0	88.9	95.0	94.7	90.2	96.4	95.3
7 to 13 years.	99.2	99.3	99.2	99.0	99.2	99.1	99.4	99.3	99.3
14 to 15 years	98.1	98.2	98.5	98.2	98.7	98.7	98.0	97.7	98.3
16 to 17 years	90.0	89.0	90.6	91.3	89.1	91.3	88.6	88.8	89.9
18 to 19 years	47.7	46.4	47.8	54.4	47.0	48.9	41.6	45.8	46.8
20 to 21 years	31.9	31.0	34.0	42.7	32.6	35.2	23.6	29.5	32.9
22 to 24 years	14.9	16.3	16.8	21.2	17.8	18.5	9.4	14.9	15.1
25 to 29 years	7.5	9.3	9.6	11.0	9.8	10.1	4.3	8.8	9.0
30 to 34 years	4.2	6.4	6.3	5.3	5.9	5.6	3.1	7.0	6.9
White, total	56.2	48.9	47.9	59.6	50.0	48.9	52.9	47.9	46.9
3 to 4 years	19.9	36.3	35.9	20.7	38.0	36.3	19.1	34.6	35.5
5 to 6 years	90.3	95.8	94.9	89.7	95.2	94.8	90.9	96.4	95.0
7 to 13 years.	99.2	99.2	99.2	99.0	99.2	99.1	99.4	99.3	99.3
14 to 15 years	98.2	98.3	98.6	98.3	98.7	98.8	98.1	97.8	98.4
16 to 17 years	90.6	88.6	90.3	92.2	88.8	91.0	89.0	88.4	89.6
18 to 19 years	48.7	46.3	47.9	56.0	47.5	48.5	41.8	45.1	47.4
20 to 21 years	33.1	31.9	35.1	45.0	33.7	36.5	24.1	30.2	33.7
22 to 24 years	15.7	16.4	16.2	22.6	18.2	18.0	9.7	14.8	14.5
25 to 29 years	7.7	9.2	9.6	11.2	9.6	10.2	4.4	8.9	9.0
30 to 34 years	4.2	6.3	6.1	5.4	5.6	5.5	3.1	7.0	6.7
Black, total	57.4	53.9	51.6	59.5	56.1	53.2	55.5	52.0	50.2
3 to 4 years	22.7	38.2	38.6	22.3	36.6	37.4	23.2	39.7	39.8
5 to 6 years	84.9	95.4	95.4	84.2	94.1	93.9	85.7	96.7	97.0
7 to 13 years.	99.3	99.4	99.1	99.2	99.5	98.7	99.5	99.3	99.3
14 to 15 years	97.6	97.9	98.1	98.8	98.5	97.8	97.2	97.4	98.3
16 to 17 years	85.7	90.6	91.6	85.4	90.8	92.2	85.9	90.4	91.0
18 to 19 years	40.1	45.7	43.6	41.3	42.8	46.5	38.9	48.2	41.0
20 to 21 years	22.8	23.4	24.3	27.8	23.0	20.9	18.9	23.7	27.2
22 to 24 years	8.0	13.6	17.0	9.6	13.3	17.4	6.7	13.9	16.6
25 to 29 years	4.8	8.8	8.4	6.1	10.6	8.4	3.6	7.4	8.4
30 to 34 years	3.4	6.8	7.0	3.6	7.3	5.6	3.3	6.5	8.1
Spanish-origin, total[a]	53.0	49.8	49.4	54.7	49.9	50.4	51.4	49.8	48.4
3 to 4 years	20.5	28.5	21.8	20.4	30.1	25.2	20.5	26.0	18.3
5 to 6 years	90.0	94.5	92.2	90.3	94.0	90.3	89.7	94.9	93.9
7 to 13 years.	98.9	99.2	98.7	99.0	98.6	98.8	98.8	99.5	98.6
14 to 15 years	96.7	94.3	96.9	98.1	96.7	96.8	95.4	92.1	97.1
16 to 17 years	83.9	81.8	85.5	87.8	81.5	87.8	80.0	82.2	82.8
18 to 19 years	41.4	37.8	39.2	40.5	36.9	39.7	42.4	38.8	38.7
20 to 21 years	17.0	19.5	22.7	20.0	21.4	21.6	14.6	17.6	23.7
22 to 24 years	9.9	11.7	10.4	13.9	10.7	11.2	6.8	12.6	9.7
25 to 29 years	5.2	6.9	8.0	5.8	6.8	8.3	4.7	6.9	7.7
30 to 34 years	3.0	5.1	4.5	2.5	6.2	4.3	3.5	4.1	4.7
Mexican-origin, total.	--	--	48.2	--	--	49.2	--	--	47.2
3 to 4 years	--	--	15.3	--	--	19.8	--	--	10.9
5 to 6 years	--	--	92.5	--	--	91.4	--	--	93.3
7 to 13 years.	--	--	98.8	--	--	99.0	--	--	98.5
14 to 15 years	--	--	97.5	--	--	97.1	--	--	98.0
16 to 17 years	--	--	83.0	--	--	86.4	--	--	78.8
18 to 19 years	--	--	31.1	--	--	33.0	--	--	29.1
20 to 21 years	--	--	18.2	--	--	18.3	--	--	18.1
22 to 24 years	--	--	7.2	--	--	7.0	--	--	7.3
25 to 29 years	--	--	6.7	--	--	6.2	--	--	7.2
30 to 34 years	--	--	3.2	--	--	3.8	--	--	2.6

[a]The 1970 Spanish-origin data are from the U.S. Bureau of the Census. "Social and Economic Characteristics of Students: October 1972." Current Population Reports (Series P-20, no. 260). Washington, DC: U.S. Government Printing Office, 1974, Table 1.

Note: -- indicates data not available.

Source: For 1970 (except for Spanish-origin) data from U.S. Bureau of the Census. "School Enrollment: October 1970." Current Population Reports (Series P-20, no. 222). 1980 and 1982 data from "School Enrollment--Social and Economic Characteristics of Students" (October 1980 and 1982). Current Population Reports (Series P-20). Washington, DC: U.S. Government Printing Office, 1971 (Table 1), 1984, and 1985.

By contrast, in 1970 far fewer black and Hispanic than white children aged fifteen and over were enrolled in elementary and high school. The race-ethnic differentials were greater at higher levels of education. At age twenty, a college attendance age, for example, enrollment of black and Spanish-origin youths was only 60 percent that of white. In 1980 the proportion had risen to 86 percent for blacks and 72 percent for Spanish-origin population. Whereas attendance rates for whites at ages over twenty improved relatively little during the decade, attendance rates for both black and Spanish-origin youths rose substantially, thereby narrowing the gap. Should this trend continue for another decade, differences in school attendance rates for the three main race-ethnic groups will be insignificant. Although the Spanish-origin population made rapid gains in school attendance at ages over fourteen during the 1970-80 decade, the gains were not sufficient to catch up to the black and white populations.

The championship in school attendance rates, by a healthy margin, is held by the Oriental population. The Asian and Pacific Island population shows school attendance rates between ages seventeen and thirty-four that are far above those for the white population; at ages twenty-one to twenty-four the rates are double those for the whites. The high rates of college and postgraduate enrollment is particularly impressive in view of the fact that a substantial portion of the youth in these ages is made up of recent immigrants.

American Indians have lower rates of school attendance after age sixteen than any other minority group. The difference seems to be a greater tendency to drop out of high school in the third or fourth year and not to attend college. As for the Spanish-origin population, rapid social change is under way, and these differentials may well shrink in the future.

When today's generation of black and other minority children reaches adulthood, their level of education will enable them to participate in every phase of the economy. Whatever handicap they suffer will be linked to the quality of their instruction and of their educational environment and not to their refusal or failure to enroll at ages above those of legal compulsion. Table 9-3 provides data that show how the sex and race differentials have continued to evolve since 1980.

Grade in Which Enrolled

Students usually enter elementary school when they are six years of age (or when they will be six within a few months). Thus, the "normal" student can expect to graduate from elementary school at the age of thirteen or fourteen, from high school at seventeen or eighteen, and from college at twenty-one or twenty-two.[1] Actually, many students deviate rather markedly from this theoretical progression. A few, whose abilities demand more challenges, are "accelerated" by being enrolled in grades whose members are older than their own age group. A larger number fall behind, either because they fail to master the materials or because of illness or other factors that prevent steady attendance. Table 9-4 (A-D) reports the actual grade distribution of students enrolled in school in 1980. The diagonal line indicates roughly the theoretical line of progress. Cells that fall to the right of this line represent acceleration, while cells that fall to the left represent slower progress. One might conclude from the data that in 1980 the population had the following overall record of progress in school, in comparison with similar data for 1950:

Age	Behind schedule		Accelerated	
	1980	1950	1980	1950
8 years . . .	4.0	6.6	2.5	3.9
9 years . . .	5.7	11.2	2.2	3.8
10 years. . .	6.8	15.7	2.4	4.2
11 years. . .	6.6	18.0	2.2	4.1
12 years. . .	7.2	21.6	2.2	4.4
13 years. . .	7.4	23.6	2.1	4.7
14 years. . .	8.3	25.0	2.2	5.9
15 years. . .	9.1	26.0	2.0	5.9
16 years. . .	9.7	24.6	2.3	6.2
17 years. . .	10.3	22.0	1.9	3.2
18 years. . .	11.2	23.4	2.5	5.6

The rough method of calculation used here indicates that at most ages only about 2 percent of the students are accelerated and that 6 to 10 percent are behind. At ages 13-14 (the normal time of graduation from elementary school), about one pupil in fourteen is behind by a year or more. (Inspection of Table 9-4 shows that about 85 percent of these students are behind by only one year. In comparison with a similar tabulation for 1950, it appears that retardation and acceleration in 1980 are both only a fraction of what was the case three decades ago. This could reflect changes in educational policy.) At the normal time of graduation from high school, a somewhat greater proportion of students are behind, presumably because some withdrew and then returned.

Table 9-5A-F is an abbreviation of Table 9-4, prepared for each age of the race-ethnicity groups. This set of data provides a profile of the educational effort each group is making at each age. These tables show the level of education in which persons at each age are enrolled. By reference to the national average, one may note magnitudes of "acceleration" or falling behind at

Table 9-4A. Year of School in Which Enrolled, by Single Years of Age, for the United States: All Races, 1980 [percent distribution]

Age	Persons enrolled in school	Year of school in which enrolled: Elementary school 1	2	3	4	5	6	7	8	High school 1	2	3	4	College 1	2	3	4	5 or more	In nursery school or kindergarten	Median school year in which enrolled
5 to 29. .	100.0	5.9	6.0	6.5	6.5	6.4	6.3	6.4	6.6	6.9	7.1	6.5	6.0	4.9	4.1	2.9	2.6	2.2	6.3	7.0
5 to 24. .	100.0	6.1	6.2	6.7	6.7	6.6	6.5	6.7	6.9	7.2	7.3	6.7	6.1	4.6	3.6	2.5	2.1	1.0	6.5	6.7
5 years. .	100.0	3.6	0.3	0.1	*	*	*	*	*	*	*	*	*	*	*	*	*	*	96.0	*
6.	100.0	55.9	2.7	0.3	0.1	*	*	*	*	*	*	*	*	*	*	*	*	*	41.0	*
7.	100.0	43.8	51.1	3.2	0.3	*	*	*	*	*	*	*	*	*	*	*	*	*	1.6	*
8.	100.0	4.0	43.0	50.5	2.3	0.2	*	*	*	*	*	*	*	*	*	*	*	*	*	2.1
9.	100.0	0.4	5.3	43.5	48.6	2.0	0.2	*	*	*	*	*	*	*	*	*	*	*	*	3.0
10	100.0	0.1	0.5	6.2	42.4	48.3	2.2	0.2	*	*	*	*	*	*	*	*	*	*	*	4.0
11	100.0	0.1	0.1	0.6	5.8	42.4	48.7	2.1	0.2	*	*	*	*	*	*	*	*	*	*	5.0
12	100.0	*	0.1	0.2	0.8	6.1	42.3	48.3	2.0	0.2	*	*	*	*	*	*	*	*	*	6.0
13	100.0	*	*	0.1	0.2	0.8	6.3	42.3	48.1	1.9	0.2	*	*	*	*	*	*	*	*	7.0
14	100.0	*	*	*	0.1	0.2	0.9	7.1	41.4	47.7	2.2	0.2	*	*	*	*	*	*	*	8.0
15	100.0	*	0.1	*	*	0.1	0.2	1.3	7.4	41.7	47.1	1.8	0.2	*	*	*	*	*	*	9.0
16 years .	100.0	0.1	0.1	*	*	*	0.1	0.3	1.4	7.7	42.4	45.5	2.1	0.2	*	*	*	*	*	9.9
17	100.0	0.1	0.1	*	*	*	0.1	0.1	0.4	1.7	7.8	41.9	45.9	1.7	0.2	*	*	*	*	10.9
18	100.0	*	*	*	*	*	0.1	0.1	0.2	0.6	2.0	8.2	50.1	36.1	2.3	0.2	*	*	*	11.8
19	100.0	*	*	*	*	*	*	0.1	0.2	0.4	0.9	2.2	11.1	43.2	39.0	2.7	0.3	*	*	12.8
20	100.0	*	*	*	*	*	*	0.1	0.1	0.3	0.6	0.9	3.0	16.0	40.3	35.4	3.2	0.2	*	13.7
21	100.0	*	*	*	*	*	*	*	0.1	0.2	0.4	0.6	1.6	10.7	16.5	34.3	34.3	1.4	*	14.6
22	100.0	*	*	*	*	*	*	0.2	0.1	0.3	0.5	0.5	1.5	11.7	14.4	17.3	39.2	14.5	*	15.1
23	100.0	*	*	*	*	*	*	0.2	0.3	0.3	0.5	0.7	1.6	14.0	15.6	15.0	23.7	28.0	*	15.1
24	100.0	*	*	*	*	*	*	0.1	0.4	0.5	0.6	0.7	1.8	14.6	16.1	13.6	19.6	32.0	*	15.1
25 to 29 .	100.0	*	*	*	*	*	*	0.1	0.3	0.5	0.8	0.9	2.0	14.7	17.0	12.5	16.8	34.4	*	15.1

Note: * indicates zero or less than 0.1.

Source: U.S. Bureau of the Census. "Detailed Population Characteristics: United States Summary." 1980 Census of Population. Washington, DC: U.S. Government Printing Office, 1984, Table 260.

Table 9-4B. Year of School in Which Enrolled, by Single Years of Age, for the United States: White Students, 1980 [percent distribution]

Age	Persons enrolled in school	Year of school in which enrolled: Elementary school 1	2	3	4	5	6	7	8	High school 1	2	3	4	College 1	2	3	4	5 or more	In nursery school or kindergarten	Median school year in which enrolled
5 to 29. .	100.0	5.7	5.9	6.4	6.5	6.3	6.2	6.4	6.5	6.9	7.0	6.5	6.1	5.0	4.2	3.0	2.8	2.3	6.2	7.0
5 to 24. .	100.0	5.9	6.1	6.6	6.7	6.6	6.5	6.6	6.8	7.1	7.3	6.7	6.3	4.7	3.7	2.7	2.3	1.1	6.5	6.8
5 years. .	100.0	2.7	0.2	*	*	*	*	*	*	*	*	*	*	*	*	*	*	*	97.0	*
6.	100.0	55.4	2.0	0.2	*	*	*	*	*	*	*	*	*	*	*	*	*	*	42.4	*
7.	100.0	44.8	50.9	2.5	0.2	*	*	*	*	*	*	*	*	*	*	*	*	*	1.5	*
8.	100.0	3.7	43.8	50.6	1.7	0.2	*	*	*	*	*	*	*	*	*	*	*	*	*	2.0
9.	100.0	0.3	4.8	44.1	49.0	1.5	0.1	*	*	*	*	*	*	*	*	*	*	*	*	3.0
10	100.0	0.1	0.4	5.5	43.1	48.8	1.8	0.2	*	*	*	*	*	*	*	*	*	*	*	4.0
11	100.0	0.1	0.1	0.5	5.0	43.1	49.4	1.7	0.2	*	*	*	*	*	*	*	*	*	*	5.0
12	100.0	*	0.1	0.1	0.6	5.3	42.7	49.3	1.7	0.2	*	*	*	*	*	*	*	*	*	6.0
13	100.0	*	*	0.1	0.1	0.6	5.5	42.7	49.1	1.6	0.2	*	*	*	*	*	*	*	*	7.0
14	100.0	*	*	*	0.1	0.1	0.7	6.1	41.8	49.0	1.9	0.2	*	*	*	*	*	*	*	8.0
15	100.0	*	0.1	*	*	0.1	0.2	1.0	6.3	41.9	48.7	1.6	0.2	*	*	*	*	*	*	9.0
16 years .	100.0	0.1	*	*	*	*	0.1	0.2	1.0	6.3	42.7	47.3	1.9	0.2	*	*	*	*	*	10.0
17	100.0	0.1	*	*	*	*	0.1	0.1	0.3	1.2	6.3	42.3	47.8	1.6	0.1	*	*	*	*	11.0
18	100.0	*	*	*	*	*	*	0.1	0.2	0.4	1.3	6.7	51.1	37.7	2.2	0.2	*	*	*	11.8
19	100.0	*	*	*	*	*	*	0.1	0.1	0.3	0.6	1.4	9.3	44.3	41.0	2.6	0.3	*	*	12.9
20	100.0	*	*	*	*	*	*	*	0.1	0.2	0.4	0.6	2.2	14.8	41.1	37.3	3.2	0.2	*	13.8
21	100.0	*	*	*	*	*	*	*	0.1	0.1	0.2	0.3	1.1	9.7	15.5	35.1	36.4	1.4	*	14.7
22	100.0	*	*	*	*	*	*	0.1	0.1	0.2	0.3	0.3	1.1	10.8	13.5	16.6	41.5	15.4	*	15.2
23	100.0	*	*	*	*	*	*	0.2	0.2	0.3	0.4	0.4	1.3	13.2	14.9	14.7	24.2	30.3	*	15.2
24	100.0	*	*	*	*	*	*	0.1	0.3	0.4	0.4	0.4	1.3	13.8	15.3	13.3	20.0	34.7	*	15.2
25 to 29 .	100.0	*	*	*	*	*	*	0.1	0.2	0.3	0.6	0.6	1.5	13.8	16.2	12.3	17.3	37.2	*	15.3

Note: * indicates zero or less than 0.1.

Source: U.S. Bureau of the Census. "Detailed Population Characteristics: United States Summary." 1980 Census of Population. Washington, DC: U.S. Government Printing Office, 1984, Table 260.

Table 9-4C. Year of School in Which Enrolled, by Single Years of Age, for the United States: Black Students, 1980 [percent distribution]

Age	Persons enrolled in school	Year of school in which enrolled: Elementary school 1	2	3	4	5	6	7	8	High school 1	2	3	4	College 1	2	3	4	5 or more	In nursery school or kindergarten	Median school year in which enrolled
5 to 29. .	100.0	6.3	6.4	6.9	6.7	6.5	6.6	6.8	7.2	7.5	7.5	6.6	5.8	4.4	3.5	2.3	1.6	0.9	6.3	6.6
5 to 24. .	100.0	6.5	6.6	7.1	6.9	6.7	6.8	7.1	7.4	7.7	7.7	6.7	5.9	3.9	2.9	1.9	1.2	0.4	6.5	6.4
5 years. .	100.0	6.9	0.7	*	*	*	*	*	*	*	*	*	*	*	*	*	*	*	92.2	*
6.	100.0	58.2	5.6	0.7	*	*	*	*	*	*	*	*	*	*	*	*	*	*	35.4	*
7.	100.0	39.8	51.6	6.0	0.6	*	*	*	*	*	*	*	*	*	*	*	*	*	1.8	*
8.	100.0	5.0	39.0	50.8	4.6	0.4	*	*	*	*	*	*	*	*	*	*	*	*	0.1	2.1
9.	100.0	0.6	7.1	40.4	47.4	4.1	0.4	*	*	*	*	*	*	*	*	*	*	*	0.1	3.0
10	100.0	0.1	0.8	8.8	39.0	46.4	4.2	0.5	0.1	*	*	*	*	*	*	*	*	*	*	4.0
11	100.0	0.1	0.1	1.0	8.7	39.0	46.7	4.0	0.4	*	*	*	*	*	*	*	*	*	*	5.0
12	100.0	0.1	*	0.3	1.4	9.0	40.1	44.8	3.7	0.4	*	*	*	*	*	*	*	*	*	6.0
13	100.0	*	*	0.1	0.3	1.6	9.6	40.1	44.4	3.4	0.4	0.1	*	*	*	*	*	*	*	7.0
14	100.0	0.1	*	0.1	0.1	0.3	1.7	11.1	39.7	42.8	3.7	0.4	*	*	*	*	*	*	*	7.9
15	100.0	*	0.1	0.1	0.1	0.1	0.4	2.6	11.9	40.3	41.2	2.9	0.3	*	*	*	*	*	*	8.9
16 years .	100.0	0.1	0.1	*	*	0.1	0.2	0.7	2.9	13.2	40.9	38.5	3.1	0.2	*	*	*	*	*	9.8
17	100.0	0.1	0.1	0.1	*	0.1	0.1	0.3	0.9	3.8	14.4	39.8	38.2	2.0	0.2	*	*	*	*	10.8
18	100.0	0.1	*	*	*	*	0.1	0.2	0.4	1.5	4.8	15.6	46.0	28.1	2.8	0.2	*	*	*	11.6
19	100.0	*	*	*	*	*	*	0.2	0.4	0.8	2.5	6.2	20.0	37.2	29.5	2.7	0.3	*	*	12.5
20	100.0	*	*	*	*	*	*	0.2	0.4	0.8	1.6	2.9	7.6	20.6	36.1	26.7	2.9	0.2	*	13.4
21	100.0	*	*	*	*	*	*	0.2	0.4	0.6	1.2	2.0	4.4	15.2	20.9	30.8	23.1	1.2	*	14.2
22	100.0	*	*	*	*	*	*	0.3	0.3	0.8	1.4	1.6	3.7	15.7	18.8	20.9	28.3	8.4	*	14.4
23	100.0	*	*	*	*	*	*	0.4	0.7	0.8	1.5	1.9	3.6	18.4	19.6	16.9	21.0	15.2	*	14.2
24	100.0	*	*	*	*	*	*	0.3	0.8	0.9	1.6	2.0	3.9	20.6	20.8	15.8	17.6	15.7	*	14.0
25 to 29 .	100.0	*	*	*	*	*	*	0.3	0.7	1.2	2.1	2.7	4.4	20.1	22.1	14.7	14.3	17.4	*	13.8

Note: * indicates zero or less than 0.1.

Source: U.S. Bureau of the Census. "Detailed Population Characteristics: United States Summary." 1980 Census of Population. Washington, DC: U.S. Government Printing Office, 1984, Table 260.

Table 9-4D. Year of School in Which Enrolled, by Single Years of Age, for the United States: Spanish-Origin Students, 1980 [percent distribution]

Age	Persons enrolled in school	Year of school in which enrolled: Elementary school 1	2	3	4	5	6	7	8	High school 1	2	3	4	College 1	2	3	4	5 or more	In nursery school or kindergarten	Median school year in which enrolled
5 to 29. .	100.0	7.4	7.3	7.5	7.1	6.9	6.8	6.8	6.9	7.1	6.7	5.6	5.0	4.0	3.1	1.9	1.4	1.1	7.4	5.9
5 to 24. .	100.0	7.6	7.5	7.7	7.4	7.1	7.0	7.0	7.1	7.3	6.8	5.7	5.0	3.6	2.6	1.5	1.0	0.5	7.7	5.7
5 years. .	100.0	6.6	0.6	0.1	*	*	*	*	*	*	*	*	*	*	*	*	*	*	92.7	*
6.	100.0	56.2	4.7	0.5	0.1	*	*	*	*	*	*	*	*	*	*	*	*	*	38.6	*
7.	100.0	43.1	49.7	4.7	0.5	*	*	*	*	*	*	*	*	*	*	*	*	*	2.0	*
8.	100.0	5.6	43.4	47.1	3.5	0.3	0.1	*	*	*	*	*	*	*	*	*	*	*	*	2.0
9.	100.0	0.6	7.7	44.0	44.2	3.0	0.3	*	*	*	*	*	*	*	*	*	*	*	*	2.9
10	100.0	0.2	1.0	9.3	42.5	43.6	3.1	0.3	0.1	*	*	*	*	*	*	*	*	*	*	3.9
11	100.0	0.1	0.2	1.2	9.0	42.8	43.4	2.9	0.3	0.1	*	*	*	*	*	*	*	*	*	4.9
12	100.0	0.1	0.1	0.4	1.5	9.7	43.2	42.0	2.6	0.3	0.1	*	*	*	*	*	*	*	*	5.9
13	100.0	*	0.1	0.1	0.4	1.6	10.4	43.3	41.3	2.5	0.3	*	*	*	*	*	*	*	*	6.9
14	100.0	0.1	0.1	0.1	0.1	0.4	1.8	11.2	42.5	40.5	2.9	0.3	*	*	*	*	*	*	*	7.9
15	100.0	0.1	0.1	0.1	0.1	0.2	0.5	2.4	12.1	43.5	38.4	2.2	0.3	*	*	*	*	*	*	8.8
16 years .	100.0	0.1	0.1	0.1	0.1	0.1	0.3	0.7	2.7	13.5	43.3	36.0	2.6	0.3	*	*	*	*	*	9.7
17	100.0	0.1	0.2	0.1	0.1	0.1	0.4	0.4	1.0	3.9	13.9	41.6	35.8	2.1	0.2	*	*	*	*	10.7
18	100.0	0.1	0.1	0.1	0.1	0.1	0.3	0.3	0.7	1.6	4.6	14.5	48.5	26.3	2.5	0.3	*	*	*	11.6
19	100.0	*	*	*	*	*	*	0.3	0.7	1.4	2.2	5.2	20.8	39.1	27.2	2.7	0.4	*	*	12.5
20	100.0	*	*	*	*	*	*	0.3	0.6	1.0	1.5	2.4	7.8	25.2	36.4	21.8	2.7	0.2	*	13.3
21	100.0	*	*	*	*	*	*	0.3	0.7	0.9	1.0	1.8	4.2	18.2	24.4	27.8	19.1	1.6	*	13.9
22	100.0	*	*	*	*	*	*	0.7	0.7	1.3	1.5	1.6	3.9	17.0	20.4	19.4	24.4	9.1	*	14.2
23	100.0	*	*	*	*	*	*	0.7	1.0	1.2	1.5	1.9	4.0	18.2	20.1	15.9	18.9	16.7	*	14.1
24	100.0	*	*	*	*	*	*	0.3	1.4	1.4	1.2	1.6	3.7	18.6	19.9	15.3	15.6	20.9	*	13.8
25 to 29 .	100.0	*	*	*	*	*	*	0.7	1.2	1.5	1.9	2.1	4.2	18.9	20.4	13.7	13.9	21.6	*	14.0

Note: * indicates zero or less than 0.1.

Source: U.S. Bureau of the Census. "Detailed Population Characteristics: United States Summary." 1980 Census of Population. Washington, DC: U.S. Government Printing Office, 1984, Table 260.

Table 9-5A. Level of School in Which Enrolled, by Sex and Age: All Races, 1980

Age	Male				Female			
	Elementary school	High school	College		Elementary school	High school	College	
			1-4 years	5 years and over			1-4 years	5 years and over
10 years	100.0	*	*	*	100.0	*	*	*
11 years	100.0	*	*	*	100.0	*	*	*
12 years	99.7	0.3	*	*	99.7	0.3	*	*
13 years	98.0	2.0	*	*	97.6	2.4	*	*
14 years	53.9	46.1	*	*	45.5	54.5	*	*
15 years	11.4	88.6	*	*	6.7	93.3	*	*
16 years	2.5	97.3	0.2	*	1.6	98.2	0.2	*
17 years	1.0	97.6	1.4	*	0.7	97.0	2.3	*
18 years	0.6	66.1	33.3	*	0.5	55.5	44.0	*
19 years	0.3	18.3	81.4	*	0.2	10.9	88.8	*
20 years	0.3	5.6	94.0	0.2	0.2	3.9	95.7	0.2
21 years	0.2	2.9	95.5	1.3	0.1	2.5	95.9	1.4
22 years	0.3	2.6	82.7	14.4	0.3	2.9	82.3	14.5
23 years	0.5	2.9	68.1	28.5	0.5	3.5	68.6	27.4
24 years	0.5	3.1	62.9	33.5	0.6	4.1	65.4	29.9
25-29 years	0.4	3.6	59.4	36.6	0.5	4.8	62.9	31.8
30-34 years	0.6	3.0	56.8	39.6	0.7	5.0	64.3	30.0
35-39 years	1.0	5.0	54.4	39.6	0.8	6.1	64.6	28.5
40-44 years	1.5	5.9	59.4	33.3	1.1	7.3	64.5	27.1
45-54 years	2.9	8.7	56.5	32.0	2.2	9.5	62.4	25.9
55-64 years	6.8	15.9	50.9	26.5	6.2	17.4	57.0	19.4
65 years and over	17.4	20.1	45.2	17.3	16.7	23.5	48.5	11.4

Source: U.S. Bureau of the Census. "Detailed Population Characteristics: United States Summary." 1980 Census of Population. Washington, DC: U.S. Government Printing Office, 1984, Table 260.

Table 9-5B. Level of School in Which Enrolled, by Sex and Age: White Students, 1980

Age	Male				Female			
	Elementary school	High school	College		Elementary school	High school	College	
			1-4 years	5 years and over			1-4 years	5 years and over
10 years	100.0	*	*	*	100.0	*	*	*
11 years	99.9	0.1	*	*	100.0	*	*	*
12 years	99.8	0.2	*	*	99.8	0.2	*	*
13 years	98.3	1.7	*	*	98.0	2.0	*	*
14 years	53.0	47.0	*	*	44.5	55.5	*	*
15 years	9.7	90.3	*	*	5.4	94.5	*	*
16 years	1.9	97.9	0.2	*	1.2	98.6	0.2	*
17 years	0.7	97.9	1.3	*	0.6	97.3	2.1	*
18 years	0.5	64.5	35.0	*	0.4	54.1	45.5	*
19 years	0.2	14.8	85.0	*	0.2	8.3	91.5	*
20 years	0.2	3.8	95.8	0.2	0.1	2.7	97.1	0.2
21 years	0.1	1.9	96.7	1.3	0.1	1.6	96.8	1.4
22 years	0.2	1.8	82.7	15.4	0.2	2.0	82.2	15.5
23 years	0.4	2.2	66.7	30.7	0.4	2.6	67.3	29.7
24 years	0.4	2.3	61.1	36.2	0.5	3.0	64.0	32.6
25-29 years	0.2	2.7	58.0	39.1	0.3	3.5	61.5	34.7
30-34 years	0.4	2.0	55.4	42.2	0.4	3.5	63.4	32.6
35-39 years	0.7	3.8	53.7	41.8	0.5	4.4	64.6	30.5
40-44 years	1.0	4.3	59.3	35.4	0.7	5.3	65.1	28.9
45-54 years	2.1	6.9	56.5	34.5	1.4	7.4	63.9	27.3
55-64 years	5.2	14.1	52.3	28.4	4.5	15.1	59.6	20.8
65 years and over	16.3	19.3	46.0	18.4	15.1	22.5	50.5	11.9

Source: U.S. Bureau of the Census. "Detailed Population Characteristics: United States Summary." 1980 Census of Population. Washington, DC: U.S. Government Printing Office, 1984, Table 260.

Table 9-5C. Level of School in Which Enrolled, by Sex and Age: Black Students, 1980

Age	Male				Female			
	Elementary school	High school	College		Elementary school	High school	College	
			1-4 years	5 years and over			1-4 years	5 years and over
10 years	100.0	*	*	*	100.0	*	*	*
11 years	99.9	0.1	*	*	99.9	0.1	*	*
12 years	99.5	0.5	*	*	99.4	0.6	*	*
13 years	96.4	3.5	*	*	95.8	4.2	*	*
14 years	57.3	42.6	*	*	48.8	51.2	*	*
15 years	18.9	81.1	*	*	11.6	88.4	*	*
16 years	5.2	94.6	0.2	*	3.0	96.8	0.2	*
17 years	1.9	96.6	1.5	*	1.3	95.8	2.9	*
18 years	1.1	75.1	23.8	*	0.8	61.2	38.1	*
19 years	0.8	37.9	61.2	*	0.5	22.4	77.1	*
20 years	0.8	17.0	82.0	0.2	0.4	9.8	89.7	0.2
21 years	0.8	10.2	88.0	1.0	0.3	6.8	91.6	1.3
22 years	0.7	8.4	83.8	7.1	0.5	6.7	83.5	9.4
23 years	1.3	8.0	76.8	13.9	0.8	7.6	75.2	16.3
24 years	1.0	8.4	75.4	15.2	1.1	8.6	74.1	16.2
25-29 years.	0.9	9.8	71.7	17.6	1.2	10.9	70.8	17.2
30-34 years.	1.2	8.5	68.7	21.6	1.7	11.2	69.6	17.5
35-39 years.	2.3	12.1	61.1	24.5	1.6	14.0	66.6	17.8
40-44 years.	3.6	13.3	63.4	19.7	2.6	16.9	62.0	18.6
45-54 years.	6.3	18.1	55.1	20.5	5.9	19.9	54.6	19.7
55-64 years.	16.3	28.5	40.1	15.2	15.3	29.7	42.9	12.0
65 years and over. . . .	26.6	27.3	38.0	8.1	28.2	30.4	34.1	7.4

Source: U.S. Bureau of the Census. "Detailed Population Characteristics: United States Summary." 1980 Census of Population. Washington, DC: U.S. Government Printing Office, 1984, Table 260.

Table 9-5D. Level of School in Which Enrolled, by Sex and Age: Spanish-Origin Students, 1980

Age	Male				Female			
	Elementary school	High school	College		Elementary school	High school	College	
			1-4 years	5 years and over			1-4 years	5 years and over
10 years	100.0	*	*	*	100.0	*	*	*
11 years	99.9	0.1	*	*	99.9	0.1	*	*
12 years	99.6	0.4	*	*	99.6	0.4	*	*
13 years	97.3	2.7	*	*	97.0	3.0	*	*
14 years	59.2	40.7	*	*	53.1	46.9	*	*
15 years	18.1	81.8	*	*	12.7	87.2	*	*
16 years	4.9	94.8	0.2	*	3.6	96.0	0.3	*
17 years	2.7	95.3	2.0	*	2.2	95.2	2.6	*
18 years	1.9	72.6	25.5	*	1.4	65.6	33.0	*
19 years	1.2	33.9	64.9	0.1	0.8	25.3	74.0	*
20 years	1.1	13.9	84.7	0.3	0.7	11.5	87.7	0.1
21 years	1.0	8.7	88.6	1.7	1.0	7.1	90.4	1.6
22 years	1.2	8.3	80.9	9.5	1.5	8.3	81.5	8.7
23 years	1.6	8.2	73.7	16.5	1.8	8.9	72.4	17.0
24 years	1.8	7.1	69.4	21.7	1.7	9.1	69.3	19.9
25-29 years.	1.8	8.7	66.6	23.0	2.1	10.9	67.1	20.0
30-34 years.	2.8	8.6	62.5	26.2	3.5	12.5	65.3	18.8
35-39 years.	3.5	11.2	58.5	26.8	4.4	14.8	63.6	17.2
40-44 years.	4.8	11.8	59.7	23.7	4.3	15.3	62.6	17.8
45-54 years.	6.8	15.8	55.4	22.1	6.0	17.8	59.1	17.2
55-64 years.	13.1	21.0	47.5	18.4	12.4	23.3	48.5	15.9
65 years and over. . . .	24.6	22.5	35.5	17.3	26.9	26.5	37.0	9.6

Source: U.S. Bureau of the Census. "Detailed Population Characteristics: United States Summary." 1980 Census of Population. Washington, DC: U.S. Government Printing Office, 1984, Table 260.

Table 9-5E. Level of School in Which Enrolled, by Sex and Age: Asian and Pacific Islander Students, 1980

Age	Male				Female			
	Elementary school	High school	College		Elementary school	High school	College	
			1-4 years	5 years and over			1-4 years	5 years and over
10 years	100.0	*	*	*	100.0	*	*	*
11 years	99.9	0.1	*	*	99.9	0.1	*	*
12 years	99.4	0.5	*	*	99.4	0.6	*	*
13 years	95.9	4.1	*	*	95.7	4.3	*	*
14 years	46.8	53.2	*	*	43.8	56.2	*	*
15 years	9.9	90.1	0.1	*	9.0	90.9	*	*
16 years	2.8	96.6	0.5	*	3.0	96.2	0.8	*
17 years	1.3	94.1	4.5	*	1.3	93.9	4.8	*
18 years	1.1	55.7	43.2	*	1.0	48.2	50.7	*
19 years	0.4	16.1	83.5	*	0.3	13.0	86.7	*
20 years	0.5	5.8	93.1	0.7	0.2	4.8	94.8	0.2
21 years	0.3	3.8	93.0	2.9	0.2	3.0	94.2	2.6
22 years	0.3	2.5	80.3	17.0	0.3	2.6	79.8	17.3
23 years	0.4	1.6	69.7	28.3	0.4	2.0	64.9	32.7
24 years	0.7	2.0	59.1	38.2	0.9	4.6	58.3	36.2
25-29 years	0.5	2.2	48.4	48.9	0.8	4.0	56.6	38.6
30-34 years	0.5	2.6	45.6	51.3	1.3	4.8	57.8	36.1
35-39 years	0.4	3.8	45.5	50.4	1.2	6.3	56.2	36.3
40-44 years	0.5	6.1	50.2	43.1	2.3	7.4	59.4	30.9
45-54 years	2.2	7.3	58.9	31.6	2.2	8.1	64.9	24.9
55-64 years	3.7	9.7	60.3	26.4	4.4	13.4	60.8	21.3
65 years and over	12.9	16.0	50.6	20.5	10.3	24.3	50.1	15.3

Source: U.S. Bureau of the Census. "Detailed Population Characteristics: United States Summary." 1980 Census of Population. Washington, DC: U.S. Government Printing Office, 1984, Table 260.

Table 9-5F. Level of School in Which Enrolled, by Sex and Age: American Indian/Eskimo/Aleut Students, 1980

Age	Male				Female			
	Elementary school	High school	College		Elementary school	High school	College	
			1-4 years	5 years and over			1-4 years	5 years and over
10 years	100.0	*	*	*	100.0	*	*	*
11 years	100.0	*	*	*	99.9	*	*	*
12 years	99.7	0.3	*	*	99.6	0.4	*	*
13 years	98.0	2.0	*	*	96.6	3.4	*	*
14 years	60.7	39.3	*	*	54.2	45.8	*	*
15 years	19.6	80.4	0.1	*	13.5	86.4	*	*
16 years	4.0	95.6	0.3	*	4.2	95.5	0.3	*
17 years	1.7	96.5	1.9	*	1.5	96.1	2.4	*
18 years	1.2	78.7	20.1	*	1.3	67.9	30.8	*
19 years	1.7	43.0	54.9	0.3	0.7	28.3	70.9	0.1
20 years	0.4	17.7	81.9	*	1.1	13.9	84.8	0.2
21 years	0.7	9.4	88.7	1.2	0.4	8.3	90.3	1.0
22 years	0.5	5.8	86.0	4.6	0.7	7.8	83.8	7.8
23 years	0.4	8.3	76.2	15.1	1.8	7.6	73.8	16.8
24 years	1.5	6.8	77.0	14.7	*	11.1	73.3	15.6
25-29 years	0.6	6.6	71.1	21.6	1.1	6.9	78.1	14.0
30-34 years	1.0	3.1	70.0	25.9	1.4	7.5	74.4	16.7
35-39 years	3.2	5.8	67.6	23.4	0.6	7.5	73.9	18.0
40-44 years	2.3	8.6	67.9	21.2	3.7	10.6	69.7	16.0
45-54 years	7.6	7.5	64.4	20.4	1.4	11.8	69.8	17.0
55-64 years	13.7	12.3	44.4	29.6	5.8	16.0	62.9	15.2
65 years and over	17.2	26.2	38.9	17.6	20.0	23.8	43.9	12.2

Source: U.S. Bureau of the Census. "Detailed Population Characteristics: United States Summary." 1980 Census of Population. Washington, DC: U.S. Government Printing Office, 1984, Table 260.

each age for each group. The following findings emerge from this table.

1. A substantial share of disadvantaged minority groups are making efforts to correct past educational deficiencies by enrolling in high school even though they are well past high school age. These may be old dropouts repairing the damage to their employment potential.

2. Minority groups appear to suffer more delay in entering and completing college, perhaps because of economic problems.

3. Female students tend to fall behind less than male students, within each race-ethnic group, up to age twenty-two.

Table 9-6. Type of School in Which Enrolled, by Age and Race-Ethnicity: 1980

Race-ethnicity and age	Type of school: Public	Church-related	Other private
All races			
3-5 years.	57.3	20.2	22.5
6-13 years	88.5	10.0	1.6
14-17 years.	91.2	7.2	1.6
White			
3-5 years.	52.8	22.4	24.8
6-13 years	87.3	11.0	1.7
14-17 years.	90.2	8.0	1.8
Black			
3-5 years.	73.7	12.1	14.2
6-13 years	93.7	5.2	1.0
14-17 years.	96.2	3.1	0.8
Spanish-origin			
3-5 years.	73.8	13.4	12.8
6-13 years	89.7	9.4	0.9
14-17 years.	91.9	7.1	1.0
Asian/Pacific Islander			
3-5 years.	50.4	23.3	26.3
6-13 years	86.1	11.4	2.4
14-17 years.	89.6	7.9	2.5
American Indian			
3-5 years.	75.7	8.7	15.6
6-13 years	92.9	4.7	2.5
14-17 years.	94.4	3.2	2.4

Source: U.S. Bureau of the Census. "Detailed Population Characteristics: United States Summary." 1980 Census of Population. Washington, DC: U.S. Government Printing Office, 1984, Table 261.

Enrollment in Public and Private Schools

In 1980 at the elementary school level about one pupil in eight was enrolled in a private school, and at the high school level only one pupil in nine was in a private school (Table 9-6). At the college level, almost one student in four was attending a private college or university. Thus private schools participate most at the lower and upper educational levels, and least at the intermediate and high school levels. The students who attend private schools can be divided into two categories: church-related schools and others. Church-related schools dominate private education at the elementary and high school levels (less at high school than at elementary levels). Nonchurch schooling is most common at the preschool level. Minority populations depend more on public schools than does the white population. Spanish-origin persons, for religious reasons, are more inclined to use church-related schools.

Table 9-7. Enrollment in Private Schools as a Percent of All Enrollment, by Race and Grade Level: 1950 to 1980 [persons 3 years of age and older]

Race and year	Total	Elementary school: Kinder-garten	Elementary school: Grades 1-8	High school grades 9-12
All races				
1980	19.5	16.0	11.3	8.9
1970	33.6	15.9	11.5	9.8
1960	41.1	14.1	14.4	11.1
1950[a].	49.0	11.3	12.2	10.4
White				
1980	20.3	16.9	12.4	9.7
1970	33.8	16.6	12.9	10.7
1960	41.6	14.9	16.1	12.0
1950	--	--	--	--
Black				
1980	14.6	12.5	6.1	4.8
1970	33.1	11.0	3.6	3.8
1960	34.0	7.6	3.5	4.0
1950	--	--	--	--

[a]1950 figures are for the 1949-1950 school year.

Source: U.S. Bureau of the Census. "General Social and Economic Characteristics." 1980 Census of Population. Washington, DC: U.S. Government Printing Office, 1983, Table 82. Data for 1950 from National Center for Education Statistics. Digest of Education Statistics, 1983-1984. Washington, DC: U.S. Government Printing Office, 1983, Table 3.

Table 9-8. Preschool Enrollment of Children Aged 3-6, by Age and Race: Type of School, 1982 and 1972

Age, level, and attendance	1982			1972			Percent change 1972-82		
	Total	White	Black	Total	White	Black	Total	White	Black
Percent in school. . .	100.0	100.0	100.0	100.0	100.0	100.0	23.4	20.2	28.4
Age:									
3 years.	17.0	16.7	18.0	12.1	11.7	15.2	73.5	72.1	52.1
4 years.	27.4	27.0	29.4	25.4	24.9	27.5	33.5	30.3	37.4
5 years.	49.2	49.6	47.1	58.3	58.8	55.1	4.1	1.4	9.7
6 years.	6.4	6.6	5.4	4.2	4.6	2.2	85.6	72.5	214.3
Level of school									
Nursery school	39.5	40.0	37.5	29.0	29.1	29.2	67.8	65.2	64.9
Public	33.9	28.3	63.0	31.3	26.4	61.1	81.3	76.8	69.9
Private.	66.1	71.7	37.0	68.7	73.6	38.9	61.5	61.1	56.9
Kindergarten	60.5	60.0	62.5	71.0	70.9	70.8	5.2	1.7	13.4
Public	83.2	81.8	91.1	84.1	83.0	89.7	4.2	0.2	15.2
Private.	16.8	18.3	8.9	15.9	17.0	10.3	10.8	9.2	-2.2
Percent attending full day									
Nursery school	29.1	23.0	61.8	31.6	24.5	74.3	54.6	55.7	38.0
Kindergarten	32.4	26.8	61.4	17.9	13.8	38.6	90.4	98.3	80.3

Source: U.S. Bureau of the Census. "Social and Economic Characteristics of Students: October, 1972." Current Population Reports (Series P-20, no. 260). Also "School Enrollment--Social and Economic Characteristics of Students: October 1982." Current Population Reports (Series P-20). Washington, DC: U.S. Government Printing Office, 1974 (Table 4) and 1985 (Table 5).

Table 9-7 reports the proportion of all enrollment at each educational level that is enrollment in private schools. (Subtraction of these statistics from 100 percent gives the proportion enrolled in public schools.) The table provides this information for four decades, separately for each race-ethnic group. A substantial decline in the proportion of enrollment in private schools is discernible at all levels except preschool.

Attendance at Nursery School and Kindergarten

It has already been noted that preschool enrollment has increased in recent years. Table 9-8 provides additional information about this phenomenon.

1. Black parents are as much, or more, inclined as whites to place their children in preschool. Approximately the same percentage of three-, four-, and five-year-old children are in school, irrespective of race.

2. Black parents are more inclined to keep their very young children in preschool for the full day.

3. Black parents are more inclined to use public schools, whereas white parents are more inclined to use private schools (nursery schools) for their very young children.

High School Dropouts

The proportion of young persons who drop out of school without completing four years of high school is a measure of the insufficiency of present schooling. Table 9-9 presents data on the proportion of persons who are not enrolled in school, yet who are not high school graduates (that is, dropouts) by age, sex, and race-ethnicity for 1982. This table permits more precise evaluation of the significance of the leveling off in enrollment rates, described earlier. During the phase of rapid improvement in enrollment, the proportion of dropouts shrank impressively. However, since 1975 progress in this direction seems to have ceased. For the nation as a whole, about 16 percent of youth are dropping out of high school. For the black population the proportion is about 25 percent, and for the Spanish-origin population it is about 40 percent or more. Among the white population the problem is slightly more prevalent among males than females. For the black population it is substantially worse for males than for females. However, among the Spanish-origin population the girls drop out of school at an even faster pace than the boys.

Table 9-9. Proportion of High School Dropouts, by Age, Sex and Race-Ethnicity: 1960, 1972, 1982
[percent of persons who are not enrolled and who have not completed four years of high school]

Race-ethnicity and age	1982			1972			1960		
	Both sexes	Male	Female	Both sexes	Male	Female	Both sexes	Male	Female
All races									
16-17 years.	7.3	7.1	7.6	8.7	8.0	9.4	16.3	16.4	16.2
18-19 years.	16.7	17.9	15.4	14.7	15.3	14.2	26.8	27.4	26.1
20-21 years.	16.0	16.9	15.2	17.6	17.7	17.5	31.7	32.8	30.7
22-24 years.	14.6	15.4	13.9	17.1	15.9	18.3	34.3	35.2	33.5
25-29 years.	13.4	14.3	12.6	19.4	18.5	20.2	37.3	38.0	36.6
White									
16-17 years.	7.6	7.3	8.0	8.7	7.8	9.6	15.3	15.4	15.1
18-19 years.	15.8	16.6	14.9	13.3	13.5	13.2	24.8	25.4	24.2
20-21 years.	14.7	15.2	14.2	16.2	16.1	16.3	29.1	30.1	28.1
22-24 years.	13.7	14.4	13.1	15.9	14.8	16.9	31.4	32.2	30.7
25-29 years.	12.6	13.8	11.4	18.0	17.3	18.8	34.4	35.1	33.7
Black									
16-17 years.	6.0	6.4	5.5	8.5	9.4	7.6	23.8	24.0	23.6
18-19 years.	22.1	26.4	18.1	23.9	27.1	21.0	40.9	42.4	39.6
20-21 years.	24.1	28.1	20.6	27.7	30.3	25.6	50.6	53.3	48.1
22-24 years.	20.5	23.3	18.2	26.9	25.1	28.5	54.7	57.1	52.5
25-29 years.	19.5	19.7	19.3	32.0	30.9	33.0	58.3	60.3	56.6
Spanish-origin									
16-17 years.	13.9	12.2	15.9	15.4	11.7	19.3	--	--	--
18-19 years.	33.0	34.9	31.1	30.7	35.5	25.9	--	--	--
20-21 years.	36.1	34.8	37.4	42.1	40.4	43.4	--	--	--
22-24 years.	40.2	39.5	40.8	46.1	47.7	44.9	--	--	--
25-29 years.	39.5	41.8	37.3	49.3	48.8	49.8	--	--	--

Source: U.S. Bureau of the Census. "Characteristics of the Population: United States Summary." 1980 Census of Population. Also U.S. Bureau of the Census. "Social and Economic Characteristics of Students: October 1972." Current Population Reports (Series P-20, no. 260). Also U.S. Bureau of the Census. "School Enrollment--Social and Economic Characteristics of Students: October 1982." Current Population Reports (Series P-20). Washington, DC: U.S. Government Printing Office, 1963 (Tables 172 and 165), 1974 (Table 1), and 1985 (Table 1).

College Enrollment

As of 1982, 12.2 million persons were enrolled in college. All but about 1,400,000 of them were between the ages of sixteen and thirty-four. Tables 9-10A, 10B, and 10C provide information about the age, grade level, residence, and degree of attendance (full time or part time), by sex and race-ethnicity. To supply a measure of recent change, Tables 9-11A, 11B, and 11C provide the same information for 1972. The following items of information are noteworthy:

1. The traditional lower participation of women has been erased; as of 1982 the number of women enrolled in college was greater than that of men. This is an important change in educational structure. If present trends continue, women will outnumber men in college enrollment by a substantial margin in future years.

2. Attendance has been extended to older ages. There is more emphasis on attendance at graduate school (fifth and higher years).

3. About 70 percent of all college students are enrolled full time. At the youngest ages full-time enrollment is nearly 100 percent, but beyond age twenty it declines rapidly with increasing age. It is also lower for those doing postgraduate work than for undergraduates.

4. Men are slightly more inclined to attend private schools than women.

5. Blacks are more likely to be attending full time than white students.

6. Women are less likely than men to be attending full time.

Table 9-10A. Characteristics of Persons Aged 16-34 Enrolled in College, by Sex: All Races: 1982

Characteristic	Percent distribution			Sex ratio	Percent attending full time		
	Both sexes	Male	Female		Both sexes	Male	Female
Age							
Total, 16-34.	100.0	100.0	100.0	98.2	70.8	74.3	67.5
16 and 17 years	2.3	2.0	2.5	80.9	91.9	88.8	94.4
18 and 19 years	26.8	25.4	28.2	88.6	90.4	92.4	88.6
20 and 21 years	24.6	24.9	24.4	100.2	86.0	87.9	84.2
22-24 years	18.9	20.6	17.2	118.0	66.0	70.3	61.0
25-29 years	17.0	17.9	16.2	108.6	45.8	50.5	40.7
30-34 years	10.3	9.1	11.6	77.2	29.4	38.8	22.1
College year							
First	27.3	25.4	29.2	85.6	69.0	72.2	66.2
Second.	24.0	23.6	24.3	95.1	76.0	80.9	71.3
Third	16.6	17.4	15.9	107.9	76.5	76.9	76.0
Fourth.	15.5	15.8	15.1	102.4	80.9	81.8	80.0
Fifth	8.2	8.2	8.2	98.0	46.2	51.8	40.8
Sixth or higher	8.4	9.6	7.3	129.8	56.2	65.4	44.9
Residence							
Metropolitan.	76.1	76.8	75.4	100.0	68.3	71.8	64.8
In central cities	31.2	31.3	31.2	98.5	67.3	71.8	62.8
Outside central cities. . .	44.9	45.5	44.2	101.0	69.1	71.9	66.2
Nonmetropolitan	23.9	23.2	24.6	92.8	78.8	82.3	75.6
Control of college							
Public.	76.5	75.9	77.1	96.8	69.4	73.5	65.5
Private	23.5	24.1	22.9	103.1	75.4	76.8	74.1

Source: U.S. Bureau of the Census. "School Enrollment--Social and Economic Characteristics of Students: October 1982." Current Population Reports (Series P-20). Washington, DC: U.S. Government Printing Office, 1985, Table 6.

Table 9-10B. Characteristics of Persons Aged 16-34 Enrolled in College, by Sex: White Students, 1982

Characteristic	Percent distribution			Sex ratio	Percent attending full time		
	Both sexes	Male	Female		Both sexes	Male	Female
Age							
Total, 16-34.	100.0	100.0	100.0	99.4	70.5	73.9	67.2
16 and 17 years	2.3	2.0	2.5	80.2	91.4	89.0	93.4
18 and 19 years	27.3	25.6	29.1	87.4	90.6	93.2	88.3
20 and 21 years	25.2	25.6	24.8	102.5	86.1	88.1	84.0
22-24 years	18.2	20.0	16.4	121.5	65.0	68.7	60.5
25-29 years	17.0	17.9	16.0	110.9	44.3	49.7	38.3
30-34 years	10.1	8.9	11.2	79.3	26.4	34.4	20.1
College year							
First	27.1	24.6	29.5	82.9	69.2	72.9	66.2
Second.	23.0	22.9	23.0	98.9	75.9	80.3	71.5
Third	16.9	18.0	15.9	112.5	77.1	76.8	77.4
Fourth.	15.8	16.2	15.4	104.6	80.7	81.4	79.8
Fifth	8.3	8.1	8.5	94.5	43.0	47.3	39.0
Sixth or higher	8.9	10.2	7.7	132.0	55.6	65.5	42.5
Residence							
Metropolitan.	74.6	75.5	73.7	101.8	67.8	71.2	64.3
In central cities	27.4	27.9	26.9	103.3	66.6	71.5	61.5
Outside central cities. . .	47.1	47.5	46.8	101.0	68.5	71.1	66.0
Nonmetropolitan	25.4	24.5	26.3	92.7	78.4	81.9	75.1
Control of college							
Public.	76.1	75.8	76.4	98.7	68.9	72.9	65.0
Private	23.9	24.1	23.6	101.6	75.5	76.7	74.2

Source: U.S. Bureau of the Census. "School Enrollment--Social and Economic Characteristics of Students: October 1982." Current Population Reports (Series P-20). Washington, DC: U.S. Government Printing Office, 1985, Table 6.

Table 9-10C. Characteristics of Persons Aged 16-34, Enrolled in College, by Sex: Black Students, 1982

Characteristic	Percent distribution			Sex ratio	Percent attending full time		
	Both sexes	Male	Female		Both sexes	Male	Female
Age							
Total, 16-34	100.0	100.0	100.0	74.8	71.0	74.1	68.7
16 and 17 years	1.9	1.9	1.7	81.8	*	*	*
18 and 19 years	24.3	25.7	23.3	82.7	91.4	89.5	92.9
20 and 21 years	21.5	19.1	23.3	61.3	86.0	85.2	86.5
22-24 years	22.3	23.9	21.1	84.6	68.6	73.9	64.0
25-29 years	17.4	18.9	16.3	86.7	48.5	50.6	46.7
30-34 years	12.6	10.6	14.3	55.4	38.4	*	28.0
College year							
First	28.2	30.7	26.2	87.6	67.6	68.4	67.0
Second	30.6	27.2	33.2	61.2	74.4	80.5	70.6
Third	15.4	15.6	15.2	76.5	68.9	70.9	67.4
Fourth	14.8	13.7	15.8	64.7	79.1	*	79.1
Fifth	6.4	8.1	5.0	121.9	*	*	*
Sixth or higher	4.6	4.8	4.5	79.3	*	*	*
Residence							
Metropolitan	84.8	83.8	85.4	73.5	68.6	71.5	66.5
In central cities	58.5	57.3	59.3	72.3	69.2	72.3	67.0
Outside central cities	26.3	26.6	26.1	76.2	67.3	69.4	65.7
Nonmetropolitan	15.2	16.2	14.6	83.0	84.1	88.0	80.9
Control of college							
Public	76.6	72.8	79.7	68.4	70.7	74.4	68.2
Private	23.4	27.4	20.3	100.8	71.9	73.1	70.7

Note: * indicates base too small to show derived measure.

Source: U.S. Bureau of the Census. "School Enrollment--Social and Economic Characteristics of Students: October 1982." Current Population Reports (Series P-20). Washington, DC: U.S. Government Printing Office, 1985, Table 6.

Table 9-11A. Characteristics of Persons Aged 16-34 Enrolled in College, by Sex: All Races, 1972

Characteristic	Percent distribution			Sex ratio	Percent attending full time		
	Both sexes	Male	Female		Both sexes	Male	Female
Age							
Total, 16-34	100.0	100.0	100.0	140.4	75.9	76.5	75.2
16-17 years	3.5	2.9	4.3	93.3	95.1	97.0	93.3
18-19 years	32.3	28.2	38.0	104.0	93.9	94.2	93.6
20-21 years	25.5	24.1	27.4	123.7	89.1	90.3	87.7
22-24 years	17.6	20.6	13.4	215.1	65.4	72.7	49.9
25-29 years	14.8	17.5	11.0	225.6	41.3	47.0	28.6
30-34 years	6.4	6.8	5.8	165.0	31.4	33.2	28.3
College year							
First	27.9	25.0	31.9	110.2	76.9	78.2	75.5
Second	23.7	23.7	23.5	141.7	82.0	81.0	83.4
Third	17.5	17.8	17.1	145.6	82.6	81.6	84.1
Fourth	15.1	15.5	14.5	150.6	86.2	85.6	86.9
Fifth	8.3	8.4	8.2	144.3	43.0	51.9	30.2
Sixth or higher	7.6	9.6	4.9	276.8	53.8	58.0	41.9
Residence							
Metropolitan	76.2	76.4	76.0	141.1	74.2	75.1	72.8
In central cities	34.5	34.4	34.7	139.4	75.4	76.4	74.0
Outside central cities	41.7	42.0	41.3	142.6	73.2	74.0	71.9
Nonmetropolitan	23.8	23.6	24.0	138.1	81.6	81.0	82.4
Control of college							
Public	76.2	75.5	77.3	137.1	74.6	75.4	73.5
Private	23.8	24.5	22.7	151.7	80.2	79.8	80.8

Source: U.S. Bureau of the Census. "Social and Economic Characteristics of Students: October, 1972." Current Population Reports (Series P-20, no. 260). Washington, DC: U.S. Government Printing Office, 1974, Table 5.

Table 9-11B. Characteristics of Persons Aged 16-34 Enrolled in College, by Sex: White Students, 1972

Characteristic	Percent distribution			Sex ratio	Percent attending full time		
	Both sexes	Male	Female		Both sexes	Male	Female
Age							
Total, 16-34	100.0	100.0	100.0	143.7	76.1	76.6	75.5
16-17 years	3.4	2.7	4.4	88.1	95.3	97.8	93.1
18-19 years	32.3	28.3	38.2	106.2	93.9	94.3	93.5
20-21 years	25.7	24.2	28.0	124.2	89.8	91.4	87.9
22-24 years	17.4	20.3	13.2	220.5	65.6	72.9	49.1
25-29 years	15.0	17.8	10.9	234.7	40.6	46.1	27.8
30-34 years	6.1	6.7	5.2	185.0	31.4	32.6	29.1
College year							
First	26.7	23.8	30.9	110.4	77.1	78.6	75.5
Second	23.6	23.7	23.5	144.8	82.7	81.2	85.0
Third	17.7	18.1	17.1	152.7	82.5	81.6	83.8
Fourth	15.7	16.0	15.3	149.7	86.4	85.9	87.1
Fifth	8.4	8.6	8.2	149.6	62.9	51.6	29.9
Sixth or higher	7.8	9.9	4.9	289.3	53.7	57.9	41.5
Residence							
Metropolitan	75.4	75.7	75.0	145.1	74.5	75.3	73.4
In central cities	31.5	31.4	31.5	143.7	75.8	77.1	74.0
Outside central cities	44.0	44.3	43.5	146.1	73.5	73.9	72.9
Nonmetropolitan	24.6	24.3	25.0	139.6	81.2	80.6	82.0
Control of college							
Public	75.7	74.9	76.7	140.4	74.9	75.8	73.8
Private	24.3	25.1	23.3	154.8	79.8	79.0	81.0

Source: U.S. Bureau of the Census. "Social and Economic Characteristics of Students: October, 1972." Current Population Reports (Series P-20, no. 260). Washington, DC: U.S. Government Printing Office, 1974, Table 5.

Table 9-11C. Characteristics of Persons Aged 16-34 Enrolled in College, by Sex: Black Students, 1972

Characteristic	Percent distribution			Sex ratio	Percent attending full time		
	Both sexes	Male	Female		Both sexes	Male	Female
Age							
Total, 16-34	100.0	100.0	100.0	112.0	72.3	74.0	70.3
16-17 years	4.4	4.7	4.1	128.6	*	*	*
18-19 years	31.5	26.6	37.0	80.3	93.7	94.1	93.4
20-21 years	23.1	23.7	22.4	118.2	80.6	77.5	84.2
22-24 years	19.7	24.5	14.3	191.8	59.9	67.1	*
25-29 years	12.0	12.8	11.1	128.9	44.7	*	*
30-34 years	9.4	7.8	11.1	78.9	*	*	*
College year							
First	38.5	37.2	39.9	104.4	72.7	72.9	72.5
Second	24.5	24.7	24.2	114.5	73.7	77.8	68.9
Third	15.4	14.8	16.0	103.6	86.2	*	*
Fourth	9.6	10.9	8.2	150.0	*	*	*
Fifth	7.2	6.8	7.9	96.3	*	*	*
Sixth or higher	4.7	5.7	3.8	169.2	*	*	*
Residence							
Metropolitan	82.6	82.3	83.1	110.9	69.1	71.2	66.7
In central cities	61.5	63.8	58.9	121.3	70.1	69.9	70.3
Outside central cities	21.3	18.5	24.2	85.5	65.8	*	57.7
Nonmetropolitan	17.2	17.7	16.6	119.3	88.3	*	*
Control of college							
Public	80.1	78.6	81.6	107.9	69.6	70.2	68.9
Private	19.9	21.4	18.4	130.2	83.2	88.3	*

Note: * indicates base too small to show derived measures.

Source: U.S. Bureau of the Census. "Social and Economic Characteristics of Students: October, 1972." Current Population Reports (Series P-20, no. 260). Washington, DC: U.S. Government Printing Office, 1974, Table 5.

Enrollment of Older Persons

A development of unusual significance is the increased attendance of persons over thirty-five years of age. Table 9-12 presents data on this group.

1. Females outnumber males by a considerable margin.

2. Only a minor portion of this enrollment is linked to completing secondary school. Almost all of it represents college enrollment.

3. Nearly 80 percent of this enrollment is part time.

4. More than three-quarters of these students are also in the labor force, at least part time.

5. More than 70 percent of these students are married and living with their spouses.

6. The college enrollment rates of older black persons are about equal to those for whites. Blacks who are enrolled are more likely to attend full time than are whites.

7. The older males who attend college are more likely to be married and living with a spouse than are females. This is particularly true for white males.

Table 9-12. College Enrollment and Attendance Status, Employment Status, and Marital Status of Persons 35 Years Old and Over, by Sex and Race: 1980

Sex and status	Total	White	Black and all other	Sex ratio	Percent white
Total enrollment (000).	1,452	1,261	191	85.2	...
Both sexes					
Percent at college level.	95.7	96.9	87.4	54.4	...
Persons enrolled in college (000)	1,389	1,222	167	--	...
Percent enrolled fulltime.	19.8	17.7	35.3	50.8	...
Percent in labor force.	75.0	75.9	68.3	69.0	...
Percent married, spouse present. . . .	70.3	72.1	56.9	68.4	...
Male					
Percent at college level.	96.5	97.1	92.5	...	87.3
Persons enrolled in college (000)	490	428	62	...	--
Percent enrolled fulltime.	19.0	15.0	46.8	...	68.8
Percent in labor force.	86.7	90.0	64.5	...	90.6
Percent married, spouse present. . . .	81.0	82.2	72.6	...	88.7
Female					
Percent at college level.	95.2	96.8	84.7	...	88.3
Persons enrolled in college (000)	900	795	105	...	--
Percent enrolled fulltime.	20.3	19.2	28.6	...	83.6
Percent in labor force.	68.4	68.2	70.5	...	88.0
Percent married, spouse present. . . .	64.4	66.5	48.6	...	91.2

Note: -- indicates data not available. ... indicates data not applicable.

Source: U.S. Bureau of the Census. "School Enrollment—Social and Economic Characteristics of Students: October 1982." Current Population Reports (Series P-20). Washington, DC: U.S. Government Printing Office, 1985.

8. A substantial portion of females attending college are wives, but compared to male enrollees a higher proportion are single, separated, divorced, or widowed; in comparison with women generally, a very high proportion are also working. Thus, the college attendance of women has the characteristics of serious career-building by working women older than thirty-five years of age.

School Enrollment and the Birth Rate

The Birth Rate and Enrollment in Primary and Secondary School

Because school attendance at primary school and the first two years of high school is compulsory by law and is nearly 100 percent, it is obvious that enrollment in these grades will be linked intimately with the number of births that occurred in previous years. In other words, with the low infant and child mortality that exists, a child born today will almost certainly be a first-grader somewhere six years hence. Once in the school system, that child will progress from grade to grade and be counted in each year's enrollment at a later age and higher grade until he either graduates or ceases attending school.

The "baby boom" of the late 1940s and the 1950s created a bulge in elementary school enrollments, beginning with the first grade about 1952 and progressing grade by grade upward. As enrollment increased, it became necessary to build new schools, hire new teachers, and make additional tax assessments to pay for the increased educational load. This expansion began to engulf high schools in the early 1950s and began to be felt in colleges and universities in 1959 and 1960. The flood of baby boom babies caused expansion in the educational system at all levels. However, as Chapter 6 has described, it began to dry up and become a "baby bust" beginning in 1957. Progressively smaller numbers of babies were born from 1960 to 1976. This meant that progressively fewer children entered school beginning in 1966 and continuing to 1981. The result was a great reduction in the need for classrooms and teachers. The "baby bust" engulfed high schools in the late 1960s and the 1970s, and began to affect college enrollment negatively in the mid-1970s. Its depressive impact has been felt most strongly at all levels of education during the 1975-83 period. The effect on colleges was less disorienting than upon elementary and high schools because of the increased rate of enrollment in colleges of women and the increased rate of college enrollment of persons older than thirty-five, as described above.

As Chapter 6 described, an "echo" to the baby boom began in the late 1970s, resulting in a new but smaller wave of youngsters, which began entering the lower elementary grades in the early 1980s. This will have the effect of forcing modest increases in enrollment at progressively higher grades. It will not be felt in high schools until about 1993 and in colleges and universities just before the year 2000.

Table 9-13 and Figure 9-3 show the roller-coaster effect of the baby boom and bust on enrollments. Because of the close ties between births and enrollments, one important task of demographers is to forecast or predict future school enrollments.

Projections of Future School Enrollments

The age distribution of the United States, twisted as it is by fluctuating birth rates and echos of such fluctuations, can be expected to generate variability in school enrollments in future years, as just described. A projection of future enrollment can be made by applying the attendance rates and the grade-distribution by age proportions for 1980 to the number of persons in each age group as projected by the Bureau of the Census (see Chapter 2). Table 9-14A provides estimates of the number of students expected to be enrolled in each level in 1985, 1990, and 2000.

Because of the baby boom echo the increase in number of births since 1978 will cause enrollment to increase in the first three grades during 1980-90 (particularly in grades one and two). During the 1990-2000 decade this growth will extend to the entire range of upper elementary grades and high school. Meanwhile, enrollments at the lower elementary grades will again have approached zero.

Because the peak of the baby bust generation is in high school between 1980 and 1990, enrollment in high schools in 1990 will be 20 percent lower than in 1980. By the year 2000 it will be about the same as in 1980.

The leading edge of the baby bust will enter the college years during the 1980-90 decade and cause substantial declines in enrollment in the first three years of the decade. This decline will continue for all college levels into the 1990-2000 decade.

Because the baby boom generation is in the ages for doing postgraduate training in the 1980-90 decade, enrollments for the fifth level and higher of universities may expect to rise by an estimated 27 percent. However, by the 1990-2000 period, the baby bust generation will be in the postgraduate ages and enrollments will not grow at all and will probably decline slightly.

The projections of Table 9-14A will prove to be too pessimistic if enrollment rates rise above 1980 levels or if the population grows faster than projected by the

Table 9-13. Percent Intercensal Change in School Enrollment, by Level, for Persons 5-34: 1950-1980

Level	1950-60	1960-70	1970-80
Elementary			
1.	34.0	1.3	-19.2
2.	38.5	5.3	-17.7
3.	44.6	12.4	-13.6
4.	46.0	17.4	-11.7
5.	54.5	18.3	-13.3
6.	55.8	18.5	-13.6
7.	68.8	16.9	-11.7
8.	52.6	31.1	-7.4
High school			
1.	52.2	49.9	0.1
2.	51.9	53.0	6.1
3.	67.4	47.7	8.1
4.	42.7	46.3	2.2
College			
1.	--	141.8	41.1
2.	--	140.4	52.3
3.	--	136.5	51.4
4.	--	125.7	52.9
5 and over .	--	137.0	79.8

Note: -- indicates data not available.

Source: U.S. Bureau of the Census. "Detailed Population Characteristics: United States Summary." 1980 Census of Population (Table 260). Data for 1970 from "Detailed Characteristics: United States Summary." 1970 Census of Population (Table 197). Data for 1960 from "Detailed Characteristics: United States Summary." 1960 Census of Population (Table 168). Data for 1950 from "Characteristics of the Population: United States Summary." 1950 Census of Population (Table 112). Washington, DC: U.S. Government Printing Office, 1983, 1973, 1963, and 1953.

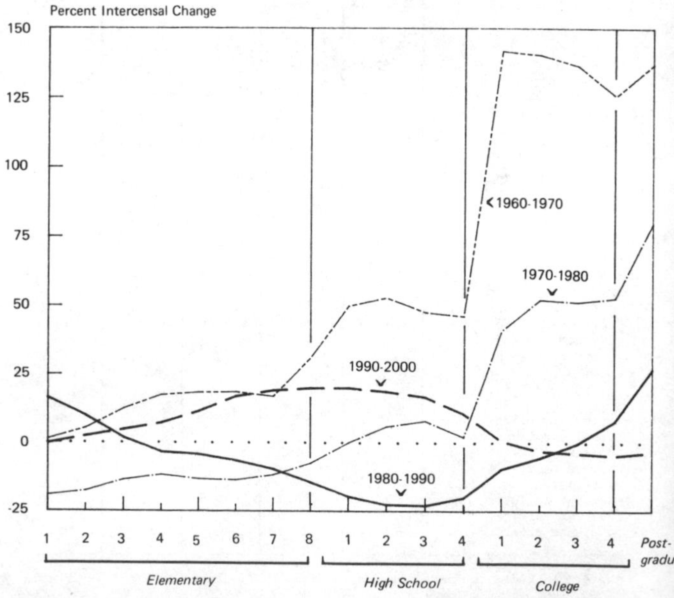

Figure 9-3. Intercensal Percent Change in School Enrollments, by Level: 1960 to 1980, with Projections to 2000

Table 9-14A. Projected School Enrollment for the United States, by Grade and Year, 1980-2000 and Intercensal Percent Change

Educational level	Enrollment (000)[a]				Percent change	
	1980	1985	1990	2000	1980-90	1990-2000
Total enrolled. . . .	61,866	58,474	59,682	61,978	-3.5	3.8
Preschool	5,640	6,443	6,910	6,607	22.5	-4.4
Elementary total. . . .	28,743	26,451	28,258	30,982	-1.7	9.6
Grade 1	3,349	3,455	3,896	3,883	16.3	-0.3
Grade 2	3,400	3,280	3,731	3,818	9.7	2.3
Grade 3	3,681	3,291	3,743	3,920	1.7	4.7
Grade 4	3,689	3,142	3,561	3,815	-3.5	7.1
Grade 5	3,608	3,146	3,451	3,840	-4.4	11.3
Grade 6	3,570	3,208	3,334	3,894	-6.6	16.8
Grade 7	3,658	3,377	3,303	3,930	-9.7	19.0
Grade 8	3,788	3,552	3,239	3,882	-14.5	19.9
High school total . . .	15,218	13,418	11,963	13,959	-21.4	16.7
Freshman.	3,970	3,691	3,188	3,827	-19.7	20.0
Sophomore	4,050	3,578	3,131	3,716	-22.7	18.7
Junior.	3,703	3,166	2,852	3,327	-23.0	16.7
Senior.	3,495	2,983	2,792	3,089	-20.1	10.6
College, undergraduate total	10,061	10,030	9,737	9,501	-3.2	-2.4
Freshman.	3,279	3,034	2,964	2,982	-9.6	0.6
Sophomore	2,860	2,747	2,704	2,623	-5.5	-3.0
Junior.	1,978	2,061	1,972	1,895	-0.3	-3.9
Senior.	1,944	2,188	2,097	2,001	7.9	-4.6
Postgraduate.	2,204	2,733	2,796	2,703	26.9	-3.3

[a]Persons 65 years and over are not included in this projection.

Source: Prepared by the author. Enrollment rates for 1980 and distribution of enrollees by age and grade for 1980 were applied to medium age-sex projections of Bureau of Census, "Projections of the Population of the United States." Current Population Reports (Series P-25, no. 952). Washington, DC: U.S. Government Printing Office, 1984.

Bureau of the Census. Conversely they will be too optimistic if the population grows more slowly than projected. (A decrease in enrollment rates is not expected.)

Table 9-14B provides more detail concerning anticipated changes in college enrollment during the 1980s. It calls for a substantial decrease in enrollment at the ages of undergraduate and early graduate enrollment, but for small increases at the older ages, as the baby boom babies reach middle age. The total net effect is for almost zero growth in college enrollment for the entire decade—simply a gradual aging of the population, with a shift from enrollment at the "normal" college-going ages 18-24 to the "returning scholar" ages.

Type of College

Colleges tend to fall into two categories: two-year colleges offering the associate degree, and four-year colleges offering the bachelor degree. Much of the increased college enrollment of recent years, especially that of black and Hispanic, female, and older students, has occurred in the two-year colleges, as the summary of Table 9-15 shows. By providing enrollment data for two dates, the table makes it possible to trace trends in enrollment at the two types of institutions.

The two-year schools have enjoyed large gains in enrollment at the younger ages and among women. As the projections provided above specify, these are the ages that are to be hard hit by declining enrollments between 1980 and 1990. As a result the two-year colleges can anticipate unusually severe cutbacks in enrollment for the remainder of this decade and into the next, unless there is a compensating increase in enrollment rates among the younger age groups. Attendance at two-year schools (which are often community colleges) is accompanied by part-time attendance. It is possible that a part of their increased enrollment has resulted from unemployment; unemployed or temporarily employed youth may have begun college at a nearby community college because of difficulties in securing satisfactory employment. Increased economic prosperity could contribute further to the financial difficulties of many two-year colleges through a possible decline in enrollment as prospective students choose to accept employment or to enroll full time in a four-year college.

Table 9-14B. Projected College Enrollment in 1990 Based on 1979 Age-Specific Enrollment Rates and Projected Population, by Age for 1990

Age	Percent enrolled 1979	Projected population 1990	Projected enrollment 1990	Estimated enrollment 1979	Difference
Total, 14-64 years . . .	7.7	161,682	11,482	11,346	136
14-24 years .	16.6	37,917	6,499	7,302	-803
14-17 years . .	1.9	12,770	243	311	-68
18-19 years . .	34.6	7,195	2,489	2,844	-355
20-21 years . .	29.1	7,311	2,128	2,353	-225
22-24 years . .	15.4	10,641	1,639	1,794	-155
25-64 years .	3.2	123,765	4,983	4,044	939
25-29 years . .	9.3	20,169	1,876	1,679	197
30-34 years . .	6.1	20,917	1,276	996	280
35-39 years . .	4.2	19,261	809	566	243
40-44 years . .	2.9	17,331	503	330	173
45-49 years . .	2.0	13,889	278	223	55
50-54 years . .	1.2	11,422	137	139	-2
55-64 years . .	0.5	20,776	104	111	-7

Source: U.S. Bureau of the Census. "School Enrollment--Social and Economic Characteristics of Students: October 1979." Current Population Report (Series P-20, no. 360). Washington, DC: U.S. Government Printing Office, 1981, Table 5.

Table 9-15. Undergraduate Enrollment at Two-Year and Four-Year College, by Age and Sex: 1980 and 1970 [in thousands]

Age, sex, and type of school	1980			1970			Percent change 1970-1980		
	Total	2-year	4-year	Total	2-year	4-year	Total	2-year	4-year
Age									
14-19 years.	3,182	1,080	2,102	2,854	895	1,959	11.5	20.7	7.3
20-21 years.	2,393	450	1,943	1,803	281	1,522	32.7	60.1	27.7
22-24 years.	1,316	417	899	866	234	632	52.0	78.2	42.2
25-34 years.	1,599	721	878	750	283	467	113.2	154.8	88.0
Sex									
Male total	4,111	1,195	2,916	3,627	1,001	2,626	13.3	19.4	11.0
Fulltime	3,192	739	2,453	3,045	726	2,319	4.8	1.8	5.8
Parttime	920	456	464	582	275	307	58.1	65.8	51.1
Female total	4,377	1,472	2,905	2,646	691	1,955	65.4	113.0	48.6
Fulltime	3,123	759	2,364	2,164	452	1,712	44.3	67.9	38.1
Parttime	1,254	713	541	482	239	243	160.2	198.3	122.6
Type									
Public	6,541[a]	2,233[a]	4,308[a]	4,911	1,559	3,352	33.2	43.2	28.5
Private.	1,746[a]	174[a]	1,572[a]	1,363	133	1,230	28.1	30.8	27.8

[a]1980 figures are for 1979.

Source: U.S. Bureau of the Census. "College Enrollment for Students 14 to 34 Years Old, by Type of College, Attendance Status, Age, and Sex: October 1970 to October 1980." Current Population Report (Series P-20, no. 362). Washington, DC: U.S. Government Printing Office, 1983.

Family Income and School Attendance

The tendency to enroll one's children in preschool and for children not to drop out of high school is strongly correlated with the income of the family in which the child is a member. This is shown in Table 9-16. The percentage of children 3-5 years of age who are in school rises progressively with family income. So does the proportion of children 14-17 years of age who are enrolled, presumably in high school. These income differentials in school enrollment are found for each race-ethnic group separately. In fact, the school enrollment differences of black and white families are almost identical at each income level. The superiority of the Asian and Pacific Island race group, noted earlier, is caused more by high income than by cultural proclivities, it would seem, because the differences with the white population are much reduced when the comparison is made by income groups. The Spanish-origin population and American Indians still have lower attendance rates than the other groups, even with income controlled, but here too the differences are much smaller than the gross comparison made earlier in this chapter.

Table 9-16. Percent of Children 3-17 Years of Age Enrolled in School, by Age of Children, Family Income, Race and Spanish-Origin: 1980

Age and race	Total	Family income							
		Under $5,000	$5,000–$9,999	$10,000–$14,999	$15,000–$19,999	$20,000–$24,999	$25,000–$34,999	$35,000–$49,999	$50,000 or more
Total	88.2	83.3	84.6	84.4	85.5	88.2	91.6	94.2	95.5
3 to 5 years.	47.2	42.5	41.4	39.8	42.1	47.7	55.3	63.2	70.6
6 to 13 years	98.7	97.5	98.0	98.4	98.7	98.9	99.1	99.2	99.2
14 to 17 years.	94.2	89.6	90.1	91.9	93.6	95.0	95.9	96.6	97.3
White, total.	88.5	82.7	83.6	83.7	85.1	88.1	91.8	94.5	95.7
3 to 5 years.	46.4	39.2	38.3	37.7	40.9	47.0	54.9	63.4	71.2
6 to 13 years	98.9	98.0	98.3	98.6	98.9	99.1	99.2	99.3	99.3
14 to 17 years.	94.7	89.1	89.6	91.9	93.7	95.2	96.1	96.8	97.5
Black, total.	88.3	85.1	87.6	88.1	88.8	89.9	91.4	92.8	92.8
3 to 5 years.	52.2	48.4	50.2	50.3	52.1	54.9	60.3	65.0	65.7
6 to 13 years	97.7	97.1	97.5	97.7	97.9	98.1	98.3	98.4	98.3
14 to 17 years.	93.3	91.2	92.2	93.1	94.0	94.7	95.4	95.6	95.0
American Indian, total	84.5	80.3	82.5	83.5	84.9	86.8	89.0	89.5	89.3
3 to 5 years.	45.2	43.6	44.9	44.3	43.8	46.8	48.9	51.1	48.5
6 to 13 years	97.2	95.9	96.7	97.1	97.7	97.8	98.2	98.3	98.2
14 to 17 years.	86.9	81.4	83.4	86.2	88.3	89.2	91.0	90.9	90.4
Asian and Pacific Islander, total . .	88.6	81.7	84.1	85.6	87.1	88.8	90.3	92.4	94.3
3 to 5 years.	54.8	42.1	44.1	46.3	49.8	55.9	59.9	64.2	72.3
6 to 13 years	98.0	93.9	97.1	97.7	97.9	98.6	98.6	99.1	99.2
14 to 17 years.	96.4	91.9	93.4	95.7	96.4	96.9	97.4	97.8	98.1
Spanish-origin, total	84.1	80.7	82.0	82.1	83.5	85.7	88.3	90.3	91.8
3 to 5 years.	41.6	38.4	38.8	38.7	40.3	44.0	49.0	53.6	59.8
6 to 13 years	97.9	97.0	97.5	97.7	98.1	98.4	98.7	98.6	98.7
14 to 17 years.	89.8	86.6	87.2	88.4	89.8	91.4	92.3	92.8	94.2

Source: U.S. Bureau of the Census. "Detailed Population Characteristics: United States Summary." 1980 Census of Population (Chapter D, Section A, Table 261). Washington, DC: U.S. Government Printing Office, 1981.

Table 9-17. College Attendance of Primary Family Members 18-24 Years Old, by Family Income, Race, and Spanish-Origin: October 1982 [numbers in thousands; civilian noninstitutional population; excludes families in which the householders are members of the armed forces]

Families, race, and Spanish-origin	Family income							
	Total	Under $10,000	$10,000–$14,999	$15,000–$19,999	$20,000–$24,999	$25,000–$34,999	$35,000 and over	Not reported
1982								
All families								
One or more members 18 to 24 years old[a]	100.0	100.0	100.0	100.0	100.0	100.0	100.0	100.0
None attending college full-time.	65.9	85.1	77.1	72.6	65.4	62.8	45.7	59.9
One or more attending college full-time	34.1	14.9	22.9	27.4	34.6	37.2	54.3	40.1
One attending college full-time	28.1	17.4	20.6	24.3	29.1	30.7	41.5	35.1
Two or more attending college full-time . . .	6.0	1.5	2.3	3.1	5.5	6.6	12.8	5.0
White families								
One or more members 18 to 24 years old[a]	100.0	100.0	100.0	100.0	100.0	100.0	100.0	100.0
None attending college full-time.	64.1	85.1	78.0	73.2	66.5	62.9	45.6	59.6
One or more attending college full-time	35.9	14.9	22.0	26.8	33.5	37.1	54.4	40.4
One attending college full-time	29.4	13.6	19.8	24.2	28.6	30.6	41.5	34.9
Two or more attending college full-time . . .	6.5	1.3	2.2	2.7	4.8	6.5	12.9	5.5
Black families								
One or more members 18 to 24 years old[a]	100.0	100.0	100.0	100.0	100.0	100.0	100.0	*
None attending college full-time.	77.0	86.4	74.7	72.1	60.3	66.0	53.2	*
One or more attending college full-time	23.0	13.6	25.3	27.9	39.7	34.0	46.8	*
One attending college full-time	20.2	12.0	23.2	23.7	32.1	29.8	40.4	*
Two or more attending college full-time . . .	2.8	1.6	2.0	4.2	7.6	4.3	6.4	*
Spanish-origin[b] families								
One or more members 18 to 24 years old[a]	100.0	100.0	100.0	100.0	*	100.0	*	*
None attending college full-time.	81.0	90.0	87.1	79.1	*	70.3	*	*
One or more attending college full-time	19.0	10.0	12.9	20.9	*	29.7	*	*
One attending college full-time	15.9	8.0	9.7	20.9	*	26.4	*	*
Two or more attending college full-time . . .	3.2	2.0	3.2	*	*	3.3	*	*

Families, race, and Spanish-origin	Total	Under $5,000	$5,000–$9,999	$10,000–$14,999	$15,000–$19,999	$20,000–$24,999	$25,000 and over	Not reported
1979								
All families								
One or more members 18 to 24 years old[a]	100.0	100.0	100.0	100.0	100.0	100.0	100.0	100.0
None attending college full-time.	66.7	86.6	79.0	73.6	68.1	65.5	50.5	67.6
One or more attending college full-time	33.3	13.4	21.0	26.4	31.9	34.5	49.5	32.4
One attending college full-time	27.3	12.1	17.9	22.7	26.3	28.5	39.3	26.5
Two or more attending college full-time . . .	6.0	1.3	3.1	3.7	5.6	6.0	10.2	5.9
White families								
One or more members 18 to 24 years old[a]	100.0	100.0	100.0	100.0	100.0	100.0	100.0	100.0
None attending college full-time.	64.9	85.9	80.5	73.5	68.2	66.2	50.4	65.0
One or more attending college full-time	35.1	14.1	19.5	26.5	31.8	33.8	49.6	35.0
One attending college full-time	28.7	12.9	16.1	23.6	26.5	28.0	39.3	28.2
Two or more attending college full-time . . .	6.4	1.2	3.4	2.8	5.3	5.9	10.3	6.8
Black families								
One or more members 18 to 24 years old[a]	100.0	100.0	100.0	100.0	100.0	100.0	100.0	100.0
None attending college full-time.	76.8	87.2	78.2	76.5	67.9	60.6	52.5	81.4
One or more attending college full-time	23.2	12.8	21.8	23.5	32.1	39.4	47.5	18.6
One attending college full-time	19.6	11.2	19.6	18.6	23.3	33.6	41.5	16.0
Two or more attending college full-time . . .	3.6	1.6	2.3	4.9	8.8	5.8	5.9	2.6
Spanish-origin[b] families								
One or more members 18 to 24 years old[a]	100.0	100.0	100.0	100.0	100.0	*	*	*
None attending college full-time.	77.3	81.3	83.3	75.6	70.8	*	*	*
One or more attending college full-time	22.7	18.7	16.7	24.4	29.2	*	*	*
One attending college full-time	18.9	15.4	15.9	19.3	26.9	*	*	*
Two or more attending college full-time . . .	3.8	3.5	0.8	5.2	2.2	*	*	*

Table 9-17. College Attendance of Primary Family Members 18-24 Years Old, by Family Income, Race, and Spanish-Origin: October 1982 [numbers in thousands; civilian noninstitutional population; excludes families in which the householders are members of the armed forces] –continued

Families, race, and Spanish-origin	Total	Family income						
		Under $3,000	$3,000-$4,999	$5,000 $7,999	$7,500-$9,999	$10,000-$14,999	$15,000-and over	Not reported
1972								
All families								
One or more members 18 to 24 years old[a]	100.0	100.0	100.0	100.0	100.0	100.0	100.0	100.0
None attending college full-time.	62.3	85.2	80.0	72.0	67.9	59.2	43.9	63.0
One or more attending college full-time	37.7	14.8	20.0	28.0	32.1	40.8	56.1	37.0
One attending college full-time	32.5	13.6	18.1	24.8	28.9	35.6	46.4	31.8
Two or more attending college full-time . . .	5.2	1.1	1.9	3.2	3.2	5.2	9.7	5.2
White families								
One or more members 18 to 24 years old[a]	100.0	100.0	100.0	100.0	100.0	100.0	100.0	100.0
None attending college full-time.	59.9	83.4	78.4	72.4	67.9	58.1	43.4	62.3
One or more attending college full-time	40.1	16.6	21.6	27.6	32.1	41.9	56.6	37.7
One attending college full-time	34.6	15.7	19.9	24.9	29.4	36.7	46.7	32.3
Two or more attending college full-time . . .	5.5	0.9	1.7	2.7	2.7	5.2	9.9	5.5
Black families								
One or more members 18 to 24 years old[a]	100.0	100.0	100.0	100.0	100.0	100.0	100.0	*
None attending college full-time.	77.4	89.1	84.4	70.7	70.5	74.5	57.7	*
One or more attending college full-time	22.6	10.9	15.6	29.3	29.5	25.5	42.3	*
One attending college full-time	19.4	9.4	13.6	24.7	24.6	20.3	41.2	*
Two or more attending college full-time . . .	3.2	1.6	2.0	4.6	4.9	5.2	3.0	*
Spanish-origin[b] families								
One or more members 18 to 24 years old[a]	100.0	*	100.0	100.0	100.0	*	*	*
None attending college full-time.	80.7	*	87.5	80.0	79.5	*	*	*
One or more attending college full-time	19.3	*	12.5	20.0	20.5	*	*	*
One attending college full-time	16.1	*	12.5	17.4	17.9	*	*	*
Two or more attending college full-time . . .	3.3	*	*	2.6	2.6	*	*	*

[a]Excludes families in which the only members 18 to 24 years old are the family householder, or other members who are married, spouse present.

[b]May be of any race.

Note: * indicates base less than 75,000, or zero.

Source: U.S. Bureau of the Census. "School Enrollment--Social and Economic Characteristics of Students." Current Population Reports (Series P-20, for October, 1972, 1979, and 1982). Washington, DC: U.S. Government Printing Office, 1974 (Table 11), 1981 (Table 19), and 1985 (Table 12).

Family Income and College Attendance

Because college attendance is much less subsidized as a public service than elementary or secondary education, family income has a strong effect upon whether or not children who graduate from high school continue on to college. Table 9-17 reports and Figure 9-4 illustrates the percentage of families that contain a college-age child (age 18-24) with such a child in school. This table shows that where family income is below $5,000 per year (1979), only 13 percent of such children were in school, but where family income is $25,000 and over, nearly one-half of the children were in college. The effect of income is equally strong on all race-ethnic groups. Figure 9-4, which charts data for 1982, shows that the black population has a higher proportion of children in school than the white population for all income categories under $25,000 (with income controlled and in 1982 dollars). In fact, the Spanish-origin population, with its considerably lower-than-average college attendance record, falls into this position primarily because of low income, and low family income explains practically all of the below-average attendance of black youth.

High income does not ensure college attendance, however. Among the most privileged group of the white population, only one-half of the children of college age elect to go to college. Whatever the causes, they appear to have worsened in recent years, as the bottom panel of Table 9-17 (with comparable data for 1972) shows.

Marital Status of College Undergraduate Students

Before World War II young persons in college usually waited until graduation before marrying. This tradition was shattered by the "baby boom," when women began to marry and have babies while they (or their husbands) were still enrolled as undergraduates. The popularity of marriage, and of early marriage, came into conflict with the desire for advanced education, and many of the college students opted to have both marriage and an advanced education.

That tradition has been modified over the years, as shown in Table 9-18. Delayed marriage has caused a decline in the percentage of undergraduates of each age who are married, in comparison with the past. Perhaps the increase of living-together arrangements without a formal marriage, to be described in Chapter 11, is a modern form of college conjugal life. However, the increased enrollment of women and of older persons of both sexes has added to the number of married people among undergraduates. Thus, overall, marriage among undergraduates is just about as common today as it was in 1960. Undergraduate education and some form of "family life" have become inextricably mixed, so that the "timing" that requires completion of college education before marriage is declining in currency.

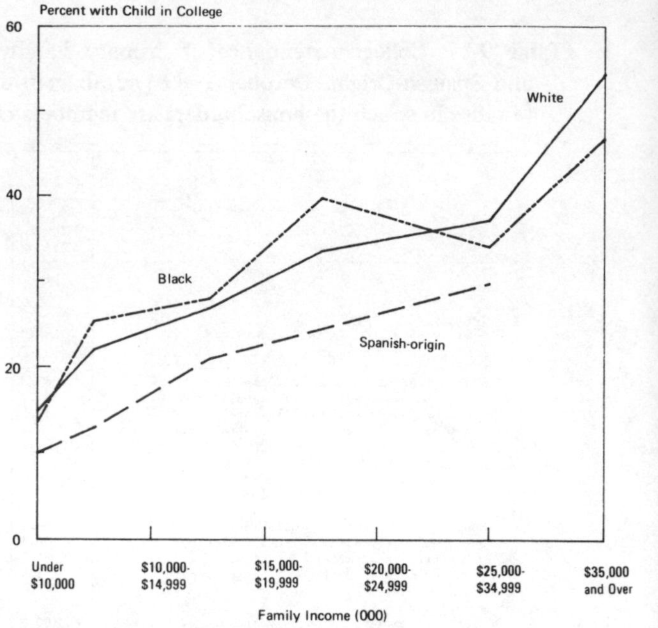

Figure 9-4. Families with a Child in College, by Family Income and Race-Ethnicity: 1980 [percent of families with a college-age child]

Table 9-18. Percent of College Undergraduates, Married With Spouse Present, by Age and Sex: 1982, 1970 and 1960

Age and status	1982			1970			1960		
	Total	Male	Female	Total	Male	Female	Total	Male	Female
Total, 14-34 years . .	19.3	17.9	20.7	23.7	27.3	18.5	23.9	28.5	15.3
14-19 years.	1.4	0.3	2.3	2.8	2.4	3.2	1.6	1.2	2.0
20-21 years.	5.6	3.8	7.3	11.4	11.8	10.9	10.3	7.8	14.6
22-24 years.	18.7	15.6	22.3	36.5	37.7	34.1	39.7	39.9	38.8
25-34 years.	51.3	50.7	52.0	72.1	74.3	67.0	73.1	76.7	59.5
Attending fulltime . .	10.0	9.7	10.2	13.9	17.3	8.8	12.3	15.1	7.2
14-19 years.	1.0	0.2	1.7	2.4	2.1	2.7	1.4	1.3	1.6
20-21 years.	4.5	2.6	6.4	9.7	10.7	8.2	8.2	5.7	12.8
22-24 years.	13.9	12.3	16.0	30.0	32.8	22.2	33.5	33.7	32.7
25-34 years.	38.0	38.2	37.8	59.8	61.1	56.0	61.1	65.4	38.2

Source: U.S. Bureau of the Census. "School Enrollment and Education of Young Adults and Their Fathers: October, 1960." Current Population Report (Series P-20, no. 110). Also U.S. Bureau of the Census. "School Enrollment: October, 1970." Current Population Report (Series P-20, no. 222). Also U.S. Bureal of the Census. "School Enrollment: October, 1982." Current Population Report (Series P-20). Washington, DC: U.S. Government Printing Office, 1964 (Table 7), 1974 (Table 11), and 1985 (Table 10).

Conclusion

Despite popular discussion to the contrary, minority groups in the United States appear to place as much or more confidence in the power of education to improve their lot in life than the white population. The differentials between the various race and ethnic groups have diminished greatly and appear to be explained more by income than by any racial or ethnic factor.

Meanwhile, white youth appear to have become less enthusiastic about school attendance. Their record of dropping out from high school and of apparent reluctance to enter college (especially for males) has improved very little or worsened in comparison with the 1960s. Even wealthy families have had poor luck in sending their children to college. Greatest enthusiasm is shown by the new immigrants from Asia. The Spanish-origin group, which traditionally has not participated in school (for cultural reasons, language problems or both), has shown remarkable increases in enrollment rates.

The sex differential in enrollment has been reversed, and women are more prone than men to acquire a college education. A higher share of college graduates are now likely to remain in school for an advanced degree, and more older college graduates are willing to return for further education—even to the most advanced ages.

Education has been riding the roller-coaster of the age pyramid, with enrollments rising and falling with the rise and fall of the size of birth cohorts. Because of the "baby bust," undergraduate and postgraduate enrollment in colleges is destined to shrink drastically in the 1980s, unless offset by higher enrollment rates.

A small "echo wave" of the baby boom began to influence elementary school enrollment in 1982-83. Whether this is a wave or a ripple, and how long it will last, will depend upon the volatile birth rates. It is very likely to be more of a swell than a breaker.

Note

1. Students who are enumerated in April of a census year have been attending school for almost eight months and hence are rather evenly divided (in the first grade, for example) between age 6 + G and 7 + G, G being the grade in which they are enrolled.

Bibliography

Abramowitz, Susan, and Rosenfeld, Stuart (eds.). *Declining Enrollment: The Challenge of the Coming Decade.* Washington, DC: National Institute of Education, 1978.

Ahlburg, D.; Crimmins, E.M.; and Easterlin, R.A. "The Outlook for Higher Education: A Cohort Size Model of Enrollment of the College Age Population, 1948-2000." *Review of Public Data Use* 9 (1981):211-27.

Alexander, K.L.; Riordan, C.; Fennessey, J.; and Pallas, A.M. "Social Background, Academic Resources and College Graduation: Recent Evidence from the National Longitudinal Survey." *American Journal of Education* 90 (1982):315-33.

Ballmer, H., and Cozby, P.C. "Family Environments of Women Who Return to College." *Sex Roles* 7 (1981): 1019-26.

Boyd, W.L. (ed.). "Declining School Enrollments: Politics and Management" (symposium). *Education and Urban Society* 11 (1979):275-430.

Brown, F., and Stent, M.D. "Black College Undergraduates, Enrollment, and Earned Degrees: Parity or Underrepresentation?" *Journal of Black Studies* 6 (1975):1-21.

Carnegie Council on Policy Studies in Higher Education. *Three Thousand Futures: The Next Twenty Years for Higher Education.* San Francisco: Jossey-Bass, 1980.

Christensen, S. et al. "Factors Affecting College Attendance." *Journal of Human Resources* 10 (1975): 174-88.

Clotfelter, C.T. "School Desegregation, Tipping, and Private School Enrollment." *Journal of Human Resources* 11 (1976):28-50.

Coleman, James S. "Recent Trends in School Integration." *Educational Researcher* 4 (1975):3-13.

Coleman, James, S.; Campbell, Ernest Q.; Hobson, Carol J. et al. *Equality of Educational Opportunity.* Washington, DC: U.S. Government Printing Office, 1966.

Coleman, James S.; Hoffer, Thomas; and Kilgore, Sally. "Achievement and Segregation in Secondary Schools: A Further Look at Public and Private School Differences." *Sociology of Education* 55 (1982):162-82.

———. *Public and Private Schools: Report to the National Center for Education Statistics.* Chicago: National Opinion Research Center, 1981.

Coleman, James S.; Kelly, Sara D.; and Moore, John A. *Trends in School Segregation, 1968-73.* Washington, DC: Urban Institute, 1975.

Cope, R.G., and Hannah, W. *Revolving College Doors: The Causes and Consequences of Dropping Out, Stopping Out, and Transferring.* New York: Wiley, 1975.

Cunningham, G.K., and Husk, W.L. "White Flight: A Closer Look at the Assumptions." *Urban Review* 12 (1980):23-30.

Davis, Nancy J., and Bumpass, Larry L. "The Continuation of Education after Marriage Among Women in the United States: 1970." *Demography* 13 (1976): 161-74.

Dentler, Robert A., and Warshauer, Mary Ellen. *Big City Dropouts and Illiterates.* New York: Praeger Press, 1968.

Edwards, L.N. "Economics of Schooling Decisions: Teenage Enrollment Rates." *Journal of Human Resources* 10 (1975):155-73.

Fromkin, Joseph; Endriss, J.R.; and Stump, Robert W. *Population, Enrollment and Costs of Public Elementary and Secondary Education: 1975-76 and 1980-81.* Washington, DC: U.S. Government Printing Office, 1972.

Grant, W. Vance, and Lind, C. George. *Digest of Education Statistics.* Washington, DC: National Center for Education Statistics, 1975.

Greeley, A.M. "Religious Factor and Academic Careers: Another Communication." *American Journal of Sociology* 78 (1973):1247-55.

Gustman, A.L., and Steinmeir, J.L. "Impact of Wages and Unemployment on Youth Enrollment and Labor Supply." *Review of Economics and Statistics* 63 (1981):553-60.

Hauser, R.M., and Featherman, D.L. "Equality of Schooling: Trends and Prospects." *Sociology of Education* 49 (1976):99-120.

Hawley, W.D. (ed.). *Effective School Desegregation.* Beverly Hills, CA: Sage Publications, 1982.

Hoenack, S.A., and Weiler, W.C. "Demand for Higher Education and Institutional Enrollment Forecasting." *Economic Inquiry* 17 (1979):89-113.

Kaplan, J.L., and Luck, E.C. "The Dropout Phenomenon as a Social Problem." *Educational Forum XL* 11 (1977):41-56.

Katznelson, Ira; Gille, K.; and Weir, M. "Public Schooling and Working Class Formation: The Case of the United States." *American Journal of Education* 90 (1982):111-43.

Jencks, C., and Riesman, D. *The Academic Revolution.* Chicago: University of Chicago Press, 1977.

Larkin, R.W. "Sympathy for the Devil: The Decline of Achievement Motivation Among Middle-Class Students." *Sociological Spectrum* 1 (1980):79-90.

Mare, Robert D. "Trends in Schooling: Demography, Performance, and Organization." *Annals of the American Academy of Political and Social Science* 453 (1981).

Mattila, J.P. "Determinants of Male School Enrollments: A Time-Series Analysis." *Review of Economics and Statistics* 64 (1982):242-51.

Nielsen, F., and Hannan, M.T. "Expansion of National Educational Systems: Tests of a Population Ecology Model." *American Sociological Review* 42 (1977): 479-90.

Pepin, A. et al. *Trends and Patterns: A Study of Enrollments in Higher Education, 1970-79.* Washington, DC: American Council on Education, 1982.

Poole, M.E., and Low, B.C. "Who Stays? Who Leaves? An Examination of Sex Differences in Staying and Leaving." *Journal of Youth and Adolescence* 11 (1982):49-63.

Porwoll, Paul J. *Indicators of Future School Enrollments: A Reference Manual for Planners.* Arlington, VA: Educational Research Service, Inc., 1980.

———. *Student Absenteeism.* Arlington, VA: Educational Research Service, Inc., 1980.

Randolph, M.L. et al. "Women in Higher Education: Trends in Enrollments and Degrees Earned." *Howard Educational Review* 52 (1982):189-202.

Research Triangle Institute. *Withdrawal from Institutions of Higher Education: An Appraisal with Longitudinal Data Involving Diverse Institutions.* Washington, DC: U.S. Government Printing Office, 1977.

Simpson, C. et al. "Conventional Failures and Unconventional Dropouts: Comparing Different Types of University Withdrawals." *Sociology of Education* 53 (1980):203-14.

Sly, D.F., and Pol, L.G. "Demographic Context of School Segregation and Desegregation." *Social Forces* 56 (1978):1072-86.

Stephan, W.G., and Feagin, J.R. (eds.). *School Desegregation: Past, Present, and Future.* New York: Plenum Press, 1980.

U.S. Commission on Civil Rights. *Reviewing a Decade of School Desegregation, 1966-1975: Report of a National Survey of School Superintendents.* Washington, DC: U.S. Government Printing Office, 1977.

———. *School Desegregation: The Courts and Suburban Migration.* Washington, DC: U.S. Government Printing Office, 1975.

Zerchykov, Ross. *A Review of the Literature and an Annotated Bibliography on Managing Decline in School Systems.* Boston: Institute for Responsive Education, 1982.

Chapter 10

Educational Attainment

Because educational attainment of the adult population has a high correlation (with causal implications) with income, with occupation, with status or social position in the community, with certain buying habits, with many attitudes and opinions, and with a great variety of other elements in human life, it is one of the most widely useful population variables. It is essential, therefore, that sociologists, economists, and analysts in other related fields comprehend the recent changes that have taken place in the level of educational attainment and the further changes that may be expected.

A question concerning educational attainment was included in a decennial census for the first time in 1940. It replaced a question on literacy, which had been abandoned because all but a very small fraction of the population was literate. The shift from a literacy question to a "years of schooling completed" question provided a much richer body of information concerning the educational attainment of the population.

By the time they have reached the age of twenty-five, most persons have completed the education to which they have aspired, or the amount they can afford or have been required to obtain, so they are no longer enrolled in school. Statistics on the educational attainment of the adult (out-of-school) population, therefore, are often gathered for the population aged twenty-five and older. This is becoming progressively less valid because of recent trends toward more postgraduate education and college enrollment at ages even beyond thirty-five, as described in the preceding chapter. Limiting the analysis to the population aged twenty-five and over omits the young persons who did not complete high school or who did not go to college but are in the labor force at ages 16-24 years.

One often-used measure involves data concerning "median years of school completed." The figure for median years of schooling completed by the population aged twenty-five and over has risen steadily during the period for which data are available:

Year	Median years of school completed
1982	12.6
1980	12.5
1970	12.1
1960	10.6
1950	9.3
1940	8.6

Definitions

Educational Attainment (Years of School Completed). Data for years of school completed are obtained by censuses or social surveys, which ask two basic questions (see questions 9 and 10 of the 1980 census questionnaire, at the end of Chapter 1). The first question calls for the highest grade attended, regardless of "skipped" or "repeated" grades. Persons whose education was received in foreign school systems or in ungraded schools are expected to report the approximate equivalent grade in the regular American school system. The second question asks whether or not the highest grade attended has been finished. It is to be answered "yes" if the person has successfully completed the entire grade or year indicated in question 9. If the person has completed only part of the year, has dropped out, or has failed to pass the last grade attended, the question is to be answered "no." If the person is still attending school in that grade, he or she answers "Now attending."

The number in each category of highest grade of school completed represents the combination of (a) persons who reported the indicated grade as the highest grade attended and that they had finished it, (b) those who had attended the next higher grade, but had not finished it, and (c) those still attending the next higher grade. Persons who have not completed the first year of elementary school are classified as having no years of school completed.

These questions on educational attainment apply only to progress in "regular" schools as defined under the definition for school enrollment. Educational attainment questions in terms of years of school completed have been included in the census since 1940.

Median School Years Completed. The median number of school years completed is computed on the basis of intervals for years under eight and a continuous series of numbers for eight years of school completed and above (e.g., completion of the first year of high school is treated as completion of the ninth year, completion of the first year of college as completion of the thirteenth, and so on). Persons completing a given school year are assumed to be distributed evenly within the interval from 0.0 to 0.9 of the year.

The rapid rise in the educational attainment of adults, to a point where the average citizen has at least some college education, is a consequence of the enrollment trends described in Chapter 9, affecting successive cohorts cumulatively over time.

Two comments can be made about these statistics: First, few other nations, if any, have achieved such a high average level of educational accomplishment. Second, the level of educational attainment has not yet reached a peak; it is still rising and may be expected to continue to rise for several decades. Only a few years before 1940 the average citizen was a graduate of elementary school. By about 1965 the average citizen was a high school graduate. By the year 2000 the average adult American will have about two years of college. This prospect has a variety of profound implications.

A much more adequate measure of educational attainment than "median years of school completed" is a percentage distribution showing the proportion of the population that has reached each level of schooling. Table 10-1 and Figure 10-1 depict succinctly the status as of 1982 and the changes that have taken place since 1940.

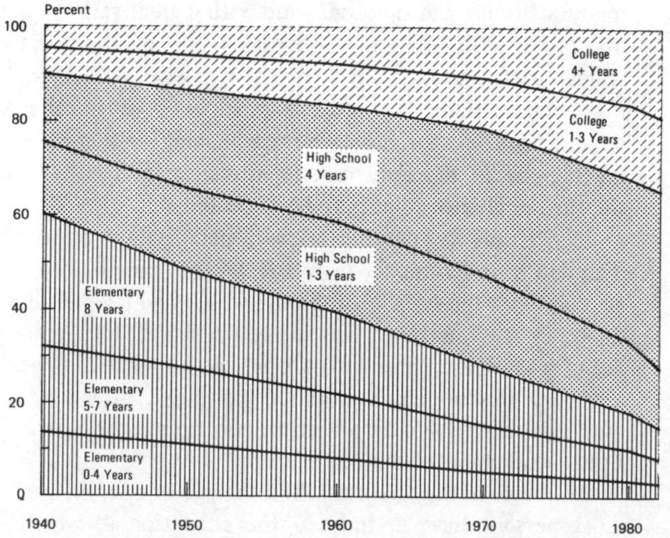

Figure 10-1. Trends in Educational Attainment Composition of the U.S. Population 25 Years of Age and Over: 1940-1982

Table 10-1. Educational Attainment of the Population 25 Years of Age and Over, by Race: 1940-1982 [percent distribution]

Educational attainment and race	1982	1980	1970	1960	1950	1940
All races	100.0	100.0	100.0	100.0	100.0	100.0
College						
4 years and over.	18.8	16.2	10.7	7.7	6.2	4.6
1-3 years	15.6	15.7	10.6	8.8	7.4	5.5
High school						
4 years	37.7	34.6	31.1	24.6	20.8	14.3
1-3 years	12.8	15.3	19.4	19.2	17.4	15.2
Elementary school						
8 years	6.8	8.0	12.8	17.5	20.8	28.2
5-7 years	5.3	6.7	10.0	13.8	16.4	18.5
0-4 years	3.0	3.6	5.5	8.3	11.1	13.7
White	100.0	100.0	100.0	100.0	100.0	100.0
College						
4 years and over.	19.5	17.1	11.3	8.1	6.6	4.9
1-3 years	15.9	16.0	11.1	9.3	7.8	5.9
High school						
4 years	38.4	35.7	32.2	25.8	22.0	15.3
1-3 years	12.1	14.6	18.8	19.3	17.8	15.8
Elementary school						
8 years	6.9	8.2	13.0	18.1	21.7	29.8
5-7 years	4.8	5.8	9.1	12.8	15.1	17.4
0-4 years	2.4	2.6	4.5	6.7	8.9	10.9
Black	100.0	100.0	100.0	100.0	100.0	100.0
College						
4 years and over.	9.5	8.4	4.4	3.1	2.1	1.3
1-3 years	13.4	13.5	5.9	4.1	2.9	1.9
High school						
4 years	33.9	29.3	21.2	12.9	8.0	4.5
1-3 years	19.9	21.8	24.8	19.0	13.6	8.7
Elementary school						
8 years	6.6	7.1	10.5	12.9	11.8	11.9
5-7 years	9.6	11.7	18.7	24.2	28.7	30.0
0-4 years	7.1	8.2	14.6	23.8	32.8	41.8

Source: U.S. Bureau of the Census. "General Social and Economic Characteristics: United States Summary." 1980 Census of Population. Washington, DC: U.S. Government Printing Office, 1983, Table 83.

In 1982, 18.8 percent of the population twenty-five and older had a complete four-year college education or more, and 15.6 percent more had completed one to three years of college. With more than 72 percent having graduated from high school and nearly one-fifth having graduated from college, the United States population can be termed educationally sophisticated. At the other end of the educational scale, only 8.3 percent had not completed elementary school in 1982, and only 3 percent had less than four years of schooling. The greatest concentration by far is in the group having completed high school without having attended college: 38 percent. This picture of high educational attainment has evolved steadily from one of high literacy but concentration of the population at lower levels of attainment. In 1940 elementary school graduates occupied the commanding proportion now held by high school graduates. Only slightly more than one-fourth had graduated from high school, and only one in twenty had a college degree. Thus the proportion of persons with at least a high school diploma has tripled over the four decades since 1940, and the proportion with a college degree has quadrupled.

The educational attainment of a particular group of

persons reflects the rates of school enrollment that its members had when they were young, modified somewhat by death and migration. The level of educational attainment today is a reflection of the rising age-specific rates of past school enrollment of successive generations. According to this principle, today's differentials in school enrollment will become tomorrow's differentials in educational attainment.

Educational Attainment Differentials

Age Pattern of Educational Attainment

In keeping with the lower rates of school enrollment they had in their youth, the older age groups have lower levels of educational attainment than the younger age groups, as indicated by the summary of the educational attainment composition in 1980 by persons of each age reported in Table 10-2 and graphed in Figure 10-2.

Persons who never completed elementary school are now predominantly concentrated in ages above sixty-five, and hence are no longer in the labor force. Persons who have no more than an elementary school education

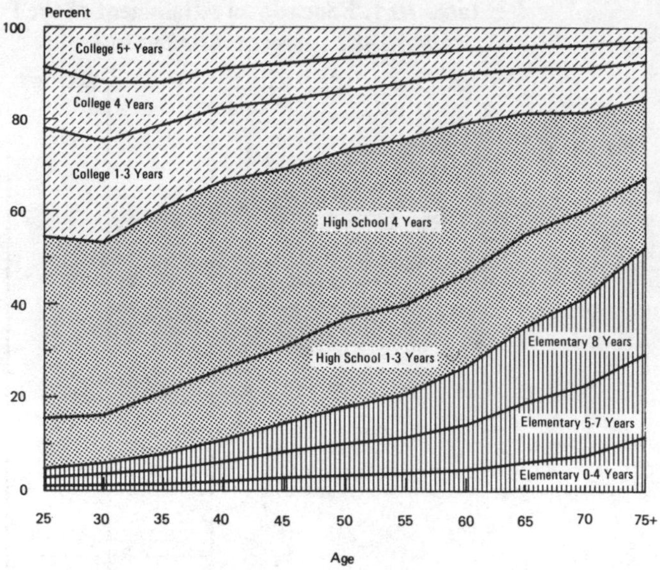

Figure 10-2. Educational Attainment Composition of the U.S. Population, by Age: 1980

Table 10-2. Years of School Completed for Persons 25 Years Old and Over, by Race: 1980 [percent distribution]

Educational attainment	Total	25–29 years	30–34 years	35–39 years	40–44 years	45–49 years	50–54 years	55–59 years	60–64 years	65–69 years	70–74 years	75 and over
Total	100.0	100.0	100.0	100.0	100.0	100.0	100.0	100.0	100.0	100.0	100.0	100.0
Elementary school												
None	1.0	0.5	0.5	0.5	0.6	0.8	0.9	0.9	1.0	1.3	1.7	3.3
1 to 4 years . .	2.6	0.6	0.8	1.0	1.5	2.1	2.5	3.0	3.6	4.8	5.9	8.3
5 and 6 years. .	3.7	1.1	1.4	1.7	2.4	3.1	3.7	4.2	5.2	6.8	8.2	10.7
7 years.	2.9	0.7	1.0	1.4	1.8	2.4	3.0	3.4	4.4	5.9	6.7	7.1
8 years.	8.0	1.9	2.3	3.3	4.6	6.1	7.8	9.2	12.4	16.2	18.9	22.9
High school												
1 year	4.6	2.8	2.9	3.8	4.5	4.8	5.5	5.3	6.0	6.6	6.5	5.8
2 years.	5.6	3.8	3.6	4.9	5.8	6.2	7.2	6.9	7.3	7.4	7.2	5.7
3 years.	5.0	4.1	3.6	4.4	4.9	5.3	6.4	7.0	6.7	5.9	5.1	3.6
4 years.	34.6	39.0	37.1	39.7	40.5	39.1	36.2	35.8	32.6	26.4	21.3	17.2
College												
1 year	5.8	9.2	8.3	6.9	6.0	5.2	4.6	4.5	3.9	3.4	3.3	2.8
2 years.	6.8	9.5	9.3	7.7	6.9	6.3	5.9	5.6	4.9	4.3	4.3	3.8
3 years.	3.1	4.8	4.4	3.5	3.1	2.8	2.5	2.2	2.0	1.9	2.0	1.6
4 years.	8.6	13.4	12.8	10.0	8.4	7.9	7.2	6.2	5.3	4.8	5.1	4.4
5 and 6 years. .	4.8	6.2	7.8	6.8	5.4	4.8	4.0	3.2	2.8	2.5	2.4	1.6
7 years or more.	2.9	2.5	4.1	4.4	3.8	3.4	2.8	2.3	1.9	1.7	1.6	1.2

Source: U.S. Bureau of the Census. "Detailed Population Characteristics: United States Summary." 1980 Census of Population. Washington, DC: U.S. Government Printing Office, 1984, Table 262.

are mostly older than fifty, and more than one-half of them are already retired or approaching retirement.

The great bulk (40 percent) of the population at ages under fifty are high school graduates who did not attend college. A much smaller proportion, somewhat larger among those thirty-five and over, began high school but did not complete it.

The upper stratum is comprised predominantly of persons under forty-five years of age, who not only completed college but have done postgraduates work. This stratum is parallelled by a considerably larger stratum consisting of persons who graduated from college but did not continue with additional education. At ages under thirty those with college degrees or post-graduate work comprise almost one-fourth of the population of those ages. College degrees are comparatively scarce among the population older than sixty-five, but even among the older work force 55-64 years of age 10 percent are college graduates. At the youngest ages the proportion of persons who began college but had not yet graduated is very substantial, almost as large as the proportion of those completing four years or more.

Sex Differences in Educational Attainment

Because of past lower rates of enrollment in college, women have slightly lower average levels of educational attainment than men. This is documented in Table 10-3, which provides data on the educational attainment composition of males and females, by age groups. Table 10-4 reports two summary indicators: the percentage having graduated from high school and the percentage having graduated from college. On the high school graduation indicator the two sexes are very nearly identical for all ages. Because there are more older women than older men, the overall percentage for all ages combined is somewhat lower for women than for men. However, on the indicator of college graduation, women are significantly less educated than men at all ages. The pre-

Table 10-3. Years of School Completed, by Sex and Age: 1980 [percent distribution]

Age and sex	Total	College			High school		Elementary school		
		5 years and over	4 years	1-3 years	4 years	1-3 years	8 years	5-7 years	0-4 years
Male									
Total, 25 and over . .	100.0	10.3	9.8	16.1	31.1	14.2	7.8	6.8	3.9
25-29 years.	100.0	10.0	13.6	24.1	36.6	10.5	2.0	1.9	1.2
30-34 years.	100.0	15.0	14.3	23.1	32.1	9.2	2.4	2.5	1.4
35-39 years.	100.0	15.0	11.1	18.2	35.1	11.9	3.6	3.5	1.7
40-44 years.	100.0	12.6	9.6	16.1	36.0	13.8	4.9	4.7	2.3
45-49 years.	100.0	11.5	9.6	14.4	34.0	14.5	6.6	6.1	3.2
50-54 years.	100.0	9.3	9.0	12.8	30.8	18.1	8.6	7.6	3.8
55-59 years.	100.0	7.9	7.9	12.1	31.1	18.4	9.7	8.3	4.5
60-64 years.	100.0	6.3	6.1	10.9	29.5	19.0	12.7	10.1	5.4
65-69 years.	100.0	5.5	5.2	9.2	24.0	18.8	16.5	13.5	7.2
70-74 years.	100.0	5.2	5.1	8.6	18.7	18.0	19.4	16.0	9.0
75 years and over. . . .	100.0	4.0	4.6	6.9	14.1	14.0	23.0	19.5	13.9
Female									
Total, 25 and over . .	100.0	5.3	7.5	15.3	37.7	16.2	8.2	6.5	3.3
25-29 years.	100.0	7.4	13.2	22.8	41.4	10.8	1.8	1.7	1.0
30-34 years.	100.0	8.9	11.3	21.0	42.1	11.0	2.3	2.3	1.2
35-39 years.	100.0	7.4	9.0	18.1	44.1	14.1	3.1	2.8	1.4
40-44 years.	100.0	5.8	7.3	15.7	44.9	16.5	4.2	3.7	1.9
45-49 years.	100.0	5.0	6.2	14.1	43.8	17.9	5.6	4.9	2.5
50-54 years.	100.0	4.3	5.6	13.1	41.2	20.0	7.0	5.9	2.9
55-59 years.	100.0	3.5	4.7	12.6	40.1	19.9	8.8	7.0	3.4
60-64 years.	100.0	3.3	4.6	10.6	35.3	20.9	12.2	9.1	4.0
65-69 years.	100.0	3.1	4.5	10.0	28.4	20.8	16.0	12.0	5.2
70-74 years.	100.0	3.1	5.0	10.3	23.1	19.4	18.5	14.1	6.5
75 years and over. . . .	100.0	2.2	4.2	9.0	18.9	15.6	22.8	16.9	10.4

Source: U.S. Bureau of the Census. "Detailed Population Characteristics: United States Summary." 1980 Census of Population. Washington, DC: U.S. Government Printing Office, 1984, Table 262.

Table 10-4. Indicators of Educational Attainment, by Sex and Age: 1980

Age	Percent high school graduates			Percent 4 years college and over		
	Both sexes	Male	Female	Both sexes	Male	Female
Total	66.5	67.3	65.8	16.2	20.1	12.8
25-29 years	84.5	84.4	84.7	22.1	23.6	20.5
30-34 years	83.8	84.4	83.3	24.6	29.2	20.2
35-39 years	79.0	79.4	78.5	21.2	26.1	16.4
40-44 years	74.0	74.3	73.6	17.5	22.2	13.1
45-49 years	69.3	69.5	69.1	16.0	21.1	11.2
50-54 years	63.1	61.9	64.2	13.9	18.4	9.9
55-59 years	60.0	59.0	60.8	11.8	15.8	8.2
60-64 years	53.3	52.8	53.8	10.0	12.4	7.8
65-69 years	45.1	43.9	46.0	9.0	10.7	7.6
70-74 years	39.8	37.6	41.5	9.0	10.3	8.1
75 years and over .	32.7	29.6	34.3	7.2	8.6	6.4

Source: U.S. Bureau of the Census. "Detailed Population Characteristics: United States Summary." 1980 Census of Population. Washington, DC: U.S. Government Printing Office, 1984, Table 262.

ceding chapter noted that enrollment of women in college surged ahead in the late 1970s to surpass that of men in the early 1980s. This is reflected in the smaller sex differential for ages 25-29 and 30-34 than for the years older than this. Because of this generational effect, future censuses will show full equality or even superiority of female educational attainment at the very youngest ages, with a progressively greater relative sex differential in educational attainment with increasing age. As of 1980 the sex differential in college graduation is greatest, both absolutely and relatively, between the ages of thirty-five and sixty. These were generations of great rise in college enrollment, but primarily for men. It will take three decades for the generations of women with this handicap to pass out of the working ages and three additional decades to disappear at the most advanced ages. Because of the generational effect, the upper-level educational attainment of women will be significantly below that of men for more than half a century, but the differences will diminish with the passage of time.

Race Differences in Educational Attainment

The educational attainment composition of the population is reported in Table 10-5 for each of the race-ethnic groups used in the census. The most educated racial group in the United States is the population from Asia. Nearly 75 percent of this group have graduated from high school and 33 percent are college graduates. The majority white population occupies second place. The least educated is the Spanish-origin population, with only 44 percent high school graduates and 8 percent college graduates. American Indians and the black population are much lower in educational attainment than the white, but significantly above the Spanish-origin population. (See Figure 10-3.)

Table 10-6 provides two indicators of educational level, by age and sex, for each racial group: graduation from high school and graduation from college. The racial differentials described above are valid for each age and sex group in general but are much diminished at the younger ages and much greater at the older ages. American Indian men are more educated at most age levels than black men, but American Indian women are less educated than black women, particularly with respect to college graduation. Older Spanish-origin males are more likely to be college graduates than black males at most ages, despite having a smaller proportion who have graduated from high school. Selective immigration is a possible explanation.

The educational disadvantages that the black population suffered in the past are reflected in the race differentials for black males and females forty and older. These are persons born before 1940, when the movement toward racial equality was gaining momentum. At those ages the percentage of persons with a high school diploma is only half that for whites, and the percentage with a college degree is less than half that for whites. The black-white differential is much greater for males than for females; black women have sought a college education more persistently than black men for many generations, with the result that they are less disadvan-

Table 10-5. Years of School Completed by Persons 25 Years and Over, by Sex and Race: 1980

Educational attainment	Sex		Race-ethnicity				
	Male	Female	White	Black	American Indian	Asian/ Pac. Is.	Spanish-origin
Total, 25 years and over. .	100.0	100.0	100.0	100.0	100.0	100.0	100.0
Elementary school							
None.	1.0	1.0	0.7	1.8	4.0	3.4	4.9
1-4 years	2.9	2.3	1.9	6.5	4.4	3.0	10.6
5-7 years	6.8	6.5	5.8	11.7	8.3	6.4	16.6
8 years	7.8	8.2	8.2	7.1	8.3	3.6	8.1
High school							
1 year.	4.4	4.8	4.4	6.2	5.9	3.1	5.7
2 years	5.2	6.1	5.4	7.8	7.2	3.1	5.3
3 years	4.6	5.4	4.7	7.8	6.3	2.6	4.8
4 years	31.1	37.7	35.7	29.3	31.3	24.7	24.4
College							
1 year.	5.5	6.1	5.9	5.4	6.6	4.9	4.6
2 years	7.3	6.2	6.9	5.6	7.0	7.8	5.0
3 years	3.3	2.9	3.1	2.5	2.9	4.5	2.4
4 years	9.8	7.5	9.1	4.4	3.9	15.0	3.6
5 and 6 years	5.7	4.0	5.0	2.6	2.4	9.4	2.3
7 years and over.	4.6	1.4	3.0	1.4	1.3	8.5	1.8

Source: U.S. Bureau of the Census. "Detailed Population Characteristics: United States Summary." 1980 Census of Population. Washington, DC: U.S. Government Printing Office, 1984, Table 262.

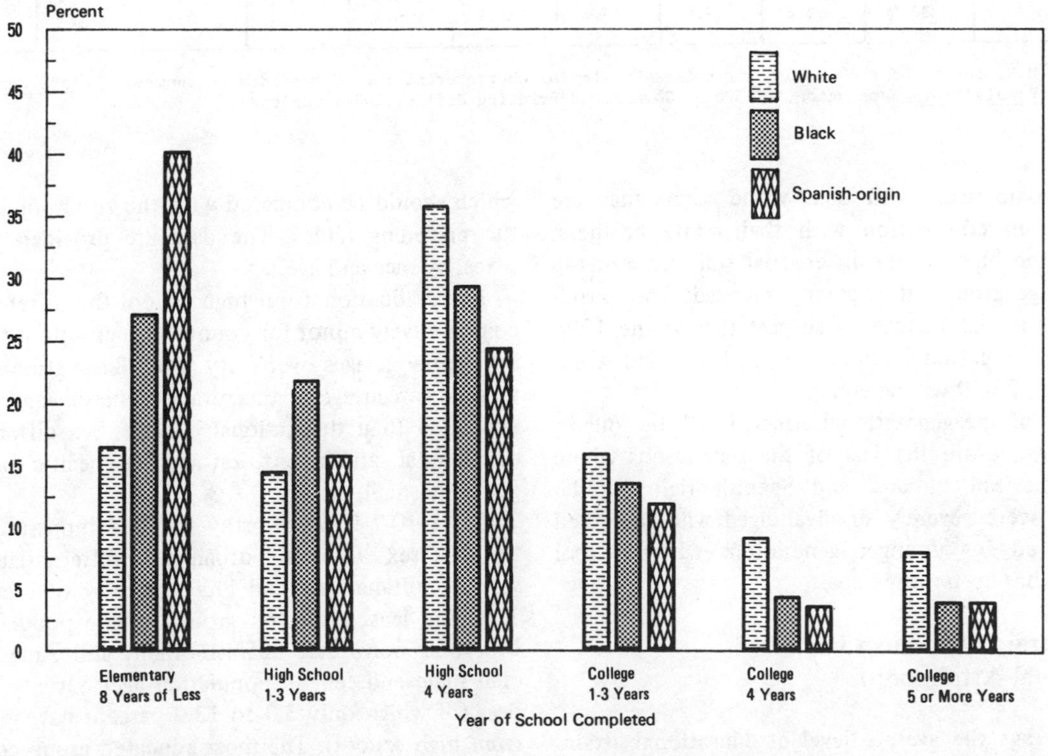

Figure 10-3. Educational Attainment of the White, Black and Spanish-Origin Population, Persons 25 Years and Over: 1980

Table 10-6. Indicators of Educational Attainment of the Total Population Age 25 and Over, by Age, Sex, and Race-Ethnicity: 1980

Age and Sex	Percent high school graduate					Percent college graduate				
	White	Black	American Indian	Asian/ Pac. Is.	Spanish-origin	White	Black	American Indian	Asian/ Pac. Is.	Spanish-origin
Male										
Total. . . .	69.6	50.8	57.0	78.8	45.4	21.3	8.4	9.2	39.8	9.4
25-29 years. .	87.0	73.8	72.7	89.2	58.4	25.8	10.7	8.5	40.5	9.7
30-34 years. .	86.9	72.4	73.7	90.1	56.3	31.5	12.5	12.0	51.1	12.1
35-39 years. .	82.0	64.4	65.3	89.0	49.6	27.7	11.0	10.9	54.5	11.0
40-44 years. .	77.3	56.0	58.6	86.6	44.8	23.6	9.1	10.4	50.9	9.8
45-49 years. .	72.7	47.9	50.7	81.4	40.9	22.6	8.4	9.5	42.1	9.2
50-54 years. .	64.9	37.8	43.2	73.4	35.5	19.7	6.9	8.1	30.9	8.2
55-59 years. .	62.2	31.6	41.8	65.7	31.9	17.0	5.5	8.9	21.6	7.2
60-64 years. .	55.8	25.0	36.0	57.6	28.0	13.2	4.6	6.6	17.8	6.6
65-69 years. .	46.6	18.7	27.9	44.0	22.1	11.4	3.7	4.8	14.1	5.2
70-74 years. .	40.0	14.6	20.4	36.0	18.8	11.1	3.1	3.8	11.5	4.6
75+ years. . .	31.4	12.2	15.6	30.6	16.1	9.1	2.7	3.4	9.7	4.2
Female										
Total. . . .	68.1	51.5	54.1	71.4	42.7	13.3	8.3	6.3	27.0	6.0
25-29 years. .	87.2	76.5	72.1	83.9	59.2	22.0	12.1	7.7	35.9	8.4
30-34 years. .	85.9	73.4	69.8	82.8	54.4	21.4	11.5	8.5	38.6	7.4
35-39 years. .	81.5	65.6	61.7	80.7	47.6	17.2	9.8	7.2	37.4	6.3
40-44 years. .	77.0	58.0	53.6	76.0	43.1	13.6	8.4	6.0	29.3	6.1
45-49 years. .	72.6	50.4	48.4	72.6	37.7	11.6	8.3	5.6	20.0	5.3
50-54 years. .	67.8	41.5	43.0	66.5	33.0	10.3	6.9	5.3	13.8	4.8
55-59 years. .	64.4	34.3	41.9	58.8	28.7	8.5	5.7	4.7	11.2	4.3
60-64 years. .	57.0	27.6	35.5	45.9	23.5	8.2	5.1	4.3	9.5	3.7
65-69 years. .	49.0	21.7	27.9	37.4	20.3	8.0	4.3	3.4	8.1	3.3
70-74 years. .	44.0	18.3	22.9	32.4	17.6	8.5	4.4	4.2	7.9	2.9
75+ years. . .	36.0	15.8	19.6	28.6	15.9	6.7	3.4	3.1	5.4	2.6

Source: U.S. Bureau of the Census. "Detailed Population Characteristics: United States Summary." 1980 Census of Population. Washington, DC: U.S. Government Printing Office, 1984, Table 262.

taged in comparison with their white sisters than are black men in comparison with their white brothers. Although the black-white differential still exists at the youngest age groups, it is greatly reduced. The enrollment statistics of Chapter 9 suggest that at the 1990 census the educational attainment of black and white persons aged 25-29 will be equal.

Because of the generational effect, it will be four to five decades before the last of the generations where blacks, American Indians, and Spanish-origin populations who were severely disadvantaged will have died out, replaced by younger generations where school enrollment has been more equal.

Urban-Rural Differences in Educational Attainment

At each age the average level of educational attainment in rural areas is considerably below that of urban areas. Table 10-7 provides data for the rural population, which should be compared with the total population of the preceding tables. The data are provided for both sexes, by race and age.

For graduation from high school the differences are comparatively minor for younger age groups but are very substantial at ages over forty. For all age groups a much smaller percentage of the rural population has a college education than the national average. Sex differences in educational attainment, on an age-specific basis, are generally small.

Table 10-7 is noteworthy for its demonstration that the age, sex, race, and urban-rural differentials are all valid simultaneously and independently of each other. Thus the least educated groups in the population are the rural nonwhite, Spanish-origin, and American Indian male and female population aged seventy-five and over (of which only 5.3 to 13.9 percent have graduated from high school). The most educated group comprises Asian males aged 35-39, of which 87 percent are high school graduates and 51 percent are college graduates.

Table 10-7. Indicators of Educational Attainment of the Rural Population, by Age, Sex and Race-Ethnicity: 1980

Age and sex	Percent high school graduate						Percent college graduate					
	All races	White	Black	American Indian	Asian/ Pac. Is.	Spanish-origin	All races	White	Black	American Indian	Asian/ Pac. Is.	Spanish-origin
Male												
Total, 25 years and over	59.6	61.5	32.0	47.3	69.1	36.2	12.8	13.4	4.1	5.4	30.0	6.7
25-29 years.	81.1	83.3	59.8	68.4	87.3	51.7	14.8	15.7	5.0	5.5	29.2	6.5
30-34 years.	80.7	82.7	55.3	67.5	88.8	51.6	20.8	21.8	6.3	7.3	44.6	10.6
35-39 years.	74.6	76.6	45.5	57.0	86.7	42.5	17.8	18.4	6.1	7.3	50.7	9.2
40-44 years.	68.6	70.7	34.8	49.1	85.2	36.7	14.3	14.8	4.6	5.7	50.2	7.1
45-49 years.	61.7	64.1	26.9	38.0	78.7	29.6	13.1	13.7	4.5	4.8	38.8	6.2
50-54 years.	51.9	54.0	18.6	33.5	65.3	24.5	10.9	11.4	3.7	4.2	23.5	5.0
55-59 years.	48.2	50.3	14.4	29.9	59.9	20.9	9.4	9.8	3.0	4.6	13.6	4.7
60-64 years.	41.6	43.5	10.6	27.8	51.1	17.3	7.6	7.9	2.4	4.2	9.8	3.4
65-69 years.	33.8	35.6	7.7	19.6	30.1	12.9	6.4	6.7	2.1	3.5	7.2	2.0
70-74 years.	27.6	29.1	6.2	13.1	23.3	9.9	6.2	6.5	1.5	3.1	4.4	2.1
75 years and over.	20.1	21.3	5.3	9.9	18.1	7.6	5.1	5.3	1.4	2.2	3.7	1.9
Female												
Total, 25 years and over	61.2	63.2	34.5	45.5	64.9	38.5	9.2	9.5	5.2	4.4	18.2	4.8
25-29 years.	82.4	84.0	67.2	68.7	77.9	58.0	14.0	14.6	7.9	4.9	23.5	6.5
30-34 years.	80.8	82.4	61.4	65.1	76.0	54.0	14.6	15.1	7.7	6.7	28.1	7.3
35-39 years.	75.6	77.6	49.3	54.8	74.6	44.6	11.4	11.7	6.3	5.2	29.0	5.3
40-44 years.	70.0	72.3	39.8	45.0	70.3	38.8	8.8	9.0	5.4	4.3	21.4	5.1
45-49 years.	63.7	66.2	30.8	35.5	71.6	31.5	7.5	7.7	5.0	3.4	14.3	3.9
50-54 years.	57.3	59.9	23.3	31.8	64.3	25.8	6.8	7.0	4.8	3.8	9.1	2.9
55-59 years.	52.5	54.9	17.6	31.8	55.9	22.6	6.0	6.1	3.9	3.5	7.2	2.6
60-64 years.	45.8	48.0	13.4	25.4	43.1	16.2	6.2	6.3	3.7	3.1	7.1	2.4
65-69 years.	39.5	41.6	11.4	19.2	31.7	15.9	6.3	6.5	3.5	2.5	4.5	2.1
70-74 years.	34.9	36.9	9.2	14.6	29.7	12.6	6.9	7.2	2.9	2.8	5.6	2.9
75 years and over.	27.6	29.0	8.5	13.9	27.7	10.5	5.3	5.5	2.5	2.3	4.4	2.1

Source: U.S. Bureau of the Census. "Detailed Population Characteristics: United States Summary." 1980 Census of Population. Washington, DC: U.S. Government Printing Office, 1984, Table 262.

Regional Differences in Educational Attainment

The age, sex, race, and urban-rural differences noted above are present in each region, as shown in Table 10-8. However, there is also a set of interregional differences. The educational attainment of the population in the South is below that of the other regions, while in the West the level of educational attainment at each age is generally higher than it is in other regions. In the South the white-black differential is unusually large, owing to past neglect with respect to educational opportunities for blacks. As Chapter 9 reports, at present blacks suffer no more neglect educationally in the South than they do in other regions. Other regional differences are due in part to differences in urban-rural composition, in part to historical differences in the quality and quantity of educational facilities provided, and in part to the fact that for many years so many of the better educated persons migrated from regions of lower opportunity to regions of higher opportunity.

In interpreting these interregional differences, one must keep in mind the fact that they are a net resultant of conditions that have existed over the past fifty to seventy-five years. The differences should not be used to evaluate the current educational programs of the various regions. Such programs are best evaluated from school enrollment data or from educational attainment data for adults under twenty-five years of age.

Educational Attainment of Out-of-School Youth

The preceding discussion has focussed exclusively on the population twenty-five years of age and over. This leaves unanswered questions concerning the educational attainment of the population under twenty-five years not enrolled in school. This information is provided by sex and race in Table 10-9. Slightly more than one-half of these youths have graduated from high school. An additional one-fifth have attended college, and a significant proportion have graduated from college (6.8 percent). Only 7 percent have failed to complete grammar school. The fact that only one young person in fifteen fails to attain 0-8 years of elementary school is due to compulsory school attendance and employment laws. However, a great many youths drop out of high school. Having complied with the legal minimum, about one youth in five attempts high school and drops out. The tendency to drop out seems stronger during the final years of high school than in the earlier years.

These findings describe both the male and female white population. The black population follows a similar pattern but with slightly higher proportions not completing grammar school greater high school dropout rates, and much less college attendance. As a result a greater proportion of the black population is less readily employable, a situation considerably more adverse for black males than for black females.

The Spanish-origin population aged 14-24 years is much less educated than the white or black. Almost 30 percent never entered high school, and the dropout rate is high for those who did. College attendance is lower than for the black population. As a consequence, only 46-48 percent completed high school, and of these 35-39 percent completed high school without entering college. According to the enrollment rates of Chapter 9, this low attainment rate is heavily concentrated among the Mexican population, much less among the Puerto Rican, and least among the Cuban.

The persons described above were not enrolled in school when the Current Population Survey was taken in November, 1979. Many of them had graduated during the preceding spring or summer and had made their decision not to continue. However, a substantial proportion will reenter school after a period of nonenrollment. The above picture, therefore, very likely understates the final educational attainment of this generation. Nonetheless, the problem of high school discontinuation, especially among the black and Spanish-origin populations as well as the white, is of major concern to modern secondary education.

Education as a Factor in Social and Economic Life

The term "socioeconomic status," widely used as an explanatory variable in social and psychological research, is an amalgam of educational attainment, occupation, and income, with educational attainment being considered a causal determinant of the other two. The re-

Table 10-8. Indicators of Educational Attainment for Regions, by Sex, Race, and Year: 1940-1980

Race, sex, and year	Percent high school graduate					Percent college graduate				
	Total	North-east	North Central	South	West	Total	North-east	North Central	South	West
All races										
1980	66.5	67.1	68.0	60.2	74.5	16.2	17.2	14.7	15.0	19.3
1970	52.3	52.9	53.7	45.1	62.3	10.7	11.2	9.6	9.8	13.2
1960	41.1	41.0	41.7	35.3	50.8	7.7	8.1	6.9	7.1	9.6
1950	34.3	35.7	35.4	26.7	45.6	6.0	6.6	5.5	5.3	7.7
1940	24.5	24.0	25.0	20.3	34.8	4.6	4.9	4.2	4.0	6.1
White										
1980	68.8	68.7	69.3	63.5	77.2	17.1	18.0	15.2	16.3	20.2
1970	54.5	54.2	55.0	49.1	63.3	11.3	11.7	10.0	10.8	13.5
1960	43.2	41.9	42.8	39.8	51.9	8.1	8.4	7.1	7.9	9.9
1950	36.4	36.7	36.4	31.6	46.7	6.4	6.8	5.6	6.2	7.9
1940	26.1	24.4	25.4	24.6	35.4	4.9	5.1	4.3	4.8	6.2
Black										
1980	51.2	56.4	54.9	44.9	68.7	8.4	8.4	7.9	8.0	11.4
1970	31.4	37.8	36.5	24.4	48.9	4.4	4.1	4.0	4.4	5.9
1960	20.1	26.9	25.3	14.7	34.3	3.1	2.9	2.9	3.1	4.1
1950	13.0	20.4	19.7	8.8	26.2	2.1	2.2	2.3	1.9	2.9
1940	7.7	11.7	12.6	5.4	18.4	1.3	1.7	1.8	1.1	2.3
Men, 1980. .	67.3	68.0	68.2	61.2	75.4	20.1	21.7	18.1	18.3	23.7
White.	69.6	69.5	69.5	64.6	77.9	21.3	22.7	18.8	20.3	25.1
Black.	50.8	56.2	53.9	44.2	69.8	8.4	9.3	8.2	7.5	12.6
Women, 1980.	65.8	66.4	67.8	59.4	73.7	12.8	13.4	11.7	12.0	15.1
White.	68.1	68.0	69.0	62.5	76.4	13.3	13.9	11.9	12.7	15.7
Black.	51.5	56.7	55.8	45.4	67.7	8.3	7.7	7.6	8.5	10.3

Source: U.S. Bureau of the Census. "General Social and Economic Characteristics: United States Summary." 1980 Census of Population. Washington, DC: U.S. Government Printing Office, 1984, Table 83.

Table 10-9. Years of School Completed of Youth Aged 14-24 Out of School for One or More Years, by Sex and Race-Ethnicity: 1979

School years completed	All races	White	Black	Spanish-origin
Male				
Total. . . .	100.0	100.0	100.0	100.0
Elementary				
8 or less years. . .	7.0	6.7	9.0	27.6
High school				
1 year . . .	5.4	5.1	8.0	8.4
2 years. . .	7.4	6.8	11.7	10.1
3 years. . .	7.6	6.8	13.6	8.3
4 years. . .	52.1	53.0	45.2	35.3
College				
1 year . . .	6.4	6.8	3.6	4.4
2 years. . .	5.7	6.0	3.8	2.8
3 years. . .	1.6	1.6	1.4	0.9
4 years. . .	6.1	6.6	3.3	2.2
5+ years . .	0.7	0.7	0.3	*
Female				
Total. . . .	100.0	100.0	100.0	100.0
Elementary				
8 or less years. . .	5.3	5.2	5.6	23.9
High school				
1 year . . .	5.5	5.2	7.3	8.7
2 years. . .	7.1	6.3	11.3	9.4
3 years. . .	6.4	5.8	10.1	9.6
4 years. . .	53.5	54.8	46.9	38.7
College				
1 year . . .	6.9	6.9	7.3	3.9
2 years. . .	6.5	6.6	5.7	3.5
3 years. . .	1.5	1.4	1.8	1.0
4 years. . .	6.8	7.3	3.8	1.3
5+ years . .	0.6	0.6	0.1	*

Note: * indicates less than 0.05.

Source: U.S. Bureau of the Census. "School Enrollment--Social and Economic Characteristics of Students, 1979." Current Population Reports (Series p-20, no. 360). Washington, DC: U.S. Government Printing Office, 1981, Table 7.

lationship of educational attainment to these other two components of socioeconomic status is discussed in Chapters 13 and 14.

Educational attainment is a principal background variable that influences "prestige" and "social status." Some researchers have theorized that providing extraordinary educational attainment is one mechanism by which high-status families transmit that status to their offspring. Attaining more education than one's parents is supposedly a routine mechanism for a child to rise from one social stratum to another. The bibliography lists important researches that have used educational attainment data to study social stratification and social mobility.

The important differences among the detailed race-ethnic groups in educational attainment are discussed in Chapter 9 as well as in this chapter. Chapter 6 documents that one of the strongest differentials in fertility is linked to educational attainment, with the number of years of schooling completed being inversely related to the number of children ever born. However, two topics not discussed in previous chapters are marital status and migration.

Marital Status and Educational Attainment

Educational attainment can affect marital status in a variety of ways. It can cause persons (especially women) to remain single until they attain the amount of education they desire. It can influence the employability and hence the financial capability (particularly of males) for getting married and establishing a family. It can influence the desirability or eligibility of a person as a marriage partner. It can provide greater freedom in choosing whether, when, and with whom to marry. Both education and marital status can be influenced jointly by external factors of a physiological or environmental nature. (For example, a person who is severely mentally retarded is incapable of normal educational achievement and normal family life.) Education can be a form of self-investment in the hope of long-term future gains at the loss of short-term income, leisure, or other benefits. Those who make such an investment tend to differ in numerous ways from those who do not, including attitude toward marriage. Education is a somewhat rigorous attrition process, in which young persons attempt (or are encouraged to attempt) to survive to the maximal extent of their intellectual, economic, and other abilities; marriage tends to occur after successful survival or as a secondary adjustment after elimination. Unforeseen events can curtail educational attainment. Important among these are premarital pregnancy followed by "forced" or "obligatory" marriage or withdrawal from school to care for a child. Death or physical incapacitation of a parent and military draft are other external events that can affect education. The availability of government funds to sponsor schooling (such as veterans' educational benefits and student loans) and the willingness of one partner of a married couple to help support the education of the other are also involved.

This chapter documents only the gross relationships between marital status and educational attainment, without evaluating the forces that determine the rela-

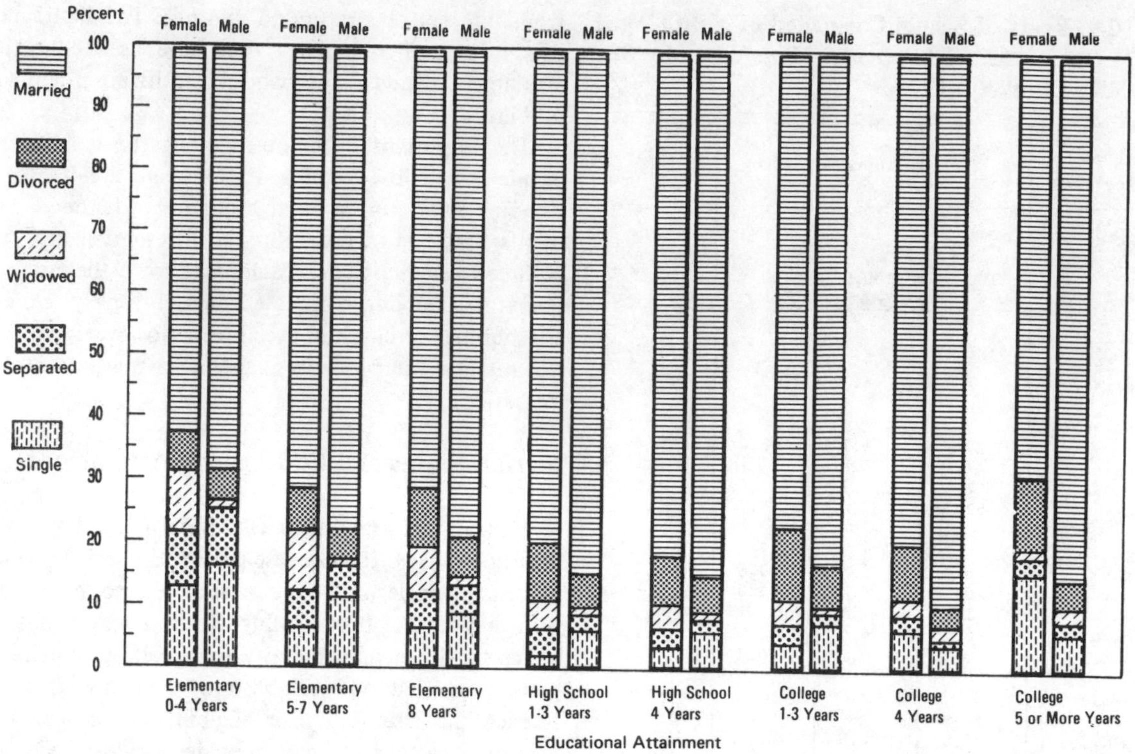

Figure 10-4. Marital Status and Educational Attainment of White Females and Males Aged 35-44 Years: 1979

tionships. (Since marital status is strongly influenced by age, race-ethnicity, and sex, these variables have been controlled.) The basic data are presented in Tables 10-10A to 10F, with one table devoted to the relationship between marital status and education (with age controlled) for six groupings of sex and age: white, black, and Spanish-origin males, and white, black, and Spanish-origin females. Figure 10-4 takes a majority group, the white population aged 35-54, to illustrates the differentials between marital status and education.

Functional Illiteracy (0-4 Years of School)

Except for the Spanish-origin population, the population with only 0-4 years of schooling is quite small and heavily concentrated in the old age category. Those young persons having little or no formal schooling are a highly select group. In order to reach adulthood with less than five years of schooling, given the laws of compulsory education, they must have been excused from school because of physical or mental handicaps, have failed repeatedly in elementary school, or have been willful dropouts or truants. It is not surprising to find that a high percentage of this group have remained single. Of those who attempted marriage, a disproportionately large share are separated. This description applies only to persons under fifty-five years of age in 1980; the older generations with less educational attainment show these propensities but to a lesser degree. It applies with special strength to those aged 25-34, both males and females and black and white. However, in 1980, having 0-4 years of schooling was normal for a significant percentage of the Spanish-origin population.

Deficient Education (5-7 Years of School)

Under present laws for compulsory school attendance completion of eight years of elementary education is the minimal acceptable achievement, and those who fail to comply are considered deficient. The causes of deficiency are similar to those enumerated above for functional illiteracy, but the selectivity is less severe; extenuating circumstances such as underprivilege can explain some of the deficiency. The effects on marital status are less noticeable than for functional illiteracy, but the propensity to remain unmarried or to be separated if ever married still exists. It applies to the white population with considerable force, less to the black population, and not at all to the Spanish-origin population (for which 5-7 years of schooling is average). Lack of sufficient income to support a family could be the important intervening variable for this group.

Table 10-10A. Marital Status by Years of School Completed, White Males, by Age, 1979

Age and marital status	Total	Elementary school 0-4 years	Elementary school 5-7 years	Elementary school 8 years	High school 1-3 years	High school 4 years	College 1-3 years	College 4 years	College 5 or more years	Median school years
25 years and over . .	100.0	100.0	100.0	100.0	100.0	100.0	100.0	100.0	100.0	12.6
Single.	10.6	13.9	8.7	7.3	7.2	9.1	12.9	14.7	14.1	12.9
Married, spouse present	78.8	67.5	74.7	78.0	81.1	81.5	77.1	77.8	76.8	12.6
Separated	2.4	4.7	3.5	2.8	2.6	1.9	2.4	1.8	2.3	*
Widowed	3.0	10.5	8.6	6.9	3.5	2.1	1.6	1.4	1.2	9.8
Divorced.	5.3	3.4	4.5	5.0	5.5	5.4	6.0	4.4	5.5	12.6
25 to 34 years. . . .	100.0	100.0	100.0	100.0	100.0	100.0	100.0	100.0	100.0	13.3
Single.	21.9	41.8	16.1	15.9	14.5	18.3	23.0	28.0	26.7	14.3
Married, spouse present	69.0	48.5	74.0	74.3	73.0	72.4	66.7	66.2	65.6	13.1
Separated	2.5	8.5	5.9	1.5	4.2	2.3	2.7	1.5	2.2	*
Widowed	0.2	*	*	*	0.4	0.3	0.1	0.1	*	*
Divorced.	6.4	1.2	4.0	8.3	7.9	6.8	7.5	4.3	5.4	13.0
35 to 54 years. . . .	100.0	100.0	100.0	100.0	100.0	100.0	100.0	100.0	100.0	12.7
Single.	7.0	16.4	10.8	8.9	6.2	5.9	7.2	6.1	7.8	12.6
Married, spouse present	83.8	68.5	78.3	79.5	84.8	85.1	84.0	86.5	82.9	12.7
Separated	2.6	8.6	4.7	4.2	2.4	2.2	2.2	2.0	2.7	*
Widowed	0.8	1.6	1.1	1.4	1.3	0.7	0.6	0.2	0.5	12.2
Divorced.	5.8	4.9	5.3	5.9	5.2	6.1	6.0	5.3	6.2	12.7
55 to 64 years. . . .	100.0	100.0	100.0	100.0	100.0	100.0	100.0	100.0	100.0	12.4
Single.	5.0	8.0	6.7	6.4	5.2	4.6	3.3	3.3	6.1	12.1
Married, spouse present	85.9	81.7	77.3	81.0	84.3	88.6	88.9	89.5	85.3	12.4
Separated	1.9	3.1	3.6	3.2	2.1	1.2	1.5	1.5	2.1	*
Widowed	2.9	2.7	5.9	3.8	2.9	2.5	2.6	2.2	2.1	12.0
Divorced.	4.2	4.6	6.4	5.6	5.5	3.1	3.6	3.3	4.5	11.9
65 years and over . .	100.0	100.0	100.0	100.0	100.0	100.0	100.0	100.0	100.0	10.1
Single.	5.3	7.6	6.6	5.3	5.0	4.4	2.5	4.8	8.7	9.0
Married, spouse present	76.3	66.0	71.1	75.6	77.5	80.5	80.1	79.7	76.9	10.4
Separated	1.9	2.4	2.2	1.9	2.3	1.0	2.7	2.7	0.6	*
Widowed	13.4	21.4	17.0	13.8	10.9	11.6	12.0	11.1	10.1	8.9
Divorced.	3.1	2.5	3.2	3.4	4.3	2.6	2.7	1.7	3.7	9.9

Note: * indicates base too small to make accurate measure. Some columns fail to add to 100.0 by a significant amount because of small sample sizes and rounding errors.

Source: U.S. Bureau of the Census. "Educational Attainment in the U.S.: March 1979." Current Population Reports (Series P-20, no. 356). Washington, DC: U.S. Government Printing Office, 1980, Table 5.

Complete Elementary Education (8 Years of School)

Unlike those with deficient education, this group with barely adequate education is more likely to marry. Among the white population the proportions of separated or divorced persons are below average for the age-race-sex group. For the black population, however, the prevalence of separation is extremely high, and for black males the proportion divorced is also high. Spanish-origin persons who have completed eight years of elementary school are, in relative terms, "middle class" and show marital status distributions about average for the age group.

Table 10-10B. Marital Status by Years of School Completed, Black Males, by Age: 1979

Age and marital status	Total	Elementary school			High school		College			Median school years
		0-4 years	5-7 years	8 years	1-3 years	4 years	1-3 years	4 years	5 or more years	
25 years and over . .	100.0	100.0	100.0	100.0	100.0	100.0	100.0	100.0	100.0	11.9
Single.	17.3	19.0	14.5	10.4	16.2	18.1	20.2	20.3	21.2	12.1
Married, spouse present	57.4	51.1	52.8	55.3	58.4	59.1	58.6	65.3	66.2	12.0
Separated	10.5	12.0	14.9	12.3	11.5	9.0	8.5	8.8	2.0	*
Widowed	5.7	14.6	8.7	7.9	4.4	3.6	2.0	0.4	4.0	8.0
Divorced.	9.1	3.3	8.9	14.1	9.4	10.3	10.8	5.2	6.6	12.1
25 to 34 years. . . .	100.0	100.0	100.0	100.0	100.0	100.0	100.0	100.0	100.0	12.6
Single.	31.9	70.0	39.0	27.9	31.5	30.6	31.4	29.0	34.9	12.5
Married, spouse present	50.3	26.7	56.1	30.2	45.3	52.5	48.6	60.9	57.8	12.6
Separated	10.4	3.3	*	34.9	15.1	8.7	11.8	6.5	2.4	*
Widowed	0.4	*	*	*	0.6	0.6	*	*	*	*
Divorced.	7.0	*	4.9	7.0	7.4	7.6	8.2	3.6	4.8	12.5
35 to 54 years. . . .	100.0	100.0	100.0	100.0	100.0	100.0	100.0	100.0	100.0	12.1
Single.	13.9	39.7	24.1	6.2	10.6	10.6	11.5	10.6	12.0	10.5
Married, spouse present	61.0	44.9	46.7	54.4	65.5	62.7	66.2	76.5	72.8	12.2
Separated	9.8	11.8	17.2	12.4	10.4	9.1	5.2	5.8	1.1	*
Widowed	3.3	3.7	1.9	6.2	1.7	4.1	3.7	*	3.3	*
Divorced.	12.0	*	10.0	20.2	11.9	13.4	13.4	7.1	10.9	12.1
55 to 64 years. . . .	100.0	100.0	100.0	100.0	100.0	100.0	100.0	100.0	100.0	8.6
Single.	7.5	12.2	4.1	19.8	6.8	1.3	10.5	4.2	*	*
Married, spouse present	61.9	59.6	59.7	52.3	63.2	68.8	60.5	50.0	100.0	8.8
Separated	13.0	15.4	17.3	8.1	8.3	12.1	7.9	37.5	*	*
Widowed	8.4	10.9	8.2	9.3	9.0	7.0	5.3	*	*	*
Divorced.	9.1	1.9	10.7	10.5	12.8	10.8	15.8	8.3	*	*
65 years and over . .	100.0	100.0	100.0	100.0	100.0	100.0	100.0	100.0	100.0	6.3
Single.	7.0	8.8	6.7	1.2	7.9	6.9	*	*	15.4	*
Married, spouse present	57.5	51.9	53.4	71.8	59.4	65.3	84.0	75.0	46.2	6.8
Separated	9.9	10.9	12.4	5.9	10.9	4.2	12.0	*	*	*
Widowed	20.4	22.8	20.7	14.1	21.8	19.4	*	25.0	38.5	6.1
Divorced.	5.0	5.6	6.7	7.1	*	4.2	4.0	*	*	*

Note: * indicates base too small to make accurate measure. Some columns fail to add to 100.0 by a significant amount because of small sample sizes and rounding errors.

Source: U.S. Bureau of the Census. "Educational Attainment in the U.S.: March 1979." Current Population Reports (Series P-20, no. 356). Washington, DC: U.S. Government Printing Office, 1980, Table 5.

High School Dropout (1-3 Years of High School)

Persons who began high school but did not complete it have very high proportions of marriage, but they also suffer extraordinarily high marital disruption. For whites this takes the form primarily of divorce; for the black population it is both separation and divorce. Persons of Spanish-origin show a pattern similar to blacks. Failure to complete high school could be linked to premarital pregnancy followed by marriage or the necessity of assuming responsibilities as a parent and with marriage to a person not chosen with due deliberation. Thus there could be an element of "social misfit" in this educational stratum, more than among those with only eight years of school.

Table 10-10C. Marital Status by Years of School Completed, Spanish-Origin Males, by Age: 1979

Age and marital status	Total	Elementary school			High school		College			Median school years
		0-4 years	5-7 years	8 years	1-3 years	4 years	1-3 years	4 years	5 or more years	
25 years and over . .	100.0	100.0	100.0	100.0	100.0	100.0	100.0	100.0	100.0	10.4
Single.	11.0	9.5	12.8	7.5	9.0	10.7	14.1	15.0	14.9	11.0
Married, spouse present	75.7	70.5	76.9	73.8	79.1	78.5	74.6	74.2	73.6	10.5
Separated	6.1	11.8	6.3	10.7	3.5	4.5	2.1	4.2	2.3	*
Widowed	2.2	5.3	2.1	2.3	1.4	1.2	1.8	0.8	*	*
Divorced.	4.9	2.9	1.9	5.6	6.8	5.2	7.4	5.8	9.2	12.1
25 to 34 years. . . .	100.0	100.0	100.0	100.0	100.0	100.0	100.0	100.0	100.0	12.2
Single.	18.9	21.9	22.2	11.1	15.0	15.2	4.6	25.0	28.1	12.3
Married, spouse present	71.0	61.5	71.1	80.0	74.4	76.2	67.1	65.4	59.4	12.2
Separated	5.2	14.6	6.7	2.2	4.5	3.9	3.0	3.8	3.1	*
Widowed	0.2	*	*	*	0.8	*	0.6	*	*	*
Divorced.	4.8	2.1	*	6.7	5.3	4.7	7.8	5.7	9.4	*
35 to 54 years. . . .	100.0	100.0	100.0	100.0	100.0	100.0	100.0	100.0	100.0	10.2
Single.	7.4	6.7	10.2	7.0	6.1	7.4	4.3	10.2	8.9	9.5
Married, spouse present	79.9	73.6	77.7	76.0	84.4	81.3	86.0	81.6	82.2	10.5
Separated	6.5	15.7	8.1	10.0	2.2	4.3	1.2	*	*	*
Widowed	0.7	0.6	0.5	1.0	0.6	1.2	*	*	*	*
Divorced.	5.6	3.4	3.6	6.0	6.7	5.9	8.6	6.1	8.9	*
55 to 64 years. . . .	100.0	100.0	100.0	100.0	100.0	100.0	*	*	*	8.5
Single.	4.5	4.5	4.4	7.0	5.1	6.5	*	*	*	*
Married, spouse present	78.4	80.3	84.4	62.8	69.2	80.4	*	*	*	8.6
Separated	8.9	9.1	2.2	23.3	7.7	4.3	*	*	*	*
Widowed	4.1	4.5	8.9	*	5.1	2.2	*	*	*	*
Divorced.	4.1	1.5	*	7.0	12.8	6.5	*	*	*	*
65 years and over . .	100.0	100.0	100.0	100.0	100.0	100.0	*	*	*	5.8
Single.	5.6	6.3	5.8	3.8	11.1	*	*	*	*	*
Married, spouse present	72.0	67.0	84.6	69.2	66.7	77.3	*	*	*	6.3
Separated	4.8	5.4	*	7.7	5.6	9.1	*	*	*	*
Widowed	14.0	17.9	7.7	11.5	5.6	13.6	*	*	*	*
Divorced.	3.6	3.6	1.9	3.8	11.1	*	*	*		*

Note: * indicates base too small to make accurate measure. Some columns fail to add to 100.0 by a significant amount because of small sample sizes and rounding errors.

Source: U.S. Bureau of the Census. "Educational Attainment in the U.S.: March 1979." Current Population Reports (Series P-20, no. 356). Washington, DC: U.S. Government Printing Office, 1980, Table 5.

Average Education (4 Years of High School)

All race-ethnic groups tend to have very high proportions of persons ever married and low proportions separated and divorced, when having four years of high school education.

College Dropouts (1-3 Years of College)

The group that began college but did not complete it for financial, academic, or personal reasons tends to have a high propensity to marry. White males in the group have low divorce and separation rates, but females

Table 10-10D. Marital Status by Years of School Completed, White Females, by Age: 1979

Age and marital status	Total	Elementary school			High school		College			Median school years
		0-4 years	5-7 years	8 years	1-3 years	4 years	1-3 years	4 years	5 or more years	
25 years and over . .	100.0	100.0	100.0	100.0	100.0	100.0	100.0	100.0	100.0	12.5
Single.	7.0	8.4	5.1	5.0	3.7	5.3	7.8	14.1	22.0	12.9
Married, spouse present	67.7	42.5	50.5	53.3	66.3	74.5	69.8	70.6	60.9	12.5
Separated	2.6	5.2	3.6	2.4	3.0	2.6	2.5	1.9	1.8	*
Widowed	15.5	39.6	36.3	34.7	18.9	10.4	10.1	7.8	6.8	10.7
Divorced.	7.2	4.3	4.5	4.6	8.1	7.2	9.8	5.7	8.5	12.6
25 to 34 years. . . .	100.0	100.0	100.0	100.0	100.0	100.0	100.0	100.0	100.0	12.8
Single.	12.7	27.1	12.3	10.0	6.6	8.5	12.1	22.5	29.9	14.5
Married, spouse present	74.2	60.4	71.1	75.2	72.4	78.2	73.9	71.2	61.5	12.8
Separated	3.7	9.7	9.2	5.6	6.2	3.9	2.9	1.8	1.4	*
Widowed	0.5	1.4	1.1	1.5	1.1	0.4	0.6	0.1	0.5	12.5
Divorced.	8.8	1.4	6.3	7.8	13.6	9.0	10.4	4.3	6.7	12.7
35 to 54 years. . . .	100.0	100.0	100.0	100.0	100.0	100.0	100.0	100.0	100.0	12.5
Single.	4.6	13.1	6.3	6.4	2.3	3.3	4.2	6.6	15.1	12.8
Married, spouse present	79.4	62.7	72.0	72.2	80.5	82.5	77.7	80.1	69.3	12.5
Separated	3.1	8.4	6.3	5.4	3.4	2.7	2.7	2.5	2.4	*
Widowed	4.2	9.2	9.2	7.4	4.8	3.9	3.5	2.5	1.4	12.3
Divorced.	8.7	6.6	6.2	8.7	9.0	7.7	11.8	8.3	11.8	12.6
55 to 64 years. . . .	100.0	100.0	100.0	100.0	100.0	100.0	100.0	100.0	100.0	12.3
Single.	4.7	6.8	5.1	4.0	2.0	4.5	4.6	6.6	18.5	12.6
Married, spouse present	69.8	53.4	60.2	68.7	68.7	73.1	68.7	75.7	63.6	12.3
Separated	1.8	8.5	3.7	1.7	1.3	1.5	1.5	1.7	0.9	*
Widowed	17.3	24.6	25.4	19.9	21.6	14.7	16.2	12.7	11.6	12.1
Divorced.	6.4	6.8	5.9	5.6	6.3	6.2	8.9	5.0	5.3	12.4
65 years and over . .	100.0	100.0	100.0	100.0	100.0	100.0	100.0	100.0	100.0	10.6
Single.	6.2	3.1	3.2	4.3	5.0	6.3	9.0	13.2	25.2	12.5
Married, spouse present	38.0	25.2	31.8	37.9	37.6	43.9	39.2	41.0	30.2	11.5
Separated	1.2	1.7	1.2	1.2	1.2	1.0	1.4	1.8	1.4	*
Widowed	51.4	67.2	61.0	54.2	52.5	45.4	47.0	41.5	37.1	9.7
Divorced.	3.2	2.9	2.7	2.4	3.8	3.3	3.4	3.6	6.1	11.7

Note: * indicates base too small to make accurate measure. Some columns fail to add to 100.0 by a significant amount because of small sample sizes and rounding errors.

Source: U.S. Bureau of the Census. "Educational Attainment in the U.S.: March 1979." Current Population Reports (Series P-20, no. 356). Washington, DC: U.S. Government Printing Office, 1980, Table 5.

have higher rates of both. Black males and females in the category have a high propensity to marry, but they also have high rates of dissolution.

College Graduates (4 Years of College)

Graduation from college is linked to delayed but stable marriage. Although the proportion remaining single is somewhat elevated, the proportions separated and divorced are low.

Postgraduate Education (5 Years of More of College)

For women postgraduate education tends to be linked to remaining single, even at ages older than

Table 10-10E. Marital Status by Years of School Completed, Black Females, by Age: 1979

Age and marital status	Total	Elementary school			High school		College			Median school years
		0-4 years	5-7 years	8 years	1-3 years	4 years	1-3 years	4 years	5 or more years	
25 years and over . .	100.0	100.0	100.0	100.0	100.0	100.0	100.0	100.0	100.0	11.9
Single.	14.2	12.1	7.3	8.1	12.9	16.7	19.2	18.2	19.6	12.3
Married, spouse present	41.8	23.3	35.7	38.7	37.3	47.7	45.4	57.0	58.9	12.2
Separated	14.0	10.4	11.4	15.4	20.3	13.5	11.6	5.8	7.6	*
Widowed	18.8	49.4	37.6	30.2	16.7	10.3	7.2	6.2	5.4	8.6
Divorced.	11.1	4.9	8.1	7.6	12.7	11.7	16.6	12.7	8.5	12.2
25 to 34 years. . . .	100.0	100.0	100.0	100.0	100.0	100.0	100.0	100.0	100.0	12.6
Single.	29.8	78.9	33.3	32.7	29.5	27.5	28.6	29.4	43.5	12.5
Married, spouse present	42.0	5.3	31.6	28.8	34.2	44.7	43.1	58.1	41.2	12.7
Separated	15.8	5.3	21.0	28.8	22.3	16.1	12.8	3.1	9.4	*
Widowed	1.3	*	1.8	3.8	1.4	1.2	1.3	1.3	*	*
Divorced.	11.1	5.3	12.3	5.8	12.6	10.6	14.3	8.1	5.9	12.6
35 to 54 years. . . .	100.0	100.0	100.0	100.0	100.0	100.0	100.0	100.0	100.0	12.1
Single.	9.8	24.7	9.6	8.7	9.4	9.8	10.5	5.0	6.5	12.0
Married, spouse present	48.1	25.9	44.2	40.0	40.8	54.8	48.6	61.4	76.1	12.3
Separated	17.4	21.2	20.7	24.3	23.5	13.4	11.8	9.9	6.5	*
Widowed	9.7	12.9	11.5	17.8	10.3	8.4	8.9	1.0	3.3	10.9
Divorced.	14.9	15.3	13.9	9.1	16.1	13.6	20.1	22.8	7.6	12.1
55 to 64 years. . . .	100.0	100.0	100.0	100.0	100.0	100.0	100.0	100.0	100.0	9.2
Single.	4.4	10.9	2.6	4.0	2.3	6.8	*	*	*	*
Married, spouse present	43.7	29.5	41.8	57.0	36.9	46.3	53.3	42.9	69.7	9.3
Separated	10.6	19.4	9.7	7.3	15.8	4.7	4.4	*	6.1	*
Widowed	32.9	38.0	38.8	26.5	36.9	28.9	22.2	50.0	12.1	8.9
Divorced.	8.4	2.3	7.1	5.3	8.1	13.2	20.0	7.1	12.1	11.7
65 years and over . .	100.0	100.0	100.0	100.0	100.0	100.0	100.0	100.0	100.0	8.0
Single.	4.9	4.9	3.3	3.8	3.2	8.8	15.0	*	7.7	*
Married, spouse present	25.1	21.1	25.6	22.6	29.6	24.5	37.5	27.8	30.8	8.3
Separated	6.0	3.6	3.7	5.7	9.0	10.9	5.0	16.7	7.7	*
Widowed	59.5	67.4	64.4	60.4	52.9	51.7	35.0	50.0	38.5	7.3
Divorced.	4.6	3.0	3.0	7.5	5.3	4.1	7.5	5.6	15.4	*

Note: * indicates base too small to make accurate measure. Some columns fail to add to 100.0 by a significant amount because of small sample sizes and rounding errors.

Source: U.S. Bureau of the Census. "Educational Attainment in the U.S.: March 1979." Current Population Reports (Series P-20, no. 356). Washington, DC: U.S. Government Printing Office, 1980, Table 5.

thirty-five. Among those who marry the proportion of separated and divorced is moderately higher than for those with four years of college, but much lower than for those with less than a complete high school education.

Synthesis

Educational attainment is closely linked to age at marriage. Those who withdraw from school early tend to marry early, and those who continue for advanced degrees tend to marry late. Completion of college ap-

Table 10-10F. Marital Status by Years of School Completed, Spanish-Origin Females, by Age: 1979

Age and marital status	Total	Elementary school			High school		College			Median school years
		0-4 years	5-7 years	8 years	1-3 years	4 years	1-3 years	4 years	5 or more years	
25 years and over . .	100.0	100.0	100.0	100.0	100.0	100.0	100.0	100.0	100.0	10.2
Single.	8.8	7.1	8.2	8.6	8.7	8.6	11.8	12.6	12.5	10.8
Married, spouse, present	65.4	55.1	65.2	64.4	66.0	71.8	64.7	65.0	70.8	10.8
Separated	8.3	10.3	10.5	8.6	8.7	6.9	4.6	3.9	4.2	*
Widowed	9.2	21.9	9.4	9.4	7.3	3.8	4.6	9.7	2.1	6.5
Divorced.	8.4	5.7	6.6	8.6	9.2	9.0	14.3	8.7	10.4	12.0
25 to 34 years. . . .	100.0	100.0	100.0	100.0	100.0	100.0	100.0	100.0	100.0	12.1
Single.	13.9	11.3	12.7	18.2	14.8	12.2	17.3	19.6	9.5	12.1
Married, spouse present	67.9	70.1	68.4	65.5	61.7	71.7	61.4	76.1	61.9	12.1
Separated	8.8	15.5	12.0	9.1	9.9	7.3	3.9	2.2	14.3	*
Widowed	1.2	2.1	0.6	1.8	3.1	*	2.4	*	*	*
Divorced.	8.3	1.0	6.3	3.6	11.1	9.0	15.0	2.2	14.3	12.4
35 to 54 years. . . .	100.0	100.0	100.0	100.0	100.0	100.0	100.0	100.0	100.0	10.4
Single.	7.1	9.8	7.5	6.5	5.1	6.2	6.0	7.3	18.2	9.6
Married, spouse present	71.2	64.7	72.8	70.1	70.4	75.1	71.4	58.5	77.3	10.6
Separated	9.3	11.4	11.4	11.2	9.7	7.9	6.0	7.3	*	*
Widowed	4.1	7.6	3.9	2.8	5.6	1.6	4.8	9.8	*	*
Divorced.	8.3	6.5	4.8	9.3	8.7	9.2	11.9	17.1	4.5	12.0
55 to 64 years. . . .	100.0	100.0	100.0	100.0	100.0	100.0	*	*	*	8.2
Single.	3.9	3.6	6.5	2.4	3.2	5.6	*	*	*	*
Married, spouse present	62.8	57.1	64.5	54.8	77.4	66.7	*	*	*	8.3
Separated	6.6	10.7	8.1	7.1	6.5	*	*	*	*	*
Widowed	16.4	19.0	12.9	16.7	6.5	20.4	*	*	*	*
Divorced.	10.5	9.5	8.1	16.7	6.5	7.4	*	*	*	*
65 years and over . .	100.0	100.0	100.0	100.0	*	*	*	*	*	5.7
Single.	3.1	3.1	3.2	6.7	*	*	*	*	*	*
Married, spouse present	34.6	28.5	31.7	53.3	*	*	*	*	*	6.9
Separated	3.5	4.6	4.8	*	*	*	*	*	*	*
Widowed	51.2	59.2	49.2	33.3	*	*	*	*	*	4.7
Divorced.	7.3	5.4	12.7	3.3	*	*	*	*	*	*

Note: * indicates base too small to make accurate measure. Some columns fail to add to 100.0 by a significant amount because of small sample sizes and rounding errors.

Source: U.S. Bureau of the Census. "Educational Attainment in the U.S.: March 1979." Current Population Reports (Series P-20, no. 356). Washington, DC: U.S. Government Printing Office, 1980, Table 5.

pears to be compatible with "normal" conjugal life, both for women and men, but postgraduate education may induce some women to remain single. Marital stability is strongly positively linked to amount of schooling; marital dissolution is less common, and when it does occur it takes the form of divorce with a very high propensity to remarry. Thus the pursuit of higher education by women, as well as by men, is neither antinuptial nor antinatal intrinsically—it involves a delay of both marriage and childbearing. For the oncoming generations, marriage among those with less education has a higher than average risk of dissolution. The risk that a marriage will end in divorce or separation appears to be inversely related to the number of years of school

Table 10-11. Education of Husband, by Education of Wife for Married Couples 14 Years Old and Over, by Age of Husband: March 1979 [noninstitutional population]

Education and age of husband	Total population	Percent distribution of education of wife							
		Elementary			High school		College		
		0 to 4 years	5 to 7 years	8 years	1 to 3 years	4 years	1 to 3 years	4 years	5 years or more
Husbands, 14 years old and over									
Total	100.0	1.8	4.2	6.4	14.7	45.6	14.8	8.5	4.1
Elementary									
0 to 4 years	100.0	32.7	26.5	16.4	12.7	8.7	2.1	0.6	0.1
5 to 7 years	100.0	6.8	27.6	17.0	23.9	20.4	3.0	1.0	0.3
8 years	100.0	2.3	8.6	27.4	24.1	31.1	4.4	1.5	0.6
High school									
1 to 3 years	100.0	0.8	4.2	8.6	35.7	43.3	5.5	1.2	0.6
4 years	100.0	0.3	1.4	3.5	13.8	65.5	11.2	3.2	1.0
College									
1 to 3 years	100.0	0.1	0.8	1.6	6.9	49.2	29.2	8.7	3.5
4 years	100.0	0.1	0.3	0.7	2.1	34.5	27.0	28.1	7.1
5 years or more	100.0	*	0.1	0.4	1.2	19.4	24.3	29.3	25.3
Husbands, 25 to 44 years old									
Total	100.0	0.9	2.2	2.2	12.2	47.1	18.4	11.6	5.5
Elementary									
0 to 4 years	100.0	43.9	21.9	6.8	10.8	10.2	5.2	1.1	*
5 to 7 years	100.0	7.7	29.5	9.2	26.6	22.6	3.0	0.9	0.6
8 years	100.0	2.6	10.0	17.0	30.2	36.4	2.0	1.1	0.7
High school									
1 to 3 years	100.0	0.9	3.6	5.2	37.5	45.3	6.0	1.2	0.3
4 years	100.0	0.2	1.1	1.8	13.7	66.5	12.5	3.3	0.8
College									
1 to 3 years	100.0	*	0.5	0.4	6.0	49.1	31.0	9.5	3.4
4 years	100.0	0.1	0.1	0.1	1.6	30.7	28.0	30.8	8.6
5 years or more	100.0	*	*	0.1	0.8	15.5	24.0	32.7	27.0
Husbands, 45 to 64 years old									
Total	100.0	1.7	4.4	7.1	16.3	47.4	12.8	6.6	3.7
Elementary									
0 to 4 years	100.0	30.5	25.9	16.9	16.1	8.7	1.3	0.4	0.2
5 to 7 years	100.0	4.3	24.8	13.7	29.3	24.2	3.0	0.6	0.1
8 years	100.0	2.0	7.0	23.1	25.8	35.2	5.1	1.3	0.6
High school									
1 to 3 years	100.0	0.6	3.9	8.2	34.3	45.4	5.8	1.0	0.8
4 years	100.0	0.4	1.5	4.7	13.8	65.8	9.6	3.1	1.2
College									
1 to 3 years	100.0	0.2	1.1	3.0	7.4	51.2	25.3	7.9	4.1
4 years	100.0	0.1	0.6	1.0	2.5	40.4	27.1	22.6	5.8
5 years or more	100.0	0.2	0.2	0.6	2.0	24.8	24.7	24.1	23.4
Husbands, 65 years old and over									
Total	100.0	5.0	10.9	18.7	16.3	32.8	8.8	5.2	2.3
Elementary									
0 to 4 years	100.0	31.2	28.3	19.4	10.5	7.9	1.8	0.6	0.2
5 to 7 years	100.0	8.7	29.8	25.0	16.8	14.6	3.2	1.5	0.3
8 years	100.0	2.7	10.0	37.2	18.7	23.9	4.9	2.0	0.6
High school									
1 to 3 years	100.0	1.4	7.3	17.4	32.8	33.4	4.5	2.2	1.0
4 years	100.0	0.5	3.3	9.7	11.6	57.2	11.3	4.5	1.9
College									
1 to 3 years	100.0	0.7	2.7	6.0	11.5	45.0	21.5	7.6	4.9
4 years	100.0	0.7	0.3	4.0	5.2	40.2	19.9	25.1	4.6
5 years or more	100.0	*	0.6	1.9	2.2	25.0	23.9	24.7	21.8

Note: * indicates zero or rounds to zero.

Source: U.S. Bureau of the Census. "Educational Attainment in the U.S.: March 1979." Current Population Reports (Series P-20, no. 356, Table 4). Washington, DC: U.S. Government Printing Office, 1980.

Table 10-12. General Mobility Rates, by Age, Sex and Years of School Completed: 1975-1980

Age and educational attainment	Male					Female				
	Non-mobile	Local mobility	Migration			Non-mobile	Local mobility	Migration		
			Total	Noncon-tiguous states	Abroad			Total	Noncon-tiguous states	Abroad
18 and over										
Total. . . .	52.3	25.2	20.3	6.7	2.2	54.5	25.1	18.8	6.0	1.6
Elementary										
0-8 years. .	67.5	19.9	10.1	2.6	2.5	68.4	19.4	9.6	2.6	2.5
High school										
1-3 years. .	57.4	25.9	15.5	4.4	1.3	56.9	27.0	15.1	4.8	1.0
4 years. . .	52.3	27.3	18.4	5.9	1.9	54.3	26.9	17.5	5.4	1.3
College										
1-3 years. .	45.5	26.6	25.5	8.3	2.4	48.0	25.3	25.2	8.5	1.5
4 years. . .	42.2	23.7	31.7	10.6	2.4	43.5	23.8	30.6	10.2	2.1
5+ years . .	41.6	23.6	31.7	13.0	3.1	45.5	21.2	30.3	11.4	3.0
18-24 years										
Total. . . .	42.5	29.8	24.0	7.3	3.6	34.8	36.4	26.5	8.0	2.3
Elementary										
0-8 years. .	31.8	35.7	17.1	2.4	15.4	21.2	42.9	20.6	5.3	15.3
High school										
1-3 years. .	44.8	33.1	19.6	5.1	2.6	32.7	42.9	22.8	8.0	1.7
4 years. . .	41.4	32.6	23.0	7.6	3.0	33.3	41.3	23.5	7.1	1.8
College										
1-3 years. .	47.7	22.8	25.9	7.8	3.7	43.6	25.7	28.9	8.1	1.8
4 years. . .	31.0	23.7	43.1	13.6	2.1	27.2	22.3	49.3	13.2	1.3
5+ years . .	23.2	23.7	45.8	16.9	7.3	30.1	15.7	51.2	21.7	3.0
25-29 years										
Total. . . .	19.6	40.2	36.1	12.5	4.1	18.9	42.6	35.4	11.2	3.1
Elementary										
0-8 years. .	24.2	44.7	18.6	5.9	12.5	22.4	39.0	23.7	6.0	14.6
High school										
1-3 years. .	23.9	44.1	29.3	9.8	2.7	21.2	47.3	29.3	9.2	2.3
4 years. . .	23.3	45.3	27.7	10.1	3.8	22.5	45.5	30.3	9.1	1.8
College										
1-3 years. .	17.8	40.8	37.5	12.5	3.9	17.2	42.7	37.4	12.4	2.7
4 years. . .	14.0	28.2	53.9	17.4	3.8	11.9	37.8	46.6	14.0	3.7
5+ years . .	10.9	30.7	54.4	20.6	4.0	10.0	28.3	56.8	21.4	5.2
30-34 years										
Total. . . .	29.2	37.7	30.2	10.2	2.9	35.8	34.5	27.3	8.9	2.3
Elementary										
0-8 years. .	34.0	38.9	17.9	4.7	9.1	41.3	33.3	17.6	4.7	7.8
High school										
1-3 years. .	33.2	41.1	24.5	8.6	1.2	38.2	40.9	18.8	5.8	2.1
4 years. . .	35.8	37.9	24.0	7.5	2.3	39.9	35.2	23.2	6.7	1.7
College										
1-3 years. .	29.0	39.1	29.8	9.2	2.2	32.2	34.1	31.8	11.6	1.9
4 years. . .	23.1	35.9	38.7	13.2	2.3	30.0	30.9	36.7	12.7	2.4
5+ years . .	17.5	34.7	42.9	17.5	4.9	25.0	29.9	41.4	15.3	3.8
35-44 years										
Total. . . .	49.5	27.3	20.9	6.8	2.2	56.5	24.6	16.9	5.9	1.9
Elementary										
0-8 years. .	52.9	28.2	15.4	3.0	3.4	53.4	28.9	13.4	3.4	4.2
High school										
1-3 years. .	54.6	29.3	15.0	3.5	1.1	58.7	26.7	13.6	4.3	1.0
4 years. . .	53.3	27.1	17.8	5.1	1.7	60.1	23.3	14.8	4.6	1.8
College										
1-3 years. .	46.0	27.6	24.6	7.7	1.8	52.9	23.6	21.9	8.7	1.7
4 years. . .	46.9	25.7	24.2	8.4	3.2	49.5	24.8	23.9	10.6	1.8
5+ years . .	38.7	26.7	31.1	14.8	3.5	49.8	26.3	20.8	8.0	3.0

Table 10-12. General Mobility Rates, by Age, Sex, and Years of School Completed: 1975-1980—continued

Age and educational attainment	Male					Female				
	Non-mobile	Local mobility	Migration			Non-mobile	Local mobility	Migration		
			Total	Noncon-tiguous states	Abroad			Total	Noncon-tiguous states	Abroad
45-64 years										
Total. . . .	71.1	16.0	12.1	3.7	0.8	73.1	15.0	11.1	3.5	0.8
Elementary										
0-8 years. .	70.5	19.3	9.1	2.7	1.1	70.4	19.1	9.0	2.4	1.5
High school										
1-3 years. .	72.6	16.9	10.2	2.7	0.4	72.5	16.8	10.3	2.9	0.5
4 years. . .	74.1	15.0	10.5	2.9	0.5	75.0	13.7	10.7	3.4	0.5
College										
1-3 years. .	68.4	15.1	15.7	5.9	0.8	70.4	13.5	15.7	5.7	0.5
4 years. . .	66.7	13.7	18.0	5.4	1.7	74.7	11.7	11.9	4.2	1.6
5+ years . .	66.8	14.1	17.8	6.5	1.3	71.9	11.6	14.4	5.1	2.0
65 and over										
Total. . . .	79.6	11.0	9.0	3.3	0.4	78.2	12.6	8.8	2.9	0.4
Elementary										
0-8 years. .	80.5	11.9	7.2	2.0	0.4	79.2	13.4	6.8	1.9	0.5
High school										
1-3 years. .	79.7	11.8	8.2	3.0	0.2	77.8	13.2	8.9	2.5	*
4 years. . .	79.0	10.5	10.0	4.2	0.6	78.4	12.3	9.0	3.4	0.3
College										
1-3 years. .	77.5	7.8	14.3	5.6	0.4	74.7	12.6	12.3	4.9	0.3
4 years. . .	78.7	10.2	10.9	6.6	0.4	76.2	8.2	14.8	5.7	0.7
5+ years . .	77.9	8.1	13.5	4.7	0.2	77.7	6.8	15.5	5.9	*

Note: * indicates less than 0.1.

Source: U.S. Bureau of the Census. "Geographical Mobility: March 1975 to March 1980." Current Population Reports (Series P-20, no. 368). Washington, DC: U.S. Government Printing Office, 1984, Table 24.

completed, up to completion of college. For the black population (for which marital dissolution is high), this correlation is less consistent. For the Spanish-origin population the correlation is practically zero, because the socioeconomic forces that affect the white and black populations apply with less force.

Educational Homogamy in Marriage

Married couples tend to be of the same educational level. Persons who failed to complete elementary school tend to marry persons who also did not complete elementary school; persons who graduated from college tend to marry college graduates. Similar tendencies to marry within one's "educational class" are found for high school dropouts, high school graduates, and college dropouts. Table 10-11 presents data from the Current Population Survey of 1979 that illustrates this tendency. The correlation is not perfect but is very high. Where there are disparities in the educational level of spouses the spouse tends to be only one category above or below the educational level of his or her partner. Extreme disparities in educational levels of couples are comparatively rare. Because older generations of women have less education, on the average, than men there is a tendency for the wife to be less educated than her husband. In the younger generations, where persons with elementary school education only are a small proportion of the total and where the educational attainment of the sexes is more equal, the educational class boundaries seem to be most rigid between graduation or nongraduation from high school. Table 10-11, which measures the homogamy of wife in comparison with the educational level of the husband, shows that men with less than a complete high school education tend to marry women who did not finish high school. Disproportionately few men sho attended college marry women who did not graduate from high school. Because of the comparative scarcity of women with complete college education, men with advanced college degrees tend to marry women who at least attended college.

To the extent that education of spouse represents

Table 10-13. General Mobility Rates, by Years of School Completed, Age and Sex: 1981-1982

Age and educational attainment	Male					Female				
	Non-mobile	Local mobility	Migration			Non-mobile	Local mobility	Migration		
			Total	Noncontiguous states	Abroad			Total	Noncontiguous states	Abroad
18 and over										
Total. . . .	82.2	10.3	6.8	2.3	0.6	83.7	9.9	6.0	2.0	0.4
Elementary										
0-8 years. .	88.7	7.3	3.3	0.9	0.8	89.4	7.2	2.7	0.8	0.7
High school										
1-3 years. .	81.4	12.2	6.1	1.8	0.3	81.9	12.3	5.7	1.6	0.2
4 years. . .	81.6	11.1	6.6	2.3	0.7	83.8	9.8	6.1	2.0	0.3
College										
1-3 years. .	79.9	11.5	8.0	2.5	0.6	81.4	11.1	7.2	2.5	0.3
4 years. . .	80.2	9.6	9.5	3.6	0.7	81.2	9.2	9.0	3.1	0.7
5+ years . .	83.0	7.7	8.6	4.1	0.8	83.9	8.3	7.1	2.7	0.8
18-24 years										
Total. . . .	69.5	17.4	11.9	4.1	1.2	65.7	21.1	12.6	4.1	0.7
Elementary										
0-8 years. .	62.4	21.3	11.2	3.7	5.1	65.3	21.3	8.7	2.3	4.9
High school										
1-3 years. .	70.0	19.1	10.5	3.2	0.3	63.0	24.7	11.7	3.4	0.6
4 years. . .	68.9	18.5	11.2	4.0	1.4	65.4	21.6	12.5	4.2	0.5
College										
1-3 years. .	74.6	14.0	10.7	3.5	0.6	71.5	18.0	10.3	3.4	0.2
4 years. . .	57.3	15.3	25.9	9.4	1.6	53.9	18.3	26.7	9.8	1.1
5+ years . .	62.2	14.0	22.0	10.4	1.2	55.4	26.9	16.2	3.8	1.5
25-29 years										
Total. . . .	67.6	19.1	12.1	4.1	1.2	70.4	17.7	11.1	3.7	0.7
Elementary										
0-8 years. .	66.5	20.6	7.7	2.1	5.2	66.3	23.1	8.9	2.0	2.0
High school										
1-3 years. .	59.2	28.5	11.8	3.1	0.5	64.6	22.8	12.4	3.8	0.3
4 years. . .	72.5	17.4	9.2	2.9	0.8	72.6	16.9	9.9	3.4	0.6
College										
1-3 years. .	66.2	19.4	13.0	4.0	1.4	70.4	17.7	11.4	3.7	0.5
4 years. . .	64.0	18.3	16.8	6.3	1.0	69.0	16.4	13.5	4.2	1.1
5+ years . .	63.1	16.4	18.7	8.3	1.7	70.4	15.6	13.1	5.3	1.1

Source: U.S. Bureau of the Census. "Geographical Mobility: March 1981 to March 1982." Current Population Reports (Series P-20, no. 384). Washington, DC: U.S. Government Printing Office, 1984 (Table 24)

social status, "upwardly mobile" men and women marry persons who have more education, and "downwardly mobile" persons marry spouses with less education. Such "nuptial mobility" is an important part of lifetime social mobility, especially for women. To the extent that there is "educational prejudice" in class intermarriage, diplomas and degrees appear to be important class-boundary delimiters.

Residential Mobility and Educational Attainment

The propensity to be residentially mobile is positively linked to educational attainment: the better educated the population, the more prone it is to be mobile. However, this is a net balance of two corollaries: (1) The higher mobility of the more educated is oriented strong-

Table 10-14. Metropolitan Mobility, by Years of School Completed, and Age: 1975-1980

Age and educational attainment	Metropolitan areas					Nonmetropolitan areas			
	Non-mobile	Mobile within SMSA	Mobile within SMSAs	Nonmetro areas		Non-mobile	Mobile within nonmetro area	Metro areas	
				Inmi-gration	Outmi-gration			Inmi-gration	Outmi-gration
18 years and over									
Total.	52.6	29.8	10.8	4.4	5.2	55.4	32.5	11.2	9.6
Elementary: 0-8 years. .	65.7	23.6	4.8	2.0	3.5	71.3	23.3	5.0	2.8
High school									
1-3 years.	57.1	30.9	7.3	3.3	4.5	57.2	33.7	8.8	6.4
4 years.	53.5	31.4	9.1	4.2	5.2	53.3	34.7	10.9	8.9
College									
1-3 years.	46.9	30.9	14.2	5.8	5.9	46.5	35.8	16.3	16.1
4 years.	42.9	29.3	18.5	6.8	6.4	42.7	37.1	18.8	19.9
5 years and over . . .	42.1	28.9	19.8	5.8	6.4	45.9	31.2	21.1	18.9
18-24 years									
Total.	39.2	37.1	12.9	7.2	5.4	37.2	48.9	12.5	16.8
Elementary: 0-8 years. .	20.9	43.8	8.0	3.9	4.4	36.8	53.9	7.4	6.4
High school									
1-3 years.	39.4	42.3	10.7	4.9	5.6	38.8	49.3	11.0	9.6
4 years.	38.6	41.1	10.8	6.7	5.7	34.0	52.4	12.3	14.3
College									
1-3 years.	45.8	28.3	14.5	8.3	4.6	45.1	39.6	13.8	25.1
4 years.	29.2	28.5	26.9	13.9	6.5	27.7	48.7	21.6	45.9
5 years and over . . .	23.6	26.0	31.3	13.5	4.2	41.8	32.7	21.8	70.9
25-29 years									
Total.	18.3	48.1	20.2	9.2	7.6	21.6	57.1	19.3	23.3
Elementary: 0-8 years. .	18.8	48.4	10.4	3.8	4.6	32.9	54.3	9.7	8.1
High school									
1-3 years.	21.0	52.6	14.3	8.6	6.5	25.4	61.9	12.4	16.4
4 years.	21.8	51.9	15.4	8.0	6.9	25.3	57.2	15.3	17.8
College									
1-3 years.	17.4	49.4	21.0	8.8	8.5	18.1	55.0	24.1	25.0
4 years.	13.3	40.2	29.4	12.7	9.2	11.9	58.2	28.6	39.5
5 years and over . . .	10.8	36.9	34.2	13.0	8.7	8.5	52.8	36.5	54.6
30-34 years									
Total.	30.7	44.0	16.6	5.5	7.2	37.0	44.6	17.0	13.2
Elementary: 0-8 years. .	32.9	41.3	9.4	3.4	5.7	44.9	45.2	8.4	5.1
High school									
1-3 years.	34.7	48.7	8.4	5.9	7.5	38.6	47.0	13.7	10.8
4 years.	36.6	43.8	12.1	5.0	6.9	41.3	43.8	14.1	10.2
College									
1-3 years.	29.7	44.8	18.3	5.2	6.8	32.8	44.8	20.1	15.3
4 years.	24.8	42.9	23.0	6.8	6.9	29.9	47.4	20.7	20.5
5 years and over . . .	18.6	42.6	26.9	6.5	9.2	25.9	40.4	31.8	22.6
35-44 years									
Total.	52.7	31.4	9.9	3.6	5.9	53.9	32.1	12.5	7.7
Elementary: 0-8 years. .	50.6	34.0	5.8	3.5	5.3	56.6	35.1	7.5	5.0
High school									
1-3 years.	56.6	33.8	5.7	2.3	4.8	57.5	33.8	8.7	4.2
4 years.	56.9	30.2	7.9	3.3	5.8	57.8	29.4	11.0	6.3
College									
1-3 years.	50.4	31.0	12.0	4.7	6.6	46.6	33.9	18.2	12.9
4 years.	48.8	30.1	13.9	4.2	6.8	46.4	34.1	18.3	11.4
5 years and over . . .	42.5	32.8	17.2	4.1	6.3	42.0	35.5	19.3	12.6

Table 10-14. Metropolitan Mobility, by Years of School Completed, and Age: 1975-1980—continued

Age and educational attainment	Metropolitan areas					Nonmetropolitan areas			
	Non-mobile	Mobile within SMSA	Mobile within SMSAs	Nonmetro areas		Non-mobile	Mobile within nonmetro area	Metro areas	
				Inmi-gration	Outmi-gration			Inmi-gration	Outmi-gration
45-64 years									
Total.	72.4	18.2	6.5	1.8	3.8	71.6	20.1	8.0	3.9
Elementary: 0-8 years. .	68.5	23.5	4.7	1.3	3.6	73.2	21.4	5.1	1.8
High school									
1-3 years.	72.8	20.0	4.9	1.7	3.0	72.0	21.6	6.3	3.6
4 years.	75.3	16.5	5.9	1.6	3.8	73.2	18.5	8.1	3.4
College									
1-3 years.	71.0	16.4	9.3	2.6	4.9	65.1	21.2	13.4	7.1
4 years.	70.8	16.2	8.8	2.2	4.0	67.5	19.3	12.6	7.1
5 years and over . . .	68.7	16.1	10.4	2.9	3.9	68.0	19.6	12.2	8.9
65 years and over									
Total.	78.4	14.4	5.0	1.7	3.2	79.4	14.9	5.6	3.0
Elementary: 0-8 years. .	79.1	15.1	3.4	1.7	2.5	80.8	15.5	3.6	2.3
High school									
1-3 years.	78.1	16.0	4.5	1.2	3.3	79.5	14.1	6.5	2.4
4 years.	78.0	14.4	5.2	2.0	2.8	79.9	13.5	6.2	4.4
College									
1-3 years.	76.9	11.7	8.6	2.4	4.9	74.0	17.2	8.9	4.4
4 years.	79.3	9.7	9.1	1.4	5.0	73.1	15.5	10.7	3.0
5 years.	78.6	11.3	8.7	1.2	5.5	75.9	10.8	13.4	3.0

Source: U.S. Bureau of the Census. "Geographical Mobility: March, 1975 to March, 1980." *Current Population Reports* (Series P-20, no. 368). Washington, DC: U.S. Government Printing Office, 1984, Table 23.

ly toward higher migration, to move across county boundaries or for great distances (the tendency to move between noncontinguous states). (2) The less educated population tends to have high local mobility, moving within the same county, but not necessarily higher than for the better educated, who are also locally mobile. These findings are verified for five-year mobility (1975-80) and for one-year mobility (1981-82) in Tables 10-12 and 10-13, respectively. These generalizations apply to each age group, but the educational differentials are greatest for ages 18-35. At older ages, lower mobility rates make the differentials smaller. These results imply that persons with more education range farther afield in making their major life-cycle adjustments, such as leaving home, attending school, marrying, and finding employment. Those with less education are more prone to make such adjustments and residential changes within the local community. Nevertheless, migration rates are far from zero for the younger age groups, regardless of educational attainment.

When age and educational attainment are both controlled, mobility differences between males and females remain comparatively small. Educated young women are slightly less inclined to migrate (including long distances) than men, and they are a little more inclined to be nonmobile. These sex differentials in mobility are more noticeable among college graduates and postgraduates than among the lower educational ranges.

Metropolitan Mobility

The pattern described above differs somewhat for mobility involving metropolitan and nonmetropolitan areas (see Table 10-14). Within nonmetropolitan areas persons with less than a complete college education tend to be less mobile than persons in metropolitan areas. Persons who leave nonmetropolitan areas in order to move to metropolitan areas tend to be more educated. There is a similar differential for outmigration from metropolitan to nonmetropolitan areas, but it is less selective with respect to education. Local mobility within SMSAs is strongly selective of those with more education. Mobility between nonmetropolitan places has little educational selectivity. Thus the metropolitan areas pull the highly educated, while sending back to

Table 10-15. Central City Mobility, by Years of School Completed, and Age: 1975-1980

Age and educational attainment	Central cities				Metropolitan rings			
	Non-mobile	Within central cities	Out to metro ring	In from metro ring	Non-mobile	Within central cities	Out to metro ring	In from metro ring
18 years and over								
Total.	50.9	33.5	17.5	8.3	53.8	27.5	12.5	5.9
Elementary school: 0-8 years. . .	64.4	26.1	8.5	3.3	67.0	18.4	8.9	3.5
High school								
1-3 years.	55.3	34.1	12.0	6.0	58.6	25.8	10.7	5.4
4 years.	51.8	33.2	18.1	8.3	54.6	28.5	11.4	5.2
College								
1-3 years.	43.7	35.3	21.8	11.7	49.0	29.4	14.4	7.7
4 years.	38.8	38.5	27.0	11.8	45.3	30.1	16.2	7.1
5 years and over	37.4	39.7	26.4	12.5	45.1	29.7	16.7	7.9
18-24 years								
Total.	34.1	40.7	17.7	12.3	43.0	34.5	13.2	9.2
Elementary school: 0-8 years. . .	17.7	45.5	10.8	6.1	25.3	37.0	15.1	8.6
High school								
1-3 years.	36.8	47.8	15.3	7.9	41.7	36.2	14.3	7.4
4 years.	34.7	41.5	19.1	12.0	41.1	38.3	12.4	7.8
College								
1-3 years.	38.2	32.1	17.0	15.7	51.1	27.3	12.0	11.1
4 years.	21.6	43.0	23.1	18.4	35.2	40.9	18.3	14.5
5 years and over	16.6	43.4	24.1	17.2	30.8	30.1	24.5	17.5
25-29 years								
Total.	17.7	53.9	30.8	13.8	18.7	44.9	23.8	10.7
Elementary school: 0-8 years. . .	21.7	47.8	19.7	8.5	15.4	38.7	22.9	9.9
High school								
1-3 years.	21.9	56.4	23.4	10.1	20.2	44.0	23.2	10.0
4 years.	21.2	53.0	30.3	14.0	22.1	47.1	20.6	9.5
College								
1-3 years.	17.4	54.0	33.2	13.8	17.3	46.7	25.6	10.7
4 years.	11.5	54.4	36.1	15.4	14.7	41.4	27.9	11.9
5 years and over	8.4	57.0	32.9	17.9	13.1	39.6	28.4	15.4
30-34 years								
Total.	30.2	49.7	31.2	11.2	30.9	39.7	20.8	7.5
Elementary school: 0-8 years. . .	35.2	39.5	14.3	8.3	29.7	35.1	19.4	11.3
High school								
1-3 years.	33.5	51.5	15.4	7.9	36.0	38.5	16.2	8.3
4 years.	36.4	47.3	30.4	9.0	36.7	37.4	18.2	5.4
College								
1-3 years.	30.1	49.4	34.5	13.3	29.4	41.9	21.4	8.2
4 years.	23.2	54.7	41.9	12.6	25.7	41.5	23.6	7.1
5 years and over	16.7	54.1	37.7	16.2	20.0	41.7	27.5	11.8
35-44 years								
Total.	50.5	34.9	20.7	8.1	54.0	28.3	11.9	4.7
Elementary school: 0-8 years. . .	48.3	38.1	16.5	3.7	52.9	23.1	15.2	3.4
High school								
1-3 years.	55.4	33.2	12.5	8.2	57.6	27.5	10.4	6.8
4 years.	55.3	32.4	19.6	6.9	57.7	27.1	10.3	3.6
College								
1-3 years.	46.8	35.5	23.3	11.0	52.4	28.4	12.7	5.9
4 years.	45.3	35.0	26.9	10.4	50.4	30.6	12.7	4.9
5 years and over	38.5	43.1	31.0	10.6	44.5	33.3	15.0	5.1

Table 10-15. Central City Mobility, by Years of School Completed, and Age: 1975-1980—continued

Age and educational attainment	Central cities				Metropolitan rings			
	Non-mobile	Within central cities	Out to metro ring	In from metro ring	Non-mobile	Within central cities	Out to metro ring	In from metro ring
45-64 years								
Total	70.5	21.8	9.7	4.7	73.7	16.8	6.6	3.2
Elementary school: 0-8 years	66.2	27.6	6.5	3.2	70.9	18.6	6.9	3.4
High school								
1-3 years	69.8	23.5	7.8	4.2	75.2	16.3	6.3	3.4
4 years	74.0	18.9	10.0	4.7	76.1	15.7	6.0	2.8
College								
1-3 years	69.9	21.4	13.4	5.5	71.7	17.0	8.0	3.3
4 years	70.8	17.6	14.7	7.1	70.8	17.7	7.5	3.6
5 years and over	66.0	20.9	12.3	6.9	70.1	19.1	6.6	3.7
65 years and over								
Total	79.0	15.9	7.7	3.2	77.9	12.6	7.0	2.9
Elementary school: 0-8 years	79.8	16.3	6.4	2.0	78.3	12.4	6.4	2.0
High school								
1-3 years	80.4	16.5	7.3	1.9	75.9	15.3	7.1	1.9
4 years	76.9	16.6	8.6	4.0	78.9	11.6	7.2	3.3
College								
1-3 years	78.1	13.9	9.1	5.5	75.9	13.3	7.6	4.6
4 years	78.5	15.2	9.0	5.4	79.9	11.7	6.0	3.6
5 years and over	79.2	9.2	14.2	10.4	78.2	9.8	10.5	7.7

Source: U.S. Bureau of the Census. "Geographical Mobility: March, 1975 to March, 1980." Current Population Reports (Series P-20, no 368). Washington, DC: U.S. Government Printing Office, 1984.

nonmetropolitan areas a token flow of highly educated people. There is much circulation of the better educated between metropolitan areas, and much internal circulation of all educational levels (especially of those with less education) within SMSAs and between nonmetropolitan places. Persons with 1-3 years of high school seem to be particularly locally mobile in comparison with other educational groups of the same age.

Central City Mobility

Within metropolitan areas residential mobility is high in both central cities and metropolitan suburban rings; it tends to be slightly higher in the central cities than in the rings. Central city mobility exhibits the following tendencies (see Table 10-15):

1. *Local circulation*—There is a greater tendency to move from one house to another within the central city than from one house to another within the ring.

2. *Suburbanization*—Within a five-year period, an estimated 17.5 percent of the central city population moves to the suburban metropolitan rings. This represents an increase of 12.5 percent for the ring population.

3. *"Regentrification" of the central city*—Inmovement from suburban rings is not a small flow. From 1975 to 1980, an estimated 5.9 percent of the ring population moved into central cities, representing a gain of 8.3 percent for central cities.

In all of these population flows, the better educated population is involved much more strongly in the suburbanward flow and the regentrification flow than the less educated population. Persons with less education are more likely to be locally mobile, both within central cities and suburban rings. However, persons with college education also have higher than average rates of local mobility, both within central cities and suburban rings. The least mobile segment of the population, both in central cities and suburban rings, are those with only a grammar school education or less.

Conclusion

This brief introduction to the subject of educational enrollment and educational attainment demonstrates that large and meaningful differences are present among the various population groups. In later chapters introduction of the educational variable will show that it is an important differentiator with respect to family status, income, occupation, and other population factors. Even though these data cannot reflect the quality of the education now available or indicate how well the various members of the population have mastered the materials presented to them, they are an excellent rough measure of the rising level of educational competence among the general population and especially among those subpopulations having low educational attainment.

Bibliography

Alexander, K.L., and Eckland, B.K. "Basic Attainment Processes: A Replication and Extension." *Sociology of Education* 48 (1975):457-95.

———. "Sex Differences in the Educational Attainment Process." *American Sociological Review* 39 (1974):668-82.

Alexander, K.L., and Reilly, T.W. "Estimating the Effects of Marriage Timing on Educational Attainment: Some Procedural Issues and Substantive Clarifications." *American Journal of Sociology* 87 (1981): 143-56.

Alwin, D.F. "College Effects on Educational and Occupational Attainments." *American Sociological Review* 39 (1974):210-23.

Andrisani, Paul, and Kohen, Andrew I. *Career Thresholds.* Volume 5 in *A Longitudinal Study of the Educational and Labor Market Experience of Male Youth.* Columbus, OH: Center for Human Resource Research, Ohio State University, 1975.

Boudon, Raymond. *Education, Opportunity, and Social Inequality: Changing Prospects in Western Society.* New York: Wiley, 1974.

Carlson, E. "Family Background, School and Early Marriage." *Journal of Marriage and the Family* 41 (1979):341-53.

Davis, Nancy J., and Bumpass, Larry L. "The Continuation of Education after Marriage Among Women in the United States: 1970." *Demography* 13 (1976): 161-74.

Dresch, Stephen P. "Demography, Technology, and Higher Education: Toward a Formal Model of Education Adaptation." *Journal of Political Economy* 83 (1975):535-69.

Duncan, O.D. "Ability and Achievement." *Social Biology* 29 (1982):208-20.

Endo, R. "Asian Americans and Higher Education." *Phylon* 41 (1980):367-78.

Featherman, D.L., and Hauser, R.M. "Changes in the Socioeconomic Stratification of the Races, 1962-73." *American Journal of Sociology* 82 (1976): 621-51.

———. *Opportunity and Change.* New York: Academic Press, 1978.

———. "Sexual Inequalities and Socioeconomic Achievement in the U.S., 1962-1973." *American Sociological Review* 41 (1976):462-83.

Felson, Marcus, and Land, Kenneth C. "Social, Demographic and Economic Interrelationships with Educational Trends in the United States, 1947-1974." In *Research in Population Economics: An Annual Compilation of Research* (Volume 1). Julian L. Simon (ed.). Greenwich, CN: Jai Press, 1978.

Gottfredson, D.C. "Black-White Differences in the Educational Attainment Process: What Have We Learned?" *American Sociological Review* 46 (1981): 542-57.

Griffin, L.J., and Alexander, K.L. "Schooling and Socioeconomic Attainments: High School and College Influences." *American Journal of Sociology* 84 (1978):319-47.

Grove, D.J. "Educational Attainment and Socioeconomic Mobility Within Ethnic Groups." *Ethnic and Racial Studies* 4 (1981):466-75.

Hauser, Robert M., and Featherman, David L. "Socioeconomic Achievements of U.S. Men, 1962 to 1972." *Science* 185 (1974):325-31.

Hogan, D.P. *Transitions and Social Change: The Early Lives of American Men.* New York: Academic Press, 1981.

Hogan, D.P., and Pazul, M. "Occupational and Earnings Returns to Education Among Black Men in the North." *American Journal of Sociology* 87 (1982): 905-20.

Hout, M., and Morgan, W.R. "Race and Sex Variations in the Causes of the Expected Attainments of High School Seniors." *American Journal of Sociology* 81 (1975):364-94.

Jencks, C.; Crouse, J.; and Mueser, P. "The Wisconsin Model of Status Attainment: A National Replication with Improved Measures of Ability and Aspiration." *Sociology of Education* 56 (1983):3-19.

Jennings, Jerry T. "Social and Economic Characteristics of Americans During Mid-Life." *Current Population Reports* (Series P-23, no. 111). Washington, DC: U.S. Government Printing Office, 1981.

Jud, G.D., and Walker, J.L. "Racial Differences in the Returns to Schooling and Experience Among Prime-

Age Males: 1967-1975." *Journal of Human Resources* 17 (1982):622-32.

Juster, F. Thomas (ed.). *Education, Income, and Human Behavior: A Report Prepared for the Carnegie Commission on Higher Education and the National Bureau of Economic Research.* New York: McGraw-Hill, 1975.

Kerckhoff, A.C., and Campbell, R.T. "Black-White Differences in the Educational Attainment Process." *Sociology of Education* 50 (1977):15-27.

Lehr, D.K., and Newton, J.M. "Time Series and Cross-Sectional Investigations of the Demand for Higher Education." *Economic Inquiry* 16 (1978):411-22.

Levine, E.M. "The Declining Educational Achievement of Middle-Class Students, the Deterioration of Educational and Social Standards, and Parents' Negligence." *Sociological Spectrum* 1 (1980):17-34.

Long, L.H. "Does Migration Interfere with Children's Progress in School?" *Sociology of Education* 48 (1975):369-81.

Mare, Robert D. "Change and Stability in Educational Stratification." *American Sociological Review* 46 (1981):72-87.

———. "Trends in Schooling: Demography, Performance, and Organization." *Annals of the American Academy of Political and Social Science,* Volume 453, 1981.

Mare, Robert D., and Winship, C. "The Paradox of Lessening Racial Inequality and Joblessness Among Black Youth: Enrollment, Enlistment and Employment, 1964-1981." *American Sociological Review* 49 (1984):39-55.

Marini, M.M. "Transition to Adulthood: Sex Differences in Educational Attainment and Age at Marriage." *American Sociological Review* 43 (1978):483-507.

Moore, Kristin A., and Waite, Linda J. "Early Childbearing and Educational Attainment." *Family Planning Perspectives* 9 (1977):220-25.

Mueller, B.J. "Rural Family Life Style and Sons' School Achievement." *Rural Sociology* 39 (1972):363-72.

Mueller, C.W. "Evidence on the Relationship Between Religion and Educational Attainment." *Sociology of Education* 53 (1980):140-52.

Porter, J.N. "Race, Socialization and Mobility in Educational and Early Occupational Attainment." *American Sociological Review* 39 (1974):303-16.

Portes, A., and Wilson, K.L. "Black-White Differences in Educational Attainment." *American Sociological Review* 41 (1976):414-31.

Rosenzweig, M.R. "Farm-Family Schooling Decisions: Determinants of the Quantity and Quality of Education in Agricultural Populations." *Journal of Human Resources* 12 (1977):71-91.

Rumberger, R.W. "The Influence of Family Background on Education, Earnings, and Wealth." *Social Forces* 61 (1983):755-73.

Sewell, W.H., and Hauser, R.M. *Education, Occupation and Earnings: Achievement in the Early Career.* New York: Academic Press, 1975.

Stolzenberg, R.M. "Education, Occupation, and Wage Differences Between White and Black Men." *American Journal of Sociology* 81 (1975):299-323.

Taylor, P.A. "Education, Ethnicity, and Cultural Assimilation in the United States." *Ethnicity* 8 (1981): 31-49.

Treiman, D.J., and Terrell, K. "Process of Status Attainment in the United States and Great Britain." *American Journal of Sociology* 81 (1975):563-83.

U.S. Bureau of the Census. "Educational Attainment in the United States." *Current Population Reports* (Series P-20). Washington, DC: U.S. Government Printing Office, selected years (nos. 274, 1973-74; 356, 1979).

Waite, L.J., and Moore, K.A. "Impact of an Early First Birth on Young Women's Educational Attainment." *Social Forces* 56 (1978):845-65.

Welch, F. "Black-White Differences in Returns to Schooling." *American Economic Review* 63 (1973): 893-907.

Wilson, K.L. "Effects of Integration and Class on Black Attainment." *Sociology of Education* 52 (1979): 814-98.

Wilson, K.L., and Portes, K. "Educational Attainment Process: Results from a National Survey." *American Journal of Sociology* 81 (1975):343-63.

Chapter 11

Household and Family

With respect to most items of census information, the members of a population are enumerated as *individuals* and the demographic characteristics for which statistics are tabulated involve such personal traits as age, sex, or educational attainment. However, information is also tabulated about certain *groups* of persons. The number of persons in the group, its type, and other characteristics (including any changes in its size or other characteristics) are the objects of investigation. If the person is considered at all in the analysis of a group, it is to ascertain his or her status in the group, the role the person plays in the group organization. Two of the most important groups about which the census collects information (and about which there is also widespread general interest) are households and families, that is, *residential* groups, clusters of people who occupy a residency jointly.

Most members of a population have a dwelling place and a set of living arrangements. The arrangements under which the members of a population live are of considerable importance to those who are concerned with research or administration in areas such as family relationships, housing problems, marketing, or city planning. In census terminology, each separate dwelling place is termed a "housing unit" (in earlier censuses it was called a "dwelling unit"), and the group of persons inhabiting it constitutes a "household." (See the Definition Box for the official definitions introduced for the 1980 census and subsequent surveys.)

The household is important as a unit of study for several reasons. Sociologists and anthropologists have a direct interest in living arrangements, in the composition of households, and in the relationships between members of a household. Economists, market analysts, public utility companies, and persons concerned with the subject of housing are especially interested in household statistics, because the household (rather than the person) is often the principal unit with which they deal. Telephone service, gas, water, and electricity are distributed to household units. Many products, such as television sets, washing machines, and home furnishings, are manufactured to satisfy the needs of household units. Information about the size, composition, and characteristics of households is very important to architects, contractors, and real estate firms as they design and sell houses and apartments.

Because children are a product of families and are wholly dependent on families for both material needs and socialization, those who are interested in children and their welfare are concerned about the families where children reside. The living arrangements of elderly persons are of interest to those who study the problems of the aged. Social agencies that are concerned with crowded housing conditions and the general quality of

Definitions

The definitions provided below are direct quotations or summaries from Current Population Reports *(Series P-20), with some modification to clarify 1980 census data.*

Household. A household consists of all the persons who occupy a housing unit. A house, an apartment or other group of rooms, or a single room is regarded as a housing unit when it is occupied or intended for occupancy as separate living quarters; that is, when the occupants do not live and eat with any other persons in the structures and there is direct access from the outside or through a common hall. A household includes the related family members and all the unrelated persons, if any, such as lodgers, foster children, wards, or employees who share the housing unit. A person living alone in a housing unit, or a group of unrelated persons sharing a housing unit as partners, is also counted as a household. The count of households excludes group quarters (see definition).

Householder. The householder refers to the person (or one of the persons) in whose name the housing unit is owned or rented (maintained) or, if there is no such person, any adult member, excluding roomers, boarders, or paid employees. (See question 2 of the 1980 census in the appendix to Chapter 1.) If the house is owned or rented jointly by a married couple, the householder may be either the husband or the wife. The person designated as the householder is the "reference person" to whom the relationship of all other household members, if any, is recorded. The term "household head" was used instead of "householder" prior to 1980 in surveys and censuses. Prior to 1980, the husband was always considered the householder in married couple households. The number of householders is equal to the number of households. Also, the number of family householders is equal to the number of families.

Head versus Householder. Beginning with the 1980 Current Population Survey, the Bureau of the Census discontinued the use of the terms "head of household" and "head of family." Instead, the terms "householder" and "family householder" are used. Recent social changes have resulted in greater sharing of household responsibilities among the adult members and, therefore, have made the term "head" increasingly inappropriate in the analysis of household and family data. Specifically, the Bureau has discontinued its longtime practice of always classifying the husband as the reference person (head) when he and his wife are living together.

The term "householder" is used in the presentation of data that had previously been presented with the designation "head." The householder is the first adult household member listed on the questionnaire. The instructions call for listing first the person (or one of the persons) in whose name the home is owned or rented. If a home is owned jointly by a married couple, either the husband or the wife may be listed first, thereby becoming the reference person, or householder, to whom the relationship of other household members is to be recorded.

Family. A family is a group of two persons or more (one of whom is the householder) related by birth, marriage, or adoption and residing together; all such persons (including related subfamily members) are considered as members of one family. Beginning with the 1980 Current Population Survey, unrelated subfamilies (referred to in the past as secondary families) are no longer included in the count of families, nor are the members of unrelated subfamilies included in the count of family members.

Family Household. A family household is a household maintained by a family (as defined above), and any unrelated persons (unrelated subfamily members and/or secondary individuals) who may be residing there are included. The number of family households is equal to the number of families. The count of family household members differs from the count of family members, however, in that the family household members include all persons living in the household, whereas family members include only the householder and his/her relatives (see definition of family).

Subfamily. A related subfamily is a married couple with or without children, or one parent with one or more own single (never married) children under 18 years old, living in a household and related to,

Continued on next page

Definitions

but not including, the person or couple who maintains the household. The most common example of a related subfamily is a young married couple sharing the home of the husband's or wife's parents. The number of related subfamilies is not included in the count of families.

Unrelated Subfamily. An unrelated subfamily (formerly called a secondary family) is a group of two persons or more who are related to each other by birth, marriage, or adoption, but who are not related to the householder. The unrelated subfamily may include persons such as guests, roomers, boarders, or resident employees and their relatives living in a household. The number of unrelated subfamily members is included in the number of household members but is not included in the count of family members.

Persons living with relatives in group quarters were formerly considered as members of unrelated subfamilies. However, the number of such unrelated subfamilies became so small (37,000 in 1967) that beginning with data for 1968 (and beginning with the census data for 1960) the Bureau of the Census includes persons in these unrelated subfamilies in the count of secondary individuals.

Married Couple. A married couple, as defined for census purposes, is a husband and wife enumerated as members of the same household. The married couple may or may not have children living with them. The expression "husband-wife" or "married-couple" before the term "household," "family," or "subfamily" indicates that the household, family, or subfamily is maintained by a husband and wife. The number of married couples equals the count of married-couple families plus related and unrelated married-couple subfamilies.

Unrelated Individuals. Unrelated individuals are persons of any age (other than inmates of institutions) who are not living with any relatives. An unrelated individual may be (a) a person living alone or with nonrelatives only, (b) a roomer, boarder, or resident employee with no relatives in the household, or (c) a group quarters member who has no relatives living with him/her. Thus, a widow who occupies her house alone or with one or more other persons not related to her, a roomer not related to anyone else in the housing unit, a maid living as a member of her employer's household but with no relatives in the household, and a resident staff member in a hospital living apart from any relatives are all examples of unrelated individuals.

Nonfamily Householder. A nonfamily householder (formerly called a primary individual) is a person maintaining a household while living alone or with nonrelatives only.

Secondary Individual. A secondary individual is a person in a household or group quarters such as a guest, roomer, boarder, or resident employee (excluding nonfamily householders and inmates of institutions) who is not related to any other person in the household or group quarters. (See section on unrelated subfamily for slight change in coverage of secondary individuals in 1968.)

Size of Household, Family, or Subfamily. The term "size of household" includes all persons occupying a housing unit. "Size of family" includes the family householder and all other persons in the living quarters who are related to the householder by birth, marriage, or adoption. "Size of related subfamily" includes the husband and wife or the lone parent and their never-married sons and daughters under 18 years of age. "Size of unrelated subfamily" includes the reference person and all other members related to the reference person. If a family has a related subfamily among its members, the size of the family includes the members of the related subfamily.

Related Persons and Family Members. In the classification of households by number of related persons, the person or couple who maintains the household or housing unit and all persons in the household related to them are included. In the classification of families by number of family members, all persons in the family are included. The number of family members is the same as the size of the family.

Own Children and Related Children. "Own" children in a family are sons and daughters, including stepchildren and adopted children, of the householder. Similarly, "own" children in a subfamily are sons and daughters of the married couple or parent in the subfamily. (All children shown as mem-

Continued on next page

Definitions

bers of related subfamilies are own children of the person(s) maintaining the subfamily.) "Related" children in a family include own children and all other children in the household who are related to the householder by birth, marriage, or adoption. For each type of family unit identified in the Current Population Survey, the count of own children under 18 years old is limited to single (never married) children; however, "own children under 25" and "own children of any age," as the terms are used here, include all children regardless of marital status. The totals include never-married children living away from home in college dormitories.

The count of related children in families was formerly restricted to single (never married) children. However, beginning with data for 1968 the Bureau of the Census includes ever-married children under the category of related children. This change added approximately 20,000 children to the category of related children in March, 1968.

Comparison of New and Old Definitions. Estimates of the number of households, families, and related units according to the new system of concepts introduced in 1980 are compared with corresponding estimates according to the former system in Figure A. Unrelated subfamilies, referred to in the past as secondary families, are no longer included in the count of families.

Persons per Household. The number of persons in households divided by the number of households (or householders).

Relationship to Householder. The data on relationship to householder were derived from answers to question 2 of the 1980 census questionnaire, which was asked of all persons in housing units. When relationship was not reported for an individual, it was allocated according to the responses for age and marital status for that person while maintaining consistency with responses for other individuals in the household.

Householder–See definitions above.

Spouse–A person married to and living with a householder. This category includes persons in formal marriages as well as persons in common-law marriages.

Child–A son, daughter, stepchild, or adopted child of the householder regardless of the child's age or marital status. The category excludes sons-in-law and daughters-in-law. "Own children" are sons and daughters, including stepchildren and adopted children, of the householder who are single (never married) and under 18 years of age. The number of children "living with two parents" includes stepchildren and adopted children as well as sons and daughters born to the couple. "Related children" in a family include own children and all other persons under 18 years of age in the household, regardless of marital status, who are related to the householder by birth, marriage, or adoption, except the spouse of the householder. In a subfamily, an "own child" is a never-married child under 18 years of age who is a son, daughter, stepchild, or adopted child of a mother in a mother-child subfamily, a father in a father-child subfamily, or either spouse in a married-couple subfamily.

Other Relative–Any person related to the householder by birth, marriage, or adoption, who is not shown separately in the particular table (e.g., "uncle," "niece," or "cousin").

Nonrelative–Any person in the household not related to the householder by birth, marriage, or adoption. Roomers, boarders, partners, roommates, paid employees, wards, and foster children are included in this category.

Unmarried Couple. An unmarried couple is composed of two unrelated adults of opposite sex (one of whom is the householder) who share a housing unit with no other persons present or with children under 15 years old.

Group Quarters. All persons not living in households are classified by the Bureau of the Census as living in group quarters. Two general categories of persons in groups quarters are recognized:

Inmates of Institutions–Persons under care or custody in institutions at the time of enumeration are classified as "patients or inmates" of an institution regardless of their length of stay in that place and regardless of the number of people in that place. Institutions include homes, schools,

Continued on next page

Definitions

hospitals, or wards for the physically or mentally handicapped; hospitals or wards for mental, tubercular, or chronic disease patients, homes for unmarried mothers; nursing, convalescent, and rest homes for the aged and dependent; orphanages; and correctional institutions.

Other–This category includes all persons living in group quarters who are not inmates of institutions. Rooming and boarding houses, communes, farm and nonfamr workers' dormitories, convents or monasteries, and other living quarters are classified as "other" group quarters if there are nine or more persons unrelated to the person listed in column 1 of the census questionnaire; or if ten or more unrelated persons share the unit. Persons residing in certain other types of living arrangements are classified as living in "other" group quarters regardless of the number or relationship of people in the unit. These include persons residing in military barracks, on ships, in college dormitories, or in sorority and fraternity houses; patients in general or maternity wards of hospitals who have no usual residence elsewhere; staff members in institutional quarters; and persons enumerated in missions, flophouses, Salvation Army shelters, railroad stations, etc. Military quarters include barracks or dormitories on base, transient quarters on base for temporary residents (both civilian and military), and military ships.

Present Terminology	*1980 (000)*	*Old Terminology*	*1980 (000)*
Households (sum of family and nonfamily households)	79,108	Households (sum of primary families and primary individuals)	79,108
Family households	58,426	Primary families	58,426
Married-couple family[a]	48,180	Husband-wife	48,180
Other family, male householder	1,706	Male head, no wife present	1,706
Other family, female householder	8,540	Female head, no husband present	8,540
Nonfamily households	20,682	Primary individuals	20,682
Male householder	8,594	Male	8,594
Female householder	12,088	Female	12,088
Families (same total as family households)	58,426	Families (sum of primary and secondary families)	58,774
Married-couple family[a]	48,180	Husband-wife	48,199
Other family, male householder	1,706	Male head, no wife present	1,742
Other family, female householder	8,540	Female head, no husband present	8,834
Unrelated subfamilies[b]	348	Secondary families[b]	348
Married couple	19	Husband-wife	19
Other, male reference person	36	Male head, no wife present	36
Other, female reference person	294	Female head, no husband present	294
Related subfamilies[c]	1,115	Subfamilies[c]	1,115
Married couple	567	Husband-wife	567
Father-child	55	Male head, no wife present	55
Mother-child	494	Female head, no husband present	494
Married couples (sum of married-couple families plus married-couple unrelated subfamilies plus married-couple related subfamilies)	48,765	Married couples (sum of husband-wife families plus husband-wife subfamilies)	48,765
Unrelated individuals (sum of nonfamily householders plus secondary individuals)	25,838	Unrelated individuals (sum of primary individuals plus secondary individuals)	25,838
Secondary individuals	5,156	Secondary individuals	5,156

[a]There were 1,631,000 women (wives) in married-couple families who identified themselves as the householder.

[b]The number of unrelated subfamilies in 1980 is the same as the number of units previously called secondary families. Unrelated subfamilies are not included in the number of families in the reports, but secondary families were previously included in the number of families.

[c]The number of related subfamilies in 1980 is the same as the number of units previously called subfamilies.

Figure A. Comparison of New and Old Definitions

living arrangements also strive to gather as much information as they can about the nation's households.

Almost all (97.5 percent) of the population lives in housing units as defined by the census. The remaining 2.5 percent live in what the census defines as "group quarters." Of this small minority, 40-45 percent are inmates of institutions and 55-60 percent are residents of dormitories, rooming and boarding houses, army barracks, convents and monasteries, and similar mass residence units (see definition of "group quarters"). This chapter deals primarily with residents of households, but there is a brief discussion of the characteristics of persons living in group quarters toward the end of the chapter.

The Bureau of the Census routinely collects data about households and families as a part of its Current Population Survey, and publishes a report, "Household and Family Characteristics," as a part of its *Current Population Reports* (Series P-20). Major changes in definitions were made in 1980 for the census and the Current Population Surveys. The reader who is not familiar with these changes should read all of the Definition Box carefully.

Growth in Households: Decline in Size

The number of households enumerated at each census since 1790, with data by race for censuses since 1890 and for survey data for recent intervening years, is provided in Table 11-1. In 1983 there were 83.9 million households housing 229.2 million persons, or 2.73 persons per household. During the decades since 1790 there has been a rather steady decline in the average size of the household. Today's household contains only 47 percent as many persons as the average household of 1790, which had 5.8 members. This decline has been due to lower fertility rates, a tendency for unmarried persons to live in housing units rather than as roomers or boarders in group quarters or with a family, a tendency for young unmarried adults to live apart from their parents instead of remaining at home until marriage, and to an increased longevity that creates a great many households occupied by elderly couples or individuals. Black households contained an average of 3.04 members, whereas white households were about 12 percent smaller

Table 11-1. Number of Households and Average Household Size: 1790-1983

Year	Number of households (in thousands)				Population per household				Percent change in number of households since preceeding date			
	Total	White	Black	Other	Total	White	Black	Other	Total	White	Black	Other
1983	83,918	73,182	8,916	1,820	2.73	2.68	3.04	3.34	0.5	0.5	-0.5	5.8
1982	83,527	72,845	8,961	1,721	2.72	2.67	2.99	3.33	1.4	1.4	1.3	4.4
1981	82,368	71,872	8,847	1,649	2.73	2.68	2.98	3.40	4.1	3.5	5.3	32.0
1980	79,108	69,454	8,405	1,249	2.75	2.71	3.01	3.35	4.0	3.8	5.4	11.6
1978	76,030	66,934	7,977	1,119	2.81	2.77	3.10	3.22	6.9	6.3	9.8	22.6
1975	71,120	62,945	7,262	913	2.94	2.89	3.27	3.44	13.1	11.9	20.0	59.3
1970	62,874	56,248	6,053	573	3.17	3.11	3.68	3.68	9.8	9.3	14.1	--[a]
1965	57,251	51,441	5,808	--[a]	3.31	3.25	3.85	--[a]	8.8	8.3	13.7	--[a]
1960	52,610	47,503	5,107	--[a]	3.35	3.28	3.95	--[a]	10.1	9.5	15.9	--[a]
1955	47,788	43,380	4,408	--[a]	3.34	3.29	3.83	--[a]	9.7	--	--	--
1950	43,554	--	--	--	3.37	--	--	--	24.6	--	--	--
1940	34,949	31,680	3,142	127	3.67	--	--	--	16.9	17.4	12.1	7.6
1930	29,905	26,983	2,804	118	4.11	--	--	--	22.8	23.6	15.3	24.2
1920	24,352	21,826	2,431	95	4.34	--	--	--	20.2	--	11.9	--
1910	20,256	--	2,173	--	4.54	--	--	--	26.9	--	18.5	--
1900	15,964	14,064	1,834	66	4.76	--	--	--	25.8	25.0	30.0	175.0
1890	12,690	11,255	1,411	24	4.93	--	--	--	27.6	--	--	--
1880	9,946	--	--	--	5.04	--	--	--	31.2	--	--	--
1870	7,579	--	--	--	5.09	--	--	--	45.4	--	--	--
1860	5,211	--	--	--	5.28	--	--	--	44.8	--	--	--
1850	3,598	--	--	--	5.55	--	--	--	544.8	--	--	--
1790	558	--	--	--	5.79	--	--	--	...	...	...	...

[a]Other included as part of black.

Note: -- indicates data not available. ... indicates data not applicable.

Source: U.S. Bureau of the Census. "Household and Family Characteristics." Current Population Reports (Series P-20, nos. 388, 381, 371, 366, 340, 291, 218, 153, 106, and 67). Washington, DC: U.S. Government Printing Office, 1984, 1983, 1982, 1981, 1979, 1976, 1971, 1966, 1961, and 1956. Data for 1790-1950 from U.S. Bureau of the Census. Historical Statistics of the United States: Colonial Times to 1970. Washington, DC: U.S. Government Printing Office, 1975.

(2.68 percent). Since 1920 the household size has declined much more rapidly among the white than among the nonwhite populations.

Because households have declined in size, the number of households has increased at a faster rate than the population. As a result there has been a steady growth in the number of households, despite recent fertility declines. However, this trend may be changing. (See Figure 11-1.)

Since 1980 there has been a significant slowdown in the formation of new households. Whereas an average of 1.6 million new households were being added each year between 1970 and 1980, since 1980 this has dropped to about 1.2 million per year. Between 1982 and 1983 the number of new households formed appears to have been less than half a million, which is very close to a growth rate of zero. This sharp decline in the formation of new households came at a time when demographers were predicting a continuation of the trends of the 1980s, because the supply of persons born during the "baby boom" who were at prime ages for household formation was still large. Also, the average size of households ceased to decline, and even rose slightly between 1982 and 1983. As of 1982, the number of households was increasing at a lower rate than the population. Thus, the post-1980 trends represent a significant departure from what has been a long-term trend. Whether this is a temporary result of the economic recession of the 1980-83 years or new arrangements is as yet unclear.

Every household is presumed to have a leader, which in earlier censuses was called "household head." In the 1980 census the euphemistic term "householder" is used to refer to this presumptive head. The Definition Box provides details of these changes.

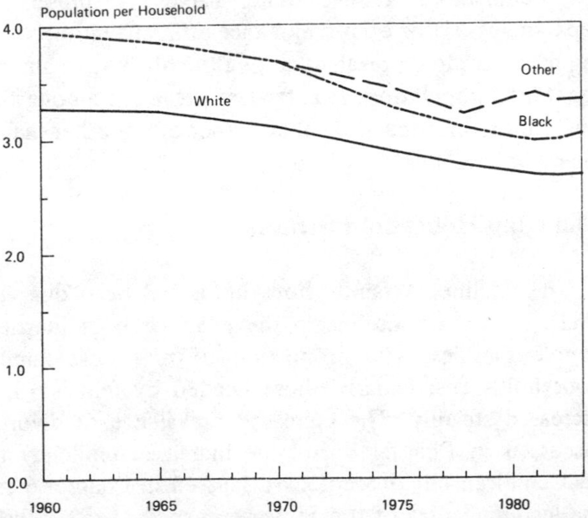

Figure 11-1. Trends in Population per Household, by Race: 1960-1983

Types of Households

The census dichotomizes all households into two categories:

• *Family households* are housing units occupied by a group of persons who are related to the householder (head) by birth, marriage, or adoption (see definition of "family").

• *Nonfamily households* are housing units occupied by a single person living alone or a householder living with one or more persons, none of whom are related to the householder by birth, marriage, or adoption.

Types of Family Households

Housing units occupied by a family are trichotomized:

• *Married couple families:* Husband and wife live together. The family includes their own or adopted children, other relatives, or nonrelative living with the family.

• *Female householder families:* A female householder living without a husband, but with one or more children or other relatives present in the household.

• *Male householder families:* A male householder living without a wife, but with one or more children or other relatives present in the household.

Types of Nonfamily Households

Nonfamily households are classified according to sex of the householder and whether or not the householder lives alone or with other nonrelatives. The four categories are

• Male householder, living alone
• Male householder, living with others
• Female householder, living alone
• Female householder, living with others.

The proportion (prevalence) within the population of each of the household types described is reported in Table 11-2 for the year 1983, for each of the major race-ethnic groups. Overall, not quite three-quarters (73 percent) of all households are occupied by families, and a little more than one-quarter (27 percent) are occupied as nonfamily households by persons either living alone or living with other unrelated persons.

Family Households

For all except black households, the married couple family is by far the dominant type of family household. About 60 percent of all households and 81 percent of all family households are of this conventional type. Within married couple families, the tradition of male

Table 11-2. Types of Households and Families, by Race-Ethnicity: 1983

Type of household	Percent distribution (vertical)					Number of house-hold	Percent distribution (horizontal)				
	Total	White	Black	Other	Spanish-origin[a]		White	Black	Other	Spanish-origin[a]	All house-holds
All households	100.0	100.0	100.0	100.0	100.0	83,918	87.2	10.6	2.2	4.9	100.0
Family households	73.2	73.0	73.2	80.0	82.5	61,393	87.0	10.6	2.4	5.5	100.0
Married couple family	59.5	61.8	39.1	64.3	59.9	49,908	90.7	7.0	2.3	4.9	100.0
Other: Male householder	2.4	2.3	3.5	3.2	3.8	2,016	81.7	15.3	2.9	7.6	100.0
Other: Female householder	11.3	8.9	30.7	12.5	18.8	9,469	68.7	28.9	2.4	8.1	100.0
Nonfamily households	26.8	27.0	26.8	19.9	17.5	22,525	87.8	10.6	1.6	3.1	100.0
Householders living alone	22.9	23.1	23.1	16.0	14.1	19,250	87.8	10.7	1.5	3.0	100.0
Male householder	8.9	8.7	10.5	7.8	6.5	7,451	85.5	12.6	1.9	3.5	100.0
Female householder	14.1	14.4	12.6	8.2	7.7	11,799	89.2	9.5	1.3	2.7	100.0
Householders living with others	3.9	3.9	3.7	3.9	3.4	3,275	87.8	10.1	2.2	4.3	100.0
Male householder	2.5	2.5	1.9	2.6	2.5	2,063	89.4	8.3	2.3	5.0	100.0
Female householder	1.4	1.4	1.8	1.3	0.9	1,212	85.0	13.0	2.0	3.0	100.0
Number of households	83,918	73,182	8,916	1,820	4,085	...	...	...	...	...	...

[a]Persons of Spanish-orign may be of any race.

Source: U.S. Bureau of the Census. "Household and Family Characteristics." Current Population Reports (Series P-20, no. 388). Washington, DC: U.S. Government Printing Office, 1984, Tables 20 and 21.

headship persists: 95 percent of all such families reported the male as "householder." Female "household heads" in married couple families are thus still quite rare and seem to be most common where the husband is elderly or extremely young.

However, a significant proportion of the households (from 10 to more than 20 percent) consist of "no-spouse" families—either a male or female living with children or other relatives, but without a spouse. In only a small share of cases (2-3 percent of all households) is this a male. The prevalence of female no-spouse families is at least four times higher (see Figure 11-2).

The phenomenon of female no-spouse family households is one of the leading concerns of this and later chapters. It is twice as prevalent among the Spanish-origin population as among the white. Among the black population, it is almost a dominant trait: 30.7 percent of all black households (42 percent of all black family households) comprise women living with their children, but without a husband.

The decline in the proportion of family households among all households, and of married couple families as a share of all families, has been underway since 1940. But the acceleration in these trends between 1970 and 1980 was sharp.

Nonfamily Households

In 1940 the ratio was 9 family to each nonfamily household. By 1983 that ratio had declined to 2.7 family to each nonfamily household. This shift from family to nonfamily household living arrangements accelerated between 1970 and 1980, but since 1980 has decelerated. Between 1980 and 1983 the average annual increase in the number of nonfamily households was less than half the annual rate of increase of 1970-80, and between 1982 and 1983 the increase was negative or zero. Thus, the economic recession and/or other factors has brought an abrupt halt to what was a phenomenal characteristic of the 1960s and 1970s.

The great preponderance of nonfamily households (86 percent) consists of persons living alone. Among one-person households, women outnumber men by a wide margin. Thus, the long-term decrease in the proportion of family households is caused not so much by persons seeking alternative forms of group living as simply by persons (primarily women) choosing or forced by circumstances to live alone. Table 11-3 presents a separate panel for each major race-ethnicity group. Living alone is more prevalent among the black than among the white population. It is far less prevalent among the Spanish-origin population than either of the other major race-ethnic groups.

Changing Household Structure

The decline in family households has been due entirely to a sharp decline in the proportion of married couple families. The proportion of no-spouse family households (particularly those headed by females) has increased steadily. The increased prevalence of divorce discussed in Chapter 4 and the increased tendency to bear children out of wedlock discussed in Chapter 6 are the leading causes of this increase in spouseless families. However, these longterm trends also seem to have been altered greatly since 1981. Between 1982 and 1983

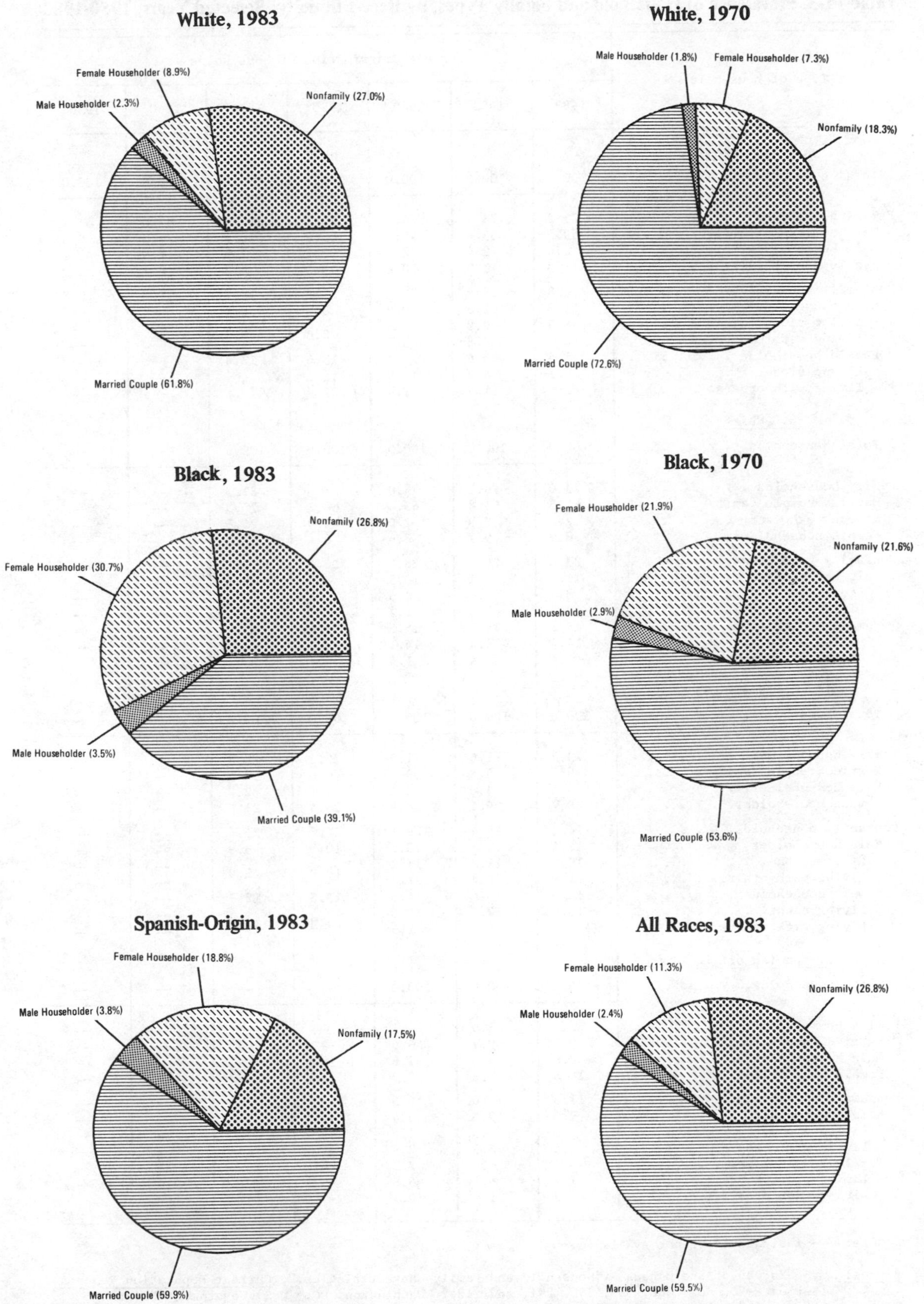

Figure 11-2. Types of Households, by Race-Ethnicity: 1970 and 1983

Table 11-3. Prevalence of Household and Family Types, by Race-Ethnicity: Selected Years, 1950-1983

Type of household	Percent distribution of households						
	1983	1982	1980	1975	1970	1960	1950
A. All races							
Total households	100.0	100.0	100.0	100.0	100.0	100.0	100.0
Family households	73.2	73.1	73.9	78.1	81.3	85.0	89.2
Married couple family	59.5	59.4	60.9	66.0	70.6	74.3	78.2
Male householder	2.4	2.4	2.2	2.1	1.9	2.3	2.7
Female householder	11.3	11.3	10.8	10.0	8.7	8.4	8.3
Nonfamily households	26.8	26.9	26.1	21.9	18.7	15.0	10.8
Male householder	11.3	11.3	10.9	8.3	6.3	--	--
Living alone	8.9	9.0	8.6	} 8.3	6.3	--	--
Living with others	2.3	2.3	2.3			--	--
Female householder	15.5	15.6	15.3	13.6	12.4	--	--
Living alone	14.1	14.2	13.9	} 13.6	12.4	--	--
Living with others	1.4	1.4	1.4			--	--
B. White							
Total households	100.0	100.0	100.0	100.0	100.0	--	--
Family households	73.0	73.1	74.0	78.4	81.7	--	--
Married couple family	61.8	61.8	63.4	68.2	72.5	--	--
Male householder	2.3	2.3	2.0	2.0	1.8	--	--
Female householder	8.9	9.1	8.6	8.1	7.3	--	--
Nonfamily households	27.0	26.9	26.0	21.6	18.3	--	--
Male householder	11.2	11.1	10.5	8.0	5.9	--	--
Living alone	8.7	8.7	8.3	} 8.0	5.9	--	--
Living with others	2.5	2.4	2.2			--	--
Female householder	15.8	15.8	15.5	13.6	12.4	--	--
Living alone	14.4	14.4	14.1	} 13.6	12.4	--	--
Living with others	1.4	1.4	1.4			--	--
C. Black							
Total households	100.0	100.0	100.0	100.0	100.0	--	--
Family households	73.2	71.6	71.9	75.3	78.4	--	--
Married couple family	39.1	39.4	39.9	46.0	53.6	--	--
Male householder	3.5	3.0	3.1	2.9	2.9	--	--
Female householder	30.7	29.1	28.9	26.4	21.9	--	--
Nonfamily households	26.8	28.4	28.1	24.7	21.6	--	--
Male householder	12.4	13.1	13.6	10.9	8.9	--	--
Living alone	10.5	11.2	11.2	} 10.9	8.9	--	--
Living with others	1.9	1.9	2.4			--	--
Female householder	14.3	15.4	14.5	13.8	12.7	--	--
Living alone	12.6	13.7	13.0	} 13.8	12.7	--	--
Living with others	1.7	1.7	1.5			--	--
D. Spanish-origin							
Total households	100.0	100.0	100.0	--	--	--	--
Family households	82.5	83.0	83.1	--	--	--	--
Married couple family	59.9	60.7	63.6	--	--	--	--
Male householder	3.8	3.6	3.6	--	--	--	--
Female householder	18.8	18.8	15.9	--	--	--	--
Nonfamily households	17.5	17.0	16.9	--	--	--	--
Male householder	9.0	9.3	9.4	--	--	--	--
Living alone	6.5	7.0	6.5	--	--	--	--
Living with others	2.5	2.3	2.9	--	--	--	--
Female householder	8.5	7.6	7.5	--	--	--	--
Living alone	7.7	6.7	6.8	--	--	--	--
Living with others	0.8	1.0	0.7	--	--	--	--

Note: -- indicates data not available.

Source: U.S. Bureau of the Census. "Household and Family Characteristics." Current Population Reports (Series P-20, nos. 388, 381, 366, 291, and 218). Washington, DC: U.S. Government Printing Office, 1984, 1983, 1981, 1976, and 1971. Data for 1950-1960 from U.S. Bureau of the Census. Historical Statistics of the United States: Colonial Times to 1970 (Part 1). Washington, DC: U.S. Government Printing Office, 1975.

there has been almost a zero increase in households headed by females without a spouse. This reversal was confined to the white population.

A dramatic way to report the impact of recent shifts in family-type composition is to compare the percentage change in the number of households and families of each type between 1970 and 1981 with the change between 1981 and 1983:

Type of household	Number of households (000)			Percent change	
	1983	1981	1970	1970-1981	1981-1983
All households	83,918	82,368	63,401	29.9	1.9
Family households. . . .	61,393	60,309	51,456	17.2	1.8
Married couple	49,908	49,294	44,728	10.2	1.2
Male (no spouse) . . .	2,016	1,933	1,228	57.4	4.3
Female (no spouse) . .	9,469	9,082	5,500	65.1	4.3
Nonfamily households . .	22,525	22,059	11,945	84.7	2.1
Male householder, living alone	7,451	7,253	3,532	105.4	2.7
Female householder, living alone	11,799	11,683	7,319	59.6	1.0
Males and females, not living alone . .	3,275	3,123	1,094	185.5	4.9

Source: U.S. Bureau of the Census. "Household and Family Characteristics: March, 1981" and "March, 1983." Current Population Reports (Series P-20, no. 371 and no. 388). Washington, DC: U.S. Government Printing Office, 1982 and 1984.

Between 1970 and 1981 there was only a very modest rate of increase in the number of conventional married couple families but an explosion of all of the other less conventional categories of families and households. By far the highest rate of increase was in the formation of nonfamily households where the occupants were not living alone. Next highest in growth rate was male householders living alone, with the formation of female no-spouse families being a strong third. The tendency for male-headed no-spouse families to proliferate was only moderately smaller than for females.

The two years 1981-83 saw these trends modified. Family households headed by females increased in 1981, but had little increase between 1982 and 1983. The long-term increase in family households headed by men continued. As explained below, these changes are concentrated among households and families where the householder is under thirty-five years of age. Meanwhile, the formation of new households by women living alone shrank to only one-half of the national rate.

Differentials in Size of Households

The average size of American households as reported above—only 2.73 persons in 1983—is quite small. This is caused in part by the large component of nonfamily households, which have the very small average size of 1.20 persons. However, family households are also comparatively small—with an average of only 3.29 per family. In the modal case, it is a husband, wife, and one child. Table 11-4 reports the average size of households according to household type, race, and Spanish-origin for selected years since 1970.

Household size and trends in household size vary by type of household. Married couples tend to have the largest households, while women living in nonfamily households tend to have the smallest. Family households where a woman householder is living without a husband are very nearly, but not quite, as large as married couple households. Family households where a male is living without a wife are the smallest of the family household types.

Black households tend to be at least 10 percent larger than white households of the same type. Black family households headed by a black female householder living with children or other relatives but without a husband are 20 percent or more larger than the same type of households in the white population.

Spanish-origin households tend to be the largest of all households. The greatest disparity is in the Spanish-origin married couple households, which are 7 percent larger than black and 25 percent larger than white married couple households.

Of special interest is the female no-spouse family householder. For white families such households are comparatively small (2.9 persons), but for both the black and the Spanish-origin households they are much larger—by more than 0.6 persons than the corresponding type of white households.

The differences between racial groups tend to be concentrated among the family households; differences among the nonfamily households tend to be minor.

Between 1982 and 1983 the average size of households increased, contrary to the long-term trends. Although small this increase was distributed among both family and nonfamily households, as Table 11-4 shows. Married couple families and men living in nonfamily households of an average size increased. For families with female householders, the size remained almost unchanged. This is a direct consequence of the slowdown in the pace of household family formation at a time when the young adult population of household-formation ages was growing moderately rapidly, described above.

Number of Persons in Families

Whereas Table 11-4 provides data only for average family size, Table 11-5 provides data on the distribution of numbers of persons in family households. By definition, a family must contain at least two persons, and for all family types for all race-ethnic groups except Spanish-origin, this is the modal size group. More than 80 percent of husband-wife (married couple) families contain two, three, or four members, and only 7 percent have six or more persons. Black families are 70 percent more prone to contain large numbers of members (five or more) than are white households. The Spanish-origin families are largest of all. The four-person family is more common among Spanish-origin married couple families than any other size. The proportion of Spanish-origin married couple families containing five or more members is more than twice the proportion for such white families and 20 percent greater than for the black married couple families.

Female and male no-spouse families tend to be even more concentrated in the two-three person span than are married couple families. This tendency is more pronounced for the male than for the female no-spouse family: The male-headed family of this type consists of two persons in almost two-thirds of the cases.

By providing data for both 1970 and 1980 Table 11-5 offers insight into how the number of persons in families has changed in the recent past. In all types of households the trend has been toward a lower proportion of households with five or more persons and a larger number of households with two or three persons. This movement has been greater among the white than among the black or Spanish-origin family households.

Age of Householders

Very few householders are under age twenty, because at these ages comparatively few males are married and comparatively few unmarried persons have the financial resources to maintain a housing unit in their own name. Few households are maintained by persons seventy-five and over, because mortality has reduced the number of such persons available to occupy households. Between these extremes, the age composition of householders re-

Table 11-4. Average Household Size: Persons per Household, by Type and Race-Ethnicity: 1970-1983

Type of household and race	1983	1982	1981	1980	1975	1970
All households	2.73	2.72	2.73	2.75	2.94	3.17
Family households	3.29	3.28	3.29	3.30	3.44	3.64
Married couple households	3.34	3.33	3.34	3.34	3.48	3.69
Male householder, no wife	2.86	2.86	2.85	2.91	3.03	3.06
Female householder, no husband	3.12	3.12	3.11	3.15	3.27	3.35
Nonfamily households	1.20	1.19	1.19	1.19	1.15	1.13
Male householder	1.31	1.28	1.30	1.29	1.25	1.19
Female householder	1.12	1.12	1.11	1.12	1.09	1.09
White households	2.68	2.67	2.68	2.71	2.89	3.11
Family households	3.23	3.21	3.22	3.24	--	--
Married couple households	3.29	3.27	3.29	3.30	--	--
Male householder, no wife	2.77	2.79	2.79	2.86	--	--
Female householder, no husband	2.91	2.92	2.90	2.93	--	--
Nonfamily households	1.19	1.18	1.19	1.19	--	--
Male householder	1.31	1.29	1.31	1.30	--	--
Female householder	1.11	1.11	1.11	1.11	--	--
Black households	3.04	2.99	2.98	3.01	3.27	3.68
Family households	3.71	3.70	3.70	3.72	--	--
Married couple households	3.84	3.82	3.85	3.78	--	--
Male householder, no wife	3.26	3.17	3.03	3.14	--	--
Female householder, no husband	3.59	3.59	3.59	3.70	--	--
Nonfamily households	1.22	1.18	1.17	1.21	--	--
Male householder	1.26	1.22	1.22	1.25	--	--
Female householder	1.18	1.19	1.12	1.17	--	--
Spanish-origin households	3.48	3.49	3.47	3.46	--	--
Family households	3.95	3.94	3.92	3.89	--	--
Married couple households	4.12	4.09	4.10	4.05	--	--
Male householder, no wife	3.30	3.36	3.32	3.30	--	--
Female householder, no husband	3.51	3.56	3.45	3.40	--	--
Nonfamily households	1.30	1.29	1.31	1.35	--	--
Male householder	1.46	1.37	1.43	1.51	--	--
Female householder	1.14	1.18	1.15	1.14	--	--

Note: -- indicates data not available.

Source: U.S. Bureau of the Census. "Household and Family Characteristics." Current Population Reports (Series P-20, nos. 388, 381, 371, 366, 291, and 218). Washington, DC: U.S. Government Printing Office, 1984, 1983, 1982, 1981, 1976, and 1971.

Table 11-5. Number of Persons in Families, by Type of Family and Race-Ethnicity: 1982, 1980, and 1970

Number of persons	Married couple families				Female householder families				Male householder families			
	Total	White	Black	Spanish-origin	Total	White	Black	Spanish-origin	Total	White	Black	Spanish-origin
1982												
Total	100.0	100.0	100.0	100.0	100.0	100.0	100.0	100.0	100.0	100.0	100.0	100.0
2 persons	38.1	39.2	28.0	18.7	45.6	50.4	33.8	33.9	63.2	65.6	56.6	47.7
3 persons	22.0	22.0	23.0	22.7	28.6	29.8	25.7	25.2	23.0	22.1	25.2	29.1
4 persons	22.4	22.4	20.8	24.9	14.3	12.2	19.4	19.3	7.3	7.0	7.8	10.0
5 persons	10.6	10.3	13.0	16.6	6.6	5.0	10.6	12.8	4.5	3.6	8.1	6.9
6 persons	4.4	4.0	7.8	8.6	2.4	1.4	4.8	3.7	1.3	1.1	2.1	1.9
7 or more persons	2.6	2.1	7.4	8.5	2.5	1.2	5.7	5.1	0.7	0.6	0.3	4.4
Average per family	3.32	3.26	3.81	4.07	3.04	2.85	3.52	3.47	2.67	2.59	2.96	3.09
1980												
Total	100.0	100.0	100.0	100.0	100.0	100.0	100.0	100.0	100.0	100.0	100.0	100.0
2 persons	37.4	38.4	28.2	20.1	44.7	49.8	32.1	33.7	62.2	63.0	61.0	54.1
3 persons	21.9	21.8	23.5	21.8	28.2	29.1	26.0	30.6	21.9	22.7	15.2	19.1
4 persons	22.3	22.3	22.3	24.1	14.7	13.1	18.9	18.8	9.6	8.6	14.3	11.4
5 persons	10.9	10.7	11.8	16.4	6.8	5.4	10.0	9.8	3.4	3.4	3.5	7.0
6 persons	4.5	4.2	7.1	8.9	2.8	1.7	5.8	4.2	2.0	1.7	4.1	6.2
7 or more persons	3.0	2.5	7.1	8.6	2.8	0.9	7.2	3.0	0.9	0.6	1.8	2.1
Average per family	3.33	3.29	3.76	4.03	3.08	2.86	3.62	3.33	2.73	2.67	2.95	3.09
1970												
Total	100.0	100.0	100.0	100.0	100.0	100.0	100.0	100.0	100.0	100.0	100.0	100.0
2 persons	32.4	32.9	27.3	--	45.3	50.2	30.2	--	59.2	62.2	42.1	--
3 persons	20.5	20.5	19.5	--	23.9	25.1	20.2	--	20.8	20.1	25.2	--
4 persons	20.2	20.6	16.4	--	13.7	13.0	15.8	--	11.0	11.0	11.7	--
5 persons	13.4	13.5	11.7	--	7.9	6.4	12.6	--	3.8	3.7	4.0	--
6 persons	7.2	6.9	10.1	--	4.5	3.1	8.7	--	1.8	1.3	4.5	--
7 or more persons	6.3	5.6	14.9	--	4.7	2.2	12.5	--	3.3	1.6	12.6	--
Average per family	3.68	3.62	4.37	--	3.29	2.98	4.22	--	2.95	2.77	3.94	--

Note: -- indicates data not available.

Source: U.S. Bureau of the Census. "Household and Family Characteristics." Current Population Reports (Series P-20, nos. 381, 366, and 218). Washington, DC: U.S. Government Printing Office, 1983, 1981, and 1971, Table 1 for all repective reports.

Table 11-6. Age Composition of Householders, by Type of Household: 1970 and 1982, and Change 1970-1982 [percent distribution]

Age of householder	All households	Family households				Nonfamily households		
		Total	Married couple	No spouse		Total	Male	Female
				Male	Female			
Total, 1982	100.0	100.0	100.0	100.0	100.0	100.0	100.0	100.0
Under 25 years	7.3	5.9	5.3	10.9	8.3	11.1	15.1	8.1
25-29 years	11.4	10.9	10.7	10.1	12.1	12.8	18.2	8.8
30-34 years	11.7	12.8	12.6	11.2	13.8	8.9	13.7	5.5
35-44 years	18.3	21.4	20.9	21.8	24.2	10.0	15.1	6.2
45-54 years	15.0	17.6	17.6	17.6	17.2	8.0	9.7	6.7
55-64 years	15.5	16.0	17.0	13.4	11.3	14.2	11.4	16.2
65-74 years	12.4	10.4	11.0	7.9	7.3	18.0	8.8	24.7
75 years and over	8.3	5.0	4.8	7.1	5.8	17.1	7.9	23.8
Median age	45.8	44.5	45.3	43.2	41.5	54.2	37.0	64.1
Total, 1970	100.0	100.0	100.0	100.0	100.0	100.0	100.0	100.0
Under 25 years	6.8	6.8	6.7	5.5	7.1	7.2	10.7	5.5
25-29 years	9.7	10.6	11.1	5.9	8.1	5.7	9.9	3.6
30-34 years	8.8	10.1	10.5	4.2	8.2	3.4	6.4	1.9
35-44 years	18.6	21.2	21.6	17.5	19.5	6.9	12.1	4.3
45-54 years	19.5	21.2	21.2	22.8	20.2	12.1	14.3	10.9
55-64 years	17.1	16.3	16.2	17.8	16.7	20.6	16.7	22.7
65-74 years	12.0	9.2	8.9	12.1	11.1	24.2	15.9	28.4
75 years and over	7.5	4.7	3.8	14.3	9.2	19.8	14.1	22.7
Median age	48.1	45.6	45.1	52.4	48.5	62.1	52.7	65.4
Percent change, 1970-82								
Under 25 years	41.9	4.8	-12.5	223.9	99.5	192.5	238.1	147.4
25-29 years	56.1	22.6	8.2	181.7	156.6	324.9	338.9	305.3
30-34 years	76.5	51.4	34.9	337.3	189.7	401.5	413.1	381.8
35-44 years	31.1	20.3	8.1	104.7	113.0	175.9	197.1	145.2
45-54 years	2.2	-1.0	-7.3	27.3	45.8	26.6	61.9	3.1
55-64 years	20.5	17.3	17.3	23.7	15.7	31.5	63.0	19.8
65-74 years	37.6	34.7	39.1	6.8	12.5	42.5	32.5	45.3
75 years and over	47.2	29.4	40.7	-18.5	7.5	65.4	33.6	75.5

Source: U.S. Bureau of the Census. "Household and Family Characteristics." Current Population Reports (Series P-20, nos. 381 and 218). Washington, DC: U.S. Government Printing Office, 1983 and 1971, Tables E and 17.

flects the age composition of the population during a particular decade. Chapter 3 showed that during the 1970-80 decade the babies born during the baby boom had aged into the 25-35 age brackets. Accordingly, one would expect much growth in the number of householders in this age group during the 1970-80 period. This is, in fact, the case, as the lower panel of Table 11-6 details. Table 11-7 shows substantial differences in age composition of the various categories of householders.

Families with no spouse tend to be headed by householders among the younger age categories, in comparison with married couple households. Female families with no spouse are particularly prone to be concentrated in the under forty-five categories.

Among male nonfamily householders (Table 11-6), the emphasis is on youth, whereas among female nonfamily householders the emphasis is on age. Almost one-third of male householders in this category are under thirty, whereas almost one-half of all females are sixty-five and over.

Table 11-7A shows the age composition, and recent changes in that composition for householders. Tables 11-7A and 11-7B report the age composition data of Table 11-6 for white, black, and Spanish-origin households. The data are for 1978 and 1983, which permits analysis of very recent trends. For all types of families, householders in white families tend to have older age composition, while householders in Spanish-origin fami-

Table 11-7A. Age Composition of Family Householders, by Type of Family and Race-Ethnicity: 1983 and 1978, and Change 1978-1983 [percent distribution]

Age of householder	Married couple households				Female householder families				Male householder families			
	Total	White	Black	Span-ish-origin	Total	White	Black	Span-ish-origin	Total	White	Black	Span-ish-origin
Total, 1983. . .	100.0	100.0	100.0	100.0	100.0	100.0	100.0	100.0	100.0	100.0	100.0	100.0
Under 20	0.2	0.2	0.3	0.2	1.0	0.8	1.3	1.0	1.0	1.1	0.3	2.6
20-24.	4.7	4.7	4.2	6.4	7.6	6.3	10.5	8.3	8.9	8.7	9.4	16.3
25-29.	10.4	10.5	9.8	15.0	12.2	10.7	15.7	14.2	10.5	10.2	10.7	13.1
30-34.	11.8	12.3	14.4	17.3	12.7	11.7	15.2	15.7	10.1	9.1	14.2	17.0
35-39.	12.5	11.7	11.9	14.8	14.0	13.9	13.8	15.9	11.4	11.4	12.6	11.8
40-44.	10.1	9.9	11.6	11.0	10.6	11.2	8.9	13.3	10.6	11.1	8.7	6.5
45-54.	17.2	17.2	16.9	17.5	16.0	16.4	15.1	17.2	17.4	17.8	14.6	11.8
55-64.	17.2	17.4	16.2	10.8	11.8	12.6	10.4	8.5	14.1	14.4	13.3	11.1
65-74.	11.0	11.1	10.3	5.0	7.7	8.7	5.4	4.2	9.5	9.0	12.3	5.2
75 and over. . . .	4.9	5.0	4.4	2.0	6.4	7.7	3.7	1.7	6.5	7.2	3.9	4.6
Median age	45.2	45.4	44.1	38.8	41.2	42.9	37.6	38.4	43.8	44.3	41.6	35.4
Total, 1978. . .	100.0	100.0	100.0	100.0	100.0	100.0	100.0	100.0	100.0	100.0	100.0	100.0
Under 20 . . . . . }	6.1	6.2	6.1	10.7	8.9	6.9	14.0	11.1	9.6	9.2	12.3	17.7
20-24.												
25-29.	11.2	11.2	10.7	16.3	11.6	10.1	15.4	20.1	8.6	7.3	14.5	10.4
30-34.	12.2	12.0	13.4	13.7	12.9	12.8	13.1	15.3	8.5	8.1	9.2	8.3
35-39. . . . . . . }	19.8	19.6	21.0	24.3	22.9	22.5	23.8	20.8	17.2	17.5	16.5	24.0
40-44.												
45-54.	19.3	19.3	19.4	17.6	17.5	18.5	14.5	20.1	21.6	22.1	19.5	18.7
55-64.	17.0	17.1	16.2	10.0	11.8	12.9	9.6	6.6	17.6	18.5	15.3	12.5
65-74.	10.0	10.1	9.7	5.6	8.6	9.4	6.5	4.6	9.3	10.2	6.2	4.2
75 and over. . . .	4.4	4.5	3.5	1.8	5.8	6.9	3.1	1.4	7.6	7.1	6.5	4.2
Median age	45.3	45.5	44.4	38.8	42.3	44.0	38.1	36.7	47.9	48.6	43.5	40.7
Percentage point change, 1978-1983												
Under 25	-1.2	-1.3	-1.6	-4.1	-0.3	0.2	-2.2	-1.8	0.3	0.6	-2.6	1.2
25-29.	-0.8	-0.7	-0.9	-1.3	0.6	0.6	0.3	-5.9	1.9	2.9	-3.8	2.7
30-34.	-0.4	0.3	1.0	3.6	-0.2	-1.1	2.1	0.4	1.6	1.0	5.0	8.7
35-44.	2.8	2.0	2.5	1.5	1.7	2.6	-1.1	8.4	4.8	5.0	4.8	-5.7
45-54.	-2.1	-2.1	-2.5	-0.1	-1.5	-2.1	0.6	-2.9	-4.2	-4.3	-4.9	-6.9
55-64.	0.2	0.3	0.0	0.8	0.0	-0.3	0.8	1.9	-3.5	-4.1	-2.0	-1.4
65-74.	1.0	1.0	0.6	-0.6	-0.9	-0.7	-1.1	-0.4	0.2	-1.2	6.1	1.0
75 and over. . . .	0.5	0.5	0.9	0.2	0.6	0.8	0.6	0.3	-1.1	0.1	-2.6	0.4

Source: U.S. Bureau of the Census. "Household and Family Characteristics." Current Population Reports (Series P-20, nos. 388 and 340). Washington, DC: U.S. Government Printing Office, 1984 and 1979, Tables 22 and 21.

lies have much younger age composition. In most cases the age composition of the black family householder is intermediate between the white and the Spanish-origin. Each race-ethnic group has an older age composition for female nonfamily householders than for male. The Spanish-origin nonfamily householders have the youngest age composition for both sexes, and the white population has the oldest age composition for both sexes. Table 11-7A shows that male no-spouse families are getting younger. The age composition of female no-spouse families appears to contain fewer women under twenty-five in 1983 than in 1978.

Tables 11-6 and 11-7 are unable to answer a very important question that needs to be answered in order to interpret the implications of recent age trends in household growth: How great are differentials in the propensity to be a householder at a particular age? In order to measure this and thereby control the effects of changing age composition, "household rates" are reported in Table 11-8. To compute these rates, the number of householders of a given age are expressed as a rate per 1,000 of the "exposed" population of the same age. This is performed separately for each sex. Table 11-8A presents these rates for males, by race-ethnicity, while Table

Table 11-7B. Age Composition of Nonfamily Householders, by Sex and Race-Ethnicity: 1983 and 1978 and Change 1978-1983 [percent distribution]

Age	Male				Female			
	Total	White	Black	Spanish-origin	Total	White	Black	Spanish-origin
Total, 1983 . . .	100.0	100.0	100.0	100.0	100.0	100.0	100.0	100.0
Under 20.	1.1	1.1	0.7	2.2	0.6	0.7	0.2	1.7
20-24 years	11.9	12.6	6.2	11.2	7.2	7.3	7.0	8.6
25-29 years	18.7	18.9	17.4	19.4	8.6	8.3	9.3	10.3
30-34 years	13.3	13.3	13.6	14.7	5.6	5.4	5.9	7.4
35-39 years	9.8	9.7	10.8	11.7	3.2	3.0	3.9	4.0
40-44 years	6.6	6.5	7.3	7.6	3.0	2.6	4.9	3.2
45-54 years	10.0	9.2	15.4	13.9	7.1	6.5	12.0	12.0
55-64 years	10.5	10.5	11.6	9.8	15.9	15.7	17.9	20.4
65-75 years	9.9	9.8	10.7	5.7	25.2	25.7	23.4	20.4
75 years and over .	8.2	8.5	6.3	3.8	23.6	24.8	15.5	12.0
Median age.	37.6	37.1	40.9	36.1	64.3	65.2	58.8	56.3
Total, 1978 . . .	100.0	100.0	100.0	100.0	100.0	100.0	100.0	100.0
Under 20. . . . . . / 20-24 years	17.6	18.4	11.9	25.4	9.6	9.6	9.8	14.2
25-29 years	17.7	17.8	16.6	18.1	7.3	7.2	8.1	9.8
30-34 years	11.5	11.8	9.1	10.5	3.6	3.4	4.3	6.3
35-39 years . . . . / 40-44 years	12.3	11.6	17.4	16.1	4.5	4.2	6.2	10.2
45-54 years	10.4	9.9	13.4	10.2	8.2	7.1	17.1	13.0
55-64 years	11.4	10.9	15.0	5.9	17.7	17.6	19.1	17.7
65-74 years	10.4	10.4	10.9	8.2	26.8	27.6	21.5	19.7
75 years and over .	8.7	9.2	5.7	5.6	22.3	23.3	13.9	9.1
Median age.	37.6	36.7	42.1	33.1	54.5	65.3	57.3	52.3
Percentage point change, 1978-1983								
Under 25.	-4.6	-4.7	-5.0	-12.0	-1.8	-1.6	-2.6	-3.9
25-29 years	1.0	1.1	0.8	1.3	1.3	1.1	1.2	0.5
30-34 years	1.8	1.5	4.5	4.2	2.0	2.0	1.6	1.1
35-44 years	4.1	4.6	0.7	3.2	1.7	1.4	2.6	-3.0
45-54 years	-0.4	-0.7	2.0	3.7	-1.1	-0.6	-5.1	-1.0
55-64 years	-0.9	-0.4	-3.4	3.9	-1.8	-1.9	-1.2	2.7
65-74 years	-0.5	-0.6	-0.2	-2.5	-1.6	-1.9	1.9	0.7
75 years and over .	-0.5	-0.7	0.6	-1.8	1.3	1.5	1.6	2.9

Source: U.S. Bureau of the Census. "Household and Family Characteristics." Current Population Reports (Series P-20, nos. 388 and 340). Washington, DC: U.S. Government Printing Office, 1984 and 1979, Tables 22 and 21.

11-8B presents comparable data for females. The tendency for the male to be declared as householder in married couple families is very strong for all age groups. Whereas female family households-no spouse tend to be highest at ages 30-54 (reaching very high levels between ages 35-39 for white and black and ages 30-34 for Spanish-origin), the male counterpart of such families tends to be distributed over all adult ages. The tendency to live alone is moderately bimodal, particularly for the white population. Figure 11-13A graphs householder rates for male race-ethnic groups by age. Figure 11-3B graphs similar information for females.

Marital Status of Householders

By definition, the marital status of married couple families is "married-spouse present." However, the other categories of householders can have any marital status except this. Table 11-9 reports the marital status for all householders and for each of the three principal race-ethnic groups. Such data for 1983 and 1978, with a measure of percentage change, permit a clearer understanding of the forces that appear to be stimulating such

Table 11-8A. Householder Rates for Males, by Age, Type of Household, and Race-Ethnicity: 1980

Age and race-ethnicity	Total	Family households		Nonfamily households	
		Married couple	No spouse	Live Alone	Multi-persons
White male					
Total	89,682,624	470.5	16.9	65.7	17.8
15-19 years	8,045,684	17.8	2.5	9.2	8.1
20-24 years	7,968,948	283.6	16.5	92.7	63.8
25-29 years	7,852,972	572.0	19.0	124.7	51.6
30-34 years	7,293,114	721.9	19.6	100.5	30.6
35-39 years	5,784,714	787.0	25.6	78.0	18.8
40-44 years	4,816,672	811.3	32.0	66.9	13.1
45-49 years	4,574,685	820.7	32.1	65.7	10.6
50-54 years	4,878,379	818.0	29.9	71.4	9.4
55-59 years	4,824,658	821.6	26.3	75.4	8.1
60-64 years	4,147,133	816.5	24.0	84.0	7.1
65-69 years	3,413,089	795.2	23.0	103.1	6.7
70-74 years	2,502,148	761.5	24.6	128.0	6.5
75-79 years	1,582,113	702.1	29.3	165.8	6.7
80-84 years	844,279	611.6	38.9	214.8	7.7
85 years and over	496,811	461.5	61.2	263.4	10.8
Black male					
Total	11,933,212	272.2	29.1	76.3	15.0
15-19 years	1,373,555	4.9	4.0	5.4	2.4
20-24 years	1,091,203	151.0	32.6	79.9	31.1
25-29 years	1,005,995	391.4	44.7	128.7	34.9
30-34 years	835,581	525.3	48.4	128.7	28.0
35-39 years	637,200	584.6	52.2	122.6	24.9
40-44 years	550,153	603.5	57.5	121.7	21.8
45-49 years	498,892	612.8	56.2	129.3	20.6
50-54 years	488,491	603.0	60.1	141.9	21.2
55-59 years	455,527	607.6	56.7	150.8	23.1
60-64 years	380,582	604.4	57.2	161.4	22.0
65-69 years	319,048	586.3	57.6	190.2	20.8
70-74 years	222,613	564.2	58.8	206.5	17.9
75-79 years	142,040	511.6	65.6	233.5	19.6
80-84 years	69,302	452.5	76.5	260.6	18.8
85 years and over	46,158	350.3	97.9	249.3	18.8
Spanish-origin male					
Total	7,074,199	336.2	23.8	42.8	14.8
15-19 years	783,692	22.2	6.9	7.7	7.1
20-24 years	748,185	282.0	37.3	55.8	41.5
25-29 years	672,613	547.5	39.7	75.4	36.9
30-34 years	555,733	676.8	38.6	73.3	25.8
35-39 years	405,109	725.9	39.6	67.1	20.6
40-44 years	341,321	743.5	46.5	66.3	18.0
45-49 years	293,503	759.1	45.4	71.7	14.1
50-54 years	262,532	758.9	45.9	76.7	12.8
55-59 years	210,284	753.8	44.5	82.1	12.2
60-64 years	142,941	726.9	43.3	102.6	10.5
65-69 years	107,825	683.2	43.1	121.5	12.1
70-74 years	78,405	643.7	46.1	149.9	10.6
75-59 years	53,864	583.3	55.0	272.7	9.2
80-84 years	24,541	505.6	64.6	372.0	8.9
85 years and over	15,381	343.7	81.7	187.0	8.8

Source: U.S. Bureau of the Census. "Detailed Population Characteristics: United States Summary." 1980 Census of Population (Chapter D, Section A). Washington, DC: U.S. Government Printing Office, 1983, Table 265.

Table 11-8B. Householder Rates for Females, by Age, Type of Household, and Race-Ethnicity: 1980

Age and race-ethnicity	Total	Family households		Nonfamily households	
		Married couple	No spouse	Live Alone	Multi-persons
White female					
Total	94,721,422	15.3	57.9	103.5	11.0
15-19 years	7,830,587	2.1	6.0	9.1	8.1
20-24 years	8,202,686	14.3	4.1	69.8	43.2
25-29 years	7,937,565	23.2	67.3	84.8	25.4
30-34 years	7,381,852	22.9	93.1	60.8	11.9
35-39 years	5,925,015	21.7	113.0	41.5	6.7
40-44 years	4,959,258	21.5	110.5	41.9	5.9
45-49 years	4,782,128	23.0	98.1	58.3	6.1
50-54 years	5,216,888	25.1	87.3	88.9	6.6
55-59 years	5,368,200	26.4	78.7	135.3	6.8
60-64 years	4,773,561	25.0	71.3	207.1	7.6
65-69 years	4,271,239	23.6	68.0	301.8	8.5
70-74 years	3,450,426	19.8	70.7	397.3	9.8
75-79 years	2,493,721	14.9	79.9	480.4	10.8
80-84 years	1,518,862	9.4	91.8	523.2	12.7
85 years and over	996,555	4.5	109.1	473.2	15.5
Black female					
Total	13,731,625	17.3	165.5	79.8	8.9
15-19 years	1,423,259	1.9	20.6	5.3	2.6
20-24 years	1,355,670	17.6	174.3	52.5	16.9
25-29 years	1,223,044	27.4	280.0	72.2	12.3
30-34 years	1,025,450	30.1	330.2	61.3	7.9
35-39 years	790,802	32.0	354.3	53.6	6.5
40-44 years	682,267	32.8	339.7	64.9	7.9
45-49 years	623,048	32.4	305.2	92.7	10.4
50-54 years	625,142	33.0	271.1	132.1	14.7
55-59 years	567,288	32.6	234.5	179.1	17.6
60-64 years	482,998	30.2	209.3	239.0	19.5
65-69 years	436,031	26.8	189.4	307.4	23.7
70-74 years	322,150	23.9	183.3	368.4	24.5
75-79 years	223,871	18.0	184.7	407.1	23.0
80-84 years	114,238	10.7	183.4	414.1	22.0
85 years and over	88,429	6.9	175.6	348.0	19.4
Spanish-origin female					
Total	7,259,180	12.5	8.8	39.7	6.3
15-19 years	763,195	3.7	15.3	5.5	3.8
20-24 years	748,655	17.9	87.1	31.6	17.5
25-29 years	677,246	23.7	132.6	38.4	13.4
30-34 years	581,876	22.9	191.9	30.7	7.0
35-39 years	440,380	23.1	188.6	25.6	5.3
40-44 years	370,192	22.3	188.9	34.1	5.7
45-49 years	323,722	22.0	183.0	48.1	6.6
50-54 years	294,527	21.8	170.5	72.9	8.0
55-59 years	236,123	21.3	161.9	109.4	8.9
60-64 years	108,501	18.8	137.3	169.8	9.0
65-69 years	142,351	16.5	126.9	231.7	11.1
70-74 years	101,521	13.2	125.8	282.4	9.8
75-79 years	70,668	9.2	128.2	316.1	12.3
80-84 years	32,741	9.4	131.0	329.1	12.2
85 years and over	24,491	4.7	140.3	256.5	12.3

Source: U.S. Bureau of the Census. "Detailed Population Characteristics: United States Summary." 1980 Census of Population (Chapter D, Section A). Washington, DC: U.S. Government Printing Office, 1983, Table 265.

Table 11-9. Marital Status of Householders, by Type of Household and Race-Ethnicity: 1983 and 1978, and Percent Change 1978-1983 [percent distribution]

Year and marital status	All households	No spouse families		Nonfamily households	
		Male	Female	Male	Female
White householders					
Total, 1983	100.0	100.0	100.0	100.0	100.0
Married, spouse present .	61.8	...	...	...	...
Married, spouse absent. .	3.5	12.7	16.4	9.7	4.0
Separated	2.7	10.6	14.1	6.6	2.9
Other reasons	0.8	2.2	2.3	3.1	1.2
Widowed	13.0	21.0	30.0	13.5	53.0
Divorced.	10.2	37.1	41.5	26.7	16.9
Single (never married). .	11.5	29.1	12.1	50.1	26.1
Total, 1978	100.0	100.0	100.0	100.0	100.0
Married, spouse present .	64.8	...	...	...	...
Married, spouse absent. .	3.7	15.1	18.6	11.6	4.5
Separated	2.6	8.9	14.8	7.8	3.1
Other reasons	1.0	6.2	3.8	3.9	1.4
Widowed	13.1	24.3	32.5	15.1	56.1
Divorced.	8.2	28.1	38.4	23.4	14.2
Single (never married). .	10.2	32.4	10.5	49.9	25.2
Change, 1978-83					
Married, spouse present	-3.0	...	...	...	...
Married, spouse absent.	-0.2	-2.4	-2.2	-1.9	-0.5
Separated	0.1	1.7	-0.7	-1.2	-0.2
Other reasons	-0.2	-4.0	-1.5	-0.8	-0.2
Widowed	-0.1	-3.3	-2.5	-1.6	-3.1
Divorced.	2.0	9.0	3.1	3.3	2.7
Single (never married).	1.3	-3.3	1.6	0.2	0.9
Black householders					
Total, 1983	100.0	100.0	100.0	100.0	100.0
Married, spouse present .	39.1	...	...	...	...
Married, spouse absent. .	12.5	20.8	23.6	22.0	12.8
Separated	11.3	18.6	21.9	19.1	10.9
Other reasons	1.2	2.2	1.7	2.9	1.9
Widowed	14.5	22.0	19.5	14.3	41.5
Divorced.	13.9	25.6	24.0	25.5	17.2
Single (never married). .	20.0	31.6	32.9	38.2	28.5
Total, 1978	100.0	100.0	100.0	100.0	100.0
Married, spouse present .	40.8	...	...	...	...
Married, spouse absent. .	15.1	27.8	29.6	25.8	17.0
Separated	13.3	22.2	26.5	22.2	14.9
Other reasons	1.8	5.6	3.1	3.6	2.1
Widowed	14.2	22.5	21.2	11.8	40.3
Divorced.	12.7	19.3	21.4	25.7	18.0
Single (never married). .	17.2	30.4	27.7	36.6	24.7
Change, 1978-83					
Married, spouse present	-1.7	...	...	...	...
Married, spouse absent.	-2.6	-7.0	-6.0	-3.8	-4.2
Separated	-2.0	-3.6	-4.6	-3.1	-4.0
Other reasons	-0.6	-3.4	-1.4	-0.7	-0.2
Widowed	0.3	-0.5	-1.7	2.5	1.2
Divorced.	1.2	6.3	2.6	-0.2	-0.8
Single (never married).	2.8	1.2	5.2	1.6	3.8
Spanish-origin					
Total, 1983	100.0	100.0	100.0	100.0	100.0
Married, spouse present .	59.9	...	...	...	...
Married, spouse absent. .	9.6	14.4	32.5	21.4	11.8
Separated	7.4	10.7	28.0	10.0	9.6
Other reasons	2.2	3.7	4.6	11.4	2.2
Widowed	6.8	18.4	15.7	4.8	32.6
Divorced.	10.6	26.3	38.2	22.8	26.3
Single (never married). .	13.0	40.9	23.5	51.1	29.3
Total, 1978	100.0	100.0	100.0	100.0	100.0
Married, spouse present .	63.6	...	...	...	...
Married, spouse absent. .	9.6	23.2	36.3	21.4	12.6
Separated	7.3	10.1	30.3	13.5	9.8
Other reasons	2.3	13.1	6.0	7.9	2.8
Widowed	6.2	16.0	16.3	8.4	30.0
Divorced.	8.8	19.6	27.7	18.4	25.1
Single (never married). .	11.7	41.2	19.7	51.9	32.3
Change, 1978-83					
Married, spouse present	-3.7	...	...	...	...
Married, spouse absent.	0.0	-8.8	-3.8	0.0	-0.8
Separated	0.1	0.6	-2.3	-3.5	-0.2
Other reasons	-0.1	-9.4	-1.4	3.5	-0.6
Widowed	0.6	2.4	-0.6	-3.6	2.6
Divorced.	1.8	6.7	0.6	4.4	1.2
Single (never married).	1.3	-0.3	3.8	-0.8	-3.0

Source: U.S. Bureau of the Census. "Household and Family Characteristics." Current Population Reports (Series P-20, nos. 388 and 340). Washington, DC: U.S. Government Printing Office, 1984 and 1979, Tables 21 and 20.

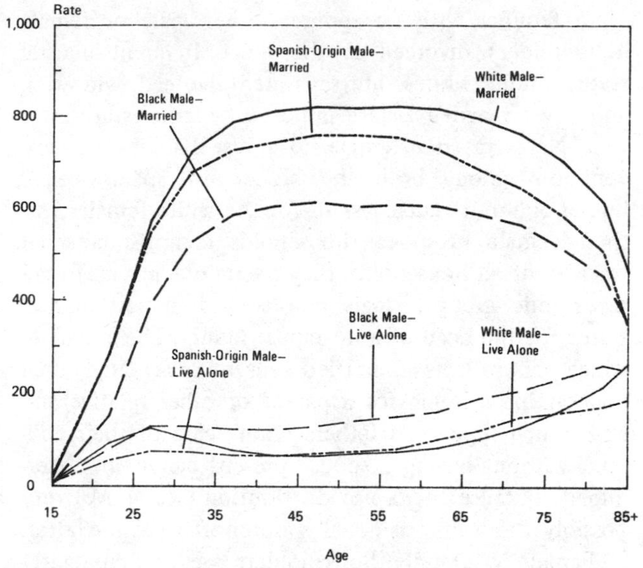

Figure 11-3A. Householder Rates for Males for Race-Ethnicity and Type of Household Groups, by Age: 1980

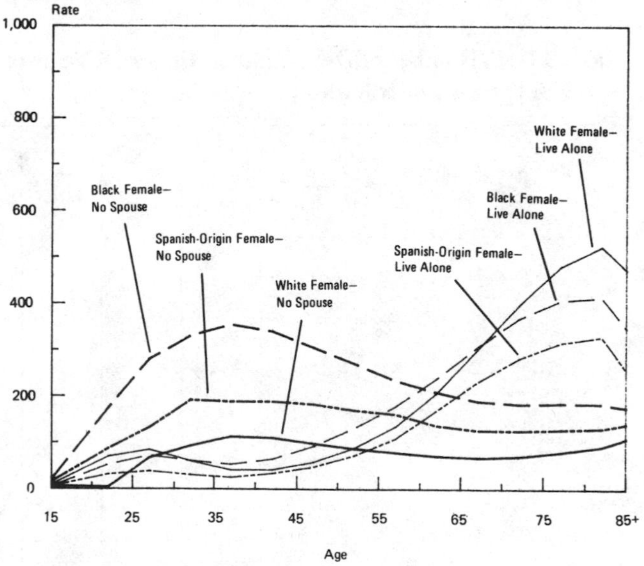

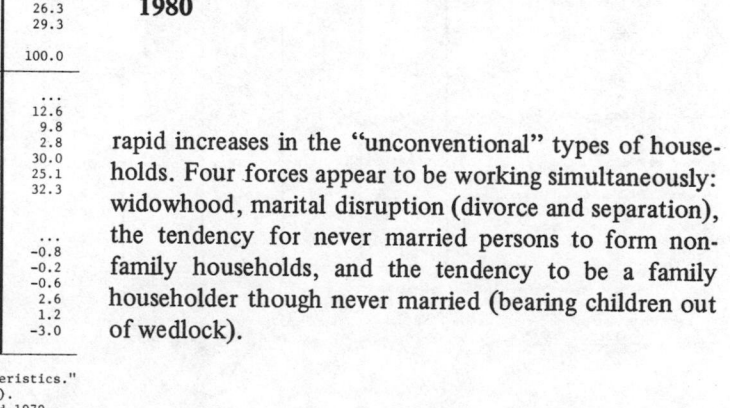

Figure 11-3B. Householder Rates for Females for Race-Ethnicity and Type of Household Groups, by Age: 1980

rapid increases in the "unconventional" types of households. Four forces appear to be working simultaneously: widowhood, marital disruption (divorce and separation), the tendency for never married persons to form nonfamily households, and the tendency to be a family householder though never married (bearing children out of wedlock).

In families with no spouse (either male or female householder) divorced is the most frequent marital status among whites, but separated/divorced, widowed, and never married all are important marital statuses as well. Never married female no-spouse families are very common among both the black and Spanish-origin households but much less so for the white females. Although male no-spouse households comprise a small fraction of all households, they are unique in that for all race-ethnic groups, singlehood is a dominant marital status for the head of a no-spouse family. The extent to which this reflects unmarried sons or other single men maintaining a home for a parent or other relative and how much represents fathers taking care of their children without having a spouse present cannot be determined. Because of its age distribution (see above) very possibly the former is equally as important as the latter.

Female nonfamily householders are predominantly widowed, while male nonfamily householders are predominantly single (never married). However, for both sexes a substantial proportion of the nonfamily householders have suffered separation or divorce.

Between 1978 and 1983 divorce became a more prevalent marital status for householders, while widowhood declined in relative importance. The increase in never married no-spouse family householders among blacks and the increase in divorced householders among all racial groups are spectacular for both sexes.

Children in Families

Barely one-half of all married couple families contained a child under eighteen years of age in 1982 (Table 11-10). Low fertility combined with longevity produce this result. By postponing childbearing or remaining childless, many couples of reproductive age reside in childless households. By surviving to an advanced age where all children have reached their eighteenth birthday and/or have left home, many older couples have "empty nest" families.

Families headed by a female without a spouse are much *more* likely to contain children. As has just been

Table 11-10. Number of Own Children Under 18 Years of Age, by Type of Family and Race-Ethnicity: 1982 and 1970 [percent distribution]

Number of own children under 18	Married couple families				Male household families				Female household families			
	Total	White	Black	Spanish-origin	Total	White	Black	Spanish-origin	Total	White	Black	Spanish-origin
1982												
Total.	100.0	100.0	100.0	100.0	100.0	100.0	100.0	100.0	100.0	100.0	100.0	100.0
No own children under 18	50.7	51.7	43.3	30.6	65.8	65.5	65.9	69.1	37.6	40.7	30.1	26.3
With own children under 18	49.3	48.3	56.7	69.4	34.2	34.5	34.1	30.9	62.4	59.3	69.9	73.7
1 own child under 18	19.4	19.2	21.0	23.3	21.0	21.7	19.4	18.5	28.6	29.6	26.2	28.6
2 own children under 18.	19.1	18.9	19.4	23.8	9.9	9.7	11.1	9.3	20.5	19.8	22.1	21.9
3 own children under 18.	7.4	7.1	9.8	12.8	2.1	2.2	1.4	1.8	8.7	6.8	13.3	12.5
4 own children under 18.	2.4	2.2	4.4	5.5	1.1	0.8	2.0	0.8	3.1	2.3	5.3	7.3
5 own children under 18.	0.7	0.6	1.4	2.3	0.1	0.1	0.2	0.0	0.9	0.5	2.1	1.7
6 or more own children under 18	0.3	0.3	0.7	1.6	0.0	0.0	0.0	0.5	0.5	0.4	0.9	1.6
1970												
Total.	100.0	100.0	100.0	100.0	100.0	100.0	100.0	100.0	100.0	100.0	100.0	100.0
No own children under 18	42.8	43.2	39.5	--	72.6	74.7	59.5	--	47.6	52.0	33.5	--
With own children under 18	57.2	56.8	60.5	--	27.4	25.3	40.5	--	52.4	48.0	66.5	--
1 own child under 18	18.3	18.3	17.6	--	13.9	13.9	14.2	--	18.8	18.8	19.1	--
2 own children under 18.	18.0	18.2	15.4	--	7.2	6.7	10.7	--	14.8	15.0	14.4	--
3 own children under 18.	11.0	11.1	9.5	--	2.9	2.6	4.7	--	8.9	7.8	12.4	--
4 own children under 18.	5.6	5.4	8.2	--	1.0	0.9	1.9	--	4.8	3.7	8.3	--
5 own children under 18.	2.4	2.2	4.4	--	1.4	0.6	5.4	--	2.6	1.7	5.4	--
6 or more own children under 18	2.0	1.7	5.4	--	1.1	0.6	3.7	--	2.5	1.0	6.9	--
Percent change 1970-1982												
No own children under 18	32.2	31.9	19.3	--	47.4	39.2	71.4	--	33.1	23.7	73.5	--
With own children under 18	-3.7	-6.2	1.9	--	102.7	116.0	31.0	--	100.6	95.6	102.8	--
1 own child under 18	18.4	15.9	30.3	--	146.7	147.2	112.0	--	156.0	149.7	164.7	--
2 own children under 18.	18.8	14.8	37.5	--	122.7	127.1	57.9	--	133.8	108.8	197.4	--
3 own children under 18.	-24.5	-28.8	12.7	--	20.0	33.3	-50.0	--	64.0	37.4	105.4	--
4 own children under 18.	-52.8	-55.7	-42.3	--	83.3	44.4	66.7	--	9.7	-1.9	24.1	--
5 own children under 18.	-68.4	-70.0	-66.4	--	-94.1	-85.7	--	--	-38.9	-54.3	-24.7	--
6 or more own children under 18	-81.0	-81.2	-85.9	--	-92.3	-83.3	--	--	-66.2	-43.2	-75.3	--

Note: -- indicates data not available.

Source: U.S. Bureau of the Census. "Household and Family Characteristics: March 1982," and "Household and Family Characteristics: March 1970." Current Population Reports (Series P-20, no. 381 and no. 218). Washington, DC: U.S. Government Printing Office, 1982 and 1971, Tables 2 and 1.

shown, these families are headed by women who have been divorced or separated, and a high percentage are still in the reproductive years. In a high proportion of cases such households constitute a family precisely because children are present.

Families headed by a male without a spouse are much *less* likely to contain children than those headed by females. Only about one-third of such families contain any children under eighteen. Thus, this type of family more frequently tends to be based on kinship other than parenthood.

Where households do contain children, a large proportion contain only one or two children. Only 11 percent of married couple families contained three or more children in 1982. As would be suspected from fertility data, Spanish-origin married couples and female no-spouse families are much more likely to contain children, and to contain three or more children, than white households. Black families in these categories also are more likely than whites to contain numerous children, but the proportions are substantially below those for the Spanish-origin population.

Families with a male no-spouse head are a little *more* likely to contain children if the householder is white, and *least* likely if the householder is of Spanish origin. Where children are present in male no-spouse households there tends to be only one child; three or more children in such families is extremely rare.

The trend since 1970 is toward an increase in childless families and a reduction in the number of children present in families. However, there has been a high rate of increase in the number of one-parent families because of the higher divorce and separation rates described in Chapter 4.

The trends in presence of children in families between 1970 and 1983 may be summarized by the following measures of percentage change over the interval:

Presence of children	Married couples	No spouse	
		Female head	Male head
Family households. .	11.6	72.2	64.2
No children.	33.1	42.0	44.2
With own children. . .	-4.6	100.1	116.1
One child.	19.2	162.7	166.5
Two children	16.9	129.5	134.5
Three or more chilren.	-43.9	16.4	-25.3

Thus, there was an absolute decline in the number of married couple families with children, caused by a very sharp decline in households with three or more children. However, the number of one-parent families doubled during this time.

Within the one-parent families the high rates of increase were in the one-child and two-child categories. The rate of increase in no-spouse families where children were not involved was only a fraction of the rate where children were involved.

Living Arrangements of Children

Because of declining fertility, there has been an absolute decline since 1970 in number of children under eighteen living in households. This loss is absorbed completely (and more) by a sharp decline in number of children living with both parents. There was a 54 percent increase in children living with one parent.

Table 11-11 provides summary information about the living arrangements of children. Increasing divorce has forced a rise in the proportions of children living with one parent, primarily the mother. Also, the rising tendency to bear children out of wedlock caused a huge percentage increase (243 percent) between 1970 and 1981 in the number of children living with a never married mother. Although the rate of increase for one-parent/father living arrangements are high, the proportion of children involved is still quite small but will accumulate to more significant proportions if these rates persist for only a few years.

Detailed information about the living arrangements of children, by race-ethnicity, for 1982 and 1970 are provided in Table 11-12. Both Tables 11-11 and 11-12 report that less than one-half of black children live with both parents. The proportion living with never married mothers (13 percent) is almost one-half as large as the proportion living with ever married mothers now separated, divorced, or widowed. Eleven percent of black children live with relatives, many as grandchildren of a mother who has assumed responsibility for care of children born by one of her children. Spanish-origin children live with both parents in 69 percent of the cases. Almost all of those not living with parents live with the mother; only 1.6 percent live with the father and 3.8 percent with neither parent. Figure 11-4 illustrates these differences and changes over time.

Information about living arrangements of children who live with one parent only is provided in Table 11-13, by race-ethnicity and age of child, and marital status/parent, with comparable data for 1970 to show change. The very great increase in the proportion of children living in a one-parent household where the parent has never married is extraordinary, not only for the black population but for the Spanish-origin and whites as well. This table shows that a spouse's service in the armed forces is a very minor reason for the increase in children living in one-parent households.

Table 11-11. Living Arrangements of Children Under 18 Years of Age: 1981 and 1970

Living arrangements of children and marital status of parent	All races					Black, 1981		
	1981		1970		Percent change 1970-81	Number	Percent	Percent of all races
	Number	Percent	Number	Percent				
Children under 18	62,918	100.0	69,162	100.0	-9.0	9,400	100.0	14.9
Living with:								
Two parents	48,040	76.4	58,939	85.2	-18.5	4,016	42.7	8.4
One parent.	12,619	20.1	8,199	11.9	53.9	4,310	45.9	34.2
Mother only	11,416	18.1	7,451	10.8	53.2	4,074	43.3	35.7
Divorced.	4,912	7.8	2,296	3.3	113.9	982	10.4	20.0
Married	3,540	5.6	3,234	4.7	9.5	1,492	15.9	42.1
Separated	3,112	4.9	2,332	3.4	33.4	1,385	14.7	44.5
Widowed	1,158	1.8	1,395	2.0	-17.0	355	3.8	30.7
Single (never married). . .	1,807	2.9	527	0.8	242.9	1,245	13.2	68.9
Father only	1,203	1.9	748	1.1	60.8	236	2.5	19.6
Divorced.	614	1.0	177	0.3	246.9	66	0.7	10.7
Married	296	0.5	287	0.4	3.1	79	0.8	26.7
Separated	261	0.4	152	0.2	71.7	65	0.7	24.9
Widowed	181	0.3	254	0.4	-28.7	40	0.4	22.1
Single (never married). . .	112	0.2	30	*	*	50	0.5	44.6
Other relatives only.	1,911	3.0	1,547	2.2	23.5	1,013	10.8	53.0
Nonrelatives only	348	0.6	477	0.7	-27.0	61	0.6	17.5

Note: * indicates numbers too small to report. All numbers are in thousands. Data exclude persons under 18 years of age who were maintaining families or subfamilies and their spouses.

Source: U.S. Bureau of the Census. "Marital Status and Living Arrangements: March, 1981." Current Population Reports (Series P-20, no. 372). Washington, DC: U.S. Government Printing Office, 1982.

Age of Youngest Child in Family

The age of the youngest child in a family places some limitations upon mothers and their ability to work or engage in other activities. The following tabulations summarize the proportion of families having children specified by ages, by family type and race, as of 1983.

Type of family and race-ethnicity	Percent with children			No child under 18 years
	Under 3	Under 6	Under 18	
All families.	13.6	22.5	50.2	49.8
Married couple. . .	14.3	23.0	48.8	51.2
Male, no spouse . .	5.5	10.0	36.5	63.5
Female, no spouse .	11.3	22.6	60.4	39.6
White families. . . .	13.2	21.7	48.7	51.3
Married couple. . .	14.1	22.5	48.0	52.0
Male, no spouse . .	5.4	9.7	36.3	63.7
Female, no spouse .	8.9	19.3	57.0	43.0
Black families. . . .	15.7	27.2	59.6	40.4
Married couple. . .	15.5	26.1	54.5	45.5
Male, no spouse . .	6.3	12.2	41.1	58.9
Female, no spouse .	17.0	30.2	68.1	31.9
Spanish-origin families.	21.4	36.5	68.4	31.6
Married couple. . .	23.7	39.4	69.2	30.8
Male, no spouse . .	8.3	12.3	34.2	65.8
Female, no spouse .	16.8	32.0	72.9	27.1

About 14 percent of all families have a child under three; 23 percent have a child under six; and 50 percent have a child under eighteen. By subtraction from 100, one can get data on percent of families with no children under three or under six. Spanish-origin families are much more likely to have very young children than white families. Black families have young children in proportions between these two extremes.

Children under three and under six are comparatively rare in families where the head is a male with no spouse; where there are children in such families, they tend to be older than six.

Unmarried Couples

In 1982 it was estimated that there were 1,863,000 couples of opposite sex sharing a housing unit while not married. Because a high proportion of them are young and of approximately the same age, it is widely assumed that they are cohabiting couples. A high percentage of them have never married. In about one-third of the cases there are children in the household. The householder is a female with a male partner in about 40 percent of the cases. Table 11-14 provides statistics about the age of

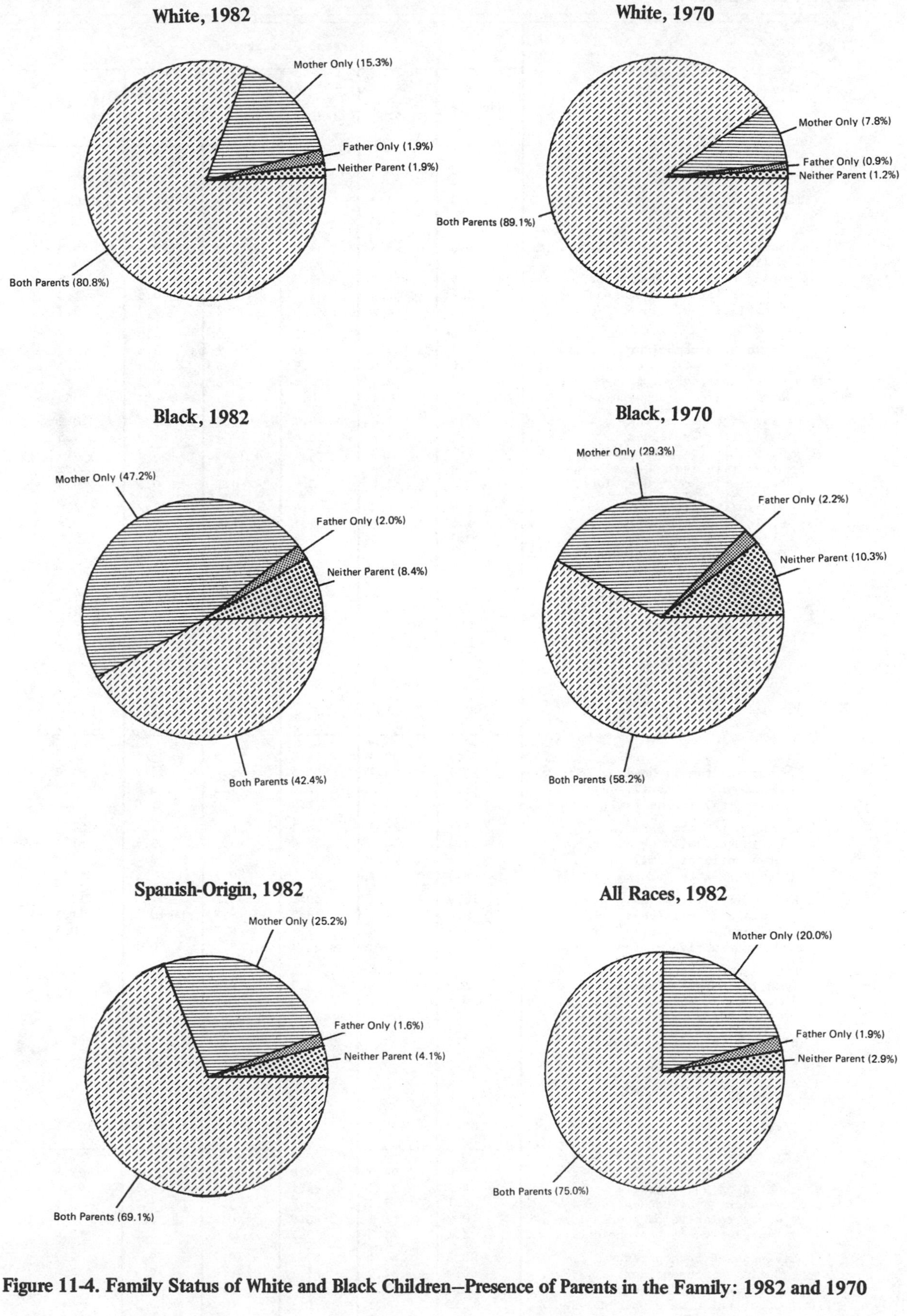

Figure 11-4. Family Status of White and Black Children–Presence of Parents in the Family: 1982 and 1970

Table 11-12. Household Relationship and Presence of Parents for Persons Under 18 Years of Age, by Age and Race-Ethnicity: 1982 and 1970

Subject	Percent distribution					
	Total under 18 years[a]	Under 3 years	3 to 5 years	6 to 9 years	10 to 14 years[b]	15 to 17 years[c]
All races--1982						
Total	100.0	100.0	100.0	100.0	100.0	100.0
In households	99.8	99.8	99.8	99.9	99.8	99.8
Child of householder.	92.7	88.0	91.7	93.3	94.5	94.6
Grandchild of householder	2.9	7.4	3.9	2.5	1.5	0.6
Other relative of householder . .	1.1	1.6	1.2	1.0	0.6	1.3
Nonrelative of householder. . . .	3.1	2.9	3.0	3.2	3.2	3.4
Living with both parents.	75.0	77.9	76.1	74.9	74.0	72.8
Child of householder.	74.1	75.7	75.0	74.1	73.6	72.7
Grandchild of householder	0.6	1.6	0.9	0.6	0.3	0.1
Other relative of householder . .	0.2	0.5	0.2	0.2	0.1	*
Nonrelative of householder. . . .	*	0.1	0.1	*	*	*
Living with mother only	20.0	18.2	19.9	20.6	20.7	20.2
Child of householder.	16.9	11.2	15.6	17.8	18.9	19.5
Grandchild of householder	2.1	5.4	2.7	1.7	1.0	0.4
Other relative of householder . .	0.4	0.9	0.7	0.5	0.2	0.1
Nonrelative of householder. . . .	0.6	0.7	0.9	0.7	0.6	0.3
Living with father only	1.9	1.5	1.5	1.6	2.2	2.6
Child of householder.	1.6	1.1	1.1	1.4	2.0	2.4
Grandchild of householder	0.2	0.3	0.3	0.2	0.1	0.1
Other relative of householder . .	*	*	*	*	*	*
Nonrelative of householder. . . .	*	*	*	*	*	*
Living with neither parent.	2.9	2.3	2.3	2.8	2.8	4.2
Relative of householder	2.5	2.0	2.0	2.5	2.6	3.1
Nonrelative of householder. . . .	0.4	0.3	0.2	0.3	0.2	1.1
In group quarters	0.2	0.2	0.2	0.1	0.2	0.2
All races--1970						
Total	100.0	100.0	100.0	100.0	100.0	100.0
In families	98.9	99.3	99.3	99.3	98.6	98.3
Child of family head.	94.7	91.7	94.6	96.0	95.7	94.2
Grandchild of family head	1.6	3.9	2.2	1.3	0.8	0.8
Other realtive of family head . .	2.6	3.6	2.5	2.0	2.0	3.3
Living with both parents.	84.7	86.3	86.3	86.0	84.3	81.4
Child of family head.	83.9	84.2	85.6	85.3	83.8	81.1
Grandchild of family head	0.6	1.9	0.6	0.5	0.4	0.2
Other relative of family head . .	0.1	0.2	0.1	0.1	0.1	*
Living with mother only	10.9	9.4	10.2	10.8	11.3	12.0
Child of family head.	9.8	7.1	8.5	9.9	10.8	11.3
Grandchild of family head	0.9	1.9	1.4	0.7	0.5	0.5
Other realtive of family head . .	0.2	0.3	0.3	0.2	0.1	0.2
Living with father only	1.1	0.5	0.6	0.9	1.2	1.9
Child of family head.	1.0	0.4	0.5	0.7	1.1	1.7
Grandchild of family head	0.1	0.1	0.1	0.1	*	*
Other relative of family head . .	*	*	*	*	*	*
Living with neither parent.	2.3	3.1	2.1	1.6	1.8	3.0
Not in families	1.1	0.7	0.7	0.7	1.4	1.7
White--1982						
Total	100.0	100.0	100.0	100.0	100.0	100.0
In households	99.9	99.9	99.8	99.9	99.9	99.9
Child of householder.	94.7	91.3	94.1	95.2	96.1	95.6
Grandchild of householder	2.1	5.2	2.7	2.0	1.2	0.5
Other relative of householder . .	0.9	1.3	0.9	0.7	0.4	1.4
Nonrelative of householder. . . .	2.1	2.0	2.1	2.0	2.2	2.4
Living with both parents.	80.8	85.1	82.3	80.7	79.6	77.7
Child of householder.	80.0	82.9	81.1	79.9	79.1	77.6
Grandchild of householder	0.7	1.6	0.9	0.6	0.3	0.1
Other relative of householder . .	0.2	0.5	0.2	0.2	0.1	*
Nonrelative of householder. . . .	*	0.1	*	*	*	*

Table 11-12. Household Relationship and Presence of Parents for Persons Under 18 Years of Age, by Age and Race-Ethnicity: 1982 and 1970–continued

Subject	Percent distribution: Total under 18 years[a]	Under 3 years	3 to 5 years	6 to 9 years	10 to 14 years[b]	15 to 17 years[c]
Living with mother only	15.3	12.1	14.9	16.1	16.4	16.2
Child of householder	13.1	7.5	11.9	13.9	14.9	15.7
Grandchild of householder	1.3	3.3	1.6	1.2	0.7	0.3
Other relative of householder	0.3	0.6	0.4	0.3	0.2	0.1
Nonrelative of householder	0.6	0.8	1.0	0.7	0.6	0.2
Living with father only	1.9	1.3	0.4	0.6	2.2	2.6
Child of householder	1.6	1.0	1.1	1.4	2.0	2.4
Grandchild of householder	0.2	0.3	0.2	0.2	0.1	0.1
Other relative of householder	*	*	*	*	*	*
Nonrelative of householder	*	*	*	*	*	*
Living with neither parent	1.9	1.4	1.2	1.5	1.7	3.4
Relative of householder	1.5	1.1	1.1	1.3	1.6	2.2
Nonrelative of householder	0.4	0.3	0.2	0.3	0.2	1.2
In group quarters	0.1	0.1	0.2	0.1	0.1	0.1
White--1970						
Total	100.0	100.0	100.0	100.0	100.0	100.0
In families	99.0	99.4	99.3	99.4	98.6	98.5
Child of family head	96.3	95.0	96.3	97.3	96.8	95.7
Grandchild of family head	1.3	3.0	1.7	1.0	0.7	0.7
Other relative of family head	1.4	1.4	1.3	1.1	1.1	2.1
Living with both parents	89.1	91.7	90.9	90.1	88.4	85.7
Child of family head	88.5	90.1	90.4	89.6	88.1	85.5
Grandchild of family head	0.5	1.5	0.5	0.5	0.3	0.2
Other relative of family head	*	0.2	*	0.1	*	*
Living with mother only	7.8	6.5	6.8	7.7	8.3	9.1
Child of family head	7.0	4.8	5.5	7.1	7.9	8.7
Grandchild of family head	0.7	1.5	1.1	0.5	0.3	0.3
Other relative of family head	0.2	0.3	0.2	0.1	0.1	0.2
Living with father only	0.9	0.2	0.6	0.7	0.9	1.7
Child of family head	0.8	0.2	0.5	0.6	0.9	1.5
Grandchild of family head	0.1	0.1	0.1	0.1	*	0.1
Other relative of family head	*	*	*	*	*	*
Living with neither parent	1.2	0.9	1.0	0.9	1.0	1.9
Not in families	1.0	0.6	0.7	0.6	1.4	1.5
Black--1982						
Total	100.0	100.0	100.0	100.0	100.0	100.0
In households	99.6	99.6	99.9	99.9	99.3	99.6
Child of householder	82.5	71.1	79.1	83.8	86.1	90.2
Grandchild of householder	7.0	18.4	10.1	4.9	3.2	1.0
Other relative of household	1.8	2.7	3.1	2.0	1.3	0.5
Nonrelative of householder	8.3	7.4	7.7	9.2	8.7	7.9
Living with both parents	42.4	40.1	41.0	42.9	42.6	45.4
Child of householder	42.0	38.8	40.5	42.6	42.4	45.3
Grandchild of householder	0.4	1.1	0.5	0.3	0.2	0.1
Other relative of householder	*	0.1	*	*	*	*
Nonrelative of householder	*	*	*	*	*	*
Living with mother only	47.2	50.5	49.3	46.5	46.0	44.4
Child of householder	38.9	30.9	37.3	40.0	41.8	42.7
Grandchild of householder	6.4	16.6	9.2	4.3	2.9	1.0
Other relative of householder	1.3	2.2	2.3	1.4	0.7	0.1
Nonrelative of householder	0.6	0.7	0.6	0.7	0.6	0.6
Living with father only	2.0	2.1	1.9	1.5	2.4	2.2
Child of householder	1.6	1.4	1.3	1.1	1.9	2.2
Grandchild of householder	0.3	0.6	0.4	0.3	0.2	*
Other realtive of householder	0.1	*	0.2	0.1	0.3	*
Nonrelative of householder	*	0.1	*	*	0.1	*
Living with neither parent	8.0	6.9	7.7	9.0	8.3	7.7
Relative fo householder	7.4	6.6	7.1	8.5	8.0	7.3
Nonrelative of householder	0.4	0.3	0.6	0.5	0.3	0.4
In group quarters	0.4	0.4	0.1	0.1	0.7	0.4

Table 11-12. Household Relationship and Presence of Parents for Persons Under 18 Years of Age, by Age and Race-Ethnicity: 1982 and 1970–continued

Subject	Percent distribution					
	Total under 18 years[a]	Under 3 years	3 to 5 years	6 to 9 years	10 to 14 years[b]	15 to 17 years[c]
Black--1970						
Total	100.0	100.0	100.0	100.0	100.0	100.0
In families	98.3	98.7	99.0	98.8	98.2	97.0
Child of family head	85.3	75.9	85.9	88.8	88.6	84.7
Grandchild of family head	3.4	7.8	4.0	2.7	1.7	2.0
Other realtive of family head	9.6	15.0	9.1	7.2	7.8	10.4
Living with both parents	58.2	58.3	61.5	61.7	57.2	52.2
Child of family head	56.8	54.7	59.8	60.6	56.5	51.8
Grandchild of family head	1.1	3.4	1.3	0.7	0.3	0.3
Other relative of family head	0.3	0.2	0.4	0.5	0.4	*
Living with mother only	29.3	24.3	28.8	29.1	31.4	31.7
Child of family head	26.5	19.4	25.3	27.0	29.5	29.4
Grandchild of family head	2.2	4.3	2.7	1.6	1.4	1.6
Other relative of family head	0.6	0.5	0.8	0.5	0.5	0.6
Living with father only	2.2	1.9	1.1	1.8	2.8	3.4
Child of family head	2.0	1.7	0.8	1.2	2.6	3.4
Grandchild of family head	0.2	0.1	0.1	0.4	0.1	0.1
Other relative of family head	0.1	*	0.2	0.1	*	*
Living with neither parent	8.6	14.2	7.7	6.1	6.8	9.7
Not in families	1.7	1.3	1.0	1.2	1.8	3.0
Spanish-origin[d]--1982						
Total	100.0	100.0	100.0	100.0	100.0	100.0
In households	99.7	99.5	99.1	99.9	99.8	99.8
Child of householder	90.7	84.8	91.1	92.7	92.6	90.9
Grandchild of householder	2.9	7.0	3.2	2.5	1.5	0.7
Other relative of householder	1.9	3.4	2.2	1.4	0.8	2.6
Nonrelative of householder	4.2	4.3	2.6	3.3	4.9	5.5
Living with both parents	69.1	73.2	71.3	70.0	65.9	65.8
Child of householder	67.2	68.3	69.7	68.6	64.9	65.2
Grandchild of householder	1.1	2.8	0.9	0.9	0.7	0.2
Other relative of householder	0.7	1.9	0.7	0.5	0.3	0.4
Nonrelative of householder	*	0.2	*	*	*	*
Living with mother only	25.2	22.0	25.3	26.0	27.2	24.6
Child of householder	22.2	15.8	21.0	23.0	25.5	23.9
Grandchild of householder	1.7	4.0	2.0	1.5	0.8	0.3
Other relative of householder	0.7	1.1	1.4	0.8	0.3	0.2
Nonrelative of householder	0.7	1.0	0.8	0.6	0.6	0.2
Living with father only	1.6	0.9	0.6	1.3	2.3	2.3
Child of householder	1.3	0.7	0.3	1.1	2.2	1.8
Grandchild of householder	0.1	0.2	0.3	0.1	0.1	0.2
Other relative of householder	0.1	*	*	*	0.1	0.3
Nonrelative of householder	0.1	*	*	0.1	0.1	0.1
Living with neither parent	3.8	3.5	1.9	2.6	4.3	7.0
Relative of householder	3.4	3.2	1.8	2.6	4.3	5.2
Nonrelative of householder	0.4	0.3	0.1	0.1	0.1	1.9
In group quarters	0.3	0.5	0.9	0.1	0.2	0.2

[a]Excludes persons under 18 years who are husbands or wives, and other persons maintaining households or related and unrelated subfamilies.

[b]10 to 13 years in 1970, 10 to 14 years in 1982.

[c]14 to 17 years in 1970, 15 to 17 years in 1982.

[d]Spanish-origin persons may be of any race.

Note: * indicates less than 0.1. Data for 1970 do not show relationship of the small fraction of children not living in family households.

Source: U.S. Bureau of the Census. "Marital Status and Living Arrangements." Current Population Reports (Series P-20, nos. 380 and 212). Washington, DC: U.S. Government Printing Office, 1983 and 1971, Table 4.

Table 11-13. Presence and Marital Status of Parent for Persons Under 18 Years of Age Living with Only One Parent, by Age and Race-Ethnicity: 1982 and 1970

Subject	Percent distribution					
	Total, under 18 years[a]	Under 3 years	3 to 5 years	6 to 9 years	10 to 14 years[b]	15 to 17 years[c]
All races--1982						
Total	100.0	100.0	100.0	100.0	100.0	100.0
Living with mother only	91.3	92.6	93.1	92.8	90.5	88.5
Single (never married)	20.2	47.6	28.4	19.6	11.2	6.4
Husband absent	25.7	25.1	27.9	26.7	25.6	23.4
Husband in armed forces	0.4	0.7	0.6	0.7	0.2	0.1
Separated	22.6	21.1	24.3	23.3	23.3	20.7
Other	2.7	3.3	3.0	2.7	2.1	2.7
Widowed	8.2	1.9	4.2	6.2	10.2	15.7
Divorced	37.2	18.0	32.6	40.4	43.6	43.1
Mother, householder	77.1	56.9	72.7	80.1	82.5	85.3
Single (never married)	13.9	24.5	20.1	15.6	9.3	5.9
Husband absent	22.3	17.6	22.8	23.2	23.5	22.8
Husband in armed forces	0.3	0.1	0.3	0.7	0.2	0.1
Separated	20.0	15.6	20.2	20.6	21.6	20.1
Other	2.0	1.9	2.2	1.9	1.8	2.6
Widowed	7.4	0.8	2.7	5.6	9.4	15.1
Divorced	33.5	14.0	27.0	35.7	40.3	41.5
Living with father only	8.7	7.4	6.9	7.2	9.5	11.5
Single (never married)	0.8	3.2	0.9	0.5	0.1	0.4
Wife absent	2.0	1.4	1.9	1.7	2.2	2.5
Separated	1.9	1.3	1.9	1.6	2.1	2.2
Other	0.1	0.1	*	0.1	0.1	0.2
Widowed	1.1	0.1	0.2	0.6	1.2	2.8
Divorced	4.8	2.8	3.9	4.4	6.0	5.8
Father, householder	7.5	5.6	5.3	6.2	8.5	10.6
Single (never married)	0.6	2.2	0.5	0.4	0.1	0.2
Wife absent	1.7	1.1	1.6	1.4	2.0	2.3
Separated	1.6	1.0	1.6	1.3	1.9	2.1
Other	0.1	0.1	*	0.1	0.1	0.2
Widowed	1.0	*	0.2	0.5	1.0	2.7
Divorced	4.3	2.4	3.0	3.9	5.4	5.4
All races--1970						
Total	100.0	100.0	100.0	100.0	100.0	100.0
Living with mother only	91.0	95.0	94.0	92.5	90.7	86.3
Single (never married)	6.7	16.0	10.8	6.5	3.5	3.1
Husband absent	39.7	56.6	47.8	39.8	36.0	30.7
Husband in armed forces	4.4	12.4	5.3	4.4	3.4	1.1
Separated	28.6	36.7	35.0	29.2	26.5	22.5
Other	6.7	7.5	7.4	6.2	6.1	6.9
Widowed	16.8	5.0	7.4	14.0	21.2	26.3
Divorced	28.3	17.4	28.1	32.1	30.1	26.2
Mother, head of family	81.8	72.1	78.3	85.2	86.2	81.2
Single (never married)	6.5	15.4	10.7	6.5	3.5	2.9
Husband absent	34.2	38.9	38.9	35.8	33.6	28.4
Husband in armed forces	3.4	7.4	3.8	3.9	3.3	1.0
Separated	24.6	25.6	29.2	26.1	24.3	20.8
Other	6.1	5.9	6.0	5.7	6.0	6.9
Widowed	16.1	4.4	6.2	13.4	20.5	25.5
Divorced	25.0	13.3	22.5	29.5	28.6	24.4
Living with father only	9.0	5.1	6.0	7.5	9.3	13.7
Single (never married)	0.4	0.5	0.7	0.2	0.1	0.7
Wife absent	3.6	3.5	2.9	3.5	3.5	4.0
Separated	1.9	1.1	1.1	1.9	2.2	2.3
Other	1.7	2.4	1.9	1.5	1.2	1.7
Widowed	3.1	0.6	0.6	2.1	3.8	6.0
Divorced	2.0	0.6	1.8	1.7	2.0	3.1
Father, head of family	8.0	4.2	4.7	6.3	8.8	12.6
Single (never married)	0.4	0.3	0.7	0.2	0.1	0.7
Wife absent	3.1	3.1	2.2	2.8	3.4	3.7
Separated	1.6	1.0	0.6	1.5	2.1	2.1
Other	1.6	2.1	1.8	1.3	1.2	1.6
Widowed	2.8	0.6	0.6	2.0	3.5	5.3
Divorced	1.7	0.3	1.2	1.4	1.8	2.9

Table 11-13. Presence and Marital Status of Parent for Persons Under 18 Years of Age Living with Only One Parent, by Age and Race-Ethnicity: 1982 and 1970—continued

Subject	Percent Distribution					
	Total, under 18 years[a]	Under 3 years	3 to 5 years	6 to 9 years	10 to 14 years[b]	15 to 17 years[c]
White--1982						
Total	100.0	100.0	100.0	100.0	100.0	100.0
Living with mother only	89.2	90.5	91.6	90.8	88.3	86.2
Single (never married)	9.0	30.2	13.3	7.3	4.2	1.4
Husband absent	24.8	31.5	29.0	26.8	22.1	19.4
Husband in armed forces	0.6	1.3	0.7	1.0	0.2	0.1
Separated	21.1	25.6	25.1	23.0	19.2	16.1
Other	3.1	4.6	3.2	2.8	2.6	3.2
Widowed	8.6	2.1	4.6	6.2	10.2	16.1
Divorced	46.7	26.7	44.6	50.5	51.9	49.4
Mother, householder	76.3	55.8	73.0	78.5	80.7	83.2
Single (never married)	5.6	14.7	9.9	5.2	2.8	1.1
Husband absent	21.1	20.2	23.4	23.1	20.7	18.7
Husband in armed forces	0.4	0.2	0.3	1.0	0.2	0.1
Separated	18.3	17.5	20.8	19.8	18.1	15.5
Other	2.5	2.5	2.3	2.2	2.3	3.1
Widowed	7.7	0.8	3.0	5.7	9.2	15.5
Divorced	41.9	20.2	36.9	44.5	47.9	47.9
Living with father only	10.8	9.5	8.4	9.2	11.7	13.8
Single (never married)	0.7	3.8	0.5	0.3	*	0.4
Wife absent	2.7	2.0	2.5	2.2	2.9	3.2
Separated	2.5	1.8	2.5	2.0	2.7	2.8
Other	0.2	0.2	*	0.2	0.2	0.3
Widowed	1.2	0.3	0.3	0.6	1.4	2.8
Divorced	6.2	3.4	5.1	6.1	7.4	7.4
Father, householder	9.5	7.4	6.8	8.1	10.8	12.6
Single (never married)	0.5	3.0	0.2	0.2	*	0.1
Wife absent	2.4	1.5	2.2	1.9	2.8	3.0
Separated	2.2	1.4	2.2	1.7	2.6	2.7
Other	0.2	0.2	*	0.2	0.2	0.3
Widowed	1.1	0.1	0.3	0.6	1.1	2.7
Divorced	5.6	2.9	4.0	5.4	6.8	6.8
White--1970						
Total	100.0	100.0	100.0	100.0	100.0	100.0
Living with mother only	89.7	96.3	92.2	91.5	89.9	84.2
Single (never married)	2.1	8.9	2.6	1.4	0.6	1.0
Husband absent	32.6	56.0	42.1	32.9	28.4	22.1
Husband in armed forces	5.5	17.0	5.7	5.9	4.4	1.2
Separated	19.9	30.3	27.8	20.7	17.5	1.2
Other	7.2	8.7	8.8	6.3	6.5	13.5
Widowed	19.3	4.6	7.7	15.8	23.3	30.0
Divorced	35.8	26.7	39.8	41.4	37.6	31.2
Mother, head of family	80.6	70.7	74.5	84.2	85.9	79.8
Single (never married)	2.1	8.7	2.6	1.4	0.6	1.0
Husband absent	28.1	37.8	34.5	30.0	26.8	20.6
Husband in armed forces	4.2	9.9	3.8	5.1	4.3	1.1
Separated	17.4	21.0	24.1	19.1	16.4	12.2
Other	6.6	7.2	6.7	5.9	6.1	7.3
Widowed	18.3	4.1	6.0	14.9	22.5	29.0
Divorced	32.1	20.1	31.4	37.9	36.0	29.1
Living with father only	10.3	3.7	7.8	8.5	10.1	15.8
Single (never married)	0.5	0.8	1.0	0.3	0.2	0.6
Wife absent	3.5	2.3	3.2	3.5	3.3	4.1
Separated	2.1	0.6	1.2	2.3	2.2	2.7
Other	1.4	1.6	2.0	1.2	1.1	1.4
Widowed	3.4	*	0.6	2.3	3.9	6.5
Divorced	3.0	0.6	3.0	2.5	2.7	4.6
Father, head of family	9.1	2.6	6.2	7.6	9.5	14.1
Single (never married)	0.4	0.5	1.0	0.3	0.1	0.6
Wife absent	3.1	1.9	2.6	3.1	3.3	3.7
Separated	1.8	0.7	0.6	2.0	2.1	2.4
Other	1.3	1.2	2.0	1.2	1.1	1.3
Widowed	3.0	*	0.6	2.2	3.5	5.5
Divorced	2.5	0.2	2.0	2.0	2.5	4.2

Table 11-13. Presence and Marital Status of Parent for Persons Under 18 Years of Age Living with Only One Parent, by Age and Race-Ethnicity: 1982 and 1970—continued

Subject	Percent distribution					
	Total, under 18 years[a]	Under 3 years	3 to 5 years	6 to 9 years	10 to 14 years[b]	15 to 17 years[c]
Black--1982						
Total.	100.0	100.0	100.0	100.0	100.0	100.0
Living with mother only.	95.8	96.0	96.3	96.9	95.1	95.2
Single (never married)	42.2	70.6	54.8	45.3	26.5	18.4
Husband absent	27.6	17.3	26.1	26.3	33.1	33.6
Husband in armed forces. . . .	0.1	*	*	*	*	*
Separated.	25.9	15.6	23.0	24.2	32.4	32.1
Other.	1.6	1.7	2.7	2.1	0.8	1.5
Widowed.	6.6	1.3	3.3	5.0	9.4	13.4
Divorced	19.4	6.7	12.1	20.2	26.0	29.8
Mother, householder.	79.1	58.8	72.8	83.5	86.4	91.8
Single (never married)	30.4	37.3	38.2	37.3	23.6	17.5
Husband absent	24.7	14.5	21.6	23.4	29.8	33.1
Husband in armed forces. . . .	0.1	*	0.4	*	*	*
Separated.	23.5	13.2	19.2	22.2	29.4	31.6
Other.	1.1	1.2	2.0	1.2	0.4	1.5
Widowed.	6.0	0.7	2.1	4.3	9.0	13.1
Divorced	17.9	6.3	10.9	18.6	23.9	28.1
Living with father only.	4.2	4.0	3.7	3.1	4.9	4.8
Single (never married)	1.1	2.3	1.5	1.1	0.3	0.4
Wife absent.	0.6	0.5	0.5	0.5	0.8	0.7
Separated.	0.6	0.5	0.5	0.5	0.8	0.7
Other.	*	*	*	*	*	*
Widowed.	0.5	*	*	0.3	0.7	1.7
Divorced	1.9	1.2	1.7	1.3	3.0	1.9
Father, householder.	3.2	2.6	2.5	2.3	3.9	4.7
Single (never married)	0.7	1.1	1.1	0.9	0.2	0.4
Wife absent.	0.3	0.5	0.2	0.1	0.3	0.7
Separated.	0.3	0.5	0.2	0.1	0.3	0.7
Other.	*	*	*	*	*	*
Widowed.	0.5	*	*	0.3	0.7	1.7
Divorced	1.7	1.0	1.2	1.1	2.7	1.9
Black--1970						
Total.	100.0	100.0	100.0	100.0	100.0	100.0
Living with mother only.	92.9	92.9	96.5	94.2	91.9	90.3
Single (never married)	14.4	25.4	22.3	14.9	8.6	7.4
Husband absent	51.3	57.1	54.8	50.8	49.3	48.0
Husband in armed forces. . . .	2.6	6.1	4.7	1.9	1.6	0.9
Separated.	42.9	44.7	44.2	43.0	42.2	41.4
Other.	5.8	6.1	5.9	6.0	5.6	5.7
Widowed.	13.1	5.7	7.6	11.5	17.1	19.0
Divorced	14.1	4.8	11.7	16.9	16.8	15.9
Mother, head of family	84.1	74.2	84.7	87.3	86.4	83.9
Single (never married)	14.1	24.3	22.1	14.8	8.7	6.9
Husband absent	44.5	40.8	46.0	45.4	45.4	43.9
Husband in armed forces. . . .	2.2	4.1	3.7	1.9	1.6	0.9
Separated.	37.0	32.4	37.0	38.1	38.2	37.1
Other.	5.4	4.3	5.3	5.4	5.6	5.7
Widowed.	12.7	5.0	7.0	11.2	17.0	18.4
Divorced	12.8	4.1	9.6	15.9	15.3	14.7
Living with father only.	7.1	7.1	3.5	5.8	8.1	9.7
Single (never married)	0.2	*	0.2	*	*	0.7
Wife absent.	3.9	5.5	2.7	3.7	3.8	3.7
Separated.	1.7	1.8	1.0	1.7	2.2	1.6
Other.	2.2	3.7	1.8	2.1	1.6	2.1
Widowed.	2.8	1.4	0.6	1.9	3.8	5.0
Divorced	0.2	0.2	*	0.1	0.4	0.3
Father, head of family	6.3	6.6	2.5	4.1	7.7	9.6
Single (never married)	0.2	*	0.2	*	*	0.7
Wife absent.	3.2	5.0	1.8	2.4	3.7	3.6
Separated.	1.3	1.4	0.2	0.9	2.1	1.4
Other.	2.0	3.5	1.6	1.5	1.6	2.1
Widowed.	2.7	1.4	0.6	1.6	3.6	5.0
Divorced	0.2	0.3	*	*	0.4	0.3

Table 11-13. Presence and Marital Status of Parent for Persons Under 18 Years of Age Living with Only One Parent, by Age and Race-Ethnicity: 1982 and 1970—continued

Subject	Percent distribution					
	Total, under 18 years[a]	Under 3 years	3 to 5 years	6 to 9 years	10 to 14 years[b]	15 to 17 years[c]
Spanish-origin[d]--1982						
Total.	100.0	100.0	100.0	100.0	100.0	100.0
Living with mother only.	94.2	96.2	97.5	95.1	92.0	91.5
Single (never married)	20.2	45.5	29.5	19.3	10.1	6.3
Husband absent	37.8	37.1	41.8	39.0	37.5	33.1
Husband in armed forces. . . .	0.3	1.3	0.7	*	*	*
Separated.	32.3	29.8	36.2	34.1	31.7	28.8
Other.	5.2	6.1	4.9	4.9	5.7	4.2
Widowed.	8.5	0.8	4.3	7.9	11.9	15.4
Divorced	27.6	12.8	21.9	29.0	32.7	36.7
Mother, householder.	82.8	69.1	81.2	84.2	86.5	88.9
Single (never married)	16.0	29.3	24.0	17.0	9.0	6.3
Husband absent	33.7	28.5	34.6	34.3	36.3	32.3
Husband in armed forces. . . .	*	*	*	*	*	*
Separated.	29.2	24.5	31.1	29.7	30.8	28.1
Other.	4.5	4.0	3.5	4.6	5.5	4.2
Widowed.	7.8	0.3	3.4	7.6	10.8	14.2
Divorced	25.3	11.1	19.2	25.3	30.4	36.1
Living with father only.	5.8	3.8	2.5	4.9	8.0	8.5
Single (never married)	0.8	2.2	0.9	0.6	*	0.9
Wife absent.	1.4	1.2	0.5	0.7	1.8	3.1
Separated.	1.2	1.0	0.5	0.2	1.8	2.7
Other.	0.2	0.2	*	0.5	*	0.4
Widowed.	1.0	*	*	1.1	1.4	2.4
Divorced	2.5	0.4	1.0	2.5	4.7	2.0
Father, householder.	4.8	2.9	1.3	4.1	7.3	6.5
Single (never married)	0.3	1.5	0.2	0.4	*	*
Wife absent.	1.1	1.0	0.1	0.6	1.6	2.0
Separated.	1.0	1.0	0.1	0.2	1.6	2.0
Other.	0.1	*	*	0.3	*	*
Widowed.	1.0	*	*	0.7	1.4	2.4
Divorced	2.4	0.4	1.0	2.5	4.3	2.0

[a]Excludes persons under 18 years who are husbands or wives, and other persons maintaining households or related and unrelated subfamilies.

[b]10 to 13 years in 1970, 10 to 14 years in 1982.

[c]14 to 17 years in 1970, 15 to 17 years in 1982.

[d]Spanish-origin persons may be of any race.

Note: * indicates less than 0.1. Due to rounding, the sum of the subcategories may not equal the main categories.

Source: U.S. Bureau of the Census. "Marital Status and Living Arrangements." Current Population Reports (Series P-20, nos. 380 and 212). Washington, DC: U.S. Government Printing Office, 1983 and 1971, Table 5.

such couples. Of all women participating in such living arrangements, 77 percent are younger than thirty-five, as are 66 percent of the men in this category. Only about 5 percent of such couples includes partners aged sixty-five or over.

Some further details of the age, marital status, and presence of children for these couples are reported in Table 11-15. The strong emphasis on youth, on single or divorced partners, and on the comparative scarcity of children is evident. Female householders in such couples tend to be a little older and to have older partners than male householders in this class.

Subfamilies

About 4 percent of all family households contain a "family within the family," or subfamily. Most common is a divorced or separated but never married daughter with one or more children living in the home of her parents. A second common situation is that of a young married couple (with or without children) living in the home of the parents of either the husband or the wife. Subfamilies can also consist of an elderly couple living in the home of one of their children. In 1983 there were 2,220,000 such families, with the composition shown in Table 11-16.

There had been a long-term decline in the share of married couple subfamilies and a steady rise in the prevalence of mother-child households. There was an unprecedented fluctuation upward between 1981 and 1983 in the number of subfamilies, and most of this was in mother-child subfamilies.

Table 11-17 shows selected characteristics of subfamilies. The lead person in the subfamily is termed a "reference person." The male reference person subfamilies are predominantly married couple subfamilies, whereas the female reference person subfamilies are predominantly mother-child families. The female reference person is therefore a divorced, separated, or never married person.

Subfamilies occur much more frequently among black and Spanish-origin populations than among white, as shown by the percent of total family households comprised of subfamilies, for each race-ethnic group.

Race-ethnicity	Sum	Type of subfamily		
		Married couple	Father-couple	Mother-couple
All races. .	3.62	1.17	0.24	2.21
White.	2.53	1.10	0.19	1.24
Black.	11.84	1.12	0.61	10.11
Spanish-origin	7.01	3.24	0.30	3.47

Source: U.S. Bureau of the Census. Current Population Reports (Series P-20, no. 388), 1984, Table 14.

A mother-child subfamily is found in 10 percent of black households—eight times the frequency for white and three times the frequency for Spanish-origin families. Spanish-origin families, in sharp contrast to both black and white families, are more likely to contain a married couple subfamily.

As Table 11-17 shows, subfamilies are not large. They usually consist of a husband and wife only or a parent and child. In most cases where the subfamily contains children, it is only one child.

Table 11-14. Unmarried Couples, by Age of Partners: 1982 [numbers in thousands]

Age of man	All unmarried couples	Age of woman				
		Under 25 years	25 to 34 years	35 to 44 years	45 to 64 years	65 years and over
Total number.	1,863	704	735	154	181	90
Under 25 years.	430	352	62	9	2	5
25 to 34 years.	804	293	467	37	4	4
35 to 44 years.	292	47	155	68	19	3
45 to 64 years.	242	10	47	40	120	24
65 years and over . . .	94	1	4	*	36	54
Percent	100.0	37.8	39.5	8.3	9.7	4.8
Under 25 years.	23.1	18.9	3.3	0.5	0.1	0.3
25 to 34 years.	43.2	15.7	25.1	2.0	0.2	0.2
35 to 44 years.	15.7	2.5	8.3	3.7	1.0	0.2
45 to 64 years.	13.0	0.5	2.5	2.1	6.4	1.3
65 years and over . . .	5.0	0.1	0.2	*	1.9	2.9

Note: * indicates insufficient numbers to report.

Source: U.S. Bureau of the Census. "Households, Families, Marital Status, and Living Arrangements: March, 1982 (Advance Report)." Current Population Reports (Series P-20, no. 376). Washington, DC: U.S. Government Printing Office, 1982.

Table 11-15. Presence of Children in Households of Two Unrelated Adults, by Marital Status, Age, and Sex of Householder: 1982

Subject	Households of two unrelated adults	Age of householder (years): Under 25	25 to 34	35 to 44	45 to 64	65 and over	Marital status of householder: Single (never married)	Married, spouse absent: Separated	Other	Widowed	Divorced
Male Householder, 1982											
Total.	100.0	100.0	100.0	100.0	100.0	100.0	100.0	100.0	100.0	100.0	100.0
No children in household											
Partner of opposite sex.	77.0	80.0	75.1	68.5	82.2	94.6	83.0	60.8	100.0	88.4	67.6
Age of partner:											
Under 25	34.4	72.1	33.1	13.7	3.7	*	45.6	22.5	9.5	*	23.3
25 to 34	27.2	7.5	39.9	37.8	17.0	3.5	29.2	21.2	47.6	4.7	26.4
35 to 44	5.1	0.4	2.0	14.2	16.3	*	3.3	10.6	4.8	4.7	7.0
45 to 64	6.9	*	*	2.7	38.5	40.3	2.1	5.3	33.3	55.8	8.6
65 and over.	3.3	*	0.2	*	6.7	50.8	2.9	1.3	4.8	23.2	2.3
Marital status of partner:											
Single (never married) . . .	50.5	75.3	55.6	32.6	20.7	12.3	67.8	28.4	35.0	4.8	31.7
Married, spouse absent . . .	4.2	2.2	3.6	5.0	8.1	8.8	3.0	10.8	50.0	4.8	2.3
Separated.	3.3	2.2	13.2	3.3	4.4	7.0	3.0	10.8	*	4.8	2.3
Widowed.	5.0	*	0.2	1.1	19.3	50.8	2.1	4.0	*	50.2	5.5
Divorced	17.3	2.5	15.8	29.8	34.1	22.8	10.0	17.6	15.0	28.7	28.1
With children in household											
Partner of opposite sex.	23.0	20.0	24.9	31.5	17.8	5.4	17.0	39.2	*	11.6	32.4
Age of partner:											
Under 25	8.7	16.4	8.7	5.5	*	1.8	9.3	13.5	*	*	8.3
25 to 34	11.1	3.6	15.3	17.1	7.4	*	7.0	13.5	*	1.9	19.2
35 to 44	2.3	*	0.8	7.7	5.9	*	0.3	9.5	*	7.8	3.6
45 to 64	0.8	*	*	1.1	3.7	3.6	0.3	2.7	*	*	1.3
65 and over.	0.1	*	*	*	0.7	*	*	*	*	1.9	*
Marital status of partner:											
Single (never married) . . .	9.4	9.6	11.2	8.7	5.2	1.8	9.0	16.2	*	*	10.1
Married, spouse absent . . .	2.6	1.8	3.0	5.4	0.7	*	1.1	10.8	*	*	3.9
Separated.	2.6	1.8	3.0	5.4	0.7	*	1.1	10.8	*	*	3.9
Widowed.	0.8	*	0.6	1.6	0.7	3.6	0.3	2.7	*	5.8	0.8
Divorced	10.2	8.6	10.0	15.7	11.1	*	6.5	9.5	*	5.8	17.6
Female Householder, 1982											
Total.	100.0	100.0	100.0	100.0	100.0	100.0	100.0	100.0	100.0	100.0	100.0
No children in household											
Partner of opposite sex.	70.4	72.8	58.2	64.7	93.5	96.2	77.8	48.3	100.0	93.0	57.8
Age of partner:											
Under 25	14.8	36.9	6.5	4.4	2.2	9.6	24.6	3.3	*	5.5	6.1
25 to 34	27.1	30.0	38.0	22.1	1.1	5.8	40.5	13.3	*	2.8	18.7
35 to 44	10.4	4.9	10.3	29.4	12.1	5.8	8.1	6.7	*	4.2	17.0
45 to 64	12.7	1.0	2.7	8.8	66.0	26.9	2.0	25.0	100.0	48.6	13.5
65 and over.	5.4	*	0.7	*	12.1	48.1	2.6	*	*	32.0	2.6
Marital status of partner:											
Single (never married) . . .	36.8	54.9	35.8	19.1	13.0	33.4	57.4	16.7	33.3	23.9	15.2
Married, spouse absent . . .	6.8	3.4	4.5	10.3	21.7	4.0	4.9	20.0	66.7	12.7	3.9
Separated.	6.1	2.4	3.4	8.8	21.7	4.0	3.5	20.0	66.7	12.7	3.9
Widowed.	3.4	*	0.3	*	10.9	25.5	0.9	*	*	19.7	2.6
Divorced	23.5	14.5	17.7	35.3	47.8	33.4	14.6	11.7	*	36.6	36.1
With children in household											
Partner of opposite sex.	29.6	27.2	41.8	35.3	6.5	3.9	22.3	51.7	*	7.0	42.2
Age of partner:											
Under 25	6.3	14.3	4.1	6.1	*	*	6.4	13.0	*	1.4	6.1
25 to 34	15.8	10.4	27.4	12.3	2.8	*	12.4	19.3	*	2.8	24.3
35 to 44	5.1	1.0	8.2	12.3	0.9	*	2.6	11.3	*	*	8.7
45 to 64	2.4	1.5	2.1	4.6	2.8	3.9	0.9	8.0	*	2.8	3.0
65 and over.	*	*	*	*	*	*	*	*	*	*	*
Marital status of partner:											
Single (never married) . . .	15.6	20.4	.18.2	19.1	2.2	3.9	16.1	21.7	*	7.0	16.5
Married, spouse absent . . .	2.4	0.5	4.8	2.9	*	*	1.4	11.7	*	*	2.6
Separated.	2.1	0.5	4.5	2.9	*	*	1.4	11.7	*	*	1.7
Widowed.	0.3	1.0	*	*	*	*	0.6	*	*	*	*
Divorced	11.3	5.3	18.8	13.2	4.3	*	4.3	18.3	*	*	23.0

Note: * indicates insufficient number of cases to report.

Source: U.S. Bureau of the Census. "Marital Status and Living Arrangements." Current Population Reports (Series P-20, no. 380, table 7). Washington, DC: U.S. Government Printing Office, 1983.

Unrelated Subfamilies

Subfamilies that are not related by kinship or marriage ties to the householder may be found both in families and in nonfamily households. However, such subfamilies are comparatively rare. In 1983 there were estimated to be only 440,000 such unrelated subfamilies, with the following characteristics:

Race	Number	Per 1,000 households	Percent distribution
White	342	4.7	77.7
Black	85	9.5	19.3
Other races . . .	13	7.1	3.0
Spanish-origin. .	45	11.0	10.2

Source: U.S. Bureau of the Census. Current Population Reports (Series P-20, no. 388), 1984, Table 14.

Table 11-16. Subfamilies Related to Family Householders: 1940-1983

Year	Number of related subfamilies (000)	Percent composition			Ratio of subfamilies to families
		Married couple	Father-child	Mother-child	
1983.	2,220	32.4	6.6	61.0	3.6
1982.	1,877	33.3	6.1	60.6	3.1
1981.	1,236	46.9	6.3	46.8	2.0
1980.	1,150	50.6	4.7	44.5	1.9
1978.	1,093	49.0	7.4	43.5	1.9
1975.	1,349	52.3	5.1	52.3	2.4
1970.	1,150	53.7	4.2	42.1	2.2
1965.	1,293	56.4	5.6	38.1	2.7
1960.	1,514	57.5	7.6	34.9	3.4
1955.	1,973	59.7	3.5	36.8	4.7
1950.	2,402	68.7	4.6	26.6	6.2
1940.	2,062	75.0	2.5	22.5	6.5

Source: U.S. Bureau of the Census. "Households, Families, Marital Status, and Living Arrangements: March 1982 (Advance Report)" and "Households and Family Characteristics: March 1983." Current Population Reports (Series P-20, no. 376 and no. 388). Washington, DC: U.S. Government Printing Office, 1982 and 1984.

Three-fourths are mother-child subfamilies:

Subfamily status	Percent
Married couple	8.9
Father-child	2.3
Mother-child	73.1
Other.	15.7

Source: U.S. Bureau of the Census. Current Population Reports (Series P-20, no. 388), 1984, Table 14.

Their marital status is primarily divorced or never married:

Marital status	Percent
Married, not separated . . .	0.9
Married, separated	17.6
Widowed.	2.0
Divorced	53.9
Single	25.6

Source: U.S. Bureau of the Census. Current Population Reports (Series P-20, no. 388), 1984, Table 14.

Summary of Subfamily Trends

In the era immediately following World War II, the subfamily was a convenient startup arrangement for young couples newly married and as a residential arrangement for an elderly dependent parent in the home of a son or daughter. In recent times, the subfamily is rapidly becoming a refuge for the one-parent family, especially for divorced and never marrried women with a child.

The rapid rise in subfamilies during 1982 and 1983, described above, may be due both to the economic recession and changes in social legislation that curtailed benefits to one-parent families. This could have forced low income families to move in with a relative and become a subfamily.

Households Containing Elderly Members

As the population ages, an increasing proportion of households contain elderly persons sixty-five and over. Elderly persons are found in about one-fifth of all families. The following summary shows differences between types of families and race-ethnicity.

Type of family	Total	White	Black	Spanish-origin
Married couple.	18.4	18.5	17.5	9.9
Male, no spouse . .	24.3	25.3	20.1	13.7
Female, no spouse . . .	17.4	20.1	11.3	10.0

Source: U.S. Bureau of the Census. Current Population Reports (Series P-20, no. 388), 1984, Table 1.

Families with a male head but no spouse are much more

Table 11-17. Subfamilies, by Characteristics and Race-Ethnicity of Subfamily Reference Person: 1982

Characteristics	Subfamilies			
	Total[a]	Married couple	Father-child	Mother-child
All races				
Number (000)	2,249	664	126	1,418
Percent	100.0	29.5	5.6	63.1
Marital status	100.0	100.0	100.0	100.0
Married, spouse present	29.5	100.0	*	*
Married, spouse absent	15.5	*	23.6	22.2
Separated	12.6	*	22.3	17.7
Spouse in armed forces	0.6	*	0.0	1.0
Other	2.3	*	1.3	3.5
Widowed	2.1	*	4.1	2.4
Divorced	20.5	*	44.9	27.8
Single (never married)	32.4	*	27.5	47.7
Age of reference person (years)	100.0	100.0	100.0	100.0
Under 20	14.1	7.4	3.2	18.2
20 to 24	31.0	24.2	31.2	34.7
25 to 29	20.5	21.5	10.4	21.2
30 to 34	13.8	14.3	18.4	13.3
35 to 39	7.2	5.5	19.2	7.2
40 to 44	3.5	3.5	10.4	2.7
45 to 54	3.9	6.3	4.0	2.1
55 to 64	2.9	7.4	3.2	0.6
65 and over	3.0	9.9	*	*
Average number of persons per subfamily	2.50	2.81	2.28	2.38
Average number of own children under 18 per subfamily	1.41	1.61	1.27	1.37
White				
Number (000)	1,511	548	91	841
Percent	100.0	36.3	6.0	55.7
Marital status	100.0	100.0	100.0	100.0
Married, spouse present	36.4	100.0	*	*
Married, spouse absent	16.8	*	19.7	27.9
Separated	13.3	*	18.0	21.8
Spouse in armed forces	1.0	*	*	1.7
Other	2.5	*	1.7	4.4
Widowed	2.1	*	5.7	2.4
Divorced	26.2	*	55.0	40.1
Single (never married)	18.5	*	19.5	29.5
Age of reference person (years)	100.0	100.0	100.0	100.0
Under 20	12.2	7.8	2.2	15.8
20 to 24	28.4	25.9	31.1	30.4
25 to 29	22.0	21.9	10.0	23.8
30 to 34	14.6	14.6	21.1	14.3
35 to 39	8.0	4.6	22.2	9.0
40 to 44	3.7	2.7	6.7	3.6
45 to 54	4.8	6.6	5.6	2.7
55 to 64	3.0	7.3	1.1	0.4
65 and over	3.2	8.7	--[c]	--[c]
Average number of persons per subfamily	2.51	2.80	2.27	2.36
Average number of own children	1.39	1.57	1.26	1.35

Characteristics	Subfamilies			
	Total[a]	Married couple	Father-child	Mother-child
Black				
Number (000)	638	55	33	544
Percent	100.0	8.6	5.2	85.3
Marital status	100.0	--[b]	--[b]	100.0
Married, spouse present	8.7	--	--	*
Married, spouse absent	13.3	--	--	13.2
Separated	12.3	--	--	12.1
Spouse in armed forces	*	--	--	*
Other	1.0	--	--	1.1
Widowed	1.6	--	--	1.9
Divorced	8.2	--	--	8.3
Single (never married)	68.2	--	--	76.5
Age of reference person (years)	100.0	100.0	100.0	100.0
Under 20	20.2	3.6	6.1	23.0
20 to 24	38.8	21.8	30.3	41.3
25 to 29	17.7	27.3	15.2	17.1
30 to 34	12.2	21.8	12.1	11.4
35 to 39	4.7	5.5	9.1	4.2
40 to 44	3.0	10.9	21.2	1.1
45 to 54	1.7	5.5	--[c]	0.9
55 to 64	1.6	1.8	6.1	0.9
65 and over	0.2	1.8	--[c]	--[c]
Average number of persons per subfamily	2.45	--[b]	--[b]	2.43
Average number of own children under 18 per subfamily	1.42	--[b]	--[b]	1.42
Spanish-origin				
Number (000)	238	107	12	113
Percent	100.0	45.0	5.0	47.5
Marital status	100.0	100.0	--[b]	100.0
Married, spouse present	45.1	100.0	--	*
Married, spouse absent	18.1	*	--	33.8
Separated	13.9	*	--	26.4
Spouse in armed forces	1.2	*	--	2.4
Other	3.0	*	--	5.0
Widowed	2.1	*	--	4.4
Divorced	12.2	*	--	21.4
Single (never married)	22.5	*	--	40.4
Age of reference person (years)	100.0	100.0	100.0	100.0
Under 20	13.0	7.6	--[c]	20.4
20 to 24	23.1	19.8	41.7	24.8
25 to 29	27.3	36.8	--[c]	21.2
30 to 34	13.9	8.5	25.0	16.5
35 to 39	7.6	6.6	8.3	8.0
40 to 44	5.9	4.7	8.3	5.3
45 to 54	2.5	2.8	--[c]	1.8
55 to 64	2.1	2.8	8.3	0.9
65 and over	4.6	10.4	--[c]	--[c]
Average number of persons per subfamily	2.70	2.98	--[b]	2.50
Average number of own children	1.55	--[b]	--[b]	1.47

[a] Total includes all married couple subfamilies, father-child and mother-child subfamilies, as well as other subfamilies not listed.

[b] Sample is too small to derive any meaningful measures.

[c] It is the practice of the Census Bureau to report numbers in thousands. Hence, zeroes and any numbers that cannot be rounded to 1 are omitted from the table.

Note: * indicates less than 0.1.

Source: U.S. Bureau of the Census. "Household and Family Characteristics: March, 1982." Current Population Reports (Series P-20, no. 381). Washington, DC: U.S. Government Printing Office, 1983, Tables 14 and 15.

likely to contain elderly persons than other types, and families with a female no-spouse head are least likely to contain elderly. Elderly persons are more likely to be found in white families of all types than in black or Spanish-origin families. Elderly persons are much less frequent in Spanish-origin than in black families.

Living Arrangements of the Elderly

Of the quarter-million persons aged sixty-five and over living in households in 1982, about two-thirds are living in families and one-third living outside families. All but a small fraction of this latter group live alone. Table 11-18 provides comparative statistical data for years since 1970. Only about 2 percent live in nonfamily households with one or more other nonrelatives. These proportions have not changed a great deal since 1970, but the number of persons involved certainly has grown as the population has aged. Also, the tendency for widowed persons living in a nonfamily context to live alone has increased substantially (from 55.2 in 1970 to 69.1 in 1982; see Figure 11-5).

Interracial and Interethnic Married Couples

Marriages between the principal ethnic groups are comparatively common for Spanish-origin persons but rare for the black and majority white population. Following is the proportion of married persons having a spouse of a different racial-ethnic group:

Racial-ethnic intermarriage	Percent
White wife with black husband.	0.26
White husband with black wife.	0.10
Black wife with white husband.	1.32
Black husband with white wife.	3.30
Spanish wife with non-Spanish husband.	17.60
Spanish husband with non-Spanish wife.	14.58

Source: U.S. Bureau of the Census. Current Population Reports (Series P-20, no. 388), 1984, Table 16.

Table 11-18. Number and Percent Distribution of Family Status and Living Alone for Persons 65 Years of Age and Older: 1982, 1980, and 1970 [numbers in thousands]

Subject	All persons 65 years and over[a]							
	Total		In families		Not in families			
							Living alone	
	Number	Percent	Number	Percent	Number	Percent	Number	Percent
1982								
Persons 65 years and over	25,232	100.0	17,090	67.7	8,141	32.3	7,673	30.4
Not widowed	16,429	100.0	14,601	88.9	1,836	11.2	1,587	9.7
Total widowed	8,803	100.0	2,489	28.3	6,315	71.7	6,086	69.1
Women	7,523	100.0	2,175	28.9	5,348	71.1	5,189	69.0
Men	1,280	100.0	314	24.5	966	75.5	897	70.1
1980								
Persons 65 years and over	24,194	100.0	16,355	67.6	7,839	32.4	7,328	30.3
Not widowed	15,556	100.0	13,776	88.6	1,780	11.4	1,520	9.8
Total widowed	8,638	100.0	2,579	29.9	6,059	70.1	5,808	67.2
Women	7,295	100.0	2,194	30.1	5,102	69.9	4,916	67.4
Men	1,342	100.0	385	28.7	958	71.4	893	66.5
1970								
Persons 65 years and over	19,061	100.0	13,347	70.0	5,716	30.0	5,071	26.6
Not widowed	11,782	100.0	10,462	88.8	1,324	11.2	1,054	8.9
Total widowed	7,279	100.0	2,885	39.6	4,392	60.3	4,017	55.2
Women	5,946	100.0	2,386	40.1	3,560	59.9	3,309	55.7
Men	1,333	100.0	499	37.4	832	62.4	708	53.1

[a]Excludes persons in institutions (nursing homes, etc.). The number of such persons age 65 years and over was estimated to be 0.8 million in 1970, 1.3 million in 1980, and 1.4 million in 1982.

Source: U.S. Bureau of the Census. "Households, Families, Marital Status, and Living Arrangements: March 1982 (Advance Report)." Current Population Reports (Series P-20, no. 376). Washington, DC: U.S. Government Printing Office, 1982, Table 5.

Because these data are collected by a sample and represent only small proportions of the population, they are subject to sampling error—in addition to possible biases in reporting.

Nonrelatives in Households

Earlier in this century it was comparatively common for families to contain nonrelatives—persons not related to the family householder or any other member. Such persons were often lodgers, boarders, or live-in servants. Nowadays such living arrangements are somewhat rare in married couple families. Persons who are not related to family members tend to live in nonfamily households, either alone or with a nonrelative.

The following tabulation shows the percent of families that contain one or more unrelated persons:

Race-ethnicity	Married couples	No-spouse families	
		Male	Female
All families . .	1.0	13.5	5.8
White.	1.0	13.3	6.1
Black.	1.4	15.6	4.4
Spanish-origin . .	1.2	16.9	4.8

Source: U.S. Bureau of the Census. Current Population Reports (Series P-20, no. 388), 1984, Table 21.

Both male and female no-spouse households (especially the male) tend to include nonrelatives much more than the married couple families. These may be lodgers or persons sharing living quarters with the householder. Unrelated persons are found more frequently in black and Spanish-origin married couple and male no-spouse households than in white.

Households and Place of Residence

The more "unconventional" types of households and families tend to be found in metropolitan areas, and especially the central cities of metropolitan areas, whereas the more "conventional" married couple families tend to be found in the suburban ring of metropolitan areas and in nonmetropolitan areas. Following is a summary of the percent living in Standard Metropolitan Statistical Areas by family type and race:

Household type	Percent living in SMSAs			
	Total	White	Black	Sp-origin
All households. . .	68.4	67.0	77.7	86.2
Family households . .	67.0	65.5	76.5	86.1
Married couple families.	65.8	64.7	74.6	84.5
Male no-spouse families.	70.4	69.8	72.5	88.2
Female no-spouse families.	72.9	70.4	79.4	90.9
Nonfamily households.	72.1	70.9	81.1	86.5
Male householders .	73.9	72.6	83.1	84.8
Female householders	70.8	69.7	79.3	88.0

Source: U.S. Bureau of the Census. Current Population Reports (Series P-20, no. 388), 1984, Table 20.

All race-ethnic groups follow the same pattern. Families with no spouse and nonfamily households headed by either males or females tend to be more metropolitanized than conventional married couple families.

Within SMSAs married couple families tend to be proportionately fewer in central cities and proportionately more in metropolitan rings than are the no-spouse families (both male and female). The following summary table presents the percent of families residing in central cities and metropolitan rings, by type of family and race, in 1983. (Percent in nonmetropolitan areas is the sum of the central city and the ring subtracted from 100.0.)

Race and family type	Central city	Metro ring
All families.	26.4	40.6
Married couples	23.6	42.2
Male, no spouse	32.8	37.6
Female, no spouse	39.9	33.0
White families.	22.7	42.8
Married couples	21.3	43.3
Male, no spouse	28.2	41.6
Female, no spouse	31.1	39.3
Black families.	54.2	22.4
Married couples	48.6	26.0
Male, no spouse	53.9	18.4
Female, no spouse	61.3	18.2
Spanish-origin families . . .	51.3	34.8
Married couples	48.1	36.4
Male, no spouse	47.4	40.3
Female, no spouse	62.5	28.4

Source: U.S. Bureau of the Census. Current Population Reports (Series P-20, no. 388), 1984, Table 4.

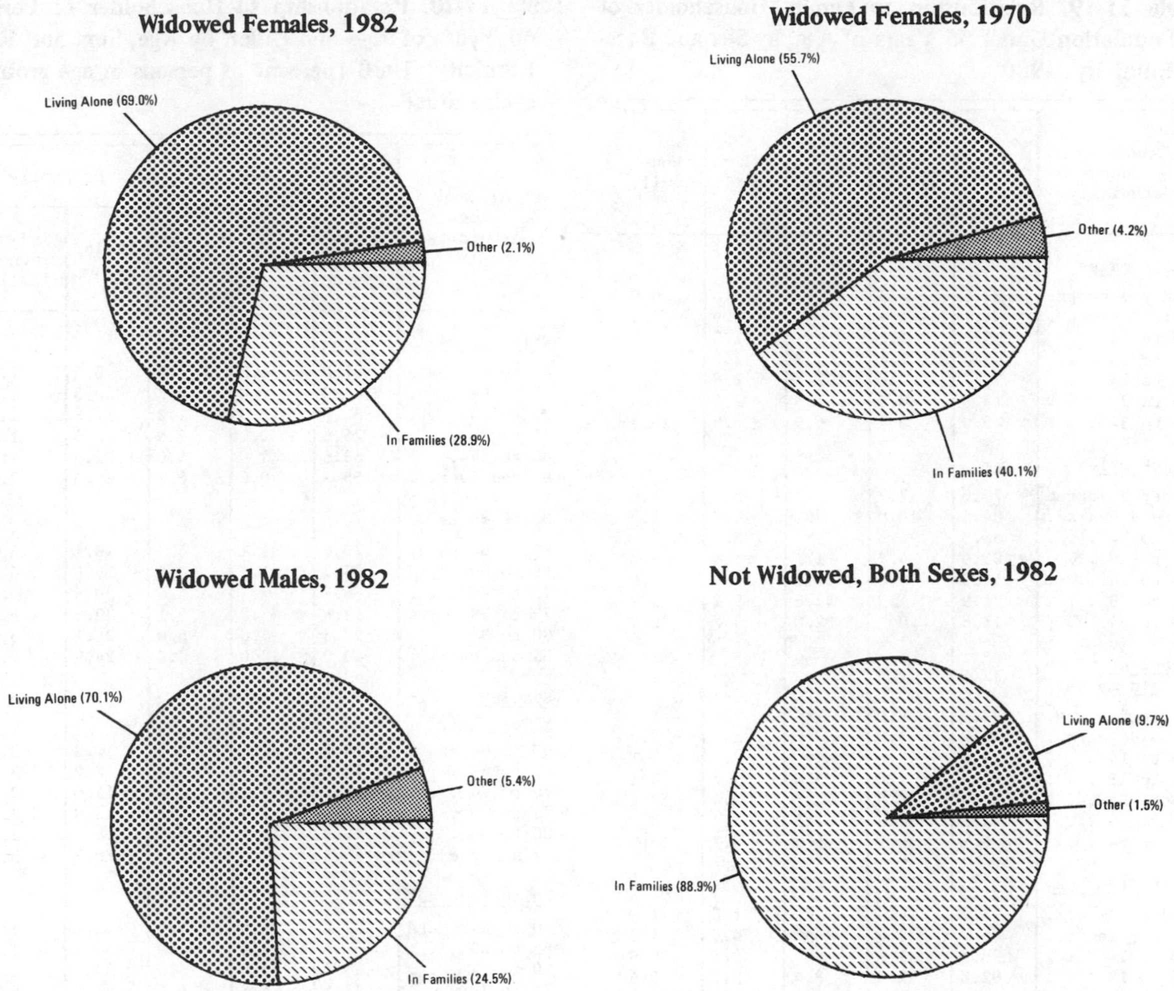

Figure 11-5. Living Arrangements of the Elderly (Population 65 Years of Age and Older), by Marital Status and Sex: 1982 and 1970

Family and Household

Every member of a family is classified according to his or her relationship to the householder (these relationships are explained in the Definition Box). Data on relationship can illuminate the structure of the family.

Family Relationship of Children

Table 11-19 provides information on the relationship of the child to the householder in order to show the significant differences that occur with age and that exist between race-ethnic groups.

The status of being a grandchild is much more prevalent among black than among other children, especially when the child is under ten years of age. Being a grandchild is moderately prevalent among Spanish-origin children, and much more rare among white children. For all groups, being a grandchild is more prevalent among very young than older children.

Being neither a child nor a grandchild but in the status of having left the parental home occurs precipitously at ages 20-24. These are the most common ages for marriage, going away to college, setting up alternative living arrangements, and so on. This break takes place at an earlier age for girls than for boys. However, many persons remain "children" to advanced ages; at age 30-34, nearly 7 percent of men and 5 percent of women are still living as dependents of a parent or grandparent. These proportions were almost double for the

Table 11-19. Relationship to Family Householder of Population Under 35 Years of Age, by Sex and Race-Ethnicity: 1980

Age and race-ethnicity	Child	Grand-child	House-holder, spouse, in-laws	Other family	Non-family
White males					
Under 5 years.	93.8	4.3	*	1.0	0.9
5 to 9 years .	95.7	2.4	*	0.9	0.9
10 to 14 . . .	96.6	1.6	*	1.0	0.8
15 to 19 . . .	89.8	1.4	2.3	2.2	4.3
20 to 24 . . .	39.7	0.8	31.7	2.8	25.1
25 to 29 . . .	13.0	0.3	61.8	1.5	23.4
30 to 34 . . .	5.9	0.1	76.9	0.8	16.3
Black males					
Under 5 years.	75.6	17.7	*	5.0	1.6
5 to 9 years .	84.6	10.0	*	3.8	1.5
10 to 14 . . .	88.2	6.6	*	3.7	1.4
15 to 19 . . .	85.9	4.7	1.1	5.6	2.8
20 to 24 . . .	51.3	3.0	20.6	7.3	17.8
25 to 29 . . .	21.9	1.3	47.8	5.2	23.7
30 to 34 . . .	11.5	0.6	62.0	3.7	22.2
Spanish-origin males					
Under 5 years.	89.1	6.9	*	2.6	1.3
5 to 9 years .	92.9	3.9	*	2.1	1.2
10 to 14 . . .	93.6	2.6	*	2.7	1.1
15 to 19 . . .	82.2	1.7	3.4	7.2	5.5
20 to 24 . . .	35.9	0.8	34.8	9.4	19.1
25 to 29 . . .	13.1	0.3	62.5	5.7	18.4
30 to 34 . . .	6.1	0.1	75.1	3.7	15.0
White females					
Under 5 years.	93.7	4.3	*	1.0	1.0
5 to 9 years .	95.7	2.4	*	0.9	1.0
10 to 14 . . .	96.5	1.6	*	1.1	0.9
15 to 19 . . .	82.8	1.2	8.4	2.1	5.6
20 to 24 . . .	27.1	0.5	48.9	2.1	21.4
25 to 29 . . .	8.1	0.2	74.2	1.1	16.5
30 to 34 . . .	4.1	0.1	85.3	0.6	10.0
Black females					
Under 5 years.	75.9	17.4	*	5.0	1.6
5 to 9 years .	84.6	9.9	*	4.0	1.6
10 to 14 . . .	88.2	6.4	*	4.0	1.4
15 to 19 . . .	81.7	4.3	4.9	5.8	3.4
20 to 24 . . .	39.1	2.1	39.6	5.9	13.3
25 to 29 . . .	15.5	0.9	66.9	3.6	13.1
30 to 34 . . .	7.9	0.4	79.0	2.5	10.2
Spanish-origin females					
Under 5 years.	89.1	6.8	*	2.8	1.3
5 to 9 years .	93.0	3.8	*	2.1	1.1
10 to 14 . . .	93.6	2.5	*	2.8	1.1
15 to 19 . . .	76.7	1.5	11.1	6.0	4.7
20 to 24 . . .	28.4	0.6	52.3	6.0	12.7
25 to 29 . . .	10.2	0.2	75.2	3.7	10.7
30 to 34 . . .	5.1	0.1	84.9	2.5	7.4

Note: * indicates not applicable.

Source: U.S. Bureau of the Census. "Detailed Population Characteristics: United States Summary." 1980 Census of Population (Chapter D, Section A). Washington, DC: U.S. Government Printing Office, 1983, Table 265.

Table 11-20. Relationship to Householder of Persons 60 Years of Age and Older, by Age, Sex, and Race-Ethnicity: 1980 [percent of persons in age group in each status]

Age and race-ethnicity	Family			Nonfamily	
	House-holder, spouse	Parent	Other rela-tive	Living alone	Other non-family
White males					
60 to 64 years	87.2	0.5	2.2	8.4	1.7
65 to 69 . . .	85.0	0.8	2.2	10.3	1.6
70 to 74 . . .	82.0	1.3	2.3	12.8	1.6
75 to 79 . . .	76.6	2.2	2.9	16.6	1.7
80 to 84 . . .	68.6	4.0	4.0	21.5	1.9
85 and over. .	55.3	9.0	6.7	26.3	2.6
Black males					
60 to 64 years	70.6	1.1	5.3	16.1	6.8
65 to 69 . . .	68.7	1.5	4.7	19.0	6.1
70 to 74 . . .	66.7	2.2	4.8	20.6	5.6
75 to 79 . . .	62.6	3.3	5.1	23.3	5.7
80 to 84 . . .	57.3	4.8	6.0	26.1	5.9
85 and over. .	49.0	10.0	10.2	24.9	5.8
Spanish-origin males					
60 to 64 years	79.7	2.6	4.3	10.3	3.2
65 to 69 . . .	75.3	3.8	5.4	12.2	3.3
70 to 74 . . .	71.2	5.1	5.6	15.0	3.1
75 to 79 . . .	66.4	7.4	7.1	15.9	3.2
80 to 84 . . .	59.9	10.1	8.7	18.8	2.5
85 and over. .	45.2	17.5	15.3	18.7	3.4
White females					
60 to 64 years	72.6	1.6	3.4	20.7	1.7
65 to 69 . . .	61.6	2.4	4.0	30.2	1.8
70 to 74 . . .	49.7	3.6	5.0	39.7	1.9
75 to 79 . . .	37.6	5.8	6.6	48.0	2.0
80 to 84 . . .	27.0	9.4	8.9	52.3	2.3
85 and over. .	18.9	17.6	13.1	47.3	3.0
Black females					
60 to 64 years	63.0	3.6	5.3	23.9	4.2
65 to 69 . . .	54.4	4.6	5.8	30.7	4.4
70 to 74 . . .	46.2	6.0	6.7	36.8	4.3
75 to 79 . . .	37.5	8.8	8.5	40.7	4.5
80 to 84 . . .	30.1	12.9	11.3	41.4	4.3
85 and over. .	23.5	20.9	16.4	34.8	4.5
Spanish-origin females					
60 to 64 years	64.4	7.7	8.0	17.0	3.0
65 to 69 . . .	53.9	9.9	9.8	23.2	3.2
70 to 74 . . .	44.4	12.7	12.1	28.2	2.6
75 to 79 . . .	34.9	15.5	15.0	31.6	3.0
80 to 84 . . .	27.1	20.2	16.7	32.9	3.0
85 and over. .	20.5	27.6	22.8	25.6	3.4

Source: U.S. Bureau of the Census. "Detailed Population Characteristics: United States Summary." 1980 Census of Population (Chapter D, Section A). Washington, DC: U.S. Government Printing Office, 1983, Table 265.

black population, while the Spanish-origin population leaves home at roughly the same ages as the white population.

The status of "other relative" is a rarer status than "grandchild" but tends to follow the same race-ethnic, sex, and age patterns. This category may be a measure of mutual aid among members of an extended family. Providing shelter to children who are not one's own is extremely rare among the white population, but is less uncommon among the black and Spanish-origin populations.

As noted earlier, only 1 percent of very young children live outside a family. Hence the nonfamily relationships are of minor significance. The small amount of extra-family living for children that does take place is relatively more common among Spanish-origin than among the black population, and it is much more frequent for blacks and Hispanics than for the white population.

Family and Household Relationships of the Elderly

As persons approach their sixtieth birthday, their family situation changes. Children have departed from home, a spouse could die, ill health might set in, financial security may be lost. The adjustment to these transitions and tragedies is reflected in the family and household relationships of the elderly. Table 11-20 reports such information by sex and race for advanced ages.

As both men and women pass their seventieth birthday, the proportion living alone, with a child, or with another relative increases rapidly at the expense of being

Table 11-21A. Number and Characteristics of the Population Living in Group Quarters: 1980

Type	Total (both sexes)	Male	Female	Per-cent male	Per-cent female	Percent black			Percent Spanish-origin		
						Total	Male	Female	Total	Male	Female
Total	5,738,423	3,152,884	2,585,539	54.9	45.1	14.2	70.4	29.6	4.7	74.0	26.0
Inmates, total.	2,492,157	1,231,468	1,260,689	49.4	50.6	15.7	75.2	24.8	3.9	76.9	23.1
Mental hospital	245,029	149,421	95,608	61.0	39.0	17.1	66.2	33.8	3.9	67.1	32.9
Home for the aged	1,426,371	422,001	1,004,370	29.6	70.4	6.3	40.9	59.1	1.5	45.6	54.5
Correctional institution.	466,371	439,228	27,143	94.2	5.8	42.6	94.3	5.7	10.0	95.6	4.4
Other institution	354,386	220,818	133,568	62.3	37.7	17.0	69.8	30.2	5.3	71.1	28.9
Noninmates, total	3,246,266	1,921,416	1,324,850	59.2	40.8	13.1	66.1	33.9	5.4	72.4	27.6
Rooming or boarding house	176,257	107,403	68,854	60.9	39.1	13.1	69.5	30.5	11.0	72.6	27.4
Military quarters	671,251	613,106	58,145	91.3	8.7	23.2	89.4	10.6	7.2	92.4	7.6
College dormitory	1,994,282	988,766	1,005,516	49.6	50.4	9.8	45.3	54.7	2.9	53.0	47.0
Other	404,476	212,141	192,335	52.4	47.6	12.9	72.4	27.6	11.7	76.1	23.9

Source: U.S. Bureau of the Census. "Detailed Population Characteristics: United States Summary." 1980 Census of Population. Washington, DC: U.S. Government Printing Office, 1983, Table 266.

Table 11-21B. Percent Distribution of Residents in Group Quarters, by Type of Quarters: 1980

Type	Percent distri-bution	Percent black			Percent Spanish-origin		
		Total	Male	Female	Total	Male	Female
Total	100.0	100.0	100.0	100.0	100.0	100.0	100.0
Inmates, total.	43.4	47.8	51.1	40.1	35.6	37.0	31.6
Mental hospital	4.3	5.1	4.8	5.8	3.5	3.2	4.4
Home for the aged	24.8	11.0	6.4	22.1	7.9	4.9	16.6
Correctional institution.	8.1	24.3	32.5	4.7	17.3	22.3	2.9
Other institution	6.2	7.4	7.3	7.5	6.9	6.6	7.7
Noninmates, total	56.6	52.2	48.9	59.9	64.4	63.0	68.4
Rooming or boarding house	3.1	2.8	2.8	2.9	7.2	7.0	7.6
Military quarters	11.7	19.1	24.2	6.8	18.0	22.4	5.3
College dormitory	34.8	23.9	15.4	44.2	21.8	15.6	39.4
Other	7.0	6.4	6.6	6.0	17.5	18.0	16.1

Source: U.S. Bureau of the Census. "Detailed Population Characteristics: United States Summary." 1980 Census of Population. Washington, DC: U.S. Government Printing Office, 1983, Table 266.

a family householder or spouse. Males retain their householder/spouse status to much more advanced ages than females.

Living with a child or other relative is more common in Spanish-origin than in black households, and it is more common in black than in white households.

Persons in Group Quarters

Earlier this chapter noted that only about 2.5 percent of the population does not live in households but in "group quarters." This small fraction of the population possesses economic, social, political, and welfare significance much greater than its proportion, however. Tables 11-21A and 11-21B present the number of persons in group quarters as well as percentage distributions on persons in group quarters by race-ethnicity and sex. Table 11-22 summarizes the age composition of such persons and their demographic composition, while Tables 11-23A and 11-23B show that the different age groups have vastly different types of institutional and noninstitutional living arrangements. Figure 11-6 illustrates sex differentials in type of quarters of those who live in group quarters.

Conclusion

Household trends may be at a turning point. Greater equality between the sexes, decreased fertility, increased labor force participation of women, and increased childbearing out of wedlock are among the forces at work. Economic prosperity seems to have been an important factor in the trends of the 1970s, which have greatly diminished, changed to zero, or even reversed between 1980 and 1983. Double-digit inflation, high unemployment, severe economic recession (which saw real incomes decline and the proportion of persons living in poverty rise), and a government policy of austerity and cutback in social programs should have an immediate, direct effect on the family formation practices of youth and their living arrangements. Young persons who formerly could afford a residence of their own (either as a single or married person) have returned to their parents' homes or started sharing living space with others.

Beginning in 1984 signs of a lessening of the recession appeared. Whether this will permit or promote a return to the family formation trends of the 1970s cannot be predicted. It appears to be very unlikely that family life and the household and family statistics will ever again resemble those of the 1950s, which may have represented an all-time high in familism in this country. It is also very unlikely that familism will diminish in popularity as an ideal. But the size, composition, and life cycle characteristics of the family will almost certainly undergo further modifications as the population searches for a better life.

Bibliography

Bane, M.J. "Is the Welfare State Replacing the Family?" *Public Interest* 70 (1983):91-101.

Becker, G.S. "A Theory of Marriage: The Economics of the Family." In *The Economic Approach to Human Behavior*. G.S. Becker (ed.). Chicago: University of Chicago Press, 1981.

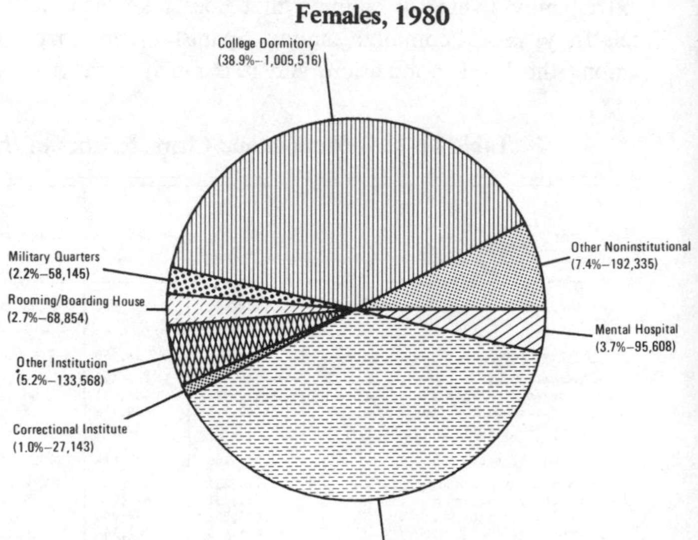

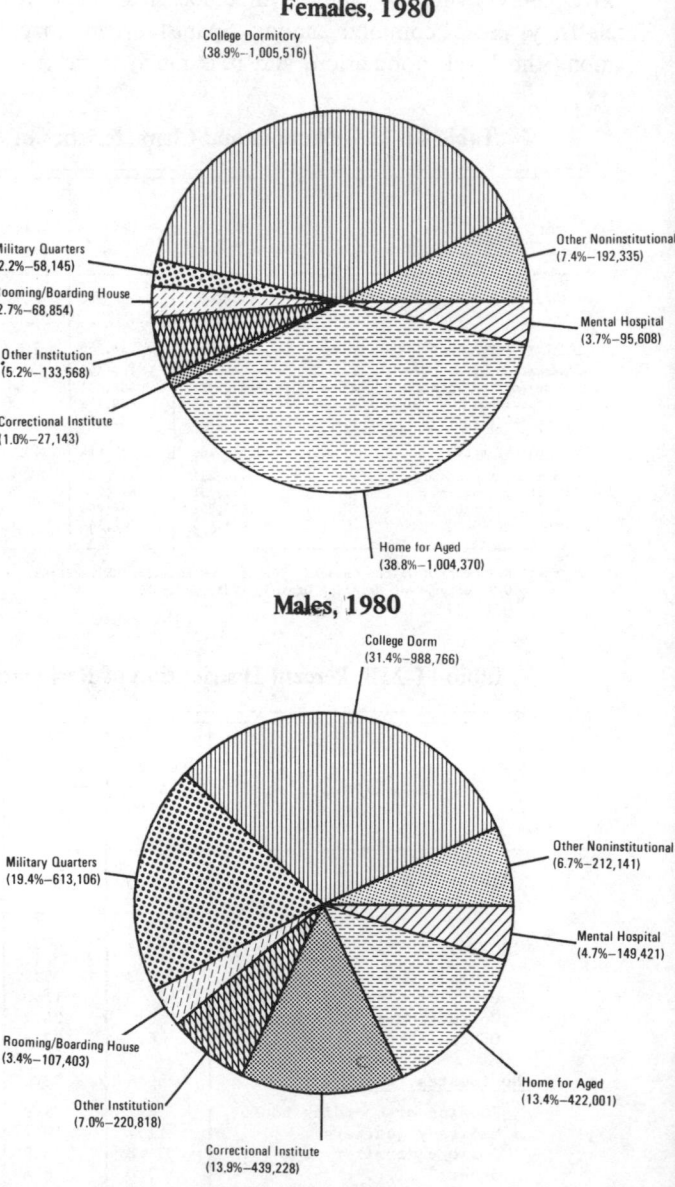

Figure 11-6. Type of Quarters–Male and Female Population Living in Group Quarters: 1980

Table 11-22. Population in Group Quarters, by Sex, Age, and Race-Ethnicity: 1980

Age	Number in group quarters (000)			Percent in group quarters							
				Total		White		Black		Spanish-origin	
	Total	Male	Female	Male	Female	Male	Female	Male	Female	Male	Female
Under 5 years. . . .	12,709	7,046	5,663	0.1	0.1	0.1	0.1	0.1	0.1	0.2	0.1
5-9 years.	21,405	13,416	7,989	0.2	0.1	0.1	0.1	0.2	0.1	0.2	0.1
10-14 years.	69,301	46,009	23,292	0.5	0.3	0.4	0.2	0.8	0.3	0.6	0.3
15-19 years.	1,432,186	808,016	624,170	7.5	6.0	7.3	6.3	8.3	4.8	5.6	2.5
20-24 years.	1,547,021	1,020,192	526,829	9.6	4.9	8.7	5.0	15.0	4.8	7.9	2.3
25-29 years.	336,648	272,331	64,317	2.8	0.7	2.0	0.6	7.5	1.0	3.8	0.6
30-34 years.	195,596	156,305	39,291	1.8	0.4	1.3	0.4	5.4	0.7	2.7	0.4
35-39 years.	130,652	99,635	31,017	1.5	0.4	1.1	0.4	3.9	0.5	2.4	0.5
40-44 years.	94,333	67,711	26,622	1.2	0.4	0.9	0.4	2.8	0.5	1.9	0.4
45-49 years.	88,195	58,135	30,060	1.1	0.5	0.9	0.5	2.2	0.5	1.9	0.4
50-54 years.	99,632	61,811	37,821	1.1	0.6	1.0	0.6	2.2	0.6	1.5	0.5
55-59 years.	114,227	66,558	47,669	1.2	0.8	1.1	0.8	2.2	0.9	1.7	0.6
60-64 years.	121,231	62,086	59,145	1.3	1.1	1.2	1.1	2.0	1.0	1.5	0.7
65-69 years.	148,766	67,110	81,656	1.7	1.7	1.6	1.7	2.4	1.6	1.5	1.1
70-74 years.	195,334	73,168	122,166	2.6	3.1	2.5	3.1	3.1	2.6	2.5	1.9
75-59 years.	265,502	79,320	186,182	4.3	6.3	4.3	6.5	4.5	4.6	3.5	3.5
80-84 years.	330,009	80,413	249,596	7.9	13.1	8.0	13.5	6.6	7.7	5.3	7.5
85 years and over. .	535,676	113,622	422,054	17.0	27.7	17.7	28.8	9.9	14.9	9.9	12.1

Source: U.S. Bureau of the Census. "Detailed Population Characteristics: United States Summary." 1980 Census of Population (Chapter D, Section A). Washington, DC: U.S. Government Printing Office, 1983, Table 266.

———. *A Treatise on the Family*. Cambridge: Harvard University Press, 1981.

Bianchi, S.M., and Farley, R. "Racial Differences in Family Living Arrangements and Economic Well-Being: An Analysis of Recent Trends." *Journal of Marriage and the Family* 41 (1979):537-51.

Billingsley, Andrew. *Black Families in White America.* Englewood Cliffs, NJ: Prentice-Hall, 1968.

Bumpass, L., and Rindfuss, R.R. "Children's Experience of Marital Disruption." *American Journal of Sociology* 85 (1979):49-65.

Burch, Thomas K. "Household and Family Demography: A Bibliographic Essay." *Population Index* 45 (1979):173-95.

Burch, Thomas K. "Household Size and Structure in Demographic Transitions." Paper presented at the American Statistical Association, 1980.

Cherlin, A. *Marriage, Divorce, Remarriage.* Cambridge: Harvard University Press, 1981.

———. "Remarriage as an Incomplete Institution." *American Journal of Sociology* 84 (1978):634-50.

Cooney, R.S., and Min, K. "Demographic Characteristics Affecting Living Arrangements Among Young Currently Unmarried Puerto Rican, Non-Spanish Black, and Non-Spanish White Mothers." *Ethicity* 8 (1981): 107-120.

Crouter, A.C. "Children of Working Parents." *Human Ecology Forum* 12 (1982):22-6.

Danziger, S., et al. "Work and Welfare as Determinants of Female Poverty and Household Headship." *Quarterly Journal of Economy* 97 (1982):519-34.

Espenshade, T.J., and Braun, R.E. "Life Course Analysis and Multistate Demography: An Application to Marriage, Divorce, and Remarriage." *Journal of Marriage and the Family* 44 (1982):1025-36.

Ferris, Abott L. *Indicators of Change in the American Family*. New York: The Russell Sage Foundation, 1970.

Frazier, Edward Franklin. *The Negro Family in the United States.* Chicago: University of Chicago Press, 1939.

Frey, William H., and Kobrin, Frances E. "Changing Families and Changing Mobility: Their Impact on the Central City." *Demography* 19 (1982):261-77.

Frisbie, W. Parker; Inman, Jan M.; Poston, Dudley L. Jr.; and Bean, Frank D. "Household and Family Demography of Hispanics: A Comparative Analysis." *Texas Population Research Center Papers no. 4.002.* Austin: University of Texas, 1982.

Glick, Paul C. *American Families.* New York: Wiley, 1957.

———. "The Future Marital Status and Living Arrangements of the Elderly." *The Gerontologist* 19 (1979):301-309.

Glick, P., and Spanier, G. "Married and Unmarried Cohabitation in the United States." *Journal of Marriage and the Family* 32 (1980):19-30.

Grossbard-Shechtman, A. "Gary Becker's Theory of the Family—Some Interdisciplinary Considerations." *Sociology and Social Research* 66 (1981):1-11.

Table 11-23A. Males in Group Quarters, by Type of Group Quarter, Age, and Race-Ethnicity: 1980

Age and race-ethnicity	Percent in group quarters	Percent distribution of group quarters population							
		Inmate of:				Noninmates			
		Mental hospital	Home for the aged	Correctional institution	Other institution	Rooming, boarding house	Military quarters	College dorm	Other
White	100.0	100.0	100.0	100.0	100.0	100.0	100.0	100.0	100.0
Under 15 years	1.9	8.5	3.4	1.9	62.5	5.4	1.3	6.2	10.8
15-19 years	26.8	1.2	0.2	3.7	6.7	1.1	22.2	62.5	2.4
20-24 years	32.0	1.6	0.4	8.6	2.0	1.5	27.6	55.5	2.8
25-29 years	6.8	7.7	2.4	28.1	8.2	5.2	25.1	13.8	9.4
30-34 years	3.9	12.0	4.2	32.3	10.9	6.4	18.0	5.0	11.2
35-39 years	2.7	13.4	7.0	27.9	11.3	8.4	15.4	2.4	14.2
40-44 years	1.9	16.9	10.8	24.1	12.0	8.7	9.2	2.3	16.0
45-49 years	1.8	16.9	16.1	17.9	13.1	11.4	3.2	2.0	19.4
50-54 years	2.0	18.1	23.2	13.1	12.8	10.5	1.1	1.2	20.0
55-59 years	2.2	17.5	31.8	6.6	13.3	10.6	0.7	1.1	18.4
60-64 years	2.2	14.6	43.9	3.0	12.6	9.4	0.4	0.9	15.1
65-69 years	2.4	12.3	60.1	2.1	9.4	6.1	0.2	0.7	9.1
70-74 years	2.7	7.7	72.9	0.4	6.6	4.8	0.1	0.4	7.2
75-79 years	3.0	5.0	81.1	0.2	4.5	3.6	0.0	0.3	5.3
80-84 years	3.1	3.7	84.0	0.1	4.6	2.2	0.1	0.1	5.3
85 years and over	4.5	2.1	89.2	*	3.4	1.4	0.1	0.1	3.8
Black	100.0	100.0	100.0	100.0	100.0	100.0	100.0	100.0	100.0
Under 15 years	2.5	8.7	3.3	3.4	67.0	4.3	1.2	2.7	9.4
15-19 years	21.7	1.4	0.3	14.2	13.7	0.8	31.0	30.8	7.8
20-24 years	33.5	2.0	0.4	29.3	1.7	1.1	38.9	23.1	3.6
25-29 years	14.3	5.0	1.0	59.1	2.5	2.9	20.3	4.1	5.1
30-34 years	8.3	7.2	1.6	64.7	3.3	4.2	9.3	2.0	7.5
35-39 years	4.5	9.0	3.4	56.7	3.5	6.2	9.0	1.5	10.7
40-44 years	2.8	11.0	5.3	49.5	5.1	6.3	8.4	1.1	13.3
45-49 years	2.0	14.5	11.7	36.7	7.5	10.2	2.6	1.0	15.9
50-54 years	1.9	16.4	19.2	29.3	9.7	9.1	1.3	0.4	14.6
55-59 years	1.8	14.6	26.6	18.7	12.2	11.4	0.5	0.6	15.3
60-64 years	1.3	16.8	39.9	8.9	13.5	10.1	0.3	0.7	9.8
65-69 years	1.4	12.2	58.0	6.6	9.3	6.5	0.3	0.1	7.0
70-74 years	1.2	10.7	67.5	2.7	8.4	5.2	*	*	5.4
75-79 years	1.2	8.3	78.7	0.4	6.3	3.8	*	0.1	2.4
80-84 years	0.8	7.4	80.6	0.1	8.8	1.4	0.1	*	1.5
85 years and over	0.9	6.0	85.4	0.5	5.6	0.8	0.1	*	1.6
Spanish-origin	100.0	100.0	100.0	100.0	100.0	100.0	100.0	100.0	100.0
Under 15 years	3.7	5.6	1.8	1.8	41.9	11.1	0.8	4.0	33.1
15-19 years	23.0	1.0	0.3	9.9	14.3	3.2	30.6	28.5	12.1
20-24 years	31.9	1.6	0.4	21.1	1.5	3.8	36.0	23.6	12.0
25-29 years	13.3	3.2	1.1	40.4	2.3	8.4	19.3	6.1	19.2
30-34 years	7.6	5.2	1.3	44.7	3.0	10.7	9.4	3.2	22.4
35-39 years	5.0	5.4	2.2	38.1	3.0	12.5	5.9	1.8	30.9
40-44 years	3.3	6.3	3.1	36.4	2.4	14.0	4.8	1.8	31.2
45-49 years	2.8	7.4	7.2	21.0	3.2	19.5	2.2	1.2	38.4
50-54 years	2.0	8.0	9.8	21.1	3.7	15.5	1.4	1.3	39.2
55-59 years	1.9	10.6	15.5	10.7	6.0	18.1	0.3	0.3	38.5
60-64 years	1.1	8.2	31.5	3.9	7.3	15.5	1.6	0.5	31.5
65-69 years	0.8	10.6	52.6	4.9	6.1	12.8	*	1.8	11.2
70-74 years	1.0	8.6	55.9	0.5	4.1	9.7	*	0.8	20.4
75-79 years	1.0	4.6	78.6	*	4.6	3.3	*	1.4	7.5
80-84 years	0.7	4.0	86.3	*	3.0	2.8	*	*	3.9
85 years and over	0.8	2.7	91.8	*	2.5	2.0	*	*	1.1

Note: * indicates less than 0.1.

Source: U.S. Bureau of the Census. "Detailed Population Characteristics: United States Summary." 1980 Census of Population (Chapter D, Section A). Washington, DC: U.S. Government Printing Office, 1983, Table 266.

Table 11-23B. Females in Group Quarters, by Type of Group Quarters, Age, and Race-Ethnicity: 1980

Age and race ethnicity	Percent in group quarters	Percent distribution of group quarters population							
		Inmate of:				Noninmates			
		Mental hospital	Home for the aged	Correctional institution	Other institution	Rooming, boarding house	Military quarters	College dorm	Other
White	100.0	100.0	100.0	100.0	100.0	100.0	100.0	100.0	100.0
Under 15 years	1.1	7.3	4.4	0.9	59.5	6.5	0.4	7.4	13.6
15-19 years	23.4	0.8	0.2	0.3	3.7	0.9	2.5	89.0	2.6
20-24 years	19.2	1.1	0.4	0.8	2.2	1.6	4.2	84.9	4.8
25-29 years	2.0	12.7	5.4	6.1	18.3	8.6	9.5	22.1	17.3
30-34 years	1.3	18.7	10.2	6.2	23.3	8.9	3.5	7.3	21.8
35-39 years	1.1	22.8	14.0	4.0	19.3	9.9	0.8	5.3	23.9
40-44 years	1.0	19.2	20.0	2.9	18.0	10.1	0.2	2.9	26.8
45-49 years	1.1	20.3	26.4	2.3	14.6	9.2	0.1	2.4	24.7
50-54 years	1.4	17.4	35.0	1.4	11.8	8.6	0.1	2.3	23.4
55-59 years	1.8	14.9	46.4	0.7	9.6	6.8	*	1.9	19.7
60-64 years	2.3	11.9	54.1	0.3	7.1	6.3	0.1	1.8	18.6
65-69 years	3.2	8.4	65.3	0.2	4.8	4.9	*	1.2	15.2
70-74 years	4.9	4.5	76.7	0.1	3.4	3.0	*	0.5	11.9
75-79 years	7.7	2.9	83.7	0.1	2.7	2.1	*	0.2	8.2
80-84 years	10.5	1.6	88.0	0.1	2.3	1.6	*	0.1	6.3
85 years and over	17.8	1.0	91.7	0.1	2.2	1.0	*	0.1	3.9
Black	100.0	100.0	100.0	100.0	100.0	100.0	100.0	100.0	100.0
Under 15 years	2.6	7.6	4.7	1.0	60.6	6.8	0.3	4.1	14.8
15-19 years	29.7	1.1	0.4	1.1	6.9	0.9	8.0	76.0	5.6
20-24 years	28.3	1.9	0.6	4.7	2.9	1.3	11.5	72.7	4.5
25-29 years	4.9	12.2	3.2	26.1	9.3	7.2	18.7	13.0	10.2
30-34 years	2.9	17.9	7.5	30.0	11.8	9.5	6.9	4.2	12.1
35-39 years	1.8	24.0	10.6	22.4	13.5	10.7	1.7	3.4	13.8
40-44 years	1.3	28.0	20.7	13.0	13.2	10.1	*	1.6	13.3
45-49 years	1.4	25.6	28.3	7.2	11.5	12.7	*	0.9	13.8
50-54 years	1.7	22.6	38.6	4.4	11.2	10.3	0.4	1.7	10.9
55-59 years	2.1	21.2	48.2	1.9	8.6	7.9	0.3	0.5	11.5
60-64 years	2.1	15.5	55.2	1.2	8.2	9.4	0.2	1.4	8.9
65-69 years	2.9	13.1	68.5	0.7	7.0	4.4	*	0.4	5.9
70-74 years	3.6	8.9	77.4	0.3	7.3	3.2	*	*	2.9
75-79 years	4.4	6.1	82.8	0.2	4.8	2.7	*	0.1	3.3
80-84 years	3.9	5.1	86.7	0.2	4.8	1.2	*	0.1	1.8
85 years and over	6.4	2.9	90.3	*	4.7	0.9	*	*	1.2
Spanish-origin	100.0	100.0	100.0	100.0	100.0	100.0	100.0	100.0	100.0
Under 15 years	5.9	3.9	2.1	0.2	32.8	13.7	0.6	4.4	42.2
15-19 years	28.4	0.9	0.2	1.0	8.6	3.1	7.0	69.9	9.4
20-24 years	25.5	1.6	0.7	3.3	2.8	4.2	9.5	66.5	11.6
25-29 years	6.3	8.7	2.4	11.1	9.4	14.6	10.5	19.6	23.6
30-34 years	3.5	8.5	5.4	14.0	12.1	16.8	4.0	8.5	30.6
35-39 years	3.0	17.9	5.2	10.5	7.8	17.6	0.6	10.8	29.6
40-44 years	2.2	16.2	8.8	6.0	5.9	22.8	*	6.3	34.0
45-49 years	2.1	16.0	14.5	4.1	9.0	18.7	*	3.2	34.5
50-54 years	2.1	12.2	19.8	0.7	5.6	18.8	0.5	3.1	39.4
55-59 years	1.9	18.0	30.6	1.0	6.3	11.5	*	3.4	29.1
60-64 years	1.7	13.9	37.6	*	6.1	17.7	*	2.4	22.3
65-69 years	2.3	7.7	56.4	0.4	9.1	12.6	*	0.9	12.9
70-74 years	2.8	6.3	66.4	*	3.0	10.8	*	2.3	11.1
75-79 years	3.7	2.2	80.5	*	3.5	5.6	*	*	8.3
80-84 years	3.8	2.8	84.8	*	3.3	2.7	*	0.4	6.1
85 years and over	4.8	2.1	88.9	*	3.4	1.6	*	*	3.9

Note: * indicates less than 0.1.

Source: U.S. Bureau of the Census. "Detailed Population Characteristics: United States Summary." 1980 Census of Population (Chapter D, Section A). Washington, DC: U. S. Government Printing Office, 1983, Table 266.

Heller, P.L. et al. "Familism in Rural and Urban America: Critique and Reconceptualization of a Construct." *Rural Sociology* 46 (1981):446-64.

Hughes, M., and Gove, W.R. "Living Alone, Social Contact and Psychological Well-Being." *American Journal of Sociology* 87 (1981):48-74.

Johnson, B.L., and Waldman, E. "Marital and Family Patterns of the Labor Force." *Monthly Labor Review* 104 (1981):36-8.

Keeley, M. "The Economics of Family Formation." *Economic Inquiry* 15 (1977):238-50.

Kent, M.O. "Remarriage: A Family Systems Perspective." *Social Casework* 61 (1980):146-53.

Kenyatta, M.L. "In Defense of the Black Family: The Impact of Racism on the Family as a Support System." *Monthly Review* 34 (1983):12-21.

Kitagawa, E.M. "New Life-Styles: Marriage Patterns, Living Arrangements, and Fertility Outside of Marriage." *American Academy of Political and Social Science Annual* 453 (1981):1-27.

Kobrin, F.E. "The Fall in Household Size and the Rise of the Primary Individual in the United States." *Demography* 13 (1976):127-38.

———. "The Primary Individual and the Family: Changes in Living Arrangements in the U.S. Since 1940." *Journal of Marriage and the Family* 38 (1976):233-39.

Krishnamoorthy, S. "Family Formation and the Life Cycle." *Demography* 16 (1979):121-29.

Levitan, S.A., and Belous, R.S. "Working Wives and Mothers: What Happens to Family Life?" *Monthly Labor Review* 104 (1981):26-30.

Long, Larry H., and Glick, Paul C. "Family Patterns in Suburban Areas: Recent Trends." In *The Changing Face of the Suburbs.* Barry Schwarts (ed.). Chicago: University of Chicago Press, 1976.

MacDonald, M., and Rindfuss, R. "Earnings, Relative Income, and Family Formation." *Demography* 18 (1981):123-36.

Masnick, George, and Bane, Mary Jo. *The Nation's Families: 1960-1990.* Boston: Auburn House, 1980.

Matthaei, J.A. "Consequences of the Rise of the Two-earner Family: The Breakdown of the Sexual Division of Labor." *American Economic Review Papers and Proceedings* 70 (1980):198-213.

McAuley, W.J., and Nutty, C.L. "Residential Preferences and Moving Behavior: A Family Life-Cycle Analysis." *Journal of Marriage and the Family* 44 (1982):301-309.

McLeod, P.B., and Ellis, J.R. "Housing Consumption over the Family Life Cycle: An Empirical Analysis." *Urban Studies* 19 (1982):177-85.

Michael, R.T. et al. "Changes in the Propensity to Live Alone: 1950-1976." *Demography* 17 (1980):39-56.

Morgan, S.P., and Rindfuss, R.R. "Household Structure and the Tempo of Family Formation in Comparative Perspective." *Carolina Population Center Working Paper No. 23.* Chapel Hill: University of North Carolina, 1982.

Nock, S.L. "Family Life Cycle: Empirical or Conceptual Tool?" *Journal of Marriage and the Family* 41 (1979):15-26.

———. "Family Life-Cycle Transitions: Longitudinal Effects on Family Members." *Journal of Marriage and the Family* 43 (1981):703-14.

Pitkin, John R. "Interactions Among Population, Household Formation and Housing Consumption." Paper presented at the meeting of the American Real Estate and Urban Economics Association. New York City, 1982.

Population Reference Bureau (Glick, P., and Norton, A.) "Marrying, Divorcing, and Living Together in the U.S. Today." *Population Bulletin* 32 (1977).

Ryder, Norman B. "Models of Family Demography." *Population Bulletin of the United Nations* 9:43-6.

Seward, Rudy R. *The American Family: A Demographic History.* Beverly Hills: Sage Publications, 1978.

Spanier, G.B. et al. "An Empirical Evaluation of the Family Life Cycle." *Journal of Marriage and the Family* 41 (1979):27-38.

Spanier, G.B., and Glick, P.C. "The Life Cycle of American Families: An Expanded Analysis." *Journal of Divorce* 3 (1980):283-298.

Sweet, J.A. "Recent Trends in the Household and Family Status of Young Adults." *CDE Working Paper 78-9.* Center for Demography and Ecology, University of Wisconsin, 1978.

Teachman, J., Polonko, K., and Scanzoni, J. "Demography of the Family: A Review of Recent Trends and Developments in the Field." In *Handbook of Marriage and the Family.* M. Sussman and S. Steinmetz (eds.). Boston: Plenum, 1982.

Treas, J. "Postwar Trends in Family Size." *Demography* 18 (1981):321-34.

Tsui, Amy O. "Family Formation Process Among U.S. Marriage Cohorts." *Demography* 19 (1982):1-27.

U.S. Bureau of the Census. "Household and Family Characteristics: March 1980." *Current Population Reports* (Series P-20, no. 366). Washington, DC: U.S. Government Printing Office, 1981.

———. "Households, Families, Marital Status, and Living Arrangements: March 1982 Advance Report." *Current Population Reports* (Series P-20, no. 376). Washington, DC: U.S. Government Printing Office, 1982.

Waite, Linda. "Working Wives: 1940-1960." *American Sociological Review* 41 (1976):65-9.

———. "Working Wives and the Family Life Cycle." *American Journal of Sociology* 86 (1980):272-94.

Wattenberg, E., and Reinhardt, H. "Female-Headed Families: Trends and Implications." *Social Work* 24 (1979):460-67.

Chapter 12

The Labor Force: Employment Status and Worker Characteristics

The labor force is that part of the population engaged in the production of economic goods and services at a particular time (see Definition Box). Information about the size and distribution of the labor force and the characteristics of its members reveals how the population has organized itself to earn its livelihood. Changes in the size, distribution, or composition of the labor force reflect shifts in the level of economic wellbeing and disclose new patterns of economic and social organization.

Statisticians, labor economists, and others interested in the field of labor have developed definitions and procedures for obtaining detailed and continuous information. A special sample survey of the labor force is made once a month. This is the Current Population Survey (CPS) of the U.S. Bureau of the Census (described in the Technical Appendix in Chapter 2). Information about each month's findings from the CPS is published by the Bureau of Labor Statistics in a monthly publication entitlted *Employment and Earnings* and also in a statistical supplement to the *Monthly Labor Review.* The censuses of 1940, 1950, 1960, 1970, and 1980 all made intensive and detailed inquiries about labor force, and they provide detailed cross-tabulations involving labor force categories and labor force data for small areas that the Current Population Survey cannot yield.

This chapter and the three following chapters undertake to summarize what is known about the United States labor force. The present chapter will concentrate on the following topics:

- Labor force participation
- Weeks worked per year
- Hours worked per week
- Multiple and part-time jobholding

(The topic of unemployment is of such importance and has such a large body of data that an entire chapter—Chapter 15—is devoted to it.) This chapter will lay the groundwork for in-depth studies of occupation, industry, income, unemployment, and poverty in subsequent chapters.

Labor Force Participation

Persons in the labor force are called collectively "labor force participants," and the proportion of the total noninstitutional population sixteen or older participating in the labor force is called the "labor force participation rate." Often it is desirable to know what percentage of the population is actually employed. This statistic is called the "population-employment

Definitions

Labor Force. Persons who, during a specified week preceding the survey ("survey week"), were defined either as "employed" or "unemployed" according to the following definitions.

Employed Persons. (a) All civilians of working age who, during the survey week, did any work at all as paid employees; in their own business or profession or on their own farm; or who worked fifteen hours or more as unpaid workers in an enterprise operated by a member of the family. (b) All those who were not working but who had jobs or businesses from which they were temporarily absent because of illness, bad weather, vacation, labor-management disputes, or personal reasons, whether they were paid for the time off or were seeking other jobs. Members of the Armed Forces stationed in the United States are also included in the employed total.

Each employed person is counted only once. Those who held more than one job are counted in the job at which they worked the greatest number of hours during the survey week.

Included in the total are employed citizens of foreign countries who are temporarily in the United States but not living on the premises of an embassy. Excluded are persons whose only activity consisted of work around the house (painting, repairing, or own home housework) or volunteer work for religious, charitable, and similar organizations.

Unemployed Persons. All civilians of working age who had no employment during the survey week, were available for work, except for temporary illness, and (a) had made specific efforts to find employment sometime during the prior four weeks, (b) were waiting to be recalled to a job from which they had been laid off, or (c) were waiting to report to a new job within thirty days.

Working Age. The minimum age at which a gainfully employed child is officially recognized as being in the labor force. Before 1967 this was fourteen years. Since 1967 it has been sixteen years. There is no official upper age limit to labor force status.

Civilian Labor Force. All civilians classified as employed or unemployed in accordance with the criteria described above.

Labor Force Participation Rates. The proportion of the population that is in the labor force. The *labor force participation rate* is the ratio of the labor force, including the resident Armed Forces, to the noninstitutional population. The *civilian labor force participation rate* is the ratio of the civilian labor force to the civilian noninstitutional population. Civilian labor force participation rates are usually published for age-sex groups, often cross-classified by other demographic characteristics such as race and educational attainment. They usually are reported as percents.

Employment-Population Ratios. The proportion of the noninstitutional population that is employed. The *total employment-population ratio* is total employment, including the resident Armed Forces, as a percentage of the noninstitutional population. The *civilian employment-population ratio* is the percentage of all employed civilians in the civilian noninstitutional population.

Unemployment Rates. The number unemployed as a percentage of the labor force, including members of the Armed Forces stationed in the United States. *Civilian unemployment rate* represents the number unemployed as a percentage of the civilian labor force. This measure can also be computed for groups within the labor force classified by sex, age, race, ethnic origin, marital status, and so on.

Hours of Work. The actual number of hours worked during the survey week. For example, persons who normally work forty hours a week but were off because of a holiday would be reported as working thirty-two hours even though they were paid for the holiday. For persons working in more than one job, the figures relate to the number of hours worked in all jobs during the week; all the hours are credited to the major job.

The distribution of employment by hours worked relates to persons at work during the survey week. At-work data differ from data on total employment because the latter include persons in the zero-hours-worked category, with a job but not at work. Included in this latter group are persons who were on vacation, ill, involved in a labor dispute, or otherwise absent from their jobs for voluntary, noneconomic reasons.

Continued on next page

Definitions

Part-Time Work. Persons who worked thirty-five hours or more in the survey week are designated as working full time. Persons who worked between one and thirty-four hours are designated as working part time. Part-time workers are classified by their usual status at their present job (either full or part time) and by their reason for working part time during the survey week (economic or other reasons). Economic reasons include slack work, material shortages, repairs to plant or equipment, start or termination of a job during the week, and inability to find full-time work. Other reasons include labor dispute, bad weather, own illness, vacation, demands of home, housework, school, no desire for full-time work, and full-time worker only during peak season. Persons on full-time schedule include, in addition to those working thirty-five hours or more, those who worked from one to thirty-four hours for noneconomic reasons and usually work full time.

Full-Time/Part-Time Labor Force. The *full-time labor force* comprises persons working on full-time schedules, persons involuntarily working part time (part time for economic reasons), and unemployed persons seeking full-time jobs. The *part-time labor force* consists of persons working part time voluntarily and unemployed persons seeking part-time work. Persons with a job but not at work during the survey week are classified according to whether they usually work full or part time.

Labor Force Time Lost. A measure of aggregate hours lost to the economy through unemployment and involuntary part-time employment, expressed as a percentage of potentially available aggregate hours. It is computed by assuming that (1) unemployed persons looking for full-time work lost an average of 37.5 hours, (2) those looking for part-time work lost the average number of hours actually worked by voluntary part-time workers during the survey week, and (3) persons on part time for economic reasons lost the difference between 37.5 hours and the actual number of hours they worked.

Weeks Worked in the Preceding Year. The number of different weeks, during the preceding calendar year, in which the person did any civilian work for pay or profit (including paid vacations and sick leave) or worked without pay on a family-operated farm or business.

Year-Round Full-Time Workers. Persons who worked primarily at full-time civilian jobs for fifty weeks or more during the preceding calendar year.

Major Activity: Going to School and Major Activity: Other. Terms used to describe whether the activity of young persons during the reference week is primarily one of going to school or not.

Duration of Unemployment. Length of time (through the current survey week) during which persons classified as unemployed had been continuously looking for work. For persons on layoff, duration of unemployment represents the number of full weeks since the termination of their most recent employment. A period of two weeks or more during which a person was employed or ceased looking for work is considered to break the continuity of the present period of seeking work. Measurements of mean and median duration are computed from a distribution of single weeks of unemployment.

Reasons for Unemployment. Unemployment is categorized according to the status of individuals at the time they began to look for work. The reasons for unemployment are divided into four major groups. (1) Job losers are persons whose employment ended involuntarily who immediately began looking for work, and persons on layoff. (2) Job leavers are persons who quit or otherwise terminated their employment voluntarily and immediately began looking for work. (3) Reentrants are persons who previously worked at a full-time job lasting two weeks or longer but were out of the labor force prior to beginning to look for work. (4) New entrants are persons who never worked at a full-time job lasting two weeks or longer. Each of these four categories of the unemployed may be expressed as an unemployment rate or proportion of the entire civilian labor force. The sum of the four rates thus equals the unemployment rate for all civilian workers.

Jobseekers are all unemployed persons who made specific efforts to find a job sometime during the four-week period preceding the survey week. Jobseekers do not include those persons unem-

Continued on next page

Definitions

ployed because they (a) were waiting to be called back to a job from which they had been laid off of (b) were waiting to report to a new job within thirty days. Jobseekers are grouped by the methods used to seek work, including going to a public or private employment agency or to an employer directly, seeking assistance from friends or relatives, placing or answering ads, or utilizing some other method. Examples of the "other" category include being on a union or professional register, obtaining assistance from a community organization, or waiting at a designated labor pickup point.

Not in the Labor Force. Includes all persons who are not classified as employed or unemployed. These persons are further classified as engaged in own-home housework, in school, unable to work because of long-term physical or mental illness, retired, and other. The "other" group includes individuals reported as too old or temporarily unable to work, the voluntarily idle, seasonal workers for whom the survey week fell in an off season and who were not reported as looking for work, and persons who did not look for work because they believed that no jobs were available in the area or that no jobs were available for which they could qualify—discouraged workers. Persons doing only incidental, unpaid family work (less than fifteen hours in the specified week) are also classified as not in the labor force.

ratio" or simply the "employment ratio" (see Definition Box).

Table 12-1 provides a historical summary of the U.S. labor force for each year since 1950. The following observations are worthy of note. (Also see Figure 12-1.)

1. Labor force growth is intimately linked to population growth. Babies born in one year grow up to enter the labor force within a reasonably short time (within five years) of their sixteenth birthday. Thus a wave or a trough in the birth rate results in an echo wave or trough in the labor force rates about two decades later.

2. The labor force has grown extremely rapidly,

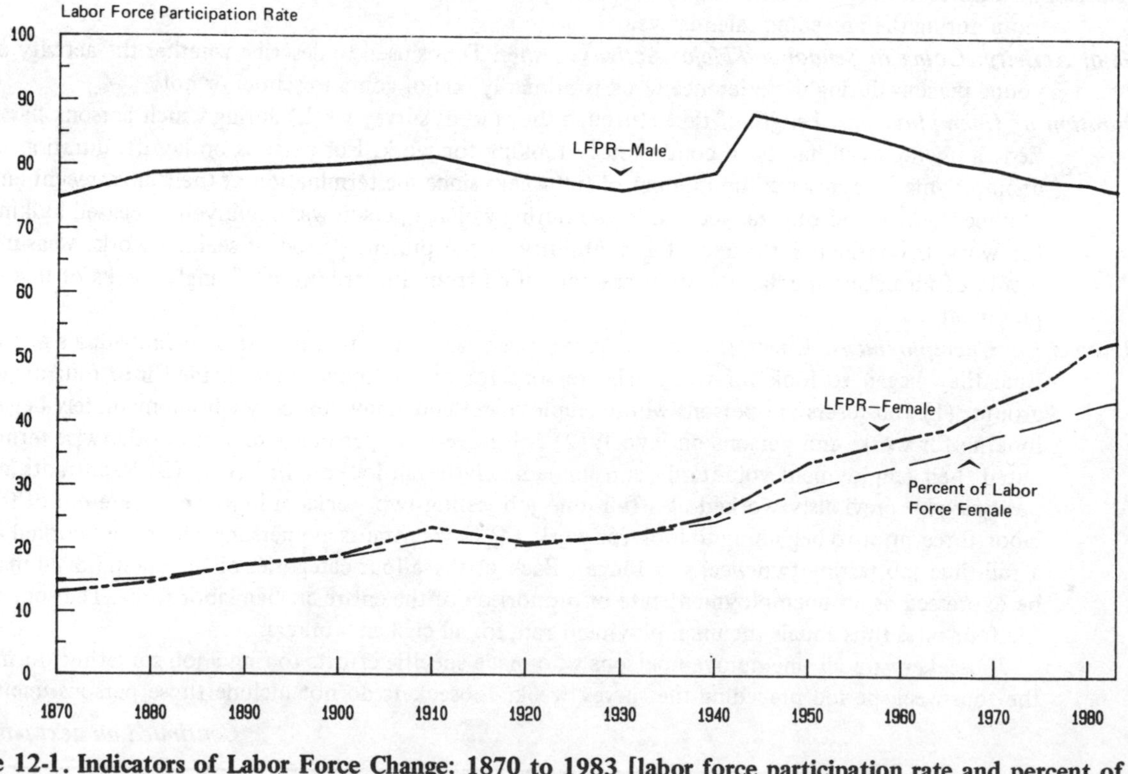

Figure 12-1. Indicators of Labor Force Change: 1870 to 1983 [labor force participation rate and percent of labor force that is female]

Table 12-1. Employment Status of the Noninstitutional Population, by Sex: 1940-1984 [civilian labor force, numbers in thousands]

Year	Labor force: both sexes			Percent Female	Participation rate			Employment/population			Annual labor force rate of growth			
	Total	Employed	Unempl.		Total	Male	Female	Total	Male	Female	Year	Total	Male	Female
1984	113,803	105,288	8,514	43.7[a]	64.6	78.3	54.2	59.8	73.2[a]	50.5[a]	1983–84	2.0	...	...
1983	111,550	100,834	10,717	43.5	64.0	76.4	52.9	57.9	68.8	48.0	1982–83	1.2	1.0	1.6
1982	110,204	99,526	10,678	43.3	64.0	76.6	52.6	57.8	69.0	47.7	1981–82	1.4	0.8	2.3
1981	108,670	100,397	8,273	43.0	63.9	77.0	52.1	59.0	71.3	48.0	1980–81	1.6	0.8	2.7
1980	106,940	99,303	7,637	42.5	63.8	77.4	51.5	59.2	72.0	47.7	1979–80	1.9	1.2	2.8
1979	104,962	98,824	6,137	42.1	63.7	77.8	50.9	59.9	73.8	47.5	1978–79	2.7	1.9	3.8
1978	102,251	96,048	6,202	41.7	63.2	77.9	50.0	59.3	73.8	46.4	1977–78	3.3	2.1	5.0
1977	99,009	92,017	6,991	41.0	62.3	77.7	48.4	57.9	72.8	44.5	1976–77	3.0	2.1	4.2
1976	96,158	88,752	7,406	40.5	61.6	77.5	47.3	56.8	72.0	43.2	1975–76	2.5	1.6	4.0
1975	93,775	85,846	7,929	40.0	61.2	77.9	46.3	56.1	71.7	42.0	1974–75	2.0	1.0	3.5
1974	91,949	86,794	5,156	39.4	61.3	78.7	45.7	57.8	74.9	42.6	1973–74	2.8	2.0	4.0
1973	89,429	85,064	4,365	38.9	60.8	78.8	44.7	57.8	75.5	42.0	1972–73	2.8	2.0	4.0
1972	87,034	82,153	4,882	38.5	60.4	78.9	43.9	57.0	75.0	41.0	1971–72	3.1	2.6	4.0
1971	84,382	79,367	5,016	38.2	60.2	79.1	43.4	56.6	74.9	40.4	1970–71	1.9	1.9	2.1
1970	82,771	78,678	4,093	38.1	60.4	79.7	43.3	57.4	76.2	40.8	1969–70	2.5	2.0	3.4
1969	80,734	77,902	2,832	37.8	60.1	79.8	42.7	58.0	77.6	40.7	1968–69	2.5	1.4	4.5
1968	78,737	75,920	2,817	37.1	59.6	80.1	41.6	57.5	77.8	39.6	1967–68	1.8	1.1	3.0
1967	77,347	74,372	2,975	36.7	59.6	80.4	41.1	57.3	78.0	39.0	1966–67	2.1	1.2	3.9
1966	75,770	72,895	2,875	36.0	59.2	80.4	40.3	56.9	77.9	38.3	1965–66	1.8	0.4	4.2
1965	74,455	71,088	3,366	35.2	58.9	80.7	39.3	56.2	77.5	37.1	1964–65	1.9	1.2	3.1
1964	73,091	69,305	3,786	34.8	58.7	81.0	38.7	55.7	77.3	36.3	1963–64	1.8	1.2	2.9
1963	71,833	67,762	4,070	34.4	58.7	81.4	38.3	55.4	77.1	35.8	1962–63	1.7	1.1	2.9
1962	70,614	66,702	3,911	34.0	58.8	82.0	37.9	55.5	77.7	35.6	1961–62	0.2	-0.1	0.9
1961	70,459	65,746	4,714	33.8	59.3	82.9	38.1	55.4	77.6	35.4	1960–61	1.2	0.6	2.4
1960	69,628	65,778	3,852	33.4	59.4	83.3	37.7	56.1	78.9	35.5	1959–60	1.8	1.1	3.4
1959	68,369	64,630	3,740	32.9	59.3	83.7	37.1	56.0	79.3	35.0	1958–59	1.2	0.8	1.7
1958	67,639	63,036	4,602	32.7	59.5	84.2	37.1	55.4	78.5	34.5	1957–58	1.2	0.7	1.8
1957	66,929	64,071	2,859	32.5	59.6	84.8	36.9	57.1	81.3	35.1	1956–57	0.6	0.2	1.3
1956	66,552	63,799	2,750	32.2	60.0	85.5	36.9	57.5	82.3	35.1	1955–56	2.4	1.4	4.4
1955	65,023	62,170	2,852	31.6	59.3	85.4	35.7	56.7	81.8	34.0	1954–55	2.2	1.2	4.4
1954	63,643	60,109	3,532	30.9	58.8	85.5	34.6	55.5	81.0	32.5	1953–54	1.0	0.8	1.5
1953	63,015	61,179	1,834	30.8	58.9	86.0	34.4	57.1	83.6	33.3	1952–53	1.4	1.8	0.6
1952	62,138	60,250	1,883	31.0	59.0	86.3	34.7	57.3	83.9	33.4	1951–52	0.2	-0.3	1.3
1951	62,017	59,961	2,055	30.7	59.2	86.3	34.6	57.3	84.0	33.1	1950–51	-0.3	-1.8	3.4
1950	62,208	58,918	3,288	29.6	59.2	86.4	33.9	56.1	82.0	32.0	1940–50	1.7	1.0	3.6
1940	52,705	45,070	7,635	24.5	52.8	78.9	25.4	45.1	67.2	22.1	...	...	...	...

[a]Civilian labor force 20 years and over.

Note: ... indicates data not applicable.

Source: U.S. Bureau of Labor Statistics. Employment and Earnings (Table A-33). Also, data for 1983 to 1950 from Employment and Earnings (Tables 1 and 2), and Handbook of Labor Statistics (Table 15). Data for 1940 from U.S. Bureau of the Census. Historical Statistics of the United States (Series D11-25). Washington, DC: U.S. Government Printing Office, 1984, 1983 and 1974.

Table 12-2A. Labor Force Participation Rates, by Age, Sex, and Race: 1930-1983 [percent in the labor force]

Years, sex, and race	Total labor force	16 to 19 years			20 to 24 years	25 to 34 years	35 to 44 years	45 to 54 years	55 to 64 years	65 and over
		Total	16 to 17 years	18 to 19 years						
Total										
Male										
1983 . . .	76.4	56.2	43.2	68.6	84.8	94.2	95.2	91.2	69.4	17.4
1982 . . .	76.6	56.7	45.4	67.9	84.9	94.7	95.3	91.2	70.2	17.8
1980 . . .	77.4	60.5	50.1	71.3	85.9	95.2	95.5	91.2	72.1	19.0
1975 . . .	77.9	59.1	48.6	70.7	84.6	95.3	95.7	92.1	75.8	21.7
1970 . . .	79.7	56.1	47.0	66.7	83.3	96.4	96.9	94.2	83.0	26.8
1965 . . .	80.7	53.8	43.9	65.9	85.8	97.3	97.3	95.6	84.6	27.9
1960 . . .	83.3	56.1	46.0	69.3	88.1	97.5	97.7	95.7	86.8	33.1
1955 . . .	85.3	58.9	48.1	72.2	86.8	97.6	98.1	96.5	87.9	39.6
1950 . . .	86.4	63.2	51.3	75.9	87.4	96.0	97.6	95.8	86.9	45.8
1944 . . .	88.2	72.2	--	--	96.4	97.0		93.2		49.4
1940 . . .	79.1	34.7	--	--	88.1	94.9		88.7		41.8
1930 . . .	82.1	40.1	--	--	88.8	95.8		91.0		54.0
Female										
1983 . . .	52.9	50.8	39.9	60.7	69.9	69.0	68.7	61.9	41.5	7.8
1982 . . .	52.6	51.4	41.0	61.2	69.8	68.0	68.0	61.6	41.8	7.9
1980 . . .	51.5	52.9	43.6	61.9	68.9	65.5	65.5	59.9	41.3	8.1
1975 . . .	46.3	49.1	40.2	58.1	64.1	54.6	55.8	54.6	41.0	8.3
1970 . . .	43.3	44.0	34.9	53.6	57.7	45.0	51.1	54.4	43.0	9.7
1965 . . .	39.3	38.0	27.7	49.3	49.9	38.5	46.1	50.9	41.1	10.0
1960 . . .	37.7	39.3	29.1	50.9	46.1	36.0	43.4	49.8	37.2	10.8
1955 . . .	35.7	39.7	28.9	50.9	45.9	34.9	41.6	43.8	32.5	10.6
1950 . . .	33.9	41.0	30.1	51.3	46.0	34.0	39.1	37.9	27.0	9.7
1944 . . .	--	--	--	--	55.6	39.3		31.1		9.5
1940 . . .	--	--	--	--	45.6	30.5		20.2		6.1
1930 . . .	--	--	--	--	41.8	24.6		18.0		7.3
White										
Male										
1983 . . .	77.1	59.4	46.9	71.3	86.1	95.2	96.0	91.9	70.0	17.7
1982 . . .	77.4	60.0	49.3	70.5	86.3	95.6	96.0	92.2	71.0	17.9
1980 . . .	78.2	63.7	53.6	74.1	87.2	95.9	96.2	92.1	73.1	19.1
1975 . . .	78.7	61.9	51.8	72.8	85.5	95.8	96.4	92.9	76.5	21.8
1970 . . .	80.0	57.5	48.9	67.4	83.3	96.7	97.3	94.9	83.3	26.7
1965 . . .	80.8	54.1	44.6	65.8	85.3	97.4	97.7	95.9	85.2	27.9
1960 . . .	83.4	55.9	46.0	69.0	87.8	97.7	97.9	96.1	87.2	33.3
1955 . . .	85.4	58.6	48.0	71.7	85.6	97.8	98.3	96.7	88.4	39.5
Female										
1983 . . .	52.7	54.5	43.9	64.1	72.1	68.7	68.2	61.9	41.1	7.8
1982 . . .	52.4	55.0	44.6	64.6	71.8	67.8	67.5	61.4	41.5	7.8
1980 . . .	51.2	56.2	47.2	65.1	70.6	64.8	65.0	59.6	40.9	7.9
1975 . . .	45.9	51.5	42.7	60.4	65.4	53.5	54.9	54.3	40.7	8.0
1970 . . .	42.6	45.6	36.6	55.0	57.7	43.2	49.9	53.7	42.6	9.5
1965 . . .	38.1	39.2	28.7	50.6	49.2	36.3	44.3	49.9	40.3	9.7
1960 . . .	36.5	40.3	30.0	51.9	45.7	34.1	41.5	48.6	36.2	10.6
1955 . . .	34.5	40.7	29.9	52.0	45.8	32.8	39.9	42.7	31.8	10.5
Black										
Male										
1983 . . .	70.6	39.9	24.7	55.0	79.4	89.0	89.7	34.5	62.6	14.0
1982 . . .	70.1	39.7	24.6	55.3	78.7	89.2	89.8	82.2	61.9	15.9
1980 . . .	70.6	43.2	31.0	56.7	79.8	90.8	89.1	83.1	61.7	16.8
1975 . . .	71.0	42.6	29.7	57.4	78.8	91.5	89.3	83.5	67.6	20.5
1970 . . .	69.8	35.8	22.2	51.8	76.4	87.6	88.1	85.0	72.4	23.5
1965 . . .	79.6	51.2	39.5	67.0	89.9	95.8	94.2	91.9	78.9	27.9
1960 . . .	83.0	57.7	45.6	71.2	90.2	96.2	95.4	92.4	82.5	31.2
1955 . . .	85.0	60.8	48.2	75.7	90.0	95.8	96.3	94.4	83.3	40.0
Female										
1983 . . .	54.2	33.0	20.8	44.4	59.1	72.3	72.6	62.3	44.8	8.2
1982 . . .	53.7	33.5	23.3	43.3	60.1	70.2	71.7	62.4	44.8	8.5
1980 . . .	53.2	34.9	24.5	45.0	60.4	70.6	68.2	61.4	44.9	9.9
1975 . . .	48.9	34.2	24.8	43.8	56.0	63.0	62.0	56.6	43.1	10.5
1970 . . .	47.5	25.4	13.9	38.1	56.3	58.9	60.4	58.0	44.9	13.2
1965 . . .	42.3	29.4	20.5	40.1	55.3	54.2	59.8	60.2	48.9	13.0
1960 . . .	48.2	32.7	22.1	44.3	48.7	49.7	59.8	60.6	47.3	12.8
1955 . . .	46.1	32.5	22.7	43.2	46.7	51.3	56.0	54.7	40.7	12.3

Note: -- indicates data not available. For white and black, data not available prior to 1955.

Source: Data for 1983 from U.S. Bureau of Labor Statistics. Employment and Earnings (Table 3). Also, Handbook of Labor Statistics (Table 4). Washington, DC: U.S. Government Printing Office, 1984 and 1983. Data for 1970 from U.S. Bureau of the Census. Characteristics of the Population (Table 216). Data for 1960 from Characteristics of the Population (Table 120). Data for 1950 from Characteristics of the Population (Table 120). Washington, DC: U.S. Government Printing Office, 1973, 1961, and 1953. Data for 1944, 1940, and 1930 from U.S. Bureau of the Census. Historical Statistics of the United States (Table Series D 29-41). Washington, DC: U.S. Government Printing Office, 1975.

especially since 1955. The growth has been caused, in part, by the maturation of the "baby boom" generation to ages at which it was seeking employment between 1960 and 1980.

3. The female component of the labor force has grown very rapidly. The female labor force participation rate rose from 25 percent in 1940 to 54 percent in 1984. Although the trend toward greater participation by women has been uniformly upward for more than a century, the most rapid advances have come since 1940, during and since World War II.

4. The labor force has tended to grow faster than

Table 12-2B. Labor Force Participation Rates, by Age, Sex, and Race-Ethnicity: 1980 [percent in the labor force]

Age and sex	Total	White	Black	American Indian	Asia and Pac. Is.	Spanish origin
Male						
16 years and over. .	75.1	76.1	66.7	69.6	76.5	78.0
16-19 years.	52.4	55.5	36.5	44.1	40.4	50.8
16 years	31.7	34.5	18.0	24.1	22.2	27.5
17 years	46.8	50.6	28.1	35.9	35.4	43.1
18 years	61.1	64.1	44.8	52.4	47.9	60.7
19 years	69.9	72.2	56.9	64.9	55.6	71.6
20-24 years.	82.7	84.3	73.5	76.9	69.4	83.5
20 years	75.5	77.4	66.4	70.7	60.6	78.4
21 years	78.7	80.1	70.4	74.6	65.3	81.4
22 years	83.3	84.9	74.7	77.7	69.0	84.4
23 years	87.2	88.9	77.9	80.7	74.5	86.4
24 years	89.0	90.7	79.3	81.7	77.7	87.5
25-29 years.	91.8	93.4	82.2	83.5	84.5	89.8
30-34 years.	94.0	95.3	85.1	85.6	91.9	91.5
35-39 years.	94.5	95.6	86.5	85.4	94.3	92.1
40-44 years.	93.7	94.8	86.1	84.1	94.6	91.4
45-49 years.	92.0	93.1	83.6	81.2	93.4	89.9
50-54 years.	88.5	89.6	78.3	74.8	91.1	86.5
55-59 years.	80.6	81.8	69.4	63.2	84.4	78.8
60-64 years.	60.4	61.0	53.7	46.8	67.6	62.6
65-69 years.	29.2	29.5	26.1	23.3	34.2	31.7
70-74 years.	18.3	18.5	16.3	15.9	21.1	18.7
75 years and over. .	9.1	9.1	8.9	7.9	11.5	9.9
Female						
16 years and over. .	49.9	49.4	53.3	48.1	57.7	49.3
16-19 years.	45.8	49.0	30.3	35.0	39.3	39.0
16 years	26.6	29.2	14.8	20.9	22.7	21.1
17 years	42.0	45.8	24.2	29.1	33.8	33.6
18 years	53.6	57.2	36.8	41.0	45.2	46.6
19 years	59.9	62.8	45.9	49.3	53.9	54.2
20-24 years.	67.8	69.5	61.4	55.8	62.4	59.1
20 years	64.0	66.4	53.4	51.8	56.5	57.8
21 years	65.7	67.5	57.9	56.3	59.9	59.2
22 years	69.3	71.0	63.4	56.7	63.7	59.9
23 years	70.3	71.9	65.3	57.1	65.5	59.4
24 years	69.7	70.7	67.7	57.5	65.8	59.5
25-29 years.	66.3	66.1	70.5	58.9	65.3	58.1
30-34 years.	63.2	62.0	73.0	61.1	65.2	56.7
35-39 years.	64.4	63.6	71.9	61.0	68.5	57.5
40-44 years.	65.0	64.6	70.0	59.8	70.6	58.2
45-49 years.	61.5	61.2	65.1	50.2	67.8	55.2
50-54 years.	56.3	56.1	58.4	48.6	64.2	50.5
55-59 years.	48.4	48.2	50.2	38.4	56.4	42.4
60-64 years.	34.0	33.8	36.9	28.8	39.0	30.3
65-69 years.	15.0	14.8	16.9	13.1	16.5	12.3
70-74 years.	7.8	7.7	9.3	6.5	9.1	6.9
75 years and over. .	3.2	3.0	4.9	3.9	4.6	4.0

Source: U.S. Bureau of the Census. "Detailed Population Characteristics: United States Summary." 1980 Census of Population. Washington, DC: U.S. Government Printing Office, 1984, Table 272.

population (accounting for a twenty-year lag after population change) because of the rising participation of women.

5. The history of labor force participation rates in the past century is graphed in Figure 12-1. It may be surprising to observe that for males the participation rates *rose* from about 75 percent in 1870 to a high of 87 percent in 1948, following which there has been a gradual decline. As of 1984 the rate stood at 78 percent—almost the same level as 113 years earlier. A high percentage of school-age population related to high fertility helped to depress the rate in earlier years; prolonged school attendance and earlier age at retirement have helped to depress it since its peak. Figure 12-1 graphs the trend toward convergence of male and female labor force participation rates and the rising percentage that females comprise of the total labor force.

6. Looking at statistics of the cumulative size of the

labor force and at participation rates tends to mask the fact that there have been very substantial fluctuations in the annual rates of labor force growth. These rates are reported in the three right-hand columns of Table 12-1.

7. It is logical to expect the trends cited above to stabilize at rates of slow growth of the labor force in the very near future. It is difficult to conceive of labor force participation rates for females as continuing to rise beyond the rates for males or for more than 50 percent of the labor force to be female. Hence they must plateau within the next decade or two. Also, because of the "baby bust" that began in 1957 and reached major proportions in the 1960s, the labor force should already be starting to grow more slowly because of fewer new entrants each year. A stage of near-zero growth in the labor force could be achieved toward the end of this century. (See the section on projected growth of the U.S. labor force, below.)

Age Differences in Labor Force Participation

Labor force participation varies a great deal with age. Table 12-2 shows that during the years of adolescence (16-19 years) only about 56 percent of the males and 53 percent of the females are in the labor force (as of 1983). For both men and women the participation rate rises rapidly as age twenty is attained, reflecting departure from school and the shift from dependency to self-support. For each sex, the labor force participation rates have a distinctive age curve. Figure 12-2 illustrates the curves for the white population with data from the 1980 and 1950 censuses. Figure 12-3 charts these age curves for the black population for 1980 and 1950. For males the curve climbs quickly toward 100 percent and remains on a high plateau through ages twenty-five to forty-four, after which it falls slowly as disabilities gradually remove men from work, although it continues to be high right up to age sixty. This pattern reflects the adherence to the cultural dictum that if an adult male is not sick or disabled he should work. Women have a lower participation rate, at all ages, than men. The rate for females climbs to its highest point at about 20-24 years, plateaus until about age forty-five, then begins to descend.

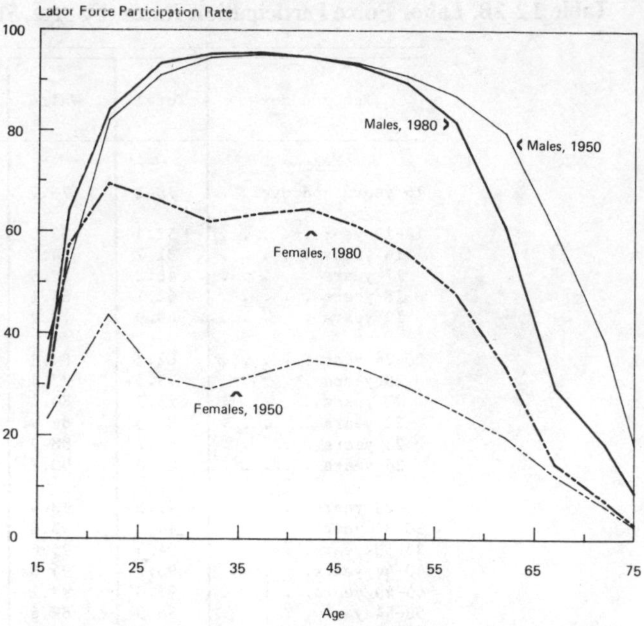

Figure 12-2. Labor Force Participation for the White Population, by Sex and Age: 1950 and 1980

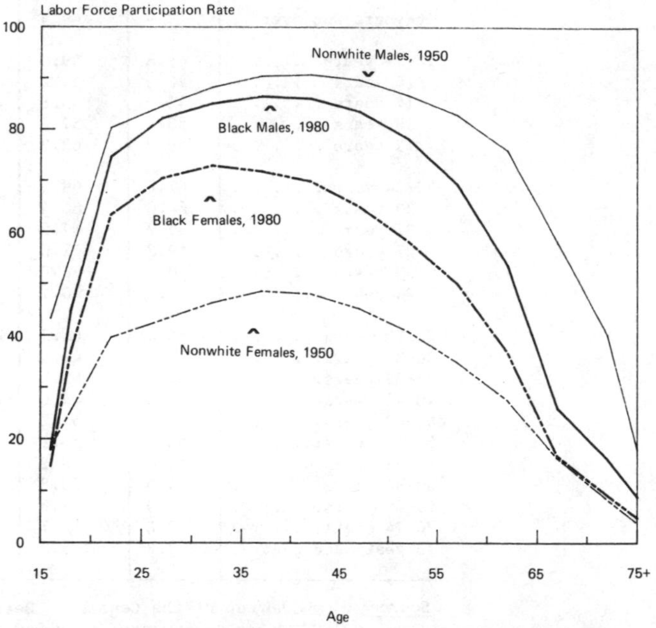

Figure 12-3. Labor Force Participation for the Black Population, by Sex and Age: 1950 and 1980

Trends in Labor Force Participation of Youth

When the United States was an agrarian society, and during the early phase of the industrial revolution, it was customary for children to begin work at a young age. In 1890 about 18 percent of the children ten to fifteen years of age were gainfully employed (26 percent of boys and 10 percent of girls). There has been a long-term decline in the participation of children in the work force. When the labor force definitions of 1940 were established, age fourteen was chosen as the youngest age for which it was worthwhile to collect employment data; that minimum age was raised to sixteen in 1967. As greater emphasis was placed upon attending secondary school and college, the labor force participation rates of persons under age eighteen declined. They reached a low point in the 1930s. However, this downward trend was reversed in the 1940s.

During the wartime emergency, the youth of the nation proved to be a most valuable source of labor. A great many teenagers worked a shift in a factory or held some other job while attending school. In 1944, 72 percent of the boys fourteen to nineteen years old and 41 percent of the girls were in the labor force. After the war's end the young teenagers began withdrawing from the labor force; their withdrawal was gradual, however, and ceased to decline in the 1950s. Instead, it rose again in the 1970s and remained high until 1982, when it again declined (perhaps because of the economic depression). Young girls reduced their labor force participation during the baby boom years of the 1950s and 1960s but reversed the decline in the 1970s. Since 1977 the participation rate for girls under twenty has been as high as or higher than during World War II.

It could have been predicted that the great emphasis upon obtaining higher education would have caused a protracted withdrawal of young people from labor force participation, even into the ages 20-24, but this has not been the case. As will be shown later, there has been a tendency to mix school attendance with work–much of it part time. This situation leaves the meaningfulness of labor force data for ages under twenty unclear and of a different dimension from the labor force data for the adult ages (ages twenty and above).

Trends in Labor Force Participation of Middle-Aged and Elderly Adults

For males there has been a steady decline in labor force participation rates at ages 55-64 and sixty-five and beyond. Whereas fully 42 percent of men aged sixty-five and over were still employed in 1940, by 1983 this proportion had shrunk to only 17 percent. Similar (though less drastic) declines in the participation rates for ages 55-64 occurred. There was even a slight reduction at ages 45-54. Programs of Social Security and disability insurance, increased prosperity, and perhaps increased employment of women have made it possible for men to retire from the labor force at younger ages than ever before.

For women the trend has been exactly the reverse of that for men. Whereas only 20 percent of women aged 45-64 were in the labor force in 1940, by 1980 this proportion had more than doubled. Since 1965 the proportion of women aged fifty-five and over in the labor force has tended to remain stationary, while the rates for younger ages continued to rise.

Labor Force Participation of Females During Childbearing Years

Peak fertility comes in the ages 25-29 and 30-34, and in the 1940s and 1950s it was customary for women to withdraw from the labor force to bear children and rear a family. This pattern has almost completely disappeared in the 1980s, when women are bearing fewer children and more are remaining in the labor force, even though they are mothers of young children. This phenomenon of working mothers will be studied in more detail in a later section of this chapter.

Age and Sex Composition of the Labor Force

The maturation of the baby boom generation, combined with comparatively high participation rates for young people (with declining rates for older men), has caused the labor force to have a much younger age composition in the 1980s than in the 1940s and 1950s. The data documenting this change are provided in Table 12-3. The transformation has been greater for the male than for the female labor force. As a consequence the age compositions of the male and female labor forces are very nearly identical today, whereas in the 1950s the female labor force was considerably younger than the male.

Because of the increased participation of women, the sex composition of the labor force has undergone great changes in the direction of approaching equality in the number of male and female workers. Table 12-4 provides statistics on sex composition for the age categories, for selected dates. The change has been much greater at the older ages than at the younger. Since it was customary for young women to work before marriage, the proportion of male and female teenage workers was not greatly different in 1950 from today. However, the greatly increased participation of women during the childbearing and middle-age years (paralleled with reduced participation of men after age fifty-five) has drastically altered the sex composition of the labor force at all ages older than twenty-five.

Race Differentials in Labor Force Participation

Table 12-2A reports participation rates for white and black workers, respectively. Figures 12-2 and 12-3 graph the age-specific participation rates for the races. The participation rates for black men are significantly below

Table 12-3. Age Composition of the Labor Force, by Sex: 1950-1983 [percent in each age group]

Year and sex	Total labor force	16 to 19 years			20-24 years	25-34 years	35-44 years	45-54 years	55-64 years	65 and over	Total 20 and over
		Total	16-17 years	18-19 years							
Total labor force											
1983	100.0	7.3	2.8	4.6	14.4	28.5	21.2	15.1	10.8	2.7	92.7
1982	100.0	7.7	3.0	4.7	14.6	28.3	20.4	15.3	10.9	2.7	92.3
1980	100.0	8.8	3.6	5.1	14.9	27.3	19.1	15.8	11.2	2.9	91.2
1975	100.0	9.5	4.0	5.5	14.7	24.4	18.0	18.2	12.1	3.2	90.5
1970	100.0	8.8	3.8	5.0	12.8	20.6	19.9	20.5	13.6	3.9	91.2
1965	100.0	7.9	3.3	4.6	11.1	19.1	22.6	21.2	13.9	4.2	92.1
1960	100.0	7.0	3.0	3.9	9.6	20.7	23.4	21.3	13.5	4.6	93.0
1955	100.0	6.3	2.6	3.7	8.7	23.2	23.7	20.0	13.1	5.1	93.7
1950	100.0	6.8	2.7	4.1	11.7	23.5	22.4	18.4	12.3	4.9	93.2
1940	100.0	7.0	2.0	5.0	14.6	25.8	21.2	17.1	10.2	4.0	93.0
Male labor force											
1983	100.0	6.8	2.6	4.3	13.6	28.6	21.3	15.5	11.3	2.9	93.2
1982	100.0	7.2	2.8	4.3	13.8	28.5	20.5	15.7	11.5	3.0	92.8
1980	100.0	8.1	3.4	4.7	14.0	27.6	19.3	16.1	11.8	3.1	91.9
1975	100.0	8.5	3.7	4.9	13.4	25.2	18.5	18.5	12.5	3.4	91.5
1970	100.0	7.8	3.5	4.3	11.2	22.1	20.4	20.3	13.9	4.2	92.2
1965	100.0	7.0	3.2	3.9	10.1	20.5	23.0	20.8	14.0	4.4	93.0
1960	100.0	6.0	2.8	3.2	8.9	22.1	23.6	20.6	13.8	4.9	94.0
1955	100.0	5.3	2.4	2.9	7.2	24.3	23.8	19.9	13.8	5.7	94.7
1950	100.0	5.7	2.4	3.3	10.6	24.0	22.3	18.5	13.2	5.6	94.3
1940	100.0	5.9	1.8	4.1	12.6	25.2	21.8	18.4	11.4	4.6	94.1
Female labor force											
1983	100.0	8.0	3.0	5.0	15.4	28.4	21.1	14.6	10.0	2.5	92.0
1982	100.0	8.5	3.3	5.2	15.7	28.0	20.2	14.9	10.2	2.5	91.5
1980	100.0	9.6	3.9	5.7	16.1	26.9	19.0	15.4	10.4	2.6	90.4
1975	100 0	10.8	4.5	6.4	16.5	23.1	17.4	17.8	11.5	2.8	89.2
1970	100.0	10.3	4.2	6.1	15.5	18.1	18.9	20.7	13.2	3.3	89.7
1965	100.0	9.6	3.6	6.0	12.8	16.5	21.8	21.8	13.7	3.7	90.4
1960	100.0	8.8	3.5	5.4	11.1	17.8	22.8	22.7	12.8	3.9	91.2
1955	100.0	8.4	3.1	5.3	11.9	20.7	23.4	20.2	11.6	3.8	91.6
1950	100.0	9.3	3.3	6.0	14.5	22.3	22.6	18.1	10.0	3.2	90.7
1940	100.0	10.3	2.5	7.9	20.8	27.8	19.3	13.0	6.6	2.1	89.7

Source: U.S. Bureau of Labor Statistics. Employment and Earnings (Table 3). Also, data for 1982-1950 from Handbook of Labor Statistics (Table 3). Data from 1940 from U.S. Bureau of the Census. "Detailed Characteristics of the Population." 1950 Census of Population (Table 120). Washington, DC: U.S. Government Printing Office, 1984, 1983 and 1953.

those for white men at all ages. This differential is of long standing and has characterized labor force statistics since they first began to be collected. The differential has grown greater in recent years and is particularly great at the very youngest and older ages.

Black women tend to have higher participation rates than white women at the adult and older ages but lower participation rates at the youngest ages. This pattern of difference is also of long standing. The difference at the youngest ages appears to be greater in 1980 than in 1950, but the difference at the intermediate and older ages has diminished sharply, as the participation rates for white women aged 30-54 have increased even faster than those for black women of the same ages. The patterns of age-race-sex differences cause the race composition of the labor force to differ substantially by age. Table 12-5 shows the race composition by sex and age for selected years. The male labor force tends to have far smaller proportions of black participants older than forty-five, whereas the race composition of the female labor force tends to have a more equal distribution. Table 12-2B provides data that show Asian adults to have higher labor force participation rates than whites. American Indians have below average participation rates, especially for older males and females of all ages.

Labor Force Participation of the Spanish-Origin Population

As a total the labor force participation rates of the

Table 12-4. Sex Composition of the Labor Force, by Race: 1950-1983 [percent female]

Year and race	Total labor force	16-19 years: Total	16-19 years: 16-17 years	16-19 years: 18-19 years	20 years and over: Total	20 years and over: 20-24 years	20 years and over: 25-34 years	20 years and over: 35-44 years	20 years and over: 45-54 years	20 years and over: 55-64 years	20 years and over: 65 and over
All races											
1983	43.5	47.3	47.3	47.4	43.2	46.4	43.3	43.3	42.2	40.6	39.4
1982	43.3	47.6	46.8	48.1	43.0	46.5	42.9	43.0	42.1	40.5	39.1
1980	42.5	46.7	45.9	47.3	42.1	45.9	41.9	42.2	41.4	39.6	38.0
1975	40.0	45.8	44.8	46.6	39.4	45.0	37.9	38.5	39.1	38.1	35.3
1970	38.1	44.7	42.3	46.6	37.5	46.1	33.5	36.3	38.5	36.8	32.8
1965	35.2	42.5	38.4	45.5	34.6	40.7	30.4	34.0	36.2	34.7	31.4
1960	33.4	42.4	38.4	45.5	32.7	38.5	28.7	32.6	35.5	31.8	28.4
1955	31.6	42.1	37.5	45.5	30.9	43.2	28.2	31.2	32.0	28.1	23.6
1950	29.6	40.6	36.8	43.1	28.8	36.6	28.0	29.8	29.1	24.1	19.2
White											
1983	42.8	47.6	47.5	47.7	42.4	46.4	42.3	42.3	41.6	39.9	38.8
1982	42.7	47.7	46.6	48.4	42.2	46.4	42.0	42.1	41.3	39.8	38.8
1980	41.8	46.8	46.1	47.3	41.3	45.7	40.9	41.3	40.6	38.8	37.4
1975	39.2	45.7	44.6	46.6	38.6	44.7	36.8	37.4	38.5	37.5	34.7
1970	37.4	44.9	42.3	46.9	36.7	46.0	32.2	35.2	37.9	36.5	32.5
1965	34.4	43.1	38.8	46.2	33.6	40.5	28.8	32.7	35.5	34.1	31.0
1960	32.6	43.1	39.1	46.2	31.8	38.5	27.3	31.4	34.8	31.2	28.2
1955	30.8	42.9	38.1	46.3	30.0	43.3	26.7	30.1	31.3	27.6	23.5
1950	--	--	--	--	--	--	--	--	--	--	--
Black and other											
1983	48.8	46.4	46.0	46.5	48.9	46.7	49.9	50.3	48.2	48.1	46.9
1982	48.8	47.0	48.9	46.0	48.9	47.9	49.3	50.0	48.8	48.1	44.4
1980	48.3	46.2	44.2	47.3	48.5	48.1	49.1	49.0	48.1	48.0	46.3
1975	45.8	46.7	46.2	46.8	45.8	46.5	46.1	46.6	45.2	44.0	41.9
1970	43.6	43.4	41.8	44.4	43.7	46.4	42.6	44.8	44.7	40.8	35.6
1965	41.6	38.1	34.7	40.4	41.9	42.5	41.4	43.5	42.6	40.0	35.7
1960	39.8	37.5	33.0	40.6	39.9	38.4	38.6	42.4	42.2	37.7	31.6
1955	38.3	36.6	32.5	39.7	38.5	42.3	39.4	40.3	38.0	33.4	24.7
1950	--	--	--	--	--	--	--	--	--	--	--

Note: -- indicates data not available.

Source: U.S. Bureau of Labor Statistics. Employment and Earnings (Table 3). Also Handbook of Labor Statistics (Table 3). Washington, DC: U.S. Government Printing Office, 1984 and 1983.

Spanish-origin population are quite similar to those for the U.S. total (Table 12-6). However, this is deceptive. When looked at by sex, the participation rate for Spanish-origin adult males (those twenty years of age and older) is considerably above average for all males in the nation, whereas that for Spanish-origin adult females is well below average for all females in the nation. The participation rates for Spanish-origin teenagers of both sexes are also below average for all teenagers in the nation. Spanish-origin adult males have much higher participation rates than adult white males, but the rates for Spanish-origin adult females are below the corresponding rates for the black population. However, Spanish-origin teenagers have higher participation rates than black teenagers.

There is considerable diversity within the Spanish-origin group. The extremely high participation rates for adult males is due almost entirely to the Mexican-origin population. Puerto Rican adult males, in contrast, have lower participation rates than white males, and Cubans are about the average for all males. Mexican adult females are also almost as likely to be in the labor force as white females, but the Puerto Rican females have extremely low participation rates—34 percent in contrast with 53 percent for all females. Cuban females have about the same participation rates as all females.

Puerto Rican teenagers also have very low participation rates in comparison with both Cuban and Mexican youths, who tend to be only moderately below the average for all youth. Puerto Rican and black youths have almost equally depressed labor force participation rates.

Thus Mexican men emerge as overparticipators when compared with other men, and Puerto Rican women and

Table 12-5. Race Composition of the Civilian Labor Force, by Age and Sex: 1975-1983 [percent black]

Year and sex	Total labor force	16 to 19 years			20–24 years	25–34 years	35–44 years	45–54 years	55–64 years	65 and over
		Total	16–17 years	18–19 years						
Total labor force										
1983	10.4	9.9	8.1	11.0	11.7	11.5	10.2	9.7	8.6	7.4
1982	10.3	9.7	8.0	10.7	11.5	11.2	10.3	9.5	8.4	8.0
1980	10.2	9.5	8.4	10.3	11.3	11.2	10.2	9.4	8.2	8.4
1975	9.9	9.4	8.3	10.2	10.7	10.8	10.5	8.9	8.2	8.7
Male labor force										
1983	9.5	10.1	8.3	11.2	11.6	10.2	8.9	8.7	7.5	6.5
1982	9.3	9.8	7.7	11.1	11.2	9.9	9.0	8.4	7.3	7.3
1980	9.1	9.6	8.6	10.3	10.9	9.8	9.0	8.4	7.0	7.3
1975	8.9	9.3	8.1	10.2	10.4	9.4	9.1	8.0	7.4	7.8
Female labor force										
1983	11.7	9.7	7.9	10.8	11.7	13.3	11.8	11.0	10.2	8.8
1982	11.6	9.5	8.4	10.3	11.8	12.9	11.9	11.1	10.0	9.1
1980	11.5	9.4	8.1	10.3	11.9	13.1	11.8	11.0	9.9	10.2
1975	11.3	9.6	8.6	10.2	11.1	13.1	12.7	10.3	9.5	10.4

Source: U.S. Bureau of Labor Statistics. Employment and Earnings (Table 3). Also, data for 1982–1975 from Handbook of Labor Statistics (Table 3). Washington, DC: U.S. Government Printing Office, 1984 and 1983.

Table 12-6. Labor Force Participation of the Spanish-Origin Population, by Sex, Age, and Place of Origin (in Comparison with U.S. Population, by Race): 1975-1983 [percent in labor force]

Sex, age, and year	Hispanic				U.S. total		
	Total	Mexican origin	Puerto Rican origin	Cuban origin	Total	White	Black
Total							
1983.	63.8	65.7	49.2	68.4	64.0	64.3	61.5
1982.	63.6	65.9	51.2	63.3	64.0	64.3	61.0
1980.	64.0	66.4	56.1	66.0	63.8	64.1	61.0
1975.	60.8	*	*	*	61.2	61.5	58.8
Males 20 years and over							
1983.	84.8	86.2	78.6	82.1	78.5	78.9	75.2
1982.	84.7	86.8	78.0	78.4	78.7	79.2	74.7
1980.	85.2	87.1	80.5	83.4	79.4	79.8	75.1
1975.	85.5	*	*	*	80.3	80.7	76.0
Females 20 years and over							
1983.	49.9	50.7	34.4	58.5	53.1	52.5	56.8
1982.	49.9	50.7	36.8	52.7	52.7	52.2	56.2
1980.	48.9	49.1	37.2	53.8	51.3	50.6	55.6
1975.	43.8	*	*	*	46.0	45.3	51.1
Both sexes 16–19 years							
1983.	45.3	49.2	27.1	58.8	53.5	56.9	36.4
1982.	44.8	49.3	30.3	48.4	54.1	57.5	36.6
1980.	50.4	55.9	30.8	50.0	56.7	60.0	38.9
1975.	46.2	*	*	*	54.0	56.7	38.2

Note: * indicates less than 60,000.

Source: U.S. Bureau of Labor Statistics. Employment and Earnings (Tables 40 and 3). Also, data for 1982–1975 from Handbook of Labor Statistics (Tables 6, 7 and 8). Washington, DC: U.S. Government Printing Office, 1984 and 1983.

Table 12-7. Labor Force Participation Rates in Metropolitan and Nonmetropolitan Areas, by Place of Residence, Age, Sex, and Race: 1980, 1982, and 1983 [percent in the labor force]

Age, sex, year, and race	Metropolitan areas			Nonmetropolitan areas		
	Total	Central cities	Suburbs	Total	Farm	Nonfarm
Total						
1983	65.1	62.8	66.7	61.8	64.2	61.6
1982	65.1	62.8	66.6	61.7	65.0	61.4
1980	64.8	62.8	66.2	61.6	63.7	61.4
Males 20 years and over						
1983	79.5	77.0	81.3	76.2	81.8	75.6
1982	79.8	77.2	81.5	76.5	82.6	76.0
1980	80.4	77.6	82.4	77.2	81.7	76.7
Females 20 years and over						
1983	54.4	53.2	55.2	50.3	48.2	50.5
1982	54.1	53.0	54.8	49.9	48.0	50.0
1980	52.6	52.2	53.0	48.5	45.8	48.7
Both sexes 16 to 19 years						
1983	53.6	47.9	57.2	53.3	54.6	53.2
1982	54.3	49.3	57.4	53.7	58.8	53.2
1980	56.7	52.7	59.3	56.7	58.8	56.5
White over 16 years						
1983	65.4	63.6	66.5	62.1	64.8	61.9
1982	65.5	63.8	66.4	62.0	65.6	61.7
1980	65.1	63.5	66.1	61.9	64.4	61.7
Black over 16 years						
1983	62.5	59.8	69.4	58.3	50.2	58.6
1982	62.1	59.3	69.2	57.3	50.7	57.5
1980	61.9	59.9	67.4	57.7	51.5	58.0

Source: U.S. Bureau of Labor Statistics. Employment and Earnings (Table 49). Also Handbook of Labor Statistics (Table 9). Washington, DC: U.S. Government Printing Office, 1984 and 1983.

youth stand out as underparticipators in comparison with other women and youth.

Participation Rates in Metropolitan and Nonmetropolitan Areas

All of the differentials discussed thus far also vary with residence of the population within metropolitan or nonmetropolitan areas. Table 12-7 provides labor force participation rates tabulated to bring out those differentials, with at least partial control of the other differences already discussed.

Participation rates are higher in metropolitan than in nonmetropolitan areas. That is true for each sex separately, for each race, and for teenage and adult groups. Although the differential is not great for males, it is substantial for females and teenagers. It is greater among the nonwhite than among the white population.

Among the population of metropolitan areas, lower participation rates are found in central cities than in suburban areas. This is particularly true for the male population (for females the differential is small). It is true for both white and black workers, but the differential is very striking for the black population. Thus the highest participation rates are found among suburban males and the lowest among females and teenagers of the central cities.

In the population of the nonmetropolitan areas, male farm residents tend to have considerably higher participation rates than male nonfarm residents. The exact reverse is true for females: The nonfarm females have higher participation rates than the farm females.

The differentials associated with residence reflect a number of complex factors. Socioeconomic status, age, opportunity for employment, and perhaps intergroup differences in "work ethic" are involved.

Urban-Rural Differences in Labor Force Participation

Males

In farm households, a higher proportion of men are participants in the labor force than the average for the nation (see Table 12-8). Farm boys and young men 20-24 begin to work at earlier ages than other boys. A great majority of farm men continue to work after they reach age sixty-five, and during the principal years of labor participation (25-64) the participation rates for farm men are considerably higher than for urban and rural nonfarm men. Figure 12-4 provides a visual comparison of the participation rates of farm, rural nonfarm, and urban workers throughout the life cycle. Several factors probably account for the lifelong high participation rate for farm men. One of the most important might be that farm workers, and particularly farm operators, have an opportunity to stay in the labor force, if they so desire, even though they may not work very intensively. A nonfarm worker usually must choose between full-time work and complete retirement. The low participation rates of rural nonfarm males may also be attributed to the ability of rural people to choose their life-style.

Urban males enter the labor force later than nonfarm rural males, probably largely because they remain in school longer. Beyond age twenty-five, however, the labor force participation rate of urban men (both white and nonwhite) is higher than that of their rural nonfarm counterparts.

Among white men living in rural nonfarm areas, labor force participation declines more rapidly after age sixty than among urban white men. This group shows evidence of much earlier retirement than does the population at large. Thus a disproportionately large share of adult males of all ages who are not in the labor force are living in rural nonfarm areas.

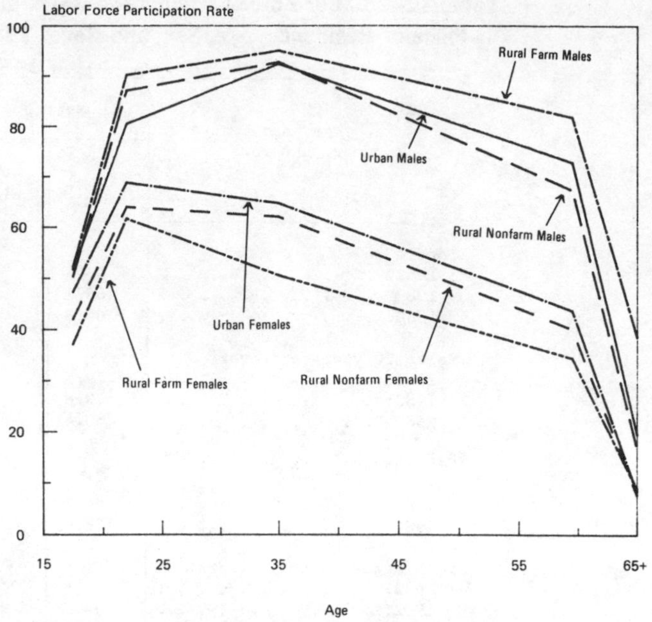

Figure 12-4. Labor Force Participation Rates, by Sex and Urban-Rural Residence: 1980

Table 12-8. Civilian Labor Force Participation Rates, by Urban-Rural and Metropolitan-Nonmetropolitan Residence by Sex and Age: 1980 [percent in the labor force]

Location	Males						Females					
	16 and over	16-19	20-24	25-54	55-64	65 and over	16 and over	16-19	20-24	25-54	55-64	65 and over
Total, United States . . .	74.7	51.2	81.8	92.4	71.3	19.3	49.8	45.6	67.6	63.1	41.6	8.2
Total urban.	75.1	51.8	80.6	92.5	72.9	19.6	51.3	47.4	68.9	64.9	43.7	8.5
Central city	72.7	48.3	77.6	90.1	70.9	19.9	51.1	43.8	40.1	65.9	45.0	9.0
Urban fringe	78.7	55.1	85.1	94.8	75.9	20.0	52.9	51.7	73.0	64.3	43.2	8.0
Places 10,000 and over . .	71.5	51.6	73.9	91.4	70.8	18.9	48.9	46.0	63.9	65.0	43.2	8.4
Places 2,500-9,999	71.1	51.4	82.0	92.3	68.2	17.4	46.2	44.8	64.1	63.2	41.0	8.1
Total rural.	73.5	49.5	85.9	92.1	66.8	18.5	45.4	40.2	62.6	57.8	35.3	7.2
Places 1,000-2,499	71.0	50.4	87.2	92.8	67.4	16.8	44.9	42.1	64.1	62.2	40.1	7.8
Farm	78.1	52.3	90.3	95.1	81.9	38.6	40.3	37.2	61.8	50.7	34.4	9.0
Total metro.	75.9	51.9	81.8	92.8	72.9	19.7	51.4	47.2	69.2	64.1	43.0	8.4
Central city	72.8	48.3	77.8	90.2	71.0	19.9	51.1	43.8	67.2	65.8	45.0	9.0
Metro rings.	78.0	54.2	85.1	94.4	74.2	18.7	51.6	49.5	71.0	63.0	41.6	7.8
Urban.	78.4	55.1	84.9	94.7	75.5	19.7	52.5	51.3	72.4	64.3	43.0	8.0
Rural.	76.8	51.6	85.8	93.6	69.8	18.7	48.2	43.9	65.5	58.6	36.6	7.2
Outside SMSA	70.9	49.2	81.6	91.1	66.4	18.3	45.1	40.8	62.1	59.9	37.6	7.7
Urban.	70.4	50.9	76.1	91.3	69.3	18.2	47.3	45.3	63.9	64.5	42.4	8.3
Rural.	71.3	48.1	85.9	91.0	64.8	18.4	43.6	37.7	60.6	57.3	34.5	7.1

Source: U.S. Bureau of the Census. "Detailed Population Characteristics: United States Summary." 1980 Census of Population. Washington, DC: U.S. Government Printing Office, 1984, Tables 103 and 114.

Females

The farm offers comparatively fewer employment opportunities to women, and for this reason women living in farm households have labor force participation rates below those of urban and rural nonfarm women. This is true for both white and nonwhite women at almost all ages (see Table 12-9). However, with modern automobile transportation, many white farm women work in nearby towns, suburban commercial or industrial places, and cities while their husbands or fathers operate the farm. As a result, urban-rural differences in labor force participation of women in 1980 were far smaller than in 1960. Labor force participation rates of white women changed as follows between 1950 and 1980:

Place of work	Labor force participation rates--white women		
	1980	1950	Change
Total. . . .	49.4	28.1	21.3
Urban.	50.8	32.2	18.6
Rural.	45.4	22.2	23.2
Farm	40.3	15.1	25.2

Labor Force Participation in Poverty and Nonpoverty Areas

In 1970 the U.S. Bureau of the Census identified certain counties and municipal divisions in the United States as "poverty areas" because 20 percent or more of their population received incomes insufficient to maintain the family or household at or above the poverty level. (For definitions of poverty, see Chapter 16.) This delimitation has been used to identify residential areas of the nation where low income and poverty are a major problem. In 1982, 15 percent of the civilian labor force resided in poverty areas and 85 percent in nonpoverty areas. Table 12-10 shows the labor force participation rates by race of the residents of the poverty areas and the remainder of the nation.

Labor force participation rates are significantly lower in the poverty than in the nonpoverty areas for both the white and the nonwhite populations. The disparity is greater for the black than for the white population. Thus poverty is linked as much or more to inability or failure to work as to low pay for those who are employed.

Labor force participation rates are lower in the metropolitan poverty areas than in the nonmetropolitan poverty areas. This is true for both the white and black populations, but the difference is greater for the black than for the white population.

Selected Facets of Labor Force

Marital Status and Labor Force Participation

A high proportion of males who are married and living with their spouses are in the labor force (79 percent)(see Table 12-11). For single men the degree of

Table 12-9. Labor Force Participation Rates, by Age, Race, Sex, and Urban-Rural Residence: 1980 [percent in the labor force]

Age and sex	White				Black			
	Total	Urban	Rural	Farm	Total	Urban	Rural	Farm
Male, 16 years and over . . .	76.1	95.8	74.7	78.4	66.7	68.0	59.3	63.7
16-19 years	54.4	55.6	51.6	52.8	34.2	34.8	31.0	34.9
20-24 years	83.6	82.2	88.0	90.7	71.0	71.9	66.1	78.7
25-54 years	93.7	93.9	93.1	95.3	83.3	84.1	78.4	85.3
55-64 years	72.1	74.1	67.2	82.1	62.2	62.7	59.6	71.8
65 years and over	19.4	19.7	18.6	38.7	17.7	17.9	16.9	31.8
Female, 16 years and over . .	49.4	50.8	45.4	40.3	53.3	54.4	46.3	40.2
16-19 years	48.9	51.5	42.1	37.7	29.9	31.0	24.2	19.6
20-24 years	69.3	71.2	63.1	62.3	61.0	61.0	60.8	54.7
25-54 years	62.5	64.5	57.5	50.6	68.9	69.5	64.8	59.1
55-64 years	41.4	43.6	35.2	34.3	44.0	45.3	36.9	35.8
65 years and over	8.0	8.2	7.1	8.9	10.4	10.8	8.5	11.1

Source: U.S. Bureau of the Census. "General Social and Economic Characteristics: United States Summary." 1980 Census of Population. Washington, DC: U.S. Government Printing Office, 1983, Table 124.

Table 12-10. Employment Status of the Civilian Noninstitutional Population in Poverty and Nonpoverty Areas, by Race: 1982

Employment status and race	Total United States		Metropolitan areas		Nonmetropolitan areas	
	Poverty areas	Nonpoverty areas	Poverty areas	Nonpoverty areas	Poverty areas	Nonpoverty areas
Total						
Civilian noninstitutional populaiton . . .	30,124	142,147	11,322	106,222	18,803	35,924
Civilian labor force	16,996	93,209	6,186	70,279	10,810	22,930
Percent of population.	56.4	65.6	54.6	66.2	57.5	63.8
Employed	14,758	84,770	5,123	64,069	9,633	20,701
Unemployed	2,240	8,439	1,063	6,210	1,177	2,228
Unemployment rate.	13.2	9.1	17.2	8.8	10.9	9.7
Men, 20 years and over	11.8	8.2	16.2	8.0	9.4	8.8
Women, 20 years and over	11.3	7.7	13.9	7.5	9.7	8.4
Both sexes, 16-19 years.	31.6	21.6	41.0	21.6	26.5	21.7
Not in labor force	13,129	48,938	5,136	35,943	7,993	12,996
White						
Civilian noninstitutional population . . .	21,202	128,239	5,749	94,075	15,453	34,164
Civilian labor force	12,274	83,869	3,275	62,089	8,999	21,780
Percent of population.	57.9	65.4	57.0	66.0	58.2	63.8
Employed	11,041	76,861	2,866	57,114	8,175	19,747
Unemployed	1,233	7,008	409	4,975	824	2,033
Unemployment rate.	10.0	8.4	12.5	8.0	9.2	9.3
Men, 20 years and over	9.0	7.6	11.6	7.3	8.0	8.5
Women, 20 years and over	8.4	7.1	10.0	6.8	7.9	8.0
Both sexes, 16-19 years.	24.6	19.8	30.4	19.4	22.7	20.9
Not in labor force	8,928	44,370	2,473	31,986	6,454	12,384
Black						
Civilian noninstitutional population . . .	8,285	10,299	5,279	9,026	3,006	1,274
Civilian labor force	4,364	6,967	2,742	6,137	1,622	829
Percent of population.	52.7	67.6	51.9	68.0	54.0	65.1
Employed	3,414	5,775	2,110	5,096	1,304	679
Unemployed	950	1,192	631	1,042	319	150
Unemployment rate.	21.8	17.1	23.0	17.0	19.6	18.1
Men, 20 years and over	20.5	16.1	22.8	16.2	16.8	15.0
Women, 20 years and over	17.9	13.9	18.0	13.6	17.7	16.6
Both sexes, 16-19 years.	50.9	45.9	52.8	46.2	47.7	44.1
Not in labor force	3,921	3,333	2,537	2,888	1,383	444

Note: Poverty areas classification consists of all census geographical divisions in which 20 percent or more of the residents were poor according to the 1970 decennial census. Persons were classified as poor or nonpoor by using income thresholds adopted by a Federal interagency committee in 1969. These thresholds vary by family size, composition, and residence (farm or nonfarm).

Source: U.S. Bureau of Labor Statistics. Handbook of Labor Statistics. Washington, DC: U.S. Government Printing Office, 1983, Table 10.

labor force participation is smaller (71 percent). For men who are separated, widowed, or divorced, it is also lower (68 percent)(Table 12-12). Among nonwhite men there is a similar but even more marked set of differences between married men and those who are single, divorced, or separated. Table 12-11 shows that there has been a long-term trend for single men to have lower participation rates and for married men to have higher participation rates. These changes are explored in more detail in Tables 12-12 and 12-13.

The reverse situation exists for females. Labor force participation rates are much lower among married women living with their husbands than among unmarried women or those whose marriages have been disrupted by separation, widowhood, or divorce (Table 12-11). Separated, widowed, or divorced women have lower participation rates than single women, possibly because some of them have dependent children or are receiving income from the ex-husband or his estate. These differences are quite large; a higher percentage of the women who do not have husbands in their households must be their own breadwinners.

Table 12-11. Labor Force Participation Rates, by Marital Status and Sex: 1950-1984 [percent in labor force]

Year	Male			Female		
	Single	Married, spouse present	Widowed, divorced, separated	Single	Married, spouse present	Widowed, divorced, separated
1984. . .	70.7	79.2	68.2	63.3	52.8	44.9
1983. . .	70.0	79.5	68.9	62.6	51.8	43.9
1982. . .	70.6	79.9	69.7	62.2	51.2	45.0
1980. . .	70.8	81.2	66.8	61.5	50.1	44.0
1975. . .	67.1	83.1	65.1	57.0	44.4	40.8
1970. . .	60.7	86.9	54.2	53.0	40.8	39.1
1965. . .	50.3	87.7	55.8	40.5	34.7	38.9
1960. . .	55.5	88.9	59.3	44.1	30.5	40.0
1955. . .	61.2	90.7	60.7	46.4	27.7	39.6
1950. . .	62.6	91.6	63.1	50.5	23.8	37.8
1940. . .	71.5	91.3	64.4	54.4	13.7	33.7

Source: Data for 1950-1982 from U.S. Bureau of Labor Statistics. Employment and Earnings (Table 50), and Handbook of Labor Statistics (Table 50). Washington, DC: U.S. Government Printing Office, 1985 and 1983. Data from 1940 census from U.S. Bureau of the Census. 1940 Census of Population. Washington, DC: U.S. Government Printing Office, 1943.

It must be emphasized, however, that the marital status differentials are far smaller in 1980 than in 1950. The participation of women in the labor force has been primarily increased by greater participation of married women. Table 12-11 shows that in 1940 only 14 percent of women living with their husbands worked; by 1984 this proportion was well above 50 percent.

Table 12-11 supports the finding that it is the nonwhite married women living with their husbands who are primarily responsible for the higher labor force participation rates of nonwhite than of white women. Single nonwhite women have *lower* rates of labor force participation than single white women, and nonwhite separated, widowed, or divorced women have about the same rates as white women of the same marital status and urban-rural residence.

By combining widowed, separated, and divorced persons in a single category, Table 12-11 covers up some important marital status differentials in labor force participation. Table 12-12 shows such rates for the widowed, divorced, and separated persons separately. Divorced persons, both male and female, tend to have much higher labor force participation rates than widowed persons. This is partially a matter of age composition. Separated persons, both male and female, tend to have comparatively high labor force participation rates, but lower than divorced persons. Women who are separated or divorced are much more likely to be in the labor force than are women married and living with the husband. The trend of labor force participation according to marital status is explored for age groups in Table 12-13.

Table 12-12. Labor Force Participation Rates of Persons with Broken Marriage, by Sex and Type of Marital Disruption: 1970-1983 [percent in the labor force]

Sex and year	Widowed, separated, divorced	Type of marital disruption		
		Widowed	Divorced	Separated
Male				
1984 . . .	68.2	25.1	82.8	76.1
1983 . . .	68.9	26.6	81.6	79.1
1982 . . .	69.7	27.9	81.7	79.6
1980 . . .	66.8	28.0	79.6	79.4
1975 . . .	65.1	33.6	76.8	79.2
1970 . . .	54.2	31.9	76.1	61.6
Female				
1984 . . .	44.9	20.4	74.3	61.1
1983 . . .	43.9	19.8	74.6	58.7
1982 . . .	45.0	21.2	74.9	60.0
1980 . . .	44.0	22.5	74.5	59.4
1975 . . .	40.8	23.9	72.1	55.3
1970 . . .	39.1	26.4	71.5	52.1

Source: U.S. Bureau of Labor Statistics. Employment and Earnings (Table 51). Also, data for 1982-1970 from Handbook of Labor Statistics (Table 51). Washington, DC: U.S. Government Printing Office, 1985 and 1983.

Presence and Age of Children and Labor Force Participation

In 1950 having a preschool child in the household was a strong barrier against a wife's participation in the labor force. Not so today! (See Figure 12-5.) Table 12-14 shows that married women with no children have only slightly higher participation rates than mothers with children under six years of age. Whereas in 1950 only 12 percent of such mothers were working, in 1983 almost one-half were in the labor force.

The presence of children of school age is less a deterrent to participation than the presence of very young children. The older children are, the greater the apparent inclination of the mother to get a job. Table 12-15 provides additional details about the characteristics of working mothers, by race-ethnicity. Married women with children now have higher labor force participation rates than married women with no children.

The fact that one mother in two who has preschool children and two mothers of every three who have an adolescent child are in the labor force has implications that touch upon family life, childrearing, and many other subjects.

Table 12-13. Labor Force Participation Rates, by Marital Status, Sex, and Age: 1960-1982 [percent of labor force]

Marital status and age	Males 1982	Males 1980	Males 1970	Males 1960	Females 1982	Females 1980	Females 1970	Females 1960
Married, spouse present								
16-19 years	91.9	91.3	92.3	91.5	50.8	49.3	37.8	27.2
20-24 years	96.3	96.9	94.7	97.1	62.2	61.4	47.9	31.7
25-44 years	97.1	97.3	98.0	98.7	62.6	60.1	42.7	33.1
45-64 years	83.2	84.3	91.2	93.7	47.8	46.9	44.0	36.0
65 years and over	19.0	20.5	29.9	36.6	7.1	7.3	7.3	6.7
Single								
16-19 years	55.9	59.9	54.6	42.6	51.5	53.6	44.7	30.2
20-24 years	80.4	81.3	73.8	80.3	75.7	75.2	73.0	77.2
25-44 years	88.4	87.9	87.4	90.5	83.0	82.0	80.5	83.2
45-64 years	64.1	66.9	75.7	80.1	64.8	65.6	73.0	79.8
65 years and over	17.6	16.8	25.2	31.2	13.0	13.3	19.7	24.3
Separated-widowed-divorced								
16-19 years	90.0	75.0	68.8	68.8	53.4	50.0	48.5	43.8
20-24 years	93.3	92.6	90.4	96.9	67.7	68.4	60.3	58.0
25-44 years	92.5	93.1	92.3	94.7	77.8	76.8	67.2	67.2
45-64 years	72.7	73.3	78.5	83.2	60.5	60.2	61.9	60.0
65 years and over	12.8	13.7	18.3	22.7	7.9	8.2	10.0	11.4

Source: U.S. Bureau of the Census. Statistical Abstract of the United States: 1984-85. Washington, DC: U.S. Government Printing Office, 1984, Table 682.

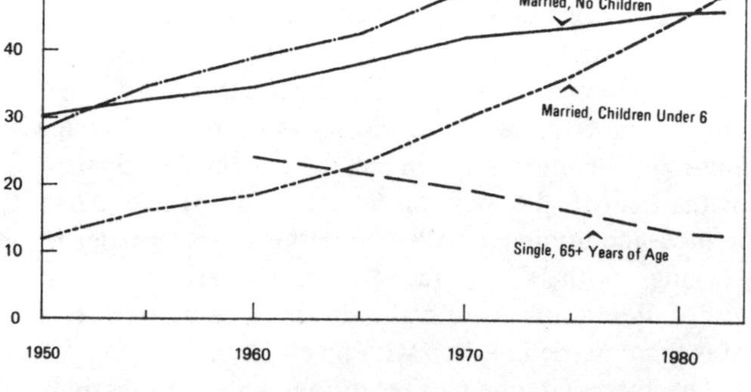

Figure 12-5. Trend in Labor Force Participation Rates of Women, by Marital Status, Age, and Presence and Age of Children: 1950 to 1983

Table 12-14. Labor Force Participation Rates of Married Women, Spouse Present, by Presence and Age of Own Children: 1948-1982 [percent in the labor force]

Year	Total	No children under 18 years	Children 6 to 17 years only	Total children under 6 years
1948	22.0	28.4	26.0	10.8
1950	23.8	30.3	28.3	11.9
1955	27.7	32.7	34.7	16.2
1960	30.5	34.7	39.0	18.6
1965	34.7	38.3	42.7	23.3
1970	40.8	42.2	49.2	30.3
1971	40.8	42.1	49.4	29.6
1972	41.5	42.7	50.2	30.1
1973	42.2	42.8	50.1	32.7
1974	43.1	43.0	51.2	34.4
1975	44.4	43.8	52.2	36.7
1976	45.1	43.7	53.6	37.5
1977	46.6	44.8	55.5	39.4
1978	47.5	44.6	57.1	41.7
1979	49.3	46.6	59.0	43.3
1980	50.1	46.0	61.7	45.1
1981	51.0	46.3	62.5	47.8
1982	51.2	46.2	63.2	48.7

Source: U.S. Bureau of Labor Statistics. Handbook of Labor Statistics. Washington, DC: U.S. Government Printing Office, 1983.

Table 12-15. Labor Force Participation Rates of Currently Married Women, by Age of Own Children and Race-Ethnicity: 1983 [percent in the labor force]

Race-ethnicity	No children	All < 6	Some < 6, some > 6	All 6-17
Total. . . .	46.6	51.4	48.5	63.9
White.	46.1	50.0	46.4	63.3
Black.	51.5	70.3	64.7	69.6
Spanish-origin . . .	46.6	38.9	43.4	53.6

Source: U.S. Bureau of the Census. "Household and Family Characteristics: March, 1983." Current Population Reports (Series P-20, no. 388). Washington, DC: U.S. Government Printing Office, 1984, Table 18.

School Enrollment and Labor Force Participation

One of the most dramatic changes in labor force demography in the recent past has been the participation of teenage youths, at least part time, while attending school. In other words, instead of choosing between continuing their education and earning money, they have chosen to do both. Table 12-16 provides statistics of this development. Whereas in 1950 only 36 percent of the boys and 28 percent of the girls aged 18-19 who were enrolled in school were also in the labor force, by 1983 these proportions had jumped to 47 and 46 percent respectively. This increase in labor force participation of those attending school also extends to young adults aged 20-24, both men and women. There has been a decline in labor force participation of persons aged 14-15 enrolled in school, but an increase for females aged 16-17.

Youth not enrolled in school tend to be in the labor force in very high proportions—70 to 90 percent for

Table 12-16. Employment Status of the Population Aged 14-24, by School Enrollment, Sex, and Age: 1949-1983 [percent in the labor force]

School enrollment and year	Total 14-24 years	Male						Female					
		Total 14-24 years	14-17 years			18-19 years	20-24 years	Total 14-24 years	14-17 years			18-19 years	20-24 years
			Total	14-15 years	16-17 years				Total	14-15 years	16-17 years		
Enrolled													
1983 . . .	35.3	35.3	24.7	14.4	35.7	46.6	55.6	35.2	25.3	14.8	36.2	46.0	56.8
1980 . . .	37.2	37.6	30.0	15.9	44.1	45.6	55.3	36.7	27.7	14.5	40.9	45.2	58.9
1975 . . .	34.3	35.3	29.2	17.7	41.7	41.9	51.2	33.2	26.2	15.0	38.9	41.1	55.1
1970 . . .	31.7	34.0	27.6	17.6	38.9	41.2	51.2	29.1	23.5	14.9	33.5	37.7	50.5
1965 . . .	27.7	32.6	27.8	19.7	37.2	36.2	49.0	22.0	18.5	11.9	26.0	29.0	39.6
1960 . . .	25.3	30.0	26.4	20.2	34.0	34.9	44.2	19.8	16.8	12.2	22.6	27.9	40.6
1955 . . .	26.5	32.5	28.9	22.3	37.3	43.9	41.7	19.4	16.4	12.6	21.4	28.1	42.0
1950 . . .	26.3	31.6	29.9	--	--	36.0	36.0	20.1	18.0	--	--	27.7	32.5
1949 . . .	21.2	24.6	22.5	--	--	27.5	31.2	17.1	15.1	--	--	24.4	33.5
Not Enrolled													
1983 . . .	80.9	90.5	58.5	*	64.3	86.4	93.1	72.1	43.0	*	49.5	70.6	73.7
1980 . . .	81.3	91.4	67.3	*	71.4	89.0	93.8	71.9	47.2	28.6	50.6	73.3	73.2
1975 . . .	77.3	91.7	68.1	*	75.6	91.2	93.5	65.4	43.0	14.5	47.4	66.9	66.6
1970 . . .	72.7	91.4	69.5	*	75.7	86.7	94.6	59.6	36.9	13.0	41.1	63.7	60.0
1965 . . .	70.2	93.7	78.2	*	81.4	91.2	96.3	54.0	41.3	*	42.9	63.3	51.8
1960 . . .	68.6	94.4	77.2	*	81.8	92.8	97.1	50.1	49.3	*	50.8	60.3	46.7
1955 . . .	68.1	94.5	81.4	52.4	88.4	94.8	96.7	51.3	44.4	*	47.3	61.9	48.6
1950 . . .	71.0	94.7	87.7	--	--	95.8	95.5	52.0	51.7	--	--	60.7	49.5
1949 . . .	96.7	94.0	85.7	--	--	94.4	95.3	50.2	50.1	--	--	60.8	47.0

Note: -- indicates data not available. * indicates that for years prior to 1967, percent not shown where base is less than 100,000; for 1967 forward, percent not shown where base is less than 75,000.

Source: U.S. Bureau of Labor Statistics. Employment and Earnings (Table 59). Data for 1982-1949 from U.S. Bureau of Labor Statistics. Handbook of Labor Statistics (Table 63). Washington, DC: U.S. Government Printing Office, 1985 and 1983.

Table 12-17. Labor Force Participation Rates, by Educational Attainment, Age, and Sex: 1970 and 1981 [percent in the labor force]

Sex and educational attainment	25–64 years		25–34 years		35–44 years		45–54 years		55–64 years	
	1970	1981	1970	1981	1970	1981	1970	1981	1970	1981
Male										
Total. . . .	93.5	89.4	96.5	94.7	97.1	95.0	94.6	91.0	83.4	71.3
High school										
Under 4 yrs.	89.3	79.3	96.1	89.3	94.7	89.0	91.5	83.7	79.4	62.1
4 years . .	96.3	91.2	98.2	96.1	98.2	95.8	96.3	92.7	88.8	73.6
College										
1-3 years. .	95.6	92.0	95.7	94.2	98.7	96.0	97.5	92.8	87.5	76.8
4 years+. .	96.3	95.4	95.4	96.1	98.8	98.3	97.4	98.2	90.0	84.3
Female										
Total. . . .	48.9	60.8	45.6	67.4	51.3	66.5	54.4	61.7	43.7	42.1
High school										
Under 4 yrs.	42.9	44.2	40.3	47.4	47.6	52.9	47.9	48.5	36.7	32.7
4 years . .	51.3	62.4	45.5	66.9	52.7	67.9	57.8	65.0	49.4	45.3
College										
1-3 years. .	50.8	68.0	45.5	71.6	52.7	72.8	57.0	66.9	50.6	50.7
4 years+. .	60.9	74.3	57.6	78.7	57.7	74.0	67.5	76.3	64.1	54.7

Source: Anne McDougall Young. "Educational Attainment of Workers, March 1981." Monthly Labor Review 105 (1982):52-55, Table 2.

males and 60 to 70 percent for females ages eighteen and above.

Table 12-16 brings out another interesting point: A considerable number of adolescent boys and girls who are not enrolled in school are not in the labor force either. For example, at ages sixteen and seventeen a very large proportion of the boys who are not in school are neither working nor looking for work. Even at ages eighteen and nineteen about 15 percent of the boys who are not in school are also not in the labor force. The corresponding proportions for girls are even higher. This indicates that a large group of young men and women in their late teens and early twenties are "floating." Table 12-16 reveals that this situation has worsened over the past three decades. Although school enrollment rates have risen, the labor force participation of the minority of teenage boys who do not attend school has declined at every age.

Educational Attainment and Labor Force Participation

For adult workers who have completed their education, the highest labor force participation rates are found among those who have completed high school or attended college. The lowest labor force participation rates are found among those with only an elementary school education. Table 12-17 provides data for the years 1981 and 1970 that show this to be true for every age group and for both males and females. Among women workers the level of educational attainment is an especially potent influence on level of participation. With each increment in educational attainment, a higher proportion of the women in every age group are found in the labor force.

This set of differentials and the rapidly rising general level of educational attainment (discussed in Chapter 10) are contributing to a progressively higher level of educational attainment in the labor force of the United States. Table 12-18 shows this trend for the years 1959-84. The proportion of semi-illiterate workers (those with less than five years of elementary school) has shrunk practically to zero, while there is a very large increase in the proportion of workers with college degrees.

In future years, as older workers with below-average educational attainment continue to retire from the labor force and are replaced by younger persons who have completed above-average amounts of education, the educational level of the labor force will continue to rise. It is a most impressive fact that in 1982 one worker in

Table 12-18. Educational Attainment of the Civilian Labor Force, by Race-Ethnicity: Selected Years, 1959-1984 [numbers in thousands]

Year, race and Spanish-origin	Total	Percent distribution							Median school years completed
		Total	Elementary		High school		College		
			Less than 5 years[a]	5 to 8 years	1 to 3 years	4 years	1 to 3 years	4 years or more	
Total									
1984	111,943	100.0	1.0	5.5	13.0	40.7	19.0	20.9	12.8
1980	105,449	100.0	1.2	7.1	15.5	40.1	17.9	18.2	12.7
1975	92,328	100.0	1.7	10.0	17.6	39.6	15.5	15.7	12.5
1970	78,955	100.0	2.4	15.1	17.3	39.0	13.3	12.9	12.4
1965	71,129	100.0	3.7	19.6	19.2	35.5	10.5	11.6	12.2
1959	65,842	100.0	5.3	25.2	19.8	30.7	9.3	9.6	12.0
White									
1984	97,617	100.0	0.8	5.2	12.4	40.9	19.1	21.6	12.8
1980	92,693	100.0	1.0	6.8	14.7	40.4	18.0	19.1	12.7
1975	81,789	100.0	1.3	9.5	16.8	40.2	15.9	16.3	12.6
1970	70,186	100.0	1.8	14.4	16.4	40.0	13.9	13.6	12.4
1965	63,261	100.0	2.7	18.9	18.4	36.8	11.0	12.2	12.3
1959	58,726	100.0	3.8	23.9	19.6	32.5	9.8	10.3	12.1
Black[b]									
1984	11,696	100.0	1.7	8.3	18.4	41.5	18.5	11.6	12.5
1980	10,472	100.0	2.7	9.7	23.1	39.3	16.1	9.1	12.4
1975	10,369	100.0	4.9	14.0	23.1	34.8	12.4	10.8	12.2
1970	8,769	100.0	7.4	20.6	24.7	31.0	9.0	7.4	11.7
1965	7,868	100.0	11.8	25.7	24.9	24.4	6.1	7.0	10.5
1959	7,116	100.0	17.8	35.5	21.1	16.5	4.9	4.1	8.6
Spanish-origin									
1984	6,249	100.0	7.4	19.2	18.2	31.8	15.1	8.3	12.2
1980	5,348	100.0	9.2	19.7	19.1	31.5	13.1	7.4	12.1
1975[c]	4,038	100.0	10.8	22.9	20.0	28.4	11.1	6.8	11.5

[a] Includes persons reporting no school years completed.

[b] Prior to 1977, data refer to black and other workers.

[c] Data not available for Spanish-origin in prior years.

Note: Data for 1972 forward refer to persons 16 years and over; 18 years and over for prior years. Data for persons whose educational attainment was not reported were distributed among the other categories.

Source: U.S. Bureau of Labor Statistics. Employment and Earnings. Washington, DC: U.S. Government Printing Office, 1985, Table 61.

five is a college graduate. As recently as about 1930 the average worker was a graduate of elementary school, and only one in twenty had completed college.

The Spanish-origin population is the only subgroup of the population with important proportions of workers with elementary (less than eight years) education or less than a full high school education.

Hours Worked per Week: Part-Time Workers

Historically there has been a long-term decline in the average length of the workweek. During the last decade of the nineteenth century the average was fifty-eight hours per week. In 1980 the average American worker

Table 12-19. Full-Time or Part-Time Work and Average Hours Worked, by Age and Sex: 1983

Sex and age	Total at work	Part time		Full time schedules			Average hours	
		Economic reasons	Voluntary	Total	40 hours or less	41 hours or more	Total at work	Full time schedules
Males, 16 and over	100.0	5.4	7.2	87.5	55.0	32.4	41.0	44.0
16-17 years.	100.0	11.9	71.4	16.7	13.6	3.1	19.2	39.2
18-19 years.	100.0	16.6	32.4	51.0	38.9	12.1	30.2	41.0
20-24 years.	100.0	9.3	11.8	79.0	53.9	25.0	38.0	42.8
25-44 years.	100.0	4.3	2.1	93.6	56.5	37.1	43.1	44.5
45-64 years.	100.0	3.6	2.8	93.6	60.2	33.4	42.5	44.0
65 years and over. . . .	100.0	4.3	42.8	53.0	35.2	17.8	31.2	43.6
Females, 16 and over . . .	100.0	8.0	21.5	70.6	56.4	14.1	34.4	40.5
16-17 years.	100.0	11.4	76.4	12.2	10.6	1.5	17.8	38.0
18-19 years.	100.0	18.3	39.9	41.8	34.9	6.9	27.6	39.9
20-24 years.	100.0	10.8	18.7	70.4	57.6	12.8	34.3	40.2
25-44 years.	100.0	6.8	17.1	76.0	60.0	16.0	35.8	40.6
45-64 years.	100.0	6.6	19.5	74.0	59.7	14.3	35.4	40.5
65 years and over. . . .	100.0	5.8	54.9	39.3	30.9	8.4	26.6	41.2

Source: U.S Bureau of Labor Statistics. Employment and Earnings. Washington, DC: U.S. Government Printing Office, 1984, Table 33.

was working forty-one hours per week, seventeen hours less than the average worker of 1890 (see Table 12-19). This decline has taken place in both agricultural and nonagricultural industries, but the nonfarm worker still works about eight hours per week less than his country cousin on the farm. As recently as 1980 the average farm workweek was more than forty-five hours.

Many persons who are employed do not have full-time jobs. Instead, they may work only a few hours per day or a few days each week. The U.S. Bureau of the Census, which collects data concerning hours worked as a part of its monthly survey of the labor force, defines full-time work as a total of thirty-five hours or more per week. Workers who work less than thirty-five hours per week are classed as part-time workers. The forty-hour week has come to be regarded as standard, and census statistics as to the number of workers who work forty-one hours or more per week are regarded as being a measure of the amount of "overtime" work.

The following summary of part-time and full-time workers presents the picture of hours worked as of 1981:

Full time	67.8
Part time	32.2
15-34 hours	27.3
1-14 hours	4.9

A much higher proportion of women than of men are part-time workers. More nonwhite males than white males, and more nonwhite females than white females, are part-time workers. The average workweek of women workers is about ten hours shorter than that of men, and the average workweek of nonwhite workers is about four hours shorter than that of white workers. In assembling this information, the Bureau of the Census also asks the reason for working part time. Two categories of reasons are recognized:

- *Economic reasons*—slack work, inability to find full-time work, material shortages, repairs to plant or equipment, beginning or termination of job during the week
- *Other reasons*—labor disputes, bad weather, own illness, vacation, demands of home housework, attendance at school, no desire for full-time work, full-time worker only during peak season, legal or religious holiday, and other such reasons.

Furthermore, the Bureau of the Census classifies the workers who were found to be working part time during the week of the census monthly survey according to whether they are usually part-time or full-time workers. The results for 1983 are reported in Tables 12-19 and 12-20.

A much higher proportion of women than of men work part-time—for both economic and voluntary reasons. That a greater proportion of nonwhite than of white workers are employed only part time may be attributed both to economic and to other reasons, but the differences between white and nonwhite workers are due more to economic reasons.

Table 12-19 presents a classification of part-time and full-time workers by age. The part-time workers, both males and females, are the very young and the very old.

Tables 12-20 and 12-21 explore the relationship

Table 12-20. Full-Time or Part-Time Work and Average Hours Worked, by Race, Marital Status, and Sex: 1983 [percent distribution]

Sex, age, race, and marital status	Total at Work	Part time		Full time schedules			Average hours	
		Economic reasons	Voluntary	Total	40 hours or less	41 hours or more	Total at work	Full time schedules
Race								
White, 16 years and over.	100.0	6.1	14.0	79.9	54.2	25.6	38.2	42.9
Men	100.0	5.0	7.3	87.7	53.7	34.0	41.2	44.3
Women	100.0	7.6	22.7	69.7	54.9	14.8	34.3	40.7
Black, 16 years and over.	100.0	10.3	8.9	80.8	67.2	13.6	36.7	40.6
Men	100.0	9.4	5.7	84.9	66.8	18.1	38.4	41.6
Women	100.0	11.3	12.2	76.5	67.6	8.9	35.0	39.5
Marital Status								
Men, 16 years and over								
Married, spouse present	100.0	3.5	3.2	93.3	56.8	36.5	42.9	44.4
Widowed, divorced, separated. .	100.0	6.4	4.9	88.7	55.8	32.9	41.4	44.1
Single (never married).	100.0	10.0	18.9	71.1	49.9	21.2	35.7	42.6
Women, 16 and over								
Married, spouse present	100.0	6.9	23.1	70.0	56.8	13.2	34.3	40.3
Widowed, divorced, separated. .	100.0	8.0	12.4	79.6	61.4	18.2	36.9	41.0
Single (never married).	100.0	10.2	24.9	64.9	52.0	12.9	32.9	40.5

Source: U.S. Bureau of Labor Statistics. Employment and Earnings. Washington, DC: U.S. Government Printing Office, 1984, Table33.

between marital status and household living arrangements and part-time employment. Voluntary part-time work is more common among single than among married or ever married men; it is also more common among single and currently married women than among divorced, separated, or widowed women.

Part-time work is also more common in households headed by women, either living alone or with their own children, no husband present. Table 12-21, which provides information for racial groups, shows that Spanish-origin and Asian populations are least inclined to work part time, and black householders are most inclined.

Weeks Worked per Year: Year-Round, Part-Year, and Intermittent Workers

The number of persons who are at work during any particular week of a year is much smaller than the total number of persons in the population who work at some time during the year. Many workers are employed for less than a full year. Throughout a year new workers continuously enter the labor force, and older workers retire; by definition, such people work less than a full year. In addition, some workers are only seasonally employed and others are sporadically employed. Many students find summer jobs that they leave when school opens. As a result of these situations, the U.S. Bureau of the Census, when conducting its annual special survey of the "work experience" of the civilian population during the preceding year, finds that part-year work is very common and during any one year there is a large turnover in the labor force personnel. Hence, some worthwhile insights concerning the labor force can be obtained by classifying the population according to the number of weeks worked during a year. The Bureau of the Census defines anyone who worked 50-52 weeks as a "year-round" worker and anyone who worked 1-49 weeks as a "part-year" worker. The workers may also be classified according to whether they worked primarily at full-time jobs (thirty-five hours or more per week during a majority of the weeks worked), or primarily at part-time jobs (less than thirty-five hours per week during a majority of the weeks worked). These classifications make it possible to arrive at tabulations of the number of year-round and part-time workers. Table 12-22 is a summary of such data for the period 1950-1983. By grouping the various items of this table it is possible to recognize a category of "nonworkers" (persons who did not work at all during the year) and the following categories of workers:

Type of worker	Percent of persons who worked in 1982	
	Male	Female
Full-time worker (35 hours or more per week).	85.4	66.9
Year-round full-time worker--worked primarily at full-time jobs for 50 or more weeks during the year.	64.2	47.7
Part-year full-time worker--worked primarily at full-time job for less than 50 weeks but more than 26 weeks	11.9	10.2
Intermittent worker--worked primarily at full-time job but for 26 weeks or less	9.4	9.0
Part-time worker (less than 35 hours per week)	14.6	33.1
Year-round part-time worker. . . .	5.0	13.1
Part-year part-time worker	11.6	20.0

Only slightly more than one-half of all workers who are employed during any year may be called year-round full-time workers. Yet all but a small fraction of jobs are full-time (full workweek) jobs. For males, there has been little change over recent years, but for women the trend has been toward a higher proportion of full-time, full-year employment and greater part-time, year-round employment with less part-year employment.

Intermittent and irregular workers are primarily very young and very old male workers and women (see Table 12-23A).

Workers give several reasons for part-time work (Table 12-23B), reasons that vary with sex, race, age, and urban/rural residence. Among males, unemployment or layoff is the primary reason, and illness or disability and going to school are the second and third most important reasons. Among women taking care of the home accounts for more than one-half of all part-time work. The other reasons given by women are much the same as those given by the men workers and are ranked in the same way.

Table 12-21. Percent of Householders Working Part-Time, by Type of Household or Family, Multiple Workers, Presence of Children, and Race: 1980

Type of household or family	All races	White	Black	American Indian	Asian and Pac. Is.	Spanish origin
All householders.	10.4	10.0	14.8	10.9	10.2	9.6
Nonfamily households.	16.4	16.2	17.8	15.7	16.6	13.9
Male householder.	11.5	11.3	12.4	12.6	14.2	11.0
Female householder.	21.9	21.7	24.6	20.3	19.9	19.3
Family households	8.8	8.3	13.9	9.6	8.5	8.7
Married couple: male HH.	6.8	6.6	9.4	7.1	7.1	6.8
Married couple: female HH.	24.7	25.5	21.2	21.0	18.9	20.1
Female householder, NHP: total	20.8	20.4	22.2	18.5	18.3	19.1
Without own children.	21.5	20.4	26.1	21.9	17.9	18.2
With children under 6	22.6	23.1	22.2	18.5	22.0	19.9
With children 6-17 only	19.5	19.3	20.1	16.8	17.3	19.2
Male householder, NWP	9.4	8.8	11.8	10.1	11.6	9.4
Multiple worker households.	8.2	7.8	12.4	9.3	8.9	8.4
Nonfamily households.	16.3	16.3	15.5	15.5	19.4	13.7
Male householder.	12.8	12.9	11.6	12.4	17.9	11.1
Female householder.	22.1	22.1	22.7	21.3	21.8	20.1
Family households	7.6	7.1	12.2	8.8	8.1	8.0
Married couple: male HH.	5.8	5.5	8.6	6.8	6.8	6.4
Married couple: female HH.	24.4	25.4	20.2	20.4	18.8	19.9
Female householder, NHP: total	20.8	20.2	23.1	18.5	17.7	18.4
Without own children.	21.2	20.4	25.1	21.9	18.0	17.7
With children under 6	21.8	22.3	21.8	17.8	21.3	18.5
With children 6-17 only	20.0	19.7	21.4	15.7	16.0	19.3
Male householder, NWP	9.7	9.2	11.6	10.4	11.9	9.6

Note: Abbreviations: HH= householder; NHP= no husband present; NWP= no wife present.

Source: U.S. Bureau of the Census. "Detailed Population Characteristics: United States Summary." 1980 Census of Population. Washington, DC: U.S. Government Printing Office, 1984, Table 274.

There is comparatively little evidence that any particular age, sex, race, or residence group works part time because it prefers part-time work, except for persons attending school and women with home responsibilities.

A Profile of Working Wives

As of 1983, 51 percent of all white wives living with their husbands were in the labor force. For black wives the proportion was even higher, 61 percent. Tables 12-24 and 12-25 show some of the characteristics of married couple families where the wife does and does not work. Part A is devoted to white wives and part B to black wives. In general, working wives are most prevalent in metropolitan areas; where there are one or two children under eighteen years of age; where children are of school age; where the husband is under forty-five years; where there are no elderly persons in the household; where both husband and wife attended college; where the family has not recently migrated, but was locally mobile; and where the wife was black. Part-time employment and unemployment of husband were only mild stimulants, and the presence of children was only a mild deterrent.

Multiple Jobholding

More than one in every twenty workers holds two or more jobs simultaneously. In its survey for 1980 the Bureau of the Census estimated that 4.8 million persons (4.9 percent of the total employed workers) were employed at two or more jobs during the week of the survey. This level of multiple jobholding is of long standing. It has fluctuated over the years but has declined only slightly. Multiple jobholding now is about equally common among agricultural workers and nonagricultural workers. Wage and salary workers in the nonagricultural sector are more inclined to hold multiple jobs than are self-employed workers.

The Status of Nonworkers

What do the people do who are not in the labor force? Why are they not working? These questions are answered, at least in part, by the data in Table 12-26,

Table 12-22. Persons with Employment During the Preceding Year, by Sex, Weeks Worked, and Employment Status: 1950-1983 [percent distribution]

Sex and year	Total	Full time[a]				Part time[b]			
		Total	50-52 weeks	27-49 weeks	1-26 weeks	Total	50-52 weeks	27-49 weeks	1-26 weeks
Male									
1983	100.0	85.4	64.2	11.9	9.4	14.6	5.0	3.1	6.4
1980	100.0	87.2	65.2	12.9	9.1	12.8	4.4	3.0	5.5
1975	100.0	87.5	63.8	13.4	10.3	12.5	4.4	3.0	5.1
1970[c]	100.0	87.5	66.1	13.0	8.4	12.5	4.4	2.6	5.4
1965	100.0	86.9	67.3	12.0	7.5	13.1	4.4	2.3	6.4
1960	100.0	86.9	63.9	15.3	7.7	13.1	4.5	2.5	6.1
1955	100.0	89.9	67.5	15.5	7.0	10.1	4.1	2.2	3.8
1950	100.0	90.2	65.4	16.7	8.0	9.8	3.1	2.2	4.6
Female									
1983	100.0	66.9	47.7	10.2	9.0	33.1	13.4	7.9	11.8
1980	100.0	67.8	44.7	12.0	11.0	32.2	11.9	8.0	12.3
1975	100.0	67.1	41.4	12.2	13.5	32.9	11.7	8.3	12.8
1970	100.0	67.9	40.7	12.8	14.4	32.1	10.0	7.5	14.6
1965	100.0	68.5	38.8	14.4	15.4	31.5	9.2	6.1	16.2
1960	100.0	67.6	36.9	14.6	16.0	32.4	10.0	6.6	15.8
1955	100.0	71.3	37.9	16.5	16.9	28.7	10.3	5.4	13.0
1950	100.0	73.4	36.8	17.9	18.7	26.6	8.2	5.1	13.2

[a]Usually worked 35 hours or more per week.

[b]Usually worked 1 to 34 hours per week.

[c]Data for 1970 forward refer to persons 16 years and over; 14 years and over for prior years.

Source: Bureau of Labor Statistics. Handbook of Labor Statistics. Washington, DC: U.S. Government Printing Office, 1984 (Table 46) and 1983 (Table 45).

Table 12-23A. Nonagricultural Workers on Voluntary Part-Time Schedules, by Selected Characteristics: 1970-1982 [percent distribution]

Characteristic	1982	1980	1975	1970
Total				
Number.	12,455	12,555	10,694	9,392
Percent.	100.0	100.0	100.0	100.0
Sex and age				
Male	29.3	30.5	31.3	32.2
16-17 years.	6.4	8.0	8.7	9.2
18-24 years.	10.7	10.2	10.3	11.0
25-44 years.	4.2	3.8	3.5	3.0
45-64 years.	3.3	3.4	3.5	3.3
65 years and over. . .	4.8	5.0	5.3	5.8
Female	70.7	69.5	68.7	67.8
16-17 years.	7.0	8.1	8.7	8.2
18-24 years.	15.0	14.3	13.6	12.2
25-44 years.	28.1	26.7	24.4	23.9
45-64 years.	16.3	16.0	17.8	19.1
65 years and over. . .	4.4	4.4	4.2	4.4
Race and sex				
White.	91.7	91.2	90.7	90.4
Male	26.6	27.5	28.2	29.4
Female	65.1	63.6	62.4	61.1
Black.	6.2	7.1	7.8	--
Male	2.0	2.4	2.4	--
Female	4.3	4.8	5.4	--
Sex and marital status				
Male				
Single	18.6	19.4	19.5	20.0
Married, spouse present.	9.1	9.5	10.1	10.6
Widowed, divorced, or separated . . .	1.7	1.6	1.7	1.5
Female				
Single	20.7	20.7	19.8	18.0
Married, spouse present.	41.9	40.4	40.5	41.5
Widowed, divorced, or separated . . .	8.2	8.3	8.5	8.6

Note: -- indicates data not available.

Source: Bureau of Labor Statistics. Handbook of Labor Statistics. Washington, DC: U.S. Government Printing Office, 1983, Table 19.

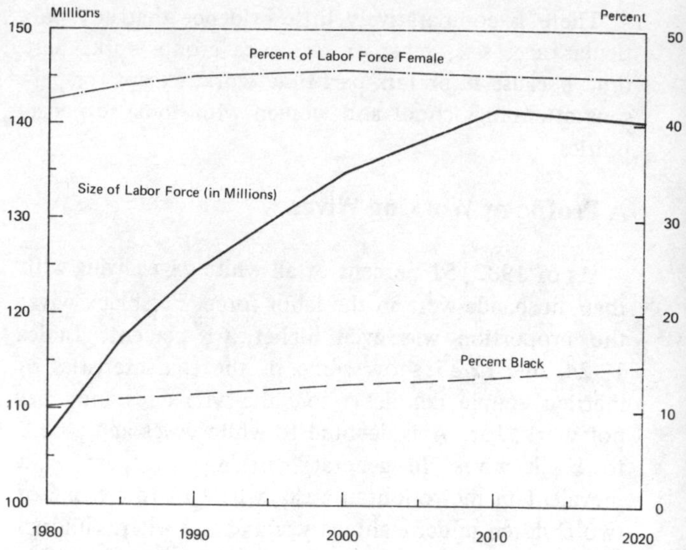

Figure 12-6A. Projected Trends in the Size and Race-Sex Composition of the Labor Force: 1980 to 2020

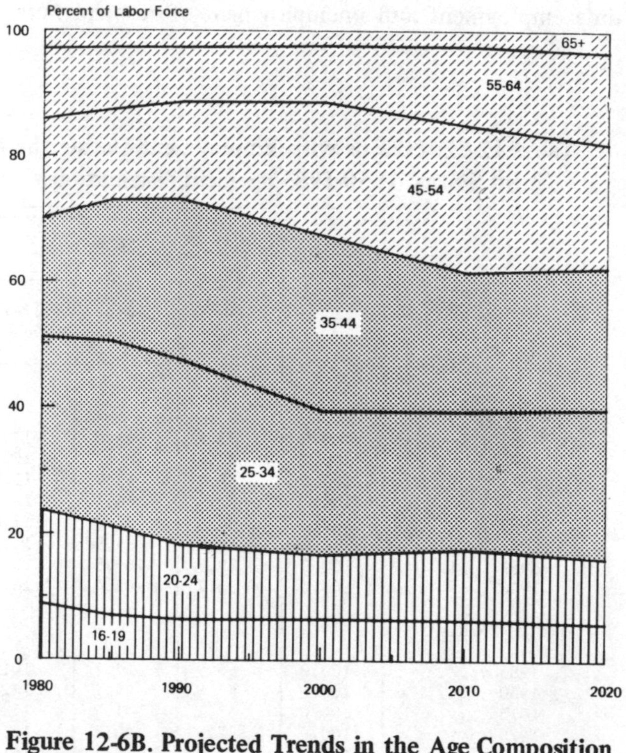

Figure 12-6B. Projected Trends in the Age Composition of the Labor Force: 1980 to 2020

which shows the status of nonworkers by age, sex, color, and urban/rural residence. Four categories of status outside the labor force were recognized in 1980; keeping house, unable to work because of age or chronic illness, inmates of institutions, and other and not reported (this last category includes students, the retired, and those too old to work). The Bureau of the Census has warned that the statistics for some of these categories have a low degree of reliability. For this reason only the largest differences are accepted here as being valid.

At ages below twenty-five almost all boys and almost all unmarried girls who are not in the labor force are

Table 12-23B. Reasons for Part-Time Work for Workers in Nonagricultural Industries, by Usual Status: 1983

Reason for working less than 35 hours	Numbers			Percent distribution		
	Total	Usually work full time	Usually work part time	Total	Usually work full time	Usually work full time
Total, 16 years and over	23,878	7,290	16,588	100.0	100.0	100.0
Economic reasons	5,997	1,826	4,171	25.1	25.0	25.1
Slack work	2,684	1,506	1,178	11.2	20.7	7.1
Material shortages or repairs to plant and equipment	57	57	--	0.2	0.8	--
New job started during week	174	174	--	0.7	2.4	--
Job terminated during week	88	88	--	0.4	1.2	--
Could find only part-time work	2,993	--	2,993	12.5	--	18.0
Other reasons	17,882	5,465	12,417	74.9	75.0	74.9
Does not want, or unavailable for, full-time work	10,341	--	10,341	43.3	--	62.3
Vacation	1,155	1,155	--	4.8	15.8	--
Illness	1,583	1,441	142	6.6	19.8	0.9
Bad weather	534	534	--	2.2	7.3	--
Industrial dispute	17	17	--	0.1	0.2	--
Legal or religious holiday	1,023	1,023	--	4.3	14.0	--
Full time for this job	1,457	--	1,457	6.1	--	8.8
All other reasons	1,773	1,295	478	7.4	17.8	2.9
Average hours						
Economic reasons	21.7	24.6	20.4	...	...	...
Other reasons	21.3	27.0	18.8	...	...	...
Worked 30-34 hours						
Economic reasons	1,798	839	957	...	...	...
Other reasons	5,400	3,215	2,185	...	...	...

Note: -- indicates data not available. ... indicates data not applicable.

Source: U.S. Bureau of Labor Statistics. Employment and Earnings. U.S. Government Printing Office, 1984, Table 31.

absent from it because of being students. Being an inmate of an institution becomes increasingly important as a reason at ages beyond thirty. A substantial portion of the men in the younger age groups who are in institutions are prisoners. Among nonwhite males, being unable to work and being an inmate are more frequent explanations for nonparticipation than they are among the white population, while being a student, being retired, or being too old to work are less frequent explanations among the nonwhite males. Nonwhite women report "keeping house" as a reason for not being in the labor force much less often than white women but report "being unable to work" much more frequently.

In rural areas being unable to work is reported much more frequently by nonwhite males than by white males. Inasmuch as many prisons, sanitariums, and other institutions are located in rural areas and are nonfarm by definition, a very high proportion of the total institutional population is rural nonfarm. It is for this reason that 15 percent of the white and 30 percent of the nonwhite rural nonfarm men who are not in the labor force are reported in Table 12-26 as being institutionalized.

Being retired or being too old to work ("other" for advanced years) are much more urban than rural phenomena. Also they are much more common among the white than among the nonwhite populations.

The Future Size of the Labor Force

Because persons born during the "baby boom" are already in the labor force ages and the oncoming generations are from the "baby bust" era, the labor force will grow more slowly for the remainder of this century. In fact, the growth of the male component will be very slow, and only a continuation of the increased participation of women will make it grow more rapidly.

Table 12-24A. Characteristics of Married Couple Families, by Joint Labor Force Characteristics of Husband and Wife: White Population, 1983

Characteristics	All married couple families	Wife in labor force			Wife not in labor force		
		Total	Husband in labor force	Husband not in labor force	Total	Husband in labor force	Husband not in labor force
Residence, total	100.0	51.0	46.9	4.1	49.0	32.8	16.2
Metropolitan	100.0	51.2	47.2	4.0	48.8	33.6	15.2
Central city	100.0	50.5	45.9	4.6	49.5	32.8	16.7
Metropolitan ring	100.0	51.5	47.8	3.7	48.5	34.0	14.5
Nonmetropolitan	100.0	50.8	46.4	4.4	49.2	31.2	18.0
Number of own children, total	100.0	51.0	46.9	4.1	49.0	32.8	16.2
No children under 18 years	100.0	46.1	39.8	6.3	53.9	24.6	29.3
1 under 18 years	100.0	61.1	58.7	2.3	38.9	36.4	2.5
2 under 18 years	100.0	56.4	55.0	1.4	43.6	42.4	1.2
3 under 18 years	100.0	49.0	47.7	1.3	51.0	49.1	1.9
4 under 18 years	100.0	46.1	44.5	1.6	53.8	51.3	2.5
5 under 18 years	100.0	34.3	32.3	2.0	66.1	58.1	8.1
6 or more under 18 years	100.0	31.3	31.3	0.0	67.0	61.6	5.4
Age of own children, total	100.0	51.0	46.9	4.1	49.0	32.8	16.2
All under 6 years	100.0	50.0	48.9	1.1	50.0	48.7	1.4
Some under 6, some 6 to 17 years	100.0	46.4	45.4	1.0	53.6	52.1	1.6
All 6 to 17 years	100.0	63.3	60.9	2.4	36.7	34.2	2.5
Age of husband, total	100.0	51.0	46.9	4.1	49.0	32.8	16.2
Under 45 years	100.0	62.3	60.9	1.4	37.7	36.6	1.1
45 years or older	100.0	40.1	33.4	6.7	59.9	29.1	30.8
With person 65 or more years in household, total	100.0	17.9	9.8	8.1	82.1	16.6	65.5
Years of school completed, total	100.0	51.0	46.9	4.1	49.0	32.8	16.2
Both less than 12 years	100.0	29.3	23.8	5.5	70.7	31.6	39.1
Husband 12 years, wife less	100.0	36.0	32.5	3.5	64.0	43.6	20.4
Wife 12 years, husband less	100.0	49.9	41.5	8.4	50.1	26.9	23.2
Both 12 years	100.0	54.1	50.9	3.2	45.9	34.2	11.6
Husband 13 to 15 years, wife less	100.0	52.9	49.3	3.6	47.1	35.6	11.5
Wife 13 to 15 years, husband less	100.0	61.6	57.2	4.4	38.4	27.0	11.4
Both 13 to 15 years	100.0	62.6	59.3	3.3	37.4	29.3	8.1
Husband 16 or more years, wife less	100.0	51.2	48.6	2.6	48.8	39.4	9.3
Wife 16 or more years, husband less	100.0	67.2	61.4	5.8	32.8	20.4	12.4
Both 16 or more years	100.0	64.5	61.8	2.7	35.5	29.5	5.9
Mobility, total	100.0	51.0	46.9	4.1	49.0	32.8	16.2
Nonmovers	100.0	50.2	45.8	4.4	47.3	32.2	15.1
Movers	100.0	57.1	54.5	2.6	42.9	36.4	6.6
Same county	100.0	60.4	58.2	2.1	39.7	33.5	6.1
Same state	100.0	56.8	53.9	2.9	43.2	34.9	8.3
Different state	100.0	47.7	43.7	4.0	52.3	46.1	6.3
Other	100.0	43.0	43.0	0.0	55.4	55.4	0.0

Source: U.S. Bureau of the Census. "Household and Family Characteristics: March, 1983." *Current Population Reports* (Series P-20, no. 388). Washington, DC: U.S. Government Printing Office, 1983, Table 18.

Table 12-24B. Characteristics of Married Couple Families, by Joint Labor Force Characteristics of Husband and Wife: Black Population, 1983

Characteristics	All married couple families	Wife in labor force			Wife not in labor force		
		Total	Husband in labor force	Husband not in labor force	Total	Husband in labor force	Husband not in labor force
Residence, total	100.0	60.7	53.1	7.6	39.3	23.2	16.1
Metropolitan	100.0	61.7	54.4	7.3	38.3	22.5	15.8
Central city	100.0	57.8	50.2	7.7	42.2	24.7	17.5
Metropolitan ring.	100.0	69.0	62.4	6.6	31.0	18.3	12.7
Nonmetropolitan.	100.0	59.1	50.4	8.7	43.4	26.0	17.3
Number of own children, total.	100.0	60.7	53.1	7.6	39.3	23.2	16.1
No children under 18 years . . .	100.0	51.5	40.6	10.9	48.5	19.5	29.0
1 under 18 years	100.0	68.6	62.5	6.1	31.6	24.0	7.6
2 under 18 years	100.0	74.4	69.8	4.6	25.6	21.8	3.8
3 under 18 years	100.0	69.2	65.4	3.8	31.0	26.6	4.4
4 under 18 years	100.0	57.9	52.1	5.8	43.0	37.2	5.8
5 under 18 years	100.0	33.3	33.3	0.0	66.7	66.7	0.0
6 or more under 18 years	100.0	42.9	42.9	0.0	57.1	57.1	0.0
Age of own children, total.	100.0	60.7	53.1	7.6	39.3	23.2	16.1
All under 6 years.	100.0	70.3	66.4	3.9	29.7	26.0	3.7
Some under 6, some 6 to 17 years	100.0	64.7	62.7	2.0	35.3	33.3	2.0
All 6 to 17 years.	100.0	69.5	62.8	6.8	30.5	23.0	7.6
Age of husband, total. . . .	100.0	60.7	53.1	7.6	39.3	23.2	16.1
Under 45 years	100.0	74.8	72.1	2.7	25.3	23.1	2.2
45 years or older.	100.0	45.6	32.7	12.9	54.4	23.3	31.1
With person 65 or more years in household, total. . . .	100.0	23.0	9.0	14.1	77.0	11.4	65.5
Years of school completed, total	100.0	60.7	53.1	7.6	39.3	23.2	16.1
Both less than 12 years.	100.0	37.0	26.8	10.2	63.0	26.7	36.3
Husband 12 years, wife less. . .	100.0	52.2	44.8	7.5	47.8	35.8	11.9
Wife 12 years, husband less. . .	100.0	58.2	46.1	12.2	41.8	24.3	17.4
Both 12 years.	100.0	70.3	66.3	4.0	29.7	24.4	5.3
Husband 13 to 15 years, wife less.	100.0	67.5	62.7	4.8	32.0	25.9	6.1
Wife 13 to 15 years, husband less	100.0	78.5	66.8	11.7	21.9	15.7	6.2
Both 13 to 15 years.	100.0	79.0	73.7	5.4	21.0	15.6	5.4
Husband 16 or more years, wife less.	100.0	68.6	67.3	1.3	31.4	24.2	7.2
Wife 16 or more years, husband less	100.0	84.2	78.7	5.5	16.4	9.8	6.6
Both 16 or more years.	100.0	77.5	73.2	4.3	23.0	13.9	9.1
Mobility, total.	100.0	60.7	53.1	7.6	39.3	23.2	16.1
Nonmovers.	100.0	59.4	51.4	8.0	40.6	23.1	17.5
Movers	100.0	68.9	64.1	4.9	31.3	24.1	7.2
Same county.	100.0	70.4	65.0	5.4	29.9	22.1	7.9
Same state	100.0	81.7	76.1	5.6	18.3	18.3	0.0
Different state.	100.0	51.7	48.3	3.4	46.6	36.2	10.3
Other.	100.0	46.2	46.2	0.0	53.8	46.2	7.7

Source: U.S. Bureau of the Census. "Household and Family Characteristics: March, 1983." Current Population Reports (Series P-20, no. 388). Washington, DC: U.S. Government Printing Office, 1983, Table 18.

Table 12-25. Work Experience of Wives in Married Couple Families, by Work Experience of Husband, Presence and Age of Own Children, and Race-Ethnicity: 1979 [percent distribution of work experience of wives]

Work experience of husband and work experience of wife	Own children under 6 years						Own children 6-17 years only					
	Total	White	Black	American Indian	Asian/ Pac. Is.	Spanish-origin	Total	White	Black	American Indian	Asian/ Pac. Is.	Spanish-origin
Husband worked 35+ hours and 40+ weeks. . . .	100.0	100.0	100.0	100.0	100.0	100.0	100.0	100.0	100.0	100.0	100.0	100.0
Wife: 35+ hours and 40+ weeks . .	21.0	18.8	42.1	25.4	34.9	23.7	32.5	30.8	51.1	38.5	48.4	34.3
Wife: 35+ hours and 1-39 weeks. .	14.1	13.6	18.4	19.2	13.2	16.6	9.3	9.1	10.2	13.8	8.5	11.2
Wife: 1-34 hours and 40+ weeks. .	7.6	8.0	5.1	4.3	5.5	4.1	12.5	13.1	8.2	7.6	8.9	7.7
Wife: 1-34 hours and 1-39 weeks .	12.5	13.1	8.3	10.3	7.7	7.9	11.4	11.9	6.5	8.7	6.9	7.9
Wife: not in labor force, not work	44.8	46.5	26.2	40.8	38.7	47.7	34.4	35.2	24.1	31.4	27.4	38.9
Husband worked 35+ hours and 1-39 weeks . . .	100.0	100.0	100.0	100.0	100.0	100.0	100.0	100.0	100.0	100.0	100.0	100.0
Wife: 35+ hours and 40+ weeks . .	18.8	17.0	32.1	17.7	22.6	16.9	31.4	30.1	42.9	30.4	36.7	25.3
Wife: 35+ hours and 1-39 weeks. .	22.9	22.1	26.4	26.8	23.4	24.8	17.4	16.9	17.7	21.5	26.4	21.6
Wife: 1-34 hours and 40+ weeks. .	4.4	4.7	3.8	3.3	3.0	2.3	7.9	8.3	6.9	4.5	5.0	4.8
Wife: 1-34 hours and 1-39 weeks .	12.3	13.1	9.5	11.5	8.0	8.0	10.0	10.5	7.6	9.2	5.8	8.0
Wife: not in labor force, not work	41.6	43.1	28.2	40.7	43.0	48.0	33.2	34.2	24.9	34.4	26.1	40.3
Husband worked 1-34 hours and 40+ weeks . . .	100.0	100.0	100.0	100.0	100.0	100.0	100.0	100.0	100.0	100.0	100.0	100.0
Wife: 35+ hours and 40+ weeks . .	18.4	16.9	27.8	18.4	23.4	16.1	27.2	25.8	34.9	25.8	38.2	22.9
Wife: 35+ hours and 1-39 weeks. .	12.4	12.1	14.6	13.9	10.9	12.5	7.9	7.7	8.0	9.6	7.0	9.0
Wife: 1-34 hours and 40+ weeks. .	10.9	10.5	14.2	12.1	12.3	8.7	16.3	16.1	18.1	13.6	18.2	14.2
Wife: 1-34 hours and 1-39 weeks .	15.2	15.7	13.6	14.4	9.1	13.4	11.3	11.7	9.6	12.1	8.0	10.2
Wife: not in labor force, not work	43.0	44.8	29.9	41.2	44.2	49.2	37.3	38.7	29.3	38.8	28.6	43.6
Husband worked 1-34 hours and 40+ weeks . . .	100.0	100.0	100.0	100.0	100.0	100.0	100.0	100.0	100.0	100.0	100.0	100.0
Wife: 35+ hours and 40+ weeks . .	20.2	19.2	34.6	21.4	20.6	14.8	30.5	30.2	33.7	25.6	36.0	21.2
Wife: 35+ hours and 1-39 weeks. .	15.7	15.6	22.5	17.2	14.5	14.6	11.5	11.5	11.7	11.9	11.7	11.1
Wife: 1-34 hours and 40+ weeks. .	6.3	6.0	5.1	5.0	6.4	4.2	9.6	9.4	11.3	7.4	8.9	7.0
Wife: 1-34 hours and 1-39 weeks .	15.8	15.8	10.2	15.1	13.2	15.8	13.1	12.8	13.3	13.1	14.5	15.3
Wife: not in labor force, not work	42.0	43.3	27.6	41.3	45.3	50.5	35.4	36.1	29.9	42.0	29.0	45.4
Husband with unemployment in 1979	100.0	100.0	100.0	100.0	100.0	100.0	100.0	100.0	100.0	100.0	100.0	100.0
Wife: 35+ hours and 40+ weeks . .	19.8	17.9	34.6	18.6	28.2	18.6	33.5	31.9	45.9	32.9	43.4	28.2
Wife: 35+ hours and 1-39 weeks. .	20.3	19.7	22.5	24.6	19.7	22.4	14.3	14.1	13.2	19.0	18.7	18.3
Wife: 1-34 hours and 40+ weeks. .	5.2	5.4	5.1	3.8	4.3	3.2	9.4	9.8	8.3	5.6	6.8	5.8
Wife: 1-34 hours and 1-39 weeks .	13.3	14.1	10.2	12.2	9.2	9.4	10.8	11.3	8.0	10.7	6.7	9.2
Wife: not in labor force, not work	41.3	42.8	27.6	40.8	38.6	46.6	32.1	32.9	24.6	31.8	24.3	38.6
Husband without unemployment in 1979	100.0	100.0	100.0	100.0	100.0	100.0	100.0	100.0	100.0	100.0	100.0	100.0
Wife: 35+ hours and 40+ weeks . .	20.9	18.7	41.0	25.3	33.8	23.3	32.1	30.5	49.4	37.2	47.2	33.4
Wife: 35+ hours and 1-39 weeks. .	13.8	13.3	18.2	18.8	13.1	16.1	9.3	9.1	10.4	13.7	8.7	11.1
Wife: 1-34 hours and 40+ weeks. .	7.8	8.2	5.5	4.5	5.7	4.2	12.6	13.1	8.7	7.7	9.2	7.9
Wife: 1-34 hours and 1-39 weeks .	12.4	13.0	8.5	10.3	7.6	8.0	11.3	11.9	6.7	8.7	7.0	7.9
Wife: not in labor force, not work	45.1	46.8	26.8	41.1	39.8	48.4	34.7	35.5	24.8	32.7	27.9	39.7

Source: U.S. Bureau of the Census. "Detailed Population Characteristics: United States Summary." 1980 Census of Population. Washington, DC: U.S. Government Printing Office, 1984, Table 275.

Table 12-27 reports the labor force participation rates expected for the next two decades, by age, race, and sex, as prepared by the Bureau of Labor Statistics in 1984. Increased participation of women, especially white women, aged 20-54 years is expected with rapid declines in labor force participation of males sixty-five and over. White males 16-19 and white females will participate even more than now, but the participation of black males and female teenagers will be about the same or less. The Bureau of Labor Statistics presents three estimates, a "high," "medium," and "low" estimate. The major differences among the three estimates are in anticipated increased participation of women, teenagers and young adults, and persons sixty-five and over.

When the rates of the medium assumptions are applied to the numbers of persons of each age predicted for the future by the Bureau of the Census middle projections (see Chapter 1), the expected size of the labor force at selected future years may be obtained; these projections are reported in Table 12-28 and illustrated

Table 12-26A. Persons Not in the Labor Force, by Reason, Sex, and Age: 1982 and 1983

Reason and sex	Total		Age							
			16-19 years		20-24 years		25-59 years		60 years and over	
	1982	1983	1982	1983	1982	1983	1982	1983	1982	1983
Total										
Total not in labor force	62,067	62,665	7,238	7,104	4,763	4,747	21,890	22,067	28,176	28,747
Do not want a job now.	55,508	56,161	5,528	5,550	3,639	3,633	18,766	18.789	27,573	28,195
Current activity:										
Going to school.	6,427	6,583	4,188	4,214	1,529	1,571	698	781	10	21
Ill, disabled.	4,034	3,915	33	40	104	106	1,912	1,871	1,985	1,898
Keeping house.	28,409	28,356	409	416	1,517	1,472	13,637	13,509	12,845	12,962
Retired.	12,326	13,019	*	*	*	*	283	340	12,043	12,679
Other activity	4,312	4,288	898	880	489	484	2,236	2,288	690	635
Want a job now	6,559	6,503	1,709	1,553	1,121	1,113	3,125	3,280	601	556
Reason for not looking:										
School attendance.	1,732	1,608	1,186	1,072	320	295	224	231	3	7
Ill health, disability	769	765	28	20	59	63	513	535	168	147
Home responsibilities.	1,391	1,413	96	90	319	322	942	964	32	37
Think cannot get a job	1,568	1,641	238	220	241	270	850	940	238	212
Job-market factors	1,181	1,248	176	155	191	218	683	766	131	109
Personal factors	386	394	62	66	50	52	166	175	107	103
Other reasons[a]	1,099	1,076	161	151	182	163	596	610	160	153
Men										
Total not in labor force	19,073	19,484	3,409	3,356	1,531	1,539	3,543	3,749	10,589	10,841
Do not want a job now.	16,862	17,274	2,551	2,571	1,147	1,153	2,860	2,963	10,302	10,590
Current activity:										
Going to school.	3,230	3,289	2,074	2,089	825	835	328	360	2	5
Ill, disabled.	2,187	2,092	17	18	60	62	1,094	1,051	1,016	963
Keeping house.	309	303	10	15	8	9	80	84	210	196
Retired.	8,824	9,230	*	*	*	*	227	279	8,597	8,951
Other activity	2,312	2,360	450	449	254	247	1,131	1,189	477	475
Want a job now	2,212	2,210	857	786	383	384	687	787	285	251
Reason for not looking:										
School attendance.	923	857	650	591	176	170	94	92	3	3
Ill health, disability	325	338	13	8	25	31	208	236	78	62
Think cannot get a job	587	650	114	118	111	125	245	295	116	112
Other reasons[a]	377	365	80	69	71	58	140	164	88	74
Women										
Total not in labor force	42,993	43,181	3,828	3,748	3,232	3,208	18,347	18,319	17,586	17,906
Do not want a job now.	38,646	38,887	2,976	2,981	2,492	2,478	15,907	15,828	17,270	17,600
Current activity:										
Going to school.	3,197	3,294	2,113	2,125	703	734	372	420	7	14
Ill, disabled.	1,847	1,823	16	22	45	44	817	823	968	933
Keeping house.	28,100	28,053	399	401	1,508	1,463	13,559	13,425	12,637	12,765
Retired.	3,502	3,789	*	*	*	*	55	61	3,446	3,728
Other activity	2,000	1,928	448	433	236	237	1,104	1,099	212	160
Want a job now	4,347	4,293	852	767	740	729	2,438	2,490	316	305
Reason not looking:										
School attendance.	809	751	536	481	145	126	129	140	*	5
Ill health, disability	444	427	15	12	34	32	305	297	90	85
Home responsibilities.	1,391	1,413	96	90	319	322	942	964	32	37
Think cannot get a job	981	991	124	102	130	145	605	643	122	100
Other reasons.	722	711	81	82	112	104	457	446	72	78

[a]Includes small number of men not looking for work because of "home responsibilities."

Note: * indicates zero or rounds to zero.

Source: U.S. Bureau of Labor Statistics. Employment and Earnings. Washington, DC: U.S. Government Printing Office, 1984, Table 35.

in Figures 12-6A and 6B. The labor force is expected to grow as follows:

Year	Thousands of workers	Intercensal percent change	Percent change since 1980
1980 . . .	106,084[a]	...	...
1985 . . .	117,257	...	10.5
1990 . . .	124,350	17.2	17.2
2000 . . .	134,830	8.4	27.1
2010 . . .	141,487	4.9	33.4
2020 . . .	140,341	-0.8	33.2

[a]Count is that of the 1980 census.

The projections are carried to the year 2020, which brings the baby boom generation completely through the labor force years and the baby bust babies into central labor force ages. The results are somewhat startling:

1. The labor force will decelerate in rate of growth during the 1980s, especially between 1985 and 1990.

2. This deceleration will continue at least until 2015, at which time labor force growth will become zero and the size will begin to decline.

3. At its peak size in 2015, the labor force will number about 142 million, or almost one-third larger than in 1980 and 20 percent larger than in 1985.

Table 12-26B. Persons Not in the Labor Force, by Reason, Race-Ethnicity, Sex, and Age: 1982 and 1983

Race-ethnicity and race	Total		Age						Sex			
			16-24 years		25-59 years		60 years and over		Male		Female	
	1982	1983	1982	1983	1982	1983	1982	1983	1982	1983	1982	1983
White												
Total.	53,298	53,784	9,270	9,112	18,610	18,761	25,417	25,911	16,078	16,441	37,220	37,342
Do not want a job now.	48,602	49,046	7,329	7,254	16,340	16,337	24,928	25,453	14,493	14,841	34,109	34,205
Current activity:												
Going to school.	5,072	5,144	4,540	4,544	523	582	7	17	2,574	2,585	2,498	2,559
Ill, disabled.	3,275	3,151	102	109	1,522	1,478	1,650	1,565	1,789	1,707	1,486	1,444
Keeping house.	25,608	25,497	1,628	1,557	12,208	12,093	11,772	11,847	253	250	25,355	25,247
Retired.	11,731	11,765	--	--	258	310	10,873	11,455	8,018	8,404	3,113	3,361
Other activity	3,516	3.489	1,059	1,044	1,829	1,874	626	569	1,859	1,895	1,657	1,594
Want a job now	4,697	4,737	1,940	1,857	2,270	2,423	490	456	1,584	1,600	3,113	3,137
Reason for not looking:.												
School attendance.	1,219	1,161	1,064	986	153	170	2	7	662	623	557	538
Ill health, disability	532	562	61	63	352	386	120	113	244	253	288	309
Home responsibilities.	1,025	1,039	260	267	738	740	26	32	--	--	1,025	1,039
Think cannot get a job	1,042	1,125	294	305	552	646	195	173	380	450	662	675
Other reasons[a]	879	850	261	236	475	481	147	131	298	274	581	576
Black												
Total.	7,254	7,278	2,277	2,279	2,589	2,564	2,389	2,434	2,480	2,482	4,773	4,796
Do not want a job now.	5,594	5,707	1,471	1,537	1,841	1,827	2,287	2,345	1,934	1,942	3,661	3,763
Current activity:												
Going to school.	984	1,050	905	957	78	91	2	3	449	475	534	574
Ill, disabled.	694	694	35	36	351	355	310	303	361	345	334	349
Keeping house.	2,209	2,238	247	271	1,039	1,006	925	962	53	46	2,158	2,191
Retired.	1,020	1,049	--	--	21	22	998	1,028	679	686	340	363
Other activity	687	676	284	273	352	353	52	49	392	390	295	286
Want a job now	1,658	1,571	807	743	749	735	100	92	546	539	1,112	1,033
Reason for not looking:												
School attendance.	434	393	390	349	43	42	--	1	214	204	220	190
Ill health, disability	222	187	24	18	152	136	45	33	74	79	148	108
Home responsibilities.	329	332	146	134	178	194	5	4	--	--	329	332
Think cannot get a job	482	470	172	172	272	265	37	35	191	179	290	291
Other reasons[a]	191	189	75	70	104	98	13	19	67	77	125	112
Spanish-origin												
Total.	3,417	3,491	1,042	1,036	1,628	1,697	747	759	897	873	2,520	2,618
Do not want a job now.	2,933	3,012	818	826	1,387	1,450	729	737	749	728	2,185	2,284
Current activity:												
Going to school.	472	489	434	443	39	43	--	2	228	220	245	269
Ill, disabled.	222	231	17	12	132	159	73	60	111	120	110	110
Keeping house.	1,645	1,706	234	256	1,085	1,110	327	341	14	14	1,632	1,692
Retired.	322	322	--	--	9	6	312	316	233	230	89	93
Other activity	272	264	133	115	122	132	17	18	163	144	109	120
Want a job now	483	477	226	211	241	246	17	20	150	146	335	332
Reason for not looking:												
School attendance.	111	118	97	98	14	21	--	--	61	60	50	58
Ill health, disability	46	59	9	9	33	42	4	8	27	26	20	34
Home responsibilities.	160	128	52	44	108	84	--	--	--	--	160	128
Think cannot get a job	98	109	37	38	51	62	10	8	38	39	60	70
Other reasons[a]	68	63	31	22	35	37	3	4	24	21	45	42

[a]Includes small number of men not looking for work because of "home responsibilities."

Source: U.S. Bureau of Labor Statistics. Employment and Earnings. Washington, DC: U.S. Government Printing Office, 1984, Table 36.

4. By 1985 the labor force will have acquired almost one-third of its projected increase between 1980 and 2020.

Because the projections are carried out by age, sex, and race, Table 12-28 can provide those details for each of the projected years. Figure 12-6A and 6B illustrate that:

1. The labor force will age progressively, with younger workers comprising a steadily declining share.

2. The percent of the labor force that is black will rise from 11 to 15 percent during these four decades.

3. The percent of the labor force that is female will rise only slightly, as the changing age composition neutralizes increasing labor force participation of women. The proportion of women in the labor force is predicted to peak in the year 2000 at 45.6 percent.

The ramifications of these changes are great for the growth of the economy, for employment prospects of oncoming generations, for retirement prospects of those generations, and for immigration from abroad.

Table 12-27. Projected Labor Force Participation Rates, by Age, Sex, Race-Ethnicity, and Level of Assumptions: 1986, 1990, and 1995

Age, sex, and race-ethnicity	Medium assumption			High assumption			Low assumption		
	1986	1990	1995	1986	1990	1995	1986	1990	1995
White female									
Total, 16 and over . .	55.9	58.1	60.0	58.4	62.4	66.4	53.7	55.0	56.2
16-19 years.	58.3	61.5	63.3	60.0	63.5	65.8	55.7	56.8	56.5
20-24 years.	76.7	80.7	84.9	78.9	83.0	87.4	74.7	77.1	79.6
25-34 years.	74.9	78.3	81.8	80.0	84.9	90.1	70.8	73.9	77.2
35-44 years.	74.3	78.4	82.7	77.8	83.6	89.7	70.8	74.1	77.4
45-54 years.	64.6	67.1	69.7	66.9	73.3	79.6	62.7	63.9	65.0
55-64 years.	40.9	41.2	42.2	41.2	46.6	53.7	40.2	39.9	40.4
65 years and over. . . .	7.6	7.4	6.9	7.9	7.9	7.7	7.4	7.0	6.4
Black/other female									
Total, 16 and over . .	57.3	59.7	61.7	61.4	65.2	68.5	55.9	57.2	58.0
16-19 years.	35.4	36.5	36.6	38.2	41.4	43.6	34.4	35.0	34.6
20-24 years.	63.8	66.7	69.8	69.6	76.1	83.1	63.6	65.6	67.8
25-34 years.	74.1	77.5	81.1	81.3	85.8	90.7	71.8	73.9	75.9
35-44 years.	76.1	79.5	83.1	81.3	85.7	90.4	73.0	74.7	76.4
45-54 years.	64.8	66.6	68.4	66.7	70.0	73.7	62.5	62.6	62.8
55-64 years.	44.0	43.6	43.7	45.0	45.6	46.8	44.7	44.3	44.5
65 years and over. . . .	8.4	8.2	7.7	8.8	8.7	8.5	8.6	8.3	7.8
White male									
Total, 16 and over . .	77.6	77.4	77.0	78.4	78.9	79.2	76.4	75.6	74.6
16-19 years.	64.6	67.5	69.1	65.3	68.7	70.8	61.5	62.1	61.2
20-24 years.	86.4	86.9	87.3	87.1	87.9	88.9	85.8	85.8	85.8
25-34 years.	95.4	95.0	94.6	95.6	96.0	96.3	94.1	93.3	92.4
35-44 years.	96.5	96.3	96.2	97.1	97.2	97.3	96.1	95.6	95.1
45-54 years.	92.4	92.3	92.1	92.7	92.8	92.9	91.5	90.7	89.9
55-64 years.	68.3	66.3	65.5	70.5	70.3	71.0	66.4	63.0	60.8
65 years and over. . . .	16.6	15.3	13.7	18.1	17.9	17.4	16.0	14.2	12.1
Black/other male									
Total, 16 and over . .	71.0	71.0	70.6	75.0	77.9	80.9	69.4	68.2	66.7
16-19 years.	39.1	37.9	35.0	47.9	54.3	61.3	38.3	36.7	33.2
20-24 years.	74.5	71.4	68.3	81.6	84.1	87.5	73.8	70.2	66.5
25-34 years.	87.3	86.7	86.0	90.9	93.0	95.6	85.0	82.6	80.1
35-44 years.	91.2	90.8	90.5	93.4	94.6	96.4	90.1	88.9	87.7
45-54 years.	84.1	84.1	84.2	86.1	87.9	90.3	81.3	79.5	77.6
55-64 years.	60.5	58.9	57.4	64.1	64.9	66.9	58.5	55.4	52.7
65 years and over. . . .	13.7	12.0	9.9	16.0	15.9	15.6	12.8	10.3	9.1

Source: U.S. Bureau of Labor Statistics. Employment Projections for 1995 (Bulletin 2197). Washington, DC: U.S. Government Printing Office, 1984, Tables A-1, A-2, A-3, and A-4.

Conclusion

The labor force is such a large and multidimensional subject that it has been possible to present in this chapter only the most basic and fundamental facts concerning statuses, differentials, and trends. A great deal of excellent research has been performed in this area. The bibliography cites works that refine the description given here. The reader is encouraged to consult the monthly reports of the Bureau of Labor Statistics *Employment and Earnings*, the *Monthly Labor Review*, and the *Statistical Abstract of the United States* in order to update the materials presented in this chapter. Because the latest data available when this chapter was written refer to a period of deep economic recession, it is quite possible that some new major trends will emerge as the business cycle changes its direction.

Table 12-28. Projections of the Future Labor Force of the United States, by Age, Race, and Sex: 1985-2020

Year and age	Number of persons (thousands)					Measures of composition and change					
	Total labor force	Male		Female		Percent black	Percent female	Percent distribution	Percent change since 1980		
		White	Black	White	Black				Total	Female	Black
Total, all ages											
1985	117,257	58,956	6,671	45,401	6,229	11.0	44.0	...	10.5	15.6	18.7
1990	124,350	61,173	7,256	48,884	7,037	11.5	45.0	...	17.2	25.2	31.5
2000	134,830	64,900	8,387	53,263	8,280	12.4	45.6	...	27.1	37.8	53.4
2010	141,487	67,814	9,715	54,668	9,290	13.4	45.2	...	33.4	43.2	74.9
2020	140,341	66,665	10,546	53,236	9,894	14.6	45.0	...	32.3	41.3	88.1
1985 total	117,257	58,956	6,671	45,401	6,229	11.0	44.0	100.0	10.5	15.6	18.7
16-19 years	8,236	3,988	425	3,440	383	9.8	46.4	7.0	-1.9	-0.6	1.1
20-24 years	16,532	7,790	1,126	6,649	967	12.7	46.1	14.1	3.2	5.5	15.1
25-34 years	34,299	16,989	2,173	13,119	2,018	12.2	44.1	29.3	17.2	24.5	28.2
35-44 years	26,401	13,276	1,423	10,299	1,403	10.7	44.3	22.5	30.1	38.4	33.8
45-54 years	16,988	8,833	875	6,441	839	10.1	42.9	14.5	1.1	5.2	7.6
55-64 years	11,657	6,359	524	4,274	500	8.8	41.0	9.9	-3.6	-1.1	2.5
65 years and over	3,144	1,721	125	1,179	119	7.8	41.3	2.7	-2.5	4.3	-11.3
1990 total	124,350	61,173	7,256	48,884	7,037	11.5	45.0	100.0	17.2	25.2	31.5
16-19 years	7,988	3,866	393	3,355	374	9.6	46.7	6.4	-4.9	-3.1	-4.0
20-24 years	14,684	6,770	970	6,036	908	12.8	47.3	11.8	-8.3	-3.8	3.3
25-34 years	36,283	17,437	2,484	14,041	2,321	13.2	45.1	29.2	24.0	34.6	47.0
35-44 years	31,848	15,547	1,810	12,661	1,830	11.4	45.5	25.6	57.0	71.4	72.3
45-54 years	19,433	9,972	983	7,508	970	10.0	43.6	15.6	15.6	22.5	22.6
55-64 years	10,845	5,831	499	4,013	502	9.2	41.6	8.7	-10.3	-6.4	0.2
65 years and over	3,269	1,750	117	1,270	132	7.6	42.9	2.6	1.4	12.7	-9.5
2000 total	134,830	64,900	8,387	53,263	8,280	12.4	45.6	100.0	27.1	37.8	53.4
16-19 years	8,850	4,255	437	3,709	449	10.0	47.0	6.5	5.4	8.1	10.9
20-24 years	13,729	6,197	875	5,766	891	12.9	48.5	10.2	-14.3	-7.8	97.1
25-34 years	30,568	14,217	2,267	11,911	2,173	14.5	46.1	22.7	4.5	15.9	35.8
35-44 years	37,574	17,600	2,547	14,936	2,491	13.4	46.4	27.9	85.2	106.1	138.5
45-54 years	28,700	14,452	1,582	11,130	1,536	10.9	44.1	21.3	70.8	83.0	95.7
55-64 years	12,167	6,483	574	4,518	592	9.6	42.0	9.0	0.6	5.9	16.7
65 years and over	3,242	1,696	105	1,293	148	7.8	44.4	2.4	0.6	15.8	-8.0
2010 total	141,487	67,814	9,715	54,668	9,290	13.4	45.2	100.0	33.4	43.2	74.9
16-19 years	8,997	4,313	457	3,757	470	10.3	47.0	6.4	7.1	9.8	16.0
20-24 years	15,865	7,045	1,130	6,547	1,143	14.3	48.5	11.2	-0.9	6.5	25.0
25-34 years	30,837	14,194	2,451	11,858	2,334	15.5	46.0	21.8	5.4	16.8	46.4
35-44 years	31,245	14,469	2,359	12,177	2,240	14.7	46.1	22.1	54.0	70.5	117.8
45-54 years	33,129	16,417	2,250	12,456	2,006	12.8	43.7	23.4	97.1	109.0	167.2
55-64 years	17,797	9,477	944	6,457	919	10.5	41.4	12.6	47.2	52.8	86.5
65 years and over	3,617	1,899	124	1,416	178	8.3	44.1	2.6	12.2	28.1	9.8
2020 total	140,341	66,665	10,546	53,236	9,894	14.6	45.0	100.0	32.3	41.3	88.1
16-19 years	8,260	3,925	453	3,418	464	11.1	47.0	5.9	-1.6	0.9	14.8
20-24 years	14,457	6,364	1,085	5,912	1,096	15.1	48.5	10.3	-9.7	-2.9	20.0
25-34 years	33,183	15,099	2,815	12,601	2,668	16.5	46.0	23.6	13.4	25.6	67.7
35-44 years	31,535	14,448	2,556	12,126	2,405	15.7	46.1	22.5	55.4	71.9	134.9
45-54 years	27,598	13,518	2,097	10,174	1,809	14.2	43.4	19.7	64.2	73.1	145.2
55-64 years	20,553	10,770	1,354	7,225	1,204	12.4	41.0	14.6	70.0	74.7	156.1
65 years and over	4,755	2,541	186	1,780	248	9.1	42.6	3.4	47.5	63.0	57.8

Note: ... indicates data not applicable.

Source: Prepared by the author, using medium participation rates of Table 12-27 and medium projections of Bureau of Census. "Projections of the Population of the United States, by Age, Sex and Race, 1909-2080." Current Population Reports (Series P-25, no. 952). Washington, DC: U.S. Government Printing Office, 1984, Table 6. (Rates assumed to remain constant after 1990.)

Bibliography

Andrisani, Paul, and Kohen, Andrew I. *Career Thresholds.* Volume 5 in *A Longitudinal Study of the Educational and Labor Market Experience of Male Youth.* Columbus, OH: Ohio State University, Center for Human Resource Research, 1975.

Bancroft, Gertrude. *The American Labor Force: Its Growth and Changing Composition.* New York: John Wiley and Sons, 1958.

Benjamin, L. "Black Women Achievers: An Isolated Elite." *Sociological Inquiry* 52 (1982):141-51.

Birch, David L.; Allman, Peter M.; and Martin, Elizabeth A. *A Model of Population and Employment Change for Metropolitan and Rural Areas in the United States.* Cambridge, MA: MIT Program on Neighborhood and Regional Change, 1978.

Brown, C. et al. "Effect of the Minimum Wage on Employment and Unemployment." *Journal of Economic Literature* 20 (1982):487-528.

———. "Time-Series Evidence of the Effect of the Minimum Wage on Youth Employment and Unemployment." *Journal of Human Resources* 18 (1983): 3-31.

Bureau of Labor Statistics. *Labor Force Statistics Derived from the Current Population Survey: A Databook.* Washington, DC: U.S. Government Printing Office, 1982.

Cantrell, R.S., and Clark, R.L. "Individual Mobility, Population Growth, and Labor Force Participation." *Demography* 19 (1982):147-59.

Clogg, C.C. "Cohort Analysis of Recent Trends in Labor Force Participants." *Demography* 19 (1982):459-79.

Davis, R.G., and Lewis, G.M. *Education and Employment.* Farnborough: Lexington Books, 1975.

DeFronzo, J. "Female Labor Force Participation and Fertility in 48 States: Cross-Sectional and Change Analyses for the 1960-70 Decade." *Sociology and Social Research* 64 (1980):263-78.

Durand, John D. *The Labor Force in the United States, 1890-1960.* New York: Social Science Research Council, 1948.

Felmlee, D. "Women's Job Mobility Processes." *American Sociological Review* 47 (1982):53-7.

Garfinkle, Stuart H. *The Length of Working Life for Males, 1900-1961.* Washington, DC: U.S. Manpower Administration, 1963.

Gilbert, L.A. et al. "Coping with Conflict Between Professional and Maternal Roles." *Family Relations* 30 (1981):419-26.

Goldstein, Harvey A. *Occupational Employment Projections for Labor Market Areas: An Analysis of Alternative Approaches.* Washington, DC: U.S. Government Printing Office, 1951.

Grant, James, and Hamermesh, Daniel. "Labor Market Competition Among Youths, White Women and Others." *Review of Economics and Statistics* 63 (1981):354-60.

Greenglass, E.R., and Defins, R. "Factors Related to Marriage and Career Plans in Unmarried Women." *Sex Roles* 8 (1982):57-71.

Hayghe, H. "Husbands and Wives as Earners: An Analysis of Family Data." *Monthly Labor Review* 104 (1981):46-59.

Hogan, D.P. *Transitions and Social Change: The Early Lives of American Men.* New York: Academic Press, 1981.

Jennings, Jerry T. "Social and Economic Characteristics of Americans During Midlife." *Current Population Reports* (Series P-23, no. 111). Washington, DC: U.S. Government Printing Office, 1981.

Johnson, B.L., and Waldman, E. "Marital and Family Patterns of the Labor Force." *Monthly Labor Review* 104 (1981):36-38.

Johnston, Denis F. "Education of Workers: Projections to 1970." *Monthly Labor Review* 96 (1973):22-31.

Lebergott, Stanley. *Manpower in Economic Growth: The American Record Since 1800.* New York: McGraw-Hill, 1964.

Li, W.L. "Note on Migration and Employment." *Demography* 13 (1976):365-70.

Lichter, D.T. "Migration of Dual-Worker Families: Does the Wife's Job Matter?" *Social Science Quarterly* 63 (1982):48-57.

Linneman, P. "Economic Impact of Minimum Wage Laws: A New Look at an Old Question." *Journal of Political Economy* 90 (1982):443-69.

Lloyd, C.; Andrews, E.S.; and Gilroy, C.L. (eds.). *Women in the Labor Market.* New York: Columbia University Press, 1979.

Madden, J.F. "Why Women Work Closer to Home." *Urban Studies* 18 (1981):181-94.

McEaddy, Beverly J. "Educational Attainment of Workers." *Monthly Labor Review* 98 (1975):64-9.

Miller, Ann R. "Components of Labor Force Growth." *Journal of Economic History* 22 (1962):47-58.

National Commission on Employment and Unemployment Statistics. *Counting the Labor Force.* Washington, DC: U.S. Government Printing Office, 1979.

Pampel, F.C. "Changes in the Labor Force Participation and Income of the Aged in the United States 1947-1976." *Social Problems* 27 (1979):125-42.

Reynolds, Lloyd G. *Labor Economics and Labor Relations.* Englewood Cliffs, NJ: Prentice Hall, 1982 (eighth edition).

Reynolds, Lloyd G.; Masters, Stanley H.; and Moser, Collette H. *Readings in Labor Economics and Labor Relations.* Englewood Cliffs, NJ: Prentice Hall,1982.

Ryscavage, P.M. "Employment Problems and Poverty: Examining the Linkages." *Monthly Labor Review* 105 (1982):55-9.

St. John, Craig, and Sandefur, Gary D. "Labor Force Participation and Labor Supply of White, Indian, and Black Females." Paper presented at the annual meeting of the Population Association of America, San Diego, 1982.

Sweezy, A., and Owens, A. "Impact of Population Growth on Employment." *American Economic Review Papers and Proceedings* 64 (1974):45-50.

Tinto, Vincent. "Higher Education and Occupational Attainment in Segmented Labor Markets: Recent Evidence from the United States." *Higher Education* 10 (1981):499-516.

Toikka, R.S.; Scanlon, W.J.; and Holt, C.C. "Extensions of a Structural Model of the Demographic Labor Market." Pp. 305-22 in *Research in Labor Economics.* R.G. Ehrenberg (ed.). Greenwich, CN: Jai Press.

Treiman, D.J., and Terrell, K. "Sex and the Process of Status Attainment: A Comparison of Working Women and Men." *American Sociological Review* 40 (1975):174-200.

U.S. Bureau of the Census. "Detailed Population Characteristics: United States Summary." *1980 Census of Population.* Washington, DC: U.S. Government Printing Office, 1983.

———. "General Social and Economic Characteristics: United States Summary." *1980 Census of Population.* Washington, DC: U.S. Government Printing Office, 1983.

U.S. Bureau of Economic Analysis. *Area Economic Projections, 1990.* Washington, DC: U.S. Government Printing Office, 1974.

U.S. Bureau of Labor Statistics. *Handbook of Labor Statistics.* Washington, DC: U.S. Government Printing Office, 1984.

———. *Monthly Report of Employment and Earnings.* Washington, DC: U.S. Government Printing Office, monthly publication.

———. *Special Labor Force Reports.* Washington, DC: U.S. Government Printing Office, periodical publication.

Waite, L.J. "Working Wives and the Family Life Cycle." *American Journal of Sociology* 86 (1980):272-94.

Wardwell, J.M., and Gilchrist, C.J. "Employment Deconcentration in the Nonmetropolitan Migration Turnaround." *Demography* 17 (1980):145-58.

White, L.K. "Note on Racial Differences in the Effect of Female Economic Opportunity on Marriage Rates." *Demography* 18 (1981):349-54.

Wolfbein, Seymour L. *Employment and Unemployment in the United States: A Study of American Labor Force.* Chicago: Science Research Associates, 1964.

Chapter 13

Occupation, Industry, and Class of Worker

The labor force concepts of Chapter 12 separate the economically active members of the population from the inactive members and determine whether or not the economically active are employed. They do not designate the kinds of jobs performed by members of the labor force, the types of organizations in which they work, or the manner in which they obtain their income, for which data concerning occupation, industry, and class of worker are needed. The present chapter discusses these three aspects of the economic composition of the population. It should be kept in mind that this discussion will deal only with the *employed* segment of the labor force, inasmuch as unemployed persons cannot have a current occupation, industry or class of worker categorization.

Occupational Composition and Trends

Census enumerators are instructed to record the exact kind of work performed by employed persons or (if the person is unemployed) the kind of work performed on the last job. Specially trained census clerks, supervised by occupational statisticians, classify and code these responses in terms of meaningful occupational groups. (For details see the Definition Box.)

The system of occupational classification now in use is a product of many years of experimentation, research, and critical review of the results yielded by earlier classifications. A pioneer among the statisticians responsible for the present relatively high quality and great usefulness of the occupational statistics was Dr. Alba M. Edwards. He was among the first to compile long lists of occupational names with the corresponding job descriptions in order to designate meaningful common elements on the basis of which occupational classifications could be established. During this painstaking labor Dr. Edwards did not lose sight of the immense sociological significance of the population's occupational characteristics. Today's specialists who use occupational data with narrow perspective to identify social strata and social classes or to build econometric models of the labor market might well pause to reflect on his words:

> The most nearly dominant single influence in a man's life is probably his occupation. More than anything else, perhaps, a man's occupation determines his course and his contribution in life. And when life's span is ended, quite likely there is no other single set of facts that will tell so well the kind of man he was and the part he played in life as will a detailed and chronological statement of

Definitions

The materials of this chapter are based on statistics generated from responses to job description questions 28-30 in the 1980 census, or corresponding questions from the previous censuses or the Current Population Surveys. Persons were instructed to describe the job they held during the reference week before the enumeration or, if not employed, the job at which the person was most recently employed. Persons working at more than one job were instructed to describe the one at which they worked the most hours during the reference week.

Industry (question 28). "(a) For whom did this person work (last week)? (b) What kind of business or industry was this? (c) Is this mainly manufacturing, wholesale trade, retail trade, or other (agriculture, construction, service, government, etc.)?" Persons working for employers engaged in more than one activity were instructed to describe only the main activity at the place or facility where the person worked. Responses to these questions were coded into 231 categories called the "detailed industry classification." An "intermediate industrial classification" of 140 categories was arrived at by combining similar or related industries from the detailed classification. These categories, in turn, were summarized in thirteen "major industry groups." Aside from changes caused by the emergence of new industries, the death of some, and the growth and decline in others–and changes in coding procedures and codebooks–industry statistics at the intermediate and major industry group levels are roughly comparable from 1940 to the present.

Occupation (question 29). "(a) What kind of work was this person doing? (b) What were this person's most important activities or duties?" These write-in responses were taken together to assign the respondent to one of 503 "detailed occupation categories," coded by specially trained coders in census processing offices. An "intermediate occupational classification" of 121 categories was arrived at by combining similar or related occupations from the detailed classification. These categories, in turn, were summarized into thirteen (sometimes fourteen) "major occupation groups." In addition, some of the intermediate and detailed occupation categories are subdivided by industry or class of worker groups. Although the enumeration procedure used in collecting occupational data at the 1980 census (and since 1972 in the Current Population Survey) is similar to those used since the census of 1940, the classification system used for coding responses (*1980 Census of Population: Classified Index of Industries and Occupations*) was substantially different in 1980 from the categories and coding systems used in the 1970 and prior enumerations. Segments of some occupational classifications of 1970 were moved to a different category in 1980, and the major occupational groups (and consequently the intermediate categories) are substantially different in the new system from the previous system. The changes create major problems of comparability. They were made so that the occupational classification would realistically reflect the current occupational structure of the United States, based on an assessment of the kind of work performed. The new system of occupational coding, used in the 1980 census, was initiated in the Current Population Survey as early as 1972. Hence, comparable data on changes in occupational composition from 1972 to the present are available from the CPS.

Occupation Divisions. The major occupation groups are often arranged in four divisions:

White collar–Professional technical, managers, and administrators, except farm; sales workers; and clerical and kindred workers.

Blue collar–Craftsmen and kindred workers; operatives, except transport; transport equipment operatives; and laborers, except farm

Farm workers–Farmers and farm managers, farm laborers, and farm foremen

Service workers–Service workers, including private household.

Class of Worker (question 30). "Was this person (a) employee of private company, business, or individual for wages, salary, or commission, (b) Federal government employee, (c) state government, (d) local government employee–city, county, etc., (e) self-employed in own business, professional practice, or farm, or (f) working without pay in family business or farm? If self-employed, specify whether

Continued on next page

Definitions

the business is incorporated or not incorporated." Responses to these questions were classified in categories as follows:

1. Private wage and salary workers—Persons who worked for a private employer for wages, salary, commission, tips, pay-in kind-, or at piece rates. Private employers include churches and other nonprofit organizations.

2. Government workers—Persons who worked for any government unit, regardless of the activity of the particular agency. This category is subdivided by the level of government: (a) Federal, (b) State, (c) Local (county and its political subdivisions such as cities, villages, and townships). Employees of the United Nations, other international organizations, and foreign governments are classified as Federal government employees. Most employees of the District of Columbia government are classified as local government employees.

3. Self-employed workers—

(a) Own business not incorporated—Persons who worked for profit or fees in their own unincorporated business, profession, or trade, or who operated a farm. Included here are the owner-operators of large stores and manufacturing establishments as well as merchants, independent craftspersons and professionals, farmers, peddlers, and other persons who conducted enterprises of their own.

(b) Own business incorporated—Persons who consider themselves self-employed but work for corporations. In most cases the respondents will own or be part of a group that owns controlling interest in the corporation. Since all workers of a corporation are defined as wage and salary workers, this category is tabulated with "private wage and salary workers" and is sometimes shown as a subcategory of that group.

4. Unpaid family workers—Persons who worked without pay on a farm or in a business operated by a person to whom they are related by blood or marriage. These are usually the children or the wife of the owner of a business or farm. About one-quarter of the unpaid family workers are farm workers.

the occupation, or occupations, he pursued. Indeed, there is no other single characteristic that tells so much about a man and his status—social, intellectual, and economic—as does his occupation. A man's occupation not only tells, for each workday, what he does during one-half of his waking hours, but it indicates, with some degree of accuracy, his manner of life during the other half—the kind of associates he will have, the kind of clothes he will wear, the kind of house he will live in, and even, to some extent, the kind of food he will eat. And, usually, it indicates, in some degree, the cultural level of this family.

In similar manner there is probably no single set of closely related facts that tell so much about a nation as do detailed statistics of the occupations of its workers. The occupations of a people influence directly their lives, their customs, their institutions—indeed, their very numbers. In fact, the social and economic status of a people is largely determined by the social and economic status of its gainful workers. And, were the figures available, the social and industrial history of a people might be traced more accurately through detailed statistics of the occupations of its gainful workers than through records of its wars, its territorial conquests, and its political struggles.[1]

In a modern industrialized nation there may be many thousands of different occupations, so complex has the division of labor become. It would be both impossible and undesirable to tabulate statistics for each item in such a long list. Because many occupations are very similar to each other, census clerks use a classification scheme that groups similar occupations into one category. In the United States occupational data are gathered by several federal agencies as well as by private organizations; so classification must be standardized if comparability is to be achieved. In fact, the need for comparability of occupational classifications is international in scope and has led to the setting up of programs to achieve an international classification scheme. Within the federal government a multiagency task force, advised by experts from universities and the private sector, has been sponsored by the Office of Management and Budget in order to promote uniformity and comparability in the presentation of statistical data collected by various agencies. The 1980 *Standard Occupational*

Classification (SOC) published by the U.S. Bureau of the Census is a product of this endeavor. For 1970 and earlier censuses, the occupational classification system used in the *Dictionary of Occupational Titles,* published by the U.S. Department of Labor, was used with some modification.

In general this system is able to present statistics on three levels of detail:

1. Detailed occupational classification. Highly specific categories of occupations, or of subgroupings of occupations, according to industry.

2. Intermediate occupational classification. Combinations of the categories of the detailed occupational classification, in which similar occupations are grouped and in which detailed occupations that contain only a few workers are merged with larger categories that they resemble.

3. Major occupational groups. Broad categories of occupation, consisting of groupings of the intermediate (and hence of the detailed) occupational categories.

New inventions, scientific discoveries, and technological progress constantly present new work tasks and need methods for performing them, causing changes in the way society is organized, so that classifications must be revised at each decennial census. Moreover, the number and proportion of workers in each of the occupations that do continue to be recognized will change with altered conditions. The new occupations must be added and old occupations must be reevaluated to ensure that they are still in the proper groupings. Hence strict comparability cannot, and should not, be maintained from census to census. Extensive and important changes were made in the occupational classification system used in the 1980 census in comparison with previous censuses.

Comparability of occupational categories between the 1980 and 1970 censuses has been established by the Bureau of the Census by combining and estimating classification (and data) into the nearest equivalent for 1980. Thus it is possible to discuss intercensal change 1970-80 in terms of the new occupational categories. The Bureau of Labor Statistics and the Current Population Survey continued to report occupations in terms of the "old" classification (as well as the new) until 1982, and hence it is possible to discuss long-term trends over several decades using the "old" categories. In order to provide a complete description of change, it is necessary to use both the old and the new systems of classification.

Major Occupational Groups

The most general occupational classification in the 1980 system consists of six summary categories, four of which have subdivisions, creating a total of thirteen major occupational groups. Table 13-1 lists these categories and provides indicators of relative size, demographic

Table 13-1. Occupational Composition of the Employed Labor Force, by Sex and Race-Ethnicity: 1980, and Percent Change, 1970-1980 [1980 occupational classification]

Occupation	Percent distribution, 1980				Percent composition, 1980			Percent change, 1970–80		
	Total	White	Black	Spanish-origin	Percent black	Percent Spanish	Percent female	Total	Black	Female
Total employed	100.0	100.0	100.0	100.0	9.6	5.6	42.6	27.5	26.8	43.9
A. Managerial and professional specialty occupations	22.7	23.9	14.1	12.2	5.9	3.0	40.4	52.5	95.8	82.6
1. Executive, administrative and managerial occupations	10.4	11.1	5.2	5.9	4.8	3.2	30.3	72.3	180.6	184.9
2. Professional specialty occupations	12.3	12.8	8.9	6.3	6.9	2.9	49.0	39.0	66.2	53.8
B. Technical, sales and administrative support occupations	30.3	31.1	25.2	24.5	7.9	4.5	64.1	32.4	75.5	44.6
1. Technicians and related support occupations	3.1	3.1	2.7	2.1	8.3	3.8	43.7	67.9	92.1	113.2
2. Sales occupations	10.0	10.7	5.0	7.2	4.8	4.0	47.9	25.6	78.7	48.1
3. Administrative support occupations, including clerical	17.3	17.3	17.5	15.2	9.7	4.9	77.1	31.7	72.4	39.0
C. Service occupations	12.9	11.6	23.1	16.3	17.1	7.0	59.0	30.1	5.5	28.8
1. Private household occupations	0.6	0.4	2.6	1.0	41.0	9.4	95.5	-48.8	-60.3	-49.3
2. Protective service occupations	1.5	1.5	1.9	1.2	12.0	4.4	11.4	42.3	121.0	150.9
3. Service occupations, except protective and household	10.8	9.8	18.6	14.1	16.5	7.3	63.6	40.5	28.4	45.9
D. Farming, forestry and fishing occupations	2.9	2.9	2.0	4.7	6.5	9.1	14.4	-3.3	-41.2	59.1
E. Precision production, draft and repair occupations	12.9	13.4	8.9	14.0	6.6	6.1	7.8	16.6	17.6	27.9
F. Operators, fabricators and laborers	18.3	17.1	26.7	28.4	14.0	8.7	27.3	9.8	9.1	18.7
1. Machine operators, assemblers and inspectors	9.3	8.6	13.5	16.0	13.8	9.6	40.1	8.5	17.7	12.6
2. Transportation and material moving occupations	4.5	4.4	6.0	4.8	12.8	5.9	7.9	17.4	15.9	123.8
3. Handlers, equipment cleaners, helpers and laborers	4.5	4.1	7.2	7.6	15.3	9.5	20.1	5.7	-8.1	23.3

Source: U.S. Bureau of the Census. "General Social and Economic Characteristics: United States Summary." 1980 Census of Population. Washington, DC: U.S. Government Printing Office, 1984, Tables 89 and 135.

characteristics of workers, and change between 1970-80 for each. Table 13-1 illustrates this composition. (The reader wishing to become more familiar with the meaning of these categories may refer to Table 13-5, where the detailed occupations falling in each category are listed.) A broad way of approaching occupations is in terms of the occupation divisions. The work force as of 1980 and 1970 had the following composition:

Category	1980	1970	Change
Total	100.0	100.0	0.0
White collar (A, B)	53.0	48.2	+4.8
Blue collar (E, F).	31.2	35.3	-4.1
Service workers (C)	12.9	12.7	+0.2
Agricultural workers (D). . .	2.9	3.8	-0.9

During the decade, the white collar occupations became an absolute majority, signalling the much-heralded shift to the "postindustrial society." Meanwhile, the blue collar and farm workers suffered proportionate declines in importance, while the service occupations remained about the same.

White Collar Workers

The white collar class has two major strata—the upper class and their middle class aides. The upper class group, termed by the census "Managerial and professional specialty occupations," is subdivided into two parts—administrators and professionals. The administrators are termed "Executive, administrative, and managerial occupations" (A-1). This class of workers increased faster than any other during the 1970-80 decade—72 percent (see "percent change 1970-80" columns of Table 13-1). The "Professional specialty occupations" (A-2) increased somewhat more slowly, but still more rapidly than the labor force as a whole. Together these "elite" occupations comprise 23 percent of the work force.

The middle class white collar aides which outnumber the upper class (they are 30 percent of the work force) fall into three categories. "Technicians and related support occupations" (B-1) is a small but very rapidly growing stratum of workers. The troops of the white collar army are of two major types, "Sales occupations" (B-2) and "Administrative support occupations, including clerical" (B-3). This latter group is the largest of the occupational groups, comprising 17 percent of the labor force. Between 1970 and 1980 the sales force grew slightly less rapidly than the work force as a whole, while the clerical-administrative support group grew slightly faster but less rapidly than the professional group.

Blue Collar Workers

These workers in shops, factories, warehouses, and on the highways and railways are divided into two subcategories, the skilled "Precision production, craft, and repair occupations" (E) and the semiskilled and unskilled "Operators, fabricators, and laborers" (F). Between 1970 and 1980 the first of these groups grew slowly—only slightly more than half as fast as the labor force. It is a sizable group (12.9 percent of the work force). The second category consists of three subgroups. "Machine operators, assemblers, and inspectors" (F-1), grew only one-third as rapidly as the work force. "Transportation and material moving occupations" (F-2) is comparatively small and grew at about the same rate as the precision production, craft and repair workers (group E). The third group, "Handlers, cleaners, helpers, and laborers" (F-3), suffered an absolute decline of nearly 6 percent during the 1970-80 decade.

Service Workers

In this heterogeneous category, private household workers (C-1) comprise less than 1 percent of the work force and declined by nearly 50 percent during the 1970-80 decade. Protective service workers (C-2) grew quite rapidly (42 percent) during the decade, but still is small. The core of the service occupations is the many attendants and workers who provide services in a wide variety of establishments. It comprises more than 10 percent of the labor force and grew rapidly during 1970-80.

Farming, Forestry and Fishing Occupations

These occupations constituted less than 3 percent of the work force. They experienced a decline of 3 percent during the 1970-80 decade.

Summary

During the 1970-80 decade there was rapid growth of managerial and technical occupations, moderately rapid growth of professional, administrative support, clerical, and service occupations other than domestic. There was slow growth in the skilled and semiskilled blue collar occupations, and absolute decline in the unskilled, the private household, and the farming occupations. Occupations demanding the exercise of power, knowledge, and skill grew, while those primarily requiring the use of muscles stagnated or declined.

Long-Term Trends in Occupation

According to the "old" occupational classification system used in the 1970 census and before (Tables 13-2 and 13-3), the trends described above have been underway since 1960. The white collar workers, especially the managers-administrators and professional-techni-

Table 13-2. Occupational Composition of Employed Civilians, by Sex: 1960-1982 ["old" occupational classification; numbers in thousands]

Occupation	Number		Percent distribution					
	1982	1980	1982	1980	1975	1970	1965	1960
Total, both sexes	99,526	99,303	100.0	100.0	100.0	100.0	100.0	100.0
Professional and technical	16,951	15,968	17.0	16.1	15.0	14.2	12.5	11.4
Managers and administrators	11,493	11,138	11.5	11.2	10.5	10.5	10.3	10.7
Sales workers	6,580	6,303	6.6	6.3	6.4	6.2	6.3	6.4
Clerical workers	18,446	18,473	18.5	18.6	17.8	17.4	15.7	14.8
Craft and kindred workers	12,272	12,787	12.3	12.9	12.9	12.9	13.0	13.0
Operatives	12,806	14,096	12.9	14.2	15.2	17.7	18.8	18.2
Nonfarm laborers	4,518	4,567	4.5	4.6	4.9	4.7	5.2	5.4
Private household workers	1,042	1,063	1.0	1.1	1.4	2.0	2.8	3.0
Other service workers	12,694	12,165	12.8	12.3	12.4	10.4	9.8	9.2
Farmers and farm managers	1,452	1,493	1.5	1.5	1.9	2.2	3.1	4.2
Farm laborers and supervisors	1,271	1,247	1.3	1.3	1.6	1.7	2.6	3.6
Males	56,271	57,186	100.0	100.0	100.0	100.0	100.0	100.0
Professional and technical	9,302	8,904	16.5	15.5	14.6	14.0	12.1	10.9
Managers and administrators	8,273	8,219	14.7	14.4	14.0	14.2	13.4	13.6
Sales workers	3,595	3,450	6.4	6.0	6.1	5.6	5.7	5.8
Clerical workers	3,556	3,687	6.3	6.4	6.5	7.1	7.1	7.1
Craft and kindred workers	11,408	12,018	20.3	21.0	20.4	20.1	19.3	19.0
Operatives	8,665	9,581	15.4	16.8	17.5	19.6	20.7	19.6
Nonfarm laborers	3,990	4,040	7.1	7.0	7.4	7.3	7.7	7.9
Private household workers	33	27	0.1	*	0.1	0.1	0.1	0.1
Other service workers	5,202	4,973	9.2	8.7	8.5	6.6	6.8	6.4
Farmers and farm managers	1,280	1,335	2.3	2.4	2.9	3.4	4.5	6.1
Farm laborers and supervisors	966	914	1.7	1.6	1.9	1.9	2.7	3.5
Females	43,256	42,117	100.0	100.0	100.0	100.0	100.0	100.0
Professional and technical	7,650	7,063	17.7	16.8	15.7	14.5	13.2	12.4
Managers and administrators	3,219	2,920	7.4	6.9	5.2	4.5	4.5	5.0
Sales workers	2.985	2,853	6.9	6.8	6.9	7.0	7.5	7.7
Clerical workers	14,890	14,787	34.4	35.1	35.1	34.5	31.8	30.3
Craft and kindred workers	864	769	2.0	1.8	1.5	1.1	1.1	1.0
Operatives	4,140	4,514	9.6	10.7	11.6	14.5	15.2	15.2
Nonfarm laborers	528	528	1.2	1.2	1.1	0.5	0.4	0.4
Private household workers	1,010	1,036	2.3	2.5	3.4	5.1	7.7	8.9
Other service workers	7,492	7,157	17.3	17.0	18.2	16.5	15.5	14.8
Farmers and farm managers	172	159	0.4	0.4	0.3	0.3	0.5	0.5
Farm laborers and supervisors	306	334	0.7	0.8	1.1	1.5	2.5	3.9

Note: * indicates less than 0.05.

Source: U.S. Bureau of Labor Statistics. Handbook of Labor Statistics. Washington, DC: U.S. Government Printing Office, 1983, Table 16.

cal workers, have grown more rapidly than the work force as a whole for decades. The unskilled blue collar workers (laborers) have grown more slowly, and farm workers and private household workers declined. However, the skilled craft and semiskilled operative workers grew at about the same rate as the work force as a whole. The unique changes in the 1970s were the stagnation of employment in skilled and semiskilled work, the quasi-stagnation of professional employment, and the zooming upward of administrative and technical workers.

Figure 13-1 charts the long-term growth of the occupations since 1900. It shows that the drift from blue collar to white collar occupations has characterized the entire century, but has accelerated since 1960.

Occupation of Employed Women

The preceding chapter pointed out that since 1960 the female component of the work force has been growing at 2.5 to 3.0 times the rate for males. Tables 13-1 and 13-3 reveal the occupations that women have enter-

Table 13-3. Percent Change in Employed Labor Force, by Occupation and Sex: 1960-1982 ["old" occupational classification]

Occupation	1980–82			1970–80			1960–70		
	Both sexes	Male	Female	Both sexes	Male	Female	Both sexes	Male	Female
Total employed labor force.	0.2	-1.6	2.7	26.2	16.7	42.0	19.6	11.6	35.7
Professional and technical. .	6.2	4.5	8.3	43.2	30.0	64.2	49.2	43.6	59.0
Managers and administrators .	3.2	0.7	10.2	34.2	17.9	120.7	17.4	16.8	20.4
Sales workers	4.4	4.2	4.6	29.8	24.8	36.4	15.2	9.1	24.4
Clerical workers.	-0.1	-3.6	0.7	34.6	5.9	44.4	40.6	11.0	54.7
Craft and kindred workers . .	-4.0	-5.1	12.4	25.8	22.2	131.6	18.7	17.9	49.5
Operatives.	-9.2	-9.6	-8.3	1.3	-0.3	4.9	16.5	10.9	29.4
Nonfarm laborers.	-1.1	-1.2	0.0	22.5	12.5	288.2	4.8	3.2	72.2
Private household workers . .	-2.0	22.2	-2.5	-31.8	-32.5	-31.8	-21.3	21.2	-22.0
Other service workers	4.3	4.6	4.7	49.1	53.2	45.7	34.9	15.2	51.9
Farmers and farm managers . .	-2.7	-4.1	8.2	-14.8	-20.2	98.8	-37.0	-37.3	-27.9
Farm laborers and supervisors	1.9	5.7	-8.4	-9.2	-1.6	-24.9	-42.3	-39.5	-47.5

Source: U.S. Bureau of Labor Statistics. Handbook of Labor Statistics. Washington, DC: U.S. Government Printing Office, 1983, Table 16.

ed and the rates of growth in female employment for those occupations. The main points are as follows:

1. Women have entered the "growth occupations" at much higher rates than men. For example, between 1970 and 1980 women in administrative (A-1) occupations increased by 185 percent. The number of women employed in the clerical fields rose at the rate of 44 percent, as against 6 percent for men. Thus the recent years have witnessed a feminization of the upper class white collar occupational strata along a much wider range of occupations in addition to teaching and secretarial positions. Meanwhile, women have maintained their well-established share of the sales occupations.

2. Since 1960 women have also entered the skilled and craft blue collar occupations at rates three to five times those for males and have equaled or surpassed men in entering the expanding category of service industries other than domestic service.

3. While making these gains, women have withdrawn from domestic service and farm laborer jobs at very rapid rates.

4. As a consequence of this differential growth between the sexes, the occupational composition of the female employed workers has tended to converge toward that of males. Women still occupy proportionately fewer managerial and administrative posts and hold fewer precision craft and kindred worker jobs in comparison with men, while having proportionately larger share of the clerical and service work tasks (see "percent female" column in Table 13-1 as well as Figure 13-2). As Chapter 14 on income shows, occupational titles can be deceptive,

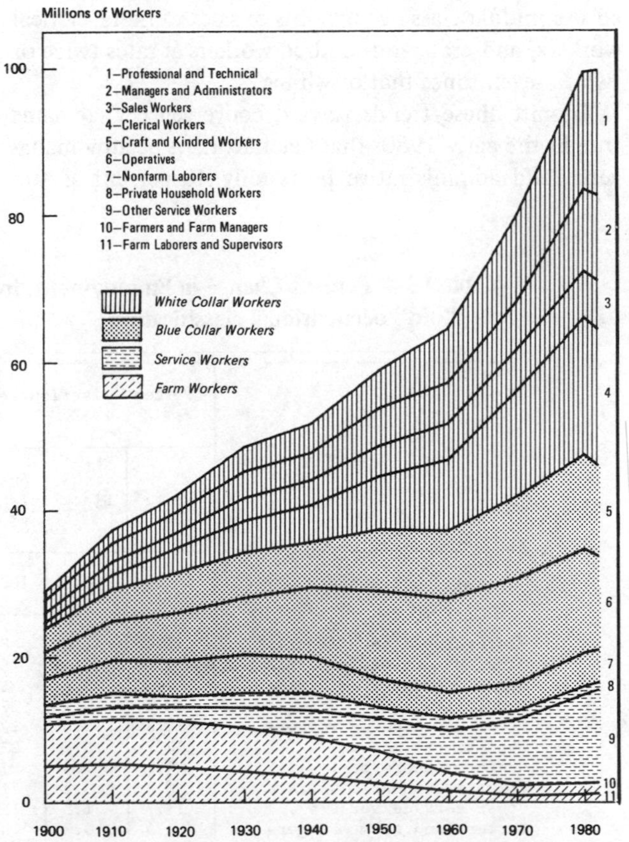

Figure 13-1. Trends in Occupational Composition of the Employed Civilian Labor Force: 1900-1983 [old definition]

and income inequalities between men and women workers are far greater than the occupational statistics might suggest.

Occupation of Race and Ethnic Groups

There are large disparities between the occupational composition of white workers on the one hand and black and Spanish-origin workers on the other (see Figure 13-2). However, recent trends have been in the direction of convergence (see Tables 13-1 or 13-4).

1. Although white workers hold a disproportionately large share of the professional, technical, and managerial jobs, the recent rates of growth for the minority groups has been twice or more that of the white majority. The Spanish-origin workers, who previously held even smaller shares of these positions than the blacks, have enjoyed the highest rate of change.
2. Meanwhile, there has been a net exodus or almost zero growth in the lowest-paying jobs of nonfarm laborer, farm laborer, and private household worker among black and Spanish-origin workers as well as among white workers.
3. Both black and Spanish-origin workers have entered the middle class occupations of sales workers, clerical workers, and craft and kindred workers at rates twice or two to seven times that of whites.

Despite these trends toward convergence, it remains true in the early 1980s that black workers occupy managerial and administrative posts only 40 percent as frequently as whites; for Spanish-origin workers the proportion is about 55 percent. In the professional and technical occupations, blacks occupy less than 70 percent of the share of positions warranted by their share in the general population; for Spanish-origin, the share is less than 50 percent. (See "percent black" and "percent Spanish-origin" columns in Table 13-1.) Meanwhile, both groups tend to be overrepresented in the lower-status jobs of laborer, service worker, and operative. The proportions occupying clerical and craft jobs have already converged toward approximate equality. If the recent patterns of change that have characterized the years since 1960 were to continue to the year 2000, the occupational composition of the U.S. labor force would show greatly reduced and comparatively minor differences linked to race and ethnicity, aside from prerequisite educational attainment.

As was stated for females, occupational titles do not reflect differences in real income very precisely, with the result that income differences between the race/ethnic groups are much wider than these data suggest (see Chapter 14).

Detailed Occupation Distribution

The overview of occupational composition and trends provided above fails to reveal the great diversity of occupations that exists within each of the major occupation groups and the great disparities in size and differences between sexes and races. There are also large differences

Table 13-4. Percent Change in Employment, by Occupation and Race-Ethnicity: 1973-1982 ["old" occupational classification]

Occupation	Percent distribution 1982			Percent distribution 1973			Percent change, 1973-82		
	White	Black	Spanish-origin	White	Black	Spanish-origin	White	Black	Spanish-origin
Total, both sexes	100.0	100.0	100.0	100.0	100.0	100.0	16.1	13.1	51.9
Professional and technical. .	17.4	11.8	8.5	14.4	8.5	6.5	39.9	57.2	100.0
Managers and administrators .	12.3	4.8	6.5	11.0	3.5	5.5	30.2	57.8	81.2
Sales workers	7.1	2.8	4.2	6.9	2.1	3.7	18.6	48.8	73.0
Clerical workers.	18.5	18.9	17.3	17.5	14.6	13.3	22.6	46.7	97.8
Craft and kindred workers . .	12.8	9.0	13.2	13.9	8.8	13.0	6.6	14.6	54.2
Operatives.	12.2	18.7	22.5	16.3	23.3	28.7	-12.6	-9.4	19.2
Nonfarm laborers.	4.2	7.4	7.2	4.6	10.2	8.1	8.1	-17.3	37.8
Private household workers . .	0.8	3.2	1.6	1.1	6.3	1.8	-12.7	-42.6	39.3
Other service workers	11.7	21.8	15.2	10.6	20.1	14.0	28.4	22.3	64.6
Farmers and farm managers . .	1.6	0.2	0.2	2.1	0.6	0.2	-11.4	-66.7	0.0
Farm laborers and supervisors	1.3	1.4	3.6	1.6	2.1	5.4	-6.0	-21.9	1.1

Source: U.S. Bureau of Labor Statistics. Handbook of Labor Statistics. Washington, DC: U.S. Government Printing Office, 1983, Table 16.

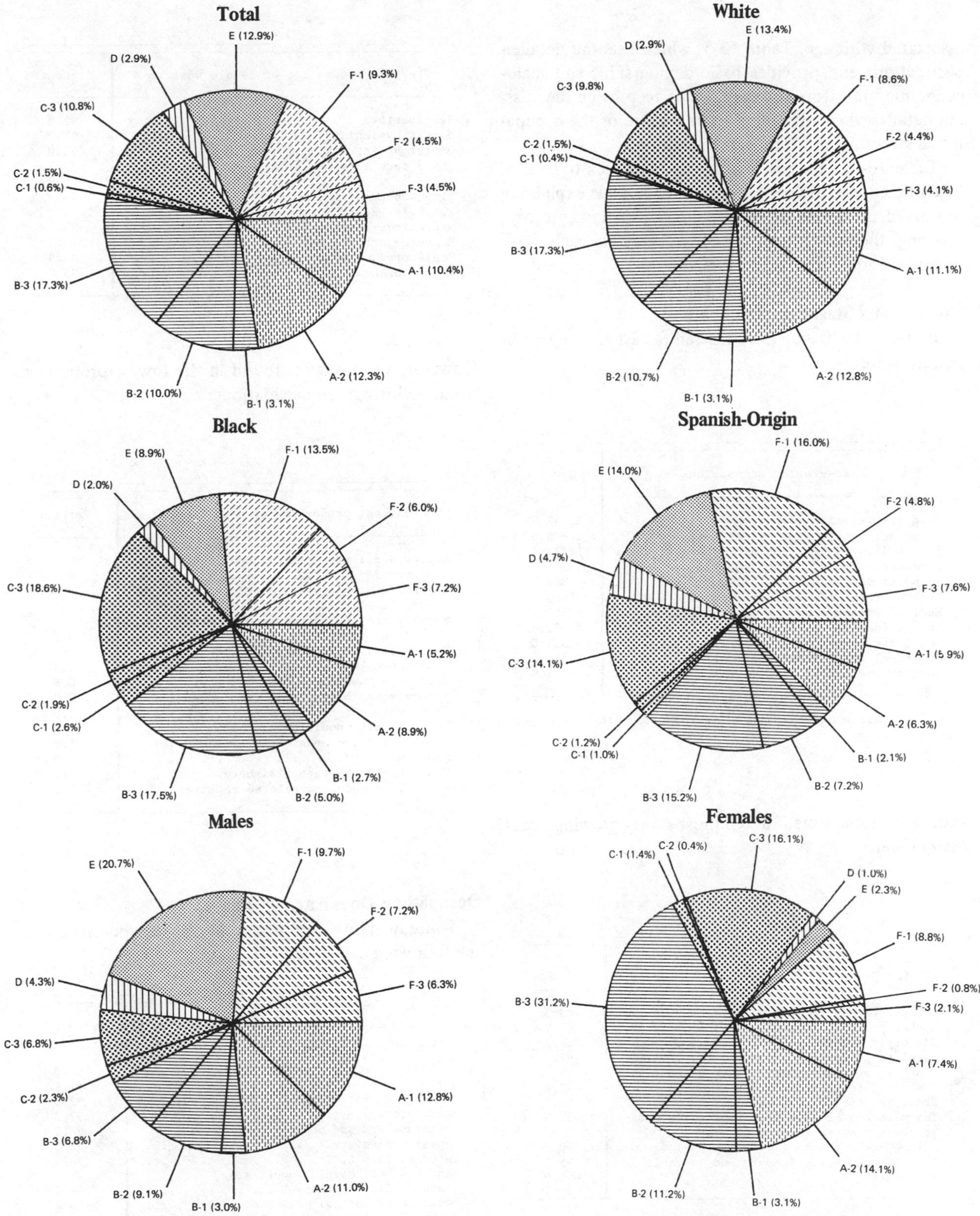

A. Managerial and Professional Specialty Occupations
A-1. Executive, Administrative, and Managerial
A-2. Professional Specialty
B. Technical, Sales, and Administrative Support
B-1. Technicians and Related Support
B-2. Sales
B-3. Administrative Support, Including Clerical
C. Service
C-1. Private Household
C-2. Protective Service
C-3. Service (Except Private and Household
D. Farming, Forestry, and Fishing
E. Precision Production, Draft, and Repair
F. Operators, Fabricators, and Laborers
F-1. Machine Operators, Assemblers, Inspectors
F-2. Transportation and Material Moving
F-3. Handlers, Equipment Cleaners, Helpers, and Laborers

Figure 13-1. Occupational Composition of the Employed Civilian Labor Force, by Race-Ethnicity and Sex: 1980

associated with age. Table 13-5, which lists the detailed occupations and provides basic demographic and socioeconomic indicators for each, helps to provide the missing details, while offering a truer picture of the occupational structure and trends of the nation.

Table 13-5 is far too lengthy and complex to be analyzed here. It is designed as a reference table explaining the detailed content of each major occupation category, showing the characteristics of workers in each. Following are some examples.

Growing and Stagnating Occupations

Between 1970 and 1980 the ten fastest growing occupations were:

Fast-growing occupations[a]	Rate
Teachers, special education	1,942.5
Managers, horticultural specialty farms	1,896.8
Eligibility clerks, social welfare	1,813.4
Personnel clerks, except payroll and timekeeping	804.5
Underwriters (management-related)	613.1
Medical scientists	450.2
Inhalation therapists	432.3
Legal assistants	339.0
Numerical control machine operators	330.2
Nuclear engineers	293.9

[a]"Not elsewhere classified" occupations are not included.

During the same time, the ten most slowly growing occupations were:

Stagnating occupations	Rate
Launderers and ironers	-83.3
Cooks, private households	-67.7
History teachers	-67.7
Samplers	-67.5
Teachers post-secondary, other social science teachers	-63.7
Precision assemblers, metal	-62.1
Teachers post-secondary, physics teachers	-61.5
Teachers post-secondary, foreign language teachers	-60.6
Private household cleaners and servants	-55.7
Stevedores	-54.0

Most Feminized and Least Feminized Occupations

In 1980 women outnumbered men by the greatest proportion in the following occupations:

Largest proportion of female workers	Percent
Secretaries	98.8
Dental hygienists	98.5
Dental assistants	98.0
Child care workers, private households	97.5
Typists	96.9
Licensed practical nurses	96.6
Teachers, kindergarten and prekindergarten	96.5
Housekeepers and butlers	96.5
Registered nurses	95.9
Receptionists	95.8

However, women were found in the lowest proportions in the following ten occupations:

Smallest proportion of female workers	Percent
Supervisors; firefighting and fire prevention	0.5
Supervisors; plumbers, pipefitters, and steamfitters	0.6
Supervisors; carpenters and related workers	0.7
Bus, truck, and stationary engine mechanics	0.7
Heavy equipment mechanics	0.8
Supervisors; brickmasons, stonemasons	0.9
Farm equipment mechanics	1.0
Heating, air conditioning, and refrigeration mechanics	1.0
Roofers	1.0
Concrete and terrazo finishers	1.1
Automobile body and related repairers	1.1

Occupations Dominated by Races

White workers comprised the highest percentage of the following categories:

Largest proportion of white workers	Percent
Airplane pilots and navigators	97.9
Sales engineers	97.9
Farmers, except horticultural	97.6
Auctioneers	97.0
Patternmakers and model makers, wood	96.8
Dental hygienists	96.8
Veterinarians	96.6
Managers, marketing, advertising, and public relations	96.4
Postmasters and mail superintendents	96.4
Other natural science teachers	96.3
Supervisors, electricians and power transmission installers	96.3
Supervisors, extractive occupations	96.3

Black workers comprised the highest percentage of the following ten occupations:

Largest proportion of black workers	Percent
Private household cleaners and servants	53.8
Cooks, private households	48.3
Housekeepers and butlers	37.8
Stevedores	35.1
Pressing machine operators	34.5
Longshore equipment operators	34.3
Garbage collectors	34.2
Baggage porters and bellhops	33.7
Nonhousehold maids and housemen	32.8
Welfare service aides	32.8

Occupations Dominated by Youth and Older Workers

The ten occupations with the highest proportion of workers 25-34 years of age were:

Highest proportions 25-34 years old	Percent
Speach therapists	59.6
Public transportation attendants	56.8
Urban planners	53.3
Clinical laboratory technologists, and technicians	52.0
Inhalation therapists	51.6
Telephone line installers and repairers	49.7
Actuaries	49.6
Dental Hygienists	49.1
Occupational therapists	48.8
Biological and life scientists	48.6

The ten occupations with the highest proportion of workers 55-64 years of age were:

Highest proportions 55-64 years old	Percent
Postmasters and mail superintendents	34.7
Cooks, private households	29.5
Launderers and ironers	28.4
Judges	28.3
Private household cleaners and servants	28.2
Elevator operators	27.9
Bridge, lock and lighthouse tenders	26.4
Optometrists	26.0
Construction inspectors	25.2
Housekeepers and butlers	25.2

Occupations with Highest and Lowest Educational Requirements

The ten occupations with the highest proportion of college graduates were:

Highest proportion of college graduates	Percent
Physicians	97.3
Lawyers	95.7
Dentists	95.4
Psychology teachers	93.3
Speech therapists	93.1
History teachers	93.1
Veterinarians	92.4
Medical science teachers	92.4
Other social science teachers	92.1
Biological science teachers	91.8

The ten occupations with the highest proportion of persons with less than a high school diploma were:

Highest proportion with 0-11 years of education	Percent
Private household cleaners and servants	68.0
Graders and sorters, agricultural products	67.0
Pressing machine operators	64.4
Cooks, private households	63.7
Housekeepers and butlers	62.6
Winding and twisting machine operators	62.3
Garbage collectors	59.0
Maids and housemen	58.8
Elevator operators	57.6
Knitting, looping, taping, and weaving machine operators	57.4

Occupations with Highest Income

The ten occupations with the highest mean income were as follows:

Highest mean income (male)	Income ($)
Physicians	57,054
Dentists	45,264
Medical scientists	39,814
Lawyers	37,546
Medical science teachers	37,038
Securities and financial services sales occupations	36,532
Airplane pilots and navigators	36,096
Podiatrists	35,825
Judges	34,108
Optometrists	32,876

Highest mean income (female)	Income ($)
Agricultural engineers	27,075
Physicians	26,963
Chief communications operators	17,930
Aerospace engineers	17,567
Computer systems analysts and scientists	17,114
Electrical and electronic engineers	17,008
Supervisors, extractive occupations	16,729
Airplane pilots and navigators	16,654
Medical science teachers	16,630
Judges	16,565

Table 13-5. Detailed Occupation of the Employed Persons in the United States, by Selected Characteristics: 1980

Occupation	Number of persons employed	Percent female	Percent white	Percent black	Percent Spanish-origin	Percent change in employment 1970–80	Percent full-time 1979	Age		Education		Mean income	
								25 to 34	55 to 64	0 to 11	16 and over	Male	Female
Persons 16 years and over	97,639,355	42.6	86.1	9.6	5.6	27.5	79.3	28.6	12.0	22.4	18.7	16,929	8,238
Managerial and professional specialty occupations	22,151,648	40.4	90.6	5.9	3.0	52.5	85.3	--	--	--	--	--	--
Executive, administrative, and managerial occupations	10,133,551	30.3	92.1	4.8	3.2	72.3	91.4	--	--	--	--	--	--
Legislators, chief executives and general administrators; public administration	45,165	25.4	84.2	11.4	3.6	356.6	86.0	--	--	--	--	--	--
Administrators and officials, public administrators	290,500	33.5	88.6	8.2	3.4	17.5	91.6	24.3	17.8	6.9	44.3	22,960	13,429
Federal	104,908	28.9	85.3	10.6	4.0	1.8	95.7	--	--	--	--	--	--
State	73,378	27.7	90.4	7.0	2.9	53.2	95.0	--	--	--	--	--	--
Local	112,214	41.5	90.7	6.8	3.1	16.6	85.5	--	--	--	--	--	--
Administrators, protective services	25,884	9.2	94.1	4.1	2.5	-0.1	96.3	17.3	17.7	12.5	14.0	19,694	10,045
Financial managers	403,507	31.2	94.3	3.1	2.8	84.9	95.8	34.1	11.1	3.1	46.9	26,856	13,849
Personnel and labor relations managers	214,749	35.8	90.4	6.5	4.2	235.5	94.1	30.5	11.9	8.4	42.9	24,566	14,383
Purchasing managers	69,982	21.1	94.2	3.5	2.5	2.9	61.6	30.3	14.1	4.1	42.5	25,737	14,737
Managers, marketing, advertising and public relations	674,364	17.4	96.4	1.9	2.1	5.3	63.4	30.8	11.9	5.5	40.6	28,596	12,691
Administrators, education and related fields	382,589	37.9	87.6	10.1	2.8	75.3	89.5	21.0	14.7	3.0	79.1	23,804	13,703
Managers, medicine and health	108,477	50.7	88.7	8.6	2.8	89.9	92.5	29.2	14.5	5.2	51.7	25,820	14,518
Managers, properties and real estate	193,863	40.8	90.3	6.3	5.1	72.2	79.4	23.6	19.8	18.4	24.4	19,785	8,950
Postmasters and mail superintendents	31,150	43.4	96.4	2.0	1.6	-15.0	89.5	8.0	34.7	13.6	8.6	22,212	13,847
Funeral directors	39,811	8.6	89.5	9.6	1.4	7.2	87.5	23.8	19.9	8.4	23.1	19,740	11,406
Managers and administrators, NEC, salaried	4,535,735	26.6	93.2	4.0	3.1	103.1	92.2	--	--	--	--	--	--
Construction	221,989	11.2	95.7	2.4	2.4	69.9	94.5	--	--	--	--	--	--
Manufacturing	1,028,650	12.7	95.9	2.0	2.6	59.3	96.6	--	--	--	--	--	--
Nondurable goods	406,643	15.8	95.3	2.5	2.9	47.7	95.9	--	--	--	--	--	--
Durable goods	622,007	10.6	96.2	1.8	2.3	67.8	97.1	--	--	--	--	--	--
Transportation	207,357	14.7	92.7	4.2	3.8	112.6	95.8	--	--	--	--	--	--
Communications, utilities and sanitary services	164,675	25.2	93.8	4.5	2.2	86.0	96.7	--	--	--	--	--	--
Wholesale trade	352,976	15.9	95.1	1.7	2.8	135.7	94.9	--	--	--	--	--	--
Retail trade	946,593	32.4	92.0	4.3	3.9	156.8	89.4	--	--	--	--	--	--
General merchandise stores	87,310	43.9	91.2	6.2	3.5	273.6	92.4	--	--	--	--	--	--
Food, bakery, and dairy stores	102,191	26.1	91.7	4.7	4.3	635.6	90.9	--	--	--	--	--	--
Automotive dealers and gasoline stations	93,128	18.6	96.9	1.6	2.3	763.6	94.9	--	--	--	--	--	--
Eating and drinking places	396,141	34.5	88.9	5.5	5.0	55.4	86.0	--	--	--	--	--	--
Other retail trade	267,823	32.9	95.0	2.7	2.8	308.0	90.9	--	--	--	--	--	--
Finance, insurance and real estate	346,712	34.4	93.9	3.8	2.8	75.2	93.7	--	--	--	--	--	--
Business and repair services	274,599	26.4	93.9	3.6	3.2	138.4	93.4	--	--	--	--	--	--
Personal services	136,395	40.2	91.0	4.8	4.3	0.0	86.9	--	--	--	--	--	--
All other industries	855,789	43.1	89.8	7.1	3.3	182.3	86.6	--	--	--	--	--	--
Managers and administrators, NEC, self-employed	561,480	26.9	92.3	2.9	3.8	16.1	83.4	--	--	--	--	--	--
Construction	63,526	5.0	95.3	2.9	3.2	-27.3	86.2	--	--	--	--	--	--
Manufacturing	67,182	17.7	95.0	1.4	4.2	-38.8	85.7	--	--	--	--	--	--
Nondurable goods	29,697	24.4	92.8	1.7	5.5	-57.3	84.8	--	--	--	--	--	--
Durable goods	37,485	12.4	96.7	1.2	3.2	-6.6	86.4	--	--	--	--	--	--
Transportation	17,899	15.8	93.7	3.4	4.0	-12.2	87.7	--	--	--	--	--	--
Communications, utilities and sanitary services	2,603	13.4	92.9	5.5	2.0	7.9	83.4	--	--	--	--	--	--
Wholesale trade	25,382	17.1	94.0	1.6	3.5	-11.6	85.7	--	--	--	--	--	--
Retail trade	208,537	35.8	89.9	3.4	4.6	465.0	84.1	--	--	--	--	--	--
General merchandise stores	2,553	33.6	96.6	1.2	1.6	24.1	82.5	--	--	--	--	--	--
Food, bakery, and dairy stores	16,005	31.5	87.1	5.6	4.9	438.2	86.1	--	--	--	--	--	--
Automotive dealers and gasoline stations	10,933	10.5	96.0	1.9	3.1	23.0	92.4	--	--	--	--	--	--
Eating and drinking places	128,184	36.8	87.8	3.9	5.7	--	84.2	--	--	--	--	--	--
Other retail trade	50,862	40.2	94.4	1.7	2.4	121.3	81.6	--	--	--	--	--	--
Finance, insurance and real estate	17,297	24.2	95.7	1.9	2.0	65.6	75.2	--	--	--	--	--	--
Business and repair services	55,896	19.4	94.8	2.8	3.5	22.1	84.5	--	--	--	--	--	--
Personal services	54,944	38.1	88.8	3.3	2.9	-34.9	78.3	--	--	--	--	--	--
All other industries	48,224	37.2	93.5	3.9	3.1	-16.4	78.2	--	--	--	--	--	--
Management related occupations	2,556,295	38.0	90.3	6.1	3.4	53.3	91.0	--	--	--	--	--	--
Accountants and auditors	993,327	37.9	90.1	5.2	3.1	55.8	91.0	37.4	11.1	2.1	57.0	21,587	11,668
Underwriters	18,220	58.0	91.0	6.4	3.2	613.1	94.7	41.8	7.9	3.1	39.2	21,669	11,440
Other financial officers	398,662	44.7	92.4	4.5	3.1	108.0	89.6	35.7	10.9	3.2	41.9	24,243	11,189

Table 13-5. Detailed Occupation of the Employed Persons in the United States, by Selected Characteristics: 1980—continued

Occupation	Number of persons employed	Percent female	Percent white	Percent black	Percent Spanish-origin	Percent change in employment 1970-80	Percent full-time 1979	Age: 25 to 34	Age: 55 to 64	Education: 0 to 11	Education: 16 and over	Mean income: Male	Mean income: Female
Managerial and professional specialty occupations (con't)													
Management analysts	115,585	25.1	93.0	4.6	2.2	263.6	85.1	29.9	13.8	3.0	65.7	28,246	14,768
Personnel, training, and labor relations specialists	410,366	46.8	85.4	10.8	4.9	66.8	91.8	34.6	11.4	7.8	37.2	21,137	12,643
Purchasing agents and buyers, farm products. . . .	18,981	7.8	95.3	3.4	2.4	-11.3	87.0	24.4	17.6	23.7	17.6	19,369	9,212
Buyers, wholesale and retail trade.	163,019	44.2	94.4	3.2	2.9	-3.7	88.9	35.9	12.4	9.8	28.2	19,988	11,033
Purchasing agents and buyers, NEC	187,126	31.8	93.7	4.2	2.7	27.4	95.6	31.4	15.6	6.3	26.9	19,521	12,176
Business and promotion agents.	19,668	32.9	92.4	5.1	3.6	62.0	84.8	30.5	13.4	12.7	32.5	21,166	11,788
Construction inspectors . .	48,543	4.6	90.5	6.1	3.5	1.3	92.9	21.9	25.2	15.7	13.7	16,296	10,761
Inspectors and compliance officers, except construction.	152,333	17.3	87.8	8.7	4.5	11.2	93.9	22.8	17.8	10.9	31.9	18,459	11,723
Management related occupations, NEC.	30,465	53.4	87.0	10.4	2.8	33.4	92.2	34.3	12.6	3.2	39.9	22,802	13,680
Professional specialty occupations	12,018,097	49.0	89.3	6.9	2.9	39.0	80.2	--	--	--	--	--	--
Engineers, architects, and surveyors	1,516,917	4.8	92.1	2.5	2.4	17.6	96.0	--	--	--	--	--	--
Architects.	105,079	8.2	92.1	2.7	4.0	98.3	91.4	38.0	9.9	2.8	75.3	23,924	12,034
Engineers	1,382,095	4.6	92.1	2.5	2.3	88.6	96.5	--	--	--	--	--	--
Aerospace	87,811	3.2	92.2	1.9	2.6	31.8	97.0	19.1	18.1	0.8	71.2	27,263	17,567
Metallurgical and materials.	24,187	5.1	93.2	2.1	1.9	-13.8	96.9	29.8	17.1	2.2	66.1	25,817	14,217
Mining.	9,786	3.4	95.8	0.9	2.8	108.3	94.7	38.0	11.5	3.1	62.3	25,587	14,394
Petroleum	22,808	3.5	95.1	1.5	1.9	98.3	95.5	39.1	12.1	2.0	74.3	30,322	16,418
Chemical.	56,916	5.0	91.7	1.9	1.9	6.1	97.0	34.3	13.7	1.1	83.3	27,519	15,249
Nuclear	9,186	3.7	90.8	1.6	2.2	293.9	96.5	42.1	8.2	0.6	81.3	26,231	15,343
Civil	200,471	2.9	90.2	2.5	2.7	8.8	96.2	32.4	12.8	2.4	66.9	24,435	14,024
Agricultural.	4,481	8.6	94.5	1.9	1.8	--	92.2	35.8	11.5	1.6	71.2	24,229	27,075
Electrical and electronic .	319,754	5.0	91.6	2.9	2.4	8.9	96.5	33.2	11.0	1.3	61.6	24,601	17,008
Industrial.	190,952	9.8	94.2	2.8	2.1	-0.8	97.3	31.5	15.0	2.9	45.0	22,140	13,233
Mechanical.	194,994	2.0	93.1	2.3	1.7	7.5	97.1	29.9	15.4	2.5	58.1	24,837	16,112
Marine and naval architects.	15,857	1.9	94.2	2.3	3.4	40.8	95.1	23.9	20.7	12.6	39.6	26,126	14,034
Engineers, NEC.	244,892	3.9	91.2	2.6	2.2	25.8	95.5	31.5	13.5	1.3	64.8	25,101	15,320
Surveyors and mapping scientists.	29,743	3.7	95.0	2.3	3.4	133.5	92.6	36.3	7.4	9.3	19.0	16,205	8,445
Mathematical and computer scientists.	326,495	26.0	90.5	5.2	2.3	58.0	95.3	--	--	--	--	--	--
Computer systems analysts and scientists.	200,684	22.4	90.8	4.7	2.3	89.1	95.8	44.6	3.8	1.3	57.7	23,464	17,114
Operations and systems researchers and analysts. . .	79,920	27.6	90.5	6.0	2.3	25.7	96.1	37.4	9.5	2.4	53.1	23,635	16,417
Actuaries	10,190	25.5	95.1	1.6	0.7	96.0	95.3	49.6	4.8	0.5	87.9	31,608	16,337
Statisticians	29,391	47.7	86.9	7.8	2.8	24.2	90.2	38.1	10.7	1.9	57.5	21,196	13,512
Mathematical scientists, NEC.	6,310	19.0	88.6	6.1	2.3	-21.3	93.1	31.2	8.9	0.8	86.6	26,837	18,208
Natural scientists.	307,295	19.6	90.5	3.7	2.3	37.5	91.9	--	--	--	--	--	--
Physicists and astronomers. .	22,310	5.4	92.1	1.6	1.6	6.7	94.6	32.5	9.4	0.6	86.0	27,606	16,326
Chemists, except biochemists.	100,458	19.9	86.5	4.9	2.5	7.0	94.0	36.9	11.7	1.7	78.5	22,101	14,788
Atmospheric and space scientists.	8,248	16.8	92.1	4.8	2.3	36.6	89.8	32.0	12.9	2.3	57.7	22,752	11,012
Geologists and geodesists . .	45,319	11.0	96.2	1.4	1.8	90.1	90.7	41.3	10.1	0.9	87.4	27,749	13,365
Physical scientists, NEC. . .	8,507	20.0	91.3	5.7	2.3	555.4	92.6	45.0	9.9	1.2	80.0	21,711	13,453
Agricultural and food scientists.	23,762	22.4	91.8	4.8	2.4	23.4	86.2	37.3	10.4	5.6	63.6	17,962	8,839
Biological and life scientists.	45,066	32.8	89.9	3.6	2.1	63.7	89.5	48.6	5.6	0.9	88.5	19,168	12,983
Forestry and conservation scientists.	33,880	9.1	94.0	2.9	2.2	24.8	93.9	40.2	8.6	7.5	62.1	16,671	9,169
Medical scientists.	19,745	40.3	88.3	4.5	3.1	450.2	91.1	38.7	9.6	1.1	81.1	39,814	15,448
Health diagnosing occupations .	643,716	11.7	88.9	2.8	3.4	42.9	88.1	--	--	--	--	--	--
Physicians.	431,418	13.3	86.1	3.1	4.3	45.8	91.5	30.8	14.1	0.4	97.3	57,054	26,963
Dentists.	124,772	6.5	93.9	2.5	1.7	31.5	79.3	29.0	16.6	0.3	95.4	45,264	14,877
Veterinarians	34,067	13.1	96.6	1.6	1.1	68.1	91.5	38.5	13.3	0.6	92.4	31,754	12,170
Optometrists.	24,443	8.0	96.1	1.0	1.7	36.0	84.4	29.1	26.0	1.4	88.6	32,876	12,951
Podiatrists	7,723	8.2	95.2	3.6	0.7	22.5	77.0	30.1	20.3	2.3	87.6	35,825	10,400
Health diagnosing practitioners, NEC.	21,293	12.2	95.7	1.2	1.4	38.7	71.6	31.1	17.2	2.7	85.0	31,093	11,975
Health assessment and occupations	1,695,436	86.0	87.8	7.8	2.4	72.3	73.1	--	--	--	--	--	--
Registered nurses	1,266,801	95.9	88.0	7.5	2.1	68.7	70.7	36.4	9.6	2.0	33.9	16,764	11,743
Pharmacists	143,490	23.9	91.4	3.2	2.4	25.2	83.3	36.4	10.7	1.1	87.2	21,282	12,611
Dietitians.	65,221	89.9	73.3	21.3	3.7	54.0	75.9	30.2	14.9	17.9	47.5	15,192	10,052
Therapists.	190,234	73.1	88.7	8.1	3.2	148.7	78.5	--	--	--	--	--	--
Inhalation therapists . . .	47,600	56.3	85.8	10.3	5.3	432.3	82.3	51.6	2.0	3.6	18.1	13,075	9,178
Occupational therapists . .	17,518	91.5	92.4	4.4	1.8	71.9	78.8	48.8	5.7	2.3	75.1	14,148	10,979
Physical therapists	42,462	74.0	89.9	6.7	2.9	138.0	77.2	46.5	5.4	4.2	71.9	19,328	11,659
Speech therapists	40,891	89.1	93.3	5.0	1.7	138.1	73.9	59.6	2.6	1.2	93.1	18,446	11,206
Therapists, NEC	41,763	67.8	84.7	11.8	3.2	87.0	80.0	46.9	5.5	5.1	56.6	13,253	9,242
Physician's assistants. . . .	29,690	39.8	85.6	9.9	5.7	--	85.6	47.7	3.9	9.1	19.8	14,601	8,458
Teachers, postsecondary	625,794	36.3	90.8	4.8	2.6	-23.9	70.9	--	--	--	--	--	--
Biological science teachers .	9,462	31.8	93.0	3.0	1.0	-50.2	74.6	30.0	10.4	0.4	91.8	19,924	10,714
Chemistry teachers.	8,257	20.2	91.9	2.1	1.9	-49.7	70.6	26.1	9.9	0.6	88.4	19,184	8,590
Physics teachers.	5,358	9.9	91.3	1.5	2.9	-61.5	73.0	22.8	9.2	1.5	88.0	19,868	10,852
Other natural science teachers.	3,045	17.7	96.3	0.5	1.7	-49.3	73.7	25.3	12.0	1.9	89.6	19,038	10,617
Psychology teachers	5,716	39.7	92.2	4.9	2.2	-53.0	75.7	32.6	9.5	1.5	93.3	24,511	13,436
Economics teachers.	4,947	19.6	91.6	2.8	1.8	-51.9	77.8	32.2	11.1	1.8	87.7	23,916	11,784
History teachers.	5,495	23.6	94.7	3.7	1.4	-67.7	81.4	21.6	13.7	2.3	93.1	20,546	12,146

Table 13-5. Detailed Occupation of the Employed Persons in the United States, by Selected Characteristics: 1980—continued

Occupation	Number of persons employed	Percent female	Percent white	Percent black	Percent Spanish-origin	Percent change in employment 1970-80	Percent full-time 1979	Age		Education		Mean income	
								25 to 34	55 to 64	0 to 11	16 and over	Male	Female
Professional specialty (con't)													
Other social science teachers	7,054	27.4	91.0	4.7	2.1	-63.7	75.1	35.4	9.1	1.5	92.1	18,689	10,730
Engineering teachers	10,759	11.3	90.6	3.4	2.0	-39.9	78.7	25.1	16.0	2.5	73.6	21,376	9,442
Mathematical and computer science teachers	18,934	31.2	88.4	5.4	2.5	-30.2	61.0	--	--	--	--	--	--
Medical science teachers	8,939	23.2	92.3	2.8	3.0	3.2	85.0	26.7	13.9	0.6	92.4	37,038	16,630
Health specialties teachers	19,147	86.7	90.9	6.3	1.9	-10.1	74.4	35.0	9.5	2.2	83.5	20,355	13,576
Business. commerce. and marketing teachers	7,447	47.2	91.1	5.5	2.1	-23.6	66.4	32.7	11.0	0.9	86.7	20,889	10,514
Art, drama, and music teachers	27,855	47.9	92.8	5.0	1.7	-33.1	56.5	32.9	11.6	1.6	84.3	16,723	8,955
English teachers	22,731	54.6	93.4	4.2	2.4	-43.6	62.1	34.5	9.6	1.1	89.8	16,634	9,697
Foreign language teachers	9,538	58.9	90.7	2.0	12.8	-60.6	49.2	31.5	11.1	1.3	82.9	14,716	8,156
Other specified teachers	32,642	34.5	91.5	6.1	1.8	-41.6	76.3	--	--	--	--	--	--
Postsecondary teachers, subject not specified	418,468	34.1	90.3	4.9	2.6	190.0	71.8	27.5	12.0	1.1	89.0	20,625	11,542
Teachers, except postsecondary	3,657,974	70.7	88.0	9.7	2.8	25.4	75.5	--	--	--	--	--	--
Teachers, prekindergarten and kindergarten	176,869	96.5	83.3	13.3	4.2	34.0	49.8	36.6	6.0	6.3	46.5	10,665	5,746
Teachers, elementary school	2,285,209	75.4	86.9	10.7	2.8	53.4	78.4	38.7	8.9	1.6	87.8	16,219	11,408
Teachers, secondary school	849,698	56.4	90.5	7.5	2.5	-19.2	81.7	40.8	8.0	1.4	89.4	16,452	11,464
Teachers, special education	31,925	69.1	88.9	9.0	2.1	1942.5	71.9	37.6	9.1	6.6	58.0	16,147	8,842
Teachers, NEC	314,373	61.4	90.8	6.1	3.0	30.2	52.8	33.0	10.2	6.6	46.9	14,100	6,367
Counselors, educational and vocational	193,456	54.3	82.0	13.7	4.2	69.0	79.7	32.2	9.1	2.1	75.5	15,869	11,961
Librarians, archivists, and curators	198,308	80.1	89.7	7.1	2.3	46.1	70.2	--	--	--	--	--	--
Librarians	183,439	82.6	89.7	7.1	2.3	42.8	69.7	27.1	15.1	3.1	65.4	12,993	10,330
Archivists and curators	14,869	49.7	90.2	7.0	3.0	105.7	76.3	38.4	10.7	3.9	62.7	16,536	9,686
Social scientists and urban planners	212,497	37.2	91.5	5.5	2.5	97.5	86.3	--	--	--	--	--	--
Economists	93,458	29.3	92.7	4.1	2.2	50.3	92.8	41.3	8.2	1.4	72.2	28,140	14,812
Psychologists	90,905	46.9	90.6	6.9	2.7	211.0	79.8	42.1	7.7	1.8	88.6	21,713	13,835
Sociologists	2,467	40.1	88.8	6.1	2.5	78.1	81.4	45.9	3.4	2.0	80.8	22,348	13,596
Social scientists, NEC	12,644	39.0	93.2	3.3	3.2	136.8	80.5	44.3	6.7	1.7	78.3	18,487	10,103
Urban planners	13,023	23.9	87.7	8.2	3.7	37.5	91.8	53.3	5.2	1.4	86.5	20,054	14,631
Social, recreation, and religious workers	806,567	44.0	83.2	13.2	4.3	49.8	83.8	--	--	--	--	--	--
Social workers	442,970	64.9	76.5	18.7	5.8	88.8	85.6	43.1	9.1	4.7	64.7	14,447	10,993
Recreation workers	33,802	68.3	80.7	15.0	4.9	-13.1	64.7	29.7	8.9	10.7	28.4	10,283	6,238
Clergy	280,965	5.8	92.3	5.7	2.1	23.6	87.0	25.0	16.9	6.1	73.4	12,157	7,625
Religious workers, NEC	48,830	57.3	92.6	4.5	3.0	30.5	62.3	26.6	13.8	7.3	56.3	11,463	5,900
Lawyers and judges	524,806	13.8	95.7	2.8	1.8	82.9	89.3	--	--	--	--	--	--
Lawyers	497,230	13.6	95.9	2.7	1.8	83.0	89.3	43.3	9.0	0.4	95.7	37,546	16,208
Judges	27,576	16.9	92.5	5.9	2.0	80.5	88.8	11.6	28.3	5.9	71.6	34,108	16,565
Writers, artists, entertainers, and athletes	1,308,736	41.9	92.4	4.3	3.6	47.5	72.4	--	--	--	--	--	--
Authors	44,032	44.3	95.4	2.6	2.0	65.1	60.6	30.6	12.9	2.5	71.4	18,955	8,821
Technical writers	48,065	37.4	93.5	4.3	1.7	293.4	88.1	35.6	12.7	1.7	58.7	19,792	13,020
Designers	325,276	49.4	93.1	3.0	3.8	44.3	77.8	34.2	10.2	8.8	32.3	18,867	8,662
Musicians and composers	128,809	30.3	90.6	5.9	4.4	39.7	37.0	42.2	7.0	10.0	34.3	11,071	5,930
Actors and directors	56,690	32.8	91.8	5.5	3.4	63.6	77.4	43.5	6.6	3.8	52.5	25,482	13,698
Painters, sculptors, craft-artists, and artist printmakers	146,144	47.9	93.2	2.9	3.6	75.3	71.7	36.9	9.7	5.6	38.7	14,689	7,362
Photographers	90,373	23.0	91.8	4.8	3.9	38.2	78.0	36.7	9.7	7.8	29.2	14,140	7,273
Dancers	11,552	75.2	85.0	7.4	6.0	83.4	54.8	42.5	1.7	19.4	18.1	10,590	7,243
Artists, performers and related workers, NEC	45,821	40.4	91.2	4.7	4.5	-7.9	61.5	37.3	8.4	14.8	27.2	14,215	7,165
Editors and reporters	202,846	49.0	93.6	3.5	3.4	34.6	80.9	38.0	10.2	2.8	63.1	18,574	10,900
Public relations specialists	115,093	48.5	92.4	5.2	2.8	47.1	84.2	33.8	11.7	3.9	54.8	22,122	11,829
Announcers	44,626	18.1	89.4	7.9	4.2	77.4	69.9	38.5	3.8	7.2	29.2	13,088	9,006
Athletes	49,409	24.0	89.9	7.2	4.5	31.9	66.2	33.5	4.2	11.1	33.1	16,438	5,675
Technical, sales, and administrative support occupations	29,593,506	64.1	88.4	7.9	4.5	32.4	75.5	--	--	--	--	--	--
Technicians and related support occupations	2,981,951	43.7	86.9	8.3	3.8	67.9	83.9	--	--	--	--	--	--
Health technologists and technicians	966,469	83.6	81.7	13.8	3.7	81.2	75.0	--	--	--	--	--	--
Clinical laboratory technologists and technicians	238,362	74.5	81.3	11.5	4.1	92.5	80.4	52.0	6.0	5.5	53.6	13,995	10,671
Dental hygienists	45,446	98.5	96.8	1.5	1.6	172.2	46.0	49.1	2.3	1.0	36.5	16,511	10,357
Health record technologists and technicians	14,803	91.3	84.6	9.7	3.9	25.6	83.7	33.9	9.7	3.0	30.4	15,142	10,563
Radiologic technicians	94,345	71.6	88.1	8.1	4.1	74.1	80.6	44.1	3.7	3.5	10.9	15,312	10,054
Licensed practical nurses	424,960	96.6	78.8	18.0	3.5	62.7	71.4	33.8	10.9	10.4	3.2	11,073	8,272
Health technologists and technicians, NEC	148,553	63.4	81.9	13.2	4.3	125.7	80.9	38.8	5.8	9.5	23.1	13,602	8,796
Engineering and related technologists and technicians	918,639	16.4	90.0	5.2	4.3	24.6	91.3	--	--	--	--	--	--
Electrical and electronic technicians	260,959	11.4	88.3	6.1	4.5	70.1	94.1	36.8	7.0	6.4	10.4	16,909	11,143
Industrial engineering technicians	10,295	20.6	93.0	5.3	3.3	-26.8	94.5	32.8	10.8	13.9	22.6	17,674	11,379
Mechanical engineering technicians	15,130	6.2	91.7	4.4	3.4	11.1	95.1	28.0	15.1	13.8	26.2	20,482	10,695
Engineering technicians, NEC	263,987	23.5	90.7	5.5	3.4	24.3	89.5	32.8	11.2	8.8	23.5	17,683	9,961
Drafting occupations	319,426	16.4	90.1	4.6	5.1	7.2	90.2	34.3	8.4	5.1	16.5	15,359	9,958
Surveying and mapping technicians	48,842	8.0	93.3	3.3	4.3	7.0	90.4	37.2	5.9	12.0	12.9	13,524	7,425

Table 13-5. Detailed Occupation of the Employed Persons in the United States, by Selected Characteristics: 1980—continued

Occupation	Number of persons employed	Percent female	Percent white	Percent black	Percent Spanish-origin	Percent change in employment 1970-80	Percent full-time 1979	Age		Education		Mean income	
								25 to 34	55 to 64	0 to 11	16 and over	Male	Female
Technical, sales, and administrative support occupations (con't)													
Science technicians	185,475	30.7	87.9	7.4	4.2	40.1	86.3	--	--	--	--	--	--
Biological technicians. . .	43,815	40.9	88.3	7.0	4.6	32.0	87.0	33.7	10.1	13.5	25.1	14,837	9,414
Chemical technicians. . . .	71,507	22.3	87.1	8.6	3.8	9.2	92.4	36.0	10.1	9.0	26.6	17,854	11,600
Science technicians, NEC. .	70,153	32.9	88.4	6.5	4.4	107.7	79.8	33.2	7.2	8.8	20.6	14,940	8,051
Technicians, except health, engineering, and science. .	911,368	31.4	89.0	5.9	3.1	144.1	85.3	--	--	--	--	--	--
Airplane pilots and navigators.	74,129	1.4	97.9	0.9	1.6	29.1	70.1	30.1	10.4	2.6	44.7	36,096	16,654
Air traffic controllers . .	40,131	14.8	90.3	6.8	3.2	51.8	95.0	38.4	6.8	4.8	17.8	25,465	12,054
Broadcast equipment operators	69,818	43.6	90.3	6.6	3.7	99.1	86.5	33.1	8.5	11.4	11.3	14,479	8,530
Computer programmers. . . .	313,179	31.1	88.7	5.6	2.7	95.0	90.2	48.0	2.1	1.7	48.0	18,089	13,348
Tool programmers, numerical control	8,426	26.1	89.6	5.3	3.3	161.2	94.1	42.8	5.6	4.4	31.3	19,608	12,937
Legal assistants.	76,392	69.0	91.7	5.4	3.5	339.0	83.9	39.3	7.6	6.2	37.0	14,886	10,045
Technicians, NEC.	329,293	29.4	86.1	7.1	3.6	349.4	82.7	39.8	7.3	5.3	42.8	16,775	10,042
Sales occupations	9,760,157	47.9	92.2	4.8	4.0	25.6	68.2	--	--	--	--	--	--
Supervisors and proprietors, sales occupations, salaried.	1,096,130	27.8	93.5	3.6	3.9	53.0	91.1	--	--	--	--	--	--
Manufacturing	49,013	17.6	93.9	3.7	4.1	111.5	92.8	--	--	--	--	--	--
Wholesale trade	109,119	8.8	95.5	2.0	3.4	1.7	95.0	--	--	--	--	--	--
Retail trade.	859,138	31.3	93.3	3.8	4.0	56.0	90.4	--	--	--	--	--	--
All other industries. . . .	78,860	21.8	93.6	4.0	3.2	124.4	92.7	--	--	--	--	--	--
Supervisors and proprietors, sales occupations, self-employed.	444,656	28.0	93.1	2.9	3.7	-15.6	84.3	--	--	--	--	--	--
Manufacturing	4,471	16.4	91.7	4.9	2.2	-94.1	83.2	--	--	--	--	--	--
Wholesale trade	40,802	11.4	94.1	2.0	3.5	2.5	84.8	--	--	--	--	--	--
Retail trade.	383,782	30.3	93.0	3.0	3.7	-18.2	84.4	--	--	--	--	--	--
All other industries. . . .	15,601	17.0	94.4	2.0	4.0	-10.5	79.0	--	--	--	--	--	--
Sales representatives, finance and business services.	1,802,715	35.1	94.7	3.3	2.5	64.9	82.1	--	--	--	--	--	--
Insurance sales occupations.	558,225	25.2	92.8	5.1	2.6	18.7	89.6	21.2	14.1	5.8	34.7	24,652	11,180
Real estates sales occupations	644,132	45.0	96.1	1.9	2.2	115.0	73.9	22.2	18.0	6.1	32.0	23,427	11,831
Securities and financial services sales occupations	130,551	18.5	95.5	2.5	2.1	23.9	87.9	32.1	10.9	3.3	59.7	36,532	14,338
Advertising and related sales occupations	110,001	41.3	95.6	2.9	2.2	65.7	84.9	36.5	10.3	5.7	39.4	20,684	11,323
Sales occupations, other business services	359,806	37.0	94.3	3.3	3.1	137.2	82.2	31.9	11.1	7.9	31.0	20,997	9,322
Sales representatives, commodities, except retail . .	1,268,214	14.1	95.8	2.4	2.8	18.0	90.4	--	--	--	--	--	--
Sales engineers	43,502	3.2	97.9	0.9	1.3	-23.3	95.7	30.2	18.1	2.7	56.1	27,426	12,130
Sales representatives, mining, manufacturing and wholesale	1,224,712	14.5	95.7	2.5	2.9	20.3	90.2	31.5	13.6	9.9	29.6	21,907	10,266
Wholesale trade	795,714	13.2	95.7	2.3	3.1	34.2	89.8	--	--	--	--	--	--
Sales workers, retail and Personal services	5,122,504	66.7	90.1	6.3	4.9	18.1	51.6	--	--	--	--	--	--
Sales workers, motor vehicles and boats. . . .	268,393	7.6	94.6	3.2	4.0	13.0	89.7	28.3	14.2	19.3	11.8	16,447	8,593
Sales workers, apparel. . .	412,851	81.8	90.8	5.9	5.1	-22.9	41.2	14.7	16.2	22.3	7.6	10,224	4,569
Sales workers, shoes. . . .	108,511	56.6	89.1	7.3	6.5	-14.0	45.5	15.8	10.4	21.9	6.3	8,807	4,786
Sales workers, furniture and home furnishings. . .	143,809	41.8	95.2	2.8	3.9	0.2	73.1	24.3	16.6	17.3	14.2	14,872	7,140
Sales workers, radio, tv, hi-fi, and appliances . .	108,404	28.1	93.3	4.2	3.8	-3.1	72.9	28.0	9.9	14.1	17.2	13,034	6,504
Sales workers, hardware and building supplies	186,001	24.6	95.4	2.3	3.6	-15.2	71.6	22.6	14.6	19.4	10.8	12,300	5,683
Sales workers, parts. . . .	190,126	8.2	95.1	2.3	4.1	5.9	90.4	31.8	9.6	17.1	5.9	13,438	8,023
Sales workers, other commodities	1,594,967	72.5	91.1	5.5	4.5	7.5	48.2	18.2	15.1	20.9	9.7	11,514	4,967
Retail trade.	1,527,469	73.4	91.2	5.5	4.5	10.0	47.6	--	--	--	--	--	--
Resonal, business and repair services	10,939	58.8	92.4	4.6	4.6	-70.9	59.6	--	--	--	--	--	--
All other industries. . .	56,559	53.0	90.5	6.3	3.6	-2.9	61.4	--	--	--	--	--	--
Sales counter clerks. . . .	89,600	73.4	88.7	7.8	4.3	-23.5	55.4	20.5	13.5	27.7	6.0	11,958	5,258
Cashiers.	1,716,318	83.2	86.0	9.3	6.0	88.4	44.8	20.3	8.4	25.3	3.4	8,718	5,406
Street and door-to-door sales workers	205,244	78.6	93.5	4.1	3.4	1.3	36.6	27.8	12.2	18.3	13.8	13,400	4,050
News vendors.	98,280	33.6	92.9	4.8	3.3	41.3	30.8	24.4	10.7	29.5	8.5	8,512	4,592
Sales related occupations . .	25,938	52.7	94.2	3.6	2.6	18.8	58.9	--	--	--	--	--	--
Demonstrators, promoters and models, sales	11,165	77.6	93.0	4.1	2.7	-4.0	37.5	28.2	12.6	16.2	14.1	14,598	3,654
Auctioneers	6,799	14.3	97.0	1.7	1.5	35.3	73.0	20.0	16.8	27.5	12.0	21,202	8,646
Sales support occupations, NEC	7,974	50.6	93.4	4.5	3.5	54.2	76.8	25.4	15.5	13.6	16.6	17,132	7,100
Administrative support occupations, including clerical . .	16,851,398	77.1	86.4	9.7	4.9	31.7	78.2	--	--	--	--	--	--
Supervisors, administrative support occupations	1,056,710	47.1	87.5	9.2	4.3	165.0	94.0	--	--	--	--	--	--
Supervisors, general office.	631,337	56.1	86.3	10.2	4.7	149.0	92.4	28.8	14.3	9.2	19.2	19,818	11,998
Supervisors, computer equipment operators.	42,142	29.4	89.3	7.3	3.6	221.2	97.1	41.1	4.5	2.9	27.4	22,925	14,792
Supervisors, financial records processing. . . .	157,409	49.0	92.5	4.7	3.0	292.8	96.2	32.5	13.6	4.0	35.0	23,058	13,474
Chief communications operators	66,765	34.3	90.0	8.0	2.8	50.9	97.7	13.8	6.5	3.6	6.4	25,346	17,930

Table 13-5. Detailed Occupation of the Employed Persons in the United States, by Selected Characteristics: 1980—continued

Occupation	Number of persons employed	Percent female	Percent white	Percent black	Percent Spanish-origin	Percent change in employment 1970-80	Percent full-time 1979	Age		Education		Mean income	
								25 to 34	55 to 64	0 to 11	16 and over	Male	Female
Technical, sales, and administrative support occupations (con't)													
Supervisors; distribution, scheduling, and adjusting clerks.	159,057	19.4	85.8	11.1	4.8	232.7	95.5	27.4	15.4	15.3	12.0	18,466	12,412
Computer equipment operators.	408,475	59.0	83.5	11.6	5.1	147.4	87.9	--	--	--	--	--	--
Computer operators.	384,392	58.9	83.5	11.6	5.1	220.8	88.1	37.4	4.3	5.6	11.1	14,389	9,478
Peripheral equipment operators	24,083	61.5	83.0	12.6	5.4	-46.8	85.4	33.1	7.2	10.4	6.9	13,711	8,935
Secretaries, stenographers, and typists	4,656,955	98.3	89.8	7.2	4.1	19.3	77.6	--	--	--	--	--	--
Secretaries	3,870,582	98.8	91.7	5.6	3.7	38.3	78.5	29.6	9.9	5.2	7.4	14,759	8,608
Stenographers	85,785	90.7	87.3	9.1	3.7	-36.5	85.2	28.5	13.2	3.7	7.0	23,685	10,907
Typists	700,588	96.9	79.4	15.4	6.1	-27.8	71.1	26.4	9.1	7.5	5.3	8,540	7,062
Information clerks.	894,178	85.4	86.9	8.9	5.6	48.1	66.3	--	--	--	--	--	--
Interviewers.	134,002	78.0	84.3	11.0	5.3	13.1	62.5	29.6	9.4	7.5	18.5	9,572	6,348
Hotel clerks.	61,217	68.2	89.5	6.0	4.3	34.6	67.7	22.0	10.4	17.6	10.0	6,728	5,593
Transportation ticket and reservation agents. . . .	99,449	57.5	84.4	10.4	6.3	23.7	86.2	38.0	6.6	6.1	18.8	17,673	12,316
Receptionists	516,498	95.8	88.2	7.9	5.8	66.8	63.8	24.2	8.9	10.8	7.1	8,005	6,205
Information clerks, NEC . .	83,012	78.6	84.3	12.1	4.8	67.1	62.6	25.9	10.1	15.3	12.7	11,068	7,017
Records processing occupations, except financial. .	965,107	77.2	82.6	12.8	5.8	41.4	72.0	--	--	--	--	--	--
Classified-ad clerks. . . .	13,552	77.6	90.2	6.4	3.5	58.7	74.7	29.7	9.9	9.9	18.9	15,896	7,873
Correspondence clerks . . .	19,309	81.5	83.7	13.4	3.7	57.2	90.2	33.0	11.4	5.3	17.0	15,357	10,144
Order clerks.	311,321	67.4	84.6	11.5	6.3	203.1	81.7	32.1	10.1	14.8	7.9	13,266	9,205
Personnel clerks, except payroll and timekeeping .	75,235	87.4	82.8	12.4	5.5	804.5	85.0	31.7	9.7	6.8	10.9	14,087	9,111
Library clerks.	140,731	81.2	84.5	10.5	4.1	8.9	43.4	19.1	10.4	6.0	20.9	4,832	5,031
File clerks	277,592	79.7	77.9	16.8	6.7	-22.3	67.0	23.3	9.4	17.0	6.8	11,310	6,290
Records clerks.	127,367	84.7	84.7	10.9	5.2	98.2	80.4	28.8	11.4	9.5	11.1	13,235	8,147
Financial records processing occupations	2,254,084	88.4	91.6	5.1	3.8	8.3	75.6	--	--	--	--	--	--
Bookkeepers, accounting and auditing clerks	1,827,890	89.7	92.5	4.3	3.4	10.0	73.7	26.2	13.6	8.5	9.1	13,487	8,392
Payroll and timekeeping clerks.	159,292	83.3	88.3	8.1	4.1	4.8	86.5	28.6	13.5	9.2	6.2	14,799	9,606
Billing clerks.	129,380	88.9	88.4	7.9	4.6	7.5	81.9	28.9	10.6	9.6	6.2	13,146	8,359
Cost and rate clerks. . . .	85,855	68.4	88.3	7.8	4.4	104.9	85.4	30.9	11.3	10.6	16.3	16,936	9,032
Billing, posting, and calculating machine operators	51,667	87.1	76.0	12.4	6.2	-50.5	76.1	27.9	7.1	9.8	5.3	11,221	7,428
Duplicating, mail, and other office machine operators. .	58,671	65.6	77.8	16.6	6.3	-2.9	75.4	--	--	--	--	--	--
Duplicating machine operators	18,822	61.0	77.1	17.0	5.9	-16.6	75.4	25.8	9.5	18.3	6.5	10,302	7,035
Mail preparing and paper handling machine operators	7,052	62.3	81.5	14.0	5.9	-49.3	72.2	20.4	15.3	30.0	4.3	11,201	6,382
Office machine operators, NEC	32,797	68.9	77.4	16.9	6.5	36.9	76.1	24.8	9.8	19.0	5.6	9,890	6,926
Communications equipment operators	308,690	89.5	82.5	14.0	4.8	-24.4	77.1	--	--	--	--	--	--
Telephone operators	292,165	91.0	82.2	14.3	4.9	-26.1	77.2	25.8	12.3	15.5	3.9	11,611	8,549
Telegraphers.	7,604	35.7	85.5	11.4	3.2	-41.2	90.1	28.4	13.2	17.3	6.3	18,935	10,134
Communications equipment operators, NEC.	8,921	84.1	89.8	7.7	3.4	--	62.3	24.3	10.6	19.6	5.7	16,332	5,568
Mail and message distributing occupations	773,826	29.6	77.7	18.1	5.2	1.8	82.7	--	--	--	--	--	--
Postal clerks, except mail carriers.	267,035	35.8	70.9	24.7	4.7	-13.1	87.9	29.2	17.9	12.9	7.5	18,083	13,993
Mail carriers, postal service	256,593	12.9	85.4	11.5	4.4	-3.3	91.5	26.7	17.8	13.5	6.4	17,894	11,834
Mail clerks, except postal service messengers. . . .	167,973	47.3	76.3	18.3	6.5	30.8	71.8	22.3	12.1	21.3	5.5	9,621	6,611
Material recording, scheduling, and distributing clerks.	1,662,256	34.4	84.2	11.5	6.4	20.7	85.2	--	--	--	--	--	--
Dispatchers	94,830	31.2	90.5	6.9	3.7	28.1	91.2	31.0	11.7	17.8	8.0	16,833	9,696
Production coordinators . .	254,625	44.2	88.1	8.4	4.7	64.3	89.8	31.1	13.1	14.7	15.4	16,835	9,948
Traffic, shipping, and receiving clerks.	481,958	23.6	81.7	13.0	8.7	12.3	87.4	28.1	11.1	27.8	4.4	11,736	8,238
Stock and inventory clerks.	570,906	34.7	83.5	12.0	5.9	20.0	80.8	26.3	12.0	22.4	6.1	11,780	8,417
Meter readers	41,407	10.2	81.2	15.0	6.5	18.7	93.2	37.0	8.1	18.4	4.2	12,637	9,303
Weighers, measurers, and checkers.	72,040	36.6	83.0	12.9	6.9	-22.8	83.7	24.4	15.0	34.3	3.5	14,414	7,279
Samplers.	2,542	45.5	88.3	9.6	3.9	-67.5	85.3	27.5	15.7	24.6	7.3	13,206	8,602
Expediters.	106,146	53.9	86.8	9.7	4.7	36.4	85.2	30.2	11.7	14.3	9.6	14,920	8,974
Material recording, scheduling, and distributing clerks, NEC	37,802	74.9	81.3	13.4	7.3	27.1	70.8	24.6	15.4	26.0	7.6	14,672	6,952
Adjusters and investigators .	515,666	62.3	85.5	10.8	4.6	48.9	88.8	--	--	--	--	--	--
Insurance adjusters, examiners, and investigators.	163,586	60.2	86.7	10.0	3.2	63.4	92.5	38.7	8.1	4.1	30.8	17,192	9,929
Investigators and adjusters, except insurance.	243,616	62.4	85.5	10.8	4.5	32.1	88.1	36.7	9.6	6.3	24.6	17,346	10,215
Eligibility clerks, social welfare	24,128	81.8	74.1	18.2	10.8	1813.4	90.1	41.4	9.7	5.1	30.7	12,092	10,231
Bill and account collectors.	84,336	60.6	86.1	10.1	6.0	39.2	82.8	34.5	9.6	11.4	12.8	12,286	8,419

Table 13-5. Detailed Occupation of the Employed Persons in the United States, by Selected Characteristics: 1980—continued

Occupation	Number of persons employed	Percent Female	Percent white	Percent black	Percent Spanish-origin	Percent change in employment 1970-80	Percent full-time 1979	Age: 25 to 34	Age: 55 to 64	Education: 0 to 11	Education: 16 and over	Mean income: Male	Mean income: Female
Technical, sales, and administrative support occupations (con't)													
Miscellaneous administrative support occupations	3,296,780	83.2	83.0	12.1	5.9	63.9	73.5	--	--	--	--	--	--
General office clerks	1,648,934	82.1	82.9	12.5	5.8	105.7	71.8	24.3	12.8	12.6	8.1	11,737	7,654
Bank tellers	494,851	91.2	88.3	7.5	5.3	77.0	74.2	26.8	5.2	6.4	6.7	8,711	6,779
Proofreading	27,321	79.1	90.1	6.9	2.6	-8.2	71.2	26.0	14.8	10.0	23.8	12,134	7,329
Data-entry keyers	378,094	92.4	77.1	16.3	6.3	28.1	83.0	36.0	4.8	8.6	4.8	12,296	8,453
Statistical clerks	139,174	75.0	83.0	12.9	4.4	-21.8	84.3	29.3	12.9	8.3	14.5	15,007	9,557
Teachers' aides	206,695	92.7	76.3	16.6	11.4	50.0	43.1	26.2	8.2	10.1	12.0	5,543	4,235
Administrative support occupations, NEC	401,711	67.2	85.6	10.2	4.6	38.8	82.5	32.4	11.1	8.1	23.6	16,681	9,269
Service occupations	12,629,425	59.0	77.3	17.1	7.0	30.1	58.9	--	--	--	--	--	--
Private household occupations	589,352	95.5	53.0	41.0	9.4	-48.8	34.8	--	--	--	--	--	--
Occupation:													
Launderers and ironers	2,193	77.0	62.8	26.3	7.5	-83.3	43.2	10.2	28.4	54.7	3.1	10,091	3,439
Cooks, private household	11,365	86.8	45.1	48.3	7.0	-67.7	48.8	9.1	29.5	63.7	2.6	7,152	4,442
Housekeepers and butlers	65,720	96.5	51.6	37.8	17.2	8.8	43.3	14.2	25.2	62.6	2.4	6,646	3,750
Childcare workers, private household	147,055	97.5	85.4	10.6	5.6	-34.2	38.7	22.3	14.4	38.7	5.9	4,366	2,414
Private household cleaners and servants	363,019	94.9	40.3	53.8	9.6	-55.7	31.3	10.6	28.2	68.0	2.1	5,608	3,217
Living arangement:													
Living in	34,405	94.7	63.6	19.1	28.3	-54.3	76.6	--	--	--	--	--	--
Living out	554,947	95.6	52.4	42.4	8.2	-48.5	32.3	--	--	--	--	--	--
Protective service occupations	1,475,315	11.4	85.0	12.0	4.4	42.3	85.5	--	--	--	--	--	--
Supervisors, protective service occupations	94,645	4.3	91.1	6.8	2.9	8.1	96.7	--	--	--	--	--	--
Supervisors, firefighting and fire prevention occupations	20,642	0.5	95.6	2.5	1.5	-25.9	98.1	17.2	10.4	11.2	7.6	22,439	13,458
Supervisors, police and detectives	50,785	3.3	92.5	5.6	2.9	4.8	97.5	23.6	8.3	6.9	23.1	21,725	13,795
Supervisors, guards	23,218	9.6	84.0	13.3	4.1	106.7	93.6	23.2	19.6	14.9	16.1	16,111	9,918
Firefighting and fire prevention occupations	210,223	1.7	91.4	6.1	3.6	28.1	96.7	--	--	--	--	--	--
Fire inspection and fire prevention occupations	21,163	8.1	92.4	4.9	3.2	67.4	93.0	27.4	12.1	18.1	18.8	15,869	7,504
Firefighting occupations	189,060	0.9	91.3	6.3	3.6	24.9	97.1	40.2	4.7	10.2	6.1	17,678	9,542
Police and detectives	557,887	7.8	86.9	10.3	4.1	32.1	95.6	--	--	--	--	--	--
Police and detectives, public service	409,792	5.8	88.8	8.5	3.9	23.3	96.3	44.9	4.0	5.9	18.4	17,846	12,360
Sheriffs, bailiffs, and other enforcement officers	61,482	12.4	88.5	8.8	4.5	40.5	93.3	36.4	10.7	12.1	13.8	14,803	10,681
Correctional institutional officers	86,613	13.9	76.6	20.1	4.7	87.9	94.0	37.6	8.9	13.0	10.3	13,757	10,399
Guards	612,560	19.2	80.1	16.2	5.1	68.8	70.7	--	--	--	--	--	--
Crossing guards	45,026	72.5	83.9	14.2	3.4	11.8	12.4	14.3	18.4	44.0	2.1	5,460	2,873
Guards and police, except public service	533,545	13.3	79.2	17.0	5.3	74.5	76.9	21.1	18.2	31.8	7.8	10,206	6,825
Protective service occupations, NEC	33,989	41.9	89.8	6.8	4.1	101.6	50.0	18.4	4.9	18.1	8.4	6,960	3,283
Service occupations, except protective and household	10,564,758	63.6	77.6	16.5	7.3	40.5	56.6	--	--	--	--	--	--
Food preparation and service occupations	4,384,936	66.2	82.8	10.7	6.8	41.6	45.7	--	--	--	--	--	--
Supervisors, food preparation and service occupations	233,539	57.2	82.7	10.1	6.1	51.6	67.7	22.4	13.1	26.7	8.6	12,358	6,213
Bartenders	289,213	43.8	92.5	3.5	4.2	41.4	67.5	30.4	9.7	27.1	7.6	8,452	5,422
Waiters and waitresses	1,362,390	87.7	90.3	4.7	4.8	25.1	40.3	24.3	5.9	30.5	5.3	6,516	4,083
Cooks, except short order	1,240,011	57.7	75.4	17.0	7.7	89.5	53.4	17.0	14.5	45.9	2.3	7,140	4,782
Short order cooks	71,351	38.3	82.4	13.3	5.3	-34.3	38.6	16.3	6.7	43.3	2.2	5,100	4,439
Food counter, fountain and related occupations	188,411	81.0	86.6	8.0	6.3	35.7	25.6	13.9	5.7	36.7	2.4	5,620	3,435
Kitchen workers, food preparation	96,984	78.3	77.0	17.6	7.2	34.4	46.0	16.8	13.8	40.8	2.7	6,569	4,703
Waiters' and waitresses' assistants	262,903	42.7	80.0	11.4	11.4	91.2	30.6	13.1	8.5	40.6	2.2	4,109	3,611
Miscellaneous food preparation	640,134	57.1	77.9	14.1	9.2	19.1	36.9	15.1	13.4	45.9	2.0	4,484	3,898
Health service occupations	1,726,875	88.1	72.3	23.4	5.3	51.0	68.8	--	--	--	--	--	--
Dental assistants	151,755	98.0	91.9	4.1	5.2	57.1	62.8	31.9	3.9	7.2	5.0	13,899	6,498
Health aides, except nursing	279,663	84.6	77.7	17.7	5.9	115.5	65.7	27.4	9.3	20.7	8.7	9,628	6,790
Nursing aides, orderlies, and attendants	1,295,457	87.7	68.8	26.9	5.2	41.2	70.2	24.6	12.1	32.1	4.6	9,578	6,298
Cleaning and building service occupations, except household	2,745,403	35.1	69.7	23.8	9.5	30.9	68.0	--	--	--	--	--	--
Supervisors, cleaning and building service workers	113,029	28.0	75.2	19.9	7.5	96.0	89.8	18.7	23.2	36.0	5.7	14,469	8,063
Maids and housemen	612,458	76.0	58.6	32.8	11.8	30.9	61.4	18.9	18.4	58.8	1.6	7,902	5,060
Janitors and cleaners	1,964,555	23.4	72.6	21.4	8.8	30.3	68.3	18.9	19.6	49.9	2.6	9,432	5,522
Elevator operators	20,279	21.7	64.6	27.9	16.1	-47.2	82.8	14.9	27.9	57.6	2.8	11,113	7,872
Pest control occupations	35,082	5.5	85.9	9.5	7.2	40.5	88.3	31.5	9.9	31.8	6.3	11,359	7,022

Table 13-5. Detailed Occupation of the Employed Persons in the United States, by Selected Characteristics: 1980—continued

Occupation	Number of persons employed	Percent female	Percent white	Percent black	Percent Spanish-origin	Percent change in employment 1970-80	Percent full-time 1979	Age: 25 to 34	Age: 55 to 64	Education: 0 to 11	Education: 16 and over	Mean income: Male	Mean income: Female
Service occupations													
Personal service occupations	1,707,544	77.9	82.4	12.5	7.0	44.5	53.7	--	--	--	--	--	--
Supervisors, personal service occupations	27,737	43.7	88.6	7.7	4.2	79.2	80.4	28.3	12.9	19.6	12.3	15,108	9,737
Barbers	103,673	13.5	85.0	10.7	8.0	-41.4	77.7	16.9	18.0	39.7	1.5	10,486	7,277
Hairdressers and cosmotologists	544,020	87.8	89.3	6.7	6.3	5.3	54.3	34.4	10.4	21.8	1.8	12,685	6,309
Attendants, amusement and recreation facilities	91,350	38.5	85.0	9.0	5.6	72.0	59.1	27.1	7.4	23.9	9.5	8,378	5,924
Guides	25,595	57.7	79.2	10.6	5.2	283.9	59.7	22.7	10.7	15.8	20.1	8,802	5,286
Ushers	21,764	32.1	86.5	9.0	6.1	-0.2	26.4	12.8	6.6	26.4	10.6	4,790	4,636
Public transportation attendants	67,775	78.5	83.7	11.3	5.3	59.9	50.9	56.8	3.5	7.0	25.2	15,353	13,868
Baggage porters and bellhops	19,682	6.9	57.8	33.7	10.5	5.4	73.2	21.7	10.2	30.2	6.2	8,467	7,525
Welfare service aides	56,120	88.8	59.3	32.8	10.0	178.2	55.9	23.4	17.0	33.1	11.0	10,582	5,379
Childcare workers, except private household	580,168	93.4	79.7	14.8	7.6	237.2	46.3	29.5	9.1	20.8	10.0	6,699	3,675
Personal service occupations, NEC	169,660	72.4	75.3	18.7	7.3	22.8	56.0	19.1	16.0	36.8	8.0	8,489	5,321
Farming, forestry, and fishing occupations	2,811,258	14.4	86.7	6.5	9.1	-3.3	78.3	--	--	--	--	--	--
Farm operators and managers	1,298,670	9.8	96.7	1.9	1.4	-8.7	84.3	--	--	--	--	--	--
Farmers, except horticultural	1,134,313	9.7	97.6	1.3	1.0	-15.5	83.8	17.6	23.0	34.8	8.7	13,317	6,105
Agricultural production crops	649,935	7.4	96.7	2.0	1.2	-11.7	83.2	--	--	--	--	--	--
Horticultural specialty farmers	13,439	16.6	90.7	4.8	3.9	12.0	81.0	28.5	15.8	28.3	16.7	13,572	5,442
Managers, farms, except horticultural	137,180	9.1	90.9	5.9	3.9	103.8	89.2	27.0	15.2	28.8	16.6	17,070	8,264
Managers, horticultural specialty farms	13,738	17.1	80.7	11.1	8,2	1896.8	83.2	29.6	8.1	32.4	12.6	11,047	6,065
Farm occupations, except managerial	875,331	21.5	76.3	9.8	19.7	-6.0	72.9	--	--	--	--	--	--
Supervisors, farm workers	51,149	16.2	79.8	7.3	17.6	35.3	90.5	25.9	15.0	38.5	12.6	14,635	8,900
Farm workers	792,503	20.8	75.9	10.1	19.9	-6.8	72.0	24.6	9.9	57.2	3.4	7,110	4,260
Agricultural production, crops	475,461	19.1	67.8	13.2	26.9	-6.7	73.4	--	--	--	--	--	--
Marine life cultivation workers	1,202	35.9	64.5	11.4	7.3	--	79.3	28.4	7.9	27.8	12.8	8,935	6,325
Nursery workers	30,477	46.3	80.5	5.2	17.6	-30.4	66.8	25.6	9.8	44.1	7.2	7,777	4,472
Related agricultural occupations	458,792	17.2	79.2	10.9	12.9	10.8	70.6	--	--	--	--	--	--
Supervisors, related agricultural occupations	19,786	7.7	90.6	5.1	7.1	-45.2	91.0	29.0	14.6	31.5	13.1	14,128	7,082
Groundskeepers and gardeners, except farm	355,206	7.1	76.8	12.3	13.9	15.4	72.0	24.5	12.2	45.4	5.3	8,123	4,765
Animal caretakers, except farm	67,234	59.0	91.2	5.8	4.4	40.5	58.6	28.1	6.5	24.2	9.1	8,764	5,195
Graders and sorters, agricultural products	15,496	77.3	67.4	8.2	34.7	-31.2	65.6	21.2	16.1	67.0	1.2	6,786	4,128
Inspectors, agricultural products	1,070	15.1	83.1	10.1	6.1	--	80.7	26.9	18.5	28.6	15.5	11,812	5,932
Forestry and logging occupations	122,745	5.4	81.6	15.1	2.4	20.8	81.1	--	--	--	--	--	--
Supervisors, forestry and logging workers	7,725	3.2	91.0	5.9	1.8	147.0	93.4	32.5	11.6	30.6	11.8	19,112	10,994
Forestry workers, except logging	22,174	17.7	83.1	10.0	6.1	181.2	81.5	29.6	7.0	33.1	12.3	9,399	5,207
Timber cutting and logging occupations	92,846	2.6	80.5	17.0	1.6	2.5	80.0	30.4	8.9	52.1	3.1	11,061	6,983
Fishers, hunters, and trappers	55,720	6.4	90.0	5.0	4.0	56.0	81.5	--	--	--	--	--	--
Captains and other officers, fishing vessels	6,209	4.1	92.0	2.6	4.9	13.5	87.0	30.6	11.9	34.7	7.9	19,272	11,013
Fishers	47,509	6.6	89.6	5.4	4.0	61.6	80.5	31.4	9.8	43.2	6.6	13,636	6,105
Hunters and trappers	2,002	9.8	93.2	2.6	2.0	132.0	89.7	27.4	15.6	21.2	16.1	14,174	8,534
Precision production, craft, and repair occupations	12,594,175	7.8	89.3	6.6	6.1	16.6	91.0	--	--	--	--	--	--
Mechanics and repairers	3,798,598	3.3	89.9	6.4	5.4	18.9	92.5	--	--	--	--	--	--
Supervisors, mechanics and repairers	158,413	2.9	94.3	3.4	3.4	23.5	96.8	25.0	16.3	21.7	6.5	20,319	12,709
Mechanics and repairers, except supervisors	3,640,185	3.3	89.8	6.5	5.5	18.7	92.3	--	--	--	--	--	--
Vehicle and mobile equipment mechanics and repairers	1,586,512	1.3	89.3	6.4	6.3	16.4	91.2	--	--	--	--	--	--
Automobile mechanics	908,961	1.2	88.7	6.9	6.4	14.5	90.1	30.5	9.1	35.8	2.2	12,752	9,422
Bus, truck, and stationary engine mechanics	146,226	0.7	89.7	7.0	5.0	82.0	94.0	31.0	10.3	36.3	1.4	15,246	10,995
Aircraft mechanics	110,287	3.3	88.5	6.3	7.0	-12.4	95.1	--	--	--	--	--	--
Small engine repairers	33,856	1.7	94.1	3.2	3.3	3.7	81.5	30.6	7.9	29.2	2.8	10,180	7,741
Automobile body and related repairers	193,023	1.1	88.9	6.0	8.3	70.0	90.1	31.9	8.3	39.2	1.7	12,751	8,977
Heavy equipment mechanics	149,828	0.8	91.2	5.5	4.7	-15,8	95.3	32.3	11.7	33.5	2.0	16,711	12,682
Farm equipment mechanics	44,331	1.0	93.7	2.8	5.1	14.2	91.6	27.3	10.5	33.4	2.7	12,397	8,801
Industrial machinery repairers	467,613	3.0	90.4	6.7	4.5	40.6	95.1	29.2	13.2	34.9	2.2	15,926	10,242
Machinery maintenance occupations	42,798	3.5	85.7	10.5	5.3	-30.0	93.5	25.0	15.8	40.3	2.4	16,103	10,041

Table 13-5. Detailed Occupation of the Employed Persons in the United States, by Selected Characteristics: 1980—continued

Occupation	Number of persons employed	Percent female	Percent white	Percent black	Percent Spanish-origin	Percent change in employment 1970-80	Percent full-time 1979	Age		Education		Mean income	
								25 to 34	55 to 64	0 to 11	16 and over	Male	Female
Precision production, craft, and repair occupations (con't)													
Electrical and electronic equipment repairers . . .	629,958	7.7	90.5	6.1	4.6	6.4	93.9	--	--	--	--	--	--
Electornic repairers, communications and industrial equipment. . .	158,775	4.9	90.5	5.5	5.2	-2.3	88.9	28.8	12.5	17.0	5.8	13,919	9,321
Data processing equipemnt repairers	46,626	8.1	90.7	5.9	3.7	59.0	95.5	42.0	3.0	4.9	11.1	18,954	11,220
Household appliance and power tool repairers. .	79,856	2.9	92.5	4.3	4.8	5.5	89.1	26.1	12.6	23.9	3.5	13,266	9,345
Telephone line installers and repairers	61,103	5.0	90.9	6.1	4.0	12.1	97.4	49.7	4.1	10.4	2.9	18,969	14,285
Telephone installers and repairers	252,469	11.4	89.8	7.0	4.4	6.3	97.5	38.7	8.8	8.9	3.2	20,303	14,664
Miscellaneous electrical and electronic equipment repairers.	31,129	9.1	89.9	6.0	5.7	-4.2	93.0	30.6	12.7	25.5	3.5	15,751	10,683
Heating, air conditioning, and refrigeration mechanics	143,626	1.0	91.9	4.8	5.4	20.7	92.0	29.9	10.6	25.4	2.8	14,808	10,052
Miscellaneous mechanics and repairers	769,678	4.7	89.5	6.9	5.4	28.8	91.5	--	--	--	--	--	--
Camera, watch, and musical instrument repairers	39,180	10.9	91.0	4.3	5.6	17.1	79.3	25.3	21.1	23.1	11.0	12,831	7,670
Locksmith and safe repairers	18,763	6.9	91.5	4.7	4.9	6.1	86.5	27.3	17.1	28.1	6.0	12,770	8,096
Office machine repairers.	38,034	5.2	89.5	6.0	5.4	-21.2	92.3	34.8	8.4	4.0	5.5	14,487	10,182
Mechanical controls and valve repairers	27,609	3.9	86.6	9.4	6.2	-24.5	94.8	29.0	14.9	27.4	2.5	15,225	9,256
Elevator installers and repairers	20,182	1.8	92.3	5.0	4.3	-12.3	96.1	31.2	10.4	20.8	3.5	20,777	10,816
Millwrights	124,392	3.2	93.1	5.1	3.0	16.3	96.6	27.6	15.8	31.0	2.3	20,293	10,300
Specified mechanics and repairers, NEC.	294,377	5.0	89.4	7.1	5.3	41.6	89.7	29.1	12.2	31.3	3.5	14,534	8,885
Not specified mechanics and repairers	207,141	4.0	87.2	8.5	6.9	67.6	92.7	29.7	12.3	33.1	3.4	15,320	9,902
Construction trades	4,247,010	2.1	89.8	6.4	5.9	25.9	88.6	--	--	--	--	--	--
Supervisors; construction occupations	741,546	1.7	93.5	3.9	4.1	53.8	93.7	--	--	--	--	--	--
Supervisors; brickmasons, stonemasons, and tile setters	4,654	0.9	91.9	4.5	5.9	-33.5	88.3	27.0	11.2	32.1	3.5	19,505	6,000
Supervisors; carpenters and related workers	32,722	0.7	94.9	2.3	3.8	-38.3	95.1	32.1	14.3	28.6	5.3	18,749	12,779
Supervisors; electricians and power transmission installers.	36,090	1.2	96.3	1.8	2.7	15.2	97.7	24.9	14.9	15.7	7.8	24,225	14,345
Supervisors; painters, paperhangers, and plasterers.	10,063	1.5	91.5	3.8	7.0	-8.0	91.5	28.7	15.4	36.6	4.5	18,197	8,924
Supervisors; plumbers, pipefitters, and steamfitters.	16,795	0.6	95.7	1.7	3.6	-37.8	96.7	27.3	14.7	25.0	4.7	23,705	13,526
Supervisors; NEC.	641,222	1.8	93.3	4.1	4.1	81.7	93.4	27.1	14.7	27.3	12.4	21,399	13,484
Construction trades, except supervisors	3,505,464	2.1	89.0	6.9	6.3	21.2	87.5	--	--	--	--	--	--
Brickmasons and stonemasons.	165,940	1.1	81.1	14.8	6.3	1.4	79.6	28.7	11.3	44.0	1.9	12,853	8,097
Tile setters, hard and soft.	29,592	1.9	88.3	6.8	9.8	-9.6	85.2	25.9	10.9	40.2	2.6	13,882	7,997
Carpet installers	80,672	1.7	90.4	5.2	8.2	50.6	81.6	36.1	5.3	36.0	2.1	12,778	7,816
Carpenters.	1,101,536	1.6	91.2	5.0	5.7	30.3	86.3	31.9	11.7	34.4	5.3	12,142	7,396
Drywall installers.	80,726	2.0	90.4	3.9	8.6	70.2	83.6	38.1	3.4	41.5	1.9	12,715	8,657
Electricians.	589,071	2.0	92.3	4.8	3.9	25.0	94.4	32.4	11.5	19.7	4.1	17,882	10,821
Electrical power installers and repairers	101,996	1.7	91.3	6.3	3.3	4.4	96.2	36.3	8.2	18.5	1.8	19,128	11,486
Painters, construction and maintenance	362,982	5.6	84.8	9.3	9.9	12.4	80.3	28.9	12.3	39.2	4.6	11,077	6,218
Paperhangers.	15,958	17.8	94.4	3.4	4.2	46.4	75.3	30.9	12.5	28.5	6.7	13,647	5,909
Plasterers.	25,110	1.6	77.0	15.7	14.2	-13.6	81.0	24.3	15.4	48.0	2.2	13,207	7,207
Plumbers, pipefitters, and steamfitters.	461,198	1.2	90.2	6.5	5.2	21.1	92.3	30.1	13.3	30.5	3.0	16,809	10,523
Concrete and terrazzo finishers	56,957	1.1	67.1	23.8	15.8	-18.2	85.0	30.8	10.3	51.0	2.3	12,537	7,400
Glaziers.	31,212	3.9	91.9	3.9	6.6	39.3	91.8	30.6	9.0	32.3	2.6	13,958	6,967
Insulation workers.	48,220	3.8	88.4	7.3	7.1	93.3	89.1	33.7	6.1	34.1	3.1	13,637	8,054
Paving, surfacing, and tamping equipment operators .	5,073	2.5	75.0	18.7	12.5	-25.2	88.4	29.9	9.0	49.4	1.8	11,803	6,467
Roofers	102,102	1.0	82.6	11.4	9.2	67.4	74.5	33.2	5.0	48.4	2.3	10,376	6,401
Sheetmetal duct installers.	26,285	1.4	94.0	2.6	4.9	47.7	93.7	32.4	9.3	28.2	2.9	15,539	10,477
Structural metal workers. .	76,584	1.3	91.1	5.0	4.8	1.5	91.5	33.2	9.6	33.3	2.6	16,171	10,796
Drillers, earth	20,702	2.2	92.4	5.0	3.7	-29.4	91.5	30.1	8.5	40.1	2.5	13,866	8,640
Construction trades, NEC. .	123,548	2.2	82.7	12.1	8.6	-4.2	87.7	30.9	8.9	43.0	2.7	11,671	7,826
Extractive occupations.	292,695	2.3	92.5	4.0	6.0	73.5	94.2	--	--	--	--	--	--
Supervisors, extractive occupations	80,535	2.1	96.3	1.7	3.7	64.9	96.2	28.4	14.0	29.2	12.8	26,278	16,729
Drillers, oil well.	68,466	1.3	92.1	3.5	7.7	86.3	93.8	32.9	4.5	40.0	3.3	15,520	10,368
Explosives workers.	9,778	3.1	85.1	9.5	7.8	-39.6	92.7	34.6	9.4	39.3	2.5	15,433	8,258
Mining machine operators. . .	84,997	2.9	91.7	4.6	5.9	158.8	93.3	37.7	7.6	41.7	2.6	16,925	11,445
Mining occupations, NEC . . .	48,919	2.7	89.7	6.4	7.1	43.5	93.1	36.4	8.0	38.7	3.2	16,787	11,465

Table 13-5. Detailed Occupation of the Employed Persons in the United States, by Selected Characteristics: 1980—continued

Occupation	Number of persons employed	Percent female	Percent white	Percent black	Percent Spanish-origin	Percent change in employment 1970-80	Percent full-time 1979	Age: 25 to 34	Age: 55 to 64	Education: 0 to 11	Education: 16 and over	Mean income: Male	Mean income: Female
Precision production, craft, and repair occupations (con't)													
Precision production occupations	4,255,872	17.8	88.1	7.3	6.8	4.7	91.8	--	--	--	--	--	--
Supervisors, production occupations	1,838,155	14.7	90.0	6.7	5.4	20.8	95.6	25.3	15.3	24.3	11.8	20,427	11,136
Nondurable goods manufacturing	486,508	18.8	89.4	7.0	6.3	17.3	96.0	--	--	--	--	--	--
Durable goods manufacturing	791,175	10.0	91.0	5.9	5.1	21.5	97.2	--	--	--	--	--	--
Transportation, communications, and other public utilities	151,234	5.7	91.5	6.2	3.8	6.1	95.8	--	--	--	--	--	--
Wholesale and retail trade	272,137	21.9	89.0	7.3	5.9	35.4	91.9	--	--	--	--	--	--
All other industries. . .	137,101	23.2	86.7	9.6	5.4	21.6	92.4	--	--	--	--	--	--
Precision metal working occupations	987,253	6.0	90.1	5.9	5.7	-0.4	94.0	--	--	--	--	--	--
Tool and die makers . . .	187,550	1.8	95.1	3.1	2.8	-5.0	96.4	23.6	20.5	22.7	3.1	19,480	11,657
Precision assemblers, metal	22,091	24.4	82.0	11.0	10.3	-62.1	93.7	27.3	14.9	29.3	2.4	15,434	9,817
Machinists.	511,469	4.6	88.6	6.9	6.1	12.1	94.4	28.7	13.9	28.7	2.4	15,664	9,063
Boilermakers.	33,000	1.6	90.4	6.4	4.3	13.3	95.2	35.0	12.7	30.9	2.1	18,348	11,779
Precision grinder, filers, tool sharpeners	18,959	5.9	93.8	3.6	3.2	-28.0	94.1	23.2	22.2	34.2	0.9	17,135	10,838
Patternmakers and model makers, metal	19,354	9.5	94.2	3.1	3.5	-40.3	95.8	21.5	22.7	20.9	5.5	19,709	10,961
Lay-out workers	21,404	10.2	83.3	12.8	4.7	65.3	94.5	31.3	13.9	31.6	3.1	14,798	10,344
Precious stones and metal workers (jewelers). . .	34,343	31.0	84.9	4.2	14.4	72.8	81.2	30.1	14.0	34.6	9.6	13,300	6,456
Engravers, metal.	14,560	37.6	91.3	4.7	6.7	33.2	76.9	22.4	15.7	24.7	5.0	14,172	6,699
Sheet metal workers . . .	122,273	3.9	91.1	4.9	6.5	-16.8	94.2	28.9	14.0	29.2	2.4	16,025	10,480
Miscellaneous precision metal workers	2,250	24.5	85.7	9.6	7.3	262.9	91.1	29.1	15.8	40.8	2.5	14,994	9,479
Precision woodworking occupations	110,356	13.5	88.9	6.9	7.2	4.9	84.7	--	--	--	--	--	--
Patternmakers and model makers, wood.	4,390	2.9	96.8	1.2	2.8	-45.3	94.8	20.0	21.9	19.1	5.6	21,384	11,804
Cabinet makers and bench carpenters.	71,905	7.3	91.3	4.6	7.4	0.9	86.1	29.5	13.3	33.4	6.1	11,630	6,904
Furniture and wood finishers	29,422	28.9	82.0	13.4	7.4	13.4	79.2	24.9	14.3	47.8	5.3	9,360	5,881
Miscellaneous precision woodworkers	4,639	23.2	88.9	6.7	7.4	--	89.1	24.1	15.6	36.1	3.7	14,434	7,568
Precision textile, apparel, and furnishings machine workers	261,346	54.7	80.6	9.8	13.7	-9.2	73.3	--	--	--	--	--	--
Dressmakers	96,815	93.5	77.8	10.8	12.4	-8.6	61.2	17.3	22.4	46.4	4.9	11,711	5,407
Tailors	57,515	39.4	78.6	10.6	16.9	-17.5	80.7	16.9	22.2	53.1	3.0	10,983	6,434
Upholsterers.	65,120	20.8	84.9	8.0	14.0	5.8	81.0	25.8	13.6	46.9	2.4	10,763	6,111
Shoe repairers.	29,752	29.7	83.6	9.2	12.3	-27.5	80.7	18.8	19.7	54.4	2.8	9,560	6,296
Apparel and fabric patternmakers	3,861	51.2	88.4	3.7	8.7	129.7	83.6	24.2	15.3	28.0	9.1	14,968	8,684
Miscellaneous precision apparel and fabric workers	8,283	63.9	79.3	12.3	11.1	6.6	71.0	19.2	18.8	45.5	5.2	12,706	6,196
Precision workers, assorted materials	306,432	46.3	82.1	8.4	10.7	-7.6	88.1	--	--	--	--	--	--
Hand molders and shapers, except jewelers	34,262	13.9	79.1	14.7	10.1	-30.4	90.4	28.0	12.8	47.6	3.4	12,813	7,680
Patternmakers, lay-out workers, and cutters. .	8,854	22.6	90.1	5.4	6.7	180.2	89.7	25.9	17.4	24.4	7.1	16,746	8,602
Optical goods workers . .	44,836	40.3	94.4	4.1	6.6	50.7	88.3	33.0	11.6	17.4	9.6	14,556	8,096
Dental laboratory and medical appliance technicians	47,012	32.1	86.4	5.6	7.7	69.5	84.7	34.3	10.3	16.0	9.9	15,832	8,147
Bookbinders	28,221	56.0	86.1	8.8	7.9	-12.9	84.6	23.7	14.1	36.9	2.7	13,604	7,697
Electrical and electronic equipment assemblers. .	104,496	76.0	73.6	9.9	16.1	-38.5	88.8	27.3	10.5	34.4	2.8	10,549	8,207
Miscellaneous precision workers, NEC.	38,751	17.2	87.0	7.4	8.3	101.7	90.7	28.1	11.6	35.1	2.7	13,173	8,540
Precision food production occupations	411,885	22.4	83.4	10.1	9.9	2.6	82.8	--	--	--	--	--	--
Butchers and meat cutters.	277,568	13.9	83.6	10.0	9.8	-3.3	87.1	26.7	12.0	38.0	1.9	14,425	7,149
Bankers	110,147	40.7	83.7	10.3	9.6	19.6	73.1	21.7	14.3	40.6	3.3	11,985	5,987
Food batchmakers.	24,170	36.5	80.3	11.1	12.7	8.6	78.2	24.2	12.4	44.3	2.6	10,762	6,012
Precision inspectors, testers, and related workers.	99,691	27.6	87.3	8.0	5.7	-51.6	94.5	--	--	--	--	--	--
Inspectors, testers and graders	96,597	26.3	87.6	7.7	5.5	-51.6	94.6	26.7	17.3	22.5	4.5	17,059	9,785
Adjusters and calibrators.	3,094	67.9	77.2	16.4	9.7	-49.6	90.6	27.7	14.1	36.1	3.0	15,185	7,361
Plant and system operators.	240,754	3.8	88.9	8.0	3.8	10.3	95.6	--	--	--	--	--	--
Water and sewage treatment plant operators. .	32,555	3.1	88.8	8.3	3.6	89.0	94.9	33.1	14.6	24.1	6.3	13,812	9,921
Power plant operators . .	27,354	4.8	91.5	6.3	2.4	31.7	97.1	31.2	15.1	15.4	4.6	19,931	11,442
Stationary engineers. . .	130,068	3.1	89.1	7.5	3.4	-11.9	95.4	25.0	20.1	23.5	12.7	19,230	12,034
Miscellaneous plant and system operators. . . .	50,777	5.3	86.8	9.7	5.5	55.9	95.6	32.6	14.1	24.9	5.0	17,890	12,791

Table 13-5. Detailed Occupation of the Employed Persons in the United States, by Selected Characteristics: 1980—continued

Occupation	Number of persons employed	Percent female	Percent white	Percent black	Percent Spanish-origin	Percent change in employment 1970-80	Percent full-time 1979	Age		Education		Mean income	
								25 to 34	55 to 64	0 to 11	16 and over	Male	Female
Operators, fabricators, and laborers	17,859,343	27.3	80.4	14.0	8.7	9.8	84.7	--	--	--	--	--	--
Machine operators, assemblers, and inspectors	9,084,988	40.1	79.7	13.8	9.6	8.5	88.9	--	--	--	--	--	--
Machine operators and tenders, except precision	5,960,505	40.4	78.9	14.6	9.9	-2.5	88.3	--	--	--	--	--	--
Metalworking and plastic working machine operators	715,441	17.4	86.2	9.5	6.9	-9.1	93.2	--	--	--	--	--	--
Lathe and turning machine set-up operators	53,191	6.4	90.0	6.8	5.2	-22.4	96.6	29.1	13.5	39.9	1.3	15,957	11,511
Lathe and turning machine operators	112,211	8.6	92.4	4.4	4.7	-5.7	94.6	30.3	12.4	28.7	2.4	15,257	9,732
Milling and planing machine operators	20,511	8.8	91.3	4.9	4.5	193.4	94.0	28.2	14.1	27.8	2.7	15,162	9,545
Punching and stamping press machine operators	150,573	31.1	84.5	11.0	7.6	-18.7	93.3	28.8	12.1	44.0	1.2	13,587	9,061
Rolling machine operators	18,106	10.8	84.7	12.3	5.2	-25.6	94.1	25.1	16.7	39.2	1.6	19,891	9,151
Drilling and boring machine operators	60,856	20.5	90.2	6.4	5.2	-36.7	92.9	28.9	13.0	36.1	1.8	14,604	8,679
Grinding, abrading, buffing, and polishing machine operators	251,840	17.0	82.4	12.0	9.1	6.7	91.2	27.5	12.6	42.9	1.5	13,379	8,650
Forging machine operators	14,575	6.9	85.6	10.6	5.9	-15.0	95.3	33.2	11.3	40.9	1.4	15,846	10,190
Numerical control machine operators	2,650	7.9	90.0	5.4	6.0	330.2	95.5	40.3	11.1	17.1	5.6	17,542	11,004
Miscellaneous metal, plastic, stone, and glass working machine operators	30,928	14.2	85.7	12.2	3.6	-7.1	95.5	27.9	13.1	37.6	1.6	18,030	9,423
Fabricating machine operators, NEC	31,820	34.2	85.5	9.6	8.5	-44.1	91.6	28.2	12.8	40.1	1.5	13,848	8,264
Metal and plastic processing machine operators	218,268	25.6	81.7	13.0	8.5	-16.1	92.3	--	--	--	--	--	--
Molding and casting machine operators	140,415	33.4	82.9	12.8	7.3	-19.5	92.0	29.0	10.4	42.0	1.7	13,205	7,776
Metal plating machine operators	40,675	15.3	80.4	11.2	13.4	10.3	91.9	28.9	9.9	41.8	2.0	12,847	8,000
Heating treating equipment operators	23,270	5.4	83.7	12.6	5.9	-23.6	95.3	24.9	17.7	41.1	1.6	17,452	10,165
Miscellaneous metal and plastic processing machine operators	13,908	10.8	70.6	21.4	11.2	-24.1	91.2	30.1	8.1	48.3	1.3	12,423	7,981
Woodworking machine operators	142,032	14.4	83.4	12.5	5.5	-5.3	88.0	--	--	--	--	--	--
Wood lathe, routing, and planing machine operators	7,223	10.1	87.7	9.0	4.7	58.5	92.4	24.7	13.7	43.1	3.5	12,514	8,576
Sawing machine operators	94,117	11.5	82.8	13.2	5.4	-16.8	88.5	27.8	11.1	52.9	1.7	10,133	7,164
Shaping and joining machine operators	8,134	38.9	82.2	13.2	5.7	127.4	89.6	29.8	9.8	44.8	1.9	10,972	7,317
Nailing and tacking machine operators	4,055	33.6	81.1	11.6	9.9	-26.8	85.2	27.8	8.0	55.3	0.4	8,094	6,245
Miscellaneous woodworking machine operators	28,503	15.7	84.7	11.2	5.3	23.2	85.2	29.9	12.2	40.9	6.4	10,453	6,915
Printing machine operators	422,477	26.5	89.1	7.0	5.9	9.9	87.7	28.0	10.1	22.9	3.9	14,466	7,827
Printing machine operators	286,807	16.5	87.4	8.2	6.8	19.6	89.8	28.0	10.1	22.9	3.9	14,466	7,827
Photoengravers and lithographers	25,088	18.9	93.4	3.8	3.8	-23.5	92.2	25.7	14.0	15.8	6.0	18,963	8,846
Typesetters and compositors	67,504	55.7	94.4	3.2	3.2	-20.4	80.1	28.2	11.0	11.1	9.5	15,989	7,940
Miscellaneous printing machine operators	43,078	52.1	89.5	7.0	5.4	59.6	82.8	24.8	12.3	29.8	3.1	13,699	7,349
Textile, apparel, and furnishings machine operators	1,487,503	81.2	72.5	18.2	12.3	-20.0	81.7	--	--	--	--	--	--
Winding and twisting machine operators	102,293	74.6	74.2	24.4	1.7	-28.6	91.5	26.9	14.1	62.3	0.5	10,374	7,694
Knitting, looping, taping and weaving machine operators	68,716	64.4	75.1	21.2	4.2	-20.1	88.9	27.0	12.5	57.4	2.0	10,233	7,969
Textile cutting machine operators	8,554	47.3	74.2	17.6	13.0	0.5	85.4	24.4	13.1	53.6	2.1	10,177	6,607
Textile sewing machine operators	829,080	94.2	73.5	14.4	15.7	-7.7	82.0	24.6	15.5	57.3	1.0	9,239	6,026
Shoe machine operators	68,388	74.0	89.9	6.4	7.2	-44.7	85.3	24.3	14.0	55.4	0.8	8,221	6,133
Pressing machine operators	97,211	75.3	55.5	34.5	14.5	-46.6	70.3	19.1	20.4	64.4	0.9	8,535	5,634
Laundering and dry cleaning machine operators	173,226	65.2	68.4	23.1	10.7	-7.5	69.6	19.6	18.4	54.5	2.1	9,530	5,627
Miscellaneous textile machine operators	140,035	47.4	72.8	23.7	6.4	-39.2	90.0	27.2	12.8	57.2	1.2	10,221	7,351
Machine operators, assorted materials	2,942,964	29.7	78.4	15.3	10.4	12.5	90.2	--	--	--	--	--	--
Cementing and gluing machine operators	31,778	47.7	80.0	14.5	8.1	-50.3	87.1	27.9	10.2	43.8	2.1	11,890	7,202
Packaging and filling machine operators	101,599	51.1	76.9	15.5	11.5	-29.4	86.3	26.8	12.7	45.3	1.9	12,369	7,351

Table 13-5. Detailed Occupation of the Employed Persons in the United States, by Selected Characteristics: 1980—continued

Occupation	Number of persons employed	Percent female	Percent white	Percent black	Percent Spanish-origin	Percent change in employment 1970–80	Percent full-time 1979	Age		Education		Mean income	
								25 to 34	55 to 64	0 to 11	16 and over	Male	Female
Operators, fabricators, and laborers (con't)													
Extruding and forming machine operators. . .	23,009	13.6	87.2	8.7	6.2	-16.1	94.7	34.3	7.3	34.4	2.0	13,213	8,383
Mixing and blending machine operators. . .	103,929	10.8	77.8	17.5	7.2	-19.9	92.3	30.2	10.7	38.4	3.3	13,305	8,817
Separating, filtering, and clarifying machine operators. . .	69,719	8.1	84.2	12.7	4.9	26.2	95.6	33.0	12.7	27.1	4.7	17,582	10,620
Compressing and compacting machine operators.	20,234	29.0	78.3	17.1	7.4	-35.0	88.5	27.5	13.7	45.7	1.5	11,824	8,074
Painting and paint spraying machine operators.	153,314	15.5	81.8	11.2	12.1	-5.2	90.7	30.4	9.1	43.7	1.8	12,608	7,665
Roasting and baking machine operators, food.	6,680	14.1	79.6	16.9	9.1	0.8	90.9	24.7	14.1	45.5	2.1	13,627	8,205
Washing, cleaning, and pickling machine operators.	8,203	23.2	78.6	15.8	8.8	-11.3	89.3	25.7	12.2	49.4	1.6	13,676	7,029
Folding machine operators.	30,402	60.0	76.5	17.9	9.2	-6.8	84.4	26.5	12.4	49.7	1.1	11,141	6,658
Furnace, kiln, and oven operators, except food.	144,071	4.7	82.2	14.4	5.5	-19.6	95.0	28.1	15.5	38.4	2.2	16,414	10,813
Crushing and grinding machine operators. . .	48,209	8.1	78.7	16.2	8.7	-18.4	91.8	27.3	13.0	45.3	1.8	13,291	8,266
Slicing and cutting machine operators. . .	189,654	28.3	80.1	13.2	11.0	-7.6	88.3	27.1	12.5	45.3	1.6	11,989	6,800
Motion picture projectionists.	13,734	9.0	91.5	5.3	4.3	-16.4	57.8	23.4	11.1	24.0	11.0	11,803	5,115
Photographic process machine operators. . .	84,650	53.0	86.2	8.3	6.4	26.6	78.8	29.6	9.0	17.8	10.5	12,056	7,268
Miscellaneous and not specified machine operators.	1,913,779	32.8	77.0	16.2	11.3	34.1	90.7	--	--	--	--	--	--
Occupation:													
Miscellaneous machine operators NEC.	639,837	32.6	80.0	14.1	9.1	-39.9	90.9	30.0	10.8	39.3	2.4	14,048	8,093
Machine operators, not specified. . .	1,273,942	32.9	75.5	17.3	12.3	250.7	90.5	28.8	11.2	43.5	2.1	13,243	8,120
Industry:													
Manufacturing. . . .	1,652,466	33.6	77.2	16.0	11.4	26.7	91.7	--	--	--	--	--	--
Nondurable goods .	663,528	36.9	76.2	17.2	11.3	31.6	91.1	--	--	--	--	--	--
Food and kindred products . . .	110,004	33.6	71.4	19.4	13.4	13.5	90.3	--	--	--	--	--	--
Tobacco manufactures . . .	13,128	39.3	61.0	38.2	2.9	27.5	94.6	--	--	--	--	--	--
Textile mill products . . .	51,705	47.6	72.8	23.7	6.6	--	90.4	--	--	--	--	--	--
Apparel and other finished textile products . . .	48,005	74.8	70.0	18.9	19.9	18.1	84.7	--	--	--	--	--	--
Paper and allied products . . .	132,216	23.4	80.5	14.3	8.7	5.8	94.6	--	--	--	--	--	--
Printing, publishing, and allied industries.	44,840	45.3	81.5	12.2	11.7	15.8	81.5	--	--	--	--	--	--
Chemicals and allied products	110,930	32.0	75.4	19.0	10.2	55.2	92.9	--	--	--	--	--	--
Pretoleum and coal products.	13,195	6.5	76.9	18.4	7.5	-0.3	95.2	--	--	--	--	--	--
Rubber and miscellaneous plastics products	118,676	35.3	79.8	13.9	10.8	24.3	92.6	--	--	--	--	--	--
Leather and leather products	20,829	61.1	79.0	10.9	23.9	69.5	87.0	--	--	--	--	--	--
Durable goods. . .	952,041	30.8	78.4	14.9	10.9	21.1	92.4	--	--	--	--	--	--
Lumber and wood products, except furniture.	47,828	18.3	73.0	21.9	7.3	46.4	91.0	--	--	--	--	--	--
Furniture and fixtures . . .	39,588	32.6	74.2	17.9	14.2	79.4	90.6	--	--	--	--	--	--
Stone, clay, glass, and concrete products.	60,067	23.3	78.4	15.2	10.4	9.1	93.3	--	--	--	--	--	--
Primary metal industries . .	131,489	11.9	76.3	17.9	10.5	12.2	94.2	--	--	--	--	--	--
Blast furnaces, steelworks, rolling and finishing mills . . .	62,679	6.4	75.1	19.8	9.5	54.0	94.1	--	--	--	--	--	--
Fabricated metal industries . . .	129,770	27.6	78.9	13.1	13.9	32.0	92.3	--	--	--	--	--	--
Machinery, except electrical . . .	166,290	21.1	83.5	10.9	8.8	45.9	92.5	--	--	--	--	--	--
Electrical machinery, equipment, and supplies . .	161,982	56.9	79.0	13.8	10.5	6.2	92.2	--	--	--	--	--	--
Transportation equipment. . . .	116,398	22.0	77.9	16.8	8.4	2.4	94.6	--	--	--	--	--	--
Motor vehicles and motor vehicle equipment.	72,301	23.2	77.5	18.7	6.3	15.4	94.7	--	--	--	--	--	--
Other transportation equipment	44,097	20.0	78.7	13.7	12.0	-13.6	94.3	--	--	--	--	--	--

Table 13-5. Detailed Occupation of the Employed Persons in the United States, by Selected Characteristics: 1980—continued

Occupation	Number of persons employed	Percent female	Percent white	Percent black	Percent Spanish-origin	Percent change in employment 1970-80	Percent full-time 1979	Age: 25 to 34	Age: 55 to 64	Education: 0 to 11	Education: 16 and over	Mean income: Male	Mean income: Female
Operators, fabricators, and laborers (con't)													
Professional and photographic eqipment and watches.	38,801	52.7	81.0	12.4	11.2	80.8	93.0	--	--	--	--	--	--
Miscellaneous manufacturing industries	59,828	54.1	73.1	16.6	18.2	0.6	86.4	--	--	--	--	--	--
Not specified manufacturing industries	36,897	45.9	63.0	23.6	26.8	178.9	83.0	--	--	--	--	--	--
Nonmanufacturing industries	261,313	27.8	76.0	17.5	10.3	111.2	84.1	--	--	--	--	--	--
Construction	27,065	4.7	80.3	14.6	8.3	570.4	89.3	--	--	--	--	--	--
Transportation, communications, and other public utilities	52,069	13.0	76.7	17.9	8.0	93.8	93.1	--	--	--	--	--	--
Wholesale trade	52,295	28.7	71.6	19.7	15.1	48.0	87.5	--	--	--	--	--	--
Retail trade	39,082	43.7	80.7	13.7	9.8	254.2	72.9	--	--	--	--	--	--
Business and repair services	26,338	31.9	79.1	13.8	11.4	70.4	82.6	--	--	--	--	--	--
Public administration	17,646	18.5	70.9	23.7	6.5	22.1	89.4	--	--	--	--	--	--
All other industries	46,818	44.4	73.6	19.1	9.9	183.1	75.3	--	--	--	--	--	--
Fabricators, assemblers, and hand working occupations	2,299,462	35.8	80.6	12.7	9.7	49.4	89.7	--	--	--	--	--	--
Welders, and cutters	712,599	5.5	84.2	10.0	8.6	26.0	93.5	33.4	8.7	38.1	1.5	14,692	9,176
Solderers, and brazers	30,510	78.3	80.5	10.1	15.6	-31.3	88.4	27.0	10.9	43.7	1.3	10,700	7,482
Assemblers	1,459,308	49.7	78.7	14.1	10.1	73.9	88.5	29.2	9.8	38.9	2.0	12,532	8,167
Hand cutting and trimming occupations	15,714	37.8	76.3	13.6	13.0	-11.1	81.5	24.7	11.0	49.2	1.7	11,593	6,015
Hand molding, casting, and forming occupations	16,949	33.3	84.3	10.1	9.8	1.2	80.7	30.9	10.8	40.2	12.1	11,206	5,771
Hand painting, coating and decorating occupations	37,764	26.3	84.7	10.0	7.9	-0.8	80.1	26.6	13.6	34.9	5.2	12,493	6,628
Hand engraving and printing occupations	2,000	31.8	87.9	7.5	6.5	-47.4	88.8	27.2	13.3	29.0	5.0	13,524	7,687
Hand grinding and polishing occupations	2,501	28.6	78.0	12.1	16.2	106.2	91.3	24.4	10.2	51.0	1.6	11,472	7,004
Miscellaneous hand working occupations	22,117	48.5	82.5	11.1	9.9	78.1	77.6	25.0	12.4	44.2	3.1	12,252	6,266
Production inspectors, testers, samplers, and weighers	825,021	50.5	83.2	11.8	6.9	14.0	91.2	--	--	--	--	--	--
Production inspectors, checkers, and examiners	669,605	51.1	84.1	11.7	5.8	16.9	93.0	25.3	17.2	34.7	3.5	16,175	8,994
Production testers	55,702	32.2	85.2	9.6	6.0	-6.9	93.4	29.6	11.9	25.6	5.5	15,563	9,335
Production samplers and weighers	8,743	41.5	82.3	11.2	14.2	43.4	89.4	24.3	16.1	43.1	3.7	12,774	7,922
Graders and sorters, except agricultural	90,971	58.1	75.3	14.5	14.7	7.3	77.0	23.7	14.5	50.4	2.4	10,545	5,591
Transportation and material moving occupations	4,389,412	7.9	83.5	12.8	5.9	17.4	87.0	--	--	--	--	--	--
Motor vehicle operators	3,017,954	9.3	83.1	13.4	5.8	15.8	84.1	--	--	--	--	--	--
Supervisors, motor vehicle operators	31,849	6.2	90.3	7.2	3.5	58.8	93.4	30.4	11.4	23.9	10.1	18,446	9,779
Truck drivers, heavy	1,713,930	2.2	84.0	12.8	5.5	18.4	92.0	29.3	10.8	45.3	1.8	15,555	8,996
Truck drivers, light	510,016	6.7	85.4	10.5	7.1	25.4	81.0	28.6	8.6	33.5	3.5	12,310	6,413
Driver-sales workers	177,373	7.2	92.3	5.5	4.0	63.3	89.9	31.6	10.0	25.3	4.2	14,900	6,703
Bus drivers	373,603	45.8	77.9	19.0	4.3	46.9	53.6	25.7	13.8	32.0	3.7	12,264	5,137
Taxicab drivers and chauffers	174,367	11.3	71.4	22.2	9.2	6.5	77.4	26.4	15.6	37.7	6.4	9,877	5,965
Parking lot attendants	33,461	8,3	68.5	22.8	12.1	1.9	58.9	10.3	10.5	42.0	4.7	6,840	4,992
Motor transportation occupations, NEC	3,355	4.8	79.9	14.2	7.6	169.0	87.9	25.4	15.3	45.4	4.3	12,594	4,923
Rail transportation occupations	203,230	1.6	90.1	8.2	2.8	-16.6	95.2	--	--	--	--	--	--
Railroad conductors and yardmasters	46,130	1.6	93.5	5.4	1.6	-14.8	96.2	25.3	23.6	23.8	4.2	24,292	13,764
Locomotive operating occupations	70,953	1.7	89.4	9.0	2.7	-11.1	95.1	29.9	20.5	22.4	5.2	23,961	16,544
Railroad brake, signal, and switch operators	77,351	1.3	89.0	8.9	3.5	-24.2	94.5	38.5	10.6	21.0	3.7	19,813	13,785
Rail vehicle operators, NEC	8,796	3.1	87.4	10.2	4.1	13.6	96.1	35.1	11.8	20.2	4.3	18,495	15,074
Water transportation occupations	68,029	2.7	90.3	6.0	4.6	17.7	90.3	--	--	--	--	--	--
Ship captains and mates, except fishing boats	31,071	1.9	94.7	2.5	2.9	19.3	91.2	27.3	14.1	37.2	11.7	22,930	9,357
Sailors and deckhands	28,583	2.6	85.3	9.6	7.1	7.8	88.6	24.4	13.8	40.7	5.3	14,079	8,871
Marine engineers	3,359	2.3	89.7	6.4	4.5	--	91.5	26.8	13.6	35.5	6.9	16,291	12,036
Bridge, lock, and lighthouse tenders	5,016	8.5	91.6	6.8	1.5	-4.1	93.4	17.9	26.4	42.1	4.0	14,186	7,652
Material moving equipment operators	1,100,199	5.6	82.9	12.6	7.1	32.5	93.1	--	--	--	--	--	--
Supervisors, material moving equipment operators	29,444	4.0	90.0	7.0	5.0	147.6	94.2	29.7	16.7	24.4	10.2	19,803	13,671
Operating engineers	194,693	1.3	89.1	6.7	5.5	73.2	94.6	29.7	12.2	42.8	2.1	15,636	10,106
Longshore equipment operators	3,971	2.3	57.1	34.3	9.8	66.0	77.2	18.4	22.4	52.6	2.8	19,814	7,643
Hoist and winch operators	28,508	2.1	89.3	5.3	10.1	39.8	93.9	34.9	5.8	43.3	1.8	15,491	10,815
Crane and tower operators	120,766	2.0	81.6	15.1	5.6	-12.0	95.6	28.0	15.1	45.9	1.3	18,370	14,041
Excavating and loading machine operators	72,462	1.8	91.1	5.5	5.5	13.1	92.0	29.9	10.2	47.0	1.4	15,425	9,524
Grader, dozer, and scaper operators	66,895	1.2	90.8	6.5	3.5	-35.4	91.6	24.5	15.4	54.8	1.5	14,213	8,587
Industrial truck and tractor equipment operators	388,654	4.6	77.1	17.6	8.7	39.4	93.7	30.9	9.1	44.6	1.4	13,093	10,644
Miscellaneous material moving equipment operators	194,806	17.9	82.0	13.3	7.9	95.3	90.0	30.1	10.8	39.8	2.3	13,596	8,009

Table 13-5. Detailed Occupation of the Employed Persons in the United States, by Selected Characteristics: 1980—continued

Occupation	Number of persons employed	Percent female	Percent white	Percent black	Percent Spanish-origin	Percent change in employment 1970-80	Percent full-time 1979	Age		Education		Mean income	
								25 to 34	55 to 64	0 to 11	16 and over	Male	Female
Operators, fabricators, and laborers (con't)													
Handlers, equipment cleaners, helpers, and laborers	4,384,943	20.1	78.6	15.3	9.5	5.7	73.9	--	--	--	--	--	--
Supervisors; handlers, equipment cleaners, and laborers, NEC	9,853	15.4	83.8	14.4	2.1	455.4	94.2	26.1	15.8	22.8	15.3	18,612	10,781
Helpers, mechanics and repairers	24,804	5.6	78.5	14.3	12.2	-17.4	73.5	24.9	7.1	44.1	1.7	9,182	7,026
Helpers, construction and extractive occupations. . . .	125,983	4.3	82.7	11.0	11.1	24.7	80.6	--	--	--	--	--	--
Helpers, construction trades.	97,697	3.7	80.9	12.5	11.8	22.4	78.7	24.6	5.7	43.1	2.1	7,910	6,129
Helpers, surveyor	9,492	6.1	91.3	4.8	5.2	-15.8	80.8	29.5	3.9	22.5	6.7	9,049	6,559
Helpers, extractive occupations	18,794	6.4	88.1	6.2	10.3	89.4	90.4	34.3	6.2	39.8	2.5	13,316	10,506
Construction laborers	661,411	3.0	76.0	17.3	11.4	29.3	83.4	27.3	8.9	46.6	3.0	10,249	6,191
Production helpers.	108,271	18.2	77.9	15.2	11.9	-24.0	80.6	27.1	8.8	41.9	2.0	11,037	7,240
Freight, stock, and material handlers.	1,259,182	15.3	81.9	13.6	6.8	-1.0	61.3	--	--	--	--	--	--
Garbage collectors.	69,719	2.8	60.5	34.2	8.5	-11.1	82.5	28.4	10.3	59.0	1.6	10,520	6,620
Stevedores.	20,135	1.4	58.9	35.1	11.9	-54.0	73.5	19.6	18.9	51.8	2.8	17,863	10,002
Stock handlers and baggers.	651,770	21.0	87.9	7.6	6.4	24.4	42.2	18.1	5.1	31.3	3.0	7,783	5,859
Machine feeders and offbearers	99,710	31.0	77.6	18.3	6.3	-8.5	87.9	28.8	9.0	45.7	1.6	11,381	7,516
Freight, stock, and material handlers, NEC.	417,848	5.4	78.2	17.4	7.1	-19.2	80.6	27.7	7.7	37.7	3.2	11,704	8,581
Garage and service station related occupations	302,606	7.9	88.1	7.9	5.5	-33.0	60.1	17.4	7.5	44.1	2.2	7,166	4,860
Vehicle washers and equipment cleaners	127,425	15.2	74.2	19.4	10.0	-3.6	67.9	22.3	8.8	49.0	1.8	8,500	6,787
Hand packers and packagers. .	543,230	66.4	76.6	14.9	13.4	-3.8	79.3	24.6	12.1	47.4	1.5	9,962	7,269
Laborers, except construction	1,222,178	19.3	75.4	18.1	10.0	30.1	81.8	27.4	9.8	42.8	2.6	10,722	6,864
Manufacturing	553,121	23.7	74.5	19.1	10.2	33.1	87.2	--	--	--	--	--	--
Nondurable goods.	232,010	29.9	73.2	20.1	10.6	29.5	84.9	--	--	--	--	--	--
Food and kindred products.	85,419	28.0	69.6	22.0	12.5	20.6	82.6	--	--	--	--	--	--
Textile mill and finished textile products.	41,024	45.3	72.0	21.3	11.0	31.0	83.9	--	--	--	--	--	--
Paper and allied products.	24,271	20.2	75.6	19.5	7.0	51.2	91.2	--	--	--	--	--	--
Chemicals and allied products.	30,649	19.5	74.3	20.1	9.2	38.5	89.1	--	--	--	--	--	--
Rubber and miscellaneous plastics products	17,311	25.4	80.8	13.1	9.4	46.8	89.7	--	--	--	--	--	--
Other nondurable goods.	33,336	34.9	76.9	17.6	9.7	23.3	81.3	--	--	--	--	--	--
Durable goods	308,328	18.7	76.1	18.1	9.6	31.9	89.1	--	--	--	--	--	--
Furniture, lumber, and wood products	48,425	18.9	72.7	21.9	8.0	32.7	84.7	--	--	--	--	--	--
Stone, clay, glass, and concrete products . .	33,090	14.1	79.3	14.2	10.6	29.1	90.3	--	--	--	--	--	--
Primary metal industries	72,099	8.5	74.1	21.4	8.7	5.8	92.6	--	--	--	--	--	--
Fabricated metal industries	36,989	19.9	78.0	14.9	11.6	39.6	89.2	--	--	--	--	--	--
Machinery, except electrical.	36,547	16.4	81.4	13.2	9.0	115.8	88.9	--	--	--	--	--	--
Electrical machinery, equipment, supplies .	24,189	41.0	79.0	13.9	10.3	75.3	90.1	--	--	--	--	--	--
Transportation equipment	35,081	15.2	72.4	22.3	8.1	10.4	90.6	--	--	--	--	--	--
Motor vehicles and motor vehical equipment	19,302	16.0	73.2	22.2	7.0	23.8	91.9	--	--	--	--	--	--
Other durable goods . .	21,908	42.2	76.2	15.8	13.3	51.7	82.4	--	--	--	--	--	--
Not specified manufacturing industries . . .	12,783	28.7	59.7	27.7	20.5	399.1	80.1	--	--	--	--	--	--
Nonmanufacturing industries.	669,057	15.7	76.1	17.2	9.8	27.6	77.4	--	--	--	--	--	--
Transportation, communications, and other public utilities	145,349	7.3	71.6	21.9	10.0	22.6	86.9	--	--	--	--	--	--
Wholesale trade	173,003	16.2	80.0	13.5	10.2	19.6	82.8	--	--	--	--	--	--
Retail trade.	134,819	19.8	80.4	13.9	8.3	41.0	70.1	--	--	--	--	--	--
Business and repair services.	39,964	14.8	79.5	14.0	9.2	47.6	68.2	--	--	--	--	--	--
Public administration . .	52,325	12.9	64.3	27.2	8.9	37.8	81.9	--	--	--	--	--	--
All other industries. . .	123,597	21.7	75.1	17.6	11.3	23.2	67.6	--	--	--	--	--	--
Experienced unemployed not classified by occupation.	339,909	62.4	--	--	--	--	--	--	--	--	--	--	--
Last job armed forces	42,878	13.2	--	--	--	--	--	--	--	--	--	--	--
Last worked 1974 or earlier . . .	297,031	69.5	--	--	--	--	--	--	--	--	--	--	--

[a]The last six columns are based on population eighteen years and older.

Note: NEC stands for "not elsewhere classified." -- indicates data not available.

Source: U.S. Bureau of the Census. "Detailed Population Characteristics: United States Summary." 1980 Census of Population. Washington, DC: U.S. Government Printing Office, 1983, Tables 276 and 278. Also, U.S. Bureau of the Census. "Special Report: Earnings by Occupation and Education." 1980 Census of Population. Washington, DC: U.S. Government Printing Office, 1984, Table 1.

The ten occupations with the lowest mean income were as follows:

Lowest mean income (male)	Income ($)
Food counters, fountain and related occupations	5,620
Private household cleaners and servants	5,608
Teachers' aides	5,543
Crossing guards	5,460
Short order cooks	5,100
Library clerks	4,832
Ushers	4,790
Miscellaneous food preparation	4,484
Childcare workers, private household	4,366
Waiters' and waitresses' assistants	4,109

Lowest mean income (female)	Income ($)
Miscellaneous food preparation	3,898
Housekeepers and butlers	3,750
Childcare workers, except private households	3,675
Demonstrators, promoters and models, sales	3,654
Waiters' and waitresses' assistants	3,611
Launderers and ironers	3,439
Food counters, fountain and related occupations	3,435
Private household cleaners and servants	3,217
Crossing guards	2,873
Childcare workers, private households	2,414

Occupational Composition of Urban and Rural Areas

Table 13-6 provides data on the occupational composition of urban and rural areas (with urban subdivided into three categories). The occupational classification is somewhat more detailed than that of Table 13-1. It shows that the highest socioeconomic status occupations are concentrated in urban fringes (as place of residence, not necessarily place of work). Central cities of urbanized areas tend to have concentrations of service workers, operators, fabricators, and laborers. Rural areas have concentrations of precision, production, craft, and repair occupations, farmers and operators–fabricators, and laborers. Table 13-6 also provides indicators of the percent of each occupation group that is black and Spanish-origin and the percent outside SMSAs, for this expanded occupational classification.

Occupational Composition of Regions and SMSAs, by Sex

Table 13-7 provides data about the occupational composition of each of the four geographic regions, subclassified by metropolitan and nonmetropolitan residence. This distribution is shown separately for male and female workers. The occupational composition of the regions is similar—especially the portions inside SMSAs. The South region, which formerly was less industrial, has nearly lost this characteristic.

Occupational Composition of Metropolitan and Nonmetropolitan Areas, by Race-Ethnicity and Sex

The occupational composition of central cities, suburban rings, and nonmetropolitan areas, by race-ethnicity and sex, is shown in Table 13-8. Suburban rings tend to have higher concentration of the upper class white collar occupations, while the central cities tend to have greater concentrations of service, clerical, as well as upper middle class white collar workers. The nonmetropolitan areas contain larger than average proportions of operators, laborers, and farm workers. However, the metropolitan-nonmetropolitan differences are not as large for the white population as for the black and Spanish-origin populations.

Summary

The process of suburbanization of both people and economic establishments and the recent growth of nonmetropolitan areas, coupled with the decline of agricultural occupations, has created a great movement toward occupational homogenization on a residential basis. Suburbs are much less exclusively the domain of the upper class white collar workers than before. Central cities, with their mixture of middle class and upper class populations, have an occupational composition that resembles the national average, except for the comparative absence of agricultural occupations.

Industry Composition and Trends

Introduction

Whereas occupation refers to the work activity of each individual worker, the industry classification refers to the establishment or organization (employer) for which the worker carries out his or her occupational tasks (for details see the "Definition Box"). Industry statistics reveal how a nation is organized to earn its livelihood. Often the economy is divided into "sectors": *primary* (extractive), *secondary* (industrial), and *tertiary* (services) industries. At other times it is dichotomized into agricultural and nonagricultural sectors. Both of these systems are summary ways of looking at the industrial composition which need to be refined.

In order to produce statistics on industry composition, standardized classifications of establishments and

Table 13-6. Occupational Composition by Urban and Rural Residence of the Employed Civilian Labor Force and Indicators of Race-Ethnicity and Residence Composition of Occupations: 1980

Occupation	Percent distribution					Percent black	Percent Spanish-origin	Percent outside SMSAs
	All areas	Central cities	Urban fringe	Other urban	Rural			
Total employed	100.0	100.0	100.0	100.0	100.0	9.6	5.6	23.1
Managerial and professional specialty occupations	22.7	23.5	26.2	21.3	17.6	5.9	3.0	18.3
Executive, administrative and managerial	10.4	10.3	12.6	9.2	7.9	4.8	3.2	17.4
Officials, administrators, public administration	0.4	0.3	0.4	0.4	0.4	8.3	3.3	26.0
Management related occupations	2.6	2.9	3.3	2.0	1.7	6.1	3.4	14.4
Professional specialty occupations	12.3	13.2	13.6	12.1	9.5	6.9	2.9	19.0
Engineers and natural scientists	2.2	2.0	3.1	1.6	1.5	3.1	2.4	12.9
Engineers	1.4	1.2	2.0	1.0	1.0	2.5	2.3	12.7
Health diagnosing occupations	0.7	0.8	0.8	0.6	0.4	2.8	3.4	15.0
Health assessment and treating occupations	1.7	1.9	1.9	1.6	1.3	7.8	2.4	18.3
Teachers, librarians, counsellors	4.8	4.7	4.7	5.8	4.5	9.1	2.8	24.5
Teachers, elementary and secondary	3.4	3.0	3.4	4.1	3.5	10.0	2.8	25.9
Technical, sales and administrative support	30.3	32.9	34.0	27.8	23.3	7.9	4.5	18.1
Health technologists and technicians	1.0	1.2	0.9	1.0	0.8	13.8	3.7	21.4
Technologists and technicians, except health	2.1	2.2	2.5	1.7	1.5	5.7	3.8	15.3
Sales occupations	10.0	10.0	11.4	10.1	8.1	4.8	4.0	19.8
Supervisors and proprietors	1.6	1.4	1.6	1.9	1.6	3.4	3.8	25.9
Sales representatives, commodities and finance	3.1	3.2	4.0	2.5	2.2	2.9	2.6	14.8
Other sales occupations	5.3	5.4	5.7	5.7	4.3	6.3	4.9	21.0
Cashiers	1.8	1.8	1.8	1.9	1.5	9.3	6.0	21.5
Administrative support occupations, including clerical	17.3	19.6	19.2	15.0	12.8	9.7	4.9	17.2
Computer equipment operators	0.4	0.5	0.5	0.3	0.3	11.6	5.1	12.6
Secretaries, stenographers and typists	4.8	5.1	5.4	4.3	3.7	7.2	4.1	17.8
Financial records processing occupations	2.3	2.4	2.5	2.3	2.1	5.1	3.7	21.2
Mail and mail distributing occupations	0.8	1.0	0.8	0.6	0.7	18.1	5.2	16.6
Service occupations	12.9	14.9	11.5	14.9	11.9	17.1	7.0	23.8
Private household occupations	0.6	0.8	0.4	0.8	0.6	41.0	9.4	27.3
Protective service occupations	1.5	1.7	1.6	1.5	1.2	12.0	4.4	19.2
Police and firefighters	0.6	0.7	0.7	0.6	0.5	7.8	3.8	17.9
Service occupations, excluding protective and household	10.8	12.4	9.5	12.6	9.9	16.5	7.3	24.2
Food service occupations	4.5	4.9	4.2	5.3	4.0	10.7	6.8	23.6
Cleaning and building service occupations	2.8	3.5	2.2	3.2	2.7	23.8	9.5	24.7
Farming, forestry and fishing occupations	2.9	0.8	0.8	2.3	8.5	6.5	9.1	59.3
Farm operators and managers	1.3	0.1	0.1	0.5	4.9	1.9	1.4	72.7
Farm workers and related occupations	1.4	0.7	0.7	1.5	3.1	10.2	17.3	45.3
Precision production, craft and repair occupations	12.9	10.8	12.4	13.3	15.9	6.6	6.1	26.0
Mechanics and repairers	3.9	3.2	3.8	4.0	4.9	6.4	5.4	26.1
Construction trades	4.3	3.6	4.1	4.4	5.6	6.4	5.9	26.6
Precision production occupations	4.4	4.0	4.5	4.3	4.7	7.3	6.8	22.5
Operators, fabricators and laborers	18.3	17.1	15.0	20.4	23.3	14.0	8.7	29.0
Machine operators and tenders, excluding precision	6.1	5.8	4.7	7.0	8.0	14.6	9.9	30.5
Fabricators, assemblers, inspectors, samplers	3.2	2.9	2.8	3.5	3.9	12.4	8.9	26.5
Transportation occupations	3.4	3.1	2.9	3.4	4.3	12.9	5.6	27.8
Motor vehicles	3.1	2.9	2.7	3.1	4.0	13.4	5.8	27.5
Material moving equipment operators	1.1	0.8	0.8	1.4	1.8	12.6	7.1	35.6
Handlers, equipment cleaners, helpers and laborers	4.5	4.4	3.8	5.1	5.3	15.3	9.5	27.8
Construction laborers	0.7	0.6	0.5	0.8	0.9	17.3	11.4	30.3
Freight, stock and material handlers	1.3	1.3	1.2	1.5	1.4	13.6	6.8	26.1

Source: U.S. Bureau of the Census. "General Social and Economic Characteristics: United States Summary." 1980 Census of Population. Washington, DC: U.S. Government Printing Office, 1983, Tables 104, 115, 125 and 135.

organizations have been developed for use not only in taking censuses, but in publishing a wide variety of other trade and economic statistics. As in the case of occupational classification, industrial classification is made at three levels:

- Major industrial group: 12 categories
- Intermediate industrial classification–150 categories
- Detailed industrial classification: 231 categories.

Space limitations have made it necessary to confine this chapter to only the first. Readers who wish data on the more detailed levels are referred to the volumes of the 1980 and 1970 censuses and to the "Special Reports" issued on occupation and industry on the basis of detailed cross-tabulations of census data.

Major Industry Groups

Table 13-9 provides data about long-term trends in industrial composition of the employed civilian labor force. Table 13-10 reports the industrial composition of the United States as detailed in the 1980 census. Figure 13-3 traces the long-term trends in industrial composition from 1900 to the 1980s. There are two facets to the industrial transformation that the American economy has undergone. The first is the shift from a predominantly agricultural to a nonagricultural economy. In 1860 nearly 60 percent of the labor force was employed in agriculture. The cross-over point at which nonagricultural workers outnumbered agricultural came about in 1880. By the start of the present century, more

Table 13-7. Occupational Composition of Employed Civilian Labor Force of Regions, by Inside and Outside of SMSA and Sex: 1980 [percent distribution]

Sex and Occupation	Regional total				Inside SMSAs				Outside SMSAs			
	North-east	North Central	South	West	North-east	North Central	South	West	North-east	North Central	South	West
Total employed, both sexes	100.0	100.0	100.0	100.0	100.0	100.0	100.0	100.0	100.0	100.0	100.0	100.0
Managerial and professional specialty occupations	24.4	21.3	21.5	24.6	25.0	22.7	23.6	25.3	20.8	17.4	16.6	21.0
Executive, administrative and managerial occupations	10.7	9.6	10.0	11.6	11.1	10.4	11.2	12.0	8.5	7.6	7.3	9.4
Professional specialty occupations	13.7	11.7	11.5	13.0	14.0	12.4	12.4	13.2	12.3	9.8	9.3	11.6
Technical, sales and administrative support occupations	31.6	29.2	29.5	31.6	32.6	31.5	32.3	32.7	25.4	23.3	23.1	25.5
Technicians and related support occupations	3.1	2.9	3.0	3.3	3.1	3.2	3.4	3.4	2.7	2.1	2.2	2.5
Sales occupations	9.5	9.7	10.1	10.8	9.7	10.1	10.8	11.0	8.4	8.5	8.5	9.4
Administrative support occupations, including clerical	19.0	16.7	16.3	17.5	19.8	18.2	18.1	18.3	14.3	12.7	12.4	13.5
Service occupations	12.9	13.3	12.5	13.2	12.8	13.0	12.6	12.9	13.5	14.0	12.3	14.9
Private household occupations	0.5	0.4	0.8	0.5	0.5	0.4	0.8	0.5	0.5	0.5	1.0	0.4
Protective service occupations	1.9	1.3	1.5	1.5	1.9	1.4	1.5	1.4	1.5	1.0	1.3	1.6
Service occupations, except protective and household	10.5	11.5	10.2	11.2	10.4	11.2	10.2	10.9	11.5	12.5	10.1	12.8
Farming, forestry and fishing occupations	1.3	3.8	2.9	3.2	0.9	1.4	1.6	2.3	3.7	10.4	6.2	8.2
Precision production, craft and repair occupations	11.8	12.6	13.9	12.9	11.4	12.3	13.2	12.6	14.2	13.4	15.5	14.5
Operators, fabricators and laborers	17.9	19.8	19.6	14.5	17.2	19.1	16.7	14.2	22.4	21.6	26.3	15.9
Machine operators, assemblers and inspectors	9.9	10.6	9.6	6.4	9.5	10.4	7.7	6.6	12.5	11.1	14.1	5.1
Transportation and material moving occupations	4.0	4.7	5.0	4.1	3.8	4.3	4.4	3.7	5.1	5.5	6.2	5.9
Handlers, equipment cleaners, helpers and laborers	4.0	4.5	5.0	4.0	3.9	4.4	4.6	3.9	4.8	5.0	6.1	4.9
Female												
Total employed	100.0	100.0	100.0	100.0	100.0	100.0	100.0	100.0	100.0	100.0	100.0	100.0
Managerial and professional specialty occupations	22.3	20.3	21.1	22.9	22.6	21.1	22.5	23.1	20.7	17.9	17.8	21.5
Executive, administrative and managerial occupations	6.9	6.5	7.3	9.2	7.1	7.0	8.2	9.4	5.8	5.1	5.2	7.7
Professional specialty occupations	15.4	13.8	13.8	13.7	15.5	14.1	14.3	13.7	14.9	12.8	12.6	13.8
Technical, sales and administrative support occupations	46.5	45.2	44.2	47.4	47.6	47.6	47.3	48.2	39.5	38.2	36.4	43.1
Technicians and related support occupations	3.1	3.1	3.2	3.0	3.1	3.3	3.4	3.1	3.0	2.8	2.0	2.7
Sales occupations	10.3	11.3	11.4	12.0	10.3	11.6	11.8	12.0	10.0	10.4	10.2	12.2
Administrative support occupations, including clerical	33.1	30.8	29.6	32.4	34.1	32.8	32.1	33.2	26.5	25.0	23.5	28.2
Service occupations	16.1	19.5	17.9	17.7	15.5	18.0	17.2	16.7	19.7	23.9	19.6	23.6
Private household occupations	1.1	1.0	1.9	1.2	1.1	0.9	1.7	1.2	1.2	1.3	2.3	1.1
Protective service occupations	0.5	0.4	0.4	0.4	0.5	0.4	0.4	0.4	0.3	0.2	0.3	0.4
Service occupations, except protective and household	14.5	18.1	15.7	16.1	13.9	16.6	15.1	15.1	18.1	22.4	17.1	22.0
Farming, forestry and fishing occupations	0.5	1.3	0.9	1.2	0.3	0.6	0.6	0.9	1.4	3.3	1.7	2.6
Precision production, craft and repair occupations	2.1	2.2	2.5	2.7	2.1	2.1	2.3	2.8	2.3	2.4	2.8	2.0
Operators, fabricators and laborers	12.5	11.6	13.4	8.1	11.9	10.6	10.0	8.3	16.4	14.2	21.6	7.3
Machine operators, assemblers and inspectors	9.7	8.4	10.3	5.5	9.2	7.6	7.3	5.8	12.6	10.5	17.6	4.0
Transportation and material moving occupations	0.7	0.9	0.9	0.8	0.7	0.8	0.8	0.7	1.0	1.0	1.0	1.2
Handlers, equipment cleaners, helpers and laborers	2.1	2.3	2.2	1.8	2.0	2.1	1.9	1.7	2.7	2.7	3.0	2.2

Source: U.S. Bureau of the Census. "General Social and Economic Characteristics: United States Summary." 1980 Census of Population. Washington, DC: U.S. Government Printing Office, 1983, Table 199.

Table 13-8. Occupational Composition of the Employed Labor Force, by Metropolitan-Nonmetropolitan Residence, Race-Ethnicity, and Sex: 1980 [percent distribution]

Sex and occupation	White				Black				Spanish-origin			
	SMSA total	Central city	Metro ring	Outside SMSA	SMSA total	Central city	Metro ring	Outside SMSA	SMSA total	Central city	Metro ring	Outside SMSA
Total employed, both sexes	100.0	100.0	100.0	100.0	100.0	100.0	100.0	100.0	100.0	100.0	100.0	100.0
Managerial and professional specialty occupations	25.5	26.3	25.1	18.7	15.0	14.3	16.6	9.4	12.2	11.6	13.4	10.7
Executive, administrative and managerial occupations	12.0	11.8	12.1	8.3	5.7	5.4	6.5	2.6	5.9	5.5	6.8	4.7
Professional specialty occupations	13.5	14.5	13.0	10.4	9.3	8.9	10.1	6.9	6.3	6.1	6.7	5.9
Technical, sales and administrative support occupations	33.1	34.5	32.4	24.8	27.9	28.3	26.9	11.6	24.5	25.3	24.9	18.8
Technicians and related support occupations	3.3	3.4	3.3	2.3	2.9	2.8	3.1	1.5	2.1	2.0	2.2	1.8
Sales occupations	11.2	11.3	11.2	9.1	5.4	5.4	5.4	3.0	7.2	7.2	7.4	6.6
Administrative support occupations, including clerical	18.6	19.8	18.0	13.4	19.6	20.2	18.3	7.1	15.2	16.2	15.3	10.4
Service occupations	11.4	12.3	10.9	12.4	23.1	24.0	20.9	23.3	16.3	17.6	14.2	17.9
Private household occupations	0.3	0.4	0.3	0.5	2.3	2.3	2.3	4.0	1.0	1.1	0.9	1.1
Protective service occupations	1.6	1.7	1.5	1.3	2.1	2.1	1.9	1.1	1.2	1.2	1.1	1.3
Service occupations, except protective and household	9.5	10.2	9.1	10.7	18.7	19.6	16.8	18.2	14.1	15.2	12.2	15.5
Farming, forestry and fishing occupations	1.5	0.7	1.8	7.4	1.1	0.7	1.9	6.5	4.7	2.1	6.1	11.2
Precision production, craft and repair occupations	12.9	11.4	13.7	14.9	8.7	8.5	9.3	10.0	14.0	13.7	14.1	15.0
Operators, fabricators and laborers	15.6	14.7	16.0	21.7	24.2	24.1	24.4	39.2	28.4	29.7	27.2	26.5
Machine operators, assemblers and inspectors	7.9	7.4	8.1	11.0	11.8	11.6	12.0	22.1	16.0	17.5	15.5	10.7
Transportation and material moving occupations	3.9	3.5	4.1	5.7	5.9	5.9	5.9	6.8	4.8	4.5	4.6	6.7
Handlers, equipment cleaners, helpers and laborers	3.8	3.8	3.9	5.0	6.6	6.6	6.5	10.3	7.6	7.7	7.1	9.1
Female												
Total employed	100.0	100.0	100.0	100.0	100.0	100.0	100.0	100.0	100.0	100.0	100.0	100.0
Managerial and professional specialty occupations	23.3	24.4	22.7	19.3	17.3	16.7	18.8	12.4	12.5	12.0	13.2	12.3
Executive, administrative and managerial occupations	8.4	8.9	8.1	5.9	5.2	5.0	5.7	2.1	4.9	4.6	5.4	4.2
Professional specialty occupations	14.9	15.5	14.6	13.4	12.1	11.7	13.1	10.3	7.6	7.4	7.8	8.1
Technical, sales and administrative support occupations	49.5	49.4	49.5	40.3	38.6	39.0	37.7	17.1	38.9	38.8	40.2	34.4
Technicians and related support occupations	3.2	3.3	3.1	2.8	3.6	3.5	3.8	2.0	2.1	2.1	2.1	2.2
Sales occupations	12.3	11.9	12.5	11.1	6.4	6.5	6.3	4.3	9.4	9.1	9.5	10.1
Administrative support occupations, including clerical	34.0	34.2	33.9	26.3	28.6	29.0	27.6	10.8	27.5	27.6	28.6	22.2
Service occupations	15.1	15.1	15.1	20.1	28.3	29.1	26.4	34.5	20.8	20.4	18.8	30.7
Private household occupations	0.8	0.8	0.7	1.1	4.4	4.4	4.4	8.2	2.4	2.6	2.1	2.9
Protective service occupations	0.4	0.4	0.4	0.3	0.7	0.8	0.6	0.3	0.3	0.4	0.3	0.3
Service occupations, except protective and household	13.9	13.8	14.0	18.7	23.2	23.9	21.4	26.0	18.0	17.4	16.4	27.4
Farming, forestry and fishing occupations	0.6	0.3	0.7	2.3	0.3	0.2	0.6	1.8	1.8	0.8	2.7	3.6
Precision production, craft and repair occupations	2.2	2.2	2.2	2.5	2.2	2.2	2.3	3.0	3.9	4.1	4.0	2.5
Operators, fabricators and laborers	9.3	8.6	9.7	15.5	13.3	12.9	14.2	31.1	22.0	23.9	21.0	16.4
Machine operators, assemblers and inspectors	6.8	6.4	7.0	11.9	9.8	9.5	10.6	25.2	17.4	19.3	16.3	11.9
Transportation and material moving occupations	0.8	0.6	0.5	1.0	0.9	0.8	1.0	1.2	0.7	0.6	0.8	1.0
Handlers, equipment cleaners, helpers and laborers	1.8	1.6	1.2	2.6	2.5	2.5	2.6	4.7	3.9	3.9	3.9	3.5

Source: U.S. Bureau of the Census. "General Social and Economic Characteristics: United States Summary." 1980 Census of Population. Washington, DC: U.S. Government Printing Office, 1983, Tables 145 and 155.

than one-third of the work force was still in agriculture. By 1980 the agricultural work force had shrunk to less than 4 percent of the total. Table 13-9 shows the rapid decline in the agricultural sector during this century.

The second facet of industrial compositional change has been the changing "mix" of industries within the nonagricultural sector. The right-hand panel of Table 13-9[2] and Figure 13-3 illustrate this remarkable change.

1. Early in this century, manufacturing dominated the nonagricultural sector, constituting almost 40 percent. Although employment in manufacturing has continued to grow, it has grown more slowly than the labor force as a whole, and hence constitutes a smaller share. In the late 1960s the size of the manufacturing labor force plateaued at about 20 million persons, which has held fairly steady to 1983, declining during economic recessions and recovering during more properous times. In 1983 manufacturing is only slightly more than 20 percent of all nonagricultural employment.

2. Since 1960 manufacturing has been replaced by "tertiary" industries involving finance, insurance, services (except domestic), and government. The 1970-80 decade appears to have continued these trends with a few modifications:

a. There was expansion of growth in the business service, professional service, and educational and recreational service sectors. Automobile services also grew rapidly in comparison with the average national rate.

b. Manufacturing was stagnant, growing at only one-fifth the national rate.

c. Retail trade, wholesale trade, construction, and

Table 13-9. Trends in Industrial Composition of the Employed Civilian Labor Force: 1900-1982

Year	Total employed[a]	Agricultural	Nonagricultural	Percent nonagricultural	Percent distribution by industry of nonagricultural workers										
					Mining	Construction	Manufacturing: Total	Manufacturing: Durable goods	Manufacturing: Nondurable goods	Transportation and utilities	Wholesale	Retail trade	Finance, insurance and real estate	Services	Government total
1982	99,526	3,401	96,125	96.6	1.3	4.4	21.0	12.4	8.7	5.7	5.9	16.9	6.0	21.3	17.6
1980	99,303	3,364	95,938	96.6	1.1	4.8	22.4	13.5	9.0	5.7	5.8	16.6	5.7	19.8	18.0
1975	85,846	3,408	82,438	96.0	1.0	4.6	23.8	13.9	9.9	5.9	5.7	16.4	5.4	18.1	19.1
1970	78,678	3,463	75,215	95.6	0.9	5.1	27.3	15.8	11.5	6.4	5.6	15.6	5.1	16.3	17.7
1965	71,088	4,361	66,726	93.9	1.0	5.3	29.7	17.1	12.6	6.6	5.7	15.2	4.9	14.9	16.6
1960	65,778	5,458	60,318	91.7	1.3	5.4	31.0	17.5	13.5	7.4	5.8	15.2	4.9	13.6	15.4
1955	62,170	6,450	55,722	89.6	1.5	5.6	33.3	18.8	14.5	8.2	5.8	15.0	4.5	12.3	13.7
1950	58,918	7,160	51,758	87.8	2.0	5.2	33.7	17.9	15.8	8.9	5.8	14.9	4.2	11.9	13.3
1940[b]	47,520	8,449	36,621	81.3	2.9	4.1	33.9	16.6	17.4	9.4	5.7	15.2	4.6	11.3	13.0
1930[b]	44,183	10,472[c]	38,358[c]	78.6	3.4	4.7	32.5	--	--	12.5	19.7		5.0	11.4	10.7
1920[b]	39,208	10,666[c]	30,948[c]	74.4	4.5	3.2	39.0	--	--	14.6	16.3		4.2	8.6	9.5
1910[b]	34,559	12,388[c]	25,779[c]	67.5	4.9	6.2	36.1	--	--	15.5	16.5		2.0	11.1	7.5
1900[b]	26,956	10,382[c]	18,691[c]	64.3	4.2	7.6	36.0	--	--	15.0	16.5		2.0	11.5	7.2

[a]Data for total employed for 1940 and prior years are designed to be comparable with the Current Population Survey and hence are not consistent with census counts, especially for 1940. (See Historical Statistics of the United States, page 126).

[b]Data are from decennial censuses.

[c]Data are for gainful workers.

Note: -- indicates data not available.

Source: Data for total, agricultural, and nonagricultural employment from U.S. Bureau of the Census. Historical Statistics of the United States (pages 126-127). Also, Statisticsl Abstract of the United States, 1984 (page 405). Washington, DC: U.S. Government Printing Office, 1975 and 1983. Distribution by industru from U.S. Bureau of Labor Statistics. Handbook of Labor Statistics. Washington, DC: U.S. Government Printing Office, 1983, Table 67. Also, from U.S. Bureau of the Census. Historical Statistics of the United States (page 137).

public services were stable, growing at rates close to the national average.

d. Sharp declines were registered in agriculture, mining, private household personal services, and employment in education. The declines were especially severe in the elementary and secondary educational levels, as the baby bust babies replaced the baby boom babies. (This decline has hit the colleges and universities in the 1980s.)

3. The economic recession of the 1980s has caused the volume of employment to become practically stationary. Meanwhile, the manufacturing industry has lost ground even faster than before, with the shift to the "growth industries" listed above continuing unabated. Disproportionate growth in the retail trade industry probably is temporary and may be a concomitant of the economic recession: As persons are unable to find employment, they attempt to create employment by going into retail activities. Recovery from the recession will bring some recovery to manufacturing, but less than to the other nonagricultural industries.

Race-Ethnicity and Industry of Employment

Unlike occupations, the race-ethnicity groups tend to have very similar industrial composition (see Table 13-10). The Spanish-origin population deviates more from the average than does the black population (excess

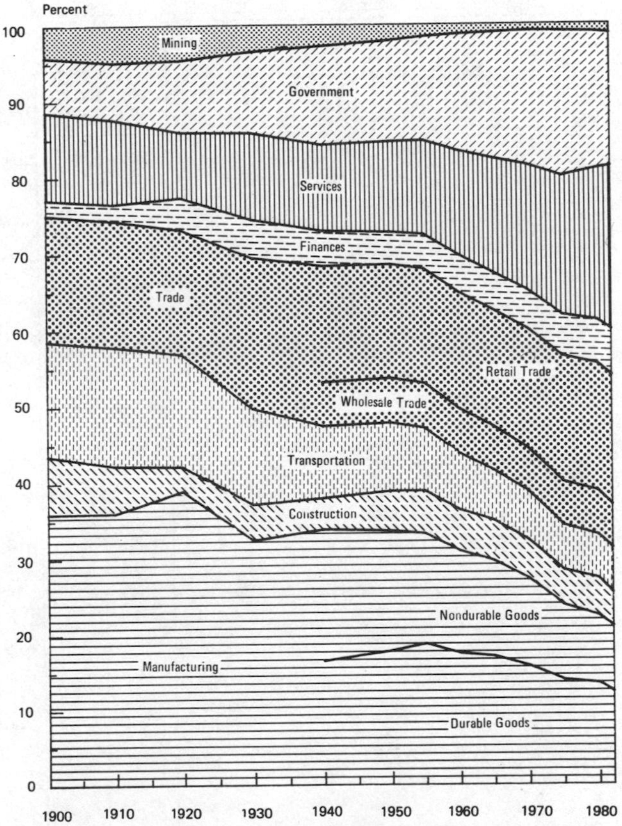

Figure 13-3. Historical Trend of Industrial Composition of the Nonagricultural Sector: 1900-1983 [based on employees on nonagricultural payrolls]

Table 13-10. Industry of the Employed Labor Force, by Sex and Race-Ethnicity: 1980, and Percent Change, 1970-1980

Industry	Percent distribution, 1980				Percent composition, 1980			Percent change, 1970-80		
	Total	White	Black	Spanish-origin	Percent black	Percent Spanish	Percent female	Total	Black	Female
Total employed	100.0	100.0	100.0	100.0	9.6	5.6	42.6	27.5	26.8	43.9
Agriculture, forestry and fisheries	3.0	3.0	1.7	4.8	5.5	9.0	17.9	2.7	-38.7	64.1
Mining	1.1	1.1	0.5	0.5	4.1	5.7	12.1	70.3	90.9	146.7
Construction	5.9	6.1	4.3	6.4	7.0	6.1	8.4	25.5	2.9	79.5
Manufacturing	22.4	22.3	23.2	27.1	9.9	6.8	31.9	10.3	20.8	23.5
Nondurable goods	8.6	8.4	10.1	11.6	11.1	7.5	41.4	5.6	26.4	11.7
Durable goods	13.8	13.9	13.1	15.5	9.1	6.3	26.0	13.5	16.8	38.1
Transportation, communication, public utilities	7.3	7.1	8.9	6.4	11.7	4.9	24.7	19.5	28.8	38.7
Wholesale and retail trade	20.4	21.2	13.9	19.8	6.5	5.4	45.8	29.6	27.4	44.2
Wholesale trade	4.3	4.5	2.8	4.3	6.2	5.5	26.9	24.4	--	45.9
Retail trade	16.1	16.7	11.1	15.5	6.6	5.4	50.9	31.1	--	44.0
Finance, insurance and real estate	6.0	6.2	4.8	4.8	7.6	4.4	58.0	53.3	101.5	78.0
Business and repair services	4.2	4.2	3.6	4.4	8.3	5.9	33.8	63.5	72.2	95.1
Personal services	3.2	2.8	6.1	4.6[a]	18.6	8.1	70.4	-11.3	-41.6	-13.5
Entertainment and recreation services	1.0	1.1	0.8	1.0	7.6	5.4	40.4	59.4	45.6	81.3
Professional and related services	20.3	19.9	24.6	15.1	11.6	4.2	66.3	48.6	62.2	55.2
Public administration	5.3	5.0	7.5	4.7	13.6	4.9	40.8	43.4	93.7	74.1

[a]Private services and other personal services.

Note: -- indicates data not available.

Source: U.S. Bureau of the Census. "General Social and Economic Characteristics: United States Summary." 1980 Census of Population. Washington, DC: U.S. Government Printing Office, 1983, Tables 90 and 136.

Table 13-11. Industry of the Employed Labor Force, by Sex and Race-Ethnicity: Inside and Outside SMSAs, 1980

Industry	White				Black				Spanish-origin			
	SMSA total	Central city	Metro ring	Outside SMSA	SMSA total	Central city	Metro ring	Outside SMSA	SMSA total	Central city	Metro ring	Outside SMSA
Total employed, both sexes	100.0	100.0	100.0	100.0	100.0	100.0	100.0	100.0	100.0	100.0	100.0	100.0
Agriculture, forestry and fisheries	1.6	0.8	2.0	7.7	0.9	0.5	1.8	6.0	3.9	2.0	6.4	12.1
Mining	0.7	0.7	0.6	2.6	0.3	0.3	0.4	1.0	0.5	0.5	0.5	5.5
Construction	5.8	5.1	6.2	6.9	4.0	3.8	4.4	6.0	6.2	6.0	6.3	8.1
Manufacturing	22.1	19.3	23.5	22.9	20.9	20.1	22.5	34.8	28.3	28.5	28.1	17.3
Nondurable goods	7.9	7.6	8.1	10.0	8.2	7.7	9.2	19.6	12.0	12.7	11.1	9.0
Durable goods	14.2	11.8	15.4	12.9	12.7	12.4	13.3	15.2	16.3	15.8	17.0	8.3
Transportation, communication, public utilities	7.3	7.2	7.4	6.5	9.7	9.8	9.4	4.8	6.5	6.3	6.8	6.0
Wholesale and retail trade	21.7	22.1	21.5	19.5	14.3	14.6	13.6	11.7	19.9	20.3	19.5	18.4
Wholesale trade	4.8	4.8	4.8	3.5	2.8	2.9	2.7	2.5	4.4	4.3	4.6	2.8
Retail trade	16.9	17.3	16.7	16.0	11.5	11.7	10.9	9.2	15.5	16.0	14.9	15.6
Finance, insurance and real estate	7.0	7.7	6.6	4.0	5.5	5.9	4.7	1.3	5.1	5.4	4.6	2.3
Business and repair services	4.7	5.0	4.6	2.7	4.0	4.2	3.7	1.7	4.6	4.9	4.2	2.9
Personal services[a]	2.8	3.0	2.5	3.0	5.9	6.3	5.2	7.0	4.6	5.0	4.0	4.5
Entertainment and recreation services	1.2	1.4	1.1	0.7	0.9	0.9	0.8	0.5	1.0	1.0	1.1	0.7
Professional and related services	20.2	22.3	19.1	19.0	25.4	25.7	24.8	20.6	14.9	15.3	14.4	16.4
Public administration	5.2	5.5	5.0	4.5	8.2	8.0	8.6	4.4	4.5	4.7	4.2	5.9
Female												
Total employed	100.0	100.0	100.0	100.0	100.0	100.0	100.0	100.0	100.0	100.0	100.0	100.0
Agriculture, forestry and fisheries	0.8	0.4	1.0	2.9	0.3	0.2	0.7	2.2	1.9	1.0	3.0	4.4
Mining	0.3	0.4	0.2	0.4	0.2	0.2	0.2	0.1	0.2	0.3	0.2	0.6
Construction	1.3	1.2	1.4	1.1	0.6	0.5	0.6	0.6	0.8	0.7	0.9	1.0
Manufacturing	15.6	14.1	16.4	19.3	14.7	13.8	16.8	31.8	26.6	27.2	25.8	15.9
Nondurable goods	7.1	7.0	7.2	11.2	6.9	6.4	8.1	22.5	14.4	15.7	12.9	10.7
Durable goods	8.4	7.1	9.2	8.1	7.8	-7.3	8.8	9.3	12.1	11.5	12.9	5.2
Transportation, communication, public utilities	4.4	4.4	4.4	3.1	5.8	5.8	5.8	1.7	4.0	3.6	4.4	2.5
Wholesale and retail trade	23.4	22.8	23.8	22.8	12.9	13.1	12.3	11.4	19.2	18.8	19.8	23.1
Wholesale trade	3.2	3.2	3.2	1.9	1.5	1.5	1.5	1.3	3.2	3.0	3.5	1.6
Retail trade	20.3	19.6	20.6	20.9	11.4	11.6	10.8	10.1	16.0	15.8	16.3	21.5
Finance, insurance and real estate	9.4	10.0	9.1	5.8	7.0	7.4	6.2	1.6	7.4	7.5	7.2	3.9
Business and repair services	3.9	4.2	3.7	1.7	3.1	3.2	3.0	1.1	3.3	3.4	3.1	1.9
Personal services[a]	4.2	4.4	4.1	5.4	9.3	9.6	8.5	12.6	7.4	8.0	6.7	9.0
Entertainment and recreation services	1.1	1.3	1.1	0.7	0.6	0.6	0.6	0.4	0.8	0.7	0.8	0.8
Professional and related services	30.9	31.9	30.3	32.2	36.8	37.1	36.3	32.2	24.0	24.1	23.8	30.3
Public administration	4.7	4.9	4.5	4.5	8.7	8.5	9.1	4.2	4.6	4.7	4.4	6.6

[a]Private households and other personal services.

Source: U.S. Bureau of the Census. "General Social and Economic Characteristics: United States Summary." 1980 Census of Population. Washington, DC: U.S. Government Printing Office, 1983, Tables 146 and 156.

of agriculture workers, deficit of professional workers). Black workers are deficient in wholesale and retail trade, agriculture, mining and construction, with surpluses in public administration, professional services, and personal services.

Industrial Composition of Metropolitan and Nonmetropolitan Areas

Table 13-11 shows that aside from the obvious (but still small) differences linked to agriculture and mining, the industrial compositions of metropolitan and nonmetropolitan areas are very much alike. Metropolitan areas tend to contain a disproportionate larger share of finance, business and repair, entertainment and professional, and related services, but all of these are found in nonmetropolitan areas in only moderately smaller proportions. The black population living in the rings of metropolitan areas or in nonmetropolitan areas tends to be engaged in manufacturing industries, while the Spanish-origin population in such residences tends to be more concentrated in agriculture.

Industrial Composition of Regions, Metropolitan and Nonmetropolitan Areas

The industrial composition of each geographic region is shown in Table 13-12. All regions have essentially the same industrial structure. There are differences in emphasis on manufacturing, agriculture, construction, and professional services, with the South and West somewhat underrepresented in manufacturing and professional services, but with larger proportions in construction, public administration, mining, transportation, and trade.

Table 13-12. Industry of the Employed Labor Force, by Inside and Outside SMSAs for Regions: 1980

Industry	Regional total				Inside SMSAs				Outside SMSAs			
	Northeast	North Central	South	West	Northeast	North Central	South	West	Northeast	North Central	South	West
Total employed, both sexes	100.0	100.0	100.0	100.0	100.0	100.0	100.0	100.0	100.0	100.0	100.0	100.0
Agriculture, forestry and fisheries	1.2	4.0	3.0	3.5	0.9	1.4	1.6	2.5	3.6	10.7	6.3	8.9
Mining	0.3	0.6	1.9	1.1	0.2	0.3	1.2	0.6	1.1	1.3	3.4	4.0
Construction	4.3	4.9	7.4	6.4	4.1	4.5	7.3	6.1	5.6	5.8	7.7	8.0
Manufacturing	25.3	25.9	20.6	17.7	24.8	26.9	18.2	18.8	27.9	23.2	26.2	11.6
Nondurable goods	10.1	7.8	10.3	5.4	10.1	7.7	8.4	5.6	10.4	8.0	14.6	4.3
Durable goods	15.2	18.1	10.3	12.3	14.8	19.3	9.8	13.2	17.5	15.2	11.6	7.3
Transportation, communication, public utilities	7.3	6.9	7.4	7.4	7.5	7.2	7.9	7.4	6.1	6.3	6.2	7.3
Wholesale and retail trade	19.4	20.7	20.4	21.2	19.5	21.1	21.3	21.4	18.3	19.7	18.0	20.5
Wholesale trade	4.2	4.3	4.4	4.3	4.4	4.5	4.7	4.6	2.9	3.8	3.4	3.1
Retail trade	15.1	16.4	16.0	16.9	15.1	16.6	16.6	16.8	15.4	15.9	14.6	17.4
Finance, insurance and real estate	6.9	5.5	5.5	6.8	7.3	6.1	6.4	7.2	4.0	3.8	3.4	4.4
Business and repair services	4.5	3.6	4.0	5.0	4.8	4.0	4.6	5.3	2.8	2.4	2.6	3.4
Personal services[a]	2.7	2.7	3.5	3.7	2.6	2.6	3.6	3.6	3.1	2.9	3.4	4.2
Entertainment and recreation services	1.0	0.8	0.9	1.6	1.1	0.9	1.1	1.6	0.8	0.6	0.6	1.1
Professional and related services	22.0	20.4	19.2	19.9	22.1	20.7	19.9	20.0	21.9	19.7	17.7	19.7
Public administration	5.0	4.1	6.2	5.7	5.0	4.2	6.8	5.5	4.9	3.7	4.6	6.8
Female												
Total employed	100.0	100.0	100.0	100.0	100.0	100.0	100.0	100.0	100.0	100.0	100.0	100.0
Agriculture, forestry and fisheries	0.6	1.5	1.2	1.6	0.4	0.7	0.8	1.3	1.8	3.8	2.2	3.8
Mining	0.1	0.1	0.6	0.3	0.1	0.1	0.6	0.2	0.1	0.2	0.5	0.8
Construction	0.8	1.0	1.4	1.4	0.8	1.0	1.6	1.4	0.7	0.9	1.1	1.6
Manufacturing	19.7	17.1	16.9	12.9	19.4	16.8	13.4	13.9	21.5	17.8	25.4	7.2
Nondurable goods	10.2	6.6	10.6	5.0	10.1	6.2	7.6	5.2	10.9	7.7	17.9	4.1
Durable goods	9.5	10.5	6.3	7.9	9.3	10.6	5.9	8.7	10.6	10.1	7.5	3.1
Transportation, communication, public utilities	4.0	3.9	4.1	4.9	4.2	4.3	4.7	5.1	3.1	2.8	2.8	4.1
Wholesale and retail trade	20.0	23.5	21.6	22.7	19.9	23.6	22.2	22.2	20.6	23.3	20.1	25.6
Wholesale trade	2.8	2.7	2.6	2.9	2.9	2.9	2.9	3.1	1.6	2.0	1.9	1.9
Retail trade	17.2	20.8	19.0	19.8	17.0	20.7	19.3	19.1	19.0	21.3	18.2	23.7
Finance, insurance and real estate	8.8	7.7	7.5	9.4	9.3	8.5	8.6	9.9	5.6	5.5	4.9	6.6
Business and repair services	3.6	2.9	3.0	4.0	3.9	3.4	3.6	4.2	1.7	1.5	1.5	2.4
Personal services[a]	4.0	4.7	6.1	5.7	3.9	4.4	6.0	5.5	5.0	5.6	6.4	7.4
Entertainment and recreation services	0.9	0.8	0.8	1.5	0.9	0.9	1.0	1.5	0.7	0.7	0.5	1.3
Professional and related services	33.0	32.6	30.7	30.1	32.7	32.2	30.9	29.7	34.6	33.9	30.2	32.1
Public administration	4.5	4.1	6.0	5.4	4.5	4.2	6.6	5.1	4.5	3.9	4.5	7.1

[a]Private households and other personal services.

Source: U.S. Bureau of the Census. "General Social and Economic Characteristics: United States Summary." 1980 Census of Population. Washington, DC: U.S. Government Printing Office, 1983, Table 200.

Class of Worker

Class-of-worker classification identifies the source from which the employees receive income or benefits. There are seven categories. The distribution of the employed labor force among these categories and the percentage change 1970-80 are shown in Table 13-13. This table shows that three-fourths of employed persons are private wage and salary workers. An additional one-sixth of the workers are employees of governments (federal, state, or local). Only 7 percent of all workers are self-employed.

Black workers tend to be more concentrated than the white population in government employment and less prevalent as self-employed workers. The Spanish-origin population is underrepresented in government industries and more concentrated in wage and salary work.

The major growth sector between 1970 and 1980 was in government employment, especially at the state and local levels. Females and black workers moved into government work at above-average rates, but not into self-employment.

Conclusion: Future Occupational Composition

It is over-simplistic to assume that the dynamic changes in occupational composition characterizing recent decades will continue with the same differentials and momentum. Alternatively, an equilibrium may be reached between agricultural and nonagricultural sectors, between the manufacturing and nonmanufacturing industries of the nonagricultural sector, and between governmental and nongovernmental employment. The slowdown in the labor force growth (now underway), coupled with the convergence of differentials in labor force participation of the sexes, of the races, and of the age groups, may also have a stabilizing effect on future occupational composition. A possible major problem for the near future will be to find suitable employment (both by occupation and industry) for the labor force that will exist. The phenomenon of chronic high unemployment may continue to shadow large numbers of workers who lack the education and skills to meet the opportunities offered by high technology, or who are victims during their youth of a combination of race, poverty, and low education.

An attempt to foresee the future occupational structure of the U.S. labor force has been made by the Bureau of Labor Statistics. In a report entitled *Occupational Projections and Training Data: 1984 Edition,* the Bureau has estimated the number of persons employed in each of the detailed occupations in the year 1995, with measures of percent change 1982-1995. These projections were made using an economic growth model, which combines assumptions about future productivity of the U.S. economy, the division of this productivity among the industrial sectors, the employment required to fulfill the necessary production in each industry, and the occupational composition of the workers in each of the industries. The future size of the labor force is taken into account. When such a series of unknowns are chained, all of them interacting in ways neither well understood nor easily predictable, the resulting predictions must be viewed with caution.

Table 13-14 presents the projections of the Bureau of Labor Statistics for selected larger occupational groups. (For projections for the individual detailed occupations, the reader should consult the source, which is revised biennially.) The projections support the idea of a trend toward less differentiation in growth rates of occupational categories, but this could be a side-effect of the projection methods. It is plausible that the Bureau's methodology has built-in assumptions about continuation of past trends, so that the amount of stabilization may be underpredicted. Despite their cautions and limitations, these projections contain some startling predictions.

Following is a listing of the twenty occupations predicted to grow at the fastest rate between 1982-95:

Twenty fastest growing occupations, 1982–95	Percent
Computer service technicians	96.8
Legal assistants	94.3
Computer systems analysts	85.3
Computer programmers	76.9
Computer operators	75.8
Office machine repairers	71.7
Physical therapy assistants	67.8
Electrical engineers	65.3
Civil engineering technicians	63.9
Peripheral EDP equipment operators	63.5
Insurance clerks, medical	62.2
Electrical and electronic technicians	60.7
Occupational therapists	59.8
Surveyor helpers	58.6
Credit clerks, banking and insurance	54.1
Physical therapists	53.6
Employment interviewers	52.5
Mechanical engineers	52.1
Mechanical engineering technicians	51.6
Compression and injection mold machine operators, plastics	50.3

The twenty occupations predicted to grow at the slowest rate (decline by the greatest rate), during 1982-95, are as follows:

Twenty most rapidly declining occupations, 1982-95	Percent
Railroad conductors	-32.0
Shoemaking machine operatives	-30.2
Aircraft structure assemblers	-21.0
Central telephone office operators	-20.0
Taxi drivers	-18.9
Postal clerks	-17.9
Private household workers	-16.9
Farm laborers	-15.9
College and university faculty	-15.0
Roustabouts	-14.4
Postmasters and mail superintendents	-13.8
Rotary drill operator helpers	-11.6
Graduate assistants	-11.2
Data entry operators	-10.6
Railroad brake operators	-9.8
Fallers and buckers	-8.7
Stenographers	-7.4
Farm owners and tenants	-7.3
Typesetters and compositors	-7.3
Butchers and meatcutters	-6.3

Close examination of Table 13-14 and the two summaries above leads to the conclusion that many occupations that require high education and special skills will not necessarily offer job security in the future to the extent they have in the past.

Notes

1. Edwards, Alba M. "Preface." *Comparative Occupation Statistics for the United States, 1870 to 1940.* Washington, DC: U.S. Census of Population, 1940, p. xi.

2. The data on industrial composition, shown in Table 13-9, are Bureau of Labor Statistics tabulations of workers on nonagricultural payrolls, used because the census enumerations before 1940 employed definitions not consistent with the present classifications. Because the payroll data are known to be incomplete, especially for early years, the trends are roughly, not precisely, indicative of long-term shifts in the nonagricultural sectors of the economy.

Bibliography

Blau, Peter M., and Ducan, Otis Dudley. *The American Occupational Structure.* New York: The Free Press, 1978.

Bureau of Labor Statistics. *Occupational Employment Patterns for 1960 and 1975.* Washington, DC: U.S. Government Printing Office, 1968.

Choldin, H.M., and Hanson, C. "Status Shifts within the City." *American Sociological Review* 47 (1982): 129-41.

Conroy, M.E. "Concept and Measurement of Regional Industrial Diversification." *Southern Economic Journal* 41 (1975):492-505.

Curry, L. "Division of Labor from Geographical Competition." *Association of American Geographers Annual* 71 (1981):133-65.

Duncan, Otis Dudley. "The Trend of Occupational Mobility in the United States." *American Sociological Review* 30 (1965): 491-98.

Table 13-13. Class of Worker of the Employed Labor Force, by Sex and Race-Ethnicity: 1980, and Percent Change, 1970-1980

Class of worker	Percent distribution, 1980				Percent composition, 1980			Percent change, 1970-80		
	Total	White	Black	Spanish-origin	Percent black	Percent Spanish	Percent female	Total	Black	Female
Total employed, 16 years+	100.0	100.0	100.0	100.0	9.6	5.6	32.0	27.5	26.8	43.9
Private wage and salary workers	75.5	76.0	70.3	80.9	8.9	6.0	42.3	27.4	18.4	42.2
Federal government workers	3.9	3.4	7.4	3.7	18.4	5.3	39.4	14.5	30.9	36.4
State government workers	4.6	4.3	6.6	3.4	13.8	4.1	52.8	48.3	102.0	66.6
Local government workers	8.7	8.2	13.1	8.0	14.4	5.2	55.5	40.4	68.6	50.1
Self-employed workers	6.8	7.5	2.4	3.8	3.4	3.1	22.9	13.0	-8.1	44.1
In agriculture	1.3	1.5	0.3	0.4	1.9	1.7	10.6	-11.6	-53.3	76.4
Unpaid family workers	0.5	0.6	0.1	0.3	2.5	3.1	68.6	23.6	1.8	20.1
In agriculture	0.1	0.2	*	*	1.8	1.4	49.5	29.6	-43.7	49.3

Note: * indicates less than 0.1.

Source: U.S. Bureau of the Census. "General Social and Economic Characteristics: United States Summary." 1980 Census of Population. Washington, DC: U.S. Government Printing Office, 1983, Tables 90 and 134.

Table 13-14. Projected Civilian Employment in Selected Occupations: 1995, and Percent Change, 1982-1995

Occupation	Number of workers 1982	Number of workers 1995	Percent distribution[a] 1982	Percent distribution[a] 1995	Percent change 1982-95 Rate	Percent change 1982-95 Ratio to nation
Total, all occupations	101,510.1	127,109.8	100.0	100.0	25.2	1.00
Professional, technical and related workers	16,583.9	21,775.0	16.3	17.1	31.3	1.24
Engineers	1,204.3	1,788.4	1.2	1.4	48.5	1.92
Life and physical sciences	271.0	341.7	0.3	0.3	26.1	1.04
Engineering and science technicians	1,243.3	1,660.8	1.2	1.3	33.6	1.33
Medical workers, except technicians	2,463.5	3,491.1	2.4	2.7	41.7	1.65
Health technologists and technicians	627.4	897.9	0.6	0.7	43.1	1.71
Technicians, except health, science, and engineering	364.3	453.1	0.4	0.4	24.4	0.97
Computer specialists	520.8	942.8	0.5	0.7	81.0	3.21
Social scientists	205.6	266.7	0.2	0.2	29.7	1.18
Teachers	3,980.0	4,706.1	3.9	3.7	18.2	0.72
College and university faculty	744.0	632.5	0.7	0.5	-15.0	...
Elementary, preschool, kindergarten	1,647.0	2,274.3	1.6	1.8	38.1	1.51
Secondary school teachers	1,024.1	1,152.2	1.0	0.9	12.5	0.50
Managers, officials and proprietors	9,532.2	12,212.4	9.4	9.6	28.1	1.12
Sales workers	6,966.7	8,771.5	6.9	6.9	25.9	1.03
Clerical workers	19,048.9	23,998.3	18.8	18.9	26.0	1.03
Craft and related workers	11,591.0	14,769.0	11.4	11.6	27.4	1.09
Construction craft workers	2,894.9	3,777.0	2.9	3.0	30.5	1.21
Mechanics, repairers and installers	3,936.0	5,107.5	3.9	4.0	29.8	1.18
Metalworking craft workers, except mechanics	817.5	1,018.8	0.8	0.8	24.6	0.98
Operatives	12,995.3	15,419.5	12.8	12.1	18.7	0.74
Assembler occupations	1,313.4	1,645.7	1.3	1.3	25.3	1.00
Metalworking operatives	1,492.2	1,812.5	1.5	1.4	21.5	0.85
Laundering, dry cleaning, and press machine operators	307.3	337.8	0.3	0.3	9.9	0.39
Mine operatives	214.8	211.4	0.2	0.2	-1.6	...
Packing and inspecting operatives	843.6	933.9	0.8	0.7	10.7	0.42
Painters, production	101.2	118.8	0.1	0.1	17.4	0.69
Sewers and stitchers	803.7	882.1	0.8	0.7	9.8	0.39
Textile operatives	312.3	351.5	0.3	0.3	12.6	0.50
Transport equipment operatives	3,551.2	4,286.9	3.5	3.4	20.7	0.82
Bus drivers	473.0	551.2	0.5	0.4	16.5	0.65
Industrial truck operators	385.1	455.1	0.4	0.4	18.2	0.72
Truck driving occupations	2,401.5	2,979.5	2.4	2.3	24.1	0.96
Fuel pump attendants and lubricators	388.3	451.0	0.4	0.4	16.1	0.64
Service workers	16,240.7	20,705.8	16.0	16.3	27.5	1.09
Building custodians	2,827.7	3,606.4	2.8	2.8	27.5	1.09
Food service workers	6,203.7	8,220.6	6.1	6.5	32.5	1.29
Selected health service workers	2,240.1	3,065.9	2.2	2.4	36.9	1.46
Selected personal service workers	1,632.1	1,960.6	1.6	1.5	20.1	0.80
Protective service workers	1,706.7	2,146.4	1.7	1.7	25.8	1.02
Private household workers	1,022.8	850.3	1.0	0.7	-16.9	...
Laborers, except farm	5,860.5	7,051.6	5.8	5.5	20.3	0.81
Construction laborers	255.1	298.7	0.3	0.2	17.1	0.68
Gardeners, groundskeepers, except farm	661.3	744.1	0.7	0.6	12.5	0.50
Helpers, trades	608.2	798.1	0.6	0.6	31.2	1.24
Stock handlers	962.5	1,150.4	0.9	0.9	19.5	0.77
Farmers and farm workers	2,690.9	2,406.7	2.7	1.9	-10.6	...
Farmers and farm managers	1,447.7	1,356.7	1.4	1.1	-6.3	...
Farm supervisors and laborers	1,243.2	1,050.0	1.2	0.8	-15.5	...

[a]Figures represent the percent which each subgroup comprises of the total. Because of duplications and omissions, the data do not sum to 100.0 percent.

Source: U.S. Bureau of Labor Statistics. Occupational Projections and Training Data, 1984. Washington, DC: U.S. Government Printing Office, 1984, pp. 80-91.

Featherman, David L., and Hauser, Robert M. *Opportunity and Change.* New York: Academic Press, 1978.

Fossett, M., and Swicegood, G. "Rediscovering City Differences in Racial Occupational Inequality." *American Sociological Review* 47 (1982): 681-89.

Fullerton, H.N. "The 1995 Labor Force: A First Look." *Monthly Labor Review* 103 (1980): 11-21.

Gory, M. la, and Magnani, R.J. "Structural Correlates of Black-White Occupational Differentiation: Will U.S. Regional Differences in Status Remain?" *Social Problems* 27 (1979): 157-69.

Hauser, Robert M. *The Process of Stratification: Trend and Analysis.* New York: Academic Press, 1977.

Hauser, Robert M. et al. *Social Structure and Behavior: Essays in Honor of William Hamilton Sweell.* New York: Academic Press, 1982.

Hodge, Robert W. "Perspectives on Occupational Mobility." Ph.D. thesis, University of Chicago, Department of Sociology, 1967.

Hodge, Robert and Duncan, Otis Dudley. "Educational and Occupational Mobility: A Regression Analysis." *American Journal of Sociology* 68 (1963): 629-44.

Hyman, D.N., and Fearn, R.M. "Influence of City Size on Labor Economics." *Quarterly Review of Economics and Business* 18 (1978): 63-73.

Jaffe,A.J., and Carleton, R.O. *Occupational Mobility in the United States, 1930-1960.* New York: King's Crown Press, Columbia University, 1954.

Kasarda, John. "The Changing Occupational Structure of the American Metropolis." In *The Changing Face of the Suburbs.* Barry Schwartz (ed.). Chicago: University of Chicago Press, 1976.

King, P.E. "Mobility of Manufacturing and the Interstate Redistribution of Employment." *Professional Geography* 27 (1975): 441-48.

Landecker, Werner S. *Class Crystallization.* New Brunswick, NJ: Rutgers University Press, 1981.

Lonsdale, Richard E., and Seyler, H.L. (eds.). *Nonmetropolitan Industrialization.* Washington, DC: Winston and Sons, 1979.

McKenzie, R.B. "Myths of Sunbelt and Frostbelt." *Policy Review* 20 (1982): 103-14.

Mickens, A. "Regional Defense Demand and Racial Response Differences in the Net Migration of Workers." *Quarterly Review of Economics and Business* 17 (1977): 65-82.

Morgan, B.S. "Occupational Segregation in Metropolitan Areas in the U.S., 1970." *Urban Studies* 17 (1980): 63-69.

National Research Council, Committee on Occupational Classification and Analysis (edited by Ann R. Miller et al.). *Work Jobs and Occupations: A Critical Review of the Dictionary of Occupational Titles.* Washington, DC: National Academy Press, 1980.

Newman, R.J. "Industry Migration and Growth in the South." *Review of Economics and Statistics* 65 (1983): 76-86.

Parnes, Herbert S. *Research in Labor Mobility: An Appraisal of Research Findings in the United States.* New York: Social Science Research Council, 1954.

Personnick, V.A. "Outlook for industry Output and Employment through 1990." *Monthly Labor ReView* 104 (1981): 28-41.

Pullum, Thomas. *Measuring Occupational Inheritance.* New York: Elsivere Press, 1975.

Rodriguez, O. "Occupational Shifts and Educational Upgrading in the American Labor Force Between 1950 and 1970." *Sociology of Education* 51 (1978): 55-67.

Scott, A.J. "Production System Dynamics and Metropolitan Development." *Association of American Geographers Annual* 72 (1982): 185-200.

Sell, R.R. "Research Note on the Demography of Occupational Relocation." *Social Forces* 60 (1982): 859-65.

Serow, W.J. "Alternative Demographic Futures and the Composition of the Demand for Labor, by Industry and by Occupation." *Research in Population Economics* 3 (1981): 209-23.

Siegel, Paul M. *Prestige in the American Occupational Structure.* Chicago: University of Chicago Press, 1971.

Singelmann, J., and Browning, H.L. "Industrial Transformation and Occupational Change in the U.S., 1960-1970." *Social Forces* 59 (1980): 246-64.

Spilerman, S., and Miller, R.E. "City Nondifferences Revisited." *American Sociological Review* 42 (1977): 979-83.

Stolzenberg, R.M., and D'Amico, R.J. "City Differences and Nondifferences in the Effect of Race and Sex on Occupational Distribution." *American Sociological Review* 42 (1977): 937-50.

U.S. Bureau of the Census (Littman, Mark S.). "Social and Economic Characteristics of the Metropolitan and Nonmetropolitan Population: 1977 and 1970." *Current Population Reports* (Series P-23, no. 75). Washington, DC: U.S. Government Printing Office, 1978.

U.S. Department of Labor (Goldstein, Harvey A.). *Occupational Employment Projections for Labor Market Areas: An Alternative Approaches.* Washington, DC: U.S. Government Printing Office, 1981.

Zuiches, James J. *Economic Function and Population Change in Nonmetropolitan Cities.* Madison, WI: University of Wisconsin, 1973.

Chapter 14

Income

Income as a Measure of Economic Wellbeing

Money income is a sensitive measure of economic wellbeing in the United States as in all technologically advanced nations. Despite exceptions for specific persons or families, on the average, income received is expended in a more or less patterned way to provide for current and prospective future needs. Income distribution is, therefore, the most adequate measure available of economic status.

In the years 1978 and 1979 the nation's population enjoyed a higher level of living than at any time in its history. Few nations in the world matched it with respect to average level of material comforts. In its *World Development Report* for 1984,[1] the World Bank estimated the per capita gross national product of the wealthiest nations in 1982, as follows:

Country	Per capita GNP
United Arab Emirates	$23,770
Kuwait	19,870
Switzerland	17,010
Saudi Arabia	16,000
Norway	14,280
Sweden	14,040
UNITED STATES	13,160
Denmark	12,470
Germany, Federal Republic	12,460
France	11,680
Canada	11,320
Australia	11,140
Netherlands	10,930
Finland	10,870
Belgium	10,760
Japan	10,080
Austria	9,880
United Kingdom	9,660
Libya	8,510
New Zealand	7,920
Italy	6,840
Trinidad and Tobago	6,840
Oman	6,090
Singapore	5,910
Spain	5,430
Hong Kong	5,340
Ireland	5,150
Israel	5,090
Greece	4,290
Venezuela	4,140

Definitions

Income. Total money receipts during the preceding calendar year from the following sources: (1) money wages or salary; (2) net income from nonfarm self-employment; (3) net income from farm self-employment; (4) Social Security or railroad retirement; (5) Supplemental Security income; (6) public assistance or welfare payments; (7) interest on savings or other investments that pay interest; (8) dividends, income from estates or trusts, or net rental income; (9) veterans payments or unemployment and workers' compensation; (10) private pensions or government employee pensions; and (11) annuities, alimony, or child support, regular contributions from persons not living in the household, and other periodic income. "Income" covers money receipts before personal income taxes, Social Security, union dues, Medicare deductions, and so forth. It does not cover noncash benefits such as food stamps, health benefits, subsidized housing, rent-free housing, and goods produced and consumed in the household.

Income Year. The twelve-month interval for which the respondent is asked to report income. In most cases this refers to the calendar year preceding the survey.

Total Money Income. The algebraic sum of money received from all of the above-listed sources.

Individual Income. Total money income received by persons aged fifteen years or older.

Household Income. The algebraic sum of total money income received by all income recipients in the household (see definitions for Chapter 11).

Family Income. The algebraic sum of the total money income received by all income recipients in the family (see definitions for Chapter 11).

Unrelated Individuals Income. The total money income received by persons classed as unrelated individuals (see definitions for Chapter 11).

Zero or Negative Income. The income tabulations for families and unrelated individuals included in the lowest income group (under $2,500), those who were classified as having no income in the income year, and those reporting a loss in net income from farm and nonfarm self-employment or in rental income.

Government Transfer Payments. The sum of income from the following sources: Social Security or railroad retirement; public assistance or welfare payments; Supplemental Security income; retirement and annuities paid from government funds; veterans payments; and unemployment and worker's compensation.

Receipts Not Counted as Income. (1) Money received from the sale of property such as stocks, bonds, house, or car, unless the person was engaged in the business of selling such property, in which case the net proceeds would be counted as income from self-employment. (2) Withdrawals of bank deposits. (3) Money borrowed. (4) Tax refunds. (5) Gifts. (6) Lump-sum inheritance or insurance payments.

Median Income. The amount that divides income distribution into two equal groups, one having incomes above the median and the other having incomes below the median. The medians for households, families, and unrelated individuals are based on all households, all families, and all unrelated individuals. The medians for persons are based on persons with income.

Mean Income. The amount obtained by dividing the total aggregate income of a group by the number of units in that group. The means for households, families, and unrelated individuals are based on all households, families, and unrelated individuals. The means for persons are based on persons with income.

Per Capita Income. The mean income computed for every man, woman, and child in a particular group. It is derived by dividing the total aggregate income of a group by the total population (excluding patients or inmates in institutional quarters) in that group.

Income Concentration (Income Inequality). The extent to which income is differentially distributed in such a way that a comparatively small proportion of the population receives a disproportionately large share of the income.

Gini Index. One of several indexes designed to measure income concentration. It varies from 0 to 1. A measure of 1 indicates perfect equality of distribution (all persons having equal shares of the wealth). An index of 0 indicates perfect inequality, with all wealth concentrated in a single person.

If per capita gross national product is accepted as a rough substitute for per capita income, then the United States is the seventh wealthiest nation in the world. If the comparison is confined to nations with industrial market economies, the United States ranks fourth. By way of comparison, following are the 1982 per capita gross national product data for the fifteen poorest countries:

Country	Per capita gross national product
Chad	80
Bangladesh	140
Ethiopia	140
Nepal	170
Mali	180
Burma	190
Zaire	190
Malawi	210
Upper Volta	210
Uganda	230
India	260
Rwanda	260
Burundi	280
Tanzania	280
Somalia	290

According to this indicator the average American is 51 times as wealthy as an average citizen of India and almost 100 times as wealthy as a citizen of Bangladesh.

A valuable statistical series, permitting one to trace changes in the level of economic wellbeing in the United States population, is the annual per capita estimate of disposable personal income prepared by the U.S. Department of Commerce in collaboration with other government agencies and with private research organizations.[2] This estimate is a measure of the number of dollars each inhabitant, on the average, can spend to satisfy his or her material needs and wants. The changing level of economic wellbeing may be traced in the following estimates of per capita disposable income for selected years, 1929 to 1982:

Year	Constant dollars (1982)
1982	9,377
1981	9,417
1980	9,212
1979	9,263
1978	9,117
1975	8,316
1970	7,524
1965	6,510
1960	5,562
1955	5,290
1950	4,898
1945	4,833
1940	3,700
1933	2,592
1929	3,534

These figures illustrate the extent to which prosperity increased after World War II; they show that in 1982, after all taxes had been paid, each man, woman, and child in the nation had $9,377 to spend for self-maintenance, education, recreation, and other goods and services. This is 3.6 times the amount the average person had during the Depression year 1933; it is 2.7 times the average amount available in 1929, the year with the all-time record for prosperity before the economic depression of 1930 to 1939. It is 90 percent more than at the close of World War II. These data reflect a real change in the purchasing power of the American public, since the adjustment of the data has taken into account changing price levels. By present-day standards, all but a small fraction of today's elderly were almost paupers in their youth.

The statistics presented show that actual purchasing power declined between 1979 and 1981—the result of the 1980-82 recession.

Income Distribution

The economic wellbeing of the population cannot be measured exclusively in terms of the average income available per citizen, however. The *distribution* of the income must also be discovered. Beginning in the mid-1940s the Bureau of the Census began to collect statistics concerning the income received from all sources by individuals, and it is these data that provide detailed information about the income distribution. The questions asked are illustrated in questions 32 and 33 in the 1980 census questionnaire (Technical Appendix 1-1). The Definition Box explains the concepts and terms employed in tabulating and reporting the results. Similar questions were included in the censuses of 1950, 1960, and 1970 and in the annual *Current Population Reports.*[3] As a consequence income data for individual earners are available on a very detailed scale decenially and on a sample basis annually.

Not included as income in these inquiries is the value of food produced and consumed in the home, the economic benefits of home ownership, and the consumption of funds from savings, borrowed money, tax refunds, gifts, or lump-sum inheritances, and insurance benefits. Also not included are goods and services provided gratis or at subsidized prices through social welfare programs for low-income persons: food stamps, Medicaid, public housing, aid to families with dependent children, senior citizen programs, and so on.

The income information is tabulated and published in two principal forms: as income of *individuals* and as income of *families* or *households*. Both of these types of data are reviewed below.

The materials of this chapter are based upon income statistics from the *Current Population Reports* published in 1984 (detailing earned income in 1982) and earlier years. Because of their greater frequency of enumeration and their comparability these income reports provide a good framework within which to study income distribution and trends. Results from decennial censuses are used to provide details not available from the *Current Population Reports.*

Income Received by Individuals

During the calendar year 1982 nine out of every ten persons fifteen and older (91.1 percent) received at least some money income. This proportion was 93.8 percent for males and 88.6 percent for females. As Table 14-1 (right-hand panel) shows the proportion of males re-

Table 14-1. Median Income and Percent Receiving Income for Persons 14 Years of Age and Over in 1947 to 1982, by Race and Sex [in constant 1982 dollars]

Year	Median income						Percent receiving income					
	All races		White		Black and other		All races		White		Black and other	
	Male	Female	Male	Female	Male	Female	Male	Female	Male	Female	Male	Female
1982	13,950	5,887	14,748	5,967	9,493	5,341	93.8	88.6	95.2	89.5	84.7	83.2
1981	14,299	5,793	15,172	5,857	9,624	5,384	94.9	89.1	96.0	89.9	87.5	83.7
1980	14,678	5,763	15,162	5,795	9,786	5,543	94.8	88.7	95.8	89.6	88.4	82.9
1979	15,664	5,787	16,363	5,842	10,604	5,440	95.3	88.9	96.3	89.7	88.3	83.8
1978	16,179	6,019	16,945	6,091	10,796	5,624	93.4	81.1	94.3	81.3	86.3	79.6
1977	16,124	6,277	16,889	6,373	10,326	5,635	92.7	74.8	93.7	74.6	85.0	76.7
1976	15,983	6,063	16,849	6,114	10,540	5,799	92.4	73.3	93.4	73.1	84.9	74.6
1975	15,877	6,071	16,679	6,134	10,511	5,664	91.8	71.6	92.8	71.2	84.6	74.0
1974	16,543	6,033	17,330	6,101	11,135	5,594	92.8	71.3	93.7	71.0	86.0	73.9
1973	17,498	6,073	18,360	6,132	11,551	5,704	92.5	69.3	93.3	68.8	86.0	72.9
1972	17,189	5,997	18,029	6,036	11,100	5,773	91.7	67.4	92.6	66.7	84.3	72.1
1971	16,452	5,739	17,248	5,834	10,351	5,224	91.7	66.1	92.4	65.4	86.0	71.9
1970	16,580	5,561	17,428	5,633	10,490	5,180	92.1	66.5	92.8	65.8	86.4	71.8
1969	16,927	5,613	17,812	5,745	10,508	4,866	92.5	65.8	93.0	65.0	88.6	72.1
1968	16,591	5,602	17,388	5,768	10,551	4,683	92.4	64.8	92.9	63.8	88.3	72.6
1967	16,054	5,207	16,901	5,363	9,653	4,305	92.4	63.7	92.9	62.7	88.3	71.2
1966	15,781	4,873	16,631	5,101	9,212	3,882	92.0	61.0	92.4	60.1	88.2	68.0
1965	15,367	4,653	16,185	4,936	8.710	3,591	91.5	59.4	92.0	58.5	87.7	66.8
1964	14,460	4,509	15,361	4,723	8,708	3,316	91.4	59.7	91.9	58.8	87.6	67.3
1963	14,221	4,326	15,151	4,535	7,874	3,036	91.4	58.7	91.8	57.9	87.9	66.1
1962	13,951	4,283	14,859	4,510	7,318	3,027	91.1	57.7	91.5	56.7	87.0	65.8
1961	13,517	4,128	14,290	4,376	7,385	2,934	91.4	57.3	91.9	56.1	87.1	67.5
1960	13,299	4,111	14,003	4,407	7,367	2,727	91.4	56.0	91.8	54.8	88.3	66.2
1959	13,237	4,050	13,937	4,343	6,561	2,676	91.4	53.7	91.7	52.6	88.3	63.4
1958	12,495	3,926	13,275	4,271	6,614	2,602	91.7	52.9	92.0	51.6	89.0	64.2
1957	12,609	4,116	13,402	4,504	7,096	2,605	91.8	52.6	92.1	51.3	89.5	63.4
1956	12,791	4,080	13,558	4,492	7,113	2,582	91.9	51.9	92.1	50.4	90.1	64.8
1955	12,104	4,037	12,776	4,512	6,724	2,354	92.1	49.3	92.3	47.9	89.8	62.3
1954	11,467	4,167	12,080	4,628	6,011	2,511	90.2	46.4	90.5	45.2	87.6	57.6
1953	11,624	4,208	12,237	4,666	6,760	2,734	91.3	46.4	91.5	44.8	89.4	61.2
1952	11,290	4,170	11,837	4,868	6,487	1,881	91.3	46.5	--	--	--	--
1951	10,968	3,882	11,524	4,536	6,346	1,926	93.9	43.7	--	--	--	--
1950	10,304	3,821	10,862	4,251	5,899	1,902	90.5	43.3	--	--	--	--
1949	9,499	3,888	10,006	4,331	4,844	2,004	90.3	41.8	--	--	--	--
1948	9,605	4,048	10,064	4,542	5,465	1,973	89.9	40.9	--	--	--	--
1947	9,635	4,394	--	--	--	--	89.2	39.1	--	--	--	--

Note: -- indicates data not available.

Source: U.S. Bureau of the Census. "Money Income of Households, Families and Persons in the United States: 1982." Current Population Reports (Series P-60, no. 142). Washington, DC: U.S. Government Printing Office, 1984, Table 40.

ceiving income has been above 90 percent since 1949, but over the past four decades the proportion of female income recipients has more than doubled, charting the lessened economic dependence of women on men. Because a large proportion of married women are now employed, a large percentage of young persons attending school are working part time, and a large percentage of persons sixty-five and older (both male and female) regularly receive pensions or other similar payments, the proportion of the adult population totally without income is small. It appears to have increased slightly during the recession of the early 1980s.

Table 14-1 documents the rise (with fluctuations) in median income, by sex and race, between 1947 and 1982. Figure 14-1 graphs these trends.

The median income for male individuals in 1982 was $13,950, or $1,162 per month; however, dispersion from the midpoint was very wide. The distribution of income among individuals is shown in Table 14-2. There is a characteristic "income curve" describing the distribution of income among individuals. It indicates that a substantial proportion of the population receive very modest incomes and a small proportion receive very large incomes. Figure 14-2 illustrates this curve (graphs are shown separately for males and females, by race-ethnicity). For centuries economists have speculated as to why the income curve for individuals has a disproportionately large proportion of income recipients concentrated toward the lower end of the income scale. Social scientists theorize that at least six factors are involved:

1. People differ widely in their ability, training, and drive to earn.

2. Various types of work command different prices in the labor market.

3. Inheritance of wealth, prestige, or influence is widely believed to explain unusually large incomes.

4. Labor turnover and part-time and part-year employment are responsible for many small incomes.

5. The system of social organization, with its accompanying power structure and traditions, also influences the pattern of income distribution.

6. The physical and mental health of workers is also an important factor influencing income.

Table 14-2 reflects the net result of the operation of all six of these forces. At the lowest end of the income scale should be the workers who were employed only part time or a part of the preceding year; who were of the lowest order of skill, intelligence, ability, or initiative; whose parents were able to give them little financial assistance in life; who were employed at jobs having the lowest market value; whose degree of bargaining power was least, or whose health was poorest. At the other extreme in the high-income groups are people with com-

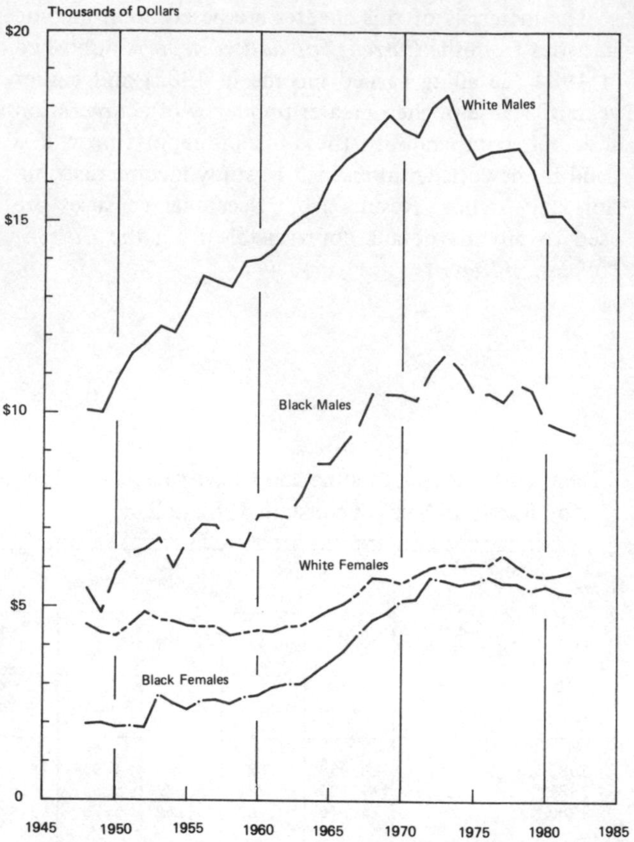

Figure 14-1. Trend in Median Income of Individuals, by Sex and Race: 1947-1982 [constant 1982 dollars]

binations of the following traits: high average intelligence, training, and ability who were employed at jobs commanding high prices in the labor market, who worked full time for a full fifty-two weeks during the preceding year, who succeeded in obtaining a great deal of supplemental income through investments resulting from the inheritance of money or previous savings, who wielded unusually great economic power by virtue of belonging to associations that helped maximize the share of the income they obtained, and/or who were in sound physical and mental health.

Tables 14-1 and 14-2 provide data about income levels and differentials in distribution of income over time. These data are adjusted for the changing purchasing power of the dollar, expressed in terms of constant 1982 dollars. The Bureau of Labor Statistics routinely adjusts time series of income data for inflation by expressing them in constant dollars for a recent year. (Also, many income tabulations are confined to that portion of the work force having year-round and full-time employment during the year for which income is measured. This eliminates the effects of part-time and

Table 14-2. Income Distribution of Persons 14 Years of Age and Over Receiving Income, by Sex and Race-Ethnicity: 1982 [in constant 1982 dollars]

Total money income	Male				Female			
	All races	White	Black	Spanish-origin	All races	White	Black	Spanish-origin
Median income	13,950	14,748	8,838	10,471	5,887	5,967	5,263	5,140
Mean income	17,381	18,071	11,050	12,786	8,195	8,295	7,349	6,820
Percent with income	93.8	95.2	83.2	89.1	88.6	89.5	83.5	74.9
Total	100.0	100.0	100.0	100.0	100.0	100.0	100.0	100.0
1 to 1,999 or loss	9.1	8.5	12.7	9.8	21.7	22.2	17.2	23.2
2,000 to 2,999	3.3	3.0	5.6	3.9	7.3	7.0	9.8	8.1
3,000 to 3,999	3.8	3.4	7.6	5.3	8.6	8.1	13.2	9.9
4,000 to 5,999	7.3	7.0	10.3	10.0	13.1	13.0	14.3	14.5
6,000 to 6,999	3.8	3.5	5.2	4.7	5.1	5.1	5.4	6.1
7,000 to 8,499	5.3	5.1	7.3	8.3	7.1	7.1	7.6	8.0
8,500 to 9,999	4.3	4.2	5.6	5.5	5.2	5.3	4.6	5.7
10,000 to 12,499	9.3	9.2	10.9	13.3	9.3	9.3	9.2	9.2
12,500 to 14,999	6.7	6.7	6.8	7.2	5.8	5.9	5.2	5.0
15,000 to 17,499	7.2	7.2	7.1	7.4	5.2	5.2	5.3	3.6
17,500 to 19,999	5.6	5.7	4.4	4.5	3.2	3.2	2.5	2.1
20,000 to 24,999	10.8	11.1	8.2	8.2	4.4	4.5	3.4	2.7
25,000 to 29,999	7.9	8.4	4.1	5.2	1.9	2.0	1.3	1.0
30,000 to 34,999	5.4	5.7	2.1	2.9	0.9	0.9	0.5	0.6
35,000 to 49,999	6.3	6.8	1.3	2.5	0.8	0.8	0.2	0.3
50,000 to 74,999	2.6	2.9	0.3	0.8	0.2	0.3	0.1	0.1
75,000 and over	1.3	1.4	0.3	0.5	0.1	0.2	*	0.1
Year-round full-time workers								
Median income	21,655	22,232	15,790	15,589	13,663	13,847	12,376	11,363
Mean income	24,809	25,413	17,499	18,277	15,142	15,347	13,645	12,614

Note: * indicates less than 0.1.

Source: U.S. Bureau of the Census. "Money Income of Households, Families and Persons in the United States: 1982." Current Population Reports (Series P-60, no. 142). Washington, DC: U.S. Government Printing Office, 1984, Table 43.

irregular employment and is useful for some analyses, but it may gloss over important problems of low income.)

Since 1947, when the collection of income statistics was firmly established, until 1982, the median income for males had risen by 45 percent and for females by 34 percent, after adjustments for inflation. For males all of this substantial improvement in individual income came between 1947 and 1962. Thereafter the trend was irregularly slightly upward to a peak in 1973 and then downward to a point in 1982 that matches the level of 1962. For females the trend was reasonably steadily upward until affected adversely by the recession of 1980-83. Figure 14-1, which charts these income trends, also reveals the year-to-year effects of business cycles upon the average income that individuals receive.

Sex Differences in Income Distribution

A smaller proportion of women than men receive incomes. This difference is due primarily to the lower rates of labor force participation among women. However, rising labor force participation by women has caused this disparity to shrink over the years, as the following summary of percent of persons aged fourteen and older who received some income in the years indicated shows:

Year	Males	Females
1982	93.8	88.6
1980	94.8	88.7
1970	92.1	66.5
1960	91.4	56.0
1950	90.5	43.3

Of those persons receiving income, women received much smaller incomes than men. The following summary of median incomes received by male and female recipients between 1947 and 1982 reveals that women receive less than half that received by men; their relative position is no better today than at the close of World War II.

Year	Median income[a]		
	Male	Female	Ratio female/male
1982. .	13,950	5,887	0.42
1980. .	14,678	5,763	0.39
1970. .	16,580	5,561	0.34
1960. .	13,299	4,111	0.31
1950. .	10,304	3,821	0.37
1947. .	9,635	4,394	0.46

[a]Constant 1982 dollars.

This results in part from more part-time employment among women and from the fact that because of marriage and childbearing more women than men left or entered the labor force, hence having only part-year employment. However, the bottom two lines of Table 14-2 report the incomes received by year-round full-time workers (persons who worked fifty weeks or more and thirty-five hours or more a week). In 1982 female workers in this category had median earnings of $13,663 while their male counterparts earned $21,655. Thus, when part-time and part-year employment are controlled, women still earned only 58 percent as much as men. Figure 14-1 graphs this sex differential in average income. A comparison of Figures 14-2A and 2B reveals how greatly skewed toward the bottom of the scale the income distribution of women still is.

Race and Spanish-Origin Differences in Income

Tables 14-1 and 14-2 document one of the greatest social problems of the United States: the abysmally low

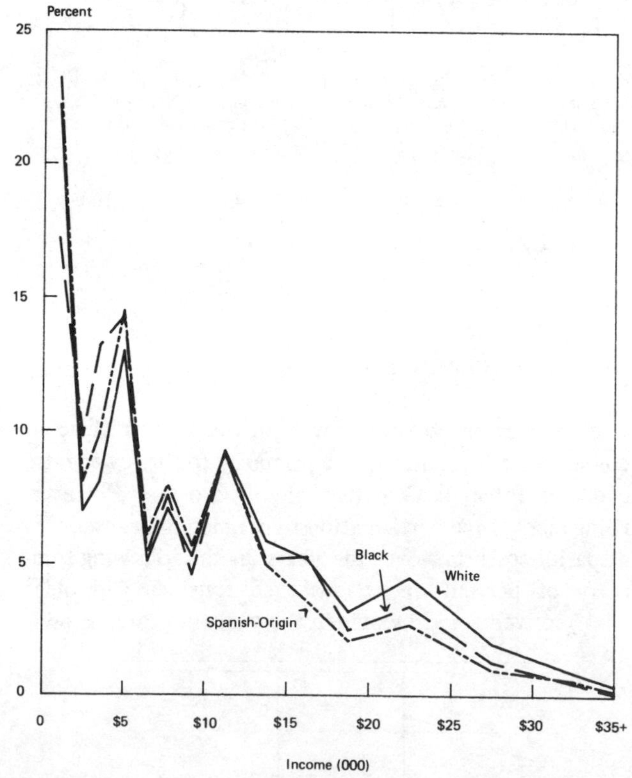

Figure 14-2A. Income Distribution of Individuals: Females, 1982

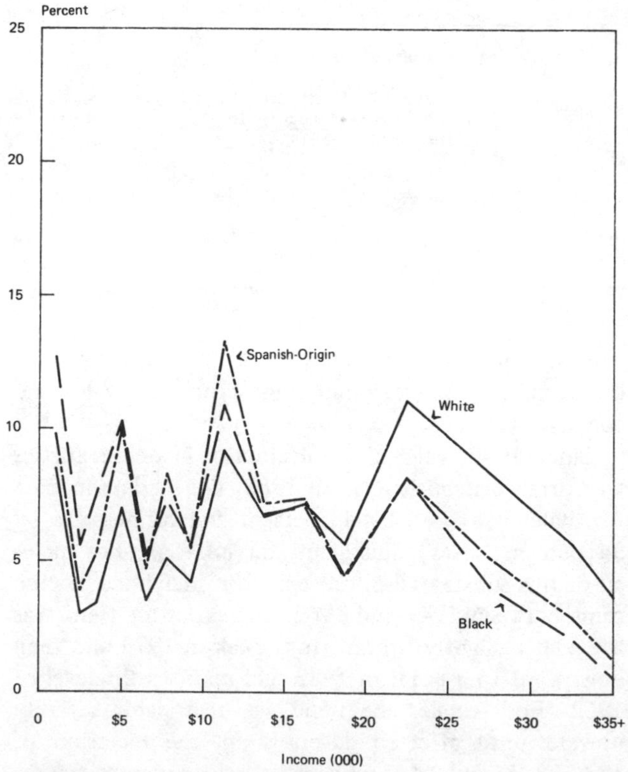

Figure 14-2B. Income Distribution of Individuals: Males, 1982

economic status of the black population in comparison with the white. The Spanish-origin population is in a condition similar to that of blacks.

The median incomes for 1982 of the three race-ethnic groups and the ratio of black and Spanish-origin populations to the white, by sex, are as follows:

Race-ethnicity	All income recipients		Year-round full-time workers	
	Male	Female	Male	Female
White	14,748	5,967	22,232	13,847
Black	8,838	5,263	15,790	12,376
Spanish-origin	10,471	5,140	15,589	11,363
Ratio to white				
Black	0.60	0.88	0.71	0.89
Spanish-origin	0.71	0.86	0.70	0.82
Ratio female to male				
White	0.40		0.62	
Black	0.60		0.78	
Spanish-origin	0.49		0.73	

In crude terms the male Spanish-origin population appears to have a smaller disadvantage than the black, but the differential disappears among individuals of both groups who work full time year-round. These workers receive 70 percent as much income as fully employed white males. Female workers, though badly handicapped by the sex disparity, suffer less because of race or ethnicity than males. Black women receive nearly 90 percent as much income as white women, on either a crude or a full-employment basis. Spanish-origin female workers who work full time received only 82 percent as much income as white females in 1982.

Thus in the income-receiving hierarchy white males stand at the top, with a median income of $22,232 in 1982 for a full year's work, while Spanish-origin females fall at the bottom with $11,363, or 52 percent as much. These ratios show that the sex differential is widest for white women and least for black women, with Spanish-origin women occupying an intermediate position.

Table 14-3. Income Distribution of Households and Families, by Race-Ethnicity: 1982

Total money income	All households				Families			
	Total	White	Black	Spanish-origin	Total	White	Black	Spanish-origin
Median income	20,171	21,117	11,966	15,178	23,614	24,763	13,917	16,376
Mean income	24,309	25,311	15,747	18,732	27,563	28,764	17,486	19,953
Total	100.0	100.0	100.0	100.0	100.0	100.0	100.0	100.0
Under 2,500	2.9	2.4	6.7	4.3	2.2	1.8	5.2	3.4
2,500-4,999	6.7	5.7	15.0	8.7	3.6	2.6	11.3	6.5
5,000-7,499	7.8	7.3	11.9	11.6	5.1	4.3	11.4	10.6
7,500-9,999	6.5	6.2	9.0	8.6	5.4	4.9	9.1	8.5
10,000-12,499	7.2	6.9	9.4	9.0	6.5	6.1	9.3	9.1
12,500-14,999	6.3	6.3	6.4	7.3	6.0	5.9	6.5	7.6
15,000-17,499	6.4	6.4	6.4	7.7	6.3	6.3	6.3	8.0
17,500-19,999	5.7	5.9	4.8	6.0	5.8	6.0	5.0	6.1
20,000-22,499	6.2	6.3	5.6	6.1	6.6	6.7	6.1	6.7
22,500-24,999	5.2	5.4	4.1	4.6	5.7	5.9	4.8	5.0
25,000-27,499	5.3	5.4	4.2	4.4	6.0	6.1	4.9	4.6
27,500-29,999	4.1	4.2	2.7	3.5	4.7	4.9	3.2	3.9
30,000-32,499	4.4	4.5	2.9	3.5	5.0	5.2	3.3	3.8
32,500-34,999	3.2	3.4	2.3	2.1	3.9	4.1	2.8	2.2
35,000-37,499	3.2	3.4	1.8	2.5	4.0	4.2	2.1	2.7
37,500-39,999	2.4	2.5	1.5	1.5	3.0	3.1	1.9	1.7
40,000-44,999	4.3	4.6	1.9	3.0	5.3	5.7	2.4	3.4
45,000-49,999	3.1	3.4	1.2	2.1	3.9	4.2	1.6	2.3
50,000-59,999	3.8	4.1	1.0	1.6	4.7	5.1	1.3	1.9
60,000-74,999	2.6	2.8	0.8	0.9	3.2	3.5	1.1	0.9
75,000 and over	2.5	2.7	0.4	1.1	3.1	3.4	0.4	1.2

Source: U.S. Bureau of the Census. "Money Income of Households, Families and Persons in the United States: 1982." Current Population Reports (Series P-60, no. 142). Washington, DC: U.S. Government Printing Office, 1984, Table 8.

Table 14-4. Income Distribution of Families and Unrelated Individuals, by Race-Ethnicity: 1950-1982 [in constant 1982 dollars]

Income	White				Black				Spanish-origin		
	1982	1979	1972	1950	1982	1979	1972	1950	1982	1979	1972
Families											
Median income. . . .	24,603	27,180	26,647	13,813	15,211	16,495	16,395	7,494	16,227	18,842	18,880
Total.	100.0	100.0	100.0	100.0	100.0	100.0	100.0	100.0	100.0	100.0	100.0
Under 2,500.	1.9	1.3	1.2	6.7	4.9	4.4	3.2	18.4	3.6	2.6	1.9
2,500-4,999.	2.7	2.7	2.1	6.4	10.2	8.8	7.3	16.7	6.5	6.3	4.1
5,000-7,499.	4.4	3.3	3.6	8.4	10.8	8.6	10.1	16.8	10.8	6.8	6.9
7,500-9,999.	4.9	4.0	4.6	9.1	8.8	8.4	9.5	14.4	8.7	7.1	8.6
10,000-12,499. . . .	6.2	5.2	5.1		8.7	8.1	8.8		9.0	7.8	8.6
12,500-14,999. . . .	5.9	5.9	5.2		6.2	7.8	7.4		7.5	8.5	7.4
15,000-19,999. . . .	12.3	11.1	15.0		11.1	11.9	15.3		14.1	13.8	19.3
20,000-24,999. . . .	12.6	11.8	9.6	69.4	10.7	9.6	8.8	33.7	11.7	12.5	10.8
25,000-34,999. . . .	20.3	22.0	28.0		14.5	15.3	18.3		14.3	17.5	21.0
35,000-49,999. . . .	16.9	19.4	13.9		9.6	11.6	7.2		10.0	11.2	7.7
50,000 and over. . .	11.9	13.3	11.7		4.6	5.7	4.0		3.9	5.9	3.8
Unrelated individuals											
Median income. . . .	10,404	10,396	8,484	4,471	6,921	7,402	6,301	3,276	7,314	8,343	7,937
Total.	100.0	100.0	100.0	100.0	100.0	100.0	100.0	100.0	100.0	100.0	100.0
Under 2,500.	5.7	4.9	8.7	26.5	13.4	10.4	14.8	36.1	12.3	9.6	17.5
2,500-4,999.	3.0	3.6	5.2	13.2	5.6	7.1	8.1	13.9	5.5	5.5	4.7
5,000-7,499.	6.3	5.7	7.5	8.0	12.9	10.6	10.3	8.0	9.7	6.9	5.5
7,500-9,999.	6.8	7.2	8.1	5.8	7.2	8.3	8.7	7.4	7.2	7.2	6.3
10,000-12,499. . . .	7.5	6.7	7.5	4.3	6.4	6.6	6.5	5.1	6.9	6.7	6.7
12,500-14,999. . . .	10.6	11.1	11.0	10.2	8.9	9.5	10.2	11.0	11.6	12.1	9.9
15,000-19,999. . . .	8.4	9.1	8.1	7.4	7.6	7.5	7.0	7.0	8.9	10.6	10.9
20,000-24,999. . . .	10.4	9.6	8.4		10.2	8.7	7.5		10.2	9.4	9.8
25,000-34,999. . . .	7.4	9.3	6.5	24.7	5.7	7.7	5.7	11.6	6.2	9.2	7.6
35,000-49,999. . . .	21.1	20.6	18.4		16.8	16.1	16.0		13.6	16.0	16.6
50,000 and over. . .	12.8	12.2	10.6		5.2	7.5	5.1		7.9	6.7	4.5

Source: U.S. Bureau of the Census. "Money Income of Households, Families and Persons in the United States: 1982." Current Population Reports (Series P-60, no. 142). Washington, DC: U.S. Government Printing Office, 1984, Table 15.

The above discussion, in terms of medians, hides the pattern of income distribution. Table 14-2, which provides these data, shows a distinctly trimodal distribution. There is a sizable concentration of persons who receive less than \$2,000 (more than one-fifth of women fall in this class). There is a second concentration around the \$4,000-5,000 level. Finally there is a third concentration at the \$10,000 level for women and \$20,000 for men. Figure 14-2 shows that each of the three race-ethnic groups follows this pattern, with "crossover" of black and Spanish-origin recipients (in comparison with white recipients) from concentrations in the low-income categories to deficits in the upper income categories; the crossover takes place at about \$15,000 for males and \$8,000 for females.

Household and Family Income

Fortunately, many individuals with low incomes are not forced to support themselves on the income they receive. As members of households (usually a family), they pool their incomes with those of other members and share in the total income. Chapter 12 has already described the high employment of married women and of two-earner (or multiearner) families. Retired persons living in a household with others are able to pool their pensions or other retirement incomes with the other members' incomes. As a consequence a much more realistic picture of the income distribution is *household income* or *family income*. This permits income to be studied in terms of the units in which it is consumed.

Table 14-5. Trends in Income Distribution in Terms of Livelihood Classes: All Races, 1950-1982

Livelihood class	Income interval (dollars)	Households		Families			
		1982	1972	1982	1972	1960	1950
Total	...	100.0	100.0	100.0	100.0	100.0	100.0
Very poor--destitute.	Under 5,000	9.6	8.7	6.0	4.0	9.2	7.7
Poor--poverty	5,000-9,999	14.3	12.7	10.6	9.5	13.3	7.3
Near-poor	10,000-14,999	13.5	11.6	12.4	10.9	15.4	9.0
Lower middle class.	15,000-19,999	12.2	14.3	12.1	15.0	22.4	9.6
Middle class.	20,000-24,999	11.4	9.0	12.3	9.6	11.6	
Upper middle class.	35,000-34,999	16.9	23.1	19.5	26.9		66.4
Lower upper class--affluent . .	35,000-49,999	13.2	11.3	16.0	13.2	28.1	
Elite--wealthy.	50,000 and over	8.9	9.2	10.9	10.9		

Source: U.S. Bureau of the Census. "Money Income of Households, Families and Persons in the United States: 1982." Current Population Reports (Series P-60, no. 142). Washington, DC: U.S. Government Printing Office, 1984, Tables 3 and 15.

Before 1980 only secondary attention was paid to household income data. Primary attention went to family income statistics. With the rapidly changing pattern of living arrangements, wherein persons live alone or two or more unrelated individuals form households and function as consumption units, in recent years data have been provided for both household and family income.

Table 14-3 provides statistics on these classes of income. They are derived by summing the individual income reported by the members of households or families to obtain a combined total income. In 1982 median household income was $20,171 and median family income was $23,614. Family income is higher than household income, because the numerous one-person households, with a maximum of one earner, are excluded from family tabulations. The following summary presents a picture of racial-ethnic differentials according to households and families as of 1982:

Race-ethnicity	All households	Families	Nonfamily households		
			Total	Living alone	Multiple-person
Total. . . .	20,171	23,614	11,420	9,884	24,426
White.	21,117	24,763	11,856	10,366	24,579
Black.	11,966	13,917	7,787	6,874	14,992
Spanish-origin	15,178	16,376	9,213	7,343	18,093
Ratio to white					
Black. . . .	0.57	0.56	0.66	0.66	0.61
Spanish-origin . .	0.72	0.66	0.78	0.71	0.74

Source: U.S. Bureau of the Census. Current Population Reports (Series P-60, no. 142). Washington, DC: U.S. Government Printing Office, 1984, Table 8.

The picture that emerges when median incomes of households and families are considered is one of overall high prosperity for the white population, whether living in family or nonfamily households. The income levels of black and Spanish-origin households in much lower. Trends in median family income are shown in Table 14-4. The details of these differences can be more fully appreciated by examining the distributions of persons among what is termed "income classes."

Income Classes

When interpreting income distribution statistics, one should consider their meaning in terms of the level of comfort and decency at which households and families exist. The statistics should indicate what part of the population is not receiving enough to support itself at a level adequate for the maintenance of health and welfare. (This is explored in detail in Chapter 16.) They should also indicate the quality of life and lifestyle in approximate increments made possible by changes in purchasing power. In an attempt to derive socioeconomic significance from income distribution figures and to combine masses of detail into fewer and more meaningful categories, income distributions have been collapsed into eight general groupings, to which income class labels have been attached for many tabulations of this chapter. The categories are defined and labeled in Table 14-5.

This table emphasizes that a large share of the individuals who receive small incomes are members of households and families that have other sources of income. Thus the livelihood picture is considerably brighter when viewed from the perspective of the household and family. By pooling two or more small incomes, a household or family can raise its economic level considerably.

Using this set of income classes to describe the income distribution of households and families of the race-ethnic groups provides a better vantage point from which to begin a more detailed analysis, as shown in Table 14-6 and Figure 14-3. Nearly half of all black and Spanish-origin and one-fourth of all white households fall in the "low income" categories.

Recent Changes in Family Income Levels and Distribution

Income distributions in terms of livelihood classes for the years 1950, 1972, and 1982 are shown for the white, black, and Spanish-origin populations in Table 14-6. The data have been adjusted for inflation and are expressed in 1982 dollars. The following significant findings may be observed from this table.

1. *1972-82.* No progress was made during the 1972-82 decade in improving the family income levels of the population. In fact conditions deteriorated. The income distribution remained almost unchanged or worsened for the Spanish-origin population. For both the black and the Spanish-origin populations, the proportion of families in the "poor" categories increased significantly. This was partially offset by a slight shifting into the highest income categories. A situation of "the rich get richer and the poor get poorer" appears to have emerged. Figure 14-3 graphs this retrogression.

2. *1950-72.* Very great improvements in the family income levels and distribution were made between 1950 and 1972. For both whites and blacks (data for the Spanish-origin population were unavailable), there was a large decline in the proportion of persons in the low-income categories and a shift toward the middle- and upper-income groups. During these two decades a substantial black middle class emerged from the low-income

Table 14-6. Livelihood Level of Families, by Race-Ethnicity: 1982, 1972, and 1950

Livelihood class	Income interval (dollars)	All races	White	Black	Spanish-origin
Livelihood level in 1982					
Total	...	100.0	100.0	100.0	100.0
Very poor--destitute.	Under 5,000	6.0	4.6	17.0	10.1
Poor--poverty	5,00-9,999	10.6	9.3	20.8	19.5
Near-poor	10,000-14,999	12.4	12.1	15.7	16.5
Lower middle class.	15,000-19,999	12.1	12.3	11.2	14.1
Middle class.	20,000-24,999	12.3	12.6	10.7	11.7
Upper middle class.	25,000-34,999	19.5	20.3	14.1	14.3
Lower upper class--affluent .	35,000-94,999	16.0	16.9	7.8	10.0
Elite--wealthy.	50,000 and over	10.9	11.9	2.6	3.9
Livelihood level in 1972					
Total	...	100.0	100.0	100.0	100.0
Very poor--destitute.	Under 5,000	4.0	3.3	11.0	6.0
Poor--poverty	5,000-9,999	9.5	8.2	20.3	15.5
Near-poor	10,000-14,999	10.9	10.3	16.5	16.0
Lower middle class.	15,000-19,999	15.0	15.0	15.5	19.3
Middle class.	20,000-24,999	9.6	9.6	8.8	10.8
Upper middle class.	25,000-34,999	26.9	28.0	17.5	21.0
Lower upper class--affluent .	35,000-49,999	13.2	13.9	6.7	7.7
Elite--wealthy.	50,000 and over	10.9	11.7	3.6	3.8
Livelihood level in 1950					
Total	...	100.0	100.0	100.0	100.0
Very poor--destitute.	Under 5,000	7.7	13.1	--	--
Poor--poverty	5,000-9,999	7.3	17.5	--	--
Near-poor	10,000-14,999	9.0	}	--	--
Lower middle class.	15,000-19,999	9.6	}	--	--
Middle class.	20,000-24,999	}	}	--	--
Upper middle class.	25,000-34,999	}	} 69.4	--	--
Lower upper class--affluent .	35,000-49,999	} 66.4	}	--	--
Elite--wealthy.	50,000 and over	}	}	--	--

Note: -- indicates data not available.

Source: U.S. Bureau of the Census. "Money Income of Households, Families and Persons in the United States: 1982." Current Population Reports (Series P-60, no. 142). Washington, DC: U.S. Government Printing Office, 1984, Tables 3 and 15.

sectors. Simultaneously, a very sizable upper-income group developed in the white population.

3. *Unrelated individuals.* Steady improvement in the income level and distribution of unrelated individuals occurred until the 1980-83 recession.

4. *Recession of 1980-83.* After periods of unusual prosperity in 1970-72 and 1975-78, the recession of 1980-83 caused a substantial increase in the size of the lower income groups and a corresponding decrease in the middle and upper income groups. The "crossover" between increases in low income and decreases in upper income was at about the $20,000 level (see Table 14-6).

5. *Bimodal income distribution for black families.* Whereas the white population tends to have a concentration in the upper-middle-class range, the black population tends to have two concentrations, one in the "poor" and "near-poor" range and another in the middle-class range. The stagnation of the 1970s and the recession of the early 1980s appear to have increased this polarization somewhat and to have widened the income gap between them.

6. *Spanish-origin trends.* Because the median family income of the Spanish-origin population declined very substantially between 1972 and 1979 and the proportion in the lowest income categories increased, it appears that the economic situation of this group worsened seriously during the 1970s. (The situation for nonfamily individuals improved over the 1972-79 interval.) During those years the size of the Spanish-origin population was growing rapidly because of immigration from Mexico and other nations, as well as from high fertility. A part or all of this apparent worsening could be due to the arrival of low-income immigrants, not a failure of those who were already resident to maintain their economic position. The 1980-83 recession exacerbated the income situation to an extremely high degree.

Peak Prosperity: 1972-73 and 1978-79

Annual values of median family income are reported in Table 14-7. It is apparent that although the monetary value of incomes has risen steadily, when corrections for inflation have been made the year 1979 had a higher median family income than 1980 and 1982. Thus the all-time peaks of American economic prosperity were reached in 1972-73 and 1978-79.

Recession Fluctuations

Because of fluctuations in the business cycle median family income tends to rise irregularly, with declines during years of recession. Although the 1980-83 reces-

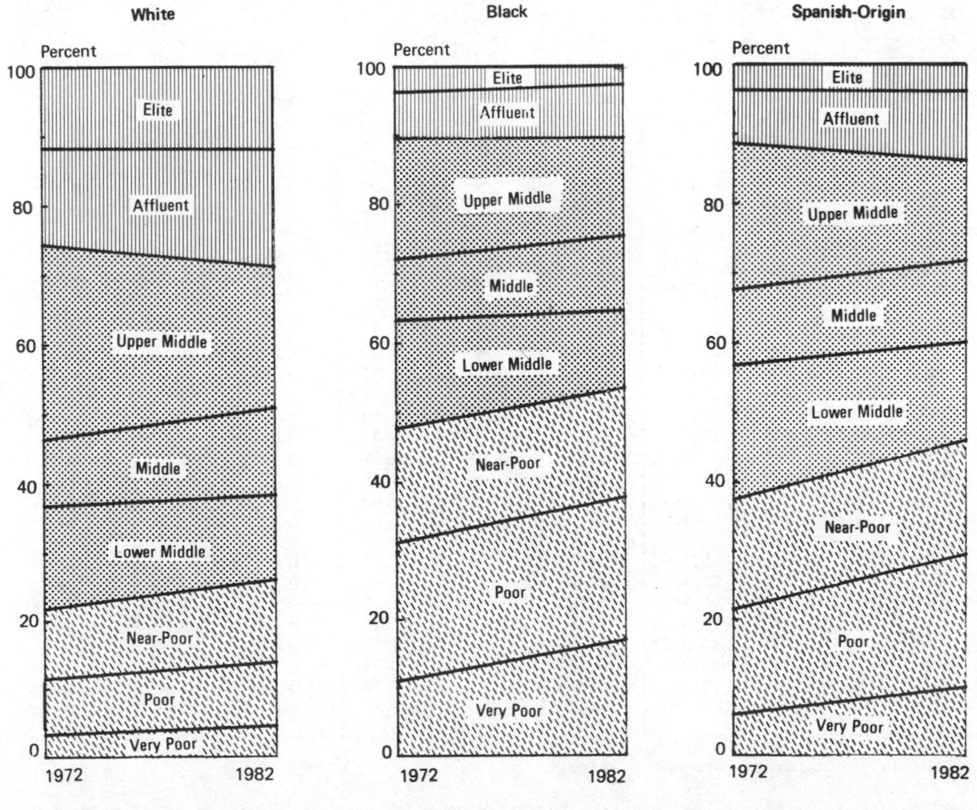

Figure 14-3. Changes in Size of Livelihood Classes in Race-Ethnic Groups: 1972-1982

sion is the sharpest and longest, significant dips may be noted for 1974-75, 1970-71, 1958, 1954, and 1947-49.

Regional and State Variations in Income

Income levels are not uniform throughout the nation. Following are indicators of median income in 1982 for the regions of the United States, by race-ethnicity, with the value for the nation set equal to 1.00.

Region	Total	White	Black
Total. . . .	1.00	1.05	0.58
Northeast. . .	1.06	1.10	0.69
North central.	1.03	1.06	0.58
South.	0.92	0.99	0.57
West	1.05	1.08	0.87

The South region is substantially below the level for the other regions, with the Northeast and West almost tied for being the most prosperous.

Table 14-7. Median Family Income of Families, by Race-Ethnicity: 1947-1982 [in constant 1982 dollars] [Index: 1982 white = 1.00]

Year	Families				Index			
	All races	White	Black	Spanish-origin	All races	White	Black	Spanish-origin
1982. . .	23,433	24,603	15,211	16,227	0.95	1.00	0.62	0.66
1981. . .	23,761	24,959	15,493	17,406	0.97	1.01	0.63	0.71
1980. . .	24,626	25,658	16,216	17,238	1.00	1.04	0.66	0.70
1979. . .	26,047	27,180	16,495	18,842	1.06	1.10	0.67	0.77
1978. . .	26,099	27,176	17,390	18,592	1.06	1.10	0.71	0.76
1977. . .	25,500	26,664	16,155	18,192	1.04	1.08	0.66	0.74
1976. . .	25,363	26,345	16,652	17,395	1.03	1.07	0.68	0.71
1975. . .	24,604	25,589	16,717	17,129	1.00	1.04	0.68	0.70
1974. . .	25,254	26,244	16,790	18,673	1.03	1.07	0.68	0.76
1973. . .	26,175	27,357	16,499	18,929	1.06	1.11	0.67	0.77
1972. . .	25,648	26,647	16,395	18,880	1.04	1.08	0.67	0.77
1971. . .	24,513	25,435	16,002	--	1.00	1.03	0.65	--
1970. . .	24,528	25,445	16,198	--	1.00	1.03	0.66	--
1969. . .	24,837	25,787	16,301	--	1.01	1.05	0.66	--
1968. . .	23,949	24,795	15,509	--	0.97	1.01	0.63	--
1967. . .	22,934	23,804	14,727	--	0.93	0.97	0.60	--
1966. . .	22,402	23,274	13,952	--	0.91	0.95	0.57	--
1965. . .	21,283	22,183	12,216	--	0.87	0.90	0.50	--
1964. . .	20,442	21,342	11,944	--	0.83	0.87	0.49	--
1963. . .	19,701	20,644	10,924	--	0.80	0.84	0.44	--
1962. . .	19,005	19,902	10,619	--	0.77	0.81	0.43	--
1961. . .	18,504	19,298	10,296	--	0.75	0.78	0.42	--
1960. . .	18,317	19,018	10,528	--	0.74	0.77	0.43	--
1959. . .	17,939	18,687	9,653	--	0.73	0.76	0.39	--
1958. . .	16,982	17,693	9,064	--	0.69	0.72	0.37	--
1957. . .	17,030	17,723	9,475	--	0.69	0.72	0.39	--
1956. . .	16,977	17,765	9,348	--	0.69	0.72	0.38	--
1955. . .	15,926	16,629	9,170	--	0.65	0.68	0.37	--
1954. . .	14,965	15,579	8,677	--	0.61	0.63	0.35	--
1953. . .	15,310	15,873	8,900	--	0.62	0.65	0.36	--
1952. . .	14,146	14,960	8,502	--	0.57	0.61	0.35	--
1951. . .	13,782	14,340	7,551	--	0.56	0.58	0.31	--
1950. . .	13,308	13,813	7,494	--	0.54	0.56	0.30	--
1949. . .	12,580	13,086	6,681	--	0.51	0.53	0.27	--
1948. . .	12,779	13,272	7,089	--	0.52	0.54	0.29	--
1947. . .	13,098	13,643	6,975	--	0.53	0.55	0.28	--

Note: -- indicates data not available.

Source: U.S. Bureau of the Census. "Money Income of Households, Families and Persons in the United States: 1982." Current Population Reports (Series P-60, no. 142). Washington, DC: U.S. Government Printing Office, 1984, Table 15.

A similar computation for the year 1955, with the national median income for that year set equal to 1.00, yields the following results:

Region	Total	White	Black
Total. . . .	1.00	1.04	0.58
Northeast. . .	1.07	1.10	0.75
North central.	1.07	1.09	0.84
South.	0.81	0.92	0.42
West	1.09	1.12	0.82

The income position of the South clearly has improved in comparison with the other regions, while that of the North Central region has declined. In the Northeast the position of the white population remains about the same, but that of the black population has declined. In the West the condition of the black population has improved while that of the white, though still well above average, has diminished.

Urban-Rural Residence, by Race-Ethnicity

According to data from the 1980 census, income levels are substantially lower in rural than in urban areas. Within urbanized areas urban fringes have considerably higher income levels than central cities. Within rural areas the rural farm population tends to have higher income than the rural nonfarm population. These differentials tend to hold for all race-ethnic groups (see Table 14-8).

Table 14-8 examines urban-rural income differences in terms of unrelated individuals as well as families. The pattern is essentially the same, except that in order to live in urban fringes unrelated individuals must have relatively higher incomes than families, where they can live in rural areas with relatively less income.

To create Table 14-8, values of median income for each subgroup were expressed as ratios to the median for the nation for the white population. Thus median income of white families and white unrelated individuals are taken as the standard of comparison for all racial groups and residential groups. This provides an opportunity to examine the income levels of the American Indian and Asian races in comparison with the white population. The American Indian group tends to be slightly more prosperous than the black population. The Asian population tends to be considerably more prosperous than the white population, which is consistent with the higher levels of educational attainment and occupational status noted in earlier chapters.

Table 14-8. Indices of Income Level of Families and Unrelated Individuals for Urban and Rural Areas, by Race-Ethnicity: 1982 [national median for white = 1.00; value of median is $20,835]

Region	White	Black	American Indian	Asian and Pac. Is.	Spanish-origin
Families					
Total.	1.00	0.60	0.66	1.09	0.71
Urban, total	1.05	0.62	0.73	1.09	0.71
Central cities . .	0.98	0.60	0.67	0.98	0.63
Urban fringe . . .	1.16	0.81	0.87	1.26	0.87
Rural, total	0.89	0.52	0.58	1.02	0.64
Farm	0.86	0.49	0.75	1.20	0.64
Unrelated individuals					
Total.	1.00	0.67	0.68	0.87	0.76
Urban, total	1.04	0.71	0.75	0.89	0.78
Central cities . .	1.01	0.71	0.76	0.87	0.77
Urban fringe . . .	1.26	0.93	0.95	1.08	0.90
Rural, total	0.86	0.42	0.54	0.70	0.61
Farm	1.07	0.50	0.64	0.79	0.73

Source: U.S. Bureau of the Census. "General Social and Economic Characteristics: United States Summary." 1980 Census of Population. Washington, DC: U.S. Government Printing Office, 1983, Tables 128 and 138.

Metropolitan-Nonmetropolitan Residence

Income levels are substantially lower outside SMSAs than inside. Within SMSAs income levels in the metropolitan rings are substantially higher than in the central cities. The differentials are summarized below in data from the 1980 census. (Values of median income were expressed as ratios to the median for the nation, separately for each group.)

Residence	Families		Unrelated individuals	
	White	Black	White	Black
Total.	1.00	1.00	1.00	1.00
Inside SMSAs . . .	1.07	1.07	1.10	1.10
Central cities .	0.98	0.99	1.01	1.05
Metro rings. . .	1.11	1.27	1.18	1.22
Outside SMSAs. . .	0.83	0.79	0.75	0.62

These differentials are valid both for families and unrelated individuals, and for black as well as white groups. However, the residential selectivity seems to be greater for blacks than for whites and greater for unrelated individuals than for families.

Table 14-9. Age Indices of Income Receipt by Persons 15 Years Old and Older, by Age, Race, and Sex: 1982 [national median for white = 1.00; value of median is $14,748]

Age	Male			Female		
	All races	White	Black	All races	White	Black
All ages. . . .	0.95	1.00	0.60	0.40	0.40	0.36
15-19 years . . .	0.12	0.12	0.11	0.12	0.12	0.12
20-24 years . . .	0.53	0.56	0.34	0.37	0.40	0.25
25-29 years . . .	1.01	1.05	0.77	0.56	0.57	0.50
30-34 years . . .	1.24	1.28	0.92	0.52	0.51	0.59
35-39 years . . .	1.45	1.50	0.93	0.53	0.52	0.56
40-44 years . . .	1.49	1.56	0.97	0.53	0.53	0.56
45-49 years . . .	1.49	1.57	0.89	0.51	0.51	0.53
50-54 years . . .	1.43	1.51	0.85	0.51	0.51	0.50
55-59 years . . .	1.37	1.43	0.54	0.42	0.42	0.42
60-64 years . . .	1.05	1.11	0.73	0.39	0.40	0.32
65-69 years . . .	0.77	0.81	0.40	0.37	0.39	0.26
70-over years . .	0.55	0.58	0.33	0.36	0.38	0.24

Source: U.S. Bureau of the Census. "Money Income of Households, Families and Persons in the United States: 1982." Current Population Reports (Series P-60, no. 142). Washington, DC: U.S. Government Printing Office, 1984, Table 46.

Age and Income Distribution

Table 14-9, which reports the median income of workers of each age, by race, shows that the age group 15-19 has a median income far below that of older workers. With increasing age, the median level of income rises until it reaches a peak at about 45-49 years of age, after which it begins a gradual decline. After the retirement age of sixty-five is reached, individual income declines considerably. Thus, the age distribution of the nation's income has the shape of an inverted "U." Figure 14-4 illustrates how median family income varies with age of householder. It must be kept in mind that each age group has its own income distribution; Table 14-10 and Figure 14-4 illustrate where the midpoints of these distributions lie.

Family Income and Family Characteristics

There is wide diversity in family income, associated with characteristics of the family. This section briefly reviews these differentials, making use only of statistics for median family income. Attention is paid only to the amount of income each category of family receives, without mention of its comparative frequency or rarity in the population—topics discussed in previous chapters.

Age of Householder

Family income follows an inverted "U" curve with age of householder, similar to but less dramatic than the curve for individual earners. Householders who are very young or very old tend to live in families with only about two-thirds as much income as the national average. Peak family income is for householders in the 45-54 year range. Table 14-10 provides data on this phenomenon. The pattern characterizes white and black households.

Type of Family: Female Householders with No Husband

Beyond a doubt, the greatest single factor in determining the level of family income is the presence or absence of both husband and wife. From the same source as Table 14-10, the following summary may be extracted:

(numbers in thousands)

Type of family	Median family income, 1982		
	Total	White	Black
Married couple families.	26.0	26.4	20.6
Male householder, no wife present.	20.1	21.4	14.7
Female householder, no husband present.	11.5	13.5	7.5

Where either the male or the female spouse is absent, family income is dramatically reduced. When the husband is absent, the reduction is nearly double the reduction when the wife is absent. Families headed by a female with no husband suffer from very low income. This is true irrespective of whether the family is white or black but is especially acute for black families.

Employment of Wife

Where the wife works, income of married-couple families is boosted by an average of about $8,000 to $10,000 per year, in comparison with families where the wife does not work (see Table 14-10, which reports these relationships as ratios).

(numbers in thousands)

Employment of Wife	Median family income, 1982		
	Total	White	Black
Wife in labor force. . . .	30.3	31.4	26.2
Wife not in labor force. .	21.3	21.8	12.5

The income boost from families with a working wife is both absolutely and relatively greater for the black than for the white family. Few events can reduce family income more than for a working couple family to separate or divorce, without remarriage. For the male the effect tends to be traumatic; for the female it is very often disastrous.

Table 14-10 provides data on ratios of median family income to white married couple families, simultaneously for head of household, type of family, and employment of wife, by race. The richest families are white married-couple families, with a male householder 45-54 years of age and a working wife. Such families had a median income of $33,400 in 1980. The poorest families are black families headed by a female with no husband, and householder aged 14-24 years of age. Such families received a median income of only $4,100 in 1980—less than one-eighth as much as the richest family type. Within each age-of-householder category, the family type effect and the working-wife effect exert themselves. Consequently, each of the following four variables has an independent effect in determining family income: age of householder, family type (presence of both spouses or only one), employment of wife, and race-ethnicity. Within all combinations, the income level of white families remains higher than for black families.

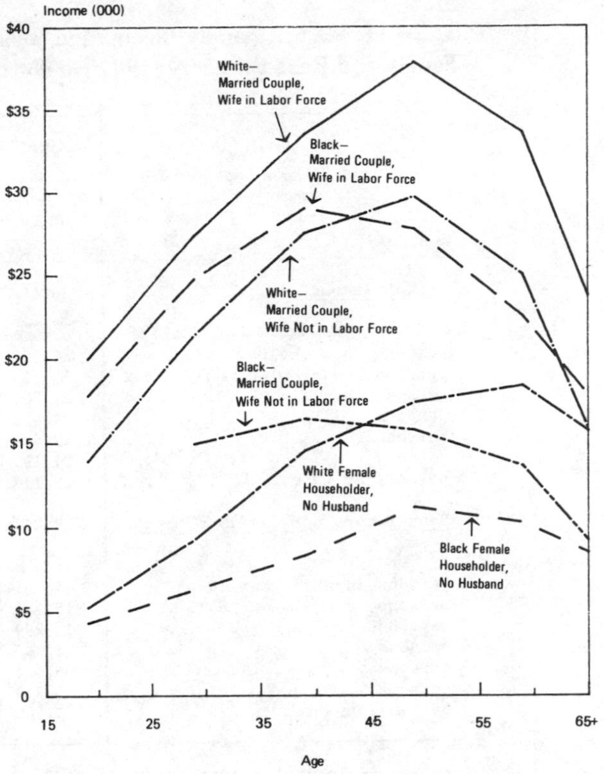

Figure 14-4. Median Family Income, by Age, Race, and Family Type: 1982

Table 14-10. Indices of Family Income, by Age of Householder, Type of Family, and Race of Householder: 1982 [national median income of married couple white families = 1.00; value of median is $26,443]

Age and race of householder	All families	Married couples			Male householder, no wife	Female householder, no husband
		Total	Wife in labor force	Wife not in labor force		
White, all ages	0.93	1.00	1.16	0.83	0.81	0.51
15-24 years . . .	0.59	0.67	0.76	0.53	0.60	0.20
25-34 years . . .	0.88	0.95	1.03	0.81	0.74	0.35
35-44 years . . .	1.09	1.19	1.27	1.04	0.89	0.55
45-54 years . . .	1.22	1.31	1.43	1.12	1.11	0.66
55-64 years . . .	1.03	1.07	1.27	0.95	0.82	0.70
65 years-over . .	0.64	0.64	0.90	0.60	0.68	0.59
Black, all ages	0.51	0.78	0.96	0.47	0.55	0.28
15-24 years . . .	0.24	0.53	0.67	--	--	0.16
25-34 years . . .	0.48	0.85	0.94	0.57	0.40	0.24
35-44 years . . .	0.65	0.99	1.10	0.62	—	0.32
45-54 years . . .	0.70	0.89	1.05	0.60	—	0.42
55-64 years . . .	0.59	0.70	0.85	0.52	—	0.39
65 years-over . .	0.36	0.37	0.67	0.35	--	0.32

Note: -- indicates data not available.

Source: U.S. Bureau of the Census. "Money Income of Households, Families and Persons in the United States: 1982." Current Population Reports (Series P-60, no. 142). Washington, DC: U.S. Government Printing Office, 1984, Table 23.

Table 14-11. Median Family Income and Mean Income per Family Member, by Size and Type of Family and Race-Ethnicity: 1982 [in dollars]

Size and type of family	Married couple families			Female householder, no husband		
	White	Black	Spanish-origin	White	Black	Spanish-origin
Median income	26,443	20,586	19,338	13,496	7,458	7,436
2 persons, householder 15-64	26,338	19,692	18,869	13,796	7,411	7,414
2 persons, householder 65+	15,825	8,485	9,436	13,849	6,749	—
3 persons	27,807	20,784	18,195	13,049	6,956	7,490
4 persons	29,659	23,864	20,575	14,059	7,646	7,160
5 persons	29,483	23,864	20,777	12,165	8,526	7,063
6 persons	31,197	22,618	21,382	9,899	7,684	—
7 persons or more	29,117	20,082	20,744	—	9,297	—
Mean income per family member	9,314	5,946	5,486	5,784	2,967	3,082
2 persons, householder 15-64	15,201	10,742	10,825	7,660	4,986	5,397
2 persons, householder 65+	10,484	5,244	6,525	8,411	3,729	--
3 persons	10,299	7,539	7,390	5,379	3,250	3,544
4 persons	8,247	6,593	5,831	4,527	2,609	2,682
5 persons	6,674	4,963	4,414	3,530	2,253	2,135
6 persons	5,759	4,211	4,040	2,207	1,868	—
7 persons or more	4,452	2,754	3,170	—	1,545	--

Note: -- indicates data not available.

Source: U.S. Bureau of the Census. "Money Income of Households, Families and Persons in the United States: 1982." Current Population Reports (Series P-60, no. 142). Washington, DC: U.S. Government Printing Office, 1984, Table 25.

Table 14-12. Median Family Income, by Type of Family and Number of Related Children Under 15 Years of Age: 1982

Number of related children under 18 years of age	All families	Married couple families	Female householder, no husband present
Total	23,433	26,019	11,484
No children	23,544	24,668	16,916
1 child	23,420	27,742	11,170
2 children	24,779	27,745	8,750
3 children	22,434	25,971	7,836
4 children	19,298	23,351	6,914
5 children	16,114	20,921	6,477
6 or more children	12,847	17,689	*

Note: * indicates insufficient data for reliable measure.

Source: U.S. Bureau of the Census. "Money Income of Households, Families and Persons in the United States: 1982." Current Population Reports (Series P-60, no. 142). Washington, DC: U.S. Government Printing Office, 1984, Table 27.

Size of Family

Table 14-11, which reports median income of families by number of persons and by type and race, shows that two-person families tend to have slightly lower incomes than families with three or more members, and that four-person families have somewhat higher incomes than three-person families. Beyond four, the level of income remains almost stationary with increasing family size. This is true for both married-couple families and families headed by a female with no husband. It is true for white, black, and Spanish-origin populations. The lower median income of two-person and three-person families could be caused by either extremely young or extremely old householders. Table 14-11 provides data showing that two-person families where the householder is sixty-five or older tend to have incomes considerably below average. The bottom panel of Table 14-11 reports the mean income per member, by family size. With increasing family size, mean income per member declines for all race and family type groups.

Table 14-13. Number of Earners—Median Family Income, by Race-Ethnicity: 1982 [in thousands of dollars]

Number of earners in family	All families				Householder year-round full-time worker			
	All races	White	Black	Spanish-origin	All races	White	Black	Spanish-origin
Total	23,495	24,654	13,507	16,254	30,480	31,088	23,156	22,856
No earners.	9,911	11,384	4,886	5,574	...	...	...	...
One earner.	18,913	20,244	11,062	12,399	23,036	24,216	14,331	15,784
Two earners	28,073	28,628	23,249	21,449	31,203	31,554	26,760	25,662
Three earners	35,798	36,824	26,992	26,255	39,078	39,893	31,093	31,186
Four or more earners. .	44,409	45,052	37,483	37,118	47,028	47,504	40,698	40,978

Note: ... indicates data not applicable.

Source: U.S. Bureau of the Census. "Money Income of Households, Families and Persons in the United States: 1982." Current Population Reports (Series P-60, no. 142). Washington, DC: U.S. Government Printing Office, 1984, Table 29.

Number of Children

The number of children has a small negative effect on family income (see Table 14-12). Married-couple families with no children have slightly lower median incomes than families with one child. However, family income in married couple families tends to decline slightly with additional numbers of children beyond the second. For families headed by females, the highest income is where there are no children; median income in such families declines with the increasing number of children. Thus having more children does not necessarily cause parents to intensify their efforts and generate more income in order to care for their offspring. Instead, large families must share a below-average income among more members, leaving the income-per-member to be only a fraction of that enjoyed by the family with one or two children.

Number of Earners

The positive effect upon family income of working wives has already been noted. Table 14-13 generalized this by reporting median family income according to the number of earners. Families with four earners or more tend to fall in the wealthy or affluent class, irrespective of race or ethnic origin, while families with no earner tend to be in low-income levels, with clear poverty for the black and Spanish-origin family and near-poverty for the white family. Income rises with each additional earner. The effect is quite marked when all earners are year-round, full-time workers.

Marital Status and Sex of Householder

Marital status tends to have comparatively little effect upon the median family income when the householder is male. Perhaps because of their youth, single (never married) men tend to have somewhat lower family incomes (see Table 14-14). Because of the lack of opportunity to have a working wife, those who are separated, widowed, or divorced have lower incomes than those who are married with wife present.

For women marital status is a critical determinant of family income. Women married with husband present enjoy peak family income, which tends to place them in the middle-class category or higher. If they are widowed or divorced, their income level is reduced by one-half. Perhaps the financial cost of obtaining a divorce influences this differential, since separated women also have incomes much below women who are divorced. Widowed women who are white and sixty-five or older have higher incomes than divorced women. Single (never married) women who are heads of families tend to have very low incomes. These marital status differences are found in white, black, and Spanish-origin families.

Educational Attainment and Income

Rich rewards are paid by the American economy to those who attain an advanced education, as Table 14-15

Table 14-14. Median Family Income by Marital Status, by Sex, Age, and Race-Ethnicity: 1982

Marital status	Age 18 to 24 years			Age 25 to 64 years			Age 65 years and over		
	White	Black	Spanish-origin	White	Black	Spanish-origin	White	Black	Spanish-origin
Male, total	6,456	3,620	6,098	19,831	12,072	12,763	9,689	5,214	6,210
Single (never married).	5,009	3,108	4,737	13,645	8,976	9,227	7,390	*	*
Married, wife present .	12,232	10,029	10,263	21,101	14,328	13,989	10,202	5,594	6,299
Married, wife absent. .	7,457	*	*	15,888	9,200	10,384	6,704	*	*
Widowed	*	*	*	16,922	7,829	*	8,340	4,706	*
Divorced.	7,975	*	*	17,172	11,938	12,958	7,834	*	*
Female, total . . .	4,569	3,279	4,231	7,397	7,479	6,361	5,594	3,605	3,671
Single (never married).	4,191	3,072	4,252	12,320	6,527	7,993	7,703	*	*
Married, husband present	5,379	5,475	4,006	5,842	8,472	5,681	4,626	2,709	2,869
Married, husband absent.	4,243	3,142	*	7,122	6,237	5,499	4,647	*	*
Widowed	*	*	*	9,597	4,933	6,534	5,965	3,772	3,851
Divorced.	6,561	*	*	12,007	9,038	8,073	5,896	*	*

Note: * indicates base too small to show derived measure.

Source: U.S. Bureau of the Census. "Money Income of Households, Families and Persons in the United States: 1982." Current Population Reports (Series P-60, no. 142). Washington, DC: U.S. Government Printing Office, 1984, Table 45.

Table 14-15. Education and Money Income, by Race and Sex for Families and Individuals: Median Income, 1982

Years of schooling completed	Families		Individuals			
			Male		Female	
	White	Black	White	Black	White	Black
All workers						
Total	25,306	14,427	17,699	10,908	6,689	6,223
Elementary						
0-7 years . .	12,708	9,798	7,748	5,424	4,030	3,484
8 years . . .	15,783	11,390	9,869	7,492	4,735	3,891
High school						
1-3 years . .	18,779	11,358	12,591	9,253	5,046	4,475
4 years . . .	24,617	16,425	17,583	12,498	6,881	7,671
College						
1-3 years . .	28,330	18,705	20,473	14,325	8,453	10,128
4 years . . .	36,370	28,805	25,368	16,532	11,472	13,811
5+ years. . .	42,030	32,268	29,068	21,902	16,635	18,469
Year-round full-time workers						
Total	31,775	23,675	23,549	16,534	14,734	12,674
Elementary						
0-7 years . .	19,679	16,902	12,762	11,288	8,176	10,346
8 years . . .	23,280	19,508	16,773	13,462	10,572	8,199
High school						
1-3 years . .	25,367	21,128	18,203	15,104	10,803	10,353
4 years . . .	29,206	23,680	21,856	16,469	13,458	12,105
College						
1-3 years . .	32,163	24,751	24,179	18,839	15,721	15,177
4 years . . .	40,236	33,124	28,745	18,829	17,596	16,183
5+ years. . .	45,607	36,764	32,542	25,204	21,474	21,112

Source: U.S. Bureau of the Census. "Money Income of Households, Families and Persons in the United States: 1982." Current Population Reports (Series P-60, no. 142). Washington, DC: U.S. Government Printing Office, 1984, Tables 32 and 47.

documents. For example, in 1982 the median income of white families whose head completed five years or more of college was $42,030, which was 3.3 times the median income of those who had completed less than eight grades ($12,708) and 70 percent greater than the median income of those who had graduated from high school ($24,617). A senior in high school, debating whether it would be worthwhile to go to college, could note from Table 14-15 that the median income of families headed by white male college graduates is $11,753 per year greater than that of high school graduates. Thus he could reasonably expect to receive a lifelong bonus of about $2,938 a year for each of the four years he would spend in college, or $45 for each working day of his life for spending the four years. The rewards that are lost by not completing elementary school or high school can also be calculated in terms of money, and the penalties are very substantial. The income benefits for additional education are substantially less for women than for men. For the black population they are less than for the white population. Although many highly educated people receive small incomes, and many people with little education receive high incomes, they only provide exceptions to what is a very marked and a very consistent relationship.

For the black population education can be an avenue for escaping poverty. Although the race differential in income remains more or less constant, the education differential works for black in the same way as for white students. Table 14-16 provides detail by age, sex, each of the races, and the Spanish-origin population.

Lifetime Earnings and Educational Attainment

One way of evaluating the impact of educational attainment on income is to compute the total lifetime earnings of individuals according to their educational attainment. This is estimated by assuming that if a person were to begin working at age eighteen and cease working at sixty-five and during his entire working life would receive an annual income that is average for a person of his age at the time and his educational attainment, one could sum the earnings for all years and obtain his lifetime earnings. These calculations have been made and reported for 1980. The estimates have been made realistic by including the probability of dying before age sixty-five. The income rates used for each age were an average of incomes for 1978 to 1980. Following are the estimates of total lifetime earnings (in thousands of dollars) under these assumptions:

Educational attainment	Average amount of employment		Full-time year-round employment	
	Men	Women	Men	Women
Less than high school. .	601	211	845	500
High school, 4 years . .	861	381	1,041	634
College, 1-3 years . . .	957	460	1,155	716
College, 4 years	1,190	523	1,392	846
College, 5+ years. . . .	1,301	699	1,503	955

Table 14-16. Median Income by Educational Attainment and Race-Ethnicity of Persons 18 Years of Age and Over in the Recent Experienced Civilian Labor Force, by Age and Sex: 1980

Educational attainment by age	All races		White		Black		American Indian		Asian/Pac.Is.		Spanish-origin	
	Male	Female	Male	Female	Male	Female	Male	Female	Male	Female	Male	Female
All ages, total.	19,943	11,051	20,574	11,158	14,136	10,328	15,807	10,119	20,536	12,583	14,881	9,706
Elementary 0-8 years	14,142	8,353	14,866	8,577	11,574	7,757	12,872	7,898	12,506	8,409	11,639	7,605
High school 1-3 years.	15,845	9,208	16,482	9,349	12,360	8,678	13,805	8,263	14,427	9,689	13,115	8,643
High school 4 years.	17,648	10,374	18,037	10,437	13,726	9,916	15,389	9,866	16,271	10,820	14,863	9,793
College 1-3 years.	19,849	11,688	20,300	11,753	15,541	11,317	16,791	11,216	17,436	11,955	16,782	10,974
College 4 years.	25,943	13,833	26,394	13,871	18,223	13,550	20,797	13,306	21,370	13,922	20,716	12,883
College 5 years or more.	31,092	16,958	31,531	16,864	23,400	16,872	23,518	15,570	28,870	19,099	27,696	15,893
Age 25-34 years, total	17,543	11,437	18,002	11,580	13,807	10,690	14,971	10,254	17,677	12,595	14,245	10,145
Elementary 0-8 years	12,034	8,032	12,693	8,155	10,009	7,985	11,270	8,159	11,635	8,346	10,710	7,423
High school 1-3 years.	13,913	8,748	14,594	8,827	11,116	8,526	13,530	8,290	12,488	9,280	12,596	8,682
High school 4 years.	16,233	10,340	16,609	10,420	13,316	9,980	14,544	9,589	14,530	10,281	14,618	10,092
College 1-3 years.	17,399	11,699	17,700	11,784	14,854	11,292	15,770	11,032	15,983	11,861	15,955	11,228
College 4 years.	19,859	13,596	20,073	13,649	16,672	13,174	16,895	13,194	18,232	13,618	18,062	13,054
College 5 years or more.	22,462	15,540	22,648	15,499	19,254	15,475	19,259	14,776	21,976	16,621	20,292	14,663
Age 35-44 years, total	22,895	11,749	23,618	11,834	15,963	11,137	17,868	10,926	24,714	14,096	17,233	10,312
Elementary 0-8 years	14,449	8,405	15,203	8,595	11,790	7,964	13,194	7,949	12,898	9,093	12,493	7,909
High school 1-3 years.	16,993	9,343	17,769	9,444	13,323	9,030	15,596	8,464	14,701	9,926	15,019	9,027
High school 4 years.	19,904	10,961	20,323	10,992	15,664	10,753	18,003	11,130	17,847	11,310	17,512	10,557
College 1-3 years.	22,862	12,746	23,370	12,778	17,919	12,616	18,696	12,322	20,433	12,977	19,599	12,245
College 4 years.	29,491	15,454	30,084	15,567	21,030	15,347	21,839	14,026	23,386	14,630	24,047	13,709
College 5 years or more.	33,919	18,462	34,389	18,254	25,311	17,939	25,230	16,659	32,299	21,887	31,020	17,531
Age 45-54 years, total	23,593	11,637	24,347	11,788	15,713	10,577	18,496	10,664	23,213	12,573	17,420	10,037
Elementary 0-8 years	15,439	8,515	16,187	8,789	12,333	7,910	14,343	7,899	12,660	8,278	13,218	7,841
High school 1-3 years.	18,264	9,735	18,833	9,905	14,281	8,985	16,326	8,795	16,490	9,998	15,879	9,345
High school 4 years.	20,869	11,347	21,213	11,421	16,077	10,562	19,104	11,024	18,806	11,493	17,751	10,698
College 1-3 years.	24,306	13,001	24,821	13,053	18,235	12,596	20,447	12,556	20,218	13,017	20,326	12,395
College 4 years.	33,864	15,312	34,448	15,378	20,898	15,243	25,918	13,927	25,172	14,554	25,219	12,995
College 5 years or more.	38,487	18,868	39,015	18,768	28,354	18,788	28,121	16,385	35,038	21,976	35,665	16,982
Age 55-64 years, total	22,012	11,446	22,646	11,610	14,271	9,847	17,161	10,526	20,227	11,912	15,864	9,582
Elementary 0-8 years	14,847	8,611	15,453	8,872	12,005	7,627	13,383	8,117	13,414	8,282	12,429	7,710
High school 1-3 years.	17,757	9.747	18,113	9,885	14,130	8,788	14,736	8,906	16,760	10,224	16,038	9,276
High school 4 years.	20,259	11,432	20,501	11,487	15,385	10,394	17,107	10,794	18,693	12,046	16,769	10,441
College 1-3 years.	24,514	13,091	24,934	13,150	16,690	12,277	18,212	12,678	19,404	13,172	19,182	11,811
College 4 years.	33,218	15,449	33,610	15,485	19,782	15,322	31,902	15,483	25,342	14,913	22,517	12,567
College 5 years or more.	37,777	19,056	38,251	19,032	25,498	19,086	27,097	16,611	33,489	20,144	32,313	17,435
Age 65 years and over, total .	19,882	10,319	20,631	10,504	11,245	8,467	12,993	8,268	16,447	10,076	13,475	8,774
Elementary 0-8 years	12,053	7,894	12,556	8,098	9,310	6,914	9,820	7,327	10,941	6,715	10,266	7,241
High school 1-3 years.	15,392	9,068	15,693	9,199	11,421	7,939	11,642	6,333	17,739	10,515	12,899	9,531
High school 4 years.	18,406	10,658	18,693	10,750	13,040	8,986	17,161	8,909	15,479	10,468	14,774	9,057
College 1-3 years.	23,228	11,810	23,750	11,851	13,464	11,153	13,502	9,889	15,376	12,444	15,107	11,788
College 4 years.	29,860	13,272	30,439	13,391	15,664	11,648	23,533	13,525	16,821	10,543	21,491	12,259
College 5 years or more.	36,838	15,941	37,410	15,824	20,680	16,074	18,800	8,676	30,795	32,529	27,583	16,472

Source: U.S. Bureau of the Census. "Subject Reports: Earnings by Occupation and Education." 1980 Census of Population. Washington, DC: U.S. Government Printing Office, 1984, Tables 2, 3, 4, 5, 6, and 7.

Table 14-17. Mean Earnings by Occupation and Race-Ethnicity of Civilian Workers 18 Years Old and Over, by Work Experience in 1982 and Sex [persons 18 years and over as of March, 1983]

Occupation of longest job	Male				Female			
	Total	White	Black	Spanish-origin	Total	White	Black	Spanish-origin
All workers (persons with earnings)								
Total	18,273	18,384	12,183	13,464	9,404	9,420	9,027	8,198
Managerial and professional specialty occupations	28,503	28,849	21,206	24,287	14,515	14,418	14,959	14,002
Executive, administrative, and managerial	28,897	29,447	20,436	21,226	15,455	15,392	16,306	14,333
Administrators and officials	30,078	30,646	20,746	20,696	15,549	15,500	17,158	*
Management related occupations	25,394	25,798	19,800	*	15,281	15,181	15,035	*
Professional specialty occupations	28,081	28,198	22,012	29,007	13,994	13,863	14,435	13,759
Technical, sales, and administrative support occupations	19,265	19,760	13,300	14,312	9,294	9,267	9,254	9,208
Technicians and related support	20,757	21,143	15,108	*	12,434	12,268	11,497	*
Sales occupations	20,680	21,094	10,544	15,133	7,031	7,114	5,655	6,492
Administrative support, including clerical	16,094	16,466	14,197	12,601	9,945	9,928	10,083	10,071
Service occupations	9,843	10,162	8,552	9,945	5,073	4,857	6,001	5,007
Private household occupations	*	*	*	*	2,433	2,194	2,922	3,760
Protective service occupations	15,908	16,575	11,920	*	8,049	7,519	*	*
Service, excluding protective and household	7,753	7,757	7,638	8,827	5,286	5,032	6,508	5,214
Farming, forestry and fishing occupations	7,420	7,676	4,716	7,652	3,190	3,312	*	3,480
Precision production, craft, and repair occupations	17,495	17,846	13,071	14,284	10,280	9,983	12,825	10,193
Mechanics and repairers	18,009	18,347	13,417	15,372	16,523	16,026	*	*
Other precision production, craft and repair occupations	17,225	17,583	12,902	13,752	9,497	9,228	11,709	*
Operators, fabricators, and laborers	13,574	13,946	11,505	11,938	8,184	8,025	9,074	6,943
Machine operators, assemblers, and inspectors	14,918	15,167	13,573	12,829	8,375	8,214	9,229	7,008
Transportation and material moving occupations	15,495	15,902	12,831	13,766	7,856	7,637	*	*
Handlers, equipment cleaners, helpers, and laborers	9,691	9,937	8,679	9,555	7,380	7,324	8,064	*
Year-round full-time workers								
Total	23,653	24,195	16,963	17,900	14,331	14,468	13,250	12,236
Managerial and professional specialty occupations	31,996	32,329	24,275	28,858	19,084	19,118	18,273	16,864
Executive, administrative, and managerial	31,803	32,307	23,468	24,339	18,763	18,769	19,338	17,196
Administrators and officials	32,931	33,426	23,414	23,696	19,190	19,188	20,849	*
Management related occupations	28,325	28,752	23,588	*	17,987	17,978	*	*
Professional specialty occupations	32,219	32,355	25,160	36,666	19,315	19,380	17,780	16,578
Technical, sales, and administrative support occupations	23,699	24,090	17,578	18,195	13,574	13,584	13,330	12,803
Technicians and related support	24,215	24,446	*	*	16,040	15,987	14,643	*
Sales occupations	25,159	25,406	16,405	19,567	12,678	12,765	11,600	10,413
Administrative support, including clerical	20,717	21,146	17,915	16,193	13,545	13,566	13,422	13,135
Service occupations	15,847	16,457	13,392	13,889	9,365	9,249	9,800	8,716
Private household occupations	*	*	*	*	5,883	5,896	*	*
Protective service occupations	20,920	21,581	16,472	*	15,595	*	*	*
Service, excluding protective and household	12,956	13,105	12,333	12,571	9,322	9,162	9,904	8,695
Farming, forestry and fishing occupations	10,367	10,401	8,824	10,955	4,886	4,804	*	*
Precision production, craft, and repair occupations	21,751	22,047	17,406	18,242	14,736	14,712	*	*
Mechanics and other repairers	20,740	20,990	16,930	18,387	18,980	*	*	*
Other precision production, craft and repair occupations	22,438	22,756	17,741	18,150	13,937	14,023	*	*
Operators, fabricators, and laborers	18,202	18,657	15,469	15,429	11,779	11,617	12,457	9,641
Machine operators, assemblers, and inspectors	18,418	18,679	16,497	15,355	11,508	11,422	11,838	9,561
Transportation and material moving occupations	19,663	20,224	16,284	17,092	15,231	15,017	*	*
Handlers, equipment cleaners, helpers, and laborers	15,534	16,016	13,348	13,904	12,246	11,654	*	*

Note: * indicates insufficient data for reliable measurement.

Source: U.S. Bureau of the Census. "Money Income of Households, Families and Persons in the United States: 1982." Current Population Reports (Series P-60, no. 142). Washington, DC: U.S. Government Printing Office, 1984, Table 52.

Thus the male who fails to complete high school suffers a lifetime loss of more than a quarter of a million dollars. By going on to complete college after high school graduation, he adds more than $300,000 to his lifetime earnings. Obtaining an advanced college degree adds more than $100,000 to his lifetime total. Although the rewards to women are smaller in size, they are proportionately similar.

Comparison of the lifetime earnings of men and women who work full-time year-round provides an important measure of the handicap women suffer because of sex differences in income, holding education constant. Following is the ratio of female to male earnings:

Education	Average employment	Full-time year-round employment
Less than high school. .	0.35	0.59
High school, 4 years . .	0.44	0.61
College, 1-3 years . . .	0.48	0.62
College, 4 years	0.44	0.61
College, 5+ years. . . .	0.54	0.64

Women who obtain additional education are able to mitigate this disparity somewhat, but not to a very substantial degree. Although they obtain more income for added years of schooling, the amount of increment for women is far less than for men, even if they devote a lifetime to full-time year-round work.

Occupation and Income

Occupations differ markedly as to the level of income they provide. The professional and managerial categories provide a very high percentage of their occupants with an upper-middle-class or higher livelihood, while a very high percentage of the nation's low-income persons who live in poverty or near-poverty are those who work as laborers or private service workers. Table 14-17 reports the income of male and female workers, by occupation of longest job held in 1981. Statistics are reported not only for all workers but also for those workers who worked full-time year-round (presumably in that occupation). The data on full-time year-round workers are a crude measure of the average share of wealth that each occupation category commands in the labor market.

In Chapter 13 Table 13-5 provided data on the median income for males and females in each of the detailed occupation groups. By referring to that table, one can learn the relative economic standing of each specific occupation in relation to all workers of the same or opposite sex.

The statistics of Table 14-17 do not report the distribution of incomes within each of the occupational categories, which is very substantial. Also, data on full-time year-round workers obscure the fact that many occupations tend to fall low in the income scale precisely because they provide only irregular employment, and the full-time workers are an unrepresentative sample. Nevertheless, these data (together with Table 13-5) reveal the income profile of the American occupational structure.

Conclusion

Income, both individual and household/family, is strongly related to almost every demographic variable. In many ways it is a *result* or effect of education, occupation, and social class. However, it can be an important causal variable in determining the living conditions (especially of dependent children). It can influence fertility (see Chapter 6), mobility (see Chapter 7), as well as marital status and housing (see Chapter 17). Table 14-18 is a succinct summary of some of the most important of the relationships, both for families as units and for family members as individuals, for the race-ethnicity groups.

On the assumption that changing educational and occupational composition will influence future income, it is plausible to predict that as the remnants of the low-education cohorts are replaced with new generations of more college graduates working at technical rather than laborer positions, all race and ethnic groups should improve their absolute level of income. Even though they may still be deprived relative to the white population, significant proportions of the other race-ethnic groups should be able to rise above the poverty level as it is now defined. However, in order to accomplish this ideal, there must also be a solution to the problems affiliated with family income in households with a female head.

Notes

1. World Bank. *World Development Report, 1984.* Washington, DC: World Bank, 1984, Annex Table 1.
2. U.S. Bureau of the Census. *Statistical Abstract of the United States: 1984.* Washington, DC: U.S. Government Printing Office, 1983, Table 739 for data from 1960 to 1982. Data for other years from corresponding tables from the same source, adjusted for inflation.
3. For a description of the *Current Population Reports,* see the technical appendix to Chapter 2.

Table 14-18. Summary Measures of Family Characteristics and Income in 1982—Selected Characteristics of Families, by Race-Ethnicity of Householder

Characteristic	Mean income per family				Income per family member			
	All races	White	Black	Spanish-origin	All races	White	Black	Spanish-origin
Type of residence								
Total	27,391	28,603	17,259	19,737	8,392	8,936	4,718	5,058
Nonfarm	27,545	28,807	17,293	19,784	8,442	9,005	4,731	5,075
Farm	21,680	21,884	*	*	6,570	6,683	*	*
In metropolitan areas	29,495	31,074	18,203	20,006	9,024	9,689	5,093	5,147
In central cities	25,628	28,239	16,661	18,030	7,919	9,066	4,665	4,637
Outside central cities	32,010	32,581	21,942	22,922	9,731	10,006	6,128	5,901
1,000,000 or more	30,971	32,979	18,597	20,249	9,433	10,235	5,265	5,301
In central cities	25,091	28,442	16,809	17,461	7,697	9,154	4,729	4,625
Outside central cities	34,206	34,833	23,182	23,782	10,378	10,654	6,671	6,137
Under 1,000,000	27,637	28,809	17,534	19,546	8,504	9,034	4,809	4,869
In central cities	26,169	28,069	16,397	18,933	8,145	8,993	4,552	4,654
Outside central cities	28,807	29,334	20,044	20,771	8,783	9,062	5,356	5,317
Outside metropolitan areas	23,115	23,905	14,176	18,068	7,102	7,495	3,606	4,522
Nonfarm	23,278	24,126	14,226	18,209	7,155	7,573	3,626	4,545
Farm	20,845	21,026	*	*	6,375	6,497	*	*
Region								
Total	27,391	28,603	17,259	19,737	8,392	8,936	4,718	5,058
Northeast	28,390	29,425	17,985	16,090	8,578	8,972	5,141	4,372
North central	27,379	28,185	17,643	22,053	8,403	8,744	4,905	5,809
South	25,851	27,723	16,425	19,904	7,973	8,864	4,352	5,067
West	29,094	29,771	19,611	20,951	8,924	9,286	5,687	5,235
Marital status and sex of householder								
Total	27,391	28,603	17,259	19,737	8,392	8,936	4,718	5,058
Male householder	29,759	30,292	22,471	22,462	8,996	9,293	6,015	5,561
Married, wife present	30,048	30,522	23,113	22,545	9,008	9,289	6,074	5,487
Married, wife absent	20,872	21,459	*	*	7,475	7,945	*	*
Separated	19,513	19,805	*	*	7,047	7,411	*	*
Other	*	*	*	*	*	*	*	*
Widowed	24,530	26,468	*	*	8,298	9,424	*	*
Divorced	24,125	24,874	18,708	*	9,299	9,685	6,656	*
Single (never married)	21,350	22,958	13,975	*	8,709	9,741	4,933	*
Female householder	17,287	19,417	11,348	12,325	5,621	6,738	3,160	3,492
Married, husband present	28,764	30,426	18,922	21,745	8,969	9,968	4,759	5,461
Married, husband absent	10,737	11,257	9,544	9,264	3,153	3,542	2,530	2,453
Separated	10,407	11,092	9,212	9,211	3,054	3,511	2,424	2,443
Other	13,182	12,280	*	*	3,894	3,729	*	*
Widowed	18,733	20,645	11,958	12,382	6,355	7,578	3,243	3,464
Divorced	15,156	15,749	12,929	11,929	5,034	5,486	3,628	3,594
Single (never married)	11,535	15,025	8,382	9,762	3,994	5,956	2,612	3,187
Age of householder								
Total	27,391	28,603	17,259	19,737	8,392	8,936	4,718	5,058
15 to 24 years	15,831	17,091	9,019	12,526	5,751	6,334	2,971	4,062
25 to 34 years	24,040	25,176	15,871	17,987	7,095	7,475	4,568	4,681
35 to 44 years	30,363	31,589	20,376	20,980	7,699	8,088	4,857	4,697
45 to 54 years	34,298	35,822	21,404	24,114	9,409	10,048	5,219	5,740
55 to 64 years	30,971	32,133	19,105	22,886	11,022	11,807	5,375	6,702
65 years and over	20,990	21,844	12,272	15,548	8,921	9,555	4,105	5,325
Size of family								
Total	27,391	28,603	17,259	19,737	8,392	8,936	4,718	5,058
2 persons	24,148	25,161	14,074	16,980	12,007	12,542	6,822	8,440
3 persons	27,401	28,804	16,804	18,812	9,022	9,498	5,456	6,230
4 persons	30,924	32,080	20,114	21,233	7,674	7,968	4,952	5,287
5 persons	30,881	32,560	20,142	20,284	6,129	6,463	3,991	4,031
6 persons	31,388	33,477	19,825	21,607	5,186	5,531	3,278	3,588
7 persons or more	29,242	33,182	18,785	23,367	3,746	4,325	2,337	2,955
Mobility status of householder								
Total	27,391	28,603	17,259	19,737	8,392	8,936	4,718	5,058
Same house (nonmover)	28,308	29,497	17,888	20,737	8,635	9,178	4,831	5,244
Different house (mover)	21,754	22,890	13,997	15,855	6,876	7,372	4,098	4,352
Same county	20,382	21,700	13,085	15,921	6,431	7,001	3,812	4,335
Different county	24,267	24,891	17,391	15,612	7,693	7,993	5,184	4,415
Within a state	24,462	24,890	20,231	17,297	7,937	8,166	6,086	4,949
Between states	24,007	24,893	13,777	*	7,386	7,768	4,059	*
Contiguous	22,049	22,591	*	*	6,890	7,282	*	*
Noncontiguous	25,034	26,061	*	*	7,640	8,002	*	*
Abroad	21,086	22,243	*	*	5,631	5,933	*	*

Table 14-18. Summary Measures of Family Characteristics and Income in 1982—Selected Characteristics of Families, by Race-Ethnicity of Householder—continued

Characteristic	Mean income per family				Income per family member			
	All races	White	Black	Spanish-origin	All races	White	Black	Spanish-origin
Occupation of longest job of householder								
Total	30,823	31,741	21,531	22,620	9,047	9,438	5,814	5,669
Managerial and professional specialty occupations	42,753	43,324	31,780	35,837	12,657	12,896	9,366	9,925
Executive, administrative, and managerial	42,704	43,276	33,430	32,577	12,533	12,786	9,183	9,034
Administrators and officials, public administrators	43,693	45,335	*	*	12,808	13,377	*	*
Other executive, administrative, and managerial	43,718	44,215	34,783	31,827	12,610	12,852	9,122	8,585
Management related occupations	39,527	40,049	32,613	*	12,236	12,456	9,723	*
Professional specialty occupations	42,807	43,378	30,236	41,408	12,800	13,025	9,564	11,441
Engineers, architects, and surveyors	45,418	45,467	*	*	13,292	13,325	*	*
Technical, sales, and administrative support occupations	31,203	32,245	20,123	24,875	9,696	10,091	6,087	6,837
Technicians and related support	33,601	34,321	22,604	*	10,558	10,941	6,382	*
Sales occupations	34,305	34,986	17,719	25,650	10,410	10,657	5,227	7,038
Administrative support, including clerical	26,660	27,744	20,461	23,447	8,507	8,973	6,315	6,536
Service occupations	20,888	22,001	17,047	17,285	6,157	6,765	4,515	4,423
Private household occupations	10,927	11,134	10,381	*	3,036	3,268	2,726	*
Protective service occupations	30,233	30,084	31,096	*	8,616	8,690	8,080	*
Service occupations, excluding protective and household	18,181	18,885	15,840	16,116	5,444	5,989	4,210	4,200
Farming, forestry, and fishing occupations	18,165	18,290	14,069	14,175	5,241	5,419	3,050	3,285
Farm operators and managers	19,335	19,243	*	*	6,004	6,006	*	*
Other agriculture, forestry, and fishing occupations	16,913	17,108	13,572	14,042	4,536	4,769	2,920	3,211
Precision production, craft, and repair occupations	28,469	28,729	23,946	23,764	8,080	8,237	6,085	5,663
Mechanics and repairers	28,681	28,935	24,111	23,554	8,144	8,289	6,233	5,832
Other precision production, craft, and repair occupations	28,357	28,621	23,864	23,873	8,045	8,210	6,013	5,580
Operators, fabricators, and laborers	24,179	24,695	21,096	19,870	6,842	7,111	5,453	4,783
Machine operators, assemblers, and inspectors	24,203	24,764	20,706	19,384	6,965	7,262	5,406	4,720
Transportation and material moving occupations	25,706	26,132	23,005	21,343	7,150	7,312	6,171	5,124
Handlers, equipment cleaners, helpers, and laborers	21,507	21,893	19,490	19,351	6,033	6,372	4,742	4,558
Work experience of householder								
Total	27,441	28,655	17,243	19,753	8,415	8,961	4,715	5,058
Worked last year	30,823	31,741	21,531	22,620	9,047	9,438	5,814	5,669
Worked at full-time jobs	31,900	32,733	23,060	23,588	9,248	9,600	6,195	5,888
50 to 52 weeks	34,471	35,222	25,476	26,374	9,945	10,272	6,834	6,572
48 and 49 weeks	28,370	28,906	21,625	*	8,255	8,458	5,958	*
40 to 47 weeks	25,797	26,299	22,462	21,063	7,526	7,791	5,903	5,265
27 to 39 weeks	21,681	22,225	16,095	15,562	6,393	6,629	4,464	3,861
14 to 26 weeks	19,592	20,347	13,908	14,032	5,857	6,184	3,795	3,530
13 weeks or less	15,824	16,675	11,472	11,056	4,759	5,206	3,026	2,853
Worked at part-time jobs	20,568	21,920	11,512	13,920	6,845	7,547	3,214	3,624
50 to 52 weeks	23,730	25,047	13,181	15,215	8,105	8,813	3,813	4,254
48 and 49 weeks	24,111	25,512	*	*	8,420	9,375	*	*
40 to 47 weeks	23,044	24,549	*	*	7,586	8,313	*	*
27 to 39 weeks	17,933	18,874	12,080	*	5,593	6,065	3,364	*
14 to 26 weeks	16,460	17,622	10,005	*	5,557	6,094	2,979	*
13 weeks or less	15,973	17,402	7,903	*	5,175	5,964	2,027	*
Did not work last year	16,028	17,466	8,743	9,832	5,793	6,725	2,452	2,720
Years of school completed by householder								
Total, 25 years and over	28,076	29,254	17,952	20,344	8,523	9,058	4,839	5,123
Elementary								
Less than 8 years	15,023	15,767	12,038	14,253	4,504	4,928	3,242	3,351
8 years	18,345	18,836	14,292	17,280	6,097	6,550	3,519	4,341
High school								
1 to 3 years	20,097	21,230	14,942	16,905	6,074	6,704	3,785	4,269
4 years	26,100	26,973	18,729	22,260	7,889	8,280	5,090	5,731
College								
1 to 3 years	30,045	30,961	21,142	27,008	9,053	9,436	5,952	7,322
4 years or more	43,485	44,139	31,815	39,472	13,092	13,350	9,957	11,205
4 years	40,268	41,134	28,905	34,920	12,267	12,593	8,967	10,451
5 years or more	47,100	47,503	36,035	45,286	13,995	14,175	11,423	12,062

Note: The metropolitan population is based on standard metropolitan statistical areas as defined in the 1970 census and does not include any subsequent additions or changes. * indicates insufficient data for reliable measure.

Source: U.S. Bureau of the Census. "Money Income of Households, Families and Persons in the United States: 1982." Current Population Reports (Series P-60, no. 142). Washington, DC: U.S. Government Printing Office, 1984, Table 19.

Bibliography

Aldrich, H., and Weiss, J. "Differentiation Within the United States Capitalist Class: Workforce Size and Income Differences." *American Sociological Review* 46 (1981): 279-90.

Alexis, M. "Economic Status of Blacks and Whites." *American Economic Review Papers and Proceedings* 68 (1978): 179-85.

Alves, W.M., and Rossi, P.H. "Who Should Get What? Fairness Judgments of the Distribution of Earnings." *American Journal of Sociology* 84 (1980): 541-64.

Angel, Ronald, and Tienda, Marta. "Living Arrangements and Components of Household Income Among Hispanics, Blacks and Non-Hispanic Whites in the U.S." *CDE Working Paper* (Series nos. 80-19 and 71-1). Madison: University of Wisconsin, Center for Demography and Ecology, 1971 and 1980.

Becker, Gary S. *Human Capital and the Personal Distribution of Income: An Analytical Approach.* Ann Arbor: University of Michigan, Institute of Public Administration, 1967.

Beller, A.H. "Impact of Equal Opportunity Policy on Sex Differentials in Earnings and Occupations." *American Economic Review Papers and Proceedings* 72 (1982): 171-5.

Bianchi, Suzanne M. "Measurement of Household Economic Well-Being." Pp. 143-48 in *1980 Proceedings of the Social Statistics Section of the American Statistical Association.* Washington, DC: American Statistical Association, 1981.

———. "Racial Differences in Per Capita Income, 1960-1976: The Importance of Household Size, Headship, and Labor Force Participation." *Demography* 17 (1980): 129-43.

Borjas, G.J. "Earnings of Male Hispanic Immigrants in the U.S." *Industrial and Labor Relations Review* 35 (1982): 343-53.

Boulier, Bryan L. "The Effects of Demographic Variables on Income Distribution." *Program in Economic Development Discussion Paper 61.* Princeton: Princeton University, Woodrow Wilson School, 1975.

Brown, R.J. et al. "Incorporating Occupational Attainment in Studies of Male-Female Earnings Differentials." *Journal of Human Resources* 15 (1980): 3-28.

Browning, K. "Trend Toward Equality in the Distribution of Net Income." *Southern Economic Journal* 43 (1976): 912-23.

Cebula, J. "Real Earnings and Human Migration in the U.S." *International Migration Review* 16 (1982): 189-96.

Cherlin, A., and Hodge, R.W. "Age Adjustment of Income Differences: A Research Note." *Social Forces* 54 (1975): 194-98.

Chiswick, B.R. "Immigrant Earnings Patterns by Sex, Race, and Ethnic Groupings." *Monthly Labor Review* 103 (1980): 22-25.

———. "Sons of Immigrants: Are They at an Earnings Disadvantage?" *American Economic Review Papers and Proceedings* 67 (1977): 376-80.

Cloutier, N.R. "Urban Residential Segragation and Black Income." *Review of Economics and Statistics* 64 (1982): 282-88.

Cogan, John F., and Berger, Franklin. *Family Formation, Labor Market Experience and the Wages of Married Women.* Santa Monica, CA: Rand Corporation, 1978.

Corcoran, M. "Structure of Female Wages." *American Economic Review Papers and Proceedings* 68 (1978): 165-70.

Corcoran, M., and Duncan, G.J. "Work History, Labor Force Attachment, and Earnings Differences between the Races and Sexes." *Journal of Human Resources* 14 (1979): 3-20.

Cottingham, P.H. "Black Income and Metropolitan Residential Dispersion." *Urban Affairs Quarterly* 10 (1975): 273-96.

Cuthbert, R.W., and Stevers, J.B. "Net Income Incentive for Illegal Mexican Migration: A Case Study." *Migration Review* 15 (1981): 543-50.

Danzinger, S. "Do Working Wives Increase Family Income Inequality?" *Journal of Human Resources* 15 (1980): 444-55.

Darity, W.A. "Illusions of Black Economic Progression." *Review of Black Political Economy* 10 (1980): 153-68.

Dauterive, J.W., and Jonish, J.E. "Wage Differences Among Black and White Career Women." *Review of Social Economics* 35 (1977):79-94.

———. "Wage Differences Among Black and White Career Women." *Review of Social Economics* 35 (1977):79-94.

DeFronzo, J. "Cross-Sectional Areal Analysis of Factors Affecting Marital Fertility: Actual Versus Relative Income." *Journal of Marriage and the Family* 38 (1976): 669-76.

Diamond, D.B. "Income and Residential Location: Muth Revisited." *Urban Studies* 17 (1980):1-12.

Dooley, M., and Gotschalk, P. "Does a Younger Male Labor Force Mean Greater Earnings Inequality?" *Monthly Labor Review* 105 (1982): 42-45.

———. *Earnings Inequality Among Males in the U.S.: Trends and the Effects of Labor Force Growth.* Hamilton, ON: McMaster University, 1982.

Easterlin, Richard A. *Birth and Fortune: The Impact*

of Numbers on Personal Welfare. New York: Basic Books, 1980.

Ewer, P.A., and Crimmins-Gardner, E. "Income in the Income and Fertility Relationship." *Journal of Marriage and the Family* 40 (1978): 291-99.

Ewer, P.A. et al. "Analysis of the Relationship between Husband's Income, Family Size, and Wife's Employment in the Early Stages of Marriage." *Journal of Marriage and the Family* 41 (1979): 727-38.

Ford, E.J. "Explaining Inter-Urban Variation in the Level and Distribution of Income." *Review of Social Economics* 35 (1977): 67-77.

Foster, A.C. "Wives' Earnings as a Factor in Family Net Worth Accumulation." *Monthly Labor Review* 104 (1981): 53-57.

Franklin, S.D., and Smith, J.D. "Black-White Differences in Income and Wealth." *American Economic Review Papers and Proceedings* 67 (1977): 405-409.

Freedman, D.S., and Thornton, A. "Income and Fertility: The Elusive Relationship." *Demography* 19 (1982): 65-78.

Freeman, R. "The Effect of Demographic Factors on Age-Earning Profiles." *Journal of Human Resources* 14 (1977): 289-318.

Frisbie, P., and Poston, D.L. "Sustenance Differentiation and Population Redistribution." *Social Forces* 57 (1978): 42-56.

Garcia, P. "Trends in the Relative Income of Mexican Origin Workers in the U.S.: The Early Seventies." *Sociology and Social Research* 66 (1981): 467-83.

Garfinkel, Irvin. *Earnings Capacity, Poverty and Inequality*. New York: Academic Press, 1977.

Gortmaker, S.L. "Poverty and Infant Mortality in the U.S." *American Sociological Review* 44 (1979): 280-97.

Hanushek, E.A. "Sources of Black-White Earnings Differences." *Social Science Research* 11 (1982): 103-26.

Harris, R.J. "Rewards of Migration for Income Change and Income Attainment, 1968-1973." *Social Science Quarterly* 62 (1981): 275-93.

Haveman, R.H. "Poverty, Income Distribution, and Social Policy: The Last Decade and the Next." *Public Policy* 25 (1977): 3-24.

Haworth, C.T. et al. "Income Distribution, City Size, and Urban Growth (Gini Concentration Ratio)." *Urban Studies* 15 (1978): 1-7.

Hill, M.S. "Wage Effects of Marital Status and Children." *Journal of Human Resources* 14 (1979): 579-93.

Hirsch, B.T. et al. "Inter-Age and Intra-Age Income Inequality: A Cross-Sectional Analysis." *Southern Economic Journal* 46 (1980): 1187-96.

Hirschman, C., and Blankenship, K. "North-South Earnings Gap: Changes During the 1960s and 1970s." *American Journal of Sociology* 87 (1981): 388-403.

Hudis, P.M. "Commitment to Work and to Family: Marital-Status Differences in Women's Earnings." *Journal of Marriage and the Family* 38 (1976): 267-78.

Hyclak, T. "Note on the Relative Earnings of Central City Blacks." *Journal of Human Resources* 16 (1981): 304-313.

Jasso, G., and Rossi, P.H. "Distributive Justice and Earned Income." *American Sociological Review* 42 (1977): 639-51.

Jeong, D.K. "Impacts of Discrimination on Black-White Earnings Differentials, 1960-1970." *Review of Black Political Economics* 10 (1980): 380-90.

Jiobu, R.M. "Earning Differentials Between Whites and Ethnic Minorities: The Cases of Asians, Blacks, and Chicanos." *Sociology and Social Research* 61 (1976): 24-38.

Johnson, Harry G. *The Theory of Income Distribution.* London: Gray-Mills Publishers, 1973.

Johnson, W.R. "Vintage Effects in the Earning of White American Men." *Review of Economic Statistics* 62 (1980): 399-417.

Juster, F. Thomas (ed.). *The Distribution of Well-Being.* Cambridge, MA: National Bureau of Economic Research, 1977.

Kaluzny, R.L. "Determinants of Household Migration: A Comparative Study by Race and Poverty Level." *Review of Economic Statistics* 57 (1975): 269-74.

Kass, R. "Recent Changes in Male Income." *Sociology Quarterly* 18 (1977): 367-77.

Kreps, J.M. "Age, Work, and Income." *Southern Economic Journal* 43 (1977): 1423-37.

Kuznets, Simon S. *Growth, Population, and Income Distribution: Selected Essays.* New York: W.W. Norton, 1979.

Larson, D.A., and Wilford, W.T. "Quality of Life and Per Capita Income in the U.S." *Review of Social Economics* 37 (1979): 111-19

Lazear, E.P., and Michael, R.T. "Family Size and the Distribution of Real Per Capita Income." *American Economic Review* 70 (1980): 91-107.

Lebergott, Stanley. *The American Economy: Income, Wealth and Want.* Princeton: Princeton University Press, 1976.

Lieberson, Stanley. "A Reconsideration of the Income Differences Found Between Migrants and the Northern-born Blacks." *American Journal of Sociology* 83 (1978):940-66.

Liu, B.C. "Differential Net Migration Rates and the Quality of Life." *Review of Economics and Statistics* 57 (1975): 329-37.

Long, J.E. et al. "Income Inequality and City Size." *Review of Economics and Statistics* 59 (1977): 224-26.

Long, L.H., and Helman, L.R. "Migration and Income

Differences Between Black and White Men in the North." *American Journal of Sociology* 80 (1975): 1391-409.

Lopreato, S.C., and Poston, D.L. "Differences in Earnings and Earnings Ability Between Black Veterans and Nonveterans in the United States." *Social Science Quarterly* 57 (1977): 750-66.

Lord, G.F., and Falk, W. "Exploratory Analysis of Individualist versus Structuralist Explanations of Income." *Social Forces* 59 (1980): 376-91.

MacDonald, Maurice M., and Rindfuss, Ronald R. "Earnings, Relative Income, and Family Formation." *Demography* 18 (1981): 123-36.

Madden, J.F. "Urban Land Use and the Growth in Two-Earner Households." *American Economic Review Papers and Proceedings* 70 (1980): 191-97.

Mallan, L.B. "Labor Force Participation, Work Experience, and the Pay Gap Between Men and Women." *Journal of Human Resources* 17 (1982): 437-48.

Masters, Stanley H. *Black-White Income Differentials: Empirical Studies and Policy Implications.* New York: Academic Press, 1975.

———. "Effect of Educational Differences and Labor-Market Discrimination on the Relative Earnings of Black Males." *Journal of Human Resources* 9 (1974): 342-60.

McGranahan, D.A. "Spatial Structure of Income Distribution in Rural Regions." *American Sociological Review* 45 (1980): 313-24.

Milkovich, G.T. "Male-Female Pay Gap: Need for Reevaluation." *Monthly Labor Review* 104 (1981): 42-44.

Miline, D. "Migration and Income Opportunities for Blacks in the South." *Southern Economic Journal* 46 (1980): 913-17.

Mount, R.I., and Bennett, R.E. "Economic and Social Factors in Income Inequality: Race and Sex Discrimination and Status as Elements in Wage Differentials." *American Journal of Economics and Sociology* 34 (1975): 161-74.

Nakosteen, R.A., and Zimmer, M.Z. "Effects on Earnings of Interregional and Interindustry Migration." *Journal of Regional Science* 22 (1982): 325-41.

———. "Migration and Income: The Questions of Self-Selection." *Southern Economic Journal* 46 (1980): 840-51.

Nord, S. "Income Inequality and City Size: An Examination of Alternative Hypotheses for Large and Small Cities." *Review of Economic Statistics* 62 (1980): 502-508.

Orcutt, Harriet. "Differential Mortality by Income and Education." Pp. 212-17 in *1980 Proceedings of the Social Statistics Section of the American Statistical Association.* Washington, D.C.: American Statistical Association, 1981.

Perucci, C.C. "Income Attainment of College Graduates: A Comparison of Employed Women and Men." *Sociology and Social Research* 62 (1978): 361-86.

Pines, D. "On the Spatial Distribution of Households According to Income." *Economic Geography* 51 (1975):142-49.

Poston, D.L. et al. "Earnings Differences Between Anglo and Mexican American Male Workers in 1960 and 1970: Changes in the Cost of Being Mexican American." *Social Science Quarterly* 57 (1976):618-31.

Poston, D.L., and White, R. "Indigenous Labor Supply, Sustenance Organization, and Population Redistribution in Metropolitan America: An Extension of the Ecological Theory of Migration." *Demography* 15 (1978):637-41.

Rainwater, Lee. *What Money Buys: Inequality and the Social Meaning of Income.* New York: Basic Books, 1974.

Reich, M. "Persistence of Racial Inequality in Urban Areas and Industries, 1950-70." *American Economic Review Papers and Proceedings* 70 (1980):128-31.

Repetto, R. "Interaction of Fertility and the Size Distribution of Income." *Journal of Development Studies* 14 (1978):22-39.

Reza, A.M. "Geographical Differences in Earnings and Unemployment Rates." *Review of Economic Statistics* 60 (1978):201-208.

Rytina, N.F. "Earnings of Mean and Women: A Look at Specific Occupations." *Monthly Labor Review* 105 (1982):25-31.

———. "Tenure as a Factor in the Male-Female Earnings Gap." *Monthly Labor Review* 105 (1982):32-4.

Sell, R.R., and Johnson, M.P. "Income and Occupational Differences between Men and Women in the U.S." *Sociology and Social Research* 62 (1977):1-20.

Shorrocks, A.F. "Age-Wealth Relationship: A Cross-Section and Cohort Analysis." *Review of Economic Statistics* 57 (1975):155-63.

Simon, Julian L. "The Overall Effect of Immigrants Upon Native's Incomes." *(College of Commerce and Business Administration) Faculty Working Paper no. 703.* Urbana, IL: University of Illinois, 1980.

———. "Puzzles and Further Explorations in the Interrelationships of Successive Births with Husband's Income, Spouse's Education, and Race." *Demography* 12 (1975):259-74.

Smith, J.P., and Ward, M.P. "Asset Accumulation and Family Size." *Demography* 17 (1980):243-60.

Smith, J.P., and Welch, F.R. "Inequality: Race Differences in the Distribution of Earnings." *International Economic Review* 20 (1979):515-26.

Stolzenberg, R.M. "Education, Occupation, and Wages

Differences Between White and Black Men." *American Journal of Sociology* 81 (1975):299-323.

———. "Occupations, Labor Markets and the Process of Wage Attainments." *American Sociological Review* 40 (1975):645-65.

Syzmanski, A. "Racial Discrimination and White Gain." *American Sociological Review* 41 (1976):403-14.

Toikka, R.S., and Holt, C.C. "Labor Force Participation and Earnings in a Demographic Model of the Labor Market." *American Economic Review Papers and Proceedings* 66 (1976):295-301.

Treas, J. "U.S. Income Stratification: Bringing Families Back In." *Sociology and Social Research* 66 (1982): 231-51.

United States Congressional Budget Office. U.S. Bureau of the Census. *Income Disparities Between Black and White Americans.* Washington, DC: U.S. Government Printing Office, 1977.

Villemez, W.J., and Kasarda, J.D. "Impact of Regional Destination on Black Migrant Income." *Social Science Quarterly* 57 (1977):767-83.

Wang, C.S.Y., and Sewell, W.H. "Residence, Migration, and Earnings." *Rural Sociology* 45 (1980):185-206.

Welch, F. "Effect of Cohort Size on Earnings: The Baby Boom Babies' Financial Bust." *Journal of Political Economy* 87 (1979):65-97.

Wheaton, W.C. "Income and Urban Residence: An Analysis of Consumer Demand for Location." *American Economic Review* 67 (1977):620-31.

Williamson, Jeffery G. *American Inequality*. New York: Academic Press, 1980.

Winkler, D.R., and Morgan, W.D. "Decline in Poverty in the U.S., 1959-74." *Review of Social Economics* 37 (1979):159-73.

Wolf, W.E., and MacDonald, M.M. "Earnings of Men and Remarriage." *Demography* 16 (1979):389-99.

Wright, Eric O. *Class Structure and Income Determination*. New York: Academic Press, 1979.

Yezer, A.M.J., and Thurston, L. "Migration Patterns and Income Change: Implications for the Human Capital Approach to Migration." *Southern Economic Journal* 42 (1976):693-702.

Zenner, W.P. (ed.). "Symposium on Economics and Ethnicity: The Case of the Middle Minorities." *Ethnic Groups* 2 (1980):185-268.

Chapter 15

Unemployment and Characteristics of the Unemployed

Some members of the labor force are unemployed—that is, seeking work. A very sensitive indicator of the economy's wellbeing is the percentage of the labor force that is employed and the percentage unemployed. (See the "Definition Box" for definitions of unemployment and unemployment rates.) Some unemployment is inevitable, and at any given instant in time a considerable number of workers will be seeking work, even in conditions of so-called full employment, due to "normal" labor turnover.

This "structural unemployment" has several causes: new workers in the labor force, migration from one community to another, quitting because of dissatisfaction, discharge for unsatisfactory performance, etc. However, this "frictional unemployment" is not very great, involving perhaps 2 to 4 percent of all workers. As soon as the unemployment rate (the percentage of the labor force that is unemployed) rises much above this minimum, it becomes a subject of immediate and serious concern. The involuntary loss of jobs due to retrenchment of operations in a firm or industry is the major cause of unemployment beyond this minimum. It is a direct indicator of significant prevalence of economic hardship that manifests itself quickly in terms of poverty and increased demands for unemployment benefits.

One of the main reasons why the Bureau of Labor Statistics and the Bureau of the Census conduct the Current Population Survey once a month is to keep a vigilant watch on the level of unemployment. Not only must this survey show the total amount of unemployment, but it must also indicate what kinds of people, and which occupations and industries, are most affected by changes in the overall unemployment level. Although the data on current unemployment collected at the time of the decennial census refer to only one week out of a total span of ten years, they are valuable in that they reveal the comparative unemployment rates of small areas and the detailed characteristics of unemployed persons.

Long-Term Trends in Unemployment

Since 1980 a high rate of unemployment has been a serious national economic problem, in some months rising above 10 percent, and for 1982 and 1983 averaging 9.5 percent. This is double or triple the rate that normal labor turnover generates in conditions of full employment. These high rates are one of the symptoms, as well as one of the causes, of the severe economic recession

Definitions

Unemployed. Civilians who, during the week used to determine labor force status in a census or survey, have no employment but are available for and desire work. They (1) have engaged in specific job-seeking activity within the preceding four weeks, such as registering at a public or private employment office, meeting with prospective employers, checking with friends or relatives, placing or answering advertisements, writing letters of application, or being on a union or professional register; (2) are waiting to be called back to a job from which they have been laid off; or (3) are waiting to report to a new wage or salary job within thirty days.

Rate of Unemployment. The percentage of persons currently in the labor force (employed plus unemployed) who are unemployed.

Duration of Unemployment. The number of weeks unemployed persons have been continuously unemployed during the twelve months preceding the survey or census.

Unemployment Work Experience. Persons who, during the preceding calendar year, were in the labor force for at least a part of the year and who also experienced unemployment during the year.

Weeks of Unemployment. The number of weeks that persons with unemployment work experience were unemployed during the preceding calendar year. This is the number of weeks during that calendar year when persons sixteen and older did not work but spent any time looking for work (trying to get a job or start a business or professional practice) or on layoff from a job. Excluded are any weeks in which the person worked, even for one hour, or any weeks during which the person received any wages or salary; or in which the person was on active duty in the Armed Forces, on paid vacation, or on paid leave. The number of weeks of unemployment is the total number of weeks accumulated during the entire calendar year, regardless of whether the periods of unemployment were continuous.

Stretches of Unemployment. The number of episodes of unemployment the person experienced during the calendar year preceding the survey or census.

that gripped the nation during the first three years of the 1980s. In 1984 sustained signs of a lowering in the rates, gives rise to hope that the downward drift will continue and accelerate for a sustained time. Figure 15-1A charts the annual fluctuations since 1900 in unemployment as adjusted for seasonal unemployment. Table 15-1 reports annual rates of unemployment (as derived from Current Population Surveys) for each year since 1950. These data document the volatile unemployment history of the U.S. economy since 1929, the last year of prosperity before the Great Depression of the 1930s.

No one knows exactly to what heights the rate of unemployment rose during the depths of the Depression in the 1930s, or how many workers were unemployed. Labor force experts estimate from the available data, that 24.9 percent of all labor force members were unemployed in 1933. These estimates indicate that when the economic depression was at its worst, approximately one worker in four was without a job. Double-digit unemployment, hovering near 20 percent, lasted for a full decade, from 1931 to 1941, after which it plunged practically to zero because of the wartime mobilization of labor.

Various labor force experts have attempted to extend estimates of unemployment backward to years before the 1930s. Among these are the estimates made by Stanley Lebergott, which are graphed as Figure 15-1.[1] A study of this graph shows that, if the estimates are correct, rates of unemployment fluctuated more violently in the pre-Depression years than they have in the post-World War II years and that some of the economic low points that occurred earlier in the century actually were quite severe and caused extensive unemployment. For example, the "hard times" of 1908 to 1911, 1914 to 1915, and 1921 to 1922 appear to have been as severe as the 1980-83 depression. Moreover, it appears that the average level of unemployment among nonfarm workers, even during "good times," was considerably higher than it has been in most years since World War II. Thus, the two decades from 1948 to 1968 are unique and stand out as the longest period of low unemployment during this century. The lowest recorded rates of unemployment occured during World War II, 1942-45, when severe manpower shortages caused unemployment rates to fall almost to 1 percent. Unemployment was moderately high during the readjustment immediately after World War II.

Unemployment During the 1980-84 Recession

The severe unemployment of the recession of 1980-83 did not burst upon the nation suddenly, but gradually gathered momentum beginning about 1973. In 1975 and 1976 there was acute unemployment, which receded for four years and then returned at even higher levels in 1980. Figure 15-1B provides a fine-grained portrait of this recession in terms of monthly unemployment rates. At its worst, the unemployment rate reached its peak of 10.7 percent when 11.9 million persons were seeking work in November of 1982.

Table 15-1. Annual Average Number of Unemployed Persons and Unemployment Rate, by Sex: 1950-1984

Year	Number of unemployed (thousands)			Unemployment rate		
	Total	Male	Female	Total	Male	Female
1984 January to June 6-month average	8,681	4,848	3,833	7.6	7.4	7.7
1983	10,717	6,260	4,457	9.5	9.9	9.2
1982	10,678	6,179	4,499	9.5	9.9	9.4
1981	8,273	4,577	3,696	7.5	7.4	7.9
1980	7,637	4,267	3,370	7.0	6.9	7.4
1979	6,137	3,120	3,018	5.8	5.1	6.8
1978	6,202	3,142	3,061	6.0	5.3	7.2
1977	6,991	3,667	3,324	6.9	6.3	8.2
1976	7,406	4,036	3,369	7.6	7.1	8.6
1975	7,929	4,442	3,486	8.3	7.9	9.3
1974	5,156	2,714	2,441	5.5	4.9	6.7
1973	4,365	2,275	2,089	4.8	4.2	6.0
1972	4,882	2,659	2,222	5.5	5.0	6.6
1971	5,016	2,789	2,227	5.8	5.3	6.9
1970	4,093	2,238	1,855	4.8	4.4	5.9
1969	2,832	1,403	1,429	3.4	2.8	4.7
1968	2,817	1,419	1,397	3.5	2.9	4.8
1967	2,975	1,508	1,468	3.7	3.1	5.2
1966	2,875	1,551	1,324	3.7	3.2	4.8
1965	3,366	1,914	1,452	4.4	4.0	5.5
1964	3,786	2,205	1,581	5.0	4.6	6.2
1963	4,070	2,472	1,598	5.5	5.2	6.5
1962	3,911	2,423	1,488	5.4	5.2	6.2
1961	4,714	2,997	1,717	6.5	6.4	7.2
1960	3,852	2,486	1,366	5.4	5.4	5.9
1959	3,740	2,420	1,320	5.3	5.2	5.9
1958	4,602	3,098	1,504	6.6	6.8	6.8
1957	2,859	1,841	1,018	4.2	4.1	4.7
1956	2,750	1,711	1,039	4.0	3.8	4.8
1955	2,852	1,854	998	4.3	4.2	4.9
1954	3,532	2,344	1,188	5.4	5.3	6.0
1953	1,834	1,202	632	2.8	2.8	3.3
1952	1,883	1,185	698	2.9	2.8	3.6
1951	2,055	1,221	834	3.2	2.8	4.4
1950	3,288	2,239	1,049	5.2	5.1	5.7

Source: U.S. Bureau of Labor Statistics. Employment and Earnings. Washington, DC: U.S. Government Printing Office, 1984, Table 1.

In long-term perspective the *rates* of unemployment for 1982-83 that are widely regarded as intolerable are close to the average annual rate for the twentieth century. However, the *volume* of suffering involved, in terms of the number of persons unemployed (10.7 million unemployed), in 1982-83 approached the all-time record of 12.8 million set in 1933. As the labor force continues to grow in size, if the rates do not decline substantially the volume will eventually surpass the 1933 record.

Seasonal Variations in Unemployment Trends

Unemployment has a rather regular seasonal cycle. The number of jobless persons and the rate of unemployment tend to rise above the yearly average during the months of January, February, and March. These are the "slow" months with respect to employment. Retail trade is at a low ebb; winter weather hampers construction; agricultural activity and many types of manufacturing are suspended or greatly curtailed because of bad weather. The arrival of spring reverses the situation, and unemployment drops sharply during April and May. Unemployment tends to rise again during June, when the schools close and pour out a new generation of graduates seeking jobs and a flood of students seeking part-time summer employment. By August or September a large part of the new workers have been absorbed into the labor force; unemployment sinks to lower levels during the last quarter, when students are in school and when retail trade and other industries are at their peak in preparation for the holidays. This seasonal pattern makes it necessary to adjust the measured rate of unemployment before comparing it with that of preceding months. The monthly fluctuations of Figure 15-1B have been adjusted for this seasonability, and hence the sawtooth changes represent monthly variations in economic conditions in comparison with the same month in preceding years.

Differentials in Unemployment

Certain categories of workers are relatively secure in their jobs, whereas others lead a more precarious existence. It is useful to answer the question, "Who are the unemployed?" This may be done by examining the differences in rates of unemployment among various subgroups of the population. Differentials will be presented for age, sex and race-ethnicity, industry and occupation. Differentials in unemployment can vary widely, both from region to region and from one stage of the business cycle to another.

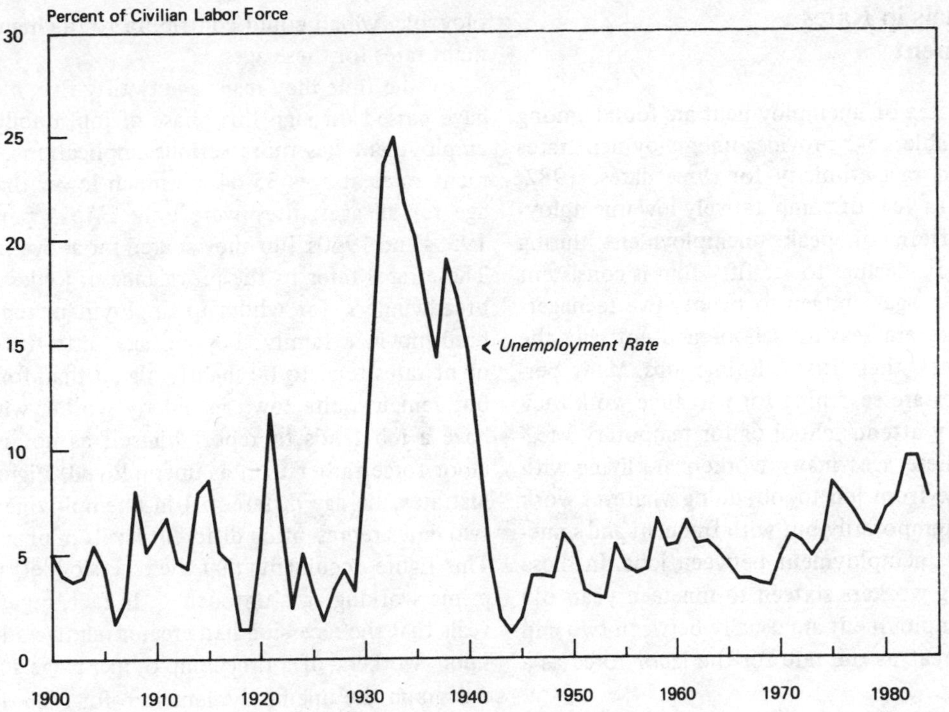

Figure 15-1A. Trend of Unemployment Rates in the Twentieth Century: 1900-1984

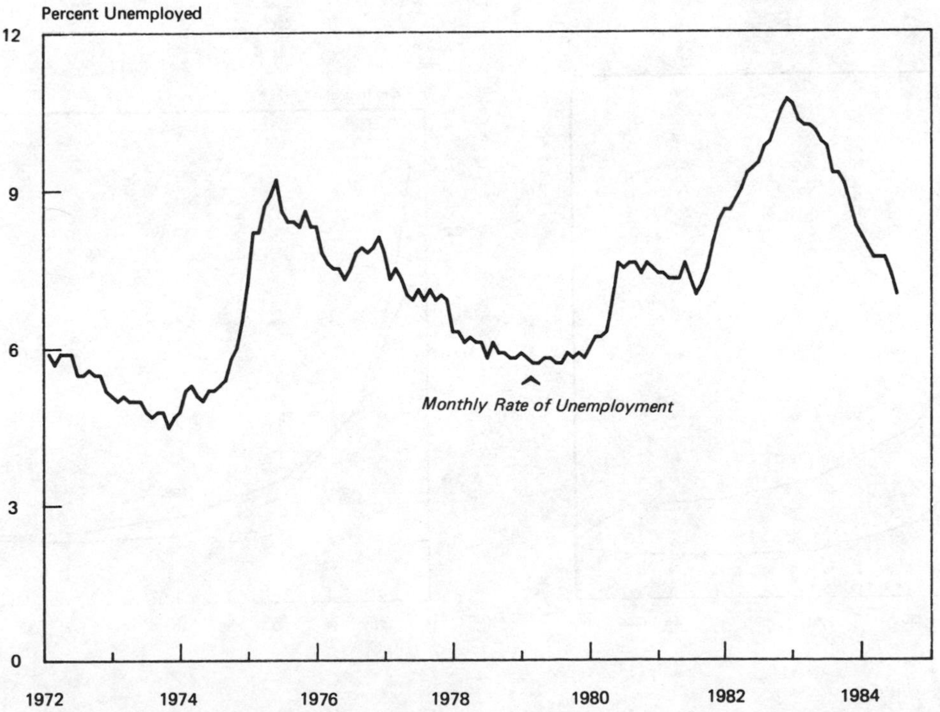

Figure 15-1B. Monthly Rates of Unemployment: January, 1972, to August, 1984 [adjusted for seasonal variation]

Age Differentials in Rates of Unemployment

The highest rates of unemployment are found among young people. Table 15-2 provides unemployment rates by age, sex, and race-ethnicity for three dates: 1982, 1980, and 1973 (a year of comparatively low unemployment). The pattern of peak unemployment during youth, with steady decline to age fifty-four is consistent for all groups. At ages sixteen to twenty-five teenagers and young adults are leaving school and entering the labor force to seek their first full-time jobs. Many persons of these ages are searching for part-time work they can do while they attend school or for temporary vacation work. At these ages many workers are living with parents and move from job to job, doing whatever work is available even temporarily but with frequent and sometimes prolonged unemployment between jobs. In these conditions among workers sixteen to nineteen years old the rates of unemployment are usually between two and three times as great as the rate for the labor force as a whole.

From one perspective, persons of this age who are seeking full-time year-round work should not be in the labor force at all but should continue in school. The fact that they are in the labor force may mean that they include school dropouts and the least educationally qualified members of their generation, hence the least employable, which could contribute to the high unemployment rates for these ages.

By the time they reach age twenty-five, most workers have passed through this phase of job mobility, and unemployment has more serious implications. Unemployment rates at ages 35-64 are much lower than the average for all ages; they were only 2 to 5 percent in the 1950s and 1960s, but they soared far above this in 1982. These rates refer to the prevalence of joblessness among breadwinners, for whom unemployment tends to mean hardship in a family. Beyond age sixty-five unemployment rates tend to be slightly higher than for ages 45-54 but remain quite low; an elderly worker who does not have a job tends to report himself as not being in the labor force rather than as unemployed. Figure 15-2A illustrates the age differential in unemployment rates for two dates representing different levels of unemployment. This figure documents that the recession left none of the prime working ages untouched. In fact, Figure 15-2B reveals that the recession had greater relative adverse effect upon workers of prime employment age (25-60). For this graph the unemployment rate for each age was expressed as a ratio of the average rate for all ages combined for that year. This was done for a year of high unemployment (1983) and for a year of moderate unemployment (1973). When unemployment is at a lower ebb, the age pattern becomes more polarized; everybody has a job except the very youngest and some of the very

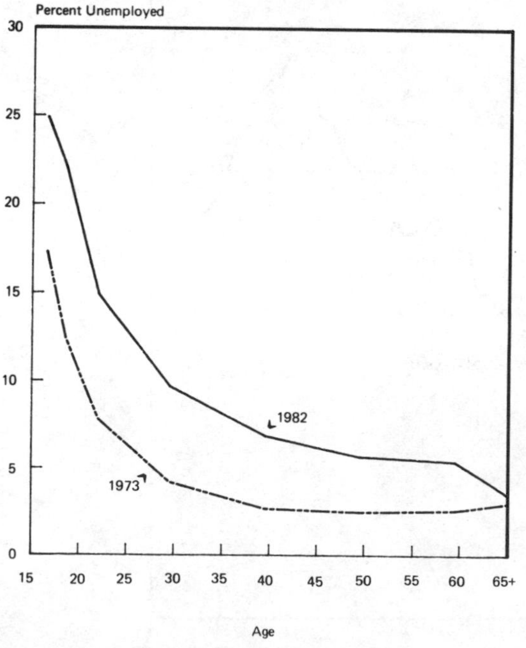

Figure 15-2A. Unemployment Rates for the U.S. Labor Force, by Age: 1973 and 1982

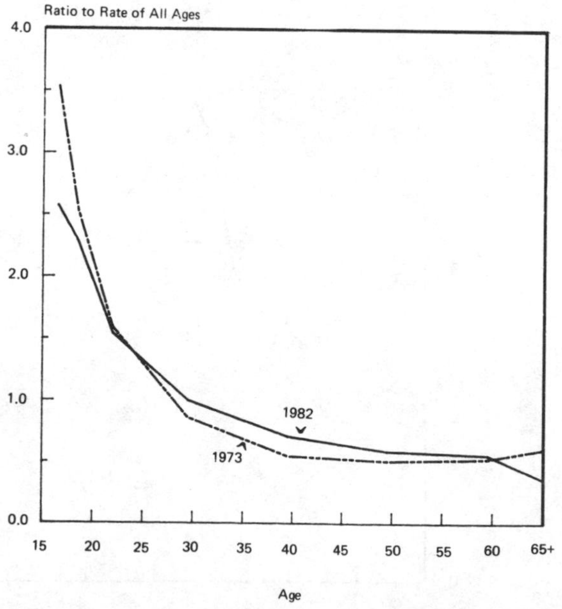

Figure 15-2B. Ratio of Age-Specific Unemployment Rates to Unemployment Rate for All Ages: U.S. Labor Force, 1973 and 1982

oldest people. Rising unemployment affects all age groups, but it causes the greatest relative increase in the central age groups 25-54 years of age. Thus, when the overall rate of unemployment rises, differentials become less sharp, because the proportional increases in joblessness are greatest among adult workers. Nevertheless, during times of recession the largest absolute (rate-point) change in unemployment rates still is found among the younger workers, as the unemployment rate in 1983 of 22.4 for persons aged 16-24 attests.

Age Differentials by Sex and Race-Ethnicity

All age groups of the black and Spanish-origin populations have higher unemployment rates than the white

Table 15-2. Unemployment Rates, by Age, Sex, and Race-Ethnicity: 1973, 1980, and 1982

Year and age	All races			Race-ethnicity: both sexes			Males			Females		
	Total	Male	Female	White	Black	Spanish-origin	White	Black	Spanish-origin	White	Black	Spanish-origin
1982												
All ages 16 and over	9.7	9.9	9.4	8.6	18.9	13.8	8.8	20.1	13.6	8.3	17.6	14.1
16 to 19 years . .	23.2	24.4	21.9	20.4	48.0	29.9	21.7	48.9	31.2	19.0	47.1	28.2
16 to 17 years .	24.9	26.4	23.2	22.8	48.6	37.9	24.2	52.7	40.0	21.2	44.2	34.8
18 to 19 years .	22.1	23.1	21.0	18.0	47.8	25.8	20.0	47.1	26.4	17.6	48.6	25.0
20 to 24 years .	14.9	16.4	13.2	12.8	30.6	17.7	14.3	31.5	18.3	10.9	29.6	17.0
25 to 34 years .	9.7	10.1	9.3	8.5	19.0	12.4	8.9	20.1	12.5	8.0	17.8	12.2
35 to 44 years .	6.9	6.9	7.0	6.3	12.1	10.7	6.2	13.4	9.8	6.4	10.7	12.1
45 to 54 years .	5.7	5.6	5.9	5.4	8.7	8.5	5.3	9.0	7.5	5.5	8.5	9.9
55 to 64 years .	5.4	5.5	5.2	5.1	8.3	10.1	5.1	10.3	10.0	5.0	6.1	10.5
65 years+. . . .	3.5	3.7	3.2	3.1	7.1	6.6	3.2	9.3	7.4	3.1	4.5	4.7
1980												
All ages 16 and over	7.1	6.9	7.4	6.3	14.3	10.1	6.1	14.5	9.7	6.5	14.0	10.7
16 to 19 years . .	17.8	18.3	17.2	15.5	38.5	22.5	16.2	37.5	21.6	14.8	39.8	23.4
16 to 17 years .	20.0	20.4	19.6	17.9	41.1	27.5	18.5	39.7	26.1	17.3	42.9	30.4
18 to 19 years .	16.2	16.7	15.6	13.8	37.1	19.5	14.5	36.2	19.1	13.1	38.2	19.7
20 years and over.	6.1	5.9	6.4	5.4	12.1	8.6	5.3	12.4	8.3	5.6	11.9	9.2
20 to 24 years .	11.5	12.5	10.4	9.9	23.6	12.1	11.1	23.7	12.3	8.5	23.5	11.9
25 to 34 years .	6.9	6.7	7.2	6.1	13.3	9.1	5.9	13.4	8.2	6.3	13.2	10.5
35 to 44 years .	4.6	4.1	5.3	4.2	8.2	7.7	3.6	8.2	7.2	4.9	8.2	8.5
45 to 54 years .	4.0	3.6	4.5	3.7	6.8	5.7	3.3	7.2	6.1	4.3	6.4	5.2
55 to 64 years .	3.3	3.4	3.3	3.1	5.4	5.9	3.1	6.2	6.2	3.1	4.5	6.3
65 years+. . . .	3.1	3.1	3.1	2.7	6.9	6.2	2.5	8.7	8.1	3.0	5.0	--
1973												
All ages 16 and over	4.9	4.1	6.0	4.3	9.4	7.5	3.7	8.0	6.7	5.3	11.1	9.0
16 to 19 years . .	14.5	13.9	15.3	12.6	31.5	19.8	12.3	27.8	19.0	13.0	36.1	20.7
16 to 17 years .	17.3	17.0	17.7	15.4	37.0	23.4	15.1	35.7	20.9	15.7	38.6	26.8
18 to 19 years .	12.4	11.4	13.5	10.4	28.1	17.3	10.0	23.0	17.7	10.9	34.2	16.7
20 years and over.	3.9	3.3	4.9	3.5	7.2	6.0	3.0	6.0	5.4	4.3	8.6	7.3
20 to 24 years	7.8	7.3	8.4	6.8	15.5	8.5	6.5	13.2	8.2	7.0	18.4	9.0
25 to 34 years .	4.2	3.3	5.8	3.7	8.1	5.7	3.0	6.2	5.0	5.1	10.3	6.9
35 to 44 years .	2.7	2.0	3.9	2.5	4.7	5.6	1.8	3.9	4.2	3.7	5.6	8.3
45 to 54 years .	2.5	2.1	3.2	2.4	3.5	4.7	2.0	3.2	4.5	3.1	3.9	5.1
55 to 64 years .	2.6	2.4	2.8	2.5	3.2	5.5	2.4	3.2	5.4	2.8	3.3	5.6
65 years+. . . .	3.0	3.0	2.9	2.9	3.5	3.9	2.9	3.3	5.5	2.8	3.8	--

Note: -- indicates data not available.

Source: U.S. Bureau of Labor Statistics. Employment and Earnings. Washington, DC: U.S. Government Printing Office, 1984, Table 44. (Ages 25 and over estimated by ratio to 1982 rates.)

Table 15-3. Ratio of the Unemployment Rates for Each Age to the Rate for All Ages Combined, by Age, Sex, and Race-Ethnicity: 1983

Age	White		Black		Spanish-origin	
	Male	Female	Male	Female	Male	Female
16 years and over.	1.00	1.00	1.00	1.00	1.00	1.00
16 to 19 years . .	2.30	2.32	2.40	2.59	2.16	2.02
16 to 17 years .	2.57	2.71	2.57	2.61	2.70	2.46
18 to 19 years .	2.13	2.08	2.33	2.58	1.91	1.81
20 to 24 years . .	1.57	1.30	1.55	1.71	1.29	1.18
25 years and over.	.78	.80	.75	.73	.82	.84
25 to 54 years .	.84	.84	.78	.78	.82	.85
55 years and over.	.58	.56	.55	.39	.81	.61

Source: U.S. Bureau of Labor Statistics. Employment and Earnings. Washington, DC: U.S. Government Printing Office, 1984, Table 44.

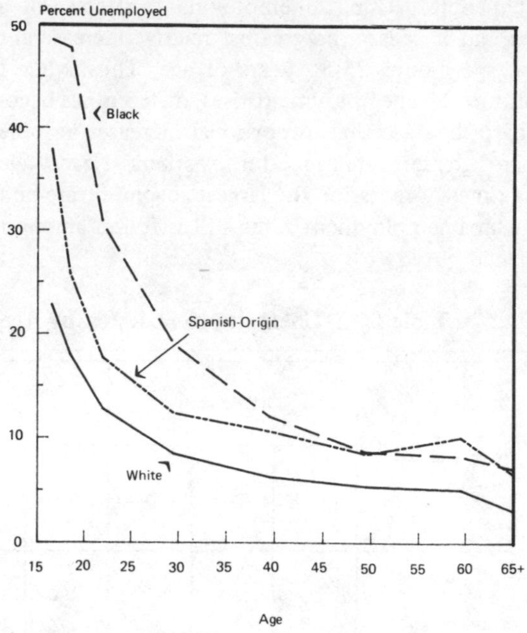

Figure 15-3. Unemployment Rates by Age, by Race-Ethnicity: 1982

population. At the same time each shows the general age differential described above. However, the age pattern is not identical for males and females or for all of the race-ethnic groups. The extent of this variation is shown in Table 15-3, which is a ratio of the rates for each age to the rate for all ages combined, for each sex/race-ethnicity grouping. The data are for 1983.

Age differentials for black workers are sharper than for either white or Spanish-origin; they tend to be extremely high in youth and unusually low in the later years of the working ages. Black females tend to have sharper age differentials than black males. Spanish-origin workers, in contrast, have less sharp differentials overall than the white population. Hispanic women tend to have smaller age differentials than Hispanic men. Thus, although each race-ethnic group tends to have its own unique level of unemployment, that risk is spread most unevenly over the ages among the black and least unevenly among the Spanish-origin populations.

Race-Ethnicity Differentials in Rates of Unemployment

Black participants in the labor force have much higher rates of unemployment than the white workers. All available evidence indicates that this phenomenon is so universal as to be almost "social law" underlying the operation of American society, as Table 15-2 demonstrates. It applies to each age group individually and to both males and females. It has persisted throughout the span of time for which unemployment statistics have been collected. Figure 15-3 graphs these differentials by age, for the year 1983. All this evidence seems to indicate that, at least on a gross basis (not considering differences in other characteristics), the cliché "Blacks are the last to be hired and the first to be fired" has a solid basis in fact. The extent to which this particular differential is due to race prejudice and how much of it is due, indirectly, to other factors associated with educational attainment, work experience, level of skill, health, and so on is a matter still being explored.

The Spanish-origin population suffers from above-average rates of unemployment also, but to a considerably lower degree. Spanish-origin males in particular suffer from unemployment less than black males.

Race Differentials by Age and Sex

The race-ethnic differentials in unemployment are not uniform by age and sex, however. Following is a set of ratios of unemployment rates of black and Spanish-origin workers to the rates for white workers of the same age and sex, separately for males and females. The data are based on the rates for 1983.

Age	Male		Female	
	Black	Spanish-origin	Black	Spanish-origin
All ages	2.3	1.6	2.4	1.8
16 to 17 years	2.3	1.6	2.2	1.6
18 to 19 years	2.5	1.4	2.9	1.6
20 to 24 years	2.3	1.3	3.1	1.6
25 to 34 years	2.2	1.4	2.4	1.7
35 to 44 years	2.1	1.6	1.8	2.0
45 to 54 years	2.0	1.4	1.8	1.8
55 to 64 years	2.0	1.9	1.6	2.0
65 years and over	3.7	2.4	2.0	1.4

Race differentials are at their highest at the youngest and oldest ages and tend to be somewhat lessened at the ages 25-54. Black and Spanish-origin women are more prone to be unemployed in comparison with white women than are black and Spanish-origin males in comparison with white males. Hispanic males particularly experience a lower differential with whites at the youthful working ages of 18-24—the very ages at which black males do worst in comparison with white males. The discrepancy between the unemployment rates of Hispanics and whites is greater for females than for males, and this disadvantage remains large at all ages.

Sex Differentials in Rates of Unemployment

During the years between 1970 and 1980 the unemployment rate for female workers was about 20 percent higher than the unemployment rate for males. A consistent pattern of higher female than male unemployment is reported for each year of the three decades 1950-1980. However, this differential was reversed in 1982 and 1983 during the severe recession, and males have had higher unemployment rates than females. This reversal occurred earlier (1980) among black workers; it had not yet occurred fully among the Spanish-origin workers by 1983. Following are the ratios of female to male employment rates for each year since 1970, by race-ethnicity:

Year	All races	White	Black	Spanish-origin
1983	0.93	0.90	0.93	1.04
1982	0.95	0.94	0.88	1.04
1981	1.07	1.06	0.99	1.06
1980	1.07	1.07	0.97	1.10
1979	1.33	1.34	1.17	1.47
1978	1.38	1.38	1.17	1.47
1977	1.32	1.33	1.12	1.32
1976	1.23	1.23	1.04	1.18
1975	1.18	1.19	1.00	1.18
1974	1.40	1.42	1.15	1.29
1973	1.46	1.43	1.39	1.34
1972	1.35	1.31	1.27	--
1971	1.30	1.29	--	--
1970	1.34	1.35	--	--

Note: -- indicates data not available.

Whether this reversal is a trend that will persist or only a temporary phenomenon linked to the high unemployment in 1982 and 1983 cannot now be determined. It is possible that discouraged female job-seekers may have tended in greater proportions than men to report themselves as not being in the labor force rather than as unemployed.

Sex Differentials by Age and Race

Following is a set of ratios of female to male unemployment rates, by age. The data are based on the rates for 1983.

Table 15-4. Rate of Unemployment and Percent Distribution of the Unemployed, by Industry: 1950-1983

Industry	1983	1980	1973	1960	1950
Total	9.6	7.1	4.9	5.5	5.3
Agriculture	16.0	11.1	7.0	8.3	9.0
Mining	17.0	6.4	2.9	9.5	6.7
Construction	18.4	14.1	8.9	13.5	12.2
Manufacturing	11.2	8.5	4.4	6.2	6.2
Durables	12.1	8.9	3.9	6.4	5.7
Nondurables	10.0	7.9	5.0	6.1	6.8
Transportation, public utilities	7.4	4.9	3.0	4.6	4.7
Wholesale and retail trade	10.0	7.4	5.7	5.9	6.0
Finance, insurance and real estate	4.5	3.4	2.7	2.4	2.2
Service industries	7.9	5.9	4.8	5.1	6.4
Government	4.2	4.1	2.7	2.4	3.0
	Percent distribution of unemployed				
Total	100.0	100.0	100.0	100.0	100.0
Agriculture	2.8	2.3	2.2	4.1	4.9
Mining	1.7	0.8	0.4	1.5	1.8
Construction	9.4	9.7	9.3	12.0	10.6
Manufacturing	22.9	26.2	21.5	28.6	29.8
Durables	14.6	16.6	11.5	16.3	14.2
Nondurables	8.3	9.6	10.1	12.4	15.6
Transportation, public utilities	4.0	3.7	3.3	5.0	5.7
Wholesale and retail trade	19.7	18.9	20.5	16.5	17.6
Finance, insurance and real estate	2.5	2.5	2.7	1.6	1.2
Service industries	15.5	14.0	14.7	12.1	13.7
Government	10.2	8.9	8.8	5.0	5.4

Source: U.S. Bureau of Labor Statistics. Handbook of Labor Statistics. Washington, DC: U.S. Government Printing Office, 1983, Table 29. U.S. Bureau of Labor Statistics. Employment and Earnings. Washington, DC: U.S. Government Printing Office, 1984, Table 11.

Age	Ratio of unemployment rate for female to male workers: 1983		
	White	Black	Spanish-origin
All ages.	0.90	0.92	1.04
16 to 17 years.	0.95	0.93	0.95
18 to 19 years.	0.88	1.01	0.99
20 to 24 years.	0.75	1.02	0.96
25 to 34 years.	0.84	0.96	0.97
35 to 44 years.	0.97	0.84	1.23
45 to 54 years.	0.96	0.87	1.31
55 to 64 years.	0.84	0.66	0.90
65 years and over . . .	0.97	0.53	0.54

The fact that the ratios are below one for all ages of the white population, almost all ages of the black population, and more than one-half of the ages of the Hispanic population makes clear that the reversal described above is just about across the board. Black women in particular have lower unemployment rates than black men at ages older than thirty-five in 1983.

Economic Characteristics of the Unemployed

Asking unemployed persons a few questions about their last job, their last employer, and some of the conditions of their employment during the preceding year makes it possible to locate unemployment within the economy. This information has been collected for sufficient years to permit identification of trends over time. Table 15-4 provides some trend data.

Industry of the Unemployed

Five sectors of the industry stand out as having above-average rates of unemployment:

Mining
Construction
Manufacturing
Agriculture
Wholesale and retail trade.

The sectors having below-average rates of unemployment are

Government
Finance-insurance
Transportation and public utilities
Service industries.

These differentials tend to be more or less stable over time. During the recent recession, the manufacturing and mining sectors had even higher ratios of unemployment in comparison with other sectors than their long-term above-average positions would predict.

Occupation of the Unemployed

Persons in some occupations are comparatively immune to unemployment, whereas persons in other occupations seem to be "sitting ducks" each time an economic downturn comes along. Table 15-5 reports unemployment rates for occupations. Occupations with below-average rates of unemployment are

Managerial and professional
Technical, sales, and administrative support
Private household service
Protective service
Mechanics and repairers.

Occupations with the above-average unemployment rates are

Operators, fabricators, laborers (all categories)
Construction trades
Service, except private household and protective.

The occupations with above-average unemployment rates are blue-collar, concentrated in the "traditional" or "low technology" industries listed above as being more prone to unemployment. Low unemployment is a trait of the white-collar occupations, especially those in high technology. Farm laborers have only moderately low rates of unemployment. Private household workers also have moderately low unemployment rates, perhaps because many may regard themselves as not being in the labor force if they do not have a job, or because of the great demand for their services.

Because of the size of the occupational group, as well as its high unemployment rate, operators are the largest single group of unemployed workers (27.6 percent). New workers with no previous work experience constituted 11 percent of the unemployed in 1983. During years of less unemployment they constitute a larger fraction.

In general women had lower rates of unemployment than men in each of the occupational groups except four:

Executive, administrative, and managerial
Sales occupations
Protective service
Machine operators and assemblers.

Because of the change in the system of occupational classification, data showing long-term trends in occupational unemployment of the unemployed cannot be reported in terms of the 1980 classification.

Table 15-5. Unemployment Rates and Distribution of Unemployed, by Occupation, Sex, and Work Experience: 1983

Occupation and work experience	Thousands of persons: Total 1983	Thousands of persons: Total Percent	Unemployment rates, 1983: Total	Men	Women
Total, 16 years and over	10,717	100.0	9.6	9.9	9.2
Managerial and professional specialty	795	7.4	3.3	3.0	3.6
Executive, administrative and managerial	396	3.7	3.5	3.1	4.5
Professional specialty	399	3.7	3.0	2.9	3.1
Technical, sales and administrative support	2,116	19.7	6.3	5.4	6.8
Technicians and related support	152	1.4	4.7	5.3	4.1
Sales occupations	850	7.9	6.7	4.7	8.8
Administrative support, including clerical	1,114	10.4	6.4	6.8	6.3
Service occupations	1,697	15.8	10.9	11.1	10.8
Private household	79	0.7	7.4	8.5	7.4
Protective service	120	1.1	6.7	6.2	9.8
Service, except private household and protective	1,498	14.0	11.8	12.8	11.2
Precision, production, craft and repair	1,466	13.7	10.6	10.7	9.8
Mechanics and repairers	344	3.2	7.6	7.6	7.6
Construction trades	709	6.6	14.2	14.2	14.1
Other precision production, craft, and repair	412	3.8	9.6	9.6	9.7
Operators, fabricators and laborers	2,955	27.6	15.5	15.5	15.5
Machine operators, assemblers, and inspectors	1,411	13.2	15.4	15.2	15.7
Transportation and material moving occupations	596	5.6	12.4	12.6	10.4
Handlers, equipment cleaners, helpers, and laborers	948	8.8	18.6	19.0	16.7
Construction laborers	207	1.9	25.8	25.5	--[a]
Other handlers, equipment cleaners, helpers, and laborers	740	6.9	17.2	17.5	16.2
Farming, forestry and fishing	407	3.8	9.9	9.6	11.5
No previous work experience	1,218	11.4	*	*	*
16 to 19 years	869	8.1	*	*	*
20 to 24 years	229	2.1	*	*	*
25 years and over	121	1.1	*	*	*

[a]Percent not shown where base is less than 35,000.

Note: * represents zero or rounds to zero.

Source: U.S. Bureau of Labor Statistics. Employment and Earnings. Washington, DC: U.S. Government Printing Office, 1984, Table 10.

Description of Unemployment

Duration of Unemployment

Some unemployed workers have been without work for a much longer time than others. Table 15-6 provides percentage distributions of duration of unemployment. It shows that during 1983 the average duration of unemployment was more than sixteen weeks. Since 1980 there has been a strong shift into the longer duration-of-unemployment categories.

Labor economists sometimes divide unemployment into "short-term unemployment" (less than fifteen weeks) and "long-term unemployment" (fifteen weeks or longer). Long-term employment as a percentage of all unemployment increases substantially during periods of high unemployment:

Table 15-6. Duration of Unemployment: 1950-1983

Duration	1983	1982	1980-81	1975-79	1970-74	1965-69	1960-64	1955-59	1950-54
Total	100.0	100.0	100.0	100.0	100.0	100.0	100.0	100.0	100.0
15 weeks and over . .	39.3	32.6	26.1	26.9	20.2	16.7	27.6	24.6	17.1
27 weeks and over . . .	23.9	16.6	12.4	13.5	8.6	7.0	14.0	11.7	7.1
15 to 26 weeks.	15.4	16.0	13.7	13.4	11.6	9.7	13.6	12.9	10.0
11 to 14 weeks.	8.0	9.4	8.7	8.6	8.1	7.3	8.7	8.4	7.7
7 to 10 weeks	19.4	13.7	14.1	13.7	13.7	12.7	12.7	12.9	12.9
5 and 6 weeks		7.9	8.9	8.6	9.1	8.9	8.4	8.3	8.5
Less than 5 weeks . . .	33.3	36.4	42.4	42.3	48.9	54.4	42.6	45.6	53.9
Mean duration	20.0	15.6	12.8	13.4	10.3	9.4	14.1	12.6	10.0
Median duration	10.1	8.7	6.7	7.0	5.6	3.7[a]	--	--	--

[a]Median duration for 1967-69.

Note: -- indicates data not available.

Source: U.S. Bureau of Labor Statistics. Handbook of Labor Statistics. Washington, DC: U.S. Government Printing Office, 1983, Table 30. Also U.S. Bureau of Labor Statistics. Employment and Earnings. Washington, DC: U.S. Government Printing Office, 1984, Table 14.

Year	Percent long-term
1983.	48.3
1982.	36.0
1981.	27.6
1980.	24.5
1979.	20.2
1975.	31.6
1970.	16.2

Prolonged recession causes the proportion of long-term unemployed to increase dramatically, as the jump from 36 to 48 percent between 1982 and 1983 indicates. Meanwhile the mean duration of unemployment rises. In 1983 it was roughly double the duration of a decade earlier.

Characteristics of the long-term unemployed, in comparison with all unemployed, are shown in Table 15-7. From this table it may be learned that persons with the longest unemployment tend to be males (both white and black) and older workers (forty-five to sixty-four) of both sexes. Women and young workers tend to be concentrated in the short-term unemployment category.

The industrial and occupational composition of the long-term unemployed, in comparison with all employed, is shown in Table 15-8. It may be noted that the long-term unemployed tend to belong to the following economic categories:

Industry: Durable goods manufacturing
Transportation and public utilities
Nondurable goods manufacturing
Occupation: Operators, fabricators, laborers
Precision production, craft, and repair
Managers and professional.

Table 15-7. Characteristics of Long-Term Unemployed in Comparison with All Unemployed, by Sex and Race: 1982, 1978, and 1972 [percent of all unemployed in each category]

Characteristics	1982		1978		1972	
	Total	Long term	Total	Long term	Total	Long term
Men.	57.9	64.4	50.4	58.0	54.5	61.7
16 to 19 years . .	10.2	6.9	13.2	8.2	14.6	9.1
16 to 17 years .	4.4	2.2	6.9	3.1	7.3	4.0
18 and 19 years.	5.8	4.6	6.3	5.1	7.3	5.1
20 to 24 years . .	13.2	13.9	12.1	12.7	12.8	12.6
25 to 44 years . .	25.0	31.1	15.9	21.5	15.2	20.5
45 to 64 years . .	8.8	11.8	7.9	13.3	10.3	16.6
65 years and over.	0.6	0.7	1.3	2.4	1.5	2.9
Women.	42.1	35.6	49.5	42.0	45.5	38.4
16 to 19 years . .	8.3	4.5	12.6	6.7	12.3	6.6
16 to 17 years .	3.4	1.3	6.0	2.5	5.7	2.5
18 and 19 years.	4.9	3.3	6.6	4.1	6.6	4.1
20 to 24 years . .	9.2	7.2	11.4	8.8	10.3	6.8
25 to 29 years . .	18.0	16.7	17.9	16.8	14.4	13.4
45 to 64 years . .	6.3	6.8	6.9	8.7	7.8	10.3
65 years and over.	0.4	0.4	0.7	0.9	0.8	1.4
White.	77.2	74.9	76.4	72.2	80.2	80.6
Men.	45.4	49.3	39.1	42.1	44.6	50.5
Women.	31.8	25.6	37.3	30.0	35.6	30.1
Black.	20.1	22.8	21.3	25.5	18.5	17.9
Men.	10.9	13.6	10.2	14.4	9.1	10.0
Women.	9.1	9.2	11.1	11.0	9.3	7.7

Source: U.S. Bureau of Labor Statistics. Handbook of Labor Statistics. Washington, DC: U.S. Government Printing Office, 1982, Table 32.

Table 15-8. Differentials in Duration of Unemployment, by Industry and Occupation: 1982 and 1983

Occupation and industry	Thousands of persons			Weeks		Percent of unemployed in group			
	Total	Less than 5 weeks	27 weeks and over	Average (mean) duration	Median duration	Unemployed less than 5 weeks		Unemployed 15 weeks and over	
	1983					1982	1983	1982	1983
Occupation									
Managerial and professional specialty	795	239	191	20.2	11.8	34.5	30.1	33.1	42.7
Technical, sales, and administrative support	2,116	760	436	17.8	9.1	38.0	35.9	30.3	36.6
Service occupations	1,697	633	345	17.8	8.7	40.1	37.3	29.0	34.5
Precision production, craft, and repair	1,466	397	430	22.9	12.9	31.8	27.1	35.7	45.6
Operators, fabricators, and laborers	2,955	816	911	24.4	13.6	32.2	27.6	38.5	47.4
Farming, forestry, and fishing	407	164	59	14.4	7.4	40.9	40.2	27.2	27.5
Industry[a]									
Agriculture	300	124	36	13.1	6.9	45.5	41.3	22.9	25.1
Construction	1,044	305	251	20.4	10.9	32.5	29.2	35.3	40.7
Manufacturing	2,461	600	865	26.6	16.7	31.3	24.4	39.4	52.5
Durable goods	1,567	333	628	29.4	20.3	28.7	21.3	42.3	57.7
Nondurable goods	894	267	237	21.7	12.0	36.0	29.9	34.0	43.4
Transportation and public utilities	475	132	141	23.4	12.9	32.3	27.8	37.2	46.2
Wholesale and retail trade	2,122	782	419	17.4	8.9	38.4	36.9	29.1	35.1
Finance and service industries	2,372	854	496	18.2	9.1	38.3	36.0	30.9	36.2
Public administration	320	98	75	21.4	10.4	31.5	30.8	41.1	39.4
No previous work experience	1,218	545	171	14.1	6.2	45.4	44.7	22.9	24.9

[a]Includes wage and salary workers only.

Source: U.S. Bureau of Labor Statistics. Employment and Earnings. Washington, DC: U.S. Government Printing Office, 1984, Table 16.

Whereas long-term unemployment formerly was linked almost exclusively to blue-collar employment, in 1982 and 1983 it included some higher echelon white-collar workers. In all occupations and industries long-term unemployment was greater in 1983 than it had been in 1982 and was most severe in the manufacturing industries.

Reasons for Unemployment

The Current Population Survey classified the unemployed population into four categories, according to the reason for being unemployed:

Job losers: persons who lost their jobs involuntarily
Job leavers: persons who left their jobs voluntarily
Reentrants: persons seeking to reenter the work force after an absence
New workers: persons seeking to enter the labor force for the first time

The distribution of these reasons by race and sex and for young workers of both sexes are shown for selected years in Table 15-9. This table shows that:

1. For adults involuntary loss of jobs is the overwhelming reason for unemployment. During the recent recession this was a still more important reason.

2. Among young workers new entrants and reentrants account for the preponderant share of the unemployed, and job loss is a comparatively minor reason for unemployment.

3. Reentrants make up an unusually large share of the unemployed women. Many women leave and reenter the labor force while men enter it and remain in it until retirement, which is reflected by above-average rates of female unemployment associated with reentrance.

4. Black workers, in comparison with white workers, seldom are job leavers but are more likely than white workers to be new workers or reentrants.

In conditions of severe unemployment (1978, 1982-83) unemployment because of job loss tends to increase, job-leaving tends to diminish, and reentrance tends to diminish in comparison with the pattern for lower unemployment. Freedom to change jobs and to withdraw and reenter the labor force at personal convenience is a luxury that workers apparently tend to forgo during economic crises.

Table 15-9. Reasons for Unemployment, by Sex, Age, and Race: 1970-1983 [percent distribution]

Sex and race	Reasons for Unemployment				
	Total	Job losers	Job leavers	Reen-trants	New workers
Total unemployed					
1983	100.0	58.4	7.7	22.5	11.3
1982	100.0	58.7	7.9	22.3	11.1
1980	100.0	51.7	11.7	25.2	11.4
1975	100.0	55.3	10.4	23.9	10.4
1970	100.0	44.2	13.4	30.0	12.3
Young workers 16 to 19					
1983	100.0	20.2	6.0	26.4	47.4
1982	100.0	23.3	6.8	25.7	44.2
1980	100.0	23.2	9.3	28.8	38.5
1975	100.0	25.5	8.8	29.9	35.9
1970	100.0	18.1	11.4	34.2	36.3
Male, 20 years+					
1983	100.0	77.8	6.4	13.2	2.6
1982	100.0	77.9	6.4	13.3	2.3
1980	100.0	71.2	10.7	15.4	2.7
1975	100.0	74.7	8.6	14.6	2.2
1970	100.0	65.1	12.8	19.4	2.7
Female 20 years+					
1983	100.0	49.6	10.6	34.0	5.8
1982	100.0	51.0	10.5	33.1	5.3
1980	100.0	44.7	14.4	35.6	5.3
1975	100.0	49.9	14.0	32.0	4.2
1970	100.0	40.5	15.9	39.4	4.3
Black					
1983	100.0	57.5	0.8	26.5	15.1
1982	100.0	59.5	0.7	24.5	15.3
1980	100.0	56.6	0.7	27.3	15.4
1975	100.0	60.2	0.4	25.8	13.7
1970	--	--	--	--	--
White					
1983	100.0	60.2	8.4	21.2	10.2
1982	100.0	60.1	8.5	21.7	9.8
1980	100.0	52.7	12.5	24.6	10.2
1975	100.0	56.0	11.0	23.5	9.6
1970	100.0	45.0	13.7	29.4	11.9

Note: -- indicates data not available.

Source: U.S. Bureau of Labor Statistics. Handbook of Labor Statistics. Washington, DC: U.S. Government Printing Office, 1983, Table 31. 1983 data from U.S. Bureau of Labor Statistics. Employment and Earnings. Washington, DC: U.S. Government Printing Office, 1984, Table 12.

Marital and Family Status of the Unemployed

Of the 10.7 million unemployed in 1982, 9.2 million (85.8 percent) lived in families; the remainder lived alone or with other nonrelatives. Conversely, of the 61.6 million families in 1982, 7.9 million (12.9 percent) contained at least one unemployed person. Thus, as members of families, many unemployed persons are able to draw on the family resources to sustain themselves while they seek work. Table 15-10 (upper panel) reports the proportion of families containing an unemployed person according to family type and presence of children. Families headed by women and families with children under eighteen are more likely to contain an unemployed person than childless families or married couple families with or without children. These differences are present for white, black, and Spanish-origin families, but among black families the proportion of families with unemployed members is almost double that for white families; Spanish-origin families show a presence of unemployed members only slightly less prevalent.

The bottom panel of Table 15-10 reports the proportion of families having at least one full-time employed person—a "safety net" that protects their unemployed members. Almost 60 percent of all families reported in the upper panel have such a net. The proportion is highest for married-couple families and is very low for families maintained by women: Only slightly more than one-third of such families with an unemployed member also contain a full-time earner. This is due because such families, almost by definition, have only one earner, if any.

The center panel of Table 15-10 shows the proportion of the families with unemployed members with no "security net" in the form of an employed person—not even one working part time. This is roughly 30 percent of all families with an unemployed member. The proportion for families maintained by women is far higher—in excess of 50 percent. This set of proportions is approximately the same in all the race-ethnic groups, although the situation is somewhat worse for black families, somewhat better for white families, and intermediate for Spanish-origin families. Overall in 1982, about one American family in twenty contained one or more unemployed members while not having any other family member with a job. For black families this was one in six.

Family Support of Unemployed

Whereas Table 15-10 viewed the "safety net" from the family's viewpoint, Table 15-11 views it from that of the unemployed person. It shows the proportion of unemployed persons who live in a family that *does not* have another employed persons to provide support. Roughly one-third of all unemployed family members are in this situation. For women who must maintain the family (without a husband), this proportion reaches 90 percent or more. It is lowest for wives, who can rely on their husbands if unemployed. Because not all wives work, about one-half of unemployed husbands have no other source of employment for the family. Because wives are less inclined to work when there are young children, the situation is worse for husbands with children in the households.

The above situation is both encouraging and discouraging. On one hand the phenomenon of the multiple-earner family and the working wife provides a high degree of protection against the disastrous effects of unemployment, which in the years before 1960 was true for a smaller fraction of the population. On the other hand, it is evidence that the very high unemployment rates of the 1980s are creating economic hardship for households that previously were economically stable and secure, leaving them wholly without income. The data also emphasize the great economic disadvantage facing working parents who must bring up children without a spouse on hand to provide an income in case of layoff.

Table 15-10. Unemployment Experience of Families, by Family Type and Race-Ethnicity: 1982

Family type	Total	White	Black	Spanish-origin
Percent of all families with unemployment in 1982				
Total families	12.9	11.7	22.4	18.3
With children under 18	15.6	14.3	23.7	18.9
Married couple families	12.0	11.1	21.7	18.6
With children under 18	15.2	14.3	25.0	20.0
Families maintained by women	17.0	14.5	23.2	17.0
With children under 18	17.1	14.5	22.4	15.4
Percent of families with underemployment containing no employed person				
Total families	30.2	27.9	39.6	33.4
With children under 18	32.2	29.3	43.6	36.6
Married couple families	23.3	23.1	13.5	27.9
With children under 18	23.7	23.5	23.5	30.2
Families maintained by women	52.8	49.1	58.5	53.7
With children under 18	61.7	57.8	66.9	63.8
Percent of families with underemployment containing at least one person employed full time				
Total families	59.5	61.7	50.6	56.1
With children under 18	57.3	59.8	47.8	54.0
Married couple families	66.5	66.6	66.5	62.2
With children under 18	65.5	65.4	67.1	60.8
Families maintained by women	36.5	39.7	31.9	32.5
With children under 18	28.8	31.0	25.5	26.3

Source: U.S. Bureau of Labor Statistics. Handbook of Labor Statistics. Washington, DC: U.S. Government Printing Office, 1983, Table 35.

Table 15-11. Family Relationship of Unemployed Persons, by Presence of Employed Members and Race-Ethnicity: 1982

Family relationship	Percent with no employed person in family			
	Total	White	Black	Spanish-origin
Total unemployed, living in families	32.7	30.5	40.9	36.3
Husbands	45.0	45.2	43.4	53.5
With children under 18	49.0	49.4	45.5	57.3
Wives	21.7	20.2	29.5	20.5
With children under 18	20.0	18.2	28.4	20.6
Women who maintain families	83.3	78.6	90.1	79.3
With children under 18	89.5	86.6	93.1	86.8
Men who maintain families	70.1	71.3	69.0	*
With children under 18	84.9	85.5	*	*
Relatives in families maintained by women	35.8	33.7	38.3	44.2
Relatives in families maintained by men	28.1	24.1	39.5	*
Relatives in married couple families	11.0	10.5	12.2	15.1

Note: * indicates data not shown where base is less than 35,000.

Source: U.S. Bureau of Labor Statistics. Handbook of Labor Statistics. Washington, DC: U.S. Government Printing Office, 1983, Table 36.

Table 15-12. Unemployment Rates, by Educational Attainment, Sex, and Race-Ethnicity: 1982

Educational attainment	Sex			Race-ethnicity		
	Both sexes	Male	Female	White	Black	Spanish-origin
Total.	9.7	10.3	8.9	8.6	18.9	13.4
Elementary:						
Less than 5 years. . .	16.9	16.7	17.4	15.2	23.4	16.2
5 to 8 years	13.6	13.2	14.6	13.2	16.1	15.4
High school:						
1 to 3 years	18.0	19.4	16.0	17.0	24.1	21.8
4 years.	10.3	11.3	9.2	9.1	20.7	11.4
College:						
1 to 3 years	6.9	7.5	6.1	5.8	15.8	7.1
4 years.	3.2	3.2	3.3	2.9	8.3	4.9

Source: U.S. Bureau of Labor Statistics. Handbook of Labor Statistics. Washington, DC: U.S. Government Printing Office, 1983, Table 66.

Educational Attainment and Unemployment

The risk of unemployment is far less among those with a high school diploma than among those who have less education. It is practically insignificant among those with a college degree. Table 15-12, which reports unemployment rates by educational attainment, sex, and race, confirms that those who have less than a complete high school education suffer from high unemployment rates, while those who have more education have less unemployment. This differential is of long standing. The prolonged and severe recession of the 1980s has eroded it somewhat, and in 1982 there was a substantial rise in rates of unemployment at the upper educational levels. The educational differential applies to men and women and to white and black workers. Although education provides less protection for black and Spanish-origin workers than for white workers, it does manage to narrow the race differential significantly.

For all groups, peak rates of unemployment are among the dropouts (high school 1-3 years). Unemployment rates are significantly lower for the small fraction of adults who attended only elementary school. These persons tend to be older workers (see Figure 15-4).

The impact of education upon the employment of youth is measured in Table 15-13, which compares unemployment rates for young persons who graduated from high school and those who dropped out. The high rates for high school dropouts document the great importance to youths of completing high school. (Chapters 10, 12, 13, and 14 all contain information on this point.)

Table 15-13. Unemployment Rates of Recent High School Graduates Not Enrolled in College and of School Dropouts 16-24 Years of Age, by Sex and Race: 1982

Characteristics	High school graduates	School dropouts
Total.	26.3	41.6
Men	24.4	43.4
Women	28.5	38.3
White	21.4	36.0
Black	58.0	73.1[a]

[a]Data for 1981.

Source: U.S. Bureau of Labor Statistics. Handbook of Labor Statistics. Washington, DC: U.S. Government Printing Office, 1983, Table 64.

Geographic Differentials in Unemployment

Unemployment is highest in the old industrial states of the Midwest and in certain states of the South and West. It is lowest in the Great Plains and certain states of the West, South, and Northeast. Table 15-14 provides the rates by states for 1982 and 1983, by sex. The states

Table 15-14. Unemployment Rates for Regions and States, by Sex, Age, and Race: 1981 and 1982

Region and state	All civilian workers		Male		Female		Both sexes, 16 to 19 years		White		Black	
	1981	1982	1981	1982	1981	1982	1981	1982	1981	1982	1981	1982
Total, United States. . . .	7.6	9.7	7.4	9.9	7.9	9.4	19.6	23.2	6.7	8.6	15.6	18.9
Northeast	7.4	9.0	7.2	9.3	7.6	8.6	20.1	22.1	6.6	8.3	15.5	16.7
New England	6.3	7.8	6.0	8.0	6.8	7.6	16.6	20.7	6.0	7.6	14.6	14.4
Connecticut	6.2	6.9	5.3	7.1	7.4	6.7	17.2	18.3	5.4	6.2	17.7	16.7
Maine	7.2	8.6	6.7	8.6	7.9	8.5	18.1	22.8	7.2	8.6	*	*
Massachusetts	6.4	7.9	6.4	8.3	6.3	7.4	15.9	21.4	6.1	7.8	11.3	11.3
New Hampshire	5.0	7.4	4.8	7.2	5.3	7.6	15.4	16.2	5.1	7.3	*	*
Rhode Island.	7.6	10.2	6.7	9.8	8.7	10.7	19.4	27.0	7.3	10.0	*	*
Vermont	5.7	6.9	4.9	6.9	6.8	6.8	13.1	17.4	5.7	6.9	*	*
Middle Atlantic	7.8	9.4	7.7	9.7	7.9	8.9	21.7	22.7	6.9	8.5	15.6	17.0
New Jersey.	7.3	9.0	6.7	8.6	8.1	9.4	23.2	22.5	6.5	7.9	14.4	18.8
New York.	7.6	8.6	7.4	8.5	7.9	8.7	21.9	22.3	6.6	7.8	14.7	13.8
Pennsylvania.	8.4	10.9	8.8	12.3	7.8	9.1	20.3	23.3	7.5	9.9	18.7	22.8
South	7.0	8.9	6.4	8.7	7.9	9.2	19.8	24.4	5.6	7.2	14.0	17.2
South Atlantic.	7.0	8.7	6.4	8.5	7.7	9.0	19.6	23.8	5.6	7.0	12.7	15.7
Delaware.	7.9	8.5	7.1	9.2	9.0	7.6	18.1	24.9	6.5	6.9	15.8	17.4
District of Columbia. . .	9.0	10.6	9.6	12.0	8.4	9.2	34.8	36.9	4.7	4.0	11.1	13.8
Florida	6.8	8.2	6.6	8.1	7.1	8.3	19.4	22.6	5.8	6.6	11.8	16.0
Georgia	6.4	7.8	5.4	7.3	7.5	8.4	18.3	21.2	5.0	6.1	12.1	13.3
Maryland.	7.3	8.4	7.1	8.6	7.5	8.3	18.6	23.6	5.5	7.1	14.5	14.8
North Carolina.	6.4	9.0	5.5	8.0	7.7	10.2	17.2	23.6	4.9	6.8	12.8	19.3
South Carolina.	8.4	10.8	7.3	10.8	9.8	10.9	20.9	24.4	5.5	8.0	15.1	17.2
Virginia.	6.1	7.7	4.9	7.1	7.6	8.4	20.4	25.8	4.9	6.2	11.5	14.7
West Virginia	10.7	13.9	11.8	15.5	8.9	11.5	30.3	32.0	10.6	13.9	*	*
East South Central.	9.2	12.1	8.5	11.8	10.1	12.4	26.3	31.3	7.2	9.6	18.2	23.7
Alabama	10.7	14.4	9.6	14.0	12.0	14.9	27.0	31.6	7.5	10.9	21.3	26.9
Kentucky.	8.4	10.6	7.9	11.0	9.0	10.1	22.5	27.6	8.0	10.1	14.5	17.9
Mississippi	8.3	11.0	7.2	10.7	9.8	11.4	25.1	31.1	4.8	6.9	16.9	21.2
Tennessee	9.1	11.8	8.7	11.1	9.6	12.7	29.4	34.3	7.4	9.3	17.2	24.1
West South Central.	5.9	7.5	5.2	7.3	7.0	7.8	16.6	21.4	4.8	6.3	13.7	15.4
Arkansas.	9.1	9.8	8.3	8.5	10.1	11.3	21.8	29.1	7.2	8.2	21.1	19.5
Louisiana	8.4	10.3	7.5	9.8	9.8	11.1	21.0	27.6	5.9	7.3	15.8	19.0
Oklahoma.	3.6	5.7	3.5	6.3	3.6	4.8	11.9	13.1	3.1	5.1	9.2	12.1
Texas	5.3	6.9	4.4	6.7	6.4	7.1	15.6	20.4	4.5	6.0	11.5	12.7
North Central	8.6	11.1	8.7	11.7	8.6	10.3	19.5	22.7	7.6	9.7	20.8	26.9
East North Central.	9.7	12.5	9.8	13.1	9.6	11.7	22.0	25.6	8.5	10.9	21.8	27.3
Illinois.	8.5	11.3	8.5	11.8	8.5	10.6	20.5	23.3	7.1	9.2	19.1	26.2
Indiana	10.1	11.9	9.7	12.5	10.6	11.3	20.6	24.8	9.1	11.0	23.4	23.7
Michigan.	12.3	15.5	12.1	15.7	12.6	15.1	25.5	28.7	10.6	13.3	26.8	33.3
Ohio.	9.6	12.5	10.1	13.4	9.0	11.3	23.1	27.5	8.6	11.2	20.4	25.0
Wisconsin	7.8	10.7	8.0	11.7	7.6	9.3	17.9	21.6	7.4	10.1	*	*
West North Central.	6.0	7.8	6.0	8.3	6.0	7.1	14.1	16.3	5.6	7.1	15.5	24.0
Iowa.	6.9	8.5	7.0	10.0	6.8	6.6	16.3	17.4	6.6	8.2	*	*
Kansas.	4.2	6.3	4.2	7.0	4.3	5.4	10.4	11.6	3.9	5.5	10.5	21.3
Minnesota	5.5	7.8	5.8	8.3	5.2	7.3	13.7	14.3	5.4	7.3	*	*
Missouri.	7.7	9.2	7.4	9.3	8.1	9.1	17.1	21.7	6.9	8.0	16.3	22.6
Nebraska.	4.1	6.1	3.8	6.5	4.4	5.6	9.9	16.2	3.6	5.6	15.9	23.3
North Dakota.	5.0	5.9	5.1	5.9	4.9	5.8	9.9	13.1	4.7	5.4	*	*
South Dakota.	5.1	5.5	5.1	5.2	5.1	5.9	12.6	12.0	4.2	4.9	*	*
West.	7.4	9.9	7.5	10.1	7.0	9.5	18.9	22.9	7.0	9.4	14.6	16.7
Mountain.	6.3	8.7	6.0	9.0	6.7	8.4	17.1	21.0	6.0	8.3	12.3	15.2
Arizona	6.1	9.9	5.7	10.1	6.7	9.7	14.5	25.2	6.1	9.5	*	*
Colorado.	5.5	7.7	5.4	8.2	5.7	7.1	18.7	18.6	5.3	7.7	8.6	8.4
Idaho	7.6	9.8	7.7	10.1	7.4	9.5	18.2	18.4	7.6	9.8	*	*
Montana	6.9	8.6	6.5	9.4	7.6	7.4	19.2	19.8	6.1	7.7	*	*
Nevada.	7.1	10.1	7.1	10.6	7.1	9.6	16.5	22.8	6.5	9.2	16.4	21.6
New Mexico.	7.3	9.2	7.1	8.6	7.5	9.9	21.9	24.2	6.2	7.9	*	*
Utah.	6.7	7.8	5.8	7.9	7.9	7.6	15.4	19.0	6.6	7.7	*	*
Wyoming	4.1	5.8	3.9	6.4	4.5	5.0	11.8	13.0	4.0	5.6	*	*
Pacific	7.8	10.2	8.0	10.6	7.7	9.9	19.7	23.7	7.4	9.8	14.9	16.9
Alaska.	9.3	9.9	10.4	11.0	7.7	8.5	15.7	17.5	7.3	8.5	12.7	15.8
California.	7.4	9.9	7.5	10.2	7.3	9.6	18.7	23.4	6.9	9.4	14.4	16.4
Hawaii.	5.4	6.7	5.8	7.3	4.9	5.9	16.9	22.3	6.5	7.7	*	*
Oregon.	9.9	11.5	10.4	11.6	9.2	11.5	22.8	25.6	9.2	11.0	*	*
Washington.	9.5	12.1	9.7	12.7	9.3	11.4	24.0	25.1	9.1	11.4	*	*

Note: * indicates insufficient data for reliable measurement.

Source: U.S. Bureau of Labor Statistics. Employment and Earnings. Washington, DC: U.S. Government Printing Office, 1984, Table 43.

with highest unemployment were

State	Percent unemployed
Michigan.	15.5
Alabama	14.4
West Virginia	13.9
Ohio.	12.5
Washington.	12.1
Indiana	11.9
Tennessee	11.8
Oregon.	11.5
Illinois.	11.3
Mississippi	11.1

Those with lowest unemployment were

State	Percent unemployed
South Dakota.	5.5
Oklahoma.	5.7
Wyoming	5.8
North Dakota.	5.9
Nebraska.	6.1
Kansas.	6.3
Hawaii.	6.7
Texas	6.9
Vermont	6.9
Connecticut	6.9

Table 15-15. Unemployment Rates for Urban and Rural Areas, by Sex, Age, and Race-Ethnicity: 1980

Sex and race-ethnicity	Total	Urban					Rural	
		Inside urbanized area			Outside urbanized area			
		Total	Central cities	Urban fringe	Place of 10,000 or more	Place of 2,500 or more	Total	Place of 1,000 to 2,500
Total, 16 years and over.	6.4	6.3	7.3	5.4	6.8	7.0	7.0	7.0
Total, males 16 years and over.	6.4	6.4	7.5	5.3	6.7	6.9	6.9	7.1
Male:								
16 to 19 years.	15.5	15.6	17.8	13.8	15.1	15.3	15.0	15.4
20 to 24 years.	11.0	11.0	12.0	9.9	11.0	11.8	12.3	12.6
25 to 54 years.	4.9	4.8	6.1	3.8	5.0	5.3	5.5	5.6
55 to 64 years.	3.8	3.8	4.3	3.4	3.8	4.2	4.7	4.7
65 years and over	5.3	5.4	5.5	5.3	4.6	5.3	4.8	5.4
Total, females 16 years and over.	6.3	6.2	7.0	5.4	6.9	7.1	7.1	6.8
Female:								
16 to 19 years.	13.0	12.9	14.9	11.3	13.7	13.8	14.4	13.7
20 to 24 years.	8.3	8.0	9.2	6.8	9.1	10.0	10.4	10.3
25 to 54 years.	5.3	5.1	5.9	4.5	5.7	6.0	5.9	5.7
55 to 64 years.	4.1	4.1	4.2	3.9	4.0	4.5	4.7	4.4
65 years and over	5.7	5.9	5.9	6.0	4.8	5.1	5.5	4.9
White								
Persons 16 years and over .	5.5	5.3	5.7	5.0	--	--	6.6	3.4
Male, 16 years and over . .	5.6	5.4	6.0	5.0	--	--	6.6	3.0
Female, 16 years and over .	5.4	5.2	5.4	5.1	--	--	6.7	4.4
Black								
Persons 16 years and over .	12.0	11.9	12.8	9.6	--	--	10.7	8.8
Male, 16 years and over . .	12.7	12.8	13.9	9.8	--	--	9.9	8.0
Female, 16 years and over .	11.2	11.1	11.7	9.3	--	--	11.7	10.1
Spanish-origin								
Persons 16 years and over .	8.8	8.6	9.3	7.6	--	--	9.9	7.0
Male, 16 years and over . .	8.5	8.3	9.0	7.2	--	--	8.8	5.2
Female, 16 years and over .	9.4	9.1	9.7	8.2	--	--	12.1	11.7

Note: -- indicates data not available.

Source: U.S. Bureau of the Census. "General Social and Economic Characteristics: United States Summary," 1980 Census of Population. Washington, DC: U.S. Government Printing Office, 1983, Tables 103, 124, and 134.

Urban-Rural and Metropolitan-Nonmetropolitan Differentials

Table 15-15 provides rates of unemployment for urban and rural areas, and Table 15-16 for the metropolitan and nonmetropolitan areas, by sex and race-ethnicity. From these tables it may be observed that:

1. Rates of unemployment are lower in rural than in urban areas; they are particularly low for the farm population.

2. Unemployment is higher in metropolitan than in nonmetropolitan areas and in central cities than in rural areas. A part (but by no means all) of this differential is caused by the concentration of black population in central cities of SMSAs.

There is very substantial place-to-place variation in unemployment rates, even within the same geographic region. These differentials are associated with the type of industries located in the area (the "economic base") as well as the race-ethnic and educational composition of the work force. Some of the metropolitan areas with very high unemployment rates are small places that are heavily dependent for employment on one or a few industries that tend to be particularly depressed. For the years 1980-83, communities specialized in the production of automobiles or parts of automobiles and other durable goods were particularly hard hit by unemployment.

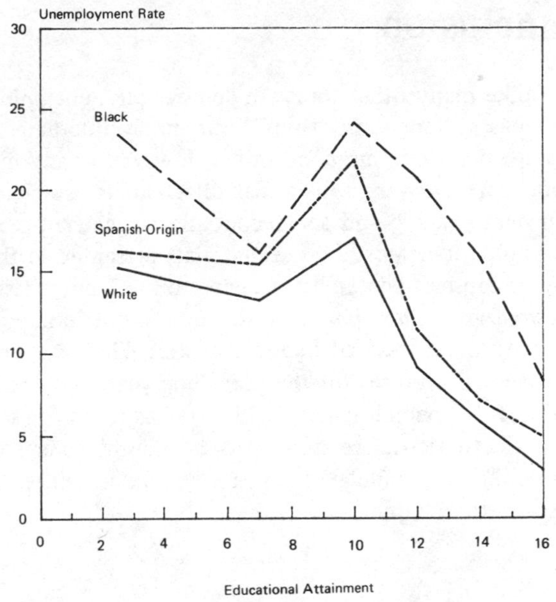

Figure 15-4. Unemployment Rates, by Educational Attainment (Years of School Completed): 1982

Table 15-16. Unemployment Rates of the Civilian Noninstitutional Population in Metropolitan and Nonmetropolitan Areas, by Sex, Age, and Race-Ethnicity: 1983

Unemployment rate	Metropolitan areas						Nonmetropolitan areas					
	Total		Central cities		Suburbs		Total		Central cities		Suburbs	
	1982	1983	1982	1983	1982	1983	1982	1983	1982	1983	1982	1983
Total. . . .	9.5	9.4	11.1	11.0	8.5	8.3	10.1	10.1	4.2	4.2	10.6	10.7
Men, 20 years and older. .	8.7	8.8	10.5	10.7	7.5	7.6	9.0	9.3	3.6	3.2	9.5	9.9
Women, 20 years and older. .	8.0	7.9	9.0	9.0	7.3	7.0	8.8	8.8	4.1	4.3	9.2	9.1
Both sexes, 16 to 19 years.	23.2	22.4	28.6	27.8	20.3	19.5	23.2	22.4	11.2	11.0	24.5	23.5
White. . . .	8.2	8.0	8.7	8.5	8.0	7.7	9.3	9.2	4.1	3.9	9.8	9.7
Black. . . .	18.8	19.7	20.1	21.2	16.1	16.3	19.1	19.0	15.5	14.6	19.2	19.1
Spanish-origin . . .	13.7	13.1	14.3	13.1	12.9	13.0	14.3	17.2	18.8	*	14.1	17.4

Note: * indicates data not shown where base is less than 35,000.

Source: U.S. Bureau of Labor Statistics. Employment and Earnings. Washington, DC: U.S. Government Printing Office, 1984, Table 49.

Conclusion

Unlike many other topics in demography, unemployment has no long-term "trend" but simply fluctuates in response to economic conditions. However, at any moment there are very substantial differentials associated with demographic and socioeconomic characteristics of the population. Most of the materials presented in this chapter can be updated by referring to the January issue of *Employment and Earnings*, the monthly bulletin published by the Bureau of Labor Statistics. This issue provides annual averages for the preceding year. Up-to-date statistics of unemployment, with rates adjusted for seasonal fluctuations, are presented in monthly issues of this publication, tabulated for most of the variables discussed in this chapter.

Note

1. Stanley Lebergott. "Annual Estimates of Unemployment in the United States." Pp. 213-390 in *The Measurement and Behavior of Unemployment.* Princeton, N.J.: National Bureau of Economic Research, Princeton University Press, 1957.

Bibliography

Adams, Arvil V. *The Lingering Crisis of Youth Unemployment.* Kalamazoo, MI: W.E. Upjohn Institute for Employment Research, 1978.

Antos, J.; Mellow, W.; and Triplett, J. "What Is a Current Equivalent to Unemployment Rates of the Past?" *Monthly Labor Review* 102 (1979):36-46.

Barnes, W.R., and Jones, E.B. "Women's Increasing Unemployment: A Cyclical Interpretation." *Quarterly Review of Economics and Business* 15 (1975):61-9.

Bowen, William G., and Harbison, Frederick (eds.). *Unemployment in a Prosperous Economy.* Princeton, NJ: Princeton University Press, 1965.

Brown, C. et al. "Time-Series Evidence of the Effect of the Minimum Wage of Youth Employment and Unemployment." *Journal of Human Resources* 18 (1983):3-31.

Cain, G.G. "The Unemployment Rate as an Economic Indicator." *Monthly Labor Review* 102 (1979): 24-35.

Cherry, R. "What Is So Natural About the Natural Rate of Unemployment?" *Journal of Economic Issues* 15 (1981):729-43.

Clark, K.B., and Summers, L.H. "Demographic Differences in Cyclical Employment Variation." *Journal of Human Resources* 16 (1981):61-79.

DiPrete, T. "Unemployment Over the Life Cycle: Racial Differences and the Effects of Changing Economic Conditions." *American Journal of Sociology* 87 (1981):286-307.

Fineman, Stephen. *White Collar Unemployment.* New York: Wiley, 1983.

Flaim, Paul O. "The Effect of Demographic Changes on the Nation's Unemployment Rate." *Monthly Labor Review* 102 (1979):13-23.

Flanagan, R.J. "Discrimination Theory, Labor Turnover, and Racial Unemployment Differentials." *Journal of Human Resources* 13 (1978):187-207.

Goldstein, Harold. *State and Local Labor Force Statistics.* Washington, DC: National Commission on Employment and Unemployment Statistics, U.S. Government Printing Office, 1978.

Gustman, A.L., and Steinmeir, T.L. "Impact of Wages and Unemployment on Youth Enrollment and Labor Supply." *Review of Economics and Statistics* 63 (1981):553-60.

Lagerfeld, S. "Distorted Unemployment Statistics." *Public Interest* 56 (1979):108-11.

Lebergott, Stanley. *Men Without Work: The Economics of Unemployment.* Englewood Cliffs, NJ: Prentice-Hall, 1964.

Lingle, R.C., and Jones, E.B. "Women's Increasing Unemployment: A Cross-Sectional Analysis" (with discussion). *American Economic Review Papers and Proceedings* 68 (1978):84-9, 95-8.

Marston, S.T. "Employment Instability and High Unemployment Rates." *Brookings Papers on Economic Activity,* no. 1 (1976):169-210.

Moen, P. "Measuring Unemployment: Family Considerations." *Human Relations* 33 (1980):183-92.

O'Neill, D.M. "Racial Differentials in Teenage Unemployment: A Note on Trends." *Journal of Human Resources* 18 (1983):295-306.

Parnes, Herbert S. *Unemployment Experiences of Individuals Over a Decade: Variations by Sex, Race, and Age.* Kalamazoo, MI: Upjohn Institute for Employment Research, 1982.

Solow, R.M. "On Theories of Unemployment." *American Economic Review* 70 (1980):1-11.

Terry, S.L. "Unemployment and Its Effects on Family Income in 1980." *Monthly Labor Review* 105 (1982): 35-43.

Wolfbein, Seymour L. *Employment and Unemployment in the United States.* Chicago: Science Research Associates, 1964.

Chapter 16

The Population Below the Poverty Level

The discussion of income (Chapter 14) emphasized that a significant proportion of the population lives in a state of poverty, with an annual money income less than the minimum required to maintain basic nutritional, health, housing, and consumption needs and services according to American consumption patterns at what would be widely accepted as a minimal socially acceptable level. Such a concept of poverty is not easy to quantify or define precisely, because the income that would define the poverty threshold varies with size of family and the characteristics of family members. Such a definition was developed in 1964 by the Social Security Administration (SSA) and was subsequently accepted—with refinements and modifications—for general use in publishing statistics. The history of that definition is explained in detail in the technical appendix to this chapter. Once each year the Bureau of the Census publishes a report, "Characteristics of the Population Below the Poverty Level," in the *Current Population Reports* (Series P-60) on consumer income. These reports, as well as the decennial censuses of 1970 and 1980, use the poverty threshold definitions to provide data about the population facing economic hardship. The Bureau of the Census emphasizes that the definition of poverty has limitations because it is based on average consumption patterns: Insofar as individual circumstances or consumption patterns differ, the dollar value of the poverty threshold for a given family size may not represent the cash income required by any particular family of that size to maintain a level of economic wellbeing equivalent to other families of the same size with similar incomes.

In 1983 the cash income at the poverty threshold was set as follows:

Type of family	Poverty threshold
For person living alone, 65 or older. .	$4,626
For person living alone, under 65 . . .	5,019
For family of three	7,693
For family of four.	9,862

The chapter appendix provides threshold levels for other sizes and types of families.

According to the Current Population Survey conducted in March, 1983, a total of 34.4 million persons were below the poverty level during 1982. This represented 15.0 percent of all individuals, which may be called the "poverty rate" (see Definition Box).

Some organizations that use poverty statistics believe the SSA thresholds are too low in the light of current values. They prefer an alternative threshold that is 1.25 percent of the official poverty thresholds. By the alternative indicator, the population below the poverty level numbered 46.5 million in 1982, making a poverty rate of 20.3 percent.

Definitions

Poverty. Persons and families defined as living in poverty received money income below a threshold amount adjusted for family or household size, age of householder, and number of children under eighteen, during the year preceding the census or enumeration. The threshold amount is based (with subsequent small modifications) on the poverty index developed by the Social Security Administration (SSA) in 1964 (see the technical appendix to this chapter).

Alternative Poverty Level. Because the poverty definition currently in use by the federal government does not meet all the needs of the analysts of the data, a variation was introduced at the same time that modifications were made to the SSA poverty index. This alternate cutoff, set at 125 percent of the official government standard, is obtained by multiplying the income cutoffs at the poverty level by 1.25. Thus, the income cutoff for a family of four at 125 percent of the poverty level was $12,328 in 1982.

Poverty Rate: Individuals. Percent of individuals living in households or families that received incomes below the specified thresholds.

Poverty Rate: Families. Percent of families that received incomes below the specified thresholds.

Poverty Areas. In 1970 the U.S. Bureau of the Census identified as poverty areas those census tracts (in metropolitan areas) or minor civil divisions (townships, districts, and so forth in nonmetropolitan areas) in which 20 percent or more of the population was below the poverty level in 1969. The same units have been used in subsequent years. For purposes of these tabulations, persons or families are identified as living inside poverty areas or outside poverty areas.

Income Deficit. The difference between the total income of families and households composed of unrelated individuals below the poverty level, and their respective poverty thresholds. Families reporting a net income loss are assigned zero dollars, making their defict equal to the poverty threshold. The income deficit is thus a measure of the degree of impoverishment of a family or household. Caution must be exercised in comparing the average deficit of families classified by the race or sex of the householder. The poverty thresholds are affected by family size and composition, so apparent differences in the average income deficits may be explained to some extent by differences in these characteristics.

Median Income Deficit. The median income deficit is the dollar amount at the midpoint of the range of income deficits. Half of the households showing an income deficit will have one greater than the median and the other half will have one smaller than the median.

Mean Income Deficit. The mean income deficit is the amount obtained by dividing the total income deficit of a group below the poverty level by the number of families or unrelated individuals (as appropriate) in that group.

Deficit per Family Member. The average amount of money necessary to raise every man, woman, and child in a family out of poverty, derived by dividing the total family income deficit of a group by the number of family members in the group.

Components of Poverty

Poverty is highly concentrated in particular race-ethnic groups and among families of particular types. Table 16-1 provides data demonstrating these fundamental components of poverty. Figure 16-1 illustrates recent trends for the race-ethnic groups.

Race-Ethnicity

Poverty rates among the black population are approximately three times as great as among the white population (35.6 as against 12.0 percent). The Spanish-origin population has a poverty rate of 29.9 percent, 2.5 times that of the white population but about 16 percent lower than that of the black population. The race differentials have persisted in roughly the same ratios since 1959, the earliest year for which poverty statistics have been prepared (Table 16-1). Even though the percentage of the poverty-level population that is black and of Spanish origin is much higher than the percentage for the white population, the overwhelming majority

Table 16-1. Persons Below the Poverty Level and Poverty Rate, by Race-Ethnicity and Type of Household: 1959-1982

Year	Number of persons (000)	Poverty rate: persons				Percent of total poor		
		Total	White	Black	Spanish-origin	White	Black	Spanish-origin
All persons								
1982	34,398	15.0	12.0	35.6	29.9	68.4	28.2	12.5
1981	31,822	14.0	11.1	34.2	26.5	67.7	28.8	11.7
1980	29,272	13.0	10.2	32.5	25.7	67.3	29.3	11.9
1979	26,072	11.7	9.0	31.0	21.8	66.0	30.9	11.2
1978	24,497	11.4	8.7	30.6	21.6	66.4	31.1	10.6
1975	25,877	12.3	9.7	31.3	26.9	68.7	29.2	11.6
1973	22,973	11.1	8.4	31.4	21.9	65.9	32.2	10.3
1970	25,420	12.6	9.9	33.5	--	68.8	29.7	--
1966	28,510	14.7	11.3	41.8	--	67.7	31.1	--
1959	39,490	22.4	18.1	55.1	--	72.1	25.1	--
Persons in households with female householder, no husband present								
1982	16,336	36.2	28.7	57.4	57.4	57.5	40.0	11.3
1981	15,378	35.2	28.4	55.8	54.0	59.4	39.5	10.9
1980	14,649	33.8	27.1	53.1	52.5	58.5	39.6	10.2
1979	13,503	32.0	24.9	52.2	48.9	56.7	41.3	9.2
1978	12,880	32.3	24.9	53.1	53.3	56.4	41.9	8.9
1975	12,268	34.6	28.1	53.6	55.6	59.7	39.0	8.7
1973	11,357	34.9	27.9	55.4	55.5	58.5	40.2	8.5
1970	11,154	38.2	31.4	58.8	--	61.3	37.8	--
1966	10,250	41.0	33.9	65.1	--	63.5	35.7	--
1959	10,390	50.2	43.8	70.0	--	68.5	28.0	--
Persons in married couple households and other households with male householder								
1982	18,063	9.8	8.7	20.0	22.0	78.2	17.5	13.6
1981	16,080	8.8	7.6	19.4	18.6	75.9	19.2	12.6
1980	14,623	8.0	6.9	17.9	18.5	76.1	19.0	13.6
1979	12,569	7.0	5.9	16.2	15.5	76.1	19.7	13.4
1976	11,617	6.6	5.7	15.1	14.6	77.4	19.2	12.5
1975	13,609	7.8	6.6	18.2	20.1	76.8	20.3	13.2
1973	11,616	6.6	5.4	18.5	15.4	73.2	24.3	12.0
1970	14,266	8.2	6.8	21.7	--	74.7	23.4	--
1966	18,260	10.8	8.5	33.4	--	70.0	28.5	--
1959	29,100	18.7	15.2	50.7	--	73.4	24.1	--

Note: -- indicates data not available.

Source: U.S. Bureau of the Census. "Characteristics of the Population Below the Poverty Level: 1982." Current Population Reports (Series P-20, no. 144). Washington, DC: U.S. Government Printing Office, 1984, Table 1.

(68 percent) of the population living below the poverty level is white. The poverty level population is 28.2 percent black (as against 11 percent of the general population), and the Spanish-origin poverty population is 12.5 percent of the whole poverty population (as against 8.1 percent of the general population).

There is wide variation dependent on country of origin among the Spanish-origin population, as the following poverty rates for 1982 show:

Origin	Rate	Percent of Spanish-origin poor
Spanish-origin total	29.9	100.0
Mexican	30.0	62.8
Puerto Rican	46.3	21.6
Cuban and other	19.8	15.6

Table 16-2. Persons Below the Poverty Level–Household and Family Status, by Race-Ethnicity: 1982 [poverty rate and percent distribution of the poor]

Family status	Number of persons (000)	Poverty rate: persons				Percent of total poor		
		Total	White	Black	Spanish-origin	White	Black	Spanish-origin
All persons below poverty								
All persons. . .	34,398	15.0	12.0	35.6	29.9	68.4	28.2	12.5
In families.	27,349	13.6	10.6	34.9	29.2	65.9	30.5	14.1
Householder. . . .	7,512	12.2	9.6	33.0	27.2	68.1	28.7	12.2
Children	13,139	21.3	16.5	47.3	38.9	63.0	33.4	16.1
Other members. . .	6,698	8.7	6.9	22.2	18.7	68.9	27.0	12.4
Unrelated individuals.	6,458	23.1	20.7	40.3	35.1	78.1	19.0	5.5
Persons in households with female householder, no husband present								
All persons. . .	16,336	36.2	28.7	57.4	57.4	57.5	40.0	11.3
In families.	11,701	40.6	30.9	58.8	60.1	48.6	48.7	13.7
Householder. . . .	3,434	36.3	27.9	56.2	55.4	52.8	44.7	12.4
Children	6,696	56.0	46.5	70.7	71.8	48.5	48.8	14.8
Other members. . .	1,571	21.2	12.8	38.2	35.9	39.7	56.9	11.8
Unrelated individuals.	4,110	26.6	24.2	48.3	41.5	80.4	17.6	4.6
Persons in married couple households and households with male householder								
All persons. . .	18,063	9.8	8.7	20.0	22.0	78.2	17.5	13.6
In families.	15,649	9.1	8.1	18.6	21.4	78.8	17.0	14.5
Householder. . . .	4,079	7.9	7.0	16.4	18.9	81.0	15.2	12.0
Children	6,443	13.0	11.6	24.1	27.8	78.1	17.4	17.5
Other members. . .	5,127	7.3	6.4	15.8	16.5	77.8	17.8	12.6
Unrelated individuals.	2,347	18.8	16.3	32.5	29.9	74.0	21.5	7.1

Source: U.S. Bureau of the Census. "Characteristics of the Population Below the Poverty Level: 1982." Current Population Reports (Series P-60, no. 144). Washington, DC: U.S. Government Printing Office, 1984, Table 1.

Over the years the poverty rates of the races have tended to fluctuate together, in unison with the business cycle, and by approximately the same relative magnitudes. As a result the racial composition of the poverty level population has changed little over time. In times of prosperity the proportion that is white tends to diminish slightly; during times of recession or depression the proportion that is white tends to increase by a small amount.

Trends in Poverty

During the 1960s great strides were made in reducing poverty. This is illustrated in Figure 16-1. The proportion of the population that was poor declined from 22.4 percent in 1959 to 12.6 percent in 1970—a reduction by almost half. The decline was just as rapid for the black as for the white population. During the 1970s the poverty rate reached a plateau, fluctuating between 11 and 12 percent. In 1973 poverty reached an all-time low of 11.1 percent, and in 1978 it dipped again to 11.4 percent, with 24.5 million persons living in poverty. With the onset of economic depression the rate began to rise, and in 1982 the number of the nation's poor stood 40 percent above the 1978 level as a result of population growth combined with a higher poverty rate (see Figure 16-1).

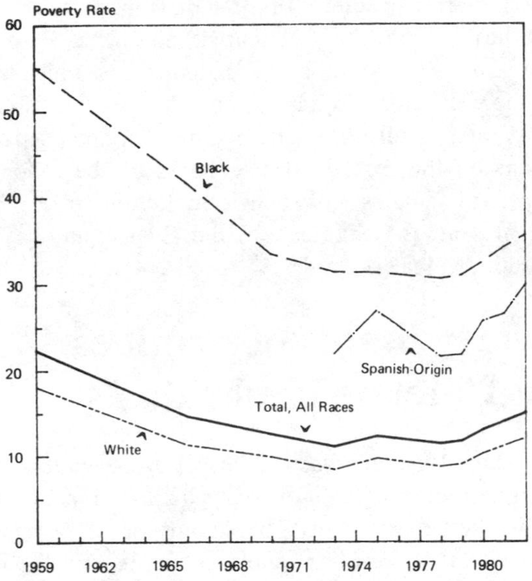

Figure 16-1. Trend in Poverty Rates, by Race-Ethnicity: 1959-1982

Family Type

Poverty rates are far higher in families where the householder is a female living with children or other relatives without a husband present (second panel of Table 16-1 and Table 16-2). This generalization holds true for the white, the black, and the Spanish-origin population. Less than 10 percent of the population living in married-couple families or families where the head is a male are living below the poverty level. For families headed by a female with no husband present, the rate is 36.2, or 3.7 times as great. Such a high rate means that persons living in female-headed families make up nearly one-half (47.5 percent) of the whole poverty-level population.

Interaction of Race and Family Type

The racial effects and the family-type effects on poverty are almost independent of each other, with the result that the poverty rates are extremely high among black and Spanish-origin populations living in families with a female householder (57.4 percent) and are extremely low (8.7 percent for 1982) among white married-couple families and families where the head is a male. The poverty rate among the former is 6.6 times the poverty rate in the latter group. Table 16-2 documents this situation.

Table 16-1 shows that some of the progress in reducing poverty during the 1960s occurred among the female-headed families as well as among those with male heads. The rapid growth of the poverty population

Table 16-3. Poverty Rates, by Age, Sex, and Race-Ethnicity: 1982

Age	All races			White		Black		Spanish-origin	
	Both sexes	Male	Female	Male	Female	Male	Female	Male	Female
Total	15.0	13.4	16.5	10.8	13.2	31.4	39.3	28.5	31.3
Under 15 years. . .	22.6	22.5	22.6	17.8	17.5	48.3	49.0	40.4	39.2
15 to 17 years. . .	18.7	18.8	18.5	14.2	14.1	43.7	41.0	38.9	35.5
18 to 21 years. . .	16.4	14.2	18.6	10.8	14.6	33.2	41.2	26.6	30.5
22 to 24 years. . .	14.7	12.4	16.9	10.7	12.9	23.0	40.8	22.7	28.6
25 to 34 years. . .	12.3	9.8	14.8	8.6	12.0	18.3	33.1	21.2	27.6
35 to 44 years. . .	11.1	8.9	13.1	8.0	10.4	16.2	33.7	18.8	27.2
45 to 54 years. . .	9.4	8.0	10.8	7.1	8.6	15.4	27.1	16.0	21.6
55 to 59 years. . .	9.9	7.8	11.8	6.1	9.4	26.3	33.4	16.8	21.9
60 to 64 years. . .	11.3	8.8	13.4	7.8	11.2	17.1	34.5	16.2	24.2
65 years and over .	14.6	10.4	17.5	8.3	15.1	31.8	42.4	19.7	31.4

Source: U.S. Bureau of the Census. "Characteristics of the Population Below the Poverty Level: 1982." Current Population Reports (Series P-60, no. 144). Washington, DC: U.S. Government Printing Office, 1984, Table 11.

in the late 1970s and since can be explained by the rapid increase in the number of households headed by females as well as by the rise since 1980 in poverty rates for households of all types.

Poverty Rates by Sex, Age, and Race

Poverty rates vary according to basic demographic characteristics, as Table 16-3 shows. From this table the following can be observed:

1. Poverty rates are consistently higher among females than among males. This is true at all ages and for all races and ethnic groups.

2. Poverty rates are highest at the childhood ages; a disproportionate share of the nation's poor are children. More detailed attention to this is given in a later section.

3. The sex difference in poverty is very small at the childhood ages, but as soon as the females reach adulthood they suffer differential increased poverty, which persists for the rest of their lives. The size of this sex differential is very great for all three race-ethnic groups.

4. The sex difference in poverty is far greater among the black population than among the white or Spanish-origin population. This becomes particularly great at the mature adult ages, where the proportion of poor among black women is nearly double that among black men. For black males aged 45-54 the poverty rate is only 15.4, very close to the national average for the total population. For black females of the same age the rate is 27.1.

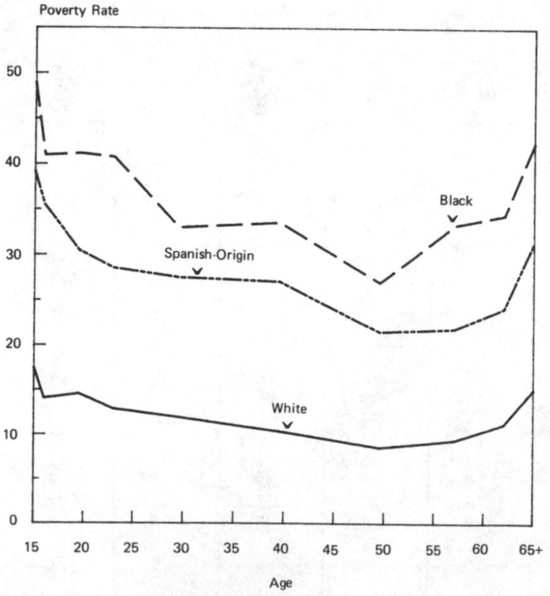

Figure 16-2. Poverty Rates for Females, by Age and Race-Ethnicity: 1982

5. Young adults are poorer than mature adults. Poverty rates reach their lowest level at ages 45-54.

6. Poverty rises moderately as people pass into retirement ages. However, poverty rates among those sixty-five and over are lower than those for young adults under twenty-five years of age.

Figure 16-2 illustrates the age curve of poverty rates for white, black, and Spanish-origin females.

These differentials pervade all of the remaining discussion of this chapter. An attempt is made to explain what lies behind the differentials and what helps to cause them. The discussion also considers the impact that these differentials have upon other aspects of community and family life. The chapter contains separate sections on the special poverty status of the following groups: (a) families with female householders, no husband present; (b) children; (c) the elderly; and (d) unrelated individuals.

Poverty Status of Families and Unrelated Individuals

It should be emphasized that poverty status, like income, is meaningful only when discussed in terms of families and households. The definition of poverty is based on family and household concepts, and the data of Tables 16-1 through 16-3 simply categorize persons in terms of their status as members of such units. Figure 16-3 shows poverty rates for selected family types by race-ethnicity. The poverty status of individuals is not determined solely by their earnings as persons but by the money income of the family or household to which they belong.

The comparison between poverty when measured in units of family and persons may be summarized as follows:

Poverty, by year	Families	Persons
Number		
1982.	7,512	34,398
1975.	5,450	25,877
Percent change, 1975-82	37.8	32.9
Rate		
1982.	12.2	15.0
1975.	9.7	12.3
Percent change, 1975-82	2.5	2.7

The rate of poverty is higher when computed for individuals than when computed for families. The number of poor families has increased more rapidly than the number of poor individual persons since 1975.

This chapter uses statistics of poverty status both for persons and for families. The reader should note carefully which unit is being used when examining the data.

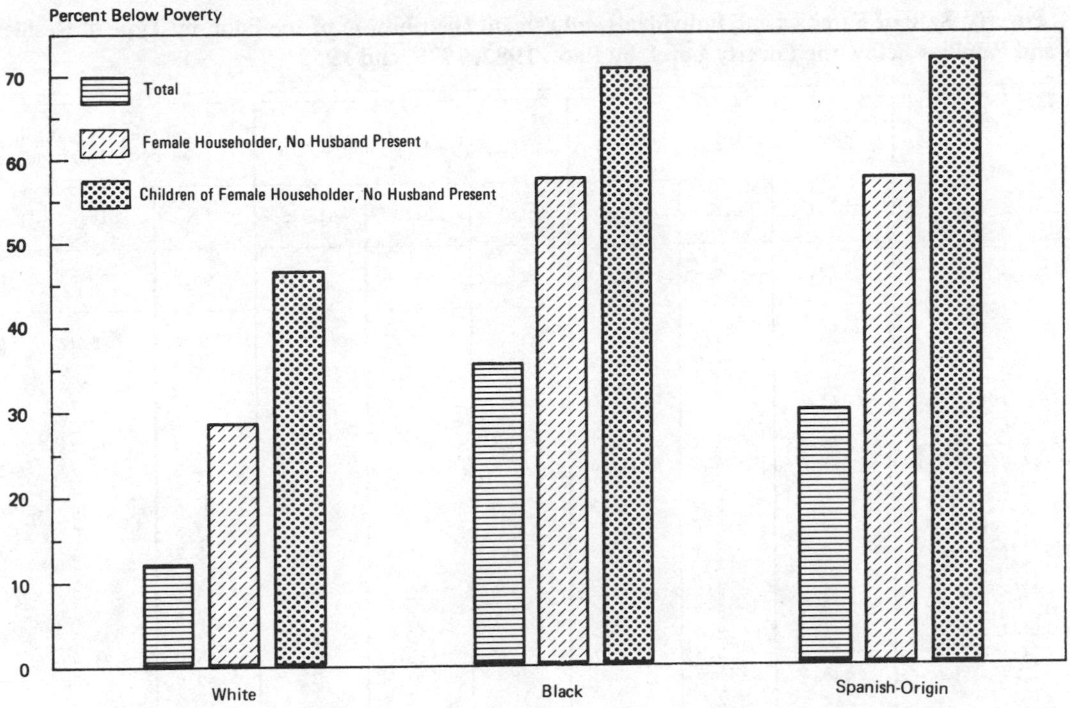

Figure 16-3. Poverty Rates, by Race-Ethnicity and Family Type: 1982

Residential Differentials in Poverty

Poverty rates differ sharply by place of residence. Table 16-4 provides an overview of the residential differentials in poverty.

Farm-Nonfarm

Poverty rates of the farm population are more than 50 percent higher than those of the nonfarm population. But because the farm population comprises such a small share of the total population, the farm poor make up only 3.6 percent of the nation's poor.

Metropolitan-Nonmetropolitan

The poverty rate of nonmetropolitan areas is significantly (30 percent) higher than that of metropolitan areas. This is true for both the white and the black populations. However, because of the highly metropolitanized nature of the population, a majority of the nation's poor reside within metropolitan areas. For the black population this proportion is very high (71 percent).

Central City-Metropolitan Ring

Within the metropolitan areas, the poverty rate in central cities is sharply higher than in the suburban metropolitan rings of the SMSA. This is true for both white and black populations. The race differential in poverty rates is greater inside the central city than outside.

Poverty Areas

Within the poverty areas (see Definition Box) poverty rates are far higher than in nonpoverty areas. Poverty rates are substantially higher in poverty areas within central cities than in poverty areas outside central cities.

Regions

Poverty rates are much higher in the South than in any other region. The black population has higher rates of poverty in the North Central region than in the South; these two regions have much higher poverty rates for the black population than the Northeast and the West. For the white population, the West has higher poverty rates than any other region outside the South, but for the black population the poverty rates are much lower in the West than in any other region except the South.

The lower panel of Table 16-4 provides data for 1975, a year of low poverty, and for 1959, the earliest date for which poverty data are available. The overall trend through the years has been a rapid shrinkage of farm poverty accompanied by a great metropolitanization of poverty, especially in the central cities. Despite

Table 16-4. Poverty Rate of Families and Individuals and Percent Distribution of the Poor, by Type of Residence of Persons and Families Below the Poverty Level, by Race: 1982, 1975, and 1959

Residence	Poverty rate: families			Poverty rate: persons			Percent distribution of the poor (persons)		
	Total	White	Black	Total	White	Black	Total	White	Black
1982, total	12.2	9.6	33.0	15.0	12.0	35.6	100.0	100.0	100.0
Nonfarm	12.1	9.3	32.9	14.8	11.7	35.5	96.4	95.2	99.0
Farm	18.6	17.8	50.0	22.1	21.0	51.1	3.6	4.8	1.0
Metropolitan areas	11.1	8.1	31.6	13.7	10.4	33.5	61.8	57.7	71.1
Inside central cities	16.7	11.4	34.7	19.9	14.5	36.9	36.9	28.7	56.1
In poverty areas	42.1	34.4	48.3	45.6	37.9	51.7	14.8	7.7	32.3
Outside central cities	7.5	6.4	24.2	9.3	8.1	25.0	24.9	28.9	15.1
In poverty areas	22.4	18.1	34.3	26.9	22.4	37.6	3.5	3.0	4.9
Nonmetropolitan areas	14.5	12.3	37.6	17.8	15.1	42.3	38.2	42.3	28.9
North and west	11.0	9.1	31.8	13.4	11.3	33.3	59.4	64.7	43.4
Northeast	10.7	8.6	29.7	13.0	10.8	31.6	18.5	19.8	15.7
North central	11.0	8.6	37.0	13.3	10.6	39.8	22.6	23.5	21.1
West	11.5	10.3	25.7	14.1	13.0	23.9	18.3	21.4	6.6
South	14.6	10.6	34.2	18.1	13.4	37.6	40.6	35.3	56.6
1975, total	9.7	7.7	27.1	12.3	9.7	31.3	100.0	100.0	100.0
Nonfarm	9.5	7.5	26.7	12.1	9.5	31.0	94.9	94.0	97.1
Farm	13.7	11.9	51.7	16.4	14.2	50.0	5.1	6.0	2.9
Metropolitan areas	8.5	6.5	24.0	10.8	8.2	27.6	59.3	56.4	65.8
Inside central cities	11.8	8.2	25.4	15.0	10.8	29.1	35.1	27.4	53.5
In poverty areas	29.5	24.3	34.4	34.9	29.8	39.6	17.2	8.8	37.5
Outside central cities	6.1	5.4	19.7	7.6	6.7	22.5	24.2	28.9	12.4
In poverty areas	15.9	12.5	26.9	20.8	16.9	32.2	3.5	3.0	4.9
Nonmetropolitan areas	12.1	10.1	37.1	15.4	12.6	42.4	40.7	43.7	34.2
North and west	8.2	7.1	21.9	10.4	9.0	25.2	57.3	64.9	37.6
Northeast	8.0	6.8	21.6	10.2	8.8	24.5	19.0	21.4	13.9
North central	7.7	6.4	22.8	9.7	8.1	25.5	21.1	23.3	16.5
West	9.3	8.5	20.7	11.7	10.6	26.2	17.2	20.2	7.1
South	12.7	9.1	31.9	16.2	11.4	36.6	42.7	35.1	62.4
1959, total	17.7	14.8	48.1	22.0	18.1	55.1	100.0	100.0	100.0
Nonfarm	15.7	12.8	45.3	--	--	--	--	--	--
Farm	42.8	38.7	88.1	--	--	--	--	--	--
Metropolitan areas	11.7	9.2	36.1	15.3	12.0	42.8	43.9	41.7	50.4
Inside cental cities	13.7	10.2	34.3	18.3	13.8	40.8	26.9	23.0	38.4
In poverty areas	--	--	--	--	--	--	--	--	--
Outside central cities	9.6	8.3	44.0	12.2	10.4	50.9	17.0	18.7	11.9
In poverty areas	--	--	--	--	--	--	--	--	--
Nonmetropolitan areas	28.2	24.3	73.2	33.2	28.2	77.7	56.1	58.3	49.6
North and west	12.5	11.5	28.9	16.0	14.8	34.3	50.7	59.5	24.4
Northeast	--	--	--	--	--	--	--	--	--
North central	--	--	--	--	--	--	--	--	--
West	--	--	--	--	--	--	--	--	--
South	29.9	23.4	62.0	35.4	26.8	68.5	49.3	40.5	75.6

Note: -- indicates data not available.

Source: U.S. Bureau of the Census. "Characteristics of the Population Below the Poverty Level: 1982." Current Population Reports (Series P-60, no. 144). Washington, DC: U.S. Government Printing Office, 1984, Table 4.

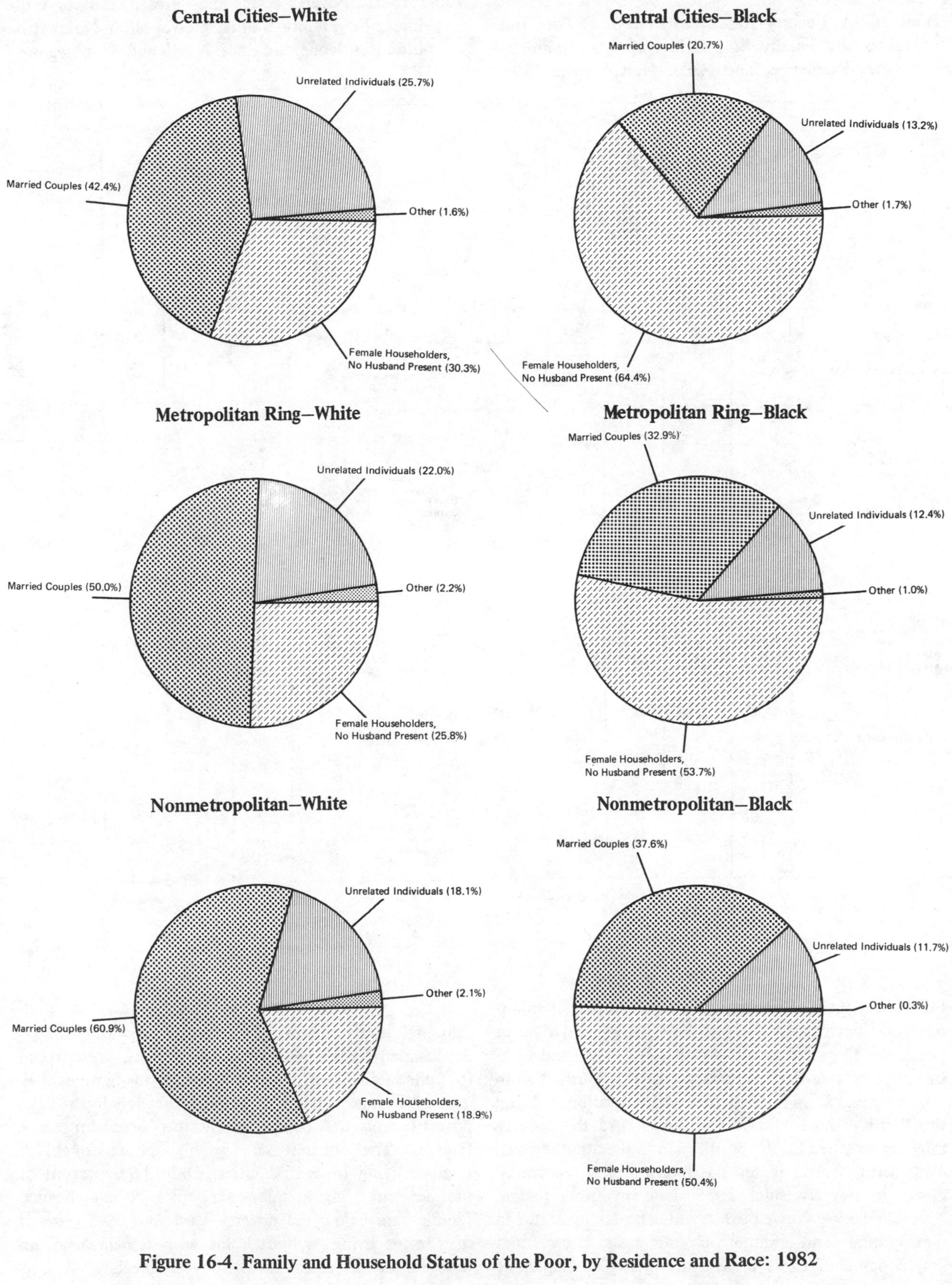

Figure 16-4. Family and Household Status of the Poor, by Residence and Race: 1982

Table 16-5A. Poverty Rates and Percent of Poor Individuals, by Family Status, Metropolitan-Nonmetropolitan Residence, and Race: United States, 1982

Race and family status	All areas	Metro-nonmetro residence: Total metropolitan	Metropolitan central city	Metropolitan ring	Nonmetropolitan
All races	15.0	13.7	19.9	9.3	17.8
In families	13.6	12.3	19.0	8.1	16.3
Female householder, no husband present	40.6	39.4	47.7	28.6	43.7
Couples and other	9.1	7.4	10.6	5.6	12.6
Unrelated individuals	23.1	21.0	23.5	18.1	29.0
White, total	12.0	10.4	14.5	8.1	15.1
In families	10.6	9.0	13.0	6.9	13.5
Female householder, no husband present	30.9	29.5	36.0	24.4	34.4
Couples and other	8.1	6.3	9.0	5.1	11.4
Unrelated individuals	20.7	18.6	20.3	16.9	26.3
Black, total	35.6	33.5	36.9	25.0	42.3
In families	34.9	32.9	36.5	24.2	40.8
Female householder, no husband present	58.8	56.9	59.5	47.4	65.4
Couples and other	18.6	15.5	16.6	13.4	27.1
Unrelated individuals	40.3	36.1	37.4	31.8	59.1
	Percent of poor people				
All races					
In families	79.5	78.2	78.5	77.7	81.7
Female householder, no husband present	34.0	38.8	44.5	30.3	26.3
Couples and other	45.5	39.4	33.9	47.4	55.4
Unrelated individuals	18.8	20.1	20.0	20.3	16.6
White					
In families	76.6	74.3	72.7	75.8	79.8
Female householder, no husband present	24.2	28.0	30.3	25.8	18.9
Couples and other	52.4	46.2	42.4	50.0	60.9
Unrelated individuals	21.4	23.9	25.7	22.0	18.1
Black					
In families	86.2	85.4	85.1	86.6	88.0
Female householder, no husband present	58.8	62.2	64.4	53.7	50.4
Couples and other	27.4	23.3	20.7	32.9	37.6
Unrelated individuals	12.7	13.1	13.2	12.4	11.7

Source: U.S. Bureau of the Census. "Characteristics of the Population Below the Poverty Level." Current Population Reports (Series P-60, no. 144). Washington, DC: U.S. Government Printing Office, 1984, Table 9.

Table 16-5B. Poverty Rates and Percent of Poor Individuals, by Family Status, Metropolitan-Nonmetropolitan Residence, and Race: North and West Regions, 1982

Race and family status	All areas	Metro-nonmetro residence: Total metropolitan	Metropolitan central city	Metropolitan ring	Nonmetropolitan
All races	13.4	13.0	19.7	8.6	14.7
In families	12.1	11.7	23.2	7.4	13.2
Female householder, no husband present	37.9	38.1	46.7	27.1	37.4
Couples or other	8.0	6.9	10.6	5.0	10.6
Unrelated individuals	20.9	20.2	23.2	16.9	23.5
White, total	11.3	10.3	14.9	7.8	13.9
In families	9.9	8.9	13.4	6.7	12.4
Female householder, no husband present	30.7	29.9	37.2	24.3	33.6
Couples and other	7.3	6.0	8.9	4.7	10.4
Unrelated individuals	19.3	18.1	20.5	15.9	22.8
Black, total	33.3	33.4	36.6	22.9	32.0
In families	32.7	32.8	36.2	21.7	31.9
Female householder, no husband present	57.5	56.9	58.2	49.8	70.0
Couples and other	14.5	14.7	16.6	9.9	13.0
Unrelated individuals	35.5	35.5	37.0	30.4	*
	Percent of poor people				
All races					
In families	78.1	77.5	77.9	76.9	79.5
Female householder, no husband present	33.6	38.6	43.9	30.5	21.6
Couples and other	44.4	38.9	34.0	46.3	57.9
Unrelated individuals	19.8	20.7	20.5	21.0	17.6
White					
In families	75.9	74.3	72.4	76.2	78.8
Female householder, no husband present	26.0	29.9	32.0	27.8	18.7
Couples and other	49.9	44.3	40.3	48.4	60.1
Unrelated individuals	21.8	23.8	26.0	21.6	18.2
Black					
In families	84.8	84.5	85.0	81.9	90.4
Female householder, no husband present	63.1	63.0	64.4	55.7	65.8
Couples and other	21.7	21.5	20.6	26.3	24.6
Unrelated individuals	13.5	13.7	13.2	16.7	9.6

Note: * indicates data not sufficient for accurate measurement.

Source: U.S. Bureau of the Census. "Characteristics of the Population Below the Poverty Level: 1982." Current Population Reports (Series P-60, no. 144). Washington, DC: U.S. Government Printing Office, 1984, Table 9.

their lower rates of poverty, the rapid growth of suburban rings has caused them to amass a greater share of poor than they had previously. Between 1959 and 1975 the poverty rate decreased faster in the South than in the other regions. This, together with migration, reduced the South's share of poverty. Since 1975 the poverty rate has risen less in the South than in the other regions. The North Central region has had a greater relative increase in poverty since 1975 than any other region.

Table 16-5A shows poverty rates by family status in metropolitan and nonmetropolitan areas. Figure 16-4 graphs some of these data. These materials emphasize that high levels of poverty are associated with (a) families headed by a female with no husband present and (b) unrelated individuals (not living in families). In married-couple families or families headed by a male, poverty rates are comparatively low—even for black families. The contrast can be highlighted for black families living in central cities: Only 16.6 percent of the persons living in married couples or male-headed families are below the poverty level, but 59.5 percent of persons living in households with female head, no husband present, are below the poverty level.

Table 16-5C. Poverty Rates and Percent of Poor Individuals, by Family Status, Metropolitan-Nonmetropolitan Residence, and Race: South Region, 1982

Race and family status	All areas	Metro-nonmetro residence: Total metropolitan	Metropolitan central city	Metropolitan ring	Nonmetropolitan
All races	18.1	15.3	20.5	11.2	21.7
In families	16.7	14.0	19.6	10.0	20.0
Female householder, no husband present	45.1	42.6	50.0	32.1	48.5
Couples and other	11.4	8.5	10.7	7.0	15.0
Unrelated individuals	28.1	23.2	24.4	21.6	36.9
White, total	13.4	10.8	13.5	9.0	16.9
In families	11.9	9.3	12.1	7.6	15.1
Female householder, no husband present	31.4	28.2	32.2	24.7	35.3
Couples and other	9.7	7.1	9.1	6.0	12.8
Unrelated individuals	24.4	19.9	19.7	20.1	32.2
Black, total	37.6	33.6	37.3	26.9	43.5
In families	36.7	33.1	37.0	26.3	41.8
Female householder, no husband present	59.9	56.8	61.6	45.6	64.9
Couples and other	21.9	16.6	16.5	16.6	28.8
Unrelated individuals	45.6	37.1	38.0	34.0	62.2
	Percent of poor people				
All races					
In families	81.6	79.6	79.8	79.4	83.5
Female householder, no husband present	34.6	39.3	45.9	29.8	30.1
Couples and other	47.0	40.3	33.8	49.6	53.3
Unrelated individuals	17.3	18.9	18.9	19.0	15.7
White					
In families	78.0	74.3	73.7	74.9	80.9
Female householder, no husband present	20.9	23.1	25.6	20.7	19.2
Couples and other	57.0	51.2	48.1	54.3	61.8
Unrelated individuals	20.7	23.9	24.9	23.1	18.1
Black					
In families	87.2	86.7	85.3	90.3	87.7
Female householder, no husband present	55.4	61.0	64.5	52.2	49.0
Couples and other	31.8	25.7	20.8	38.0	38.7
Unrelated individuals	12.0	12.1	13.4	9.1	11.9

Source: U.S. Bureau of the Census. "Characteristics of the Population Below the Poverty Level: 1982." Current Population Reports (Series P-60, no. 144). Washington, DC: U.S. Government Printing Office, 1984, Table 9.

The lower panel of Table 16-5A shows a percentage distribution of the poor by family status, race, and metropolitan-nonmetropolitan residence. It shows the family status of the black and white poor in metropolitan and nonmetropolitan areas. Table 16-5B reports for the North and West regions combined the same information as Table 16-5A, while Table 16-5C reports it for the South region. These tables reveal the high central city concentration of poverty outside the South and the more dispersed distribution in the South.

Characteristics of the Poor

Educational Attainment

Educational Attainment is most dramatically linked to poverty. Table 16-6 not only shows a strong inverse relationship between poverty status and educational attainment but also emphasizes the importance of a high school diploma and of college education as a protection against poverty. Poverty rates are highest among the tiny fraction of the population that has less than five years of elementary schooling. These rates are very high (above 30 percent) for both the white and black populations. With each increment of educational attainment, the poverty rate declines. This is true for both males and females and for both the black and white populations (see Figure 16-5).

But educational attainment is not able to wipe out the sex and race differentials in poverty. Females have a higher poverty rate than males at all educational levels. The black population has far higher poverty rates at each educational level than does the white population. Within both the white and the black populations, females have higher poverty rates than males. Thus, the sex and race differentials remain intact while reflecting the fundamental importance of education.

Thanks to the fact that (as Chapter 10 has described) the proportion of population having less than a grammar

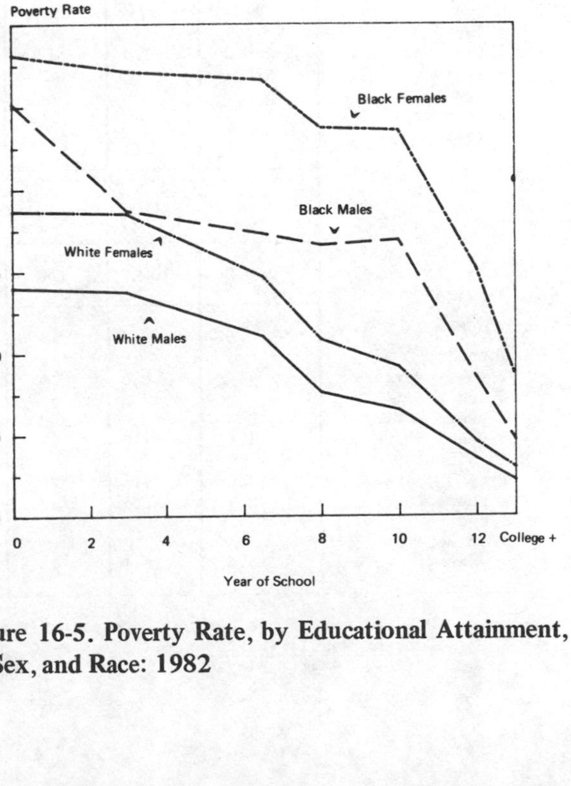

Figure 16-5. Poverty Rate, by Educational Attainment, Sex, and Race: 1982

school education is now comparatively small, the high poverty rates for these groups do not translate into a majority of the overall poverty-level population. Because the educational attainment of the population is now so high, nearly a majority of persons below the poverty level are high school graduates. The lower panel of Table 16-6 reports the percentage distribution of the poor across the educational attainment levels. Because of lower average educational attainment and extraordinarily high poverty rates among the lowest educational levels, the poor black population is more concentrated toward the lower end of the income distribution range than is the white. It is erroneous, however, to combine poverty with lack of schooling in a stereotype. More than 40 percent of all poor people in 1982 had a high school diploma. An impressive and increasing share of those who do not "make it" in America's technological society have good educational credentials on paper.

Joint Effects of Education and Age

It has already been shown that poverty rates tend to be higher at the youngest and oldest ages, which could be attributed to age differences in educational attainment. But, in fact, as Table 16-7 demonstrates, age, sex, race, and educational attainment all contribute to differences in poverty levels. The analysis is restricted to two educational groups—those who have completed high school only and those with at least some college completed. (These are the groups that show greatest success in averting poverty.) From this table the following information may be inferred:

The *age effect* persists for each education-sex-race group but is reduced in range. Clearly, a part of the age differentials (particularly at the older ages) is due to age differences in educational attainment. Nevertheless,

Table 16-6. Poverty Rates and Percent Distribution of Poor Persons Aged 15 and Over, by Educational Attainment, Sex, and Race: 1982

Educational attainment	All races			White			Black		
	Both sexes	Male	Female	Both sexes	Male	Female	Both sexes	Male	Female
Total	12.8	10.5	14.9	10.5	8.8	12.0	30.4	23.8	35.8
None.	37.8	33.9	41.4	32.9	28.1	37.4	52.6	50.4	56.3
Elementary									
1 to 5 years. .	35.5	30.4	41.1	32.2	27.6	37.1	45.7	37.5	54.3
6 and 7 years	29.2	24.3	33.6	26.0	22.2	29.5	45.0	34.7	53.3
8 years	21.4	17.4	24.9	18.7	15.3	21.8	41.2	33.3	47.5
High school									
1 to 3 years. .	20.2	16.6	23.4	15.9	13.1	18.4	41.2	33.9	47.2
4 years	10.1	8.3	11.4	8.3	7.1	9.2	24.7	17.1	30.4
College									
1 or more years	5.9	4.8	7.0	5.1	4.4	6.0	13.7	9.4	17.2
	Percent distribution of poor persons								
Total	100.0	100.0	100.0	100.0	100.0	100.0	100.0	100.0	100.0
None.	1.9	2.1	1.8	1.7	1.7	1.6	1.9	3.2	1.2
Elementary									
1 to 5 years. .	7.4	8.3	6.7	6.8	7.6	6.3	8.9	10.8	7.9
6 and 7 years	8.4	8.4	8.4	8.5	8.5	8.4	8.6	8.4	8.6
8 years	11.1	11.0	11.2	11.9	11.6	12.1	9.1	9.2	9.0
High school									
1 to 3 years. .	27.8	27.6	28.0	25.4	24.8	25.8	34.9	37.0	33.8
4 years	28.8	26.5	30.3	29.6	27.6	30.9	27.0	23.1	29.2
College									
1 or more years	14.6	16.1	13.6	16.1	18.1	14.8	9.6	8.3	10.3

Source: U.S. Bureau of the Census. "Characteristics of the Population Below the Poverty Level: 1982." Current Population Reports (Series P-60, no. 144). Washington, DC: U.S. Government Printing Office, 1984, Table 13.

the age effect persists: Poverty rates for high school graduates are lowest at ages 45-54, and poverty rates for college attendees are lowest at ages 55-59. Poverty rates tend to increase for ages over fifty-nine and to be considerably higher as well for the ages younger than forty-five.

The *sex differential* is very little reduced by controlling for age. Female high school graduates are poverty-stricken substantially more than their male counterparts at all ages. In absolute terms the differential is greatest at the youngest and oldest ages. This holds true for both white and nonwhite females.

The *race differential* is greater by far than the differentials for age and sex, when educational attainment is specified. When sex, race, and amount of education are held constant, the proportion of black persons below the poverty level varies between two and four times that of their white counterparts. The absolute differential between the races is least among those 45-59 years of age and greatest at the younger and older ages. Whereas having some college education is a strong deterrent to poverty for whites (both males and females), it is a very weak protection for blacks: Poverty rates for black college graduates at age sixty-five and older are higher even than for black youngsters of the same sex just entering the work force. Controlling for all of the demographic variables does little to diminish the race inequality in poverty status linked to education on either an absolute or a relative basis.

Marital Status

Next to high educational attainment, the most important factor in avoiding poverty is being married and living with a spouse. Table 16-8, which reports poverty rates by marital status, shows that for white females poverty rates among the never married population are double those for the married, and this disparity triples at ages forty-five and over. For black females the average disparity is triple, with some age groups having quad-

Table 16-7. Poverty Rates for Persons Who Have Completed High School, and for Persons with One Year or More of College, by Age, Sex, and Race: 1982

Age	All races			White			Black		
	Both sexes	Male	Female	Both sexes	Male	Female	Both sexes	Male	Female
Persons who have completed 4 years of high school									
All ages. . . .	10.1	8.3	11.4	8.3	7.1	9.2	24.7	17.1	30.4
15 to 17 years. . .	17.7	15.5	19.6	14.2	*	*	*	*	*
18 to 21 years. . .	12.9	10.4	15.2	9.9	8.2	11.6	30.3	21.9	37.2
22 to 34 years. . .	12.3	10.0	14.4	9.8	8.5	11.0	27.6	18.8	34.9
35 to 44 years. . .	10.0	7.8	11.7	8.3	7.1	9.2	22.1	11.9	30.4
45 to 54 years. . .	6.8	6.2	7.2	5.7	5.4	6.0	16.8	13.6	18.7
55 to 59 years. . .	7.2	6.2	7.8	6.4	5.3	7.0	20.6	17.9	22.3
60 to 64 years. . .	6.7	5.9	7.2	6.2	5.5	6.7	16.5	13.9	18.2
65 years and over .	8.2	5.7	9.7	7.9	5.2	9.5	16.7	14.1	18.2
Persons who have completed 1 year or more of college									
All ages. . . .	5.9	4.8	7.0	5.1	4.4	6.0	13.7	9.4	17.2
15 to 17 years. . .	*	*	*	*	*	*	*	*	*
18 to 21 years. . .	8.4	7.0	9.6	7.4	6.2	8.5	16.5	12.1	19.2
22 to 34 years. . .	6.7	5.8	7.7	5.7	5.1	6.3	15.3	10.6	19.2
35 to 44 years. . .	4.8	4.4	5.4	4.4	4.4	4.5	9.7	4.8	14.0
45 to 54 years. . .	4.0	3.2	5.0	3.7	2.9	4.7	7.5	5.8	9.1
55 to 59 years. . .	3.3	2.7	4.1	3.0	2.4	3.8	9.8	*	6.6
60 to 64 years. . .	5.2	4.2	6.3	4.7	3.8	5.7	14.7	*	*
65 years and over .	6.5	3.9	8.7	5.8	3.4	7.7	21.5	*	24.6

Note: * indicates insufficent data for accurate measurement.

Source: U.S. Bureau of the Census. "Characteristics of the Population Below the Poverty Level: 1982." Current Population Reports (Series P-60, no. 144). Washington, DC: U.S. Government Printing Office, 1984, Table 13.

Table 16-8. Poverty Rates for Persons, by Marital Status, Age, Sex, and Race: 1982

Age	White females						Black females					
	All ages	Single	Married[a]	Separated	Widowed	Divorced	All ages	Single	Married[a]	Separated	Widowed	Divorced
Total	12.0	13.8	6.9	44.7	20.2	23.2	35.8	43.4	15.6	57.7	48.7	39.8
15 to 19 years. . .	14.6	13.7	20.3	*	*	*	41.3	41.3	*	*	*	*
20 to 24 years. . .	13.4	13.1	9.1	49.1	*	35.1	40.7	42.9	19.1	*	*	*
25 to 29 years. . .	12.7	11.5	8.8	45.0	*	29.3	34.6	43.8	12.5	58.1	*	54.0
30 to 34 years. . .	11.3	14.7	7.2	51.0	*	23.0	31.2	42.1	11.8	55.4	*	43.5
35 to 44 years. . .	10.4	12.8	6.7	39.8	22.7	21.2	33.7	53.0	12.4	66.2	49.5	42.9
45 to 54 years. . .	8.6	15.0	5.4	36.2	19.7	18.1	27.1	43.1	13.8	40.0	52.2	27.9
55 to 64 years. . .	10.2	17.8	5.3	51.5	20.8	19.7	33.9	57.4	21.0	55.1	42.4	31.1
65 years and over .	15.1	21.3	6.7	42.4	19.8	25.3	42.4	*	23.0	*	49.3	*
	White males						Black males					
	All ages	Single	Married[a]	Separated	Widowed	Divorced	All ages	Single	Married[a]	Separated	Widowed	Divorced
Total	8.8	11.2	6.9	16.7	13.8	13.1	23.8	30.9	15.5	24.5	37.5	19.7
15 to 19 years. . .	12.9	12.7	27.7	*	*	*	41.6	41.5	*	*	*	*
20 to 24 years. . .	10.6	10.3	10.6	15.3	*	16.8	24.9	25.6	22.2	*	*	*
25 to 29 years. . .	8.8	7.8	8.7	16.7	*	10.4	19.1	23.5	12.4	*	*	*
30 to 34 years. . .	8.4	10.1	7.1	19.2	*	12.8	17.2	22.3	13.2	*	*	18.6
35 to 44 years. . .	8.0	11.0	7.2	15.7	*	10.8	16.2	26.5	11.4	24.0	*	17.7
45 to 54 years. . .	7.1	15.4	5.7	10.6	18.8	14.3	15.4	19.9	13.5	21.6	*	13.7
55 to 64 years. . .	6.9	18.7	5.5	16.1	13.0	16.7	21.9	*	15.2	30.7	*	29.0
65 years and over .	8.3	14.6	6.5	*	13.4	16.6	31.8	*	26.9	*	41.1	*

[a]Spouse present.

Note: * indicates base too small to make accurate measurement.

Source: U.S. Bureau of the Census. "Characteristics of the Population Below the Poverty Level: 1982." Current Population Reports (Series P-60, no. 144). Washington, DC: U.S. Government Printing Office, 1984, Table 21.

ruple the poverty rates for single as for the married/spouse-present group. Although the differential is negligible for males in the young adult ages, it becomes almost as great as for females for ages thirty-five and over. Poverty rates of even greater dimensions are found for women who are separated. Although widowed and divorced persons of both sexes also have much higher poverty rates than the married, they fare somewhat better than those reported as separated. The linkage between the unmarried statuses and poverty is not due simply to age but is more adverse at older than at younger ages.

The causal factors that lie behind these impressively large differences are numerous. On the one hand there must be a direct causal relationship involving the presence of two or more earners in the family, or the higher salary of a single male earner, given the information provided in Chapter 14 about family incomes. Separated persons have not only lost this connection but are also less likely than divorced or widowed persons to be receiving supplemental support payments or pensions. However, there is probably a great deal of selectivity at work also: Persons who have low incomes may tend never to marry or may be more prone to separation, divorce, and even widowhood, given the emotional and physical stresses of poverty.

The following percentage distributions reveal how the poverty population is disproportionately represented by those outside the married/spouse-present status. The excess for females is 27 percent and for males 16 percent.

Marital status, both sexes, all races	Percent of total population	Percent of poverty population	Difference
Female			
Single	22.9	29.8	+6.9
Separated. . . .	3.5	10.9	+7.4
Widowed.	11.7	18.6	+6.9
Divorced	7.5	12.9	+5.4
Sum.	45.6	72.2	+26.6
Married, spouse present. . . .	54.4	27.8	-26.6
Male			
Single	30.0	41.1	+11.1
Separated. . . .	2.6	4.5	+1.9
Widowed.	2.3	3.9	+1.6
Divorced	5.5	7.3	+1.8
Sum.	40.4	56.8	+16.4
Married, spouse present. . . .	59.6	43.2	-16.4

Table 16-9. Poverty Rates of Families by Size of Family and Type of Family, by Race: 1982

Size and type of family	All races	White	Black
All families . . .	12.2	9.6	33.0
2 persons.	10.0	8.0	29.3
3 persons.	12.1	9.5	32.3
4 persons.	10.8	8.6	30.5
5 persons.	16.1	12.8	35.1
6 persons.	21.8	17.4	43.0
7 persons.	27.0	22.4	39.8
8 persons.	34.5	27.2	54.8
9 and more persons .	48.1	35.4	70.9
Families with female householder, no husband present.	36.3	27.9	56.2
2 persons.	26.1	20.7	45.0
3 persons.	37.2	30.3	55.6
4 persons.	47.2	38.1	62.3
5 persons.	56.0	45.9	66.7
6 persons.	70.1	63.1	74.6
7 persons.	55.1	*	*
8 persons.	*	*	*
9 and more persons .	*	*	*
Married couples and other families	7.9	7.0	16.4
2 persons.	6.5	5.8	16.6
3 persons.	6.2	5.7	11.6
4 persons.	6.6	6.3	9.9
5 persons.	11.5	10.6	18.1
6 persons.	15.8	14.5	24.3
7 persons.	22.6	20.5	28.3
8 persons.	29.7	25.5	*
9 and more persons .	38.7	33.7	*

Note: * indicates insufficient data.

Source: U.S. Bureau of the Census. "Characteristics of the Population Below the Poverty Level: 1982." Current Population Reports (Series P-60, no. 144). Washington DC: U.S. Government Printing Office, 1984, Table 17.

Table 16-10. Poverty Rates of Unrelated Individuals 16 Years Old and Over, by Living Arrangement, Sex, Age, and Race: 1982

Age and race	Males		Females	
	Living alone	Nonrelatives	Living alone	Nonrelatives
White, 16 years and over . . .	13.9	20.1	21.8	31.1
16 to 21 years . .	33.7	43.0	27.1	54.6
22 to 34 years . .	10.2	16.8	8.9	20.5
35 to 54 years . .	12.9	17.8	18.9	32.7
55 to 64 years . .	17.2	14.2	25.3	46.6
65 years and over	16.7	19.1	24.8	29.4
Black, 16 years and over . . .	29.6	35.0	47.0	52.2
16 to 21 years . .	*	*	*	*
22 to 34 years . .	21.4	31.0	22.0	31.2
35 to 54 years . .	23.7	28.3	34.9	66.3
55 to 64 years . .	38.8	*	42.8	*
65 years and over	47.5	*	65.6	*

Note: * indicates insufficient data.

Source: U.S. Bureau of the Census. "Characteristics of the Population Below the Poverty Level: 1982." Current Population Reports (Series P-60, no. 144). Washington, DC: U.S. Government Printing Office, 1984, Table 22.

Size of Family

Poverty is directly related to family size (see Table 16-9). Lowest poverty rates are found in families of four or fewer members. Poverty rates rise by large increments with each increase in family size beyond four. At five members the rate is about double that of the small family with minimum rates. At seven the poverty rate is triple the minimum, and the nine-person family has a poverty rate (48 percent) quintuple the minimum. These tendencies are no less sharp for married couple families than for families with a female householder, no husband present. Although they characterize both the black and white populations, they are much sharper for the white population than for the black. These differentials result from two factors: (1) In large families the income must be shared among more persons, thereby driving many families below the poverty level. (2) Those who receive low incomes tend to have larger families (see Chapter 14).

Living Arrangements of Unrelated Adult Individuals

Unrelated individuals, who by definition do not live as members of a family, have substantially higher poverty rates than do persons who live in families. Table 16-10, which reports the poverty rates of these unrelated individuals, may be compared with the poverty rate of married persons of similar age (Table 16-8). At all ages, those who live outside families have higher poverty rates than persons of the same sex, race, and age who are married and living with a spouse.

These persons who live outside families either live alone or live in households with one or more persons unrelated to them (see Chapter 11). Poverty rates are lower for those who live alone than for those who live with others. White males who live alone tend to have relatively low poverty rates at all ages except the very young. Even at ages of retirement, only 17 percent of white males are defined as living in poverty. The rates are much higher for females and for blacks of both sexes. Females who live alone have substantially higher poverty rates than males who live alone, and females who live with nonrelatives tend to have extraordinarily high poverty rates. Black males who live alone have poverty rates that are only moderately higher than for all black males, but black females who live outside families (either alone or with others) are extremely disadvantaged; their poverty rates tend to be 50 percent or higher.

Thus, living outside families and particularly living alone is not a very important indicator of poverty for the white population, especially not for males. Living outside families is a very strong indicator of poverty for black females. Living with other nonrelatives is a strong indicator of poverty for white as well as black females. These differentials are correlated with the data for marital status. By definition, unrelated individuals living together are single, separated, widowed, or divorced—all high poverty groups.

Employment Status of Householder

Poverty rates are low where the householder or individual is employed; they are very high where the householder is unemployed or not in the labor force. Among black and Spanish-origin households, lack of employment or failure to have a householder in the labor force leads to poverty rates in excess of 50 percent, and rising as high as 75 percent or more. Highest poverty is encountered among female black family householders who are unemployed and female Spanish-origin family householders who are not in the labor force. Table 16-11 presents poverty rates for householders by employment status.

Number of Workers

The importance of employment in averting or reducing poverty may be amplified by noting poverty levels according to the number of persons in the family who worked at any time during the year preceding the interview (Table 16-12). Families who had no earners invariably have high poverty rates. Families with two earners have very low poverty rates. Having a third or fourth worker tends to depress the poverty rate further, but the effect is small and irregular; families that have large numbers of earners tend to receive low rates of pay. The effect of having an earner in the household is more dramatic for black than for white householders, especially for black households with female heads. In such households, where there is no earner, 92 percent are below the poverty level. Where there are two earners, the rate tumbles to less than one-fourth of this level. Married-couple black families with two workers have poverty levels as low as average white married-couple families.

Work Experience Last Year

Some of the situations and conditions that tend to create poverty are measured in Table 16-13, which summarizes the work experience during the year preceding

Table 16-11. Poverty Rates by Employment Status of of Family Householders and Unrelated Individuals, by Sex and Race-Ethnicity: 1982

Sex, race-ethnicity and family type of householder	Employment status		
	Employed	Unemployed	Not in labor force
White			
Female household, no husband present . . .	10.8	51.2	37.4
Married couple, and other families. . . .	5.0	19.1	10.9
Male unrelated individuals	9.6	35.8	30.8
Female unrelated individuals	12.9	41.2	33.2
Black			
Female household, no husband present . . .	26.7	76.5	73.5
Married couple, and other families. . . .	9.2	32.7	28.1
Male unrelated individuals	14.6	57.4	56.7
Female unrelated individuals	16.0	61.3	74.7
Spanish-origin			
Female household, no husband present . . .	22.1	*	71.9
Married couple, and other families. . . .	14.0	36.8	33.0
Male unrelated individuals	18.7	*	58.2
Female unrelated individuals	14.8	*	67.5

Note: * indicates insufficient data. The above table refers to the poverty status of householders.

Source: U.S. Bureau of the Census. "Characteristics of the Population Below the Poverty Level: 1982." Current Population Reports (Series P-60, no. 144). Washington, DC: U.S. Government Printing Office, 1984, Table 24.

the interview for persons fifteen years of age or over, by sex and race. Among these factors are the following:

1. *Part-year employment.* Persons who worked full time for more than fifty weeks have a poverty rate of only 3.1 percent. Even for the black population the rate for full-time year-round workers is only 6.7 percent. With each decrease in the number of weeks worked, the poverty rate increases by substantial amounts.

2. *Part-time work.* Poverty rates are substantially higher among those who worked part time (thirty-five hours or less a week) than among those who worked full time. When part-time work is combined with part-year work, rates are even higher.

3. *Unemployment.* One leading reason for part-year work is unemployment. The longer the duration of unemployment during the preceding year, the higher the poverty rates tended to be. For those who were unemployed for more than half of the year, poverty rates for white adults were above 25 percent and for black adults approached 50 percent.

4. *Reasons for not working.* People who did not work at all during the preceding year tended to vary in poverty rate according to the reason for not working. Those who were ill or unable to find work tended to have very high poverty rates. Women who did not work because they were "keeping house" also tended to be poor—especially among the black population. Persons who were "retired" did not have poverty rates that were above average for their sex and race groups. Full-time students tended to show intermediate poverty rates. Retired persons appear to have chosen retirement because of reasonable protection from poverty. The unemployed who are poor, on the other hand, have persisted in efforts to find work even though chronically unemployed or else are involuntarily out of the labor force for reasons of illness or the need to care for children.

Table 16-12. Poverty Rates for Families, by Number of Workers, Family Type, and Race: 1982

Number or workers and family type	All races	White	Black
All families.	12.3	9.7	33.3
No worker	33.9	25.3	76.0
1 worker.	15.5	12.5	35.8
2 workers	5.0	4.5	9.4
3 workers	4.6	3.6	14.3
4 or more workers .	2.8	2.7	4.1
Married couple families	7.7	6.9	15.7
No worker	17.3	14.6	43.4
1 worker.	10.9	9.8	24.9
2 workers	4.4	4.2	6.3
3 or more workers .	3.6	3.3	6.5
Female householder, no husband present.	36.3	27.9	56.1
No worker	74.5	63.8	91.5
1 worker.	30.0	23.9	45.1
2 or more workers .	11.1	7.3	22.8

Source: U.S. Bureau of the Census. "Characteristics of the Population Below the Poverty Level: 1982." Current Population Reports (Series P-60, no. 144). Washington, DC: U.S. Government Printing Office, 1984, Table 25.

The Poverty Status of Children

Children, more than adults, tend to be the victims of poverty. This is consistent with the fact that poverty rates are often lowest in families where there are no chil-

Table 16-13. Poverty Rates by Work Experience of Persons 15 Years of Age and Over, by Sex and Race: 1982

Work experience	Total	White		Black	
		Male	Female	Male	Female
Total	12.8	8.8	12.0	23.8	35.8
Worked last year.	7.8	6.4	7.2	14.6	18.8
Worked full-time. . . .	6.0	5.2	5.5	10.5	12.9
50 to 52 weeks. . . .	3.1	3.0	2.6	4.5	6.7
40 to 49 weeks. . . .	5.2	5.0	4.7	6.4	10.2
27 to 39 weeks. . . .	11.1	10.2	9.8	21.1	16.9
26 weeks or less. . .	20.0	17.1	18.0	30.6	39.3
Worked part-time. . . .	13.5	13.0	10.3	34.2	35.6
50 to 52 weeks. . . .	8.9	9.1	7.0	21.2	24.2
40 to 49 weeks. . . .	10.4	10.3	7.5	27.6	33.7
27 to 39 weeks. . . .	13.4	13.5	10.5	23.3	36.8
26 weeks or less. . .	18.9	16.9	14.6	43.7	44.0
Worked less than 50 weeks	14.4	12.6	12.2	26.9	32.3
Main reasons for working part year					
Ill or disabled . . .	14.9	14.1	10.9	27.0	28.2
Keeping house	13.3	22.2	11.6	*	33.9
Unable to find work .	16.7	14.3	15.4	26.5	34.4
Other	12.3	10.1	10.5	28.0	30.0
Number of weeks unemployed					
1 to 4 weeks.	11.1	7.2	12.7	11.6	30.4
5 to 14 weeks	11.9	8.4	13.5	21.1	25.2
15 to 26 weeks. . . .	18.3	14.8	17.5	27.0	39.3
27 weeks or more. . .	27.7	26.1	23.4	38.9	45.5
Did not work last year. .	22.7	17.8	18.4	40.9	55.1
Main reason for not working					
Ill or disabled . . .	34.0	25.8	30.6	41.3	65.7
Keeping house	19.9	33.2	16.4	*	55.9
Going to school . . .	23.4	18.1	17.0	40.8	42.7
Unable to find work .	48.2	45.1	36.7	53.4	71.1
Retired	13.2	8.8	14.4	29.0	40.0
Other	32.1	30.8	29.0	33.8	*
In armed forces	2.6	2.1	*	4.2	*

Note: * indicates zero or rounds to zero.

Source: U.S. Bureau of the Census. "Characteristics of the Population Below the Poverty Level: 1982." Current Population Reports (Series P-60, no. 144). Washington, DC: U.S. Government Printing Office, 1984, Table 14.

Table 16-14. Poverty Rates for Families by Number of Children, by Family Type and Race: 1982

Family type and number of children	Total	White	Black
Married couples and other families. .	12.2	9.6	33.0
No children	6.2	5.4	16.4
1 child	13.4	10.6	31.7
2 children.	14.9	11.8	38.5
3 children.	24.0	19.7	43.9
4 children.	36.2	28.6	64.5
5 children.	48.2	38.7	67.6
6 children.	64.3	54.0	*
7 or more children.	61.4	*	*
Female householder, no husband present.	36.3	27.9	56.2
No children	12.2	9.2	25.1
1 child	35.2	29.3	49.8
2 children.	49.1	40.6	66.2
3 children.	64.6	59.6	71.3
4 children.	78.6	71.5	85.7
5 children.	84.8	*	85.1
6 children.	*	*	*
7 or more children.	*	*	*

Note: * indicates base too small to make accurate measurement.

Source: U.S. Bureau of the Census. "Characteristics of the Population Below the Poverty Level: 1982." Current Population Reports (Series P-60, no. 144). Washington, DC: U.S. Government Printing Office, 1984, Table 18.

Table 16-15. Poverty Rates for Children, by Age, Type of Family, and Race-Ethnicity: 1982

Age and type of family	All races	White	Black	Spanish-origin
Total.	21.3	16.5	47.3	38.9
Under 3 years. . .	23.6	17.9	51.1	40.7
3 to 5 years . . .	23.0	18.7	47.2	42.7
6 to 13 years. . .	21.6	16.8	48.0	38.0
14 and 15 years. .	19.4	14.9	43.7	38.5
16 and 17 years. .	16.5	11.7	42.6	34.4
In families with female heads, no husband present				
Total.	56.0	46.5	70.7	71.8
Under 3 years. . .	72.1	66.9	77.2	85.0
3 to 5 years . . .	62.4	57.3	70.8	82.1
6 to 13 years. . .	55.5	45.8	71.1	69.9
14 and 15 years. .	46.6	37.3	64.9	60.2
16 and 17 years. .	41.4	28.5	64.1	61.3
In married couple and other families				
Total.	13.0	11.6	24.1	27.8
Under 3 years. . .	14.6	13.0	26.2	29.1
3 to 5 years . . .	13.7	12.8	22.0	30.2
6 to 13 years. . .	13.1	11.8	24.5	27.4
14 and 15 years. .	11.8	10.3	23.2	28.1
16 and 17 years. .	10.1	8.6	22.7	22.1

Source: U.S. Bureau of the Census. "Characteristics of the Population Below the Poverty Level: 1982." Current Population Reports (Series P-60, no. 144). Washington, DC: U.S. Government Printing Office, 1984, Table 11.

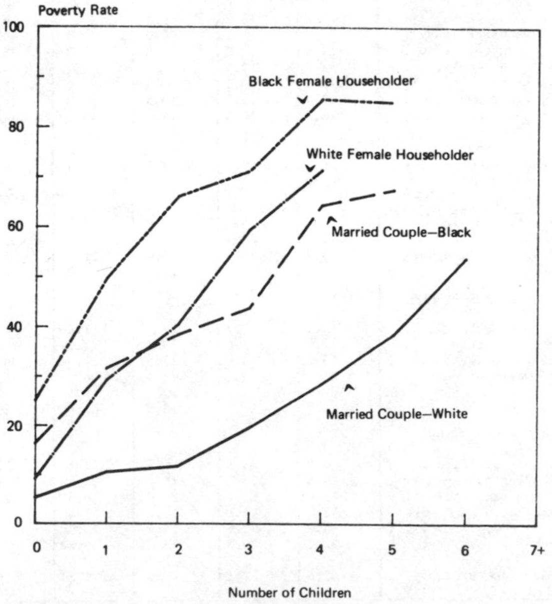

Figure 16-6. Poverty Rate of Families, by Number of Children, Family Type, and Race: 1982

dren and highest in families with many children (see Table 16-14 and Figure 16-6). For both white and nonwhite families and for husband-wife and female householder families, the greater the number of children the higher the poverty level tends to be. This is the well-known dependency effect. Children are not earners but tend to claim a share of the income; the more children, the less income per capita in the family, so that a higher proportion of families with children are pushed below the poverty line. The concentration of children below the poverty line is especially strong for families with female householders, no husband present. Even among white families, an overwhelming majority of the female-headed households with three children or more are below the poverty level, and for black families more than 75 percent are below the poverty level if there are three or more children.

The differential impact of poverty upon children is shown in the following comparison of percentage distributions:

Impact of povery upon children	White	Black	Total
Children's share in the general population.	25.7	34.1	26.8
Percent of the population in poverty.	35.2	45.3	38.2
Difference (excess of poverty).	+9.5	+11.2	+11.4

Although children under eighteen years of age account for only 27 percent of the population, they constitute 38 percent of the poor. A very substantial part of this excess is in families with female heads and in two-parent families with three children or more.

Age of Children

Very young children have a higher probability of being in a poverty family than older children. Poverty rates for children, by age, are shown in Table 16-15. For white, black, and Spanish-origin populations alike, children under three years of age have highest poverty rates, and children sixteen and seventeen have the lowest. The differences are not large, but they suggest that because young parents tend to have smaller incomes their children are more exposed to the risk of poverty. Also, children under three have a higher probability of having older brothers and sisters (large family size) than do older children. Thus, the age-of-children differential in poverty rate is a diluted reflection of the number-of-children differential.

Age of Householder with Children

Very young and very old householders with dependent children have higher rates of poverty than householders at the intermediate ages, as is shown in Table 16-16. The higher poverty rates among young families with children are manifest for both white and nonwhite families and for all family types. This age effect does not greatly modify the basic differentials between the races and between family types. Thus families with a householder who is female, black, under twenty-five, and with children have a poverty rate of 85 percent. Married couples where the householder is white, aged 45-64 years, and without children have a poverty rate of 4.5 percent—less than one-twentieth as great. At all age ranges, the absence of children is linked to lower poverty rates. This holds true for both races and all family types. The combined implications of Tables 16-15 and 16-16 are that for any given age of householder, as the number of children in the family increases, so does the poverty rate.

Table 16-16. Poverty Rates for Families, by Type of Family, Age and Race of Householder, and Presence of Children: 1982

Race and age of householder	Married couples		Female householder		Male householder	
	With children	Without children	With children	Without children	With children	Without children
White householder . . .	9.0	4.8	39.3	9.2	17.4	8.5
Under 25 years. . .	18.9	3.7	72.1	*	*	4.9
25 to 44 years. . .	8.5	3.5	38.1	9.4	18.9	10.2
45 to 64 years. . .	7.8	4.5	27.6	9.0	9.9	10.7
65 years and over . . .	14.9	6.3	28.8	9.5	*	4.6
Black householder . . .	17.2	13.1	63.7	25.1	32.7	16.1
Under 25 years. . .	25.8	*	85.2	*	*	*
25 to 44 years. . .	13.6	4.1	62.6	33.1	38.0	*
45 to 64 years. . .	20.5	9.5	51.0	25.5	*	*
65 years and over . . .	38.2	24.7	66.7	21.1	*	*

Note: * indicates base too small to make accurate measurement.

Source: U.S. Bureau of the Census. "Characteristics of the Population Below the Poverty Level: 1982." Current Population Reports (Series P-60, no. 144). Washington, DC: U.S. Government Printing Office, 1984, Table 19.

Table 16-17. Poverty Rates for Children, by Work Experience of Mother in 1981, Family Type, and Race: 1982

Race and age of children	Married couples		Female householder	
	Mother worked[a]	Mother did not work	Mother worked[a]	Mother did not work
White householder				
Total	3.5	14.5	6.1	83.2
Under 6 years only. .	1.3	15.3	8.7	92.8
Under 6, and 6 to 17 years.	7.1	19.1	16.3	92.3
6 to 17 years only. .	3.6	11.6	4.4	74.0
Black householder				
Total	3.9	38.6	18.6	93.8
Under 6 years only. .	*	42.2	13.5	98.0
Under 6, and 6 to 17 years.	7.8	42.7	24.1	96.6
6 to 17 years only. .	3.7	35.1	18.3	89.8

[a]Mother worked full time, 50 to 52 weeks.

Source: U.S. Bureau of the Census. "Characteristics of the Population Below the Poverty Level: 1982." Current Population Reports (Series P-60, no. 144). Washington, DC: U.S. Government Printing Office, 1984, Table 29.

Work of Mother

Children whose mothers are employed have lower poverty rates (Table 16-17). Table 16-18 shows the poverty rates for children in families where the mother worked full-time for fifty or more weeks during the preceding year and for women who did not work at all during the preceding year. In married-couple families the full-time employment of the mother virtually assured the absence of poverty. The rates for black families where the mother worked are almost as low as for the white families. The effect upon families with only young children or only older children is especially marked. In families where the mother was the head of household, with no husband, poverty rates were quite low when the mother worked full time but almost 100 percent when she did not. Even in black families with female heads, the poverty rates for the children were only 14-19 percent when the mother worked full time but 90-98 percent when she did not. Thus the employment of mothers is a powerful factor in reducing the poverty condition of children.

Table 16-17 contrasts nonwork with full-time year-round employment, and Table 16-18 indicates that the poverty rates of children are highly inversely related to the amount of time their mothers worked during the preceding year. Thus, one way for mothers to protect their offspring from poverty is to work outside the home, at least part time or part of the year.

Table 16-18. Poverty Rates Among Children, by Amount of Employment of Mother in 1981, Family Type, and Race: 1982

Race and number of weeks worked[a]	Married couple families	Female householder families
White householders . . .	11.3	47.7
50 to 52 weeks	4.9	12.3
40 to 49 weeks	5.4	19.9
27 to 29 weeks	5.9	48.5
14 to 27 weeks	10.0	69.8
1 to 13 weeks.	16.3	82.6
Did not work	17.6	86.2
Black householders . . .	21.1	71.9
50 to 52 weeks	8.9	30.6
40 to 49 weeks	13.7	55.6
27 to 29 weeks	12.4	76.9
14 to 27 weeks	28.3	74.9
1 to 13 weeks.	19.0	91.8
Did not work	40.7	94.9

[a]Includes employment at less than full time (less than 35 hours per week).

Source: U.S. Bureau of the Census. "Characteristics of the Population Below the Poverty Level: 1982." Current Population Reports (Series P-60, no. 144). Washington, DC: U.S. Government Printing Office, 1984, Table 30.

Table 16-19. Poverty Rates for Persons 65 Years or Older, by Family Status, Sex, and Race: 1970-1982

Family status and year	All races			White			Black		
	Both sexes	Male	Female	Both sexes	Male	Female	Both sexes	Male	Female
Total									
1982	14.6	10.4	17.5	12.4	8.3	15.1	38.2	31.7	42.4
1980	15.7	10.9	19.0	13.6	9.0	16.8	38.1	31.4	42.6
1978	14.0	10.0	16.7	12.1	8.3	14.7	33.9	26.7	39.0
1975	15.3	11.4	18.1	13.4	9.5	16.1	36.3	31.0	40.2
1970	24.5	19.0	28.5	22.5	17.0	26.5	48.0	41.3	53.2
In families									
1982	8.5	8.1	8.9	6.9	6.6	7.2	25.9	25.6	26.1
1980	8.5	8.2	8.8	6.9	6.8	7.1	26.2	25.6	26.6
1978	7.6	7.7	7.5	6.2	6.5	6.0	22.5	22.3	22.6
1975	8.0	8.1	8.0	6.7	6.9	6.4	23.9	23.6	24.2
1970	14.7	14.9	14.5	12.9	13.2	12.6	36.7	36.1	37.2
Unrelated individuals									
1982	27.1	21.2	28.7	23.6	16.9	25.4	61.6	50.2	66.3
1980	30.6	24.4	32.3	27.7	21.1	29.3	59.5	45.1	66.5
1978	27.0	20.7	28.8	24.1	17.4	25.9	54.0	37.8	62.0
1975	31.0	27.8	31.9	28.0	23.8	29.1	61.1	51.8	65.8
1970	47.1	38.9	49.7	44.8	36.0	47.5	73.2	59.7	79.2

Source: U.S. Bureau of the Census. "Characteristics of the Population Below the Poverty Level: 1982." Current Population Reports (Series P-60, no. 144). Washington, DC: U.S. Government Printing Office, 1984, Table 3.

The Poverty Status of the Elderly

Preceding sections have shown that the poverty rates for persons aged sixty-five and over are somewhat higher than those of the working-age population, but not substantially so. The poverty situation of the elderly, taken as a group, is better than that of children. However, there are some significant differentials in poverty rates within the elderly group, and these are explored in this section.

Trends

Table 16-19, which shows poverty rates for selected dates, indicates that contrary to the general trend, the elderly are less poor in 1982 than they were in 1980; the economic recession has affected them less adversely than it has the other age segments of the population (see Figure 16-7). Moreover, the elderly have experienced a substantial decline in poverty between 1970 and 1975, at a time when the general population was making almost no improvement. Although poverty rates are somewhat higher in 1980 and 1982 than in the prosperous year 1978, the increase is very small (from 14.0 to 14.6 percent, as against 11.4 to 15.0 for the general population). In consequence, in 1982, for the first time in history, the poverty rate of the elderly was below the national average, as the following summary reveals:

Year	General population	Persons 65 and over	Difference
1982. . . .	15.0	14.6	-0.4
1981. . . .	14.0	15.3	1.3
1980. . . .	13.0	15.7	2.7
1979. . . .	11.7	15.2	3.5
1978. . . .	11.4	14.0	3.6
1977. . . .	11.6	14.1	3.5
1976. . . .	11.8	15.0	3.2
1975. . . .	12.3	15.3	3.0
1974. . . .	11.2	14.6	3.4
1973. . . .	11.1	16.3	5.2
1972. . . .	11.9	18.6	6.7
1971. . . .	12.5	21.6	8.1
1970. . . .	12.6	24.5	11.9
1966. . . .	14.7	28.6	13.9
1959. . . .	22.4	35.2	12.8

This is not a temporary aberration but the result of a long-term trend in which the poverty status of the elderly has gradually improved in comparison with the general population. As a group the elderly are not any more disadvantaged than the general population.

Table 16-19 shows some large disparities in poverty status among the elderly, however. These are, for the most part, the same differentials that have already been noted for all age groups:

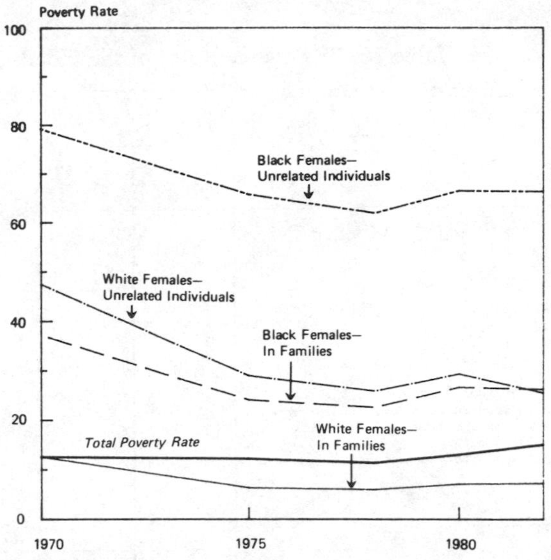

Figure 16-7. Trend in Poverty Rate of Elderly Females, by Race and Living Arrangements: 1970-1982

1. Elderly who live in families have much lower poverty rates than those who live alone or with unrelated individuals.
2. Black elderly persons have poverty rates 3.0 times those of the white elderly.
3. Female elderly persons have poverty rates 70 percent higher than those of the male elderly.

Nevertheless, the improvement over time noted above has affected all sex, race, and family-status groups favorably. The recent improvement (1978-82) has affected females more favorably than males, and blacks more favorably than whites. The improvement has been confined almost entirely to elderly persons living within families. Poverty rates for white unrelated elderly persons have remained practically unchanged since 1978, but there has been a substantial worsening in the poverty status of black unrelated elderly individuals since 1978.

Characteristics of the Elderly Poor

Table 16-20 provides poverty rates for the elderly poor subdivided into three age groups, those 62-64, those 67-71, and those seventy-two and over. Rates for all persons aged sixty and over are provided for comparison. For each of these age groups, poverty rates are shown for a wide variety of characteristics. This table provides information about differentials discussed previously for the general population. Unfortunately the detail is not available by race or by family type. This table does permit the reader to pinpoint those subgroups among the elderly where poverty rates are high, intermediate, and low.

Table 16-20. Poverty Rates of the Elderly, by Selected Characteristics, Age, and Sex: 1982

Characteristic	Both sexes				Female				Percent of male persons 60 and over
	Age 60 and over	62 to 64 years	65 to 71 years	72 years and over	Age 60 and over	62 to 64 years	65 to 71 years	72 years and over	
Family status and composition									
Total	13.6	15.7	11.4	17.3	16.3	13.6	14.4	19.9	30.8
In families	8.2	7.4	6.8	10.3	8.6	8.0	7.9	10.1	47.3
Householder	9.1	8 1	7.2	11.6	16.2	17.2	15.4	15.5	72.2
With related children under 18 years	25.4	21.6	28.5	34.2	42.3	41.7	40.0	44.6	50.9
Spouse of householder	7.0	6.0	6.4	9.6	7.0	5.9	6.4	9.7	5.1
Other family members	7.4	11.8	6.5	6.9	7.3	11.5	7.7	6.4	21.3
In related subfamilies	33.0	19.5	26.1	39.7	35.5	18.2	31.0	42.3	50.6
Unrelated individuals	27.3	27.3	24.9	28.3	29.1	29.8	26.9	29.7	18.2
Living alone	26.5	25.5	24.3	27.6	28.0	27.3	26.2	28.8	17.3
Living with nonrelatives	38.4	40.9	32.7	39.3	47.1	57.3	40.4	45.0	26.6
Marital status									
Total	13.6	11.3	11.4	17.3	16.3	13.6	14.4	19.9	30.8
Single	21.3	26.1	17.2	23.7	23.4	27.6	19.9	25.5	32.3
Married, spouse present	7.4	6.3	5.9	10.2	7.1	6.0	6.2	9.7	58.2
Married, spouse absent	35.6	28.6	32.3	44.6	45.5	40.2	43.8	51.4	29.0
Separated	39.9	33.6	40.5	49.0	50.0	46.6	48.8	58.8	27.1
Other	28.2	15.2	17.9	40.4	36.6	20.0	32.4	42.6	33.8
Widowed	22.0	20.2	21.6	22.1	22.8	21.5	22.8	22.7	12.0
Divorced	24.5	27.4	21.8	27.4	26.9	29.2	24.2	30.8	30.5
Work experience[a]									
All persons	13.6	11.3	11.4	17.3	16.3	13.6	14.4	19.9	30.8
Worked last year	4.9	4.7	3.7	8.3	6.0	6.0	4.6	10.6	51.1
50 to 52 weeks	3.6	3.2	3.1	7.8	4.0	4.2	3.1	8.8	57.7
full-time	2.7	2.4	2.8	6.6	2.5	3.2	2.7	6.5	68.3
49 weeks or less	7.2	7.8	4.5	8.8	8.9	9.0	6.1	12.4	45.3
full-time	6.5	6.9	3.7	4.8	10.0	11.2	6.4	7.7	43.4
Main reason for working part year									
Ill or disabled	12.7	17.8	9.2	18.2	12.8	13.7	14.5	18.5	48.0
Keeping house	8.9	8.5	6.6	11.3	8.8	9.2	7.1	12.0	7.5
Unable to find work	8.5	9.2	3.9	7.7	9.1	11.2	4.3	*	61.4
Retired	4.0	3.1	3.0	7.2	5.9	5.0	4.0	13.0	55.9
Other	9.0	12.1	4.2	7.7	10.7	10.6	3.4	14.3	44.0
Did not work last year	16.7	17.3	13.9	18.2	18.7	18.1	16.4	20.4	28.7
Main reason for not working									
Ill or disabled	31.0	27.5	28.0	33.2	35.1	35.2	35.0	34.2	30.1
Keeping house	14.4	12.7	13.5	16.3	14.5	12.7	13.5	16.5	0.4
Unable to find work	33.2	28.2	23.8	53.8	36.1	28.9	36.8	64.3	47.0
Retired	13.1	14.1	10.5	14.7	16.1	17.4	13.1	17.8	43.2
Other	27.0	40.0	23.1	20.5	24.4	35.5	25.0	20.8	26.7
Source of income									
All persons	13.6	11.3	11.4	17.3	16.3	13.6	14.4	19.9	30.8
Earnings only	12.9	12.2	13.5	28.6	15.1	14.6	14.7	30.8	48.5
Wage or salary income only	9.8	9.3	12.0	15.4	14.2	14.8	16.4	30.8	29.5
Self-employed income only	32.6	29.3	26.1	66.7	33.3	12.5	14.3	*	84.8
Wage or salary and self-employed income	*	*	*	*	*	*	*	*	*
Earnings and income other than earnings	3.9	3.5	3.2	7.5	4.7	4.6	3.9	9.7	52.8
Earnings and social security income only	12.9	16.8	8.8	16.2	17.6	21.6	11.2	23.2	32.6
Earnings and supplemental security income only	42.1	20.0	42.9	50.0	16.7	*	33.3	*	87.5
Earnings and social security and supplemental security income only	58.3	100.0	54.5	70.0	50.0	100.0	53.3	40.0	42.9
Earnings and other income only	2.8	2.5	1.9	4.7	2.8	2.8	1.9	5.2	61.5
Other combinations	40.0	*	*	75.0	66.7	*	*	75.0	0.0
Income other than earnings	16.1	16.5	13.4	17.7	18.1	17.6	15.8	19.9	28.8
Social security income only	32.5	37.4	29.3	33.6	32.4	36.7	30.1	33.2	30.9
Supplemental security income only	56.3	66.2	54.7	50.2	54.3	64.6	54.8	48.3	24.9
Other income only	23.2	13.2	22.9	53.5	20.5	11.3	22.1	50.4	30.1
Other transfer payments only	57.1	48.5	58.8	57.1	79.0	72.7	100.0	63.6	35.5
Social security and supplemental security income only	63.9	61.0	58.9	67.6	64.5	58.5	61.5	67.8	27.2
Social security and other income only	7.7	8.9	6.0	8.5	9.4	10.1	7.4	10.6	26.3
Social security income and other transfer payments only[b]	15.7	6.6	14.5	20.3	26.3	8.3	24.7	30.0	11.4
Social security and "all other" income only[c]	7.4	9.0	5.8	8.1	9.0	10.0	7.1	10.0	27.1
Other combinations	12.5	10.4	12.8	22.7	11.8	10.6	14.8	24.2	41.3
No income	36.5	25.5	45.1	56.7	32.0	21.5	41.1	53.7	27.6

Table 16-20. Poverty Rates of the Elderly, by Selected Characteristics, Age, and Sex: 1982—continued

Characteristic	Both sexes				Female				Percent of male persons 60 and over
	Age 60 and over	62 to 64 years	65 to 71 years	72 years and over	Age 60 and over	62 to 64 years	65 to 71 years	72 years and over	
Type of residence									
Total	13.6	11.3	11.4	17.3	16.3	13.6	14.4	19.9	30.8
Metropolitan areas	11.8	10.1	10.0	15.0	14.6	12.8	13.0	17.8	28.1
Inside central cities	15.3	14.5	13.6	17.7	18.5	17.1	17.6	20.5	27.6
Outside central cities	9.0	6.8	7.4	12.5	11.4	9.1	9.4	15.3	28.6
Nonmetropolitan areas	17.0	13.7	13.9	21.4	19.6	15.4	16.9	23.8	34.4
Tenure and living arrangements									
All persons	13.6	11.3	11.4	17.3	16.3	13.6	14.4	19.9	30.8
Living with relatives	8.2	7.4	6.8	10.3	8.6	8.0	7.9	10.1	47.3
Owner-occupied units	6.9	6.0	6.0	8.8	7.1	6.0	6.8	8.3	49.4
Renter-occupied units	16.3	18.4	12.5	18.2	17.2	21.6	14.0	18.3	42.0
Public	31.5	41.9	33.7	27.1	32.3	41.4	29.7	28.9	42.3
Private	14.7	16.5	10.8	17.0	15.6	19.8	12.4	17.2	41.9
Family householders	9.1	8.1	7.2	11.6	16.2	17.2	15.4	15.5	72.2
Owner-occupied units	7.5	6.4	6.1	9.9	12.2	11.9	12.3	11.7	77.7
Renter-occupied units	18.8	19.8	15.1	19.9	28.0	33.7	25.5	26.7	58.7
Public	36.0	48.0	52.3	24.8	51.6	54.5	57.1	42.9	52.9
Private	17.0	17.6	12.1	19.2	25.1	30.3	20.7	25.1	60.0
Living with nonrelatives only	38.0	40.3	32.3	39.2	46.1	53.8	39.6	44.6	27.4
Owner-occupied units	31.7	35.7	31.3	31.3	39.6	46.5	35.3	38.8	25.9
Renter-occupied units	46.4	44.9	33.3	52.3	54.5	62.2	45.5	51.5	28.8
Public	44.4	100.0	33.3	33.3	*	*	*	*	*
Private	46.5	42.4	33.3	53.7	56.8	62.2	48.8	54.7	24.8
Living alone	26.5	25.5	24.3	27.6	28.0	27.3	26.2	28.8	17.3
Owner-occupied units	23.1	22.9	21.4	23.9	24.4	24.1	22.9	24.9	15.6
Renter-occupied units	31.9	30.1	29.2	33.5	34.3	35.2	32.4	35.0	19.3
Public	47.2	71.4	38.1	47.6	48.8	73.3	40.2	48.8	13.5
Private	28.7	24.9	27.6	29.9	30.8	29.4	30.8	31.2	21.2
Type of income									
All persons[d]	13.6	11.3	11.4	17.3	16.3	13.6	14.4	19.9	30.8
Earnings[d]	4.9	4.7	3.7	8.2	5.9	5.9	4.6	10.3	51.6
Wage and salary income	4.1	4.0	3.5	6.6	5.8	5.9	4.6	10.1	38.3
Nonfarm self-employment income	8.1	8.5	2.9	11.2	7.9	9.2	5.5	9.9	73.5
Farm self-employment income	10.2	8.1	9.5	13.3	*	*	*	*	*
Income other than earnings[d]	13.1	10.6	11.0	16.8	15.8	12.9	13.9	19.4	30.5
Social security income	13.6	13.4	10.9	15.6	16.2	15.6	13.6	18.2	29.2
Supplemental security income	58.3	62.0	55.6	58.8	58.8	61.0	57.5	58.8	26.6
Other transfer payments[b]	15.4	13.3	12.2	21.0	24.3	21.2	20.8	30.0	40.3
Dividends, interest, and rent	6.0	4.5	4.6	8.4	7.5	5.5	5.9	10.3	29.7
Private pensions, government employee pensions, alimony, annuities, etc.	3.8	4.2	2.4	4.2	6.3	8.0	4.2	6.5	33.0
No income	36.5	25.5	45.1	56.7	32.0	21.5	41.1	53.7	27.6

[a]Includes members of the armed forces, not shown separately.

[b]Other transfer payments include public assistance, unemployment compensation, workmen's compensation and veteran's payments.

[c]"all other" income includes dividends, interest, rent, private pensions, government employee pensions, alimony, and annuity income.

[d]Detail does not add to total since some persons receive more than one of the specified types of income.

Note: * indicates zero or rounds to zero.

Source: U.S. Bureau of the Census. "Characteristics of the Population Below the Poverty Level: 1982." Current Population Reports (Series P-60, no. 144). Washington, DC: U.S. Government Printing Office, 1984, Table 15.

Sources of Income of the Poverty Population

Rates of poverty according to source of income are specified in Table 16-21. As would be expected, the highest poverty rates (75 percent) are found for families (75 percent) and individuals (78 percent) who receive income solely from public assistance. Poverty rates are also high, but less extreme, for persons who receive supplemental assistance. The lowest poverty rates are found for persons who receive income from dividends, interests, and rents (4.1 percent for families and 11.4 percent for unrelated individuals). Poverty rates also tend to be low where there is income from wages and salaries. Where there is income from self-employment, poverty rates are moderately high (17 percent).

Social Security appears to be performing its intended function quite well. Both families and individuals who received Social Security income had poverty rates almost as low as those of the general population. Also, those on private or government pensions have very low poverty rates. In addition to these institutionalized sources of income, several individual activities are instrumental in keeping poverty in the United States relatively low. The following five characteristics provide the most significant protection against poverty:

1. Employment at a wage or salary job full time
2. Living in a family
3. Qualifying for Social Security or having a pension
4. Accumulating savings to pay interest and dividends
5. Attaining a minimum level of education (preferably some college).

Any person who manages to achieve all five of these states has almost a zero probability of being in poverty, irrespective of race, age, sex, or ethnicity.

Conclusion

The combination of high unemployment, inflation, economic recession, and other economic problems that plagued the American economy in the late 1970s and early 1980s brought to a grinding halt, and even reversed, the reduction of poverty. When the correlates of poverty are exposed, it seems likely that the long-term trend in reduction will be resumed as the business cycle turns upward again. Rising levels of educational attainment, rising levels of occupation, a stronger positive correlation between education and income, and prospects for greater family stability, for smaller families, and for greater socioeconomic equality among the race-ethnic groups have all been predicted in preceding chapters. These are all indicative of further shrinking in the prevalence of poverty. If these favorable predictions occur at about the pace that has been the recent trend, and if the spectre of chronic unemployment and recession can be banished, the dream of eliminating poverty could come very close to being realized.

Table 16-21. Poverty Rates for Families and Unrelated Individuals, by Source of Income, Family Type, and Race: 1982

Source of income	All families	White		Black		Both sexes	White		Black	
		Married couple[a]	Female head[b]	Married couple[a]	Female head[b]		Male	Female	Male	Female
Total	12.2	7.0	27.9	16.4	56.2	23.1	16.3	24.2	32.5	48.3
Earnings.	8.5	5.8	17.0	12.1	37.9	13.5	11.6	14.1	18.8	17.8
Wage and salary income.	8.0	5.1	16.7	11.9	37.7	12.9	10.7	13.8	18.1	17.6
Nonfarm self-employment. . .	10.2	9.7	16.3	13.4	*	20.4	18.8	21.4	*	*
Farm self-employment. . .	16.7	17.0	*	*	*	29.6	31.0	*	*	*
Income other than earnings.	11.3	6.0	27.2	15.7	59.4	21.5	13.8	22.6	31.3	52.1
Social security income.	10.4	6.9	12.9	21.8	44.0	27.3	18.2	25.6	44.8	68.0
Public assistance income.	75.1	55.5	82.4	52.7	88.0	78.2	76.4	74.9	78.5	*
Supplemental security income .	39.0	34.5	35.5	46.3	54.9	75.9	69.0	74.0	81.0	88.1
Other transfer payments. . . .	8.9	6.9	14.0	12.6	34.9	17.5	11.8	23.9	17.3	39.0
Dividends, interest and rent. .	4.1	3.1	9.9	5.3	21.7	11.4	8.1	12.8	10.3	22.8
Pensions: private, government, and alimony	8.1	3.8	17.0	11.4	44.7	14.9	12.8	13.3	28.6	30.5

[a] Families with female householder, no husband present.

[b] All other families.

Source: U.S. Bureau of the Census. "Characteristics of the Population Below the Poverty Level: 1982." Current Population Reports (Series P-60, no. 144). Washington, DC: U.S. Government Printing Office, 1984, Table 34.

Bibliography

Bane, M.J. "Is the Welfare State Replacing the Family?" *Public Interest* 70 (1983):91-101.

Blume, S.S. "Explanation and Social Policy: The Problem of Social Inequalities in Health." *Journal of Social Policy* 11 (1982):7-31.

Bronfenbrenner, M. "Poverty–Exploitation–Alienation." *American Behavioral Science* 23 (1980):383-92.

Chambers, D.E. "U.S. Poverty Line: A Time for Change." *Social Work* 27 (1982):354-58.

Corcoran, Mary; Duncan, Greg J.; and Gurin, Patricia. "Psychological and Demographic Aspects of the Underclass." Paper prepared for the Population Association of America, 1983.

Corcoran, Mary, and Hill, M.S. "Unemployment and Poverty." *Social Service Review* 54 (1980):407-13.

Covello, Vincent T. (ed.) *Poverty and Public Policy: An Evaluation of Social Science Research.* Cambridge, MA: Schenkman Publishing Co., 1980 (published for the National Academy of Science).

Cowell, Frank A. *Measuring Inequality: Techniques for the Social Sciences.* New York: Wiley, 1977.

Danziger, S. et al. "Work and Welfare as Determinants of Female Poverty and Household Headship." *Quarterly Journal of Economics* 97 (1982):519-34.

Davis, F.G. "What to Do about Urban Poverty: The Black Ghetto Case." *Journal of Economic Issues* 16 (1982):877-87.

Dellaportas, G. "Effectiveness of Public Assistance Payments in Reducing Poverty." *American Journal of Economics and Sociology* 39 (1980):113-21.

Gans, H.J. "What Can be Done about Poverty? Egalitarian Social Policy in the 1980s." *Dissent* 28 (1981): 40-46.

Garfinkel, Irwin, and Haveman, Robert H. *Earnings Capacity, Poverty, and Inequality.* New York: Academic Press, 1977.

Gottschalk. P. "Transfer Scenarios and Projections of Poverty into the 1980s." *Journal of Human Resources* 16 (1981):41-60.

Gronberg, Kirsten A.; Sheet, David; and Suttles, Gerald D. *Poverty and Social Change.* Chicago: The University of Chicago Press, 1978.

Hannon, M.; Tuma, N.; and Groeneveld, L. "Income and Marital Events: Evidence from an Income Maintenance Experiment." *American Journal of Sociology* 89 (1977):1186-1211.

Holman, Robert. *Poverty: Explanations of Social Deprivation.* New York: St. Martin's Press, 1978.

Huber, Joan and Chalfant, H. Paul. *The Sociology of American Poverty.* Cambridge, MA: Schenkman Publishing Co., 1974.

Hunt, Joseph McVicker. "The Challenge of Incompetence and Poverty." Papers on the role of early Education. Urbana: University of Illinois Press, 1969.

Hurley, Rodger L. *Poverty and Mental Retardation: A Causal Relationship.* New York: Random House, 1969.

Keyfitz, N. "Development and the Elimination of Poverty." *Economic Development and Cultural Change* 30 (1982):649-70.

Kilson, M. "Black Social Classes and Intergenerational Poverty." *Public Interest* 64 (1981):58-78.

Kosa, John; Antonovsky, Aaron; and Zola, Irving K. *Poverty and Health: A Sociological Analysis.* Cambridge, MA: Harvard University Press, 1969.

Miller, Herman P. (ed.) *Poverty, American Style.* Belmont, CA: Wadsworth Publishing Co., 1966.

Moon, Marilyn L. and Smolensky, Eugene (eds.). *Improving Measures of Economic Well-Being.* New York: Academic Press, 1977.

Moynihan, Daniel P. (ed.) *On Understanding Poverty.* New York: Basic Books, 1969.

Murray, C.A. "Two Wars Against Poverty: Economic Growth and the Great Society." *Public Interest* 69 (1982):3-16.

Myrdal, Gunnar (ed.). *Poverty as a Public Issue.* New York: Free Press, 1965.

Orcutt, Ben Avis (comp.). *Poverty and Social Casework Services.* Metuchen, NJ: Scarecrow Press, 1974.

Rein, M., and Rainwater, L. "Patterns of Welfare Use." *Social Science Review* ((1978):511-34.

Ribich, Thomas I. *Education and Poverty.* Washington, DC: Brookings Institution, 1968.

Rich, S. "Poor America." *Public Interest* 60 (1980):148-149.

Schiller, Bradley R. "Empirical Studies of Welfare Dependency: A Survey." *Journal of Human Resources* VIII Supplement (1973):19-32.

Segalman, Ralph. *Poverty in America: The Welfare Dilemma.* Westport, CT: Greenwood Press, 1981.

Stoez, D. "Wake for the Welfare State: Social Welfare and the Neoconservative Challenge." *Social Service Review* 55 (1981):398-410.

Thornton, J.R. et al. "Poverty and Economic Growth: Trickle Down Peters Out." *Economic Inquiry* 16 (1978):385-94.

Thurow, Lester C. *Poverty and Discrimination.* Washington, DC: Brookings Institution, 1969.

Trader, H.P. "Welfare Policies and Black Families." *Social Work* 24 (1979):548-52.

Will, Robert E. *Poverty in Affluence.* New York: Harcourt, Brace, and World, 1970.

Wolch, J.R. "Residential Location of the Service-Dependent Poor." *Association of American Geographers Annual* 70 (1980):330-41.

Technical Appendix 16-1

The SSA Poverty Threshold

At the core of the poverty index developed by the Social Security Administration (SSA) in 1964 was the economy food plan, the least costly of four nutritionally adequate food plans designed by the Department of Agriculture. It was determined from the Department of Agriculture's 1955 survey of food consumption that families of three or more spent approximately one-third of their income on food; the poverty level for such families was therefore set at three times the cost of the economy food plan. For smaller families and persons living alone, the cost of the economy food plan was multiplied by slightly higher coefficients to compensate for the relatively larger fixed expenses of smaller households. Annual revisions of the SSA poverty cutoffs were based on price changes of the items in the economy food budget.

As a result of deliberations of a Federal Interagency Committee in 1969, the following two modifications to the original SSA definitions of poverty were recommended: (1) that the SSA thresholds for nonfarm families be retained for the base year 1963, but annual adjustments in the levels be based on changes in the Consumer Price Index (CPI) rather than changes in the cost of food included in the economy food plan; and (2) that the farm thresholds be raised from 70 to 85 percent of the corresponding nonfarm levels. The combined impact of these two modifications resulted in an increase of 360,000 poor families and 1.6 million poor persons in 1967.

The poverty thresholds change each year by the same percentage as the annual average Consumer Price Index. Table 16-A shows the change in the CPI between 1959 and 1982 and the corresponding thresholds for a family of four.

In 1980 another interagency committee recommended three additional modifications that were implemented in the March, 1982, Current Population Survey as well as in the 1980 census: (1) elimination of separate thresholds for farm families, (2) averaging of thresholds for female-householder and "all other" families, and (3) extension of the poverty matrix to families with nine or more members.

Size-Composition Matrix. The poverty cutoffs used by the Bureau of the Census to determine the poverty status of families and unrelated individuals consist of a set of forty-eight thresholds arranged in a two-dimensional matrix consisting of family size (from one person—unrelated individuals—to nine or more persons) cross-classified by presence and number of family members under eighteen years old (from no children present to eight or more children present). Unrelated individuals and two-person families are further differentiatied by the age of the individual or family householder (under sixty-five and sixty-five and over). The total family income of each family in the sample is tested against the appropriate dollar threshold to determine the poverty status of that family. If the family's total income is less than its corresponding cutoff, the family is classified as below the poverty level. The average thresholds were weighted by the number of children. For a given size of family, the weighted average threshold for that group is obtained by multiplying the threshold for each presence and the number of children category within the given family size by the number of families in that category. These products are then aggregated across the entire range of presence and number of children categories, and the total aggregate is divided by the total number of families in the group to yield the weighted average threshold at the poverty level for that size family.

Table 16-A. Changes Between 1959 and 1982 in the Consumer Price Index and the Average Poverty Threshold for a Family of Four

Year	Consumer Price Index (1967=100)	Average threshold for a family of four[a] ($)
1982	289.1	9,862
1981	272.4	9,287
1980	246.8	8,414
1979	217.4	7,412
1978	195.4	6,662
1977	181.5	6,191
1976	170.5	5,815
1975	161.2	5,500
1974	147.7	5,038
1973	133.1	4,540
1972	125.3	4,275
1971	121.3	4,137
1970	116.3	3,968
1969	109.8	3,743
1968	104.2	3,553
1967	100.0	3,410
1966	97.2	3,317
1965	94.5	3,223
1964	92.9	3,169
1963	91.7	3,128
1962	90.6	3,089
1961	89.6	3,054
1960	88.7	3,022
1959	87.3	2,973

[a]For years prior to 1981, average threshold for a nonfarm family of four is shown.

Source: U.S. Bureau of the Census. "Characteristics of the Population Below the Poverty Level: 1982." Current Population Reports (Series P-60, no. 144). Washington, DC: U.S. Government Printing Office, 1984, Appendix Table A-1, page 180.

Chapter 17

Population and Housing

Since population trends bear a close relationship to housing trends, the demographer needs information about the residential situation and the living arrangements of the population, and the housing specialist must look to demography for an understanding of many of the forces that underlie changes in the quantity and distribution of housing. The processes of family formation and dissolution and other social and economic processes that affect the number and the composition of households are a part of the demographic foundation upon which housing analysis is built. The present chapter is aimed at meeting some of the joint needs of demographers and housing experts.

Key concepts in housing analysis are "living quarters" and "housing units" (see Definition Box). Excluding group quarters, there is a one-to-one correspondence between households and living units: A living unit is the housing aspect of a household, and a household is the demographic aspect of a housing unit. The number of householders is equal to the number of housing units.

It is common to refer to the totality of housing units as the "housing inventory," just as demographers refer to the totality of a population count as "the population." Housing units are "born" and "die" (demolition), and some can migrate. Hence, it is just as meaningful to speak of trends, composition, and distribution for housing as it is for demography.

This chapter will provide an overview of the numerous themes that link housing and demography. It is, in several aspects, a supplement to Chapter 11; materials already presented under the household rubric are not repeated here under their living unit counterparts.

Sources of Housing Data

At each census since 1940 a housing census and a population census have been taken together. The census form, filled out by the occupants of each household or used by an enumerator to enumerate a household, has a set of housing census questions about the living unit. Another source of housing data is the Annual Housing Survey, sponsored since 1973 by the Department of Housing and Urban Development. A special cycle of this survey, called the Components of Inventory Change (CINCH) Survey, was coordinated with the 1980 housing census. A CINCH survey was also taken in 1973. The materials of this chapter are almost entirely from these sources, for 1980 and earlier years.

Definitions

The reader should review the Definition Box in Chapter 11, since several household and family concepts employed in this chapter are defined there.

Living Quarters. Housing units in structures intended for residential use (e.g. one-family home, apartment home, hotel, motel, or boarding house), but also in structures intended for nonresidential use (e.g. the rooms in a warehouse where a night guard lives). Mobile homes or trailers, boats, tents, caves, vans, etc., may also be used as living quarters.

Housing Units. A house, an apartment, a group of rooms, or a single room occupied or intended for occupancy as separate living quarters, that is, quarters in which the occupants live and eat separately from other persons in the building and which have (a) direct access from the outside of the building or through a common hall used or intended to be used by the occupants of another unit or by the general public, and (b) complete kitchen facilities for the exclusive use of the occupants. The occupants may be a single family, one person living alone, two or more families living together, or any other group of related or unrelated persons who share living arrangements (except those defined as living in group quarters). Both occupied and vacant housing units are included, except that tents, caves, boats, railroad cars, and the like, are included only if they are occupied as someone's usual place of residence. Vacant mobile homes are included only if intended for occupancy on the site where they stand; vacant mobile homes on dealers' sales lots, at the factory, or in storage are excluded.

Occupied Housing Unit. A housing unit that is the usual place of residence of at least one of the persons living in it at the time of the interview or only temporarily absent—e.g. away on vacation. A unit occupied at the time of the survey solely by persons whose usual place of residence is elsewhere is classified as "vacant."

Household. All the persons who occupy a housing unit as their usual place of residence.

Year-Round Housing Units. All occupied units plus vacant units intended for year-round use. Units intended for seasonal occupancy and units held for migratory labor are excluded.

Components of Change (CINCH Survey). Components into which the housing stock is divided to reflect units that remain the same as well as the several kinds of changes that occur, designed to explain the source of the 1980 housing inventory and the disposition of the 1973 housing inventory. In terms of the 1980 inventory the components of change are same units, units added through new construction, units added through other sources, units changed by conversion, and units changed by merger. In terms of the 1973 inventory: units lost through demolition or disaster, units lost through other means, units changed by conversion, and units changed by merger. The classifications were obtained by interviewers by making comparisons between units as listed in 1973 and units as listed in 1980, and by a more detailed computer comparison of housing unit status and characteristics.

Same units. Living quarters that existed in 1973 and remained unchanged in number in 1980, hence units common to both the 1973 and 1980 inventories.

Units changed by conversion. Units of 1973 increased to a larger number of 1980 housing units through structural alteration or change in use.

Units changed by merger. The result of combining two or more 1973 housing units into fewer 1980 units through structural alteration (e.g. the removal of walls or dismantling of kitchen facilities) or changes in use.

Units added through new construction. Any housing unit built in 1974 or later, including occupied and vacant trailers and mobile homes if the model year is 1974 or later.

Units added through other sources. Any housing unit added to the inventory through sources other than new construction or conversion.

Housing Growth versus Population Growth

As of April, 1980, the housing stock of the nation consisted of 86,758,717 units intended for year-round occupancy. Of these, 80,389,673 were occupied and 6,369,144 were vacant. For nine decades the number of dwelling units has increased faster than the population, with the result that the average number of persons per housing unit has declined. Data to support this finding are given in Table 17-1. Between 1970 and 1980 the number of occupied housing units increased by 26.7 percent, whereas the population in housing units increased by 11.9 percent. In this one period the supply of living quarters increased 2.2 times as fast as the number of people. A similar change took place between 1960 and 1970; during that decade the number of dwelling units increased at a rate nearly 50 percent faster than the rate of population growth. Over the years this trend has been impressively consistent. In 1890 there were five persons per household; by 1980 the average household

Table 17-1. Comparative Trends in Housing and Population, by Race of Occupants: 1890-1982

Race of occupants and year	Housing-occupied dwelling units: Number (000)	Housing-occupied dwelling units: Percent increase over preceding period	Total population in housing units: Number (000)	Total population in housing units: Percent increase over preceding period	Population per occupied dwelling unit	Ratio of housing growth to population growth
Total						
1980.	80,390	26.7	220,807	11.9	2.74	2.24
1970.	63,450	19.7	197,400	13.2	3.11	1.49
1960.	53,024	23.8	174,373	15.7	3.28	1.52
1950.	42,826	22.9	150,697	14.5	3.53	1.58
1940.	34,855	16.6	131,669	7.2	3.77	2.31
1930.	29,905	22.8	122,775	16.1	4.11	1.42
1920.	24,352	20.2	105,711	14.9	4.34	1.36
1910.	20,256	26.9	91,972	21.0	4.54	1.28
1900.	15,964	25.8	75,995	20.7	4.76	1.25
1890.	12,690	...	62,948	...	4.93	...
White						
1980.	68,982	22.0	184,654	6.9	2.67	3.19
1970.	56,529	18.1	172,729	11.8	3.05	1.53
1960.	47,880	22.6	154,552	14.5	3.22	1.56
1950.	39,044	23.7	134,942	14.1	3.46	1.68
1940.	31,561	17.0	118,215	7.2	3.75	2.36
1930.	26,983	23.6	110,287	16.3	4.09	1.45
1920.	21,826	--	94,821	16.0	4.34	--
1910.	--	--	81,732	22.3	--	--
1900.	14,064	25.0	66,809	21.2	4.75	1.18
1890.	11,255	...	55,101	...	4.90	...
Nonwhite						
1980.	11,408	64.9	36,154	46.5	3.17	1.40
1970.	6,920	34.5	24,671	24.5	3.56	1.41
1960.	5,144	36.0	19,822	25.8	3.85	1.40
1950.	3,783	14.9	15,755	17.1	4.16	0.87
1940.	3,293	12.7	13,454	7.7	4.09	1.65
1930.	2,922	15.7	12,488	14.7	4.27	1.07
1920.	2,526	--	10,890	6.3	4.31	--
1910.	--	--	10,240	11.5	--	--
1900.	1,900	32.4	9,185	17.1	4.83	1.89
1890.	1,435	...	7,846	...	5.47	...

Note: Data for 1950 and earlier refers to total population divided by total number of occupied dwelling units. -- indicates data not available.

Source: Housing data from U.S. Bureau of the Census. "Characteristics of Housing Units" (Tables 80, 83, and 84). 1980 Census of Housing. Also "Housing Characteristics for States, Cities, and Counties: United States Summary" (Table 3). 1970 Census of Housing. Also "States and Small Areas: United States Summary" (Table 3). 1960 Census of Housing. Washington, DC: U.S. Government Printing Office, 1983, 1972, and 1962. Population data from U.S. Bureau of the Census. "Metropolitan Housing Characteristics" (Table A-7). 1980 Census of Housing. Also "Characteristics of the Population: United States Summary" (Table 54). 1970 Census of Population. Also "Characteristics of the Population: United States Summary" (Table 50). 1960 Census of Population. Washington, DC: U.S. Government Printing Office, 1983, 1973, and 1963.

contained only 56 percent as many persons as it had in 1890.

The decline in average size of household continued right through the baby boom and its resulting increase in the number of families having two, three, or four children. It has greatly accelerated during the baby bust. The factors that have caused the demand for more living units to outstrip population growth are described in more detail in Chapter 11, but among them are:

1. Greater longevity, meaning that more elderly people are surviving to live in their own households after their children have grown and departed

2. Greater economic security for elderly and widowed people, enabling them to live apart rather than with a child or other relative

3. The recent decline in fertility, resulting in more families with no children or only one child

4. An increase in the tendency for unmarried persons to live in their own apartments, either alone or with someone else, with a decline in the proportion of unmarried persons who live with their parents or as lodgers in private homes or rooming houses

5. A decline in the number of subfamilies and secondary families (In the past young married couples tended to live with their parents more frequently than now. The decline may have been reversed during the economic recession of the 1980s.)

6. Increased divorce and separation, most often creating two households where one existed before

7. Aging of the population, so that an increased share of the population is now concentrated in the age groups where childless households are most common, age forty-five and over.

There is a limit, however, to how far the population is willing or able to extend several of the above changes, and apparently that limit is rapidly being approached. The long-term trend toward smaller households therefore seems destined to be halted or reversed in the near future. Chapter 11 and data of this chapter give evidence that this has already occurred since 1980, at least temporarily.

Table 17-2 provides measures of the distribution and growth of housing and population and the ratio of housing growth to population growth for regions, urban-rural areas, and metropolitan and nonmetropolitan areas. It shows the following:

1. Housing and population are distributed in almost identical proportions between regions, between urban and rural areas, between metropolitan and nonmetropolitan areas, and between central cities and metropolitan rings. The percentage distribution of population and the percentage distribution of housing are practically identical (columns 8 and 9).

2. This distribution implies, in turn, that the average number of persons per dwelling unit is roughly the same in all of these areas. This is verified by the two right-hand columns.

3. The pattern of housing growth is similar to the pattern of population growth. Regions that had high population growth also had high housing growth. Growth trends in urban-rural and metropolitan-nonmetropolitan areas are mirrored by housing trends.

Table 17-2. Relation of Housing Growth to Population Growth, by Place of Residence: 1970-1980

Area	Occupied housing units			Population			Ratio housing to population growth	Percent distribution: 1980		Population per housing unit	
	1980 (000)	1970 (000)	Percent change	1980 (000)	1970 (000)	Percent change		Housing	Population	1980	1970
United States. . . .	80,390	63,450	26.7	220,807	197,400	11.9	2.2	100.0	100.0	2.7	3.1
Regions											
Northeast.	17,471	15,483	12.8	47,845	47,701	0.3	42.7	21.7	21.7	2.7	3.1
North Central.	20,859	17,537	18.9	57,369	55,037	4.2	4.5	25.9	26.0	2.8	3.1
South.	26,486	19,258	37.5	73,444	60,911	20.6	1.8	32.9	33.3	2.8	3.2
West	15,574	11,172	39.4	42,150	33,751	24.9	1.6	19.4	19.1	2.7	3.0
Urban-rural residence											
Urban.	60,557	47,563	27.3	162,242	144,610	12.2	2.2	75.3	73.5	2.7	3.0
Rural.	19,833	15,887	24.8	58,565	52,790	10.9	2.3	24.7	26.5	3.0	3.3
Metropolitan (SMSAs)											
Metropolitan inside SMSAs.	60,498	43,863	37.9	165,291	135,719	21.8	1.7	75.3	74.9	2.7	3.1
Central cities . . .	25,527	21,382	19.4	65,770	61,946	6.2	3.1	31.8	29.8	2.6	2.9
Metropolitan rings .	34,971	22,481	55.6	99,521	73,773	34.9	1.6	43.5	45.1	2.8	3.3
Nonmetropolitan. . . .	19,892	19,587	1.6	55,516	61,707	-10.0	*	24.7	25.1	2.8	3.2

Note: * indicates data not sufficient for accurate measurement.

Source: U.S. Bureau of the Census. "Detailed Housing Characteristics: United States Summary" (Table 81); and "Metropolitan Housing Characteristics" (Tables B-7, C-7, G-7, J-7, and M-7). 1980 Census of Housing. Also "Housing Characteristics for States, Cities, and Counties: United States Summary" (Tables 1 and 6). 1970 Census of Housing. Washington, DC: U.S. Government Printing Office, 1983 and 1972. Also "General Social and Economic Characteristics: United States Summary" (Table 100). 1980 Census of Population. Also "Characteristics of the Population: United States Summary (Tables 54, 58, and 107). 1970 Census of Population. Washington, DC: U.S. Government Printing Office, 1983 and 1973.

Table 17-3. Structural Characteristics of Housing: 1950-1980

Characteristics	Percent distribution				Percent change			New construction 1973-1980
	1980	1970	1960	1950	1970-1980	1960-1970	1950-1960	
Age of structure								
Total.	100.0	100.0	100.0	100.0	...	...	...	100.0
15 months prior. . . .	3.5	3.4	3.9	13.4 (15 months prior and 5 years or less prior combined)	30.3	2.6	42.8 (15 months prior and 5 years or less prior combined)	100.0
5 years or less prior. .	9.6	9.7	10.7		27.7	5.2		
6 to 10 years prior. . .	13.1	11.9	13.0	7.3	40.4	7.0	134.1	...
11 to 20 years prior . .	19.7	21.4	14.8	13.3	17.8	67.8	46.5	...
21 to 30 years prior . .	17.1	13.0	11.2	20.1	69.3	34.9	-26.8	...
31 to 40 years prior . .	11.1	40.6 (31 to 40 years and 40 years and over combined)	46.5	45.8	16.7	1.2	33.8	...
40 years and over prior.	25.8							...
Units in structure								
Total.	100.0	100.0	100.0	100.0	...	...	...	100.0
1 - detached	61.8	66.2	68.8	63.3	19.6	11.7	37.7	61.4
1 - attached	4.1	2.9	6.3	2.6	80.3	-45.6	202.2	4.7
2 units.	6.1	8.0	7.7	15.0[a]	-2.5	21.9	-35.2	7.0 (2 units and 3 or 4 units combined)
3 or 4 units	5.0	5.3	5.3	7.3	22.7	15.4	-8.5	
5 to 9 units	4.4	14.5 (5 to 9, 10 to 49, and 50 or more units combined)		4.6	57.5 (5 to 9, 10 to 49, and 50 or more units combined)			
10 to 49 units	8.2		10.7	4.9		57.6	22.8	15.9
50 or more units	5.3			1.5				
Mobile home or trailer .	5.1	3.1	1.3	0.7	113.0	170.4	143.2	10.9
Bedrooms								
Total.	100.0	100.0	100.0	--	...	...	...	100.0
None	2.1	2.4	4.2	--	13.5	-33.4	--	0.7
1 bedroom.	14.9	15.8	17.4	--	21.3	5.7	--	10.1
2 bedrooms	32.4	33.9	36.1	--	22.8	8.9	--	25.9
3 bedrooms	36.9	35.4	31.3	--	33.8	31.3	--	47.2
4 or more bedrooms . . .	13.6	12.6	11.0	--	38.1	33.5	--	16.1

[a] Two categories are combined: (1) 1 and 2 dwelling unit, semidetached, and (2) 2 dwelling units, other.

Note: -- indicates data not available. ... indicated data not applicable.

Source: U.S. Bureau of the Census. "Detailed Housing Characteristics: United States Summary" (Table 80). 1980 Census of Housing. Also U.S. Bureau of the Census. "Housing Characteristics for States, Cities and Counties: United States Summary" (Tables 22 and 24). 1970 Census of Housing. Also U.S. Bureau of the Census. "States and Small Areas: United States Summary" (Tables 4 and 5). 1960 Census of Housing. Also U.S. Bureau of the Census. "General Characteristics: United States Summary" (Tables 5 and 6). 1950 Census of Housing. Washington, DC: U.S. Government Printing Office, 1983, 1973, 1963 and 1953. Also U.S. Bureau of the Census. "Components of Inventory Change (CINCH)." 1980 Census of Housing (Part I: "United States Summary"). Washington, DC: U.S. Government Printing Office, 1983, Table A-1.

4. The decline in average household size has occurred everywhere—in all regions, in both urban and rural areas, in the central cities and suburbs of metropolitan areas, and in nonmetropolitan areas.

Components of Change in the Housing Inventory

Because the housing inventory of the nation is a set of physical facilities that have accumulated over several decades, as an aggregate it can change in size and composition only slowly. In order to learn what the latest trends are, one must focus on the units being added and deleted. It became possible to do this with the emergence of housing surveys. A CINCH housing survey taken in 1973 and repeated in 1980 made it possible to identify unit by unit those housing units that had been added to the housing stock between 1973 and 1980 and the number that had been deleted (see "Components of Change" in the Definition Box). The effect upon the number of housing units of the various types of additions and deletions were as follows:

Housing units	Number (000)
Additions	
New construction	13,119
Conversion	925
Mobile homes moved in. . . .	2,784
Merger	469
From nonresidential, other.	1,271
Total.	18,568
Same units	70,725
Housing stock, 1980. . .	89,292
Deletions	
Conversion or merger	1,264
Demolition or disaster . . .	1,808
Mobile homes moved out . . .	2,170
To other use, condemnation, other.	1,278
Total.	6,521
Same units	70,725
Housing stock, 1973. . .	77,246

Thus, 70,725,000, or 79 percent, of the 1980 inventory comprises housing units that already existed in 1973. Of the net gain of 12,047,000, by far the largest component was new construction. There was a great deal of circulation of mobile homes from one site to another, with a net addition of 614,000 homes. Only 3.1 million units, or 4 percent of the 1973 inventory, were lost through demolition, disaster, condemnation, or other causes. Very little net change resulted from the conversion or merger of 1,264,000 units to produce 1,394,000 different units through conversion or merger.

In summary, the main component of growth to the housing inventory is new construction, and this is counterbalanced by a small annual loss from demolition, disaster, condemnation, or transfer to nonresidential use. In order to know the essential elements of change in the housing inventory, one must focus on new construction. Wherever possible in the remainder of this chapter, statistics on the characteristics of new construction are provided. By comparing these data with data for the total inventory, most recent changes are revealed.

Characteristics of Housing Units

Age of Structure

The housing boom of the 1970s and 1960s has caused a remarkable change to take place in the average age of housing. No less than one-fourth of all the living units in existence in 1980 had been erected since 1970, and nearly one-half (45 percent) were less than twenty years old. This is in sharp contrast to the situation as it was in 1940, or even in 1950, as Table 17-3 (first panel) and the following summary show:

Approximate age of structure	Percent distribution, selected dates		
	1980	1960	1940
Total	100.0	100.0	100.0
10 years or less. . . .	26.2	27.6	15.9
10 to 19 years.	19.7	14.8	24.6
20 to 29 years.	17.1	11.2	18.6
30 to 39 years.	11.1	} 46.5	17.6
40 years or more. . . .	25.8		23.3

Source: Estimated by the author, using data from National Housing Inventory and Census of Housing for respective years.

Comparatively little housing was built during the Depression of the 1930s and during World War II, when materials for housing were scarce, so most of the units reported in Table 17-3 as having been built in 1939 or earlier were built during the 1920s, and most of those reported as having been built during 1940-49 were actually built in 1945-49.

A well-designed and well-constructed dwelling unit can easily last for a hundred years, if well maintained. Ill-designed and poorly constructed living units quickly become obsolete and undesirable places in which to live. Decades of federally funded programs of clearance and renewal have attempted to preserve the best and demolish the worst of the older housing stock. As a consequence, on balance the U.S. population is well housed in "young" housing or in structurally sound older housing. The quality of housing is discussed later.

Table 17-4 (first panel) shows that the oldest housing is in rural farm areas, in villages of less than 2,500 people, and in cities of less than 10,000 in 1980. Places that remain small have had less new housing constructed, and the housing stock has aged. By failing to grow or even losing population, central cities also tend to have older housing stock. In contrast, urban fringes have comparatively little housing older than thirty years.

Table 17-5 (first panel) shows that the black population lives in housing that is considerably older, on the average, than does the white population. The traditional "filtering down" process means that lower-income groups are able to afford the housing that commands the least rent or purchase price, which is the older and obsolescent housing being vacated by those moving into better units. Special programs for building new public

Table 17-4. Structural Characteristics of Housing, by Place of Residence: 1980

Characteristics	Total	Urban total	Central cities	Urban fringe	Places 10,000+	2,500–9,999	Rural total	1,000–2,499	Rural farm	Inside SMSA	Outside SMSA
Year structure built											
Total	100.0	100.0	100.0	100.0	100.0	100.0	100.0	100.0	100.0	100.0	100.0
1979–80	3.5	3.1	2.3	3.8	3.5	3.6	4.7	3.2	1.8	3.4	3.7
1975–78	9.6	8.3	5.9	10.3	9.2	9.8	13.5	9.5	6.6	9.1	11.2
1970–74	13.1	12.1	9.4	15.0	11.2	12.1	16.0	12.0	8.3	12.8	13.8
1960–69	19.7	20.4	17.6	24.5	17.5	16.8	17.7	15.5	11.6	20.7	16.8
1950–59	17.1	18.8	17.9	20.9	16.6	15.4	12.2	13.6	10.0	18.4	13.5
1940–49	11.1	11.9	14.1	9.8	12.2	11.3	8.7	10.6	8.7	11.4	10.4
1939 and earlier	25.8	25.4	32.8	15.8	29.8	31.0	27.1	35.4	52.9	24.2	30.6
Units in structure											
Total	100.0	100.0	100.0	100.0	100.0	100.0	100.0	100.0	100.0	100.0	100.0
1-detached	61.8	56.0	44.5	62.6	65.8	70.3	78.8	75.2	91.8	57.4	74.5
1-attached	4.1	5.2	6.5	4.7	3.0	3.1	1.1	1.9	0.6	5.0	1.6
2	6.1	7.3	9.5	5.2	7.6	6.4	2.7	5.4	1.9	6.7	4.3
3 or 4	5.0	6.2	7.9	4.8	5.9	4.7	1.7	3.6	1.1	5.7	3.2
5 to 9	4.4	5.5	6.7	4.7	4.7	3.6	1.4	2.6	--	5.1	2.5
10 to 49	8.2	10.4	13.1	9.6	6.5	4.8	1.6	3.0	--	9.9	3.1
50 or more	5.3	6.9	10.5	5.3	2.7	1.4	0.4	0.6	--	6.7	1.0
Mobile home or trailer	5.1	2.6	1.3	3.1	3.8	5.6	12.3	7.6	4.6	3.5	9.8
Bedrooms											
Total	100.0	100.0	100.0	100.0	100.0	100.0	100.0	100.0	100.0	100.0	100.0
None	2.1	2.5	4.0	1.5	1.7	1.3	0.9	1.1	0.2	2.4	1.2
1	14.9	17.5	22.5	13.9	14.7	12.6	7.5	10.7	3.0	16.5	10.2
2	32.4	32.3	33.5	29.8	35.2	35.6	32.9	36.0	22.1	31.5	35.2
3	36.9	34.7	30.1	38.2	36.8	38.6	43.3	39.4	45.9	35.8	40.3
4 or more	13.6	13.0	9.9	16.6	11.5	11.8	15.3	12.8	28.8	13.7	13.1

Note: -- indicated data not available.

Source: U.S. Bureau of the Census. "Detailed Housing Characteristics: United States Summary" (Table 80). 1980 Census of Housing. Washington, DC: U.S. Government Printing Office, 1983.

Table 17-5. Structural Characteristics of Housing, by Race: 1980

Characteristic	White	Black	American Indian	Japanese	Chinese	Filipino	Asian Indian	Vietnamese
Year structure built	100.0	100.0	100.0	100.0	100.0	100.0	100.0	100.0
1979–80	3.1	1.5	4.1	2.7	4.4	4.8	5.1	4.8
1975–78	10.1	5.2	11.7	9.6	11.9	14.7	13.8	10.2
1970–74	13.3	11.1	16.6	15.1	13.2	15.5	16.1	14.1
1960–69	20.1	19.3	20.6	27.3	21.5	22.6	22.6	26.1
1950–59	17.4	18.6	15.5	19.8	15.2	16.1	13.9	16.6
1940–49	10.4	16.5	10.9	9.9	9.9	10.2	9.0	10.7
1939 and earlier	25.7	27.6	20.7	15.6	24.0	15.9	19.4	17.5
Units in structure	100.0	100.0	100.0	100.0	100.0	100.0	100.0	100.0
1 unit, detached	65.6	46.5	59.8	56.7	43.5	52.5	44.5	35.4
1 unit, attached	3.6	8.3	3.5	3.8	7.2	6.6	5.1	7.8
2 units	5.7	8.7	5.6	4.1	6.0	5.8	4.9	6.0
3–4 units	4.4	7.7	6.0	5.5	7.6	7.1	5.9	10.6
5–9 units	3.8	7.1	4.9	6.5	7.5	6.8	6.9	9.7
10–49 units	7.0	11.5	8.0	13.1	17.1	12.2	17.2	19.7
50 units or more	4.6	8.1	3.3	9.4	10.7	7.9	14.2	8.7
Mobile home or trailer	5.2	2.2	8.9	0.9	0.4	1.0	1.3	2.0
Bedrooms	100.0	100.0	100.0	100.0	100.0	100.0	100.0	100.0
None	1.7	2.5	5.2	5.0	7.8	8.2	5.4	10.6
1 bedroom	13.4	18.8	17.5	18.2	24.0	21.4	25.5	28.6
2 bedrooms	31.4	34.8	33.6	25.0	23.1	23.7	26.6	29.8
3 bedrooms	38.8	33.3	33.4	36.5	27.3	28.6	25.4	22.4
4 bedrooms or more	14.6	10.6	10.4	15.3	17.8	18.2	17.1	8.6

Source: U.S. Bureau of the Census. "Detailed Housing Characteristics: United States Summary" (Table 83 and 84). 1980 Census of Housing. Washington, DC: U.S. Government Printing Office, 1983.

housing units to be occupied by lower-income residents have somewhat modified that process, so that not all who live in younger housing units are affluent and not all who occupy old housing are poor. American Indians, Japanese, Chinese, Filipinos, Asian Indians, and Vietnamese, for example, all occupy housing that is on the average younger than that occupied by the white population. Table 17-6 (first panel) shows in addition that Puerto Ricans tend to occupy very old housing, while Mexicans and Cubans occupy younger housing. Within the Spanish-origin group, the population that reported itself as racially white lives in younger housing than the small fraction of the population that classified itself as racially black.

Type of Structure

The single-family house, detached from all other structures, is by far the nation's most popular living arrangement (see Table 17-3, second panel). More than 60 percent of American families live in such houses, and most of the new housing being built is of this type (see components section below). The preference for detached dwellings makes housing in the United States unlike that of many other nations, where multiple-unit dwellings are more prevalent. However, recent trends in construction have favored multiple-unit structures, with the result that one-family detached housing units are less prevalent than in 1960, and large buildings with as many as fifty or more units in the structure account for more of the housing total.

Housing construction during the baby boom of the 1950s was characterized by the building of relatively fewer apartments. That trend has been strongly altered as inflation rates and housing costs have soared and lifestyles have changed. Mobile homes, an insignificant proportion in 1950, now comprise one-twentieth of the housing stock.

Table 17-4 (second panel) shows that in central cities the detached single-family unit is no longer in the

Table 17-6. Structural Characteristics of Housing of Spanish-Origin Population, by Type of Origin and Race: 1980

Characteristic	Spanish-origin total	By origin				Spanish-origin, by race		
		Mexican	Puerto Rican	Cuban	Other Spanish	White	Black	Unclassified
Year structure built								
Total	100.0	100.0	100.0	100.0	100.0	100.0	100.0	100.0
1979-80	2.5	2.7	1.4	2.9	2.9	2.7	1.5	2.3
1975-78	7.4	7.6	4.0	9.0	8.6	8.0	4.7	6.3
1970-74	11.0	11.1	7.2	15.7	11.8	11.7	10.3	9.8
1960-69	18.9	20.5	12.6	20.8	18.7	19.5	18.3	17.9
1950-59	20.5	23.2	14.8	19.1	18.1	20.5	16.6	20.8
1940-49	15.6	16.2	17.8	12.4	14.0	14.7	16.9	17.2
1939 and earlier	24.0	18.9	42.1	20.1	26.1	22.8	31.7	25.8
Units in structure								
Total	100.0	100.0	100.0	100.0	100.0	100.0	100.0	100.0
1-detached	47.1	58.7	15.4	37.2	43.0	51.0	29.9	42.3
1-attached	4.8	4.6	5.3	5.8	4.6	4.6	6.5	5.0
2	7.0	5.5	11.7	8.6	6.9	6.7	9.6	7.2
3 or 4	8.1	6.9	12.8	8.4	7.8	7.4	9.4	9.2
5 to 9	7.7	6.4	12.5	8.6	7.2	6.9	9.1	8.7
10 to 49	14.3	10.1	23.9	18.4	16.8	12.8	18.9	16.2
50 or more	8.2	4.3	17.7	12.0	10.3	7.7	14.3	8.6
Mobile home or trailer	2.9	3.4	0.8	1.0	3.4	3.0	2.3	2.8
Bedrooms								
Total	100.0	100.0	100.0	100.0	100.0	100.0	100.0	100.0
None	4.9	4.4	4.0	7.8	5.7	4.6	5.0	5.2
1	22.8	21.3	25.5	27.6	23.0	21.5	25.0	24.5
2	33.8	34.1	36.4	31.3	32.0	33.1	34.6	35.0
3	29.3	31.1	26.2	24.9	28.6	30.8	26.4	27.3
4 or 5	9.2	9.1	8.0	8.3	10.7	10.0	8.9	7.9

Source: U.S. Bureau of the Census. "Detailed Housing Characteristics: United States Summary" (Table 87). 1980 Census of Housing. Washington, DC: U.S. Government Printing Office, 1983.

majority, while urban fringes share the emphasis on the single-family structure with the rural areas and small towns.

Because of large multiunit public housing projects and the occupancy of older multiple-unit structures at the core of central cities, the black population tends to be the most concentrated of any racial group in multiple-unit structures, and the white population tends to be the least. This is documented in Table 17-5 (second panel). Among the Spanish-origin population, Puerto Ricans and Cubans are among the groups least likely to be found living in single-family detached units, whereas the Mexican population appears to prefer it strongly (Table 17-6, second panel).

In suburban areas nearly two-thirds of all housing is of the single-family type. Outside the SMSAs more than three-fourths of the housing is of the single-family type; large multiunit structures are very scarce. However, during the 1970s multiple-unit construction invaded the suburbs, with the result that there is much more apartment living there than formerly.

Size of Living Unit

The big, old-fashioned house with seven or more rooms fell into disfavor after World War I, when fertility declined and families became smaller. The later age at marriage, the larger number of childless couples, and the small-size families that characterized the late 1920s and the 1930s made the small "efficiency" or "kitchenette" apartment and the four-room house or apartment popular. The baby boom reversed this trend,

Table 17-7. Number of Rooms and Number of Persons in Housing Units: 1950-1980, and Intercensal Percent Change

Number	Percent distribution				Intercensal percent change			New construction 1973-80
	1980	1970	1960	1950	1970-1980	1960-1970	1950-1960	
Number of rooms in unit								
Total	100.0	100.0	100.0	100.0	...	...	...	100.0
1 room	1.6	1.7	2.3	2.6	17.5	-9.2	12.4	0.6
2 rooms	3.3	3.4	4.0	7.0	24.3	-0.7	-27.2	2.0
3 rooms	9.9	10.7	11.3	14.5	17.9	12.5	-1.7	8.1
4 rooms	18.9	20.5	21.1	21.7	16.9	16.3	21.9	17.5
5 rooms	23.2	25.2	25.2	21.6	16.5	19.9	46.5	24.4
6 rooms	20.1	20.5	19.9	17.4	24.1	23.0	44.5	19.8
7 rooms	11.6	9.7	9.0	7.7	50.3	30.2	47.2	27.7
8 or more rooms	11.5	8.3	7.2	7.6	74.6	38.7	19.2	
Median rooms								
Owner-occupied units	5.8	5.6	5.5	--	...	...	...	...
Renter-occupied units	4.0	4.0	3.9	--	...	...	...	...
Persons in unit								
Total	100.0	100.0	100.0	100.0	...	...	...	100.0
1 person	22.7	17.6	13.3	9.3	63.7	57.5	77.2	15.5
2 persons	31.3	29.6	28.0	28.1	34.0	26.4	23.6	29.1
3 persons	17.4	17.2	18.9	22.8	28.1	9.0	2.5	20.1
4 persons	15.4	15.4	17.2	18.4	26.2	7.4	15.9	21.6
5 persons	7.6	9.8	11.1	10.4	-1.3	5.4	31.6	8.9
6 persons	3.2	5.3	5.9	5.3	-22.6	7.4	38.6	3.1
7 persons	1.6	2.7	2.7	2.7	-26.0	18.1	24.0	1.7
8 or more persons	0.8	2.4	2.8	3.0	-58.4	3.0	17.3	
Median persons in unit								
Owner-occupied units	2.60	3.0	3.1	3.2	...	...	...	...
Renter-occupied units	1.99	2.3	2.6	2.9	...	...	...	...

Note: -- indicates data not available. ... indicates data not applicable.

Source: U.S. Bureau of the Census. "General Housing Characteristics: United States Summary" (Table 4). 1980 Census of Housing. Also "Housing Characteristics for States, Cities, and Counties" (Table 4). 1970 Census of Housing. Also "States and Small Areas: United States Summary" (Tables 4 and 6). 1960 Census of Housing. Also "General Characteristics: United States Summary" (Tables 9 and 19). 1950 Census of Housing. Washington, DC: U.S. Government Printing Office, 1983, 1973, 1963, and 1953. Also U.S. Bureau of the Census. "Components of Inventory Change (CINCH)." 1980 Census of Housing (Part I: "United States Summary"). Washington, DC: U.S. Government Printing Office, 1983, Table A-3.

Table 17-8. Number of Rooms and Number of Persons in Housing Units, by Place of Residence: 1980

Number	National total	Urban total	Central cities	Urban fringe	Places 10,000+	2,500-9,999	Rural total	1,000-2,499	Rural farm	Inside SMSA	Outside SMSA
Total, percent distribution.	100.0	100.0	100.0	100.0	100.0	100.0	100.0	100.0	100.0	100.0	100.0
Number of rooms in unit (owner and renter)											
1 room.	1.6	1.9	3.0	1.1	1.3	1.0	0.7	0.7	0.6	1.9	0.9
2 rooms	3.3	3.9	5.4	2.7	3.1	2.6	1.6	2.1	1.5	3.7	2.2
3 rooms	9.9	11.5	14.6	9.2	9.8	8.5	5.2	7.1	4.9	10.8	7.0
4 rooms	18.9	18.9	20.2	17.0	20.4	20.5	18.7	20.2	18.5	18.4	20.3
5 rooms	23.2	22.3	21.8	21.5	25.0	25.9	26.0	26.2	26.0	22.1	26.4
6 rooms	20.1	19.5	18.1	20.5	20.0	20.5	22.0	21.1	22.1	19.8	21.0
7 rooms	11.6	11.1	8.9	13.4	10.6	11.0	13.0	11.7	13.2	11.6	11.5
8 or more rooms	11.5	11.0	7.9	14.5	9.7	10.0	12.9	10.9	13.2	11.7	10.7
Median rooms:											
Owner occupied units.	5.8	5.9	5.8	6.1	5.7	5.6	5.6	5.6	5.6	5.9	5.5
Renter occupied units	4.0	3.9	3.8	4.0	4.1	4.1	4.6	4.2	4.6	3.9	4.3
Total, percent distribution.	100.0	100.0	100.0	100.0	100.0	100.0	100.0	100.0	100.0	100.0	100.0
Persons in unit (owner and renter combined)											
1 person.	22.7	24.7	29.1	20.3	25.2	24.1	16.7	23.5	15.7	23.3	21.0
2 persons	31.3	31.2	30.5	31.6	32.2	32.1	31.6	32.3	31.5	31.0	32.3
3 persons	17.4	17.1	16.1	18.1	16.9	16.7	18.3	16.6	18.6	17.4	17.4
4 persons	15.4	14.6	12.5	16.7	14.3	14.8	20.7	14.9	18.2	15.3	15.7
5 persons	7.6	7.1	6.3	8.1	6.7	7.1	9.0	7.4	9.3	7.5	7.8
6 persons	3.2	3.0	2.9	3.2	2.7	3.0	3.8	3.1	3.9	3.2	3.3
7 persons	1.6	1.5	1.7	1.4	1.3	1.4	1.8	1.4	1.8	1.5	1.6
8 or more persons . . .	0.8	0.7	0.9	0.6	0.7	0.8	1.0	0.7	1.0	0.8	0.9
Median persons in unit:											
Owner occupied units.	2.60	2.58	2.46	2.77	2.41	2.40	2.66	2.39	2.71	2.66	2.47
Renter occupied units	1.99	1.93	1.87	1.97	1.99	2.05	2.37	2.07	2.43	1.95	2.16

Source: U.S. Bureau of the Census. "General Housing Characteristics: United States Summary" (Table 4). 1980 Census of Housing. Washington, DC: U.S. Government Printing Office, 1983.

Table 17-9. Number of Rooms and Number of Persons in Housing Units, by Race: 1980

Number	All races	White	Black	American Indian	Japanese	Chinese	Filipino	Asian Indian	Vietnamese
Number of rooms in unit									
Total.	100.0	100.0	100.0	100.0	100.0	100.0	100.0	100.0	100.0
1 room	1.6	1.4	2.2	4.8	4.4	6.9	7.0	4.7	8.9
2 rooms.	3.3	2.9	4.4	6.5	8.1	11.1	9.9	10.4	16.5
3 rooms.	9.9	9.0	14.2	12.8	13.9	17.3	17.1	18.6	21.6
4 rooms.	18.9	18.3	22.6	22.9	16.3	15.8	17.2	17.6	21.5
5 rooms.	23.2	23.3	23.6	24.9	20.3	14.3	16.9	13.5	14.9
6 rooms.	20.1	20.6	18.3	15.6	17.4	13.4	13.4	11.9	9.5
7 rooms.	11.6	12.2	8.2	7.0	10.5	9.4	8.8	9.4	4.2
8 or more rooms.	11.5	12.3	6.5	5.5	9.1	11.8	9.7	13.8	3.0
Median rooms									
Owner-occupied units . .	5.8	5.8	5.7	5.1	5.7	5.9	5.5	6.2	5.1
Renter-occupied units. .	4.0	4.0	4.0	4.1	3.4	3.0	3.2	3.2	3.2
Persons in unit									
Total.	100.0	100.0	100.0	100.0	100.0	100.0	100.0	100.0	100.0
1 person	22.7	22.8	24.0	18.1	24.0	18.8	12.4	20.1	10.5
2 persons.	31.3	32.8	23.3	23.2	28.5	24.2	18.5	19.9	14.3
3 persons.	17.4	17.3	17.7	18.0	18.9	18.0	17.5	19.7	16.2
4 persons.	15.4	15.4	14.5	16.7	17.3	18.4	19.1	23.6	15.3
5 persons.	7.6	7.3	9.0	10.5	7.5	10.8	14.3	10.2	12.4
6 persons.	3.2	2.8	5.2	6.2	2.5	5.5	8.8	3.8	10.1
7 persons.	1.6	1.1	3.9	4.0	0.9	3.0	6.0	1.9	11.1
8 or more persons. . . .	0.8	0.5	2.4	3.4	0.3	1.3	3.4	0.8	10.0
Median persons in unit									
Owner-occupied units . .	2.60	2.53	3.08	3.29	2.91	3.49	4.20	3.64	4.79
Renter-occupied units. .	1.99	1.88	2.30	2.66	1.81	2.19	2.64	2.34	3.81

Source: U.S. Bureau of the Census. "General Housing Characteristics: United States Summary" (Tables 4, 11 and 12). 1980 Census of Housing. Washington, DC: U.S. Government Printing Office, 1983.

Table 17-10. Number of Rooms and Number of Persons in Housing Units for Spanish-Origin Population, by Type of Origin and Race: 1980

Number of rooms and persons	Spanish-origin total	Type of origin				Spanish-origin, by race		
		Mexican	Puerto Rican	Cuban	Other Spanish	White	Black	Unclassified
Number of rooms in unit	100.0	100.0	100.0	100.0	100.0	100.0	100.0	100.0
1 room	4.2	3.7	3.8	7.0	4.9	4.0	4.4	4.4
2 rooms	8.1	8.3	5.9	11.4	8.2	7.7	7.2	8.7
3 rooms	17.0	15.9	20.1	19.3	17.0	16.1	19.2	18.1
4 rooms	23.9	23.5	29.7	20.5	22.0	22.8	25.2	25.3
5 rooms	21.5	22.9	21.4	16.1	19.9	21.6	20.8	21.5
6 rooms	14.2	15.2	11.5	12.3	14.0	15.0	13.5	13.0
7 rooms	6.4	6.4	4.2	7.3	7.4	7.1	5.4	5.3
8 rooms or more	4.7	4.1	3.4	6.1	6.8	5.6	4.4	3.6
Median rooms								
Owner-occupied units	5.3	5.2	5.7	5.4	5.6	5.4	5.5	5.3
Renter-occupied units	3.7	3.7	3.9	3.4	3.6	3.7	3.8	3.7
Persons in unit	100.0	100.0	100.0	100.0	100.0	100.0	100.0	100.0
1 person	15.1	12.9	17.1	17.5	18.6	16.2	22.6	13.1
2 persons	21.2	19.0	21.4	28.0	24.6	22.9	22.2	18.9
3 persons	19.0	18.2	20.6	20.9	19.2	18.8	18.2	19.4
4 persons	18.3	18.6	18.5	17.9	17.4	18.0	14.6	18.9
5 persons	11.9	13.1	11.4	9.1	10.3	11.4	9.6	12.8
6 persons	6.9	8.1	5.9	4.0	5.3	6.3	5.8	7.7
7 persons	4.7	6.0	3.5	1.9	3.1	4.1	4.8	5.6
8 persons or more	2.9	4.1	1.6	0.5	1.5	2.3	2.3	3.7
Median persons in unit								
Owner-occupied units	3.67	3.84	3.73	3.42	3.26	3.50	3.29	3.98
Renter-occupied units	2.89	3.15	2.89	2.24	2.54	2.71	2.57	3.10

Source: U.S. Bureau of the Census. "General Housing Characteristics: United States Summary" (Table 15). 1980 Census of Population. Washington, DC: U.S. Government Printing Office, 1983.

and builders again emphasized units with six or seven rooms or more. Table 17-7 (first panel) shows the increase in larger units and the decrease in units with less than five rooms during the years since 1950.

This resurgence of large homes has occurred primarily in the suburban fringe, where most of the new construction has taken place. Table 17-8 shows that the homes with seven or more rooms tend to be concentrated in the suburbs or in farm and older small-town areas. The central city contains a concentration of the units with four rooms or less.

There are substantial racial differences in size-of-unit (Table 17-9). Because of its greater concentration in nonmetropolitan, rural, and suburban areas, the white population occupies a disproportionately large share of the larger units. All of the minority races tend to be concentrated in smaller units. The Vietnamese, Filipinos, Japanese, Chinese, and Asian Indians all show a tendency toward small apartment living, although some of these groups tend also to occupy larger units. Table 17-10 shows that Puerto Ricans and Cubans are concentrated in housing units with three rooms or less, while Mexicans tend to occupy units of intermediate size.

Number of Bedrooms

As houses become more and more modern in design, the size and adequacy of a house may come to be rated in terms of the number of bedrooms. A trend in this direction is indicated by the fact that the proportion of housing units with three or four bedrooms has risen steadily, despite declining average size of household. The results, reported in Table 17-3 (bottom panel), show that the three-bedroom unit is now the most common (37 percent), displacing the two-bedroom unit most common in the 1950s. Only about one-fifth of the living units have one bedroom. Four-bedroom units comprised 14 percent of the total in 1980, when they had definitely increased over the decades. The urban-rural differences, the racial differences, and the Spanish-origin differences in number of bedrooms follow those described above for number of rooms (for details, see

Table 17-11. Equipment and Plumbing Facilities: 1950-1980 and Intercensal Percent Change

Facilities and equipment	Percent distribution			Change in percent		New construction 1973-80
	1980	1970	1960	1970-1980	1960-1970	
Bathrooms	100.0	100.0	100.0	...	...	100.0
None or half a bath	2.7	6.5	14.7	-3.8	-8.2	1.1
1 complete bathroom	58.0	65.4	69.8	-7.4	-4.4	33.9
1 plus half bathroom. . . .	14.6	11.8		2.8		14.4
2 complete bathrooms. . . .	24.7	16.3	15.5	8.4	12.6	50.6
Source of water	100.0	100.0	100.0	...	...	100.0
Public system or company. .	83.9	82.4	--	1.5	--	80.5
Individually-drilled well .	12.8		--		--	
Individually-dug well . . .	2.1	16.0	--	-1.1	--	18.2
Other source.	1.2	1.7	--	-0.5	--	1.3
Heating equipment	100.0	100.0	100.0	...	...	100.0
Built-in unit	83.3	78.1	68.1	5.2	10.0	94.2
Other	16.7	21.9	31.9	-5.2	-10.0	5.8
Selected characteristics						
No telephone.	7.1	13.0	21.5	-5.9	-8.5	6.1
No complete kitchen facilities.	2.5	4.4	--	-1.9	--	0.6
Lacking air conditioning. .	44.2	63.3	87.6	-19.1	-24.3	27.9
Lacking public sewer. . . .	25.6	35.0	--	-9.4	--	34.3
No automobile available . .	14.8	17.5	21.5	-2.7	-4.0	7.7
1.01 or more persons per room						
Owner-occupied units. . . .	3.2	6.4	8.7	-3.2	-2.3	2.9
Renter-occupied units . . .	7.0	10.6	16.1	-3.6	-5.5	2.5

Note: -- indicates data not available. ... indicates data not applicable.

Source: U.S. Bureau of the Census. "Detailed Housing Characteristics: United States Summary" (Tables 81 and 87). 1980 Census of Housing. Also "Housing Characteristics for States, Cities, and Counties: United States Summary" (Tables 3, 4, 22, and 23). 1970 Census of Housing. Also "Metropolitan Housing Characteristics: United States and Regions" (Tables A-3 and A-4). 1970 Census of Housing. Also "Metropolitan Housing: United States and Divisions" (Tables A-3 and A-6). 1960 Census of Housing. Washington, DC: U.S. Government Printing Office, 1963, 1973, and 1963. Also U.S. Bureau of the Census. "Components of Inventory Change (CINCH)." 1980 Census of Housing (Part I: "United States Summary"). Washington, DC: U.S. Government Printing Office, 1983, Table A-3. Also U.S. Bureau of the Census. Statistical Abstracts of the United States, 1984. Washington, DC: U.S. Government Printing Office, 1983, Table 1348.

Tables 17-4, 17-5, and 17-6). The large proportion of housing units with three and four bedrooms, coupled with average size of household of less than three persons, suggests that most middle- and upper-income families are very well supplied, if not oversupplied, with sleeping space.

Facilities: Sanitation, Water, and Heat

A description of housing facilities is incomplete without measuring the presence or absence of essential facilities of sanitation, water, and heat. Table 17-11 provides that information. The picture emerging is one of almost complete adequacy. In 1980 only 3 percent of all housing units in the nation lacked a complete bathroom, only 3.3 percent relied for water from a dug well or some source other than piped water, and more than three-fourths of the units were heated by built-in units. Because built-in heating units are not an essential facility in the southernmost portions of the nation, only a comparatively small proportion of the units could be said to have inadequate heating facilities. Although inadequacy is low, such as does exist is distributed according to the pattern already elaborated above: highest for the black population; highest in rural and small-town areas, with significant prevalence in central cities; higher for the black than for the white population, and lower for the Cuban than for the Mexican or

Puerto Rican populations. Table 17-11 also documents how significantly deficiencies in these facilities have declined since 1960.

In summary, in terms of age of housing, number of rooms, number of bedrooms, sanitary facilities, water supply, and heating facilities, a very high proportion (well above 90 percent) of the U.S. housing stock must be rated as adequate for the number of persons who occupy it. Such inadequacies as do exist tend to be linked to remnants of old housing (rural areas and central cities). Only a small portion of any racial, ethnic, or income group can be termed absolutely inadequately housed, despite the fact that black residents tend to occupy a disproportionately large share of the comparatively few units that are deficient. To the extent that they exist, "slums" in America are more a social climate and insufficiency of maintenance than a structural deficiency in housing units.

Owner-Renter Status

More than 65 percent of all occupied dwelling units are occupied by owners; renters are now a shrinking minority, comprising only 35 percent of all householders. The situation today has changed sharply since 1940, when the proportions were almost reversed, nearly 60 percent of occupied dwelling units being rented. Between 1940 and 1970 the various governmental home financing programs of the Housing and Home Finance Agency, the loans for veterans' housing, income tax regulations on mortgage interest, and so forth, caused a steady and dramatic increase in the amount of home ownership. The rising level of living and the higher real income of the average working person are also partially responsible. Almost all of the gain in the renter-occupied units has come since 1960. Between 1940 and 1960 there was almost zero growth in renter units; all housing growth was in owner-occupied units. Table 17-12 provides a detailed history of the trend, by race of the householder.

To provide more information about ownership and rental Table 17-13 reports the percentage of population living in owner-occupied units by selected characteristics of the housing unit. Table 17-14 provides information about the proportion of population living in owner-

Table 17-12. Housing Tenure: Percent Change in Home Ownership and Home Rentership, 1940-1980

Decade	Percent change in home ownership			Percent change in home rentership		
	Total	White	Black/ other	Total	White	Black/ other
1970-80	2.4	3.7	5.0	-4.0	-6.9	-3.6
1960-70	1.6	1.6	9.6	-2.6	-2.8	-6.0
1950-60	12.6	13.0	10.0	-15.3	-17.2	-5.4
1940-50	26.1	24.7	47.9	-20.2	-20.8	-14.8
	Percent change in number of homes owned			Percent change in number of homes rented		
1970-80	29.9	26.1	77.9	21.4	12.9	63.1
1960-70	21.6	20.1	45.9	16.5	14.9	24.9
1950-60	39.2	38.6	49.7	5.0	1.5	28.7
1940-50	55.0	54.3	69.5	-2.0	-2.0	-2.1

Source: U.S. Bureau of the Census. Statistical Abstract of the United States, 1984. Washington, DC: U.S. Government Printing Office, 1983, Table 1344.

Table 17-13. Percent Owner-Occupied Units, by Characteristics of Units and Socioeconomic Status: 1980

Characteristic	Inventory 1973	Inventory 1980	New construction 1973-80
Units in structure			
1 unit, detached	84.2	85.7	94.8
1 unit, attached	52.1	62.5	69.1
2-4 units.	24.5	23.3	25.7
5 or more units.	6.2	7.3	11.8
Mobile home or trailer .	83.8	79.4	91.5
Year structure built			
Since 1973	...	75.2	...
1970-73.	65.0	60.7	...
1965-70.	65.0	65.0	...
1960-64.	71.2	69.3	...
1950-59.	76.2	75.5	...
1940-49.	65.4	65.5	...
1939 or earlier.	56.0	56.2	...
Number of rooms			
1 room	6.2	10.0	24.7
2 rooms.	10.9	15.8	24.3
3 rooms.	18.5	15.9	17.5
4 rooms.	44.5	42.3	50.5
5 rooms.	72.4	72.1	81.2
6 rooms.	83.2	84.0	89.9
7 rooms or more.	90.8	92.0	96.4
Education of householder			
No school completed. . .	--	45.6	61.9
Elementary: under 8 yrs	--	58.9	66.0
: 8 yrs . . .	--	70.3	70.7
High school: 1-3 yrs. .	--	61.6	74.5
: 4 yrs. . .	--	66.4	74.9
College: 1-3 yrs. . . .	--	63.8	71.8
: 4 yrs or more.	--	70.1	80.0
Income of householder			
Under $5,000	51.4	43.8	46.5
$5,000-9,999	55.7	51.7	56.0
$10,000-14,999	69.6	56.6	64.2
$15,000-19,999	78.7	66.1	71.8
$20,000-29,999	82.6	77.4	81.8
$30,000-39,000	86.7	87.3	90.8
$40,000-49,000	88.1	89.5	89.6
$50,000 and over	88.4	92.3	92.6

Note: -- indicates data not available. ... indicates data not applicable.

Source: U.S. Bureau of the Census. "Components of Inventory Change (CINCH)." 1980 Census of Housing (Part I: "United States Summary"). Washington, DC: U.S. Government Printing Office, 1983, Tables A-1 and A-3.

occupied units by characteristics of the householder. All tables also show ownership status of new units constructed between 1973 and 1980.

Number of Persons in Housing Unit

Over the years there has been a remarkable change in the number of persons occupying dwelling units. More detail on numbers of persons in housing units is provided in Tables 17-7, 17-8, 17-9, and 17-10 (lower panels).

While one-person units have grown explosively, units with three or more persons have declined. The baby boom buoyed the three- and four-person units during the 1950s until 1960, but thereafter they went into decline, while units with five or more persons have declined more or less steadily since 1940.

One-person housing units are most common in central cities and are rarest in rural areas and urban fringe areas. Large households (six or more members) are scarce everywhere but are more common in urban fringe and rural farm areas.

Black households are inclined to have a concentration of one-person households and also of larger households. Large households are also found among the Vietnamese (Table 17-9). American Indians, Chinese, and Filipinos tend to have a higher proportion of larger households and a below-average proportion of one-person households. The one-person household is also comparatively scarce among the Spanish-origin group: Mexicans tend to have a higher proportion of larger households, and Cubans the lowest.

Table 17-14. Socioeconomic Differentials in Home Ownership, 1973 and 1980 [percent of units owner-occupied]

Characteristic	Inventory		New construction
	1973	1980	1973-80
Race-ethnicity			
White	67.2	68.7	76.5
Black	43.5	43.9	54.2
Spanish-origin	44.4	42.3	60.9
Age of householder			
Married couple families	74.1	78.8	85.9
15-24 years	30.7	36.8	58.9
25-29 years	54.7	58.4	79.4
30-34 years	70.9	75.2	89.4
35-44 years	79.5	84.1	93.0
45-64 years	84.5	88.0	90.8
65 years and over	81.9	84.6	74.9
Other male householder	41.7	41.8	50.8
15-44 years	26.9	31.0	46.9
45-64 years	53.6	52.9	68.6
65 years and over	56.7	61.2	45.1
Other female householder	48.3	46.8	45.4
15-44 years	23.8	25.8	40.0
45-64 years	58.2	59.5	67.4
65 years and over	61.5	61.5	37.3

Source: U.S. Bureau of the Census. "Components of Inventory Change (CINCH)." 1980 Census of Housing (Part I: "United States Summary"). Washington, DC: U.S. Government Printing Office, 1983, Tables A-1, A-3, A-7, A-9, A-13, A-15, A-19, and A-21.

Persons per Room: Overcrowding

By taking into account simultaneously the number of rooms and the number of persons in a household, it is possible to measure the intensity with which housing is used. The most conventional measure is the "number of persons per room," obtained for each household individually by dividing the number of occupants by the number of rooms. A ratio of 1.0 persons per room is regarded as the maximum desirable under present standards, while 1.51 or more persons per room is regarded as evidence of definite overcrowding. The trends in overcrowding are reported in Table 17-15. Obviously overcrowding, which was a moderately common problem in 1940, is practically nonexistent in 1980. In fact, "undercrowding" could almost be said to be a problem, since 61 percent of all units were occupied at less than 0.5 persons per room.

The pattern differs by tenure. Renters tend to make use of their space more intensively, and their proportion with more than 1.01 persons per room at the national level is 7 percent, as against 3.1 percent for owners, in 1980.

Quality of Housing

The bottom panel of Table 17-11 presents certain negative indicators of quality in housing. These statistics reemphasize that truly substandard housing, as defined by lack of bath, lack of piped water, and incomplete kitchen facilities is now rare in the United States and affects much less than 10 percent of the population. Such amenities as telephones or vehicles are available to almost 90 percent of the population or more. Air conditioning is available to a majority (55 percent). To the extent that necessities are lacking, the deficit tends to be concentrated in rural areas, where the housing is older

Table 17-15. Persons Per Room: 1950-1980, and Intercensal Percent Change

Persons per room	Percent distribution				Intercensal percent change		
	1980	1970	1960	1950	1970-1980	1960-1970	1950-1960
All occupied rooms. . .	100.0	100.0	100.0	100.0	26.7	19.7	25.8
0.50 or less.	61.4	49.8	41.8	60.2 (0.50 or less and 0.51 to 0.75)	56.3	42.3	36.6 (0.50 or less and 0.51 to 0.75)
0.51 to 0.75.	20.5	22.7	23.5		14.4	15.5	
0.76 to 1.00.	13.6	19.4	23.1	24.1	-10.8	0.2	20.6
1.01 to 1.50.	3.1	6.0	7.9	9.5	-33.9	-9.7	4.7
1.51 or more.	1.4	2.2	3.6	6.2	-19.4	-26.0	-27.0
Owner occupied units. .	100.0	100.0	100.0	100.0	29.9	21.6	41.4
0.50 or less.	63.9	52.7	46.6	67.9 (0.50 or less and 0.51 to 0.75)	57.5	37.4	45.9 (0.50 or less and 0.51 to 0.75)
0.51 to 0.75.	21.0	22.5	23.5		21.1	16.4	
0.76 to 1.00.	12.0	18.2	21.2	21.0	-14.3	4.2	42.6
1.01 to 1.50.	2.4	5.3	6.6	7.3	-40.1	-3.6	28.0
1.51 or more.	0.7	1.4	2.0	3.7	-32.8	-16.3	-22.3
Renter occupied units .	100.0	100.0	100.0	100.0	21.3	16.5	6.7
0.50 or less.	56.8	44.8	34.1	50.6 (0.50 or less and 0.51 to 0.75)	53.9	53.0	21.4 (0.50 or less and 0.51 to 0.75)
0.51 to 0.75.	19.6	23.0	23.5		3.3	14.0	
0.76 to 1.00.	16.6	21.4	26.3	27.9	-5.9	-5.0	0.3
1.01 to 1.50.	4.4	7.2	10.0	12.2	-26.3	-16.2	-12.3
1.51 or more.	2.6	3.6	6.1	9.2	-10.6	-31.3	-29.4

Source: U.S. Bureau of the Census. "General Housing Characteristics: United States Summary" (Table 4). 1980 Census of Housing. Also "Housing Characteristics for States, Cities, and Counties: United States Summary" (Table 4). 1970 Census of Housing. Also "States and Small Areas" (Table 6). 1960 Census of Housing. Also "General Characteristics: United States Summary" (Table 11). 1950 Census of Housing. Washington, DC: U.S. Government Printing Office, 1983, 1973, 1963, and 1953.

Table 17-16. Equipment and Plumbing Facilities Indicators of Poor Housing Quality: 1960-1980

Indicator	CINCH Inventory			Census		
	1980	1973	New construction 1973-1980	1980	1970	1960
Year-round housing units						
Lack complete kitchen facilities. .	2.3	3.3	0.6	2.5	4.4	--[a]
No bath or only half-bath	3.1	5.2	0.8	2.7	7.5	14.7[a]
Individual dug well or other source.	16.7	18.2	13.7	16.1[a]	18.3	--
No public sewer, cesspool, or septic tank	1.2	2.3	0.1	1.8	4.3	--
No air conditioning	42.4	51.7	23.6	44.2	64.2	87.6
No built-in heating	13.4	15.5	4.5	16.7[a]	21.9[a]	31.9[a]
Percent dilapidated	--	--	--	--	--	5.0
Occupied housing units						
No telephone.	8.3	--	4.2	7.1	12.7	21.5
No auto available	16.7	17.4	5.4	14.8	17.5	21.5
Occupancy:						
1.01 or more persons per room . .	4.2	5.5	2.4	4.5	8.2	11.5

[a]Percent of occupied housing units.

Note: -- indicates data not available.

Source: U.S. Bureau of the Census. "Detailed Housing Characteristics: United States Summary" (Table 81). 1980 Census of Housing. Also, "Housing Characteristics for States, Cities, and Counties: United States Summary" (Tables 1, 3, and 22). 1970 Census of Housing. Also, "States and Small Areas: United States Summary" (Tables 1, 3, and 7). 1960 Census of Housing. Also, "Metropolitan Housing: United States and Divisions" (Table A-5). 1960 Census of Housing. Washington, DC: U.S. Government Printing Office, 1983, 1973, and 1963. Also, U.S. Bureau of the Census. "Component of Inventory Change (CINCH)." 1980 Census of Housing (Part I: "United States Summary"). Washington, DC: U.S. Government Printing Office, 1983, Tables A-1 and A-3.

and the water supply and sanitation facilities are less modern. Blacks and American Indians are more prone to have low-quality housing units than other racial groups. However, the comparative scarcity of low-quality housing everywhere must be emphasized.

Table 17-16 provides similar information from the CINCH to show the decline of these indicators between 1973 and 1980 and their practical nonexistence in the housing units constructed between those dates. As new housing units are added to the inventory, they tend to be not only adequate but provided with modern amenities. Demolition, condemnation, and change to other uses are gradually removing the small proportion of remaining substandard units. While there is no doubt that practically every metropolis has a "blighted area" where the indicators of substandard housing reach meaningful percentages, it is nonetheless true that the proportion of such units in comparison with all units (and in comparison with even the recent past) is minuscule.

The Cost of Housing: Value and Rent

Housing is a consumption good and costs money. For owners it is also an investment with value. For renters the rent that must be paid each month is a large component in the cost of living. The range of values of owner-occupied housing and of rent paid for renter-occupied housing is quite wide. Table 17-17 shows these ranges in the form of percentage distributions. These distributions reflect the workings of the housing market and represent the comparative utility that can be derived from occupying a given unit at a given site. They reflect type of structure, number of rooms, age, and the quality of the housing unit itself. Units in the low-value range are the least desirable, while units in the upper value ranges are the more desirable. Undoubtedly a large proportion of the 10 percent of housing units that lack one or more of the essential facilities are to be found in the lowest 10 percent of the rent and value ranges. The luxury housing would be found in the upper 10 percent or so.

Income in Relation to Housing

The higher a person's income, the more money that person spends for housing and the better the quality of housing is. There is widespread interest in the relationship between income and housing and in the amounts of additional housing that are purchased as additional income is received. Housing statisticians are fond of using the "rent-income ratio," which is determined by dividing the annual gross rent by the annual family income and multiplying the result by 100 to form a percentage. Table 17-18 shows that poor people must spend a larger percentage of their total income for rent than the well-to-do; in other words, low rent-income ratios are generally found among high-income families, while high rent-income ratios are usually found among low-income families.

Table 17-17. Rent Paid for Housing Units, by Location of Unit: 1973 and 1980 [percent distribution]

Rent	1980 total	Central city	Metropolitan ring	Nonmetro-politan	New construction	
					1973	1980
Total, percent distribution. .	100.0	100.0	100.0	100.0	100.0	100.0
Less than $99 . . .	7.5	8.3	3.8	11.2	27.5	6.4
$100 - $149	9.2	9.6	5.3	14.1	28.7	4.9
$150 - $199	15.0	16.1	10.1	19.7	22.8	5.4
$200 - $249	18.5	20.6	15.6	18.5	8.8	11.1
$250 - $299	17.1	17.9	19.4	12.1	3.0	17.1
$300 - $349	11.2	10.7	15.2	6.4	1.4	18.2
$350 - $399	6.7	6.1	9.6	3.6	0.5	11.3
$400 - $499	6.0	4.8	9.7	2.7	0.3	11.3
$500 - $599	2.3	1.7	4.1	0.9	0.1	6.0
$600 - $749	1.0	0.9	1.6	0.2	0.1	2.8
$750 or more. . . .	0.6	0.8	0.7	0.1	*	1.9
No cash rent. . . .	5.0	2.4	4.9	10.4	6.7	3.5

Note: * indicates insufficient data to make accurate measurement.

Source: U.S. Bureau of the Census. "Components of Inventory Change (CINCH)." 1980 Census of Housing (Part I: "United States Summary"). Washington, DC: U.S. Government Printing Office, 1983 Tables A-2 and A-4.

Table 17-18. Gross Rent as Percent of Household Income, by Income in 1979

Income level	Gross rent as percentage of income								
	Total	Under 15 percent	15-19 percent	20-24 percent	25-29 percent	30-34 percent	35-49 percent	50+ percent	Not computed
Total.	100.0	17.6	15.4	13.8	10.3	7.2	12.1	17.2	6.4
Less than $5,000	100.0	0.9	2.7	5.3	4.6	3.8	11.9	57.2	13.7
$5,000-9,999	100.0	3.6	6.0	10.2	13.1	13.4	29.4	19.3	5.0
$10,000-12,499	100.0	7.0	13.4	21.1	21.4	14.6	15.0	3.1	4.4
$12,500-14,999	100.0	11.7	21.3	26.9	18.3	9.3	7.2	1.0	4.2
$15,000-19,999	100.0	21.3	30.9	24.2	11.2	4.7	3.6	0.1	3.9
$20,000-24,999	100.0	38.5	33.4	15.0	6.0	2.4	0.8	*	3.8
$25,000-34,999	100.0	57.9	24.8	9.8	3.1	0.5	*	*	3.9
$35,000-49,999	100.0	74.3	17.9	3.2	0.2	*	*	*	4.5
$50,000 and over	100.0	91.0	2.6	*	*	*	*	*	6.3

Source: U.S. Bureau of the Census. "Metropolitan Housing Characteristics: United States Summary." 1980 Census of Housing. Washington, DC: U.S. Government Printing Office, 1983, Table A-4.

Future Housing Trends

For a number of reasons, demographers interested in housing had predicted a housing boom for the 1980s. The persons born during the baby boom years are in their late twenties, thirties, and early forties, the prime ages for purchasing new housing. Greater survival of the elderly was expected to cause the demand for one-person households to grow steadily. The small number of housing starts in 1981 and 1982, with only modest recovery in 1983, and the reversal of many of the trends discussed in this chapter (such as average number of persons per housing unit) comes as a surprise. The extent to which it is a temporary phenomenon due to the economic recession, and the extent to which it represents the exhaustion of the forces that have long been at work to create these trends require a great deal of intensive research, using the housing inventory data for additional years as they become available. In conducting this research, careful and precise demographic analysis will be perhaps even more important than in the past. Instead of simply assuming that housing trends will continue out of inertia or with momentum, demographers must participate more actively in understanding what factors (demographic, economic, and social) create the distributions and changes in distributions.

Bibliography

Bourne, Larry S. *Geography of Housing.* New York: Wiley, 1981.

Brueckner, J.K., and Colwell, P.F. "Spatial Model of Housing Attributes: Theory and Evidence." *Land Economy* 59 (1983):58-69.

Buttler, H.J., and Beckmann, M.J. "Design Parameters in Housing Construction and the Market for Urban Housing." *Econometrica* 48 (1980):201-25.

Carlinger, Geoffrey. *Income Elasticity of Housing Demand.* Madison: University of Wisconsin Institute for Research on Poverty, 1972.

Chevan, A. "Age, Housing Choice, and Neighborhood Age Structure." *American Journal of Sociology* 87 (1982):1133-49.

Dahmann, Donald C. "Housing Opportunities for Black and White Households." *Special Demographic Analyses.* Washington, DC: U.S. Government Printing Office, 1982.

Farley, Reynolds. "Racial Residential Segregation: It is Caused by Misinformation about Housing Costs." *Social Science Quarterly* 61 (1980):623-37.

Follain, J.R., Jr., and Malpezzi, S. "Another Look at Racial Differences in Housing Prices." *Urban Studies* 18 (1981):195-203.

Frieden, Bernard J., and Nash, William W. (eds.) *Shaping an Urban Future: Essays in Memory of Catherine Bauer Wurster.* Cambridge, MIT Press, 1968.

Galster, G.C., and Hesser, G.W. "Social Neighborhood: An Unspecified Factor in Homeowner Maintenance." *Urban Affairs Quarterly* 18 (1982):235-54.

Goetze, R. "Housing Post-Reagan: Policies for a New Era." *Journal of Housing* 39 (1982):177-80.

Jackman, M.R., and Jackman, R.W. "Racial Inequalities in Home Ownership." *Social Forces* 58 (1980):1221-34.

Jud, G.D., and Watts, J.M. "Schools and Housing Values." *Land Economy* 57 (1981):459-70.

Kilbridge, Maurice D.; O'Block, Robert; and Teplitz, Paul V. *Urban Analysis.* Boston: Graduate School of Business Administration, Harvard University, 1970.

Muth, Richard F. *Cities and Housing: The Spatial Pattern of Urban Residential Use.* Chicago: The University of Chicago Press, 1969.

Newman, Sandra J., et al. *Housing Adjustments of Older People.* Ann Arbor, MI: Institute for Social Research, University of Michigan, 1976.

Parcel, T.L. "Wealth Accumulation of Black and White Men: The Case of Housing Equity." *Social Problems* 30 (1982):199-211.

Reid, Margaret G. *Housing and Income.* Chicago: The University of Chicago Press, 1969.

Rosen, H.S. "Estimating Inter-City Differences in the Price of Housing Services." *Urban Studies* 15 (1978): 351-5.

Smith, Wallace F. (ed.) *Housing America.* Beverly Hills, CA: Sage Publications, 1983.

Solomon, Arthur P. *Housing and the Urban Poor.* Cambridge, MA: MIT Press, 1974.

Stutz, F.P., and Kartman, A.E. "Housing Affordability and Spatial Price Variations in the United States." *Economic Geography* 58 (1982):221-35.

U.S. Bureau of the Census. "Components of Inventory Change (CINCH)." *1980 Census of Population* (Part I: "United States and Regions"). Washington, DC: U.S. Government Printing Office, 1983.

Varady, D.P. "Indirect Benefits of Subsidized Housing Programs." *American Planning Association Journal* 48 (1982):432-40.

White, Michael J. *Urban Renewal and the Changing Residential Structure of the City.* Chicago: Community and Family Study Center, 1980.

Wood, Edith Elmer. *Slums and Blighted Areas in the United States.* Washington, DC: U.S. Government Printing Office, 1935.

Chapter 18

Religious Affiliation

Like educational attainment, occupation, and income, religion is an axis around which much of a person's life is oriented. Even for the purposes of formal demography the religious affiliations of the population are important as a component of the cultural factors that help explain the level and trend of fertility, the willingness of some persons to migrate to particular localities, and other behaviors. Many nations of the world collect statistics concerning religious affiliation and report them as a part of the regular official census,[1] but the United States does not.[2]

In March, 1957, the U.S. Bureau of the Census included the question "What is your religion?" on its monthly Current Population Survey. The Census Bureau wanted to determine the attitude of the public toward answering such a question and also to experiment with the wording in case the question should become an item on the 1960 census. Very few people refused to answer, and much valuable information (reported in this chapter) was obtained concerning the general religious affiliation of the population. Sample surveys made by private research organizations routinely ask questions concerning religion. Their experience has been that it is an easy question to enumerate and causes no more anxiety or resentment than questions on such matters as age or marital status. Thus the absence of a question on religious affiliation from census questionnaires is due to policy considerations, not technical problems.

This brief chapter summarizes existing information about the demography of religions. It is based primarily on tabulations of data concerning religious preference collected by the National Opinion Research Center (NORC) of the University of Chicago in its nationwide surveys.[3] Surveys taken in the years between 1972 and 1983 were pooled to create a large sample of about 15,000 cases, which could be subjected to cross-tabulation. The midyear of these data is about 1977. For an earlier edition of this book, the National Opinion Research Center prepared special tabulations by combining the results of two sample surveys taken about 1957-58,[4] and some of those materials are used in this chapter. These tabulations are supplemented by the results of the Census Bureau's survey of March, 1957[5] and by membership compilations made of the National Council of Churches of Christ in the United States of America for their annual publication *Yearbook of American Churches*.

Definitions

No standardized definitions have been developed for collecting and analyzing data on religion. At least three definitions, only roughly comparable with each other, have widest use.

Membership in Religious Bodies. The total number of living persons registered as members of an organization recognized as a religious body by the National Council of Churches of Christ in the United States of America in its *Yearbook of American Churches.*

Religious Identification. The question "What is your (his/her) religion?" elicits a response that identifies the person with religious categories provided by the respondent. Responses such as "Protestant" or "Catholic" can be made more specific by probing questions concerning denominations or branches. This approach was used by the U.S. Bureau of the Census in a survey in 1957. The report of this survey was contained in U.S. Bureau of the Census. "Religion Reported by the Civilian Population of the United States, 1957." *Current Population Reports* (Series P-20, no. 79). Washington, DC: U.S. Government Printing Office, 1958.

Religious Preference. The questions, "What is your (his/her) religious preference? Is it Protestant, Catholic, Jewish, some other religion, or no religion?" and (if Protestant) "What specific denomination is that, if any?" were used by the National Opinion Research Center in its *General Social Surveys* dataset. It is presumed that there is an extremely high correlation between religious identification and religious preference definitions, when used in sample surveys. Membership data, collected from the religious organizations themselves, can be compared only in aggregate form with survey data, because no information about the characteristics of individual members is obtained.

Table 18-1. Estimated Religious Affiliation of the U.S. Population, by Major Religious Groups and Principal Protestant Denominations: 1957 and 1980

Religion	Estimate: 1980			Bureau of Census (1957 report)			Implied percent change, 1957–80		
	Total	Black and other	White	Total	Nonwhite	White	Total	Black and other	White
Total 15 years and over[a]	175,255	27,011	148,244	119,333	11,972	107,361	46.9	125.6	38.1
Protestant	112,801	21,779	91,022	78,952	10,477	68,475	42.9	107.9	32.9
Baptist	39,255	14,406	24,849	23,525	7,253	16,272	66.9	98.6	52.7
Lutheran	14,664	283	14,381	8,417	32	8,385	74.2	784.4	71.5
Methodist	22,222	3,289	18,933	16,676	2,067	14,609	33.3	59.1	29.6
Presbyterian	8,460	359	8,101	6,656	107	6,549	27.1	235.5	23.7
Episcopal-Anglican	4,850	390	4,460	3,746	145	3,601	29.5	169.0	23.9
Other Protestant	23,350	3,052	20,298	19,932	873	19,059	17.1	249.6	6.5
Roman Catholic	43,851	3,084	40,767	30,669	774	29,895	43.0	298.4	36.4
Jewish	4,141	138	4,003	3,868	9	3,859	7.1	...	3.7
Other religion	2,357	430	1,927	1,545	181	1,364	52.6	137.6	41.3
No religion	12,105	1,580	10,525	3,195	414	2,781	278.9	281.6	278.5
Religion not reported	--	--	--	1,104	117	987	--	--	--

[a]15 years and over in 1980; 14 years and over in 1957.

Note: -- indicates data not available.

Source: The 1980 data for this table were based on a dataset defined by the National Opinion Research Center (NORC). General Social Surveys, 1972-83: Cumulative Codebook. Chicago: National Opinion Research Center, University of Chicago, 1983. Data for 1980 were estimated using the 1980 census statistics for population and the NORC percent distributions of religious preference (1977). Data for 1957 are from U.S. Bureau of the Census. "Religion Reported by the Civilian Population of the United States: March, 1957." Current Population Reports (Series P-20, no. 79). Washington, DC: U.S. Government Printing Office, 1958.

Membership and Religious Preference

About two-thirds of the U.S. population fifteen years of age and over identify themselves with the Protestant religion; about one-fourth are Roman Catholic. Of the remainder of the population (about 10 percent) two-third report they have no religious identification. Jewish affiliation is expressed by 2.4 percent. All other religions combined constitute slightly more than 1 percent (see Figure 18-1). These proportions, derived from the NORC surveys, are substantiated in their general magnitude by the Bureau of the Census survey of 1957 (the fact that twenty years separate these sources should be kept in mind).

Religion	NORC (1977)	NORC (1958)	Census Bureau (1957)	Difference, NORC (77)/Census (57)
Total	100.0	100.0	100.0	--
Protestant.	64.4	71.5	66.2	-1.8
Roman Catholic. . . .	25.0	21.0	25.7	-0.7
Jewish.	2.4	3.0	3.2	-0.8
Other religion. . . .	1.3	1.4	1.3	0.0
No religion	6.9	2.8	2.7	+4.2
No information. . . .	--	--	0.9	--

The NORC materials for 1958 appear to have overestimated Protestants and underestimated Roman Catholics, while counting Jewish, other religions, and no religion in the correct magnitudes. Limitations of sampling variability make statements about trends of dubious reliability. As reported, the data suggest that the Protestant sector has grown at about the same rate as the population, that the Roman Catholic and Jewish sectors have grown at about the same rate as the general population, and that there has been a substantial increase in the proportion of the public reporting no religious preference or membership. This latter group of disbelievers-agnostics-nonreligious persons appears to comprise about one person in twenty, making it the third largest category of religious preference.

Within the Protestant sector (see Figure 18-1), the following denominations may be identified:

Denomination	NORC (1977)	NORC (1958)	Census Bureau (1957)	Difference, NORC (77)/Census (57)
Total	100.0	100.0	100.0	--
Baptist	34.8	30.7	29.8	5.0
Methodist	19.7	24.3	21.1	-1.4
Lutheran.	13.0	10.6	10.7	+2.3
Presbyterian.	7.5	9.4	8.4	-0.9
Episcopal-Anglican. .	4.3	3.9	--	--
Other	20.7	20.8	30.0	-9.3

The Baptist denominations comprise one-third of all Protestants, followed by Methodists with 20 percent. Lutherans and Presbyterians combined are about as numerous as Methodists, while Episcopalians-Anglicans are a distant fifth in rank size. About one-fifth of the Protestant sector is affiliated with the many dozens of

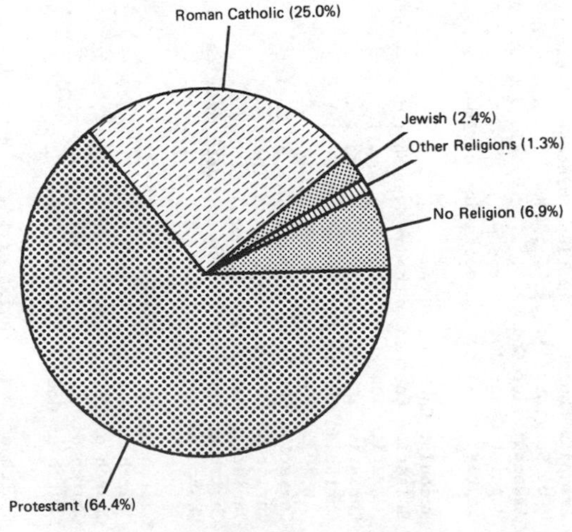

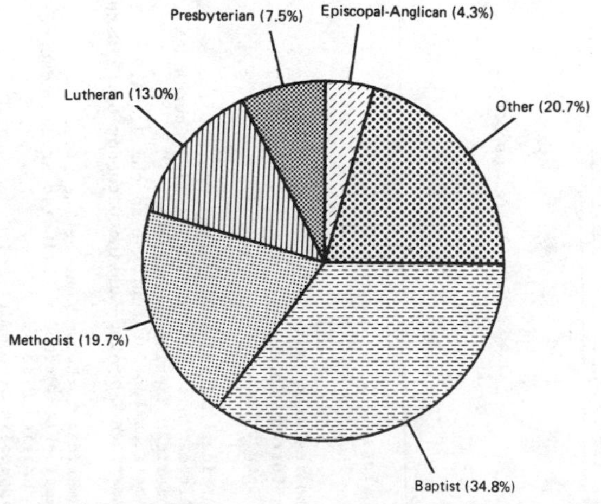

Figure 18-1. Percentage Distribution of Religious Preference: All Religons and Protestant Denominations

Table 18-2. Membership and Number of Churches of Religious Bodies Having a Membership of 50,000 or More in 1980: 1960, 1970, and 1980

Religious body	Circa 1980			Circa 1970			Circa 1960		
	Year	Churches reported	Membership (1,000)	Year	Churches reported	Membership (1,000)	Year	Churches reported	Membership (1,000)
Total	...	336,281	134,817	...	328,657	131,046	...	318,697	114,449
Bodies with membership of 50,000 or more	...	322,485	133,350	...	314,083	129,470	...	300,384	112,757
Current data	...	247,407	114,791	...	238,575	114,591	--	--	--
Noncurrent data	...	75,078	18,559	...	75,508	14,879	--	--	--
African Methodist Episcopal Church	1980	6,000	2,050	1951	5,878	1,166	1951	5,878	1,166
African Methodist Episcopal Zion Church	1980	6,020	1,134	1970	4,500	940	1959	4,083	770
American Baptist Association	1981	5,000	1,500	1971	3,295	790	1960	3,091	648
American Baptist Churches in the U.S.A.	1979	5,814	1,601	1970	6,090	1,472	1959	6,262	1,543
American Carpatho-Russian Orthodox Greek Catholic Church	1976	70	100	1971	69	107	1960	64	100
American Lutheran Church, The	1980	4,864	2,353	1970	4,822	2,543	1960	4,625	2,242
Antiochian Orthodox Christian Archdiocese of North America, The	1977	110	152	1970	92	100	--	--	--
Apostolic Overcoming Holy Church of God	1956	300	75	1956	300	75	1956	300	75
Armenian Apostolic Church of America	1972	29	125	1970	34	125	--	--	--
Armenian Church of America, Diocese of the (incl. Diocese of California)	1979	66	450	1971	58	300	1960	51	125
Assemblies of God	1980	9,773	1,732	1971	8,734	1,065	1960	8,233	509
Baptist General Conference	1980	779	133	1970	677	104	1960	536	72
Baptist Missionary Association of America	1980	1,415	225	1970	1,408	187	--	--	--
Buddhist Churches of America	1975	60	60	1970	60	100	--	--	--
Bulgarian Eastern Orthodox Church (Diocese of N. and S. America and Australia)	1971	13	86	1962	23	86	1960	22	86
Christian and Missionary Alliance	1980	1,382	190	1970	1,112	113	1960	1,016	60
Christian Church (Disciples of Christ)	1980	4,295	1,178	197	5,114	1,424	1960	8,001	1,802
Christian Churches and Churches of Christ	1981	5,605	1,063	1970	4,688	1,020	--	--	--
Christian Congregation, Inc., The	1980	1,266	89	--	--	--	--	--	--
Christian Methodist Episcopal Church	1981	2,883	787	1965	2,598	467	1951	2,469	392
Christian Reformed Church in North America	1980	626	214	1970	660	286	1960	549	243
Church of God, The	1978	2,035	76	1971	2,025	76	1959	1,901	74
Church of God (Anderson, Ind.)	1980	2,271	176	1970	2,282	150	1960	2,278	143
Church of God (Cleveland, Tenn.)	1980	5,178	435	1970	4,024	272	1960	3,280	170
Church of God in Christ, The	1965	4,500	425	1965	4,500	425	1960	3,800	393
Church of God in Christ, International, The	1971	1,041	501	1970	1,006	500	--	--	--
Church of God of Prophecy, The	1961	1,977	73	1970	1,561	51	--	--	--
Church of Jesus Christ of Latter-day Saints, The	1980	7,369	2,811	1970	4,828	2,073	1960	3,491	1,487
Church of the Brethren	1980	1,063	171	1970	1,038	183	1960	1,074	200
Church of the Nazarene	1980	4,853	484	1970	4,636	383	1960	4,458	308
Churches of Christ	1979	12,700	1,600	1968	18,000	2,400	1960	18,680	2,163
Community Churches, National Council of	1979	185	190	--	--	--	--	--	--

Table 18-2. Membership and Number of Churches of Religious Bodies Having a Membership of 50,000 or More in 1980: 1960, 1970, and 1980–continued

Religious body	Circa 1980			Circa 1970			Circa 1960		
	Year	Churches reported	Membership (1,000)	Year	Churches reported	Membership (1,000)	Year	Churches reported	Membership (1,000)
Congregational Christian Churches, National Association of	1981	443	104	1970	327	85	1960	5,401	1,428
Conservative Baptist Association of America	1980	1,126	225	1970	1,127	300	1960	1,350	300
Coptic Orthodox Church	1980	25	100	--	--	--	--	--	--
Cumberland Presbyterian Church	1980	857	97	1970	901	92	1960	975	88
Episcopal Church, The	1980	7,215	2,786	1970	7,069	3,28	--	--	--
Evangelical Covenant Church of America	1980	539	78	1970	527	67	1960	510	60
Evangelical Free Church of America	1979	732	78	1971	562	70	--	--	--
Evangelical Lutheran Churches, The Association of	1980	268	108	--	--	--	--	--	--
Free Methodist Church of North America	1979	1,013	67	1970	1,095	65	1960	1,193	55
Free Will Baptists	1980	2,452	228	1970	2,163	186	1960	2,232	191
Friends United Meeting	1980	530	61	1970	517	68	--	--	--
Full Gospel Fellowship of Churches and Ministers, International	1980	394	59	--	--	--	--	--	--
General Association of Regular Baptist Churches	1981	1,571	243	1971	1,426	210	1960	934	136
General Baptist (General Association of)	1980	894	74	1971	854	65	1960	792	59
Greek Orthodox Archdiocese of North and South America	1977	535	1,950	1971	482	1,950	1960	382	1,200
Independent Fundamental Churches of America	1980	1,019	120	1970	901	112	1960	754	90
International Association of the Foursquare Gospel	1963	714	89	1963	741	89	1960	721	83
Jehovah's Witnesses	1980	7,515	565	1970	5,492	389	1960	4,170	250
Jews	1980	3,500	5,921	1970	5,000	5,870	1960	4,079	5,367
Lutheran Church in America	1980	5,800	2,923	1970	5,812	3,107	--	--	--
Lutheran Church--Missouri Synod, The	1980	5,694	2,626	1970	5,690	2,789	1960	5,215	2,391
Mennonite Church	1980	1,140	100	1970	1,181	89	1960	869	73
National Baptist Covention of America	1956	11,398	2,669	1956	11,398	2,669	1956	11,398	2,669
National Baptist Convention, U.S.A., Inc.	1958	26,000	5,500	1958	26,000	5,500	1958	26,000	5,500
National Primitive Baptist Convention, Inc.	1975	606	250	1970	2,196	1,523	1957	1,100	81
North American Old Roman Catholic Church	1980	134	61	1971	117	59	1960	64	85
Old Order Amish Church	1980	535	80	--	--	--	--	--	--
Orthodox Church in America	1978	440	1,000	1970	312	1,000	--	--	--
Pentecostal Church of God	1980	1,147	113	1967	975	115	1955	900	104
Pentecostal Holiness Church	1977	2,340	86	1970	1,318	67	1960	1,239	53
Plymouth Brethren	1980	1,100	98	--	--	--	--	--	--
Polish National Catholic Church of America	1960	162	282	1960	162	282	1960	162	282
Presbyterian Church in America	1980	487	91	--	--	--	--	--	--
Presbyterian Church in the U.S.	1980	4,159	838	1970	4,063	958	1960	3,995	903
Primitive Baptists	1960	1,000	72	1950	1,000	72	1950	1,000	72
Progressive National Baptist Convention, Inc.	1967	655	522	1967	655	522	--	--	--
Reformed Church in America	1980	902	346	1970	923	368	1960	867	226
Reorganized Church of Jesus Christ of Latter-day Saints	1980	1,056	190	1970	1,025	153	1960	848	155
Roman Catholic Church, The	1980	24,188	50,450	1970	23,708	48,215	1960	23,393	42,105

Table 18-2. Membership and Number of Churches of Religious Bodies Having a Membership of 50,000 or More in 1980: 1960, 1970, and 1980—continued

Religious body	Circa 1980			Circa 1970			Circa 1960		
	Year	Churches reported	Membership (1,000)	Year	Churches reported	Membership (1,000)	Year	Churches reported	Membership (1,000)
Russian Orthodox Church in the U.S.A., Patriarchal Parishes of the	1975	41	52	1965	67	153	--	--	--
Russian Orthodox Church Outside Russia, The	1955	81	55	1955	81	55	1955	81	55
Salvation Army, The	1980	1,056	417	1970	1,115	327	1960	1,255	254
Serbian Eastern Orthodox Church for the U.S.A. and Canada	1967	52	65	1967	52	65	1960	71	125
Seventh-day Adventists	1980	3,730	571	1970	3,218	420	1960	3,032	318
Southern Baptist Convention	1980	35,778	13,600	1970	34,340	11,628	1960	32,251	9,732
Triumph the Church and the Kingdom of God in Christ International	1972	475	54	1971	498	55	1960	670	67
Ukrainian Orthodox Church in the U.S.A.	1966	107	88	1966	107	88	1960	96	85
Unitarian Universalist Association	1979	968	139	1969	1,076	265	--	--	--
United Church of Christ	1980	6,642	1,736	1970	6,727	1,961	--	--	--
United Free Will Baptist Church	1952	836	100	1958	836	100	1958	836	100
United Methodist Church, The	1980	38,444	9,585	1970	40,653	10,672	--	--	--
United Pentecostal Church, International	1980	2,829	465	--	--	--	--	--	--
United Presbyterian Church in the U.S.A., The	1980	8,770	2,424	1970	8,610	3,087	1960	9,383	3,259
Wesleyan Church, The	1980	1,710	103	1970	1,898	84	--	--	--
Wisconsin Evangelical Lutheran Synod	1980	1,139	407	1970	967	381	1960	829	235
Bodies with membership of less than 50,000	...	13,796	1,467	...	14,574	1,576	...	18,313	1,692

Note: -- indicates data not available. ... indicates data not applicable.

Source: National Council of the Churches of Christ in the United States of America. Yearbook of the American and Canadian Churches (annual), as reported in U.S. Bureau of the Census. Statistical Abstract of the United States, 1982-83. Washington, DC: U.S. Government Printing Office, 1982, (Table 80) and corresponding issues for earlier years.

smaller denominations and hundreds of sects that exist. (See below for membership of some of these.)

Overlooking sampling error and possible differences in classification of small Baptist and Methodist sects, it appears that Baptists and Lutherans have grown more rapidly than the general population, while Methodists appear to have declined. The NORC data for 1958 are consistent with this inference, despite the fact that they appear to have overestimated the Methodist group.

Using the NORC estimated proportions for 1977 and the 1980 population statistics as a base, the religious preference/affiliation of the U.S. public may be estimated as shown in Table 18-1. The estimates of 113 million Protestants, 44 million Catholics, 4 million Jews, and 12 million "no-religion" for 1980 (population aged fifteen and over) should be accepted only as indications of approximate magnitude.

Membership of Religious Bodies

There are hundreds of religious bodies, many having a membership of only a few hundred or even a few dozen persons. Table 18-2 lists the membership of religious bodies with 50,000 or more members. Because these data are obtained from the individual organizations, there is considerable variation in the counting of members, particularly with respect to age. (Some count all baptized infants, while others count only persons above a certain minimum age who have been enrolled as full members.) The listing is alphabetical and provides membership statistics for the latest year specified in the column ranges. Eight Protestant religious groups, in addition to the "big four" (Baptist, Methodist, Lutheran, and Presbyterian), claim 1 million or more members:

Assemblies of God
Churches of Christ
Congregational Christian Churches
Disciples of Christ
Episcopal Church
Greek Archdiocese of North and South America ("Greek Orthodox")
Latter Day Saints ("Mormons")
United Church of Christ.

Table 18-3. Membership of Major Religious Groups, 1950-1980, and Number of Churches: 1980

Religious body	Membership						Number of churches, 1980	Percent change 1960-80	Percent distribution, 1980
	1950	1960	1965	1970	1975	1980			
Total.	86,830	114,449	124,682	131,046	131,012	134,817	336,281	17.8	100.0
Members as percent of population[a] . . .	57	64	64	63	61	59	...	...	...
Average members per local church	304	359	382	399	393	401	...	...	...
Buddhist Churches of America.	73	20	92	100	60	60	60	200.0	*
Eastern Churches	1,650	2,699	3,172	3,850	3,696	3,823	1,606	41.6	2.8
Jews[b].	5,000	5,367	5,600	5,870	6,115	5,920	3,500	10.3	4.4
Old Catholic, Polish National Catholic, and Armenian Churches. . .	250	590	484	848	846	924	436	56.6	0.7
The Roman Catholic Church	28,635	42,105	46,246	48,215	48,882	50,450	24,188	19.8	37.4
Protestants[c]	51,080	63,669	69,088	71,713	71,043	73,479	305,273	15.7	54.5
Miscellaneous[d]	142			449	372	161	1,218		0.1

[a]Based on Bureau of the Census estimated total population as of July 1.

[b]Estimates of the Jewish community including those identified with Orthodox, Conservative and Reformed synagogues or temples.

[c]Includes nonprotestant bodies such as "Latter-day Saints" and "Jehovah's Witnesses."

[d]Includes non-Christian bodies such as "Spiritualists," "Ethical Culture Movement," and "Unitarian-Universalists."

Note: ... indicates data not applicable. * indicates less than 0.1.

Source: National Council of the Churches of Christ in the United States of America. Yearbook of the American and Canadian Churches (annual), as reported in the U.S. Bureau of the Census. Statistical Abstract of the United States, 1982-83. Washington, DC: U.S. Government Printing Office, 1982, Table 81.

The data compiled by the National Council of the Churches of Christ in the United States of America are the main source of information on religious membership. The data have been extracted from reports a decade apart, and changes in membership should be interpreted cautiously because of the possibility of changes in organizations caused by combination or division, as well as change in reporting procedures. This table also does not include religious bodies that reported a membership of more than 50,000 members in an earlier period and now are combined with other religious groups or now have less than 50,000 members.

Table 18-3 reports the membership of the major religious groups, summarized from the data of Table 18-2. These data report a substantially higher proportion of Roman Catholic and Jewish membership than the Census Bureau and the NORC survey data, and a faster rate of growth for both in comparison with growth in the national total membership (as reported in Table 18-1). The differences appear to be due primarily to the fact that both Jewish and Catholic membership data include young children and infants, whereas the NORC/Census Bureau data refer to persons fifteen years of age and over. As a measure of religious affiliation of adults, the NORC data for 1977 are to be preferred.

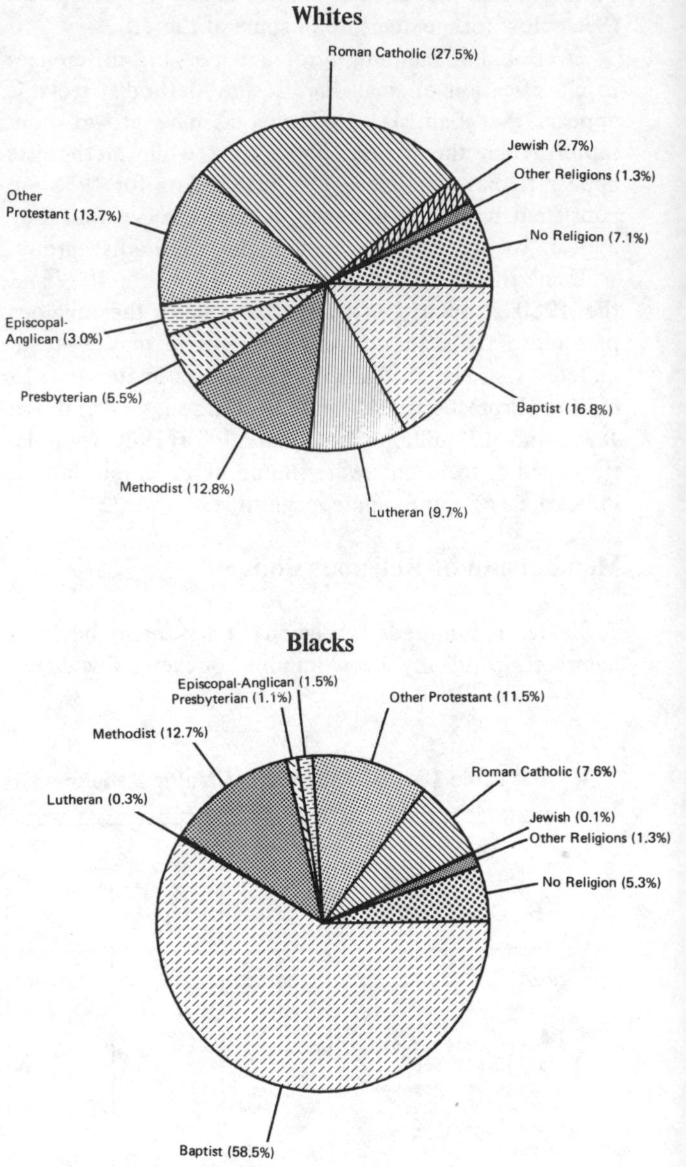

Figure 18-2. Religious Preference and Protestant Denominations, by Race: 1980

Demographic Composition of Religious Bodies

Racial Composition

The racial composition of the principal religious groups is shown in Table 18-4 and illustrated in Figure 18-2. The black population is almost exclusively Protestant (85.7 percent). Only about one black person in thirteen is a Roman Catholic. However, during the two decades 1960-80, very substantial increases in black membership in the Roman Catholic Church took place. About 60 percent of the black population belongs to one denomination, the Baptist, and an additional 13 percent belongs to the Methodist denomination. (Approximately 37 percent of all Baptists are nonwhite.) Hence more than 60 percent of all nonwhites belong to these two denominations. A very small percentage of the membership of the Lutheran, Presbyterian, Roman Catholic, and Jewish groups is nonwhite; however, between 1957 and 1980 all made substantial percentage increases in their black membership. The remaining nonwhite population tends to belong to one of the many minor sects or small denominations. Black persons are less inclined than whites to report that they have no religion.

Sex Composition

The ratio of the sexes is approximately the same in all major religious groups and denominations. The only noteworthy sex differential is that, among those reporting no religion, there was a greater proportion of men (62 percent) than women (38 percent). A similar differential also was evident in the Bureau of the Census survey of 1957.

Table 18-4. Percent Distribution of Religious Affiliation, by Race: 1980 and 1957

Religion	1980			1957			Percent black 1980	Percent nonwhite 1957
	Total[a]	Black	White	Total	Nonwhite	White		
Total	100.0	100.0	100.0	100.0	100.0	100.0	10.8	10.0
Protestant.	64.4	85.7	61.4	66.2	87.5	63.8	14.4	13.3
Baptist	22.4	58.5	16.8	19.7	60.6	15.2	28.2	30.8
Lutheran.	8.4	0.3	9.7	7.1	0.3	7.8	0.4	0.4
Methodist	12.7	12.7	12.8	14.0	17.3	13.6	10.8	12.4
Presbyterian.	4.8	1.1	5.5	5.6	0.9	6.1	2.5	1.6
Episcopal-Anglican.	2.8	1.5	3.0	3.1	1.2	3.4	6.0	3.9
Other Protestant.	13.3	11.5	13.7	16.7	7.3	17.8	9.3	4.4
Roman Catholic.	25.0	7.6	27.5	25.7	6.5	27.8	3.3	2.5
Jewish.	2.4	0.1	2.7	3.2	0.1	3.6	0.5	0.2
Other religion.	1.3	1.3	1.3	1.3	1.5	1.3	10.4	11.7
No religion	6.9	5.3	7.1	2.7	3.4	2.6	8.3	13.0
Religion not reported	--	--	--	0.9	1.0	0.9	--	10.6

[a] Total indicates all races, including other races not listed above.

Note: -- indicates data not available.

Source: The 1980 data for this table were based on a dataset defined by the National Opinion Research Center (NORC). General Social Surveys, 1972-83: Cumulative Codebook. Chicago: National Opinion Research Center, University of Chicago, 1983. Data for 1980 were estimated using the 1980 census statistics for population and the NORC percent distributions of religious preference (1977). Data for 1957 are from U.S. Bureau of the Census. "Religion Reported by the Civilian Population of the United States: March, 1957." Current Population Reports (Series P-20, no. 79). Washington, DC: U.S. Government Printing Office, 1958.

Table 18-5. Religious Preference of the U.S. Population, by Age: 1977

Religion	Total	Under 20 years	20-24 years	25-34 years	35-44 years	45-64 years	65 years and over
Total, 18 years and over . . .	100.0	2.2	10.7	23.8	17.0	29.6	16.7
Protestant	100.0	1.9	9.5	21.4	16.9	31.4	18.9
Baptist.	100.0	2.4	11.4	23.2	17.5	29.3	16.3
Lutheran	100.0	1.1	8.9	21.0	17.7	33.6	17.8
Methodist.	100.0	1.7	6.8	19.1	15.0	34.7	22.8
Presbyterian	100.0	1.8	8.2	16.9	16.3	34.3	22.4
Episcopal-Anglican	100.0	1.7	6.6	21.3	15.4	34.8	20.1
Other Protestant	100.0	1.6	10.6	21.9	17.6	29.4	19.0
Roman Catholic	100.0	2.6	11.6	25.9	17.5	29.0	13.5
Jewish	100.0	0.6	6.4	24.0	15.9	32.3	20.9
Other religion	100.0	2.9	18.2	29.2	17.7	23.0	9.1
No religion.	100.0	5.0	18.9	36.5	16.3	15.9	7.4

Source: The data for this table were tabulated from a dataset defined by the National Opinion Research Center. General Social Surveys, 1972-83: Cumulative Codebook. Chicago: National Opinion Research Center, University of Chicago, 1983.

Age Composition

In general the Protestant and Jewish populations tend to have an older age composition, while the Catholic and "no-religion" groups have a younger age composition. Within the Protestant group, Methodists, Presbyterians, and Episcopalians tend to have older age compositions, whereas the Baptists and Lutherans have younger age compositions. Table 18-5 provides data on age composition.

Proportionately few persons change their religious affiliation after they reach maturity. Any differences between religious groups with respect to age composition must therefore result primarily from the operation of basic demographic processes–fertility, mortality, immigration–within the groups. Assuming that mortality has only a minor differentiating effect, being roughly the same in all groups, fertility and migration seem the logical factors by means of which to explain age differences.

The Roman Catholic Church contains disproportionately large numbers of persons aged fourteen to thirty-four in comparison with the general population. This situation is due in part to higher fertility in former years. More importantly it results from the large migration of Puerto Rican, Mexican, and other Latin Americans to the continental United States in recent years. Because of very low fertility and lack of any recent migration, the Jewish population has the oldest age composition; 21 percent of all adult members are sixty-five and over, as against 17 percent for the general population.

Claiming to have no religion is distinctly a phenomenon of youth. Among those under twenty years of age, twice the average proportion claimed to have no religion. At ages forty-five and above only about one-half of the average proportion made this claim. The progressive decline in irrelegiosity with age could be a permanent generational effect, a temporary phenomenon linked to the life cycle, or a mixture of both.

Table 18-6. Religious Preference of the U.S. Population, by Region: 1977

Religion	Total	New England	Middle Atlantic	East North Central	West North Central	South Atlantic	East South Central	West South Central	Mountain	Pacific
Religious composition of regions										
Total	100.0	100.0	100.0	100.0	100.0	100.0	100.0	100.0	100.0	100.0
Protestant	64.4	31.4	44.6	62.3	69.2	83.6	90.9	72.2	65.8	57.3
Baptist	34.8	25.8	17.7	23.7	20.1	51.6	54.5	51.6	17.1	25.1
Lutheran	13.0	7.2	20.3	23.8	29.0	3.8	1.5	5.0	12.0	11.1
Methodist	19.7	13.4	16.5	22.0	20.9	23.0	17.7	16.6	18.4	16.1
Presbyterian	7.5	7.7	14.3	7.1	8.5	5.8	4.3	3.9	7.1	9.6
Episcopal-Anglican	4.3	15.3	9.8	2.2	1.4	3.3	2.1	2.8	7.4	6.6
Other Protestant	20.7	30.6	21.3	21.2	20.0	12.4	20.0	20.2	38.0	31.6
Roman Catholic	25.0	55.0	39.7	28.9	22.9	9.7	4.1	22.9	21.8	23.8
Jewish	2.4	3.0	7.2	1.2	1.2	1.1	0.5	0.7	0.3	2.6
Other religion	1.3	1.7	1.9	1.4	0.3	0.8	0.1	0.5	1.9	2.8
No religion	6.9	8.9	6.7	6.2	6.3	4.7	4.3	3.6	10.2	13.4
Regional distribution of religion										
Total	100.0	4.5	17.2	21.2	7.5	18.5	5.9	8.4	4.2	12.7
Protestant	100.0	2.2	11.9	20.5	8.0	24.0	8.4	9.4	4.3	11.3
Baptist	100.0	1.6	6.2	13.8	4.7	36.6	13.5	14.1	2.0	7.5
Lutheran	100.0	1.2	18.8	37.1	18.3	7.2	1.0	3.7	3.8	8.9
Methodist	100.0	1.5	10.1	22.7	8.7	28.9	7.8	8.0	3.9	8.5
Presbyterian	100.0	2.3	23.1	19.3	9.3	19.1	4.9	4.9	3.9	13.2
Episcopal-Anglican	100.0	7.8	27.3	10.2	2.7	19.0	4.1	6.1	7.1	15.8
Other Protestant	100.0	3.3	12.4	20.7	7.9	14.8	8.3	9.3	7.6	15.8
Roman Catholic	100.0	10.0	27.2	24.4	6.8	7.2	1.0	7.7	3.6	12.1
Jewish	100.0	5.7	52.0	10.9	3.8	9.0	1.4	2.5	0.5	14.2
Other religion	100.0	5.7	23.9	21.5	1.9	11.0	0.5	3.3	5.7	26.4
No religion	100.0	5.9	16.8	19.0	6.8	12.7	3.7	4.4	6.2	24.5

Source: The data for this table were tabulated from a dataset defined by the National Opinion Research Center. General Social Surveys, 1972-83: Cumulative Codebook. Chicago: National Opinion Research Center, University of Chicago, 1983.

Spatial Distribution

Geographic Divisions

The religious preference of the residents of each geographic division is reported in Table 18-6. The percentages are shown both vertically (religious composition of each division) and horizontally (distribution of religions across divisions). There is great diversity among the regions in religious composition and distribution. In New England more than half of the population is *Roman Catholic;* this is the only part of the nation where Catholics outnumber Protestants. However, Catholics are disproportionately concentrated in the Middle Atlantic and the East North Central divisions. Everywhere except in the Deep South they constitute 20 percent or more of the population, however. In the Southwest and West the Roman Catholic Church is important because of the Hispanic population as well as persons of European background.

Protestants outnumber all other religions in the Deep South—the South Atlantic and the East South Central regions. Throughout the South, Baptists are an absolute majority of the population, with Methodists as the only other major Protestant denomination. Lutherans are disproportionately concentrated in three regions: Middle Atlantic, East North Central, and West North Central. Presbyterians are widely distributed, with small concentrations in Middle Atlantic and Pacific divisions. The "other Protestant" groups are heavily concentrated in New England and the West, with a comparative scarcity in the South.

Jewish affiliation is linked strongly to only one area: the Middle Atlantic division. In this division the proportion of Jewish is triple the national average, and 52 percent of all Jewish members reside here. California and New England have small above-average concentrations also.

The *"other religions"* are located in the regions of the greatest migration from Asia and the Middle East: New England, Middle Atlantic, East North Central, Mountain, and Pacific. *No religion* is an outstanding characteristic of the Mountain and Pacific divisions, followed by New England. It is at its lowest in the South and Southwest, where Protestants and Catholics make up about 95 percent of the population.

Regional distribution of religion, as surveyed by the Bureau of the Census in 1957, is reported in Table 18-7. It shows that the pattern described above is of long

Table 18-7. Region of Residence of Persons 14 Years of Age and Older, by Reported Religion: Civilian Population, 1957

Religion	United States (000)	North-east (000)	North Central (000)	South (000)	West (000)
Percent by religion					
Total, 14 years old and over	100.0	100.0	100.0	100.0	100.0
Protestant	66.2	42.3	69.0	82.8	68.6
White	57.4	37.3	63.1	65.8	64.6
Nonwhite	8.8	5.0	5.9	17.0	4.0
Roman Catholic	25.7	45.1	24.7	11.6	22.3
Jewish	3.2	8.5	1.3	0.8	2.6
Other religion	1.3	2.1	1.2	0.7	1.3
No religion	2.7	1.1	2.9	3.0	4.2
Religion not reported	0.9	0.8	0.9	1.0	0.9
Percent by residence					
Total, 14 years old and over	100.0	26.2	29.2	30.6	14.0
Protestant	100.0	16.8	30.4	38.3	14.5
White	100.0	17.1	32.1	35.1	15.8
Nonwhite	100.0	14.8	19.5	59.3	6.4
Roman Catholic	100.0	46.0	28.0	13.9	12.1
Jewish	100.0	69.1	11.9	7.7	11.3
Other religion	100.0	41.9	26.5	17.4	14.2
No religion	100.0	11.2	32.1	34.7	22.1
Religion not reported	100.0	23.3	28.9	33.7	14.1

Source: U.S. Bureau of the Census. "Religion Reported by the Civilian Population of the United States: March, 1957." Current Population Reports (Series P-20, no. 79). Washington, DC: U.S. Government Printing Office, 1958.

Table 18-8. Religious Preference, by Size of Place: 1977 [percent distribution, by size of place]

Size of place	Total	Protestant	Catholic	Jewish	Other	None
Distribution by size of place						
Total	100.0	100.0	100.0	100.0	100.0	100.0
City larger than 250,000	20.4	17.6	21.4	49.3	35.4	30.8
Suburb of city of 250,000 or more	16.3	14.1	21.1	21.8	22.0	15.8
Unincorporated area of large city	7.7	6.9	9.8	10.9	6.2	7.5
City 50,000 to 249,999	10.2	9.9	11.3	3.3	9.1	11.2
Suburbs of such cities	5.8	5.2	7.2	4.9	5.7	6.8
Unincorporated surrounding area	7.7	8.5	6.4	2.7	7.7	6.5
Cities of 10,000 to 49,999	6.4	7.3	5.4	1.6	3.8	4.0
Places 2,500 to 9,999	6.2	6.6	6.3	1.1	6.2	3.3
Places under 2,500	3.7	4.9	2.1	0.3	0.5	1.1
Open country	15.6	19.0	9.1	4.1	3.3	13.0
Distribution by religion						
Total	100.0	64.4	25.0	2.4	1.3	6.9
City larger than 250,000	100.0	55.4	26.1	5.7	2.3	10.4
Suburb of city of 250,000 or more	100.0	55.8	32.5	3.2	1.8	6.7
Unincorporated area of large city	100.0	57.3	31.6	3.3	1.1	6.7
City 50,000 to 249,999	100.0	62.7	27.8	0.8	1.2	7.6
Suburbs of such cities	100.0	57.5	31.1	2.0	1.3	8.1
Unincorporated surrounding area	100.0	71.3	20.7	0.8	1.3	5.9
Cities of 10,000 to 49,999	100.0	73.3	21.1	0.6	0.8	4.3
Places 2,500 to 9,999	100.0	69.0	25.5	0.4	1.4	3.7
Places under 2,500	100.0	83.5	14.1	0.2	0.2	2.1
Open country	100.0	78.7	14.6	0.6	0.3	5.8

Source: The data for this table were tabulated from a dataset defined by the National Opinion Research Center. General Social Surveys, 1972-83: Cumulative Codebook. Chicago: National Opinion Research Center, University of Chicago, 1983.

standing. It has been modified somewhat by immigration from Latin America and Asia since that date.

Size of Place

The religious groups differ markedly in their size of place distribution, as shown in Table 18-8. *Protestants* are a majority in all size categories but reach their highest proportions in the open country, small rural places, small cities, and suburban areas of smaller metropolises. In the largest places the large black population maintains the Protestant proportion above the 50-percent mark.

Catholics are concentrated in the suburbs of large metropolitan areas and in medium-size cities; they are scarce in rural areas. They maintain about national average proportions in the largest central cities. This pattern reflects suburbanization of the successful immigrants and second-generation Catholic ethnic groups from Europe, as well as the residential pattern of the Hispanic population.

Jews are highly concentrated in the very largest cities and their suburbs. More than 90 percent are located in the largest cities, their immediate suburbs, or the unincorporated parts of the metropolitan areas of these largest places. Less than 10 percent are found in places with less than 50,000 population.

Socioeconomic Characteristics

Educational Attainment

Two religious groups stand out above all others as well educated: Jews and Episcopalians. One Jewish person in six has a postgraduate degree; among Episcopal members, the proportion is one in ten. For both groups, more than one-third have graduated from college. Three other groups (the Presbyterians, those with "other religion," and those with "no religion") attain an educational level considerably above the average. More than one-fourth of the members of these

Table 18-9. Religious Preference by Race, by Educational Attainment: 1977 [percent distribution, by educational attainment]

Religion, by race	Total	Less than 4 years high school	4 years high school	1-3 years college	Bachelor college	Post-graduate
All races						
Total, 18 years and over. . .	100.0	33.8	49.8	2.4	9.7	4.3
Protestant.	100.0	36.5	48.9	2.0	8.7	3.9
Baptist	100.0	47.7	43.3	1.5	5.2	2.3
Lutheran.	100.0	29.9	56.4	2.1	8.0	3.5
Methodist	100.0	29.4	54.3	1.7	10.4	4.2
Presbyterian.	100.0	21.6	51.2	3.3	16.7	7.2
Episcopal-Anglican.	100.0	15.6	46.3	4.4	23.7	10.0
Other Protestant.	100.0	38.7	48.3	2.1	7.5	3.4
Roman Catholic.	100.0	31.6	53.2	3.1	8.8	3.2
Jewish.	100.0	15.3	45.8	1.9	21.1	15.9
Other religion.	100.0	23.7	49.8	2.9	15.0	8.7
No religion	100.0	24.9	46.9	3.5	17.1	7.7
White						
Total, 18 years and over. . .	100.0	31.5	51.1	2.5	10.3	4.6
Protestant.	100.0	33.5	50.7	2.1	9.5	4.2
Baptist	100.0	43.8	46.4	1.3	5.9	2.6
Lutheran.	100.0	30.1	56.2	2.1	8.1	3.4
Methodist	100.0	27.0	56.1	1.9	10.8	4.3
Presbyterian.	100.0	21.0	51.3	3.4	16.9	7.4
Episcopal-Anglican.	100.0	14.1	46.7	4.8	24.1	10.3
Other Protestant.	100.0	38.1	48.4	1.8	7.9	3.7
Roman Catholic.	100.0	31.4	53.5	3.0	8.8	3.3
Jewish.	100.0	15.5	45.6	1.9	21.3	15.7
Other religion.	100.0	22.2	49.1	3.6	16.2	9.0
No religion	100.0	23.4	46.9	3.5	18.1	8.1
Black						
Total, 18 years and over. . .	100.0	48.8	41.7	2.2	4.9	2.3
Protestant.	100.0	50.8	40.3	1.9	4.8	2.2
Baptist	100.0	54.7	37.7	1.8	3.9	1.9
Lutheran.	100.0	0.0	85.7	0.0	0.0	14.3
Methodist	100.0	44.6	43.8	0.8	7.2	3.6
Presbyterian.	100.0	31.8	54.5	0.0	9.1	4.5
Episcopal-Anglican.	100.0	35.5	41.9	0.0	19.4	3.2
Other Protestant.	100.0	44.6	47.2	3.9	3.5	0.9
Roman Catholic.	100.0	35.7	48.7	5.2	6.5	3.9
Jewish.	100.0	*	*	*	*	*
Other religion.	100.0	29.6	63.0	0.0	7.4	0.0
No religion	100.0	41.9	47.6	3.8	4.8	1.9

Note: * indicates sample too small for accurate reporting.

Source: The data for this table were tabulated from a dataset defined by the National Opinion Research Center. General Social Surveys, 1972-83: Cumulative Codebook. Chicago: National Opinion Research Center, University of Chicago, 1983.

groups were college graduates, and only a comparatively small percent had less than twelve years of schooling. Protestants with the lowest levels of educational attainment are the Baptist, Methodist, and "other Protestant" groups. The black population, with high membership in the first two of these groups, tends to lower the average with below-average educational attainment because of race, not religion.

Table 18-9, which shows the educational attainment of white and black persons in each religious group, indicates that the average level of educational attainment is much lower among nonwhite household heads

Table 18-10. Religious Preference of the U.S. Population, by Occupation: 1977
[percent distribution, by occupation]

Religion	Total	Prof/ tech	Man- ager	Sales	Cleri- cal	Craft	Opera- tive	Non- farm labor	Farmer	Farm labor	Service
Total.	100.0	15.1	9.4	5.6	19.8	12.4	16.6	3.7	1.9	0.7	14.9
Protestant	100.0	14.1	9.1	5.5	18.4	12.4	17.4	3.7	2.4	0.8	16.3
Baptist.	100.0	9.0	6.1	4.4	15.8	12.1	23.2	5.0	2.2	1.2	21.1
Lutheran	100.0	14.9	9.1	4.4	20.6	13.7	14.9	2.7	3.9	0.3	15.4
Methodist.	100.0	16.1	11.5	6.0	19.4	12.8	14.7	3.2	2.6	0.6	13.0
Presbyterian	100.0	22.6	13.9	7.6	21.8	9.2	9.7	2.3	2.1	0.6	10.2
Episcopal-Anglican . .	100.0	27.1	17.4	7.8	21.6	7.6	6.0	1.8	0.5	0.3	9.9
Other Protestant . . .	100.0	13.6	7.5	5.7	18.5	13.0	18.3	3.7	2.2	1.0	16.5
Roman Catholic	100.0	14.0	8.9	5.5	24.1	12.4	16.3	3.3	0.9	0.6	14.0
Jewish	100.0	25.2	18.2	12.6	29.6	3.2	5.6	0.6	0.0	0.0	5.0
Other religion	100.0	21.5	13.1	5.2	11.5	14.7	16.2	5.2	0.0	1.0	11.5
No religion.	100.0	23.0	10.3	5.0	15.4	14.4	14.5	5.5	1.5	0.4	10.0

Source: The data for this table were tabulated from a dataset defined by the National Opinion Research Center. General Social Surveys, 1972-83: Cumulative Codebook. Chicago: National Opinion Research Center, University of Chicago, 1983.

where the person is a Baptist than where he is a member of some other denomination. This suggests that as blacks attain more education, they or their children tend to change their religious preference. Among the white population, Baptists have the lowest educational attainment, followed by "other Protestants."

Undoubtedly the "other Protestant" category hides some denominations that, if tabulated separately using samples large enough to be reliable, would rank near the top with the Episcopal and Jewish groups. Unitarians, for example, might well outrank both. Such groups as Christian Scientist and Congregationalist might rank near, or even above, the Presbyterian and Methodist groups.

Occupational Composition

Table 18-10 shows the diverse occupational composition of the various religious groups. Five religions stand out distinctively as having large percentages of their groups in "white collar" employment: Episcopal, Jewish, Presbyterian, "other religion," and "no religion." These data reflect the above-average level of educational attainment reported in the preceding section. The Episcopal group contains the largest percentage of professional and technical persons, while the Jewish group has substantial proportions in managerial and proprietary jobs. At the other extreme are three religions with above-average proportions of "blue collar" workers: Baptists, Methodists, and "other Protestants." All three groups contain substantial numbers of farmers, craftsmen, operatives, and unskilled workers.

Roman Catholics and Protestants tend to have very similar occupational compositions. In the past there was a tendency to think of Catholics as being considerably lower in socioeconomic status than Protestants. Upward mobility of Catholic immigrants coupled with growing black membership in Protestant denominations has largely erased this distinction. A close examination of Table 18-10 will show that in the Catholic group the proportion who are professional, proprietary, sales, and clerical workers is fully as large as it is among Protestants. The main difference is that such Protestant religions as Baptist, Methodist, and Lutheran contain a large proportion of farmers; Catholics have a disproportionate number of urban working-class persons, which compensates for the scarcity of Catholic farmers.

To what extent are these religious differentials in occupation due to religious doctrine, to cultural differences, to class status and the tendency to transmit socioeconomic advantage or disadvantage from one generation to another—or simply to differences in educational attainment? Answering that questions requires multivariate research. The answer seems to be that educational attainment, independent of religion, is a much more powerful factor in determining occupation than is religious preference, independent of education. To the extent that some religious groups appear to overachieve while others tend to underachieve, the mechanism seems to be primarily in the amount of education they tend to provide for their children or inspire their children to attain. Certainly the occupational differences between Catholics and Protestants are now much too small to attribute very much by way of occupational achievement to a "Protestant ethic" or to a lower "need for achievement" among Catholics.

Income Distribution

There is a high concentration of poverty among the Baptist population. People in the upper income brackets tend to be Episcopalian, Jewish, and Presbyterian (see Table 18-11 and Figure 18-3). Methodists, Roman Catholics, Lutherans, and other Protestants seem to be in the middle-income grades. In comparison with the general population, persons who claim no religion are disproportionately concentrated at the extremely high and the extremely low income levels.

How much of this income difference between religious groups is due to the differences in occupational composition described above? Here again, an answer requires a multivariate analysis. Since the measure of income employed here is family income, such items as the number of earners in the family, the occupational and educational level of the secondary earners, and so on, could also affect the comparisons. Even such aspects of family structure and composition as age of head of household and family reaction to poverty (some groups support elderly low-income parents in their own households, while other groups may allow them to live apart) may affect these data to a marked degree.

In view of the large and consistent differentials in educational attainment and occupational composition noted in the preceding sections, it is highly plausible that the substantial income differentials observed in Table 18-11 are primarily reflections of the level of education achieved and the resulting occupation entered and maintained. If any religious group experiences a class privilege or disadvantage, it most plausibly is linked to education, occupation, region of residence, and other factors that affect success in the labor force, more than to religion itself.

Family and Fertility

Age at Marriage

Table 18-12 reports age at first marriage for religious groups. It shows that precocious marriage is linked to the Protestant religion, and delayed marriage to the

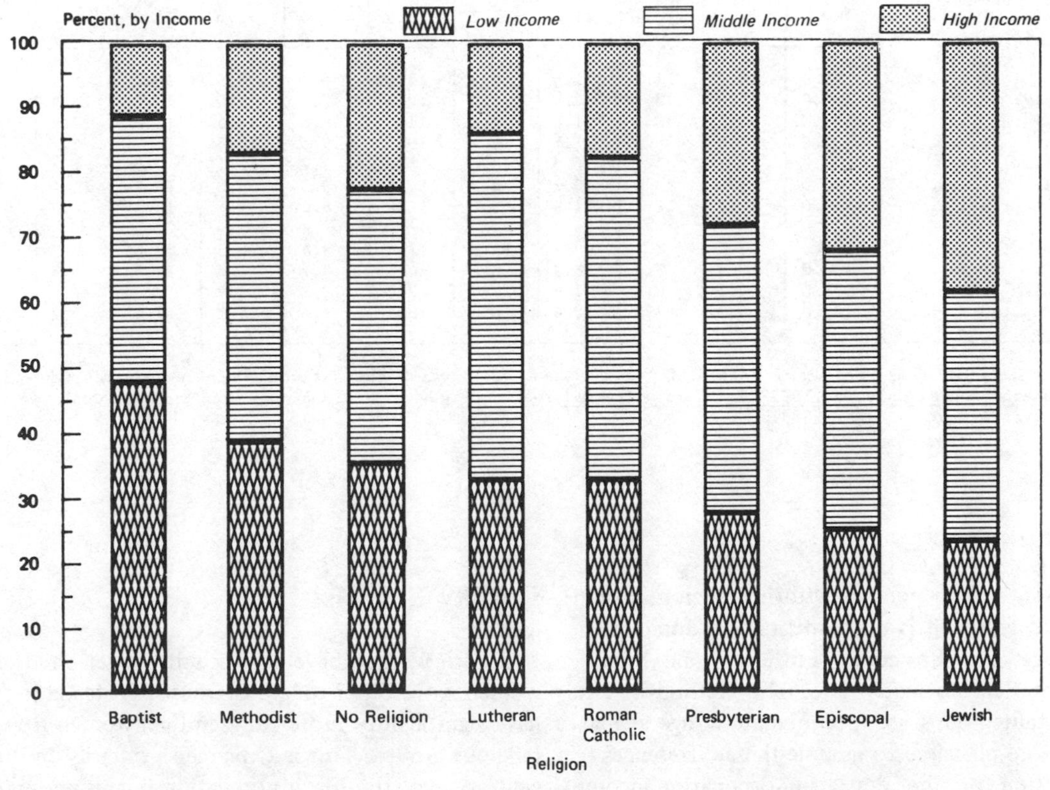

Figure 18-3. Religious Preference of the U.S. Population, by Low, Middle, and High Income: 1977

Table 18-11. Religious Preference of the U.S. Population, by Income: 1977 [percent distribution]

Religion	Total	Under $5,000	$5,000–$9,999	$10,000–$14,999	$15,000–$19,999	$20,000–$24,999	$25,000–over
Total, 18 years and over. .	100.0	16.5	20.9	20.4	14.0	10.8	17.4
Protestant.	100.0	18.2	21.8	20.4	13.5	10.0	16.1
Baptist	100.0	23.8	23.8	20.8	12.1	7.8	11.7
Lutheran.	100.0	12.9	19.9	24.1	14.8	13.7	14.6
Methodist	100.0	17.2	21.5	18.6	15.2	10.0	17.5
Presbyterian.	100.0	10.2	17.5	18.7	12.9	12.1	28.6
Episcopal-Anglican.	100.0	8.5	16.5	18.5	13.4	10.5	32.5
Other Protestant.	100.0	19.4	22.4	20.1	13.2	10.2	14.8
Roman Catholic.	100.0	12.8	19.9	21.3	15.0	13.0	18.1
Jewish.	100.0	10.2	13.1	15.1	13.2	9.4	38.9
Other	100.0	16.2	19.2	18.7	12.7	10.2	22.9
No religion	100.0	16.8	18.2	19.0	15.3	11.1	19.7

Source: The data for this table were tabulated from a dataset defined by the National Opinion Research Center. General Social Surveys, 1972-83: Cumulative Codebook. Chicago: National Opinion Research Center, University of Chicago, 1983.

Table 18-12. Age at Marriage, by Religious Affiliation: 1977 [percent distribution, by age at marriage]

Religion	Total	Under 18	18	19	20	21	22	23-24	25-29	30-44	45 and over
Total, 18 years and over	100.0	11.1	10.4	11.1	10.2	12.9	8.8	13.5	15.5	6.2	0.4
Protestant	100.0	12.7	11.7	11.8	9.9	13.0	8.4	12.5	14.1	5.6	0.4
Baptist.	100.0	18.5	13.9	12.4	10.3	12.3	7.0	9.9	10.2	4.9	0.5
Lutheran	100.0	5.5	10.0	11.5	9.4	11.6	9.6	16.5	18.0	7.5	0.4
Methodist.	100.0	9.8	10.8	11.5	9.4	13.7	9.5	13.9	15.3	5.7	0.4
Presbyterian	100.0	6.1	8.7	10.3	9.8	14.4	9.7	13.7	19.5	7.3	0.5
Episcopal-Anglican . . .	100.0	3.4	9.5	10.1	8.9	14.8	9.5	14.8	18.7	10.1	0.3
Other Protestant	100.0	14.3	11.4	11.9	10.4	13.8	8.6	11.2	14.1	4.0	0.3
Roman Catholic	100.0	8.1	8.2	9.7	11.0	12.4	9.4	15.5	18.0	7.2	0.4
Jewish	100.0	3.3	3.3	8.9	8.2	14.4	9.2	21.0	22.0	9.8	0.0
Other religion	100.0	9.5	6.3	7.6	12.0	12.0	10.8	11.4	17.7	11.4	1.3
No religion.	100.0	9.2	7.7	10.4	10.2	13.4	9.5	15.1	17.4	6.7	0.4

Source: The data for this table were tabulated from a dataset defined by the National Opinion Research Center. General Social Surveys, 1972-83: Cumulative Codebook. Chicago: National Opinion Research Center, University of Chicago, 1983.

Jewish religion and to persons with no religion. Within the Protestant group, it is the Baptists who dominate in early marriage. The Episcopal, Lutheran, and Presbyterian groups tend to marry late. The Methodists and other Protestant groups are intermediate in age at marriage. It is more plausible to assume these differences to be a reflection of the education-occupation-income differences, noted above, rather than any intrinsic tendencies rooted in religious beliefs.

Fertility

Jewish women have significantly fewer children than women from other religious groups. Protestants tend to have significantly more children than women from other religious groups. This is explained primarily by the concentration of the black population in this group. Catholics have a fertility history very similar to that of the national average, with a slight surplus of third and fourth

Table 18-13. Children Ever Born to Female Respondents 18 Years of Age and Older, by Religious Affiliation: 1977 [percent distribution, by number of children ever born]

Religion	Children ever born									
	Total	0	1	2	3	4	5	6	7	8 and over
Total	100.0	22.3	16.5	23.6	15.7	9.3	5.0	3.0	1.7	2.8
Protestant.	100.0	19.5	17.1	24.0	16.2	9.7	5.2	3.3	1.8	3.2
Baptist	100.0	18.4	17.6	22.0	15.2	8.7	6.2	4.3	2.5	5.2
Lutheran.	100.0	19.4	17.2	25.1	16.1	9.5	5.6	2.8	1.9	2.4
Methodist	100.0	20.7	17.3	24.8	16.7	9.7	4.5	2.6	1.3	2.3
Presbyterian.	100.0	26.5	15.8	23.0	18.4	9.9	3.8	1.5	0.5	0.5
Episcopal-Anglican. . .	100.0	21.9	20.2	25.9	13.8	11.3	2.4	2.0	1.2	1.2
Other Protestant. . . .	100.0	17.0	16.4	25.0	17.1	10.9	5.4	3.8	1.5	3.0
Roman Catholic.	100.0	25.3	14.4	22.1	15.9	9.3	5.6	3.0	1.9	2.5
Jewish.	100.0	23.2	16.6	38.9	13.3	6.6	0.0	0.9	0.5	0.0
Other religion.	100.0	42.7	11.2	16.9	14.6	7.9	4.5	0.0	0.0	2.2
No religion	100.0	40.4	21.1	18.9	9.3	5.9	1.7	1.0	0.5	1.2

Source: The data for this table were tabulated from the dataset defined by the National Opinion Research Center. General Social Surveys, 1972-83: Cumulative Codebook. Chicago: National Opinion Research Center, University of Chicago, 1983.

children but no sign of a large-family pattern. Any tendency toward higher fertility could be attributed to the Spanish-origin population rather than to Catholicism. The data of Table 18-13 verify imprecisely what more refined analyses have shown: that religion is of minor importance in influencing fertility in the United States. The cult of the small family outweighs religious beliefs—or has been incorporated as a part of the religious value system. The no-religion group also has small families. This is consistent with its higher education, youth, and occupational composition.

Intermarriage

All religious groups exhibit a high degree of within-religion marriage (Table 18-14). Even persons with no religion tend to marry other persons with no religion. Intramarriage is highest in the Jewish religion, in spite of its small proportion of the total population and consequent high exposure to opportunity for exogamous marriage.

Yet marriage outside one's own religious preference is very common, particularly when denominations are taken into account among Protestants. Between 15 and 20 percent of all marriages involving Catholic or Jewish persons are marriages to a person with a different religious preference. These differences are as of the time of the interview, and hence do not include conversion to a different religion as a result of marriage.

Conclusion

The various religious groups differ greatly from each other in their distribution among regions, metropolitan and nonmetropolitan areas, and with respect to the size of place in which they live. They also differ as to age of the family head, ethnic composition, and income levels. However, these differences are not due solely to religious affiliation as such. For example, it has been demonstrated in this chapter that occupational differences and educational differences each "explain" a large part of the income difference between religious groups. (Data were not available with which to measure how much of the total income differences between religious groups would be explained by both occupation and education considered simultaneously, but these factors probably would explain by far the larger part of these differences, if detailed occupation and education categories were used in the analysis.) There is little evidence that any particular group is receiving favored social or economic treatment simply on the basis of its religious affiliation. Neither is there much evidence to support a conclusion that any major religious group is being economically persecuted or disadvantaged solely because of its religious affiliation or beliefs.

The analysis in this chapter concerning the interrelationships between religious affiliation and other population variables has perforce been based on incomplete data. These materials have enabled the analysis to

Table 18-14. Intermarriage of Religious Groups; Percent Distribution of Religion of Spouse, by Religion of Husbands and Wives: 1977

Religion	Total	Religion of spouse: Protestant: Total Prot	Bapt	Luth	Meth	Pres	Epis	Other Prot	Catholic	Jewish	Other rel	No rel
Religion of husband												
Protestant	100.0	91.1	32.3	12.9	19.7	8.2	4.0	22.9	7.3	0.2	1.0	0.4
Baptist.	100.0	93.3	87.6	1.2	4.4	1.3	0.6	4.9	5.3	0.2	0.8	0.4
Lutheran	100.0	87.3	2.0	87.8	4.3	2.6	1.0	2.3	10.8	0.0	0.6	1.4
Methodist. . . .	100.0	92.6	9.3	2.3	80.4	1.9	2.3	3.8	6.6	0.2	0.0	0.6
Prebyterian. . .	100.0	86.0	5.0	3.9	5.0	81.2	2.2	2.8	10.3	0.0	0.9	2.8
Episcopal-Anglican . . .	100.0	90.9	5.7	3.4	6.8	5.7	75.0	3.4	8.1	0.0	0.0	1.0
Other Protestant	100.0	91.5	4.0	1.3	3.8	0.8	0.8	89.2	7.0	0.2	0.0	1.4
Roman Catholic . .	100.0	15.6	23.3	26.7	20.5	7.5	8.2	13.7	82.0	0.2	2.0	0.2
Jewish	100.0	6.9	20.0	0.0	20.0	0.0	20.0	40.0	6.9	85.1	0.0	1.1
Other religion . .	100.0	13.8	16.7	16.7	16.7	0.0	16.7	33.3	13.8	1.7	65.5	5.2
No religion. . . .	100.0	47.6	26.8	18.7	17.9	7.3	3.3	26.0	21.4	3.1	2.1	25.9
Religion of wife												
Protestant	100.0	87.0	35.4	12.3	20.1	8.1	3.7	20.5	6.7	0.4	0.3	5.6
Baptist.	100.0	90.6	86.2	1.0	6.6	1.8	0.9	3.5	4.3	0.1	0.4	4.5
Lutheran.	100.0	81.1	3.1	85.4	5.3	3.1	0.6	2.5	11.4	0.2	0.0	7.2
Methodist. . . .	100.0	87.5	9.7	1.9	80.4	1.7	1.3	5.1	7.1	0.7	0.2	4.5
Presbyterian . .	100.0	90.8	6.1	0.6	5.5	85.1	0.0	2.8	5.3	1.4	0.0	2.4
Episcopal-Anglican . . .	100.0	75.9	5.2	3.1	5.2	4.2	76.0	6.3	13.5	0.8	0.0	9.8
Other Protestant	100.0	86.2	7.8	2.1	5.5	1.3	0.6	82.8	6.1	0.3	0.6	6.7
Roman Catholic . .	100.0	17.5	23.9	23.9	19.3	14.7	8.6	9.6	76.0	0.4	0.6	5.5
Jewish	100.0	4.6	50.0	0.0	25.0	25.0	0.0	0.0	7.3	85.3	0.9	1.8
Other religion . .	100.0	24.4	25.0	0.0	25.0	25.0	0.0	25.0	4.9	0.0	58.5	12.2
No religion. . . .	100.0	26.6	24.4	17.1	19.5	12.2	7.3	19.5	13.6	1.6	1.1	57.1

Source: The data for this table were tabulated from a dataset defined by the National Opinion Research Center. General Social Surveys, 1972-83: Cumulative Codebook. Chicago: National Opinion Research Center, University of Chicago, 1983.

demonstrate only that some highly meaningful relationships exist. As data with which to measure the magnitude of these relationships, however, they have permitted only approximate conclusions. It is to be hoped that the Bureau of the Census will give a high priority to including religion as an item in the 1990 census.

Notes

1. "Among the countries with 500,000 or more inhabitants for which censuses have been published in recent years . . . about half have included at least one question on religion. By continental divisions, these totaled seven in North America, three in South America, twelve in Europe (including all the German governments as one), sixteen in Africa, and two in Oceania." Dorothy Good. "Questions on Religion in the United States Census." *Population Index*, January, 1959.

2. Despite strong appeals from a wide array of analysts and administrators (including leaders of religious groups), a question on religious affiliation has never been included in the regular decennial census enumerations. For example, the American Sociological Society, the Census Users Advisory Committee (representing more than seventy-five professional organizations), and the Population Association of America have all supported the asking of a question on religious affiliation in the census. The Bureau of the Census has received strong representation directly and indirectly through purse-string-holding Congressmen not to include questions on religion in its enumerations. It has been held by some that to ask a census question on religious affiliation would violate those Constitutional rights of the citizen assuring freedom of religious belief. A small minority has feared that, at some future date, census records showing religious affiliation could be used as a weapon

against persons belonging to particular religious groups. This is a fallacious argument. The religious affiliation of almost every citizen is already recorded or indicated in a number of different places.

3. Most of the data for this chapter have been tabulated from the National Opinion Survey (NORC) dataset *General Social Surveys, 1973-1983,* prepared as part of the National Data Program for the Social Sciences, supported by the National Science Foundation and distributed by Roper Public Opinion Research Center, University of Connecticut. Surveys were taken during February, March, and April of each year, 1972-1978, 1980, 1982, and 1983. There are a total of 15,579 completed interviews. Each survey is an independently drawn sample of English-speaking persons eighteen years of age or over, living in noninstitutional arrangements within the continental United States. Block quota sampling was used in 1972-74 surveys and for half of the 1975 and 1976 surveys. Full probability sampling was employed in the remainder. In order to obtain sufficient cases for the analysis, data from all surveys (1972 to 1983) were pooled into a single file. In the analysis it is assumed that the resulting data refer to the year 1977, midpoint of that period. The author acknowledges with thanks the assistance of the National Opinion Research Center in the use of these datasets. Odalia Ho, senior research assistant, Department of Sociology, University of Chicago, made the tabulations.

4. See Donald J. Bogue. "Religious Affiliation." Chapter 18 in *The Population of the United States.* New York: The Free Press, 1959. Jacob L. Feldman prepared these special tabulations.

5. In February, 1958, the Bureau of the Census published a report, "Religion Reported by the Civilian Population of the United States: March, 1957." *Current Population Reports* (Series P-20, no. 79). Washington, DC: U.S. Government Printing Office, 1958.

Bibliography

Alston, J.P., and McIntosh, W.A. "Assessment of the Determinants of Religious Participation." *Sociological Quarterly* 20 (1979):49-62.

Beeghley, L. et al. "Correlates of Religiosity Among Black and White Americans." *Sociological Quarterly* 22 (1981):403-12.

Bouvier, Leon F., and Weller, Robert H. "Residence and Religious Participation in a Catholic Setting." *Sociological Analysis* 35 (1974):273-81.

Cohen, M., and Kapsis, R.E. "Religion, Ethnicity, and Party Affiliation in the U.S.: Evidence from Pooled Electoral Surveys, 1968-72." *Social Forces* 56 (1977): 637-53.

Glenn, N.D., and Gotard, E. "Religion of Blacks in the United States: Some Recent Trends and Current Characteristics." *American Journal of Sociology* 83 (1977):443-51.

Goldberg, Nathan. "Demographic Characteristics of American Jews." In *Jews in the Modern World,* by Jacob Fried (ed.). New York: Twayne, 1962.

Good, Dorothy. "Questions on Religion in the United States Census." *Population Index* 25 (1959):3-16.

Greeley, Andrew M. *The American Catholic: A Social Portrait.* New York: Basic Books, 1977.

Hadaway, C.K. "Demographic Environment and Church Membership Change." *Journal for the Scientific Study of Religion* 20 (1981):77-89.

Janssen, S.G., and Hauser, R.M. "Religion, Socialization, and Fertility." *Demography* 18 (1981):511-28.

Knoke, D. "Religion, Stratification and Politics: America in the 1960s." *American Journal of Political Science* 18 (1974):331-45.

Lenski, Gerhard E. *The Religion Factor: A Sociological Study of Religion's Impact on Politics, Economics and Family Life.* Garden City, NJ: Doubleday, 1963.

Mueller, C.W. "Evidence on the Relationship Between Religion and Educational Attainment." *Sociology of Education* 53 (1980):140-52.

Newman, W.M., and Halvorson, P.L. "American Jews: Patterns of Geographic Distribution and Change, 1952-1974." *Journal for the Scientific Study of Religion* 18 (1979):183-93.

Parson, T. "Religion in Postindustrial America: The Problem of Secularization." *Social Research* 41 (1974):193-225.

Roof, W.C. "Socioeconomic Differentials Among White Socioreligious Groups in the United States." *Social Forces* 58 (1979):280-89.

Shortridge, J.R. "New Regionalization of American Religion." *Journal for the Scientific Study of Religion* 16 (1977):143-53.

Smith, T.L. "Religion and Ethnicity in America." *American Historical Review* 83 (1978):1155-85.

Stark, Rodney, and Glock, Charles. *American Piety: The Nature of Religious Commitment.* Berkeley, CA: University of California Press, 1968.

Wingrove, C.R., and Alston, J.P. "Cohort Analysis of Church Attendance, 1939-69." *Social Forces* 53 (1974):324-31.

Wuthnow, Robert. "Recent Patterns of Secularization: A Problem of Generations?" *American Sociological Review* 41 (1976):850-67.

Chapter 19

Political Demography

Research and everyday observation confirm that most citizens develop a characteristic politcal stance on particular issues and a voting pattern in elections. A political stance may consist in identification with a particular political party or location along a political outlook scale ranging, for example, from radical conservatism to radical liberalism. The stance is expressed behaviorally at times of election by voting for particular candidates or by failing or refusing to vote.

Political demography asks whether stance varies with the standard variables with which demography is concerned: sex, age, race-ethnicity, marital status, educational attainment, occupation, income, urban-rural residence, and region of residence. The answer is clearly affirmative. A standard description of the profile of public opinion on any issue or of election results will show distribution of politcal behavior according to these demographic variables, perhaps supplemented by political science variables (e.g. past voting, party affiliation) cross-tabulated with opinions on other issues. Despite this strong intersection of demography and politics, demographers have not given sufficient attention to political science, and political scientists often are inadequately informed about demography. There is need for more systematic study of the interaction between political processes and demographic processes to test the various popular beliefs about the existence, direction, and strength of correlation between the two. Among the services demographer can perform are to check those beliefs regularly against empirical data and to apply demographic methods to the study of changing political climates. The present chapter is an exploratory effort in this direction.

Identification with Political Parties

One principal characteristic of election statistics is that within particular precincts or other small areas, the proportion of the vote that goes to the Republican or the Democratic party tends to remain more or less constant over time. If the Republicans in a particular district win one election, they are more likely to win there again in the next. The underlying phenomenon is that a great many voters have party attachments that persist from one election to the next. Longitudinal surveys of panels of respondents demonstrate that all but a comparatively small fraction of citizens form an identification with one or the other of the two major parties. The following comment on this phenomenon provides the basis for a more scientific study of politcal processes:

> Few factors are of greater importance for our national elections than the lasting attachment of tens of millions of Americans to one of the parties. These loyalties establish a basic division of electoral strength within which the competition of particular campaigns take place. And they are an important factor in assuring the stability of the party system itself. . . . Only in the exceptional case does the sense of individual attachment to party reflect a formal membership or an active connection with a party apparatus. Nor does it simply denote a voting record, although the influence of party allegiance on electoral behavior is strong. Generally, this tie is a psychological identification, which can persist without legal recognition or evidence of formal membership and even

Definitions

Political Party Affiliation. A question with three parts, developed by the Michigan Center for Political Studies, is widely accepted as the standard operational definition: "Generally speaking, do you usually think of yourself as a Republic, Democrat, independent, or what? [Republican (ask A); Democrat (ask A); independent (ask B); other (specify and ask B); or no preference]" "A. *If Republican or Democrat:* Would you call yourself a strong (Republican/Democrat) or not a very strong (Republican/Democrat)?" "B. *If independent/no preference/other:* Do you think of yourself as closer to the Republican or Democratic party? [Republican; Democratic; or neither]" These questions are recoded in eight categories, reported in Table 19-1.

without a consistent record of party support. Most Americans have this sense of attachment with one party or the other.[1]

A quantifiable measurement of party identification, based on self-classification by respondents in sample surveys, was developed by the Center for Political Studies (CPS) at the University of Michigan (details are given in the Definition Box). This system permits the categorization of individuals into one of seven categories along a dimension representing both the direction and strength of party identification. The continuum permits a separation of those with strong Republican or Democratic party attachment from those of weaker identification with one of the parties. Those who are independent may be divided according to whether or not they "lean toward" one or the other of the parties or whether they truly lack any party identification. The Center for Political Studies has collected information about political preferences using this set of questions since 1950. In 1972 the University of Chicago's National Opinion Research Center (NORC) added the identical questions to its General Social Surveys conducted annually. Table 19-1A shows the distribution of party identification

Table 19-1A. Trends in Identification of the U.S. Population with Political Parties: Both Sexes, 1952-1983 [percent distribution, by party affiliation]

Year	Total	Democrat				Independent						Republican				Apolitical[a]	
		Strong		Weak		Lean Democrat		Fully independent		Lean Republican		Weak		Strong			
		CPS	NORC	CPS	NORC	CPS	NORC	CPS	NORC	CPS	NORC	CPS	NORC	CPS	NORC	CPS	NORC
1983. . .	100	--	15	--	24	--	14	--	12	--	9	--	16	--	9	--	1
1982. . .	100	--	16	--	25	--	13	--	13	--	10	--	14	--	9	--	1
1980. . .	100	18	13	23	26	11	13	13	17	10	8	14	15	9	8	2	1
1978. . .	100	15	14	24	26	14	13	14	15	10	9	13	16	8	7	3	1
1976. . .	100	15	15	25	27	12	14	15	16	10	7	14	14	9	6	1	*
1974. . .	100	18	17	21	26	13	14	15	10	9	7	14	15	8	8	3	4
1972. . .	100	15	20	26	27	11	10	13	10	11	6	13	14	10	8	1	4
1970. . .	100	20	--	24	--	10	--	13	--	8	--	15	--	9	--	1	--
1968. . .	100	20	--	25	--	10	--	11	--	9	--	15	--	10	--	1	--
1966. . .	100	18	--	28	--	9	--	12	--	7	--	15	--	10	--	1	--
1964. . .	100	27	--	25	--	9	--	8	--	6	--	14	--	11	--	1	--
1962. . .	100	23	--	23	--	7	--	8	--	6	--	16	--	12	--	4	--
1960. . .	100	20	--	25	--	6	--	10	--	7	--	14	--	16	--	3	--
1958. . .	100	27	--	22	--	7	--	7	--	5	--	17	--	11	--	4	--
1956. . .	100	21	--	23	--	6	--	9	--	8	--	14	--	15	--	4	--
1954. . .	100	22	--	26	--	9	--	7	--	6	--	14	--	13	--	4	--
1952. . .	100	22	--	25	--	10	--	6	--	7	--	14	--	14	--	3	--

[a]"Apolitical" in the CPS data indicates those without party identification. "Apolitical" in the NORC data indicates those with party identifications other than those listed.

Note: -- indicates data not available. * indicates less than 1.0. Due to extensive rounding, row totals may not sum up to 100.

Source: University of Michigan Center for Political Studies identified as CPS; National Opinion Research Center identified as NORC. The CPS data for 1952-78 from Miller, Warren E.; Miller, Arthur H.; and Snyder, Edward J. American National Election Studies Data Sourcebook, 1952-1978. Cambridge, MA: Harvard University Press, 1980, Table 2.1. CPS data for 1980 provided by the Center for Political Studies, University of Michigan, "American National Election Studies, 1980." The NORC data were tabulated from a dataset defined by the National Opinion Research Center. General Social Surveys, 1972-83: Cumulative Codebook. Chicago: National Opinion Research Center, University of Chicago, 1983.

among the electorate for alternate years, 1952 to 1983. The data from 1952 to 1980 are from the University of Michigan surveys. The data from 1972 to 1983 are from the National Opinion Research Center's sample. (The overlap to the years 1972-1980 provide evidence that the two surveys obtained very similar results, with the Center for Political Studies showing a little less "independent" responses than NORC.) This table reveals a comparatively stable pattern, in which allegiance to the Democratic party is expressed by three persons for every two who identify themselves with the Republican party. The one important trend that has emerged is the increased tendency for persons to report themselves as independents. This gain has been made at the expense of the proportions professing to be either strong Democrats or strong Republicans, because the proportions classifying themselves as being weak Democrats or weak Republicans have remained almost constant over the entire three decades.

Actual voting behavior from 1952 to 1982 has been much more variable than the picture of stable party affiliation shown in Table 19-1A. Below is a summary of the vote cast for each party in recent presidential elections:

Year	Percentage of popular vote		Person elected President	President's party
	Democrat	Republican		
1948. . .	49.5	45.1	Truman	Democrat
1952. . .	44.4	55.1	Eisenhower	Republican
1956. . .	42.0	57.4	Eisenhower	Republican
1960. . .	49.7	49.6	Kennedy	Democrat
1964. . .	61.1	38.5	Johnson	Democrat
1968. . .	42.7	43.4	Nixon	Republican
1972. . .	37.5	60.7	Nixon	Republican
1976. . .	50.1	48.0	Carter	Democrat
1980. . .	41.0	50.7	Reagan	Republican

Note: Percentage of popular vote for parties or candidates other than Democrat and Republican are not reported.

Source: U.S. Bureau of the Census. Statistical Abstract of the United States, 1984. Washington, DC: U.S. Government Printing Office, 1983, Table 415.

Table 19-1B. Trends in Identification of the U.S. Population with Political Parties: Male Population, 1952-1983 [percent distribution, by party affiliation]

Year	Total	Democrat				Independent						Republican				Apolitical[a]	
		Strong		Weak		Lean Democrat		Fully independent		Lean Republican		Weak		Strong			
		CPS	NORC	CPS	NORC	CPS	NORC	CPS	NORC	CPS	NORC	CPS	NORC	CPS	NORC	CPS	NORC
1983. . .	100	--	16	--	22	--	15	--	11	--	11	--	15	--	9	--	1
1982. . .	100	--	15	--	21	--	15	--	14	--	11	--	14	--	8	--	2
1980. . .	100	20	12	18	25	12	14	15	17	12	10	14	15	7	7	2	1
1978. . .	100	14	14	24	24	15	15	16	16	12	10	12	14	6	7	2	1
1976. . .	100	15	15	22	22	13	17	16	17	12	6	14	15	8	7	1	*
1974. . .	100	17	18	18	24	15	16	15	10	12	8	13	15	9	6	1	4
1972. . .	100	15	21	22	26	12	10	15	11	13	8	13	14	10	8	1	3
1970. . .	100	20	--	23	--	12	--	13	--	9	--	13	--	10	--	1	--
1968. . .	100	20	--	23	--	11	--	10	--	10	--	16	--	9	--	1	--
1966. . .	100	20	--	26	--	9	--	12	--	9	--	13	--	11	--	1	--
1964. . .	100	28	--	22	--	11	--	8	--	6	--	12	--	11	--	1	--
1962. . .	100	25	--	24	--	8	--	9	--	6	--	15	--	11	--	2	--
1960. . .	100	23	--	22	--	9	--	10	--	7	--	14	--	14	--	1	--
1958. . .	100	29	--	19	--	9	--	7	--	5	--	15	--	13	--	3	--
1956. . .	100	22	--	23	--	9	--	10	--	9	--	13	--	13	--	2	--
1954. . .	100	25	--	25	--	10	--	8	--	6	--	13	--	12	--	2	--
1952. . .	100	24	--	23	--	11	--	7	--	7	--	13	--	13	--	2	--

[a]"Apolitical" in the CPS data indicates those without party identification. "Apolitical" in the NORC data indicates those with party identifications other than those listed.

Note: -- indicates data not available. * indicates less than 1.0. Due to extensive rounding, row totals may not sum up to 100.

Source: University of Michigan Center for Political Studies identified as CPS; National Opinion Research Center identified as NORC. The CPS data for 1952-78 from Miller, Warren E.; Miller, Arthur H.; and Snyder, Edward J. American National Election Studies Data Sourcebook, 1952-1978. Cambridge, MA: Harvard University Press, 1980, Table 2.10. CPS data for 1980 provided by the Center for Political Studies, University of Michigan, "American National Election Studies, 1980." The NORC data were tabulated from a dataset defined by the National Opinion Research Center. General Social Surveys, 1972-83: Cumulative Codebook. Chicago: National Opinion Research Center, University of Chicago, 1983.

Despite the fact that the public identified itself with the Democratic party more than the Republican, of the eight presidential elections that occurred since these data began to be collected, Republicans have won five. Republican victories have been achieved by capturing almost all of the votes of both strong and weak Republicans, a majority of independents, and a substantial minority of the votes of weak and even strong Democrats. The fact that this identification persists over time, despite changes in administration and party-in-power suggests that it is a fairly stable part of the individual's value system, rather than a response to particular events or political personalities.

It should be noted from Table 19-1A that a majority of both Democrats and Republicans classify themselves as "weak Democrats" or "weak Republicans" rather than as having strong affiliations. Also, only about 40 percent of the "independents" are truly independent of any politcal party but admit to tendencies toward one party or the other. The picture that emerges is one not of fixed and inflexible party identification but of a continuum with only about one-fourth of the voting public more or less inflexibly or strongly linked to a particular political party.

Correlates of Political Identification

To shed light on the direction and degree of association between demographic variables and identification with political parties, computations were prepared especially for this book.

Table 19-1C. Trends in Identification of the U.S. Population with Political Parties: Female Population, 1952-1983 [percent distribution, by party affiliation]

Year	Total	Democrat				Independent						Republican				Apolitical[a]	
		Strong		Weak		Lean Democrat		Fully independent		Lean Republican		Weak		Strong			
		CPS	NORC	CPS	NORC	CPS	NORC	CPS	NORC	CPS	NORC	CPS	NORC	CPS	NORC	CPS	NORC
1983. . .	100	--	15	--	26	--	12	--	13	--	7	--	17	--	9	--	1
1982. . .	100	--	16	--	28	--	12	--	12	--	9	--	13	--	9	--	1
1980. . .	100	16	13	27	26	11	13	11	17	9	7	14	15	9	8	2	1
1978. . .	100	16	15	25	27	14	12	12	13	8	8	13	18	9	7	3	*
1976. . .	100	16	15	27	31	10	12	13	15	8	8	15	14	11	6	1	*
1974. . .	100	19	16	22	27	11	13	13	10	7	7	15	15	9	9	3	4
1972. . .	100	14	19	29	29	11	10	12	9	9	5	13	15	11	8	2	5
1970. . .	100	20	--	25	--	9	--	13	--	7	--	17	--	8	--	1	--
1968. . .	100	20	--	27	--	9	--	11	--	8	--	13	--	10	--	2	--
1966. . .	100	17	--	29	--	9	--	12	--	6	--	17	--	9	--	2	--
1964. . .	100	26	--	27	--	8	--	8	--	5	--	15	--	11	--	1	--
1962. . .	100	22	--	23	--	6	--	7	--	6	--	18	--	13	--	6	--
1960. . .	100	23	--	26	--	3	--	8	--	6	--	14	--	16	--	3	--
1958. . .	100	24	--	25	--	5	--	7	--	5	--	18	--	11	--	5	--
1956. . .	100	19	--	23	--	5	--	8	--	8	--	15	--	17	--	5	--
1954. . .	100	20	--	26	--	8	--	7	--	6	--	15	--	14	--	5	--
1952. . .	100	21	--	27	--	8	--	5	--	7	--	15	--	14	--	4	--

[a]"Apolitical" in the CPS data indicates those without party identification. "Apolitical" in the NORC data indicates those with party identifications other than those listed.

Note: -- indicates data not available. * indicates less than 1.0. Due to extensive rounding, row totals may not sum up to 100.

Source: University of Michigan Center for Political Studies identified as CPS; National Opinion Research Center identified as NORC. The CPS data for 1952-78 from Miller, Warren E.; Miller, Arthur H.; and Snyder, Edward J. American National Election Studies Data Sourcebook, 1952-1978. Cambridge, MA: Harvard University Press, 1980, Table 2.10. CPS data for 1980 provided by the Center for Political Studies, University of Michigan, "American National Election Studies, 1980." The NORC data were tabulated from a dataset defined by the National Opinion Research Center. General Social Surveys, 1972-83: Cumulative Codebook. Chicago: National Opinion Research Center, University of Chicago, 1983.

Table 19-2. Party Affiliation, by Age and Sex of Respondent: Pooled NORC Data, 1972-1983 [percent distribution, by party affiliation]

Age and sex	Total	Democrat		Independent			Republican	
		Strong	Weak	Lean Democrat	Fully independent	Lean Republican	Weak	Strong
Both sexes . . .	100.0	16.4	26.0	13.4	12.9	8.4	15.2	7.7
18-19 years. .	100.0	9.6	24.4	16.6	19.6	11.7	14.8	3.3
20-24 years. .	100.0	8.3	26.6	18.3	18.6	9.9	14.4	3.8
25-34 years. .	100.0	11.2	27.4	17.9	16.4	9.7	13.4	4.0
35-44 years. .	100.0	15.2	28.8	13.3	13.2	8.8	15.0	5.7
45-64 years. .	100.0	20.6	25.5	11.0	9.6	8.0	15.8	9.6
65 years+. . .	100.0	23.6	21.9	7.6	9.1	5.4	17.6	14.7
Male	100.0	16.7	23.7	14.8	13.4	9.5	14.4	7.5
18-19 years. .	100.0	9.5	23.8	15.5	20.2	11.9	14.3	4.8
20-24 years. .	100.0	8.9	23.3	20.9	18.1	10.4	13.8	4.6
25-34 years. .	100.0	11.1	23.5	19.6	18.3	10.8	12.6	4.2
35-44 years. .	100.0	15.1	25.9	13.8	14.7	10.9	13.5	6.1
45-64 years. .	100.0	20.8	24.8	12.3	9.3	9.3	15.1	8.4
65 years+. . .	100.0	25.4	20.1	9.5	8.1	5.5	17.2	14.2
Female	100.0	16.2	27.8	12.2	12.5	7.5	15.9	7.9
18-19 years. .	100.0	9.8	25.0	17.7	18.9	11.6	15.2	1.8
20-24 years. .	100.0	7.9	29.4	16.1	19.1	9.5	14.9	3.1
25-34 years. .	100.0	11.3	30.4	16.6	14.9	8.9	14.1	3.8
35-44 years. .	100.0	15.2	31.3	13.0	11.9	7.0	16.1	5.4
45-64 years. .	100.0	20.5	26.1	9.8	9.8	6.8	16.4	10.6
65 years+. . .	100.0	22.3	23.3	6.2	9.9	5.2	18.0	15.1

Source: The data for this table were tabulated from a dataset defined by the National Opinion Research Center. General Social Surveys, 1972-83: Cumulative Codebook. Chicago: National Opinion Research Center, University of Chicago, 1983.

Sex and Political Orientation

Both the CPS and the NORC data show no large difference between the sexes in their political identification (Tables 19-1B and 19-1C). Figure 19-1 illustrates the various party affiliations by selected demographic characteristics. Males were somewhat more inclined than females to declare themselves independent, whereas females were more inclined to identify with one political party or the other, even though they may have characterized the identification as weak. Earlier surveys showed females to be somewhat more inclined than males to identify with the Republican party, but this tendency has not been manifest since about 1974.

In order to obtain sufficient number of cases to study characteristics of party identification in more detail, the data of the National Opinion Research Center for 1972 to 1983 were pooled, yielding responses for 15,225 persons. These pooled data were used to prepare Tables 19-2, 19-3, and 19-5 to 19-12.

Age and Political Orientation

There is practically zero correlation in the NORC data between age and identification with one of the two major political parties (see Table 19-2). However, there is a very strong tendency for younger persons to declare themselves to be independent of party affiliation. Moreover, if they did identify with a political party, far fewer of the younger persons declared a strong identification. This may be clarified by combining the responses for Democrats and Republicans to show only the strength of the party identifications:

Age	Independent		Party identification	
	No leaning	Leaning	Weak	Strong
Total. . . .	12.9	21.8	41.2	24.1
18-19 years. .	19.6	28.3	39.2	12.9
20-24 years. .	18.6	28.2	41.0	12.1
25-34 years. .	16.4	27.6	40.8	15.2
35-44 years. .	13.2	22.1	43.8	20.9
45-64 years. .	9.6	19.0	41.3	30.2
65 years and over	9.1	13.0	39.5	38.3

About 40 percent of persons of all ages declared their party identification, whatever it was, to be weak. Only a small fraction of voters (12 to 15 percent) under thirty-

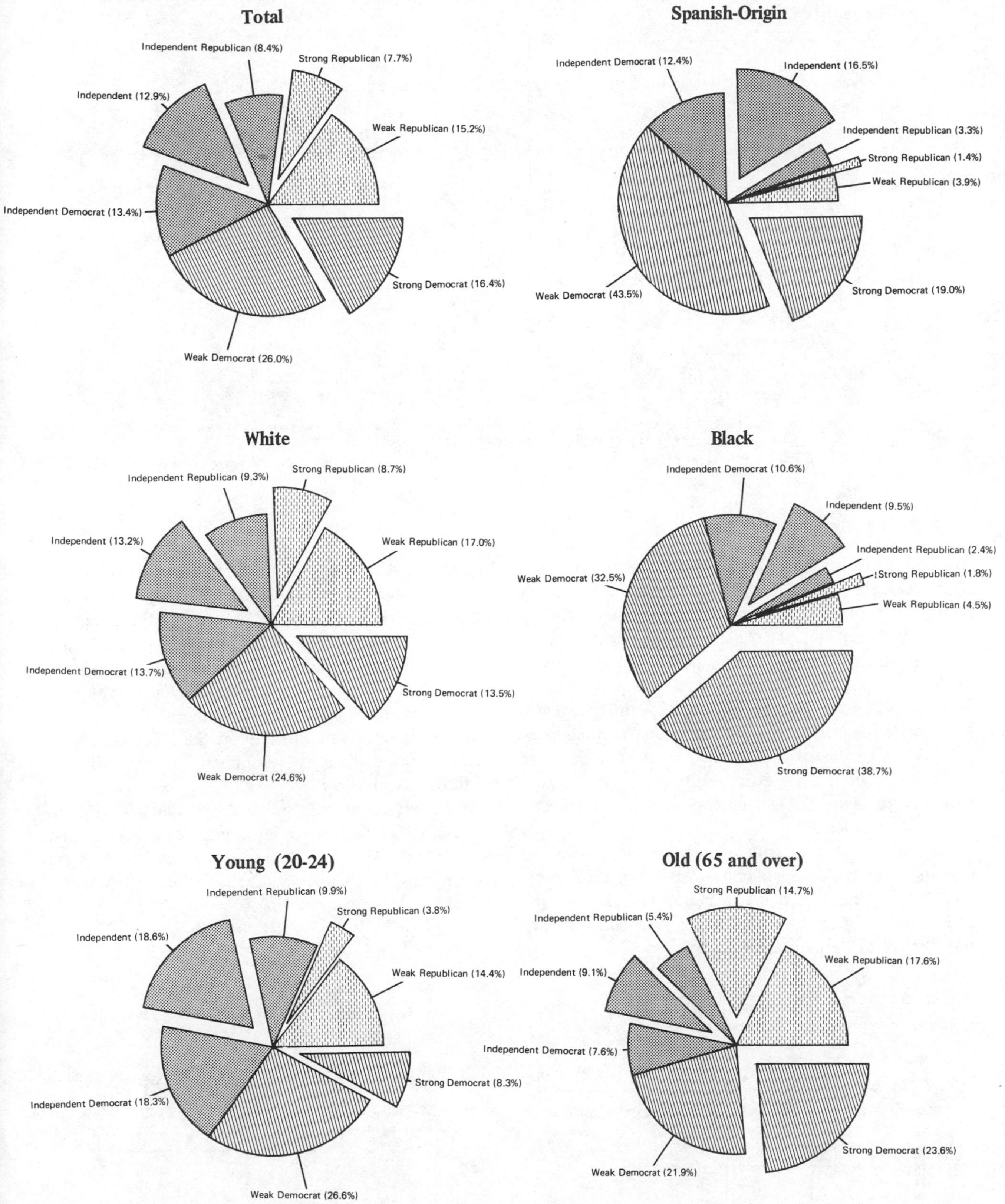
Total
Independent Republican (8.4%)
Strong Republican (7.7%)
Independent (12.9%)
Weak Republican (15.2%)
Independent Democrat (13.4%)
Strong Democrat (16.4%)
Weak Democrat (26.0%)
Spanish-Origin
Independent Democrat (12.4%)
Independent (16.5%)
Independent Republican (3.3%)
Strong Republican (1.4%)
Weak Republican (3.9%)
Weak Democrat (43.5%)
Strong Democrat (19.0%)
White
Strong Republican (8.7%)
Independent Republican (9.3%)
Independent (13.2%)
Weak Republican (17.0%)
Independent Democrat (13.7%)
Strong Democrat (13.5%)
Weak Democrat (24.6%)
Black
Independent Democrat (10.6%)
Independent (9.5%)
Independent Republican (2.4%)
Weak Democrat (32.5%)
Strong Republican (1.8%)
Weak Republican (4.5%)
Strong Democrat (38.7%)
Young (20-24)
Independent Republican (9.9%)
Strong Republican (3.8%)
Independent (18.6%)
Weak Republican (14.4%)
Strong Democrat (8.3%)
Independent Democrat (18.3%)
Weak Democrat (26.6%)
Old (65 and over)
Strong Republican (14.7%)
Independent Republican (5.4%)
Weak Republican (17.6%)
Independent (9.1%)
Independent Democrat (7.6%)
Strong Democrat (23.6%)
Weak Democrat (21.9%)

Figure 19-1. Party Affiliation, by Selected Demographic Characteristics

Table 19-3. Party Identification, by Race and Sex: Pooled NORC Data, 1972-1983 [percent distribution, by party affiliation]

Race and sex	Total	Democrat		Independent			Republican	
		Strong	Weak	Lean Democrat	Fully independent	Lean Republican	Weak	Strong
White (non-Spanish), both sexes.	100.0	13.5	24.6	13.7	13.2	9.3	17.0	8.7
Male.	100.0	13.7	22.9	14.8	13.9	10.6	16.0	8.2
Female.	100.0	13.4	26.1	12.8	12.6	8.3	17.8	9.1
Black (non-Spanish), both sexes.	100.0	38.7	32.5	10.6	9.5	2.4	4.5	1.8
Male.	100.0	40.5	28.6	13.7	8.9	2.3	3.9	2.0
Female.	100.0	37.4	35.3	8.3	10.0	2.5	4.9	1.7
Spanish-origin (white black), both sexes.	100.0	19.0	43.5	12.4	16.5	3.3	3.9	1.4
Male.	100.0	25.8	34.2	20.0	12.3	1.9	3.9	1.9
Female.	100.0	13.9	50.5	6.7	19.7	4.3	3.8	1.0

Source: The data for this table were tabulated from a dataset defined by the National Opinion Research Center. General Social Surveys, 1972-83: Cumulative Codebook. Chicago: National Opinion Research Center, University of Chicago, 1983.

five had a strong identification with either party, and only after age sixty-five did the number professing a strong party identification match the number claiming weak identification. The percentage of voters who classified themselves as independent, even those professing a "political leaning" toward one party or the other, tended to be very high through age thirty-five and then to decline rather sharply with age. When independent voters expressed a "leaning" toward one party or the other (rather than strict neutrality), there was a tendency to favor the Democratic party in the ratio of 1.6 to 1 Republican.

Removing the independent vote from consideration permits a clearer understanding of party affiliation by age. By combining Democratic and Republican identification into a dichotomy (omitting independents) the following results are obtained:

Age	Percentage		Ratio Democrat to Republican, total
	Democrat	Republican	
Total.	42.4	22.9	1.85
18-20 years. . . .	34.0	18.1	1.88
20-24 years. . . .	34.9	18.2	1.92
25-34 years. . . .	38.6	17.4	2.21
35-44 years. . . .	44.0	20.7	2.13
45-64 years. . . .	46.1	25.4	1.81
65 years and over	45.5	32.3	1.41

The notion that younger generations tend to be Democratic and older ones Republican not only was invalid in the late 1970s and early 1980s but was the reverse of the actual situation. The NORC data show that Democrats outnumber Republicans strongly at all ages and come close to being an absolute majority at ages beyond forty-five years. While it is true that Republicans were comparatively less in a minority at the older ages, their absolute minority status is impressive, as the ratios of the third column show.

Moreover, young persons who expressed allegiance to the Republican party were more inclined to report their identification as "weak" than young persons showing allegiance to the Democrats, as the following tabulation shows:

Age	Ratio of "weak" to "strong" party identification	
	Democrat	Republican
All ages.	1.58	1.97
Under 18 years. . .	2.54	4.48
18-24 years	3.20	3.79
25-34 years	2.45	3.35
35-44 years	1.89	2.63
45-64 years	1.24	1.65
65 years and over .	0.93	1.20

Table 19-4A. Trends in Identification of the U.S. Population with Political Parties: White Population, 1952-1983 [percent distribution, by party affiliation]

Year	Total	Democrat				Independent						Republican				Apolitical[a]	
		Strong		Weak		Lean Democrat		Fully independent		Lean Republican		Weak		Strong			
		CPS	NORC	CPS	NORC	CPS	NORC	CPS	NORC	CPS	NORC	CPS	NORC	CPS	NORC	CPS	NORC
1983. . . .	100	--	13	--	24	--	13	--	12	--	10	--	18	--	10	--	1
1982. . . .	100	--	13	--	24	--	14	--	14	--	11	--	15	--	10	--	1
1980. . . .	100	14	10	23	25	12	14	14	17	11	9	16	16	9	9	2	1
1978. . . .	100	12	12	24	25	14	13	14	14	10	10	14	17	9	8	2	1
1976. . . .	100	13	14	23	26	11	14	15	16	11	8	16	15	10	7	1	*
1974. . . .	100	16	15	20	24	12	14	14	11	10	8	15	16	10	8	2	4
1972. . . .	100	12	15	25	27	12	11	13	11	11	7	14	16	11	9	1	4
1970. . . .	100	17	--	23	--	11	--	13	--	9	--	16	--	10	--	1	--
1968. . . .	100	16	--	25	--	10	--	11	--	10	--	16	--	11	--	1	--
1966. . . .	100	17	--	27	--	9	--	12	--	8	--	16	--	11	--	1	--
1964. . . .	100	24	--	25	--	9	--	8	--	6	--	15	--	12	--	1	--
1962. . . .	100	22	--	23	--	8	--	8	--	7	--	17	--	13	--	3	--
1960. . . .	100	23	--	25	--	6	--	9	--	7	--	14	--	16	--	1	--
1958. . . .	100	26	--	23	--	7	--	7	--	5	--	17	--	12	--	2	--
1956. . . .	100	20	--	23	--	6	--	9	--	9	--	14	--	16	--	3	--
1954. . . .	100	22	--	25	--	9	--	8	--	6	--	15	--	13	--	3	--
1952. . . .	100	21	--	26	--	10	--	6	--	7	--	14	--	14	--	2	--

[a]"Apolitical" in the CPS data indicates those without party identification. "Apolitical" in the NORC data indicates those with party identifications other than those listed.

Note: -- indicates data not available. * indicates less than 1.0. Due to extensive rounding, row totals may not sum up to 100.

Source: University of Michigan Center for Political Studies identified as CPS; National Opinion Research Center identified as NORC. The CPS data for 1952-78 from Miller, Warren E.; Miller, Arthur H.; and Snyder, Edward J. American National Election Studies Data Sourcebook, 1952-1978. Cambridge, MA: Harvard University Press, 1980, Table 2.12. CPS data for 1980 provided by the Center for Political Studies, University of Michigan, "American National Election Studies, 1980." The NORC data were tabulated from a dataset defined by the National Opinion Research Center. General Social Surveys, 1972-83: Cumulative Codebook. Chicago: National Opinion Research Center, University of Chicago, 1983.

At the oldest ages, the strong Democrats outnumber the weak, whereas among Republicans at those ages the weak Republicans are still a majority of Republicans.

In summary the older age groups are considerably more strongly Democrat than Republican, with a high loyalty index. Are the old people simply the "New Deal" generation, which will gradually age and fade out of the picture, or is it a political stance that accompanies and is a part of the aging process? Younger generations tend to be more flexible in their party identification as well as more inclined to be independent. The "baby boom" generations, represented by the 25-34 and 35-44 age groups above, seem to be more strongly Democrats and to be more loyally Democrat than the "baby bust" generation, which only recently has become eligible to vote. Identification as independent occurs more fequently in both generations than among their elders. Are these age differences cohort changes or secular changes? That is a question worthy of careful demographic study.

Race and Party Identification

Black citizens are far more inclined to be Democrat and less inclined to be Republican or independent than are white citizens:

Party identification	White	Black
Total.	100.0	100.0
Democrat	38.1	71.2
Independent. . . .	36.2	22.5
Republican	25.7	6.3

The above summary of the 1972-82 NORC pooled data is portrayed in full party identification detail, by race and sex, in Table 19-3. Trends in race identification over the years since 1952 are provided separately for white

Table 19-4B. Trends in Identification of the U.S. Population with Political Parties: Black Population, 1952-1983 [percent distribution, by party affiliation]

Year	Total	Democrat				Independent						Republican				Apolitical[a]	
		Strong		Weak		Lean Democrat		Fully independent		Lean Republican		Weak		Strong			
		CPS	NORC	CPS	NORC	CPS	NORC	CPS	NORC	CPS	NORC	CPS	NORC	CPS	NORC	CPS	NORC
1983. . . .	100	--	34	--	29	--	16	--	13	--	4	--	2	--	1	--	1
1982. . . .	100	--	46	--	33	--	8	--	6	--	3	--	3	--	0	--	1
1980. . . .	100	45	38	27	32	9	9	7	13	3	3	2	4	3	1	4	1
1978. . . .	100	37	31	30	33	15	11	9	14	2	4	3	6	3	1	2	0
1976. . . .	100	35	32	36	35	14	14	8	11	1	2	3	4	2	2	1	0
1974. . . .	100	43	30	25	34	15	14	10	5	1	2	1	8	3	3	3	0
1972. . . .	100	37	48	31	30	8	5	12	5	3	*	4	5	4	1	2	5
1970. . . .	100	43	--	34	--	8	--	10	--	0	--	4	--	0	--	1	--
1968. . . .	100	56	--	29	--	7	--	3	--	1	--	1	--	1	--	3	--
1966. . . .	100	30	--	31	--	11	--	14	--	2	--	7	--	2	--	3	--
1964. . . .	100	52	--	22	--	8	--	6	--	1	--	5	--	2	--	5	--
1962. . . .	100	35	--	25	--	4	--	6	--	2	--	7	--	6	--	15	--
1960. . . .	100	27	--	21	--	5	--	12	--	4	--	10	--	7	--	14	--
1958. . . .	100	30	--	21	--	6	--	5	--	3	--	9	--	7	--	19	--
1956. . . .	100	27	--	23	--	6	--	7	--	1	--	12	--	7	--	18	--
1954. . . .	100	24	--	29	--	6	--	5	--	6	--	5	--	11	--	15	--
1952. . . .	100	31	--	22	--	10	--	4	--	4	--	8	--	5	--	17	--

[a]"Apolitical" in the CPS data indicates those without party identification. "Apolitical" in the NORC data indicates those with party identifications other than those listed.

Note: -- indicates data not available. * indicates less than 1.0. Due to extensive rounding, row totals may not sum up to 100.

Source: University of Michigan Center for Political Studies identified as CPS; National Opinion Research Center identified as NORC. The CPS data for 1952-78 from Miller, Warren E.; Miller, Arthur H.; and Snyder, Edward J. American National Election Studies Data Sourcebook, 1952-1978. Cambridge, MA: Harvard University Press, 1980, Table 2.12. CPS data for 1980 provided by the Center for Political Studies, University of Michigan, "American National Election Studies, 1980." The NORC data were tabulated from a dataset defined by the National Opinion Research Center. General Social Surveys, 1972-83: Cumulative Codebook. Chicago: National Opinion Research Center, University of Chicago, 1983.

and black in Tables 19-4A and 19-4B. Race-ethnic categories by age are provided in Table 19-5. Only 3 percent of the black population reported itself in 1983 as Republican, while 34 percent reported itself as strong Democrat and an additional 29 percent as weak Democrat. Whatever small support the Republican party gets from the black population seems to be concentrated among older blacks, who may still carry the remnants of the tradition of the post-Civil War era of the Republican party as the party that freed the slaves. However, there also seems to be a small surge of weak support for Republican affiliation among young black persons aged 18-24 years. Clearly, a large part of the present party loyalty for the Democratic party, described above, is contributed by the black population. The overlap in data between the CPS and NORC surveys confirm the validity of the race differential and its general magnitude. Because the data for the black population are based on a comparatively small number of cases when tabulated for single years, inferences about trends are risky. However, since 1980 there appears to have been a slight lessening of support for the Democratic party and a tendency for a higher proportion of independents to lean toward the Republican party than at any time since 1952. Although this shift to the right is clearly noticeable for the white population, it appears to be more of a shift toward the center for the black population. For both races, this movement away from open identification with Democrats involves about 5-8 percent of both the white and the black population.

However, even allowing for secular shifts, Democrat identification is also still paramount among the white population, including a tendency for more independents to lean toward the Democratic than toward the Republican side. The tendency for more young citizens to declare themselves is evident for all race groups but more characteristic of the white than the black population.

The Spanish-origin population tends to be strongly

Table 19-5. Party Affiliation, by Age and Race-Ethnicity of Respondents: Pooled NORC Data, 1972-1983 [percent distribution horizontally and vertically]

Race and age	Total	Democrat		Independent			Republican		Democrat		Independent			Republican	
		Weak	Strong	Lean Demo-crat	Fully inde-pendent	Lean Repub-lican	Weak	Strong	Strong	Weak	Lean Demo-crat	Fully inde-pendent	Lean Repub-lican	Weak	Strong
White (non-Spanish)	100.0	...	...	...	...	...	...	...	100.0	100.0	100.0	100.0	100.0	100.0	100.0
18-19 years	100.0	7.5	21.6	17.9	19.8	13.1	16.4	3.7	1.2	1.8	2.7	3.2	3.0	2.0	0.9
20-24 years	100.0	6.3	23.6	19.2	19.3	10.8	16.6	4.3	4.7	9.7	14.2	14.9	11.7	9.9	5.0
25-34 years	100.0	8.7	25.7	18.0	16.9	10.9	15.3	4.5	14.8	24.1	30.3	29.8	27.2	20.8	12.0
35-44 years	100.0	12.0	27.7	13.8	13.5	10.1	16.5	6.4	15.1	19.0	17.1	17.4	18.3	16.5	12.7
45-64 years	100.0	17.1	24.6	11.6	9.8	8.9	17.4	10.6	38.2	30.1	25.6	22.5	28.8	31.0	37.2
65 years and over	100.0	20.2	21.4	7.9	9.3	5.9	19.3	15.9	26.0	15.1	10.1	12.3	11.0	19.8	32.2
Black (non-Spanish)	100.0	...	...	...	...	...	...	...	100.0	100.0	100.0	100.0	100.0	100.0	100.0
18-19 years	100.0	22.9	33.3	10.4	16.7	6.3	8.3	2.1	1.7	3.0	2.9	5.2	7.5	5.4	3.3
20-24 years	100.0	23.0	38.0	15.5	11.5	5.5	5.0	1.5	7.3	14.3	17.9	14.8	27.5	13.5	10.0
25-34 years	100.0	27.5	36.3	17.5	10.7	3.6	3.2	1.2	17.9	28.0	41.6	28.4	37.5	17.6	16.7
35-44 years	100.0	41.3	31.8	9.8	9.1	1.5	5.3	1.1	17.2	15.8	15.0	15.5	10.0	18.9	10.0
45-64 years	100.0	47.4	30.9	6.0	7.9	1.1	4.7	1.9	35.0	27.0	16.2	23.9	12.5	29.7	30.0
65 years and over	100.0	53.2	25.8	4.4	7.7	0.8	4.4	3.6	20.9	12.0	6.4	12.3	5.0	14.9	30.0
Spanish-origin (white and black).	100.0	...	...	...	...	...	...	...	100.0	100.0	100.0	100.0	100.0	100.0	100.0
18-19 years	100.0	0.0	46.2	15.4	30.8	7.7	0.0	0.0	0.0	3.8	4.4	6.7	8.3	0.0	0.0
20-24 years	100.0	5.3	48.7	10.5	25.0	6.6	3.9	0.0	5.8	23.6	17.8	31.7	41.7	21.4	0.0
25-34 years	100.0	16.7	38.3	15.0	19.2	3.3	5.8	1.7	29.0	29.3	40.0	38.3	33.3	50.0	40.0
35-44 years	100.0	15.7	52.9	14.3	11.4	0.0	5.7	0.0	15.9	23.6	22.2	13.3	0.0	28.6	0.0
45-64 years	100.0	41.2	36.8	8.8	7.4	2.9	0.0	2.9	40.6	15.9	13.3	8.3	16.7	0.0	40.0
65 years and over	100.0	40.0	40.0	6.7	6.7	0.0	0.0	6.7	8.7	3.8	2.2	1.7	0.0	0.0	20.0

Source: The data for this table were tabulated from a dataset defined by the National Opinion Research Center. General Social Surveys, 1972-83: Cumulative Codebook. Chicago: National Opinion Research Center, University of Chicago, 1983.

Democratic but less so than the black population. There appears to be a generation difference within the Spanish speaking groups. The older generations seem to be strongly Democratic, with also a small Republican minority. In contrast, the younger Spanish speaking groups tend to be weak Democrats or independents, with almost zero identification with the Republican party, but with an increased propensity for independents to lean in that direction.

Educational Attainment

Identification with the Republican party is strongest among persons who have attended college or who have graduated with four years of college but have not obtained an advanced degree. Table 19-6A provides data on education by political identification separately for males and females. Among those with four years of college, Republicans are as numerous as Democrats, with a very substantial share of independents leaning toward the Republican position. Persons with postgraduate college education tend to be somewhat less pro-Republican. At the lowest levels of educational attainment, the population is overwhelmingly Democrat, and at the very highest level of persons with a graduate degree, Democrats also outnumber Republicans in the ratio of 33 to 27 percent. That this is not simply a matter of race is shown in Tables 19-6B and 19-6C, which provide summary data by education for each race, by sex. The pattern just described for the general population is valid for the white population. For the black population with education at the high school level or above, support for the Republican party is less than five percent. At these levels the black respondents tend to report themselves as weak Democrat or as independents with Democrat leanings, but show even less support for the Republicans than those black citizens with less than a high school education.

Total independence of party identification is strongest among high school graduates and those with an incomplete college education. Independence with an indication of "leaning" toward one party or the other is moderately positively correlated with educational attainment. As a consequence, among those with some college training or a college degree, independent (with or without leaning) is the major political identification, outnumbering both parties.

Table 19-7A shows percentages of respondents reporting party identification with the Democratic party by educational attainment, age, and race. Table 19-7B provides the same information with respect to identification with the Republican party. A similar tabulation with respect to independents is provided in Table 19-7C. Figure 19-2 illustrates these differences.

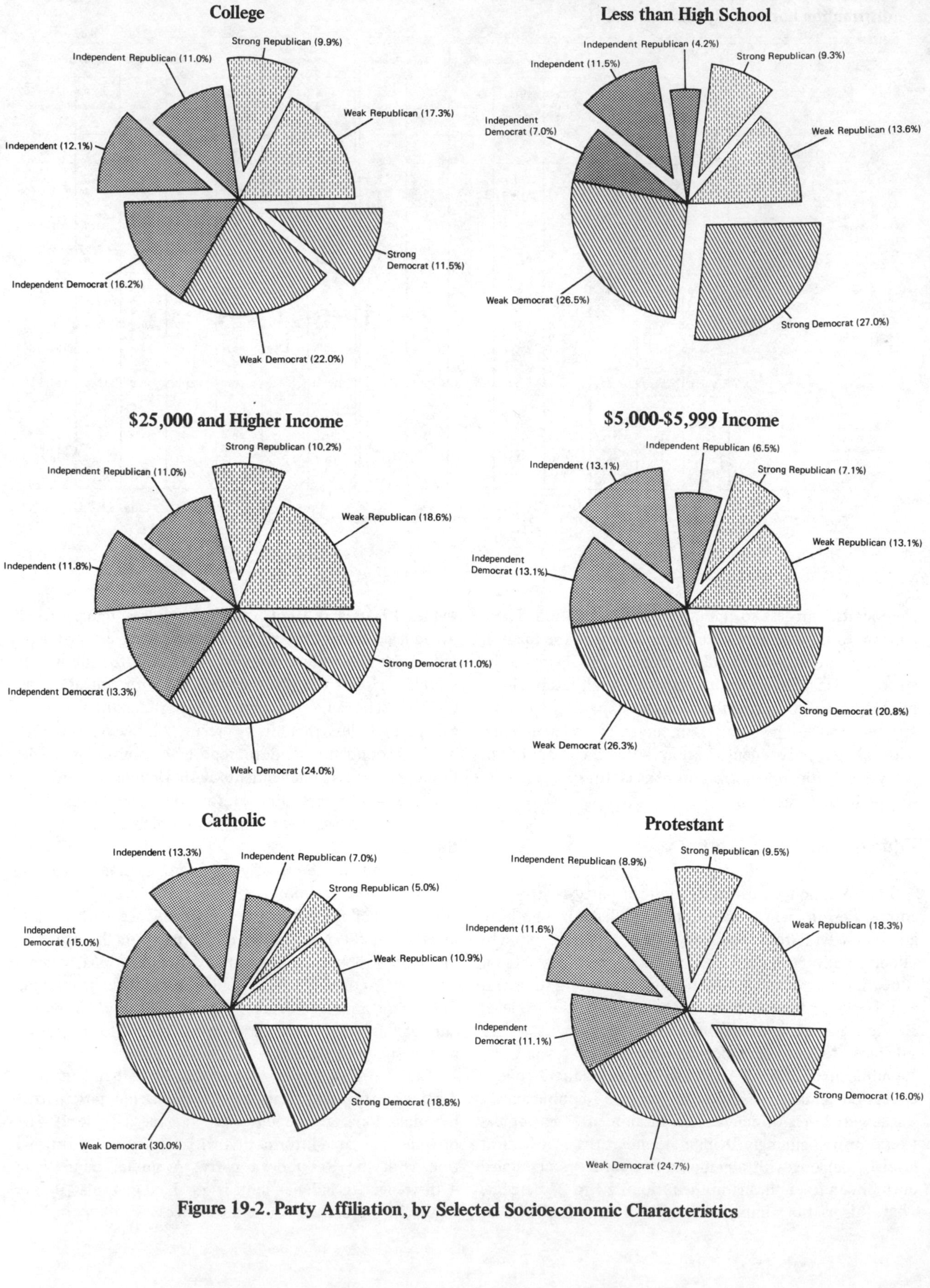

Figure 19-2. Party Affiliation, by Selected Socioeconomic Characteristics

Table 19-6A. Educational Attainment and Party Affiliation, by Sex: Total Population, Pooled NORC Data, 1972-1983 [percent distribution horizontally and vertically]

Educational attainment and sex	Total	Democrat		Independent			Republican		Democrat		Independent			Republican	
		Strong	Weak	Lean Demo-crat	Fully inde-pendent	Lean Repub-lican	Weak	Strong	Strong	Weak	Lean Demo-crat	Fully inde-pendent	Lean Repub-lican	Weak	Strong
Both sexes	...	...	...	...	...	...	...	...	100.0	100.0	100.0	100.0	100.0	100.0	100.0
Less than high school	100.0	27.0	26.5	7.9	11.5	4.2	13.6	9.3	26.6	16.6	9.5	14.4	8.2	14.5	19.4
High school	100.0	16.2	28.2	13.3	13.9	8.1	14.5	5.9	51.0	56.3	51.5	55.4	49.7	49.1	39.3
College: 1-3 years	100.0	12.7	22.4	15.3	14.1	9.4	17.4	8.7	13.5	15.0	20.0	19.0	19.5	19.8	19.6
4 years	100.0	9.7	20.6	17.4	9.2	13.3	17.8	12.0	5.2	7.0	11.5	6.3	14.0	10.3	13.7
more than 4 years	100.0	10.5	22.7	17.1	10.6	12.3	16.4	10.5	3.8	5.2	7.6	4.8	8.7	6.4	8.0
Male	...	...	...	...	...	...	...	...	100.0	100.0	100.0	100.0	100.0	100.0	100.0
Less than high school	100.0	29.3	25.0	9.4	10.0	4.4	12.5	9.3	30.3	18.2	10.9	12.9	8.0	15.0	21.6
High school	100.0	16.8	26.4	14.9	14.7	9.2	12.9	5.1	46.0	51.0	46.0	50.3	44.1	41.0	31.7
College	100.0	10.7	19.7	17.3	13.3	12.3	17.2	9.4	23.7	30.8	43.1	36.8	47.9	44.0	46.7
Female	...	...	...	...	...	...	...	...	100.0	100.0	100.0	100.0	100.0	100.0	100.0
Less than high school	100.0	24.8	28.0	6.5	12.9	4.1	14.6	9.2	23.5	15.5	8.2	15.8	8.3	14.1	17.8
High school	100.0	15.8	29.4	12.2	13.3	7.4	15.5	6.4	55.1	59.9	57.0	59.8	55.6	55.1	45.0
College	100.0	12.3	24.3	15.0	10.8	9.6	17.4	10.5	21.4	24.6	34.8	24.4	36.1	30.8	37.2

Source: The data for this table were tabulated from a dataset defined by the National Opinion Research Center. General Social Surveys, 1972-83: Cumulative Codebook. Chicago: National Opinion Research Center, University of Chicago, 1983.

Table 19-6B. Educational Attainment and Party Affiliation, by Sex: White Population, Pooled NORC Data, 1972-1983 [percent distribution horizontally and vertically]

Educational attainment and sex	Total	Democrat		Independent			Republican		Democrat		Independent			Republican	
		Strong	Weak	Lean Demo-crat	Fully inde-pendent	Lean Repub-lican	Weak	Strong	Strong	Weak	Lean Demo-crat	Fully inde-pendent	Lean Repub-lican	Weak	Strong
Both sexes	...	...	...	...	...	...	...	...	100.0	100.0	100.0	100.0	100.0	100.0	100.0
Less than high school	100.0	22.9	26.1	8.3	12.4	4.9	15.2	10.3	25.2	15.7	9.1	14.0	8.0	13.8	18.4
High school	100.0	13.5	27.6	13.6	14.2	8.8	15.8	6.4	51.0	57.0	51.7	55.5	49.5	49.1	39.4
College: 1-3 years	100.0	10.5	20.9	15.3	14.4	10.2	19.1	9.7	13.5	14.7	19.7	19.0	19.5	20.1	20.1
4 years	100.0	8.5	19.6	17.1	9.1	14.1	18.9	12.7	5.8	7.3	11.6	6.3	14.2	10.5	13.9
more than 4 years	100.0	9.8	21.5	17.1	10.8	12.8	17.0	11.0	4.5	5.4	7.9	5.1	8.8	6.4	8.2
Male	...	...	...	...	...	...	...	...	100.0	100.0	100.0	100.0	100.0	100.0	100.0
Less than high school	100.0	26.1	23.9	9.9	10.9	5.3	13.9	10.0	29.8	16.5	10.6	12.5	8.1	14.2	20.1
High school	100.0	13.9	26.3	14.8	15.3	10.0	14.1	5.5	45.4	51.9	45.1	50.1	43.7	41.0	31.6
College	100.0	9.0	19.0	17.2	13.5	13.0	18.3	10.0	24.8	31.6	44.3	37.4	48.2	44.8	48.3
Female	...	...	...	...	...	...	...	...	100.0	100.0	100.0	100.0	100.0	100.0	100.0
Less than high school	100.0	20.0	28.1	6.7	13.7	4.5	16.5	10.5	21.3	15.1	7.6	15.4	7.8	13.5	17.1
High school	100.0	13.2	28.4	12.9	13.6	8.0	16.9	7.0	55.9	60.6	58.1	60.4	55.5	55.2	45.2
College	100.0	10.6	22.5	15.0	10.8	10.4	19.0	11.6	22.8	24.3	34.3	24.2	36.7	31.3	37.7

Source: The data for this table were tabulated from a dataset defined by the National Opinion Research Center. General Social Surveys, 1972-83: Cumulative Codebook. Chicago: National Opinion Research Center, University of Chicago, 1983.

Self-Employment

People employed by others tend to identify themselves with the Democratic party, while those who work for themselves (self-employed) are considerably more inclined to identify themselves as Republican. But even among the self-employed group the Democrats very nearly equal Republicans, and strong Democrats are almost as common as strong Republicans:

Party preference	*Self-employed*	*Work for others*
Strong Democrat	14.0	16.7
Weak Democrat	21.6	26.2
Independent–lean Democrat	11.8	13.9
Independent	12.9	12.7
Independent–lean Republican	10.3	8.2
Weak Republican	17.7	15.0
Strong Republican	11.8	7.3

Table 19-6C. Educational Attainment and Party Affiliation, by Sex: Black Population, Pooled NORC Data, 1972-1983 [percent distribution horizontally and vertically]

Educational attainment and sex	Total	Democrat		Independent			Republican		Democrat		Independent			Republican	
		Strong	Weak	Lean Demo-crat	Fully inde-pendent	Lean Repub-lican	Weak	Strong	Strong	Weak	Lean Demo-crat	Fully inde-pendent	Lean Repub-lican	Weak	Strong
Both sexes	...	...	...	...	...	...	...	...	100.0	100.0	100.0	100.0	100.0	100.0	100.0
Less than high school	100.0	46.7	28.2	5.8	7.7	1.4	6.0	4.1	30.5	21.9	13.6	20.6	15.0	34.2	56.7
High school	100.0	37.8	32.9	10.8	10.6	2.6	4.1	1.3	50.7	52.5	52.0	58.7	55.0	47.9	36.7
College: 1-3 years	100.0	33.6	34.4	14.5	10.7	3.1	3.8	0.0	13.8	16.8	21.5	18.1	20.0	13.7	0.0
4 years	100.0	30.7	37.3	21.3	4.0	2.7	2.7	1.3	3.6	5.2	9.0	1.9	5.0	2.7	3.3
more than 4 years	100.0	22.5	47.5	17.5	2.5	5.0	2.5	2.5	1.4	3.6	4.0	0.6	5.0	1.4	3.3
Male	...	...	...	...	...	...	...	...	100.0	100.0	100.0	100.0	100.0	100.0	100.0
Less than high school	100.0	45.9	30.4	6.7	5.7	0.5	6.2	4.6	32.0	30.3	13.5	18.3	6.3	42.9	64.3
High school	100.0	39.7	26.6	15.8	10.7	2.7	3.3	1.2	47.8	45.6	55.2	60.0	56.3	39.3	28.6
College	100.0	35.4	29.7	19.0	8.2	3.8	3.2	0.6	20.2	24.1	31.3	21.7	37.4	17.8	7.1
Female	...	...	...	...	...	...	...	...	100.0	100.0	100.0	100.0	100.0	100.0	100.0
Less than high school	100.0	47.5	26.2	5.0	9.5	2.3	5.9	3.6	29.2	17.1	13.6	22.1	20.8	28.9	50.0
High school	100.0	36.5	36.9	7.5	10.6	2.5	4.6	1.3	52.9	56.5	48.1	57.9	54.2	53.3	43.8
College	100.0	29.2	41.1	14.2	8.7	2.7	3.7	0.5	17.9	26.4	38.3	20.0	25.0	17.8	6.2

Note: ... indicates data not applicable.

Source: The data for this table were tabulated from a dataset defined by the National Opinion Research Center. General Social Surveys, 1972-83: Cumulative Codebook. Chicago: National Opinion Research Center, University of Chicago, 1983.

Table 19-7A. Party Identification of the U.S. Population, by Educational Attainment, Age, and Sex: Pooled NORC Data, 1972-1983 [percent distribution, by educational level]

Sex and age	Democrat			Independent			Republican		
	Less than high school	High school	College	Less than high school	High school	College	Less than high school	High school	College
Both sexes									
18-19 years	2.4	90.5	7.1	4.6	90.8	4.6	2.4	90.5	7.1
20-24 years	1.5	57.6	40.9	3.1	70.7	26.2	1.5	57.6	40.9
25-34 years	3.7	53.4	42.8	5.9	54.6	39.4	3.7	53.4	42.8
35-44 years	10.5	56.8	32.7	10.0	53.8	36.2	10.5	56.8	32.7
45-64 years	23.3	56.5	20.2	23.5	51.8	24.7	23.3	56.5	20.2
65 years and over	49.1	37.3	13.6	42.9	37.1	20.1	49.1	37.3	13.6
Male									
18-19 years	1.2	87.8	11.0	0.0	94.1	5.9	1.2	87.8	11.0
20-24 years	1.5	56.8	41.6	2.3	65.4	32.3	1.5	56.8	41.6
25-34 years	3.8	46.0	50.2	4.9	46.8	48.2	3.8	46.0	50.2
35-44 years	13.0	48.5	38.6	10.3	46.1	43.6	13.0	48.5	38.6
45-64 years	26.7	51.2	22.1	23.5	47.6	28.9	26.7	51.2	22.1
65 years and over	52.0	33.9	14.1	42.4	36.5	21.2	52.0	33.9	14.1
Female									
18-19 years	3.5	93.0	3.5	9.7	87.1	3.2	3.5	93.0	3.5
20-24 years	1.5	58.3	40.2	3.7	75.2	21.1	1.5	58.3	40.2
25-34 years	3.7	58.9	37.4	6.9	62.3	30.8	3.7	58.9	37.4
35-44 years	8.7	63.1	28.2	9.8	61.6	28.7	8.7	63.1	28.2
45-64 years	20.4	61.1	18.5	23.5	55.1	21.4	20.4	61.1	18.5
65 years and over	46.8	39.9	13.3	43.2	37.4	19.4	46.8	39.9	13.3

Source: The data for this table were tabulated from a dataset defined by the National Opinion Research Center. General Social Surveys, 1972-83: Cumulative Codebook. Chicago: National Opinion Research Center, University of Chicago, 1983.

Occupation and Party Identification

Strong political preferences are linked to occupation. Managers and administrators, like self-employed persons, are evenly divided between Republican and Democrat (Table 19-8). Professionals and technical workers, and sales workers also show above-average identification with the Republican party, although a majority of both groups is Democrat. Among operatives, nonfarm laborers, and service workers, political identification is overwhelmingly with the Democratic party, but within each group a significant proportion (15-18 percent) shows a

Table 19-7B. Party Identification of the U.S. Population, by Educational Attainment, Age, and Sex: White Population, Pooled NORC Data, 1972-1983 [percent distribution, by educational level]

Sex and age	Democrat			Independent			Republican		
	Less than high school	High school	College	Less than high school	High school	College	Less than high school	High school	College
Both sexes									
18-19 years. . . .	2.3	91.7	6.0	5.3	91.2	3.5	2.2	93.3	4.4
20-24 years. . . .	1.8	57.4	40.9	2.6	70.9	26.5	1.7	57.2	41.1
25-34 years. . . .	3.3	52.5	44.2	5.8	54.3	39.9	3.2	44.4	52.5
35-44 years. . . .	10.1	57.0	32.9	10.5	54.1	35.5	5.2	48.2	46.6
45-64 years. . . .	20.9	57.9	21.3	22.4	51.8	25.8	12.6	48.7	38.7
65 years and over.	45.2	39.2	15.6	42.2	37.9	19.9	37.7	36.2	26.0
Male									
18-19 years. . . .	1.5	89.2	9.2	0.0	93.5	6.5	4.3	93.5	2.2
20-24 years. . . .	1.9	55.5	42.7	1.6	66.7	31.7	2.0	54.0	44.0
25-34 years. . . .	3.2	44.3	52.6	4.2	46.0	49.8	2.4	38.4	59.2
35-44 years. . . .	12.2	49.2	38.5	11.3	45.3	43.3	5.6	36.6	57.8
45-64 years. . . .	24.4	51.7	23.9	22.8	46.8	30.4	13.4	37.8	48.8
65 years and over.	48.3	35.5	16.2	42.5	37.5	20.0	41.2	32.7	26.1
Female									
18-19 years. . . .	2.9	94.1	2.9	11.5	88.5	0.0	0.0	93.2	6.8
20-24 years. . . .	1.7	59.1	39.3	3.5	74.6	21.8	1.4	60.2	38.4
25-34 years. . . .	3.5	58.7	37.9	7.3	62.7	30.0	3.8	49.3	46.9
35-44 years. . . .	8.5	63.1	28.4	9.6	63.0	27.4	4.8	58.6	36.6
45-64 years. . . .	17.8	63.2	19.0	22.0	56.0	22.0	11.9	57.4	30.6
65 years and over.	42.8	42.2	15.0	42.1	38.1	19.8	35.3	38.7	26.0

Source: The data for this table were tabulated from a dataset defined by the National Opinion Research Center. General Social Surveys, 1972-83: Cumulative Codebook. Chicago: National Opinion Research Center, University of Chicago, 1983.

Table 19-7C. Party Identification of the U.S. Population, by Educational Attainment, Age, and Sex: Black Population, Pooled NORC Data, 1972-1983 [percent distribution, by educational level]

Sex and age	Democrat			Independent			Republican		
	Less than high school	High school	College	Less than high school	High school	College	Less than high school	High school	College
Both sexes									
18-19 years. . . .	3.1	84.4	12.5	0.0	87.5	12.5	0.0	100.0	0.0
20-24 years. . . .	0.7	58.2	41.2	8.7	69.6	21.7	8.7	56.5	34.8
25-34 years. . . .	5.0	59.1	35.9	9.1	65.9	25.0	14.7	70.6	14.7
35-44 years. . . .	12.7	57.0	30.3	8.3	62.5	29.2	25.0	45.0	30.0
45-64 years. . . .	36.0	50.3	13.7	35.1	51.4	13.5	55.6	27.8	16.7
65 years and over.	70.1	26.5	3.4	52.9	29.4	17.6	72.7	18.2	9.1
Male									
18-19 years. . . .	0.0	82.4	17.6	0.0	100.0	0.0	0.0	100.0	0.0
20-24 years. . . .	0.0	61.9	38.1	16.7	33.3	50.0	25.0	50.0	25.0
25-34 years. . . .	7.6	56.1	36.4	14.3	61.9	23.8	0.0	69.2	30.8
35-44 years. . . .	17.1	45.1	37.8	0.0	72.7	27.3	40.0	20.0	40.0
45-64 years. . . .	39.2	48.6	12.2	28.6	64.3	7.1	55.6	22.2	22.2
65 years and over.	71.7	25.0	3.3	50.0	25.0	25.0	88.9	11.1	0.0
Female									
18-19 years. . . .	6.7	86.7	6.7	0.0	80.0	20.0	0.0	100.0	0.0
20-24 years. . . .	1.1	55.6	43.3	5.9	82.4	11.8	0.0	60.0	40.0
25-34 years. . . .	3.4	61.0	35.6	4.3	69.6	26.1	23.8	71.4	4.8
35-44 years. . . .	10.1	64.0	25.9	15.4	53.8	30.8	20.0	53.3	26.7
45-64 years. . . .	33.3	51.6	15.0	39.1	43.5	17.4	55.6	33.3	11.1
65 years and over.	68.8	27.7	3.6	53.8	30.8	15.4	61.5	23.1	15.4

Source: The data for this table were tabulated from a dataset defined by the National Opinion Research Center. General Social Surveys, 1972-83: Cumulative Codebook. Chicago: National Opinion Research Center, University of Chicago, 1983.

preference for the Republican party. Clerical workers, craftsmen, and farm laborers are more Democrat than Republican, but less markedly so than laborers and operatives. Thus, the Republican party commands no absolute majority among any occupation group, but it most nearly approaches equality in the upper economic levels of managers, technicians, and educated white-collar and clerical workers. Among the white upper class white-collars, Republicans outnumber Democrats by a small margin.

One might have expected black workers who have succeeded in reaching upper levels of the occupational scale to absorb the political views of their white counterparts. This appears not to have happened, as Table 19-9 shows. Black managers, officials, and professional and technical workers tend to be only slightly less pro-Democrat than black workers lower in the socioeconomic scale. In short, the black population tends to be Democrat or independent, almost irrespective of its occupation. The chief variation is among weak Democrats, strong Democrats, and independents. Occupational variations in political identification are therefore primarily accounted for by the white population.

Table 19-9 shows how party identification is simultaneously influenced by occupation, age, sex, and race.

Income and Party Affiliation

Being a strong Democrat is associated with having an income of less than $8,000 per year, and being a strong Republican is associated with having an income of more than $25,000 per year (Table 19-10 and Figure 19-2). However, the income-political affiliation correlation is not strong. Instead, the tendency to be an independent is almost equally strong at all income levels, and the tendency to be a weak Democrat also remains constant at almost all levels. In view of popular stereotypes, the substantial support for the Republican party at the very lowest levels of the income scale is surprising. The proportions that report themselves to be Republican is almost the same at the very bottom as at all other income categories below $20,000. The white population and the black population alike show substantial support for the Republican party among the very poorest group (under $10,000 for whites and under $7,000 for blacks). That support sags in the intermediate income groups and reemerges at the income level of $20,000 or above for whites but not for blacks (instead, wealthier blacks tend to be independent).

Thus, the stereotype that the Republican party is the party of the affluent is true only in a relative way. Identification with both parties runs the entire range of the

Table 19-8. Occupation and Party Identification, by Sex and Race: Pooled NORC Data, 1972-1983 [percent distribution horizontally and vertically]

Occupation, race and sex	Total	Democrat		Independent			Republican		Democrat		Independent			Republican	
		Strong	Weak	Lean Democrat	Fully independent	Lean Republican	Weak	Strong	Strong	Weak	Lean Democrat	Fully independent	Lean Republican	Weak	Strong
Occupation total	...	...	...	...	...	...	...	...	100.0	100.0	100.0	100.0	100.0	100.0	100.0
Professional and technical	100.0	10.8	22.5	16.4	12.1	11.4	17.1	9.8	10.0	13.3	18.3	14.5	20.4	17.0	19.3
Managers and administrators	100.0	11.8	21.1	12.8	11.1	11.8	18.2	13.1	6.8	7.8	8.9	8.3	13.3	11.3	16.1
Sales workers	100.0	10.9	22.1	13.8	13.3	10.4	19.3	10.2	3.8	4.9	5.8	6.0	7.0	7.2	7.5
Clerical workers	100.0	13.1	26.8	13.9	12.3	8.9	17.5	7.6	15.9	20.8	20.3	19.3	20.9	22.8	19.5
Craftment	100.0	16.5	26.5	15.9	14.5	8.2	12.8	5.7	12.4	12.8	14.4	14.1	12.0	10.4	9.2
Operatives	100.0	23.7	28.7	11.1	13.1	6.0	12.1	5.2	23.7	18.4	13.4	16.9	11.7	13.0	11.2
Nonfarm laborers	100.0	22.6	26.8	13.4	14.8	6.5	12.2	3.7	5.0	3.8	3.6	4.2	2.8	2.9	1.7
Farm operators	100.0	17.0	20.9	5.1	8.7	7.1	24.9	16.2	1.9	1.5	0.7	1.3	1.6	3.0	3.9
Farm laborers	100.0	20.2	34.0	10.6	5.3	5.3	16.0	8.5	0.8	0.9	0.5	0.3	0.4	0.7	0.8
Service workers	100.0	22.2	27.8	13.1	13.2	5.7	12.2	5.7	19.7	15.8	14.1	15.1	9.8	11.7	10.9
White males	...	...	...	...	...	...	...	...	100.0	100.0	100.0	100.0	100.0	100.0	100.0
White collar, upper	100.0	10.1	19.2	14.1	12.5	13.2	19.5	11.4	29.0	33.9	38.4	37.0	52.0	50.6	57.5
White collar, lower	100.0	14.3	25.9	16.5	14.4	9.2	13.6	6.0	30.9	34.2	33.9	32.1	27.4	26.5	23.0
Blue collar	100.0	19.7	25.8	14.3	14.8	7.4	12.5	5.5	40.1	32.0	27.7	30.9	20.6	22.9	19.5
White females	...	...	...	...	...	...	...	...	100.0	100.0	100.0	100.0	100.0	100.0	100.0
White collar, upper	100.0	10.5	24.1	14.2	10.9	9.5	18.6	12.2	23.4	26.8	31.9	25.9	33.9	31.1	40.8
White collar, lower	100.0	11.7	26.3	13.2	12.3	8.9	19.4	8.3	32.3	36.4	36.7	36.2	39.1	40.2	34.4
Blue collar	100.0	17.3	28.8	12.1	13.9	6.6	14.9	6.4	44.3	36.8	31.3	37.9	26.9	28.7	24.7
Black males	...	...	...	...	...	...	...	...	100.0	100.0	100.0	100.0	100.0	100.0	100.0
White collar, upper	100.0	33.9	29.6	19.1	6.1	3.5	5.2	2.6	14.5	18.0	23.4	12.1	26.7	22.2	21.4
White collar, lower	100.0	39.1	28.8	17.3	10.3	2.6	1.9	0.0	22.7	23.8	28.7	27.6	26.7	11.1	0.0
Blue collar	100.0	42.8	27.8	11.4	8.9	1.8	4.6	2.8	62.8	58.2	47.9	60.3	46.7	66.7	78.6
Black females	...	...	...	...	...	...	...	...	100.0	100.0	100.0	100.0	100.0	100.0	100.0
White collar, upper	100.0	34.2	39.6	11.4	8.7	0.7	4.0	1.3	16.1	20.5	24.3	16.5	6.3	14.6	16.7
White collar, lower	100.0	31.5	37.7	12.3	11.7	3.7	2.5	0.6	16.1	21.2	28.6	24.1	37.5	9.8	8.3
Blue collar	100.0	41.9	32.9	6.4	9.2	1.8	6.1	1.8	67.7	58.3	47.1	59.5	56.3	75.6	75.0

Note: ... indicates data not applicable.

Source: The data for this table were tabulated from a dataset defined by the National Opinion Research Center. General Social Surveys, 1972-83: Cumulative Codebook. Chicago: National Opinion Research Center, University of Chicago, 1983.

income scale, with greater concentration in favor of Democrats at the lower end of the scale and greater concentration in favor of Republicans at the upper income end.

Religion

Although there are systematic and statistically significant differences in party identification according to religion, the size of these differences are, in most cases, comparatively small (Table 19-11 and Figure 19-2). In general, despite the fact that a majority of Protestants tend to be Democrat, a larger proportion of Protestants tend to report themselves as strong Republicans or weak Republicans than any of the other religious groups. Least inclined to have a Republican identification are Jewish respondents, who tend to declare themselves either Democrat or independent. Catholics occupy an intermediate position between Protestants and Jews. Persons with no religion tend to be overwhelmingly independent, with a strong leaning toward the Democratic party.

Among the Protestant denominations, the Lutherans, Presbyterians and Episcopal-Anglican groups tend to be predominantly Republican. The Baptists, because of their large black membership and lower socioeconomic status, tend to be most heavily inclined toward the Democratic party. Methodists and other denominations show a political preference pattern that is almost average for the nation: predominantly Democrat, but with sizable minority support for the Republican party.

Registration and Voting

Party identification, as described above, does not always translate itself into voting behavior. Many persons of voting age do not register to vote, and many of those who register do not go to the polls to vote. The proportions registering and voting tend to change over time. For example, a higher proportion vote during presidential elections than during the biennial interim congressional elections. Only very general statistics on the proportions registering and voting can be created by

Table 19-9. Percent of the U.S. Population Identified with Various Political Positions, by Occupation Type, Age, and Race: Pooled NORC Data, 1972-1983

Political preference and age	Total			White			Black		
	White collar		Blue collar	White collar		Blue collar	White collar		Blue collar
	Upper	Lower		Upper	Lower		Upper	Lower	
Democratic									
18-19 years.	18.7	27.1	54.2	19.1	25.8	55.1	18.8	31.3	50.0
20-24 years.	21.2	38.2	40.6	22.2	39.0	38.8	15.0	35.0	50.0
25-34 years.	33.5	33.7	32.8	35.9	34.3	29.8	21.9	30.3	47.7
35-44 years.	31.6	34.1	34.3	33.4	36.5	30.1	22.5	20.6	56.9
45-64 years.	25.8	31.4	42.8	38.0	34.2	37.8	14.9	16.8	68.3
65 years and over. . . .	26.9	26.7	46.4	29.1	30.1	40.8	15.3	9.5	75.1
Republican									
18-19 years.	16.4	26.0	57.5	16.9	29.2	53.8	14.3	0.0	85.7
20-24 years.	26.2	40.5	33.2	27.5	41.3	31.2	5.6	27.8	66.7
25-34 years.	39.9	36.0	24.1	40.5	36.6	22.9	23.3	20.0	56.7
35-44 years.	47.3	32.9	19.8	48.1	33.2	18.7	11.8	23.5	64.7
45-64 years.	46.0	30.6	23.4	46.7	31.0	22.3	21.9	6.3	71.9
65 years and over. . . .	43.4	25.6	30.9	44.2	26.1	29.7	19.0	4.8	76.2
Independent									
18-19 years.	9.8	31.7	58.5	10.5	31.6	57.9	0.0	33.3	66.7
20-24 years.	17.6	33.5	49.0	18.1	33.2	48.7	11.8	41.2	47.0
25-34 years.	31.6	37.3	31.1	32.5	37.1	30.4	18.6	37.2	44.2
35-44 years.	35.4	32.5	32.2	36.7	33.9	29.3	9.1	22.7	68.2
45-64 years.	32.3	31.5	36.2	34.2	33.2	32.5	12.1	12.1	75.8
65 years and over. . . .	35.8	28.9	35.3	37.2	30.1	32.8	23.5	11.8	64.7

Source: The data for this table were tabulated from a dataset defined by the National Opinion Research Center. General Social Surveys, 1972-83: Cumulative Codebook. Chicago: National Opinion Research Center, University of Chicago, 1983.

Table 19-10. Party Identification, by Income and Race: Pooled NORC Data, 1972-1983 [percent distribution, by party affiliation]

Income and race	Total	Democrat		Independent			Republican		Other[a]
		Strong	Weak	Lean Demo-crat	Fully inde-pendent	Lean Repub-lican	Weak	Strong	
White									
Under $1,000	100.0	14.5	20.6	9.2	16.8	10.7	18.3	7.6	2.3
$1,000-2,999	100.0	18.6	25.1	13.2	16.4	3.8	12.8	8.0	2.0
$3,000-3,999	100.0	22.8	21.7	10.4	14.6	7.0	11.7	10.4	1.5
$4,000-4,999	100.0	17.6	22.6	14.6	14.2	5.5	14.8	9.1	1.6
$5,000-5,999	100.0	18.0	23.7	13.4	12.4	7.5	15.5	8.2	1.3
$6,000-6,999	100.0	15.4	22.5	11.8	16.5	9.0	15.6	7.6	1.7
$7,000-7,999	100.0	12.3	27.7	12.1	14.4	7.4	18.3	7.0	0.8
$8,000-9,999	100.0	17.1	24.3	13.0	14.5	7.1	13.9	8.1	2.1
$10,000-14,999	100.0	13.5	26.3	15.9	12.2	9.8	14.6	6.6	1.2
$15,000-19,999	100.0	10.9	26.2	16.2	12.3	10.5	16.5	6.1	1.2
$20,000-24,999	100.0	10.8	25.0	13.7	13.2	9.9	19.3	7.3	0.8
$25,000 and over	100.0	9.3	23.0	13.0	10.8	11.7	20.1	10.9	1.1
Black									
Under $1,000	100.0	29.8	27.4	17.9	9.5	2.4	8.3	2.4	2.4
$1,000-2,999	100.0	39.4	29.4	8.3	6.1	3.9	5.6	5.0	2.2
$3,000-3,999	100.0	43.5	26.7	8.4	9.9	1.5	7.6	0.8	1.5
$4,000-4,999	100.0	39.6	30.2	10.4	9.4	2.8	4.7	0.9	1.9
$5,000-5,999	100.0	34.7	37.8	12.2	9.2	2.0	2.0	1.0	1.0
$6,000-6,999	100.0	37.8	36.9	8.1	1.8	1.8	6.3	4.5	2.7
$7,000-7,999	100.0	41.7	27.4	11.9	11.9	2.4	2.4	1.2	1.2
$8,000-9,999	100.0	39.5	32.3	11.3	10.5	1.6	3.2	1.6	0.0
$10,000-14,999	100.0	33.9	32.3	16.3	9.2	3.2	2.8	1.2	1.2
$15,000-19,999	100.0	41.3	30.0	12.0	9.3	2.7	3.3	0.7	0.7
$20,000-24,999	100.0	33.3	35.2	11.1	13.9	2.8	0.9	1.9	0.9
$25,000 and over	100.0	32.4	37.1	17.1	8.2	3.5	1.2	0.6	0.0

[a]"Other" indicates those with party identification other than those listed.

Source: The data for this table were tablulated from a dataset defined by the National Opinion Research Center. General Social Surveys, 1972-83: Cumulative Codebook. Chicago: National Opinion Research Center, University of Chicago, 1983.

Table 19-11. Party Identification of the U.S. Population, by Religious Preference: Pooled NORC Data, 1972-1983 [percent distribution, by party affiliation]

Religion and denomination	Total	Democrat		Independent			Republican	
		Strong	Weak	Lean Demo-crat	Fully inde-pendent	Lean Repub-lican	Weak	Strong
Religion								
Protestant	100.0	16.0	24.7	11.1	11.6	8.9	18.3	9.5
Catholic	100.0	18.8	30.0	15.0	13.3	7.0	10.9	5.0
Jewish	100.0	20.3	38.1	18.4	11.0	4.5	5.6	2.0
Other religion	100.0	14.9	19.0	25.6	15.9	9.7	6.7	8.2
No religion.	100.0	10.7	20.3	23.8	23.9	9.8	7.7	3.7
Protestant denomination								
Baptist.	100.0	23.6	29.3	11.1	10.5	6.7	11.8	6.9
Methodist.	100.0	14.2	24.1	10.3	10.0	9.0	21.7	10.7
Episcopalian, Lutheran, and Presbyterian	100.0	10.3	20.3	10.6	10.9	11.0	24.7	12.1
Other Protestant	100.0	14.1	23.4	11.2	14.1	8.9	18.3	10.0

Source: The data for this table were tabulated from a dataset defined by the National Opinion Research Center. General Social Surveys, 1972-83: Cumulative Codebook. Chicago: National Opinion Research Center, University of Chicago, 1983.

using official voting data as numerators and population estimates as denominators; the official counts provide no demographic information about the voting and non-voting population. However, the Current Population Survey asks a series of questions to persons of voting age approximately two weeks after each congressional or presidential election concerning registration and voting (no questions are asked concerning for what party or for whom votes were cast). This survey makes it possible to provide demographic and socioeconomic characteristics for those who reported that they registered to vote in comparison with those who did not, and for those who reported that they voted in comparison with nonvoters. Table 19-12 summarizes some of the results of these surveys.

In the congressional elections of 1982, 40 percent of

Table 19-12. Percent Reported Having Voted, by Region and Race-Ethnicity: November, 1964, to November, 1982 [numbers in thousands; civilian noninstitutional population]

Region, race, and Spanish-origin	Congressional elections					Presidential elections				
	1982	1978	1974	1970	1966	1980	1976	1972	1968	1964
United States										
Total, voting age	165,483	151,646	141,299	120,701	112,800	157,085	146,548	136,203	116,535	110,604
Percent voted	48.5	45.9	44.7	54.6	55.4	59.2	59.2	63.0	67.8	69.3
White	49.9	47.3	46.3	56.0	57.0	60.9	60.9	64.5	69.1	70.7
Black	43.0	37.2	33.8	43.5	41.7	50.5	48.7	52.1	57.6	58.5[a]
Spanish-origin[b]	25.3	23.5	22.9	--	--	29.9	31.8	37.5	--	--
Male	48.7	46.6	46.2	56.8	58.2	59.1	59.6	64.1	69.8	71.9
Female	48.4	45.3	43.4	52.7	53.0	59.4	58.8	62.0	66.0	67.0
18 to 24 years old	24.8	23.5	23.8	30.4[c]	31.1[c]	39.9	42.2	49.6	50.4[c]	50.9[c]
25 to 44 years old	45.4	43.1	42.2	51.9	53.1	58.7	58.7	62.7	66.6	69.0
45 to 64 years old	62.2	58.5	56.9	64.2	64.5	69.3	68.7	70.8	74.9	75.9
65 years and over	59.9	55.9	51.4	57.0	56.1	65.1	62.2	63.5	65.8	66.3
North and West										
Total, voting age	110,126	102,894	96,505	83,515	78,355	106,524	99,403	93,653	81,594	78,174
Percent voted	51.9	48.9	48.8	59.0	60.9	61.0	61.2	66.4	71.0	74.6
White	53.1	50.0	50.0	59.8	61.7	62.4	62.6	67.5	71.8	74.7
Black	48.5	41.3	37.9	51.4	52.1	52.8	52.2	56.7	64.8	72.0[a]
South										
Total, voting age	55,357	48,752	44,794	37,186	34,445	50,561	47,145	42,550	34,941	32,429
Percent voted	41.8	39.6	36.0	44.7	43.0	55.6	54.9	55.4	60.1	56.7
White	42.9	41.1	37.4	46.4	45.1	57.4	57.1	57.0	61.9	59.5
Black	38.3	33.5	30.0	36.8	32.9	48.2	45.7	47.8	51.6	44.0[a]

[a]Black and other races in 1964.

[b]Persons of Spanish-origin may be of any race.

[c]Prior to 1972, includes persons 18 to 20 years old in Georgia and Kentucky, 19 and 20 in Alaska, and 20 years old in Hawaii.

Note: -- indicates data not available.

Source: U.S. Bureau of the Census. "Voting and Registration in the Election of November, 1982." Current Population Reports (Series P-20, nos. 143, 174, 192, 228, 253, 293, 332, 344, 370, and 383). Washington, DC: U.S. Government Printing Office, 1984, Table A.

Table 19-13. Characteristics of the Voting-Age Population Having Registered or Voted: November, 1982 [civilian noninstitutional population]

Characteristic	Percent registered	Percent voted
Total, 18 years and over	64.1	48.5
Race of Spanish-origin		
White	65.6	49.9
Black	59.1	43.0
Spanish-origin[a]	35.3	25.3
Sex		
Male	63.7	48.7
Female	64.4	48.4
Age		
18 to 24 years	42.4	24.8
25 to 44 years	61.5	45.4
45 to 64 years	75.6	62.2
65 years and over	75.2	59.9
Region		
Northeast	62.5	49.8
North Central	71.1	54.7
South	61.7	41.8
West	60.6	50.7
Residence		
Metropolitan	62.6	48.3
In SMSAs of 1 million or more	62.8	48.5
In SMSAs of under 1 million or more	62.3	48.0
Nonmetropolitan	67.2	49.1
Years of school completed		
Elementary		
0 to 8 years	52.3	35.7
High school		
1 to 3 years	53.3	37.7
4 years	62.9	47.1
College		
1 to 3 years	70.0	53.3
4 years or more	79.4	66.5
Labor force status and class of worker		
In civilian labor force	63.9	48.4
Employed	65.5	50.0
Agriculture	63.5	48.1
Nonagricultural industries	65.6	50.1
Private wage and salary workers	61.7	45.7
Government workers	79.8	66.5
Self-employed workers[b]	72.1	57.0
Unemployed	49.8	34.1
Not in labor force	64.3	48.7
Occupation[c]		
White collar workers	72.7	57.8
Blue collar workers	55.8	39.1
Service workers	56.9	41.1
Farm workers	66.7	51.3
Family income[d]		
Under $5,000	47.9	30.5
$5,000 to $9,999	54.5	38.7
$10,000 to $14,999	59.4	43.1
$15,000 to $19,999	62.8	47.5
$20,000 to $24,999	68.2	52.3
$25,000 to $34,999	70.6	55.6
$35,000 and over	76.8	62.0
Income not reported	62.1	49.4
Tenure[e]		
Owner occupied	77.2	62.2
Renter occupied	47.4	31.9

[a]Persons of Spanish-origin may be of any race.

[b]Includes unpaid family workers.

[c]Includes all employed persons in the civilian labor force.

[d]Restricted to members of families.

[e]Restricted to householders.

Source: U.S. Bureau of the Census. "Voting and Registration in the Election of November, 1982." Current Population Reports (Series P-20, no. 383). Washington, DC: U.S. Government Printing Office, 1984, Table B.

the voting-age population (eighteen years and over) cast ballots, according to the official election statistics. Results from the November, 1982, Current Population Survey indicated that 49 percent of the eligible population voted, revealing a tendency for more persons to report that they voted than actually did vote. However, despite this bias, the time series of data for the Census Bureau Current Population Survey tend to follow the same trends in voting rates as computed from voting records. Both sets of data indicate, for example, that since 1976 a higher percentage of eligible voters participate in elections, reversing an earlier downward trend. Table 19-12 provides data on reported voting behavior since 1964, with the years of presidential elections separated from the years of congressional elections only. This table also provides information which shows:

1. *Sex*. A previous tendency for males to participate more than females apparently ended with the presidential election of 1980. In that election and again in 1982 females participated at almost identical or slightly higher rates than men.

2. *Age*. Young persons (those 18-24 years of age) tend to participate less than half as frequently as older adults. Persons 25-44 are much more likely to vote than the youth, but themselves are less politically active than the age group 45-64. This latter age group is more active than any other. The elderly are moderately less likely to vote than those 45 to 64.

3. *Race-ethnicity*. A substantially smaller proportion of the black than of the white population votes. During the years since 1964 the differential has averaged 10 to 12 percentage points, even in years of presidential elections. In 1982 the gap narrowed to 7 percentage points, which showed greater black participation in comparison with whites. The Spanish-origin population has a history of extremely low participation rates, about one-half the national rates.

4. *Regions*. Political participation is higher in the North and West than in the South. This is true not only for the black population, where problems of registration and voting have been long-standing, but also for the white population. In fact the North-South differential in political participation is almost as great in recent elections for the white as for the black population.

Socioeconomic Characteristics of Voters

Table 19-13 reports the proportion of persons who registered to vote and those who voted in 1982, classified according to socioeconomic characteristics.

1. *Education*. There is a direct relationship between amount of education and propensity to vote. Persons who have four years or more years of college are 40 percent more likely to have voted than high school gradu-

ates. High school graduates, in turn, are more than 30 percent more likely to have voted than persons with elementary education or less.

2. *Labor force status*. Those who have a job are more likely to have voted than those who are unemployed. (This undoubtedly is partially a result of race and education.) Those who are government workers or self-employed workers are considerably more likely to have voted than wage and salary workers and nongovernment workers.

3. *Occupation*. White collar workers and farm workers are more likely to have registered and voted than blue collar and service workers.

4. *Family income*. Persons who live in families with incomes in excess of $35,000 per year vote with more than twice the frequency of those with incomes less than $5,000. Between these extremes there is a steady progression in increasing income and percent who voted.

5. *Tenure*. Those who own their homes are twice as likely to have voted as those who rent.

Conclusion

In this chapter it has been possible to examine only the gross differentials in party affiliation and voting behavior. There is a great deal of variation according to race-ethnicity, age, educational attainment, income, religion, tenure, labor force status, occupation, and region. A more thorough demographic analysis would identify the relative independent contribution of each of these variables and the apparent trend in its explanatory effects over time.

Note

1. Angus Campbell, Philip E. Converse, Warren E. Miller, and Donald E. Stokes. *The American Voter*. Chicago: John Wiley and Sons, 1960.

Bibliography

Agger, Robert E. *American Voting Behavior*. (Chapter 17, "Independents and Party Identifiers: Characteristics and Behavior in 1952.") Glencoe, IL: The Free Press, 1959.

Alford, Robert R. *Party and Society: The Anglo-American Democracies*. (Chapter 8, "The United States: The Politics of Diversity.") Chicago: Rand McNally & Co., 1963.

Campbell, Angus, Converse, Philip E., Miller, Warren E., and Stokes, Donald E. *The American Voter*. (Chapter 6, "The Impact of Party Identification.") Chicago: University of Chicago Press, 1960.

Clubb, Jerome H., Flanigan, William, Zingale, and Nancy H. (eds.). *Analyzing Electoral History*. Beverly Hills, CA: Sage Publications, 1981.

de Vries, Walter. *The Ticket-Splitter: A New Force in American Politics*. Grand Rapids, MI: Erdmans, 1972.

Fiorina, Morris P. *Restrospective Voting in American National Elections*. New Haven, CN: Yale University Press, 1981.

Levy, Mark R., and Kramer, Michael S. *The Ethnic Factor: How America's Minorities Decide Elections*. New York: Simon and Schuster, 1973.

Lipset, Seymour M. *Political Man: The Social Basis of Politics*. Baltimore, MD: Johns Hopkins Press, 1981.

Miller, Warren E., Miller, Arthur H., and Schneider, Edward J. *American National Election Studies Data Sourcebook, 1952-1978*. Cambridge, MA: Harvard University Press, 1980.

Nie, Norman H., Verba, Sidney, and Petrocik, John R. *The Changing American Voter*. (Chapter 4, "The Decline of Partisanship.") Cambridge, MA: Harvard University Press, 1976.

Pomper, G.M. *Voter's Choice: Varieties of American Electoral Behavior*. New York: Dodd-Mead, 1975.

Rothenberg, Stuart; Licht, Eric; with Newport, Frank. *Ethnic Voters and National Issues: Coalitions in the 1980s*. (Chapter 2, "Ethnics and Coalitions," and Chapter 7, "The Historical Context.") Washington, DC: Free Congress Research and Education Foundation, 1982.

Scammon, Richard M. *America Votes*. New York: Macmillan, issued biennially by Government Affairs Institute.

Taylor, Peter J. *Geography of Elections*. New York: Holmes & Meier Publishers, 1979.

Chapter 20

Puerto Rico: Demographically a State

Donald J. Bogue and José L. Vázquez

The "outlying areas under the jurisdiction of the United States" had a total population of 3,565,376 in 1980. Of this, 3,196,520 (or 90 percent) consisted of the population of the Commonwealth of Puerto Rico. Under commonwealth status residents of Puerto Rico have the right of unrestricted movement to and from the mainland of the United States. They are exempt from immigration regulations that constitute a demographic barrier to other nations and territories. U.S. citizens may travel freely to Puerto Rico without a visa, may accept extended employment there, or may retire there without being considered outside the United States for Social Security, public assistance, Medicare, or other citizen benefits purposes. The population of Puerto Rico is about the same size as that of South Carolina, which ranks twenty-third among the states in population, which means Puerto Rico is more populous than twenty-seven of the fifty states. The 1980 census counted as permanent residents of the United States 1,003,000 persons who reported they were born in Puerto Rico and 2,014,000 who identified themselves as of Spanish-origin with Puerto Rico as the mother country. Of all living persons born in Puerto Rico, then, one-fourth were living in the United States, and of all persons who called themselves or by residence were identified as Puerto Rican, nearly 40 percent were residing in the United States and only 60 percent in Puerto Rico (assuming zero migration to other places in the world). Because of its comparatively large size and the "openness" of its demographic interaction with the United States, Puerto Rico is the equivalent of a state. One cannot precisely comprehend the growth patterns of the United States without taking into account the growth pattern of Puerto Rico, because the two populations interact so intimately.

Numerous books and essays document how completely the economy and political life of Puerto Rico are entwined with those of the United States, to the extent that statehood is seriously proposed and approved by a large proportion of Puerto Ricans and possibly by nearly a majority of voting Americans. For economic, social, and demographic reasons, those who study the U.S. population should know, at least in broad outline, the demography of Puerto Rico. Such an overview is attempted in this chapter. Since this presentation is confined primarily to the demographic aspects of Puerto Rico, with only a brief résumé of its physical characteristics and economic base as they affect population, the interested reader is encouraged to supplement the materials in this chapter by reading other sources' expositions of Puerto Rico's geography, economy, culture, and history.

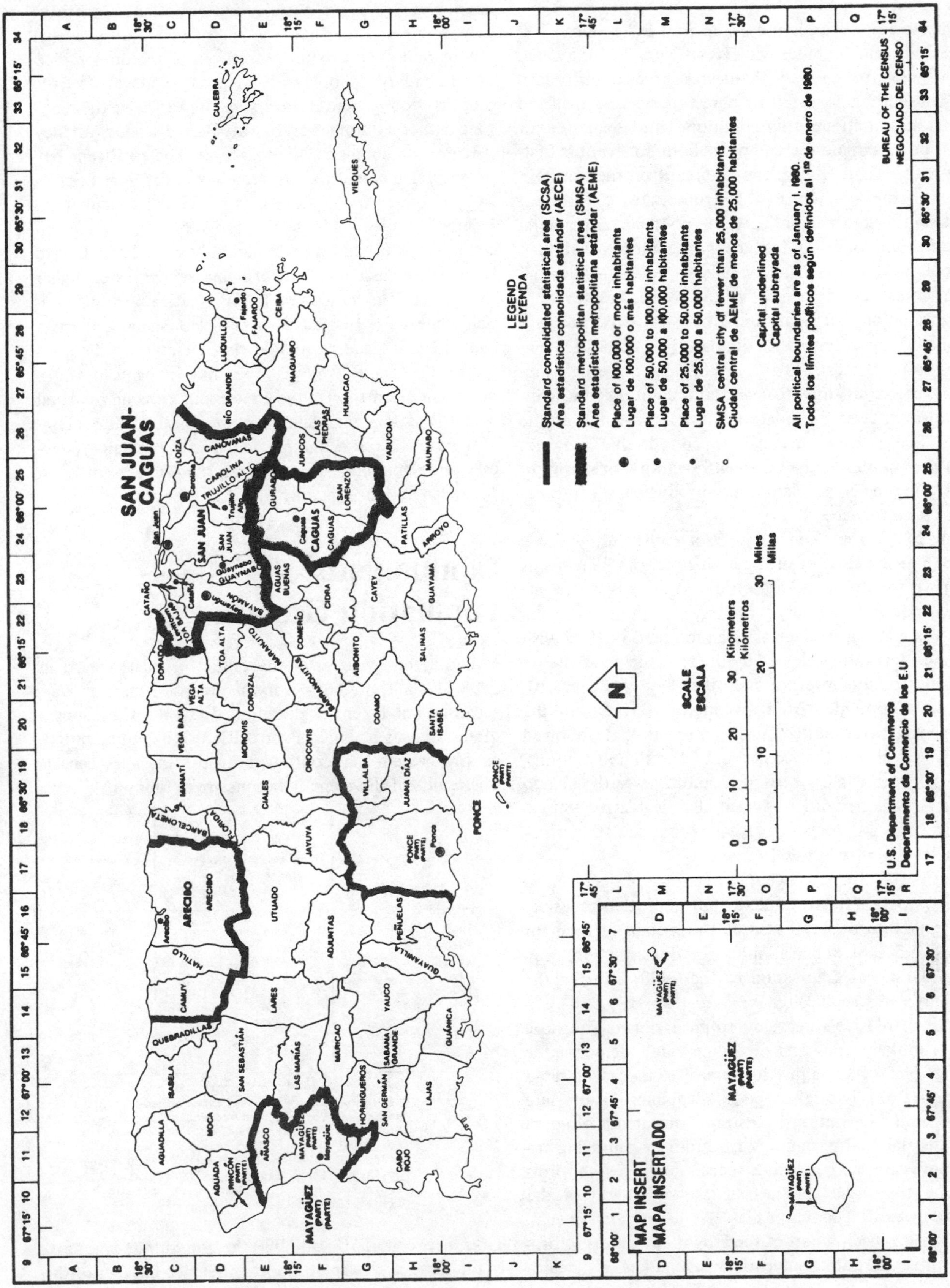

Figure 20-1. Standard Consolidated Statistical Areas, Standard Metropolitan Statistical Areas, Municipios, and Selected Places of Puerto Rico

Brief Description

Puerto Rico is an island in the West Indies about 100 miles long and 35 miles wide (see Figure 20-1), located 1,050 miles from Miami, the nearest point of entry into the United States. At least three-quarters of the land area is mountainous, only about one-third is suitable for any type of agriculture, and only about 5 percent is first-class arable land. Rainfall is abundant on the northern slopes of the mountains (which run east-west) but deficient on the south coast. There are no important mineral deposits and only limited energy resources other than hydroelectric power, already fully exploited. Almost all of the forests of commercial value have been removed.

As a colony of Spain until 1898, Puerto Rico was populated by black slaves, Indians and colonial Spaniards who intermarried to form a Spanish-speaking population, predominantly Roman Catholic in religion, with a culture that is an amalgam of its racial and ethnic roots. Slaves were imported in considerable numbers until the middle of the nineteenth century, primarily to meet the needs of plantations producing sugar cane, coffee, and tobacco.

Puerto Rico was ceded by Spain to the United States in 1898 at the close of the Spanish-American War. It was governed for the next half-century as an "organized but unincorporated territory" (colony). Although citizenship was granted to Puerto Rican residents in 1917 with a limited legislature elected by the residents to advise on local affairs, the governor and other key executive officials were appointed from Washington, D.C. During the rising worldwide anticolonial sentiment that followed World War II and the formation of the United Nations, in 1952 Puerto Rico became a commonwealth (*Estado Libre Asociado*) with power to elect legislative and executive officials to govern itself within the framework of the U.S. Constitution.

Until well into the twentieth century the great mass of the population was illiterate and poor, tied to a sluggish agrarian economy based on production of food for export and subsistence farming for domestic consumption. The Great Depression of the 1930s affected the economy catastrophically.

In Puerto Rico's heavenly tropical climate—but in a most unlikely physical resource and demographic setting—one of the most impressive examples of rapid modernization has taken place. Beginning in the late 1940s with "Operation Bootstrap," an intense program to industrialize the economy (including encouraging private investors and granting special privileges to firms locating there) has induced a rate of growth of the commonwealth economy that has been phenomenal. Tourism has been a part of the growth. Programs to provide universal public education and nationwide health care (including a strong emphasis on family planning) have brought rapid social modernization. English is taught as a second language in all elementary and high school grades, and there is strong emphasis on completing secondary school and attending college. As U.S. citizens, young school-leavers are free to seek their fortune either at home or in the United States, as they perceive the comparative advantages. Puerto Ricans pay no federal income tax and are eligible for Social Security, Medicare, food stamps, public welfare, and other federally funded social selfare programs. The average income per family has risen remarkably since 1950. Puerto Rico today has a standard of living as high as or higher than any of the nations of Latin America, including oil-rich Venezuela. Instead of a two-class society, it has a sizable and expanding middle class (relative to the average for the island), which, despite huge streams of return migration from the United States and growing bilingual communication, maintains a strong local culture. Many of Puerto Rico's economic and social problems, however, have common elements with the problems of Latin American nations, one of which still is poverty.

Components of Population Growth

Within one year after the taking of Puerto Rico in 1898 by the United States in the Spanish-American War, a census was taken. Beginning in 1910 the U.S. Bureau of the Census included Puerto Rico in its enumeration, an arrangement that continued through the 1980 census. The results of these enumerations are as follows:

Year	Population (000)	Rate of growth during interval	Annual average
1899	953.2	--	--
1910	1,118.0	17.3	1.5
1920	1,299.8	16.3	1.6
1930	1,543.0	18.7	1.7
1940	1,869.3	21.1	1.9
1950	2,210.7	18.3	1.7
1960	2,349.5	6.3	0.6
1970	2,712.0	15.4	1.4
1980	3,196.5	17.9	1.6

Source: Vázquez, José. "The Demographic Evolution of Puerto Rico." Ph.D. Dissertation, University of Chicago, Department of Sociology, 1964, page 28, for 1899-1960. U.S. Bureau of the Census. "General Population Characteristics: United States Summary." 1980 Census Population (Area Report 53, "Puerto Rico"). Washington, DC: U.S. Government Printing Office, 1983, page 34.

Thus, between 1970 and 1980 the growth rate was nearly the same as it was during the first two decades of the century, after having risen to a peak in the 1930-40 decade, fallen to a very low growth trough in the 1950-60 decade, and then recovered in the years since 1960. Such a roller-coaster effect can be understood only be examining simultaneously the components of growth.

Birth Rates

The number of births and deaths, with corresponding birth and death rates, from the early 1940s to 1982 are provided in Table 20-1. Puerto Rico's birth rate in the 1940s was that of a more or less typical developing part of Latin America and appeared to be rising, reaching a peak of 43.2 per 1,000 in 1947. Thereafter it began a somewhat irregular but nevertheless fairly steady and swift downward drift, to attain a rate of 22.8 in 1980 (see Figure 20-2). The birth rate nearly reached its 1980 level by 1975 and has remained on this plateau or drifted slightly downward since. Thus, within a short period of twenty-eight years (1947 to 1975), the crude birth rate of Puerto Rico fell by nearly 50 percent.

Table 20-1. Births, Deaths, and Natural Increase in Puerto Rico: Numbers and Rates, 1940-1982

Years	Number of events			Rate per 1,000 population			
	Births	Deaths	Natural increase	Births	Deaths	Reproductive increase	Infant mortality rate
1982. . .	69,336	21,522	47,814	21.2	6.5	14.7	17.2
1981. . .	71,365	21,197	50,168	22.0	6.5	15.5	18.6
1980. . .	73,060	20,530	52,530	22.8	6.4	16.4	19.0
1979. . .	73,781	20,390	53,391	23.4	6.4	17.0	19.9
1978. . .	75,066	19,876	55,190	22.4	5.9	16.5	18.5
1977. . .	75,151	19,895	55,256	22.6	6.0	16.6	20.1
1976. . .	72,883	19,893	52,990	22.6	6.2	16.4	20.2
1975. . .	69,691	19,073	50,618	22.3	6.1	16.2	20.9
1974. . .	70,082	19,490	50,592	23.1	6.4	16.7	23.0
1973. . .	68,821	19,257	49,564	23.3	6.5	16.8	24.2
1972. . .	68,914	19,011	49,903	24.0	6.6	17.4	27.1
1971. . .	71,117	18,144	52,973	25.6	6.5	19.1	27.5
1970. . .	67,438	18,080	49,358	24.8	6.7	18.1	28.6
1969. . .	67,577	17,669	49,908	25.0	6.5	18.5	29.7
1968. . .	69,989	17,481	50,508	25.5	6.6	18.9	29.2
1967. . .	70,735	16,780	53,955	26.9	6.4	20.5	32.8
1966. . .	75,735	17,506	58,229	29.0	6.7	22.3	37.6
1965. . .	79,586	17,719	61,867	30.8	6.9	23.9	43.0
1964. . .	78,837	18,556	60,281	31.0	7.3	23.7	51.7
1963. . .	77,382	17,386	59,996	31.1	7.0	24.0	44.8
1962. . .	76,667	16,575	60,102	31.3	6.8	24.5	41.6
1961. . .	75,563	16,361	59,202	31.5	6.8	24.7	41.3
1960. . .	76,015	15,841	60,174	32.2	6.7	25.5	43.7
1959. . .	74,933	15,870	59,063	32.3	6.8	25.5	48.1
1958. . .	76,128	16,099	60,029	33.1	7.0	26.1	53.7
1957. . .	76,068	16,022	60,046	33.7	7.1	26.6	50.3
1956. . .	78,177	16,607	61,570	34.8	7.4	27.4	55.4
1955. . .	79,221	16,243	62,978	35.2	7.2	28.0	55.1
1954. . .	78,008	16,871	61,137	35.2	7.6	27.6	57.8
1953. . .	77,380	17,966	59,414	35.1	8.2	26.9	63.3
1952. . .	80,200	20,504	59,696	36.0	9.2	26.8	66.6
1951. . .	84,007	22,371	61,636	37.6	10.0	27.6	67.1
1950. . .	85,455	21,917	63,538	38.5	9.9	28.6	68.3
1949. . .	85,638	23,391	62,247	39.2	10.7	28.5	67.6
1948. . .	87,746	26,204	61,542	40.8	12.2	28.6	78.5
1947. . .	91,496	25,411	66,085	43.2	12.0	31.2	71.5
1946. . .	88,723	27,570	61,153	42.6	13.2	29.4	83.8
1945. . .	86,582	28,886	57,696	42.3	14.1	28.2	93.4
1944. . .	82,585	29,843	52,742	41.0	14.8	26.2	99.4
1943. . .	78,393	29,065	49,328	39.6	14.7	24.9	95.3
1942. . .	78,405	32,218	46,187	40.3	16.6	23.7	103.4
1941. . .	76,130	35,551	40,579	39.8	16.6	23.2	116.2
1940. . .	72,388	34,477	37,911	38.5	18.4	20.1	113.4

Source: Department of Health of Puerto Rico. Informe Anual de Estadísticas Vitales. San Juan: Department of Health, 1979 and 1982, Table 1.

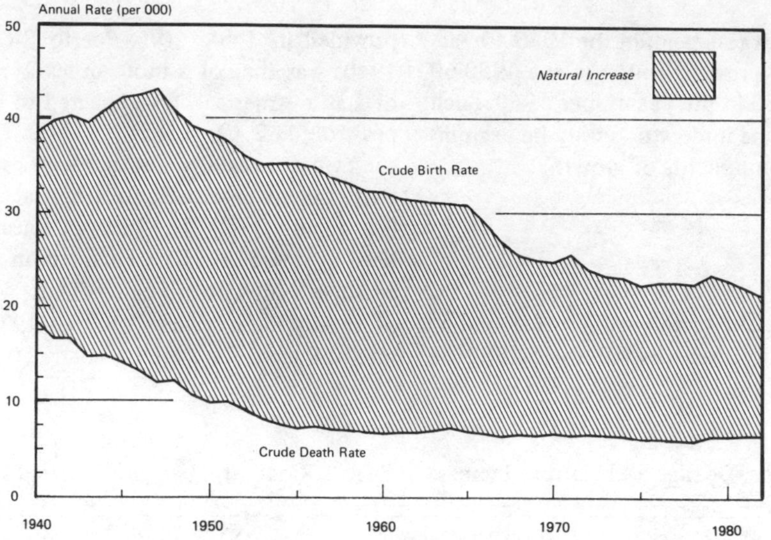

Figure 20-2. Trend in Crude Birth Rate, Crude Death Rate, and Rate of Natural Increase in Puerto Rico: 1940-1982

A more refined measure of fertility, the total fertility rate has changed as follows:

Year	Total fertility rate
1950.	5,312
1955.	4,787
1960.	4,755
1965.	3,614
1970.	3,143
1975.	2,960
1980.	2,772
1981.	2,715

(Age-specific fertility for selected dates are reported in Table 20-2.) Thus the total fertility rate has similarly nearly halved. Within only two decades Puerto Rico moved down the entire fertility scale from the extremely high fertility of an underdeveloped nation all the way to near replacement level. That accomplishment has been matched by very few populations, almost none previously.

The transition from a five-child to a two-plus-child family, very close to the replacement level, took only twenty years in Puerto Rico, thanks to a combination of rapid social and economic development accompanied by intensive government-sponsored special programs of organized family planning information and services.

Death Rates

Meanwhile, Puerto Rico's crude death rate plunged steadily from 18 per 1,000 to 6 per 1,000, or by two-thirds, in the four decades from 1940 to 1980 (see Table 20-1 and Figure 20-2). Rapidly rising levels of living, rising literacy, improved health care, and the use of modern health technology to control malaria and other environmental infections combined to produce this result.

The present very low crude death rate of Puerto Rico is partially a statistical artifact of extremley young age composition and is only an approximate indicator of trends. Expectation of life at birth, a more refined measure of mortality, has been computed as follows:

Year	Both sexes	Males	Females
1902-3.	30.4	29.8	31.0
1909-11	38.2	37.7	38.6
1919-21	38.5	38.2	38.9
1929-31	40.6	40.1	41.5
1939-41	46.0	45.1	47.1
1949-51	60.9	59.4	62.4
1959-61	67.1	67.1	71.9
1969-71	71.9	68.9	75.1
1979-81	74.1	70.5	77.6

Source: Vázquez, José. "The Demographic Evolution of Puerto Rico." Ph.D. Dissertation, University of Chicago, Department of Sociology, 1964, page 245 for 1902-61. Data for 1969-71 and 1979-81 from Vázquez, José. "La Longevidad de los Puertorriqueños." Revista de Salud Pública de Puerto Rico (Vol. 4, 1983).

By 1960 the great difference in life expectancy (fifteen years) between the United States and Puerto Rico at the turn of the century had virtually disappeared, and since then the survival of the Puerto Rican population fully matches that of the United States.

Table 20-2. Age-Specific and Total Fertility Rates for Puerto Rico: 1950-1981

Age	1950	1955	1960	1965	1970	1975	1978	1979	1980	1981
Total fertility rate, 15 to 44 years. . .	5312.0	4787.5	4755.0	3614.5	3143.0	2960.0	2955.5	2867.5	2772.0	2715.0
15-19 years. .	105.1	99.0	101.6	48.6	73.0	77.0	78.3	72.6	70.6	68.8
20-24 years. .	291.6	268.9	287.2	255.3	193.8	186.7	192.4	180.9	177.6	173.7
25-29 years. .	265.3	230.9	243.2	191.9	181.7	177.0	173.9	176.9	169.9	167.9
30-34 years. .	201.8	172.8	157.5	113.3	103.1	94.6	93.7	93.0	88.7	88.6
35-39 years. .	146.7	127.9	110.0	81.8	56.2	43.4	40.3	38.8	37.6	34.4
40-44 years. .	51.9	58.0	51.5	32.0	20.8	13.3	12.5	11.3	10.0	9.6

Source: Department of Health of Puerto Rico. Informe Anual de Estadísticas Vitales. San Juan: Department of Health, 1975 to 1981 and other years cited in table.

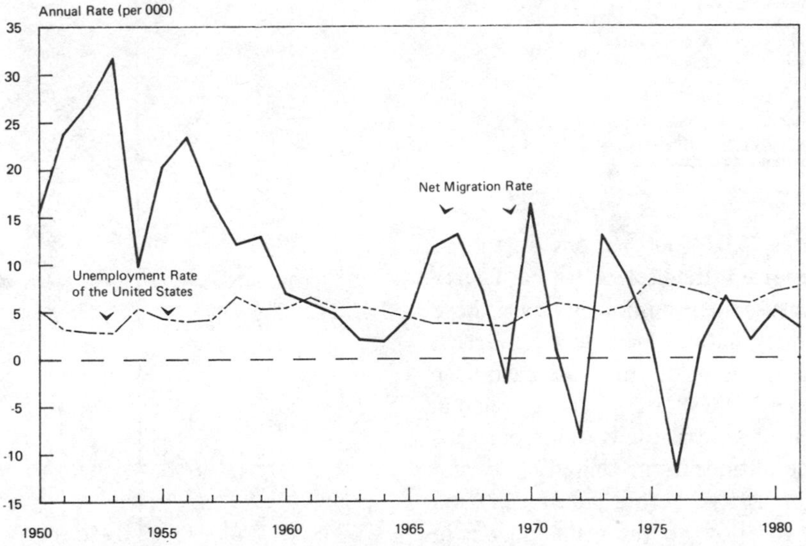

Figure 20-3. Annual Rate of Net Emigration from Puerto Rico and Annual Rate of Unemployment in the United States: 1950-1982

An impressive aspect of this mortality decline in Puerto Rico has been the conquest of infant mortality. The right-hand column of Table 20-1 reports annual rates of infant mortality, charting the fall from 113 infant deaths per 1,000 live births in 1940 to 17.2 in 1982.

Natural Increase

Subtracting deaths from births and death rates from birth rates (Table 20-1 and Figure 20-2) yields estimates of Puerto Rico's population growth through natural increase over the years. At the time of peak fertility in 1947, a total of 66,000 persons were being added to the population annually, for a growth through natural increase of 2.12 percent per year. By 1980, even with a much larger population, this annual increase had declined to 52,500 per year and an annual growth rate of 1.64 percent. Because of the lowered fertility and slow increase in life expectancy, the crude death rate of the island population will certainly begin to rise in future years despite continued improvements in life expectancy. With good prospects for further declines in the birth rate, it is very plausible that the annual rate of natural increase will be in the vicinity of 1.0 percent by the year 2000.

Emigration

Had Puerto Rico provided residence for all of the natural increase since the turn of the century, the population would be far greater than it actually is. However, large numbers moved to the mainland, primarily to New York City, Chicago, and other large metropolitan centers. The number of persons born in Puerto Rico and living in the United States at the respective censuses is as follows:

Year	Number of persons
1940.	69,967[a]
1950.	226,110[b]
1960.	617,056[b]
1970.	810,087[b]
1980.	1,003,000[c]

[a] U.S. Bureau of the Census. "Special Reports: Puerto Ricans in the United States" (Part 3, Chapter D). U.S. Census of Population, 1950. Washington, DC: U.S. Government Printing Office, 1953.

[b] U.S. Bureau of the Census. "Subject Reports: Puerto Ricans in the United States." 1970 Census of Population. Washington, DC: U.S. Government Printing Office, 1973, page xi.

[c] U.S. Bureau of the Census. 1980 Census of Population. Washington, DC: U.S. Government Printing Office, 1983.

Since, as has been noted, 2,014,000 persons residing in the United States reported themselves to be Puerto Rican at the 1980 census, these million emigrants have doubled their numbers by natural increase after arrival.

Estimates of the net number of emigrants have been prepared and are reported in Table 20-3 and graphed in Figure 20-3. There are substantial fluctuations, correlated with employment conditions in the United States and in Puerto Rico. In the 1950s, before industrialization had really developed, the flow to the mainland was in excess of 40,000 annually. In the 1960s, when the economy of the island was strong, migration dropped and is estimated to have even become negative for the single year 1969. The flow of migration reversed itself during the years 1972-76. Because air travel between the mainland and the island is fast, cheap, and uninhibited by passport requirements, there is much return migration and even shuttling back and forth. Many arrive each year to work as seasonal agricultural workers, and many return after having saved money, acquired work skills, decided to marry, or decided to retire—or after having been laid off from a full-time job because of economic conditions.

As a consequence of fluctuating net emigration, the census count in Puerto Rico represents natural increase minus net migration loss. When the volume of emigration is high, the growth rate is small; when emigration is low, growth rates are higher. So volatile and migratory is the population that even the birth rates are affected by fluctuations in the number of men and women of reproductive age who remain on the island.

Table 20-3. Net Emigration from Puerto Rico: 1910-1981 [annual rate per thousand]

Year	Number	Annual rate
1910-1919. . .	5,588	0.5
1920-1929. . .	35,638	2.5
1930-1939. . .	12,645	0.7
1940-1944. . .	15,826	1.6
1945-1949. . .	134,589	12.5
1950-1954. . .	237,390	21.6
1955-1959. . .	193,200	16.8
1960-1964. . .	35,070	2.9
1965-1969. . .	86,655	6.7
1970-1974. . .	84,999	6.1
1975-1979. . .	199	0.0
1950	34,703	15.6
1951	52,900	23.8
1952	59,132	26.9
1953	69,124	31.7
1954	21,531	9.8
1955	45,464	20.3
1956	52,315	23.4
1957	37,704	16.7
1958	27,728	12.1
1959	29,989	12.9
1960	16,298	6.9
1961	13,800	5.8
1962	11,362	4.7
1963	4,798	2.0
1964	4,366	1.8
1965	10,758	4.3
1966	30,089	11.7
1967	34,174	13.1
1968	18,681	7.1
1969	-7,047	-2.6
1970	44,082	16.3
1971	2,525	0.9
1972	-23,648	-8.4
1973	37,069	13.0
1974	24,971	8.6
1975	5,430	1.8
1976	-36,201	-12.1
1977	4,610	1.5
1978	20,282	6.5
1979	6,078	1.9
1980	16,101	5.0
1981	10,460	3.2

Source: José L. Vázquez. "The Demographic Evolution of Puerto Rico." Ph.D. Dissertation, University of Chicago, Department of Sociology, 1964, page 118. Also Junta de Planificación de Puerto Rico, Area de Análisis y Asesoramiento Económico.

Spatial Distribution of the Population

With a gross area of only 3,459 square miles, Puerto Rico has a high and rapidly rising population density:

Year	Population per square mile	
	Puerto Rico	United States
1980.	924.1	64.0
1970.	784.1	57.5
1960.	679.3	50.6
1950.	639.1	60.1
1940.	540.4	50.7

Source: U.S. Bureau of the Census. "Number of Inhabitants: United States Summary." 1980 Census of Population (Area Report 53, "Puerto Rico"). Washington, DC: U.S. Government Printing Office, 1983.

Thus, the population density is about fourteen times the average for the United States and is further intensified by the mountainous and semiarid condition of a large part of the territory.

Urban-Rural Residence

All of the population growth of Puerto Rico for the past half-century has flowed into urban areas. The size of the rural population in 1980 was almost exactly the same as in 1930, whereas the size of the urban population in 1980 was five times that of 1930. The steady trend toward urbanization is shown in Table 20-4. In 1980, 67 percent of the population was urban and 33 percent rural. At the start of the movement toward industrialization (1940) these proportions were reversed: 70 percent of the population was rural and 30 percent urban. Growth rates for the rural population have been practically zero or negative for each of the three decades 1950-80. Hence, all of the natural increase for the entire nation accrued to the cities or emigrated to the mainland United States. This implies very substantial internal migration from rural to urban areas in addition to the emigration to the United States.

About 80 percent of the urban population is located in cities of 50,000 or more inhabitants plus their suburban fringes (Table 20-5). Like cities in the United States, these places have experienced rapid suburban growth, with the result that the population of the urban fringe is equal to that of the central cities, and recent metropolitan growth has been concentrated largely in the fringe. Outside the urbanized areas, which contain the important industrial and commercial enterprises, growth has been slower. It should be kept in mind that the 1970-80 urban growth pattern took place under conditions of low movement to the mainland, and hence some of the urbanward movement could be a substitute for what otherwise would have been emigration.

Metropolitan Population

Five cities in Puerto Rico qualify as standard metropolitan statistical areas by census definitions. They are, in order of size in 1980:

City	Population (000)
San Juan.	1,086
Ponce	253
Caguas.	174
Arecibo	141
Mayaguez.	134

Table 20-4. Urban and Rural Population of Puerto Rico: 1899-1980

Date	Population			Percent urban	Percent change over preceding census		
	Total	Urban	Rural		Total	Urban	Rural
1980 . .	3,196,520	2,134,792	1,061,728	66.8	17.9	35.5	-6.6
1970 . .	2,712,033	1,575,491	1,136,542	58.1	15.4	51.6	-13.3
1960[a] . .	2,349,544	1,039,301	1,310,243	44.2	6.3	61.9	-0.4
1950 . .	2,210,703	894,813	1,315,890	40.5	18.3	26.4	1.0
1940 . .	1,869,255	566,357	1,302,898	30.3	21.1	50.5	16.7
1930 . .	1,543,913	427,221	1,116,692	27.7	18.8	32.6	9.9
1920 . .	1,299,809	283,934	1,015,875	21.8	16.3	58.0	13.7
1910 . .	1,118,012	224,620	893,392	20.1	17.3	16.1	9.7
1899 . .	953,243	138,703	814,540	14.6	--	--	--

[a]Current urban definition.

Note: -- indicates data not available.

Source: U.S. Bureau of the Census. "Number of Inhabitants: United States Summary." 1980 Census of Population (Area Report 53: "Puerto Rico"). Washington, DC: U.S. Government Printing Office, 1983, Table 1.

Table 20-5. Distribution of Population in Puerto Rico: 1980 Sex Ratio and Percent Change 1970-1980

Place of residence 1980	1980					Percent change total population 1970-80
	Both sexes	Male	Female	Percent distribution	Sex ratio	
Total, Puerto Rico	3,196,520	1,556,842	1,639,678	100.0	94.9	17.9
Urban and rural and size of place						
Urban	2,134,792	1,823,599	1,111,193	66.8	92.1	35.5
Inside urbanized areas	1,719,995	823,403	896,592	53.8	91.8	58.7
Central cities	862,671	406,775	455,896	27.0	89.2	21.0
Urban fringe	857,324	416,628	440,696	26.8	94.5	--
Outside urbanized areas	414,797	200,196	214,601	13.0	93.3	-15.6
Places of 10,000 or more	195,775	93,775	102,000	6.1	91.9	-5.8
Places of 2,500 to 10,000	219,022	106,421	112,601	6.9	94.5	-22.8
Rural	1,061,728	533,243	528,485	33.2	100.9	-6.6
Places of 1,000 to 2,500	147,720	73,871	73,849	4.6	100.0	7.7
Other rural	914,008	459,372	454,636	28.6	101.0	-8.5
Rural farm	42,202	21,818	20,384	1.3	107.0	--
Inside and outside SMSAs						
Inside SMSAs	1,787,727	859,562	928,165	55.9	92.6	50.0
Urban	1,558,712	744,248	814,464	48.8	91.4	46.6
Central cities	805,185	379,095	426,090	25.2	89.0	12.9
Not in central cities	753,527	365,153	388,374	23.6	94.0	115.2
Rural	229,015	115,314	113,701	7.1	101.4	78.3
Outside SMSAs	1,408,793	697,280	711,513	44.1	98.0	-7.3
Urban	576,080	279,351	296,729	18.0	94.1	12.5
Rural	832,713	417,929	414,784	26.1	100.8	-17.4
SCSAs						
San Juan-Caguas, P.R.	1,260,337	603,096	657,241	39.4	91.8	--
Urban	1,182,256	563,397	618,859	37.0	91.0	--
Rural	78,081	39,699	38,382	2.4	103.4	--
SMSAs						
Arecibo, P.R.	140,608	68,505	72,103	4.4	95.0	--
Urban	79,619	38,071	41,548	2.5	91.6	--
Rural	60,989	30,434	30,555	1.9	99.6	--
Caguas, P.R.	173,961	84,962	88,999	5.4	95.5	81.9
Urban	137,443	66,295	71,148	4.3	93.2	--
Rural	36,518	18,667	17,851	1.1	104.6	--
Mayaguez, P.R.	133,497	64,907	68,590	4.2	94.6	55.5
Urban	103,627	49,969	53,658	3.3	93.1	--
Rural	29,870	14,938	14,932	0.9	100.0	--
Ponce, P.R.	253,285	123,054	130,231	7.9	94.5	97.5
Urban	193,210	92,811	100,399	6.0	92.4	--
Rural	60,075	30,243	29,832	1.9	101.4	--
San Juan, P.R.	1,086,376	518,134	568,242	34.0	91.2	32.4
Urban	1,044,813	497,102	547,711	32.7	90.8	--
Rural	41,563	21,032	20,531	1.3	102.4	--

Note: -- indicates data not available.

Source: U.S. Bureau of the Census. "General Population Characteristics: United States Summary." 1980 Census of Population (Area Report 53: "Puerto Rico"). Washington, DC: U.S. Government Printing Office, 1983, Table 53. Also "Number of Inhabitants: United States Summary." 1970 Census of Population. Washington, DC: U.S. Government Printing Office, 1973, Tables 17 and 18.

Because San Juan and Caguas are contiguous, together they form a supermetropolitan area (standard consolidated statistical area) of 1.26 million persons, or 40 percent of the national population. Together the five metropolitan areas contain more than half the total population of the nation (56 percent). A substantial amount of rural population is found within the orbit of each SMSA, which reveals that a very substantial share of the rural population is not truly rural but semimetropolitan. Between 1970 and 1980 all of the metropolitan areas grew rapidly, particularly the portion outside central cities (Table 20-5). As a consequence the urban population of nonmetropolitan areas grew only slowly, and a large negative growth took place in rural nonmetropolitan territory.

Demographic Composition of the Population

Trends in the age distribution of the Puerto Rican population reflect both the fertility and migration history of the commonwealth (see Table 20-6). Because birth rates were high, until 1960 more than 40 percent of the population was below fifteen years of age. However, in 1970 the proportion had declined to 36.5 percent and by 1980 had shrunk to 31.6 percent. The number of infants born each year has tended to decline or remain the same, with the result that the age pyramid in 1980 for the first twenty years of life is almost vertical (see Figure 20-4).

Because of the episodes of strong emigration to the United States, in some censuses the age groups 20-39, the prime ages for mobility, show unusually small proportions, while in other censuses they are larger. (In the absence of migration, these age groups tend to maintain a fairly constant proportion of the total population, irrespective of birth and death rates.) The following pattern implies that there was strong outmigration beginning in 1940 that reached major proportions in the 1950-60 period, followed by deceleration in the 1960-70 period.

Year	Percent 20-39 years of age
1980.	29.2
1970.	26.5
1960.	24.1
1950.	27.8
1940.	29.8
1930.	28.3
1920.	29.2
1910.	30.2

The fact that the 1980 proportion is similar to that of the 1910-30 period suggests that migration during the 1970-80 decade was nearly zero or even slightly nega-

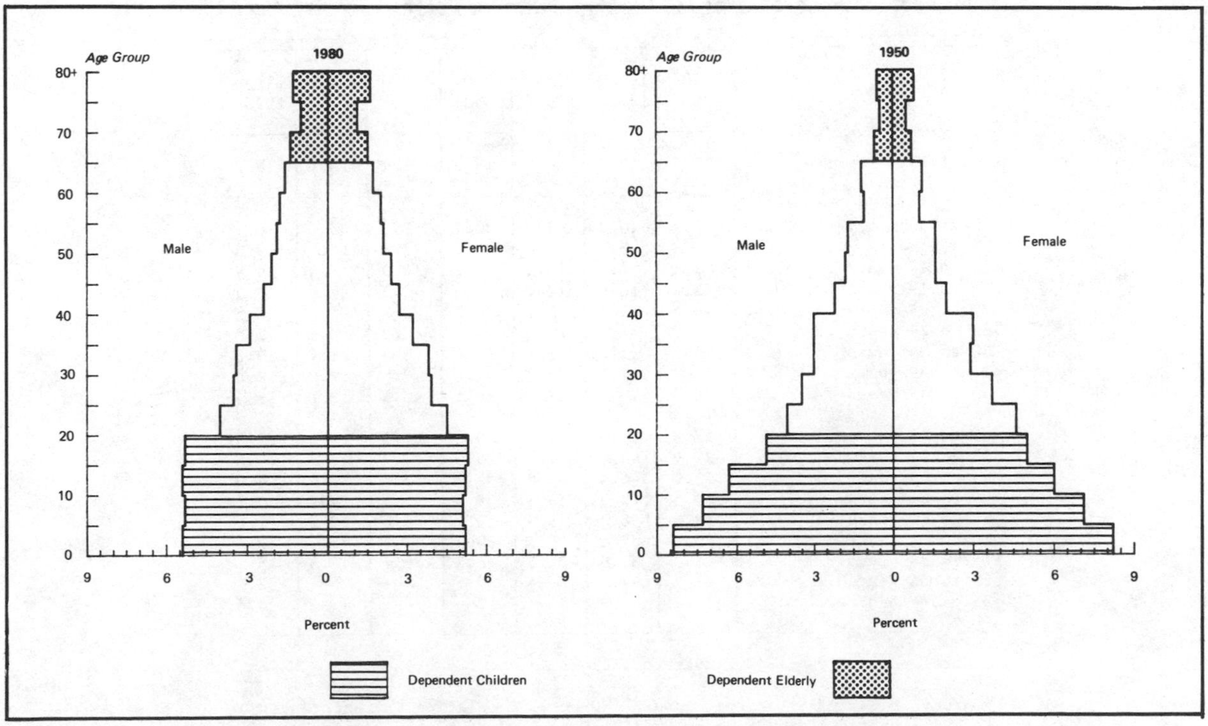

Figure 20-4. Age Pyramids for Puerto Rico: 1980 and 1950

Table 20-6. Age Composition of the Population of Puerto Rico: 1910-1980

Age	1980	1970	1960	1950	1940	1930	1920	1910
Total, both sexes. . .	100.0	100.0	100.0	100.0	100.0	100.0	100.0	100.0
Under 5 years.	10.7	11.7	15.1	16.6	15.0	14.7	15.4	16.6
5 to 9 years	10.3	12.5	13.9	14.4	13.5	14.5	15.0	13.5
10 to 14 years	10.6	12.3	13.7	12.2	12.1	12.9	12.9	12.9
15 to 19 years	10.5	10.7	10.5	10.0	11.0	12.1	9.7	10.2
20 to 24 years	8.5	8.6	7.3	8.7	11.0	9.7	9.9	9.7
25 to 29 years	7.4	6.7	5.8	7.1	7.9	6.5	7.4	8.4
30 to 34 years	7.2	5.8	5.4	6.0	5.5	6.1	6.0	6.3
35 to 39 years	6.1	5.4	5.6	6.0	5.4	6.0	5.9	5.8
40 to 44 years	5.2	4.8	4.6	4.1	4.6	4.7	4.7	4.7
45 to 49 years	4.5	4.5	4.5	3.4	3.7	3.6	3.9	3.3
50 to 54 years	4.1	3.9	3.2	3.2	3.0	3.1	3.2	3.0
55 to 59 years	3.7	3.6	2.8	2.1	1.8	1.7	1.7	1.7
60 to 64 years	3.3	3.0	2.5	2.2	1.9	2.0	1.9	1.7
65 to 69 years	3.0	2.4	2.0	1.5	1.4	0.9	0.8	0.9
70 to 74 years	2.0	1.6	1.3	1.0	0.9	0.8	0.7	0.7
75 to 79 years	1.4	1.0	0.9				0.3	0.3
80 to 84 years	0.8	0.7	0.4	1.4	1.1	0.9	0.3	0.3
85 years and over. . . .	0.7	0.7	0.5				0.2	0.2

Source: U.S. Bureau of the Census. "General Population Characteristics: United States Summary." 1980 Census of Population. Washington, DC: U.S. Government Printing Office, 1983, Table 17.

Table 20-7. Intercensal Percent Change in the Population of Puerto Rico, by Age: 1910-1980

Age	1970–1980	1960–1970	1950–1960	1940–1950	1930–1940	1920–1930	1910–1920
Total, both sexes. . .	17.9	15.4	6.3	18.3	21.1	18.8	16.3
Under 5 years.	7.1	-10.2	-3.3	30.7	23.8	13.1	8.1
5 to 9 years	-2.3	3.3	3.0	26.4	12.3	14.8	29.0
10 to 14 years	1.1	4.2	18.6	19.2	13.9	18.6	16.9
15 to 19 years	15.7	18.0	12.1	6.8	10.7	47.4	10.9
20 to 24 years	16.5	36.2	-11.0	-6.5	38.2	16.2	18.5
25 to 29 years	29.3	34.1	-13.8	6.7	48.3	3.9	2.0
30 to 34 years	46.7	23.6	-3.8	28.4	8.3	21.4	10.8
35 to 39 years	33.9	11.1	-1.8	31.6	9.5	19.8	19.9
40 to 44 years	28.6	20.0	17.7	6.1	18.5	18.1	17.4
45 to 49 years	18.9	15.5	39.4	9.8	23.3	11.3	35.3
50 to 54 years	22.9	40.4	5.6	25.0	20.7	13.4	24.8
55 to 59 years	23.9	46.4	41.6	35.1	32.4	20.5	14.9
60 to 64 years	28.6	40.5	18.3	38.8	16.4	24.7	27.5
65 to 69 years	42.4	38.0	45.9	30.1	79.6	28.7	11.6
70 to 74 years	50.8	37.8	45.7	30.4	41.4	28.0	23.6
75 to 79 years	60.0	33.6	-31.5	46.2	56.2	242.3	15.1
80 to 84 years	21.2	97.6	--	--	--	--	32.7
85 years and over. . . .	21.1	68.3	--	--	--	--	30.6

Note: -- indicates data not available.

Source: U.S. Bureau of the Census. "General Population Characteristics: United States Summary." 1980 Census of Population (Area Report 53: "Puerto Rico"). Washington, DC: U.S. Government Printing Office, 1983, Table 17.

Table 20-8. Age Composition of Urban and Rural Areas of Puerto Rico: 1980 [percent distribution]

Age	Puerto Rico total	Urbanized areas			Other urban		Rural		
		Urban total	Central city	Urban fringe	10,000 and over	2,500-9,999	Rural total	1,000-2,499	Rural farm
Total number of persons. . . .	3,196,520	2,134,792	862,671	857,324	195,775	219,022	1,061,728	147,720	42,202
Total percent distribution . .	100.0	100.0	100.0	100.0	100.0	100.0	100.0	100.0	100.0
Under 5 years.	10.7	10.2	9.5	10.7	10.3	11.3	11.5	11.4	7.8
5 to 9 years	10.4	10.0	9.1	10.5	10.1	10.9	11.2	11.1	9.1
10 to 14 years	10.5	10.1	9.3	10.5	10.8	10.9	11.5	12.1	12.4
15 to 19 years	10.5	10.2	10.0	10.4	10.1	10.4	11.3	11.4	14.1
20 to 24 years	8.5	8.6	8.9	8.3	8.2	8.2	8.5	8.3	8.3
25 to 29 years	7.4	7.4	7.5	7.7	6.8	7.2	7.3	7.1	4.9
30 to 34 years	7.2	7.3	7.0	7.8	7.2	7.2	6.8	6.7	4.6
35 to 39 years	6.1	6.2	5.8	6.7	6.2	6.0	5.8	5.7	4.4
40 to 44 years	5.2	5.4	5.3	5.8	5.0	4.8	4.6	4.7	4.8
45 to 49 years	4.5	4.8	4.9	4.9	4.6	4.2	3.9	3.8	4.7
50 to 54 years	4.0	4.3	4.7	4.2	4.0	3.5	3.4	3.4	4.5
55 to 59 years	3.8	4.0	4.5	3.6	4.0	3.6	3.4	3.6	5.0
60 to 64 years	3.3	3.4	3.9	2.8	3.5	3.3	3.2	3.3	4.5
65 to 69 years	2.9	3.0	3.4	2.4	3.4	3.0	2.9	2.9	4.5
70 to 74 years	2.1	2.1	2.6	1.5	2.5	2.3	2.0	1.9	3.0
75 to 79 years	1.4	1.5	1.8	1.1	1.6	1.5	1.3	1.4	1.6
80 to 84 years	0.8	0.8	1.0	0.6	0.9	0.9	0.7	0.6	1.0
85 years and over.	0.7	0.7	0.8	0.5	0.8	0.8	0.7	0.6	0.8
Median age	24.6	25.7	27.2	24.7	25.4	24.0	22.6	22.3	23.7

Source: U.S. Bureau of the Census. "General Population Characteristics: United States Summary." 1980 Census of Population (Area Report 53: "Puerto Rico"). Washington, DC: U.S. Government Printing Office, 1983, Table 44.

tive, to compensate for earlier deficiencies in the age interval.

Meanwhile, there has been a fairly steady increase in the proportion of the population aged sixty-five and over, primarily because of declining fertility and greater longevity. But the rapidity of the increase suggests that there may also be substantial return migration to Puerto Rico from the United States of persons sixty-five and older, coming home to retire.

Further insight into the growth dynamics of the Puerto Rican population is provided by Table 20-7, which reports the intercensal percentage change in the size of age groups for each decade since 1910. The rapid decline in fertility (plus the emigration of families with young children) caused the growth rates for ages 0-5 and 5-9 to be negative or very low from 1950 to 1960. In the next decade this spread to the first three age groups and by 1980 encompassed all ages under twenty years. However, rapid emigration to the United States of young adults during the 1950-60 decade (as shown by negative rates for ages 20-39) must have been an important factor in that early fertility decline. The more rapid growth rates of these age groups, especially in the 1970-80 decade, imply in still another way that emigration slackened. High rates of growth for ages sixty-five and above are further evidence of return migration for retirement. The fact that these rates were especially high for persons aged 50-64 in the 1960-70 decade of curtailed migration suggests the repatriation of mature workers who were being attracted back to the island by expanding industrial and commercial employment.

Age Composition in Urban and Rural Areas

Table 20-8 reports the age distribution of urban and rural populations of several categories. Unusally low percentages of children under twenty indicate the fertility decline has been greatest in central cities, while the above-average proportion for the rural population suggest that fertility tends to be higher in rural than urban areas. The decimation of the rural farm population is indicated by the extreme shortage of young adults from age twenty to thirty-nine in comparison with national averages, and the surplus of older persons above fifty years of age. So severe has been the loss of young rural farm people that the proportion of children under ten years of age has also been affected. Some persons have hypothesized that much of the emigration to the mainland comprised not urbanites who were prepared by living in San Juan or other major cities to participate in the life of New York, but agricultural workers, who were displaced directly from the land to the mainland, where they competed for unskilled jobs, temporary jobs as farm laborers, and (by some accounts) access to welfare rolls to relieve their miserable plight. The rural population of Puerto Rico today primarily resides in small villages and not on farms.

Sex Composition

Despite its young age composition, the Puerto Rican population has a strong predominance of females in the population (sex ratio of 95 females per 100 males). This results from the tendency for males to outnumber females in the emigration to the United States. Table 20-9, which shows sex ratios for age groups, reveals a drop of nearly ten points between ages 15-19 and 20-24, which mark the onset of migration. At ages forty and above, the sex ratios rise again, marking the return of migrants from the United States. Thus, the sex ratios for the ages 20-39, like the age composition, are indicators of migration. The fact that in 1980 the sex ratios for ages 20-24 and 25-29 are higher than in 1970 betokens reduced emigration during the decade.

It should not be inferred that there was little net movement of women to the mainland, however. Both sexes moved in large numbers; males outnumbered females moderately.

This tendency for sex ratios to drop and then rise again may be observed as early as 1910, for Puerto Rico has a long history of migration to other parts of Latin America, as well as to the mainland United States even before 1940. However, the 1960 census in particular shows the effects of the departure of large numbers of males.

The sex ratios for ages above sixty-five are unusually high for most populations and are not affected by migration. On the basis of differential death rates and greater survival of females, one would expect a greater preponderance of women at these ages. Instead, since 1950 they tend to hover around 100 for the ages 65-74. This suggests that a higher percentage of older men than of older women are returning from the mainland to retire.

Table 20-9. Sex Ratios of the Puerto Rican Population, by Age: 1910-1980

Age	1980	1970	1960	1950	1940	1930	1920	1910
Total	94.9	96.2	98.0	101.0	100.8	99.9	99.4	99.4
Under 5 years	103.5	102.9	102.8	102.2	103.0	101.4	101.6	103.6
5 to 9 years.	103.7	102.3	102.7	102.7	103.2	102.8	103.3	102.6
10 to 14 years.	104.0	103.0	102.1	105.0	101.7	103.5	104.1	106.9
15 to 19 years.	99.8	97.5	98.7	97.8	93.2	89.5	91.1	88.4
20 to 24 years.	90.3	85.9	86.9	89.4	98.7	99.4	93.5	97.2
25 to 29 years.	88.4	86.5	83.5	93.5	95.4	90.9	85.0	94.7
30 to 34 years.	87.8	88.4	86.3	102.2	102.8	97.4	92.8	100.7
35 to 39 years.	88.9	88.6	89.2	101.8	99.8	97.3	99.4	100.9
40 to 44 years.	89.1	91.4	97.8	109.8	103.6	108.0	103.0	102.8
45 to 49 years.	89.1	95.1	103.8	111.3	110.3	115.1	129.5	104.3
50 to 54 years.	89.2	100.9	112.6	105.4	116.3	108.3	110.8	102.3
55 to 59 years.	91.6	103.9	109.3	114.2	122.0	119.7	116.4	96.7
60 to 64 years.	93.3	99.4	100.4	111.0	102.1	105.6	103.0	88.7
65 to 69 years.	94.7	98.3	104.0	99.8	95.1	97.4	97.6	88.5
70 to 74 years.	94.4	101.3	108.2	101.1	92.0	94.0	82.5	74.3
75 to 79 years.	91.4	95.5	93.7				85.6	79.4
80 to 84 years.	85.0	87.1	84.5	78.5	73.2	78.3	73.3	65.0
85 years and over . . .	71.4	69.9	61.6				60.9	59.8

Source: U.S. Bureau of the Census. "General Population Characteristics: United States Summary." 1980 Census of Population (Area Report 53: "Puerto Rico"). Washington, DC: U.S. Government Printing Office, 1983, Table 17.

Place of Birth

The high mobility of the Puerto Rican population is revealed in Table 20-10, which reports places of birth for urban and rural residence groups. More than 6 percent reported being born in the United States; this is a measure of return migration (6.5 percent of 3.2 million is 208,000 American-born Puerto Ricans who returned with parents or for other reasons). High internal mobility is revealed by the fact that less than half of the popu-

Table 20-10. Place of Birth and U.S. Citizenship of the Puerto Rican Population: 1980 [percent distribution]

Place of birth	Puerto Rico total	Urbanized areas					Rural		
		Urban total	Central city	Urban fringe	Other urban		Rural total	1,000-2,499	Rural farm
					10,000 over	2,500-9,999			
Total persons	100.0	100.0	100.0	100.0	100.0	100.0	100.0	100.0	100.0
Born in Puerto Rico	90.1	89.3	88.5	89.1	91.8	90.7	91.9	92.4	94.4
In municipio of residence . .	48.3	43.4	53.5	28.1	56.5	51.6	58.4	57.3	62.4
In a different municipio. . .	41.8	45.9	35.0	61.0	35.3	39.1	33.6	35.1	32.0
Born in United States	6.5	6.7	6.1	7.1	6.4	7.8	6.0	6.3	3.2
Born elsewhere.	2.0	2.9	4.2	2.6	0.9	0.5	0.2	0.2	0.1
Naturalized U.S. citizen. . .	1.0	1.4	2.0	1.3	0.5	0.3	0.1	0.1	0.1
Not citizen of U.S.	1.0	1.5	2.2	1.3	0.4	0.2	0.1	0.1	0.0
Place of birth not reported . .	1.4	1.1	1.2	1.2	0.9	1.0	1.9	1.1	2.3

Source: U.S. Bureau of the Census. "General Social and Economic Characteristics: United States Summary." 1980 Census of Population. (Area Report 53: "Puerto Rico"). Washington, DC: U.S. Government Printing Office, 1983, Table 45.

Table 20-11. Mobility of the Puerto Rican Population: Residence in 1957 [percent distribution]

Residence in 1975	Puerto Rico total	Urbanized areas			Other urban		Rural		
		Urban total	Central city	Urban fringe	10,000 and over	2,500-9,999	Rural total	1,000-2,499	Rural farm
Total, 5 years and over	100.0	100.0	100.0	100.0	100.0	100.0	100.0	100.0	100.0
Same house	68.6	66.9	66.0	68.0	66.2	67.0	72.1	77.2	77.0
Different house.	23.9	25.7	27.1	24.9	26.5	22.9	20.2	15.3	19.6
Same municipio	15.1	15.5	18.5	11.9	17.7	16.1	14.2	11.0	15.8
Different municipio. .	8.8	10.2	8.6	13.0	8.8	6.8	6.0	4.3	3.8
Outside Puerto Rico. . .	5.2	5.0	4.3	5.0	5.2	7.2	5.6	5.5	1.6
United States.	4.8	4.5	3.7	4.6	4.8	7.0	5.5	5.3	1.6
Other places	0.4	0.5	0.6	0.4	0.4	0.2	0.1	0.2	--
Residence not reported .	2.3	2.4	2.6	2.1	2.1	2.9	2.1	2.0	1.8

Note: -- indicates data not sufficient for reliable measurement.

Source: U.S. Bureau of the Census. "General Population Characteristics: United States Summary." 1980 Census of Population (Area Report 53: "Puerto Rico"). Washington, DC: U.S. Government Printing Office, 1983, Table 17.

lation resided in 1980 in *municipio* of birth. This proportion is highest in the urban fringe of urbanized areas and is lowest in rural farm areas. Persons born outside Puerto Rico but residing there in 1980 were much more likely to be found living in the fringes of urbanized areas or in small cities than in central cities or rural farm areas.

Table 20-12A. Marital Status of the Population 15 Years of Age and Over, by Sex: Puerto Rico, 1950-1980 [percent distribution, by marital status]

Marital status and sex	1950	1960	1970	1980
Males				
Single.	38.6	34.6	33.6	31.7
Married[a].	57.0	61.1	61.7	62.7
Widowed	3.6	3.1	2.9	2.5
Divorced.	0.8	1.2	1.8	3.9
Females				
Single.	27.3	25.6	26.8	24.7
Married[a].	59.4	61.4	60.0	58.6
Widowed	11.2	10.3	9.3	9.3
Divorced.	2.1	2.7	3.9	7.2

[a]Includes consensually married and separated.

Source: José L. Vázquez Calzada. La Población de Puerto Rico y Su Trayectoria Histórica (The Population of Puerto Rico and its Historical Trends). San Juan: School of Public Health, 1978, Table 32. U.S. Bureau of the Census. "General Population Characteristics: United States Summary." 1980 Census of Population (Area Report: "Puerto Rico"). Washington, DC: U.S. Government Printing Office, 1983, Table 18.

Place of Residence in 1975

The question concerning place of residence in 1975, analyzed in Chapter 7, was also asked in Puerto Rico (see Table 20-11). The principal finding is that mobility in Puerto Rico is considerably less than in the United States. (Whereas 54 percent of the U.S. population was residing in the same house in 1980 as in 1975, the proportion of Puerto Rico was 60 percent.) Migration (moving across a *municipio* boundary, including residence abroad as well as internal movement) involved only 14.0 percent of the population (as compared with nearly 20 percent of the U.S. population that moved across a county boundary). Of those who were migrants, more than one-third had moved from the United States. The statistics for migration may be summarized as follows:

Migration	Percent of 1980 population	Percent of migration
Total	13.6	100.0
Migrated within Puerto Rico .	8.8	64.7
Migrated from United States .	4.8	35.3

Internal migration was highest in urban fringes (suburbanization). Return migration from the United States was rather evenly spread among all residence groups except the rural farm and central cities, which had proportions below average. Those who returned from the United States tended to settle most in small urban places or in rural villages of less than 2,500 inhabitants.

Table 20-12B. Marital Status of the Population of Puerto Rico, by Sex and Age: 1970 [percent distribution]

Age	Single	Married spouse present	Common law marriage	Separated	Divorced	Widowed
Females						
15-19 years. .	84.4	11.0	1.7	1.1	0.3	0.1
20-24 years. .	45.3	43.6	4.0	2.8	2.0	0.5
25-29 years. .	18.7	67.7	5.3	3.3	3.8	0.8
30-34 years. .	10.2	75.0	5.4	3.6	4.9	1.3
35-39 years. .	7.7	74.6	5.4	4.0	5.9	2.3
40-44 years. .	7.2	72.9	4.7	4.5	6.6	3.8
45-49 years. .	6.5	71.4	4.6	4.3	6.5	6.6
50-54 years. .	6.8	66.7	4.2	4.5	6.0	11.5
55-59 years. .	6.7	61.6	3.6	4.5	5.6	16.9
60-64 years. .	6.9	54.7	3.0	3.9	4.9	25.6
65-69 years. .	7.9	43.5	2.3	3.5	4.5	37.5
70-74 years. .	7.7	33.6	1.4	3.0	3.7	48.6
75 years and over	7.7	23.8	0.9	2.2	2.2	66.4
Males						
15-19 years. .	95.4	3.2	0.6	0.3	0.1	*
20-24 years. .	61.9	32.2	3.3	1.2	0.7	0.1
25-29 years. .	26.6	65.8	5.0	1.7	1.6	0.2
30-34 years. .	14.7	77.1	5.4	1.8	2.1	0.2
35-39 years. .	11.7	79.8	5.4	1.6	2.3	0.5
40-44 years. .	10.1	79.8	5.6	1.9	2.9	1.0
45-49 years. .	9.7	79.7	5.7	2.1	2.8	1.5
50-54 years. .	9.4	78.7	6.1	2.4	2.6	2.6
55-59 years. .	9.8	76.5	5.7	2.7	2.7	4.1
60-64 years. .	9.6	73.1	5.0	3.3	3.2	6.6
65-69 years. .	9.3	69.2	3.6	3.2	3.0	10.6
70-74 years. .	8.5	65.7	2.9	3.3	2.8	15.4
75 years and over	8.0	54.6	2.6	2.8	2.1	26.7

Note: * indicates less than 0.1.

Source: U.S. Bureau of the Census. "Detailed Characteristics of the Population." 1970 Census of Population (Area Report: "Puerto Rico"). Washington, DC: U.S. Government Printing Office, 1973, Table 121.

Table 20-13. Family Type of Puerto Rican Population Living in Families, by Presence of Own Children: 1980 [percent distribution]

Family type and presence of children	Puerto Rico total	Urbanized areas			Other urban		Rural		
		Urban total	Central city	Urban fringe	10,000 and over	2,500-9,999	Rural total	1,000-2,499	Rural farm
Percent distribution.	100.0	100.0	100.0	100.0	100.0	100.0	100.0	100.0	100.0
Married couple families	77.2	75.5	72.4	79.1	74.4	75.0	80.8	78.0	86.1
With own children under 18.	63.8	61.9	56.8	65.7	62.8	65.6	67.7	66.4	58.7
With own children under 6	36.2	34.4	31.1	36.4	35.0	37.9	39.8	37.3	27.2
Female householder, no husband present.	18.9	20.7	23.5	17.6	21.6	20.6	14.9	17.5	7.8
With own children under 18.	51.4	51.4	50.7	53.5	49.0	49.6	51.5	52.2	41.9
With own children under 6	19.3	19.5	20.1	19.3	18.6	17.9	18.7	18.7	17.6
Other families.	3.9	3.8	4.1	3.3	4.0	7.4	4.3	4.5	6.1
Percents									
Percent subfamilies of all families . .	5.7	5.7	5.4	5.7	6.1	6.4	5.7	7.4	7.0
Percent subfamilies mother-child. . . .	47.2	49.3	51.7	47.8	46.5	48.4	42.8	40.1	35.0
Percent persons under 18 living with two parents	74.5	72.2	68.0	75.7	72.8	72.4	78.5	74.2	81.9

Source: U.S. Bureau of the Census. "General Population Characteristics: United States Summary." 1980 Census of Population (Area Report 53: "Puerto Rico"). Washington, DC: U.S. Government Printing Office, 1983, Table 46.

Marital Status

The marital status distribution by age of Puerto Rico's population is very similar to that of the United States (Table 20-12A). Women tend to delay marriage until age twenty or shortly thereafter, and men lag about two years behind. This "modern" pattern has been achieved over the past several decades, as the following data on median age at marriage reveal:

Year	Female	Male
1940.	20.2	24.5
1950.	20.0	23.9
1960.	20.6	23.2
1970.	21.3	23.1
1980.	21.8	23.1

Note: This is the "singulate mean age at marriage," computed from census data (1940 to 1970). Also, for 1980, data computed from marriage statistics.

The proportion of the population divorced or separated is very nearly typical of the white population in the United States but is high by the standards of some Latin American countries. Thus, Puerto Rico has "inherited" some of the family dissolution tendencies linked to Caribbean and North American peoples (see Table 20-12B).

A uniquely Latin American statistical custom is to enumerate separately those couples living together in consensual unions (common law marriages). This is a very common marriage form in much of Latin America, and has characterized rural as well as urban populations for many decades. In general, its occurrence diminishes with rising standards of living, increased urbanization, and later age at marriage. Only about 5 percent of the Puerto Rican population reports itself in this type of union, a considerably lower percentage than found in Venezuela, El Salvador, or other nations of Central America.

Because of dramatic improvements in mortality, widowhood is not nearly so high in Puerto Rico as in most Latin American countries, but is higher than in the United States. This could result from a tendency for widows not to remarry as readily as in the United States and from higher death rates in previous decades.

Family Type

In 1980 the living arrangements of Puerto Rican families were quite similar to those of the U.S. population (Table 20-13). The percentage of families headed by a female householder living alone with no husband in Puerto Rico is almost identical with that of the white population in the United States. Female-headed households are more common in urban than in rural areas and more prevalent in central cities than in urban fringes.

Subfamilies (married children living with parents, etc.) occur in about 6 percent of families, which does not differ greatly from the situation in the United States. The percentage of children living with both parents (75 percent) is much higher than for the black population of the United States, though slightly less than for the white population.

Overall, the picture one obtains of Puerto Rican family life shows stable married-couple families, with a degree of separation or estrangement of couples similar to that existing in the United States. It is quite possible that there is greater family stability in Puerto Rico than in the United States.

School Enrollment

The strong emphasis on education in Puerto Rico for the past several decades is clearly evident in the data of Table 20-14, showing the percentage of persons of each age enrolled in school. These rates compare favorably with those of the United States:

Age	Puerto Rico 1980	United States 1980
5 and 6 years	74.9	95.7
7-13 years.	96.4	99.3
14-15 years	88.9	98.2
16-17 years	76.3	89.0
18-19 years	52.9	46.4
20-21 years	34.2	31.0
22-24 years	16.5	16.3

There is nearly 100 percent attendance in the elementary school years but significantly less attendance in the high school years than in the United States. But the percentage of students persisting beyond high school and even through the college attendance years is higher in Puerto Rico than in the United States. Part of the difference could be students completing secondary school, but it nevertheless indicates high interest in educational achievement. Table 20-14 shows that high enrollment rates are more persistent in urban areas and decline substantially after age thirteen in the rural areas. In rural areas at least 15 percent of the youth do not even enter high school and an additional 15 percent do not complete high school. Yet even with these lower rates, the educational attainment of oncoming generations in Puerto Rico will be quite high, with median education above the high school level.

Table 20-14. School Enrollment of the Puerto Rican Population, by Age: 1980 [percent distribution]

Age	Puerto Rico total	Urbanized areas			Other urban		Rural		
		Urban total	Central city	Urban fringe	10,000 and over	2,500-9,999	Rural total	1,000-2,499	Rural farm
School enrollment rates (percent enrolled in school)									
3 and 4 years. . .	9.6	12.0	14.1	12.1	9.0	7.3	5.4	5.7	3.0
5 and 6 years. . .	74.9	79.8	80.7	80.4	79.4	74.5	65.9	75.1	59.4
7-13 years	96.4	97.1	97.3	97.1	97.3	96.6	95.1	94.8	94.0
14-15 years. . . .	88.9	90.9	91.5	90.9	91.2	89.1	85.3	84.3	81.0
16-17 years. . . .	76.3	79.8	80.5	79.8	80.4	76.7	70.0	70.5	63.9
18-19 years. . . .	52.9	58.3	62.6	55.9	58.6	49.8	42.5	38.5	46.1
20-21 years. . . .	34.2	40.1	47.6	35.7	39.2	26.3	22.2	21.8	25.3
22-24 years. . . .	16.5	20.0	24.3	17.3	18.9	13.2	9.6	7.9	15.3
25-34 years. . . .	6.2	7.6	8.9	6.9	8.0	5.5	3.4	3.1	4.2

Source: U.S. Bureau of the Census. "General Social and Economic Characteristics: United States Summary." 1980 Census of Population (Area Report 53: "Puerto Rico"). Washington, DC: U.S. Government Printing Office, 1983, Table 49.

Educational Attainment of the Adult Population

Because large numbers of persons older than forty in 1980 lacked the educational opportunities younger generations enjoy, a quarter of the population twenty-five and older lack an elementary school education (Table 20-15). However, 40 percent of these adults are high school graduates, and nearly 10 percent have four years or more of college. These proportions of the more educated persons are considerably higher in urban areas, and considerably lower in rural areas, where college graduates are particularly scarce. Table 20-15 provides this information separately for each sex, to show that female attainment is fully equal to that of males right through four years of college. In fact, among the younger generation aged 18-24 years, the educational attainment of women is substantially higher than that of men, as the bottom two panels of Table 20-15 show.

Ability to Speak English

Despite the fact that English is taught in elementary schools, beginning with the first grade, more than one-half of Puerto Ricans (56.8 percent in 1980) report they cannot speak English (Table 20-16). About one-fifth reported themselves as able to speak English easily, and an additional one-fifth stated they could speak it only with difficulty. Ability to speak English easily is considerably higher in central cities and urban fringes of the large cities. It is much weaker in rural areas, where more than 70 percent reported they were unable to speak English.

Literacy in Spanish, however, is almost universal, as the bottom panel of Table 20-16 shows. Persons 10-44 years of age are 93 percent literate, and those 45-64 are 90 percent literate. It is only in the elderly population that high rates of illiteracy are found, particularly among the elderly population residing in rural areas. Illiteracy is very scarce among adults under forty-five years of age who live in urban areas.

Economic Characteristics

Industrial Composition

The size of employment in each of the principal industrial sectors of the Puerto Rican economy is portrayed in Table 20-17, for urban and rural areas. Perhaps surprisingly, in 1980 only 3.4 percent of all employment was in agriculture. On the other hand, 20 percent of the employment came from manufacturing, 18 percent from commerce, 13 percent from public administration, and a whopping 28 percent from services, of which education is a substantial part. Thus, the economy of Puerto Rico is not only "industrial" but "postindustrial" in that professional services employ more persons than manufacturing. According to Table 20-17, the smaller cities and small towns tend to house more manufacturing personnel than do the urbanized areas, which tend to have more emphasis on services, finance, wholesale trade, and transportation. It should be noted that a minority of even the small rural farm population in Puerto Rico is employed in the agricultural sector.

Female Labor Force Participation

Because a high and nearly constant percentage of males between the ages of sixteen and sixty-five who are not in school are in the labor force, very little can be learned by studying labor force participation rates for Puerto Rican males. However, much can be learned from analyzing such data for females (Tables 20-18A and

Table 20-15. Educational Attainment of the Puerto Rican Population: 1980 [percent distribution, by educational attainment]

Educational attainment	Puerto Rico total	Urbanized areas			Other urban		Rural		
		Urban total	Central city	Urban fringe	10,000 and over	2,500–9,999	Rural total	1,000–2,499	Rural farm
Males 25 years old and over	100.0	100.0	100.0	100.0	100.0	100.0	100.0	100.0	100.0
Elementary:									
0 to 4 years	24.6	19.2	17.9	19.0	20.9	24.5	35.5	34.7	47.5
5 and 6 years	11.0	9.1	8.8	9.1	9.8	10.0	14.7	14.1	18.0
7 years	4.1	3.8	3.8	3.9	3.7	4.2	4.8	5.4	5.0
8 years	6.8	6.9	7.1	6.7	7.3	7.1	6.6	7.4	6.0
High school:									
1 to 3 years	13.4	13.5	12.3	14.5	13.7	14.1	13.2	13.8	9.0
4 years	21.5	23.6	22.0	24.8	24.3	24.3	17.1	18.2	9.2
College:									
1 to 3 years	8.7	10.7	11.1	11.0	9.8	8.4	4.6	4.2	2.8
4 years	5.6	7.3	8.8	6.5	5.8	4.9	2.3	1.5	1.7
5 or more years	4.3	5.9	8.2	4.5	4.7	2.5	1.2	0.7	0.8
Females 25 years old and over	100.0	100.0	100.0	100.0	100.0	100.0	100.0	100.0	100.0
Elementary:									
0 to 4 years	26.9	21.9	20.5	21.2	25.1	28.0	39.0	37.9	51.0
5 and 6 years	11.9	10.3	9.7	10.4	11.2	11.9	15.6	15.8	18.5
7 years	3.8	3.6	3.5	3.5	3.9	4.5	4.5	4.7	3.3
8 years	6.3	6.5	6.8	6.2	6.6	6.4	5.6	6.3	4.9
High school:									
1 to 3 years	12.1	12.2	11.5	13.0	12.0	12.3	11.8	12.4	7.1
4 years	20.7	23.1	22.4	24.5	22.5	20.4	15.2	16.2	7.9
College:									
1 to 3 years	9.4	11.4	12.1	11.6	9.7	9.0	4.7	4.0	3.5
4 years	6.4	7.8	9.2	7.0	6.7	5.9	2.9	2.2	2.8
5 or more years	2.5	3.2	4.3	2.6	2.3	1.6	0.7	0.5	1.0
Summary									
Both sexes, 25 years and over	1,577,682	1,088,725	459,808	424,005	99,056	105,856	488,957	67,591	20,334
Percent less than 5 years elementary	25.8	20.7	19.3	20.2	23.2	26.4	37.2	36.3	49.1
Percent high school graduates	39.5	46.4	49.0	46.2	42.8	38.5	24.3	23.8	14.9
Percent with 4 or more years college	9.4	12.0	15.1	10.3	9.7	7.5	3.6	2.5	3.1
Males, 18–24 years	189,319	125,112	52,015	49,432	11,024	12,641	64,207	8,798	2,823
Percent high school graduates	52.4	57.8	61.1	55.3	57.7	54.6	41.9	41.2	40.1
Percent with 4 or more years college	3.3	4.1	5.6	3.2	3.0	2.4	1.7	1.8	4.0
Females 18–24 years	206,120	138,241	58,761	53,915	12,358	13,207	67,879	9,336	2,874
Percent high school graduates	61.8	67.3	69.5	66.8	66.1	60.5	50.7	48.0	47.1
Percent with 4 or more years college	5.8	7.1	8.5	6.4	6.0	4.5	3.2	2.3	3.0

Source: U.S. Bureau of the Census. "General Population Characteristics: United States Summary." 1980 Census of Population (Area Report 53: "Puerto Rico"). Washington, DC: U.S. Government Printing Office, 1983, Table 49.

Table 20-16. Ability to Speak English and Literacy in Puerto Rico, by Age: 1980

Ability, by age	Puerto Rico total	Urbanized areas			Other urban		Rural		
		Urban total	Central city	Urban fringe	10,000 and over	2,500–9,999	Rural total	1,000–2,499	Rural farm
Ability to speak Spanish and English									
Persons 5+ years (percent)	100.0	100.0	100.0	100.0	100.0	100.0	100.0	100.0	100.0
Able to speak Spanish	98.2	98.4	98.5	98.6	98.4	97.0	98.0	98.0	97.5
Speak English easily	18.9	23.2	26.4	22.9	19.7	15.1	10.2	10.1	6.8
Speak English with difficulty	22.5	25.2	26.3	24.6	25.1	22.7	17.2	18.0	16.2
Unable to speak English	56.8	50.0	45.8	51.1	53.6	59.2	70.6	69.9	74.5
Unable to speak Spanish	1.8	1.6	1.5	1.4	1.6	3.0	2.0	2.0	2.5
Speaks English easily	0.4	0.4	0.3	0.3	0.3	1.6	0.2	0.1	*
Speak English with difficulty	0.1	0.1	0.1	0.1	0.1	0.1	0.1	0.2	0.1
Unable to speak English	1.3	1.1	1.1	1.0	1.2	1.3	1.7	1.7	2.4
Ability to read and write									
Percent unable to read and write: total persons 10 years and over	10.3	8.4	7.6	7.9	10.2	12.3	14.1	13.8	17.5
Persons 10–17 years	6.0	5.3	4.6	5.1	6.1	7.6	7.2	7.0	7.8
Persons 18–44 years	7.2	5.8	5.2	5.5	6.5	8.9	10.1	9.5	15.9
Persons 45–64 years	12.8	9.9	8.4	10.1	11.8	14.6	19.9	20.2	22.1
Persons 65 years and over	29.7	24.8	20.6	26.6	29.7	33.4	40.0	40.7	33.5

Note: * indicates less than 0.1.

Source: U.S. Bureau of the Census. "General Social and Economic Characteristics: United States Summary." 1980 Census of Population (Area Report 53: "Puerto Rico"). Washington, DC: U.S. Government Printing Office, 1983, Table 45.

Table 20-17. Industrial Composition of the Employed Population of Puerto Rico: 1980 [percent distribution]

Industry	Puerto Rico total	Urbanized areas			Other urban		Rural		
		Urban total	Central city	Urban fringe	10,000 and over	2,500-9,999	Rural total	1,000-2,499	Rural farm
Employed persons, total	100.0	100.0	100.0	100.0	100.0	100.0	100.0	100.0	100.0
Agriculture	3.4	1.2	0.7	1.1	2.1	3.0	9.6	6.7	38.9
Forestry and fisheries	0.1	0.1	*	0.1	*	0.1	0.1	0.2	*
Mining	0.1	0.1	0.1	0.1	0.1	0.1	0.2	0.2	*
Construction	7.4	6.1	5.1	7.1	6.0	6.8	10.8	11.9	6.4
Manufacturing	19.7	17.6	15.6	17.0	21.2	26.2	25.9	27.7	14.5
Nondurable goods	12.4	10.7	10.0	9.6	13.0	17.0	17.2	18.4	11.7
Food and kindred products	2.7	2.6	2.7	2.1	2.0	4.4	3.2	4.6	1.9
Textile mill and finished textile products	4.5	3.5	3.0	3.2	5.3	5.7	7.3	7.1	5.0
Printing, publishing, and allied industries	0.6	0.7	0.7	0.8	0.4	0.2	0.2	0.3	*
Chemicals and allied products	2.6	2.3	2.2	2.0	2.7	4.1	3.3	3.4	2.9
Durable goods	7.3	6.9	5.6	7.4	8.2	9.2	8.7	9.3	2.8
Furniture, lumber, and wood products	0.6	0.6	0.5	0.7	0.4	0.6	0.6	0.5	0.5
Primary metal industries	0.3	0.3	0.2	0.4	0.2	0.2	0.2	0.4	*
Fabricated metal industries, including ordnance	0.5	0.5	0.4	0.6	0.3	0.4	0.4	0.5	*
Machinery, except electrical	0.7	0.6	0.7	0.5	0.9	0.8	0.8	0.8	0.4
Electrical machinery, equipment, and supplies	2.5	2.3	1.8	2.3	3.6	3.6	3.1	3.5	0.8
Transportation equipment	0.2	0.2	0.2	0.2	0.1	0.1	0.2	0.1	0.2
Transportation, communications, and other public utilities	7.3	7.9	7.3	9.4	6.0	4.7	5.6	6.0	2.8
Railroads	*	*	*	*	*	*	*	*	*
Trucking service and warehousing	0.9	0.9	0.8	1.2	0.6	0.6	0.7	0.7	0.5
Other transportation	2.9	3.1	3.0	3.9	1.8	1.8	2.4	2.7	1.3
Communications	1.2	1.4	1.4	1.9	0.8	0.4	0.5	0.3	0.1
Utilities and sanitary services	2.3	2.3	2.2	2.5	2.8	1.9	2.1	2.3	0.9
Wholesale trade	4.0	4.6	4.8	5.4	2.0	2.2	2.3	2.0	1.4
Retail trade	14.0	14.9	16.1	14.3	14.4	12.7	11.2	10.2	8.9
General merchandise stores	1.5	1.8	2.0	1.9	1.1	1.0	0.6	0.4	0.4
Food, bakery, and dairy stores	3.3	3.3	3.2	3.2	3.8	3.7	3.5	3.2	4.3
Automotive dealers and gasoline stations	1.5	1.5	1.7	1.5	1.2	1.1	1.3	1.0	1.0
Eating and drinking places	2.4	2.5	2.9	2.4	1.9	1.7	1.9	1.4	0.9
Finance, insurance, and real estate	3.8	4.6	5.3	5.0	2.7	2.0	1.3	1.1	1.0
Banking and credit agencies	2.1	2.6	3.0	2.7	1.8	1.3	0.7	0.5	0.6
Insurance, real estate, and other finance	1.7	2.0	2.3	2.3	0.9	0.7	0.6	0.7	0.4
Services	27.7	29.7	31.7	27.4	32.7	28.4	22.0	22.0	18.7
Business services	1.7	2.0	2.2	2.0	1.1	0.9	0.9	1.1	0.2
Repair services	2.0	2.1	2.1	2.3	2.0	1.6	1.7	1.6	0.5
Private households	0.7	0.7	0.9	0.6	0.5	0.5	0.5	0.6	0.5
Other personal services	2.2	2.4	2.3	2.7	2.5	1.6	1.5	1.9	0.4
Entertainment and recreation services	0.7	0.9	1.0	0.9	0.6	0.6	0.4	0.4	0.7
Professional and related services	20.3	21.6	23.1	18.8	25.9	23.2	17.0	16.5	16.4
Hospitals	5.0	5.4	5.9	4.7	6.4	5.3	3.8	4.0	2.9
Health services, except hospitals	1.4	1.7	2.1	1.4	1.5	1.2	0.7	0.9	0.4
Elementary and secondary schools and colleges	10.7	11.0	11.1	9.3	14.8	13.8	10.2	9.3	11.9
Other educational services	0.2	0.2	0.3	0.2	0.3	0.2	0.1	0.1	*
Social services, religious, and membership organizations	1.7	1.7	1.6	1.6	2.1	2.2	1.6	1.9	1.0
Legal, engineering, and other professional services	1.3	1.6	2.1	1.5	0.8	0.5	0.4	0.3	0.1
Public administration	12.6	13.2	13.4	13.1	12.7	13.8	10.9	12.0	7.5

Note: * indicates less than 0.1.

Source: U.S. Bureau of the Census. "General Social and Economic Characteristics." 1980 Census of Population (Area Report 53: "Puerto Rico"). Washington, DC: U.S. Government Printing Office, 1983, Table 52.

18B). Participation rates for women are high (38-40 percent for ages 20-54). As a result, more than one-third of the labor force is female. This is a development very similar to that of the United States. Female employment tends to be quite high in rural as well as urban areas, although it is higher in the latter. Participation rates for youths 16-19 years old tend to be below 20 percent, which is quite low even for a fully developed and industrialized nation. There may be less inclination or opportunity to combine employment part time with school attendance than in the United States.

Occupational Composition of Employed

From the exposition above, it is not surprising to find the occupational composition of workers in Puerto Rico to be heavily concentrated in managerial, technical, and operative posts (see Table 20-19). Only 8 percent of the workforce is classified "laborer." Less than 1 percent is in private household occupations. This "postindustrial" picture is more dominant in the large urban areas and their suburbs but tends to be characteristic of all urban areas; even the rural areas have comparatively small portions of what one might call "subsistence" or "submarginal" occupations.

Table 20-20 reports what proportion of the persons in each occupational group are female. This shows the occupations in which women hold a numerical advantage over men and the occupations that they tend not to enter or from which they are excluded. The total statistic at the head of each column of the table is the reference number for comparison. In general, the division is fairly conventional.

Unemployment

Despite its rapid economic growth and declining birth rate, Puerto Rico has had great difficulty in providing employment to all who enter the labor force. Double-digit unemployment rates were a chronic condition, even before the recession of the 1980s. Table 20-21 reports age-specific unemployment rates for 1980, by sex. More than a quarter of workers 20-24 years old were unemployed. The rates for females tend to be higher than for males. They are high for the population older than sixty-five. They are also higher in rural than in urban areas, and higher in the smaller urban places than in the urbanized areas. The pressure of unemployment is the motivating force behind the emigration to the mainland.

Puerto Rico's fertility declines of the past twenty years are just now beginning to affect the growth of the labor force. In future years fewer youths will be leaving school and seeking work because of smaller birth cohorts 15-20 years earlier. This should ease the pressure for 3 percent per year expansion, which has been required in the past. The indirect effect of the fertility decline could well be greater ability of the economy to absorb its own natural increase, with lessened emigration to the mainland.

Table 20-18A. Labor Force Participation Rates, by Age and Sex in Puerto Rico: 1950-1980

Age	1950	1960	1970	1980
Males				
14-19 years[a]. . . .	45.2	29.1	34.3	24.0
20-24 years	89.3	81.4	78.2	69.5
25-34 years	89.0	91.5	91.7	86.8
35-44 years	96.1	93.0	90.3	85.2
45-54 years	95.3	91.1	85.7	75.8
55-64 years	87.0	84.1	73.8	50.6
65 years and over .	57.7	37.5	28.6	15.1
Females				
14-19 years[a]. . . .	24.9	9.8	14.1	9.9
20-24 years	39.1	35.2	41.3	36.1
25-34 years	37.3	32.3	40.5	45.5
35-44 years	36.9	28.1	37.8	39.8
45-54 years	26.2	21.6	26.7	30.0
55-64 years	15.4	14.2	16.1	13.4
65 years and over .	6.3	4.2	4.1	2.4

[a]For 1970 and 1980 population 16-19 years of age.

Source: José L. Vázquez Calzada. La Población de Puerto Rico y Su Trayectoria Histórica. University of Puerto Rico, School of Public Health, 1978, Table 65. Department of Work of Puerto Rico. Serie Estadísticas Sobre el Estado de Empleo: 1970-1982. San Juan: Department of Work of Puerto Rico, 1983, Tables VIII and IX.

Income Distribution

Despite the modernity of the industrial composition, the occupational composition, and the high participation of women, incomes in Puerto Rico are far lower than in the United States (Table 20-22). The median income of households for the entire island was only $5,348 and for families $5,923 in 1980. For the mainland United States median family income was $20,745, or 3.5 times as great. One household in eight received less than $1,000 in 1979, and a quarter of all households received incomes of less than $2,500. One of the "secrets" of the economic growth of the Puerto Rican economy has been the low wage bill that employers are required to pay,

Table 20-18B. Labor Force Characteristics of Puerto Rico: 1980

Characteristics	Puerto Rico total	Urbanized areas			Other urban		Rural		
		Urban total	Central city	Urban fringe	10,000 and over	2,500-9,999	Rural total	1,000-2,499	Rural farm
Total civilian labor force (number). . . .	865,719	626,252	260,535	257,184	52,297	56,236	239,467	33,749	9,073
Male.	544,239	382,418	155,399	161,259	31,656	34,104	161,821	22,603	6,444
Female.	321,480	243,834	105,136	95,925	20,641	22,132	77,646	11,146	2,629
Percent female. .	37.1	38.9	40.4	37.3	39.5	39.4	32.4	33.0	29.0
Participation rates									
Males:									
16-19 years . . .	19.0	19.8	20.2	21.3	14.4	17.4	17.4	16.1	21.7
20-24 years . . .	58.5	58.0	54.6	62.2	55.3	58.3	59.6	61.1	58.2
25-54 years . . .	74.0	77.1	77.4	78.5	73.9	72.2	67.5	68.8	62.1
55-64 years . . .	44.9	49.5	52.2	49.9	43.3	40.3	35.2	39.6	40.5
65+ years	12.4	13.9	14.7	13.4	12.6	13.7	9.8	10.4	17.4
Females:									
16-19 years . . .	12.9	13.9	14.6	14.8	9.9	11.4	11.0	8.7	11.2
20-24 years . . .	37.5	39.1	38.7	40.5	35.4	38.2	34.2	31.7	39.7
25-54 years . . .	39.6	43.4	45.2	41.7	43.2	42.4	30.8	33.2	24.7
55-64 years . . .	13.9	16.4	18.4	14.7	14.8	14.8	7.8	39.9	7.1
65+ years	2.8	3.2	3.4	3.2	2.5	2.9	1.9	2.1	1.3

Source: U.S. Bureau of the Census. "General Population Characteristics: United States Summary." 1980 Census of Population (Area Report 53: "Puerto Rico"). Washington, DC: U.S. Government Printing Office, 1983, Table 50.

Table 20-19. Occupation of Employed Persons in Puerto Rico: 1980

Occupation	Puerto Rico total	Urbanized areas			Other urban		Rural		
		Urban total	Central city	Urban fringe	10,000 and over	2,500-9,999	Rural total	1,000-2,499	Rural farm
Percent total	100.0	100.0	100.0	100.0	100.0	100.0	100.0	100.0	100.0
Managerial and professional specialty occupations	20.3	23.3	26.7	20.9	23.2	19.1	11.8	9.0	10.9
Executive, administrative and managerial occupations	8.4	10.0	11.5	9.8	8.0	5.7	3.8	3.0	3.0
Officials and administrators, public administration	0.6	0.7	0.8	0.7	0.6	0.6	0.4	0.3	0.2
Management related occupations	3.1	3.8	4.3	3.8	2.7	1.9	1.3	1.0	1.1
Professional specialty occupations	11.9	13.3	15.1	11.1	15.1	13.4	8.1	6.0	8.0
Engineers and natural scientists	1.0	1.2	1.4	1.1	0.8	0.8	0.5	0.4	0.3
Engineers	0.6	0.7	0.9	0.7	0.5	0.4	0.3	0.2	0.2
Health diagnosing occupations	0.8	1.0	1.4	0.6	1.0	0.3	0.2	0.1	*
Health assessment and treating occupations	1.3	1.6	1.9	1.2	1.4	1.7	0.7	0.6	0.2
Teachers, librarians and counselors	6.2	6.6	6.8	5.5	9.3	8.6	5.1	3.9	6.1
Teachers, elementary and secondary schools	4.9	5.1	4.6	4.4	7.8	7.8	4.6	3.6	5.7
Technical, sales and administrative support occupations	27.2	30.6	32.6	31.2	25.4	22.6	17.6	16.6	13.4
Health technologists and technicians	0.7	0.8	0.9	0.7	0.9	0.7	0.5	0.4	0.8
Technologists and technicians, except health	1.3	1.5	1.6	1.5	1.4	1.1	0.9	0.9	0.6
Sales occupations	10.1	11.1	12.0	10.8	10.2	8.5	7.3	6.9	6.3
Supervisors and proprietors, sales occupations	2.1	2.3	2.3	2.1	2.7	2.3	1.7	1.5	2.3
Sales representatives, commodities and finance	2.3	2.7	3.1	2.9	1.6	0.9	1.0	1.0	0.5
Other sales occupations	5.7	6.1	6.6	5.8	5.9	5.3	4.6	4.4	3.5
Cashiers	2.0	2.1	2.2	2.0	2.2	1.7	1.7	1.7	1.8
Administrative support occupations, including clerical	15.0	17.2	18.2	18.1	12.9	12.3	8.9	8.5	5.8
Computer equipment operators	0.3	0.3	0.3	0.4	0.1	0.2	0.1	0.1	0.2
Secretaries, stenographers and typists	5.9	6.8	7.4	6.9	5.0	5.1	3.3	2.7	2.1
Financial records processing occupations	1.1	1.3	1.5	1.4	0.8	0.7	0.5	0.6	0.6
Mail and message distributing occupations	0.6	0.7	0.7	0.9	0.5	0.5	0.4	0.4	0.2
Service occupations	14.6	14.2	13.8	13.7	16.0	16.6	15.7	17.6	11.1
Private household occupations	0.5	0.6	0.8	0.5	0.4	0.4	0.4	0.4	0.4
Protective service occupations	3.2	3.1	2.6	3.1	3.7	4.3	3.5	3.7	2.0
Police and firefighters	1.3	1.2	0.9	1.2	1.8	1.8	1.5	1.5	1.1
Service occupations, except protective and household	10.8	10.5	10.4	10.0	12.0	11.9	11.8	13.5	8.7
Food service occupations	3.7	3.5	3.4	3.4	4.5	4.0	4.3	4.4	3.3
Cleaning and building service occupations	4.3	4.0	3.9	3.8	4.4	4.8	5.1	6.0	3.3
Farming, forestry and fishing occupations	3.5	1.3	0.8	1.4	2.1	3.0	9.5	6.2	38.1
Farm operators and managers	0.6	0.2	0.1	0.2	0.4	0.4	1.7	0.4	20.9
Farm workers and related occupations	2.8	1.1	0.6	1.1	1.6	2.5	7.6	5.5	17.2
Precision production, craft and repair occupations	12.5	11.9	10.8	12.9	12.3	12.5	14.3	15.9	6.8
Mechanics and repairers	4.2	4.4	3.9	5.0	4.0	3.9	3.9	4.3	1.5
Construction trades	4.7	4.0	3.4	4.4	4.2	4.6	6.8	8.0	3.5
Precision production occupations	3.6	3.6	3.5	3.5	4.1	4.0	3.5	3.7	1.7
Operators, fabricators and laborers	22.0	18.7	15.3	20.0	21.0	26.2	31.2	34.7	19.7
Machine operators and teachers, except precision	8.6	7.0	5.5	7.1	9.4	11.3	13.2	14.4	8.8
Fabricators, assemblers, inspectors and samplers	2.1	2.0	1.6	2.0	2.5	3.1	2.7	2.9	2.0
Transportation occupations	4.4	3.9	3.2	4.8	3.4	4.0	5.5	6.2	3.1
Motor vehicle operators	4.3	3.8	3.1	4.7	3.3	3.9	5.5	6.1	3.1
Material moving equipment operators	0.8	0.7	0.5	0.7	0.6	1.0	1.0	1.1	0.5
Handlers, equipment cleaners, helpers and laborers	6.1	5.1	4.5	5.4	5.2	6.8	8.7	10.1	5.4
Construction laborers	1.5	1.0	0.7	1.2	1.5	1.5	2.7	3.1	2.1
Freight, stock and material handlers	1.1	1.1	1.1	1.1	0.8	1.2	1.0	1.2	0.5

Note: * indicates less than 0.1.

Source: U.S. Bureau of the Census. "General Social and Economic Characteristics." 1980 Census of Population (Area Report 53: "Puerto Rico"). Washington, DC: U.S. Government Printing Office, 1983, Table 51.

which reflected in the income statistics. Because prices of commodities in Puerto Rico tend to be comparable to those on the mainland (durable goods are more expensive), it can only be presumed that the standard of living is much more modest.

When the U.S. standards of poverty are applied to the families, the results reported in Table 20-23 are obtained. Considerably more than one-half (58 percent) of the families are below the poverty line by this standard. Nearly two-thirds of persons (62 percent) are below the poverty level. The proportions are much higher in rural areas and small cities and are lowest in central cities and urban fringes of urbanized areas. This is absolute deprivation, applying the U.S. standards of living to the incomes of Puerto Ricans. What this means in terms of relative deprivation is difficult to say. Nevertheless, it must be concluded that despite the fantastic economic growth of the past thirty years, a very large share of Puerto Rican families and individuals still live in absolute poverty, however defined. Unlike the situation in the United States it does not appear to be unusually concentrated among families with female householders, no husband present, or among people receiving public assistance or Social Security. It does tend to be concentrated in households with larger families; dividing a small income among several people automatically defines a family as poor.

Table 20-20. Percent Female of Employed Population of Puerto Rico, by Occupation: 1980

Occupation	Puerto Rico total	Urbanized areas			Other urban		Rural		
		Urban total	Central city	Urban fringe	10,000 and over	2,500–9,999	Rural total	1,000–2,499	Rural farm
Percent female, total	36.6	38.4	40.0	36.5	39.2	39.1	31.4	31.8	27.8
Managerial and professional specialty occupations	44.5	44.0	43.1	43.1	47.3	51.2	47.4	52.3	56.4
Executive, administrative and managerial occupations	26.2	26.7	27.9	26.3	23.6	22.4	22.6	23.4	24.2
Officials and administrators, public administration	31.1	32.1	36.0	31.8	18.0	21.4	25.7	19.8	*
Management-related occupations	29.0	29.7	31.7	29.8	19.6	20.7	23.6	19.9	22.9
Professional specialty occupations	57.5	57.1	54.7	58.0	59.8	63.6	59.1	66.5	68.5
Engineers and natural scientists	13.3	13.7	12.9	13.3	18.2	18.8	10.4	24.5	*
Engineers	6.3	5.8	3.8	7.2	8.5	12.3	10.6	39.6	*
Health diagnosing occupations	18.1	18.5	19.9	17.2	11.8	20.0	11.9	16.2	100.0
Health assessment and treating occupations	82.8	83.1	82.1	86.8	73.3	82.8	81.2	100.0	100.0
Teachers, librarians, and counselors	71.6	72.8	71.7	76.1	70.7	68.8	67.5	71.4	76.3
Teachers, elementary and secondary schools	75.4	77.4	78.6	79.4	75.3	70.9	69.3	73.0	76.8
Technical, sales, and administrative support occupations	49.6	51.3	52.7	50.6	48.0	49.9	41.4	40.8	42.4
Health technologists and technicians	73.8	73.2	74.3	69.2	85.0	72.2	76.9	71.6	86.0
Technologists and technicians, except health	24.5	24.4	27.7	21.3	23.0	23.8	25.2	28.0	27.9
Sales occupations	27.7	29.6	31.3	28.3	29.4	27.1	19.3	22.4	20.4
Supervisors and proprietors, sales occupations	14.6	16.3	17.5	13.8	20.2	16.7	8.3	12.3	11.8
Sales representatives, commodities and finance	15.3	16.3	18.5	14.4	15.0	11.7	7.9	10.5	*
Other sales occupations	37.4	40.5	42.2	40.4	37.5	34.4	25.9	28.4	28.8
Cashiers	49.5	54.4	56.5	54.9	49.4	43.4	33.0	35.9	27.1
Administrative support occupations, including clerical	65.4	66.5	67.7	65.8	63.0	66.7	59.5	55.8	61.9
Computer equipment operators	48.8	49.8	50.0	47.6	47.4	73.2	37.7	*	100.0
Secretaries, stenographers, and typists	96.7	97.0	96.6	97.4	95.3	99.2	94.7	97.4	84.1
Financial records processing occupations	48.6	49.8	51.9	48.8	38.1	50.0	40.5	40.1	40.4
Mail and message distributing occupations	7.0	6.7	4.2	7.8	10.2	11.1	8.2	9.4	*
Service occupations	40.7	41.2	42.3	39.6	41.8	42.6	39.3	40.8	55.3
Private household occupations	94.5	94.7	95.0	93.4	97.7	97.1	93.7	100.0	73.3
Protective service occupations	3.9	4.5	4.0	5.9	3.3	2.0	2.6	1.7	4.8
Police and firefighters	3.8	4.9	4.5	6.4	3.1	2.4	1.7	*	*
Service occupations, except protective and household	48.7	48.9	48.1	47.3	51.9	55.4	48.3	49.7	65.9
Food service occupations	59.4	55.4	52.0	51.8	65.8	72.8	68.7	69.3	93.0
Cleaning and building service occupations	24.8	26.8	27.0	26.6	24.4	29.2	20.2	22.8	21.8
Farming, forestry, and fishing occupations	3.3	5.2	5.3	5.0	6.1	5.0	2.6	1.2	2.6
Farm operators and managers	3.3	5.2	9.8	5.1	2.3	*	2.7	*	3.1
Farm workers and related occupations	3.4	5.4	4.5	5.1	7.1	6.0	2.6	1.4	2.1
Precision production, craft, and repair occupations	9.0	9.0	11.0	7.0	9.1	10.0	9.2	9.8	14.1
Mechanics and repairers	2.6	2.6	2.7	2.7	2.6	2.2	2.5	1.9	*
Construction trades	2.0	2.1	2.5	1.8	1.9	2.2	1.8	3.5	*
Precision production occupations	26.1	24.2	28.4	19.7	23.1	26.7	31.5	32.9	55.1
Operators, fabricators, and laborers	31.4	29.5	27.9	26.9	38.5	36.6	34.7	33.1	39.8
Machine operators and teachers, except precision	59.0	55.7	54.3	53.5	63.1	60.1	63.9	63.2	65.4
Fabricators, assemblers, inspectors, and samplers	49.5	47.2	45.9	43.8	53.8	55.5	54.3	51.6	39.7
Transportation occupations	1.7	1.9	2.0	2.1	1.6	0.6	1.2	*	9.3
Motor vehicle operators	1.7	2.0	2.1	2.2	1.6	0.6	1.2	*	9.3
Material moving equipment operators	5.6	6.9	7.4	6.1	11.2	5.8	3.3	2.0	*
Handlers, equipment cleaners, helpers, and laborers	10.4	11.0	10.0	10.4	13.6	14.1	9.4	8.0	19.1
Construction laborers	1.0	1.1	1.7	0.7	*	2.2	0.9	1.2	9.7
Freight, stock, and material handlers	3.9	3.4	2.1	1.9	15.1	8.0	5.6	7.3	16.7

Note: * indicates less than 0.1.

Source: U.S. Bureau of the Census. "General Social and Economic Characteristics: United States Summary." 1980 Census of Population (Area Report 53: "Puerto Rico"). Washington, DC: U.S. Government Printing Office, 1983, Table 51.

Conclusion

This rapid overview of the population of Puerto Rico may evoke a mixed reaction. By all but the income indicators, the island is extremely modern even in comparison with the United States. It is, at most, only a decade or two behind the mainland and apparently making up the gap quickly. On the income side it is somewhat poor, but in comparison with the rest of Latin America it is wealthy. Compared with the individual states of the U.S., Puerto Rico could well emerge as modern and prosperous as one-fifth of them. If the time comes that statehood is an imminent possibility, the impact of admitting Puerto Rico to statehood would be scarcely noticeable. The population has made so much progress that it differs from the U.S. white population far less than four decades ago, and the demographic, economic, and social interaction is so little restricted that already Puerto Rico is almost a *de facto*, though not *de jure*, state.

Bibliography

Alvarado, Carmen, and Tietze, Christopher. "Birth Control in Puerto Rico." *Human Biology* 12 (1947).

Bournier, Leon F., and Macisco, John. "Education of Husband and Wife and Fertility in Puerto Rico." *Social and Economic Studies* 17 (1968), no. 1.

Bruckman, Walter H. "Rechazo y Atracción como Causas de la Migración Interna en Puerto Rico: Un Modelo Económico." *Revista de Ciencias Sociales* XX (1978), no. 2.

Corrada, Rafael. *Economic Dependency and Income Distribution in Puerto Rico: 1950-1977.* San Juan: Centro de Investigaciones Sociales, Universidad de Puerto Rico, 1979.

Cofresí, Emilio. *Realidad Poblacional de Puerto Rico.* San Juan, 1951.

Coombs, J.W., and Davis, Kingsley. "The Patterns of Puerto Rican Fertility." *Population Studies* 4 (1951), no. 4.

Departamento de Salud de Puerto Rico. *Informe Anual de Estadísticas Vitales.* San Juan: Departamento de Salud, annual reports series 1958.

Departamento del Trabajo de Puerto Rico. *Ingresos y Gastos de las Familias en Puerto Rico.* San Juan: Departamento del Trabajo, 1953, 1963, and 1977.

———. *Serie Estadística Sobre el Estado de Empleo.* San Juan: Departamento del Trabajo, 1970-82 and 1983.

Earnhardt, Kent C. "Population Growth and Educational Investment in Puerto Rico, 1970-1990." Masters thesis, School of Planning, University of Puerto Rico, 1968.

Fernández de Cintrón, Celia E., and Vales, Pedro A. *Return Migration to Puerto Rico.* San Juan: Social Sciences Research Center, University of Puerto Rico, 1974.

Gutierrez, Horacio F. "Algunos Factores Asociados con la Fecundidad en Puerto Rico." *Actas de la Conferencia Regional de Latinoamerica de Población* 1 (Mexico, 1970).

Hatt, Paul K. *Backgrounds of Human Fertility in Puerto Rico.* Princeton, NJ: Princeton University Press, 1952.

Hernández Alvarez, Celia Ines. *Matrimonio en Puerto Rico.* San Juan: Editorial Río Piedras, 1971.

Hernández Alvarez, José. *Return Migration to Puerto Rico.* Berkeley, CA: Berkeley Institute of International Studies, University of California, 1967.

Hill, Reuben; Stycos, J. Mayone; and Back, Kurt W. *The Family and Population Control: A Puerto Rican Experiment in Social Change.* Chapel Hill, NC: University of North Carolina Press, 1959.

History Task Force, Centro de Estudios Puertorriqueños. *Labor Migration Under Capitalism: The Puerto Rican Experience.* New York: Monthly Review Press, 1979.

Holback, Karel, and Swage, Philip L. *Industrialization and Employment in Puerto Rico.* Austin, TX: University of Texas Press, 1974.

Table 20-21. Unemployment in Puerto Rico: 1980

Unemployment	Puerto Rico total	Urbanized areas			Other urban		Rural		
		Urban total	Central city	Urban fringe	10,000 and over	2,500-9,999	Rural total	1,000-2,499	Rural farm
Total number of unemployed.	131,797	85,294	34,834	33,072	7,812	9,576	46,503	6,938	1,733
Male	78,913	49,380	20,035	19,042	4,605	5,698	29,533	4,311	1,142
Female	52,884	35,914	14,799	14,030	3,207	3,878	16,970	2,627	591
Percent female	40.1	42.1	42.5	42.4	41.1	40.5	36.5	37.9	34.1
Unemployment rates									
Males:									
16 to 19 years	49.9	49.7	52.7	45.9	49.9	54.9	50.3	47.0	52.0
20 to 24 years	26.0	24.4	24.5	22.8	27.3	28.1	29.1	33.1	31.3
25 to 54 years	10.8	9.3	9.3	8.1	11.3	13.0	14.4	15.0	13.3
55 to 64 years	9.0	8.1	7.2	8.4	9.7	9.8	11.6	11.9	7.1
65 years and over	10.2	10.2	9.8	9.9	9.7	12.8	10.4	15.2	2.3
Females:									
16 to 19 years	54.7	53.9	55.0	51.1	60.3	58.2	56.6	57.8	67.1
20 to 24 years	24.5	22.6	21.5	21.9	27.5	26.4	29.1	30.2	22.2
25 to 54 years	12.0	10.7	10.4	10.2	11.4	13.4	16.5	19.8	16.9
55 to 64 years	11.2	10.1	8.3	12.3	10.1	10.3	16.7	20.1	4.7
65 years and over	21.3	18.9	12.8	28.0	13.2	29.9	31.8	18.5	18.2

Source: U.S. Bureau of the Census. "General Population Characteristics: United States Summary." 1980 Census of Population (Area Report 53: "Puerto Rico"). Washington, DC: U.S. Government Printing Office, 1983, Table 50.

Table 20-22. Income Distribution in Puerto Rico: 1979

Income in 1979	Puerto Rico total	Urbanized areas			Other urban		Rural		
		Urban total	Central city	Urban fringe	10,000 and over	2,500–9,999	Rural total	1,000–2,499	Rural farm
Households									
Median income.	5,348	6,238	6,306	6,781	5,128	4,882	3,886	3,903	3,893
Mean income.	7,738	8,836	9,444	9,137	7,269	6,481	5,300	5,071	5,871
Percent distribution	100.0	100.0	100.0	100.0	100.0	100.0	100.0	100.0	100.0
Less than $1,000	12.9	11.1	11.5	10.7	12.9	13.7	15.8	17.1	12.9
$1,000 to $2,499	15.0	11.8	12.5	11.0	16.1	16.0	20.2	18.5	21.4
$2,500 to $4,999	19.8	17.4	17.9	16.6	20.1	21.2	24.1	24.1	25.7
$5,000 to $7,499	16.5	16.0	15.5	16.7	16.1	17.6	17.2	18.5	16.7
$7,500 to $9,999	10.0	10.5	10.0	11.1	10.1	10.6	9.0	8.8	8.5
$10,000 to $12,499	7.5	8.6	7.9	9.4	7.4	7.4	5.5	5.3	5.0
$12,500 to $14,999	4.7	5.7	5.3	6.1	5.0	4.5	2.9	3.2	3.3
$15,000 to $24,999	9.4	12.5	12.2	12.9	9.2	7.4	4.3	3.8	4.6
$25,000 or more.	4.2	6.4	7.2	5.5	3.1	1.6	1.0	0.7	1.9
Families									
Median income.	5,923	6,845	7,061	7,199	5,917	5,544	4,354	4,370	4,241
Mean income.	8,271	9,462	10,293	9,571	7,931	7,008	5,693	5,438	6,197
Percent distribution	100.0	100.0	100.0	100.0	100.0	100.0	100.0	100.0	100.0
Less than $1,000	11.3	10.1	9.9	9.4	11.4	12.0	14.0	15.4	12.1
$1,000 to $2,499	12.4	10.1	9.8	9.2	12.3	12.8	17.3	15.7	18.6
$2,500 to $4,999	19.7	17.4	17.0	16.2	20.1	21.1	24.9	24.7	26.5
$5,000 to $7,499	17.5	17.0	16.1	17.3	17.2	19.0	18.7	20.0	17.6
$7,500 to $9,999	10.9	11.3	10.8	11.7	11.3	11.8	10.0	9.7	9.2
$10,000 to $12,499	8.2	9.1	8.7	10.0	8.2	8.2	6.1	5.9	5.8
$12,500 to $14,999	5.2	6.0	5.9	6.5	5.6	5.1	3.2	3.6	3.3
$15,000 to $24,999	10.3	12.9	13.7	13.8	10.3	8.2	4.7	4.1	4.8
$25,000 or more.	4.6	6.1	8.1	5.8	3.6	1.7	1.1	0.8	2.1

Source: U.S. Bureau of the Census. "General Population Characteristics: United States Summary." 1980 Census of Population (Area Report 53: "Puerto Rico"). Washington, DC: U.S. Government Printing Office, 1983, Table 54.

Table 20-23. Poverty Status of the Population of Puerto Rico: 1980

Characteristics	Puerto Rico total	Urbanized areas			Other urban		Rural		
		Urban total	Central city	Urban fringe	10,000 and over	2,500–9,999	Rural total	1,000–2,499	Rural farm
Families									
Number of families below poverty level	439,567	262,916	101,436	102,343	27,500	31,637	176,651	24,616	6,573
Percent of all families.	58.0	50.7	47.8	49.4	57.8	61.6	73.8	74.7	75.4
Mean income deficit.	$4,285	$4,066	$4,016	$4,073	$4,035	$4,236	$4,610	$4,648	$5,017
Percent of poverty families:									
With Social Security income.	29.5	28.2	28.2	25.9	33.1	31.3	31.4	32.0	38.2
With public assistance income.	21.1	19.5	20.4	18.6	18.1	20.5	23.6	20.7	27.5
Householder worked in 1979	43.3	42.8	40.5	46.5	39.4	41.7	44.0	43.6	61.5
With related children under 18 years	74.4	73.7	71.2	76.2	71.4	75.1	75.5	76.5	72.1
Female householder, no husband present	23.1	27.4	32.0	23.5	27.6	25.2	16.7	19.1	8.7
With related children under 18 years	17.3	20.6	24.2	17.9	19.8	18.6	12.3	14.8	5.6
With related children under 6 years.	7.6	9.2	11.2	7.8	8.5	7.9	5.2	6.0	2.8
Householder 65 years and over.	16.5	16.0	17.0	13.7	19.1	17.7	17.2	17.3	26.0
Unrelated individuals									
Number of unrelated individuals.	100,258	70,268	37,316	18,385	7,439	7,128	29,990	4,235	1,003
Percent below poverty level.	71.1	66.4	63.1	65.1	78.9	78.7	85.4	84.6	82.0
Mean income deficit.	$2,402	$2,406	$2,432	$2,378	$2,401	$2,349	$2,393	$2,418	$2,209
Percent with Social Security income.	40.9	38.7	36.8	38.5	43.2	44.4	46.2	43.6	48.0
Percent with public assistance income.	15.3	13.5	11.6	15.1	14.4	18.0	19.8	18.4	16.6
Percent worked in 1979	16.2	17.0	18.5	16.9	14.0	12.7	14.5	13.5	41.2
Percent 65 years and over.	40.1	37.4	34.8	37.0	42.8	46.0	46.4	41.3	50.1
Persons									
Number of persons below poverty level.	1,983,201	1,162,467	443,457	455,507	119,890	143,613	820,734	115,507	33,483
Percent below poverty level.	62.4	54.9	52.0	53.4	61.6	66.0	77.6	78.4	79.4
Percent of poverty children under 18 years . . .	42.3	41.3	39.4	42.9	40.4	42.9	43.8	44.2	41.7
Percent of poverty persons 65 years and over . .	8.1	8.3	9.5	6.6	9.8	8.7	7.7	7.4	9.8

Source: U.S. Bureau of the Census. "General Social and Economic Characteristics: United States Summary." 1980 Census of Population (Area Report 53: "Puerto Rico"). Washington, DC: U.S. Government Printing Office, 1983, Table 55.

Janer, José L. "Population Growth in Puerto Rico and Its Relation to Time Changes in Vital Statistics." *Human Biology* 17 (1945), no. 4.

Junta de Planificación de Puerto Rico. *Informe Económico al Gobernador.* San Juan: Junta de Planificación, annual reports series 1950.

———. *Serie Histórica del Empleo, del Desempleo y Grupos Trabajadores en Puerto Rico.* San Juan: Junta de Planificación, 1981.

Mills, C. Wright et al. *The Puerto Rican Journey: New York's Newest Migrants.* New York: Harper and Land Brothers, 1950.

Morales del Valle, Zoraida. "Cambios en la Estructura Industrial y Ocupacional de Puerto Rico y sus Implicaciones en la Salud." *Revista de Salud Pública de Puerto Rico* 2 (1980).

———. "El Tipo de Matrimonio y su Relación con la Fecundidad en Puerto Rico." *Revista Interamericana* XI (Inter-American University Press, 1981-82), no. 4.

Muñoz Vázquez, Mayra M. "Matrimonio y Divorcio en Puerto Rico." In *La Mujer en la Sociedad Puertorriqueña*, by Edna Acosta (ed.). San Juan: Ediciones Huracán, Río Piedras, 1980.

Ramírez de Arellano, Annette B., and Seipp, Conrad. *Colonialism, Catholicism, and Contraception: A History of Birth Control in Puerto Rico.* Chapel Hill, NC: University of North Carolina Press, 1983.

Rivera de Morales, Nidia. *Mortalidad en Puerto Rico: 1888 a 1967.* San Juan: Escuela de Salud Pública, Universidad de Puerto Rico, 1970.

———. *Tendencias de la Natalidad y Diferenciales de la Fecundidad en Puerto Rico: 1888-1972.* San Juan: Escuela de Salud Pública, Universidad de Puerto Rico, 1974.

Roberts, Lydia, and Stefani, Rosa L. *Patterns of Living of Puerto Rican Families.* San Juan: University of Puerto Rico, 1949.

Powers, Mary G., and Macisco, John J. *Los Puertorriqueños en Nueva York: Un Analisis de su Participación Laboral y Migratoria.* San Juan: Centro de Investigaciones Sociales, Universidad de Puerto Rico, 1982.

Presser, Harriet B. "The Role of Sterilization in Controlling Puerto Rican Fertility." *Population Studies* 23 (1969), no. 3.

Torruellas, Luz M., and Vázquez, José L. *Los Puertorriqueños que Regresaron: Un Análisis de su Participación Laboral.* San Juan: Centro de Investigaciones Sociales, Universidad de Puerto Rico, 1982.

U.S. Bureau of the Census. *Thirteenth Census of the United States (1910); Fourteenth Census of the United States (1920)* ("Population: Puerto Rico"); *Fifteenth Census of the United States (1930)* ("Outlying Territories and Possessions"); *16th Census of the United States (1940)* ("Puerto Rico"); *1950 United States Census of Population* (Bulletins P-A53, P-B53, P-C53, and H-A53); *United States Census of Population: 1960* (Final Reports PC(1)-53A, PC(1)-C53, and PC(1)-D53, Puerto Rico); *Census of Population: 1970* (Final Reports PC(1)-A53, PC(1)-B53, PC(1)-C53, and PC(1)-D53, Puerto Rico); and *Census of Population: 1980* (PC80-1-A53, PC80-1-B53, and PC80-1-C53, Puerto Rico). Washington, DC: U.S. Government Printing Office, various years cited.

U.S. Commission on Civil Rights. *Puerto Ricans in the United States: An Uncertain Future.* Washington, DC: U.S. Government Printing Office, 1976.

Vázquez, José L. "The Demographic Evolution of Puerto Rico." Ph.D. dissertation, Department of Sociology, University of Chicago, 1964.

———. "Fertility Decline in Puerto Rico: Extent and Causes." *Demography* 5 (1968), no. 2.

Vázquez Calzada, José L. "La Emigración Puertorriqueña: ¿Solución o Problema? " *Revista de Ciencias Sociales* VII (1963).

———. "La Esterilización Femenina en Puerto Rico." *Revista de Ciencias Sociales* XVII (1973), no. 3.

———. "La Distribución Geográfica de la Población de Puerto Rico." *Revista de Ciencias Sociales* XXIII (1981), nos. 1-2.

———. "La Ociosidad y el Desempleo en Puerto Rico." *Revista de Salud Pública de Puerto Rico* 2 (1980).

———. *La Poblacion de Puerto Rico y su Trayectoria Histórica.* San Juan: Centro de Investigaciones Demográficas, Escuela de Salud Pública, Universidad de Puerto Rico, 1978.

Vázquez Calzada, José L., and Morales del Valle, Zoraida. "Características Socio-demográficas de los Norteamericanos, Cubanos y Dominicanos Residentes en Puerto Rico." *Revista de Ciencias Sociales* XXII (1979), nos. 1-2.

———. "La Población de Ascendencia Puertorriqueña Nacida en el Exterior." *Revista de Ciencias Sociales* XXII (1980), nos. 1-2.

———. "Female Sterilization in Puerto Rico and Its Demographic Effectiveness." *Puerto Rico Health Sciences Journal* 1 (1982), no. 2.

Vázquez Calzadas, José L. et al. "Patrones de Nupcialidad en Puerto Rico." *Revista Interamericana* XI (1981), no. 3.

———. *Tablas de Vida Abreviadas para Puerto Rico.* San Juan: Escuela de Medicina, Universidad de Puerto Rico, 1963.

Appendix Table 1-A. Population of the United States, by Age and Sex: Total Population, 1940-1980

Age	Both sexes					Male					Female				
	1980	1970	1960	1950	1940	1980	1970	1960	1950	1940	1980	1970	1960	1950	1940
Total.	226,545,805	203,211,926	179,323,175	151,325,798	132,165,129	110,053,161	98,912,192	88,331,494	75,186,606	66,349,730	116,492,644	104,299,734	90,991,681	76,139,192	65,815,399
Under 5 years. . .	16,348,254	17,154,337	20,320,901	16,243,141	10,589,220	8,362,009	8,745,499	10,329,729	8,276,952	5,379,108	7,986,245	8,408,838	9,991,172	7,966,189	5,210,112
Under 1 year .	3,533,692	3,485,277	4,111,949	3,163,019	2,020,174	1,806,338	1,777,915	2,089,909	1,610,371	1,026,800	1,727,354	1,707,362	2,022,040	1,552,648	993,374
1 year	3,269,557	3,377,502	4,106,252	6,809,376	2,056,762	1,674,095	1,721,763	2,085,354	3,470,798	1,046,770	1,595,462	1,655,739	2,020,898	3,338,578	1,009,992
2 years.	3,223,816	3,290,419	4,098,876		2,197,488	1,648,044	1,678,842	2,084,452		1,116,478	1,575,772	1,611,577	2,014,424		1,081,010
3 years.	3,179,441	3,418,679	4,015,598	6,270,746	2,116,290	1,625,693	1,740,906	2,040,591	3,195,783	1,068,821	1,553,748	1,677,773	1,975,007	3,074,963	1,047,469
4 years.	3,141,748	3,582,460	3,988,226		2,150,810	1,607,839	1,826,073	2,029,423		1,095,939	1,533,909	1,756,387	1,958,803		1,054,871
5 to 9 years . . .	16,699,956	19,956,247	18,691,780	13,262,123	10,734,852	8,539,080	10,168,496	9,504,368	6,746,568	5,444,271	8,160,876	9,787,751	9,187,412	6,515,555	5,290,581
5 years.	3,162,691	3,811,077	3,953,528	2,727,292	2,142,407	1,618,300	1,941,004	2,011,362	1,388,404	1,087,811	1,544,391	1,870,073	1,942,166	1,338,888	1,054,596
6 years.	3,109,095	3,952,146	3,819,827	2,778,907	2,054,385	1,589,501	2,012,834	1,939,097	1,414,528	1,041,757	1,519,594	1,939,312	1,880,730	1,364,379	1,012,628
7 years.	3,273,052	4,012,474	3,786,783	7,755,924	2,094,129	1,672,647	2,043,834	1,924,076	3,943,636	1,058,929	1,600,405	1,968,640	1,862,707	3,812,288	1,035,200
8 years.	3,394,998	4,052,265	3,649,334		2,203,365	1,735,956	2,065,571	1,857,230		1,116,907	1,659,042	1,986,694	1,792,104		1,086,458
9 years.	3,760,120	4,128,285	3,482,308		2,190,336	1,922,676	2,105,253	1,772,603		1,113,419	1,837,444	2,023,032	1,709,705		1,076,917
10 to 14 years . .	18,242,129	20,789,468	16,773,492	11,167,478	11,799,526	9,316,221	10,590,737	8,524,289	5,684,922	5,979,562	8,925,908	10,198,731	8,249,203	5,482,556	5,819,964
10 years	3,716,530	4,282,106	3,481,131	9,019,104	2,308,369	1,901,610	2,183,371	1,770,747	4,590,821	1,173,032	1,814,920	2,098,735	1,710,384	4,428,283	1,135,337
11 years	3,580,644	4,126,685	3,472,908		2,217,092	1,828,934	2,100,739	1,765,126		1,118,729	1,751,710	2,025,946	1,707,782		1,098,363
12 years	3,518,982	4,183,341	3,573,854		2,425,400	1,796,333	2,132,903	1,817,916		1,234,629	1,722,649	2,050,438	1,755,938		1,190,771
13 years	3,643,189	4,101,977	3,506,557		2,389,344	1,856,566	2,088,820	1,781,553		1,207,823	1,786,623	2,013,157	1,725,004		1,181,521
14 years	3,782,784	4,095,359	2,739,042	2,148,374	2,405,730	1,932,778	2,084,904	1,388,947	1,094,101	1,218,116	1,850,006	2,010,455	1,350,095	1,054,273	1,187,614
15 to 19 years . .	21,168,124	19,070,348	13,219,243	10,671,321	12,387,471	10,755,409	9,633,847	6,633,661	5,342,290	6,209,432	10,412,715	9,436,501	6,585,582	5,329,031	6,178,039
15 years	4,059,898	4,029,034	2,756,616	2,124,747	2,422,519	2,069,726	2,053,643	1,398,066	1,075,988	1,222,337	1,990,172	1,975,391	1,358,550	1,048,759	1,200,182
16 years	4,180,875	3,889,652	2,797,216	4,169,955	2,489,096	2,135,125	1,979,619	1,416,200	2,106,710	1,249,166	2,045,750	1,910,033	1,381,016	2,063,245	1,239,930
17 years	4,223,848	3,825,343	2,862,005		2,403,074	2,160,114	1,944,907	1,443,277		1,213,277	2,063,734	1,880,436	1,418,728		1,189,797
18 years	4,251,779	3,766,102	2,528,953	4,376,619	2,582,648	2,153,292	1,893,207	1,261,572	2,159,592	1,281,638	2,098,487	1,872,895	1,267,381	2,217,027	1,301,010
19 years	4,451,724	3,560,217	2,274,453		2,436,186	2,237,152	1,762,471	1,114,546		1,213,735	2,214,572	1,797,746	1,159,907		1,222,451
20-24 years. . . .	21,318,704	16,371,021	10,800,761	11,549,355	11,645,184	10,663,231	7,917,269	5,272,340	5,646,699	5,728,069	10,655,473	8,453,752	5,528,421	5,902,656	5,917,115
25-29 years. . . .	19,520,919	13,476,993	10,869,124	12,305,951	11,145,741	9,705,107	6,621,567	5,333,075	6,006,520	5,481,762	9,815,812	6,855,426	5,536,049	6,299,431	5,663,979
30-34 years. . . .	17,560,920	11,430,436	11,949,186	11,572,337	10,281,662	8,676,796	5,595,790	5,846,224	5,655,538	5,095,365	8,884,124	5,834,646	6,102,962	5,916,799	5,186,297
35-39 years. . . .	13,965,302	11,106,851	12,481,109	11,294,478	9,579,430	6,861,509	5,412,423	6,079,512	5,546,565	4,766,737	7,103,793	5,694,428	6,401,597	5,747,913	4,812,693
40-44 years. . . .	11,669,408	11,980,954	11,600,243	10,240,671	8,813,993	5,708,210	5,818,813	5,675,881	5,093,005	4,434,622	5,961,198	6,162,141	5,924,362	5,147,666	4,379,371
45-49 years. . . .	11,089,755	12,115,939	10,879,485	9,101,778	8,276,759	5,388,249	5,851,334	5,357,925	4,545,606	4,221,445	5,701,506	6,264,605	5,521,560	4,556,172	4,055,314
50-54 years. . . .	11,710,032	11,104,018	9,605,954	8,295,580	7,275,863	5,620,670	5,347,916	4,734,829	4,142,277	3,764,840	6,089,362	5,756,102	4,871,125	4,153,303	3,511,023
55-59 years. . . .	11,615,254	9,973,028	8,429,865	7,252,524	5,858,395	5,481,863	4,765,821	4,127,245	3,639,761	3,020,691	6,133,391	5,207,207	4,302,620	3,612,763	2,837,704
60-64 years. . . .	10,087,621	8,616,784	7,142,452	6,074,363	4,740,298	4,669,892	4,026,972	3,409,319	3,047,212	2,405,768	5,417,729	4,589,812	3,733,133	3,027,151	2,334,530
65-69 years. . . .	8,782,481	6,991,625	6,257,910	5,013,490	3,815,355	3,902,955	3,122,084	2,931,088	2,431,035	1,902,057	4,879,526	3,869,541	3,326,822	2,582,455	1,913,298
70-74 years. . . .	6,798,124	5,443,831	4,738,932	3,419,208	2,574,111	2,853,547	2,315,000	2,185,216	1,633,382	1,274,152	3,944,577	3,128,831	2,553,716	1,785,826	1,299,959
75-79 years. . . .	4,793,722	3,834,834	3,053,559	3,284,061	2,646,863	1,847,661	1,560,661	1,359,424	1,510,794	1,241,583	2,946,061	2,274,173	1,694,135	1,773,267	1,405,280
80-84 years. . . .	2,935,033	2,284,311	1,579,927	--	--	1,019,227	875,584	665,093	--	--	1,915,806	1,408,727	914,834	--	--
85 years + over. .	2,240,067	1,510,901	929,252	577,939	--	681,525	542,379	362,276	237,480	--	1,558,542	968,522	566,976	340,459	--

Note: -- indicates data included in the preceding age category.

Source: Five-year interval from U.S. Bureau of the Census. "General Population Characteristics: United States Summary." 1980 Census of Population. Washington, DC: U.S. Government Printing Office, 1983, Table 45. Single-year data for 1960 and 1950 from U.S. Bureau of the Census. 1960 Census of Population. Washington, DC: U.S. Government Printing Office, 1961, Table 46. Single-year data for 1940 from U.S. Bureau of the Census. 1940 Census of Population. Washington, DC: U.S. Government Printing Office, 1941, Table 2.

Appendix Table 1-B. Population of the United States, by Age and Sex: White Population, 1940-1980

Age	Both sexes					Male					Female				
	1980	1970	1960	1950	1940	1980	1970	1960	1950	1940	1980	1970	1960	1950	1940
Total.	188,371,622	177,748,975	158,831,732	135,149,629	118,357,831	91,685,333	86,720,987	78,367,149	67,254,991	59,538,616	96,686,289	91,027,988	80,464,583	67,894,638	58,819,215
Under 5 years. . .	12,634,075	14,423,140	17,358,552	14,206,738	9,238,708	6,484,021	7,374,333	8,849,181	7,255,723	4,706,173	6,150,054	7,048,807	8,509,371	6,951,015	4,532,535
Under 1 year . .	2,719,445	2,935,089	3,498,211	2,745,353	1,778,233	1,395,560	1,501,250	1,784,033	1,402,032	906,897	1,323,885	1,433,839	1,714,178	1,343,321	871,336
1 year	2,528,598	2,851,928	3,504,621	5,951,221	1,816,224	1,299,045	1,458,143	1,785,112	3,038,740	926,398	1,229,553	1,393,785	1,719,509	2,912,481	889,826
2 years.	2,497,249	2,762,530	3,505,733		1,920,139	1,280,931	1,414,274	1,786,979		978,470	1,216,318	1,348,256	1,718,754		941,669
3 years.	2,460,551	2,872,719	3,435,586	5,510,164	1,844,809	1,261,857	1,466,847	1,750,963	2,814,951	935,050	1,198,694	1,405,872	1,684,623	2,695,213	909,759
4 years.	2,428,232	3,000,874	3,414,401		1,870,100	1,246,628	1,533,819	1,742,094		954,655	1,181,604	1,467,055	1,672,307		915,445
5 to 9 years . . .	13,032,966	16,897,426	16,087,542	11,611,025	9,337,381	6,685,142	8,633,093	8,202,157	5,922,422	4,748,802	6,347,824	8,264,333	7,885,385	5,688,603	4,588,579
5 years.	2,456,167	3,208,463	3,389,585	2,382,243	1,868,995	1,260,475	1,638,441	1,729,558	1,216,265	951,805	1,195,692	1,570,022	1,660,027	1,165,978	917,190
6 years.	2,410,344	3,338,213	3,284,884	2,434,433	1,778,068	1,236,396	1,704,717	1,671,880	1,242,682	904,934	1,173,948	1,633,496	1,613,004	1,191,751	873,134
7 years.	2,539,701	3,394,875	3,263,270	6,794,349	1,823,959	1,301,581	1,734,099	1,622,702	3,463,475	924,604	1,238,120	1,660,776	1,600,568	3,330,874	899,355
8 years.	2,658,627	3,444,037	3,154,029		1,926,523	1,364,028	1,760,037	1,609,106		979,140	1,294,599	1,684,000	1,544,923		947,383
9 years.	2,968,127	3,511,838	2,995,774		1,931,406	1,522,662	1,795,799	1,528,911		984,054	1,445,465	1,716,039	1,466,863		947,352
10 to 14 years . .	14,460,922	17,681,117	14,638,892	9,703,895	10,361,068	7,408,443	9,033,725	7,456,573	4,949,357	5,263,245	7,052,479	8,647,392	7,182,319	4,754,538	5,097,823
10 years	2,946,378	3,624,787	3,004,268	7,835,520	2,025,079	1,511,857	1,853,786	1,531,758	3,994,792	1,030,854	1,434,521	1,771,001	1,472,510	3,840,728	994,225
11 years	2,846,168	3,512,236	3,012,363		1,968,292	1,457,937	1,793,731	1,534,396		996,041	1,388,231	1,718,505	1,477,967		972,251
12 years	2,786,155	3,563,400	3,133,082		2,131,313	1,427,928	1,821,354	1,597,038		1,086,784	1,358,227	1,742,046	1,536,044		1,044,529
13 years	2,889,432	3,495,074	3,103,660		2,103,565	1,477,087	1,785,238	1,580,542		1,065,831	1,412,345	1,709,836	1,523,118		1,037,734
14 years	2,992,789	3,485,620	2,385,519	1,868,375	2,124,446	1,533,634	1,779,616	1,212,839	954,565	1,079,497	1,459,155	1,706,004	1,172,680	913,810	1,044,949
15 to 19 years . .	16,962,102	16,370,360	11,608,229	9,345,432	10,976,539	8,634,142	8,291,270	5,837,093	4,696,766	5,524,189	8,327,960	8,079,090	5,771,136	4,648,666	5,452,350
15 years	3,232,449	3,440,465	2,408,133	1,854,790	2,150,945	1,652,399	1,758,578	1,224,164	942,521	1,089,253	1,580,050	1,681,887	1,183,969	912,269	1,061,692
16 years	3,343,837	3,332,604	2,460,188	3,635,419	2,206,995	1,710,931	1,700,014	1,248,003	1,843,193	1,112,397	1,632,906	1,632,590	1,212,185	1,792,226	1,094,598
17 years	3,380,772	3,287,148	2,525,118		2,137,551	1,731,264	1,675,393	1,275,695		1,081,852	1,649,508	1,611,755	1,249,423		1,055,699
18 years	3,417,053	3,247,187	2,221,444	3,855,223	2,290,573	1,733,097	1,636,643	1,109,762	1,911,052	1,142,185	1,683,956	1,610,544	1,111,682	1,944,171	1,148,388
19 years	3,587,991	3,062,956	1,993,346		2,177,983	1,806,451	1,520,642	979,469		1,090,233	1,781,540	1,542,314	1,013,877		1,087,750
20-24 years. . . .	17,288,774	14,281,827	9,470,779	10,206,919	10,363,924	8,683,292	6,940,820	4,645,822	5,023,563	5,132,242	8,605,482	7,341,007	4,824,957	5,183,356	5,231,682
25-29 years. . . .	15,984,830	11,811,914	9,555,585	10,950,004	9,921,640	8,005,295	5,849,792	4,721,783	5,364,484	4,903,341	7,979,535	5,962,122	4,833,802	5,585,520	5,018,299
30-34 years. . . .	14,644,799	9,967,437	10,588,830	10,379,700	9,220,301	7,299,659	4,925,069	5,218,188	5,094,766	4,581,410	7,345,140	5,042,368	5,370,642	5,284,934	4,638,891
35-39 years. . . .	11,761,107	9,720,869	11,140,841	10,077,161	8,528,053	5,831,107	4,784,375	5,446,833	4,966,995	4,261,143	5,930,000	4,936,494	5,694,008	5,110,166	4,266,910
40-44 years. . . .	9,825,833	10,606,832	10,423,020	9,204,318	7,944,954	4,849,516	5,194,497	5,117,038	4,581,568	4,000,403	4,976,317	5,412,335	5,305,982	4,622,750	3,944,551
45-49 years. . . .	9,456,991	10,844,642	9,785,162	8,180,192	7,540,584	4,638,737	5,257,619	4,828,179	4,086,557	3,847,267	4,818,254	5,587,023	4,956,983	4,093,635	3,693,317
50-54 years. . . .	10,157,561	10,001,857	8,693,528	7,543,650	6,686,917	4,918,060	4,832,555	4,286,023	3,760,945	3,455,867	5,239,501	5,169,302	4,407,505	3,782,705	3,231,050
55-59 years. . . .	10,237,758	9,006,502	7,626,211	6,702,037	5,431,917	4,852,744	4,310,921	3,728,599	3,354,638	2,793,345	5,385,014	4,695,581	3,897,612	3,347,399	2,638,572
60-64 years. . . .	8,975,711	7,804,710	6,550,673	5,657,376	4,420,406	4,173,113	3,647,243	3,121,664	2,832,328	2,234,912	4,802,598	4,157,467	3,429,009	2,825,048	2,185,494
65-69 years. . . .	7,812,247	6,299,054	5,739,224	4,588,995	3,501,691	3,481,640	2,807,974	2,684,132	2,225,073	1,738,750	4,330,607	3,491,080	3,055,092	2,363,922	1,762,941
70-74 years. . . .	6,095,352	4,982,083	4,391,042	3,183,570	2,402,174	2,552,321	2,107,552	2,018,350	1,514,530	1,184,383	3,543,031	2,874,531	2,372,692	1,669,040	1,217,791
75-79 years. . . .	4,310,284	3,552,571	2,835,318	3,076,174	2,481,368	1,650,386	1,437,628	1,255,281	1,406,930	1,163,006	2,659,898	2,114,943	1,580,037	1,669,244	1,318,362
80-84 years. . . .	2,685,349	2,119,822	1,480,689	--	--	923,308	805,564	619,338	--	--	1,762,041	1,314,258	861,351	--	--
85 years + over. .	2,044,961	1,376,812	857,615	532,443	--	614,407	486,957	330,915	218,346	--	1,430,554	889,855	526,700	314,097	--

Note: -- indicates data included in the preceding age category.

Source: Same as Appendix Table 1-A.

Appendix Table 1-C. Population of the United States, by Age and Sex: Black Population, 1940-1980

Age	Both sexes 1980	Both sexes 1970	Both sexes 1960	Both sexes 1950	Both sexes 1940	Male 1980	Male 1970	Male 1960	Male 1950	Male 1940	Female 1980	Female 1970	Female 1960	Female 1950	Female 1940
Total.	26,495,025	22,580,289	18,848,619	15,026,675	12,865,518	12,519,189	10,748,316	9,097,704	7,269,170	6,269,038	13,975,836	11,831,973	9,750,915	7,757,505	6,596,480
Under 5 years. . .	2,436,169	2,432,638	2,722,400	1,890,620	1,249,080	1,227,900	1,219,567	1,362,831	947,740	621,689	1,208,269	1,213,071	1,359,569	942,880	627,391
Under 1 year . .	530,964	487,199	564,025	388,057	230,335	267,044	244,504	281,556	193,458	114,390	263,920	242,695	282,467	194,599	116,241
1 year	486,890	466,446	552,899	797,118	229,000	245,307	233,632	276,371	401,097	114,391	241,583	232,814	276,528	396,021	114,458
2 years.	477,708	469,964	545,099		264,044	240,629	235,078	273,821		131,176	237,079	234,886	271,281		132,722
3 years.	470,660	487,809	533,031	705,446	258,458	237,612	244,653	266,600	353,186	127,446	233,048	243,156	266,431	352,260	131,168
4 years.	469,947	521,220	527,345		267,244	237,308	261,700	264,484		134,286	232,639	259,520	262,862		132,803
5 to 9 years . . .	2,490,717	2,747,428	2,390,638	1,529,830	1,294,546	1,255,253	1,377,355	1,195,123	761,430	643,781	1,235,464	1,370,073	1,195,515	768,400	650,765
5 years.	468,080	540,061	525,940	318,330	261,084	236,209	270,724	258,631	158,440	129,757	231,871	269,337	259,059	160,081	131,231
6 years.	467,645	550,724	502,034	318,453	263,858	235,737	276,000	245,242	158,501	130,536	231,908	274,724	245,825	160,204	133,226
7 years.	498,320	555,169	478,128	893,047	257,989	251,220	278,026	239,880	444,489	128,630	247,100	277,143	240,695	448,115	129,740
8 years.	506,709	546,786	454,221		264,360	255,098	274,276	227,719		131,437	251,611	272,510	226,960		132,825
9 years.	549,963	554,688	430,315		247,255	276,989	278,329	223,652		123,421	272,974	276,359	222,976		123,743
10 to 14 years . .	2,673,272	2,809,869	1,972,932	1,352,445	1,330,660	1,344,324	1,406,715	989,360	674,480	661,351	1,328,948	1,403,154	983,572	677,965	669,309
10 years	536,456	593,719	440,747	1,095,882	270,565	270,689	297,458	221,450	546,529	135,622	265,767	296,261	219,299	547,232	134,941
11 years	513,788	554,764	425,665		237,626	258,838	277,098	213,797		117,030	254,950	277,666	211,869		120,597
12 years	517,587	560,273	407,389		280,877	259,055	281,327	204,669		141,027	258,532	278,946	202,723		139,847
13 years	537,569	548,936	372,383		272,943	270,002	274,426	186,259		135,445	267,567	274,510	186,121		137,498
14 years	567,872	552,177	326,448	256,564	268,649	285,740	276,406	163,185	127,951	132,227	282,132	275,771	163,560	130,733	136,426
15 to 19 years . .	2,984,863	2,423,045	1,496,991	1,226,135	1,304,606	1,489,065	1,201,605	740,971	591,550	630,079	1,495,798	1,221,440	756,020	634,585	674,527
15 years	595,146	531,985	323,818	253,843	258,710	299,219	266,309	161,764	122,467	126,241	295,927	265,676	162,057	127,387	132,458
16 years	600,439	502,731	313,174	500,543	268,738	302,757	252,145	156,458	241,488	129,736	297,682	250,586	156,720	252,654	139,002
17 years	600,169	483,695	313,043		252,945	302,629	241,838	155,886		124,667	297,540	241,857	157,159		128,257
18 years	589,101	463,572	285,744	471,748	278,240	291,685	228,318	141,214	227,595	132,283	297,416	235,254	144,530	254,544	145,975
19 years	600,008	441,062	261,212		245,972	292,775	212,995	125,649		117,152	307,233	228,067	135,554		128,835
20-24 years. . . .	2,724,806	1,814,220	1,211,713	1,231,545	1,195,227	1,300,253	839,848	569,398	563,730	550,193	1,424,553	974,372	642,315	667,815	645,034
25-29 years. . . .	2,321,319	1,428,257	1,178,799	1,249,175	1,145,284	1,084,442	657,544	547,941	579,880	529,613	1,236,877	770,713	630,858	669,295	615,671
30-34 years. . . .	1,888,713	1,252,935	1,226,594	1,103,540	992,879	870,997	568,086	563,502	510,970	467,887	1,017,716	684,849	663,092	592,570	524,992
35-39 years. . . .	1,457,747	1,195,727	1,221,328	1,138,860	985,833	662,338	540,539	569,133	530,210	462,559	795,409	655,188	652,195	608,650	523,274
40-44 years. . . .	1,251,067	1,197,865	1,086,511	972,555	815,096	566,539	543,737	508,082	468,595	400,249	684,528	654,128	578,429	503,960	414,847
45-49 years. . . .	1,142,948	1,122,779	1,013,343	862,905	692,807	515,277	520,095	479,629	418,690	348,251	627,671	602,684	533,714	444,215	344,556
50-54 years. . . .	1,128,926	989,467	851,582	702,235	550,435	504,531	458,526	406,991	350,255	283,120	624,395	530,941	444,591	351,980	267,315
55-59 years. . . .	1,036,784	873,528	758,741	515,365	397,219	466,506	404,704	365,302	264,085	207,220	570,278	468,824	393,439	251,280	189,999
60-64 years. . . .	870,836	733,777	549,167	384,840	295,904	385,052	334,425	258,918	195,155	154,245	485,784	399,352	290,249	189,685	141,659
65-69 years. . . .	776,997	626,917	487,406	406,930	296,737	331,725	277,117	229,067	191,435	151,990	445,272	349,800	258,339	215,495	144,747
70-74 years. . . .	563,567	415,903	324,320	220,650	162,948	234,315	183,822	151,112	108,390	83,835	329,252	232,081	173,208	112,260	79,113
75-79 years. . . .	387,399	254,487	203,119	130,605	156,257	152,755	109,959	94,216	64,885	72,976	234,644	144,528	108,903	65,720	83,281
80-84 years. . . .	199,975	144,063	90,399	65,325	--	74,951	58,674	39,841	30,825	--	125,024	85,389	50,558	34,500	--
85 years + over. .	158,920	117,384	62,636	43,115	--	52,966	45,998	26,287	16,865	--	105,954	71,386	36,349	26,250	--

Note: -- indicates data included in the preceding age category.

Source: Same as Appendix Table 1-A.

Appendix Table 1-D. Population of the United States, by Age and Sex: Spanish-Origin Population, 1970-1980

Age	Both sexes					Male					Female				
	1980	1970	1960	1950	1940	1980	1970	1960	1950	1940	1980	1970	1960	1950	1940
Total.	14,608,673	9,072,602	--	--	--	7,279,831	4,452,978	--	--	--	7,328,842	4,619,624	--	--	--
Under 5 years. . .	1,663,173	1,110,642	--	--	--	848,043	558,387	--	--	--	815,130	552,255	--	--	--
Under 1 year . .	368,045	230,823	--	--	--	187,087	117,042	--	--	--	180,958	113,781	--	--	--
1 year	328,216	217,137	--	--	--	168,208	106,454	--	--	--	160,008	110,683	--	--	--
2 years.	324,950	211,678	--	--	--	165,699	107,057	--	--	--	159,251	104,621	--	--	--
3 years.	324,066	217,108	--	--	--	165,061	110,060	--	--	--	159,005	107,048	--	--	--
4 years.	317,896	233,896	--	--	--	161,988	117,774	--	--	--	155,908	116,122	--	--	--
5 to 9 years . . .	1,537,181	1,197,322	--	--	--	782,955	605,133	--	--	--	754,226	592,189	--	--	--
5 years.	311,256	238,428	--	--	--	158,585	121,070	--	--	--	152,671	117,358	--	--	--
6 years.	299,199	243,353	--	--	--	152,065	123,143	--	--	--	147,134	120,210	--	--	--
7 years.	305,492	240,055	--	--	--	156,284	121,274	--	--	--	149,208	118,781	--	--	--
8 years.	301,298	238,292	--	--	--	153,284	121,192	--	--	--	148,014	117,100	--	--	--
9 years.	319,936	237,194	--	--	--	162,737	118,454	--	--	--	157,199	118,740	--	--	--
10 to 14 years . .	1,474,998	1,103,630	--	--	--	746,975	558,504	--	--	--	728,023	545,126	--	--	--
10 years	309,824	235,751	--	--	--	157,277	119,944	--	--	--	152,547	115,807	--	--	--
11 years	292,372	224,005	--	--	--	148,068	112,451	--	--	--	144,304	111,554	--	--	--
12 years	285,634	219,901	--	--	--	144,506	110,850	--	--	--	141,128	109,051	--	--	--
13 years	289,555	213,031	--	--	--	146,028	107,726	--	--	--	143,527	105,305	--	--	--
14 years	297,613	210,942	--	--	--	151,096	107,533	--	--	--	146,517	103,409	--	--	--
15 to 19 years . .	1,606,328	941,562	--	--	--	826,725	470,676	--	--	--	779,603	470,886	--	--	--
15 years	311,277	210,175	--	--	--	157,826	106,938	--	--	--	153,451	103,237	--	--	--
16 years	316,742	195,002	--	--	--	162,034	98,002	--	--	--	154,708	97,000	--	--	--
17 years	324,585	189,494	--	--	--	167,678	94,518	--	--	--	156,907	94,976	--	--	--
18 years	319,622	177,647	--	--	--	166,356	88,735	--	--	--	153,266	88,912	--	--	--
19 years	334,102	169,244	--	--	--	172,831	82,483	--	--	--	161,271	86,761	--	--	--
20-24 years. . . .	1,585,863	773,012	--	--	--	819,189	363,454	--	--	--	766,674	409,558	--	--	--
25-29 years. . . .	1,375,914	671,910	--	--	--	697,371	321,490	--	--	--	678,543	350,420	--	--	--
30-34 years. . . .	1,128,545	612,745	--	--	--	558,171	292,740	--	--	--	570,374	320,005	--	--	--
35-39 years. . . .	854,218	559,707	--	--	--	415,802	270,658	--	--	--	438,416	289,049	--	--	--
40-44 years. . . .	712,271	514,862	--	--	--	344,790	252,563	--	--	--	367,481	262,299	--	--	--
45-49 years. . . .	621,589	422,163	--	--	--	300,140	207,584	--	--	--	321,449	214,579	--	--	--
50-54 years. . . .	564,376	303,030	--	--	--	270,070	146,896	--	--	--	294,306	156,134	--	--	--
55-59 years. . . .	454,368	255,739	--	--	--	217,193	121,140	--	--	--	237,175	134,599	--	--	--
60-64 years. . . .	320,969	202,008	--	--	--	147,203	95,990	--	--	--	173,766	106,018	--	--	--
65-69 years. . . .	263,683	163,893	--	--	--	115,548	78,652	--	--	--	148,135	85,241	--	--	--
70-74 years. . . .	193,463	105,294	--	--	--	84,754	49,397	--	--	--	108,709	55,897	--	--	--
75-79 years. . . .	136,390	67,803	--	--	--	58,968	30,987	--	--	--	77,422	36,816	--	--	--
80-84 years. . . .	66,506	39,382	--	--	--	27,381	16,652	--	--	--	39,125	22,730	--	--	--
85 years + over. .	48,838	27,898	--	--	--	18,553	12,075	--	--	--	30,285	15,823	--	--	--

Note: -- indicates data not available.

Source: 1980 data from U.S. Bureau of the Census. "General Population Characteristics: United States Summary." 1980 Census of Population. Washington, DC: U.S. Government Printing Office, 1983, Table 43. 1970 data from U.S. Bureau of the Census. "Subject Reports: Persons of Spanish-Origin." 1970 Census of Population. Washington, DC: U.S. Government Printing Office, 1973, Table 3.

Appendix Table 2. Population Growth in Individual Standard Metropolitan Statistical Areas: 1960-1980

Name of SMSA	Total SMSA				Central cities					Metropolitan rings					
	Population		Percent change		Population		Percent change		Density per square mile	Population		Percent change		Density per square mile	Percent 1980
	1980	1970	1970-80	1960-70	1980	1970	1970-80	1960-70		1980	1970	1970-80	1960-70		
Abilene, TX	139,192	122,164	13.9	-4.8	98,315	89,653	9.7	-0.8	1,293.6	40,877	32,511	25.7	-14.3	15.3	29.4
Akron, OH	660,328	679,239	-2.8	12.2	237,177	275,452	-13.9	-5.1	4,089.3	423,151	403,818	4.8	28.2	499.0	64.1
Albany, GA.	112,402	96,683	16.3	18.1	74,059	72,623	2.0	29.9	1,722.3	38,343	24,060	59.4	-7.4	59.4	34.1
Albany-Schenectady-Troy, NY	795,019	777,977[a]	2.2	8.8	226,337	256,657[a]	-11.8	-8.0	5,389.0	568,682	521,320[a]	9.1	19.6	222.5	71.5
Albuquerque, NM	454,499	333,266	36.4	20.6	331,767	244,501[a]	35.7	21.5	3,492.3	122,732	88,765[a]	38.3	18.0	25.7	27.0
Alexandria, LA.	151,985	131,749	15.4	5.7	51,565	41,811[a]	23.3	3.8	2,864.7	100,420	89,938[a]	11.7	6.6	50.8	66.1
Allentown-Bethlehem-Easton, PA-NJ	635,481	594,382[a]	6.9	9.0	200,204	212,007[a]	-5.6	-1.7	4,883.0	435,277	382,375[a]	13.8	16.1	305.0	68.5
Altoona, PA	136,621	135,356	0.9	-1.4	57,078	63,115[a]	-9.6	-9.1	6,342.0	79,543	72,241[a]	10.1	6.5	153.6	58.2
Amarillo, TX.	173,699	144,396	20.3	-3.4	149,230	127,010	17.5	-7.9	1,865.4	24,469	17,386	40.7	50.9	14.1	14.1
Anaheim-Santa Ana-Garden Grove, CA	1,932,709	1,421,233[a]	36.0	101.9	546,331	443,273[a]	23.2	53.5	6,279.7	1,386,378	977,960[a]	41.8	135.6	1,949.9	71.7
Anchorage, AK	174,431	126,385[a]	38.0	52.6	174,431	48,081[a]	262.8	8.7	100.7	--	78,304[a]	-100.0	102.9	--	--
Anderson, IN.	139,336	138,522[a]	0.6	10.1	64,695	70,787	-8.6	44.3	1,748.5	74,641	67,735[a]	10.2	-11.8	179.4	53.6
Anderson, SC.	133,235	105,474	26.3	7.1	27,313	27,556	-0.9	-33.3	2,276.1	105,922	77,918	35.9	36.3	149.8	79.5
Ann Arbor, MI	264,748	234,103	13.1	35.8	107,966	100,035[a]	7.9	48.6	4,318.6	156,782	134,068[a]	16.9	27.6	228.5	59.2
Anniston, AL.	119,761	103,092	16.2	7.5	29,523	31,533	-6.4	-6.3	1,405.9	90,238	71,559	26.1	15.0	152.9	75.3
Appleton-Oshkosh, WI.	291,369	276,948[a]	5.2	19.4	108,652	109,459	-0.7	17.0	3,746.6	182,717	167,489[a]	9.1	21.0	131.5	62.7
Asheville, NC	177,761	161,059	10.4	9.3	53,583	57,820[a]	-7.3	-3.9	1,847.7	124,178	103,239	20.3	18.5	114.8	69.9
Athens, GA.	130,015	107,702	20.7	32.3	42,549	44,342	-4.0	41.4	2,659.3	87,466	63,360	38.0	26.6	95.1	67.3
Atlanta, GA	2,029,710	1,595,517[a]	27.2	36.5	425,022	495,039[a]	-14.1	1.6	3,244.4	1,604,688	1,100,478	45.8	61.5	381.1	79.1
Atlantic City, NJ	194,119	175,043	10.9	8.8	40,199	47,859	-16.0	-19.6	3,654.5	153,920	127,184	21.0	25.5	276.3	79.3
Augusta, GA-SC	327,372	275,787	18.7	19.9	47,532	59,864	-20.6	-15.2	2,796.0	279,840	215,923	29.6	35.4	165.5	85.5
Austin, TX.	536,688	360,463	48.9	34.9	345,496	253,539[a]	36.3	35.9	2,978.4	191,192	106,924[a]	78.8	32.7	71.1	35.6
Bakersfield, CA	403,089	330,234[a]	22.1	13.1	105,611	69,515	51.9	22.3	1,427.2	297,478	260,719[a]	14.1	10.9	36.9	73.8
Baltimore, MD	2,174,023	2,071,016[a]	5.0	14.8	786,775	905,787[a]	-13.1	-3.5	9,834.7	1,387,248	1,165,229[a]	19.1	34.8	640.2	63.8
Bangor, ME.	83,919	79,933	5.0	-2.3	31,643	33,168	-4.6	-14.8	904.1	52,276	46,765	11.8	9.0	159.9	62.2
Baton Rouge, LA	494,151	375,628	31.6	25.3	219,419	165,921	32.2	8.9	3,539.0	274,732	209,707	31.0	42.0	177.6	55.6
Battle Creek, MI.	187,338	180,129	4.0	5.6	35,724	38,931	-8.2	-11.9	2,101.4	151,614	141,198	7.4	11.7	120.9	81.0
Bay City, MI.	119,881	117,339	2.2	9.6	41,593	49,449	-15.9	-7.8	3,781.2	78,288	67,890	15.3	27.0	179.1	65.3
Beaumont-Port Arthur-Orange, TX	375,497	347,568	8.0	5.1	202,981	199,376	1.8	-5.7	1,380.8	172,516	148,192	16.4	24.3	84.1	50.0
Bellingham, WA.	106,701	81,983	30.2	16.6	45,794	39,375	16.3	13.5	1,991.0	60,907	42,608	42.9	19.6	29.0	57.1
Benton Harbor, MI	171,276	163,940	4.5	9.4	14,707	16,481	-10.8	-13.9	2,941.4	156,569	147,459	6.2	12.8	273.7	91.4
Billings, MT.	108,035	87,367	23.7	10.6	66,798	61,581	8.5	16.5	3,339.9	41,237	25,786	59.9	-1.4	15.8	38.2
Biloxi, Gulfport, MS.	191,918	160,070	19.9	13.9	88,987	89,277	-0.3	20.2	2,224.7	102,931	70,793	45.4	6.8	70.3	53.6
Binghamton, NY-PA	301,336	302,672	-0.4	6.7	55,860	64,123	-12.9	-15.6	5,586.0	245,476	238,549	2.9	14.9	120.0	81.5
Birmingham, AL.	847,487	767,230	10.5	2.8	284,413	300,910	-5.5	-11.7	2,872.9	563,074	466,320	20.7	14.9	172.1	66.4
Bismarck, ND.	79,988	61,024	31.1	10.9	44,485	34,703	28.2	25.4	2,341.3	35,503	26,321	34.9	-3.7	10.1	44.4
Bloomington, IN	98,785	85,221	15.9	43.9	52,044	43,262	20.3	38.0	4,731.3	46,741	41,959	11.4	50.6	125.0	47.3
Bloomington-Normal, IL.	119,149	104,389	14.1	24.5	79,861	66,388	20.3	33.8	3,472.2	39,288	38,001	3.4	11.0	33.8	33.0
Boise City, ID.	173,036	112,230	54.2	20.1	102,451	74,990	36.6	117.3	2,626.9	70,585	37,240	89.5	-36.9	69.7	40.8
Boston, MA.	2,763,357	2,899,101	-4.7	7.9	562,994	641,071	-12.2	-8.1	11,978.6	2,200,363	2,258,030	-2.6	13.4	1,849.0	79.6
Bradenton, FL	148,442	97,115	52.9	40.4	30,170	21,040	43.4	8.6	3,017.0	118,272	76,075	55.5	52.8	160.5	79.7
Bremerton, WA	147,152	101,732	44.6	20.9	36,208	35,307	2.6	22.1	1,905.7	110,944	66,425	67.0	20.2	296.6	75.4
Bridgeport, CT.	395,455	401,752	-1.6	14.7	142,546	156,542	-8.9	-0.1	9,503.1	252,909	245,210	3.1	26.8	1,338.1	64.0
Bristol, CT	73,762	69,878	5.6	22.0	57,370	55,487	3.4	22.0	321.4	16,392	14,391	0.1	22.1	321.4	22.2
Brockton, MA.	169,374	150,416	12.6	25.6	95,172	89,040	6.9	22.3	4,326.0	74,202	61,376	20.9	30.8	634.2	43.8
Brownsville-Harlingen-San Benito, TX.	209,727	140,368	49.4	-7.1	146,528	101,201	44.8	-4.2	2,187.0	63,199	39,167	61.4	-13.8	75.4	30.1
Bryan-College Station, TX	93,588	57,978	61.4	29.1	81,609	51,395	58.8	32.0	1,736.4	11,979	6,583	82.0	10.5	22.1	12.8
Buffalo, NY	1,242,826	1,349,211	-7.9	3.2	357,870	462,768	-22.7	-13.1	8,520.7	884,956	886,443	-0.2	14.5	578.4	71.2
Burlington, NC.	99,319	96,502	2.9	12.6	37,266	35,930	3.7	8.2	2,192.1	62,053	60,572	2.4	15.4	149.2	62.5
Burlington, VT.	114,070	98,336	16.0	33.0	33,712	38,633	-2.4	8.7	3,428.4	76,358	59,703	27.9	55.4	179.2	67.0
Canton, OH.	404,421	393,789	2.7	9.0	94,730	110,053	-13.9	-3.1	4,736.5	309,691	283,736	9.1	14.6	326.7	76.6
Casper, WY.	71,856	51,264	40.2	3.3	51,016	39,361	29.6	1.1	3,644.0	20,840	11,903	75.1	11.3	3.9	29.0
Cedar Rapids, IA.	169,775	163,213	4.0	19.2	110,243	110,642	-0.4	20.2	2,041.5	59,532	52,571	13.2	17.2	88.9	35.0
Champaign-Urbana-Rantoul, IL.	168,392	163,281	3.1	23.3	114,272	116,375	-1.8	17.6	4,761.3	54,120	49,906	15.4	40.3	55.6	32.1
Charleston-North Charleston, SC	430,462	336,125	28.1	20.5	132,044	69,945	97.2	1.5	2,400.8	298,418	269,180	10.9	26.4	116.3	69.3

Appendix Table 2. Population Growth in Individual Standard Metropolitan Statistical Areas: 1960-1980—continued

Name of SMSA	Total SMSA				Central cities					Metropolitan rings					
	Population		Percent change		Population		Percent change		Density per square mile	Population		Percent change		Density per square mile	Percent 1980
	1980	1970	1970-80	1960-70	1980	1970	1970-80	1960-70		1980	1970	1970-80	1960-70		
Charleston, WV	269,595	257,140	4.8	-7.0	63,968	71,505	-10.5	-16.7	2,284.6	205,627	185,635	10.8	-2.7	168.5	76.3
Charlotte-Gastonia, NC	637,218	557,785	14.2	25.7	361,780	288,742	25.3	20.9	2,247.1	275,438	269,043	2.4	31.2	202.1	43.2
Charlottesville, VA.	113,568	89,529	26.9	23.8	39,916	38,880	2.7	32.1	3,991.6	73,652	50,649	45.4	18.0	62.8	65.0
Chattanooga, TN-GA	426,540	370,857	15.0	9.1	169,565	119,923	41.4	-7.8	1,367.5	256,975	250,934	2.4	19.6	130.0	60.2
Chicago, IL.	7,103,624	6,974,755	1.8	12.1	3,005,072	3,369,357	-10.8	-5.1	13,180.1	4,098,552	3,605,398	13.7	35.0	1,172.7	57.7
Chico, CA.	143,851	101,969	41.1	24.3	26,603	19,580	35.9	32.7	1,900.2	117,248	82,389	42.3	22.5	71.8	81.5
Cincinnati, OH-KY-IN	1,401,491	1,387,207	1.0	9.4	385,457	453,514	-15.0	-9.8	4,941.8	1,016,034	933,693	8.8	21.9	493.0	72.5
Clarksville-Hopkinsville, TN-KY.	150,220	118,945	26.3	5.7	82,095	53,114	54.6	28.0	1,391.4	68,125	65,831	3.5	-7.4	56.7	43.4
Cleveland, OH.	1,898,825	2,063,729	-8.0	8.1	573,822	750,879	-23.6	-14.3	7,263.6	1,325,003	1,312,850	0.9	27.0	919.5	69.8
Colorado Springs, CO	317,458	239,288	32.7	63.6	215,150	135,517	58.8	93.1	2,088.8	102,308	103,771	-1.4	36.5	39.6	32.2
Columbia, MO	100,376	80,935	24.0	46.6	62,061	58,812	5.5	60.5	1,477.6	38,315	22,123	73.2	19.2	59.4	38.2
Columbia, SC	410,088	322,880	27.0	23.8	101,208	113,542	-10.9	16.5	945.9	308,880	209,338	47.6	28.1	226.8	75.3
Columbus, GA-AL.	239,196	238,584	0.3	9.4	169,441	155,028	9.3	32.8	777.3	69,755	83,556	-16.5	-17.4	78.9	29.2
Columbus, OH	1,093,316	1,017,847	7.4	20.4	564,871	540,025	4.6	14.6	3,120.8	528,445	477,822	10.6	27.8	231.7	48.3
Corpus Christi, TX	326,228	284,832	14.5	6.8	231,999	204,525	13.4	22.0	2,230.8	94,229	80,307	17.3	-18.8	65.6	28.9
Cumberland, MD-WV.	107,782	107,153	0.6	0.6	25,933	29,724	-12.8	-11.0	3,241.6	81,849	77,429	5.7	5.9	110.3	76.0
Dallas-Fort Worth, TX.	2,974,805	2,377,623	25.1	36.8	1,289,242	1,237,856	4.2	19.5	2,250.0	1,685,563	1,139,767	47.9	62.4	217.4	56.7
Danbury, CN.	146,405	115,538	26.7	49.3	60,470	50,781	19.1	121.5	1,286.6	85,935	64,757	32.7	18.9	419.2	58.7
Danville, VA	111,789	105,180	6.3	0.3	45,642	46,391	-1.6	-0.4	2,684.8	66,147	58,789	12.5	0.8	66.5	59.2
Davenport-Rock Island-Moline, IA-IL.	383,958	362,638	5.9	13.5	196,009	194,872	0.6	6.2	2,117.9	187,949	167,766	12.0	23.5	116.3	49.0
Dayton, OH	830,070	852,531	-2.6	17.2	203,371	243,023	-16.3	-7.4	4,236.9	626,699	609,508	2.8	31.1	377.5	75.5
Daytona Beach, FL.	258,762	169,487	52.7	35.2	54,176	45,327	19.5	21.2	1,934.9	204,586	124,160	64.8	41.2	188.6	79.1
Decatur, IL.	131,375	125,010	5.1	5.7	94,081	90,397	4.1	15.9	2,542.7	37,294	34,613	7.7	-14.0	68.6	28.4
Denver-Boulder, CO	1,620,902	1,239,545	30.8	32.6	569,050	581,548	-2.1	9.4	4,377.3	1,051,852	657,997	59.9	63.2	232.9	64.9
Des Moines, IA	338,048	313,562	7.8	9.2	191,003	201,404	-5.2	-3.6	2,894.0	147,045	112,158	31.1	43.5	135.2	43.5
Detroit, MI.	4,353,413	4,435,051	-1.8	12.3	1,203,339	1,514,063	-20.5	-9.3	8,848.1	3,150,074	2,920,988	7.8	28.1	828.3	72.3
Dubuque, IA.	93,745	90,609	3.5	13.2	62,321	62,309	--	10.1	2,709.6	31,424	28,300	11.0	20.7	53.8	33.5
Duluth-Superior, MN-WI	266,650	265,350	0.5	-4.1	122,382	132,815	-7.9	-5.4	1,154.5	144,268	132,535	8.9	-2.7	19.7	54.1
Eau Claire, WI	130,932	114,936	13.9	11.2	51,509	44,619	15.4	17.5	1,907.1	79,423	70,317	12.9	7.5	48.8	60.7
El Paso, TX.	479,899	359,291	33.6	14.4	425,259	322,261	32.0	16.5	1,779.3	54,640	37,030	47.6	-0.9	70.5	11.4
Elkhart, IN.	137,330	126,529	8.5	18.5	41,305	43,152	-4.3	7.1	2,581.6	96,025	83,377	15.2	25.3	213.4	69.9
Elmira, NY	97,656	101,537	-3.8	2.9	35,327	39,945	-11.6	-14.1	5,046.7	62,329	61,592	1.2	18.0	154.3	63.8
Enid, OK	62,820	56,343	11.5	6.4	50,363	44,986	12.0	15.8	680.6	12,457	11,357	9.7	-19.5	12.6	19.8
Erie, PA	279,780	263,654	6.1	5.2	119,123	129,265	-7.8	-6.6	5,414.7	160,657	134,389	19.5	19.7	205.4	57.4
Eugene-Springfield, OR	275,226	215,401	27.8	32.2	147,245	105,902	39.0	50.0	3,201.0	105,624	79,028	33.7	55.0	3,200.7	38.4
Evansville, IN-KY.	309,408	284,959	8.6	4.7	130,496	138,764	-6.0	-2.0	3,526.9	178,912	146,195	22.4	12.0	92.8	57.8
Fall River, MA-RI.	176,831	169,549	4.3	11.6	92,574	96,898	-4.5	-3.0	2,722.8	84,257	72,651	16.0	39.9	465.5	47.6
Fargo-Moorhead, ND-MN.	137,574	120,261	14.4	13.4	91,381	83,052	10.0	19.3	2,610.9	29,998	29,687	1.0	29.4	3,333.1	21.8
Fayetteville, NC	247,160	212,042	16.6	42.9	59,507	53,510	11.2	13.6	1,803.2	187,653	158,532	18.4	56.5	300.7	75.9
Fayetteville-Springdale, AK.	178,609	127,846	39.7	38.9	60,066	47,512	26.4	56.5	1,072.6	118,543	80,334	47.6	30.2	68.2	66.4
Fitchburg-Leominster, MA	99,957	97,164	2.9	7.8	74,088	76,282	-2.9	7.5	1,323.0	25,869	20,882	23.9	8.7	237.3	25.9
Flint, MI.	521,589	508,664	2.5	18.9	159,611	193,317	-17.4	-1.8	4,987.8	361,978	315,347	14.8	36.6	314.8	69.4
Florence, AL	135,065	117,743	14.7	8.9	37,029	34,031	8.8	7.5	1,763.3	98,036	83,712	17.1	9.5	79.8	72.6
Florence, SC	110,163	89,636	22.9	6.2	30,062	25,997	15.6	5.2	2,505.2	80,101	63,639	25.9	6.6	101.1	72.7
Fort Collins, CO	149,184	89,900	65.9	68.5	65,092	43,337	50.2	73.2	2,958.7	84,092	46,563	80.6	64.4	32.6	56.4
Fort Lauderdale-Hollywood, FL.	1,018,200	620,100	64.2	85.7	274,602	246,463	11.4	107.3	4,992.8	743,598	373,637	99.0	73.7	73.0	73.0
Fort Myers-Cape Coral, FL.	205,266	105,216	95.1	92.9	68,741	27,351	151.3	21.4	563.5	136,525	77,865	75.3	143.2	200.5	66.5
Fort Smith, AK-OK.	203,511	160,421	26.9	18.7	71,626	62,802	14.1	18.5	1,557.1	131,885	97,619	35.1	18.9	39.4	64.8
Fort Walton Beach, FL.	109,920	88,187	24.6	44.2	20,829	19,994	4.2	64.6	2,975.6	89,091	68,193	30.6	39.1	95.9	81.1
Fort Wayne, IN	382,961	361,984	5.8	18.2	172,196	178,269	-3.4	10.2	3,249.0	210,765	183,715	14.7	27.1	125.5	55.0
Fresno, CA	514,621	413,329	24.5	12.9	218,202	165,655	31.7	23.7	3,306.1	296,419	247,674	19.7	6.7	50.1	57.6
Gadsden, AL.	103,057	94,144	9.5	-2.9	47,565	53,928	-11.8	-7.2	1,359.0	55,492	40,216	38.0	3.4	109.5	53.8
Gainesville, FL.	151,348	104,764	44.5	41.4	81,371	64,510	26.1	117.2	2,542.8	69,977	40,254	73.8	-9.3	80.5	46.2
Galveston-Texas City, TX	195,940	169,812	15.4	21.0	103,305	100,717	2.6	1.5	930.7	92,635	69,095	34.1	68.0	321.6	47.3
Gary-Hammond-East Chicago, IN.	642,781	633,367	1.5	10.4	285,453	330,380	-13.6	-5.0	3,857.5	357,328	302,987	17.9	34.1	422.9	55.6

Appendix Table 2. Population Growth in Individual Standard Metropolitan Statistical Areas: 1960-1980–continued

Name of SMSA	Total SMSA				Central cities					Metropolitan rings					
	Population		Percent change		Population		Percent change		Density per square mile	Population		Percent change		Density per square mile	Percent 1980
	1980	1970	1970-80	1960-70	1980	1970	1970-80	1960-70		1980	1970	1970-80	1960-70		
Glens Falls, NY.	109,649	102,127	7.4	10.4	15,897	17,222	-7.7	-7.3	3,974.3	93,752	84,905	10.4	14.9	54.7	85.5
Grand Forks, ND-MN	100,944	95,537	5.7	12.6	43,765	39,008	12.2	13.2	3,366.5	57,179	56,529	1.1	12.1	16.8	56.6
Grand Rapids, MI	601,680	539,225	11.6	16.7	181,843	197,649	-8.0	11.5	4,228.9	419,837	341,576	22.9	20.0	302.9	69.8
Great Falls, MT.	80,696	81,804	-1.4	11.4	56,725	60,691	-5.6	8.8	3,545.3	23,971	21,713	10.4	19.5	8.9	29.7
Greeley, CO.	123,438	89,297	38.2	23.4	53,006	38,902	36.3	47.8	3,786.1	70,432	50,395	39.8	9.5	17.7	57.1
Green Bay, WI.	175,280	158,244	10.8	26.5	87,899	87,809	0.1	39.6	1,758.0	87,381	70,435	24.1	13.3	184.0	49.9
Greensboro-Winston-Salem-High Point, NC	827,252	724,129	14.2	16.4	350,907	340,988	2.9	16.5	2,293.5	476,345	383,141	24.3	16.4	156.9	57.6
Greenville-Spartanburg, SC	569,066	473,454	20.2	14.7	102,210	105,982	-3.6	-4.1	2,147.7	446,856	367,472	27.0	21.6	226.5	78.5
Hagerstown, MD	113,086	103,829	8.9	13.8	34,132	35,862	-4.8	-2.2	3,792.4	78,954	67,967	16.2	24.6	177.0	69.8
Hamilton-Middletown, OH.	258,787	226,207	14.4	13.6	106,908	116,632	-8.3	1.9	2,741.2	151,879	109,575	38.6	29.5	353.2	58.7
Harrisburg, PA	446,576	410,505	8.8	10.5	53,264	68,061	-21.7	-14.6	6,658.0	393,312	342,444	14.9	17.3	242.3	88.1
Hartford, CT	726,114	720,581	0.8	22.5	136,392	158,017	-13.7	-2.6	7,577.3	589,722	562,564	4.8	32.0	581.0	81.2
Hickory, NC.	130,207	110,339	18.0	24.2	20,684	20,459	1.1	5.9	1,723.7	109,523	89,880	21.9	29.3	170.6	84.1
Honolulu, HI	762,565	630,528	20.9	26.0	365,048	324,871	12.4	10.4	4,196.0	397,517	305,657	30.1	48.2	781.0	52.1
Houston, TX.	2,905,353	1,999,316	45.3	39.8	1,595,138	1,233,535	29.3	31.5	2,869.0	1,310,215	765,781	71.1	55.6	211.5	45.1
Huntington-Ashland, WV-KY-OH . . .	311,350	286,935	8.5	1.0	90,748	103,560	-12.4	-9.9	3,361.0	220,602	183,375	20.3	8.4	127.7	70.9
Huntsville, AL	308,593	282,450	9.3	39.9	142,513	139,282	2.3	92.5	1,250.1	166,080	143,168	16.0	10.5	91.4	53.8
Indianapolis, IN	1,166,575	1,111,352	5.0	17.7	700,807	736,856	-4.9	54.7	1,990.9	465,768	374,496	24.4	-20.0	170.9	39.9
Iowa City, IA.	81,717	72,127	13.3	34.4	50,508	46,850	7.8	40.1	2,295.8	31,209	25,277	23.5	25.0	52.7	38.2
Jackson, MI.	151,495	143,274	5.7	8.5	39,739	45,484	-12.6	-10.3	3,612.6	111,756	97,790	14.3	20.3	161.0	73.8
Jackson, MS.	320,425	258,906	23.8	17.0	202,895	153,968	31.8	6.6	1,914.1	117,530	104,938	12.0	36.4	75.8	36.7
Jacksonville, FL	737,541	621,827	18.6	17.4	540,920	504,265	7.3	150.8	711.7	196,621	117,562	67.2	-64.2	79.9	26.7
Jacksonville, NC	112,784	103,126	9.4	19.6	17,056	16,289	4.7	20.7	2,132.0	95,728	86,837	10.2	19.4	126.8	84.9
Janesville-Beloit, WI.	139,420	131,970	5.6	15.9	86,278	82,155	5.0	20.8	2,396.6	53,142	49,815	6.7	8.5	77.4	38.1
Jersey City, NJ.	556,972	607,839	-8.4	-0.5	223,532	260,350	-14.1	-5.7	17,194.8	333,440	347,489	-4.0	3.8	10,104.2	59.9
Johnson City-Kingsport-Bristol, TN-VA	433,638	373,591	16.1	7.6	95,766	85,722	11.7	14.2	1,544.6	337,872	287,819	17.4	5.8	120.6	77.9
Johnstown, PA.	264,506	262,822	0.6	-6.4	35,496	42,476	-16.4	-21.3	5,916.0	229,010	220,346	3.9	-2.8	130.2	86.6
Joplin, MO	127,513	112,833	13.0	3.6	38,893	39,256	-0.9	0.8	1,341.1	88,620	73,577	20.4	5.1	71.5	69.5
Kalamazoo-Portage, MI.	279,192	257,723	8.3	18.2	117,879	119,145	-1.1	45.1	2,105.0	161,313	138,578	16.4	1.9	144.4	57.8
Kankakee, IL	102,926	97,250	5.8	5.6	30,141	30,944	-2.6	11.8	2,740.1	72,785	66,306	9.8	3.0	109.0	70.7
Kansas City, MO-KS	1,327,106	1,273,926	4.2	14.9	448,159	507,330	-11.7	6.7	1,418.2	878,947	766,596	14.7	21.1	291.4	66.2
Kenosha, WI.	123,137	117,917	4.4	17.2	77,685	78,805	-1.4	16.1	5,179.0	45,452	39,112	16.2	19.6	176.9	36.9
Killeen-Temple, TX	214,656	159,794	34.3	35.4	88,779	68,938	28.8	28.1	1,409.2	125,877	90,856	38.5	41.4	61.4	58.6
Knoxville, TN.	476,517	409,409	16.4	8.7	175,030	174,587	0.3	56.1	2,273.1	301,487	234,822	28.4	-11.3	195.3	63.3
Kokomo, IN	103,715	89,848	3.9	17.0	47,808	44,042	8.6	-6.7	3,187.2	55,907	55,806	0.2	46.2	103.7	53.9
La Crosse, WI.	91,056	80,468	13.2	11.0	48,347	50,286	-3.9	5.7	2,843.9	42,709	30,182	41.5	21.3	96.8	46.9
Lafayette, LA.	150,017	111,643	34.4	31.9	81,961	68,908	18.9	70.6	3,035.6	68,056	42,735	59.3	-3.4	280.1	45.4
Lafayette-West Lafayette, IN . . .	121,702	109,378	11.3	22.7	64,258	64,112	0.2	16.5	4,016.1	57,444	45,266	26.9	32.7	118.2	47.2
Lake Charles, LA	167,223	145,415	15.0	--	75,226	77,998	-3.6	23.0	2,786.1	91,997	67,417	36.5	-17.9	87.3	55.0
Lakeland-Winter Haven, FL.	321,652	228,515	40.8	17.1	68,525	58,939	16.3	2.3	2,362.9	253,127	169,576	49.3	23.3	141.1	78.7
Lancaster, PA.	362,346	320,079	13.2	15.0	54,725	57,690	-5.1	-5.5	9,120.8	307,621	262,389	17.2	20.7	325.2	84.9
Lansing-East Lansing, MI	471,565	424,271	11.1	24.0	181,806	178,943	1.6	29.7	4,132.0	289,759	245,328	18.1	20.2	129.1	61.4
Laredo, TX	99,258	72,859	36.2	12.5	91,449	69,024	32.5	13.8	4,572.5	7,809	3,835	103.6	-6.8	2.3	7.9
Las Cruces, NM	96,340	69,773	38.1	16.4	45,086	37,857	19.1	28.9	1,960.3	51,254	31,916	60.6	4.4	13.5	53.2
Las Vegas, NV.	463,087	273,288	69.5	115.2	164,674	125,787	30.9	95.3	2,994.1	298,413	147,501	102.3	135.6	38.1	64.4
Lawrence, KS	67,640	57,932	16.8	32.5	52,738	45,698	15.4	39.1	2,775.7	14,902	12,234	21.8	12.6	33.7	22.0
Lawrence-Haverhill, MA-NH.	281,981	258,564	9.1	18.4	110,040	113,035	-2.6	-3.6	2,895.8	171,941	145,529	18.1	44.0	641.6	61.0
Lawton, OK	112,456	108,144	4.0	19.1	80,054	74,470	7.5	20.7	1,790.0	32,402	33,674	-3.8	15.7	31.4	28.8
Lewiston-Auburn, ME.	72,378	72,474	-0.1	3.1	63,609	65,930	-3.5	1.0	655.8	8,769	6,544	34.0	29.8	350.8	12.1
Lexington-Fayette, KY.	317,629	266,701	19.1	25.8	204,165	108,137	88.8	72.2	716.4	113,464	158,564	-28.4	6.2	94.6	35.7
Lima, OH	218,244	210,074	3.9	6.6	47,381	53,734	-11.8	5.3	3,948.4	170,863	156,340	9.3	7.1	101.4	78.3
Lincoln, NB.	192,884	167,972	14.8	8.2	171,932	149,518	15.0	16.3	2,865.5	20,952	18,454	13.5	-31.0	26.9	10.9
Little Rock-North Little Rock, AR.	393,774	323,296	21.8	18.9	222,749	192,523	15.7	16.1	2,043.6	171,025	130,773	30.8	23.3	123.7	43.4
Long Branch-Asbury Park, NJ. . . .	503,173	461,849	8.9	38.1	46,834	48,307	-3.0	10.8	6,690.6	456,339	413,542	10.3	42.2	979.3	90.7
Longview-Marshall, TX.	151,752	120,770	25.7	5.0	87,683	68,484	28.0	7.2	1,349.0	64,096	52,286	22.5	2.3	57.4	42.2

Appendix Table 2. Population Growth in Individual Standard Metropolitan Statistical Areas: 1960-1980–continued

Name of SMSA	Total SMSA				Central cities					Metropolitan rings					
	Population		Percent change		Population		Percent change		Density per square mile	Population		Percent change		Density per square mile	Percent 1980
	1980	1970	1970-80	1960-70	1980	1970	1970-80	1960-70		1980	1970	1970-80	1960-70		
Lorain-Elyria, OH.	274,909	256,843	7.0	18.1	132,954	131,612	1.0	16.8	3,092.0	141,955	125,231	13.4	19.5	314.1	51.6
Los Angeles-Long Beach, CA	7,477,503	7,041,980	6.2	16.6	3,328,184	3,170,680	5.0	12.3	6,462.5	4,149,319	3,871,300	7.2	20.4	1,166.9	55.5
Louisville, KY-IN.	906,152	867,330	4.5	15.0	298,451	361,706	-17.5	-7.4	4,974.2	607,701	505,624	20.2	39.1	452.8	67.1
Lowell, MA-NH.	233,410	218,268	6.9	30.8	92,418	94,239	-1.9	2.3	7,109.1	140,992	124,029	13.7	65.9	854.5	60.4
Lubbock, TX.	211,651	179,295	18.0	14.7	173,979	149,101	16.7	15.9	1,911.9	37,672	30,194	24.8	9.5	46.5	17.8
Lynchburg, VA.	153,260	133,258	15.0	11.2	66,743	54,083	23.4	-1.3	1,334.9	86,517	79,175	9.3	21.7	65.5	56.5
Macon, GA.	253,794	226,782	11.9	15.2	116,896	122,423	-4.5	75.5	2,337.9	136,898	104,359	31.2	-17.9	102.2	53.9
Madison, WI.	323,545	290,272	11.5	30.7	170,616	171,809	-0.7	35.6	3,159.6	152,929	118,463	29.1	24.2	132.9	47.3
Manchester, NH	160,767	132,512	21.3	12.7	90,936	87,754	3.6	-0.6	2,841.8	69,831	44,758	56.0	52.6	307.6	43.4
Mansfield, OH.	131,205	129,997	0.9	10.4	53,927	55,047	-2.0	16.3	2,074.1	77,278	74,950	3.1	6.4	163.7	58.9
McAllen-Pharr-Edinburg, TX	283,229	181,535	56.0	0.3	111,737	70,628	58.2	7.8	2,539.5	171,492	110,907	54.6	-3.9	112.4	60.5
Medford, OR.	132,456	94,533	40.1	27.8	39,603	28,973	36.7	18.6	2,329.6	92,853	65,560	41.6	32.3	33.5	70.1
Melbourne-Titusville-Cocoa, FL	272,959	230,006	18.7	106.4	94,542	86,861	8.8	183.1	1,853.8	178,417	143,145	24.6	77.3	189.0	65.4
Memphis, TN-AK-MS.	913,472	834,103	9.5	14.7	646,356	623,988	3.6	25.4	2,448.3	267,116	210,115	27.1	-8.5	130.7	29.2
Meriden, CN.	57,118	55,959	2.1	7.9	57,118	55,959	2.1	7.9	2,483.4	--	--	--	--	--	--
Miami, FL.	1,625,781	1,267,792	28.2	35.6	346,865	334,859	3.6	14.8	10,201.9	1,278,916	932,933	37.1	45.0	665.8	78.7
Meidland, TX	82,636	65,433	26.3	-3.4	70,525	59,463	18.6	-5.0	2,074.3	12,111	5,970	102.9	17.2	14.0	14.7
Milwaukee, WI.	1,397,143	1,403,884	-0.5	9.8	636,212	717,372	-11.3	-3.2	6,627.2	760,931	686,512	10.8	27.7	557.5	54.5
Minneapolis-St. Paul, MN-WI.	2,113,533	1,965,391	7.5	23.0	641,181	744,266	-13.9	-6.5	5,936.9	1,472,352	1,221,125	20.6	52.3	327.1	69.7
Mobile, AL	443,536	376,690	17.7	3.7	200,452	190,026	5.5	-2.5	1,629.7	243,084	186,664	30.2	10.8	89.9	54.8
Modesto, CA.	265,900	194,506	36.7	23.7	106,602	61,712	72.7	68.7	4,264.1	159,298	132,794	20.0	10.0	107.6	59.9
Monroe, LA	139,241	115,387	20.7	13.5	57,597	56,374	2.2	8.0	2,303.9	81,644	59,013	38.3	19.4	135.6	58.6
Montgomery, AL	272,687	225,911	20.7	3.4	177,857	133,386	33.3	-0.7	1,389.5	94,830	92,525	2.5	10.0	50.3	34.8
Muncie, IN	128,587	129,219	-0.5	16.5	77,216	69,082	11.8	0.7	3,509.8	51,371	60,137	-14.6	42.1	138.8	40.0
Muskegon-Norton Shores-Muskegon Heights, MI.	179,591	175,410	2.4	5.4	77,459	84,206	-8.0	27.5	1,760.4	102,132	91,204	12.0	-9.2	101.7	56.9
Nashua, NH	114,221	86,280	32.4	57.2	67,865	55,820	21.6	42.8	2,189.2	46,356	30,460	52.2	93.0	380.0	40.6
Nashville-Davidson, TN	850,505	699,271	21.6	17.2	455,651	426,029	7.0	175.6	949.3	394,854	273,242	44.5	-38.2	110.3	46.4
Nassau-Suffolk, NY	2,605,813	2,555,868	2.0	29.9	--	--	--	--	--	2,605,813	2,555,868	2.0	29.9	2,175.1	100.0
New Bedford, MA.	169,425	161,288	5.0	7.9	98,478	101,777	-3.2	-0.7	5,183.1	70,947	59,511	19.2	26.8	381.4	41.9
New Britain, CN.	142,241	145,269	-2.1	12.3	73,840	83,441	-11.5	1.5	5,274.3	68,401	61,828	10.6	31.0	937.0	48.1
New Brunswick-Perth Amboy-Sayreville, NJ	595,893	583,813	2.1	34.6	110,362	113,191	-2.5	12.4	4,414.5	485,531	470,622	3.2	41.3	1,668.5	81.5
New Haven-West Haven, CN	417,592	411,287	1.5	14.4	179,293	190,558	-5.9	-2.3	6,182.5	238,299	220,729	8.0	34.2	773.7	57.1
New London-Norwich, CN-RI.	248,554	241,862	2.8	23.2	66,916	73,369	-8.8	0.9	1,968.1	181,638	168,493	7.8	36.3	407.3	73.1
New Orleans, LA.	1,187,073	1,046,470	13.4	15.4	557,515	593,471	-6.1	-5.4	2,801.6	629,558	452,999	39.0	62.0	368.8	53.0
New York, NY-NJ.	9,120,346	9,973,716	-8.6	4.6	7,071,639	7,895,563	-10.4	1.5	23,416.0	2,048,707	2,078,153	-1.4	18.2	1,897.0	22.5
Newark, NJ	1,965,969	2,057,468	-4.4	12.2	329,248	381,930	-13.8	-5.7	13,718.7	1,636,721	1,675,538	-2.3	17.3	1,668.4	83.3
Newark, OH	120,981	107,799	12.2	19.5	41,200	41,836	-1.5	0.1	2,423.5	79,781	65,963	20.9	36.1	119.3	66.0
Newburgh-Middletown, NY.	259,603	221,657	17.1	20.6	44,892	48,826	-8.1	-10.3	4,988.0	214,711	172,831	24.2	33.7	262.8	82.7
Newport News-Hampton, VA	364,449	333,140	9.4	30.7	267,520	258,956	3.3	27.6	2,286.5	96,929	74,184	30.7	43.0	188.6	26.6
Norfolk-Virginia Beach City-Portsmouth, VA-NC.	806,951	732,600	10.1	16.5	633,755	591,020	7.2	38.2	1,869.5	173,196	141,580	22.3	-29.7	172.3	21.5
Northeast, PA.	640,396	621,882	3.0	0.1	166,986	191,978	-13.0	-7.3	4,394.4	473,410	429,904	10.1	3.8	246.2	74.0
Norwalk, CN.	126,692	127,595	-0.7	26.6	77,767	79,288	-1.9	17.0	3,534.9	48,925	48,307	1.3	46.3	730.2	38.6
Ocala, FL.	122,488	69,030	77.4	33.7	37,170	22,583	64.6	66.1	1,376.7	85,318	46,447	83.7	22.2	53.9	69.7
Odessa, TX	115,374	92,660	24.5	1.8	90,027	78,380	14.9	-2.4	3,104.4	25,347	14,280	77.5	34.0	29.0	22.0
Oklahoma City, OK.	834,088	699,092	19.3	23.5	403,213	368,164	9.5	13.5	667.6	430,875	330,928	30.2	36.9	148.6	51.7
Olympia, WA.	124,264	76,894	61.6	79.7	27,447	23,296	17.8	27.5	1,614.5	96,817	53,598	80.6	45.7	136.4	78.0
Omaha, NE-IO	569,614	542,646	5.0	18.5	314,255	346,929	-9.4	15.0	3,453.4	255,359	195,717	30.5	25.2	178.2	44.8
Orlando, FL.	700,055	453,270	54.4	34.3	128,291	99,006	29.6	12.3	3,207.3	571,764	354,264	61.4	42.1	227.0	81.7
Owensboro, KY.	85,949	79,486	8.1	12.6	54,450	50,329	8.2	18.5	4,950.0	31,499	29,157	8.0	3.7	69.8	36.6
Oxnard-Simi Valley-Ventura, CA	529,174	378,497	39.8	90.1	260,088	189,021	37.6	172.4	3,824.8	269,086	189,476	42.0	46.0	150.0	50.9
Panama City, FL.	97,740	75,283	29.8	12.1	33,346	32,096	3.9	-3.5	2,084.1	64,394	43,187	49.1	27.6	86.8	65.9
Parkersburg-Marietta, WV-OH.	162,836	148,132	9.9	10.2	56,434	61,069	-7.6	-0.9	2,970.2	106,402	87,063	22.2	19.6	86.9	65.3
Pascagoula-Moss Point, MS.	118,015	87,975	34.1	58.5	48,316	46,585	3.7	95.9	1,610.5	69,699	41,390	68.4	30.4	99.4	59.1
Paterson-Clifton-Passaic, NJ	447,585	460,782	-2.9	13.3	264,821	284,385	-6.2	1.0	11,514.0	182,764	178,397	2.4	40.6	1,114.4	40.8
Pensacola, FL.	289,782	243,075	19.2	19.5	57,619	59,507	-3.2	4.9	2,400.8	232,163	183,568	26.5	25.2	139.9	80.1

Appendix Table 2. Population Growth in Individual Standard Metropolitan Statistical Areas: 1960-1980–continued

Name of SMSA	Total SMSA				Central cities					Metropolitan rings					
	Population		Percent change		Population		Percent change		Density per square mile	Population		Percent change		Density per square mile	Percent 1980
	1980	1970	1970-80	1960-70	1980	1970	1970-80	1960-70		1980	1970	1970-80	1960-70		
Peoria, IL	365,864	341,979	7.0	9.1	124,160	126,963	-2.2	23.1	3,028.3	241,704	215,016	12.4	2.3	137.6	66.1
Petersburg-Colonial Heights-Hopewell, VA	129,296	128,809	0.4	20.7	80,961	74,671	8.4	16.3	1,974.7	48,335	54,138	-10.7	27.5	62.5	37.4
Philadelphia, PA-NJ	4,716,818	4,824,110	-2.2	11.1	1,688,210	1,949,996	-13.4	-2.6	12,413.3	3,028,608	2,874,114	5.4	22.8	891.8	64.2
Phoenix, AR	1,509,052	971,228	55.4	46.4	789,704	584,303	35.2	33.0	2,437.4	719,348	386,925	35.2	33.0	81.7	47.7
Pine Bluff, AK	90,718	85,329	6.3	4.9	56,636	57,389	-1.3	30.3	2,574.4	34,082	27,940	22.0	-25.2	39.6	37.6
Pittsburgh, PA	2,263,894	2,401,362	-5.7	-0.2	423,938	520,089	-18.5	-13.9	7,708.0	1,839,956	1,881,273	-2.2	4.5	613.5	83.1
Pittsfield, MA	90,505	96,817	-6.5	3.2	51,974	57,020	-8.8	-1.5	1,267.7	38,531	39,797	-3.2	10.8	225.3	42.6
Portland, ME	183,625	170,081	8.0	4.5	61,572	65,116	-5.4	-10.3	2,677.0	122,053	104,965	16.3	16.4	357.9	66.5
Portland, OR-WA.	1,242,594	1,007,130	23.4	22.5	366,383	379,967	-3.6	2.0	3,557.1	876,211	627,163	39.7	39.6	246.8	70.5
Portsmouth-Dover-Rochester, NH-ME.	163,880	142,264	15.2	13.3	70,191	64,505	8.8	4.1	797.6	93,689	77,759	20.5	22.3	230.8	57.2
Poughkeepsie, NY	245,055	222,295	10.2	26.3	215,298	190,266	13.2	38.2	7,439.3	215,298	190,266	13.2	26.3	304.8	87.9
Providence-Warwick-Pawtucket, RI-MA.	919,216	908,887	1.1	10.7	315,131	339,794	-7.4	-4.8	5,002.1	604,085	569,093	6.1	22.6	869.2	65.7
Provo-Orem, UT	218,106	137,776	58.3	28.8	126,507	78,860	60.4	44.9	2,432.8	91,559	58,916	55.5	12.1	46.6	42.0
Pueblo, CO	125,972	118,238	6.5	-0.4	101,686	97,774	4.0	7.2	3,081.4	24,286	20,464	18.7	-25.7	10.4	19.3
Racine, WI	173,132	170,838	1.3	20.5	85,725	95,162	-9.9	6.8	6,123.2	87,407	75,676	15.5	43.8	272.3	50.5
Raleigh-Durham, NC	531,167	419,254	26.7	29.4	251,086	218,268	15.0	26.7	2,671.1	280,081	200,986	39.4	32.4	192.1	52.7
Reading, PA.	312,509	296,382	5.4	7.6	78,686	87,643	-10.2	-10.7	7,868.6	233,823	208,739	12.0	17.8	274.8	74.8
Redding, CA.	115,715	77,640	49.0	30.6	41,995	16,659	152.1	30.4	1,448.1	73,720	60,981	20.9	30.6	19.6	63.7
Reno, NV	193,623	121,068	59.9	42.9	100,756	72,863	38.3	41.6	3,250.2	92,867	48,205	14.8	92.7	44.9	48.0
Richland-Kennewick-Pasco, WA	144,469	93,356	54.8	9.3	85,919	55,422	55.0	5.9	1,481.4	58,550	37,934	54.3	14.6	20.2	40.5
Richmond, VA	632,015	547,542	15.4	18.5	219,214	249,332	-12.1	13.4	3,653.6	412,801	298,210	38.4	23.2	198.7	65.3
Riverside-San Bernardino-Ontario, CA.	1,558,182	1,139,149	36.8	40.7	377,186	311,076	21.3	39.6	2,342.8	1,180,996	828,073	42.6	41.1	43.6	75.8
Roanoke, VA.	224,331	203,153	10.4	4.2	100,220	92,115	8.8	-5.1	2,330.7	124,121	111,038	11.8	13.5	108.9	55.3
Rochester, MN.	92,006	84,104	9.4	28.3	57,890	53,766	7.7	32.2	3,046.8	34,116	30,338	12.5	22.0	53.6	37.1
Rochester, NY.	971,230	961,516	1.0	20.1	241,741	295,011	-18.1	-7.4	7,110.0	729,489	666,505	9.4	38.3	251.4	75.1
Rockford, IL	279,514	272,063	2.7	18.2	139,712	147,370	-5.2	16.3	3,582.4	139,802	124,693	12.1	20.6	184.2	50.0
Rock Hill, SC.	106,720	85,216	25.2	8.2	35,344	33,846	4.4	15.1	2,209.0	71,376	51,370	38.9	4.1	106.7	66.9
Sacramento, CA	1,014,002	803,793	26.2	28.5	275,741	257,105	7.2	34.1	2,872.3	738,261	546,688	35.0	26.0	223.3	72.8
Saginaw, MI.	228,059	219,743	3.8	15.2	77,508	91,849	-15.6	-6.5	4,559.3	150,551	127,894	17.7	38.3	188.7	66.0
St. Cloud, MN.	163,256	134,585	21.3	21.8	42,556	39,691	7.2	17.4	2,837.7	120,690	94,894	27.2	23.8	55.7	74.0
St. Joseph, MO	101,868	98,828	3.1	-2.8	76,691	72,748	5.4	-8.7	1,743.0	25,177	26,080	-3.5	18.7	31.5	24.7
St. Louis, MO-IL	2,356,460	2,410,884	-2.3	12.4	453,085	622,236	-27.2	-17.0	7,427.6	1,903,375	1,788,648	6.4	28.3	388.0	80.8
Salem, OR.	249,895	186,658	33.9	26.6	89,233	68,725	29.8	39.8	2,411.7	160,662	117,933	36.2	20.0	85.1	64.3
Salinas-Seaside-Monterey, CA	290,444	247,450	17.4	24.8	144,604	122,081	18.4	72.1	4,381.9	145,840	125,369	16.3	-1.6	44.6	50.2
Salisbury-Concord, NC.	185,081	164,664	12.4	9.1	39,619	40,979	-3.3	4.8	1,800.9	145,462	123,685	17.6	10.6	168.7	78.6
Salt Lake City-Ogden, UT	936,255	705,458	32.7	22.4	227,440	245,363	-7.3	-5.5	2,251.9	708,815	460,095	54.1	45.3	84.0	75.7
San Angelo, TX	84,784	71,047	19.3	9.9	73,240	63,884	14.6	8.6	1,927.4	11,544	7,163	61.2	23.2	7.8	13.6
San Antonio, TX.	1,071,954	888,179	20.7	20.7	785,880	654,153	20.1	11.3	2,988.1	286,074	234,026	22.2	57.8	127.0	26.7
San Diego, CA.	1,861,846	1,357,854	37.1	31.4	875,538	697,471	25.5	21.7	2,736.1	986,308	660,383	49.4	43.6	253.4	53.0
San Francisco-Oakland, CA.	3,250,630	3,109,249	4.5	17.4	1,018,311	1,077,235	-5.5	-2.8	10,183.1	2,232,319	2,032,014	9.9	31.9	937.6	68.7
San Jose, CA	1,295,071	1,065,313	21.6	65.9	629,442	459,913	36.9	125.2	3,983.8	665,629	605,400	9.9	38.2	586.5	51.4
Santa Barbara-Santa Maria-Lompoc, CA	298,694	264,324	13.0	56.4	140,366	128,248	9.4	37.6	3,119.2	158,328	136,076	16.4	79.6	58.6	53.0
Santa Cruz, CA	188,141	123,790	52.0	47.0	41,483	32,076	29.3	25.3	3,456.9	146,658	91,714	59.9	56.4	337.1	78.0
Santa Rosa, CA	299,681	204,885	46.3	39.0	83,320	50,006	66.6	61.2	3,085.9	216,361	154,879	39.7	33.1	137.2	72.2
Sarasota, FL	202,251	120,413	68.0	56.6	48,868	40,237	21.5	18.1	3,490.6	153,383	80,176	91.3	87.3	274.4	75.8
Savannah, GA	230,728	207,987	10.9	1.6	141,390	118,349	19.5	-20.7	2,480.5	89,338	89,638	-0.3	61.7	68.2	38.7
Seattle-Everett, WA.	1,607,469	1,424,605	12.8	28.7	548,259	584,453	-6.2	-2.2	3,263.4	1,059,210	840,152	26.1	64.8	261.0	65.9
Sharon, PA	128,299	127,225	0.8	-0.2	19,057	22,653	-15.9	-10.3	4,764.3	109,242	104,572	4.5	2.3	163.5	85.1
Sheboygan, WI.	100,935	96,660	4.4	11.8	48,085	48,484	-0.8	6.0	4,371.4	52,850	48,176	9.7	18.3	104.7	52.4
Sherman-Denison, TX.	89,796	83,225	7.9	13.9	54,297	53,984	0.6	13.1	1,234.0	35,499	29,241	21.4	15.5	39.8	39.5
Shreveport, LA	376,710	336,000	12.1	4.6	205,820	182,064	13.0	10.8	2,541.0	170,890	153,936	11.0	-1.8	75.6	45.4
Sioux City, IA-NB.	117,457	116,189	1.1	-3.2	82,003	85,925	-4.6	-3.6	1,577.0	35,454	30,264	17.1	-1.9	32.8	30.2
Sioux Falls, SD.	109,435	95,209	14.9	10.0	81,182	72,488	12.0	10.7	1,980.0	28,253	22,721	24.3	7.6	36.7	25.8
South Bend, IN	280,772	279,813	0.3	3.2	109,727	125,580	-12.6	-5.2	3,048.0	171,045	154,233	10.9	11.3	197.3	60.9
Spokane, WA.	341,835	287,487	18.9	3.3	171,300	170,516	0.5	-6.1	3,294.2	170,535	116,971	45.8	20.9	99.7	49.9

Appendix Table 2. Population Growth in Individual Standard Metropolitan Statistical Areas: 1960-1980—continued

Name of SMSA	Total SMSA				Central cities					Metropolitan rings					
	Population		Percent change		Population		Percent change		Density per square mile	Population		Percent change		Density per square mile	Percent 1980
	1980	1970	1970-80	1960-70	1980	1970	1970-80	1960-70		1980	1970	1970-80	1960-70		
Springfield, IL.	187,789	171,020	9.8	9.8	99,637	91,753	8.6	10.2	2,490.9	88,152	79,267	11.2	9.3	77.3	46.9
Springfield, MO.	207,704	168,053	23.6	21.2	133,116	120,096	10.8	25.3	2,047.9	74,588	47,957	55.5	12.1	63.4	35.9
Springfield, OH.	183,885	187,606	-2.0	16.4	72,563	81,941	-11.4	-0.9	4,031.3	111,322	105,665	5.4	34.7	137.6	60.5
Springfield-Chicopee-Holyoke, MA-CT.	530,668	541,752	-2.0	7.5	252,109	280,693	-10.2	-2.8	3,361.5	278,559	261,059	6.7	21.4	502.8	52.5
Stamford, CT	198,854	206,340	-3.6	15.7	102,453	108,798	-5.8	17.3	2,696.1	96,401	97,542	-1.2	13.8	1,071.1	48.5
State College, PA.	112,760	99,267	13.6	26.3	36,130	32,833	10.0	46.5	7,226.0	76,630	66,434	15.3	18.3	69.6	68.0
Steubenville-Weirton, OH-WV.	163,099	166,385	-2.0	-0.8	51,136	57,902	-11.7	-4.6	1,893.9	111,963	108,483	3.2	1.3	201.0	68.6
Stockton, CA	347,342	291,073	19.3	16.4	149,779	109,963	36.2	27.4	3,744.5	197,563	181,110	9.1	10.7	143.7	56.8
Syracuse, NY	642,971	636,596	1.0	12.9	170,105	197,297	-13.8	-8.7	7,087.7	472,866	439,299	7.6	26.3	199.4	73.5
Tacoma, WA	485,643	412,344	17.8	28.2	158,501	154,407	2.7	4.3	3,302.1	327,142	257,937	26.8	48.6	200.9	67.4
Tallahassee, FL.	159,542	109,355	45.9	37.6	81,548	72,624	12.3	50.8	2,912.4	77,994	36,731	112.3	17.3	62.4	48.9
Tampa-St. Petersburg, FL	1,569,134	1,088,549	44.1	34.5	510,170	493,873	3.3	8.2	3,644.1	1,058,964	594,676	78.1	68.5	548.4	67.5
Terre Haute, IN.	176,583	175,143	0.8	1.8	61,125	70,335	-13.1	-3.0	2,351.0	115,458	104,808	10.2	5.3	79.6	65.4
Texarkana, TX-AR	127,019	113,488	11.9	12.5	52,730	52,179	1.1	4.3	1,550.9	74,289	61,309	21.2	20.5	37.3	58.5
Toledo, OH-MI.	791,599	762,658	3.8	9.7	354,635	383,062	-7.4	20.5	4,221.8	436,964	379,596	15.1	0.6	208.8	55.2
Topeka, KS	185,442	180,619	2.7	9.2	115,266	125,011	-7.8	4.6	2,352.4	70,176	55,608	26.2	21.0	40.6	37.8
Trenton, NJ.	307,863	304,116	1.2	14.2	92,124	104,786	-12.1	-8.2	13,160.6	215,739	199,330	8.2	30.9	980.6	70.1
Tucson, AZ	531,443	351,667	51.1	32.4	330,537	262,933	25.7	23.5	3,338.8	200,906	88,734	126.4	68.2	22.1	37.8
Tulsa, OK.	689,434	549,154	25.5	15.5	360,919	330,350	9.3	26.2	1,940.4	328,515	218,804	50.1	2.4	60.1	47.6
Tuscaloosa, AL	137,541	116,029	18.5	6.4	75,211	65,773	14.3	3.8	1,749.1	62,330	50,256	24.0	10.0	48.2	45.3
Tyler, TX.	128,366	97,096	32.2	12.4	70,508	57,770	22.0	12.8	2,014.5	50,858	39,326	47.1	12.0	64.5	39.6
Utica-Rome, NY	320,180	340,477	-6.0	2.9	119,458	141,521	-15.6	-6.9	1,342.2	200,722	198,956	0.9	11.3	78.8	62.7
Vallejo-Fairfield-Napa, CA	334,402	251,129	33.2	25.3	189,281	151,959	24.6	55.0	2,825.1	145,121	99,170	46.3	-3.2	96.0	43.4
Victoria, TX	68,807	53,766	28.0	15.7	50,695	41,349	22.6	25.1	2,668.2	18,112	12,417	45.9	-7.5	20.9	26.3
Vineland-Millville-Bridgeton, NJ	132,866	121,374	9.5	13.6	97,363	89,200	9.2	14.7	839.3	35,503	32,174	10.3	10.6	92.9	26.7
Visalia-Tulare-Porterville, CA	245,738	188,322	30.5	11.8	91,962	55,967	64.3	48.8	2,189.6	153,776	132,355	16.2	1.2	32.3	62.6
Waco, TX	170,755	147,553	15.7	-1.7	101,261	95,326	6.2	-2.5	1,368.4	69,494	147,533	15.7	-1.7	165.6	40.7
Washington, DC-MD-VA	3,060,922	2,910,111	5.2	37.1	638,333	756,668	-15.6	-1.0	10,132.3	2,422,589	2,153,443	12.5	58.5	881.9	79.1
Waterbury, CN.	228,178	216,808	5.2	13.7	103,266	108,033	-4.4	0.8	3,560.9	124,912	108,775	14.8	30.1	557.6	54.7
Waterloo-Cedar Falls, IA	137,961	132,916	3.8	8.5	112,307	105,130	6.8	13.1	1,247.9	25,654	27,786	-7.7	-5.9	53.2	18.6
Wausau, WI	111,270	97,457	14.2	9.7	32,426	32,806	-1.2	2.7	2,702.2	78,844	64,651	22.0	13.6	51.0	70.9
West Palm Beach-Boca Raton, FL	576,863	348,993	65.3	53.0	112,810	85,881	31.4	36.0	1,659.0	464,053	263,112	76.4	59.5	240.9	80.4
Wheeling, WV-OH.	185,566	181,954	2.0	-4.4	43,070	48,188	-10.6	-9.8	3,313.1	142,496	133,766	6.5	-2.3	152.4	76.8
Wichita, KS.	411,313	389,352	5.6	2.0	279,272	276,554	1.0	8.6	2,765.1	132,041	112,798	17.1	-11.1	56.2	32.1
Wichita Falls, KS.	130,664	128,642	1.6	-2.5	94,201	96,265	-2.1	-5.4	1,922.5	36,463	32,377	12.6	7.4	22.2	27.9
Williamsport, PA	118,416	113,296	4.5	3.6	33,401	37,918	-11.9	-9.6	3,711.2	85,015	75,378	12.8	11.8	69.2	71.8
Wilmington, DE-NJ-MD	523,221	499,493	4.8	20.5	70,195	80,386	-12.7	-16.1	6,381.4	453,026	419,107	8.1	31.5	418.3	86.6
Wilmington, NC	139,248	107,219	29.9	16.5	44,000	46,169	-4.7	4.9	2,000.0	95,248	61,050	56.0	27.2	93.0	68.4
Worcester, MA.	372,940	372,144	0.2	5.1	161,799	176,572	-8.4	-5.4	4,372.9	211,141	195,572	8.0	16.8	406.0	56.6
Yakima, WA	172,508	145,212	18.8	0.1	49,826	45,588	9.3	5.3	4,152.2	122,682	99,624	23.1	-2.2	28.7	71.1
York, PA	381,255	329,540	15.7	13.5	44,619	50,335	-11.4	-7.6	8,923.8	336,636	279,205	20.6	18.4	236.7	88.3
Youngstown-Warren, OH.	531,350	537,124	-1.1	5.5	172,065	204,403	-15.8	-9.7	3,511.5	359,285	332,721	8.0	17.7	367.0	67.6
Yuba City, CA.	101,979	86,671	17.7	28.9	18,736	13,986	34.0	21.5	3,747.2	83,243	72,685	14.5	30.4	67.3	71.3

[a]Indicates: (1) the count has been revised since publication of the 1970 census reprint; (2) the area was erroneously omitted; or (3) the area was not shown in the correct geographic relationship in the 1970 census reprints.

Source: U.S. Bureau of the Census. "Number of Inhabitants: United States Summary." 1980 Census of Population. Washington, DC: U.S. Government Printing Office, 1983, Table 30.

Appendix Table 3. Demographic Characteristics of Standard Metropolitan Statistical Areas, Central Cities, and Metropolitan Rings: 1980

Name of standard metropolitan statistical area (SMSA)	SMSA total					Central cities					Metropolitan rings				
	Percent black	Percent Spanish-origin	Sex ratio	Percent 0-14 years	Percent 65+ years	Percent black	Percent Spanish-origin	Sex ratio	Percent 0-14 years	Percent 65+ years	Percent black	Percent Spanish-origin	Sex ratio	Percent 0-14 years	Percent 65+ years
Abilene, TX	5.4	11.6	94.3	22.6	12.4	6.7	12.6	94.6	22.7	10.3	2.1	9.0	93.7	22.6	17.4
Akron, OH	9.1	0.5	93.6	22.1	10.4	22.2	0.6	88.1	21.4	13.5	1.8	0.5	96.9	22.6	8.7
Albany, GA	40.8	1.1	92.0	27.7	7.2	47.7	1.2	88.2	27.5	8.5	27.3	0.9	99.6	28.1	4.6
Albany-Schnectady-Troy, NY	3.7	1.0	92.1	21.1	12.9	10.4	1.4	87.0	17.9	16.1	0.9	0.9	94.2	22.4	11.6
Albuquerque, NM	2.2	36.1	95.6	23.6	8.2	2.4	33.8	94.1	22.3	8.4	1.4	42.5	99.9	27.0	7.7
Alexandria, LA	25.8	1.2	92.5	25.5	11.0	47.8	1.1	84.3	25.3	12.3	14.3	1.2	97.1	25.5	10.4
Allentown-Bethlehem-Easton, PA-NJ	1.4	2.4	93.2	20.3	12.9	3.3	5.9	90.1	17.9	15.3	0.5	0.8	94.6	21.3	11.8
Altoona, PA	0.7	0.3	89.2	22.1	14.3	1.4	0.3	84.5	20.9	16.5	0.2	0.3	92.7	44.2	12.6
Amarillo, TX	4.9	8.6	93.6	23.7	9.7	5.5	9.2	93.0	24.2	10.1	1.1	5.0	97.3	21.2	7.3
Anaheim-Santa Ana-Garden Grove, CA	1.3	14.8	97.4	21.6	8.3	2.1	26.5	98.4	23.1	7.5	0.9	10.2	97.1	21.0	8.6
Anchorage, AK	5.3	3.0	107.7	26.1	2.0	5.2	3.0	107.7	26.1	2.0	--	--	--	--	--
Anderson, IN	6.9	0.6	94.7	23.9	10.9	13.6	0.6	89.2	22.9	12.6	1.1	0.5	99.7	24.8	9.4
Anderson, SC	17.2	0.6	92.2	23.6	10.8	29.5	0.8	81.5	20.9	15.8	13.9	0.6	95.2	24.2	9.5
Ann Arbor, MI	10.7	1.5	99.5	19.8	6.4	9.2	2.1	101.2	15.6	5.9	11.6	1.2	98.3	22.7	6.7
Anniston, AK	17.6	1.1	96.1	23.0	9.7	40.3	0.7	85.1	23.5	14.2	10.1	1.2	100.0	22.8	8.2
Appleton-Oshkosh, WI	0.2	0.5	96.5	23.7	10.7	0.3	0.5	90.6	20.5	12.4	0.1	0.5	100.2	25.5	9.7
Asheville, NC	8.0	0.6	90.6	20.7	13.8	21.0	0.8	81.9	18.4	18.3	2.2	0.6	94.7	21.6	11.9
Athens, GA	18.1	1.0	93.2	20.7	8.9	27.4	1.4	87.5	13.5	10.0	13.4	0.9	96.1	24.2	8.4
Atlanta, GA	24.6	1.2	93.2	23.8	7.6	66.6	1.4	87.4	21.7	11.5	13.3	1.1	94.8	24.3	6.6
Atlantic City, NJ	17.6	3.9	88.5	21.0	15.9	49.8	5.8	76.0	19.4	23.5	9.0	3.4	92.1	21.5	13.9
Augusta, GA-SC	30.6	1.5	96.5	24.0	8.3	53.5	1.0	79.6	19.3	18.1	26.4	1.6	99.7	24.8	6.7
Austin, TX	9.4	17.6	98.3	21.7	7.8	12.0	18.7	97.6	20.1	7.5	4.1	15.5	99.7	24.6	8.3
Bakersfield, CA	5.2	21.6	99.3	25.3	9.7	10.5	15.0	93.0	24.3	9.2	3.3	23.9	101.6	25.6	9.9
Baltimore, MD	25.6	1.0	93.4	21.3	10.1	54.8	1.0	87.6	21.2	12.8	17.7	1.0	96.8	21.4	8.6
Bangor, ME	0.3	0.4	94.5	19.9	10.6	0.5	0.4	89.4	19.1	13.1	0.1	0.3	97.7	20.5	9.1
Baton Rouge, LA	27.8	1.7	94.9	25.7	7.0	36.2	1.8	91.3	21.9	8.7	20.7	1.6	97.9	28.7	5.7
Battle Creek, MI	7.3	1.5	95.6	23.7	11.0	22.6	1.9	86.0	24.2	14.0	3.6	1.4	98.1	23.6	10.3
Bay City, MI	0.9	2.6	95.4	24.6	10.1	1.8	4.7	91.3	22.2	13.5	0.3	1.6	97.6	25.8	8.3
Beaumont-Port Arthur-Orange, TX	21.8	3.4	95.1	24.1	10.3	36.5	4.2	92.0	23.4	11.9	4.0	2.4	98.8	24.8	8.4
Bellingham, WA	0.3	1.9	96.8	21.7	11.2	0.5	1.6	90.9	16.6	13.4	0.2	2.2	101.6	25.6	9.6
Benton Harbor, MI	14.5	1.2	93.2	24.8	11.0	86.3	0.9	86.4	37.4	7.8	7.7	1.2	93.9	23.6	11.3
Billings, MT	0.3	2.7	95.9	23.9	9.1	0.3	3.1	92.6	21.3	10.8	0.1	2.0	101.6	28.3	6.3
Biloxi-Gulfport, MS	18.3	1.9	100.7	24.8	9.2	20.8	2.3	102.5	9.7	10.1	15.7	1.5	99.2	37.8	8.4
Binghamton, NY-PA	1.1	0.7	93.8	21.8	12.3	3.2	0.9	84.5	17.5	18.3	0.7	0.6	96.1	22.7	11.0
Birmingham, AL	28.3	0.7	89.8	22.7	11.7	55.6	0.8	84.4	21.5	13.9	14.3	0.6	92.7	23.4	10.6
Bismarck, ND	0.1	0.4	97.3	25.1	9.1	0.1	0.4	92.6	23.6	8.9	--	0.3	103.5	27.1	9.5
Bloomington, IN	2.6	1.1	97.1	17.0	7.2	4.3	1.6	95.2	11.3	6.5	0.7	0.6	99.2	23.4	8.0
Bloomington-Normal, IL	4.0	0.9	90.9	20.0	9.7	5.8	1.1	87.2	17.6	9.2	0.1	0.6	98.8	24.9	10.8
Boise City, ID	0.4	2.2	96.9	25.0	8.6	0.5	2.3	93.3	21.9	10.2	0.2	2.1	102.3	29.6	6.1
Boston, MA	5.8	2.4	90.1	18.9	12.5	22.4	6.4	89.3	17.0	12.7	1.5	1.4	90.3	19.4	12.4
Bradenton, FL	8.9	2.1	87.4	16.8	27.1	17.9	2.2	83.7	17.9	26.9	6.6	2.1	88.4	16.3	27.1
Bremerton, WA	1.8	2.6	105.5	23.6	9.9	4.2	3.6	115.4	18.7	12.5	1.0	2.2	102.4	25.1	9.0
Bridgeport, CT	8.8	7.7	91.3	21.0	12.2	21.0	18.7	86.9	22.8	13.4	1.9	1.5	93.9	20.1	11.6
Bristol, CT	1.4	1.5	94.5	22.2	10.3	1.6	1.7	93.3	21.4	10.9	0.6	0.9	99.0	24.8	8.2
Brockton, MA	3.4	1.6	93.4	24.1	10.7	5.0	2.3	91.3	24.3	11.9	1.1	0.7	96.1	23.8	9.2
Brownsville-Harlingen-San Benito, TX	0.3	77.1	92.2	31.8	9.6	0.3	79.2	90.2	31.5	9.6	0.1	72.1	96.9	32.4	9.5
Bryan-College Station, TX	11.1	10.1	112.5	18.5	6.8	11.0	10.7	113.2	18.0	6.6	10.6	5.9	106.5	22.5	8.1
Buffalo, NY	9.2	1.3	91.2	21.2	12.3	26.3	2.7	85.6	20.3	15.0	2.1	0.8	93.6	21.6	11.3
Burlington, NC	19.2	0.6	90.8	20.7	11.5	20.7	0.6	85.6	19.9	12.9	18.1	0.6	94.1	21.1	10.7
Burlington, VT	0.4	0.8	94.2	21.8	7.7	0.6	0.8	83.4	15.2	10.8	0.3	0.8	100.1	25.1	6.1
Canton, OH	6.0	0.9	93.1	23.1	11.1	15.8	1.3	85.9	22.1	14.4	2.9	0.7	95.4	23.4	10.1
Casper, WY	0.7	3.5	103.6	24.9	6.3	0.8	3.9	100.7	23.3	7.3	0.3	2.7	111.0	28.8	4.0
Cedar Rapids, IA	1.6	0.8	93.9	23.4	10.1	2.3	0.9	91.2	22.4	11.0	0.3	0.5	99.1	25.4	8.4
Champaign-Urbana-Rantoul, IL	8.7	1.4	105.0	18.4	7.2	11.5	1.8	108.2	15.5	7.0	2.6	0.6	98.5	24.7	7.6
Charleston-North Charleston, SC	31.0	1.5	101.8	24.6	6.9	36.1	1.7	111.6	20.4	8.5	28.2	1.4	97.7	26.4	6.2
Charleston, WV	5.1	0.5	92.3	21.7	11.5	12.2	0.6	83.3	17.8	16.2	2.9	0.5	95.3	22.9	10.0
Charlotte-Gastonia, NC	21.8	0.9	92.3	23.2	8.9	29.5	1.0	89.2	22.5	9.1	11.0	0.7	96.5	24.1	8.6
Charlottesville, VA	15.0	0.8	95.2	18.5	9.6	18.1	0.9	88.1	15.4	11.4	13.1	0.7	99.2	20.2	8.6
Chattanooga, TN-GA	14.0	0.7	92.2	23.0	10.9	31.7	0.8	87.9	21.6	12.7	2.3	0.6	95.1	23.9	9.6
Chicago, IL	20.1	8.2	93.9	23.0	10.0	39.8	14.0	90.5	23.1	11.4	5.6	3.9	96.4	23.0	9.0
Chico, CA	1.2	5.2	95.2	18.6	15.5	1.7	5.5	91.2	13.9	9.0	1.0	5.2	96.2	19.7	16.9
Cincinnati, OH-KY-IN	12.4	0.6	92.0	23.5	10.9	33.6	0.8	85.5	20.6	14.5	4.2	0.5	94.6	24.6	9.6
Clarksville-Hopkinsville, TN-KY	21.2	2.6	109.1	23.7	8.1	22.1	2.3	98.6	23.0	8.7	19.4	3.0	123.3	24.8	7.5
Cleveland, OH	18.2	1.4	91.3	21.6	11.7	43.8	3.1	88.4	22.6	13.0	7.1	0.6	92.5	21.1	11.2
Colorado Springs, CO	6.0	7.9	101.8	23.7	6.8	5.4	8.5	94.5	22.9	8.3	6.8	6.7	119.4	25.4	3.8

Appendix Table 3. Demographic Characteristics of Standard Metropolitan Statistical Areas, Central Cities, and Metropolitan Rings: 1980—continued

Name of standard metropolitan statistical area (SMSA)	SMSA total					Central cities					Metropolitan rings				
	Percent black	Percent Spanish-origin	Sex ratio	Percent 0-14 years	Percent 65+ years	Percent black	Percent Spanish-origin	Sex ratio	Percent 0-14 years	Percent 65+ years	Percent black	Percent Spanish-origin	Sex ratio	Percent 0-14 years	Percent 65+ years
Columbia, MO	6.4	1.0	95.2	18.1	7.6	8.7	1.1	92.1	14.0	7.6	2.5	0.7	100.5	24.8	7.5
Columbia, SC	28.8	1.3	96.7	22.4	7.3	40.2	2.2	98.1	15.7	10.4	24.8	1.0	96.3	24.5	6.4
Columbus, GA-AL	34.9	2.3	102.5	23.4	8.5	33.9	2.1	94.9	23.5	8.9	36.3	2.9	123.7	23.4	7.6
Columbus, OH	12.3	0.7	94.2	22.6	8.8	22.0	0.8	92.8	21.3	8.9	1.8	0.6	95.6	24.1	8.7
Corpus Christi, TX	4.0	48.5	96.1	27.4	8.4	5.0	46.6	96.0	26.5	8.2	1.3	53.0	96.5	29.7	8.6
Cumberland, MD-WV	2.0	0.4	90.6	20.8	14.5	3.4	0.5	81.8	18.1	20.4	1.5	0.4	93.5	21.6	12.6
Dallas-Fort Worth, TX	14.1	8.4	95.2	23.9	8.3	27.2	12.4	92.9	22.0	10.2	3.9	5.3	97.1	25.3	6.9
Danbury, CT	2.9	2.1	96.4	24.0	9.3	5.6	3.3	94.6	22.0	10.7	0.9	1.2	97.6	25.5	8.4
Danville, VA	30.0	0.7	90.5	21.3	12.7	29.5	0.7	82.9	19.2	15.4	29.8	0.7	96.1	22.7	10.8
Davenport-Rock Island-Moline, IA-IL	4.4	3.0	95.7	24.1	10.7	7.1	3.5	93.0	22.7	11.8	1.6	2.5	98.5	25.5	9.5
Dayton, OH	12.7	0.7	93.6	23.0	9.6	36.7	0.9	90.1	22.6	11.8	4.8	0.6	94.8	23.1	8.9
Daytona Beach, FL	11.2	1.6	90.1	16.8	22.3	32.5	1.6	88.5	16.7	21.6	4.8	1.4	114.3	14.9	20.0
Decatur, IL	10.5	0.6	93.1	23.7	11.7	14.4	0.6	90.3	22.6	13.1	0.2	0.5	100.3	26.5	8.0
Denver-Boulder, CO	4.8	10.7	97.3	22.3	7.8	10.5	16.8	94.7	17.7	11.8	1.6	7.5	98.7	24.8	5.6
Des Moines, IA	4.1	1.4	91.4	22.8	10.3	6.8	1.8	88.3	21.1	12.5	6.1	0.8	95.5	25.0	7.4
Detroit, MI	20.5	1.6	94.0	23.8	9.5	63.1	2.4	89.8	25.1	11.7	4.2	1.4	95.6	23.2	8.7
Dubuque, IA	0.3	0.5	93.6	25.3	11.1	0.3	0.6	88.7	22.6	12.8	0.1	0.3	104.0	30.6	7.7
Duluth-Superior, MN-WI	0.4	0.3	96.3	21.7	13.6	0.7	0.4	90.2	14.6	11.7	0.1	0.3	101.9	27.8	15.3
Eau Claire, WI	0.1	0.3	93.7	22.9	11.7	0.2	0.4	85.9	18.1	11.7	--	0.3	99.1	26.0	11.6
El Paso, TX	3.8	61.9	96.0	28.9	6.6	3.1	62.5	92.8	28.6	6.9	8.4	57.1	125.1	31.2	3.9
Elkhart, IN	4.2	1.3	93.6	25.3	9.6	12.5	1.3	87.9	23.6	12.3	0.6	1.2	96.2	26.1	8.5
Elmira, NY	4.0	0.9	92.5	22.3	12.8	9.8	1.7	91.7	20.8	14.6	0.7	0.4	92.9	23.1	11.8
Enid, OK	3.3	1.1	95.1	22.6	13.1	4.0	1.2	94.2	21.9	13.2	0.2	0.7	98.4	25.2	12.6
Erie, PA	4.4	0.7	93.2	23.4	10.9	9.6	1.1	88.9	22.3	13.4	0.5	0.4	96.5	5.5	9.1
Eugene-Springfield, OR	0.6	2.0	97.8	21.9	9.6	0.9	2.1	95.8	20.1	9.2	0.2	1.9	100.2	24.0	10.0
Evansville, IN-KY	5.2	0.5	92.1	22.3	12.5	8.8	0.5	86.3	19.9	15.2	2.6	0.4	96.6	24.0	11.0
Fall River, MA-RI	0.4	1.7	90.2	22.5	13.8	0.4	2.4	85.2	21.9	16.6	0.3	0.9	96.2	23.1	10.8
Fargo-Moorhead, ND-MN	0.2	0.7	96.9	21.2	9.7	0.3	0.7	93.5	18.2	9.7	0.1	0.7	103.9	27.0	9.9
Fayetteville, NC	30.6	3.7	111.3	25.5	4.5	40.3	1.8	88.4	22.8	8.7	27.2	4.3	119.7	26.4	3.2
Fayetteville-Springdale, AR	0.9	0.8	97.9	21.3	13.0	2.4	1.0	99.4	18.6	10.4	0.1	0.7	97.1	22.7	14.3
Fitchburg-Leominster, MA	1.5	2.7	90.1	21.9	11.8	1.5	3.3	87.0	20.8	13.2	1.5	0.9	99.6	25.0	7.9
Flint, MI	15.1	1.6	94.2	26.0	8.1	41.1	2.5	89.6	26.3	10.0	3.5	1.2	96.3	25.8	7.2
Florence, AL	12.6	0.6	92.5	22.3	11.0	15.7	0.6	85.8	20.4	12.4	11.2	0.6	95.2	23.6	10.5
Florence, SC	37.5	0.8	90.1	26.2	8.6	47.2	0.8	83.3	24.9	10.2	33.5	0.8	92.8	26.7	8.0
Fort Collins, CO	0.4	5.9	98.5	21.1	8.5	0.7	6.8	98.5	17.3	7.3	0.2	5.1	98.5	24.0	9.4
Fort Lauderdale-Hollywood, FL	11.2	4.0	90.4	16.7	22.0	13.2	4.7	90.4	15.4	21.8	10.1	3.7	90.5	17.2	22.0
Fort Myers-Cape Coral, FL	8.0	2.8	92.5	17.5	22.3	16.7	2.5	90.6	18.6	20.3	3.4	2.9	93.4	16.9	23.4
Fort Smith, AK-OK	3.5	0.8	94.2	24.2	13.1	6.7	1.0	89.5	22.5	13.2	1.7	0.7	96.9	25.1	13.0
Fort Walton Beach, FL	8.6	2.3	103.1	23.9	5.8	12.4	1.9	96.2	22.2	6.5	7.6	2.4	104.8	24.3	5.6
Fort Wayne, IN	6.9	1.6	94.6	25.1	9.9	14.4	2.2	90.2	22.9	11.9	0.6	1.1	98.4	27.0	8.3
Fresno, CA	4.9	29.3	96.9	24.2	10.1	9.5	23.6	92.0	23.1	10.9	1.5	33.5	100.6	25.0	9.4
Gadsden, AL	13.4	0.5	91.4	23.3	12.7	24.4	0.6	85.2	20.9	16.0	3.8	0.4	97.0	25.5	9.9
Gainesville, FL	19.1	3.2	100.3	19.0	7.1	20.4	4.0	100.3	17.3	7.0	17.1	2.4	100.2	21.0	7.2
Galveston-Texas City, TX	18.5	12.0	96.8	24.0	9.1	26.2	15.6	93.9	22.6	11.1	9.6	8.1	100.1	25.5	6.8
Gary-Hammond-East Chicago, IN	19.7	7.3	95.3	25.5	8.4	43.6	12.4	92.4	26.5	9.3	0.2	3.1	97.6	24.8	7.7
Glens Falls, NY	1.1	0.9	94.6	24.1	12.8	1.0	0.8	82.2	22.9	15.7	1.0	0.9	96.9	24.3	12.3
Grand Forks, ND-MN	1.2	1.5	102.0	23.3	10.5	0.6	1.0	96.8	20.2	8.4	1.6	1.9	106.2	25.7	12.1
Grand Rapids, MI	5.3	2.3	94.0	24.4	9.8	15.5	3.2	88.6	22.4	13.4	0.8	1.9	96.5	25.3	8.3
Great Falls, MT	1.2	1.7	99.9	23.4	9.9	0.6	1.5	94.8	21.8	11.5	2.5	2.1	113.1	27.1	6.1
Greeley, CO	0.5	17.0	96.1	24.1	8.8	0.8	15.6	89.4	20.6	9.8	0.2	18.1	101.4	26.7	8.1
Green Bay, WI	0.3	0.5	95.6	24.9	9.6	0.2	0.7	90.3	22.2	12.0	0.3	0.4	101.2	27.6	7.2
Greensboro-Winston-Salem-High Point, NC	19.3	0.7	91.3	21.8	10.2	34.5	0.8	85.5	20.7	11.3	7.8	0.6	95.9	22.6	9.3
Greenville-Spartanburg, SC	17.1	0.8	93.4	22.6	9.8	37.6	1.0	82.4	20.0	13.7	12.4	0.7	96.0	23.2	9.0
Hagerstown, MD	4.2	0.6	99.0	20.8	11.9	5.7	0.8	85.7	19.4	16.1	3.5	0.5	105.3	21.4	10.1
Hamilton-Middletown, OH	4.7	0.6	94.0	23.4	8.9	4.4	1.2	91.7	19.7	11.0	4.8	--	96.1	26.8	6.9
Harrisburg, PA	7.6	1.0	92.5	21.0	11.6	43.6	4.3	82.4	22.8	15.3	2.7	0.6	94.0	20.7	11.1
Hartford, CT	8.5	4.7	92.4	20.9	11.4	33.9	20.5	88.0	23.4	11.4	2.6	1.1	93.5	20.3	11.4
Hickory, NC	8.8	0.6	94.6	23.5	9.5	18.7	0.6	84.6	19.3	13.3	6.8	0.6	96.7	24.2	8.8
Honolulu, HI	2.2	7.2	105.7	23.0	7.3	1.1	5.2	97.5	18.6	10.4	3.1	8.9	113.9	27.0	4.4
Houston, TX	18.2	14.6	100.4	25.2	6.2	27.4	17.6	98.7	23.2	6.9	6.6	11.0	102.6	27.5	5.4
Huntington-Ashland, WV-KY-OH	2.3	0.5	93.1	23.2	11.7	5.5	0.5	84.2	18.3	16.7	1.0	0.5	97.0	25.2	9.7
Huntsville, AL	15.1	0.9	95.2	23.5	8.8	20.6	1.0	93.6	22.7	7.0	10.2	0.8	96.6	24.2	10.2
Indianapolis, IN	13.5	0.8	92.8	23.7	9.8	21.7	0.9	90.7	23.0	10.3	1.0	0.6	96.2	24.8	9.0
Iowa City, IA	1.5	1.0	96.6	18.1	7.1	1.9	1.2	94.5	15.3	6.6	0.6	0.8	100.1	22.7	8.0
Jackson, MI	7.2	1.2	102.3	23.5	9.9	15.2	2.0	88.5	24.0	13.3	4.2	0.9	107.7	23.3	8.7

Appendix Table 3. Demographic Characteristics of Standard Metropolitan Statistical Areas, Central Cities, and Metropolitan Rings: 1980—continued

Name of standard metropolitan statistical area (SMSA)	SMSA total					Central cities					Metropolitan rings				
	Percent black	Percent Spanish-origin	Sex ratio	Percent 0-14 years	Percent 65+ years	Percent black	Percent Spanish-origin	Sex ratio	Percent 0-14 years	Percent 65+ years	Percent black	Percent Spanish-origin	Sex ratio	Percent 0-14 years	Percent 65+ years
Jackson, MS.	39.4	0.8	89.7	24.9	9.2	47.0	0.7	86.7	24.3	9.7	26.0	0.8	95.0	26.1	8.4
Jacksonville, FL	21.5	1.8	93.6	23.6	9.7	25.4	1.8	93.0	23.4	9.6	10.5	3.6	95.3	24.3	9.9
Jacksonville, NC	20.2	3.9	146.8	22.2	3.7	16.2	2.8	95.5	24.0	5.2	20.5	4.1	158.9	21.9	3.4
Janesville-Beloit, WI.	3.4	0.7	96.3	24.4	11.0	4.7	0.8	93.5	24.3	10.8	1.1	0.5	100.9	24.5	11.2
Jersey City, NJ.	12.6	26.1	89.8	20.8	12.6	27.7	18.6	88.2	24.0	11.8	1.7	31.0	90.8	18.7	13.1
Johnson City-Kingsport-Bristol, TN-VA.	2.1	0.5	93.7	22.0	11.4	5.2	0.5	87.3	18.8	13.8	1.2	0.4	95.6	22.9	10.8
Johnstown, PA.	1.3	0.4	93.4	22.1	13.6	7.6	1.0	83.8	19.4	18.2	0.3	0.4	95.0	22.5	12.8
Joplin, MO	0.9	0.7	91.3	22.3	14.5	2.0	0.9	84.5	19.8	15.9	0.4	0.6	94.5	23.3	13.8
Kalamazoo-Portage, MI.	7.5	1.5	94.4	22.6	9.7	11.0	1.6	91.5	20.7	8.9	4.8	1.4	96.6	24.0	10.3
Kankakee, IL	14.5	1.2	93.9	25.0	10.8	28.0	1.1	87.0	23.9	14.4	8.8	1.3	96.8	25.4	9.3
Kansas City, MO-KS	13.0	2.4	92.2	22.9	10.4	10.3	3.7	89.6	22.0	12.2	15.3	1.3	94.5	23.6	8.9
Kenosha, WI.	2.3	2.9	96.4	23.2	10.8	3.6	4.0	93.6	22.7	11.6	0.2	1.0	101.2	24.2	9.4
Killeen-Temple, TX	17.1	10.3	117.7	24.0	7.2	19.2	11.7	98.5	23.8	8.5	15.1	9.3	133.7	24.1	6.3
Knoxville, TN.	7.0	0.6	92.9	20.8	11.2	14.5	0.7	87.9	17.6	13.8	2.5	0.6	95.9	22.6	9.7
Kokomo, IN	4.1	1.0	93.4	24.9	9.4	8.1	1.4	89.1	24.2	11.3	0.7	0.7	97.2	25.6	7.8
La Crosse, WI.	0.2	0.4	90.6	20.8	12.1	0.3	0.5	82.3	15.2	15.2	0.1	0.3	101.0	27.1	8.5
Lafayette, LA.	20.2	2.5	97.0	25.0	6.7	27.9	2.5	94.0	22.1	8.1	10.8	2.5	100.6	28.4	5.1
Lafayette-West Lafayette, IN	1.7	1.1	102.0	18.7	8.2	1.7	1.2	98.9	17.6	10.1	1.6	1.1	105.6	20.0	6.0
Lake Charles, LA	21.7	1.3	95.5	25.5	8.7	37.8	1.5	90.8	23.3	9.9	8.4	1.2	99.5	27.2	7.7
Lakeland-Winter Haven, FL.	15.0	3.0	96.7	21.8	14.3	22.0	2.1	85.7	18.2	19.4	12.9	3.2	100.0	22.7	12.9
Lancaster, PA.	1.9	2.5	93.7	22.8	11.7	8.9	12.0	89.0	21.7	13.6	0.6	0.8	94.7	23.1	11.4
Lansing-East Lansing, MI	5.3	3.0	96.7	23.4	7.8	12.7	5.0	92.8	36.2	7.3	0.6	1.7	99.2	25.4	8.1
Laredo, TX	0.1	91.5	91.5	32.6	8.4	0.1	93.0	90.5	32.6	8.6	0.1	73.8	104.4	33.0	5.5
Las Cruces, NM	1.7	52.1	97.7	26.2	7.2	1.8	45.5	95.5	23.6	8.9	1.5	58.0	99.6	28.5	5.7
Las Vegas, NV.	10.0	7.6	101.7	22.4	7.6	12.7	7.8	100.6	22.5	8.3	8.4	7.5	102.4	22.4	7.2
Lawrence, KS	4.5	2.3	100.8	17.0	7.5	5.4	2.7	101.0	15.8	6.4	1.0	0.8	99.8	21.5	11.1
Lawrence-Haverhill, MA-NH.	0.9	4.4	91.4	23.2	12.3	1.2	10.2	86.9	22.9	15.4	0.3	0.8	94.4	23.3	10.3
Lawton, OK	15.9	5.3	115.1	24.3	6.5	15.7	5.4	97.9	26.0	7.0	15.6	5.1	180.4	20.1	5.2
Lewiston-Auburn, ME.	0.3	0.5	88.3	21.9	14.2	0.3	0.5	87.3	21.1	15.0	0.2	0.4	95.9	28.2	8.3
Lexington-Fayette, KY.	11.0	0.7	93.9	22.1	9.2	13.2	0.7	93.2	20.7	8.6	6.7	0.6	95.3	24.6	10.2
Lima, OH	5.1	1.2	95.3	25.2	11.5	20.2	1.1	89.1	25.7	12.7	0.9	1.2	97.1	25.1	11.2
Lincoln, NB.	1.8	1.5	95.8	19.9	10.1	2.0	1.6	94.7	19.2	10.3	0.4	0.6	105.2	25.4	8.7
Little Rock-North Little Rock, AR.	21.0	0.9	92.2	24.2	9.7	28.0	0.8	87.2	22.8	11.4	11.6	1.0	99.2	26.1	7.5
Long Branch-Asbury Park, NJ.	8.5	2.6	92.6	22.6	11.8	30.4	7.5	83.6	21.1	16.3	6.1	2.1	93.5	22.7	11.4
Longview-Marshall, TX.	22.6	1.9	94.1	24.1	12.2	24.4	2.2	93.0	23.4	12.3	19.5	1.4	95.7	25.2	12.0
Lorain-Elyria, OH.	7.2	4.8	95.3	25.9	8.5	12.2	8.6	92.5	25.6	9.7	2.3	1.2	98.1	26.2	7.3
Los Angeles-Long Beach, CA	12.6	27.6	95.3	22.0	9.9	16.1	24.5	95.8	20.3	11.0	9.4	30.1	94.8	23.5	9.1
Louisville, KY-IN.	13.0	0.6	92.1	23.1	10.4	28.0	0.7	85.7	20.0	15.3	5.5	0.6	95.5	24.6	8.0
Lowell, MA-NH.	0.8	2.3	95.0	24.6	9.3	1.2	5.0	89.8	22.4	13.0	0.4	0.6	98.6	26.1	6.8
Lubbock, TX.	7.5	19.6	98.1	23.6	7.9	8.1	18.8	97.0	22.8	7.8	4.0	22.9	103.1	27.4	8.4
Lynchburg, VA.	20.5	0.6	89.8	21.7	11.6	23.5	0.7	83.2	19.5	14.0	17.8	0.6	95.3	23.3	9.8
Macon, GA.	33.0	0.9	91.3	24.6	8.9	44.2	0.7	83.7	23.3	11.9	22.8	1.1	98.4	25.7	6.4
Madison, WI.	1.8	1.0	96.6	20.0	8.4	2.7	1.3	94.5	16.3	8.7	0.7	0.7	98.9	24.2	7.9
Manchester, NH	0.3	0.8	92.2	22.6	11.1	0.3	1.1	87.8	20.3	13.4	0.3	0.5	98.3	25.5	8.0
Mansfield, OH.	7.1	0.8	97.5	23.6	10.2	15.8	1.1	95.9	21.7	13.3	0.9	0.5	98.7	24.9	8.1
McAllen-Pharr-Edinburg, TX	0.2	81.3	92.3	32.6	9.2	0.2	76.9	90.4	30.9	9.2	0.1	84.2	93.5	33.7	9.2
Medford, OR.	0.1	3.0	98.5	22.4	12.6	0.1	3.0	92.5	22.8	13.7	0.1	3.0	101.3	22.2	12.2
Melbourne-Titusville-Cocoa, FL	8.7	2.0	97.8	19.1	12.7	13.6	2.0	95.4	19.5	13.8	6.0	1.9	99.1	18.8	12.1
Memphis, TN-AR-MS.	39.9	0.9	91.9	24.7	9.3	47.2	0.8	88.1	23.5	10.4	20.9	1.1	101.8	27.6	6.6
Meriden, CT.	3.4	8.2	90.4	21.2	12.7	3.3	8.2	90.4	21.2	12.7	--	--	--	--	--
Miami, FL.	17.2	35.7	89.5	18.9	15.7	25.1	55.9	88.0	16.8	17.0	14.7	30.3	89.9	19.5	15.3
Midland, TX.	8.6	14.9	96.4	24.5	7.4	9.8	15.9	95.5	24.3	7.8	0.8	9.3	101.9	25.9	4.7
Milwaukee, WI.	10.8	2.5	93.2	22.6	11.1	23.1	4.1	89.9	22.1	12.5	0.5	1.1	96.1	23.0	10.0
Minneapolis-St. Paul, MN-WI.	2.4	1.1	94.7	22.7	9.5	6.4	2.0	88.2	17.6	15.2	0.6	0.7	97.6	25.0	7.1
Mobile, AL	28.6	1.0	92.9	25.3	10.2	36.2	1.1	89.7	23.2	11.1	22.1	1.0	95.7	27.1	9.3
Modesto, CA.	1.2	15.0	95.3	24.2	11.0	2.0	10.5	93.4	24.2	9.7	0.6	18.0	96.6	24.3	11.8
Monroe, LA	29.1	0.9	90.7	26.2	10.0	48.6	1.1	84.2	25.5	12.1	15.4	0.8	95.6	26.7	8.5
Montgomery, AL	34.7	0.9	90.8	24.8	10.1	39.2	0.9	87.2	24.7	10.1	0.9	27.2	98.1	25.1	10.2
Muncie, IN	5.9	0.6	91.1	21.8	10.0	9.5	0.8	87.7	19.5	10.8	0.4	0.4	96.4	25.2	8.9
Muskegon-Norton Shores-Muskegon-Heights, MI.	10.7	2.2	93.9	24.7	10.9	23.1	2.3	90.5	23.8	12.6	1.1	2.1	96.6	25.3	9.7
Nashua, NH	0.8	0.8	95.6	25.3	8.0	0.9	1.1	93.5	23.0	9.5	0.5	0.4	98.7	28.7	6.0
Nashville-Davidson, TN	16.1	0.7	92.8	22.0	10.4	23.1	0.8	89.5	20.0	11.0	7.9	0.6	96.9	24.3	9.7
Nassau-Suffolk, NY	6.2	3.9	93.7	22.2	9.8	--	--	--	--	--	6.1	3.9	93.7	22.2	9.8
New Bedford, MA.	1.8	3.1	89.9	21.3	14.6	2.6	4.6	86.3	21.2	16.2	0.6	1.0	95.2	21.4	12.4
New Britain, CT.	3.4	5.0	93.3	19.2	12.4	5.6	8.7	91.4	17.1	14.4	0.9	1.0	95.3	21.5	10.2

Appendix Table 3. Demographic Characteristics of Standard Metropolitan Statistical Areas, Central Cities, and Metropolitan Rings: 1980—continued

Name of standard metropolitan statistical area (SMSA)	SMSA total					Central cities					Metropolitan rings				
	Percent black	Percent Spanish-origin	Sex ratio	Percent 0-14 years	Percent 65+ years	Percent black	Percent Spanish-origin	Sex ratio	Percent 0-14 years	Percent 65+ years	Percent black	Percent Spanish-origin	Sex ratio	Percent 0-14 years	Percent 65+ years
New Brunswick-Perth Amboy-Sayreville, NJ	6.0	5.7	93.4	20.3	8.8	13.3	19.3	91.2	19.7	10.6	4.2	2.6	97.6	20.4	8.5
New Haven-West Haven, CT	12.0	3.2	90.6	20.0	12.3	24.8	6.1	87.8	19.9	13.1	2.1	1.1	92.7	20.1	11.8
New London-Norwich, CT-RI.	3.6	1.9	100.6	21.6	10.8	8.2	3.6	96.7	19.5	13.2	1.8	1.3	102.1	22.4	9.9
New Orleans, LA.	32.6	4.1	92.4	24.5	9.3	55.3	3.4	88.1	23.4	11.7	12.4	4.6	96.3	25.4	7.1
New York, NY-NJ.	21.3	16.4	87.4	20.1	13.2	24.0	19.9	86.3	20.1	13.5	7.4	4.3	91.2	19.8	12.1
Newark, NJ	21.3	6.7	90.8	21.4	11.1	58.2	18.6	86.5	27.8	8.8	13.6	4.3	91.7	20.2	11.5
Newark, OH	1.7	0.4	95.7	23.6	10.2	3.0	0.5	89.1	21.9	14.1	1.0	0.4	99.3	24.5	8.2
Newburgh-Middletown, NY.	6.2	4.3	97.6	24.6	10.9	20.2	11.2	82.6	23.9	14.3	3.1	2.9	101.0	24.8	10.1
Newport News-Hampton, VA	28.6	1.5	97.9	22.8	7.7	32.5	1.6	97.7	23.0	4.3	17.0	1.1	98.4	22.1	17.1
Norfolk-Virginia Beach-Portsmouth, VA-NC.	27.7	1.7	103.5	23.1	7.7	26.2	1.9	105.6	22.7	7.5	32.1	0.9	95.8	48.5	8.6
Northeast Pennsylvania	0.7	0.4	88.6	19.5	16.0	1.4	0.5	84.1	17.7	18.8	0.5	0.4	89.9	20.0	15.2
Norwalk, CT.	8.9	4.1	93.4	20.3	9.9	13.7	5.8	91.6	19.9	10.8	0.8	1.3	96.2	21.0	8.4
Ocala, FL.	16.6	1.6	92.6	20.7	17.1	28.2	1.4	87.3	23.2	15.0	11.3	1.7	95.1	19.7	17.9
Odessa, TX	4.5	21.5	99.5	25.7	7.0	5.5	23.2	98.7	25.1	7.4	0.3	15.5	102.6	27.8	5.5
Oklahoma City, OK.	9.0	2.2	94.4	23.0	9.9	14.5	2.8	92.0	22.2	11.3	3.7	1.7	96.8	23.8	8.5
Olympia, WA.	0.8	2.1	96.3	24.0	9.8	0.7	1.9	91.8	20.0	13.3	0.8	2.1	97.6	25.1	8.9
Omaha, NB-IA	7.7	2.1	93.6	24.4	9.6	12.0	2.3	90.0	21.8	12.2	2.4	1.7	98.1	27.7	6.3
Orlando, FL.	12.9	3.7	94.1	21.7	10.9	30.0	3.9	93.4	19.0	12.7	9.0	3.7	94.3	22.3	10.5
Owensboro, KY.	3.9	0.5	92.2	24.3	10.9	6.0	0.5	87.4	22.9	12.2	0.4	0.4	101.2	26.8	8.6
Oxnard-Simi Valley-Ventura, CA	2.1	21.4	99.1	25.2	8.3	3.9	29.8	99.6	28.4	5.3	1.1	16.9	98.8	23.5	9.9
Panama City, FL.	12.0	1.6	96.7	23.3	9.5	23.8	1.2	89.1	22.1	13.2	5.7	1.8	100.8	23.9	7.5
Parkersburg-Marietta, WV-OH.	1.0	0.4	93.2	23.5	11.8	1.5	0.5	86.7	20.0	15.9	0.7	0.4	96.8	25.3	9.6
Pascagoula-Moss Point, MS.	18.7	1.3	100.2	28.1	6.3	35.6	1.2	100.5	27.3	7.2	6.8	1.3	100.1	28.7	5.7
Paterson-Clifton-Passaic, NJ	13.2	13.9	90.5	22.0	11.9	3.7	22.3	88.5	8.9	7.2	25.9	1.6	93.5	41.0	18.6
Pensacola, FL.	16.7	1.6	96.1	23.3	8.6	33.9	1.4	85.9	21.3	13.2	12.3	1.7	98.8	23.9	7.4
Peoria, IL	6.0	0.9	94.2	23.9	10.9	16.5	1.4	89.7	22.7	12.3	0.5	0.7	96.5	24.5	10.2
Petersburg-Colonial Heights-Hopewell, VA	36.3	1.5	97.6	22.5	9.4	36.5	1.0	88.6	22.1	10.9	35.0	2.3	114.8	23.0	7.1
Philadelphia, PA-NJ.	18.8	2.5	91.4	21.5	11.7	37.5	3.8	86.4	20.7	14.1	8.0	1.7	94.4	22.0	10.4
Phoenix, AZ.	3.2	13.2	96.2	22.8	11.6	4.7	14.8	96.1	23.5	9.3	1.4	11.4	96.2	22.0	14.1
Pine Bluff, AR	40.6	0.8	94.0	24.9	12.2	49.0	0.9	88.0	24.4	13.9	26.4	0.6	104.9	25.8	9.3
Pittsburgh, PA	7.8	0.5	91.1	19.5	13.3	23.9	0.8	86.7	10.6	16.0	4.0	0.5	92.1	21.5	12.7
Pittsfield, MA	1.5	0.5	89.8	20.5	14.2	2.4	0.5	88.1	21.0	14.1	0.3	0.4	92.2	19.9	14.2
Portland, ME	0.4	0.5	89.2	20.8	13.2	0.8	0.6	83.1	18.3	16.6	0.2	0.4	92.5	22.0	11.5
Portland, OR-WA.	2.7	2.0	95.3	22.2	10.9	7.5	2.1	91.7	17.9	15.3	0.6	1.9	96.8	24.1	9.1
Portsmouth-Dover-Rochester, NH-ME.	0.9	0.7	95.7	20.8	10.8	0.0	1.6	94.0	21.5	11.7	0.8	0.1	96.9	20.3	10.1
Poughkeepsie, NY	7.0	2.4	91.4	22.0	11.1	25.6	1.7	86.8	19.9	16.6	4.3	2.5	99.7	22.3	10.3
Providence-Warwick-Pawtucket, RI-MA.	2.7	2.1	90.3	20.3	13.4	0.1	6.1	87.9	19.4	14.9	2.0	0.0	91.6	20.8	12.6
Provo-Orem, UT	0.1	2.3	96.3	32.8	6.1	0.1	2.5	94.0	28.8	5.3	0.0	2.1	99.4	38.2	7.2
Pueblo, CO	1.8	33.0	94.7	23.5	11.6	2.0	35.5	93.1	22.9	12.3	0.4	22.9	102.0	25.6	8.5
Racine, WI	8.0	4.2	95.8	24.6	10.2	14.6	6.4	91.5	23.9	12.0	1.4	1.9	100.2	25.3	8.3
Raleigh-Durham, NC	25.3	0.8	93.0	20.3	8.2	35.1	0.9	89.9	18.2	9.8	16.1	0.7	95.8	22.2	6.9
Reading, PA.	2.5	2.9	92.7	20.1	14.1	8.0	9.8	85.5	20.0	17.8	0.6	0.6	95.3	20.1	12.9
Redding, CA.	0.6	3.0	96.1	23.1	11.1	1.1	2.8	93.3	21.2	12.0	0.3	3.1	98.5	24.2	10.6
Reno, NV	1.8	4.8	101.4	19.1	8.5	2.6	5.1	101.5	15.9	10.5	0.9	4.6	101.2	22.4	6.3
Richland-Kennewick-Pasco, WA	1.6	6.9	102.8	26.2	6.8	2.3	6.8	101.3	24.9	7.6	0.5	7.1	105.1	28.2	5.8
Richmond, VA	27.6	0.8	90.5	21.2	10.0	51.3	1.0	83.0	18.0	14.1	15.0	0.7	94.8	23.0	7.9
Riverside-San Bernardino-Ontario, CA	5.0	18.6	96.9	23.9	12.1	8.4	21.6	94.9	24.6	9.4	3.8	17.7	97.5	23.6	12.9
Roanoke, VA.	11.6	0.6	89.6	20.5	12.8	21.8	0.7	84.8	19.8	15.6	3.1	0.5	93.7	21.1	10.5
Rochester, MN.	0.4	0.6	90.4	23.6	9.3	0.6	0.7	83.6	21.2	10.7	0.1	0.4	103.2	27.8	7.0
Rochester, NY.	8.0	2.0	93.6	22.2	11.0	25.8	5.4	89.2	21.9	14.0	2.1	0.8	95.1	22.3	10.0
Rockford, IL	7.6	2.4	94.7	24.1	10.2	13.1	2.9	90.3	22.6	12.6	1.9	1.9	99.4	25.6	7.8
Rock Hill, SC.	22.3	0.6	91.9	24.5	8.7	36.2	0.7	82.0	22.6	10.4	15.2	0.5	97.2	25.4	7.8
Sacramento, CA	6.0	10.0	95.9	21.4	9.6	13.1	14.2	92.4	19.8	13.6	3.3	8.5	97.3	21.9	8.1
Saginaw, MI.	15.7	5.4	93.5	26.2	9.2	35.3	9.0	87.8	26.9	11.2	5.4	3.6	96.6	25.9	8.2
St. Cloud, MN.	0.2	0.4	100.4	25.5	9.7	0.5	0.4	92.2	17.1	10.9	0.1	0.3	103.4	28.5	9.2
St. Joseph, MO	2.6	1.6	90.5	22.0	15.2	3.4	1.9	87.9	21.5	15.9	0.0	0.8	98.9	23.5	13.2
St. Louis, MO-IL	17.3	0.9	91.0	22.9	11.7	45.2	1.2	81.7	21.0	17.6	10.5	0.9	93.4	23.4	10.3
Salem, OR.	0.6	4.5	96.6	22.9	12.6	1.1	3.5	96.7	20.0	13.2	0.3	5.1	96.5	24.6	12.2
Salinas-Seaside-Monterey, CA	6.5	25.9	105.0	23.3	9.2	8.9	24.9	105.1	23.5	8.3	3.8	26.9	104.9	23.1	10.1
Salisbury-Concord, NC.	15.0	0.6	93.1	21.5	12.5	27.2	0.6	87.2	17.6	17.3	11.6	0.6	94.8	22.5	11.2
Salt Lake City-Ogden, UT	0.9	5.0	98.3	31.0	7.2	1.8	8.2	93.5	21.5	14.2	0.6	4.0	100.0	34.0	5.0
San Angelo, TX	4.0	21.2	92.8	22.2	12.1	4.4	23.1	91.6	22.2	12.4	0.7	9.2	100.9	22.2	10.4
San Antonio, TX.	6.8	44.9	94.3	25.8	9.0	7.2	53.7	91.5	26.2	9.5	5.2	20.8	102.5	24.6	7.8
San Diego, CA.	5.6	14.8	103.6	20.6	10.3	8.7	14.9	106.1	19.5	9.7	2.6	14.7	101.5	21.7	10.8
San Francisco-Oakland, CA.	12.0	10.8	95.8	18.7	11.2	23.8	11.4	96.0	15.7	14.6	6.4	10.6	95.7	20.1	9.6

Appendix Table 3. Demographic Characteristics of Standard Metropolitan Statistical Areas, Central Cities, and Metropolitan Rings: 1980–continued

Name of standard metropolitan statistical area (SMSA)	SMSA total					Central cities					Metropolitan rings				
	Percent black	Percent Spanish-origin	Sex ratio	Percent 0-14 years	Percent 65+ years	Percent black	Percent Spanish-origin	Sex ratio	Percent 0-14 years	Percent 65+ years	Percent black	Percent Spanish-origin	Sex ratio	Percent 0-14 years	Percent 65+ years
San Jose, CA	3.4	17.5	98.1	22.0	7.5	4.5	22.3	97.9	25.2	6.2	2.1	12.9	98.3	19.0	8.6
Santa Barbara-Santa Maria-Lompoc, CA	2.6	18.5	97.0	19.2	11.3	3.1	24.6	93.8	18.4	14.2	2.0	13.1	99.9	19.8	8.8
Santa Cruz, CA	0.8	14.7	95.9	19.5	13.2	1.8	8.7	92.2	15.1	14.3	0.4	16.4	96.9	20.7	12.9
Santa Rosa, CA	1.2	6.9	93.9	21.1	13.5	1.3	5.6	87.9	20.2	15.8	1.1	7.5	96.3	21.5	12.6
Sarasota, FL	5.2	1.5	86.2	13.7	30.0	16.2	2.6	83.4	14.8	26.1	1.6	1.1	87.1	13.3	31.2
Savannah, GA	35.9	1.1	91.9	24.6	10.1	49.0	1.3	88.4	23.9	11.4	15.2	0.8	97.7	25.8	8.1
Seattle-Everett, WA	3.6	2.0	97.6	20.6	9.9	8.5	2.5	95.5	14.7	15.3	1.0	1.7	99.2	23.6	7.1
Sharon, PA	4.2	0.3	94.1	7.9	13.0	6.4	0.3	86.3	20.1	15.8	1.0	1.8	98.6	5.8	12.5
Sheboygan, WI	0.3	1.0	97.0	23.3	13.3	0.1	1.6	91.9	21.5	15.8	0.5	0.5	102.0	25.0	11.1
Sherman-Denison, TX	7.0	1.5	91.4	21.3	15.6	10.5	1.8	89.2	21.3	15.2	1.7	1.0	94.9	21.4	16.1
Shreveport, LA	33.0	1.5	90.7	24.9	10.9	41.1	1.3	86.3	24.8	11.7	22.9	1.6	96.4	25.0	9.9
Sioux City, IA-NB	1.0	1.4	91.3	24.1	12.9	1.3	1.3	88.4	23.2	13.5	0.2	1.5	98.4	26.1	11.4
Sioux Falls, SD	0.3	0.4	91.6	23.2	10.6	0.3	0.5	87.8	21.6	11.1	0.1	0.3	103.6	27.8	9.2
South Bend, IN	7.7	1.5	93.9	22.4	12.1	18.2	2.4	89.3	21.9	14.8	0.9	1.0	96.9	22.8	10.4
Spokane, WA	1.3	1.4	94.2	22.9	11.5	1.6	1.5	89.5	20.1	15.3	0.9	1.3	99.1	23.9	7.8
Springfield, IL	6.1	0.6	89.0	22.2	12.6	10.7	0.7	83.7	20.6	14.3	0.7	0.5	95.4	23.9	10.7
Springfield, MO	1.5	0.7	91.5	21.3	11.9	2.1	0.7	88.1	19.1	13.2	0.2	0.5	98.0	25.3	9.5
Springfield, OH	7.7	0.6	92.7	23.6	11.5	17.1	0.7	86.9	22.7	14.1	1.5	0.5	96.7	24.2	9.8
Springfield-Chicopee-Holyoke, MA-CT	5.4	4.5	89.3	20.9	12.8	10.3	8.2	87.1	21.5	14.4	0.7	1.1	91.3	20.3	11.3
Stamford, CT	8.4	3.7	90.1	19.0	12.4	14.7	5.6	89.1	19.0	12.0	1.4	1.7	91.0	19.0	12.7
State College, PA	1.3	0.7	105.7	17.3	7.6	2.3	1.3	114.3	6.1	4.4	0.8	0.5	101.8	22.5	9.1
Steubenville-Weirton, OH-WV	3.9	0.5	93.9	21.9	12.2	9.3	0.7	88.6	18.4	15.5	12.9	4.1	96.4	23.5	10.6
Stockton, CA	5.5	19.2	97.9	23.6	11.3	10.4	22.1	94.5	24.1	11.0	1.7	17.0	100.5	23.2	11.6
Syracuse, NY	4.8	0.9	93.2	22.6	10.7	15.5	1.7	86.4	18.9	14.6	0.9	0.6	95.7	23.9	9.2
Tacoma, WA	6.1	2.7	101.7	23.0	9.4	9.0	2.4	92.2	21.8	13.5	4.6	2.8	106.6	23.6	7.4
Tallahassee, FL	24.1	1.6	93.2	21.1	6.9	31.5	1.8	89.8	17.0	7.4	15.9	1.3	96.8	25.4	6.3
Tampa-St. Petersburg, FL	9.3	5.1	89.2	17.7	21.4	20.2	7.9	86.8	10.7	7.9	3.8	3.7	90.4	21.1	28.0
Terre Haute, IN	3.6	0.6	92.4	21.1	14.1	8.5	0.8	85.5	18.2	15.8	0.9	0.5	96.3	22.6	13.2
Texarkana, TX- Texarkana, AK	22.9	1.1	91.8	24.7	13.3	29.9	1.0	84.4	23.4	15.9	17.5	1.1	97.4	25.7	6.1
Toledo, OH-MI	8.6	2.5	93.7	23.9	10.6	17.3	3.0	90.8	23.0	12.5	1.4	2.1	96.1	24.6	9.0
Topeka, KS	6.4	3.4	94.1	22.2	12.5	9.4	4.6	90.4	20.3	13.9	1.3	1.5	100.5	25.3	10.3
Trenton, NJ	18.0	3.4	91.4	20.3	11.4	45.4	8.0	88.8	23.6	12.6	6.2	1.5	92.5	18.8	10.9
Tucson, AZ	2.8	21.0	95.3	21.7	11.7	3.6	24.9	93.6	20.6	11.7	1.4	14.5	98.2	23.6	11.8
Tulsa, OK	7.4	1.4	94.5	23.5	10.3	11.7	1.7	92.0	21.1	10.8	2.6	1.1	97.3	26.1	9.9
Tuscaloosa, AL	27.2	0.9	94.3	22.1	9.7	35.0	1.1	92.5	19.4	9.8	17.5	0.7	96.4	25.4	9.6
Tyler, TX	22.0	3.1	92.2	23.7	12.5	26.0	4.6	88.6	23.0	13.1	16.8	1.4	96.7	24.5	11.8
Utica-Rome, NY	2.4	0.9	93.4	22.2	13.5	5.9	1.7	89.1	12.2	11.3	0.4	0.4	95.8	28.2	14.8
Vallejo-Fairfield-Napa, CA	8.6	10.0	100.9	23.3	9.9	11.7	8.8	98.5	23.8	9.3	4.1	11.5	104.1	22.8	10.5
Victoria, TX	6.8	30.4	96.8	26.4	8.5	7.7	33.8	94.4	26.1	8.7	3.9	21.1	103.8	27.7	8.0
Vineland-Millville-Bridgeton, NJ	15.0	9.4	90.2	24.4	11.7	12.8	12.0	86.7	24.5	11.8	19.6	2.3	100.7	24.1	11.3
Visalia-Tulare-Porterville, CA	1.4	29.8	97.9	26.6	10.7	2.3	22.5	92.5	25.1	11.3	0.9	34.2	101.3	27.5	10.4
Waco, TX	16.0	8.8	93.1	21.7	13.2	21.6	11.1	90.6	20.0	14.3	7.4	5.4	96.7	24.2	11.7
Washington, DC-MD-VA	27.9	3.1	93.3	21.3	7.5	69.7	2.8	86.1	17.7	11.6	16.5	3.1	95.3	22.3	6.5
Waterbury, CT	5.8	3.6	91.7	21.5	13.8	11.5	6.7	88.3	20.8	15.5	1.0	1.0	94.6	22.1	12.4
Waterloo-Cedar Falls, IA	6.2	0.7	93.9	22.9	10.2	7.6	0.7	92.2	21.9	10.7	0.1	0.5	101.6	27.5	8.2
Wausau, WI	--	0.3	98.8	25.1	10.8	0.1	0.3	88.3	19.5	15.6	--	0.2	103.5	27.4	8.9
West Palm Beach-Boca Raton, FL	13.4	4.9	91.1	17.0	23.3	16.3	6.8	89.2	15.8	21.8	12.5	4.5	91.6	17.3	23.7
Wheeling, WV-OH	2.1	0.5	91.2	21.3	14.0	2.1	0.5	83.1	18.2	17.7	2.1	0.5	93.8	22.3	12.8
Wichita, KS	7.8	2.9	95.7	23.0	9.9	10.7	3.5	93.8	21.7	10.6	1.4	1.4	99.8	25.7	8.3
Wichita Falls, TX	8.4	6.0	97.6	21.7	11.8	11.0	7.6	97.8	21.4	11.2	1.3	2.0	95.8	22.4	13.2
Williamsport, PA	1.5	0.3	93.0	22.2	12.8	3.9	0.5	88.2	21.0	14.5	0.5	0.3	94.9	22.7	12.1
Wilmington, DE-NJ-MD	14.0	1.6	93.5	22.3	9.7	50.5	4.9	81.2	22.5	15.7	8.1	1.1	95.6	22.2	8.7
Wilmington, NC	22.0	0.8	92.7	23.0	10.3	39.2	1.0	82.9	20.8	14.2	13.9	0.7	97.6	24.0	8.4
Worcester, MA	1.4	2.2	91.5	21.1	13.4	2.8	4.3	87.7	18.7	16.3	0.4	0.5	94.5	22.8	11.3
Yakima, WA	0.9	14.8	98.0	24.9	12.1	2.2	7.0	90.6	20.9	15.4	0.4	17.9	101.1	26.6	10.8
York, PA	2.6	0.9	94.7	22.3	11.5	17.3	3.4	84.7	21.6	15.6	0.6	0.5	96.1	22.4	10.9
Youngstown-Warren, OH	10.5	1.3	92.7	22.4	11.4	28.1	2.4	87.8	21.9	14.1	1.9	0.7	95.0	22.6	10.1
Yuba City, CA	2.7	10.3	100.2	24.3	9.8	1.7	9.5	91.9	21.3	12.0	3.1	11.5	102.1	25.0	9.3

Note: -- indicates data not available.

Source: U.S. Bureau of the Census. "General Population Characteristics: United States Summary" (Tables 68 and 69). Also "Census Trends" (Table 1, 3, and 6). 1980 Census of Population. Washington, DC: U.S. Government Printing Office, 1983.

Index